ENGLISH • PORTUGUESE
PORTUGUE
DICTIONARY

John Whitlam   Vitoria Davies
Mike Harland

First published 1991

Latest reprint 1998

ers
reat Britain

NY 10022

rback)

Distribuído pela Agência Siciliano de Livros, Jornais e Revistas Ltda.
Av. Raimundo Pereira de Magalhães 3305 – CEP 05145-200 – São Paulo – Brasil
Editora Siciliano, 1991

First HarperCollins edition published 1997

Library of Congress Cataloging-in-Publication Data

Whitlam, John.
Harper Collins Portuguese dictionary : English-Portuguese Portuguese-English / John Whitlam, Vitoria Davies, Mike Harland, – College ed.
p. cm.
Updated ed. of: Collins Portuguese dictionary. 1991.
ISBN 0-06-273662-0
1. Portuguese language–Dictionaries-English. 2. English language–Dictionaries–Portuguese. I. Davies, Vitoria. II. Harland, Mike. III. Whitlam, John. Collins Portuguese dictionary. IV. Title.
PC5333.W45 1997
469.3'21–dc20 96-44948

98 99 00 01 02 CIBM 10 9 8 7 6 5 4

Printed and bound in Great Britain by
Caledonian International Book Manufacturing Ltd, Glasgow, G64

ÍNDICE

CONTENTS

---

contributors/colaboradores
Carlos Ramires,
Nelly Wanderley Fernandes Porto,
Ana Maria de Mello e Souza,
Adriana Ceschin Rieche, Lígia Xavier,
Amos Maidantchik, Helio Leoncio Martins,
Jane Horwood

consultant/assessor
Dr Euzi Rodrigues Moraes

editorial staff/redação
Gerry Breslin, Lesley Johnston,
Irene Lakhani

INTRODUÇÃO

Para compreender o inglês

Este novo dicionário, completamente atualizado, fornece ao leitor uma cobertura ampla e prática dos usos lingüísticos mais comuns, incluindo a terminologia relativa à área empresarial e à microinformática, além de uma seleção abrangente de abreviaturas, siglas e topônimos encontrados freqüentemente na imprensa. Para facilitar as consultas do leitor, as formas irregulares de verbos e substantivos ingleses foram incluídas, com indicações que fazem referência à forma básica, onde uma tradução é dada.

Para expressar-se em inglês

A fim de ajudar o leitor a expressar-se correta e idiomaticamente em inglês, foram incluídas várias indicações para orientá-lo quanto à tradução mais apropriada em um determinado contexto. Todas as palavras de uso mais comum receberam um tratamento detalhado, com muitos exemplos de utilização típica.

Um companheiro de trabalho

Todo o cuidado foi tomado para fazer deste novo dicionário da editora Collins uma obra totalmente confiável, fácil de ser usada e útil para o trabalho e estudos do leitor. Esperamos que ele seja um companheiro de longos anos no atendimento das necessidades de expressão numa língua estrangeira.

Understanding Portuguese

This new and thoroughly up-to-date dictionary provides the user with wide-ranging, practical coverage of current usage, including terminology relevant to business and office automation, and a comprehensive selection of abbreviations, acronyms and geographical names commonly found in the press. You will also find, for ease of consultation, irregular forms of Portuguese verbs and nouns with a cross-reference to the basic form where a translation is given.

Self-expression in Portuguese

To help you express yourself correctly and idiomatically in Portuguese, numerous indications — think of them as signposts — guide you to the most appropriate translation for your context. All the most commonly used words are given detailed treatment, with many examples of typical usage.

A working companion

Much care has been taken to make this new Collins dictionary thoroughly reliable, easy to use and relevant to your work and study. We hope it will become a long-serving companion for all your foreign language needs.

ABREVIATURAS		ABBREVIATIONS
abreviatura	**ab(b)r**	abbreviation
adjetivo	**adj**	adjective
administração	**ADMIN**	administration
advérbio, locução adverbial	**adv**	adverb, adverbial phrase
aeronáutica	**AER**	flying, air travel
agricultura	**AGR**	agricultura
anatomia	**ANAT**	anatomy
arquitetura	**ARQ, ARCH**	architecture
artigo definido	**art def**	definite article
artigo indefinido	**art indef**	indefinite article
uso atributivo do substantivo	**atr**	compound element
automobilismo	**AUT(O)**	the motor car and motoring
auxiliar	**aux**	auxiliary
aeronáutica	**AVIAT**	flying, air travel
biologia	**BIO**	biology
botânica, flores	**BOT**	botany
português do Brasil	**BR**	Brazilian
inglês britânico	**BRIT**	British English
química	**CHEM**	chemistry
linguagem coloquial (! chulo)	**col(!)**	colloquial usage (! particularly offensive)
comércio, finanças, bancos	**COM(M)**	commerce, finance, banking
comparativo	**compar**	comparative
computação	**COMPUT**	computing
conjunção	**conj**	conjunction
construção	**CONSTR**	building
uso atributivo do substantivo	**cpd**	compound element
cozinha	**CULIN**	cookery
artigo definido	**def art**	definite article
economia	**ECON**	economics
educação, escola e universidade	**EDUC**	schooling, schools and universities
eletricidade, eletrônica	**ELET, ELEC**	electricity, electronics
especialmente	**esp**	especially
exclamação	**excl**	exclamation
feminino	**f**	feminine
ferrovia	**FERRO**	railways
uso figurado	**fig**	figurative use
física	**FÍS**	physics
fisiologia	**FISIOL**	physiology
fotografia	**FOTO**	photography
(verbo inglês) do qual a partícula é inseparável	**fus**	(phrasal verb) where the particle is inseparable
geralmente	**gen**	generally
geografia, geologia	**GEO**	geography, geology
geometria	**GEOM**	geometry
geralmente	**ger**	generally
impessoal	**impess, impers**	impersonal
artigo indefinido	**indef art**	indefinite article
linguagem coloquial (! chulo)	**inf (!)**	informal usage (! particularly offensive)
infinitivo	**infin**	infinitive
invariável	**inv**	invariable
irregular	**irreg**	irregular

ABREVIATURAS		ABBREVIATIONS
jurídico	**JUR**	law
gramática, lingüística	**LING**	grammar, linguistics
masculino	**m**	masculine
matemática	**MAT(H)**	mathematics, calculus
medicina	**MED**	medicine
ou masculino ou feminino, dependendo do sexo da pessoa	**m/f**	masculine/feminine
militar, exército	**MIL**	military matters
música	**MÚS, MUS**	music
substantivo	**n**	noun
navegação, náutica	**NÁUT, NAUT**	sailing, navigation
adjetivo ou substantivo numérico	**num**	numeral adjective or noun
	o.s.	oneself
pejorativo	**pej**	pejorative
fotografia	**PHOT**	photography
física	**PHYS**	physics
fisiologia	**PHYSIOL**	physiology
plural	**pl**	plural
política	**POL**	politics
particípio passado	**pp**	past participle
preposição	**prep**	preposition
pronome	**pron**	pronoun
psicologia, psiquiatria	**PSICO, PSYCH**	psychology, psychiatry
português de Portugal	**PT**	European Portuguese
pretérito	**pt**	past tense
química	**QUÍM**	chemistry
religião e cultos	**REL**	religion, church services
	sb	somebody
educação, escola e universidade	**SCH**	schooling, schools and universities
singular	**sg**	singular
	sth	something
sujeito (gramatical)	**su(b)j**	(grammatical) subject
subjuntivo, conjuntivo	**sub(jun)**	subjunctive
superlativo	**superl**	superlative
também	**tb**	also
técnica, tecnologia	**TEC(H)**	technical term, technology
telecomunicações	**TEL**	telecommunications
tipografia, imprensa	**TIP**	typography, printing
televisão	**TV**	television
tipografia, imprensa	**TYP**	typography, printing
inglês americano	**US**	American English
ver	**V**	see
verbo	**vb**	verb
verbo intransitivo	**vi**	intransitive verb
verbo reflexivo	**vr**	reflexive verb
verbo transitivo	**vt**	transitive verb
zoologia	**ZOOL**	zoology
marca registrada	®	registered trademark
indica um equivalente cultural	≈	introduces a cultural equivalent

PORTUGUESE PRONUNCIATION

The rules given below refer to Portuguese as spoken in the city and surrounding region of Rio de Janeiro, Brazil. In general, the pronunciation of each entry is given in square brackets in the text after the word in question. However, where an entry is composed of two or more words, each of which is given elsewhere in the dictionary, you will find the pronunciation of each word in its alphabetical position.

Consonants

c	[k]	*c*afé	*c* before *a*, *o*, *u* is pronounced as in *c*at
ce, ci	[s]	*c*ego	*c* before *e* or *i*, as in receive
ç	[s]	ra*ç*a	*ç* is pronounced as in receive
ch	[ʃ]	*ch*ave	*ch* is pronounced as in *sh*ock
d	[d]	*d*ata	as in English *EXCEPT*
de, di	[dʒ]	*di*fícil cida*de*	*d* before an *i* sound or final unstressed *e* is pronounced as in ju*dg*e
g	[g]	*g*ado	*g* before *a*, *o* or *u*, as in *g*ap
ge, gi	[ʒ]	*g*iria	*g* before *e* or *i*, as *s* in leisure
h		*h*umano	*h* is always silent in Portuguese
j	[ʒ]	*j*ogo	*j* is pronounced as *s* in lei*s*ure
l	[w]	fa*l*ta, tota*l*	*l* after a vowel tends to become *w*
lh	[ʎ]	traba*lh*o	*lh* is pronounced like the *lli* in mi*lli*on
m	[m] [ãw] [ĩ]	ani*m*al, *m*assa cant*am* s*im*	as in English *EXCEPT* *m* at the end of a syllable preceded by a vowel nasalizes the preceding vowel
n	[n] [ã] [ẽ]	*n*adar, pe*n*al c*an*sar al*en*to	as in English *EXCEPT* *n* at the end of a syllable, preceded by a vowel and followed by a consonant, nasalizes the preceding vowel
nh	[ɲ]	tama*nh*o	*nh* is pronounced like the *ni* in o*ni*on
q	[k]	*qu*eijo	*qu* before *e* or *i* is pronounced as in *k*ick
q	[kw]	*qu*anto cin*qü*enta	*qu* before *a* or *o*, or *qü* before *e* or *i*, is proncounced as in *qu*oits
-r-	[r]	comp*r*a	*r* preceded by a consonant (except *n*) and followed by a vowel is pronounced with a single trill
r-, -r- rr	[x] [x]	*r*ato, a*r*pão bexe*rr*o	initial *r*, *r* followed by a consonant and *rr* are pronounced similar to the Scottish *ch* in lo*ch*
-r	[*]	pinta*r*, dize*r*	word-final *r* before a word beginning with a consonant or at the end of a sentence is pronounced [x]; before a word beginning with a vowel it is pronounced [r]. In colloquial speech this variable sound is often not pronounced at all.
s-	[s]	*s*ol	as in English *EXCEPT*
-s-	[z]	me*s*a	intervocalic *s* is pronounced as in ro*s*e
-s-	[ʒ]	ra*s*gar, de*s*maio	*s* before *b*, *d*, *g*, *l*, *m*, *n*, *r* and *v*, as in lei*s*ure
-s-, -s	[ʃ]	e*s*cada, livro*s*	*s* before *c*, *f*, *p*, *qu*, *t* and finally, as in *s*ugar
-ss-	[s]	no*ss*o	double *s* is always pronounced as in bo*ss*

t	[t]	*t*odo	as in English, *EXCEPT*
te, ti	[tʃ]	aman*te* *t*ipo	*t* followed by an *i* sound or final unstressed *e* is pronounced as *ch* in *ch*eer
x-	[ʃ]	xarope explorar	initial *x* or *x* before a consonant (except *c*) is pronounced as in *s*ugar
-xce-, -xci-	[s]	ex*c*eto, ex*c*itar	*x* before *ce* or *ci* is unpronounced
ex-	[z]	exame	*x* in the prefix *ex* before a vowel is pronounced as *z* in squee*z*e
-x-	[ʃ] [ks] [s]	rixa fixo auxiliar	*x* in any other position may be pronounced as in *s*ugar, axe or *s*ail
z-, -z-	[z]	zangar	as in English *EXCEPT*
-z	[ʒ]	carta*z*	final *z* is pronounced as in lei*s*ure

b, f, k, p, v, w are prounced as in English.

Vowels

a, á, à, â	[a]	m*a*ta	*a* is normally pronounced as in f*a*ther
ã	[ã]	irm*ã*	*ã* is pronounced approximately as in s*u*ng
e	[e]	v*e*jo	unstressed (except final) *e* is pronounced like *e* in th*ey*; stressed *e* is pronounced either as in th*ey* or as in b*e*t
-e	[i]	fom*e*	final *e* is pronounced as in mon*ey*
é	[ɛ]	mis*é*ria	*é* is pronounced as in b*e*t
ê	[e]	p*ê*lo	*ê* is pronounced as in th*ey*
i	[i]	v*i*da	*i* is pronounced as in m*ea*n
o	[o] [ɔ] [o]	l*o*c*o*motiva l*o*ja gl*o*bo	unstressed (except final) *o* is pronounced as in l*o*cal; stressed *o* can be pronounced either as in l*o*cal or as in r*o*ck
-o	[u]	livr*o*	final *o* is pronounced as in f*oo*t
ó	[ɔ]	*ó*leo	*o* is pronounced as in r*o*ck
ô	[o]	col*ô*nia	*ô* is pronounced as in l*o*cal
u	[u]	l*u*va	*u* is pronounced as in r*u*le; it is silent in *gue*, *gui*, *que* and *qui*

Semivowels

e	[j]	t*e*atro	occasionally before a stressed *a*, *e* is pronounced as *y* in *y*acht
i	[j]	c*i*úme, silênc*i*o	unstressed *i* before a vowel is pronounced as *y* in *y*acht
u	[w]	ág*u*a, aq*u*ático ag*ü*entar	*u* is pronounced *w* in *qua*, *quo* and *gua*, and when marked with a dieresis

Dipthongs

ãe	[aj]	m*ãe*	nasalized, approximately as in fl*y*ing
ai	[aj]	v*ai*	as in r*i*de
ao, au	[aw]	*ao*s, *au*xílio	as in sh*ou*t
ão	[ãw]	v*ão*	nasalized, approximately as in r*ou*nd
ei	[ej]	f*ei*ra	as in th*ey*
eu	[ew]	d*eu*sa	both elements pronounced
oi	[oj]	b*oi*	as in t*oy*
ou	[o]	cen*ou*ra	as in l*o*cal
õe	[õj]	avi*õe*s	nasalized, approximately as in "b*oi*ng!"

Stress

The rules of stress in Portuguese are as follows:

(a) when a word ends in *a*, *e*, *o*, *m* (except *im*, *um* and their plural forms) or *s*, the second last syllable is stressed; camar*a*da, camar*a*das, *par*te, *par*tem
(b) when a word ends in *i*, *u*, *im* (and plural), *um* (and plural), *n* or a consonant other than *m* or *s*, the stress falls on the last syllable: ven*di*, al*gum*, al*guns*, fa*lar*
(c) when the rules set out in (a) and (b) are not applicable, an acute or circumflex accent appears over the stressed vowel: *ó*tica, *â*nimo, ingl*ê*s

In the phonetic transcription, the symbol ['] precedes the syllable on which the stress falls.

EUROPEAN PRONUNCIATION

The pronunciation of Brazilian Portuguese differs quite markedly from the Portuguese spoken in Portugal itself and in the African and island states. The more phonetic nature of Brazilian means that words nearly always retain their set pronunciation; in European Portuguese, on the other hand, vowels can often be unpronounced or weakened and consonants can change their sound, all depending on their position within a word or whether they are being elided with a following word. The major differences in pronunciation of European Portuguese are as follows:

Consonants: as in Brazilian, except:

-b-	[β]	cu*b*a	*b* between vowels is a softer sound, closer to ha*v*e
d	[d]	*d*ança, *d*ifícil	as in English, *EXCEPT*
-d-	[ð]	fa*d*o, ci*dad*e	*d* between vowels is softer, approximately as in *th*e
-g-	[ɣ]	sa*g*a	*g* between vowels is a softer sound, approximately as in la*g*er
gu	[ɣw]	a*gu*entar	in certain words *gu* is pronounced as in *Gw*ent
qu	[kw]	tran*qu*ilo	in certain words *qu* is pronounced as in *qu*oits
r-, rr	[ʀ] [rr]		initial *r* and double *r* are pronounced either like the French *r* or strongly trilled as in Scottish *R*o*r*y; pronunciation varies according to region
-r-, -r	[r]	*r*ato, a*r*ma	*r* in any other position is slightly trilled
t	[t]	*t*odo, aman*t*e	*t* is pronounced as in English
z	[z]	*z*angar	as in English *EXCEPT*
	[ʃ]	carta*z*	final *z* is pronounced as *sh* in fla*sh*

Vowels: as in Brazilian, except:

a	[a] [ɐ]	fal*a*r c*a*ma	stressed *a* is pronounced either as in f*a*ther or as *u* in f*u*rther
-a-, -a	[ə]	f*a*lar, fal*a*	unstressed or final *a* is pronounced as *e* in furth*e*r
e	[ə]	m*e*dir	unstressed *e* is a very short *i* sound as in rabb*i*t
-e	[ə]	art*e*, regim*e*	final *e* is barely pronounced; these would sound like English *art* and *regime*
o	[u]	poç*o*, p*o*der	unstressed or final *o* is pronounced as in f*oo*t

PRONÚNCIA INGLESA

Em geral, damos a pronúncia de cada verbete em colchetes logo após a palavra em questão. Todavia, quando a verbete for composto de duas ou mais palavras, e cada uma delas aparecer em outro lugar no dicionário, o leitor encontrará a pronúncia de cada palavra na sua posição alfabética.

Vogais e ditongos

	Exemplo Inglês	*Explicação*
[aː]	f*a*ther	Entre o *a* de p*a*dre e o *o* de n*ó*; como en f*a*d*a*
[ʌ]	b*u*t, c*o*me	Aproximadamente como o primeiro *a* de c*a*ma
[æ]	m*a*n, c*a*t	Som entre o *a* de l*á* e o *e* de p*é*
[ə]	fath*er*, *a*go	Som parecido com o *e* final pronunciado em Portugal
[əː]	b*i*rd, h*ea*rd	Entre o *e* aberto e o *o* fechado
[ɛ]	g*e*t, b*e*d	Como em p*é*
[ɪ]	*i*t, b*i*g	Mais breve do que em s*i*
[iː]	t*ea*, s*ee*	Como em f*i*no
[ɔ]	h*o*t, w*a*sh	Como em p*ó*
[ɔː]	s*aw*, *a*ll	Como o *o* de p*o*rte
[u]	p*u*t, b*oo*k	Som breve e mais fechado do que em b*u*rro
[uː]	t*oo*, y*ou*	Som aberto como em j*u*ro
[aɪ]	fl*y*, h*igh*	Como em b*ai*le
[au]	h*ow*, h*ou*se	Como em c*au*sa
[ɛə]	th*ere*, b*ear*	Como o *e* de a*e*roporte
[eɪ]	d*ay*, ob*ey*	Como o *ei* de l*ei*
[ɪə]	h*ere*, h*ear*	Como *ia* de companh*ia*
[əu]	g*o*, n*o*te	[ə] seguido de um *u* breve
[ɔɪ]	b*oy*, *oi*l	Como em b*ói*a
[uə]	p*oor*, s*ure*	Como *ua* em s*ua*

Consoantes

	Exemplo Inglés	*Explicação*
[d]	men*ded*	Como em *dado*, an*d*ar
[g]	*g*et, bi*g*	Como em *g*rande
[dʒ]	*g*in, *judge*	Como em ida*d*e
[ŋ]	si*ng*	Como em ci*n*co
[h]	*h*ouse, *h*e	*h* aspirado
[j]	*y*oung, *y*es	Como em *io*gurte
[k]	*c*ome, mo*ck*	Como em *c*ama
[r]	*r*ed, t*r*ead	*r* como em pa*r*a, mas pronunciado no céu da boca
[s]	*s*and, ye*s*	Como em *s*ala
[z]	ro*s*e, *z*ebra	Como em *z*ebra
[ʃ]	*sh*e, ma*ch*ine	Como em *ch*apéu
[tʃ]	*ch*in, ri*ch*	Como *t* em *t*imbre
[w]	*w*ater, *w*hich	Como o *u* em ág*u*a
[ʒ]	vi*s*ion	Como em *j*á
[θ]	*th*ink, my*th*	Sem equivalente, aproximadamente como um *s* pronunciado entre os dentes
[ð]	*th*is, *th*e	Sem equivalente, aproximadamente como um *z* pronunciado entre os dentes

b, f, l, m, n, p, t, v pronunciam-se como em português.

O signo [*] indica que o r final escrito pronuncia-se apenas em inglês britânico, excepto quando a palavra seguinte começa por uma vogal. O signo ['] indica a sílaba acentuada.

EUROPEAN PORTUGUESE

The spelling of European Portuguese differs significantly from that of Brazilian. The differences, which affect consonant groups and accents, follow general patterns but do not on the whole conform to fixed rules. Limited space makes it impossible to cover all European forms in the dictionary text, but major differences in spelling and vocabulary have been included. In addition, the following guide is intended as a broad outline of these differences.

The following orthographic changes are consistent:

Brazilian *gü* and *qü* become European *gu* and *qu*, e.g. ag*ü*entar (BR), ag*u*entar (PT), cinq*ü*enta (BR), cinq*u*enta (PT)
Brazilian *-éia* becomes European *-eia*, e.g. id*éia* (BR), id*eia* (PT)
European spelling links forms of the verb *haver de* with a hyphen, e.g. *hei de* (BR), *hei-de* (PT)
The numbers dez*e*sseis (BR), dez*e*ssete (BR), dez*e*nove (BR) become dez*a*sseis (PT), dez*a*ssete (PT), dez*a*nove (PT)
Adverbial forms of adjectives ending in *m* take double *m* in European spelling, single *m* in Brazilian, e.g. comu*m*ente (BR), comu*mm*ente (PT)
European spelling adds an acute accent to the final *a* in first person plural preterite forms of regular *-ar* verbs to distinguish them from the present tense, e.g. am*a*mos (BR), am*á*mos (PT)
Brazilian co*n*osco becomes European co*nn*osco.

The following changes may take place, but are not consistent:

Consonant changes

Brazilian *c* and *ç* double to *cc* and *cç*, e.g. a*c*ionista (BR), a*cc*ionista (PT), se*ç*ão (BR), se*cç*ão (PT)
Brazilian *t* becomes *ct*, e.g. fa*t*o (BR), fa*ct*o (PT), edi*t*o (BR), edi*ct*o (PT)
European spelling adds *b* to certain words, e.g. sú*d*to (BR), su*bd*ito (PT), su*t*ilizar (BR), su*bt*ilizar (PT)
European spelling changes *ç*, *t* to *pç*, *pt*, e.g. exce*ç*ão (BR), exce*pç*ão (PT), ó*t*ico (BR), ó*pt*ico (PT)
Brazilian *-n-* becomes *-mn-*, e.g. a*n*istia (BR), a*mn*istia (PT)
Brazilian *tr* becomes *t*, e.g. regis*tr*o (BR), regis*t*o (PT)

Accentuation changes

Brazilian *ôo* loses circumflex accent, e.g. v*ôo* (BR), v*oo* (PT)
European spelling changes circumflex accent on *e* and *o* to acute, e.g. t*ê*nis (BR), t*é*nis (PT), abd*ô*men (BR), abd*ó*men (PT)

PORTUGUESE VERB FORMS

1 Gerund. **2** Imperative. **3** Present. **4** Imperfect. **5** Preterite. **6** Future. **7** Present subjunctive. **8** Imperfect subjunctive. **9** Future subjunctive. **10** Past participle. **11** Pluperfect. **12** Personal infinitive.

Etc indicates that the irregular root is used for all persons of the tense, e.g. **ouvir: 7** ouça, ouças, ouça, ouçamos, ouçais, ouçam.

abrir 10 aberto
acudir 2 acode **3** acudo, acodes, acode, acodem
aderir 3 adiro **7** adira
aduzir 2 aduz **3** aduzo, aduzes, aduz
advertir 3 advirto **7** advirta *etc*
agir 3 ajo **7** aja *etc*
agradecer 3 agradeço **7** agradeça *etc*
agredir 2 agride **3** agrido, agrides, agride, agridem **7** agrida *etc*
AMAR 1 amando **2** ama, amai **3** amo, amas, ama, amamos, amais, amam **4** amava, amavas, amava, amávamos, amáveis, amavam **5** amei, amaste, amou, amamos (*PT*: amá-), amastes, amaram **6** amarei, amarás, amará, amaremos, amareis, amarão **7** ame, ames, ame, amemos, ameis, amem **8** amasse, amasses, amasse, amássemos, amásseis, amassem **9** amar, amares, amar, ámarmos, amardes, amarem **10** amado **11** amara, amaras, amara, amáramos, amáreis, amaram **12** amar, amares, amar, amarmos, amardes, amarem
ansiar 2 anseia **3** anseio, anseias, anseia, anseiam **7** anseie *etc*
aprazer 2 apraz **3** aprazo, aprazes, apraz **5** aprouve *etc* **8** aprouvesse *etc* **9** aprouver *etc* **11** aprouvera *etc*
apreçar 7 aprece *etc*
arrancar 7 arranque *etc*
arruinar 2 arruína **3** arruíno, arruínas, arruína, arruínam **7** arruíne, arruínes, arruíne, arruínem
aspergir 3 aspirjo **7** aspirja *etc*
averiguar 7 averigúe, avergúes, averigúe, averigúem
boiar 2 bóia, bóias, bóia, bóiam **7** bóie, bóies, bóie, bóiem
bulir 2 bole **3** bulo, boles, bole, bolem
caber 3 caibo **5** coube *etc* **7** caiba *etc* **8** coubesse *etc* **9** couber *etc*
cair 2 cai **3** caio, cais, cai, caímos, caís, caem **4** caía *etc* **5** caí, caíste **7** caia *etc* **8** caísse *etc*
cobrir 3 cubro **7** cubra *etc* **10** coberto
colorir 3 coluro **7** colura *etc*
compelir 3 compilo **7** compila *etc*
crer 2 crê **3** creio, crês, crê, cremos, credes, crêem **5** cri, creste, creu, cremos, crestes, creram **7** creia *etc*
cuspir 2 cospe **3** cuspo, cospes, cospe, cospem
dar 2 dá **3** dou, dás, dá, damos, dais, dão **5** dei, deste, deu, demos, destes, deram **7** dê, dês, dê, demos, deis, dêem **8** desse *etc* **9** der *etc* **11** dera *etc*
denegrir 2 denigre **3** denigro, denigres, denigre, denigrem **7** denigra *etc*
despir 3 dispo **7** dispa *etc*
dizer 2 diz (dize) **3** digo, dizes, diz, dizemos, dizeis, dizem **5** disse *etc* **6** direi *etc* **7** diga *etc* **8** dissesse *etc* **9** disser *etc* **10** dito
doer 2 dói **3** dôo (*BR*), doo (*PT*), dóis, dói
dormir 3 durmo **7** durma *etc*
escrever 10 escrito
ESTAR 2 está **3** estou, estás, está, estamos, estais, estão **4** estava *etc* **5** estive, estiveste, esteve, estivemos, estivestes, estiveram **7** esteja *etc* **8** estivesse *etc* **9** estiver *etc* **11** estivera *etc*
extorquir 3 exturco **7** exturca *etc*
FAZER 3 faço **5** fiz, fizeste, fez, fizemos, fizestes, fizeram **6** farei *etc* **7** faça *etc* **8** fizesse *etc* **9** fizer *etc* **10** feito **11** fizera *etc*
ferir 3 firo **7** fira *etc*
flectir 3 flito **7** flita *etc*
fluir 3 fluo, fluis, flui, fluímos, fluís, fluem
fremir 3 frimo **7** frima *etc*
fruir 3 fruo, fruis, frui, fruímos, fruís, fruem
fugir 2 foge **3** fujo, foges, foge, fogem, fogem **7** fuja *etc*
ganhar 10 ganho
gastar 10 gasto
gerir 3 giro **7** gira *etc*
haver 2 há **3** hei, hás, há, havemos, haveis, hão **4** havia *etc* **5** houve, houveste, houve, houvemos, houvestes, houveram **7** haja *etc* **8** houvesse *etc* **9** houver *etc* **11** houvera *etc*
ir 1 indo **2** vai **3** vou, vais, vai, vamos, ides, vão **4** ia *etc* **5** fui, foste, foi, fomos, fostes, foram **7** vá, vás, vá, vamos, vades, vão **8** fosse, fosses, fosse, fôssemos, fôsseis, fossem **9** for *etc* **10** ido **11** fora *etc*
jazar 3 jazo, jazes, jaz
ler 2 lê **3** leio, lês, lê, lemos, ledes, lêem **5** li, leste, leu, lemos, lestes, leram **7** leia *etc*
medir 3 meço **7** meça *etc*
mentir 3 minto **7** minta *etc*
ouvir 3 ouço **7** ouça *etc*

pagar 10 pago
parar 2 pára **3** paro, paras, pára
parir 3 pairo **7** paira *etc*
pecar 7 peque *etc*
pedir 3 peço **7** peça *etc*
perder 3 perco **7** perca *etc*
poder 3 pesso **5** pude, pudeste, pôde, pudemos, pudestes, puderam **7** possa *etc* **8** pudesse *etc* **9** puder *etc* **11** pudera *etc*
polir 2 pule **3** pulo, pules, pule, pulem **7** pula *etc*
pôr 1 pondo **2** põe **3** ponho, pões, põe, pomos, pondes, põem **4** punha *etc* **5** pus, puseste, pôs, pusemos, pusestes, puseram **6** porei *etc* **7** ponha *etc* **8** pusesse *etc* **9** puser *etc* **10** posto **11** pusera *etc*
preferir 3 prefiro **7** prefire *etc*
premir 2 prime **3** primo, primes, prime, primem **7** prima *etc*
prevenir 2 previne **3** previno, prevines, previne, previnem **7** previna *etc*
prover 2 provê **3** provejo, provês, provê, provemos, provedes, provêem **5** provi, proveste, proveu, provemos, provestes, proveram **7** proveja *etc* **8** provesse *etc* **9** prover *etc*
provir 2 provém **3** provenho, provéns, provém, provimos, provindes, provêm **4** provinha *etc* **5** provim, provieste, proveio, proviemos, proviestes, provieram **7** provenha *etc* **8** proviesse *etc* **9** provier **10** provindo **11** proviera *etc*
querer 3 quero, queres, quer **5** quis, quiseste, quis, quisemos, quisestes, quiseram **7** queira *etc* **8** quisesse *etc* **9** quiser *etc* **11** quisera *etc*
repetir 3 repito **7** repita *etc*
requerer 3 requeiro, requeres, requer **7** requeira *etc*
retorquir 3 returco **7** returca *etc*
reunir 2 reúne **3** reúno, reúnes, reúne, reúnem **7** reúna *etc*
rir 2 ri **3** rio, ris, ri, rimos, rides, riem **5** ri, riste, riu, rimos, ristes, riram **7** ria *etc*
saber 3 sei, sabes, sabe, sabemos, sabeis, sabem **5** soube, soubeste, soube, soubemos, soubestes, souberam **7** saiba *etc* **8** soubesse *etc* **9** souber *etc* **11** soubera *etc*
seguir 3 sigo **7** siga *etc*
sentir 3 sinto **7** sinta *etc*
ser 2 sê **3** sou, és, é, somos, sois, são **4** era *etc* **5** fui, foste, foi, fomos, fostes, foram **7** seja *etc* **8** fosse *etc* **9** for *etc* **11** fora *etc*
servir 3 sirvo **7** sirva *etc*
subir 2 sobe **3** subo, sobes, sobe, sobem
suster 2 sustém **3** sustenho, sustens, sustém, sustendes, sustêm **5** sustive, sustiveste, susteve, sustivemos, sustivestes, sustiveram **7** sustenha *etc*
ter 2 tem **3** tenho, tens, tem, temos, tendes, têm **4** tinha *etc* **5** tive, tiveste, teve, tivemos, tivestes, tiveram **6** terei *etc* **7** tenha *etc* **8** tivesse *etc* **8** tiver *etc* **11** tivera *etc*
torcer 3 torço **7** torça *etc*
tossir 3 tusso **7** tussa *etc*
trair 2 trai **3** traio, trais, trai, traímos, traís, traem **7** traia *etc*
trazer 2 (traze) traz **3** trago, trazes, traz **5** trouxe, trouxeste, trouxe, trouxemos, trouxestes, trouxeram **6** trarei *etc* **7** traga *etc* **8** trouxesse *etc* **9** trouxer *etc* **11** trouxera *etc*
UNIR 1 unindo **2** une, uni **3** uno, unes, une, unimos, unis, unem **4** unia, unias, unia, uníamos, uníeis, uniam **5** uni, uniste, uniu, unimos, unistes, uniram **6** unirei, unirás, unirá, uniremos, unireis, unirão **7** una, unas, una, unamos, unais, unam **8** unisse, unisses, unisse, uníssemos, unísseis, unissem **9** unir, unires, unir, unirmos, unirdes, unirem **10** unido **11** unira, uniras, unira, uníramos, uníreis, uniram **12** unir, unires, unir, unirmos, unirdes, unirem
valer 3 valho **7** valha *etc*
ver 2 vê **3** vejo, vês, vê, vemos, vedes, vêem **4** via *etc* **5** vi, viste, viu, vimos, vistes, viram **7** veja *etc* **8** visse *etc* **9** vir *etc* **10** visto **11** vira
vir 1 vindo **2** vem **3** venho, vens, vem, vimos, vindes, vêm **4** vinha *etc* **5** vim, vieste, veio, viemos, viestes, vieram **7** venha *etc* **8** viesse *etc* **9** vier *etc* **10** vindo **11** viera *etc*
VIVER 1 vivendo **2** vive, vivei **3** vivo, vives, vive, vivemos, viveis, vivem **4** vivia, vivias, vivia, vivíamos, vivíeis, viviam **5** vivi, viveste, viveu, vivemos, vivestes, viveram **6** viverei, viverás, viverá, viveremos, vivereis, viverão **7** viva, vivas, viva, vivamos, vivais, vivam **8** vivesse, vivesses, vivesse, vivêssemos, vivêsseis, vivessem **9** viver, viveres, viver, vivermos, viverdes, viverem **10** vivido **11** vivera, viveras, vivera, vivêramos, vivêreis, viveram **12** viver, viveres, viver, vivermos, viverdes, viverem

VERBOS INGLESES

present	pt	pp
arise (arising)	arose	arisen
awake (awaking)	awoke	awaked
be (am, is, are, being)	was, were	been
bear	bore	born(e)
beat	beat	beaten
become (becoming)	became	become
befall	befell	befallen
begin (beginning)	began	begun
behold	beheld	beheld
bend	bent	bent
beseech	besought	besought
beset (besetting)	beset	beset
bet (betting)	bet (*also* betted)	bet (*also* betted)
bid (bidding)	bid (*also* bade)	bid (*also* bidden)
bind	bound	bound
bite (biting)	bit	bitten
bleed	bled	bled
blow	blew	blown
break	broke	broken
breed	bred	bred
bring	brought	brought
build	built	built
burn	burnt (*also* burned)	burnt (*also* burned)
burst	burst	burst
buy	bought	bought
can	could	(been able)
cast	cast	cast
catch	caught	caught
choose (choosing)	chose	chosen
cling	clung	clung
come (coming)	came	come
cost	cost	cost
creep	crept	crept
cut (cutting)	cut	cut
deal	dealt	dealt
dig (digging)	dug	dug
do (3rd person: he/she/it/does)	did	done
draw	drew	drawn
dream	dreamed (*also* dreamt)	dreamed *also* dreamt)
drink	drank	drunk
drive (driving)	drove	driven
dwell	dwelt	dwelt

present	pt	pp
eat	ate	eaten
fall	fell	fallen
feed	fed	fed
feel	felt	felt
fight	fought	fought
find	found	found
flee	fled	fled
fling	flung	flung
fly (flies)	flew	flown
forbid (forbidding)	forbade	forbidden
forecast	forecast	forecast
forego	forewent	foregone
foresee	foresaw	foreseen
foretell	foretold	foretold
forget (forgetting)	forgot	forgotten
forgive (forgiving)	forgave	forgiven
forsake (forsaking)	forsook	forsaken
freeze (freezing)	froze	frozen
get (getting)	got	got, (*US*) gotten
give (giving)	gave	given
go (goes)	went	gone
grind	ground	ground
grow	grew	grown
hang	hung (*also* hanged)	hung (*also* hanged)
have (has; having)	had	had
hear	heard	heard
hide (hiding)	hid	hidden
hit (hitting)	hit	hit
hold	held	held
hurt	hurt	hurt
keep	kept	kept
kneel	knelt (*also* kneeled)	knelt (*also* kneeled)
know	knew	known
lay	laid	laid
lead	led	led
lean	leant (*also* leaned)	leant (*also* leaned)
leap	leapt (*also* leaped)	leapt (*also* leaped)
learn	learnt (*also* learned)	learnt (*also* learned)
leave (leaving)	left	left
lend	lent	lent
let (letting)	let	let
lie (lying)	lay	lain
light	lit (*also* lighted)	lit (*also* lighted)
lose (losing)	lost	lost

present	pt	pp	present	pt	pp
make (making)	made	made	**spell**	spelt (*also* spelled)	spelt (*also* spelled)
may	might	—	**spend**	spent	spent
mean	meant	meant	**spill**	spilt (*also* spilled)	spilt (*also* spilled)
meet	met	met	**spin (spinning)**	spun	spun
mistake (mistaking)	mistook	mistaken	**spit (spitting)**	spat	spat
mow	mowed	mown (*also* mowed)	**split (splitting)**	split	split
must	(had to)	(had to)	**spoil**	spoiled (*also* spoilt)	spoiled (*also* spoilt)
pay	paid	paid	**spread**	spread	spread
put (putting)	put	put	**spring**	sprang	sprung
quit (quitting)	quit (*also* quitted)	quit (*also* quitted)	**stand**	stood	stood
read	read	read	**steal**	stole	stolen
rend	rent	rent	**stick**	stuck	stuck
rid (ridding)	rid	rid	**sting**	stung	stung
ride (riding)	rode	ridden	**stink**	stank	stunk
ring	rang	rung	**stride (striding)**	strode	stridden
rise (rising)	rose	risen	**strike (striking)**	struck	struck (*also* stricken)
run (running)	ran	run	**strive (striving)**	strove	striven
saw	sawed	sawn	**swear**	swore	sworn
say	said	said	**sweep**	swept	swept
see	saw	seen	**swell**	swelled	swollen (*also* swelled)
seek	sought	sought	**swim (swimming)**	swam	swum
sell	sold	sold	**swing**	swung	swung
send	sent	sent	**take (taking)**	took	taken
set (setting)	set	set	**teach**	taught	taught
shake (shaking)	shook	shaken	**tear**	tore	torn
shall	should	—	**tell**	told	told
shear	sheared	shorn (*also* sheared)	**think**	thought	thought
shed (shedding)	shed	shed	**throw**	threw	thrown
shine (shining)	shone	shone	**thrust**	thrust	thrust
shoot	shot	shot	**tread**	trod	trodden
show	showed	shown	**wake (waking)**	woke (*also* waked)	woken (*also* waked)
shrink	shrank	shrunk	**waylay**	waylaid	waylaid
shut (shutting)	shut	shut	**wear**	wore	worn
sing	sang	sung	**weave (weaving)**	wove (*also* weaved)	woven (*also* weaved)
sink	sank	sunk	**wed (wedding)**	wedded (*also* wed)	wedded (*also* wed)
sit (sitting)	sat	sat	**weep**	wept	wept
slay	slew	slain	**win (winning)**	won	won
sleep	slept	slept	**wind**	wound	wound
slide (sliding)	slid	slid	**withdraw**	withdrew	withdrawn
sling	slung	slung	**withhold**	withheld	withheld
slit (slitting)	slit	slit	**withstand**	withstood	withstood
smell	smelled, (*BRIT*) smelt	smelled, (*BRIT*) smelt	**wring**	wrung	wrung
sow	sowed	sown (*also* sowed)	**write (writing)**	wrote	written
speak	spoke	spoken			
speed	sped (*also* speeded)	sped (*also* speeded)			

NÚMEROS — NUMBERS

um (uma)*	**1**	one
dois (duas)*	**2**	two
três	**3**	three
quatro	**4**	four
cinco	**5**	five
seis	**6**	six
sete	**7**	seven
oito	**8**	eight
nove	**9**	nine
dez	**10**	ten
onze	**11**	eleven
doze	**12**	twelve
treze	**13**	thirteen
catorze	**14**	fourteen
quinze	**15**	fifteen
dezesseis (*BR*), dezasseis (*PT*)	**16**	sixteen
dezessete (*BR*), dezassete (*PT*)	**17**	seventeen
dezoito	**18**	eighteen
dezenove (*BR*), dezanove (*PT*)	**19**	nineteen
vinte	**20**	twenty
vinte e um (uma)*	**21**	twenty-one
trinta	**30**	thirty
quarenta	**40**	forty
cinqüenta (*BR*), cinquenta (*PT*)	**50**	fifty
sessenta	**60**	sixty
setenta	**70**	seventy
oitenta	**80**	eighty
noventa	**90**	ninety
cem (cento)**	**100**	a hundred
cem e um (uma)*	**101**	a hundred and one
duzentos/as*	**200**	two hundred
trezentos/as*	**300**	three hundred
quinhentos/as*	**500**	five hundred
mil	**1 000**	a thousand
un milhão	**1 000 000**	a million

primeiro/a, 1º/1ª	first, 1st	trigésimo/a	thirtieth
segundo/a, 2º/2ª	second, 2nd	quadragésimo/a	fortieth
terceiro/a, 3º/3ª	third, 3rd	qüinquagésimo/a (*BR*), quinquagésimo/a (*PT*)	fiftieth
quarto/a, 4º/4ª	fourth, 4th	sexagésimo/a	sixtieth
quinto/a	fifth	setuagésimo/a (*BR*), septuagésimo/a (*PT*)	seventieth
sexto/a	sixth	octagésimo/a	eightieth
sétimo/a	seventh	nonagésimo/a	ninetieth
oitavo/a	eighth	centésimo/a	hundredth
nono/a	ninth	milésimo/a	thousandth
décimo/a	tenth		
décimo primeiro/a	eleventh		
vigésimo/a	twentieth		

* "um" *etc*, "dois" *etc* and the hundreds (duzentos *etc*) agree in gender with their noun: trinta e uma pessoas. NB: 2 000 is **duas** mil before a feminine noun.

** "cem" is used when not followed by a lower number: cem mil, cem mulheres *etc*; "cento e" is used when a lower follows: cento e vinte dias.

ENGLISH-PORTUGUESE
INGLÊS-PORTUGUÊS

A

A, a [eɪ] *n* (*letter*) A, a *m*; (*MUS*): **A** lá *m*; **A for Andrew** (*BRIT*) *or* **Able** (*US*) A de Antônio; **A road** (*BRIT*: *AUT*) via expressa; **A shares** (*BRIT*: *STOCK EXCHANGE*) ações *fpl* preferenciais.

a [eɪ, ə] (*before vowel or silent h*: **an**) *indef art* um(a); **an apple** uma maçã; **I haven't got ~ car** não tenho carro; **he's ~ doctor** ele é médico; **3 a day/week** 3 por dia/semana; **10 km an hour** 10 km por hora.

a. *abbr* = **acre**.

AA *n abbr* (*BRIT*: = *Automobile Association*) ≈ TCB *m* (*BR*), ≈ ACP *m* (*PT*); (*US*: = *Associate in/of Arts*) *título universitário*; (= *Alcoholics Anonymous*) AA *m*; (= *anti-aircraft*) AA.

AAA *n abbr* (= *American Automobile Association*) ≈ TCB *m* (*BR*), ≈ ACP *m* (*PT*); (*BRIT*) = **Amateur Athletics Association**.

AAUP *n abbr* (= *American Association of University Professors*) *sindicato universitário*.

AB *abbr* (*BRIT*) = **able-bodied seaman**; (*CANADA*) = **Alberta**.

aback [ə'bæk] *adv*: **to be taken ~** ficar surpreendido, sobressaltar-se.

abaci ['æbəsaɪ] *npl of* **abacus**.

abacus ['æbəkəs] (*pl* **abaci**) *n* ábaco.

abandon [ə'bændən] *vt* abandonar ♦ *n* desenfreamento; **to ~ ship** abandonar o navio.

abandoned [ə'bændənd] *adj* (*child, house*) abandonado; (*unrestrained*) desenfreado.

abase [ə'beɪs] *vt*: **to ~ o.s. (so far as to do)** rebaixar-se (até o ponto de fazer).

abashed [ə'bæʃt] *adj* envergonhado.

abate [ə'beɪt] *vi* (*lessen*) diminuir; (*calm down*) acalmar-se.

abatement [ə'beɪtmənt] *n see* **noise**.

abattoir ['æbətwɑ:*] (*BRIT*) *n* matadouro.

abbey ['æbɪ] *n* abadia, mosteiro.

abbot ['æbət] *n* abade *m*.

abbreviate [ə'bri:vɪeɪt] *vt* abreviar.

abbreviation [əbri:vɪ'eɪʃən] *n* (*short form*) abreviatura; (*act*) abreviação *f*.

ABC *n abbr* (= *American Broadcasting Company*) *rede de televisão*.

abdicate ['æbdɪkeɪt] *vt* abdicar, renunciar a ♦ *vi* abdicar, renunciar ao trono.

abdication [æbdɪ'keɪʃən] *n* abdicação *f*.

abdomen ['æbdəmən] *n* abdômen *m*.

abdominal [æb'dɔmɪnl] *adj* abdominal.

abduct [æb'dʌkt] *vt* seqüestrar.

abduction [æb'dʌkʃən] *n* seqüestro.

Aberdonian [æbə'dəunɪən] *adj* de Aberdeen ♦ *n* natural *m/f* de Aberdeen.

aberration [æbə'reɪʃən] *n* aberração *f*; **in a moment of mental ~** num momento de desatino.

abet [ə'bɛt] *vt see* **aid**.

abeyance [ə'beɪəns] *n*: **in ~** (*law*) em desuso; (*matter*) suspenso.

abhor [əb'hɔ:*] *vt* detestar, odiar.

abhorrent [əb'hɔrənt] *adj* detestável, repugnante.

abide [ə'baɪd] *vt* agüentar, suportar.

abide by *vt fus* (*promise, word*) cumprir; (*law, rules*) ater-se a.

ability [ə'bɪlɪtɪ] *n* habilidade *f*, capacidade *f*; (*talent*) talento; **to the best of my ~** o melhor que eu puder *or* pudesse.

abject ['æbdʒɛkt] *adj* (*poverty*) miserável; (*coward*) desprezível, vil; **an ~ apology** um pedido de desculpa humilde.

ablaze [ə'bleɪz] *adj* em chamas; **~ with light** resplandecente.

able ['eɪbl] *adj* capaz; (*skilled*) hábil, competente; **to be ~ to do sth** poder fazer alguma coisa.

able-bodied [-'bɔdɪd] *adj* são/sã; **~ seaman** (*BRIT*) marinheiro experimentado.

ably ['eɪblɪ] *adv* habilmente.

ABM *n abbr* = **anti-ballistic missile**.

abnormal [æb'nɔ:məl] *adj* anormal.

abnormality [æbnɔ:'mælɪtɪ] *n* anormalidade *f*.

aboard [ə'bɔ:d] *adv* a bordo ♦ *prep* a bordo de; (*train*) dentro de.

abode [ə'bəud] *n* (*old*) residência, domicílio; (*LAW*): **of no fixed ~** sem domicílio fixo.

abolish [ə'bɔlɪʃ] *vt* abolir.

abolition [æbə'lɪʃən] *n* abolição *f*.

abominable [ə'bɔmɪnəbl] *adj* abominável, detestável.

aborigine [æbə'rɪdʒɪnɪ] *n* aborígene *m/f*.

abort [ə'bɔ:t] *vt* abortar.

abortion [ə'bɔ:ʃən] *n* aborto; **to have an ~** fazer um aborto.

abortive [ə'bɔ:tɪv] *adj* (*failed*) fracassado; (*fruitless*) inútil.

abound [ə'baund] *vi*: **to ~ (in)** abundar (em).

about [ə'baut] *prep* (*subject*) acerca de, sobre; (*place*) em redor de, por ♦ *adv* mais ou menos; **do something ~ it!** faça alguma coisa!; **it takes ~ 10 hours** leva mais ou menos 10 horas; **at ~ 2 o'clock** aproximadamente às duas; **it's just ~ finished** está quase

***NB:** European Portuguese adds the following consonants to certain words:* **b** (sú(b)dito, su(b)til); **c** (a(c)ção, a(c)cionista, a(c)to); **m** (inde(m)ne); **p** (ado(p)ção, ado(p)tar); *for further details see p. xiii.*

terminado; **is Paul ~?** (*BRIT*) o Paulo está por aí?; **it's the other way ~** (*BRIT*) está pelo avesso; **it's ~ here** é por aqui; **to walk ~ the town** andar pela cidade; **to run ~** (*BRIT*) correr por todos os lados; **they left all their things lying ~** eles deixaram suas coisas espalhadas por toda parte; **to be ~ to** estar a ponto de; **I'm not ~ to do all that for nothing** (*inf*) não estou disposto a fazer tudo isso de graça; **what** *or* **how ~ doing this?** que tal se fizermos isso?

about face *n* (*MIL*) meia-volta; (*fig*) reviravolta.

about turn *n* (*MIL*) meia-volta; (*fig*) reviravolta.

above [ə'bʌv] *adv* em/por cima, acima ♦ *prep* acima de, por cima de; **mentioned ~** acima mencionado; **costing ~ £10** que custa mais de £10; **~ all** sobretudo.

aboveboard [ə'bʌv'bɔːd] *adj* legítimo, limpo.

abrasion [ə'breɪʒən] *n* (*on skin*) esfoladura.

abrasive [ə'breɪzɪv] *adj* abrasivo; (*fig*) cáustico, mordaz.

abreast [ə'brɛst] *adv* lado a lado; **to keep ~ of** estar a par de.

abridge [ə'brɪdʒ] *vt* resumir, abreviar.

abroad [ə'brɔːd] *adv* (*to be*) no estrangeiro; (*to go*) ao estrangeiro; **there is a rumour ~ that ...** (*fig*) corre o boato de que ....

abrupt [ə'brʌpt] *adj* (*sudden*) brusco, inesperado; (*gruff*) áspero.

abruptly [ə'brʌptlɪ] *adv* bruscamente.

abscess ['æbsɪs] *n* abscesso (*BR*), abcesso (*PT*).

abscond [əb'skɔnd] *vi* fugir, sumir.

absence ['æbsəns] *n* ausência; **in the ~ of** (*person*) na ausência de; (*thing*) na falta de.

absent ['æbsənt] *adj* ausente; **~ without leave** ausente sem permissão oficial; **to be ~** faltar.

absentee [æbsən'tiː] *n* ausente *m/f*.

absenteeism [æbsən'tiːɪzəm] *n* absenteísmo.

absent-minded *adj* distraído.

absent-mindedness [-'maɪndɪdnɪs] *n* distração *f*.

absolute ['æbsəluːt] *adj* absoluto.

absolutely [æbsə'luːtlɪ] *adv* absolutamente; **oh, yes, ~!** claro que sim!

absolve [əb'zɔlv] *vt*: **to ~ sb (from)** (*sin etc*) absolver alguém (de); **to ~ sb from** (*oath*) desobrigar alguém de.

absorb [əb'zɔːb] *vt* absorver; **to be ~ed in a book** estar absorvido num livro.

absorbent [əb'zɔːbənt] *adj* absorvente.

absorbent cotton (*US*) *n* algodão *m* hidrófilo.

absorbing [əb'zɔːbɪŋ] *adj* (*book, film etc*) absorvente, cativante.

absorption [əb'zɔːpʃən] *n* absorção *f*.

abstain [əb'steɪn] *vi*: **to ~ (from)** abster-se (de).

abstemious [əb'stiːmɪəs] *adj* abstinente.

abstention [əb'stɛnʃən] *n* abstenção *f*.

abstinence ['æbstɪnəns] *n* abstinência, sobriedade *f*.

abstract [*adj, n* 'æbstrækt, *vt* æb'strækt] *adj* abstrato ♦ *n* resumo ♦ *vt* (*remove*) abstrair; (*summarize*) resumir; (*steal*) surripiar.

absurd [əb'səːd] *adj* absurdo.

absurdity [əb'səːdɪtɪ] *n* absurdo.

ABTA ['æbtə] *n abbr* = **Association of British Travel Agents.**

Abu Dhabi ['æbuː'dɑːbɪ] *n* Abu Dabi (*no article*).

abundance [ə'bʌndəns] *n* abundância.

abundant [ə'bʌndənt] *adj* abundante.

abuse [*n* ə'bjuːs, *vt* ə'bjuːz] *n* (*insults*) insultos *mpl*, injúrias *fpl*; (*misuse*) abuso ♦ *vt* (*ill-treat*) maltratar; (*take advantage of*) abusar de; **open to ~** aberto ao abuso.

abusive [ə'bjuːsɪv] *adj* ofensivo.

abysmal [ə'bɪzməl] *adj* (*ignorance*) profundo, total; (*very bad*) péssimo.

abyss [ə'bɪs] *n* abismo.

AC *n abbr* (*US*) = **athletic club** ♦ *abbr* (= *alternating current*) CA.

a/c *abbr* (*BANKING etc*: = *account*) c/.

academic [ækə'dɛmɪk] *adj* acadêmico, universitário; (*pej*: *issue*) teórico ♦ *n* universitário/a; **~ freedom** liberdade de cátedra.

academic year *n* ano letivo.

academy [ə'kædəmɪ] *n* (*learned body*) academia; (*school*) instituto, academia, colégio; **military/naval ~** academia militar/escola naval; **~ of music** conservatório.

ACAS ['eɪkæs] (*BRIT*) *n abbr* (= *Advisory, Conciliation and Arbitration Service*) ≈ Justiça do Trabalho.

accede [æk'siːd] *vi*: **to ~ to** (*request*) consentir em, aceder a; (*throne*) subir a.

accelerate [æk'sɛləreɪt] *vt* acelerar ♦ *vi* apressar-se.

acceleration [æksɛlə'reɪʃən] *n* aceleração *f*.

accelerator [æk'sɛləreɪtə*] *n* acelerador *m*.

accent ['æksɛnt] *n* (*stress, written*) acento; (*pronunciation*) sotaque *m*.

accentuate [æk'sɛntjueɪt] *vt* (*syllable*) acentuar; (*need, difference etc*) ressaltar, salientar.

accept [ək'sɛpt] *vt* aceitar.

acceptable [ək'sɛptəbl] *adj* aceitável.

acceptance [ək'sɛptəns] *n* aceitação *f*; **to meet with general ~** ter aprovação geral.

access ['æksɛs] *n* acesso ♦ *vt* (*COMPUT*) acessar; **to have ~ to** ter acesso a; **the burglars gained ~ through a window** os ladrões conseguiram entrar por uma janela.

accessible [æk'sɛsəbl] *adj* acessível.

accession [æk'sɛʃən] *n* acessão *f*; (*of king*) elevação *f* ao trono; (*to library*) aquisição *f*.

accessory [æk'sɛsərɪ] *n* acessório; **toilet accessories** (*BRIT*) artigos de toalete.

access road *n* via de acesso.

access time *n* (*COMPUT*) tempo de acesso.

accident ['æksɪdənt] *n* acidente *m*; (*chance*) casualidade *f*; **to meet with** *or* **have an ~** sofrer *or* ter um acidente; **~s at work** acidentes de trabalho; **by ~** (*unintentionally*) sem querer; (*by coincidence*) por acaso.

accidental [æksɪ'dɛntl] *adj* acidental.

accidentally [æksɪ'dɛntəlɪ] *adv* (*by accident*) sem querer; (*by chance*) casualmente.
accident insurance *n* seguro contra acidentes.
accident-prone *adj* com tendência para sofrer *or* causar acidente, desastrado.
acclaim [ə'kleɪm] *vt* aclamar ♦ *n* aclamação *f*.
acclamation [æklə'meɪʃən] *n* (*approval*) aclamação *f*; (*applause*) aplausos *mpl*.
acclimate [ə'klaɪmət] (*US*) *vt* = **acclimatize.**
acclimatize [ə'klaɪmətaɪz] (*BRIT*) *vt*: **to become ~d** aclimatar-se.
accolade ['ækəleɪd] *n* louvor *m*, honra.
accommodate [ə'kɔmədeɪt] *vt* alojar, hospedar; (*reconcile*) conciliar; (*oblige, help*) comprazer a; (*adapt*): **to ~ one's plans to** acomodar seus projetos a; **this car ~s 4 people** este carro tem lugar para 4 pessoas.
accommodating [ə'kɔmədeɪtɪŋ] *adj* complacente, serviçal.
accommodation [əkɔmə'deɪʃən] (*BRIT*) *n* alojamento; (*space*) lugar *m* (*BR*), sítio (*PT*); **he's found ~** ele já encontrou um lugar para morar; **"~ to let"** "aluga-se (apartamento *etc*)"; **they have ~ for 500** têm lugar para 500 pessoas; **seating ~** lugares *mpl* sentados.
accommodations [əkɔmə'deɪʃənz] (*US*) *npl* = **accommodation.**
accompaniment [ə'kʌmpənɪmənt] *n* acompanhamento.
accompanist [ə'kʌmpənɪst] *n* acompanhador(a) *m/f*, acompanhante *m/f*.
accompany [ə'kʌmpənɪ] *vt* acompanhar.
accomplice [ə'kʌmplɪs] *n* cúmplice *m/f*.
accomplish [ə'kʌmplɪʃ] *vt* (*achieve*) realizar, levar a cabo.
accomplished [ə'kʌmplɪʃt] *adj* ilustre, talentoso.
accomplishment [ə'kʌmplɪʃmənt] *n* (*bringing about*) realização *f*; (*achievement*) proeza; **~s** *npl* (*skills*) talentos *mpl*.
accord [ə'kɔːd] *n* acordo ♦ *vt* conceder; **of his own ~** por sua iniciativa; **with one ~** de comum acordo.
accordance [ə'kɔːdəns] *n*: **in ~ with** de acordo com, conforme.
according [ə'kɔːdɪŋ]: **~ to** *prep* segundo; (*in accordance with*) conforme; **~ to plan** como previsto.
accordingly [ə'kɔːdɪŋlɪ] *adv* (*thus*) por conseguinte, conseqüentemente.
accordion [ə'kɔːdɪən] *n* acordeão *m*.
accost [ə'kɔst] *vt* abordar.
account [ə'kaunt] *n* (*COMM*) conta; (*report*) relato; **~s** *npl* (*books, department*) contabilidade *f*; **"~ payee only"** (*BRIT*) "cheque não endossável" (*a ser creditado na conta do favorecido*); **to keep an ~ of** anotar, registrar; **to bring sb to ~ for sth/for having done sth** chamar alguém a contas por algo/por ter feito algo; **by all ~s** segundo dizem todos; **of little ~** sem importância; **on his own ~** por sua conta; **to pay £5 on ~** pagar £5 por conta; **to buy sth on ~** comprar algo a crédito; **on no ~** de modo nenhum; **on ~ of** por causa de; **to take into ~, take ~ of** levar em conta.
account for *vt fus* prestar contas de; **all the children were ~ed for** nenhuma das crianças faltava; **4 people are still not ~ed for** 4 pessoas ainda não foram encontradas.
accountability [əkauntə'bɪlɪtɪ] *n* responsabilidade *f*.
accountable [ə'kauntəbl] *adj* responsavel.
accountancy [ə'kauntənsɪ] *n* contabilidade *f*.
accountant [ə'kauntənt] *n* contador(a) *m/f* (*BR*), contabilista *m/f* (*PT*).
accounting [ə'kauntɪŋ] *n* contabilidade *f*.
accounting period *n* exercício.
account number *n* número de conta.
account payable *n* conta a pagar.
account receivable *n* conta a receber.
accredited [ə'krɛdɪtɪd] *adj* (*person*) autorizado.
accretion [ə'kriːʃən] *n* acresção *f*.
accrue [ə'kruː] *vi* aumentar; (*mount up*) acumular-se; **to ~ to** advir a; **~d interest** juros *mpl* acumulados.
accumulate [ə'kjuːmjuleɪt] *vt* acumular, amontoar ♦ *vi* acumular-se.
accumulation [əkjuːmju'leɪʃən] *n* acumulação *f*.
accuracy ['ækjurəsɪ] *n* exatidão *f*, precisão *f*.
accurate ['ækjurɪt] *adj* (*number*) exato; (*answer*) correto; (*shot*) certeiro.
accurately ['ækjurətlɪ] *adv* com precisão.
accusation [ækju'zeɪʃən] *n* acusação *f*.
accusative [ə'kjuːzətɪv] *n* (*LING*) acusativo.
accuse [ə'kjuːz] *vt* acusar.
accused [ə'kjuːzd] *n* acusado/a.
accustom [ə'kʌstəm] *vt* acostumar; **to ~ o.s. to sth** acostumar-se a algo.
accustomed [ə'kʌstəmd] *adj* (*usual*) habitual; **~ to** acostumado a.
AC/DC *abbr* (= *alternating current/direct current*) CA/CC.
ACE [eɪs] *n abbr* = **American Council on Education.**
ace [eɪs] *n* ás *m*; **to be** *or* **come within an ~ of doing** (*BRIT*) não fazer por um triz.
acerbic [ə'səːbɪk] *adj* (*also fig*) acerbo.
acetate ['æsɪteɪt] *n* acetato.
ache [eɪk] *n* dor *f* ♦ *vi* doer; (*yearn*): **to ~ to do sth** ansiar por fazer algo; **I've got (a) stomach ~** eu estou com dor de barriga; **my head ~s** dói-me a cabeça; **I'm aching all over** estou todo dolorido.
achieve [ə'tʃiːv] *vt* (*reach*) alcançar; (*realize*) realizar; (*victory, success*) obter.
achievement [ə'tʃiːvmənt] *n* (*of aims*) realização *f*; (*success*) proeza.
acid ['æsɪd] *adj* ácido; (*bitter*) azedo ♦ *n* ácido.
acidity [ə'sɪdɪtɪ] *n* acidez *f*.
acid rain *n* chuva ácida.

***NB:** European Portuguese adds the following consonants to certain words:* **b** (sú(b)dito, su(b)til); **c** (a(c)ção, a(c)cionista, a(c)to); **m** (inde(m)ne); **p** (ado(p)ção, ado(p)tar); *for further details see p. xiii.*

acknowledge [ək'nɔlɪdʒ] *vt* reconhecer; (*also*: ~ *receipt of*) acusar o recebimento de (*BR*) *or* a recepção de (*PT*); (*fact*) admitir.
acknowledgement [ək'nɔlɪdʒmənt] *n* reconhecimento, notificação *f* de recebimento; **~s** *npl* (*in book*) agradecimentos *mpl*.
ACLU *n abbr* (= *American Civil Liberties Union*) *associação que defende os direitos humanos*.
acme ['ækmɪ] *n* acme *m*.
acne ['æknɪ] *n* acne *f*.
acorn ['eɪkɔːn] *n* bolota.
acoustic [ə'kuːstɪk] *adj* acústico.
acoustic coupler *n* (*COMPUT*) acoplador *m* acústico.
acoustics [ə'kuːstɪks] *n*, *npl* acústica.
acoustic screen *n* divisória.
acquaint [ə'kweɪnt] *vt*: **to ~ sb with sth** (*inform*) pôr alguém ao corrente de alguma coisa; **to be ~ed with** (*person*) conhecer; (*fact*) saber.
acquaintance [ə'kweɪntəns] *n* conhecimento; (*person*) conhecido/a; **to make sb's ~** conhecer alguém.
acquiesce [ækwɪ'ɛs] *vi*: **to ~ (in)** condescender (com).
acquire [ə'kwaɪə*] *vt* adquirir.
acquired [ə'kwaɪəd] *adj* adquirido; **an ~ taste** um gosto cultivado.
acquisition [ækwɪ'zɪʃən] *n* aquisição *f*.
acquisitive [ə'kwɪzɪtɪv] *adj* cobiçoso.
acquit [ə'kwɪt] *vt* absolver; **to ~ o.s. well** desempenhar-se bem.
acquittal [ə'kwɪtəl] *n* absolvição *f*.
acre ['eɪkə*] *n* acre *m* (= *4047m²*).
acreage ['eɪkərɪdʒ] *n* extensão *f* (em acres).
acrid ['ækrɪd] *adj* (*smell*) acre, pungente; (*fig*) mordaz.
acrimonious [ækrɪ'məunɪəs] *adj* (*remark*) mordaz; (*argument*) acrimonioso.
acrobat ['ækrəbæt] *n* acrobata *m/f*.
acrobatic [ækrə'bætɪk] *adj* acrobático.
acrobatics [ækrə'bætɪks] *npl* acrobacia.
Acropolis [ə'krɔpəlɪs] *n*: **the ~** a Acrópole.
across [ə'krɔs] *prep* (*on the other side of*) no outro lado de; (*crosswise*) através de ♦ *adv* transversalmente, de um lado ao outro; **to walk ~ (the road)** atravessar (a rua); **to run/swim ~** atravessar correndo/a nado; **the lake is 12 km ~** o lago tem 12 km de largura; **~ from** em frente de; **to get sth ~ (to sb)** conseguir comunicar algo (a alguém).
acrylic [ə'krɪlɪk] *adj*, *n* acrílico.
ACT *n abbr* (= *American College Test*) ≈ vestibular *m*.
act [ækt] *n* ação *f*; (*THEATRE*) ato; (*in music-hall etc*) número; (*LAW*) lei *f* ♦ *vi* (*THEATRE*) representar; (*pretend*) fingir; (*take action*) tomar atitude ♦ *vt* (*part*) representar; **~ of God** (*LAW*) força maior; **to catch sb in the ~** apanhar alguém em flagrante, flagrar alguém; **it's only an ~** é só encenação; **to ~ Hamlet** (*BRIT*) representar Hamlet; **to ~ the fool** (*BRIT*) fazer-se de bobo; **to ~ as** servir de; **it ~s as a deterrent** serve para dissuadir; **~ing in my capacity as chairman, I ...** na qualidade de presidente, eu ....
act on *vt fus*: **to ~ on sth** agir de acordo com algo.
act out *vt* (*event*) representar; (*fantasy*) realizar.
acting ['æktɪŋ] *adj* interino ♦ *n* (*performance*) representação *f*, atuação *f*; (*activity*): **to do some ~** fazer teatro.
action ['ækʃən] *n* ação *f*; (*MIL*) batalha, combate *m*; (*LAW*) ação judicial; **to bring an ~ against sb** (*LAW*) intentar ação judicial contra alguém; **killed in ~** (*MIL*) morto em combate; **out of ~** fora de combate; (*machine*) com defeito; **to take ~** tomar atitude; **to put a plan into ~** pôr um plano em ação.
action replay (*BRIT*) *n* (*TV*) replay *m*.
activate ['æktɪveɪt] *vt* (*mechanism*) acionar; (*CHEM*, *PHYS*) ativar.
active ['æktɪv] *adj* ativo; (*volcano*) em atividade.
active duty (*US*) *n* (*MIL*) ativa.
actively ['æktɪvlɪ] *adv* ativamente.
active partner *n* (*COMM*) comanditado/a.
active service (*BRIT*) *n* (*MIL*) ativa.
activist ['æktɪvɪst] *n* ativista *m/f*, militante *m/f*.
activity [æk'tɪvɪtɪ] *n* atividade *f*.
actor ['æktə*] *n* ator *m*.
actress ['æktrɪs] *n* atriz *f*.
ACTT (*BRIT*) *n abbr* (= *Association of Cinematographic, Television and Allied Technicians*) *sindicato dos técnicos do cinema e da televisão*.
actual ['æktjuəl] *adj* real.
actually ['æktjuəlɪ] *adv* realmente; (*in fact*) de fato.
actuary ['æktjuərɪ] *n* atuário/a.
actuate ['æktjueɪt] *vt* atuar, acionar.
acuity [ə'kjuːɪtɪ] *n* acuidade *f*.
acumen ['ækjumən] *n* perspicácia; **business ~** tino para os negócios.
acupuncture ['ækjupʌŋktʃə*] *n* acupuntura.
acute [ə'kjuːt] *adj* agudo.
AD *adv abbr* (= *Anno Domini*) d.C. ♦ *n abbr* (*US*: *MIL*) = **active duty**.
ad [æd] *n abbr* = **advertisement**.
adamant ['ædəmənt] *adj* inflexível.
Adam's apple ['ædəmz-] *n* pomo-de-Adão *m* (*BR*), maçã-de-Adão *f* (*PT*).
adapt [ə'dæpt] *vt* adaptar ♦ *vi*: **to ~ (to)** adaptar-se (a).
adaptability [ədæptə'bɪlɪtɪ] *n* adaptabilidade *f*.
adaptable [ə'dæptəbl] *adj* (*device*) ajustável; (*person*) adaptável.
adaptation [ædæp'teɪʃən] *n* adaptação *f*.
adapter [ə'dæptə*] *n* (*ELEC*) adaptador *m*.
ADC *n abbr* (*MIL*) = **aide-de-camp**; (*US*: = *Aid to Dependent Children*) *auxílio a crianças dependentes*.
add [æd] *vt* acrescentar; (*figures*: *also*: ~ *up*) somar ♦ *vi*: **to ~ to** (*increase*) aumentar.
add on *vt* acrescentar, adicionar.
add up *vt* (*figures*) somar ♦ *vi* (*fig*): **it doesn't ~ up** não faz sentido; **it doesn't ~**

up to much é pouca coisa.
adder ['ædə*] *n* víbora.
addict ['ædɪkt] *n* viciado/a; **heroin ~** viciado/a em heroína; **drug ~** toxicômano/a.
addicted [ə'dɪktɪd] *adj*: **to be/become ~ to** ser/ficar viciado em.
addiction [ə'dɪkʃən] *n* (*MED*) dependência.
adding machine ['ædɪŋ-] *n* máquina de somar.
Addis Ababa ['ædɪs'æbəbə] *n* Adis-Abeba.
addition [ə'dɪʃən] *n* (*adding up*) adição *f*; (*thing added*) acréscimo; **in ~** além disso; **in ~ to** além de.
additional [ə'dɪʃənl] *adj* adicional.
additive ['ædɪtɪv] *n* aditivo.
addled ['ædld] (*BRIT*) *adj* (*egg*) podre, estragado.
address [ə'drɛs] *n* endereço; (*speech*) discurso ♦ *vt* (*letter*) endereçar; (*speak to*) dirigir-se a, dirigir a palavra a; **form of ~** tratamento; **to ~ (o.s. to)** (*problem, issue*) enfocar; **absolute/relative ~** (*COMPUT*) endereço absoluto/relativo.
addressee [ædrɛ'siː] *n* destinatário/a.
Aden ['eɪdən] *n* Áden (*no article*); **Gulf of ~** golfo de Áden.
adenoids ['ædɪnɔɪdz] *npl* adenóides *fpl*.
adept ['ædɛpt] *adj*: **~ at** hábil *or* competente em.
adequate ['ædɪkwɪt] *adj* (*enough*) suficiente; (*suitable*) adequado; **to feel ~ to the task** sentir-se à altura da tarefa.
adequately ['ædɪkwɪtlɪ] *adv* adequadamente.
adhere [əd'hɪə*] *vi*: **to ~ to** aderir a; (*fig*: *abide by*) ater-se a.
adherent [əd'hɪərənt] *n* partidário/a.
adhesion [əd'hiːʒən] *n* adesão *f*.
adhesive [əd'hiːzɪv] *adj*, *n* adesivo; **~ tape** (*BRIT*) durex *m* ®, fita adesiva; (*US*) esparadrapo.
ad hoc [-hɔk] *adj* (*decision*) para o caso; (*committee*) ad hoc.
ad infinitum [-ɪnfɪ'naɪtəm] *adv* ad infinitum.
adjacent [ə'dʒeɪsənt] *adj*: **~ (to)** adjacente (a), contíguo (a).
adjective ['ædʒɛktɪv] *n* adjetivo.
adjoin [ə'dʒɔɪn] *vt* ser contíguo a.
adjoining [ə'dʒɔɪnɪŋ] *adj* adjacente, contíguo.
adjourn [ə'dʒəːn] *vt* (*postpone*) adiar; (*session*) suspender ♦ *vi* encerrar a sessão; (*go*) deslocar-se; **they ~ed to the pub** (*BRIT*: *inf*) deslocaram-se para o bar.
adjournment [ə'dʒəːnmənt] *n* (*period*) recesso.
Adjt *abbr* (*MIL*: = *adjutant*) Ajte.
adjudicate [ə'dʒuːdɪkeɪt] *vt*, *vi* julgar.
adjudication [ədʒuːdɪ'keɪʃən] *n* julgamento.
adjudicator [ə'dʒuːdɪkeɪtə*] *n* juíza *m/f*.
adjust [ə'dʒʌst] *vt* (*change*) ajustar; (*clothes*) arrumar; (*machine*) regular ♦ *vi*: **to ~ (to)** adaptar-se (a).
adjustable [ə'dʒʌstəbl] *adj* ajustável.
adjuster [ə'dʒʌstə*] *n see* **loss**.
adjustment [ə'dʒʌstmənt] *n* ajuste *m*; (*of engine*) regulagem *f*; (*of prices, wages*) reajuste *m*; (*of person*) adaptação *f*.
adjutant ['ædʒətənt] *n* ajudante *m*.
ad-lib [-lɪb] *vt*, *vi* improvisar ♦ *n* improviso; (*THEATRE*) caco ♦ *adv*: **ad lib** à vontade.
adman ['ædmæn] (*inf*; *irreg*) *n* publicitário.
admin ['ædmɪn] (*inf*) *n abbr* = **administration**.
administer [əd'mɪnɪstə*] *vt* administrar.
administration [ədmɪnɪs'treɪʃən] *n* administração *f*; (*US*: *government*) governo.
administrative [əd'mɪnɪstrətɪv] *adj* administrativo.
administrator [əd'mɪnɪstreɪtə*] *n* administrador(a) *m/f*.
admirable ['ædmərəbl] *adj* admirável.
admiral ['ædmərəl] *n* almirante *m*.
Admiralty ['ædmərəltɪ] (*BRIT*) *n* (*also*: **~** *Board*) Ministério da Marinha, Almirantado.
admiration [ædmə'reɪʃən] *n* admiração *f*.
admire [əd'maɪə*] *vt* admirar.
admirer [əd'maɪrə*] *n* admirador(a) *m/f*.
admission [əd'mɪʃən] *n* (*entry*) entrada, ingresso; (*enrolment*) admissão *f*; (*confession*) confissão *f*; **"~ free"**, **"free ~"** "entrada gratuita", "ingresso gratuito"; **by his own ~ he drinks too much** ele mesmo reconhece que bebe demais.
admit [əd'mɪt] *vt* admitir; (*acknowledge*) reconhecer; (*accept*) aceitar; (*confess*) confessar; **"children not ~ted"** "entrada proibida a menores de idade"; **this ticket ~s two** este ingresso é válido para duas pessoas; **I must ~ that ...** devo admitir *or* reconhecer que ....
admit of *vt fus* admitir.
admit to *vt fus* confessar.
admittance [əd'mɪtəns] *n* entrada; **"no ~"** "entrada proibida".
admittedly [əd'mɪtədlɪ] *adv* evidentemente.
admonish [əd'mɔnɪʃ] *vt* admoestar.
ad nauseam [æd'nɔːsɪæm] *adv* sem parar.
ado [ə'duː] *n*: **without further** *or* **(any) more ~** sem mais cerimônias.
adolescence [ædəu'lɛsns] *n* adolescência.
adolescent [ædəu'lɛsnt] *adj*, *n* adolescente *m/f*.
adopt [ə'dɔpt] *vt* adotar.
adopted [ə'dɔptɪd] *adj* adotivo.
adoption [ə'dɔpʃən] *n* adoção *f*.
adorable [ə'dɔːrəbl] *adj* encantador(a).
adoration [ædə'reɪʃən] *n* adoração *f*.
adore [ə'dɔː*] *vt* adorar.
adoring [ə'dɔːrɪŋ] *adj* devotado.
adoringly [ə'dɔːrɪŋlɪ] *adv* com adoração.
adorn [ə'dɔːn] *vt* adornar, enfeitar.
adornment [ə'dɔːnmənt] *n* enfeite *m*, adorno.
ADP *n abbr* = **automatic data processing**.
adrenalin [ə'drɛnəlɪn] *n* adrenalina.
Adriatic (Sea) [eɪdrɪ'ætɪk-] *n* (mar *m*) Adriático.

***NB**: European Portuguese adds the following consonants to certain words:* **b** (sú(b)dito, su(b)til); **c** (a(c)ção, a(c)cionista, a(c)to); **m** (inde(m)ne); **p** (ado(p)ção, ado(p)tar); *for further details see p. xiii.*

adrift [ə'drɪft] *adv* à deriva; **to come ~** desprender-se.
adroit [ə'drɔɪt] *adj* hábil.
ADT (*US*) *abbr* (= *Atlantic Daylight Time*) *hora de verão de Nova Iorque*.
adult ['ædʌlt] *n* adulto/a.
adult education *n* educação *f* de adultos.
adulterate [ə'dʌltəreɪt] *vt* adulterar.
adulterer [ə'dʌltərə*] *n* adúltero.
adulteress [ə'dʌltərɪs] *n* adúltera.
adultery [ə'dʌltərɪ] *n* adultério.
adulthood ['ædʌlthud] *n* idade *f* adulta.
advance [əd'vɑːns] *n* avanço; (*money*: *payment in advance*) adiantamento; (: *loan*) empréstimo; (*MIL*) avançada ♦ *vt* (*develop*) desenvolver, promover; (*lend*) adiantar ♦ *vi* avançar; **in ~** com antecedência; (*pay*) adiantado; **to make ~s to sb** (*gen*) fazer propostas a alguém; (*amorously*) fazer propostas amorosas a alguém.
advanced [əd'vɑːnst] *adj* avançado; (*SCH*: *studies*) adiantado; **~ in years** de idade avançada.
advancement [əd'vɑːnsmənt] *n* avanço, progresso; (*in rank*) promoção *f*, ascenção *f*.
advance notice *n* aviso prévio.
advantage [əd'vɑːntɪdʒ] *n* vantagem *f*; **to take ~ of** (*use*) aproveitar, aproveitar-se de; (*gain by*) tirar proveito de; **it's to our ~ (to do)** é vantajoso para nós (fazer).
advantageous [ædvən'teɪdʒəs] *adj* vantajoso.
advent ['ædvənt] *n* vinda, chegada; **A~** (*REL*) Advento.
Advent calendar *n* calendário do Advento.
adventure [əd'vɛntʃə*] *n* aventura.
adventurer [əd'vɛntʃərə*] *n* aventureiro/a.
adventurous [əd'vɛntʃərəs] *adj* aventuroso; (*person*) aventureiro.
adverb ['ædvəːb] *n* advérbio.
adversary ['ædvəsərɪ] *n* adversário/a.
adverse ['ædvəːs] *adj* adverso, contrário; **~ to** contrário a.
adversity [əd'vəːsɪtɪ] *n* adversidade *f*.
advert ['ædvəːt] (*BRIT*) *n abbr* = **advertisement**.
advertise ['ædvətaɪz] *vi* anunciar, fazer propaganda; (*in newspaper etc*) anunciar ♦ *vt* (*in newspaper*) anunciar; (*product*) fazer a propaganda de; **to ~ for** (*staff*) procurar.
advertisement [əd'vəːtɪsmənt] *n* (*classified*) anúncio; (*display*, *TV*) propaganda, anúncio.
advertiser ['ædvətaɪzə*] *n* anunciante *m/f*.
advertising ['ædvətaɪzɪŋ] *n* publicidade *f*.
advertising agency *n* agência de publicidade.
advertising campaign *n* campanha publicitária.
advice [əd'vaɪs] *n* conselhos *mpl*; (*notification*) aviso; **piece of ~** conselho; **to ask (sb) for ~** pedir conselho (a alguém); **to take legal ~** consultar um advogado.
advice note (*BRIT*) *n* aviso.
advisable [əd'vaɪzəbl] *adj* aconselhável.
advise [əd'vaɪz] *vt* aconselhar; (*inform*): **to ~ sb of sth** avisar alguém de algo; **to ~ sb against sth** desaconselhar algo a alguém; **to ~ sb against doing sth** aconselhar alguém a não fazer algo; **you would be well/ill ~d to go** seria melhor você ir/você não ir.
advisedly [əd'vaɪzɪdlɪ] *adv* de propósito.
adviser [əd'vaɪzə*] *n* conselheiro/a; (*business adviser*) consultor(a) *m/f*; (*political*) assessor(a) *m/f*.
advisory [əd'vaɪzərɪ] *adj* consultivo; **in an ~ capacity** na qualidade de assessor(a) *or* consultor(a).
advocate [*vt* 'ædvəkeɪt, *n* 'ædvəkɪt] *vt* advogar, defender ♦ *n* advogado/a, defensor(a) *m/f*.
advt. *abbr* = **advertisement**.
AEA (*BRIT*) *n abbr* (= *Atomic Energy Authority*) ≈ CNEN *f*.
AEC (*US*) *n abbr* (= *Atomic Energy Commission*) ≈ CNEN *f*.
Aegean (Sea) [iː'dʒiːən-] *n* (mar *m*) Egeu *m*.
aegis ['iːdʒɪs] *n*: **under the ~ of** sob a égide de.
aeon ['iːən] *n* eternidade *f*.
aerial ['ɛərɪəl] *n* antena ♦ *adj* aéreo.
aerobatics [ɛərəu'bætɪks] *npl* acrobacias *fpl* aéreas.
aerobics [ɛə'rəubɪks] *n* ginástica.
aerodrome ['ɛərədrəum] (*BRIT*) *n* aeródromo.
aerodynamic [ɛərəudaɪ'næmɪk] *adj* aerodinâmico.
aerodynamics [ɛərəudaɪ'næmɪks] *n*, *npl* aerodinâmica.
aeronautics [ɛərə'nɔːtɪks] *n* aeronáutica.
aeroplane ['ɛərəpleɪn] *n* avião *m*.
aerosol ['ɛərəsɔl] *n* aerossol *m*.
aerospace industry ['ɛərəuspeɪs-] *n* indústria aeroespacial.
aesthetic [iːs'θɛtɪk] *adj* estético.
aesthetics [iːs'θɛtɪks] *n*, *npl* estética.
AEU (*BRIT*) *n abbr* (= *Amalgamated Engineering Union*) *sindicato dos operários técnicos*.
afar [ə'fɑː*] *adv*: **from ~** de longe.
AFB (*US*) *n abbr* = **Air Force Base**.
AFDC (*US*) *n abbr* (= *Aid to Families with Dependent Children*) auxílio-família *m*.
affable ['æfəbl] *adj* afável, simpático.
affair [ə'fɛə*] *n* negócio; (*also*: *love ~*) caso; **~s** (*matters*) assuntos *mpl*; (*personal concerns*) vida; **that is my ~** isso é comigo; **the Watergate ~** o caso Watergate.
affect [ə'fɛkt] *vt* afetar; (*move*) comover.
affectation [æfɛk'teɪʃən] *n* afetação *f*.
affected [ə'fɛktɪd] *adj* afetado.
affection [ə'fɛkʃən] *n* afeto, afeição *f*.
affectionate [ə'fɛkʃənət] *adj* afetuoso, carinhoso.
affectionately [ə'fɛkʃənətlɪ] *adv* carinhosamente.
affidavit [æfɪ'deɪvɪt] *n* (*LAW*) declaração *f* escrita e juramentada.
affiliated [ə'fɪlɪeɪtɪd] *adj*: **~ (to)** afiliado (a); **~ company** filial *f*.
affinity [ə'fɪnɪtɪ] *n* afinidade *f*.
affirm [ə'fəːm] *vt* afirmar.
affirmation [æfə'meɪʃən] *n* afirmação *f*.

affirmative [əˈfəːmətɪv] *adj* afirmativo ♦ *n*: **in the ~** afirmativamente.
affix [əˈfɪks] *vt* (*signature*) apor; (*stamp*) afixar, colar.
afflict [əˈflɪkt] *vt* afligir; **to be ~ed with** sofrer de.
affliction [əˈflɪkʃən] *n* aflição *f*; (*illness*) doença.
affluence [ˈæfluəns] *n* riqueza, opulência.
affluent [ˈæfluənt] *adj* rico, opulento; (*person*) rico; **the ~ society** a sociedade de abundância.
afford [əˈfɔːd] *vt* (*provide*) fornecer, dar; (*goods etc*) ter o dinheiro *or* os recursos para; **can we ~ a car?** temos dinheiro para comprar um carro?; **I can't ~ the time** não tenho tempo; **we can ~ to wait** podemos permitir-nos esperar.
affray [əˈfreɪ] (*BRIT*) *n* (*LAW*) desordem *f*, tumulto.
affront [əˈfrʌnt] *n* afronta, ofensa.
affronted [əˈfrʌntɪd] *adj* afrontado, ofendido.
Afghan [ˈæfgæn] *adj*, *n* afegão/gã *m/f*.
Afghanistan [æfˈgænɪstæn] *n* Afeganistão *m*.
afield [əˈfiːld] *adv*: **far ~** muito longe.
AFL-CIO *n abbr* (= *American Federation of Labor and Congress of Industrial Organizations*) *confederação sindical.*
afloat [əˈfləut] *adv* (*floating*) flutuando; (*at sea*) no mar; **to stay ~** continuar flutuando; **to keep/get ~** (*business*) manter financeiramente equilibrado/estabelecer.
afoot [əˈfut] *adv*: **there is something ~** está acontecendo algo.
aforementioned [əˈfɔːmɛnʃənd] *adj* acima mencionado.
aforesaid [əˈfɔːsɛd] *adj* supracitado, referido.
afraid [əˈfreɪd] *adj* (*frightened*) assustado; (*fearful*) receoso; **to be ~ of/to** ter medo de; **I am ~ that** lamento que; **I'm ~ so/not** receio que sim/não.
afresh [əˈfrɛʃ] *adv* de novo, outra vez.
Africa [ˈæfrɪkə] *n* África.
African [ˈæfrɪkən] *adj*, *n* africano/a.
Afrikaans [æfrɪˈkɑːns] *n* (*LING*) afrikaan *m*.
Afrikaner [æfrɪˈkɑːnə*] *n* africânder *m/f*.
Afro-American [ˈæfrəu-] *adj* afro-americano.
AFT *n abbr* (= *American Federation of Teachers*) *sindicato dos professores.*
aft [ɑːft] *adv* a ré.
after [ˈɑːftə*] *prep* (*time*) depois de ♦ *adv* depois ♦ *conj* depois que; **~ dinner** depois do jantar; **the day ~ tomorrow** depois de amanhã; **day ~ day** dia após dia; **time ~ time** repetidas vezes; **a quarter ~ two** (*US*) duas e quinze; **what are you ~?** o que você quer?; **who are you ~?** quem procura?; **the police are ~ him** a polícia está atrás dele; **to ask ~ sb** perguntar por alguém; **~ all** afinal (de contas); **~ you!** passe primeiro!
afterbirth [ˈɑːftəbəːθ] *n* placenta.
aftercare [ˈɑːftəkɛə*] (*BRIT*) *n* (*MED*) assistência pós-operatória.
after-effects *npl* repercussões *fpl*; (*of drug*) efeitos *mpl* secundários.
afterlife [ˈɑːftəlaɪf] *n* vida após a morte.
aftermath [ˈɑːftəmæθ] *n* conseqüências *fpl*; **in the ~ of** no período depois de.
afternoon [ɑːftəˈnuːn] *n* tarde *f*; **good ~!** boa tarde!
afters [ˈɑːftəz] (*BRIT*: *inf*) *n* (*dessert*) sobremesa.
after-sales service *n* serviço pós-vendas; (*of computers etc*) assistência técnica.
after-shave (lotion) *n* loção *f* após-barba.
aftershock [ˈɑːftəʃɔk] *n* abalo secundário.
afterthought [ˈɑːftəθɔːt] *n* reflexão *f* posterior *or* tardia.
afterwards [ˈɑːftəwədz] *adv* depois; **immediately ~** logo depois.
again [əˈgɛn] *adv* outra vez, de novo; **to do sth ~** voltar a fazer algo; **~ and ~** repetidas vezes; **now and ~** de vez em quando.
against [əˈgɛnst] *prep* contra; **~ a blue background** sobre um fundo azul; **(as) ~** (*BRIT*) em contraste com.
age [eɪdʒ] *n* idade *f*; (*old ~*) velhice *f*; (*period*) época ♦ *vt*, *vi* envelhecer; **he's 20 years of ~** ele tem 20 anos de idade; **at the ~ of 20** aos 20 anos de idade; **under ~** menor de idade; **to come of ~** atingir a maioridade; **it's been ~s since I saw him** faz muito tempo *or* um tempão (*BR*: *inf*) que eu não o vejo.
aged[1] [eɪdʒd] *adj*: **~ 10** de 10 anos de idade.
aged[2] [ˈeɪdʒɪd] *adj* idoso ♦ *npl*: **the ~** os idosos.
age group *n* faixa etária; **the 40 to 50 ~** a faixa etária dos 40 aos 50 anos.
ageless [ˈeɪdʒlɪs] *adj* (*eternal*) eterno; (*ever young*) sempre jovem.
age limit *n* idade *f* mínima/máxima.
agency [ˈeɪdʒənsɪ] *n* agência; **through** *or* **by the ~ of** por meio de.
agenda [əˈdʒɛndə] *n* ordem *f* do dia.
agent [ˈeɪdʒənt] *n* agente *m/f*.
aggravate [ˈægrəveɪt] *vt* agravar; (*annoy*) irritar.
aggravation [ægrəˈveɪʃən] *n* irritação *f*.
aggregate [ˈægrɪgət] *n* (*whole*) conjunto; **on ~** (*SPORT*) no total dos pontos.
aggression [əˈgrɛʃən] *n* agressão *f*.
aggressive [əˈgrɛsɪv] *adj* agressivo.
aggressiveness [əˈgrɛsɪvnɪs] *n* agressividade *f*.
aggrieved [əˈgriːvd] *adj* aflito.
aghast [əˈgɑːst] *adj* horrorizado.
agile [ˈædʒaɪl] *adj* ágil.
agitate [ˈædʒɪteɪt] *vt* (*shake*) agitar; (*trouble*) perturbar ♦ *vi*: **to ~ for** fazer agitação em prol de *or* a favor de.
agitation [ædʒɪˈteɪʃən] *n* agitação *f*.
agitator [ˈædʒɪteɪtə*] *n* agitador(a) *m/f*.
AGM *n abbr* (= *annual general meeting*)

NB: European Portuguese adds the following consonants to certain words: **b** (sú(b)dito, su(b)til); **c** (a(c)ção, a(c)cionista, a(c)to); **m** (inde(m)ne); **p** (ado(p)ção, ado(p)tar); *for further details see p. xiii.*

AGO *f*.

ago [ə'gəu] *adv*: **2 days ~** há 2 dias (atrás); **not long ~** há pouco tempo; **as long ~ as 1960** já em 1960; **how long ~?** há quanto tempo?

agog [ə'gɔg] *adj* (*impatient*): **~ to** ansioso para; (*excited*): **(all) ~** empolgado, entusiasmado.

agonize ['ægənaɪz] *vi*: **to ~ over sth** agoniar-se *or* angustiar-se com algo.

agonizing ['ægənaɪzɪŋ] *adj* (*pain*) agudo; (*suspense*) angustiante.

agony ['ægənɪ] *n* (*pain*) dor *f*; (*distress*) angústia; **to be in ~** sofrer dores terríveis.

agony column *n* correspondência sentimental.

agree [ə'gri:] *vt* (*price*) combinar, ajustar ♦ *vi* (*statements etc*) combinar; **to ~ (with)** (*person*, LING) concordar (com); **to ~ to do** aceitar fazer; **to ~ to sth** consentir algo; **to ~ that** (*admit*) concordar *or* admitir que; **it was ~d that ...** foi combinado que ...; **they ~ on this** concordam *or* estão de acordo nisso; **garlic doesn't ~ with me** não me dou bem com o alho.

agreeable [ə'gri:əbl] *adj* agradável; (*willing*) disposto; **are you ~ to this?** você concorda *or* está de acordo com isso?

agreed [ə'gri:d] *adj* (*time, place*) combinado; **to be ~** concordar, estar de acordo.

agreement [ə'gri:mənt] *n* acordo; (COMM) contrato; **in ~** de acordo; **by mutual ~** de comum acordo.

agricultural [ægrɪ'kʌltʃərəl] *adj* (*of crops*) agrícola; (*of crops and cattle*) agropecuário.

agriculture ['ægrɪkʌltʃə*] *n* (*of crops*) agricultura; (*of crops and cattle*) agropecuária.

aground [ə'graund] *adv*: **to run ~** encalhar.

ahead [ə'hɛd] *adv* adiante; **go right** *or* **straight ~** continue sempre em frente; **go ~!** (*fig*) vá lá!; (: *speak*) pode falar!; **~ of** à frente de; (*fig*: *schedule etc*) antes de; **~ of time** antes do tempo; **to go ~ (with)** prosseguir (com); **to be ~ of sb** (*fig*) ter vantagem sobre alguém.

AI *n abbr* = **Amnesty International**; (COMPUT) = **artificial intelligence**.

AIB (BRIT) *n abbr* (= *Accident Investigation Bureau*) *comissão de inquérito sobre acidentes*.

AID *n abbr* = **artificial insemination by donor**; (US) = **Agency for International Development**.

aid [eɪd] *n* ajuda, auxílio ♦ *vt* ajudar, auxiliar; **with the ~ of** com a ajuda de; **in ~ of** em benefício de; **to ~ and abet** (LAW) ser cúmplice de.

aide [eɪd] *n* (*person*) assessor(a) *m/f*.

AIDS [eɪdz] *n abbr* (= *acquired immune deficiency syndrome*) AIDS *f* (BR), SIDA *f* (PT).

AIH *n abbr* = **artificial insemination by husband**.

ailment ['eɪlmənt] *n* achaque *m*.

aim [eɪm] *vt*: **to ~ sth at** (*gun, camera, blow*) apontar algo para; (*missile, remark*) dirigir algo a ♦ *vi* (*also*: *take ~*) apontar ♦ *n* (*accuracy*) pontaria; (*objective*) objetivo, meta; **to ~ at** (*objective*) visar; **to ~ to do** pretender fazer.

aimless ['eɪmlɪs] *adj* à toa.

aimlessly ['eɪmlɪslɪ] *adv* à toa.

ain't [eɪnt] (*inf*) = **am not; aren't; isn't**.

air [ɛə*] *n* ar *m*; (*appearance*) aparência, aspeto ♦ *vt* arejar; (*grievances, ideas*) discutir ♦ *cpd* (*currents, attack etc*) aéreo; **by ~** (*travel*) de avião; (*send*) por via aérea; **to be on the ~** (RADIO, TV: *programme, station*) estar no ar.

air base *n* base *f* aérea.

airbed ['ɛəbɛd] (BRIT) *n* colchão *m* de ar.

airborne ['ɛəbɔ:n] *adj* (*in the air*) no ar; (*plane*) em vôo; (*troops*) aerotransportado.

air cargo *n* frete *m* aéreo.

air-conditioned [-kən'dɪʃənd] *adj* com ar condicionado.

air conditioning [-kən'dɪʃənɪŋ] *n* ar condicionado.

air-cooled [-ku:ld] *adj* refrigerado a ar.

aircraft ['ɛəkrɑ:ft] *n inv* aeronave *f*.

aircraft carrier *n* porta-aviões *m inv*.

air cushion *n* almofada de ar.

airfield ['ɛəfi:ld] *n* campo de aviação.

Air Force *n* Força Aérea, Aeronáutica.

air freight *n* frete *m* aéreo.

airgun ['ɛəgʌn] *n* espingarda de ar comprimido.

air hostess (BRIT) *n* aeromoça (BR), hospedeira (PT).

airily ['ɛərɪlɪ] *adv* levianamente.

airing ['ɛərɪŋ] *n*: **to give an ~ to** arejar; (*fig*: *ideas, views*) discutir.

air letter (BRIT) *n* aerograma *m*.

airlift ['ɛəlɪft] *n* ponte aérea.

airline ['ɛəlaɪn] *n* linha aérea.

airliner ['ɛəlaɪnə*] *n* avião *m* de passageiros.

airlock ['ɛəlɔk] *n* (*blockage*) entupimento de ar.

airmail ['ɛəmeɪl] *n*: **by ~** por via aérea.

air mattress *n* colchão *m* de ar.

airplane ['ɛəpleɪn] (US) *n* avião *m*.

air pocket *n* bolsa de ar.

airport ['ɛəpɔ:t] *n* aeroporto.

air raid *n* ataque *m* aéreo.

airsick ['ɛəsɪk] *adj*: **to be ~** enjoar-se (no avião).

airstrip ['ɛəstrɪp] *n* pista (de aterrissar).

air terminal *n* terminal *m* aéreo.

airtight ['ɛətaɪt] *adj* hermético.

air traffic control *n* controle *m* de tráfego aéreo.

air traffic controller *n* controlador(a) *m/f* de tráfego aéreo.

air waybill *n* conhecimento aéreo.

airy ['ɛərɪ] *adj* (*room*) arejado, ventilado; (*person*) leviano.

aisle [aɪl] *n* (*of church*) nave *f*; (*of theatre, plane*) corredor *m*, coxia.

ajar [ə'dʒɑ:*] *adj* entreaberto.

AK (US) *abbr* (POST) = **Alaska**.

aka *abbr* (= *also known as*) vulgo.
akin [ə'kɪn] *adj*: ~ **to** parecido com.
AL (*US*) *abbr* (*POST*) = **Alabama.**
ALA *n abbr* = **American Library Association.**
à la carte [ælɑː'kɑːt] *adj*, *adv* à la carte.
alacrity [ə'lækrɪtɪ] *n*: **with** ~ prontamente.
alarm [ə'lɑːm] *n* alarme *m*; (*anxiety*) inquietação *f* ♦ *vt* alarmar, inquietar.
alarm clock *n* despertador *m*.
alarming [ə'lɑːmɪŋ] *adj* alarmante.
alarmist [ə'lɑːmɪst] *adj*, *n* alarmista *m/f*.
alas [ə'læs] *excl* ai, ai de mim.
Alaska [ə'læskə] *n* Alasca *m*.
Albania [æl'beɪnɪə] *n* Albânia.
Albanian [æl'beɪnɪən] *adj* albanês/esa ♦ *n* albanês/esa *m/f*; (*LING*) albanês *m*.
albeit [ɔːl'biːɪt] *conj* embora.
album ['ælbəm] *n* álbum *m*; (*record*) elepê *m*, álbum.
albumen ['ælbjumɪn] *n* albumina; (*of egg*) albume *m*.
alchemy ['ælkɪmɪ] *n* alquimia.
alcohol ['ælkəhɔl] *n* álcool *m*.
alcoholic [ælkə'hɔlɪk] *adj* alcoólico ♦ *n* alcoólatra *m/f*.
alcoholism ['ælkəhɔlɪzəm] *n* alcoolismo.
alcove ['ælkəuv] *n* alcova.
Ald. *abbr* = **alderman.**
alderman ['ɔːldəmən] (*irreg*) *n* vereador *m*.
ale [eɪl] *n* cerveja.
alert [ə'ləːt] *adj* atento; (*sharp*) esperto; (*watchful*) vigilante ♦ *n* alerta ♦ *vt*: **to** ~ **sb (to sth)** alertar alguém (de *or* sobre algo); **on the** ~ de sobreaviso *or* alerta.
Aleutian Islands [ə'luːʃən-] *npl* ilhas *fpl* Aleútas.
Alexandria [ælɪg'zɑːndrɪə] *n* Alexandria.
alfresco [æl'frɛskəu] *adj*, *adv* ao ar livre.
Algarve [æl'gɑːv] *m*: **the** ~ o Algarve.
algebra ['ældʒɪbrə] *n* álgebra.
Algeria [æl'dʒɪərɪə] *n* Argélia.
Algerian [æl'dʒɪərɪən] *adj*, *n* argelino/a.
Algiers [æl'dʒɪəz] *n* Argel.
algorithm ['ælgərɪðəm] *n* algoritmo.
alias ['eɪlɪəs] *adv* também chamado ♦ *n* outro nome, pseudônimo.
alibi ['ælɪbaɪ] *n* álibi *m*.
alien ['eɪlɪən] *n* estrangeiro/a; (*from space*) alienígena *m/f* ♦ *adj*: ~ **to** estranho a, alheio a.
alienate ['eɪlɪəneɪt] *vt* alienar.
alienation [eɪlɪə'neɪʃən] *n* alienação *f*.
alight [ə'laɪt] *adj* aceso ♦ *vi* (*passenger*) apear; (*bird*) pousar.
align [ə'laɪn] *vt* alinhar.
alignment [ə'laɪnmənt] *n* alinhamento.
alike [ə'laɪk] *adj* (*identical*) igual; (*similar*) parecido ♦ *adv* igualmente, do mesmo modo; **to look** ~ parecer-se.
alimony ['ælɪmənɪ] *n* (*payment*) pensão *f* alimentícia, sustento.
alive [ə'laɪv] *adj* vivo; **to be** ~ **with** fervilhar de; ~ **to** sensível a.
alkali ['ælkəlaɪ] *n* álcali *m*.
all [ɔːl] *adj* todo; (*pl*) todos/as ♦ *pron* tudo; (*pl*: *pessoas*) todos/as ♦ *adv* todo, completamente; ~ **alone** completamente só; ~ **the time/his life** o tempo todo/toda a sua vida; ~ **five (of them)** todos os cinco; ~ **of them** todos eles; ~ **of it** tudo; **we** ~ **went**, ~ **of us went** nós fomos todos; ~ **day** o dia inteiro; **is that** ~**?** é só isso?; **for** ~ **their efforts** apesar de seus esforços; **not as hard** *etc* **as** ~ **that** não tão difícil *etc* assim; **not at** ~ (*in answer to question*) em absoluto, absolutamente não; (*after thanks*) de nada; **I'm not at** ~ **tired** não estou nada cansada; **anything at** ~ **will do** qualquer coisa serve; ~ **but** quase; **to be** ~ **in** (*BRIT*: *inf*) estar exausto; ~ **in** ~ ao todo; ~ **out** com toda a energia; **it's** ~ **the same** dá no mesmo.
allay [ə'leɪ] *vt* (*fears*) acalmar; (*pain*) aliviar.
all clear *n* sinal *m* de tudo limpo; (*after air raid*) sinal de fim de alerta aérea.
allegation [ælɪ'geɪʃən] *n* alegação *f*, afirmação *f*.
allege [ə'lɛdʒ] *vt* alegar, afirmar; **he is** ~**d to have said** afirma-se que ele disse.
alleged [ə'lɛdʒd] *adj* pretenso.
allegedly [ə'lɛdʒɪdlɪ] *adv* segundo dizem.
allegiance [ə'liːdʒəns] *n* lealdade *f*.
allegory ['ælɪgərɪ] *n* alegoria.
all-embracing [-ɪm'breɪsɪŋ] *adj* universal.
allergic [ə'ləːdʒɪk] *adj*: ~ **to** alérgico a.
allergy ['ælədʒɪ] *n* alergia.
alleviate [ə'liːvɪeɪt] *vt* aliviar.
alley ['ælɪ] *n* (*street*) viela, beco; (*in garden*) passeio.
alliance [ə'laɪəns] *n* aliança.
allied ['ælaɪd] *adj* aliado; (*related*) afim, aparentado.
alligator ['ælɪgeɪtə*] *n* aligátor *m*; (*in Brazil*) jacaré *m*.
all-important *adj* importantíssimo.
all-in (*BRIT*) *adj*, *adv* (*charge*) tudo incluído.
all-in wrestling (*BRIT*) *n* luta livre.
alliteration [əlɪtə'reɪʃən] *n* aliteração *f*.
all-night *adj* (*café*) aberto toda a noite; (*party*) que dura toda a noite.
allocate ['æləkeɪt] *vt* (*share out*) distribuir; (*devote*) designar.
allocation [ælə'keɪʃən] *n* (*of money*) repartição *f*; (*distribution*) distribuição *f*; (*money*) verbas *fpl*.
allot [ə'lɔt] *vt* distribuir, repartir; (*devote*) designar; **in the** ~**ted time** no tempo designado.
allotment [ə'lɔtmənt] *n* distribuição *f*, partilha; (*garden*) lote *m*.
all-out *adj* (*effort etc*) máximo; (*attack etc*) irrestrito.
allow [ə'lau] *vt* (*practice*, *behaviour*) permitir; (*sum to spend etc*) dar, conceder; (*claim*) admitir; (*sum*, *time estimated*) calcular;

NB: *European Portuguese adds the following consonants to certain words:* **b** (sú(b)dito, su(b)til); **c** (a(c)ção, a(c)cionista, a(c)to); **m** (inde(m)ne); **p** (ado(p)ção, ado(p)tar); *for further details see p. xiii.*

(*concede*): **to ~ that** reconhecer que; **to ~ sb to do** permitir a alguém fazer; **he is ~d to do** é permitido que ele faça, ele pode fazer; **smoking is not ~ed** é proibido fumar; **we must ~ 3 days for the journey** temos que calcular três dias para a viagem.
allow for *vt fus* levar em conta.
allowance [ə'lauəns] *n* concessão *f*; (*payment*) pensão *f*, subsídio; (: *for expenses*) ajuda de custo; (*discount*) desconto; (*TAX*) abatimento; **to make ~s for** levar em consideração.
alloy ['ælɔı] *n* liga.
all right *adv* (*well*) bem; (*as answer*) está bem!
all-round *adj* (*view*) geral, amplo; (*person*) consumado.
all-rounder (*BRIT*) *n*: **to be a good ~** ser homem/mulher para tudo.
allspice ['ɔːlspaıs] *n* pimenta da Jamaica.
all-time *adj* (*record*) de todos os tempos.
allude [ə'luːd] *vi*: **to ~ to** aludir a.
alluring [ə'ljuərıŋ] *adj* tentador(a), sedutor(a).
allusion [ə'luːʒən] *n* alusão *f*.
alluvium [ə'luːvıəm] *n* aluvião *m*.
ally [*n* 'ælaı, *vt* ə'laı] *n* aliado ♦ *vt*: **to ~ o.s. with** aliar-se com.
almighty [ɔːl'maıtı] *adj* onipotente, todo-poderoso.
almond ['ɑːmənd] *n* (*fruit*) amêndoa; (*tree*) amendoeira.
almost ['ɔːlməust] *adv* quase.
alms [ɑːmz] *npl* esmolas *fpl*, esmola.
aloft [ə'lɔft] *adv* em cima, no alto.
alone [ə'ləun] *adj* só, sozinho ♦ *adv* só, somente; **to leave sb ~** deixar alguém em paz; **to leave sth ~** não tocar em algo; **let ~** ... sem falar em ....
along [ə'lɔŋ] *prep* por, ao longo de ♦ *adv*: **is he coming ~?** ele vem conosco?; **he was limping ~** ia coxeando; **~ with** junto com.
alongside [əlɔŋ'saıd] *prep* ao lado de ♦ *adv* (*NAUT*) encostado.
aloof [ə'luːf] *adj* afastado, altivo ♦ *adv*: **to stand ~** afastar-se.
aloofness [ə'luːfnıs] *n* afastamento, altivez *f*.
aloud [ə'laud] *adv* em voz alta.
alphabet ['ælfəbɛt] *n* alfabeto.
alphabetical [ælfə'bɛtıkəl] *adj* alfabético; **in ~ order** em ordem alfabética.
alphanumeric ['ælfənjuː'mɛrık] *adj* alfanumérico.
alpine ['ælpaın] *adj* alpino, alpestre.
Alps [ælps] *npl*: **the ~** os Alpes.
already [ɔːl'rɛdı] *adv* já.
alright ['ɔːl'raıt] (*BRIT*) *adv* = **all right**.
Alsatian [æl'seıʃən] (*BRIT*) *n* (*dog*) pastor *m* alemão.
also ['ɔːlsəu] *adv* também.
altar ['ɔltə*] *n* altar *m*.
alter ['ɔltə*] *vt* alterar, modificar ♦ *vi* alterar-se, modificar-se.
alteration [ɔltə'reıʃən] *n* alteração *f*, modificação *f*; **~s** *npl* (*SEWING*) consertos *mpl*; (*ARCHIT*) reformas *fpl*; **timetable subject to ~** horário sujeito a mudanças.
alternate [*adj* ɔl'təːnıt, *vi* 'ɔltəːneıt] *adj* alternado ♦ *vi* alternar-se; **on ~ days** em dias alternados.
alternately [ɔl'təːnıtlı] *adv* alternadamente.
alternating ['ɔltəːneıtıŋ] *adj*: **~ current** corrente *f* alternada.
alternative [ɔl'təːnətıv] *adj* alternativo ♦ *n* alternativa.
alternatively [ɔl'təːnətıvlı] *adv*: **~ one could** ... por outro lado se podia ....
alternator ['ɔltəːneıtə*] *n* (*AUT*) alternador *m*.
although [ɔːl'ðəu] *conj* embora; (*given that*) se bem que.
altitude ['æltıtjuːd] *n* altitude *f*.
alto ['æltəu] *n* (*female*) contralto *f*; (*male*) alto.
altogether [ɔːltə'gɛðə*] *adv* (*completely*) totalmente, de todo; (*on the whole, in all*) no total, ao todo; **how much is that ~?** qual é a soma total?
altruistic [æltru'ıstık] *adj* (*person*) altruísta; (*act*) altruístico.
aluminium [ælju'mınıəm] (*BRIT*) *n* alumínio.
aluminum [ə'luːmınəm] (*US*) *n* = **aluminium**.
always ['ɔːlweız] *adv* sempre.
AM *abbr* = **amplitude modulation**.
am [æm] *vb see* **be**.
a.m. *adv abbr* (= *ante meridiem*) da manhã.
AMA *n abbr* = **American Medical Association**.
amalgam [ə'mælgəm] *n* amálgama *m*.
amalgamate [ə'mælgəmeıt] *vi* amalgamar-se, unir-se ♦ *vt* amalgamar, unir.
amalgamation [əmælgə'meıʃən] *n* (*COMM*) amalgamação *f*, união *f*.
amass [ə'mæs] *vt* acumular, amontoar.
amateur ['æmətə*] *adj, n* amador(a) *m/f*; **~ dramatics** teatro amador.
amateurish ['æmətərıʃ] (*pej*) *adj* amador(a).
amaze [ə'meız] *vt* assombrar, espantar; **to be ~d (at)** espantar-se (de *or* com).
amazement [ə'meızmənt] *n* assombro, espanto; **to my ~** para o meu espanto.
amazing [ə'meızıŋ] *adj* (*surprising*) surpreendente; (*incredible*) incrível.
amazingly [ə'meızıŋlı] *adv* (*surprisingly*) surpreendentemente; (*incredibly*) incrivelmente.
Amazon ['æməzən] *n* (*GEO*) Amazonas *m*; (*MYTHOLOGY*) amazona *f* ♦ *cpd* amazônico, do Amazonas; **the ~ basin** a bacia amazônica; **the ~ jungle** a selva amazônica.
Amazonian [æmə'zeunıən] *adj* (*of river, region*) amazônico; (*of state*) amazonense ♦ *n* amazonense *m/f*.
ambassador [æm'bæsədə*] *n* embaixador/embaixatriz *m/f*.
amber ['æmbə*] *n* âmbar *m*; **at ~** (*BRIT*: *AUT*) em amarelo.
ambidextrous [æmbı'dɛkstrəs] *adj* ambidestro.
ambience ['æmbıəns] *n* ambiente *m*.
ambiguity [æmbı'gjuıtı] *n* ambigüidade *f*.
ambiguous [æm'bıgjuəs] *adj* ambíguo.
ambition [æm'bıʃən] *n* ambição *f*.

ambitious [æm'bɪʃəs] *adj* ambicioso; (*plan*) grandioso.
ambivalent [æm'bɪvələnt] *adj* ambivalente; (*pej*) equívoco.
amble ['æmbl] *vi* (*also*: ~ *along*) andar a furta-passo.
ambulance ['æmbjuləns] *n* ambulância.
ambush ['æmbuʃ] *n* emboscada ♦ *vt* emboscar.
ameba [ə'miːbə] (*US*) *n* = **amoeba**.
ameliorate [ə'miːlɪəreɪt] *vt* melhorar.
amen ['ɑː'mɛn] *excl* amém.
amenable [ə'miːnəbl] *adj*: ~ **to** (*advice etc*) receptivo a.
amend [ə'mɛnd] *vt* (*law, text*) emendar; (*habits*) corrigir.
amendment [ə'mɛndmənt] *n* (*to law etc*) emenda; (*in text*) correção *f*.
amends [ə'mɛndz] *n*: **to make** ~ reparar seus erros; **to make** ~ **to sb for sth** compensar alguém por algo.
amenity [ə'miːnɪtɪ] *n* amenidade *f*; **amenities** *npl* atrações *fpl*, comodidades *fpl*.
America [ə'mɛrɪkə] *n* (*continent*) América; (*USA*) Estados Unidos *mpl*.
American [ə'mɛrɪkən] *adj* americano; (*from USA*) norte-americano, estadunidense ♦ *n* americano/a; (*from USA*) norte-americano/a.
americanize [ə'mɛrɪkənaɪz] *vt* americanizar.
amethyst ['æmɪθɪst] *n* ametista.
Amex ['æmɛks] *n abbr* = **American Stock Exchange**.
amiable ['eɪmɪəbl] *adj* amável, simpático.
amicable ['æmɪkəbl] *adj* amigável; (*person*) amigo.
amid(st) [ə'mɪd(st)] *prep* em meio a.
amiss [ə'mɪs] *adv*: **to take sth** ~ levar algo a mal; **there's something** ~ aí tem coisa.
ammo ['æməu] (*inf*) *n abbr* = **ammunition**.
ammonia [ə'məunɪə] *n* (*gas*) amoníaco; (*liquid*) amônia.
ammunition [æmju'nɪʃən] *n* munição *f*; (*fig*) argumentos *mpl*.
ammunition dump *n* depósito de munições.
amnesia [æm'niːzɪə] *n* amnésia.
amnesty ['æmnɪstɪ] *n* anistia; **to grant an** ~ **to** anistiar.
amoeba [ə'miːbə] (*US* **ameba**) *n* ameba.
amok [ə'mɔk] *adv*: **to run** ~ enlouquecer.
among(st) [ə'mʌŋ(st)] *prep* entre, no meio de.
amoral [æ'mɔrəl] *adj* amoral.
amorous ['æmərəs] *adj* amoroso; (*in love*) apaixonado, enamorado.
amorphous [ə'mɔːfəs] *adj* amorfo.
amortization [əmɔːtaɪ'zeɪʃən] *n* amortização *f*.
amount [ə'maunt] *n* quantidade *f*; (*of money etc*) quantia, importância, montante *m* ♦ *vi*: **to** ~ **to** (*reach*) chegar a; (*total*) montar a; (*be same as*) equivaler a, significar; **this** ~**s to a refusal** isto equivale a uma recusa; **the total** ~ (*of money*) o total.
amp(ère) ['æmp(ɛə*)] *n* ampère *m*; **a 13 amp plug** um pino de tomada de 13 ampères.
ampersand ['æmpəsænd] *n* "e" *m* comercial.
amphibian [æm'fɪbɪən] *n* anfíbio.
amphibious [æm'fɪbɪəs] *adj* anfíbio.
amphitheatre ['æmfɪθɪətə*] (*US* **amphitheater**) *n* anfiteatro.
ample ['æmpl] *adj* amplo; (*enough*) suficiente; **this is** ~ isso é mais do que suficiente; **to have** ~ **time/room** ter tempo/lugar de sobra.
amplifier ['æmplɪfaɪə*] *n* amplificador *m*.
amplify ['æmplɪfaɪ] *vt* amplificar.
amply ['æmplɪ] *adv* amplamente.
ampoule ['æmpuːl] (*US* **ampule**) *n* (*MED*) ampola.
amputate ['æmpjuteɪt] *vt* amputar.
Amsterdam ['æmstədæm] *n* Amsterdã (*BR*), Amsterdão (*PT*).
amt *abbr* = **amount**.
amuck [ə'mʌk] *adv* = **amok**.
amuse [ə'mjuːz] *vt* divertir; **to** ~ **o.s. with sth/by doing sth** divertir-se com algo/em fazer algo; **to be** ~**d at** achar graça em; **he was not** ~**d** ele ficou sem graça.
amusement [ə'mjuːzmənt] *n* diversão *f*, divertimento; (*pastime*) passatempo; (*laughter*) riso; **much to my** ~ para grande diversão minha.
amusement arcade *n* fliperama *m*.
amusing [ə'mjuːzɪŋ] *adj* divertido.
an [æn, ən, n] *indef art see* **a**.
ANA *n abbr* = **American Newspaper Association**; **American Nurses Association**.
anachronism [ə'nækrənɪzəm] *n* anacronismo.
anaemia [ə'niːmɪə] (*US* **anemia**) *n* anemia.
anaemic [ə'niːmɪk] (*US* **anemic**) *adj* anêmico.
anaesthetic [ænɪs'θɛtɪk] (*US* **anesthetic**) *adj*, *n* anestésico; **under** ~ sob anestesia; **local/general** ~ anestesia local/geral.
anaesthetist [æ'niːsθɪtɪst] (*US* **anesthetist**) *n* anestesista *m/f*.
anagram ['ænəgræm] *n* anagrama *m*.
analgesic [ænæl'dʒiːsɪk] *adj*, *n* analgésico.
analog(ue) ['ænəlɔg] *adj* (*watch, computer*) analogico.
analogy [ə'nælədʒɪ] *n* analogia; **to draw** *or* **make an** ~ **between** fazer uma analogia entre.
analyse ['ænəlaɪz] (*US* **analyze**) *vt* analizar.
analyses [ə'næləsiːz] *npl of* **analysis**.
analysis [ə'næləsɪs] (*pl* **analyses**) *n* análise *f*; **in the last** *or* **final** ~ em última análise.
analyst ['ænəlɪst] *n* analista *m/f*; (*psychoanalyst*) psicanalista *m/f*.
analytic(al) [ænə'lɪtɪk(əl)] *adj* analítico.
analyze ['ænəlaɪz] (*US*) *vt* = **analyse**.
anarchic [ə'nɑːkɪk] *adj* anárquico.
anarchist ['ænəkɪst] *adj*, *n* anarquista *m/f*.
anarchy ['ænəkɪ] *n* anarquia.
anathema [ə'næθɪmə] *n*: **it is** ~ **to him** ele tem horror disso.
anatomical [ænə'tɔmɪkəl] *adj* anatômico.
anatomy [ə'nætəmɪ] *n* anatomia.

***NB**: European Portuguese adds the following consonants to certain words:* **b** (sú(b)dito, su(b)til); **c** (a(c)ção, a(c)cionista, a(c)to); **m** (inde(m)ne); **p** (ado(p)ção, ado(p)tar); *for further details see p. xiii.*

ANC *n abbr* (= *African National Congress*) CNA *m*.
ancestor ['ænsɪstə*] *n* antepassado.
ancestral [æn'sɛstrəl] *adj* ancestral.
ancestry ['ænsɪstrɪ] *n* ascendência, ancestrais *mpl*.
anchor ['æŋkə*] *n* âncora ♦ *vi* (*also*: *to drop* ~) ancorar, fundear ♦ *vt* (*boat*) ancorar; (*fig*) segurar, firmar; **to weigh** ~ levantar âncoras; **to drop** ~ fundear.
anchorage ['æŋkərɪdʒ] *n* ancoradouro.
anchovy ['æntʃəvɪ] *n* enchova.
ancient ['eɪnʃənt] *adj* antigo, velho; ~ **monument** monumento antigo.
ancillary [æn'sɪlərɪ] *adj* auxiliar.
and [ænd] *conj* e; ~ **so on** e assim por diante; **try** ~ **come** tente vir; **come** ~ **sit here** vem sentar aqui; **better** ~ **better** cada vez melhor; **more** ~ **more** cada vez mais.
Andes ['ændi:z] *npl*: **the** ~ os Andes.
anecdote ['ænɪkdəut] *n* anedota.
anemia [ə'ni:mɪə] (*US*) *n* = **anaemia**.
anemic [ə'ni:mɪk] (*US*) *adj* = **anaemic**.
anemone [ə'nɛmənɪ] *n* (*BOT*) anêmona.
anesthetic [ænɪs'θɛtɪk] (*US*) *adj*, *n* = **anaesthetic**.
anesthetist [æ'ni:sθɪtɪst] (*US*) *n* = **anaesthetist**.
anew [ə'nju:] *adv* de novo, novamente.
angel ['eɪndʒəl] *n* anjo.
anger ['æŋgə*] *n* raiva ♦ *vt* zangar.
angina [æn'dʒaɪnə] *n* angina (de peito).
angle ['æŋgl] *n* ângulo ♦ *vi*: **to** ~ **for** (*fish*, *compliments*) pescar; **from their** ~ do ponto de vista deles.
angler ['æŋglə*] *n* pescador(a) *m/f* de vara (*BR*), pescador(a) *m/f* à linha (*PT*).
Anglican ['æŋglɪkən] *adj*, *n* anglicano/a.
anglicize ['æŋglɪsaɪz] *vt* anglicizar.
angling ['æŋglɪŋ] *n* pesca à vara (*BR*), pesca à linha (*PT*).
Anglo- ['æŋgləu] *prefix* anglo-.
Anglo-Brazilian *adj* anglo-brasileiro.
Anglo-Portuguese *adj* anglo-português/esa.
Anglo-Saxon [-'sæksən] *adj* anglo-saxão/xôni(c)a ♦ *n* anglo-saxão/xôni(c)a *m/f*; (*LING*) anglo-saxão *m*.
Angola [æŋ'gəulə] *n* Angola (*no article*).
Angolan [æŋ'gəulən] *adj*, *n* angolano/a.
angrily ['æŋgrɪlɪ] *adv* com raiva, zangadamente.
angry ['æŋgrɪ] *adj* zangado; **to be** ~ **with sb/at sth** estar zangado com alguém/algo; **to get** ~ zangar-se; **to make sb** ~ zangar alguém.
anguish ['æŋgwɪʃ] *n* (*physical*) dor *f*, sofrimento; (*mental*) angústia.
angular ['æŋgjulə*] *adj* (*shape*) angular; (*features*) anguloso.
animal ['ænɪməl] *n* animal *m*, bicho ♦ *adj* animal.
animal spirits *npl* vivacidade *f*.
animate [*vt* 'ænɪmeɪt, *adj* 'ænɪmɪt] *vt* animar ♦ *adj* animado.
animated ['ænɪmeɪtɪd] *adj* animado.
animation [ænɪ'meɪʃən] *n* animação.
animosity [ænɪ'mɔsɪtɪ] *n* animosidade *f*.
aniseed ['ænɪsi:d] *n* erva-doce *f*, anis *f*.
Ankara ['æŋkərə] *n* Ancara.
ankle ['æŋkl] *n* tornozelo.
ankle socks *npl* soquetes *fpl*.
annex [*n* 'ænɛks, *vt* æ'nɛks] *n* (*also*: *BRIT*: *annexe*) (*building*) anexo ♦ *vt* anexar.
annexation [ænɛks'eɪʃən] *n* anexação *f*.
annexe ['ænɛks] (*BRIT*) *n* = **annex**.
annihilate [ə'naɪəleɪt] *vt* aniquilar.
anniversary [ænɪ'və:sərɪ] *n* aniversário.
annotate ['ænəuteɪt] *vt* anotar.
announce [ə'nauns] *vt* anunciar; **he ~ed that he wasn't going** ele declarou que não iria.
announcement [ə'naunsmənt] *n* anúncio; (*official*) comunicação *f*; (*letter*, *card*) aviso; **to make an** ~ anunciar alguma coisa.
announcer [ə'naunsə*] *n* (*RADIO*, *TV*) locutor(a) *m/f*.
annoy [ə'nɔɪ] *vt* aborrecer, irritar; **to be ~ed (at sth/with sb)** aborrecer-se *or* irritar-se (com algo/alguém); **don't get ~ed!** não se aborreça!
annoyance [ə'nɔɪəns] *n* aborrecimento; (*thing*) moléstia.
annoying [ə'nɔɪɪŋ] *adj* aborrecido; (*person*) importuno.
annual ['ænjuəl] *adj* anual ♦ *n* (*BOT*) anual *f*; (*book*) anuário.
annual general meeting (*BRIT*) *n* assembléia geral ordinária.
annually ['ænjuəlɪ] *adv* anualmente, cada ano.
annual report *n* relatório anual.
annuity [ə'nju:ɪtɪ] *n* anuidade *f or* renda anual; **life** ~ renda vitalícia.
annul [ə'nʌl] *vt* anular; (*law*) revogar.
annulment [ə'nʌlmənt] *n* anulação *f*; (*of law*) revogação *f*.
annum ['ænəm] *n see* **per annum**.
Annunciation [ənʌnsɪ'eɪʃən] *n* Anunciação *f*.
anode ['ænəud] *n* anodo.
anoint [ə'nɔɪnt] *vt* ungir.
anomalous [ə'nɔmələs] *adj* anômalo.
anomaly [ə'nɔməlɪ] *n* anomalia.
anon [ə'nɔn] *adv* daqui a pouco.
anon. [ə'nɔn] *abbr* = **anonymous**.
anonymity [ænə'nɪmɪtɪ] *n* anonimato.
anonymous [ə'nɔnɪməs] *adj* anônimo; **to remain** ~ ficar no anonimato.
anorak ['ænəræk] *n* anoraque *m* (*BR*), anorak *m* (*PT*).
anorexia [ænə'rɛksɪə] *n* (*MED*: *also*: ~ *nervosa*) anorexia.
another [ə'nʌðə*] *adj*: ~ **book** (*one more*) outro livro, mais um livro; (*a different one*) um outro livro, um livro diferente ♦ *pron* outro; ~ **drink?** outra bebida?, mais uma bebida?; **in** ~ **5 years** daqui a 5 anos; *see also* **one**.
ANSI *n abbr* (= *American National Standards Institute*) *instituto de padrões*.
answer ['ɑ:nsə*] *n* resposta; (*to problem*) solução *f* ♦ *vi* responder ♦ *vt* (*reply to*) responder a; (*problem*) resolver; **to** ~ **the phone** atender o telefone; **in** ~ **to your letter**

em resposta *or* respondendo à sua carta; **to ~ the bell** *or* **the door** atender à porta.
answer back *vi* replicar, retrucar.
answer for *vt fus* responder por, responsabilizar-se por.
answer to *vt fus* (*description*) corresponder a; (*needs*) satisfazer.
answerable ['ɑ:nsərəbl] *adj*: ~ **(to sb/for sth)** responsável (perante alguém/por algo); **I am ~ to no-one** não tenho que dar satisfações a ninguém.
answering machine ['ɑ:nsərɪŋ-] *n* secretária eletrônica.
ant [ænt] *n* formiga.
ANTA *n abbr* = **American National Theatre and Academy**.
antacid [ænt'æsɪd] *adj* antiácido.
antagonism [æn'tægənɪzəm] *n* antagonismo.
antagonist [æn'tægənɪst] *n* antagonista *m/f*, adversário/a.
antagonistic [æntægə'nɪstɪk] *adj* antagônico, hostil; (*opposed*) oposto, contrário.
antagonize [æn'tægənaɪz] *vt* contrariar, hostilizar.
Antarctic [ænt'ɑ:ktɪk] *adj* antártico ♦ *n*: **the ~** o Antártico.
Antarctica [æn'tɑ:ktɪkə] *n* Antártica.
Antarctic Circle *n* Círculo Polar Antártico.
Antarctic Ocean *n* oceano Antártico.
ante ['æntɪ] *n*: **to up the ~** apostar mais alto.
ante... ['æntɪ] *prefix* ante..., pré....
anteater ['ænti:tə*] *n* tamanduá *m*.
antecedent [æntɪ'si:dənt] *n* antecedente *m*.
antechamber ['æntɪtʃeɪmbə*] *n* antecâmara.
antelope ['æntɪləup] *n* antílope *m*.
antenatal ['æntɪ'neɪtl] *adj* pré-natal; **~ clinic** clínica pré-natal.
antenna [æn'tɛnə] (*pl* **~e**) *n* antena.
antennae [æn'tɛni:] *npl of* **antenna**.
anthem ['ænθəm] *n* motete *m*; *see also* **national anthem**.
ant hill *n* formigueiro.
anthology [æn'θɔlədʒɪ] *n* antologia.
anthropologist [ænθrə'pɔlədʒɪst] *n* antropologista *m/f*, antropólogo/a.
anthropology [ænθrə'pɔlədʒɪ] *n* antropologia.
anti... [æntɪ] *prefix* anti....
anti-aircraft *adj* antiaéreo.
anti-aircraft defence *n* defesa antiaérea.
anti-ballistic missile ['æntɪbə'lɪstɪk-] *n* míssil *m* antimíssil.
antibiotic [æntɪbaɪ'ɔtɪk] *adj*, *n* antibiótico.
antibody ['æntɪbɔdɪ] *n* anticorpo.
anticipate [æn'tɪsɪpeɪt] *vt* (*foresee*) prever; (*expect*) esperar; (*forestall*) antecipar; (*look forward to*) aguardar, esperar; **this is worse than I ~d** isso é pior do que eu esperava; **as ~d** como previsto.
anticipation [æntɪsɪ'peɪʃən] *n* expectativa; **thanking you in ~** antecipadamente grato(s), agradeço (*or* agradecemos) antecipadamente a atenção de V.Sª.
anticlimax [æntɪ'klaɪmæks] *n* desapontamento, desilusão *f*.
anticlockwise [æntɪ'klɔkwaɪz] *adv* em sentido anti-horário.
antics ['æntɪks] *npl* bobices *fpl*; (*of child*) travessuras.
anticyclone [æntɪ'saɪkləun] *n* anticiclone *m*.
antidote ['æntɪdəut] *n* antídoto.
antifreeze ['æntɪfri:z] *n* anticongelante *m*.
antihistamine [æntɪ'hɪstəmi:n] *n* anti-histamínico.
Antilles [æn'tɪli:z] *npl*: **the ~** as Antilhas.
antipathy [æn'tɪpəθɪ] *n* antipatia.
Antipodean [æntɪpə'di:ən] *adj* australiano e neozelandês.
Antipodes [æn'tɪpədi:z] *npl*: **the ~** a Austrália e a Nova Zelândia.
antiquarian [æntɪ'kwɛərɪən] *adj*: **~ bookshop** livraria de livros usados, sebo (*BR*) ♦ *n* antiquário/a.
antiquated ['æntɪkweɪtɪd] *adj* antiquado.
antique [æn'ti:k] *n* antiguidade *f*, antigualha ♦ *adj* antigo.
antique dealer *n* antiquário/a.
antique shop *n* loja de antiguidades.
antiquity [æn'tɪkwɪtɪ] *n* antiguidade *f*.
anti-Semitic [-sɪ'mɪtɪk] *adj* (*person*) anti-semita; (*views, publications etc*) anti-semítico.
anti-Semitism [-'sɛmɪtɪzəm] *n* anti-semitismo.
antiseptic [æntɪ'sɛptɪk] *adj*, *n* anti-séptico.
antisocial [æntɪ'səuʃəl] *adj* insociável; (*against society*) anti-social.
antitank ['æntɪ'tæŋk] *adj* antitanque *inv*.
antitheses [æn'tɪθɪsi:z] *npl of* **antithesis**.
antithesis [æn'tɪθɪsɪs] (*pl* **antitheses**) *n* antítese *f*.
antitrust legislation ['æntɪ'trʌst-] *n* legislação *f* antitruste.
antlers ['æntləz] *npl* esgalhos *mpl*, chifres *mpl*.
Antwerp ['æntwə:p] *n* Antuérpia.
anus ['eɪnəs] *n* ânus *m*.
anvil ['ænvɪl] *n* bigorna.
anxiety [æŋ'zaɪətɪ] *n* (*worry*) inquietude *f*; (*eagerness*) ânsia; (*MED*) ansiedade *f*; **~ to do** ânsia de fazer.
anxious ['æŋkʃəs] *adj* (*worried*) inquieto, apreensivo; (*moment*) angustiante; (*keen*) ansioso; **~ to do/for sth** ansioso para fazer/por algo; **to be ~ that** desejar que; **I'm very ~ about you** estou muito preocupado com você.
anxiously ['æŋkʃəslɪ] *adv* ansiosamente.
any ['ɛnɪ] *adj* (*in negative and interrogative sentences = some*) algum(a); (*negative sense*) nenhum(a); (*no matter which*) qualquer; (*each and every*) todo/a ♦ *pron* (*some*) algum(a); (*none*) nenhum(a) ♦ *adv* (*in negative sentences*) nada; (*in interrogative and conditional constructions*) algo; **I haven't ~ money/books** não tenho dinheiro/livros; **have you ~ butter/children?** você

NB: *European Portuguese adds the following consonants to certain words:* **b** (sú(b)dito, su(b)til); **c** (a(c)ção, a(c)cionista, a(c)to); **m** (inde(m)ne); **p** (ado(p)ção, ado(p)tar); *for further details see p. xiii.*

tem manteiga/filhos?; **without ~ difficulty** sem problema nenhum; **at ~ moment** a qualquer momento; **come (at) ~ time** venha a qualquer hora; **~ day now** qualquer dia desses; **in ~ case** em todo o caso; **at ~ rate** de qualquer modo; **I haven't ~** não tenho nenhum; **have you got ~?** tem algum?; **can ~ of you sing?** algum de vocês sabe cantar?; **I can't hear him ~ more** não consigo mais ouvi-lo; **do you want ~ more soup?** quer mais sopa?; **are you feeling ~ better?** você se está sentindo melhor?
anybody ['ɛnɪbɔdɪ] *pron* qualquer um, qualquer pessoa; (*in interrogative sentences*) alguém; (*in negative sentences*): **I don't see ~** não vejo ninguém.
anyhow ['ɛnɪhau] *adv* de qualquer modo; (*carelessly*) descuidadamente; **I shall go ~** eu irei de qualquer jeito.
anyone ['ɛnɪwʌn] *pron* qualquer um, qualquer pessoa; (*in interrogative sentences*) alguém; (*in negative sentences*): **I don't see ~** não vejo ninguém.
anyplace ['ɛnɪpleɪs] (*US*) *adv* em qualquer parte; (*negative sense*) em parte nenhuma; (*everywhere*) em *or* por toda a parte.
anything ['ɛnɪθɪŋ] *pron* qualquer coisa; (*in interrogative sentences*) alguma coisa; (*in negative sentences*) nada; (*everything*) tudo.
anytime ['ɛnɪtaɪm] *adv* (*at any moment*) a qualquer momento; (*whenever*) não importa quando.
anyway ['ɛnɪweɪ] *adv* de qualquer modo.
anywhere ['ɛnɪwɛə*] *adv* em qualquer parte; (*negative sense*) em parte nenhuma; (*everywhere*) em *or* por toda a parte; **I don't see him ~** não o vejo em parte nenhuma; **~ in the world** em qualquer lugar do mundo.
Anzac ['ænzæk] *n abbr* (= *Australia-New Zealand Army Corps*) *soldado da tropa ANZAC.*
apart [ə'pɑːt] *adv* à parte, de lado; (*separately*) separado; **10 miles ~** separados por 10 milhas; **they are living ~** estão separados; **~ from** além de, à parte de.
apartheid [ə'pɑːteɪt] *n* apartheid *m.*
apartment [ə'pɑːtmənt] (*US*) *n* apartamento.
apartment building (*US*) *n* prédio *or* edifício (de apartamentos).
apathetic [æpə'θɛtɪk] *adj* apático, indiferente.
apathy ['æpəθɪ] *n* apatia, indiferença.
APB (*US*) *n abbr* (= *all points bulletin*) *expressão usada pela polícia significando "descubram e prendam o suspeito".*
ape [eɪp] *n* macaco ♦ *vt* macaquear, imitar.
Apennines ['æpənaɪnz] *npl*: **the ~** os Apeninos.
aperitif [ə'pɛrɪtɪv] *n* aperitivo.
aperture ['æpətʃjuə*] *n* orifício; (*PHOT*) abertura.
APEX ['eɪpɛks] *n* (*BRIT*: = *Association of Professional, Executive, Clerical and Computer Staff*) *sindicato de funcionários comerciais;* (*AVIAT*: = *advance passenger excursion*) APEX *f.*
apex ['eɪpɛks] *n* ápice *m.*
aphid ['eɪfɪd] *n* pulgão *m.*
aphrodisiac [æfrəu'dɪzɪæk] *adj, n* afrodisíaco.
API *n abbr* = **American Press Institute.**
apiece [ə'piːs] *adv* (*for each person*) cada um, por cabeça; (*for each item*) cada.
aplomb [ə'plɔm] *n* desenvoltura.
APO (*US*) *n abbr* (= *Army Post Office*) *serviço postal do exército.*
apocalypse [ə'pɔkəlɪps] *n* apocalipse *m.*
apolitical [eɪpə'lɪtɪkl] *adj* apolítico.
apologetic [əpɔlə'dʒɛtɪk] *adj* cheio de desculpas.
apologetically [əpɔlə'dʒɛtɪklɪ] *adv* (*say*) desculpando-se; (*smile*) como quem pede desculpas.
apologize [ə'pɔlədʒaɪz] *vi*: **to ~ (for sth to sb)** desculpar-se *or* pedir desculpas (por *or* de algo a alguém).
apology [ə'pɔlədʒɪ] *n* desculpas *fpl*; **please accept my apologies for ...** peço desculpas por ...; **to send one's apologies** apresentar desculpas.
apoplectic [æpə'plɛktɪk] *adj* (*MED*) apopléctico; (*inf*): **~ with rage** enraivecido.
apoplexy ['æpəplɛksɪ] *n* (*MED*) apoplexia.
apostle [ə'pɔsl] *n* apóstolo.
apostrophe [ə'pɔstrəfɪ] *n* apóstrofo.
appal [ə'pɔːl] *vt* horrorizar.
Appalachian Mountains [æpə'leɪʃən-] *npl*: **the ~** os montes Apalaches.
appalling [ə'pɔːlɪŋ] *adj* horrível; **she's an ~ cook** ela é uma péssima cozinheira.
apparatus [æpə'reɪtəs] *n* aparelho; (*in gym*) aparelhos *mpl.*
apparel [ə'pærl] (*US*) *n* vestuário, roupa.
apparent [ə'pærənt] *adj* aparente; (*obvious*) claro, patente; **it is ~ that ...** é claro *or* evidente que ....
apparently [ə'pærəntlɪ] *adv* aparentemente, pelo(s) visto(s).
apparition [æpə'rɪʃən] *n* aparição *f*; (*ghost*) fantasma *m.*
appeal [ə'piːl] *vi* (*LAW*) apelar, recorrer ♦ *n* (*LAW*) recurso, apelação *f*; (*request*) pedido; (*plea*) súplica; (*charm*) encanto, atração *f*; **to ~ for** solicitar; **to appeal to** (*subj*: *person*) suplicar a; (: *thing*) atrair, agradar a; **to ~ to sb for mercy** pedir misericórdia a alguém; **it doesn't ~ to me** não me atrai; **right of ~** direito a recorrer *or* apelar.
appealing [ə'piːlɪŋ] *adj* (*nice*) atraente; (*touching*) comovedor(a), comovente.
appear [ə'pɪə*] *vi* (*come into view*) aparecer; (*be present*) comparecer; (*LAW*) apresentar-se, comparecer; (*publication*) ser publicado; (*seem*) parecer; **it would ~ that** pareceria que; **to ~ in Hamlet** trabalhar em Hamlet; **to ~ on TV** (*person, news item*) sair na televisão; (*programme*) passar na televisão.
appearance [ə'pɪərəns] *n* (*coming into view*) aparecimento; (*presence*) comparecimento; (*look, aspect*) aparência; **to put in** *or* **make an ~** comparecer; **in order of ~** (*THEATRE*) por ordem de entrar em cena; **to keep up**

~s manter as aparências; **to all ~s** ao que tudo indica.
appease [ə'pi:z] *vt* (*pacify*) apaziguar; (*satisfy*) satisfazer.
appeasement [ə'pi:zmənt] *n* apaziguamento.
append [ə'pɛnd] *vt* anexar.
appendage [ə'pɛndɪdʒ] *n* apêndice *m*.
appendices [ə'pɛndɪsi:z] *npl of* **appendix**.
appendicitis [əpɛndɪ'saɪtɪs] *n* apendicite *f*.
appendix [ə'pɛndɪks] (*pl* **appendices**) *n* apêndice *m*; **to have one's ~ out** tirar o apêndice.
appetite ['æpɪtaɪt] *n* apetite *m*; **that walk has given me an ~** essa caminhada me abriu o apetite.
appetizer ['æpɪtaɪzə*] *n* (*food*) tira-gosto; (*drink*) aperitivo.
appetizing ['æpɪtaɪzɪŋ] *adj* apetitoso.
applaud [ə'plɔ:d] *vt*, *vi* aplaudir.
applause [ə'plɔ:z] *n* aplausos *mpl*.
apple ['æpl] *n* maçã *f*; (*also*: *~ tree*) macieira; **she's the ~ of his eye** ela é a menina dos olhos dele.
apple tree *n* macieira.
apple turnover *n* pastel *m* de maçã.
appliance [ə'plaɪəns] *n* (*TECH*) aparelho; **electrical** *or* **domestic ~s** eletrodomésticos *mpl*.
applicable [ə'plɪkəbl] *adj* aplicável; (*relevant*) apropriado; **the law is ~ from January** a lei entrará em vigor a partir de janeiro; **to be ~ to** valer para.
applicant ['æplɪkənt] *n*: **~ (for)** (*for post*) candidato/a (a); (*ADMIN*: *for benefit etc*) requerente *m/f* (de).
application [æplɪ'keɪʃən] *n* aplicação *f*; (*for a job, a grant etc*) candidatura, requerimento; **on ~** a pedido.
application form *n* (formulário de) requerimento.
application program *n* (*COMPUT*) aplicativo.
applications package *n* (*COMPUT*) pacote *m* de aplicações.
applied [ə'plaɪd] *adj* aplicado.
apply [ə'plaɪ] *vt*: **to ~ (to)** aplicar (a) ♦ *vi*: **to ~ to** apresentar-se a; (*be suitable for*) ser aplicável a; (*be relevant to*) dizer respeito a; **to ~ for** (*permit, grant, job*) solicitar, pedir; **to ~ the brakes** frear (*BR*), travar (*PT*); **to ~ o.s. to** aplicar-se a, dedicar-se a.
appoint [ə'pɔɪnt] *vt* (*to post*) nomear; (*date, place*) marcar.
appointee [əpɔɪn'ti:] *n* nomeado/a.
appointment [ə'pɔɪntmənt] *n* (*engagement*) encontro, marcado, compromisso; (*at doctors etc*) hora marcada; (*act*) nomeação *f*; (*post*) cargo; **to make an ~ (with)** marcar um encontro (com); (*with doctor, hairdresser etc*) marcar hora (com); **"~s (vacant)"** (*PRESS*) "ofertas de emprego"; **by ~** com hora marcada.
apportion [ə'pɔ:ʃən] *vt* repartir, distribuir; (*blame*) pôr; **to ~ sth to sb** atribuir algo a alguém.
appraisal [ə'preɪzl] *n* avaliação *f*, estimatura.
appraise [ə'preɪz] *vt* avaliar.
appreciable [ə'pri:ʃəbl] *adj* apreciável, notável.
appreciate [ə'pri:ʃɪeɪt] *vt* (*like*) apreciar, estimar; (*be grateful for*) agradecer; (*be aware of*) compreender, perceber ♦ *vi* (*COMM*) valorizar-se; **I ~ your help** agradeço-lhe a *or* pela sua ajuda.
appreciation [əpri:ʃɪ'eɪʃən] *n* apreciação *f*, estima; (*gratitude*) agradecimento; (*FINANCE*) valorização *f*.
appreciative [ə'pri:ʃɪətɪv] *adj* (*person*) agradecido; (*comment*) elogioso.
apprehend [æprɪ'hɛnd] *vt* (*understand*) perceber, compreender; (*arrest*) prender.
apprehension [æprɪ'hɛnʃən] *n* apreensão *f*.
apprehensive [æprɪ'hɛnsɪv] *adj* apreensivo, receoso.
apprentice [ə'prɛntɪs] *n* aprendiz *m/f* ♦ *vt*: **to be ~d to** ser aprendiz de.
apprenticeship [ə'prɛntɪsʃɪp] *n* aprendizado, aprendizagem *f*; **to serve one's ~** fazer seu aprendizado.
appro. ['æprəu] (*BRIT*: *inf*) *abbr* (*COMM*) = **approval**.
approach [ə'prəutʃ] *vi* aproximar-se ♦ *vt* aproximar-se de; (*be approximate*) aproximar-se a; (*ask, apply to*) dirigir-se a; (*subject, passer-by*) abordar ♦ *n* aproximação *f*; (*access*) acesso; (*proposal*) proposição *f*; (*way of handling*) enfoque *m*; **to ~ sb about sth** falar com alguém sobre algo.
approachable [ə'prəutʃəbl] *adj* (*person*) tratável; (*place*) acessível.
approach road *n* via de acesso.
approbation [æprə'beɪʃən] *n* aprovação *f*.
appropriate [*vt* ə'prəuprɪeɪt, *adj* ə'prəuprɪɪt] *vt* (*take*) apropriar-se de; (*allot*): **to ~ sth for** destinar algo a ♦ *adj* (*apt*) apropriado, próprio; (*relevant*) adequado; **it would not be ~ for me to comment** não seria conveniente eu comentar.
appropriately [ə'prəuprɪɪtlɪ] *adv* adequadamente.
appropriation [əprəuprɪ'eɪʃən] *n* (*confiscation*) apropriação *f*; (*of funds for sth*) dotação *f*.
approval [ə'pru:vəl] *n* aprovação *f*; **on ~** (*COMM*) a contento; **to meet with sb's ~** (*proposal etc*) ser aprovado por alguém, obter a aprovação de alguém.
approve [ə'pru:v] *vt* aprovar.
  approve of *vt fus* aprovar.
approved school [ə'pru:vd-] (*BRIT*) *n* reformatório.
approvingly [ə'pru:vɪŋlɪ] *adv* com aprovação.
approx. *abbr* = **approximately**.
approximate [*adj* ə'prɔksɪmɪt, *vt* ə'prɔksɪmeɪt] *adj* aproximado ♦ *vt* aproximar.
approximately [ə'prɔksɪmɪtlɪ] *adv* aproxima-

damente.

approximation [əprɔksɪ'meɪʃən] *n* aproximação *f*.

apr *n abbr* (= *annual percentage rate*) *taxa de juros anual*.

Apr. *abbr* = **April**.

apricot ['eɪprɪkɔt] *n* damasco.

April ['eɪprəl] *n* abril *m*; *see also* **July**.

April Fool's Day *n* Primeiro-de-abril *m*.

apron ['eɪprən] *n* avental *m*; (*AVIAT*) pátio de estacionamento.

apse [æps] *n* (*ARCHIT*) abside *f*.

APT (*BRIT*) *n abbr* = **advanced passenger train**.

apt [æpt] *adj* (*suitable*) adequado; (*appropriate*) a propósito, apropriado; (*likely*): ~ **to do** sujeito a fazer.

Apt. *abbr* (= *apartment*) ap., apto.

aptitude ['æptɪtjuːd] *n* aptidão *f*, talento.

aptitude test *n* teste *m* de aptidão.

aptly ['æptlɪ] *adv* (*express*) acertadamente; ~ **named** apropriadamente chamado.

aqualung ['ækwəlʌŋ] *n* aparelho respiratório autônomo.

aquarium [ə'kwɛərɪəm] *n* aquário.

Aquarius [ə'kwɛərɪəs] *n* Aquário.

aquatic [ə'kwætɪk] *adj* aquático.

aqueduct ['ækwɪdʌkt] *n* aqueduto.

AR (*US*) *abbr* (*POST*) = **Arkansas**.

ARA (*BRIT*) *n abbr* = **Associate of the Royal Academy**.

Arab ['ærəb] *adj*, *n* árabe *m/f*.

Arabia [ə'reɪbɪə] *n* Arábia.

Arabian [ə'reɪbɪən] *adj* árabe.

Arabian Desert *n* deserto da Arábia.

Arabian Sea *n* mar *m* Arábico.

Arabic ['ærəbɪk] *n* árabe *m* ♦ *adj* árabe.

Arabic numerals *npl* algarismos *mpl* arábicos.

arable ['ærəbl] *adj* cultivável.

ARAM (*BRIT*) *n abbr* = **Associate of the Royal Academy of Music**.

arbiter ['ɑːbɪtə*] *n* árbitro.

arbitrary ['ɑːbɪtrərɪ] *adj* arbitrário.

arbitrate ['ɑːbɪtreɪt] *vi* arbitrar.

arbitration [ɑːbɪ'treɪʃən] *n* arbitragem *f*; **the dispute went to** ~ o litígio foi submetido a arbitragem.

arbitrator ['ɑːbɪtreɪtə*] *n* árbitro.

ARC *n abbr* = **American Red Cross**.

arc [ɑːk] *n* arco.

arcade [ɑː'keɪd] *n* arcada; (*round a square*) arcos *mpl*; (*passage with shops*) galeria.

arch [ɑːtʃ] *n* arco ♦ *vt* arquear, curvar ♦ *adj* malicioso ♦ *prefix*: ~**(-)** arce..., arqui...; **pointed** ~ ogiva.

archaeological [ɑːkɪə'lɔdʒɪkl] (*US* **archeological**) *adj* arqueológico.

archaeologist [ɑːkɪ'ɔlədʒɪst] (*US* **archeologist**) *n* arqueólogo/a.

archaeology [ɑːkɪ'ɔlədʒɪ] (*US* **archeology**) *n* arqueologia.

archaic [ɑː'keɪɪk] *adj* arcaico.

archangel ['ɑːkeɪndʒəl] *n* arcanjo.

archbishop [ɑːtʃ'bɪʃəp] *n* arcebispo.

arch-enemy *n* arquiinimigo/a.

archeology *etc* [ɑːkɪ'ɔlədʒɪ] (*US*) = **archaeology** *etc*.

archer ['ɑːtʃə*] *n* arqueiro/a.

archery ['ɑːtʃərɪ] *n* tiro de arco.

archetypal ['ɑːkɪtaɪpəl] *adj* arquetípico.

archetype ['ɑːkɪtaɪp] *n* arquétipo.

archipelago [ɑːkɪ'pɛlɪgəu] *n* arquipélago.

architect ['ɑːkɪtɛkt] *n* arquiteto/a.

architectural [ɑːkɪ'tɛktʃərəl] *adj* arquitetônico.

architecture ['ɑːkɪtɛktʃə*] *n* arquitetura.

archives ['ɑːkaɪvz] *npl* arquivo.

archivist ['ɑːkɪvɪst] *n* arquivista *m/f*.

archway ['ɑːtʃweɪ] *n* arco.

ARCM (*BRIT*) *n abbr* = **Associate of the Royal College of Music**.

Arctic ['ɑːktɪk] *adj* ártico ♦ *n*: **the** ~ o Ártico.

Arctic Circle *n* Círculo Polar Ártico.

Arctic Ocean *n* oceano Ártico.

ARD (*US*) *n abbr* (*MED*) = **acute respiratory disease**.

ardent ['ɑːdənt] *adj* (*passionate*) ardente, apaixonado; (*fervent*) fervoroso.

ardour ['ɑːdə*] (*US* **ardor**) *n* (*passion*) ardor *m*; (*fervour*) fervor *m*.

arduous ['ɑːdjuəs] *adj* árduo.

are [ɑː*] *vb see* **be**.

area ['ɛərɪə] *n* área; (*MAT*) superfície *f*, extensão *f*; (*zone*) zona, região *f*; **dining** ~ área de jantar; **the London** ~ a região de Londres.

area code (*US*) *n* (*TEL*) código DDD *or* de área.

arena [ə'riːnə] *n* arena; (*of circus*) picadeiro (*BR*), pista (*PT*); (*for bullfight*) arena (*BR*), praça (*PT*).

aren't [ɑːnt] = **are not**.

Argentina [ɑːdʒən'tiːnə] *n* Argentina.

Argentinian [ɑːdʒən'tɪnɪən] *adj*, *n* argentino/a.

arguable ['ɑːgjuəbl] *adj* discutível.

arguably ['ɑːgjuəblɪ] *adv* possivelmente.

argue ['ɑːgjuː] *vi* (*quarrel*) discutir; (*reason*) argumentar; **to ~ about sth (with sb)** discutir sobre algo (com alguém); **to ~ that** sustentar que.

argument ['ɑːgjumənt] *n* (*reasons*) argumento; (*quarrel*) briga, discussão *f*; (*debate*) debate *m*; ~ **for/against** argumento a favor de/contra.

argumentative [ɑːgju'mɛntətɪv] *adj* discutidor(a).

aria ['ɑːrɪə] *n* (*MUS*) ária.

ARIBA (*BRIT*) *n abbr* = **Associate of the Royal Institute of British Architects**.

arid ['ærɪd] *adj* árido.

aridity [ə'rɪdɪtɪ] *n* aridez *f*.

Aries ['ɛərɪz] *n* Áries *m*.

arise [ə'raɪz] (*irreg*: *like* **rise**) *vi* (*rise up*) levantar-se, erguer-se; (*emerge*) surgir; **to ~ from** resultar de; **should the need ~** se for necessário.

aristocracy [ærɪs'tɔkrəsɪ] *n* aristocracia.

aristocrat ['ærɪstəkræt] *n* aristocrata *m/f*.

aristocratic [ærɪstə'krætɪk] *adj* aristocrático.

arithmetic [ə'rɪθmətɪk] *n* aritmética.

arithmetical [ærɪθ'mɛtɪkl] *adj* aritmético.
ark [ɑːk] *n*: **Noah's A~** arca de Noé.
arm [ɑːm] *n* (*ANAT*) braço ♦ *vt* armar; **~s** *npl* (*weapons*) armas *fpl*; (*HERALDRY*) brasão *m*; **~ in ~** de braços dados.
armaments ['ɑːməmənts] *npl* (*weapons*) armamento.
armband ['ɑːmbænd] *n* faixa de braço, braçadeira; (*for swimming*) bóia de braço.
armchair ['ɑːmtʃɛə*] *n* poltrona.
armed [ɑːmd] *adj* armado; **the ~ forces** as forças armadas.
armed robbery *n* assalto à mão armada.
Armenia [ɑː'miːnɪə] *n* Armênia.
Armenian [ɑː'miːnɪən] *adj* armênio ♦ *n* armênio/a; (*LING*) armênio.
armful ['ɑːmful] *n* braçada.
armistice ['ɑːmɪstɪs] *n* armistício.
armour ['ɑːmə*] (*US* **armor**) *n* armadura; (*also*: **~** *plating*) blindagem *f*.
armo(u)red car ['ɑːməd-] *n* carro blindado.
armo(u)ry ['ɑːmərɪ] *n* arsenal *m*.
armpit ['ɑːmpɪt] *n* sovaco.
armrest ['ɑːmrɛst] *n* braço (de poltrona).
arms control *n* controle *m* de armas.
arms race *n* corrida armamentista.
army ['ɑːmɪ] *n* exército.
aroma [ə'rəumə] *n* aroma.
aromatic [ærə'mætɪk] *adj* aromático.
arose [ə'rəuz] *pt of* **arise**.
around [ə'raund] *adv* em volta; (*in the area*) perto ♦ *prep* em redor de, em volta de; (*fig*: *about*) cerca de; **is he ~?** ele está por aí?
arouse [ə'rauz] *vt* despertar.
arpeggio [ɑː'pɛdʒɪəu] *n* arpejo.
arrange [ə'reɪndʒ] *vt* arranjar; (*programme*) organizar ♦ *vi*: **we have ~d for a car to pick you up** providenciamos um carro para buscá-lo; **it was ~d that ...** foi combinado que ...; **to ~ to do sth** combinar em *or* ficar de fazer algo.
arrangement [ə'reɪndʒmənt] *n* arranjo; (*agreement*) acordo; **~s** *npl* (*plans*) planos *mpl*; (*preparations*) preparativos *mpl*; **to come to an ~ (with sb)** chegar a um acordo (com alguém); **home deliveries by ~** entregas a domicílio por convênio; **I'll make all the necessary ~s** eu vou tomar todas as providências necessárias.
array [ə'reɪ] *n* (*variety*) leque *m*; (*MATH*, *COMPUT*) tabela.
arrears [ə'rɪəz] *npl* atrasos *mpl*; **to be in ~ with one's rent** atrasar o aluguel.
arrest [ə'rɛst] *vt* prender, deter; (*sb's attention*) chamar, prender ♦ *n* detenção *f*, prisão *f*; **under ~** preso.
arresting [ə'rɛstɪŋ] *adj* (*fig*: *beauty*) cativante; (: *painting*, *novel*) impressionante.
arrival [ə'raɪvəl] *n* chegada; **new ~** recém-chegado.
arrive [ə'raɪv] *vi* chegar.
arrive at *vt fus* (*fig*) chegar a.
arrogance ['ærəgəns] *n* arrogância.
arrogant ['ærəgənt] *adj* arrogante.
arrow ['ærəu] *n* flecha, seta.
arse [ɑːs] (*BRIT*: *inf!*) *n* cu *m* (*!*).
arsenal ['ɑːsɪnl] *n* arsenal *m*.
arsenic ['ɑːsnɪk] *n* arsênico.
arson ['ɑːsn] *n* incêndio premeditado.
art [ɑːt] *n* arte *f*; (*craft*) ofício; (*skill*) habilidade *f*, jeito; **~s** *npl* (*SCH*) letras *fpl*; **work of ~** obra de arte.
artefact ['ɑːtɪfækt] *n* artefato.
arterial [ɑː'tɪərɪəl] *adj* (*ANAT*) arterial; **~ road** estrada mestra.
artery ['ɑːtərɪ] *n* (*MED*) artéria; (*fig*) estrada principal.
artful ['ɑːtful] *adj* ardiloso, esperto.
art gallery *n* museu *m* de belas artes; (*small*, *private*) galeria de arte.
arthritis [ɑː'θraɪtɪs] *n* artrite *f*.
artichoke ['ɑːtɪtʃəuk] *n* alcachofra; *see also* **Jerusalem**.
article ['ɑːtɪkl] *n* artigo; (*BRIT*: *LAW*: *training*): **~s** *npl* contrato de aprendizagem; **~s of clothing** peças *fpl* de vestuário.
articles of association *npl* (*COMM*) estatutos *mpl* sociais.
articulate [*adj* ɑː'tɪkjulɪt, *vt* ɑː'tɪkjuleɪt] *adj* (*person*) que se expressa com clareza e desenvoltura; (*speech*) bem articulado ♦ *vt* articular, pronunciar.
articulated lorry [ɑː'tɪkjuleɪtɪd-] (*BRIT*) *n* caminhão (*PT*: camião) *m* articulado, jamanta.
artifice ['ɑːtɪfɪs] *n* ardil *m*, artifício.
artificial [ɑːtɪ'fɪʃəl] *adj* artificial; (*teeth etc*) postiço.
artificial insemination [-ɪnsɛmɪ'neɪʃən] *n* inseminação *f* artificial.
artificial intelligence *n* inteligência artificial.
artificial respiration *n* respiração *f* artificial.
artillery [ɑː'tɪlərɪ] *n* artilharia.
artisan ['ɑːtɪzæn] *n* artesão/sã *m/f*.
artist ['ɑːtɪst] *n* artista *m/f*; (*MUS*) intérprete *m/f*.
artistic [ɑː'tɪstɪk] *adj* artístico.
artistry ['ɑːtɪstrɪ] *n* arte *f*, mestria.
artless ['ɑːtlɪs] *adj* (*innocent*) natural, simples; (*clumsy*) desajeitado.
art school *n* ≈ escola de artes.
ARV *n abbr* (= *American Revised Version*) *tradução norte-americana da Bíblia*.
AS (*US*) *n abbr* (*SCH*: = *Associate in/of Science*) *título universitário* ♦ *abbr* (*POST*) = **American Samoa**.
as [æz, əz] *conj* (*cause*) como, já que; (*time*: *moment*) quando; (*duration*) enquanto; (*manner*) como ♦ *prep* (*in the capacity of*) como; **~ big ~** tão grande como; **twice ~ big ~** duas vezes maior que; **much ~ I like them, I ...** por mais que eu goste deles, eu ...; **strong ~ he is, he won't be able to ...** por mais forte que seja, não poderá ...; **~ the years went by** no decorrer dos anos; **~ she**

NB*: European Portuguese adds the following consonants to certain words:* **b** (sú(b)dito, su(b)til); **c** (a(c)ção, a(c)cionista, a(c)to); **m** (inde(m)ne); **p** (ado(p)ção, ado(p)tar); *for further details see p. xiii.*

said como ela disse; **he gave me this ~ a present** ele me deu isso de presente; **~ if** *or* **though** como se; **~ for** *or* **to** quanto a; **~** *or* **so long ~** desde que, contanto que; **~ much/many ... (~)** tanto/s ... (como); **~ soon ~** logo que, assim que; **~ soon ~ possible** o mais cedo possível; **~ such** como tal; **~ well** também; **~ well ~** assim como; *see also* **so**; **such**.

ASA *n abbr* (= *American Standards Association*) *associação de padronização*.

a.s.a.p. *abbr* = **as soon as possible**.

asbestos [æz'bɛstəs] *n* asbesto, amianto.

ascend [ə'sɛnd] *vt* ascender, subir.

ascendancy [ə'sɛndənsɪ] *n* predomínio, ascendência.

ascendant [ə'sɛndənt] *n*: **to be in the ~** estar em alta.

Ascension [ə'sɛnʃən] *n* (REL): **the ~** a Ascensão.

Ascension Island *n* ilha da Ascensão.

ascent [ə'sɛnt] *n* subida; (*slope*) rampa; (*promotion*) ascensão *f*.

ascertain [æsə'teɪn] *vt* averiguar, verificar.

ascetic [ə'sɛtɪk] *adj* ascético.

asceticism [ə'sɛtɪsɪzəm] *n* ascetismo.

ASCII ['æski:] *n abbr* (= *American Standard Code for Information Interchange*) ASCII *m*.

ascribe [ə'skraɪb] *vt*: **to ~ sth to** atribuir algo a.

ASCU (US) *n abbr* = **Association of State Colleges and Universities**.

ASE *n abbr* = **American Stock Exchange**.

ASH [æʃ] (BRIT) *n abbr* (= *Action on Smoking and Health*) *liga antitabagista*.

ash [æʃ] *n* cinza; (*also*: **~** *tree*) freixo.

ashamed [ə'ʃeɪmd] *adj* envergonhado; **to be ~ of** ter vergonha de; **to be ~ (of o.s.) for having done** ter vergonha de ter feito.

ashen ['æʃn] *adj* cinzento.

ashore [ə'ʃɔ:*] *adv* em terra; **to go ~** descer à terra, desembarcar.

ashtray ['æʃtreɪ] *n* cinzeiro.

Ash Wednesday *n* quarta-feira de cinzas.

Asia ['eɪʃə] *n* Ásia.

Asia Minor *n* Ásia Menor.

Asian ['eɪʃən] *adj, n* asiático/a.

Asiatic [eɪsɪ'ætɪk] *adj* asiático/a.

aside [ə'saɪd] *adv* à parte, de lado ♦ *n* aparte *m*; **~ from** além de.

ask [ɑ:sk] *vt* perguntar; (*invite*) convidar; **to ~ sb sth** perguntar algo a alguém; **to ~ sb for sth** pedir algo a alguém; **to ~ sb to do sth** pedir para alguém fazer algo; **to ~ sb the time** perguntar as horas a alguém; **to ~ sb about sth** perguntar a alguém sobre algo; **to ~ about the price** perguntar pelo preço; **to ~ (sb) a question** fazer uma pergunta (a alguém); **to ~ sb out to dinner** convidar alguém para jantar.

ask after *vt fus* perguntar por.

ask for *vt fus* pedir; **it's just ~ing for it** *or* **trouble** é procurar encrenca.

askance [ə'skɑ:ns] *adv*: **to look ~ at sb** olhar alguém de soslaio.

askew [ə'skju:] *adv* torto, de esguelha.

asking price ['ɑ:skɪŋ-] *n* preço pedido.

asleep [ə'sli:p] *adj* dormindo; **to fall ~** dormir, adormecer.

ASLEF ['æzlɛf] (BRIT) *n abbr* (= *Associated Society of Locomotive Engineers and Firemen*) *sindicato dos ferroviários*.

asp [æsp] *n* áspide *f or m*.

asparagus [əs'pærəgəs] *n* aspargo (PT: esp-).

asparagus tips *npl* aspargos *mpl*.

ASPCA *n abbr* = **American Society for the Prevention of Cruelty to Animals**.

aspect ['æspɛkt] *n* aspecto; (*direction in which a building etc faces*) orientação *f*.

aspersions [əs'pə:ʃənz] *npl*: **to cast ~ on** difamar, caluniar.

asphalt ['æsfælt] *n* asfalto.

asphyxiate [æs'fɪksɪeɪt] *vt* asfixiar ♦ *vi* asfixiar-se.

asphyxiation [æsfɪksɪ'eɪʃən] *n* asfixia.

aspirate [*vt* 'æspəreɪt, *adj* 'æspərɪt] *vt* aspirar ♦ *adj* aspirado.

aspiration [æspə'reɪʃən] *n* aspiração *f*.

aspire [əs'paɪə*] *vi*: **to ~ to** aspirar a.

aspirin ['æsprɪn] *n* aspirina.

ass [æs] *n* jumento, burro; (*inf*) imbecil *m/f*; (*US*: *inf!*) cu *m* (*!*).

assail [ə'seɪl] *vt* assaltar, atacar.

assailant [ə'seɪlənt] *n* (*attacker*) assaltante *m/f*, atacante *m/f*; (*aggressor*) agressor(a) *m/f*.

assassin [ə'sæsɪn] *n* assassino/a.

assassinate [ə'sæsɪneɪt] *vt* assassinar.

assassination [əsæsɪ'neɪʃən] *n* assassinato, assassínio.

assault [ə'sɔ:lt] *n* assalto; (LAW): **~ (and battery)** vias *fpl* de fato ♦ *vt* assaltar, atacar; (*sexually*) agredir, violar.

assemble [ə'sɛmbl] *vt* reunir; (TECH) montar ♦ *vi* reunir-se.

assembly [ə'sɛmblɪ] *n* (*meeting*) reunião *f*, assembléia; (*people*) congregação *f*; (*construction*) montagem *f*.

assembly language *n* (COMPUT) linguagem *f* de montagem.

assembly line *n* linha de montagem.

assent [ə'sɛnt] *n* assentimento, aprovação *f* ♦ *vi*: **to ~ (to sth)** consentir *or* assentir (em algo).

assert [ə'sə:t] *vt* afirmar; (*claim etc*) fazer valer; **to ~ o.s.** impor-se.

assertion [ə'sə:ʃən] *n* afirmação *f*.

assertive [ə'sə:tɪv] *adj* (*vigorous*) enérgico; (*forceful*) agressivo; (*dogmatic*) peremptório.

assess [ə'sɛs] *vt* avaliar; (*tax, damages*) fixar; (*property etc*: *for tax*) taxar.

assessment [ə'sɛsmənt] *n* avaliação *f*.

assessor [ə'sɛsə*] *n* avaliador(a) *m/f*; (*of tax*) avaliador(a) do fisco.

asset ['æsɛt] *n* (*property*) bem *m*; (*quality*) vantagem *f*, trunfo; **~s** *npl* (*of company*) ativo; (*of person*) bens *mpl*.

asset-stripping [-'strɪpɪŋ] *n* (COMM) venda em parcelas do patrimônio social.

assiduous [ə'sɪdjuəs] *adj* assíduo.

assign [ə'saɪn] *vt* (*date*) fixar; **to ~ sth to** (*task*) designar algo a; (*resources*) destinar algo a; (*cause*, *meaning*) atribuir algo a.
assignment [ə'saɪnmənt] *n* tarefa.
assimilate [ə'sɪmɪleɪt] *vt* assimilar.
assimilation [əsɪmɪ'leɪʃən] *n* assimilação *f*.
assist [ə'sɪst] *vt* ajudar; (*progress etc*) auxiliar; (*injured person etc*) socorrer.
assistance [ə'sɪstəns] *n* ajuda, auxílio; (*welfare*) subsídio; (*to injured person*) socorro.
assistant [ə'sɪstənt] *n* assistente *m/f*, auxiliar *m/f*; (*BRIT*: *also*: *shop* ~) vendedor(a) *m/f*.
assistant manager *n* subgerente *m/f*.
assizes [ə'saɪzɪz] *npl* sessão *f* de tribunal superior.
associate [*adj*, *n* ə'səuʃɪɪt, *vt*, *vi* ə'səuʃɪeɪt] *adj* associado ♦ *n* (*colleague*) colega *m/f*; (*partner*) sócio/a; (*in crime*) cúmplice *m/f*; (*member*) sócio/a ♦ *vt* associar ♦ *vi*: **to ~ with sb** associar-se com alguém; **~ company** companhia ligada; **~ director** diretor(a) *m/f* associado/a.
associated company [ə'səuʃɪeɪtɪd-] *n* companhia ligada.
association [əsəusɪ'eɪʃən] *n* associação *f*; (*COMM*) sociedade *f*; **in ~ with** em parceria com.
association football (*BRIT*) *n* futebol *m*.
assorted [ə'sɔːtɪd] *adj* sortido; **in ~ sizes** em vários tamanhos.
assortment [ə'sɔːtmənt] *n* sortimento.
Asst. *abbr* = **assistant**.
assuage [ə'sweɪdʒ] *vt* (*grief*, *pain*) aliviar, abrandar; (*thirst*) matar.
assume [ə'sjuːm] *vt* (*suppose*) supor, presumir; (*responsibilities etc*) assumir; (*attitude*, *name*) adotar, tomar.
assumed name [ə'sjuːmd-] *n* nome *m* falso.
assumption [ə'sʌmpʃən] *n* (*supposition*) suposição *f*, presunção *f*; **on the ~ that** na suposição *or* hipótese que; (*on condition that*) com a condição de que.
assurance [ə'ʃuərəns] *n* garantia; (*confidence*) confiança; (*insurance*) seguro.
assure [ə'ʃuə*] *vt* assegurar; **to ~ sb that** garantir *or* assegurar a alguém que.
AST (*US*) *abbr* (= *Atlantic Standard Time*) *hora de inverno de Nova Iorque*.
asterisk ['æstərɪsk] *n* asterisco.
astern [ə'stəːn] *adv* à popa; (*direction*) à ré.
asteroid ['æstərɔɪd] *n* asteróide *m*.
asthma ['æsmə] *n* asma.
asthmatic [æs'mætɪk] *adj*, *n* asmático/a.
astigmatism [ə'stɪgmətɪzəm] *n* astigmatismo.
astir [ə'stəː*] *adv* em agitação.
ASTMS (*BRIT*) *n abbr* (= *Association of Scientific, Technical and Managerial Staffs*) *sindicato dos empregados científicos, técnicos e administrativos*.
astonish [ə'stɔnɪʃ] *vt* assombrar, espantar.
astonishing [ə'stɔnɪʃɪŋ] *adj* espantoso, surpreendente.
astonishingly [ə'stɔnɪʃɪŋlɪ] *adv* surpreendentemente.
astonishment [ə'stɔnɪʃmənt] *n* assombro, espanto; **to my ~** para minha grande surpresa.
astound [ə'staund] *vt* pasmar, estarrecer.
astray [ə'streɪ] *adv*: **to go ~** (*person*) perder-se; (*letter etc*) extraviar-se; **to go ~ in one's calculations** cometer um erro em seus cálculos; **to lead ~** desencaminhar.
astride [ə'straɪd] *prep* a cavalo *or* montado sobre.
astringent [ə'strɪndʒənt] *adj* adstringente ♦ *n* adstringente *m*.
astrologer [əs'trɔlədʒə*] *n* astrólogo/a.
astrology [əs'trɔlədʒɪ] *n* astrologia.
astronaut ['æstrənɔːt] *n* astronauta *m/f*.
astronomer [əs'trɔnəmə*] *n* astrônomo/a.
astronomical [æstrə'nɔmɪkəl] *adj* astronômico.
astronomy [əs'trɔnəmɪ] *n* astronomia.
astrophysics ['æstrəu'fɪzɪks] *n* astrofísica.
astute [əs'tjuːt] *adj* astuto, esperto.
asunder [ə'sʌndə*] *adv*: **to put ~** separar; **to tear ~** rasgar.
ASV *n abbr* (= *American Standard Version*) *tradução da Bíblia*.
asylum [ə'saɪləm] *n* (*refuge*) asilo; (*hospital*) manicômio; *see also* **political asylum**.
asymmetric(al) [eɪsɪ'mɛtrɪk(l)] *adj* assimétrico.
at [æt] *prep* em, a; (*because of*): **he was surprised/annoyed ~** ele ficou surpreso/chateado com; **~ the top** em cima; **~ John's** na casa de João; **~ the baker's** na padaria; **~ times** às vezes; **~ 4 o'clock** às quatro; **~ night** à noite; **~ £1 a kilo** a uma libra o quilo; **~ a stroke** de um golpe; **two ~ a time** de dois em dois.
ate [eɪt] *pt of* **eat**.
atheism ['eɪθɪɪzəm] *n* ateísmo.
atheist ['eɪθɪɪst] *n* ateu/atéia *m/f*.
Athenian [ə'θiːnɪən] *adj*, *n* ateniense *m/f*.
Athens ['æθɪnz] *n* Atenas.
athlete ['æθliːt] *n* atleta *m/f*.
athletic [æθ'lɛtɪk] *adj* atlético.
athletics [æθ'lɛtɪks] *n* atletismo.
Atlantic [ət'læntɪk] *adj* atlântico ♦ *n*: **the ~ (Ocean)** o (oceano) Atlântico.
atlas ['ætləs] *n* atlas *m*.
Atlas Mountains *npl*: **the ~** os montes Atlas.
A.T.M. *abbr* (= *Automatic Telling Machine*) caixa automática *or* eletrônica.
atmosphere ['ætməsfɪə*] *n* atmosfera; (*fig*) ambiente *m*.
atmospheric [ætməs'fɛrɪk] *adj* atmosférico.
atmospherics [ætməs'fɛrɪks] *npl* (*RADIO*) estática.
atoll ['ætɔl] *n* atol *m*.
atom ['ætəm] *n* átomo.
atomic [ə'tɔmɪk] *adj* atômico.
atom(ic) bomb *n* bomba atômica.

NB: *European Portuguese adds the following consonants to certain words:* **b** (sú(b)dito, su(b)til); **c** (a(c)ção, a(c)cionista, a(c)to); **m** (inde(m)ne); **p** (ado(p)ção, ado(p)tar); *for further details see p. xiii.*

atomizer ['ætəmaɪzə*] *n* atomizador *m*, pulverizador *m*.
atone [ə'təun] *vi*: **to ~ for** expiar.
atonement [ə'təunmənt] *n* expiação *f*.
ATP *n abbr* (= *Association of Tennis Professionals*) Associação *f* de Tenistas Profissionais.
atrocious [ə'trəuʃəs] *adj* atroz; (*very bad*) péssimo.
atrocity [ə'trɔsɪtɪ] *n* atrocidade *f*.
atrophy ['ætrəfɪ] *n* atrofia ♦ *vt* atrofiar ♦ *vi* atrofiar-se.
attach [ə'tætʃ] *vt* (*fix*) prender; (*document, letter*) juntar, anexar; (*employee, troops*) adir; **to be ~ed to sb/sth** (*to like*) ter afeição por alguém/algo; **the ~ed letter** a carta junta *or* anexa.
attaché [ə'tæʃeɪ] *n* adido/a.
attaché case *n* pasta.
attachment [ə'tætʃmənt] *n* (*tool*) acessório; (*love*): **~ (to)** afeição *f* (por).
attack [ə'tæk] *vt* atacar; (*subj*: *criminal*) assaltar; (*task etc*) empreender ♦ *n* ataque *m*; (*mugging etc*) assalto; (*on sb's life*) atentado; (*also*: *heart ~*) ataque cardíaco *or* de coração.
attacker [ə'tækə*] *n* agressor(a) *m/f*; (*criminal*) assaltante *m/f*.
attain [ə'teɪn] *vt* (*also*: *~ to*) alcançar, atingir.
attainments [ə'teɪnmənts] *npl* dotes *mpl*, talento.
attempt [ə'tɛmpt] *n* tentativa ♦ *vt* tentar; **~ed theft** *etc* (*LAW*) tentativa de roubo *etc*; **to make an ~ on sb's life** atentar contra a vida de alguém; **he made no ~ to help** ele não fez nada para ajudar.
attend [ə'tɛnd] *vt* (*meeting, talk*) assistir a; (*party*) presenciar; (*school*) cursar; (*church*) ir a; (*course*) fazer; (*patient*) tratar; **to ~ (up)on** acompanhar, servir.
attend to *vt fus* (*matter*) encarregar-se de; (*speech etc*) prestar atenção a; (*needs, customer*) atender a.
attendance [ə'tɛndəns] *n* (*being present*) comparecimento; (*people present*) assistência.
attendant [ə'tɛndənt] *n* servidor(a) *m/f*; (*THEATRE*) arrumador(a) *m/f* ♦ *adj* concomitante.
attention [ə'tɛnʃən] *n* atenção *f*; **~!** (*MIL*) sentido!; **at ~** (*MIL*) em posição de sentido; **for the ~ of ...** (*ADMIN*) atenção ...; **it has come to my ~ that ...** constatei que ....
attentive [ə'tɛntɪv] *adj* atento; (*polite*) cortês.
attentively [ə'tɛntɪvlɪ] *adv* atentamente.
attenuate [ə'tɛnjueɪt] *vt* atenuar ♦ *vi* atenuar-se.
attest [ə'tɛst] *vi*: **to ~ to** atestar.
attic ['ætɪk] *n* sótão *m*.
attire [ə'taɪə*] *n* traje *m*, roupa.
attitude ['ætɪtju:d] *n* atitude *f*; (*view*): **~ (to)** atitude (para com).
attorney [ə'tə:nɪ] *n* (*US*: *lawyer*) advogado/a; (*having proxy*) procurador(a) *m/f*.
Attorney General *n* procurador(a) *m/f* geral da Justiça.
attract [ə'trækt] *vt* atrair; (*attention*) chamar.
attraction [ə'trækʃən] *n* atração *f*; (*good point*) atrativo; **~ towards sth** atração por algo.
attractive [ə'træktɪv] *adj* atraente.
attribute [*n* 'ætrɪbju:t, *vt* ə'trɪbju:t] *n* atributo ♦ *vt*: **to ~ sth to** atribuir algo a.
attrition [ə'trɪʃən] *n see* **war**.
Atty. Gen. *abbr* = **Attorney General**.
ATV *n abbr* (= *all terrain vehicle*) veículo todo-terreno.
aubergine ['əubəʒi:n] *n* berinjela.
auburn ['ɔ:bən] *adj* castanho-avermelhado.
auction ['ɔ:kʃən] *n* (*also*: *sale by ~*) leilão *m* ♦ *vt* leiloar; **to sell by ~** vender em leilão; **to put up for ~** pôr em leilão.
auctioneer [ɔ:kʃə'nɪə*] *n* leiloeiro/a.
auction room *n* local *m* de leilão.
audacious [ɔ:'deɪʃəs] *adj* audaz, atrevido; (*pej*) descarado.
audacity [ɔ:'dæsɪtɪ] *n* audácia, atrevimento; (*pej*) descaramento.
audible ['ɔ:dɪbl] *adj* audível.
audience ['ɔ:dɪəns] *n* (*in theatre, concert etc*) platéia; (*of TV, radio programme*) audiência; (*of speech etc*) auditório; (*of writer, magazine*) público; (*interview*) audiência.
audio typist ['ɔ:dɪəu-] *n* datilógrafo/a (*de textos ditados em fita*).
audiovisual [ɔ:dɪəu'vɪzjuəl] *adj* audiovisual; **~ aids** recursos *mpl* audiovisuais.
audit ['ɔ:dɪt] *vt* fazer a auditoria de ♦ *n* auditoria.
audition [ɔ:'dɪʃən] *n* audição *f*.
auditor ['ɔ:dɪtə*] *n* auditor(a) *m/f*.
auditoria [ɔ:dɪ'tɔ:rɪə] *npl of* **auditorium**.
auditorium [ɔ:dɪ'tɔ:rɪəm] (*pl* **~s** *or* **auditoria**) *n* auditório.
AUEW (*BRIT*) *n abbr* (= *Amalgamated Union of Engineering Workers*) *sindicato das indústrias mecânicas*.
Aug. *abbr* = **August**.
augment [ɔ:g'mɛnt] *vt, vi* aumentar.
augur ['ɔ:gə*] *vi*: **it ~s well** é de bom augúrio ♦ *vt* (*be a sign of*) augurar, pressagiar.
August ['ɔ:gəst] *n* agosto; *see also* **July**.
august [ɔ:'gʌst] *adj* augusto, imponente.
aunt [ɑ:nt] *n* tia.
auntie ['ɑ:ntɪ] *n* titia.
aunty ['ɑ:ntɪ] *n* = **auntie**.
au pair ['əu'pɛə*] *n* (*also*: *~ girl*) au pair *f*.
aura ['ɔ:rə] *n* (*of person*) ar *m*, aspecto; (*of place*) ambiente *m*.
auspices ['ɔ:spɪsɪz] *npl*: **under the ~ of** sob os auspícios de.
auspicious [ɔ:s'pɪʃəs] *adj* propício.
Aussie ['ɔzɪ] (*inf*) *adj, n* australiano/a.
austere [ɔs'tɪə*] *adj* austero; (*manner*) severo.
austerity [ɔ'stɛrətɪ] *n* austeridade *f*.
Australasia [ɔ:strə'leɪzɪə] *n* Australásia.
Australia [ɔs'treɪlɪə] *n* Austrália.
Australian [ɔs'treɪlɪən] *adj, n* australiano/a.
Austria ['ɔstrɪə] *n* Áustria.

Austrian ['ɔstrɪən] *adj*, *n* austríaco/a.
AUT (*BRIT*) *n abbr* (= *Association of University Teachers*) *sindicato universitário*.
authentic [ɔː'θɛntɪk] *adj* autêntico.
authenticate [ɔː'θɛntɪkeɪt] *vt* autenticar.
authenticity [ɔːθɛn'tɪsɪtɪ] *n* autenticidade *f*.
author ['ɔːθə] *n* autor(a) *m/f*.
authoritarian [ɔːθɔrɪ'tɛərɪən] *adj* autoritário.
authoritative [ɔː'θɔrɪtətɪv] *adj* autorizado; (*manner*) autoritário.
authority [ɔː'θɔrɪtɪ] *n* autoridade *f*; (*permission*) autorização *f*; **the authorities** *npl* as autoridades; **to have ~ to do sth** ter autorização para fazer algo.
authorization [ɔːθəraɪ'zeɪʃən] *n* autorização *f*.
authorize ['ɔːθəraɪz] *vt* autorizar.
authorized capital ['ɔːθəraɪzd-] *n* (*COMM*) capital *m* autorizado.
authorship ['ɔːθəʃɪp] *n* autoria.
autistic [ɔː'tɪstɪk] *adj* autista.
auto ['ɔːtəu] (*US*) *n* carro, automóvel *m* ♦ *cpd* (*industry*) automobilístico.
autobiographical [ɔːtəbaɪə'græfɪkl] *adj* autobiográfico.
autobiography [ɔːtəbaɪ'ɔgrəfɪ] *n* autobiografia.
autocratic [ɔːtə'krætɪk] *adj* autocrático.
autograph ['ɔːtəgrɑːf] *n* autógrafo ♦ *vt* (*photo etc*) autografar.
automat ['ɔːtəmæt] *n* (*vending machine*) autômato; (*US*: *restaurant*) restaurante *m* automático.
automata [ɔː'tɔmətə] *npl of* **automaton**.
automated ['ɔːtəmeɪtɪd] *adj* automatizado.
automatic [ɔːtə'mætɪk] *adj* automático ♦ *n* (*gun*) pistola automática; (*washing machine*) máquina de lavar roupa automática; (*BRIT*: *AUT*) carro automático.
automatically [ɔːtə'mætɪklɪ] *adv* automaticamente.
automatic data processing *n* processamento automático de dados.
automation [ɔːtə'meɪʃən] *n* automação *f*.
automaton [ɔː'tɔmətən] (*pl* **automata**) *n* autômato.
automobile ['ɔːtəməbiːl] (*US*) *n* carro, automóvel *m* ♦ *cpd* (*industry*, *accident*) automobilístico.
autonomous [ɔː'tɔnəməs] *adj* autônomo.
autonomy [ɔː'tɔnəmɪ] *n* autonomia.
autopsy ['ɔːtɔpsɪ] *n* autópsia.
autumn ['ɔːtəm] *n* outono.
auxiliary [ɔːg'zɪlɪərɪ] *adj*, *n* auxiliar *m/f*.
AV *n abbr* (= *Authorized Version*) *tradução inglesa da Bíblia* ♦ *abbr* = **audiovisual**.
Av. *abbr* (= *avenue*) Av., Avda.
avail [ə'veɪl] *vt*: **to ~ o.s. of** aproveitar, valer-se de ♦ *n*: **to no ~** em vão, inutilmente.
availability [əveɪlə'bɪlɪtɪ] *n* disponibilidade *f*.
available [ə'veɪləbl] *adj* disponível; **every ~ means** todos os recursos à sua (*or* nossa *etc*) disposição; **is the manager ~?** o gerente pode me atender?; (*on phone*) queria falar com o gerente; **to make sth ~ to sb** pôr algo à disposição de alguém.
avalanche ['ævəlɑːnʃ] *n* avalanche *f*, alude *m*.
avant-garde ['ævãŋ'gɑːd] *adj* de vanguarda.
avaricious [ævə'rɪʃəs] *adj* avarento, avaro.
avdp. *abbr* = **avoirdupois**.
Ave. *abbr* (= *avenue*) Av., Avda.
avenge [ə'vɛndʒ] *vt* vingar.
avenue ['ævənjuː] *n* avenida; (*fig*) caminho.
average ['ævərɪdʒ] *n* média ♦ *adj* (*mean*) médio; (*ordinary*) regular ♦ *vt* (*calculate*) calcular a média de; (*a certain figure*) alcançar uma média de; **on ~** em média; **above/below (the) ~** acima/abaixo da média.
average out *vt* calcular a média de ♦ *vi*: **to ~ out at** dar uma média de.
averse [ə'vəːs] *adj*: **to be ~ to sth/doing** ser avesso *or* pouco disposto a algo/a fazer algo; **I wouldn't be ~ to a drink** eu aceitaria uma bebida.
aversion [ə'vəːʃən] *n* aversão *f*.
avert [ə'vəːt] *vt* prevenir; (*blow*, *one's eyes*) desviar.
aviary ['eɪvɪərɪ] *n* aviário, viveiro de aves.
aviation [eɪvɪ'eɪʃən] *n* aviação *f*.
avid ['ævɪd] *adj* ávido.
avidly ['ævɪdlɪ] *adv* avidamente.
avocado [ævə'kɑːdəu] *n* (*also*: *BRIT*: ~ *pear*) abacate *m*.
avoid [ə'vɔɪd] *vt* evitar.
avoidable [ə'vɔɪdəbl] *adj* evitável.
avoidance [ə'vɔɪdəns] *n* evitação *f*.
avowed [ə'vaud] *adj* confesso, declarado.
AVP (*US*) *n abbr* = **assistant vice-president**.
AWACS ['eɪwæks] *n abbr* (= *airborne warning and control system*) AWACS *m* (*sistema aerotransportado de alerta e de controle*).
await [ə'weɪt] *vt* esperar, aguardar; **~ing attention/delivery** (*COMM*) a ser(em) atendido(s)/entregue(s); **long ~ed** longamente esperado.
awake [ə'weɪk] (*pt* **awoke**, *pp* **awoken** *or* **~d**) *adj* acordado ♦ *vt* despertar, acordar ♦ *vi* despertar, acordar; **~ to** atento a.
awakening [ə'weɪkənɪŋ] *n* despertar *m*.
award [ə'wɔːd] *n* (*prize*) prêmio, condecoração *f*; (*LAW*) sentença; (*act*) concessão *f* ♦ *vt* (*prize*) outorgar, conceder; (*LAW*: *damages*) adjudicar.
aware [ə'wɛə*] *adj*: **~ of** (*conscious*) consciente de; (*informed*) informado de *or* sobre; **to become ~ of** reparar em, saber de; **politically/socially ~** conscientizado politicamente/socialmente; **I am fully ~ that** ... eu compreendo perfeitamente que ....
awareness [ə'wɛənɪs] *n* consciência; (*knowledge*) conhecimento; **to develop people's ~ (of)** conscientizar o público (de).
awash [ə'wɔʃ] *adj* inundado.
away [ə'weɪ] *adv* fora; (*far* ~) muito longe;

NB: *European Portuguese adds the following consonants to certain words:* **b** (sú(b)dito, su(b)til); **c** (a(c)ção, a(c)cionista, a(c)to); **m** (inde(m)ne); **p** (ado(p)ção, ado(p)tar); *for further details see p. xiii.*

two kilometres ~ a dois quilômetros de distância; **two hours** ~ **by car** a duas horas de carro; **the holiday was two weeks** ~ faltavam duas semanas para as férias; ~ **from** longe de; **he's** ~ **for a week** está ausente uma semana; **he's** ~ **in Miami** ele foi para Miami; **to take** ~ levar; **to work/pedal** ~ trabalhar/pedalar sem parar; **to fade** ~ desvanecer-se.
away game *n* (*SPORT*) jogo de fora.
away match *n* (*SPORT*) jogo de fora.
awe [ɔː] *n* temor *m* respeitoso.
awe-inspiring *adj* imponente.
awesome ['ɔːsəm] *adj* imponente.
awestruck ['ɔːstrʌk] *adj* pasmado.
awful ['ɔːfəl] *adj* terrível, horrível; **an** ~ **lot of** um monte de.
awfully ['ɔːfəlɪ] *adv* (*very*) muito.
awhile [ə'waɪl] *adv* por algum tempo, um pouco.
awkward ['ɔːkwəd] *adj* (*clumsy*) desajeitado; (*shape*) incômodo; (*problem*) difícil; (*embarrassing*) embaraçoso, delicado.
awkwardness ['ɔːkwədnəs] *n* (*embarrassment*) embaraço.
awl [ɔːl] *n* sovela.
awning ['ɔːnɪŋ] *n* toldo.
awoke [ə'wəuk] *pt of* **awake**.
awoken [ə'wəukən] *pp of* **awake**.
AWOL ['eɪwɔl] *abbr* (*MIL*) = **absent without leave**.
awry [ə'raɪ] *adv*: **to be** ~ estar de viés *or* de esguelha; **to go** ~ sair mal.
axe [æks] (*US* **ax**) *n* machado ♦ *vt* (*employee*) despedir; (*project etc*) abandonar; (*jobs*) reduzir; **to have an** ~ **to grind** (*fig*) ter interesse pessoal, puxar a brasa para a sua sardinha (*inf*).
axes[1] ['æksɪz] *npl* of **axe**; **ax**.
axes[2] ['æksiːz] *npl of* **axis**.
axiom ['æksɪəm] *n* axioma *m*.
axiomatic [æksɪəu'mætɪk] *adj* axiomático.
axis ['æksɪs] (*pl* **axes**) *n* eixo.
axle ['æksl] *n* (*also*: ~ *tree*) eixo.
ay(e) [aɪ] *excl* (*yes*) sim ♦ *n*: **the ayes** os votos a favor.
AYH *n abbr* = **American Youth Hostels**.
AZ (*US*) *abbr* (*POST*) = **Arizona**.
azalea [ə'zeɪlɪə] *n* azaléia.
Azores [ə'zɔːz] *npl*: **the** ~ os Açores.
Aztec ['æztɛk] *adj*, *n* asteca *m/f*.
azure ['eɪʒə*] *adj* azul-celeste *inv*.

B

B, b [biː] *n* (*letter*) B, b *m*; (*MUS*): **B** si *m*; **B for Benjamin** (*BRIT*) *or* **Baker** (*US*) B de Beatriz; **B road** (*BRIT*: *AUT*) via secundária.
b. *abbr* = **born**.
BA *n abbr* = **British Academy**; (*SCH*) = **Bachelor of Arts**.
babble ['bæbl] *vi* balbuciar ♦ *n* balbucio.
baboon [bə'buːn] *n* babuíno.
baby ['beɪbɪ] *n* neném *m/f*, nenê *m/f*, bebê *m/f*.
baby carriage (*US*) *n* carrinho de bebê.
baby grand *n* (*also*: ~ *piano*) piano de ¼ de cauda.
babyhood ['beɪbɪhud] *n* primeira infância.
babyish ['beɪbɪɪʃ] *adj* infantil.
baby-minder (*BRIT*) *n* ≈ babá *f*.
baby-sit (*irreg*) *vi* tomar conta da(s) criança(s).
baby-sitter *n* baby-sitter *m/f*.
bachelor ['bætʃələ*] *n* solteiro; (*SCH*): **B~ of Arts/Science** ≈ bacharel *m* em Letras/Ciências; **B~ of Arts/Science degree** ≈ bacharelado em Letras/Ciências.
bachelorhood ['bætʃələhud] *n* celibato.
bachelor party (*US*) *n* despedida de solteiro.
back [bæk] *n* (*of person*) costas *fpl*; (*of animal*) lombo; (*of hand*) dorso; (*of car, train*) parte *f* traseira; (*of house*) fundos *mpl*; (*of chair*) encosto; (*of page*) verso; (*of coin*) reverso; (*FOOTBALL*) zagueiro (*BR*), defesa *m* (*PT*) ♦ *vt* (*financially*) patrocinar; (*candidate*: *also*: ~ *up*) apoiar; (*horse*: *at races*) apostar em; (*car*) recuar ♦ *vi* (*car etc*) recuar, dar ré (*BR*), fazer marcha atrás (*PT*) ♦ *adj* (*in compounds*) traseiro, de trás ♦ *adv* (*not forward*) para trás; (*returned*) de volta; **he's** ~ ele voltou; **when will you be** ~**?** quando você estará de volta?; **he ran** ~ recuou correndo; **throw the ball** ~ devolva a bola; **can I have it** ~**?** pode devolvê-lo?; **he called** ~ chamou de novo; **to have one's** ~ **to the wall** (*fig*) estar acuado; **to break the** ~ **of a job** (*BRIT*) fazer o mais difícil de um trabalho; **at the** ~ **of my mind was the thought that ...** no meu íntimo havia a idéia que ...; ~ **to front** pelo avesso, às avessas; ~ **garden/room** jardim *m*/quarto dos fundos; ~ **seats/wheels** (*AUT*) assentos *mpl*/rodas *fpl* de trás; **to take a** ~ **seat** (*fig*) colocar-se em segundo plano; ~ **payments/rent** pagamentos *mpl* atrasados/aluguel *m* atrasado.
back down *vi* desistir.
back on to *vt fus*: **the house** ~**s on to the golf course** a casa dá fundas para o campo de golfe.
back out *vi* (*of promise*) voltar atrás, recuar.
back up *vt* (*COMPUT*) tirar um backup de.
backache ['bækeɪk] *n* dor *f* nas costas.
backbencher [bæk'bɛntʃə*] (*BRIT*) *n membro do parlamento sem pasta.*
backbiting ['bækbaɪtɪŋ] *n* maledicência.
backbone ['bækbəun] *n* coluna vertebral; **he's the** ~ **of the organization** ele é o pilar *or* esteio da organização.
backchat ['bæktʃæt] (*BRIT*: *inf*) *n* insolências *fpl*.
back-cloth (*BRIT*) *n* pano de fundo.
backcomb ['bækkəum] (*BRIT*) *vt* encrespar.

backdate [bæk'deɪt] *vt* (*letter*) antedatar; **~d pay rise** aumento de vencimento com efeito retroativo.
backdrop ['bækdrɔp] *n* pano de fundo.
backer ['bækə*] *n* (*supporter*) partidário/a; (*COMM*: *in partnership*) comanditário/a; (: *financier*) financiador(a) *m/f*.
backfire [bæk'faɪə*] *vi* (*AUT*) engasgar; (*plan*) sair pela culatra.
backgammon [bæk'gæmən] *n* gamão *m*.
background ['bækgraund] *n* fundo; (*of events*) antecedentes *mpl*; (*basic knowledge*) bases *fpl*; (*experience*) conhecimentos *mpl*, experiência ♦ *cpd* (*noise*, *music*) de fundo; **~ reading** leitura de fundo; **family ~** antecedentes *mpl* familiares.
backhand ['bækhænd] *n* (*TENNIS*: *also*: *~ stroke*) revés *m*.
backhanded ['bækhændɪd] *adj* (*fig*) ambíguo, insincero.
backhander ['bækhændə*] (*BRIT*) *n* (*bribe*) propina, peita (*PT*).
backing ['bækɪŋ] *n* (*fig*) apoio; (*COMM*) patrocínio; (*MUS*) fundo (musical).
backlash ['bæklæʃ] *n* reação *f*.
backlog ['bæklɔg] *n*: **~ of work** atrasos *mpl*.
back number *n* (*of magazine etc*) número atrasado.
backpack ['bækpæk] *n* mochila.
backpacker ['bækpækə*] *n* excursionista *m/f* com mochila.
back pay *n* salário atrasado.
backpedal ['bækpɛdl] *vi* (*fig*) recuar, voltar atrás.
backside [bæk'saɪd] (*inf*) *n* traseiro.
backslash ['bækslæʃ] *n* contrabarra.
backslide ['bækslaɪd] (*irreg*) *vi* ter uma recaída.
backsliding ['bækslaɪdɪŋ] *n* recaídas *fpl*.
backspace ['bækspeɪs] *vi* (*TYPING*) retroceder.
backstage [bæk'steɪdʒ] *adv* nos bastidores.
back-street *adj* (*abortion*) clandestino; **~ abortionist** aborteiro/a.
backstroke ['bækstrəuk] *n* nado de costas.
backtrack ['bæktræk] *vi* (*fig*) = **backpedal**.
backup ['bækʌp] *adj* (*train*, *plane*) reserva *inv*; (*COMPUT*) de backup ♦ *n* (*support*) apoio; (*COMPUT*: *also*: *~ file*) backup *m*; (*US*: *congestion*) congestionamento.
backward ['bækwəd] *adj* (*movement*) para trás; (*person*, *country*) atrasado; (*shy*) tímido; **~ and forward movement** movimento de vaivém.
backwards ['bækwədz] *adv* (*move*, *go*) para trás; (*read a list*) às avessas; (*fall*) de costas; **to know sth ~** (*BRIT*) *or* **~ and forwards** (*US*) (*inf*) saber algo de cor e salteado.
backwater ['bækwɔːtə*] *n* (*fig*: *backward place*) lugar *m* atrasado; (: *remote place*) fim-do-mundo *m*.
backyard [bæk'jɑːd] *n* quintal *m*.
bacon ['beɪkən] *n* toucinho, bacon *m*.
bacteria [bæk'tɪərɪə] *npl* bactérias *fpl*.
bacteriology [bæktɪərɪ'ɔlədʒɪ] *n* bacteriologia.
bad [bæd] *adj* mau/má, ruim; (*child*) levado; (*serious*) grave; (*meat*, *food*) estragado; **his ~ leg** sua perna machucada; **to go ~** estragar-se; **to have a ~ time of it** passar um mau pedaço; **I feel ~ about it** (*guilty*) eu me sinto culpado (por isso); **in ~ faith** de má fé.
bade [bæd] *pt of* **bid**.
badge [bædʒ] *n* (*emblem*) emblema *m*; (*to wear*) crachá *m*.
badger ['bædʒə*] *n* texugo ♦ *vt* acossar.
badly ['bædlɪ] *adv* (*work*, *dress etc*) mal; **~ wounded** gravemente ferido; **he needs it ~** faz-lhe grande falta; **things are going ~** as coisas vão mal; **to be ~ off (for money)** estar com pouco dinheiro.
bad-mannered [-'mænəd] *adj* mal-educado, sem modas.
badminton ['bædmɪntən] *n* badminton *m*.
bad-tempered *adj* mal humorado; (*temporary*) de mau humor.
baffle ['bæfl] *vt* (*puzzle*) deixar perplexo, desconcertar.
baffled ['bæfld] *adj* perplexo.
baffling ['bæflɪŋ] *adj* desconcertante.
bag [bæg] *n* saco, bolsa; (*handbag*) bolsa; (*satchel*, *shopping ~*) sacola; (*case*) mala; (*of hunter*) caça ♦ *vt* (*inf*: *take*) pegar; (*game*) matar; (*TECH*) ensacar; **~s of** ... (*inf*: *lots of*) ... de sobra; **to pack one's ~s** fazer as malas; **~s under the eyes** olheiras *fpl*.
bagful ['bægful] *n* saco cheio.
baggage ['bægɪdʒ] *n* bagagem *f*.
baggage checkroom [-'tʃɛkruːm] (*US*) *n* depósito de bagagem.
baggage claim *n* (*at airport*) recebimento de bagagem.
baggy ['bægɪ] *adj* folgado, largo.
bagpipes ['bægpaɪps] *npl* gaita de foles.
Baghdad [bæg'dæd] *n* Bagdá *f*.
bag-snatcher [-'snætʃə*] (*BRIT*) *n* trombadinha *m*.
bag-snatching [-'snætʃɪŋ] (*BRIT*) *n* roubo de bolsa.
Bahamas [bə'hɑːməz] *npl*: **the ~** as Bahamas.
Bahrain [bɑː'reɪn] *n* Barein *m*.
bail [beɪl] *n* fiança ♦ *vt* (*prisoner*: *also*: *grant ~ to*) libertar sob fiança; (*boat*: *also*: *~ out*) baldear a água de; **to be released on ~** ser posto em liberdade mediante fiança; *see also* **bale**.
bail out *vt* (*prisoner*) afiançar; (*fig*: *help out*) socorrer.
bailiff ['beɪlɪf] *n* oficial *m/f* de justiça (*BR*) *or* de diligências (*PT*).
bait [beɪt] *n* isca, engodo ♦ *vt* iscar, cevar; (*fig*) apoquentar.
bake [beɪk] *vt* cozinhar ao forno ♦ *vi* (*cook*:

NB: *European Portuguese adds the following consonants to certain words:* **b** (sú(b)dito, su(b)til); **c** (a(c)ção, a(c)cionista, a(c)to); **m** (inde(m)ne); **p** (ado(p)ção, ado(p)tar); *for further details see p. xiii.*

cake, person) cozinhar; (*be hot*) fazer um calor terrível.
baked beans [beɪkt-] *npl* feijão *m* cozido com molho de tomate.
baker ['beɪkə*] *n* padeiro/a.
bakery ['beɪkərɪ] *n* (*for bread*) padaria; (*for cakes*) confeitaria.
baking ['beɪkɪŋ] *n* (*act*) cozimento; (*batch*) fornada.
baking powder *n* fermento em pó.
baking tin *n* (*for cake*) fôrma; (*for meat*) assadeira.
baking tray *n* tabuleiro.
balaclava [bælə'klɑːvə] *n* (*also*: ~ *helmet*) capuz *f*.
balance ['bæləns] *n* equilíbrio; (*scales*) balança; (*COMM*) balanço; (*remainder*) resto, saldo ♦ *vt* equilibrar; (*budget*) nivelar; (*account*) fazer o balanço de; (*compensate*) contrabalançar; (*pros and cons*) pesar; **~ of trade/payments** balança comercial/balanço de pagamentos; **~ carried forward** transporte; **~ brought forward** transporte; **to ~ the books** fazer o balanço dos livros.
balanced ['bælənst] *adj* (*personality, diet*) equilibrado.
balance sheet *n* balanço geral.
balance wheel *n* balanceiro.
balcony ['bælkənɪ] *n* (*open*) varanda; (*closed*) galeria.
bald [bɔːld] *adj* calvo, careca; (*tyre*) careca.
baldness ['bɔːldnɪs] *n* calvície *f*.
bale [beɪl] *n* (*AGR*) fardo.
bale out *vi* (*of a plane*) atirar-se de pára-quedas ♦ *vt* (*NAUT*: *water*) baldear; (: *boat*) baldear a água de.
Balearic Islands [bælɪ'ærɪk-] *npl*: **the ~** as ilhas Baleares.
baleful ['beɪlful] *adj* (*look*) triste; (*sinister*) funesto, sinistro.
balk [bɔːk] *vi*: **to ~ (at)** (*subj*: *person*) relutar (contra); (: *horse*) refugar, empacar (diante de); **to ~ at doing** relutar em fazer.
Balkan ['bɔːlkən] *adj* balcânico ♦ *n*: **the ~s** os Balcãs.
ball [bɔːl] *n* bola; (*dance*) baile *m*; **~s** *npl* (*inf!*) colhões *mpl* (*!*), ovos *mpl* (*!*); **to play ~ with sb** jogar bola com alguém; (*fig*) fazer o jogo de alguém; **to be on the ~** (*fig*: *competent*) ser competente *or* batuta (*inf*); (: *alert*) estar alerta; **to start the ~ rolling** (*fig*) dar começo, dar o pontapé inicial; **the ~ is in their court** (*fig*) é a vez deles de agir.
ballad ['bæləd] *n* balada.
ballast ['bæləst] *n* lastro.
ball bearing *n* rolamento de esferas, rolimã *m*.
ball cock *n* torneira com bóia.
ballerina [bælə'riːnə] *n* bailarina.
ballet ['bæleɪ] *n* balé *m*.
ballet dancer *n* bailarino/a.
ballistic [bə'lɪstɪk] *adj* balístico.
ballistics [bə'lɪstɪks] *n* balística.
balloon [bə'luːn] *n* balão *m* ♦ *vi* (*sails etc*) inflar(-se); (*prices*) disparar.
balloonist [bə'luːnɪst] *n* aeróstata *m/f*.
ballot ['bælət] *n* votação *f*.
ballot box *n* urna.
ballot paper *n* cédula eleitoral.
ballpark ['bɔːlpɑːk] (*US*) *n* estádio de beisebol.
ballpark figure (*inf*) *n* número aproximado.
ball-point pen *n* (caneta) esferográfica.
ballroom ['bɔːlrum] *n* salão *m* de baile.
balm [bɑːm] *n* bálsamo.
balmy ['bɑːmɪ] *adj* (*breeze, air*) suave, fragrante; (*BRIT*: *inf*) = **barmy**.
BALPA ['bælpə] *n abbr* (= *British Airline Pilots' Association*) *sindicato dos aeronautas*.
balsam ['bɔːlsəm] *n* bálsamo.
balsa (wood) ['bɔːlsə-] *n* pau-de-balsa *m*.
Baltic ['bɔːltɪk] *n*: **the ~ (Sea)** o (mar) Báltico.
balustrade ['bæləstreɪd] *n* balaustrada.
bamboo [bæm'buː] *n* bambu *m*.
bamboozle [bæm'buːzl] (*inf*) *vt* embromar, trapacear.
ban [bæn] *n* proibição *f*, interdição *f* ♦ *vt* proibir, interditar; (*exclude*) excluir; **he was ~ned from driving** (*BRIT*) cassaram-lhe a carteira de motorista.
banal [bə'nɑːl] *adj* banal, vulgar.
banana [bə'nɑːnə] *n* banana.
band [bænd] *n* (*group*) bando, banda; (*gang*) quadrilha, bando; (*strip*) faixa, cinta; (*at a dance*) orquestra; (*MIL*) banda.
band together *vi* juntar-se, associar-se.
bandage ['bændɪdʒ] *n* atadura (*BR*), ligadura (*PT*) ♦ *vt* enfaixar.
Band-Aid ['bændeɪd] ® (*US*) *n* esparadrapo.
bandit ['bændɪt] *n* bandido.
bandstand ['bændstænd] *n* coreto.
bandwagon ['bændwægən] *n*: **to jump on the ~** (*fig*) entrar na roda, ir na onda.
bandy ['bændɪ] *vt* (*jokes, insults*) trocar.
bandy about *vt* usar a torto e a direito.
bandy-legged *adj* cambaio, de pernas tortas.
bane [beɪn] *n*: **it** (*or* **he** *etc*) **is the ~ of my life** é a maldição da minha vida.
bang [bæŋ] *n* estalo; (*of door*) estrondo; (*blow*) pancada ♦ *vt* bater com força; (*door*) fechar com violência ♦ *vi* produzir estrondo; (*door*) bater ♦ *adv* (*BRIT*: *inf*): **to be ~ on time** chegar na hora exata; **~s** *npl* (*US*: *fringe*) franja; **to ~ at the door** bater à porta com violência; **to ~ into sth** bater em algo.
banger ['bæŋə*] *n* (*BRIT*: *car*: *also*: *old* ~) calhambeque *m*, lata-velha; (: *inf*: *sausage*) salsicha; (*firework*) bomba (de São João).
Bangkok [bæŋ'kɔk] *n* Bangcoc.
Bangladesh [bæŋglə'dɛʃ] *n* Bangladesh *m* (*no article*).
bangle ['bæŋgl] *n* bracelete *m*, pulseira.
banish ['bænɪʃ] *vt* banir.
banister(s) ['bænɪstə(z)] *n*(*pl*) corrimão *m*.
banjo ['bændʒəu] (*pl* **~es** *or* **~s**) *n* banjo.
bank [bæŋk] *n* (*COMM*) banco; (*of river, lake*) margem *f*; (*of earth*) rampa, ladeira ♦ *vi* (*AVIAT*) ladear-se; (*COMM*): **they ~ with Pitt's** eles têm conta no banco Pitt's.

bank on *vt fus* contar com, apostar em.
bank account *n* conta bancária.
bank card *n* cartão *m* de garantia de cheques.
bank charges (*BRIT*) *npl* encargos *mpl* bancários.
bank draft *n* saque *m* bancário.
banker ['bæŋkə*] *n* banqueiro/a; **~'s card** (*BRIT*) cartão *m* de garantia de cheques; **~'s order** (*BRIT*) ordem *f* bancária.
bank giro *n* transferência bancária.
Bank holiday (*BRIT*) *n* feriado nacional.
banking ['bæŋkɪŋ] *n* transações *fpl* bancárias; (*job*) profissão *f* de banqueiro.
banking hours *npl* horário de banco.
bank loan *n* empréstimo bancário.
bank manager *n* gerente *m/f* de banco.
banknote ['bæŋknəut] *n* nota (bancária).
bank rate *n* taxa bancária.
bankrupt ['bæŋkrʌpt] *n* falido/a, quebrado/a ♦ *adj* falido, quebrado; **to go ~** falir; **to be ~** estar falido/quebrado.
bankruptcy ['bæŋkrʌptsɪ] *n* falência; (*fraudulent*) bancarrota.
bank statement *n* extrato bancário.
banner ['bænə*] *n* bandeira; (*in demonstration*) estandarte *m*.
bannister(s) ['bænɪstə(z)] *n* (*pl*) = **banister(s)**.
banns [bænz] *npl* proclamas *fpl*.
banquet ['bæŋkwɪt] *n* banquete *m*.
bantam-weight ['bæntəm-] *n* peso-galo.
banter ['bæntə*] *n* caçoada.
BAOR *n abbr* (= *British Army of the Rhine*) *forças armadas britânicas na Alemanha*.
baptism ['bæptɪzəm] *n* batismo.
Baptist ['bæptɪst] *n* batista *m/f*.
baptize [bæp'taɪz] *vt* batizar.
bar [bɑː*] *n* (*gen*, *MUS*, *of chocolate*) barra; (*of window etc*) tranca; (*fig*: *hindrance*) obstáculo; (*prohibition*) impedimento; (*pub*) bar *m*; (*counter*: *in pub*) balcão *m* ♦ *vt* (*road*) obstruir; (*window*) trancar; (*person*) excluir; (*activity*) proibir ♦ *prep*: **~ none** sem exceção; **~ of soap** sabonete *m*; **behind ~s** (*prisoner*) atrás das grades; **the B~** (*LAW*) (*profession*) a advocacia; (*people*) o corpo de advogados.
Barbados [bɑː'beɪdɔs] *n* Barbados *m* (*no article*).
barbaric [bɑː'bærɪk] *adj* bárbaro.
barbarous ['bɑːbərəs] *adj* bárbaro.
barbecue ['bɑːbɪkjuː] *n* churrasco.
barbed wire ['bɑːbd-] *n* arame *m* farpado.
barber ['bɑːbə*] *n* barbeiro, cabeleireiro.
barbiturate [bɑː'bɪtjurɪt] *n* barbitúrico.
Barcelona [bɑːsə'ləunə] *n* Barcelona.
bar chart *n* gráfico de barras.
bar code *n* código de barras.
bare [bɛə*] *adj* nu; (*head*) descoberto ♦ *vt* desnudar, descobrir; **to ~ one's teeth** mostrar os dentes; **the ~ essentials** o imprescindível.
bareback ['bɛəbæk] *adv* em pêlo, sem arreios.
barefaced ['bɛəfeɪst] *adj* descarado.
barefoot ['bɛəfut] *adj*, *adv* descalço.
bareheaded [bɛə'hɛdɪd] *adj*, *adv* de cabeça descoberta.
barely ['bɛəlɪ] *adv* apenas, mal.
Barents Sea ['bærənts-] *n*: **the ~** o mar de Barents.
bargain ['bɑːgɪn] *n* (*deal*) negócio; (*good buy*) pechincha ♦ *vi* (*trade*) negociar; (*haggle*) regatear; **into the ~** ainda por cima.
bargain for (*inf*) *vt fus*: **he got more than he ~ed for** ele conseguiu mais do que pediu.
bargaining ['bɑːgənɪŋ] *n* (*haggling*) regateio; (*talks*) negociações *fpl*.
barge [bɑːdʒ] *n* barcaça.
barge in *vi* irromper.
barge into *vt fus* (*collide with*) atropelar; (*interrupt*) intrometer-se em.
baritone ['bærɪtəun] *n* barítono.
barium meal ['bɛərɪəm-] *n* contraste *m* de bário.
bark [bɑːk] *n* (*of tree*) casca; (*of dog*) latido ♦ *vi* latir.
barley ['bɑːlɪ] *n* cevada.
barley sugar *n* maltose *f*.
barmaid ['bɑːmeɪd] *n* garçonete *f* (*BR*), empregada (de bar) (*PT*).
barman ['bɑːmən] (*irreg*) *n* garçom *m* (*BR*), empregado (de bar) (*PT*).
barmy ['bɑːmɪ] (*BRIT*: *inf*) *adj* maluco.
barn [bɑːn] *n* celeiro.
barnacle ['bɑːnəkl] *n* craca.
barometer [bə'rɔmɪtə*] *n* barômetro.
baron ['bærən] *n* barão *m*; **the press/oil ~s** os magnatas da imprensa/do petróleo.
baroness ['bærənɪs] *n* baronesa.
barracks ['bærəks] *npl* quartel *m*, caserna.
barrage ['bærɑːʒ] *n* (*MIL*) fogo de barragem; (*dam*) barragem *f*; **a ~ of questions** uma saraivada de perguntas.
barrel ['bærəl] *n* barril *m*, barrica; (*of gun*) cano.
barrel organ *n* realejo.
barren ['bærən] *adj* (*sterile*) estéril; (*land*) árido.
barricade [bærɪ'keɪd] *n* barricada ♦ *vt* barricar.
barrier ['bærɪə*] *n* barreira; (*obstacle*) obstáculo; (*BRIT*: *also*: *crash ~*) cerca entre as pistas.
barrier cream (*BRIT*) *n* creme *m* protetor.
barring ['bɑːrɪŋ] *prep* exceto, salvo.
barrister ['bærɪstə*] (*BRIT*) *n* advogado/a, causídico/a.
barrow ['bærəu] *n* (*cart*) carrinho (de mão).
barstool ['bɑːstuːl] *n* tamborete *m* de bar.
Bart. (*BRIT*) *abbr* = **baronet**.
bartender ['bɑːtɛndə*] (*US*) *n* garçom *m* (*BR*), empregado (de bar) (*PT*).
barter ['bɑːtə*] *n* permuta, troca ♦ *vt*: **to ~ sth for sth** trocar algo por algo.

base [beɪs] *n* base *f* ♦ *vt* (*troops*): **to be ~d at** estar estacionado em; (*opinion, belief*): **to ~ sth on** basear *or* fundamentar algo em ♦ *adj* baixo, vil; **coffee-~d** à base de café; **a Rio-~d firm** uma empresa sediada no Rio; **I'm ~d in London** estou sediado em Londres.
baseball ['beɪsbɔːl] *n* beisebol *m*.
baseboard ['beɪsbɔːd] (*US*) *n* rodapé *m*.
base camp *n* base *f* de operações.
Basel ['bɑːzl] *n* = **Basle**.
basement ['beɪsmənt] *n* (*in house*) porão *m*; (*in shop etc*) subsolo.
base rate *n* taxa de base.
bases[1] ['beɪsɪz] *npl of* **base**.
bases[2] ['beɪsiːz] *npl of* **basis**.
bash [bæʃ] (*inf*) *vt* (*with fist*) dar soco *or* murro em; (*with object*) bater em ♦ *n* (*BRIT*): **I'll have a ~ (at it)** vou tentar (fazê-lo); **~ed in** amassado.
bash up (*inf*) *vt* (*car*) arrebentar; (*BRIT*: *person*) dar uma surra em, espancar.
bashful ['bæʃful] *adj* tímido, envergonhado.
bashing ['bæʃɪŋ] (*inf*) *n* surra; **Paki-~** *espancamento de asiáticos por motivos racistas*; **queer-~** espancamento de homossexuais.
BASIC ['beɪsɪk] *n* (*COMPUT*) BASIC *m*.
basic ['beɪsɪk] *adj* básico; (*vocabulary, rate*) de base.
basically ['beɪsɪkəlɪ] *adv* fundamentalmente, basicamente; (*really*) no fundo.
basic rate *n* (*of tax*) alíquota de base.
basil ['bæzl] *n* manjericão *m*.
basin ['beɪsn] *n* (*vessel*) bacia; (*dock, GEO*) bacia; (*also*: *wash~*) pia.
basis ['beɪsɪs] (*pl* **bases**) *n* base *f*; **on the ~ of what you've said** com base no que você disse.
bask [bɑːsk] *vi*: **to ~ in the sun** tomar sol.
basket ['bɑːskɪt] *n* cesto; (*with handle*) cesta.
basketball ['bɑːskɪtbɔːl] *n* basquete(bol) *m*.
basketball player *n* jogador(a) *m/f* de basquete.
basketwork ['bɑːskɪtwəːk] *n* obra de verga, trabalho de vime.
Basle [bɑːl] *n* Basiléia.
Basque [bæsk] *adj*, *n* basco/a.
Basque Country *n*: **the ~** o País Basco.
bass [beɪs] *n* (*MUS*) baixo.
bass clef *n* clave *f* de fá.
bassoon [bə'suːn] *n* fagote *m*.
bastard ['bɑːstəd] *n* bastardo/a; (*inf!*) filho-da-puta (*!*).
baste [beɪst] *vt* (*CULIN*) untar; (*SEWING*) alinhavar.
bastion ['bæstɪən] *n* baluarte *m*.
BASW *n abbr* (= *British Association of Social Workers*) *sindicato dos assistentes sociais*.
bat [bæt] *n* (*ZOOL*) morcego; (*for ball games*) bastão *m*; (*for table tennis*) raquete *f* ♦ *vt*: **he didn't ~ an eyelid** ele nem pestanejou; **off one's own ~** por iniciativa própria.
batch [bætʃ] *n* (*of bread*) fornada; (*pile of papers*) monte *m*; (*lot*) remessa, lote *m*.
batch processing *n* (*COMPUT*) processamento batch *or* em lote.
bated ['beɪtɪd] *adj*: **with ~ breath** contendo a respiração.
bath [bɑːθ, *pl* bɑːðz] *n* banho; (*bathtub*) banheira ♦ *vt* banhar; **~s** *npl* banhos *mpl* públicos; (*also*: *swimming ~s*) piscina; **to have a ~** tomar banho (de banheira).
bathchair [bɑːθ'tʃɛə*] *n* cadeira de rodas.
bathe [beɪð] *vi* banhar-se ♦ *vt* banhar; (*wound*) lavar.
bather ['beɪðə*] *n* banhista *m/f*.
bathing ['beɪðɪŋ] *n* banho.
bathing cap *n* touca de banho.
bathing costume (*US* **bathing suit**) *n* (*woman's*) maiô *m* (*BR*), fato de banho (*PT*).
bathmat ['bɑːθmæt] *n* tapete *m* de banheiro.
bathrobe ['bɑːθrəub] *n* roupão *m* de banho.
bathroom ['bɑːθrum] *n* banheiro (*BR*), casa de banho (*PT*).
bath towel *n* toalha de banho.
bathtub ['bɑːθtʌb] *n* banheira.
batman ['bætmən] (*irreg*) (*BRIT*) *n* ordenança *m*.
baton ['bætən] *n* (*MUS*) batuta; (*truncheon*) cassetete *m*.
battalion [bə'tælɪən] *n* batalhão *m*.
batten ['bætn] *n* (*CARPENTRY*) caibro.
batten down *vt* (*NAUT*): **to ~ down the hatches** correr as escotilhas.
batter ['bætə*] *vt* espancar, bater em; (*wife, child*) seviciar ♦ *n* massa (mole).
battered ['bætəd] *adj* (*hat, pan*) amassado, surrado; **~ wife/child** mulher/criança seviciada.
battering ram ['bætərɪŋ] *n* aríete *m*.
battery ['bætərɪ] *n* bateria; (*of torch*) pilha.
battery charger *n* carregador *m* de bateria.
battery farming *n* criação *f* intensiva.
battle ['bætl] *n* batalha; (*fig*) luta ♦ *vi* lutar; **that's half the ~** (*fig*) é meio caminho andado; **it's a** *or* **we're fighting a losing ~** estamos lutando em vão.
battle dress *n* uniforme *m* de combate.
battlefield ['bætlfiːld] *n* campo de batalha.
battlements ['bætlmənts] *npl* ameias *fpl*.
battleship ['bætlʃɪp] *n* couraçado.
bauble ['bɔːbl] *n* bugiganga.
baud [bɔːd] *n* (*COMPUT*) baud *m*.
baud rate *n* (*COMPUT*) índice *m* de baud, taxa de transmissão.
baulk [bɔːlk] *vi* = **balk**.
bauxite ['bɔːksaɪt] *n* bauxita.
bawdy ['bɔːdɪ] *adj* indecente; (*joke*) imoral.
bawl [bɔːl] *vi* gritar, berrar.
bay [beɪ] *n* (*GEO*) baía; (*BOT*) louro; (*BRIT*: *for parking*) área de estacionamento; (: *for loading*) vão *m* de carregamento ♦ *vi* ladrar; **to hold sb at ~** manter alguém a distância; **the B~ of Biscay** o golfo de Biscaia.
bay leaf (*irreg*) *n* louro.
bayonet ['beɪənɪt] *n* baioneta.
bay tree *n* loureiro.
bay window *n* janela saliente.
bazaar [bə'zɑː*] *n* bazar *m*.
bazooka [bə'zuːkə] *n* bazuca.

BB (*BRIT*) *n abbr* (= *Boys' Brigade*) *movimento de meninos*.
B & B *n abbr* = **bed and breakfast**.
BBB (*US*) *n abbr* (= *Better Business Bureau*) *organização de defesa ao consumidor*.
BBC *n abbr* (= *British Broadcasting Corporation*) *companhia britânica de rádio e televisão*.
BBE (*US*) *n abbr* (= *Benevolent and Protective Order of Elks*) *associação beneficente*.
BC *adv abbr* (= *before Christ*) a.C. ♦ *abbr* (*CANADA*) = **British Columbia**.
BCG *n abbr* (= *Bacillus Calmette-Guérin*) BCG *m*.
BD *n abbr* (= *Bachelor of Divinity*) *título universitário*.
B/D *abbr* = **bank draft**.
BDS *n abbr* (= *Bachelor of Dental Surgery*) *título universitário*.
be [bi:] (*pt* **was, were**, *pp* **been**) *vi* (*of permanent place/state*) ser; (*of temporary place/condition*) estar; **I am English** sou inglês; **I am tired** estou cansado; **how are you?** como está?; **who is it?** quem é?; **it's me** sou eu; **it is raining** está chovendo (*BR*) *or* a chover (*PT*); **I am warm** estou com calor; **it is cold** está frio; **where is the bank?** onde é o banco?; **how much is it?** quanto é *or* custa?; **he is four (years old)** ele tem quatro anos; **it's 8 o'clock** são 8 horas; **2 and 2 are 4** dois e dois são quatro; **where have you been?** (*recently*) onde você tem estado?; (*at a certain time*) onde você estava?; **I've been waiting for her for two hours** há *or* faz duas horas que eu espero por ela; **to ~ killed** ser morto; **he is nowhere to ~ found** ninguém sabe o paradeiro dele; **the car is to ~ sold** o carro está a venda; **he was to have come yesterday** ele devia ter vindo ontem, era para ele vir ontem; **if I were you, I ...** se eu fosse você, eu ...; **am I to understand that ...?** devo então concluir que ...?
B/E *abbr* = **bill of exchange**.
beach [bi:tʃ] *n* praia ♦ *vt* puxar para a terra *or* praia, encalhar.
beachcomber ['bi:tʃkəumə*] *n* vagabundo/a de praia.
beachwear ['bi:tʃwɛə*] *n* roupa de praia.
beacon ['bi:kən] *n* (*lighthouse*) farol *m*; (*marker*) baliza; (*also*: *radio ~*) radiofarol *m*.
bead [bi:d] *n* (*of necklace*) conta; (*of sweat*) gota; **~s** *npl* (*necklace*) colar *m*.
beady ['bi:dɪ] *adj*: **~ eyes** olhinhos vivos.
beagle ['bi:gl] *n* bigle *m*.
beak [bi:k] *n* bico.
beaker ['bi:kə*] *n* copo com bico.
beam [bi:m] *n* (*ARCH*) viga; (*of light*) raio; (*NAUT*) través *m*; (*RADIO*) feixe *m* direcional ♦ *vi* brilhar; (*smile*) sorrir; **to drive on full** *or* **main ~** (*BRIT*), **to drive on high ~** (*US*) transitar com os faróis altos.
beaming ['bi:mɪŋ] *adj* (*sun, smile*) radiante.
bean [bi:n] *n* feijão *m*; (*of coffee*) grão *m*.
beanshoots ['bi:nʃu:ts] *npl* brotos *mpl* de feijão.
beansprouts ['bi:nsprauts] *npl* brotos *mpl* de feijão.
bear [bɛə*] (*pt* **bore**, *pp* **borne**) *n* urso; (*STOCK EXCHANGE*) baixista *m/f* ♦ *vt* (*carry*) carregar; (*cost*) arcar com; (*endure, support*) suportar, agüentar; (*fruit*) dar; (*name, title*) trazer; (*traces, signs*) apresentar, trazer; (*children*) ter, dar à luz; (*COMM*: *interest*) render ♦ *vi*: **to ~ right/left** virar à direita/à esquerda; **to ~ the responsibility of** assumir a responsabilidade de; **to ~ comparison with** comparar-se a; **I can't ~ him** eu não o agüento; **to bring pressure to ~ on sb** exercer pressão sobre alguém.
bear out *vt* (*theory, suspicion*) confirmar, corroborar.
bear up *vi* agüentar, resistir.
bear with *vt fus* (*sb's moods, temper*) ter paciência com; **~ with me a minute** só um momentinho, por favor.
bearable ['bɛərəbl] *adj* suportável, tolerável.
beard [bɪəd] *n* barba.
bearded ['bɪədɪd] *adj* barbado, barbudo.
bearer ['bɛərə*] *n* portador(a) *m/f*.
bearing ['bɛərɪŋ] *n* porte *m*, comportamento; (*connection*) relação *f*; (*TECH*): **(ball) ~** rolamento de esferas; **to take a ~** fazer marcação; **to find one's ~s** orientar-se.
beast [bi:st] *n* besta, bicho; (*inf*) fera.
beastly ['bi:stlɪ] *adj* horrível.
beat [bi:t] (*pt* **beat**, *pp* **beaten**) *n* (*of heart*) batida; (*MUS*) ritmo, compasso; (*of policeman*) ronda ♦ *vt* (*hit*) bater em; (*eggs*) bater; (*defeat*) vencer, derrotar; (*better*) superar, ultrapassar; (*drum*) tocar; (*rhythm*) marcar ♦ *vi* (*heart*) bater; **off the ~en track** fora de mão; **to ~ about the bush** falar com rodeios (*BR*), fazer rodeios (*PT*); **to ~ it** (*inf*) cair fora; **to ~ time** marcar o compasso; **that ~s everything!** isso é o cúmulo!
beat down *vt* (*door*) arrombar; (*price*) conseguir que seja abatido; (*seller*) conseguir que abata o preço ♦ *vi* (*rain*) cair a cântaros; (*sun*) bater de chapa.
beat off *vt* repelir.
beat up *vt* (*inf*: *person*) espancar; (*eggs*) bater.
beaten ['bi:tn] *pp of* **beat**.
beater ['bi:tə*] *n* (*for eggs, cream*) batedeira.
beating ['bi:tɪŋ] *n* batida; (*of person*) sova, surra; **to take a ~** levar uma surra.
beat-up (*inf*) *adj* (*car*) caindo aos pedaços; (*suitcase etc*) surrado.
beautician [bju:'tɪʃən] *n* esteticista *m/f*.
beautiful ['bju:tɪful] *adj* belo, lindo, formoso.
beautifully ['bju:tɪfulɪ] *adv* maravilhosamente, lindamente.
beautify ['bju:tɪfaɪ] *vt* embelezar.

NB: European Portuguese adds the following consonants to certain words: **b** (sú(b)dito, su(b)til); **c** (a(c)ção, a(c)cionista, a(c)to); **m** (inde(m)ne); **p** (ado(p)ção, ado(p)tar); *for further details see p. xiii.*

beauty ['bju:tɪ] *n* beleza; (*person*) beldade *f*, beleza; **the ~ of it is that ...** o atrativo disso é que ....
beauty contest *n* concurso de beleza.
beauty queen *n* miss *f*, rainha de beleza.
beauty salon [-sælɔ̃:ŋ] *n* salão *m* de beleza.
beauty spot *n* sinal *m* (*de beleza na pele*); (*BRIT*: *TOURISM*) lugar *m* de beleza excepcional.
beaver ['bi:və*] *n* castor *m*.
becalmed [bɪ'kɑ:md] *adj* parado devido a calmaria.
became [bɪ'keɪm] *pt of* **become**.
because [bɪ'kɔz] *conj* porque; **~ of** por causa de.
beck [bɛk] *n*: **to be at sb's ~ and call** estar às ordens de alguém.
beckon ['bɛkən] *vt* (*also*: **~** *to*) chamar com sinais, acenar para.
become [bɪ'kʌm] (*irreg*: *like* **come**) *vt* (*suit*) favorecer a ♦ *vi* (+ *n*) virar, fazer-se, tornar-se; (+ *adj*) tornar-se, ficar; **to ~ fat** engordar, ficar gordo; **to ~ angry** zangar-se, ficar com raiva; **it became known that** soube-se que; **what has ~ of him?** o que é feito dele?, o que aconteceu a ele?
becoming [bɪ'kʌmɪŋ] *adj* (*behaviour*) decoroso; (*clothes*) favorecedor(a), elegante.
BEd *n abbr* (= *Bachelor of Education*) *habilitação ao magistério*.
bed [bɛd] *n* cama; (*of flowers*) canteiro; (*of coal, clay*) camada, base *f*; (*of sea, lake*) fundo; (*of river*) leito; **to go to ~** ir dormir, deitar(-se).
  bed down *vi* dormir.
bed and breakfast *n* (*terms*) cama e café da manhã (*BR*) *or* pequeno almoço (*PT*); (*place*) pensão *f*.
bedbug ['bɛdbʌg] *n* percevejo.
bedclothes ['bɛdkləuðz] *npl* roupa de cama.
bedcover ['bɛdkʌvə*] *n* colcha.
bedding ['bɛdɪŋ] *n* roupa de cama.
bedevil [bɪ'dɛvl] *vt* (*harass*) acossar; **to be ~led by** ser vítima de.
bedfellow ['bɛdfɛləu] *n*: **they are strange ~s** (*fig*) eles formam uma dupla estranha.
bedlam ['bɛdləm] *n* confusão *f*.
bedpan ['bɛdpæn] *n* comadre *f*.
bedpost ['bɛdpəust] *n* pé *m* de cama.
bedraggled [bɪ'drægld] *adj* molhado, ensopado; (*dirty*) enlameado.
bedridden ['bɛdrɪdn] *adj* acamado.
bedrock ['bɛdrɔk] *n* (*fig*) fundamento, alicerce *m*; (*GEO*) leito de rocha firme.
bedroom ['bɛdrum] *n* quarto, dormitório.
Beds (*BRIT*) *abbr* = **Bedfordshire**.
bedside ['bɛdsaɪd] *n*: **at sb's ~** à cabeceira de alguém ♦ *cpd* (*book, lamp*) de cabeceira.
bedsit(ter) ['bɛdsɪt(ə*)] (*BRIT*) *n* conjugado.
bedspread ['bɛdsprɛd] *n* colcha.
bedtime ['bɛdtaɪm] *n*: **it's ~** está na hora de ir para a cama.
bee [bi:] *n* abelha; **to have a ~ in one's bonnet (about sth)** estar obcecado (por algo).
beech [bi:tʃ] *n* faia.
beef [bi:f] *n* carne *f* de vaca.
  beef up (*inf*) *vt* (*support*) reforçar; (*essay*) desenvolver mais.
beefburger ['bi:fbə:gə*] *n* hambúrguer *m*.
beefeater ['bi:fi:tə*] *n alabardeiro* (*da guarda da Torre de Londres*).
beehive ['bi:haɪv] *n* colméia.
beeline ['bi:laɪn] *n*: **to make a ~ for** ir direto a.
been [bi:n] *pp of* **be**.
beer [bɪə*] *n* cerveja.
beer can *n* lata de cerveja.
beet [bi:t] (*US*) *n* beterraba.
beetle ['bi:tl] *n* besouro.
beetroot ['bi:tru:t] (*BRIT*) *n* beterraba.
befall [bɪ'fɔ:l] (*irreg*: *like* **fall**) *vt* acontecer a.
befit [bɪ'fɪt] *vt* convir a.
before [bɪ'fɔ:*] *prep* (*of time*) antes de; (*of space*) diante de ♦ *conj* antes que ♦ *adv* (*time*) antes, anteriormente; **~ going** antes de sair; **~ she goes** antes dela sair; **the week ~** a semana anterior; **I've seen it ~** eu já vi isso (antes); **I've never seen it ~** nunca vi isso antes.
beforehand [bɪ'fɔ:hænd] *adv* antes.
befriend [bɪ'frɛnd] *vt* fazer amizade com.
befuddled [bɪ'fʌdld] *adj* atordoado, aturdido.
beg [bɛg] *vi* mendigar, pedir esmola ♦ *vt* (*as beggar*) mendigar; (*favour*) pedir; (*entreat*) suplicar; **that ~s the question of ...** isso dá por resolvida a questão de ....
began [bɪ'gæn] *pt of* **begin**.
beggar ['bɛgə*] *n* (*also*: *~man*; *~woman*) mendigo/a.
begin [bɪ'gɪn] (*pt* **began**, *pp* **begun**) *vt*, *vi* começar, iniciar; **to ~ doing** *or* **to do sth** começar a fazer algo; **~ning (from) Monday** a partir de segunda-feira; **I can't ~ to thank you** não sei como agradecer-lhe; **to ~ with** em primeiro lugar.
beginner [bɪ'gɪnə*] *n* principiante *m/f*.
beginning [bɪ'gɪnɪŋ] *n* início, começo; **right from the ~** desde o início.
begrudge [bɪ'grʌdʒ] *vt*: **to ~ sb sth** (*envy*) invejar algo de alguém; (*give grudgingly*) dar algo a alguém de má vontade.
beguile [bɪ'gaɪl] *vt* (*enchant*) encantar.
beguiling [bɪ'gaɪlɪŋ] *adj* (*charming*) sedutor(a), encantador(a).
begun [bɪ'gʌn] *pp of* **begin**.
behalf [bɪ'hɑ:f] *n*: **on** (*BRIT*) *or* **in** (*US*) **~ of** em nome de; (*in aid of*) em favor de.
behave [bɪ'heɪv] *vi* comportar-se; (*well*: *also*: **~** *o.s.*) comportar-se (bem).
behaviour [bɪ'heɪvjə*] (*US* **behavior**) *n* comportamento.
behead [bɪ'hɛd] *vt* decapitar, degolar.
beheld [bɪ'hɛld] *pt, pp of* **behold**.
behind [bɪ'haɪnd] *prep* atrás de ♦ *adv* atrás; (*move*) para trás ♦ *n* traseiro; **~ (time)** atrasado; **~ the scenes** nos bastidores; **to leave sth ~** (*forget*) esquecer algo; (*run ahead of*) deixar algo para trás; **to be ~ (schedule) with sth** estar atrasado *or* com atraso em

algo.
behold [bɪ'həuld] (*irreg*: *like* **hold**) *vt* contemplar.
beige [beɪʒ] *adj* bege.
being ['bi:ɪŋ] *n* (*state*) existência; (*entity*) ser *m*; **to come into ~** nascer, aparecer.
Beirut [beɪ'ru:t] *n* Beirute.
belated [bɪ'leɪtɪd] *adj* atrasado, tardio.
belch [bɛltʃ] *vi* arrotar ♦ *vt* (*also*: *~ out*: *smoke etc*) vomitar.
beleaguered [bɪ'li:gəd] *adj* (*city*, *fig*) assediado; (*army*) cercado.
Belfast ['bɛlfa:st] *n* Belfast.
belfry ['bɛlfrɪ] *n* campanário.
Belgian ['bɛldʒən] *adj*, *n* belga *m/f*.
Belgium ['bɛldʒəm] *n* Bélgica.
Belgrade [bɛl'greɪd] *n* Belgrado.
belie [bɪ'laɪ] *vt* (*invalidate*) desmentir; (*obscure*) ocultar.
belief [bɪ'li:f] *n* (*opinion*) opinião *f*; (*trust*, *faith*) fé *f*; (*acceptance as true*) crença, convicção *f*; **it's beyond ~** é inacreditável; **in the ~ that** na convicção de que.
believable [bɪ'li:vəbl] *adj* crível, acreditável.
believe [bɪ'li:v] *vt*: **to ~ sth/sb** acreditar algo/em alguém ♦ *vi*: **to ~ in** (*God*, *ghosts*) crer em; (*method*, *person*) acreditar em; **I believe (that)** ... (*think*) eu acho que ...; **I don't ~ in corporal punishment** não sou partidário de castigos corporais; **he is ~d to be abroad** acredita-se que ele esteja no exterior.
believer [bɪ'li:və*] *n* (REL) crente *m/f*, fiel *m/f*; (*in idea*, *activity*): **~ in** partidário/a de.
belittle [bɪ'lɪtl] *vt* diminuir, depreciar.
Belize [bɛ'li:z] *n* Belize *m* (*no article*).
bell [bɛl] *n* sino; (*small*, *door~*) campainha; (*animal's*, *on toy*) guizo, sininho; **that rings a ~** (*fig*) tenho uma vaga lembrança disso; **the name rings a ~** o nome não me é estranho.
bell-bottoms *npl* calça boca-de-sino.
bellboy ['bɛlbɔɪ] (BRIT) *n* boy *m* (de hotel) (BR), groom *m* (PT).
bellhop ['bɛlhɔp] (US) *n* = **bellboy**.
belligerent [bɪ'lɪdʒərənt] *adj* (*at war*) beligerante; (*fig*) agressivo.
bellow ['bɛləu] *vi* berrar, mugir; (*person*) bramar ♦ *vt* (*orders*) gritar, berrar; **~s** *npl* fole *m*.
bell push (BRIT) *n* botão *m* de campainha.
belly ['bɛlɪ] *n* barriga, ventre *m*.
bellyache ['bɛlɪeɪk] (*inf*) *n* dor *f* de barriga ♦ *vi* bufar.
belly button ['bɛlɪbʌtn] *n* umbigo.
belong [bɪ'lɔŋ] *vi*: **to ~ to** pertencer a; (*club etc*) ser sócio de; **the book ~s on the shelf** o livro fica guardado na estante.
belongings [bɪ'lɔŋɪŋz] *npl* pertences *mpl*.
beloved [bɪ'lʌvɪd] *adj* querido, amado ♦ *n* bem-amado/a.
below [bɪ'ləu] *prep* (*lower than*, *less than*) abaixo de; (*covered by*) debaixo de ♦ *adv* em baixo; **see ~** ver abaixo; **temperatures ~ normal** temperaturas abaixo da normal.
belt [bɛlt] *n* cinto; (*area*) faixa; (TECH) correia ♦ *vt* (*thrash*) surrar ♦ *vi* (BRIT: *inf*): **to ~ along** ir a toda, correr; **industrial ~** zona industrial.
belt out *vt* (*song*) cantar a plenos pulmões.
belt up (BRIT: *inf*) *vi* calar a boca.
beltway ['bɛltweɪ] (US) *n* via circular.
bemoan [bɪ'məun] *vt* lamentar.
bemused [bɪ'mju:zd] *adj* bestificado, estupidificado.
bench [bɛntʃ] *n* banco; **the B~** (LAW) o tribunal; (*people*) os magistrados, o corpo de magistrados.
bench mark *n* referência.
bend [bɛnd] (*pt*, *pp* **bent**) *vt* dobrar, curvar; (*leg*, *arm*) dobrar ♦ *vi* dobrar-se, inclinar-se ♦ *n* curva; **~s** *n* mal-dos-mergulhadores *m*.
bend down *vi* abaixar-se; (*squat*) agachar-se.
bend over *vi* debruçar-se.
beneath [bɪ'ni:θ] *prep* (*lower than*, *less than*) abaixo de; (*covered by*) debaixo de; (*unworthy of*) indigno de ♦ *adv* em baixo.
benefactor ['bɛnɪfæktə*] *n* benfeitor(a) *m/f*.
benefactress ['bɛnɪfæktrɪs] *n* benfeitora.
beneficial [bɛnɪ'fɪʃəl] *adj*: **~ (to)** benéfico (a).
beneficiary [bɛnɪ'fɪʃərɪ] *n* (LAW) beneficiário/a.
benefit ['bɛnɪfɪt] *n* benefício, proveito; (*as part of salary etc*) benefício; (*money*) subsídio, auxílio ♦ *vt* beneficiar ♦ *vi*: **to ~ from sth** beneficiar-se de algo.
benefit (performance) *n* apresentação *f* beneficente.
Benelux ['bɛnɪlʌks] *n* Benelux *m*.
benevolent [bɪ'nɛvələnt] *adj* benévolo.
BEng *n abbr* (= *Bachelor of Engineering*) *título universitário*.
benign [bɪ'naɪn] *adj* (*person*, *smile*) afável, bondoso; (MED) benigno.
bent [bɛnt] *pt*, *pp of* **bend** ♦ *n* inclinação *f* ♦ *adj* (*wire*, *pipe*) torto; (*inf*: *dishonest*) corrupto; **to be ~ on** estar empenhado em; **to have a ~ for** ter queda para.
bequeath [bɪ'kwi:ð] *vt* legar.
bequest [bɪ'kwɛst] *n* legado.
bereaved [bɪ'ri:vd] *npl*: **the ~** os enlutados ♦ *adj* enlutado.
bereavement [bɪ'ri:vmənt] *n* luto.
beret ['bɛreɪ] *n* boina.
Bering Sea ['beɪrɪŋ-] *n*: **the ~** o mar de Bering.
Berks (BRIT) *abbr* = **Berkshire**.
Berlin [bə:'lɪn] *n* Berlim; **East/West ~** Berlim Oriental/Ocidental.
berm [bə:m] (US) *n* acostamento (BR), berma (PT).
Bermuda [bə:'mju:də] *n* Bermudas *fpl*.
Bermuda shorts *npl* bermuda.
Bern [bə:n] *n* Berna.

***NB**: European Portuguese adds the following consonants to certain words:* **b** (sú(b)dito, su(b)til); **c** (a(c)ção, a(c)cionista, a(c)to); **m** (inde(m)ne); **p** (ado(p)ção, ado(p)tar); *for further details see* *p. xiii.*

berry ['bɛrɪ] *n* baga.

berserk [bə'sə:k] *adj*: **to go ~** perder as estribeiras.

berth [bə:θ] *n* (*on ship*) beliche *m*; (*on train*) leito; (*for ship*) ancoradouro ♦ *vi* (*in harbour*) atracar, encostar-se; (*at anchor*) ancorar; **to give sb a wide ~** (*fig*) evitar alguém.

beseech [bɪ'si:tʃ] (*pt, pp* **besought**) *vt* suplicar, implorar.

beset [bɪ'sɛt] (*irreg*: *like* **set**) *vt* (*subj*: *problems, difficulties*) acossar ♦ *adj*: **a policy ~ with dangers** uma política cercada de perigos.

besetting [bɪ'sɛtɪŋ] *adj*: **his ~ sin** seu grande vício.

beside [bɪ'saɪd] *prep* (*next to*) junto de, ao lado de, ao pé de; (*compared with*) em comparação com; **that's ~ the point** isso não tem nada a ver; **to be ~ o.s. (with anger)** estar fora de si.

besides [bɪ'saɪdz] *adv* além disso ♦ *prep* (*as well as*) além de; (*except*) salvo, exceto.

besiege [bɪ'si:dʒ] *vt* (*town*) sitiar, pôr cerco a; (*fig*) assediar.

besotted [bɪ'sɔtɪd] (*BRIT*) *adj*: **~ with** gamado em, louco por.

besought [bɪ'sɔ:t] *pt, pp of* **beseech**.

bespectacled [bɪ'spɛktɪkld] *adj* de óculos.

bespoke [bɪ'spəuk] (*BRIT*) *adj* (*garment*) feito sob medida; **~ software** software *m* sob medida; **~ tailor** alfaiate *m* que confecciona roupa sob medida.

best [bɛst] *adj* melhor ♦ *adv* (o) melhor; **the ~ part of** (*quantity*) a maior parte de; **at ~** na melhor das hipóteses; **to make the ~ of sth** tirar o maior partido possível de algo; **to do one's ~** fazer o possível; **to the ~ of my knowledge** que eu saiba; **to the ~ of my ability** o melhor que eu puder; **he's not exactly patient at the ~ of times** mesmo nos seus melhores momentos ele não é muito paciente; **the ~ thing to do is ...** o melhor é ....

best man *n* padrinho de casamento.

bestow [bɪ'stəu] *vt* outorgar; (*affection*) dar, oferecer.

bestseller ['bɛst'sɛlə*] *n* (*book*) best-seller *m*.

bet [bɛt] (*pt, pp* **bet** *or* **~ted**) *n* aposta ♦ *vt, vi*: **to ~ (on)** apostar (em); **it's a safe ~** (*fig*) é coisa segura, é dinheiro ganho.

Bethlehem ['bɛθlɪhɛm] *n* Belém.

betray [bɪ'treɪ] *vt* trair, atraiçoar; (*denounce*) delatar.

betrayal [bɪ'treɪəl] *n* traição *f*.

better ['bɛtə*] *adj, adv* melhor ♦ *vt* melhorar; (*go above*) superar ♦ *n*: **to get the ~ of sb** vencer alguém; **you had ~ do it** é melhor você fazer isso; **he thought ~ of it** pensou melhor, mudou de opinião; **to get ~** melhorar; **that's ~!** isso!; **~ off** em melhor situação; **you'd be ~ off this way** (*fig*) seria melhor para você assim.

betting ['bɛtɪŋ] *n* jogo.

betting shop (*BRIT*) *n* agência de apostas.

between [bɪ'twi:n] *prep* no meio de, entre ♦ *adv* no meio; **the road ~ here and London** a estrada daqui a Londres; **we only had 5 ~ us** juntos só tínhamos 5; **~ you and me** cá entre nós.

bevel ['bɛvəl] *n* (*also*: **~ edge**) bisel *m*.

beverage ['bɛvərɪdʒ] *n* bebida.

bevy ['bɛvɪ] *n*: **a ~ of** um grupo *or* bando de.

bewail [bɪ'weɪl] *vt* lamentar.

beware [bɪ'wɛə*] *vt, vi*: **to ~ (of)** precaver-se (de), ter cuidado (com) ♦ *excl* cuidado!

bewildered [bɪ'wɪldəd] *adj* confuso, desnorteado.

bewildering [bɪ'wɪldərɪŋ] *adj* atordoador(a), desnorteante.

bewitching [bɪ'wɪtʃɪŋ] *adj* encantador(a), sedutor(a).

beyond [bɪ'jɔnd] *prep* (*in space*) além de; (*exceeding*) acima de, fora de ♦ *adv* além.

b/f *abbr* = **brought forward**.

BFPO *n abbr* (= *British Forces Post Office*) *serviço postal do exército*.

bhp *n abbr* (*AUT*: *brake horsepower*) potência efetiva ao freio.

bi... [baɪ] *prefix* bi....

biannual [baɪ'ænjuəl] *adj* semestral.

bias ['baɪəs] *n* (*prejudice*) preconceito; (*preference*) prevenção *f*.

bias(s)ed ['baɪəst] *adj* parcial; **to be ~ against** ter preconceito contra.

bib [bɪb] *n* babadouro, babador *m*.

Bible ['baɪbl] *n* Bíblia.

bibliography [bɪblɪ'ɔgrəfɪ] *n* bibliografia.

bicarbonate of soda [baɪ'kɑ:bənɪt-] *n* bicarbonato de sódio.

bicentenary [baɪsɛn'ti:nərɪ] *n* bicentenário.

bicentennial [baɪsɛn'tɛnɪəl] *n* bicentenário.

biceps ['baɪsɛps] *n* bíceps *m inv*.

bicker ['bɪkə*] *vi* brigar.

bicycle ['baɪsɪkl] *n* bicicleta.

bicycle path *n* ciclovia.

bicycle pump *n* bomba de bicicleta.

bicycle track *n* ciclovia.

bid [bɪd] (*pt* **bade** *or* **bid**, *pp* **bidden** *or* **bid**) *n* oferta; (*at auction*) lance *m*; (*attempt*) tentativa ♦ *vi* fazer uma oferta; (*COMM*) licitar, fazer uma licitação ♦ *vt* (*price*) oferecer; (*order*) mandar, ordenar; **to ~ sb good day** dar bom dia a alguém.

bidder ['bɪdə*] *n* (*COMM*) licitante *m*; **the highest ~** quem oferece mais.

bidding ['bɪdɪŋ] *n* (*at auction*) lances *mpl*; (*COMM*) licitação *f*; (*order*) ordem *f*.

bide [baɪd] *vt*: **to ~ one's time** esperar o momento adequado.

bidet ['bi:deɪ] *n* bidê *m*.

bidirectional ['baɪdɪ'rɛkʃənl] *adj* bidirecional.

biennial [baɪ'ɛnɪəl] *adj* bienal ♦ *n* (*plant*) planta bienal.

bier [bɪə*] *n* féretro.

bifocals [baɪ'fəuklz] *npl* óculos *mpl* bifocais.

big [bɪg] *adj* grande; **to do things in a ~ way** fazer as coisas em grande escala.

bigamy ['bɪgəmɪ] *n* bigamia.

big business *n* alto comércio.

big dipper [-'dɪpə*] *n* montanha-russa.
big end *n* (*AUT*) cabeça de biela.
bigheaded ['bɪg'hɛdɪd] *adj* vaidoso.
big-hearted ['bɪg'hɑ:tɪd] *adj* magnânimo.
bigot ['bɪgət] *n* fanático, intolerante *m/f*.
bigoted ['bɪgətɪd] *adj* fanático, intolerante.
bigotry ['bɪgətrɪ] *n* fanatismo, intolerância.
big toe *n* dedão *m* do pé.
big top *n* tenda de circo.
big wheel *n* (*at fair*) roda gigante.
bigwig ['bɪgwɪg] (*inf*) *n* mandachuva *m*.
bike [baɪk] *n* bicicleta.
bikini [bɪ'ki:nɪ] *n* biquíni *m*.
bilateral [baɪ'lætrəl] *adj* bilateral.
bile [baɪl] *n* bílis *f*.
bilingual [baɪ'lɪŋgwəl] *adj* bilíngüe.
bilious ['bɪlɪəs] *adj* bilioso.
bill [bɪl] *n* (*account*) conta; (*invoice*) fatura; (*POL*) projeto de lei; (*US*: *banknote*) bilhete *m*, nota; (*in restaurant*) conta, notinha; (*notice*) cartaz *m*; (*of bird*) bico ♦ *vt* (*item*) faturar; (*customer*) enviar fatura a; **may I have the ~ please?** a conta *or* a notinha, por favor?; **"stick** *or* **post no ~s"** "é proibido afixar cartazes"; **to fit** *or* **fill the ~** (*fig*) servir; **~ of exchange** letra de câmbio; **~ of lading** conhecimento de carga; **~ of sale** nota de venda; (*formal*) escritura de venda.
billboard ['bɪlbɔ:d] *n* quadro para cartazes.
billet ['bɪlɪt] *n* alojamento ♦ *vt* alojar, quartelar.
billfold ['bɪlfəuld] (*US*) *n* carteira (para notas).
billiards ['bɪlɪədz] *n* bilhar *m*.
billion ['bɪlɪən] *n* (*BRIT*: *= 1,000,000,000,000*) trilhão *m*; (*US*: *= 1,000,000,000*) bilhão *m*.
billow ['bɪləu] *n* (*of smoke*) bulcão *m* ♦ *vi* (*smoke*) redemoinhar; (*sail*) enfunar-se.
billy goat ['bɪlɪ-] *n* bode *m*.
bin [bɪn] *n* caixa; (*BRIT*: *also*: *dust~*; *litter ~*) lata de lixo; *see also* **breadbin**.
binary ['baɪnərɪ] *adj* binário.
bind [baɪnd] (*pt*, *pp* **bound**) *vt* atar, amarrar; (*wound*) enfaixar; (*book*) encadernar; (*oblige*) obrigar.
bind over *vt* (*LAW*) pôr em liberdade condicional.
bind up *vt* (*wound*) enfaixar; **to be bound up with** estar vinculado a.
binder ['baɪndə*] *n* (*file*) fichário.
binding ['baɪndɪŋ] *adj* (*contract*) sujeitante ♦ *n* (*of book*) encadernação *f*.
binge [bɪndʒ] (*inf*) *n*: **(to go on a) ~** (cair na) farra.
bingo ['bɪŋgəu] *n* bingo.
binoculars [bɪ'nɔkjuləz] *npl* binóculo.
biochemistry [baɪə'kɛmɪstrɪ] *n* bioquímica.
biodegradable ['baɪəudɪ'greɪdəbl] *adj* biodegradável.
biographer [baɪ'ɔgrəfə*] *n* biógrafo/a.
biographic(al) [baɪə'græfɪk(l)] *adj* biográfico.
biography [baɪ'ɔgrəfɪ] *n* biografia.
biological [baɪə'lɔdʒɪkəl] *adj* biológico.
biologist [baɪ'ɔlədʒɪst] *n* biólogo/a.
biology [baɪ'ɔlədʒɪ] *n* biologia.
biophysics ['baɪəu'fɪzɪks] *n* biofísica.
biopsy ['baɪɔpsɪ] *n* biopsia.
biotechnology ['baɪəutɛk'nɔlədʒɪ] *n* biotecnia.
birch [bə:tʃ] *n* bétula; (*cane*) vara de vidoeiro.
bird [bə:d] *n* ave *f*, pássaro; (*BRIT*: *inf*: *girl*) gatinha.
birdcage ['bə:dkeɪdʒ] *n* gaiola.
bird's-eye view *n* vista aérea; (*fig*) vista geral.
bird watcher [-'wɔtʃə*] *n* ornitófilo/a.
Biro ['baɪərəu] ® *n* caneta esferográfica.
birth [bə:θ] *n* nascimento; (*MED*) parto; **to give ~ to** dar à luz, parir.
birth certificate *n* certidão *f* de nascimento.
birth control *n* controle *m* de natalidade; (*methods*) métodos *mpl* anticoncepcionais.
birthday ['bə:θdeɪ] *n* aniversário (*BR*), dia *m* de anos (*PT*).
birthmark ['bə:θmɑ:k] *n* nevo.
birthplace ['bə:θpleɪs] *n* lugar *m* de nascimento.
birth rate *n* (índice *m* de) natalidade *f*.
Biscay ['bɪskeɪ] *n*: **the Bay of ~** o golfo de Biscaia.
biscuit ['bɪskɪt] *n* (*BRIT*) bolacha, biscoito; (*US*) pão *m* doce.
bisect [baɪ'sɛkt] *vt* dividir ao meio.
bishop ['bɪʃəp] *n* bispo.
bit [bɪt] *pt of* **bite** ♦ *n* pedaço, bocado; (*of tool*) broca; (*of horse*) freio; (*COMPUT*) bit *m*; **a ~ of** (*a little*) um pouco de; **a ~ mad** um pouco *or* meio doido; **~ by ~** pouco a pouco; **to come to ~s** (*break*) cair aos pedaços; **bring all your ~s and pieces** traz todos os teus troços; **to do one's ~** fazer sua parte.
bitch [bɪtʃ] *n* (*dog*) cadela, cachorra; (*inf!*) cadela (*!*), vagabunda (*!*).
bite [baɪt] (*pt* **bit**, *pp* **bitten**) *vt*, *vi* morder; (*insect etc*) picar ♦ *n* mordida; (*insect ~*) picada; (*mouthful*) bocado; **let's have a ~ (to eat)** vamos comer algo; **to ~ one's nails** roer as unhas.
biting ['baɪtɪŋ] *adj* (*wind*) penetrante; (*wit*) mordaz.
bit part *n* (*THEATRE*) ponta.
bitten ['bɪtn] *pp of* **bite**.
bitter ['bɪtə*] *adj* amargo; (*wind*, *criticism*) cortante, penetrante; (*battle*) encarniçado ♦ *n* (*BRIT*: *beer*) cerveja amarga; **to the ~ end** até o fim.
bitterly ['bɪtəlɪ] *adv* (*complain*, *weep*) amargamente; (*criticize*) asperamente; (*oppose*) implacavelmente; (*jealous*, *disappointed*) extremamente; **it's ~ cold** faz um frio glacial.
bitterness ['bɪtənɪs] *n* amargor *m*; (*anger*) rancor *m*.
bittersweet ['bɪtəswi:t] *adj* agridoce.
bitty ['bɪtɪ] (*BRIT*: *inf*) *adj* sem nexo.
bitumen ['bɪtjumɪn] *n* betume *m*.
bivouac ['bɪvuæk] *n* bivaque *m*.

NB*: European Portuguese adds the following consonants to certain words:* **b** (sú(b)dito, su(b)til); **c** (a(c)ção, a(c)cionista, a(c)to); **m** (inde(m)ne); **p** (ado(p)ção, ado(p)tar); *for further details see p. xiii.*

bizarre [bɪ'zɑ:*] *adj* esquisito.
bk *abbr* = **bank**; **book**.
BL *n abbr* (= *Bachelor of Laws*; *Bachelor of Letters*) *título universitário*; (*US*: = *Bachelor of Literature*) *título universitário*.
bl *abbr* = **bill of lading**.
blab [blæb] *vi* dar *or* bater com a língua nos dentes ♦ *vt* (*also*: ~ *out*) revelar, badalar.
black [blæk] *adj* preto ♦ *n* (*colour*) cor *f* preta; (*person*): **B~** negro/a, preto/a ♦ *vt* (*shoes*) lustrar (*BR*), engraxar (*PT*); (*BRIT*: *INDUSTRY*) boicotar; **to give sb a ~ eye** esmurrar alguém e deixá-lo de olho roxo; **~ coffee** café *m* preto; **there it is in ~ and white** (*fig*) aí está preto no branco; **to be in the ~** (*in credit*) estar com saldo credor; **~ and blue** contuso, contundido.
black out *vi* (*faint*) desmaiar.
black belt (*US*) *n* zona de negros.
blackberry ['blækbərɪ] *n* amora preta (*BR*), amora silvestre (*PT*).
blackbird ['blækbə:d] *n* melro.
blackboard ['blækbɔ:d] *n* quadro(-negro).
black box *n* (*AVIAT*) caixa preta.
Black Country (*BRIT*) *n*: **the ~** *zona industrial na região central da Inglaterra*.
blackcurrant [blæk'kʌrənt] *n* groselha negra.
black economy (*BRIT*) *n* economia invisível.
blacken ['blækən] *vt* enegrecer; (*fig*) denegrir.
Black Forest *n*: **the ~** a Floresta Negra.
blackhead ['blækhɛd] *n* cravo.
black ice *n* gelo negro.
blackjack ['blækdʒæk] *n* (*CARDS*) vinte-e-um *m*; (*US*: *truncheon*) cassetete *m*.
blackleg ['blæklɛg] (*BRIT*) *n* fura-greve *m/f*.
blacklist ['blæklɪst] *n* lista negra ♦ *vt* colocar na lista negra.
blackmail ['blækmeɪl] *n* chantagem *f* ♦ *vt* fazer chantagem a.
blackmailer ['blækmeɪlə*] *n* chantagista *m/f*.
black market *n* mercado *or* câmbio negro.
blackout ['blækaut] *n* blecaute *m*; (*fainting*) desmaio; (*of radio signal*) desvanecimento.
Black Sea *n*: **the ~** o mar Negro.
black sheep *n* (*fig*) ovelha negra.
blacksmith ['blæksmɪθ] *n* ferreiro.
black spot *n* (*AUT*) lugar *m* perigoso.
bladder ['blædə*] *n* bexiga.
blade [bleɪd] *n* folha; (*cutting edge*) lâmina; (*of oar*, *rotor*) pá *f*; **a ~ of grass** uma folha de relva.
blame [bleɪm] *n* culpa ♦ *vt*: **to ~ sb for sth** culpar alguém por algo; **to be to ~** ter a culpa.
blameless ['bleɪmlɪs] *adj* (*person*) inocente.
blanch [blɑ:ntʃ] *vi* (*person*, *face*) empalidecer ♦ *vt* (*CULIN*) escaldar.
bland [blænd] *adj* suave; (*taste*) brando.
blank [blæŋk] *adj* em branco; (*shot*) sem bala; (*look*) sem expressão ♦ *n* lacuna, espaço em branco; (*cartridge*) bala de festim; **we drew a ~** (*fig*) chegamos a lugar nenhum.
blank cheque (*US* **blank check**) *n* cheque *m* em branco; **to give sb a ~ to do ...** dar carta branca a alguém para fazer ....
blanket ['blæŋkɪt] *n* (*for bed*) cobertor *m*; (*for travelling etc*) manta ♦ *adj* (*statement*, *agreement*) global, geral; **to give ~ cover** (*subj*: *insurance policy*) dar cobertura geral.
blare [blɛə*] *vi* (*horn*, *radio*) clangorar.
blarney ['blɑ:nɪ] *n* bajulação *f*.
blasé ['blɑ:zeɪ] *adj* indiferente.
blasphemous ['blæsfɪməs] *adj* blasfemo.
blasphemy ['blæsfɪmɪ] *n* blasfêmia.
blast [blɑ:st] *n* (*of wind*) rajada; (*of whistle*) toque *m*; (*of explosive*) explosão *f*; (*shock wave*) sopro; (*of air*, *steam*) jato ♦ *vt* (*blow up*) fazer voar; (*blow open*) abrir com uma carga explosiva ♦ (*BRIT*: *inf*) *excl* droga!; **(at) full ~** (*play music etc*) no volume máximo; (*fig*) a todo vapor.
blast off *vi* (*SPACE*) decolar.
blast furnace *n* alto forno.
blast-off *n* (*SPACE*) lançamento.
blatant ['bleɪtənt] *adj* descarado.
blatantly ['bleɪtəntlɪ] *adv* (*lie*) descaradamente; **it's ~ obvious** é de toda a evidência, está na cara.
blaze [bleɪz] *n* (*fire*) fogo; (*in building etc*) incêndio; (*flames*) chamas *fpl*; (*of sun etc*) esplendor *m*; (*fig*) explosão *f* ♦ *vi* (*fire*) arder; (*fig*) resplandecer ♦ *vt*: **to ~ a trail** (*fig*) abrir (um) caminho; **in a ~ of publicity** numa explosão de publicidade.
blazer ['bleɪzə*] *n* casaco esportivo, blazer *m*.
bleach [bli:tʃ] *n* (*also*: *household* ~) água sanitária ♦ *vt* (*linen*) branquear.
bleached [bli:tʃt] *adj* (*hair*) oxigenado; (*linen*) branqueado, alvejado.
bleachers ['bli:tʃəz] (*US*) *npl* (*SPORT*) arquibancada descoberta.
bleak [bli:k] *adj* (*countryside*) desolado; (*prospect*) desanimador(a), sombrio; (*weather*) ruim; (*smile*) sem graça, amarelo.
bleary-eyed ['blɪərɪ'aɪd] *adj* de olhos injetados.
bleat [bli:t] *vi* balir ♦ *n* balido.
bled [blɛd] *pt*, *pp of* **bleed**.
bleed [bli:d] (*pt*, *pp* **bled**) *vt*, *vi* sangrar; **my nose is ~ing** eu estou sangrando do nariz.
bleeper ['bli:pə*] *n* (*of doctor etc*) bip *m*.
blemish ['blɛmɪʃ] *n* mancha, falha.
blend [blɛnd] *n* mistura ♦ *vt* misturar ♦ *vi* (*colours etc*) combinar-se, misturar-se.
blender ['blɛndə*] *n* (*CULIN*) liquidificador *m*.
bless [blɛs] (*pt*, *pp* **blessed** *or* **blest**) *vt* abençoar.
blessed[1] [blɛst] *pt*, *pp of* **bless**; **to be ~ with** estar dotado de.
blessed[2] ['blɛsɪd] *adj* (*REL*: *holy*) bendito, bento; (*happy*) afortunado; **it rains every ~ day** chove cada santo dia.
blessing ['blɛsɪŋ] *n* bênção *f*; (*advantage*) benefício, vantagem *f*; **to count one's ~s** dar graças a Deus; **it was a ~ in disguise** Deus escreve certo por linhas tortas.
blest [blɛst] *pt*, *pp of* **bless**.
blew [blu:] *pt of* **blow**.
blight [blaɪt] *vt* (*hopes etc*) frustrar, gorar ♦ *n*

(*of plants*) ferrugem *f*.
blimey ['blaɪmɪ] (*BRIT*: *inf*) *excl* nossa!
blind [blaɪnd] *adj* cego ♦ *n* (*for window*) persiana ♦ *vt* cegar; (*dazzle*) deslumbrar; **to turn a ~ eye (on** *or* **to)** fazer vista grossa (a).
blind alley *n* beco-sem-saída *m*.
blind corner (*BRIT*) *n* curva sem visibilidade.
blindfold ['blaɪndfəuld] *n* venda ♦ *adj*, *adv* com os olhos vendados, às cegas ♦ *vt* vendar os olhos a.
blindly ['blaɪndlɪ] *adv* às cegas, cegamente.
blindness ['blaɪndnɪs] *n* cegueira.
blind spot *n* ponto cego; (*fig*) cegueira.
blink [blɪŋk] *vi* piscar ♦ (*inf*) *n*: **the TV's on the ~** a TV está com defeito.
blinkers ['blɪŋkəz] *npl* antolhos *mpl*.
blinking ['blɪŋkɪŋ] (*BRIT*: *inf*) *adj*: **this ~ ...** este danado ....
bliss [blɪs] *n* felicidade *f*.
blissful ['blɪsful] *adj* (*event*, *day*) maravilhoso; (*sigh*, *smile*) contente; **in ~ ignorance** numa bendita ignorância.
blissfully ['blɪsfulɪ] *adj* (*smile*) ditosamente; (*happy*) maravilhosamente.
blister ['blɪstə*] *n* (*on skin*) bolha, empola ♦ *vi* (*paint*) empolar-se.
blistering ['blɪstərɪŋ] *adj* (*heat*) causticante.
blithe [blaɪð] *adj* alegre.
blithely ['blaɪðlɪ] *adv* (*unconcernedly*) tranqüilamente; (*joyfully*) alegremente.
blithering ['blɪðərɪŋ] (*inf*) *adj*: **this ~ idiot** esta besta quadrada.
BLit(t) *n abbr* (= *Bachelor of Literature*) *título universitário*.
blitz [blɪts] *n* bombardeio aéreo; (*fig*): **to have a ~ on sth** dar um jeito em algo.
blizzard ['blɪzəd] *n* nevasca.
BLM (*US*) *n abbr* = **Bureau of Land Management**.
bloated ['bləutɪd] *adj* inchado.
blob [blɔb] *n* (*drop*) gota; (*stain*, *spot*) mancha.
bloc [blɔk] *n* (*POL*) bloco.
block [blɔk] *n* bloco; (*in pipes*) entupimento; (*toy*) cubo; (*of buildings*) quarteirão *m* ♦ *vt* obstruir, bloquear; (*pipe*) entupir; (*progress*) impedir; (*COMPUT*) blocar; **~ of flats** (*BRIT*) prédio (de apartamentos); **3 ~s from here** a três quarteirões daqui; **mental ~** bloqueio; **~ and tackle** (*TECH*) talha.
block up *vt* (*hole*) tampar; (*pipe*) entupir; (*road*) bloquear.
blockade [blɔ'keɪd] *n* bloqueio ♦ *vt* bloquear.
blockage ['blɔkɪdʒ] *n* obstrução *f*.
block booking *n* reserva em bloco.
blockbuster ['blɔkbʌstə*] *n* grande sucesso.
block capitals *npl* letras *fpl* de forma.
blockhead ['blɔkhɛd] *n* imbecil *m/f*.
block letters *npl* letras *fpl* maiúsculas.
block release (*BRIT*) *n* licença para fins de aperfeiçoamento profissional.
block vote (*BRIT*) *n* voto em bloco.
bloke [bləuk] (*BRIT*: *inf*) *n* cara *m* (*BR*), gajo (*PT*).
blond(e) [blɔnd] *adj*, *n* louro/a.
blood [blʌd] *n* sangue *m*.
bloodcurdling ['blʌdkəːdlɪŋ] *adj* horripilante, de fazer gelar o sangue nas veias.
blood donor *n* doador(a) *m/f* de sangue.
blood group *n* grupo sangüíneo.
bloodhound ['blʌdhaund] *n* sabujo.
bloodless ['blʌdlɪs] *adj* (*victory*) incruento; (*pale*) pálido.
bloodletting ['blʌdlɛtɪŋ] *n* (*MED*) sangria; (*fig*) derramamento de sangue.
blood poisoning *n* toxemia.
blood pressure *n* pressão *f* arterial *or* sangüínea.
bloodshed ['blʌdʃɛd] *n* matança, carnificina.
bloodshot ['blʌdʃɔt] *adj* (*eyes*) injetado.
bloodstained ['blʌdsteɪnd] *adj* manchado de sangue.
bloodstream ['blʌdstriːm] *n* corrente *f* sangüínea.
blood test *n* exame *m* de sangue.
bloodthirsty ['blʌdθəːstɪ] *adj* sangüinário.
blood transfusion *n* transfusão *f* de sangue.
blood vessel *n* vaso sangüíneo.
bloody ['blʌdɪ] *adj* sangrento; (*BRIT*: *inf!*): **this ~ ...** essa droga de ..., esse maldito ... ♦ *adv* (*BRIT*: *inf!*): **~ strong/good** forte/bom pra burro (*inf*).
bloody-minded ['blʌdɪ'maɪndɪd] (*BRIT*: *inf*) *adj* espírito de porco *inv*.
bloom [bluːm] *n* flor *f*; (*fig*) florescimento, viço ♦ *vi* florescer.
blooming ['bluːmɪŋ] (*inf*) *adj*: **this ~ ...** esse maldito ..., esse miserável ....
blossom ['blɔsəm] *n* flor *f* ♦ *vi* florescer; (*fig*) desabrochar-se; **to ~ into** (*fig*) tornar-se.
blot [blɔt] *n* borrão *m* ♦ *vt* borrar; (*ink*) secar; **a ~ on the landscape** um aleijão na paisagem; **to ~ one's copy book** (*fig*) manchar sua reputação.
blot out *vt* (*view*) tapar; (*memory*) apagar.
blotchy ['blɔtʃɪ] *adj* (*complexion*) cheio de manchas.
blotter ['blɔtə*] *n* mata-borrão *m*.
blotting paper ['blɔtɪŋ-] *n* mata-borrão *m*.
blouse [blauz] *n* blusa.
blow [bləu] (*pt* **blew**, *pp* **blown**) *n* golpe *m* ♦ *vi* soprar ♦ *vt* (*glass*) soprar; (*fuse*) queimar; (*instrument*) tocar; **to ~ one's nose** assoar o nariz; **to come to ~s** chegar às vias de fato.
blow away *vt* levar, arrancar ♦ *vi* ser levado pelo vento.
blow down *vt* derrubar.
blow off *vt* levar ♦ *vi* ser levado.
blow out *vi* (*candle*) apagar; (*tyre*) estourar ♦ *vt* (*candle*) apagar.
blow over *vi* passar, ser esquecido.

***NB:** European Portuguese adds the following consonants to certain words:* **b** (sú(b)dito, su(b)til); **c** (a(c)ção, a(c)cionista, a(c)to); **m** (inde(m)ne); **p** (ado(p)ção, ado(p)tar); *for further details see p. xiii.*

blow up *vi* explodir; (*fig*) perder a paciência ♦ *vt* dinamitar; (*tyre*) encher; (*PHOT*) ampliar.
blow-dry *n* escova ♦ *vt* fazer escova em.
blowlamp ['bləulæmp] (*BRIT*) *n* maçarico.
blow-out *n* (*of tyre*) furo, estouro; (*inf*: *big meal*) rega-bofe *m*.
blowtorch ['bləutɔ:tʃ] *n* maçarico.
blowzy ['blauzɪ] (*BRIT*) *adj* balofa.
BLS (*US*) *n abbr* = **Bureau of Labor Statistics.**
blubber ['blʌbə*] *n* óleo de baleia ♦ *vi* (*pej*) choramingar.
blue [blu:] *adj* azul; **~s** *npl*: **the ~s** (*MUS*) o blues; **to have the ~s** (*inf*: *feeling*) estar na fossa, estar de baixo astral; **~ film/joke** filme/anedota picante; **(only) once in a ~ moon** uma vez na vida e outra na morte; **out of the ~** (*fig*) de estalo, inesperadamente.
blue baby *n* criança azul.
bluebell ['blu:bɛl] *n* campainha (azul), campânula.
bluebottle ['blu:bɔtl] *n* varejeira azul.
blue cheese *n* queijo tipo roquefort.
blue-chip *adj*: **~ investment** investimento de primeira ordem.
blue-collar worker *n* operário/a.
blue jeans *npl* jeans *m* (*BR*), jeans *mpl* (*PT*).
blueprint ['blu:prɪnt] *n* anteprojeto; (*fig*): **~ (for)** esquema *m* (de).
bluff [blʌf] *vi* blefar ♦ *n* blefe *m*; (*crag*) penhasco ♦ *adj* (*person*) brusco; **to call sb's ~** pagar para ver alguém.
blunder ['blʌndə*] *n* gafe *f* ♦ *vi* cometer *or* fazer uma gafe; **to ~ into sb/sth** esbarrar com alguém/algo.
blunt [blʌnt] *adj* (*blade*) cego, embotado; (*pencil*) rombudo; (*person*) franco, direto ♦ *vt* embotar; **~ instrument** (*LAW*) arma imprópria.
bluntly ['blʌntlɪ] *adv* sem rodeios.
bluntness ['blʌntnɪs] *n* (*of person*) franqueza, rudeza.
blur [blə:*] *n* borrão *m*, nebulosidade *f* ♦ *vt* borrar, nublar.
blurb [blə:b] *n* (*for book*) dizeres *mpl* de propaganda.
blurred [blə:d] *adj* indistinto, borrado.
blurt [blə:t]: **to ~ out** *vt* (*reveal*) deixar escapar; (*say*) balbuciar.
blush [blʌʃ] *vi* corar, ruborizar-se ♦ *n* rubor *m*, vermelhidão *f*.
blusher ['blʌʃə*] *n* blusher *m*.
bluster ['blʌstə*] *n* fanfarronada, bazófia ♦ *vi* fanfarronar.
blustering ['blʌstərɪŋ] *adj* (*person*) fanfarrão/rona.
blustery ['blʌstərɪ] *adj* (*weather*) borrascoso, tormentoso.
Blvd *abbr* = **boulevard.**
BM *n abbr* = **British Museum**; (*SCH*: = *Bachelor of Medicine*) *título universitário.*
BMA *n abbr* = **British Medical Association.**
BMJ *n abbr* = **British Medical Journal.**
BMus *n abbr* (= *Bachelor of Music*) *título universitário.*
BO *n abbr* (*inf*: = *body odour*) fartum *m*, c.c. *m*; (*US*) = **box office.**
boar [bɔ:*] *n* javali *m*.
board [bɔ:d] *n* tábua; (*on wall*) quadro; (*for chess etc*) tabuleiro; (*committee*) junta, conselho; (*in firm*) diretoria, conselho administrativo ♦ *vt* embarcar em; **on ~** (*NAUT*, *AVIAT*) a bordo; **full ~** (*BRIT*) pensão *f* completa; **half ~** (*BRIT*) meia-pensão; **~ and lodging** casa e comida; **above ~** (*fig*) limpo; **across the ~** *adj* geral ♦ *adv* de uma maneira geral; **to go by the ~** ficar abandonado, dançar (*inf*).
board up *vt* (*door*) entabuar.
boarder ['bɔ:də*] *n* hóspede *m/f*; (*SCH*) interno/a.
board game *n* jogo de tabuleiro.
boarding card ['bɔ:dɪŋ-] *n* (*AVIAT*, *NAUT*) cartão *m* de embarque.
boarding house ['bɔ:dɪŋ-] (*irreg*) *n* pensão *m*.
boarding pass ['bɔ:dɪŋ-] (*BRIT*) *n* cartão *m* de embarque.
boarding school ['bɔ:dɪŋ-] *n* internato.
board meeting *n* reunião *f* da diretoria.
board room *n* sala da diretoria.
boardwalk ['bɔ:dwɔ:k] (*US*) *n* passeio de tábuas.
boast [bəust] *vi* contar vantagem; **to ~ (about *or* of)** gabar-se (de), jactar-se (de) ♦ *vt* ostentar ♦ *n* jactância, bazófia.
boastful ['bəustful] *adj* vaidoso, jactancioso.
boastfulness ['bəustfulnɪs] *n* bazófia, jactância.
boat [bəut] *n* barco; (*small*) bote *m*; (*big*) navio; **to go by ~** ir de barco; **to be in the same ~** (*fig*) estar no mesmo barco.
boater ['bəutə*] *n* (*hat*) chapéu *m* de palha.
boating ['bəutɪŋ] *n* passeio de barco.
boatman ['bəutmən] (*irreg*) *n* barqueiro.
boatswain ['bəusn] *n* contramestre *m*.
bob [bɔb] *vi* (*boat, cork on water*: *also*: *~ up and down*) balouçar-se ♦ *n* (*BRIT*: *inf*) = **shilling.**
bob up *vi* aparecer, surgir.
bobbin ['bɔbɪn] *n* bobina, carretel *m*.
bobby ['bɔbɪ] (*BRIT*: *inf*) *n* policial *m/f* (*BR*), polícia *m* (*PT*).
bobsleigh ['bɔbsleɪ] *n* bob *m*, trenó *m* duplo.
bode [bəud] *vi*: **to ~ well/ill (for)** ser de bom/mau agouro (para).
bodice ['bɔdɪs] *n* corpete *m*.
bodily ['bɔdɪlɪ] *adj* corpóreo, corporal; (*pain*) físico; (*needs*) material ♦ *adv* (*lift*) em peso.
body ['bɔdɪ] *n* corpo; (*corpse*) cadáver *m*; (*of car*) carroceria; (*of plane*) fuselagem *f*; (*fig*: *society*) órgão *m*; (: *quantity*) conjunto; (*of wine*) corpo; **in a ~** todos juntos.
body-building *n* musculação *f*.
bodyguard ['bɔdɪgɑ:d] *n* guarda-costas *m inv*.
body repairs *npl* lanternagem *f*.
bodywork ['bɔdɪwə:k] *n* lataria.
boffin ['bɔfɪn] (*BRIT*) *n* cientista *m/f*.
bog [bɔg] *n* pântano, atoleiro ♦ *vt*: **to get ~ged down (in)** (*fig*) atolar-se (em).

bogey ['bəugɪ] *n* (*worry*) espectro; (*BRIT*: *inf*: *dried mucus*) meleca.
boggle ['bɔgl] *vi*: **the mind ~s** (*wonder*) não dá para imaginar; (*innuendo*) nem quero pensar.
bogie ['bəugɪ] *n* (*RAIL*) truque *m*.
Bogotá [bɔgə'tɑː] *n* Bogotá.
bogus ['bəugəs] *adj* falso; (*person*) fingido, farsante.
Bohemia [bəu'hiːmɪə] *n* Boêmia.
Bohemian [bəu'hiːmɪən] *adj*, *n* boêmio/a.
boil [bɔɪl] *vt* ferver; (*eggs*) cozinhar ♦ *vi* ferver ♦ *n* (*MED*) furúnculo; **to come to the** (*BRIT*) *or* **a** (*US*) ~ começar a ferver; **to bring to the** (*BRIT*) *or* **a** (*US*) ~ deixar ferver; **~ed egg** (*hard*) ovo cozido; (*soft*) ovo quente; **~ed potatoes** batatas *fpl* cozidas.
boil down *vi* (*fig*): **to ~ down to** reduzir-se a.
boil over *vi* transbordar.
boiler ['bɔɪlə*] *n* caldeira; (*for central heating*) boiler *m*.
boiler suit (*BRIT*) *n* macacão *m* (*BR*), fato macaco (*PT*).
boiling ['bɔɪlɪŋ] *adj*: **it's ~** (*weather*) está um calor horrível; **I'm ~ (hot)** (*inf*) estou morrendo de calor.
boiling point *n* ponto de ebulição.
boisterous ['bɔɪstərəs] *adj* (*noisy*) barulhento; (*excitable*) agitado; (*crowd*) turbulento.
bold [bəuld] *adj* audacioso, corajoso; (*pej*) atrevido, insolente; (*outline*, *colour*) forte.
boldness ['bəuldnɪs] *n* arrojo, coragem *f*; (*cheek*) audácia, descaramento.
bold type *n* (*TYP*) negrito.
Bolivia [bə'lɪvɪə] *n* Bolívia.
Bolivian [bə'lɪvɪən] *adj*, *n* boliviano/a.
bollard ['bɔləd] *n* (*BRIT*: *AUT*) poste *m* de sinalização; (*NAUT*) poste de amarração.
bolster ['bəulstə*] *n* travesseiro.
bolster up *vt* sustentar.
bolt [bəult] *n* (*lock*) trinco, ferrolho; (*with nut*) parafuso, cavilha ♦ *adv*: **~ upright** direito como um fuso ♦ *vt* (*door*) fechar a ferrolho, trancar; (*food*) engolir às pressas ♦ *vi* fugir; (*horse*) disparar; **to be a ~ from the blue** (*fig*) cair como uma bomba, ser uma bomba.
bomb [bɔm] *n* bomba ♦ *vt* bombardear.
bombard [bɔm'bɑːd] *vt* bombardear.
bombardment [bɔm'bɑːdmənt] *n* bombardeio.
bombastic [bɔm'bæstɪk] *adj* empolado, bombástico; (*person*) pomposo.
bomb disposal *n*: **~ expert** perito/a em desmontagem de explosivos; **~ unit** unidade *f* de desmontagem de explosivos.
bomber ['bɔmə*] *n* (*AVIAT*) bombardeiro; (*terrorist*) terrorista *m/f*.
bombing ['bɔmɪŋ] *n* bombardeio; (*by terrorists*) atentado a bomba.
bombshell ['bɔmʃɛl] *n* granada de artilharia; (*fig*) bomba.
bomb site *n* zona bombardeada.
bona fide ['bəunə'faɪdɪ] *adj* genuíno, autêntico.
bonanza [bə'nænzə] *n* boom *m*.
bond [bɔnd] *n* (*binding promise*) compromisso; (*FINANCE*) obrigação *f*; (*link*) vínculo, laço; **in ~** (*goods*) retido sob caução na alfândega.
bondage ['bɔndɪdʒ] *n* escravidão *f*.
bonded warehouse ['bɔndɪd-] (*irreg*) *n* depósito da alfândega, entreposto aduaneiro.
bone [bəun] *n* osso; (*of fish*) espinha ♦ *vt* (*fish*) tirar as espinhas de; (*meat*) desossar.
bone china *n* porcelana com mistura de cinza de ossos.
bone-dry *adj* completamente seco.
bone idle *adj* preguiçoso.
boner ['bəunə*] (*US*) *n* gafe *f*.
bonfire ['bɔnfaɪə*] *n* fogueira.
Bonn [bɔn] *n* Bonn.
bonnet ['bɔnɪt] *n* toucado; (*BRIT*: *of car*) capô *m*.
bonny ['bɔnɪ] (*SCOTTISH*) *adj* bonitinho.
bonus ['bəunəs] *n* bônus *m*, prêmio; (*on salary*) prêmio, gratificação *f*.
bony ['bəunɪ] *adj* (*arm*, *face*, *MED*: *tissue*) ossudo; (*meat*) cheio de ossos; (*fish*) cheio de espinhas.
boo [buː] *vt* vaiar ♦ *n* vaia ♦ *excl* ruuh!, bu!
boob [buːb] (*inf*) *n* (*breast*) seio; (*BRIT*: *mistake*) besteira, gafe *f*.
booby prize ['buːbɪ-] *n* prêmio de consolação.
booby trap ['buːbɪ-] *n* armadilha explosiva.
booby-trapped ['buːbɪtræpt] *adj* que tem armadilha explosiva.
book [buk] *n* livro; (*notebook*) caderno; (*COMM*): **~s** *npl* contas *fpl*, contabilidade *f* ♦ *vt* reservar; (*driver*) autuar; (*football player*) mostrar o cartão amarelo a; **to keep the ~s** fazer a escrituração *or* contabilidade; **by the ~** de acordo com o regulamento, corretamente; **to throw the ~ at sb** condenar alguém à pena máxima.
book in (*BRIT*) *vi* (*at hotel*) registrar (*BR*), registar (*PT*).
book up *vt* reservar; **all seats are ~ed up** todos os lugares estão tomados; **the hotel is ~ed up** o hotel está lotado.
bookable ['bukəbl] *adj*: **seats are ~** lugares podem ser reservados.
bookcase ['bukkeɪs] *n* estante *f* (para livros).
book ends *npl* suportes *mpl* de livros.
booking ['bukɪŋ] (*BRIT*) *n* reserva.
booking office (*BRIT*) *n* (*RAIL*, *THEATRE*) bilheteria (*BR*), bilheteira (*PT*).
book-keeping *n* escrituração *f*, contabilidade *f*.
booklet ['buklɪt] *n* livrinho, brochura.
bookmaker ['bukmeɪkə*] *n* book(maker) *m* (*BR*), agenciador *m* de apostas (*PT*).
bookseller ['buksɛlə*] *n* livreiro/a.

bookshop ['bukʃɔp] *n* livraria.
bookstall ['bukstɔːl] *n* banca de livros.
bookstore ['bukstɔː*] *n* livraria.
book token *n* vale *m* para livro.
book value *n* valor *m* contábil.
boom [buːm] *n* (*noise*) barulho, estrondo; (*in sales etc*) aumento rápido; (*ECON*) boom *m*, fase *f* or aumento de prosperidade ♦ *vi* (*sound*) retumbar, ribombar; (*business*) tomar surto.
boomerang ['buːməræŋ] *n* bumerangue *m*.
boom town *n* cidade *f* de rápido crescimento econômico.
boon [buːn] *n* benefício.
boorish ['buərɪʃ] *adj* rude.
boost [buːst] *n* estímulo ♦ *vt* estimular; **to give a ~ to sb's spirits** *or* **to sb** dar uma força a alguém.
booster ['buːstə*] *n* (*MED*) revacinação *f*; (*TV*) amplificador *m* (de sinal); (*ELEC*) sobrevoltador *m*; (*also*: ~ *rocket*) foguete *m* auxiliar.
booster seat *n* (*AUT*: *for children*) *assento de carro para crianças maiores.*
boot [buːt] *n* bota; (*for football*) chuteira; (*ankle* ~) botina; (*BRIT*: *of car*) porta-malas *m* (*BR*), mala (*BR*: *inf*), porta-bagagem *m* (*PT*) ♦ *vt* (*kick*) dar pontapé em; (*COMPUT*) dar carga em; **to ~** (*in addition*) ainda por cima; **to give sb the ~** (*inf*) botar alguém na rua.
booth [buːð] *n* (*at fair*) barraca; (*telephone* ~, *voting* ~) cabine *f*.
bootleg ['buːtlɛg] *adj* de contrabando; **~ recording** gravação *f* pirata.
booty ['buːtɪ] *n* despojos *mpl*, pilhagem *f*.
booze [buːz] (*inf*) *n* bebida alcoólica ♦ *vi* embebedar-se.
boozer ['buːzə*] (*inf*) *n* (*person*) beberrão/beberrona *m/f*; (*BRIT*: *pub*) pub *m*.
border ['bɔːdə*] *n* margem *f*, borda; (*of a country*) fronteira ♦ *cpd* (*town*, *region*) fronteiriço; **the B~s** *a região fronteiriça entre a Escócia e a Inglaterra.*
border on *vt fus* limitar-se com; (*fig*) chegar às raias de.
borderline ['bɔːdəlaɪn] *n* (*fig*) fronteira ♦ *adj*: **~ case** caso-limite *m*.
bore [bɔː*] *pt of* **bear** ♦ *vt* (*hole*) abrir; (*person*) aborrecer ♦ *n* (*person*) chato, maçante; (*of gun*) calibre *m*; **what a ~!** que chato! (*BR*), que saco! (*BR*), que maçada! (*PT*); **to be ~d to tears** *or* **~d to death** *or* **~d stiff** estar muito entediado.
bored [bɔːd] *adj* entediado.
boredom ['bɔːdəm] *n* tédio, aborrecimento.
boring ['bɔːrɪŋ] *adj* chato, maçante.
born [bɔːn] *adj*: **to be ~** nascer; **I was ~ in 1960** nasci em 1960; **~ blind** cego de nascença; **a ~ leader** um líder nato.
borne [bɔːn] *pp of* **bear**.
Borneo ['bɔːnɪəu] *n* Bornéu.
borough ['bʌrə] *n* município.
borrow ['bɔrəu] *vt*: **to ~ sth (from sb)** pedir algo emprestado a alguém; **may I ~ your car?** você pode me emprestar o seu carro?
borrower ['bɔrəuə*] *n* tomador(a) *m/f* de empréstimo.
borrowing ['bɔrəuɪŋ] *n* empréstimo(s) *m(pl)*.
borstal ['bɔːstl] (*BRIT*) *n* reformatório (de menores).
bosom ['buzəm] *n* peito.
bosom friend *n* amigo/a íntimo/a *or* do peito.
boss [bɔs] *n* chefe *m/f*; (*employer*) patrão/troa *m/f*; (*in agriculture, industry etc*) capataz *m* ♦ *vt* (*also*: ~ *about*; ~ *around*) mandar em.
bossy ['bɔsɪ] *adj* mandão/dona.
bosun ['bəusn] *n* contramestre *m*.
botanical [bə'tænɪkl] *adj* botânico.
botanist ['bɔtənɪst] *n* botânico/a.
botany ['bɔtənɪ] *n* botânica.
botch [bɔtʃ] *vt* (*also*: ~ *up*) estropiar, atamancar.
both [bəuθ] *adj*, *pron* ambos/as, os dois/as duas ♦ *adv*: **~ A and B** tanto A como B; **~ of us went, we ~ went** nós dois fomos, ambos fomos.
bother ['bɔðə*] *vt* (*worry*) preocupar; (*irritate*) incomodar, molestar; (*disturb*) atrapalhar ♦ *vi* (*also*: ~ *o.s.*) preocupar-se ♦ *n*: **it is a ~ to have to do** é chato ter que fazer ♦ *excl* bolas!; **to ~ doing** dar-se ao trabalho de fazer; **to ~ about** preocupar-se com; **I'm sorry to ~ you** lamento incomodá-lo; **please don't ~** por favor, não se preocupe, não se dê ao trabalho; **don't ~** não vale a pena; **it's no ~** não tem problema.
Botswana [bɔt'swɑːnə] *n* Botsuana.
bottle ['bɔtl] *n* garrafa; (*of perfume, medicine*) frasco; (*baby's*) mamadeira (*BR*), biberão *m* (*PT*) ♦ *vt* engarrafar.
bottle up *vt* conter, refrear.
bottleneck ['bɔtlnɛk] *n* (*traffic*) engarrafamento; (*of bottle, fig*) gargalo.
bottle-opener *n* abridor *m* (de garrafas) (*BR*), abre-garrafas *m inv* (*PT*).
bottom ['bɔtəm] *n* (*of box, sea*) fundo; (*buttocks*) traseiro, bunda (*inf*); (*of page, list*) pé *m*; (*of mountain, hill*) sopé *m* ♦ *adj* (*low*) inferior, mais baixo; (*last*) último; **to get to the ~ of sth** (*fig*) tirar algo a limpo.
bottomless ['bɔtəmlɪs] *adj* sem fundo; (*fig*) insondável.
bough [bau] *n* ramo.
bought [bɔːt] *pt, pp of* **buy**.
boulder ['bəuldə*] *n* pedregulho, matacão *m*.
bounce [bauns] *vi* (*ball*) saltar, quicar; (*cheque*) ser devolvido (*por insuficiência de fundos*) ♦ *vt* fazer saltar ♦ *n* (*rebound*) salto; **he's got plenty of ~** (*fig*) ele tem pique.
bouncer ['baunsə*] (*inf*) *n* leão-de-chácara *m*.
bound [baund] *pt, pp of* **bind** ♦ *n* (*leap*) pulo, salto; (*gen pl*: *limit*) limite *m* ♦ *vt* (*limit*) limitar ♦ *vi* (*leap*) pular, saltar ♦ *adj*: **~ by** (*limited by*) limitado por; **to be ~ to do sth** (*obliged*) ter a obrigação de fazer algo; (*likely*) na certa ir fazer algo; **~ for** com destino a; **out of ~s** fora dos limites.
boundary ['baundrɪ] *n* limite *m*, fronteira.
boundless ['baundlɪs] *adj* ilimitado.
bountiful ['bauntɪful] *adj* (*person*) generoso;

(*supply*) farto.
bounty ['bauntı] *n* (*generosity*) generosidade *f*; (*wealth*) fartura.
bouquet ['bukeı] *n* (*of flowers*) buquê *m*, ramalhete *m*; (*of wine*) buquê *m*, aroma *m*.
bourbon ['buəbən] (*US*) *n* (*also*: ~ *whiskey*) uísque *m* (*BR*) *or* whisky (*PT*) (norte-americano).
bourgeois ['bueʒwɑ:] *adj* burguês/guesa.
bout [baut] *n* período; (*of malaria etc*) ataque *m*; (*BOXING etc*) combate *m*.
boutique [bu:'ti:k] *n* butique *f*.
bow[1] [bəu] *n* (*knot*) laço; (*weapon, MUS*) arco.
bow[2] [bau] *n* (*of the body*) reverência; (*of the head*) inclinação *f*; (*NAUT*: *also*: ~*s*) proa ♦ *vi* curvar-se, fazer uma reverência; (*yield*): **to ~ to** *or* **before** ceder ante, submeter-se a; **to ~ to the inevitable** curvar-se ao inevitável.
bowels ['bauəlz] *npl* intestinos *mpl*, tripas *fpl*; (*fig*) entranhas *fpl*.
bowl [bəul] *n* tigela; (*for washing*) bacia; (*ball*) bola; (*of pipe*) fornilho; (*US*: *stadium*) estádio ♦ *vi* (*CRICKET*) arremessar a bola; **~s** *n* (*game*) jogo de bolas.
bowl over *vt* (*fig*) impressionar, comover.
bow-legged *adj* cambaio, de pernas tortas.
bowler ['bəulə*] *n* jogador(a) *m/f* de bolas; (*CRICKET*) lançador *m* (da bola); (*BRIT*: *also*: ~ *hat*) chapéu-coco *m*.
bowling ['bəulıŋ] *n* (*game*) boliche *m*.
bowling alley *n* boliche *m*.
bowling green *n* gramado (*BR*) *or* relvado (*PT*) para jogo de bolas.
bow tie ['bəu-] *n* gravata-borboleta.
box [bɔks] *n* caixa; (*crate*) caixote *m*; (*for jewels*) estojo; (*for money*) cofre *m*; (*THEATRE*) camarote *m* ♦ *vt* encaixotar; (*SPORT*) boxear contra ♦ *vi* (*SPORT*) boxear.
boxer ['bɔksə*] *n* (*person*) boxeador *m*, pugilista *m*; (*dog*) boxer *m*.
boxer shorts *npl* cueca samba-canção.
boxing ['bɔksıŋ] *n* (*SPORT*) boxe *m*, pugilismo.
Boxing Day (*BRIT*) *n Dia de Santo Estêvão, 26 de dezembro*.
boxing gloves *npl* luvas *fpl* de boxe.
boxing ring *n* ringue *m* de boxe.
box number *n* (*for advertisements*) caixa postal.
box office *n* bilheteria (*BR*), bilheteira (*PT*).
boxroom ['bɔksrum] *n* quarto pequeno.
boy [bɔı] *n* (*young*) menino, garoto; (*older*) moço, rapaz *m*; (*servant*) criado.
boycott ['bɔıkɔt] *n* boicote *m*, boicotagem *f* ♦ *vt* boicotar.
boyfriend ['bɔıfrɛnd] *n* namorado.
boyish ['bɔııʃ] *adj* de menino, pueril.
Bp *abbr* = **bishop.**
BR *abbr* = **British Rail.**
bra [brɑ:] *n* sutiã (*PT*: soutien) *m*.
brace [breıs] *n* reforço, braçadeira; (*on teeth*) aparelho; (*tool*) arco de pua; (*TYP*: *also*: ~ *bracket*) chave *f* ♦ *vt* firmar, reforçar; **~s** *npl* (*BRIT*) suspensórios *mpl*; **to ~ o.s.** (*fig*) preparar-se.
bracelet ['breıslıt] *n* pulseira.
bracing ['breısıŋ] *adj* tonificante.
bracken ['brækən] *n* samambaia (*BR*), feto (*PT*).
bracket ['brækıt] *n* (*TECH*) suporte *m*; (*group*) classe *f*, categoria; (*also*: *brace* ~) chave *f*; (*also*: *round* ~) parêntese *m*; (*gen*: *square* ~) colchete *m* ♦ *vt* pôr entre parênteses; (*fig*: *also*: ~ *together*) agrupar; **in ~s** entre parênteses (*or* colchetes).
brackish ['brækıʃ] *adj* (*water*) salobro.
brag [bræg] *vi* gabar-se, contar vantagem.
braid [breıd] *n* (*trimming*) galão *m*; (*of hair*) trança.
Braille [breıl] *n* braile *m*.
brain [breın] *n* cérebro; **~s** *npl* inteligência, miolos *mpl*; **he's got ~s** ele é inteligente.
brainchild ['breıntʃaıld] *n* idéia original.
brainless ['breınlıs] *adj* estúpido, desmiolado.
brainstorm ['breınstɔ:m] *n* (*fig*) momento de distração; (*US*: *brainwave*) idéia luminosa.
brainwash ['breınwɔʃ] *vt* fazer uma lavagem cerebral em.
brainwave ['breınweıv] *n* inspiração *f*, idéia luminosa *or* brilhante.
brainy ['breını] *adj* inteligente.
braise [breız] *vt* estufar.
brake [breık] *n* (*on vehicle*) freio (*BR*), travão *m* (*PT*) ♦ *vt, vi* frear (*BR*), travar (*PT*).
brake drum *n* tambor *m* de freio (*BR*) *or* de travão (*PT*).
brake fluid *n* óleo de freio (*BR*) *or* dos travões (*PT*).
brake light *n* farol *m* do freio (*BR*), farolim *m* de travagem (*PT*).
brake pedal *n* pedal *m* do freio (*BR*), travão *m* de pé (*PT*).
bramble ['bræmbl] *n* amora-preta.
bran [bræn] *n* farelo.
branch [brɑ:ntʃ] *n* ramo, galho; (*road*) ramal *m*; (*COMM*) sucursal *f*, filial *f*; (: *bank*) agência ♦ *vi* bifurcar-se.
branch out *vi* diversificar suas atividades; **to ~ out into** estender suas atividades a.
branch line *n* (*RAIL*) ramal *m*.
branch manager *n* gerente *m/f* de sucursal *or* filial.
brand [brænd] *n* marca ♦ *vt* (*cattle*) marcar com ferro quente; (*fig*: *pej*): **to ~ sb a communist** *etc* estigmatizar alguém de comunista *etc*.
brandish ['brændıʃ] *vt* brandir.
brand name *n* marca de fábrica, griffe *f*.
brand-new *adj* novo em folha, novinho.
brandy ['brændı] *n* conhaque *m*.
brash [bræʃ] *adj* (*rough*) grosseiro; (*cheeky*) descarado.
Brasilia [brə'zılıə] *n* Brasília.

NB*: European Portuguese adds the following consonants to certain words:* **b** (sú(b)dito, su(b)til); **c** (a(c)ção, a(c)cionista, a(c)to); **m** (inde(m)ne); **p** (ado(p)ção, ado(p)tar); *for further details see p. xiii.*

brass [brɑːs] *n* latão *m*; **the ~** (*MUS*) os metais; **the top ~** as altas patentes.
brass band *n* banda de música.
brassiere ['bræsɪə*] *n* sutiã *m* (*BR*), soutien *m* (*PT*).
brass tacks *npl*: **to get down to ~** passar ao que interessa, entrar no assunto principal.
brat [bræt] (*pej*) *n* pirralho, fedelho, malcriado.
bravado [brə'vɑːdəu] *n* bravata.
brave [breɪv] *adj* valente, corajoso ♦ *n* guerreiro pele-vermelha ♦ *vt* (*challenge*) desafiar; (*resist*) encarar.
bravery ['breɪvərɪ] *n* coragem *f*, bravura.
bravo [brɑː'vəu] *excl* bravo!
brawl [brɔːl] *n* briga, pancadaria ♦ *vi* brigar.
brawn [brɔːn] *n* força; (*meat*) patê *m* de carne.
brawny ['brɔːnɪ] *adj* musculoso, carnudo.
bray [breɪ] *n* zurro, ornejo ♦ *vi* zurrar, ornejar.
brazen ['breɪzn] *adj* descarado ♦ *vt*: **to ~ it out** defender-se descaradamente.
brazier ['breɪzɪə*] *n* braseiro.
Brazil [brə'zɪl] *n* Brasil *m*.
Brazilian [brə'zɪljən] *adj*, *n* brasileiro/a.
Brazil nut *n* castanha-do-pará *f*.
breach [briːtʃ] *vt* abrir brecha em ♦ *n* (*gap*) brecha; (*estrangement*) rompimento; (*breaking*): **~ of contract** inadimplência (*BR*), inadimplemento (*PT*); **~ of the peace** perturbação *f* da ordem pública; **~ of trust** abuso de confiança.
bread [brɛd] *n* pão *m*; (*inf*: *money*) grana; **~ and butter** pão com manteiga; (*fig*) ganha-pão *m*; **to earn one's daily ~** ganhar o pão *or* a vida; **to know which side one's ~ is buttered (on)** saber o que lhe convém.
breadbin ['brɛdbɪn] (*BRIT*) *n* caixa de pão.
breadboard ['brɛdbɔːd] *n* tábua de pão; (*COMPUT*) breadboard *m*.
breadbox ['brɛdbɔks] (*US*) *n* caixa de pão.
breadcrumbs ['brɛdkrʌmz] *npl* migalhas *fpl*; (*CULIN*) farinha de rosca.
breadline ['brɛdlaɪn] *n*: **to be on the ~** viver na miséria.
breadth [brɛtθ] *n* largura; (*fig*) amplitude *f*.
breadwinner ['brɛdwɪnə*] *n* arrimo de família.
break [breɪk] (*pt* **broke**, *pp* **broken**) *vt* quebrar (*BR*), partir (*PT*); (*split*) partir; (*promise*) quebrar; (*word*) faltar a; (*fall*) amortecer; (*journey*) interromper; (*law*) violar, transgredir; (*record*) bater; (*news*) revelar ♦ *vi* quebrar-se, partir-se; (*storm*) estalar ♦ *n* (*gap*) abertura; (*crack*) fenda; (*fracture*) fratura; (*breakdown*) ruptura, rompimento; (*rest*) descanso; (*time*) intervalo; (*at school*) recreio; (*chance*) oportunidade *f*; **to ~ one's leg** *etc* quebrar a perna *etc*; **to ~ with sb** romper com alguém; **to ~ even** sair sem ganhar nem perder; **to ~ free** *or* **loose** soltar-se; **to take a ~** (*few minutes*) descansar um pouco, fazer uma pausa; (*holiday*) tirar férias para descansar; **without a ~** sem parar.
break down *vt* (*door etc*) arrombar; (*figures*, *data*) analisar; (*resistance*) acabar com ♦ *vi* (*go awry*) desarranjar-se; (*machine*, *AUT*) enguiçar, pifar (*inf*); (*MED*) sofrer um colapso; (*cry*) desatar a chorar.
break in *vt* (*horse etc*) domar; (*US*: *car*) fazer a rodagem de ♦ *vi* (*burglar*) forçar uma entrada.
break into *vt fus* (*house*) arrombar.
break off *vi* (*speaker*) parar-se, deter-se; (*branch*) partir ♦ *vt* (*talks*) suspender; (*relations*) cortar; (*engagement*) terminar, acabar com.
break open *vt* (*door etc*) arrombar.
break out *vi* (*war*) estourar; (*prisoner*) libertar-se; **to ~ out in spots** aparecer coberto de manchas.
break through *vi*: **the sun broke through** o sol apareceu, o tempo abriu ♦ *vt fus* (*defences*, *barrier*) transpor; (*crowd*) abrir passagem por.
break up *vi* despedaçar-se; (*partnership*) acabar; (*marriage*) desmanchar-se; (*friends*) separar-se, brigar ♦ *vt* romper; (*intervene*) intervir em; (*marriage*) desmanchar.
breakable ['breɪkəbl] *adj* quebradiço, frágil ♦ *n*: **~s** artigos *mpl* frágeis.
breakage ['breɪkɪdʒ] *n* quebradura; (*COMM*) quebra; **to pay for ~s** pagar indenização por quebras.
breakaway ['breɪkəweɪ] *adj* (*group etc*) dissidente.
breakdown ['breɪkdaun] *n* (*AUT*) enguiço, avaria; (*in communications*) interrupção *f*; (*machine*) enguiço; (*MED*: *also*: *nervous ~*) esgotamento nervoso; (*of figures*) discriminação *f*, desdobramento.
breakdown service (*BRIT*) *n* auto-socorro (*BR*), pronto socorro (*PT*).
breakdown van (*BRIT*) *n* reboque *m* (*BR*), pronto socorro (*PT*).
breaker ['breɪkə*] *n* onda grande.
breakeven ['breɪk'iːvn] *cpd*: **~ chart** gráfico do ponto de equilíbrio; **~ point** ponto de equilíbrio.
breakfast ['brɛkfəst] *n* café *m* da manhã (*BR*), pequeno almoço (*PT*).
breakfast cereal *n* cereais *mpl*.
break-in *n* roubo com arrombamento.
breaking point ['breɪkɪŋ-] *n* limite *m*.
breakthrough ['breɪkθruː] *n* ruptura; (*fig*) avanço.
break-up *n* (*of partnership*, *marriage*) dissolução *f*.
break-up value *n* (*COMM*) valor *m* de liquidação.
breakwater ['breɪkwɔːtə*] *n* quebra-mar *m*.
breast [brɛst] *n* (*of woman*) peito, seio; (*chest*) peito.
breast-feed (*irreg*) *vt*, *vi* amamentar.
breast pocket *n* bolso sobre o peito.
breaststroke ['brɛststrəuk] *n* nado de peito.
breath [brɛθ] *n* fôlego, hálito, respiração *f*; **to go out for a ~ of air** sair para tomar fôlego; **out of ~** ofegante, sem fôlego.
Breathalyser ['brɛθəlaɪzə*] ® *n* bafômetro.

breathe [bri:ð] *vt, vi* respirar; **I won't ~ a word about it** não vou abrir a boca, eu sou um túmulo.
breathe in *vt, vi* inspirar.
breathe out *vt, vi* expirar.
breather ['bri:ðə*] *n* pausa.
breathing ['bri:ðɪŋ] *n* respiração *f*.
breathing space *n* (*fig*) descanso, repouso.
breathless ['brɛθlɪs] *adj* sem fôlego, ofegante.
breathtaking ['brɛθteɪkɪŋ] *adj* empolgante.
bred [brɛd] *pt, pp of* **breed**.
-bred [brɛd] *suffix*: **well/ill~** bem-/mal-educado.
breed [bri:d] (*pt, pp* **bred**) *vt* (*animals*) criar; (*hate, suspicion*) gerar ♦ *vi* reproduzir-se, procriar-se ♦ *n* raça.
breeder ['bri:də*] *n* (*person*) criador(a) *m/f*; (*PHYS*: *also*: *~ reactor*) reator *m* regenerador.
breeding ['bri:dɪŋ] *n* reprodução *f*; (*raising*) criação *f*; (*of person*: *culture*) educação *f*, cultura.
breeze [bri:z] *n* brisa, aragem *f*.
breezeblock ['bri:zblɔk] (*BRIT*) *n* bloco pré-moldado.
breezy ['bri:zɪ] *adj* ventoso; (*person*) despreocupado, animado.
Breton ['brɛtən] *adj* bretão/tã ♦ *n* bretão/tã; (*LING*) bretão *m*.
brevity ['brɛvɪtɪ] *n* brevidade *f*.
brew [bru:] *vt* (*tea*) fazer; (*beer*) fermentar; (*plot*) armar, tramar ♦ *vi* (*tea*) fazer-se, preparar-se; (*beer*) fermentar; (*fig*) armar-se.
brewer ['bru:ə*] *n* cervejeiro/a.
brewery ['bruərɪ] *n* cervejaria.
briar ['braɪə*] *n* (*thorny bush*) urze-branca *f*; (*wild rose*) roseira-brava.
bribe [braɪb] *n* suborno ♦ *vt* subornar; **to ~ sb to do sth** subornar alguém para fazer algo.
bribery ['braɪbərɪ] *n* suborno.
bric-a-brac ['brɪkəbræk] *n* bricabraque *m*.
brick [brɪk] *n* tijolo.
bricklayer ['brɪkleɪə*] *n* pedreiro.
brickwork ['brɪkwə:k] *n* alvenaria.
brickworks ['brɪkwə:kz] *n* fábrica de tijolos.
bridal ['braɪdl] *adj* nupcial.
bride [braɪd] *n* noiva.
bridegroom ['braɪdgrum] *n* noivo.
bridesmaid ['braɪdzmeɪd] *n* dama de honra.
bridge [brɪdʒ] *n* ponte *f*; (*NAUT*) ponte de comando; (*CARDS*) bridge *m*; (*of nose*) cavalete *m*; (*DENTISTRY*) ponte *f* ♦ *vt* (*river*) lançar uma ponte sobre; (*gap*) transpor.
bridgehead ['brɪdʒhɛd] *n* cabeça-de-ponte *f*.
bridging loan ['brɪdʒɪŋ-] (*BRIT*) *n* empréstimo a curto prazo.
bridle ['braɪdl] *n* cabeçada, freio ♦ *vt* enfrear; (*fig*) refrear, conter.
bridle path *n* senda.
brief [bri:f] *adj* breve ♦ *n* (*LAW*) causa ♦ *vt* (*inform*) informar; (*instruct*) instruir; **~s** *npl* (*for men*) cueca (*BR*), cuecas *fpl* (*PT*); (*for women*) calcinha (*BR*), cuecas *fpl* (*PT*); **in ~** ... em resumo ...; **to ~ sb about sth** informar alguém sobre algo.
briefcase ['bri:fkeɪs] *n* pasta.
briefing ['bri:fɪŋ] *n* (*PRESS*) instruções *fpl*.
briefly ['bri:flɪ] *adv* brevemente; **to glimpse ~** vislumbrar.
briefness ['bri:fnɪs] *n* brevidade *f*.
Brig. *abbr* (= *brigadier*) brig.
brigade [brɪ'geɪd] *n* (*MIL*) brigada.
brigadier [brɪgə'dɪə*] *n* general *m* de brigada, brigadeiro.
bright [braɪt] *adj* claro, brilhante; (*weather*) resplandecente; (*person*: *clever*) inteligente; (: *lively*) alegre, animado; (*colour*) vivo; **to look on the ~ side** considerar o lado positivo.
brighten ['braɪtən] *vt* (*room*: *also*: *~ up*) tornar mais alegre ♦ *vi* (*weather*) clarear; (*person*: *also*: *~ up*) animar-se, alegrar-se.
brightly ['braɪtlɪ] *adv* brilhantemente.
brightness ['braɪtnɪs] *n* claridade *f*.
brilliance ['brɪljəns] *n* brilho, claridade *f*.
brilliant ['brɪljənt] *adj* brilhante; (*clever*) inteligente; (*inf*: *great*) sensacional.
brim [brɪm] *n* borda; (*of hat*) aba.
brimful ['brɪmful] *adj* cheio até as bordas; (*fig*) repleto.
brine [braɪn] *n* (*CULIN*) salmoura.
bring [brɪŋ] (*pt, pp* **brought**) *vt* trazer; **to ~ sth to an end** acabar com algo; **I can't ~ myself to fire him** não posso me resolver a despedi-lo.
bring about *vt* ocasionar, produzir.
bring back *vt* trazer de volta; (*return*) devolver.
bring down *vt* (*lower*) abaixar; (*shoot down*) abater; (*government*) derrubar.
bring forward *vt* adiantar; (*BOOKKEEPING*) transportar.
bring in *vt* (*person*) fazer entrar; (*object*) trazer; (*POL*: *legislation*) introduzir; (: *bill*) apresentar; (*LAW*: *verdict*) pronunciar; (*produce*: *income*) render; (*harvest*) recolher.
bring off *vt* (*task, plan*) levar a cabo; (*deal*) fechar.
bring out *vt* (*object*) tirar; (*meaning*) salientar; (*new product, book*) lançar.
bring round *vt* (*unconscious person*) fazer voltar a si; (*convince*) convencer.
bring to *vt* (*unconscious person*) fazer voltar a si.
bring up *vt* (*person*) educar, criar; (*carry up*) subir; (*question*) introduzir; (*food*) vomitar.
brink [brɪŋk] *n* beira; **on the ~ of doing** a ponto de fazer, à beira de fazer; **she was on the ~ of tears** ela estava à beira de desatar em prantos.
brisk [brɪsk] *adj* vigoroso; (*speedy*) rápido; (*trade, business*) ativo.

NB*: European Portuguese adds the following consonants to certain words:* **b** (sú(b)dito, su(b)til); **c** (a(c)ção, a(c)cionista, a(c)to); **m** (inde(m)ne); **p** (ado(p)ção, ado(p)tar); *for further details see p. xiii.*

brisket ['brɪskɪt] *n* carne *f* de vaca para assar.
bristle ['brɪsl] *n* cerda ♦ *vi* eriçar-se; **to ~ with** estar cheio de.
bristly ['brɪslɪ] *adj* (*beard, hair*) eriçado.
Brit [brɪt] (*inf*) *n abbr* (= *British person*) britânico/a.
Britain ['brɪtən] *n* (*also*: *Great* ~) Grã-Bretanha; **in ~** na Grã-Bretanha.
British ['brɪtɪʃ] *adj* britânico; **the ~** *npl* os britânicos; **the ~ Isles** as ilhas Britânicas.
British Rail *n companhia ferroviária britânica.*
Briton ['brɪtən] *n* britânico/a.
Brittany ['brɪtənɪ] *n* Bretanha.
brittle ['brɪtl] *adj* quebradiço, frágil.
Br(o). *abbr* (*REL*: = *brother*) Fr.
broach [brəutʃ] *vt* (*subject*) abordar, tocar em.
broad [brɔːd] *adj* amplo, largo; (*distinction, outline*) geral; (*accent*) carregado ♦ *n* (*US*: *inf*) sujeita; **~ hint** indireta transparente; **in ~ daylight** em pleno dia.
broad bean *n* fava.
broadcast ['brɔːdkɑːst] (*pt, pp* **broadcast**) *n* transmissão *f* ♦ *vt* (*RADIO, TV*) transmitir ♦ *vi* transmitir.
broadcasting ['brɔːdkɑːstɪŋ] *n* radiodifusão *f*, transmissão *f*.
broadcasting station *n* emissora.
broaden ['brɔːdən] *vt* alargar ♦ *vi* alargar-se, ampliar-se.
broadly ['brɔːdlɪ] *adv* em geral.
broad-minded *adj* tolerante, liberal.
broccoli ['brɔkəlɪ] *n* brócolis *mpl* (*BR*), brócolos *mpl* (*PT*).
brochure ['brəuʃjuə*] *n* folheto, brochura.
brogue [brəug] *n* (*accent*) sotaque *m* regional; (*shoe*) chanca.
broil [brɔɪl] (*US*) *vt* grelhar.
broiler ['brɔɪlə*] *n* (*fowl*) ave *f* (*a ser grelhada*).
broke [brəuk] *pt of* **break** ♦ *adj* (*inf*) sem um vintém, duro; **to go ~** (*business*) quebrar.
broken ['brəukən] *pp of* **break** ♦ *adj* (*leg, promise etc*) quebrado; (*marriage*) desfeito; **a ~ home** um lar desfeito; **children from ~ homes** filhos de pais separados; **in ~ English** num inglês mascavado.
broken-down *adj* (*car*) enguiçado; (*machine*) com defeito; (*house*) desmoronado, caindo aos pedaços.
broken-hearted *adj* com o coração partido.
broker ['brəukə*] *n* corretor(a) *m/f*.
brokerage ['brəukrɪdʒ] *n* corretagem *f*.
brolly ['brɔlɪ] (*BRIT*: *inf*) *n* guarda-chuva *m*.
bronchitis [brɔŋ'kaɪtɪs] *n* bronquite *f*.
bronze [brɔnz] *n* bronze *m*.
bronzed ['brɔnzd] *adj* bronzeado.
brooch [brəutʃ] *n* broche *m*.
brood [bruːd] *n* ninhada; (*children*) filhos *mpl*; (*pej*) prole *f* ♦ *vi* (*hen*) chocar; (*person*) cismar, parafusar, matutar.
broody ['bruːdɪ] *adj* (*fig*) taciturno, melancólico.
brook [bruk] *n* arroio, ribeiro.
broom [brum] *n* vassoura; (*BOT*) giesta.
broomstick ['brumstɪk] *n* cabo de vassoura.
Bros. *abbr* (*COMM*: = *brothers*) Irmãos.
broth [brɔθ] *n* caldo.
brothel ['brɔθl] *n* bordel *m*.
brother ['brʌðə*] *n* irmão *m*.
brotherhood ['brʌðəhud] *n* (*association, REL*) confraria.
brother-in-law (*pl* **brothers-in-law**) *n* cunhado.
brotherly ['brʌðəlɪ] *adj* fraternal, fraterno.
brought [brɔːt] *pt, pp of* **bring**.
brow [brau] *n* (*forehead*) fronte *f*, testa; (*rare*: *gen*: *eye~*) sobrancelha; (*of hill*) cimo, cume *m*.
browbeat ['braubiːt] (*irreg*: *like* **beat**) *vt* intimidar, amedrontar.
brown [braun] *adj* marrom (*BR*), castanho (*PT*); (*hair*) castanho; (*tanned*) bronzeado, moreno; (*rice, bread, flour*) integral ♦ *n* (*colour*) cor *f* marrom (*BR*) *or* castanha (*PT*) ♦ *vt* tostar; (*tan*) bronzear; (*CULIN*) dourar; **to go ~** (*person*) bronzear-se, ficar moreno; (*leaves*) secar.
brownie ['braunɪ] *n* fadinha de bandeirante.
brown paper *n* papel *m* pardo.
brown sugar *n* açúcar *m* mascavo.
browse [brauz] *vi* (*in shop*) dar uma olhada; (*among books*) folhear livros; (*animal*) pastar; **to ~ through a book** folhear um livro.
bruise [bruːz] *n* hematoma *m*, contusão *f* ♦ *vt* machucar, contundir; (*fig*) magoar ♦ *vi* (*fruit*) amassar.
Brum [brʌm] (*inf*) *n abbr* = **Birmingham**.
Brummagem ['brʌmədʒəm] (*inf*) *n* = **Birmingham**.
Brummie ['brʌmɪ] (*inf*) *n* natural *m/f* de Birmingham.
brunch [brʌntʃ] *n* brunch *m*.
brunette [bruː'nɛt] *n* morena.
brunt [brʌnt] *n*: **the ~ of** (*greater part*) a maior parte de.
brush [brʌʃ] *n* escova; (*for painting, shaving etc*) pincel *m*; (*BOT*) mato rasteiro; (*quarrel*) bate-boca *m* ♦ *vt* escovar; (*also*: *~ past, ~ against*) tocar ao passar, roçar; **to have a ~ with sb** bater boca com alguém; **to have a ~ with the police** ser indiciado pela polícia.
brush aside *vt* afastar, não fazer caso de.
brush up *vt* (*knowledge*) retocar, revisar.
brushed [brʌʃt] *adj* (*TECH*: *steel, chrome etc*) escovado; (*nylon, denim etc*) felpudo.
brush-off (*inf*) *n*: **to give sb the ~** dar o fora em alguém.
brushwood ['brʌʃwud] *n* (*bushes*) mato; (*sticks*) lenha, gravetos *mpl*.
brusque [bruːsk] *adj* brusco, áspero.
Brussels ['brʌslz] *n* Bruxelas.
Brussels sprout *n* couve-de-bruxelas *f*.
brutal ['bruːtl] *adj* brutal.
brutality [bruː'tælɪtɪ] *n* brutalidade *f*.
brute [bruːt] *n* bruto; (*person*) animal *m* ♦ *adj*: **by ~ force** por força bruta.
brutish ['bruːtɪʃ] *adj* grosseiro, bruto.

BS (*US*) *n abbr* = **Bachelor of Science**.
bs *abbr* = **bill of sale**.
BSA *n abbr* = **Boy Scouts of America**.
BSc *n abbr* = **Bachelor of Science**.
BSI *n abbr* (= *British Standards Institution*) *instituto britânico de padrões*.
BST *abbr* (= *British Summer Time*) hora de verão.
Bt. (*BRIT*) *abbr* = **baronet**.
btu *n abbr* (= *British thermal unit*) BTU *f* (= *1054.2 joules*).
bubble ['bʌbl] *n* bolha (*BR*), borbulha (*PT*) ♦ *vi* borbulhar.
bubble bath *n* banho de espuma.
bubble gum *n* chiclete *m* (de bola) (*BR*), pastilha elástica (*PT*).
Bucharest [bu:kə'rɛst] *n* Bucareste.
buck [bʌk] *n* macho; (*US*: *inf*) dólar *m* ♦ *vi* corcovear; **to pass the ~** fazer o jogo de empurra.
buck up *vi* (*cheer up*) animar-se, cobrar ânimo ♦ *vt*: **to ~ one's ideas up** tomar jeito.
bucket ['bʌkɪt] *n* balde *m* ♦ *vi* (*BRIT*: *inf*): **the rain is ~ing down** está chovendo a cântaros.
buckle ['bʌkl] *n* fivela ♦ *vt* afivelar ♦ *vi* torcer-se, cambar-se.
buckle down *vi* empenhar-se.
Bucks [bʌks] (*BRIT*) *abbr* = **Buckinghamshire**.
bud [bʌd] *n* broto, rebento; (*of flower*) botão *m* ♦ *vi* brotar, desabrochar; (*fig*) florescer.
Budapest [bju:də'pɛst] *n* Budapeste.
Buddha ['budə] *n* Buda *m*.
Buddhism ['budɪzəm] *n* budismo.
Buddhist ['budɪst] *adj* (*person*) budista; (*scripture, thought etc*) budístico ♦ *n* budista *m/f*.
budding ['bʌdɪŋ] *adj* (*flower*) em botão; (*passion etc*) nascente; (*poet etc*) em ascensão.
buddy ['bʌdɪ] (*US*) *n* camarada *m*, companheiro.
budge [bʌdʒ] *vt* mover ♦ *vi* mexer-se.
budgerigar ['bʌdʒərɪgɑ:*] *n* periquito.
budget ['bʌdʒɪt] *n* orçamento ♦ *vi*: **to ~ for sth** incluir algo no orçamento; **I'm on a tight ~** estou com o orçamento apertado.
budgie ['bʌdʒɪ] *n* = **budgerigar**.
Buenos Aires ['bwɛnə'saɪrɪz] *n* Buenos Aires.
buff [bʌf] *adj* (*colour*) cor *f* de camurça ♦ *n* (*enthusiast*) aficionado/a.
buffalo ['bʌfələu] (*pl* ~ *or* **~es**) *n* búfalo.
buffer ['bʌfə*] *n* pára-choque *m*; (*COMPUT*) buffer *m*, memória intermediária.
buffering ['bʌfərɪŋ] *n* (*COMPUT*) buffering *m*, armazenamento intermediário.
buffer state *n* estado-tampão *m*.
buffet [*n* 'bufeɪ, *vt* 'bʌfɪt] *n* (*BRIT*: *bar*) bar *m*, cafeteria; (*food*) bufê *m* ♦ *vt* (*strike*) esbofetear; (*subj*: *wind etc*) fustigar.
buffet car (*BRIT*) *n* vagão-restaurante *m*.
buffet lunch *n* almoço americano.
buffoon [bə'fu:n] *n* bufão *m*.
bug [bʌg] *n* (*insect*) bicho; (*fig*: *germ*) micróbio; (*spy device*) microfone *m* oculto; (*tap*) escuta clandestina; (*COMPUT*: *of program*) erro; (: *of equipment*) defeito ♦ *vt* (*inf*: *annoy*) apoquentar, incomodar; (*room*) colocar microfones em; (*phone*) grampear; **I've got the travel ~** peguei a mania de viajar.
bugbear ['bʌgbɛə*] *n* pesadelo, fantasma *m*.
bugger ['bʌgə*] (*inf!*) *n* filho-da-puta *m* (*!*) ♦ *vt*: **~ (it)!** merda! (*!*); **~ all** (*nothing*) chongas (*!*).
bugger off (*inf!*) *vi*: **~ off!** vai a merda! (*!*).
bugle ['bju:gl] *n* trompa, corneta.
build [bɪld] (*pt, pp* **built**) *n* (*of person*) talhe *m*, estatura ♦ *vt* construir, edificar.
build on *vt fus* (*fig*) explorar, aproveitar.
build up *vt* (*MED*) fortalecer; (*stocks*) acumular; (*business*) desenvolver; (*reputation*) estabelecer.
builder ['bɪldə*] *n* (*contractor*) construtor(a) *m/f*, empreiteiro/a *m/f*; (*worker*) pedreiro.
building ['bɪldɪŋ] *n* (*act*) construção *f*; (*residential, offices*) edifício, prédio.
building contractor *n* empreiteiro/a de obras; (*company*) construtora.
building industry *n* construção *f*.
building site *n* terreno de construção.
building society (*BRIT*) *n* sociedade *f* de crédito imobiliário, financiadora.
building trade *n* construção *f*.
build-up *n* (*of gas etc*) acumulação *f*; (*publicity*): **to give sb/sth a good ~** fazer muita propaganda de alguém/algo.
built [bɪlt] *pt, pp of* **build**.
built-in *adj* (*cupboard*) embutido; (*device*) incorporado, embutido.
built-up area *n* zona urbanizada.
bulb [bʌlb] *n* (*BOT*) bulbo; (*ELEC*) lâmpada.
bulbous ['bʌlbəs] *adj* bojudo.
Bulgaria [bʌl'gɛərɪə] *n* Bulgária.
Bulgarian [bʌl'gɛərɪən] *adj* búlgaro ♦ *n* búlgaro/a; (*LING*) búlgaro.
bulge [bʌldʒ] *n* bojo, saliência; (*in birth rate, sales*) disparo ♦ *vi* inchar-se; (*pocket etc*) fazer bojo; **to be bulging with** estar abarrotado de.
bulk [bʌlk] *n* (*mass*) massa, volume *m*; **in ~** (*COMM*) a granel; **the ~ of** a maior parte de.
bulk buying [-'baɪɪŋ] *n* compra a granel.
bulkhead ['bʌlkhɛd] *n* anteparo.
bulky ['bʌlkɪ] *adj* volumoso; (*person*) corpulento.
bull [bul] *n* touro; (*STOCK EXCHANGE*) altista *m/f*; (*REL*) bula.
bulldog ['buldɔg] *n* buldogue *m*.
bulldoze ['buldəuz] *vt* arrasar (com buldôzer); **I was ~d into doing it** (*fig*: *inf*) fui forçado *or* obrigado a fazê-lo.
bulldozer ['buldəuzə*] *n* buldôzer *m*, escavadora.
bullet ['bulɪt] *n* bala.
bulletin ['bulɪtɪn] *n* boletim *m*.

***NB**: European Portuguese adds the following consonants to certain words:* **b** (sú(b)dito, su(b)til); **c** (a(c)ção, a(c)cionista, a(c)to); **m** (inde(m)ne); **p** (ado(p)ção, ado(p)tar); *for further details see p. xiii.*

bulletin board *n* (*US*) quadro de anúncios; (*COMPUT*) informativo.
bulletproof ['bulıtpru:f] *adj* à prova de balas; ~ **vest** colete *m* à prova de balas.
bullet wound *n* ferida de bala.
bullfight ['bulfaıt] *n* tourada.
bullfighter ['bulfaıtə*] *n* toureiro.
bullfighting ['bulfaıtıŋ] *n* (*art*) tauromaquia.
bullion ['buljən] *n* ouro (*or* prata) em barras.
bullock ['bulək] *n* boi *m*, novilho.
bullring ['bulrıŋ] *n* praça de touros.
bull's-eye *n* centro do alvo, mosca (do alvo) (*BR*).
bully ['bulı] *n* fanfarrão *m*, valentão *m* ♦ *vt* intimidar, tiranizar.
bullying ['bulııŋ] *n* provocação *f*, implicância.
bum [bʌm] *n* (*inf*: *backside*) traseiro, bunda; (*tramp*) vagabundo/a, vadio/a.
bum around (*inf*) *vi* vadiar.
bumblebee ['bʌmblbi:] *n* (*ZOOL*) mamangaba.
bumf [bʌmf] (*inf*) *n* (*forms etc*) papelada.
bump [bʌmp] *n* (*blow*) choque *m*, embate *m*, baque *m*; (*jolt*) sacudida; (*on head*) galo, inchaço; (*sound*) baque ♦ *vt* (*strike*) bater contra, dar encontrão em ♦ *vi* dar sacudidas.
bump along *vi* mover-se aos solavancos.
bump into *vt fus* chocar-se com *or* contra, colidir com; (*inf*: *person*) dar com, topar com.
bumper ['bʌmpə*] *n* (*BRIT*) pára-choque *m* ♦ *adj*: ~ **crop/harvest** supersafra.
bumper cars *npl* carros *mpl* de trombada.
bumph [bʌmf] *n* = **bumf**.
bumptious ['bʌmpʃəs] *adj* presunçoso.
bumpy ['bʌmpı] *adj* (*road*) acidentado, cheio de altos e baixos; (*journey*) cheio de solavancos; (*flight*) turbulento.
bun [bʌn] *n* pão *m* doce (*BR*), pãozinho (*PT*); (*in hair*) coque *m*.
bunch [bʌntʃ] *n* (*of flowers*) ramo; (*of keys*) molho; (*of bananas, grapes*) cacho; (*of people*) grupo.
bundle ['bʌndl] *n* trouxa; (*tied up*) embrulho; (*of sticks*) feixe *m*; (*of papers*) maço ♦ *vt* (*also*: ~ *up*) embrulhar, atar; (*put*): **to ~ sth/sb into** meter *or* enfiar algo/alguém correndo em.
bundle off *vt* (*person*) despachar sem cerimônia.
bundle out *vt* expulsar sem cerimônia.
bung [bʌŋ] *n* tampão *m*, batoque *m* ♦ *vt* (*also*: ~ *up*: *pipe*, *hole*) tapar; (*BRIT*: *inf*: *throw*) jogar; **my nose is ~ed up** estou com o nariz entupido.
bungalow ['bʌŋgələu] *n* bangalô *m*, chalé *m*.
bungle ['bʌŋgl] *vt* estropear, estragar.
bunion ['bʌnjən] *n* joanete *m*.
bunk [bʌŋk] *n* beliche *m*.
bunk beds *npl* beliche *m*, cama-beliche *f*.
bunker ['bʌŋkə*] *n* (*coal store*) carvoeira; (*MIL*) abrigo, casamata; (*GOLF*) bunker *m*.
bunny ['bʌnı] *n* (*also*: ~ *rabbit*) coelhinho.
bunny girl (*BRIT*) *n* coelhinha.
bunny hill (*US*) *n* (*SKI*) pista para principiantes.
bunting ['bʌntıŋ] *n* bandeiras *fpl*.
buoy [bɔı] *n* bóia.
buoy up *vt* fazer boiar; (*fig*) animar.
buoyancy ['bɔıənsı] *n* flutuabilidade *f*.
buoyant ['bɔıənt] *adj* flutuante; (*person*) alegre; (*COMM*: *market*) animado; (: *currency*, *prices*) firme.
burden ['bə:dn] *n* carga; (*fig*) fardo ♦ *vt* carregar; (*oppress*) sobrecarregar; **to be a ~ to sb** ser um fardo para alguém.
bureau [bjuə'rəu] (*pl* ~**x**) *n* (*BRIT*: *desk*) secretária, escrivaninha; (*US*: *chest of drawers*) cômoda; (*office*) escritório, agência.
bureaucracy [bjuə'rɔkrəsı] *n* burocracia.
bureaucrat ['bjuərəkræt] *n* burocrata *m/f*.
bureaucratic [bjuərə'krætık] *adj* burocrático.
bureaux [bjuə'rəuz] *npl of* **bureau**.
burgeon ['bə:dʒən] *vi* florescer.
burglar ['bə:glə*] *n* ladrão/ladrona *m/f*.
burglar alarm *n* alarma de roubo.
burglarize ['bə:gləraız] (*US*) *vt* assaltar, arrombar.
burglary ['bə:glərı] *n* roubo.
burgle ['bə:gl] *vt* assaltar, arrombar.
Burgundy ['bə:gəndı] *n* (*wine*) borgonha *m*.
burial ['bɛrıəl] *n* enterro.
burial ground *n* cemitério.
burlesque [bə:'lɛsk] *n* paródia.
burly ['bə:lı] *adj* robusto, forte.
Burma ['bə:mə] *n* Birmânia.
Burmese [bə:'mi:z] *adj* birmanês/esa ♦ *n inv* birmanês/esa *m/f*; (*LING*) birmanês *m*.
burn [bə:n] (*pt*, *pp* ~**ed** *or* **burnt**) *vt* queimar ♦ *vi* queimar-se, arder; (*sting*) arder, picar ♦ *n* queimadura; **the cigarette ~t a hole in her dress** o cigarro fez um buraco no vestido dela; **I've ~t myself!** eu me queimei!
burn down *vt* incendiar.
burn out *vt* (*subj*: *writer etc*): **to ~ o.s. out** desgastar-se.
burner ['bə:nə*] *n* (*gas*) bico de gás, fogo.
burning ['bə:nıŋ] *adj* ardente.
burnish ['bə:nıʃ] *vt* polir, lustrar.
burnt [bə:nt] *pt*, *pp of* **burn**.
burnt sugar (*BRIT*) *n* caramelo.
burp [bə:p] (*inf*) *n* arroto ♦ *vi* arrotar.
burrow ['bʌrəu] *n* toca, lura ♦ *vt* fazer uma toca, cavar.
bursar ['bə:sə*] *n* tesoureiro/a; (*BRIT*: *student*) bolsista *m/f* (*BR*), bolseiro/a (*PT*).
bursary ['bə:sərı] (*BRIT*) *n* (*grant*) bolsa.
burst [bə:st] (*pt*, *pp* **burst**) *vt* (*balloon*, *pipe*) arrebentar; (*banks etc*) romper ♦ *vi* estourar; (*bomb*) estourar, explodir ♦ *n* estouro *m*; (*of shots*) rajada; **a ~ of energy** uma explosão de energia; **a ~ of applause** uma salva de palmas; **a ~ of speed** uma arrancada; **to ~ into flames** incendiar-se de repente; **to ~ out laughing** cair na gargalhada; **to ~ into tears** desatar a chorar; **to be ~ing with** (*crammed with*) estar abarrotado de; **to be ~ing with health/energy** estar esbanjando saúde/energia; **the door ~ open** a porta abriu-se de repente.
burst into *vt fus* (*room etc*) irromper em.

burst out of *vt fus* sair precipitadamente de.

bury ['bɛrɪ] *vt* enterrar; (*body*) enterrar, sepultar; **to ~ one's head in one's hands** cobrir o rosto com as mãos; **to ~ one's head in the sand** (*fig*) bancar avestruz; **to ~ the hatchet** (*fig*) fazer as pazes.

bus [bʌs] *n* ônibus *m inv* (*BR*), autocarro (*PT*).

bush [buʃ] *n* arbusto, mata; (*scrub land*) sertão *m*.

bushel ['buʃl] *n* alqueire *m*.

bushy ['buʃɪ] *adj* (*thick*) espesso, denso.

busily ['bɪzɪlɪ] *adv* atarefadamente.

business ['bɪznɪs] *n* (*matter*) negócio; (*trading*) comércio, negócios *mpl*; (*firm*) empresa; (*occupation*) profissão *f*; (*affair*) assunto; **to travel on ~** viajar a negócios; **he's in the insurance ~** ele trabalha com seguros; **to do ~ with sb** fazer negócios com alguém; **it's my ~ to ...** encarrego-me de ...; **it's none of my ~** eu não tenho nada com isto; **that's my ~** isso é cá comigo; **he means ~** fala a sério.

business address *n* endereço profissional.

business card *n* cartão *m* de visita.

businesslike ['bɪznɪslaɪk] *adj* eficiente, metódico, sério.

businessman ['bɪznɪsmən] (*irreg*) *n* homem *m* de negócios.

business trip *n* viagem *f* de negócios.

businesswoman ['bɪznɪswumən] (*irreg*) *n* mulher *f* de negócios.

busker [bʌskə*] (*BRIT*) *n* artista *m/f* de rua.

bus lane *n* pista reservada aos ônibus (*BR*) *or* autocarros (*PT*).

bus shelter *n* abrigo.

bus station *n* rodoviária.

bus stop *n* ponto de ônibus (*BR*), paragem *f* de autocarro (*PT*).

bust [bʌst] *n* (*ANAT*) busto ♦ *adj* (*inf*: *broken*) quebrado ♦ *vt* (*inf*: *POLICE*: *arrest*) prender, grampear; **to go ~** falir.

bustle ['bʌsl] *n* animação *f*, movimento ♦ *vi* apressar-se, andar azafamado.

bustling ['bʌslɪŋ] *adj* (*town*) animado, movimentado.

bust-up (*BRIT*: *inf*) *n* bate-boca *m*.

busy ['bɪzɪ] *adj* (*person*) ocupado, atarefado; (*shop*, *street*) animado, movimentado; (*US*: *TEL*) ocupado (*BR*), impedido (*PT*) ♦ *vt*: **to ~ o.s. with** ocupar-se em *or* de.

busybody ['bɪzɪbɔdɪ] *n* intrometido/a.

busy signal (*US*) *n* sinal *m* de ocupado (*BR*) *or* impedido (*PT*).

but [bʌt] *conj* mas ♦ *prep* exceto, menos; **nothing ~** só, somente; **~ for** sem, se não fosse; **no-one ~ him** só ele, ninguém a não ser ele; **the last ~ one** (*BRIT*) o/a penúltimo/a; **all ~ finished** quase acabado; **anything ~ finished** tudo menos acabado.

butane ['bju:teɪn] *n* butano.

butcher ['butʃə*] *n* açougueiro (*BR*), homem *m* do talho (*PT*) ♦ *vt* chacinar; (*cattle etc for meat*) abater e carnear; **~'s (shop)** açougue *m* (*BR*), talho (*PT*).

butler ['bʌtlə*] *n* mordomo.

butt [bʌt] *n* (*cask*) tonel *m*; (*for rain*) barril *m*; (*thick end*) cabo, extremidade *f*; (*of gun*) coronha; (*of cigarette*) toco (*BR*), ponta (*PT*); (*BRIT*: *fig*: *target*) alvo ♦ *vt* dar uma cabeçada em.

butt in *vi* (*interrupt*) interromper.

butter ['bʌtə*] *n* manteiga ♦ *vt* untar com manteiga.

butter bean *n* fava.

buttercup ['bʌtəkʌp] *n* botão-de-ouro *m*, ranúnculo.

butter dish *n* manteigueira.

butterfingers ['bʌtəfɪŋgəz] (*inf*) *n* mão-furada *m/f*.

butterfly ['bʌtəflaɪ] *n* borboleta; (*SWIMMING*: *also*: *~ stroke*) nado borboleta.

buttocks ['bʌtəks] *npl* nádegas *fpl*.

button ['bʌtn] *n* botão *m* ♦ *vt* (*also*: *~ up*) abotoar ♦ *vi* ter botões.

buttonhole ['bʌtnhəul] *n* casa de botão, botoeira; (*flower*) flor *f* na lapela ♦ *vt* obrigar a ouvir.

buttress ['bʌtrɪs] *n* contraforte *m*.

buxom ['bʌksəm] *adj* (*baby*) saudável; (*woman*) rechonchudo.

buy [baɪ] (*pt*, *pp* **bought**) *vt* comprar ♦ *n* compra; **to ~ sb sth/sth from sb** comprar algo para alguém/algo a alguém.

buy back *vt* comprar de volta; (*COMM*) recomprar.

buy in (*BRIT*) *vt* (*goods*) comprar, abastecer-se com.

buy into (*BRIT*) *vt fus* (*COMM*) comprar ações de.

buy off *vt* (*partner*) comprar a parte de; (*business*) comprar o fundo de comércio de.

buy up *vt* comprar em grande quantidade.

buyer ['baɪə*] *n* comprador(a) *m/f*; **~'s market** mercado de comprador.

buzz [bʌz] *n* zumbido; (*inf*: *phone call*) ligada ♦ *vi* zumbir ♦ *vt* (*call on intercom*) chamar no interfone; (*AVIAT*: *plane*, *building*) voar baixo sobre.

buzz off (*inf*) *vi* cair fora.

buzzard ['bʌzəd] *n* abutre *m*, urubu *m*.

buzzer ['bʌzə*] *n* cigarra; (*doorbell*) campainha.

buzz word *n* modismo.

by [baɪ] *prep* por; (*beside*) perto de, ao pé de, ao lado de; (*according to*) segundo, de acordo com; (*before*): **~ 4 o'clock** antes das quatro ♦ *adv see* **pass, go** *etc*; **a picture ~ Picasso** um quadro de Picasso; **surrounded ~ enemies** cercado de inimigos; **~ bus/car** de ônibus/carro; **paid ~ the hour** pago por hora; **to increase** *etc* **~ the hour** aumentar *etc* de hora em hora; **~ the kilo/metre** por quilo/metro; **~ night/day** de noite/dia; **to**

NB: *European Portuguese adds the following consonants to certain words:* **b** (sú(b)dito, su(b)til); **c** (a(c)ção, a(c)cionista, a(c)to); **m** (inde(m)ne); **p** (ado(p)ção, ado(p)tar); *for further details see p. xiii.*

pay ~ cheque pagar com cheque; **a room 3 metres ~ 4** um cômodo medindo 3 metros por 4; **the bullet missed him ~ inches** por pouco a bala não acertou nele; **~ saving hard, he ...** economizando muito, ele ...; **(all) ~ oneself** (completamente) só, sozinho; **~ the way** a propósito; **~ and large** em geral; **~ and ~** logo, mais tarde; **~ this time tomorrow** esta mesma hora amanhã.

bye(-bye) ['baɪ('baɪ)] *excl* até logo (*BR*), tchau (*BR*), adeus (*PT*).

by(e)-law *n* lei *f* de município.

by-election (*BRIT*) *n* eleição *f* parlamentar complementar.

bygone ['baɪgɔn] *adj* passado, antigo ♦ *n*: **let ~s be ~s** que passou passou, águas passadas não movem moinhos.

bypass ['baɪpɑːs] *n* via secundária, desvio; (*MED*) ponte *f* de safena ♦ *vt* evitar.

by-product *n* subproduto, produto derivado.

byre ['baɪə*] (*BRIT*) *n* estábulo (de vacas).

bystander ['baɪstændə*] *n* circunstante *m/f*; (*observer*) espectador(a); **a crowd of ~s** um grupo de curiosos.

byte [baɪt] *n* (*COMPUT*) byte *m*.

byway ['baɪweɪ] *n* caminho secundário.

byword ['baɪwəːd] *n*: **to be a ~ for** ser sinônimo de.

by-your-leave *n*: **without so much as a ~** sem mais aquela.

C

C, c [siː] *n* (*letter*) C, c *m*; (*SCH*: *mark*) ≈ 5, 6; (*MUS*): **C** dó *m*; **C for Charlie** C de Carlos.

C *abbr* (= *Celsius*; *centigrade*) C.

c *abbr* (= *century*) séc.; (= *circa*) ca.; (*US etc*: = *cent*) cent.

CA *n abbr* = **Central America**; (*BRIT*) = **chartered accountant** ♦ *abbr* (*US*: *POST*) = **California**.

ca. *abbr* (= *circa*) ca.

c/a *abbr* = **capital account**; **credit account**; (= *current account*) c/c.

CAA *n abbr* (= *Civil Aviation Authority* (*BRIT*); *Civil Aeronautics Authority* (*US*)) ≈ DAC *m*.

CAB (*BRIT*) *n abbr* (= *Citizens' Advice Bureau*) *serviço de informação do consumidor*.

cab [kæb] *n* táxi *m*; (*of truck*) boléia; (*horse-drawn*) cabriolé *m*.

cabaret ['kæbəreɪ] *n* cabaré *m*.

cabbage ['kæbɪdʒ] *n* repolho (*BR*), couve *f* (*PT*).

cabin ['kæbɪn] *n* cabana; (*on ship*) camarote *m*.

cabin cruiser *n* lancha a motor com cabine.

cabinet ['kæbɪnɪt] *n* (*POL*) gabinete *m*; (*furniture*) armário; (*also*: *display ~*) armário com vitrina; **~ reshuffle** reforma ministerial.

cabinet-maker *n* marceneiro/a.

cabinet minister *n* ministro/a (*integrante do gabinete*).

cable ['keɪbl] *n* cabo; (*telegram*) cabograma *m* ♦ *vt* enviar cabograma para.

cable-car *n* bonde *m* (*BR*), teleférico (*PT*).

cablegram ['keɪblgræm] *n* cabograma *m*.

cable railway (*BRIT*) *n* funicular *m*.

cable television *n* televisão *f* a cabo.

cache [kæʃ] *n* esconderijo; **a ~ of arms** *etc* um depósito secreto de armas *etc*.

cackle ['kækl] *vi* cacarejar.

cacti ['kæktaɪ] *npl of* **cactus**.

cactus ['kæktəs] (*pl* **cacti**) *n* cacto.

CAD *n abbr* (= *computer-aided design*) CAD *m*.

caddie ['kædɪ] *n* caddie *m*.

cadet [kə'dɛt] *n* (*MIL*) cadete *m*.

cadge [kædʒ] (*inf*) *vt* filar.

cadger ['kædʒə*] *n* filante *m/f*.

cadre ['kɑːdə*] *n* funcionários *mpl* qualificados.

Caesarean [siː'zɛərɪən] (*US* **Cesarean**) *adj*, *n*: **~ (section)** cesariana.

CAF (*BRIT*) *abbr* (= *cost and freight*) custo e frete.

café ['kæfeɪ] *n* café *m*.

cafeteria [kæfɪ'tɪərɪə] *n* lanchonete *f*.

caffein(e) ['kæfiːn] *n* cafeína.

cage [keɪdʒ] *n* (*bird ~*) gaiola; (*for large animals*) jaula ♦ *vt* engaiolar; enjaular.

cagey ['keɪdʒɪ] (*inf*) *adj* cuidadoso, reservado, desconfiado.

cagoule [kə'guːl] *n* casaco de náilon.

CAI *n abbr* (= *computer-aided instruction*) CAI *m*.

Cairo ['kaɪərəu] *n* o Cairo.

cajole [kə'dʒəul] *vt* lisonjear.

cake [keɪk] *n* (*large*) bolo; (*small*) doce *m*, bolinho; **~ of soap** sabonete *m*; **it's a piece of ~** (*inf*) é moleza *or* sopa; **he wants to have his ~ and eat it (too)** (*fig*) ele quer chupar cana e assoviar ao mesmo tempo; **~ mix** massa pronta de bolo.

caked [keɪkt] *adj*: **~ with** empastado de.

cake shop *n* confeitaria.

calamitous [kə'læmɪtəs] *adj* calamitoso.

calamity [kə'læmɪtɪ] *n* calamidade *f*.

calcium ['kælsɪəm] *n* cálcio.

calculate ['kælkjuleɪt] *vt* calcular; (*estimate*: *chances*, *effect*) avaliar.

calculate on *vt fus*: **to ~ on sth/on doing sth** contar com algo/em fazer algo.

calculated ['kælkjuleɪtɪd] *adj* (*insult*, *action*) intencional; **a ~ risk** um risco calculado.

calculating ['kælkjuleɪtɪŋ] *adj* (*clever*) matreiro, calculista; (*devious*) esperto.

calculation [kælkju'leɪʃən] *n* cálculo.

calculator ['kælkjuleɪtə*] *n* calculador *m*.

calculus ['kælkjuləs] *n* cálculo; **integral/differential ~** cálculo integral/diferencial.

calendar ['kæləndə*] *n* calendário.

calendar month *n* mês *m* civil.

calendar year *n* ano civil.
calf [kɑːf] (*pl* **calves**) *n* (*of cow*) bezerro, vitela; (*of other animals*) cria; (*also*: **~skin**) pele *f or* couro de bezerro; (ANAT) barriga-da-perna.
caliber ['kælɪbə*] (US) *n* = **calibre**.
calibrate ['kælɪbreɪt] *vt* calibrar.
calibre ['kælɪbə*] (US **caliber**) *n* calibre *m*.
calico ['kælɪkəu] *n* (BRIT) morim *m*; (US) chita.
California [kælɪ'fɔːnɪə] *n* Califórnia.
calipers ['kælɪpəz] (US) *npl* = **callipers**.
call [kɔːl] *vt* chamar; (*telephone*) telefonar a, ligar para; (*announce*: *flight*) anunciar; (*meeting*, *strike*) convocar ♦ *vi* chamar; (*visit*: *also*: *~ in*, *~ round*) dar um pulo ♦ *n* (*shout*, *announcement*) chamada; (*also*: *telephone ~*) telefonema *m*; (*of bird*) canto; (*visit*) visita; (*fig*: *appeal*) chamamento, apelo; **to ~ (for)** passar (para buscar); **to be on ~** estar de prontidão; **she's ~ed Suzana** ela se chama Suzana; **who is ~ing?** (TEL) quem fala?; **London ~ing** (RADIO) aqui fala Londres; **please give me a ~ at 7** acorde-me às 7.00 por favor; **to make a ~** telefonar; **to pay a ~ on sb** visitar alguém, dar um pulo na casa de alguém; **there's not much ~ for these items** não há muita procura para esses artigos.
call at *vt fus* (*subj*: *ship*) fazer escala em; (: *train*) parar em.
call back *vi* (*return*) voltar, passar de novo; (TEL) ligar de volta ♦ *vt* (TEL) ligar de volta para.
call for *vt fus* (*demand*) requerer, exigir; (*fetch*) ir buscar.
call in *vt* (*doctor*, *expert*, *police*) chamar.
call off *vt* (*cancel*) cancelar.
call on *vt fus* (*visit*) visitar; (*turn to*) recorrer a; **to ~ on sb to do** pedir para alguém fazer.
call out *vi* gritar, bradar ♦ *vt* (*doctor*, *police*, *troops*) chamar.
call up *vt* (MIL) chamar às fileiras.
callbox ['kɔːlbɔks] (BRIT) *n* cabine *f* telefônica.
caller ['kɔːlə*] *n* visita *m/f*; (TEL) chamador(a) *m/f*.
call girl *n* call girl *f*, prostituta.
call-in (US) *n* (RADIO) *programa com participação dos ouvintes*; (TV) *programa com participação dos espectadores*.
calling ['kɔːlɪŋ] *n* vocação *f*; (*trade*) profissão *f*.
calling card (US) *n* cartão *m* de visita.
callipers ['kælɪpəz] (US **calipers**) *npl* (MATH) compasso de calibre; (MED) aparelho ortopédico.
callous ['kæləs] *adj* cruel, insensível.
callousness ['kæləsnɪs] *n* crueldade *f*, insensibilidade *f*.
callow ['kæləu] *adj* inexperiente.
calm [kɑːm] *n* calma ♦ *vt* acalmar ♦ *adj* tranqüilo; (*sea*) calmo, sereno.
calm down *vi* acalmar-se, tranqüilizar-se ♦ *vt* acalmar, tranqüilizar.
calmly ['kɑːmlɪ] *adv* tranqüilamente, com calma.
calmness ['kɑːmnɪs] *n* tranqüilidade *f*.
Calor gas ['kælə*-] ® (BRIT) *n* butano.
calorie ['kælərɪ] *n* caloria.
calve [kɑːv] *vi* parir.
calves [kɑːvz] *npl of* **calf**.
CAM *n abbr* (= *computer-aided manufacture*) CAM *m*.
camber ['kæmbə*] *n* (*of road*) abaulamento.
Cambodia [kæm'bəudjə] *n* Camboja.
Cambodian [kæm'bəudɪən] *adj*, *n* cambojano/a.
Cambs (BRIT) *abbr* = **Cambridgeshire**.
came [keɪm] *pt of* **come**.
camel ['kæməl] *n* camelo.
cameo ['kæmɪəu] *n* camafeu *m*.
camera ['kæmərə] *n* máquina fotográfica; (CINEMA, TV) câmera; **in ~** em câmara.
cameraman ['kæmərəmən] (*irreg*) *n* camaraman *m*.
Cameroon [kæmə'ruːn] *n* Camarões *m*.
Cameroun [kæmə'ruːn] *n* = **Cameroon**.
camouflage ['kæməflɑːʒ] *n* camuflagem *f* ♦ *vt* camuflar.
camp [kæmp] *n* campo, acampamento ♦ *vi* acampar ♦ *adj* afetado, afeminado; **to go ~ing** fazer camping (BR), fazer campismo (PT).
campaign [kæm'peɪn] *n* (MIL, POL *etc*) campanha ♦ *vi* fazer campanha.
campaigner [kæm'peɪnə*] *n*: **~ for** partidário/a de; **~ against** oponente *m/f* de.
campbed ['kæmpbɛd] *n* cama de campanha.
camper ['kæmpə*] *n* campista *m/f*; (*vehicle*) reboque *m*.
camping ['kæmpɪŋ] *n* camping *m* (BR), campismo (PT).
camping site *n* camping *m* (BR), parque *m* de campismo (PT).
campsite ['kæmpsaɪt] *n* camping *m* (BR), parque *m* de campismo (PT).
campus ['kæmpəs] *n* campus *m*, cidade *f* universitária.
camshaft ['kæmʃɑːft] *n* eixo de ressaltos.
can[1] [kæn] *n* (*of oil*, *food*) lata ♦ *vt* enlatar; (*preserve*) conservar em latas; **to carry the ~** (BRIT: *inf*) assumir a responsabilidade.
can[2] [kæn] (*conditional* **could**) *aux vb* (*gen*) poder; (*know how to*) saber; **I ~ swim** eu sei nadar; **I ~ speak Portuguese** eu falo português; **~ you hear me?** você está me ouvindo?; **could I have a word with you?** será que eu podia falar com você?; **he could be in the library** ele talvez esteja na biblioteca; **they could have forgotten** eles podiam ter esquecido.
Canada ['kænədə] *n* Canadá *m*.
Canadian [kə'neɪdɪən] *adj*, *n* canadense *m/f*.
canal [kə'næl] *n* canal *m*.

NB*: European Portuguese adds the following consonants to certain words:* **b** (sú(b)dito, su(b)til); **c** (a(c)ção, a(c)cionista, a(c)to); **m** (inde(m)ne); **p** (ado(p)ção, ado(p)tar); *for further details see p. xiii.*

Canaries [kə'nɛərɪz] *npl* = **Canary Islands**.
canary [kə'nɛərɪ] *n* canário.
Canary Islands *npl*: **the ~** as (ilhas) Canárias.
Canberra ['kænbərə] *n* Canberra.
cancel ['kænsəl] *vt* (*gen, train, cheque*) cancelar; (*appointment*) desmarcar; (*cross out*) riscar, invalidar; (*stamp*) contra-selar.
cancel out *vt* anular; **they ~ each other out** eles se anulam.
cancellation [kænsə'leɪʃən] *n* cancelamento; (*of contract*) anulação *f*.
cancer ['kænsə*] *n* câncer *m* (*BR*), cancro (*PT*); **C~** (*ASTROLOGY*) Câncer.
cancerous ['kænsrəs] *adj* canceroso.
cancer patient *n* canceroso/a.
cancer research *n* pesquisa sobre o câncer (*BR*) *or* cancro (*PT*).
C and F (*BRIT*) *abbr* (= *cost and freight*) custo e frete.
candid ['kændɪd] *adj* franco, sincero.
candidacy ['kændɪdəsɪ] *n* candidatura.
candidate ['kændɪdeɪt] *n* candidato/a.
candidature ['kændɪdətʃə*] (*BRIT*) *n* = **candidacy**.
candied ['kændɪd] *adj* cristalizado; **~ apple** (*US*) maçã *f* do amor.
candle ['kændl] *n* vela; (*in church*) círio.
candle holder *n* (*single*) castiçal *m*; (*bigger, more ornate*) candelabro, lustre *m*.
candlelight ['kændllaɪt] *n*: **by ~** à luz de vela; (*dinner*) à luz de velas.
candlestick ['kændlstɪk] *n* (*single*) castiçal *m*; (*bigger, ornate*) candelabro, lustre *m*.
candour ['kændə*] (*US* **candor**) *n* franqueza.
candy ['kændɪ] *n* açúcar *m* cristalizado; (*US*) bala (*BR*), rebuçado (*PT*).
candy floss [-flɔs] (*BRIT*) *n* algodão-doce *m*.
candy store (*US*) *n* confeitaria.
cane [keɪn] *n* (*BOT*) cana; (*stick*) bengala; (*for chairs etc*) palhinha ♦ *vt* (*BRIT*: *SCH*) castigar (com bengala).
canine ['kænaɪn] *adj* canino.
canister ['kænɪstə*] *n* lata.
cannabis ['kænəbɪs] *n* (*also*: ~ *plant*) cânhamo; (*drug*) maconha.
canned [kænd] *adj* (*food*) em lata, enlatado; (*inf*: *music*) gravado; (*BRIT*: *inf*: *drunk*) bêbado; (*US*: *inf*: *worker*) despedido.
cannibal ['kænɪbəl] *n* canibal *m/f*.
cannibalism ['kænɪbəlɪzəm] *n* canibalismo.
cannon ['kænən] (*pl inv or* **~s**) *n* canhão *m*.
cannonball ['kænənbɔːl] *n* bala (de canhão).
cannon fodder *n* bucha para canhão.
cannot ['kænɔt] = **can not**.
canny ['kænɪ] *adj* astuto.
canoe [kə'nuː] *n* canoa.
canoeing [kə'nuːɪŋ] *n* (*SPORT*) canoagem *f*.
canoeist [kə'nuːɪst] *n* canoísta *m/f*.
canon ['kænən] *n* (*clergyman*) cônego; (*standard*) cânone *m*.
canonize ['kænənaɪz] *vt* canonizar.
can opener *n* abridor *m* de latas (*BR*), abre-latas *m inv* (*PT*).
canopy ['kænəpɪ] *n* dossel *m*; (*ARCH*) baldaquino.
cant [kænt] *n* jargão *m*.
can't [kaːnt] = **can not**.
Cantab. (*BRIT*) *abbr* (= *cantabrigiensis*) = **of Cambridge**.
cantankerous [kæn'tæŋkərəs] *adj* rabugento, irritável.
canteen [kæn'tiːn] *n* cantina; (*bottle*) cantil *m*; (*of cutlery*) jogo (de talheres).
canter ['kæntə*] *n* meio galope ♦ *vi* ir a meio galope.
cantilever ['kæntɪliːvə*] *n* cantiléver *m*.
canvas ['kænvəs] *n* (*material*) lona; (*for painting*) tela; (*NAUT*) velas *fpl*; **under ~** (*camping*) em barracas.
canvass ['kænvəs] *vt* (*POL*: *district*) fazer campanha em; (: *person*) angariar; (: *opinion*) sondar.
canvasser ['kænvəsə*] *n* cabo eleitoral.
canvassing ['kænvəsɪŋ] *n* (*POL*) angariação *f* de votos; (*COMM*) pesquisa de mercado.
canyon ['kænjən] *n* canhão *m*, garganta, desfiladeiro.
CAP *n abbr* (= *Common Agricultural Policy*) PAC *f*.
cap [kæp] *n* gorro; (*peaked*) boné *m*; (*of pen, bottle*) tampa; (*BRIT*: *contraceptive*: *also*: *Dutch* ~) diafragma *m*; (: *FOOTBALL*): **he won his England ~** ele foi escalado para jogar na seleção inglesa ♦ *vt* rematar; (*outdo*) superar; **and to ~ it all, he ...** (*BRIT*) e para completar *or* culminar, ele ....
capability [keɪpə'bɪlɪtɪ] *n* capacidade *f*.
capable ['keɪpəbl] *adj* (*of sth*) capaz; (*competent*) competente, hábil; **~ of** (*interpretation etc*) susceptível de, passível de.
capacious [kə'peɪʃəs] *adj* vasto.
capacity [kə'pæsɪtɪ] *n* capacidade *f*; (*role*) condição *f*; **filled to ~** lotado; **in his ~ as** em sua condição de; **this work is beyond my ~** este trabalho está além das minhas limitações; **in an advisory ~** na condição de consultor; **to work at full ~** trabalhar com máximo rendimento.
cape [keɪp] *n* capa; (*GEO*) cabo.
Cape of Good Hope *n* Cabo da Boa Esperança.
caper ['keɪpə*] *n* (*CULIN*: *gen*: *~s*) alcaparra; (*prank*) travessura.
Cape Town *n* Cidade *f* do Cabo.
capita ['kæpɪtə] *see* **per capita**.
capital ['kæpɪtl] *n* (*also*: ~ *city*) capital *f*; (*money*) capital *m*; (*also*: ~ *letter*) maiúscula.
capital account *n* conta de capital.
capital allowance *n* desconto para depreciação.
capital assets *npl* bens *mpl* imobilizados, ativo fixo.
capital expenditure *n* despesas *fpl or* dispêndio de capital.
capital gains tax *n* imposto sobre ganhos de capital.
capital goods *npl* bens *mpl* de capital.
capital-intensive *adj* intensivo de capital.

capitalism ['kæpɪtəlɪzəm] *n* capitalismo.
capitalist ['kæpɪtəlɪst] *adj, n* capitalista *m/f*.
capitalize ['kæpɪtəlaɪz] *vt* capitalizar.
capitalize on *vt fus* (*fig*) aproveitar, explorar.
capital punishment *n* pena de morte.
capital transfer tax (BRIT) *n* imposto sobre transferências de capital.
capitulate [kə'pɪtjuleɪt] *vi* capitular.
capitulation [kəpɪtju'leɪʃən] *n* capitulação *f*.
capricious [kə'prɪʃəs] *adj* caprichoso.
Capricorn ['kæprɪkɔːn] *n* Capricórnio.
caps [kæps] *abbr* = **capital letters**.
capsize [kæp'saɪz] *vt, vi* emborcar, virar.
capstan ['kæpstən] *n* cabrestante *m*.
capsule ['kæpsjuːl] *n* cápsula.
Capt. *abbr* (= *captain*) Cap.
captain ['kæptɪn] *n* capitão *m* ♦ *vt* capitanear, ser o capitão de.
caption ['kæpʃən] *n* (*heading*) título; (*to picture*) legenda.
captivate ['kæptɪveɪt] *vt* cativar.
captive ['kæptɪv] *adj, n* cativo/a.
captivity [kæp'tɪvɪtɪ] *n* cativeiro.
captor ['kæptə*] *n* capturador(a) *m/f*.
capture ['kæptʃə*] *vt* prender, aprisionar; (*place*) tomar; (*attention*) captar, chamar ♦ *n* captura; (*of place*) tomada; (*thing taken*) presa.
car [kɑː*] *n* carro, automóvel *m*; (US: RAIL) vagão *m*; **by ~** de carro.
Caracas [kə'rækəs] *n* Caracas.
carafe [kə'ræf] *n* garrafa de mesa.
caramel ['kærəməl] *n* caramelo.
carat ['kærət] *n* quilate *m*; **18 ~ gold** ouro de 18 quilates.
caravan ['kærəvæn] *n* reboque *m* (BR), trailer *m* (BR), rulote *f* (PT); (*of camels*) caravana.
caravan site (BRIT) *n* camping *m* para reboques (BR), parque *m* de campismo (PT).
caraway ['kærəweɪ] *n*: **~ seed** sementes *fpl* de alcaravia.
carbohydrate [kɑːbəu'haɪdreɪt] *n* hidrato de carbono; (*food*) carboidrato.
carbolic acid [kɑː'bɔlɪk-] *n* ácido carbólico, fenol *m*.
carbon ['kɑːbən] *n* carbono.
carbonated ['kɑːbeneɪtɪd] *adj* (*drink*) gasoso.
carbon copy *n* cópia de papel carbono.
carbon dioxide *n* dióxido de carbono.
carbon monoxide *n* monóxido de carbono.
carbon paper *n* papel *m* carbono.
carbon ribbon *n* fita carbono.
carburettor [kɑːbju'rɛtə*] (US **carburetor**) *n* carburador *m*.
carcass ['kɑːkəs] *n* carcaça.
carcinogenic [kɑːsɪnə'dʒɛnɪk] *adj* carcinogênico.
card [kɑːd] *n* (*also*: *playing ~*) carta; (*visiting ~, post~ etc*) cartão *m*; (*membership ~ etc*) carteira; (*thin cardboard*) cartolina; **to play ~s** jogar cartas.
cardamom ['kɑːdəməm] *n* cardamomo.
cardboard ['kɑːdbɔːd] *n* cartão *m*, papelão *m*.
cardboard box *n* caixa de papelão.
card-carrying member [-'kærɪɪŋ-] *n* membro ativo.
card game *n* jogo de cartas.
cardiac ['kɑːdɪæk] *adj* cardíaco.
cardigan ['kɑːdɪgən] *n* casaco de lã, cardigã *m*.
cardinal ['kɑːdɪnl] *adj* cardeal; (MATH) cardinal ♦ *n* (REL) cardeal *m*; (MATH) número cardinal.
card index *n* fichário.
Cards (BRIT) *abbr* = **Cardiganshire**.
cardsharp ['kɑːdʃɑːp] *n* batoteiro/a, trapaceiro/a.
card vote (BRIT) *n* votação *f* de delegados.
CARE [kɛə*] *n abbr* (= *Cooperative for American Relief Everywhere*) *associação beneficente*.
care [kɛə*] *n* cuidado; (*worry*) preocupação *f*; (*charge*) encargo, custódia ♦ *vi*: **to ~ about** preocupar-se com, ter interesse em; **would you ~ to/for ...?** você quer ...?; **I wouldn't ~ to do it** eu não gostaria de fazê-lo; **in sb's ~** a cargo de alguém; **~ of** (*on letter*) aos cuidados de; **"with ~"** "frágil"; **to take ~ to** cuidar-se *or* ter o cuidado de; **to take ~ of** cuidar de; **the child has been taken into ~** a criança foi entregue aos cuidados da Assistência Social; **I don't ~** não me importa; **I couldn't ~ less** não dou a mínima.
care for *vt fus* cuidar de; (*like*) gostar de.
careen [kə'riːn] *vi* (*ship*) dar de quilha, querenar ♦ *vt* querenar.
career [kə'rɪə*] *n* carreira ♦ *vi* (*also*: *~ along*) correr a toda velocidade.
career girl *n* moça disposta a fazer carreira.
careers officer *n* orientador(a) *m/f* vocacional.
carefree ['kɛəfriː] *adj* despreocupado.
careful ['kɛəful] *adj* cuidadoso; (*cautious*) cauteloso; **(be) ~!** tenha cuidado!
carefully ['kɛəfulɪ] *adv* com cuidado, cuidadosamente; (*cautiously*) cautelosamente.
careless ['kɛəlɪs] *adj* descuidado; (*heedless*) desatento.
carelessly ['kɛəlɪslɪ] *adv* sem cuidado; (*without worry*) sem preocupação.
carelessness ['kɛəlɪsnɪs] *n* descuido, falta de atenção.
caress [kə'rɛs] *n* carícia ♦ *vt* acariciar.
caretaker ['kɛəteɪkə*] *n* zelador(a) *m/f*.
caretaker government (BRIT) *n* governo interino.
car-ferry *n* barca para carros (BR), barco de passagem (PT).
cargo ['kɑːgəu] (*pl* **~es**) *n* carregamento, carga; (*freight*) frete *m*.
cargo boat *n* cargueiro.
cargo plane *n* avião *m* de carga.

***NB**: European Portuguese adds the following consonants to certain words:* **b** (sú(b)dito, su(b)til); **c** (a(c)ção, a(c)cionista, a(c)to); **m** (inde(m)ne); **p** (ado(p)ção, ado(p)tar); *for further details see p. xiii.*

car hire (*BRIT*) *n* aluguel *m* (*BR*) *or* aluguer *m* (*PT*) de carros.
Caribbean [kærɪ'bi:ən] *adj* caraíba; **the ~ (Sea)** o Caribe.
caricature ['kærɪkətjuə*] *n* caricatura.
caring ['kɛərɪŋ] *adj* (*person*) bondoso; (*society*) humanitário.
carnage ['kɑ:nɪdʒ] *n* carnificina, matança.
carnal ['kɑ:nl] *adj* carnal.
carnation [kɑ:'neɪʃən] *n* cravo.
carnival ['kɑ:nɪvəl] *n* carnaval *m*; (*US*: *funfair*) parque *m* de diversões.
carnivore ['kɑ:nɪvɔ:*] *n* carnívoro.
carnivorous [kɑ:'nɪvərəs] *adj* carnívoro.
carol ['kærəl] *n*: **(Christmas) ~** cântico de Natal.
carouse [kə'rauz] *vi* farrear.
carousel [kærə'sɛl] (*US*) *n* carrossel *m*.
carp [kɑ:p] *n inv* (*fish*) carpa.
carp at *vt fus* criticar.
car park *n* estacionamento.
carpenter ['kɑ:pɪntə*] *n* carpinteiro.
carpentry ['kɑ:pɪntrɪ] *n* carpintaria.
carpet ['kɑ:pɪt] *n* tapete *m* ♦ *vt* atapetar; (*with fitted ~*) acarpetar; **fitted ~** (*BRIT*) carpete *m*.
carpet slippers *npl* chinelos *mpl*.
carpet sweeper [-'swi:pə*] *n* limpador *m* de tapetes.
car rental (*US*) *n* aluguel *m* (*BR*) *or* aluguer *m* (*PT*) de carros.
carriage ['kærɪdʒ] *n* carruagem *f*, coche *m*; (*RAIL*) vagão *m*; (*of goods*) transporte *m*; (: *cost*) porte *m*; (*of typewriter*) carro; (*bearing*) porte *m*; **~ forward** frete a pagar; **~ free** franco de porte; **~ paid** frete *or* porte pago.
carriage return *n* retorno do carro.
carriageway ['kærɪdʒweɪ] (*BRIT*) *n* (*part of road*) pista.
carrier ['kærɪə*] *n* transportador(a) *m/f*; (*company*) empresa de transportes, transportadora; (*MED*) portador(a) *m/f*; (*NAUT*) porta-aviões *m inv*.
carrier bag *n* saco, sacola.
carrier pigeon *n* pombo-correio.
carrion ['kærɪən] *n* carniça.
carrot ['kærət] *n* cenoura.
carry ['kærɪ] *vt* carregar; (*take*) levar; (*transport*) transportar; (*a motion, bill*) aprovar; (*involve*: *responsibilities etc*) implicar; (*MATH*: *figure*) levar; (*COMM*: *interest*) render ♦ *vi* (*sound*) projetar-se; **to get carried away** (*fig*) exagerar.
carry forward *vt* transportar.
carry on *vi* (*continue*) seguir, continuar; (*inf*: *complain*) queixar-se, criar caso ♦ *vt* prosseguir, continuar.
carry out *vt* (*orders*) cumprir; (*investigation*) levar a cabo, realizar; (*idea, threat*) executar.
carrycot ['kærɪkɔt] (*BRIT*) *n* moisés *m inv*.
carry-on (*inf*) *n* alvoroço, rebuliço.
cart [kɑ:t] *n* carroça, carreta; (*US*: *for luggage*) carrinho ♦ *vt* transportar (em carroça).
carte blanche ['kɑ:t'blɔŋʃ] *n*: **to give sb ~** dar carta branca a alguém.
cartel [kɑ:'tɛl] *n* (*COMM*) cartel *m*.
cartilage ['kɑ:tɪlɪdʒ] *n* cartilagem *f*.
cartographer [kɑ:'tɔgrəfə*] *n* cartógrafo/a.
cartography [kɑ:'tɔgrəfɪ] *n* cartografia.
carton ['kɑ:tən] *n* (*box*) caixa (de papelão); (*of yogurt*) pote *m*; (*packet*) pacote *m*.
cartoon [kɑ:'tu:n] *n* (*PRESS*) charge *f*; (*satirical*) caricatura; (*comic strip*) história em quadrinhos (*BR*), banda desenhada (*PT*); (*film*) desenho animado.
cartoonist [kɑ:'tu:nɪst] *n* caricaturista *m/f*, cartunista *m/f*; (*PRESS*) chargista *m/f*.
cartridge ['kɑ:trɪdʒ] *n* cartucho; (*of record player*) cápsula.
cartwheel ['kɑ:twi:l] *n* pirueta, cabriola; **to turn a ~** fazer uma pirueta.
carve [kɑ:v] *vt* (*meat*) trinchar; (*wood, stone*) cinzelar, esculpir; (*on tree*) gravar; **to ~ up** dividir, repartir.
carving ['kɑ:vɪŋ] *n* (*in wood etc*) escultura, obra de talha *or* de entalhe.
carving knife (*irreg*) *n* trinchante *m*, faca de trinchar.
car wash *n* lavagem *f* de carros.
cascade [kæs'keɪd] *n* cascata ♦ *vi* cascatear, cair em cascata.
case [keɪs] *n* (*container*) caixa, estojo; (*instance, affair, MED*) caso; (*for jewels etc*) estojo; (*LAW*) causa; (*BRIT*: *also*: *suit~*) mala; (*TYP*): **lower/upper ~** caixa baixa/alta; **to have a good ~** ter bons argumentos; **there's a strong ~ for ...** há bons argumentos para ...; **in ~ (of)** em caso (de); **in any ~** em todo o caso; **just in ~** *conj* se por acaso ♦ *adv* por via das dúvidas.
case-hardened *adj* calejado.
case history *n* (*MED*) anamnese *f*.
case study *n* (*MED*) caso clínico; (*SOCIOLOGY*) estudo sociológico.
cash [kæʃ] *n* dinheiro (em espécie) ♦ *vt* descontar; **to pay (in) ~** pagar em dinheiro; **~ on delivery** pagamento contra entrega; **to be short of ~** estar sem dinheiro.
cash in *vt* (*insurance policy etc*) resgatar.
cash in on *vt fus* lucrar com, explorar.
cash account *n* conta de caixa.
cashbook ['kæʃbuk] *n* livro-caixa *m*.
cash box *n* cofre *m*.
cash card *n* cartão *m* de saque.
cashdesk ['kæʃdɛsk] (*BRIT*) *n* caixa.
cash discount *n* desconto por pagamento à vista.
cash dispenser *n* caixa automática *or* eletrônica.
cashew [kæ'ʃu:] *n* (*also*: *~ nut*) castanha de caju.
cash flow *n* fluxo de caixa.
cashier [kæ'ʃɪə*] *n* caixa *m/f* ♦ *vt* (*MIL*) exonerar.
cashmere ['kæʃmɪə*] *n* caxemira, cachemira.
cash payment *n* (*in money*) pagamento em dinheiro; (*in one go*) pagamento à vista.
cash price *n* preço à vista.

cash register *n* caixa registradora.
cash sale *n* venda à vista.
casing ['keɪsɪŋ] *n* invólucro; (*of boiler etc*) revestimento.
casino [kə'si:nəu] *n* casino.
cask [kɑ:sk] *n* barril *m*, casco.
casket ['kɑ:skɪt] *n* cofre *m*, porta-jóias *m inv*; (*US*: *coffin*) caixão *m*.
Caspian Sea ['kæspɪən-] *n*: **the ~** o mar Cáspio.
casserole ['kæsərəul] *n* panela de ir ao forno; (*food*) ensopado (*BR*) no forno, guisado (*PT*) no forno.
cassette [kæ'sɛt] *n* fita-cassete *f*.
cassette deck *n* toca-fitas *m inv*.
cassette player *n* toca-fitas *m inv*.
cassette recorder *n* gravador *m*.
cassock ['kæsək] *n* sotaina, batina.
cast [kɑ:st] (*pt*, *pp* **cast**) *vt* (*throw*) lançar, atirar; (*skin*) mudar, perder; (*metal*) fundir; (*THEATRE*): **to ~ sb as Hamlet** dar a alguém o papel de Hamlet ♦ *vi* (*FISHING*) lançar ♦ *n* (*THEATRE*) elenco; (*mould*) forma, molde *m*; (*also*: *plaster ~*) gesso; **to ~ loose** soltar; **to ~ one's vote** votar.
cast aside *vt* rejeitar.
cast away *vt* desperdiçar.
cast down *vt* abater, desalentar.
cast off *vi* (*NAUT*) soltar o cabo; (*KNITTING*) rematar os pontos ♦ *vt* (*KNITTING*) rematar.
cast on *vt* (*KNITTING*) montar ♦ *vi* montar os pontos.
castanets [kæstə'nɛts] *npl* castanholas *fpl*.
castaway ['kɑ:stəwəɪ] *n* náufrago/a.
caste [kɑ:st] *n* casta.
caster sugar ['kɑ:stə*-] (*BRIT*) *n* acuçar *m* branco refinado.
casting vote ['kɑ:stɪŋ-] (*BRIT*) *n* voto decisivo, voto de minerva.
cast iron *n* ferro fundido ♦ *adj*: **cast-iron** (*fig*: *will*) de ferro; (: *alibi*) forte.
castle ['kɑ:sl] *n* castelo; (*CHESS*) torre *f*.
castor ['kɑ:stə*] *n* (*wheel*) rodízio.
castor oil *n* óleo de rícino.
castor sugar (*BRIT*) *n* = **caster sugar**.
castrate [kæs'treɪt] *vt* castrar.
casual ['kæʒjul] *adj* (*by chance*) fortuito; (*irregular*: *work etc*) eventual; (*unconcerned*) despreocupado; (*informal*: *atmosphere etc*) descontraído; **~ wear** roupas *fpl* esportivas.
casual labour *n* mão-de-obra *f* ocasional.
casually ['kæʒjulɪ] *adv* (*by chance*) casualmente; (*informally*) informalmente.
casualty ['kæʒjultɪ] *n* (*wounded*) ferido/a; (*dead*) morto/a; (*MIL*) baixa; **casualties** *npl* perdas *fpl*.
casualty ward (*BRIT*) *n* setor *m* de emergência, pronto-socorro.
cat [kæt] *n* gato.
catacombs ['kætəku:mz] *npl* catacumbas *fpl*.
Catalan ['kætəlæn] *adj* catalão/lã ♦ *n* catalão/lã *m/f*; (*LING*) catalão *m*.
catalogue ['kætəlɔg] (*US* **catalog**) *n* catálogo ♦ *vt* catalogar.
Catalonia [kætə'ləunɪə] *n* Catalunha.
catalyst ['kætəlɪst] *n* catalisador *m*.
catapult ['kætəpʌlt] *n* catapulta; (*child's toy*) atiradeira.
cataract ['kætərækt] *n* (*also*: *MED*) catarata.
catarrh [kə'tɑ:*] *n* catarro.
catastrophe [kə'tæstrəfɪ] *n* catástrofe *f*.
catastrophic [kætə'strɔfɪk] *adj* catastrófico.
catcall ['kætkɔ:l] *n* assobio.
catch [kætʃ] (*pt*, *pp* **caught**) *vt* (*ball*, *train*, *flu*) pegar (*BR*), apanhar (*PT*); (*arrest*) deter; (*person*: *by surprise*) flagrar, surpreender; (*understand*) compreender; (*get entangled*) prender; (*also*: *~ up*) alcançar ♦ *vi* (*fire*) pegar; (*in branches etc*) ficar preso, prender-se ♦ *n* (*fish etc*) pesca; (*act of ~ing*) captura; (*trap*) manha, armadilha; (*of lock*) trinco, lingüeta; **to ~ sb's attention** *or* **eye** chamar a atenção de alguém; **to ~ fire** pegar fogo; (*building*) incendiar-se; **to ~ sight of** avistar.
catch on *vi* (*understand*) entender (*BR*), perceber (*PT*); (*grow popular*) pegar.
catch out (*BRIT*) *vt* (*with trick question*) apanhar em erro.
catch up *vi* equiparar-se; (*make up for lost time*) recuperar o tempo perdido ♦ *vt* (*also*: *~ up with*) alcançar.
catching ['kætʃɪŋ] *adj* (*MED*) contagioso.
catchment area ['kætʃmənt-] *n área atendida por um hospital, uma escola etc.*
catch phrase *n* clichê *m*, slogan *m*.
catch-22 [-twentɪ'tu:] *n*: **it's a ~ situation** é uma situação do tipo se correr, o bicho pega, se ficar, o bicho come.
catchy ['kætʃɪ] *adj* (*tune*) que pega fácil, que gruda no ouvido.
catechism ['kætɪkɪzəm] *n* (*REL*) catecismo.
categoric(al) [kætɪ'gɔrɪk(əl)] *adj* categórico, terminante.
categorize ['kætɪgəraɪz] *vt* classificar.
category ['kætɪgərɪ] *n* categoria.
cater ['keɪtə*] *vi* preparar comida.
cater for *vt fus* (*needs*) atender a; (*consumers*) satisfazer.
caterer ['keɪtərə*] *n* (*service*) serviço de bufê.
catering ['keɪtərɪŋ] *n* serviço de bufê; (*trade*) abastecimento.
caterpillar ['kætəpɪlə*] *n* lagarta ♦ *cpd* (*vehicle*) de lagartas; **~ track** lagarta.
cathedral [kə'θi:drəl] *n* catedral *f*.
cathode ['kæθəud] *n* cátodo.
cathode ray tube *n* tubo de raios catódicos.
Catholic ['kæθəlɪk] *adj*, *n* (*REL*) católico/a.
catholic ['kæθəlɪk] *adj* eclético.
cat's eye (*BRIT*) *n* (*AUT*) catadióptrico.
catsup ['kætsəp] (*US*) *n* ketchup *m*.
cattle ['kætl] *npl* gado.
catty ['kætɪ] *adj* malicioso, rancoroso.

NB*: European Portuguese adds the following consonants to certain words:* **b** (sú(b)dito, su(b)til); **c** (a(c)ção, a(c)cionista, a(c)to); **m** (inde(m)ne); **p** (ado(p)ção, ado(p)tar); *for further details see p. xiii.*

Caucasian [kɔː'keɪʒn] *adj, n* caucasóide *m/f*.
Caucasus ['kɔːkəsəs] *n* Cáucaso.
caucus ['kɔːkəs] *n* (*US*: *POL*) comitê *m* eleitoral (para indicar candidatos); (*BRIT*: *POL*: *group*) panelinha (de políticos).
caught [kɔːt] *pt, pp of* **catch**.
cauliflower ['kɔlɪflauə*] *n* couve-flor *f*.
cause [kɔːz] *n* causa; (*reason*) motivo, razão *f* ♦ *vt* causar, provocar; **there is no ~ for concern** não há motivo de preocupação; **to ~ sth to be done** fazer com que algo seja feito; **to ~ sb to do sth** fazer com que alguém faça algo.
causeway ['kɔːzweɪ] *n* (*road*) calçada; (*embankment*) banqueta.
caustic ['kɔːstɪk] *adj* cáustico; (*fig*) mordaz.
caution ['kɔːʃən] *n* cautela, prudência; (*warning*) aviso ♦ *vt* acautelar, avisar.
cautious ['kɔːʃəs] *adj* cauteloso, prudente, precavido.
cautiously ['kɔːʃəslɪ] *adv* com cautela.
cautiousness ['kɔːʃəsnɪs] *n* cautela, prudência.
cavalier [kævə'lɪə*] *adj* arrogante, descortês ♦ *n* (*knight*) cavaleiro.
cavalry ['kævəlrɪ] *n* cavalaria.
cave [keɪv] *n* caverna, gruta ♦ *vi*: **to go caving** fazer espeleologia.
cave in *vi* dar de si; (*roof etc*) ceder.
caveman ['keɪvmæn] (*irreg*) *n* troglodita *m*, homem *m* das cavernas.
cavern ['kævən] *n* caverna.
caviar(e) ['kævɪɑː*] *n* caviar *m*.
cavity ['kævɪtɪ] *n* cavidade *f*.
cavort [kə'vɔːt] *vi* cabriolar.
caw [kɔː] *vi* grasnar.
cayenne [keɪ'ɛn] *n* (*also*: *~ pepper*) pimenta-de-caiena.
CB *n abbr* = **Citizens' Band (Radio)**; (*BRIT*: = *Companion of (the Order of) the Bath*) *título honorífico*.
CBC *n abbr* = **Canadian Broadcasting Corporation**.
CBE *n abbr* (= *Companion of (the Order of) the British Empire*) *título honorífico*.
CBI *n abbr* (= *Confederation of British Industry*) *federação de indústria*.
CBS (*US*) *n abbr* (= *Columbia Broadcasting System*) *emissora de televisão*.
CC (*BRIT*) = **County Council**.
cc *abbr* (= *cubic centimetre*) cc; (*on letter etc*) = **carbon copy**.
CCA (*US*) *n abbr* (= *Circuit Court of Appeals*) *tribunal de recursos itinerante*.
CCU (*US*) *n abbr* (= *coronary care unit*) *unidade de cardiologia*.
CD *n abbr* (= *compact disc*) disco laser; (*MIL*) = **Civil Defence (Corps)** (*BRIT*); **Civil Defense** (*US*) ♦ *abbr* (*BRIT*: = *Corps Diplomatique*) CD.
CDC (*US*) *n abbr* = **center for disease control**.
CD player *n* toca-discos *m inv* laser.
Cdr. *abbr* (= *commander*) Com.
CDT (*US*) *n abbr* (= *Central Daylight Time*) *hora de verão do centro*.
cease [siːs] *vt, vi* cessar.
ceasefire [siːs'faɪə*] *n* cessar-fogo *m*.
ceaseless ['siːslɪs] *adj* contínuo, incessante.
ceaselessly ['siːslɪslɪ] *adv* sem parar, sem cessar.
CED (*US*) *n abbr* = **Committee for Economic Development**.
cedar ['siːdə*] *n* cedro.
cede [siːd] *vt* ceder.
cedilla [sɪ'dɪlə] *n* cedilha.
CEEB (*US*) *n abbr* (= *College Entry Examination Board*) *comissão de admissão ao ensino superior*.
ceiling ['siːlɪŋ] *n* (*also fig*) teto.
celebrate ['sɛlɪbreɪt] *vt* celebrar ♦ *vi* celebrar, festejar.
celebrated ['sɛlɪbreɪtɪd] *adj* célebre.
celebration [sɛlɪ'breɪʃən] *n* (*act*) celebração *f*; (*party*) festa.
celebrity [sɪ'lɛbrɪtɪ] *n* celebridade *f*.
celeriac [sə'lɛrɪæk] *n* aipo-rábano.
celery ['sɛlərɪ] *n* aipo.
celestial [sɪ'lɛstɪəl] *adj* (*of sky*) celeste; (*divine*) celestial.
celibacy ['sɛlɪbəsɪ] *n* celibato.
cell [sɛl] *n* cela; (*BIO*) célula; (*ELEC*) pilha, elemento.
cellar ['sɛlə*] *n* porão *m*; (*for wine*) adega.
'cellist ['tʃɛlɪst] *n* violoncelista *m/f*.
'cello ['tʃɛləu] *n* violoncelo.
cellophane ['sɛləfeɪn] *n* celofane *m*.
cellular ['sɛljulə*] *adj* celular.
Celluloid ['sɛljulɔɪd] ® *n* celulóide *m* ®.
cellulose ['sɛljuləus] *n* celulose *f*.
Celsius ['sɛlsɪəs] *adj* Célsius *inv*.
Celt [kɛlt, sɛlt] *adj, n* celta *m/f*.
Celtic ['kɛltɪk, 'sɛltɪk] *adj* celta ♦ *n* (*LING*) celta *m*.
cement [sə'mɛnt] *n* cimento ♦ *vt* cimentar; (*fig*) cimentar, fortalecer.
cement mixer *n* betoneira.
cemetery ['sɛmɪtrɪ] *n* cemitério.
cenotaph ['sɛnətɑːf] *n* cenotáfio.
censor ['sɛnsə*] *n* (*person*) censor(a) *m/f*; (*concept*): **the ~** a censura ♦ *vt* censurar.
censorship ['sɛnsəʃɪp] *n* censura.
censure ['sɛnʃə*] *vt* censurar.
census ['sɛnsəs] *n* censo.
cent [sɛnt] (*US*) *n* (*coin*) cêntimo; *see also* **per**.
centenary [sɛn'tiːnərɪ] *n* centenário.
centennial [sɛn'tɛnɪəl] *n* centenário.
center *etc* ['sɛntə*] (*US*) = **centre** *etc*.
centigrade ['sɛntɪgreɪd] *adj* centígrado.
centilitre ['sɛntɪliːtə*] (*US* **centiliter**) *n* centilitro.
centimetre ['sɛntɪmiːtə*] (*US* **centimeter**) *n* centímetro.
centipede ['sɛntɪpiːd] *n* centopéia.
central ['sɛntrəl] *adj* central.
Central African Republic *n* República Centro-Africana.
Central America *n* América Central.
Central American *adj* centro-americano.
central heating *n* aquecimento central.
centralize ['sɛntrəlaɪz] *vt* centralizar.

central processing unit *n* (*COMPUT*) unidade *f* central de processamento.
central reservation (*BRIT*) *n* (*AUT*) canteiro divisor.
centre ['sɛntə*] (*US* **center**) *n* centro ♦ *vt* centrar ♦ *vi* (*concentrate*): **to ~ (on)** concentrar (em).
centrefold ['sɛntəfəuld] (*US* **centerfold**) *n* poster *m* central.
centre-forward *n* (*SPORT*) centro-avante *m*, centro.
centre-half *n* (*SPORT*) (centro)médio.
centrepiece ['sɛntəpi:s] (*US* **centerpiece**) *n* centro de mesa.
centre spread (*BRIT*) *n* páginas *fpl* centrais.
centrifugal [sɛntrɪ'fju:gl] *adj* centrífugo.
centrifuge ['sɛntrɪfju:ʒ] *n* centrífuga.
century ['sɛntjurɪ] *n* século; **20th ~** século vinte.
CEO (*US*) *n abbr* = **chief executive officer**.
ceramic [sɪ'ræmɪk] *adj* cerâmico.
ceramics [sɪ'ræmɪks] *n* cerâmica.
cereal ['si:rɪəl] *n* cereal *m*.
cerebral ['sɛrɪbrəl] *adj* cerebral.
ceremonial [sɛrɪ'məunɪəl] *n* cerimonial *m*; (*rite*) rito.
ceremony ['sɛrɪmənɪ] *n* cerimônia; **to stand on ~** fazer cerimônia.
cert [sə:t] (*BRIT*: *inf*) *n*: **it's a dead ~** é barbada, é coisa certa.
certain ['sə:tən] *adj* certo; (*person*: *sure*) seguro; **to make ~ of** assegurar-se de; **for ~** com certeza.
certainly ['sə:tənlɪ] *adv* certamente, com certeza.
certainty ['sə:təntɪ] *n* certeza.
certificate [sə'tɪfɪkɪt] *n* certificado.
certified letter ['sə:tɪfaɪd-] (*US*) *n* carta registrada.
certified public accountant ['sə:tɪfaɪd-] (*US*) *n* perito-contador *m*/perita-contadora *f*.
certify ['sə:tɪfaɪ] *vt* certificar ♦ *vi*: **to ~ to** atestar.
cervical ['sə:vɪkl] *adj*: **~ cancer** câncer *m* (*BR*) *or* cancro (*PT*) do colo do útero; **~ smear** exame *m* de lâmina, esfregaço.
cervix ['sə:vɪks] *n* cerviz *f*.
Cesarean [sɪ'zɛərɪən] (*US*) *adj*, *n* = **Caesarean**.
cessation [sə'seɪʃən] *n* cessação *f*, suspensão *f*.
cesspit ['sɛspɪt] *n* fossa séptica.
CET *abbr* (= *Central European Time*) *hora da Europa Central*.
Ceylon [sɪ'lɔn] *n* (*old*) Ceilão *m*.
cf. *abbr* (= *compare*) cf.
c/f *abbr* (*COMM*: = *carry forward*) a transportar.
CG (*US*) *n abbr* = **coastguard**.
cg *abbr* (= *centigram*) cg.
CH (*BRIT*) *n abbr* (= *Companion of Honour*) *título honorífico*.
ch (*BRIT*) *abbr* = **central heating**.
ch. *abbr* (= *chapter*) cap.
Chad [tʃæd] *n* Chad *m*.
chafe [tʃeɪf] *vt* (*rub*) roçar; (*wear*) gastar; (*irritate*) irritar ♦ *vi* (*fig*): **to ~ at sth** irritar-se com algo.
chaffinch ['tʃæfɪntʃ] *n* tentilhão *m*.
chagrin ['ʃægrɪn] *n* desgosto.
chain [tʃeɪn] *n* corrente *f*; (*of shops*) cadeia ♦ *vt* (*also*: **~ up**) encadear.
chain reaction *n* reação *f* em cadeia.
chain-smoke *vi* fumar um (cigarro) atrás do outro.
chain store *n* magazine *m* (*BR*), grande armazem *f* (*PT*).
chair [tʃɛə*] *n* cadeira; (*armchair*) poltrona; (*of university*) cátedra ♦ *vt* (*meeting*) presidir; **the ~** (*US*: *electric ~*) a cadeira elétrica.
chairlift ['tʃɛəlɪft] *n* teleférico.
chairman ['tʃɛəmən] (*irreg*) *n* presidente *m*.
chairperson ['tʃɛəpə:sn] *n* presidente *m/f*.
chairwoman ['tʃɛəwumən] (*irreg*) *n* presidenta, presidente *f*.
chalet ['ʃæleɪ] *n* chalé *m*.
chalice ['tʃælɪs] *n* cálice *m*.
chalk [tʃɔ:k] *n* (*GEO*) greda; (*for writing*) giz *m*.
  chalk up *vt* escrever a giz; (*fig*: *success*) obter.
challenge ['tʃælɪndʒ] *n* desafio ♦ *vt* desafiar; (*statement*, *right*) disputar, contestar; **to ~ sb to sth/to do sth** desafiar alguém para algo/a fazer algo.
challenger ['tʃælɪndʒə*] *n* (*SPORT*) competidor(a) *m/f*.
challenging ['tʃælɪndʒɪŋ] *adj* desafiante; (*tone*) de desafio.
chamber ['tʃeɪmbə*] *n* câmara; **~ of commerce** câmara de comércio.
chambermaid ['tʃeɪmbəmeɪd] *n* arrumadeira (*BR*), empregada (*PT*).
chamber music *n* música de câmara.
chamberpot ['tʃeɪmbəpɔt] *n* urinol *m*.
chameleon [kə'mi:lɪən] *n* camaleão *m*.
chamois ['ʃæmwɑ:] *n* camurça.
chamois leather ['ʃæmɪ-] *n* camurça.
champagne [ʃæm'peɪn] *n* champanhe *m or f*.
champion ['tʃæmpɪən] *n* campeão/peã *m/f* ♦ *vt* defender, lutar por.
championship ['tʃæmpɪənʃɪp] *n* campeonato.
chance [tʃɑ:ns] *n* (*luck*) acaso, casualidade *f*; (*opportunity*) oportunidade, ocasião *f*; (*likelihood*) chance *f*; (*risk*) risco ♦ *vt* arriscar ♦ *adj* fortuito, casual; **there is little ~ of his coming** é pouco provável que ele venha; **to take a ~** arriscar-se; **it's the ~ of a lifetime** é uma chance que só se tem uma vez na vida; **by ~** por acaso **to ~ it** arriscar-se; **to ~ to do** fazer por acaso.
  chance (up)on *vt fus* dar com, encontrar por acaso.
chancel ['tʃɑ:nsəl] *n* coro, capela-mor *f*.
chancellor ['tʃɑ:nsələ*] *n* chanceler *m*; **C~ of**

***NB**: European Portuguese adds the following consonants to certain words:* **b** (sú(b)dito, su(b)til); **c** (a(c)ção, a(c)cionista, a(c)to); **m** (inde(m)ne); **p** (ado(p)ção, ado(p)tar); *for further details see p. xiii.*

the Exchequer (*BRIT*) Ministro da Economia (Fazenda e Planejamento).
chandelier [ʃændəˈlɪə*] *n* lustre *m*.
change [tʃeɪndʒ] *vt* (*move, alter*) mudar; (*exchange*) trocar; (*replace*) substituir; (*gear, clothes, house*) mudar de, trocar de; (*transform*): **to ~ sb into** transformar alguém em ♦ *vi* (*gen*) mudar(-se); (*change clothes*) trocar de roupa; (*trains*) fazer baldeação (*BR*), mudar (*PT*) ♦ *n* mudança; (*exchange, money returned*) troca; (*modification*) modificação *f*; (*transformation*) transformação *f*; (*coins*: *also*: *small ~*) trocado; **for a ~** para variar; **to ~ into** transformar-se em; **to ~ one's mind** mudar de idéia; **she ~d into an old skirt** ela (trocou de roupa e) vestiu uma saia velha; **a ~ of clothes** uma muda de roupa; **to give sb ~ for** *or* **of £10** trocar £10 para alguém.
changeable [ˈtʃeɪndʒəbl] *adj* (*weather*) variável, instável; (*person*) inconstante, volúvel.
changeless [ˈtʃeɪndʒlɪs] *adj* imutável.
change machine *n máquina que fornece trocado.*
changeover [ˈtʃeɪndʒəuvə*] *n* (*to new system*) mudança.
changing [ˈtʃeɪndʒɪŋ] *adj* variável.
changing room (*BRIT*) *n* (*SPORT*) vestiário; (*in shop*) cabine *f* de provas.
channel [ˈtʃænl] *n* (*TV*) canal *m*; (*of river*) leito; (*of sea*) canal, estreito; (*groove*) ranhura; (*fig*: *medium*) meio, via ♦ *vt* (*also fig*): **to ~ (into)** canalizar (para); **to go through the usual ~s** seguir os trâmites normais; **green/red ~** (*CUSTOMS*) canal verde/vermelho; **the (English) C~** o Canal da Mancha.
Channel Islands *npl*: **the ~** as ilhas Anglo-Normandas.
chant [tʃɑːnt] *n* cântico ♦ *vt* cantar; (*fig*) entoar.
chaos [ˈkeɪɔs] *n* caos *m*.
chaotic [keɪˈɔtɪk] *adj* caótico.
chap [tʃæp] *n* (*BRIT*: *inf*: *man*) sujeito (*BR*), tipo (*PT*); (*term of address*): **old ~** meu velho ♦ *vt* (*skin*) rachar.
chapel [ˈtʃæpəl] *n* capela.
chaperon(e) [ˈʃæpərəun] *n* mulher *f* acompanhante ♦ *vt* acompanhar.
chaplain [ˈtʃæplɪn] *n* capelão *m*.
chapter [ˈtʃæptə*] *n* capítulo.
char [tʃɑː*] *vt* (*burn*) tostar, queimar ♦ *vi* (*BRIT*) trabalhar como diarista ♦ *n* (*BRIT*) = **charlady**.
character [ˈkærɪktə*] *n* caráter *m*; (*in novel, film*) personagem *m/f*; (*role*) papel *m*; (*eccentric*): **to be a (real) ~** ser um número; **a person of good ~** uma pessoa de bom caráter.
character code *n* (*COMPUT*) código de caráter.
characteristic [kærɪktəˈrɪstɪk] *adj* característico ♦ *n* característica.
characterize [ˈkærɪktəraɪz] *vt* caracterizar.
charade [ʃəˈrɑːd] *n* charada.
charcoal [ˈtʃɑːkəul] *n* carvão *m* de lenha; (*ART*) carvão *m*.
charge [tʃɑːdʒ] *n* (*of gun, electrical, MIL*: *attack*) carga; (*LAW*) encargo, acusação *f*; (*cost*) preço, custo; (*responsibility*) encargo; (*task*) incumbência ♦ *vt* (*LAW*): **to ~ sb (with)** acusar alguém (de); (*gun, battery*) carregar; (*MIL*: *enemy*) atacar; (*price*) cobrar; (*customer*) cobrar dinheiro de; (*sb with task*) incumbir, encarregar ♦ *vi* precipitar-se; (*make pay*) cobrar; **~s** *npl*: **bank/labour ~s** taxas *fpl* cobradas pelo banco/custos *mpl* de mão-de-obra; **free of ~** grátis; **is there a ~?** se tem que pagar?; **there's no ~** é de graça; **extra ~** sobretaxa; **to reverse the ~s** (*BRIT*: *TEL*) ligar a cobrar; **to take ~ of** encarregar-se de, tomar conta de; **to be in ~ of** estar a cargo de *or* encarregado de; **they ~d us £10 for the dinner** eles nos cobraram £10 pelo jantar; **how much do you ~?** quanto você cobra?; **to ~ an expense (up) to sb's account** pôr a despesa na conta de alguém; **to ~ in/out** precipitar-se para dentro/fora.
charge account *n* conta de crédito.
charge card *n* cartão *m* de crédito (*emitido por uma loja*).
chargé d'affaires [ˈʃɑːʒeɪdæˈfɛə*] *n* encarregado/a de negócios.
chargehand [ˈtʃɑːdʒhænd] (*BRIT*) *n* capataz *m*.
charger [ˈtʃɑːdʒə*] *n* (*also*: *battery ~*) carregador *m*; (*old*: *warhorse*) cavalo de batalha.
charitable [ˈtʃærɪtəbl] *adj* caritativo; (*organization*) beneficente.
charity [ˈtʃærɪtɪ] *n* caridade *f*; (*sympathy*) compaixão *f*; (*organization*) obra *f* de caridade.
charlady [ˈtʃɑːleɪdɪ] (*BRIT*) *n* diarista.
charm [tʃɑːm] *n* (*quality*) charme *m*; (*attraction*) encanto, atrativo; (*spell*) feitiço; (*object*) amuleto ♦ *vt* encantar, enfeitiçar.
charm bracelet *n* pulseira de berloques.
charming [ˈtʃɑːmɪŋ] *adj* encantador(a), simpático, charmoso.
chart [tʃɑːt] *n* (*table*) quadro; (*graph*) gráfico; (*map*) carta de navegação; (*weather ~*) carta meteorológica *or* de tempo ♦ *vt* fazer um gráfico de; (*course, progress*) traçar; **to be in the ~s** (*record, pop group*) estar nas paradas (de sucesso).
charter [ˈtʃɑːtə*] *vt* fretar ♦ *n* (*document*) carta, alvará *m*; **on ~** (*plane*) fretado.
chartered accountant [ˈtʃɑːtəd-] (*BRIT*) *n* perito-contador *m*/perita-contadora *f*.
charter flight *n* vôo charter *or* fretado.
charwoman [ˈtʃɑːwumən] (*BRIT*: *irreg*) *n* diarista.
chase [tʃeɪs] *vt* (*follow*) perseguir; (*hunt*) caçar, dar caça a ♦ *vi*: **to ~ after** correr atrás de ♦ *n* perseguição *f*, caça.
chase down (*US*) *vt* = **chase up**.
chase up (*BRIT*) *vt* (*person*) ficar atrás de; (*information*) pesquisar.
chasm [ˈkæzəm] *n* abismo.
chassis [ˈʃæsɪ] *n* chassi *m*.

chaste [tʃeɪst] *adj* casto.
chastened ['tʃeɪsnd] *adj*: **to be ~ by an experience** aprender uma lição com uma experiência.
chastening ['tʃeɪsnɪŋ] *adj*: **it was a ~ experience** foi uma lição.
chastise [tʃæs'taɪz] *vt* castigar.
chastity ['tʃæstɪtɪ] *n* castidade *f*.
chat [tʃæt] *vi* (*also*: *have a ~*) conversar, bater papo (BR), cavaquear (PT) ♦ *n* conversa, bate-papo *m* (BR), cavaqueira (PT).
chat up (BRIT: *inf*) *vt* (*girl*) paquerar.
chat show (BRIT) *n* programa *m* de entrevistas.
chattel ['tʃætl] *n see* **goods**.
chatter ['tʃætə*] *vi* (*person*) tagarelar; (*teeth*) tiritar ♦ *n* (*of birds*) chilro; (*of people*) tagarelice *f*.
chatterbox ['tʃætəbɔks] *n* tagarela *m/f*.
chatty ['tʃætɪ] *adj* (*style*) informal; (*person*) conversador(a).
chauffeur ['ʃəufə*] *n* chofer *m*, motorista *m/f*.
chauvinism ['ʃəuvɪnɪzəm] *n* (*also*: *male ~*) machismo; (*nationalism*) chauvinismo.
chauvinist ['ʃəuvɪnɪst] *n* (*also*: *male ~*) machista *m*; (*nationalist*) chauvinista *m/f*.
ChE *abbr* = **chemical engineer**.
cheap [tʃi:p] *adj* barato; (*ticket etc*) a preço reduzido; (*joke*) de mau gosto; (*poor quality*) barato, de pouca qualidade ♦ *adv* barato; **a ~ trick** uma sujeira, uma sacanagem.
cheapen ['tʃi:pən] *vt* baixar o preço de, rebaixar; **to ~ o.s.** rebaixar-se.
cheaply ['tʃi:plɪ] *adv* barato, por baixo preço.
cheat [tʃi:t] *vi* trapacear; (*at cards*) roubar (BR), fazer batota (PT); (*in exam*) colar (BR), cabular (PT) ♦ *vt* defraudar, enganar ♦ *n* fraude *f*; (*person*) trapaceiro/a; **to ~ on sb** (*inf*: *husband, wife etc*) passar alguém para trás.
cheating ['tʃi:tɪŋ] *n* trapaça.
check [tʃɛk] *vt* (*examine*) controlar; (*facts*) verificar; (*count*) contar; (*halt*) impedir, deter; (*restrain*) parar, refrear ♦ *vi* verificar ♦ *n* (*inspection*) controle *m*, inspeção *f*; (*curb*) freio; (*bill*) conta; (CHESS) xeque *m*; (*token*) ficha, talão *m*; (*pattern*: *gen pl*) xadrez *m*; (US) = **cheque** ♦ *adj* (*also*: *~ed*: *pattern, cloth*) xadrez *inv*; **to ~ with sb** perguntar a alguém; **to keep a ~ on sb/sth** controlar alguém/algo.
check in *vi* (*in hotel*) registrar-se; (*in airport*) apresentar-se ♦ *vt* (*luggage*) entregar.
check off *vt* checar.
check out *vi* (*of hotel*) pagar a conta e sair ♦ *vt* (*story*) verificar; (*person*) investigar; **~ it out** (*see for yourself*) confira.
check up *vi*: **to ~ up on sth** verificar algo; **to ~ up on sb** investigar alguém.
checkbook ['tʃɛkbuk] (US) *n* = **chequebook**.
checkered ['tʃɛkəd] (US) *adj* = **chequered**.
checkers ['tʃɛkəz] (US) *n* (jogo de) damas *fpl*.
check guarantee card (US) *n* cartão *m* (de garantia) de cheques.
check-in *n* (*also*: *~ desk*: *at airport*) check-in *m*.
checking account ['tʃɛkɪŋ-] (US) *n* conta corrente.
checklist ['tʃɛklɪst] *n* lista de conferência.
checkmate ['tʃɛkmeɪt] *n* xeque-mate *m*.
checkout ['tʃɛkaut] *n* caixa.
checkpoint ['tʃɛkpɔɪnt] *n* (ponto de) controle *m*.
checkup ['tʃɛkʌp] *n* (MED) check-up *m*; (*of machine*) revisão *f*.
cheek [tʃi:k] *n* bochecha; (*impudence*) folga, descaramento; **what a ~!** que folga!
cheekbone ['tʃi:kbəun] *n* maçã *f* do rosto.
cheeky ['tʃi:kɪ] *adj* insolente, descarado.
cheep [tʃi:p] *n* (*of bird*) pio ♦ *vi* piar.
cheer [tʃɪə*] *vt* dar vivas a, aplaudir; (*gladden*) alegrar, animar ♦ *vi* aplaudir, gritar com entusiasmo ♦ *n* (*gen pl*) aplausos *mpl*; **~s!** saúde!
cheer on *vt* torcer por.
cheer up *vi* animar-se, alegrar-se ♦ *vt* alegrar, animar.
cheerful ['tʃɪəful] *adj* alegre.
cheerfulness ['tʃɪəfulnɪs] *n* alegria.
cheerio [tʃɪərɪ'əu] (BRIT) *excl* tchau (BR), adeus (PT).
cheerless ['tʃɪəlɪs] *adj* triste, sombrio.
cheese [tʃi:z] *n* queijo.
cheeseboard ['tʃi:zbɔ:d] *n* (*in restaurant*) sortimento de queijos.
cheesecake ['tʃi:zkeɪk] *n* queijada, torta de queijo.
cheetah ['tʃi:tə] *n* chitá *m*.
chef [ʃɛf] *n* cozinheiro-chefe/cozinheira-chefe *m/f*.
chemical ['kɛmɪkəl] *adj* químico ♦ *n* produto químico.
chemist ['kɛmɪst] *n* (BRIT: *pharmacist*) farmacêutico/a; (*scientist*) químico/a; **~'s (shop)** (BRIT) farmácia.
chemistry ['kɛmɪstrɪ] *n* química.
cheque [tʃɛk] (US **check**) *n* cheque *m*; **to pay by ~** pagar com cheque.
chequebook ['tʃɛkbuk] (US **checkbook**) *n* talão *m* (BR) *or* livro (PT) de cheques.
cheque card (BRIT) *n* cartão *m* (de garantia) de cheques.
chequered ['tʃɛkəd] (US **checkered**) *adj* (*fig*) variado, acidentado.
cherish ['tʃɛrɪʃ] *vt* (*love*) apreciar; (*protect*) cuidar; (*hope etc*) acalentar.
cheroot [ʃə'ru:t] *n* charuto.
cherry ['tʃɛrɪ] *n* cereja.
Ches (BRIT) *abbr* = **Cheshire**.
chess [tʃɛs] *n* xadrez *m*.
chessboard ['tʃɛsbɔ:d] *n* tabuleiro de xadrez.
chessman ['tʃɛsmæn] (*irreg*) *n* peça, pedra (de xadrez).

***NB**: European Portuguese adds the following consonants to certain words:* **b** (sú(b)dito, su(b)til); **c** (a(c)ção, a(c)cionista, a(c)to); **m** (inde(m)ne); **p** (ado(p)ção, ado(p)tar); *for further details see p. xiii.*

chessplayer ['tʃɛspleɪə*] *n* xadrezista *m/f*.
chest [tʃɛst] *n* (ANAT) peito; (*box*) caixa, cofre *m*; **to get sth** *or* **it off one's ~** (*inf*) desabafar; **~ of drawers** cômoda.
chest measurement *n* medida de peito.
chestnut ['tʃɛsnʌt] *n* castanha; (*also*: ~ *tree*) castanheiro; (*colour*) castanho ♦ *adj* castanho.
chew [tʃu:] *vt* mastigar.
chewing gum ['tʃu:ɪŋ-] *n* chiclete *m* (BR), pastilha elástica (PT).
chic [ʃɪk] *adj* elegante, chique.
chick [tʃɪk] *n* pinto; (US: *inf*) broto.
chicken ['tʃɪkɪn] *n* galinha; (*food*) galinha, frango; (*inf*: *coward*) covarde *m/f*, galinha.
chicken out (*inf*) *vi* agalinhar-se.
chicken feed *n* (*fig*) dinheiro miúdo.
chickenpox ['tʃɪkɪnpɔks] *n* catapora (BR), varicela (PT).
chickpea ['tʃɪkpi:] *n* grão-de-bico *m*.
chicory ['tʃɪkərɪ] *n* chicória.
chide [tʃaɪd] *vt* repreender, censurar.
chief [tʃi:f] *n* chefe *m/f* ♦ *adj* principal; **C~ of Staff** (MIL) chefe *m* do Estado-Maior.
chief constable (BRIT) *n* chefe *m/f* de polícia.
chief executive (US **chief executive officer**) *n* diretor(a) *m/f* geral.
chiefly ['tʃi:flɪ] *adv* principalmente.
chiffon ['ʃɪfɔn] *n* gaze *f*.
chilblain ['tʃɪlbleɪn] *n* frieira.
child [tʃaɪld] (*pl* **~ren**) *n* criança; (*offspring*) filho/a.
childbirth ['tʃaɪldbə:θ] *n* parto.
childhood ['tʃaɪldhud] *n* infância.
childish ['tʃaɪldɪʃ] *adj* infantil, pueril.
childless ['tʃaɪldlɪs] *adj* sem filhos.
childlike ['tʃaɪldlaɪk] *adj* infantil, ingênuo.
childminder ['tʃaɪld'maɪndə*] (BRIT) *n* cuidadora de crianças.
children ['tʃɪldrən] *npl of* **child**.
Chile ['tʃɪlɪ] *n* Chile *m*.
Chilean ['tʃɪlɪən] *adj*, *n* chileno/a.
chili ['tʃɪlɪ] (US) *n* = **chilli**.
chill [tʃɪl] *n* frio; (MED) resfriamento ♦ *vt* esfriar; (CULIN) semi-congelar ♦ *adj* frio, glacial; **"serve ~ed"** "servir fresco".
chilli ['tʃɪlɪ] (US **chili**) *n* pimentão *m* picante.
chilly ['tʃɪlɪ] *adj* frio; (*sensitive to cold*) friorento; **to feel ~** estar com frio.
chime [tʃaɪm] *n* (*peal*) repique *m*, som *m* ♦ *vi* repicar, soar.
chimney ['tʃɪmnɪ] *n* chaminé *f*.
chimney sweep *n* limpador *m* de chaminés.
chimpanzee [tʃɪmpæn'zi:] *n* chimpanzé *m*.
chin [tʃɪn] *n* queixo.
China ['tʃaɪnə] *n* China.
china ['tʃaɪnə] *n* porcelana; (*crockery*) louça fina.
Chinese [tʃaɪ'ni:z] *adj* chinês/esa ♦ *n inv* chinês/esa *m/f*; (LING) chinês *m*.
chink [tʃɪŋk] *n* (*opening*) fresta, abertura; (*noise*) tinir *m*.
chip [tʃɪp] *n* (*gen pl*: BRIT: CULIN) batata frita; (: US: *also*: *potato* ~) batatinha frita; (*of wood*) lasca; (*of glass*, *stone*) lasca, pedaço; (*at poker*) ficha; (*also*: *micro~*) chip *m* ♦ *vt* (*cup*, *plate*) lascar; **when the ~s are down** (*fig*) na hora H.
chip in (*inf*) *vi* interromper; (*contribute*) compartilhar as despesas.
chipboard ['tʃɪpbɔ:d] *n* compensado.
chipmunk ['tʃɪpmʌŋk] *n* tâmia *m*.
chippings ['tʃɪpɪŋz] *npl*: **"loose ~"** "projeção de cascalho".
chiropodist [kɪ'rɔpədɪst] (BRIT) *n* pedicuro/a.
chiropody [kɪ'rɔpədɪ] (BRIT) *n* quiropodia.
chirp [tʃə:p] *vi* chilrar, piar; (*cricket*) chilrear ♦ *n* chilro.
chirpy ['tʃə:pɪ] *adj* alegre, animado.
chisel ['tʃɪzl] *n* (*for wood*) formão *m*; (*for stone*) cinzel *m*.
chit [tʃɪt] *n* talão *m*.
chitchat ['tʃɪttʃæt] *n* conversa fiada.
chivalrous ['ʃɪvəlrəs] *adj* cavalheiresco.
chivalry ['ʃɪvəlrɪ] *n* cavalaria.
chives [tʃaɪvz] *npl* cebolinha.
chloride ['klɔ:raɪd] *n* cloreto.
chlorinate ['klɔrɪneɪt] *vt* clorar.
chlorine ['klɔ:ri:n] *n* cloro.
chock [tʃɔk] *n* cunha.
chock-a-block *adj* abarrotado, apinhado.
chock-full *adj* abarrotado, apinhado.
chocolate ['tʃɔklɪt] *n* chocolate *m*.
choice [tʃɔɪs] *n* escolha; (*preference*) preferência ♦ *adj* seleto, escolhido; **by** *or* **from ~** de preferência; **a wide ~** uma grande variedade.
choir ['kwaɪə*] *n* coro.
choirboy ['kwaɪəbɔɪ] *n* menino de coro.
choke [tʃəuk] *vi* sufocar-se; (*on food*) engasgar ♦ *vt* afogar, sufocar; (*block*) obstruir ♦ *n* (AUT) afogador *m* (BR), ar *m* (PT).
choker ['tʃəukə*] *n* (*necklace*) colar *m* curto.
cholera ['kɔlərə] *n* cólera *m*.
cholesterol [kə'lɛstərɔl] *n* colesterol *m*.
choose [tʃu:z] (*pt* **chose**, *pp* **chosen**) *vt* escolher ♦ *vi*: **to ~ between** escolher entre; **to ~ to do** optar por fazer.
choosy ['tʃu:zɪ] *adj* exigente.
chop [tʃɔp] *vt* (*wood*) cortar, talhar; (CULIN: *also*: ~ *up*) cortar em pedaços; (*meat*) picar ♦ *n* golpe *m*; (CULIN) costeleta; **~s** *npl* (*jaws*) beiços *mpl*; **to get the ~** (BRIT: *inf*: *project*) ser cancelado; (: *person*: *be sacked*) ser posto na rua.
chop down *vt* (*tree*) abater, derrubar.
chopper ['tʃɔpə*] *n* (*helicopter*) helicóptero.
choppy ['tʃɔpɪ] *adj* (*sea*) agitado.
chopsticks ['tʃɔpstɪks] *npl* pauzinhos *mpl*, palitos *mpl*.
choral ['kɔ:rəl] *adj* coral.
chord [kɔ:d] *n* (MUS) acorde *m*.
chore [tʃɔ:*] *n* tarefa; (*routine task*) trabalho de rotina; **household ~s** afazeres *mpl* domésticos.
choreographer [kɔrɪ'ɔgrəfə*] *n* coreógrafo/a.
chorister ['kɔrɪstə*] *n* corista *m/f*.
chortle ['tʃɔ:tl] *vi* rir, gargalhar.
chorus ['kɔ:rəs] *n* coro; (*repeated part of song*) estribilho.

chose [tʃəuz] *pt of* **choose**.
chosen ['tʃəuzn] *pp of* **choose**.
chow [tʃau] *n* (*dog*) chow *m* (*raça de cão*).
chowder ['tʃaudə*] *n* sopa (de peixe).
Christ [kraɪst] *n* Cristo.
christen ['krɪsn] *vt* batizar.
christening ['krɪsnɪŋ] *n* batismo.
Christian ['krɪstɪən] *adj*, *n* cristão/tã *m/f*.
Christianity [krɪstɪ'ænɪtɪ] *n* cristianismo.
Christian name *n* prenome *m*, nome *m* de batismo.
Christmas ['krɪsməs] *n* Natal *m*; **happy** *or* **merry** ~! Feliz Natal!
Christmas card *n* cartão *m* de Natal.
Christmas Day *n* dia *m* de Natal.
Christmas Eve *n* véspera de Natal.
Christmas Island *n* ilha de Christmas.
Christmas tree *n* árvore *f* de Natal.
chrome [krəum] *n* cromo.
chromium ['krəumɪəm] *n* cromo.
chromosome ['krəuməsəum] *n* cromossomo.
chronic ['krɔnɪk] *adj* crônico; (*fig*: *smoker*, *liar*) inveterado.
chronicle ['krɔnɪkl] *n* crônica.
chronological [krɔnə'lɔdʒɪkəl] *adj* cronológico.
chrysanthemum [krɪ'sænθəməm] *n* crisântemo.
chubby ['tʃʌbɪ] *adj* roliço, gorducho.
chuck [tʃʌk] *vt* jogar (*BR*), deitar (*PT*); **to** ~ **(up** *or* **in)** (*BRIT*: *job*) largar; (: *person*) acabar com.
chuck out *vt* (*thing*) jogar (*BR*) *or* deitar (*PT*) fora; (*person*) expulsar.
chuckle ['tʃʌkl] *vi* rir.
chug [tʃʌg] *vi* andar fazendo ruído da descarga.
chug along *vi* (*fig*) ir indo.
chum [tʃʌm] *n* camarada *m/f*.
chump [tʃʌmp] (*inf*) *n* imbecil *m/f*, boboca *m/f*.
chunk [tʃʌŋk] *n* pedaço, naco.
chunky ['tʃʌŋkɪ] *adj* (*furniture*) pesado; (*person*) atarracado; (*knitwear*) grosso.
church [tʃəːtʃ] *n* igreja; **the C~ of England** a Igreja Anglicana.
churchyard ['tʃəːtʃjɑːd] *n* adro, cemitério.
churlish ['tʃəːlɪʃ] *adj* grosseiro, rude.
churn [tʃəːn] *n* (*for butter*) batedeira; (*for milk*) lata, vasilha ♦ *vt* bater, agitar.
churn out *vt* produzir em série.
chute [ʃuːt] *n* rampa; (*also*: *rubbish* ~) despejador *m*.
chutney ['tʃʌtnɪ] *n* conserva picante.
CIA (*US*) *n abbr* (= *Central Intelligence Agency*) CIA *f*.
CID (*BRIT*) *n abbr* = **Criminal Investigation Department**.
cider ['saɪdə*] *n* sidra.
CIF *abbr* (= *cost, insurance and freight*) CIF.
cigar [sɪ'gɑː*] *n* charuto.
cigarette [sɪgə'rɛt] *n* cigarro.
cigarette case *n* cigarreira.
cigarette end *n* ponta de cigarro, guimba (*BR*).
cigarette holder *n* piteira (*BR*), boquilha (*PT*).
C-in-C *abbr* = **commander-in-chief**.
cinch [sɪntʃ] (*inf*) *n*: **it's a** ~ é sopa, é moleza.
cinder ['sɪndə*] *n* cinza.
Cinderella [sɪndə'rɛlə] *n* Gata Borralheira.
cine-camera ['sɪnɪ-] (*BRIT*) *n* câmera (cinematográfica).
cine-film ['sɪnɪ-] (*BRIT*) *n* filme *m* cinematográfico.
cinema ['sɪnəmə] *n* cinema *m*.
cine-projector ['sɪnɪ-] (*BRIT*) *n* projetor *m* cinematográfico.
cinnamon ['sɪnəmən] *n* canela.
cipher ['saɪfə*] *n* cifra; **in** ~ cifrado.
circa ['səːkə] *prep* cerca de.
circle ['səːkl] *n* círculo; (*in cinema*) balcão *m* ♦ *vi* dar voltas ♦ *vt* (*surround*) rodear, cercar; (*move round*) dar a volta de.
circuit ['səːkɪt] *n* circuito; (*tour*, *lap*) volta; (*track*) pista.
circuit board *n* placa.
circuitous [səː'kjuɪtəs] *adj* tortuoso, indireto.
circular ['səːkjulə*] *adj* circular ♦ *n* circular *f*.
circulate ['səːkjuleɪt] *vi* circular ♦ *vt* pôr em circulação, espalhar.
circulation [səːkju'leɪʃən] *n* circulação *f*; (*of newspaper*) tiragem *f*.
circumcise ['səːkəmsaɪz] *vt* circuncidar.
circumference [sə'kʌmfərəns] *n* circunferência.
circumflex ['səːkəmflɛks] *n* (*also*: ~ *accent*) (acento) circunflexo.
circumscribe ['səːkəmskraɪb] *vt* circunscrever.
circumspect ['səːkəmspɛkt] *adj* circunspeto, prudente.
circumstances ['səːkəmstənsɪz] *npl* circunstâncias *fpl*; (*financial condition*) situação *f* econômica; **in the** ~ em tais circunstâncias, assim sendo, neste caso; **under no** ~ de modo algum, de jeito nenhum.
circumstantial [səːkəm'stænʃl] *adj* (*report*) circunstanciado; ~ **evidence** prova circunstancial.
circumvent [səːkəm'vɛnt] *vt* (*rule etc*) driblar, burlar.
circus ['səːkəs] *n* circo; (*also*: *C~*: *in place names*) praça.
cistern ['sɪstən] *n* tanque *m*, reservatório; (*in toilet*) caixa d'água.
citation [saɪ'teɪʃən] *n* (*commendation*) menção *f*; (*US*: *LAW*) intimação *f*; (*quotation*) citação *f*.
cite [saɪt] *vt* citar.
citizen ['sɪtɪzn] *n* (*POL*) cidadão/dã *m/f*; (*resident*) habitante *m/f*.
citizenship ['sɪtɪznʃɪp] *n* cidadania.
citric acid ['sɪtrɪk-] *n* ácido cítrico.
citrus fruit ['sɪtrəs-] *n* citrino.

NB: European Portuguese adds the following consonants to certain words: **b** (sú(b)dito, su(b)til); **c** (a(c)ção, a(c)cionista, a(c)to); **m** (inde(m)ne); **p** (ado(p)ção, ado(p)tar); *for further details see p. xiii.*

city ['sɪtɪ] *n* cidade *f*; **the C~** *centro financeiro de Londres.*
city centre *n* centro (da cidade).
civic ['sɪvɪk] *adj* cívico, municipal.
civic centre (*BRIT*) *n* sede *f* do município.
civil ['sɪvɪl] *adj* civil; (*polite*) delicado, cortês.
civil disobedience *n* resistência passiva.
civil engineer *n* engenheiro/a civil.
civil engineering *n* engenharia civil.
civilian [sɪ'vɪlɪən] *adj*, *n* civil *m/f*, paisano/a.
civilization [sɪvɪlaɪ'zeɪʃən] *n* civilização *f*.
civilized ['sɪvɪlaɪzd] *adj* civilizado.
civil law *n* direito civil.
civil rights *npl* direitos *mpl* civis.
civil servant *n* funcionário/a público/a.
Civil Service *n* administração *f* pública.
civil war *n* guerra civil.
cl *abbr* (= *centilitre*) cl.
clad [klæd] *adj*: ~ **(in)** vestido (de).
claim [kleɪm] *vt* exigir, reclamar; (*rights etc*) reivindicar; (*assert*) afirmar, alegar ♦ *vi* (*for insurance*) reclamar ♦ *n* reclamação *f*; (*LAW*) direito; (*pretension*) pretensão *f*; (*wage ~ etc*) reivindicação *f*; **(insurance)** ~ reclamação *f*; **to put in a ~ for** (*pay rise etc*) reivindicar.
claimant ['kleɪmənt] *n* (*ADMIN*, *LAW*) requerente *m/f*.
claim form *n* formulário de requerimento; (*INSURANCE*) formulário para reclamações.
clairvoyant [klɛə'vɔɪənt] *n* clarividente *m/f*.
clam [klæm] *n* molusco.
clam up (*inf*) *vi* ficar calado.
clamber ['klæmbə*] *vi* subir.
clammy ['klæmɪ] *adj* (*cold*) frio e úmido; (*sticky*) pegajoso.
clamour ['klæmə*] (*US* **clamor**) *n* clamor *m* ♦ *vi*: **to ~ for sth** clamar algo.
clamp [klæmp] *n* grampo ♦ *vt* segurar.
clamp down on *vt fus* suprimir, proibir.
clan [klæn] *n* clã *m*.
clandestine [klæn'dɛstɪn] *adj* clandestino.
clang [klæŋ] *n* retintim *m*, som metálico ♦ *vi* retinir.
clansman ['klænzmən] (*irreg*) *n* membro de um clã escocês.
clap [klæp] *vi* bater palmas, aplaudir ♦ *vt* (*performer*) aplaudir ♦ *n* (*of hands*) palmas *fpl*; **to ~ one's hands** bater palmas; **a ~ of thunder** uma trovoada.
clapping ['klæpɪŋ] *n* aplausos *mpl*, palmas *fpl*.
claret ['klærət] *n* clarete *m*.
clarification [klærɪfɪ'keɪʃən] *n* esclarecimento.
clarify ['klærɪfaɪ] *vt* esclarecer, aclarar.
clarinet [klærɪ'nɛt] *n* clarinete *m*.
clarity ['klærɪtɪ] *n* claridade *f*.
clash [klæʃ] *n* (*of metal*) estridor *m*; (*with police*, *fig*) choque *m* ♦ *vi* (*fight*) chocar-se; (*disagree*) entrar em conflito, ter uma desavença; (*colours*) não combinar; (*dates*, *events*) coincidir.
clasp [klɑːsp] *n* fecho ♦ *vt* afivelar; (*hand*) apertar; (*embrace*) abraçar.
class [klɑːs] *n* classe *f*; (*lesson*) aula ♦ *cpd* de classe ♦ *vt* classificar.
class-conscious *adj* que tem consciência de classe.
class consciousness *n* consciência de classe.
classic ['klæsɪk] *adj* clássico ♦ *n* (*author*, *work*, *race etc*) clássico; **~s** *npl* (*SCH*) línguas *fpl* clássicas.
classical ['klæsɪkl] *adj* clássico.
classification [klæsɪfɪ'keɪʃən] *n* classificação *f*.
classified ['klæsɪfaɪd] *adj* (*information*) secreto; ~ **ads** classificados *mpl*.
classify ['klæsɪfaɪ] *vt* classificar.
classmate ['klæsmeɪt] *n* colega *m/f* de aula.
classroom ['klæsrum] *n* sala de aula.
classy ['klɑːsɪ] (*inf*) *adj* (*person*) classudo; (*flat*, *clothes*) chique, incrementado.
clatter ['klætə*] *n* ruído, estrépito ♦ *vi* fazer barulho *or* ruído.
clause [klɔːz] *n* cláusula; (*LING*) oração *f*.
claustrophobia [klɔːstrə'fəubɪə] *n* claustrofobia.
claw [klɔː] *n* (*of cat*) pata, unha; (*of bird of prey*) garra; (*of lobster*) pinça; (*TECH*) unha ♦ *vt* arranhar.
claw at *vt fus* arranhar; (*tear*) rasgar.
clay [kleɪ] *n* argila.
clean [kliːn] *adj* limpo; (*clear*) nítido, bem definido ♦ *vt* limpar ♦ *adv*: **he ~ forgot** ele esqueceu completamente; **to come ~** (*inf*: *own up*) abrir o jogo; **to ~ one's teeth** (*BRIT*) escovar os dentes; **~ driving licence** (*BRIT*), **~ record** (*US*) carteira de motorista sem infrações.
clean off *vt* tirar.
clean out *vt* limpar.
clean up *vt* limpar, assear ♦ *vi* (*fig*: *make profit*): **to ~ up on** faturar com, lucrar com.
clean-cut *adj* (*person*) alinhado.
cleaner ['kliːnə*] *n* (*person*) faxineiro/a; (*also*: *dry ~*) tintureiro/a; (*product*) limpador *m*.
cleaning ['kliːnɪŋ] *n* limpeza.
cleaning lady *n* faxineira.
cleanliness ['klɛnlɪnɪs] *n* limpeza.
cleanly ['kliːnlɪ] *adv* perfeitamente; (*without mess*) limpamente.
cleanse [klɛnz] *vt* limpar; (*fig*) purificar.
cleanser ['klɛnzə*] *n* limpador *m*; (*for face*) creme *m* de limpeza.
clean-shaven [-'ʃeɪvn] *adj* sem barba, de cara raspada.
cleansing department ['klɛnzɪŋ-] (*BRIT*) *n* departamento de limpeza.
clean-up *n* limpeza geral.
clear [klɪə*] *adj* claro; (*road*, *way*) limpo, livre; (*profit*) líquido; (*majority*) absoluto ♦ *vt* (*space*) abrir; (*desk etc*) limpar; (*room*) esvaziar; (*LAW*: *suspect*) absolver; (*obstacle*) salvar, passar sobre; (*debt*) liquidar; (*woodland*) desmatar; (*cheque*) compensar; (*COMM*: *goods*) liquidar ♦ *vi* (*weather*) abrir, clarear; (*fog etc*) dissipar-se ♦ *adv*: **~ of** a salvo de ♦ *n*: **to be in the ~** (*out of debt*) estar sem dívidas; (*out of suspicion*) estar livre de suspeita; (*out of danger*) estar fora de perigo; **to ~ the table** tirar a mesa; **to ~**

one's throat pigarrear; **to ~ a profit** fazer um lucro líquido; **let me make myself ~** deixe-me explicar melhor; **do I make myself ~?** entendeu?; **to make o.s. ~** fazer-se entender bem; **to make it ~ to sb that ...** deixar bem claro para alguém que; **I have a ~ day tomorrow** (*BRIT*) não tenho compromisso amanhã; **to keep ~ of sb/sth** evitar alguém/algo.
clear off (*inf*) *vi* (*leave*) cair fora.
clear up *vt* limpar; (*mystery*) resolver, esclarecer.
clearance ['klɪərəns] *n* (*removal*) despejo; (*permission*) permissão *f*.
clearance sale *n* (*COMM*) liquidação *f*.
clear-cut *adj* bem definido, nítido.
clearing ['klɪərɪŋ] *n* (*in wood*) clareira; (*BRIT*: *BANKING*) compensação *f*.
clearing bank (*BRIT*) *n* câmara de compensação.
clearly ['klɪəlɪ] *adv* claramente.
clearway ['klɪəweɪ] (*BRIT*) *n estrada onde não se pode estacionar.*
cleavage ['kli:vɪdʒ] *n* (*of dress*) decote *m*; (*of woman*) colo.
cleaver ['kli:və] *n* cutelo (de açougueiro).
clef [klɛf] *n* (*MUS*) clave *f*.
cleft [klɛft] *n* (*in rock*) fissura.
clemency ['klɛmənsɪ] *n* clemência.
clement ['klɛmənt] *adj* (*weather*) ameno.
clench [klɛntʃ] *vt* apertar, cerrar.
clergy ['klə:dʒɪ] *n* clero.
clergyman ['klə:dʒɪmən] (*irreg*) *n* clérigo, pastor *m*.
clerical ['klɛrɪkəl] *adj* de escritório; (*REL*) clerical.
clerk [klɑ:k, (*US*) klə:rk] *n* auxiliar *m/f* de escritório; (*US*: *salesman/woman*) balconista *m/f*; **C~ of Court** (*LAW*) escrivão/vã *m/f* (do tribunal).
clever ['klɛvə*] *adj* (*mentally*) inteligente; (*deft, crafty*) hábil; (*device, arrangement*) engenhoso.
clew [klu:] (*US*) *n* = **clue**.
cliché ['kli:ʃeɪ] *n* clichê *m*, frase *f* feita.
click [klɪk] *vt* (*tongue*) estalar; (*heels*) bater ♦ *vi* estalar.
client ['klaɪənt] *n* cliente *m/f*.
clientele [kli:ɑ:n'tɛl] *n* clientela.
cliff [klɪf] *n* penhasco.
cliffhanger ['klɪfhæŋə*] *n* (*TV, fig*) história de suspense.
climactic [klaɪ'mæktɪk] *adj* culminante.
climate ['klaɪmɪt] *n* clima *m*.
climax ['klaɪmæks] *n* clímax *m*, ponto culminante; (*sexual*) clímax.
climb [klaɪm] *vi* subir, trepar; (*plane*) ganhar altitude ♦ *vt* (*stairs*) subir; (*tree*) trepar em; (*hill*) escalar ♦ *n* subida; **to ~ over a wall** passar por cima de um muro.
climb down *vi* descer; (*BRIT*: *fig*) recuar, ceder.
climbdown ['klaɪmdaun] (*BRIT*) *n* recuo.
climber ['klaɪmə*] *n* alpinista *m/f*.
climbing ['klaɪmɪŋ] *n* alpinismo.
clinch [klɪntʃ] *vt* (*deal*) fechar; (*argument*) decidir, resolver.
cling [klɪŋ] (*pt, pp* **clung**) *vi*: **to ~ to** pegar-se a, aderir a; (*hold on to*: *object, idea*) agarrar-se a; (*clothes*) ajustar-se a.
clinic ['klɪnɪk] *n* clínica; (*consultation*) consulta.
clinical ['klɪnɪkl] *adj* clínico; (*fig*) frio, impessoal.
clink [klɪŋk] *vi* tinir.
clip [klɪp] *n* (*for hair*) grampo (*BR*), gancho (*PT*); (*also*: *paper ~*) mola, clipe *m*; (*on necklace etc*) fecho; (*AUT*: *holding hose etc*) braçadeira ♦ *vt* (*cut*) cortar; (*shorten, trim*) aparar; (*also*: *~ together*: *papers*) grampear.
clippers ['klɪpəz] *npl* (*for gardening*) podadeira; (*for hair*) máquina; (*for nails*) alicate *m* de unhas.
clipping ['klɪpɪŋ] *n* recorte *m*.
clique [kli:k] *n* panelinha.
cloak [kləuk] *n* capa, manto ♦ *vt* (*fig*) encobrir.
cloakroom ['kləukrum] *n* vestiário; (*BRIT*: *WC*) sanitários *mpl* (*BR*), lavatórios *mpl* (*PT*).
clock [klɔk] *n* relógio; (*in taxi*) taxímetro; **round the ~** (*work etc*) dia e noite, ininterruptamente; **30,000 on the ~** (*BRIT*: *AUT*) 30,000 km rodados; **to work against the ~** trabalhar contra o tempo.
clock in (*BRIT*) *vi* assinar o ponto na entrada.
clock off (*BRIT*) *vi* assinar o ponto na saída.
clock on (*BRIT*) *vi* assinar o ponto na entrada.
clock out (*BRIT*) *vi* assinar o ponto na saída.
clock up *vt* (*miles, hours etc*) fazer.
clockwise ['klɔkwaɪz] *adv* em sentido horário.
clockwork ['klɔkwə:k] *n* mecanismo de relógio ♦ *adj* de corda.
clog [klɔg] *n* tamanco ♦ *vt* entupir ♦ *vi* entupir-se, emperrar.
cloister ['klɔɪstə*] *n* claustro.
clone [kləun] *n* clone *m*.
close [*adj, adv* kləus, *vb, n* kləuz] *adj* próximo; (*print, weave*) denso, compacto; (*friend*) íntimo; (*connection*) estreito; (*examination*) minucioso; (*weather*) abafado; (*atmosphere*) sufocante; (*room*) mal arejado ♦ *adv* perto ♦ *vt* (*shut*) fechar; (*end*) acabar, concluir ♦ *vi* (*shop, door etc*) fechar; (*end*) concluir-se, terminar-se ♦ *n* (*end*) fim *m*, conclusão *f*, terminação *f*; **~ by, ~ at hand** perto, pertinho; **how ~ is Edinburgh to Glasgow?** qual é a distância entre Edimburgo e Glasgow?; **to have a ~ shave** (*fig*) livrar-se por um triz; **at ~ quarters** de perto; **to bring sth to a ~** dar fim a algo.

***NB**: European Portuguese adds the following consonants to certain words:* **b** (sú(b)dito, su(b)til); **c** (a(c)ção, a(c)cionista, a(c)to); **m** (inde(m)ne); **p** (ado(p)ção, ado(p)tar); *for further details see p. xiii.*

close down *vt, vi* fechar definitivamente.
close in *vi* (*hunters*) apertar o cerco; (*night, fog*) cair; **the days are closing in** os dias estão ficando mais curtos; **to ~ in on sb** aproximar-se de alguém, cercar alguém.
close off *vt* (*area*) isolar.
closed [kləuzd] *adj* (*shop etc*) fechado.
closed-circuit *adj*: **~ television** televisão *f* de circuito fechado.
closed shop *n estabelecimento industrial que só admite empregados sindicalizados.*
close-knit *adj* (*family, community*) muito unido.
closely ['kləuslı] *adv* (*exactly*) fielmente; (*carefully*) rigorosamente; (*watch*) de perto; **we are ~ related** somos parentes próximos; **a ~ guarded secret** um segredo bem guardado.
closet ['klɔzıt] *n* (*cupboard*) armário; (*walk-in*) closet *m*.
close-up [kləus-] *n* close *m*, close-up *m*.
closing ['kləuzıŋ] *adj* (*stages, remarks*) final; **~ price** (STOCK EXCHANGE) cotação *f* de fechamento.
closing-down sale (BRIT) *n* liquidação *f* (por motivo de fechamento).
closure ['kləuʒə*] *n* (*close-down*) encerramento, fechamento.
clot [klɔt] *n* (*gen*: *blood* ~) coágulo; (*inf*: *idiot*) imbecil *m/f* ♦ *vi* (*blood*) coagular-se, coalhar-se.
cloth [klɔθ] *n* (*material*) tecido, fazenda; (*rag*) pano; (*also*: *table~*) toalha.
clothe [kləuð] *vt* vestir; (*fig*) revestir.
clothes [kləuðz] *npl* roupa; **to put one's ~ on** vestir-se; **to take one's ~ off** tirar a roupa.
clothes brush *n* escova (para a roupa).
clothes line *n* corda (para estender a roupa).
clothes peg (US **clothes pin**) *n* pregador *m*.
clothing ['kləuðıŋ] *n* vestuário.
clotted cream ['klɔtıd-] (BRIT) *n* creme *m* coalhado.
cloud [klaud] *n* nuvem *f* ♦ *vt* (*liquid*) turvar; **to ~ the issue** confundir *or* complicar as coisas; **every ~ has a silver lining** (*proverb*) Deus escreve certo por linhas tortas.
cloud over *vi* (*also*: *fig*) fechar.
cloudburst ['klaudbə:st] *n* aguaceiro.
cloud-cuckoo-land (BRIT) *n*: **to live in ~** viver no mundo da lua.
cloudy ['klaudı] *adj* nublado; (*liquid*) turvo.
clout [klaut] *vt* dar uma bofetada em ♦ *n* (*blow*) bofetada; (*fig*) influência.
clove [kləuv] *n* cravo; **~ of garlic** dente *m* de alho.
clover ['kləuvə*] *n* trevo.
cloverleaf ['kləuvəli:f] (*irreg*) *n* (AUT) trevo rodoviário.
clown [klaun] *n* palhaço ♦ *vi* (*also*: *~ about*; *~ around*) fazer palhaçadas.
cloying ['klɔııŋ] *adj* (*taste, smell*) enjoativo, nauseabundo.
club [klʌb] *n* (*society*) clube *m*; (*weapon*) cacete *m*; (*also*: *golf* ~) taco ♦ *vt* esbordoar ♦ *vi*: **to ~ together** cotizar-se; **~s** *npl* (CARDS) paus *mpl*.
club car (US) *n* vagão-restaurante *m*.
clubhouse ['klʌbhaus] (*irreg*) *n* sede *f* do clube.
cluck [klʌk] *vi* cacarejar.
clue [klu:] *n* indício, pista; (*in crossword*) definição *f*; **I haven't a ~** não faço idéia.
clued in [klu:d-] (US **clued in**) (*inf*) *adj* entendido.
clueless ['klu:lıs] (*inf*) *adj* burro.
clump [klʌmp] *n* (*of trees*) grupo.
clumsy ['klʌmzı] *adj* (*person*) desajeitado; (*movement*) deselegante, mal-feito.
clung [klʌŋ] *pt, pp of* **cling**.
cluster ['klʌstə*] *n* grupo; (BOT) cacho, ramo ♦ *vi* agrupar-se, apinhar-se.
clutch [klʌtʃ] *n* (*grip, grasp*) garra; (AUT) embreagem *f* (BR), embraiagem *f* (PT); (*pedal*) pedal *m* de embreagem (BR) *or* embraiagem (PT) ♦ *vt* empunhar, pegar em ♦ *vi*: **to ~ at** agarrar-se a.
clutter ['klʌtə*] *vt* abarrotar, encher desordenadamente ♦ *n* bagunça, desordem *f*.
CM (US) *abbr* (POST) = **North Mariana Islands.**
cm *abbr* (= *centimetre*) cm.
CNAA (BRIT) *n abbr* (= *Council for National Academic Awards*) *órgão não universitário que outorga diplomas.*
CND *n abbr* = **Campaign for Nuclear Disarmament.**
CO *n abbr* (= *commanding officer*) Com.; (BRIT) = **Commonwealth Office** ♦ *abbr* (US: POST) = **Colorado.**
Co. *abbr* = **county**; (= *company*) Cia.
c/o *abbr* (= *care of*) a/c.
coach [kəutʃ] *n* (*bus*) ônibus *m* (BR), autocarro (PT); (*horse-drawn*) carruagem *f*, coche *m*; (*of train*) vagão *m*; (SPORT) treinador(a) *m/f*, instrutor(a) *m/f* ♦ *vt* (SPORT) treinar; (*student*) preparar, ensinar.
coach trip *n* passeio de ônibus (BR) *or* autocarro (PT).
coagulate [kəu'ægjuleıt] *vi* coagular-se ♦ *vt* coagular.
coal [kəul] *n* carvão *m*.
coal face *n* frente *f* de carvão.
coalfield ['kəulfi:ld] *n* região *f* carbonífera.
coalition [kəuə'lıʃən] *n* coalizão *f*, coligação *f*.
coalman ['kəulmæn] (*irreg*) *n* carvoeiro.
coal merchant *n* carvoeiro.
coalmine ['kəulmaın] *n* mina de carvão.
coal miner *n* mineiro de carvão.
coal mining *n* mineração *f* de carvão.
coarse [kɔ:s] *adj* grosso, áspero; (*vulgar*) grosseiro, ordinário.
coast [kəust] *n* costa, litoral *m* ♦ *vi* (AUT) ir em ponto morto.
coastal ['kəustəl] *adj* costeiro, litorâneo.
coaster ['kəustə*] *n* embarcação *f* costeira, barco de cabotagem; (*for glass*) descanso.
coastguard ['kəustgɑ:d] *n* guarda costeira.
coastline ['kəustlaın] *n* litoral *m*.
coat [kəut] *n* (*jacket*) casaco; (*overcoat*) sobretudo; (*of animal*) pelo; (*of paint*) demão *f*, camada ♦ *vt* cobrir, revestir.

coat hanger *n* cabide *m*.
coating ['kəutɪŋ] *n* camada, revestimento.
coat of arms *n* brasão *m*.
co-author [kəu-] *n* co-autor(a) *m/f*.
coax [kəuks] *vt* persuadir com meiguice.
cob [kɔb] *n see* **corn**.
cobbler ['kɔblə*] *n* sapateiro.
cobbles ['kɔblz] *npl* pedras *fpl* arredondadas.
cobblestones ['kɔblstəunz] *npl* pedras *fpl* arredondadas.
COBOL ['kəubɔl] *n* COBOL *m*.
cobra ['kəubrə] *n* naja.
cobweb ['kɔbwɛb] *n* teia de aranha.
cocaine [kɔ'keɪn] *n* cocaína.
cock [kɔk] *n* (*rooster*) galo; (*male bird*) macho ♦ *vt* (*gun*) engatilhar; **to ~ one's ears** (*fig*) prestar atenção.
cock-a-hoop *adj* exultante, eufórico.
cockatoo [kɔkə'tu:] *n* cacatua.
cockerel ['kɔkərəl] *n* frango, galo pequeno.
cock-eyed [-aɪd] *adj* (*crooked*) torto; (*fig: scheme*) absurdo.
cockle ['kɔkl] *n* berbigão *m*.
cockney ['kɔknɪ] *n* londrino/a (*nativo dos bairros populares do leste de Londres*).
cockpit ['kɔkpɪt] *n* (*in aircraft*) cabina.
cockroach ['kɔkrəutʃ] *n* barata.
cocktail ['kɔkteɪl] *n* coquetel (*PT*: cocktail) *m*; **prawn** (*BRIT*) *or* **shrimp** (*US*) **~** coquetel de camarão (*BR*), cocktail de gambas (*PT*).
cocktail cabinet *n* móvel-bar *m*.
cocktail party *n* coquetel (*PT*: cocktail) *m*.
cocktail shaker [-ʃeɪkə*] *n* coqueteleira.
cocoa ['kəukəu] *n* cacau *m*; (*drink*) chocolate *m*.
coconut ['kəukənʌt] *n* coco.
cocoon [kə'ku:n] *n* casulo.
COD *abbr* = **cash** (*BRIT*) *or* **collect** (*US*) **on delivery**.
cod [kɔd] *n inv* bacalhau *m*.
code [kəud] *n* código; **~ of behaviour** código de comportamento; **~ of practice** deontologia.
codeine ['kəudi:n] *n* codeína.
code name *n* codinome *m*.
codicil ['kɔdɪsɪl] *n* codicilo.
codify ['kəudɪfaɪ] *vt* codificar.
cod-liver oil *n* óleo de fígado de bacalhau.
co-driver [kəu-] *n* (*in race*) co-piloto; (*in lorry*) segundo motorista *m*.
co-ed ['kəu'ɛd] *adj abbr* = **coeducational** ♦ *n* (*US: female student*) *aluna de escola mista*; (*BRIT: school*) escola mista.
coeducational ['kəuɛdju'keɪʃənl] *adj* misto.
coerce [kəu'ə:s] *vt* coagir.
coercion [kəu'ə:ʃən] *n* coerção *f*.
coexistence ['kəuɪg'zɪstəns] *n* coexistência.
C. of C. *n abbr* = **chamber of commerce**.
C of E *abbr* = **Church of England**.
coffee ['kɔfɪ] *n* café *m*; **white ~** (*BRIT*) *or* **~ with cream** (*US*) café com leite.
coffee bar (*BRIT*) *n* café *m*, lanchonete *f*.
coffee bean *n* grão *m* de café.
coffee break *n* hora do café.
coffeecake ['kɔfɪkeɪk] (*US*) *n* pão *m* doce com passas.
coffee cup *n* xícara (*BR*) *or* chávena (*PT*) de café.
coffee grounds *npl* borras *fpl* de café.
coffee plant *n* pé *m* de café.
coffee plantation *n* cafezal *m*.
coffeepot ['kɔfɪpɔt] *n* cafeteira.
coffee table *n* mesinha de centro.
coffin ['kɔfɪn] *n* caixão *m*.
C of I *abbr* = **Church of Ireland**.
C of S *abbr* = **Church of Scotland**.
cog [kɔg] *n* (*tooth*) dente *m*; (*wheel*) roda dentada.
cogent ['kəudʒənt] *adj* convincente.
cognac ['kɔnjæk] *n* conhaque *m*.
cogwheel ['kɔgwi:l] *n* roda dentada.
cohabit [kəu'hæbɪt] *vi* (*formal*): **to ~ (with sb)** coabitar (com alguém).
coherent [kəu'hɪərənt] *adj* coerente.
cohesion [kəu'hi:ʒən] *n* coesão *f*.
cohesive [kəu'hi:sɪv] *adj* coeso.
COHSE ['kəuzɪ] (*BRIT*) *n abbr* (= *Confederation of Health Service Employees*) *sindicato dos empregados do serviço de saúde*.
COI (*BRIT*) *n abbr* (= *Central Office of Information*) *serviço de informação governamental*.
coil [kɔɪl] *n* rolo; (*rope*) corda enrolada; (*of smoke*) espiral *f*; (*ELEC*) bobina; (*contraceptive*) DIU *m* ♦ *vt* enrolar, enroscar ♦ *vi* enrolar-se, espiralar-se.
coin [kɔɪn] *n* moeda ♦ *vt* (*word*) cunhar, criar.
coinage ['kɔɪnɪdʒ] *n* moeda, sistema *m* monetário.
coin-box (*BRIT*) *n* telefone *m* público.
coincide [kəuɪn'saɪd] *vi* coincidir.
coincidence [kəu'ɪnsɪdəns] *n* coincidência.
coin-operated [-'ɔpəreɪtɪd] *adj* (*machine, laundry*) automático, que funciona com moedas.
Coke [kəuk] ® *n* (*drink*) coca.
coke [kəuk] *n* (*coal*) coque *m*.
Col. *abbr* (= *colonel*) Cel.
COLA (*US*) *n abbr* (= *cost-of-living adjustment*) ≈ URP *f*.
colander ['kɔləndə*] *n* coador *m*, passador *m*.
cold [kəuld] *adj* frio ♦ *n* frio; (*MED*) resfriado (*BR*), constipação *f* (*PT*); **it's ~** está frio; **to be ~** estar com frio; **to catch ~** resfriar-se (*BR*), apanhar constipação (*PT*); **in ~ blood** a sangue frio; **to have ~ feet** (*fig*) estar com medo; **to give sb the ~ shoulder** tratar alguém com frieza, dar uma fria em alguém (*inf*).
cold-blooded [-'blʌdɪd] *adj* (*ZOOL*) de sangue frio; (*murder*) a sangue frio.
cold cream *n* creme *m* de limpeza.
coldly ['kəuldlɪ] *adv* friamente.
cold sore *n* herpes *m* labial.

NB: *European Portuguese adds the following consonants to certain words:* **b** (sú(b)dito, su(b)til); **c** (a(c)ção, a(c)cionista, a(c)to); **m** (inde(m)ne); **p** (ado(p)ção, ado(p)tar); *for further details see p. xiii.*

coleslaw ['kəulslɔː] *n* salada de repolho cru.
colic ['kɔlɪk] *n* cólica.
collaborate [kə'læbəreɪt] *vi* colaborar.
collaboration [kəlæbə'reɪʃən] *n* colaboração *f*.
collaborator [kə'læbəreɪtə*] *n* colaborador(a) *m/f*.
collage [kɔ'lɑːʒ] *n* colagem *f*.
collagen ['kɔlədʒən] *n* colágeno.
collapse [kə'læps] *vi* cair, tombar; (*roof*) dar de si, desabar; (*building*) desabar; (MED) desmaiar ♦ *n* desabamento, desmoronamento; (*of government*) queda; (MED) colapso.
collapsible [kə'læpsəbl] *adj* dobrável.
collar ['kɔlə*] *n* (*of shirt*) colarinho; (*of coat etc*) gola; (*for dog*) coleira; (TECH) aro, colar *m* ♦ *vt* (*inf*: *person*) prender.
collarbone ['kɔləbəun] *n* clavícula.
collate [kɔ'leɪt] *vt* cotejar.
collateral [kə'lætrəl] *n* garantia subsidiária *or* pignoratícia.
collation [kə'leɪʃən] *n* colação *f*.
colleague ['kɔliːg] *n* colega *m/f*.
collect [kə'lɛkt] *vt* reunir; (*as a hobby*) colecionar; (*pick up*) recolher; (*wages, debts*) cobrar; (*donations, subscriptions*) colher; (*mail*) coletar; (BRIT: *call for*) (ir) buscar ♦ *vi* (*people*) reunir-se; (*dust, dirt*) acumular-se ♦ *adv*: **to call ~** (US: TEL) ligar a cobrar; **to ~ one's thoughts** refletir; **~ on delivery** (US: COMM) pagamento na entrega.
collected [kə'lɛktɪd] *adj*: **~ works** obra completa.
collection [kə'lɛkʃən] *n* coleção *f*; (*of people*) reunião *f*, grupo; (*of donations*) arrecadação *f*; (*of post, in church*) coleta; (*of writings*) coletânea.
collective [kə'lɛktɪv] *adj* coletivo.
collective bargaining *n* negociação *f* coletiva.
collector [kə'lɛktə*] *n* colecionador(a) *m/f*; (*of taxes etc*) cobrador(a) *m/f*; **~'s item** *or* **piece** peça de coleção.
college ['kɔlɪdʒ] *n* colégio; (*faculty*) faculdade *f*; (*of technology, agriculture*) instituto, escola; **to go to ~** fazer faculdade; **~ of education** ≈ faculdade *f* de educação.
collide [kə'laɪd] *vi*: **to ~ (with)** colidir (com).
collie ['kɔlɪ] *n* collie *m*.
colliery ['kɔlɪərɪ] (BRIT) *n* mina de carvão.
collision [kə'lɪʒən] *n* choque *m*; **to be on a ~ course** estar em curso de colisão.
colloquial [kə'ləukwɪəl] *adj* familiar, coloquial.
collusion [kə'luːʒən] *n* colusão *f*, conluio; **in ~ with** em conluio com.
cologne [kə'ləun] *n* (*also*: *eau-de-~*) (água de) colônia.
Colombia [kə'lɔmbɪə] *n* Colômbia.
Colombian [kə'lɔmbɪən] *adj, n* colombiano/a.
colon ['kəulən] *n* (*sign*) dois pontos; (MED) cólon *m*.
colonel ['kəːnl] *n* coronel *m*.
colonial [kə'ləunɪəl] *adj* colonial.
colonize ['kɔlənaɪz] *vt* colonizar.
colony ['kɔlənɪ] *n* colônia.
color *etc* ['kʌlə*] (US) = **colour** *etc*.
Colorado beetle [kɔlə'rɑːdəu-] *n* besouro da batata, dorífora.
colossal [kə'lɔsl] *adj* colossal.
colour ['kʌlə*] (US **color**) *n* cor *f* ♦ *vt* colorir; (*with crayons*) colorir, pintar; (*dye*) tingir; (*news*) falsear ♦ *vi* (*blush*) corar ♦ *cpd* (*photograph etc*) a cores; **~s** *npl* (*of party, club*) cores *fpl*.
colo(u)r bar *n* discriminação *f* racial.
colo(u)r-blind ['kʌləblaɪnd] *adj* daltônico.
colo(u)red ['kʌləd] *adj* colorido; (*person*) de cor.
colo(u)reds ['kʌlədz] *npl* gente *f* de cor.
colo(u)r film *n* filme *m* a cores.
colo(u)rful ['kʌləful] *adj* colorido; (*personality*) vivo, animado.
colo(u)ring ['kʌlərɪŋ] *n* colorido; (*complexion*) tez *f*.
colo(u)rless ['kʌləlɪs] *adj* sem cor, pálido.
colo(u)r scheme *n* distribuição *f* de cores.
colour supplement (BRIT) *n* (PRESS) revista, suplemento a cores.
colo(u)r television *n* televisão *f* a cores.
colt [kəult] *n* potro.
column ['kɔləm] *n* coluna; **the editorial ~** o editorial.
columnist ['kɔləmnɪst] *n* cronista *m/f*.
coma ['kəumə] *n* coma *m*.
comb [kəum] *n* pente *m*; (*of cock*) crista ♦ *vt* (*hair*) pentear; (*area*) vasculhar.
combat ['kɔmbæt] *n* combate *m* ♦ *vt* combater.
combination [kɔmbɪ'neɪʃən] *n* combinação *f*; (*of safe*) segredo.
combination lock *n* fechadura de combinação.
combine [*vt, vi* kəm'baɪn, *n* 'kɔmbaɪn] *vt* combinar; (*qualities*) reunir ♦ *vi* combinar-se ♦ *n* (ECON) associação *f*; (*pej*) monopólio; **a ~d effort** um esforço conjunto.
combine (harvester) *n* ceifeira debulhadora.
combo ['kɔmbəu] *n* (JAZZ *etc*) conjunto.
combustible [kəm'bʌstɪbl] *adj* combustível.
combustion [kəm'bʌstʃən] *n* combustão *f*.
come [kʌm] (*pt* **came**, *pp* **come**) *vi* vir; (*inf*: *sexually*) gozar; **he is coming with us to Paris** ele vai a Paris com a gente; **... what might ~ of it** ... o que poderia resultar disso; **to ~ into sight** *or* **view** aparecer; **to ~ to** (*conclusion etc*) chegar a; **to ~ undone/loose** desfazer-se/soltar-se; **coming!** já vou!; **it if ~s to it** em último caso.
come about *vi* suceder, acontecer.
come across *vt fus* (*person*) topar com; (*thing*) encontrar ♦ *vi*: **to ~ across well/badly** fazer uma boa/má impressão.
come along *vi* (*pupil, work*) ir bem; **~ along!** vem!
come apart *vi* desfazer-se.
come away *vi* ir-se embora; (*become detached*) desprender-se, soltar-se.
come back *vi* voltar; (*reply*): **can I ~ back to you on that one?** posso lhe dar uma resposta sobre isso mais tarde?

come by *vt fus* (*acquire*) conseguir.
come down *vi* descer; (*prices*) baixar; (*crash*) desabar; (*buildings*) desmoronar-se; (: *be demolished*) ser derrubado.
come forward *vi* apresentar-se; (*move forward*) avançar.
come from *vt fus* vir de; (*place*: *subj*: *person*) ser de; (: *thing*) originar-se de.
come in *vi* entrar; (*train*) chegar; (*fashion*) entrar na moda.
come in for *vt fus* (*criticism etc*) merecer.
come into *vt fus* (*money*) herdar.
come off *vi* (*button*) desprender-se, soltar-se; (*attempt*) dar certo.
come on *vi* (*pupil, undertaking*) avançar, fazer progressos; (*lights, heating*) ser ligado ♦ *vt fus* (*find*) encontrar; ~ **on!** vamos!, vai!
come out *vi* sair; (*book*) ser publicado; (*be revealed*) revelar-se; (*strike*) entrar em greve; **to ~ out for/against** declarar-se por/contra.
come over *vt fus*: **I don't know what's ~ over him!** eu não sei o que deu nele.
come round *vi* (*after faint etc*) voltar a si.
come through *vi* (*survive*) sobreviver; (*telephone call*) ser completado.
come to *vi* voltar a si ♦ *vt fus* (*total*) somar.
come under *vt fus* (*heading*) incluir-se em, estar sob; (*influence*) estar sujeito a.
come up *vi* subir; (*sun*) nascer; (*problem*) surgir.
come up against *vt fus* (*resistance, difficulties*) tropeçar com, esbarrar em.
come up to *vt fus* alcançar; (*expectations*) corresponder a.
come up with *vt fus* (*idea*) propor, sugerir.
come upon *vt fus* encontrar, achar.
comeback ['kʌmbæk] *n* (*THEATRE*) reaparição *f*; (*reaction*) reação *f*; (*response*) resposta.
Comecon ['kɔmɪkɔn] *n abbr* (= *Council for Mutual Economic Aid*) COMECON *m*.
comedian [kə'miːdɪən] *n* cômico, humorista *m*.
comedienne [kəmiːdɪ'ɛn] *n* cômica, humorista.
comedown ['kʌmdaun] (*inf*) *n* revés *m*, humilhação *f*.
comedy ['kɔmɪdɪ] *n* comédia.
comet ['kɔmɪt] *n* cometa *m*.
comeuppance [kʌm'ʌpəns] *n*: **to get one's ~ (for sth)** pagar (por algo).
comfort ['kʌmfət] *n* comodidade *f*, conforto; (*well-being*) bem-estar *m*; (*solace*) consolo; (*relief*) alívio ♦ *vt* consolar, confortar; **~s** *npl* conforto.
comfortable ['kʌmfətəbl] *adj* confortável; **I don't feel very ~ about it** não estou completamente conformado com isso.
comfortably ['kʌmfətəblɪ] *adv* confortavelmente.
comforter ['kʌmfətə*] (*US*) *n* edredom (*PT*: -dão) *m*.
comfort station (*US*) *n* banheiro (*BR*), lavatórios *mpl* (*PT*).
comic ['kɔmɪk] *adj* cômico ♦ *n* (*person*) cômico/a, humorista *m/f*; (*magazine*) revista em quadrinhos (*BR*), revista de banda desenhada (*PT*), gibi *m* (*BR*: *inf*).
comical ['kɔmɪkl] *adj* engraçado, cômico.
comic strip *n* história em quadrinhos (*BR*), banda desenhada (*PT*).
coming ['kʌmɪŋ] *n* vinda, chegada ♦ *adj* que vem, vindouro; **~(s) and going(s)** *n*(*pl*) vaivém *m*, azáfama; **in the ~ weeks** nas próximas semanas.
Comintern ['kɔmɪntəːn] *n* Comintern *m*.
comma ['kɔmə] *n* vírgula.
command [kə'mɑːnd] *n* ordem *f*, mandado; (*MIL*: *authority*) comando; (*mastery*) domínio; (*COMPUT*) comando ♦ *vt* (*troops*) mandar; (*give orders to*) mandar, ordenar; (*dispose of*) dispor de; (*deserve*) merecer; **to ~ sb to do** mandar alguém fazer; **to have/take ~ of** ter/assumir o controle de; **to have at one's ~** (*money, resources etc*) dispor de.
commandeer [kɔmən'dɪə*] *vt* requisitar.
commander [kə'mɑːndə*] *n* (*MIL*) comandante *m/f*.
commander-in-chief *n* (*MIL*) comandante-em-chefe *m/f*, comandante-chefe *m/f*.
commanding [kə'mɑːndɪŋ] *adj* (*appearance*) imponente; (*voice, tone*) autoritário, imperioso; (*lead, position*) dominante.
commanding officer *n* comandante *m/f*.
commandment [kə'mɑːndmənt] *n* (*REL*) mandamento.
command module *n* (*SPACE*) módulo de comando.
commando [kə'mɑːndəu] *n* comando.
commemorate [kə'mɛməreɪt] *vt* comemorar.
commemoration [kəmɛmə'reɪʃən] *n* comemoração *f*.
commemorative [kə'mɛmərətɪv] *adj* comemorativo.
commence [kə'mɛns] *vt, vi* começar, iniciar.
commend [kə'mɛnd] *vt* (*praise*) elogiar, louvar; (*recommend*) recomendar; (*entrust*) encomendar.
commendable [kə'mɛndəbl] *adj* louvável.
commendation [kɔmɛn'deɪʃən] *n* elogio, louvor *m*.
commensurate [kə'mɛnʃərɪt] *adj*: **~ with** compatível com.
comment ['kɔmɛnt] *n* comentário ♦ *vi* fazer comentários, comentar; **to ~ on sth** comentar algo; **to ~ that** observar que; **"no ~"** "sem comentário".
commentary ['kɔməntərɪ] *n* comentário.
commentator ['kɔmənteɪtə*] *n* comentarista *m/f*.
commerce ['kɔməːs] *n* comércio.
commercial [kə'məːʃəl] *adj* comercial ♦ *n*

NB: European Portuguese adds the following consonants to certain words: **b** (sú(b)dito, su(b)til); **c** (a(c)ção, a(c)cionista, a(c)to); **m** (inde(m)ne); **p** (ado(p)ção, ado(p)tar); *for further details see p. xiii.*

anúncio, comercial *m*; ~ **break** intervalo para os comerciais.
commercial bank *n* banco comercial.
commercial college *n* escola de comércio.
commercialism [kə'mə:ʃəlɪzəm] *n* mercantilismo.
commercialize [kə'mə:ʃəlaɪz] *vt* comercializar.
commercial television *n* televisão *f* comercial.
commercial traveller *n* caixeiro/a-viajante *m/f*.
commercial vehicle *n* (veículo) utilitário.
commiserate [kə'mɪzəreɪt] *vi*: **to ~ with** comiserar-se de, condoer-se de.
commission [kə'mɪʃən] *n* (*body, fee*) comissão *f*; (*act*) incumbência; (*order for work of art etc*) empreitada, encomenda ♦ *vt* (*MIL*) dar patente oficial a; (*work of art*) encomendar; (*artist*) incumbir; **out of ~** (*NAUT*) fora do serviço ativo; (*machine*) com defeito; **to ~ sb to do sth** mandar alguém fazer algo; **to ~ sth from sb** encomendar algo a alguém; **~ of inquiry** (*BRIT*) comissão de inquérito.
commissionaire [kəmɪʃə'nɛə*] (*BRIT*) *n* porteiro.
commissioner [kə'mɪʃənə*] *n* comissário/a.
commit [kə'mɪt] *vt* (*act*) cometer; (*to sb's care*) entregar; **to ~ o.s. (to do)** comprometer-se (a fazer); **to ~ suicide** suicidar-se; **to ~ to writing** pôr por escrito, pôr no papel; **to ~ sb for trial** levar alguém a julgamento.
commitment [kə'mɪtmənt] *n* (*obligation*) compromisso; (*political etc*) engajamento.
committed [kə'mɪtɪd] *adj* (*writer, politician etc*) engajado.
committee [kə'mɪtɪ] *n* comitê *m*; **to be on a ~** ser membro de um comitê.
committee meeting *n* reunião *f* de comitê.
commodity [kə'mɔdɪtɪ] *n* mercadoria; **commodities** *npl* (*COMM*) commodities *mpl*.
commodity exchange *n* bolsa de mercadorias.
common ['kɔmən] *adj* comum; (*pej*) ordinário ♦ *n* terrenos baldios *mpl*; **C~s** *npl* (*BRIT*: *POL*): **the (House of) C~s** a Câmara dos Comuns; **in ~** em comum; **in ~ use** de uso corrente; **it's ~ knowledge that** todos sabem que; **to the ~ good** para o bem comum.
commoner ['kɔmənə*] *n* plebeu/béia *m/f*.
common ground *n* (*fig*) consenso.
common law *n* lei *f* consuetudinária ♦ *adj*: **common-law wife** concubina.
commonly ['kɔmənlɪ] *adv* geralmente.
Common Market *n* Mercado Comum.
commonplace ['kɔmənpleɪs] *adj* vulgar, trivial ♦ *n* lugar-comum *m*.
common room *n* sala comum; (*SCH*) sala dos professores (*or* estudantes).
common sense *n* bom senso.
Commonwealth ['kɔmənwɛlθ] *n*: **the ~** a Comunidade Britânica.
commotion [kə'məuʃən] *n* tumulto, confusão *f*.
communal ['kɔmju:nl] *adj* (*life*) comunal; (*bathroom etc*) social.
commune [*n* 'kɔmju:n, *vi* kə'mju:n] *n* (*group*) comuna ♦ *vi*: **to ~ with** conversar com.
communicate [kə'mju:nɪkeɪt] *vt* comunicar ♦ *vi*: **to ~ (with)** comunicar-se (com).
communication [kəmju:nɪ'keɪʃən] *n* comunicação *f*.
communication cord (*BRIT*) *n* sinal *m* de alarme.
communications network *n* rede *f* de comunicações.
communications satellite *n* satélite *m* de comunicações.
communicative [kə'mju:nɪkətɪv] *adj* comunicativo.
communion [kə'mju:nɪən] *n* (*also*: *Holy C~*) comunhão *f*.
communiqué [kə'mju:nɪkeɪ] *n* comunicado.
communism ['kɔmjunɪzəm] *n* comunismo.
communist ['kɔmjunɪst] *adj*, *n* comunista *m/f*.
community [kə'mju:nɪtɪ] *n* comunidade *f*.
community centre *n* centro social.
community chest (*US*) *n* fundo de assistência social.
community health centre *n* centro de saúde comunitário.
community service *n* serviços *mpl* comunitários.
community spirit *n* espírito comunitário.
commutation ticket [kɔmju'teɪʃən-] (*US*) *n* passe *m*, bilhete *m* de assinatura.
commute [kə'mju:t] *vi* viajar diariamente ♦ *vt* comutar.
commuter [kə'mju:tə*] *n* viajante *m/f* habitual.
compact [*adj* kəm'pækt, *n* 'kɔmpækt] *adj* compacto; (*style*) conciso ♦ *n* (*pact*) pacto; (*for powder*) estojo.
compact disk *n* disco laser.
companion [kəm'pænɪən] *n* companheiro/a.
companionship [kəm'pænɪənʃɪp] *n* companhia; (*spirit*) camaradagem *f*.
companionway [kəm'pænjənweɪ] *n* (*NAUT*) escada de tombadilho.
company ['kʌmpənɪ] *n* companhia; (*COMM*) sociedade *f*, companhia; **he's good ~** ele é uma boa companhia; **we have ~** temos visita; **to keep sb ~** fazer companhia a alguém; **to part ~ with** separar-se de; **Smith and C~** Smith e Companhia.
company car *n* carro da companhia.
company director *n* administrador(a) *m/f* de companhia.
company secretary (*BRIT*) *n* (*COMM*) secretário/a geral (*de uma companhia*).
comparable ['kɔmpərəbl] *adj* comparável.
comparative [kəm'pærətɪv] *adj* comparativo; (*relative*) relativo.
comparatively [kəm'pærətɪvlɪ] *adj* (*relatively*) relativamente.
compare [kəm'pɛə*] *vt* (*set side by side*) cotejar; (*contrast*): **to ~ (to/with)** comparar (a/com) ♦ *vi*: **to ~ with** comparar-se com; **how**

do the prices ~? qual é a diferença entre os preços?; **~d with** *or* **to** em comparação com.
comparison [kəm'pærɪsn] *n* comparação *f*; **in ~ with** em comparação com, comparado com.
compartment [kəm'pɑːtmənt] *n* (*also*: RAIL) compartimento.
compass ['kʌmpəs] *n* bússola; **within the ~ of** no âmbito de.
compasses ['kʌmpəsɪz] *npl* compasso.
compassion [kəm'pæʃən] *n* compaixão *f*.
compassionate [kəm'pæʃənət] *adj* compassivo; **on ~ grounds** por motivos humanitários.
compatibility [kɔmpætɪ'bɪlɪtɪ] *n* compatibilidade *f*.
compatible [kəm'pætɪbl] *adj* compatível.
compel [kəm'pɛl] *vt* obrigar.
compelling [kəm'pɛlɪŋ] *adj* (*fig*: *argument*) convincente.
compendium [kəm'pɛndɪəm] *n* compêndio.
compensate ['kɔmpənseɪt] *vt* (*financially*) indenizar ♦ *vi*: **to ~ for** compensar.
compensation [kɔmpən'seɪʃən] *n* compensação *f*; (*damages*) indenização *f*.
compère ['kɔmpɛə*] *n* apresentador(a) *m/f*.
compete [kəm'piːt] *vi* (*take part*) competir, concorrer; (*vie*): **to ~ (with)** competir (com), fazer competição (com).
competence ['kɔmpɪtəns] *n* competência, capacidade *f*.
competent ['kɔmpɪtənt] *adj* competente.
competition [kɔmpɪ'tɪʃən] *n* (*contest*) concurso; (ECON) concorrência; (*rivalry*) competição *f*; **in ~ with** em competição com.
competitive [kəm'pɛtɪtɪv] *adj* (ECON, *sport*) competitivo; (*spirit*) competidor(a), de rivalidade.
competitive examination *n* concurso.
competitor [kəm'pɛtɪtə*] *n* (*rival*) competidor(a) *m/f*; (*participant*, ECON) concorrente *m/f*; **our ~s** (COMM) a (nossa) concorrência.
compile [kəm'paɪl] *vt* compilar, compor.
complacency [kəm'pleɪsnsɪ] *n* satisfação *f* consigo mesmo.
complacent [kəm'pleɪsənt] *adj* relaxado, acomodado.
complain [kəm'pleɪn] *vi*: **to ~ (about)** queixar-se (de); (*in shop etc*) reclamar (de).
complain of *vt fus* (MED) sofrer de.
complaint [kəm'pleɪnt] *n* queixa; (*in shop etc*) reclamação *f*; (JUR) querela; (MED) achaque *m*, doença.
complement ['kɔmplɪmənt] *n* complemento; (*esp ship's crew*) tripulação *f* ♦ *vt* complementar.
complementary [kɔmplɪ'mɛntərɪ] *adj* complementar.
complete [kəm'pliːt] *adj* (*full*) completo; (*finished*) acabado ♦ *vt* (*fulfil*) completar; (*finish*) acabar; (*a form*) preencher; **a ~ disaster** um desastre total.
completely [kəm'pliːtlɪ] *adv* completamente.
completion [kəm'pliːʃən] *n* conclusão *f*, término; (*of contract etc*) realização *f*; **to be nearing ~** estar quase pronto; **on ~ of contract** na assinatura do contrato; (*for house*) na escritura.
complex ['kɔmplɛks] *adj* complexo ♦ *n* (PSYCH, *of ideas etc*) complexo; (*of buildings*) conjunto.
complexion [kəm'plɛkʃən] *n* (*of face*) cor *f*, tez *f*; (*fig*) aspecto.
complexity [kəm'plɛksɪtɪ] *n* complexidade *f*.
compliance [kəm'plaɪəns] *n* (*submission*) submissão *f*; (*agreement*) conformidade *f*; **in ~ with** de acordo com, conforme.
compliant [kəm'plaɪənt] *adj* complacente, submisso.
complicate ['kɔmplɪkeɪt] *vt* complicar.
complicated ['kɔmplɪkeɪtɪd] *adj* complicado.
complication [kɔmplɪ'keɪʃən] *n* complicação *f*.
complicity [kəm'plɪsɪtɪ] *n* cumplicidade *f*.
compliment [*n* 'kɔmplɪmənt, *vt* 'kɔmplɪmɛnt] *n* (*formal*) cumprimento; (*praise*) elogio ♦ *vt* elogiar; **~s** *npl* cumprimentos *mpl*; **to pay sb a ~** elogiar alguém; **to ~ sb (on sth/on doing sth)** cumprimentar *or* elogiar alguém (por algo/por ter feito algo).
complimentary [kɔmplɪ'mɛntərɪ] *adj* lisonjeiro; (*free*) gratuito.
complimentary ticket *n* entrada de favor *or* de cortesia.
compliments slip *n* memorando.
comply [kəm'plaɪ] *vi*: **to ~ with** cumprir com.
component [kəm'pəunənt] *adj* componente ♦ *n* (TECH) peça; (*element*) componente *m*.
compose [kəm'pəuz] *vt* compor; **to be ~d of** compor-se de; **to ~ o.s.** tranqüilizar-se.
composed [kəm'pəuzd] *adj* calmo.
composer [kəm'pəuzə*] *n* (MUS) compositor(a) *m/f*.
composite ['kɔmpəzɪt] *adj* composto.
composition [kɔmpə'zɪʃən] *n* composição *f*.
compost ['kɔmpɔst] *n* adubo.
composure [kəm'pəuʒə*] *n* serenidade *f*, calma.
compound [*n*, *adj* 'kɔmpaund, *vt* kəm'paund] *n* (CHEM, LING) composto; (*enclosure*) recinto ♦ *adj* composto; (*fracture*) complicado ♦ *vt* (*fig*: *problem etc*) agravar.
compound interest *n* juro composto.
comprehend [kɔmprɪ'hɛnd] *vt* compreender.
comprehension [kɔmprɪ'hɛnʃən] *n* compreensão *f*.
comprehensive [kɔmprɪ'hɛnsɪv] *adj* abrangente.
comprehensive insurance policy *n* apólice *f* de seguro com cobertura total.
comprehensive (school) (BRIT) *n* *escola secundária de amplo programa.*
compress [*vt* kəm'prɛs, *n* 'kɔmprɛs] *vt* comprimir ♦ *n* (MED) compressa.
compression [kəm'prɛʃən] *n* compressão *f*.

***NB**: European Portuguese adds the following consonants to certain words:* **b** (sú(b)dito, su(b)til); **c** (a(c)ção, a(c)cionista, a(c)to); **m** (inde(m)ne); **p** (ado(p)ção, ado(p)tar); *for further details see p. xiii.*

comprise [kəm'praɪz] *vt* (*also*: *be ~d of*) compreender, constar de.
compromise ['kɔmprəmaɪz] *n* meio-termo ♦ *vt* comprometer ♦ *vi* chegar a um meio-termo ♦ *cpd* (*decision, solution*) de meio-termo.
compulsion [kəm'pʌlʃən] *n* compulsão *f*; **under ~** sob coação, à força.
compulsive [kəm'pʌlsɪv] *adj* (*PSYCH*) compulsório; **he's a ~ smoker** ele não pode deixar de fumar.
compulsory [kəm'pʌlsərɪ] *adj* obrigatório.
compulsory purchase *n* compra compulsória.
compunction [kəm'pʌŋkʃən] *n* compunção; **to have no ~ about doing sth** não hesitar em fazer algo.
computer [kəm'pju:tə*] *n* computador *m*.
computerize [kəm'pju:təraɪz] *vt* informatizar, computadorizar.
computer language *n* linguagem *f* de máquina.
computer peripheral *n* periférico.
computer program *n* programa *m* de computador.
computer progra(m)mer *n* programador(a) *m/f*.
computer program(m)ing *n* programação *f*.
computer science *n* informática, computação *f*.
computer scientist *n* cientista *m/f* da computação.
computing [kəm'pju:tɪŋ] *n* informática, computação *f*.
comrade ['kɔmrɪd] *n* camarada *m/f*.
comradeship ['kɔmrɪdʃɪp] *n* camaradagem *f*.
comsat ['kɔmsæt] *n abbr* = **communications satellite**.
con [kɔn] *vt* enganar ♦ *n* vigarice *f*; **~s** *npl see* **convenience**; **pro**; **to ~ sb into doing sth** convencer alguém a fazer algo (por artimanhas).
concave [kɔn'keɪv] *adj* côncavo.
conceal [kən'si:l] *vt* ocultar.
concede [kən'si:d] *vt* conceder ♦ *vi* ceder.
conceit [kən'si:t] *n* presunção *f*.
conceited [kən'si:tɪd] *adj* presunçoso.
conceivable [kən'si:vəbl] *adj* concebível; **it is ~ that** é possível que.
conceivably [kən'si:vəblɪ] *adv*: **he may ~ be right** é possível que ele tenha razão.
conceive [kən'si:v] *vt* conceber ♦ *vi*: **to ~ of sth/of doing sth** conceber algo/fazer idéia de fazer algo.
concentrate ['kɔnsəntreɪt] *vi* concentrar-se ♦ *vt* concentrar.
concentration [kɔnsən'treɪʃən] *n* concentração *f*.
concentration camp *n* campo de concentração.
concentric [kɔn'sɛntrɪk] *adj* concêntrico.
concept ['kɔnsɛpt] *n* conceito.
conception [kən'sɛpʃən] *n* (*idea*) conceito, idéia; (*BIO*) concepção *f*.
concern [kən'sə:n] *n* (*matter*) assunto; (*COMM*) empresa; (*anxiety*) preocupação *f* ♦ *vt* dizer respeito a; **to be ~ed (about)** preocupar-se (com); **"to whom it may ~"** "a quem interessar possa"; **as far as I'm ~ed** no que me diz respeito, quanto a mim; **to be ~ed with** (*person*: *involved with*) ocupar-se de; (*book*: *be about*) tratar de; **the department ~ed** (*under discussion*) o departamento em questão; (*relevant*) o departamento competente.
concerning [kən'sə:nɪŋ] *prep* sobre, a respeito de, acerca de.
concert ['kɔnsət] *n* concerto; **in ~** de comum acordo.
concerted [kən'sə:tɪd] *adj* (*joint*) conjunto; (*strong*) sério.
concert hall *n* sala de concertos.
concertina [kɔnsə'ti:nə] *n* sanfona, concertina ♦ *vi* engavetar-se.
concert master (*US*) *n* primeiro violino de uma orquestra.
concerto [kən'tʃə:təu] *n* concerto.
concession [kən'sɛʃən] *n* concessão *f*.
concessionaire [kənsɛʃə'nɛə*] *n* concessionário/a.
concessionary [kən'sɛʃənrɪ] *adj* (*ticket, fare*) a preço reduzido.
conciliation [kənsɪlɪ'eɪʃən] *n* conciliação *f*.
conciliatory [kən'sɪlɪətrɪ] *adj* conciliador(a).
concise [kən'saɪs] *adj* conciso.
conclave ['kɔnkleɪv] *n* conclave *m*.
conclude [kən'klu:d] *vt* (*finish*) acabar, concluir; (*treaty etc*) firmar; (*agreement*) chegar a; (*decide*): **to ~ that** chegar à conclusão de que ♦ *vi* terminar, acabar.
conclusion [kən'klu:ʒən] *n* conclusão *f*; **to come to the ~ that** chegar à conclusão de que.
conclusive [kən'klu:sɪv] *adj* conclusivo, decisivo.
concoct [kən'kɔkt] *vt* confeccionar; (*plot*) fabricar, tramar.
concoction [kən'kɔkʃən] *n* (*food, drink*) mistura.
concord ['kɔŋkɔ:d] *n* (*harmony*) concórdia; (*treaty*) acordo.
concourse ['kɔŋkɔ:s] *n* (*hall*) saguão *m*; (*crowd*) multidão *f*.
concrete ['kɔnkri:t] *n* concreto (*BR*), betão *m* (*PT*) ♦ *adj* concreto.
concrete mixer *n* betoneira.
concur [kən'kə:*] *vi* estar de acordo, concordar.
concurrently [kən'kʌrntlɪ] *adv* ao mesmo tempo, simultaneamente.
concussion [kən'kʌʃən] *n* (*MED*) concussão *f* cerebral.
condemn [kən'dɛm] *vt* condenar.
condemnation [kɔndɛm'neɪʃən] *n* condenação *f*; (*blame*) censura.
condensation [kɔndɛn'seɪʃən] *n* condensação *f*.
condense [kən'dɛns] *vi* condensar-se ♦ *vt* condensar.
condensed milk [kən'dɛnst-] *n* leite *m*

condensado.
condescend [kɔndɪ'sɛnd] *vi* condescender, dignar-se; **to ~ to do sth** condescender a fazer algo.
condescending [kɔndɪ'sɛndɪŋ] *adj* condescendente.
condition [kən'dɪʃən] *n* condição *f*; (*health*) estado de saúde ♦ *vt* condicionar; **on ~ that** com a condição (de) que; **in good/poor ~** em bom/mau estado (de conservação); **a heart ~** um problema no coração; **weather ~s** condições *fpl* meteorológicas.
conditional [kən'dɪʃənl] *adj* condicional; **to be ~ upon** depender de.
conditioner [kən'dɪʃənə*] *n* (*for hair*) condicionador *m*.
condo ['kɔndəu] (*US*: *inf*) *n abbr* = **condominium**.
condolences [kən'dəulənsɪz] *npl* pêsames *mpl*.
condom ['kɔndɔm] *n* preservativo, camisa-de-Venus *f*.
condominium [kɔndə'mɪnɪəm] (*US*) *n* (*building*) edifício; (*rooms*) apartamento.
condone [kən'dəun] *vt* admitir, aceitar.
conducive [kən'djuːsɪv] *adj*: **~ to** conducente para *or* a.
conduct [*n* 'kɔndʌkt, *vt, vi* kən'dʌkt] *n* conduta, comportamento ♦ *vt* (*lead*) conduzir; (*manage*) dirigir; (*MUS*) reger ♦ *vi* (*MUS*) reger uma orquestra; **to ~ o.s.** comportar-se.
conducted tour [kən'dʌktɪd-] *n* viagem *f* organizada; (*of building etc*) visita guiada.
conductor [kən'dʌktə*] *n* (*of orchestra*) regente *m/f*; (*on bus*) cobrador(a) *m/f*; (*RAIL*) revisor(a) *m/f*; (*ELEC*) condutor *m*.
conductress [kən'dʌktrɪs] *n* (*on bus*) cobradora.
conduit ['kɔndɪt] *n* conduto.
cone [kəun] *n* cone *m*; (*for ice-cream*) casquinha; **pine ~** pinha.
confectioner [kən'fɛkʃənə*] *n* confeiteiro/a (*BR*), pasteleiro/a (*PT*); **~'s (shop)** confeitaria (*BR*), pastelaria (*PT*); (*sweet shop*) confeitaria.
confectionery [kən'fɛkʃnərɪ] *n* (*cakes*) bolos *mpl*; (*sweets*) doces *mpl*.
confederate [kən'fɛdrɪt] *adj* confederado ♦ *n* cúmplice *m/f*; (*US*: *HISTORY*) confederado/a (sulista).
confederation [kənfɛdə'reɪʃən] *n* confederação *f*.
confer [kən'fəː*] *vt*: **to ~ on** outorgar a ♦ *vi* conferenciar.
conference ['kɔnfərns] *n* (*meeting*) congresso; **to be in ~** estar em conferência.
conference room *n* sala de conferência.
confess [kən'fɛs] *vt* confessar ♦ *vi* confessar-se.
confession [kən'fɛʃən] *n* confissão *f*.
confessional [kən'fɛʃənl] *n* confessionário.
confessor [kən'fɛsə*] *n* confessor *m*.
confetti [kən'fɛtɪ] *n* confete *m*.
confide [kən'faɪd] *vi*: **to ~ in** confiar em, fiar-se em.
confidence ['kɔnfɪdns] *n* confiança; (*secret*) confidência; **to have (every) ~ that** ter certeza de que; **motion of no ~** moção de não confiança; **in ~** em confidência.
confidence trick *n* conto do vigário.
confident ['kɔnfɪdnt] *adj* confiante, convicto.
confidential [kɔnfɪ'dɛnʃəl] *adj* confidencial; (*secretary*) de confiança.
confidentiality ['kɔnfɪdɛnʃɪ'ælɪtɪ] *n* sigilo.
configuration [kən'fɪgju'reɪʃən] *n* (*also*: *COMPUT*) configuração *f*.
confine [kən'faɪn] *vt* (*limit*) limitar; (*shut up*) encarcerar; **to ~ o.s. to (doing) sth** limitar-se a (fazer) algo.
confined [kən'faɪnd] *adj* (*space*) reduzido, retido.
confinement [kən'faɪnmənt] *n* (*prison*) prisão *f*; (*enclosure*) reclusão *f*; (*MED*) parto.
confines ['kɔnfaɪnz] *npl* confins *mpl*.
confirm [kən'fəːm] *vt* confirmar.
confirmation [kɔnfə'meɪʃən] *n* confirmação *f*.
confirmed [kən'fəːmd] *adj* inveterado.
confiscate ['kɔnfɪskeɪt] *vt* confiscar.
confiscation [kɔnfɪs'keɪʃən] *n* confiscação *f*.
conflagration [kɔnflə'greɪʃən] *n* conflagração *f*.
conflict [*n* 'kɔnflɪkt, *vi* kən'flɪkt] *n* conflito ♦ *vi* estar em conflito; (*opinions*) divergir.
conflicting [kən'flɪktɪŋ] *adj* (*views*) divergente; (*interests*) oposto; (*account*) discrepante.
conform [kən'fɔːm] *vi* conformar-se; **to ~ to** ajustar-se a, acomodar-se a.
conformist [kən'fɔːmɪst] *n* conformista *m/f*.
confound [kən'faund] *vt* confundir; (*amaze*) desconcertar.
confounded [kən'faundɪd] *adj* maldito.
confront [kən'frʌnt] *vt* (*problems*) enfrentar; (*enemy, danger*) defrontar-se com.
confrontation [kɔnfrən'teɪʃən] *n* confrontação *f*.
confuse [kən'fjuːz] *vt* (*perplex*) desconcertar; (*mix up*) confundir, misturar.
confused [kən'fjuːzd] *adj* confuso; (*person*) perplexo, confuso.
confusing [kən'fjuːzɪŋ] *adj* confuso.
confusion [kən'fjuːʒən] *n* confusão *f*.
congeal [kən'dʒiːl] *vi* (*freeze*) congelar-se; (*coagulate*) coagular-se.
congenial [kən'dʒiːnɪəl] *adj* simpático, agradável.
congenital [kən'dʒɛnɪtl] *adj* congênito.
conger eel ['kɔŋge*-] *n* congro.
congested [kən'dʒɛstɪd] *adj* (*gen*) congestionado.
congestion [kən'dʒɛstʃən] *n* (*MED*) congestão *f*; (*traffic*) congestionamento.
conglomerate [kən'glɔmərɪt] *n* (*COMM*) conglomerado.
conglomeration [kənglɔmə'reɪʃən] *n* conglo-

***NB**: European Portuguese adds the following consonants to certain words:* **b** (sú(b)dito, su(b)til); **c** (a(c)ção, a(c)cionista, a(c)to); **m** (inde(m)ne); **p** (ado(p)ção, ado(p)tar); *for further details see p. xiii.*

meração *f*, aglomeração *f*.
Congo ['kɔŋgəu] *n* (*state*) Congo.
congratulate [kən'grætjuleɪt] *vt*: **to ~ sb (on)** felicitar *or* parabenizar alguém (por).
congratulations [kəngrætju'leɪʃənz] *npl*: **~ (on)** parabéns *mpl* (por) ♦ *excl* parabéns!
congregate ['kɔŋgrɪgeɪt] *vi* reunir-se.
congregation [kɔŋgrɪ'geɪʃən] *n* (*in church*) fiéis *mpl*; (*assembly*) congregação *f*, reunião *f*.
congress ['kɔŋgrɛs] *n* congresso.
congressman ['kɔŋgrɛsmən] (*US*: *irreg*) *n* deputado.
congresswoman ['kɔŋgrɛswumən] (*US*: *irreg*) *n* deputada.
conical ['kɔnɪkl] *adj* cônico.
conifer ['kɔnɪfə*] *n* conífera.
coniferous [kə'nɪfərəs] *adj* (*forest*) conífero.
conjecture [kən'dʒɛktʃə*] *n* conjetura ♦ *vt*, *vi* conjeturar.
conjugal ['kɔndʒugl] *adj* conjugal.
conjugate ['kɔndʒugeɪt] *vt* conjugar.
conjugation [kɔndʒu'geɪʃən] *n* conjugação *f*.
conjunction [kən'dʒʌŋkʃən] *n* conjunção *f*; **in ~ with** junto com.
conjunctivitis [kəndʒʌŋktɪ'vaɪtɪs] *n* conjuntivite *f*.
conjure ['kʌndʒə*] *vi* fazer truques ♦ *vt* fazer aparecer.
conjure up *vt* (*ghost*, *spirit*) fazer aparecer, invocar; (*memories*) evocar.
conjurer ['kʌndʒərə*] *n* mágico/a, prestidigitador(a) *m/f*.
conjuring trick ['kʌndʒərɪŋ-] *n* mágica.
conker ['koŋkə*] (*BRIT*) *n* castanha-da-índia.
conk out [kɔŋk-] (*inf*) *vi* pifar.
con man ['kɔn-] (*irreg*) *n* vigarista *m*.
connect [kə'nɛkt] *vt* juntar, unir; (*ELEC*) ligar, conectar; (*fig*) relacionar, unir ♦ *vi*: **to ~ with** (*train*) conectar com; **to be ~ed with** estar relacionado com; **I'm trying to ~ you** (*TEL*) estou tentando completar a ligação.
connection [kə'nɛkʃən] *n* ligação *f*; (*ELEC*, *RAIL*) conexão *f*; (*TEL*) ligação *f*; (*fig*) relação *f*; **in ~ with** com relação a; **what is the ~ between them?** qual é a relação entre eles?; **business ~s** contatos de trabalho.
connexion [kə'nɛkʃən] (*BRIT*) *n* = **connection**.
conning tower ['kɔnɪŋ-] *n* torre *f* de comando.
connive [kə'naɪv] *vi*: **to ~ at** ser conivente em.
connoisseur [kɔnɪ'sə*] *n* conhecedor(a) *m/f*, apreciador(a) *m/f*.
connotation [kɔnə'teɪʃən] *n* conotação *f*.
connubial [kə'nju:bɪəl] *adj* conjugal.
conquer ['kɔŋkə*] *vt* conquistar; (*enemy*) vencer; (*feelings*) superar.
conqueror ['kɔŋkərə*] *n* conquistador(a) *m/f*.
conquest ['kɔŋkwɛst] *n* conquista.
conscience ['kɔnʃəns] *n* consciência; **in all ~** em sã consciência.
conscientious [kɔnʃɪ'ɛnʃəs] *adj* consciencioso; (*objection*) de consciência.
conscientious objector *n* *aquele que faz uma objeção de consciência à sua participação nas forças armadas*.
conscious ['kɔnʃəs] *adj* consciente; (*deliberate*: *insult*, *error*) intencional; **to become ~ of** tornar-se consciente de, conscientizar-se de.
consciousness ['kɔnʃəsnɪs] *n* consciência; **to lose/regain ~** perder/recuperar os sentidos.
conscript ['kɔnskrɪpt] *n* recruta *m/f*.
conscription [kən'skrɪpʃən] *n* serviço militar obrigatório.
consecrate ['kɔnsɪkreɪt] *vt* consagrar.
consecutive [kən'sɛkjutɪv] *adj* consecutivo, sucessivo, seguido.
consensus [kən'sɛnsəs] *n* consenso; **the ~ (of opinion)** o consenso (de opiniões).
consent [kən'sɛnt] *n* consentimento ♦ *vi*: **to ~ to** consentir em; **age of ~** maioridade; **by common ~** de comum acordo.
consequence ['kɔnsɪkwəns] *n* conseqüência; **in ~** por conseqüência.
consequently ['kɔnsɪkwəntlɪ] *adv* por conseguinte.
conservation [kɔnsə'veɪʃən] *n* conservação *f*; (*also*: *nature* ~) proteção *f* do meio ambiente; **energy ~** conservação da energia.
conservationist [kɔnsə'veɪʃənɪst] *n* conservacionista *m/f*.
Conservative [kən'sə:vətɪv] (*BRIT*) *adj*, *n* (*POL*) conservador(a) *m/f*.
conservative [kən'sə:vətɪv] *adj* conservador(a); (*cautious*) moderado.
conservatory [kən'sə:vətrɪ] *n* conservatório; (*greenhouse*) estufa.
conserve [kən'sə:v] *vt* conservar ♦ *n* conserva.
consider [kən'sɪdə*] *vt* considerar; (*take into account*) levar em consideração; (*study*) estudar, examinar; **to ~ doing sth** pensar em fazer algo; **~ yourself lucky** dê-se por sortudo; **all things ~ed** afinal de contas.
considerable [kən'sɪdərəbl] *adj* considerável; (*sum*) importante.
considerably [kən'sɪdərəblɪ] *adv* consideravelmente.
considerate [kən'sɪdərɪt] *adj* atencioso.
consideration [kənsɪdə'reɪʃən] *n* consideração *f*; (*reward*) remuneração *f*; **out of ~ for** em consideração a; **to be under ~** estar em apreciação; **my first ~ is my family** minha maior preocupação é a minha família.
considering [kən'sɪdərɪŋ] *prep* em vista de ♦ *conj*: **~ (that)** apesar de que, considerando que.
consign [kən'saɪn] *vt* consignar.
consignee [kɔnsaɪ'ni:] *n* consignatário/a.
consignment [kən'saɪnmənt] *n* consignação *f*.
consignment note *n* (*COMM*) guia de remessa.
consignor [kən'saɪnə*] *n* consignador(a) *m/f*.
consist [kən'sɪst] *vi*: **to ~ of** consistir em, compor-se de.
consistency [kən'sɪstənsɪ] *n* (*of person etc*) coerência; (*thickness*) consistência.
consistent [kən'sɪstənt] *adj* (*person*) compatí-

vel, coerente; (*even*) constante; ~ **with** compatível com, de acordo com.
consolation [kɔnsə'leɪʃən] *n* consolação *f*, consolo.
console [*vt* kən'səul, *n* 'kɔnsəul] *vt* consolar ♦ *n* consolo.
consolidate [kən'sɔlɪdeɪt] *vt* consolidar.
consols ['kɔnsɔlz] (*BRIT*) *npl* (*STOCK EXCHANGE*) consolidados *mpl*.
consommé [kən'sɔmeɪ] *n* consomê *m*, caldo.
consonant ['kɔnsənənt] *n* consoante *f*.
consort [*n* 'kɔnsɔːt, *vi* kən'sɔːt] *n* consorte *m/f* ♦ *vi*: **to ~ with** ter ligações com, conviver com; **prince ~** príncipe *m* consorte.
consortia [kən'sɔːtɪə] *npl of* **consortium**.
consortium [kən'sɔːtɪəm] (*pl* **~s** *or* **consortia**) *n* consórcio.
conspicuous [kən'spɪkjuəs] *adj* (*visible*) visível; (*garish*) berrante; (*outstanding*) notável; **to make o.s. ~** fazer-se notar.
conspiracy [kən'spɪrəsɪ] *n* conspiração *f*, trama.
conspiratorial [kən'spɪrə'tɔːrɪəl] *adj* conspirador(a).
conspire [kən'spaɪə*] *vi* conspirar.
constable ['kʌnstəbl] (*BRIT*) *n* policial *m/f* (*BR*), polícia *m/f* (*PT*); **chief ~** chefe *m/f* de polícia.
constabulary [kən'stæbjulərɪ] *n* polícia (distrital).
constant ['kɔnstənt] *adj* constante; (*loyal*) leal, fiel.
constantly ['kɔnstəntlɪ] *adv* constantemente.
constellation [kɔnstə'leɪʃən] *n* constelação *f*.
consternation [kɔnstə'neɪʃən] *n* consternação *f*.
constipated ['kɔnstɪpeɪtəd] *adj* com prisão de ventre.
constipation [kɔnstɪ'peɪʃən] *n* prisão *f* de ventre.
constituency [kən'stɪtjuənsɪ] *n* (*POL*) distrito eleitoral; (*people*) eleitorado.
constituency party *n* partido local.
constituent [kən'stɪtjuənt] *n* (*POL*) eleitor(a) *m/f*; (*part*) componente *m*.
constitute ['kɔnstɪtjuːt] *vt* constituir.
constitution [kɔnstɪ'tjuːʃən] *n* constituição *f*.
constitutional [kɔnstɪ'tjuːʃənl] *adj* constitucional.
constrain [kən'streɪn] *vt* obrigar.
constrained [kən'streɪnd] *adj*: **to feel ~ to ...** sentir-se compelido a ....
constraint [kən'streɪnt] *n* (*force*) força, coação *f*; (*restraint*) limitação *f*; (*shyness*) constrangimento.
constrict [kən'strɪkt] *vt* apertar, constringir.
construct [kən'strʌkt] *vt* construir.
construction [kən'strʌkʃən] *n* construção *f*; (*fig*: *interpretation*) interpretação *f*; **under ~** em construção.
construction industry *n* construção *f*.
constructive [kən'strʌktɪv] *adj* construtivo.
construe [kən'struː] *vt* interpretar.
consul ['kɔnsl] *n* cônsul *m/f*.
consulate ['kɔnsjulɪt] *n* consulado.
consult [kən'sʌlt] *vt*, *vi* consultar.
consultancy [kən'sʌltənsɪ] *n* consultoria.
consultancy fee *n* honorário de consultor.
consultant [kən'sʌltənt] *n* (*MED*) (médico/a) especialista *m/f*; (*other specialist*) assessor(a) *m/f*, consultor(a) *m/f* ♦ *cpd*: **~ engineer** engenheiro-consultor/engenheira-consultora *m/f*; **~ paediatrician** pediatra *m/f*; **legal/management ~** assessor jurídico/consultor em administração.
consultation [kɔnsəl'teɪʃən] *n* consulta; **in ~ with** em consulta com.
consulting room [kən'sʌltɪŋ-] (*BRIT*) *n* consultório.
consume [kən'sjuːm] *vt* (*eat*) comer; (*drink*) beber; (*fire etc*, *COMM*) consumir.
consumer [kən'sjuːmə*] *n* consumidor(a) *m/f*.
consumer credit *n* crédito ao consumidor.
consumer durables *npl* bens *mpl* de consumo duráveis.
consumer goods *npl* bens *mpl* de consumo.
consumerism [kən'sjuːmərɪzəm] *n* (*ECON*) consumismo; (*consumer protection*) proteção *f* ao consumidor.
consumer society *n* sociedade *f* de consumo.
consummate ['kɔnsʌmeɪt] *vt* consumar.
consumption [kən'sʌmpʃən] *n* consumo; (*MED*) tuberculose *f*; **not fit for human ~** impróprio para consumo.
cont. *abbr* = **continued**.
contact ['kɔntækt] *n* contato ♦ *vt* entrar *or* pôr-se em contato com; **to be in ~ with sb** estar em contato com alguém; **he has good ~s** tem boas relações.
contact lenses *npl* lentes *fpl* de contato.
contagious [kən'teɪdʒəs] *adj* contagioso.
contain [kən'teɪn] *vt* conter; **to ~ o.s.** conter-se.
container [kən'teɪnə*] *n* recipiente *m*; (*for shipping etc*) container *m*, cofre *m* de carga.
containerize [kən'teɪnəraɪz] *vt* containerizar.
contaminate [kən'tæmɪneɪt] *vt* contaminar.
contamination [kəntæmɪ'neɪʃən] *n* contaminação *f*.
cont'd *abbr* = **continued**.
contemplate ['kɔntəmpleɪt] *vt* contemplar; (*expect*) contar com; (*intend*) pretender, pensar em.
contemplation [kɔntəm'pleɪʃən] *n* contemplação *f*.
contemporary [kən'tɛmpərərɪ] *adj* contemporâneo; (*design*) moderno ♦ *n* contemporâneo/a.
contempt [kən'tɛmpt] *n* desprezo; **~ of court** (*LAW*) desacato à autoridade do tribunal.
contemptible [kən'tɛmptəbl] *adj* desprezível.
contemptuous [kən'tɛmptjuəs] *adj* desdenhoso.
contend [kən'tɛnd] *vt* (*argue*) afirmar ♦ *vi*

***NB**: European Portuguese adds the following consonants to certain words:* **b** (sú(b)dito, su(b)til); **c** (a(c)ção, a(c)cionista, a(c)to); **m** (inde(m)ne); **p** (ado(p)ção, ado(p)tar); *for further details see p. xiii.*

(*struggle*) lutar; **to have to ~ with** arcar com, lidar com; **he has a lot to ~ with** ele tem muito o que enfrentar.

contender [kən'tɛndə*] *n* contendor(a) *m/f*.

content [*adj, vt* kən'tɛnt, *n* 'kɔntɛnt] *adj* (*happy*) contente; (*satisfied*) satisfeito ♦ *vt* contentar, satisfazer ♦ *n* conteúdo; **~s** *npl* conteúdo; **(table of) ~s** índice *m* das matérias; **to be ~ with** estar contente *or* satisfeito com; **to ~ o.s. with sth/with doing sth** contentar-se com algo/em fazer algo.

contented [kən'tɛntɪd] *adj* contente, satisfeito.

contentedly [kən'tɛntɪdlɪ] *adv* contentemente.

contention [kən'tɛnʃən] *n* contenda; (*argument*) afirmação *f*; **bone of ~** pomo da discórdia.

contentious [kən'tɛnʃəs] *adj* controvertido.

contentment [kən'tɛntmənt] *n* contentamento.

contest [*n* 'kɔntɛst, *vt* kən'tɛst] *n* contenda; (*competition*) concurso ♦ *vt* (*dispute*) disputar; (*legal case*) defender; (*POL*) ser candidato a, disputar.

contestant [kən'tɛstənt] *n* competidor(a) *m/f*; (*in fight*) adversário/a.

context ['kɔntɛkst] *n* contexto; **in/out of ~** em/fora de contexto.

continent ['kɔntɪnənt] *n* continente *m*; **the C~** (*BRIT*) o continente europeu; **on the C~** na Europa (continental).

continental [kɔntɪ'nɛntl] *adj* continental ♦ *n* (*BRIT*) europeu/péia *m/f*.

continental breakfast *n* café *m* da manhã (*BR*), pequeno almoço (*PT*) (*de pão, geléia e café*).

continental quilt (*BRIT*) *n* edredom (*PT*: -dão) *m*.

contingency [kən'tɪndʒənsɪ] *n* contingência.

contingency plan *n* plano de contingência.

contingent [kən'tɪndʒənt] *n* contingente *m* ♦ *adj* contingente; **to be ~ upon** depender de.

continual [kən'tɪnjuəl] *adj* contínuo.

continually [kən'tɪnjuəlɪ] *adv* constantemente.

continuation [kəntɪnju'eɪʃən] *n* prolongamento; (*after interruption*) continuação *f*, retomada.

continue [kən'tɪnju:] *vi* prosseguir, continuar ♦ *vt* continuar; (*start again*) recomeçar, retomar; **to be ~d** (*story*) segue; **~d on page 10** continua na página 10.

continuity [kɔntɪ'njuɪtɪ] *n* (*also*: *CINEMA*) continuidade *f*.

continuity girl *n* (*CINEMA*) continuista.

continuous [kən'tɪnjuəs] *adj* contínuo; **~ performance** (*CINEMA*) sessão *f* contínua; **~ stationery** (*COMPUT*) formulários *mpl* contínuos.

continuously [kən'tɪnjuəslɪ] *adv* (*repeatedly*) repetidamente; (*uninterruptedly*) continuamente.

contort [kən'tɔ:t] *vt* retorcer.

contortion [kən'tɔ:ʃən] *n* contorção *f*.

contortionist [kən'tɔ:ʃənɪst] *n* contorcionista *m/f*.

contour ['kɔntuə*] *n* contorno; (*also*: *~ line*) curva de nível.

contraband ['kɔntrəbænd] *n* contrabando ♦ *adj* de contrabando, contrabandeado.

contraception [kɔntrə'sɛpʃən] *n* anticoncepção *f*.

contraceptive [kɔntrə'sɛptɪv] *adj* anticoncepcional ♦ *n* anticoncepcional *f*.

contract [*n, cpd* 'kɔntrækt, *vt, vi* kən'trækt] *n* contrato ♦ *cpd* (*price, date*) contratual; (*work*) de empreitada ♦ *vi* (*become smaller*) contrair-se, encolher-se; (*COMM*): **to ~ to do sth** comprometer-se por contrato a fazer algo ♦ *vt* contrair; **~ of employment** *or* **service** contrato de trabalho, ≈ vínculo empregatício.

contract in *vi* comprometer-se por contrato.

contract out *vi* desobrigar-se por contrato; (*from pension scheme*) optar por não participar.

contraction [kən'trækʃən] *n* contração *f*.

contractor [kən'træktə*] *n* contratante *m/f*.

contractual [kən'træktʃuəl] *adj* contratual.

contradict [kɔntrə'dɪkt] *vt* (*deny*) desmentir; (*be contrary to*) contradizer.

contradiction [kɔntrə'dɪkʃən] *n* contradição *f*; **to be in ~ with** contradizer.

contradictory [kɔntrə'dɪktərɪ] *adj* contraditório.

contralto [kən'træltəu] *n* contralto.

contraption [kən'træpʃən] (*pej*) *n* engenhoca, geringonça.

contrary[1] ['kɔntrərɪ] *adj, n* contrário; **on the ~** muito pelo contrário; **unless you hear to the ~** salvo aviso contrário; **~ to what we thought** ao contrário do que pensamos.

contrary[2] [kən'trɛərɪ] *adj* teimoso.

contrast [*n* 'kɔntrɑ:st, *vt* kən'trɑ:st] *n* contraste *m* ♦ *vt* contrastar, comparar; **in ~ to** *or* **with** em contraste com, ao contrário de.

contrasting [kən'trɑ:stɪŋ] *adj* oposto.

contravene [kɔntrə'vi:n] *vt* infringir.

contravention [kəntrə'vɛnʃən] *n* contravenção *f*, infração *f*.

contribute [kən'trɪbju:t] *vt* contribuir ♦ *vi*: **to ~ to** contribuir para; (*newspaper*) escrever para; (*discussion*) participar de.

contribution [kɔntrɪ'bju:ʃən] *n* (*money*) contribuição *f*; (*to debate*) intervenção *f*; (*to journal*) colaboração *f*.

contributor [kən'trɪbju:tə*] *n* (*to newspaper*) colaborador(a) *m/f*.

contributory [kən'trɪbjutərɪ] *adj*: **it was a ~ factor in ...** era um fator que contribuiu para ....

contributory pension scheme (*BRIT*) *n* sistema *m* de pensão contributária.

contrite ['kɔntraɪt] *adj* arrependido, contrito.

contrivance [kən'traɪvəns] *n* (*scheme*) maquinação *f*; (*device*) aparelho, dispositivo.

contrive [kən'traɪv] *vt* (*invent*) idealizar; (*carry out*) efetuar; (*plot*) tramar ♦ *vi*: **to ~ to do** chegar a fazer.

control [kən'trəul] *vt* controlar; (*traffic etc*) dirigir; (*machinery*) regular; (*temper*) dominar ♦ *n* (*command*) controle *m*, autoridade *f*; (*of car*) direção *f* (*BR*), condução *f* (*PT*); (*check*) freio, controle; **~s** *npl* mando; **to**

take ~ of assumir o controle de; **to be in ~ of** ter o controle de; (*in charge of*) ser responsável por; **to ~ o.s.** controlar-se; **out of/under ~** descontrolado/sob controle; **through circumstances beyond our ~** por motivos alheios à nossa vontade.
control key *n* (COMPUT) tecla de controle.
controller [kən'trəulə*] *n* controlador(a) *m/f*.
controlling interest [kən'trəulɪŋ-] *n* (COMM) controle *m* acionário.
control panel *n* painel *m* de instrumentos.
control point *n* ponto de controle.
control room *n* sala de comando; (RADIO, TV) sala de controle.
control tower *n* (AVIAT) torre *f* de controle.
control unit *n* (COMPUT) unidade *f* de controle.
controversial [kɔntrə'vəːʃl] *adj* controvertido, polêmico.
controversy ['kɔntrəvəːsɪ] *n* controvérsia, polêmica.
conurbation [kɔnə'beɪʃən] *n* conurbação *f*.
convalesce [kɔnvə'lɛs] *vi* convalescer.
convalescence [kɔnvə'lɛsns] *n* convalescença.
convalescent [kɔnvə'lɛsnt] *adj*, *n* convalescente *m/f*.
convector [kən'vɛktə*] *n* (*heater*) aquecedor *m* de convecção.
convene [kən'viːn] *vt* convocar ♦ *vi* reunir-se.
convener [kən'viːnə*] *n* organizador(a) *m/f*.
convenience [kən'viːnɪəns] *n* (*comfort*) comodidade *f*; (*advantage*) vantagem *f*, conveniência; **at your ~** quando lhe convier; **at your earliest ~** (COMM) o mais cedo que lhe for possível; **all modern ~s** (*also*: BRIT: *all mod cons*) com todos os confortos.
convenience foods *npl* alimentos *mpl* semiprontos.
convenient [kən'viːnɪənt] *adj* cômodo; (*useful*) útil; (*place*) acessível; (*time*) oportuno, conveniente; **if it is ~ to you** se isso lhe convier, se isso não lhe for incômodo.
conveniently [kən'viːnɪəntlɪ] *adv* convenientemente.
convent ['kɔnvənt] *n* convento.
convention [kən'vɛnʃən] *n* convenção *f*; (*meeting*) assembléia.
conventional [kən'vɛnʃənl] *adj* convencional.
convent school *n* colégio de freiras.
converge [kən'vəːdʒ] *vi* convergir.
conversant [kən'vəːsnt] *adj*: **to be ~ with** estar familiarizado com.
conversation [kɔnvə'seɪʃən] *n* conversação *f*, conversa.
conversational [kɔnvə'seɪʃənl] *adj* (*familiar*) familiar; (*talkative*) loquaz; (COMPUT) conversacional, interativo.
conversationalist [kɔnvə'seɪʃnəlɪst] *n* conversador(a) *m/f*; **she's a good ~** ela tem muita conversa.
converse [*n* 'kɔnvəːs, *vi* kən'vəːs] *n* inverso ♦ *vi* conversar.
conversely [kɔn'vəːslɪ] *adv* pelo contrário, inversamente.
conversion [kən'vəːʃən] *n* conversão *f*; (BRIT: *of house*) transformação *f*.
conversion table *n* tabela de conversão.
convert [*vt* kən'vəːt, *n* 'kɔnvəːt] *vt* (REL, COMM) converter; (*alter*) transformar ♦ *n* convertido/a.
convertible [kən'vəːtəbl] *adj* convertível ♦ *n* conversível *m*.
convex [kɔn'vɛks] *adj* convexo.
convey [kən'veɪ] *vt* transportar, levar; (*thanks*) comunicar; (*idea*) exprimir.
conveyance [kən'veɪəns] *n* (*of goods*) transporte *m*; (*vehicle*) meio de transporte, veículo.
conveyancing [kən'veɪənsɪŋ] *n* (LAW) transferência de bens imóveis.
conveyor belt [kənveɪə*-] *n* correia transportadora.
convict [*vt* kən'vɪkt, *n* 'kɔnvɪkt] *vt* condenar; (*sentence*) declarar culpado ♦ *n* presidiário.
conviction [kən'vɪkʃən] *n* condenação *f*; (*belief*) convicção *f*.
convince [kən'vɪns] *vt* convencer; **to ~ sb of sth/that** convencer alguém de algo/de que.
convincing [kən'vɪnsɪŋ] *adj* convincente.
convincingly [kən'vɪnsɪŋlɪ] *adv* convincentemente.
convivial [kən'vɪvɪəl] *adj* jovial, alegre.
convoluted ['kɔnvəluːtɪd] *adj* (*shape*) curvilíneo; (*argument*) complicado.
convoy ['kɔnvɔɪ] *n* escolta.
convulse [kən'vʌls] *vt* convulsionar; **to be ~d with laughter** morrer de rir.
convulsion [kən'vʌlʃən] *n* convulsão *f*; (*laughter*) ataque *m*, acesso.
coo [kuː] *vi* arrulhar.
cook [kuk] *vt* cozinhar; (*meal*) preparar ♦ *vi* cozinhar ♦ *n* cozinheiro/a.
cook up (*inf*) *vt* (*excuse, story*) bolar.
cookbook ['kukbuk] *n* livro de receitas.
cooker ['kukə*] *n* fogão *m*.
cookery ['kukərɪ] *n* (*dishes*) cozinha; (*art*) (arte *f*) culinária.
cookery book (BRIT) *n* livro de receitas.
cookie ['kukɪ] (US) *n* bolacha, biscoito.
cooking ['kukɪŋ] *n* cozinha ♦ *cpd* (*apples, chocolate*) para cozinhar; (*utensils, salt*) de cozinha.
cookout ['kukaut] (US) *n* churrasco.
cool [kuːl] *adj* fresco; (*not hot*) tépido; (*not afraid*) calmo; (*unfriendly*) frio ♦ *vt, vi* esfriar; **it's ~** (*weather*) está fresco.
cool down *vi* esfriar; (*fig*: *person, situation*) acalmar-se.
cool box (BRIT) *n* mala frigorífica.
cooler ['kuːlə*] (US) *n* mala frigorífica.
cooling tower ['kuːlɪŋ-] *n* torre *f* de esfriamento.
coolly ['kuːlɪ] *adv* (*calmly*) calmamente; (*audaciously*) descaradamente; (*unenthusiasti-*

cally) friamente.
coolness ['ku:lnɪs] *n* frescura; (*hostility*) frieza; (*indifference*) indiferença.
coop [ku:p] *n* galinheiro, capoeira.
coop up *vt* (*fig*) confinar.
co-op ['kəuɔp] *n abbr* = **cooperative (society)**.
cooperate [kəu'ɔpəreɪt] *vi* cooperar, colaborar.
cooperation [kəuɔpə'reɪʃən] *n* cooperação *f*, colaboração *f*.
cooperative [kəu'ɔpərətɪv] *adj* cooperativo ♦ *n* cooperativa.
coopt [kəu'ɔpt] *vt*: **to ~ sb onto a committee** cooptar alguém para fazer parte de um comitê.
coordinate [*vt* kəu'ɔ:dɪneɪt, *n* kəu'ɔdɪnət] *vt* coordenar ♦ *n* (*MATH*) coordenada *f*; **~s** *npl* (*clothes*) coordenados *mpl*.
coordination [kəuɔ:dɪ'neɪʃən] *n* coordenação *f*.
coot [ku:t] *n* galeirão *m*.
co-ownership [kəu-] *n* co-propriedade *f*, condomínio.
cop [kɔp] (*inf*) *n* policial *m/f* (*BR*), polícia *m/f* (*PT*), tira *m* (*inf*).
cope [kəup] *vi* sair-se, dar-se; **to ~ with** poder com, arcar com; (*problem*) estar à altura de.
Copenhagen ['kəupn'heɪgən] *n* Copenhague.
copier ['kɔpɪə*] *n* (*also*: *photo~*) copiador *m*.
co-pilot [kəu-] *n* co-piloto/a.
copious ['kəupɪəs] *adj* copioso, abundante.
copper ['kɔpə*] *n* (*metal*) cobre *m*; (*inf*: *policeman*) polícia *m*; **~s** *npl* moedas *fpl* de pouco valor.
copper sulphate *n* sulfato de cobre.
coppice ['kɔpɪs] *n* bosquete *m*.
copse [kɔps] *n* bosquete *m*.
copulate ['kɔpjuleɪt] *vi* copular.
copulation [kɔpju'leɪʃən] *n* cópula.
copy ['kɔpɪ] *n* cópia; (*of book etc*) exemplar *m*; (*of writing*) originais *mpl* ♦ *vt* copiar; (*imitate*) imitar; **to make good ~** (*PRESS*) fazer uma boa matéria.
copy out *vt* copiar.
copycat ['kɔpɪkæt] (*inf*) *n* macaco.
copyright ['kɔpɪraɪt] *n* direitos *mpl* de autor, direitos autorais, copirraite *m*; **~ reserved** todos os direitos reservados.
copy typist *n* datilógrafo/a.
copywriter ['kɔpɪraɪtə*] *n* redator(a) *m/f* de material publicitário.
coral ['kɔrəl] *n* coral *m*.
coral reef *n* recife *m* de coral.
Coral Sea *n*: **the ~** o mar de Coral.
cord [kɔ:d] *n* corda; (*ELEC*) fio, cabo; (*fabric*) veludo cotelê; **~s** *npl* (*trousers*) calça (*BR*) *or* calças *fpl* (*PT*) de veludo cotelê.
cordial ['kɔ:dɪəl] *adj* cordial ♦ *n* cordial *m*.
cordless ['kɔ:dlɪs] *adj* sem fio.
cordon ['kɔ:dn] *n* cordão *m*.
cordon off *vt* isolar.
corduroy ['kɔ:dərɔɪ] *n* veludo cotelê.
CORE [kɔ:*] (*US*) *n abbr* = **Congress of Racial Equality**.
core [kɔ:*] *n* centro, núcleo; (*of fruit*) caroço; (*of problem*) âmago ♦ *vt* descaroçar; **rotten to the ~** completamente podre.
Corfu [kɔ:'fu:] *n* Corfu *f* (*no article*).
coriander [kɔrɪ'ændə*] *n* coentro.
cork [kɔ:k] *n* rolha; (*tree*) cortiça.
corkage ['kɔ:kɪdʒ] *n taxa cobrada num restaurante pela abertura das garrafas levadas pelo cliente*.
corked [kɔ:kt] (*BRIT*) *adj* que tem gosto de rolha.
corkscrew ['kɔ:kskru:] *n* saca-rolhas *m inv*.
corky ['kɔ:kɪ] (*US*) *adj* que tem gosto de rolha.
corm [kɔ:m] *n* cormo.
cormorant ['kɔ:mərnt] *n* cormorão *m*, corvo marinho.
Corn (*BRIT*) *abbr* = **Cornwall**.
corn [kɔ:n] *n* (*BRIT*: *wheat*) trigo; (*US*: *maize*) milho; (*cereals*) grão *m*, cereal *m*; (*on foot*) calo; **~ on the cob** (*CULIN*) espiga de milho.
cornea ['kɔ:nɪə] *n* córnea.
corned beef ['kɔ:nd-] *n* carne *f* de boi enlatada.
corner ['kɔ:nə*] *n* (*outside*) esquina; (*inside*) canto; (*in road*) curva; (*FOOTBALL*) córner *m* ♦ *vt* (*trap*) encurralar; (*COMM*) açambarcar, monopolizar ♦ *vi* (*in car*) fazer uma curva; **to cut ~s** (*fig*) matar o serviço.
corner flag *n* (*FOOTBALL*) bandeira de escanteio.
corner kick *n* (*FOOTBALL*) córner *m*.
cornerstone ['kɔ:nəstəun] *n* pedra angular.
cornet ['kɔ:nɪt] *n* (*MUS*) cornetim *m*; (*BRIT*: *of ice-cream*) casquinha.
cornflakes ['kɔ:nfleɪks] *npl* flocos *mpl* de milho.
cornflour ['kɔ:nflauə*] (*BRIT*) *n* farinha de milho, maisena ®.
cornice ['kɔ:nɪs] *n* cornija.
Cornish ['kɔ:nɪʃ] *adj* de Cornualha ♦ *n* (*LING*) córnico.
corn oil *n* óleo de milho.
cornstarch ['kɔ:nstɑ:tʃ] (*US*) *n* farinha de milho, maisena ®.
cornucopia [kɔ:nju'kəupɪə] *n* cornucópia.
Cornwall ['kɔ:nwəl] *n* Cornualha.
corny ['kɔ:nɪ] (*inf*) *adj* velho, gasto.
corollary [kə'rɔlərɪ] *n* corolário.
coronary ['kɔrənərɪ] *n*: **~ (thrombosis)** trombose *f* (coronária).
coronation [kɔrə'neɪʃən] *n* coroação *f*.
coroner ['kɔrənə*] *n magistrado que investiga mortes suspeitas*.
coronet ['kɔrənɪt] *n* coroa aberta, diadema *m*.
Corp. *abbr* = **corporation**.
corporal ['kɔ:pərl] *n* cabo ♦ *adj* corpóreo; **~ punishment** castigo corporal.
corporate ['kɔ:pərɪt] *adj* corporativo; (*COMM*: *of a company*) da empresa.
corporate body *n* (*LAW*) pessoa jurídica.
corporate identity *n* imagem *f* da empresa.
corporate image *n* imagem *f* da empresa.
corporation [kɔ:pə'reɪʃən] *n* (*of town*) município, junta; (*COMM*) sociedade *f*.
corporation tax *n* imposto sobre a renda de

sociedades.

corps [kɔ:*, *pl* kɔ:z] (*pl* **corps**) *n* corpo; **the press** ~ a imprensa.

corpse [kɔ:ps] *n* cadáver *m*.

corpuscle ['kɔ:pʌsl] *n* corpúsculo.

corral [kə'rɑ:l] *n* curral *m*.

correct [kə'rɛkt] *adj* correto ♦ *vt* corrigir; **you are** ~ você tem razão.

correction [kə'rɛkʃən] *n* correção *f*, retificação *f*; (*erasure*) emenda.

correlate ['kɔrɪleɪt] *vt* correlacionar ♦ *vi*: **to** ~ **with** corresponder a.

correlation [kɔrɪ'leɪʃən] *n* correlação *f*.

correspond [kɔrɪs'pɔnd] *vi* (*write*) corresponder-se, escrever-se; (*be equal to*): **to** ~ **to** *or* **with** corresponder a.

correspondence [kɔrɪs'pɔndəns] *n* correspondência.

correspondence column *n* (PRESS) seção *f* de cartas.

correspondence course *n* curso por correspondência.

correspondent [kɔrɪs'pɔndənt] *n* correspondente *m/f*.

corresponding [kɔrɪs'pɔndɪŋ] *adj* correspondente.

corridor ['kɔrɪdɔ:*] *n* corredor *m*.

corroborate [kə'rɔbəreɪt] *vt* corroborar.

corrode [kə'rəud] *vt* corroer ♦ *vi* corroer-se.

corrosion [kə'rəuʒən] *n* corrosão *f*.

corrosive [kə'rəuzɪv] *adj* corrosivo.

corrugated ['kɔrəgeɪtɪd] *adj* ondulado.

corrugated iron *n* chapa ondulada *or* corrugada.

corrupt [kə'rʌpt] *adj* corrupto ♦ *vt* corromper; (*bribe*) subornar; (*data*) corromper, destruir; ~ **practices** corrupção *f*.

corruption [kə'rʌpʃən] *n* corrupção *f*; (*of data*) destruição *f*.

corset ['kɔ:sɪt] *n* espartilho.

Corsica ['kɔ:sɪkə] *n* Córsega.

Corsican ['kɔ:sɪkən] *adj*, *n* córsico/a.

cortège [kɔ:'tɛ:ʒ] *n* séquito, cortejo.

cortisone ['kɔ:tɪzəun] *n* cortisona.

coruscating ['kɔrəskeɪtɪŋ] *adj* cintilante.

c.o.s. *abbr* (= *cash on shipment*) pagamento na expedição.

cosh [kɔʃ] (BRIT) *n* cassetete *m*.

cosignatory ['kəu'sɪgnətərɪ] *n* co-signatário/a.

cosiness ['kəuzɪnɪs] (US **coziness**) *n* conforto; (*atmosphere*) aconchego, conforto.

cos lettuce [kɔs-] *n* alface *m* (cos).

cosmetic [kɔz'mɛtɪk] *n* cosmético ♦ *adj* (*preparation*) cosmético; (*fig*: *reforms*) simbólico, superficial; ~ **surgery** cirurgia plástica embelezadora.

cosmic ['kɔzmɪk] *adj* cósmico.

cosmonaut ['kɔzmənɔ:t] *n* cosmonauta *m/f*.

cosmopolitan [kɔzmə'pɔlɪtn] *adj* cosmopolita.

cosmos ['kɔzmɔs] *n* cosmo.

cost [kɔst] (*pt*, *pp* **cost**) *n* (*gen*) custo; (*price*) preço ♦ *vi* custar ♦ *vt* custar; (*determine cost of*) determinar o custo de; ~**s** *npl* (LAW) custas *fpl*; **at the** ~ **of** à custa de; **how much does it** ~? quanto custa?; **it** ~**s £5/too much** custa £5/é muito caro; **it** ~ **him his life/job** custou-lhe a vida/o emprego; **the** ~ **of living** o custo de vida; **at all** ~**s** custe o que custar.

cost accountant *n* contador(a) *m/f* de custos.

co-star [kəu-] *n* co-estrela *m/f*.

Costa Rica ['kɔstə'ri:kə] *n* Costa Rica.

Costa Rican ['kɔstə'ri:kən] *adj*, *n* costarriquenho/a.

cost centre *n* centro de custo.

cost control *n* controle *m* dos custos.

cost-effective *adj* rentável.

cost-effectiveness *n* rentabilidade *f*.

costly ['kɔstlɪ] *adj* (*expensive*) caro, custoso; (*valuable*) suntuoso.

cost-of-living *adj*: ~ **allowance** ajuda de custo; ~ **index** índice *m* de preços ao consumidor.

cost price (BRIT) *n* preço de custo.

costume ['kɔstju:m] *n* traje *m*; (BRIT: *also*: *swimming* ~) (*woman's*) maiô *m* (BR), fato de banho (PT); (*man's*) calção *m* (de banho) (BR), calções *mpl* de banho (PT).

costume jewellery *n* bijuteria.

cosy ['kəuzɪ] (US **cozy**) *adj* cômodo; (*atmosphere*) aconchegante; (*life*) folgado, confortável.

cot [kɔt] *n* (BRIT: *child's*) cama (de criança), berço; (US: *campbed*) cama de lona.

Cotswolds ['kɔtswəuldz] *npl*: **the** ~ *região de colinas em Gloucestershire*.

cottage ['kɔtɪdʒ] *n* casa de campo; (*rustic*) cabana.

cottage cheese *n* ricota (BR), queijo creme (PT).

cottage industry *n* indústria artesanal.

cottage pie *n prato de carne picada com batata*.

cotton ['kɔtn] *n* algodão *m*; (*thread*) fio, linha ♦ *cpd* de algodão.

cotton on (*inf*) *vi*: **to** ~ **on (to sth)** sacar (algo).

cotton wool (BRIT) *n* algodão *m* (hidrófilo).

couch [kautʃ] *n* sofá *m*; (*doctor's*) cama; (*psychiatrist's*) divã *m* ♦ *vt* formular.

couchette [ku:'ʃɛt] *n* leito.

cough [kɔf] *vi* tossir ♦ *n* tosse *f*.

cough up *vt* expelir; (*inf*: *money*) desembolsar.

cough drop *n* pastilha para a tosse.

cough mixture *n* xarope *m* (para a tosse).

cough syrup *n* xarope *m* (para a tosse).

could [kud] *conditional of* **can**.

couldn't ['kudnt] = **could not**.

council ['kaunsl] *n* conselho; **city** *or* **town** ~ câmara municipal; **C**~ **of Europe** Conselho da Europa.

council estate (BRIT) *n* conjunto habitacio-

NB: *European Portuguese adds the following consonants to certain words:* **b** (sú(b)dito, su(b)til); **c** (a(c)ção, a(c)cionista, a(c)to); **m** (inde(m)ne); **p** (ado(p)ção, ado(p)tar); *for further details see p. xiii.*

nal.
council house (*BRIT*: *irreg*) *n* casa popular.
councillor ['kaunsələ*] *n* vereador(a) *m/f*.
counsel ['kaunsl] *n* (*advice*) conselho; (*lawyer*) advogado/a ♦ *vt*: **to ~ sth/sb to do sth** aconselhar algo/alguém a fazer algo; **~ for the defence/the prosecution** advogado/a de defesa/promotor(a) *m/f* público/a.
counsellor ['kaunsələ*] *n* (*US* **counselor**) conselheiro/a; (*US*: *LAW*) advogado/a.
count [kaunt] *vt* contar ♦ *vi* contar ♦ *n* conta; (*of votes*) contagem *f*; (*nobleman*) conde *m*; (*sum*) total *m*, soma; **not ~ing the children** sem contar as crianças; **10 ~ing him** 10 contando com ele; **it ~s for very little** conta muito pouco; **~ yourself lucky** considere-se sortudo; **that doesn't ~!** isso não vale!
count on *vt fus* contar com; **to ~ on doing sth** contar em fazer algo.
count up *vt* contar.
countdown ['kauntdaun] *n* contagem *f* regressiva.
countenance ['kauntınəns] *n* expressão *f* ♦ *vt* aprovar.
counter ['kauntə*] *n* (*in shop*) balcão *m*; (*in post office etc*: *window*) guichê *m*; (*in games*) ficha ♦ *vt* contrariar; (*blow*) parar ♦ *adv*: **~ to** ao contrário de; **to buy under the ~** (*fig*) comprar por baixo do pano *or* da mesa.
counteract [kauntər'ækt] *vt* neutralizar.
counterattack ['kauntərətæk] *n* contra-ataque *m* ♦ *vi* contra-atacar.
counterbalance [kauntə'bæləns] *n* contrapeso.
counter-clockwise *adv* ao contrário dos ponteiros do relógio.
counter-espionage *n* contra-espionagem *f*.
counterfeit ['kauntəfıt] *n* falsificação *f* ♦ *vt* falsificar ♦ *adj* falso, falsificado.
counterfoil ['kauntəfɔıl] *n* canhoto (*BR*), talão *m* (*PT*).
counterintelligence ['kauntərın'tɛlıdʒəns] *n* contra-informacão *f*.
countermand ['kauntəmɑːnd] *vt* revogar.
countermeasure ['kauntəmɛʒə*] *n* contramedida.
counteroffensive ['kauntərə'fɛnsıv] *n* contra-ofensiva.
counterpane ['kauntəpeın] *n* colcha.
counterpart ['kauntəpɑːt] *n* contrapartida; (*of person*) sósia *m/f*; (: *opposite number*) homólogo/a.
counterproductive ['kauntəprə'dʌktıv] *adj* contraproducente.
counterproposal ['kauntəprə'pəuzl] *n* contraproposta.
counter-revolution *n* contra-revolução *f*.
countersign ['kauntəsaın] *vt* referendar.
countersink ['kauntəsıŋk] (*irreg*: *like* **sink**) *vt* escarear.
countess ['kauntıs] *n* condessa.
countless ['kauntlıs] *adj* inumerável.
countrified ['kʌntrıfaıd] *adj* bucólico, rústico.
country ['kʌntrı] *n* país *m*; (*native land*) terra; (*as opposed to town*) campo; (*region*) região *f*, terra; **in the ~** no campo; (*esp in Brazil*) no interior; **mountainous ~** região montanhosa.
country and western (music) *n* música country.
country dancing (*BRIT*) *n* dança regional.
country house (*irreg*) *n* casa de campo.
countryman ['kʌntrımən] (*irreg*) *n* (*national*) compatriota *m*; (*rural*) camponês *m*.
countryside ['kʌntrısaıd] *n* campo.
country-wide *adj* em todo o país; (*problem*) de escala nacional ♦ *adv* em todo o país.
county ['kauntı] *n* condado.
county town (*BRIT*) *n* capital *f* do condado.
coup [kuː] *n* golpe *m* de mestre; (*also*: **~ d'état**) golpe (de estado).
coupé ['kuːpeı] *n* (*AUT*) cupê *m*.
couple ['kʌpl] *n* (*of things, people*) par *m*; (*married ~, courting ~*) casal *m* ♦ *vt* (*ideas, names*) unir, juntar; (*machinery*) ligar, juntar; **a ~ of** um par de; (*a few*) alguns/algumas.
couplet ['kʌplıt] *n* dístico.
coupling ['kʌplıŋ] *n* (*RAIL*) engate *m*.
coupon ['kuːpɔn] *n* cupom (*PT*: -pão) *m*; (*pools ~*) talão *m*; (*voucher*) vale *m*; (*FINANCE*) cupom (*PT*: -pão).
courage ['kʌrıdʒ] *n* coragem *f*.
courageous [kə'reıdʒəs] *adj* corajoso, valente.
courgette [kuə'ʒɛt] (*BRIT*) *n* abobrinha.
courier ['kurıə*] *n* correio; (*diplomatic*) mala; (*for tourists*) guia *m/f*, agente *m/f* de turismo.
course [kɔːs] *n* (*direction*) direção *f*, caminho; (*of river, SCH*) curso; (*of ship*) rumo; (*of bullet*) trajetória; (*fig*) procedimento; (*GOLF*) campo; (*part of meal*) prato; **of ~** claro, naturalmente; **of ~!** claro!, lógico!; **(no) of ~ not!** claro que não!; **in due ~** oportunamente, no devido tempo; **first ~** entrada; **in the ~ of the next few days** no decorrer dos próximos dias; **~ (of action)** atitude *f*; **the best ~ would be to do ...** o melhor seria fazer ...; **we have no other ~ but to ...** não temos nenhuma outra opção, senão ...; **~ of lectures** série de palestras; **~ of treatment** (*MED*) tratamento.
court [kɔːt] *n* (*royal*) corte *f*; (*LAW*) tribunal *m*; (*TENNIS*) quadra ♦ *vt* (*woman*) cortejar, namorar; (*danger etc*) procurar; **out of ~** (*LAW*: *settle*) extrajudicialmente; **to take to ~** demandar, levar a julgamento; **~ of appeal** tribunal de recursos.
courteous ['kəːtıəs] *adj* cortês/esa.
courtesan [kɔːtı'zæn] *n* cortesã *f*.
courtesy ['kəːtəsı] *n* cortesia; **by ~ of** com permissão de.
courtesy coach *n* ônibus *m* (*BR*) *or* autocarro (*PT*) gratuito.
courtesy light *n* (*AUT*) luz *f* interior.
court-house (*US*: *irreg*) *n* palácio de justiça.
courtier ['kɔːtıə*] *n* cortesão *m*.
court martial (*pl* **courts martial**) *n* conselho de guerra ♦ *vt* submeter a conselho de guerra.
courtroom ['kɔːtrum] *n* sala de tribunal.

court shoe *n* escarpim *m*.
courtyard ['kɔ:tjɑ:d] *n* pátio.
cousin ['kʌzn] *n* primo/a *m/f*; **first ~** primo/a irmão/mã.
cove [kəuv] *n* angra, enseada.
covenant ['kʌvənənt] *n* convênio ♦ *vt*: **to ~ £2000 per year to a charity** comprometer-se a doar £2000 por ano para uma obra de caridade.
Coventry ['kɔvəntrı] *n*: **to send sb to ~** (*fig*) relegar alguém ao ostracismo.
cover ['kʌvə*] *vt* (*gen*, *PRESS*, *costs*) cobrir; (*with lid*) tapar; (*chairs etc*) revestir; (*distance*) percorrer; (*include*) abranger; (*protect*) abrigar; (*issues*) tratar ♦ *n* (*gen*, *PRESS*, *COMM*) cobertura; (*lid*) tampa; (*for chair etc*) capa; (*for bed*) cobertor *m*; (*envelope*) envelope *m*; (*for book*) capa, forro; (*of magazine*) capa; (*shelter*) abrigo; (*insurance*) cobertura; **to take ~** abrigar-se; **under ~** (*indoors*) abrigado; **under ~ of** sob o abrigo de; (*fig*) sob capa de; **under separate ~** (*COMM*) em separado; **£10 will ~ everything** £10 vão dar para tudo.
cover up *vt* (*person*, *object*): **to ~ up (with)** cobrir (com); (*fig*: *truth*, *facts*) abafar, encobrir ♦ *vi*: **to ~ up for sb** (*fig*) cobrir alguém.
coverage ['kʌvərıdʒ] *n* (*PRESS*, *INSURANCE*) cobertura.
cover charge *n* couvert *m*.
covering ['kʌvərıŋ] *n* cobertura, invólucro.
covering letter (*US* **cover letter**) *n* carta de cobertura.
cover note *n* (*INSURANCE*) nota de cobertura.
cover price *n* preço de capa.
covert ['kəuvə:t] *adj* (*threat*) velado; (*action*) oculto, secreto.
cover-up *n* encobrimento (dos fatos).
covet ['kʌvıt] *vt* cobiçar.
cow [kau] *n* vaca ♦ *cpd* fêmea ♦ *vt* intimidar.
coward ['kauəd] *n* covarde *m/f*.
cowardice ['kauədıs] *n* covardia.
cowardly ['kauədlı] *adj* covarde.
cowboy ['kaubɔı] *n* vaqueiro.
cower ['kauə*] *vi* encolher-se (de medo).
cowshed ['kauʃɛd] *n* estábulo.
cowslip ['kauslıp] *n* (*BOT*) primavera.
cox [kɔks] *n abbr* = **coxswain**.
coxswain ['kɔksn] *n* timoneiro/a *m/f*.
coy [kɔı] *adj* tímido.
coyote [kɔı'əutı] *n* coiote *m*.
coziness ['kəuzınıs] (*US*) *n* = **cosiness**.
cozy ['kəuzı] (*US*) *adj* = **cosy**.
CP *n abbr* (= *Communist Party*) PC *m*.
cp. *abbr* (= *compare*) cp.
c/p (*BRIT*) *abbr* = **carriage paid**.
CPA (*US*) *n abbr* = **certified public accountant**.
CPI *n abbr* (= *Consumer Price Index*) IPC *m*.
Cpl. *abbr* = **Corporal**.
CP/M *n abbr* (= *Central Program for Microprocessors*) CP/M *m*.
c.p.s. *abbr* (= *characters per second*) c.p.s.
CPSA (*BRIT*) *n abbr* (= *Civil and Public Services Association*) *sindicato dos funcionários públicos*.
CPU *n abbr* (= *Central Processing Unit*) CPU *f*.
cr. *abbr* = **credit**; **creditor**.
crab [kræb] *n* caranguejo.
crab apple *n* maçã ácida.
crack [kræk] *n* rachadura, arranhão *m*; (*noise*) estalo; (*joke*) piada; (*DRUGS*) crack *m*; (*inf*: *attempt*): **to have a ~ (at sth)** tentar (fazer algo) ♦ *vt* quebrar; (*nut*) partir, descascar; (*safe*) arrombar; (*whip etc*) estalar; (*knuckles*) estalar, partir; (*joke*) soltar; (*mystery*) resolver; (*code*) decifrar ♦ *cpd* (*expert*) excelente; **to get ~ing** (*inf*) pôr mãos à obra.
crack down on *vt fus* (*crime*) ser linha dura com; (*spending*) cortar.
crack up *vi* (*MED*) sofrer um colapso nervoso.
crackdown ['krækdaun] *n*: **~ (on)** (*on crime*) endurecimento (em relação a); (*on spending*) arrocho (a).
cracked [krækt] (*inf*) *adj* doido.
cracker ['krækə*] *n* (*biscuit*) biscoito; (*Christmas ~*) busca-pé-surpresa *m*; (*firework*) busca-pé *m*; **a ~ of a ...** (*BRIT*: *inf*) um(a) ... sensacional.
crackers ['krækəz] (*BRIT*: *inf*) *adj*: **he's ~** ele é maluco.
crackle ['krækl] *vi* crepitar.
crackling ['kræklıŋ] *n* (*of fire*) crepitação *f*; (*of leaves etc*) estalidos *mpl*; (*of pork*) torresmo.
cradle ['kreıdl] *n* berço ♦ *vt* (*child*) embalar; (*object*) segurar com cuidado.
craft [krɑ:ft] *n* (*skill*) arte *f*; (*trade*) ofício; (*cunning*) astúcia; (*boat*) barco.
craftsman ['krɑ:ftsmən] (*irreg*) *n* artífice *m*, artesão *m*.
craftsmanship ['krɑ:ftsmənʃıp] *n* artesanato.
craftsmen ['krɑ:ftsmɛn] *npl of* **craftsman**.
crafty ['krɑ:ftı] *adj* astuto, malandro, esperto.
crag [kræg] *n* penhasco.
craggy ['krægı] *adj* escarpado.
cram [kræm] *vt* (*fill*): **to ~ sth with** encher *or* abarrotar algo de; (*put*): **to ~ sth into** enfiar algo em.
crammed [kræmd] *adj* abarrotado.
cramming ['kræmıŋ] *n* (*for exams*) virada final.
cramp [kræmp] *n* (*MED*) cãibra; (*TECH*) grampo ♦ *vt* (*limit*) restringir; (*annoy*) estorvar.
cramped [kræmpt] *adj* apertado, confinado.
crampon ['kræmpən] *n* gato de ferro.
cranberry ['krænbərı] *n* oxicoco.
crane [kreın] *n* (*TECH*) guindaste *m*; (*bird*) grou *m* ♦ *vt*, *vi*: **to ~ forward, to ~ one's**

NB: *European Portuguese adds the following consonants to certain words:* **b** (sú(b)dito, su(b)til); **c** (a(c)ção, a(c)cionista, a(c)to); **m** (inde(m)ne); **p** (ado(p)ção, ado(p)tar); *for further details see p. xiii.*

neck espichar-se, espichar o pescoço.
crania ['kreɪnɪə] *npl* of **cranium.**
cranium ['kreɪnɪəm] (*pl* **crania**) *n* crânio.
crank [kræŋk] *n* manivela; (*person*) excêntrico/a.
crankshaft ['kræŋkʃɑːft] *n* virabrequim *m*.
cranky ['kræŋkɪ] *adj* (*eccentric*) excêntrico; (*bad-tempered*) irritadiço.
cranny ['krænɪ] *n see* **nook.**
crap [kræp] (*inf!*) *n* papo furado; **to have a ~** cagar (*!*).
crash [kræʃ] *n* (*noise*) estrondo; (*of cars etc*) choque *m*, batida; (*of plane*) desastre *m* de avião; (COMM) falência, quebra; (STOCK EXCHANGE) craque *m* ♦ *vt* (*plane*) espatifar ♦ *vi* (*plane*) cair, espatifar-se; (*two cars*) colidir, bater; (*fall noisily*) cair (com estrondo); (*fig*) despencar; **to ~ into** bater em; **he ~ed into a wall** ele bateu com o carro num muro.
crash barrier (BRIT) *n* (AUT) cerca de proteção.
crash course *n* curso intensivo.
crash helmet *n* capacete *m*.
crash landing *n* aterrissagem *f* forçada (BR), aterragem *f* forçosa (PT).
crass [kræs] *adj* crasso.
crate [kreɪt] *n* caixote *m*; (*inf*: *old car*) lata-velha; (*of beer*) engradado.
crater ['kreɪtə*] *n* cratera.
cravat(e) [krə'væt] *n* gravata.
crave [kreɪv] *vt*, *vi*: **to ~ for** ansiar por.
craving ['kreɪvɪŋ] *n* (*of pregnant woman*) desejo.
crawl [krɔːl] *vi* arrastar-se; (*child*) engatinhar; (*vehicle*) arrastar-se a passo de tartaruga ♦ *n* rastejo; (SWIMMING) crawl *m*; **to ~ to sb** (*inf*) puxar o saco de alguém.
crayfish ['kreɪfɪʃ] *n inv* lagostim *m*.
crayon ['kreɪən] *n* lápis *m* de cera, crayon *m*.
craze [kreɪz] *n* mania; (*fashion*) moda.
crazed [kreɪzd] *adj* (*look*, *person*) enlouquecido; (*pottery*, *glaze*) craquelê.
crazy ['kreɪzɪ] *adj* (*person*) louco, maluco, doido; (*idea*) disparatado; **to go ~** enlouquecer; **to be ~ about sth** (*inf*) ser louco por algo.
crazy paving (BRIT) *n* pavimento irregular.
creak [kriːk] *vi* chiar, ranger; (*door etc*) ranger.
cream [kriːm] *n* (*of milk*) nata; (*gen*) creme *m*; (*fig*): **the ~ of** a fina flor de ♦ *adj* (*colour*) creme *inv*.
cream off *vt* (*fig*) tirar.
cream cake *n* bolo de creme.
cream cheese *n* ricota (BR), queijo creme (PT).
creamery ['kriːmərɪ] *n* (*shop*) leiteria; (*factory*) fábrica de laticínios.
creamy ['kriːmɪ] *adj* cremoso.
crease [kriːs] *n* (*fold*) dobra, vinco; (*in trousers*) vinco; (*wrinkle*) ruga ♦ *vt* (*fold*) dobrar, vincar; (*wrinkle*) amassar, amarrotar ♦ *vi* (*wrinkle up*) amassar-se, amarrotar-se.
crease-resistant *adj*: **a ~ fabric** um tecido que não amarrota.
create [kriː'eɪt] *vt* criar.
creation [kriː'eɪʃən] *n* criação *f*.
creative [kriː'eɪtɪv] *adj* criativo.
creativity [kriːeɪ'tɪvɪtɪ] *n* criatividade *f*.
creator [kriː'eɪtə*] *n* criador(a) *m/f*.
creature ['kriːtʃə*] *n* (*animal*) animal *m*, bicho; (*living thing*) criatura.
creche [krɛʃ] *n* creche *f*.
crèche [krɛʃ] *n* = **creche.**
credence ['kriːdns] *n* crédito.
credentials [krɪ'dɛnʃlz] *npl* credenciais *fpl*.
credibility [krɛdɪ'bɪlɪtɪ] *n* credibilidade *f*.
credible ['krɛdɪbl] *adj* crível.
credit ['krɛdɪt] *n* (*gen*, SCH) crédito; (*merit*) mérito, honra ♦ *vt* (*believe*: *also*: *give ~ to*) acreditar; (COMM) creditar ♦ *cpd* creditício; **~s** *npl* (CINEMA) crédito; **to ~ sb with sth** (*fig*) atribuir algo a alguém; **to ~ £5 to sb** creditar £5 a alguém; **to be in ~** (*person*, *bank account*) ter fundos; **on ~** a crédito; **to one's ~** honra lhe seja; **to take the ~ for sth** atribuir-se o mérito de; **it does him ~** é motivo de honra para ele; **he's a ~ to his family** ele é um orgulho para a família.
creditable ['krɛdɪtəbl] *adj* louvável.
credit account *n* conta de crédito.
credit agency (BRIT) *n* agência de crédito.
credit balance *n* saldo credor.
credit bureau (US: *irreg*) *n* agência de crédito.
credit card *n* cartão *m* de crédito.
credit control *n* controle *m* de crédito.
credit facilities *npl* crediário.
credit limit *n* limite *m* de crédito.
credit note *n* nota de crédito.
creditor ['krɛdɪtə*] *n* credor(a) *m/f*.
credit transfer *n* transferência.
creditworthy ['krɛdɪtwəːðɪ] *adj* merecedor(a) de crédito.
credulity [krɪ'djuːlɪtɪ] *n* credulidade *f*.
creed [kriːd] *n* credo.
creek [kriːk] *n* enseada; (US) riacho.
creel [kriːl] *n* cesto de pescador.
creep [kriːp] (*pt*, *pp* **crept**) *vi* (*animal*) rastejar; (*person*) deslizar(-se), andar na ponta dos pés; (*plant*) trepar ♦ *n* (*inf*) puxa-saco *m*; **it gives me the ~s** me dá arrepios; **to ~ up on sb** pegar alguém de surpresa.
creeper ['kriːpə*] *n* trepadeira; **~s** *npl* (US: *for baby*) macacão *m* (BR), fato macaco (PT).
creepy ['kriːpɪ] *adj* (*frightening*) horripilante.
creepy-crawly [-'krɔːlɪ] (*inf*) *n* bichinho.
cremate [krɪ'meɪt] *vt* cremar.
cremation [krɔ'meɪʃən] *n* cremação *f*.
crematoria [krɛmə'tɔːrɪə] *npl of* **crematorium.**
crematorium [krɛmə'tɔːrɪəm] (*pl* **crematoria**) *n* crematório.
creosote ['krɪəsəut] *n* creosoto.
crêpe [kreɪp] *n* (*fabric*) crepe *m*; (*paper*) papel crepom *m*.
crêpe bandage *n* atadura de crepe.
crêpe paper *n* papel *m* crepom.
crêpe sole *n* sola de crepe.
crept [krɛpt] *pt*, *pp of* **creep.**
crescendo [krɪ'ʃɛndəu] *n* crescendo.
crescent ['krɛsnt] *n* meia-lua; (*street*) rua se-

micircular.
cress [krɛs] *n* agrião *m.*
crest [krɛst] *n* (*of bird*) crista; (*of hill*) cimo, topo; (*of helmet*) cimeira; (*of coat of arms*) timbre *m.*
crestfallen ['krɛstfɔːlən] *adj* abatido, cabisbaixo.
Crete [kriːt] *n* Creta.
crevasse [krɪ'væs] *n* fenda.
crevice ['krɛvɪs] *n* fenda, greta.
crew [kruː] *n* (*of ship etc*) tripulação *f*; (*gang*) bando, quadrilha; (*MIL*) guarnição *f*; (*CINEMA*) equipe *f.*
crew-cut *n* corte *m* à escovinha.
crew-neck *n* gola arredondada.
crib [krɪb] *n* manjedoira, presépio; (*US*: *cot*) berço ♦ *vt* (*inf*) colar.
cribbage ['krɪbɪdʒ] *n jogo de cartas.*
crick [krɪk] *n* câibra; ~ **in the neck** torcicolo.
cricket ['krɪkɪt] *n* (*insect*) grilo; (*game*) criquete *m*, cricket *m.*
cricketer ['krɪkɪtə*] *n* jogador(a) *m/f* de criquete.
crime [kraɪm] *n* crime *m*; (*less serious*) delito; (~ *in general*) criminalidade *f.*
crime wave *n* onda de criminalidade.
criminal ['krɪmɪnl] *n* criminoso ♦ *adj* criminal; (*law*) penal; **the C~ Investigation Department** (*BRIT*) a Brigada de Investigação Criminal.
crimp [krɪmp] *vt* (*hair*) frisar.
crimson ['krɪmzn] *adj* carmesim *inv.*
cringe [krɪndʒ] *vi* agachar-se, encolher-se.
crinkle ['krɪŋkl] *vt* amassar, enrugar.
cripple ['krɪpl] *n* coxo/a, aleijado/a ♦ *vt* aleijar; (*ship, plane*) inutilizar; (*industry, exports*) paralisar.
crippling ['krɪplɪŋ] *adj* (*disease*) devastador(a); (*taxation, debts*) excessivo.
crises ['kraɪsiːz] *npl of* **crisis**.
crisis ['kraɪsɪs] (*pl* **crises**) *n* crise *f.*
crisp [krɪsp] *adj* (*crunchy*) crocante; (*vegetables, fruit*) fresco; (*cooked*) torrado; (*manner*) seco.
crisps [krɪsps] (*BRIT*) *npl* batatinhas *fpl* fritas.
criss-cross [krɪs-] *adj* (*lines*) entrecruzado; (*pattern*) em xadrez ♦ *vt* entrecruzar; ~ **pattern** (padrão *m* em) xadrez *m.*
criteria [kraɪ'tɪərɪə] *npl of* **criterion**.
criterion [kraɪ'tɪərɪən] (*pl* **criteria**) *n* critério.
critic ['krɪtɪk] *n* crítico/a.
critical ['krɪtɪkl] *adj* crítico; (*illness*) grave; **to be ~ of sth/sb** criticar algo/alguém.
critically ['krɪtɪkəlɪ] *adv* (*examine*) criteriosamente; (*speak*) criticamente; (*ill*) gravemente.
criticism ['krɪtɪsɪzm] *n* crítica.
criticize ['krɪtɪsaɪz] *vt* criticar.
critique [krɪ'tiːk] *n* crítica.
croak [krəuk] *vi* (*frog*) coaxar; (*raven*) crocitar ♦ *n* grasnido.
crochet ['krəuʃeɪ] *n* crochê *m.*
crock [krɔk] *n* jarro; (*inf*: *also*: *old* ~: *person*) caco velho; (: *car*) calhambeque *m.*
crockery ['krɔkərɪ] *n* louça.
crocodile ['krɔkədaɪl] *n* crocodilo.
crocus ['krəukəs] *n* açafrão-da-primavera *m.*
croft [krɔft] (*BRIT*) *n* pequena chácara.
crofter ['krɔftə*] (*BRIT*) *n* arrendatário.
croissant ['krwasã] *n* croissant *m.*
crone [krəun] *n* velha encarquilhada.
crony ['krəunɪ] *n* camarada *m/f*, compadre *m.*
crook [kruk] *n* (*inf*: *criminal*) vigarista *m/f*; (*of shepherd*) cajado; (*of arm*) curva.
crooked ['krukɪd] *adj* torto; (*path*) tortuoso; (*action*) desonesto.
crop [krɔp] *n* (*species*) colheita; (*quantity*) safra; (*riding* ~) chicotinho; (*of bird*) papo ♦ *vt* cortar, ceifar.
crop up *vi* surgir.
cropper ['krɔpə*] *n*: **to come a ~** (*inf*) dar com os burros n'água, entrar pelo cano.
crop spraying [-'spreɪɪŋ] *n* pulverização *f* das culturas.
croquet ['krəukeɪ] *n* croquet *m*, croquê *m.*
croquette [krə'kɛt] *n* croquete *m.*
cross [krɔs] *n* cruz *f*; (*BIO*) cruzamento ♦ *vt* cruzar; (*street etc*) atravessar; (*thwart*: *person, plan*) contrariar ♦ *vi* atravessar ♦ *adj* zangado, mal-humorado; **to ~ o.s.** persignar-se; **they've got their lines ~ed** eles têm um mal-entendido.
cross out *vt* riscar.
cross over *vi* atravessar.
crossbar ['krɔsbɑː*] *n* travessa; (*SPORT*) barra transversal.
crossbreed ['krɔsbriːd] *n* raça cruzada.
cross-Channel ferry *n* barca que faz a travessia do Canal da Mancha.
cross-check *n* conferição *f* ♦ *vt* conferir.
cross-country (race) *n* corrida pelo campo.
cross-examination *n* interrogatório; (*LAW*) repergunta.
cross-examine *vt* interrogar; (*LAW*) reperguntar.
cross-eyed [-aɪd] *adj* vesgo.
crossfire ['krɔsfaɪə*] *n* fogo cruzado.
crossing ['krɔsɪŋ] *n* (*road*) cruzamento; (*rail*) passagem *f* de nível; (*sea-passage*) travessia; (*also*: *pedestrian* ~) faixa (para pedestres) (*BR*), passadeira (*PT*).
cross-purposes *npl*: **to be at ~ (with sb)** não entender-se (com alguém); **we're (talking) at ~** não falamos da mesma coisa.
cross-reference *n* referência remissiva.
crossroads ['krɔsrəudz] *n* cruzamento.
cross section *n* (*BIO*) corte *m* transversal; (*of population*) grupo representativo.
crosswalk ['krɔswɔːk] (*US*) *n* faixa (para pedestres) (*BR*), passadeira (*PT*).
crosswind ['krɔswɪnd] *n* vento costal.
crosswise ['krɔswaɪz] *adv* transversalmente.
crossword ['krɔswəːd] *n* palavras *fpl* cruzadas.

NB: *European Portuguese adds the following consonants to certain words:* **b** (sú(b)dito, su(b)til); **c** (a(c)ção, a(c)cionista, a(c)to); **m** (inde(m)ne); **p** (ado(p)ção, ado(p)tar); *for further details see p. xiii.*

crotch [krɔtʃ] *n* (*of garment*) fundilho.
crotchet ['krɔtʃɪt] *n* (*MUS*) semínima.
crotchety ['krɔtʃɪtɪ] *adj* (*person*) rabugento.
crouch [krautʃ] *vi* agachar-se.
croup [kru:p] *n* (*MED*) crupe *m*.
croupier ['kru:pɪə] *n* crupiê *m/f*.
crouton ['kru:tɔn] *n* crouton *m*.
crow [krəu] *n* (*bird*) corvo; (*of cock*) canto, cocoricó *m* ♦ *vi* (*cock*) cantar, cocoricar; (*fig*) contar vantagem.
crowbar ['krəuba:*] *n* pé-de-cabra *m*.
crowd [kraud] *n* multidão *f*; (*SPORT*) público, galera (*inf*); (*unruly*) tropel *m*; (*common herd*) turba, vulgo ♦ *vt* (*fill*) apinhar ♦ *vi* (*gather*) reunir-se; **~s of people** um grande número de pessoas.
crowded ['kraudɪd] *adj* (*full*) lotado; (*well-attended*) concorrido.
crowd scene *n* (*CINEMA, THEATRE*) cena de multidão.
crown [kraun] *n* coroa; (*of head*) topo, alta; (*of hat*) copa; (*of hill*) cume *m* ♦ *vt* coroar; (*tooth*) pôr uma coroa artificial em.
crown court (*BRIT*) *n* Tribunal *m* de Justiça.
crowning ['kraunɪŋ] *adj* (*achievement, glory*) supremo.
crown jewels *npl* jóias *fpl* reais.
crown prince *n* príncipe *m* herdeiro.
crow's-feet *npl* pés-de-galinha *mpl*.
crow's-nest *n* (*on ship*) cesto de gávea.
crucial ['kru:ʃl] *adj* decisivo; **~ to** vital para.
crucifix ['kru:sɪfɪks] *n* crucifixo.
crucifixion [kru:sɪ'fɪkʃən] *n* crucificação *f*.
crucify ['kru:sɪfaɪ] *vt* crucificar.
crude [kru:d] *adj* (*materials*) bruto; (*fig*: *basic*) tosco; (: *vulgar*) grosseiro.
crude (oil) *n* petróleo em bruto.
cruel ['kruəl] *adj* cruel.
cruelty ['kruəltɪ] *n* crueldade *f*.
cruet ['kru:ɪt] *n* galheta.
cruise [kru:z] *n* cruzeiro ♦ *vi* (*ship*) fazer um cruzeiro; (*aircraft*) voar; (*car*): **to ~ at ... km/h** ir a ... km por hora.
cruise missile *n* míssil *m* Cruise.
cruiser ['kru:zə*] *n* cruzador *m*.
cruising speed ['kru:zɪŋ-] *n* velocidade *f* de cruzeiro.
crumb [krʌm] *n* migalha.
crumble ['krʌmbl] *vt* esmigalhar ♦ *vi* desintegrar-se; (*building, fig*) desmoronar-se.
crumbly ['krʌmblɪ] *adj* friável.
crummy ['krʌmɪ] (*inf*) *adj* mixa; (*unwell*) podre.
crumpet ['krʌmpɪt] *n* *bolo leve*.
crumple ['krʌmpl] *vt* (*paper*) amassar; (*material*) amarrotar.
crunch [krʌntʃ] *vt* (*food etc*) mastigar; (*underfoot*) esmagar ♦ *n* (*fig*) crise *f*.
crunchy ['krʌntʃɪ] *adj* crocante.
crusade [kru:'seɪd] *n* cruzada ♦ *vi* (*fig*): **to ~ for/against** batalhar por/contra.
crusader [kru:'seɪdə*] *n* cruzado; (*fig*): **~ (for)** batalhador(a) *m/f* (por).
crush [krʌʃ] *n* (*people*) esmagamento; (*crowd*) aglomeração *f*; (*love*): **to have a ~ on sb** ter um rabicho por alguém; (*drink*): **lemon ~** limonada ♦ *vt* (*gen*) esmagar; (*paper*) amassar; (*cloth*) enrugar; (*fruit*) espremer.
crushing ['krʌʃɪŋ] *adj* (*burden*) esmagador(a).
crust [krʌst] *n* côdea; (*MED*) crosta.
crustacean [krʌs'teɪʃən] *n* crustáceo.
crusty ['krʌstɪ] *adj* cascudo.
crutch [krʌtʃ] *n* muleta; (*of garment*: *also*: *crotch*) fundilho.
crux [krʌks] *n* ponto crucial.
cry [kraɪ] *vi* chorar; (*shout*) gritar ♦ *n* grito; **to ~ for help** gritar por socorro; **it's a far ~ from ...** (*fig*) é totalmente diferente de ....
cry off *vi* desistir.
crying ['kraɪɪŋ] *adj* (*fig*) flagrante.
crypt [krɪpt] *n* cripta.
cryptic ['krɪptɪk] *adj* enigmático.
crystal ['krɪstl] *n* cristal *m*.
crystal-clear *adj* cristalino, claro.
crystallize ['krɪstəlaɪz] *vt* cristalizar ♦ *vi* cristalizar-se.
CSA *n abbr* = **Confederate States of America**.
CSC *n abbr* (= *Civil Service Commission*) *comissão de recrutamento de funcionários públicos*.
CSE (*BRIT*) *n abbr* = **Certificate of Secondary Education**.
CSEU (*BRIT*) *n abbr* (= *Confederation of Shipbuilding and Engineering Unions*) *confederação dos sindicatos da construção naval e da engenharia*.
CS gas (*BRIT*) *n* gás *m* CS.
CST (*US*) *n abbr* (= *Central Standard Time*) *fuso horário*.
CSU (*BRIT*) *n abbr* (= *Civil Service Union*) *sindicato de funcionários públicos*.
CT (*US*) *abbr* (*POST*) = **Connecticut**.
ct *abbr* = **carat**.
cu. *abbr* = **cubic**.
cub [kʌb] *n* filhote *m*; (*also*: *~ scout*) lobinho.
Cuba ['kju:bə] *n* Cuba.
Cuban ['kju:bən] *adj, n* cubano/a.
cubbyhole ['kʌbɪhəul] *n* esconderijo.
cube [kju:b] *n* cubo ♦ *vt* (*MATH*) elevar ao cubo.
cube root *n* raiz *f* cúbica.
cubic ['kju:bɪk] *adj* cúbico; **~ metre** *etc* metro *etc* cúbico; **~ capacity** (*AUT*) cilindrada.
cubicle ['kju:bɪkl] *n* cubículo; (*shower ~*) boxe *m*.
cuckoo ['kuku:] *n* cuco.
cuckoo clock *n* relógio de cuco.
cucumber ['kju:kʌmbə*] *n* pepino.
cud [kʌd] *n*: **to chew the ~** ruminar.
cuddle ['kʌdl] *vt* abraçar ♦ *vi* abraçar-se.
cuddly ['kʌdlɪ] *adj* fofo.
cudgel ['kʌdʒəl] *n* cacete *m* ♦ *vt*: **to ~ one's brains** quebrar a cabeça.
cue [kju:] *n* (*SNOOKER*) taco; (*THEATRE etc*) deixa.
cuff [kʌf] *n* (*of shirt, coat etc*) punho; (*US*: *on trousers*) bainha; (*blow*) bofetada ♦ *vt* esbofetear; **off the ~** de improviso.

cufflinks ['kʌflɪŋks] *npl* abotoaduras *fpl*.
cu. in. *abbr* = **cubic inches**.
cuisine [kwɪ'zi:n] *n* cozinha.
cul-de-sac ['kʌldəsæk] *n* beco sem saída.
culinary ['kʌlɪnərɪ] *adj* culinário.
cull [kʌl] *vt* (*flowers*) escolher; (*select*) selecionar; (*kill*) matar seletivamente.
culminate ['kʌlmɪneɪt] *vi*: **to ~ in** terminar em; (*lead to*) resultar em.
culmination [kʌlmɪ'neɪʃən] *n* culminação *f*, auge *m*.
culottes [kju:'lɔts] *npl* saia-calça.
culpable ['kʌlpəbl] *adj* culpável.
culprit ['kʌlprɪt] *n* culpado/a.
cult [kʌlt] *n* culto.
cult figure *n* ídolo.
cultivate ['kʌltɪveɪt] *vt* (*also fig*) cultivar.
cultivation [kʌltɪ'veɪʃən] *n* cultivo; (*fig*) cultura.
cultural ['kʌltʃərəl] *adj* cultural.
culture ['kʌltʃə*] *n* (*also fig*) cultura.
cultured ['kʌltʃəd] *adj* culto.
cumbersome ['kʌmbəsəm] *adj* pesado, incômodo.
cumin ['kʌmɪn] *n* cominho.
cumulative ['kju:mjulətɪv] *adj* cumulativo.
cunning ['kʌnɪŋ] *n* astúcia ♦ *adj* astuto, malandro; (*clever*: *device*, *idea*) engenhoso.
cup [kʌp] *n* xícara (*BR*), chávena (*PT*); (*prize, event*) taça.
cupboard ['kʌbəd] *n* armário; (*for crockery*) guarda-louça.
cup final (*BRIT*) *n* final *f*.
Cupid ['kju:pɪd] *n* Cupido.
cupidity [kju:'pɪdɪtɪ] *n* cupidez *f*.
cupola ['kju:pələ] *n* cúpula.
cup-tie *n* jogo eliminatório.
cur [kə:] *n* cão *m* vadio, vira-latas *m inv*; (*person*) patife *m/f*.
curable ['kjuərəbl] *adj* curável.
curate ['kjuə:rɪt] *n* coadjutor *m*.
curator [kjuə'reɪtə*] *n* diretor(a) *m/f*, curador(a) *m/f*.
curb [kə:b] *vt* refrear ♦ *n* freio; (*US*) = **kerb**.
curdle ['kə:dl] *vi* coalhar.
curds [kə:dz] *npl* coalho.
cure [kjuə*] *vt* curar ♦ *n* tratamento, cura; **to be ~d of sth** sarar(-se) de algo.
cure-all *n* (*also*: *fig*) panacéia.
curfew ['kə:fju:] *n* hora de recolher.
curio ['kjuərɪəu] *n* antiguidade *f*.
curiosity [kjuərɪ'ɔsɪtɪ] *n* curiosidade *f*.
curious ['kjuərɪəs] *adj* curioso.
curiously ['kjuərɪəslɪ] *adv* curiosamente; **~ enough, ...** por estranho que pareça, ...
curl [kə:l] *n* anel *m*, caracol *m* ♦ *vt* (*hair*) frisar, encrespar; (*paper*) enrolar; (*lip*) torcer ♦ *vi* (*hair*) encaracolar.
curl up *vi* frisar-se; (*person*) encaracolar-se.
curler ['kə:lə*] *n* rolo, bobe *m*.
curlew ['kə:lu:] *n* maçarico.
curling ['kə:lɪŋ] *n* (*SPORT*) curling *m*.
curling tongs (*US* **curling irons**) *npl* ferros *mpl* de frisar cabelo.
curly ['kə:lɪ] *adj* frisado, crespo.
currant ['kʌrnt] *n* passa de corinto; (*black, red*) groselha.
currency ['kʌrnsɪ] *n* moeda; **foreign ~** câmbio, divisas; **to gain ~** (*fig*) consagrar-se.
current ['kʌrnt] *n* (*ELEC*) corrente *f*; (*in river*) correnteza ♦ *adj* corrente; (*present*) atual; **in ~ usage** de uso corrente.
current account *n* conta corrente.
current affairs *npl* atualidades *fpl*.
current assets *npl* (*COMM*) ativo corrente.
current liabilities *npl* (*COMM*) passivo corrente.
currently ['kʌrntlɪ] *adv* atualmente.
curricula [kə'rɪkjulə] *npl of* **curriculum**.
curriculum [kə'rɪkjuləm] (*pl* **~s** *or* **curricula**) *n* programa *m* de estudos.
curriculum vitae [-'vi:taɪ] *n* curriculum vitae *m*, currículo.
curry ['kʌrɪ] *n* caril *m* ♦ *vt*: **to ~ favour with** captar simpatia de.
curry powder *n* pós *mpl* de caril, curry *m*.
curse [kə:s] *vi* xingar (*BR*), praguejar (*PT*) ♦ *vt* amaldiçoar, xingar (*BR*) ♦ *n* maldição *f*; (*swearword*) palavrão *m* (*BR*), baixo calão *m* (*PT*).
cursor ['kə:sə*] *n* (*COMPUT*) cursor *m*.
cursory ['kə:sərɪ] *adj* rápido, superficial.
curt [kə:t] *adj* seco, brusco.
curtail [kə:'teɪl] *vt* (*visit etc*) abreviar, encurtar; (*expenses etc*) reduzir.
curtain ['kə:tn] *n* cortina; (*THEATRE*) pano.
curtain call *n* (*THEATRE*) chamada à ribalta.
curtain ring *n* argola.
curts(e)y ['kə:tsɪ] *n* mesura, reverência ♦ *vi* fazer reverência.
curvature ['kə:vətʃə*] *n* curvatura.
curve [kə:v] *n* curva ♦ *vt* encurvar, torcer ♦ *vi* encurvar-se, torcer-se; (*road*) fazer (uma) curva.
curved [kə:vd] *adj* curvado, curvo.
cushion ['kuʃən] *n* almofada; (*SNOOKER*) tabela ♦ *vt* (*seat*) escorar com almofada; (*shock*) amortecer.
cushy ['kuʃɪ] (*inf*) *adj*: **a ~ job** uma boca; **to have a ~ time** estar na moleza.
custard ['kʌstəd] *n* (*for pouring*) nata, creme *m*.
custard powder (*BRIT*) *n* pó *m* para fazer creme.
custodian [kʌs'təudɪən] *n* guarda *m/f*.
custody ['kʌstədɪ] *n* custódia; (*for offenders*) prisão *f* preventiva; **to take into ~** deter.
custom ['kʌstəm] *n* costume *m*; (*COMM*) clientela; **~s** *npl* alfândega.
customary ['kʌstəmərɪ] *adj* costumeiro; **it is ~ to do it** é costume fazê-lo.
custom-built *adj* feito sob encomenda.

***NB**: European Portuguese adds the following consonants to certain words:* **b** (sú(b)dito, su(b)til); **c** (a(c)ção, a(c)cionista, a(c)to); **m** (inde(m)ne); **p** (ado(p)ção, ado(p)tar); *for further details see p. xiii.*

customer ['kʌstəmə*] *n* cliente *m/f*; **he's an awkward ~** (*inf*) ele é um cara difícil.
custom-made *adj* feito sob encomenda; (*clothes*) feito sob medida.
Customs and Excise (BRIT) *n* autoridades *fpl* alfandegárias.
customs duty *n* imposto alfandegário.
customs officer *n* inspetor(a) *m/f* da alfândega, aduaneiro/a.
cut [kʌt] (*pt, pp* **cut**) *vt* cortar; (*price*) baixar; (*record*) gravar; (*reduce*) reduzir; (*inf: class*) matar ♦ *vi* cortar; (*intersect*) interceptar-se ♦ *n* corte *m*; **cold ~s** *npl* (US) frios *mpl* sortidos; **to ~ a tooth** estar com um dente nascendo; **to ~ one's finger** cortar o dedo; **to get one's hair ~** cortar o cabelo; **to ~ sth short** abreviar algo; **to ~ sb dead** fingir que não conhece alguém.
cut back *vt* (*plants*) podar; (*production, expenditure*) cortar.
cut down *vt* (*tree*) derrubar; (*reduce*) reduzir; **to ~ sb down to size** (*fig*) abaixar a crista de alguém, colocar alguém no seu lugar.
cut in *vi*: **to ~ in (on)** interromper; (AUT) cortar.
cut off *vt* cortar; (*retreat*) impedir; (*troops*) cercar; **we've been ~ off** (TEL) fomos cortados.
cut out *vt* (*shape*) recortar; (*delete*) suprimir.
cut through *vi* abrir caminho.
cut up *vt* cortar em pedaços.
cut-and-dried *adj* (*also: cut-and-dry*) todo resolvido.
cutaway ['kʌtəweɪ] *adj, n*: **~ (drawing)** vista diagramática.
cutback ['kʌtbæk] *n* redução *f*, corte *m*.
cute [kjuːt] *adj* bonitinho, gracinha; (*shrewd*) astuto.
cut glass *n* cristal *m* lapidado.
cuticle ['kjuːtɪkl] *n* cutícula; **~ remover** produto para tirar as cutículas.
cutlery ['kʌtlərɪ] *n* talheres *mpl*.
cutlet ['kʌtlɪt] *n* costeleta.
cutoff ['kʌtɔf] *n* (*also: ~ point*) ponto de corte.
cutoff switch *n* interruptor *m*.
cutout ['kʌtaut] *n* figura para recortar; (ELEC) interruptor *m*.
cut-price (US **cut-rate**) *adj* a preço reduzido.
cut-throat *n* assassino/a ♦ *adj* impiedoso, feroz.
cutting ['kʌtɪŋ] *adj* cortante; (*remark*) mordaz ♦ *n* (BRIT: *from newspaper*) recorte *m*; (: RAIL) corte *m*; (CINEMA) corte *m*.
cuttlefish ['kʌtlfɪʃ] (*pl inv or* **~es**) *n* sita.
cut-up *adj* arrasado, aflito.
CV *n abbr* = **curriculum vitae**.
C & W *n abbr* = **country and western (music)**.
cwo *abbr* (COMM) = **cash with order**.
cwt *abbr* = **hundredweight**.
cyanide ['saɪənaɪd] *n* cianeto.
cybernetics [saɪbə'nɛtɪks] *n* cibernética.
cyclamen ['sɪkləmən] *n* cíclame *m*.
cycle ['saɪkl] *n* ciclo; (*bicycle*) bicicleta ♦ *vi* andar de bicicleta.
cycle race *n* corrida de bicicletas.
cycle rack *n* engradado para guardar bicicletas.
cycling ['saɪklɪŋ] *n* ciclismo.
cyclist ['saɪklɪst] *n* ciclista *m/f*.
cyclone ['saɪkləun] *n* ciclone *m*.
cygnet ['sɪgnɪt] *n* cisne *m* novo.
cylinder ['sɪlɪndə*] *n* cilindro.
cylinder block *n* bloco de cilindros.
cylinder capacity *n* capacidade *f* cilíndrica, cilindrada.
cylinder head *n* cilíndrico.
cylinder-head gasket *n* culatra.
cymbals ['sɪmblz] *npl* pratos *mpl*.
cynic ['sɪnɪk] *n* cínico/a.
cynical ['sɪnɪkl] *adj* cínico, sarcástico.
cynicism ['sɪnɪsɪzəm] *n* cinismo.
CYO (US) *n abbr* = **Catholic Youth Organization**.
cypress ['saɪprɪs] *n* cipreste *m*.
Cypriot ['sɪprɪət] *adj, n* cipriota *m/f*.
Cyprus ['saɪprəs] *n* Chipre *f*.
cyst [sɪst] *n* cisto.
cystitis [sɪs'taɪtɪs] *n* cistite *f*.
CZ (US) *n abbr* (= *Canal Zone*) zona do canal do Panamá.
czar [zɑː*] *n* czar *m*.
Czech [tʃɛk] *adj* tcheco ♦ *n* tcheco/a; (LING) tcheco.
Czechoslovak [tʃɛkə'sləuvæk] *adj, n* = **Czechoslovakian**.
Czechoslovakia [tʃɛkəslə'vækɪə] *n* Tchecoslováquia.
Czechoslovakian [tʃɛkəslə'vækɪən] *adj, n* tchecoslovaco/a.

D

D, d [diː] *n* (*letter*) D, d *m*; (MUS): **D** ré *m*; **D for David** (BRIT) *or* **Dog** (US) D de dado.
D (*US*) *abbr* (POL) = **democrat(ic)**.
d (BRIT) *abbr* (*old*) = **penny**.
d. *abbr* = **died**.
DA (US) *n abbr* = **district attorney**.
dab [dæb] *vt* (*eyes, wound*) tocar (de leve); (*paint, cream*) aplicar de leve ♦ *n* (*of paint*) pincelada; (*of liquid*) gota; (*amount*) pequena quantidade *f*.
dabble ['dæbl] *vi*: **to ~ in** interessar-se por.
dachshund ['dækshund] *n* bassê *m*.
dad [dæd] *n* papai *m*.
daddy ['dædɪ] *n* = **dad**.
daddy-long-legs *n inv* pernilongo.
daffodil ['dæfədɪl] *n* narciso-dos-prados *m*.
daft [dɑːft] *adj* bobo, besta; **to be ~ about** ser louco por.

dagger ['dægə*] *n* punhal *m*, adaga; **to look ~s at sb** olhar feio para alguém; **to be at ~s drawn with sb** andar às turras com alguém.
dahlia ['deɪljə] *n* dália.
daily ['deɪlɪ] *adj* diário, cotidiano ♦ *n* (*paper*) diário; (*BRIT*: *domestic help*) diarista (*BR*), mulher *f* a dias (*PT*) ♦ *adv* diariamente, todo dia; **twice ~** duas vezes por dia.
dainty ['deɪntɪ] *adj* delicado; (*tasteful*) elegante, gracioso.
dairy ['dɛərɪ] *n* leiteria ♦ *adj* (*industry*) de laticínios; (*cattle*) leiteiro.
dairy cow *n* vaca leiteira.
dairy farm *n* fazenda de gado leiteiro.
dairy produce *n* laticínios *mpl*.
dais ['deɪɪs] *n* estrado.
daisy ['deɪzɪ] *n* margarida.
daisy wheel *n* (*on printer*) margarida.
daisy-wheel printer *n* impressora margarida.
Dakar ['dækə*] *n* Dacar.
dale [deɪl] *n* vale *m*.
dally ['dælɪ] *vi* vadiar.
dalmatian [dæl'meɪʃən] *n* (*dog*) dálmata *m*.
dam [dæm] *n* represa, barragem *f* ♦ *vt* represar.
damage ['dæmɪdʒ] *n* (*physical*) danos *mpl*; (*harm*) prejuízo; (*to machine*) avaria ♦ *vt* (*physically*) danificar; (*harm*) prejudicar; **~s** *npl* (*LAW*) indenização *f* por perdas e danos; **to pay £5,000 in ~s** pagar £5,000 de indenização; **~ to property** danos materiais.
damaging ['dæmɪdʒɪŋ] *adj*: **~ (to)** prejudicial (a).
Damascus [də'mɑːskəs] *n* Damasco.
dame [deɪm] *n* (*title*) *título honorífico dado a uma membra da Ordem do Império Britânico*; *título honorífico dado à esposa de um cavalheiro ou baronete*; (*US*: *inf*) dona; (*THEATRE*) dama.
damn [dæm] *vt* condenar; (*curse*) maldizer ♦ *n* (*inf*): **I don't give a ~** não dou a mínima, estou me lixando ♦ *adj* (*inf*) (que) droga de; **~ (it)!** (que) droga!
damnable ['dæmnəbl] (*inf*) *adj* (*behaviour*) condenável; (*weather*) horrível.
damnation [dæm'neɪʃən] *n* (*REL*) danação *f* ♦ *excl* (*inf*) droga!
damning ['dæmɪŋ] *adj* (*evidence*) prejudicial; (*criticism*) condenador(a).
damp [dæmp] *adj* úmido ♦ *n* umidade *f* ♦ *vt* (*also*: **~en**: *cloth, rag*) umedecer; (*enthusiasm etc*) jogar água fria em.
dampcourse ['dæmpkɔːs] *n* impermeabilização *f*.
damper ['dæmpə*] *n* (*MUS*) abafador *m*; (*of fire*) registro; **to put a ~ on** (*fig*: *atmosphere*) criar um mal-estar em; (: *party*) acabar com a animação de; (: *enthusiasm*) cortar.
dampness ['dæmpnɪs] *n* umidade *f*.
damson ['dæmzən] *n* ameixa pequena.
dance [dɑːns] *n* dança; (*party*) baile *m* ♦ *vi* dançar; **to ~ about** saltitar.
dance hall *n* salão *m* de baile.
dancer ['dɑːnsə*] *n* dançarino/a; (*professional*) bailarino/a.
dancing ['dɑːnsɪŋ] *n* dança.
D and C *n abbr* (*MED*: = *dilation and curettage*) dilatação *f* e curetagem *f*.
dandelion ['dændɪlaɪən] *n* dente-de-leão *m*.
dandruff ['dændrəf] *n* caspa.
dandy ['dændɪ] *n* dândi *m* ♦ *adj* (*US*: *inf*) bacana.
Dane [deɪn] *n* dinamarquês/esa *m/f*.
danger ['deɪndʒə*] *n* perigo; **to be in ~ of** correr o risco de; **in ~** em perigo; **out of ~** fora de perigo; **~ money** (*BRIT*) adicional *m* por insalubridade.
danger list *n* (*MED*): **on the ~** na lista dos pacientes graves.
dangerous ['deɪndʒərəs] *adj* perigoso.
dangerously ['deɪndʒərəslɪ] *adv* perigosamente; **~ ill** gravemente doente.
danger zone *n* zona de perigo.
dangle ['dæŋgl] *vt* balançar ♦ *vi* pender balançando.
Danish ['deɪnɪʃ] *adj* dinamarquês/esa ♦ *n* (*LING*) dinamarquês *m*.
Danish pastry *n* doce *m* (*de massa com frutas*).
dank [dæŋk] *adj* frio e úmido.
Danube ['dænjuːb] *n*: **the ~** o Danúbio.
dapper ['dæpə*] *adj* garboso.
dare [dɛə*] *vt*: **to ~ sb to do sth** desafiar alguém a fazer algo ♦ *vi*: **to ~ (to) do sth** atrever-se a fazer algo, ousar fazer algo; **I ~n't tell him** (*BRIT*) eu não ouso dizê-lo a ele; **I ~ say he'll turn up** acho provável que ele venha.
daredevil ['dɛədɛvl] *n* intrépido, atrevido.
Dar-es-Salaam ['dɑːrɛssə'lɑːm] *n* Dar-es-Salaam.
daring ['dɛərɪŋ] *adj* atrevido, ousado ♦ *n* atrevimento, audácia, ousadia.
dark [dɑːk] *adj* (*gen, hair*) escuro; (*complexion*) moreno; (*cheerless*) triste, sombrio; (*fig*) sombrio ♦ *n* escuro; **in the ~** no escuro; **in the ~ about** (*fig*) no escuro sobre; **after ~** depois de escurecer; **it is/is getting ~** está escuro/está escurecendo.
dark chocolate *n* chocolate *m* amargo.
darken ['dɑːkən] *vt* escurecer; (*colour*) fazer mais escuro ♦ *vi* escurecer(-se).
dark glasses *npl* óculos *mpl* escuros.
darkly ['dɑːklɪ] *adv* (*gloomily*) sombriamente; (*in a sinister way*) sinistramente.
darkness ['dɑːknɪs] *n* escuridão *f*, trevas *fpl*.
dark room *n* câmara escura.
darling ['dɑːlɪŋ] *adj*, *n* querido/a.
darn [dɑːn] *vt* remendar, cerzir.
dart [dɑːt] *n* dardo; ♦ *vi* precipitar-se; **~s** *n* jogo de dardos; **to ~ away/along** ir-se/seguir

NB: European Portuguese adds the following consonants to certain words: **b** (sú(b)dito, su(b)til); **c** (a(c)ção, a(c)cionista, a(c)to); **m** (inde(m)ne); **p** (ado(p)ção, ado(p)tar); *for further details see p. xiii.*

precipitadamente.

dartboard ['dɑːtbɔːd] *n* alvo (para jogo de dardos).

dash [dæʃ] *n* (*sign*) hífen *m*; (: *long*) travessão *m*; (*rush*) correria; (*small quantity*) pontinha ♦ *vt* (*throw*) arremessar; (*hopes*) frustrar ♦ *vi* precipitar-se, ir depressa.

dash away *vi* sair apressado.

dash off *vt* (*letter, essay*) escrever a toda ♦ *vi* sair apressado.

dashboard ['dæʃbɔːd] *n* painel *m* de instrumentos.

dashing ['dæʃɪŋ] *adj* arrojado.

dastardly ['dæstədlɪ] *adj* vil.

data ['deɪtə] *npl* dados *mpl*.

database ['deɪtəbeɪs] *n* banco de dados.

data capture *n* entrada de dados.

data processing *n* processamento de dados.

data transmission *n* transmissão *f* de dados.

date [deɪt] *n* (*day*) data; (*with friend*) encontro; (*fruit*) tâmara; (*tree*) tamareira ♦ *vt* datar; (*inf*: *go out with*) namorar; **what's the ~ today?** que dia é hoje?; **~ of birth** data de nascimento; **closing ~** data de encerramento; **to ~** até agora; **out of ~** desatualizado; **up to ~** (*correspondence etc*) em dia; (*dictionary, phone book etc*) atualizado; (*method, technology*) moderno; **to bring up to ~** (*correspondence, person*) pôr em dia; (*method*) modernizar; **letter ~d 5th July** (*BRIT*) *or* **July 5th** (*US*) carta datada de 5 de julho.

dated ['deɪtɪd] *adj* antiquado.

dateline ['deɪtlaɪn] *n* meridiano *or* linha de data.

date stamp *n* carimbo datador.

daub [dɔːb] *vt* borrar.

daughter ['dɔːtə*] *n* filha.

daughter-in-law (*pl* **daughters-in-law**) *n* nora.

daunt [dɔːnt] *vt* desalentar, desencorajar.

daunting ['dɔːntɪŋ] *adj* desalentador(a).

dauntless ['dɔːntlɪs] *adj* intrépido, destemido.

dawdle ['dɔːdl] *vi* (*waste time*) fazer cera; (*go slow*) vadiar.

dawn [dɔːn] *n* alvorada, amanhecer *m* ♦ *vi* (*day*) amanhecer; (*fig*): **it ~ed on him that ...** começou a perceber que ...; **at ~** ao amanhecer; **from ~ to dusk** de manhã à noite.

dawn chorus (*BRIT*) *n* canto dos pássaros na alvorada.

day [deɪ] *n* dia *m*; (*working ~*) jornada, dia útil; **the ~ before** a véspera; **the ~ after, the following ~** o dia seguinte; **the ~ before yesterday** anteontem; **the ~ after tomorrow** depois de amanhã; **(on) the ~ that ...** (n)o dia em que ...; **~ by ~** dia a dia; **by ~** de dia; **paid by the ~** pago por dia; **these ~s, in the present ~** hoje em dia.

daybook ['deɪbuk] (*BRIT*) *n* diário.

day boy *n* (*SCH*) externo.

daybreak ['deɪbreɪk] *n* amanhecer *m*.

daydream ['deɪdriːm] *n* devaneio ♦ *vi* devanear.

day girl *n* (*SCH*) externa.

daylight ['deɪlaɪt] *n* luz *f* (do dia).

Daylight Saving Time (*US*) *n* hora de verão.

day release *n*: **to be on ~** ter licença de um dia por semana para fins de aperfeiçoamento profissional.

day return (ticket) (*BRIT*) *n* bilhete *m* de ida e volta no mesmo dia.

day shift *n* turno diurno.

daytime ['deɪtaɪm] *n* dia *m* ♦ *adj* de dia, diurno.

day-to-day *adj* (*life, expenses*) cotidiano; **the ~ routine** o dia-a-dia; **on a ~ basis** dia a dia, diariamente.

day trip *n* excursão *f* (de um dia).

day tripper *n* excursionista *m/f*.

daze [deɪz] *vt* (*stun*) aturdir ♦ *n*: **in a ~** aturdido.

dazzle ['dæzl] *vt* deslumbrar, ofuscar.

dazzling ['dæzlɪŋ] *adj* deslumbrante, ofuscante.

DC *abbr* (*ELEC*) = **direct current**; (*US*: *POST*) = **District of Columbia**.

DD *n abbr* (= *Doctor of Divinity*) *título universitário*.

dd. *abbr* (*COMM*: = *delivered*) entregue.

D/D *abbr* = **direct debit**.

D-day ['diːdeɪ] *n* o dia D.

DDS (*US*) *n abbr* (= *Doctor of Dental Science*; *Doctor of Dental Surgery*) *títulos universitários*.

DDT *n abbr* (= *dichlorodiphenyltrichloroethane*) DDT *m*.

DE (*US*) *abbr* (*POST*) = **Delaware**.

DEA (*US*) *n abbr* (= *Drug Enforcement Administration*) ≈ Conselho Nacional de Entorpecentes.

deacon ['diːkən] *n* diácono.

dead [dɛd] *adj* morto; (*deceased*) falecido; (*telephone*) cortado; (*ELEC*) sem corrente ♦ *adv* (*very*) totalmente; (*exactly*) absolutamente ♦ *npl*: **the ~** os mortos; **~ tired** morto de cansado; **to stop ~** estacar; **he was shot ~** ele foi morto a tiro; **~ on time** na hora em ponto; **the line has gone ~** (*TEL*) caiu a ligação.

deaden ['dɛdn] *vt* (*blow, sound*) amortecer; (*make numb*) anestesiar.

dead end *n* beco sem saída ♦ *adj*: **a dead-end job** um emprego sem perspectivas.

dead heat *n* (*SPORT*) empate *m*; **to finish in a ~** (*race*) ser empatado.

dead-letter office *n* seção *f* de cartas não reclamadas.

deadline ['dɛdlaɪn] *n* prazo final; **to work to a ~** trabalhar com prazo estabelecido.

deadlock ['dɛdlɔk] *n* impasse *m*.

dead loss (*inf*) *n*: **to be a ~** não ser de nada.

deadly ['dɛdlɪ] *adj* mortal, fatal; (*weapon*) mortífero ♦ *adv*: **~ dull** tediosíssimo, chatíssimo.

deadpan [dɛd'pæn] *adj* sem expressão.

Dead Sea *n*: **the ~** o mar Morto.

dead season *n* (*TOURISM*) baixa estação *f*.

deaf [dɛf] *adj* surdo.

deaf-aid (*BRIT*) *n* aparelho para a surdez.

deaf-and-dumb *adj* surdo-mudo; ~ **alphabet** alfabeto de surdos-mudos.
deafen ['dɛfn] *vt* ensurdecer.
deafening ['dɛfnɪŋ] *adj* ensurdecedor(a).
deaf-mute *n* surdo-mudo/surda-muda.
deafness ['dɛfnɪs] *n* surdez *f*.
deal [di:l] (*pt, pp* **dealt**) *n* (*agreement*) acordo; (*business*) negócio ♦ *vt* (*cards, blows*) dar; **to strike a ~ with sb** fechar um negócio com alguém; **it's a ~!** (*inf*) negócio fechado; **he got a fair/bad ~ from them** ele foi/não foi bem tratado por eles; **a good ~** bastante; **a good** *or* **great ~ (of)** bastante, muito.
deal in *vt fus* (COMM) negociar em *or* com.
deal with *vt fus* (*people*) tratar com; (*problem*) ocupar-se de; (*be about*: *book etc*) tratar de; (COMM) negociar com; (*punish*) castigar.
dealer ['di:lə*] *n* negociante *m/f*; (*for cars*) concessionário/a; (*for products*) revendedor(a) *m/f*; (CARDS) carteador(a) *m/f*, banqueiro/a.
dealership ['di:ləʃɪp] *n* concesionária.
dealings ['di:lɪŋz] *npl* transações *fpl*; (*relations*) relações *fpl*.
dealt [dɛlt] *pt, pp of* **deal**.
dean [di:n] *n* (REL) decano; (BRIT: SCH) reitor(a) *m/f*; (US: SCH) orientador(a) *m/f* de estudos.
dear [dɪə*] *adj* querido; (*expensive*) caro ♦ *n*: **my ~** meu querido/minha querida; **~ me!** ai, meu Deus!; **D~ Sir/Madam** (*in letter*) Ilmo. Senhor/Exma. Senhora (BR), Exmo. Senhor/ Exma. Senhora (PT).
dearly ['dɪəlɪ] *adv* (*love*) ternamente; (*pay*) caro.
dearth [də:θ] *n* escassez *f*.
death [dɛθ] *n* morte *f*; (ADMIN) óbito.
deathbed ['dɛθbɛd] *n* leito de morte.
death certificate *n* certidão *f* de óbito.
death duties *npl* (BRIT) impostos *mpl* sobre inventário.
deathly ['dɛθlɪ] *adj* mortal; (*silence*) profundo ♦ *adv* (*quiet*) completamente.
death penalty *n* pena de morte.
death rate *n* (índice *m* de) mortalidade *f*.
death sentence *n* sentença de morte.
deathtrap ['dɛθtræp] *n* perigo.
deb [dɛb] (*inf*) *n abbr* = **debutante**.
debar [dɪ'bɑ:*] *vt* (*exclude*) excluir; **to ~ sb from doing sth** proibir a alguém fazer algo *or* que faça algo.
debase [dɪ'beɪs] *vt* degradar; (*currency*) desvalorizar.
debatable [dɪ'beɪtəbl] *adj* discutível.
debate [dɪ'beɪt] *n* debate *m* ♦ *vt* debater ♦ *vi* (*consider*): **to ~ whether** perguntar-se se.
debauchery [dɪ'bɔ:tʃərɪ] *n* libertinagem *f*.
debenture [dɪ'bɛntʃə*] *n* (COMM) debênture *f*.
debilitate [dɪ'bɪlɪteɪt] *vt* debilitar.
debit ['dɛbɪt] *n* débito ♦ *vt*: **to ~ a sum to sb** *or* **to sb's account** lançar uma quantia ao débito de alguém *or* à conta de alguém.
debit balance *n* saldo devedor.
debit note *n* nota de débito.
debrief [di:'bri:f] *vt* interrogar.
debriefing [di:'bri:fɪŋ] *n* interrogatório.
debris ['dɛbri:] *n* escombros *mpl*.
debt [dɛt] *n* dívida; **to be in ~** ter dívidas, estar endividado; **bad ~** dívida incobrável.
debt collector *n* cobrador(a) *m/f* de dívidas.
debtor ['dɛtə*] *n* devedor(a) *m/f*.
debug ['di:'bʌg] *vt* (COMPUT) depurar.
debunk [di:'bʌŋk] *vt* (*theory, claim*) desacreditar, desmerecer.
début ['deɪbju:] *n* estréia.
debutante ['dɛbjutænt] *n* debutante *f*.
Dec. *abbr* (= *December*) dez.
decade ['dɛkeɪd] *n* década.
decadence ['dɛkədəns] *n* decadência.
decadent ['dɛkədənt] *adj* decadente.
decaffeinated [dɪ'kæfɪneɪtɪd] *adj* descafeinado.
decamp [dɪ'kæmp] (*inf*) *vi* safar-se.
decant [dɪ'kænt] *vt* (*wine*) decantar.
decanter [dɪ'kæntə*] *n* garrafa ornamental.
decarbonize [di:'kɑ:bənaɪz] *vt* (AUT) descarbonizar.
decay [dɪ'keɪ] *n* decadência; (*of building*) ruína; (*fig*) deterioração *f*; (*rotting*) podridão *f*; (*also*: *tooth ~*) cárie *f* ♦ *vi* (*rot*) apodrecer-se; (*fig*) decair.
decease [dɪ'si:s] *n* falecimento, óbito.
deceased [dɪ'si:st] *n*: **the ~** o/a falecido/a.
deceit [dɪ'si:t] *n* engano.
deceitful [dɪ'si:tful] *adj* enganador(a).
deceive [dɪ'si:v] *vt* enganar.
decelerate [di:'sɛləreɪt] *vt* moderar a marcha de, desacelerar ♦ *vi* diminuir a velocidade.
December [dɪ'sɛmbə*] *n* dezembro; *see also* **July**.
decency ['di:sənsɪ] *n* decência.
decent ['di:sənt] *adj* (*proper*) decente; (*person*) honesto, amável.
decently ['di:səntlɪ] *adv* (*respectably*) decentemente; (*kindly*) gentilmente.
decentralization ['di:sɛntrəlaɪ'zeɪʃən] *n* descentralização *f*.
decentralize [di:'sɛntrəlaɪz] *vt* descentralizar.
deception [dɪ'sɛpʃən] *n* engano, fraude *f*.
deceptive [dɪ'sɛptɪv] *adj* enganador(a).
decibel ['dɛsɪbɛl] *n* decibel *m*.
decide [dɪ'saɪd] *vt* (*person*) decidir; (*question, argument*) resolver ♦ *vi* decidir; **to ~ to do/ that** decidir fazer/que; **to ~ on sth** decidir-se por algo; **to ~ on doing** decidir fazer; **to ~ against doing** decidir não fazer.
decided [dɪ'saɪdɪd] *adj* (*resolute*) decidido; (*clear, definite*) claro, definido.
decidedly [dɪ'saɪdɪdlɪ] *adv* decididamente.
deciding [dɪ'saɪdɪŋ] *adj* decisivo.
deciduous [dɪ'sɪdjuəs] *adj* decíduo, caduco.
decimal ['dɛsɪməl] *adj* decimal ♦ *n* decimal *m*;

NB: European Portuguese adds the following consonants to certain words: **b** (sú(b)dito, su(b)til); **c** (a(c)ção, a(c)cionista, a(c)to); **m** (inde(m)ne); **p** (ado(p)ção, ado(p)tar); *for further details see p. xiii.*

to 3 ~ places com 3 casas decimais.
decimalize ['dɛsɪməlaɪz] (*BRIT*) *vt* decimalizar.
decimal point *n* vírgula de decimais.
decimate ['dɛsɪmeɪt] *vt* dizimar.
decipher [dɪ'saɪfə*] *vt* decifrar.
decision [dɪ'sɪʒən] *n* decisão *f*; **to make a ~** tomar uma decisão.
decisive [dɪ'saɪsɪv] *adj* decisivo; (*conclusive*) decidido, terminante; (*manner, reply*) categórico.
deck [dɛk] *n* (*NAUT*) convés *m*; (*of bus*) andar *m*; (*of cards*) baralho; **to go up on ~** subir ao convés; **below ~** abaixo do convés principal; **record/cassette ~** toca-discos *m inv*/ toca-fitas *m inv*.
deckchair ['dɛktʃɛə*] *n* cadeira de lona, espreguiçadeira.
deck hand *n* taifeiro/a.
declaration [dɛklə'reɪʃən] *n* declaração *f*.
declare [dɪ'klɛə*] *vt* declarar.
declassify [diː'klæsɪfaɪ] *vt* tornar público.
decline [dɪ'klaɪn] *n* declínio, decadência; (*lessening*) diminuição *f*, baixa ♦ *vt* recusar ♦ *vi* decair, diminuir; (*fall*) baixar; **~ in living standards** queda dos padrões de vida; **to ~ to do sth** recusar-se a fazer algo.
declutch ['diː'klʌtʃ] (*BRIT*) *vi* debrear.
decode [diː'kəud] *vt* decifrar; (*TV signal etc*) decodificar.
decoder [diː'kəudə*] *n* decodificador *m*.
decompose [diːkəm'pəuz] *vi* decompor-se.
decomposition [diːkɔmpə'zɪʃən] *n* decomposição *f*.
decompression [diːkəm'prɛʃən] *n* descompressão *f*.
decompression chamber *n* câmara de descompressão.
decongestant [diːkən'dʒɛstənt] *n* descongestionante *m*.
decontaminate [diːkən'tæmɪneɪt] *vt* descontaminar.
decontrol [diːkən'trəul] *vt* (*prices etc*) liberar.
décor ['deɪkɔː*] *n* decoração *f*; (*THEATRE*) cenário.
decorate ['dɛkəreɪt] *vt* (*adorn*) enfeitar, decorar; (*give medal to*) condecorar; (*paint*) pintar; (*paper*) decorar com papel.
decoration [dɛkə'reɪʃən] *n* decoração *f*, adorno; (*act*) decoração; (*medal*) condecoração *f*.
decorative ['dɛkərətɪv] *adj* decorativo.
decorator ['dɛkəreɪtə*] *n* (*painter*) pintor(a) *m/f*.
decorum [dɪ'kɔːrəm] *n* decoro.
decoy ['diːkɔɪ] *n* engodo, chamariz *m*.
decrease [*n* 'diːkriːs, *vt, vi* diː'kriːs] *n* diminuição *f* ♦ *vt* diminuir, reduzir ♦ *vi* diminuir; **to be on the ~** estar diminuindo.
decreasing [diː'kriːsɪŋ] *adj* decrescente.
decree [dɪ'kriː] *n* decreto ♦ *vt*: **to ~ (that)** decretar (que); **~ absolute** sentença final de divórcio; **~ nisi** ordem *f* provisória de divórcio.
decrepit [dɪ'krɛpɪt] *adj* decrépito, caduco; (*building*) (que está) caindo aos pedaços.
decry [dɪ'kraɪ] *vt* execrar; (*disparage*) denegrir.
dedicate ['dɛdɪkeɪt] *vt* dedicar.
dedicated ['dɛdɪkeɪtɪd] *adj* (*person, COMPUT*) dedicado; **~ word processor** processador *m* de texto dedicado.
dedication [dɛdɪ'keɪʃən] *n* (*devotion*) dedicação *f*; (*in book*) dedicatória.
deduce [dɪ'djuːs] *vt* deduzir.
deduct [dɪ'dʌkt] *vt* deduzir; (*from wage etc*) descontar.
deduction [dɪ'dʌkʃən] *n* (*deducting*) redução *f*, dedução *f*; (*from wage etc*) desconto; (*conclusion*) conclusão *f*, dedução *f*.
deed [diːd] *n* feito, ato; (*feat*) façanha; (*LAW*) escritura, título; **~ of covenant** escritura de transferência.
deem [diːm] *vt* julgar, estimar; **to ~ it wise to do** julgar prudente fazer.
deep [diːp] *adj* profundo; (*voice*) baixo, grave; (*person*) fechado ♦ *adv*: **the spectators stood 20 ~** os espectadores formaram-se em 20 fileiras; **knee-~ in water** com água até os joelhos; **to be 4 metres ~** ter 4 metros de profundidade; **he took a ~ breath** ele respirou fundo.
deepen ['diːpən] *vt* aprofundar ♦ *vi* (*mystery*) aumentar.
deep-freeze (*irreg*) *vt* congelar ♦ *n* congelador *m*, freezer *m* (*BR*).
deep-fry *vt* fritar em recipiente fundo.
deeply ['diːplɪ] *adv* profundamente.
deep-rooted [-'ruːtɪd] *adj* (*prejudice*) enraizado; (*affection*) profundo.
deep-sea diver *n* escafandrista *m/f*.
deep-sea diving *n* mergulho com escafandro.
deep-sea fishing *n* pesca de alto-mar.
deep-seated [-'siːtɪd] *adj* (*beliefs*) arraigado.
deep-set *adj* (*eyes*) fundo.
deer [dɪə*] *n inv* veado, cervo.
deerskin ['dɪəskɪn] *n* camurça, pele *f* de cervo.
deerstalker ['dɪəstɔːkə*] *n tipo de chapéu, como o de Sherlock Holmes*.
deface [dɪ'feɪs] *vt* desfigurar, deformar.
defamation [dɛfə'meɪʃən] *n* difamação *f*.
defamatory [dɪ'fæmətrɪ] *adj* difamatório.
default [dɪ'fɔːlt] *vi* (*LAW*) inadimplir; (*SPORT*) não comparecer ♦ *n* (*COMPUT*) default *m*; **by ~** (*LAW*) à revelia; (*SPORT*) por ausência; **to ~ on a debt** deixar de pagar uma dívida.
defaulter [dɪ'fɔːltə*] *n* (*in debt*) devedor(a) *m/f* inadimplente.
default option *n* (*COMPUT*) opção *f* de default.
defeat [dɪ'fiːt] *n* derrota ♦ *vt* derrotar, vencer; (*fig: efforts*) frustrar.
defeatism [dɪ'fiːtɪzm] *n* derrotismo.
defeatist [dɪ'fiːtɪst] *adj, n* derrotista *m/f*.
defect [*n* 'diːfɛkt, *vi* dɪ'fɛkt] *n* defeito ♦ *vi* desertar; **physical/mental ~** defeito físico/ mental.
defective [dɪ'fɛktɪv] *adj* defeituoso.
defector [dɪ'fɛktə*] *n* trânsfuga *m/f*.
defence [dɪ'fɛns] (*US* **defense**) *n* defesa; **in ~ of** em defesa de; **witness for the ~** testemu-

nha de defesa; **the Ministry of D~** (*BRIT*), **the Department of Defense** (*US*) o Ministério da Defesa.
defenceless [dɪ'fɛnslɪs] *adj* indefeso.
defend [dɪ'fɛnd] *vt* defender.
defendant [dɪ'fɛndənt] *n* acusado/a; (*in civil case*) réu/ré *m/f*.
defender [dɪ'fɛndə*] *n* defensor(a) *m/f*.
defending champion [dɪ'fɛndɪŋ-] *n* (*SPORT*) atual campeão/peã *m/f*.
defending counsel [dɪ'fɛndɪŋ-] *n* (*LAW*) advogado/a de defesa.
defense [dɪ'fɛns] (*US*) *n* = **defence**.
defensive [dɪ'fɛnsɪv] *adj* defensivo ♦ *n*: **on the ~** na defensiva.
defer [dɪ'fəː*] *vt* (*postpone*) adiar ♦ *vi* (*submit*): **to ~ to** submeter-se a.
deference ['dɛfərəns] *n* deferência, respeito; **out of** *or* **in ~ to** por *or* em deferência a.
defiance [dɪ'faɪəns] *n* desafio, desrespeito; **in ~ of** sem respeito por; (*despite*) a despeito de.
defiant [dɪ'faɪənt] *adj* (*insolent*) desafiante, insolente; (*challenging*) desafiador(a).
defiantly [dɪ'faɪəntlɪ] *adv* desafiadoramente.
deficiency [dɪ'fɪʃənsɪ] *n* (*lack*) deficiência, falta; (*defect*) defeito; (*COMM*) déficit *m*.
deficiency disease *n* doença de carência.
deficient [dɪ'fɪʃənt] *adj* (*lacking*) deficiente; (*incomplete*) incompleto; (*defective*) imperfeito; **~ in** falto de, carente de.
deficit ['dɛfɪsɪt] *n* déficit *m*.
defile [*vt, vi* dɪ'faɪl, *n* 'diːfaɪl] *vt* sujar, profanar ♦ *vi* desfilar ♦ *n* desfile *m*.
define [dɪ'faɪn] *vt* definir.
definite ['dɛfɪnɪt] *adj* (*fixed*) definitivo; (*clear, obvious*) claro, categórico; (*LING*) definido; **he was ~ about it** ele foi categórico.
definitely ['dɛfɪnɪtlɪ] *adv* sem dúvida.
definition [dɛfɪ'nɪʃən] *n* definição *f*.
definitive [dɪ'fɪnɪtɪv] *adj* definitivo.
deflate [diː'fleɪt] *vt* esvaziar; (*person*) fazer perder o rebolado; (*ECON*) deflacionar.
deflation [diː'fleɪʃən] *n* (*ECON*) deflação *f*.
deflationary [diː'fleɪʃənrɪ] *adj* (*ECON*) deflacionário.
deflect [dɪ'flɛkt] *vt* desviar.
defog ['diː'fɔg] (*US*) *vt* desembaçar.
defogger ['diː'fɔgə*] (*US*) *n* (*AUT*) desembaçador *m*.
deform [dɪ'fɔːm] *vt* deformar.
deformed [dɪ'fɔːmd] *adj* deformado.
deformity [dɪ'fɔːmɪtɪ] *n* deformidade *f*.
defraud [dɪ'frɔːd] *vt* defraudar.
defray [dɪ'freɪ] *vt* (*costs, expenses*) correr com.
defrost [diː'frɔst] *vt* descongelar.
deft [dɛft] *adj* destro, hábil.
defunct [dɪ'fʌŋkt] *adj* extinto.
defuse [diː'fjuːz] *vt* tirar o estopim *or* a espoleta de.
defy [dɪ'faɪ] *vt* (*resist*) opor-se a; (*challenge*) desafiar; (*order*) desobedecer.
degenerate [*vi* dɪ'dʒɛnəreɪt, *adj* dɪ'dʒɛnərɪt] *vi* degenerar ♦ *adj* degenerado.
degradation [dɛgrə'deɪʃən] *n* degradação *f*.
degrade [dɪ'greɪd] *vt* degradar.
degrading [dɪ'greɪdɪŋ] *adj* degradante.
degree [dɪ'griː] *n* grau *m*; (*SCH*) diploma *m*, título; **~ in maths** formatura em matemática; **10 ~s below (zero)** 10 graus abaixo de zero; **a considerable ~ of risk** um grau considerável de risco; **by ~s** (*gradually*) pouco a pouco; **to some ~, to a certain ~** até certo ponto.
dehydrated [diːhaɪ'dreɪtɪd] *adj* desidratado; (*milk*) em pó.
dehydration [diːhaɪ'dreɪʃən] *n* desidratação *f*.
de-ice *vt* (*windscreen*) descongelar.
de-icer [-'aɪsə*] *n* descongelador *m*.
deign [deɪn] *vi*: **to ~ to do** dignar-se a fazer.
deity ['diːɪtɪ] *n* divindade *f*, deidade *f*.
dejected [dɪ'dʒɛktɪd] *adj* abatido, desanimado; (*face*) triste.
dejection [dɪ'dʒɛkʃən] *n* desânimo.
del. *abbr* = **delete**.
delay [dɪ'leɪ] *vt* retardar, atrasar; (*trains*) atrasar ♦ *vi* retardar-se ♦ *n* demora, atraso; **without ~** sem demora *or* atraso.
delayed-action [dɪ'leɪd-] *adj* de retardo, de ação retardada.
delectable [dɪ'lɛktəbl] *adj* deleitável.
delegate [*n* 'dɛlɪgɪt, *vt* 'dɛlɪgeɪt] *n* delegado/a ♦ *vt* delegar; **to ~ sth to sb/sb to do sth** delegar algo a alguém/alguém para fazer algo.
delegation [dɛlɪ'geɪʃən] *n* delegação *f*.
delete [dɪ'liːt] *vt* eliminar, riscar; (*COMPUT*) deletar.
Delhi ['dɛlɪ] *n* Délhi.
deliberate [*adj* dɪ'lɪbərɪt, *vi* dɪ'lɪbəreɪt] *adj* (*intentional*) intencional; (*slow*) pausado, lento ♦ *vi* deliberar.
deliberately [dɪ'lɪbərɪtlɪ] *adv* (*on purpose*) de propósito; (*slowly*) lentamente.
deliberation [dɪlɪbə'reɪʃən] *n* deliberação *f*.
delicacy ['dɛlɪkəsɪ] *n* delicadeza; (*choice food*) iguaria.
delicate ['dɛlɪkɪt] *adj* delicado; (*fragile*) frágil; (*skilled*) fino.
delicately ['dɛlɪkɪtlɪ] *adv* delicadamente.
delicatessen [dɛlɪkə'tɛsn] *n* delicatessen *m*.
delicious [dɪ'lɪʃəs] *adj* delicioso, saboroso.
delight [dɪ'laɪt] *n* (*feeling*) prazer *m*, deleite *m*; (*object*) encanto, delícia ♦ *vt* encantar, deleitar; **to take ~ in** deleitar-se com.
delighted [dɪ'laɪtɪd] *adj*: **~ (at** *or* **with sth)** encantado (com algo); **to be ~ to do sth/that** ter muito prazer em fazer algo/ficar muito contente que; **I'd be ~** eu adoraria.
delightful [dɪ'laɪtful] *adj* encantador(a), delicioso.
delimit [diː'lɪmɪt] *vt* delimitar.
delineate [dɪ'lɪnɪeɪt] *vt* delinear; (*fig: describe*) descrever, definir.

***NB:** European Portuguese adds the following consonants to certain words:* **b** (sú(b)dito, su(b)til); **c** (a(c)ção, a(c)cionista, a(c)to); **m** (inde(m)ne); **p** (ado(p)ção, ado(p)tar); *for further details see p. xiii.*

delinquency [dɪ'lɪŋkwənsɪ] *n* delinqüência.
delinquent [dɪ'lɪŋkwənt] *adj*, *n* delinqüente *m/f*.
delirious [dɪ'lɪrɪəs] *adj* delirante; **to be ~** delirar.
delirium [dɪ'lɪrɪəm] *n* delírio.
deliver [dɪ'lɪvə*] *vt* (*mail*) distribuir; (*goods*) entregar; (*message*) comunicar; (*speech*) proferir; (*free*) livrar; (*MED*) partejar; **to ~ the goods** (*fig*) dar conta do recado.
deliverance [dɪ'lɪvrəns] *n* libertação *f*, livramento.
delivery [dɪ'lɪvərɪ] *n* entrega; (*of mail*) distribuição *f*; (*of speaker*) enunciação *f*; (*MED*) parto; **to take ~ of** receber.
delivery note *n* guia *or* nota de entrega.
delivery van (*US* **delivery truck**) *n* furgão *m* de entrega.
delouse ['diː'laus] *vt* espiolhar.
delta ['dɛltə] *n* delta *m*.
delude [dɪ'luːd] *vt* iludir, enganar; **to ~ o.s.** iludir-se.
deluge ['dɛljuːdʒ] *n* dilúvio ♦ *vt* (*fig*): **to ~ (with)** inundar (de).
delusion [dɪ'luːʒən] *n* ilusão *f*; **to have ~s of grandeur** ter mania de grandeza.
de luxe [də'lʌks] *adj* de luxo.
delve [dɛlv] *vi*: **to ~ into** investigar, pesquisar.
Dem. (*US*) *abbr* (*POL*) = **democrat(ic)**.
demagogue ['dɛməgɔg] *n* demagogo/a.
demand [dɪ'mɑːnd] *vt* exigir; (*rights*) reivindicar, reclamar ♦ *n* exigência; (*claim*) reivindicação *f*; (*ECON*) procura; **to ~ sth (from** *or* **of sb)** exigir algo (de alguém); **to be in ~** ser muito solicitado; **on ~** à vista.
demanding [dɪ'mɑːndɪŋ] *adj* (*boss*) exigente; (*work*) absorvente.
demarcation [diːmɑː'keɪʃən] *n* demarcação *f*.
demarcation dispute *n* (*INDUSTRY*) dissídio coletivo.
demean [dɪ'miːn] *vt*: **to ~ o.s.** rebaixar-se.
demeanour [dɪ'miːnə*] (*US* **demeanor**) *n* conduta, comportamento.
demented [dɪ'mɛntɪd] *adj* demente, doido.
demilitarized zone [diː'mɪlɪtəraɪzd-] *n* zona desmilitarizada.
demise [dɪ'maɪz] *n* falecimento.
demist [diː'mɪst] (*BRIT*) *vt* desembaçar.
demister [diː'mɪstə*] (*BRIT*) *n* (*AUT*) desembaçador *m* de pára-brisa.
demo ['dɛməu] (*inf*) *n abbr* (= *demonstration*) passeata.
demobilize [diː'məubɪlaɪz] *vt* desmobilizar.
democracy [dɪ'mɔkrəsɪ] *n* democracia.
democrat ['dɛməkræt] *n* democrata *m/f*.
democratic [dɛmə'krætɪk] *adj* democrático.
demography [dɪ'mɔgraəfɪ] *n* demografia.
demolish [dɪ'mɔlɪʃ] *vt* demolir, derrubar.
demolition [dɛmə'lɪʃən] *n* demolição *f*.
demon ['diːmən] *n* demônio ♦ *cpd*: **a ~ squash player** um(a) craque em squash.
demonstrate ['dɛmənstreɪt] *vt* demonstrar ♦ *vi*: **to ~ (for/against)** manifestar-se (a favor de/contra).
demonstration [dɛmən'streɪʃən] *n* (*POL*) manifestação *f*; (: *march*) passeata; (*proof*) demonstração *f*; **to hold a ~** realizar uma passeata.
demonstrative [dɪ'mɔnstrətɪv] *adj* demonstrativo.
demonstrator ['dɛmənstreɪtə*] *n* (*POL*) manifestante *m/f*; (*COMM*: *sales person*) demonstrador(a) *m/f*; (: *car, computer etc*) modelo de demonstração
demoralize [dɪ'mɔrəlaɪz] *vt* desmoralizar.
demote [dɪ'məut] *vt* rebaixar de posto.
demotion [dɪ'məuʃən] *n* rebaixamento.
demur [dɪ'məː*] *vi*: **to ~ (at sth)** objetar (a algo), opor-se (a algo) ♦ *n*: **without ~** sem objeção.
demure [dɪ'mjuə*] *adj* recatado.
demurrage [dɪ'mʌrɪdʒ] *n* sobreestadia.
den [dɛn] *n* (*of animal*) covil *m*; (*room*) aposento privado, cantinho.
denationalization ['diːnæʃnəlaɪ'zeɪʃən] *n* desnacionalização *f*, desestatização *f*.
denationalize [diː'næʃnəlaɪz] *nt* desnacionalizar, desestatizar.
denial [dɪ'naɪəl] *n* (*refusal*) negativa; (*of report etc*) desmentido.
denier ['dɛnɪə*] *n* denier *m*; **15 ~ stockings** meias de 15 denieres.
denigrate ['dɛnɪgreɪt] *vt* denegrir.
denim ['dɛnɪm] *n* brim *m*, zuarte *m*; **~s** *npl* jeans *m* (*BR*), jeans *mpl* (*PT*).
denim jacket *n* jaqueta de brim.
denizen ['dɛnɪzn] *n* habitante *m/f*.
Denmark ['dɛnmɑːk] *n* Dinamarca.
denomination [dɪnɔmɪ'neɪʃən] *n* valor *m*, denominação *f*; (*REL*) confissão *f*, seita.
denominator [dɪ'nɔmɪneɪtə*] *n* denominador *m*.
denote [dɪ'nəut] *vt* (*indicate*) denotar, indicar; (*mean*) significar.
denounce [dɪ'nauns] *vt* denunciar.
dense [dɛns] *adj* (*thick*) denso, espesso; (: *foliage etc*) denso; (*inf*: *stupid*) estúpido, bronco.
densely ['dɛnslɪ] *adv*: **~ populated** com grande densidade de população; **~ wooded** coberto de florestas densas.
density ['dɛnsɪtɪ] *n* densidade *f*; **single/double ~ disk** (*COMPUT*) disco de densidade simples/dupla.
dent [dɛnt] *n* amolgadura, depressão *f* ♦ *vt* (*also*: *make a ~ in*) amolgar, dentar; **to make a ~ in** (*fig*) reduzir.
dental ['dɛntl] *adj* dental.
dental surgeon *n* cirurgião/giã *m/f* dentista.
dentifrice ['dɛntɪfrɪs] *n* dentifrício.
dentist ['dɛntɪst] *n* dentista *m/f*; **~'s surgery** (*BRIT*) consultório dentário.
dentistry ['dɛntɪstrɪ] *n* odontologia.
dentures ['dɛntʃəz] *npl* dentadura.
denunciation [dɪnʌnsɪ'eɪʃən] *n* denúncia.
deny [dɪ'naɪ] *vt* negar; (*report*) desmentir; **he denies having said it** ele nega ter dito isso.
deodorant [diː'əudərənt] *n* desodorante *m* (*BR*), desodorizante *m* (*PT*).

depart [dɪ'pɑːt] *vi* ir-se, partir; (*train*) sair; **to ~ from** (*fig*: *differ from*) afastar-se de.

department [dɪ'pɑːtmənt] *n* departamento; (COMM) seção *f*; (POL) repartição *f*; **that's not my ~** (*fig*) este não é o meu departamento; **D~ of State** (US) Departamento de Estado.

departmental [diːpɑːt'mɛntl] *adj* departamental; **~ manager** chefe *m/f* de serviço.

department store *n* magazine *m* (BR), grande armazém *m* (PT).

departure [dɪ'pɑːtʃə*] *n* partida, ida; (*of train*) saída; (*fig*): **~ from** afastamento de; **a new ~** uma nova orientação.

departure lounge *n* sala de embarque.

departures board (US **departure board**) *n* horário de saídas.

depend [dɪ'pɛnd] *vi*: **to ~ (up)on** depender de; (*rely on*) contar com; **it ~s** depende; **~ing on the result ...** dependendo do resultado ....

dependable [dɪ'pɛndəbl] *adj* (*person*) de confiança, seguro.

dependant [dɪ'pɛndənt] *n* dependente *m/f*.

dependence [dɪ'pɛndəns] *n* dependência.

dependent [dɪ'pɛndənt] *adj*: **to be ~ (on)** depender (de), ser dependente (de) ♦ *n* = **dependant.**

depict [dɪ'pɪkt] *vt* (*in picture*) retratar, representar; (*describe*) descrever.

depilatory [dɪ'pɪlətrɪ] *n* (*also*: *~ cream*) depilatório.

depleted [dɪ'pliːtɪd] *adj* depauperado.

deplorable [dɪ'plɔːrəbl] *adj* (*disgraceful*) deplorável; (*regrettable*) lamentável.

deplore [dɪ'plɔː*] *vt* (*condemn*) deplorar; (*regret*) lamentar.

deploy [dɪ'plɔɪ] *vt* dispor; (*missiles*) instalar.

depopulate [diː'pɔpjuleɪt] *vt* despovoar.

depopulation ['diːpɔpju'leɪʃən] *n* despovoamento.

deport [dɪ'pɔːt] *vt* deportar.

deportation [dɪpɔː'teɪʃən] *n* deportação *f*.

deportation order *n* ordem *f* de deportação.

deportment [dɪ'pɔːtmənt] *n* comportamento.

depose [dɪ'pəuz] *vt* depor.

deposit [dɪ'pɔzɪt] *n* (COMM, GEO) depósito; (CHEM) sedimento; (*of ore, oil*) jazida; (*part payment*) sinal *m*; (*for hired goods etc*) caução *f* ♦ *vt* depositar; **to put down a ~ of £50** pagar um sinal de £50.

deposit account *n* conta de depósito a prazo.

depositor [dɪ'pɔzɪtə*] *n* depositante *m/f*.

depository [dɪ'pɔzɪtərɪ] *n* (*person*) depositário/a; (*place*) depósito.

depot ['dɛpəu] *n* (*storehouse*) depósito, armazém *m*; (*for vehicles*) garagem *f*, parque *m*.

depraved [dɪ'preɪvd] *adj* depravado, viciado.

depravity [dɪ'prævɪtɪ] *n* depravação *f*, vício.

deprecate ['dɛprɪkeɪt] *vt* desaprovar.

deprecating ['dɛprɪkeɪtɪŋ] *adj* desaprovador(a).

depreciate [dɪ'priːʃɪeɪt] *vt* depreciar ♦ *vi* depreciar-se, desvalorizar-se.

depreciation [dɪpriːʃɪ'eɪʃən] *n* depreciação *f*.

depress [dɪ'prɛs] *vt* deprimir; (*press down*) apertar.

depressant [dɪ'prɛsnt] *n* (MED) depressor *m*.

depressed [dɪ'prɛst] *adj* (*person*) deprimido; (*area, market, trade*) em depressão.

depressing [dɪ'prɛsɪŋ] *adj* deprimente.

depression [dɪ'prɛʃən] *n* (*also*: ECON) depressão *f*.

deprivation [dɛprɪ'veɪʃən] *n* privação *f*; (*loss*) perda.

deprive [dɪ'praɪv] *vt*: **to ~ sb of** privar alguém de.

deprived [dɪ'prəɪvd] *adj* carente.

dept. *abbr* (= *department*) depto.

depth [dɛpθ] *n* profundidade *f*; (*of room etc*) comprimento; **in the ~s of** nas profundezas de; **at a ~ of 3 metres** a uma profundidade de 3 metros; **to be out of one's ~** (BRIT: *swimmer*) estar sem pé; (*fig*) estar voando; **to study sth in ~** estudar algo em profundidade.

depth charge *n* carga de profundidade.

deputation [dɛpju'teɪʃən] *n* delegação *f*.

deputize ['dɛpjutaɪz] *vi*: **to ~ for sb** substituir alguém.

deputy ['dɛpjutɪ] *adj*: **~ chairman** vice-presidente/a *m/f* ♦ *n* (*replacement*) substituto/a, suplente *m/f*; (POL: *MP*) deputado/a; (*second in command*) vice *m/f*; **~ head** (SCH) diretor adjunto/diretora adjunta *m/f*; **~ leader** (BRIT: POL) vice-líder *m/f*.

derail [dɪ'reɪl] *vt* descarrilhar; **to be ~ed** descarrilhar.

derailment [dɪ'reɪlmənt] *n* descarrilhamento.

deranged [dɪ'reɪndʒd] *adj* (*person*) louco, transtornado.

derby ['dəːbɪ] (US) *n* chapéu-coco.

Derbys (BRIT) *abbr* = **Derbyshire.**

deregulate [dɪ'rɛgjuleɪt] *vt* liberar.

deregulation [dɪ'rɛgju'leɪʃən] *n* liberação *f*.

derelict ['dɛrɪlɪkt] *adj* abandonado.

deride [dɪ'raɪd] *vt* ridicularizar, zombar de.

derision [dɪ'rɪʒən] *n* irrisão *f*, escárnio.

derisive [dɪ'raɪsɪv] *adj* zombeteiro.

derisory [dɪ'raɪsərɪ] *adj* (*sum*) irrisório; (*person, smile*) zombeteiro.

derivation [dɛrɪ'veɪʃən] *n* derivação *f*.

derivative [dɪ'rɪvətɪv] *n* derivado ♦ *adj* derivado; (*work*) pouco original.

derive [dɪ'raɪv] *vt* derivar ♦ *vi*: **to ~ from** derivar-se de.

dermatitis [dəːmə'taɪtɪs] *n* dermatite *f*.

dermatology [dəːmə'tɔlədʒɪ] *n* dermatologia.

derogatory [dɪ'rɔgətərɪ] *adj* depreciativo.

derrick ['dɛrɪk] *n* (*crane*) guindaste *m*; (*oil ~*) torre *f* de perfurar.

derv [dəːv] (BRIT) *n* gasóleo.

DES (BRIT) *n abbr* (= *Department of Education and Science*) *Ministério da Educação e*

***NB:** European Portuguese adds the following consonants to certain words:* **b** (sú(b)dito, su(b)til); **c** (a(c)ção, a(c)cionista, a(c)to); **m** (inde(m)ne); **p** (ado(p)ção, ado(p)tar); *for further details see p. xiii.*

das Ciências.

desalination [diːsælɪ'neɪʃən] *n* dessalinização *f*.

descend [dɪ'sɛnd] *vt, vi* descer; **to ~ from** descer de; **in ~ing order** em ordem decrescente.

descend on *vt fus* (*subj*: *enemy, angry person*) cair sobre; (: *misfortune*) abater-se sobre; (: *gloom, silence*) invadir; **visitors ~ed (up)on us** visitas invadiram nossa casa.

descendant [dɪ'sɛndənt] *n* descendente *m/f*.

descent [dɪ'sɛnt] *n* descida; (*slope*) declive *m*, ladeira; (*origin*) descendência.

describe [dɪs'kraɪb] *vt* descrever.

description [dɪs'krɪpʃən] *n* descrição *f*; (*sort*) classe *f*, espécie *f*; **of every ~** de toda a sorte, de todo o tipo.

descriptive [dɪs'krɪptɪv] *adj* descritivo.

desecrate ['dɛsɪkreɪt] *vt* profanar.

desert [*n* 'dɛzət, *vt, vi* dɪ'zəːt] *n* deserto ♦ *vt* abandonar ♦ *vi* (*MIL*) desertar.

deserter [dɪ'zəːtə*] *n* desertor *m*.

desertion [dɪ'zəːʃən] *n* deserção *f*.

desert island *n* ilha deserta.

deserts [dɪ'zəːts] *npl*: **to get one's just ~** receber o que merece.

deserve [dɪ'zəːv] *vt* merecer.

deservedly [dɪ'zəːvɪdlɪ] *adj* merecidamente.

deserving [dɪ'zəːvɪŋ] *adj* (*person*) merecedor(a), digno; (*action, cause*) meritório.

desiccated ['dɛsɪkeɪtɪd] *adj* dessecado.

design [dɪ'zaɪn] *n* (*sketch*) desenho, esboço; (*layout, shape*) plano, projeto; (*pattern*) desenho, padrão *m*; (*of dress, car etc*) modelo; (*art*) design *m*; (*intention*) propósito, intenção *f* ♦ *vt* desenhar; (*plan*) projetar; **to have ~s on** ter a mira em; **well-~ed** bem projetado; **to be ~ed for sb/sth** (*intended*) ser destinado a alguém/algo.

designate [*vt* 'dɛzɪgneɪt, *adj* 'dɛzɪgnɪt] *vt* (*point to*) apontar; (*appoint*) nomear; (*destine*) designar ♦ *adj* designado.

designation [dɛzɪg'neɪʃən] *n* (*appointment*) nomeação *f*; (*name*) designação *f*.

designer [dɪ'zaɪnə*] *n* (*ART*) artista *m/f* gráfico/a; (*TECH*) desenhista *m/f*, projetista *m/f*; (*fashion* ~) estilista *m/f*.

desirability [dɪzaɪrə'bɪlɪtɪ] *n* necessidade *f*.

desirable [dɪ'zaɪərəbl] *adj* (*proper*) desejável; (*attractive*) atraente.

desire [dɪ'zaɪə*] *n* desejo ♦ *vt* desejar; **to ~ to do sth/that** desejar fazer algo/que.

desirous [dɪ'zaɪərəs] *adj*: **~ of** desejoso de.

desk [dɛsk] *n* (*in office*) mesa, secretária; (*for pupil*) carteira *f*; (*at airport*) balcão *m*; (*in hotel*) recepção *f*; (*BRIT*: *in shop, restaurant*) caixa.

desk-top publishing *n* editoração *f* eletrônica, desktop publishing *m*.

desolate ['dɛsəlɪt] *adj* (*place*) deserto; (*person*) desolado.

desolation [dɛsə'leɪʃən] *n* (*of place*) desolação *f*; (*of person*) aflição *f*.

despair [dɪs'pɛə*] *n* desespero ♦ *vi*: **to ~ of** desesperar-se de; **to be in ~** estar desesperado.

despatch [dɪs'pætʃ] *n, vt* = **dispatch**.

desperate ['dɛspərɪt] *adj* desesperado.

desperately ['dɛspərɪtlɪ] *adv* desesperadamente; (*very*) terrívelmente, gravemente.

desperation [dɛspə'reɪʃən] *n* desespero, desesperança; **in ~** desesperado.

despicable [dɪs'pɪkəbl] *adj* desprezível.

despise [dɪs'paɪz] *vt* desprezar.

despite [dɪs'paɪt] *prep* apesar de, a despeito de.

despondent [dɪs'pɔndənt] *adj* abatido, desanimado.

despot ['dɛspɔt] *n* déspota *m/f*.

dessert [dɪ'zəːt] *n* sobremesa.

dessertspoon [dɪ'zəːtspuːn] *n* colher *f* de sobremesa.

destabilize [diː'steɪbɪlaɪz] *vt* desestabilizar.

destination [dɛstɪ'neɪʃən] *n* destino.

destine ['dɛstɪn] *vt* destinar.

destined ['dɛstɪnd] *adj*: **~ to do sth** destinado a fazer algo; **~ for London** com destino a Londres.

destiny ['dɛstɪnɪ] *n* destino.

destitute ['dɛstɪtjuːt] *adj* indigente, necessitado; **~ of** desprovido de.

destroy [dɪs'trɔɪ] *vt* destruir.

destroyer [dɪs'trɔɪə*] *n* (*NAUT*) contratorpedeiro.

destruction [dɪs'trʌkʃən] *n* destruição *f*.

destructive [dɪs'trʌktɪv] *adj* destrutivo, destruidor(a).

desultory ['dɛsəltərɪ] *adj* (*reading, conversation*) desconexo; (*contact*) irregular.

detach [dɪ'tætʃ] *vt* separar; (*unstick*) desprender.

detachable [dɪ'tætʃəbl] *adj* separável; (*TECH*) desmontável.

detached [dɪ'tætʃt] *adj* (*attitude*) imparcial, objetivo; (*house*) independente, isolado.

detachment [dɪ'tætʃmənt] *n* separação *f*; (*MIL*) destacamento; (*fig*) objetividade *f*, imparcialidade *f*.

detail ['diːteɪl] *n* detalhe *m*; (*MIL*) destacamento ♦ *vt* detalhar; (*MIL*): **to ~ sb (for)** destacar alguém (para); **in ~** pormenorizado, em detalhe; **to go into ~(s)** entrar em detalhes.

detailed ['diːteɪld] *adj* detalhado.

detain [dɪ'teɪn] *vt* deter; (*in hospital*) hospitalizar.

detainee [dɪːteɪ'niː] *n* detido/a.

detect [dɪ'tɛkt] *vt* descobrir; (*MED, POLICE*) identificar; (*MIL, RADAR, TECH*) detectar.

detection [dɪ'tɛkʃən] *n* descobrimento; (*MED, POLICE*) identificação *f*; (*MIL, RADAR, TECH*) detecção *f*; **to escape ~** evitar ser descoberto; **crime ~** investigação *f* de crimes.

detective [dɪ'tɛktɪv] *n* detetive *m/f*; **private ~** detetive particular.

detective story *n* romance *m* policial.

detector [dɪ'tɛktə*] *n* detetor *m*.

détente [deɪ'tɑːnt] *n* distensão *f* (de relações), détente *f*.

detention [dɪ'tɛnʃən] *n* detenção *f*, prisão *f*;

(*SCH*) castigo.
deter [dɪ'tə:*] *vt* (*discourage*) desanimar; (*dissuade*) dissuadir; (*prevent*) impedir.
detergent [dɪ'tə:dʒənt] *n* detergente *m*.
deteriorate [dɪ'tɪərɪəreɪt] *vi* deteriorar-se.
deterioration [dɪtɪərɪə'reɪʃən] *n* deterioração *f*.
determination [dɪtə:mɪ'neɪʃən] *n* determinação *f*; (*resolve*) resolução *f*.
determine [dɪ'tə:mɪn] *vt* determinar; **to ~ to do** resolver fazer, determinar-se de fazer.
determined [dɪ'tə:mɪnd] *adj* (*person*) resoluto, decidido; (*quantity*) determinado; (*effort*) grande.
deterrence [dɪ'tɛrəns] *n* dissuasão *f*.
deterrent [dɪ'tɛrənt] *n* dissuasivo.
detest [dɪ'tɛst] *vt* detestar.
detestable [dɪ'tɛstəbl] *adj* detestável.
detonate ['dɛtəneɪt] *vi* explodir, estalar ♦ *vt* detonar.
detonator ['dɛtəneɪtə*] *n* detonador *m*.
detour ['di:tuə*] *n* desvio.
detract [dɪ'trækt] *vi*: **to ~ from** (*merits, reputation*) depreciar; (*quality, pleasure*) diminuir.
detractor [dɪ'trəæktə*] *n* detrator(a) *m/f*.
detriment ['dɛtrɪmənt] *n*: **to the ~ of** em detrimento de; **without ~ to** sem detrimento de.
detrimental [dɛtrɪ'mɛntl] *adj*: **~ (to)** prejudicial (a).
deuce [dju:s] *n* (*TENNIS*) empate *m*, iguais.
devaluation [dɪvælju'eɪʃən] *n* desvalorização *f*.
devalue [dɪ'vælju:] *vt* desvalorizar.
devastate ['dɛvəsteɪt] *vt* devastar; **he was ~d by the news** as notícias deixaram-no desolado.
devastating ['dɛvəsteɪtɪŋ] *adj* devastador(a); (*fig*) assolador(a).
devastation [dɛvəs'teɪʃən] *n* devastação *f*.
develop [dɪ'vɛləp] *vt* desenvolver; (*PHOT*) revelar; (*disease*) contrair; (*resources*) explotar; (*engine trouble*) começar a ter ♦ *vi* desenvolver-se; (*advance*) progredir; (*appear*) aparecer.
developer [dɪ'vɛləpə*] *n* (*PHOT*) revelador *m*; (*also*: *property* **~**) empresário/a de imóveis.
developing country [dɪ'vɛləpɪŋ-] país *m* em desenvolvimento.
development [dɪ'vɛləpmənt] *n* desenvolvimento; (*advance*) progresso; (*of land*) urbanização *f*.
development area *n* zona a ser urbanizada.
deviate ['di:vɪeɪt] *vi* desviar-se.
deviation [di:vɪ'eɪʃən] *n* desvio.
device [dɪ'vaɪs] *n* (*scheme*) estratagema *m*, plano; (*apparatus*) aparelho, dispositivo; **explosive ~** dispositivo explosivo.
devil ['dɛvl] *n* diabo.
devilish ['dɛvlɪʃ] *adj* diabólico.
devil-may-care *adj* despreocupado.
devious ['di:vɪəs] *adj* (*means*) intricado, indireto; (*person*) malandro, esperto.
devise [dɪ'vaɪz] *vt* idear, inventar.
devoid [dɪ'vɔɪd] *adj*: **~ of** destituído de.
devolution [di:və'lu:ʃən] *n* (*POL*) descentralização *f*.
devolve [dɪ'vɔlv] *vi*: **to ~ (up)on** passar a ser da competência de.
devote [dɪ'vəut] *vt*: **to ~ sth to** dedicar algo a.
devoted [dɪ'vəutɪd] *adj* (*loyal*) leal, fiel; **the book is ~ to politics** o livro trata de política; **to be ~ to** (*love*) estar devotado a.
devotee [dɛvəu'ti:] *n* adepto/a, entusiasta *m/f*.
devotion [dɪ'vəuʃən] *n* dedicação *f*; (*REL*) devoção *f*.
devour [dɪ'vauə*] *vt* devorar.
devout [dɪ'vaut] *adj* devoto.
dew [dju:] *n* orvalho.
dexterity [dɛks'tɛrɪtɪ] *n* destreza.
dext(e)rous ['dɛkstrəs] *adj* destro.
dg *abbr* (= *decigram*) dg.
Dhaka ['dækə] *n* Daca.
diabetes [daɪə'bi:ti:z] *n* diabete *f*.
diabetic [da'ə'bɛtɪk] *adj* (*person*) diabético; (*chocolate*, *jam*) para diabéticos ♦ *n* diabético/a.
diabolical [daɪə'bɔlɪkl] *adj* diabólico; (*inf*: *dreadful*) terrível, horrível.
diaeresis [daɪ'ɛrɪsɪs] *n* diérese *f*.
diagnose [daɪəg'nəuz] *vt* diagnosticar.
diagnoses [daɪəg'nəsi:z] *npl of* **diagnosis**.
diagnosis [daɪəg'nəusɪs] (*pl* **diagnoses**) *n* diagnóstico.
diagonal [daɪ'ægənl] *adj* diagonal ♦ *n* diagonal *f*.
diagram ['daɪəgræm] *n* diagrama *m*, esquema *m*.
dial ['daɪəl] *n* disco ♦ *vt* (*number*) discar (*BR*), marcar (*PT*); **to ~ a wrong number** discar (*BR*) *or* marcar (*PT*) um número errado; **can I ~ London direct?** é possível discar direto para Londres?
dial. *abbr* = **dialect**.
dial code (*US*) *n* = **dialling code**.
dialect ['daɪəlɛkt] *n* dialeto.
dialling code ['daɪəlɪŋ-] (*BRIT*) *n* código.
dialling tone ['daɪəlɪŋ-] (*BRIT*) *n* sinal *m* de discar (*BR*) *or* de marcar (*PT*).
dialogue ['daɪəlɔg] *n* diálogo.
dial tone (*US*) *n* = **dialling tone**.
dialysis [daɪ'ælɪsɪs] *n* diálise *f*.
diameter [daɪ'æmɪtə*] *n* diâmetro.
diametrically [daɪə'mɛtrɪklɪ] *adv*: **~ opposed (to)** diametralmente oposto (a).
diamond ['daɪəmənd] *n* diamante *m*; (*shape*) losango, rombo; **~s** *npl* (*CARDS*) ouros *mpl*.
diamond ring *n* anel *m* de brilhante.
diaper ['daɪəpə*] (*US*) *n* fralda.
diaphragm ['daɪəfræm] *n* diafragma *m*.
diarrhoea [daɪə'ri:ə] (*US* **diarrhea**) *n* diarréia.
diary ['daɪərɪ] *n* (*daily account*) diário; (*book*)

__NB__: European Portuguese adds the following consonants to certain words: **b** (sú(b)dito, su(b)til); **c** (a(c)ção, a(c)cionista, a(c)to); **m** (inde(m)ne); **p** (ado(p)ção, ado(p)tar); *for further details see p. xiii.*

agenda; **to keep a ~** ter um diário.
diatribe ['daɪətraɪb] *n* diatribe *f*.
dice [daɪs] *npl of* **die** ♦ *n inv* dado ♦ *vt* (*CULIN*) cortar em cubos.
dicey ['daɪsɪ] (*inf*) *adj*: **it's a bit ~** é um pouco arriscado.
dichotomy [daɪ'kɔtəmɪ] *n* dicotomia.
Dictaphone ['dɪktəfəun] ® *n* ditafone *m* ®, máquina de ditar.
dictate [dɪk'teɪt] *vt* ditar ♦ *vi*: **to ~ to** (*person*) dar ordens a; **I won't be ~d to** não vou acatar ordens.
dictates ['dɪkteɪts] *npl* ditames *npl*.
dictation [dɪk'teɪʃən] *n* ditado; **at ~ speed** com a velocidade de ditado.
dictator [dɪk'teɪtə*] *n* ditador(a) *m/f*.
dictatorship [dɪk'teɪtəʃɪp] *n* ditadura.
diction ['dɪkʃən] *n* dicção *f*.
dictionary ['dɪkʃənrɪ] *n* dicionário.
did [dɪd] *pt of* **do**.
didactic [daɪ'dæktɪk] *adj* didático.
die [daɪ] (*pl* **dice**) *vi* morrer ♦ *n* dado; (*pl*: **dies**) cunho, molde *m*; **to ~ of** *or* **from** morrer de; **to be dying for sth** estar louco por algo; **to be dying to do sth** estar morrendo de vontade de fazer algo.
die away *vi* (*sound, light*) extinguir-se lentamente.
die down *vi* apagar-se; (*wind*) abrandar.
die out *vi* desaparecer, apagar-se.
diehard ['daɪhɑːd] *n* reacionário/a, reaça *m/f* (*inf*).
diesel ['diːzl] *n* diesel *m*.
diesel engine ['diːzəl-] *n* motor *m* diesel.
diesel (fuel) *n* óleo diesel.
diesel (oil) *n* óleo diesel.
diet ['daɪət] *n* dieta; (*restricted food*) regime *m* ♦ *vi* (*also*: *be on a ~*) estar de dieta, fazer regime; **to live on a ~ of** alimentar-se de.
dietician [daɪə'tɪʃən] *n* dietista *m/f*.
differ ['dɪfə*] *vi*: **to ~ from sth** (*be different*) ser diferente de algo, diferenciar-se de algo; **to ~ from sb over sth** discordar de alguém em algo.
difference ['dɪfərəns] *n* diferença; (*quarrel*) desacordo; **it makes no ~ to me** não faz diferença para mim, para mim dá no mesmo; **to settle one's ~s** resolver as diferenças.
different ['dɪfərənt] *adj* diferente.
differential [dɪfə'rɛnʃəl] *n* (*AUT*) diferencial *m*; **wage/price ~s** diferenças de salário/preço.
differentiate [dɪfə'rɛnʃɪeɪt] *vt* diferenciar, distinguir ♦ *vi* diferenciar-se; **to ~ between** distinguir entre.
differently ['dɪfərəntlɪ] *adv* de outro modo, de forma diferente.
difficult ['dɪfɪkəlt] *adj* difícil; **~ to understand** difícil de (se) entender.
difficulty ['dɪfɪkəltɪ] *n* dificuldade *f*; **to have difficulties with** ter problemas com; **to be in ~** estar em dificuldade.
diffidence ['dɪfɪdəns] *n* timidez *f*.
diffident ['dɪfɪdənt] *adj* tímido.
diffuse [*adj* dɪ'fjuːs, *vt* dɪ'fjuːz] *adj* difuso ♦ *vt* difundir.
dig [dɪg] (*pt, pp* **dug**) *vt* (*hole, garden*) cavar; (*coal*) escavar; (*nails etc*) cravar ♦ *n* (*prod*) pontada; (*archaeological*) excavação *f*; (*remark*) alfinetada; **~s** *npl* (*BRIT*: *inf*) pensão *f*, alojamento; **to ~ into one's pockets for sth** enfiar as mãos nos bolsos à procura de algo; **to ~ one's nails into** cravar as unhas em.
dig in *vi* (*MIL*) cavar trincheiras; (*inf*: *eat*) atacar ♦ *vt* (*compost*) misturar; (*knife, claw*) cravar; **to ~ in one's heels** (*fig*) bater o pé; **~ in!** vai lá!
dig out *vt* escavar.
dig up *vt* desenterrar; (*plant*) arrancar.
digest [*vt* daɪ'dʒɛst, *n* 'daɪdʒɛst] *vt* (*food*) digerir; (*facts*) assimilar ♦ *n* sumário.
digestible [dɪ'dʒɛstəbl] *adj* digerível.
digestion [dɪ'dʒɛstʃən] *n* digestão *f*.
digestive [dɪ'dʒɛstɪv] *adj* digestivo.
digit ['dɪdʒɪt] *n* (*MATH, finger*) dígito.
digital ['dɪdʒɪtəl] *adj* digital.
dignified ['dɪgnɪfaɪd] *adj* digno.
dignitary ['dɪgnɪtərɪ] *n* dignitário/a.
dignity ['dɪgnɪtɪ] *n* dignidade *f*.
digress [daɪ'grɛs] *vi*: **to ~ from** afastar-se de.
digression [daɪ'grɛʃən] *n* digressão *f*.
dilapidated [dɪ'læpɪdeɪtɪd] *adj* arruinado.
dilate [daɪ'leɪt] *vt* dilatar ♦ *vi* dilatar-se.
dilatory ['dɪlətərɪ] *adj* retardio.
dilemma [daɪ'lɛmə] *n* dilema *m*; **to be in a ~** estar num dilema.
diligent ['dɪlɪdʒənt] *adj* diligente.
dill [dɪl] *n* endro, aneto.
dilly-dally ['dɪlɪ'dælɪ] *vi* (*loiter*) vadiar; (*hesitate*) vacilar.
dilute [daɪ'luːt] *vt* diluir ♦ *adj* diluído.
dim [dɪm] *adj* (*light, eyesight*) fraco; (*outline*) indistinto; (*memory*) vago; (*stupid*) burro; (*room*) escuro ♦ *vt* (*light*) diminuir; (*US*: *AUT*: *headlights*) baixar; **to take a ~ view of sth** desaprovar algo.
dime [daɪm] (*US*) *n moeda de dez centavos.*
dimension [dɪ'mɛnʃən] *n* dimensão *f*.
-dimensional [dɪ'mɛnʃənl] *suffix*: **two~** bidimensional.
diminish [dɪ'mɪnɪʃ] *vt, vi* diminuir.
diminished [dɪ'mɪnɪʃt] *adj*: **~ responsibility** (*LAW*) responsabilidade *f* reduzida.
diminutive [dɪ'mɪnjutɪv] *adj* diminuto ♦ *n* (*LING*) diminutivo.
dimly ['dɪmlɪ] *adv* fracamente; (*not clearly*) indistintamente.
dimmers ['dɪməz] (*US*) *npl* (*AUT*) faróis *mpl* baixos.
dimple ['dɪmpl] *n* covinha.
dim-witted [-'wɪtɪd] (*inf*) *adj* burro.
din [dɪn] *n* zoeira ♦ *vt*: **to ~ sth into sb** (*inf*) meter algo na cabeça de alguém, repisar algo a alguém.
dine [daɪn] *vi* jantar.
diner ['daɪnə*] *n* (*person*) comensal *m/f*; (*RAIL*) vagão-restaurante *m*; (*US*: *eating place*) lanchonete *f*.
dinghy ['dɪŋgɪ] *n* dingue *m*, bote *m*; **rubber ~**

bote de borracha; (*also*: *sailing* ~) barco a vela.
dingy ['dɪndʒɪ] *adj* (*room*) sombrio, lúgubre; (*dirty*) esquálido; (*dull*) descolorido.
dining car ['daɪnɪŋ-] *n* vagão-restaurante *m*.
dining room ['daɪnɪŋ-] *n* sala de jantar.
dinner ['dɪnə*] *n* (*evening meal*) jantar *m*; (*lunch*) almoço; (*public*) jantar, banquete *m*; **~'s ready!** está na mesa!
dinner jacket *n* smoking *m*.
dinner party *n* jantar *m*.
dinner time *n* hora de jantar *or* almoçar.
dinosaur ['daɪnəsɔː*] *n* dinossauro.
dint [dɪnt] *n*: **by ~ of (doing) sth** à força de (fazer) algo.
diocese ['daɪəsɪs] *n* diocese *f*.
dioxide [daɪ'ɔksaɪd] *n* dióxido.
Dip. (*BRIT*) *abbr* = **diploma**.
dip [dɪp] *n* (*slope*) inclinação *f*; (*in sea*) mergulho ♦ *vt* (*in water*) mergulhar; (*ladle etc*) meter; (*BRIT*: *AUT*: *lights*) baixar ♦ *vi* mergulhar.
diphtheria [dɪf'θɪərɪə] *n* difteria.
diphthong ['dɪfθɔŋ] *n* ditongo.
diploma [dɪ'pləumə] *n* diploma *m*.
diplomacy [dɪ'pləuməsɪ] *n* diplomacia.
diplomat ['dɪpləmæt] *n* diplomata *m/f*.
diplomatic [dɪplə'mætɪk] *adj* diplomático; **to break off ~ relations (with)** romper relações diplomáticas (com).
dipstick ['dɪpstɪk] *n* (*AUT*) vareta medidora.
dipswitch ['dɪpswɪtʃ] (*BRIT*) *n* (*AUT*) interruptor *m* de luz alta e baixa.
dire [daɪə*] *adj* terrível; (*very bad*) péssimo.
direct [daɪ'rɛkt] *adj* direto ♦ *vt* dirigir; **can you ~ me to ...?** pode me indicar o caminho a ...?; **to ~ sb to do sth** mandar alguém fazer algo.
direct cost *n* (*COMM*) custo direto.
direct current *n* (*ELEC*) corrente *f* contínua.
direct debit *n* (*BANKING*) débito direto.
direct dialling *n* (*TEL*) discagem *f* direta (*BR*), marcação *f* directa (*PT*).
direct hit *n* (*MIL*) acerto direto.
direction [dɪ'rɛkʃən] *n* direção *f*; **~s** *npl* (*to a place*) indicação *f*; (*instructions*) instruções *fpl*; **~s for use** modo de usar; **to ask for ~s** pedir uma indicação, perguntar o caminho; **sense of ~** senso de direção; **in the ~ of** na direção de.
directive [dɪ'rɛktɪv] *n* diretriz *f*.
direct labour *n* mão-de-obra direta.
directly [dɪ'rɛktlɪ] *adv* (*in straight line*) diretamente; (*at once*) imediatamente.
direct mail *n* mala direta.
direct mailshot (*BRIT*) *n* mailing *m*.
directness [daɪ'rɛktnɪs] *n* (*of person, speech*) franqueza.
director [dɪ'rɛktə*] *n* diretor *m*; **D~ of Public Prosecutions** (*BRIT*) ≈ procurador(a) *m/f* da República.
directory [dɪ'rɛktərɪ] *n* (*TEL*) lista (telefônica); (*also*: *street* ~) lista de endereços; (*also*: *trade* ~) anuário comercial; (*COMPUT*) diretório.
directory enquiries (*US* **directory assistance**) *n* (serviço de) informações *fpl* (*BR*), serviço informativo (*PT*).
dirt [dəːt] *n* sujeira (*BR*), sujidade (*PT*); **to treat sb like ~** espezinhar alguém.
dirt-cheap *adj* baratíssimo.
dirt road *n* estrada de terra.
dirty ['dəːtɪ] *adj* sujo; (*joke*) indecente ♦ *vt* sujar; **~ trick** golpe *m* baixo, sujeira.
disability [dɪsə'bɪlɪtɪ] *n* incapacidade *f*.
disability allowance *n* pensão *f* de invalidez.
disable [dɪs'eɪbl] *vt* (*subj*: *illness, accident*) incapacitar; (*tank, gun*) inutilizar.
disabled [dɪs'eɪbld] *adj* incapacitado, deficiente.
disadvantage [dɪsəd'vɑːntɪdʒ] *n* desvantagem *f*, inconveniente *m*.
disadvantaged [dɪsəd'vɑːntɪdʒd] *adj* (*person*) menos favorecido.
disadvantageous [dɪsædvɑːn'teɪdʒəs] *adj* desvantajoso.
disaffected [dɪsə'fɛktɪd] *adj*: **~ (to** *or* **towards)** descontente (de).
disaffection [dɪsə'fɛkʃən] *n* descontentamento.
disagree [dɪsə'griː] *vi* (*differ*: *accounts*) diferir; (*be against, think otherwise*): **to ~ (with)** não concordar (com), discordar (de); **garlic ~s with me** o alho me faz mal, o alho não me convém.
disagreeable [dɪsə'grɪəbl] *adj* desagradável.
disagreement [dɪsə'griːmənt] *n* desacordo; (*quarrel*) desavença.
disallow ['dɪsə'lau] *vt* não admitir; (*BRIT*: *goal*) anular.
disappear [dɪsə'pɪə*] *vi* desaparecer, sumir.
disappearance [dɪsə'pɪərəns] *n* desaparecimento, desaparição *f*.
disappoint [dɪsə'pɔɪnt] *vt* (*cause to regret*) desapontar; (*let down*) decepcionar; (*hopes*) frustrar.
disappointed [dɪsə'pɔɪntɪd] *adj* decepcionado; (*with oneself*) desapontado.
disappointing [dɪsə'pɔɪntɪŋ] *adj* decepcionante.
disappointment [dɪsə'pɔɪntmənt] *n* decepção *f*; (*regret*) desapontamento.
disapproval [dɪsə'pruːvəl] *n* desaprovação *f*.
disapprove [dɪsə'pruːv] *vi*: **to ~ of** desaprovar.
disapproving [dɪsə'pruːvɪŋ] *adj* desaprovativo, de desaprovação.
disarm [dɪs'ɑːm] *vt* desarmar.
disarmament [dɪs'ɑːməmənt] *n* desarmamento.
disarming [dɪs'ɑːmɪŋ] *adj* (*smile*) encantador(a).
disarray [dɪsə'reɪ] *n* desordem *f*; **in ~** (*troops*) desbaratado; (*thoughts*) confuso; (*clothes*) em desalinho; **to throw into ~** (*troops*)

***NB**: European Portuguese adds the following consonants to certain words:* **b** (sú(b)dito, su(b)til); **c** (a(c)ção, a(c)cionista, a(c)to); **m** (inde(m)ne); **p** (ado(p)ção, ado(p)tar); *for further details see p. xiii.*

desbaratar; (*government etc*) deixar em polvorosa.
disaster [dɪ'zɑːstə*] *n* (*accident*) desastre *m*; (*natural*) catástrofe *f*.
disastrous [dɪ'zɑːstrəs] *adj* desastroso.
disband [dɪs'bænd] *vt* dispersar ♦ *vi* dispersar-se, desfazer-se.
disbelief [dɪsbə'liːf] *n* incredulidade *f*; **in** ~ com incredulidade, incrédulo.
disbelieve ['dɪsbə'liːv] *vt* não acreditar em.
disc [dɪsk] *n* disco.
disc. *abbr* (COMM) = **discount**.
discard [dɪs'kɑːd] *vt* (*old things*) desfazer-se de; (*fig*) descartar.
disc brake *n* freio de disco (BR), travão *m* de discos (PT).
discern [dɪ'səːn] *vt* perceber.
discernible [dɪ'səːnəbl] *adj* perceptível; (*object*) visível.
discerning [dɪ'səːnɪŋ] *adj* perspicaz.
discharge [*vt* dɪs'tʃɑːdʒ, *n* 'dɪstʃɑːdʒ] *vt* (*duties*) cumprir, desempenhar; (*settle*: *debt*) saldar, quitar; (*patient*) dar alta a; (*employee*) despedir; (*soldier*) dar baixa em, dispensar; (*defendant*) pôr em liberdade; (*waste etc*) descarregar, despejar ♦ *n* (ELEC) descarga; (*dismissal*) despedida; (*of duty*) desempenho; (*of debt*) quitação *f*; (*from hospital*) alta; (*from army*) baixa; (LAW) absolvição *f*; (MED) secreção *f*; (*also*: *vaginal* ~) corrimento; **to** ~ **one's gun** descarregar a arma, disparar; **~d bankrupt** falido/a reabilitado/a.
disciple [dɪ'saɪpl] *n* discípulo/a.
disciplinary ['dɪsɪplɪnərɪ] *adj* disciplinar; **to take** ~ **action against sb** mover ação disciplinar contra alguém.
discipline ['dɪsɪplɪn] *n* disciplina ♦ *vt* disciplinar; (*punish*) punir; **to** ~ **o.s. to do sth** disciplinar-se para fazer algo.
disc jockey *n* (*on radio*) radialista *m/f*; (*in discothèque*) discotecário/a.
disclaim [dɪs'kleɪm] *vt* negar.
disclaimer [dɪs'kleɪmə*] *n* desmentido; **to issue a** ~ publicar um desmentido.
disclose [dɪs'kləuz] *vt* revelar.
disclosure [dɪs'kləuʒə*] *n* revelação *f*.
disco ['dɪskəu] *n abbr* = **discothèque**.
discolour [dɪs'kʌlə*] (US **discolor**) *vt* descolorar; (*fade*: *fabric*) desbotar; (*yellow*: *teeth*) amarelar; (*stain*) manchar ♦ *vi* (*fabric*) desbotar; (*teeth etc*) amarelar.
discolo(u)ration [dɪskʌlə'reɪʃən] *n* (*of fabric*) desbotamento; (*stain*) mancha.
discolo(u)red [dɪs'kʌləd] *adj* descolorado; (*teeth etc*) amarelado.
discomfort [dɪs'kʌmfət] *n* desconforto; (*unease*) inquietação *f*; (*physical*) mal-estar *m*.
disconcert [dɪskən'səːt] *vt* desconcertar.
disconnect [dɪskə'nɛkt] *vt* desligar; (*gas, water*) cortar.
disconnected [dɪskə'nɛktɪd] *adj* (*speech, thoughts*) desconexo, incoerente.
disconsolate [dɪs'kɔnsəlɪt] *adj* desconsolado, inconsolável.
discontent [dɪskən'tɛnt] *n* descontentamento.
discontented [dɪskən'tɛntɪd] *adj* descontente.
discontinue [dɪskən'tɪnjuː] *vt* interromper; (*payments*) suspender; **"~d"** (COMM) "fora de linha".
discord ['dɪskɔːd] *n* discórdia; (MUS) dissonância.
discordant [dɪs'kɔːdənt] *adj* dissonante.
discothèque ['dɪskəutɛk] *n* discoteca.
discount [*n* 'dɪskaunt, *vt* dɪs'kaunt] *n* desconto ♦ *vt* descontar; **to give sb a** ~ **on sth** dar *or* conceder um desconto a alguém por algo; ~ **for cash** desconto por pagamento à vista; **at a** ~ com desconto.
discount house (*irreg*) *n* (FINANCE) agência corretora de descontos; (COMM: *also*: *discount store*) loja de descontos.
discount rate *n* taxa de desconto.
discourage [dɪs'kʌrɪdʒ] *vt* (*dishearten*) desanimar; (*dissuade*) dissuadir; (*deter*) desincentivar; (*theft etc*) desencorajar.
discouragement [dɪs'kʌrɪdʒmənt] *n* (*depression*) desânimo, desalento; **to act as a** ~ **to sb** dissuadir alguém.
discouraging [dɪs'kʌrɪdʒɪŋ] *adj* desanimador(a).
discourteous [dɪs'kəːtɪəs] *adj* descortês.
discover [dɪs'kʌvə*] *vt* descobrir.
discovery [dɪs'kʌvərɪ] *n* (*act*) descobrimento, descoberta; (*thing discovered*) descoberta.
discredit [dɪs'krɛdɪt] *vt* desacreditar ♦ *n* descrédito.
discreet [dɪ'skriːt] *adj* discreto.
discreetly [dɪ'skriːtlɪ] *adv* discretamente.
discrepancy [dɪ'skrɛpənsɪ] *n* (*difference*) diferença; (*disagreement*) discrepância.
discretion [dɪ'skrɛʃən] *n* discrição *f*; **use your** ~ aja segundo o seu critério.
discretionary [dɪ'skrɛʃənrɪ] *adj* (*powers*) discricionário.
discriminate [dɪ'skrɪmɪneɪt] *vi*: **to** ~ **between** fazer distinção entre; **to** ~ **against** discriminar contra.
discriminating [dɪ'skrɪmɪneɪtɪŋ] *adj* acurado, criterioso.
discrimination [dɪskrɪmɪ'neɪʃən] *n* (*discernment*) discernimento; (*bias*) discriminaçaõ *f*; **racial/sexual** ~ discriminação racial/sexual.
discus ['dɪskəs] *n* disco; (*event*) arremesso do disco.
discuss [dɪ'skʌs] *vt* discutir.
discussion [dɪ'skʌʃən] *n* discussão *f*; **under** ~ em discussão.
disdain [dɪs'deɪn] *n* desdém *m* ♦ *vt* desdenhar.
disease [dɪ'ziːz] *n* moléstia.
diseased [dɪ'ziːzd] *adj* doente.
disembark [dɪsɪm'bɑːk] *vt, vi* desembarcar.
disembarkation [dɪsembɑː'keɪʃən] *n* desembarque *m*.
disembodied ['dɪsɪm'bɔdɪd] *adj* desencarnado.
disembowel ['dɪsɪm'bauəl] *vt* estripar, eviscerar.
disenchanted ['dɪsɪn'tʃɑːntɪd] *adj*: ~ **(with)** desencantado (de).
disenfranchise ['dɪsɪn'fræntʃaɪz] *vt* privar do

privilégio do voto; (COMM) retirar a concessão de.
disengage [dısın'geıdʒ] *vt* soltar; (TECH) desengrenar; **to ~ the clutch** (AUT) desembrear.
disengagement [dısın'geıdʒmənt] *n* (POL) desengajamento.
disentangle [dısın'tæŋgl] *vt* desenredar.
disfavour [dıs'feıvə*] (US **disfavor**) *n* desfavor *m*.
disfigure [dıs'fıgə*] *vt* desfigurar.
disgorge [dıs'gɔːdʒ] *vt* descarregar, despejar.
disgrace [dıs'greıs] *n* ignomínia; (*downfall*) queda; (*shame*) vergonha, desonra ♦ *vt* desonrar.
disgraceful [dıs'greısful] *adj* vergonhoso; (*behaviour*) escandaloso.
disgruntled [dıs'grʌntld] *adj* descontente.
disguise [dıs'gaız] *n* disfarce *m* ♦ *vt* disfarçar; **in ~** disfarçado; **to ~ o.s. as** disfarçar-se de; **there's no disguising the fact that ...** não há como esconder o fato de que ....
disgust [dıs'gʌst] *n* repugnância ♦ *vt* repugnar a, dar nojo em.
disgusting [dıs'gʌstıŋ] *adj* repugnante, nojento.
dish [dıʃ] *n* prato; (*serving ~*) travessa; **to do** *or* **wash the ~es** lavar os pratos *or* a louça.
dish out *vt* repartir.
dish up *vt* servir; (*facts, statistics*) apresentar.
dishcloth ['dıʃklɔθ] *n* pano de prato *or* de louça.
dishearten [dıs'hɑːtn] *vt* desalentar.
dishevelled [dı'ʃɛvəld] (US **disheveled**) *adj* despenteado, desgrenhado.
dishonest [dıs'ɔnıst] *adj* (*person*) desonesto; (*means*) fraudulento.
dishonesty [dıs'ɔnıstı] *n* desonestidade *f*.
dishonour [dıs'ɔnə*] (US **dishonor**) *n* desonra.
dishono(u)rable [dıs'ɔnərəbl] *adj* desonroso.
dish soap (US) *n* detergente *m*.
dishtowel [dıʃ'tauəl] (US) *n* pano de prato.
dishwasher ['dıʃwɔʃə*] *n* máquina de lavar louça *or* pratos.
disillusion [dısı'luːʒən] *vt* desiludir ♦ *n* desilusão *f*; **to become ~ed** ficar desiludido, desiludir-se.
disillusionment [dısı'luːʒənmənt] *n* desilusão *f*.
disincentive [dısın'sɛntıv] *n* desincentivo; **to be a ~ to sb** desincentivar alguém.
disinclined ['dısın'klaınd] *adj*: **to be ~ to do** estar pouco disposto a fazer.
disinfect [dısın'fɛkt] *vt* desinfetar.
disinfectant [dısın'fɛktənt] *n* desinfetante *m*.
disinflation [dısın'fleıʃən] *n* desinflação *f*.
disinherit [dısın'hɛrıt] *vt* deserdar.
disintegrate [dıs'ıntıgreıt] *vi* desagregar-se, desintegrar-se.
disinterested [dıs'ıntrəstıd] *adj* desinteressado.
disjointed [dıs'dʒɔıntıd] *adj* desconexo.
disk [dısk] *n* (COMPUT) disco; **single-/double-sided ~** disquete de face simples/dupla.
disk drive *n* unidade *f* de disco.
diskette [dıs'kɛt] *n* (COMPUT) disquete *m*.
disk operating system *n* sistema *m* operacional residente em disco.
dislike [dıs'laık] *n* antipatia, aversão *f* ♦ *vt* antipatizar com, não gostar de; **to take a ~ to sb/sth** tomar antipatia por alguém/algo; **I ~ the idea** não gosto da idéia.
dislocate ['dısləkeıt] *vt* deslocar; **he has ~d his shoulder** ele deslocou o ombro.
dislodge [dıs'lɔdʒ] *vt* desentocar; (*enemy*) desalojar.
disloyal [dıs'lɔıəl] *adj* desleal.
dismal ['dızml] *adj* (*dull*) sombrio, lúgubre; (*depressing*) deprimente; (*very bad*) horrível.
dismantle [dıs'mæntl] *vt* desmontar, desmantelar.
dismay [dıs'meı] *n* consternação *f* ♦ *vt* consternar; **much to my ~** para minha grande consternação.
dismiss [dıs'mıs] *vt* (*worker*) despedir; (*official*) demitir; (*idea*) descartar; (LAW, *possibility*) rejeitar ♦ *vi* (MIL) sair de forma.
dismissal [dıs'mısəl] *n* (*of worker*) despedida; (*of official*) demissão *f*.
dismount [dıs'maunt] *vi* desmontar.
disobedience [dısə'biːdıəns] *n* desobediência.
disobedient [dısə'biːdıənt] *adj* desobediente.
disobey [dısə'beı] *vt* desobedecer a; (*rules*) transgredir, desrespeitar.
disorder [dıs'ɔːdə*] *n* desordem *f*; (*rioting*) distúrbios *mpl*, tumulto; (MED) distúrbio; **stomach ~** problema estomacal.
disorderly [dıs'ɔːdəlı] *adj* (*untidy*) desordenado; (*crowd*) tumultuado; (*behaviour*) escandaloso.
disorderly conduct *n* (LAW) perturbação *f* da ordem, ofensa à moral.
disorganized [dıs'ɔːgənaızd] *adj* desorganizado.
disorientated [dıs'ɔːrıɛnteıtəd] *adj* desorientado.
disown [dıs'əun] *vt* repudiar.
disparaging [dıs'pærıdʒıŋ] *adj* depreciativo; **to be ~ about sb/sth** fazer pouco de alguém/algo, depreciar alguém/algo.
disparate ['dıspərıt] *adj* diverso, desigual.
disparity [dıs'pærıtı] *n* desigualdade *f*.
dispassionate [dıs'pæʃənət] *adj* (*calm*) calmo, controlado; (*impartial*) desinteressado, imparcial.
dispatch [dıs'pætʃ] *vt* (*person, business*) despachar; (*send: parcel etc*) expedir ♦ *n* (*sending*) remessa; (*speed*) rapidez *f*, urgência; (PRESS) comunicado; (MIL) parte *f*.
dispatch department *n* (serviço de) expedição *f*.
dispatch rider *n* (MIL) estafeta *m/f*.

***NB:** European Portuguese adds the following consonants to certain words:* **b** (sú(b)dito, su(b)til); **c** (a(c)ção, a(c)cionista, a(c)to); **m** (inde(m)ne); **p** (ado(p)ção, ado(p)tar); *for further details see p. xiii.*

dispel [dɪs'pɛl] *vt* dissipar.
dispensary [dɪs'pɛnsərɪ] *n* dispensário, farmácia.
dispense [dɪs'pɛns] *vt* (*give out*) dispensar; (*medicine*) preparar (e vender); **to ~ sb from** dispensar alguém de.
dispense with *vt fus* prescindir de.
dispenser [dɪs'pɛnsə*] *n* (*device*) distribuidor *m* automático.
dispensing chemist [dɪs'pɛnsɪŋ-] (*BRIT*) *n* farmacêutico/a.
dispersal [dɪs'pəːsl] *n* dispersão *f*.
disperse [dɪs'pəːs] *vt* dispersar ♦ *vi* dispersar-se.
dispirited [dɪs'pɪrɪtɪd] *adj* desanimado.
displace [dɪs'pleɪs] *vt* (*shift*) deslocar.
displaced person [dɪs'pleɪst-] *n* (*POL*) deslocado/a de guerra.
displacement [dɪs'pleɪsmənt] *n* deslocamento.
display [dɪs'pleɪ] *n* (*exhibition*) exposição *f*; (*computer ~*: *information*) apresentação *f* visual; (: *device*) display *m*; (*MIL*) parada; (*of feeling*) manifestação *f*; (*pej*) ostentação *f*; (*show*, *spectacle*) espetáculo ♦ *vt* (*goods*) expor; (*feelings*, *tastes*) manifestar; (*ostentatiously*) ostentar; (*results*, *departure times*) expor; **on ~** (*visible*) à mostra; (*goods*, *paintings etc*) em exposição.
display advertising *n* anúncios *mpl*.
displease [dɪs'pliːz] *vt* desagradar, desgostar; **~d with** descontente com.
displeasure [dɪs'plɛʒə*] *n* desgosto.
disposable [dɪs'pəuzəbl] *adj* (*pack etc*) descartável; (*income*) disponível; **~ nappy** (*BRIT*) fralda descartável.
disposal [dɪs'pəuzl] *n* (*availability*, *arrangement*) disposição *f*; (*of rubbish*) destruição *f*; (*of property etc*: *by selling*) venda, traspasse *m*; (: *by giving away*) cessão *f*; **at sb's ~** à disposição de alguém; **to put sth at sb's ~** pôr algo à disposição de alguém.
dispose [dɪs'pəuz] *vt* dispor.
dispose of *vt fus* (*time*, *money*) dispor de; (*unwanted goods*) desfazer-se de; (*throw away*) jogar (*BR*) *or* tirar (*PT*) fora; (*COMM*: *stock*) vender; (*problem*, *task*) expedir.
disposed [dɪs'pəuzd] *adj*: **~ to do** disposto a fazer.
disposition [dɪspə'zɪʃən] *n* disposição *f*; (*temperament*) índole *f*.
dispossess ['dɪspəzɛs] *vt*: **to ~ sb (of)** despojar alguém (de).
disproportion [dɪsprə'pɔːʃən] *n* desproporção *f*.
disproportionate [dɪsprə'pɔːʃənət] *adj* desproporcionado.
disprove [dɪs'pruːv] *vt* refutar.
dispute [dɪs'pjuːt] *n* disputa; (*verbal*) discussão *f*; (*also*: *industrial ~*) conflito, disputa ♦ *vt* disputar; (*argue*) discutir; (*question*) questionar; **to be in** *or* **under ~** (*matter*) estar em discussão; (*territory*) estar em disputa, ser disputado.
disqualification [dɪskwɔlɪfɪ'keɪʃən] *n* (*LAW*) inabilitação *f*, incapacitação *f*; (*SPORT*) desclassificação *f*; **~ (from driving)** (*BRIT*) cassação *f* da carteira (de motorista).
disqualify [dɪs'kwɔlɪfaɪ] *vt* (*SPORT*) desclassificar; **to ~ sb for sth/from doing sth** desqualificar alguém para algo/de fazer algo; **to ~ sb (from driving)** (*BRIT*) cassar a carteira (de motorista) a alguém.
disquiet [dɪs'kwaɪət] *n* inquietação *f*.
disquieting [dɪs'kwaɪətɪŋ] *adj* inquietante, alarmante.
disregard [dɪsrɪ'gɑːd] *vt* desconsiderar ♦ *n* (*indifference*): **~ (for)** (*feelings*) desconsideração *f* (por); (*danger*) indiferença (a); (*money*) menosprezo (por).
disrepair [dɪsrɪ'pɛə*] *n*: **to fall into ~** ficar dilapidado.
disreputable [dɪs'rɛpjutəbl] *adj* (*person*) de má fama; (*behaviour*) vergonhoso.
disrepute ['dɪsrɪ'pjuːt] *n* descrédito, desonra; **to bring into ~** desacreditar, desprestigiar.
disrespect [dɪsrɪ'spɛkt] *n*: **~ (for)** desrespeito (por).
disrespectful [dɪsrɪ'spɛktful] *adj* desrespeitoso.
disrupt [dɪs'rʌpt] *vt* (*plans*) desfazer; (*meeting*, *process*) perturbar, interromper.
disruption [dɪs'rʌpʃən] *n* transtorno, perturbação *f*.
disruptive [dɪs'rʌptɪv] *adj* (*influence*) maléfico; (*strike*) perturbador(a).
dissatisfaction [dɪssætɪs'fækʃən] *n* descontentamento.
dissatisfied [dɪs'sætɪsfaɪd] *adj*: **~ (with)** descontente (com).
dissect [dɪ'sɛkt] *vt* dissecar.
disseminate [dɪ'sɛmɪneɪt] *vt* disseminar.
dissent [dɪ'sɛnt] *n* dissensão *f*.
dissenter [dɪ'sɛntə*] *n* (*REL*, *POL etc*) dissidente *m/f*.
dissertation [dɪsə'teɪʃən] *n* (*SCH*) dissertação *f*, tese *f*.
disservice [dɪs'səːvɪs] *n*: **to do sb a ~** prejudicar alguém.
dissident ['dɪsɪdnt] *adj*, *n* dissidente *m/f*.
dissimilar [dɪ'sɪmɪlə*] *adj*: **~ (to)** dessemelhante (de), diferente (de).
dissipate ['dɪsɪpeɪt] *vt* dissipar ♦ *vi* dissipar-se.
dissipated ['dɪsɪpeɪtɪd] *adj* (*person*) dissoluto.
dissociate [dɪ'səuʃɪeɪt] *vt* dissociar, separar; **to ~ o.s. from** desassociar-se de, distanciar-se de.
dissolute ['dɪsəluːt] *adj* dissoluto.
dissolution [dɪsə'luːʃən] *n* dissolução *f*.
dissolve [dɪ'zɔlv] *vt* dissolver ♦ *vi* dissolver-se; (*fig*: *problem etc*) desaparecer.
dissuade [dɪ'sweɪd] *vt*: **to ~ sb (from)** dissuadir alguém (de).
distaff ['dɪstɑːf] *n*: **~ side** lado materno.
distance ['dɪstns] *n* distância; **in the ~** ao longe; **what's the ~ to London?** qual é a distância daqui a Londres?; **it's within walking ~** pode-se ir a pé, dá para ir a pé (*inf*).
distant ['dɪstnt] *adj* distante; (*manner*) afastado, reservado.

distaste [dɪs'teɪst] *n* repugnância.
distasteful [dɪs'teɪstful] *adj* repugnante, desagradável.
Dist. Atty. (*US*) *abbr* = **district attorney.**
distemper [dɪs'tɛmpə*] *n* (*paint*) tinta plástica; (*of dogs*) cinomose *f*.
distended [dɪs'tɛndɪd] *adj* inchado.
distil [dɪs'tɪl] *vt* destilar.
distillery [dɪs'tɪlərɪ] *n* destilaria.
distinct [dɪs'tɪŋkt] *adj* (*different*) distinto; (*clear*) claro; (*unmistakeable*) nítido; **as ~ from** em oposição a.
distinction [dɪs'tɪŋkʃən] *n* distinção *f*; **to draw a ~ between** fazer distinção entre; **a writer of ~** um escritor de destaque.
distinctive [dɪs'tɪŋktɪv] *adj* distintivo.
distinctly [dɪs'tɪŋktlɪ] *adv* claramente, nitidamente.
distinguish [dɪs'tɪŋgwɪʃ] *vt* distinguir ♦ *vi*: **to ~ between** (*concepts*) distinguir entre, fazer distinção entre; **to ~ o.s.** distinguir-se.
distinguished [dɪs'tɪŋgwɪʃt] *adj* (*eminent*) eminente, distinto; (*career*) notável.
distinguishing [dɪs'tɪŋgwɪʃɪŋ] *adj* (*feature*) distintivo.
distort [dɪs'tɔːt] *vt* alterar.
distortion [dɪs'tɔːʃən] *n* deformação *f*; (*of sound*) deturpação *f*.
distract [dɪs'trækt] *vt* distrair; (*attention*) desviar; (*bewilder*) aturdir.
distracted [dɪs'træktɪd] *adj* distraído.
distraction [dɪs'trækʃən] *n* distração *f*; (*confusion*) aturdimento, perplexidade *f*; (*amusement*) divertimento; **to drive sb to ~** deixar alguém louco.
distraught [dɪs'trɔːt] *adj* desesperado.
distress [dɪs'trɛs] *n* (*anguish*) angústia; (*misfortune*) desgraça; (*want*) miséria; (*pain*) dor *f* ♦ *vt* (*cause anguish*) afligir; **in ~** (*ship*) em perigo; **~ed area** (*BRIT*) área de baixo nível socio-econômico.
distressing [dɪs'trɛsɪŋ] *adj* aflitivo, angustioso.
distress signal *n* sinal *m* de socorro.
distribute [dɪs'trɪbjuːt] *vt* distribuir.
distribution [dɪstrɪ'bjuːʃən] *n* distribuição *f*.
distribution cost *n* custo de distribuição.
distributor [dɪ'strɪbjutə*] *n* (*AUT*) distribuidor *m*; (*COMM*) distribuidor(a) *m/f*; (: *company*) distribuidora.
district ['dɪstrɪkt] *n* (*of country*) região *f*; (*of town*) zona; (*ADMIN*) distrito.
district attorney (*US*) *n* promotor(a) *m/f* público/a.
district council (*BRIT*) *n* ≈ município (*BR*), câmara municipal (*PT*).
district nurse (*BRIT*) *n* *enfermeiro/a do Serviço Nacional que visita os pacientes em casa.*
distrust [dɪs'trʌst] *n* desconfiança ♦ *vt* desconfiar de.
distrustful [dɪs'trʌstful] *adj* desconfiado.
disturb [dɪs'təːb] *vt* perturbar; (*bother*) incomodar; (*interrupt*) atrapalhar; **sorry to ~ you** desculpe incomodá-lo.
disturbance [dɪs'təːbəns] *n* perturbação *f*; (*political etc*) distúrbio; (*violence*) agitação *f*; (*of mind*) transtorno; **to cause a ~** perturbar a ordem.
disturbed [dɪs'təːbd] *adj* perturbado; **to be mentally/emotionally ~** ter problemas psicológicos/emocionais.
disturbing [dɪs'təːbɪŋ] *adj* perturbador(a), inquietante.
disuse [dɪs'juːs] *n*: **to fall into ~** cair em desuso.
disused [dɪs'juːzd] *adj* desusado, abandonado.
ditch [dɪtʃ] *n* fosso; (*irrigation ~*) rego ♦ *vt* (*inf*) desfazer-se de.
dither ['dɪðə*] *vi* vacilar.
ditto ['dɪtəu] *adv* idem.
divan [dɪ'væn] *n* divã *m*.
divan bed *n* divã *m*.
dive [daɪv] *n* (*from board*) salto; (*underwater, of submarine*) mergulho; (*AVIAT*) picada; (*pej*: *café, bar etc*) espelunca ♦ *vi* saltar; mergulhar; picar.
diver ['daɪvə*] *n* (*SPORT*) saltador(a) *m/f*; (*underwater*) mergulhador(a) *m/f*.
diverge [daɪ'vəːdʒ] *vi* divergir.
divergent [daɪ'vəːdʒənt] *adj* divergente.
diverse [daɪ'vəːs] *adj* diverso; (*group*) heterogêneo.
diversification [daɪvəːsɪfɪ'keɪʃən] *n* diversificação *f*.
diversify [daɪ'vəːsɪfaɪ] *vt, vi* diversificar.
diversion [daɪ'vəːʃən] *n* (*BRIT*: *AUT*) desvio; (*distraction, MIL*) diversão *f*.
diversity [daɪ'vəːsɪtɪ] *n* diversidade *f*.
divert [daɪ'vəːt] *vt* (*change course of*) desviar; (*amuse*) divertir.
divest [daɪ'vɛst] *vt*: **to ~ sb of sth** privar alguém de algo.
divide [dɪ'vaɪd] *vt* dividir; (*separate*) separar ♦ *vi* dividir-se; (*road*) bifurcar-se; **to ~ (between *or* among)** dividir *or* repartir (entre); **40 ~d by 5** 40 dividido por 5.
divide out *vt*: **to ~ out (between *or* among)** distribuir *or* repartir (entre).
divided [dɪ'vaɪdɪd] *adj* (*fig*) dividido.
divided highway (*US*) *n* pista dupla.
divided skirt *n* saia-calça.
dividend ['dɪvɪdɛnd] *n* dividendo; (*fig*) lucro.
dividend cover *n* cobertura para pagamento de dividendos.
dividers [dɪ'vaɪdəz] *npl* compasso de ponta seca; (*between pages*) divisórias *fpl*.
divine [dɪ'vaɪn] *adj* divino ♦ *vt* (*future, truth*) adivinhar; (*water, metal*) descobrir.
diving ['daɪvɪŋ] *n* (*SPORT*) salto; (*underwater*) mergulho.
diving board *n* trampolim *m*.
diving suit *n* escafandro.
divinity [dɪ'vɪnɪtɪ] *n* divindade *f*; (*SCH*) teologia.

***NB:** European Portuguese adds the following consonants to certain words:* **b** (sú(b)dito, su(b)til); **c** (a(c)ção, a(c)cionista, a(c)to); **m** (inde(m)ne); **p** (ado(p)ção, ado(p)tar); *for further details see p. xiii.*

division [dɪ'vɪʒən] *n* (*also*: *BRIT*: *FOOTBALL*) divisão *f*; (*sharing out*) repartição *f*; (*disagreement*) discórdia; (*BRIT*: *POL*) votação *f*; ~ **of labour** divisão do trabalho.
divisive [dɪ'vaɪsɪv] *adj* que causa divisão.
divorce [dɪ'vɔːs] *n* divórcio ♦ *vt* divorciar-se de.
divorced [dɪ'vɔːst] *adj* divorciado.
divorcee [dɪvɔː'siː] *n* divorciado/a.
divulge [daɪ'vʌldʒ] *vt* divulgar, revelar.
DIY (*BRIT*) *adj*, *n abbr* = **do-it-yourself**.
dizziness ['dɪzɪnɪs] *n* vertigem *f*, tontura.
dizzy ['dɪzɪ] *adj* (*person*) tonto; (*height*) vertiginoso; **to feel** ~ sentir-se tonto, sentir-se atordoado; **to make sb** ~ dar vertigem a alguém.
DJ *n abbr* = **disc jockey**.
Djakarta [dʒə'kɑːtə] *n* Jacarta.
DJIA (*US*) *n abbr* (*STOCK EXCHANGE*) = **Dow Jones Industrial Average**.
dl *abbr* (= *decilitre*) dl.
DLit(t) *n abbr* (= *Doctor of Literature*; *Doctor of Letters*) *títulos universitários*.
DLO *n abbr* = **dead-letter office**.
dm *abbr* (= *decimetre*) dm.
DMus *n abbr* (= *Doctor of Music*) *título universitário*.
DMZ *n abbr* = **demilitarized zone**.
DNA *n abbr* (= *deoxyribonucleic acid*) ADN *m*.
do [duː] (*pt* **did**, *pp* **done**) *vt*, *vi* (*gen*) fazer; (*speed*) ir a; (*visit*: *city*, *museum*) visitar; (*THEATRE*) representar ♦ *n* (*inf*: *party*) festa; (: *formal gathering*) recepção *f*; **he didn't laugh** ele não riu; ~ **you want any?** você quer?; **she swims better than I** ~ ela nada melhor que eu; **he laughed, didn't he?** ele riu, não foi?; ~ **they?** ah, é?; **who broke it? — I did** quem quebrou isso? — (fui) eu; ~ **you agree? — I** ~ você concorda? — concordo; **so does he** ele também; **DO come!** venha mesmo!; **I DO wish I could go** eu gostaria tanto de ir; **but I DO like it!** mas claro que eu gosto!; **to** ~ **one's nails/teeth** fazer as unhas/escovar os dentes; **to** ~ **one's hair** (*comb*) pentear-se; (*style*) fazer um penteado; **will it** ~**?** (*is it enough?*) dá?, chega?; (*is it suitable?*) serve?; **that will** ~**!** basta!, chega!; **to** ~ **well** prosperar, ter êxito; **to make** ~ **with** contentar-se com; **to** ~ **without sth** passar sem algo; **what did he** ~ **with the cat?** o que é que ele fez com o gato?; **what has that got to** ~ **with it?** o que é que isso tem a ver?
do away with *vt fus* (*kill*) matar; (*suppress*) suprimir.
do for (*BRIT*: *inf*) *vt fus* (*clean for*) fazer o serviço de casa para.
do up *vt* (*laces*) atar; (*room*) arrumar, renovar; **to** ~ **o.s. up** arrumar-se.
do with *vt fus*: **I could** ~ **with a drink** eu bem que gostaria de tomar alguma coisa; **I could** ~ **with some help** eu bem que precisaria de uma ajuda; **it could** ~ **with a wash** seria bom lavá-lo.
do. *abbr* = **ditto**.
DOA *abbr* (= *dead on arrival*) ≈ já era cadáver.
d.o.b. *abbr* = **date of birth**.
docile ['dəusaɪl] *adj* dócil.
dock [dɔk] *n* (*NAUT*) doca; (*wharf*) cais *m*; (*LAW*) banco (dos réus); ~**s** *npl* docas *fpl* ♦ *vi* (*arrive*) chegar; (*enter* ~) entrar no estaleiro ♦ *vt* (*pay etc*) deduzir.
dock dues *npl* direitos *mpl* portuários.
docker ['dɔkə*] *n* portuário, estivador *m*.
docket ['dɔkɪt] *n* (*of delivery etc*) guia.
dockyard ['dɔkjɑːd] *n* estaleiro.
doctor ['dɔktə*] *n* médico/a; (*Ph.D. etc*) doutor(a) *m/f* ♦ *vt* (*fig*) tratar, falsificar; (*drink etc*) falsificar; (*cat*) castrar; ~**'s office** (*US*) consultório; **D**~ **of Philosophy** (*degree*) doutorado; (*person*) doutor(a) *m/f*.
doctorate ['dɔktərɪt] *n* doutorado.
doctrine ['dɔktrɪn] *n* doutrina.
document [*n* 'dɔkjumənt, *vt* 'dɔkjumɛnt] *n* documento ♦ *vt* documentar.
documentary [dɔkju'mɛntərɪ] *adj* documental ♦ *n* documentário.
documentation [dɔkjumɛn'teɪʃən] *n* documentação *f*.
DOD (*US*) *n abbr* = **Department of Defense**.
doddering ['dɔdərɪŋ] *adj* (*senile*) caquético, caduco.
Dodecanese (Islands) [dəudɪkə'niːz-] *n(pl)* (ilhas *fpl* do) Dodecaneso.
dodge [dɔdʒ] *n* (*of body*) evasiva; (*fig*) trapaça ♦ *vt* esquivar-se de, evitar; (*blow*) furtar-se a ♦ *vi*: **to** ~ **out of the way** esquivar-se; **to** ~ **the traffic** ziguezaguear por entre os carros.
dodgems ['dɔdʒəmz] (*BRIT*) *npl* carros *mpl* de choque.
dodgy ['dɔdʒɪ] *adj* arriscado.
DOE *n abbr* (*BRIT*) = **Department of the Environment**; (*US*) = **Department of Energy**.
doe [dəu] *n* corça.
does [dʌz] *see* **do**.
doesn't ['dʌznt] = **does not**.
dog [dɔg] *n* cachorro, cão *m* ♦ *vt* acossar; **to go to the** ~**s** (*nation etc*) degringolar.
dog biscuits *npl* biscoitos *mpl* para cachorro.
dog collar *n* coleira de cachorro; (*fig*: *of priest*) gola de padre.
dog-eared [-ɪəd] *adj* surrado.
dog food *n* ração *f* para cachorro.
dogged ['dɔgɪd] *adj* tenaz, persistente.
dogma ['dɔgmə] *n* dogma *m*.
dogmatic [dɔg'mætɪk] *adj* dogmático.
do-gooder [-'gudə*] (*pej*) *n* bom/boa samaritano/a.
dogsbody ['dɔgzbɔdɪ] (*BRIT*) *n* faz-tudo *m/f*.
doing ['duɪŋ] *n*: **this is your** ~ foi você que fez isso; ~**s** *npl* (*events*) acontecimentos *mpl*; (*acts*) atos *mpl*.
do-it-yourself *n* sistema *m* faça-você-mesmo ♦ *adj* do tipo faça-você-mesmo.
doldrums ['dɔldrəmz] *npl*: **to be in the** ~ (*person*) estar abatido; (*business*) estar parado *or* estagnado.

dole [dəul] (*BRIT*) *n* (*payment*) subsídio de desemprego; **on the ~** desempregado.
dole out *vt* repartir.
doleful ['dəulful] *adj* triste, lúgubre.
doll [dɔl] *n* boneca.
doll up *vt*: **to ~ o.s. up** embonecar-se (*BR*), ataviar-se (*PT*).
dollar ['dɔlə*] *n* dólar *m*.
dollar area *n* zona do dólar.
dolphin ['dɔlfɪn] *n* golfinho.
domain [də'meɪn] *n* domínio; (*fig*) campo.
dome [dəum] *n* (*ARCH*) cúpula; (*shape*) abóbada.
domestic [də'mɛstɪk] *adj* (*gen*) doméstico; (*national*) nacional; (*home-loving*) caseiro; (*strife*) interno.
domesticated [də'mɛstɪkeɪtɪd] *adj* domesticado; **he's very ~** ele é muito prendado (no lar).
domesticity [dɔmɛs'tɪsɪtɪ] *n* vida caseira.
domestic servant *n* empregado/a doméstico/a.
domicile ['dɔmɪsaɪl] *n* domicílio.
dominant ['dɔmɪnənt] *adj* dominante.
dominate ['dɔmɪneɪt] *vt* dominar.
domination [dɔmɪ'neɪʃən] *n* dominação *f*.
domineering [dɔmɪ'nɪərɪŋ] *adj* dominante, mandão/dona.
Dominican Republic [də'mɪnɪkən-] *n* República Dominicana.
dominion [də'mɪnɪən] *n* domínio.
domino ['dɔmɪnəu] (*pl* **~es**) *n* peça de dominó; **~es** *n* (*game*) dominó *m*.
don [dɔn] *n* (*BRIT*) professor(a) *m/f* universitário/a ♦ *vt* vestir.
donate [də'neɪt] *vt* doar.
donation [də'neɪʃən] *n* doação *f*.
done [dʌn] *pp of* **do**.
donkey ['dɔŋkɪ] *n* burro.
donkey-work (*BRIT*: *inf*) *n* labuta.
donor ['dəunə*] *n* doador(a) *m/f*.
don't [dəunt] = **do not**.
doodle ['du:dl] *n* rabisco ♦ *vi* rabiscar.
doom [du:m] *n* (*fate*) destino; (*ruin*) ruína ♦ *vt*: **to be ~ed to failure** estar destinado *or* fadado ao fracasso.
doomsday ['du:mzdeɪ] *n* o Juízo Final.
door [dɔ:*] *n* porta; (*entry*) entrada; **next ~** na casa ao lado; **to go from ~ to ~** ir de porta em porta.
doorbell ['dɔ:bɛl] *n* campainha.
door handle *n* maçaneta (*BR*), puxador *m* (*PT*); (*of car*) maçaneta.
door knocker *n* aldrava.
doorman ['dɔ:mæn] (*irreg*) *n* porteiro.
doormat ['dɔ:mæt] *n* capacho.
doormen ['dɔ:mɛn] *npl of* **doorman**.
doorpost ['dɔ:pəust] *n* batente *m* de porta.
doorstep ['dɔ:stɛp] *n* degrau *m* da porta, soleira.
door-to-door *adj*: **~ selling** venda de porta em porta.
doorway ['dɔ:weɪ] *n* vão *m* da porta, entrada.
dope [dəup] *n* (*inf*: *person*) imbecil *m/f* (: *drugs*) maconha; (: *information*) dica, macete *m* ♦ *vt* (*horse etc*) dopar.
dopey ['dəupɪ] *adj* (*dizzy*) zonzo.
dormant ['dɔ:mənt] *adj* inativo; (*latent*) latente.
dormer ['dɔ:mə*] *n* (*also*: *~ window*) água-furtada, trapeira.
dormice ['dɔ:maɪs] *npl of* **dormouse**.
dormitory ['dɔ:mɪtrɪ] *n* dormitório.
dormouse ['dɔ:maus] (*pl* **dormice**) *n* rato (de campo).
Dors (*BRIT*) *abbr* = **Dorset**.
DOS [dɔs] *n abbr* (= *disk operating system*) DOS *m*.
dosage ['dəusɪdʒ] *n* dose *f*; (*on label*) posologia.
dose [dəus] *n* dose *f*; (*BRIT*: *bout*) ataque *m* ♦ *vt*: **to ~ o.s.** medicar-se; **a ~ of flu** uma gripe.
doss house ['dɔs-] (*BRIT*: *irreg*) *n* pensão *f* barata *or* de malta (*PT*).
dossier ['dɔsɪeɪ] *n* dossiê.
DOT (*US*) *n abbr* = **Department of Transportation**.
dot [dɔt] *n* ponto ♦ *vt*: **~ted with** salpicado de; **on the ~** em ponto.
dot command *n* (*COMPUT*) comando precedido de um ponto.
dote on [dəut-] *vt fus* adorar, idolatrar.
dot-matrix printer *n* impressora matricial.
dotted line ['dɔtɪd-] *n* linha pontilhada; **to sign on the ~** (*fig*) firmar o compromisso.
dotty ['dɔtɪ] (*inf*) *adj* lelé, doido.
double ['dʌbl] *adj* duplo ♦ *adv* (*twice*): **to cost ~ (sth)** custar o dobro (de algo) ♦ *n* dobro; (*person*) duplo/a; (*CINEMA*) substituto/a ♦ *vt* dobrar; (*efforts*) duplicar ♦ *vi* duplicar(-se); (*have two uses*): **to ~ as** servir também de; **~s** *n* (*TENNIS*) dupla; **~ five two six (5526)** (*BRIT*: *TEL*) cinco cinco dois meia; **it's spelt with a ~ "l"** escreve-se com dois ls; **at the ~** (*BRIT*), **on the ~** em passo acelerado.
double back *vi* (*person*) voltar atrás.
double up *vi* (*bend over*) dobrar-se; (*share room*) dividir o quarto.
double bass *n* contrabaixo.
double bed *n* cama de casal.
double bend (*BRIT*) *n* curva dupla, curva em "s".
double-breasted [-'brɛstɪd] *adj* trespassado.
double-check *vt*, *vi* verificar de novo.
double-clutch (*US*) *vi* fazer embreagem dupla.
double cream (*BRIT*) *n* creme *m* de leite.
doublecross [dʌbl'krɔs] *vt* (*trick*) enganar; (*betray*) atraiçoar.
doubledecker [dʌbl'dɛkə*] *n* ônibus *m* (*BR*) *or* autocarro (*PT*) de dois andares.
double declutch (*BRIT*) *vi* fazer embreagem

NB: *European Portuguese adds the following consonants to certain words:* **b** (sú(b)dito, su(b)til); **c** (a(c)ção, a(c)cionista, a(c)to); **m** (inde(m)ne); **p** (ado(p)ção, ado(p)tar); *for further details see p. xiii.*

dupla.

double exposure *n* (PHOT) dupla exposição *f*.

double glazing [-'gleɪzɪŋ] (BRIT) *n* (janelas *fpl* de) vidro duplo.

double-page spread *n* anúncio (*or* reportagem *f etc*) de página dupla.

double-park *vi*, *vt* estacionar em fila dupla.

double room *n* quarto de casal.

doubly ['dʌblɪ] *adv* duplamente.

doubt [daut] *n* dúvida ♦ *vt* duvidar; (*suspect*) desconfiar de; **without (a)** ~ sem dúvida; **beyond** ~ *adv* sem dúvida alguma ♦ *adj* indubitável; **there is no ~ that** não há dúvida que; **to ~ that** duvidar que; **I ~ it very much** duvido muito.

doubtful ['dautful] *adj* duvidoso; **to be ~ about sth** ter dúvidas *or* estar em dúvida sobre algo; **I'm a bit ~** duvido.

doubtless ['dautlɪs] *adv* sem dúvida.

dough [dəu] *n* massa; (*inf*: *money*) grana.

doughnut ['dəunʌt] *n* sonho (BR), bola de Berlim (PT).

dour [duə*] *adj* austero.

douse [dauz] *vt* (*with water*) encharcar; (*flames*) apagar.

dove [dʌv] *n* pomba.

dovetail ['dʌvteɪl] *vi* (*fig*) encaixar-se ♦ *n*: ~ **joint** sambladura em cauda de andorinha.

dowager ['dauədʒə*] *n* *mulher que herda o título do marido falecido*.

dowdy ['daudɪ] *adj* desalinhado; (*inelegant*) deselegante, pouco elegante.

Dow-Jones average ['dau'dʒəunz-] (US) *n* índice *m* da bolsa de valores de Nova Iorque.

down [daun] *n* (*fluff*) lanugem *f*; (*feathers*) penugem *f*; (*hill*) colina ♦ *adv* abaixo; (*~wards*) para baixo; (*on the ground*) por terra ♦ *prep* por, abaixo ♦ *vt* (*inf*: *drink*) tomar de um gole só; (: *food*) devorar; **D~s** *npl* (BRIT): **the ~** *chapada gredosa do sul da Inglaterra*; ~ **there** lá em baixo; ~ **here** aqui em baixo; **the price of meat is ~** o preço da carne baixou; **I've got it ~ in my diary** já o anotei na minha agenda; **to pay £2 ~** pagar £2 de entrada; **England are two goals ~** a Inglaterra está perdendo por dois gols; **to ~ tools** (BRIT) cruzar os braços; **~ with X!** abaixo X!

down-and-out *n* (*tramp*) vagabundo/a.

down-at-heel *adj* descuidado, desmazelado; (*appearance*) deselegante.

downbeat ['daunbi:t] *n* (MUS) tempo forte ♦ *adj* sombrio, negativo.

downcast ['daunkɑ:st] *adj* abatido.

downer ['daunə*] (*inf*) *n* (*drug*) calmante *m*; **to be on a ~** (*depressed*) estar na fossa, estar de baixo astral.

downfall ['daunfɔ:l] *n* queda, ruína.

downgrade ['daungreɪd] *vt* (*reduce*) reduzir; (*devalue*) desvalorizar, depreciar.

downhearted [daun'hɑ:tɪd] *adj* desanimado.

downhill ['daun'hɪl] *adv* para baixo ♦ *n* (SKI: *also*: ~ *race*) descida; **to go ~** descer, ir morro abaixo; (*fig*: *business*) degringolar.

Downing Street ['daunɪŋ-] (BRIT) *n*: **10 ~** *residência do primeiro-ministro*.

download ['daunləud] *vt* (COMPUT) baixar.

down-market *adj* destinado a consumidores de renda baixa.

down payment *n* entrada, sinal *m*.

downplay ['daunpleɪ] (US) *vt* minimizar.

downpour ['daunpɔ:*] *n* aguaceiro.

downright ['daunraɪt] *adj* (*lie*) patente ♦ *adv* francamente.

downstairs ['daun'stɛəz] *adv* (*below*) (lá) em baixo; (*downwards*) para baixo; **to come ~, to go ~** descer.

downstream ['daun'stri:m] *adv* água *or* rio abaixo.

downtime ['dauntaɪm] *n* (*of machine*, *person*) tempo ocioso.

down-to-earth *adj* prático, realista.

downtown ['daun'taun] *adv* no centro da cidade ♦ *adj* (US): ~ **Chicago** o centro comercial de Chicago.

downtrodden ['dauntrɔdn] *adj* oprimido.

down under *adv* na Austrália (*or* Nova Zelândia).

downward ['daunwəd] *adj* para baixo; **a ~ trend** uma tendência para a baixa.

downward(s) ['daunwəd(z)] *adv* para baixo.

dowry ['daurɪ] *n* dote *m*.

doz. *abbr* (= *dozen*) dz.

doze [dəuz] *vi* dormitar.

doze off *vi* cochilar.

dozen ['dʌzn] *n* dúzia; **a ~ books** uma dúzia de livros; **80p a ~** 80p a dúzia; **~s of times** milhares de vezes.

DPh *n abbr* (= *Doctor of Philosophy*) *título universitário*.

DPhil *n abbr* = **DPh**.

DPP (BRIT) *n abbr* = **Director of Public Prosecutions**.

DPT *n abbr* (MED: = *diphtheria*, *pertussis*, *tetanus*) *espécie de vacina*.

DPW (US) *n abbr* = **Department of Public Works**.

Dr *abbr* (= *doctor*) Dr(a).

Dr. *abbr* (*in street names*) = **drive**; (= *doctor*) Dr(a).

dr *abbr* (COMM) = **debtor**.

drab [dræb] *adj* monótono, sombrio.

draft [drɑ:ft] *n* (*first copy*) rascunho; (COMM) saque *m*, letra; (US: *call-up*) recrutamento ♦ *vt* (*plan*) esboçar; (*speech*, *letter*) rascunhar; *see also* **draught**.

draftsman *etc* ['drɑ:ftsmən] (US) *n* = **draughtsman** *etc*.

drag [dræg] *vt* arrastar; (*river*) dragar ♦ *vi* arrastar-se ♦ *n* (*inf*) chatice *f* (BR), maçada (PT); (*of cigarette*) tragada; (AVIAT, NAUT) resistência; (*women's clothing*): **in ~** em travesti.

drag away *vt*: **to ~ away (from)** desgrudar (de).

drag on *vi* arrastar-se.

dragnet ['drægnɛt] *n* rede *f* de arrasto; (*by police*) diligência policial.

dragon ['drægən] *n* dragão *m*.

dragonfly ['drægənflaı] *n* libélula.
dragoon [drə'gu:n] *n* (*cavalryman*) dragão *m* ♦ *vt*: **to ~ sb into doing sth** (*BRIT*) forçar alguém a fazer algo.
drain [dreın] *n* (**~** *pipe*) cano de esgoto; (*underground*) esgoto; (*in street*) bueiro; (*on resources*) sorvedouro ♦ *vt* (*land*, *marshes*, *MED*) drenar; (*reservoir*) esvaziar; (*vegetables*) coar; (*fig*) esgotar ♦ *vi* (*water*) escorrer, escoar-se; **to feel ~ed** sentir-se esgotado *or* estafado.
drainage ['dreınıdʒ] *n* (*act*) drenagem *f*; (*MED*, *AGR*) dreno; (*sewage*) esgoto.
drainboard ['dreınbɔ:d] (*US*) *n* = **draining board**.
draining board ['dreınıŋ-] (*BRIT*) *n* escorredor *m*.
drainpipe ['dreınpaıp] *n* cano de esgoto.
drake [dreık] *n* pato (macho).
dram [dræm] *n* (*drink*) trago.
drama ['dra:mə] *n* (*art*) teatro; (*play*, *event*) drama *m*.
dramatic [drə'mætık] *adj* dramático.
dramatically [drə'mætıklı] *adv* dramaticamente.
dramatist ['dræmətıst] *n* dramaturgo/a.
dramatize ['dræmətaız] *vt* dramatizar.
drank [dræŋk] *pt of* **drink**.
drape [dreıp] *vt* ornar, cobrir ♦ *vi* cair.
draper ['dreıpə*] (*BRIT*) *n* fanqueiro/a.
drapes [dreıps] (*US*) *npl* cortinas *fpl*.
drastic ['dræstık] *adj* drástico.
drastically ['dræstıklı] *adv* drasticamente.
draught [dra:ft] (*US* **draft**) *n* (*of air*) corrente *f*; (*drink*) trago; (*NAUT*) calado; (*beer*) chope *m*; **~s** *n* (*BRIT*) (jogo de) damas *fpl*; **on ~** (*beer*) de barril.
draughtboard ['dra:ftbɔ:d] (*BRIT*) *n* tabuleiro de damas.
draughtsman ['dra:ftsmən] (*US* **draftsman**) (*irreg*) *n* desenhista *m/f* industrial.
draughtsmanship ['dra:ftsmənʃıp] (*US* **draftsmanship**) *n* (*art*) desenho industrial; (*technique*) habilidade *f* de desenhista.
draughtsmen ['dra:ftsmɛn] (*US* **draftsmen**) *npl of* **draughtsman**.
draw [drɔ:] (*pt* **drew**, *pp* **drawn**) *vt* (*pull*) tirar; (*take out*) retirar; (*attract*) atrair; (*picture*) desenhar; (*money*) tirar, receber (: *from bank*) sacar; (*comparison*, *distinction*) fazer ♦ *vi* (*SPORT*) empatar ♦ *n* (*SPORT*) empate *m*; (*lottery*) sorteio; (*attraction*) atração *f*; **to ~ to a close** tender para o fim; **to ~ near** aproximar-se.
  draw back *vi* (*move back*): **to ~ back (from)** recuar (de).
  draw in *vi* (*BRIT*: *car*) encostar; (: *train*) entrar na estação ♦ *vt* (*involve*) envolver.
  draw on *vt fus* (*resources*) recorrer a, lançar mão de; (*person*, *imagination*) recorrer a.
  draw out *vi* (*car*, *train*) sair ♦ *vt* (*lengthen*) esticar, alargar; (*money*) sacar; (*confession*, *truth*) arrancar; (*shy person*) desacanhar, desinibir.
  draw up *vi* (*stop*) parar(-se) ♦ *vt* (*document*) redigir; (*plans*) esboçar.
drawback ['drɔ:bæk] *n* inconveniente *m*, desvantagem *f*.
drawbridge ['drɔ:brıdʒ] *n* ponte *f* levadiça.
drawee [drɔ:'i:] *n* sacado.
drawer[1] [drɔ:*] *n* gaveta.
drawer[2] ['drɔ:ə*] *n* (*of cheque*) sacador(a) *m/f*, emitente *m/f*.
drawing ['drɔ:ıŋ] *n* desenho.
drawing board *n* prancheta.
drawing pin (*BRIT*) *n* tachinha (*BR*), pionés *m* (*PT*).
drawing room *n* sala de visitas.
drawl [drɔ:l] *n* fala arrastada.
drawn [drɔ:n] *pp of* **draw** ♦ *adj* (*haggard*) abatido.
drawstring ['drɔ:strıŋ] *n* cordão *m*.
dread [drɛd] *n* medo, pavor *m* ♦ *vt* temer, recear, ter medo de.
dreadful ['drɛdful] *adj* terrível.
dream [dri:m] (*pt*, *pp* **~ed** *or* **dreamt**) *n* sonho ♦ *vt*, *vi* sonhar; **to have a ~ about sb/sth**, **to ~ about sb/sth** sonhar com alguém/algo; **sweet ~s!** sonha com os anjos!
  dream up *vt* inventar, bolar (*inf*).
dreamer ['dri:mə*] *n* sonhador(a) *m/f*.
dreamt [drɛmt] *pt*, *pp of* **dream**.
dream world *n* mundo da fantasia.
dreamy ['dri:mı] *adj* (*distracted*) sonhador(a), distraído; (*music*) sentimental.
dreary ['drıərı] *adj* (*boring*) monótono; (*bad*) sombrio.
dredge [drɛdʒ] *vt* dragar.
  dredge up *vt* tirar do fundo; (*fig*: *unpleasant facts*) trazer à tona, descobrir.
dredger ['drɛdʒə*] *n* (*ship*) draga; (*BRIT*: *also*: *sugar ~*) polvilhador *m*.
dregs [drɛgz] *npl* lia.
drench [drɛntʃ] *vt* encharcar; **to get ~ed** encharcar-se.
dress [drɛs] *n* vestido; (*clothing*) traje *m* ♦ *vt* vestir; (*wound*) pensar; (*CULIN*) preparar, temperar ♦ *vi* vestir-se; **to ~ o.s.**, **to get ~ed** vestir-se; **to ~ a shop window** adornar uma vitrina.
  dress up *vi* vestir-se com elegância; (*in fancy dress*) fantasiar-se.
dress circle *n* balcão *m* nobre.
dress designer *n* estilista *m/f*.
dresser ['drɛsə*] *n* (*THEATRE*) camareiro/a; (*also*: *window ~*) vitrinista *m/f*; (*furniture*) aparador *m*; (: *US*) cômoda de espelho.
dressing ['drɛsıŋ] *n* (*MED*) penso; (*CULIN*) molho.
dressing gown (*BRIT*) *n* roupão *m*; (*woman's*) peignoir *m*.
dressing room *n* (*THEATRE*) camarim *m*; (*SPORT*) vestiário.

***NB**: European Portuguese adds the following consonants to certain words:* **b** (sú(b)dito, su(b)til); **c** (a(c)ção, a(c)cionista, a(c)to); **m** (inde(m)ne); **p** (ado(p)ção, ado(p)tar); *for further details see p. xiii.*

dressing table *n* penteadeira (*BR*), toucador *m* (*PT*).
dressmaker ['drɛsmeɪkə*] *n* costureiro/a.
dressmaking ['drɛsmeɪkɪŋ] *n* (arte *f* da) costura.
dress rehearsal *n* ensaio geral.
dress shirt *n* camisa social.
dressy ['drɛsɪ] (*inf*) *adj* (*clothes*) chique.
drew [dru:] *pt of* **draw**.
dribble ['drɪbl] *vi* gotejar, pingar; (*baby*) babar ♦ *vt* (*ball*) driblar.
dried [draɪd] *adj* seco; (*eggs, milk*) em pó.
drier ['draɪə*] *n* = **dryer**.
drift [drɪft] *n* (*of current etc*) força; (*of snow, sand etc*) monte *m*; (*distance off course*) deriva; (*meaning*) sentido ♦ *vi* (*boat*) derivar; (*sand, snow*) amontoar-se; **to let things ~** deixar o barco correr; **to ~ apart** (*friends, lovers*) afastar-se um do outro; **I get** *or* **catch your ~** eu entendo mais ou menos o que você está dizendo.
drifter ['drɪftə*] *n* nômade *m/f*.
driftwood ['drɪftwud] *n* madeira flutuante.
drill [drɪl] *n* furadeira; (*bit, of dentist*) broca; (*for mining etc*) broca, furadeira; (*MIL*) exercícios *mpl* militares ♦ *vt* furar, brocar; (*MIL*) exercitar ♦ *vi* (*for oil*) perfurar.
drilling ['drɪlɪŋ] *n* (*for oil*) perfuração *f*.
drilling rig *n* torre *f* de perfurar.
drily ['draɪlɪ] *adv* = **dryly**.
drink [drɪŋk] (*pt* **drank**, *pp* **drunk**) *n* bebida ♦ *vt, vi* beber; **to have a ~** tomar uma bebida; **a ~ of water** um copo d'água; **would you like something to ~?** você quer beber *or* tomar alguma coisa?; **to ~ to sb/sth** brindar alguém/algo.
drink in *vt* embeber-se em.
drinkable ['drɪŋkəbl] *adj* (*not dangerous*) potável; (*palatable*) bebível.
drinker ['drɪŋkə*] *n* bebedor(a) *m/f*.
drinking ['drɪŋkɪŋ] *n* (*drunkenness*) alcoolismo.
drinking fountain *n* bebedouro.
drinking water *n* água potável.
drip [drɪp] *n* (*act*) gotejar *m*; (*one ~*) gota, pingo; (*MED*) gota a gota *m*; (*inf: person*) mané *m*, banana *m* ♦ *vi* gotejar, pingar.
drip-dry *adj* (*shirt*) de lavar e vestir.
drip-feed (*irreg*) *vt* alimentar intravenosamente.
dripping ['drɪpɪŋ] *n* gordura ♦ *adj*: **~ wet** encharcado.
drive [draɪv] (*pt* **drove**, *pp* **driven**) *n* passeio (de automóvel); (*journey*) trajeto, percurso; (*also*: *~way*) entrada; (*energy*) energia, vigor *m*; (*PSYCH*) impulso; (*SPORT*) drive *m*; (*push*) campanha; (*TECH*) propulsão *f*; (*COMPUT*: *also*: *disk ~*) unidade *f* de disco ♦ *vt* conduzir; (*car*) dirigir (*BR*), guiar (*PT*); (*urge*) fazer trabalhar; (*by power*) impelir; (*nail*) cravar; (*push*) empurrar; (*TECH*: *motor*) acionar ♦ *vi* (*AUT*: *at controls*) dirigir (*BR*), guiar (*PT*); (: *travel*) ir de carro; **to go for a ~** dar um passeio (de carro); **it's 3 hours' ~ from London** são 3 horas de carro de lá a Londres; **left-/right-hand ~** direção à esquerda/direita; **front-/rear-wheel ~** (*AUT*) tração dianteira/traseira; **to ~ sb to do sth** impelir alguém a fazer algo; **to ~ sb mad** deixar alguém louco.
drive at *vt fus* (*fig*: *intend, mean*) querer dizer; **what are you driving at?** onde é que voce queria chegar?
drive on *vi* seguir adiante ♦ *vt* impelir.
drive-in *adj* drive-in ♦ *n* (*cinema*) drive-in *m*.
drive-in window (*US*) *n* balcão *m* drive-in.
drivel ['drɪvl] (*inf*) *n* bobagem *f*, besteira.
driven ['drɪvn] *pp of* **drive**.
driver ['draɪvə*] *n* motorista *m/f*.
driver's license (*US*) *n* carteira de motorista (*BR*), carta de condução (*PT*).
driveway ['draɪvweɪ] *n* entrada.
driving ['draɪvɪŋ] *n* direção *f* (*BR*), condução *f* (*PT*) ♦ *adj*: **~ rain** chuva torrencial.
driving belt *n* correia de transmissão.
driving force *n* (*fig*) mola.
driving instructor *n* instrutor(a) *m/f* de auto-escola (*BR*) *or* de condução (*PT*).
driving lesson *n* aula de direção (*BR*) *or* de condução (*PT*).
driving licence (*BRIT*) *n* carteira de motorista (*BR*), carta de condução (*PT*).
driving mirror (*BRIT*) *n* retrovisor *m*.
driving school *n* auto-escola *f*.
driving test *n* exame *m* de motorista.
drizzle ['drɪzl] *n* chuvisco ♦ *vi* chuviscar.
droll [drəul] *adj* engraçado.
dromedary ['drɔmədərɪ] *n* dromedário.
drone [drəun] *n* (*sound*) zumbido; (*male bee*) zangão *m* ♦ *vi* (*bee, engine*) zumbir; (*also*: *~ on*) falar monotonamente.
drool [dru:l] *vi* babar(-se); **to ~ over sth** babar por algo.
droop [dru:p] *vi* pender.
drop [drɔp] *n* (*of water*) gota; (*fall*: *in prices*) baixa, queda; (: *in salary*) redução *f*; (*of cliff*) escarpa, declive *m*; (*also*: *parachute ~*) salto ♦ *vt* (*allow to fall*) deixar cair; (*voice, eyes, price*) baixar; (*set down from car*) deixar (saltar/descer); (*omit*) omitir ♦ *vi* cair; (*price, temperature*) baixar; (*wind*) parar; **~s** *npl* (*MED*) gotas *fpl*; **cough ~s** pastilhas para tosse; **a ~ of 10%** uma queda de 10%; **to ~ sb a line** escrever (umas linhas) para alguém.
drop in (*inf*) *vi* (*visit*): **to ~ in (on)** dar um pulo (na casa de).
drop off *vi* (*sleep*) cochilar ♦ *vt* (*passenger*) deixar (saltar).
drop out *vi* (*withdraw*) retirar-se; (*student etc*) largar tudo.
droplet ['drɔplɪt] *n* gotícula.
drop-out *n pessoa que abandona o trabalho/os estudos, etc.*
dropper ['drɔpə*] *n* conta-gotas *m inv*.
droppings ['drɔpɪŋz] *npl* fezes *fpl* (de animal).
dross [drɔs] *n* escória.
drought [draut] *n* seca.
drove [drəuv] *pt of* **drive** ♦ *n*: **~s of people** uma quantidade de gente.

drown [draun] *vt* afogar; (*also*: ~ *out*: *sound*) encobrir ♦ *vi* afogar-se.
drowse [drauz] *vi* dormitar.
drowsy ['drauzı] *adj* sonolento; **to be** ~ estar com sono.
drudge [drʌdʒ] *n* burro-de-carga *m*.
drudgery ['drʌdʒərı] *n* labuta.
drug [drʌg] *n* remédio, medicamento; (*narcotic*) droga; (: *MED*, *ADMIN*) entorpecente *m* ♦ *vt* drogar; **he's on ~s** (*an addict*) ele é um viciado em drogas; (*MED*) ele está sob medicação.
drug addict *n* toxicômano/a.
druggist ['drʌgıst] (*US*) *n* farmacêutico/a.
drug peddler *n* traficante *m/f* de drogas.
drugstore ['drʌgstɔ:] (*US*) *n* drogaria.
drum [drʌm] *n* tambor *m*; (*large*) bombo; (*for oil, petrol*) tambor, barril *m* ♦ *vi* (*with fingers*) tamborilar ♦ *vt*: **to ~ sth into sb** incutir algo em alguém; **~s** *npl* (*in band*) bateria.
drum up *vt* (*enthusiasm, support*) angariar.
drummer ['drʌmə*] *n* baterista *m/f*.
drum roll *n* rufo de tambor.
drumstick ['drʌmstık] *n* (*MUS*) baqueta; (*of chicken*) perna.
drunk [drʌŋk] *pp of* **drink** ♦ *adj* bêbado ♦ *n* bêbado/a; **to get ~** ficar bêbado, encher a cara (*inf*).
drunkard ['drʌŋkəd] *n* beberrão/beberrona *m/f*.
drunken ['drʌŋkən] *adj* bêbado; ~ **driving** embriaguez *f* no volante.
drunkenness ['drʌŋkənnıs] *n* embriaguez *f*.
dry [draı] *adj* seco; (*day*) sem chuva; (*uninteresting*) insípido; (*humour*) irônico; ♦ *vt* secar, enxugar; (*tears*) limpar ♦ *vi* secar; **on ~ land** em terra firme; **to ~ one's hands/hair/eyes** enxugar as maõs o cabelo/as lágrimas.
dry up *vi* secar completamente; (*supply*) esgotar-se; (*in speech*) calar-se; (*dishes*) enxugar (a louça).
dry-clean *vt* lavar a seco.
dry-cleaner *n* tintureiro/a.
dry-cleaner's *n* tinturaria, lavanderia.
dry-cleaning *n* lavagem *f* a seco.
dry dock *n* (*NAUT*) dique *m* seco.
dryer ['draıə*] *n* secador *m*; (*also*: *spin-~*) secadora.
dry goods *npl* (*COMM*) fazendas *fpl* e artigos *mpl* de armarinho.
dry goods store (*US*) *n* armarinho.
dry ice *n* gelo seco.
dryness ['draınıs] *n* secura.
dry rot *n* putrefação *f* fungosa.
dry run *n* (*fig*) ensaio, prova.
dry ski slope *n* pista de esqui artificial.
DSc *n abbr* (= *Doctor of Science*) *título universitário*.
DSS (*BRIT*) *n abbr* (= *Department of Social Security*) ≈ INAMPS *m*.
DST (*US*) *abbr* (= *Daylight Saving Time*) *hora de verão*.
DT *n abbr* (*COMPUT*) = **data transmission**.
DTI (*BRIT*) *n* = **Department of Trade and Industry**.
DT's (*inf*) *npl abbr* (= *delirium tremens*) delirium tremens *m*.
dual ['djuəl] *adj* dual, duplo.
dual carriageway (*BRIT*) pista dupla.
dual-control *adj* de duplo comando.
dual nationality *n* dupla nacionalidade *f*.
dual-purpose *adj* de duplo uso.
dubbed [dʌbd] *adj* (*CINEMA*) dublado; (*nicknamed*) apelidado.
dubious ['dju:bıəs] *adj* duvidoso; (*reputation, company*) suspeitoso; **I'm very ~ about it** eu tenho muitas dúvidas a respeito.
Dublin ['dʌblın] *n* Dublin.
Dubliner ['dʌblınə*] *n* natural *m/f* de Dublin.
duchess ['dʌtʃıs] *n* duquesa.
duck [dʌk] *n* pato ♦ *vi* abaixar-se repentinamente ♦ *vt* mergulhar.
duckling ['dʌklıŋ] *n* patinho.
duct [dʌkt] *n* conduto, canal *m*; (*ANAT*) ducto.
dud [dʌd] *n* (*shell*) bomba falhada; (*object, tool*): **it's a ~** não presta ♦ *adj* (*BRIT*: *coin, note*) falso; ~ **cheque** cheque sem fundos, cheque voador (*inf*).
due [dju:] *adj* (*proper*) devido; (*expected*) esperado; (*fitting*) conveniente, oportuno ♦ *n* (*deserts*) aquilo que foi merecido ♦ *adv*: ~ **north** exatamente ao norte; **~s** *npl* (*for club, union*) quota; (*in harbour*) direitos *mpl*; **in ~ course** no devido tempo; ~ **to** devido a; **the rent is ~ on the 30th** o aluguel vence no dia 30; **the train is ~ at 8** o trem deve chegar às 8; **I am ~ 6 days' leave** eu tenho direito a 6 dias de folga.
due date *n* (data de) vencimento.
duel ['djuəl] *n* duelo.
duet [dju:'ɛt] *n* dueto.
duff [dʌf] (*BRIT*: *inf*) *adj* de nada.
duffelbag ['dʌflbæg] *n* mochila.
duffelcoat ['dʌflkəut] *n* casaco de baeta.
duffer ['dʌfə*] (*inf*) *n* zero (à esquerda).
duffle bag ['dʌfl-] *n* = **duffelbag**.
duffle coat ['dʌfl-] *n* = **duffelcoat**.
dug [dʌg] *pt, pp of* **dig**.
duke [dju:k] *n* duque *m*.
dull [dʌl] *adj* (*light*) sombrio; (*slow*) lento; (*boring*) enfadonho; (*sound, pain*) surdo; (*weather, day*) nublado, carregado; (*blade*) embotado, cego ♦ *vt* (*pain, grief*) aliviar; (*mind, senses*) entorpecer.
duly ['dju:lı] *adv* devidamente; (*on time*) no devido tempo.
dumb [dʌm] *adj* mudo; (*stupid*) estúpido; **to be struck ~** (*fig*) ficar pasmo.
dumbbell ['dʌmbɛl] *n* (*SPORT*) haltere *m*.
dumbfounded [dʌm'faundıd] *adj* pasmado.
dummy ['dʌmı] *n* (*tailor's model*) boneco, manequim *m*; (*BRIT*: *for baby*) chupeta; (*CARDS*)

***NB:** European Portuguese adds the following consonants to certain words:* **b** (sú(b)dito, su(b)til); **c** (a(c)ção, a(c)cionista, a(c)to); **m** (inde(m)ne); **p** (ado(p)ção, ado(p)tar); *for further details see p. xiii.*

morto ♦ *adj* falso, postiço.
dummy run *n* prova, ensaio.
dump [dʌmp] *n* (*heap*) montão *m*; (*place*) depósito de lixo; (*inf*) chiqueiro; (MIL) depósito; (COMPUT) dump *m*, descarga ♦ *vt* (*put down*) depositar, descarregar; (*get rid of*) desfazer-se de; (COMM: *goods*) fazer dumping de; (COMPUT) tirar um dump de; **to be (down) in the ~s** (*inf*) estar na fossa.
dumping ['dʌmpɪŋ] *n* (ECON) dumping *m*; (*of rubbish*): **"no ~"** "proibido jogar lixo" (BR), "proibido deitar lixo" (PT).
dumpling ['dʌmplɪŋ] *n* bolinho cozido.
dumpy ['dʌmpɪ] *adj* gorducho.
dunce [dʌns] *n* burro, ignorante.
dune [dju:n] *n* duna.
dung [dʌŋ] *n* estrume *m*.
dungarees [dʌŋgə'ri:z] *npl* macacão *m* (BR), fato macaco (PT).
dungeon ['dʌndʒən] *n* calabouço.
dunk [dʌŋk] *vt* mergulhar.
duo ['dju:əu] *n* (MUS) duo; (*gen*) dupla.
duodenal [dju:ə'di:nl] *adj* duodenal.
dupe [dju:p] *n* (*victim*) otário/a, trouxa *m/f* ♦ *vt* enganar.
duplex ['dju:plɛks] (US) *n* (*also*: ~ *apartment*) duplex *m*.
duplicate [*n* 'dju:plɪkət, *vt* 'dju:plɪkeɪt] *n* duplicado, duplicata ♦ *vt* duplicar; (*on machine*) multigrafar; (*reproduce*) reproduzir; **in ~** em duplicata; ~ **key** cópia de chave.
duplicating machine ['dju:plɪkeɪtɪŋ-] *n* duplicador *m*.
duplicator ['dju:plɪkeɪtə*] *n* duplicador *m*.
duplicity [dju:'plɪsɪtɪ] *n* duplicidade *f*, falsidade *f*.
Dur (BRIT) *abbr* = **Durham**.
durability [djuərə'bɪlɪtɪ] *n* durabilidade *f*, solidez *f*.
durable ['djuərəbl] *adj* durável; (*clothes, metal*) resistente.
duration [djuə'reɪʃən] *n* duração *f*.
duress [djuə'rɛs] *n*: **under ~** sob coação.
Durex ['djuərɛks] ® (BRIT) *n* preservativo, camisinha (*inf*), camisa-de-venus *f*.
during ['djuərɪŋ] *prep* durante.
dusk [dʌsk] *n* crepúsculo, anoitecer *m*.
dusky ['dʌskɪ] *adj* (*sky, room*) sombrio; (*person, complexion*) moreno.
dust [dʌst] *n* pó *m*, poeira ♦ *vt* (*furniture*) tirar o pó de; (*cake etc*): **to ~ with** polvilhar com.
dust off *vt* (*dirt*) tirar.
dustbin ['dʌstbɪn] *n* (BRIT) lata de lixo.
duster ['dʌstə*] *n* espanador *m* de pó, pano de pó.
dust jacket *n* sobrecapa.
dustman ['dʌstmən] (BRIT: *irreg*) *n* lixeiro, gari *m* (BR: *inf*).
dustpan ['dʌstpæn] *n* pá *f* de lixo.
dusty ['dʌstɪ] *adj* empoeirado.
Dutch [dʌtʃ] *adj* holandês/esa ♦ *n* (LING) holandês *m* ♦ *adv*: **let's go ~** *or* **d~** cada um paga o seu, vamos rachar; **the ~** *npl* os holandeses.
Dutch auction *leilão m em que os ofertantes oferecem cada vez menos.*
Dutchman ['dʌtʃmən] (*irreg*) *n* holandês *m*.
Dutchwoman ['dʌtʃwumən] (*irreg*) *n* holandesa.
dutiable ['dju:tɪəbl] *adj* (*taxable*) tributável; (*by customs*) sujeito a impostos alfandegários.
dutiful ['dju:tɪful] *adj* (*child*) respeitoso; (*husband, wife*) atencioso; (*employee*) zeloso, consciente.
duty ['dju:tɪ] *n* dever *m*; (*tax*) taxa; (*customs*) taxa alfandegária; **duties** *npl* funções *fpl*; **to make it one's ~ to do sth** dar-se a responsabilidade de fazer algo; **to pay ~ on sth** pagar imposto sobre algo; **on ~** de serviço; (*at night etc*) de plantão; **off ~** de folga.
duty-free *adj* livre de impostos; ~ **shop** duty-free *f*.
duty officer *n* (MIL *etc*) oficial *m* de serviço.
duvet ['du:veɪ] (BRIT) *n* edredom (PT: -dão) *m*.
DV *abbr* (= *Deo volente*) se Deus quiser.
DVLC (BRIT) *n abbr* (= *Driver and Vehicle Licensing Centre*) ≈ Contran *m*.
DVM (US) *n abbr* (= *Doctor of Veterinary Medicine*) *título universitário.*
dwarf [dwɔ:f] (*pl* **dwarves**) *n* anão/anã *m/f* ♦ *vt* ananicar.
dwarves [dwɔ:vz] *npl of* **dwarf**.
dwell [dwɛl] (*pt, pp* **dwelt**) *vi* morar.
dwell on *vt fus* estender-se sobre.
dweller ['dwɛlə*] *n* habitante *m/f*.
dwelling ['dwɛlɪŋ] *n* residência.
dwelt [dwɛlt] *pt, pp of* **dwell**.
dwindle ['dwɪndl] *vi* minguar, diminuir.
dwindling ['dwɪndlɪŋ] *adj* descrescente, minguante.
dye [daɪ] *n* tintura, tinta ♦ *vt* tingir; **hair ~** tintura para o cabelo.
dyestuffs ['daɪstʌfs] *npl* corantes *mpl*.
dying ['daɪɪŋ] *adj* moribundo, agonizante; (*moments*) final; (*words*) último.
dyke [daɪk] *n* (*embankment*) dique *m*.
dynamic [daɪ'næmɪk] *adj* dinâmico.
dynamics [daɪ'næmɪks] *n, npl* dinâmica.
dynamite ['daɪnəmaɪt] *n* dinamite *f* ♦ *vt* dinamitar.
dynamo ['daɪnəməu] *n* dínamo.
dynasty ['dɪnəstɪ] *n* dinastia.
dysentery ['dɪsntrɪ] *n* disenteria.
dyslexia [dɪs'lɛksɪə] *n* dislexia.
dyslexic [dɪs'lɛksɪk] *adj, n* dislético/a, disléxico/a.
dyspepsia [dɪs'pɛpsɪə] *n* dispepsia.
dystrophy ['dɪstrəfɪ] *n* distrofia; *see also* **muscular dystrophy**.

E

E, e [iː] *n* (*letter*) E, e *m*; (*MUS*): **E** mi *m*; **E for Edward** (*BRIT*) *or* **Easy** (*US*) E de Eliane.
E *abbr* (= *east*) E.
E111 *n abbr* (*also*: *form* ~) formulário E111.
ea. *abbr* = **each**.
E.A. (*US*) *n abbr* (= *educational age*) *idade educacional*.
each [iːtʃ] *adj* cada *inv* ♦ *pron* cada um(a); ~ **one** cada um; ~ **other** um ao outro; **they hate ~ other** (eles) se odeiam; **you are jealous of ~ other** vocês têm ciume um do outro; ~ **day** cada dia; **they have 2 books ~** eles têm 2 livros cada um; **they cost £5 ~** custam £5 cada; ~ **of us** cada um de nós.
eager ['iːgə*] *adj* ávido; (*hopeful*) desejoso; (*ambitious*) ambicioso; (*pupil*) empolgado; **to be ~ to do sth** ansiar por fazer algo; **to be ~ for** ansiar por.
eagle ['iːgl] *n* águia.
E and OE *abbr* (= *errors and omissions excepted*) SEO.
ear [ɪə*] *n* (*external*) orelha; (*inner*, *fig*) ouvido; (*of corn*) espiga; **to play by ~** tocar de ouvido; **up to one's ~s in debt** endividado até o pescoço.
earache ['ɪəreɪk] *n* dor *f* de ouvidos.
eardrum ['ɪədrʌm] *n* tímpano.
earl [əːl] *n* conde *m*.
earlier ['əːlɪə*] *adj* (*date etc*) mais adiantado; (*edition etc*) anterior ♦ *adv* mais cedo.
early ['əːlɪ] *adv* cedo; (*before time*) com antecedência ♦ *adj* prematuro; (*reply*) pronto; (*Christians*, *settlers*) primeiro; (*man*) primitivo; (*life*, *work*) juvenil; **have an ~ night/start** vá para cama cedo/saia de manhã cedo; **in the ~** *or* **~ in the spring/19th century** no princípio da primavera/do século dezenove; **as ~ as possible** o mais cedo possível; **you're ~!** você chegou cedo!; **~ in the morning** de manhã cedo; **she's in her ~ forties** ela tem pouco mais de 40 anos; **at your earliest convenience** (*COMM*) o mais cedo que lhe for possível.
early retirement *n* aposentadoria antecipada.
early warning system *n* sistema *m* de alerta antecipado.
earmark ['ɪəmɑːk] *vt*: **to ~ sth for** reservar *or* destinar algo para.
earn [əːn] *vt* ganhar; (*COMM*: *yield*) render; (*praise*, *reward*) merecer; **to ~ one's living** ganhar a vida.
earned income [əːnd-] *n* rendimento do trabalho individual.
earnest ['əːnɪst] *adj* sério ♦ *n* (*also*: ~ *money*) sinal *m* em dinheiro; **in ~** a sério.
earnings ['əːnɪŋz] *npl* (*personal*) vencimentos *mpl*, salário, ordenado; (*of company*) lucro.
ear nose and throat specialist *n* otorrinolaringologista *m/f*, otorrino *m/f*.
earphones ['ɪəfəunz] *npl* fones *mpl* de ouvido.
earplugs ['ɪəplʌgz] *npl* borrachinhas *fpl* (de ouvido).
earring ['ɪərɪŋ] *n* brinco.
earshot ['ɪəʃɔt] *n*: **out of/within ~** fora do/ao alcance do ouvido *or* da voz.
earth [əːθ] *n* terra; (*BRIT*: *ELEC*) fio terra ♦ *vt* (*BRIT*: *ELEC*) ligar à terra; **what on ~!** que diabo!
earthenware ['əːθənwɛə*] *n* louça de barro ♦ *adj* de barro.
earthly ['əːθlɪ] *adj* terrestre; **~ paradise** paraíso terrestre; **there is no ~ reason to think ...** não há a mínima razão para se pensar que ....
earthquake ['əːθkweɪk] *n* terremoto (*BR*), terramoto (*PT*).
earth tremor tremor *m*, abalo sísmico.
earthworks ['əːθwəːks] *npl* trabalhos *mpl* de terraplenagem.
earthworm ['əːθwəːm] *n* minhoca.
earthy ['əːθɪ] *adj* (*fig*: *vulgar*) grosseiro; (: *natural*) natural.
earwax ['ɪəwæks] *n* cerume *m*.
earwig ['ɪəwɪg] *n* lacrainha.
ease [iːz] *n* facilidade *f*; (*relaxed state*) sossego ♦ *vt* facilitar; (*relieve*: *pressure*) afrouxar; (*soothe*) aliviar; (*help pass*): **to ~ sth in/out** meter/tirar algo com cuidado ♦ *vi* (*situation*) abrandar; **at ~!** (*MIL*) descansar!; **to be at ~** estar à vontade; **with ~** com facilidade.
  ease off *vi* acalmar-se; (*at work*) deixar de trabalhar tanto; (*wind*) baixar; (*rain*) moderar-se.
  ease up *vi* acalmar-se; (*at work*) deixar de trabalhar tanto; (*wind*) baixar; (*rain*) moderar-se.
easel ['iːzl] *n* cavalete *m*.
easily ['iːzɪlɪ] *adv* facilmente, fácil (*inf*).
easiness ['iːzɪnɪs] *n* facilidade *f*; (*of manner*) desenvoltura.
east [iːst] *n* leste *m*, este *m* ♦ *adj* oriental, do leste ♦ *adv* para o leste; **the E~** o Oriente; (*POL*) o leste.
Easter ['iːstə*] *n* Páscoa ♦ *adj* (*holidays*) da Páscoa; (*traditions*) pascal.
Easter egg *n* ovo de Páscoa.
Easter Island *n* ilha da Páscoa.
easterly ['iːstəlɪ] *adj* (*to the east*) para o leste; (*from the east*) do Leste.
Easter Monday *n* Segunda-Feira da Páscoa.
eastern ['iːstən] *adj* do leste, oriental; **E~ Europe** a Europa Oriental; **the E~ bloc** (*POL*) o Bloco Oriental.

NB*: European Portuguese adds the following consonants to certain words:* **b** (sú(b)dito, su(b)til); **c** (a(c)ção, a(c)cionista, a(c)to); **m** (inde(m)ne); **p** (ado(p)ção, ado(p)tar); *for further details see p. xiii.*

Easter Sunday *n* Domingo da Páscoa.
East Germany *n* Alemanha Oriental.
eastward(s) ['i:stwəd(z)] *adv* ao leste.
easy ['i:zɪ] *adj* fácil; (*comfortable*) folgado, cômodo; (*relaxed*) natural, complacente ♦ *adv*: **to take it** *or* **things** ~ (*not worry*) levar as coisas com calma; (*go slowly*) ir devagar; (*rest*) descansar; **payment on ~ terms** (COMM) pagamento facilitado; **that's easier said than done** é mais fácil falar do que fazer; **I'm ~** (*inf*) para mim, tanto faz.
easy chair *n* poltrona.
easy-going *adj* pacato, fácil.
eat [i:t] (*pt* **ate**, *pp* **eaten**) *vt*, *vi* comer.
eat away *vt* corroer.
eat away at *vt fus* corroer.
eat into *vt fus* corroer.
eat out *vi* jantar fora.
eat up *vt* (*food*) acabar; **it ~s up electricity** consome eletricidade demais.
eatable ['i:təbl] *adj* comestível.
eau-de-cologne [əudə-] *n* (água de) Colônia.
eaves [i:vz] *npl* beira, beiral *m*.
eavesdrop ['i:vzdrɔp] *vi*: **to ~ (on sb)** escutar (alguém) às escondidas.
ebb [ɛb] *n* refluxo ♦ *vi* baixar; (*fig*: *also*: ~ *away*) declinar; **the ~ and flow** o fluxo e refluxo; **to be at a low ~** (*fig*: *person*) estar de maré baixa; (: *business*, *relations etc*) ir mal.
ebb tide *n* baixa-mar *f*, maré *f* vazante.
ebony ['ɛbənɪ] *n* ébano.
ebullient [ɪ'bʌlɪənt] *adj* vivo, enérgico.
EC *n abbr* (= *European Community*) CE *f*.
eccentric [ɪk'sɛntrɪk] *adj*, *n* excêntrico/a.
ecclesiastic(al) [ɪkli:zɪ'æstɪk(əl)] *adj* eclesiástico.
ECG *n abbr* (= *electrocardiogram*) eletro.
ECGD *n abbr* (= *Export Credits Guarantee Department*) *serviço de garantia financeira para exportações*.
echo ['ɛkəu] (*pl* **~es**) *n* eco ♦ *vt* (*sound*) ecoar, repetir ♦ *vi* ressoar, repetir.
éclair [eɪ'klɛə*] *n* (CULIN) bomba.
eclipse [ɪ'klɪps] *n* eclipse *m* ♦ *vt* eclipsar.
ECM (US) *n abbr* = **European Common Market**.
ecologist [ɪ'kɔlədʒɪst] *n* ecologista *m/f*.
ecology [ɪ'kɔlədʒɪ] *n* ecologia.
economic [i:kə'nɔmɪk] *adj* econômico; (*proposition etc*) rentável.
economical [i:kə'nɔmɪkəl] *adj* econômico; (*proposition etc*) rentável.
economically [i:kə'nɔmɪklɪ] *adv* economicamente.
economics [i:kə'nɔmɪks] *n* economia ♦ *npl* aspectos *mpl* econômicos.
economist [ɪ'kɔnəmɪst] *n* economista *m/f*.
economize [ɪ'kɔnəmaɪz] *vi* economizar, fazer economias.
economy [ɪ'kɔnəmɪ] *n* economia; **economies of scale** economias de escala.
economy class *n* (AVIAT *etc*) classe *f* econômica.
economy size *n* tamanho econômico.
ECSC *n abbr* (= *European Coal and Steel Community*) CECA *f*.
ecstasy ['ɛkstəsɪ] *n* êxtase *m*; **to go into ecstasies over** extasiar-se com.
ecstatic [ɛks'tætɪk] *adj* extasiado.
ECT *n abbr* = **electroconvulsive therapy**.
ECU *n abbr* (= *European Currency Unit*) ECU *f*.
Ecuador ['ɛkwədɔ:*] *n* Equador *m*.
Ecuadorian [ɛkwə'dɔ:rɪən] *adj*, *n* equatoriano/a.
ecumenical [i:kju'mɛnɪkl] *adj* ecumênico.
eczema ['ɛksɪmə] *n* eczema *m*.
eddy ['ɛdɪ] *n* rodamoinho.
edge [ɛdʒ] *n* (*of knife etc*) fio; (*of object*) borda; (*of lake etc*) margem *f* ♦ *vt* (SEWING) embainhar ♦ *vi*: **to ~ forward** avançar pouco a pouco; **to ~ away from** afastar-se pouco a pouco de; **on ~** (*fig*) nervoso, inquieto; **to have the ~ on** (*fig*) levar vantagem sobre.
edgeways ['ɛdʒweɪz] *adv* lateralmente; **he couldn't get a word in ~** não pôde entrar na conversa.
edging ['ɛdʒɪŋ] *n* (SEWING) debrum *m*; (*of path*) borda.
edgy ['ɛdʒɪ] *adj* nervoso, inquieto.
edible ['ɛdɪbl] *adj* comestível.
edict ['i:dɪkt] *n* édito.
edifice ['ɛdɪfɪs] *n* edifício.
edifying ['ɛdɪfaɪɪŋ] *adj* edificante.
Edinburgh ['ɛdɪnbərə] *n* Edimburgo.
edit ['ɛdɪt] *vt* (*be editor of*) dirigir; (*cut*) cortar, redigir; (COMPUT, TV) editar; (CINEMA) montar.
edition [ɪ'dɪʃən] *n* (*gen*) edição *f*; (*number printed*) tiragem *f*.
editor ['ɛdɪtə*] *n* redator(a) *m/f*; (*of newspaper*) diretor(a) *m/f*; (*of book*) organizador(a) *m/f* da edição; (*also*: *film* ~) montador(a) *m/f*.
editorial [ɛdɪ'tɔ:rɪəl] *adj* editorial ♦ *n* editorial *m*; **the ~ staff** a redação.
EDP *n abbr* = **electronic data processing**.
EDT (US) *abbr* (= *Eastern Daylight Time*) *hora de verão de Nova Iorque*.
educate ['ɛdjukeɪt] *vt* educar; **~d at ...** que cursou ....
education [ɛdju'keɪʃən] *n* educação *f*; (*schooling*) ensino; (*science*) pedagogia; **primary** (BRIT) *or* **elementary** (US)/ **secondary ~** ensino de 1°/2° grau.
educational [ɛdju'keɪʃənl] *adj* (*policy etc*) educacional; (*teaching*) docente; (*instructive*) educativo; **~ technology** tecnologia educacional.
Edwardian [ɛd'wɔ:dɪən] *adj* da época do rei Eduardo VII, dos anos 1900.
EE *abbr* = **electrical engineer**.
EEC *n abbr* (= *European Economic Community*) CEE *f*.
EEG *n abbr* (= *electroencephalogram*) eletro.
eel [i:l] *n* enguia.
EENT (US) *n abbr* (MED) = **eye, ear, nose and throat**.
EEOC (US) *n abbr* = **Equal Employment**

Opportunity Commission.
eerie ['ɪərɪ] *adj* (*strange*) estranho; (*mysterious*) misterioso.
EET *n abbr* (= *Eastern European Time*) *hora da Europa Oriental.*
effect [ɪ'fɛkt] *n* efeito ♦ *vt* efetuar; **~s** *npl* (*THEATRE*) efeitos *mpl*; (*property*) bens *mpl* móveis, pertences *mpl*; **to take ~** (*LAW*) entrar em vigor; (*drug*) fazer efeito; **to put into ~** (*plan*) pôr em ação *or* prática; **to have an ~ on sb/sth** produzir efeito em alguém/algo; **in ~** na realidade; **his letter is to the ~ that ...** a carta dele informa que ....
effective [ɪ'fɛktɪv] *adj* eficaz; (*striking*) impressionante; (*real*) efetivo; **to become ~** (*LAW*) entrar em vigor; **~ date** data de entrada em vigor.
effectively [ɪ'fɛktɪvlɪ] *adv* (*efficiently*) eficazmente; (*in reality*) efetivamente.
effectiveness [ɪ'fɛktɪvnɪs] *n* eficácia.
effeminate [ɪ'fɛmɪnɪt] *adj* efeminado.
effervescent [ɛfə'vɛsnt] *adj* efervescente.
efficacy ['ɛfɪkəsɪ] *n* eficácia.
efficiency [ɪ'fɪʃənsɪ] *n* eficiência; (*of machine*) rendimento.
efficiency apartment (*US*) *n* kitchenette *f*.
efficient [ɪ'fɪʃənt] *adj* eficiente.
efficiently [ɪ'fɪʃəntlɪ] *adv* eficientemente.
effigy ['ɛfɪdʒɪ] *n* efígie *f*.
effluent ['ɛfluənt] *n* efluente *m*.
effort ['ɛfət] *n* esforço; **to make an ~ to** esforçar-se para.
effortless ['ɛfətlɪs] *adj* com desenvoltura.
effrontery [ɪ'frʌntərɪ] *n* descaramento.
effusive [ɪ'fju:sɪv] *adj* efusivo; (*welcome*) caloroso.
EFL *n abbr* (*SCH*) = **English as a foreign language.**
EFTA ['ɛftə] *n abbr* (= *European Free Trade Association*) AELC *f*.
e.g. *adv abbr* (= *exempli gratia*) p. ex.
egalitarian [ɪgælɪ'tɛərɪən] *adj* igualitário.
egg [ɛg] *n* ovo.
egg on *vt* incitar.
eggcup ['ɛgkʌp] *n* oveiro.
eggplant ['ɛgplɑ:nt] (*US*) *n* beringela.
eggshell ['ɛgʃɛl] *n* casca de ovo.
egg white *n* clara (de ovo).
egg yolk *n* gema.
ego ['i:gəu] *n* ego.
egoism ['i:gəuɪzəm] *n* egoísmo.
egoist ['i:gəuɪst] *n* egoísta *m/f*.
egotism ['ɛgəutɪzəm] *n* egotismo *m*.
egotist ['ɛgəutɪst] *n* egotista *m/f*.
Egypt ['i:dʒɪpt] *n* Egito.
Egyptian [ɪ'dʒɪpʃən] *adj*, *n* egípcio/a.
eiderdown ['aɪdədaun] *n* edredom (*PT*: -dão) *m*.
eight [eɪt] *num* oito; *see also* **five.**
eighteen ['eɪ'ti:n] *num* dezoito; *see also* **five.**
eighth [eɪtθ] *num* oitavo; *see also* **fifth.**
eighty ['eɪtɪ] *num* oitenta; *see also* **fifty.**

Eire ['ɛərə] *n* (República da) Irlanda.
EIS *n abbr* (= *Educational Institute of Scotland*) *sindicato dos professores escoceses.*
either ['aɪðə*] *adj* (*each*) cada; (*any*) qualquer; (*both*) ambos ♦ *pron*: **~ (of them)** qualquer (dos dois) ♦ *adv*: **no, I don't ~** eu também não ♦ *conj*: **~ yes or no** ou sim ou não; **on ~ side** de ambos os lados; **I don't like ~** não gosto nem de um nem do outro; **I haven't seen ~ one or the other** eu não vi nem um nem o outro.
ejaculation [ɪdʒækju'leɪʃən] *n* (*PHYSIOLOGY*) ejaculação *f*.
eject [ɪ'dʒɛkt] *vt* expulsar ♦ *vi* (*pilot*) ser ejetado.
ejector seat [ɪ'dʒɛktə*-] *n* assento ejetor.
eke [i:k]: **to ~ out** *vt* (*money*) economizar; (*food*) economizar em; (*add to*) complementar.
EKG (*US*) *n abbr* (= *electrocardiogram*) eletro.
el [ɛl] (*US*: *inf*) *n abbr* = **elevated railroad.**
elaborate [*adj* ɪ'læbərɪt, *vt*, *vi* ɪ'læbəreɪt] *adj* complicado; (*decorated*) rebuscado ♦ *vt* elaborar ♦ *vi* entrar em detalhes.
elapse [ɪ'læps] *vi* decorrer.
elastic [ɪ'læstɪk] *adj*, *n* elástico.
elastic band (*BRIT*) *n* elástico.
elasticity [ɪlæs'tɪsɪtɪ] *n* elasticidade *f*.
elated [ɪ'leɪtɪd] *adj*: **to be ~** rejubilar-se.
elation [ɪ'leɪʃən] *n* exaltação *f*.
elbow ['ɛlbəu] *n* cotovelo ♦ *vt*: **to ~ one's way through the crowd** abrir passagem pela multidão com os cotovelos.
elbow room *n* (*fig*) liberdade *f*.
elder ['ɛldə*] *adj* mais velho ♦ *n* (*tree*) sabugueiro; (*person*) o/a mais velho/a; (*of tribe*) ancião; (*of church*) presbítero.
elderly ['ɛldəlɪ] *adj* idoso, de idade ♦ *npl*: **the ~** as pessoas de idade, os idosos.
eldest ['ɛldɪst] *adj* mais velho ♦ *n* o/a mais velho/a.
elect [ɪ'lɛkt] *vt* eleger; (*choose*): **to ~ to do** optar por fazer ♦ *adj*: **the president ~** o presidente eleito.
election [ɪ'lɛkʃən] *n* eleição *f*; **to hold an ~** realizar uma eleição.
election campaign *n* campanha eleitoral.
electioneering [ɪlɛkʃə'nɪərɪŋ] *n* campanha *or* propaganda eleitoral.
elector [ɪ'lɛktə*] *n* eleitor(a) *m/f*.
electoral [ɪ'lɛktərəl] *adj* eleitoral.
electoral college *n* colégio eleitoral.
electoral roll (*BRIT*) *n* lista de eleitores.
electorate [ɪ'lɛktərɪt] *n* eleitorado.
electric [ɪ'lɛktrɪk] *adj* elétrico.
electrical [ɪ'lɛktrɪkəl] *adj* elétrico.
electrical engineer *n* engenheiro/a eletricista.
electrical failure *n* pane *f* elétrica.
electric blanket *n* cobertor *m* elétrico.
electric chair *n* cadeira elétrica.
electric cooker *n* fogão *m* elétrico.

NB: *European Portuguese adds the following consonants to certain words:* **b** (sú(b)dito, su(b)til); **c** (a(c)ção, a(c)cionista, a(c)to); **m** (inde(m)ne); **p** (ado(p)ção, ado(p)tar); *for further details see p. xiii.*

electric current *n* corrente *f* elétrica.
electric fire (*BRIT*) *n* aquecimento elétrico.
electrician [ɪlɛk'trɪʃən] *n* eletricista *m/f*.
electricity [ɪlɛk'trɪsɪtɪ] *n* eletricidade *f*.
electricity board (*BRIT*) *n* empresa de energia elétrica.
electric light *n* luz *f* elétrica.
electric shock *n* choque *m* elétrico.
electrify [ɪ'lɛktrɪfaɪ] *vt* (*RAIL*) eletrificar; (*audience*) eletrizar.
electro... [ɪ'lɛktrəu] *prefix* eletro....
electrocardiogram [ɪ'lɛktrəu'kɑːdɪəgræm] *n* eletrocardiograma *m*.
electro-convulsive therapy *n* eletrochoques *mpl*.
electrocute [ɪ'lɛktrəkjuːt] *vt* eletrocutar.
electrode [ɪ'lɛktrəud] *n* eletrodo (*BR*), eléctrodo (*PT*).
electroencephalogram [ɪ'lɛktrəuɛn'sɛfələgræm] *n* eletroencefalograma *m*.
electrolysis [ɪlɛk'trɔlɪsɪs] *n* eletrólise *f*.
electromagnetic [ɪlɛktrəumæg'nɛtɪk] *adj* eletromagnético.
electron [ɪ'lɛktrɔn] *n* elétron *m* (*BR*), electrão *m* (*PT*).
electronic [ɪlɛk'trɔnɪk] *adj* eletrônico.
electronic data processing *n* processamento de dados eletrônico.
electronic mail *n* correio eletrônico.
electronics [ɪlɛk'trɔnɪks] *n* eletrônica.
electron microscope *n* microscópio eletrônico.
electroplated [ɪ'lɛktrəu'pleɪtɪd] *adj* galvanizado.
electrotherapy [ɪ'lɛktrəu'θɛrəpɪ] *n* eletroterapia.
elegance ['ɛlɪgəns] *n* elegância.
elegant ['ɛlɪgənt] *adj* elegante.
element ['ɛlɪmənt] *n* elemento; **to brave the ~s** enfrentar intempérie.
elementary [ɛlɪ'mɛntərɪ] *adj* (*gen*) elementar; (*primitive*) rudimentar; (*school, education*) primário.
elephant ['ɛlɪfənt] *n* elefante *m*.
elevate ['ɛlɪveɪt] *vt* elevar; (*in rank*) promover.
elevated railroad (*US*) *n* ferrovia elevada.
elevation [ɛlɪ'veɪʃən] *n* elevação *f*; (*land*) eminência; (*height*) altura.
elevator ['ɛlɪveɪtə*] (*US*) *n* elevador *m*.
eleven [ɪ'lɛvn] *num* onze; *see also* **five**.
elevenses [ɪ'lɛvənzɪz] (*BRIT*) *npl refeição leve da manhã*.
eleventh [ɪ'lɛvnθ] *num* décimo-primeiro; **at the ~ hour** (*fig*) no último momento, na hora H; *see also* **fifth**.
elf [ɛlf] (*pl* **elves**) *n* elfo, duende *m*.
elicit [ɪ'lɪsɪt] *vt*: **to ~ (from)** arrancar (de), eliciar (de).
eligible ['ɛlɪdʒəbl] *adj* elegível, apto; **to be ~ for sth** (*job etc*) ter qualificações para algo; (*pension etc*) ter direito a algo.
eliminate [ɪ'lɪmɪneɪt] *vt* eliminar; (*strike out*) suprimir; (*suspect*) eliminar, excluir.
elimination [ɪlɪmɪ'neɪʃən] *n* eliminação *f*; **by a process of ~** por eliminação.
élite [eɪ'liːt] *n* elite *f*.
élitist [eɪ'liːtɪst] (*pej*) *adj* elitista.
elixir [ɪ'lɪksə*] *n* elixir *m*.
Elizabethan [ɪlɪzə'biːθən] *adj* elisabetano.
ellipse [ɪ'lɪps] *n* elipse *f*.
elliptical [ɪ'lɪptɪkl] *adj* elíptico.
elm [ɛlm] *n* olmo.
elocution [ɛlə'kjuːʃən] *n* elocução *f*.
elongated ['iːlɔŋgeɪtɪd] *adj* alongado.
elope [ɪ'ləup] *vi* fugir.
elopement [ɪ'ləupmənt] *n* fuga do lar paterno.
eloquence ['ɛləkwəns] *n* eloqüência.
eloquent ['ɛləkwənt] *adj* eloqüente.
else [ɛls] *adv* outro, mais; **something ~** outra coisa; **somewhere ~** em outro lugar (*BR*), noutro sítio (*PT*); **everywhere ~** por todo o lado (menos aqui); **everyone ~** todos os outros; **where ~?** onde mais?; **what ~ can we do?** que mais podemos fazer?; **or ~** senão; **there was little ~ to do** não havia outra coisa a fazer; **nobody ~ spoke** ninguém mais falou.
elsewhere [ɛls'wɛə*] *adv* (*be*) em outro lugar (*BR*), noutro sítio (*PT*); (*go*) para outro lugar (*BR*), a outro sítio (*PT*).
ELT *n abbr* (*SCH*) = **English Language Teaching**.
elucidate [ɪ'luːsɪdeɪt] *vt* esclarecer, elucidar.
elude [ɪ'luːd] *vt* (*pursuer*) escapar de, esquivar-se de; (*question*) evadir.
elusive [ɪ'luːsɪv] *adj* esquivo; (*answer*) evasivo.
elves [ɛlvz] *npl of* **elf**.
emaciated [ɪ'meɪsɪeɪtɪd] *adj* emaciado, macilento.
emanate ['ɛməneɪt] *vi* emanar.
emancipate [ɪ'mænsɪpeɪt] *vt* emancipar.
emancipated [ɪ'mænsɪpeɪtɪd] *adj* emancipado.
emancipation [ɪmænsɪ'peɪʃən] *n* emancipação *f*.
emasculate [ɪ'mæskjuleɪt] *vt* emascular.
embalm [ɪm'bɑːm] *vt* embalsamar.
embankment [ɪm'bæŋkmənt] *n* aterro; (*riverside*) dique *m*.
embargo [ɪm'bɑːgəu] (*pl* **~es**) *n* (*NAUT*) embargo; (*COMM*) proibição *f* ♦ *vt* boicotear; **to put an ~ on sth** proibir algo.
embark [ɪm'bɑːk] *vi* embarcar ♦ *vt* embarcar; **to ~ on** (*fig*) empreender, começar.
embarkation [ɛmbɑː'keɪʃən] *n* (*of people, goods*) embarque *m*.
embarkation card *n* cartão *m* de embarque.
embarrass [ɪm'bærəs] *vt* embaraçar, constranger; **to be financially ~ed** estar com dificuldades financeiras.
embarrassing [ɪm'bærəsɪŋ] *adj* embaraçoso, constrangedor(a).
embarrassment [ɪm'bærəsmənt] *n* embaraço, constrangimento; (*financial*) dificuldades *fpl*.
embassy ['ɛmbəsɪ] *n* embaixada.
embed [ɪm'bɛd] *vt* embutir; (*teeth etc*) cravar.
embellish [ɪm'bɛlɪʃ] *vt* embelezar; (*fig: story*) florear.

embers ['ɛmbəz] *npl* brasa, borralho, cinzas *fpl*.
embezzle [ɪm'bɛzl] *vt* desviar.
embezzlement [ɪm'bɛzlmənt] *n* desvio (de fundos).
embezzler [ɪm'bɛzlə*] *n* malversador(a) *m/f*.
embitter [ɪm'bɪtə*] *vt* (*person*) amargurar; (*relations*) azedar.
embittered [ɪm'bɪtəd] *adj* amargurado.
emblem ['ɛmbləm] *n* emblema *m*.
embodiment [ɪm'bɔdɪmənt] *n* encarnação *f*.
embody [ɪm'bɔdɪ] *vt* (*features*) incorporar; (*ideas*) expressar.
embolden [ɪm'bəuldn] *vt* encorajar, animar.
embolism ['ɛmbəlɪzəm] *n* embolia.
embossed [ɪm'bɔst] *adj* realçado; ~ **with** ornado com relevos de.
embrace [ɪm'breɪs] *vt* abraçar, dar um abraço em; (*include*) abarcar, abranger; (*adopt: idea*) adotar ♦ *vi* abraçar-se ♦ *n* abraço.
embroider [ɪm'brɔɪdə*] *vt* bordar; (*fig: story*) florear.
embroidery [ɪm'brɔɪdərɪ] *n* bordado.
embroil [ɪm'brɔɪl] *vt*: **to become ~ed (in sth)** ficar envolvido (em algo).
embryo ['ɛmbrɪəu] *n* (*also: fig*) embrião *m*.
emend [ɪ'mɛnd] *vt* emendar.
emerald ['ɛmərəld] *n* esmeralda.
emerge [ɪ'mə:dʒ] *vi* sair, aparecer; (*arise*) surgir; **it ~s that ...** (*BRIT*) veio à tona que ....
emergence [ɪ'mə:dʒəns] *n* surgimento, aparecimento; (*of a nation*) nascimento.
emergency [ɪ'mə:dʒənsɪ] *n* emergência; **in an ~** em caso de urgência; **state of ~** estado de emergência.
emergency exit *n* saída de emergência.
emergency landing *n* aterrissagem *f* forçada (*BR*), aterragem *f* forçosa (*PT*).
emergency lane (*US*) *n* (*AUT*) acostamento (*BR*), berma (*PT*).
emergency meeting *n* reunião *f* extraordinária.
emergency road service (*US*) *n* auto-socorro (*BR*), pronto socorro (*PT*).
emergency service *n* serviço de emergência.
emergency stop (*BRIT*) *n* (*AUT*) parada de emergência.
emergent [ɪ'mə:dʒənt] *adj*: ~ **nation** país *m* em desenvolvimento.
emery board ['ɛmərɪ-] *n* lixa de unhas.
emery paper ['ɛmərɪ-] *n* lixa *or* papel *m* de esmeril.
emetic [ɪ'mɛtɪk] *n* emético.
emigrant ['ɛmɪgrənt] *n* emigrante *m/f*.
emigrate ['ɛmɪgreɪt] *vi* emigrar.
emigration [ɛmɪ'greɪʃən] *n* emigração *f*.
émigré ['ɛmɪgreɪ] *n* emigrado/a.
eminence ['ɛmɪnəns] *n* eminência.
eminent ['ɛmɪnənt] *adj* eminente.
eminently ['ɛmɪnəntlɪ] *adv* eminentemente.
emirate ['ɛmɪrɪt] *n* emirado.
emission [ɪ'mɪʃən] *n* emissão *f*.
emit [ɪ'mɪt] *vt* (*gen*) emitir; (*smoke*) soltar; (*smell*) exalar; (*sound*) produzir.
emolument [ɪ'mɔljumənt] *n* (*often pl: formal: fee*) honorário; (*salary*) remuneração *f*.
emotion [ɪ'məuʃən] *n* emoção *f*.
emotional [ɪ'məuʃənəl] *adj* (*person*) sentimental, emotivo; (*scene*) comovente; (*problem*) emocional; (*tone*) emocionante.
emotionally [ɪ'məuʃənəlɪ] *adv* (*disturbed, involved*) emocionalmente; (*behave*) emotivamente; (*speak*) com emoção.
emotive [ɪ'məutɪv] *adj* que sensibiliza; ~ **power** capacidade *f* de comover.
empathy ['ɛmpəθɪ] *n* empatia; **to feel ~ with sb** ter afinidade com alguém.
emperor ['ɛmpərə*] *n* imperador *m*.
emphases ['ɛmfəsi:z] *npl of* **emphasis**.
emphasis ['ɛmfəsɪs] (*pl* **emphases**) *n* ênfase *f*; **to lay** *or* **place ~ on sth** dar ênfase a; **the ~ is on reading** a leitura ocupa um lugar de destaque.
emphasize ['ɛmfəsaɪz] *vt* (*word, point*) enfatizar, acentuar; (*feature*) salientar.
emphatic [ɛm'fætɪk] *adj* (*strong*) enérgico; (*unambiguous, clear*) enfático.
emphatically [ɛm'fætɪkəlɪ] *adv* com ênfase.
empire ['ɛmpaɪə*] *n* império.
empirical [ɛm'pɪrɪkl] *adj* empírico.
employ [ɪm'plɔɪ] *vt* empregar; **he's ~ed in a bank** ele trabalha num banco.
employee [ɪmplɔɪ'i:] *n* empregado/a.
employer [ɪm'plɔɪə*] *n* empregador(a) *m/f*, patrão/troa *m/f*.
employment [ɪm'plɔɪmənt] *n* (*gen*) emprego; (*work*) trabalho; **to find ~** encontrar um emprego; **without ~** sem emprego, desempregado; **place of ~** local de trabalho.
employment agency *n* agência de empregos.
employment exchange (*BRIT*) *n* bolsa de trabalho.
empower [ɪm'pauə*] *vt*: **to ~ sb to do sth** autorizar alguém para fazer algo.
empress ['ɛmprɪs] *n* imperatriz *f*.
emptiness ['ɛmptɪnɪs] *n* vazio, vácuo.
empty ['ɛmptɪ] *adj* vazio; (*place*) deserto; (*house*) desocupado; (*threat*) vão/vã ♦ *n* (*bottle*) vazio ♦ *vt* esvaziar; (*place*) evacuar ♦ *vi* esvaziar-se; (*place*) ficar deserto; **on an ~ stomach** em jejum, com o estômago vazio; **to ~ into** (*river*) desaguar em.
empty-handed [-'hændɪd] *adj* de mãos vazias.
empty-headed [-'hɛdɪd] *adj* de cabeça oca.
EMS *n abbr* (= *European Monetary System*) SME *m*.
EMT *n abbr* = **emergency medical technician**.
emulate ['ɛmjuleɪt] *vt* (*person*) emular com.
emulsion [ɪ'mʌlʃən] *n* emulsão *f*; (*also: ~ paint*) tinta plástica.

NB: *European Portuguese adds the following consonants to certain words:* **b** (sú(b)dito, su(b)til); **c** (a(c)ção, a(c)cionista, a(c)to); **m** (inde(m)ne); **p** (ado(p)ção, ado(p)tar); *for further details see p. xiii.*

enable [ɪ'neɪbl] *vt*: **to ~ sb to do sth** (*allow*) permitir que alguém faça algo; (*prepare*) capacitar alguém para fazer algo.
enact [ɪn'ækt] *vt* (*LAW*) pôr em vigor, promulgar; (*play*) representar; (*role*) fazer.
enamel [ɪ'næməl] *n* esmalte *m*.
enamel paint *n* esmalte *m*.
enamoured [ɪ'næməd] *adj*: **to be ~ of** (*person*) estar apaixonado por; (*activity etc*) ser louco por; (*idea*) encantar-se com.
encampment [ɪn'kæmpmənt] *n* acampamento.
encased [ɪn'keɪst] *adj*: **~ in** (*enclosed*) encaixado em; (*covered*) revestido de.
encash [ɪn'kæʃ] (*BRIT*) *vt* descontar.
enchant [ɪn'tʃɑːnt] *vt* encantar.
enchanting [ɪn'tʃɑːntɪŋ] *adj* encantador(a).
encircle [ɪn'səːkl] *vt* cercar, circundar; (*waist*) rodear.
enc(l). *abbr* (*in letters etc*) = **enclosed; enclosure**.
enclose [ɪn'kləuz] *vt* (*land*) cercar; (*with letter etc*) anexar (*BR*), enviar junto (*PT*); **please find ~d** segue junto.
enclosure [ɪn'kləuʒə*] *n* cercado; (*COMM*) documento anexo.
encoder [ɪn'kəudə*] *n* (*COMPUT*) codificador *m*.
encompass [ɪn'kʌmpəs] *vt* abranger, encerrar.
encore [ɔŋ'kɔː*] *excl* bis!, outra! ♦ *n* bis *m*.
encounter [ɪn'kauntə*] *n* encontro ♦ *vt* encontrar, topar com; (*difficulty*) enfrentar.
encourage [ɪn'kʌrɪdʒ] *vt* encorajar, animar; (*growth*) estimular; **to ~ sb to do sth** animar alguém a fazer algo.
encouragement [ɪn'kʌrɪdʒmənt] *n* estímulo.
encouraging [ɪn'kʌrɪdʒɪŋ] *adj* animador(a).
encroach [ɪn'krəutʃ] *vi*: **to ~ (up)on** invadir; (*time*) ocupar.
encrusted [ɪn'krʌstəd] *adj*: **~ with** incrustado de.
encumber [ɪn'kʌmbə*] *vt*: **to be ~ed with** (*carry*) estar carregado de; (*debts*) estar sobrecarregado de.
encyclop(a)edia [ɛnsaɪkləu'piːdɪə] *n* enciclopédia.
end [ɛnd] *n* (*in time*; *also*: *aim*) fim *m*; (*of table*, *line*, *rope etc*) ponta; (*of street*) final *m*; (*SPORT*) ponta ♦ *vt* acabar, terminar; (*also*: *bring to an ~*, *put an ~ to*) acabar com, pôr fim a ♦ *vi* terminar, acabar; **from ~ to ~** de ponta a ponta; **to come to an ~** acabar; **to be at an ~** estar no fim, estar terminado; **in the ~** ao fim, por fim, finalmente; **on ~** (*object*) na ponta; **to stand on ~** (*hair*) arrepiar-se; **for hours on ~** por horas a fio; **at the ~ of the day** (*BRIT*: *fig*) no final das contas; **to this ~, with this ~ in view** a este fim.
end up *vi*: **to ~ up in** terminar em; (*place*) ir parar em.
endanger [ɪn'deɪndʒə*] *vt* pôr em perigo; **an ~ed species** uma espécie ameaçada de extinção.
endear [ɪn'dɪə*] *vt*: **to ~ o.s. to sb** conquistar a afeição de alguém, cativar alguém.
endearing [ɪn'dɪərɪŋ] *adj* simpático, atrativo.
endearment [ɪn'dɪəmənt] *n*: **to whisper ~s** sussurrar palavras carinhosas; **term of ~** palavra carinhosa.
endeavour [ɪn'dɛvə*] (*US* **endeavor**) *n* esforço; (*attempt*) tentativa; (*striving*) empenho ♦ *vi*: **to ~ to do** esforçar-se para fazer; (*try*) tentar fazer.
endemic [ɛn'dɛmɪk] *adj* endêmico.
ending ['ɛndɪŋ] *n* fim *m*, conclusão *f*; (*of book*) desenlace *m*; (*LING*) terminação *f*.
endive ['ɛndaɪv] *n* (*curly*) chicória; (*smooth*, *flat*) endívia.
endless ['ɛndlɪs] *adj* interminável; (*possibilities*) infinito.
endorse [ɪn'dɔːs] *vt* (*cheque*) endossar; (*approve*) aprovar.
endorsee [ɪndɔː'siː] *n* endossado/a, endossatário/a.
endorsement [ɪn'dɔːsmənt] *n* (*BRIT*: *on driving licence*) descrição *f* das multas; (*approval*) aval *m*; (*signature*) endosso.
endorser [ɪn'dɔːsə*] *n* endossante *m/f*, endossador(a) *m/f*.
endow [ɪn'dau] *vt* (*provide with money*) dotar; (: *institution*) fundar; **to be ~ed with** ser dotado de.
endowment [ɪn'daumənt] *n* dotação *f*.
endowment assurance *n* seguro dotal.
end product *n* (*INDUSTRY*) produto final; (*fig*) resultado.
end result *n* resultado final.
endurable [ɪn'djuərəbl] *adj* suportável.
endurance [ɪn'djuərəns] *n* resistência.
endurance test teste *m* de resistência.
endure [ɪn'djuə*] *vt* (*bear*) agüentar, suportar ♦ *vi* (*last*) durar; (*resist*) resistir.
end user *n* (*COMPUT*) usuário/a (*BR*) *or* utente *m/f* (*PT*) final.
enema ['ɛnɪmə] *n* (*MED*) enema *m*, clister *m*.
enemy ['ɛnəmɪ] *adj*, *n* inimigo/a; **to make an ~ of sb** fazer de alguém um inimigo.
energetic [ɛnə'dʒɛtɪk] *adj* energético.
energy ['ɛnədʒɪ] *n* energia; **Department of E~** Ministério da Energia.
energy crisis *n* crise *f* de energia.
energy-saving *adj* (*policy*) de economia de energia; (*device*) que economiza energia.
enervating ['ɛnəveɪtɪŋ] *adj* enervante.
enforce [ɪn'fɔːs] *vt* (*LAW*) fazer cumprir.
enforced [ɪn'fɔːst] *adj* forçoso.
enfranchise [ɪn'fræntʃaɪz] *vt* conferir o direito de voto a; (*set free*) emancipar.
engage [ɪn'geɪdʒ] *vt* (*attention*) chamar; (*lawyer*) contratar; (*clutch*) engrenar ♦ *vi* (*TECH*) engrenar; **to ~ in** dedicar-se a, ocupar-se com; **to ~ sb in conversation** travar conversa com alguém.
engaged [ɪn'geɪdʒd] *adj* (*BRIT*: *phone*) ocupado (*BR*), impedido (*PT*); (: *toilet*) ocupado; (*betrothed*) noivo; **to get ~** ficar noivo; **he is ~ in research** dedica-se à pesquisa.
engaged tone (*BRIT*) *n* (*TEL*) sinal *m* de ocupado (*BR*) *or* de impedido (*PT*).

engagement [ɪn'geɪdʒmənt] *n* (*appointment*) encontro; (*battle*) combate *m*; (*to marry*) noivado; **I have a previous ~** já tenho compromisso.
engagement ring *n* aliança de noivado.
engaging [ɪn'geɪdʒɪŋ] *adj* atraente, simpático.
engender [ɪn'dʒɛndə*] *vt* engendrar, gerar.
engine ['ɛndʒɪn] *n* (AUT) motor *m*; (RAIL) locomotiva.
engine driver (BRIT) *n* maquinista *m/f*.
engineer [ɛndʒɪ'nɪə*] *n* engenheiro/a; (US: RAIL) maquinista *m/f*; (BRIT: *for domestic appliances*) consertador(a) *m/f* (de aparelhos domésticos).
engineering [ɛndʒɪ'nɪərɪŋ] *n* engenharia ♦ *cpd*: **~ works** *or* **factory** fábrica de construção de máquinas.
engine failure *n* falha do motor.
engine trouble *n* enguiço.
England ['ɪŋglənd] *n* Inglaterra.
English ['ɪŋglɪʃ] *adj* inglês/esa ♦ *n* (LING) inglês *m*; **the ~** *npl* os ingleses; **an ~ speaker** uma pessoa de língua inglesa.
English Channel *n*: **the ~** o Canal da Mancha.
Englishman ['ɪŋglɪʃmən] (*irreg*) *n* inglês *m*.
English-speaking *adj* de língua inglesa.
Englishwoman ['ɪŋglɪʃwumən] (*irreg*) *n* inglesa.
engrave [ɪn'greɪv] *vt* gravar.
engraving [ɪn'greɪvɪŋ] *n* gravura, gravação *f*.
engrossed [ɪn'grəust] *adj*: **~ in** absorto em.
engulf [ɪn'gʌlf] *vt* engolfar, tragar.
enhance [ɪn'hɑ:ns] *vt* (*gen*) ressaltar, salientar; (*beauty*) realçar; (*position*) melhorar; (*add to*) aumentar.
enigma [ɪ'nɪgmə] *n* enigma *m*.
enigmatic [ɛnɪg'mætɪk] *adj* enigmático.
enjoy [ɪn'dʒɔɪ] *vt* (*like*) gostar de; (*have*: *health, privilege*) desfrutar de; (*food*) comer com gosto; **to ~ o.s.** divertir-se.
enjoyable [ɪn'dʒɔɪəbl] *adj* (*pleasant*) agradável; (*amusing*) divertido.
enjoyment [ɪn'dʒɔɪmənt] *n* (*joy*) prazer *m*; (*use*) gozo.
enlarge [ɪn'lɑ:dʒ] *vt* aumentar; (*broaden*) estender, alargar; (PHOT) ampliar ♦ *vi*: **to ~ on** (*subject*) desenvolver, estender-se sobre.
enlarged [ɪn'lɑ:dʒd] *adj* (*edition*) ampliado; (MED: *organ, gland*) dilatado, hipertrofiado.
enlargement [ɪn'lɑ:dʒmənt] *n* (PHOT) ampliação *f*.
enlighten [ɪn'laɪtn] *vt* (*inform*) informar, instruir.
enlightened [ɪn'laɪtnd] *adj* (*cultured*) culto; (*knowledgeable*) bem informado; (*tolerant*) compreensivo.
enlightening [ɪn'laɪtnɪŋ] *adj* esclarecedor(a).
enlightenment [ɪn'laɪtənmənt] *n* esclarecimento; (HISTORY): **the E~** o Século das Luzes.
enlist [ɪn'lɪst] *vt* alistar; (*support*) conseguir, aliciar ♦ *vi* alistar-se; **~ed man** (US: MIL) praça *m*.
enliven [ɪn'laɪvn] *vt* animar, agitar.
enmity ['ɛnmɪtɪ] *n* inimizade *f*.
ennoble [ɪ'nəubl] *vt* (*with title*) nobilitar.
enormity [ɪ'nɔ:mɪtɪ] *n* enormidade *f*.
enormous [ɪ'nɔ:məs] *adj* enorme.
enormously [ɪ'nɔ:məslɪ] *adv* imensamente.
enough [ɪ'nʌf] *adj*: **~ time/books** tempo suficiente/livros suficientes ♦ *n*: **have you got ~?** você tem o suficiente? ♦ *adv*: **big ~** suficientemente grande; **will 5 be ~?** 5 chegam?; **~!** basta!, chega!; **that's ~, thanks** chega, obrigado; **I've had ~!** não agüento mais!; **I've had ~ of him** estou farto dele; **he has not worked ~** não tem trabalhado o suficiente; **it's hot ~ (as it is)!** já está tão quente!; **he was kind ~ to lend me the money** ele teve a gentileza de me emprestar o dinheiro; **which, funnily ~ ...** o que, por estranho que pareça ....
enquire [ɪn'kwaɪə*] *vt, vi* = **inquire**.
enrage [ɪn'reɪdʒ] *vt* enfurecer, enraivecer.
enrich [ɪn'rɪtʃ] *vt* enriquecer.
enrol [ɪn'rəul] (US **enroll**) *vt* inscrever; (SCH) matricular ♦ *vi* inscrever-se; (SCH) matricular-se.
enrol(l)ment [ɪn'rəulmənt] *n* inscrição *f*; (SCH) matrícula.
en route [ɔn-] *adv* (*on the way*) no caminho; **~ for** *or* **to** a caminho de.
ensconced [ɪn'skɔnst] *adj*: **~ in** acomodado em.
enshrine [ɪn'ʃraɪn] *vt* (*fig*) conservar, resguardar.
ensign ['ɛnsaɪn] *n* (*flag*) bandeira; (MIL) insígnia; (US: NAUT) guarda-marinha *m*.
enslave [ɪn'sleɪv] *vt* escravizar.
ensue [ɪn'sju:] *vi* seguir-se; (*result*) resultar; (*happen*) acontecer.
ensure [ɪn'ʃuə*] *vt* assegurar; **to ~ that** verificar-se que.
ENT *n abbr* (= *Ear, Nose & Throat*) otorrinolaringologia.
entail [ɪn'teɪl] *vt* (*imply*) implicar; (*result in*) acarretar.
entangle [ɪn'tæŋgl] *vt* enredar, emaranhar; **to get ~d in sth** (*fig*) ficar enrolado em algo.
entanglement [ɪn'tæŋglmənt] *n* emaranhado.
enter ['ɛntə*] *vt* (*room*) entrar em; (*club*) ficar *or* fazer-se sócio de; (*army*) alistar-se em; (*competition*) inscrever-se em; (*sb for a competition*) inscrever; (*write down*) anotar; (COMPUT) entrar com ♦ *vi* entrar.
enter for *vt fus* inscrever-se em.
enter into *vt fus* (*relations*) estabelecer; (*plans*) fazer parte de; (*debate, negotiations*) entrar em; (*agreement*) chegar a, firmar.
enter up *vt* lançar.
enter (up)on *vt fus* (*career*) entrar para.
enteritis [ɛntə'raɪtɪs] *n* enterite *f*.
enterprise ['ɛntəpraɪz] *n* empresa; (*spirit*) ini-

***NB**: European Portuguese adds the following consonants to certain words:* **b** (sú(b)dito, su(b)til); **c** (a(c)ção, a(c)cionista, a(c)to); **m** (inde(m)ne); **p** (ado(p)ção, ado(p)tar); *for further details see p. xiii.*

ciativa.

enterprising ['ɛntəpraɪzɪŋ] *adj* empreendedor(a).

entertain [ɛntə'teɪn] *vt* (*amuse*) divertir, entreter; (*receive: guest*) receber (em casa); (*idea, plan*) estudar.

entertainer [ɛntə'teɪnə*] *n* artista *m/f*.

entertaining [ɛntə'teɪnɪŋ] *adj* divertido ♦ *n*: **to do a lot of ~** receber com freqüência.

entertainment [ɛntə'teɪnmənt] *n* (*amusement*) entretenimento, diversão *f*; (*show*) espetáculo.

entertainment allowance *n* verba de representação.

enthralled [ɪn'θrɔːld] *adj* encantado, cativado.

enthralling [ɪn'θrɔːlɪŋ] *adj* cativante, encantador(a).

enthuse [ɪn'θuːz] *vi*: **to ~ about** *or* **over** entusiasmar-se com *or* por.

enthusiasm [ɪn'θuːzɪæzəm] *n* entusiasmo.

enthusiast [ɪn'θuːzɪæst] *n* entusiasta *m/f*; **a jazz** *etc* **~** um(a) aficionado/a de jazz *etc*.

enthusiastic [ɪnθuːzɪ'æstɪk] *adj* entusiástico; **to be ~ about** entusiasmar-se por.

entice [ɪn'taɪs] *vt* atrair, tentar; (*seduce*) seduzir.

enticing [ɪn'taɪsɪŋ] *adj* sedutor(a), tentador(a).

entire [ɪn'taɪə*] *adj* inteiro.

entirely [ɪn'taɪəlɪ] *adv* totalmente, completamente.

entirety [ɪn'taɪərətɪ] *n*: **in its ~** na sua totalidade.

entitle [ɪn'taɪtl] *vt*: **to ~ sb to sth** dar a alguém direito a algo; **to ~ sb to do** dar a alguém direito de fazer.

entitled [ɪn'taɪtld] *adj* (*book*) intitulado; **to be ~ to sth/to do sth** ter direito a algo/de fazer algo.

entity ['ɛntɪtɪ] *n* ente *m*.

entourage [ɔntu'rɑːʒ] *n* séquito.

entrails ['ɛntreɪlz] *npl* entranhas *fpl*.

entrance [*n* 'ɛntrəns, *vt* ɪn'trɑːns] *n* entrada ♦ *vt* encantar, fascinar; **to gain ~ to** (*university etc*) ser admitido em.

entrance examination *n* exame *m* de admissão.

entrance fee *n* jóia; (*to museum etc*) (preço da) entrada.

entrance ramp (*US*) *n* (*AUT*) entrada (para a rodovia).

entrancing [ɪn'trɑːnsɪŋ] *adj* encantador(a), fascinante.

entrant ['ɛntrənt] *n* participante *m/f*; (*BRIT: in exam*) candidato/a.

entreat [ɛn'triːt] *vt* rogar, suplicar.

entreaty [ɛn'triːtɪ] *n* rogo, súplica.

entrée ['ɔntreɪ] *n* (*CULIN*) entrada.

entrenched [ɛn'trɛntʃd] *adj* entrincheirado.

entrepreneur [ɔntrəprə'nəː] *n* empresário/a.

entrepreneurial [ɔntrəprə'nəːrɪəl] *adj* empreendedor(a).

entrust [ɪn'trʌst] *vt*: **to ~ sth to sb** confiar algo a alguém.

entry ['ɛntrɪ] *n* entrada; (*permission to enter*) acesso; (*in register*) registro, assentamento; (*in account*) lançamento; (*in dictionary*) verbete *m*; **"no ~"** "entrada proibida"; (*AUT*) "contramão" (*BR*), "entrada proibida" (*PT*); **single/double ~ book-keeping** escrituração por partidas simples/dobradas.

entry form *n* formulário de inscrição.

entry phone (*BRIT*) *n* interfone *m* (*em apartamento*).

entwine [ɪn'twaɪn] *vt* entrelaçar.

enumerate [ɪ'njuːməreɪt] *vt* enumerar.

enunciate [ɪ'nʌnsɪeɪt] *vt* pronunciar; (*principle etc*) enunciar.

envelop [ɪn'vɛləp] *vt* envolver.

envelope ['ɛnvələup] *n* envelope *m*.

enviable ['ɛnvɪəbl] *adj* invejável.

envious ['ɛnvɪəs] *adj* invejoso; (*look*) de inveja.

environment [ɪn'vaɪərnmənt] *n* meio ambiente *m*; **Department of the E~** (*BRIT*) ≈ Ministério da Habitação, Urbanismo e Meio Ambiente.

environmental [ɪnvaɪərn'mɛntl] *adj* ambiental; **~ studies** (*SCH*) ecologia.

environmentalist [ɪnvaɪərn'mɛntəlɪst] *n* ecologista *m/f*.

Environmental Protection Agency (*US*) *n* ≈ Secretaria Especial do Meio Ambiente.

envisage [ɪn'vɪzɪdʒ] *vt* (*foresee*) prever; (*imagine*) conceber, imaginar.

envision [ɪn'vɪʒən] (*US*) *vt* = **envisage**.

envoy ['ɛnvɔɪ] *n* enviado/a.

envy ['ɛnvɪ] *n* inveja ♦ *vt* ter inveja de; **to ~ sb sth** invejar alguém por algo, cobiçar algo de alguém.

enzyme ['ɛnzaɪm] *n* enzima.

EPA (*US*) *n abbr* (= *Environmental Protection Agency*) ≈ SEMA.

ephemeral [ɪ'fɛmərl] *adj* efêmero.

epic ['ɛpɪk] *n* epopéia ♦ *adj* épico.

epicentre ['ɛpɪsɛntə*] (*US* **epicenter**) *n* epicentro.

epidemic [ɛpɪ'dɛmɪk] *n* epidemia.

epilepsy ['ɛpɪlɛpsɪ] *n* epilepsia.

epileptic [ɛpɪ'lɛptɪk] *adj*, *n* epilético/a.

epilogue ['ɛpɪlɔg] *n* epílogo.

episcopal [ɪ'pɪskəpl] *adj* episcopal.

episode ['ɛpɪsəud] *n* episódio.

epistle [ɪ'pɪsl] *n* epístola.

epitaph ['ɛpɪtɑːf] *n* epitáfio.

epithet ['ɛpɪθɛt] *n* epíteto.

epitome [ɪ'pɪtəmɪ] *n* epítome *m*.

epitomize [ɪ'pɪtəmaɪz] *vt* epitomar, resumir.

epoch ['iːpɔk] *n* época.

epoch-making *adj* que marca época, marcante.

eponymous [ɪ'pɔnɪməs] *adj* epônimo.

equable ['ɛkwəbl] *adj* uniforme, igual; (*character*) tranqüilo, calmo.

equal ['iːkwl] *adj* igual; (*treatment*) equitativo, equivalente ♦ *n* igual *m/f* ♦ *vt* ser igual a; **to be ~ to** (*task*) estar à altura de; **~ to doing** capaz de fazer.

equality [iː'kwɔlɪtɪ] *n* igualdade *f*.

equalize ['iːkwəlaɪz] *vt*, *vi* igualar; (*SPORT*)

empatar.
equalizer ['iːkwəlaɪzə*] *n* gol (*PT*: golo) *m* de empate.
equally ['iːkwəlɪ] *adv* igualmente; (*share etc*) por igual.
Equal Opportunities Commission (*US* **Equal Employment Opportunity Commission**) *n comissão para a não-discriminação no trabalho.*
equal(s) sign *n* sinal *m* de igualdade.
equanimity [ɛkwə'nɪmɪtɪ] *n* equanimidade *f.*
equate [ɪ'kweɪt] *vt*: **to ~ sth with** equiparar algo com; **to ~ sth to** igualar algo a.
equation [ɪ'kweɪʒən] *n* (*MATH*) equação *f.*
equator [ɪ'kweɪtə*] *n* equador *m.*
equatorial [ɛkwə'tɔːrɪəl] *adj* equatorial.
Equatorial Guinea *n* Guiné *f* Equatorial.
equestrian [ɪ'kwɛstrɪən] *adj* eqüestre; (*sport*) hípico ♦ *n* (*man*) ginete *m*; (*woman*) amazona.
equilibrium [iːkwɪ'lɪbrɪəm] *n* equilíbrio.
equinox ['iːkwɪnɔks] *n* equinócio.
equip [ɪ'kwɪp] *vt* equipar; (*person*) prover, munir; **to ~ sb/sth with** equipar alguém/algo com, munir alguém/algo de; **to be well ~ped** estar bem preparado *or* equipado.
equipment [ɪ'kwɪpmənt] *n* equipamento; (*machines etc*) equipamentos *mpl*, aparelhagem *f.*
equitable ['ɛkwɪtəbl] *adj* equitativo.
equities ['ɛkwɪtɪz] (*BRIT*) *npl* (*COMM*) ações *fpl* ordinárias.
equity capital *n* capital *m* próprio.
equivalent [ɪ'kwɪvəlnt] *adj* equivalente ♦ *n* equivalente *m*; **to be ~ to** ser equivalente a.
equivocal [ɪ'kwɪvəkl] *adj* equívoco; (*open to suspicion*) ambíguo.
equivocate [ɪ'kwɪvəkeɪt] *vi* sofismar.
equivocation [ɪkwɪvə'keɪʃən] sofismas *mpl.*
ER (*BRIT*) *abbr* (= *Elizabeth Regina*) *a rainha Elisabete.*
ERA (*US*) *n abbr* (*POL*: = *equal rights amendment*) *emenda sobre a igualdade das mulheres.*
era ['ɪərə] *n* era, época.
eradicate [ɪ'rædɪkeɪt] *vt* erradicar, eliminar.
erase [ɪ'reɪz] *vt* apagar.
eraser [ɪ'reɪzə*] *n* borracha (de apagar).
erect [ɪ'rɛkt] *adj* erguido, ereto ♦ *vt* erigir, levantar; (*assemble*) montar; (*tent*) armar.
erection [ɪ'rɛkʃən] *n* construção *f*; (*assembly*) montagem *f*; (*structure*) edifício; (*PHYSIOLOGY*) ereção *f.*
ergonomics [əːgə'nɔmɪks] *n* ergonomia.
ERISA (*US*) *n abbr* (= *Employee Retirement Income Security Act*) *lei referente às aposentadorias.*
ermine ['əːmɪn] *n* arminho.
ERNIE ['əːnɪ] (*BRIT*) *n abbr* (= *Electronic Random Number Indicator Equipment*) *computador que serve para o sorteio dos "premium bonds".*
erode [ɪ'rəud] *vt* (*GEO*) causar erosão em; (*salary*) corroer.
erosion [ɪ'rəuʒən] *n* erosão *f*; (*fig*) corrosão *f.*
erotic [ɪ'rɔtɪk] *adj* erótico.
eroticism [ɪ'rɔtɪsɪzm] *n* erotismo.
err [əː*] *vi* errar, enganar-se; (*REL*) pecar.
errand ['ɛrnd] *n* recado, mensagem *f*; **to run ~s** fazer incumbências; **~ of mercy** missão *f* de caridade.
errand boy *n* mensageiro.
erratic [ɪ'rætɪk] *adj* irregular.
erroneous [ɪ'rəunɪəs] *adj* errôneo.
error ['ɛrə*] *n* erro; **typing/spelling ~** erro de datilografia/ortografia; **in ~** por engano; **~s and omissions excepted** salvo erro ou omissão.
error message *n* (*COMPUT*) mensagem *f* de erro.
erstwhile ['əːstwaɪl] *adj* antigo.
erudite ['ɛrjudaɪt] *adj* erudito.
erupt [ɪ'rʌpt] *vi* entrar em erupção; (*fig*) explodir, estourar.
eruption [ɪ'rʌpʃən] *n* erupção *f*; (*fig*) explosão *f.*
ESA *n abbr* (= *European Space Agency*) AEE *f.*
escalate ['ɛskəleɪt] *vi* intensificar-se; (*costs, prices*) disparar.
escalation [ɛskə'leɪʃən] *n* escalada, intensificação *f.*
escalation clause *n* cláusula de reajustamento.
escalator ['ɛskəleɪtə*] *n* escada rolante.
escapade [ɛskə'peɪd] *n* peripécia.
escape [ɪ'skeɪp] *n* fuga; (*from duties*) escapatória; (*from chase*) fuga, evasão *f* ♦ *vi* escapar; (*flee*) fugir, evadir-se; (*leak*) vazar, escapar ♦ *vt* evitar, fugir de; (*consequences*) fugir de; **to ~ from** (*place*) escapar de; (*person*) escapulir de; (*clutches*) livrar-se de; **to ~ to** fugir para; **to ~ to safety** salvar-se; **to ~ notice** passar despercebido.
escape artist *n* ilusionista *m/f.*
escape clause cláusula que permite revogação do contrato.
escape key *n* (*COMPUT*) tecla de saída.
escape route *n* (*from fire*) saída de emergência; (*of prisoners*) roteiro da fuga.
escapism [ɪ'skeɪpɪzəm] *n* escapismo, fuga à realidade.
escapist [ɪ'skeɪpɪst] *adj* (*person*) que foge da realidade; (*literature*) de evasão.
escapologist [ɛskə'pɔlədʒɪst] (*BRIT*) *n* ilusionista *m/f.*
escarpment [ɪs'kɑːpmənt] *n* escarpa.
eschew [ɪs'tʃuː] *vt* evitar.
escort [*n* 'ɛskɔːt, *vt* ɪ'skɔːt] *n* acompanhante *m/f*; (*MIL, NAUT*) escolta ♦ *vt* acompanhar; (*MIL, NAUT*) escoltar.
escort agency *n* agência de escorte.
Eskimo ['ɛskɪməu] *adj* esquimó ♦ *n* esquimó *m/f*; (*LING*) esquimó *m.*

ESL *n abbr* (*SCH*) = **English as a Second Language.**
esophagus [iː'sɔfəgəs] (*US*) *n* = **oesophagus.**
esoteric [ɛsə'tɛrɪk] *adj* esotérico.
ESP *n abbr* = **extrasensory perception.**
esp. *abbr* = **especially.**
especially [ɪ'spɛʃlɪ] *adv* (*gen*) especialmente; (*above all*) sobretudo; (*particularly*) em particular.
espionage ['ɛspɪənɑːʒ] *n* espionagem *f.*
esplanade [ɛsplə'neɪd] *n* (*by sea*) avenida beira-mar, esplanada.
espouse [ɪ'spauz] *vt* (*cause*) abraçar.
Esq. (*BRIT*) *abbr* (= *Esquire*) Sr.
Esquire [ɪ'skwaɪə*] (*BRIT*) *n*: **J. Brown,** ~ Sr. J. Brown.
essay ['ɛseɪ] *n* (*SCH*) ensaio.
essence ['ɛsns] *n* essência; **in** ~ em sua essência; **speed is of the** ~ a rapidez é fundamental.
essential [ɪ'sɛnʃl] *adj* (*necessary*) indispensável; (*basic*) essencial ♦ *n* elemento essencial; **it is** ~ **that** é indispensável que + *sub.*
essentially [ɪ'sɛnʃəlɪ] *adv* essencialmente.
EST (*US*) *abbr* (= *Eastern Standard Time*) *hora de inverno de Nova Iorque.*
est. *abbr* = **established; estimate(d).**
establish [ɪ'stæblɪʃ] *vt* estabelecer; (*facts*) verificar; (*proof*) demonstrar; (*relations*) fundar.
established [ɪ'stæblɪʃt] *adj* consagrado; (*staff*) fixo.
establishment [ɪ'stæblɪʃmənt] *n* estabelecimento; **the E**~ a classe dirigente.
estate [ɪ'steɪt] *n* (*land*) fazenda (*BR*), propriedade *f* (*PT*); (*property*) propriedade; (*inheritance*) herança; (*POL*) estado; (*BRIT*: *also*: *housing* ~) conjunto habitacional.
estate agency (*BRIT*) *n* imobiliária, corretora de imóveis.
estate agent (*BRIT*) *n* corretor(a) *m/f* de imóveis (*BR*), agente *m/f* imobiliário/a (*PT*).
estate car (*BRIT*) *n* perua (*BR*), canadiana (*PT*).
esteem [ɪ'stiːm] *n* estima ♦ *vt* estimar; **to hold sb in high** ~ estimar muito alguém.
esthetic [ɪs'θɛtɪk] (*US*) *adj* **aesthetic.**
estimate [*n* 'ɛstɪmət, *vt, vi* 'ɛstɪmeɪt] *n* estimativa; (*assessment*) avaliação *f*, cálculo; (*COMM*) orçamento ♦ *vt* estimar, avaliar, calcular ♦ *vi* (*BRIT*: *COMM*): **to** ~ **for a job** orçar uma obra; **at a rough** ~ numa estimativa aproximada.
estimation [ɛstɪ'meɪʃən] *n* estimação *f*, opinião *f*; (*esteem*) apreço; **in my** ~ na minha opinião.
estimator ['ɛstɪmeɪtə*] *n* avaliador(a) *m/f.*
Estonia [ɛ'stəunɪə] *n* Estônia.
estranged [ɪ'streɪndʒd] *adj* (*couple*) separado; (*husband, wife*) de quem se separou.
estrangement [ɪ'streɪndʒmənt] *n* separação *f.*
estrogen ['iːstrəudʒɛn] (*US*) *n* = **oestrogen.**
estuary ['ɛstjuərɪ] *n* estuário.
ET (*US*) *abbr* (= *Eastern Time*) *hora de Nova Iorque.*
ETA *n abbr* = **estimated time of arrival.**
et al. *abbr* (= *et alii*: *and others*) e outras pessoas.
etc. *abbr* (= *et cetera*) etc.
etch [ɛtʃ] *vt* gravar com água-forte.
etching ['ɛtʃɪŋ] *n* água-forte *f.*
ETD *n abbr* = **estimated time of departure.**
eternal [ɪ'təːnl] *adj* eterno.
eternity [ɪ'təːnɪtɪ] *n* eternidade *f.*
ether ['iːθə*] *n* éter *m.*
ethereal [ɪ'θɪərɪəl] *adj* etéreo.
ethical ['ɛθɪkl] *adj* ético; (*honest*) honrado.
ethics ['ɛθɪks] *n* ética ♦ *npl* moral *f.*
Ethiopia [iːθɪ'əupɪə] *n* Etiópia.
Ethiopian [iːθɪ'əupɪən] *adj, n* etíope *m/f.*
ethnic ['ɛθnɪk] *adj* étnico; (*clothes*) folclórico; (*food*) exótico.
ethnology [ɛθ'nɔlədʒɪ] *n* etnologia.
ethos ['iːθɔs] *n* sistema *m* de valores.
etiquette ['ɛtɪkɛt] *n* etiqueta.
ETU (*BRIT*) *n abbr* (= *Electrical Trades Union*) *sindicato dos eletricistas.*
ETV (*US*) *n abbr* (= *Educational Television*) TV *f* educativa.
etymology [ɛtɪ'mɔlədʒɪ] *n* etimologia.
eucalyptus [juːkə'lɪptəs] *n* eucalipto.
euphemism ['juːfəmɪzm] *n* eufemismo.
euphemistic [juːfə'mɪstɪk] *adj* eufêmico.
euphoria [juː'fɔːrɪə] *n* euforia.
Eurasia [juə'reɪʃə] *n* Eurásia.
Eurasian [juə'reɪʃən] *adj* (*person*) eurasiático; (*continent*) eurásio ♦ *n* eurasiático/a.
Euratom [juə'rætəm] *n abbr* (= *European Atomic Energy Community*) EURATOM *f.*
Eurocheque ['juərəutʃɛk] *n* eurocheque *m.*
Eurocrat ['juərəukræt] *n* eurocrata *m/f*, funcionário/a da CEE.
Eurodollar ['juərəudɔlə*] *n* eurodólar *m.*
Europe ['juərəp] *n* Europa.
European [juərə'piːən] *adj, n* europeu/péia.
European Court of Justice *n* Tribunal *m* Europeu de Justiça.
euthanasia [juːθə'neɪzɪə] *n* eutanásia.
evacuate [ɪ'vækjueɪt] *vt* evacuar.
evacuation [ɪvækju'eɪʃən] *n* evacuação *f.*
evade [ɪ'veɪd] *vt* evadir, evitar; (*duties*) esquivar-se de, escapar a.
evaluate [ɪ'væljueɪt] *vt* avaliar; (*evidence*) interpretar.
evangelist [ɪ'vændʒəlɪst] *n* evangelista *m/f*; (*preacher*) evangelizador(a) *m/f.*
evangelize [ɪ'vændʒəlaɪz] *vt* evangelizar.
evaporate [ɪ'væpəreɪt] *vi* evaporar-se ♦ *vt* evaporar.
evaporated milk [ɪ'væpəreɪtɪd-] *n* leite *m* condensado.
evaporation [ɪvæpə'reɪʃən] *n* evaporação *f.*
evasion [ɪ'veɪʒən] *n* evasão *f*, fuga; (*fig*) evasiva.
evasive [ɪ'veɪsɪv] *adj* evasivo.
eve [iːv] *n*: **on the** ~ **of** na véspera de.
even ['iːvn] *adj* (*level*) plano; (*smooth*) liso; (*speed, temperature*) uniforme; (*number*) par; (*nature*) equilibrado; (*SPORT*) igual ♦ *adv* até, mesmo; ~ **if** mesmo que; ~ **though**

mesmo que, embora; ~ **more** ainda mais; ~ **faster** ainda mais rápido, mais rápido ainda; ~ **so** mesmo assim; **never** ~ nem sequer; **not** ~ nem; ~ **he was there** até ele esteve ali; ~ **on Sundays** até nos domingos; **to get** ~ **with sb** ficar quite com alguém; **to break** ~ sair sem lucros nem prejuízos.

even out *vi* nivelar-se.

evening ['i:vnɪŋ] *n* noite *f*; (*before six*) tarde *f*; (*event*) noitada; **in the** ~ à noite; **this** ~ hoje à noite; **tomorrow/yesterday** ~ amanhã/ontem à noite.

evening class *n* aula noturna.

evening dress *n* (*man's*) traje *m* de rigor (*BR*) *or* de cerimónia (*PT*); (*woman's*) vestido de noite.

evenly ['i:vnlɪ] *adv* uniformemente; (*space*) regularmente; (*divide*) por igual.

evensong ['i:vnsɔŋ] *n* oração *f* da tarde.

event [ɪ'vɛnt] *n* acontecimento; (*SPORT*) prova; **in the course of ~s** no decorrer dos acontecimentos; **in the** ~ **of** no caso de; **in the** ~ de fato, na realidade; **at all ~s** (*BRIT*), **in any** ~ em todo o caso.

eventful [ɪ'vɛntful] *adj* cheio de acontecimentos; (*game etc*) cheio de emoção, agitado.

eventing [ɪ'vɛntɪŋ] *n* (*HORSERIDING*) concurso completo (*hipismo*).

eventual [ɪ'vɛntʃuəl] *adj* (*last*) final; (*resulting*) definitivo.

eventuality [ɪvɛntʃu'ælɪtɪ] *n* eventualidade *f*.

eventually [ɪ'vɛntʃuəlɪ] *adv* (*finally*) finalmente; (*in time*) por fim.

ever ['ɛvə*] *adv* já, alguma vez; (*in negative*) nunca, jamais; (*at all times*) sempre; **the best** ~ o melhor que já se viu; **have you** ~ **seen it?** você alguma vez já viu isto?; **better than** ~ melhor que nunca; **for** ~ para sempre; **hardly** ~ quase nunca; ~ **since** *adv* desde então ♦ *conj* depois que; ~ **so pretty** tão bonitinho; **thank you** ~ **so much** muitíssimo obrigado, obrigadão (*inf*); **yours** ~ (*BRIT*: *in letters*) sempre seu/sua.

Everest ['ɛvərɪst] *n* (*also*: *Mount* ~) o monte Everest.

evergreen ['ɛvəgri:n] *n* sempre-verde *f*.

everlasting [ɛvə'lɑ:stɪŋ] *adj* eterno, perpétuo.

every ['ɛvrɪ] *adj* (*each*) cada; (*all*) todo; ~ **day** todo dia; ~ **other/third day** cada dois/três dias; ~ **other car** cada dois carros; ~ **now and then** de vez em quando; ~ **3 weeks** de 3 em 3 semanas; **I have** ~ **confidence in him** tenho absoluta confiança nele.

everybody ['ɛvrɪbɔdɪ] *pron* todos, todo mundo (*BR*), toda a gente (*PT*); ~ **knows about it** todo o mundo já sabe; ~ **else** todos os outros.

everyday ['ɛvrɪdeɪ] *adj* (*daily*) diário; (*usual*) corrente; (*common*) comum; (*routine*) rotineiro.

everyone ['ɛvrɪwʌn] *pron* todos, todo o mundo (*BR*), toda a gente (*PT*).

everything ['ɛvrɪθɪŋ] *pron* tudo; ~ **is ready** tudo está pronto; **he did** ~ **possible** ele fez todo o possível.

everywhere ['ɛvrɪwɛə*] *adv* (*be*) em todo lugar (*BR*), em toda a parte (*PT*); (*go*) a todo lugar (*BR*), a toda a parte (*PT*); ~ **you go you meet** ... aonde quer que se vá, encontra-se ....

evict [ɪ'vɪkt] *vt* despejar.

eviction [ɪ'vɪkʃən] *n* despejo.

eviction notice *n* notificação *f* de despejo.

evidence ['ɛvɪdəns] *n* (*proof*) prova(s) *f*(*pl*); (*of witness*) testemunho, depoimento; (*facts*) dados *mpl*, evidência; **to give** ~ testemunhar, prestar depoimento; **in** ~ (*obvious*) em evidência, evidente.

evident ['ɛvɪdənt] *adj* evidente.

evidently ['ɛvɪdəntlɪ] *adv* evidentemente.

evil ['i:vl] *adj* mau/má; (*influence*) funesto; (*smell*) horrível ♦ *n* mal *m*, maldade *f*.

evildoer ['i:vldu:ə*] *n* malfeitor(a) *m/f*.

evince [ɪ'vɪns] *vt* evidenciar.

evocative [ɪ'vɔkətɪv] *adj* evocativo, sugestivo.

evoke [ɪ'vəuk] *vt* evocar.

evolution [i:və'lu:ʃən] *n* evolução *f*.

evolve [ɪ'vɔlv] *vt* desenvolver ♦ *vi* desenvolver-se.

ewe [ju:] *n* ovelha.

ex- [ɛks] *prefix* (*former*) ex-; (*out of*): **the price** ~ **works** o preço na porta da fábrica.

exacerbate [ɛks'æsəbeɪt] *vt* (*pain, illness*) exacerbar; (*fig*) agravar.

exact [ɪg'zækt] *adj* exato ♦ *vt*: **to** ~ **sth (from)** exigir algo (de).

exacting [ɪg'zæktɪŋ] *adj* exigente; (*conditions*) difícil.

exactitude [ɪg'zæktɪtju:d] *n* exatidão *f*.

exactly [ɪg'zæktlɪ] *adv* exatamente; (*time*) em ponto.

exaggerate [ɪg'zædʒəreɪt] *vt, vi* exagerar.

exaggeration [ɪgzædʒə'reɪʃən] *n* exagero.

exalted [ɪg'zɔ:ltɪd] *adj* exaltado.

exam [ɪg'zæm] *n abbr* = **examination**.

examination [ɪgzæmɪ'neɪʃən] *n* (*SCH, MED*) exame *m*; (*LAW*) inquirição *f*; (*inquiry*) investigação *f*; **to sit** (*BRIT*) *or* **take an** ~ submeter-se a um exame; **the matter is under** ~ o assunto está sendo examinado.

examine [ɪg'zæmɪn] *vt* examinar; (*inspect*) inspecionar; (*SCH, LAW*: *person*) interrogar; (*at customs*: *luggage*) revistar; (*passport*) controlar.

examiner [ɪg'zæmɪnə*] *n* examinador(a) *m/f*.

example [ɪg'zɑ:mpl] *n* exemplo; **for** ~ por exemplo; **to set a good/bad** ~ dar um bom/mau exemplo.

exasperate [ɪg'zɑ:spəreɪt] *vt* exasperar, irritar.

exasperating [ɪg'zɑ:spəreɪtɪŋ] *adj* irritante.

exasperation [ɪgzɑ:spə'reɪʃən] *n* exasperação *f*, irritação *f*.

excavate ['ɛkskəveɪt] *vt* escavar.

NB*: European Portuguese adds the following consonants to certain words:* **b** (sú(b)dito, su(b)til); **c** (a(c)ção, a(c)cionista, a(c)to); **m** (inde(m)ne); **p** (ado(p)ção, ado(p)tar); *for further details see p. xiii.*

excavation [ɛkskə'veɪʃən] *n* escavação *f*.
excavator ['ɛkskəveɪtə*] *n* (*machine*) escavadeira.
exceed [ɪk'si:d] *vt* exceder; (*number*) ser superior a; (*speed limit*) ultrapassar; (*limits*) ir além de; (*powers*) exceder-se em; (*hopes*) superar.
exceedingly [ɪk'si:dɪŋlɪ] *adv* extremamente.
excel [ɪk'sɛl] *vi* sobressair, distinguir-se ♦ *vt* superar; **to ~ o.s.** (*BRIT*) destacar-se.
excellence ['ɛksələns] *n* excelência.
Excellency ['ɛksələnsɪ] *n*: **His ~** Sua Excelência.
excellent ['ɛksələnt] *adj* excelente.
except [ɪk'sɛpt] *prep* (*also*: ~ *for*, ~*ing*) exceto, a não ser ♦ *vt* excetuar, excluir; **~ if/when** a menos que, a não ser que; **~ that** exceto que.
exception [ɪk'sɛpʃən] *n* exceção *f*; **to take ~ to** ressentir-se de; **with the ~ of** à exceção de; **to make an ~** fazer exceção.
exceptional [ɪk'sɛpʃənl] *adj* excepcional.
excerpt ['ɛksə:pt] *n* trecho.
excess [ɪk'sɛs] *n* excesso; (*COMM*) excedente *m*; **in ~ of** mais de.
excess baggage *n* excesso de bagagem.
excess fare *n* sobretaxa de excesso.
excessive [ɪk'sɛsɪv] *adj* excessivo.
excess supply *n* oferta excedente.
exchange [ɪks'tʃeɪndʒ] *n* permuta, câmbio; (*of goods*, *of ideas*) troca; (*also*: *telephone* ~) estação *f* telefônica (*BR*), central *f* telefónica (*PT*) ♦ *vt*: **to ~ (for)** trocar (por); **in ~ for** em troca de; **foreign ~** (*COMM*) divisas *fpl*, câmbio.
exchange control *n* controle *m* de câmbio.
exchange market *n* mercado cambial *or* de câmbio.
exchange rate *n* (taxa de) câmbio.
exchequer [ɪks'tʃɛkə*] (*BRIT*) *n* ≈ Tesouro Nacional.
excisable [ɪk'saɪzəbl] *adj* tributável.
excise [*n* 'ɛksaɪz, *vt* ɛk'saɪz] *n* imposto de consumo ♦ *vt* cortar (fora).
excise duties *npl* impostos *mpl* indiretos.
excitable [ɪk'saɪtəbl] *adj* excitável; (*edgy*) nervoso.
excite [ɪk'saɪt] *vt* (*stimulate*) excitar; (*awaken*) despertar; (*move*) entusiasmar; **to get ~d** entusiasmar-se.
excitement [ɪk'saɪtmənt] *n* emoções *fpl*; (*anticipation*) expectativa; (*agitation*) agitação *f*.
exciting [ɪk'saɪtɪŋ] *adj* emocionante, empolgante.
excl. *abbr* = **excluding**; **exclusive (of)**.
exclaim [ɪk'skleɪm] *vi* exclamar.
exclamation [ɛksklə'meɪʃən] *n* exclamação *f*.
exclamation mark *n* ponto de exclamação.
exclude [ɪk'sklu:d] *vt* excluir; (*except*) excetuar.
excluding [ɪk'sklu:dɪŋ] *prep*: **~ tax** imposto excluído.
exclusion [ɪk'sklu:ʒən] *n* exclusão *f*; **to the ~ of** a ponto de excluir.
exclusion clause *n* cláusula de exclusão.
exclusive [ɪk'sklu:sɪv] *adj* exclusivo; (*club*, *district*) privativo; (*item of news*) com exclusividade ♦ *adv* (*COMM*): **~ of tax** sem incluir os impostos; **~ of postage** tarifas postais excluídas; **from 1st to 15th March ~** entre o dia 1º e 15 de março; **~ rights** (*COMM*) exclusividade *f*.
exclusively [ɪk'sklu:sɪvlɪ] *adv* unicamente.
excommunicate [ɛkskə'mju:nɪkeɪt] *vt* excomungar.
excrement ['ɛkskrəmənt] *n* excremento.
excrete [ɪk'skri:t] *vi* excretar.
excruciating [ɪk'skru:ʃɪeɪtɪŋ] *adj* (ex)cruciante, torturante.
excursion [ɪk'skə:ʃən] *n* excursão *f*.
excursion ticket *n* passagem *f* de excursão.
excusable [ɪk'skju:zəbl] *adj* perdoável, excusável.
excuse [*n* ɪk'skju:s, *vt* ik'skju:z] *n* desculpa; (*evasion*) pretexto ♦ *vt* desculpar, perdoar; **to ~ sb from doing sth** dispensar alguém de fazer algo; **~ me!** (*calling attention*) desculpe!; (*asking permission*) (com) licença; **if you will ~ me** com a sua licença; **to make ~s for sb** apresentar desculpas por alguém; **to ~ o.s. for sth/for doing sth** desculpar-se de algo/de fazer algo.
ex-directory (*BRIT*) *adj*: **~ (phone) number** número que não figura na lista telefônica.
execute ['ɛksɪkju:t] *vt* (*plan*) realizar; (*order*) cumprir; (*person*) executar.
execution [ɛksɪ'kju:ʃən] *n* realização *f*; (*killing*) execução *f*.
executioner [ɛksɪ'kju:ʃənə*] *n* verdugo, carrasco.
executive [ɪg'zɛkjutɪv] *n* (*COMM*, *POL*) executivo ♦ *adj* executivo.
executive director *n* diretor(a) *m/f* executivo/a.
executor [ɪg'zɛkjutə*] *n* executor(a) *m/f* testamentário/a, testamenteiro/a.
exemplary [ɪg'zɛmplərɪ] *adj* exemplar.
exemplify [ɪg'zɛmplɪfaɪ] *vt* exemplificar.
exempt [ɪg'zɛmpt] *adj*: **~ from** isento de ♦ *vt*: **to ~ sb from** dispensar *or* isentar alguém de.
exemption [ɪg'zɛmpʃən] *n* (*from taxes etc*) isenção *f*; (*from military service*) dispensa; (*immunity*) imunidade *f*.
exercise ['ɛksəsaɪz] *n* exercício ♦ *vt* exercer; (*right*) valer-se de; (*dog*) levar para passear ♦ *vi* (*also*: *to take* ~) fazer exercício.
exercise book *n* caderno.
exert [ɪg'zə:t] *vt* exercer; **to ~ o.s.** esforçar-se, empenhar-se.
exertion [ɪg'zə:ʃən] *n* esforço.
ex gratia [-'greɪʃə] *adj*: **~ payment** gratificação *f*.
exhale [ɛks'heɪl] *vt*, *vi* expirar.
exhaust [ɪg'zɔ:st] *n* (*pipe*) escape *m*, exaustor *m*; (*fumes*) escapamento (de gás) ♦ *vt* esgotar; **to ~ o.s.** esgotar-se; **~ manifold** (*AUT etc*) cano de descarga.
exhausted [ɪg'zɔ:stɪd] *adj* esgotado.
exhausting [ɪg'zɔ:stɪŋ] *adj* exaustivo, esta-

fante.

exhaustion [ɪg'zɔːstʃən] *n* exaustão *f*.

exhaustive [ɪg'zɔːstɪv] *adj* exaustivo.

exhibit [ɪg'zɪbɪt] *n* (*ART*) obra exposta; (*LAW*) objeto exposto ♦ *vt* (*courage etc*) manifestar, mostrar; (*emotion*) demonstrar; (*film*) apresentar; (*paintings*) expor.

exhibition [ɛksɪ'bɪʃən] *n* exposição *f*.

exhibitionist [ɛksɪ'bɪʃənɪst] *n* exibicionista *m/f*.

exhibitor [ɪg'zɪbɪtə*] *n* expositor(a) *m/f*.

exhilarating [ɪg'zɪləreɪtɪŋ] *adj* estimulante, tônico.

exhilaration [ɪgzɪlə'reɪʃən] *n* euforia.

exhort [ɪg'zɔːt] *vt* exortar.

exile ['ɛksaɪl] *n* exílio; (*person*) exilado/a ♦ *vt* desterrar, exilar; **in ~** em exílio, exilado.

exist [ɪg'zɪst] *vi* existir; (*live*) viver.

existence [ɪg'zɪstəns] *n* existência; (*life*) vida; **to be in ~** existir.

existentialism [ɛgzɪs'tɛnʃlɪzəm] *n* existencialismo.

existing [ɪg'zɪstɪŋ] *adj* (*laws*) existente; (*system, regime*) atual.

exit ['ɛksɪt] *n* saída ♦ *vi* (*COMPUT, THEATRE*) sair.

exit ramp (*US*) *n* (*AUT*) saída da rodovia.

exit visa *n* visto de saída.

exodus ['ɛksədəs] *n* êxodo.

ex officio [-ə'fɪʃɪəu] *adj, adv* ex-officio, por dever do cargo.

exonerate [ɪg'zɔnəreɪt] *vt*: **to ~ from** absolver de.

exorbitant [ɪg'zɔːbɪtənt] *adj* exorbitante.

exorcize ['ɛksɔːsaɪz] *vt* exorcizar.

exotic [ɪg'zɔtɪk] *adj* exótico.

expand [ɪk'spænd] *vt* (*widen*) ampliar; (*number*) aumentar; (*influence etc*) estender ♦ *vi* (*population, production*) aumentar; (*trade, gas, etc*) expandir-se; (*metal*) dilatar-se; **to ~ on** (*notes, story etc*) estender-se sobre.

expanse [ɪk'spæns] *n* extensão *f*.

expansion [ɪk'spænʃən] *n* (*of town*) desenvolvimento; (*of trade*) expansão *f*; (*of population*) aumento; (*of metal*) dilatação *f*.

expansionism [ɪk'spænʃənɪzəm] *n* expansionismo.

expansionist [ɪk'spænʃənɪst] *adj* expansionista.

expatriate [*n* ɛks'pætrɪət, *vt* ɛks'pætrɪeɪt] *n* expatriado/a ♦ *vt* expatriar.

expect [ɪk'spɛkt] *vt* (*gen*) esperar; (*count on*) contar com; (*suppose*) supor; (*require*) exigir ♦ *vi*: **to be ~ing** estar grávida; **to ~ sb to do** (*anticipate*) esperar que alguém faça; (*demand*) esperar de alguém que faça; **to ~ to do sth** esperar fazer algo; **as ~ed** como previsto; **I ~ so** suponho que sim.

expectancy [ɪks'pɛktənsɪ] *n* expectativa; **life ~** expectativa de vida.

expectant [ɪk'spɛktənt] *adj* expectante; **~ mother** gestante *f*.

expectantly [ɪk'spɛktəntlɪ] *adv* cheio de expectativa.

expectation [ɛkspɛk'teɪʃən] *n* esperança, expectativa; **in ~ of** na expectativa de; **against** *or* **contrary to all ~(s)** contra todas as expectativas; **to come** *or* **live up to one's ~s** corresponder à expectativa de alguém.

expedience [ɛk'spiːdɪəns] *n* conveniência; **for the sake of ~** por ser mais conveniente.

expediency [ɛk'spiːdɪənsɪ] *n* = **expedience**.

expedient [ɛk'spiːdɪənt] *adj* conveniente, oportuno ♦ *n* expediente *m*, recurso.

expedite ['ɛkspədaɪt] *vt* acelerar.

expedition [ɛkspə'dɪʃən] *n* expedição *f*.

expeditionary force [ɛkspə'dɪʃənrɪ-] *n* força expedicionária.

expeditious [ɛkspə'dɪʃəs] *adj* eficiente.

expel [ɪk'spɛl] *vt* expelir; (*SCH*) expulsar.

expend [ɪk'spɛnd] *vt* gastar; (*use up*) consumir.

expendable [ɪk'spɛndəbl] *adj* prescindível.

expenditure [ɪk'spɛndɪtʃə*] *n* gastos *mpl*.

expense [ɪk'spɛns] *n* gasto, despesa; (*high cost*) custo; **~s** *npl* (*COMM*: *costs*) despesas *fpl*; (: *paid to employee*) ajuda de custo; **at the ~ of** à custa de; **to go to the ~ of** fazer a despesa de; **to meet the ~ of** arcar com a despesa de.

expense account *n* relatório de despesas.

expensive [ɪk'spɛnsɪv] *adj* caro.

experience [ɪk'spɪərɪəns] *n* experiência ♦ *vt* experimentar; (*suffer*) sofrer; **to learn by ~** aprender com a experiência.

experienced [ɪk'spɪərɪənst] *adj* experimentado, experiente.

experiment [ɪk'spɛrɪmənt] *n* experimento, experiência ♦ *vi* fazer experiências.

experimental [ɪkspɛrɪ'mɛntl] *adj* experimental.

expert ['ɛkspəːt] *adj* hábil, perito ♦ *n* perito/a; (*specialist*) especialista *m/f*; **~ in** *or* **at doing sth** perito em fazer algo; **an ~ on sth** um perito em algo; **~ witness** (*LAW*) perito/a.

expertise [ɛkspəː'tiːz] *n* perícia.

expire [ɪk'spaɪə*] *vi* (*gen*) expirar; (*end*) terminar; (*run out*) vencer.

expiry [ɪk'spaɪərɪ] *n* expiração *f*, vencimento.

explain [ɪk'spleɪn] *vt* explicar; (*clarify*) esclarecer; (*demonstrate*) expor.

explain away *vt* justificar.

explanation [ɛksplə'neɪʃən] *n* explicação *f*; **to find an ~ for sth** achar uma explicação para algo.

explanatory [ɪk'splænətrɪ] *adj* explicativo.

explicit [ɪk'splɪsɪt] *adj* explícito.

explode [ɪk'spləud] *vi* estourar, explodir; (*with anger*) rebentar ♦ *vt* detonar, fazer explodir; (*fig*: *theory*) derrubar; (: *myth*) destruir.

exploit [*n* 'ɛksplɔɪt, *vt* ɪk'splɔɪt] *n* façanha ♦ *vt* explorar.

exploitation [ɛksplɔɪ'teɪʃən] *n* exploração *f*.

exploration [ɛksplə'reɪʃən] *n* exploração *f*.
exploratory [ɪk'splɔrətrɪ] *adj* (*fig*: *talks*) exploratório, de pesquisa; (*MED*: *operation*) exploratório.
explore [ɪk'splɔː*] *vt* explorar; (*fig*) examinar, pesquisar.
explorer [ɪk'splɔːrə*] *n* explorador(a) *m/f*.
explosion [ɪk'spləuʒən] *n* explosão *f*.
explosive [ɪk'spləusɪv] *adj*, *n* explosivo.
exponent [ɪk'spəunənt] *n* representante *m/f*, expoente *m/f*; (*MATH*) expoente *m*.
export [*vt* ɛk'spɔːt, *n*, *cpd* 'ɛkspɔːt] *vt* exportar ♦ *n* exportação *f* ♦ *cpd* de exportação.
exportation [ɛkspɔː'teɪʃən] *n* exportação *f*.
exporter [ɛk'spɔːtə*] *n* exportador(a) *m/f*.
export licence *n* licença de exportação.
expose [ɪk'spəuz] *vt* expor; (*unmask*) desmascarar.
exposed [ɪk'spəuzd] *adj* exposto; (*position*) desabrigado; (*wire*) descascado; (*pipes*, *beams*) aparente.
exposition [ɛkspə'zɪʃən] *n* exposição *f*.
exposure [ɪk'spəuʒə*] *n* exposição *f*; (*PHOT*) revelação *f*; (: *shot*) fotografia; **to die from ~** (*MED*) morrer de frio.
exposure meter *n* fotômetro.
expound [ɪk'spaund] *vt* expor, explicar.
express [ɪk'sprɛs] *adj* (*definite*) expresso, explícito; (*BRIT*: *letter etc*) urgente ♦ *n* (*train*) rápido ♦ *adv* (*send*) por via expressa ♦ *vt* exprimir, expressar; **to ~ o.s.** expressar-se.
expression [ɪk'sprɛʃən] *n* expressão *f*.
expressionism [ɪk'sprɛʃənɪzəm] *n* expressionismo.
expressive [ɪk'sprɛsɪv] *adj* expressivo.
expressly [ɪk'sprɛslɪ] *adv* expressamente.
expressway [ɪk'sprɛsweɪ] (*US*) *n* rodovia (*BR*), auto-estrada (*PT*).
expropriate [ɛks'prəuprɪeɪt] *vt* expropriar.
expulsion [ɪk'spʌlʃən] *n* expulsão *f*.
exquisite [ɛk'skwɪzɪt] *adj* requintado.
ex-serviceman (*irreg*) *n* veterano (de guerra).
ext. *abbr* (*TEL*: = *extension*) r. (*BR*), int. (*PT*).
extemporize [ɪk'stɛmpəraɪz] *vi* improvisar.
extend [ɪk'stɛnd] *vt* (*visit*, *street*) prolongar; (*building*) aumentar; (*offer*) fazer; (*COMM*: *credit*) conceder; (: *period of loan*) prorrogar ♦ *vi* (*land*) estender-se.
extension [ɪk'stɛnʃən] *n* extensão *f*; (*building*) acréscimo, expansão *f*; (*TEL*) ramal *m* (*BR*), extensão *f* (*PT*); (*of deadline*) prolongamento, prorrogação *f*.
extension cable *n* cabo de extensão.
extensive [ɪk'stɛnsɪv] *adj* extenso; (*damage*) considerável; (*broad*) vasto, amplo; (*frequent*) geral, comum.
extensively [ɪk'stɛnsɪvlɪ] *adv* (*altered*, *damaged etc*) amplamente; **he's travelled ~** ele já viajou bastante.
extent [ɪk'stɛnt] *n* (*breadth*) extensão *f*; (*of damage etc*) dimensão *f*; (*scope*) alcance *m*; **to some** *or* **to a certain ~** até certo ponto; **to the ~ of** ... a ponto de ...; **to a large ~** em grande parte; **to what ~?** até que ponto?; **to such an ~ that** ... a tal ponto que ...; **debts to the ~ of £5,000** dívidas da ordem de £5,000.
extenuating [ɪks'tɛnjueɪtɪŋ]: **~ circumstances** circunstâncias *fpl* atenuantes.
exterior [ɛk'stɪərɪə*] *adj* exterior, externo ♦ *n* exterior *m*; (*appearance*) aspecto.
exterminate [ɪk'stəːmɪneɪt] *vt* exterminar.
extermination [ɪkstəːmɪ'neɪʃən] *n* extermínio.
external [ɛk'stəːnl] *adj* externo; (*foreign*) exterior ♦ *n*: **the ~s** as aparências; **for ~ use only** (*MED*) exclusivamente para uso externo.
externally [ɛk'stəːnəlɪ] *adv* por fora.
extinct [ɪk'stɪŋkt] *adj* extinto.
extinction [ɪk'stɪŋkʃən] *n* extinção *f*.
extinguish [ɪk'stɪŋgwɪʃ] *vt* extinguir.
extinguisher [ɪk'stɪŋgwɪʃə*] *n* extintor *m*.
extol [ɪk'stəul] (*US* **extoll**) *vt* (*merits*) exaltar; (*person*) elogiar.
extort [ɪk'stɔːt] *vt*: **to ~ sth (from sb)** extorquir algo (a *or* de alguém).
extortion [ɪk'stɔːʃən] *n* extorsão *f*.
extortionate [ɪk'stɔːʃnət] *adj* extorsivo, excessivo.
extra ['ɛkstrə] *adj* adicional; (*excessive*) de mais, extra; (*bonus*: *payment*) extraordinário ♦ *adv* (*in addition*) adicionalmente ♦ *n* (*addition*) extra *m*, suplemento; (*THEATRE*) figurante *m/f*; (*newspaper*) edição *f* extra; **the wine will cost ~** o vinho não está incluído no preço; **~ large sizes** tamanhos extra grandes.
extra... [ɛkstrə] *prefix* extra....
extract [*vt* ɪk'strækt, *n* 'ɛkstrækt] *vt* tirar, extrair; (*tooth*) arrancar; (*confession*) arrancar, obter ♦ *n* extrato.
extraction [ɪk'strækʃən] *n* extração *f*; (*of tooth*) arrancamento; (*descent*) descendência.
extracurricular ['ɛkstrəkə'rɪkjulə*] *adj* (*SCH*) extracurricular.
extradite ['ɛkstrədaɪt] *vt* (*from country*) extraditar; (*to country*) obter a extradição de.
extradition [ɛkstrə'dɪʃən] *n* extradição *f*.
extramarital [ɛkstrə'mærɪtl] *adj* extramatrimonial.
extramural [ɛkstrə'mjuərl] *adj* (*course*) de extensão universitária.
extraneous [ɛk'streɪnɪəs] *adj*: **~ to** alheio a.
extraordinary [ɪk'strɔːdnrɪ] *adj* extraordinário; (*odd*) estranho.
extraordinary general meeting *n* assembléia geral extraordinária.
extrapolation [ɛkstræpə'leɪʃən] *n* extrapolação *f*.
extrasensory perception ['ɛkstrə'sɛnsərɪ-] *n* percepção *f* extra-sensorial.
extra time *n* (*FOOTBALL*) prorrogação *f*.
extravagance [ɪk'strævəgəns] *n* extravagância; (*spending*) esbanjamento.
extravagant [ɪk'strævəgənt] *adj* (*lavish*) extravagante; (*wasteful*) gastador(a), esbanjador(a); (*price*) exorbitante; (*praise*) excessivo; (*odd*) excêntrico, estranho.

extreme [ɪk'striːm] *adj* extremo; (*case*) excessivo ♦ *n* extremo, extremidade *f*; **the ~ left/right** (*POL*) a extrema esquerda/direita; **~s of temperature** temperaturas extremas.

extremely [ɪk'striːmlɪ] *adv* muito, extremamente.

extremist [ɪk'striːmɪst] *adj*, *n* extremista *m/f*.

extremity [ɪk'strɛmətɪ] *n* extremidade *f*; (*need*) apuro, necessidade *f*.

extricate ['ɛkstrɪkeɪt] *vt*: **to ~ sth (from)** soltar algo (de).

extrovert ['ɛkstrəvəːt] *n* extrovertido/a.

exuberance [ɪg'zjuːbərəns] *n* exuberância.

exuberant [ɪg'zjuːbərnt] *adj* (*person*) eufórico; (*style*) exuberante.

exude [ɪg'zjuːd] *vt* exsudar; (*fig*) esbanjar; **the charm** *etc* **he ~s** o charme *etc* que emana dele.

exult [ɪg'zʌlt] *vi* regozijar-se.

exultant [ɪg'zʌltənt] *adj* exultante, triunfante.

exultation [ɛgzʌl'teɪʃən] *n* exultação *f*, regozijo.

eye [aɪ] *n* olho; (*of needle*) buraco ♦ *vt* olhar, observar; **as far as the ~ can see** a perder de vista; **to keep an ~ on** vigiar, ficar de olho em; **to have an ~ for sth** ter faro para algo; **in the public ~** conhecido pelo público; **with an ~ to doing** (*BRIT*) com vista a fazer; **there's more to this than meets the ~** a coisa é mais complicada do que parece.

eyeball ['aɪbɔːl] *n* globo ocular.

eyebath ['aɪbɑːθ] (*BRIT*) *n* copinho (*para lavar o olho*).

eyebrow ['aɪbrau] *n* sobrancelha.

eyebrow pencil *n* lápis *m* de sobrancelha.

eye-catching *adj* chamativo, vistoso.

eye cup (*US*) *n* copinho (*para lavar o olho*).

eyedrops ['aɪdrɔps] *npl* gotas *fpl* para os olhos.

eyeglass ['aɪglɑːs] *n* monóculo; **~es** *npl* (*US*) óculos *mpl*.

eyelash ['aɪlæʃ] *n* cílio.

eyelet ['aɪlɪt] *n* ilhós *m*.

eye-level *adj* à altura dos olhos.

eyelid ['aɪlɪd] *n* pálpebra.

eyeliner ['aɪlaɪnə*] *n* delineador *m*.

eye-opener *n* revelação *f*, grande surpresa.

eyeshadow ['aɪʃædəu] *n* sombra de olhos.

eyesight ['aɪsaɪt] *n* vista, visão *f*.

eyesore ['aɪsɔː*] *n* monstruosidade *f*.

eyestrain ['aɪstreɪn] *n* cansaço ocular.

eyetooth ['aɪtuːθ] (*irreg*) *n* dente *m* canino superior; **to give one's eyeteeth for sth/to do sth** (*fig*) dar tudo por algo/para fazer algo.

eyewash ['aɪwɔʃ] *n* colírio; (*fig*) disparates *mpl*, maluquices *fpl*.

eye witness *n* testemunha *f* ocular.

eyrie ['ɪərɪ] *n* ninho de ave de rapina.

F

F, f [ɛf] *n* (*letter*) F, f *m*; (*MUS*): **F** fá *m*; **F for Frederick** (*BRIT*) *or* **Fox** (*US*) F de Francisco.

F *abbr* = **Fahrenheit**.

FA (*BRIT*) *n abbr* (= *Football Association*) *confederação de futebol*.

FAA (*US*) *n abbr* = **Federal Aviation Administration**.

fable ['feɪbl] *n* fábula.

fabric ['fæbrɪk] *n* tecido, pano; (*of building*) estrutura.

fabricate ['fæbrɪkeɪt] *vt* inventar.

fabrication [fæbrɪ'keɪʃən] *n* invencionice *f*.

fabric conditioner *n* amaciante *m* de pano.

fabulous ['fæbjuləs] *adj* fabuloso; (*inf*: *super*) sensacional.

façade [fə'sɑːd] *n* fachada.

face [feɪs] *n* (*ANAT*) cara, rosto; (*grimace*) careta; (*of clock*) mostrador *m*; (*side, surface*) superfície *f* ♦ *vt* (*person, reality, facts*) encarar; (*subj*: *building*) dar para, ter frente para; (*problems*) enfrentar; **to lose ~** perder o prestígio; **to save ~** salvar as aparências, livrar a cara; **to pull a ~** fazer careta; **in the ~ of** (*difficulties etc*) diante de, à vista de; **on the ~ of it** a julgar pelas aparências, à primeira vista; **~ to ~** cara a cara; **~ down** (*person*) de bruços; (*card*) virado para baixo; **we are ~d with serious problems** estamos enfrentando sérios problemas, temos sérios problemas pela frente.

face up to *vt fus* enfrentar.

face cloth (*BRIT*) *n* pano de rosto.

face cream *n* creme *m* facial.

face lift *n* (operação *f*) plástica; (*of façade*) remodelamento.

face powder *n* pó *m* de arroz.

face-saving *adj* para salvar as aparências.

facet ['fæsɪt] *n* faceta.

facetious [fə'siːʃəs] *adj* engraçado, faceto.

face-to-face *adv* face a face, cara a cara.

face value *n* (*of stamp*) valor *m* nominal; **to take sth at ~** (*fig*) tomar algo em sentido literal.

facia ['feɪʃə] *n* = **fascia**.

facial ['feɪʃəl] *adj* facial.

facile ['fæsaɪl] *adj* superficial.

facilitate [fə'sɪlɪteɪt] *vt* facilitar.

facility [fə'sɪlɪtɪ] *n* facilidade *f*; **facilities** *npl* facilidades *fpl*, instalações *fpl*; **credit facilities** crediário.

facing ['feɪsɪŋ] *prep* de frente para ♦ *n* (*of wall etc*) revestimento; (*SEWING*) forro.

***NB:** European Portuguese adds the following consonants to certain words:* **b** (sú(b)dito, su(b)til); **c** (a(c)ção, a(c)cionista, a(c)to); **m** (inde(m)ne); **p** (ado(p)ção, ado(p)tar); *for further details see p. xiii.*

facsimile [fæk'sımılı] *n* (*copy, machine, document*) fac-símile *m*.
fact [fækt] *n* fato; **in ~** realmente, na verdade; **to know for a ~ that ...** saber com certeza que ...; **~s and figures** dados e números.
fact-finding *adj*: **a ~ tour** *or* **mission** uma missão de pesquisa.
faction ['fækʃən] *n* facção *f*.
factor ['fæktə*] *n* fator *m*; (*COMM*) comissário financiador, empresa que compra contas a receber; (: *agent*) corretor(a) *m/f* ♦ *vi* comprar contas a receber; **safety ~** fator de segurança.
factory ['fæktərı] *n* fábrica.
factory farming (*BRIT*) *n* criação *f* intensiva.
factory ship *n* navio-fábrica *m*.
factual ['fæktjuəl] *adj* real, fatual.
faculty ['fækəltı] *n* faculdade *f*; (*US*: *teaching staff*) corpo docente.
fad [fæd] (*inf*) *n* mania, modismo.
fade [feıd] *vi* (*colour, cloth*) desbotar; (*sound, hope*) desvanecer-se; (*light*) apagar-se; (*flower*) murchar.
fade in *vt* (*sound*) subir; (*picture*) clarear.
fade out *vt* (*sound*) abaixar; (*picture*) escurecer.
faeces ['fi:si:z] (*US* **feces**) *npl* fezes *fpl*.
fag [fæg] (*inf*) *n* (*cigarette*) cigarro; (*US*: *homosexual*) bicha; (*chore*): **what a ~!** que saco!
fag end (*BRIT*: *inf*) *n* ponta de cigarro, guimba.
fagged out [fægd-] (*BRIT*: *inf*) *adj* estafado.
fail [feıl] *vt* (*candidate*) reprovar; (*exam*) não passar em, ser reprovado em ♦ *vi* (*person*) fracassar; (*business*) falir; (*supply*) acabar; (*engine, brakes, voice*) falhar; (*patient*) enfraquecer-se; **to ~ to do sth** (*neglect*) deixar de fazer algo; (*be unable*) não conseguir fazer algo; **without ~** sem falta.
failing ['feılıŋ] *n* defeito ♦ *prep* na *or* à falta de; **~ that** senão.
failsafe ['feılseıf] *adj* (*device etc*) de segurança contra falhas.
failure ['feıljə*] *n* fracasso; (*in exam*) reprovação *f*; (*of crop*) perda; (*mechanical etc*) falha; **his ~ to turn up** o fato dele não ter vindo; **heart ~** parada cardíaca; **~ rate** taxa de reprovados.
faint [feınt] *adj* fraco; (*recollection*) vago; (*mark*) indistinto; (*smell, trace*) leve; (*dizzy*) tonto ♦ *n* desmaio ♦ *vi* desmaiar.
faint-hearted *adj* pusilânime.
faintly ['feıntlı] *adv* indistintamente, vagamente.
faintness ['feıntnıs] *n* fraqueza.
fair [fɛə*] *adj* justo; (*colour*: *hair*) louro; (: *complexion*) branco; (*weather*) bom; (*good enough*) razoável; (*sizeable*) considerável ♦ *adv*: **to play ~** fazer jogo limpo ♦ *n* feira; (*BRIT*: *funfair*) parque *m* de diversões; **a ~ amount of time** bastante tempo; **it's not ~!** não é justo!
fair copy *n* cópia a limpo.
fair-haired *adj* (de cabelo) louro.
fairly ['fɛəlı] *adv* (*justly*) com justiça; (*share*) igualmente; (*quite*) bastante; **I'm ~ sure** tenho quase certeza.
fairness ['fɛənıs] *n* justiça; (*impartiality*) imparcialidade *f*; **in all ~** com toda a justiça.
fair play *n* jogo limpo.
fairy ['fɛərı] *n* fada.
fairy godmother *n* fada-madrinha.
fairy lights (*BRIT*) *npl* lâmpadas *fpl* coloridas de enfeite.
fairy tale *n* conto de fadas.
faith [feıθ] *n* fé *f*; (*trust*) confiança; (*denomination*) seita; **to have ~ in sb/sth** ter fé *or* confiança em alguém/algo.
faithful ['feıθful] *adj* fiel.
faithfully ['feıθfulı] *adv* fielmente; **yours ~** (*BRIT*: *in letters*) atenciosamente.
faith healer *n* curandeiro/a.
fake [feık] *n* (*painting etc*) falsificação *f*; (*person*) impostor(a) *m/f* ♦ *adj* falso ♦ *vt* fingir; (*painting etc*) falsificar; **his illness is a ~** sua doença é fingimento *or* um embuste.
falcon ['fɔ:lkən] *n* falcão *m*.
Falkland Islands ['fɔ:lklənd-] *npl*: **the ~** as (ilhas) Malvinas *or* Falkland.
fall [fɔ:l] (*pt* **fell**, *pp* **fallen**) *n* queda; (*US*: *autumn*) outono ♦ *vi* cair; (*price*) baixar; **~s** *npl* (*waterfall*) cascata, queda d'água; **to ~ flat** (*on one's face*) cair de cara no chão; (*plan*) falhar; (*joke*) não agradar; **to ~ short of** (*sb's expectations*) não corresponder a, ficar abaixo de; **a ~ of snow** (*BRIT*) uma nevasca.
fall apart *vi* cair aos pedaços; (*inf*: *emotionally*) descontrolar-se completamente.
fall back *vi* retroceder.
fall back on *vt fus* (*remedy etc*) recorrer a.
fall behind *vi* ficar para trás.
fall down *vi* (*person*) cair; (*building*) desabar; (*hopes*) cair por terra.
fall for *vt fus* (*trick*) cair em; (*person*) enamorar-se de.
fall in *vi* (*roof*) ruir; (*MIL*) alinhar-se.
fall in with *vt fus* (*sb's plans etc*) conformar-se com.
fall off *vi* cair; (*diminish*) declinar, diminuir.
fall out *vi* (*friends etc*) brigar; (*MIL*) sair da fila.
fall over *vi* cair por terra, tombar.
fall through *vi* (*plan, project*) furar.
fallacy ['fæləsı] *n* (*error*) erro; (*lie*) mentira, falácia.
fallback ['fɔ:lbæk] *adj*: **~ position** alternativa.
fallen ['fɔ:lən] *pp of* **fall**.
fallible ['fæləbl] *adj* falível.
falling-off ['fɔ:lıŋ-] *n* declínio.
fallopian tube [fə'ləupıən-] *n* (*ANAT*) trompa de Falópio.
fallout ['fɔ:laut] *n* chuva radioativa.
fallout shelter *n* refúgio contra chuva radioativa.
fallow ['fæləu] *adj* alqueivado, de pousio.
false [fɔ:ls] *adj* falso; (*hair, teeth etc*) postiço;

(*disloyal*) desleal, traidor(a); **under ~ pretences** sob falsos pretextos.
false alarm *n* alarme *m* falso.
falsehood ['fɔːlshud] *n* (*lie*) mentira; (*falseness*) falsidade *f*.
falsely ['fɔːlslɪ] *adv* falsamente.
false teeth (BRIT) *npl* dentadura postiça.
falsify ['fɔːlsɪfaɪ] *vt* falsificar.
falter ['fɔːltə*] *vi* vacilar.
fame [feɪm] *n* fama.
familiar [fə'mɪlɪə*] *adj* (*well-known*) conhecido; (*tone*) familiar, íntimo; **to be ~ with** (*subject*) estar familiarizado com; **to make o.s. ~ with sth** familiarizar-se com algo; **to be on ~ terms with sb** ter intimidade com alguém.
familiarity [fəmɪlɪ'ærɪtɪ] *n* familiaridade *f*.
familiarize [fə'mɪlɪəraɪz] *vt*: **to ~ o.s. with** familiarizar-se com.
family ['fæmɪlɪ] *n* família.
family allowance (BRIT) *n* abono-família *m*.
family business *n* negócio familiar.
family doctor *n* médico/a da família.
family life *n* vida familiar.
family planning *n* planejamento familiar; **~ clinic** clínica de planejamento familiar.
family tree *n* árvore *f* genealógica.
famine ['fæmɪn] *n* fome *f*.
famished ['fæmɪʃt] *adj* faminto; **I'm ~!** (*inf*) estou morrendo de fome.
famous ['feɪməs] *adj* famoso, célebre.
famously ['feɪməslɪ] *adv* (*get on*) maravilhosamente.
fan [fæn] *n* (*hand-held*) leque *m*; (ELEC) ventilador *m*; (*person*) fã (PT: fan) *m/f*; (SPORT) torcedor(a) *m/f* (BR), adepto/a (PT) ♦ *vt* abanar; (*fire, quarrel*) atiçar.
 fan out *vi* espalhar-se.
fanatic [fə'nætɪk] *n* fanático/a.
fanatical [fə'nætɪkəl] *adj* fanático.
fan belt *n* correia do ventilador (BR) *or* da ventoinha (PT).
fancied ['fænsɪd] *adj* imaginário.
fanciful ['fænsɪful] *adj* fantástico; (*imaginary*) imaginário.
fancy ['fænsɪ] *n* (*whim*) capricho; (*taste*) inclinação *f*, gosto; (*imagination*) imaginação *f* ♦ *adj* (*decorative*) ornamental; (*luxury*) luxuoso; (*as decoration*) como decoração ♦ *vt* (*feel like, want*) desejar, querer; (*imagine*) imaginar; **to take a ~ to** tomar gosto por; **it took** *or* **caught my ~** gostei disso; **when the ~ takes him** quando lhe dá na veneta; **to ~ that** ... imaginar que ...; **he fancies her** ele está a fim dela.
fancy dress *n* fantasia.
fancy-dress ball *n* baile *m* à fantasia.
fancy goods *npl* artigos *mpl* de fantasia.
fanfare ['fænfɛə*] *n* fanfarra.
fanfold paper ['fænfəuld-] *n* formulários *mpl* contínuos.
fang [fæŋ] *n* presa.
fan heater (BRIT) *n* aquecedor *m* de ventoinha.
fanlight ['fænlaɪt] *n* (*window*) basculante *f*.
fantasize ['fæntəsaɪz] *vi* fantasiar.
fantastic [fæn'tæstɪk] *adj* fantástico.
fantasy ['fæntəsɪ] *n* fantasia.
FAO *n abbr* (= *Food and Agriculture Organization*) FAO *f*.
FAQ *abbr* (= *free at quay*) posto no cais.
far [fɑː*] *adj* (*distant*) distante ♦ *adv* (*also ~ away*; *~ off*) longe; **the ~ side/end** o lado de lá/a outra ponta; **the ~ left/right** (POL) a extrema esquerda/direita; **is it ~ to London?** Londres é longe daqui?; **it's not ~ (from here)** não é longe (daqui); **~ better** muito melhor; **~ from** longe de; **by ~** de longe; **go as ~ as the farm** vá até a (BR) *or* à (PT) fazenda; **as ~ as I know** que eu saiba; **as ~ as possible** na medida do possível; **how ~?** até onde?; (*fig*) até que ponto?
faraway ['fɑːrəweɪ] *adj* remoto, distante.
farce [fɑːs] *n* farsa.
farcical ['fɑːsɪkəl] *adj* farsante.
fare [fɛə*] *n* (*on trains, buses*) preço (da passagem); (*in taxi: cost*) tarifa; (: *passenger*) passageiro/a; (*food*) comida ♦ *vi* sair-se.
Far East *n*: **the ~** o Extremo Oriente.
farewell [fɛə'wɛl] *excl* adeus ♦ *n* despedida ♦ *cpd* (*party etc*) de despedida.
far-fetched [-fɛtʃt] *adj* inverossímil.
farm [fɑːm] *n* fazenda (BR), quinta (PT) ♦ *vt* cultivar.
 farm out *vt* (*work etc*) dar de empreitada.
farmer ['fɑːmə*] *n* fazendeiro/a, agricultor *m*.
farmhand ['fɑːmhænd] *n* lavrador(a) *m/f*, trabalhador(a) *m/f* rural.
farmhouse ['fɑːmhaus] (*irreg*) *n* casa da fazenda (BR) *or* da quinta (PT).
farming ['fɑːmɪŋ] *n* agricultura; (*tilling*) cultura; **intensive ~** cultura intensiva; **sheep ~** criação de ovelhas, ovinocultura.
farm labourer *n* lavrador(a) *m/f*, trabalhador(a) *m/f* rural.
farmland ['fɑːmlænd] *n* terra de cultivo.
farm produce *n* produtos *mpl* agrícolas.
farm worker *n* lavrador(a) *m/f*, trabalhador(a) *m/f* rural.
farmyard ['fɑːmjɑːd] *n* curral *m*.
Faroe Islands ['fɛərəu-] *npl*: **the ~** as (ilhas) Faroë.
Faroes ['fɛərəuz] *npl* = **Faroe Islands**.
far-reaching [-'riːtʃɪŋ] *adj* de grande alcance, abrangente.
far-sighted *adj* presbita; (*fig*) previdente.
fart [fɑːt] (*inf!*) *n* peido (*!*) ♦ *vi* soltar um peido (*!*), peidar (*!*).
farther ['fɑːðə*] *adv* mais longe ♦ *adj* mais distante, mais afastado.
farthest ['fɑːðɪst] *superl of* **far**.
FAS (BRIT) *abbr* (= *free alongside ship*) FAS.
fascia ['feɪʃə] *n* (AUT) painel *m*.
fascinate ['fæsɪneɪt] *vt* fascinar.

NB*: European Portuguese adds the following consonants to certain words:* **b** (sú(b)dito, su(b)til); **c** (a(c)ção, a(c)cionista, a(c)to); **m** (inde(m)ne); **p** (ado(p)ção, ado(p)tar); *for further details see p. xiii.*

fascinating ['fæsɪneɪtɪŋ] *adj* fascinante.
fascination [fæsɪ'neɪʃən] *n* fascinação *f*, fascínio.
fascism ['fæʃɪzəm] *n* fascismo.
fascist ['fæʃɪst] *adj*, *n* fascista *m/f*.
fashion ['fæʃən] *n* moda; (*manner*) maneira ♦ *vt* amoldar; **in ~** na moda; **out of ~** fora da moda; **in the Greek ~** à grega, à maneira dos gregos; **after a ~** (*finish, manage etc*) até certo ponto.
fashionable ['fæʃənəbl] *adj* na moda, elegante; (*writer, café*) da moda.
fashion designer *n* estilista *m/f*.
fashion parade (*BRIT*) *n* desfile *m* de modas.
fashion show *n* desfile *m* de modas.
fast [fɑːst] *adj* rápido; (*dye, colour*) firme, permanente; (*PHOT*: *film*) de alta sensibilidade; (*clock*): **to be ~** estar adiantado ♦ *adv* rápido, rapidamente, depressa; (*stuck, held*) firmemente ♦ *n* jejum *m* ♦ *vi* jejuar; **my watch is 5 minutes ~** meu relógio está 5 minutos adiantado; **~ asleep** dormindo profundamente; **as ~ as I can** o mais rápido possível; **to make a boat ~** (*BRIT*) amarrar um barco.
fasten ['fɑːsn] *vt* fixar, prender; (*coat*) fechar; (*belt*) apertar, atar ♦ *vi* prender-se, fixar-se.
fasten (up)on *vt fus* (*idea*) agarrar-se a.
fastener ['fɑːsnə*] *n* presilha, fecho; (*of door etc*) fechadura; **zip ~** (*BRIT*) fecho ecler (*BR*) *or* éclair (*PT*).
fastening ['fɑːsnɪŋ] *n* presilha, fecho; (*of door etc*) fechadura.
fast food *n* fast food *f*.
fastidious [fæs'tɪdɪəs] *adj* (*fussy*) meticuloso; (*demanding*) exigente.
fast lane *n* (*AUT*) pista de velocidade.
fat [fæt] *adj* gordo; (*meat*) com muita gordura; (*greasy*) gorduroso ♦ *n* (*on person*) gordura; (*lard*) banha, gordura; **to live off the ~ of the land** viver na abundância.
fatal ['feɪtl] *adj* fatal; (*injury*) mortal; (*consequence*) funesto.
fatalism ['feɪtəlɪzəm] *n* fatalismo.
fatality [fə'tælɪtɪ] *n* (*road death etc*) vítima *m/f*.
fatally ['feɪtəlɪ] *adv*: **~ injured** mortalmente ferido.
fate [feɪt] *n* destino; (*of person*) sorte *f*.
fated ['feɪtɪd] *adj* (*person*) condenado; (*project*) fadado ao fracasso.
fateful ['feɪtful] *adj* fatídico.
father ['fɑːðə*] *n* pai *m*.
Father Christmas *n* Papai *m* Noel.
fatherhood ['fɑːðəhud] *n* paternidade *f*.
father-in-law (*pl* **fathers-in-law**) *n* sogro.
fatherland ['fɑːðəlænd] *n* pátria.
fatherly ['fɑːðəlɪ] *adj* paternal.
fathom ['fæðəm] *n* braça ♦ *vt* (*NAUT*) sondar; (*unravel*) penetrar, deslindar; (*understand*) compreender.
fatigue [fə'tiːg] *n* fadiga, cansaço; (*MIL*) faxina; **metal ~** fadiga do metal.
fatness ['fætnɪs] *n* gordura.
fatten ['fætn] *vt*, *vi* engordar; **chocolate is ~ing** o chocolate engorda.
fatty ['fætɪ] *adj* (*food*) gorduroso ♦ *n* (*inf*) gorducho/a.
fatuous ['fætjuəs] *adj* fátuo.
faucet ['fɔːsɪt] (*US*) *n* torneira.
fault [fɔːlt] *n* (*error*) defeito, falta; (*blame*) culpa; (*defect*) defeito; (*GEO*) falha ♦ *vt* criticar; **it's my ~** é minha culpa; **to find ~ with** criticar, queixar-se de; **at ~** culpado; **to a ~** em demasia.
faultless ['fɔːltlɪs] *adj* (*action*) impecável; (*person*) irrepreensível.
faulty ['fɔːltɪ] *adj* defeituoso.
fauna ['fɔːnə] *n* fauna.
faux pas ['fəu'pɑː] *n inv* gafe *f*.
favour ['feɪvə*] (*US* **favor**) *n* favor *m* ♦ *vt* (*proposition*) favorecer, aprovar; (*person etc*) favorecer; (*assist*) auxiliar; **to ask a ~ of** pedir um favor a; **to do sb a ~** fazer favor a alguém; **to be in ~ of sth/of doing sth** estar a favor de algo/de fazer algo; **to find ~ with** cair nas boas graças de; **in ~ of** em favor de.
favo(u)rable ['feɪuərəbl] *adj* favorável.
favo(u)rably ['feɪvərəblɪ] *adv* favoravelmente.
favo(u)rite ['feɪvərɪt] *adj* predileto ♦ *n* favorito/a.
favo(u)ritism ['feɪvərɪtɪzəm] *n* favoritismo.
fawn [fɔːn] *n* cervo novo, cervato ♦ *adj* (*also*: *~-coloured*) castanho-claro *inv* ♦ *vi*: **to ~ (up)on** bajular.
fax [fæks] *n* (*document, machine*) fax *m*, fac-símile *m* ♦ *vt* enviar por fax *or* fac-símile.
FBI (*US*) *n abbr* (= *Federal Bureau of Investigation*) FBI *m*.
FCC (*US*) *n abbr* = **Federal Communications Commission**.
FCO (*BRIT*) *n abbr* (= *Foreign and Commonwealth Office*) *ministério das Relações Exteriores*.
FD (*US*) *n abbr* = **fire department**.
FDA (*US*) *n abbr* (= *Food and Drug Administration*) *órgão controlador de medicamentos e gêneros alimentícios*.
fear [fɪə*] *n* medo; (*misgiving*) temor *m* ♦ *vt* ter medo de, temer ♦ *vi*: **to ~ for** recear *or* temer por; **to ~ that** temer que; **~ of heights** medo das alturas, vertigem *f*; **for ~ of** com medo de.
fearful ['fɪəful] *adj* medonho, temível; (*cowardly*) medroso; (*awful*) terrível; **to be ~ of** temer, ter medo de.
fearfully ['fɪəfəlɪ] *adv* (*timidly*) timidamente; (*inf*: *very*) muito, terrivelmente.
fearless ['fɪəlɪs] *adj* sem medo, intrépido; (*bold*) audaz.
fearsome ['fɪəsəm] *adj* (*opponent*) medonho, temível; (*sight*) espantoso.
feasibility [fiːzə'bɪlɪtɪ] *n* viabilidade *f*.
feasibility study *n* estudo de viabilidade.
feasible ['fiːzəbl] *adj* viável, praticável.
feast [fiːst] *n* banquete *m*; (*REL*: *also*: *~ day*) festa ♦ *vi* banquetear-se.
feat [fiːt] *n* façanha, feito.
feather ['fɛðə*] *n* pena ♦ *vt*: **to ~ one's nest**

(*fig*) acumular riquezas ♦ *cpd* (*bed etc*) de penas.
feather-weight *n* (*BOXING*) peso-pena *m*.
feature ['fi:tʃə*] *n* característica; (*ANAT*) feição *f*, traço; (*article*) reportagem *f* ♦ *vt* (*subj*: *film*) apresentar ♦ *vi* figurar; **~s** *npl* (*of face*) feições *fpl*; **it ~d prominently in ...** ocupou um lugar de destaque em ....
feature film *n* longa-metragem *m*.
featureless ['fi:tʃəlɪs] *adj* anônimo.
Feb. *abbr* (= *February*) fev.
February ['fɛbruərɪ] *n* fevereiro; *see also* **July**.
feces ['fi:si:z] (*US*) *npl* = **faeces**.
feckless ['fɛklɪs] *adj* displicente.
Fed (*US*) *abbr* = **federal**; **federation**.
fed [fɛd] *pt, pp of* **feed**; **to be ~ up** estar (de saco) cheio (*BR*), estar farto (*PT*).
Fed. [fɛd] (*US*: *inf*) *n abbr* = **Federal Reserve Board**.
federal ['fɛdərəl] *adj* federal.
Federal Reserve Board (*US*) *n órgão controlador do banco central dos EUA*.
Federal Trade Commission (*US*) *n órgão regulador de práticas comerciais*.
federation [fɛdə'reɪʃən] *n* federação *f*.
fee [fi:] *n* taxa (*BR*), propina (*PT*); (*of school*) matrícula; (*of doctor, lawyer*) honorários *mpl*; **entrance ~** (*to club*) jóia; (*to museum etc*) entrada; **membership ~** (*to join*) jóia; (*annual etc*) quota; **for a small ~** em troca de uma pequena taxa.
feeble ['fi:bl] *adj* fraco, débil.
feeble-minded *adj* imbecil.
feed [fi:d] (*pt, pp* **fed**) *n* comida; (*of baby*) alimento infantil; (*of animal*) ração *f*; (*on printer*) mecanismo alimentador ♦ *vt* (*gen, machine*) alimentar; (*baby*: *breastfeed*) amamentar; (*animal*) dar de comer a; (*data, information*): **to ~ into** introduzir em.
feed on *vt fus* alimentar-se de.
feedback ['fi:dbæk] *m* (*ELEC*) feedback *m*; (*from person*) reação *f*.
feeder ['fi:də*] *n* (*bib*) babador *m*.
feeding bottle ['fi:dɪŋ-] (*BRIT*) *n* mamadeira.
feel [fi:l] (*pt, pp* **felt**) *n* (*sensation*) sensação *f*; (*sense of touch*) tato ♦ *vt* (*touch*) tocar, apalpar; (*cold, pain etc*) sentir; (*think, believe*) achar, acreditar; **to get the ~ of sth** (*fig*) acostumar-se a algo; **to ~ (that)** achar (que); **I ~ that you ought to do it** eu acho que você deveria fazê-lo; **to ~ hungry/cold** estar com fome/frio (*BR*), ter fome/frio (*PT*); **to ~ lonely/better** sentir-se só/melhor; **to ~ sorry for** ter pena de; **it ~s soft** é macio; **it ~s colder here** sente-se mais frio aqui; **it ~s like velvet** parece veludo; **to ~ like** (*want*) querer; **to ~ about** *or* **around** apalpar, tatear; **I'm still ~ing my way** (*fig*) ainda estou me ambientando.
feeler ['fi:lə*] *n* (*of insect*) antena; **to put out ~s** *or* **a ~** (*fig*) sondar opiniões, lançar um balão-de-ensaio.
feeling ['fi:lɪŋ] *n* sensação *f*; (*foreboding*) pressentimento; (*opinion*) opinião *f*; (*emotion*) sentimento; **to hurt sb's ~s** magoar alguém; **~s ran high about it** os sentimentos se esquentaram a respeito disso; **what are your ~s about the matter?** qual é a sua opinião sobre o assunto?; **my ~ is that ...** eu acho que ...; **I have a ~ that ...** tenho a impressão de que ....
feet [fi:t] *npl of* **foot**.
feign [feɪn] *vt* fingir.
felicitous [fɪ'lɪsɪtəs] *adj* feliz.
feline ['fi:laɪn] *adj* felino.
fell [fɛl] *pt of* **fall** ♦ *vt* (*tree*) lançar por terra, derrubar ♦ *n* (*BRIT*: *mountain*) montanha; (: *moorland*): **the ~s** a charneca ♦ *adj*: **with one ~ blow** de um só golpe.
fellow ['fɛləu] *n* (*gen*) camarada *m/f*; (*inf*: *man*) cara *m* (*BR*), tipo (*PT*); (*of learned society*) membro; (*of university*) membro do conselho universitário ♦ *cpd*: **~ students** colegas *m/fpl* de curso; **his ~ workers** seus colegas de trabalho.
fellow citizen *n* concidadão/dã *m/f*.
fellow countryman (*irreg*) *n* compatriota *m*.
fellow feeling *n* simpatia.
fellow men *npl* semelhantes *mpl*.
fellowship ['fɛləuʃɪp] *n* (*comradeship*) amizade *f*; (*grant*) bolsa de estudo; (*society*) associação *f*.
fellow traveller (*US* **fellow traveler**) *n* companheiro/a de viagem; (*POL*) simpatizante *m/f*.
fell-walking (*BRIT*) *n* caminhadas *fpl* nas montanhas.
felon ['fɛlən] *n* (*LAW*) criminoso/a.
felony ['fɛlənɪ] *n* (*LAW*) crime *m*.
felt [fɛlt] *pt, pp of* **feel** ♦ *n* feltro.
felt-tip pen *n* caneta pilot ® (*BR*) *or* de feltro (*PT*).
female ['fi:meɪl] *n* (*woman*) mulher *f*; (*ZOOL*) fêmea ♦ *adj* (*BIO, ELEC*) fêmeo/a; (*sex, character*) feminino; (*vote etc*) das mulheres; (*child etc*) de sexo feminino; **male and ~ teachers** professores e professoras.
female impersonator *n* (*THEATRE*) travesti *m*.
feminine ['fɛmɪnɪn] *adj* feminino; (*womanly*) feminil ♦ *n* feminino.
femininity [fɛmɪ'nɪnɪtɪ] *n* feminilidade *f*.
feminism ['fɛmɪnɪzəm] *n* feminismo.
feminist ['fɛmɪnɪst] *n* feminista *m/f*.
fen [fɛn] (*BRIT*) *n*: **the F~s** os pântanos de Norfolk.
fence [fɛns] *n* cerca; (*SPORT*) obstáculo; (*inf*: *person*) receptor(a) *m/f* ♦ *vt* (*also*: **~** *in*) cercar ♦ *vi* esgrimir; **to sit on the ~** (*fig*) ficar no muro.
fencing ['fɛnsɪŋ] *n* (*sport*) esgrima.
fend [fɛnd] *vi*: **to ~ for o.s.** defender-se, virar-se.

***NB:** European Portuguese adds the following consonants to certain words:* **b** (sú(b)dito, su(b)til); **c** (a(c)ção, a(c)cionista, a(c)to); **m** (inde(m)ne); **p** (ado(p)ção, ado(p)tar); *for further details see p. xiii.*

fend off *vt* (*attack, attacker*) defender-se de.
fender ['fɛndə*] *n* (*of fireplace*) guarda-fogo *m*; (*US*: *AUT*) pára-lama *m*; (: *RAIL*) limpa-trilhos *m inv*.
fennel ['fɛnl] *n* erva-doce *f*, funcho.
ferment [*vi* fə'mɛnt, *n* 'fə:mɛnt] *vi* fermentar ♦ *n* (*fig*) agitação *f*.
fermentation [fə:mən'teɪʃən] *n* fermentação *f*.
fern [fə:n] *n* samambaia (*BR*), feto (*PT*).
ferocious [fə'rəuʃəs] *adj* feroz.
ferocity [fə'rɔsɪtɪ] *n* ferocidade *f*.
ferret ['fɛrɪt] *n* furão *m*.
ferret about (*BRIT*) *vi* = **ferret around**.
ferret around *vi*: **to ~ around in sth** vasculhar algo.
ferret out *vt* (*information*) desenterrar, descobrir.
ferry ['fɛrɪ] *n* (*small*) barco (de travessia); (*ship*) balsa ♦ *vt* transportar; **to ~ sth/sb across** *or* **over** transportar algo/alguém para o outro lado.
ferryman ['fɛrɪmən] (*irreg*) *n* barqueiro, balseiro.
fertile ['fə:taɪl] *adj* fértil; (*BIO*) fecundo.
fertility [fə'tɪlɪtɪ] *n* fertilidade *f*; (*BIO*) fecundidade *f*.
fertility drug *n* droga que propicia a fecundação.
fertilize ['fə:tɪlaɪz] *vt* fertilizar, fecundar; (*AGR*) adubar.
fertilizer ['fə:tɪlaɪzə*] *n* adubo, fertilizante *m*.
fervent ['fə:vənt] *adj* ardente, apaixonado.
fervour ['fə:və*] (*US* **fervor**) *n* fervor *m*.
fester ['fɛstə*] *vi* inflamar-se.
festival ['fɛstɪvəl] *n* (*REL*) festa; (*ART, MUS*) festival *m*.
festive ['fɛstɪv] *adj* festivo; **the ~ season** (*BRIT*: *Christmas*) a época do Natal.
festivities [fɛs'tɪvɪtɪz] *npl* festas *fpl*, festividades *fpl*.
festoon [fɛs'tu:n] *vt*: **to ~ with** engrinaldar de *or* com.
fetch [fɛtʃ] *vt* ir buscar, trazer; (*BRIT*: *sell for*) alcançar; **how much did it ~?** quanto rendeu?, por quanto foi vendido?
fetch up (*US*) *vi* ir parar.
fetching ['fɛtʃɪŋ] *adj* atraente.
fête [feɪt] *n* festa.
fetid ['fɛtɪd] *adj* fétido.
fetish ['fɛtɪʃ] *n* fetiche *m*.
fetter ['fɛtə*] *vt* restringir, refrear.
fetters ['fɛtəz] *npl* grilhões *mpl*.
fettle ['fɛtl] (*BRIT*) *n*: **in fine ~** (*car etc*) em bom estado; (*person*) em forma.
fetus ['fi:təs] (*US*) *n* = **foetus**.
feud [fju:d] *n* (*hostility*) inimizade *f*; (*quarrel*) disputa, rixa ♦ *vi* brigar; **a family ~** uma briga de família.
feudal ['fju:dl] *adj* feudal.
feudalism ['fju:dəlɪzəm] *n* feudalismo.
fever ['fi:və*] *n* febre *f*; **he has a ~** ele está com febre.
feverish ['fi:vərɪʃ] *adj* febril.
few [fju:] *adj, pron* poucos/as; **a ~** ... alguns/algumas ...; **I know a ~** conheço alguns; **quite a ~** ... vários/as ...; **in the next ~ days** nos próximos dias; **in the past ~ days** nos últimos dias; **every ~ days/months** cada dois ou três dias/meses; **a ~ more** ... mais alguns/algumas ....
fewer ['fju:ə*] *adj, pron* menos.
fewest ['fju:ɪst] *adj* o menor número de.
FFA *n abbr* = **Future Farmers of America**.
FH (*BRIT*) *abbr* = **fire hydrant**.
FHA (*US*) *n abbr* (= *Federal Housing Administration*) *secretaria federal da habitação*.
fiancé [fɪ'ã:ŋseɪ] *n* noivo.
fiancée [fɪ'ã:ŋseɪ] *n* noiva.
fiasco [fɪ'æskəu] *n* fiasco.
fib [fɪb] *n* lorota.
fibre ['faɪbə*] (*US* **fiber**) *n* fibra.
fibreboard ['faɪbəbɔ:d] (*US* **fiberboard**) *n* madeira compensada, compensado.
fibre-glass (*US* **fiber-glass**) *n* fibra de vidro.
fibrositis [faɪbrə'saɪtɪs] *n* aponeurosite *f*.
FICA (*US*) *n abbr* = **Federal Insurance Contributions Act**.
fickle ['fɪkl] *adj* inconstante.
fiction ['fɪkʃən] *n* ficção *f*.
fictional ['fɪkʃənl] *adj* de ficção.
fictionalize ['fɪkʃnəlaɪz] *vt* romancear.
fictitious [fɪk'tɪʃəs] *adj* fictício.
fiddle ['fɪdl] *n* (*MUS*) violino; (*cheating*) fraude *f*, embuste *m*; (*swindle*) trapaça ♦ *vt* (*BRIT*: *accounts*) falsificar.
fiddle with *vt fus* brincar com.
fiddler ['fɪdlə*] *n* violinista *m/f*.
fiddly ['fɪdlɪ] *adj* (*task*) espinhoso.
fidelity [fɪ'dɛlɪtɪ] *n* fidelidade *f*.
fidget ['fɪdʒɪt] *vi* estar irrequieto, mexer-se.
fidgety ['fɪdʒɪtɪ] *adj* inquieto, nervoso.
fiduciary [fɪ'dju:ʃɪərɪ] *n* fiduciário/a.
field [fi:ld] *n* campo; (*fig*) área, esfera, especialidade *f*; **to lead the ~** (*SPORT*) tomar a dianteira; (*COMM*) liderar; **to have a ~ day** (*fig*) fazer a festa.
field glasses *npl* binóculo.
field marshal *n* marechal-de-campo.
fieldwork ['fi:ldwə:k] *n* trabalho de campo.
fiend [fi:nd] *n* demônio.
fiendish ['fi:ndɪʃ] *adj* diabólico.
fierce [fɪəs] *adj* feroz; (*wind, attack*) violento; (*heat*) intenso; (*fighting, enemy*) feroz, violento.
fiery ['faɪərɪ] *adj* (*burning*) ardente; (*temperament*) fogoso.
FIFA ['fi:fə] *n abbr* (= *Fédération Internationale de Football Association*) FIFA.
fifteen [fɪf'ti:n] *num* quinze; *see also* **five**.
fifth [fɪfθ] *num* quinto; **I was (the) ~ to arrive** eu fui o quinto a chegar; **he came ~ in the competition** ele tirou o quinto lugar; (*in race*) ele chegou em quinto lugar; **Henry the F~** Henrique Quinto; **the ~ of July, July the ~** dia cinco de julho; **I wrote to him on the ~** eu lhe escrevi no dia cinco.
fiftieth ['fɪftɪɪθ] *num* qüinquagésimo; *see also* **fifth**.
fifty ['fɪftɪ] *num* cinqüenta; **about ~ people**

umas cinqüenta pessoas; **he'll be ~ (years old) next birthday** ele fará cinqüenta anos no seu próximo aniversário; **he's about ~** ele tem uns cinqüenta anos; **the fifties** os anos 50; **to be in one's fifties** estar na casa dos cinqüenta anos; **the temperature was in the fifties** a temperatura estava na faixa dos cinqüenta graus; **to do ~** (*AUT*) ir a 50 (quilômetros por hora).

fifty-fifty ['fɪftɪ'fɪftɪ] *adv*: **to share** *or* **go ~ with sb** dividir meio a meio com alguém, rachar com alguém ♦ *adj*: **to have a ~ chance** ter 50% de chance.

fig [fɪg] *n* figo.

fight [faɪt] (*pt, pp* **fought**) *n* briga; (*MIL*) combate *m*; (*struggle*: *against illness etc*) luta ♦ *vt* lutar contra; (*cancer, alcoholism*) combater; (*LAW*: *case*) defender ♦ *vi* brigar, bater-se; (*fig*): **to ~ (for/against)** lutar (por/contra).

fight back *vi* revidar; (*SPORT, from illness etc*) reagir ♦ *vt* (*tears*) tentar reter.

fight off *vt* (*attack, attacker*) repelir; (*illness, sleep, urge*) lutar contra.

fight out *vt*: **to ~ it out** resolver a questão pela briga.

fighter ['faɪtə*] *n* combatente *m/f*; (*fig*) lutador(a) *m/f*; (*plane*) caça *m*.

fighter pilot *n* piloto de caça.

fighting ['faɪtɪŋ] *n* luta, briga; (*battle*) batalha.

figment ['fɪgmənt] *n*: **a ~ of the imagination** um produto da imaginação.

figurative ['fɪgjurətɪv] *adj* figurado, figurativo.

figure ['fɪgə*] *n* (*DRAWING, MATH*) figura, desenho; (*numeral*) algarismo; (*number, cipher*) número, cifra; (*outline*) forma; (*of woman*) corpo; (*person*) personagem *m* ♦ *vt* (*esp US*) imaginar ♦ *vi* (*appear*) figurar; (*US*: *make sense*) fazer sentido; **public ~** personalidade *f*; **~ of speech** figura de linguagem.

figure on (*US*) *vt fus*: **to ~ on doing** contar em fazer.

figure out *vt* (*understand*) compreender.

figurehead ['fɪgəhɛd] *n* (*NAUT*) carranca de proa; (*fig*) chefe *m* nominal.

figure skating *n* movimentos *mpl* de patinação.

Fiji (Islands) ['fiːdʒiː-] *n(pl)* (ilhas *fpl*) Fiji (*no article*).

filament ['fɪləmənt] *n* filamento.

filch [fɪltʃ] (*inf*) *vt* furtar, abafar.

file [faɪl] *n* (*tool*) lixa; (*dossier*) dossiê *m*, pasta; (*folder*) pasta; (: *binder*) fichário; (*COMPUT*) arquivo; (*row*) fila, coluna ♦ *vt* lixar; (*papers*) arquivar; (*LAW*: *claim*) apresentar, dar entrada em; (*store*) arquivar ♦ *vi*: **to ~ in/out** entrar/sair em fila; **to ~ past** desfilar em frente de; **to ~ a suit against sb** (*LAW*) abrir processo contra alguém.

file name *n* (*COMPUT*) nome *m* do arquivo.

filibuster ['fɪlɪbʌstə*] (*esp US*) *n* (*POL*) obstrucionista *m/f* ♦ *vi* obstruir.

filing ['faɪlɪŋ] *n* arquivamento; **~s** *npl* (*of iron etc*) limalha.

filing cabinet *n* fichário, arquivo.

filing clerk *n* arquivista *m/f*.

Filipino [fɪlɪ'piːnəu] *n* (*person*) filipino/a; (*LING*) filipino.

fill [fɪl] *vt* encher; (*vacancy*) preencher; (*order*) atender ♦ *n*: **to eat one's ~** encher-se *or* fartar-se de comer; **~ed with admiration** cheio de admiração.

fill in *vt* (*form*) preencher; (*hole*) tapar; (*details, report*) escrever ♦ *vi*: **to ~ in for sb** substituir alguém; **to ~ sb in on sth** (*inf*) dar as dicas a alguém sobre algo.

fill out *vt* preencher.

fill up *vt* encher ♦ *vi* (*AUT*) abastecer o carro; **~ it up, please** (*AUT*) pode encher (o tanque), por favor.

fillet ['fɪlɪt] *n* filete *m*, filé *m* ♦ *vt* preparar em filés.

fillet steak *n* filé *m*.

filling ['fɪlɪŋ] *n* (*CULIN*) recheio; (*for tooth*) obturação *f* (*BR*), chumbo (*PT*).

filling station *n* posto de gasolina.

fillip ['fɪlɪp] *n* estimulo, incentivo.

filly ['fɪlɪ] *n* potranca.

film [fɪlm] *n* filme *m* ♦ *vt* (*scene*) rodar, filmar ♦ *vi* filmar.

film star *n* astro/estrela do cinema.

filmstrip ['fɪlmstrɪp] *n* diafilme *m*.

film studio *n* estúdio (de cinema).

filter ['fɪltə*] *n* filtro ♦ *vt* filtrar.

filter coffee *n* café *m* filtro.

filter lane (*BRIT*) *n* (*AUT*) pista para se dobrar à esquerda (*or* à direita).

filter tip *n* filtro.

filth [fɪlθ] *n* sujeira (*BR*), sujidade *f* (*PT*).

filthy ['fɪlθɪ] *adj* sujo; (*language*) indecente, obsceno.

fin [fɪn] *n* barbatana.

final ['faɪnl] *adj* (*last*) final, último; (*definitive*) definitivo ♦ *n* (*SPORT*) final *f*; **~s** *npl* (*SCH*) exames *mpl* finais; **~ demand** (*on invoice etc*) demanda final.

finale [fɪ'nɑːlɪ] *n* final *m*.

finalist ['faɪnəlɪst] *n* (*SPORT*) finalista *m/f*.

finalize ['faɪnəlaɪz] *vt* concluir, completar.

finally ['faɪnəlɪ] *adv* (*lastly*) finalmente, por fim; (*eventually*) por fim; (*irrevocably*) definitivamente.

finance [faɪ'næns] *n* (*money*) fundos *mpl* ♦ *vt* financiar; **~s** *npl* finanças *fpl*.

financial [faɪ'nænʃəl] *adj* financeiro; **~ statement** demonstração financeira.

financially [faɪ'nænʃəlɪ] *adv* financeiramente.

financial year *n* ano fiscal, exercício.

financier [fɪ'nænsɪə*] *n* financista *m/f*; (*backer*) financiador(a) *m/f*.

find [faɪnd] (*pt, pp* **found**) *vt* encontrar, achar ♦ *n* achado, descoberta; **to ~ sb guilty** (*LAW*) declarar alguém culpado.

NB: *European Portuguese adds the following consonants to certain words:* **b** (sú(b)dito, su(b)til); **c** (a(c)ção, a(c)cionista, a(c)to); **m** (inde(m)ne); **p** (ado(p)ção, ado(p)tar); *for further details see p. xiii.*

find out *vt* descobrir; (*person*) desmascarar ♦ *vi*: **to ~ out about** informar-se sobre; (*by chance*) saber de.
findings ['faɪndɪŋz] *npl* (*LAW*) veredito, decisão *f*; (*of report*) constatações *fpl*.
fine [faɪn] *adj* (*delicate, refined, thin*) fino; (*good*) bom/boa; (*beautiful*) bonito ♦ *adv* (*well*) muito bem ♦ *n* (*LAW*) multa ♦ *vt* (*LAW*) multar; **to be ~** (*weather*) estar bom; **you're doing ~** você se dá bem; **to cut it ~** deixar pouca margem; (*arrive just in time*) chegar em cima da hora.
fine arts *npl* belas artes *fpl*.
finely ['faɪnlɪ] *adv* (*tune*) finamente; **~ chopped** picado.
finery ['faɪnərɪ] *n* enfeites *mpl*.
finesse [fɪ'nɛs] *n* sutileza.
fine-tooth comb *n*: **to go through sth with a ~** (*fig*) passar o pente fino em algo.
finger ['fɪŋgə*] *n* dedo ♦ *vt* (*touch*) manusear; (*MUS*) dedilhar; **little/index ~** dedo mínimo/indicador.
fingering ['fɪŋgərɪŋ] *n* (*MUS*) dedilhado.
fingermark ['fɪŋgəmɑːk] *n* dedada.
fingernail ['fɪŋgəneɪl] *n* unha.
fingerprint ['fɪŋgəprɪnt] *n* impressão *f* digital ♦ *vt* (*person*) tirar as impressões digitais de.
fingerstall ['fɪŋgəstɔːl] *n* dedeira.
fingertip ['fɪŋgətɪp] *n* ponta do dedo; **to have sth at one's ~s** ter algo à sua disposição, dispor de algo; (*knowledge*) saber algo na ponta da língua.
finicky ['fɪnɪkɪ] *adj* (*fussy*) fresco, cheio de coisas.
finish ['fɪnɪʃ] *n* (*end*) fim *m*; (*SPORT*) chegada; (*on wood etc*) acabamento ♦ *vt*, *vi* terminar, acabar; **to ~ doing sth** terminar de fazer algo; **to ~ with sb** (*end relationship*) acabar com alguém; **to ~ third** chegar no terceiro lugar.
finish off *vt* terminar; (*kill*) liquidar.
finish up *vt* acabar ♦ *vi* acabar; (*in place*) ir parar.
finished product ['fɪnɪʃt-] *n* produto acabado.
finishing line ['fɪnɪʃɪŋ-] *n* linha de chegada, meta.
finishing school ['fɪnɪʃɪŋ-] *n* escola de aperfeiçoamento (para moças).
finishing touches ['fɪnɪʃɪŋ-] *npl* últimos retoques *mpl*.
finite ['faɪnaɪt] *adj* finito.
Finland ['fɪnlənd] *n* Finlândia.
Finn [fɪn] *n* finlandês/esa *m/f*.
Finnish ['fɪnɪʃ] *adj* finlandês/esa ♦ *n* (*LING*) finlandês *m*.
fiord [fjɔːd] *n* fiorde *m*.
fir [fəː*] *n* abeto.
fire ['faɪə*] *n* fogo; (*accidental*) incêndio ♦ *vt* (*gun*) disparar; (*interest*) despertar; (*dismiss*) despedir; (*excite*): **to ~ sb with enthusiasm** encher alguém de entusiasmo ♦ *vi* disparar ♦ *cpd*: **~ hazard**, **~ risk** perigo *or* risco de incêndio; **on ~** em chamas; **to set ~ to sth, set sth on ~** incendiar algo; **insured against ~** segurado contra fogo; **to come under ~ (from)** (*fig*) ser atacado (por).
fire alarm *n* alarme *m* de incêndio.
firearm ['faɪərɑːm] *n* arma de fogo.
fire brigade *n* (corpo de) bombeiros *mpl*.
fire chief (*US*) *n* = **fire master**.
fire department (*US*) *n* = **fire brigade**.
fire drill *n* treinamento de incêndio.
fire engine *n* carro de bombeiro.
fire escape *n* escada de incêndio.
fire extinguisher *n* extintor *m* de incêndio.
fireguard ['faɪəgɑːd] (*BRIT*) *n* guarda-fogo *m*.
fire insurance *n* seguro contra fogo.
fireman ['faɪəmɛn] (*irreg*) *n* bombeiro.
fire master (*BRIT*) *n* capitão *m* dos bombeiros.
firemen ['faɪəmɛn] *npl of* **fireman**.
fireplace ['faɪəpleɪs] *n* lareira.
fireproof ['faɪəpruːf] *adj* à prova de fogo.
fire regulations *npl* normas *fpl* preventivas contra incêndio.
fire screen *n* guarda-fogo *m*.
fireside ['faɪəsaɪd] *n* lugar *m* junto à lareira.
fire station *n* posto de bombeiros.
firewood ['faɪəwud] *n* lenha.
fireworks ['faɪəwəːks] *npl* fogos *mpl* de artifício.
firing ['faɪərɪŋ] *n* (*MIL*) tiros *mpl*, tiroteio.
firing line *n* (*MIL*) linha de fogo; **to be in the ~** (*fig*) estar na linha de frente.
firing squad *n* pelotão *m* de fuzilamento.
firm [fəːm] *adj* firme ♦ *n* firma; **to be a ~ believer in sth** ser partidário perseverante de algo; **to stand ~** *or* **take a ~ stand on sth** (*fig*) manter-se firme em algo.
firmly ['fəːmlɪ] *adv* firmemente.
firmness ['fəːmnɪs] *n* firmeza.
first [fəːst] *adj* primeiro ♦ *adv* (*before others*) primeiro; (*when listing reasons etc*) em primeiro lugar ♦ *n* (*person: in race*) primeiro/a; (*AUT*) primeira; (*BRIT: SCH*) menção *f* honrosa; **the ~ of January** primeiro de janeiro (*BR*), dia um de Janeiro (*PT*); **at ~** no início; **~ of all** antes de tudo, antes de mais nada; **in the ~ place** em primeiro lugar; **I'll do it ~ thing tomorrow** vou fazê-lo amanhã cedo; **head ~** com a cabeça para a frente; **for the ~ time** pela primeira vez; **from the (very) ~** desde o início; *see also* **fifth**.
first aid *n* pronto socorro.
first-aid kit *n* estojo de pronto socorro.
first-aid post *n* pronto-socorro.
first-class *adj* de primeira classe.
first-class mail *n* correspondência prioritária.
first-hand *adj* de primeira mão.
first lady (*US*) *n* primeira dama.
firstly ['fəːstlɪ] *adv* primeiramente, em primeiro lugar.
first name *n* primeiro nome *m*.
first night *n* (*THEATRE*) estréia.
first-rate *adj* de primeira categoria.
fir tree *n* abeto.
FIS (*BRIT*) *n abbr* (= *Family Income Supplement*) abono-família *m*.
fiscal ['fɪskəl] *adj* fiscal; **~ year** ano-fiscal.

fish [fɪʃ] *n inv* peixe *m* ♦ *vt, vi* pescar; **to go ~ing** ir pescar.
fish out *vt* (*from water*) pescar; (*from box etc*) tirar.
fishbone ['fɪʃbəun] *n* espinha de peixe.
fisherman ['fɪʃəmən] (*irreg*) *n* pescador *m*.
fishery ['fɪʃərɪ] *n* pescaria.
fish factory (*BRIT*) *n* fábrica de processamento de pescados.
fish farm *n* viveiro (de piscicultura).
fish fingers (*BRIT*) *npl* filezinhos *mpl* de peixe.
fish hook *n* anzol *m*.
fishing boat ['fɪʃɪŋ-] *n* barco de pesca.
fishing industry ['fɪʃɪŋ-] *n* indústria da pesca.
fishing line ['fɪʃɪŋ-] *n* linha de pesca.
fishing net ['fɪʃɪŋ-] *n* rede *f* de pesca.
fishing rod ['fɪʃɪŋ-] *n* vara (de pesca).
fishing tackle ['fɪʃɪŋ-] *n* apetrechos *mpl* (de pesca).
fish market *n* mercado de peixe.
fishmonger ['fɪʃmʌŋgə*] *n* peixeiro/a; **~'s (shop)** peixaria.
fish sticks (*US*) *npl* filezinhos *mpl* de peixe.
fishy ['fɪʃɪ] *adj* (*fig*) suspeito.
fission ['fɪʃən] *n* fissão *f*; **nuclear ~** fissão nuclear.
fissure ['fɪʃə*] *n* fenda, fissura.
fist [fɪst] *n* punho.
fistfight ['fɪstfaɪt] *n* briga de socos.
fit [fɪt] *adj* (*MED, SPORT*) em (boa) forma; (*proper*) adequado, apropriado ♦ *vt* (*clothes*) caber em; (*try on: clothes*) experimentar, provar; (*facts*) enquadrar-se *or* condizer com; (*accommodate*) ajustar, adaptar; (*correspond exactly*) encaixar em; (*put in, attach*) colocar; (*equip*) equipar ♦ *vi* (*clothes*) servir; (*in space, gap*) caber; (*correspond*) encaixar-se ♦ *n* (*MED*) ataque *m*; **~ to** bom para; **~ for** adequado para; **this dress is a good/tight ~** este vestido tem um bom corte/está um pouco justo; **a ~ of anger** um acesso de raiva; **to have a ~** (*MED*) sofrer *or* ter um ataque; (*fig: inf*) fazer escândalo; **do as you think** *or* **see ~** faça como você achar melhor; **by ~s and starts** espasmodicamente.
fit in *vi* encaixar-se; (*fig: person*) dar-se bem (com todos).
fit out (*BRIT*) *vt* (*also: ~ up*) equipar.
fitful ['fɪtful] *adj* espasmódico, intermitente.
fitment ['fɪtmənt] *n* móvel *m*.
fitness ['fɪtnɪs] *n* (*MED*) saúde *f*, boa forma; (*of remark*) conveniência.
fitted ['fɪtɪd] *adj* (*cupboards*) embutido; (*kitchen*) com armários embutidos; **~ carpet** carpete *m*.
fitter ['fɪtə*] *n* ajustador(a) *m/f*, montador(a) *m/f*; (*also: gas ~*) gasista *m/f*.
fitting ['fɪtɪŋ] *adj* próprio, apropriado ♦ *n* (*of dress*) prova; **~s** *npl* instalações *fpl*, acessórios *mpl*.
fitting room *n* (*in shop*) cabine *f* (para experimentar roupa).
five [faɪv] *num* cinco; **she is ~ (years old)** ela tem cinco anos; **they live at number ~/at ~ Green Street** eles moram no número cinco/na Green Street número cinco; **there are ~ of us** somos cinco; **all ~ of them came** todos os cinco vieram; **it costs ~ pounds** custa cinco libras; **~ and a quarter/half** cinco e um quarto/e meio; **it's ~ (o'clock)** são cinco horas; **to divide sth into ~** dividir algo em cinco partes; **they are sold in ~s** eles são vendidos em pacotes de cinco.
five-day week *n* semana de cinco dias.
fiver ['faɪvə*] (*inf*) *n* (*BRIT*) nota de cinco libras; (*US*) nota de cinco dólares.
fix [fɪks] *vt* (*secure*) fixar, colocar; (*arrange*) arranjar; (*mend*) consertar; (*meal, drink*) preparar; (*inf: game etc*) arranjar ♦ *n*: **to be in a ~** estar em apuros; **the fight was a ~** a luta foi uma marmelada; **to ~ sth in one's mind** gravar algo.
fix up *vt* (*meeting*) marcar; **to ~ sb up with sth** arranjar algo para alguém.
fixation [fɪk'seɪʃən] *n* fixação *f*.
fixative ['fɪksətɪv] *n* fixador *m*.
fixed [fɪkst] *adj* (*prices etc*) fixo; **how are you ~ for money?** (*inf*) a quantas anda você em matéria de dinheiro?
fixed assets *npl* ativo fixo.
fixture ['fɪkstʃə*] *n* coisa fixa; (*furniture*) móvel *m* fixo; (*SPORT*) desafio, encontro.
fizz [fɪz] *vi* efervescer.
fizzle ['fɪzl] *vi* chiar.
fizzle out *vi* fracassar, falhar.
fizzy ['fɪzɪ] *adj* (*drink*) com gás, gasoso; (*gen*) efervescente.
fjord [fjɔːd] *n* = **fiord**.
FL (*US*) *abbr* (*POST*) = **Florida**.
flabbergasted ['flæbəgɑːstɪd] *adj* pasmado.
flabby ['flæbɪ] *adj* flácido.
flag [flæg] *n* bandeira; (*stone*) laje *f* ♦ *vi* acabar-se, descair; **~ of convenience** bandeira de conveniência.
flag down *vt*: **to ~ sb down** fazer sinais a alguém para que pare.
flagon ['flægən] *n* garrafão *m*.
flagpole ['flægpəul] *n* mastro de bandeira.
flagrant ['fleɪgrənt] *adj* flagrante.
flagship ['flægʃɪp] *n* nau *f* capitânia.
flag stop (*US*) *n* (*for bus*) parada facultativa.
flair [flɛə*] *n* jeito, habilidade *f*.
flak [flæk] *n* (*MIL*) fogo antiaéreo; (*inf: criticism*) críticas *fpl*.
flake [fleɪk] *n* (*of rust, paint*) lasca; (*of snow, soap powder*) floco ♦ *vi* (*also: ~ off*) lascar, descamar-se.
flaky ['fleɪkɪ] *adj* (*paintwork*) laminoso; (*skin*) escamoso; (*pastry*) folhado.
flamboyant [flæm'bɔɪənt] *adj* (*dress*) espalhafatoso; (*person*) extravagante.

***NB**: European Portuguese adds the following consonants to certain words:* **b** (sú(b)dito, su(b)til); **c** (a(c)ção, a(c)cionista, a(c)to); **m** (inde(m)ne); **p** (ado(p)ção, ado(p)tar); *for further details see p. xiii.*

flame [fleɪm] *n* chama; **to burst into ~s** irromper em chamas; **old ~** (*inf*) velha paixão *f*.
flamingo [flə'mɪŋgəu] (*pl* **~es**) *n* flamingo.
flammable ['flæməbl] *adj* inflamável.
flan [flæn] *n* torta.
flange [flændʒ] *n* flange *m*.
flank [flæŋk] *n* flanco; (*of person*) lado ♦ *vt* ladear.
flannel ['flænl] *n* (*also*: *face ~*) pano; (*fabric*) flanela; (BRIT: *inf*) conversa fiada; **~s** *npl* calça (BR) *or* calças *fpl* (PT) de flanela.
flannelette [flænə'lɛt] *n* baetilha.
flap [flæp] *n* (*of pocket, table*) aba; (*of envelope*) dobra; (*wing movement*) bater *m*; (AVIAT) flap *m* ♦ *vt* (*wings*) bater ♦ *vi* (*sail, flag*) ondular; (*inf*: *also*: *be in a ~*) estar atarantado.
flapjack ['flæpdʒæk] *n* (US: *pancake*) panqueca; (BRIT: *biscuit*) biscoito de aveia.
flare [flɛə*] *n* fogacho, chama; (MIL) sinal *m* luminoso; (*in skirt etc*) folga.
flare up *vi* chamejar; (*fig*: *person*) encolerizar-se; (: *revolt*) irromper.
flared ['flɛəd] *adj* (*trousers*) com roda; (*skirt*) rodado.
flash [flæʃ] *n* relâmpago; (*also*: *news ~*) notícias *fpl* de última hora; (PHOT) flash *m*; (*of inspiration*) lampejo ♦ *vt* (*light, headlights*) piscar; (*torch*) acender; (*send*: *message*) transmitir ♦ *vi* brilhar, relampejar; **in a ~** num instante; **he ~ed by** *or* **past** passou como um raio; **to ~ sth about** (*fig*: *inf*) ostentar *or* exibir algo.
flashback ['flæʃbæk] *n* flashback *m*.
flashbulb ['flæʃbʌlb] *n* lâmpada de flash.
flash card *n* (SCH) cartão *m*.
flashcube ['flæʃkju:b] *n* cubo de flash.
flasher ['flæʃə*] *n* (AUT) pisca-pisca *m*.
flashlight ['flæʃlaɪt] *n* lanterna de bolso.
flashpoint ['flæʃpɔɪnt] *n* ponto de centelha.
flashy ['flæʃɪ] (*pej*) *adj* espalhafatoso.
flask [flɑ:sk] *n* frasco; (*also*: *vacuum ~*) garrafa térmica (BR), termo (PT).
flat [flæt] *adj* chato, plano; (*smooth*) liso; (*battery*) descarregado; (*tyre*) vazio; (*beer*) choco; (*denial*) categórico; (MUS) abemolado; (: *voice*) desafinado ♦ *n* (BRIT: *apartment*) apartamento; (MUS) bemol *m*; (AUT) pneu *m* furado; **~ out** (*work*) a toque de caixa; (*race*) a toda; **~ rate of pay** (COMM) salário fixo.
flat-footed [-'futɪd] *adj* de pés chatos.
flatly ['flætlɪ] *adv* terminantemente.
flatmate ['flætmeɪt] (BRIT) *n* companheiro/a de apartamento.
flatness ['flætnɪs] *n* (*of land*) planura, lisura.
flatten ['flætən] *vt* (*also*: *~ out*) aplanar; (*smooth out*) alisar; (*demolish*) arrasar; (*defeat*) derrubar.
flatter ['flætə*] *vt* lisonjear; (*show to advantage*) favorecer.
flatterer ['flætərə*] *n* lisonjeador(a) *m/f*.
flattering ['flætərɪŋ] *adj* lisonjeiro; (*clothes etc*) favorecedor(a).
flattery ['flætərɪ] *n* bajulação *f*.
flatulence ['flætjuləns] *n* flatulência.
flaunt [flɔ:nt] *vt* ostentar, pavonear.
flavour ['fleɪvə*] (US **flavor**) *n* sabor *m* ♦ *vt* condimentar, aromatizar; **vanilla-~ed** com sabor de baunilha.
flavo(u)ring ['fleɪvərɪŋ] *n* condimento; (*synthetic*) aromatizante *m*.
flaw [flɔ:] *n* defeito.
flawless ['flɔ:lɪs] *adj* impecável.
flax [flæks] *n* linho.
flaxen ['flæksən] *adj* de cor de linho.
flea [fli:] *n* pulga.
flea market *n* feira de quinquilharias.
fleapit ['fli:pɪt] *n* (*cinema*) pulgueiro.
fleck [flɛk] *n* (*of dust*) partícula; (*of mud*) salpico; (*of paint*) pontinho ♦ *vt* salpicar; **brown ~ed with white** marrom salpicado de branco.
fled [flɛd] *pt, pp of* **flee**.
fledg(e)ling ['flɛdʒlɪŋ] *n* ave *f* recém-emplumada.
flee [fli:] (*pt, pp* **fled**) *vt* fugir de ♦ *vi* fugir.
fleece [fli:s] *n* velo; (*wool*) lã *f* ♦ *vt* (*inf*) pelar, depenar.
fleecy ['fli:sɪ] *adj* (*blanket*) felpudo; (*cloud*) fofo.
fleet [fli:t] *n* (*gen, of lorries etc*) frota; (*of ships*) esquadra.
fleeting ['fli:tɪŋ] *adj* fugaz.
Flemish ['flɛmɪʃ] *adj* flamengo ♦ *n* (LING) flamengo; **the ~** *npl* os flamengos.
flesh [flɛʃ] *n* carne *f*; (*of fruit*) polpa; **of ~ and blood** de carne e osso.
flesh wound *n* ferimento de superfície.
flew [flu:] *pt of* **fly**.
flex [flɛks] *n* fio ♦ *vt* (*muscles*) flexionar.
flexibility [flɛksɪ'bɪlɪtɪ] *n* flexibilidade *f*.
flexible ['flɛksɪbl] *adj* flexível.
flick [flɪk] *n* pancada leve; (*with finger*) peteleco, piparote *m*; (*with whip*) chicotada ♦ *vt* dar pancada leve em; **~s** *npl* (BRIT: *inf*) cinema *m*.
flick through *vt fus* folhear.
flicker ['flɪkə*] *vi* (*light*) tremeluzir; (*flame*) tremular ♦ *n* tremulação *f*; **a ~ of light** um fio de luz.
flick knife (BRIT: *irreg*) *n* canivete *m* de mola.
flier ['flaɪə*] *n* aviador(a) *m/f*.
flight [flaɪt] *n* vôo *m*; (*escape*) fuga; (*of steps*) lance *m*; **to take ~** fugir, pôr-se em fuga; **to put to ~** pôr em fuga.
flight attendant (US) *n* comissário/a de bordo.
flight crew *n* tripulação *f*.
flight deck *n* (AVIAT) cabine *f* do piloto; (NAUT) pista de aterrissagem (BR) *or* aterragem (PT).
flight recorder *n* gravador *m* de vôo.
flimsy ['flɪmzɪ] *adj* (*thin*) delgado, franzino; (*weak*) débil; (*excuse*) fraco.
flinch [flɪntʃ] *vi* encolher-se; **to ~ from sth/from doing sth** vacilar diante de algo/em fazer algo.

fling [flɪŋ] (*pt, pp* **flung**) *vt* lançar ♦ *n* (*love affair*) caso.
flint [flɪnt] *n* pederneira; (*in lighter*) pedra.
flip [flɪp] *vt* (*turn over*) dar a volta em; (*throw*) jogar; **to ~ a coin** tirar cara ou coroa.
flip through *vt fus* folhear.
flippant ['flɪpənt] *adj* petulante, irreverente.
flipper ['flɪpə*] *n* (*of animal*) nadadeira; (*for swimmer*) pé-de-pato, nadadeira.
flip side *n* (*of record*) outro lado.
flirt [flə:t] *vi* flertar ♦ *n* namorador(a) *m/f*, paquerador(a) *m/f*.
flirtation [flə:'teɪʃən] *n* flerte *m*, paquera.
flit [flɪt] *vi* esvoaçar.
float [fləut] *n* bóia; (*in procession*) carro alegórico; (*sum of money*) caixa ♦ *vi* flutuar; (*swimmer*) boiar ♦ *vt* fazer flutuar; (*company*) lançar (na Bolsa).
floating ['fləutɪŋ] *adj* flutuante; **~ vote** voto oscilante; **~ voter** indeciso/a.
flock [flɔk] *n* (*of sheep*) rebanho; (*of birds*) bando; (*of people*) multidão *f*.
floe [fləu] *n* (*also*: *ice ~*) banquisa.
flog [flɔg] *vt* açoitar; (*inf*) vender.
flood [flʌd] *n* enchente *f*, inundação *f*; (*of words, tears etc*) torrente *m* ♦ *vt* inundar, alagar; (*AUT*: *carburettor*) afogar; **to ~ the market** (*COMM*) inundar o mercado; **in ~** transbordante.
flooding ['flʌdɪŋ] *n* inundação *f*.
floodlight ['flʌdlaɪt] (*irreg*: *like* **light**) *n* refletor *m*, holofote *m* ♦ *vt* iluminar com holofotes.
floodlit ['flʌdlɪt] *pt, pp of* **floodlight** ♦ *adj* iluminado (por holofotes).
flood tide *n* maré *f* enchente.
floor [flɔ:*] *n* chão *m*; (*in house*) soalho; (*storey*) andar *m*; (*of sea*) fundo; (*dance ~*) pista de dança ♦ *vt* (*fig*: *confuse*) confundir, pasmar; **ground ~** (*BRIT*) *or* **first ~** (*US*) andar térreo (*BR*), rés-do-chão (*PT*); **first ~** (*BRIT*) *or* **second ~** (*US*) primeiro andar; **top ~** último andar; **to have the ~** (*speaker*) ter a palavra.
floorboard ['flɔ:bɔ:d] *n* tábua de assoalho.
flooring ['flɔ:rɪŋ] *n* piso.
floor lamp (*US*) *n* abajur *m* de pé.
floor show *n* show *m*.
floorwalker ['flɔ:wɔ:kə*] (*esp US*) *n* supervisor(a) *m/f* (numa loja de departamentos).
flop [flɔp] *n* fracasso ♦ *vi* (*fail*) fracassar.
floppy ['flɔpɪ] *adj* frouxo, mole.
floppy disk *n* disquete *m*.
flora ['flɔ:rə] *n* flora.
floral ['flɔ:rl] *adj* floral.
Florence ['flɔrəns] *n* Florença.
florid ['flɔrɪd] *adj* (*style*) florido; (*complexion*) corado.
florist ['flɔrɪst] *n* florista *m/f*; **~'s (shop)** floricultura.
flotation [fləu'teɪʃən] *n* (*of shares*) emissão *f*; (*of company*) lançamento (na Bolsa).
flounce [flauns] *n* babado, debrum *m*.
flounce out *vi* sair indignado.
flounder ['flaundə*] (*pl* ~ *or* **~s**) *n* (*ZOOL*) linguado ♦ *vi* atrapalhar-se.
flour ['flauə*] *n* farinha.
flourish ['flʌrɪʃ] *vi* florescer ♦ *vt* brandir, menear ♦ *n* floreio; (*of trumpets*) fanfarra.
flourishing ['flʌrɪʃɪŋ] *adj* próspero.
flout [flaut] *vt* (*law*) desrespeitar; (*offer*) desprezar.
flow [fləu] *n* (*movement, tide*) fluxo; (*direction*) curso; (*of river*) corrente *f*; (*ELEC, of blood*) circulação *f* ♦ *vi* correr, fluir; (*traffic, blood*) circular; (*robes, hair*) flutuar.
flow chart *n* fluxograma *m*.
flow diagram *n* fluxograma *m*.
flower ['flauə*] *n* flor *f* ♦ *vi* florescer, florir; **in ~** em flor.
flower bed *n* canteiro.
flowerpot ['flauəpɔt] *n* vaso.
flowery ['flauərɪ] *adj* florido.
flown [fləun] *pp of* **fly**.
flu [flu:] *n* gripe *f*.
fluctuate ['flʌktjueɪt] *vi* flutuar, variar.
fluctuation [flʌktju'eɪʃən] *n* flutuação *f*, oscilação *f*.
flue [flu:] *n* fumeiro.
fluency ['flu:ənsɪ] *n* fluência.
fluent ['flu:ənt] *adj* (*speech*) fluente; **he speaks ~ French, he's ~ in French** ele fala francês fluentemente.
fluently ['flu:əntlɪ] *adv* fluentemente.
fluff [flʌf] *n* felpa, penugem *f*.
fluffy ['flʌfɪ] *adj* macio, fofo; **~ toy** brinquedo de pelúcia.
fluid ['flu:ɪd] *adj* fluido ♦ *n* fluido; (*in diet*) líquido.
fluid ounce (*BRIT*) *n = 0.028 l; 0.05 pints*.
fluke [flu:k] (*inf*) *n* sorte *f*.
flummox ['flʌməks] *vt* desconcertar.
flung [flʌŋ] *pt, pp of* **fling**.
flunky ['flʌŋkɪ] *n* lacaio.
fluorescent [fluə'rɛsnt] *adj* fluorescente.
fluoride ['fluəraɪd] *n* fluoreto ♦ *cpd*: **~ toothpaste** pasta de dentes com flúor.
fluorine ['fluəri:n] *n* flúor *m*.
flurry ['flʌrɪ] *n* (*of snow*) lufada; (*haste*) agitação *f*; **~ of activity** muita atividade.
flush [flʌʃ] *n* (*on face*) rubor *m*; (*plenty*) abundância ♦ *vt* lavar com água; (*also*: *~ out*) levantar ♦ *vi* ruborizar-se; **~ with** rente com; **to ~ the toilet** dar descarga; **hot ~es** (*MED*) calores.
flushed [flʌʃt] *adj* ruborizado, corado.
fluster ['flʌstə*] *n* agitação *f* ♦ *vt* atrapalhar, desconcertar.
flustered ['flʌstəd] *adj* atrapalhado.
flute [flu:t] *n* flauta.
fluted ['flu:tɪd] *adj* acanelado.
flutter ['flʌtə*] *n* agitação *f*; (*of wings*) bater *m*; (*inf*: *bet*) aposta ♦ *vi* esvoaçar.

***NB**: European Portuguese adds the following consonants to certain words:* **b** (sú(b)dito, su(b)til); **c** (a(c)ção, a(c)cionista, a(c)to); **m** (inde(m)ne); **p** (ado(p)ção, ado(p)tar); *for further details see p. xiii.*

flux [flʌks] *n* fluxo; **in a state of ~** mudando continuamente.

fly [flaɪ] (*pt* **flew**, *pp* **flown**) *n* (*insect*) mosca; (*on trousers*: *also*: *flies*) braguilha ♦ *vt* (*plane*) pilotar; (*passengers, cargo*) transportar (de avião); (*flag*) hastear; (*distances*) percorrer; (*kite*) soltar, empinar ♦ *vi* voar; (*passengers*) ir de avião; (*escape*) fugir; (*flag*) hastear-se; **to ~ open** abrir-se bruscamente; **to ~ off the handle** perder as estribeiras.

fly away *vi* ir-se.

fly in *vi* chegar.

fly off *vi* ir-se.

fly out *vi* sair (de avião).

fly-fishing *n* pesca com iscas artificiais.

flying ['flaɪɪŋ] *n* (*activity*) aviação *f* ♦ *adj*: **~ visit** visita de médico; **with ~ colours** brilhantemente; **he doesn't like ~** ele não gosta de andar de avião.

flying buttress *n* arcobotante *m*.

flying saucer *n* disco voador.

flying start *n*: **to get off to a ~** (*in race*) disparar; (*fig*) começar muito bem.

fly leaf ['flaɪliːf] (*irreg*) *n* guarda (*num livro*).

flyover ['flaɪəuvə*] (BRIT) *n* (*bridge*) viaduto.

flypast ['flaɪpɑːst] *n* desfile *m* aéreo.

flysheet ['flaɪʃiːt] *n* (*for tent*) duplo teto.

flywheel ['flaɪwiːl] *n* volante *m*.

FM *abbr* (BRIT: MIL) = **field marshal**; (RADIO: = *frequency modulation*) FM.

FMB (US) *n abbr* = **Federal Maritime Board**.

FMCS (US) *n abbr* (= *Federal Mediation and Conciliation Service*) ≈ *Justiça do Trabalho*.

FO (BRIT) *n abbr* = **Foreign Office**.

foal [fəul] *n* potro.

foam [fəum] *n* espuma ♦ *vi* espumar.

foam rubber *n* espuma de borracha.

FOB *abbr* (= *free on board*) FOB.

fob [fɔb] *vt*: **to ~ sb off with sth** despachar alguém com algo; **to ~ sth off on sb** impingir algo a alguém.

foc (BRIT) *abbr* = **free of charge**.

focal ['fəukəl] *adj* focal.

focal point *n* foco.

focus ['fəukəs] (*pl* **~es**) *n* foco ♦ *vt* (*field glasses etc*) enfocar ♦ *vi*: **to ~ on** enfocar, focalizar; **in/out of ~** enfocado/desenfocado, em foco/fora de foco.

fodder ['fɔdə*] *n* forragem *f*.

FOE *n abbr* (= *Friends of the Earth*) *organizacão ecologista;* (US: = *Fraternal Order of Eagles*) *associação beneficente*.

foe [fəu] *n* inimigo.

foetus ['fiːtəs] (US **fetus**) *n* feto.

fog [fɔg] *n* nevoeiro.

fogbound ['fɔgbaund] *adj* imobilizado pelo nevoeiro.

foggy ['fɔgɪ] *adj* nevoento.

fog lamp (US **fog light**) *n* farol *m* de neblina.

foible ['fɔɪbl] *n* fraqueza, ponto fraco.

foil [fɔɪl] *vt* frustrar ♦ *n* folha metálica; (*also*: *kitchen ~*) folha *or* papel *m* de alumínio; (FENCING) florete *m*; **to act as a ~ to** (*fig*) dar realce a.

foist [fɔɪst] *vt*: **to ~ sth on sb** impingir algo a alguém.

fold [fəuld] *n* (*bend, crease*) dobra, vinco, prega; (*of skin*) ruga; (AGR) redil *m*, curral *m* ♦ *vt* dobrar; **to ~ one's arms** cruzar os braços.

fold up *vi* (*map etc*) dobrar; (*business*) abrir falência ♦ *vt* (*map etc*) dobrar.

folder ['fəuldə*] *n* (*for papers*) pasta; (: *binder*) fichário; (*brochure*) folheto.

folding ['fəuldɪŋ] *adj* (*chair, bed*) dobrável.

foliage ['fəulɪɪdʒ] *n* folhagem *f*.

folk [fəuk] *npl* gente *f* ♦ *adj* popular, folclórico; **~s** *npl* (*family*) família, parentes *mpl*; (*people*) gente *f*.

folklore ['fəuklɔː*] *n* folclore *m*.

folksong ['fəuksɔŋ] *n* canção *f* popular *or* folclórica.

follow ['fɔləu] *vt* seguir ♦ *vi* seguir; (*result*) resultar; **to ~ sb's advice** seguir o conselho de alguém; **I don't quite ~ you** não consigo acompanhar o seu raciocínio; **to ~ in sb's footsteps** seguir os passos de alguém; **it doesn't ~ that ...** (isso) não quer dizer que ...; **he ~ed suit** ele fez o mesmo.

follow out *vt* (*idea, plan*) levar a cabo, executar.

follow through *vt* levar a cabo, executar.

follow up *vt* (*letter*) responder a; (*offer*) levar adiante; (*case*) acompanhar.

follower ['fɔləuə*] *n* seguidor(a) *m/f*; (POL) partidário/a.

following ['fɔləuɪŋ] *adj* seguinte ♦ *n* séquito, adeptos *mpl*.

follow-up *n* continuação *f* ♦ *cpd*: **~ letter** carta suplementar de reforço.

folly ['fɔlɪ] *n* loucura.

fond [fɔnd] *adj* (*loving*) amoroso, carinhoso; **to be ~ of** gostar de.

fondle ['fɔndl] *vt* acariciar.

fondly ['fɔndlɪ] *adv* (*lovingly*) afetuosamente; (*naïvely*): **he ~ believed that ...** ele acreditava piamente que ....

fondness ['fɔndnɪs] *n* (*for things*) gosto, afeição *f*; (*for people*) carinho.

font [fɔnt] *n* (REL) pia batismal; (TYP) fonte *f*, família.

food [fuːd] *n* comida.

food mixer *n* batedeira.

food poisoning *n* intoxicação *f* alimentar.

food processor *n* multiprocessador *m* de cozinha.

foodstuffs ['fuːdstʌfs] *npl* gêneros *mpl* alimentícios.

fool [fuːl] *n* tolo/a; (HISTORY: *of king*) bobo; (CULIN) puré *m* de frutas com creme ♦ *vt* enganar ♦ *vi* (*gen*: *~ around*) brincar; (*waste time*) fazer bagunça; **to make a ~ of sb** (*ridicule*) ridicularizar alguém; (*trick*) fazer alguém de bobo; **to make a ~ of o.s.** fazer papel de bobo, fazer-se de bobo; **you can't ~ me** você não pode me fazer de bobo.

fool about (*pej*) *vi* (*waste time*) fazer bagunça; (*behave foolishly*) fazer-se de bobo.

fool around (*pej*) *vi* (*waste time*) fazer bagunça; (*behave foolishly*) fazer-se de

bobo.
foolhardy ['fu:lhɑ:dɪ] *adj* temerário.
foolish ['fu:lɪʃ] *adj* bobo; (*stupid*) burro; (*careless*) imprudente.
foolishly ['fu:lɪʃlɪ] *adv* imprudentemente.
foolishness ['fu:lɪʃnɪs] *n* tolice *f*.
foolproof ['fu:lpru:f] *adj* (*plan etc*) infalível.
foolscap ['fu:lskæp] *n* papel *m* ofício.
foot [fut] (*pl* **feet**) *n* pé *m*; (*measure*) pé (*=304 mm; 12 inches*); (*of animal*) pata ♦ *vt* (*bill*) pagar; **on ~** a pé; **to find one's feet** (*fig*) ambientar-se; **to put one's ~ down** (*AUT*) acelerar; (*say no*) bater o pé.
footage ['futɪdʒ] *n* (*CINEMA*: *length*) ≈ metragem *f*; (: *material*) seqüências *fpl*.
foot and mouth (disease) *n* febre *f* aftosa.
football ['futbɔ:l] *n* bola; (*game*: *BRIT*) futebol *m*; (: *US*) futebol norte-americano.
footballer ['futbɔ:lə*] *n* futebolista *m*, jogador *m* de futebol.
football ground *n* campo de futebol.
football match (*BRIT*) *n* partida de futebol.
football player *n* jogador *m* de futebol.
footbrake ['futbreɪk] *n* freio (*BR*) *or* travão *m* (*PT*) de pé.
footbridge ['futbrɪdʒ] *n* passarela.
foothills ['futhɪlz] *npl* contraforte *m*.
foothold ['futhəuld] *n* apoio para o pé.
footing ['futɪŋ] *n* (*fig*) posição *f*; **to lose one's ~** escorregar; **on an equal ~** em pé de igualdade.
footlights ['futlaɪts] *npl* ribalta.
footman ['futmən] (*irreg*) *n* lacaio.
footnote ['futnəut] *n* nota ao pé da página, nota de rodapé.
footpath ['futpɑ:θ] *n* senda, vereda, caminho; (*pavement*) calçada.
footprint ['futprɪnt] *n* pegada.
footrest ['futrɛst] *n* suporte *m* para os pés.
footsore ['futsɔ:*] *adj* com os pés doloridos.
footstep ['futstɛp] *n* passo.
footwear ['futwɛə*] *n* calçados *mpl*.
FOR *abbr* (= *free on rail*) franco sobre vagão.
for [fɔ:*] *prep* (*gen*) para; (*as, in exchange for, because of*) por; (*during*) durante; (*in spite of*): **~ all that** apesar de tudo isso ♦ *conj* pois, porque; **I haven't seen him ~ a week** faz uma semana que não o vejo; **he was away ~ 2 years** esteve fora 2 anos; **he went ~ the paper** foi pegar o jornal; **it was sold ~ £100** foi vendido por £100; **~ sale** vende-se; **the train ~ London** o trem para Londres; **it's time ~ lunch** é hora de almoçar; **what ~?** (*why*) por quê?; (*to what end*) para quê?; **what's it ~?** para que serve?; **there's nothing ~ it but to jump** (*BRIT*) não há outra solução senão saltar; **the campaign ~** a campanha pró *or* a favor de.
forage ['fɔrɪdʒ] *n* forragem *f* ♦ *vi* ir à procura de alimentos.
forage cap *n* casquete *m*.
foray ['fɔreɪ] *n* incursão *f*.
forbad(e) [fə'bæd] *pt of* **forbid**.
forbearing [fɔ:'bɛərɪŋ] *adj* indulgente.
forbid [fə'bɪd] (*pt* **forbad(e)**, *pp* **forbidden**) *vt* proibir; **to ~ sb to do** proibir alguém de fazer.
forbidden [fə'bɪdn] *pp of* **forbid** ♦ *adj* proibido.
forbidding [fə'bɪdɪŋ] *adj* (*gloomy*) lúgubre; (*severe*) severo.
force [fɔ:s] *n* força ♦ *vt* (*gen, smile*) forçar; (*confession*) arrancar à força; **the F~s** *npl* (*BRIT*) as Forças Armadas; **to ~ sb to do** forçar alguém a fazer; **in ~** em vigor; **to come into ~** entrar em vigor; **a ~ 5 wind** um vento força 5; **the sales ~** (*COMM*) a equipe de vendas; **to join ~s** unir forças; **by ~** à força.
force back *vt* (*crowd, enemy*) fazer recuar; (*tears*) reprimir.
force down *vt* (*food*) forçar-se a comer.
forced [fɔ:st] *adj* forçado.
force-feed ['fɔ:sfi:d] (*irreg*) *vt* alimentar à força.
forceful ['fɔ:sful] *adj* enérgico, vigoroso.
forcemeat ['fɔ:smi:t] (*BRIT*) *n* (*CULIN*) recheio.
forceps ['fɔ:sɛps] *npl* fórceps *m inv*.
forcibly ['fɔ:səblɪ] *adv* à força.
ford [fɔ:d] *n* vau *m* ♦ *vt* vadear.
fore [fɔ:*] *n*: **to bring to the ~** pôr em evidência; **to come to the ~** (*person*) salientar-se.
forearm ['fɔ:rɑ:m] *n* antebraço.
forebear ['fɔ:bɛə*] *n* antepassado.
foreboding [fɔ:'bəudɪŋ] *n* mau presságio.
forecast ['fɔ:kɑ:st] (*irreg*: *like* **cast**) *n* prognóstico, previsão *f*; (*also*: *weather ~*) previsão do tempo ♦ *vt* prognosticar, prever.
foreclose [fɔ:'kləuz] *vt* (*LAW*: *also*: *~ on*) executar.
foreclosure [fɔ:'kləuʒə*] *n* execução *f* de uma hipoteca.
forecourt ['fɔ:kɔ:t] *n* (*of garage*) área de estacionamento.
forefathers ['fɔ:fɑ:ðəz] *npl* antepassados *mpl*.
forefinger ['fɔ:fɪŋgə*] *n* (dedo) indicador *m*.
forefront ['fɔ:frʌnt] *n*: **in the ~ of** em primeiro plano em.
forego (*irreg*: *like* **go**) *vt* = **forgo**.
foregoing ['fɔ:gəuɪŋ] *adj* acima mencionado ♦ *n*: **the ~** o supracitado.
foregone ['fɔ:gɔn] *pp of* **forego** ♦ *adj*: **it's a ~ conclusion** é uma conclusão inevitável.
foreground ['fɔ:graund] *n* primeiro plano ♦ *cpd* (*COMPUT*) de primeiro plano.
forehand ['fɔ:hænd] *n* (*TENNIS*) golpe *m* de frente.
forehead ['fɔrɪd] *n* testa.
foreign ['fɔrɪn] *adj* estrangeiro; (*trade*) exterior.
foreign body *n* corpo estranho.
foreign currency *n* câmbio, divisas *fpl*.
foreigner ['fɔrɪnə*] *n* estrangeiro/a.

***NB**: European Portuguese adds the following consonants to certain words:* **b** (sú(b)dito, su(b)til); **c** (a(c)ção, a(c)cionista, a(c)to); **m** (inde(m)ne); **p** (ado(p)ção, ado(p)tar); *for further details see p. xiii.*

foreign exchange *n* (*system*) câmbio; (*money*) divisas *fpl*.
foreign exchange market *n* mercado de câmbio.
foreign exchange rate *n* taxa de câmbio.
foreign investment *n* investimento estrangeiro.
Foreign Office (BRIT) *n* Ministério das Relações Exteriores.
foreign secretary (BRIT) *n* ministro das Relações Exteriores.
foreleg ['fɔːlɛg] *n* perna dianteira.
foreman ['fɔːmən] (*irreg*) *n* capataz *m*; (*in construction*) contramestre *m*; (LAW: *of jury*) primeiro jurado.
foremost ['fɔːməust] *adj* principal ♦ *adv*: **first and ~** antes de mais nada.
forename ['fɔːneɪm] *n* prenome *m*.
forensic [fə'rɛnsɪk] *adj* forense; **~ medicine** medicina legal; **~ expert** perito/a criminal.
forerunner ['fɔːrʌnə*] *n* precursor(a) *m/f*.
foresee [fɔː'siː] (*irreg*: *like* **see**) *vt* prever.
foreseeable [fɔː'siːəbl] *adj* previsível.
foreshadow [fɔː'fædəu] *vt* prefigurar.
foreshorten [fɔː'ʃɔːtn] *vt* escorçar.
foresight ['fɔːsaɪt] *n* previdência.
foreskin ['fɔːskɪn] *n* (ANAT) prepúcio.
forest ['fɔrɪst] *n* floresta.
forestall [fɔː'stɔːl] *vt* prevenir.
forestry ['fɔrɪstrɪ] *n* silvicultura.
foretaste ['fɔːteɪst] *n* antegosto, antegozo; (*sample*) amostra.
foretell [fɔː'tɛl] (*irreg*: *like* **tell**) *vt* predizer, profetizar.
forethought ['fɔːθɔːt] *n* previdência.
forever [fə'rɛvə*] *adv* para sempre; (*a long time*) muito tempo, um tempão (*inf*); **he's ~ forgetting my name** ele vive esquecendo o meu nome.
forewarn [fɔː'wɔːn] *vt* prevenir.
forewent *pt of* **forego**.
foreword ['fɔːwəːd] *n* prefácio.
forfeit ['fɔːfɪt] *n* prenda, perda; (*fine*) multa ♦ *vt* perder (direito a); (*one's life, health*) pagar com.
forgave [fə'geɪv] *pt of* **forgive**.
forge [fɔːdʒ] *n* forja; (*smithy*) ferraria ♦ *vt* (*signature, money*) falsificar; (*metal*) forjar.
forge ahead *vi* avançar constantemente.
forger ['fɔːdʒə*] *n* falsificador(a) *m/f*.
forgery ['fɔːdʒərɪ] *n* falsificação *f*.
forget [fə'gɛt] (*pt* **forgot**, *pp* **forgotten**) *vt, vi* esquecer.
forgetful [fə'gɛtful] *adj* esquecido.
forgetfulness [fə'gɛtfulnɪs] *n* esquecimento.
forget-me-not *n* miosótis *m*.
forgive [fə'gɪv] (*irreg*: *like* **give**) *vt* perdoar; **to ~ sb for sth** perdoar algo a alguém, perdoar alguém de algo.
forgiveness [fə'gɪvnɪs] *n* perdão *m*.
forgiving [fə'gɪvɪŋ] *adj* clemente.
forgo [fɔː'gəu] (*irreg*: *like* **go**) *vt* (*give up*) renunciar a; (*go without*) abster-se de.
forgot [fə'gɔt] *pt of* **forget**.
forgotten [fə'gɔtn] *pp of* **forget**.
fork [fɔːk] *n* (*for eating*) garfo; (*for gardening*) forquilha; (*of roads*) bifurcação *f* ♦ *vi* (*road*) bifurcar-se.
fork out (*inf*) *vt* (*pay*) desembolsar, morrer em ♦ *vi* (*pay*) descolar uma grana.
forked [fɔːkt] *adj* (*lightning*) em ziguezague.
fork-lift truck *n* empilhadeira.
forlorn [fə'lɔːn] *adj* desesperado; (*abandoned*) abandonado; (*attempt*) desesperado; (*hope*) último.
form [fɔːm] *n* forma; (SCH) série *f*; (*questionnaire*) formulário ♦ *vt* formar; **in the ~ of** na forma de; **to ~ part of sth** fazer parte de algo; **to ~ a queue** (BRIT) fazer fila; **to be in good ~** (SPORT, *fig*) estar em forma; **in top ~** em plena forma.
formal ['fɔːməl] *adj* (*offer, receipt*) oficial; (*person etc*) cerimonioso; (*occasion, dinner*) formal; (*dress*) a rigor (BR), de cerimônia (PT); (ART, PHILOSOPHY) formal.
formality [fɔː'mælɪtɪ] *n* (*of person*) formalismo; (*formal requirement*) formalidade *f*; (*ceremony*) cerimônia; **formalities** *npl* formalidades.
formalize ['fɔːməlaɪz] *vt* formalizar.
formally ['fɔːməlɪ] *adv* oficialmente, formalmente; (*in a formal way*) formalmente.
format ['fɔːmæt] *n* formato ♦ *vt* (COMPUT) formatar.
formation [fɔː'meɪʃən] *n* formação *f*.
formative ['fɔːmətɪv] *adj* (*years*) formativo.
former ['fɔːmə*] *adj* anterior; (*earlier*) antigo; (*ex*) ex-; **the ~ ... the latter ...** aquele ... este ...; **the ~ president** o ex-presidente.
formerly ['fɔːməlɪ] *adv* antigamente.
form feed *n* (*on printer*) alimentar formulário.
formidable ['fɔːmɪdəbl] *adj* terrível, temível.
formula ['fɔːmjulə] *n* fórmula; **F~ One** (AUT) Fórmula Um.
formulate ['fɔːmjuleɪt] *vt* formular.
fornicate ['fɔːnɪkeɪt] *vi* fornicar.
forsake [fə'seɪk] (*pt* **forsook**, *pp* **forsaken**) *vt* abandonar; (*plan*) renunciar a.
forsaken [fə'seɪkən] *pp of* **forsake**.
forsook [fə'suk] *pt of* **forsake**.
fort [fɔːt] *n* forte *m*; **to hold the ~** (*fig*) agüentar a mão.
forte ['fɔːtɪ] *n* forte *m*.
forth [fɔːθ] *adv* para adiante; **back and ~** de cá para lá; **and so ~** e assim por diante.
forthcoming ['fɔːθ'kʌmɪŋ] *adj* próximo, que está para aparecer; (*character*) comunicativo; (*book*) a ser publicado.
forthright ['fɔːθraɪt] *adj* franco.
forthwith ['fɔːθ'wɪθ] *adv* em seguida.
fortieth ['fɔːtɪɪθ] *num* quadragésimo; *see also* **fifth**.
fortification [fɔːtɪfɪ'keɪʃən] *n* fortificação *f*.
fortified wine ['fɔːtɪfaɪd-] *n* vinho generoso.
fortify ['fɔːtɪfaɪ] *vt* fortalecer.
fortitude ['fɔːtɪtjuːd] *n* fortaleza.
fortnight ['fɔːtnaɪt] *n* quinzena, quinze dias *mpl*.
fortnightly ['fɔːtnaɪtlɪ] *adj* quinzenal ♦ *adv*

quinzenalmente.
FORTRAN ['fɔːtræn] *n* FORTRAN *m*.
fortress ['fɔːtrɪs] *n* fortaleza.
fortuitous [fɔː'tjuːɪtəs] *adj* fortuito.
fortunate ['fɔːtʃənɪt] *adj*: **to be ~** ter sorte; **it is ~ that** ... é uma sorte que ....
fortunately ['fɔːtʃənɪtlɪ] *adv* felizmente.
fortune ['fɔːtʃən] *n* sorte *f*; (*wealth*) fortuna; **to make a ~** fazer fortuna.
fortune-teller *n* adivinho/a.
forty ['fɔːtɪ] *num* quarenta; *see also* **fifty**.
forum ['fɔːrəm] *n* foro.
forward ['fɔːwəd] *adj* (*movement*) para a frente; (*position*) avançado; (*front*) dianteiro; (*not shy*) imodesto, presunçoso; (COMM: *delivery*) futuro; (: *sales, exchange*) a termo ♦ *n* (SPORT) atacante *m* ♦ *adv* para a frente ♦ *vt* (*letter*) remeter; (*goods, parcel*) expedir; (*career*) promover; **to move ~** avançar; **"please ~"** "por favor remeta a novo endereço"; **~ planning** planejamento para o futuro.
forward(s) ['fɔːwəd(z)] *adv* para a frente.
forwent [fɔː'wɛnt] *pt of* **forgo**.
fossil ['fɔsl] *n* fóssil *m*; **~ fuel** combustível *m* fóssil.
foster ['fɔstə*] *vt* fomentar.
foster brother *n* irmão *m* de criação.
foster child (*irreg*) *n* filho adotivo.
foster mother *n* mãe *f* adotiva.
fought [fɔːt] *pt, pp of* **fight**.
foul [faul] *adj* sujo, porco; (*food*) podre; (*weather*) horrível; (*smell etc*) nojento; (*language*) obsceno; (*deed*) infame ♦ *n* (FOOTBALL) falta ♦ *vt* (*dirty*) sujar; (*block*) entupir; (*football player*) cometer uma falta contra; (*entangle: anchor, propeller*) enredar.
foul play *n* (SPORT) jogada suja; (LAW) crime *m*.
found [faund] *pt, pp of* **find** ♦ *vt* (*establish*) fundar.
foundation [faun'deɪʃən] *n* (*act*) fundação *f*; (*basis*) base *f*; (*also*: **~** *cream*) creme *m* base; **~s** *npl* (*of building*) alicerces *mpl*; **to lay the ~s** (*fig*) lançar os alicerces.
foundation stone *n* pedra fundamental.
founder ['faundə*] *n* fundador(a) *m/f* ♦ *vi* naufragar.
founding ['faundɪŋ] *n* fundação *f* ♦ *adj* fundador(a).
foundry ['faundrɪ] *n* fundição *f*.
fount [faunt] *n* fonte *f*.
fountain ['fauntɪn] *n* chafariz *m*.
fountain pen *n* caneta-tinteiro *f*.
four [fɔː*] *num* quatro; **on all ~s** de quatro; *see also* **five**.
four-poster *n* (*also*: **~** *bed*) cama com colunas.
foursome ['fɔːsəm] *n* grupo de quatro pessoas.
fourteen ['fɔː'tiːn] *num* catorze; *see also* **five**.
fourteenth ['fɔː'tiːnθ] *num* décimo-quarto; *see also* **fifth**.
fourth [fɔːθ] *adj* quarto ♦ *n* (AUT: *also*: **~** *gear*) quarta; *see also* **fifth**.
four-wheel drive *n* (AUT): **with ~** com tração nas quatro rodas.
fowl [faul] *n* ave *f* (doméstica).
fox [fɔks] *n* raposa ♦ *vt* deixar perplexo.
fox fur *n* raposa.
foxglove ['fɔksglʌv] *n* (BOT) dedaleira.
fox-hunting *n* caça à raposa.
foxtrot ['fɔkstrɔt] *n* foxtrote *m*.
foyer ['fɔɪeɪ] *n* vestíbulo, saguão *m*.
FP *n abbr* (BRIT) = **former pupil**; (US) = **fireplug**.
FPA (BRIT) *n abbr* = **Family Planning Association**.
Fr. *abbr* (REL: = *father*) P.; (: = *friar*) Fr.
fr. *abbr* (= *franc*) fr.
fracas ['frækɑː] *n* desordem *f*, rixa.
fraction ['frækʃən] *n* fração *f*.
fractionally ['frækʃnəlɪ] *adv*: **~ smaller** *etc* um pouquinho menor *etc*.
fractious ['frækʃəs] *adj* irascível.
fracture ['fræktʃə*] *n* fratura ♦ *vt* fraturar.
fragile ['frædʒaɪl] *adj* frágil.
fragment ['frægmənt] *n* fragmento.
fragmentary ['frægməntərɪ] *adj* fragmentário.
fragrance ['freɪgrəns] *n* fragrância.
fragrant ['freɪgrənt] *adj* fragrante, perfumado.
frail [freɪl] *adj* (*fragile*) frágil, quebradiço; (*weak*) delicado.
frame [freɪm] *n* (*of building*) estrutura; (*body*) corpo; (TECH) armação *f*; (*of picture, door*) moldura; (*of spectacles*: *also*: **~s**) armação *f*, aro ♦ *vt* enquadrar, encaixilhar; (*reply*) formular; (*inf*) incriminar; **~ of mind** estado de espírito.
framework ['freɪmwəːk] *n* armação *f*; (*fig*) sistema *m*, quadro.
France [frɑːns] *n* França.
franchise ['fræntʃaɪz] *n* (POL) direito de voto; (COMM) concessão *f*.
franchisee [fræntʃaɪ'ziː] *n* concessionário/a.
franchiser ['fræntʃaɪzə*] *n* concedente *m/f*.
frank [fræŋk] *adj* franco ♦ *vt* (*letter*) franquear.
Frankfurt ['fræŋkfəːt] *n* Frankfurt (BR), Francoforte (PT).
frankfurter ['fræŋkfəːtə*] *n* salsicha de cachorro quente.
franking machine ['fræŋkɪŋ-] *n* máquina de selagem.
frankly ['fræŋklɪ] *adv* francamente.
frankness ['fræŋknɪs] *n* franqueza.
frantic ['fræntɪk] *adj* frenético; (*person*) fora de si.
frantically ['fræntɪklɪ] *adv* freneticamente.
fraternal [frə'təːnl] *adj* fraterno.
fraternity [frə'təːnɪtɪ] *n* (*club*) fraternidade *f*; (US) clube *m* de estudantes; (*guild*) confraria.
fraternize ['frætənaɪz] *vi* confraternizar.

NB: *European Portuguese adds the following consonants to certain words:* **b** (sú(b)dito, su(b)til); **c** (a(c)ção, a(c)cionista, a(c)to); **m** (inde(m)ne); **p** (ado(p)ção, ado(p)tar); *for further details see p. xiii.*

fraud [frɔ:d] *n* fraude *f*; (*person*) impostor(a) *m/f*.
fraudulent ['frɔ:djulənt] *adj* fraudulento.
fraught [frɔ:t] *adj* tenso; ~ **with** repleto de.
fray [freɪ] *n* combate *m*, luta ♦ *vt* esfiapar ♦ *vi* esfiapar-se; **tempers were ~ed** estavam com os nervos em frangalhos.
FRB (*US*) *n abbr* = **Federal Reserve Board.**
FRCM (*BRIT*) *n abbr* = **Fellow of the Royal College of Music.**
FRCO (*BRIT*) *n abbr* = **Fellow of the Royal College of Organists.**
FRCP (*BRIT*) *n abbr* = **Fellow of the Royal College of Physicians.**
FRCS (*BRIT*) *n abbr* = **Fellow of the Royal College of Surgeons.**
freak [fri:k] *n* (*person*) anormal *m/f*; (*event*) anomalia; (*thing*) aberração *f*; (*inf*: *enthusiast*): **health** ~ maníaco/a com a saúde.
freak out (*inf*) *vi* (*on drugs*) baratinar-se; (*get angry*) ficar uma fera.
freakish ['fri:kɪʃ[*adj* anormal.
freckle ['frɛkl] *n* sarda.
free [fri:] *adj* livre; (*not fixed*) solto; (*gratis*) gratuito; (*liberal*) generoso ♦ *vt* (*prisoner etc*) pôr em liberdade; (*jammed object*) soltar; **to give sb a ~ hand** dar carta branca a alguém; **~ and easy** informal; **admission ~** entrada livre; **~ (of charge)** grátis, de graça.
freebie ['fri:bɪ] (*inf*) *n* brinde *m*; (*trip etc*): **it's a ~** está tudo pago.
freedom ['fri:dəm] *n* liberdade *f*.
freedom fighter *n* lutador(a) *m/f* pela liberdade.
free enterprise *n* livre iniciativa.
free-for-all *n* quebra-quebra *m*.
free gift *n* brinde *m*.
freehold ['fri:həuld] *n* propriedade *f* livre e alodial.
free kick *n* (tiro) livre *m*.
freelance ['fri:la:ns] *adj* autônomo.
freelancer ['fri:lɑ:nsə*] *n* free-lance *m/f*.
freeloader ['fri:ləudə*] (*pej*) *n* sanguessuga *m*.
freely ['fri:lɪ] *adv* livremente.
freemason ['fri:meɪsən] *n* maçom *m*.
freemasonry ['fri:meɪsnrɪ] *n* maçonaria.
freepost ['fri:pəust] *n* porte *m* pago.
free-range *n* (*egg*) caseiro.
free sample *n* amostra grátis.
free speech *n* liberdade *f* de expressão.
free trade *n* livre comércio.
freeway ['fri:weɪ] (*US*) *n* auto-estrada.
freewheel [fri:'wi:l] *vi* ir em ponto morto.
freewheeling [fri:'wi:lɪŋ] *adj* independente, livre.
free will *n* livre arbítrio; **of one's own ~** por sua própria vontade.
freeze [fri:z] (*pt* **froze**, *pp* **frozen**) *vi* gelar (-se), congelar-se ♦ *vt* gelar; (*prices, food, salaries*) congelar ♦ *n* geada, congelamento.
freeze over *vi* (*lake, river*) gelar; (*windscreen*) cobrir-se de gelo.
freeze up *vi* gelar.
freeze-dried *adj* liofilizado.
freezer ['fri:zə*] *n* congelador *m*, freezer *m* (*BR*).
freezing ['fri:zɪŋ] *adj*: ~ **(cold)** (*room etc*) glacial; (*person, hands*) gelado ♦ *n*: **3 degrees below ~** 3 graus abaixo de zero.
freezing point *n* ponto de congelamento.
freight [freɪt] *n* (*goods*) carga; (*money charged*) frete *m*; ~ **forward** frete pago na chegada; ~ **inward** frete incluído no preço.
freight car (*US*) *n* vagão *m* de carga.
freighter ['freɪtə*] *n* cargueiro.
freight forwarder [-'fɔ:wədə*] *n* despachante *m/f*.
freight train (*US*) *n* trem *m* de carga.
French [frɛntʃ] *adj* francês/esa ♦ *n* (*LING*) francês *m*; **the ~** *npl* os franceses.
French bean (*BRIT*) *n* feijão *m* comum.
French-Canadian *adj* franco-canadense ♦ *n* canadense *m/f* francês/esa *or* da parte francesa; (*LING*) francês *m* do Canadá.
French dressing *n* (*CULIN*) molho francês (de salada).
French fried potatoes (*US* **French fries**) *npl* batatas *fpl* fritas.
French Guiana [-gaɪ'ænə] *n* Guiana Francesa.
Frenchman ['frɛntʃmən] (*irreg*) *n* francês *m*.
French Riviera *n*: **the ~** a Costa Azul.
French window *n* porta-janela, janela de batente.
Frenchwoman ['frɛntʃwumən] (*irreg*) *n* francesa.
frenetic [frə'nɛtɪk[*adj* frenético.
frenzy ['frɛnzɪ] *n* frenesi *m*.
frequency ['fri:kwənsɪ] *n* freqüência.
frequency modulation *n* freqüência modulada.
frequent [*adj* 'fri:kwənt, *vt* frɪ'kwɛnt] *adj* freqüente ♦ *vt* freqüentar.
frequently ['fri:kwəntlɪ] *adv* freqüentemente, a miúdo.
fresco ['frɛskəu] *n* fresco.
fresh [frɛʃ] *adj* fresco; (*new*) novo; (*cheeky*) atrevido; **to make a ~ start** começar de novo.
freshen ['frɛʃən] *vi* (*wind, air*) tornar-se mais forte.
freshen up *vi* (*person*) lavar-se, refrescar-se.
freshener ['frɛʃnə*] *n*: **skin ~** refrescante *m* da pele; **air ~** purificador *m* de ar.
fresher ['frɛʃə*] (*BRIT*: *inf*) *n* (*SCH*) calouro/a.
freshly ['frɛʃlɪ] *adv* (*newly*) novamente; (*recently*) recentemente.
freshman ['frɛʃmən] (*irreg*) *n* (*SCH*) calouro/a.
freshness ['frɛʃnɪs] *n* frescura.
freshwater ['frɛʃwɔ:tə*] *adj* de água doce.
fret [frɛt] *vi* afligir-se.
fretful ['frɛtful] *adj* irritável.
Freudian ['frɔɪdɪən] *adj* freudiano; ~ **slip** ato falho.
FRG *n abbr* (= *Federal Republic of Germany*) RFA *f*.
Fri. *abbr* (= *Friday*) sex.
friar ['fraɪə*] *n* frade *m*; (*before name*) frei *m*.
friction ['frɪkʃən] *n* fricção *f*.

friction feed *n* (*on printer*) alimentação *f* por fricção.
Friday ['fraɪdɪ] *n* sexta-feira *f*; *see also* **Tuesday**.
fridge [frɪdʒ] *n* geladeira (*BR*), frigorífico (*PT*).
fried [fraɪd] *pt*, *pp of* **fry** ♦ *adj* frito; ~ **egg** ovo estrelado *or* frito.
friend [frɛnd] *n* amigo/a; **to make ~s with sb** fazer amizade com alguém.
friendliness ['frɛndlɪnɪs] *n* simpatia.
friendly ['frɛndlɪ] *adj* (*kind*) simpático; (*relations, behaviour*) amigável ♦ *n* (*also*: ~ *match*) amistoso; **to be ~ with** ser amigo de; **to be ~ to** ser simpático com.
friendly society *n* sociedade *f* mutuante, mútua.
friendship ['frɛndʃɪp] *n* amizade *f*.
frieze [fri:z] *n* friso.
frigate ['frɪgɪt] *n* fragata.
fright [fraɪt] *n* susto; **to take ~** assustar-se.
frighten ['fraɪtən] *vt* assustar.
frighten away *vt* espantar.
frighten off *vt* espantar.
frightened ['fraɪtnd] *adj*: **to be ~ of** ter medo de.
frightening ['fraɪtnɪŋ] *adj* assustador(a).
frightful ['fraɪtful] *adj* terrível, horrível.
frightfully ['fraɪtfulɪ] *adv* terrivelmente.
frigid ['frɪdʒɪd] *adj* (*MED*) frígido, frio.
frigidity [frɪ'dʒɪdɪtɪ] *n* (*MED*) frigidez *f*.
frill [frɪl] *n* babado; **without ~s** (*fig*: *car*) sem nenhum luxo; (: *dinner*) simples; (: *service*) sem mordomias; (: *holiday*) sem extras.
fringe [frɪndʒ] *n* franja; (*edge*: *of forest etc*) orla, margem *f*; (*fig*): **on the ~ of** à margem de.
fringe benefits *npl* benefícios *mpl* adicionais.
fringe theatre *n* teatro de vanguarda.
frisk [frɪsk] *vt* revistar.
frisky ['frɪskɪ] *adj* alegre, brincalhão/lhona.
fritter ['frɪtə*] *n* bolinho frito.
fritter away *vt* desperdiçar.
frivolity [frɪ'vɔlɪtɪ] *n* frivolidade *f*.
frivolous ['frɪvələs] *adj* frívolo.
frizzy ['frɪzɪ] *adj* frisado.
fro [frəu] *see* **to**.
frock [frɔk] *n* vestido.
frog [frɔg] *n* rã *f*; **to have a ~ in one's throat** ter pigarro.
frogman ['frɔgmən] (*irreg*) *n* homem-rã *m*.
frogmarch ['frɔgmɑ:tʃ] (*BRIT*) *vt*: **to ~ sb in/out** arrastar alguém para dentro/para fora.
frogmen ['frɔgmən] *npl of* **frogman**.
frolic ['frɔlɪk] *vi* brincar.
from [frɔm] *prep* de; **~ January (on)** a partir de janeiro; **where ~?** de onde?, daonde? (*inf*); **where is he ~?** ele é de onde?; **(as) ~ Friday** a partir de sexta-feira; **prices range ~ £10 to £50** os preços vão de £10 a £50; **~ what he says** pelo que ele diz.
frond [frɔnd] *n* fronde *f*.
front [frʌnt] *n* (*foremost part*) frente *f*, parte *f* dianteira; (*of house*) fachada; (*of book*) capa; (*promenade*: *also*: *sea* ~) orla marítima; (*MIL, POL, METEOROLOGY*) frente *f*; (*fig*: *appearances*) fachada ♦ *adj* dianteiro, da frente ♦ *vi*: **to ~ onto sth** dar para algo; **in ~ (of)** em frente (de).
frontage ['frʌntɪdʒ] *n* frontaria.
frontal ['frʌntəl] *adj* frontal.
front bench (*BRIT*) *n* (*POL*) *os dirigentes do partido no poder ou da oposição.*
front desk (*US*) *n* (*in hotel, at doctor's*) recepção *f*.
front door *n* porta principal; (*of car*) porta dianteira.
frontier ['frʌntɪə*] *n* fronteira.
frontispiece ['frʌntɪspi:s] *n* frontispício.
front page *n* primeira página.
front room (*BRIT*) *n* salão *m*, sala de estar.
front runner *n* (*fig*) favorito/a.
front-wheel drive *n* tração *f* dianteira.
frost [frɔst] *n* geada; (*also*: *hoar~*) gelo.
frostbite ['frɔstbaɪt] *n* ulceração *f* produzida pelo frio.
frosted ['frɔstɪd] *adj* (*glass*) fosco; (*esp US*: *cake*) com cobertura.
frosting ['frɔstɪŋ] (*esp US*) *n* (*on cake*) glace *f*.
frosty ['frɔstɪ] *adj* (*window*) coberto de geada; (*welcome*) glacial.
froth [frɔθ] *n* espuma.
frown [fraun] *n* olhar *m* carrancudo, cara amarrada ♦ *vi* franzir as sobrancelhas, amarrar a cara.
frown on *vt fus* (*fig*) desaprovar, não ver com bons olhos.
froze [frəuz] *pt of* **freeze**.
frozen ['frəuzn] *pp of* **freeze** ♦ *adj* congelado; **~ foods** congelados *mpl*.
FRS *n abbr* (*BRIT*: = *Fellow of the Royal Society*) *membro de associação promovedora de pesquisa científica*; (*US*: = *Federal Reserve System*) *banco central dos EUA*.
frugal ['fru:gəl] *adj* frugal.
fruit [fru:t] *n inv* fruta; (*fig*: *pl* **~s**) fruto.
fruiterer ['fru:tərə*] *n* fruteiro/a; **~'s (shop)** fruterio (*BR*), frutaria (*PT*).
fruitful ['fru:tful] *adj* proveitoso.
fruition [fru:'ɪʃən] *n*: **to come to ~** realizar-se.
fruit juice *n* suco (*BR*) *or* sumo (*PT*) de frutas.
fruitless ['fru:tlɪs] *adj* inútil, vão/vã.
fruit machine *n* caça-níqueis *m inv* (*BR*), máquina de jogo (*PT*).
fruit salad *n* salada de frutas.
frump [frʌmp] *n* careta (*mulher antiquada*).
frustrate [frʌs'treɪt] *vt* frustrar.
frustrated [frʌs'treɪtɪd] *adj* frustrado.
frustrating [frʌs'treɪtɪŋ] *adj* frustrante.
frustration [frʌs'treɪʃən] *n* frustração *f*.
fry [fraɪ] (*pt, pp* **fried**) *vt* fritar ♦ *npl*: **small ~** gente *f* insignificante.
frying pan ['fraɪɪŋ-] *n* frigideira.
FT (*BRIT*) *n abbr* (= *Financial Times*) *jornal*

NB: *European Portuguese adds the following consonants to certain words:* **b** (sú(b)dito, su(b)til); **c** (a(c)ção, a(c)cionista, a(c)to); **m** (inde(m)ne); **p** (ado(p)ção, ado(p)tar); *for further details see p. xiii.*

financeiro; **the ~ index** o índice da Bolsa de Valores de Londres.

ft. *abbr* = **foot; feet.**

FTC (*US*) *n abbr* = **Federal Trade Commission.**

fuchsia ['fju:ʃə] *n* fúcsia.

fuck [fʌk] (*inf!*) *vi* trepar(*!*) ♦ *vt* trepar com (*!*); ~ **off**! vai tomar no cu! (*!*).

fucking ['fʌkɪŋ] (*inf!*) *adj*: **this ~ ...** essa merda de ... (*!*); ~ **hell** puta que pariu (*!*).

fuddled ['fʌdld] *adj* (*muddled*) confuso, enrolado.

fuddy-duddy ['fʌdɪdʌdɪ] *adj, n* careta *m/f*.

fudge [fʌdʒ] *n* (*CULIN*) ≈ doce *m* de leite ♦ *vt* (*issue, problem*) evadir.

fuel [fjuəl] *n* (*gen, for heating*) combustível *m*; (*for propelling*) carburante *m*.

fuel oil *n* óleo combustível.

fuel pump *n* (*AUT*) bomba de gasolina.

fuel tank *n* depósito de combustível.

fug [fʌg] (*BRIT*) *n* bafio.

fugitive ['fju:dʒɪtɪv] *n* fugitivo/a.

fulfil [ful'fɪl] (*US* **fulfill**) *vt* (*function*) cumprir; (*condition*) satisfazer; (*wish, desire*) realizar.

fulfilled [ful'fɪld] *adj* (*person*) realizado.

fulfil(l)ment [ful'fɪlmənt] *n* satisfação *f*; (*of wish, desire*) realização *f*.

full [ful] *adj* cheio; (*fig*) pleno; (*complete*) completo; (*information*) detalhado; (*price*) integral; (*skirt*) folgado ♦ *adv*: ~ **well** perfeitamente; **I'm ~** estou satisfeito; ~ **(up)** (*hotel etc*) lotado; ~ **employment** pleno emprego; ~ **fare** passagem completa; **a ~ two hours** duas horas completas; **at ~ speed** a toda a velocidade; **in ~** (*reproduce, quote*) integralmente; (*name*) por completo.

fullback ['fulbæk] *n* zagueiro (*BR*), defesa *m* (*PT*).

full-blooded [-'blʌdɪd] *adj* (*vigorous*) vigoroso.

full-cream (*BRIT*) *adj*: ~ **milk** leite *m* integral.

full-grown *adj* crescido, adulto.

full-length *adj* (*portrait*) de corpo inteiro; ~ **(feature) film** longa-metragem *m*.

full moon *n* lua cheia.

full-scale *adj* (*model*) em tamanho natural; (*search, retreat*) em grande escala.

full-sized [-saɪzd] *adj* (*portrait etc*) em tamanho natural.

full stop *n* ponto (final).

full-time *adj* (*work*) de tempo completo *or* integral ♦ *n*: **full time** (*SPORT*) final *m*.

fully ['fulɪ] *adv* completamente; (*at least*): ~ **as big as** pelo menos tão grande como.

fully-fledged [-flɛdʒd] *adj* (*teacher, barrister*) diplomado; (*citizen, member*) verdadeiro.

fulsome ['fulsəm] (*pej*) *adj* extravagante.

fumble ['fʌmbl] *vi* atrapalhar-se ♦ *vt* (*ball*) atrapalhar-se com, apanhar de (*inf*).

fumble with *vt fus* atrapalhar-se com, apanhar de (*inf*).

fume [fju:m] *vi* fumegar; (*be angry*) estar com raiva; **~s** *npl* gases *mpl*.

fumigate ['fju:mɪgeɪt] *vt* fumigar; (*against pests etc*) pulverizar.

fun [fʌn] *n* (*amusement*) divertimento; (*joy*) alegria; **to have ~** divertir-se; **for ~** de brincadeira; **it's not much ~** não tem graça; **to make ~ of** fazer troça de, zombar de.

function ['fʌŋkʃən] *n* função *f*; (*reception, dinner*) recepção *f* ♦ *vi* funcionar; **to ~ as** funcionar como.

functional ['fʌŋkʃənəl] *adj* funcional.

function key *n* (*COMPUT*) tecla de função.

fund [fʌnd] *n* fundo; (*source, store*) fonte *f*; **~s** *npl* fundos *mpl*.

fundamental [fʌndə'mɛntl] *adj* fundamental.

fundamentalist [fʌndə'mɛntəlɪst] *n* fundamentalista *m/f*.

fundamentally [fʌndə'mɛntəlɪ] *adv* fundamentalmente.

fundamentals [fʌndə'mɛntlz] *npl* fundamentos *mpl*.

fund-raising [-'reɪzɪŋ] *n* angariação *f* de fundos.

funeral ['fju:nərəl] *n* (*burial*) enterro; (*ceremony*) exéquias *fpl*.

funeral director *n* agente *m/f* funerário/a.

funeral parlour *n* casa funerária.

funeral service *n* missa fúnebre.

funereal [fju:'nɪərɪəl] *adj* fúnebre, funéreo.

funfair ['fʌnfɛə*] (*BRIT*) *n* parque *m* de diversões.

fungi ['fʌŋgaɪ] *npl of* **fungus**.

fungus ['fʌŋgəs] (*pl* **fungi**) *n* fungo; (*mould*) bolor *m*, mofo.

funicular [fju:'nɪkjulə*] *n* (*also*: ~ *railway*) funicular *m*.

funnel ['fʌnl] *n* funil *m*; (*of ship*) chaminé *m*.

funnily ['fʌnɪlɪ] *adv*: ~ **enough** por incrível que pareça.

funny ['fʌnɪ] *adj* engraçado, divertido; (*strange*) esquisito, estranho.

funny bone *n parte sensível do cotovelo.*

fur [fə:*] *n* pele *f*; (*BRIT*: *in kettle etc*) depósito, crosta.

fur coat *n* casaco de peles.

furious ['fjuərɪəs] *adj* furioso; (*effort*) violento.

furiously ['fjuərɪəslɪ] *adv* com fúria; (*argue*) com violência.

furl [fə:l] *vt* enrolar; (*NAUT*) colher.

furlong ['fə:lɔŋ] *n* = *201.17m.*

furlough ['fə:ləu] *n* licença.

furnace ['fə:nɪs] *n* forno.

furnish ['fə:nɪʃ] *vt* mobiliar (*BR*), mobilar (*PT*); (*supply*): **to ~ with** fornecer de; **~ed flat** (*BRIT*) *or* **apartment** (*US*) apartamento mobiliado (*BR*) *or* mobilado (*PT*).

furnishings ['fə:nɪʃɪŋz] *npl* mobília.

furniture ['fə:nɪtʃə*] *n* mobília, móveis *mpl*; **piece of ~** móvel.

furniture polish *n* cera de lustrar móveis.

furore [fjuə'rɔ:rɪ] *n* furor *m*.

furrier ['fʌrɪə*] *n* peleiro/a.

furrow ['fʌrəu] *n* sulco.

furry ['fə:rɪ] *adj* peludo; (*toy*) de pelúcia.

further ['fə:ðə*] *adj* (*new*) novo, adicional ♦ *adv* mais longe; (*more*) mais; (*moreover*) além disso ♦ *vt* promover; **how much ~ is**

it? quanto mais tem que se ir?; **until ~ notice** até novo aviso; **~ to your letter of ...** (*COMM*) em resposta à sua carta do ....
further education *n* educação *f* superior.
furthermore [fəːðə'mɔː*] *adv* além disso.
furthermost ['fəːðəməust] *adj* mais distante.
furthest ['fəːðɪst] *superl of* **far**.
furtive ['fəːtɪv] *adj* furtivo.
furtively ['fəːtɪvlɪ] *adv* furtivamente.
fury ['fjuərɪ] *n* fúria.
fuse [fjuːz] (*US* **fuze**) *n* fusível *m*; (*for bomb etc*) espoleta, mecha ♦ *vt* (*metal*) fundir; (*fig*) unir ♦ *vi* (*metal*) fundir-se; (*fig*) unir-se; (*ELEC*): **to ~ the lights** queimar as luzes; **a ~ has blown** queimou um fusível.
fuse box *n* caixa de fusíveis.
fuselage ['fjuːzəlɑːʒ] *n* fuselagem *f*.
fuse wire *n* fio fusível.
fusillade [fjuːzɪ'leɪd] *n* fuzilada; (*fig*) saraivada.
fusion ['fjuːʒən] *n* fusão *f*.
fuss [fʌs] *n* (*uproar*) rebuliço; (*excitement*) espalhafato; (*complaining*) escândalo ♦ *vi* criar caso; **to make a ~** criar caso; **to make a ~ of sb** paparicar alguém.
fuss over *vt fus* (*person*) paparicar.
fussy ['fʌsɪ] *adj* (*person*) exigente, complicado, cheio de coisas (*inf*); (*dress, style*) espalhafatoso; **I'm not ~** (*inf*) para mim, tanto faz.
futile ['fjuːtaɪl] *adj* (*frivolous*) fútil; (*useless*) inútil, vão/vã.
futility [fjuː'tɪlɪtɪ] *n* inutilidade *f*.
future ['fjuːtʃə*] *adj*, *n* futuro **~s** *npl* (*COMM*) operações *fpl* a termo; **in (the) ~** no futuro; **in the near/immediate ~** em futuro próximo/imediato.
futuristic [fjuːtʃə'rɪstɪk] *adj* futurístico.
fuze [fjuːz] (*US*) *n*, *vi*, *vt* = **fuse**.
fuzzy ['fʌzɪ] *adj* (*PHOT*) indistinto; (*hair*) frisado, encrespado.
fwd. *abbr* = **forward**.
fwy (*US*) *abbr* = **freeway**.
FY *abbr* = **fiscal year**.
FYI *abbr* (= *for your information*) para seu conhecimento.

G

G, g [dʒiː] *n* (*letter*) G, g *m*; (*MUS*): **G** sol *m*; **G for George** G de Gomes.
G *n abbr* (*BRIT*: *SCH*) = **good**; (*US*: *CINEMA*: = *general (audience)*) livre.
g *abbr* (= *gram*; *gravity*) g.
GA (*US*) *abbr* (*POST*) = **Georgia**.
gab [gæb] (*inf*) *n*: **to have the gift of the ~** ter lábia, ser bom de bico.
gabble ['gæbl] *vi* tagarelar.
gaberdine [gæbə'diːn] *n* gabardina, gabardine *f*.
gable ['geɪbl] *n* cumeeira.
Gabon [gə'bɔn] *n* Gabão *m*.
gad about [gæd-] (*inf*) *vi* badalar.
gadget ['gædʒɪt] *n* aparelho, engenhoca; (*in kitchen*) pequeno utensílio.
Gaelic ['geɪlɪk] *adj* gaélico/a ♦ *n* (*LING*) gaélico.
gaffe [gæf] *n* gafe *f*.
gag [gæg] *n* (*on mouth*) mordaça; (*joke*) piada ♦ *vt* amordaçar.
gaga ['gɑːgɑː] *adj*: **to go ~** ficar gagá.
gaiety ['geɪɪtɪ] *n* alegria.
gaily ['geɪlɪ] *adv* alegremente.
gain [geɪn] *n* lucro, ganho ♦ *vt* ganhar ♦ *vi* (*watch*) adiantar-se; **to ~ by sth** tirar proveito de algo; **to ~ on sb** aproximar-se de alguém; **to ~ 3lbs (in weight)** engordar 3 libras; **to ~ ground** ganhar terreno.
gainful ['geɪnful] *adj* lucrativo, proveitoso.
gainsay [geɪn'seɪ] (*irreg*: *like* **say**) *vt* (*contradict*) contradizer; (*deny*) negar.
gait [geɪt] *n* modo de andar.
gal. *abbr* = **gallon**.
gala ['gɑːlə] *n* festa, gala; **swimming ~** festival de natação.
Galapagos (Islands) [gə'læpəgəs-] *npl*: **the ~** as ilhas Galápagos.
galaxy ['gæləksɪ] *n* galáxia.
gale [geɪl] *n* (*wind*) ventania; **~ force 10** vento de força 10.
gall [gɔːl] *n* (*ANAT*) fel *m*, bílis *f*; (*fig*) descaramento ♦ *vt* irritar.
gall. *abbr* = **gallon**.
gallant ['gælənt] *adj* valente; (*towards ladies*) galante.
gallantry ['gæləntrɪ] *n* valentia; (*courtesy*) galanteria.
gall-bladder *n* vesícula biliar.
galleon ['gælɪən] *n* galeão *m*.
gallery ['gælərɪ] *n* (*in theatre etc*) galeria; (*also*: *art ~*) galeria (de arte).
galley ['gælɪ] *n* (*ship's kitchen*) cozinha; (*ship*) galé *f*; (*also*: *~ proof*) paquê *m*.
Gallic ['gælɪk] *adj* francês/esa.
galling ['gɔːlɪŋ] *adj* irritante.
gallon ['gæln] *n* galão *m* (*BRIT* = *4.543 l*; *US* = *3.785 l*).
gallop ['gæləp] *n* galope *m* ♦ *vi* galopar; **~ing inflation** inflação galopante.
gallows ['gæləuz] *n* forca.
gallstone ['gɔːlstəun] *n* cálculo biliar.
galore [gə'lɔː*] *adv* à beça.
galvanize ['gælvənaɪz] *vt* galvanizar; (*fig*): **to ~ sb into action** galvanizar *or* eletrizar alguém.
Gambia ['gæmbɪə] *n* Gâmbia (*no article*).
gambit ['gæmbɪt] *n* (*fig*): (**opening**) **~** início (de conversa).

***NB**: European Portuguese adds the following consonants to certain words:* **b** (sú(b)dito, su(b)til); **c** (a(c)ção, a(c)cionista, a(c)to); **m** (inde(m)ne); **p** (ado(p)ção, ado(p)tar); *for further details see p. xiii.*

gamble ['gæmbl] *n* (*risk*) risco; (*bet*) aposta ♦ *vt*: **to ~ on** apostar em; ♦ *vi* jogar, arriscar; (*COMM*) especular.
gambler ['gæmblə*] *n* jogador(a) *m/f*.
gambling ['gæmblɪŋ] *n* jogo.
gambol ['gæmbl] *vi* cabriolar.
game [geɪm] *n* jogo; (*of cards, football*) partida; (*HUNTING*) caça ♦ *adj* valente; (*ready*): **to be ~ for anything** topar qualquer parada; **~s** *npl* (*SCH*) esporte *m* (*BR*), desporto (*PT*); **I'm ~** eu topo; **big ~** caça grossa.
game bird *n* ave *f* de caça.
gamekeeper ['geɪmki:pə*] *n* guarda-caça *m*.
gamely ['geɪmlɪ] *adv* valentemente.
game reserve *n* reserva de caça.
gamesmanship ['geɪmzmənʃɪp] *n* tática.
gammon ['gæmən] *n* (*bacon*) toucinho (defumado); (*ham*) presunto.
gamut ['gæmət] *n* gama.
gang [gæŋ] *n* bando, grupo; (*of workmen*) turma ♦ *vi*: **to ~ up on sb** conspirar contra alguém.
Ganges ['gændʒi:z] *n*: **the ~** o Ganges.
gangling ['gæŋglɪŋ] *adj* desengonçado.
gangplank ['gæŋplæŋk] *n* prancha (de desembarque).
gangrene ['gæŋgri:n] *n* gangrena.
gangster ['gæŋstə*] *n* gângster *m*, bandido.
gangway ['gæŋweɪ] *n* (*in theatre etc*) passagem *f*, coxia; (*on ship*) passadiço; (*on dock*) portaló *m*.
gantry ['gæntrɪ] *n* pórtico; (*for rocket*) guindaste *m*.
GAO (*US*) *n abbr* (= *General Accounting Office*) ≈ Tribunal *m* de Contas da União.
gaol [dʒeɪl] (*BRIT*) *n*, *vt* = **jail**.
gap [gæp] *n* brecha, fenda; (*in trees, traffic*) abertura; (*in time*) intervalo; (*fig*) lacuna.
gape [geɪp] *vi* estar *or* ficar boquiaberto.
gaping ['geɪpɪŋ] *adj* (*hole*) muito aberto.
garage ['gærɑ:ʒ] *n* garagem *f*.
garb [gɑ:b] *n* traje *m*.
garbage ['gɑ:bɪdʒ] *n* lixo; (*fig*: *inf*) disparates *mpl*; **the book/film is ~** o livro/filme é uma droga.
garbage can (*US*) *n* lata de lixo.
garbage disposal (unit) *n* triturador *m* de lixo.
garbled ['gɑ:bld] *adj* (*distorted*) adulterado, deturpado.
garden ['gɑ:dn] *n* jardim *m* ♦ *vi* jardinar; **~s** *npl* jardim público, parque *m*.
garden centre *n* loja de jardinagem.
gardener ['gɑ:dnə*] *n* jardineiro/a.
gardening ['gɑ:dnɪŋ] *n* jardinagem *f*.
gargle ['gɑ:gl] *vi* gargarejar ♦ *n* gargarejo.
gargoyle ['gɑ:gɔɪl] *n* gárgula.
garish ['gɛərɪʃ] *adj* vistoso, chamativo; (*colour*) berrante.
garland ['gɑ:lənd] *n* guirlanda.
garlic ['gɑ:lɪk] *n* alho.
garment ['gɑ:mənt] *n* peça de roupa.
garner ['gɑ:nə*] *vt* acumular, amontoar.
garnish ['gɑ:nɪʃ] *vt* adornar; (*CULIN*) enfeitar.
garret ['gærət] *n* mansarda.
garrison ['gærɪsn] *n* guarnição *f* ♦ *vt* guarnecer.
garrulous ['gærjuləs] *adj* tagarela.
garter ['gɑ:tə*] *n* liga.
garter belt (*US*) *n* cinta-liga.
gas [gæs] *n* gás *m*; (*US*: *gasoline*) gasolina ♦ *vt* asfixiar com gás; (*MIL*) gasear.
gas cooker (*BRIT*) *n* fogão *m* a gás.
gas cylinder *n* bujão *m* de gás.
gaseous ['gæsɪəs] *adj* gasoso.
gas fire (*BRIT*) *n* aquecedor *m* a gás.
gash [gæʃ] *n* talho; (*on face*) corte *m* ♦ *vt* talhar; (*with knife*) cortar.
gasket ['gæskɪt] *n* (*AUT*) junta, gaxeta.
gas mask *n* máscara antigás.
gas meter *n* medidor *m* de gás.
gasoline ['gæsəli:n] (*US*) *n* gasolina.
gasp [gɑ:sp] *n* arfada ♦ *vi* arfar.
  gasp out *vt* (*say*) dizer com voz entrecortada.
gas ring *n* boca de gás.
gas station (*US*) *n* posto de gasolina.
gas stove *n* (*cooker*) fogão *m* a gás; (*heater*) aquecedor *m* a gás.
gassy ['gæsɪ] *adj* gasoso.
gas tank (*US*) *n* (*AUT*) tanque *m* de gasolina.
gas tap *n* torneira do gás.
gastric ['gæstrɪk] *adj* gástrico.
gastric ulcer *n* úlcera gástrica.
gastroenteritis ['gæstrəuɛntə'raɪtɪs] *n* gastrenterite *f*.
gastronomy [gæs'trɔnəmɪ] *n* gastronomia.
gasworks ['gæswə:ks] *n*, *npl* usina de gás, gasômetro.
gate [geɪt] *n* portão *m*; (*RAIL*) barreira; (*of town, castle*) porta; (*at airport*) portão *m*; (*of lock*) comporta.
gateau ['gætəu] (*pl* **-x**) *n* bolo com creme e frutas.
gateaux ['gætəuz] *npl of* **gateau**.
gatecrash ['geɪtkræʃ] *vt* entrar de penetra em.
gatecrasher ['geɪtkræʃə*] *n* penetra *m/f*.
gateway ['geɪtweɪ] *n* portão *m*, passagem *f*.
gather ['gæðə*] *vt* (*flowers, fruit*) colher; (*assemble*) reunir; (*pick up*) colher; (*SEWING*) franzir; (*understand*) compreender ♦ *vi* (*assemble*) reunir-se; (*dust, clouds*) acumular-se; **to ~ (from/that)** concluir *or* depreender (de/que); **as far as I can ~** ao que eu entendo; **to ~ speed** acelerar(-se).
gathering ['gæðərɪŋ] *n* reunião *f*, assembléia.
GATT [gæt] *n* (= *General Agreement on Tariffs and Trade*) GATT *m*.
gauche [gəuʃ] *adj* desajeitado.
gaudy ['gɔ:dɪ] *adj* chamativo; (*pej*) cafona.
gauge [geɪdʒ] *n* (*instrument*) medidor *m*; (*measure, fig*) medida; (*RAIL*) bitola; ♦ *vt* medir; (*fig*: *sb's capabilities, character*) avaliar; **to ~ the right moment** calcular o momento azado; **petrol** (*BRIT*) *or* **gas** (*US*) **~** medidor de gasolina.
Gaul [gɔ:l] *n* (*country*) Gália; (*person*) gaulês/esa *m/f*.
gaunt [gɔ:nt] *adj* descarnado; (*grim, desolate*) desolado.

gauntlet ['gɔːntlɪt] *n* (*fig*): **to throw down the ~** lançar um desafio; **to run the ~** expôr-se (à crítica).
gauze [gɔːz] *n* gaze *f*.
gave [geɪv] *pt of* **give**.
gavel ['gævl] *n* martelo.
gawky ['gɔːkɪ] *adj* desengonçado.
gawp [gɔːp] *vi*: **to ~ at** olhar boquiaberto para.
gay [geɪ] *adj* (*homosexual*) gay; (*old-fashioned*: *person*) alegre; (*colour*) vistoso, vivo.
gaze [geɪz] *n* olhar *m* fixo ♦ *vi*: **to ~ at sth** fitar algo.
gazelle [gə'zɛl] *n* gazela.
gazette [gə'zɛt] *n* (*newspaper*) jornal *m*; (*official publication*) boletim *m* oficial.
gazetteer [gæzə'tɪə*] *n* dicionário geográfico.
gazumping [gə'zʌmpɪŋ] *n o fato de um vendedor quebrar uma promessa de venda para conseguir um preço mais alto*.
GB *abbr* = **Great Britain**.
GBH (*BRIT*: *inf*) *n abbr* (*LAW*) = **grievous bodily harm**.
GC (*BRIT*) *n abbr* (= *George Cross*) *distinção militar*.
GCE (*BRIT*) *n abbr* = **General Certificate of Education**.
GCHQ (*BRIT*) *n abbr* (= *Government Communications Headquarters*) *centro de intercepção de radiotransmissões estrangeiras*.
GCSE (*BRIT*) *n abbr* = **General Certificate of Secondary Education**.
Gdns *abbr* = **gardens**.
GDP *n abbr* = **gross domestic product**.
GDR *n abbr* (= *German Democratic Republic*) RDA *f*.
gear [gɪə*] *n* equipamento; (*TECH*) engrenagem *f*; (*AUT*) velocidade *f*, marcha (*BR*), mudança (*PT*) ♦ *vt*: **our service is ~ed to meet the needs of the disabled** o nosso serviço está adequado às necessidades dos deficientes físicos; **top** (*BRIT*) *or* **high** (*US*)**/low ~** quarta/primeira (marcha); **in ~** engrenado; **out of ~** desengrenado.
gear up *vi*: **to ~ up to do** preparar-se para fazer.
gear box *n* caixa de mudança (*BR*) *or* velocidades (*PT*).
gear lever (*US* **gear shift**) *n* alavanca de mudança (*BR*) *or* mudanças (*PT*).
gear wheel *n* roda de engrenagem.
GED (*US*) *n abbr* (*SCH*) = **general educational development**.
geese [giːs] *npl of* **goose**.
Geiger counter ['gaɪgə-] *n* contador *m* Geiger.
gel [dʒɛl] *n* gel *m*.
gelatin(e) ['dʒɛlətiːn] *n* gelatina.
gelignite ['dʒɛlɪgnaɪt] *n* gelignite *f*.
gem [dʒɛm] *n* jóia, gema.
Gemini ['dʒɛmɪnaɪ] *n* Gêminis *m*, Gêmeos *mpl*.
gen [dʒɛn] (*BRIT*: *inf*) *n*: **to give sb the ~ on sth** pôr alguém a par de algo.
Gen. *abbr* (*MIL*: = *general*) Gen.
gen. *abbr* (= *general*; *generally*) ger.
gender ['dʒɛndə*] *n* gênero.
gene [dʒiːn] *n* (*BIO*) gene *m*.
genealogy [dʒiːnɪ'ælədʒɪ] *n* genealogia.
general ['dʒɛnərl] *n* general *m* ♦ *adj* geral; **in ~** em geral; **the ~ public** o grande público; **~ audit** (*COMM*) exame *m* geral de auditoria.
general anaesthetic (*US* **general anesthetic**) *n* anestesia geral.
general election *n* eleições *fpl* gerais.
generalization [dʒɛnrəlaɪ'zeɪʃən] *n* generalização *f*.
generalize ['dʒɛnrəlaɪz] *vi* generalizar.
generally ['dʒənrəlɪ] *adv* geralmente.
general manager *n* diretor(a) *m/f* geral.
general practitioner *n* clínico/a geral.
general strike *n* greve *f* geral.
generate ['dʒɛnəreɪt] *vt* (*ELEC*) gerar; (*fig*) produzir.
generation [dʒɛnə'reɪʃən] *n* geração *f*.
generator ['dʒɛnəreɪtə*] *n* gerador *m*.
generic [dʒə'nɛrɪk] *adj* genérico.
generosity [dʒɛnə'rɔsɪtɪ] *n* generosidade *f*.
generous ['dʒɛnərəs] *adj* generoso; (*helping etc*) abundante.
genesis ['dʒɛnəsɪs] *n* gênese *f*.
genetic [dʒə'nɛtɪk] *adj* genético; **~ engineering** engenharia genética.
genetics [dʒɪ'nɛtɪks] *n* genética.
Geneva [dʒɪ'niːvə] *n* Genebra.
genial ['dʒiːnɪəl] *adj* jovial, simpático.
genitals ['dʒɛnɪtlz] *npl* órgãos *mpl* genitais.
genitive ['dʒɛnətɪv] *n* genitivo.
genius ['dʒiːnɪəs] *n* gênio.
genocide ['dʒɛnəusaɪd] *n* genocídio.
gent [dʒɛnt] (*BRIT*: *inf*) *n abbr* = **gentleman**.
genteel [dʒɛn'tiːl] *adj* fino, elegante.
gentle ['dʒɛntl] *adj* (*sweet*) amável, doce; (*touch etc*) leve, suave; (*animal*) manso.
gentleman ['dʒɛntlmən] (*irreg*) *n* senhor *m*; (*well-bred man*) cavalheiro; **~'s agreement** acordo de cavalheiros.
gentlemanly ['dʒɛntlmənlɪ] *adj* cavalheiresco.
gentlemen ['dʒɛntlmen] *npl of* **gentleman**.
gentleness ['dʒɛntlnɪs] *n* doçura, meiguice *f*; (*of touch*) suavidade *f*; (*of animal*) mansidão *f*.
gently ['dʒɛntlɪ] *adv* suavemente.
gentry ['dʒɛntrɪ] *n* pequena nobreza.
gents [dʒɛnts] *n* banheiro de homens (*BR*), casa de banho dos homens (*PT*).
genuine ['dʒɛnjuɪn] *adj* autêntico; (*person*) sincero.
genuinely ['dʒɛnjuɪnlɪ] *adj* sinceramente, realmente.
geographer [dʒɪ'ɔgrəfə*] *n* geógrafo/a.
geographic(al) [dʒɪə'græfɪk(l)] *adj* geográfico.

NB: European Portuguese adds the following consonants to certain words: **b** (sú(b)dito, su(b)til); **c** (a(c)ção, a(c)cionista, a(c)to); **m** (inde(m)ne); **p** (ado(p)ção, ado(p)tar); *for further details see p. xiii.*

geography [dʒɪ'ɔgrəfɪ] *n* geografia.
geological [dʒɪə'lɔdʒɪkl] *adj* geológico.
geologist [dʒɪ'ɔlədʒɪst] *n* geólogo/a.
geology [dʒɪ'ɔlədʒɪ] *n* geologia.
geometric(al) [dʒɪə'mɛtrɪk(l)] *adj* geométrico.
geometry [dʒɪ'ɔmətrɪ] *n* geometria.
Geordie ['dʒɔ:dɪ] (*BRIT*: *inf*) *n* natural *m/f* da cidade de Newcastle-upon-Tyne.
geranium [dʒɪ'reɪnjəm] *n* gerânio.
geriatric [dʒɛrɪ'ætrɪk] *adj* geriátrico.
germ [dʒə:m] *n* micróbio, bacilo; (*BIO*, *fig*) germe *m*.
German ['dʒə:mən] *adj* alemão/mã ♦ *n* alemão/mã *m/f*; (*LING*) alemão *m*.
German measles *n* rubéola.
Germany ['dʒə:mənɪ] *n* Alemanha.
germination [dʒə:mɪ'neɪʃən] *n* germinação *f*.
germ warfare *n* guerra bacteriológica.
gerrymandering ['dʒɛrɪmændərɪŋ] *n* *reorganização dos distritos eleitorais para garantir a vitória do próprio partido*.
gestation [dʒɛs'teɪʃən] *n* gestação *f*.
gesticulate [dʒɛs'tɪkjuleɪt] *vi* gesticular.
gesture ['dʒɛstjə*] *n* gesto; **as a ~ of friendship** em sinal de amizade.
get [gɛt] (*pt*, *pp* **got**, (*US*) *pp* **gotten**) *vt* (*obtain*) obter, arranjar; (*receive*) receber; (*achieve*) conseguir; (*find*) encontrar; (*catch*) pegar; (*fetch*) ir buscar; (*understand*) compreender; (*inf*: *annoy*): **he really ~s me!** ele me enche o saco! ♦ *vi* (*become*) ficar, tornar-se; (*go*): **to ~ to** (*place*) chegar a ♦ *modal aux vb*: **you've got to do it** você tem que fazê-lo; **to have got** ter; **to ~ old** envelhecer; **he got under the fence** passou por baixo da cerca; **to ~ sth for sb** arranjar algo para alguém; (*fetch*) ir buscar algo para alguém; **~ me Mr Jones, please** (*TEL*) pode chamar o Sr Jones por favor; **can I ~ you a drink?** você está servido?; **to ~ ready** preparar-se; **to ~ washed** lavar-se; **to ~ sth done** (*do*) fazer algo; (*have done*) mandar fazer algo; **to ~ one's hair cut** cortar o cabelo; **to ~ sb to do sth** convencer alguém a fazer algo; **I can't ~ it in/out/through** não consigo enfiá-lo/tirá-lo/passá-lo; **to ~ sth out of sth** (*fig*) tirar proveito de algo; **let's ~ going** *or* **started** vamos lá!
get about *vi* sair muito, viajar muito; (*news*) espalhar-se.
get across *vt*: **to ~ across (to)** (*message*, *meaning*) comunicar (a) ♦ *vi*: **to ~ across to** (*subj*: *speaker*) fazer-se entender por.
get along *vi* (*agree*) entender-se; (*depart*) ir embora; (*manage*) = **get by**.
get at *vt fus* (*attack*) atacar; (*reach*) alcançar; (*the truth*) descobrir; **what are you ~ting at?** o que você está querendo dizer?
get away *vi* partir; (*on holiday*) ir-se de férias; (*escape*) escapar.
get away with *vt fus* conseguir fazer impunemente.
get back *vi* (*return*) regressar, voltar ♦ *vt* receber de volta, recobrar; **to ~ back to** (*return*) voltar a; (*contact again*) estar em contato novamente com.
get back at (*inf*) *vt fus*: **to ~ back at sb** ir à forra com alguém.
get by *vi* (*manage*) virar-se; **I can ~ by in Dutch** eu me viro em holandês.
get down *vi* descer ♦ *vt* (*object*) abaixar, descer; (*depress*) deprimir.
get down to *vt fus* (*work*) pôr-se a (fazer); **to ~ down to business** entrar no assunto.
get in *vi* (*train*) chegar; (*arrive home*) voltar para casa ♦ *vt* (*bring in*: *harvest*) colher; (: *supplies*) abastecer-se de *or* com ♦ *vt fus* (*car etc*) subir em.
get into *vt fus* entrar em; (*vehicle*) subir em; (*clothes*) pôr, vestir, enfiar; **to ~ into bed** meter-se na cama; **to ~ into a rage** ficar com raiva.
get off *vi* (*from train etc*) saltar (*BR*), descer (*PT*); (*depart*: *person*, *car*) sair ♦ *vt* (*remove*: *clothes*, *stain*) tirar; (*send off*) mandar; (*have as leave*: *day*, *time*): **we got 2 days off** tivemos 2 dias de folga ♦ *vt fus* (*train*, *bus*) saltar de (*BR*), sair de (*PT*); **to ~ off to a good start** (*fig*) começar bem.
get on *vi* (*at exam etc*) ter sucesso; (*agree*) entender-se ♦ *vt fus* (*train etc*) subir em (*BR*), subir para (*PT*); (*horse*) montar em; **how are you ~ting on?** como vai?
get on to (*BRIT*) *vt fus* (*deal with*: *problem*) lidar com; (*contact*: *person*) entrar em contato com.
get out *vi* (*of place*, *vehicle*) sair; (*news*) vir a público ♦ *vt* (*take out*) tirar.
get out of *vt fus* sair de; (*duty etc*) escapar de.
get over *vt fus* (*illness*) restabelecer-se de ♦ *vt* (*communicate*: *idea etc*) fazer compreender, comunicar; (*finish*): **let's ~ it over (with)** vamos acabar com isso.
get round *vt fus* rodear; (*fig*: *person*) convencer ♦ *vi*: **to ~ round to doing sth** conseguir fazer algo.
get through *vi* (*TEL*) completar a ligação ♦ *vt fus* (*finish*: *work*, *book*) terminar.
get through to *vt fus* (*TEL*) comunicar-se com.
get together *vi* reunir-se ♦ *vt* reunir.
get up (*inf*) *vi* (*rise*) levantar(-se) ♦ *vt fus* levantar.
get up to *vt fus* (*reach*) chegar a; (*BRIT*: *prank etc*) fazer.
getaway ['gɛtəweɪ] *n* fuga, escape *m*.
getaway car *n* carro de fuga.
get-together *n* reunião *f*.
get-up (*inf*) *n* (*outfit*) roupa.
get-well card *n* cartão *m* com votos de melhoras.
geyser ['gi:zə*] *n* aquecedor *m* de água; (*GEO*) gêiser *m*.
Ghana ['gɑ:nə] *n* Gana (*no article*).
Ghanaian [gɑ:'neɪən] *adj*, *n* ganense *m/f*.
ghastly ['gɑ:stlɪ] *adj* horrível; (*pale*) pálido.

gherkin ['gəːkɪn] *n* pepino em vinagre.
ghetto ['gɛtəu] *n* gueto.
ghost [gəust] *n* fantasma *m* ♦ *vt* (*sb else's book*) escrever.
ghostly ['gəustlɪ] *adj* fantasmal.
ghostwriter ['gəustraɪtə*] *n* escritor(a) *m/f* cujos trabalhos são assinados por outrem.
ghoul [guːl] *n* assombração *f*.
ghoulish ['guːlɪʃ] *adj* (*tastes etc*) macabro.
GHQ *n abbr* (*MIL*) = **general headquarters**.
GI (*US*: *inf*) *n abbr* (= *government issue*) *soldado do exército americano*.
giant ['dʒaɪənt] *n* gigante *m* ♦ *adj* gigantesco, gigante; ~ **(size) packet** pacote tamanho gigante.
gibber ['dʒɪbə*] *vi* algaraviar.
gibberish ['dʒɪbərɪʃ] *n* algaravia.
gibe [dʒaɪb] *n* deboche *m* ♦ *vi*: **to ~ at** debochar de.
giblets ['dʒɪblɪts] *npl* miúdos *mpl*.
Gibraltar [dʒɪ'brɔːltə*] *n* Gibraltar *m* (*no article*).
giddiness ['gɪdɪnɪs] *n* vertigem *f*.
giddy ['gɪdɪ] *adj* (*dizzy*) tonto; (*speed*) vertiginoso; (*frivolous*) frívolo; **it makes me ~** me dá vertigem; **to be ~** estar com vertigem.
gift [gɪft] *n* presente *m*, dádiva; (*offering*) oferta; (*ability*) dom *m*, talento; (*COMM*: *also*: *free* ~) brinde *m*; **to have a ~ for sth** ter o dom de algo, ter facilidade para algo.
gifted ['gɪftɪd] *adj* dotado.
gift token *n* vale *m* para presente.
gift voucher *n* vale *m* para presente.
gig [gɪg] (*inf*) *n* (*of musician*) show *m*.
gigantic [dʒaɪ'gæntɪk] *adj* gigantesco.
giggle ['gɪgl] *vi* dar risadinha boba ♦ *n* risadinha boba.
GIGO ['gaɪgəu] (*inf*) *abbr* (*COMPUT*: = *garbage in, garbage out*) qualidade de entrada, qualidade de saída.
gild [gɪld] *vt* dourar.
gill [dʒɪl] *n* (*measure*) = *0.25 pints* (*BRIT* = *0.148 l*; *US* = *0.118 l*).
gills [gɪlz] *npl* (*of fish*) guelras *fpl*, brânquias *fpl*.
gilt [gɪlt] *adj*, *n* dourado.
gilt-edged [-'ɛdʒd] *adj* (*stocks, securities*) do Estado, de toda confiança.
gimlet ['gɪmlɪt] *n* verruma.
gimmick ['gɪmɪk] *n* truque *m or* macete *m* (publicitário).
gin [dʒɪn] *n* gim *m*, genebra.
ginger ['dʒɪndʒə*] *n* gengibre *m*.
ginger up *vt* animar.
ginger ale *n* cerveja de gengibre.
ginger beer *n* cerveja de gengibre.
gingerbread ['dʒɪndʒəbrɛd] *n* pão *m* de gengibre.
ginger-haired *adj* ruivo.
gingerly ['dʒɪndʒəlɪ] *adv* cuidadosamente.
gingham ['gɪŋəm] *n* riscadinho.
gipsy ['dʒɪpsɪ] *n* cigano ♦ *cpd* (*caravan, camp*) de ciganos.
giraffe [dʒɪ'rɑːf] *n* girafa.
girder ['gəːdə*] *n* viga, trave *f*.
girdle ['gəːdl] *n* (*corset*) cinta ♦ *vt* cintar.
girl [gəːl] *n* (*small*) menina (*BR*), rapariga (*PT*); (*young woman*) jovem *f*, moça; **an English ~** uma moça inglesa.
girlfriend ['gəːlfrɛnd] *n* (*of girl*) amiga; (*of boy*) namorada.
girlish ['gəːlɪʃ] *adj* ameninado, de menina.
Girl Scout (*US*) *n* escoteira.
Giro ['dʒaɪrəu] *n*: **the National ~** (*BRIT*) serviço bancário do correio.
giro ['dʒaɪrəu] *n* (*bank* ~) transferência bancária; (*post office* ~) transferência postal.
girth [gəːθ] *n* circunferência; (*stoutness*) gordura; (*of horse*) cilha.
gist [dʒɪst] *n* essencial *m*.
give [gɪv] (*pt* **gave**, *pp* **given**) *vt* dar; (*deliver*) entregar; (*as gift*) oferecer ♦ *vi* (*break*) dar folga; (*stretch*: *fabric*) dar de si; **to ~ sb sth, ~ sth to sb** dar algo a alguém; **to ~ a cry/sigh** dar um grito/suspiro; **how much did you ~ for it**? quanto você pagou por isso?; **12 o'clock, ~ or take a few minutes** por volta do meio-dia; **to ~ way** ceder; (*BRIT*: *AUT*) dar a preferência (*BR*), dar prioridade (*PT*).
give away *vt* (*give free*) dar de graça; (*betray*) traiçoar; (*disclose*) revelar; (*bride*) conduzir ao altar.
give back *vt* devolver.
give in *vi* ceder ♦ *vt* entregar.
give off *vt* soltar.
give out *vt* (*food etc*) distribuir; (*news*) divulgar ♦ *vi* (*be exhausted*: *strength, supplies*) esgotar-se; (*fail*) falhar.
give up *vi* desistir, dar-se por vencido ♦ *vt* renunciar a; **to ~ up smoking** deixar de fumar; **to ~ o.s. up** entregar-se.
give-and-take *n* toma-lá-dá-cá *m*.
giveaway ['gɪvəweɪ] *cpd*: ~ **prices** preços de liquidação ♦ *n* (*inf*): **her expression was a ~** a expressão dela a atraiçoava; **the exam was a ~**! o exame foi sopa!
given ['gɪvn] *pp of* **give** ♦ *adj* (*fixed*: *time, amount*) dado, determinado ♦ *conj*: ~ **the circumstances** ... dadas as circunstâncias ...; ~ **that** ... dado que ..., já que ....
glacial ['gleɪsɪəl] *adj* (*GEO*) glaciário; (*wind, weather*) glacial.
glacier ['glæsɪə*] *n* glaciar *m*, geleira.
glad [glæd] *adj* contente; **to be ~ about sth/that** estar contente com algo/contente que; **I was ~ of his help** eu lhe agradeci (por) sua ajuda.
gladden ['glædən] *vt* alegrar.
glade [gleɪd] *n* clareira.
gladioli [glædɪ'əulaɪ] *npl* gladíolos *mpl*.
gladly ['glædlɪ] *adv* com muito prazer.
glamorous ['glæmərəs] *adj* encantador(a), glamoroso.

NB: *European Portuguese adds the following consonants to certain words:* **b** (sú(b)dito, su(b)til); **c** (a(c)ção, a(c)cionista, a(c)to); **m** (inde(m)ne); **p** (ado(p)ção, ado(p)tar); *for further details see p. xiii.*

glamour ['glæmə*] *n* encanto, glamour *m*.
glance [glɑːns] *n* relance *m*, vista de olhos ♦ *vi*: **to ~ at** olhar (de relance).
glance off *vt fus* (*bullet*) ricochetear de.
glancing ['glɑːnsɪŋ] *adj* (*blow*) oblíquo.
gland [glænd] *n* glândula.
glandular fever ['glændjulə*-] (*BRIT*) *adj* mononucleose *f* infecciosa.
glare [glɛə*] *n* luz *f*, brilho ♦ *vi* deslumbrar; **to ~ at** olhar furiosamente para.
glaring ['glɛərɪŋ] *adj* (*mistake*) notório.
glass [glɑːs] *n* vidro, cristal *m*; (*for drinking*) copo; (: *with stem*) cálice *m*; (*also*: *looking ~*) espelho; **~es** *npl* óculos *mpl*.
glass-blowing [-bləuɪŋ] *n* modelagem *f* de vidro a quente.
glass fibre *n* fibra de vidro.
glasshouse ['glɑːshaus] (*irreg*) *n* estufa.
glassware ['glɑːswɛə*] *n* objetos *mpl* de cristal.
glassy ['glɑːsɪ] *adj* (*eyes*) vidrado.
Glaswegian [glæs'wiːdʒən] *adj* de Glasgow ♦ *n* natural *m/f* de Glasgow.
glaze [gleɪz] *vt* (*door*) envidraçar; (*pottery*) vitrificar; (*CULIN*) glaçar ♦ *n* verniz *m*; (*CULIN*) glacê *m*.
glazed [gleɪzd] *adj* (*eye*) vidrado; (*pottery*) vitrificado.
glazier ['gleɪzɪə*] *n* vidraceiro/a.
GLC (*BRIT*) *n abbr* (*old*: = *Greater London Council*) *o município de Grande Londres*.
gleam [gliːm] *n* brilho ♦ *vi* brilhar; **a ~ of hope** um fio de esperança.
gleaming ['gliːmɪŋ] *adj* brilhante.
glean [gliːn] *vt* (*information*) colher.
glee [gliː] *n* alegria, regozijo.
gleeful ['gliːful] *adj* alegre.
glen [glɛn] *n* vale *m*.
glib [glɪb] *adj* (*answer*) pronto; (*politician*) labioso.
glibness ['glɪbnɪs] *n* verbosidade *f*, lábia; (*of answer*) facilidade *f*.
glide [glaɪd] *vi* deslizar; (*AVIAT*, *birds*) planar ♦ *n* deslizamento; (*AVIAT*) vôo planado.
glider ['glaɪdə*] *n* (*AVIAT*) planador *m*.
gliding ['glaɪdɪŋ] *n* (*AVIAT*) vôo sem motor.
glimmer ['glɪmə*] *n* luz *f* trêmula ♦ *vi* tremeluzir.
glimpse [glɪmps] *n* olhar *m* de relance, vislumbre *m* ♦ *vt* vislumbrar, ver de relance; **to catch a ~ of** vislumbrar.
glint [glɪnt] *n* brilho; (*in the eye*) cintilação *f* ♦ *vi* cintilar.
glisten ['glɪsn] *vi* cintilar, resplandecer.
glitter ['glɪtə*] *vi* reluzir, brilhar ♦ *n* brilho.
glitz [glɪts] (*inf*) *n* cafonice *f*.
gloat [gləut] *vi*: **to ~ (over)** exultar (com).
global ['gləubl] *adj* (*worldwide*) mundial; (*overall*) global.
globe [gləub] *n* globo, esfera.
globetrotter ['gləubtrɔtə*] *n* pessoa que corre mundo.
globule ['glɔbjuːl] *n* glóbulo.
gloom [gluːm] *n* escuridão *f*; (*sadness*) tristeza.
gloomy ['gluːmɪ] *adj* (*dark*) escuro; (*sad*) triste; (*pessimistic*) pessimista; **to feel ~** estar abatido.
glorification [glɔːrɪfɪ'keɪʃən] *n* glorificação *f*.
glorify ['glɔːrɪfaɪ] *vt* glorificar; (*praise*) adorar.
glorious ['glɔːrɪəs] *adj* glorioso; (*splendid*) excelente.
glory ['glɔːrɪ] *n* glória ♦ *vi*: **to ~ in** gloriar-se de.
glory hole (*inf*) *n* zona.
Glos (*BRIT*) *abbr* = **Gloucestershire**.
gloss [glɔs] *n* (*shine*) brilho; (*also*: *~ paint*) pintura brilhante, esmalte *m*.
gloss over *vt fus* encobrir.
glossary ['glɔsərɪ] *n* glossário.
glossy ['glɔsɪ] *adj* lustroso ♦ *n* (*also*: *~ magazine*) revista de luxo.
glove [glʌv] *n* luva.
glove compartment *n* (*AUT*) porta-luvas *m inv*.
glow [gləu] *vi* (*shine*) brilhar; (*fire*) arder ♦ *n* brilho.
glower ['glauə*] *vi*: **to ~ at** olhar de modo ameaçador.
glowing ['gləuɪŋ] *adj* (*fire*) ardente; (*complexion*) afogueado; (*report*, *description etc*) entusiástico.
glow-worm *n* pirilampo, vaga-lume *m*.
glucose ['gluːkəus] *n* glicose *f*.
glue [gluː] *n* cola ♦ *vt* colar.
glue-sniffing [-'snɪfɪŋ] *n* cheira-cola *m*.
glum [glʌm] *adj* (*mood*) abatido; (*person*, *tone*) triste.
glut [glʌt] *n* abundância, fartura ♦ *vt* (*market*) saturar.
glutinous ['gluːtɪnəs] *adj* glutinoso.
glutton ['glʌtn] *n* glutão/ona *m/f*; **a ~ for work** um trabalhador incansável.
gluttonous ['glʌtənəs] *adj* glutão/ona.
gluttony ['glʌtənɪ] *n* gula.
glycerin(e) ['glɪsəriːn] *n* glicerina.
gm *abbr* (= *gram*) g.
GMAT (*US*) *n abbr* (= *Graduate Management Admissions Test*) *exame de admissão aos cursos de pós-graduação*.
GMB (*BRIT*) *n abbr* (= *General Municipal Boilermakers and Allied Trade Union*) *sindicato dos empregados dos municípios*.
GMT *abbr* (= *Greenwich Mean Time*) GMT *m*.
gnarled [nɑːld] *adj* nodoso.
gnash [næʃ] *vt*: **to ~ one's teeth** ranger os dentes.
gnat [næt] *n* mosquito.
gnaw [nɔː] *vt* roer.
gnome [nəum] *n* gnomo.
GNP *n abbr* = **gross national product**.
go [gəu] (*pt* **went**, *pp* **gone**, *pl* **~es**) *vi* ir; (*travel*) viajar; (*depart*) partir, ir-se; (*work*) funcionar; (*be sold*): **to ~ for £10** ser vendido por £10; (*time*) passar; (*become*) ficar; (*break*) romper-se; (*suit*): **to ~ with** acompanhar, combinar com ♦ *n*: **to have a ~ (at)** tentar a sorte (com); **to be on the ~** ter

muito para fazer; **whose ~ is it?** de quem é a vez?; **to ~ by car/on foot** ir de carro/a pé; **he's ~ing to do it** ele vai fazê-lo; **to ~ for a walk** ir passear; **to ~ dancing** ir dançar; **to ~ to sleep** adormecer, dormir; **to ~ and see sb, to ~ to see sb** ir visitar alguém; **how is it ~ing?** como vai?; **how did it ~?** como foi?; **my voice has gone** fiquei afônico; **the cake is all gone** o bolo acabou; **I'll take whatever is ~ing** (*BRIT*) eu aceito o que tem; **... to ~** (*US*: *food*) ... para levar.
go about *vi* (*also*: *~ around*) andar por aí; (*rumour*) espalhar-se ♦ *vt fus*: **how do I ~ about this?** como é que eu faço isso?; **to ~ about one's business** ocupar-se de seus afazeres.
go after *vt fus* (*pursue*) perseguir, ir atrás de; (*job, record etc*) tentar conseguir.
go against *vt fus* (*be unfavourable to*) ser desfavorável a; (*be contrary to*) ser contrário a.
go ahead *vi* (*make progress*) progredir; (*be realized*) efetuar-se.
go along *vi* (*go too*) ir também; (*continue*) continuar, prosseguir ♦ *vt fus* ladear; **correct as you ~ along** corrija na hora; **to ~ along with** (*accompany*) acompanhar; (*agree with*) concordar com.
go away *vi* ir-se, ir embora.
go back *vi* voltar.
go back on *vt fus* (*promise*) faltar com.
go by *vi* (*years, time*) passar ♦ *vt fus* guiar-se por; (*believe*) acreditar em.
go down *vi* descer, baixar; (*ship*) afundar; (*sun*) pôr-se ♦ *vt fus* descer; **that should ~ down well with him** (*fig*) isso deve agradar-lhe.
go for *vt fus* (*fetch*) ir buscar; (*like*) gostar de; (*attack*) atacar.
go in *vi* entrar.
go in for *vt fus* (*competition*) inscrever-se em; (*like*) gostar de.
go into *vt fus* entrar em; (*investigate*) investigar; (*embark on*) embarcar em.
go off *vi* ir-se; (*food*) estragar, apodrecer; (*explode*) explodir; (*lights etc*) apagar-se; (*event*) realizar-se ♦ *vt fus* deixar de gostar de; **the gun went off** o revólver disparou; **to ~ off to sleep** adormecer; **the party went off well** a festa foi um sucesso.
go on *vi* seguir, continuar; (*happen*) acontecer, ocorrer; (*lights*) acender-se ♦ *vt fus* (*be guided by*: *evidence etc*) basear-se em; **to ~ on doing** continuar fazendo *or* a fazer; **what's ~ing on here?** o que é que está acontecendo aqui?
go on at *vt fus* (*nag*) bronquear com.
go on with *vt fus* continuar com.
go out *vi* sair; (*fire, light*) apagar-se; (*tide*) baixar; **to ~ out with sb** (*boyfriend, girlfriend*) namorar alguém.
go over *vi* (*ship*) soçobrar ♦ *vt fus* (*check*) revisar; **to ~ over sth in one's mind** refletir sobre algo.
go round *vi* (*circulate*: *news, rumour*) circular; (*revolve*) girar; (*suffice*) bastar, dar (para todos); (*visit*): **to ~ round to sb's** ir à casa de alguém; (*make a detour*): **to ~ round (by)** fazer um desvio (por).
go through *vt fus* (*town etc*) atravessar; (*search through*) vasculhar; (*examine*: *list, book*) percorrer de cabo a rabo: (*carry out*) executar.
go through with *vt fus* (*plan, crime*) levar a cabo.
go together *vi* combinar.
go under *vi* (*sink*) afundar; (*fail*: *company*) falir; (: *person*) sucumbir.
go up *vi* subir; (*price*) aumentar ♦ *vt fus* subir; **to ~ up in flames** incendiar-se, pegar fogo.
go without *vt fus* passar sem.
goad [gəud] *vt* aguilhoar.
go-ahead *adj* empreendedor(a), dinâmico ♦ *n* luz *f* verde.
goal [gəul] *n* meta, alvo; (*SPORT*) gol *m* (*BR*), golo (*PT*).
goalkeeper ['gəulki:pə*] *n* goleiro/a (*BR*), guarda-redes *m/f inv* (*PT*).
goal post *n* trave *f*.
goat [gəut] *n* cabra; (*also*: *billy ~*) bode *m*.
gobble ['gɔbl] *vt* (*also*: *~ down, ~ up*) engolir rapidamente, devorar.
go-between *n* intermediário/a.
Gobi Desert ['gəubɪ-] *n* Deserto de Gobi.
goblet ['gɔblɪt] *n* cálice *m*.
goblin ['gɔblɪn] *n* duende *m*.
go-cart *n* kart *m* ♦ *cpd*: **~ racing** kartismo.
god [gɔd] *n* deus *m*; **G~** Deus.
godchild ['gɔdtʃaɪld] (*irreg*) *n* afilhado/a.
goddaughter ['gɔddɔ:tə*] *n* afilhada.
goddess ['gɔdɪs] *n* deusa.
godfather ['gɔdfɑ:ðə*] *n* padrinho.
godforsaken ['gɔdfəseɪkən] *adj* miserável, abandonado.
godmother ['gɔdmʌðə*] *n* madrinha.
godparents ['gɔdpɛərənts] *npl* padrinhos *mpl*.
godsend ['gɔdsɛnd] *n* dádiva do céu.
godson ['gɔdsʌn] *n* afilhado.
goes [gəuz] *vb see* **go**.
go-getter [-'gɛtə*] *n* pessoa dinâmica, pessoa furona (*inf*).
goggle ['gɔgl] *vi*: **to ~ at** olhar de olhos esbugalhados.
goggles ['gɔglz] *npl* óculos *mpl* de proteção.
going ['gəuɪŋ] *n* (*conditions*) estado do terreno ♦ *adj*: **the ~ rate** tarifa corrente *or* em vigor; **a ~ concern** empresa em funcionamento, empresa com fundo de comérico; **it was slow ~** ia devagar.
goings-on (*inf*) *npl* maquinações *fpl*.
go-kart [-kɑ:t] *n* = **go-cart**.
gold [gəuld] *n* ouro ♦ *adj* de ouro.
golden ['gəuldən] *adj* (*made of gold*) de ouro;

NB: European Portuguese adds the following consonants to certain words: **b** (sú(b)dito, su(b)til); **c** (a(c)ção, a(c)cionista, a(c)to); **m** (inde(m)ne); **p** (ado(p)ção, ado(p)tar); *for further details see p. xiii.*

(*gold in colour*) dourado.
golden age *n* idade *f* de ouro.
golden handshake (*BRIT*) *n* bolada.
golden rule *n* regra de ouro.
goldfish ['gəuldfɪʃ] *n inv* peixe-dourado *m*.
gold leaf *n* ouro em folha.
gold medal *n* (*SPORT*) medalha de ouro.
goldmine ['gəuldmaɪn] *n* mina de ouro.
gold-plated [-'pleɪtɪd] *adj* plaquê *inv*.
gold-rush *n* corrida do ouro.
goldsmith ['gəuldsmɪθ] *n* ourives *m/f inv*.
gold standard *n* padrão-ouro *m*.
golf [gɔlf] *n* golfe *m*.
golf ball *n* bola de golfe; (*on typewriter*) esfera.
golf club *n* clube *m* de golfe; (*stick*) taco.
golf course *n* campo de golfe.
golfer ['gɔlfə*] *n* jogador(a) *m/f* de golfe, golfista *m/f*.
gondola ['gɔndələ] *n* gôndola.
gondolier [gɔndə'lɪə*] *n* gondoleiro.
gone [gɔn] *pp of* **go**.
gong [gɔŋ] *n* gongo.
gonorrhea [gɔnə'rɪə] *n* gonorréia.
good [gud] *adj* bom/boa; (*kind*) bom, bondoso; (*well-behaved*) educado; (*useful*) útil ♦ *n* bem *m*; **~s** *npl* (*possessions*) bens *mpl*; (*COMM*) mercadorias *fpl*; **~s and chattels** bens móveis; **~!** bom!; **to be ~ at** ser bom em; **to be ~ for** servir para; **it's ~ for you** faz-lhe bem; **it's a ~ thing you were there** ainda bem que você estava lá; **she is ~ with children/her hands** ela tem habilidade com crianças/com as mãos; **to feel ~** sentir-se bem, estar bom; **it's ~ to see you** é bom ver você; (*formal*) prazer em vê-lo; **he's up to no ~** ele tem más intenções; **it's no ~ complaining** não adianta se queixar; **for the common ~** para o bem comum; **would you be ~ enough to ...?** podia fazer-me o favor de ...?, poderia me fazer a gentileza de ...?; **that's very ~ of you** é muita bondade sua; **is this any ~?** (*will it do?*) será que isso serve?; (*what's it like?*) será que vale a pena?; **a ~ deal (of)** muito; **a ~ many** muitos; **to make ~** reparar; **for ~** (*forever*) para sempre, definitivamente; (*once and for all*) de uma vez por todas; **~ morning/afternoon!** bom dia/boa tarde!; **~ evening!** boa noite!; **~ night!** boa noite!
goodbye [gud'baɪ] *excl* até logo (*BR*), adeus (*PT*); **to say ~** despedir-se.
good faith *n* boa fé.
good-for-nothing *adj* imprestável.
Good Friday *n* Sexta-Feira Santa.
good-humoured [-'hju:məd] *adj* (*person*) alegre; (*remark, joke*) sem malícia.
good-looking [-'lukɪŋ] *adj* bonito.
good-natured *adj* (*person*) de bom gênio; (*discussion*) cordial.
goodness ['gudnɪs] *n* (*of person*) bondade *f*; **for ~ sake!** pelo amor de Deus!; **~ gracious!** meu Deus do céu!, nossa (senhora)!
goods train (*BRIT*) *n* trem *m* de carga.
goodwill [gud'wɪl] *n* boa vontade *f*; (*COMM*) fundo de comércio, aviamento.
goody-goody ['gudɪgudɪ] (*pej*) *n* puxa-saco *m*.
goose [gu:s] (*pl* **geese**) *n* ganso.
gooseberry ['guzbərɪ] *n* groselha; **to play ~** ficar de vela, segurar a vela.
gooseflesh ['gu:sflɛʃ] *n* pele *f* arrepiada.
goosepimples ['gu:spɪmplz] *npl* pele *f* arrepiada.
goose step *n* (*MIL*) passo de ganso.
GOP (*US*: *inf*) *n abbr* (*POL*: = *Grand Old Party*) partido republicano.
gore [gɔ:*] *vt* escornar ♦ *n* sangue *m*.
gorge [gɔ:dʒ] *n* desfiladeiro ♦ *vt*: **to ~ o.s. (on)** empanturrar-se (de).
gorgeous ['gɔ:dʒəs] *adj* magnífico, maravilhoso; (*woman*) lindo.
gorilla [gə'rɪlə] *n* gorila *m*.
gormless ['gɔ:mlɪs] (*BRIT*: *inf*) *adj* burro.
gorse [gɔ:s] *n* tojo.
gory ['gɔ:rɪ] *adj* sangrento.
go-slow (*BRIT*) *n* greve *f* de trabalho lento, operação *f* tartaruga.
gospel ['gɔspl] *n* evangelho.
gossamer ['gɔsəmə*] *n* (*cobweb*) teia de aranha; (*cloth*) tecido diáfano, gaze *f* fina.
gossip ['gɔsɪp] *n* (*scandal*) fofocas *fpl* (*BR*), mexericos *mpl* (*PT*); (*chat*) conversa; (*scandalmonger*) fofoqueiro/a (*BR*), mexeriqueiro/a (*PT*) ♦ *vi* (*spread scandal*) fofocar (*BR*), mexericar (*PT*); (*chat*) bater (um) papo (*BR*), cavaquear (*PT*); **a piece of ~** uma fofoca (*BR*), um mexerico (*PT*).
gossip column *n* (*PRESS*) coluna social.
got [gɔt] *pt, pp of* **get**.
Gothic ['gɔθɪk] *adj* gótico.
gotten ['gɔtn] (*US*) *pp of* **get**.
gouge [gaudʒ] *vt* (*also*: **~** *out*: *hole etc*) abrir; (: *initials*) talhar: **to ~ sb's eyes out** arrancar os olhos de alguém.
gourd [guəd] *n* cabaça, cucúrbita.
gourmet ['guəmeɪ] *n* gourmet *m*, gastrônomo/a.
gout [gaut] *n* gota.
govern ['gʌvən] *vt* governar.
governess ['gʌvənɪs] *n* governanta.
governing ['gʌvənɪŋ] *adj* (*POL*) no governo, ao poder; **~ body** conselho de administração.
government ['gʌvnmənt] *n* governo ♦ *cpd* (*of administration*) governamental; (*of state*) do Estado; **local ~** governo municipal.
governmental [gʌvn'mɛntl] *adj* governamental.
government housing (*US*) *n* casas *fpl* populares.
government stock *n* títulos *mpl* do governo.
governor ['gʌvənə*] *n* governador(a) *m/f*; (*of school, hospital, jail*) diretor(a) *m/f*.
Govt *abbr* = **government**.
gown [gaun] *n* vestido; (*of teacher, judge*) toga.
GP *n abbr* (*MED*) = **general practitioner**.
GPO *n abbr* (*BRIT*: *old*) = **General Post Office**; (*US*) = **Government Printing Office**.
gr. *abbr* (*COMM*) = **gross**.

grab [græb] *vt* agarrar ♦ *vi*: **to ~ at** tentar agarrar.
grace [greɪs] *n* (*REL*) graça; (*gracefulness*) elegância, fineza ♦ *vt* (*favour*) honrar; **5 days'** ~ um prazo de 5 dias; **to say** ~ dar graças (antes de comer); **with a good/bad** ~ de bom/mau grado; **his sense of humour is his saving** ~ seu único mérito é seu senso de humor.
graceful ['greɪsful] *adj* elegante, gracioso.
gracious ['greɪʃəs] *adj* gracioso, afável; (*benevolent*) bondoso, complacente; (*formal*: *God*) misericordioso ♦ *excl*: **(good)** ~! meu Deus do céu!, nossa (senhora)!
gradation [grə'deɪʃn] *n* gradação *f*.
grade [greɪd] *n* (*quality*) classe *f*, qualidade *f*; (*degree*) grau *m*; (*US*: *SCH*) série f, classe; (: *gradient*) declive *m* ♦ *vt* classificar; **to make the** ~ (*fig*) ter sucesso.
grade crossing (*US*) *n* passagem *f* de nível.
grade school (*US*) *n* escola primária.
gradient ['greɪdɪənt] *n* declive *m*; (*GEOM*) gradiente *m*.
gradual ['grædjuəl] *adj* gradual, gradativo.
gradually ['grædjuəlɪ] *adv* gradualmente, gradativamente, pouco a pouco.
graduate [*n* 'grædjuɪt, *vi* 'grædjueɪt] *n* graduado, licenciado; (*US*) diplomado do colégio ♦ *vi* formar-se, licenciar-se.
graduated pension ['grædjueɪtɪd-] *n aposentadoria calculada em função dos últimos salários.*
graduation [grædju'eɪʃən] *n* formatura.
graffiti [grə'fi:tɪ] *n* pichações *fpl*.
graft [grɑ:ft] *n* (*AGR*, *MED*) enxerto; (*bribery*) suborno ♦ *vt* enxertar; **hard** ~ (*inf*) labuta.
grain [greɪn] *n* grão *m*; (*corn*) cereais *mpl*; (*US*: *corn*) trigo; (*in wood*) veio, fibra; **it goes against the** ~ é contra a sua (*or* minha *etc*) natureza.
gram [græm] *n* grama *m*.
grammar ['græmə*] *n* gramática.
grammar school *n* (*BRIT*) ≈ liceo, ≈ ginásio.
grammatical [grə'mætɪkl] *adj* gramatical.
gramme [græm] *n* = **gram**.
gramophone ['græməfəun] (*BRIT*) *n* toca-discos *m inv* (*BR*), gira-discos *m inv* (*PT*).
granary ['grænərɪ] *n* celeiro.
grand [grænd] *adj* grande, magnífico ♦ *n* (*inf*: *thousand*) mil libras *fpl* (*or* dólares *mpl*).
grandchild ['græntʃaɪld] (*irreg*) *n* neto/a.
granddad ['grændæd] *n* vovô *m*.
granddaughter ['grændɔ:tə*] *n* neta.
grandeur ['grændjə*] *n* grandeza, magnificência; (*of event*) grandiosidade *f*; (*of house*, *style*) imponência.
grandfather ['grænfɑ:ðə*] *n* avô *m*.
grandiose ['grændɪəuz] *adj* grandioso; (*pej*) pomposo; (*house*, *style*) imponente.
grand jury (*US*) *n* júri *m* de instrução.
grandma ['grænmɑ:] *n* avó *f*, vovó *f*.
grandmother ['grænmʌðə*] *n* avó *f*.
grandpa ['grænpɑ:] *n* = **granddad**.
grandparents ['grændpɛərənts] *npl* avós *mpl*.
grand piano *n* piano de cauda.
Grand Prix ['grɑ̃:'pri:] *n* (*AUT*) Grande Prêmio.
grandson ['grænsʌn] *n* neto.
grandstand ['grænstænd] *n* (*SPORT*) tribuna principal.
grand total *n* total *m* geral *or* global.
granite ['grænɪt] *n* granito.
granny ['grænɪ] *n* avó *f*, vovó *f*.
grant [grɑ:nt] *vt* (*concede*) conceder; (*a request etc*) anuir a; (*admit*) admitir ♦ *n* (*SCH*) bolsa; (*ADMIN*) subvenção *f*, subsídio; **to take sth for ~ed** dar algo por certo; **to ~ that** admitir que.
granulated sugar ['grænjuleɪtɪd-] *n* açúcar *m* granulado.
granule ['grænju:l] *n* grânulo.
grape [greɪp] *n* uva; **sour ~s** (*fig*) inveja; **a bunch of ~s** um cacho de uvas.
grapefruit ['greɪpfru:t] *n* toranja, grapefruit *m* (*BR*).
grapevine ['greɪpvaɪn] *n* parreira; **I heard it on** *or* **through the** ~ (*fig*) um passarinho me contou.
graph [grɑ:f] *n* gráfico.
graphic ['græ:fɪk] *adj* gráfico.
graphic designer *n* desenhista *m/f* industrial.
graphics ['græfɪks] *n* (*art*) artes *fpl* gráficas ♦ *npl* (*drawings*) dessenhos *mpl*; (: *COMPUT*) gráficos *mpl*.
graphite ['græfaɪt] *n* grafita.
graph paper *n* papel *m* quadriculado.
grapple ['græpl] *vi*: **to ~ with sth** estar às voltas com algo.
grappling iron ['græplɪŋ-] *n* (*NAUT*) arpéu *m*.
grasp [grɑ:sp] *vt* agarrar, segurar; (*understand*) compreender, entender ♦ *n* (*grip*) agarramento; (*reach*) alcance *m*; (*understanding*) compreensão *f*; **to have sth within one's** ~ ter algo ao seu alcance; **to have a good ~ of sth** (*fig*) ter um bom domínio de algo, dominar algo.
grasp at *vt fus* (*rope etc*) tentar agarrar; (*opportunity*) agarrar.
grasping ['grɑ:spɪŋ] *adj* avaro.
grass [grɑ:s] *n* grama (*BR*), relva (*PT*); (*uncultivated*) cupim *m*; (*lawn*) gramado (*BR*), relvado (*PT*); (*BRIT*: *inf*: *informer*) dedo-duro *m*.
grasshopper ['grɑ:shɔpə*] *n* gafanhoto.
grassland ['grɑ:slænd] *n* pradaria.
grass roots *npl* (*fig*) raízes *fpl*, base *f* ♦ *adj*: **grass-roots** popular.
grass snake *n* serpente *f*.
grassy ['grɑ:sɪ] *adj* coberto de grama (*BR*) *or* de relva (*PT*).
grate [greɪt] *n* (*fireplace*) lareira; (*of iron*) grelha ♦ *vi* ranger ♦ *vt* (*CULIN*) ralar.
grateful ['greɪtful] *adj* agradecido, grato.
gratefully ['greɪtfəlɪ] *adv* agradecidamente.

***NB**: European Portuguese adds the following consonants to certain words:* **b** (sú(b)dito, su(b)til); **c** (a(c)ção, a(c)cionista, a(c)to); **m** (inde(m)ne); **p** (ado(p)ção, ado(p)tar); *for further details see p. xiii.*

grater ['greɪtə*] *n* ralador *m*, ralo.
gratification [grætɪfɪ'keɪʃən] *n* satisfação *f*.
gratify ['grætɪfaɪ] *vt* gratificar; (*whim*) satisfazer.
gratifying ['grætɪfaɪɪŋ] *adj* gratificante.
grating ['greɪtɪŋ] *n* (*iron bars*) grade *f* ♦ *adj* (*noise*) áspero.
gratitude ['grætɪtju:d] *n* agradecimento.
gratuitous [grə'tju:ɪtəs] *adj* gratuito.
gratuity [grə'tju:ɪtɪ] *n* gratificação *f*, gorjeta.
grave [greɪv] *n* cova, sepultura ♦ *adj* sério, grave.
gravedigger ['greɪvdɪgə*] *n* coveiro.
gravel ['grævl] *n* cascalho.
gravely ['greɪvlɪ] *adv* gravemente; ~ **ill** gravemente doente.
gravestone ['greɪvstəun] *n* lápide *f*.
graveyard ['greɪvjɑ:d] *n* cemitério.
gravitate ['grævɪteɪt] *vi*: **to ~ towards** ser atraído por.
gravity ['grævɪtɪ] *n* (*PHYS*) gravidade *f*; (*seriousness*) seriedade *f*, gravidade *f*.
gravy ['greɪvɪ] *n* molho (de carne).
gravy boat *n* molheira.
gravy train (*inf*) *n*: **to be on** *or* **ride the ~** ter achado uma mina.
gray [greɪ] *adj* = **grey**.
graze [greɪz] *vi* pastar ♦ *vt* (*touch lightly*) roçar; (*scrape*) raspar; (*MED*) esfolar ♦ *n* (*MED*) esfoladura, arranhadura.
grazing ['greɪzɪŋ] *n* (*pasture*) pasto, pastagem *f*.
grease [gri:s] *n* (*fat*) gordura; (*lubricant*) graxa, lubrificante *m* ♦ *vt* (*CULIN*: *dish*) untar; (*TECH*: *brakes etc*) lubrificar, engraxar.
grease gun *n* bomba de graxa.
greasepaint [gri:speɪnt] *n* maquilagem *f* (para o teatro).
greaseproof paper ['gri:spru:f-] *n* papel *m* de cera (vegetal).
greasy ['gri:zɪ] *adj* gordurento, gorduroso; (*hands*, *clothes*) engordurado; (*BRIT*: *road*, *surface*) escorregadio.
great [greɪt] *adj* grande; (*inf*) ótimo; (*pain*, *heat*) forte; **they're ~ friends** eles são grandes amigos; **we had a ~ time** nos divertimos à beça; **it was ~!** foi ótimo, foi um barato (*inf*); **the ~ thing is that ...** o melhor é que ....
Great Barrier Reef *n*: **the ~** a Grande Barreira.
Great Britain *n* Grã-Bretanha.
great-grandchild (*irreg*) *n* bisneto/a.
great-grandfather *n* bisavô *m*.
great-grandmother *n* bisavó *f*.
Great Lakes *npl*: **the ~** os Grandes Lagos.
greatly ['greɪtlɪ] *adv* imensamente, muito.
greatness ['greɪtnɪs] *n* grandeza.
Grecian ['gri:ʃən] *adj* grego.
Greece [gri:s] *n* Grécia.
greed [gri:d] *n* (*also*: *~iness*) avidez *f*, cobiça; (*for food*) gula.
greedily ['gri:dɪlɪ] *adv* com avidez; (*eat*) gulosamente.
greedy ['gri:dɪ] *adj* avarento; (*for food*) guloso.
Greek [gri:k] *adj* grego ♦ *n* grego/a; (*LING*) grego; **ancient/modern ~** grego clássico/moderno.
green [gri:n] *adj* verde; (*inexperienced*) inexperiente, ingênuo ♦ *n* verde *m*; (*stretch of grass*) gramado (*BR*), relvado (*PT*); (*on golf course*) green *m*; (*also*: *village ~*) ≈ praça; **~s** *npl* verduras *fpl*; **to have ~ fingers** (*BRIT*) *or* **a ~ thumb** (*US*) ter mão boa (para plantar).
green belt *n* (*round town*) cinturão *m* verde.
green card *n* (*BRIT*: *AUT*) carta verde; (*US*) autorização *f* de residência.
greenery ['gri:nərɪ] *n* verdura.
greenfly ['gri:nflaɪ] (*BRIT*) *n* pulgão *m*.
greengage ['gri:ngeɪdʒ] *n* rainha-cláudia.
greengrocer ['gri:ngrəusə*] *n* (*BRIT*) verdureiro/a.
greenhouse ['gri:nhaus] (*irreg*) *n* estufa.
greenish ['gri:nɪʃ] *adj* esverdeado.
Greenland ['gri:nlənd] *n* Groenlândia.
Greenlander ['gri:nləndə*] *n* groenlandês/esa *m/f*.
green pepper *n* pimentão *m* verde.
greet [gri:t] *vt* saudar; (*welcome*) acolher.
greeting ['gri:tɪŋ] *n* cumprimento; (*welcome*) acolhimento; **Christmas/birthday ~s** votos de boas festas/feliz aniversário.
greeting(s) card *n* cartão *m* comemorativo.
gregarious [grə'gɛərɪəs] *adj* gregário.
grenade [grə'neɪd] *n* (*also*: *hand ~*) granada.
grew [gru:] *pt of* **grow**.
grey [greɪ] *adj* cinzento; (*dismal*) sombrio; **to go ~** (*hair*, *person*) ficar grisalho.
grey-haired *adj* grisalho.
greyhound ['greɪhaund] *n* galgo.
grid [grɪd] *n* grade *f*; (*ELEC*) rede *f*; (*US*: *AUT*) cruzamento.
griddle [grɪdl] *n* (*on cooker*) chapa de assar.
gridiron ['grɪdaɪən] *n* grelha; (*US*: *FOOTBALL*) campo.
grief [gri:f] *n* dor *f*, pena; **to come to ~** fracassar.
grievance ['gri:vəns] *n* motivo de queixa, agravo.
grieve [gri:v] *vi* afligir-se, sofrer ♦ *vt* dar pena a, afligir; **to ~ for** chorar por.
grievous ['gri:vəs] *adj* penoso; ~ **bodily harm** (*LAW*) lesão *f* corporal (grave).
grill [grɪl] *n* (*on cooker*) grelha ♦ *vt* (*BRIT*) grelhar; (*question*) interrogar cerradamente.
grille [grɪl] *n* grade *f*; (*AUT*) grelha.
grill(room) ['grɪl(rum)] *n* grill-room *m*, ≈ churrascaria.
grim [grɪm] *adj* sinistro, lúgubre; (*inf*: *dreadful*) horrível.
grimace [grɪ'meɪs] *n* careta ♦ *vi* fazer caretas.
grime [graɪm] *n* sujeira (*BR*), sujidade *f* (*PT*).
grimy ['graɪmɪ] *adj* sujo, encardido.
grin [grɪn] *n* sorriso largo ♦ *vi* sorrir abertamente; **to ~ (at)** dar um sorriso largo (para).
grind [graɪnd] (*pt*, *pp* **ground**) *vt* (*mangle*) triturar; (*coffee*, *pepper etc*) moer; (*make*

sharp) afiar; (*US*: *meat*) picar; (*polish*: *gem*) lapidar; (: *lens*) polir ♦ *vi* (*car gears*) ranger ♦ *n* (*work*) labuta; **to ~ one's teeth** ranger os dentes; **to ~ to a halt** (*vehicle*) parar com um ranger de freios; (*fig*: *work*, *production*) paralisar-se; (: *talks*, *process*) empacar; **the daily ~** (*inf*) a labuta diária.

grinder ['graɪndə*] *n* (*machine*: *for coffee*) moinho; (: *for waste disposal*) triturador *m*.

grindstone ['graɪndstəun] *n*: **to keep one's nose to the ~** trabalhar sem descanso.

grip [grɪp] *n* (*of hands*) aperto; (*handle*) punho; (*of racquet etc*) cabo; (*holdall*) valise *f* ♦ *vt* agarrar; **to come** *or* **get to ~s with** arcar com; **to ~ the road** (*AUT*) aderir à estrada; **to lose one's ~** perder a pega; (*fig*) perder a eficiência.

gripe [graɪp] *n* (*MED*) cólicas *fpl*; (*inf*: *complaint*) queixa ♦ *vi* (*inf*) bufar.

gripping ['grɪpɪŋ] *adj* absorvente, emocionante.

grisly ['grɪzlɪ] *adj* horrendo, medonho.

grist [grɪst] *n* (*fig*): **it's (all) ~ to his mill** ele se vale de tudo.

gristle ['grɪsl] *n* cartilagem *f*.

grit [grɪt] *n* areia, grão *m* de areia; (*courage*) coragem *f* ♦ *vt* (*road*) pôr areia em; **~s** *npl* (*US*) canjica; **to ~ one's teeth** cerrar os dentes; **to have a piece of ~ in one's eye** ter uma pedrinha no olho.

grizzle ['grɪzl] (*BRIT*) *vi* choramingar.

grizzly ['grɪzlɪ] *n* (*also*: **~** *bear*) urso pardo.

groan [grəun] *n* gemido ♦ *vi* gemer.

grocer ['grəusə*] *n* dono/a de mercearia.

grocer's (shop) *n* mercearia.

grocery ['grəusərɪ] *n* mercearia; **groceries** *npl* comestíveis *mpl*.

grog [grɔg] grogue *m*.

groggy ['grɔgɪ] *adj* grogue.

groin [grɔɪn] *n* virilha.

groom [gru:m] *n* cavalariço; (*also*: *bride~*) noivo ♦ *vt* (*horse*) tratar; (*fig*): **to ~ sb for sth** preparar alguém para algo; **well-~ed** bem-posto.

groove [gru:v] *n* ranhura, entalhe *m*.

grope [grəup] *vi* tatear.

grope for *vt fus* procurar às cegas.

grosgrain ['grəugreɪn] *n* gorgorão *m*.

gross [grəus] *adj* grosso; (*COMM*) bruto ♦ *n inv* (*twelve dozen*) grosa ♦ *vt* (*COMM*): **to ~ £500,000** dar uma receita bruta de £500,000.

gross domestic product *n* produto interno bruto.

grossly ['grəuslɪ] *adv* (*greatly*) enormemente, gritantemente.

gross national product *n* produto nacional bruto.

grotesque [grə'tɛsk] *adj* grotesco.

grotto ['grɔtəu] *n* gruta.

grotty ['grɔtɪ] (*BRIT*: *inf*) *adj* (*room etc*) mixa; **I'm feeling ~** estou me sentindo podre.

grouch [grautʃ] (*inf*) *vi* ralhar ♦ *n* (*person*) pessoa geniosa, rabugento/a.

ground [graund] *pt*, *pp of* **grind** ♦ *n* terra, chão *m*; (*SPORT*) campo; (*land*) terreno; (*reason*: *gen pl*) motivo, razão *f* (*US*: *also*: *~wire*) (ligacão *f* à) terra, fio-terra *m* ♦ *vt* (*plane*) manter em terra; (*US*: *ELEC*) ligar à terra ♦ *vi* (*ship*) encalhar ♦ *adj* (*coffee etc*) moído; (*US*: *meat*) picado; **~s** *npl* (*of coffee etc*) borra; (*gardens etc*) jardins *mpl*, parque *m*; **on the ~** no chão; **to the ~** por terra; **below ~** embaixo da terra; **to gain/lose ~** ganhar/perder terreno; **common ~** consenso; **he covered a lot of ~ in his lecture** sua palestra cobriu uma área considerável.

ground cloth (*US*) *n* = **groundsheet**.

ground control *n* (*AVIAT*, *SPACE*) controle *m* de solo *or* terra.

ground floor *n* andar *m* térreo (*BR*), rés-do-chão *m* (*PT*).

grounding ['graundɪŋ] *n* (*SCH*) conhecimentos *mpl* básicos.

groundless ['graundlɪs] *adj* infundado.

groundnut ['graundnʌt] *n* amendoim *m*.

ground rent (*BRIT*) *n* foro.

groundsheet ['graundʃi:t] *n* capa impermeável.

groundskeeper ['graundzki:pə*] (*US*) *n* (*SPORT*) zelador *m* de um campo esportivo.

groundsman ['graundzmən] (*irreg*) *n* (*SPORT*) zelador *m* de um campo esportivo.

ground staff *n* pessoal *m* de terra.

groundswell ['graundswɛl] *n* vagalhão *m*.

ground-to-ground missile *n* míssil *m* terra-terra.

groundwork ['graundwə:k] *n* base *f*, preparação *f*.

group [gru:p] *n* grupo; (*musical*) conjunto ♦ *vt* (*also*: **~** *together*) agrupar ♦ *vi* (*also*: **~** *together*) agrupar-se.

grouse [graus] *n inv* (*bird*) tetraz *m*, galo-silvestre *m* ♦ *vi* (*complain*) queixar-se, resmungar.

grove [grəuv] *n* arvoredo.

grovel ['grɔvl] *vi* (*fig*) humilhar-se; **to ~ (before)** abaixar-se (diante de).

grow [grəu] (*pt* **grew**, *pp* **grown**) *vi* crescer; (*increase*) aumentar; (*become*) tornar-se ♦ *vt* cultivar; **to ~ rich/weak** enriquecer(-se)/enfraquecer-se.

grow apart *vi* (*fig*) afastar-se (um do outro).

grow away from *vt fus* (*fig*) afastar-se de.

grow on *vt fus*: **that painting is ~ing on me** estou gostando cada vez mais daquele quadro.

grow out of *vt fus* (*clothes*) ficar muito grande para; (*habit*) superar com *or* perder o tempo.

grow up *vi* crescer, fazer-se homem/mulher.

grower ['grəuə*] *n* cultivador(a) *m/f*, produtor(a) *m/f*.

NB: *European Portuguese adds the following consonants to certain words:* **b** (sú(b)dito, su(b)til); **c** (a(c)ção, a(c)cionista, a(c)to); **m** (inde(m)ne); **p** (ado(p)ção, ado(p)tar); *for further details see p. xiii.*

growing ['grəuɪŋ] *adj* crescente; ~ **pains** (*MED*) dores *fpl* do crescimento; (*fig*) dificuldades *fpl* iniciais.
growl [graul] *vi* rosnar.
grown [grəun] *pp of* **grow** ♦ *adj* crescido, adulto.
grown-up *n* adulto/a, pessoa mais velha.
growth [grəuθ] *n* crescimento, desenvolvimento; (*what has grown*) crescimento; (*increase*) aumento; (*MED*) abcesso, tumor *m*.
growth rate *n* taxa de crescimento.
GRSM (*BRIT*) *n abbr* = **Graduate of the Royal Schools of Music**.
grub [grʌb] *n* larva, lagarta; (*inf*: *food*) comida, rango (*BR*).
grubby ['grʌbɪ] *adj* encardido.
grudge [grʌdʒ] *n* motivo de rancor ♦ *vt*: **to ~ sb sth** dar algo a alguém de má vontade, invejar algo a alguém; **to bear sb a ~ for sth** guardar rancor a alguém por algo; **he ~s (giving) the money** ele dá dinheiro de má vontade.
grudgingly ['grʌdʒɪŋlɪ] *adv* de má vontade.
gruelling ['gruəlɪŋ] *adj* duro, árduo.
gruesome ['gru:səm] *adj* horrível.
gruff [grʌf] *adj* (*voice*) rouco; (*manner*) brusco.
grumble ['grʌmbl] *vi* resmungar, bufar.
grumpy ['grʌmpɪ] *adj* rabugento.
grunt [grʌnt] *vi* grunhir ♦ *n* grunhido.
G-string *n* (*garment*) tapa-sexo *m*.
GSUSA *n abbr* = **Girl Scouts of the United States of America**.
GU (*US*) *abbr* (*POST*) = **Guam**.
guarantee [gærən'ti:] *n* garantia ♦ *vt* garantir.
guarantor [gærən'tɔ:*] *n* fiador(a) *m/f*.
guard [gɑ:d] *n* guarda; (*one man*) guarda *m*; (*BRIT*: *RAIL*) guarda-freio; (*safety device*) dispositivo de segurança; (*also*: *fire* ~) guarda-fogo ♦ *vt* guardar; (*protect*): **to ~ sth (against** *or* **from)** proteger algo de *or* contra; **to be on one's ~** estar prevenido.
guard against *vt fus*: **to ~ against doing sth** guardar-se de fazer algo.
guard dog *m* cão *m* de guarda.
guarded ['gɑ:dɪd] *adj* (*fig*) cauteloso.
guardian ['gɑ:dɪən] *n* protetor(a) *m/f*; (*of minor*) tutor(a) *m/f*.
guard's van (*BRIT*) *n* (*RAIL*) vagão *m* de freio.
Guatemala [gwɔtə'mɑ:lə] *n* Guatemala.
Guatemalan [gwɔtə'mɑ:lən] *adj*, *n* guatemalteco/a.
Guernsey ['gə:nzɪ] *n* Guernsey *f* (*no article*).
guerrilla [gə'rɪlə] *n* guerrilheiro/a.
guerrilla warfare *n* guerrilha.
guess [gɛs] *vt*, *vi* adivinhar; (*US*: *suppose*) achar, supor ♦ *n* suposição *f*, conjetura; **to take** *or* **have a ~** adivinhar, chutar (*inf*); **to keep sb ~ing** não contar a alguém; **my ~ is that ...** meu palpite é que ...; **to ~ right/wrong** acertar/errar.
guesstimate ['gɛstɪmɪt] (*inf*) *n* estimativa aproximada.
guesswork ['gɛswə:k] *n* conjeturas *fpl*; **I got the answer by ~** obtive a resposta por adivinhação.
guest [gɛst] *n* convidado/a; (*in hotel*) hóspede *m/f*; **be my ~** fique à vontade.
guest-house (*irreg*) *n* pensão *f*.
guest room *n* quarto de hóspedes.
guffaw [gʌ'fɔ:] *n* gargalhada ♦ *vi* dar gargalhadas.
guidance ['gaɪdəns] *n* orientação *f*; (*advice*) conselhos *mpl*; **under the ~ of** sob a direção de, orientado por; **vocational** *or* **careers ~** orientação vocacional; **marriage ~** aconselhamento conjugal.
guide [gaɪd] *n* (*person*) guia *m/f*; (*book*, *fig*) guia *m*; (*also*: *girl* ~) escoteira ♦ *vt* guiar; **to be ~d by sb/sth** orientar-se com alguém/ por algo.
guidebook ['gaɪdbuk] *n* guia *m*.
guided missile ['gaɪdɪd-] *n* (*internally controlled*) míssil *m* guiado; (*remote-controlled*) míssil *m* teleguiado.
guide dog *n* cão *m* de guia.
guidelines ['gaɪdlaɪnz] *npl* (*fig*) princípios *mpl* gerais, diretrizes *fpl*.
guild [gɪld] *n* grêmio.
guildhall ['gɪldhɔ:l] (*BRIT*) *n* sede *f* da prefeitura.
guile [gaɪl] *n* astúcia.
guileless ['gaɪllɪs] *adj* ingênuo, cândido.
guillotine ['gɪləti:n] *n* guilhotina.
guilt [gɪlt] *n* culpa.
guilty ['gɪltɪ] *adj* culpado; **to plead ~/not ~** declarar-se culpado/inocente.
Guinea ['gɪnɪ] *n*: **Republic of ~** (República da) Guiné *f*.
guinea ['gɪnɪ] (*BRIT*) *n* guinéu *m* (= *21 shillings*: *antiga unidade monetária equivalente a £1.05*).
guinea pig ['gɪnɪpɪg] *n* porquinho-da-Índia *m*, cobaia; (*fig*) cobaia.
guise [gaɪz] *n*: **in** *or* **under the ~ of** sob a aparência de.
guitar [gɪ'tɑ:*] *n* violão *m*.
guitarist [gɪ'tɑ:rɪst] *n* violonista *m/f*.
gulch [gʌltʃ] (*US*) *n* ravina.
gulf [gʌlf] *n* golfo; (*abyss*) abismo; **the (Persian) G ~** o Golfo Pérsico.
Gulf States *npl*: **the ~** (*in Middle East*) os países do Golfo Pérsico.
Gulf Stream *n*: **the ~** a corrente do Golfo.
gull [gʌl] *n* gaivota.
gullet ['gʌlɪt] *n* esôfago.
gullibility [gʌlə'bɪlɪtɪ] *n* credulidade *f*.
gullible ['gʌlɪbl] *adj* crédulo.
gully ['gʌlɪ] *n* barranco.
gulp [gʌlp] *vi* engolir em seco ♦ *vt* (*also*: ~ *down*) engolir ♦ *n* (*of drink*) gole *m*; **at one ~** de um gole só.
gum [gʌm] *n* (*ANAT*) gengiva; (*glue*) goma; (*also*: *chewing-~*) chiclete *m* (*BR*), pastilha elástica (*PT*) ♦ *vt* colar.
gum up *vt*: **to ~ up the works** (*inf*) estragar tudo.
gumboil ['gʌmbɔɪl] *n* abscesso gengival, parúlide *f*.

gumboots ['gʌmbu:ts] (*BRIT*) *npl* botas *fpl* de borracha, galochas *fpl*.
gumption ['gʌmpʃən] *n* juízo, bom senso.
gun [gʌn] *n* (*gen*) arma (de fogo); (*revolver*) revólver *m*; (*small*) pistola; (*rifle*) espingarda; (*cannon*) canhão *m* ♦ *vt* (*also*: ~ *down*) balear; **to stick to one's ~s** (*fig*) não dar o braço a torcer, ser durão (*inf*).
gunboat ['gʌnbəut] *n* canhoneira.
gun dog *n* cão *m* de caça.
gunfire ['gʌnfaɪə*] *n* tiroteio.
gunk [gʌŋk] (*inf*) *n* sujeira (*BR*), sujidade *f* (*PT*).
gunman ['gʌnmən] (*irreg*) *n* pistoleiro.
gunner ['gʌnə*] *n* artilheiro.
gunpoint ['gʌnpɔɪnt] *n*: **at ~** sob a ameaça de uma arma.
gunpowder ['gʌnpaudə*] *n* pólvora.
gunrunner ['gʌnrʌnə*] *n* contrabandista *m/f* de armas.
gunrunning ['gʌnrʌnɪŋ] *n* contrabando de armas.
gunshot ['gʌnʃɔt] *n* tiro (de arma de fogo); **within ~** ao alcance do tiro.
gunsmith ['gʌnsmɪθ] *n* armeiro/a.
gurgle ['gə:gl] *vi* gorgolejar ♦ *n* gorgolejo.
guru ['guru:] *n* guru *m*.
gush [gʌʃ] *vi* jorrar; (*fig*) alvoroçar-se ♦ *n* jorro.
gusset ['gʌsɪt] *n* nesga; (*of tights, pants*) entreperna.
gust [gʌst] *n* (*of wind*) rajada.
gusto ['gʌstəu] *n* entusiasmo, garra.
gut [gʌt] *n* intestino, tripa; (*MUS etc*) corda de tripa ♦ *vt* (*poultry, fish*) estripar; (*building*) destruir o interior de; **~s** *npl* (*courage*) coragem *f*, raça (*inf*); **to hate sb's ~s** ter alguém atravessado na garganta, não poder ver alguém nem pintado.
gut reaction *n* reação *f* instintiva.
gutter ['gʌtə*] *n* (*of roof*) calha; (*in street*) sarjeta.
guttural ['gʌtərl] *adj* gutural.
guy [gaɪ] *n* (*also*: *~rope*) corda; (*inf*: *man*) cara *m* (*BR*), tipo (*PT*).
Guyana [gaɪ'ænə] *n* Guiana.
Guyanese [gaɪə'ni:z] *adj*, *n* guianense *m/f*.
guzzle ['gʌzl] *vi* comer *or* beber com gula ♦ *vt* engolir com gula.
gym [dʒɪm] *n* (*also*: *gymnasium*) ginásio; (*also*: *gymnastics*) ginástica.
gymkhana [dʒɪm'kɑ:nə] *n* gincana.
gymnasium [dʒɪm'neɪzɪəm] *n* ginásio.
gymnast ['dʒɪmnæst] *n* ginasta *m/f*.
gymnastics [dʒɪm'næstɪks] *n* ginástica.
gym shoes *npl* tênis *mpl*.
gym slip (*BRIT*) *n* uniforme *m* escolar.
gynaecologist [gaɪnɪ'kɔlədʒɪst] (*US* **gynecologist**) *n* ginecologista *m/f*.
gynaecology [gaɪnə'kɔlədʒɪ] (*US* **gynecology**) *n* ginecologia.
gypsy ['dʒɪpsɪ] *n*, *cpd* = **gipsy**.
gyrate [dʒaɪ'reɪt] *vi* girar.
gyroscope ['dʒaɪərəskəup] *n* giroscópio.

H

H, h [eɪtʃ] *n* (*letter*) H, h *m*; **H for Harry** (*BRIT*) *or* **How** (*US*) H de Henrique.
habeas corpus ['heɪbɪəs'kɔ:pəs] *n* (*LAW*) habeas-corpus *m*.
haberdashery ['hæbə'dæʃərɪ] (*BRIT*) *n* armarinho.
habit ['hæbɪt] *n* hábito, costume *m*; (*costume*) hábito; **to get out of/into the ~ of doing sth** perder/criar o hábito de fazer algo.
habitable ['hæbɪtəbl] *adj* habitável.
habitat ['hæbɪtæt] *n* habitat *m*.
habitation [hæbɪ'teɪʃən] *n* habitação *f*.
habitual [hə'bɪtjuəl] *adj* habitual, costumeiro; (*drinker, liar*) inveterado.
habitually [hə'bɪtjuəlɪ] *adv* habitualmente.
hack [hæk] *vt* (*cut*) cortar; (*chop*) talhar ♦ *n* corte *m*; (*axe blow*) talho; (*pej*: *writer*) escrevinhador(a) *m/f*; (*old horse*) metungo.
hackles ['hæklz] *npl*: **to make sb's ~ rise** (*fig*) enfurecer alguém.
hackney cab ['hæknɪ-] *n* fiacre *m*.
hackneyed ['hæknɪd] *adj* corriqueiro, batido.
had [hæd] *pt*, *pp of* **have**.
haddock ['hædək] (*pl inv or* **~s**) *n* hadoque *m* (*BR*), eglefim *m* (*PT*).
hadn't ['hædnt] = **had not**.
haematology ['hi:mə'tɔlədʒɪ] (*US* **hematology**) *n* hematologia.
haemoglobin ['hi:mə'gləubɪn] (*US* **hemoglobin**) *n* hemoglobina.
haemophilia ['hi:mə'fɪlɪə] (*US* **hemophilia**) *n* hemofilia.
haemorrhage ['hɛmərɪdʒ] (*US* **hemorrhage**) *n* hemorragia.
haemorrhoids ['hɛmərɔɪdz] (*US* **hemorrhoids**) *npl* hemorróidas *fpl*.
hag [hæg] *n* (*ugly*) bruxa; (*nasty*) megera; (*witch*) bruxa.
haggard ['hægəd] *adj* emaciado, macilento.
haggis ['hægɪs] *n* *miúdos de carneiro com aveia, cozidos no estômago do animal.*
haggle ['hægl] *vi* (*bargain*) pechinchar, regatear; **to ~ over** discutir sobre.
haggling ['hæglɪŋ] *n* regateio.
Hague [heɪg] *n*: **The ~** Haia.
hail [heɪl] *n* (*weather*) granizo ♦ *vt* (*greet*) cumprimentar, saudar; (*call*) chamar ♦ *vi* chover granizo; (*originate*): **he ~s from Scotland** ele é originário da Escócia.
hailstone ['heɪlstəun] *n* pedra de granizo.

NB: *European Portuguese adds the following consonants to certain words:* **b** (sú(b)dito, su(b)til); **c** (a(c)ção, a(c)cionista, a(c)to); **m** (inde(m)ne); **p** (ado(p)ção, ado(p)tar); *for further details see p. xiii.*

hailstorm ['heɪlstɔːm] *n* tempestade *f* de granizo.
hair [hɛə*] *n* (*of human*) cabelo; (*of animal, on legs*) pêlo; (*one* ~) fio de cabelo, pêlo; (*head of* ~) cabeleira; **grey** ~ cabelo grisalho; **to do one's** ~ pentear-se.
hairbrush ['hɛəbrʌʃ] *n* escova de cabelo.
haircut ['hɛəkʌt] *n* corte *m* de cabelo.
hairdo ['hɛəduː] *n* penteado.
hairdresser ['hɛədrɛsə*] *n* cabeleireiro/a.
hairdresser's *n* cabeleireiro.
hair-dryer *n* secador *m* de cabelo.
-haired [hɛəd] *suffix*: **fair/long~** de cabelo louro/comprido.
hairgrip ['hɛəgrɪp] *n* grampo (*BR*), gancho (*PT*).
hairline ['hɛəlaɪn] *n* contorno do couro cabeludo.
hairline fracture *n* fratura muito fina.
hairnet ['hɛənɛt] *n* rede *f* de cabelo.
hair oil *n* óleo para o cabelo.
hairpiece ['hɛəpiːs] *n* aplique *m*.
hairpin ['hɛəpɪn] *n* grampo (*BR*), gancho (*PT*), pinça.
hairpin bend (*US* **hairpin curve**) *n* curva fechada.
hair-raising [-'reɪzɪŋ] *adj* horripilante, de arrepiar os cabelos.
hair remover *n* (creme *m*) depilatório.
hair spray *n* laquê *m* (*BR*), laca (*PT*).
hairstyle ['hɛəstaɪl] *n* penteado.
hairy ['hɛərɪ] *adj* cabeludo, peludo; (*fig*) perigoso.
Haiti ['heɪtɪ] *n* Haiti *m*.
hake [heɪk] (*pl inv or* **~s**) *n* abrótea.
halcyon ['hælsɪən] *adj* tranqüilo.
hale [heɪl] *adj*: ~ **and hearty** robusto, em ótima forma.
half [hɑːf] (*pl* **halves**) *n* metade *f*; (*SPORT*: *of match*) tempo; (*of ground*) lado ♦ *adj* meio ♦ *adv* meio, pela metade; **~-an-hour** meia hora; ~ **a pound** meia libra; **two and a** ~ dois e meio; **a week and a** ~ uma semana e meia; ~ **(of it)** a metade; ~ **(of)** a metade de; ~ **the amount of** a metade de; **to cut sth in** ~ cortar algo ao meio; ~ **past three** três e meia; ~ **asleep/empty/closed** meio adormecido/vazio/fechado; **to go halves (with sb)** rachar as despesas (com alguém).
half-back *n* (*SPORT*) meio-de-campo.
half-baked (*inf*) *adj* (*idea, scheme*) mal planejado.
half-breed *n* mestiço/a.
half-brother *n* meio-irmão *m*.
half-caste *n* mestiço/a.
half-hearted *adj* irresoluto, indiferente.
half-hour *n* meia hora.
half-mast *n*: **at** ~ (*flag*) a meio-pau.
halfpenny ['heɪpnɪ] *n* meio pêni *m*.
half-price *adj* pela metade do preço ♦ *adv* (*also*: *at* ~) pela metade do preço.
half term (*BRIT*) *n* (*SCH*) *dias de folga no meio do semestre*.
half-time *n* meio tempo.
halfway [hɑːf'weɪ] *adv* a meio caminho; **to meet sb** ~ (*fig*) chegar a um meio-termo com alguém.
half-yearly *adv* semestralmente ♦ *adj* semestral.
halibut ['hælɪbət] *n inv* hipoglosso.
halitosis [hælɪ'təusɪs] *n* halitose *f*, mau hálito.
hall [hɔːl] *n* (*for concerts*) sala; (*entrance way*) hall *m*, entrada; (*corridor*) corredor *m*; **town** ~ prefeitura (*BR*), câmara municipal (*PT*); ~ **of residence** (*BRIT*) residência universitária.
hallmark ['hɔːlmɑːk] *n* (*also fig*) marca.
hallo [hə'ləu] *excl* = **hello**.
Hallowe'en ['hæləu'iːn] *n* Dia *m* das Bruxas (*31 de outubro*).
hallucination [həluːsɪ'neɪʃən] *n* alucinação *f*.
hallway ['hɔːlweɪ] *n* hall *m*, entrada; (*corridor*) corredor *m*.
halo ['heɪləu] *n* (*of saint*) auréola; (*of sun*) halo.
halt [hɔːlt] *n* (*stop*) parada (*BR*), paragem *f* (*PT*); (*RAIL*) pequena parada; (*MIL*) alto ♦ *vi* parar; (*MIL*) fazer alto ♦ *vt* deter; (*process*) interromper; **to call a** ~ **to sth** (*fig*) pôr um fim a algo.
halter ['hɔːltə*] *n* (*for horse*) cabresto.
halterneck ['hɔːltənɛk] *adj* (*dress*) frente-única *inv*.
halve [hɑːv] *vt* (*divide*) dividir ao meio; (*reduce by half*) reduzir à metade.
halves [hɑːvz] *npl of* **half**.
ham [hæm] *n* presunto, fiambre *m* (*PT*); (*inf*: *actor, actress*) canastrão/trona *m/f*; (: *also*: *radio* ~) rádio-amador(a) *m/f*.
hamburger ['hæmbəːgə*] *n* hambúrguer *m*.
ham-fisted [-'fɪstɪd] (*BRIT*) *adj* desajeitado.
ham-handed [-'hændɪd] (*US*) *adj* desajeitado.
hamlet ['hæmlɪt] *n* aldeola, lugarejo.
hammer ['hæmə*] *n* martelo ♦ *vt* martelar; (*fig*) dar uma surra em ♦ *vi* (*on door*) bater insistentemente; **to** ~ **a point home to sb** fincar uma idéia na mente de alguém.
hammer out *vt* (*metal*) malhar; (*fig*: *solution*) elaborar.
hammock ['hæmək] *n* rede *f*.
hamper ['hæmpə*] *vt* dificultar, atrapalhar ♦ *n* cesto.
hamster ['hæmstə*] *n* hamster *m*.
hamstring ['hæmstrɪŋ] *n* (*ANAT*) tendão *m* do jarrete.
hand [hænd] *n* mão *f*; (*of clock*) ponteiro; (*writing*) letra; (*applause*) aplauso; (*at cards*) cartas *fpl*; (*worker*) trabalhador *m*; (*measurement*) palmo ♦ *vt* (*give*) dar, passar; (*deliver*) entregar; **to give sb a** ~ dar uma mãozinha a alguém, dar uma ajuda a alguém; **at** ~ à mão, disponível; **in** ~ sob controle; (*COMM*) em caixa, à disposição; **to be on** ~ (*person*) estar disponível; (*emergency services*) estar num estado de prontidão; **to** ~ (*information*) à mão; **to force sb's** ~ forçar alguém a agir; **to have a free** ~ ter carta branca; **to have sth in one's** ~ ter algo na mão; **on the one** ~ ..., **on the other** ~ ... por um lado ..., por outro

(lado) ....

hand down *vt* passar; (*tradition, heirloom*) transmitir; (*US*: *sentence, verdict*) proferir.

hand in *vt* entregar.

hand out *vt* distribuir.

hand over *vt* (*deliver*) entregar; (*surrender*) ceder; (*powers etc*) transmitir.

hand round (*BRIT*) *vt* (*information*) fazer circular; (*chocolates*) oferecer.

handbag ['hændbæg] *n* bolsa.

handball ['hændbɔːl] *n* handebol *m*.

handbasin ['hændbeɪsn] *n* pia (*BR*), lavatório (*PT*).

handbook ['hændbuk] *n* manual *m*.

handbrake ['hændbreɪk] *n* freio (*BR*) *or* travão *m* (*PT*) de mão.

hand cream *n* creme *m* para as mãos.

handcuffs ['hændkʌfs] *npl* algemas *fpl*.

handful ['hændful] *n* punhado.

handicap ['hændɪkæp] *n* (*MED*) incapacidade *f*; (*disadvantage*) desvantagem *f* ♦ *vt* prejudicar; **mentally/physically ~ped** deficiente mental/físico.

handicraft ['hændɪkrɑːft] *n* artesanato, trabalho manual.

handiwork ['hændɪwəːk] *n* obra; **this looks like his ~** (*pej*) isso parece coisa dele.

handkerchief ['hæŋkətʃɪf] *n* lenço.

handle ['hændl] *n* (*of door etc*) maçaneta; (*of bag etc*) alça; (*of cup etc*) asa; (*of knife etc*) cabo; (*for winding*) manivela; (*inf*: *name*) título ♦ *vt* (*touch*) manusear; (*deal with*) tratar de; (*treat*: *people*) lidar com; **"~ with care"** "cuidado — frágil"; **to fly off the ~** perder as estribeiras.

handlebar(s) ['hɑːndlbɑː(z)] *n*(*pl*) guidom (*PT*: -dão) *m*.

handling charges ['hændlɪŋ-] *npl* taxa de manuseio; (*BANKING*) comissão *f*.

hand-luggage *n* bagagem *f* de mão.

handmade ['hændmeɪd] *adj* feito a mão.

handout ['hændaut] *n* (*charity*) doação *f*, esmola; (*leaflet*) folheto; (*university*) apostila.

hand-picked [-'pɪkt] *adj* (*fruit*) colhido à mão; (*staff*) escolhido a dedo.

handrail ['hændreɪl] *n* (*on staircase*) corrimão *m*.

handshake ['hændʃeɪk] *n* aperto de mão; (*COMPUT*) handshake *m*.

handsome ['hænsəm] *adj* bonito; (*gift*) generoso; (*profit*) considerável.

handstand ['hændstænd] *n*: **to do a ~** plantar bananeira.

hand-to-mouth *adj* (*existence*) ao deus-dará.

handwriting ['hændraɪtɪŋ] *n* letra, caligrafia.

handwritten ['hændrɪtn] *adj* escrito à mão, manuscrito.

handy ['hændɪ] *adj* (*close at hand*) à mão; (*convenient*) útil, prático; (*skilful*) habilidoso, hábil; **to come in ~** ser útil.

handyman ['hændɪmæn] (*irreg*) *n* biscateiro, faz-tudo *m*.

hang [hæŋ] (*pt, pp* **hung**) *vt* pendurar; (*on wall etc*) prender; (*head*) baixar; (*criminal*: *pt, pp* **~ed**) enforcar ♦ *vi* estar pendurado; (*hair, drapery*) cair ♦ *n* (*inf*): **to get the ~ of (doing) sth** pegar o jeito de (fazer) algo.

hang about *vi* vadiar, vagabundear; **~ about!** (*inf*) 'pera aí!

hang back *vi* (*hesitate*): **to ~ back from (doing) sth** vacilar em (fazer) algo.

hang on *vi* (*wait*) esperar ♦ *vt fus* (*depend on*) depender de; **to ~ on to** (*keep hold of*) não soltar, segurar; (*keep*) ficar com.

hang out *vt* (*washing*) estender ♦ *vi* (*be visible*) aparecer; (*inf*: *spend time*) fazer ponto.

hang together *vi* (*argument etc*) ser coerente.

hang up *vi* (*TEL*) desligar ♦ *vt* (*coat*) pendurar; **to ~ up on sb** (*TEL*) bater o telefone na cara de alguém.

hangar ['hæŋə*] *n* hangar *m*.

hangdog ['hæŋdɔg] *adj* (*look, expression*) envergonhado.

hanger ['hæŋə*] *n* cabide *m*.

hanger-on *n* parasita *m/f*, filão/filona *m/f*.

hang-gliding *n* vôo livre.

hanging ['hæŋɪŋ] *n* enforcamento.

hangman ['hæŋmən] (*irreg*) *n* carrasco.

hangover ['hæŋəuvə*] *n* (*after drinking*) ressaca; **to have a ~** estar de ressaca.

hang-up *n* mania, grilo.

hank [hæŋk] *n* meada.

hanker ['hæŋkə*] *vi*: **to ~ after** (*miss*) sentir saudade de; (*long for*) ansiar por.

hankie ['hæŋkɪ] *n abbr* = **handkerchief**.

hanky ['hæŋkɪ] *n abbr* = **handkerchief**.

Hants (*BRIT*) *abbr* = **Hampshire**.

haphazard [hæp'hæzəd] *adj* (*random*) fortuito; (*disorganized*) desorganizado.

hapless ['hæplɪs] *adj* desafortunado.

happen ['hæpən] *vi* acontecer; **what's ~ing?** o que é que está acontecendo?; **she ~ed to be in London** aconteceu que estava em Londres; **if anything ~ed to him** se lhe acontecesse alguma coisa; **as it ~s ...** acontece que ....

happen (up)on *vt fus* dar com.

happening ['hæpənɪŋ] *n* acontecimento, ocorrência.

happily ['hæpɪlɪ] *adv* (*luckily*) felizmente; (*cheerfully*) alegremente.

happiness ['hæpɪnɪs] *n* felicidade *f*; (*joy*) alegria.

happy ['hæpɪ] *adj* feliz, contente; **to be ~ (with)** estar contente (com); **to be ~** ser feliz; **yes, I'd be ~ to** sim, com muito prazer; **~ birthday!** feliz aniversário; (*said to somebody*) parabéns!; **~ Christmas/New Year** feliz Natal/Ano Novo.

happy-go-lucky *adj* despreocupado.

harangue [hə'ræŋ] *vt* arengar.

harass ['hærəs] *vt* (*bother*) importunar;

***NB**: European Portuguese adds the following consonants to certain words:* **b** (sú(b)dito, su(b)til); **c** (a(c)ção, a(c)cionista, a(c)to); **m** (inde(m)ne); **p** (ado(p)ção, ado(p)tar); *for further details see p. xiii.*

(*pursue*) acossar.
harassed ['hærəst] *adj* chateado.
harassment ['hærəsmənt] *n* perseguição *f*; (*worry*) preocupação *f*.
harbour ['hɑːbə*] (*US* **harbor**) *n* porto ♦ *vt* (*hope etc*) abrigar; (*hide*) esconder; **to ~ a grudge against sb** guardar rancor a alguém.
harbo(u)r dues *npl* direitos *mpl* portuários.
harbo(u)r master *n* capitão *m* do porto.
hard [hɑːd] *adj* duro; (*difficult*) difícil; (*work*) árduo; (*person*) severo, cruel ♦ *adv* (*work*) muito, diligentemente; (*think, try*) seriamente; **to look ~ at** olhar firme *or* fixamente para; **~ luck!** azar!; **no ~ feelings!** sem ressentimentos!; **to be ~ of hearing** ser surdo; **to be ~ done by** ser tratado injustamente; **to be ~ on sb** ser rigoroso com alguém; **I find it ~ to believe that ...** acho difícil acreditar que ....
hard-and-fast *adj* rígido.
hardback ['hɑːdbæk] *n* livro de capa dura.
hardboard ['hɑːdbɔːd] *n* madeira compensada.
hard-boiled egg [-'bɔɪld-] *n* ovo cozido.
hard cash *n* dinheiro vivo *or* em espécie.
hard copy *n* (*COMPUT*) cópia impressa.
hard-core *adj* (*pornography*) pesado; (*supporters*) ferrenho.
hard court *n* (*TENNIS*) quadra de cimento.
hard disk *n* (*COMPUT*) disco rígido.
harden ['hɑːdən] *vt* endurecer; (*steel*) temperar; (*fig*) tornar insensível ♦ *vi* endurecer-se.
hardened ['hɑːdnd] *adj* (*criminal, drinker*) inveterado; **to be ~ to sth** ser insensível a algo.
hardening ['hɑːdnɪŋ] *n* endurecimento.
hard-headed [-'hɛdɪd] *adj* prático, pouco sentimental.
hard-hearted *adj* empedernido, insensível.
hard labour *n* trabalhos *mpl* forçados.
hardliner [hɑːd'laɪnə*] *n* intransigente *m/f*.
hardly ['hɑːdlɪ] *adv* (*scarcely*) apenas, mal; **that can ~ be true** dificilmente pode ser verdade; **~ ever** quase nunca; **I can ~ believe it** mal posso acreditar nisso.
hardness ['hɑːdnɪs] *n* dureza.
hard sell *n* venda agressiva.
hardship ['hɑːdʃɪp] *n* (*troubles*) sofrimento; (*financial*) privação *f*.
hard shoulder (*BRIT*) *n* (*AUT*) acostamento (*BR*), berma (*PT*).
hard-up (*inf*) *adj* duro (*BR*), liso (*PT*).
hardware ['hɑːdwɛə*] *n* ferragens *fpl*, maquinaria; (*COMPUT*) hardware *m*.
hardware shop *n* loja de ferragens.
hard-wearing [-'wɛərɪŋ] *adj* resistente.
hard-working *adj* trabalhador(a).
hardy ['hɑːdɪ] *adj* forte; (*plant*) resistente.
hare [hɛə*] *n* lebre *f*.
hare-brained [-breɪnd] *adj* estonteado, desatinado.
harelip ['hɛəlɪp] *n* (*MED*) lábio leporino.
harem [hɑː'riːm] *n* harém *m*.
hark back [hɑːk-] *vi*: **to ~ back to** (*reminisce*) recordar; (*be reminiscent of*) lembrar.
harm [hɑːm] *n* mal *m*, dano ♦ *vt* (*person*) fazer mal a, prejudicar; (*thing*) danificar; **to mean no ~** ter boas intenções; **there's no ~ in trying** não faz mal tentar; **out of ~'s way** a salvo.
harmful ['hɑːmful] *adj* prejudicial; (*plant, weed*) daninho.
harmless ['hɑːmlɪs] *adj* inofensivo.
harmonic [hɑː'mɔnɪk] *adj* harmônico.
harmonica [hɑː'mɔnɪkə] *n* gaita de boca, harmônica.
harmonics [hɑː'mɔnɪks] *npl* harmônicos *mpl*.
harmonious [hɑː'məunɪəs] *adj* harmonioso.
harmonium [hɑː'məunɪəm] *n* harmônio.
harmonize ['hɑːmənaɪz] *vt, vi* harmonizar.
harmony ['hɑːmənɪ] *n* harmonia.
harness ['hɑːnɪs] *n* arreios *mpl* ♦ *vt* (*horse*) arrear, pôr arreios em; (*resources*) aproveitar.
harp [hɑːp] *n* harpa ♦ *vi*: **to ~ on about** bater sempre na mesma tecla sobre.
harpist ['hɑːpɪst] *n* harpista *m/f*.
harpoon [hɑː'puːn] *n* arpão *m* ♦ *vt* arpoar.
harpsichord ['hɑːpsɪkɔːd] *n* cravo, clavecino.
harrow ['hærəu] *n* (*AGR*) grade *f*, rastelo.
harrowing ['hærəuɪŋ] *adj* doloroso, pungente.
harry ['hærɪ] *vt* (*MIL, fig*) assolar.
harsh [hɑːʃ] *adj* (*hard*) duro, severo; (*rough: surface, taste*) áspero; (: *sound*) desarmonioso.
harshly ['hɑːʃlɪ] *adv* severamente.
harshness ['hɑːʃnɪs] *n* dureza, severidade *f*; (*roughness*) aspereza.
harvest ['hɑːvɪst] *n* colheita; (*of grapes*) vindima ♦ *vt, vi* colher.
harvester ['hɑːvɪstə*] *n* (*machine*) segadora; (*also*: *combine ~*) ceifeira-debulhadora; (*person*) segador(a) *m/f*.
has [hæz] *vb see* **have**.
has-been (*inf*) *n* (*person*): **he/she's a ~** ele/ela já era.
hash [hæʃ] *n* (*CULIN*) picadinho; (*fig*: *mess*) confusão *f*, bagunça ♦ *n abbr* (*inf*) = **hashish**.
hashish ['hæʃɪʃ] *n* haxixe *m*.
hasn't ['hæznt] = **has not**.
hassle ['hæsl] (*inf*) *n* (*fuss, problems*) complicação *f* ♦ *vt* molestar, chatear.
haste [heɪst] *n* pressa; **in ~** às pressas.
hasten ['heɪsn] *vt* acelerar ♦ *vi* apressar-se; **I ~ to add that ...** eu me apresso a acrescentar que ....
hastily ['heɪstɪlɪ] *adv* depressa.
hasty ['heɪstɪ] *adj* apressado.
hat [hæt] *n* chapéu *m*.
hatbox ['hætbɔks] *n* chapeleira.
hatch [hætʃ] *n* (*NAUT*: *also*: *~way*) escotilha; (*BRIT*: *also*: *service ~*) comunicação *f* entre a cozinha e a sala de jantar ♦ *vi* sair do ovo, chocar ♦ *vt* chocar; (*plot*) tramar, arquitetar.
hatchback ['hætʃbæk] *n* (*AUT*) camionete *f*, hatch *m*.
hatchet ['hætʃɪt] *n* machadinha.
hate [heɪt] *vt* odiar, detestar ♦ *n* ódio; **to ~ to do** *or* **doing** odiar *or* detestar fazer; **I ~ to trouble you, but ...** desculpe incomodá-lo,

mas ....

hateful ['heɪtful] *adj* odioso.

hatred ['heɪtrɪd] *n* ódio.

hat trick (*BRIT*) *n* (*SPORT, also fig*) três vitórias (*or* gols *etc*) consecutivas.

haughty ['hɔːtɪ] *adj* soberbo, arrogante.

haul [hɔːl] *vt* puxar; (*by lorry*) carregar, fretar; (*NAUT*) levar à orça ♦ *n* (*of fish*) redada; (*of stolen goods etc*) pilhagem *f*, presa.

haulage ['hɔːlɪdʒ] *n* transporte *m* (rodoviário); (*costs*) gasto com transporte.

haulage contractor (*BRIT*) *n* (*firm*) transportadora; (*person*) transportador(a) *m/f*.

hauler ['hɔːlə*] (*US*) *n* = **haulier**.

haulier ['hɔːljə*] (*BRIT*) *n* (*firm*) transportadora; (*person*) transportador(a) *m/f*.

haunch [hɔːntʃ] *n* anca, quadril *m*; (*of meat*) quarto traseiro.

haunt [hɔːnt] *vt* (*subj: ghost*) assombrar; (*frequent*) freqüentar; (*obsess*) obcecar ♦ *n* lugar *m* freqüentado.

haunted ['hɔːntɪd] *adj* (*castle etc*) mal-assombrado.

haunting ['hɔːntɪŋ] *adj* (*sight, music*) obcecante.

Havana [hə'vænə] *n* Havana.

have [hæv] (*pt, pp* **had**) *vt* ter; (*possess*) possuir; (*shower*) tomar; (*meal*) comer ♦ *aux vb*: **he has gone** foi embora ♦ *n*: **the ~s and ~-nots** (*inf*) os ricos e os pobres; **I don't ~ any money (on me)** estou sem dinheiro; **to ~ breakfast** tomar café (*BR*), tomar o pequeno almoço (*PT*); **to ~ lunch** almoçar; **to ~ dinner** jantar; **I'll ~ a coffee** vou tomar um café; **to ~ a baby** dar à luz, ter um nenê (*BR*) *or* bebé (*PT*); **to ~ an operation** fazer uma operação; **to ~ a party** fazer uma festa; **to ~ sth done** mandar fazer algo; **he had a suit made** ele mandou fazer um terno; **let me ~ a try** deixe-me tentar; **she has to do it** ela tem que fazê-lo; **I had better leave** é melhor que eu vá embora; **I won't ~ it** não vou agüentar isso; **he's been had** (*inf*) ele comprou gato por lebre; **rumour has it (that)** ... dizem os boatos que ....

have in *vt*: **to ~ it in for sb** (*inf*) estar com implicância *or* de pinimba com alguém.

have on *vt*: **~ you anything on tomorrow?** (*BRIT*) você tem compromisso amanhã?; **to ~ sb on** (*BRIT*) brincar com alguém.

have out *vt*: **to ~ it out with sb** explicar-se com alguém.

haven ['heɪvn] *n* porto; (*fig*) abrigo, refúgio.

haven't ['hævnt] = **have not**.

haversack ['hævəsæk] *n* mochila.

havoc ['hævək] *n* destruição *f*: **to play ~ with** (*fig*) estragar.

Hawaii [hə'waiiː] *n* Havaí *m*.

Hawaiian [ha'waɪjən] *adj, n* havaiano/a.

hawk [hɔːk] *n* falcão *m* ♦ *vt* (*goods for sale*) mascatear.

hawker ['hɔːkə*] *n* camelô *m*, mascate *m*.

hawthorn ['hɔːθɔːn] *n* pilriteiro, estripeiro.

hay [heɪ] *n* feno.

hay fever *n* febre *f* do feno.

haystack ['heɪstæk] *n* palheiro.

haywire ['heɪwaɪə*] (*inf*) *adj*: **to go ~** (*person*) ficar maluco; (*plan*) desorganizar-se, degringolar.

hazard ['hæzəd] *n* (*danger*) perigo, risco; (*chance*) acaso ♦ *vt* aventurar, arriscar; **to be a health/fire ~** ser um risco para a saúde/de incêndio; **to ~ a guess** arriscar um palpite.

hazardous ['hæzədəs] *adj* (*dangerous*) perigoso; (*risky*) arriscado.

hazard pay (*US*) *n* adicional *m* por insalubridade.

hazard warning lights *npl* (*AUT*) pisca-alerta *m*.

haze [heɪz] *n* névoa, neblina.

hazel [heɪzl] *n* (*tree*) aveleira ♦ *adj* (*eyes*) castanho-claro *inv*.

hazelnut ['heɪzlnʌt] *n* avelã *f*.

hazy ['heɪzɪ] *adj* nublado; (*idea*) confuso.

H-bomb *n* bomba de hidrogênio.

h & c (*BRIT*) *abbr* = **hot and cold (water)**.

HE *abbr* = **high explosive**; (*REL, DIPLOMACY*) = **His (*or* Her) Excellency**.

he [hiː] *pron* ele; **~ who ...** quem ..., aquele que ....; **~-bear** *etc* urso *etc* macho.

head [hɛd] *n* cabeça; (*leader*) chefe *m/f*, líder *m/f* ♦ *vt* (*list*) encabeçar; (*group*) liderar; **~s or tails** cara ou coroa; **~ first** de cabeça; **~ over heels** de pernas para o ar; **~ over heels in love** apaixonadíssimo; **to ~ the ball** cabecear a bola; **£10 a** *or* **per ~** £10 por pessoa *or* cabeça; **to sit at the ~ of the table** sentar-se à cabeceira da mesa; **to have a ~ for business** ter tino para negócios; **to have no ~ for heights** não suportar alturas; **to come to a ~** (*fig: situation etc*) chegar a um ponto crítico; **on your ~ be it** você que arque com as conseqüências.

head for *vt fus* dirigir-se a.

head off *vt* (*danger, threat*) desviar.

headache ['hɛdeɪk] *n* dor *f* de cabeça; **to have a ~** estar com dor de cabeça.

head cold *n* resfriado (*BR*), constipação *f* (*PT*).

headdress ['hɛddrɛs] *n* (*of Indian etc*) cocar *m*; (*of bride*) grinalda.

header ['hɛdə*] *n* (*BRIT: inf: FOOTBALL*) cabeçada; (*on page*) cabeçalho.

headhunter ['hɛdhʌntə*] *n* caçador *m* de cabeças.

heading ['hɛdɪŋ] *n* título, cabeçalho; (*subject title*) rubrica.

headlamp ['hɛdlæmp] (*BRIT*) *n* farol *m*.

headland ['hɛdlənd] *n* promontório.

headlight ['hɛdlaɪt] *n* farol *m*.

headline ['hɛdlaɪn] *n* manchete *f*.

headlong ['hɛdlɔŋ] *adv* (*fall*) de cabeça;

***NB:** European Portuguese adds the following consonants to certain words:* **b** (sú(b)dito, su(b)til); **c** (a(c)ção, a(c)cionista, a(c)to); **m** (inde(m)ne); **p** (ado(p)ção, ado(p)tar); *for further details* *see p. xiii.*

(*rush*) precipitadamente.

headmaster [hɛd'mɑːstə*] *n* diretor *m* (de escola).

headmistress [hɛd'mɪstrɪs] *n* diretora *f* (de escola).

head office *n* matriz *f*.

head-on *adj* (*collision*) de frente.

headphones ['hɛdfəunz] *npl* fones *mpl* de ouvido.

headquarters [hɛd'kwɔːtəz] *npl* (*of business etc*) sede *f*; (*MIL*) quartel *m* general.

head-rest *n* apoio para a cabeça.

headroom ['hɛdrum] *n* (*in car*) espaço (para a cabeça); (*under bridge*) vão *m* livre.

headscarf ['hɛdskɑːf] (*irreg*) *n* lenço de cabeça.

headset ['hɛdsɛt] *n* fones *mpl* de ouvido.

headstone ['hɛdstəun] *n* lápide *f* de ponta cabeça.

headstrong ['hɛdstrɔŋ] *adj* voluntarioso, teimoso.

head waiter *n* maitre *m* (*BR*), chefe *m* de mesa (*PT*).

headway ['hɛdweɪ] *n* progresso; **to make ~** avançar.

headwind ['hɛdwɪnd] *n* vento contrário.

heady ['hɛdɪ] *adj* (*exciting*) emocionante; (*intoxicating*) estonteante.

heal [hiːl] *vt* curar ♦ *vi* cicatrizar.

health [hɛlθ] *n* saúde *f*; **good ~!** saúde!; **Department of H~** (*US*) ≈ Ministério da Saúde.

health centre (*BRIT*) *n* posto de saúde.

health food(s) *n(pl)* alimentos *mpl* naturais.

health food shop *n* loja de comida natural.

health hazard *n* risco para a saúde.

Health Service (*BRIT*) *n*: **the ~** o Serviço Nacional da Saúde, ≈ a Previdência Social.

healthy ['hɛlθɪ] *adj* saudável, sadio; (*economy*) próspero, forte.

heap [hiːp] *n* pilha, montão *m* ♦ *vt* amontoar, empilhar; (*plate*) encher; **~s (of)** (*inf*: *lots*) um monte de; **to ~ favours/praise/gifts** *etc* **on sb** cobrir *or* cumular alguém de favores/elogios/presentes *etc*.

hear [hɪə*] (*pt, pp* **heard**) *vt* ouvir; (*listen to*) escutar; (*news*) saber; (*lecture*) assistir a ♦ *vi* ouvir; **to ~ about** ouvir falar de; **when did you ~ about this?** quando você soube disso?; **to ~ from sb** ter notícias de alguém; **I've never heard of the book** eu nunca ouvi falar no livro.

hear out *vt* ouvir sem interromper.

heard [həːd] *pt, pp of* **hear**.

hearing ['hɪərɪŋ] *n* (*sense*) audição *f*; (*LAW*) audiência; **to give sb a ~** (*BRIT*) ouvir alguém.

hearing aid *n* aparelho para a surdez.

hearsay ['hɪəseɪ] *n* boato, ouvir-dizer *m*; **by ~** por ouvir dizer.

hearse [həːs] *n* carro fúnebre.

heart [hɑːt] *n* coração *m*; **~s** *npl* (*CARDS*) copas *fpl*; **at ~** no fundo; **by ~** (*learn, know*) de cor; **to lose ~** perder o ânimo; **to take ~** criar coragem; **to set one's ~ on sth/on doing sth** decidir-se por algo/a fazer algo; **the ~ of the matter** a essência da questão.

heart attack *n* ataque *m* de coração.

heartbeat ['hɑːtbiːt] *n* batida do coração.

heartbreak ['hɑːtbreɪk] *n* desgosto, dor *f*.

heartbreaking ['hɑːtbreɪkɪŋ] *adj* desolador(a).

heartbroken ['hɑːtbrəukən]: **to be ~** estar inconsolável.

heartburn ['hɑːtbəːn] *n* azia.

-hearted ['hɑːtɪd] *suffix*: **kind~** bondoso.

heartening ['hɑːtnɪŋ] *adj* animador(a).

heart failure *n* parada cardíaca.

heartfelt ['hɑːtfɛlt] *adj* (*cordial*) cordial; (*deeply felt*) sincero.

hearth [hɑːθ] *n* lar *m*; (*fireplace*) lareira.

heartily ['hɑːtɪlɪ] *adv* sinceramente, cordialmente; (*laugh*) a gargalhadas, com vontade; (*eat*) apetitosamente; **I ~ agree** concordo completamente; **to be ~ sick of** (*BRIT*) estar farto de.

heartland ['hɑːtlænd] *n* coração *m* (do país).

heartless ['hɑːtlɪs] *adj* cruel, sem coração.

heart-to-heart *adj* (*conversation*) franco, sincero ♦ *n* conversa franca.

heart transplant *n* transplante *m* de coração.

heartwarming ['hɑːtwɔːmɪŋ] *adj* emocionante.

hearty ['hɑːtɪ] *adj* cordial, sincero.

heat [hiːt] *n* calor *m*; (*ardour*) ardor *m*; (*SPORT*: *also*: *qualifying ~*) (prova) eliminatória; (*ZOOL*): **in ~, on ~** (*BRIT*) no cio ♦ *vt* esquentar; (*room, house*) aquecer; (*fig*) acalorar.

heat up *vi* aquecer-se, esquentar ♦ *vt* esquentar.

heated ['hiːtɪd] *adj* aquecido; (*fig*) acalorado.

heater ['hiːtə*] *n* aquecedor *m*.

heath [hiːθ] (*BRIT*) *n* charneca.

heathen ['hiːðn] *adj, n* pagão/pagã *m/f*.

heather ['hɛðə*] *n* urze *f*.

heating ['hiːtɪŋ] *n* aquecimento, calefação *f*.

heat-resistant *adj* resistente ao calor.

heatstroke ['hiːtstrəuk] *n* insolação *f*.

heatwave ['hiːtweɪv] *n* onda de calor.

heave [hiːv] *vt* (*pull*) puxar; (*push*) empurrar (com esforço); (*lift*) levantar (com esforço) ♦ *vi* (*water*) agitar-se; (*retch*) ter ânsias de vômito ♦ *n* puxão *m*; empurrão *m*; **to ~ a sigh** soltar um suspiro.

heave to *vi* (*NAUT*) capear.

heaven ['hɛvn] *n* céu *m*, paraíso; **~ forbid!** Deus me livre!; **thank ~!** graças a Deus!; **for ~'s sake!** pelo amor de Deus!

heavenly ['hɛvnlɪ] *adj* celestial; (*REL*) divino.

heavily ['hɛvɪlɪ] *adv* pesadamente; (*drink, smoke*) excessivamente; (*sleep, sigh*) profundamente.

heavy ['hɛvɪ] *adj* pesado; (*work*) duro; (*sea*) violento; (*rain, meal*) forte; (*drinker, smoker*) inveterado; **it's ~ going** é difícil.

heavy cream (*US*) *n* creme *m* de leite.

heavy-duty *adj* de serviço pesado.

heavy goods vehicle (*BRIT*) *n* caminhão *m* de carga pesada.

heavy-handed [-'hændɪd] *adj* (*fig*) desajeita-

do, sem tato.
heavyweight ['hɛvɪweɪt] *n* (*SPORT*) peso-pesado.
Hebrew ['hiːbruː] *adj* hebreu/hebréia; (*LING*) hebraico ♦ *n* (*LING*) hebraico.
Hebrides ['hɛbrɪdiːz] *n*: **the ~** as (ilhas) Hébridas.
heckle ['hɛkl] *vt* apartear.
heckler ['hɛklə*] *n* pessoa que aparteia.
hectare ['hɛktɛə*] (*BRIT*) *n* hectare *m*.
hectic ['hɛktɪk] *adj* febril, agitado.
hector ['hɛktə*] *vt* importunar, implicar com.
he'd [hiːd] = **he would; he had**.
hedge [hɛdʒ] *n* cerca viva, sebe *f* ♦ *vi* dar evasivas ♦ *vt*: **to ~ one's bets** (*fig*) resguardar-se; **as a ~ against inflation** para precaver-se da inflação.
hedge in *vt* cercar com uma sebe.
hedgehog ['hɛdʒhɔg] *n* ouriço.
hedgerow ['hɛdʒrəu] *n* cercas *fpl* vivas, sebes *fpl*.
hedonism ['hiːdənɪzm] *n* hedonismo.
heed [hiːd] *vt* (*also*: *take ~ of*: *attend to*) prestar atenção a; (: *bear in mind*) levar em consideração.
heedless ['hiːdlɪs] *adj* desatento, negligente.
heel [hiːl] *n* (*of shoe*) salto; (*of foot*) calcanhar *m* ♦ *vt* (*shoe*) pôr salto em; **to take to one's ~s** dar no pé *or* aos calcanhares.
hefty ['hɛftɪ] *adj* (*person*) robusto; (*piece*) grande; (*price*) alto.
heifer ['hɛfə*] *n* novilha, bezerra.
height [haɪt] *n* (*of person*) estatura; (*of building*) altura; (*high ground*) monte *m*; (*altitude*) altitude *f*; (*fig*: *of glory*) cume *m*; (: *of stupidity*) cúmulo; **what ~ are you?** quanto você tem de altura?; **of average ~** de estatura mediana; **to be afraid of ~s** ter medo de alturas; **it's the ~ of fashion** é a última palavra *or* moda.
heighten ['haɪtən] *vt* elevar; (*fig*) aumentar.
heinous ['hiːnəs] *adj* hediondo, abominável.
heir [ɛə*] *n* herdeiro.
heir apparent *n* herdeiro presuntivo.
heiress ['ɛərɪs] *n* herdeira.
heirloom ['ɛəluːm] *n* relíquia de família.
heist [haɪst] (*US*: *inf*) *n* (*hold-up*) assalto.
held [hɛld] *pt, pp of* **hold**.
helicopter ['hɛlɪkɔptə*] *n* helicóptero.
heliport ['hɛlɪpɔːt] *n* (*AVAIT*) heliporto.
helium ['hiːlɪəm] *n* hélio.
hell [hɛl] *n* inferno; **a ~ of a ...** (*inf*) um ... danado; **oh ~!** (*inf*) droga!
he'll [hiːl]= **he will; he shall**.
hellish ['hɛlɪʃ] *adj* infernal; (*inf*) terrível.
hello [hə'ləu] *excl* oi! (*BR*), olá! (*PT*); (*on phone*) alô! (*BR*), está! (*PT*); (*surprise*) ora essa!
helm [hɛlm] *n* (*NAUT*) timão *m*, leme *m*.
helmet ['hɛlmɪt] *n* capacete *m*.
helmsman ['hɛlmzmən] (*irreg*) *n* timoneiro.
help [hɛlp] *n* ajuda; (*charwoman*) faxineira; (*assistant etc*) auxiliar *m/f* ♦ *vt* ajudar; **~!** socorro!; **~ yourself** sirva-se; **can I ~ you?** (*in shop*) deseja alguma coisa?; **with the ~ of** com a ajuda de; **to be of ~ to sb** ajudar alguém, ser útil a alguém; **to ~ sb (to) do sth** ajudar alguém a fazer algo; **he can't ~ it** não tem culpa.
helper ['hɛlpə*] *n* ajudante *m/f*.
helpful ['hɛlpful] *adj* (*thing*) útil, benéfico; (*person*) prestativo.
helping ['hɛlpɪŋ] *n* porção *f*.
helpless ['hɛlplɪs] *adj* (*incapable*) incapaz; (*defenceless*) indefeso; (*baby*) desamparado.
helplessly ['hɛlplɪslɪ] *adv* (*watch*) sem poder fazer nada.
Helsinki [hɛl'sɪŋkɪ] *n* Helsinque.
helter-skelter ['hɛltə'skɛltə*] (*BRIT*) *n* (*at amusement park*) tobogã *m*.
hem [hɛm] *n* bainha ♦ *vt* embainhar.
hem in *vt* cercar, encurralar; **to feel ~med in** sentir-se acuado.
he-man (*irreg*) *n* macho.
hematology ['hiːmə'tɔlədʒɪ] (*US*) *n* = **haematology**.
hemisphere ['hɛmɪsfɪə*] *n* hemisfério.
hemlock ['hɛmlɔk] *n* cicuta.
hemoglobin ['hiːmə'gləubɪn] (*US*) *n* = **haemoglobin**.
hemophilia ['hiːmə'fɪlɪə] (*US*) *n* = **haemophilia**.
hemorrhage ['hɛmərɪdʒ] (*US*) *n* = **haemorrhage**.
hemorrhoids ['hɛmərɔɪdʒ] (*US*) *npl* = **haemorrhoids**.
hemp [hɛmp] *n* cânhamo.
hen [hɛn] *n* galinha; (*female bird*) fêmea.
hence [hɛns] *adv* (*therefore*) daí, portanto; **2 years ~** daqui a 2 anos.
henceforth ['hɛns'fɔːθ] *adv* de agora em diante, doravante.
henchman ['hɛntʃmən] (*irreg*) *n* jagunço, capanga *m*.
henna ['hɛnə] *n* hena.
hen party (*inf*) *n* reunião *f* de mulheres.
henpecked ['hɛnpɛkt] *adj* dominado pela esposa.
hepatitis [hɛpə'taɪtɪs] *n* hepatite *f*.
her [həː*] *pron* (*direct*) a; (*indirect*) lhe; (*stressed, after prep*) ela ♦ *adj* seu/sua, dela; **~ name** o nome dela; **I see ~** vejo-a, vejo ela (*BR*: *inf*); **give ~ a book** dá-lhe um livro, dá um livro a ela.
herald ['hɛrəld] *n* (*forerunner*) precursor(a) *m/f* ♦ *vt* anunciar.
heraldic [hɛ'rældɪk[*adj* heráldico.
heraldry ['hɛrəldrɪ] *n* heráldica.
herb [həːb] *n* erva.
herbaceous [həː'beɪʃəs] *adj* herbáceo.
herbal ['həːbəl] *adj* herbáceo; **~ tea** tisana.
herd [həːd] *n* rebanho ♦ *vt* (*drive*: *animals, people*) conduzir; (*gather*) arrebanhar.
here [hɪə*] *adv* aqui; (*to this place*) para cá ♦

***NB**: European Portuguese adds the following consonants to certain words:* **b** (sú(b)dito, su(b)til); **c** (a(c)ção, a(c)cionista, a(c)to); **m** (inde(m)ne); **p** (ado(p)ção, ado(p)tar); *for further details see p. xiii.*

excl toma!; ~! (*present*) presente!; ~ **he/she is** aqui está ele/ela; ~ **she comes** lá vem ela; **come** ~! vem cá!; ~ **and there** aqui e ali.
hereabouts ['hɪərə'bauts] *adv* por aqui.
hereafter [hɪər'ɑːftə*] *adv* daqui por diante ♦ *n*: **the** ~ a vida de além-túmulo.
hereby [hɪə'baɪ] *adv* (*in letter*) por este meio.
hereditary [hɪ'rɛdɪtrɪ] *adj* hereditário.
heredity [hɪ'rɛdɪtɪ] *n* hereditariedade *f*.
heresy ['hɛrəsɪ] *n* heresia.
heretic ['hɛrətɪk] *n* herege *m/f*.
heretical [hɪ'rɛtɪkl] *adj* herético.
herewith [hɪə'wɪð] *adv* em anexo, junto.
heritage ['hɛrɪtɪdʒ] *n* herança; (*fig*) patrimônio; **our national** ~ nosso patrimônio nacional.
hermetically [həː'mɛtɪklɪ] *adv* hermeticamente; ~ **sealed** hermeticamente fechado.
hermit ['həːmɪt] *n* eremita *m/f*.
hernia ['həːnɪə] *n* hérnia.
hero ['hɪərəu] (*pl* ~**es**) *n* herói *m*; (*of book, film*) protagonista *m*.
heroic [hɪ'rəuɪk] *adj* heróico.
heroin ['hɛrəuɪn] *n* heroína.
heroin addict *n* viciado/a em heroína.
heroine ['hɛrəuɪn] *n* heroína; (*of book, film*) protagonista.
heroism ['hɛrəuɪzm] *n* heroísmo.
heron ['hɛrən] *n* garça.
hero worship *n* culto de heróis.
herring ['hɛrɪŋ] (*pl inv or* ~**s**) *n* arenque *m*.
hers [həːz] *pron* (o) seu/(a) sua, (o/a) dela; **a friend of** ~ uma amiga dela; **this is** ~ isto é dela.
herself [həː'sɛlf] *pron* (*reflexive*) se; (*emphatic*) ela mesma; (*after prep*) si (mesma).
Herts (*BRIT*) *abbr* = **Hertfordshire**.
he's [hiːz] = **he is; he has**.
hesitant ['hɛzɪtənt] *adj* hesitante, indeciso; **to be** ~ **about doing sth** hesitar em fazer algo.
hesitate ['hɛzɪteɪt] *vi* hesitar; **to** ~ **to do** hesitar em fazer; **don't** ~ **to phone** não deixe de telefonar.
hesitation [hɛzɪ'teɪʃən] *n* hesitação *f*, indecisão *f*; **I have no** ~ **in saying (that)** ... não hesito em dizer (que) ....
hessian ['hɛsɪən] *n* aniagem *f*.
heterogeneous ['hɛtərə'dʒiːnɪəs] *adj* heterogêneo.
heterosexual ['hɛtərəu'sɛksjuəl] *adj, n* heterossexual *m/f*.
het up [hɛt-] (*inf*) *adj* excitado.
HEW (*US*) *n abbr* (= *Department of Health, Education and Welfare*) *ministério da saúde, da educação e da previdência social*.
hew [hjuː] *vt* cortar (com machado).
hex [hɛks] (*US*) *n* feitiço ♦ *vt* enfeitiçar.
hexagon ['hɛksəgən] *n* hexágono.
hexagonal [hɛk'sægənl] *adj* hexagonal.
hey [heɪ] *excl* eh! ei!
heyday ['heɪdeɪ] *n*: **the** ~ **of** o auge *or* apogeu de.
HF *n abbr* (= *high frequency*) HF *f*.
HGV (*BRIT*) *n abbr* = **heavy goods vehicle**.
HI (*US*) *abbr* (*POST*) = **Hawaii**.
hi [haɪ] *excl* oi!
hiatus [haɪ'eɪtəs] *n* hiato.
hibernate ['haɪbəneɪt] *vi* hibernar.
hibernation [haɪbə'neɪʃən] *n* hibernação *f*.
hiccough ['hɪkʌp] *vi* soluçar ♦ *n* soluço; **to have (the)** ~**s** estar com soluço.
hiccup ['hɪkʌp] *vi, n* = **hiccough**.
hid [hɪd] *pt of* **hide**.
hidden ['hɪdn] *pp of* **hide** ♦ *adj* (*costs*) oculto.
hide [haɪd] (*pt* **hid**, *pp* **hidden**) *n* (*skin*) pele *f* ♦ *vt* esconder, ocultar ♦ *vi*: **to** ~ **(from sb)** esconder-se *or* ocultar-se (de alguém).
hide-and-seek *n* esconde-esconde *m*.
hideaway ['haɪdəweɪ] *n* esconderijo.
hideous ['hɪdɪəs] *adj* horrível.
hide-out *n* esconderijo.
hiding ['haɪdɪŋ] *n* (*beating*) surra; **to be in** ~ (*concealed*) estar escondido.
hiding place *n* esconderijo.
hierarchy ['haɪərɑːkɪ] *n* hierarquia.
hieroglyphic [haɪərə'glɪfɪk] *adj* hieroglífico.
hieroglyphics [haɪərə'glɪfɪks] *npl* hieroglifos *mpl*.
hi-fi ['haɪfaɪ] *abbr* (= *high fidelity*) *n* alta-fidelidade *f*; (*system*) som *m* ♦ *adj* de alta-fidelidade.
higgledy-piggledy ['hɪgldɪ'pɪgldɪ] *adv* desordenadamente.
high [haɪ] *adj* (*gen, speed*) alto; (*number*) grande; (*price*) alto, elevado; (*wind*) forte; (*voice*) agudo; (*inf*: *person*: *on drugs*) alto, baratinado; (*BRIT*: *CULIN*: *meat, game*) faisandé *inv*; (: *spoilt*) estragado ♦ *adv* alto, a grande altura ♦ *n*: **exports have reached a new** ~ as exportações atingiram um novo pico; **it is 20 m** ~ tem 20 m de altura; ~ **in the air** nas alturas; **to pay a** ~ **price for sth** pagar caro por algo.
highball ['haɪbɔːl] (*US*) *n* uísque com soda.
highboy ['haɪbɔɪ] (*US*) *n* comoda alta.
highbrow ['haɪbrau] *adj* intelectual, erudito.
highchair ['haɪtʃɛə*] *n* cadeira alta (para criança).
high-class *adj* (*neighbourhood*) nobre; (*hotel*) de primeira categoria; (*person*) da classe alta; (*performance etc*) de alto nível.
high court *n* (*LAW*) tribunal *m* superior.
higher ['haɪə*] *adj* (*form of life, study etc*) superior ♦ *adv* mais alto.
higher education *n* ensino superior.
high finance *n* altas finanças *fpl*.
high-flier *n* estudante *m/f* (*or* empregado/a) talentoso/a e ambicioso/a.
high-flying *adj* (*fig*) ambicioso, talentoso.
high-handed [-'hændɪd] *adj* despótico.
high-heeled [-'hiːld] *adj* de salto alto.
highjack ['haɪdʒæk] *n, vt* = **hijack**.
high jump *n* (*SPORT*) salto em altura.
highlands ['haɪləndz] *npl* serrania, serra; **the H**~ (*in Scotland*) a Alta Escócia.
high-level *adj* de alto nível; ~ **language** (*COMPUT*) linguagem *f* de alto nível.
highlight ['haɪlaɪt] *n* (*fig*: *of event*) ponto alto ♦ *vt* realçar, ressaltar; ~**s** *npl* (*in hair*) me-

chas *fpl*; **the ~s of the match** os melhores lances do jogo.
highlighter ['haɪlaɪtə*] *n* (*pen*) caneta marca-texto.
highly ['haɪlɪ] *adv* altamente; (*very*) muito; ~ **paid** muito bem pago; **to speak ~ of** falar elogiosamente de.
highly-strung *adj* tenso, irritadiço.
High Mass *n* missa cantada.
highness ['haɪnɪs] *n* altura; **Her H~** Sua Alteza.
high-pitched *adj* agudo.
high-powered *adj* (*engine*) muito potente, de alta potência; (*fig*: *person*) dinâmico; (: *job, businessman*) muito importante.
high-pressure *adj* de alta pressão.
high-rise block *n* edifício alto, espigão *m*.
high school *n* (*BRIT*) escola secundária; (*US*) científico.
high season (*BRIT*) *n* alta estação *f*.
high spirits *npl* alegria; **to be in ~** estar alegre.
high street (*BRIT*) *n* rua principal.
highway ['haɪweɪ] *n* estrada, rodovia.
Highway Code (*BRIT*) *n* Código Nacional de Trânsito.
highwayman ['haɪweɪmən] (*irreg*) *n* salteador *m* de estrada.
hijack ['haɪdʒæk] *vt* seqüestrar ♦ *n* (*also*: *~ing*) seqüestro (de avião).
hijacker ['haɪdʒækə*] *n* seqüestrador(a) *m/f* (de avião).
hike [haɪk] *vi* (*go walking*) caminhar; ♦ *n* caminhada, excursão *f* a pé; (*inf*: *in prices etc*) aumento ♦ *vt* (*inf*) aumentar.
hiker ['haɪkə*] *n* caminhante *m/f*, andarilho/a.
hiking ['haɪkɪŋ] *n* excursões *fpl* a pé, caminhar *m*.
hilarious [hɪ'lɛərɪəs] *adj* (*behaviour, event*) hilariante.
hilarity [hɪ'lærɪtɪ] *n* hilaridade *f*.
hill [hɪl] *n* colina; (*high*) montanha; (*slope*) ladeira, rampa.
hillbilly ['hɪlbɪlɪ] (*US*) *n* montanhês/esa *m/f*; (*pej*) caipira *m/f*, jeca *m/f*.
hillock ['hɪlək] *n* morro pequeno.
hillside ['hɪlsaɪd] *n* vertente *f*.
hill start *n* (*AUT*) partida em ladeira.
hilly ['hɪlɪ] *adj* montanhoso; (*uneven*) acidentado.
hilt [hɪlt] *n* (*of sword*) punho, guarda; **to the ~** plenamente.
him [hɪm] *pron* (*direct*) o; (*indirect*) lhe; (*stressed, after prep*) ele; **I see ~** vejo-o, vejo ele (*BR*: *inf*); **give ~ a book** dá-lhe um livro, dá um livro a ele.
Himalayas [hɪmə'leɪəz] *npl*: **the ~** o Himalaia.
himself [hɪm'sɛlf] *pron* (*reflexive*) se; (*emphatic*) ele mesmo; (*after prep*) si (mesmo).
hind [haɪnd] *adj* traseiro ♦ *n* corça.
hinder ['hɪndə*] *vt* atrapalhar; (*delay*) retardar.
hindquarters ['haɪnd'kwɔːtəz] *npl* (*ZOOL*) quartos *mpl* traseiros.
hindrance ['hɪndrəns] *n* impedimento, estorvo.
hindsight ['haɪndsaɪt] *n*: **with the benefit of ~** em retrospecto.
Hindu ['hɪnduː] *n* hindu *m/f*.
hinge [hɪndʒ] *n* dobradiça ♦ *vi* (*fig*): **to ~ on** depender de.
hint [hɪnt] *n* insinuação *f*; (*advice*) palpite *m*, dica ♦ *vt*: **to ~ that** insinuar que ♦ *vi* dar indiretas; **to ~ at** fazer alusão a; **to drop a ~** dar uma indireta; **give me a ~** (*clue*) me dá uma pista.
hip [hɪp] *n* quadril *m*.
hip flask *n* cantil *m*.
hippie ['hɪpɪ] *n* hippie *m/f*.
hip pocket *n* bolso traseiro.
hippopotami [hɪpə'pɔtəmaɪ] *npl of* **hippopotamus**.
hippopotamus [hɪpə'pɔtəməs] (*pl* **~es** *or* **hippopotami**) *n* hipopótamo.
hippy ['hɪpɪ] *n* = **hippie**.
hire ['haɪə*] *vt* (*BRIT*: *car, equipment*) alugar; (*worker*) contratar ♦ *n* aluguel *m*; (*of person*) contratação *f*; **for ~** aluga-se; (*taxi*) livre; **on ~** alugado.
hire out *vt* alugar.
hire(d) car ['haɪə(d)-] (*BRIT*) *n* carro alugado.
hire purchase (*BRIT*) *n* compra a prazo; **to buy sth on ~** comprar algo a prazo *or* pelo crediário.
his [hɪz] *pron* (o) seu/(a) sua, (o/a) dele ♦ *adj* seu/sua *or* dele; **~ name** o nome dele; **it's ~** é dele.
Hispanic [hɪs'pænɪk] *adj* hispânico.
hiss [hɪs] *vi* silvar; (*boo*) vaiar ♦ *n* silvo; vaia.
histogram ['hɪstəgræm] *n* histograma *m*.
historian [hɪ'stɔːrɪən] *n* historiador(a) *m/f*.
historic(al) [hɪ'stɔrɪk(l)] *adj* histórico.
history ['hɪstərɪ] *n* história; (*of illness etc*) histórico; **medical ~** (*of patient*) histórico médico.
histrionics [hɪstrɪ'ɔnɪks] *n* teatro.
hit [hɪt] (*pt, pp* **hit**) *vt* (*strike*) bater em; (*reach*: *target*) acertar, alcançar; (*collide with*: *car*) bater em, colidir com; (*fig*: *affect*) atingir ♦ *n* (*blow*) golpe *m*; (*success*) sucesso, grande êxito; (*song*) sucesso; **to ~ it off with sb** dar-se bem com alguém; **to ~ the headlines** virar *or* fazer manchete; **to ~ the road** (*inf*) dar o fora, mandar-se.
hit back *vi*: **to ~ back at sb** revidar ao ataque (*or* à crítica *etc*) de alguém.
hit out at *vt fus* tentar bater em; (*fig*) criticar veementemente.
hit (up)on *vt fus* (*answer*) descobrir.
hit-and-run driver *n motorista que atropela alguém e foge da cena do acidente.*
hitch [hɪtʃ] *vt* (*fasten*) atar, amarrar; (*also*: ~ *up*) levantar ♦ *n* (*difficulty*) dificuldade *f*; **to ~ a lift** pegar carona (*BR*), arranjar uma bo-

leia (*PT*); **technical ~** probleminha técnico.
hitch up *vt* (*horse, cart*) atrelar; *see also* **hitch.**
hitch-hike *vi* pegar carona (*BR*), andar à boleia (*PT*).
hitch-hiker *n* pessoa que pega carona (*BR*) *or* anda à boleia (*PT*).
hi-tech *adj* tecnologicamente avançado ♦ *n* alta tecnologia.
hitherto [hɪðə'tuː] *adv* até agora.
hitman ['hɪtmæn] (*irreg*) *n* sicário.
hit-or-miss *adj* aleatório; **it's ~ whether ...** não é nada certo que ....
hit parade *n* parada de sucessos.
hive [haɪv] *n* colméia; **the shop was a ~ of activity** (*fig*) a loja fervilhava de atividade.
hive off (*inf*) *vt* transferir.
hl *abbr* (= *hectolitre*) hl.
HM *abbr* (= *His* (*or Her*) *Majesty*) SM.
HMG (*BRIT*) *abbr* = **His** (*or* **Her**) **Majesty's Government.**
HMI (*BRIT*) *abbr* (*SCH*) = **His** (*or* **Her**) **Majesty's Inspector.**
HMO (*US*) *n abbr* (= *health maintenance organization*) *órgão que garante a manutenção de sáude.*
HMS (*BRIT*) *abbr* = **His** (*or* **Her**) **Majesty's Ship.**
HMSO *n abbr* (= *His* (*or Her*) *Majesty's Stationery Office*) *imprensa do governo.*
HNC (*BRIT*) *n abbr* = **Higher National Certificate.**
HND (*BRIT*) *n abbr* = **Higher National Diploma.**
hoard [hɔːd] *n* provisão *f*; (*of money*) tesouro ♦ *vt* acumular.
hoarding ['hɔːdɪŋ] (*BRIT*) *n* tapume *m*, outdoor *m*.
hoarfrost ['hɔːfrɔst] *n* geada.
hoarse [hɔːs] *adj* rouco.
hoax [həuks] *n* trote *m*.
hob [hɔb] *n* mesa (do fogão).
hobble ['hɔbl] *vi* coxear.
hobby ['hɔbɪ] *n* hobby *m*, passatempo predileto.
hobby-horse *n* cavalinho-de-pau; (*fig*) tema *m* favorito.
hobnob ['hɔbnɔb] *vi*: **to ~ with** ter intimidade com.
hobo ['həubəu] (*pl* **~s** *or* **~es**) (*US*) *n* vagabundo.
hock [hɔk] *n* (*BRIT*: *wine*) vinho branco do Reno; (*of animal, CULIN*) jarrete *m*; (*inf*): **to be in ~** (*person*) estar endividado; (*object*) estar no prego *or* empenhado.
hockey ['hɔkɪ] *n* hóquei *m*.
hocus-pocus ['həukəs'pəukəs] *n* (*trickery*) tapeação *f*; (*words*) embromação *f*.
hodgepodge ['hɔdʒpɔdʒ] *n* = **hotchpotch.**
hoe [həu] *n* enxada ♦ *vt* trabalhar com enxada, capinar.
hog [hɔg] *n* porco; (*person*) glutão/ona *m/f* ♦ *vt* (*fig*) monopolizar; **to go the whole ~** ir até o fim.
hoist [hɔɪst] *n* (*lift*) guincho; (*crane*) guindaste *m* ♦ *vt* içar.
hold [həuld] (*pt, pp* **held**) *vt* segurar; (*contain*) conter; (*keep back*) reter; (*believe*) sustentar; (*have*) ter; (*record etc*) deter; (*take weight*) agüentar; (*meeting*) realizar ♦ *vi* (*withstand pressure*) resistir; (*be valid*) ser válido ♦ *n* (*handle*) apoio (para a mão); (*fig*: *grasp*) influência, domínio; (*NAUT*) porão *m* de navio; **to catch** *or* **get (a) ~ of** agarrar, pegar; **to get ~ of** (*fig*) arranjar; **to get ~ of o.s.** controlar-se; **~ the line!** (*TEL*) não desligue!; **to ~ one's own** (*fig*) virar-se, sair-se bem; **to ~ office** (*POL*) exercer um cargo; **to ~ firm** *or* **fast** agüentar; **he ~s the view that ...** ele sustenta que ...; **to ~ sb responsible for sth** responsabilizar alguém por algo.
hold back *vt* reter; (*secret*) manter, guardar; **to ~ sb back from doing sth** impedir alguém de fazer algo.
hold down *vt* (*person*) segurar; (*job*) manter.
hold forth *vi* discursar, deitar falação.
hold off *vt* (*enemy*) afastar, repelir ♦ *vi* (*rain*): **if the rain ~s off** se não chover.
hold on *vi* agarrar-se; (*wait*) esperar; **~ on!** espera aí!; (*TEL*) não desligue!
hold on to *vt fus* agarrar-se a; (*keep*) guardar, ficar com.
hold out *vt* estender ♦ *vi* (*resist*) resistir; **to ~ out (against)** defender-se (contra).
hold over *vt* (*meeting etc*) adiar.
hold up *vt* (*raise*) levantar; (*support*) apoiar; (*delay*) atrasar; (*traffic*) reter; (*rob*) assaltar.
holdall ['həuldɔːl] (*BRIT*) *n* bolsa de viagem.
holder ['həuldə*] *n* (*of ticket*) portador(a) *m/f*; (*of record*) detentor(a) *m/f*; (*of office, title etc*) titular *m/f*.
holding ['həuldɪŋ] *n* (*share*) participação *f*; **~s** *npl* posses *fpl*.
holding company *n* holding *f*.
holdup ['həuldʌp] *n* (*robbery*) assalto; (*delay*) demora; (*BRIT*: *in traffic*) engarrafamento.
hole [həul] *n* buraco ♦ *vt* esburacar; **~ in the heart** (*MED*) defeito na membrana cardíaca; **to pick ~s (in)** (*fig*) botar defeito (em).
hole up *vi* esconder-se.
holiday ['hɔlədɪ] *n* (*BRIT*: *vacation*) férias *fpl*; (*day off*) dia *m* de folga; (*public*) feriado; **to be on ~** estar de férias; **tomorrow is a ~** amanhã é feriado.
holiday camp (*BRIT*) *n* colônia de férias.
holiday-maker (*BRIT*) *n* pessoa (que está) de férias.
holiday pay salário de férias.
holiday resort *n* local *m* de férias.
holiday season *n* temporada de férias.
holiness ['həulɪnɪs] *n* santidade *f*.
Holland ['hɔlənd] *n* Holanda.
hollow ['hɔləu] *adj* oco, vazio; (*eyes*) fundo; (*sound*) surdo; (*doctrine*) falso ♦ *n* buraco; (*in ground*) cavidade *f*, depressão *f* ♦ *vt*: **to ~ out** escavar.
holly ['hɔlɪ] *n* azevinho.

hollyhock ['hɔlɪhɔk] *n* malva-rosa.
holocaust ['hɔləkɔːst] *n* holocausto.
holster ['həulstə*] *n* coldre *m*.
holy ['həulɪ] *adj* santo, sagrado; (*water*) bento.
Holy Communion *n* Sagrada Comunhão *f*.
Holy Ghost *n* Espírito Santo.
Holy Land *n*: **the ~** a Terra Santa.
holy orders *npl* ordens *fpl* sacras.
Holy Spirit *n* = **Holy Ghost**.
homage ['hɔmɪdʒ] *n* homenagem *f*; **to pay ~ to** prestar homenagem a, homenagear.
home [həum] *n* casa, lar *m*; (*country*) pátria; (*institution*) asilo ♦ *cpd* (*domestic*) caseiro, doméstico; (*of family*) familiar; (*heating, computer etc*) residencial; (*ECON, POL*) nacional, interno (*SPORT*: *team*) de casa; (: *win, match*) no próprio campo ♦ *adv* (*direction*) para casa; (*right in*: *nail etc*) até o fundo; **at ~** em casa; **to go/come ~** ir/vir para casa; **make yourself at ~** fique à vontade; **near my ~** perto da minha casa.
home in on *vt fus* (*missiles*) dirigir-se automaticamente para.
home address *n* endereço residencial.
home-brew *n* (*wine*) vinho feito em casa; (*beer*) cerveja feita em casa.
homecoming ['həumkʌmɪŋ] *n* regresso ao lar.
home computer *n* computador *m* residencial.
Home Counties *npl os condados por volta de Londres*.
home economics *n* economia doméstica.
home-grown *adj* (*not foreign*) nacional; (*from garden*) plantado em casa.
homeland ['həumlænd] *n* terra (natal).
homeless ['həumlɪs] *adj* sem casa, desabrigado ♦ *npl*: **the ~** os desabrigados.
home loan *n* crédito imobiliário, financiamento habitacional.
homely ['həumlɪ] *adj* (*domestic*) caseiro; (*simple*) simples *inv*.
home-made *adj* caseiro.
Home Office (*BRIT*) *n* Ministério do Interior.
homeopathy *etc* [həumɪ'ɔpəθɪ] (*US*) = **homoeopathy** *etc*.
home rule *n* autonomia.
Home Secretary (*BRIT*) *n* Ministro do Interior.
homesick ['həumsɪk] *adj*: **to be ~** estar com saudades (do lar).
homestead ['həumstɛd] *n* propriedade *f*; (*farm*) fazenda.
home town *n* cidade *f* natal.
homeward ['həumwəd] *adj* (*journey*) para casa, para a terra natal.
homeward(s) ['həumwəd(z)] *adv* para casa.
homework ['həumwəːk] *n* dever *m* de casa.
homicidal [hɔmɪ'saɪdl] *adj* homicida.
homicide ['hɔmɪsaɪd] (*US*) *n* homicídio.
homily ['hɔmɪlɪ] *n* homilia.
homing ['həumɪŋ] *adj* (*device, missile*) de correção de rumo; **~ pigeon** pombo- correio.
homoeopath ['həumɪəpæθ] (*US* **homeopath**) *n* homeopata *m/f*.
homoeopathic [həumɪə'pæθɪk] (*US* **homeopathic**) *adj* homeopático.
homoeopathy [həumɪ'ɔpəθɪ] (*US* **homeopathy**) *n* homeopatia.
homogeneous [hɔməu'dʒiːnɪəs] *adj* homogêneo.
homogenize [hə'mɔdʒənaɪz] *vt* homogeneizar.
homosexual [hɔməu'sɛksjuəl] *adj, n* homossexual *m/f*.
homosexuality [hɔməsɛksju'ælətɪ] *n* homossexualismo.
Hon. *abbr* = **honourable**; **honorary**.
Honduran [hɔn'djuərən] *adj, n* hondurenho/a.
Honduras [hɔn'djuərəs] *n* Honduras (*no article*).
hone [həun] *vt* amolar, afiar.
honest ['ɔnɪst] *adj* honesto; (*sincere*) sincero, franco; **to be quite ~ with you** ... para falar a verdade ....
honestly ['ɔnɪstlɪ] *adv* honestamente, francamente.
honesty ['ɔnɪstɪ] *n* honestidade *f*, sinceridade *f*.
honey ['hʌnɪ] *n* mel *m*; (*US*: *inf*: *darling*) querido/a.
honeycomb ['hʌnɪkəum] *n* favo de mel; (*pattern*) em forma de favo ♦ *vt* (*fig*): **to ~ with** crivar de.
honeymoon ['hʌnɪmuːn] *n* lua-de-mel *f*; (*trip*) viagem *f* de lua-de-mel.
honeysuckle ['hʌnɪsʌkl] *n* madressilva.
Hong Kong ['hɔŋ'kɔŋ] *n* Hong Kong (*no article*).
honk [hɔŋk] *n* buzinada ♦ *vi* (*AUT*) buzinar.
Honolulu [hɔnə'luːluː] *n* Honolulu.
honor ['ɔnə*] (*US*) *vt, n* = **honour**.
honorary ['ɔnərərɪ] *adj* (*unpaid*) não remunerado; (*duty, title*) honorário.
honour ['ɔnə*] (*US* **honor**) *vt* honrar ♦ *n* honra; **in ~ of** em honra de.
hono(u)rable ['ɔnərəbl] *adj* honrado.
hono(u)r-bound *adj*: **to be ~ to do** estar moralmente obrigado a fazer.
hono(u)rs degree *n* (*SCH*) diploma *m* com distinção.
Hons. *abbr* (*SCH*) = **hono(u)rs degree**.
hood [hud] *n* capuz *m*, touca; (*BRIT*: *AUT*) capota; (*US*: *AUT*) capô *m*; (*inf*: *hoodlum*) pinta-brava *m*.
hooded ['hudɪd] *adj* encapuzado, mascarado.
hoodlum ['huːdləm] *n* pinta-brava *m*.
hoodwink ['hudwɪŋk] *vt* tapear.
hoof [huːf] (*pl* **~s** *or* **hooves**) *n* casco, pata.
hook [huk] *n* gancho; (*on dress*) colchete *m*; (*for fishing*) anzol *m* ♦ *vt* enganchar, fisgar; **~ and eye** colchete *m*; **by ~ or by crook** custe o que custar; **to be ~ed (on)** (*inf*) estar viciado (em); (*person*) estar fissurado (em).
hook up *vt* ligar.

NB: *European Portuguese adds the following consonants to certain words:* **b** (sú(b)dito, su(b)til); **c** (a(c)ção, a(c)cionista, a(c)to); **m** (inde(m)ne); **p** (ado(p)ção, ado(p)tar); *for further details see p. xiii.*

hooligan ['hu:lɪgən] *n* desordeiro/a, baguceiro/a.
hooliganism ['hu:ligənɪzm] *n* vandalismo.
hoop [hu:p] *n* arco.
hoot [hu:t] *vi* (AUT) buzinar; (*siren*) tocar; (*owl*) piar ♦ *vt* (*jeer at*) vaiar ♦ *n* buzinada; toque *m* de sirena; **to ~ with laughter** morrer de rir.
hooter ['hu:tə*] *n* (BRIT: AUT) buzina; (NAUT, *factory*) sirena.
hoover ['hu:və*] (BRIT) ® *n* aspirador *m* (de pó) ♦ *vt* passar o aspirador em.
hooves [hu:vz] *npl of* **hoof**.
hop [hɔp] *vi* saltar, pular; (*on one foot*) pular num pé só ♦ *n* salto, pulo; **~s** *npl* lúpulo.
hope [həup] *vi* esperar ♦ *n* esperança; **I ~ so/not** espero que sim/não.
hopeful ['həupful] *adj* (*person*) otimista, esperançoso; (*situation*) promissor(a); **I'm ~ that she'll manage to come** acredito que ela conseguirá vir.
hopefully ['həupfulɪ] *adv* (*with hope*) esperançosamente; **~, they'll come back** é de esperar *or* esperamos que voltem.
hopeless ['həuplɪs] *adj* desesperado, irremediável; (*useless*) inútil; (*bad*) péssimo.
hopelessly ['həupləslɪ] *adv* (*confused, involved*) irremediavelmente.
hopper ['hɔpə*] *n* tremonha.
horde [hɔ:d] *n* horda.
horizon [hə'raɪzn] *n* horizonte *m*.
horizontal [hɔrɪ'zɔntl] *adj* horizontal.
hormone ['hɔ:məun] *n* hormônio.
horn [hɔ:n] *n* corno, chifre *m*; (MUS) trompa; (AUT) buzina.
horned [hɔ:nd] *adj* (*animal*) com chifres, chifrudo.
hornet ['hɔ:nɪt] *n* vespão *m*.
horn-rimmed [-rɪmd] *adj* com aro de chifre *or* de tartaruga.
horny ['hɔ:nɪ] *adj* (*material*) córneo; (*hands*) calejado; (*inf*: *aroused*) tarado, com tesão (BR: *!*).
horoscope ['hɔrəskəup] *n* horóscopo.
horrendous [hə'rɛndɔs] *adj* horrível, terrível.
horrible ['hɔrɪbl] *adj* horrível.
horrid ['hɔrɪd] *adj* antipático, horrível.
horrific [hə'rɪfɪk] *adj* horroroso.
horrify ['hɔrɪfaɪ] *vt* horrorizar.
horrifying ['hɔrɪfaɪɪŋ] *adj* horripilante.
horror ['hɔrə*] *n* horror *m*.
horror film *n* filme *m* de terror.
horror-striken *adj* = **horror-struck**.
horror-struck *adj* horrorizado.
hors d'œuvre [ɔ:'də:vrə] *n* entrada.
horse [hɔ:s] *n* cavalo.
horseback ['hɔ:sbæk] : **on ~** *adv* a cavalo.
horsebox ['hɔ:sbɔks] *n* reboque *m* (para transportar cavalos).
horse chestnut *n* castanha-da-índia.
horse-drawn *adj* puxado a cavalo.
horsefly ['hɔ:sflaɪ] *n* mutuca.
horseman ['hɔ:smən] (*irreg*) *n* cavaleiro; (*skilled*) ginete *m*.
horsemanship ['hɔ:smənʃɪp] *n* equitação *f*.
horsemen ['hɔ:smən] *npl of* **horseman**.
horseplay ['hɔ:spleɪ] *n* zona, bagunça (*brincadeiras etc*).
horsepower ['hɔ:spauə*] *n* cavalo-vapor *m*.
horse-racing *n* corridas *fpl* de cavalo, turfe *m*.
horseradish ['hɔ:srædɪʃ] *n* rábano-bastardo.
horseshoe ['hɔ:sʃu:] *n* ferradura.
horse show *n* concurso hípico.
horse-trading *n* regateio.
horse trials *npl* = **horse show**.
horsewhip ['hɔ:swɪp] *vt* chicotear.
horsewoman ['hɔ:swumən] (*irreg*) *n* amazona.
horsey ['hɔ:sɪ] *adj* aficionado por cavalos; (*appearance*) com cara de cavalo.
horticulture ['hɔ:tɪkʌltʃə*] *n* horticultura.
hose [həuz] *n* (*also*: *~pipe*) mangueira.
hose down *vt* lavar com mangueira.
hosiery ['həuzɪərɪ] *n* meias *fpl* e roupa de baixo.
hospice ['hɔspɪs] *n* asilo.
hospitable ['hɔspɪtəbl] *adj* hospitaleiro.
hospital ['hɔspɪtl] *n* hospital *m*.
hospitality [hɔspɪ'tælɪtɪ] *n* hospitalidade *f*.
hospitalize ['hɔspɪtəlaɪz] *vt* hospitalizar.
host [həust] *n* anfitrião *m*; (*in hotel etc*) hospedeiro; (TV) animador(a) *m/f*; (REL) hóstia; (*large number*): **a ~ of** uma multidão de ♦ *vt* (*TV programme*) apresentar, animar.
hostage ['hɔstɪdʒ] *n* refém *m*.
host country *n* país *m* anfitrião.
hostel ['hɔstl] *n* hospedaria; (*for students, tramps*) residência; (*also*: *youth ~*) albergue *m* de juventude.
hostelling ['hɔstlɪŋ] *n*: **to go (youth) ~** *viajar de férias pernoitando em albergues de juventude.*
hostess ['həustɪs] *n* anfitriã *f*; (*air ~*) aeromoça (BR), hospedeira de bordo (PT); (*in nightclub*) taxi-girl *f*.
hostile ['hɔstaɪl] *adj* hostil.
hostility [hɔ'stɪlɪtɪ] *n* hostilidade *f*.
hot [hɔt] *adj* quente; (*as opposed to only warm*) muito quente, ardente; (*spicy*) picante; (*fig*) ardente, veemente; **to be ~** (*person*) estar com calor; (*thing, weather*) estar quente.
hot up (BRIT: *inf*) *vi* (*party, debate*) esquentar ♦ *vt* (*pace*) acelerar; (*engine*) envenenar.
hot-air balloon *n* balão *m* de ar quente.
hotbed ['hɔtbɛd] *n* (*fig*) faco, ninho.
hotchpotch ['hɔtʃpɔtʃ] (BRIT) *n* mixórdia, salada.
hot dog *n* cachorro-quente *m*.
hotel [həu'tɛl] *n* hotel *m*.
hotelier [hɔ'tɛljeɪ] *n* hoteleiro/a.
hotel industry *n* indústria hoteleira.
hotel room *n* quarto de hotel.
hotfoot ['hɔtfut] *adv* a mil, a toda.
hotheaded [hɔt'hɛdɪd] *adj* impetuoso, fogoso.
hothouse ['hɔthaus] (*irreg*) *n* estufa.
hot line *n* (POL) telefone *m* vermelho, linha direta.

hotly ['hɔtlɪ] *adv* ardentemente, apaixonadamente.
hotplate ['hɔtpleɪt] *n* (*on cooker*) chapa elétrica.
hotpot ['hɔtpɔt] (*BRIT*) *n* (*CULIN*) ragu *m*.
hot seat *n* (*fig*) posição *f* de responsabilidade.
hot spot *n* área de tensão.
hot spring *n* fonte *f* termal.
hot-tempered *adj* esquentado, de pavio curto.
hot-water bottle *n* bolsa de água quente.
hound [haund] *vt* acossar, perseguir ♦ *n* cão *m* de caça, sabujo.
hour ['auə*] *n* hora; **at 30 miles an** ~ ≈ a 50 km por hora; **lunch** ~ hora do almoço; **to pay sb by the** ~ pagar alguém por hora.
hourly ['auəlɪ] *adv* de hora em hora ♦ *adj* de hora em hora; (*rate*) por hora.
house [*n* haus, *pl* hauziz, *vt* hauz] *n* (*gen, firm*) casa; (*POL*) câmara; (*THEATRE*) assistência, lotação *f* ♦ *vt* (*person*) alojar; **to/at my** ~ para a/na minha casa; **the H** ~ **(of Commons)** (*BRIT*) a Câmara dos Comuns; **the H** ~ **(of Representatives)** (*US*) a Câmara de Deputados; **on the** ~ (*fig*) por conta da casa.
house arrest *n* prisão *f* domiciliar.
houseboat ['hausbəut] *n* casa flutuante.
housebound ['hausbaund] *adj* preso em casa.
housebreaking ['hausbreɪkɪŋ] *n* arrombamento de domicílio.
house-broken (*US*) *adj* = **house-trained**.
housecoat ['hauskəut] *n* roupão *m*.
household ['haushəuld] *n* família; (*house*) casa; ~ **name** nome *m* conhecido por todos.
householder ['haushəuldə*] *n* (*owner*) dono/a de casa; (*head of family*) chefe *m/f* de família.
househunting ['haushʌntɪŋ] *n*: **to go** ~ procurar casa para morar.
housekeeper ['hauski:pə*] *n* governanta.
housekeeping ['hauski:pɪŋ] *n* (*work*) trabalhos *mpl* domésticos; (*also*: ~ *money*) economia doméstica; (*COMPUT*) gestão *f* dos discos.
houseman ['hausmən] (*BRIT*: *irreg*) *n* (*MED*) interno.
house-proud *adj* preocupado com a aparência da casa.
house-to-house *adj* (*enquiries*) de porta em porta; (*search*) de casa em casa.
house-trained (*BRIT*) *adj* (*animal*) domesticado.
house-warming (party) [-'wɔ:mɪŋ-] *n* festa de inauguração de uma casa.
housewife ['həuswaɪf] (*irreg*) *n* dona de casa.
housework ['hauswə:k] *n* trabalhos *mpl* domésticos.
housing ['hauzɪŋ] *n* (*act*) alojamento; (*houses*) residências *fpl*; (*as issue*) habitação *f* ♦ *cpd* (*problem, shortage*) habitacional.
housing association *n organização beneficente que vende ou alaga casas.*
housing conditions *npl* condições *fpl* de habitação.
housing development (*BRIT* **housing estate**) *n* conjunto residencial.
hovel ['hɔvl] *n* choupana, casebre *m*.
hover ['hɔvə*] *vi* pairar; (*person*) rondar.
hovercraft ['hɔvəkrɑ:ft] *n* aerobarco.
hoverport ['hɔvəpɔ:t] *n* porto para aerobarcos.
how [hau] *adv* como; ~ **are you?** como vai?; ~ **do you do?** (muito) prazer; ~ **far is it to ...?** qual é a distância daqui a ...?; ~ **long have you been here?** quanto tempo você está aqui?; ~ **lovely!** que lindo!; ~ **many/much?** quantos/quanto?; ~ **old are you?** quantos anos você tem?; ~**'s school?** como vai a escola?; ~ **about a drink?** que tal beber alguma coisa?; ~ **is it that ...?** por que é que ...?
however [hau'ɛvə*] *adv* de qualquer modo; (+ *adj*) por mais ... que; (*in questions*) como ♦ *conj* no entanto, contudo, todavia.
howitzer ['hauɪtsə*] *n* (*MIL*) morteiro, obus *m*.
howl [haul] *n* uivo ♦ *vi* uivar.
howler ['haulə*] *n* besteira, erro.
HP (*BRIT*) *n abbr* = **hire purchase**.
hp *abbr* (*AUT*: = *horsepower*) CV.
HQ *n abbr* (= *headquarters*) QG *m*.
HR (*US*) *n abbr* = **House of Representatives**.
HRH *abbr* (= *His (or Her) Royal Highness*) SAR.
hr(s) *abbr* (= *hour(s)*) h(s).
HS (*US*) *abbr* = **high school**.
HST (*US*) *abbr* (= *Hawaiian Standard Time*) *hora do Havaí*.
hub [hʌb] *n* (*of wheel*) cubo; (*fig*) centro.
hubbub ['hʌbʌb] *n* algazarra, vozerio.
hubcap ['hʌbkæp] *n* (*AUT*) calota.
HUD (*US*) *n abbr* (= *Department of Housing and Urban Development*) *ministério do urbanismo e da habitação*.
huddle ['hʌdl] *vi*: **to** ~ **together** aconchegar-se.
hue [hju:] *n* cor *f*, matiz *m*; ~ **and cry** clamor *m* público.
huff [hʌf] *n*: **in a** ~ com raiva; **to take the** ~ ficar sem graça.
hug [hʌg] *vt* abraçar ♦ *n* abraço; **to give sb a** ~ dar um abraço em alguém, abraçar alguém.
huge [hju:dʒ] *adj* enorme, imenso.
hulk [hʌlk] *n* (*wreck*) navio velho; (*hull*) casco, carcaça; (*person*) brutamontes *m inv*.
hulking ['hʌlkɪŋ] *adj* pesado, grandão/ona.
hull [hʌl] *n* (*of ship*) casco.
hullabaloo ['hʌləbə'lu:] (*inf*) *n* algazarra.
hullo [hə'ləu] *excl* = **hello**.
hum [hʌm] *vt* (*tune*) cantarolar ♦ *vi* cantarolar; (*insect, machine etc*) zumbir ♦ *n* zumbido.
human ['hju:mən] *adj* humano ♦ *n* (*also*: ~ *being*) ser *m* humano.
humane [hju:'meɪn] *adj* humano, humanitário.

***NB**: European Portuguese adds the following consonants to certain words:* **b** (sú(b)dito, su(b)til); **c** (a(c)ção, a(c)cionista, a(c)to); **m** (inde(m)ne); **p** (ado(p)ção, ado(p)tar); *for further details see p. xiii.*

humanism ['hju:mənɪzm] *n* humanismo.
humanitarian [hju:mænɪ'tɛərɪən] *adj* humanitário.
humanity [hju:'mænɪtɪ] *n* humanidade *f*.
humanly ['hju:mən'lɪ] *adv* humanamente.
humanoid ['hju:mənɔɪd] *adj*, *n* humanóide *m/f*.
humble ['hʌmbl] *adj* humilde ♦ *vt* humilhar.
humbly ['hʌmblɪ] *adv* humildemente.
humbug ['hʌmbʌg] *n* fraude *f*, embuste *m*; (BRIT: *sweet*) bala de hortelã.
humdrum ['hʌmdrʌm] *adj* (*boring*) monótono, enfadonho; (*routine*) rotineiro.
humid ['hju:mɪd] *adj* úmido.
humidifier [hju:'mɪdɪfaɪə*] *n* umidificador *m*.
humidity [hju:'mɪdɪtɪ] *n* umidade *f*.
humiliate [hju:'mɪlɪeɪt] *vt* humilhar.
humiliation [hju:mɪlɪ'eɪʃən] *n* humilhação *f*.
humility [hju:'mɪlɪtɪ] *n* humildade *f*.
humorist ['hju:mərɪst] *n* humorista *m/f*.
humor ['hju:mə*] (*US*) *n*, *vt* = **humour**.
humorous ['hju:mərəs] *adj* humorístico.
humour ['hju:mə*] (*US* **humor**) *n* humorismo, senso de humor; (*mood*) humor *m* ♦ *vt* (*person*) fazer a vontade de; **sense of ~** senso de humor; **to be in a good/bad ~** estar de bom/mau humor.
humo(u)rless ['hju:məlɛs] *adj* sem senso de humor.
hump [hʌmp] *n* (*in ground*) elevação *f*; (*camel's*) corcova, giba.
humpback ['hʌmpbæk] *n* corcunda *m/f* ♦ *cpd*: **~ bridge** (BRIT) *ponte pequena e muito arqueada.*
humus ['hju:məs] *n* húmus *m*, humo.
hunch [hʌntʃ] *n* (*premonition*) pressentimento, palpite *m*.
hunchback ['hʌntʃbæk] *n* corcunda *m/f*.
hunched [hʌntʃt] *adj* corcunda.
hundred ['hʌndrəd] *num* cem; (*before lower numbers*) cento; (*collective*) centena; **~s of people** centenas de pessoas; **I'm a ~ per cent sure** tenho certeza absoluta.
hundredweight ['hʌndrədweɪt] *n* (BRIT) = *50.8 kg*; *112 lb*; (*US*) = *45.3 kg*; *100 lb*.
hung [hʌŋ] *pt*, *pp of* **hang**.
Hungarian [hʌŋ'gɛərɪən] *adj* húngaro ♦ *n* húngaro/a; (LING) húngaro.
Hungary ['hʌŋgərɪ] *n* Hungria.
hunger ['hʌŋgə*] *n* fome *f* ♦ *vi*: **to ~ for** ter fome de; (*desire*) desejar ardentemente.
hunger strike *n* greve *f* de fome.
hungrily ['hʌŋgrəlɪ] *adv* (*eat*) vorazmente; (*fig*) avidamente.
hungry ['hʌŋgrɪ] *adj* faminto, esfomeado; **to be ~** estar com fome; **~ for** (*fig*) ávido de, ansioso por.
hung up (*inf*) *adj* complexado, grilado.
hunk [hʌŋk] *n* naco; (*inf*: *man*) gatão *m*.
hunt [hʌnt] *vt* (*seek*) buscar, perseguir; (SPORT) caçar ♦ *vi* caçar ♦ *n* caça, caçada.
  hunt down *vt* acossar.
hunter ['hʌntə*] *n* caçador(a) *m/f*; (BRIT: *horse*) cavalo de caça.
hunting ['hʌntɪŋ] *n* caça.
hurdle ['hə:dl] *n* (SPORT) barreira; (*fig*) obstáculo.
hurl [hə:l] *vt* arremessar, lançar.
hurrah [hu'rɑ:] *excl* viva!, hurra!
hurray [hu'reɪ] *excl* = **hurrah**.
hurricane ['hʌrɪkən] *n* furacão *m*.
hurried ['hʌrɪd] *adj* (*fast*) apressado; (*rushed*) feito às pressas.
hurriedly ['hʌrɪdlɪ] *adv* depressa, apressadamente.
hurry ['hʌrɪ] *n* pressa ♦ *vi* apressar-se ♦ *vt* (*person*) apressar; (*work*) acelerar; **to be in a ~** estar com pressa; **to do sth in a ~** fazer algo às pressas; **to ~ in/out** entrar/sair correndo; **to ~ home** correr para casa.
  hurry along *vi* andar às pressas.
  hurry away *vi* sair correndo.
  hurry off *vi* sair correndo.
  hurry up *vi* apressar-se.
hurt [hə:t] (*pt*, *pp* **hurt**) *vt* machucar; (*injure*) ferir; (*damage*: *business etc*) prejudicar; (*fig*) magoar ♦ *vi* doer ♦ *adj* machucado, ferido; **I ~ my arm** machuquei o braço; **where does it ~?** onde é que dói?
hurtful ['hə:tful] *adj* (*remark*) que magoa, ofensivo.
hurtle ['hə:tl] *vi* correr; **to ~ past** passar como um raio; **to ~ down** cair com violência.
husband ['hʌzbənd] *n* marido, esposo.
hush [hʌʃ] *n* silêncio, quietude *f* ♦ *vt* silenciar, fazer calar; **~!** silêncio!, psiu!
  hush up *vt* (*fact*) abafar, encobrir.
hushed [hʌʃt] *adj* (*tone*) baixo.
hush-hush *adj* secreto.
husk [hʌsk] *n* (*of wheat*) casca; (*of maize*) palha.
husky ['hʌskɪ] *adj* rouco; (*burly*) robusto ♦ *n* cão *m* esquimó.
hustings ['hʌstɪŋz] (BRIT) *npl* (POL) campanha (eleitoral).
hustle ['hʌsl] *vt* (*push*) empurrar; (*hurry*) apressar ♦ *n* agitação *f*, atividade *f* febril; **~ and bustle** grande movimento.
hut [hʌt] *n* cabana, choupana; (*shed*) alpendre *m*.
hutch [hʌtʃ] *n* coelheira.
hyacinth ['haɪəsɪnθ] *n* jacinto.
hybrid ['haɪbrɪd] *adj*, *n* híbrido.
hydrant ['haɪdrənt] *n* (*also*: *fire ~*) hidrante *m*.
hydraulic [haɪ'drɔ:lɪk] *adj* hidráulico.
hydraulics [haɪ'drɔ:lɪks] *n* hidráulica.
hydrochloric acid ['haɪdrəu'klɔrɪk-] *n* ácido clorídrico.
hydroelectric [haɪdrəuɪ'lɛktrɪk] *adj* hidroelétrico.
hydrofoil ['haɪdrəfɔɪl] *n* hidrofoil *m*, aliscafo.
hydrogen ['haɪdrədʒən] *n* hidrogênio.
hydrogen bomb *n* bomba de hidrogênio.
hydrolysis [haɪ'drɔləsɪs] *n* hidrólise *f*.
hydrophobia ['haɪdrə'fəubɪə] *n* hidrofobia.
hydroplane ['haɪdrəpleɪn] *n* lancha planadora.
hyena [haɪ'i:nə] *n* hiena.
hygiene ['haɪdʒi:n] *n* higiene *f*.

hygienic [haɪ'dʒiːnɪk] *adj* higiênico.
hymn [hɪm] *n* hino.
hype [haɪp] (*inf*) *n* tititi *m*, falatório.
hyperactive ['haɪpər'æktɪv] *adj* hiperativo.
hypermarket ['haɪpəmɑːkɪt] *n* hipermercado.
hypertension ['haɪpə'tɛnʃən] *n* (*MED*) hipertensão *f*.
hyphen ['haɪfn] *n* hífen *m*.
hypnosis [hɪp'nəusɪs] *n* hipnose *f*.
hypnotic [hɪp'nɔtɪk] *adj* hipnótico.
hypnotism ['hɪpnətɪzm] *n* hipnotismo.
hypnotist ['hɪpnətɪst] *n* hipnotizador(a) *m/f*.
hypnotize ['hɪpnətaɪz] *vt* hipnotizar.
hypoallergenic ['haɪpəuælə'dʒɛnɪk] *adj* hipoalergênico.
hypochondriac [haɪpə'kɔndrɪæk] *n* hipocondríaco/a.
hypocrisy [hɪ'pɔkrɪsɪ] *n* hipocrisia.
hypocrite ['hɪpəkrɪt] *n* hipócrita *m/f*.
hypocritical [hɪpə'krɪtɪkl] *adj* hipócrita.
hypodermic [haɪpə'dəːmɪk] *adj* hipodérmico ♦ *n* seringa hipodérmica.
hypothermia [haɪpə'θəːmɪa] *n* hipotermia.
hypotheses [haɪ'pɔθɪsiːz] *npl of* **hypothesis**.
hypothesis [haɪ'pɔθɪsɪs] (*pl* **hypotheses**) *n* hipótese *f*.
hypothetic(al) [haɪpəu'θɛtɪk(l)] *adj* hipotético.
hysterectomy [hɪstə'rɛktəmɪ] *n* histerectomia.
hysteria [hɪ'stɪərɪə] *n* histeria.
hysterical [hɪ'stɛrɪkl] *adj* histérico.
hysterics [hɪ'stɛrɪks] *npl* (*nervous*) crise *f* histérica; (*laughter*) ataque *m* de riso.
Hz *abbr* (= *hertz*) Hz.

I

I, i [aɪ] *n* (*letter*) I, i *m*; **I for Isaac** (*BRIT*) *or* **Item** (*US*) I de Irene.
I [aɪ] *pron* eu ♦ *abbr* (= *island*; *isle*) I.
IA (*US*) *abbr* (*POST*) = **Iowa**.
IAEA *n abbr* (= *International Atomic Energy Agency*) IAEA *f*.
IBA (*BRIT*) *n* (= *Independent Broadcasting Authority*) *órgão que supervisiona as emissoras comerciais de TV*.
Iberian [aɪ'bɪərɪən] *adj* ibérico.
Iberian Peninsula *n*: **the** ~ a península Ibérica.
IBEW (*US*) *n abbr* (= *International Brotherhood of Electrical Workers*) *sindicato internacional dos eletricistas*.
i/c (*BRIT*) *abbr* = **in charge**.
ICC *n abbr* = **International Chamber of Commerce**; (*US*) = **Interstate Commerce Commission**.
ice [aɪs] *n* gelo ♦ *vt* (*cake*) cobrir com glacê; (*drink*) gelar ♦ *vi* (*also*: ~ *over*, ~ *up*) gelar; **to put sth on** ~ (*fig*) engavetar algo.
ice age *n* era glacial.
ice axe *n* picareta para o gelo.
iceberg ['aɪsbəːg] *n* iceberg *m*; **this is just the tip of the** ~ isso é só a ponta do iceberg.
icebox ['aɪsbɔks] *n* (*US*) geladeira; (*BRIT*: *in fridge*) congelador *m*.
icebreaker ['aɪsbreɪkə*] *n* navio quebra-gelo *m*.
ice bucket *n* balde *m* de gelo.
ice-cold *adj* gelado.
ice cream *n* sorvete *m* (*BR*), gelado (*PT*).
ice cube *n* pedra de gelo.
iced [aɪst] *adj* (*drink*) gelado; (*cake*) glaçado.
ice hockey *n* hóquei *m* sobre o gelo.
Iceland ['aɪslənd] *n* Islândia.
Icelander ['aɪsləndə*] *n* islandês/esa *m/f*.
Icelandic [aɪs'lændɪk] *adj* islandês/esa ♦ *n* (*LING*) islandês *m*.
ice lolly (*BRIT*) *n* picolé *m*.
ice pick *n* furador *m* de gelo.
ice rink *n* pista de gelo, rinque *m*.
ice-skate *n* patim *m* (para o gelo) ♦ *vi* patinar no gelo.
ice-skating *n* patinação *f* no gelo.
icicle ['aɪsɪkl] *n* pingente *m* de gelo.
icing ['aɪsɪŋ] *n* (*CULIN*) glacê *m*; (*AVIAT etc*) formação *f* de gelo.
icing sugar (*BRIT*) *n* açúcar *m* glacê.
ICJ *n abbr* = **International Court of Justice**.
icon ['aɪkɔn] *n* ícone *m*.
ICR (*US*) *n abbr* = **Institute for Cancer Research**.
ICU *n abbr* (= *intensive care unit*) UTI *f*.
icy ['aɪsɪ] *adj* (*road*) gelado; (*fig*) glacial, indiferente.
ID (*US*) *abbr* (*POST*) = **Idaho**.
I'd [aɪd] = **I would**; **I had**.
ID card *n* = **identity card**.
IDD (*BRIT*) *n abbr* (*TEL*: = *international direct dialling*) DDI *f*.
idea [aɪ'dɪə] *n* idéia; **good** ~! boa idéia!; **to have an** ~ **that** ... ter a impressão de que ...; **I haven't the least** ~ não tenho a mínima idéia.
ideal [aɪ'dɪəl] *n* ideal *m* ♦ *adj* ideal.
idealist [aɪ'dɪəlɪst] *n* idealista *m/f*.
ideally [aɪ'dɪəlɪ] *adv* de preferência; ~ **the book should have** ... seria ideal que o livro tivesse ....
identical [aɪ'dɛntɪkl] *adj* idêntico.
identification [aɪdɛntɪfɪ'keɪʃən] *n* identificação *f*; **means of** ~ documentos pessoais.
identify [aɪ'dɛntɪfaɪ] *vt* identificar ♦ *vi*: **to** ~ **with** identificar-se com.
Identikit picture [aɪ'dɛntɪkɪt-] ® *n* retrato falado.
identity [aɪ'dɛntɪtɪ] *n* identidade *f*.
identity card *n* carteira de identidade.
identity parade (*BRIT*) *n* identificação *f*.

***NB:** European Portuguese adds the following consonants to certain words:* **b** (sú(b)dito, su(b)til); **c** (a(c)ção, a(c)cionista, a(c)to); **m** (inde(m)ne); **p** (ado(p)ção, ado(p)tar); *for further details see p. xiii.*

ideological [aɪdɪə'lɔdʒɪkəl] *adj* ideológico.
ideology [aɪdɪ'ɔlədʒɪ] *n* ideologia.
idiocy ['ɪdɪəsɪ] *n* idiotice *f*; (*stupid act*) estupidez *f*.
idiom ['ɪdɪəm] *n* expressão *f* idiomática; (*style of speaking*) idioma *m*, linguagem *f*.
idiomatic [ɪdɪə'mætɪk] *adj* idiomático.
idiosyncrasy [ɪdɪəu'sɪŋkrəsɪ] *n* idiossincrasia.
idiot ['ɪdɪət] *n* idiota *m/f*.
idiotic [ɪdɪ'ɔtɪk] *adj* idiota.
idle ['aɪdl] *adj* ocioso; (*lazy*) preguiçoso; (*unemployed*) desempregado; (*pointless*) inútil, vão/vã ♦ *vi* (*machine*) funcionar com a transmissão desligada.
idle away *vt*: **to ~ away the time** perder *or* desperdiçar tempo.
idleness ['aɪdlnɪs] *n* ociosidade *f*; preguiça; (*pointlessness*) inutilidade *f*.
idler ['aɪdlə*] *n* preguiçoso/a.
idle time *n* (COMM) tempo ocioso.
idol ['aɪdl] *n* ídolo.
idolize ['aɪdəlaɪz] *vt* idolatrar.
idyllic [ɪ'dɪlɪk] *adj* idílico.
i.e. *abbr* (= *id est*: *that is*) i.e., isto é.
if [ɪf] *conj* se ♦ *n*: **there are a lot of ~s and buts** não está nada decidido; **I'd be pleased ~ you could do it** ficaria satisfeito se você pudesse fazê-lo; **~ necessary** se necessário; **~ only he were here** se pelo menos ele estivesse aqui; **even ~** mesmo que.
igloo ['ɪglu:] *n* iglu *m*.
ignite [ɪg'naɪt] *vt* acender; (*set fire to*) incendiar ♦ *vi* acender.
ignition [ɪg'nɪʃən] *n* (AUT) ignição *f*; **to switch on/off the ~** ligar/desligar o motor.
ignition key *n* (AUT) chave *f* de ignição.
ignoble [ɪg'nəubl] *adj* ignóbil.
ignominious [ɪgnə'mɪnɪəs] *adj* vergonhoso, humilhante.
ignoramus [ɪgnə'reɪməs] *n* ignorante *m/f*.
ignorance ['ɪgnərəns] *n* ignorância; **to keep sb in ~ of sth** deixar alguém na ignorância de algo.
ignorant ['ɪgnərənt] *adj* ignorante; **to be ~ of** ignorar.
ignore [ɪg'nɔ:*] *vt* (*person*) não fazer caso de; (*fact*) não levar em consideração, ignorar.
ikon ['aɪkɔn] *n* = **icon**.
IL (*US*) *abbr* (POST) = **Illinois**.
ILA (*US*) *n abbr* (= *International Longshoremen's Association*) *sindicato internacional dos portuários*.
ILEA ['ɪlɪə] (*BRIT*) *n abbr* (= *Inner London Education Authority*) *órgão administrador de ensino em Grande Londres*.
ILGWU (*US*) *n abbr* (= *International Ladies' Garment Workers' Union*) *sindicato dos trabalhadores na área de roupa feminina*.
I'll [aɪl] = **I will; I shall**.
ill [ɪl] *adj* doente; (*slightly ~*) indisposto; (*bad*) mau/má ♦ *n* mal *m*; (*fig*) desgraça ♦ *adv*: **to speak/think ~ of sb** falar/pensar mal de alguém; **to take** *or* **be taken ~** ficar doente.
ill-advised [-əd'vaɪzd] *adj* pouco recomendado; (*misled*) mal aconselhado.
ill-at-ease *adj* constrangido, pouco à vontade.
ill-considered [-kən'sɪdəd] *adj* (*plan*) imponderado.
ill-disposed *adj*: **to be ~ towards sb/sth** ser desfavorável a alguém/algo.
illegal [ɪ'li:gl] *adj* ilegal.
illegally [ɪ'li:gəlɪ] *adv* ilegalmente.
illegible [ɪ'lɛdʒɪbl] *adj* ilegível.
illegitimate [ɪlɪ'dʒɪtɪmət] *adj* ilegítimo.
ill-fated *adj* malfadado, azarento.
ill-favoured [-'feɪvəd] (*US* **ill-favored**) *adj* desagradável.
ill feeling *n* má vontade *f*, rancor *m*.
ill-gotten *adj* (*gains etc*) mal adquirido.
illicit [ɪ'lɪsɪt] *adj* ilícito.
ill-informed *adj* mal informado.
illiterate [ɪ'lɪtərət] *adj* analfabeto.
ill-mannered [-'mænəd] *adj* mal-educado, grosseiro.
illness ['ɪlnɪs] *n* doença.
illogical [ɪ'lɔdʒɪkl] *adj* ilógico.
ill-suited [-'su:tɪd] *adj* (*couple*) desajustado; **he is ~ to the job** ele é inadequado para o cargo.
ill-timed [-taɪmd] *adj* inoportuno.
ill-treat *vt* maltratar.
ill-treatment *n* maus tratos *mpl*.
illuminate [ɪ'lu:mɪneɪt] *vt* (*room, street*) iluminar, clarear; (*subject*) esclarecer; **~d sign** anúncio luminoso.
illuminating [ɪ'lu:mɪneɪtɪŋ] *adj* esclarecedor.
illumination [ɪlu:mɪ'neɪʃən] *n* iluminação *f*; **~s** *npl* luminárias *fpl*.
illusion [ɪ'lu:ʒən] *n* ilusão *f*; **to be under the ~ that ...** estar com a ilusão de que ....
illusive [ɪ'lu:sɪv] *adj* ilusório.
illusory [ɪ'lu:sərɪ] *adj* ilusório.
illustrate ['ɪləstreɪt] *vt* ilustrar; (*subject*) esclarecer; (*point*) exemplificar.
illustration [ɪlə'streɪʃən] *n* (*example*) exemplo; (*explanation*) esclarecimento; (*in book*) gravura, ilustração *f*.
illustrator ['ɪləstreɪtə*] *n* ilustrador(a) *m/f*.
illustrious [ɪ'lʌstrɪəs] *adj* ilustre.
ill will *n* animosidade *f*, má vontade *f*.
ILO *n abbr* (= *International Labour Organization*) OIT *f*.
ILWU (*US*) *n abbr* (= *International Longshoremen's and Warehousemen's Union*) *sindicato dos portuários*.
I'm [aɪm] = **I am**.
image ['ɪmɪdʒ] *n* imagem *f*.
imagery ['ɪmɪdʒərɪ] *n* imagens *fpl*.
imaginable [ɪ'mædʒɪnəbl] *adj* imaginável, concebível.
imaginary [ɪ'mædʒɪnərɪ] *adj* imaginário.
imagination [ɪmædʒɪ'neɪʃən] *n* imaginação *f*; (*inventiveness*) inventividade *f*; (*illusion*) fantasia.
imaginative [ɪ'mædʒɪnətɪv] *adj* imaginativo.
imagine [ɪ'mædʒɪn] *vt* imaginar; (*delude o.s.*) fantasiar.
imbalance [ɪm'bæləns] *n* desequilíbrio; (*inequality*) desigualdade *f*.
imbecile ['ɪmbəsi:l] *n* imbecil *m/f*.

imbue [ɪm'bjuː] *vt*: **to ~ sth with** imbuir *or* impregnar algo de.
IMF *n abbr* (= *International Monetary Fund*) FMI *m*.
imitate ['ɪmɪteɪt] *vt* imitar.
imitation [ɪmɪ'teɪʃən] *n* imitação *f*; (*copy*) cópia; (*mimicry*) mímica.
imitator ['ɪmɪteɪtə*] *n* imitador(a) *m/f*.
immaculate [ɪ'mækjulət] *adj* impecável; (REL) imaculado.
immaterial [ɪmə'tɪərɪəl] *adj* imaterial; **it is ~ whether ...** é indiferente se ....
immature [ɪmə'tjuə*] *adj* (*person*) imaturo; (*of one's youth*) juvenil.
immaturity [ɪmə'tjuərɪtɪ] *n* imaturidade *f*.
immeasurable [ɪ'mɛʒrəbl] *adj* incomensurável, imensurável.
immediacy [ɪ'miːdɪəsɪ] *n* (*of events etc*) proximidade *f*; (*of needs*) urgência.
immediate [ɪ'miːdɪət] *adj* imediato; (*pressing*) urgente, premente.
immediately [ɪ'miːdɪətlɪ] *adv* (*at once*) imediatamente; **~ next to** bem junto a.
immense [ɪ'mɛns] *adj* imenso, enorme.
immensity [ɪ'mɛnsətɪ] *n* imensidade *f*.
immerse [ɪ'məːs] *vt* (*submerge*) submergir; (*sink*) imergir, mergulhar; **to be ~d in** (*fig*) estar absorto em.
immersion heater [ɪ'məːʃn-] (BRIT) *n* aquecedor *m* de imersão.
immigrant ['ɪmɪgrənt] *n* imigrante *m/f*.
immigrate ['ɪmɪgreɪt] *vi* imigrar.
immigration [ɪmɪ'greɪʃən] *n* imigração *f*.
immigration authorities *npl* fiscais *mpl* de imigração, ≈ polícia federal.
immigration laws *npl* leis *fpl* imigratórias.
imminent ['ɪmɪnənt] *adj* iminente.
immobile [ɪ'məubaɪl] *adj* imóvel.
immobilize [ɪ'məubɪlaɪz] *vt* imobilizar.
immoderate [ɪ'mɔdərət] *adj* imoderado.
immodest [ɪ'mɔdɪst] *adj* (*indecent*) indecente, impudico; (*person*: *boasting*) presumido, arrogante.
immoral [ɪ'mɔrl] *adj* imoral.
immorality [ɪmə'rælɪtɪ] *n* imoralidade *f*.
immortal [ɪ'mɔːtl] *adj* imortal.
immortalize [ɪ'mɔːtəlaɪz] *vt* imortalizar.
immovable [ɪ'muːvəbl] *adj* (*object*) imóvel, fixo; (*person*) inflexível.
immune [ɪ'mjuːn] *adj*: **~ to** imune a, imunizado contra.
immunity [ɪ'mjuːnɪtɪ] *n* (MED) imunidade *f*; (COMM) isenção *f*; **diplomatic ~** imunidade diplomática.
immunization [ɪmjunaɪ'zeɪʃən] *n* imunização *f*.
immunize ['ɪmjunaɪz] *vt* imunizar.
imp [ɪmp] *n* diabinho, criança levada.
impact ['ɪmpækt] *n* impacto (PT: impacte *m*).
impair [ɪm'pɛə*] *vt* prejudicar.
impale [ɪm'peɪl] *vt* perfurar, empalar.
impart [ɪm'pɑːt] *vt* dar, comunicar.
impartial [ɪm'pɑːʃl] *adj* imparcial.
impartiality [ɪmpɑːʃɪ'ælɪtɪ] *n* imparcialidade *f*.
impassable [ɪm'pɑːsəbl] *adj* (*barrier, river*) intransponível; (*road*) intransitável.
impasse [æm'pɑːs] *n* (*fig*) impasse *m*.
impassioned [ɪm'pæʃənd] *adj* ardente, veemente.
impassive [ɪm'pæsɪv] *adj* impassível.
impatience [ɪm'peɪʃəns] *n* impaciência.
impatient [ɪm'peɪʃənt] *adj* impaciente; **to get** *or* **grow ~** impacientar-se.
impeach [ɪm'piːtʃ] *vt* impugnar; (*public official*) levar a juízo.
impeachment [ɪm'piːtʃmənt] *n* (LAW) impeachment *m*.
impeccable [ɪm'pɛkəbl] *adj* impecável.
impecunious [ɪmpə'kjuːnɪəs] *adj* impecunioso, sem recursos.
impede [ɪm'piːd] *vt* impedir, estorvar.
impediment [ɪm'pɛdɪmənt] *n* obstáculo, impedimento; (*also*: *speech ~*) defeito (de fala).
impel [ɪm'pɛl] *vt* (*force*): **to ~ sb (to do sth)** impelir alguém (a fazer algo).
impending [ɪm'pɛndɪŋ] *adj* (*near*) iminente, próximo.
impenetrable [ɪm'pɛnɪtrəbl] *adj* impenetrável; (*unfathomable*) incompreensível.
imperative [ɪm'pɛrətɪv] *adj* (*tone*) imperioso, obrigatório; (*necessary*) indispensável; (*pressing*) premente ♦ *n* (LING) imperativo.
imperceptible [ɪmpə'sɛptɪbl] *adj* imperceptível.
imperfect [ɪm'pəːfɪkt] *adj* imperfeito; (*goods etc*) defeituoso ♦ *n* (LING: *also*: ~ *tense*) imperfeito.
imperfection [ɪmpə'fɛkʃən] *n* (*blemish*) defeito; (*state*) imperfeição *f*.
imperial [ɪm'pɪərɪəl] *adj* imperial.
imperialism [ɪm'pɪərɪəlɪzəm] *n* imperialismo.
imperil [ɪm'pɛrɪl] *vt* pôr em perigo, arriscar.
imperious [ɪm'pɪərɪəs] *adj* imperioso.
impersonal [ɪm'pəːsənl] *adj* impessoal.
impersonate [ɪm'pəːsəneɪt] *vt* fazer-se passar por, personificar; (THEATRE) imitar.
impersonation [ɪmpəːsə'neɪʃən] *n* (LAW) impostura; (THEATRE) imitacão *f*.
impersonator [ɪm'pəːsəneɪtə*] *n* impostor(a) *m/f*; (THEATRE) imitador(a) *m/f*.
impertinence [ɪm'pəːtɪnəns] *n* impertinência, insolência.
impertinent [ɪm'pəːtɪnənt] *adj* impertinente, insolente.
imperturbable [ɪmpə'təːbəbl] *adj* imperturbável, inabalável.
impervious [ɪm'pəːvɪəs] *adj* impenetrável; (*fig*): **~ to** insensível a.
impetuous [ɪm'pɛtjuəs] *adj* impetuoso, precipitado.
impetus ['ɪmpətəs] *n* ímpeto; (*fig*) impulso.
impinge [ɪm'pɪndʒ]: **to ~ on** *vt fus* impressionar, impingir em; (*affect*) afetar.
impish ['ɪmpɪʃ] *adj* levado, travesso.

***NB**: European Portuguese adds the following consonants to certain words:* **b** (sú(b)dito, su(b)til); **c** (a(c)ção, a(c)cionista, a(c)to); **m** (inde(m)ne); **p** (ado(p)ção, ado(p)tar); *for further details see p. xiii.*

implacable [ɪm'plækəbl] *adj* implacável, impiedoso.
implant [*vt* ɪm'plɑːnt, *n* 'ɪmplɑːnt] *vt* (*MED*) implantar; (*fig*) inculcar ♦ *n* implante *m*.
implausible [ɪm'plɔːzɪbl] *adj* inverossímil (*PT*: -osí-).
implement [*n* 'ɪmplɪmənt, *vt* 'ɪmplɪmɛnt] *n* instrumento, ferramenta; (*for cooking*) utensílio ♦ *vt* efetivar; (*carry out*) realizar, executar.
implicate ['ɪmplɪkeɪt] *vt* (*compromise*) comprometer; (*involve*) implicar, envolver.
implication [ɪmplɪ'keɪʃən] *n* implicação *f*, conseqüência; **by ~** por conseqüência.
implicit [ɪm'plɪsɪt] *adj* implícito; (*complete*) absoluto.
implicitly [ɪm'plɪsɪtlɪ] *adv* implicitamente; (*completely*) completamente.
implore [ɪm'plɔː*] *vt* (*person*) implorar, suplicar.
imply [ɪm'plaɪ] *vt* (*involve*) implicar; (*mean*) significar; (*hint*) dar a entender que; **it is implied** se subentende.
impolite [ɪmpə'laɪt] *adj* indelicado, ineducado.
imponderable [ɪm'pɔndərəbl] *adj* imponderável.
import [*vt* ɪm'pɔːt, *n*, *cpd* 'ɪmpɔːt] *vt* importar ♦ *n* (*COMM*) importação *f*; (: *article*) mercadoria importada; (*meaning*) significado, sentido ♦ *cpd* (*duty*, *licence etc*) de importação.
importance [ɪm'pɔːtəns] *n* importância; **to be of great/little ~** ser de grande/pouca importância.
important [ɪm'pɔːtənt] *adj* importante; **it is ~ that ...** é importante *or* importa que ...; **it's not ~** não tem importância, não importa.
importantly [ɪm'pɔːtəntlɪ] *adv*: **but, more ~ ...** mas, o que é mais importante, ...
importation [ɪmpɔː'teɪʃən] *n* importação *f*.
imported [ɪm'pɔːtɪd] *adj* importado.
importer [ɪm'pɔːtə*] *n* importador(a) *m/f*.
impose [ɪm'pəuz] *vt* impor ♦ *vi*: **to ~ on sb** abusar de alguém.
imposing [ɪm'pəuzɪŋ] *adj* imponente.
imposition [ɪmpə'zɪʃən] *n* (*of tax etc*) imposição *f*; **to be an ~ on sb** (*person*) abusar de alguém.
impossibility [ɪmpɔsɪ'bɪlɪtɪ] *n* impossibilidade *f*.
impossible [ɪm'pɔsɪbl] *adj* impossível; (*person*) insuportável; **it's ~ for me to leave** é-me impossível sair, não dá para eu sair (*inf*).
impostor [ɪm'pɔstə*] *n* impostor(a) *m/f*.
impotence ['ɪmpətəns] *n* impotência.
impotent ['ɪmpətənt] *adj* impotente.
impound [ɪm'paund] *vt* confiscar.
impoverished [ɪm'pɔvərɪʃt] *adj* empobrecido; (*land*) esgotado.
impracticable [ɪm'præktɪkəbl] *adj* impraticável, inexeqüível.
impractical [ɪm'præktɪkl] *adj* pouco prático.
imprecise [ɪmprɪ'saɪs] *adj* impreciso, vago.
impregnable [ɪm'prɛgnəbl] *adj* invulnerável; (*castle*) inexpugnável.
impregnate ['ɪmprɛgneɪt] *vt* (*gen*) impregnar; (*soak*) embeber; (*fertilize*) fecundar.
impresario [ɪmprɪ'sɑːrɪəu] *n* empresário/a.
impress [ɪm'prɛs] *vt* impressionar; (*mark*) imprimir ♦ *vi* causar boa impressão; **to ~ sth on sb** inculcar algo em alguém; **it ~ed itself on me** fiquei com isso gravado (na memória).
impression [ɪm'prɛʃən] *n* impressão *f*; (*footprint etc*) marca; (*print run*) edição *f*; **to make a good/bad ~ on sb** fazer boa/má impressão em alguém; **to be under the ~ that** estar com a impressão de que.
impressionable [ɪm'prɛʃənəbl] *adj* impressionável; (*sensitive*) sensível.
impressionist [ɪm'prɛʃənɪst] *n* impressionista *m/f*.
impressive [ɪm'prɛsɪv] *adj* impressionante.
imprint ['ɪmprɪnt] *n* impressão *f*, marca; (*PUBLISHING*) nome *m* (da coleção).
imprinted [ɪm'prɪntɪd] *adj*: **~ on** imprimido em; (*fig*) gravado em.
imprison [ɪm'prɪzn] *vt* encarcerar.
imprisonment [ɪm'prɪzənmənt] *n* prisão *f*.
improbable [ɪm'prɔbəbl] *adj* improvável; (*story*) inverossímil (*PT*: -osí-).
impromptu [ɪm'prɔmptjuː] *adj* improvisado ♦ *adv* de improviso.
improper [ɪm'prɔpə*] *adj* (*incorrect*) impróprio; (*unseemly*) indecoroso; (*indecent*) indecente.
impropriety [ɪmprə'praɪətɪ] *n* falta de decoro, inconveniência; (*indecency*) indecência; (*of language*) impropriedade *f*.
improve [ɪm'pruːv] *vt* melhorar ♦ *vi* melhorar; (*pupils*) progredir.
improve (up)on *vt fus* melhorar.
improvement [ɪm'pruːvmənt] *n* melhora; (*of pupils*) progresso; **to make ~s to** melhorar.
improvisation [ɪmprəvaɪ'zeɪʃən] *n* improvisação *f*.
improvise ['ɪmprəvaɪz] *vt*, *vi* improvisar.
imprudence [ɪm'pruːdns] *n* imprudência.
imprudent [ɪm'pruːdnt] *adj* imprudente.
impudent ['ɪmpjudnt] *adj* insolente, impudente.
impugn [ɪm'pjuːn] *vt* impugnar, contestar.
impulse ['ɪmpʌls] *n* impulso, ímpeto; **to act on ~** agir sem pensar *or* num impulso.
impulse buy *n* compra por impulso.
impulsive [ɪm'pʌlsɪv] *adj* impulsivo.
impunity [ɪm'pjuːnɪtɪ] *n*: **with ~** impunemente.
impure [ɪm'pjuə*] *adj* (*adulterated*) adulterado; (*not pure*) impuro.
impurity [ɪm'pjuərɪtɪ] *n* impureza.
IN (*US*) *abbr* (*POST*) = **Indiana**.
in [ɪn] *prep* em; (*within*) dentro de; (*with time*: *during, within*): **~ 2 days** em *or* dentro de 2 dias; (: *after*): **~ 2 weeks** daqui a 2 semanas; (*with town, country*): **it's ~ France** é *or* fica na França ♦ *adv* dentro, para dentro; (*fashionable*) na moda ♦ *n*: **the ~s and outs** os cantos e recantos, os pormenores; **is he ~?** ele está?; **~ the United States** nos Esta-

dos Unidos; ~ **1986** em 1986; ~ **May** em maio; ~ **spring/autumn** na primavera/no outono; ~ **the morning** de manhã; ~ **the distance** ao longe; ~ **the country** no campo; ~ **town** no centro (da cidade); ~ **the sun** ao *or* sob o sol; ~ **the rain** na chuva; ~ **French** em francês; ~ **writing** por escrito; **written** ~ **pencil** escrito a lápis; **to pay** ~ **dollars** pagar em dólares; **1** ~ **10** 1 em 10, 1 em cada 10; ~ **hundreds** às centenas; **the best pupil** ~ **the class** o melhor aluno da classe; **to be** ~ **teaching/publishing** ser professor/ trabalhar numa editora; ~ **saying this** ao dizer isto; ~ **that ...** já que ...; **their party is** ~ seu partido chegou ao poder; **to ask sb** ~ convidar alguém para entrar; **to run/limp** ~ entrar correndo/mancando.

in. *abbr* = **inch(es)**.

inability [ɪnə'bɪlɪtɪ] *n* incapacidade *f*; ~ **to pay** impossibilidade de pagar.

inaccessible [ɪnək'sɛsɪbl] *adj* inacessível.

inaccuracy [ɪn'ækjurəsɪ] *n* inexatidão *f*, imprecisão *f*.

inaccurate [ɪn'ækjurət] *adj* inexato, impreciso.

inaction [ɪn'ækʃən] *n* inação *f*.

inactivity [ɪnæk'tɪvɪtɪ] *n* inatividade *f*.

inadequacy [ɪn'ædɪkwəsɪ] *adj* (*insufficiency*) insuficiência.

inadequate [ɪn'ædɪkwət] *adj* (*insufficient*) insuficiente; (*unsuitable*) inadequado; (*person*) impróprio.

inadmissible [ɪnəd'mɪsəbl] *adj* inadmissível.

inadvertent [ɪnəd'vəːtənt] *adj* (*mistake*) cometido sem querer.

inadvertently [ɪnəd'vəːtntlɪ] *adv* inadvertidamente, sem querer.

inadvisable [ɪnəd'vaɪzəbl] *adj* não aconselhável, inoportuno.

inane [ɪ'neɪn] *adj* tolo; (*fatuous*) vazio.

inanimate [ɪn'ænɪmət] *adj* inanimado.

inapplicable [ɪn'æplɪkəbl] *adj* inaplicável.

inappropriate [ɪnə'prəuprɪət] *adj* inadequado, inconveniente; (*word, expression*) impróprio.

inapt [ɪn'æpt] *adj* inapto.

inaptitude [ɪn'æptɪtjuːd] *n* incapacidade *f*, inaptidão *f*.

inarticulate [ɪnɑː'tɪkjulət] *adj* (*person*) incapaz de expressar-se (bem); (*speech*) inarticulado.

inasmuch as [ɪnəz'mʌtʃ-] *conj* (*given that*) visto que; (*since*) desde que, já que.

inattention [ɪnə'tɛnʃən] *n* inatenção *f*.

inattentive [ɪnə'tɛntɪv] *adj* desatento.

inaudible [ɪn'ɔːdɪbl] *adj* inaudível.

inaugural [ɪ'nɔːgjurəl] *adj* (*speech*) inaugural; (: *of president*) de posse.

inaugurate [ɪ'nɔːgjureɪt] *vt* inaugurar; (*president, official*) empossar.

inauguration [ɪnɔːgju'reɪʃən] *n* inauguração *f*; (*of president, official*) posse *f*.

inauspicious [ɪnɔːs'pɪʃəs] *adj* infausto.

in-between *adj* intermediário, entre dois extremos.

inborn [ɪn'bɔːn] *adj* (*feeling*) inato; (*defect*) congênito.

inbred [ɪn'brɛd] *adj* inato; (*family*) de procriação consangüínea.

inbreeding [ɪn'briːdɪŋ] *n* endogamia.

Inc. *abbr* = **incorporated**.

Inca ['ɪŋkə] *adj* (*also*: ~*n*) inca, incaico ♦ *n* inca *m/f*.

incalculable [ɪn'kælkjuləbl] *adj* incalculável.

incapability [ɪnkeɪpə'bɪlɪtɪ] *n* incapacidade *f*.

incapable [ɪn'keɪpəbl] *adj* incapaz.

incapacitate [ɪnkə'pæsɪteɪt] *vt* incapacitar.

incapacitated [ɪnkə'pæsɪteɪtɪd] *adj* (LAW) incapacitado.

incapacity [ɪnkə'pæsɪtɪ] *n* (*inability*) incapacidade *f*.

incarcerate [ɪn'kɑːsəreɪt] *vt* encarcerar.

incarnate [*adj* ɪn'kɑːnɪt, *vt* 'ɪnkɑːneɪt] *adj* encarnado, personificado ♦ *vt* encarnar.

incarnation [ɪnkɑː'neɪʃən] *n* encarnação *f*.

incendiary [ɪn'sɛndɪərɪ] *adj* incendiário ♦ *n* (*bomb*) bomba incendiária.

incense [*n* 'ɪnsɛns, *vt* ɪn'sɛns] *n* incenso ♦ *vt* (*anger*) exasperar, enraivecer.

incense burner *n* incensório.

incentive [ɪn'sɛntɪv] *n* incentivo, estímulo.

incentive scheme *n* plano de incentivos.

inception [ɪn'sɛpʃən] *n* começo, início.

incessant [ɪn'sɛsnt] *adj* incessante, contínuo.

incessantly [ɪn'sɛsntlɪ] *adv* constantemente.

incest ['ɪnsɛst] *n* incesto.

inch [ɪntʃ] *n* polegada (= *25 mm*; *12 in a foot*); **to be within an** ~ **of** estar a um passo de; **he didn't give an** ~ ele não cedeu nem um milímetro.

inch forward *vi* avançar palmo a palmo.

inch tape (BRIT) *n* fita métrica.

incidence ['ɪnsɪdns] *n* (*of crime, disease*) incidência.

incident ['ɪnsɪdnt] *n* incidente *m*, evento; (*in book*) episódio.

incidental [ɪnsɪ'dɛntl] *adj* acessório, não essencial; (*unplanned*) acidental, casual; ~ **expenses** despesas *fpl* adicionais.

incidentally [ɪnsɪ'dɛntəlɪ] *adv* (*by the way*) a propósito.

incidental music *n* música de cena *or* de fundo.

incinerate [ɪn'sɪnəreɪt] *vt* incinerar.

incinerator [ɪn'sɪnəreɪtə*] *n* incinerador *m*.

incipient [ɪn'sɪpɪənt] *adj* incipiente.

incision [ɪn'sɪʒən] *n* incisão *f*.

incisive [ɪn'saɪsɪv] *adj* (*mind*) penetrante, perspicaz; (*tone*) mordaz, sarcástico; (*remark etc*) incisivo.

incisor [ɪn'saɪzə*] *n* incisivo.

incite [ɪn'saɪt] *vt* incitar, provocar.

incl. *abbr* = **including**; **inclusive (of)**.

inclement [ɪn'klɛmənt] *adj* (*weather*) inclemente.

inclination [ɪnklɪ'neɪʃən] *n* (*tendency*)

NB: *European Portuguese adds the following consonants to certain words:* **b** (sú(b)dito, su(b)til); **c** (a(c)ção, a(c)cionista, a(c)to); **m** (inde(m)ne); **p** (ado(p)ção, ado(p)tar); *for further details see p. xiii.*

tendência, inclinação *f*.

incline [*n* 'ınklaın, *vt*, *vi* ın'klaın] *n* inclinação *f*, ladeira ♦ *vt* (*slope*) inclinar; (*head*) curvar, inclinar ♦ *vi* inclinar-se; **to be ~d to** (*tend*) tender a, ser propenso a; (*be willing*) estar disposto a.

include [ın'klu:d] *vt* incluir; **the service is/is not ~d** o serviço está/não está incluído.

including [ın'klu:dıŋ] *prep* inclusive; **~ tip** gorjeta incluída.

inclusion [ın'klu:ʒən] *n* inclusão *f*.

inclusive [ın'klu:sıv] *adj* incluído, incluso ♦ *adv* inclusive; **£50 ~ of all surcharges** £50, incluídas todas as sobretaxas.

inclusive terms (BRIT) *npl* preço global.

incognito [ınkɔg'ni:təu] *adv* incógnito.

incoherent [ınkəu'hıərənt] *adj* incoerente.

income ['ıŋkʌm] *n* (*earnings*) renda, rendimentos; (*unearned*) renda; (*profit*) lucro; **gross/net ~** renda bruta/líquida; **~ and expenditure account** conta de receitas e despesas; **~ bracket** faixa salarial.

income tax *n* imposto de renda (BR), imposto complementar (PT).

income tax inspector *n* fiscal *m/f* do imposto de renda.

income tax return *n* declaração *f* do imposto de renda.

incoming ['ınkʌmıŋ] *adj* (*flight*, *passenger*) de chegada; (*mail*) de entrada; (*government*, *tenant*) novo; **~ tide** maré enchente.

incommunicado [ınkəmjunı'kɑ:dəu] *adj* incomunicável.

incomparable [ın'kɔmpərəbl] *adj* incomparável.

incompatible [ınkəm'pætıbl] *adj* incompatível.

incompetence [ın'kɔmpıtəns] *n* incompetência.

incompetent [ın'kɔmpıtənt] *adj* incompetente.

incomplete [ınkəm'pli:t] *adj* incompleto; (*unfinished*) por terminar.

incomprehensible [ınkɔmprı'hɛnsıbl] *adj* incompreensível.

inconceivable [ınkən'si:vəbl] *adj* inconcebível.

inconclusive [ınkən'klu:sıv] *adj* inconclusivo; (*argument*) pouco convincente.

incongruous [ın'kɔŋgruəs] *adj* (*foolish*) ridículo, absurdo; (*remark*, *act*) incongruente, ilógico.

inconsequential [ınkɔnsı'kwɛnʃl] *adj* sem importância.

inconsiderable [ınkən'sıdərəbl] *adj*: **not ~** importante.

inconsiderate [ınkən'sıdərət] *adj* sem consideração; **how ~ of him!** que falta de consideração (de sua parte)!

inconsistency [ınkən'sıstənsı] *n* inconsistência.

inconsistent [ınkən'sıstnt] *adj* inconsistente, incompatível; **~ with** (que) não está de acordo com.

inconsolable [ınkən'səuləbl] *adj* inconsolável.

inconspicuous [ınkən'spıkjuəs] *adj* não conspícuo; (*modest*) modesto; **to make o.s. ~** não chamar a atenção.

inconstant [ın'kɔnstnt] *adj* inconstante.

incontinence [ın'kɔntınəns] *n* incontinência.

incontinent [ın'kɔntınənt] *adj* incontinente.

incontrovertible [ınkɔntrə'və:təbl] *adj* incontestável.

inconvenience [ınkən'vi:njəns] *n* (*quality*) inconveniência; (*problem*) inconveniente *m* ♦ *vt* incomodar; **don't ~ yourself** não se incomode.

inconvenient [ınkən'vi:njənt] *adj* inconveniente, incômodo; (*time, place*) inoportuno; **that time is very ~ for me** esse horário me é muito inconveniente.

incorporate [ın'kɔ:pəreıt] *vt* incorporar; (*contain*) compreender; (*add*) incluir.

incorporated company [ın'kɔ:pəreıtıd-] (US) *n* ≈ sociedade *f* anônima.

incorrect [ınkə'rɛkt] *adj* incorreto.

incorrigible [ın'kɔrıdʒıbl] *adj* incorrigível.

incorruptible [ınkə'rʌptıbl] *adj* incorruptível; (*not open to bribes*) insubornável.

increase [*n* 'ınkri:s, *vi*, *vt* ın'kri:s] *n* aumento ♦ *vi*, *vt* aumentar; **an ~ of 5%** um aumento de 5%; **to be on the ~** estar em crescimento *or* alta.

increasing [ın'kri:sıŋ] *adj* (*number*) crescente, em aumento.

increasingly [ın'kri:sıŋlı] *adv* cada vez mais.

incredible [ın'krɛdıbl] *adj* incrível.

incredulous [ın'krɛdjuləs] *adj* incrédulo.

increment ['ınkrımənt] *n* aumento, incremento.

incriminate [ın'krımıneıt] *vt* incriminar.

incriminating [ın'krımıneıtıŋ] *adj* incriminador(a).

incrust [ın'krʌst] *vt* = **encrust**.

incubate ['ınkjubeıt] *vt*, *vi* incubar.

incubation [ınkju'beıʃən] *n* incubação *f*.

incubation period *n* período de incubação.

incubator ['ınkjubeıtə*] *n* incubadora; (*for eggs*) chocadeira.

inculcate ['ınkʌlkeıt] *vt*: **to ~ sth in sb** inculcar algo a alguém.

incumbent [ın'kʌmbənt] *n* titular *m/f* ♦ *adj*: **it is ~ on him to ...** cabe a ele ....

incur [ın'kə:*] *vt* incorrer em; (*expenses*) contrair.

incurable [ın'kjuərəbl] *adj* incurável; (*fig*) irremediável.

incursion [ın'kə:ʃən] *n* incursão *f*.

indebted [ın'dɛtıd] *adj*: **to be ~ to sb** estar em dívida com alguém, dever obrigação a alguém.

indecency [ın'di:snsı] *n* indecência.

indecent [ın'di:snt] *adj* indecente.

indecent assault (BRIT) *n* atentado contra o pudor.

indecent exposure *n* exibição *f* obscena, exibicionismo.

indecipherable [ındı'saıfərəbl] *adj* indecifrável.

indecision [ındı'sıʒən] *n* indecisão *f*.

indecisive [ındı'saısıv] *adj* indeciso; (*discussion*) inconcludente, sem resultados.

indeed [ın'di:d] *adv* de fato, realmente;

(*furthermore*) aliás; **yes ~!** claro que sim!
indefatigable [ɪndɪ'fætɪgəbl] *adj* incansável.
indefensible [ɪndɪ'fɛnsɪbl] *adj* indefensível.
indefinable [ɪndɪ'faɪnəbl] *adj* indefinível.
indefinite [ɪn'dɛfɪnɪt] *adj* indefinido; (*uncertain*) impreciso; (*period, number*) indeterminado.
indefinitely [ɪn'dɛfɪnɪtlɪ] *adv* (*wait*) indefinidamente.
indelible [ɪn'dɛlɪbl] *adj* indelével.
indelicate [ɪn'dɛlɪkɪt] *adj* (*tactless*) inábil; (*not polite*) indelicado, rude.
indemnify [ɪn'dɛmnɪfaɪ] *vt* indenizar, compensar.
indemnity [ɪn'dɛmnɪtɪ] *n* (*insurance*) garantia, seguro; (*compensation*) indenização *f*.
indent [ɪn'dɛnt] *vt* (*text*) recolher ♦ *vi*: **to ~ for sth** (*COMM*) encomendar algo.
indentation [ɪndɛn'teɪʃən] *n* entalhe *m*, recorte *m*; (*TYP*) parágrafo, recuo.
indenture [ɪn'dɛntʃə*] *n* contrato de aprendizagem.
independence [ɪndɪ'pɛndns] *n* independência.
independent [ɪndɪ'pɛndnt] *adj* independente; **to become ~** tornar-se independente.
independently [ɪndɪ'pɛndntlɪ] *adv* independentemente.
indescribable [ɪndɪ'skraɪbəbl] *adj* indescritível.
indestructible [ɪndɪ'strʌktəbl] *adj* indestrutível.
indeterminate [ɪndɪ'tə:mɪnɪt] *adj* indeterminado.
index ['ɪndɛks] (*pl* **~es**) *n* (*in book*) índice *m*; (: *in library etc*) catálogo; (*pl*: *indices*: *ratio, sign*) índice *m*, expoente *m*.
index card *n* ficha de arquivo.
indexed ['ɪndɛkst] (*US*) *adj* = **index-linked**.
index finger *n* dedo indicador.
index-linked [-lɪŋkt] (*BRIT*) *adj* vinculado ao índice (do custo de vida).
India ['ɪndɪə] *n* Índia.
Indian ['ɪndɪən] *adj, n* (*from India*) indiano/a; (*American, Brazilian*) índio/a.
Indian ink *n* tinta nanquim.
Indian Ocean *n*: **the ~** o oceano Índico.
Indian summer *n* (*fig*) veranico.
India paper *n* papel *m* da China.
India rubber *n* borracha.
indicate ['ɪndɪkeɪt] *vt* indicar ♦ *vi* (*BRIT*: *AUT*): **to ~ left/right** indicar para a esquerda/direita.
indication [ɪndɪ'keɪʃən] *n* indício, sinal *m*.
indicative [ɪn'dɪkətɪv] *adj* indicativo ♦ *n* (*LING*) indicativo; **to be ~ of sth** ser sintomático de algo.
indicator ['ɪndɪkeɪtə*] *n* indicador *m*; (*on car*) pisca-pisca *m*.
indices ['ɪndɪsi:z] *npl of* **index**.
indict [ɪn'daɪt] *vt* acusar.
indictable [ɪn'daɪtəbl] *adj* (*person*) culpado; **~ offence** crime sujeito às penas da lei.
indictment [ɪn'daɪtmənt] *n* acusação *f*, denúncia.
indifference [ɪn'dɪfrəns] *n* indiferença.
indifferent [ɪn'dɪfrənt] *adj* indiferente; (*poor*) regular, medíocre.
indigenous [ɪn'dɪdʒɪnəs] *adj* indígena, nativo.
indigestible [ɪndɪ'dʒɛstɪbl] *adj* indigesto.
indigestion [ɪndɪ'dʒɛstʃən] *n* indigestão *f*.
indignant [ɪn'dɪgnənt] *adj*: **to be ~ about sth** estar indignado com algo, indignar-se de algo.
indignation [ɪndɪg'neɪʃən] *n* indignação *f*.
indignity [ɪn'dɪgnɪtɪ] *n* indignidade *f*; (*insult*) ultraje *m*, afronta.
indigo ['ɪndɪgəu] *adj* cor de anil *inv* ♦ *n* anil *m*.
indirect [ɪndɪ'rɛkt] *adj* indireto.
indirectly [ɪndɪ'rɛktlɪ] *adv* indiretamente.
indiscreet [ɪndɪ'skri:t] *adj* indiscreto; (*rash*) imprudente.
indiscretion [ɪndɪ'skrɛʃən] *n* indiscrição *f*; imprudência.
indiscriminate [ɪndɪ'skrɪmɪnət] *adj* indiscriminado.
indispensable [ɪndɪ'spɛnsəbl] *adj* indispensável, imprescindível.
indisposed [ɪndɪ'spəuzd] *adj* (*unwell*) indisposto.
indisposition [ɪndɪspə'zɪʃən] *n* (*illness*) mal-estar *m*, indisposição *f*.
indisputable [ɪndɪ'spju:təbl] *adj* incontestável.
indistinct [ɪndɪ'stɪŋkt] *adj* indistinto; (*memory, noise*) confuso, vago.
indistinguishable [ɪndɪ'stɪŋwɪʃəbl] *adj* indistinguível.
individual [ɪndɪ'vɪdjuəl] *n* indivíduo ♦ *adj* individual; (*personal*) pessoal; (*for/of one only*) particular.
individualist [ɪndɪ'vɪdjuəlɪst] *n* individualista *m/f*.
individuality [ɪndɪvɪdju'ælɪtɪ] *n* individualidade *f*.
individually [ɪndɪ'vɪdjuəlɪ] *adv* individualmente, particularmente.
indivisible [ɪndɪ'vɪzɪbl] *adj* indivisível.
Indo-China ['ɪndəu-] *n* Indochina.
indoctrinate [ɪn'dɔktrɪneɪt] *vt* doutrinar.
indoctrination [ɪndɔktrɪ'neɪʃən] *n* doutrinação *f*.
indolent ['ɪndələnt] *adj* indolente, preguiçoso.
Indonesia [ɪndə'ni:zɪə] *n* Indonésia.
Indonesian [ɪndə'ni:zɪən] *adj* indonésio ♦ *n* indonésio/a; (*LING*) indonésio.
indoor ['ɪndɔ:*] *adj* (*inner*) interno, interior; (*inside*) dentro de casa; (*swimming pool*) coberto; (*games, sport*) de salão.
indoors [ɪn'dɔ:z] *adv* em lugar fechado; (*at home*) em casa.
indubitable [ɪn'dju:bɪtəbl] *adj* indubitável.
induce [ɪn'dju:s] *vt* induzir; (*bring about*) causar, produzir; (*provoke*) provocar; **to ~ sb to do sth** induzir alguém a fazer algo.

NB*: European Portuguese adds the following consonants to certain words:* **b** (sú(b)dito, su(b)til); **c** (a(c)ção, a(c)cionista, a(c)to); **m** (inde(m)ne); **p** (ado(p)ção, ado(p)tar); *for further details see p. xiii.*

inducement [ɪn'dju:smənt] *n* (*incentive*) incentivo, estímulo.
induct [ɪn'dʌkt] *vt* instalar.
induction [ɪn'dʌkʃən] *n* (*MED*: *of birth*) indução *f*.
induction course (*BRIT*) *n* curso de indução.
indulge [ɪn'dʌldʒ] *vt* (*desire*) satisfazer; (*whim*) condescender com; (*person*) comprazer; (*child*) fazer a vontade de ♦ *vi*: **to ~ in** entregar-se a, satisfazer-se com.
indulgence [ɪn'dʌldʒəns] *n* (*of desire*) satisfação *f*; (*leniency*) indulgência, tolerância.
indulgent [ɪn'dʌldʒənt] *adj* indulgente.
industrial [ɪn'dʌstrɪəl] *adj* industrial; (*injury*) de trabalho; (*dispute*) trabalhista.
industrial action *n* greve *f*.
industrial design *n* desenho industrial.
industrial estate (*BRIT*) *n* zona industrial.
industrialist [ɪn'dʌstrɪəlɪst] *n* industrial *m/f*.
industrialize [ɪn'dʌstrɪəlaɪz] *vt* industrializar.
industrial park (*US*) *n* parque *m* industrial.
industrial relations *npl* relações *fpl* industriais.
industrial tribunal (*BRIT*) *n* ≈ tribunal *m* do trabalho.
industrial unrest (*BRIT*) *n* agitação *f* operária.
industrious [ɪn'dʌstrɪəs] *adj* trabalhador(a); (*student*) aplicado.
industry ['ɪndəstrɪ] *n* indústria; (*diligence*) aplicação *f*, diligência.
inebriated [ɪ'ni:brɪeɪtɪd] *adj* embriagado, bêbado.
inedible [ɪn'ɛdɪbl] *adj* não-comestível.
ineffective [ɪnɪ'fɛktɪv] *adj* ineficaz.
ineffectual [ɪnɪ'fɛktʃuəl] *adj* ineficaz.
inefficiency [ɪnɪ'fɪʃənsɪ] *n* ineficiência.
inefficient [ɪnɪ'fɪʃənt] *adj* ineficiente.
inelegant [ɪn'ɛlɪgənt] *adj* deselegante.
ineligible [ɪn'ɛlɪdʒɪbl] *adj* (*candidate*) inelegível; **to be ~ for sth** não estar qualificado para algo.
inept [ɪ'nɛpt] *adj* inepto.
ineptitude [ɪ'nɛptɪtju:d] *n* inépcia, incompetência.
inequality [ɪnɪ'kwɔlɪtɪ] *n* desigualdade *f*.
inequitable [ɪn'ɛkwɪtəbl] *adj* injusto, iníquo.
ineradicable [ɪnɪ'rædɪkəbl] *adj* inerradicável.
inert [ɪ'nə:t] *adj* inerte; (*immobile*) imóvel.
inertia [ɪ'nə:ʃə] *n* inércia; (*laziness*) lerdeza.
inertia-reel seat belt *n* cinto de segurança retrátil.
inescapable [ɪnɪ'skeɪpəbl] *adj* inevitável.
inessential [ɪnɪ'sɛnʃl] *adj* desnecessário.
inestimable [ɪn'ɛstɪməbl] *adj* inestimável, incalculável.
inevitable [ɪn'ɛvɪtəbl] *adj* inevitável; (*necessary*) forçoso, necessário.
inevitably [ɪn'ɛvɪtəblɪ] *adv* inevitavelmente.
inexact [ɪnɪg'zækt] *adj* inexato.
inexcusable [ɪnɪks'kju:zəbl] *adj* imperdoável, indesculpável.
inexhaustible [ɪnɪg'zɔ:stɪbl] *adj* inesgotável, inexaurível.
inexorable [ɪn'ɛksərəbl] *adj* inexorável.
inexpensive [ɪnɪk'spɛnsɪv] *adj* barato, econômico.
inexperience [ɪnɪk'spɪərɪəns] *n* inexperiência, falta de experiência.
inexperienced [ɪnɪk'spɪərɪənst] *adj* inexperiente.
inexplicable [ɪnɪk'splɪkəbl] *adj* inexplicável.
inexpressible [ɪnɪk'sprɛsɪbl] *adj* inexprimível.
inextricable [ɪnɪk'strɪkəbl] *adj* inextricável.
infallibility [ɪnfælə'bɪlɪtɪ] *n* infalibilidade *f*.
infallible [ɪn'fælɪbl] *adj* infalível.
infamous ['ɪnfəməs] *adj* infame, abominável.
infamy ['ɪnfəmɪ] *n* infâmia.
infancy ['ɪnfənsɪ] *n* infância.
infant ['ɪnfənt] *n* (*baby*) bebê *m*; (*young child*) criança.
infantile ['ɪnfəntaɪl] *adj* infantil; (*pej*) acriançado.
infant mortality *n* mortalidade *f* infantil.
infantry ['ɪnfəntrɪ] *n* infantaria.
infantryman ['ɪnfəntrɪmən] (*irreg*) *n* soldado de infantaria.
infant school (*BRIT*) *n* pré-escola.
infatuated [ɪn'fætjueɪtɪd] *adj*: **~ with** apaixonado por.
infatuation [ɪnfætju'eɪʃən] *n* gamação *f*, paixão *f* louca.
infect [ɪn'fɛkt] *vt* (*wound*) infeccionar, infetar; (*person*) contagiar; (*fig*: *pej*) corromper, contaminar; **~ed with** (*illness*) contagiado por; **to become ~ed** (*wound*) infeccionar(-se), infetar(-se).
infection [ɪn'fɛkʃən] *n* infecção *f*; (*fig*) contágio.
infectious [ɪn'fɛkʃəs] *adj* contagioso; (*also*: *fig*) infeccioso.
infer [ɪn'fə:*] *vt* deduzir, inferir.
inference ['ɪnfərəns] *n* dedução *f*, inferência.
inferior [ɪn'fɪərɪə*] *adj* inferior; (*goods*) de qualidade inferior ♦ *n* inferior *m/f*; (*in rank*) subalterno/a; **to feel ~** sentir-se inferior.
inferiority [ɪnfɪərɪ'ɔrətɪ] *n* inferioridade *f*.
inferiority complex *n* complexo de inferioridade.
infernal [ɪn'fə:nl] *adj* infernal.
infernally [ɪn'fə:nəlɪ] *adv* (*very*) muito.
inferno [ɪn'fə:nəu] *n* inferno; (*fig*) inferno de chamas.
infertile [ɪn'fə:taɪl] *adj* infértil, estéril.
infertility [ɪnfə'tɪlɪtɪ] *n* infertilidade *f*, esterilidade *f*.
infested [ɪn'fɛstɪd] *adj*: **~ (with)** infestado (de), assolado (por).
infidelity [ɪnfɪ'dɛlɪtɪ] *n* infidelidade *f*.
in-fighting *n* (*fig*) lutas *fpl* internas, conflitos *mpl* internos.
infiltrate ['ɪnfɪltreɪt] *vt* (*troops etc*) infiltrar-se em ♦ *vi* infiltrar-se.
infinite ['ɪnfɪnɪt] *adj* infinito; (*time, money*) ilimitado.
infinitely ['ɪnfɪnɪtlɪ] *adv* infinitamente.
infinitesimal [ɪnfɪnɪ'tɛsɪməl] *adj* infinitésimo.
infinitive [ɪn'fɪnɪtɪv] *n* infinitivo.
infinity [ɪn'fɪnɪtɪ] *n* (*also*: *MATH*) infinito; (*an ~*) infinidade *f*.

infirm [ɪn'fə:m] *adj* enfermo, fraco.
infirmary [ɪn'fə:mərɪ] *n* enfermaria, hospital *m*.
infirmity [ɪn'fə:mɪtɪ] *n* fraqueza; (*illness*) enfermidade *f*, achaque *m*.
inflame [ɪn'fleɪm] *vt* inflamar.
inflamed [ɪn'fleɪmd] *adj* inflamado.
inflammable [ɪn'flæməbl] (*BRIT*) *adj* inflamável.
inflammation [ɪnflə'meɪʃən] *n* inflamação *f*.
inflammatory [ɪn'flæmətərɪ] *adj* (*speech*) incendiário.
inflatable [ɪn'fleɪtəbl] *adj* inflável.
inflate [ɪn'fleɪt] *vt* (*tyre, balloon*) inflar, encher; (*fig*) inchar.
inflated [ɪn'fleɪtɪd] *adj* (*style*) empolado, pomposo; (*value*) excessivo.
inflation [ɪn'fleɪʃən] *n* (*ECON*) inflação *f*.
inflationary [ɪn'fleɪʃənərɪ] *adj* inflacionário.
inflexible [ɪn'flɛksɪbl] *adj* inflexível.
inflict [ɪn'flɪkt] *vt*: **to ~ on** infligir em; (*tax etc*) impor a.
infliction [ɪn'flɪkʃən] *n* imposição *f*, inflição *f*.
in-flight *adj* (*refuelling*) em vôo; (*movie*) exibido durante o vôo; (*service*) de bordo.
inflow ['ɪnfləu] *n* afluência.
influence ['ɪnfluəns] *n* influência ♦ *vt* influir em, influenciar; (*persuade*) persuadir; **under the ~ of alcohol** sob o efeito do álcool.
influential [ɪnflu'ɛnʃl] *adj* influente.
influenza [ɪnflu'ɛnzə] *n* gripe *f*.
influx ['ɪnflʌks] *n* afluxo, influxo.
inform [ɪn'fɔ:m] *vt*: **to ~ sb of sth** informar alguém de algo; (*warn*) avisar alguém de algo; (*communicate*) comunicar algo a alguém ♦ *vi*: **to ~ on sb** delatar alguém; **to ~ sb about** informar alguém sobre.
informal [ɪn'fɔ:ml] *adj* (*person, manner*) sem formalidade; (*language*) informal; (*visit, discussion*) extra-oficial; (*intimate*) familiar; **"dress ~"** "traje de passeio".
informality [ɪnfɔ:'mælɪtɪ] *n* falta de cerimônia; (*intimacy*) intimidade *f*; (*familiarity*) familiaridade *f*; (*ease*) informalidade *f*.
informally [ɪn'fɔ:məlɪ] *adv* sem formalidade; (*unofficially*) não oficialmente.
informant [ɪn'fɔ:mənt] *n* informante *m/f*; (*to police*) delator(a) *m/f*.
information [ɪnfə'meɪʃən] *n* informação *f*, informações *fpl*; (*news*) notícias *fpl*; (*knowledge*) conhecimento; **a piece of ~** uma informação; **for your ~** para a sua informação, para o seu governo.
information bureau *n* balcão *m* de informações.
information processing *n* processamento de informações.
information retrieval *n* recuperação *f* de informações.
information technology *n* informática.
informative [ɪn'fɔ:mətɪv] *adj* informativo.
informed [ɪn'fɔ:md] *adj* informado; **an ~ guess** um palpite baseado em conhecimento dos fatos.
informer [ɪn'fɔ:mə*] *n* delator(a) *m/f*.
infra dig ['ɪnfrə-] (*inf*) *adj abbr* (= *infra dignitatem*) abaixo da minha (*or* sua *etc*) dignidade.
infra-red ['ɪnfrə-] *adj* infravermelho.
infrastructure ['ɪnfrəstrʌktʃə*] *n* infra-estrutura.
infrequent [ɪn'fri:kwənt] *adj* infreqüente.
infringe [ɪn'frɪndʒ] *vt* infringir, transgredir ♦ *vi*: **to ~ on** invadir, violar.
infringement [ɪn'frɪndʒmənt] *n* transgressão *f*; (*of rights*) violação *f*; (*SPORT*) infração *f*.
infuriate [ɪn'fjuərɪeɪt] *vt* enfurecer, enraivecer.
infuriating [ɪn'fjuərɪeɪtɪŋ] *adj* de dar raiva, enfurecedor(a).
infuse [ɪn'fju:z] *vt*: **to ~ sb with sth** (*fig*) inspirar *or* infundir algo em alguém.
infusion [ɪn'fju:ʒən] *n* (*tea etc*) infusão *f*.
ingenious [ɪn'dʒi:njəs] *adj* engenhoso.
ingenuity [ɪndʒɪ'nju:ɪtɪ] *n* engenho, habilidade *f*.
ingenuous [ɪn'dʒɛnjuəs] *adj* ingênuo.
ingot ['ɪŋgət] *n* lingote *m*.
ingrained [ɪn'greɪnd] *adj* arraigado, enraizado.
ingratiate [ɪn'greɪʃɪeɪt] *vt*: **to ~ o.s. with** cair nas (boas) graças de.
ingratiating [ɪn'greɪʃɪeɪtɪŋ] *adj* insinuante.
ingratitude [ɪn'grætɪtju:d] *n* ingratidão *f*.
ingredient [ɪn'gri:dɪənt] *n* ingrediente *m*.
ingrowing toenail ['ɪngrəuɪŋ-] *n* unha encravada.
ingrown toenail ['ɪngrəun-] *n* = **ingrowing toenail**.
inhabit [ɪn'hæbɪt] *vt* habitar; (*occupy*) ocupar.
inhabitable [ɪn'hæbɪtəbl] *adj* habitável.
inhabitant [ɪn'hæbɪtənt] *n* habitante *m/f*.
inhale [ɪn'heɪl] *vt* inalar ♦ *vi* (*in smoking*) aspirar.
inherent [ɪn'hɪərənt] *adj*: **~ in** *or* **to** inerente a.
inherently [ɪn'hɪərəntlɪ] *adv* inerentemente, em si.
inherit [ɪn'hɛrɪt] *vt* herdar.
inheritance [ɪn'hɛrɪtəns] *n* herança; (*fig*) patrimônio.
inhibit [ɪn'hɪbɪt] *vt* inibir; **to ~ sb from doing sth** impedir alguém de fazer algo.
inhibited [ɪn'hɪbɪtɪd] *adj* inibido.
inhibiting [ɪn'hɪbɪtɪŋ] *adj* constrangedor(a).
inhibition [ɪnhɪ'bɪʃən] *n* inibição *f*.
inhospitable [ɪnhɔs'pɪtəbl] *adj* (*person*) inospitaleiro; (*place*) inóspito.
inhuman [ɪn'hju:mən] *adj* inumano, desumano.
inhumane [ɪnhju:'meɪn] *adj* desumano.
inimitable [ɪ'nɪmɪtəbl] *adj* inimitável.
iniquity [ɪ'nɪkwɪtɪ] *n* iniqüidade *f*; (*injustice*) injustiça.
initial [ɪ'nɪʃl] *adj* inicial; (*first*) primeiro ♦ *n* inicial *f* ♦ *vt* marcar com iniciais; **~s** *npl* iniciais *fpl*; (*abbreviation*) abreviatura, sigla.

***NB**: European Portuguese adds the following consonants to certain words:* **b** (sú(b)dito, su(b)til); **c** (a(c)ção, a(c)cionista, a(c)to); **m** (inde(m)ne); **p** (ado(p)ção, ado(p)tar); *for further details see p. xiii.*

initialize [ɪ'nɪʃəlaɪz] *vt* (*COMPUT*) inicializar.
initially [ɪ'nɪʃəlɪ] *adv* inicialmente, no início.
initiate [ɪ'nɪʃɪeɪt] *vt* (*start*) iniciar, começar; (*person*) iniciar; **to ~ sb into a secret** revelar um segredo a alguém; **to ~ proceedings against sb** (*LAW*) abrir um processo contra alguém.
initiation [ɪnɪʃɪ'eɪʃən] *n* (*into secret etc*) iniciação *f*; (*beginning*) começo, início.
initiative [ɪ'nɪʃətɪv] *n* iniciativa; **to take the ~** tomar a iniciativa.
inject [ɪn'dʒɛkt] *vt* (*liquid, fig: money*) injetar; (*person*) dar uma injeção em; (*fig: put in*) introduzir.
injection [ɪn'dʒɛkʃən] *n* injeção *f*; **to have an ~** tomar uma injeção.
injudicious [ɪndʒu'dɪʃəs] *adj* imprudente.
injunction [ɪn'dʒʌŋkʃən] *n* injunção *f*, ordem *f*.
injure ['ɪndʒə*] *vt* ferir; (*damage: reputation etc*) prejudicar; (*offend*) ofender, magoar; **to ~ o.s.** ferir-se.
injured ['ɪndʒəd] *adj* (*person, leg*) ferido; (*feelings*) ofendido, magoado; **~ party** (*LAW*) parte *f* lesada.
injurious [ɪn'dʒuərɪəs] *adj*: **~ (to)** prejudicial (a).
injury ['ɪndʒərɪ] *n* ferida; (*wrong*) dano, prejuízo; **to escape without ~** escapar ileso.
injury time *n* (*SPORT*) desconto.
injustice [ɪn'dʒʌstɪs] *n* injustiça; **to do sb an ~** fazer mau juízo de alguém.
ink [ɪŋk] *n* tinta.
ink-jet printer *n* impressora a tinta.
inkling ['ɪŋklɪŋ] *n* suspeita; (*idea*) idéia vaga.
inkpad ['ɪŋkpæd] *n* almofada de tinta.
inky ['ɪŋkɪ] *adj* manchado de tinta.
inlaid ['ɪnleɪd] *adj* embutido; (*table etc*) marchetado.
inland [*adj* 'ɪnlənd, *adv* ɪn'lænd] *adj* interior, interno ♦ *adv* para o interior; **~ waterways** hidrovias *fpl*.
Inland Revenue (*BRIT*) *n* ≈ fisco, ≈ receita federal (*BR*).
in-laws *npl* sogros *mpl*.
inlet ['ɪnlɛt] *n* (*GEO*) enseada, angra; (*TECH*) entrada.
inlet pipe *n* tubo de admissão.
inmate ['ɪnmeɪt] *n* (*in prison*) presidiário/a; (*in asylum*) internado/a.
inmost ['ɪnməust] *adj* mais íntimo.
inn [ɪn] *n* hospedaria, taberna.
innards ['ɪnədʒ] (*inf*) *npl* entranhas *fpl*.
innate [ɪ'neɪt] *adj* inato.
inner ['ɪnə*] *adj* interno, interior.
inner city *n* aglomeração *f* urbana, metrópole *f*.
innermost ['ɪnəməust] *adj* mais íntimo.
inner tube *n* (*of tyre*) câmara de ar.
innings ['ɪnɪŋz] *n* (*SPORT*) turno; (*BRIT: fig*): **he's had a good ~** ele aproveitou bem a vida.
innocence ['ɪnəsns] *n* inocência.
innocent ['ɪnəsnt] *adj* inocente.
innocuous [ɪ'nɔkjuəs] *adj* inócuo.
innovation [ɪnəu'veɪʃən] *n* inovação *f*, novidade *f*.
innuendo [ɪnju'ɛndəu] (*pl* **~es**) *n* insinuação *f*, indireta.
innumerable [ɪ'nju:mrəbl] *adj* inumerável.
inoculate [ɪ'nɔkjuleɪt] *vt*: **to ~ sb with sth** inocular algo em alguém; **to ~ sb against sth** vacinar alguém contra algo.
inoculation [ɪnɔkju'leɪʃən] *n* inoculação *f*, vacinação *f*.
inoffensive [ɪnə'fɛnsɪv] *adj* inofensivo.
inopportune [ɪn'ɔpətju:n] *adj* inoportuno.
inordinate [ɪn'ɔ:dɪnət] *adj* desmesurado, excessivo.
inordinately [ɪ'nɔ:dɪnətlɪ] *adv* desmedidamente, excessivamente.
inorganic [ɪnɔ:'gænɪk] *adj* inorgânico.
in-patient *n* paciente *m/f* interno/a.
input ['ɪnput] *n* (*ELEC, COMPUT*) entrada; (*COMM*) investimento ♦ *vt* (*COMPUT*) entrar com.
inquest ['ɪnkwɛst] *n* inquérito policial; (*coroner's*) inquérito judicial.
inquire [ɪn'kwaɪə*] *vi* pedir informação ♦ *vt* (*ask*) perguntar; **to ~ about** pedir informações sobre; **to ~ when/where/whether** perguntar quando/onde/se.
inquire after *vt fus* (*person*) perguntar por.
inquire into *vt fus* investigar, indagar.
inquiring [ɪn'kwaɪərɪŋ] *adj* (*mind*) inquiridor(a); (*look*) interrogativo.
inquiry [ɪn'kwaɪərɪ] *n* pergunta; (*LAW*) investigação *f*, inquérito; (*commission*) comissão *f* de inquérito; **to hold an ~ into sth** realizar uma investigação sobre algo.
inquiry desk (*BRIT*) *n* balcão *m* de informações.
inquiry office (*BRIT*) *n* seção *f* de informações.
inquisition [ɪnkwɪ'zɪʃən] *n* inquérito; (*REL*): **the I~** a Inquisição.
inquisitive [ɪn'kwɪzɪtɪv] *adj* (*curious*) curioso, perguntador(a); (*prying*) indiscreto, intrometido.
inroads ['ɪnrəudz] *npl*: **to make ~ into** (*savings, supplies*) consumir parte de.
ins. *abbr* = **inches**.
insane [ɪn'seɪn] *adj* louco, doido; (*MED*) demente, insano.
insanitary [ɪn'sænɪtərɪ] *adj* insalubre.
insanity [ɪn'sænɪtɪ] *n* (*MED*) insanidade *f*, demência; (*folly*) loucura.
insatiable [ɪn'seɪʃəbl] *adj* insaciável.
inscribe [ɪn'skraɪb] *vt* inscrever; (*book etc*): **to ~ (to sb)** dedicar (a alguém).
inscription [ɪn'skrɪpʃən] *n* inscrição *f*; (*in book*) dedicatória.
inscrutable [ɪn'skru:təbl] *adj* inescrutável, impenetrável.
inseam measurement ['ɪnsi:m-] (*US*) *n* altura de entrepernas.
insect ['ɪnsɛkt] *n* inseto.
insect bite *n* picada de inseto.
insecticide [ɪn'sɛktɪsaɪd] *n* inseticida *m*.
insect repellent *n* repelente *m* contra inse-

tos, insetífugo.
insecure [ɪnsɪ'kjuə*] *adj* inseguro.
insecurity [ɪnsɪ'kjuərətɪ] *n* insegurança.
insensible [ɪn'sɛnsɪbl] *adj* impassível, insensível; (*unconscious*) inconsciente.
insensitive [ɪn'sɛnsɪtɪv] *adj* insensível.
insensitivity [ɪnsɛnsɪ'tɪvɪtɪ] *n* insensibilidade *f*.
inseparable [ɪn'sɛprəbl] *adj* inseparável.
insert [*vt* ɪn'səːt, *n* 'ɪnsəːt] *vt* (*between things*) intercalar; (*into sth*) introduzir, inserir; (*in paper*) publicar; (: *advert*) pôr ♦ *n* folha solta.
insertion [ɪn'səːʃən] *n* inserção *f*; (*publication*) publicação *f*; (*of pages*) matéria inserida.
in-service *adj* (*training*) contínuo; (*course*) de aperfeiçoamento, de reciclagem.
inshore [ɪn'ʃɔː*] *adj* perto da costa, costeiro ♦ *adv* (*be*) perto da costa; (*move*) em direção à costa.
inside ['ɪn'saɪd] *n* interior *m*; (*lining*) forro; (*of road*: *in Britain*) lado esquerdo (da estrada); (: *in US*, *Europe etc*) lado direito (da estrada) ♦ *adj* interior, interno; (*secret*) secreto ♦ *adv* (*within*) (por) dentro; (*with movement*) para dentro; (*inf*: *in prison*) na prisão ♦ *prep* dentro de; (*of time*): **~ 10 minutes** em menos de 10 minutos; **~s** *npl* (*inf*) entranhas *fpl*; **~ out** às avessas; **to turn sth ~ out** virar algo pelo avesso; **to know sth ~ out** conhecer algo como a palma da mão; (*book etc*) conhecer algo a fundo; **~ information** informação privilegiada; **the ~ story** a verdade sobre os fatos.
inside forward *n* (*SPORT*) centro avante.
inside lane *n* (*AUT*: *in Britain*) pista da esquerda; (: *in US*, *Europe etc*) pista da direita.
inside leg measurement (*BRIT*) *n* altura de entrepernas.
insider [ɪn'saɪdə*] *n* iniciado/a.
insider dealing *n* (*STOCK EXCHANGE*) uso de informações privilegiadas.
insidious [ɪn'sɪdɪəs] *adj* insidioso; (*underground*) clandestino.
insight ['ɪnsaɪt] *n* (*quality*) discernimento; **an ~ into sth** uma idéia de algo.
insignia [ɪn'sɪgnɪə] *npl* insígnias *fpl*.
insignificant [ɪnsɪg'nɪfɪknt] *adj* insignificante.
insincere [ɪnsɪn'sɪə*] *adj* insincero.
insincerity [ɪnsɪn'sɛrɪtɪ] *n* insinceridade *f*.
insinuate [ɪn'sɪnjueɪt] *vt* insinuar.
insinuation [ɪnsɪnju'eɪʃən] *n* insinuação *f*; (*hint*) indireta.
insipid [ɪn'sɪpɪd] *adj* insípido, insosso; (*person*) sem graça.
insist [ɪn'sɪst] *vi* insistir; **to ~ on doing** insistir em fazer; (*stubbornly*) teimar em fazer; **to ~ that** insistir em que; (*claim*) cismar que.
insistence [ɪn'sɪstəns] *n* insistência; (*stubbornness*) teimosia.
insistent [ɪn'sɪstənt] *adj* insistente, pertinaz.
insole ['ɪnsəul] *n* palmilha.
insolence ['ɪnsələns] *n* insolência, atrevimento.
insolent ['ɪnsələnt] *adj* insolente, atrevido.
insoluble [ɪn'sɔljubl] *adj* insolúvel.
insolvency [ɪn'sɔlvənsɪ] *n* insolvência.
insolvent [ɪn'sɔlvənt] *adj* insolvente.
insomnia [ɪn'sɔmnɪə] *n* insônia.
insomniac [ɪn'sɔmnɪæk] *n* insone *m/f*.
inspect [ɪn'spɛkt] *vt* inspecionar; (*building*) vistoriar; (*tickets*) fiscalizar; (*troops*) passar revista em.
inspection [ɪn'spɛkʃən] *n* inspeção *f*; vistoria; fiscalização *f*.
inspector [ɪn'spɛktə*] *n* inspetor(a) *m/f*; (*RAIL*) fiscal *m*.
inspiration [ɪnspə'reɪʃən] *n* inspiração *f*.
inspire [ɪn'spaɪə*] *vt* inspirar.
inspired [ɪn'spaɪəd] *adj* (*writer*, *book etc*) inspirado; **in an ~ moment** num momento de inspiração.
inspiring [ɪn'spaɪərɪŋ] *adj* inspirador(a).
inst. (*BRIT*) *abbr* (*COMM*) = **instant**.
instability [ɪnstə'bɪlɪtɪ] *n* instabilidade *f*.
install [ɪn'stɔːl] *vt* instalar.
installation [ɪnstə'leɪʃən] *n* instalação *f*.
installment [ɪn'stɔːlmənt] (*US*) *n* = **instalment**.
installment plan (*US*) *n* crediário.
instalment [ɪn'stɔːlmənt] (*BRIT*) *n* (*of money*) prestação *f*; (*of story*) fascículo; (*of TV serial etc*) capítulo; **in ~s** (*pay*) a prestações; (*receive*) em várias vezes.
instance ['ɪnstəns] *n* (*example*) exemplo; (*case*) caso; **for ~** por exemplo; **in many ~s** em muitos casos; **in that ~** naquele caso; **in the first ~** em primeiro lugar.
instant ['ɪnstənt] *n* instante *m*, momento ♦ *adj* instantâneo, imediato; (*coffee*) instantâneo; **of the 10th ~** (*BRIT*: *COMM*) de 10 do corrente.
instantaneous [ɪnstən'teɪnɪəs] *adj* instantâneo.
instantly ['ɪnstəntlɪ] *adv* imediatamente.
instant replay (*US*) *n* (*TV*) replay *m*.
instead [ɪn'stɛd] *adv* em vez disso; **~ of** em vez de, em lugar de.
instep ['ɪnstɛp] *n* peito do pé.
instigate ['ɪnstɪgeɪt] *vt* (*rebellion*, *strike*) fomentar; (*new ideas*) suscitar.
instigation [ɪnstɪ'geɪʃən] *n* instigação *f*; **at sb's ~** por incitação de alguém.
instil [ɪn'stɪl] *vt*: **to ~ (into)** infundir *or* incutir (em).
instinct ['ɪnstɪŋkt] *n* instinto.
instinctive [ɪn'stɪŋktɪv] *adj* instintivo.
instinctively [ɪn'stɪŋktɪvlɪ] *adv* por instinto, instintivamente.
institute ['ɪnstɪtjuːt] *n* instituto; (*professional body*) associação *f* ♦ *vt* (*inquiry*) começar, iniciar; (*proceedings*) instituir, estabelecer.
institution [ɪnstɪ'tjuːʃən] *n* instituição *f*; (*be-*

NB*: European Portuguese adds the following consonants to certain words:* **b** (sú(b)dito, su(b)til); **c** (a(c)ção, a(c)cionista, a(c)to); **m** (inde(m)ne); **p** (ado(p)ção, ado(p)tar); *for further details see p. xiii.*

ginning) início; (*organization*) instituto; (*MED*: *home*) asilo; (*asylum*) manicômio; (*custom*) costume *m*.

institutional [ɪnstɪ'tju:ʃənəl] *adj* institucional.

instruct [ɪn'strʌkt] *vt*: **to ~ sb in sth** instruir alguém em *or* sobre algo; **to ~ sb to do sth** dar instruções a alguém para fazer algo.

instruction [ɪn'strʌkʃən] *n* (*teaching*) instrução *f*; **~s** *npl* ordens *fpl*; **~s (for use)** modo de usar.

instruction book *n* livro de instruções.

instructive [ɪn'strʌktɪv] *adj* instrutivo.

instructor [ɪn'strʌktə*] *n* instrutor(a) *m/f*.

instrument ['ɪnstrumənt] *n* instrumento.

instrumental [ɪnstru'mɛntl] *adj* (*MUS*) instrumental; **to be ~ in** contribuir para.

instrumentalist [ɪnstru'mɛntəlɪst] *n* instrumentalista *m/f*.

instrument panel *n* painel *m* de instrumentos.

insubordinate [ɪnsə'bɔ:dənɪt] *adj* insubordinado.

insubordination [ɪnsəbɔ:də'neɪʃən] *n* insubordinação *f*.

insufferable [ɪn'sʌfrəbl] *adj* insuportável.

insufficient [ɪnsə'fɪʃənt] *adj* insuficiente.

insufficiently [ɪnsə'fɪʃəntlɪ] *adv* insuficientemente.

insular ['ɪnsjulə*] *adj* insular; (*outlook*) estreito; (*person*) de mente limitada.

insulate ['ɪnsjuleɪt] *vt* isolar.

insulating tape ['ɪnsjuleɪtɪŋ-] *n* fita isolante.

insulation [ɪnsju'leɪʃən] *n* isolamento.

insulin ['ɪnsjulɪn] *n* insulina.

insult [*n* 'ɪnsʌlt, *vt* ɪn'sʌlt] *n* insulto; (*offence*) ofensa ♦ *vt* insultar, ofender.

insulting [ɪn'sʌltɪŋ] *adj* insultante, ofensivo.

insuperable [ɪn'sju:prəbl] *adj* insuperável.

insurance [ɪn'ʃuərəns] *n* seguro; **fire ~** seguro contra incêndio; **life ~** seguro de vida; **to take out ~ (against)** segurar-se *or* fazer seguro (contra).

insurance agent *n* agente *m/f* de seguros.

insurance broker *n* corretor(a) *m/f* de seguros.

insurance company *n* seguradora.

insurance policy *n* apólice *f* de seguro.

insurance premium *n* prêmio de seguro.

insure [ɪn'ʃuə*] *vt* segurar; **to ~ sb/sb's life** segurar alguém/a vida de alguém; **to be ~d for £5000** estar segurado em £5000.

insured [ɪn'ʃuəd] *n*: **the ~** o/a segurado/a.

insurer [ɪn'ʃuərə*] *n* (*person*) segurador(a) *m/f*; (*company*) seguradora.

insurgent [ɪn'sə:dʒənt] *adj*, *n* insurgente *m/f*.

insurmountable [ɪnsə'mauntəbl] *adj* insuperável.

insurrection [ɪnsə'rɛkʃən] *n* insurreição *f*.

intact [ɪn'tækt] *adj* intacto, íntegro; (*unharmed*) ileso, são e salvo.

intake ['ɪnteɪk] *n* (*TECH*) entrada, tomada; (: *pipe*) tubo de entrada; (*of food*) quantidade *f* ingerida; (*SCH*): **an ~ of 200 a year** 200 matriculados por ano.

intangible [ɪn'tændʒɪbl] *adj* intangível.

integral ['ɪntɪgrəl] *adj* (*whole*) integral, total; (*part*) integrante.

integrate ['ɪntɪgreɪt] *vt* integrar ♦ *vi* integrar-se.

integrated circuit ['ɪntɪgreɪtɪd-] *n* (*COMPUT*) circuito integrado.

integration [ɪntɪ'greɪʃən] *n* integração *f*; **racial ~** integração racial.

integrity [ɪn'tɛgrɪtɪ] *n* integridade *f*, honestidade *f*, retidão *f*.

intellect ['ɪntəlɛkt] *n* intelecto.

intellectual [ɪntə'lɛktjuəl] *adj*, *n* intelectual *m/f*.

intelligence [ɪn'tɛlɪdʒəns] *n* inteligência; (*MIL etc*) informações *fpl*.

intelligence quotient *n* quociente *m* de inteligência.

Intelligence Service *n* Serviço de Informações.

intelligence test *n* teste *m* de inteligência.

intelligent [ɪn'tɛlɪdʒənt] *adj* inteligente.

intelligently [ɪn'tɛlɪdʒəntlɪ] *adv* inteligentemente.

intelligible [ɪn'tɛlɪdʒɪbl] *adj* inteligível, compreensível.

intemperate [ɪn'tɛmpərət] *adj* imoderado; (*with alcohol*) intemperado.

intend [ɪn'tɛnd] *vt* (*gift etc*): **to ~ sth for** destinar algo a; **to ~ to do sth** tencionar *or* pretender fazer algo.

intended [ɪn'tɛndɪd] *adj* (*effect*) desejado ♦ *n* noivo/a.

intense [ɪn'tɛns] *adj* intenso; (*person*) muito emotivo.

intensely [ɪn'tɛnslɪ] *adv* intensamente; (*very*) extremamente.

intensify [ɪn'tɛnsɪfaɪ] *vt* intensificar; (*increase*) aumentar.

intensity [ɪn'tɛnsɪtɪ] *n* intensidade *f*; (*of emotion*) força, veemência.

intensive [ɪn'tɛnsɪv] *adj* intensivo.

intensive care *n*: **to be in ~** estar na UTI.

intensive care unit *n* unidade *f* de tratamento intensivo.

intent [ɪn'tɛnt] *n* intenção *f* ♦ *adj* (*absorbed*) absorto; (*attentive*) atento; **to all ~s and purposes** para todos os efeitos; **to be ~ on doing sth** estar resolvido a fazer algo.

intention [ɪn'tɛnʃən] *n* intenção *f*, propósito.

intentional [ɪn'tɛnʃənl] *adj* intencional, proposital.

intentionally [ɪn'tɛnʃənəlɪ] *adv* de propósito.

intently [ɪn'tɛntlɪ] *adv* atentamente.

inter [ɪn'tə:*] *vt* enterrar.

interact [ɪntər'ækt] *vi* interagir.

interaction [ɪntər'ækʃən] *n* interação *f*, ação *f* recíproca.

interactive [ɪntər'æktɪv] *adj* interativo.

intercede [ɪntə'si:d] *vi*: **to ~ with sb/on behalf of sb** interceder junto a alguém/em favor de alguém.

intercept [ɪntə'sɛpt] *vt* interceptar; (*person*) deter.

interception [ɪntə'sɛpʃən] *n* interceptação *f*; (*of person*) detenção *f*.

interchange [*n* 'ɪntətʃeɪndʒ, *vt* ɪntə'tʃeɪndʒ] *n* intercâmbio; (*exchange*) troca, permuta; (*on motorway*) trevo ♦ *vt* intercambiar, trocar.
interchangeable [ɪntə'tʃeɪndʒəbl] *adj* permutável.
intercity (train) [ɪntə'sɪtɪ-] *n* expresso.
intercom ['ɪntəkɔm] *n* interfone *m*.
interconnect [ɪntəkə'nɛkt] *vi* interligar.
intercontinental [ɪntəkɔntɪ'nɛntl] *adj* intercontinental.
intercourse ['ɪntəkɔːs] *n* (*social*) relacionamento; **sexual ~** relações *fpl* sexuais.
interdependent [ɪntədɪ'pɛndənt] *adj* interdependente.
interest ['ɪntrɪst] *n* interesse *m*; (*COMM*: *on loan etc*) juros *mpl*; (: *share*) participação *f* ♦ *vt* interessar; **compound/simple ~** juros compostos/simples; **British ~s in the Middle East** os interesses britânicos no Oriente Médio.
interested ['ɪntrɛstɪd] *adj* interessado; **to be ~ in** interessar-se por, estar interessado em.
interest-free *adj* sem juros.
interesting ['ɪntrɪstɪŋ] *adj* interessante.
interest rate *n* taxa de juros.
interface ['ɪntəfeɪs] *n* (*COMPUT*) interface *f*.
interfere [ɪntə'fɪə*] *vi*: **to ~ in** (*quarrel, other people's business*) interferir *or* intrometer-se em; **to ~ with** (*objects*) mexer em; (*hinder*) impedir; **don't ~** não se meta.
interference [ɪntə'fɪərəns] *n* intromissão *f*; (*RADIO, TV*) interferência.
interfering [ɪntə'fɪərɪŋ] *adj* intrometido.
interim ['ɪntərɪm] *adj* interino, provisório ♦ *n*: **in the ~** neste ínterim, nesse meio tempo.
interior [ɪn'tɪərɪə*] *n* interior *m* ♦ *adj* interior.
interior decorator *n* decorador(a) *m/f*, arquiteto/a de interiores.
interior designer *n* arquiteto/a de interiores.
interject [ɪntə'dʒɛkt] *vt* inserir, interpor.
interjection [ɪntə'dʒɛkʃən] *n* interjeição *f*, exclamação *f*.
interlock [ɪntə'lɔk] *vi* entrelaçar-se; (*wheels etc*) engatar-se, engrenar-se ♦ *vt* engrenar.
interloper ['ɪntələupə*] *n* intruso/a.
interlude ['ɪntəluːd] *n* interlúdio; (*rest*) descanso; (*THEATRE*) intervalo.
intermarry [ɪntə'mærɪ] *vi* ligar-se por casamento.
intermediary [ɪntə'miːdɪərɪ] *n* intermediário/a.
intermediate [ɪntə'miːdɪət] *adj* intermédio, intermediário.
interminable [ɪn'təːmɪnəbl] *adj* interminável.
intermission [ɪntə'mɪʃən] *n* (*THEATRE*) intervalo.
intermittent [ɪntə'mɪtnt] *adj* intermitente.
intermittently [ɪntə'mɪtntlɪ] *adv* intermitentemente, a intervalos.
intern [*vt* ɪn'təːn, *n* 'ɪntəːn] *vt* internar; (*enclose*) encerrar ♦ *n* (*US*) médico-interno/médica-interna.
internal [ɪn'təːnl] *adj* interno; **~ injuries** ferimentos *mpl* internos.
internally [ɪn'təːnəlɪ] *adv* interiormente; **"not to be taken ~"** "uso externo".
Internal Revenue (Service) (*US*) *n* ≈ fisco, ≈ receita federal (*BR*).
international [ɪntə'næʃənl] *adj* internacional ♦ (*BRIT*) *n* (*SPORT*: *game*) jogo internacional; (: *player*) jogador(a) *m/f* internacional.
International Atomic Energy Agency *n* Agência Internacional de Energia Atômica.
International Court of Justice *n* Corte *f* Internacional de Justiça.
international date line *n* linha internacional de mudança de data.
internationally [ɪntə'næʃnəlɪ] *adv* internacionalmente.
International Monetary Fund *n* Fundo Monetário Internacional.
internecine [ɪntə'niːsaɪn] *adj* mutuamente destrutivo.
internee [ɪntəː'niː] *n* internado/a.
internment [ɪn'təːnmənt] *n* internamento.
interplay ['ɪntəpleɪ] *n* interação *f*.
Interpol ['ɪntəpɔl] *n* Interpol *m*.
interpret [ɪn'təːprɪt] *vt* interpretar; (*translate*) traduzir ♦ *vi* interpretar.
interpretation [ɪntəːprɪ'teɪʃən] *n* interpretação *f*; (*translation*) tradução *f*.
interpreter [ɪn'təːprɪtə*] *n* intérprete *m/f*.
interpreting [ɪn'təːprɪtɪŋ] *n* (*profession*) interpretação *f*.
interrelated [ɪntərɪ'leɪtɪd] *adj* inter-relacionado.
interrogate [ɪn'tɛrəugeɪt] *vt* interrogar.
interrogation [ɪntɛrə'geɪʃən] *n* interrogatório.
interrogative [ɪntə'rɔgətɪv] *adj* interrogativo ♦ *n* (*LING*) interrogativo.
interrogator [ɪn'tɛrəgeɪtə*] *n* interrogador(a) *m/f*.
interrupt [ɪntə'rʌpt] *vt, vi* interromper.
interruption [ɪntə'rʌpʃən] *n* interrupção *f*.
intersect [ɪntə'sɛkt] *vt* cruzar ♦ *vi* (*roads*) cruzar-se.
intersection [ɪntə'sɛkʃən] *n* intersecção *f*; (*of roads*) cruzamento.
intersperse [ɪntə'spəːs] *vt* entremear; **to ~ with** entremear com *or* de.
intertwine [ɪntə'twaɪn] *vt* entrelaçar ♦ *vi* entrelaçar-se.
interval ['ɪntəvl] *n* intervalo; (*BRIT*: *SCH*) recreio; (*THEATRE, SPORT*) intervalo; **sunny ~s** (*in weather*) períodos de melhoria; **at ~s** a intervalos.
intervene [ɪntə'viːn] *vi* intervir; (*occur*) ocorrer.
intervention [ɪntə'vɛnʃən] *n* intervenção *f*.
interview ['ɪntəvjuː] *n* entrevista ♦ *vt* entrevistar.
interviewee [ɪntəvjuː'iː] *n* entrevistado/a.
interviewer ['ɪntəvjuːə*] *n* entrevistador(a) *m/f*.
intestate [ɪn'tɛsteɪt] *adj* intestado.

***NB:** European Portuguese adds the following consonants to certain words:* **b** (sú(b)dito, su(b)til); **c** (a(c)ção, a(c)cionista, a(c)to); **m** (inde(m)ne); **p** (ado(p)ção, ado(p)tar); *for further details see p. xiii.*

intestinal [ɪn'tɛstɪnl] *adj* intestinal.
intestine [ɪn'tɛstɪn] *n*: **large/small ~** intestino grosso/delgado.
intimacy ['ɪntɪməsɪ] *n* intimidade *f*.
intimate [*adj* 'ɪntɪmət, *vt* 'ɪntɪmeɪt] *adj* íntimo; (*knowledge*) profundo ♦ *vt* insinuar, sugerir.
intimately ['ɪntɪmətlɪ] *adv* intimamente.
intimation [ɪntɪ'meɪʃən] *n* insinuação *f*, sugestão *f*.
intimidate [ɪn'tɪmɪdeɪt] *vt* intimidar, amedrontar.
intimidation [ɪntɪmɪ'deɪʃən] *n* intimidação *f*.
into ['ɪntu] *prep* em; **~ 3 pieces/French** em 3 pedaços/para o francês; **to change pounds ~ dollars** trocar libras por dólares.
intolerable [ɪn'tɔlərəbl] *adj* intolerável, insuportável.
intolerance [ɪn'tɔlərəns] *n* intolerância.
intolerant [ɪn'tɔlərənt] *adj*: **~ of** intolerante com *or* para com.
intonation [ɪntəu'neɪʃən] *n* entonação *f*, inflexão *f*.
intoxicate [ɪn'tɔksɪkeɪt] *vt* embriagar.
intoxicated [ɪn'tɔksɪkeɪtɪd] *adj* embriagado.
intoxication [ɪntɔksɪ'keɪʃən] *n* intoxicação *f*, embriaguez *f*.
intractable [ɪn'træktəbl] *adj* (*child*) intratável; (*material*) difícil de trabalhar; (*problem*) espinhoso; (*illness*) intratável.
intransigent [ɪn'trænsɪdʒənt] *adj* intransigente.
intransitive [ɪn'trænsɪtɪv] *adj* intransitivo.
intra-uterine device ['ɪntrə'ju:təraɪn-] *n* dispositivo intra-uterino.
intravenous [ɪntrə'vi:nəs] *adj* intravenoso.
in-tray *n* cesta para correspondência de entrada.
intrepid [ɪn'trɛpɪd] *adj* intrépido.
intricacy ['ɪntrɪkəsɪ] *n* complexidade *f*.
intricate ['ɪntrɪkət] *adj* complexo, complicado.
intrigue [ɪn'tri:g] *n* intriga ♦ *vt* intrigar ♦ *vi* fazer intriga.
intriguing [ɪn'tri:gɪŋ] *adj* intrigante.
intrinsic [ɪn'trɪnsɪk] *adj* intrínseco.
introduce [ɪntrə'dju:s] *vt* introduzir, inserir; **to ~ sb (to sb)** apresentar alguém (a alguém); **to ~ sb to** (*pastime, technique*) iniciar alguém em; **may I ~ ...?** permita-me apresentar ....
introduction [ɪntrə'dʌkʃən] *n* introdução *f*; (*of person*) apresentação *f*; **a letter of ~** uma carta de recomendação.
introductory [ɪntrə'dʌktərɪ] *adj* introdutório, preliminar; **~ remarks** observações preliminares; **~ offer** oferta de lançamento.
introspection [ɪntrəu'spɛkʃən] *n* introspecção *f*.
introspective [ɪntrəu'spɛktɪv] *adj* introspectivo.
introvert ['ɪntrəuvə:t] *adj*, *n* introvertido/a.
intrude [ɪn'tru:d] *vi*: **to ~ on** *or* **into** intrometer-se em.
intruder [ɪn'tru:də*] *n* intruso/a.
intrusion [ɪn'tru:ʒən] *n* intromissão *f*.
intrusive [ɪn'tru:sɪv] *adj* intruso.
intuition [ɪntju:'ɪʃən] *n* intuição *f*.
intuitive [ɪn'tju:ɪtɪv] *adj* intuitivo.
inundate ['ɪnʌndeɪt] *vt*: **to ~ with** inundar de.
inure [ɪn'juə*] *vt*: **to ~ (to)** habituar (a).
invade [ɪn'veɪd] *vt* invadir.
invader [ɪn'veɪdə*] *n* invasor(a) *m/f*.
invalid [*n* 'ɪnvəlɪd, *adj* ɪn'vælɪd] *n* inválido/a ♦ *adj* (*not valid*) inválido, nulo.
invalidate [ɪn'vælɪdeɪt] *vt* invalidar, anular.
invalid chair ['ɪnvəlɪd-] (BRIT) *n* cadeira de rodas.
invaluable [ɪn'væljuəbl] *adj* inestimável, impagável.
invariable [ɪn'vɛərɪəbl] *adj* invariável.
invariably [ɪn'vɛərɪəblɪ] *adv* invariavelmente; **she is ~ late** ela sempre chega atrasada.
invasion [ɪn'veɪʒən] *n* invasão *f*.
invective [ɪn'vɛktɪv] *n* invectiva.
inveigle [ɪn'vi:gl] *vt*: **to ~ sb into (doing) sth** aliciar alguém para (fazer) algo.
invent [ɪn'vɛnt] *vt* inventar.
invention [ɪn'vɛnʃən] *n* invenção *f*; (*inventiveness*) engenho; (*lie*) ficção *f*, mentira.
inventive [ɪn'vɛntɪv] *adj* engenhoso.
inventiveness [ɪn'vɛntɪvnɪs] *n* engenhosidade *f*, inventiva.
inventor [ɪn'vɛntə*] *n* inventor(a) *m/f*.
inventory ['ɪnvəntrɪ] *n* inventário, relação *f*.
inventory control *n* (COMM) controle *m* de estoques.
inverse [ɪn'və:s] *adj*, *n* inverso; **in ~ proportion to** em proporção inversa a.
inversely [ɪn'və:slɪ] *adv* inversamente.
invert [ɪn'və:t] *vt* inverter.
invertebrate [ɪn'və:tɪbrət] *n* invertebrado.
inverted commas [ɪn'və:tɪd-] (BRIT) *npl* aspas *fpl*.
invest [ɪn'vɛst] *vt* investir; (*endow*): **to ~ sb with sth** conferir algo a alguém, investir alguém de algo ♦ *vi* investir; **to ~ in** investir em; (*acquire*) comprar.
investigate [ɪn'vɛstɪgeɪt] *vt* investigar; (*study*) estudar, examinar.
investigation [ɪnvɛstɪ'geɪʃən] *n* investigação *f*.
investigative journalism [ɪn'vɛstɪgətɪv-] *n* jornalismo de investigação.
investigator [ɪn'vɛstɪgeɪtə*] *n* investigador(a) *m/f*; **private ~** detetive particular.
investiture [ɪn'vɛstɪtʃə*] *n* investidura.
investment [ɪn'vɛstmənt] *n* investimento.
investment income *n* rendimento de investimentos.
investment trust *n* fundo mútuo.
investor [ɪn'vɛstə*] *n* investidor(a) *m/f*.
inveterate [ɪn'vɛtərət] *adj* inveterado.
invidious [ɪn'vɪdɪəs] *adj* injusto; (*task*) desagradável.
invigilate [ɪn'vɪdʒɪleɪt] (BRIT) *vt* fiscalizar ♦ *vi* fiscalizar o exame.
invigilator [ɪn'vɪdʒɪleɪtə*] (BRIT) *n* fiscal *m/f* (de exame).
invigorating [ɪn'vɪgəreɪtɪŋ] *adj* revigorante.
invincible [ɪn'vɪnsɪbl] *adj* invencível.
inviolate [ɪn'vaɪələt] *adj* inviolado.
invisible [ɪn'vɪzɪbl] *adj* invisível.

invisible assets (*BRIT*) *npl* ativo intangível.
invisible ink *n* tinta invisível.
invisible mending *n* cerzidura.
invitation [ɪnvɪ'teɪʃən] *n* convite *m*; **by ~ only** estritamente mediante convite; **at sb's ~** a convite de alguém.
invite [ɪn'vaɪt] *vt* convidar; (*opinions etc*) solicitar, pedir; (*trouble*) pedir; **to ~ sb to do** convidar alguém para fazer; **to ~ sb to dinner** convidar alguém para jantar.
invite out *vt* convidar *or* chamar para sair.
invite over *vt* chamar.
inviting [ɪn'vaɪtɪŋ] *adj* convidativo.
invoice ['ɪnvɔɪs] *n* fatura ♦ *vt* faturar; **to ~ sb for goods** faturar mercadorias em nome de alguém.
invoke [ɪn'vəuk] *vt* invocar; (*aid*) implorar; (*law*) apelar para.
involuntary [ɪn'vɔləntrɪ] *adj* involuntário.
involve [ɪn'vɔlv] *vt* (*entail*) implicar; (*require*) exigir; **to ~ sb (in)** envolver alguém (em).
involved [ɪn'vɔlvd] *adj* envolvido; (*emotionally*) comprometido; (*complex*) complexo; **to be/get ~ in sth** estar/ficar envolvido em algo.
involvement [ɪn'vɔlvmənt] *n* envolvimento; (*obligation*) compromisso.
invulnerable [ɪn'vʌlnərəbl] *adj* invulnerável.
inward ['ɪnwəd] *adj* (*movement*) interior, interno; (*thought, feeling*) íntimo.
inwardly ['ɪnwədlɪ] *adv* (*feel, think etc*) para si, para dentro.
inward(s) ['ɪnwəd(z)] *adv* para dentro.
i/o *abbr* (*COMPUT*: = *input/output*) E/S, I/O.
IOC *n abbr* (= *International Olympic Committee*) COI *m*.
iodine ['aɪəudi:n] *n* iodo.
ion ['aɪən] *n* íon *m*, ião *m* (*PT*).
Ionian Sea [aɪ'əunɪən-] *n*: **the ~** o mar Iônico.
iota [aɪ'əutə] *n* (*fig*) pouquinho, tiquinho.
IOU *n abbr* (= *I owe you*) vale *m*.
IOW (*BRIT*) *abbr* = **Isle of Wight**.
IPA *n abbr* (= *International Phonetic Alphabet*) AFI *m*.
IQ *n abbr* (= *intelligence quotient*) QI *m*.
IRA *n abbr* (= *Irish Republican Army*) IRA *m*; (*US*) = **individual retirement account**.
Iran [ɪ'rɑ:n] *n* Irã (*PT*: Irão) *m*.
Iranian [ɪ'reɪnɪən] *adj* iraniano ♦ *n* iraniano/a; (*LING*) iraniano.
Iraq [ɪ'rɑ:k] *n* Iraque *m*.
Iraqi [ɪ'rɑ:kɪ] *adj, n* iraquiano/a.
irascible [ɪ'ræsɪbl] *adj* irascível.
irate [aɪ'reɪt] *adj* irado, enfurecido.
Ireland ['aɪələnd] *n* Irlanda; **Republic of ~** República da Irlanda.
iris ['aɪrɪs] (*pl* **~es**) *n* íris *f*.
Irish ['aɪrɪʃ] *adj* irlandês/esa ♦ *n* (*LING*) irlandês *m*; **the ~** *npl* os irlandeses.
Irishman ['aɪrɪʃmən] (*irreg*) *n* irlandês *m*.
Irish Sea *n*: **the ~** o mar da Irlanda.
Irishwoman ['aɪrɪʃwumən] (*irreg*) *n* irlandesa.
irk [ə:k] *vt* aborrecer.
irksome ['ə:ksəm] *adj* aborrecido.
IRN (*BRIT*) *n abbr* (= *Independent Radio News*) *agência de notícias radiofônicas*.
IRO (*US*) *n abbr* = **International Refugee Organization**.
iron ['aɪən] *n* ferro; (*for clothes*) ferro de passar roupa ♦ *adj* de ferro ♦ *vt* (*clothes*) passar; **~s** *npl* (*chains*) grilhões *mpl*.
iron out *vt* (*crease*) tirar; (*fig*: *problem*) resolver.
Iron Curtain *n*: **the ~** a cortina de ferro.
iron foundry *n* fundição *f*.
ironic(al) [aɪ'rɔnɪk(l)] *adj* irônico.
ironically [aɪ'rɔnɪklɪ] *adv* ironicamente.
ironing ['aɪənɪŋ] *n* (*ironed clothes*) roupa passada; (*to be ironed*) roupa a ser passada.
ironing board *n* tábua de passar roupa.
ironmonger ['aɪənmʌŋgə*] (*BRIT*) *n* ferreiro/a; **~'s (shop)** loja de ferragens.
iron ore *n* minério de ferro.
ironworks ['aɪənwə:ks] *n* siderúrgica.
irony ['aɪrənɪ] *n* ironia; **the ~ of it is that ...** o irônico é que ....
irrational [ɪ'ræʃənl] *adj* irracional.
irreconcilable [ɪrɛkən'saɪləbl] *adj* irreconciliável, incompatível.
irredeemable [ɪrɪ'di:məbl] *adj* (*COMM*) irresgatável.
irrefutable [ɪrɪ'fju:təbl] *adj* irrefutável.
irregular [ɪ'rɛgjulə*] *adj* irregular; (*surface*) desigual; (*illegal*) ilegal.
irregularity [ɪrɛgju'lærɪtɪ] *n* irregularidade *f*; (*of surface*) desigualdade *f*.
irrelevance [ɪ'rɛləvəns] *n* irrelevância.
irrelevant [ɪ'rɛləvənt] *adj* irrelevante, descabido.
irreligious [ɪrɪ'lɪdʒəs] *adj* irreligioso.
irreparable [ɪ'rɛprəbl] *adj* irreparável.
irreplaceable [ɪrɪ'pleɪsəbl] *adj* insubstituível.
irrepressible [ɪrɪ'prɛsəbl] *adj* irreprimível, irrefreável.
irreproachable [ɪrɪ'prəutʃəbl] *adj* irrepreensível.
irresistible [ɪrɪ'zɪstɪbl] *adj* irresistível.
irresolute [ɪ'rɛzəlu:t] *adj* irresoluto.
irrespective [ɪrɪ'spɛktɪv]: **~ of** *prep* independente de, sem considerar.
irresponsible [ɪrɪ'spɔnsɪbl] *adj* (*act, person*) irresponsável.
irretrievable [ɪrɪ'tri:vəbl] *adj* (*object*) irrecuperável; (*loss, damage*) irreparável.
irreverent [ɪ'rɛvərnt] *adj* irreverente, desrespeitoso.
irrevocable [ɪ'rɛvəkəbl] *adj* irrevogável.
irrigate ['ɪrɪgeɪt] *vt* irrigar.
irrigation [ɪrɪ'geɪʃən] *n* irrigação *f*.
irritable ['ɪrɪtəbl] *adj* irritável; (*mood*) de mal humor, nervoso.
irritate ['ɪrɪteɪt] *vt* irritar.

irritation [ɪrɪ'teɪʃən] *n* irritação *f*.
IRS (*US*) *n abbr* = **Internal Revenue Service**.
is [ɪz] *vb see* **be**.
ISBN *n abbr* (= *International Standard Book Number*) ISBN *m*.
Islam ['ɪzlɑːm] *n* islamismo.
island ['aɪlənd] *n* ilha; (*also*: *traffic* ~) abrigo.
islander ['aɪləndə*] *n* ilhéu/ilhoa *m/f*.
isle [aɪl] *n* ilhota, ilha.
isn't ['ɪznt] = **is not**.
isolate ['aɪsəleɪt] *vt* isolar.
isolated ['aɪsəleɪtɪd] *adj* isolado.
isolation [aɪsə'leɪʃən] *n* isolamento.
isolationism [aɪsə'leɪʃənɪzm] *n* isolacionismo.
isotope ['aɪsəutəup] *n* isótopo.
Israel ['ɪzreɪl] *n* Israel *m* (*no article*).
Israeli [ɪz'reɪlɪ] *adj*, *n* israelense *m/f*.
issue ['ɪsjuː] *n* questão *f*, tema *m*; (*outcome*) resultado; (*of banknotes etc*) emissão *f*; (*of newspaper etc*) número; (*offspring*) sucessão *f*, descendência ♦ *vt* (*rations, equipment*) distribuir; (*orders*) dar; (*certificate*) emitir; (*decree*) promulgar; (*book*) publicar; (*cheques, banknotes, stamps*) emitir ♦ *vi*: **to ~ from** (*smell, liquid*) emanar de; **at ~** em debate; **to avoid the ~** contornar o problema; **to take ~ with sb (over sth)** discordar de alguém (sobre algo); **to make an ~ of sth** criar caso com algo; **to confuse** *or* **obscure the ~** complicar as coisas.
Istanbul [ɪstæn'buːl] *n* Istambul.
isthmus ['ɪsməs] *n* istmo.
IT *n abbr* = **information technology**.
it [ɪt] *pron* (*subject*) ele/ela; (*direct object*) o/a; (*indirect object*) lhe; (*impers*) isto, isso; (*after prep*) ele, ela; **in front of/behind ~** em frente/atrás; **who is ~?** quem é?; **~'s me** sou eu; **what is ~?** o que é que é? **where is ~?** onde está? **~'s Friday tomorrow** amanhã é sexta-feira; **~'s raining** está chovendo (*BR*) *or* a chover (*PT*); **~'s six o'clock** são seis horas; **~'s two hours by train** são duas horas de trem; **he's proud of ~** ele orgulha-se disso; **he agreed to ~** ele consentiu.
ITA (*BRIT*) *n abbr* (= *initial teaching alphabet*) *alfabeto modificado utilizado na alfabetização*.
Italian [ɪ'tæljən] *adj* italiano ♦ *n* italiano/a; (*LING*) italiano.
italic [ɪ'tælɪk] *adj* itálico.
italics [ɪ'tælɪks] *npl* itálico.
Italy ['ɪtəlɪ] *n* Itália.
itch [ɪtʃ] *n* comichão *f*, coceira ♦ *vi* (*person*) estar com *or* sentir comichão *or* coceira; (*part of body*) comichar, coçar; **I'm ~ing to do sth** estou louco para fazer algo.
itching ['ɪtʃɪŋ] *n* comichão *f*, coceira.
itchy ['ɪtʃɪ] *adj* que coça; **to be ~** coçar.
it'd ['ɪtd] = **it would**; **it had**.
item ['aɪtəm] *n* item *m*; (*on agenda*) assunto; (*in programme*) número; (*also*: *news* ~) notícia; **~s of clothing** artigos de vestuário.
itemize ['aɪtəmaɪz] *vt* detalhar, especificar.
itinerant [ɪ'tɪnərənt] *adj* itinerante.
itinerary [aɪ'tɪnərərɪ] *n* itinerário.
it'll ['ɪtl] = **it will**; **it shall**.
ITN (*BRIT*) *n abbr* (= *Independent Television News*) *agência de notícias televisivas*.
its [ɪts] *adj* seu/sua, dele/dela ♦ *pron* (o) seu/(a) sua, o dele/a dela.
it's [ɪts] = **it is**; **it has**.
itself [ɪt'sɛlf] *pron* (*reflexive*) si mesmo/a; (*emphatic*) ele mesmo/ela mesma.
ITV (*BRIT*) *n abbr* (= *Independent Television*) *canal de televisão comercial*.
IUD *n abbr* (= *intra-uterine device*) DIU *m*.
I've [aɪv] = **I have**.
ivory ['aɪvərɪ] *n* marfim *m*.
Ivory Coast *n* Costa do Marfim.
ivory tower *n* (*fig*) torre *f* de marfim.
ivy ['aɪvɪ] *n* hera.
Ivy League (*US*) *n as grandes faculdades do nordeste dos EUA* (*Harvard, Yale, Princeton etc*).

J

J, j [dʒeɪ] *n* (*letter*) J, j *m*; **J for Jack** (*BRIT*) *or* **Jig** (*US*) J de José.
JA *n abbr* = **judge advocate**.
J/A *abbr* = **joint account**.
jab [dʒæb] *vt* (*elbow*) cutucar; (*punch*) esmurrar, socar ♦ *n* cotovelada, murro; (*MED*: *inf*) injeção *f*; **to ~ sth into sth** cravar algo em algo.
jabber ['dʒæbə*] *vt*, *vi* tagarelar.
jack [dʒæk] *n* (*AUT*) macaco; (*BOWLS*) bola branca; (*CARDS*) valete *m*.
 jack in (*inf*) *vt* largar.
 jack up *vt* (*AUT*) levantar com macaco; (*raise*: *prices*) aumentar.
jackel ['dʒækl] *n* chacal *m*.
jackass ['dʒækæs] *n* (*also*: *fig*) burro.
jackdaw ['dʒækdɔː] *n* gralha.
jacket ['dʒækɪt] *n* jaqueta, casaco curto; (*of boiler etc*) capa, forro; (*of book*) sobrecapa; **potatoes in their ~s** (*BRIT*) batatas com casca.
jack-in-the-box *n* caixa de surpresas.
jack-knife (*irreg*: *like* **knife**) *n* canivete *m* ♦ *vi*: **the lorry ~d** o reboque do caminhão deu uma guinada.
jack-of-all-trades *n* pau *m* para toda obra, homem *m* dos sete instrumentos.
jack plug (*BRIT*) *n* pino.
jackpot ['dʒækpɔt] *n* bolada, sorte *f* grande.
jacuzzi [dʒə'kuːzɪ] ® *n* jacuzzi *m* ®, banheira de hidromassagem.
jade [dʒeɪd] *n* (*stone*) jade *m*.
jaded ['dʒeɪdɪd] *adj* (*tired*) cansado; (*fed-up*) aborrecido, amolado.
JAG *n abbr* = **Judge Advocate General**.
jagged ['dʒægɪd] *adj* dentado, denteado.

jaguar ['dʒægjuə*] *n* jaguar *m*.
jail [dʒeɪl] *n* prisão *f*, cadeia ♦ *vt* encarcerar.
jailbird ['dʒeɪlbə:d] *n* criminoso inveterado.
jailbreak ['dʒeɪlbreɪk] *n* fuga da prisão.
jailer ['dʒeɪlə*] *n* carcereiro.
jalopy [dʒə'lɔpɪ] (*inf*) *n* calhambeque *m*.
jam [dʒæm] *n* geléia; (*also*: *traffic* ~) engarrafamento; (*difficulty*) apuro ♦ *vt* (*passage etc*) obstruir, atravancar; (*mechanism*) emperrar; (*RADIO*) bloquear, interferir ♦ *vi* (*mechanism, drawer etc*) emperrar; **to get sb out of a ~** (*inf*) tirar alguém de uma enrascada; **to ~ sth into sth** forçar algo dentro de algo; **the telephone lines are ~med** as linhas telefônicas estão congestionadas.
Jamaica [dʒə'meɪkə] *n* Jamaica.
Jamaican [dʒə'meɪkən] *adj*, *n* jamaicano/a *m/f*.
jamb ['dʒæm] *n* umbral *m*.
jam-packed *adj*: ~ **(with)** abarrotado (de).
jam session *n* jam session *m*.
Jan. *abbr* (= *January*) jan.
jangle ['dʒæŋgl] *vi* soar estridentemente, desafinar.
janitor ['dʒænɪtə*] *n* (*caretaker*) zelador *m*; (*doorman*) porteiro.
January ['dʒænjuərɪ] *n* janeiro; *see also* **July**.
Japan [dʒə'pæn] *n* Japão *m*.
Japanese [dʒæpə'ni:z] *adj* japonês/esa ♦ *n inv* japonês/esa *m/f*; (*LING*) japonês *m*.
jar [dʒɑ:*] *n* (*glass*: *large*) jarro; (: *small*) pote *m* ♦ *vi* (*sound*) ranger, chiar; (*colours*) destoar ♦ *vt* (*shake*) abalar.
jargon ['dʒɑ:gən] *n* jargão *m*.
jarring ['dʒɑ:rɪŋ] *adj* (*sound*, *colour*) destoante.
Jas. *abbr* = **James**.
jasmin(e) ['dʒæzmɪn] *n* jasmim *m*.
jaundice ['dʒɔ:ndɪs] *n* icterícia.
jaundiced ['dʒɔ:ndɪst] *adj* (*fig*: *embittered*) amargurado, despeitado; (: *disillusioned*) desiludido.
jaunt [dʒɔ:nt] *n* excursão *f*.
jaunty ['dʒɔ:ntɪ] *adj* alegre, jovial.
Java ['dʒɑ:və] *n* Java (*no article*).
javelin ['dʒævlɪn] *n* dardo de arremesso.
jaw [dʒɔ:] *n* mandíbula, maxilar *m*.
jawbone ['dʒɔ:bəun] *n* osso maxilar, maxila.
jay [dʒeɪ] *n* gaio.
jaywalker ['dʒeɪwɔ:kə*] *n* pedestre *m/f* imprudente (*BR*), peão *m* imprudente (*PT*).
jazz [dʒæz] *n* jazz *m*.
jazz up *vt* (*liven up*) animar, avivar.
jazz band *n* banda de jazz.
jazzy ['dʒæzɪ] *adj* (*of jazz*) jazzístico; (*bright*) de cor berrante.
JCS (*US*) *n abbr* = **Joint Chiefs of Staff**.
JD (*US*) *n abbr* (= *Doctor of Laws*) *título universitário*; (= *Justice Department*) *ministério da Justiça*.
jealous ['dʒɛləs] *adj* ciumento; (*envious*) invejoso; **to be ~** estar com ciúmes.
jealously ['dʒɛləslɪ] *adv* (*enviously*) invejosamente; (*guard*) zelosamente.
jealousy ['dʒɛləsɪ] *n* ciúmes *mpl*; (*envy*) inveja.
jeans [dʒi:nz] *npl* jeans *m* (*BR*), jeans *mpl* (*PT*).
jeep [dʒi:p] *n* jipe *m*.
jeer [dʒɪə*] *vi*: **to ~ (at)** (*boo*) vaiar; (*mock*) zombar (de).
jeering ['dʒɪərɪŋ] *adj* vaiador(a) ♦ *n* vaias *fpl*.
jeers ['dʒɪəz] *npl* (*boos*) vaias *fpl*; (*mocking*) zombarias *fpl*.
jelly ['dʒɛlɪ] *n* geléia, gelatina.
jellyfish ['dʒɛlɪfɪʃ] *n inv* água-viva.
jeopardize ['dʒɛpədaɪz] *vt* arriscar, pôr em perigo.
jeopardy ['dʒɛpədɪ] *n*: **to be in ~** estar em perigo, estar correndo risco.
jerk [dʒə:k] *n* (*jolt*) solavanco, sacudida; (*wrench*) puxão *m*; (*inf*) babaca *m* ♦ *vt* sacudir ♦ *vi* (*vehicle*) dar um solavanco.
jerkin ['dʒə:kɪn] *n* jaqueta.
jerky ['dʒə:kɪ] *adj* espasmódico, aos arrancos.
jerry-built ['dʒɛrɪ-] *adj* mal construído.
jerry can ['dʒɛrɪ-] *n* lata.
Jersey ['dʒə:zɪ] *n* Jersey (*no article*).
jersey ['dʒə:zɪ] *n* suéter *m or f* (*BR*), camisola (*PT*); (*fabric*) jérsei *m*, malha.
Jerusalem [dʒə'ru:sələm] *n* Jerusalém; ~ **artichoke** topinambo.
jest [dʒɛst] *n* gracejo, brincadeira; **in ~** de brincadeira.
jester ['dʒɛstə*] *n* (*HISTORY*) bobo.
Jesus ['dʒi:zəs] *n* Jesus *m*; ~ **Christ** Jesus Cristo.
jet [dʒɛt] *n* (*of gas, liquid*) jato; (*AVIAT*) (avião *m* a) jato.
jet-black *adj* da cor do azeviche.
jet engine *n* motor *m* a jato.
jet lag *n* cansaço devido à diferença de fuso horário.
jetsam ['dʒɛtsəm] *n* objetos *mpl* alijados ao mar.
jettison ['dʒɛtɪsn] *vt* alijar.
jetty ['dʒɛtɪ] *n* quebra-mar *m*, cais *m*.
Jew [dʒu:] *n* judeu/dia *m/f*.
jewel ['dʒu:əl] *n* jóia; (*in watch*) rubi *m*.
jeweller ['dʒu:ələ*] (*US* **jeweler**) *n* joalheiro/a; **~'s (shop)** joalheria.
jewellery ['dʒu:əlrɪ] (*US* **jewelry**) *n* jóias *fpl*, pedrarias *fpl*.
Jewess ['dʒu:ɪs] *n* (*offensive*) judia.
Jewish ['dʒu:ɪʃ] *adj* judeu/judia.
JFK (*US*) *n abbr* = **John Fitzgerald Kennedy International Airport**.
jib [dʒɪb] *n* (*NAUT*) bujarrona; (*of crane*) lança ♦ *vi* (*horse*) empacar; **to ~ at doing sth** relutar em fazer algo.
jibe [dʒaɪb] *n* zombaria.
jiffy ['dʒɪfɪ] (*inf*) *n*: **in a ~** num instante.
jig [dʒɪg] *n* jiga.
jigsaw ['dʒɪgsɔ:] *n* (*also*: ~ *puzzle*) quebra-

***NB**: European Portuguese adds the following consonants to certain words:* **b** (sú(b)dito, su(b)til); **c** (a(c)ção, a(c)cionista, a(c)to); **m** (inde(m)ne); **p** (ado(p)ção, ado(p)tar); *for further details see p. xiii.*

cabeça *m*; (*tool*) serra de vaivém.
jilt [dʒɪlt] *vt* dar o fora em.
jingle ['dʒɪŋgl] *n* (*advert*) música de propaganda ♦ *vi* tilintar, retinir.
jingoism ['dʒɪŋgəuɪzm] *n* jingoísmo.
jinx [dʒɪŋks] (*inf*) *n* caipora, pé *m* frio.
jitters ['dʒɪtəz] (*inf*) *npl*: **to get the ~** ficar muito nervoso.
jittery ['dʒɪtərɪ] (*inf*) *adj* nervoso.
jiu-jitsu [dʒuː'dʒɪtsuː] *n* jiu-jítsu *m*.
job [dʒɔb] *n* trabalho; (*task*) tarefa; (*duty*) dever *m*; (*post*) emprego; (*inf*: *difficulty*): **you'll have a ~ to do that** não vai ser fácil você fazer isso; **a part-time/full-time ~** um trabalho de meio-expediente/de tempo integral; **it's a good ~ that ...** ainda bem que ...; **just the ~!** justo o que queria!
jobber ['dʒɔbə*] (*BRIT*) *n* (*STOCK EXCHANGE*) operador(a) *m/f* intermediário/a.
jobbing ['dʒɔbɪŋ] (*BRIT*) *adj* (*workman*) tarefeiro, pago por tarefa.
Jobcentre ['dʒɔbsɛntə*] *n* agência de emprego.
job creation scheme *n* plano para a criação de empregos.
job description *n* descrição *f* do cargo.
jobless ['dʒɔblɪs] *adj* desempregado.
job lot *n* lote *m* (de mercadorias variadas).
job satisfaction *n* satisfação *f* profissional.
job security *n* estabilidade *f* de emprego.
job specification *n* especificação *f* do cargo.
jockey ['dʒɔkɪ] *n* jóquei *m* ♦ *vi*: **to ~ for position** manobrar para conseguir uma posição.
jockey box (*US*) *n* (*AUT*) porta-luvas *m inv*.
jocular ['dʒɔkjulə*] *adj* (*humorous*) jocoso, divertido; (*merry*) alegre.
jog [dʒɔg] *vt* empurrar, sacudir ♦ *vi* (*run*) fazer jogging *or* cooper; **to ~ along** ir levando; **to ~ sb's memory** refrescar a memória de alguém.
jogger ['dʒɔgə*] *n* corredor(a) *m/f*, praticante *m/f* de jogging.
jogging ['dʒɔgɪŋ] *n* jogging *m*.
join [dʒɔɪn] *vt* (*things*) juntar, unir; (*become member of*) associar-se a, afiliar-se a; (*meet*) encontrar-se com; (*accompany*) juntar-se a ♦ *vi* (*roads, rivers*) confluir ♦ *n* junção *f*; **will you ~ us for dinner?** você janta conosco?; **I'll ~ you later** vou me encontrar com você mais tarde; **to ~ forces (with)** associar-se (com).
join in *vi* participar ♦ *vt fus* participar em.
join up *vi* unir-se; (*MIL*) alistar-se.
joiner ['dʒɔɪnə*] *n* marceneiro.
joinery ['dʒɔɪnərɪ] *n* marcenaria.
joint [dʒɔɪnt] *n* (*TECH*) junta, união *f*; (*wood*) encaixe *m*; (*ANAT*) articulação *f*; (*CULIN*) quarto; (*inf*: *place*) espelunca; (: *marijuana cigarette*) baseado ♦ *adj* (*common*) comum; (*combined*) conjunto; (*committee*) misto; **by ~ agreement** por comum acordo; **~ responsibility** co-responsabilidade *f*.
joint account *n* conta conjunta.
jointly ['dʒɔɪntlɪ] *adv* em comum; (*collectively*) coletivamente; (*together*) conjuntamente.
joint ownership *n* co-propriedade *f*, condomínio.
joint-stock company *n* sociedade *f* anônima por ações.
joint venture *n* joint venture *m*.
joist [dʒɔɪst] *n* barrote *m*.
joke [dʒəuk] *n* piada; (*also*: *practical ~*) brincadeira, peça ♦ *vi* brincar; **to play a ~ on** pregar uma peça em.
joker ['dʒəukə*] *n* piadista *m/f*, brincalhão/lhona *m/f*; (*CARDS*) curingão *m*.
joking ['dʒəukɪŋ] *n* brincadeira.
jollity ['dʒɔlɪtɪ] *n* alegria.
jolly ['dʒɔlɪ] *adj* (*merry*) alegre; (*enjoyable*) divertido ♦ *adv* (*BRIT*: *inf*) muito, extremamente ♦ *vt* (*BRIT*): **to ~ sb along** animar alguém; **~ good!** (*BRIT*) excelente!
jolt [dʒəult] *n* (*shake*) sacudida, solavanco; (*shock*) susto ♦ *vt* sacudir, abalar.
Jordan ['dʒɔːdən] *n* Jordânia; (*river*) Jordão *m*.
Jordanian [dʒɔː'deɪnɪən] *adj*, *n* jordaniano/a.
joss stick [dʒɔs-] *n* palito perfumado.
jostle ['dʒɔsl] *vt* acotovelar, empurrar.
jot [dʒɔt] *n*: **not one ~** nem um pouquinho.
jot down *vt* anotar.
jotter ['dʒɔtə*] (*BRIT*) *n* bloco (de anotações).
journal ['dʒəːnl] *n* (*paper*) jornal *m*; (*magazine*) revista; (*diary*) diário.
journalese [dʒəːnə'liːz] (*pej*) *n* linguagem *f* jornalística.
journalism ['dʒəːnəlɪzəm] *n* jornalismo.
journalist ['dʒəːnəlɪst] *n* jornalista *m/f*.
journey ['dʒəːnɪ] *n* viagem *f*; (*distance covered*) trajeto ♦ *vi* viajar; **return ~** volta; **a 5-hour ~** 5 horas de viagem.
jovial ['dʒəuvɪəl] *adj* jovial, alegre.
jowl [dʒaul] *n* papada.
joy [dʒɔɪ] *n* alegria.
joyful ['dʒɔɪful] *adj* alegre.
joyous ['dʒɔɪəs] *adj* alegre.
joy ride *n* passeio de carro; (*illegal*) passeio (*com veículo roubado*).
joystick ['dʒɔɪstɪk] *n* (*AVIAT*) manche *m*, alavanca de controle; (*COMPUT*) joystick *m*.
JP *n abbr* = **Justice of the Peace**.
Jr. *abbr* = **junior**.
JTPA (*US*) *n abbr* (= *Job Training Partnership*) *programa governamental de aprendizagem*.
jubilant ['dʒuːbɪlnt] *adj* jubilante.
jubilation [dʒuːbɪ'leɪʃən] *n* júbilo, regozijo.
jubilee ['dʒuːbɪliː] *n* jubileu *m*; **silver ~** jubileu de prata.
judge [dʒʌdʒ] *n* juiz/juíza *m/f* ♦ *vt* julgar; (*estimate*: *weight, size etc*) avaliar; (*consider*) considerar ♦ *vi*: **judging** *or* **to ~ by ...** a julgar por ...; **as far as I can ~** ao que me parece, no meu entender; **I ~d it necessary to inform him** julguei necessário informá-lo.
judge advocate *n* (*MIL*) auditor *m* de guerra.
Judge Advocate General *n* (*MIL*) procurador *m* geral da Justiça Militar.
judg(e)ment ['dʒʌdʒmənt] *n* juízo; (*pun-*

ishment) decisão *f*, sentença; **in my ~** na minha opinião; **to pass ~ on** (*LAW*) julgar, dar sentença sobre.
judicial [dʒuːˈdɪʃl] *adj* judicial; (*fair*) imparcial.
judiciary [dʒuːˈdɪʃɪərɪ[*n* poder *m* judiciário.
judicious [dʒuːˈdɪʃəs] *adj* judicioso.
judo [ˈdʒuːdəu] *n* judô *m*.
jug [dʒʌg] *n* jarro.
jugged hare [dʒʌgd-] (*BRIT*) *n* guisado de lebre.
juggernaut [ˈdʒʌgənɔːt] (*BRIT*) *n* (*huge truck*) jamanta.
juggle [ˈdʒʌgl] *vi* fazer malabarismos.
juggler [ˈdʒʌglə*] *n* malabarista *m/f*.
Jugoslav [ˈjuːgəuslɑːv] *adj*, *n* = **Yugoslav**.
jugular (vein) [ˈdʒʌgjulə*-] *n* veia jugular.
juice [dʒuːs] *n* suco (*BR*), sumo (*PT*); (*inf*: *petrol*): **we've run out of ~** estamos sem gasolina.
juicy [ˈdʒuːsɪ] *adj* suculento.
jukebox [ˈdʒuːkbɔks] *n* juke-box *m*.
Jul. *abbr* (= *July*) jul.
July [dʒuːˈlaɪ] *n* julho; **the first of ~** dia primeiro de julho; **(on) the eleventh of ~** (no) dia onze de julho; **in the month of ~** no mês de julho; **at the beginning/end of ~** no começo/fim de julho; **in the middle of ~** em meados de julho; **during ~** durante o mês de julho; **in ~ of next year** em julho do ano que vem; **each** *or* **every ~** todo ano em julho; **~ was wet this year** choveu muito em julho deste ano.
jumble [ˈdʒʌmbl] *n* confusão *f*, mixórdia ♦ *vt* (*also*: **~** *up*: *mix up*) misturar; (: *disarrange*) desorganizar.
jumble sale (*BRIT*) *n* venda de objetos usados, bazar *m*.
jumbo [ˈdʒʌmbəu] *adj*: **~ jet** avião *m* jumbo; **~ size** tamanho gigante.
jump [dʒʌmp] *vi* saltar, pular; (*start*) sobressaltar-se; (*increase*) disparar ♦ *vt* pular, saltar ♦ *n* pulo, salto; (*increase*) alta; (*fence*) obstáculo; **to ~ the queue** (*BRIT*) furar a fila (*BR*), pôr-se à frente (*PT*); **to ~ for joy** pular de alegria.
jump about *vi* saltitar.
jump at *vt fus* (*accept*) aceitar imediatamente; (*chance*) agarrar.
jump down *vi* pular para baixo.
jump up *vi* levantar-se num ímpeto.
jumped-up [dʒʌmpt-] (*BRIT*: *pej*) *adj* arrivista.
jumper [ˈdʒʌmpə*] *n* (*BRIT*: *pullover*) suéter *m or f* (*BR*), camisola (*PT*); (*US*: *pinafore dress*) avental *m*; (*SPORT*) saltador(a) *m/f*.
jump leads (*US* **jumper cables**) *npl* cabos *mpl* para ligar a bateria.
jumpy [ˈdʒʌmpɪ] *adj* nervoso.
Jun. *abbr* = **June; junior**.
junction [ˈdʒʌŋkʃən] *n* (*BRIT*: *of roads*) cruzamento; (: *on motorway*) trevo; (*RAIL*) entroncamento.
juncture [ˈdʒʌŋktʃə*] *n*: **at this ~** neste momento, nesta conjuntura.
June [dʒuːn] *n* junho; *see also* **July**.
jungle [ˈdʒʌŋgl] *n* selva, mato.
junior [ˈdʒuːnɪə*] *adj* (*in age*) mais novo *or* moço; (*competition*) juvenil; (*position*) subalterno ♦ *n* jovem *m/f*; (*SPORT*) júnior *m*; **he's ~ to me (by 2 years), he's (2 years) my ~** ele é (dois anos) mais novo do que eu; **he's ~ to me** (*seniority*) tenho mais antiguidade do que ele.
junior executive *n* executivo/a júnior.
junior high school (*US*) *n* ≈ colégio (*2º e 3º ginasial*).
junior minister (*BRIT*) *n* ministro/a subalterno/a.
junior partner *n* sócio/a minoritário/a.
junior school (*BRIT*) *n* escola primária.
junior sizes *npl* (*COMM*) tamanhos *mpl* para crianças.
juniper [ˈdʒuːnɪpə*] *n* junípero.
junk [dʒʌŋk] *n* (*cheap goods*) tranqueira, velharias *fpl*; (*lumber*) trastes *mpl*; (*rubbish*) lixo; (*ship*) junco ♦ *vt* (*inf*) jogar no lixo.
junk dealer *n* belchior *m*.
junket [ˈdʒʌŋkɪt] *n* (*CULIN*) coalhada; (*BRIT*: *inf*): **to go on a ~** viajar à custa do governo ♦ *vi* (*BRIT*: *inf*): **to go ~ing** = **to go on a ~**.
junk food *n* lanches *mpl*.
junkie [ˈdʒʌŋkɪ] (*inf*) *n* drogado/a.
junk room (*US*) *n* quarto de despejo.
junk shop *n* loja de objetos usados.
Junr *abbr* = **junior**.
junta [ˈdʒʌntə] *n* junta.
Jupiter [ˈdʒuːpɪtə*] *n* Júpiter *m*.
jurisdiction [dʒuərɪsˈdɪkʃən] *n* jurisdição *f*; **it falls** *or* **comes within/outside our ~** é/não é da nossa competência.
jurisprudence [dʒuərɪsˈpruːdəns] *n* jurisprudência.
juror [ˈdʒuərə*] *n* jurado/a.
jury [ˈdʒuərɪ] *n* júri *m*.
jury box *n* banca dos jurados.
juryman [ˈdʒuərɪmən] (*irreg*) *n* = **juror**.
just [dʒʌst] *adj* justo ♦ *adv* (*exactly*) justamente, exatamente; (*only*) apenas, somente; **he's ~ done it/left** ele acabou (*PT*: acaba) de fazê-lo/ir; **~ as I expected** exatamente como eu esperava; **~ right** perfeito; **~ two o'clock** duas (horas) em ponto; **I was ~ about to phone** eu já ia telefonar; **we were ~ leaving** estávamos de saída; **~ as he was leaving** no momento em que ele saía; **~ before/enough** justo antes/o suficiente; **~ here** bem aqui; **it's ~ a mistake** não passa de um erro; **he ~ missed** falhou por pouco; **~ listen** escute aqui!; **~ ask someone the way** é só pedir uma indicação; **it's ~ as good** é igualmente bom; **~ as well that ...** ainda bem que ...; **not ~ now** não neste momento; **~ a minute!**, **~ one moment!** só um

***NB**: European Portuguese adds the following consonants to certain words:* **b** (sú(b)dito, su(b)til); **c** (a(c)ção, a(c)cionista, a(c)to); **m** (inde(m)ne); **p** (ado(p)ção, ado(p)tar); *for further details see p. xiii.*

minuto!, espera aí!, peraí! (*inf*).
justice ['dʒʌstɪs] *n* justiça; **Lord Chief J~** (*BRIT*) presidente do tribunal de recursos; **this photo doesn't do you ~** esta foto não te faz justiça.
Justice of the Peace *n* juiz/juíza *m/f* de paz.
justifiable [dʒʌstɪ'faɪəbl] *adj* justificável.
justifiably [dʒʌstɪ'faɪəblɪ] *adv* justificadamente.
justification [dʒʌstɪfɪ'keɪʃən] *n* (*reason*) justificativa; (*action*) justificação *f*.
justify ['dʒʌstɪfaɪ] *vt* justificar; **to be justified in doing sth** ter razão de fazer algo.
justly ['dʒʌstlɪ] *adv* justamente; (*with reason*) com razão.
justness ['dʒʌstnɪs] *n* justiça.
jut [dʒʌt] *vi* (*also*: ~ *out*) sobressair.
jute [dʒu:t] *n* juta.
juvenile ['dʒu:vənaɪl] *adj* juvenil; (*court*) de menores ♦ *n* jovem *m/f*; (*LAW*) menor *m/f* de idade.
juvenile delinquency *n* delinqüência juvenil.
juvenile delinquent *n* delinqüente *m/f* juvenil.
juxtapose ['dʒʌkstəpəuz] *vt* justapor.
juxtaposition [dʒʌkstəpə'zɪʃən] *n* justaposição *f*.

K

K, k [keɪ] *n* (*letter*) K, k *m*; **K for King** K de Kátia.
K *abbr* (= *kilobyte*) K; (*BRIT*: = *Knight*) *título honorífico* ♦ *n abbr* = **one thousand**.
kaftan ['kæftæn] *n* cafetã *m*.
Kalahari Desert [kælə'hɑ:rɪ-] *n* deserto de Kalahari.
kale [keɪl] *n* couve *f*.
kaleidoscope [kə'laɪdəskəup] *n* calidoscópio, caleidoscópio.
Kampala [kæm'pɑ:lə] *n* Campala.
Kampuchea [kæmpu'tʃɪə] *n* Kampuchea *m*, Camboja *m*.
kangaroo [kæŋgə'ru:] *n* canguru *m*.
kaput [kə'put] (*inf*) *adj* pifado.
karate [kə'rɑ:tɪ] *n* karatê *m*.
Kashmir [kæʃ'mɪə*] *n* Cachemira.
KC (*BRIT*) *n abbr* (*LAW*: = *King's Counsel*) *título dado a certos advogados*.
kd *abbr* (= *knocked down*) em pedaços.
kebab [kə'bæb] *n* churrasquinho, espetinho.
keel [ki:l] *n* quilha; **on an even ~** (*fig*) em equilíbrio.
keel over *vi* (*NAUT*) emborcar; (*person*) desmaiar.
keen [ki:n] *adj* (*interest, desire*) grande, vivo; (*eye, intelligence*) penetrante; (*competition*) acirrado, intenso; (*edge*) afiado; (*eager*) entusiasmado; **to be ~ to do** *or* **on doing sth** sentir muita vontade de fazer algo; **to be ~ on sth/sb** gostar de algo/alguém; **I'm not ~ on going** não estou a fim de ir.
keenly ['ki:nlɪ] *adv* (*enthusiastically*) com entusiasmo; (*feel*) profundamente, agudamente.
keenness ['ki:nnɪs] *n* (*eagerness*) entusiasmo, interesse *m*; **~ to do** vontade de fazer.
keep [ki:p] (*pt, pp* **kept**) *vt* (*retain*) ficar com; (*look after*) guardar; (*preserve*) conservar; (*hold back*) reter; (*shop, diary*) ter; (*feed: family etc*) manter; (*promise*) cumprir; (*chickens, bees etc*) criar ♦ *vi* (*food*) conservar-se; (*remain*) ficar ♦ *n* (*of castle*) torre *f* de menagem; (*food etc*): **to earn one's ~** ganhar a vida; **~s** *n*: **for ~s** (*inf*) para sempre; **to ~ doing sth** continuar fazendo algo; **to ~ sb from doing sth** impedir alguém de fazer algo; **to ~ sth from happening** impedir que algo aconteça; **to ~ sb happy** fazer alguém feliz; **to ~ a place tidy** manter um lugar limpo; **to ~ sb waiting** deixar alguém esperando; **to ~ an appointment** manter um compromisso; **to ~ a record of sth** anotar algo; **to ~ sth to o.s.** guardar algo para si mesmo; **to ~ sth (back) from sb** ocultar algo de alguém; **to ~ time** (*clock*) marcar a hora exata.
keep away *vt*: **to ~ sth/sb away from sb** manter algo/alguém afastado de alguém ♦ *vi*: **to ~ away (from)** manter-se afastado (de).
keep back *vt* (*crowd, tears*) conter; (*money*) reter ♦ *vi* manter-se afastado.
keep down *vt* (*control: prices, spending*) limitar, controlar ♦ *vi* não se levantar; **I can't ~ my food down** o que como não pára no estômago.
keep in *vt* (*invalid, child*) não deixar sair; (*SCH*) reter ♦ *vi*: **to ~ in with sb** manter boas relações com alguém.
keep off *vi* não se aproximar ♦ *vt* afastar; **"~ off the grass"** "não pise na grama"; **~ your hands off!** tira a mão!
keep on *vi*: **to ~ on doing** continuar fazendo.
keep out *vt* impedir de entrar ♦ *vi* (*stay out*) permanecer fora; **"~ out"** "entrada proibida".
keep up *vt* manter ♦ *vi* não atrasar-se, acompanhar; **to ~ up with** (*pace*) acompanhar; (*level*) manter-se ao nível de.
keeper ['ki:pə*] *n* guarda *m*, guardião/diã *m/f*.
keep-fit *n* ginástica.
keeping ['ki:pɪŋ] *n* (*care*) cuidado; **in ~ with** de acordo com.
keepsake ['ki:pseɪk] *n* lembrança.
keg [kɛg] *n* barrilete *m*, barril *m* pequeno.
kennel ['kɛnl] *n* casa de cachorro; **~s** *npl* canil *m*.
Kenya ['kɛnjə] *n* Quênia *m*.
Kenyan ['kɛnjən] *adj, n* queniano/a *m/f*.
kept [kɛpt] *pt, pp of* **keep**.
kerb [kə:b] (*BRIT*) *n* meio-fio (*BR*), borda do passeio (*PT*).

kernel ['kə:nl] *n* amêndoa.
kerosene ['kɛrəsi:n] *n* querosene *m*.
ketchup ['kɛtʃəp] *n* molho de tomate, catsup *m*.
kettle ['kɛtl] *n* chaleira.
kettle drums *npl* tímpanos *mpl*.
key [ki:] *n* chave *f*; (MUS) clave *f*; (*of piano, typewriter*) tecla; (*on map*) legenda ♦ *cpd* (-) chave.
key in *vt* (*text*) digitar, teclar.
keyboard ['ki:bɔ:d] *n* teclado ♦ *vt* (*text*) teclar, digitar.
keyed up [ki:d-] *adj*: **to be (all)** ~ estar excitado *or* ligado (*inf*).
keyhole ['ki:həul] *n* buraco da fechadura.
keynote ['ki:nəut] *n* (MUS) tônica; (*fig*) idéia fundamental ♦ *cpd*: ~ **speech** discurso programático.
keypad ['ki:pæd] *n* teclado complementar.
keyring ['ki:rɪŋ] *n* chaveiro.
keystone ['ki:stəun] *n* pedra angular.
keystroke ['ki:strəuk] *n* batida de tecla.
kg *abbr* (= *kilogram*) kg.
KGB *n abbr* KGB *f*.
khaki ['kɑ:kɪ] *adj* cáqui.
kibbutz [kɪ'buts] (*pl* ~**im**) *n* kibutz *m*.
kibbutzim [kɪ'butsɪm] *npl of* **kibbutz**.
kick [kɪk] *vt* (*person*) dar um pontapé em; (*ball*) chutar ♦ *vi* (*horse*) dar coices ♦ *n* pontapé *m*, chute *m*; (*of rifle*) recuo; (*inf: thrill*): **he does it for ~s** faz isso para curtir.
kick around (*inf*) *vi* ficar por aí.
kick off *vi* (SPORT) dar o pontapé inicial.
kick-off *n* (SPORT) pontapé *m* inicial.
kick-start *n* (*also*: ~*er*) arranque *m* ♦ *vt* dar partida em.
kid [kɪd] *n* (*child*) criança; (*animal*) cabrito; (*leather*) pelica ♦ *vi* (*inf*) brincar.
kidnap ['kɪdnæp] *vt* seqüestrar.
kidnapper ['kɪdnæpə*] *n* seqüestrador(a) *m/f*.
kidnapping ['kɪdnæpɪŋ] *n* seqüestro.
kidney ['kɪdnɪ] *n* rim *m*.
kidney bean *n* feijão *m* roxo.
kidney machine *n* (MED) aparelho de hemodiálise.
Kilimanjaro [kɪlɪmən'dʒɑ:rəu] *n*: **Mount** ~ Kilimanjaro.
kill [kɪl] *vt* matar; (*murder*) assassinar; (*destroy*) destruir; (*finish off*) acabar com, aniquilar ♦ *n* ato de matar; **to** ~ **time** matar o tempo.
kill off *vt* aniquilar; (*fig*) eliminar.
killer ['kɪlə*] *n* assassino/a.
killing ['kɪlɪŋ] *n* (*one*) assassinato; (*several*) matança; (*inf*): **to make a** ~ faturar uma boa nota ♦ *adj* (*funny*) divertido, engraçado.
kill-joy *n* desmancha-prazeres *m inv*.
kiln [kɪln] *n* forno.
kilo ['ki:ləu] *n* quilo.
kilobyte ['ki:ləubaɪt] *n* kilobyte *m*.
kilogram(me) ['kɪləugræm] *n* quilograma *m*.
kilometre ['kɪləmi:tə*] (US **kilometer**) *n* quilômetro.
kilowatt ['kɪləuwɔt] *n* quilowatt *m*.
kilt [kɪlt] *n* saiote *m* escocês.
kimono [kɪ'məunəu] *n* quimono.
kin [kɪn] *n* parentela; *see* **next**; **kith**.
kind [kaɪnd] *adj* (*friendly*) gentil; (*generous*) generoso; (*good*) bom/boa, bondoso, amável ♦ *n* espécie *f*, classe *f*; (*species*) gênero; **a** ~ **of** uma espécie de; **two of a** ~ dois da mesma espécie; **would you be** ~ **enough to ...?, would you be so** ~ **as to ...?** pode me fazer a gentileza de ...?; **it's very** ~ **of you (to do)** é muito gentil da sua parte (fazer); **in** ~ (COMM) em espécie; **to repay sb in** ~ (*fig*) pagar alguém na mesma moeda.
kindergarten ['kɪndəgɑ:tn] *n* jardim *m* de infância.
kind-hearted *adj* de bom coração, bondoso.
kindle ['kɪndl] *vt* acender.
kindling ['kɪndlɪŋ] *n* gravetos *mpl*.
kindly ['kaɪndlɪ] *adj* (*good*) bom/boa, bondoso; (*gentle*) gentil, carinhoso ♦ *adv* bondosamente, amavelmente; **will you** ~ ... você pode fazer o favor de ...; **he didn't take it** ~ não gostou.
kindness ['kaɪndnɪs] *n* bondade *f*, gentileza.
kindred ['kɪndrɪd] *adj* aparentado; ~ **spirit** pessoa com os mesmos gostos.
kinetic [kɪ'nɛtɪk[*adj* cinético.
king [kɪŋ] *n* rei *m*.
kingdom ['kɪŋdəm] *n* reino.
kingfisher ['kɪŋfɪʃə*] *n* martim-pescador *m*.
kingpin ['kɪŋpɪn] *n* (TECH) pino mestre; (*fig*) mandachuva *m*.
king-size(d) [-saɪʒ(d)] *adj* tamanho grande; (*cigarettes*) king-size.
kink [kɪŋk] *n* (*of rope*) dobra, coca; (*inf: fig*) mania.
kinky ['kɪŋkɪ] *adj* (*odd*) excêntrico, esquisito; (*pej*) pervertido.
kinship ['kɪnʃɪp] *n* parentesco.
kinsman ['kɪnzmən] (*irreg*) *n* parente *m*.
kinswoman ['kɪnzwumən] (*irreg*) *n* parenta.
kiosk ['ki:ɔsk] *n* banca (BR), quiosque *m* (PT); (BRIT: *also*: *telephone* ~) cabine *f*.
kipper ['kɪpə*] *n tipo de arenque defumado*.
kiss [kɪs] *n* beijo ♦ *vt* beijar; **to** ~ **(each other)** beijar-se; **to** ~ **sb goodbye** despedir-se de alguém com beijos; ~ **of life** (BRIT) respiração *f* boca-a-boca.
kit [kɪt] *n* apetrechos *mpl*; (*equipment*) equipamento; (*set of tools etc*) caixa de ferramentas; (*for assembly*) kit *m* para montar.
kit out (BRIT) *vt* equipar.
kitbag ['kɪtbæg] *n* saco de viagem.
kitchen ['kɪtʃɪn] *n* cozinha.
kitchen garden *n* horta.
kitchen sink *n* pia (de cozinha).
kitchen unit (BRIT) *n* módulo de cozinha.
kitchenware ['kɪtʃɪnwɛə*] *n* bateria de cozinha.
kite [kaɪt] *n* (*toy*) papagaio, pipa; (ZOOL) mi-

lhafre *m*.
kith [kɪθ] *n*: ~ **and kin** amigos e parentes *mpl*.
kitten ['kɪtn] *n* gatinho.
kitty ['kɪtɪ] *n* (*pool of money*) fundo comum, vaquinha; (CARDS) bolo.
KKK (US) *n abbr* = **Ku Klux Klan.**
Kleenex ['kli:nɛks] ® *n* lenço de papel.
kleptomaniac [klɛptəu'meɪnɪæk] *n* cleptomaníaco/a.
km *abbr* (= *kilometre*) km.
km/h *abbr* (= *kilometres per hour*) km/h.
knack [næk] *n*: **to have the ~ of doing sth** ter um jeito *or* queda para fazer algo; **there's a ~ (to it)** tem um jeito.
knapsack ['næpsæk] *n* mochila.
knave [neɪv] *n* (CARDS) valete *m*.
knead [ni:d] *vt* amassar.
knee [ni:] *n* joelho.
kneecap ['ni:kæp] *n* rótula.
knee-deep *adj*: **the water was ~** a água batia no joelho.
kneel [ni:l] (*pt, pp* **knelt**) *vi* (*also*: ~ *down*) ajoelhar-se.
kneepad ['ni:pæd] *n* joelheira.
knell [nɛl] *n* dobre *m* de finados.
knelt [nɛlt] *pt, pp of* **kneel**.
knew [nju:] *pt of* **know**.
knickers ['nɪkəz] *npl* calcinha (BR), cuecas *fpl* (PT).
knick-knack ['nɪk-] *n* bibelô *m*.
knife [naɪf] (*pl* **knives**) *n* faca ♦ *vt* esfaquear; **~, fork and spoon** talher *m*.
knight [naɪt] *n* cavaleiro; (CHESS) cavalo.
knighthood ['naɪthud] *n* cavalaria; (*title*): **to get a ~** receber o título de Sir.
knit [nɪt] *vt* tricotar; (*brows*) franzir ♦ *vi* tricotar (BR), fazer malha (PT); (*bones*) consolidar-se; **to ~ together** (*fig*) unir, juntar.
knitted ['nɪtɪd] *adj* de malha.
knitting ['nɪtɪŋ] *n* trabalho de tricô (BR), malha (PT).
knitting machine *n* máquina de tricotar.
knitting needle *n* agulha de tricô (BR) *or* de malha (PT).
knitting pattern *n* molde *m* para tricotar.
knitwear ['nɪtwɛə*] *n* roupa de malha.
knives [naɪvz] *npl of* **knife**.
knob [nɔb] *n* (*of door*) maçaneta; (*of drawer*) puxador *m*; (*of stick*) castão *m*; (*lump*) calombo; **a ~ of butter** (BRIT) uma porção de manteiga.
knobbly ['nɔblɪ] (BRIT) *adj* (*wood, surface*) nodoso; (*knees*) ossudo.
knobby ['nɔbɪ] (US) *adj* = **knobbly**.
knock [nɔk] *vt* (*strike*) bater em; (*bump into*) colidir com; (*fig*: *inf*) criticar, malhar ♦ *n* pancada, golpe *m*; (*on door*) batida ♦ *vi*: **to ~ at** *or* **on the door** bater à porta; **to ~ a hole in sth** abrir um buraco em algo; **to ~ a nail into** pregar um prego em.
knock down *vt* derrubar; (*price*) abater; (*pedestrian*) atropelar.
knock off *vi* (*inf*: *finish*) terminar ♦ *vt* (*inf*: *steal*) abafar; (*vase*) derrubar; (*fig*: *from price etc*): **to ~ off £10** fazer um desconto de £10.
knock out *vt* pôr nocaute, nocautear.
knock over *vt* (*object*) derrubar; (*pedestrian*) atropelar.
knockdown ['nɔkdaun] *adj* (*price*) de liqüidação, de queima (*inf*).
knocker ['nɔkə*] *n* (*on door*) aldrava.
knock-for-knock (BRIT) *adj*: ~ **agreement** *acordo entre seguradoras pelo qual cada uma se compromete a indenizar seu próprio cliente*.
knocking ['nɔkɪŋ] *n* pancadas *fpl*.
knock-kneed [-ni:d] *adj* cambaio.
knockout ['nɔkaut] *n* (BOXING) nocaute *m*.
knockout competition (BRIT) *n* competição *f* com eliminatórias.
knock-up *n* (TENNIS) bate-bola *m*.
knot [nɔt] *n* nó *m* ♦ *vt* dar nó em; **to tie a ~** dar *or* fazer um nó.
knotty ['nɔtɪ] *adj* (*fig*) cabeludo, espinhoso.
know [nəu] (*pt* **knew**, *pp* **known**) *vt* saber; (*person, author, place*) conhecer ♦ *vi*: **to ~ about** *or* **of sth** saber de algo; **to ~ that ...** saber que ...; **to ~ how to swim** saber nadar; **to get to ~ sth** (*fact*) saber, descobrir; (*place*) conhecer; **I don't ~ him** não o conheço; **to ~ right from wrong** saber distinguir o bem e o mal; **as far as I ~ ...** que eu saiba ....
know-all (BRIT: *pej*) *n* sabichão/chona *m/f*.
know-how *n* know-how *m*, experiência.
knowing ['nəuɪŋ] *adj* (*look*: *of complicity*) de cumplicidade.
knowingly ['nəuɪŋlɪ] *adv* (*purposely*) de propósito; (*spitefully*) maliciosamente.
know-it-all (US) *n* = **know-all.**
knowledge ['nɔlɪdʒ] *n* conhecimento; (*range of learning*) saber *m*, conhecimentos *mpl*; **to have no ~ of** não ter conhecimento de; **not to my ~** que eu saiba, não; **without my ~** sem eu saber; **to have a working ~ of Portuguese** ter um conhecimento básico do português; **it's common ~ that ...** todos sabem que ...; **it has come to my ~ that ...** chegou ao meu conhecimento que ....
knowledgeable ['nɔlɪdʒəbl] *adj* entendido, versado.
known [nəun] *pp of* **know** ♦ *adj* (*thief*) famigerado; (*fact*) conhecido.
knuckle ['nʌkl] *n* nó *m*.
knuckle under (*inf*) *vi* ceder.
knuckleduster ['nʌkldʌstə*] *n* soco inglês.
KO *n abbr* = **knockout** ♦ *vt* nocautear, pôr nocaute.
koala [kəu'ɑ:lə] *n* (*also*: ~ *bear*) coala *m*.
kook [ku:k] (US: *inf*) *n* maluco/a, biruta (*inf*).
Koran [kɔ'rɑ:n] *n* Alcorão *m*.
Korea [kə'rɪə] *n* Coréia; **North/South ~** Coréia do Norte/Sul.
Korean [kə'rɪən] *adj* coreano ♦ *n* coreano/a; (LING) coreano.
kosher ['kəuʃə*] *adj* kosher *inv*.
kowtow ['kau'tau] *vi*: **to ~ to sb** bajular alguém.

Kremlin ['krɛmlın] *n*: **the ~** o Kremlin.
KS (*US*) *abbr* (*POST*) = **Kansas**.
Kt (*BRIT*) *abbr* (= *Knight*) *título honorífico*.
Kuala Lumpur ['kwɑːlə'lumpuə*] *n* Cuala Lumpur.
kudos ['kjuːdɔs] *n* glória, fama.
Kuwait [ku'weıt] *n* Kuweit *m*.
Kuwaiti [ku'weıtı] *adj*, *n* kuweitiano/a.
kW *abbr* (= *kilowatt*) kW.
KY (*US*) *abbr* (*POST*) = **Kentucky**.

L

L, l [ɛl] *n* (*letter*) L, l *m*; **L for Lucy** (*BRIT*) *or* **Love** (*US*) L de Lúcia.
L *abbr* (= *lake*) L; (= *large*) G; (= *left*) esq; (*BRIT*: *AUT*: = *learner*) (condutor(a) *m/f*) aprendiz *m/f*.
l *abbr* (= *litre*) l.
LA (*US*) *n abbr* = **Los Angeles** ♦ *abbr* (*POST*) = **Louisiana**.
lab [læb] *n abbr* = **laboratory**.
label ['leıbl] *n* etiqueta, rótulo; (*brand*: *of record*) selo ♦ *vt* etiquetar, rotular; **to ~ sb a ...** rotular alguém de ....
labor *etc* ['leıbə*] (*US*) = **labour** *etc*.
laboratory [lə'bɔrətərı] *n* laboratório.
Labor Day (*US*) *n* Dia *m* do Trabalho.
laborious [lə'bɔːrıəs] *adj* laborioso.
labor union (*US*) *n* sindicato.
Labour ['leıbə*] (*BRIT*) *n* (*POL*: *also*: *the ~ Party*) o partido trabalhista, os trabalhistas.
labour ['leıbə*] (*US* **labor**) *n* (*task*) trabalho; (*~ force*) mão-de-obra; (*workers*) trabalhadores *mpl*; (*MED*) (trabalho de) parto ♦ *vi*: **to ~ (at)** trabalhar (em) ♦ *vt* insistir em; **in ~** (*MED*) em trabalho de parto.
labo(u)r camp *n* campo de trabalhos forçados.
labo(u)r cost *n* custo de mão-de-obra.
labo(u)red ['leıbəd] *adj* (*movement*) forçado; (*style*) elaborado.
labo(u)rer ['leıbərə*] *n* operário; (*on farm*) trabalhador *m* rural, peão *m*; (*day ~*) diarista *m*.
labo(u)r force *n* mão-de-obra *f*.
labo(u)r-intensive *adj* intensivo de mão-de-obra.
labo(u)r market *n* mercado de trabalho.
labo(u)r pains *npl* dores *fpl* do parto.
labo(u)r relations *npl* relações *fpl* trabalhistas.
labo(u)r-saving *adj* que poupa trabalho.
labo(u)r unrest *n* agitação *f* operária.
labyrinth ['læbırınθ] *n* labirinto.
lace [leıs] *n* renda; (*of shoe etc*) cordão *m* ♦ *vt* (*shoe*) amarrar; (*drink*) misturar aguardente a.
lacemaking ['leısmeıkıŋ] *n* feitura de renda.
laceration [læsə'reıʃən] *n* laceração *f*.
lace-up *adj* (*shoes etc*) de cordões.
lack [læk] *n* falta ♦ *vt* carecer de; **through** *or* **for ~ of** por falta de; **to be ~ing** faltar; **to be ~ing in** carecer de.
lackadaisical [lækə'deızıkl] *adj* (*careless*) descuidado; (*indifferent*) apático, aéreo.
lackey ['lækı] *n* (*also*: *fig*) lacaio.
lacklustre ['læklʌstə*] *adj* sem brilho, insosso.
laconic [lə'kɔnık] *adj* lacônico.
lacquer ['lækə*] *n* laca; (*for hair*) fixador *m*.
lacy ['leısı] *adj* rendado.
lad [læd] *n* menino, rapaz *m*, moço; (*BRIT*: *in stable etc*) empregado.
ladder ['lædə*] *n* escada de mão *f*; (*BRIT*: *in tights*) defeito (em forma de escada) ♦ *vt* (*BRIT*: *tights*) desfiar ♦ *vi* (*BRIT*: *tights*) desfiar.
laden ['leıdn] *adj*: **~ (with)** carregado (de); **fully ~** (*truck*, *ship*) completamente carregado, com a carga máxima.
ladle ['leıdl] *n* concha (de sopa).
lady ['leıdı] *n* senhora; (*distinguished*, *noble*) dama; **young ~** senhorita; **L~ Smith** a lady Smith; **"ladies' (toilets)"** "senhoras"; **a ~ doctor** uma médica.
ladybird ['leıdıbəːd] (*BRIT*) *n* joaninha.
ladybug ['leıdıbʌg] (*US*) *n* joaninha.
lady-in-waiting *n* dama de companhia.
ladykiller ['leıdıkılə*] *n* mulherengo.
ladylike ['leıdılaık] *adj* elegante, refinado.
ladyship ['leıdıʃıp] *n*: **her ~** Sua Senhoria.
lag [læg] *n* = **time lag** ♦ *vi* (*also*: *~ behind*) ficar para trás ♦ *vt* (*pipes*) revestir com isolante térmico.
lager ['lɑːgə*] *n cerveja leve e clara*.
lagging ['lægıŋ] *n* revestimento.
lagoon [lə'guːn] *n* lagoa.
Lagos ['leıgɔs] *n* Lagos.
laid [leıd] *pt*, *pp of* **lay**.
laid-back (*inf*) *adj* descontraído.
lain [leın] *pp of* **lie**.
lair [lɛə*] *n* covil *m*, toca.
laissez-faire [lɛseı'fɛə*] *n* laissez-faire *m*.
laity ['leıətı] *n* leigos *mpl*.
lake [leık] *n* lago.
Lake District (*BRIT*) *n*: **the ~** a região dos Lagos.
lamb [læm] *n* cordeiro.
lamb chop *n* costeleta de cordeiro.
lambskin ['læmskın] *n* pele *f* de cordeiro.
lambswool ['læmzwul] *n* lã *f* de cordeiro.
lame [leım] *adj* coxo, manco; (*weak*) pouco convincente, fraco; **~ duck** (*fig*) pessoa incapaz.
lamely ['leımlı] *adv* (*fig*) sem convicção.
lament [lə'mɛnt] *n* lamento, queixa ♦ *vt* lamentar-se de.

***NB**: European Portuguese adds the following consonants to certain words:* **b** (sú(b)dito, su(b)til); **c** (a(c)ção, a(c)cionista, a(c)to); **m** (inde(m)ne); **p** (ado(p)ção, ado(p)tar); *for further details see p. xiii.*

lamentable ['læməntəbl] *adj* lamentável.
laminated ['læmɪneɪtɪd] *adj* laminado.
lamp [læmp] *n* lâmpada.
lamplight ['læmplaɪt] *n*: **by ~** à luz da lâmpada.
lampoon [læm'puːn] *vt* satirizar.
lamppost ['læmppəust] (BRIT) *n* poste *m*.
lampshade ['læmpʃeɪd] *n* abajur *m*, quebra-luz *m*.
lance [lɑːns] *n* lança ♦ *vt* (MED) lancetar.
lance corporal (BRIT) *n* cabo.
lancet ['lɑːnsɪt] *n* (MED) bisturi, lanceta.
Lancs [læŋks] (BRIT) *abbr* = **Lancashire**.
land [lænd] *n* terra; (*country*) país *m*; (*piece of* ~) terreno; (*estate*) terras *fpl*, propriedades *fpl*; (AGR) solo ♦ *vi* (*from ship*) desembarcar; (AVIAT) pousar, aterrissar (BR), aterrar (PT); (*fig*: *fall*) cair, terminar ♦ *vt* (*obtain*) conseguir; (*passengers, goods*) desembarcar; **to go/travel by ~** ir/viajar por terra; **to own ~** ter propriedades; **to ~ on one's feet** (*fig*) dar-se bem, cair de pé.
land up *vi* ir parar.
landed gentry ['lændɪd-] *n* proprietários *mpl* de terras.
landing ['lændɪŋ] *n* (*from ship*) desembarque *m*; (AVIAT) pouso, aterrissagem *f* (BR), aterragem *f* (PT); (*of staircase*) patamar *m*.
landing card *n* cartão *m* de desembarque.
landing craft *n* navio para desembarque.
landing gear *n* trem *m* de aterrissagem (BR) *or* de aterragem (PT).
landing stage (BRIT) *n* cais *m* de desembarque.
landing strip *n* pista de aterrissagem (BR) *or* de aterragem (PT).
landlady ['lændleɪdɪ] *n* (*of boarding house*) senhoria; (*owner*) proprietária.
landlocked ['lændlɔkt] *adj* cercado de terra.
landlord ['lændlɔːd] *n* senhorio, locador *m*; (*of pub etc*) dono, proprietário.
landlubber ['lændlʌbə*] *n* *pessoa desacostumada ao mar*.
landmark ['lændmɑːk] *n* lugar *m* conhecido; (*fig*) marco.
landowner ['lændəunə*] *n* latifundiário/a.
landscape ['lændskeɪp] *n* paisagem *f*.
landscape architect *n* paisagista *m/f*.
landscaped ['lændskeɪpt] *adj* projetado paisagisticamente.
landscape gardener *n* paisagista *m/f*.
landscape painting *n* (ART: *genre*) paisagismo; (: *picture*) paisagem *f*.
landslide ['lændslaɪd] *n* (GEO) desmoronamento, desabamento; (*fig*: POL) vitória esmagadora.
lane [leɪn] *n* (*in country*) senda; (*in town*) ruela; (AUT) pista; (*in race*) raia; (*for air or sea traffic*) rota.
language ['læŋgwɪdʒ] *n* língua; (*way one speaks*, COMPUT) linguagem *f*; **bad ~** palavrões *mpl*.
language laboratory *n* laboratório de línguas.
languid ['læŋgwɪd] *adj* lânguido.
languish ['læŋgwɪʃ] *vi* elanguescer, debilitar-se.
lank [læŋk] *adj* (*hair*) liso.
lanky ['læŋkɪ] *adj* magricela.
lanolin(e) ['lænəlɪn] *n* lanolina.
lantern ['læntn] *n* lanterna.
Laos [laus] *n* Laos *m*.
lap [læp] *n* (*of track*) volta; (*of body*): **to sit on sb's ~** sentar-se no colo de alguém ♦ *vt* (*also*: ~ *up*) lamber ♦ *vi* (*waves*) marulhar.
lap up *vt* (*fig*: *food*) comer sofregamente; (: *compliments etc*) receber com sofreguidão.
La Paz [læ'pæz] *n* La Paz.
lapdog ['læpdɔg] *n* cãozinho de estimação.
lapel [lə'pɛl] *n* lapela.
Lapland ['læplænd] *n* Lapônia.
Lapp [læp] *adj*, *n* lapão/ona *m/f*.
lapse [læps] *n* lapso; (*in behaviour*) lapso, deslize *m* ♦ *vi* (*expire*) caducar; (LAW) prescrever; (*morally*) decair; **to ~ into bad habits** adquirir maus hábitos; **~ of time** lapso, intervalo; **a ~ of memory** um lapso de memória.
larceny ['lɑːsənɪ] *n* furto; **petty ~** delito leve.
lard [lɑːd] *n* banha de porco.
larder ['lɑːdə*] *n* despensa.
large [lɑːdʒ] *adj* grande; (*fat*) gordo; **at ~** (*free*) em liberdade; (*generally*) em geral; **to make ~r** ampliar; **a ~ number of people** um grande número de pessoas; **by and ~** de modo geral; **on a ~ scale** em grande escala.
largely ['lɑːdʒlɪ] *adv* em grande parte.
large-scale *adj* (*map*) em grande escala; (*fig*) importante, de grande alcance.
lark [lɑːk] *n* (*bird*) cotovia; (*joke*) brincadeira, peça.
lark about *vi* divertir-se, brincar.
larva ['lɑːvə] (*pl* **-vae**) *n* larva.
larvae ['lɑːviː] *npl of* **larva**.
laryngitis [lærɪn'dʒaɪtɪs] *n* laringite *f*.
larynx ['lærɪŋks] *n* laringe *f*.
lascivious [lə'sɪvɪəs] *adj* lascivo.
laser ['leɪzə*] *n* laser *m*.
laser beam *n* raio laser.
laser printer *n* impressora a laser.
lash [læʃ] *n* chicote *m*, açoite *m*; (*blow*) chicotada; (*also*: *eyelash*) pestana, cílio ♦ *vt* chicotear, açoitar; (*tie*) atar.
lash down *vt* atar, amarrar ♦ *vi* (*rain*) cair em bátegas.
lash out *vi*: **to ~ out at** *or* **against sb** atacar alguém violentamente; **to ~ out (on sth)** (*inf*: *spend*) esbanjar dinheiro (em algo).
lashings ['læʃɪŋz] (BRIT: *inf*) *npl*: **~ of** (*cream etc*) montes *mpl* de, um montão de.
lass [læs] *n* moça.
lasso [læ'suː] *n* laço ♦ *vt* laçar.
last [lɑːst] *adj* (*gen*) último; (*final*) derradeiro ♦ *adv* em último lugar ♦ *vi* (*endure*) durar; (*continue*) continuar; **~ week** na semana passada; **~ night** ontem à noite; **at ~** finalmente; **at ~!** até que enfim!; **~ but one** penúltimo; **the ~ time** a última vez; **it ~s (for) 2 hours** dura 2 horas.
last-ditch *adj* desesperado, derradeiro.

lasting ['lɑːstɪŋ] *adj* durável, duradouro.
lastly ['lɑːstlɪ] *adv* por fim, por último.
last-minute *adj* de última hora.
latch [lætʃ] *n* trinco, fecho, tranca.
latch on to *vt fus* (*cling to*: *person*) grudar em; (: *idea*) agarrar-se a.
latchkey ['lætʃkiː] *n* chave *f* de trinco.
late [leɪt] *adj* (*not on time*) atrasado; (*far on in day etc*) tardio; (*hour*) avançado; (*recent*) recente; (*former*) antigo, ex-, anterior; (*dead*) falecido ♦ *adv* tarde; (*behind time, schedule*) atrasado; **to be ~** estar atrasado, atrasar; **to be 10 minutes ~** estar atrasado dez minutos; **to work ~** trabalhar até tarde; **~ in life** com idade avançada; **it was too ~** já era tarde; **of ~** recentemente; **in ~ May** no final de maio; **the ~ Mr X** o falecido Sr X.
latecomer ['leɪtkʌmə*] *n* retardatário/a.
lately ['leɪtlɪ] *adv* ultimamente.
lateness ['leɪtnɪs] *n* (*of person*) atraso; (*of event*) hora avançada.
latent ['leɪtnt] *adj* latente.
later ['leɪtə*] *adj* (*date etc*) posterior; (*version etc*) mais recente ♦ *adv* mais tarde, depois; **~ on today** hoje mais tarde.
lateral ['lætərl] *adj* lateral.
latest ['leɪtɪst] *adj* último; **the ~ news** as últimas novidades; **at the ~** no mais tardar.
latex ['leɪtɛks] *n* látex *m*.
lath [læθ, *pl* læðz] *n* ripa.
lathe [leɪð] *n* torno.
lather ['lɑːðə*] *n* espuma (de sabão) ♦ *vt* ensaboar ♦ *vi* fazer espuma.
Latin ['lætɪn] *n* latim *m* ♦ *adj* latino.
Latin America *n* América Latina.
Latin-American *adj*, *n* latino-americano/a.
latitude ['lætɪtjuːd] *n* (*also fig*) latitude *f*.
latrine [lə'triːn] *n* latrina.
latter ['lætə*] *adj* último; (*of two*) segundo ♦ *n*: **the ~** o último, este.
latterly ['lætəlɪ] *adv* ultimamente.
lattice ['lætɪs] *n* treliça.
lattice window *n* janela com treliça de chumbo.
Latvia ['lætvɪə] *n* Letônia.
laudable ['lɔːdəbl] *adj* louvável.
laudatory ['lɔːdətrɪ] *adj* laudatório, elogioso.
laugh [lɑːf] *n* riso, risada; (*loud*) gargalhada ♦ *vi* rir, dar risada (*or* gargalhada).
laugh at *vt fus* rir de.
laugh off *vt* disfarçar sorrindo.
laughable ['lɑːfəbl] *adj* risível, ridículo.
laughing ['lɑːfɪŋ] *adj* risonho; **this is no ~ matter** isto não é para rir.
laughing gas *n* gás *m* hilariante.
laughing stock *n* alvo de riso.
laughter ['lɑːftə*] *n* riso, risada; (*people laughing*) risos *mpl*.
launch [lɔːntʃ] *n* (*boat*) lancha; (*of rocket, book etc*) lançamento ♦ *vt* (*ship, rocket, plan*) lançar.
launch out *vi*: **to ~ out (into)** lançar-se (a).
launching ['lɔːntʃɪŋ] *n* (*of rocket etc*) lançamento.
launch(ing) pad *n* plataforma de lançamento.
launder ['lɔːndə*] *vt* lavar e passar; (*money*) lavar.
launderette [lɔːn'drɛt] (BRIT) *n* lavanderia automática.
laundromat ['lɔːndrəmæt] (US) *n* lavanderia automática.
laundry ['lɔːndrɪ] *n* lavanderia; (*clothes*) roupa para lavar; **to do the ~** lavar a roupa.
laureate ['lɔːrɪət] *adj see* **poet**.
laurel ['lɔrl] *n* louro; (BOT) loureiro; **to rest on one's ~s** dormir sobre os louros.
lava ['lɑːvə] *n* lava.
lavatory ['lævətərɪ] *n* privada (BR), casa de banho (PT); **lavatories** *npl* sanitários *mpl* (BR), lavabos *mpl* (PT).
lavatory paper (BRIT) *n* papel *m* higiênico.
lavender ['lævəndə*] *n* lavanda.
lavish ['lævɪʃ] *adj* profuso, perdulário; (*giving freely*): **~ with** pródigo em, generoso com ♦ *vt*: **to ~ sth on sb** encher *or* cobrir alguém de algo.
lavishly ['lævɪʃlɪ] *adv* (*give, spend*) prodigamente; (*furnished*) luxuosamente.
law [lɔː] *n* lei *f*; (*study*) direito; **against the ~** contra a lei; **to study ~** estudar direito; **to go to ~** (BRIT) recorrer à justiça; **~ and order** a ordem pública.
law-abiding [-ə'baɪdɪŋ] *adj* obediente à lei.
lawbreaker ['lɔːbreɪkə*] *n* infrator(a) *m/f* (da lei).
law court *n* tribunal *m* de justiça.
lawful ['lɔːful] *adj* legal, lícito.
lawfully ['lɔːfulɪ] *adv* legalmente.
lawless ['lɔːlɪs] *adj* (*act*) ilegal; (*person*) rebelde; (*country*) sem lei, desordenado.
lawmaker ['lɔːmeɪkə*] *n* legislador(a) *m/f*.
lawn [lɔːn] *n* gramado (BR), relvado (PT).
lawnmower ['lɔːnməuə*] *n* cortador *m* de grama (BR) *or* de relva (PT).
lawn tennis *n* tênis *m* de gramado (BR) *or* de relvado (PT).
law school *n* faculdade *f* de direito.
law student *n* estudante *m/f* de direito.
lawsuit ['lɔːsuːt] *n* ação *f* judicial, processo; **to bring a ~ against** mover processo contra.
lawyer ['lɔːjə*] *n* advogado/a; (*for sales, wills etc*) notário/a, tabelião/liã *m/f*.
lax [læks] *adj* (*discipline*) relaxado; (*person*) negligente.
laxative ['læksətɪv] *n* laxante *m*.
laxity ['læksɪtɪ] *n*: **moral ~** falta de escrúpulo *or* caráter.
lay [leɪ] (*pt, pp* **laid**) *pt of* **lie** ♦ *adj* leigo ♦ *vt* (*place*) colocar; (*eggs, table*) pôr; (*trap*) armar; (*plan*) traçar; **to ~ the table** pôr a mesa; **to ~ the facts/one's proposals before**

NB: *European Portuguese adds the following consonants to certain words:* **b** (sú(b)dito, su(b)til); **c** (a(c)ção, a(c)cionista, a(c)to); **m** (inde(m)ne); **p** (ado(p)ção, ado(p)tar); *for further details see p. xiii.*

sb apresentar os fatos/suas propostas a alguém; **to get laid** (*inf!*) trepar (*!*).
lay aside *vt* pôr de lado.
lay by *vt* pôr de lado.
lay down *vt* (*pen etc*) depositar; (*flat*) deitar; (*arms*) depor; (*policy*) estabelecer; **to ~ down the law** impor regras.
lay in *vt* armazenar, abastecer-se de.
lay into (*inf*) *vt fus* (*attack*) surrar, espancar; (*scold*) dar uma bronca em.
lay off *vt* (*workers*) dispensar.
lay on *vt* (*water, gas*) instalar; (*provide*) prover; (*paint*) aplicar.
lay out *vt* (*design*) planejar; (*display*) expor; (*spend*) esbanjar.
lay up *vt* (*store*) estocar; (*ship*) pôr fora de serviço; (*subj*: *illness*) acometer.
layabout ['leɪəbaut] *n* vadio/a, preguiçoso/a.
lay-by (*BRIT*) *n* acostamento.
lay days *npl* (*NAUT*) dias *mpl* de estadia.
layer ['leɪə*] *n* camada.
layette [leɪ'ɛt] *n* enxoval *m* de bebê.
layman ['leɪmən] (*irreg*) *n* leigo.
lay-off *n* demissão *f*.
layout ['leɪaut] *n* (*design*) leiaute *m*, esquema *m*; (*disposition*) disposição *f*; (*PRESS*) composição *f*.
laze [leɪz] *vi* descansar; (*pej*) vadiar.
laziness ['leɪzɪnɪs] *n* preguiça.
lazy ['leɪzɪ] *adj* preguiçoso.
LB (*CANADA*) *abbr* = **Labrador**.
lb. *abbr* = **pound** (*weight*).
lbw *abbr* (*CRICKET*: = *leg before wicket*) *falta em que o batedor está com a perna em frente da meta.*
LC (*US*) *n abbr* = **Library of Congress**.
LCD *n abbr* = **liquid crystal display**.
Ld (*BRIT*) *abbr* (= *lord*) *título honorífico.*
LDS *n abbr* (= *Licentiate in Dental Surgery*) *diploma universitário*; (= *Latter-day Saints*) *os Santos dos Últimos Dias.*
LEA (*BRIT*) *n abbr* (= *local education authority*) *departamento de ensino do município.*
lead[1] [li:d] (*pt, pp* **led**) *n* (*front position*) dianteira; (*SPORT*) liderança; (*distance, time ahead*) vantagem *f*; (*clue*) pista; (*ELEC*) fio; (*for dog*) correia; (*THEATRE*) papel *m* principal ♦ *vt* conduzir; (*induce*) levar, induzir; (*be leader of*) chefiar, dirigir; (*SPORT*) liderar; (*orchestra*: *BRIT*) ser a primeira figura de; (: *US*) reger ♦ *vi* encabeçar; **to ~ to** levar a, conduzir a; (*result in*) resultar em; **to ~ sb astray** desencaminhar alguém; **to be in the ~** (*SPORT*: *in race*) estar na frente; (: *in match*) estar ganhando; **to take the ~** (*SPORT*) disparar na frente; (*fig*) tomar a dianteira; **to ~ sb to believe that ...** levar alguém a acreditar que ...; **to ~ sb to do sth** levar alguém a fazer algo.
lead away *vt* levar.
lead back *vt* levar de volta.
lead off *vi* (*in game etc*) começar.
lead on *vt* (*tease*) provocar; **to ~ sb on to** induzir alguém a.
lead up to *vt fus* conduzir a.
lead[2] [lɛd] *n* chumbo; (*in pencil*) grafite *f*.
leaded ['lɛdɪd] *adj* (*petrol*) com chumbo; **~ window** *janela com pequenas lâminas de vidro presas por tiras de chumbo.*
leader ['li:də*] *n* líder *m/f*, chefe *m/f*; (*of party, union etc*) líder *m/f*; (*of gang*) cabeça *m/f*; (*of newspaper*) artigo de fundo; **they are ~s in their field** são os líderes na área em que atuam; **the L~ of the House** (*BRIT*) o chefe dos ministros na Câmara.
leadership ['li:dəʃɪp] *n* liderança, direção *f*; (*quality*) poder *m* de liderança; **under the ~ of ...** sob a liderança de ...; (*army*) sob o comando de ...; **qualities of ~** qualidades de liderança.
lead-free [lɛd-] *adj* sem chumbo.
leading ['li:dɪŋ] *adj* (*main*) principal; (*outstanding*) de destaque, notável; (*front*) dianteiro; **a ~ question** uma pergunta capciosa; **~ role** papel de destaque.
leading lady *n* (*THEATRE*) primeira atriz *f*.
leading light *n* (*person*) figura principal, destaque *m*.
leading man (*irreg*) *n* (*THEATRE*) ator *m* principal.
lead pencil [lɛd-] *n* lápis *f* de grafite.
lead poisoning [lɛd-] *n* saturnismo.
lead time [li:d-] *n* (*COMM*) prazo de entrega.
lead weight [lɛd-] *n* peso de chumbo.
leaf [li:f] (*pl* **leaves**) *n* folha; (*of table*) aba; **to turn over a new ~** mudar de vida, partir para outra (*inf*); **to take a ~ out of sb's book** (*fig*) seguir o exemplo de alguém.
leaf through *vt fus* (*book*) folhear.
leaflet ['li:flɪt] *n* folheto.
leafy ['li:fɪ] *adj* folhoso, folhudo.
league [li:g] *n* liga; (*FOOTBALL*: *championship*) campeonato; (: *table*) classificação *f*; **to be in ~ with** estar de comum acordo com.
leak [li:k] *n* (*of liquid, gas*) escape *m*, vazamento; (*hole*) buraco, rombo; (*in roof*) goteira; (*fig*: *of information*) vazamento ♦ *vi* (*ship*) fazer água; (*shoe*) deixar entrar água; (*roof*) gotejar; (*pipe, container, liquid etc*) vazar; (*gas*) escapar; (*fig*: *news*) vazar ♦ *vt* vazar; **the information was ~ed to the enemy** as informações foram passadas para o inimigo.
leak out *vi* vazar.
leakage ['li:kɪdʒ] *n* (*also*: *fig*) vazamento.
leaky ['li:kɪ] *adj* (*pipe, shoe, boat*) furado; (*roof*) com goteira.
lean [li:n] (*pt, pp* **~ed** *or* **leant**) *adj* magro ♦ *n* (*of meat*) carne *f* magra ♦ *vt*: **to ~ sth on** encostar *or* apoiar algo em ♦ *vi* (*slope*) inclinar-se; (*rest*): **to ~ against** encostar-se *or* apoiar-se contra; **to ~ on** encostar-se *or* apoiar-se em.
lean back *vi* (*move body*) inclinar-se para trás; (*against wall, in chair*) recostar-se.
lean forward *vi* inclinar-se para frente.
lean out *vi*: **to ~ out (of)** inclinar-se para fora (de).
lean over *vi* debruçar-se ♦ *vt fus* debruçar-

se sobre.

leaning ['li:nɪŋ] *adj* inclinado ♦ *n*: ~ **(towards)** inclinação *f* (para); **the L~ Tower of Pisa** a torre inclinada de Pisa.

leant [lɛnt] *pt, pp of* **lean**.

lean-to *n* alpendre *m*.

leap [li:p] (*pt, pp* **~ed** or **leapt**) *n* salto, pulo ♦ *vi* saltar.

leap at *vt fus*: **to ~ at an offer** agarrar uma oferta.

leap up *vi* (*person*) levantar-se num ímpeto.

leapfrog ['li:pfrɔg] *n* jogo de pular carniça.

leapt [lɛpt] *pt, pp of* **leap**.

leap year *n* ano bissexto.

learn [lə:n] (*pt, pp* **~ed** *or* **learnt**) *vt* aprender; (*come to know of*) saber, ficar sabendo ♦ *vi* aprender; **to ~ how to do sth** aprender a fazer algo; **we were sorry to ~ that** ... sentimos tomar conhecimento de que ...; **to ~ about sth** (*SCH*) instruir-se sobre algo; (*hear*) saber de algo.

learned ['lə:nɪd] *adj* erudito.

learner ['lə:nə*] *n* principiante *m/f*; (*BRIT*: *also*: *~ driver*) (condutor(a) *m/f*) aprendiz *m/f*.

learning ['lə:nɪŋ] *n* (*process*) aprendizagem *f*; (*quality*) erudição *f*; (*knowledge*) saber *m*.

lease [li:s] *n* arrendamento ♦ *vt* arrendar, alugar; **on ~** em arrendamento.

lease back *vt* vender e alugar do comprador.

leaseback ['li:sbæk] *n venda de uma propriedade com a condição do comprador alugá-la ao vendedor*.

leasehold ['li:shəuld] *n* (*contract*) arrendamento ♦ *adj* arrendado.

leash [li:ʃ] *n* correia.

least [li:st] *adj*: **the** ~ + *n* o/a menor; (*smallest amount of*) a menor quantidade de ♦ *adv*: **the** ~ + *adj* o/a menos ♦ *pron*: **not in the ~** de maneira nenhuma; **the ~ money** o menos dinheiro de todos; **the ~ expensive** o/a menos caro/a; **the ~ possible effort** o menor esforço possível; **at ~** pelo menos.

leather ['lɛðə*] *n* couro ♦ *cpd* de couro; **~ goods** artigos *mpl* de couro.

leave [li:v] (*pt, pp* **left**) *vt* deixar; (*go away from*) abandonar ♦ *vi* ir-se, sair; (*train*) sair ♦ *n* (*consent*) permissão *f*, licença; (*time off, MIL*) licença; **to be left** sobrar; **there's some milk left over** sobrou um pouco de leite; **to ~ school** sair da escola; **~ it to me!** deixe comigo!; **on ~** de licença; **to take one's ~ of** despedir-se de; **~ of absence** licença excepcional.

leave behind *vt* (*also fig*) deixar para trás; (*forget*) esquecer.

leave off *vt* (*lid, cover*) não colocar; (*heating*) não ligar; (*light*) deixar apagado; (*BRIT*: *inf*: *stop*): **to ~ off (doing sth)** parar (de fazer algo).

leave on *vt* (*coat etc*) ficar com, não tirar; (*lid*) não tirar; (*light, fire*) deixar aceso; (*radio*) deixar ligado.

leave out *vt* omitir.

leaves [li:vz] *npl of* **leaf**.

leavetaking ['li:vteɪkɪŋ] *n* despedida.

Lebanese [lɛbə'ni:z] *adj, n inv* libanês/esa *m/f*.

Lebanon ['lɛbənən] *n* Líbano.

lecherous ['lɛtʃərəs] *adj* lascivo.

lectern ['lɛktə:n] *n* atril *m*.

lecture ['lɛktʃə*] *n* conferência, palestra; (*SCH*) aula ♦ *vi* dar aulas, lecionar ♦ *vt* (*scold*) passar um sermão em; **to give a ~ on** dar uma conferência sobre.

lecture hall *n* salão *m* de conferências, anfiteatro.

lecturer ['lɛktʃərə*] *n* conferencista *m/f* (*BR*), conferente *m/f* (*PT*); (*BRIT*: *at university*) professor(a) *m/f*; **assistant ~** (*BRIT*) assistente *m/f*; **senior ~** (*BRIT*) lente *m/f*.

lecture theatre *n* = **lecture hall**.

LED *n abbr* (= *light-emitting diode*) LED *m*.

led [lɛd] *pt, pp of* **lead**.

ledge [lɛdʒ] *n* (*of window*) peitoril *m*; (*of mountain*) saliência, proeminência.

ledger ['lɛdʒə*] *n* livro-razão *m*, razão *m*.

lee [li:] *n* sotavento; **in the ~ of** ao abrigo de.

leech [li:tʃ] *n* sanguessuga.

leek [li:k] *n* alho-poró *m*.

leer [lɪə*] *vi*: **to ~ at sb** olhar maliciosamente para alguém.

leeward ['li:wəd] *adj* de sotavento ♦ *adv* a sotavento ♦ *n* sotavento; **to ~** para sotavento.

leeway ['li:weɪ] *n* (*fig*): **to make up ~** reduzir o atraso; **to have some ~** ter certa liberdade de ação.

left [lɛft] *pt, pp of* **leave** ♦ *adj* esquerdo ♦ *n* esquerda ♦ *adv* à esquerda; **on the ~** à esquerda; **to the ~** para a esquerda; **the L~** (*POL*) a Esquerda.

left-hand drive (*BRIT*) *n* direção *f* do lado esquerdo.

left-handed [-'hændɪd] *adj* canhoto; (*scissors etc*) para canhotos.

left-hand side *n* esquerda, lado esquerdo.

leftist ['lɛftɪst] *adj* (*POL*) esquerdista.

left-luggage (office) (*BRIT*) *n* depósito de bagagem.

left-overs *npl* sobras *fpl*.

left wing *n* (*MIL, SPORT*) ala esquerda; (*POL*) esquerda ♦ *adj*: **left-wing** (*POL*) de esquerda, esquerdista.

left-winger *n* (*POL*) esquerdista *m/f*; (*SPORT*) ponta-esquerda *m/f*.

leg [lɛg] *n* perna; (*of animal*) pata; (*of chair*) pé *m*; (*CULIN*: *of meat*) perna; (*of journey*) etapa; **lst/2nd ~** (*SPORT*) primeiro/segundo turno; **to pull sb's ~** brincar *or* mexer com alguém; **to stretch one's ~s** esticar as pernas.

legacy ['lɛgəsɪ] *n* legado.

legal ['li:gl] *adj* (*lawful, of law*) legal; (*terminology, enquiry etc*) jurídico; **to take ~**

***NB**: European Portuguese adds the following consonants to certain words:* **b** (sú(b)dito, su(b)til); **c** (a(c)ção, a(c)cionista, a(c)to); **m** (inde(m)ne); **p** (ado(p)ção, ado(p)tar); *for further details see p. xiii.*

proceedings *or* **action against sb** instaurar processo contra alguém.
legal adviser *n* consultor(a) *m/f* jurídico/a.
legality [lɪ'gælɪtɪ] *n* legalidade *f*.
legalize ['li:gəlaɪz] *vt* legalizar.
legally ['li:gəlɪ] *adv* legalmente; (*in terms of law*) de acordo com a lei.
legal tender *n* moeda corrente.
legation [lə'geɪʃən] *n* legação *f*.
legend ['lɛdʒənd] *n* lenda.
legendary ['lɛdʒəndərɪ] *adj* legendário.
-legged ['lɛgɪd] *suffix*: **two~** de duas patas (*or* pernas).
leggings ['lɛgɪŋz] *npl* (*overtrousers*) perneiras *fpl*; (*women's*) legging *f*.
legibility [lɛdʒɪ'bɪlɪtɪ] *n* legibilidade *f*.
legible ['lɛdʒəbl] *adj* legível.
legibly ['lɛdʒəblɪ] *adv* legivelmente.
legion ['li:dʒən] *n* legião *f*.
legionnaire [li:dʒə'nɛə*] *n* legionário; **~'s disease** *doença rara parecida à pneumonia*.
legislate ['lɛdʒɪsleɪt] *vi* legislar.
legislation [lɛdʒɪs'leɪʃən] *n* legislação *f*; **a piece of ~** uma lei.
legislative ['lɛdʒɪslətɪv] *adj* legislativo.
legislator ['lɛdʒɪsleɪtə*] *n* legislador(a) *m/f*.
legislature ['lɛdʒɪslətʃə*] *n* legislatura.
legitimacy [lɪ'dʒɪtɪməsɪ] *n* legitimidade *f*.
legitimate [lɪ'dʒɪtɪmət] *adj* legítimo.
legitimize [lɪ'dʒɪtɪmaɪz] *vt* legitimar.
leg-room *n* espaço para as pernas.
Leics (*BRIT*) *abbr* = **Leicestershire**.
leisure ['lɛʒə*] *n* lazer *m*; **at ~** desocupado, livre.
leisure centre *n* centro de lazer.
leisurely ['lɛʒəlɪ] *adj* calmo, vagaroso.
leisure suit (*BRIT*) *n* jogging *m*.
lemon ['lɛmən] *n* limão(-galego) *m*.
lemonade [lɛmə'neɪd] *n* limonada.
lemon cheese *n* coalho *or* pasta de limão.
lemon curd *n* coalho *or* pasta de limão.
lemon juice *n* suco (*BR*) *or* sumo (*PT*) de limão.
lemon squeezer [-'skwi:zə*] *n* espremedor *m* de limão.
lemon tea *n* chá *m* de limão.
lend [lɛnd] (*pt, pp* **lent**) *vt*: **to ~ sth to sb** emprestar algo a alguém; **to ~ a hand** dar uma ajuda.
lender ['lɛndə*] *n* emprestador(a) *m/f*.
lending library ['lɛndɪŋ] *n* biblioteca circulante.
length [lɛŋθ] *n* comprimento, extensão *f*; (*section*: *of road, pipe etc*) trecho; **~ of time** duração; **what ~ is it?** de que comprimento é?; **it is 2 metres in ~** tem dois metros de comprimento; **to fall full ~** cair estirado; **at ~** (*at last*) finalmente, afinal; (*lengthily*) por extenso; **to go to any ~(s) to do sth** fazer qualquer coisa para fazer algo.
lengthen ['lɛŋθən] *vt* encomprida, alongar ♦ *vi* encompridar-se.
lengthways ['lɛŋθweɪz] *adv* longitudinalmente, ao comprido.
lengthy ['lɛŋθɪ] *adj* comprido, longo; (*meeting*) prolongado.
leniency ['li:nɪənsɪ] *n* indulgência.
lenient ['li:nɪənt] *adj* indulgente, clemente.
leniently ['li:nɪəntlɪ] *adv* com indulgência.
lens [lɛnz] *n* (*of spectacles*) lente *f*; (*of camera*) objetiva.
Lent [lɛnt] *n* Quaresma.
lent [lɛnt] *pt, pp of* **lend**.
lentil ['lɛntl] *n* lentilha.
Leo ['li:əu] *n* Leão *m*.
leopard ['lɛpəd] *n* leopardo.
leotard ['li:əta:d] *n* collant *m*.
leper ['lɛpə*] *n* leproso/a.
leper colony *n* leprosário.
leprosy ['lɛprəsɪ] *n* lepra.
lesbian ['lɛzbɪən] *adj* lésbico ♦ *n* lésbica.
lesion ['li:ʒən] *n* (*MED*) lesão *f*.
Lesotho [lɪ'su:tu:] *n* Lesoto.
less [lɛs] *adj* menos ♦ *pron, adv* menos; **~ than that/you** menos que isso/você; **~ than half** menos da metade; **~ than 1/a kilo/3 metres** menos de um/um quilo/3 metros; **~ and ~** cada vez menos; **the ~ he works ...** quanto menos trabalha ...; **income ~ expenses** renda menos despesas.
lessee [lɛ'si:] *n* arrendatário/a, locatário/a.
lessen ['lɛsn] *vi* diminuir, minguar ♦ *vt* diminuir, reduzir.
lesser ['lɛsə*] *adj* menor; **to a ~ extent** *or* **degree** nem tanto.
lesson ['lɛsn] *n* aula; (*in book etc*) lição *f*; **a maths ~** uma aula *or* uma lição de matemática; **to give ~s in** dar aulas de; **it taught him a ~** (*fig*) serviu-lhe de lição.
lessor ['lɛsə*] *n* arrendador(a) *m/f*, locador(a) *m/f*.
lest [lɛst] *conj*: **~ it happen** para que não aconteça; **I was afraid ~ he forget** temi que ele esquecesse.
let [lɛt] (*pt, pp* **let**) *vt* (*allow*) deixar; (*lease*) alugar; **to ~ sb do sth** deixar alguém fazer algo; **to ~ sb know sth** avisar alguém de algo; **he ~ me go** ele me deixou ir; **~ the water boil and ...** deixe ferver a água e ...; **~'s go!** vamos!; **~ him come!** deixa ele vir!; **"to ~"** "aluga-se".
let down *vt* (*lower*) abaixar; (*dress*) encompridar; (*BRIT*: *tyre*) esvaziar; (*hair*) soltar; (*disappoint*) desapontar.
let go *vt, vi* soltar.
let in *vt* deixar entrar; (*visitor etc*) fazer entrar; **what have you ~ yourself in for?** onde você foi se meter?
let off *vt* (*allow to leave*) deixar ir; (*not punish*) perdoar; (*subj*: *bus driver*) deixar (saltar); (*firework etc*) soltar; **to ~ off steam** (*fig*) desabafar.
let on (*inf*) *vt*: **to ~ on that ...** dizer por aí que ..., contar que ....
let out *vt* deixar sair; (*dress*) alargar; (*scream*) soltar; (*rent out*) alugar.
let up *vi* cessar, afrouxar.
let-down *n* (*disappointment*) decepção *f*.
lethal ['li:θl] *adj* letal; (*wound*) mortal.
lethargic [lɛ'θa:dʒɪk] *adj* letárgico.

lethargy ['lɛθədʒɪ] *n* letargia.
letter ['lɛtə*] *n* (*of alphabet*) letra; (*correspondence*) carta; **small/capital** ~ minúscula/maiúscula; ~ **of credit** carta de crédito.
letter bomb *n* carta-bomba.
letterbox ['lɛtəbɔks] (*BRIT*) *n* caixa do correio.
letterhead ['lɛtəhɛd] *n* cabeçalho.
lettering ['lɛtərɪŋ] *n* letras *fpl*.
letter opener *n* corta-papel *m*.
letterpress ['lɛtəprɛs] *n* (*method*) impressão *f* tipográfica.
letter quality *n* qualidade *f* carta.
letters patent *n* carta patente.
lettuce ['lɛtɪs] *n* alface *f*.
let-up *n* diminuição *f*, afrouxamento.
leukaemia [lu:'ki:mɪə] (*US* **leukemia**) *n* leucemia.
level ['lɛvl] *adj* (*flat*) plano; (*flattened*) nivelado; (*uniform*) uniforme ♦ *adv* no mesmo nível ♦ *n* nível *m*; (*flat place*) plano; (*also*: *spirit* ~) nível de bolha ♦ *vt* nivelar, aplanar; (*gun*) apontar; (*accusation*): **to** ~ **(against)** dirigir *or* lançar (contra) ♦ *vi* (*inf*): **to** ~ **with sb** ser franco com alguém; **"A"** ~**s** *npl* (*BRIT*) ≈ vestibular *m*; **"O"** ~**s** *npl* (*BRIT*) *exames optativos feitos após o término do 1º Grau*; **a** ~ **spoonful** (*CULIN*) uma colherada rasa; **to be** ~ **with** estar no mesmo nível que; **to draw** ~ **with** (*team*) empatar com; (*runner, car*) alcançar; **on the** ~ em nível; (*fig*: *honest*) sincero.
level off *vi* (*prices etc*) estabilizar-se ♦ *vt* (*ground*) nivelar, aplanar.
level out *vi* (*prices etc*) estabilizar-se ♦ *vt* (*ground*) nivelar, aplanar.
level crossing (*BRIT*) *n* passagem *f* de nível.
level-headed [-'hɛdɪd] *adj* sensato.
levelling ['lɛvlɪŋ] (*US* **leveling**) *adj* (*process*) de nivelamento; (*effect*) nivelador(a).
lever ['li:və*] *n* alavanca ♦ *vt*: **to** ~ **up** levantar com alavanca.
leverage ['li:vərɪdʒ] *n* (*fig*: *influence*) influência.
levity ['lɛvɪtɪ] *n* leviandade *f*, frivolidade *f*.
levy ['lɛvɪ] *n* imposto, tributo ♦ *vt* arrecadar, cobrar.
lewd [lu:d] *adj* obsceno, lascivo.
LI (*US*) *abbr* = **Long Island.**
liability [laɪə'bɪlətɪ] *n* responsabilidade *f*; (*handicap*) desvantagem *f*; **liabilities** *npl* (*COMM*) exigibilidades *fpl*, obrigações *fpl*; (*on balance sheet*) passivo.
liable ['laɪəbl] *adj* (*subject*): ~ **to** sujeito a; (*responsible*): **to be** ~ **for** ser responsável por; **to be** ~ **to** (*likely*) ser capaz de; **to be** ~ **to a fine** ser passível de *or* sujeito a uma multa.
liaise [li:'eɪz] *vi*: **to** ~ **with** cooperar com.
liaison [li:'eɪzɔn] *n* (*coordination*) ligação *f*; (*affair*) relação *f* amorosa.
liar ['laɪə*] *n* mentiroso/a.
libel ['laɪbl] *n* difamação *f* ♦ *vt* caluniar, difamar.
libellous ['laɪbləs] (*US* **libelous**) *adj* difamatório.
liberal ['lɪbərl] *adj* liberal; (*generous*): ~ **with** generoso com ♦ *n*: **L**~ (*POL*) Liberal *m/f*.
liberality [lɪbə'rælɪtɪ] *n* (*generosity*) generosidade *f*.
liberalize ['lɪbərəlaɪz] *vt* liberalizar.
liberal-minded *adj* liberal.
liberate ['lɪbəreɪt] *vt* liberar, libertar.
liberation [lɪbə'reɪʃən] *n* liberação *f*, libertação *f*.
Liberia [laɪ'bɪərɪə] *n* Libéria.
Liberian [laɪ'bɪərɪən] *adj*, *n* liberiano/a.
liberty ['lɪbətɪ] *n* liberdade *f*; **to be at** ~ **to do** ser livre de fazer; **to take the** ~ **of doing sth** tomar a liberdade de fazer algo.
libido [lɪ'bi:dəu] *n* libido *f*.
Libra ['li:brə] *n* Libra, Balança.
librarian [laɪ'brɛərɪən] *n* bibliotecário/a.
library ['laɪbrərɪ] *n* biblioteca.
library book *n* livro de biblioteca.
libretto [lɪ'brɛtəu] *n* libreto.
Libya ['lɪbɪə] *n* Líbia.
Libyan ['lɪbɪən] *adj*, *n* líbio/a.
lice [laɪs] *npl of* **louse**.
licence ['laɪsns] (*US* **license**) *n* (*gen*, *COMM*) licença; (*also*: *driving* ~ (*BRIT*), *driver's license* (*US*)) carteira de motorista (*BR*), carta de condução (*PT*); (*excessive freedom*) libertinagem *f*; **import** ~ licença de importação; **produced under** ~ fabricado sob licença.
licence number (*BRIT*) *n* (*AUT*) número da placa.
license ['laɪsns] *n* (*US*) = **licence** ♦ *vt* autorizar, licenciar; (*car*) licenciar.
licensed ['laɪsnst] *adj* (*for alcohol*) autorizado para vender bebidas alcoólicas.
licensee [laɪsən'si:] (*BRIT*) *n* (*in a pub*) dono/a.
license plate (*esp US*) *n* (*AUT*) placa (de identificação) (*do carro*).
licentious [laɪ'sɛnʃəs] *adj* licencioso.
lichen ['laɪkən] *n* líquen *m*.
lick [lɪk] *vt* lamber; (*inf*: *defeat*) arrasar, surrar ♦ *n* lambida; **a** ~ **of paint** uma mão de pintura.
licorice ['lɪkərɪs] *n* = **liquorice**.
lid [lɪd] *n* (*of box, case, pan*) tampa; **to take the** ~ **off sth** (*fig*) desvendar algo.
lido ['laɪdəu] *n piscina pública ao ar livre*.
lie [laɪ] (*pt*, *pp* ~**d**) *n* mentira ♦ *vi* (*tell untruths*) mentir; (*pt* **lay**, *pp* **lain**) (*act*) deitar-se; (*state*) estar deitado; (*of object*: *be situated*) estar, encontrar-se; **to** ~ **low** (*fig*) esconder-se; **to tell** ~**s** dizer mentiras, mentir.
lie about *vi* (*things*) estar espalhado; (*people*) vadiar.
lie around *vi* (*things*) estar espalhado; (*people*) vadiar.
lie back *vi* recostar-se.

***NB:** European Portuguese adds the following consonants to certain words:* **b** (sú(b)dito, su(b)til); **c** (a(c)ção, a(c)cionista, a(c)to); **m** (inde(m)ne); **p** (ado(p)ção, ado(p)tar); *for further details see p. xiii.*

lie down *vi* deitar-se.
Liechtenstein ['lɪktənstaɪn] *n* Liechtenstein *m*.
lie detector *n* detector *m* de mentiras.
lie-down (*BRIT*) *n*: **to have a ~** descansar.
lie-in (*BRIT*) *n*: **to have a ~** dormir até tarde.
lieu [lu:]: **in ~ of** *prep* em vez de.
Lieut. *abbr* (= *lieutenant*) Ten.
lieutenant [lɛf'tɛnənt, (*US*) lu:'tɛnənt] *n* (*MIL*) tenente *m*.
lieutenant-colonel *n* tenente-coronel *m*.
life [laɪf] (*pl* **lives**) *n* vida ♦ *cpd* (*imprisonment*) perpétuo; (*style*) de vida; **true to ~** fiel à realidade; **to paint from ~** pintar copiando a natureza; **to be sent to prison for ~** ser condenado a prisão perpétua; **country/city ~** vida campestre/urbana.
life annuity *n* renda vitalícia.
life assurance (*BRIT*) *n* seguro de vida.
lifebelt ['laɪfbɛlt] (*BRIT*) *n* cinto salva-vidas.
lifeblood ['laɪfblʌd] *n* (*fig*) força vital.
lifeboat ['laɪfbəut] *n* barco salva-vidas.
lifebuoy ['laɪfbɔɪ] *n* bóia salva-vidas.
life expectancy *n* expectativa de vida.
lifeguard ['laɪfgɑ:d] *n* (guarda *m*) salva-vidas *m/f*.
life imprisonment *n* prisão *f* perpétua.
life insurance *n* seguro de vida.
life jacket *n* colete *m* salva-vidas.
lifeless ['laɪflɪs] *adj* sem vida; (*dull*) sem graça.
lifelike ['laɪflaɪk] *adj* natural.
lifeline ['laɪflaɪn] *n* corda salva-vidas.
lifelong ['laɪflɔŋ] *adj* vitalício, perpétuo.
life preserver [-prɪ'zə:və*] (*US*) *n* colete *m* salva-vidas.
life-raft *n* balsa salva-vidas.
life-saver [-'seɪvə*] *n* (guarda *m*) salva-vidas *m/f*.
life sentence *n* pena de prisão perpétua.
life-sized [-saɪzd] *adj* de tamanho natural.
life span *n* vida, duração *f*.
life style *n* estilo de vida.
life support system *n* (*MED*) sistema *m* de respiração artificial.
lifetime ['laɪftaɪm] *n*: **in his ~** durante a sua vida; **once in a ~** uma vez na vida; **the chance of a ~** uma oportunidade única.
lift [lɪft] *vt* levantar; (*steal*) roubar ♦ *vi* (*fog*) dispersar-se, dissipar-se ♦ *n* (*BRIT*: *elevator*) elevador *m*; **to give sb a ~** (*BRIT*) dar uma carona para alguém (*BR*), dar uma boleia a alguém (*PT*).
lift off *vi* (*rocket, helicopter*) decolar.
lift out *vt* tirar; (*troops etc*) evacuar de avião *or* helicóptero.
lift up *vt* levantar.
lift-off ['lɪftɔf] *n* decolagem *f*.
ligament ['lɪgəmənt] *n* ligamento.
light [laɪt] (*pt, pp* **~ed** *or* **lit**) *n* luz *f*; (*lamp*) luz, lâmpada; (*daylight*) (luz do) dia *m*; (*headlight*) farol *m*; (*rear ~*) luz traseira; (*traffic ~*) sinal *m*; (*for cigarette etc*): **have you got a ~?** tem fogo? ♦ *vt* (*candle, cigarette, fire*) acender; (*room*) iluminar ♦ *adj* (*colour, room*) claro; (*not heavy, also: fig*) leve ♦ *adv* (*travel*) com pouca bagagem; **to turn the ~ on/off** acender/apagar a luz; **to cast** *or* **shed** *or* **throw ~ on** esclarecer; **to come to ~** vir à tona; **in the ~ of ...** à luz de ...; **to make ~ of sth** (*fig*) não levar algo a sério, fazer pouco caso de algo.
light up *vi* (*smoke*) acender um cigarro; (*face*) iluminar-se ♦ *vt* (*illuminate*) iluminar; (*cigarette etc*) acender.
light bulb *n* lâmpada.
lighten ['laɪtən] *vi* (*grow light*) clarear ♦ *vt* (*give light to*) iluminar; (*make lighter*) clarear; (*make less heavy*) tornar mais leve.
lighter ['laɪtə*] *n* (*also*: *cigarette ~*) isqueiro, acendedor *m*; (*boat*) chata.
light-fingered [-'fɪŋgəd] *adj* gatuno; **to be ~** ter mão leve.
light-headed [-'hɛdɪd] *adj* (*dizzy*) aturdido, tonto; (*excited*) exaltado; (*by nature*) estouvado.
light-hearted *adj* alegre, despreocupado.
lighthouse ['laɪthaus] (*irreg*) *n* farol *m*.
lighting ['laɪtɪŋ] *n* (*act, system*) iluminação *f*.
lighting-up time (*BRIT*) *n* *hora oficial do anoitecer*.
lightly ['laɪtlɪ] *adv* (*touch*) ligeiramente; (*thoughtlessly*) despreocupadamente; (*slightly*) levemente; (*not seriously*) levianamente; **to get off ~** conseguir se safar, livrar a cara (*inf*).
light meter *n* (*PHOT*) fotômetro.
lightness ['laɪtnɪs] *n* claridade *f*; (*in weight*) leveza.
lightning ['laɪtnɪŋ] *n* relâmpago, raio.
lightning conductor (*US* **lightning rod**) *n* pára-raios *m inv*.
lightning strike (*BRIT*) *n* greve *f* relâmpago.
light pen *n* caneta leitora.
lightship ['laɪtʃɪp] *n* navio-farol *m*.
lightweight ['laɪtweɪt] *adj* (*suit*) leve; (*BOXING*) peso-leve.
light year *n* ano-luz *m*.
like [laɪk] *vt* gostar de ♦ *prep* como ♦ *adj* parecido, semelhante ♦ *n*: **the ~** coisas *fpl* parecidas; **his ~s and dislikes** seus gostos e aversões; **I would ~, I'd ~** (eu) gostaria de; **would you ~ a coffee?** você quer um café?; **to be** *or* **look ~ sb/sth** parecer-se com alguém/algo, parecer alguém/algo; **what's he ~?** como é que ele é?; **what's the weather ~?** como está o tempo?; **that's just ~ him** é típico dele; **something ~ that** uma coisa dessas; **I feel ~ a drink** estou com vontade de tomar um drinque; **if you ~** se você quiser; **it is nothing ~ ...** não se parece nada com ....
likeable ['laɪkəbl] *adj* simpático, agradável.
likelihood ['laɪklɪhud] *n* probabilidade *f*.
likely ['laɪklɪ] *adj* provável; (*excuse*) plausível; **he's ~ to leave** é provável que ele se vá; **not ~!** (*inf*) nem morto!
like-minded *adj* da mesma opinião.
liken ['laɪkən] *vt*: **to ~ sth to sth** comparar algo com algo.
likeness ['laɪknɪs] *n* semelhança.

likewise ['laɪkwaɪz] *adv* igualmente.
liking ['laɪkɪŋ] *n*: **to take a ~ to sb** simpatizar com alguém; **to his ~** ao seu gosto.
lilac ['laɪlək] *n* lilás *m* ♦ *adj* (*colour*) de cor lilás.
lilt [lɪlt] *n* cadência.
lilting ['lɪltɪŋ] *n* cadenciado.
lily ['lɪlɪ] *n* lírio, açucena; **~ of the valley** lírio-do-vale *m*.
Lima ['li:mə] *n* Lima.
limb [lɪm] *n* membro; **to be out on a ~** (*fig*) estar isolado.
limber up ['lɪmbə*-] *vi* (*SPORT*) fazer aquecimento.
limbo ['lɪmbəu] *n*: **to be in ~** (*fig*) viver na expectativa.
lime [laɪm] *n* (*tree*) limeira; (*fruit*) limão *m*; (*GEO*) cal *f*.
lime juice *n* suco (*BR*) *or* sumo (*PT*) de limão.
limelight ['laɪmlaɪt] *n*: **to be in the ~** (*fig*) ser o centro das atenções.
limerick ['lɪmərɪk] *n* quintilha humorística.
limestone ['laɪmstəun] *n* pedra calcária.
limit ['lɪmɪt] *n* limite *m* ♦ *vt* limitar; **weight/speed ~** limite de peso/de velocidade.
limitation [lɪmɪ'teɪʃən] *n* limitação *f*.
limited ['lɪmɪtɪd] *adj* limitado; **to be ~ to** limitar-se a; **~ edition** edição *f* limitada.
limited (liability) company (*BRIT*) *n* ≈ sociedade *f* anônima.
limitless ['lɪmɪtlɪs] *adj* ilimitado.
limousine ['lɪməzi:n] *n* limusine *f*.
limp [lɪmp] *n*: **to have a ~** mancar, ser coxo ♦ *vi* mancar ♦ *adj* frouxo.
limpet ['lɪmpɪt] *n* lapa.
limpid ['lɪmpɪd] *adj* límpido, cristalino.
linchpin ['lɪntʃpɪn] *n* cavilha; (*fig*) pivô *m*.
Lincs [lɪŋks] (*BRIT*) *abbr* = **Lincolnshire**.
line [laɪn] *n* linha; (*straight* ~) reta; (*rope*) corda; (*for fishing*) linha; (*US*: *queue*) fila (*BR*), bicha (*PT*); (*wire*) fio; (*row*) fila, fileira; (*of writing*) linha; (*on face*) ruga; (*speciality*) ramo (de negócio); (*COMM*: *type of goods*) linha ♦ *vt*: **to ~ (with)** (*coat etc*) forrar (de); **to ~ the streets** ladear as ruas; **to cut in ~** (*US*) furar a fila (*BR*), pôr-se à frente (*PT*); **in his ~ of business** no ramo dele; **on the right ~s** no caminho certo; **a new ~ in cosmetics** uma nova linha de cosméticos; **hold the ~ please** (*BRIT*: *TEL*) não desligue; **to be in ~ for sth** estar na bica para algo; **in ~ with** de acordo com; **to bring sth into ~ with sth** alinhar algo com algo; **to draw the ~ at doing sth** (*fig*) recusar-se a fazer algo; **to take the ~ that ...** ser de opinião que ....
line up *vi* enfileirar-se ♦ *vt* enfileirar; (*set up, have ready*) preparar, arranjar; **to have sth/sb ~d up** ter algo programado/alguém em vista.
linear ['lɪnɪə*] *adj* linear.
lined [laɪnd] *adj* (*face*) enrugado; (*paper*) pautado; (*clothes*) forrado.
line feed *n* (*COMPUT*) entrelinha.
linen ['lɪnɪn] *n* roupa branca *or* de cama; (*cloth*) linho.
line printer *n* impressora de linha.
liner ['laɪnə*] *n* navio de linha regular.
linesman ['laɪnzmən] (*irreg*) *n* (*SPORT*) juiz *m* de linha.
line-up *n* formação *f* em linha, alinhamento; (*players*) escalação *f*.
linger ['lɪŋgə*] *vi* demorar-se, retardar-se; (*smell, tradition*) persistir.
lingerie ['lænʒəri:] *n* lingerie *f*, roupa de baixo (de mulher).
lingering ['lɪŋgərɪŋ] *adj* persistente; (*death*) lento, vagaroso.
lingo ['lɪŋgəu] (*pl* **~es**) (*pej*) *n* língua.
linguist ['lɪŋgwɪst] *n* lingüista *m/f*.
linguistic [lɪŋ'gwɪstɪk] *adj* lingüístico.
linguistics [lɪŋ'gwɪstɪks] *n* lingüística.
lining ['laɪnɪŋ] *n* forro; (*TECH*) revestimento; (: *of brakes*) lona.
link [lɪŋk] *n* (*of a chain*) elo; (*connection*) conexão *f*; (*bond*) vínculo, laço ♦ *vt* vincular, unir; **~s** *npl* campo de golfe; **rail ~** ligação ferroviária.
link up *vt* acoplar ♦ *vi* unir-se.
link-up *n* ligação *f*; (*in space*) acoplamento; (*of roads*) junção *f*, confluência; (*RADIO, TV*) transmissão *f* em rede.
lino ['laɪnəu] *n* = **linoleum**.
linoleum [lɪ'nəulɪəm] *n* linóleo.
linseed oil ['lɪnsi:d-] *n* óleo de linhaça.
lint [lɪnt] *n* fibra de algodão; (*thread*) fio.
lintel ['lɪntl] *n* verga.
lion ['laɪən] *n* leão *m*.
lion cub *n* filhote *m* de leão.
lioness ['laɪənɪs] *n* leoa.
lip [lɪp] *n* lábio; (*of jug*) bico; (*of cup etc*) borda; (*insolence*) insolência.
lipread ['lɪpri:d] (*irreg*) *vi* ler os lábios.
lip salve *n* pomada para os lábios.
lip service *n*: **to pay ~ to sth** devotar-se a *or* elogiar algo falsamente.
lipstick ['lɪpstɪk] *n* batom *m*.
liquefy ['lɪkwɪfaɪ] *vt* liquefazer ♦ *vi* liquefazer-se.
liqueur [lɪ'kjuə*] *n* licor *m*.
liquid ['lɪkwɪd] *adj*, *n* líquido.
liquid assets *npl* ativo disponível, disponibilidades *fpl*.
liquidate ['lɪkwɪdeɪt] *vt* liquidar.
liquidation [lɪkwɪ'deɪʃən] *n*: **to go into ~** entrar em liquidação.
liquidation sale (*US*) *n* liquidação *f* (por motivo de fechamento).
liquidator ['lɪkwɪdeɪtə*] *n* liquidador(a) *m/f*.
liquid crystal display *n* display *m* digital em cristal líquido.
liquidity [lɪ'kwɪdətɪ] *n* (*COMM*) liquidez *f*.
liquidize ['lɪkwɪdaɪz] (*BRIT*) *vt* (*CULIN*) liqüidificar, passar no liqüidificador.

***NB**: European Portuguese adds the following consonants to certain words:* **b** (sú(b)dito, su(b)til); **c** (a(c)ção, a(c)cionista, a(c)to); **m** (inde(m)ne); **p** (ado(p)ção, ado(p)tar); *for further details see p. xiii.*

liquidizer ['lɪkwɪdaɪzə*] (*BRIT*) *n* (*CULIN*) liqüidificador *m*.
liquor ['lɪkə*] *n* licor *m*, bebida alcoólica.
liquorice ['lɪkərɪs] (*BRIT*) *n* alcaçuz *m*.
Lisbon ['lɪzbən] *n* Lisboa.
lisp [lɪsp] *n* ceceio ♦ *vi* cecear, falar com a língua presa.
lissom ['lɪsəm] *adj* gracioso, ágil.
list [lɪst] *n* lista; (*of ship*) inclinação *f* ♦ *vt* (*write down*) fazer uma lista *or* relação de; (*enumerate*) enumerar; (*COMPUT*) listar ♦ *vi* (*ship*) inclinar-se, adernar; **shopping ~** lista de compras.
listed building ['lɪstɪd-] *n* prédio tombado.
listed company ['lɪstɪd-] *n* ≈ sociedade *f* de capital aberto, sociedade cotada na Bolsa.
listen ['lɪsn] *vi* escutar, ouvir; (*pay attention*) prestar atenção; **to ~ to** escutar.
listener ['lɪsnə*] *n* ouvinte *m/f*.
listing ['lɪstɪŋ] *n* (*COMPUT*) listagem *f*.
listless ['lɪstlɪs] *adj* apático, indiferente.
listlessly ['lɪstlɪslɪ] *adv* apaticamente.
list price *n* preço de tabela.
lit [lɪt] *pt, pp of* **light**.
litany ['lɪtənɪ] *n* ladainha, litania.
liter ['li:tə*] (*US*) *n* = **litre**.
literacy ['lɪtərəsɪ] *n* capacidade *f* de ler e escrever, alfabetização *f*; **~ campaign** campanha de alfabetização.
literal ['lɪtərl] *adj* literal.
literally ['lɪtərəlɪ] *adv* literalmente.
literary ['lɪtərərɪ] *adj* literário.
literate ['lɪtərət] *adj* alfabetizado, instruído; (*fig*) culto, letrado.
literature ['lɪtərɪtʃə*] *n* literatura; (*brochures etc*) folhetos *mpl*.
lithe [laɪð] *adj* ágil, flexível.
lithography [lɪ'θɔgrəfɪ] *n* litografia.
Lithuania [lɪθju'eɪnɪə] *n* Lituânia.
litigate ['lɪtɪgeɪt] *vt, vi* litigar.
litigation [lɪtɪ'geɪʃən] *n* litígio.
litmus paper ['lɪtməs-] *n* papel *m* de tornassol.
litre ['li:tə*] (*US* **liter**) *n* litro.
litter ['lɪtə*] *n* (*rubbish*) lixo; (*paper*) papéis *mpl*; (*young animals*) ninhada; (*stretcher*) maca, padiola ♦ *vt* (*subj*: *person*) jogar lixo em; (: *papers etc*) estar espalhado por; **~ed with** (*scattered*) semeado de; (*covered*) coberto de.
litter bin (*BRIT*) *n* lata de lixo.
litterbug ['lɪtəbʌg] *n* sujismundo.
litter lout (*BRIT*) *n* = **litterbug**.
little ['lɪtl] *adj* (*small*) pequeno; (*not much*) pouco; *often translated by suffix*: *eg* **~ house** casinha ♦ *adv* pouco; **a ~** um pouco (de); **~ milk** pouco leite; **a ~ milk** um pouco de leite; **for a ~ while** por um instante; **with ~ difficulty** com pouca dificuldade; **as ~ as possible** o menos possível; **~ by ~** pouco a pouco; **to make ~ of** fazer pouco de.
little finger *n* dedo mindinho.
liturgy ['lɪtədʒɪ] *n* liturgia.
live [*vi, vt* lɪv, *adj* laɪv] *vi* viver; (*reside*) morar ♦ *vt* (*a life*) levar; (*experience*) viver ♦ *adj* (*animal*) vivo; (*wire*) eletrizado; (*broadcast*) ao vivo; (*shell*) carregado; **to ~ in London** morar em Londres; **to ~ together** viver juntos; **~ ammunition** munição de guerra.
live down *vt* redimir.
live in *vi* (*maid*) dormir no emprego; (*student, nurse*) ser interno/a.
live off *vt fus* (*land, fish etc*) viver de; (*pej*: *parents etc*) viver às custas de.
live on *vt fus* (*food*) viver de, alimentar-se de ♦ *vi* continuar vivo; **to ~ on £50 a week** viver com £50 por semana.
live out *vi* (*BRIT*: *student*) ser externo ♦ *vt*: **to ~ out one's days** *or* **life** viver o resto de seus dias.
live up (*inf*) *vt*: **to ~ it up** cair na farra.
live up to *vt fus* (*fulfil*) cumprir; (*justify*) justificar.
livelihood ['laɪvlɪhud] *n* meio de vida, subsistência.
liveliness ['laɪvlɪnɛs] *n* vivacidade *f*.
lively ['laɪvlɪ] *adj* vivo; (*talk*) animado; (*pace*) rápido; (*party, tune*) alegre.
liven up ['laɪvn-] *vt* (*room*) dar nova vida a; (*discussion, evening*) animar.
liver ['lɪvə*] *n* (*ANAT*) fígado.
liverish ['lɪvərɪʃ] *adj* (*fig*) rabugento, mal-humorado.
Liverpudlian [lɪvə'pʌdlɪən] *adj* de Liverpool ♦ *n* natural *m/f* de Liverpool.
livery ['lɪvərɪ] *n* libré *f*.
lives [laɪvz] *npl of* **life**.
livestock ['laɪvstɔk] *n* gado.
livid ['lɪvɪd] *adj* lívido; (*furious*) furioso.
living ['lɪvɪŋ] *adj* (*alive*) vivo ♦ *n*: **to earn** *or* **make a ~** ganhar a vida; **cost of ~** custo de vida; **within ~ memory** na memória de pessoas ainda vivas.
living conditions *npl* condições *fpl* de vida.
living expenses *npl* despesas *fpl* para sobrevivência quotidiana.
living room *n* sala de estar.
living standards *npl* padrão *m or* nível *m* de vida.
living wage *n* salário de subsistência.
lizard ['lɪzəd] *n* lagarto.
llama ['lɑ:mə] *n* lhama.
LLB *n abbr* (= *Bachelor of Laws*) *título universitário*.
LLD *n abbr* (= *Doctor of Laws*) *título universitário*.
LMT (*US*) *abbr* (= *Local Mean Time*) *hora local*.
load [ləud] *n* carga; (*weight*) peso ♦ *vt* (*gen, COMPUT*) carregar; (*fig*) cumular, encher; **a ~ of, ~s of** (*fig*) um monte de, uma porção de.
loaded ['ləudɪd] *adj* (*dice*) viciado; (*question, word*) intencionado; (*inf*: *rich*) cheio da nota; (: *drunk*) de porre.
loading bay ['ləudɪŋ-] *n* vão *m* de carregamento.
loaf [ləuf] (*pl* **loaves**) *n* (bisnaga de) pão *m* ♦ *vi* (*also*: *~ about, ~ around*) vadiar, vaga-

bundar.
loam [ləum] *n* marga.
loan [ləun] *n* empréstimo ♦ *vt* emprestar; **on ~** emprestado; **to raise a ~** levantar um empréstimo.
loan account *n* conta de empréstimo.
loan capital *n* capital-obrigações *m*.
loath [ləuθ] *adj*: **to be ~ to do sth** estar pouco inclinado a *or* relutar em fazer algo.
loathe [ləuð] *vt* detestar, odiar.
loathing ['ləuðɪŋ] *n* ódio; **it fills me with ~** me dá (um) ódio.
loathsome ['ləuðsəm] *adj* repugnante, asqueroso.
loaves [ləuvz] *npl of* **loaf**.
lob [lɔb] *n* (TENNIS) lobe *m* ♦ *vt*: **to ~ the ball** dar um lobe.
lobby ['lɔbɪ] *n* vestíbulo, saguão *m*; (POL: *pressure group*) grupo de pressão, lobby *m* ♦ *vt* pressionar.
lobbyist ['lɔbɪɪst] *n* membro de um grupo de pressão.
lobe [ləub] *n* lóbulo.
lobster ['lɔbstə*] *n* lagostim *m*; (*large*) lagosta.
lobster pot *n* armadilha para pegar lagosta.
local ['ləukl] *adj* local ♦ *n* (BRIT: *inf*: *pub*) bar *m* (local); **the ~s** *npl* os moradores locais.
local anaesthetic (US **local anesthetic**) *n* anestesia local.
local authority *n* município.
local call *n* (TEL) ligação *f* local.
local government *n* administração *f* municipal.
locality [ləu'kælɪtɪ] *n* localidade *f*.
localize ['ləukəlaɪz] *vt* localizar.
locally ['ləukəlɪ] *adv* nos arredores, na vizinhança.
locate [ləu'keɪt] *vt* (*find*) localizar, situar; (*situate*) colocar.
location [ləu'keɪʃən] *n* local *m*, posição *f*; **on ~** (CINEMA) em externas.
loch [lɔx] *n* lago.
lock [lɔk] *n* (*of door, box*) fechadura; (*of canal*) eclusa; (*of hair*) anel *m*, mecha ♦ *vt* (*with key*) trancar; (*immobilize*) travar ♦ *vi* (*door etc*) fechar-se à chave; (*wheels*) travar-se; **~ stock and barrel** (*fig*) com tudo; **on full ~** (BRIT: AUT) com o volante virado ao máximo.
lock away *vt* (*valuables*) guardar a sete chaves; (*person*) encarcerar.
lock in *vt* trancar dentro.
lock out *vt* trancar do lado de fora; (*on purpose*) deixar na rua; (: *workers*) recusar trabalho a.
lock up *vi* fechar tudo.
locker ['lɔkə*] *n* compartimento com chave.
locket ['lɔkɪt] *n* medalhão *m*.
lockjaw ['lɔkdʒɔː] *n* trismo.
lockout ['lɔkaut] *n* greve *f* de patrões, lockout *m*.
locksmith ['lɔksmɪθ] *n* serralheiro/a.
lock-up *n* (*prison*) prisão *f*; (*cell*) cela; (*also*: *~ garage*) compartimento seguro.
locomotive [ləukə'məutɪv] *n* locomotiva.
locum ['ləukəm] *n* (MED) (médico/a) interino/a.
locust ['ləukəst] *n* gafanhoto.
lodge [lɔdʒ] *n* casa do guarda, guarita; (*porter's*) portaria; (FREEMASONRY) loja ♦ *vi* (*person*): **to ~ (with)** alojar-se (na casa de) ♦ *vt* (*complaint*) apresentar; **to ~ (itself) in/between** cravar-se em/entre.
lodger ['lɔdʒə*] *n* inquilino/a, hóspede *m/f*.
lodging ['lɔdʒɪŋ] *n* alojamento; **~s** *npl* quarto (mobiliado); *see also* **board**.
lodging house (BRIT: *irreg*) *n* casa de hóspedes.
loft [lɔft] *n* sótão *m*.
lofty ['lɔftɪ] *adj* alto, elevado; (*haughty*) altivo, arrogante; (*sentiments, aims*) nobre.
log [lɔg] *n* (*of wood*) tronco, lenho; (*book*) = **logbook** ♦ *n abbr* (= *logarithm*) log *m* ♦ *vt* registrar.
log in *vi* (COMPUT) iniciar o uso, logar.
log on *vi* (COMPUT) iniciar o uso, logar.
log off *vi* (COMPUT) encerrar o uso, dar logoff.
log out *vi* (COMPUT) encerrar o uso, dar logoff.
logarithm ['lɔgərɪðəm] *n* logaritmo.
logbook ['lɔgbuk] *n* (NAUT) diário de bordo; (AVIAT) diário de vôo; (*of car*) documentação *f* (do carro).
log cabin *n* cabana de madeira.
log fire *n* fogueira.
loggerheads ['lɔgəhɛdz] *npl*: **at ~ (with)** às turras (com).
logic ['lɔdʒɪk] *n* lógica.
logical ['lɔdʒɪkl] *adj* lógico.
logically ['lɔdʒɪkəlɪ] *adv* logicamente.
logistics [lɔ'dʒɪstɪks] *n* logística.
logo ['ləugəu] *n* logotipo.
loin [lɔɪn] *n* (CULIN) (carne de) lombo; **~s** *npl* lombos *mpl*.
loin cloth *n* tanga.
loiter ['lɔɪtə*] *vi* perder tempo; (*pej*) vadiar, vagabundar.
loll [lɔl] *vi* (*also*: *~ about*) refestelar-se, reclinar-se.
lollipop ['lɔlɪpɔp] *n* pirulito (BR), chupa-chupa *m* (PT); (*iced*) picolé *m*.
lollipop lady (BRIT) *n mulher que ajuda as crianças a atravessarem a rua.*
lollipop man (BRIT: *irreg*) *n homem que ajuda as crianças a atravessarem a rua.*
lollop ['lɔləp] (BRIT) *vi* andar com pachorra.
London ['lʌndən] *n* Londres.
Londoner ['lʌndənə*] *n* londrino/a.
lone [ləun] *adj* solitário.
loneliness ['ləunlɪnɪs] *n* solidão *f*, isolamento.
lonely ['ləunlɪ] *adj* (*person*) só; (*place, childhood*) solitário, isolado; **to feel ~**

NB: European Portuguese adds the following consonants to certain words: **b** (sú(b)dito, su(b)til); **c** (a(c)ção, a(c)cionista, a(c)to); **m** (inde(m)ne); **p** (ado(p)ção, ado(p)tar); *for further details see p. xiii.*

sentir-se só.
loner ['ləunə*] *n* solitário/a.
lonesome ['ləunsəm] *adj* (*person*) só; (*place*, *childhood*) solitário.
long [lɔŋ] *adj* comprido, longo ♦ *adv* muito tempo ♦ *n*: **the ~ and the short of it is that ...** (*fig*) em poucas palavras ... ♦ *vi*: **to ~ for sth** ansiar *or* suspirar por algo; **he had ~ understood that ...** fazia muito tempo que ele entendia ...; **how ~ is the street?** qual é a extensão da rua?; **how ~ is the lesson?** quanto dura a lição?; **6 metres ~** de 6 metros de extensão, que mede 6 metros; **6 months ~** de 6 meses de duração, que dura 6 meses; **all night ~** a noite inteira; **he no ~er comes** ele não vem mais; **~ before** muito antes; **before ~** (+ *future*) dentro de pouco; (+ *past*) pouco tempo depois; **~ ago** há muito tempo atrás; **don't be ~!** não demore!; **I shan't be ~** não vou demorar; **at ~ last** por fim, no final; **in the ~ run** no final de contas; **so** *or* **as ~ as** contanto que.
long-distance *adj* (*race*) de longa distância; (*call*) interurbano.
long-haired *adj* (*person*) cabeludo; (*animal*) peludo.
longhand ['lɔŋhænd] *n* escrita usual.
longing ['lɔŋɪŋ] *n* desejo, anseio; (*nostalgia*) saudade *f* ♦ *adj* saudoso.
longingly ['lɔŋɪŋlɪ] *adv* ansiosamente; (*nostalgically*) saudosamente.
longitude ['lɔŋgɪtju:d] *n* longitude *f*.
long johns [-dʒɔnz] *npl* ceroulas *fpl*.
long jump *n* salto em distância.
long-lost *adj* perdido há muito (tempo).
long-playing record [-'pleɪɪŋ-] *n* elepê *m* (*BR*), LP *m* (*PT*).
long-range *adj* de longo alcance; (*weather forecast*) a longo prazo.
longshoreman ['lɔŋʃɔ:mən] (*US*: *irreg*) *n* estivador *m*, portuário.
long-sighted *adj* (*BRIT*) presbita; (*fig*) previdente.
long-standing *adj* de muito tempo.
long-suffering *adj* paciente, resignado.
long-term *adj* a longo prazo.
long wave *n* (*RADIO*) onda longa.
long-winded [-'wɪndɪd] *adj* prolixo, cansativo.
loo [lu:] (*BRIT*: *inf*) *n* banheiro (*BR*), casa de banho (*PT*).
loofah ['lu:fə] *n* tipo de esponja.
look [luk] *vi* olhar; (*seem*) parecer; (*building etc*): **to ~ south/on to the sea** dar para o sul/o mar ♦ *n* olhar *m*; (*glance*) olhada, vista de olhos; (*appearance*) aparência, aspecto; (*style*) visual *m*; **~s** *npl* físico, aparência; **to ~ like sb** parecer-se com alguém; **it ~s like him** parece ele; **it ~s about 4 metres long** parece ter uns 4 metros de comprimento; **it ~s all right to me** para mim está bem; **to have a ~ at sth** dar uma olhada em algo; **to have a ~ for sth** procurar algo; **to ~ ahead** olhar para a frente; (*fig*) pensar no futuro.
look after *vt fus* cuidar de; (*luggage etc*: *watch over*) ficar de olho em.
look around *vi* olhar em torno; (*in shop*) dar uma olhada.
look at *vt fus* olhar (para); (*consider*) considerar.
look back *vi*: **to ~ back at sth/sb** voltar-se para ver algo/alguém; **to ~ back on** (*event*, *period*) recordar, rever.
look down on *vt fus* (*fig*) desdenhar, desprezar.
look for *vt fus* procurar.
look forward to *vt fus* aguardar com prazer, ansiar por; **to ~ forward to doing sth** não ver a hora de fazer algo; **I'm not ~ing forward to it** não estou nada animado com isso; **~ing forward to hearing from you** (*in letter*) no aguardo de suas notícias.
look in *vi*: **to ~ in on sb** dar uma passada na casa de alguém.
look into *vt fus* investigar.
look on *vi* assistir.
look out *vi* (*beware*): **to ~ out (for)** tomar cuidado (com).
look out for *vt fus* (*seek*) procurar; (*await*) esperar.
look over *vt* (*essay*) dar uma olhada em; (*town*, *building*) visitar; (*person*) olhar da cabeça aos pés.
look round *vi* virar a cabeça, voltar-se; **to ~ round for sth** procurar algo.
look through *vt fus* (*papers*, *book*) examinar; (: *briefly*) folhear; (*telescope*) olhar através de.
look to *vt fus* cuidar de; (*rely on*) contar com.
look up *vi* levantar os olhos; (*improve*) melhorar ♦ *vt* (*word*) procurar; (*friend*) visitar.
look up to *vt fus* admirar, respeitar.
look-out *n* (*tower etc*) posto de observação, guarita; (*person*) vigia *m*; **to be on the ~ for sth** estar na expectativa de algo.
look-up table *n* (*COMPUT*) tabela de pesquisa.
LOOM (*US*) *n abbr* (= *Loyal Order of Moose*) *associação beneficente*.
loom [lu:m] *n* tear *m* ♦ *vi* assomar-se; (*threaten*) ameaçar.
loony ['lu:nɪ] (*inf*) *adj* meio doido ♦ *n* débil *m*/*f* mental.
loony bin (*inf*) *n* hospício, manicômio.
loop [lu:p] *n* laço; (*bend*) volta, curva; (*contraceptive*) DIU *m*.
loophole ['lu:phəul] *n* escapatória.
loose [lu:s] *adj* (*not fixed*) solto; (*not tight*) frouxo; (*animal*) solto; (*clothes*) folgado; (*morals*, *discipline*) relaxado; (*sense*) impreciso ♦ *vt* (*free*) soltar; (*slacken*) afrouxar; **~ connection** (*ELEC*) conexão solta; **to be at a ~ end** (*BRIT*) *or* **at ~ ends** (*US*) (*fig*) não ter o que fazer; **to tie up ~ ends (of sth)** (*fig*) amarrar (algo).
loose change *n* trocado.
loose-fitting *adj* (*clothes*) folgado, largo.
loose-leaf *adj*: **~ binder** *or* **folder** pasta de folhas soltas.
loose-limbed [-'lɪmd] *adj* ágil.
loosely ['lu:slɪ] *adv* frouxamente, folgada-

mente; (*not closely*) aproximativamente.
loosen ['lu:sən] *vt* (*free*) soltar; (*untie*) desatar; (*slacken*) afrouxar.
loosen up *vi* (*before game*) aquecer; (*inf: relax*) descontrair-se.
loot [lu:t] *n* saque *m*, despojo ♦ *vt* saquear, pilhar.
looter ['lu:tə*] *n* saqueador(a) *m/f*.
looting ['lu:tɪŋ] *n* saque *m*, pilhagem *f*.
lop off [lɔp-] *vt* cortar; (*branches*) podar.
lop-sided [-'saɪdɪd] *adj* desequilibrado, torto.
lord [lɔ:d] *n* senhor *m*; **L~ Smith** Lord Smith; **the L~** (*REL*) o Senhor; **the (House of) L~s** (*BRIT*) a Câmara dos Lordes.
lordly ['lɔ:dlɪ] *adj* senhorial; (*arrogant*) arrogante.
lordship ['lɔ:dʃɪp] (*BRIT*) *n*: **Your L~** Vossa senhoria.
lore [lɔ:*] *n* sabedoria popular, tradições *fpl*.
lorry ['lɔrɪ] (*BRIT*) *n* caminhão *m* (*BR*), camião *m* (*PT*).
lorry driver (*BRIT*) *n* caminhoneiro (*BR*), camionista *m/f* (*PT*).
lorry load (*BRIT*) *n* carga de caminhão.
lose [lu:z] (*pt, pp* **lost**) *vt, vi* perder; **to ~ (time)** (*clock*) atrasar-se; **to ~ no time (in doing sth)** não demorar (a fazer algo); **to get lost** (*person*) perder-se; (*thing*) extraviar-se.
loser ['lu:zə*] *n* perdedor(a) *m/f*; **to be a good/bad ~** ser bom/mau perdedor.
loss [lɔs] *n* perda; **to cut one's ~es** reduzir os prejuízos; **to make a ~** sair com prejuízo; **to sell sth at a ~** vender algo com prejuízo; **to be at a ~** estar perplexo; **to be at a ~ to do** ser incapaz de fazer; **to be a dead ~** ser totalmente inútil.
loss adjuster *n* (*INSURANCE*) árbitro regulador de avarias.
loss leader *n* (*COMM*) chamariz *m*.
lost [lɔst] *pt, pp of* **lose** ♦ *adj* perdido; **~ in thought** perdido em seus pensamentos; **~ and found property** (*US*) (objetos *mpl*) perdidos e achados *mpl*; **~ and found** (*US*) (seção *f* de) perdidos e achados *mpl*.
lost property (*BRIT*) *n* (objetos *mpl*) perdidos e achados *mpl*; **~ office** *or* **department** (seção *f* de) perdidos e achados *mpl*.
lot [lɔt] *n* (*at auctions*) lote *m*; (*destiny*) destino, sorte *f*; **the ~** tudo, todos/as; **a ~** muito, bastante; **a ~ of, ~s of** muito(s); **to draw ~s** tirar à sorte; **I read a ~** leio bastante; **parking ~** (*US*) estacionamento.
lotion ['ləuʃən] *n* loção *f*.
lottery ['lɔtərɪ] *n* loteria.
loud [laud] *adj* (*voice*) alto; (*shout*) forte; (*noisy*) barulhento; (*gaudy*) berrante ♦ *adv* alto; **out ~** alto.
loudhailer [laud'heɪlə*] (*BRIT*) *n* megafone *m*.
loudly ['laudlɪ] *adv* (*noisily*) ruidosamente; (*aloud*) em voz alta.
loudspeaker [laud'spi:kə*] *n* alto-falante *m*.
lounge [laundʒ] *n* sala de estar *f*; (*of airport*) salão *m* ♦ *vi* recostar-se, espreguiçar-se.
lounge bar *n* bar *m* social.
lounge suit (*BRIT*) *n* terno (*BR*), fato (*PT*).
louse [laus] (*pl* **lice**) *n* piolho.
louse up (*inf*) *vt* estragar.
lousy ['lauzɪ] *adj* (*fig*) ruim, péssimo.
lout [laut] *n* rústico, grosseiro.
louvre ['lu:və*] (*US* **louver**) *adj*: **~ door** porta de veneziana; **~ window** veneziana.
lovable ['lʌvəbl] *adj* adorável, simpático.
love [lʌv] *n* amor *m* ♦ *vt* amar, adorar; **I ~ coffee** adoro o café; **to ~ to do** gostar muito de fazer; **I'd ~ to come** gostaria muito de ir; **"15 ~"** (*TENNIS*) "15 a zero"; **to be in ~ with** estar apaixonado por; **to fall in ~ with sb** apaixonar-se por alguém; **to make ~** fazer amor; **~ at first sight** amor à primeira vista; **for the ~ of** pelo amor de; **to send one's ~ to sb** mandar um abraço para alguém; **~ from Anne, ~, Anne** um abraço *or* um beijo, Anne.
love affair *n* aventura (amorosa), caso (de amor).
love letter *n* carta de amor.
love life (*irreg*) *n* vida sentimental.
lovely ['lʌvlɪ] *adj* (*delightful*) encantador(a), delicioso; (*beautiful*) lindo, belo; (*holiday, surprise*) muito agradável, maravilhoso; **we had a ~ time** foi maravilhoso, nós nos divertimos muito.
lover ['lʌvə*] *n* amante *m/f*; (*amateur*): **a ~ of** um(a) apreciador(a) de *or* um(a) amante de.
lovesick ['lʌvsɪk] *adj* perdido de amor.
lovesong ['lʌvsɔŋ] *n* canção *f* de amor.
loving ['lʌvɪŋ] *adj* carinhoso, afetuoso.
low [ləu] *adj, adv* baixo ♦ *n* (*METEOROLOGY*) área de baixa pressão ♦ *vi* (*cow*) mugir; **to feel ~** sentir-se deprimido; **to turn (down) ~** *vt* baixar, diminuir; **to reach a new** *or* **an all-time ~** cair para o seu nível mais baixo.
lowbrow ['ləubrau] *adj* sem pretensões intelectuais.
low-calorie *adj* baixo em calorias, de baixo teor calórico.
low-cut *adj* (*dress*) decotado.
low-down *n* (*inf*): **he gave me the ~ on it** me deu a dica sobre isso ♦ *adj* (*mean*) vil, desprezível.
lower[1] ['ləuə*] *vt* abaixar; (*reduce*) reduzir, diminuir; **to ~ o.s. to** (*fig*) rebaixar-se a.
lower[2] ['lauə*] *vi* (*sky, clouds*) escurecer; (*person*): **to ~ at sb** olhar para alguém com raiva.
low-fat *adj* magro.
low-grade *adj* de baixa qualidade.
low-key *adj* discreto.
lowland ['ləulənd] *n* planície *f*.
low-level *adj* de baixo nível, baixo; (*flying*) a baixa altura.
lowly ['ləulɪ] *adj* humilde.

NB: European Portuguese adds the following consonants to certain words: **b** (sú(b)dito, su(b)til); **c** (a(c)ção, a(c)cionista, a(c)to); **m** (inde(m)ne); **p** (ado(p)ção, ado(p)tar); *for further details see p. xiii.*

low-lying *adj* de baixo nível.
low-paid *adj* (*person*) de renda baixa; (*work*) mal pago.
loyal ['lɔɪəl] *adj* leal.
loyalist ['lɔɪəlɪst] *n* legalista *m/f*.
loyalty ['lɔɪəltɪ] *n* lealdade *f*.
lozenge ['lɔzɪndʒ] *n* (MED) pastilha; (GEOM) losango, rombo.
LP *n abbr* = **long-playing record.**
L-plates ['ɛlpleɪts] (BRIT) *npl* placas *fpl* de aprendiz de motorista.
LPN (US) *n abbr* (= *Licensed Practical Nurse*) enfermeiro/a diplomado/a.
LRAM (BRIT) *n abbr* = **Licentiate of the Royal Academy of Music.**
LSAT (US) *n abbr* = **Law Schools Admissions Test.**
LSD *n abbr* (= *lysergic acid diethylamide*) LSD *m*; (BRIT: = *pounds, shillings and pence*) *sistema monetário usado na Grã-Bretanha até 1971.*
LSE *n abbr* = **London School of Economics.**
LT *abbr* (ELEC: = *low tension*) BT.
Lt. *abbr* (= *lieutenant*) Ten.
Ltd (BRIT) *abbr* (= *limited* (*liability*) *company*) SA.
lubricant ['lu:brɪkənt] *n* lubrificante *m*.
lubricate ['lu:brɪkeɪt] *vt* lubrificar.
lucid ['lu:sɪd] *adj* lúcido.
lucidity [lu:'sɪdɪtɪ] *n* lucidez *f*.
luck [lʌk] *n* sorte *f*; **bad ~** azar *m*; **to be in ~** ter *or* dar sorte; **to be out of ~** ter azar; **good ~!** boa sorte!
luckily ['lʌkɪlɪ] *adv* por sorte, felizmente.
lucky ['lʌkɪ] *adj* (*person*) sortudo; (*coincidence*) feliz; (*number etc*) da sorte.
lucrative ['lu:krətɪv] *adj* lucrativo.
ludicrous ['lu:dɪkrəs] *adj* ridículo.
ludo ['lu:dəu] *n* ludo.
lug [lʌg] *vt* (*drag*) arrastar; (*pull*) puxar.
luggage ['lʌgɪdʒ] *n* bagagem *f*.
luggage car (US) *n* (RAIL) vagão *m* de bagagens.
luggage rack *n* (*in train*) rede *f* para bagagem; (*on car*) porta-bagagem *m*, bagageiro.
luggage van (BRIT) *n* (RAIL) vagão *m* de bagagens.
lugubrious [lu'gu:brɪəs] *adj* lúgubre.
lukewarm ['lu:kwɔ:m] *adj* morno, tépido; (*fig*) indiferente.
lull [lʌl] *n* calmaria ♦ *vt* (*child*) embalar, acalentar; (*person, fear*) acalmar.
lullaby ['lʌləbaɪ] *n* canção *f* de ninar.
lumbago [lʌm'beɪgəu] *n* lumbago.
lumber ['lʌmbə*] *n* (*junk*) trastes *mpl* velhos; (*wood*) madeira serrada, tábua ♦ *vt* (BRIT: *inf*): **to ~ sb with sth/sb** empurrar algo/alguém para cima de alguém ♦ *vi* (*also*: ~ *about*, ~ *along*) mover-se pesadamente.
lumberjack ['lʌmbədʒæk] *n* madeireiro, lenhador *m*.
lumber room (BRIT) *n* quarto de despejo.
lumber yard *n* depósito de madeira.
luminous ['lu:mɪnəs] *adj* luminoso.
lump [lʌmp] *n* torrão *m*; (*fragment*) pedaço; (*in sauce*) caroço; (*in throat*) nó *m*; (*swelling*) galo, caroço ♦ *vt* (*also*: ~ *together*) amontoar.
lump sum *n* quantia global.
lumpy ['lʌmpɪ] *adj* (*sauce*) encaroçado.
lunacy ['lu:nəsɪ] *n* loucura.
lunar ['lu:nə*] *adj* lunar.
lunatic ['lu:nətɪk] *adj*, *n* louco/a.
lunatic asylum *n* manicômio, hospício.
lunch [lʌntʃ] *n* almoço ♦ *vi* almoçar; **to invite sb for ~** convidar alguém para almoçar.
luncheon ['lʌntʃən] *n* almoço formal.
luncheon meat *n* bolo de carne.
luncheon voucher *n* vale *m* para refeição, ticket *m* restaurante.
lunch hour *n* hora do almoço.
lunchtime ['lʌntʃtaɪm] *n* hora do almoço.
lung [lʌŋ] *n* pulmão *m*.
lung cancer *n* câncer *m* (BR) *or* cancro (PT) de pulmão.
lunge [lʌndʒ] *vi* (*also*: ~ *forward*) dar estocada *or* bote; **to ~ at** arremeter-se contra.
lupin ['lu:pɪn] *n* tremoço.
lurch [lə:tʃ] *vi* balançar ♦ *n* sacudida, solavanco; **to leave sb in the ~** deixar alguém em apuros, deixar alguém na mão (*inf*).
lure [luə*] *n* (*bait*) isca; (*decoy*) chamariz *m*, engodo ♦ *vt* atrair, seduzir.
lurid ['luərɪd] *adj* (*account*) sensacional; (*detail*) horrível.
lurk [lə:k] *vi* (*hide*) esconder-se; (*wait*) estar à espreita.
luscious ['lʌʃəs] *adj* delicioso.
lush [lʌʃ] *adj* exuberante.
lust [lʌst] *n* luxúria; (*greed*) cobiça.
lust after *vt fus* cobiçar.
luster ['lʌstə*] (US) *n* = **lustre.**
lustful ['lʌstful] *adj* lascivo, sensual.
lustre ['lʌstə*] (US **luster**) *n* lustre *m*, brilho.
lusty ['lʌstɪ] *adj* robusto, forte.
lute [lu:t] *n* alaúde *m*.
Luxembourg ['lʌksəmbə:g] *n* Luxemburgo.
luxuriant [lʌg'zjuərɪənt] *adj* luxuriante, exuberante.
luxurious [lʌg'zjuərɪəs] *adj* luxuoso.
luxury ['lʌkʃərɪ] *n* luxo ♦ *cpd* de luxo.
LV (BRIT) *n abbr* = **luncheon voucher.**
LW *abbr* (RADIO: = *long wave*) OL.
lying ['laɪɪŋ] *n* mentira(s) *f(pl)* ♦ *adj* mentiroso, falso.
lynch [lɪntʃ] *vt* linchar.
lynching ['lɪntʃɪŋ] *n* linchamento.
lynx [lɪŋks] *n* lince *m*.
lyre ['laɪə*] *n* lira.
lyric ['lɪrɪk] *adj* lírico.
lyrical ['lɪrɪkəl] *adj* lírico.
lyricism ['lɪrɪsɪzəm] *n* lirismo.
lyrics ['lɪrɪks] *npl* (*of song*) letra.

M

M, m [ɛm] *n* (*letter*) M, m *m*; **M for Mary** (*BRIT*) *or* **Mike** (*US*) M de Maria.
M *n abbr* (*BRIT*: = *motorway*): **the M8** ≈ BR 8 *f*; (= *medium*) M.
m *abbr* (= *metre*) m; (= *mile*) mil.; = **million**.
MA *abbr* (*SCH*) = **Master of Arts**; (*US*) = **military academy**; (: *POST*) = **Massachusetts**.
mac [mæk] (*BRIT*) *n* capa impermeável.
macabre [mə'kɑːbrə] *adj* macabro.
Macao [mə'kau] *n* Macau.
macaroni [mækə'rəunɪ] *n* macarrão *m*.
macaroon [mækə'ruːn] *n* biscoitinho de amêndoas.
mace [meɪs] *n* (*BOT*) macis *m*; (*sceptre*) bastão *m*.
machinations [mækɪ'neɪʃənz] *npl* maquinações *fpl*, intrigas *fpl*.
machine [mə'ʃiːn] *n* máquina ♦ *vt* (*dress etc*) costurar à máquina; (*TECH*) usinar.
machine code *n* (*COMPUT*) código de máquina.
machine gun *n* metralhadora.
machine language *n* (*COMPUT*) linguagem *f* de máquina.
machine readable *adj* (*COMPUT*) legível por máquina.
machinery [mə'ʃiːnərɪ] *n* maquinaria; (*fig*) mecanismo.
machine shop *n* oficina mecânica.
machine tool *n* máquina-ferramenta *f*.
machine washable *adj* (*garment*) lavável à máquina.
machinist [mə'ʃiːnɪst] *n* operário/a (de máquina); (*RAIL*) maquinista *m/f*.
macho ['mætʃəu] *adj* machista.
mackerel ['mækrl] *n inv* cavala.
mackintosh ['mækɪntɔʃ] (*BRIT*) *n* capa impermeável.
macro... ['mækrəu] *prefix* macro....
macro-economics *n* macroeconomia.
mad [mæd] *adj* louco; (*angry*) furioso, brabo; **to go ~** enlouquecer; **to be ~ (keen) about** *or* **on sth** (*inf*) ser louco por algo.
madam ['mædəm] *n* senhora, madame *f*; **yes, ~** sim, senhora; **M~ Chairman** Senhora Presidente; **can I help you, ~?** a senhora já foi atendida?
madden ['mædn] *vt* exasperar.
maddening ['mædnɪŋ] *adj* exasperante.
made [meɪd] *pt, pp of* **make**.
Madeira [mə'dɪərə] *n* (*GEO*) Madeira; (*wine*) (vinho) Madeira *m*.
Madeiran [mə'dɪərən] *adj*, *n* madeirense *m/f*.
made-to-measure (*BRIT*) *adj* feito sob medida.
madly ['mædlɪ] *adv* loucamente.
madman ['mædmən] (*irreg*) *n* louco.
madness ['mædnɪs] *n* loucura.
Madrid [mə'drɪd] *n* Madri (*BR*), Madrid (*PT*).
Mafia ['mæfɪə] *n* máfia.
mag. [mæg] (*BRIT*: *inf*) *n abbr* = **magazine** (*PRESS*).
magazine [mægə'ziːn] *n* (*PRESS*) revista; (*MIL*: *store*) depósito; (*of firearm*) câmara.
magazine rack *n* porta-revistas *m inv*.
maggot ['mægət] *n* larva de inseto.
magic ['mædʒɪk] *n* magia, mágica ♦ *adj* mágico.
magical ['mædʒɪkl] *adj* mágico.
magician [mə'dʒɪʃən] *n* mago/a; (*entertainer*) mágico/a.
magistrate ['mædʒɪstreɪt] *n* magistrado/a, juiz/juíza *m/f*.
magnanimous [mæg'nænɪməs] *adj* magnânimo.
magnate ['mægneɪt] *n* magnata *m*.
magnesium [mæg'niːzɪəm] *n* magnésio.
magnet ['mægnɪt] *n* ímã *m*, iman *m* (*PT*).
magnetic [mæg'nɛtɪk] *adj* magnético.
magnetic disk *n* (*COMPUT*) disco magnético.
magnetic tape *n* fita magnética.
magnetism ['mægnɪtɪzəm] *n* magnetismo.
magnification [mægnɪfɪ'keɪʃən] *n* aumento.
magnificence [mæg'nɪfɪsns] *n* magnificência.
magnificent [mæg'nɪfɪsnt] *adj* magnífico.
magnify ['mægnɪfaɪ] *vt* aumentar.
magnifying glass ['mægnɪfaɪɪŋ-] *n* lupa, lente *f* de aumento.
magnitude ['mægnɪtjuːd] *n* magnitude *f*.
magnolia [mæg'nəulɪə] *n* magnólia.
magpie ['mægpaɪ] *n* pega.
mahogany [mə'hɔgənɪ] *n* mogno, acaju *m* ♦ *cpd* de mogno *or* acaju.
maid [meɪd] *n* empregada; **old ~** (*pej*) solteirona.
maiden ['meɪdn] *n* moça, donzela ♦ *adj* (*aunt etc*) solteirona; (*speech*, *voyage*) inaugural.
maiden name *n* nome *m* de solteira.
mail [meɪl] *n* correio; (*letters*) cartas *fpl* ♦ *vt* (*post*) pôr no correio; (*send*) mandar pelo correio; **by ~** pelo correio.
mailbox ['meɪlbɔks] *n* (*US*: *for letters*) caixa do correio; (*COMPUT*) caixa de entrada.
mailing list ['meɪlɪŋ-] *n* lista de clientes, mailing list *m*.
mailman ['meɪlmæn] (*US*: *irreg*) *n* carteiro.
mail order *n* pedido por reembolso postal; (*business*) venda por correspondência ♦ *cpd*: **mail-order firm** *or* **house** firma de vendas por correspondência.
mailshot ['meɪlʃɔt] (*BRIT*) *n* mailing *m*.
mail train *n* trem-correio, trem *m* postal.

***NB:** European Portuguese adds the following consonants to certain words:* **b** (sú(b)dito, su(b)til); **c** (a(c)ção, a(c)cionista, a(c)to); **m** (inde(m)ne); **p** (ado(p)ção, ado(p)tar); *for further details see p. xiii.*

mail truck (*US*) *n* (*AUT*) = **mail van.**
mail van (*BRIT*) *n* (*AUT*) furgão *m* do correio; (*RAIL*) vagão *m* postal.
maim [meɪm] *vt* mutilar, aleijar.
main [meɪn] *adj* principal ♦ *n* (*pipe*) cano *or* esgoto principal; **the ~s** *npl* (*ELEC*) a rede elétrica; **in the ~** na maior parte.
main course *n* (*CULIN*) prato principal.
mainframe ['meɪnfreɪm] *n* (*also*: *~ computer*) mainframe *m*.
mainland ['meɪnlənd] *n* continente *m*.
mainline ['meɪnlaɪn] (*inf*) *vt* (*heroin*) picar-se com ♦ *vi* picar-se, aplicar-se.
main line *n* (*RAIL*) linha-tronco *f* ♦ *adj*: **main-line** de linha-tronco.
mainly ['meɪnlɪ] *adv* principalmente.
main road *n* estrada principal.
mainstay ['meɪnsteɪ] *n* (*fig*) esteio.
mainstream ['meɪnstri:m] *n* (*fig*) corrente *f* principal.
maintain [meɪn'teɪn] *vt* manter; (*keep up*) conservar (em bom estado); (*affirm*) sustentar, afirmar; **to ~ that ...** afirmar que ....
maintenance ['meɪntənəns] *n* manutenção *f*; (*LAW*: *alimony*) alimentos *mpl*, pensão *f* alimentícia.
maintenance contract *n* contrato de assistência técnica.
maintenance order *n* (*LAW*) ordem *f* de pensão.
maisonette [meɪzə'nɛt] (*BRIT*) *n* duplex *m*.
maize [meɪz] *n* milho.
Maj. *abbr* (*MIL*) = **major.**
majestic [mə'dʒɛstɪk] *adj* majestoso.
majesty ['mædʒɪstɪ] *n* majestade *f*.
major ['meɪdʒə*] *n* (*MIL*) major *m* ♦ *adj* (*main*) principal; (*considerable*) importante; (*great*) grande; (*MUS*) maior ♦ *vi* (*US*: *SCH*): **to ~ (in)** especializar-se (em); **a ~ operation** (*MED*) uma operação séria.
Majorca [mə'jɔ:kə] *n* Maiorca.
major general *n* (*MIL*) general-de-divisão *m*.
majority [mə'dʒɔrɪtɪ] *n* maioria ♦ *cpd* (*verdict*, *holding*) majoritário.
make [meɪk] (*pt*, *pp* **made**) *n* marca ♦ *vt* fazer; (*manufacture*) fabricar, produzir; (*cause to be*): **to ~ sb sad** entristecer alguém, fazer alguém ficar triste; (*force*): **to ~ sb do sth** fazer com que alguém faça algo; (*equal*): **2 and 2 ~ 4** dois e dois são quatro; **to ~ do with** contentar-se com; **to ~ it** (*in time etc*) chegar; (*succeed*) ter sucesso; **what time do you ~ it?** que horas você tem?; **to ~ good** *vi* (*succeed*) dar-se bem ♦ *vt* (*losses*) indenizar; **to ~ a profit/loss** ter um lucro/uma perda.
make for *vt fus* (*place*) dirigir-se a.
make off *vi* fugir.
make out *vt* (*decipher*) decifrar; (*understand*) compreender; (*see*) divisar, avistar; (*write out*: *prescription*) escrever; (: *form*, *cheque*) preencher; (*claim*, *imply*) afirmar; (*pretend*) fazer de conta; **to ~ out a case for sth** argumentar em favor de algo, defender algo.
make over *vt* (*assign*): **to ~ over (to)** transferir (para).
make up *vt* (*invent*) inventar; (*parcel*) embrulhar ♦ *vi* reconciliar-se; (*with cosmetics*) maquilar-se (*PT*: -lha-); **to be made up of** compor-se de, ser composto de; **to ~ up one's mind** decidir-se.
make up for *vt fus* compensar.
make-believe *adj* fingido, simulado ♦ *n*: **a world of ~** um mundo de faz-de-conta; **it's just ~** é pura ilusão.
maker ['meɪkə*] *n* fabricante *m/f*.
makeshift ['meɪkʃɪft] *adj* provisório.
make-up ['meɪkʌp] *n* maquilagem (*PT*: -lha-) *f*.
make-up bag *n* bolsa de maquilagem (*PT*: -lha-).
make-up remover *n* desmaquilante (*PT*: -lha-) *m*.
making ['meɪkɪŋ] *n* (*fig*): **in the ~** em vias de formação; **he has the ~s of an actor** ele tem tudo para ser ator.
maladjusted [mælə'dʒʌstɪd] *adj* inadaptado, desajustado.
malaise [mæ'leɪz] *n* mal-estar *m*, indisposição *f*.
malaria [mə'lɛərɪə] *n* malária.
Malawi [mə'lɑ:wɪ] *n* Malavi *m*.
Malay [mə'leɪ] *adj* malaio ♦ *n* malaio/a; (*LING*) malaio.
Malaya [mə'leɪə] *n* Malaia.
Malayan [mə'leɪən] *adj*, *n* = **Malay.**
Malaysia [mə'leɪzɪə] *n* Malaísia (*BR*), Malásia (*PT*).
Malaysian [mə'leɪzɪən] *adj*, *n* malásio/a.
Maldives ['mɔ:ldaɪvz] *npl*: **the ~** as ilhas Maldivas.
male [meɪl] *n* (*BIO*, *ELEC*) macho ♦ *adj* (*sex*, *attitude*) masculino; (*animal*) macho; (*child etc*) do sexo masculino.
male chauvinist *n* machista *m*.
male nurse *n* enfermeiro.
malevolence [mə'lɛvələns] *n* malevolência.
malevolent [mə'lɛvələnt] *adj* malévolo.
malfunction [mæl'fʌŋkʃən] *n* funcionamento defeituoso.
malice ['mælɪs] *n* (*ill will*) malícia; (*rancour*) rancor *m*.
malicious [mə'lɪʃəs] *adj* malicioso, mal-intencionado; (*LAW*) com intenção criminosa.
malign [mə'laɪn] *vt* caluniar, difamar.
malignant [mə'lɪgnənt] *adj* (*MED*) maligno.
malingerer [mə'lɪŋgərə*] *n* doente *m/f* fingido/a.
mall [mɔ:l] *n* (*also*: *shopping ~*) shopping *m*.
malleable ['mælɪəbl] *adj* maleável.
mallet ['mælɪt] *n* maço, marreta.
malnutrition [mælnju:'trɪʃən] *n* desnutrição *f*.
malpractice [mæl'præktɪs] *n* falta profissional.
malt [mɔ:lt] *n* malte *m* ♦ *cpd*: **~ whisky** uísque *m* de malte.
Malta ['mɔ:ltə] *n* Malta.
Maltese [mɔ:l'ti:z] *adj* maltês/esa ♦ *n inv* maltês/esa *m/f*; (*LING*) maltês *m*.

maltreat [mæl'triːt] *vt* maltratar.
mammal ['mæml] *n* mamífero.
mammoth ['mæməθ] *n* mamute *m* ♦ *adj* gigantesco, imenso.
man [mæn] (*pl* **men**) *n* homem *m*; (*CHESS*) peça ♦ *vt* (*NAUT*) tripular; (*MIL*) guarnecer; **an old** ~ um velho; **a young** ~ um jovem; ~ **and wife** marido e mulher.
manacles ['mænəklz] *npl* grilhões *mpl*.
manage ['mænɪdʒ] *vi* arranjar-se, virar-se ♦ *vt* (*be in charge of*) dirigir, administrar; (*business*) gerenciar; (*device*) manusear; (*carry*) carregar; **to** ~ **to do sth** conseguir fazer algo; **to** ~ **without sb/sth** passar sem alguém/algo; **can you** ~**?** você consegue?
manageable ['mænɪdʒəbl] *adj* manejável; (*task etc*) viável.
management ['mænɪdʒmənt] *n* administração *f*, direção *f*, gerência; **"under new** ~**"** "sob nova direção".
management accounting *n* contabilidade *f* administrativa *or* gerencial.
management consultant *n* consultor(a) *m/f* em administração.
manager ['mænɪdʒə*] *n* gerente *m/f*; (*SPORT*) técnico/a; (*of project*) superintendente *m/f*; (*of department, unit*) chefe *m/f*, diretor(a) *m/f*; (*of artist*) empresário/a; **sales** ~ gerente de vendas.
manageress [mænɪdʒə'rɛs] *n* gerente *f*.
managerial [mænə'dʒɪerɪəl] *adj* administrativo, gerencial.
managing director ['mænɪdʒɪŋ-] *n* diretor(a) *m/f* geral, diretor-gerente/diretora-gerente *m/f*.
Mancunian [mæŋ'kjuːnɪən] *adj* de Manchester ♦ *n* natural *m/f* de Manchester.
mandarin ['mændərɪn] *n* (*also*: ~ *orange*) tangerina; (*person*) mandarim *m*.
mandate ['mændeɪt] *n* mandato.
mandatory ['mændətərɪ] *adj* obrigatório; (*powers etc*) mandatário.
mandolin(e) ['mændəlɪn] *n* bandolim *m*.
mane [meɪn] *n* (*of horse*) crina; (*of lion*) juba.
maneuver *etc* [mə'nuːvə*] (*US*) = **manoeuvre** *etc*.
manfully ['mænfəlɪ] *adv* valentemente.
manganese ['mæŋgəniːz] *n* manganês *m*.
mangle ['mæŋgl] *vt* mutilar, estropiar ♦ *n* calandra.
mango ['mæŋgəu] (*pl* ~**es**) *n* manga.
mangrove ['mæŋgrəuv] *n* mangue *m*.
mangy ['meɪndʒɪ] *adj* sarnento, esfarrapado.
manhandle ['mænhændl] *vt* (*mistreat*) maltratar; (*move by hand*) manipular.
manhole ['mænhəul] *n* poço de inspeção.
manhood ['mænhud] *n* (*adulthood*) idade *f* adulta; (*masculinity*) virilidade *f*.
man-hour *n* hora-homem *f*.
manhunt ['mænhʌnt] *n* caça ao homem.
mania ['meɪnɪə] *n* mania.
maniac ['meɪnɪæk] *n* maníaco/a; (*fig*) louco/a.
manic ['mænɪk] *adj* maníaco.
manic-depressive *adj, n* maníaco-depressivo/a.
manicure ['mænɪkjuə*] *n* manicure (*PT*: -cura) *f* ♦ *vt* (*person*) fazer as unhas a.
manicure set *n* estojo de manicure (*PT*: -cura).
manifest ['mænɪfɛst] *vt* manifestar, mostrar ♦ *adj* manifesto, evidente ♦ *n* (*AVIAT, NAUT*) manifesto.
manifestation [mænɪfɛs'teɪʃən] *n* manifestação *f*.
manifesto [mænɪ'fɛstəu] (*pl* ~**s** *or* ~**es**) *n* manifesto.
manifold ['mænɪfəuld] *adj* múltiplo ♦ *n* (*AUT etc*) *see* **exhaust**.
Manila [mə'nɪlə] *n* Manilha.
manila [mə'nɪlə] *adj*: ~ **paper** papel-manilha *m*.
manipulate [mə'nɪpjuleɪt] *vt* manipular, manejar.
manipulation [mənɪpju'leɪʃən] *n* manipulação *f*.
mankind [mæn'kaɪnd] *n* humanidade *f*, raça humana.
manliness ['mænlɪnɪs] *n* virilidade *f*.
manly ['mænlɪ] *adj* másculo, viril.
man-made *adj* sintético, artificial.
manna ['mænə] *n* maná *m*.
mannequin ['mænɪkɪn] *n* manequim *m*.
manner ['mænə*] *n* modo, maneira; (*behaviour*) conduta, comportamento; (*type*) espécie *f*, gênero; **(good)** ~**s** *npl* boas maneiras *fpl*, educação *f*; **bad** ~**s** falta de educação; **all** ~ **of** todo tipo de.
mannerism ['mænərɪzəm] *n* maneirismo, hábito.
mannerly ['mænəlɪ] *adj* polido, educado.
manoeuvrable [mə'nuːvrəbl] (*US* **maneuverable**) *adj* manobrável.
manoeuvre [mə'nuːvə*] (*US* **maneuver**) *vt, vi* manobrar ♦ *n* manobra; **to** ~ **sb into doing sth** induzir alguém a fazer algo.
manor ['mænə*] *n* (*also*: ~ *house*) casa senhorial, solar *m*.
manpower ['mænpauə*] *n* potencial *m* humano, mão-de-obra.
manservant ['mænsəːvənt] (*pl* **menservants**) *n* criado.
mansion ['mænʃən] *n* mansão *f*, palacete *m*.
manslaughter ['mænslɔːtə*] *n* homicídio involuntário.
mantelpiece ['mæntlpiːs] *n* consolo da lareira.
mantle ['mæntl] *n* manto; (*fig*) camada.
man-to-man *adj, adv* de homem para homem.
manual ['mænjuəl] *adj* manual ♦ *n* manual *m*; (*MUS*) teclado.
manual worker *n* trabalhador(a) *m/f* braçal.
manufacture [mænju'fæktʃə*] *vt* manufaturar, fabricar ♦ *n* fabricação *f*.
manufactured goods [mænju'fæktʃəd-] *npl*

***NB**: European Portuguese adds the following consonants to certain words:* **b** (sú(b)dito, su(b)til); **c** (a(c)ção, a(c)cionista, a(c)to); **m** (inde(m)ne); **p** (ado(p)ção, ado(p)tar); *for further details see p. xiii.*

produtos *mpl* industrializados.
manufacturer [mænju'fæktʃərə*] *n* fabricante *m/f*.
manufacturing industries [mænju'fæktʃərɪŋ] *npl* indústrias *fpl* de transformação.
manure [mə'njuə*] *n* estrume *m*, adubo.
manuscript ['mænjuskrɪpt] *n* manuscrito.
many ['mɛnɪ] *adj, pron* muitos/as; **how ~?** quantos/as?; **a great ~** muitíssimos; **twice as ~** *adj* duas vezes mais ♦ *pron* o dobro; **~ a time** muitas vezes.
map [mæp] *n* mapa *m* ♦ *vt* fazer o mapa de.
map out *vt* traçar; (*fig*: *career, holiday*) planejar.
maple ['meɪpl] *n* bordo.
mar [mɑː*] *vt* estragar.
Mar. *abbr* = **March.**
marathon ['mærəθən] *n* maratona ♦ *adj*: **a ~ session** uma sessão exaustiva.
marathon runner *n* corredor(a) *m/f* de maratona, maratonista *m/f*.
marauder [mə'rɔːdə*] *n* saqueador(a) *m/f*.
marble ['mɑːbl] *n* mármore *m*; (*toy*) bola de gude; **~s** *n* (*game*) jogo de gude.
March [mɑːtʃ] *n* março; *see also* **July**.
march [mɑːtʃ] *vi* (MIL) marchar; (*demonstrators*) desfilar ♦ *n* marcha; (*demonstration*) passeata; **to ~ out of/into** *etc* sair de/entrar em *etc* marchando.
marcher ['mɑːtʃə*] *n* (*demonstrator*) manifestante *m/f*.
marching ['mɑːtʃɪŋ] *n*: **to give sb his ~ orders** (*fig*) dar um bilhete azul a alguém, mandar passear alguém.
march-past *n* desfile *m*.
mare [mɛə*] *n* égua.
marg. [mɑːdʒ] (*inf*) *n abbr* = **margarine**.
margarine [mɑːdʒə'riːn] *n* margarina.
margin ['mɑːdʒɪn] *n* margem *f*.
marginal ['mɑːdʒɪnl] *adj* marginal; **~ seat** (POL) cadeira ganha por pequena maioria.
marginally ['mɑːdʒɪnəlɪ] *adv* ligeiramente.
marigold ['mærɪgəuld] *n* malmequer *m*.
marijuana [mærɪ'wɑːnə] *n* maconha.
marina [mə'riːnə] *n* marina.
marinade [*n* mærɪ'neɪd, *vt* 'mærɪneɪd] *n* escabeche *m* ♦ *vt* = **marinate**.
marinate ['mærɪneɪt] *vt* marinar, pôr em escabeche.
marine [mə'riːn] *adj* (*in the sea*) marinho; (*of seafaring*) marítimo ♦ *n* fuzileiro naval.
marine insurance *n* seguro marítimo.
marital ['mærɪtl] *adj* matrimonial, marital; **~ status** estado civil.
maritime ['mærɪtaɪm] *adj* marítimo.
maritime law *n* direito marítimo.
marjoram ['mɑːdʒərəm] *n* manjerona.
mark [mɑːk] *n* marca, sinal *m*; (*imprint*) impressão *f*; (*stain*) mancha; (BRIT: SCH) nota; (*currency*) marco; (BRIT: TECH): **M~ 2** 2ª versão ♦ *vt* (*also*: SPORT: *player*) marcar; (*stain*) manchar; (BRIT: SCH: *grade*) dar nota em; (: *correct*) corrigir; **to ~ time** marcar passo; **to be quick off the ~ (in doing)** (*fig*) não perder tempo (para fazer); **up to the ~** (*in efficiency*) à altura das exigências.
mark down *vt* (*prices, goods*) rebaixar, remarcar para baixo.
mark off *vt* (*tick off*) ticar.
mark out *vt* (*trace*) traçar; (*designate*) destinar.
mark up *vt* (*price*) aumentar, remarcar.
marked [mɑːkt] *adj* marcado.
markedly ['mɑːkɪdlɪ] *adv* marcadamente.
marker ['mɑːkə*] *n* (*sign*) marcador *m*, marca; (*bookmark*) marcador.
market ['mɑːkɪt] *n* mercado ♦ *vt* (COMM) comercializar; **to be on the ~** estar à venda; **on the open ~** no mercado livre; **to play the ~** especular na bolsa de valores.
marketable ['mɑːkɪtəbl] *adj* comercializável.
market analysis *n* análise *f* de mercado.
market day *n* dia *m* de mercado.
market demand *n* procura de mercado.
market forces *npl* forças *fpl* do mercado.
market garden (BRIT) *n* horta.
marketing ['mɑːkɪtɪŋ] *n* marketing *m*.
market leader *n* líder *m* do mercado.
marketplace ['mɑːkɪtpleɪs] *n* mercado.
market price *n* preço de mercado.
market research *n* pesquisa de mercado.
market value *n* valor *m* de mercado.
marking ['mɑːkɪŋ] *n* (*on animal*) marcação *f*; (*on road*) marca.
marksman ['mɑːksmən] (*irreg*) *n* bom atirador *m*.
marksmanship ['mɑːksmənʃɪp] *n* boa pontaria.
marksmen ['mɑːksmɛn] *npl of* **marksman**.
mark-up *n* (COMM: *margin*) margem *f* (de lucro), markup *m*; (: *increase*) remarcação *f*, aumento.
marmalade ['mɑːməleɪd] *n* geléia de laranja.
maroon [mə'ruːn] *vt*: **to be ~ed** ficar abandonado (numa ilha) ♦ *adj* de cor castanho-avermelhado, vinho *inv*.
marquee [mɑː'kiː] *n* toldo, tenda.
marquess ['mɑːkwɪs] *n* marquês *m*.
marquis ['mɑːkwɪs] *n* = **marquess**.
marriage ['mærɪdʒ] *n* casamento.
marriage bureau (*irreg*) *n* agência matrimonial.
marriage certificate *n* certidão *f* de casamento.
marriage counselling (US) *n* orientação *f* matrimonial.
marriage guidance (BRIT) *n* orientação *f* matrimonial.
married ['mærɪd] *adj* casado; (*life, love*) conjugal; **to get ~** casar(-se).
marrow ['mærəu] *n* medula; (*vegetable*) abóbora.
marry ['mærɪ] *vt* casar(-se) com; (*subj*: *father, priest etc*) casar, unir ♦ *vi* casar(-se).
Mars [mɑːz] *n* (*planet*) Marte *m*.
marsh [mɑːʃ] *n* pântano; (*salt ~*) marisma.
marshal ['mɑːʃl] *n* (MIL) marechal *m*; (*at sports meeting etc*) oficial *m* ♦ *vt* (*facts*) dispor, ordenar; (*soldiers*) formar.
marshalling yard ['mɑːʃlɪŋ-] *n* (RAIL) local *m*

de manobras.
marshmallow [mɑːʃ'mæləu] *n espécie de doce de malvavisco.*
marshy ['mɑːʃɪ] *adj* pantanoso.
marsupial [mɑː'suːpɪəl] *adj* marsupial ♦ *n* marsupial *m*.
martial ['mɑːʃl] *adj* marcial.
martial law *n* lei *f* marcial.
Martian ['mɑːʃən] *n* marciano/a.
martin ['mɑːtɪn] *n* (*also*: *house* ~) andorinha-de-casa.
martyr ['mɑːtə*] *n* mártir *m/f* ♦ *vt* martirizar.
martyrdom ['mɑːtədəm] *n* martírio.
marvel ['mɑːvl] *n* maravilha ♦ *vi*: **to ~ (at)** maravilhar-se (de *or* com).
marvellous ['mɑːvələs] (*US* **marvelous**) *adj* maravilhoso.
Marxism ['mɑːksɪzəm] *n* marxismo.
Marxist ['mɑːksɪst] *adj*, *n* marxista *m/f*.
marzipan ['mɑːzɪpæn] *n* maçapão *m*.
mascara [mæs'kɑːrə] *n* rímel *m*.
mascot ['mæskət] *n* mascote *f*.
masculine ['mæskjulɪn] *adj*, *n* masculino.
masculinity [mæskju'lɪnɪtɪ] *n* masculinidade *f*.
MASH [mæʃ] (*US*) *n abbr* (*MIL*) = **mobile army surgical hospital**.
mash [mæʃ] *vt* (*CULIN*) fazer um purê de; (*crush*) amassar.
mashed potatoes [mæʃt-] *n* purê *m* de batatas.
mask [mɑːsk] *n* máscara ♦ *vt* mascarar.
masochism ['mæsəkɪzəm] *n* masoquismo.
masochist ['mæsəkɪst] *n* masoquista *m/f*.
mason ['meɪsn] *n* (*also*: *stone*~) pedreiro/a; (*also*: *free*~) maçom *m*.
masonic [mə'sɔnɪk] *adj* maçônico.
masonry ['meɪsənrɪ] *n* (*also*: *free*~) maçonaria; (*building*) alvenaria.
masquerade [mæskə'reɪd] *n* baile *m* de máscaras; (*fig*) farsa, embuste *m* ♦ *vi*: **to ~ as** disfarçar-se de, fazer-se passar por.
mass [mæs] *n* (*people*) multidão *f*; (*PHYS*) massa; (*REL*) missa; (*great quantity*) montão *m* ♦ *vi* reunir-se; (*MIL*) concentrar-se; **the ~es** *npl* as massas; **to go to ~** ir à missa.
massacre ['mæsəkə*] *n* massacre *m*, carnificina ♦ *vt* massacrar.
massage ['mæsɑːʒ] *n* massagem *f* ♦ *vt* fazer massagem em, massagear.
masseur [mæ'səː*] *n* massagista *m*.
masseuse [mæ'səːz] *n* massagista.
massive ['mæsɪv] *adj* (*large*) enorme; (*support*) massivo.
mass market *n* mercado de consumo em massa.
mass media *npl* meios *mpl* de comunicação de massa, mídia.
mass meeting *n* concentração *f* de massa.
mass-produce *vt* produzir em massa, fabricar em série.
mass-production *n* produção *f* em massa, fabricação *f* em série.
mast [mɑːst] *n* (*NAUT*) mastro; (*RADIO etc*) antena.
master ['mɑːstə*] *n* mestre *m*; (*landowner*) senhor *m*, dono; (*in secondary school*) professor *m*; (*title for boys*): **M~ X** o menino X ♦ *vt* dominar; (*learn*) conhecer a fundo; **~ of ceremonies** mestre de cerimônias; **M~ of Arts/Science** detentor(a) *m/f* de mestrado em letras/ciências; **M~ of Arts/Science degree** mestrado; **M~'s degree** mestrado.
master disk *n* (*COMPUT*) disco mestre.
masterful ['mɑːstəful] *adj* autoritário, imperioso.
master key *n* chave *f* mestra.
masterly ['mɑːstəlɪ] *adj* magistral.
mastermind ['mɑːstəmaɪnd] *n* (*fig*) cabeça ♦ *vt* dirigir, planejar.
masterpiece ['mɑːstəpiːs] *n* obra-prima.
master plan *n* plano piloto.
master stroke *n* golpe *m* de mestre.
mastery ['mɑːstərɪ] *n* domínio.
mastiff ['mæstɪf] *n* mastim *m*.
masturbate ['mæstəbeɪt] *vi* masturbar-se.
masturbation [mæstə'beɪʃən] *n* masturbação *f*.
mat [mæt] *n* esteira; (*also*: *door*~) capacho ♦ *adj* = **matt**.
match [mætʃ] *n* fósforo; (*game*) jogo, partida; (*fig*) igual *m/f* ♦ *vt* casar, emparelhar; (*go well with*) combinar com; (*equal*) igualar ♦ *vi* casar-se, combinar; **to be a good ~** (*people*) formar um bom casal; (*colours*) combinar.
match up *vt* casar, emparelhar.
matchbox ['mætʃbɔks] *n* caixa de fósforos.
matching ['mætʃɪŋ] *adj* que combina (com).
matchless ['mætʃlɪs] *adj* sem igual, incomparável.
mate [meɪt] *n* (*also*: *inf*) colega *m/f*; (*assistant*) ajudante *m/f*; (*CHESS*) mate *m*; (*animal*) macho/fêmea; (*in merchant navy*) imediato ♦ *vi* acasalar-se ♦ *vt* acasalar.
material [mə'tɪərɪəl] *n* (*substance*) matéria; (*equipment*) material *m*; (*cloth*) pano, tecido; (*data*) dados *mpl* ♦ *adj* material; (*important*) importante; **~s** *npl* material; **reading ~** (material de) leitura.
materialistic [mətɪərɪə'lɪstɪk] *adj* materialista.
materialize [mə'tɪərɪəlaɪz] *vi* materializar-se, concretizar-se.
materially [mə'tɪərɪəlɪ] *adv* materialmente.
maternal [mə'təːnl] *adj* maternal.
maternity [mə'təːnɪtɪ] *n* maternidade *f* ♦ *cpd* de maternidade, de gravidez.
maternity benefit *n* auxílio-maternidade *m*.
maternity dress *n* vestido de gestante.
maternity hospital *n* maternidade *f*.
matey ['meɪtɪ] (*BRIT*: *inf*) *adj* chapinha.
math. [mæθ] (*US*) *n abbr* = **mathematics**.
mathematical [mæθə'mætɪkl] *adj* matemático.
mathematician [mæθəmə'tɪʃən] *n* matemático/a.

NB: European Portuguese adds the following consonants to certain words: **b** (sú(b)dito, su(b)til); **c** (a(c)ção, a(c)cionista, a(c)to); **m** (inde(m)ne); **p** (ado(p)ção, ado(p)tar); *for further details see p. xiii.*

mathematics [mæθə'mætɪks] *n* matemática.
maths [mæθs] (*BRIT*) *n abbr* = **mathematics**.
matinée ['mætɪneɪ] *n* matinê *f*.
mating ['meɪtɪŋ] *n* acasalamento.
mating call *n* chamado do macho.
mating season *n* época de cio.
matriarchal [meɪtrɪ'ɑːkl] *adj* matriarcal.
matrices ['meɪtrɪsiːz] *npl of* **matrix**.
matriculation [mətrɪkju'leɪʃən] *n* matrícula.
matrimonial [mætrɪ'məunɪəl] *adj* matrimonial.
matrimony ['mætrɪmənɪ] *n* matrimônio, casamento.
matrix ['meɪtrɪks] (*pl* **matrices**) *n* matriz *f*.
matron ['meɪtrən] *n* (*in hospital*) enfermeira-chefe *f*; (*in school*) inspetora.
matronly ['meɪtrənlɪ] *adj* matronal; (*fig*: *figure*) corpulento.
matt [mæt] *adj* fosco, sem brilho.
matted ['mætɪd] *adj* emaranhado.
matter ['mætə*] *n* questão *f*, assunto; (*PHYS*) matéria, substância; (*content*) conteúdo; (*MED*: *pus*) pus *m* ♦ *vi* importar; **it doesn't ~** não importa; (*I don't mind*) tanto faz; **what's the ~?** o que (é que) há?, qual é o problema?; **no ~ what** aconteça o que acontecer; **as a ~ of course** o que é de se esperar; (*routine*) por rotina; **as a ~ of fact** na realidade, de fato; **it's a ~ of habit** é uma questão de hábito; **printed ~** impressos; **reading ~** (*BRIT*) (material de) leitura.
matter-of-fact [mætərə'fækt] *adj* prosaico, prático.
matting ['mætɪŋ] *n* esteira.
mattress ['mætrɪs] *n* colchão *m*.
mature [mə'tjuə*] *adj* maduro ♦ *vi* amadurecer.
maturity [mə'tjuərɪtɪ] *n* maturidade *f*.
maudlin ['mɔːdlɪn] *adj* (*film*, *book*) piegas *inv*; (*person*) chorão/rona.
maul [mɔːl] *vt* machucar, maltratar.
Mauritania [mɔːrɪ'teɪnɪə] *n* Mauritânia.
Mauritius [mə'rɪʃəs] *n* Maurício *f* (*no article*).
mausoleum [mɔːsə'lɪəm] *n* mausoléu *m*.
mauve [məuv] *adj* cor de malva *inv*.
maverick ['mævrɪk] *n* (*fig*) dissidente *m/f*.
mawkish ['mɔːkɪʃ] *adj* piegas *inv*.
max. *abbr* = **maximum**.
maxim ['mæksɪm] *n* máxima.
maxima ['mæksɪmə] *npl of* **maximum**.
maximize ['mæksɪmaɪz] *vt* maximizar.
maximum ['mæksɪməm] (*pl* **maxima**) *adj*, *n* máximo.
May [meɪ] *n* maio; *see also* **July**.
may [meɪ] (*pt*, *conditional* **might**) *aux vb* (*indicating possibility*): **he ~ come** pode ser que ele venha, é capaz de vir; (*be allowed to*): **~ I smoke?** posso fumar?; (*wishes*): **~ God bless you!** que Deus lhe abençoe; **he might be there** ele poderia estar lá, ele é capaz de estar lá; **I might as well go** mais vale que eu vá; **you might like to try** talvez você queira tentar.
maybe ['meɪbiː] *adv* talvez; **~ he'll come** talvez ele venha; **~ not** talvez não.
May Day *n* dia *m* primeiro de maio.
mayday ['meɪdeɪ] *n* S.O.S. *m* (*chamada de socorro internacional*).
mayhem ['meɪhɛm] *n* caos *m*.
mayonnaise [meɪə'neɪz] *n* maionese *f*.
mayor [mɛə*] *n* prefeito (*BR*), presidente *m* do município (*PT*).
mayoress ['mɛərɪs] *n* prefeita (*BR*), presidenta do município (*PT*).
maypole ['meɪpəul] *n mastro erguido no dia primeiro de maio*.
maze [meɪz] *n* labirinto.
MB *abbr* (*COMPUT*) = **megabyte**; (*CANADIAN*) = **Manitoba**.
MBA *n abbr* (= *Master of Business Administration*) *grau universitário*.
MBBS (*BRIT*) *n abbr* (= *Bachelor of Medicine and Surgery*) *grau universitário*.
MBChB (*BRIT*) *n abbr* (= *Bachelor of Medicine and Surgery*) *grau universitário*.
MBE (*BRIT*) *n abbr* (= *Member of the Order of the British Empire*) *título honorífico*.
MC *n abbr* = **master of ceremonies**.
MCAT (*US*) *n abbr* = **Medical College Admissions Test**.
MCP (*BRIT*: *inf*) *n abbr* (= *male chauvinist pig*) machista *m*.
MD *n abbr* = **Doctor of Medicine**; (*COMM*) = **managing director** ♦ *abbr* (*US*: *POST*) = **Maryland**.
MDT (*US*) *abbr* (= *Mountain Daylight Time*) *hora de verão nas montanhas Rochosas*.
ME (*US*) *abbr* (*POST*) = **Maine** ♦ *n abbr* (*MED*) = **medical examiner**.
me [miː] *pron* me; (*stressed*, *after prep*) mim; **with ~** comigo; **it's ~** sou eu.
meadow ['mɛdəu] *n* prado, campina.
meagre ['miːgə*] (*US* **meager**) *adj* escasso.
meal [miːl] *n* refeição *f*; (*flour*) farinha; **to go out for a ~** jantar fora.
mealtime ['miːltaɪm] *n* hora da refeição.
mealy-mouthed ['miːlimauðd] *adj* insincero.
mean [miːn] (*pt*, *pp* **meant**) *adj* (*with money*) sovina, avarento, pão-duro *inv* (*BR*); (*unkind*) mesquinho; (*shabby*) surrado, miserável; (*of poor quality*) inferior; (*average*) médio ♦ *vt* (*signify*) significar, querer dizer; (*intend*): **to ~ to do sth** pretender *or* tencionar fazer algo ♦ *n* meio, meio termo; **~s** *npl* meio; **by ~s of** por meio de, mediante; **by all ~s!** claro que sim!, pois não; **to be meant for** estar destinado a; **do you ~ it?** você está falando sério?; **what do you ~?** o que você quer dizer?
meander [mɪ'ændə*] *vi* (*river*) serpentear; (*person*) vadiar, perambular.
meaning ['miːnɪŋ] *n* sentido, significado.
meaningful ['miːnɪŋful] *adj* significativo; (*relationship*) sério.
meaningless ['miːnɪŋlɪs] *adj* sem sentido.
meanness ['miːnnɪs] *n* (*with money*) avareza, sovinice *f*; (*shabbiness*) vileza, baixeza; (*unkindness*) maldade *f*, mesquinharia.
means test *n* (*ADMIN*) avaliação *f* de rendimento.
meant [mɛnt] *pt*, *pp of* **mean**.

meantime ['mi:ntaɪm] *adv* (*also*: *in the* ~) entretanto, enquanto isso.
meanwhile ['mi:nwaɪl] *adv* (*also*: *in the* ~) entretanto, enquanto isso.
measles ['mi:zlz] *n* sarampo.
measly ['mi:zlɪ] (*inf*) *adj* miserável.
measure ['mɛʒə*] *vt* medir; (*for clothes etc*) tirar as medidas de; (*consider*) avaliar, ponderar ♦ *vi* medir ♦ *n* medida; (*ruler*) régua; **a litre** ~ um litro; **some** ~ **of success** certo grau de sucesso; **to take** ~**s to do sth** tomar medidas *or* providências para fazer algo.
measure up *vi*: **to** ~ **up (to)** corresponder (a).
measured ['mɛʒəd] *adj* medido, calculado; (*tone*) ponderado.
measurement ['mɛʒəmənt] *n* (*act*) medição *f*; (*dimension*) medida; ~**s** *npl* medidas *fpl*; **to take sb's** ~**s** tirar as medidas de alguém; **chest/hip** ~ medida de peito/quadris.
meat [mi:t] *n* carne *f*; **cold** ~**s** (*BRIT*) frios; **crab** ~ caranguejo.
meatball ['mi:tbɔ:l] *n* almôndega.
meat pie *n* bolo de carne.
meaty ['mi:tɪ] *adj* carnudo; (*fig*) substancial.
Mecca ['mɛkə] *n* Meca; (*fig*): **a** ~ **(for)** a meca (de).
mechanic [mɪ'kænɪk] *n* mecânico; ~**s** *n* mecânica ♦ *npl* mecanismo.
mechanical [mɪ'kænɪkl] *adj* mecânico.
mechanical engineer *n* engenheiro/a mecânico/a.
mechanical engineering *n* (*science*) mecânica; (*industry*) engenharia mecânica.
mechanism ['mɛkənɪzəm] *n* mecanismo.
mechanization [mɛkənaɪ'zeɪʃən] *n* mecanização *f*.
MEd *n abbr* (= *Master of Education*) *grau universitário*.
medal ['mɛdl] *n* medalha.
medalist ['mɛdəlɪst] (*US*) *n* = **medallist**.
medallion [mɪ'dælɪən] *n* medalhão *m*.
medallist ['mɛdəlɪst] (*US* **medalist**) *n* (*SPORT*) ganhador(a) *m/f* de medalha.
meddle ['mɛdl] *vi*: **to** ~ **in** meter-se em, intrometer-se em; **to** ~ **with sth** mexer em algo.
meddlesome ['mɛdlsəm] *adj* intrometido.
meddling ['mɛdlɪŋ] *adj* intrometido.
media ['mi:dɪə] *npl* meios *mpl* de comunicação, mídia.
mediaeval [mɛdɪ'i:vl] *adj* = **medieval**.
median ['mi:dɪən] (*US*) *n* (*also*: ~ *strip*) canteiro divisor.
media research *n* pesquisa de audiência.
mediate ['mi:dɪeɪt] *vi* mediar.
mediation [mi:dɪ'eɪʃən] *n* mediação *f*.
mediator ['mi:dɪeɪtə*] *n* mediador(a) *m/f*.
medical ['mɛdɪkl] *adj* médico ♦ *n* (*also*: ~ *examination*) exame *m* médico.
medical certificate *n* atestado médico.
medical student *n* estudante *m/f* de medicina.
Medicare ['mɛdɪkɛə*] (*US*) *n sistema federal de seguro saúde*.
medicated ['mɛdɪkeɪtɪd] *adj* medicinal, higienizado.
medication [mɛdɪ'keɪʃən] *n* (*drugs etc*) medicação *f*.
medicinal [mɛ'dɪsɪnl] *adj* medicinal.
medicine ['mɛdsɪn] *n* medicina; (*drug*) remédio, medicamento.
medicine chest *n* armário de remédios.
medicine man (*irreg*) *n* curandeiro *m*, pajé *m*.
medieval [mɛdɪ'i:vl] *adj* medieval.
mediocre [mi:dɪ'əukə*] *adj* medíocre.
mediocrity [mi:dɪ'ɔkrɪtɪ] *n* mediocridade *f*.
meditate ['mɛdɪteɪt] *vi* meditar.
meditation [mɛdɪ'teɪʃən] *n* meditação *f*.
Mediterranean [mɛdɪtə'reɪnɪən] *adj* mediterrâneo; **the** ~ **(Sea)** o (mar) Mediterrâneo.
medium ['mi:dɪəm] (*pl* ~**s**) *adj* médio ♦ *n* (*pl*: **media**: *means*) meio; (*person*) médium *m/f*; **the happy** ~ o justo meio.
medium-sized [-saɪzd] *adj* de tamanho médio.
medium wave *n* (*RADIO*) onda média.
medley ['mɛdlɪ] *n* mistura; (*MUS*) pot-pourri *m*.
meek [mi:k] *adj* manso, dócil.
meet [mi:t] (*pt, pp* **met**) *vt* (*gen*) encontrar; (*accidentally*) topar com, dar de cara com; (*by arrangement*) encontrar-se com, ir ao encontro de; (*for the first time*) conhecer; (*go and fetch*) ir buscar; (*opponent*) enfrentar; (*obligations*) cumprir ♦ *vi* encontrar-se; (*in session*) reunir-se; (*join: objects*) unir-se; (*get to know*) conhecer-se ♦ *n* (*BRIT: HUNTING*) reunião *f* de caçadores; (*US: SPORT*) promoção *f*, competição *f*; **pleased to** ~ **you!** prazer em conhecê-lo/-la.
meet up *vi*: **to** ~ **up with sb** encontrar-se com alguém.
meet with *vt fus* reunir-se com; (*face: difficulty*) encontrar.
meeting ['mi:tɪŋ] *n* encontro; (*session: of club etc*) reunião *f*; (*interview*) entrevista; (*formal*) assembléia; (*SPORT*) corrida; **she's in** *or* **at a** ~ ela está em conferência; **to call a** ~ convocar uma reunião.
meeting place *n* ponto de encontro.
megabyte ['mɛgəbaɪt] *n* (*COMPUT*) megabyte *m*.
megalomaniac [mɛgələu'meɪnɪæk] *adj, n* megalomaníaco/a.
megaphone ['mɛgəfəun] *n* megafone *m*.
melancholy ['mɛlənkəlɪ] *n* melancolia ♦ *adj* melancólico.
melee ['mɛleɪ] *n* briga, refrega.
mellow ['mɛləu] *adj* (*sound*) melodioso, suave; (*colour*) suave; (*fruit*) maduro ♦ *vi* (*person*) amadurecer.

***NB**: European Portuguese adds the following consonants to certain words:* **b** (sú(b)dito, su(b)til); **c** (a(c)ção, a(c)cionista, a(c)to); **m** (inde(m)ne); **p** (ado(p)ção, ado(p)tar); *for further details see p. xiii.*

melodious [mɪ'ləudɪəs] *adj* melodioso.
melodrama ['mɛləudrɑːmə] *adj* melodrama *m.*
melodramatic [mɛlədrə'mætɪk] *adj* melodramático.
melody ['mɛlədɪ] *n* melodia.
melon ['mɛlən] *n* melão *m.*
melt [mɛlt] *vi* (*metal*) fundir-se; (*snow*) derreter; (*fig*) desvanecer-se ♦ *vt* derreter.
melt away *vi* desaparecer.
melt down *vt* fundir.
meltdown ['mɛltdaun] *n* fusão *f.*
melting point ['mɛltɪŋ-] *n* ponto de fusão.
melting pot ['mɛltɪŋ-] *n* (*fig*) cadinho.
member ['mɛmbə*] *n* (*gen*) membro/a; (*of club*) sócio/a ♦ *cpd*: ~ **state** estado membro; **M~ of Parliament** (BRIT) deputado/a; **M~ of the European Parliament** Membro/a do Parlamento Europeu; **M~ of the House of Representatives** (US) membro/a da Câmara dos representantes.
membership ['mɛmbəʃɪp] *n* (*being a member*) adesão *f*, condição *f* de membro; (*of club*) associação *f*; (*members*) número de sócios; **to seek ~ of** candidatar-se a sócio de.
membership card *n* carteira de sócio.
membrane ['mɛmbreɪn] *n* membrana.
memento [mə'mɛntəu] (*pl* **~s** *or* **~es**) *n* lembrança.
memo ['mɛməu] *n* memorando, nota.
memoirs ['mɛmwɑːz] *npl* memórias *fpl.*
memo pad *n* bloco de memorando.
memorable ['mɛmərəbl] *adj* memorável.
memoranda [mɛmə'rændə] *npl of* **memorandum.**
memorandum [mɛmə'rændəm] (*pl* **memoranda**) *n* memorando.
memorial [mɪ'mɔːrɪəl] *n* memorial *m*, monumento comemorativo ♦ *adj* comemorativo.
memorize ['mɛməraɪz] *vt* decorar, aprender de cor.
memory ['mɛmərɪ] *n* (*faculty*) memória; (*recollection*) lembrança; **to have a good/bad ~** ter memória boa/ruim; **loss of ~** perda de memória; **in ~ of** em memória de.
men [mɛn] *npl of* **man.**
menace ['mɛnəs] *n* ameaça; (*inf*: *nuisance*) droga ♦ *vt* ameaçar.
menacing ['mɛnəsɪŋ] *adj* ameaçador(a).
menagerie [mə'nædʒərɪ] *n* coleção *f* de animais.
mend [mɛnd] *vt* consertar, reparar; (*darn*) remendar ♦ *n* remendo; **to be on the ~** estar melhorando.
mending ['mɛndɪŋ] *n* reparação *f*; (*clothes*) roupas *fpl* por consertar.
menial ['miːnɪəl] *adj* doméstico; (*pej*) baixo.
meningitis [mɛnɪn'dʒaɪtɪs] *n* meningite *f.*
menopause ['mɛnəupɔːz] *n* menopausa.
menservants ['mɛnsəːvənts] *npl of* **manservant.**
menstruate ['mɛnstrueɪt] *vi* menstruar.
menstruation [mɛnstru'eɪʃən] *n* menstruação *f.*
mental ['mɛntl] *adj* mental; ~ **illness** doença mental.
mentality [mɛn'tælɪtɪ] *n* mentalidade *f.*
mentally ['mɛntlɪ] *adv*: **to be ~ handicapped** ser deficiente mental.
menthol ['mɛnθɔl] *n* mentol *m.*
mention ['mɛnʃən] *n* menção *f* ♦ *vt* mencionar; (*speak of*) falar de; **don't ~ it!** não tem de quê!, de nada!; **I need hardly ~ that** ... não preciso dizer que ...; **not to ~ ..., without ~ing** ... para não falar de ..., sem falar de ....
mentor ['mɛntɔː*] *n* mentor *m.*
menu ['mɛnjuː] *n* (*set* ~, COMPUT) menu *m*; (*printed*) cardápio (BR), ementa (PT).
menu-driven *adj* (COMPUT) que se navega através de menus.
MEP *n abbr* = **Member of the European Parliament.**
mercantile ['məːkəntaɪl] *adj* mercantil; (*law*) comercial.
mercenary ['məːsɪnərɪ] *adj, n* mercenário.
merchandise ['məːtʃəndaɪz] *n* mercadorias *fpl* ♦ *vt* comercializar.
merchandiser ['məːtʃəndaɪzə*] *n* comerciante *m/f.*
merchant ['məːtʃənt] *n* comerciante *m/f*; **timber/wine ~** negociante de madeira/vinhos.
merchant bank (BRIT) *n* banco mercantil.
merchantman ['məːtʃəntmən] (*irreg*) *n* navio mercante.
merchant navy (US **merchant marine**) *n* marinha mercante.
merciful ['məːsɪful] *adj* piedoso, misericordioso.
mercifully ['məːsɪflɪ] *adv* misericordiosamente, generosamente; (*fortunately*) graças a Deus, felizmente.
merciless ['məːsɪlɪs] *adj* desapiedado, impiedoso.
mercurial [məː'kjuərɪəl] *adj* volúvel; (*lively*) vivo.
mercury ['məːkjurɪ] *n* mercúrio.
mercy ['məːsɪ] *n* piedade *f*; (REL) misericórdia; **to have ~ on sb** apiedar-se de alguém; **at the ~ of** à mercê de.
mercy killing *n* eutanásia.
mere [mɪə*] *adj* mero, simples *inv.*
merely ['mɪəlɪ] *adv* simplesmente, somente, apenas.
merge [məːdʒ] *vt* (*join*) unir; (*mix*) misturar; (COMM) fundir; (COMPUT) intercalar ♦ *vi* unir-se; (COMM) fundir-se.
merger ['məːdʒə*] *n* (COMM) fusão *f.*
meridian [mə'rɪdɪən] *n* meridiano.
meringue [mə'ræŋ] *n* suspiro, merengue *m.*
merit ['mɛrɪt] *n* mérito ♦ *vt* merecer.
meritocracy [mɛrɪ'tɔkrəsɪ] *n* sistema *m* social baseado no mérito.
mermaid ['məːmeɪd] *n* sereia.
merrily ['mɛrɪlɪ] *adv* alegremente, com alegria.
merriment ['mɛrɪmənt] *n* alegria.
merry ['mɛrɪ] *adj* alegre; **M~ Christmas!** Fe-

liz Natal!
merry-go-round *n* carrossel *m*.
mesh [mɛʃ] *n* malha; (*TECH*) engrenagem *f* ♦ *vi* (*gears*) engrenar.
mesmerize ['mɛzməraɪz] *vt* hipnotizar.
mess [mɛs] *n* (*gen*) confusão *f*; (*of objects*) desordem *f*; (*tangle*) bagunça; (*MIL*) rancho; **to be (in) a ~** (*house, room*) ser uma bagunça, estar numa bagunça; (*fig*: *marriage, life*) estar bagunçado; **to be/get o.s. in a ~** (*fig*) meter-se numa encrenca.
mess about (*inf*) *vi* perder tempo; (*pass the time*) vadiar.
mess about with (*inf*) *vt fus* mexer com.
mess around (*inf*) *vi* perder tempo; (*pass the time*) vadiar.
mess around with (*inf*) *vi* mexer com.
mess up *vt* (*disarrange*) desarrumar; (*spoil*) estragar; (*dirty*) sujar.
message ['mɛsɪdʒ] *n* recado, mensagem *f*; **to get the ~** (*fig*: *inf*) sacar, pescar.
message switching [-'swɪtʃɪŋ] *n* (*COMPUT*) troca de mensagens.
messenger ['mɛsɪndʒə*] *n* mensageiro/a.
Messiah [mɪ'saɪə] *n* Messias *m*.
Messrs(.) ['mɛsəz] *abbr* (*on letters*: = *messieurs*) Srs.
messy ['mɛsɪ] *adj* (*dirty*) sujo; (*untidy*) desarrumado; (*confused*) bagunçado.
Met [mɛt] (*US*) *n abbr* = **Metropolitan Opera**.
met [mɛt] *pt, pp of* **meet** ♦ *adj abbr* = **meteorological**.
metabolism [mɛ'tæbəlɪzəm] *n* metabolismo.
metal ['mɛtl] *n* metal *m* ♦ *vt* (*road*) empedrar.
metallic [mɛ'tælɪk] *adj* metálico.
metallurgy [mɛ'tælədʒɪ] *n* metalurgia.
metalwork ['mɛtlwəːk] *n* (*craft*) trabalho em metal.
metamorphoses [mɛtə'mɔːfəsiːz] *npl of* **metamorphosis**.
metamorphosis [mɛtə'mɔːfəsɪs] (*pl* **metamorphoses**) *n* metamorfose *f*.
metaphor ['mɛtəfə*] *n* metáfora.
metaphysics [mɛtə'fɪzɪks] *n* metafísica.
mete out [miːt-] *vt fus* infligir.
meteor ['miːtɪə*] *n* meteoro.
meteoric [miːtɪ'ɔrɪk] *adj* (*fig*) meteórico.
meteorite ['miːtɪəraɪt] *n* meteorito.
meteorological [miːtɪərə'lɔdʒɪkl] *adj* meteorológico.
meteorology [miːtɪə'rɔlədʒɪ] *n* meteorologia.
meter ['miːtə*] *n* (*instrument*) medidor *m*; (*also*: *parking ~*) parcômetro; (*US*) = **metre**.
methane ['miːθeɪn] *n* metano.
method ['mɛθəd] *n* método; **~ of payment** modalidade de pagamento.
methodical [mɪ'θɔdɪkl] *adj* metódico.
Methodist ['mɛθədɪst] *adj*, *n* metodista *m/f*.
methylated spirit ['mɛθɪleɪtɪd-] *n* (*also*: *BRIT*: *meths*) álcool *m* metílico *or* desnaturado.
meticulous [mɛ'tɪkjuləs] *adj* meticuloso.
metre ['miːtə*] (*US* **meter**) *n* metro.
metric ['mɛtrɪk] *adj* métrico; **to go ~** adotar o sistema métrico decimal.
metrical ['mɛtrɪkl] *adj* métrico.
metrication [mɛtrɪ'keɪʃən] *n* conversão *f* ao sistema métrico decimal.
metric system *n* sistema *m* métrico decimal.
metric ton *n* tonelada (métrica).
metronome ['mɛtrənəum] *n* metrônomo.
metropolis [mɪ'trɔpəlɪs] *n* metrópole *f*.
metropolitan [mɛtrə'pɔlɪtən] *adj* metropolitano.
Metropolitan Police (*BRIT*) *n*: **the ~** a polícia de Londres.
mettle ['mɛtl] *n* (*spirit*) caráter *m*, têmpera; (*courage*) coragem *f*.
mew [mjuː] *vi* (*cat*) miar.
mews [mjuːz] (*BRIT*) *n*: **~ cottage** *pequena casa resultante de reforma de antigos estábulos*.
Mexican ['mɛksɪkən] *adj*, *n* mexicano/a.
Mexico ['mɛksɪkəu] *n* México.
Mexico City *n* Cidade *f* do México.
mezzanine ['mɛtsəniːn] *n* sobreloja, mezanino.
MFA (*US*) *n abbr* (= *Master of Fine Arts*) *grau universitário*.
mfr *abbr* = **manufacture**; **manufacturer**.
mg *abbr* (= *milligram*) mg.
Mgr *abbr* = **Monseigneur**; **Monsignor**; (= *manager*) dir.
MHR (*US*) *n abbr* = **Member of the House of Representatives**.
MHz *abbr* (= *megahertz*) MHz.
MI (*US*) *abbr* (*POST*) = **Michigan**.
MI5 (*BRIT*) *n abbr* (= *Military Intelligence 5*) ≈ SNI *m*.
MI6 (*BRIT*) *n abbr* (= *Military Intelligence 6*) ≈ SNI *m*.
MIA *abbr* = **missing in action**.
miaow [miː'au] *vi* miar.
mice [maɪs] *npl of* **mouse**.
microbe ['maɪkrəub] *n* micróbio.
microbiology [maɪkrəubaɪ'ɔlədʒɪ] *n* microbiologia.
microchip ['maɪkrəutʃɪp] *n* (*ELEC*) microchip *m*.
micro(computer) ['maɪkrəu(kəm'pjuːtə*)] *n* micro(computador) *m*.
microcosm ['maɪkrəukɔzəm] *n* microcosmo.
microeconomics [maɪkrəuiːkə'nɔmɪks] *n* microeconomia.
microfiche ['maɪkrəufiːʃ] *n* microficha.
microfilm ['maɪkrəufɪlm] *n* microfilme *m* ♦ *vt* microfilmar.
microlight ['maɪkrəulaɪt] *n* ultraleve *m*.
micrometer [maɪ'krɔmɪtə*] *n* micrômetro.
microphone ['maɪkrəfəun] *n* microfone *m*.
microprocessor [maɪkrəu'prəusɛsə*] *n* microprocessador *m*.
microscope ['maɪkrəskəup] *n* microscópio; **under the ~** com microscópio.
microscopic [maɪkrə'skɔpɪk] *adj* microscópico.
microwave ['maɪkrəuweɪv] *n* (*also*: *~ oven*)

NB: *European Portuguese adds the following consonants to certain words:* **b** (sú(b)dito, su(b)til); **c** (a(c)ção, a(c)cionista, a(c)to); **m** (inde(m)ne); **p** (ado(p)ção, ado(p)tar); *for further details see p. xiii.*

forno microondas.

mid [mɪd] *adj*: **in ~ May** em meados de maio; **in ~ afternoon** no meio da tarde; **in ~ air** em pleno ar; **he's in his ~ thirties** ele tem por volta de trinta e cinco anos.

midday ['mɪddeɪ] *n* meio-dia *m*.

middle ['mɪdl] *n* meio; (*waist*) cintura ♦ *adj* meio; (*quantity, size*) médio, mediano; **in the ~ of the night** no meio da noite; **I'm in the ~ of reading it** estou no meio da leitura.

middle age *n* meia-idade *f* ♦ *cpd*: **middle-age spread** barriga de meia-idade.

middle-aged *adj* de meia-idade.

Middle Ages *npl*: **the ~** a Idade Média.

middle class *n*: **the ~(es)** a classe média ♦ *adj* (*also*: *middle-class*) de classe média.

Middle East *n*: **the ~** o Oriente Médio.

middleman ['mɪdlmæn] (*irreg*) *n* intermediário; (COMM) atravessador *m*.

middle management *n* escalão gerencial intermediário.

middlemen ['mɪdlmɛn] *npl of* **middleman**.

middle name *n* segundo nome *m*.

middle-of-the-road *adj* (*policy*) de meio-termo; (*music*) romântico.

middleweight ['mɪdlweɪt] *n* (BOXING) peso médio.

middling ['mɪdlɪŋ] *adj* mediano.

Middx (BRIT) *abbr* = **Middlesex**.

midge [mɪdʒ] *n* mosquito.

midget ['mɪdʒɪt] *n* anão/anã *m/f* ♦ *adj* minúsculo.

Midlands ['mɪdləndz] *npl região central da Inglaterra*.

midnight ['mɪdnaɪt] *n* meia-noite *f*; **at ~** à meia-noite.

midriff ['mɪdrɪf] *n* barriga.

midst [mɪdst] *n*: **in the ~ of** no meio de, entre.

midsummer [mɪd'sʌmə*] *n*: **a ~ day** um dia em pleno verão.

midway [mɪd'weɪ] *adj, adv*: **~ (between)** no meio do caminho (entre).

midweek [mɪd'wiːk] *adv* no meio da semana.

midwife ['mɪdwaɪf] (*irreg*) *n* parteira.

midwifery ['mɪdwɪfərɪ] *n* trabalho de parteira, obstetrícia.

midwinter [mɪd'wɪntə*] *n*: **in ~** em pleno inverno.

midwives ['mɪdwaɪvz] *npl of* **midwife**.

might [maɪt] *pt, conditional of* **may** ♦ *n* poder *m*, força.

mighty ['maɪtɪ] *adj* poderoso, forte ♦ *adv* (*inf*): **~ ... ...** pra burro.

migraine ['miːgreɪn] *n* enxaqueca.

migrant ['maɪgrənt] *n* (*bird*) ave *f* de arribação; (*person*) emigrante *m/f*; (*fig*) nômade *m/f* ♦ *adj* migratório; (*worker*) emigrante.

migrate [maɪ'greɪt] *vi* emigrar; (*birds*) arribar.

migration [maɪ'greɪʃən] *n* emigração *f*; (*of birds*) arribação *f*.

mike [maɪk] *n abbr* = **microphone**.

mild [maɪld] *adj* (*character*) pacífico; (*climate*) temperado; (*slight*) ligeiro; (*taste*) suave; (*illness*) leve, benigno ♦ *n* cerveja ligeira.

mildew ['mɪldjuː] *n* mofo; (BOT) míldio.

mildly ['maɪldlɪ] *adv* brandamente; (*slightly*) ligeiramente, um tanto; **to put it ~** (*inf*) para não dizer coisa pior.

mildness ['maɪldnɪs] *n* (*softness*) suavidade *f*; (*gentleness*) doçura; (*quiet character*) brandura.

mile [maɪl] *n* milha (= *1609 m*); **to do 30 ~s per gallon** ≈ fazer 10.64 quilômetros por litro.

mileage ['maɪlɪdʒ] *n* número de milhas; (AUT) ≈ quilometragem *f*.

mileage allowance *n* ≈ ajuda de custo com base na quilometragem rodada.

mileometer [maɪ'lɔmɪtə*] (BRIT) *n* ≈ conta-quilômetros *m inv*.

milestone ['maɪlstəun] *n* marco miliário; (*event*) marco.

milieu ['miːljəː] (*pl* **~s** *or* **~x**) *n* meio, meio social.

milieux ['miːljəːz] *npl of* **milieu**.

militant ['mɪlɪtnt] *adj, n* militante *m/f*.

militarism ['mɪlɪtərɪzəm] *n* militarismo.

militaristic [mɪlɪtə'rɪstɪk] *adj* militarista.

military ['mɪlɪtərɪ] *adj* militar ♦ *n*: **the ~** as forças armadas, os militares.

militate ['mɪlɪteɪt] *vi*: **to ~ against** militar contra.

militia [mɪ'lɪʃə] *n* milícia.

milk [mɪlk] *n* leite *m* ♦ *vt* (*cow*) ordenhar; (*fig*) explorar, chupar.

milk chocolate *n* chocolate *m* de leite.

milk float (BRIT) *n* furgão *m* de leiteiro.

milking ['mɪlkɪŋ] *n* ordenhação *f*, ordenha.

milkman ['mɪlkmən] (*irreg*) *n* leiteiro.

milk shake *n* milk-shake *m*, leite *m* batido com sorvete.

milk tooth (*irreg*) *n* dente *m* de leite.

milk truck (US) *n* = **milk float**.

milky ['mɪlkɪ] *adj* leitoso.

Milky Way *n* Via Láctea.

mill [mɪl] *n* (*windmill etc*) moinho; (*coffee ~*) moedor *m* de café; (*factory*) moinho, engenho; (*spinning ~*) fábrica de tecelagem, fiação *f* ♦ *vt* moer ♦ *vi* (*also*: *~ about*) aglomerar-se, remoinhar.

millennia [mɪ'lɛnɪə] *npl of* **millennium**.

millennium [mɪ'lɛnɪəm] (*pl* **~s** *or* **millennia**) *n* milênio, milenário.

miller ['mɪlə*] *n* moleiro/a.

millet ['mɪlɪt] *n* milhete *m*.

milli... ['mɪlɪ] *prefix* mili....

milligram(me) ['mɪlɪgræm] *n* miligrama *m*.

millilitre ['mɪlɪliːtə*] (US **milliliter**) *n* mililitro.

millimetre ['mɪlɪmiːtə*] (US **millimeter**) *n* milímetro.

milliner ['mɪlɪnə*] *n* chapeleiro/a de senhoras.

millinery ['mɪlɪnərɪ] *n* chapelaria de senhoras.

million ['mɪljən] *n* milhão *m*; **a ~ times** um milhão de vezes.

millionaire [mɪljə'nɛə*] *n* milionário/a.

millipede ['mɪlɪpiːd] *n* embuá *m*.

millstone ['mɪlstəun] *n* mó *f*, pedra (de moinho).

millwheel ['mɪlwiːl] *n* roda de azenha.
milometer [maɪ'lɔmɪtə*] *n* = **mileometer**.
mime [maɪm] *n* mimo; (*actor*) mímico/a, comediante *m/f* ♦ *vt* imitar ♦ *vi* fazer mímica.
mimic ['mɪmɪk] *n* mímico/a, imitador(a) *m/f* ♦ *vt* imitar, parodiar.
mimicry ['mɪmɪkrɪ] *n* imitação *f*; (ZOOL) mimetismo.
Min. (*BRIT*) *abbr* (*POL*) = **ministry**.
min. *abbr* (= *minute*; *minimum*) min.
minaret [mɪnə'rɛt] *n* minarete *m*.
mince [mɪns] *vt* moer ♦ *vi* (*in walking*) andar com afetação ♦ *n* (*BRIT*: *CULIN*) carne *f* moída; **he does not ~ (his) words** ele não tem papas na língua.
mincemeat ['mɪnsmiːt] *n recheio de sebo e frutas picadas*.
mince pie *n pastel com recheio de sebo e frutas picadas*.
mincer ['mɪnsə*] *n* moedor *m* de carne.
mincing ['mɪnsɪŋ] *adj* afetado (*PT*: -ct-).
mind [maɪnd] *n* mente *f* ♦ *vt* (*attend to, look after*) tomar conta de, cuidar de; (*be careful of*) ter cuidado com; (*object to*): **I don't ~ the noise** não me importa o ruído; **do you ~ if ...?** você se incomoda se ...?; **I don't ~** (*it doesn't worry me*) eu nem ligo; (*it's all the same to me*) para mim tanto faz; **~ you, ...** se bem que ...; **never ~!** não faz mal, não importa!; (*don't worry*) não se preocupe!; **it is on my ~** não me sai da cabeça; **to change one's ~** mudar de idéia; **to be in two ~s about sth** (*BRIT*) estar dividido em relação a algo; **to my ~** a meu ver; **to be out of one's ~** estar fora de si; **to bear** *or* **keep sth in ~** levar algo em consideração, não esquecer-se de algo; **to have sb/sth in ~** ter alguém/algo em mente; **to have in ~ to do** pretender fazer; **it went right out of my ~** saiu-me totalmente da cabeça; **to bring** *or* **call sth to ~** lembrar algo; **to make up one's ~** decidir-se; **"~ the step"** "cuidado com o degrau".
-minded ['maɪndɪd] *suffix*: **fair~** imparcial, justo; **an industrially~ nation** uma nação de vocação industrial.
minder ['maɪndə*] *n* (*child~*) cuidadora de crianças; (*bodyguard*) guarda-costas *m/f inv*.
mindful ['maɪndful] *adj*: **~ of** consciente de, atento a.
mindless ['maɪndlɪs] *adj* estúpido; (*violence, crime*) insensato.
mine [maɪn] *pron* (o) meu/(a) minha *etc* ♦ *n* mina ♦ *vt* (*coal*) extrair, explorar; (*ship, beach*) minar.
mine detector *n* detector *m* de minas.
minefield ['maɪnfiːld] *n* campo minado.
miner ['maɪnə*] *n* mineiro.
mineral ['mɪnərəl] *adj* mineral ♦ *n* mineral *m*; **~s** *npl* (*BRIT*: *soft drinks*) refrigerantes *mpl*.
mineralogy [mɪnə'rælədʒɪ] *n* mineralogia.
mineral water *n* água mineral.
minesweeper ['maɪnswiːpə*] *n* caça-minas *m inv*.
mingle ['mɪŋgl] *vt* misturar ♦ *vi*: **to ~ with** misturar-se com.
mingy ['mɪndʒɪ] (*inf*) *adj* sovina, pão-duro (*BR*) *inv*.
miniature ['mɪnətʃə*] *adj* em miniatura ♦ *n* miniatura.
minibus ['mɪnɪbʌs] *n* microônibus *m*.
minicab ['mɪnɪkæb] (*BRIT*) *n* ≈ (táxi *m*) cooperativado.
minicomputer ['mɪnɪkəm'pjuːtə*] *n* minicomputador *m*, míni *m*.
minim ['mɪnɪm] *n* (*MUS*) mínima.
minima ['mɪnɪmə] *npl of* **minimum**.
minimal ['mɪnɪml] *adj* mínimo.
minimize ['mɪnɪmaɪz] *vt* minimizar.
minimum ['mɪnɪməm] (*pl* **minima**) *adj*, *n* mínimo; **to reduce to a ~** reduzir ao mínimo.
minimum lending rate *n* (*ECON*) taxa mínima de empréstimos.
minimum wage *n* salário mínimo.
mining ['maɪnɪŋ] *n* exploração *f* de minas ♦ *adj* mineiro.
minion ['mɪnjən] (*pej*) *n* lacaio.
miniskirt ['mɪnɪskəːt] *n* minissaia.
minister ['mɪnɪstə*] *n* (*POL*) ministro/a; (*REL*) pastor *m* ♦ *vi*: **to ~ to sb** prestar assistência a alguém; **to ~ to sb's needs** atender às necessidades de alguém.
ministerial [mɪnɪs'tɪərɪəl] *adj* (*POL*) ministerial.
ministry ['mɪnɪstrɪ] *n* ministério; (*REL*): **to go into the ~** ingressar no sacerdócio.
mink [mɪŋk] *n* marta.
mink coat *n* casaco de marta.
minnow ['mɪnəu] *n* peixinho (de água doce).
minor ['maɪnə*] *adj* menor; (*unimportant*) de pouca importância; (*inferior*) inferior; (*MUS*) menor ♦ *n* (*LAW*) menor *m/f* de idade.
Minorca [mɪ'nɔːkə] *n* Minorca.
minority [maɪ'nɔrɪtɪ] *n* minoria; (*age*) menoridade *f*; **to be in a ~** estar em minoria.
minster ['mɪnstə*] *n* catedral *f*.
minstrel ['mɪnstrəl] *n* menestrel *m*.
mint [mɪnt] *n* (*plant*) hortelã *f*; (*sweet*) bala de hortelã ♦ *vt* (*coins*) cunhar; **the (Royal) M~** (*BRIT*) *or* **the (US) M~** (*US*) ≈ a Casa da Moeda; **in ~ condition** em perfeito estado.
mint sauce *n* molho de hortelã.
minuet [mɪnju'ɛt] *n* minueto.
minus ['maɪnəs] *n* (*also*: **~** *sign*) sinal *m* de subtração ♦ *prep* menos; (*without*) sem.
minute [*n* 'mɪnɪt, *adj* maɪ'njuːt] *n* minuto; (*official record*) ata ♦ *adj* miúdo, diminuto; (*search*) minucioso; **~s** *npl* atas *fpl*; **it is 5 ~s past 3** são 3 e 5; **wait a ~!** (espere) um minuto *or* minutinho!; **at the last ~** no último momento; **to leave sth till the last ~** deixar algo até em cima da hora; **up to the ~** (*fashion*) último; (*news*) de última hora; **up to the ~ technology** a última tecnologia; **in**

~ **detail** por miúdo, em miúdos.
minute book *n* livro de atas.
minute hand *n* ponteiro dos minutos.
minutely [maɪ'nju:tlɪ] *adv* (*by a small amount*) ligeiramente; (*in detail*) minuciosamente.
miracle ['mɪrəkl] *n* milagre *m*.
miraculous [mɪ'rækjuləs] *adj* milagroso.
mirage ['mɪrɑ:ʒ] *n* miragem *f*.
mire ['maɪə*] *n* lamaçal *m*.
mirror ['mɪrə*] *n* espelho; (*in car*) retrovisor *m* ♦ *vt* refletir.
mirror image *n* imagem *f* de espelho.
mirth [mə:θ] *n* alegria; (*laughter*) risada.
misadventure [mɪsəd'vɛntʃə*] *n* desgraça, infortúnio; **death by** ~ (*BRIT*) morte acidental.
misanthropist [mɪ'zænθrəpɪst] *n* misantropo/a.
misapply [mɪsə'plaɪ] *vt* empregar mal.
misapprehension [mɪsæprɪ'hɛnʃən] *n* malentendido, equívoco.
misappropriate [mɪsə'prəuprɪeɪt] *vt* desviar.
misappropriation [mɪsəprəuprɪ'eɪʃən] *n* desvio.
misbehave [mɪsbɪ'heɪv] *vi* comportar-se mal.
misbehaviour [mɪsbɪ'heɪvjə*] (*US* **misbehavior**) *n* mau comportamento.
misc. *abbr* = **miscellaneous**.
miscalculate [mɪs'kælkjuleɪt] *vt* calcular mal.
miscalculation [mɪskælkju'leɪʃən] *n* erro de cálculo.
miscarriage ['mɪskærɪdʒ] *n* (*MED*) aborto (espontâneo); ~ **of justice** erro judicial.
miscarry [mɪs'kærɪ] *vi* (*MED*) abortar espontaneamente; (*fail: plans*) fracassar.
miscellaneous [mɪsɪ'leɪnɪəs] *adj* (*items, expenses*) diverso; (*selection*) variado.
miscellany [mɪ'sɛlənɪ] *n* coletânea.
mischance [mɪs'tʃɑ:ns] *n* infelicidade *f*, azar *m*.
mischief ['mɪstʃɪf] *n* (*naughtiness*) travessura; (*harm*) dano, prejuízo; (*maliciousness*) malícia.
mischievous ['mɪstʃɪvəs] *adj* malicioso; (*naughty*) travesso.
misconception [mɪskən'sɛpʃən] *n* concepção *f* errada, conceito errado.
misconduct [mɪs'kɔndʌkt] *n* comportamento impróprio; **professional** ~ má conduta profissional.
misconstrue [mɪskən'stru:] *vt* interpretar mal.
miscount [mɪs'kaunt] *vt, vi* contar mal.
misdeed [mɪs'di:d] *n* delito, ofensa.
misdemeanour [mɪsdɪ'mi:nə*] (*US* **misdemeanor**) *n* má ação, contravenção *f*.
misdirect [mɪsdɪ'rɛkt] *vt* (*person*) orientar *or* informar mal; (*letter*) endereçar mal.
miser ['maɪzə*] *n* avaro/a, sovina *m/f*.
miserable ['mɪzərəbl] *adj* (*unhappy, of weather*) triste; (*wretched*) miserável; (*despicable*) desprezível; **to feel** ~ estar na fossa, estar de baixo astral.
miserably ['mɪzərəblɪ] *adv* (*smile, answer*) tristemente; (*fail, live, pay*) miseravelmente.
miserly ['maɪzəlɪ] *adj* avarento, mesquinho.
misery ['mɪzərɪ] *n* (*unhappiness*) tristeza; (*wretchedness*) miséria.
misfire [mɪs'faɪə*] *vi* falhar.
misfit ['mɪsfɪt] *n* (*person*) inadaptado/a, deslocado/a.
misfortune [mɪs'fɔ:tʃən] *n* desgraça, infortúnio.
misgiving(s) [mɪs'gɪvɪŋ(z)] *n(pl)* (*mistrust*) desconfiança, receio; (*apprehension*) mau pressentimento; **to have ~s about sth** ter desconfianças em relação a algo.
misguided [mɪs'gaɪdɪd] *adj* enganado.
mishandle [mɪs'hændl] *vt* (*treat roughly*) maltratar; (*mismanage*) manejar mal.
mishap ['mɪshæp] *n* desgraça, contratempo.
mishear [mɪs'hɪə*] (*irreg*) *vt* ouvir mal.
mishmash ['mɪʃmæʃ] (*inf*) *n* mixórdia, salada.
misinform [mɪsɪn'fɔ:m] *vt* informar mal.
misinterpret [mɪsɪn'tə:prɪt] *vt* interpretar mal.
misinterpretation [mɪsɪntə:prɪ'teɪʃən] *n* interpretação *f* errônea.
misjudge [mɪs'dʒʌdʒ] *vt* fazer um juízo errado de, julgar mal.
mislay [mɪs'leɪ] (*irreg*) *vt* extraviar, perder.
mislead [mɪs'li:d] (*irreg*) *vt* induzir em erro, enganar.
misleading [mɪs'li:dɪŋ] *adj* enganoso, errôneo.
misled [mɪs'lɛd] *pt, pp of* **mislead**.
mismanage [mɪs'mænɪdʒ] *vt* administrar mal.
mismanagement [mɪs'mænɪdʒmənt] *n* má administração *f*.
misnomer [mɪs'nəumə*] *n* termo impróprio *or* errado.
misogynist [mɪ'sɔdʒɪnɪst] *n* misógino.
misplace [mɪs'pleɪs] *vt* (*lose*) extraviar, perder; (*wrongly*) colocar em lugar errado; **to be ~d** (*trust etc*) ser imerecido.
misprint ['mɪsprɪnt] *n* erro tipográfico.
mispronounce [mɪsprə'nauns] *vt* pronunciar mal.
misquote [mɪs'kwəut] *vt* citar incorretamente.
misread [mɪs'ri:d] (*irreg*) *vt* interpretar *or* ler mal.
misrepresent [mɪsrɛprɪ'zɛnt] *vt* desvirtuar, deturpar.
Miss [mɪs] *n* Senhorita (*BR*), a menina (*PT*); **Dear ~ Smith** Ilma. Srta. Smith (*BR*), Exma. Sra. Smith (*PT*).
miss [mɪs] *vt* (*train, appointment, class*) perder; (*fail to hit*) errar, não acertar em; (*notice loss of: money etc*) dar por falta de; (*regret the absence of*): **I ~ him** sinto a falta dele ♦ *vi* falhar ♦ *n* (*shot*) tiro perdido *or* errado; (*fig*): **that was a near ~** (*near accident*) essa foi por pouco; **the bus just ~ed the wall** o ônibus por pouco não bateu no muro; **you're ~ing the point** você não está entendendo.
miss out (*BRIT*) *vt* omitir.
miss out on *vt fus* perder, ficar por fora de.
missal ['mɪsl] *n* missal *m*.
misshapen [mɪs'ʃeɪpən] *adj* disforme.

missile ['mɪsaɪl] *n* (*AVIAT*) míssil *m*; (*object thrown*) projétil *m*.
missile base *n* base *f* de mísseis.
missile launcher [-'lɔːntʃə*] *n* plataforma para lançamento de mísseis.
missing ['mɪsɪŋ] *adj* (*pupil*) ausente; (*thing*) perdido; (*after escape, disaster: person*) desaparecido; **to go ~** desaparecer; **~ person** pessoa desaparecida.
mission ['mɪʃən] *n* missão *f*; **on a ~ to sb** em missão a alguém.
missionary ['mɪʃənərɪ] *n* missionário/a.
missive ['mɪsɪv] *n* missiva.
misspell [mɪs'spɛl] *vt* (*irreg: like* **spell**) escrever errado, errar na ortografia de.
misspent [mɪs'spɛnt] *adj*: **his ~ youth** sua juventude desperdiçada.
mist [mɪst] *n* (*light*) neblina; (*heavy*) névoa; (*at sea*) bruma ♦ *vi* (*also*: *~ over*; *~ up*) enevoar-se; (*BRIT*: *windows*) embaçar.
mistake [mɪs'teɪk] (*irreg: like* **take**) *n* erro, engano ♦ *vt* entender *or* interpretar mal; **to ~ A for B** confundir A com B; **by ~** por engano; **to make a ~** fazer *or* cometer um erro; **to make a ~ about sb/sth** enganar-se a respeito de alguém/algo.
mistaken [mɪs'teɪkən] *pp of* **mistake** ♦ *adj* (*idea etc*) errado; (*person*) enganado; **to be ~** enganar-se, equivocar-se.
mistaken identity *n* identidade *f* errada.
mistakenly [mɪs'teɪkənlɪ] *adv* por engano.
mister ['mɪstə*] (*inf*) *n* senhor *m*; *see* **Mr.**
mistletoe ['mɪsltəu] *n* visco.
mistook [mɪs'tuk] *pt of* **mistake**.
mistranslation [mɪstræns'leɪʃən] *n* erro de tradução, tradução *f* incorreta.
mistreat [mɪs'triːt] *vt* maltratar.
mistreatment [mɪs'triːtmənt] *n* maus tratos *mpl*.
mistress ['mɪstrɪs] *n* (*lover*) amante *f*; (*of house*) dona (da casa); (*BRIT*: *in school*) professora, mestra; *see* **Mrs.**
mistrust [mɪs'trʌst] *vt* desconfiar de ♦ *n*: **~ (of)** desconfiança (em relação a).
mistrustful [mɪs'trʌstful] *adj*: **~ (of)** desconfiado (em relação a).
misty ['mɪstɪ] *adj* enevoado, nebuloso; (*day*) nublado; (*glasses*) embaçado.
misty-eyed [-aɪd] *adj* (*fig*) sentimental.
misunderstand [mɪsʌndə'stænd] (*irreg*) *vt, vi* entender *or* interpretar mal.
misunderstanding [mɪsʌndə'stændɪŋ] *n* mal-entendido.
misunderstood [mɪsʌndə'stud] *pt, pp of* **misunderstand**.
misuse [*n* mɪs'juːs, *vt* mɪs'juːz] *n* uso impróprio; (*of power*) abuso ♦ *vt* (*use wrongly*) empregar mal; (*power*) abusar de; (*funds*) desviar.
MIT (*US*) *n abbr* = **Massachusetts Institute of Technology**.
mite [maɪt] *n* (*small quantity*) pingo; (*BRIT*: *small child*) criancinha.
miter ['maɪtə*] (*US*) *n* = **mitre**.
mitigate ['mɪtɪgeɪt] *vt* mitigar, atenuar; **mitigating circumstances** circunstâncias *fpl* atenuantes.
mitigation [mɪtɪ'geɪʃən] *n* abrandamento, mitigação *f*.
mitre ['maɪtə*] (*US* **miter**) *n* mitra; (*CARPENTRY*) meia-esquadria.
mitt(en) ['mɪt(n)] *n* mitene *f*.
mix [mɪks] *vt* (*gen*) misturar; (*combine*) combinar ♦ *vi* misturar-se; (*people*) entrosar-se ♦ *n* mistura; **to ~ sth with sth** misturar algo com algo; **to ~ business with pleasure** misturar trabalho com divertimento.
mix in *vt* misturar.
mix up *vt* misturar; (*confuse*) confundir, misturar; **to be ~ed up in sth** estar envolvido *or* metido em algo.
mixed [mɪkst] *adj* (*assorted*) sortido, variado; (*school etc*) misto.
mixed doubles *npl* (*SPORT*) duplas *fpl* mistas.
mixed economy *n* economia mista.
mixed grill (*BRIT*) *n* carnes *fpl* grelhadas.
mixed-up *adj* (*confused*) confuso.
mixer ['mɪksə*] *n* (*for food*) batedeira; (*person*) pessoa sociável.
mixture ['mɪkstʃə*] *n* mistura; (*MED*) preparado.
mix-up *n* trapalhada, confusão *f*.
Mk (*BRIT*) *abbr* (*TECH*) = **mark**.
mk *abbr* = **mark** (*currency*).
mkt *abbr* = **market**.
MLitt *n abbr* (= *Master of Literature*; *Master of Letters*) *grau universitário*.
MLR (*BRIT*) *n abbr* = **minimum lending rate**.
mm *abbr* (= *millimetre*) mm.
MN *abbr* (*BRIT*) = **merchant navy**; (*US*: *POST*) = **Minnesota**.
MO *n abbr* (*MED*) = **medical officer**; (*US*: *inf*: = *modus operandi*) método ♦ *abbr* (*US*: *POST*) = **Missouri**.
M.O. *abbr* = **money order**.
moan [məun] *n* gemido ♦ *vi* gemer; (*inf*: *complain*): **to ~ (about)** queixar-se (de), bufar (sobre) (*inf*).
moaning ['məunɪŋ] *n* gemidos *mpl*; (*inf*: *complaining*) queixas *fpl*.
moat [məut] *n* fosso.
mob [mɔb] *n* multidão *f*; (*pej*): **the ~** (*masses*) o povinho; (*mafia*) a máfia ♦ *vt* cercar.
mobile ['məubaɪl] *adj* móvel ♦ *n* móvel *m*; **applicants must be ~** (*BRIT*) os candidatos devem estar dispostos a aceitar qualquer deslocamento.
mobile home *n* trailer *m*, casa móvel.
mobile shop (*BRIT*) *n* loja circulante.
mobility [məu'bɪlɪtɪ] *n* mobilidade *f*.
mobilize ['məubɪlaɪz] *vt* mobilizar ♦ *vi*

NB*: European Portuguese adds the following consonants to certain words:* **b** (sú(b)dito, su(b)til); **c** (a(c)ção, a(c)cionista, a(c)to); **m** (inde(m)ne); **p** (ado(p)ção, ado(p)tar); *for further details see p. xiii.*

mobilizar-se; (*MIL*) ser mobilizado.
moccasin ['mɔkəsɪn] *n* mocassim *m*.
mock [mɔk] *vt* (*make ridiculous*) ridicularizar; (*laugh at*) zombar de, gozar de ♦ *adj* falso, fingido.
mockery ['mɔkərɪ] *n* zombaria; **to make a ~ of sth** ridicularizar algo.
mocking ['mɔkɪŋ] *adj* zombeteiro.
mockingbird ['mɔkɪŋbəːd] *n* tordo-dos-remédios *m*.
mock-up *n* maqueta, modelo.
MOD (*BRIT*) *n abbr* = **Ministry of Defence**.
mod cons (*BRIT*) *npl abbr* (= *modern conveniences*) *see* **convenience**.
mode [məud] *n* modo; (*of transport*) meio.
model ['mɔdl] *n* (*gen*) modelo; (*ARCH*) maqueta; (*person: for fashion, ART*) modelo *m/f* ♦ *adj* (*car, toy*) de brinquedo; (*child, factory*) modelar ♦ *vt* modelar ♦ *vi* servir de modelo; (*in fashion*) trabalhar como modelo; **~ railway** trenzinho de brinquedo; **to ~ clothes** desfilar apresentando modelos; **to ~ sb/sth on** modelar alguém/algo a *or* por.
modeller ['mɔdlə*] (*US* **modeler**) *n* modelador(a) *m/f*; (*model maker*) maquetista *m/f*.
modem ['məudɛm] *n* modem *m*.
moderate [*adj, n* 'mɔdərət, *vi, vt* 'mɔdəreɪt] *adj, n* moderado/a ♦ *vi* moderar-se, acalmar-se ♦ *vt* moderar.
moderately ['mɔdərətlɪ] *adv* (*act*) com moderação, moderadamente; (*pleased, happy*) razoavelmente; **~ priced** de preço médio *or* razoável.
moderation [mɔdə'reɪʃən] *n* moderação *f*; **in ~** com moderação.
modern ['mɔdən] *adj* moderno; **~ languages** línguas *fpl* vivas.
modernization [mɔdənaɪ'zeɪʃən] *n* modernização *f*.
modernize ['mɔdənaɪz] *vt* modernizar, atualizar.
modest ['mɔdɪst] *adj* modesto.
modesty ['mɔdɪstɪ] *n* modéstia.
modicum ['mɔdɪkəm] *n*: **a ~ of** um mínimo de.
modification [mɔdɪfɪ'keɪʃən] *n* modificação *f*.
modify ['mɔdɪfaɪ] *vt* modificar.
Mods [mɔdz] (*BRIT*) *n abbr* (= (*Honour*) *Moderations*) *primeiro exame universitário* (*em Oxford*).
modular ['mɔdjulə*] *adj* (*filing, unit*) modular.
modulate ['mɔdjuleɪt] *vt* modular.
modulation [mɔdju'leɪʃən] *n* modulação *f*.
module ['mɔdjuːl] *n* módulo.
mogul ['məugl] *n* (*fig*) magnata *m*.
MOH (*BRIT*) *n abbr* = **Medical Officer of Health**.
mohair ['məuhɛə*] *n* mohair *m*, angorá *m*.
Mohammed [mə'hæmɪd] *n* Maomé *m*.
moist [mɔɪst] *adj* úmido (*PT*: hú-), molhado.
moisten ['mɔɪsn] *vt* umedecer (*PT*: hu-).
moisture ['mɔɪstʃə*] *n* umidade *f* (*PT*: hu-).
moisturize ['mɔɪstʃəraɪz] *vt* (*skin*) hidratar.
moisturizer ['mɔɪstʃəraɪzə*] *n* creme *m* hidratante.
molar ['məulə*] *n* molar *m*.
molasses [məu'læsɪz] *n* melaço, melado.
mold [məuld] (*US*) *n, vt* = **mould**.
mole [məul] *n* (*animal*) toupeira; (*spot*) sinal *m*, lunar *m*.
molecule ['mɔlɪkjuːl] *n* molécula.
molehill ['məulhɪl] *n* montículo (feito por uma toupeira).
molest [məu'lɛst] *vt* molestar, importunar.
mollusc ['mɔləsk] *n* molusco.
mollycoddle ['mɔlɪkɔdl] *vt* mimar.
molt [məult] (*US*) *vi* = **moult**.
molten ['məultən] *adj* fundido; (*lava*) liquefeito.
mom [mɔm] (*US*) *n* = **mum**.
moment ['məumənt] *n* momento; (*importance*) importância; **at the ~** neste momento; **for the ~** por enquanto; **in a ~** num instante; **"one ~ please"** (*TEL*) "não desligue".
momentarily ['məuməntrɪlɪ] *adv* momentaneamente; (*US: soon*) daqui a pouco.
momentary ['məuməntərɪ] *adj* momentâneo.
momentous [məu'mɛntəs] *adj* importantíssimo.
momentum [məu'mɛntəm] *n* momento; (*fig*) ímpeto; **to gather ~** ganhar ímpeto.
mommy ['mɔmɪ] (*US*) *n* = **mummy**.
Mon. *abbr* (= *Monday*) seg., 2ª.
Monaco ['mɔnəkəu] *n* Mônaco (*no article*).
monarch ['mɔnək] *n* monarca *m/f*.
monarchist ['mɔnəkɪst] *n* monarquista *m/f*.
monarchy ['mɔnəkɪ] *n* monarquia.
monastery ['mɔnəstərɪ] *n* mosteiro, convento.
monastic [mə'næstɪk] *adj* monástico.
Monday ['mʌndɪ] *n* segunda-feira; *see also* **Tuesday**.
monetarist ['mʌnɪtərɪst] *n* monetarista *m/f*.
monetary ['mʌnɪtərɪ] *adj* monetário.
money ['mʌnɪ] *n* dinheiro; **to make ~** ganhar dinheiro; **I've got no ~ left** não tenho mais dinheiro.
moneyed ['mʌnɪd] *adj* rico, endinheirado.
moneylender ['mʌnɪlɛndə*] *n* agiota *m/f*.
moneymaking ['mʌnɪmeɪkɪŋ] *adj* lucrativo, rendoso.
money market *n* mercado financeiro.
money order *n* vale *m* (postal).
money-spinner (*inf*) *n* mina.
money supply *n* meios *mpl* de pagamento, suprimento monetário.
Mongol ['mɔŋgəl] *n* mongol *m/f*; (*LING*) mongol *m*.
mongol ['mɔŋgəl] *adj, n* (*offensive*) mongolóide *m/f*.
Mongolia [mɔŋ'gəulɪə] *n* Mongólia.
Mongolian [mɔŋ'gəulɪən] *adj* mongol ♦ *n* mongol *m/f*; (*LING*) mongol *m*.
mongoose ['mɔŋguːs] *n* mangusto.
mongrel ['mʌŋgrəl] *n* (*dog*) vira-lata *m*.
monitor ['mɔnɪtə*] *n* (*SCH*) monitor(a) *m/f*; (*TV, COMPUT*) terminal *m* de vídeo ♦ *vt* controlar; (*foreign station*) controlar, monitorar.
monk [mʌŋk] *n* monge *m*.
monkey ['mʌŋkɪ] *n* macaco.

monkey business *n* trapaça, travessura.
monkey nut (*BRIT*) *n* amendoim *m*.
monkey tricks *npl* trapaça, travessura.
monkey wrench *n* chave *f* inglesa.
mono ['mɔnəu] *adj* mono *inv*.
mono... ['mɔnəu] *prefix* mono....
monochrome ['mɔnəkrəum] *adj* monocromático.
monocle ['mɔnəkl] *n* monóculo.
monogram ['mɔnəgræm] *n* monograma *m*.
monolith ['mɔnəlɪθ] *n* monólito.
monologue ['mɔnəlɔg] *n* monólogo.
monoplane ['mɔnəpleɪn] *n* monoplano.
monopolize [mə'nɔpəlaɪz] *vt* monopolizar.
monopoly [mə'nɔpəlɪ] *n* monopólio; **Monopolies and Mergers Commission** (*BRIT*) *comissão de inquérito sobre os monopólios*.
monorail ['mɔnəureɪl] *n* monotrilho.
monosodium glutamate [mɔnə'səudɪəm 'glu:təmeɪt] *n* glutamato de monossódio.
monosyllabic [mɔnəusɪ'læbɪk] *adj* monossilábico; (*person*) lacônico.
monosyllable ['mɔnəsɪləbl] *n* monossílabo.
monotone ['mɔnətəun] *n* monotonia; **to speak in a ~** falar num tom monótono.
monotonous [mə'nɔtənəs] *adj* monótono.
monotony [mə'nɔtənɪ] *n* monotonia.
monoxide [mɔ'nɔksaɪd] *n see* **carbon monoxide**.
monsoon [mɔn'su:n] *n* monção *f*.
monster ['mɔnstə*] *n* monstro.
monstrosity [mɔns'trɔsɪtɪ] *n* monstruosidade *f*.
monstrous ['mɔnstrəs] *adj* (*huge*) descomunal; (*atrocious*) monstruoso.
montage [mɔn'tɑ:ʒ] *n* montagem *f*.
Mont Blanc [mɔ̃blɑ̃] *n* Monte *m* Branco.
Montevideo ['mɔnteɪvɪ'deɪəu] *n* Montevidéu.
month [mʌnθ] *n* mês *m*; **every ~** todo mês; **300 dollars a ~** 300 dólares mensais *or* por mês.
monthly ['mʌnθlɪ] *adj* mensal ♦ *adv* mensalmente ♦ *n* (*magazine*) revista mensal; **twice ~** duas vezes por mês.
monument ['mɔnjumənt] *n* monumento.
monumental [mɔnju'mɛntl] *adj* monumental.
monumental mason *n* marmorista *m/f*.
moo [mu:] *vi* mugir.
mood [mu:d] *n* humor *m*; **to be in a good/bad ~** estar de bom/mau humor; **to be in the ~ for** estar a fim *or* com vontade de.
moody ['mu:dɪ] *adj* (*variable*) caprichoso, de veneta; (*sullen*) rabugento.
moon [mu:n] *n* lua.
moonbeam ['mu:nbi:m] *n* raio de lua.
moon landing *n* alunissagem *f*.
moonlight ['mu:nlaɪt] *n* luar *m* ♦ *vi* ter dois empregos, ter um bico.
moonlighting ['mu:nlaɪtɪŋ] *n* trabalho adicional, bico.
moonlit ['mu:nlɪt] *adj* enluarado; **a ~ night** uma noite de lua.
moonshot ['mu:nʃɔt] *n* (*SPACE*) lançamento de nave para a lua.
moonstruck ['mu:nstrʌk] *adj* lunático, aluado.
Moor [muə*] *n* mouro/a.
moor [muə*] *n* charneca ♦ *vt* (*ship*) amarrar ♦ *vi* fundear, atracar.
mooring ['muərɪŋ] *n* (*place*) ancoradouro; **~s** *npl* (*chains*) amarras *fpl*.
Moorish ['muərɪʃ] *adj* mouro; (*architecture*) mourisco.
moorland ['muələnd] *n* charneca.
moose [mu:s] *n inv* alce *m*.
moot [mu:t] *vt* levantar ♦ *adj*: **~ point** ponto discutível.
mop [mɔp] *n* esfregão *m*; (*of hair*) grenha ♦ *vt* esfregar.
  mop up *vt* limpar.
mope [məup] *vi* estar *or* andar deprimido *or* desanimado.
  mope about *vi* andar por aí desanimado.
  mope around *vi* andar por aí desanimado.
moped ['məupɛd] (*BRIT*) *n* moto *f* pequena (*BR*), motorizada (*PT*).
moquette [mɔ'kɛt] *n* moquete *f*.
moral ['mɔrl] *adj* moral ♦ *n* moral *f*; **~s** *npl* moralidade *f*, costumes *mpl*.
morale [mɔ'rɑ:l] *n* moral *f*, estado de espírito.
morality [mə'rælɪtɪ] *n* moralidade *f*.
moralize ['mɔrəlaɪz] *vi*: **to ~ (about)** dar lições de moral (sobre).
morally ['mɔrəlɪ] *adv* moralmente.
morass [mə'ræs] *n* pântano, brejo.
moratoria [mɔrə'tɔ:rɪə] *npl of* **moratorium**.
moratorium [mɔrə'tɔ:rɪəm] (*pl* **~s** *or* **moratoria**) *n* moratória.
morbid ['mɔ:bɪd] *adj* mórbido.
more [mɔ:*] *adj, adv* mais; **~ money** mais dinheiro; **I want ~** quero mais; **is there any ~?** tem ainda?; **many/much ~** muitos/muito mais; **~ and ~** cada vez mais; **once ~** outra vez; **no ~, not any ~** não ... mais; **and what's ~** ... além do mais ..., aliás ...; **~ dangerous than** mais perigoso do que; **~ or less** mais ou menos; **~ than ever** mais do que nunca.
moreover [mɔ:'rəuvə*] *adv* além do mais, além disso.
morgue [mɔ:g] *n* necrotério.
MORI ['mɔrɪ] (*BRIT*) *n abbr* (= *Market and Opinion Research Institute*) ≈ IBOPE *m*.
moribund ['mɔrɪbʌnd] *adj* moribundo, agonizante.
Mormon ['mɔ:mən] *n* mórmon *m/f*.
morning ['mɔ:nɪŋ] *n* manhã *f*; (*early ~*) madrugada; **good ~** bom dia; **in the ~** de manhã; **7 o'clock in the ~** (as) 7 da manhã; **3 o'clock in the ~** (as) 3 da madrugada; **tomorrow ~** amanhã de manhã; **this ~** hoje de manhã.
morning sickness *n* náusea matinal.
Moroccan [mə'rɔkən] *adj, n* marroquino/a.
Morocco [mə'rɔkəu] *n* Marrocos *m*.
moron ['mɔ:rɔn] *n* débil mental *m/f*, idiota *m/*

***NB**: European Portuguese adds the following consonants to certain words:* **b** (sú(b)dito, su(b)til); **c** (a(c)ção, a(c)cionista, a(c)to); **m** (inde(m)ne); **p** (ado(p)ção, ado(p)tar); *for further details see p. xiii.*

f.
moronic [mə'rɔnɪk] *adj* imbecil, idiota.
morose [mə'rəus] *adj* taciturno, rabugento.
morphine ['mɔːfiːn] *n* morfina.
Morse [mɔːs] *n* (*also*: ~ *code*) código Morse.
morsel ['mɔːsl] *n* (*of food*) bocado.
mortal ['mɔːtl] *adj*, *n* mortal *m/f*.
mortality [mɔː'tælɪtɪ] *n* mortalidade *f*.
mortality rate *n* (taxa de) mortalidade *f*.
mortar ['mɔːtə*] *n* argamassa; (*dish*) pilão *m*, almofariz *m*.
mortgage ['mɔːgɪdʒ] *n* hipoteca; (*for house*) financiamento ♦ *vt* hipotecar; **to take out a** ~ fazer um crédito imobiliário.
mortgage company (*US*) *n* sociedade *f* de crédito imobiliário.
mortgagee [mɔːgə'dʒiː] *n* credor(a) *m/f* hipotecário/a.
mortgagor ['mɔːgədʒə*] *n* devedor(a) *m/f* hipotecário/a.
mortician [mɔː'tɪʃən] (*US*) *n* agente *m/f* funerário/a.
mortified ['mɔːtɪfaɪd] *adj* morto de vergonha.
mortise lock ['mɔːtɪs-] *n* fechadura embutida.
mortuary ['mɔːtjuərɪ] *n* necrotério.
mosaic [məu'zeɪɪk] *n* mosaico.
Moscow ['mɔskəu] *n* Moscou (*BR*), Moscovo (*PT*).
Moslem ['mɔzləm] *adj*, *n* = **Muslim**.
mosque [mɔsk] *n* mesquita.
mosquito [mɔs'kiːtəu] (*pl* ~**es**) *n* mosquito.
mosquito net *n* mosquiteiro.
moss [mɔs] *n* musgo.
mossy ['mɔsɪ] *adj* musgoso, musguento.
most [məust] *adj* a maior parte de, a maioria de ♦ *pron* a maior parte, a maioria ♦ *adv* o mais; (*very*) muito; **the** ~ (*also*: + *adj*) o mais; ~ **fish** a maioria dos peixes; ~ **of them** a maioria deles; **I saw (the)** ~ vi mais; **at the (very)** ~ quando muito, no máximo; **to make the** ~ **of** aproveitar ao máximo; **a** ~ **interesting book** um livro interessantíssimo.
mostly ['məustlɪ] *adv* principalmente, na maior parte.
MOT (*BRIT*) *n abbr* (= *Ministry of Transport*): **the** ~ **(test)** *vistoria anual dos veículos automotores.*
motel [məu'tɛl] *n* motel *m*.
moth [mɔθ] *n* mariposa; (*clothes* ~) traça.
mothball ['mɔθbɔːl] *n* bola de naftalina.
moth-eaten *adj* roído pelas traças.
mother ['mʌðə*] *n* mãe *f* ♦ *adj* materno ♦ *vt* (*care for*) cuidar de (como uma mãe).
mother board *n* (*COMPUT*) placa-base *f*.
motherhood ['mʌðəhud] *n* maternidade *f*.
mother-in-law (*pl* **mothers-in-law**) *n* sogra.
motherly ['mʌðəlɪ] *adj* maternal.
mother-of-pearl *n* madrepérola.
mother's help *n* babá *f*.
mother-to-be (*pl* **mothers-to-be**) *n* futura mamãe *f*.
mother tongue *n* língua materna.
mothproof ['mɔθpruːf] *adj* à prova de traças.
motif [məu'tiːf] *n* motivo.
motion ['məuʃən] *n* movimento; (*gesture*) gesto, sinal *m*; (*at meeting*) moção *f*; (*BRIT*: *of bowels*) fezes *fpl* ♦ *vt*, *vi*: **to** ~ **(to) sb to do sth** fazer sinal a alguém para que faça algo; **to be in** ~ (*vehicle*) estar em movimento; **to set in** ~ pôr em movimento; **to go through the** ~**s of doing sth** (*fig*) fazer algo automaticamente *or* sem convicção.
motionless ['məuʃənlɪs] *adj* imóvel.
motion picture *n* filme *m* (cinematográfico).
motivate ['məutɪveɪt] *vt* motivar.
motivated ['məutɪveɪtɪd] *adj* motivado.
motivation [məutɪ'veɪʃən] *n* motivação *f*.
motive ['məutɪv] *n* motivo ♦ *adj* motor/motriz; **from the best (of)** ~**s** com as melhores intenções.
motley ['mɔtlɪ] *adj* variado, heterogêneo.
motor ['məutə*] *n* motor *m*; (*BRIT*: *inf*: *vehicle*) carro, automóvel *m* ♦ *adj* motor/motriz.
motorbike ['məutəbaɪk] *n* moto(cicleta) *f*, motoca (*inf*).
motorboat ['məutəbəut] *n* barco a motor.
motorcar ['məutəkɑː] (*BRIT*) *n* carro, automóvel *m*.
motorcoach ['məutəkəutʃ] *n* ônibus *m* turístico.
motorcycle ['məutəsaɪkl] *n* motocicleta.
motorcyclist ['məutəsaɪklɪst] *n* motociclista *m/f*.
motoring ['məutərɪŋ] (*BRIT*) *n* automobilismo ♦ *adj* (*accident*, *offence*) de trânsito; ~ **holiday** passeio de carro.
motorist ['məutərɪst] *n* motorista *m/f*.
motorize ['məutəraɪz] *vt* motorizar.
motor oil *n* óleo de motor.
motor racing (*BRIT*) *n* corrida de carros, automobilismo.
motor scooter *n* lambreta (*BR*), motoreta (*PT*).
motor vehicle *n* automóvel *m*, veículo automotor.
motorway ['məutəweɪ] (*BRIT*) *n* rodovia (*BR*), autoestrada (*PT*).
mottled ['mɔtld] *adj* mosqueado, em furtacores.
motto ['mɔtəu] (*pl* ~**es**) *n* lema *m*.
mould [məuld] (*US* **mold**) *n* molde *m*; (*mildew*) mofo, bolor *m* ♦ *vt* moldar; (*fig*) modelar, plasmar.
mo(u)lder ['məuldə*] *vi* (*decay*) desfazer-se.
mo(u)lding ['məuldɪŋ] *n* moldura.
mo(u)ldy ['məuldɪ] *adj* mofado.
moult [məult] (*US* **molt**) *vi* mudar (de penas *etc*).
mound [maund] *n* montão *m*, montículo.
mount [maunt] *n* monte *m*; (*horse*) montaria; (*for jewel etc*) engaste *m*; (*for picture*) moldura ♦ *vt* (*horse etc*) montar em, subir a; (*stairs*) subir; (*exhibition*) montar; (*attack*) montar, desfechar; (*picture*) emoldurar ♦ *vi* (*also*: ~ *up*) aumentar.
mountain ['mauntɪn] *n* montanha ♦ *cpd* de montanha; **to make a** ~ **out of a molehill** (*fig*) fazer um bicho de sete cabeças *or* um cavalo de batalha (de algo).

mountaineer [mauntɪ'nɪə*] *n* alpinista *m/f*, montanhista *m/f*.
mountaineering [mauntɪ'nɪərɪŋ] *n* alpinismo; **to go ~** praticar o alpinismo.
mountainous ['mauntɪnəs] *adj* montanhoso.
mountain rescue team *n* equipe *m* de socorro para alpinistas.
mountainside ['mauntɪnsaɪd] *n* lado da montanha.
mounted ['mauntɪd] *adj* montado.
Mount Everest *n* monte *m* Everest.
mourn [mɔːn] *vt* chorar, lamentar ♦ *vi*: **to ~ for** chorar *or* lamentar a morte de.
mourner ['mɔːnə*] *n* parente/a *m/f or* amigo/a do defunto.
mournful ['mɔːnful] *adj* desolado, triste.
mourning ['mɔːnɪŋ] *n* luto ♦ *cpd* (*dress*) de luto; **(to be) in ~** (estar) de luto.
mouse [maus] (*pl* **mice**) *n* camundongo (*BR*), rato (*PT*).
mousetrap ['maustræp] *n* ratoeira.
mousse [muːs] *n* musse *f*.
moustache [məs'tɑːʃ] *n* bigode *m*.
mousy ['mausɪ] *adj* (*person*) tímido; (*hair*) pardacento.
mouth [mauθ, *pl* mauðz] *n* boca; (*of river*) desembocadura.
mouthful ['mauθful] *n* bocado.
mouth organ *n* gaita.
mouthpiece ['mauθpiːs] *n* (*of musical instrument*) bocal *m*; (*representative*) porta-voz *m/f*.
mouth-to-mouth *adj*: **~ resuscitation** respiração *f* boca-a-boca.
mouthwash ['mauθwɔʃ] *n* colutório.
mouth-watering *adj* de dar água na boca.
movable ['muːvəbl] *adj* móvel.
move [muːv] *n* (*movement*) movimento; (*in game*) lance *m*, jogada; (: *turn to play*) turno, vez *f*; (*change of house*) mudança ♦ *vt* (*hand etc*) mexer, mover; (*from one place to another*) deslocar; (*emotionally*) comover; (*POL*: *resolution etc*) propor ♦ *vi* (*gen*) mexer-se, mover-se; (*traffic*) circular; (*also*: *~ house*) mudar-se; **to ~ sb to do sth** convencer alguém a fazer algo; **to get a ~ on** apressar-se; **to be ~d** (*emotionally*) ficar comovido.
move about *vi* (*fidget*) mexer-se; (*travel*) deslocar-se.
move along *vi* avançar.
move around *vi* (*fidget*) mexer-se; (*travel*) deslocar-se.
move away *vi* afastar-se.
move back *vi* (*step back*) recuar; (*return*) voltar.
move down *vt* abaixar; (*demote*) rebaixar.
move forward *vi* avançar ♦ *vt* adiantar.
move in *vi* (*to a house*) instalar-se (numa casa).
move off *vi* partir.
move on *vi* ir andando ♦ *vt* (*onlookers*) afastar.
move out *vi* (*of house*) sair (de uma casa).
move over *vi* afastar-se; **~ over!** (*towards speaker*) chega mais para cá!; (*away from speaker*) chega mais para lá!
move up *vi* subir; (*employee*) ser promovido; (*~ aside*) chegar mais para lá *or* cá.
movement ['muːvmənt] *n* movimento; (*TECH*) mecanismo; (*MED*: *also*: *bowel ~*) defecação *f*.
mover ['muːvə*] *n* autor(a) *m/f* de proposta.
movie ['muːvɪ] *n* filme *m*; **the ~s** o cinema.
movie camera *n* câmara cinematográfica.
moviegoer ['muːvɪgəuə*] (*US*) *n* freqüentador(a) *m/f* de cinema.
moving ['muːvɪŋ] *adj* (*emotional*) comovente; (*mobile*) móvel; (*in motion*) em movimento ♦ *n* (*US*) mudança.
mow [məu] (*pt* **~ed**, *pp* **~ed** *or* **mown**) *vt* (*grass*) cortar; (*corn*) ceifar.
mow down *vt* ceifar; (*massacre*) chacinar.
mower ['məuə*] *n* ceifeira; (*also*: *lawn~*) cortador *m* de grama (*BR*) *or* de relva (*PT*).
mown [məun] *pp of* **mow**.
Mozambique [məuzəm'biːk] *n* Moçambique *m* (*no article*) ♦ *adj* moçambicano.
MP *n abbr* (= *Military Police*) PM *f*; (*BRIT*) = **Member of Parliament**; (*CANADIAN*) = **Mounted Police**.
mpg *n abbr* = **miles per gallon** (*30 mpg = 10.64 km/l*).
mph *abbr* = **miles per hour** (*60 mph = 96 km/h*).
MPhil *n abbr* (= *Master of Philosophy*) *grau universitário*.
MPS (*BRIT*) *n abbr* = **Member of the Pharmaceutical Society**.
Mr(.) ['mɪstə*] *n*: **~ Smith** (o) Sr. Smith.
MRC (*BRIT*) *n abbr* = **Medical Research Council**.
MRCP (*BRIT*) *n abbr* = **Member of the Royal College of Physicians**.
MRCS (*BRIT*) *n abbr* = **Member of the Royal College of Surgeons**.
MRCVS (*BRIT*) *n abbr* = **Member of the Royal College of Veterinary Surgeons**.
Mrs(.) ['mɪsɪz] *n*: **~ Smith** (a) Sra. Smith.
MS *n abbr* (= *manuscript*) ms; = **multiple sclerosis**; (*US*: = *Master of Science*) *grau universitário* ♦ *abbr* (*US*: *POST*) = **Mississippi**.
Ms(.) [mɪz] *n* (= *Miss or Mrs*): **~ X** (a) Sa X.
MSA (*US*) *n abbr* (= *Master of Science in Agriculture*) *grau universitário*.
MSc *n abbr* = **Master of Science**.
MSG *n abbr* = **monosodium glutamate**.
MST (*US*) *abbr* (= *Mountain Standard Time*) *hora de inverno das montanhas Rochosas*.
MSW (*US*) *n abbr* (= *Master of Social Work*) *grau universitário*.
MT *n abbr* = **machine translation** ♦ *abbr* (*US*:

***NB**: European Portuguese adds the following consonants to certain words:* **b** (sú(b)dito, su(b)til); **c** (a(c)ção, a(c)cionista, a(c)to); **m** (inde(m)ne); **p** (ado(p)ção, ado(p)tar); *for further details see p. xiii.*

POST) = **Montana.**
Mt *abbr* (GEO: = *mount*) Mt.
much [mʌtʃ] *adj, adv, pron* muito ♦ *n* muito, grande parte *f*; **how ~ is it?** quanto é?, quanto custa?; **it's not ~** não é muito; **too ~** demais; **so ~** tanto; **as ~ as** tanto como; **I like it very/so ~** gosto muito/tanto disso; **thank you very ~** muito obrigado/a; **however ~ he tries** por mais que tente.
muck [mʌk] *n* (*dirt*) sujeira (BR), sujidade *f* (PT); (*manure*) estrume *m*; (*fig*) porcaria.
muck about (*inf*) *vi* (*be silly*) fazer besteiras; (*waste time*) fazer cera; (*tinker*) mexer.
muck in (BRIT: *inf*) *vi* dar uma ajuda.
muck out *vt* (*stable*) limpar.
muck up (*inf*) *vt* (*ruin*) estragar; (*dirty*) sujar.
muckraking ['mʌkreɪkɪŋ] (*inf*) *n* (PRESS) sensacionalismo.
mucky ['mʌkɪ] *adj* (*dirty*) sujo.
mucus ['mju:kəs] *n* muco.
mud [mʌd] *n* lama.
muddle ['mʌdl] *n* confusão *f*, bagunça; (*mix-up*) trapalhada ♦ *vt* (*also*: ~ *up*) confundir, misturar; **to be in a ~** (*person*) estar confuso; **to get in a ~** (*while explaining etc*) enrolar-se.
muddle along *vi* viver sem rumo.
muddle through *vi* virar-se.
muddle-headed [-'hɛdɪd] *adj* (*person*) confuso.
muddy ['mʌdɪ] *adj* (*road*) lamacento; (*person, clothes*) enlameado.
mud flats *npl* extensão *f* de terra lamacenta.
mudguard ['mʌdgɑ:d] *n* pára-lama *m*.
mudpack ['mʌdpæk] *n* máscara (de beleza).
mud-slinging [-slɪŋɪŋ] *n* difamação *f*, injúria.
muff [mʌf] *n* regalo ♦ *vt* (*chance*) desperdiçar, perder; (*lines*) estropiar.
muffin ['mʌfɪn] *n bolinho redondo e chato.*
muffle ['mʌfl] *vt* (*sound*) abafar; (*against cold*) agasalhar.
muffled ['mʌfld] *adj* abafado, surdo.
muffler ['mʌflə*] *n* (*scarf*) cachecol *m*; (US: AUT) silencioso (BR), panela de escape (PT).
mufti ['mʌftɪ] *n*: **in ~** vestido à paisana.
mug [mʌg] *n* (*cup*) caneca; (: *for beer*) caneco, canecão; (*inf*: *face*) careta; (: *fool*) bobo/a ♦ *vt* (*assault*) assaltar.
mug up (BRIT: *inf*) *vt* (*also*: ~ *up on*) decorar.
mugger ['mʌgə*] *n* assaltante *m/f*.
mugging ['mʌgɪŋ] *n* assalto.
muggy ['mʌgɪ] *adj* abafado.
mulatto [mju:'lætəu] (*pl* **~es**) *n* mulato/a.
mulberry ['mʌlbrɪ] *n* (*fruit*) amora; (*tree*) amoreira.
mule [mju:l] *n* mula.
mull over [mʌl-] *vt* meditar sobre.
mulled [mʌld] *adj*: **~ wine** quentão *m*.
multi... [mʌltɪ] *prefix* multi....
multi-access *adj* (COMPUT) de múltiplo acesso.
multicoloured ['mʌltɪkʌləd] (US **multicolored**) *adj* multicolor.
multifarious [mʌltɪ'fɛərɪəs] *adj* diverso, variado.
multilateral [mʌltɪ'lætrəl] *adj* (POL) multilateral.
multi-level (US) *adj* de vários andares.
multimillionaire [mʌltɪmɪljə'nɛə*] *n* multimilionário/a.
multinational [mʌltɪ'næʃənl] *n* multinacional *f* ♦ *adj* multinacional.
multiple ['mʌltɪpl] *adj, n* múltiplo.
multiple choice *n* múltipla escolha.
multiple crash *n* engavetamento.
multiple sclerosis *n* esclerose *f* múltipla.
multiple store *n* cadeia de lojas.
multiplication [mʌltɪplɪ'keɪʃən] *n* multiplicação *f*.
multiplication table *n* tabela de multiplicação.
multiplicity [mʌltɪ'plɪsɪtɪ] *n* multiplicidade *f*.
multiply ['mʌltɪplaɪ] *vt* multiplicar ♦ *vi* multiplicar-se.
multiracial [mʌltɪ'reɪʃl] *adj* multirracial.
multistorey ['mʌltɪ'stɔ:rɪ] (BRIT) *adj* de vários andares.
multitude ['mʌltɪtju:d] *n* multidão *f*.
mum [mʌm] *n* (BRIT) mamãe *f* ♦ *adj*: **to keep ~** ficar calado; **~'s the word!** bico calado!
mumble ['mʌmbl] *vt, vi* resmungar, murmurar.
mummify ['mʌmɪfaɪ] *vt* mumificar.
mummy ['mʌmɪ] *n* (BRIT: *mother*) mamãe *f*; (*embalmed*) múmia.
mumps [mʌmps] *n* caxumba.
munch [mʌntʃ] *vt, vi* mascar.
mundane [mʌn'deɪn] *adj* banal, mundano.
municipal [mju:'nɪsɪpl] *adj* municipal.
municipality [mju:nɪsɪ'pælɪtɪ] *n* municipalidade *f*; (*area*) município.
munitions [mju:'nɪʃənz] *npl* munições *fpl*.
mural ['mjuərl] *n* mural *m*.
murder ['mə:də*] *n* assassinato; (LAW) homicídio ♦ *vt* assassinar; (*spoil*) estragar; **to commit ~** cometer um assassinato.
murderer ['mə:dərə*] *n* assassino.
murderess ['mə:dərɪs] *n* assassina.
murderous ['mə:dərəs] *adj* homicida.
murk [mə:k] *n* escuridão *f*.
murky ['mə:kɪ] *adj* escuro; (*fig*) sombrio.
murmur ['mə:mə*] *n* murmúrio ♦ *vt, vi* murmurar; **heart ~** (MED) sopro cardíaco *or* no coração.
MusB(ac) *n abbr* (= *Bachelor of Music*) *grau universitário.*
muscle ['mʌsl] *n* músculo; (*fig*: *strength*) força (muscular).
muscle in *vi* imiscuir-se, impor-se.
muscular ['mʌskjulə*] *adj* muscular; (*person*) musculoso.
muscular dystrophy *n* distrofia muscular.
MusD(oc) *n abbr* (= *Doctor of Music*) *grau universitário.*
muse [mju:z] *vi* meditar ♦ *n* musa.
museum [mju:'zɪəm] *n* museu *m*.
mush [mʌʃ] *n* pasta, papa; (*fig*) pieguice *f*.
mushroom ['mʌʃrum] *n* cogumelo ♦ *vi* (*fig*)

crescer da noite para o dia, pipocar.
mushy ['mʌʃɪ] *adj* mole; (*pej*) piegas *inv*.
music ['mju:zɪk] *n* música.
musical ['mju:zɪkl] *adj* (*of music, person*) musical; (*harmonious*) melodioso ♦ *n* (*show*) musical *m*.
music(al) box *n* caixinha de música.
musical instrument *n* instrumento musical.
music hall *n* teatro de variedades.
musician [mju:'zɪʃən] *n* músico/a.
music stand *n* atril *m*, estante *f* de música.
musk [mʌsk] *n* almíscar *m*.
musket ['mʌskɪt] *n* mosquete *m*.
muskrat ['mʌskræt] *n* rato almiscarado.
musk rose *n* (BOT) rosa-moscada.
Muslim ['mʌzlɪm] *adj*, *n* muçulmano/a.
muslin ['mʌzlɪn] *n* musselina.
musquash ['mʌskwɔʃ] *n* rato almiscarado; (*fur*) pele *f* de rato almiscarado.
mussel ['mʌsl] *n* mexilhão *m*.
must [mʌst] *aux vb* (*obligation*): **I ~ do it** tenho que *or* devo fazer isso; (*probability*): **he ~ be there by now** ele já deve estar lá ♦ *n* (*necessity*): **it's a ~** é imprescindível; **I ~ have made a mistake** eu devo ter feito um erro.
mustache ['mʌstæʃ] (US) *n* = **moustache**.
mustard ['mʌstəd] *n* mostarda.
mustard gas *n* gás *m* de mostarda.
muster ['mʌstə*] *vt* reunir, juntar; (*also*: ~ *up*: *strength, courage*) criar, juntar.
mustiness ['mʌstɪnɪs] *n* mofo.
mustn't ['mʌsnt] = **must not**.
musty ['mʌstɪ] *adj* mofado, com cheiro de bolor.
mutant ['mju:tənt] *adj*, *n* mutante *m/f*.
mutate [mju:'teɪt] *vi* sofrer mutação genética.
mutation [mju:'teɪʃən] *n* mutação *f*.
mute [mju:t] *adj*, *n* mudo/a.
muted ['mju:tɪd] *adj* (*noise*, MUS) abafado; (*criticism*) velado.
mutilate ['mju:tɪleɪt] *vt* mutilar.
mutilation [mju:tɪ'leɪʃən] *n* mutilação *f*.
mutinous ['mju:tɪnəs] *adj* (*troops*) amotinado; (*attitude*) rebelde.
mutiny ['mju:tɪnɪ] *n* motim *m*, rebelião *f* ♦ *vi* amotinar-se.
mutter ['mʌtə*] *vt*, *vi* resmungar, murmurar.
mutton ['mʌtn] *n* carne *f* de carneiro.
mutual ['mju:tʃuəl] *adj* mútuo; (*shared*) comum.
mutually ['mju:tʃuəlɪ] *adv* mutuamente, reciprocamente.
muzzle ['mʌzl] *n* (*of animal*) focinho; (*protective device*) focinheira; (*of gun*) boca ♦ *vt* (*press etc*) amordaçar; (*dog*) pôr focinheira em.
MVP (US) *n abbr* (SPORT) = **most valuable player**.
MW *abbr* (= *medium wave*) OM.
my [maɪ] *adj* meu/minha ♦ *excl*: **~!** meu Deus!
mynah bird ['maɪnə-] *n* mainá *m*.
myopic [maɪ'ɔpɪk] *adj* míope.
myriad ['mɪrɪəd] *n* miríade *f*.
myself [maɪ'sɛlf] *pron* (*reflexive*) me; (*emphatic*) eu mesmo; (*after prep*) mim mesmo.
mysterious [mɪs'tɪərɪəs] *adj* misterioso.
mystery ['mɪstərɪ] *n* mistério.
mystery story *n* romance *m* policial.
mystic ['mɪstɪk] *adj*, *n* místico/a.
mystical ['mɪstɪkl] *adj* místico.
mystify ['mɪstɪfaɪ] *vt* (*perplex*) mistificar, confundir; (*disconcert*) desconcertar.
mystique [mɪs'ti:k] *n* mística.
myth [mɪθ] *n* mito.
mythical ['mɪθɪkəl] *adj* mítico.
mythological [mɪθə'lɔdʒɪkl] *adj* mitológico.
mythology [mɪ'θɔlədʒɪ] *n* mitologia.

N

N, n [ɛn] *n* (*letter*) N, n *m*; **N for Nellie** (BRIT) *or* **Nan** (US) N de Nair.
N *abbr* (= *north*) N.
NA (US) *n abbr* (= *Narcotics Anonymous*) *associação de assistência aos toxicômanos*; = **National Academy**.
n/a *abbr* = **not applicable**; (COMM *etc*) = **no account**.
NAACP (US) *n abbr* = **National Association for the Advancement of Colored People**.
NAAFI ['næfɪ] (BRIT) *n abbr* (= *Navy, Army & Air Force Institute*) *órgão responsável pelas lojas e cantinas do exército*.
nab [næb] (*inf*) *vt* pegar, prender.
NACU (US) *n abbr* = **National Association of Colleges and Universities**.
nadir ['neɪdɪə*] *n* (ASTRONOMY, *fig*) nadir *m*.
nag [næg] *n* (*pej*: *horse*) rocim *m* ♦ *vt* ralhar, apoquentar.
nagging ['nægɪŋ] *adj* (*doubt*) persistente; (*pain*) contínuo ♦ *n* queixas *fpl*, censuras *fpl*, apoquentação *f*.
nail [neɪl] *n* (*human*) unha; (*metal*) prego ♦ *vt* pregar; **to ~ sb down to a date/price** conseguir que alguém se defina sobre a data/o preço; **to pay cash on the ~** (BRIT) pagar na bucha.
nailbrush ['neɪlbrʌʃ] *n* escova de unhas.
nailfile ['neɪlfaɪl] *n* lixa de unhas.
nail polish *n* esmalte *m* (BR) *or* verniz *m* (PT) de unhas.
nail polish remover *n* dissolvente *m* de esmalte (BR) *or* verniz (PT).
nail scissors *npl* tesourinha de unhas.
nail varnish (BRIT) *n* esmalte *m* (BR) *or*

NB: European Portuguese adds the following consonants to certain words: **b** (sú(b)dito, su(b)til); **c** (a(c)ção, a(c)cionista, a(c)to); **m** (inde(m)ne); **p** (ado(p)ção, ado(p)tar); *for further details see p. xiii.*

verniz *m* (*PT*) de unhas.
Nairobi [naɪ'rəubɪ] *n* Nairóbi.
naïve [naɪ'i:v] *adj* ingênuo.
naïveté [naɪ'i:vteɪ] *n* = **naivety**.
naïvety [naɪ'i:vətɪ] *n* ingenuidade *f*.
naked ['neɪkɪd] *adj* (*nude*) nu/nua; **with the ~ eye** a olho nu.
nakedness ['neɪkɪdnɪs] *n* nudez *f*.
NALGO ['nælgəu] (*BRIT*) *n abbr* (= *National and Local Government Officers' Association*) *sindicato dos funcionários públicos*.
NAM (*US*) *n abbr* = **National Association of Manufacturers**.
name [neɪm] *n* nome *m*; (*surname*) sobrenome *m*; (*reputation*) reputação *f*, fama ♦ *vt* (*child*) pôr nome em; (*criminal*) apontar; (*appoint*) nomear; (*price*) fixar; (*date*) marcar; **by ~** de nome; **in the ~ of** em nome de; **what's your ~?** qual é o seu nome?, como (você) se chama?; **my ~ is Peter** eu me chamo Peter; **to take sb's ~ and address** anotar o nome e o endereço de alguém; **to make a ~ for o.s.** fazer nome; **to get (o.s.) a bad ~** fazer má reputação; **to call sb ~s** xingar alguém.
name-dropping [-'drɔpɪŋ] *n*: **she loves ~** ela adora esnobar conhecimento de gente importante.
nameless ['neɪmlɪs] *adj* sem nome, anônimo.
namely ['neɪmlɪ] *adv* a saber, isto é.
nameplate ['neɪmpleɪt] *n* (*on door etc*) placa.
namesake ['neɪmseɪk] *n* xará *m/f* (*BR*), homónimo/a (*PT*).
nanny ['nænɪ] *n* babá *f*.
nanny goat *n* cabra.
nap [næp] *n* (*sleep*) soneca; (*cloth*) felpa ♦ *vi*: **to be caught ~ping** ser pego de surpresa.
NAPA (*US*) *n abbr* (= *National Association of Performing Artists*) *sindicato dos artistas de teatro e de cinema*.
napalm ['neɪpɑ:m] *n* napalm *m*.
nape [neɪp] *n*: **~ of the neck** nuca.
napkin ['næpkɪn] *n* (*also*: *table ~*) guardanapo.
nappy ['næpɪ] (*BRIT*) *n* fralda.
nappy liner (*BRIT*) *n* gaze *f*.
nappy rash (*BRIT*) *n* assadura.
narcissi [nɑ:'sɪsaɪ] *npl of* **narcissus**.
narcissistic [nɑ:sɪ'sɪstɪk] *adj* narcisista.
narcissus [nɑ:'sɪsəs] (*pl* **narcissi**) *n* narciso.
narcotic [nɑ:'kɔtɪk] *n* (*MED*) narcótico; **~s** *npl* (*drugs*) entorpecentes *mpl*.
nark [nɑ:k] (*BRIT*: *inf*) *vt* encher o saco de.
narrate [nə'reɪt] *vt* narrar, contar.
narration [nə'reɪʃən] *n* narração *f*.
narrative ['nærətɪv] *n* narrativa ♦ *adj* narrativo.
narrator [nə'reɪtə*] *n* narrador(a) *m/f*.
narrow ['nærəu] *adj* estreito; (*shoe*) apertado; (*fig*) intolerante, limitado ♦ *vi* estreitar-se; **to have a ~ escape** escapar por um triz; **to ~ sth down to** restringir *or* reduzir algo a.
narrow gauge *adj* (*RAIL*) de bitola estreita.
narrowly ['nærəulɪ] *adv* (*miss*) por pouco; **he ~ missed injury/the tree** por pouco não se machucou/não bateu na árvore.
narrow-minded [-'maɪndɪd] *adj* de visão limitada, bitolado.
NAS (*US*) *n abbr* = **National Academy of Sciences**.
NASA ['næsə] (*US*) *n abbr* (= *National Aeronautics and Space Administration*) NASA *f*.
nasal ['neɪzl] *adj* nasal.
Nassau ['næsɔ:] *n* (*in Bahamas*) Nassau.
nastily ['nɑ:stɪlɪ] *adv* (*say*, *act*) maldosamente.
nastiness ['nɑ:stɪnɪs] *n* (*malice*) maldade *f*; (*rudeness*) grosseria.
nasturtium [nəs'tə:ʃəm] *n* chagas *fpl*, capuchinha.
nasty ['nɑ:stɪ] *adj* (*unpleasant*: *remark*) desagradável; (: *person*) mau, ruim; (*malicious*) maldoso; (*rude*) grosseiro, obsceno; (*revolting*: *taste*, *smell*) repugnante, asqueroso; (*wound*, *disease etc*) grave, sério; **to turn ~** (*situation*, *weather*) ficar feio; (*person*) engrossar.
NAS/UWT (*BRIT*) *n abbr* (= *National Association of Schoolmasters/Union of Women Teachers*) *sindicato dos professores*.
nation ['neɪʃən] *n* nação *f*.
national ['næʃənl] *adj*, *n* nacional *m/f*.
national anthem *n* hino nacional.
national debt *n* dívida pública.
national dress *n* traje *m* nacional.
National Guard (*US*) *n* guarda nacional.
National Health Service (*BRIT*) *n serviço nacional de saúde*, ≈ Instituto Nacional de Assistência Médica e Previdência Social.
National Insurance (*BRIT*) *n* previdência social.
nationalism ['næʃənəlɪzəm] *n* nacionalismo.
nationalist ['næʃənəlɪst] *adj*, *n* nacionalista *m/f*.
nationality [næʃə'nælɪtɪ] *n* nacionalidade *f*.
nationalization [næʃənəlaɪ'zeɪʃən] *n* nacionalização *f*.
nationalize ['næʃənəlaɪz] *vt* nacionalizar.
nationally ['næʃənəlɪ] *adv* (*nationwide*) de âmbito nacional; (*as a nation*) nacionalmente, como nação.
national park *n* parque *m* nacional.
national press *n* imprensa nacional.
National Security Council (*US*) *n* conselho nacional de segurança.
national service *n* (*MIL*) serviço militar.
nationwide ['neɪʃənwaɪd] *adj* de âmbito *or* a nível nacional ♦ *adv* em todo o país.
native ['neɪtɪv] *n* (*local inhabitant*) natural *m/f*, nativo/a; (*in colonies*) indígena *m/f*, nativo/a ♦ *adj* (*indigenous*) indígena; (*of one's birth*) natal; (*language*) materno; (*innate*) inato, natural; **a ~ of Russia** um natural da Rússia; **a ~ speaker of Portuguese** uma pessoa de língua materna portuguesa.
Nativity [nə'tɪvɪtɪ] *n* (*REL*): **the ~** a Natividade.
NATO ['neɪtəu] *n abbr* (= *North Atlantic Treaty Organization*) OTAN *f*.
NATSOPA [næt'səupə] (*BRIT*) *n abbr* (= *National Society of Operative Printers*,

Graphical and Media Personnel) sindicato da imprensa e das indústrias gráficas.
natter ['nætə*] (*BRIT*) *vi* conversar fiado.
NATTKE (*BRIT*) *n abbr* (= *National Association of Television, Theatrical and Kinematographic Employees*) *sindicato dos empregados de televisão, de teatro e de cinema.*
natural ['nætʃrəl] *adj* natural; **death from ~ causes** morte *f* natural.
natural childbirth *n* parto natural.
natural gas *n* gás *m* natural.
naturalist ['nætʃrəlɪst] *n* naturalista *m/f*.
naturalization [nætʃrəlaɪ'zeɪʃən] *n* naturalização *f*.
naturalize ['nætʃrəlaɪz] *vt*: **to become ~d** (*person*) naturalizar-se.
naturally ['nætʃrəlɪ] *adv* naturalmente; (*of course*) claro, evidentemente; (*instinctively*) por instinto, espontaneamente.
naturalness ['nætʃrəlnɪs] *n* naturalidade *f*.
natural resources *npl* recursos *mpl* naturais.
natural wastage *n* (*INDUSTRY*) afastamentos *mpl* naturais e voluntários.
nature ['neɪtʃə*] *n* natureza; (*character*) caráter *m*, índole *f*; **by ~** por natureza; **documents of a confidential ~** documentos de caráter confidencial.
-natured ['neɪtʃəd] *suffix*: **ill~** de mau caráter.
nature reserve (*BRIT*) *n* reserva natural.
nature trail *n trilha de descoberta da natureza.*
naturist ['neɪtʃərɪst] *n* naturista *m/f*.
naught [nɔːt] *n* = **nought**.
naughtiness ['nɔːtɪnɪs] *n* (*of child*) travessura, mau comportamento; (*of story etc*) picante *m*.
naughty ['nɔːtɪ] *adj* (*child*) travesso, levado; (*story, film*) picante.
nausea ['nɔːsɪə] *n* náusea.
nauseate ['nɔːsɪeɪt] *vt* dar náuseas a; (*fig*) repugnar.
nauseating ['nɔːsɪeɪtɪŋ] *adj* nauseabundo, enjoativo; (*fig*) nojento, repugnante.
nauseous ['nɔːsɪəs] *adj* (*nauseating*) nauseabundo, enjoativo; (*feeling sick*): **to be ~** estar enjoado.
nautical ['nɔːtɪkl] *adj* náutico.
nautical mile *n* milha marítima (= *1853 m*).
naval ['neɪvl] *adj* naval.
naval officer *n* oficial *m* de marinha.
nave [neɪv] *n* nave *f*.
navel ['neɪvl] *n* umbigo.
navigable ['nævɪgəbl] *adj* navegável.
navigate ['nævɪgeɪt] *vt* (*ship*) pilotar; (*sea*) navegar ♦ *vi* navegar; (*AUT*) ler o mapa.
navigation [nævɪ'geɪʃən] *n* (*action*) navegação *f*; (*science*) náutica.
navigator ['nævɪgeɪtə*] *n* navegante *m/f*, navegador(a) *m/f*.
navvy ['nævɪ] (*BRIT*) *n* trabalhador *m* braçal, cavouqueiro.
navy ['neɪvɪ] *n* marinha (de guerra); (*ships*) armada, frota; **Department of the N~** (*US*) ministério da Marinha.
navy(-blue) *adj* azul-marinho *inv*.
Nazareth ['næzərəθ] *n* Nazaré.
Nazi ['nɑːtsɪ] *adj, n* nazista *m/f*.
Nazism ['nɑːtsɪzəm] *n* nazismo.
NB *abbr* (= *nota bene*) NB; (*CANADA*) = **New Brunswick**.
NBA (*US*) *n abbr* = **National Basketball Association; National Boxing Association**.
NBC (*US*) *n abbr* (= *National Broadcasting Company*) *rede de televisão.*
NBS (*US*) *n abbr* (= *National Bureau of Standards*) *órgão de padronização.*
NC *abbr* (*COMM etc*) = **no charge**; (*US: POST*) = **North Carolina**.
NCB (*BRIT*) *n abbr* (*old*) = **National Coal Board**.
NCC *n abbr* (*BRIT*: = *Nature Conservancy Council*) *órgão de proteção à natureza*; (*US*) = **National Council of Churches**.
NCCL (*BRIT*) *n abbr* (= *National Council for Civil Liberties*) *associação de defesa das liberdades civis.*
NCO *n abbr* = **non-commissioned officer**.
ND (*US*) *abbr* (*POST*) = **North Dakota**.
NE (*US*) *abbr* (*POST*) = **Nebraska; New England**.
NEA (*US*) *n abbr* = **National Education Association**.
neap tide [niːp-] *n* maré *f* morta.
near [nɪə*] *adj* (*place*) vizinho; (*time*) próximo; (*relation*) íntimo ♦ *adv* perto ♦ *prep* (*also*: *~ to*) (*space*) perto de; (*time*) perto de, quase ♦ *vt* aproximar-se de, abeirar-se de; **~ here/there** aqui/ali perto; **£25,000 or ~est offer** (*BRIT*) £25,000 ou melhor oferta; **in the ~ future** no próximo futuro; **the building is ~ing completion** o edifício está quase pronto; **to come ~** aproximar-se.
nearby [nɪə'baɪ] *adj* próximo, vizinho ♦ *adv* à mão, perto.
Near East *n*: **the ~** o Oriente Próximo.
nearer ['nɪərə*] *adj* que fica mais perto ♦ *adv* mais perto.
nearly ['nɪəlɪ] *adv* quase; **I ~ fell** quase que caí; **it's not ~ big enough** é pequeno demais.
near miss *n* (*of planes*) quase-colisão *f*; (*shot*) tiro que passou de raspão.
nearness ['nɪənɪs] *n* proximidade *f*; (*relationship*) intimidade *f*.
nearside ['nɪəsaɪd] *n* (*AUT*: *right-hand drive*) lado esquerdo (: *left-hand drive*) lado direito ♦ *adj* esquerdo; direito.
near-sighted [-'saɪtɪd] *adj* míope.
neat [niːt] *adj* (*place*) arrumado, em ordem; (*person*) asseado, arrumado; (*skilful*) hábil; (*plan*) engenhoso, bem bolado; (*spirits*) puro.
neatly ['niːtlɪ] *adv* caprichosamente, com capricho; (*avoid etc*) habilmente.
neatness ['niːtnɪs] *n* (*tidiness*) asseio;

***NB:** European Portuguese adds the following consonants to certain words:* **b** (sú(b)dito, su(b)til); **c** (a(c)ção, a(c)cionista, a(c)to); **m** (inde(m)ne); **p** (ado(p)ção, ado(p)tar); *for further details see p. xiii.*

(*skilfulness*) habilidade *f*.
nebulous ['nɛbjuləs] *adj* nebuloso; (*fig*) vago, confuso.
necessarily ['nɛsɪsrɪlɪ] *adv* necessariamente; **not ~** não necessariamente.
necessary ['nɛsɪsrɪ] *adj* necessário; **he did all that was ~** fez tudo o que foi necessário; **if ~** se necessário for.
necessitate [nɪ'sɛsɪteɪt] *vt* exigir, tornar necessário.
necessity [nɪ'sɛsɪtɪ] *n* (*thing needed*) necessidade *f*, requisito; (*compelling circumstances*) necessidade; **necessities** *npl* artigos *mpl* de primeira necessidade; **in case of ~** em caso de necessidade.
neck [nɛk] *n* (ANAT) pescoço; (*of garment*) gola; (*of bottle*) gargalo ♦ *vi* (*inf*) ficar de agarramento; **~ and ~** emparelhados; **to stick one's ~ out** (*inf*) arriscar-se.
necklace ['nɛklɪs] *n* colar *m*.
neckline ['nɛklaɪn] *n* decote *m*.
necktie ['nɛktaɪ] (*esp US*) *n* gravata.
nectar ['nɛktə*] *n* néctar *m*.
nectarine ['nɛktərɪn] *n* nectarina.
NEDC (BRIT) *n abbr* = **National Economic Development Council**.
Neddy ['nɛdɪ] (BRIT: *inf*) *n abbr* = **NEDC**.
née [neɪ] *adj*: **~ Scott** em solteira Scott.
need [ni:d] *n* (*lack*) falta, carência; (*necessity*) necessidade *f*; (*thing needed*) requisito, necessidade ♦ *vt* (*require*) precisar de; **I ~ to do it** preciso fazê-lo; **you don't ~ to go** você não precisa ir; **a signature is ~ed** é necessária uma assinatura; **to be in ~ of** *or* **have ~ of** estar precisando de; **£10 will meet my immediate ~s** £10 atenderão minhas necessidades mais prementes; **in case of ~** em caso de necessidade; **there's no ~ to do ...** não é preciso fazer ...; **there's no ~ for that** isso não é necessário.
needle ['ni:dl] *n* agulha ♦ *vt* (*inf*) provocar, picar, alfinetar.
needlecord ['ni:dlkɔ:d] (BRIT) *n* veludo cotelê.
needless ['ni:dlɪs] *adj* inútil, desnecessário; **~ to say ...** desnecessário dizer que ....
needlessly ['ni:dlɪslɪ] *adv* desnecessariamente, à toa.
needlework ['ni:dlwə:k] *n* trabalho de agulha, costura.
needn't ['ni:dnt] = **need not**.
needy ['ni:dɪ] *adj* necessitado, carente.
negation [nɪ'geɪʃən] *n* negação *f*.
negative ['nɛgətɪv] *n* (PHOT) negativo; (*answer*) negativa ♦ *adj* negativo; **to answer in the ~** responder negativamente.
neglect [nɪ'glɛkt] *vt* (*one's duty*) negligenciar, não cumprir com; (*child*) descuidar, esquecer-se de ♦ *n* descuido, desatenção *f*; (*personal*) desleixo; (*of duty*) negligência; **(state of) ~** abandono; **to ~ to do sth** omitir de fazer algo.
neglected [nɪ'glɛktɪd] *adj* abandonado.
neglectful [nɪ'glɛktful] *adj* negligente; **to be ~ of sb/sth** descuidar de alguém/algo.
negligee ['nɛglɪʒeɪ] *n* négligé *m*.
negligence ['nɛglɪdʒəns] *n* negligência, descuido.
negligent ['nɛglɪdʒənt] *adj* negligente.
negligently ['nɛglɪdʒəntlɪ] *adv* por negligência; (*offhandedly*) negligentemente.
negligible ['nɛglɪdʒɪbl] *adj* insignificante, desprezível, ínfimo.
negotiable [nɪ'gəuʃɪəbl] *adj* (*cheque*) negociável; (*road*) transitável.
negotiate [nɪ'gəuʃɪeɪt] *vi* negociar ♦ *vt* (*treaty*) negociar; (*obstacle*) contornar; **to ~ with sb for sth** negociar com alguém para obter algo.
negotiation [nɪgəuʃɪ'eɪʃən] *n* negociação *f*; **to enter into ~s with sb** entrar em negociações com alguém.
negotiator [nɪ'gəuʃɪeɪtə*] *n* negociador(a) *m/f*.
Negress ['ni:grɪs] *n* negra.
Negro ['ni:grəu] (*pl* **~es**) *adj* negro ♦ *n* negro/a.
Negroes ['ni:grəuz] *npl of* **Negro**.
neigh [neɪ] *n* relincho ♦ *vi* relinchar.
neighbour ['neɪbə*] (US **neighbor**) *n* vizinho/a.
neighbo(u)rhood ['neɪbəhud] *n* (*place*) vizinhança, bairro; (*people*) vizinhos *mpl*.
neighbo(u)ring ['neɪbərɪŋ] *adj* vizinho.
neighbo(u)rly ['neɪbəlɪ] *adj* amistoso, prestativo.
neither ['naɪðə*] *conj*: **I didn't move and ~ did he** não me movi nem ele ♦ *adj*, *pron* nenhum (dos dois), nem um nem outro ♦ *adv*: **~ good nor bad** nem bom nem mau.
neo... [ni:əu] *prefix* neo-.
neolithic [ni:əu'lɪθɪk] *adj* neolítico.
neologism [nɪ'ɔlədʒɪzəm] *n* neologismo.
neon ['ni:ɔn] *n* neônio, néon *m*.
neon light *n* luz *f* de neônio.
neon sign *n* anúncio luminoso a neônio.
Nepal [nɪ'pɔ:l] *n* Nepal *m*.
nephew ['nɛvju:] *n* sobrinho.
nepotism ['nɛpətɪzm] *n* nepotismo.
nerve [nə:v] *n* (ANAT) nervo; (*courage*) coragem *f*; (*impudence*) descaramento, atrevimento; **he gets on my ~s** ele me irrita, ele me dá nos nervos; **to have a fit of ~s** ter uma crise nervosa; **to lose one's ~** (*self-confidence*) perder o sangue frio.
nerve centre (US **nerve center**) *n* (ANAT) centro nervoso; (*fig*) centro de operações.
nerve gas *n* gás *m* tóxico.
nerve-racking [-'rækɪŋ] *adj* angustiante.
nervous ['nə:vəs] *adj* (*anxious*, ANAT) nervoso; (*timid*) tímido, acanhado; **~ exhaustion** esgotamento nervoso.
nervous breakdown *n* esgotamento nervoso.
nervously ['nə:vəslɪ] *adv* nervosamente; (*timidly*) timidamente.
nervousness ['nə:vəsnɪs] *n* nervosismo; (*timidity*) timidez *f*.
nest [nɛst] *vi* aninhar-se ♦ *n* (*of bird*) ninho; (*of wasp*) vespeiro; **~ of tables** jogo de mesinhas.
nest egg *n* (*fig*) pé-de-meia *m*.
nestle ['nɛsl] *vi*: **to ~ up to sb** aconchegar-se a alguém.

nestling ['nɛstlɪŋ] *n* filhote *m* (de passarinho).

net [nɛt] *n* rede *f* ♦ *adj* (COMM) líquido ♦ *vt* pegar na rede; (*money*: *subj*: *person*) faturar; (: *deal*, *sale*) render; **~ of tax** isento de impostos; **he earns £10,000 ~ per year** ele ganha £10,000 líquidas por ano.

netball ['nɛtbɔːl] *n* (*espécie de*) *basquetebol*.

net curtains *npl* cortinas *fpl* de voile.

Netherlands ['nɛðələndz] *npl*: **the ~** os Países Baixos.

net profit *n* lucro líquido.

nett [nɛt] *adj* = **net**.

netting ['nɛtɪŋ] *n* rede *f*, redes *fpl*; (*fabric*) voile *m*.

nettle ['nɛtl] *n* urtiga.

network ['nɛtwəːk] *n* rede *f* ♦ *vt* (RADIO, TV) transmitir em rede; (*computers*) interligar.

neuralgia [njuə'rældʒə] *n* neuralgia.

neuroses [njuə'rəusiːz] *npl of* **neurosis**.

neurosis [njuə'rəusɪs] (*pl* **neuroses**) *n* neurose *f*.

neurotic [njuə'rɔtɪk] *adj*, *n* neurótico/a.

neuter ['njuːtə*] *adj* neutro ♦ *n* neutro ♦ *vt* (*cat etc*) castrar, capar.

neutral ['njuːtrəl] *adj* neutro ♦ *n* (AUT) ponto morto.

neutrality [njuː'trælɪtɪ] *n* neutralidade *f*.

neutralize ['njuːtrəlaɪz] *vt* neutralizar.

neutron ['njuːtrɔn] *n* nêutron (PT: neutrão) *m*.

neutron bomb *n* bomba de nêutrons (PT: neutrões).

never ['nɛvə*] *adv* nunca; **I ~ went** nunca fui; **~ again** nunca mais; **~ in my life** nunca na minha vida; *see also* **mind**.

never-ending [-'ɛndɪŋ] *adj* sem fim, interminável.

nevertheless [nɛvəðə'lɛs] *adv* todavia, contudo.

new [njuː] *adj* novo; **as good as ~** tal como novo.

newborn ['njuːbɔːn] *adj* recém-nascido.

newcomer ['njuːkʌmə*] *n* recém-chegado/a.

new-fangled [-'fæŋgld] (*pej*) *adj* ultramoderno.

new-found *adj* (*friend*) novo; (*enthusiasm*) recente.

Newfoundland ['njuːfənlənd] *n* Terra Nova.

New Guinea *n* Nova Guiné *f*.

newly ['njuːlɪ] *adv* recém, novamente.

newly-weds *npl* recém-casados *mpl*.

new moon *n* lua nova.

newness ['njuːnɪs] *n* novidade *f*.

news [njuːz] *n* notícias *fpl*; (RADIO, TV) noticiário; **a piece of ~** uma notícia; **good/bad ~** boa/má notícia; **financial ~** noticiário financeiro.

news agency *n* agência de notícias.

newsagent ['njuːzeɪdʒənt] (BRIT) *n* jornaleiro/a.

news bulletin *n* (RADIO, TV) noticiário.

newscaster ['njuːzkɑːstə*] *n* (RADIO, TV) noticiarista *m/f*.

newsdealer ['njuːzdiːlə*] (US) *n* jornaleiro/a.

news flash *n* notícia de última hora.

newsletter ['njuːzlɛtə*] *n* boletim *m* informativo.

newspaper ['njuːzpeɪpə*] *n* jornal *m*; (*material*) papel *m* de jornal; **daily ~** diário; **weekly ~** semanário.

newsprint ['njuːzprɪnt] *n* papel *m* de jornal.

newsreader ['njuːzriːdə*] *n* noticiarista.

newsreel ['njuːzriːl] *n* jornal *m* cinematográfico, atualidades *fpl*.

newsroom ['njuːzruːm] *n* (PRESS) sala da redação; (TV) estúdio.

newsstand ['njuːzstænd] *n* banca de jornais.

newt [njuːt] *n* tritão *m*.

New Year *n* ano novo; **Happy ~!** Feliz Ano Novo!; **to wish sb a happy ~** desejar feliz ano novo a alguém.

New Year's Day *n* dia *m* de ano novo.

New Year's Eve *n* véspera de ano novo.

New York [-jɔːk] *n* Nova Iorque.

New Zealand [-'ziːlənd] *n* Nova Zelândia ♦ *cpd* neozelandês/esa.

New Zealander [-'ziːləndə*] *n* neozelandês/esa *m/f*.

next [nɛkst] *adj* (*in space*) próximo, vizinho; (*in time*) seguinte, próximo ♦ *adv* (*place*) depois; (*time*) depois, logo; **~ to** ao lado de; **~ to nothing** quase nada; **~ time** na próxima vez; **the ~ day** o dia seguinte; **~ year** (n)o ano que vem; **"turn to the ~ page"** "vire para a página seguinte"; **who's ~?** quem é o próximo?; **the week after ~** sem ser a semana que vem, a outra; **when do we meet ~?** quando é que nós nos reencontramos?

next door *adv* na casa do lado ♦ *adj* vizinho.

next-of-kin *n* parentes *mpl* mais próximos.

NF *n abbr* (BRIT: POL: = *National Front*) *partido político da extrema direita* ♦ *abbr* (CANADA) = **Newfoundland**.

NFL (US) *n abbr* = **National Football League**.

NFU (BRIT) *n abbr* (= *National Farmers' Union*) *sindicato dos fazendeiros*.

NG (US) *abbr* = **National Guard**.

NGA (BRIT) *n abbr* (= *National Graphical Association*) *sindicato das indústrias gráficas*.

NGO (US) *n abbr* = **non-governmental organization**.

NH (US) *abbr* (POST) = **New Hampshire**.

NHL (US) *n abbr* = **National Hockey League**.

NHS (BRIT) *n abbr* = **National Health Service**.

NI *abbr* = **Northern Ireland**; (BRIT) = **National Insurance**.

Niagara Falls [naɪ'ægrə-] *npl*: **the ~** as cataratas do Niagara.

nib [nɪb] *n* ponta *or* bico da pena.

nibble ['nɪbl] *vt* mordiscar, beliscar; (ZOOL) roer.

Nicaragua [nɪkə'rægjuə] *n* Nicarágua.

Nicaraguan [nɪkə'rægjuən] *adj*, *n* nicaragüense *m/f*.

***NB:** European Portuguese adds the following consonants to certain words:* **b** (sú(b)dito, su(b)til); **c** (a(c)ção, a(c)cionista, a(c)to); **m** (inde(m)ne); **p** (ado(p)ção, ado(p)tar); *for further details see p. xiii.*

nice [naɪs] *adj* (*likeable*) simpático; (*kind*) amável, atencioso; (*pleasant*) agradável; (*flat, picture*) bonito; (*subtle*) sutil, fino.
nice-looking [-'lukɪŋ] *adj* bonito.
nicely ['naɪslɪ] *adv* agradavelmente, bem; **that will do ~** isso será perfeito.
niceties ['naɪsɪtɪz] *npl* sutilezas *fpl*.
niche [ni:ʃ] *n* nicho.
nick [nɪk] *n* (*wound*) corte *m*; (*cut, indentation*) entalhe *m*, incisão *f*; (*BRIT*: *inf*): **in good ~** em bom estado ♦ *vt* (*cut*) entalhar; (*inf*: *steal*) furtar; (: *BRIT*: *arrest*) prender, arrochar; **in the ~ of time** na hora H, no momento exato; **to ~ o.s.** cortar-se.
nickel ['nɪkl] *n* níquel *m*; (*US*) moeda de 5 centavos.
nickname ['nɪkneɪm] *n* apelido (*BR*), alcunha (*PT*) ♦ *vt* apelidar de (*BR*), alcunhar de (*PT*).
Nicosia [nɪkə'si:ə] *n* Nicósia.
nicotine ['nɪkəti:n] *n* nicotina.
niece [ni:s] *n* sobrinha.
nifty ['nɪftɪ] (*inf*) *adj* (*car, jacket*) chique; (*gadget, tool*) jeitoso.
Niger ['naɪdʒə*] *n* (*country, river*) Níger *m*.
Nigeria [naɪ'dʒɪərɪə] *n* Nigéria.
Nigerian [naɪ'dʒɪərɪən] *adj, n* nigeriano/a.
niggardly ['nɪgədlɪ] *adj* (*person*) avarento, sovina; (*amount*) miserável.
nigger ['nɪgə*] (*inf!*) *n* (*highly offensive*) crioulo/a, baiano/a.
niggle ['nɪgl] *vi* (*find fault*) botar defeito; (*fuss*) fazer histórias ♦ *vt* irritar.
niggling ['nɪglɪŋ] *adj* (*trifling*) insignificante, mesquinho; (*annoying*) irritante; (*pain, doubt*) persistente.
night [naɪt] *n* noite *f*; **at** *or* **by ~** à *or* de noite; **in** *or* **during the ~** durante a noite; **last ~** ontem à noite; **the ~ before last** anteontem à noite; **good ~!** boa noite!
night-bird *n* (*ZOOL*) ave *f* noturna; (*fig*) noctívago/a.
nightcap ['naɪtkæp] *n* (*drink*) *bebida tomada antes de dormir*.
night club *n* boate *f*.
nightdress ['naɪtdrɛs] *n* camisola (*BR*), camisa de noite (*PT*).
nightfall ['naɪtfɔ:l] *n* anoitecer *m*.
nightgown ['naɪtgaun] *n* camisola (*BR*), camisa de noite (*PT*).
nightie ['naɪtɪ] *n* camisola (*BR*), camisa de noite (*PT*).
nightingale ['naɪtɪŋgeɪl] *n* rouxinol *m*.
night life *n* vida noturna.
nightly ['naɪtlɪ] *adj* noturno, de noite ♦ *adv* todas as noites, cada noite.
nightmare ['naɪtmɛə*] *n* pesadelo.
night porter *n* porteiro da noite.
night safe *n* cofre *m* noturno.
night school *n* escola noturna.
nightshade ['naɪtʃeɪd] *n*: **deadly ~** (*BOT*) beladona.
nightshift ['naɪtʃɪft] *n* turno da noite.
night-time *n* noite *f*.
night watchman (*irreg*) *n* vigia *m*, guarda-noturno *m*.
nihilism ['naɪɪlɪzm] *n* niilismo.
nil [nɪl] *n* nada; (*BRIT*: *SPORT*) zero.
Nile [naɪl] *n*: **the ~** o Nilo.
nimble ['nɪmbl] *adj* (*agile*) ágil, ligeiro; (*skilful*) hábil, esperto.
nine [naɪn] *num* nove; *see also* **five**.
nineteen [naɪn'ti:n] *num* dezenove (*BR*), dezanove (*PT*); *see also* **five**.
ninety ['naɪntɪ] *num* noventa; *see also* **fifty**.
ninth [naɪnθ] *num* nono; *see also* **fifth**.
nip [nɪp] *vt* (*pinch*) beliscar; (*bite*) morder ♦ *vi* (*BRIT*: *inf*): **to ~ out/down/up** dar uma saidinha/descida/subida ♦ *n* (*drink*) gole *m*, trago; **to ~ into a shop** dar um pulo numa loja.
nipple ['nɪpl] *n* (*ANAT*) bico do seio, mamilo; (*of bottle*) bocal *m*, bico; (*TECH*) bocal (roscado).
nippy ['nɪpɪ] (*BRIT*) *adj* (*person*) rápido, ágil; (*cold*) friozinho.
nit [nɪt] *n* (*in hair*) lêndea, ovo de piolho; (*inf*: *idiot*) imbecil *m/f*, idiota *m/f*.
nit-pick (*inf*) *vi* ser implicante.
nitrate ['naɪtreɪt] *n* nitrato.
nitrogen ['naɪtrədʒən] *n* nitrogênio.
nitroglycerin(e) [naɪtrəu'glɪsəri:n] *n* nitroglicerina.
nitty-gritty ['nɪtɪ'grɪtɪ] (*inf*) *n*: **to get down to the ~** chegar ao âmago.
nitwit ['nɪtwɪt] (*inf*) *n* pateta *m/f*, bobalhão/ona *m/f*.
NJ (*US*) *abbr* (*POST*) = **New Jersey**.
NLF *n abbr* = **National Liberation Front**.
NLQ *abbr* (= *near letter quality*) qualidade *f* carta.
NLRB (*US*) *n abbr* (= *National Labor Relations Board*) *órgão de proteção aos trabalhadores*.
NM (*US*) *abbr* (*POST*) = **New Mexico**.
no [nəu] *adv* não ♦ *adj* nenhum(a), não ... algum ♦ *n* não *m*, negativa; **I have ~ more wine** não tenho mais vinho; **"~ entry"** "entrada proibida"; **"~ dogs"** "proibido a cães"; **I won't take ~ for an answer** não aceitarei um não como resposta.
no. *abbr* (= *number*) nº.
nobble ['nɔbl] (*BRIT*: *inf*) *vt* (*bribe*) subornar; (*person*: *speak to*) agarrar; (*RACING*: *horse*) incapacitar (*com drogas*).
Nobel prize [nəu'bɛl-] *n* prêmio Nobel.
nobility [nəu'bɪlɪtɪ] *n* nobreza.
noble ['nəubl] *adj* (*person*) nobre; (*title*) de nobreza.
nobleman ['nəublmən] (*irreg*) *n* nobre *m*, fidalgo.
nobly ['nəublɪ] *adv* nobremente.
nobody ['nəubədɪ] *pron* ninguém (*with negative*).
no-claims bonus *n* bonificação *f* (*por não ter reclamado indenização*).
nocturnal [nɔk'tə:nəl] *adj* noturno.
nod [nɔd] *vi* (*greeting*) cumprimentar com a cabeça; (*in agreement*) acenar (que sim) com a cabeça; (*doze*) cochilar, dormitar ♦ *vt*: **to ~ one's head** inclinar a cabeça ♦ *n* in-

clinação *f* da cabeça; **they ~ded their agreement** inclinaram a cabeça afirmando seu acordo.
nod off *vi* cochilar.
noise [nɔɪz] *n* barulho; **~ abatement** luta contra a poluição sonora.
noiseless ['nɔɪzlɪs] *adj* silencioso.
noisily ['nɔɪzɪlɪ] *adv* ruidosamente, com muito barulho.
noisy ['nɔɪzɪ] *adj* barulhento.
nomad ['nəumæd] *n* nômade *m/f*.
nomadic [nəu'mædɪk] *adj* nômade.
no man's land *n* terra de ninguém.
nominal ['nɔmɪnl] *adj* nominal.
nominate ['nɔmɪneɪt] *vt* (*propose*) propor; (*appoint*) nomear.
nomination [nɔmɪ'neɪʃən] *n* nomeação *f*; (*proposal*) proposta.
nominee [nɔmɪ'ni:] *n* pessoa nomeada, candidato/a.
non- [nɔn] *prefix* não-, des..., in..., anti-....
non-alcoholic *adj* não-alcoólico.
nonaligned [-ə'laɪnd] *adj* não-alinhado.
non-breakable *adj* inquebrável.
nonce word ['nɔns-] *n* palavra criada para a ocasião.
nonchalant ['nɔnʃələnt] *adj* despreocupado.
non-commissioned [-kə'mɪʃənd] *adj*: **~ officer** oficial *m* subalterno.
non-committal [-kə'mɪtl] *adj* (*uncommitted*) evasivo.
nonconformist [nɔnkən'fɔ:mɪst] *adj* não-conformista, dissidente ♦ *n* não-conformista *m/f*.
non-contributory *adj*: **~ pension scheme** (*BRIT*) *or* **plan** (*US*) caixa de aposentadoria não-contributária.
non-cooperation *n* não-cooperação *f*.
nondescript ['nɔndɪskrɪpt] *adj* qualquer; (*pej*) medíocre.
none [nʌn] *pron* (*person*) ninguém; (*thing*) nenhum(a), nada; **~ of you** nenhum de vocês; **I have ~** não tenho; **I have ~ left** não tenho mais; **~ at all** (*not one*) nem um só; **how much milk? - ~ at all** quanto leite? - nada; **he's ~ the worse for it** isso não o afetou.
nonentity [nɔ'nɛntɪtɪ] *n* nulidade *f*, zero à esquerda *m*.
non-essential *adj* não essencial, dispensável ♦ *npl*: **~s** desnecessários *mpl*.
nonetheless [nʌnðə'lɛs] *adv* no entanto, apesar disso, contudo.
non-executive *adj*: **~ director** administrador(a) *m/f*, conselheiro/a.
non-existent [-ɪg'zɪstənt] *adj* inexistente.
non-fiction *n* literatura de não-ficção.
non-flammable *adj* não inflamável.
non-intervention *n* não-intervenção *f*.
non obst. *abbr* (= *non obstante*; *notwithstanding*) não obstante.
non-payment *n* falta de pagamento.
nonplussed [nɔn'plʌst] *adj* perplexo, pasmado.
non-profit-making *adj* sem fins lucrativos.
nonsense ['nɔnsəns] *n* disparate *m*, besteira, absurdo; **~!** bobagem!, que nada!; **it's ~ to say ...** é um absurdo dizer que ....
non-shrink (*BRIT*) *adj* que não encolhe.
non-skid *adj* antiderrapante.
non-smoker *n* não-fumador(a) *m/f*.
non-stick *adj* tefal ®, não-aderente.
non-stop *adj* ininterrupto; (*RAIL*) direto; (*AVIAT*) sem escala ♦ *adv* sem parar.
non-taxable income *n* renda não-tributável.
non-U (*BRIT*: *inf*) *adj abbr* (= *non-upper class*) que não se diz (*or* se faz).
non-volatile memory *n* (*COMPUT*) memória não volátil.
non-voting shares *npl* ações *fpl* sem direito de voto.
non-white *adj*, *n* não-branco/a.
noodles ['nu:dlz] *npl* talharim *m*.
nook [nuk] *n* canto, recanto; **~s and crannies** esconderijos *mpl*.
noon [nu:n] *n* meio-dia *m*.
no-one *pron* (*with negative*) ninguém.
noose [nu:s] *n* laço corrediço; (*hangman's*) corda da forca.
nor [nɔ:*] *conj* = **neither** ♦ *adv see* **neither**.
Norf (*BRIT*) *abbr* = **Norfolk**.
norm [nɔ:m] *n* norma.
normal ['nɔ:ml] *adj* normal ♦ *n*: **to return to ~** normalizar-se.
normality [nɔ:'mælɪtɪ] *n* normalidade *f*.
normally ['nɔ:məlɪ] *adv* normalmente.
Normandy ['nɔ:məndɪ] *n* Normandia.
north [nɔ:θ] *n* norte *m* ♦ *adj* do norte, setentrional ♦ *adv* ao *or* para o norte.
North Africa *n* Africa do Norte.
North African *adj*, *n* norte-africano/a.
North America *n* América do Norte.
North American *adj*, *n* norte-americano/a.
Northants [nɔ:'θænts] (*BRIT*) *abbr* = **Northamptonshire**.
northbound ['nɔ:θbaund] *adj* em direção norte.
Northd (*BRIT*) *abbr* = **Northumberland**.
north-east *n* nordeste *m*.
northerly ['nɔ:ðəlɪ] *adj* (*wind*, *course*) norte.
northern ['nɔ:ðən] *adj* do norte, setentrional.
Northern Ireland *n* Irlanda do Norte.
North Pole *n*: **the ~** o Pólo Norte.
North Sea *n*: **the ~** o Mar do Norte.
North Sea oil *n* petróleo do Mar do Norte.
northward(s) ['nɔ:θwəd(z)] *adv* em direção norte.
north-west *n* noroeste *m*.
Norway ['nɔ:weɪ] *n* Noruega.
Norwegian [nɔ:'wi:dʒən] *adj* norueguês/esa ♦ *n* norueguês/esa *m/f*; (*LING*) norueguês *m*.
nos. *abbr* (= *numbers*) nº.
nose [nəuz] *n* (*ANAT*) nariz *m*; (*ZOOL*) focinho; (*sense of smell*) faro, olfato ♦ *vi* (*also*: **~** *one's way*) avançar cautelosamente; **to turn**

***NB:** European Portuguese adds the following consonants to certain words:* **b** (sú(b)dito, su(b)til); **c** (a(c)ção, a(c)cionista, a(c)to); **m** (inde(m)ne); **p** (ado(p)ção, ado(p)tar); *for further details see p. xiii.*

up one's ~ at desdenhar; to pay through the ~ (for sth) (*inf*) pagar os olhos da cara (por algo).
nose about *vi* bisbilhotar.
nose around *vi* bisbilhotar.
nosebleed ['nəuzbli:d] *n* hemorragia nasal.
nose-dive *n* (*deliberate*) vôo picado; (*involuntary*) parafuso.
nose drops *npl* gotas *fpl* para o nariz.
nosey ['nəuzɪ] *adj* intrometido, abelhudo.
nostalgia [nɔs'tældʒɪə] *n* nostalgia.
nostalgic [nɔs'tældʒɪk] *adj* nostálgico.
nostril ['nɔstrɪl] *n* narina.
nosy ['nəuzɪ] *adj* = **nosey**.
not [nɔt] *adv* não; ~ **at all** não ... de modo nenhum; (*after thanks*) de nada; ~ **that he knows** não que ele o saiba; ~ **yet** ainda não; ~ **now** agora não; **why** ~? por que não?; **I hope** ~ espero que não.
notable ['nəutəbl] *adj* notável.
notably ['nəutəblɪ] *adv* notavelmente.
notary ['nəutərɪ] *n* (*also*: ~ *public*) tabelião/ tabelioa *m/f*, notário/a.
notation [nəu'teɪʃən] *n* notação *f*.
notch [nɔtʃ] *n* entalhe *m*, corte *m*.
notch up *vt* (*score*) marcar; (*victory*) registrar.
note [nəut] *n* (MUS, *bank* ~) nota; (*letter*) nota, bilhete *m*; (*record*) nota, anotação *f*; (*tone*) tom *m* ♦ *vt* (*observe*) observar, reparar em; (*also*: ~ *down*) anotar, tomar nota de; **just a quick ~ to let you know ...** apenas um bilhete rápido para avisá-lo ...; **to take ~s** tomar notas; **to compare ~s** (*fig*) trocar impressões; **to take ~ of** fazer caso de; **a person of ~** uma pessoa eminente.
notebook ['nəutbuk] *n* caderno.
note-case (BRIT) *n* carteira.
noted ['nəutɪd] *adj* célebre, conhecido.
notepad ['nəutpæd] *n* bloco de anotações.
notepaper ['nəutpeɪpə*] *n* papel *m* de carta.
noteworthy ['nəutwə:θɪ] *adj* notável.
nothing ['nʌθɪŋ] *n* nada; (*zero*) zero; **he does ~** ele não faz nada; ~ **new** nada de novo; **for ~** (*free*) de graça, grátis; (*in vain*) em vão, por nada; ~ **at all** absolutamente nada, coisa nenhuma.
notice ['nəutɪs] *n* (*sign*) aviso, anúncio; (*warning*) aviso; (*of leaving*) aviso prévio; (BRIT: *review*: *of play etc*) resenha ♦ *vt* (*observe*) reparar em, notar; **without ~** sem aviso prévio; **advance ~** aviso prévio, preaviso; **to give sb ~ of sth** dar aviso a alguém de algo; **at short ~** a curto prazo; **until further ~** até nova ordem; **to hand in** *or* **give one's ~** (*subj*: *employee*) demitir, pedir a demissão; **to take ~ of** prestar atenção a, fazer caso de; **to bring sth to sb's ~** levar algo ao conhecimento de alguém; **it has come to my ~ that ...** tornei-me ciente que ...; **to escape** *or* **avoid ~** passar desapercebido.
noticeable ['nəutɪsəbl] *adj* evidente, sensível.
notice board (BRIT) *n* quadro de avisos.
notification [nəutɪfɪ'keɪʃən] *n* aviso, notificação *f*.
notify ['nəutɪfaɪ] *vt* avisar, notificar; **to ~ sth to sb** notificar algo a alguém; **to ~ sb of sth** avisar alguém de algo.
notion ['nəuʃən] *n* noção *f*, idéia.
notions ['nəuʃənz] (US) *npl* miudezas *fpl*.
notoriety [nəutə'raɪətɪ] *n* notoriedade *f*, má fama.
notorious [nəu'tɔ:rɪəs] *adj* notório.
notoriously [nəu'tɔ:rɪəslɪ] *adv* notoriamente.
Notts [nɔts] (BRIT) *abbr* = **Nottinghamshire**.
notwithstanding [nɔtwɪθ'stændɪŋ] *adv* no entanto, não obstante ♦ *prep*: ~ **this** apesar disto.
nougat ['nu:gɑ:] *n* torrone *m*, nugá *m*.
nought [nɔ:t] *n* zero.
noun [naun] *n* substantivo.
nourish ['nʌrɪʃ] *vt* nutrir, alimentar; (*fig*) fomentar, alentar.
nourishing ['nʌrɪʃɪŋ] *adj* nutritivo, alimentício.
nourishment ['nʌrɪʃmənt] *n* alimento, nutrimento.
Nov. *abbr* (= *November*) nov.
Nova Scotia ['nəuvə'skəuʃə] *n* Nova Escócia.
novel ['nɔvl] *n* romance *m*; (*short*) novela ♦ *adj* (*new*) novo, recente; (*unexpected*) insólito.
novelist ['nɔvəlɪst] *n* romancista *m/f*.
novelty ['nɔvəltɪ] *n* novidade *f*.
November [nəu'vɛmbə*] *n* novembro; *see also* **July**.
novice ['nɔvɪs] *n* principiante *m/f*, novato/a; (REL) noviço/a.
NOW [nau] (US) *n abbr* = **National Organization for Women**.
now [nau] *adv* (*at the present time*) agora; (*these days*) atualmente, hoje em dia ♦ *conj*: ~ **(that)** agora que; **right ~** agora mesmo; **that's the fashion just ~** é a moda atualmente; **I saw her just ~** eu a vi agora, acabei de vê-la; ~ **and then,** ~ **and again** de vez em quando; **from ~ on** de agora em diante; **in 3 days from ~** daqui a 3 dias; **between ~ and Monday** até segunda-feira; **that's all for ~** por agora é tudo.
nowadays ['nauədeɪz] *adv* hoje em dia.
nowhere ['nəuwɛə*] *adv* (*direction*) a lugar nenhum; (*location*) em nenhum lugar; ~ **else** em nenhum outro lugar.
noxious ['nɔkʃəs] *adj* nocivo.
nozzle ['nɔzl] *n* bico, bocal *m*; (TECH) tubeira; (: *hose*) agulheta.
NP *n abbr* = **notary public**.
NS (CANADA) *abbr* = **Nova Scotia**.
NSC (US) *n abbr* = **National Security Council**.
NSF (US) *n abbr* = **National Science Foundation**.
NSPCC (BRIT) *n abbr* = **National Society for the Prevention of Cruelty to Children**.
NSW (AUSTRALIA) *abbr* = **New South Wales**.
NT *n abbr* (= *New Testament*) NT.
nth [ɛnθ] *adj*: **for the ~ time** pela enésima vez.
NUAAW (BRIT) *n abbr* (= *National Union of*

Agricultural and Allied Workers) sindicato da agropecuária.

nuance ['nju:ɑ̃:ns] *n* nuança, matiz *m*.

NUBE (*BRIT*) *n abbr* (= *National Union of Bank Employees*) *sindicato dos bancários*.

nubile ['nju:baɪl] *adj* (*attractive*) jovem e bela.

nuclear ['nju:klɪə*] *adj* nuclear.

nuclear disarmament *n* desarmamento nuclear.

nuclei ['nju:klɪaɪ] *npl of* **nucleus**.

nucleus ['nju:klɪəs] (*pl* **nuclei**) *n* núcleo.

nude [nju:d] *adj* nu/nua ♦ *n* (*ART*) nu *m*; **in the ~** nu, pelado.

nudge [nʌdʒ] *vt* acotovelar, cutucar (*BR*).

nudist ['nju:dɪst] *n* nudista *m/f*.

nudist colony *n* colonia nudista.

nudity ['nju:dɪtɪ] *n* nudez *f*.

nugget ['nʌgɪt] *n* pepita.

nuisance ['nju:sns] *n* amolação *f*, aborrecimento; (*person*) chato; **what a ~!** que saco! (*BR*), que chatice! (*PT*).

NUJ (*BRIT*) *n abbr* (= *National Union of Journalists*) *sindicato dos jornalistas*.

nuke [nju:k] (*inf*) *n* usina nuclear.

null [nʌl] *adj*: **~ and void** írrito e nulo.

nullify ['nʌlɪfaɪ] *vt* anular, invalidar.

NUM (*BRIT*) *n abbr* (= *National Union of Mineworkers*) *sindicato dos mineiros*.

numb [nʌm] *adj* dormente, entorpecido; (*fig*) insensível ♦ *vt* adormecer, entorpecer; **~ with cold** tolhido de frio; **~ with fear** paralisado de medo.

number ['nʌmbə*] *n* número; (*numeral*) algarismo ♦ *vt* (*pages etc*) numerar; **a ~ of** vários, muitos; **to be ~ed among** figurar entre; **they were ten in ~** eram em número de dez; **wrong ~** (*TEL*) engano.

numbered account ['nʌmbəd-] *n* (*in bank*) conta numerada.

number plate (*BRIT*) *n* placa (do carro).

Number Ten (*BRIT*) *n* (= *10 Downing Street*) *residência do primeiro-ministro*.

numbness ['nʌmnɪs] *n* torpor *m*, dormência; (*fig*) insensibilidade *f*.

numeral ['nju:mərəl] *n* algarismo.

numerate ['nju:mərɪt] (*BRIT*) *adj*: **to be ~** ter uma noção básica da aritmética.

numerical [nju:'mɛrɪkl] *adj* numérico.

numerous ['nju:mərəs] *adj* numeroso.

nun [nʌn] *n* freira.

NUPE ['nju:pɪ] (*BRIT*) *n abbr* (= *National Union of Public Employees*) *sindicato dos funcionários públicos*.

nuptial ['nʌpʃəl] *adj* nupcial.

NUR (*BRIT*) *n abbr* (= *National Union of Railwaymen*) *sindicato dos ferroviários*.

nurse [nə:s] *n* enfermeiro/a; (*nanny*) ama-seca, babá *f* ♦ *vt* (*patient*) cuidar de, tratar de; (*baby*: *feed*) criar, amamentar; (: *BRIT*: *rock*) embalar; (*fig*) alimentar; **wet ~** ama de leite.

nursery ['nə:sərɪ] *n* (*institution*) creche *f*; (*room*) quarto das crianças; (*for plants*) viveiro.

nursery rhyme *n* poesia infantil.

nursery school *n* escola maternal.

nursery slope (*BRIT*) *n* (*SKI*) rampa para principiantes.

nursing ['nə:sɪŋ] *n* (*profession*) enfermagem *f*; (*care*) cuidado, assistência ♦ *adj* (*mother*) amamentadora.

nursing home *n* sanatório, clínica de repouso.

nurture ['nə:tʃə*] *vt* alimentar.

NUS (*BRIT*) *n abbr* (= *National Union of Seamen*) *sindicato dos marinheiros*; (= *National Union of Students*) *sindicato dos estudantes*.

NUT (*BRIT*) *n abbr* (= *National Union of Teachers*) *sindicato dos professores*.

nut [nʌt] *n* (*TECH*) porca; (*BOT*) noz *f* ♦ *cpd* (*chocolate etc*) de nozes.

nutcase ['nʌtkeɪs] (*inf*) *n* doido/a, biruta *m/f*.

nutcrackers ['nʌtkrækəz] *npl* quebra-nozes *m inv*.

nutmeg ['nʌtmɛg] *n* noz-moscada.

nutrient ['nju:trɪənt] *n* nutrimento ♦ *adj* nutritivo.

nutrition [nju:'trɪʃən] *n* nutrição *f*, alimentação *f*.

nutritionist [nju:'trɪʃənɪst] *n* nutricionista *m/f*.

nutritious [nju:'trɪʃəs] *adj* nutritivo.

nuts [nʌts] (*inf*) *adj*: **he's ~** ele é doido.

nutshell ['nʌtʃɛl] *n* casca de noz; **in a ~** em poucas palavras.

nuzzle ['nʌzl] *vi*: **to ~ up to** aconchegar-se com.

NV (*US*) *abbr* (*POST*) = **Nevada**.

NWT (*CANADA*) *abbr* = **Northwest Territories**.

NY (*US*) *abbr* (*POST*) = **New York**.

NYC (*US*) *abbr* (*POST*) = **New York City**.

nylon ['naɪlɔn] *n* náilon *m* (*BR*), nylon *m* (*PT*) ♦ *adj* de náilon; **~s** *npl* meias *fpl* (de náilon).

nymph [nɪmf] *n* ninfa.

nymphomaniac [nɪmfəu'meɪnɪæk] *n* ninfômana.

NYSE (*US*) *n abbr* = **New York Stock Exchange**.

NZ *abbr* = **New Zealand**.

O

O, o [əu] *n* (*letter*) O, o *m*; (*US*: *SCH*) = **outstanding**; **O for Olive** (*BRIT*) *or* **Oboe** (*US*) O de Osvaldo.

oaf [əuf] *n* imbecil *m/f*.

oak [əuk] *n* carvalho ♦ *cpd* de carvalho.

OAP (*BRIT*) *n abbr* = **old-age pensioner**.

NB: European Portuguese adds the following consonants to certain words: **b** (sú(b)dito, su(b)til); **c** (a(c)ção, a(c)cionista, a(c)to); **m** (inde(m)ne); **p** (ado(p)ção, ado(p)tar); *for further details see* *p. xiii.*

oar [ɔː*] *n* remo; **to put** *or* **shove one's ~ in** (*fig*: *inf*) meter o bedelho *or* a colher.
oarsman ['ɔːzmən] (*irreg*) *n* remador *m*.
oarswoman ['ɔːzwumən] (*irreg*) *n* remadora.
OAS *n abbr* (= *Organization of American States*) OEA *f*.
oases [əu'eɪsiːz] *npl of* **oasis**.
oasis [əu'eɪsɪs] (*pl* **oases**) *n* oásis *m inv*.
oath [əuθ] *n* juramento; (*swear word*) palavrão *m*; (*curse*) praga; **on** (BRIT) *or* **under ~** sob juramento; **to take an ~** prestar juramento.
oatmeal ['əutmiːl] *n* farinha *or* mingau *m* de aveia.
oats [əuts] *n* aveia.
OAU *n abbr* (= *Organization of African Unity*) OUA *f*.
obdurate ['ɔbdjurɪt] *adj* (*obstinate*) teimoso; (*sinner*) empedernido; (*unyielding*) inflexível.
obedience [ə'biːdɪəns] *n* obediência; **in ~ to** em conformidade com.
obedient [ə'biːdɪənt] *adj* obediente; **to be ~ to sb/sth** obedecer a alguém/algo.
obelisk ['ɔbɪlɪsk] *n* obelisco.
obese [əu'biːs] *adj* obeso.
obesity [əu'biːsɪtɪ] *n* obesidade *f*.
obey [ə'beɪ] *vt* obedecer a; (*instructions, regulations*) cumprir ♦ *vi* obedecer.
obituary [ə'bɪtjuərɪ] *n* necrológio.
object [*n* 'ɔbdʒɪkt, *vi* əb'dʒɛkt] *n* (*gen*, LING) objeto; (*purpose*) objetivo ♦ *vi*: **to ~ to** (*attitude*) desaprovar, objetar a; (*proposal*) opor-se a; **I ~!** protesto!; **he ~ed that ...** ele objetou que ...; **do you ~ to my smoking?** você se incomoda que eu fume?; **what's the ~ of doing that?** qual o objetivo de fazer isso?; **money is no ~** o dinheiro não tem importância.
objection [əb'dʒɛkʃən] *n* objeção *f*; (*drawback*) inconveniente *m*; **I have no ~ to ...** não tenho nada contra ...; **to make** *or* **raise an ~** fazer *or* levantar uma objeção.
objectionable [əb'dʒɛkʃənəbl] *adj* desagradável; (*conduct*) censurável.
objective [əb'dʒɛktɪv] *adj*, *n* objetivo.
objectivity [ɔbdʒɪk'tɪvɪtɪ] *n* objetividade *f*.
object lesson *n* (*fig*): **~ (in)** demonstração *f* (de).
objector [əb'dʒɛktə*] *n* opositor(a) *m/f*.
obligation [ɔblɪ'geɪʃən] *n* obrigação *f*; (*debt*) dívida (de gratidão); **without ~** sem compromisso; **to be under an ~ to do sth** ser obrigado a fazer algo.
obligatory [ə'blɪgətərɪ] *adj* obrigatório.
oblige [ə'blaɪdʒ] *vt* (*do a favour for*) obsequiar, fazer um favor a; (*force*): **to ~ sb to do sth** obrigar *or* forçar alguém a fazer algo; **I should be ~d if ...** agradeceria muito se ...; **anything to ~!** (*inf*) estou à sua disposição!
obliging [ə'blaɪdʒɪŋ] *adj* amável, prestativo.
oblique [ə'bliːk] *adj* oblíquo; (*allusion*) indireto ♦ *n* (BRIT: TYP): **~ (stroke)** barra.
obliterate [ə'blɪtəreɪt] *vt* (*erase*) apagar; (*destroy*) destruir.
oblivion [ə'blɪvɪən] *n* esquecimento.
oblivious [ə'blɪvɪəs] *adj*: **~ of** inconsciente de, esquecido de.
oblong ['ɔblɔŋ] *adj* oblongo, retangular ♦ *n* retângulo.
obnoxious [əb'nɔkʃəs] *adj* odioso, detestável; (*smell*) enjoativo.
o.b.o (US) *abbr* (= *or best offer*) ou melhor oferta.
oboe ['əubəu] *n* oboé *m*.
obscene [əb'siːn] *adj* obsceno.
obscenity [əb'sɛnɪtɪ] *n* obscenidade *f*.
obscure [əb'skjuə*] *adj* obscuro, pouco claro ♦ *vt* ocultar, escurecer; (*hide*: *sun etc*) esconder.
obscurity [əb'skjuərɪtɪ] *n* obscuridade *f*; (*darkness*) escuridão *f*.
obsequious [əb'siːkwɪəs] *adj* obsequioso, servil.
observable [əb'zəːvəbl] *adj* observável; (*appreciable*) perceptível.
observance [əb'zəːvns] *n* observância, cumprimento; (*ritual*) prática, hábito; **religious ~s** observância religiosa.
observant [əb'zəːvnt] *adj* observador(a).
observation [ɔbzə'veɪʃən] *n* observação *f*; (*by police etc*) vigilância; (MED) exame *m*.
observation post *n* (MIL) posto de observação.
observatory [əb'zəːvətrɪ] *n* observatório.
observe [əb'zəːv] *vt* observar; (*rule*) cumprir.
observer [əb'zəːvə*] *n* observador(a) *m/f*.
obsess [əb'sɛs] *vt* obsedar, obcecar; **to be ~ed by** *or* **with sb/sth** estar obcecado por *or* com alguém/algo.
obsession [əb'sɛʃən] *n* obsessão *f*, idéia fixa.
obsessive [əb'sɛsɪv] *adj* obsessivo.
obsolescence [ɔbsə'lɛsns] *n* obsolescência; **built-in** *or* **planned ~** (COMM) obsolescência pré-incorporada.
obsolescent [ɔbsə'lɛsnt] *adj* obsolescente, antiquado.
obsolete ['ɔbsəliːt] *adj* obsoleto; **to become ~** cair em desuso.
obstacle ['ɔbstəkl] *n* obstáculo; (*hindrance*) estorvo, impedimento.
obstacle race *n* corrida de obstáculos.
obstetrician [ɔbstə'trɪʃən] *n* obstetra *m/f*.
obstetrics [ɔb'stɛtrɪks] *n* obstetrícia.
obstinacy ['ɔbstɪnəsɪ] *n* teimosia, obstinação *f*.
obstinate ['ɔbstɪnɪt] *adj* teimoso, obstinado; (*determined*) pertinaz.
obstreperous [əb'strɛpərəs] *adj* turbulento.
obstruct [əb'strʌkt] *vt* obstruir; (*block*: *pipe*) entupir; (*hinder*) estorvar.
obstruction [əb'strʌkʃən] *n* obstrução *f*; (*hindrance*) estorvo, obstáculo.
obstructive [əb'strʌktɪv] *adj* obstrutor(a).
obtain [əb'teɪn] *vt* (*get*) obter; (*achieve*) conseguir ♦ *vi* prevalecer.
obtainable [əb'teɪnəbl] *adj* disponível.
obtrusive [əb'truːsɪv] *adj* (*person*) intrometido, intruso; (*building etc*) que dá muito na vista.
obtuse [əb'tjuːs] *adj* obtuso.

obverse ['ɔbvəːs] *n* (*of medal, coin*) obverso; (*fig*) contrapartida.
obviate ['ɔbvɪeɪt] *vt* obviar a, prevenir.
obvious ['ɔbvɪəs] *adj* (*clear*) óbvio, evidente; (*unsubtle*) nada sutil.
obviously ['ɔbvɪəslɪ] *adv* evidentemente; **~, he was not drunk** *or* **he was ~ not drunk** certamente ele não estava bêbado; **he was not ~ drunk** ele não aparentava estar bêbado; **~!** claro!, lógico!; **~ not!** (é) claro que não!
OCAS *n abbr* (= *Organization of Central American States*) ODECA *f*.
occasion [ə'keɪʒən] *n* ocasião *f*; (*event*) acontecimento ♦ *vt* ocasionar, causar; **on that ~** naquela ocasião; **to rise to the ~** mostrar-se à altura da situação.
occasional [ə'keɪʒənl] *adj* (feito *etc*) de vez em quando.
occasionally [ə'keɪʒənəlɪ] *adv* de vez em quando; **very ~** raramente.
occasional table *n* mesinha.
occult [ɔ'kʌlt] *adj* oculto ♦ *n*: **the ~** as ciências ocultas.
occupancy ['ɔkjupənsɪ] *n* ocupação *f*, posse *f*.
occupant ['ɔkjupənt] *n* (*of house*) inquilino/a; (*of car*) ocupante *m/f*.
occupation [ɔkju'peɪʃən] *n* ocupação *f*; (*job*) profissão *f*; **unfit for ~** (*house*) inabitável.
occupational [ɔkju'peɪʃənl] *adj* (*accident*) de trabalho; (*disease*) profissional.
occupational guidance (*BRIT*) *n* orientação *f* vocacional.
occupational hazard *n* risco profissional.
occupational pension *n* pensão *f* profissional.
occupational therapy *n* terapia ocupacional.
occupier ['ɔkjupaɪə*] *n* inquilino/a.
occupy ['ɔkjupaɪ] *vt* ocupar; (*house*) morar em; (*time*) encher; **to ~ o.s. with** *or* **by doing** (*as job*) dedicar-se a fazer; (*to pass time*) ocupar-se de fazer; **to be occupied with sth** ocupar-se de algo.
occur [ə'kəː*] *vi* ocorrer, acontecer; (*difficulty, opportunity*) surgir; (*phenomenon*) encontrar-se; **to ~ to** ocorrer a, vir à mente de; **it ~s to me that ...** ocorre-me que ....
occurrence [ə'kʌrəns] *n* (*event*) ocorrência, acontecimento; (*existence*) existência.
ocean ['əuʃən] *n* oceano; **~s of** (*inf*) um monte de.
ocean bed *n* fundo do oceano.
ocean-going [-'gəuɪŋ] *adj* de longo curso.
Oceania [əuʃɪ'eɪnɪə] *n* Oceania.
ocean liner *n* transatlântico.
ochre ['əukə*] (*US* **ocher**) *adj* cor de ocre *inv*.
o'clock [ə'klɔk] *adv*: **it is 5 ~** são cinco horas.
OCR *n abbr* = **optical character reader**; **optical character recognition**.
Oct. *abbr* (= *October*) out.
octagonal [ɔk'tægənl] *adj* octogonal.
octane ['ɔkteɪn] *n* octano; **high-~ petrol** (*BRIT*) *or* **gas** (*US*) gasolina de alto índice de octana.
octave ['ɔktɪv] *n* oitava.
October [ɔk'təubə*] *n* outubro; *see also* **July**.
octogenarian [ɔktəudʒɪ'nɛərɪən] *n* octogenário/a.
octopus ['ɔktəpəs] *n* polvo.
odd [ɔd] *adj* (*strange*) estranho, esquisito; (*number*) ímpar; (*left over*) avulso, de sobra; **60-~** 60 e tantos; **at ~ times** às vezes, de vez em quando; **to be the ~ one out** ficar sobrando, ser a exceção.
oddball ['ɔdbɔːl] (*inf*) *n* excêntrico/a, esquisitão/ona *m/f*.
oddity ['ɔdɪtɪ] *n* coisa estranha, esquisitice *f*; (*person*) excêntrico/a.
odd-job man (*irreg*) *n* faz-tudo *m*.
odd jobs *npl* biscates *mpl*, bicos *mpl*.
oddly ['ɔdlɪ] *adv* curiosamente.
oddments ['ɔdmənts] (*BRIT*) *npl* (*COMM*) retalhos *mpl*.
odds [ɔdz] *npl* (*in betting*) pontos *mpl* de vantagem; **the ~ are against his coming** é pouco provável que ele venha; **it makes no ~** dá no mesmo; **to succeed against all the ~** conseguir contra todas as expectativas; **~ and ends** miudezas *fpl*; **at ~** brigados/as, de mal.
ode [əud] *n* ode *f*.
odious ['əudɪəs] *adj* odioso.
odometer [əu'dɔmɪtə*] *n* conta-quilômetros *m inv*.
odour ['əudə*] (*US* **odor**) *n* odor *m*, cheiro.
odo(u)rless ['əudəlɪs] *adj* inodoro.
OECD *n abbr* (= *Organization for Economic Cooperation and Development*) OCDE *f*.
oesophagus [iː'sɔfəgəs] (*US* **esophagus**) *n* esôfago.
oestrogen ['iːstrəudʒən] (*US* **estrogen**) *n* estrogênio.
of [ɔv, əv] *prep* de; **a friend ~ ours** um amigo nosso; **3 ~ them** 3 deles; **the 5th ~ July** dia 5 de julho; **a boy ~ 10** um menino de 10 anos; **made ~ wood** feito de madeira; **a kilo ~ flour** um quilo de farinha; **that was very kind ~ you** foi muito gentil da sua parte; **a quarter ~ 4** (*US*) quinze para as 4.
off [ɔf] *adj, adv* (*engine, radio*) desligado; (*light*) apagado; (*tap*) fechado; (*BRIT*: *food*: *bad*) passado; (: *milk*) talhado; (*cancelled*) anulado; (*removed*): **the lid was ~** estava destampado ♦ *prep* de; **to be ~** (*to leave*) ir(-se) embora; **I must be ~** devo ir-me; **to be ~ sick** estar ausente por motivo de saúde; **a day ~** um dia de folga *or* livre; **today I had an ~ day** hoje não foi o meu dia; **he had his coat ~** ele havia tirado o casaco; **10% ~** (*COMM*) 10% de abatimento *or* desconto; **to be 5 km ~** estar a 5 km de distância; **5 km ~ (the road)** a 5 km (da estrada); **~ the coast** em frente à costa; **a house ~ the main road** uma casa afastada

NB: *European Portuguese adds the following consonants to certain words:* **b** (sú(b)dito, su(b)til); **c** (a(c)ção, a(c)cionista, a(c)to); **m** (inde(m)ne); **p** (ado(p)ção, ado(p)tar); *for further details see p. xiii.*

da estrada principal; **it's a long way ~** fica bem longe; **I'm ~ meat** não como mais carne; **on the ~ chance** ao acaso; **to be well/badly ~** estar em boa/má situação; **~ and on, on and ~** de vez em quando; **I'm afraid the chicken is ~** (*BRIT*: *not available*) sinto muito, mas frango não tem mais; **that's a bit ~** (*fig*: *inf*) o que é que isso?, isso não se faz.

offal ['ɔfl] *n* (*CULIN*) sobras *fpl*, restos *mpl*.

offbeat ['ɔfbi:t] *adj* excêntrico.

off-centre (*US* **off-center**) *adj* descentrado, excêntrico.

off-colour (*BRIT*) *adj* (*ill*) indisposto.

offence [ə'fɛns] (*US* **offense**) *n* (*crime*) delito; (*insult*) insulto, ofensa; **to give ~ to** ofender; **to take ~ at** ofender-se com, melindrar-se com; **to commit an ~** cometer uma infração.

offend [ə'fɛnd] *vt* (*person*) ofender ♦ *vi*: **to ~ against** (*law*, *rule*) pecar contra, transgredir.

offender [ə'fɛndə*] *n* delinqüente *m/f*; (*against regulations*) infrator(a) *m/f*.

offense [ə'fɛns] (*US*) *n* = **offence**.

offensive [ə'fɛnsɪv] *adj* (*weapon*, *remark*) ofensivo; (*smell etc*) repugnante ♦ *n* (*MIL*) ofensiva.

offer ['ɔfə*] *n* oferta; (*proposal*) proposta ♦ *vt* oferecer; (*opportunity*) proporcionar; **to make an ~ for sth** fazer uma oferta por algo; **to ~ sth to sb, ~ sb sth** oferecer algo a alguém; **to ~ to do sth** oferecer-se para fazer algo; **"on ~"** (*COMM*) "em oferta".

offering ['ɔfərɪŋ] *n* oferenda.

offertory ['ɔfətərɪ] *n* (*REL*) ofertório.

offhand [ɔf'hænd] *adj* informal ♦ *adv* de improviso; **I can't tell you ~** não posso te dizer assim de improviso.

office ['ɔfɪs] *n* (*place*) escritório; (*room*) gabinete *m*; (*position*) cargo, função *f*; **to take ~** tomar posse; **doctor's ~** (*US*) consultório; **through his good ~s** (*fig*) graças aos grandes préstimos dele; **O~ of Fair Trading** (*BRIT*) *órgão de proteção ao consumidor*.

office automation *n* automação *f* de escritórios.

office bearer *n* (*of club etc*) detentor(a) *m/f* de um cargo.

office block (*BRIT*) *n* conjunto de escritórios.

office boy *n* contínuo, bói *m*.

office building (*US*) *n* conjunto de escritórios.

office hours *npl* (horas *fpl* de) expediente *m*; (*US*: *MED*) horas *fpl* de consulta.

office manager *n* gerente *m/f* de escritório.

officer ['ɔfɪsə*] *n* (*MIL etc*) oficial *m/f*; (*of organization*) diretor(a) *m/f*; (*also*: *police ~*) agente *m/f* policial *or* de polícia.

office work *n* trabalho de escritório.

office worker *n* empregado/a *or* funcionário/a de escritório.

official [ə'fɪʃl] *adj* oficial ♦ *n* oficial *m/f*; (*civil servant*) funcionário/a (público/a).

officialdom [ə'fɪʃldəm] *n* burocracia.

officially [ə'fɪʃəlɪ] *adv* oficialmente.

official receiver *n* síndico/a de massa falida.

officiate [ə'fɪʃɪeɪt] *vi* (*REL*) oficiar; **to ~ as Mayor** exercer as funções de prefeito; **to ~ at a marriage** celebrar um casamento.

officious [ə'fɪʃəs] *adj* intrometido.

offing ['ɔfɪŋ] *n*: **in the ~** (*fig*) em perspectiva.

off-key *adj*, *adv* desafinado.

off-licence (*BRIT*) *n* (*shop*) *loja de bebidas alcoólicas*.

off-limits (*esp US*) *adj* proibido.

off line *adj* (*COMPUT*) fora de linha; (: *switched off*) desligado.

off-load *vt*: **to ~ sth (onto)** (*goods*) descarregar algo (sobre); (*job*) descarregar algo (em).

off-peak *adj* de temporada de pouco consumo *or* pouca atividade.

off-putting [-'putɪŋ] (*BRIT*) *adj* desconcertante.

off-season *adj*, *adv* fora de estação *or* temporada.

offset ['ɔfsɛt] (*irreg*: *like* **set**) *vt* (*counteract*) compensar, contrabalançar ♦ *n* (*also*: *~ printing*) ofsete *m*.

offshoot ['ɔfʃu:t] (*fig*) *n* desdobramento.

offshore [ɔf'ʃɔ:*] *adv* a pouca distância da costa, ao largo ♦ *adj* (*breeze*) de terra; (*island*) perto do litoral; (*fishing*) costeiro; **~ oilfield** campo petrolífero ao largo.

offside ['ɔf'saɪd] *n* (*AUT*) lado do motorista ♦ *adj* (*SPORT*) impedido; (*AUT*) do lado do motorista.

offspring ['ɔfsprɪŋ] *n* descendência, prole *f*.

offstage ['ɔf'steɪdʒ] *adv* nos bastidores.

off-the-cuff *adj* improvisado ♦ *adv* de improviso.

off-the-job training *n* treinamento fora do local de trabalho.

off-the-peg (*US* **off-the-rack**) *adj* pronto.

off-white *adj* quase branco.

often ['ɔfn] *adv* muitas vezes, freqüentemente; **how ~ do you go?** quantas vezes *or* com que freqüência você vai?; **as ~ as not** quase sempre; **very ~** com muita freqüência.

ogle ['əugl] *vt* comer com os olhos.

ogre ['əugə*] *n* ogre *m*.

OH (*US*) *abbr* (*POST*) = **Ohio**.

oh [əu] *excl* oh!, ô!, ah!

OHMS (*BRIT*) *abbr* = **On His** (*or* **Her**) **Majesty's Service**.

oil [ɔɪl] *n* óleo; (*petroleum*) petróleo; (*CULIN*) azeite *m* ♦ *vt* (*machine*) lubrificar.

oilcan ['ɔɪlkæn] *n* almotolia; (*for storing*) lata.

oil change *n* mudança de óleo.

oilfield ['ɔɪlfi:ld] *n* campo petrolífero.

oil filter *n* (*AUT*) filtro de óleo.

oil-fired [-'faɪəd] *adj* que usa óleo combustível.

oil gauge *n* indicador *m* do nível de óleo.

oil industry *n* indústria petroleira.

oil level *n* nível *m* de óleo.

oil painting *n* pintura a óleo.

oil refinery *n* refinaria de petróleo.

oil rig *n* torre *f* de perfuração.

oilskins ['ɔɪlskɪnz] *npl* capa de oleado.

oil slick *n* mancha de óleo.

oil tanker *n* petroleiro.

oil well *n* poço petrolífero.
oily ['ɔɪlɪ] *adj* oleoso; (*food*) gorduroso.
ointment ['ɔɪntmənt] *n* pomada.
OK (*US*) *abbr* (*POST*) = **Oklahoma**.
O.K. = **okay**.
okay ['əu'keɪ] *excl* está bem, está bom, tá (bem *or* bom) (*inf*) ♦ *adj* bom; (*correct*) certo ♦ *vt* aprovar ♦ *n*: **to give sth the ~** dar luz verde a algo; **is it ~?** tá bom?; **are you ~?** você está bem?; **are you ~ for money?** você está bem de dinheiro?; **it's ~ with** *or* **by me** para mim tudo bem.
old [əuld] *adj* velho; (*former*) antigo, anterior; **how ~ are you?** quantos anos você tem?; **he's 10 years ~** ele tem 10 anos; **~er brother** irmão mais velho; **any ~ thing will do** qualquer coisa serve.
old age *n* velhice *f*.
old-age pensioner (*BRIT*) *n* aposentado/a (*BR*), reformado/a (*PT*).
old-fashioned [-'fæʃnd] *adj* antiquado, fora de moda; (*person*) careta.
old maid *n* solteirona.
old people's home *n* asilo de velhos.
old-time *adj* antigo, do tempo antigo.
old-timer *n* veterano.
old wives' tale *n* conto da carochinha.
olive ['ɔlɪv] *n* (*fruit*) azeitona; (*tree*) oliveira ♦ *adj* (*also*: *~-green*) verde-oliva *inv*.
olive oil *n* azeite *m* de oliva.
Olympic [əu'lɪmpɪk] *adj* olímpico; **the ~ Games, the ~s** os Jogos Olímpicos, as Olimpíadas.
OM (*BRIT*) *n abbr* (= *Order of Merit*) *título honorífico*.
O&M *n abbr* = **organization and method**.
Oman [əu'mɑːn] *n* Omã (*PT*: Oman) *m*.
OMB (*US*) *n abbr* (= *Office of Management and Budget*) *serviço que assessora o presidente em assuntos orçamentários*.
omelet(te) ['ɔmlɪt] *n* omelete *f* (*BR*), omeleta (*PT*).
omen ['əumən] *n* presságio, agouro.
ominous ['ɔmɪnəs] *adj* (*menacing*) ameaçador(a); (*event*) de mau agouro.
omission [əu'mɪʃən] *n* omissão *f*; (*error*) descuido, negligência.
omit [əu'mɪt] *vt* omitir; (*by mistake*) esquecer; **to ~ to do sth** deixar de fazer algo.
omnivorous [ɔm'nɪvərəs] *adj* onívoro.
ON (*CANADA*) *abbr* = **Ontario**.
on [ɔn] *prep* sobre, em (cima de) ♦ *adv* (*machine*) em funcionamento; (*light*) aceso; (*radio*) ligado; (*tap*) aberto; **~ to** em, para, em direção a; **is the meeting still ~?** ainda vai haver reunião?; **when is this film ~?** quando vão passar este filme?; **~ the train** no trem; **~ the wall** na parede; **~ television** na televisão; **~ the Continent** no continente; **a book ~ physics** um livro sobre física; **~ seeing this** ao ver isto; **~ arrival** ao chegar; **~ the left** à esquerda; **~ Friday** na sexta-feira; **~ Fridays** nas sextas-feiras; **a week ~ Friday** sem ser esta sexta-feira, a outra; **~ holiday** (*BRIT*) *or* **vacation** (*US*) de férias; **I haven't any money ~ me** estou sem dinheiro; **this round's ~ me** esta rodada é por minha conta; **to have one's coat ~** estar de casaco; **to go ~** continuar (em frente); **from that day ~** daquele dia em diante; **it was well ~ in the evening** a noite estava adiantada; **we're ~ irregular verbs** estamos tratando de verbos irregulares; **she's ~ £20,000 a year** ela ganha £20,000 por ano; **it's not ~!** isso não se faz!; **~ and off** de vez em quando.
ONC (*BRIT*) *n abbr* = **Ordinary National Certificate**.
once [wʌns] *adv* uma vez; (*formerly*) outrora ♦ *conj* depois que; **~ he had left** depois que ele saiu; **at ~** imediatamente; (*simultaneously*) de uma vez, ao mesmo tempo; **all at ~** de repente; **~ a week** uma vez por semana; **~ more** mais uma vez; **I knew him ~** eu o conheci antigamente; **~ and for all** uma vez por todas, definitivamente; **~ upon a time** era uma vez.
oncoming ['ɔnkʌmɪŋ] *adj* (*traffic*) que vem de frente.
OND (*BRIT*) *n abbr* = **Ordinary National Diploma**.
one [wʌn] *adj*, *num* um/uma ♦ *pron* um/uma; (+ *vb*: *impers*) se; **this ~** este/esta; **that ~** esse/essa, aquele/aquela; **~ by ~** um por um; **~ never knows** nunca se sabe; **~ another** um ao outro; **the ~ book which ...** o único livro que ...; **it's ~ (o'clock)** é uma (hora); **which ~ do you want?** qual você quer?; **to be ~ up on sb** levar vantagem a alguém; **to be at ~ (with sb)** estar de acordo (com alguém); *see also* **five**.
one-armed bandit *n* caça-níqueis *m inv*.
one day excursion (*US*) *n* bilhete *m* de ida e volta.
one-man *adj* (*business*) individual.
one-man band *n* homem-orquestra *m*.
one-off (*BRIT*: *inf*) *n* exemplar *m* único ♦ *adj* único.
one-piece *adj*: **~ bathing suit** maiô inteiro.
onerous ['əunərəs] *adj* (*task, duty*) incômodo; (*responsibility*) pesado.
oneself [wʌn'sɛlf] *pron* se; (*after prep, also emphatic*) si (mesmo/a); **by ~** sozinho/a.
one-sided [-'saɪdɪd] *adj* (*decision*) unilateral; (*judgement, account*) parcial; (*contest*) desigual.
one-time *adj* antigo.
one-to-one *adj* (*relationship*) individual.
one-upmanship [-'ʌpmənʃɪp] *n*: **the art of ~** a arte de aparentar ser melhor do que os outros.
one-way *adj* (*street, traffic*) de mão única (*BR*), de sentido único (*PT*).
ongoing ['ɔngəuɪŋ] *adj* contínuo, em anda-

***NB**: European Portuguese adds the following consonants to certain words:* **b** (sú(b)dito, su(b)til); **c** (a(c)ção, a(c)cionista, a(c)to); **m** (inde(m)ne); **p** (ado(p)ção, ado(p)tar); *for further details see p. xiii.*

mento.
onion ['ʌnjən] *n* cebola.
on line *adj* (COMPUT) on-line, em linha; (: *switched on*) ligado.
onlooker ['ɔnlukə*] *n* espectador(a) *m/f*.
only ['əunlɪ] *adv* somente, apenas ♦ *adj* único, só ♦ *conj* só que, porém; **an ~ child** um filho único; **not ~ ... but also ...** não só ... mas também ...; **I ~ ate one** eu comi só um; **I saw her ~ yesterday** apenas ontem eu a vi; **I'd be ~ too pleased to help** eu teria muitíssimo prazer em ajudar; **I would come, ~ I'm very busy** eu iria, porém estou muito ocupado.
ono *abbr* (= *or nearest offer*) ou melhor oferta.
onset ['ɔnsɛt] *n* (*beginning*) começo; (*attack*) ataque *m*.
onshore ['ɔnʃɔ:*] *adj* (*wind*) do mar.
onslaught ['ɔnslɔ:t] *n* investida, arremetida.
on-the-job training *n* treinamento no serviço.
onto ['ɔntu] *prep* = **on to**.
onus ['əunəs] *n* responsabilidade *f*; **the ~ is upon him to prove it** cabe a ele comprová-lo.
onward(s) ['ɔnwəd(z)] *adv* (*move*) para diante, para a frente; **from this time ~** de (ag)ora em diante.
onyx ['ɔnɪks] *n* ônix *m*.
ooze [u:z] *vi* ressumar, filtrar-se; **to ~ a feeling** mostrar um sentimento exagerado.
opacity [əu'pæsɪtɪ] *n* opacidade *f*.
opal ['əupl] *n* opala.
opaque [əu'peɪk] *adj* opaco, fosco.
OPEC ['əupɛk] *n abbr* (= *Organization of Petroleum-Exporting Countries*) OPEP *f*.
open ['əupn] *adj* aberto; (*car*) descoberto; (*road*) livre; (*meeting*) público; (*admiration*) declarado; (*question*) discutível; (*enemy*) assumido ♦ *vt* abrir ♦ *vi* (*gen*) abrir(-se); (*shop*) abrir; (*book etc*: *commence*) começar; **in the ~ (air)** ao ar livre; **the ~ sea** o largo; **~ ground** (*among trees*) clareira, abertura; (*waste ground*) terreno baldio; **to have an ~ mind (on sth)** ter uma cabeça aberta (a respeito de algo).
open on to *vt fus* (*subj*: *room, door*) dar para.
open out *vt* abrir ♦ *vi* abrir-se.
open up *vt* abrir; (*blocked road*) desobstruir ♦ *vi* abrir-se.
open-air *adj* a céu aberto.
open-and-shut *adj*: **~ case** caso evidente.
open day (BRIT) *n* dia *m* de visita.
open-ended [-'ɛndɪd] *adj* (*fig*) não limitado.
opener ['əupnə*] *n* (*also*: *can ~, tin ~*) abridor *m* de latas (BR), abre-latas *m inv* (PT).
open-heart surgery *n* cirurgia de coração aberto.
opening ['əupnɪŋ] *n* abertura; (*start*) início; (*opportunity*) oportunidade *f*; (*job*) vaga.
opening night *n* (THEATRE) estréia.
openly ['əupənlɪ] *adv* abertamente.
open-minded [-'maɪndɪd] *adj* aberto, imparcial.
open-necked [-nɛkt] *adj* aberto no colo.
openness ['əupnnɪs] *n* abertura, sinceridade *f*.
open-plan *adj* sem paredes divisórias.
open sandwich *n* canapê *m*.
open shop *n empresa que admite trabalhadores não sindicalizados*.
Open University (BRIT) *n universidade que oferece curso universitário por correspondência*.
opera ['ɔpərə] *n* ópera.
opera glasses *npl* binóculo de teatro.
opera house (*irreg*) *n* teatro lírico *or* de ópera.
opera singer *n* cantor(a) *m/f* de ópera.
operate ['ɔpəreɪt] *vt* (*machine*) fazer funcionar, pôr em funcionamento; (*company*) dirigir ♦ *vi* funcionar; (*drug*) fazer efeito; **to ~ on sb** (MED) operar alguém.
operatic [ɔpə'rætɪk] *adj* lírico, operístico.
operating ['ɔpəreɪtɪŋ] *adj* (COMM: *costs, profit*) operacional.
operating system *n* (COMPUT) sistema *m* operacional.
operating table *n* mesa de operações.
operating theatre *n* sala de operações.
operation [ɔpə'reɪʃən] *n* operação *f*; (*of machine*) funcionamento; **to have an ~** fazer uma operação; **to be in ~** (*system*) estar em vigor; (*machine*) estar funcionando.
operational [ɔpə'reɪʃənl] *adj* operacional; **when the service is fully ~** quando o serviço estiver com toda a sua eficácia.
operative ['ɔpərətɪv] *adj* (*measure*) em vigor ♦ *n* (*in factory*) operário/a; **the ~ word** a palavra mais importante *or* atuante.
operator ['ɔpəreɪtə*] *n* (*of machine*) operador(a) *m/f*, manipulador(a) *m/f*; (TEL) telefonista *m/f*.
operetta [ɔpə'rɛtə] *n* opereta.
ophthalmic [ɔf'θælmɪk] *adj* oftálmico.
ophthalmologist [ɔfθæl'mɔlədʒɪst] *n* oftalmologista *m/f*, oftalmólogo/a.
opinion [ə'pɪnɪən] *n* opinião *f*; **in my ~** na minha opinião, a meu ver; **to seek a second ~** procurar uma segunda opinião.
opinionated [ə'pɪnɪəneɪtɪd] *adj* opinioso.
opinion poll *n* pesquisa, levantamento.
opium ['əupɪəm] *n* ópio.
opponent [ə'pəunənt] *n* adversário/a, oponente *m/f*.
opportune ['ɔpətju:n] *adj* oportuno.
opportunist [ɔpə'tju:nɪst] *n* oportunista *m/f*.
opportunity [ɔpə'tju:nɪtɪ] *n* oportunidade *f*; **to take the ~ to do** *or* **of doing** aproveitar a oportunidade para fazer.
oppose [ə'pəuz] *vt* opor-se a; **to be ~d to sth** opor-se a algo, estar contra algo; **as ~d to** em oposição a.
opposing [ə'pəuzɪŋ] *adj* (*side*) oposto, contrário.
opposite ['ɔpəzɪt] *adj* oposto; (*house etc*) em frente ♦ *adv* (lá) em frente ♦ *prep* em frente de, defronte de ♦ *n* oposto, contrário.
opposite number (BRIT) *n* homólogo/a.

opposite sex *n*: **the ~** o sexo oposto.
opposition [ɔpə'zɪʃən] *n* oposição *f*.
oppress [ə'prɛs] *vt* oprimir.
oppression [ə'prɛʃən] *n* opressão *f*.
oppressive [ə'prɛsɪv] *adj* opressivo.
opprobrium [ə'prəubrɪəm] *n* (*formal*) opróbrio.
opt [ɔpt] *vi*: **to ~ for** optar por; **to ~ to do** optar por fazer; **to ~ out of doing sth** optar por não fazer algo.
optical ['ɔptɪkl] *adj* ótico.
optical character reader *n* leitora de caracteres óticos.
optical character recognition *n* reconhecimento de caracteres óticos.
optical fibre *n* fibra ótica.
optician [ɔp'tɪʃən] *n* oculista *m/f*.
optics ['ɔptɪks] *n* ótica.
optimism ['ɔptɪmɪzəm] *n* otimismo.
optimist ['ɔptɪmɪst] *n* otimista *m/f*.
optimistic [ɔptɪ'mɪstɪk] *adj* otimista.
optimum ['ɔptɪməm] *adj* ótimo.
option ['ɔpʃən] *n* opção *f*; **to keep one's ~s open** (*fig*) manter as opções em aberto; **I have no ~** não tenho opção *or* escolha.
optional ['ɔpʃənəl] *adj* opcional, facultativo; **~ extras** acessórios *mpl* opcionais.
opulence ['ɔpjuləns] *n* opulência.
opulent ['ɔpjulənt] *adj* opulento.
OR (*US*) *abbr* (*POST*) = **Oregon**.
or [ɔ:*] *conj* ou; (*with negative*): **he hasn't seen ~ heard anything** ele não viu nem ouviu nada; **~ else** senão; **either ..., ~ else** *ou* ..., ou (então).
oracle ['ɔrəkl] *n* oráculo.
oral ['ɔ:rəl] *adj* oral ♦ *n* exame *m* oral.
orange ['ɔrɪndʒ] *n* (*fruit*) laranja ♦ *adj* cor de laranja *inv*, alaranjado.
orangeade [ɔrɪndʒ'eɪd] *n* laranjada.
oration [ɔ:'reɪʃən] *n* oração *f*.
orator ['ɔrətə*] *n* orador(a) *m/f*.
oratorio [ɔrə'tɔ:rɪəu] *n* oratório.
orb [ɔ:b] *n* orbe *m*.
orbit ['ɔ:bɪt] *n* órbita ♦ *vt, vi* orbitar; **to be/go into ~ (around)** estar/entrar em órbita (em torno de).
orchard ['ɔ:tʃəd] *n* pomar *m*; **apple ~** pomar de macieiras.
orchestra ['ɔ:kɪstrə] *n* orquestra; (*US*: *seating*) platéia.
orchestral [ɔ:'kɛstrəl] *adj* orquestral; (*concert*) sinfônico.
orchestrate ['ɔ:kɪstreɪt] *vt* (*MUS*, *fig*) orquestrar.
orchid ['ɔ:kɪd] *n* orquídea.
ordain [ɔ:'deɪn] *vt* (*REL*) ordenar, decretar; (*decide*) decidir, mandar.
ordeal [ɔ:'di:l] *n* experiência penosa, provação *f*.
order ['ɔ:də*] *n* (*gen*) ordem *f*; (*COMM*) encomenda ♦ *vt* (*also*: *put in ~*) pôr em ordem, arrumar; (*in restaurant*) pedir; (*COMM*) encomendar; (*command*) mandar, ordenar; **in ~** em ordem; **out of ~** com defeito, enguiçado; **a machine in working ~** uma máquina em bom estado; **in ~ of preference** por ordem de preferência; **in ~ to do/that** para fazer/que + *sub*; **to ~ sb to do sth** mandar alguém fazer algo; **to place an ~ for sth with sb** fazer uma encomenda a alguém para algo, encomendar algo a alguém; **made to ~** feito sob encomenda; **to be under ~s to do sth** ter ordens para fazer algo; **a point of ~** uma questão de ordem; **to the ~ of** (*BANKING*) à ordem de.
order book *n* livro de encomendas.
order form *n* impresso para encomendas.
orderly ['ɔ:dəlɪ] *n* (*MIL*) ordenança *m*; (*MED*) servente *m/f* ♦ *adj* (*room*) arrumado, ordenado; (*person*) metódico.
order number *n* número de encomenda.
ordinal ['ɔ:dɪnl] *adj* (*number*) ordinal.
ordinary ['ɔ:dnrɪ] *adj* comum, usual; (*pej*) ordinário, medíocre; **out of the ~** fora do comum, extraordinário.
ordinary seaman (*BRIT*: *irreg*) *n* marinheiro de segunda classe.
ordinary shares *npl* ações *fpl* ordinárias.
ordination [ɔ:dɪ'neɪʃən] *n* ordenação *f*.
ordnance ['ɔ:dnəns] *n* (*MIL*: *unit*) artilharia.
Ordnance Survey (*BRIT*) *n serviço oficial de topografia e cartografia.*
ore [ɔ:*] *n* minério.
organ ['ɔ:gən] *n* (*gen*) órgão *m*.
organic [ɔ:'gænɪk] *adj* orgânico.
organism ['ɔ:gənɪzəm] *n* organismo.
organist ['ɔ:gənɪst] *n* organista *m/f*.
organization [ɔ:gənaɪ'zeɪʃən] *n* organização *f*.
organization chart *n* organograma *m*.
organize ['ɔ:gənaɪz] *vt* organizar; **to get ~d** organizar-se.
organized labour ['ɔ:gənaɪzd-] *n* mão-de-obra sindicalizada.
organizer ['ɔ:gənaɪzə*] *n* organizador(a) *m/f*.
orgasm ['ɔ:gæzəm] *n* orgasmo.
orgy ['ɔ:dʒɪ] *n* orgia.
Orient ['ɔ:rɪənt] *n*: **the ~** o Oriente.
oriental [ɔ:rɪ'ɛntl] *adj, n* oriental *m/f*.
orientate ['ɔ:rɪənteɪt] *vt* orientar.
orifice ['ɔrɪfɪs] *n* orifício.
origin ['ɔrɪdʒɪn] *n* origem *f*; (*point of departure*) procedência; **country of ~** país de origem.
original [ə'rɪdʒɪnl] *adj* original ♦ *n* original *m*.
originality [ərɪdʒɪ'nælɪtɪ] *n* originalidade *f*.
originally [ə'rɪdʒɪnəlɪ] *adv* (*at first*) originalmente; (*with originality*) com originalidade.
originate [ə'rɪdʒɪneɪt] *vi*: **to ~ from** originar-se de, surgir de; **to ~ in** ter origem em.
originator [ə'rɪdʒɪneɪtə*] *n* iniciador(a) *m/f*.
Orkneys ['ɔ:knɪz] *npl*: **the ~** (*also*: *the Orkney Islands*) as ilhas Órcadas.
ornament ['ɔ:nəmənt] *n* ornamento; (*trinket*)

***NB**: European Portuguese adds the following consonants to certain words:* **b** (sú(b)dito, su(b)til); **c** (a(c)ção, a(c)cionista, a(c)to); **m** (inde(m)ne); **p** (ado(p)ção, ado(p)tar); *for further details see p. xiii.*

quinquilharia.
ornamental [ɔːnə'mɛntl] *adj* decorativo, ornamental.
ornamentation [ɔːnəmɛn'teɪʃən] *n* ornamentação *f*.
ornate [ɔː'neɪt] *adj* enfeitado, requintado.
ornithologist [ɔːnɪ'θɔlədʒɪst] *n* ornitólogo/a.
ornithology [ɔːnɪ'θɔlədʒɪ] *n* ornitologia.
orphan ['ɔːfn] *n* órfão/órfã *m/f* ♦ *vt*: **to be ~ed** ficar orfão.
orphanage ['ɔːfənɪdʒ] *n* orfanato.
orthodox ['ɔːθədɔks] *adj* ortodoxo.
orthodoxy ['ɔːθədɔksɪ] *n* ortodoxia.
orthopaedic [ɔːθə'piːdɪk] (*US* **orthopedic**) *adj* ortopédico.
orthop(a)edics [ɔːθə'piːdɪks] *n* ortopedia.
OS (*BRIT*) *abbr* = **Ordnance Survey**; (*NAUT*) = **ordinary seaman**; (*DRESS*) = **outsize**.
O/S *abbr* = **out of stock**.
oscillate ['ɔsɪleɪt] *vi* oscilar; (*person*) vacilar, hesitar.
OSHA (*US*) *n abbr* (= *Occupational Safety and Health Administration*) *órgão que supervisiona a higiene e a segurança do trabalho*.
Oslo ['ɔzləu] *n* Oslo.
ostensible [ɔs'tɛnsɪbl] *adj* aparente.
ostensibly [ɔs'tɛnsɪblɪ] *adv* aparentemente.
ostentation [ɔstɛn'teɪʃən] *n* ostentação *f*.
ostentatious [ɔstɛn'teɪʃəs] *adj* aparatoso, pomposo; (*person*) ostentoso.
osteopath ['ɔstɪəpæθ] *n* osteopata *m/f*.
ostracize ['ɔstrəsaɪz] *vt* condenar ao ostracismo.
ostrich ['ɔstrɪtʃ] *n* avestruz *m/f*.
OT *n abbr* (= *Old Testament*) AT *m*.
OTB (*US*) *n abbr* (= *off-track betting*) *apostas tomadas fora da pista de corridas*.
other ['ʌðə*] *adj* outro ♦ *pron*: **the ~ (one)** o outro/a outra; **~s** (**~** *people*) outros; **some ~ people have still to arrive** outras pessoas ainda não chegaram; **the ~ day** outro dia; **~ than** (*in another way*) de outro modo que; (*apart from*) além de; **some actor or ~** um certo ator; **somebody or ~** não sei quem, alguém; **the car was none ~ than John's** o carro não era nenhum outro senão o de João.
otherwise ['ʌðəwaɪz] *adv* de outra maneira ♦ *conj* (*if not*) senão; **an ~ good piece of work** sob outros aspectos, um trabalho bem feito.
OTT (*inf*) *abbr* = **over the top**; *see* **top**.
otter ['ɔtə*] *n* lontra.
OU (*BRIT*) *n abbr* = **Open University**.
ouch [autʃ] *excl* ai!
ought [ɔːt] (*pt* **ought**) *aux vb*: **I ~ to do it** eu deveria fazê-lo; **this ~ to have been corrected** isto deveria ter sido corrigido; **he ~ to win** (*probability*) ele deve ganhar; **you ~ to go and see it** você deveria ir vê-lo.
ounce [auns] *n* onça (= *28.35g*; *16 in a pound*).
our ['auə*] *adj* nosso.
ours ['auəz] *pron* (o) nosso/(a) nossa *etc*.
ourselves [auə'sɛlvz] *pron pl* (*reflexive, after prep*) nós; (*emphatic*) nós mesmos/as; **we did it (all) by ~** nós fizemos isso sozinhos.
oust [aust] *vt* desalojar, expulsar.
out [aut] *adv* fora; (*not at home*) fora (de casa); (*light, fire*) apagado; (*on strike*) em greve; **~ there** lá fora; **~ here** aqui fora; **he's ~** (*absent*) não está, saiu; (*unconscious*) está inconsciente; **get ~!** fora!; **to be ~ in one's calculations** enganar-se nos cálculos; **to run ~** sair correndo; **to be ~ and about** (*BRIT*) *or* **around** (*US*) **again** estar com a saúde refeita; **before the week was ~** antes da semana acabar; **the journey ~** a ida; **the boat was 10 km ~** o barco estava a 10 km da costa; **~ loud** em voz alta; **~ of** (*outside*) fora de; (*because of*: *anger etc*) por; **~ of petrol** sem gasolina; **"~ of order"** "não funciona", "avariado"; **made ~ of wood** de madeira; **~ of stock** (*COMM*) esgotado.
outage ['autɪdʒ] (*esp US*) *n* (*power failure*) blecaute *m*.
out-and-out *adj* acabado, rematado.
outback ['autbæk] *n* interior *m*.
outbid [aut'bɪd] (*pt, pp* **outbid** *or* **~ded**) *vt* sobrepujar.
outboard motor ['autbɔːd-] *n* motor *m* de popa.
outbreak ['autbreɪk] *n* (*of war*) deflagração *f*; (*of disease*) surto; (*of violence etc*) explosão *f*.
outbuilding ['autbɪldɪŋ] *n* dependência.
outburst ['autbəːst] *n* explosão *f*.
outcast ['autkɑːst] *n* pária *m/f*.
outclass [aut'klɑːs] *vt* ultrapassar, superar.
outcome ['autkʌm] *n* resultado.
outcrop ['autkrɔp] *n* afloramento.
outcry ['autkraɪ] *n* clamor *m* (de protesto).
outdated [aut'deɪtɪd] *adj* antiquado, fora de moda.
outdistance [aut'dɪstəns] *vt* deixar para trás.
outdo [aut'duː] (*irreg*) *vt* ultrapassar, exceder.
outdoor [aut'dɔː*] *adj* ao ar livre.
outdoors [aut'dɔːz] *adv* ao ar livre.
outer ['autə*] *adj* exterior, externo.
outer space *n* espaço (exterior).
outfit ['autfɪt] *n* equipamento; (*clothes*) roupa, traje *m*; (*inf*: *COMM*) firma.
outfitter's ['autfɪtəz] (*BRIT*) *n* fornecedor *m* de roupas.
outgoing ['autgəuɪŋ] *adj* (*president, tenant*) de saída; (*character*) extrovertido, sociável.
outgoings ['autgəuɪŋz] (*BRIT*) *npl* despesas *fpl*.
outgrow [aut'grəu] (*irreg*) *vt*: **he has ~n his clothes** a roupa ficou pequena para ele.
outhouse ['authaus] (*irreg*) *n* anexo.
outing ['autɪŋ] *n* (*going out*) saída; (*excursion*) excursão *f*.
outlandish [aut'lændɪʃ] *adj* estranho, bizarro.
outlast [aut'lɑːst] *vt* sobreviver a.
outlaw ['autlɔː] *n* fora-da-lei *m/f* ♦ *vt* (*person*) declarar fora da lei; (*practice*) declarar ilegal.
outlay ['autleɪ] *n* despesas *fpl*.
outlet ['autlɛt] *n* saída, escape *m*; (*of pipe*) desagüe *m*, escoadouro; (*US*: *ELEC*) tomada;

(*also*: *retail* ~) posto de venda.

outline ['autlaɪn] *n* (*shape*) contorno, perfil *m*; (*of plan*) traçado; (*sketch*) esboço, linhas *fpl* gerais.

outlive [aut'lɪv] *vt* sobreviver a.

outlook ['autluk] *n* perspectiva; (*opinion*) ponto de vista.

outlying ['autlaɪɪŋ] *adj* afastado, remoto.

outmanoeuvre [autmə'nuːvə*] (*US* **outmaneuver**) *vt* (*rival etc*) passar a perna em.

outmoded [aut'məudɪd] *adj* antiquado, fora de moda, obsoleto.

outnumber [aut'nʌmbə*] *vt* exceder em número.

out-of-date *adj* (*passport, ticket*) sem validade; (*theory, idea*) antiquado, superado; (*custom*) antiquado; (*clothes*) fora de moda.

out-of-the-way *adj* remoto, afastado; (*fig*) insólito.

outpatient ['autpeɪʃənt] *n* paciente *m/f* externo/a *or* de ambulatório.

outpost ['autpəust] *n* posto avançado.

output ['autput] *n* (volume *m* de) produção *f*; (*TECH*) rendimento ♦ *vt* (*COMPUT*) liberar.

outrage ['autreɪdʒ] *n* (*scandal*) escândalo; (*atrocity*) atrocidade *f* ♦ *vt* ultrajar.

outrageous [aut'reɪdʒəs] *adj* ultrajante, escandaloso.

outrider ['autraɪdə*] *n* (*on motorcycle*) batedor(a) *m/f*.

outright [*adv* aut'raɪt, *adj* 'autraɪt] *adv* completamente ♦ *adj* completo.

outrun [aut'rʌn] (*irreg*) *vt* ultrapassar.

outset ['autsɛt] *n* início, princípio.

outshine [aut'ʃaɪn] (*irreg*) *vt* (*fig*) eclipsar.

outside [aut'saɪd] *n* exterior *m* ♦ *adj* exterior, externo; (*contractor etc*) de fora ♦ *adv* (lá) fora ♦ *prep* fora de; (*beyond*) além (dos limites) de; **at the** ~ (*fig*) no máximo; **an** ~ **chance** uma possibilidade remota; ~ **left/right** (*FOOTBALL*) ponta *m* esquerdo/direito.

outside broadcast *n* (*RADIO, TV*) transmissão *f* de exteriores.

outside lane *n* (*AUT*: *in Britain*) pista da direita; (: *in US, Europe etc*) pista da esquerda.

outside line *n* (*TEL*) linha de saída.

outsider [aut'saɪdə*] *n* (*stranger*) estranho/a, forasteiro/a; (*in race etc*) outsider *m*.

outsize ['autsaɪz] *adj* enorme; (*clothes*) de tamanho extra-grande *or* especial.

outskirts ['autskəːts] *npl* arredores *mpl*, subúrbios *mpl*.

outsmart [aut'smɑːt] *vt* passar a perna em.

outspoken [aut'spəukən] *adj* franco, sem rodeios.

outspread [aut'sprɛd] *adj* estendido.

outstanding [aut'stændɪŋ] *adj* excepcional, saliente; (*unfinished, debt*) pendente; **your account is still** ~ a sua conta ainda não está liquidada.

outstay [aut'steɪ] *vt*: **to** ~ **one's welcome** abusar da hospitalidade (demorando mais tempo).

outstretched [aut'strɛtʃt] *adj* (*hand*) estendido; (*body*) esticado.

outstrip [aut'strɪp] *vt* (*also*: *fig*) ultrapassar.

out-tray *n* cesta de saída.

outvote [aut'vəut] *vt*: **to** ~ **sb (by ...)** vencer alguém (por ... votos); **to** ~ **sth (by ...)** rejeitar algo (por ... votos).

outward ['autwəd] *adj* (*sign, appearances*) externo; (*journey*) de ida.

outwardly ['autwədlɪ] *adv* para fora.

outweigh [aut'weɪ] *vt* ter mais valor do que.

outwit [aut'wɪt] *vt* passar a perna em.

oval ['əuvl] *adj* ovalado ♦ *n* oval *m*.

ovary ['əuvərɪ] *n* ovário.

ovation [əu'veɪʃən] *n* ovação *f*.

oven ['ʌvn] *n* forno.

ovenproof ['ʌvnpruːf] *adj* refratário.

oven-ready *adj* pronto para o forno.

ovenware ['ʌvnwɛə*] *n* louça refratária.

over ['əuvə*] *adv* por cima; (*excessively*) muito, demais ♦ *adj* (*or adv*) (*finished*) acabado; (*too much*) a mais ♦ *prep* por cima de; (*above*) acima de; (*on the other side of*) do outro lado de; (*more than*) mais de; (*during*) durante; (*about, concerning*): **they fell out** ~ **money** eles se desentenderam por dinheiro; ~ **here** por aqui, cá; ~ **there** por ali, lá; **all** ~ (*everywhere*) por todos os lados; (*finished*) acabado; ~ **and** ~ **(again)** repetidamente; ~ **and above** além de; **to ask sb** ~ convidar alguém; **to bend** ~ inclinar-se (sobre); **to go** ~ **to sb's** passar na casa de alguém; **now** ~ **to our Paris correspondent** com a palavra o nosso correspondente em Paris; **the world** ~ no mundo inteiro; **she's not** ~ **intelligent** (*BRIT*) ela não é superdotada.

over... [əuvə*] *prefix* sobre..., super....

overabundant [əuvərə'bʌndənt] *adj* superabundante.

overact [əuvər'ækt] *vi* (*THEATRE*) exagerar.

overall [*n, adj* 'əuvərɔːl, *adv* əuvər'ɔːl] *adj* (*length*) total; (*study*) global ♦ *adv* globalmente; ~**s** *npl* macacão *m* (*BR*), (fato) macaco (*PT*).

overanxious [əuvər'æŋkʃəs] *adj* muito ansioso.

overawe [əuvər'ɔː] *vt* intimidar.

overbalance [əuvə'bæləns] *vi* perder o equilíbrio, desequilibrar-se.

overbearing [əuvə'bɛərɪŋ] *adj* autoritário, dominador(a); (*arrogant*) arrogante.

overboard ['əuvəbɔːd] *adv* (*NAUT*) ao mar; **man** ~! homem ao mar!; **to go** ~ **for sth** (*fig*) empolgar-se com algo.

overbook [əuvə'buk] *vi* fazer reservas em excesso.

overcapitalize [əuvə'kæpɪtəlaɪz] *vt* sobrecapitalizar.

overcast ['əuvəkɑːst] *adj* nublado, fechado.

overcharge [əuvə'tʃɑːdʒ] *vt*: **to** ~ **sb** cobrar

***NB**: European Portuguese adds the following consonants to certain words:* **b** (sú(b)dito, su(b)til); **c** (a(c)ção, a(c)cionista, a(c)to); **m** (inde(m)ne); **p** (ado(p)ção, ado(p)tar); *for further details see p. xiii.*

em excesso a alguém.

overcoat ['əuvəkəut] *n* sobretudo.

overcome [əuvə'kʌm] (*irreg*) *vt* vencer, dominar; (*difficulty*) superar ♦ *adj* (*emotionally*) assolado; ~ **with grief** tomado pela dor.

overconfident [əuvə'kɔnfɪdənt] *adj* confiante em excesso.

overcrowded [əuvə'kraudɪd] *adj* superlotado; (*country*) superpovoado.

overcrowding [əuvə'kraudɪŋ] *n* superlotação *f*; (*in country*) superpovoamento .

overdo [əuvə'du:] (*irreg*) *vt* exagerar; (*overcook*) cozinhar demais; **to ~ it, to ~ things** (*work too hard*) exceder-se; (*go too far*) exagerar.

overdose ['əuvədəus] *n* overdose *f*, dose *f* excessiva.

overdraft ['əuvədrɑ:ft] *n* saldo negativo.

overdrawn [əuvə'drɔ:n] *adj* (*account*) sem fundos, a descoberto.

overdue [əuvə'dju:] *adj* atrasado; (*COMM*) vencido; (*recognition*) tardio; **that change was long ~** essa mudança foi muito protelada.

overestimate [əuvər'ɛstɪmeɪt] *vt* sobrestimar.

overexcited [əuvərɪk'saɪtɪd] *adj* superexcitado.

overexertion [əuvərɪg'zə:ʃən] *n* estafa.

overexpose [əuvərɪk'spəuz] *vt* (*PHOT*) expor demais (à luz).

overflow [*vi* əuvə'fləu, *n* 'əuvəfləu] *vi* transbordar ♦ *n* (*excess*) excesso; (*also*: ~ *pipe*) tubo de descarga, ladrão *m*.

overfly [əuvə'flaɪ] (*irreg*) *vt* sobrevoar.

overgenerous [əuvə'dʒɛnərəs] *adj* pródigo; (*offer*) excessivo.

overgrown [əuvə'grəun] *adj* (*garden*) coberto de vegetação; **he's just an ~ schoolboy** (*fig*) ele é apenas um garotão de escola.

overhang [*vt*, *vi* əuvə'hæŋ, *n* 'əuvəhæŋ] (*irreg*) *vt* sobrepairar ♦ *vi* sobressair ♦ *n* saliência, ressalto.

overhaul [*vt* əuvə'hɔ:l, *n* 'əuvəhɔ:l] *vt* examinar, revisar ♦ *n* revisão *f*.

overhead [*adv* əuvə'hɛd, *adj*, *n* 'əuvəhɛd] *adv* por cima, em cima ♦ *adj* aéreo, elevado; (*railway*) suspenso ♦ *n* (*US*) (*also*: *BRIT*: **~s** *npl*) despesas *fpl* gerais.

overhear [əuvə'hɪə*] (*irreg*) *vt* ouvir por acaso.

overheat [əuvə'hi:t] *vi* ficar superaquecido; (*engine*) aquecer demais.

overjoyed [əuvə'dʒɔɪd] *adj* maravilhado, cheio de alegria.

overkill ['əuvəkɪl] *n* (*fig*): **it would be ~** seria exagero, seria matar mosquito com tiro de canhão.

overland ['əuvəlænd] *adj*, *adv* por terra.

overlap [*vi* əuvə'læp, *n* 'əuvəlæp] *vi* coincidir *or* sobrepor-se em parte ♦ *n* sobreposição *f*.

overleaf [əuvə'li:f] *adv* no verso.

overload [əuvə'ləud] *vt* sobrecarregar.

overlook [əuvə'luk] *vt* (*have view on*) dar para; (*miss*) omitir; (*forgive*) fazer vista grossa a.

overlord ['əuvəlɔ:d] *n* suserano.

overmanning [əuvə'mænɪŋ] *n* excesso de pessoal.

overnight [*adv* əuvə'naɪt, *adj* 'əuvənaɪt] *adv* durante a noite; (*fig*: *suddenly*) da noite para o dia ♦ *adj* de uma (*or* de) noite; (*decision*) tomada da noite para o dia; **to stay ~** passar a noite, pernoitar; **if you travel ~** ... se você viajar de noite ...; **he'll be away ~** ele não voltará hoje.

overpaid [əuvə'peɪd] *pt*, *pp of* **overpay**.

overpass ['əuvəpɑ:s] *n* (*road*) viaduto; (*US*) passagem *f* superior.

overpay [əuvə'peɪ] (*irreg*) *vt*: **to ~ sb by £50** pagar £50 em excesso a alguém.

overpower [əuvə'pauə*] *vt* dominar, subjugar; (*fig*) assolar.

overpowering [əuvə'pauərɪŋ] *adj* (*heat*, *stench*) sufocante.

overproduction [əuvəprə'dʌkʃən] *n* superprodução *f*.

overrate [əuvə'reɪt] *vt* sobrestimar, supervalorizar.

overreach [əuvə'ri:tʃ] *vt*: **to ~ o.s.** exceder-se.

overreact [əuvəri:'ækt] *vi* reagir com exagero.

override [əuvə'raɪd] (*irreg*) *vt* (*order*, *objection*) não fazer caso de, ignorar; (*decision*) anular.

overriding [əuvə'raɪdɪŋ] *adj* primordial.

overrule [əuvə'ru:l] *vt* (*decision*) anular; (*claim*) indeferir.

overrun [əuvə'rʌn] (*irreg*) *vt* (*MIL*: *country etc*) invadir; (*time limit*) ultrapassar, exceder ♦ *vi* ultrapassar o devido tempo; **the town is ~ with tourists** a cidade está infestada de turistas.

overseas [əuvə'si:z] *adv* ultra-mar; (*abroad*) no estrangeiro, no exterior ♦ *adj* (*trade*) exterior; (*visitor*) estrangeiro.

overseer ['əuvəsɪə*] *n* (*in factory*) superintendente *m/f*; (*foreman*) capataz *m*.

overshadow [əuvə'ʃædəu] *vt* (*fig*) eclipsar, ofuscar.

overshoot [əuvə'ʃu:t] (*irreg*) *vt* passar.

oversight ['əuvəsaɪt] *n* descuido; **due to an ~** devido a um descuido *or* uma inadvertência.

oversimplify [əuvə'sɪmplɪfaɪ] *vt* simplificar demais.

oversleep [əuvə'sli:p] (*irreg*) *vi* dormir além da hora.

overspend [əuvə'spɛnd] (*irreg*) *vi* gastar demais; **we have overspent by $5000** gastamos $5000 além dos nossos recursos.

overspill ['əuvəspɪl] *n* excesso (de população).

overstaffed [əuvə'stɑ:ft] *adj*: **to be ~** ter um excesso de pessoal.

overstate [əuvə'steɪt] *vt* exagerar.

overstatement [əuvə'steɪtmənt] *n* exagero.

overstep [əuvə'stɛp] *vt*: **to ~ the mark** ultrapassar o limite.

overstock [əuvə'stɔk] *vt* estocar em excesso.

overstrike [*n* 'əuvəstraɪk, *vt* əuvə'straɪk] (*irreg*: *like* **strike**) *n* (*on printer*) batida múltipla ♦ *vt* sobreimprimir.

overt [əu'vəːt] *adj* aberto, indissimulado.
overtake [əuvə'teɪk] *(irreg) vt* ultrapassar.
overtaking [əuvə'teɪkɪŋ] *n* (AUT) ultrapassagem *f*.
overtax [əuvə'tæks] *vt* (ECON) sobrecarregar de impostos; (*fig*: *strength, patience*) abusar de; (: *person*) exigir demais de; **to ~ o.s.** exceder-se.
overthrow [əuvə'θrəu] *(irreg) vt* (*government*) derrubar.
overtime ['əuvətaɪm] *n* horas *fpl* extras; **to do** *or* **work ~** fazer horas extras.
overtime ban *n* recusa de fazer horas extras.
overtone ['əuvətəun] *n* (*fig*) implicação *f*, tom *m*.
overture ['əuvətʃuə*] *n* (MUS) abertura; (*fig*) proposta, oferta.
overturn [əuvə'təːn] *vt* virar; (*accidentally*) derrubar; (*decision*) anular ♦ *vi* virar; (*car*) capotar.
overweight [əuvə'weɪt] *adj* gordo demais, com excesso de peso; (*luggage*) com excesso de peso.
overwhelm [əuvə'wɛlm] *vt* esmagar, assolar.
overwhelming [əuvə'wɛlmɪŋ] *adj* (*victory, defeat*) esmagador(a); (*desire*) irresistível; **one's ~ impression is of heat** a impressão mais forte é de calor.
overwhelmingly [əuvə'wɛlmɪŋlɪ] *adv* (*vote*) em massa; (*win*) esmagadoramente.
overwork [əuvə'wəːk] *n* excesso de trabalho ♦ *vt* sobrecarregar de trabalho ♦ *vi* trabalhar demais.
overwrite [əuvə'raɪt] *(irreg) vt* (COMPUT) gravar em cima de.
overwrought [əuvə'rɔːt] *adj* extenuado, superexcitado.
ovulation [ɔvju'leɪʃən] *n* ovulação *f*.
owe [əu] *vt* dever; **to ~ sb sth, to ~ sth to sb** dever algo a alguém.
owing to ['əuɪŋ-] *prep* devido a, por causa de.
owl [aul] *n* coruja.
own [əun] *adj* próprio ♦ *vi* (BRIT): **to ~ to (having done) sth** confessar (ter feito) algo ♦ *vt* possuir, ter; **a room of my ~** meu próprio quarto; **can I have it for my (very) ~?** posso ficar com isso para mim?; **to get one's ~ back** ir à forra; **on one's ~** sozinho; **to come into one's ~** revelar-se.
own up *vi*: **to ~ up to sth** confessar algo; **to ~ up to having done sth** confessar ter feito algo.
own brand *n* (COMM) marca de distribuidora.
owner ['əunə*] *n* dono/a, proprietário/a.
owner-occupier *n* proprietário/a com posse e uso.
ownership ['əunəʃɪp] *n* posse *f*; **it's under new ~** (*shop etc*) está sob novo proprietário.
ox [ɔks] (*pl* **~en**) *n* boi *m*.
oxen ['ɔksn] *npl of* **ox**.
Oxfam ['ɔksfæm] (BRIT) *n abbr* (= *Oxford Committee for Famine Relief*) *associação de assistência*.
oxide ['ɔksaɪd] *n* óxido.
Oxon. ['ɔksn] (BRIT) *abbr* (= *Oxoniensis*) = *of Oxford*.
oxtail soup ['ɔksteɪl-] *n* rabada.
oxyacetylene [ɔksɪə'sɛtɪliːn] *n* oxiacetileno ♦ *cpd*: **~ burner, ~ torch** maçarico oxiacetilênico.
oxygen ['ɔksɪdʒən] *n* oxigênio.
oxygen mask *n* máscara de oxigênio.
oxygen tent *n* tenda de oxigênio.
oyster ['ɔɪstə*] *n* ostra.
oz. *abbr* = **ounce(s)**.
ozone ['əuzəun] *n* ozônio.
ozone layer *n* camada de ozônio.

P

P, p [piː] *n* (*letter*) P, p *m*; **P for Peter** P de Pedro.
P *abbr* = **president; prince**.
p [piː] *abbr* (= *page*) p; (BRIT) = **penny; pence**.
PA *n abbr* = **personal assistant; public address system** ♦ *abbr* (US: POST) = **Pennsylvania**.
pa [pɑː] (*inf*) *n* papai *m*.
p.a. *abbr* = **per annum**.
PAC (US) *n abbr* = **political action committee**.
pace [peɪs] *n* (*step*) passo; (*rhythm*) ritmo ♦ *vi*: **to ~ up and down** andar de um lado para o outro; **to keep ~ with** acompanhar o passo de; (*events*) manter-se inteirado de *or* atualizado com; **to set the ~** (*running*) regular a marcha; (*fig*) dar o tom; **to put sb through his ~s** (*fig*) pôr alguém à prova.
pacemaker ['peɪsmeɪkə*] *n* (MED) marca-passo *m*.
pacific [pə'sɪfɪk] *adj* pacífico ♦ *n*: **the P~ (Ocean)** o (Oceano) Pacífico.
pacification [pæsɪfɪ'keɪʃən] *n* pacificação *f*.
pacifier ['pæsɪfaɪə*] (US) *n* chupeta.
pacifist ['pæsɪfɪst] *n* pacifista *m/f*.
pacify ['pæsɪfaɪ] *vt* (*soothe*) acalmar, serenar; (*country*) pacificar.
pack [pæk] *n* pacote *m*, embrulho; (US: *packet*) pacote *m*; (*of cigarettes*) maço; (*of hounds*) matilha; (*of thieves etc*) bando, quadrilha; (*of cards*) baralho; (*bundle*) trouxa; (*back ~*) mochila ♦ *vt* (*wrap*) empacotar, embrulhar; (*fill*) encher; (*in suitcase etc*) arrumar (na mala); (*cram*) entupir, entulhar; (*fig*: *room etc*) lotar; (COMPUT) compactar ♦ *vi*: **to ~ (one's bags)** fazer as

***NB**: European Portuguese adds the following consonants to certain words:* **b** (sú(b)dito, su(b)til); **c** (a(c)ção, a(c)cionista, a(c)to); **m** (inde(m)ne); **p** (ado(p)ção, ado(p)tar); *for further details see p. xiii.*

malas; **to ~ into** (*room, stadium*) apinhar-se em; **to send sb ~ing** (*inf*) dar o fora em alguém.
pack in (*BRIT*: *inf*) *vi* (*machine*) pifar ♦ *vt* (*boyfriend*) dar o fora em; **~ it in!** pára com isso!
pack off *vt* (*person*) despedir.
pack up *vi* (*BRIT*: *inf*: *machine*) pifar; (: *person*) desistir, parar ♦ *vt* (*belongings*) arrumar; (*goods, presents*) empacotar, embrulhar.
package ['pækɪdʒ] *n* pacote *m*; (*bulky*) embrulho, fardo; (*also*: **~** *deal*) acordo global, pacote; (*COMPUT*) pacote ♦ *vt* (*goods*) empacotar, acondicionar.
package holiday (*BRIT*) *n* férias *fpl* organizadas.
package tour *n* excursão *f* organizada.
packaging ['pækɪdʒɪŋ] *n* embalagem *f*.
packed [pækt] *adj* (*crowded*) lotado, apinhado; **~ lunch** (*BRIT*) merenda.
packer ['pækə*] *n* (*person*) empacotador(a) *m/f*.
packet ['pækɪt] *n* pacote *m*; (*of cigarettes*) maço; (*NAUT*) paquete *m*.
packet switching [-'swɪtʃɪŋ] *n* (*COMPUT*) chaveamento de pacote.
pack ice *n* gelo flutuante.
packing ['pækɪŋ] *n* embalagem *f*; (*internal*) enchimento.
packing case *n* caixa de embalagem.
pact [pækt] *n* pacto; (*COMM*) convênio.
pad [pæd] *n* (*of paper*) bloco; (*for inking*) almofada; (*launching* ~) plataforma (de lançamento); (*inf*: *home*) casa ♦ *vt* acolchoar, enchumaçar ♦ *vi*: **to ~ in/about** *etc* entrar/andar *etc* sem ruído.
padding ['pædɪŋ] *n* enchimento, recheio; (*fig*) palavreado inútil.
paddle ['pædl] *n* (*oar*) remo curto ♦ *vt* remar ♦ *vi* (*with feet*) patinhar.
paddle steamer *n* vapor *m* movido a rodas.
paddling pool ['pædlɪŋ-] *n* lago de recreação.
paddock ['pædək] *n* cercado, paddock *m*.
paddy ['pædɪ] *n* (*also*: ~ *field*) arrozal *m*.
padlock ['pædlɔk] *n* cadeado ♦ *vt* fechar com cadeado.
padre ['pɑːdrɪ] *n* capelão *m*, padre *m*.
paediatrics [piːdɪ'ætrɪks] (*US* **pediatrics**) *n* pediatria.
pagan ['peɪgən] *adj*, *n* pagão/pagã *m/f*.
page [peɪdʒ] *n* página; (*also*: ~ *boy*) mensageiro; (*at wedding*) pajem *m* ♦ *vt* (*in hotel etc*) mandar chamar.
pageant ['pædʒənt] *n* (*procession*) cortejo suntuoso; (*show*) desfile *m* alegórico.
pageantry ['pædʒəntrɪ] *n* pompa, fausto.
page break *n* quebra de página.
pager ['peɪdʒə*] *n* bip *m*.
paginate ['pædʒɪneɪt] *vt* paginar.
pagination [pædʒɪ'neɪʃən] *n* paginação *f*.
pagoda [pə'gəudə] *n* pagode *m*.
paid [peɪd] *pt, pp of* **pay** ♦ *adj* (*work*) remunerado; (*official*) assalariado; **to put ~ to** (*BRIT*) acabar com.
paid-up (*US* **paid-in**) *adj* (*member*) efetivo; (*shares*) integralizado; **~ capital** capital *m* realizado.
pail [peɪl] *n* balde *m*.
pain [peɪn] *n* dor *f*; **to be in ~** sofrer *or* sentir dor; **to have a ~ in** estar com uma dor em; **on ~ of death** sob pena de morte; **to take ~s to do sth** dar-se ao trabalho de fazer algo.
pained [peɪnd] *adj* (*expression*) magoado, aflito.
painful ['peɪnful] *adj* doloroso; (*difficult*) penoso; (*disagreeable*) desagradável.
painfully ['peɪnfulɪ] *adv* (*fig*: *very*) terrivelmente.
painkiller ['peɪnkɪlə*] *n* analgésico, calmante *m*.
painless ['peɪnlɪs] *adj* sem dor, indolor.
painstaking ['peɪnzteɪkɪŋ] *adj* esmerado, meticuloso.
paint [peɪnt] *n* pintura ♦ *vt* pintar; **to ~ the door blue** pintar a porta de azul; **to ~ the town red** (*fig*) cair na farra.
paintbox ['peɪntbɔks] *n* estojo de tintas.
paintbrush ['peɪntbrʌʃ] *n* (*artist's*) pincel *m*; (*decorator's*) broxa.
painter ['peɪntə*] *n* pintor(a) *m/f*.
painting ['peɪntɪŋ] *n* pintura; (*picture*) tela, quadro.
paint-stripper *n* removedor *m* de tinta.
paintwork ['peɪntwəːk] (*BRIT*) *n* pintura.
pair [pɛə*] *n* (*of shoes, gloves etc*) par *m*; (*of people*) casal *m*; (*twosome*) dupla; **a ~ of scissors** uma tesoura; **a ~ of trousers** uma calça (*BR*), umas calças (*PT*).
pair off *vi* formar pares.
pajamas [pɪ'dʒɑːməz] (*US*) *npl* pijama *m*.
Pakistan [pɑːkɪ'stɑːn] *n* Paquistão *m*.
Pakistani [pɑːkɪ'stɑːnɪ] *adj*, *n* paquistanês/esa *m/f*.
PAL [pæl] *n abbr* (*TV*: *phase alternation line*) PAL *m*.
pal [pæl] (*inf*) *n* camarada *m/f*, colega *m/f*.
palace ['pæləs] *n* palácio.
palatable ['pælɪtəbl] *adj* saboroso, apetitoso; (*acceptable*) aceitável.
palate ['pælɪt] *n* paladar *m*.
palatial [pə'leɪʃəl] *adj* suntuoso, magnífico.
palaver [pə'lɑːvə*] *n* (*fuss*) confusão *f*; (*hindrances*) complicação *f*.
pale [peɪl] *adj* pálido; (*colour*) claro ♦ *vi* empalidecer ♦ *n*: **to be beyond the ~** passar dos limites; **to grow** *or* **turn ~** empalidecer; **~ blue** azul claro *inv*; **to ~ into insignificance (beside)** perder a importância (diante de).
paleness ['peɪlnɪs] *n* palidez *f*.
Palestine ['pælɪstaɪn] *n* Palestina.
Palestinian [pælɪs'tɪnɪən] *adj*, *n* palestino/a.
palette ['pælɪt] *n* palheta.
paling ['peɪlɪŋ] *n* (*stake*) estaca; (*fence*) cerca.
palisade [pælɪ'seɪd] *n* paliçada.
pall [pɔːl] *n* (*of smoke*) manto ♦ *vi* perder a graça.

pallet ['pælɪt] *n* (*for goods*) paleta.
pallid ['pælɪd] *adj* pálido, descorado.
pallor ['pælə*] *n* palidez *f*.
pally ['pælɪ] (*inf*) *adj* chapinha.
palm [pɑːm] *n* (*hand, leaf*) palma; (*also*: ~ *tree*) palmeira ♦ *vt*: **to ~ sth off on sb** (*inf*) impingir algo a alguém.
palmist ['pɑːmɪst] *n* quiromante *m/f*.
Palm Sunday *n* Domingo de Ramos.
palpable ['pælpəbl] *adj* palpável.
palpitation [pælpɪ'teɪʃən] *n* palpitação *f*; **to have ~s** sentir palpitações.
paltry ['pɔːltrɪ] *adj* irrisório.
pamper ['pæmpə*] *vt* paparicar, mimar.
pamphlet ['pæmflət] *n* panfleto.
pan [pæn] *n* (*also*: *sauce~*) panela (*BR*), caçarola (*PT*); (*also*: *frying ~*) frigideira; (*of lavatory*) vaso ♦ *vi* (*CINEMA*) tomar uma panorâmica ♦ *vt* (*inf*: *book, film*) arrasar com; **to ~ for gold** batear à procura de ouro.
panacea [pænə'sɪə] *n* panacéia.
Panama ['pænəmɑː] *n* Panamá *m*.
Panama Canal *n* canal *m* do Panamá.
pancake ['pænkeɪk] *n* panqueca.
Pancake Day (*BRIT*) *n* terça-feira de Carnaval.
pancreas ['pæŋkrɪəs] *n* pâncreas *m inv*.
panda ['pændə] *n* panda *m/f*.
panda car (*BRIT*) *n* patrulhinha, carro policial.
pandemonium [pændɪ'məunɪəm] *n* (*noise*) pandemônio; (*mess*) caos *m*.
pander ['pændə*] *vi*: **to ~ to** favorecer.
pane [peɪn] *n* vidraça, vidro.
panel ['pænl] *n* (*of wood, RADIO, TV*) painel *m*; (*of cloth*) pano.
panel game (*BRIT*) *n* jogo em painel.
panelling ['pænəlɪŋ] (*US* **paneling**) *n* painéis *mpl*.
panellist ['pænəlɪst] (*US* **panelist**) *n* convidado/a, integrante *m/f* do painel.
pang [pæŋ] *n*: **~s of conscience** dor *f* de consciência; **~s of hunger** fome aguda.
panic ['pænɪk] *n* pânico ♦ *vi* entrar em pânico.
panicky ['pænɪkɪ] *adj* (*person*) assustadiço, apavorado.
panic-stricken [-'strɪkən] *adj* tomado de pânico.
pannier ['pænɪə*] *n* (*on bicycle*) cesta; (*on mule etc*) cesto, alcofa.
panorama [pænə'rɑːmə] *n* panorama *m*.
panoramic [pænə'ræmɪk] *adj* panorâmico.
pansy ['pænzɪ] *n* (*BOT*) amor-perfeito; (*inf*) bicha (*BR*), maricas *m* (*PT*).
pant [pænt] *vi* arquejar, ofegar.
pantechnicon [pæn'tɛknɪkən] (*BRIT*) *n* caminhão *m* de mudanças.
panther ['pænθə*] *n* pantera.
panties ['pæntɪz] *npl* calcinha (*BR*), cuecas *fpl* (*PT*).
pantihose ['pæntɪhəuz] (*US*) *n* meia-calça (*BR*), collants *mpl* (*PT*).
pantomime ['pæntəmaɪm] (*BRIT*) *n* pantomima, *revista musical montada na época de Natal, baseada em contos de fada.*
pantry ['pæntrɪ] *n* despensa.
pants [pænts] *npl* (*BRIT*: *woman's*) calcinha (*BR*), cuecas *fpl* (*PT*); (: *man's*) cueca (*BR*), cuecas (*PT*); (*US*: *trousers*) calça (*BR*), calças *fpl* (*PT*).
pantsuit ['pæntsuːt] (*US*) *n* terninho (de mulher).
papacy ['peɪpəsɪ] *n* papado.
papal ['peɪpəl] *adj* papal.
paper ['peɪpə*] *n* papel *m*; (*also*: *news~*) jornal *m*; (*study, article*) artigo, dissertação *f*; (*exam*) exame *m*, prova ♦ *adj* de papel ♦ *vt* empapelar; **~s** *npl* (*also*: *identity ~s*) documentos *mpl*; **a piece of ~** um papel; **to put sth down on ~** pôr algo por escrito.
paper advance *n* (*on printer*) avançar formulário.
paperback ['peɪpəbæk] *n* livro de capa mole ♦ *adj*: **~ edition** edição *f* brochada.
paper bag *n* saco de papel.
paperboy ['peɪpəbɔɪ] *n* jornaleiro.
paper clip *n* clipe *m*.
paper handkerchief *n* lenço de papel.
paper mill *n* fábrica de papel.
paper money *n* papel-moeda *m*.
paper profit *n* lucro fictício.
paperweight ['peɪpəweɪt] *n* pesa-papéis *m inv*.
paperwork ['peɪpəwəːk] *n* trabalho burocrático; (*pej*) papelada.
papier-mâché ['pæpɪeɪ'mæʃeɪ] *n* papel *m* machê.
paprika ['pæprɪkə] *n* páprica, pimentão-doce *m*.
Pap smear [pæp-] *n* (*MED*) esfregaço.
Pap test [pæp-] *n* (*MED*) esfregaço.
par [pɑː*] *n* par *m*; (*GOLF*) média *f*; **to be on a ~ with** estar em pé de igualdade com; **at ~** ao par; **above/below ~** acima/abaixo do par; **to feel below** *or* **under** *or* **not up to ~** estar aquém das suas possibilidades.
parable ['pærəbl] *n* parábola.
parabola [pə'ræbələ] *n* parábola.
parachute ['pærəʃuːt] *n* pára-quedas *m inv* ♦ *vi* saltar de pára-quedas.
parachute jump *n* salto de pára-quedas.
parachutist ['pærəʃuːtɪst] *n* pára-quedista *m/f*.
parade [pə'reɪd] *n* desfile *m* ♦ *vt* desfilar; (*show off*) exibir ♦ *vi* desfilar; (*MIL*) passar revista.
parade ground *n* praça de armas.
paradise ['pærədaɪs] *n* paraíso.
paradox ['pærədɔks] *n* paradoxo.
paradoxical [pærə'dɔksɪkl] *adj* paradoxal.
paradoxically [pærə'dɔksɪklɪ] *adv* paradoxalmente.
paraffin ['pærəfɪn] (*BRIT*) *n*: **~ (oil)** querosene *m*; **liquid ~** óleo de parafina.
paraffin heater (*BRIT*) *n* aquecedor *m* a pa-

rafina.
paraffin lamp (*BRIT*) *n* lâmpada de parafina.
paragon ['pærəgən] *n* modelo.
paragraph ['pærəgrɑːf] *n* parágrafo.
Paraguay ['pærəgwaɪ] *n* Paraguai *m*.
Paraguayan [pærə'gwaɪən] *adj*, *n* paraguaio/a.
parallel ['pærəlɛl] *adj*: ~ **(with** *or* **to)** paralelo (a); (*fig*) correspondente (a) ♦ *n* (*line*) paralela; (*fig, GEO*) paralelo.
paralyses [pə'rælɪsiːz] *npl of* **paralysis**.
paralysis [pə'rælɪsɪs] (*pl* **paralyses**) *n* paralisia.
paralytic [pærə'lɪtɪk] *adj* paralítico; (*BRIT*: *inf*: *drunk*) de cara cheia.
paralyze ['pærəlaɪz] *vt* paralisar.
parameter [pə'ræmɪtə*] *n* parâmetro.
paramilitary [pærə'mɪlɪtərɪ] *adj* paramilitar.
paramount ['pærəmaunt] *adj*: **of** ~ **importance** de suma importância, primordial.
paranoia [pærə'nɔɪə] *n* paranóia.
paranoid ['pærənɔɪd] *adj* paranóico.
paranormal [pærə'nɔːməl] *adj* paranormal.
paraphernalia [pærəfə'neɪlɪə] *n* (*gear*) acessórios *mpl*, equipamento.
paraphrase ['pærəfreɪz] *vt* parafrasear.
paraplegic [pærə'pliːdʒɪk] *n* paraplégico/a.
parapsychology [pærəsaɪ'kɔlədʒɪ] *n* parapsicologia.
parasite ['pærəsaɪt] *n* parasito/a.
parasol ['pærəsɔl] *n* guarda-sol *m*, sombrinha.
paratrooper ['pærətruːpə*] *n* pára-quedista *m/f*.
parcel ['pɑːsl] *n* pacote *m* ♦ *vt* (*also*: ~ *up*) embrulhar, empacotar.
parcel out *vt* repartir, distribuir.
parcel bomb (*BRIT*) *n* pacote-bomba *m*.
parcel post *n* serviço de encomenda postal.
parch [pɑːtʃ] *vt* secar, ressecar.
parched [pɑːtʃt] *adj* (*person*) morto de sede.
parchment ['pɑːtʃmənt] *n* pergaminho.
pardon ['pɑːdn] *n* perdão *m*; (*LAW*) indulto ♦ *vt* perdoar; (*LAW*) indultar; ~! desculpe!; ~ **me!, I beg your** ~ (*apologizing*) desculpe(-me); **(I beg your)** ~**?** (*BRIT*), ~ **me?** (*US*) (*not hearing*) como?, como disse?
pare [pɛə*] *vt* (*BRIT*: *nails*) aparar; (*fruit etc*) descascar; (*fig*: *costs etc*) reduzir, cortar.
parent ['pɛərənt] *n* pai *m* (*or* mãe *f*); ~**s** *npl* pais *mpl*.
parentage ['pɛərəntɪdʒ] *n* ascendência; **of unknown** ~ de pais desconhecidos.
parental [pə'rɛntl] *adj* paternal (*or* maternal), dos pais.
parent company *n* (empresa) matriz *f*.
parentheses [pə'rɛnθɪsiːz] *npl of* **parenthesis**.
parenthesis [pə'rɛnθɪsɪs] (*pl* **parentheses**) *n* parêntese *m*; **in parentheses** entre parênteses.
parenthood ['pɛərənthud] *n* paternidade *f* (*or* maternidade *f*).
parenting ['pɛərəntɪŋ] *n* trabalho de ser pai (*or* mãe).
Paris ['pærɪs] *n* Paris.
parish ['pærɪʃ] *n* paróquia, freguesia ♦ *adj* paroquial.
parish council (*BRIT*) *n* ≈ junta da freguesia.
parishioner [pə'rɪʃənə*] *n* paroquiano/a.
Parisian [pə'rɪzɪən] *adj*, *n* parisiense *m/f*.
parity ['pærɪtɪ] *n* paridade *f*, igualdade *f*.
park [pɑːk] *n* parque *m* ♦ *vt*, *vi* estacionar.
parka ['pɑːkə] *n* parka *m*.
parking ['pɑːkɪŋ] *n* estacionamento; **"no** ~**"** "estacionamento proibido".
parking lights *npl* luzes *fpl* de estacionamento.
parking lot (*US*) *n* (parque de) estacionamento.
parking meter *n* parquímetro.
parking offence (*BRIT*) *n* infração *f* por estacionamento não permitido.
parking place *n* vaga.
parking ticket *n* multa por estacionamento proibido.
parking violation (*US*) *n* infração *f* por estacionamento não permitido.
parkway ['pɑːkweɪ] (*US*) *n* rodovia arborizada.
parlance ['pɑːləns] *n*: **in common/modern** ~ na linguagem cotidiana *or* corrente/moderna.
parliament ['pɑːləmənt] *n* parlamento.
parliamentary [pɑːlə'mɛntərɪ] *adj* parlamentar.
parlour ['pɑːlə*] (*US* **parlor**) *n* sala de visitas, salão *m*, saleta.
parlous ['pɑːləs] *adj* (*formal*) precário.
Parmesan [pɑːmɪ'zæn] *n* (*also*: ~ *cheese*) parmesão *m*.
parochial [pə'rəukɪəl] *adj* paroquial; (*pej*) provinciano.
parody ['pærədɪ] *n* paródia ♦ *vt* parodiar.
parole [pə'rəul] *n*: **on** ~ em liberdade condicional, sob promessa.
paroxysm ['pærəksɪzəm] *n* (*MED*, *of grief*) paroxismo; (*of anger*, *coughing*) acesso.
parquet ['pɑːkeɪ] *n*: ~ **floor(ing)** parquete *m*, assoalho de tacos.
parrot ['pærət] *n* papagaio.
parrot fashion *adv* mecanicamente, feito papagaio.
parry ['pærɪ] *vt* aparar, desviar.
parsimonious [pɑːsɪ'məunɪəs] *adj* parco.
parsley ['pɑːslɪ] *n* salsa.
parsnip ['pɑːsnɪp] *n* cherivia, pastinaga.
parson ['pɑːsn] *n* padre *m*, clérigo; (*Church of England*) pastor *m*.
parsonage ['pɑːsnɪdʒ] *n* presbitério.
part [pɑːt] *n* (*gen*, *MUS*) parte *f*; (*of machine*) peça; (*THEATRE etc*) papel *m*; (*of serial*) capítulo; (*US*: *in hair*) risca, repartido ♦ *adj* parcial ♦ *adv* em parte ♦ *vt* dividir; (*break*) partir; (*hair*) repartir ♦ *vi* (*people*) separar-se; (*roads*) bifurcar-se; (*crowd*) dispersar-se; (*break*) partir-se; **to take** ~ **in** participar de, tomar parte em; **to take sb's** ~ defender alguém; **on his** ~ da sua parte; **for my** ~ pela minha parte; **for the most** ~ na maior parte; **for the better** ~ **of the day** durante a maior parte do dia; **to be** ~ **and parcel of** fazer parte de; **to take sth in good** ~ não se ofender com algo; ~ **of speech** (*LING*) cate-

goria gramatical.

part with *vt fus* ceder, entregar; (*money*) pagar.

partake [pɑː'teɪk] (*irreg*) *vi* (*formal*): **to ~ of sth** participar de algo.

part exchange (*BRIT*) *n*: **in ~** como parte do pagamento.

partial ['pɑːʃl] *adj* parcial; **to be ~ to** gostar de, ser apreciador(a) de.

partially ['pɑːʃəlɪ] *adv* parcialmente.

participant [pɑː'tɪsɪpənt] *n* (*in competition*) participante *m/f*.

participate [pɑː'tɪsɪpeɪt] *vi*: **to ~ in** participar de.

participation [pɑːtɪsɪ'peɪʃən] *n* participação *f*.

participle ['pɑːtɪsɪpl] *n* particípio.

particle ['pɑːtɪkl] *n* partícula; (*of dust*) grão *m*.

particular [pə'tɪkjulə*] *adj* (*special*) especial; (*specific*) específico; (*given*) determinado; (*fussy*) exigente, minucioso; **in ~** em particular; **I'm not ~** para mim tanto faz.

particularly [pə'tɪkjuləlɪ] *adv* em particular, especialmente.

particulars [pə'tɪkjuləz] *npl* detalhes *mpl*.

parting ['pɑːtɪŋ] *n* (*act of*) separação *f*; (*farewell*) despedida; (*BRIT*: *in hair*) risca, repartido ♦ *adj* de despedida; **~ shot** (*fig*) flecha de parto.

partisan [pɑːtɪ'zæn] *adj* partidário ♦ *n* partidário/a; (*in war*) guerrilheiro/a.

partition [pɑː'tɪʃən] *n* (*POL*) divisão *f*; (*wall*) tabique *m*, divisória ♦ *vt* separar com tabique; (*fig*) dividir.

partly ['pɑːtlɪ] *adv* em parte.

partner ['pɑːtnə*] *n* (*COMM*) sócio/a; (*SPORT*) parceiro/a; (*at dance*) par *m*; (*spouse*) cônjuge *m/f*; (*friend etc*) companheiro/a ♦ *vt* acompanhar.

partnership ['pɑːtnəʃɪp] *n* associação *f*, parceria; (*COMM*) sociedade *f*; **to go into** *or* **form a ~ (with)** associar-se (com), formar sociedade (com).

partook [pɑː'tuk] *pt of* **partake**.

part payment *n* parcela, prestação *f*.

partridge ['pɑːtrɪdʒ] *n* perdiz *f*.

part-time *adj*, *adv* de meio expediente.

part-timer *n* (*also*: *part-time worker*) trabalhador(a) *m/f* de meio expediente.

party ['pɑːtɪ] *n* (*POL*) partido; (*celebration*) festa; (*group*) grupo; (*LAW*) parte *f* interessada, litigante *m/f* ♦ *adj* (*POL*) do partido, partidário; (*dress etc*) de gala, de luxo; **dinner ~** jantar *m*; **to give** *or* **have** *or* **throw a ~** dar uma festa; **to be a ~ to a crime** ser cúmplice num crime.

party line *n* (*POL*) linha partidária; (*TEL*) linha compartilhada.

par value *n* (*of share, bond*) valor *m* nominal.

pass [pɑːs] *vt* (*time, object*) passar; (*exam*) passar em; (*place*) passar por; (*overtake, surpass*) ultrapassar; (*approve*) aprovar; (*candidate*) aprovar ♦ *vi* passar; (*SCH*) ser aprovado, passar ♦ *n* (*permit*) passe *m*; (*membership card*) carteira; (*in mountains*) desfiladeiro; (*SPORT*) passe *m*; (*SCH*: *also*: ~ *mark*): **to get a ~ in** ser aprovado em; **she could ~ for 25/a singer** ela podia passar por 25 anos/cantora; **to ~ sth through sth** passar algo por algo; **things have come to a pretty ~** (*BRIT*) as coisas ficaram pretas; **to make a ~ at sb** tomar liberdade com alguém.

pass away *vi* falecer.

pass by *vi* passar ♦ *vt* (*ignore*) passar por cima de.

pass down *vt* (*customs, inheritance*) passar.

pass on *vi* (*die*) falecer ♦ *vt* (*hand on*): **to ~ on (to)** transmitir (a); (: *price rises*) repassar (a).

pass out *vi* desmaiar; (*BRIT*: *MIL*) sair (*de uma escola militar*).

pass over *vt* (*ignore*) passar por cima de.

pass up *vt* deixar passar.

passable ['pɑːsəbl] *adj* (*road*) transitável; (*work*) aceitável.

passage ['pæsɪdʒ] *n* (*also*: *~way*) corredor *m*; (*act of passing*) trânsito; (*in book*) passagem *f*, trecho; (*fare*) passagem (*BR*), bilhete *m* (*PT*); (*by boat*) travessia; (*MECHANICS, MED*) conduto.

passbook ['pɑːsbuk] *n* caderneta.

passenger ['pæsɪndʒə*] *n* passageiro/a.

passer-by ['pɑːsə*-] *n* transeunte *m/f*.

passing ['pɑːsɪŋ] *adj* (*fleeting*) passageiro, fugaz; **in ~** de passagem.

passing place *n* trecho de ultrapassagem.

passion ['pæʃən] *n* paixão *f*; **to have a ~ for sth** ser aficionado/a de algo.

passionate ['pæʃənɪt] *adj* apaixonado.

passive ['pæsɪv] *adj* (*also*: *LING*) passivo.

passkey ['pɑːskiː] *n* chave *f* mestra.

Passover ['pɑːsəuvə*] *n* Páscoa (dos judeus).

passport ['pɑːspɔːt] *n* passaporte *m*.

passport control *n* controle *m* dos passaportes.

password ['pɑːswəːd] *n* senha, contra-senha.

past [pɑːst] *prep* (*further than*) para além de; (*later than*) depois de ♦ *adj* passado; (*president etc*) ex-, anterior ♦ *n* passado; **quarter/half ~ four** quatro e quinze/meia; **ten/twenty ~ four** quatro e dez/vinte; **he's ~ forty** ele tem mais de quarenta anos; **for the ~ few days** nos últimos dias; **to run ~** passar correndo (por); **it's ~ midnight** é mais de meia-noite; **in the ~** no passado; **I'm ~ caring** já não ligo mais; **he's ~ it** (*BRIT*: *inf*: *person*) ele já passou da idade.

pasta ['pæstə] *n* massa.

paste [peɪst] *n* (*gen*) pasta; (*glue*) grude *m*, cola; (*jewellery*) vidro ♦ *vt* (*stick*) grudar; (*glue*) colar; **tomato ~** massa de tomate.

pastel ['pæstl] *adj* pastel; (*painting*) a pastel.

pasteurized ['pæstəraɪzd] *adj* pasteurizado.

***NB**: European Portuguese adds the following consonants to certain words:* **b** (sú(b)dito, su(b)til); **c** (a(c)ção, a(c)cionista, a(c)to); **m** (inde(m)ne); **p** (ado(p)ção, ado(p)tar); *for further details see p. xiii.*

pastille ['pæstl] *n* pastilha.
pastime ['pɑːstaɪm] *n* passatempo.
past master (*BRIT*) *n*: **to be a ~ at** ser perito em.
pastor ['pɑːstə*] *n* pastor(a) *m/f*.
pastoral ['pɑːstərl] *adj* pastoral.
pastry ['peɪstrɪ] *n* massa; (*cake*) bolo.
pasture ['pɑːstʃə*] *n* (*grass*) pasto; (*land*) pastagem *f*, pasto.
pasty [*n* 'pæstɪ, *adj* 'peɪstɪ] *n* empadão *m* de carne ♦ *adj* pastoso; (*complexion*) pálido.
pat [pæt] *vt* dar palmadinhas em; (*dog etc*) fazer festa em ♦ *n* (*of butter*) porção *f* ♦ *adv*: **he knows it off ~** (*BRIT*), **he has it down ~** (*US*) ele sabe isso de cor; **to give sb a ~ on the back** (*fig*) animar alguém.
patch [pætʃ] *n* (*of material*) retalho; (*spot*) mancha; (*mend*) remendo; (*of land*) lote *m*, terreno ♦ *vt* (*clothes*) remendar; **a bad ~** (*BRIT*) um mau pedaço.
patch up *vt* (*mend temporarily*) consertar provisoriamente; (*quarrel*) resolver.
patchwork ['pætʃwəːk] *n* colcha de retalhos ♦ *adj* (feito) de retalhos.
patchy ['pætʃɪ] *adj* desigual.
pate [peɪt] *n*: **a bald ~** uma calva, uma careca.
pâté ['pæteɪ] *n* patê *m*.
patent ['peɪtnt] *n* patente *f* ♦ *vt* patentear ♦ *adj* patente, evidente.
patent leather *n* verniz *m*.
patently ['peɪtntlɪ] *adv* claramente.
patent medicine *n* medicamento registrado.
patent office *n* escritório de registro de patentes.
paternal [pə'təːnl] *adj* paternal; (*relation*) paterno.
paternity [pə'təːnɪtɪ] *n* paternidade *f*.
paternity suit *n* (*LAW*) processo de paternidade.
path [pɑːθ] *n* caminho; (*trail, track*) trilha, senda; (*of missile*) trajetória; (*of planet*) órbita.
pathetic [pə'θɛtɪk] *adj* (*pitiful*) patético, digno de pena; (*very bad*) péssimo; (*moving*) comovente.
pathological [pæθə'lɔdʒɪkl] *adj* patológico.
pathologist [pə'θɔlədʒɪst] *n* patologista *m/f*.
pathology [pə'θɔlədʒɪ] *n* patologia.
pathos ['peɪθɔs] *n* patos *m*, patético.
pathway ['pɑːθweɪ] *n* caminho, trilha.
patience ['peɪʃns] *n* paciência; **to lose one's ~** perder a paciência.
patient ['peɪʃnt] *n* paciente *m/f* ♦ *adj* paciente.
patiently ['peɪʃntlɪ] *adv* pacientemente.
patio ['pætɪəu] *n* pátio.
patriot ['peɪtrɪət] *n* patriota *m/f*.
patriotic [pætrɪ'ɔtɪk] *adj* patriótico.
patriotism ['pætrɪətɪzəm] *n* patriotismo.
patrol [pə'trəul] *n* patrulha ♦ *vt* patrulhar; **to be on ~** fazer ronda, patrulhar.
patrol boat *n* barco de patrulha.
patrol car *n* carro de patrulha, radiopatrulha.
patrolman [pə'trəulmən] (*US*: *irreg*) guarda *m*, policial *m* (*BR*), polícia *m* (*PT*).
patron ['peɪtrən] *n* (*in shop*) cliente *m/f*; (*of charity*) benfeitor(a) *m/f*; **~ of the arts** mecenas *m*.
patronage ['pætrənɪdʒ] *n* patrocínio *m*.
patronize ['pætrənaɪz] *vt* (*shop*) ser cliente de; (*business*) patrocinar; (*look down on*) tratar com ar de superioridade.
patronizing ['pætrənaɪzɪŋ] *adj* condescendente.
patron saint *n* (santo/a) padroeiro/a.
patter ['pætə*] *n* tamborilada; (*of feet*) passos miúdos *mpl*; (*sales talk*) jargão *m* profissional ♦ *vi* correr dando passinhos; (*rain*) tamborilar.
pattern ['pætən] *n* modelo, padrão *m*; (*SEWING*) molde *m*; (*design*) desenho; (*sample*) amostra; **behaviour ~** modo de comportamento.
patterned ['pætənd] *adj* padronizado.
paucity ['pɔːsɪtɪ] *n* penúria, escassez *f*.
paunch [pɔːntʃ] *n* pança, barriga.
pauper ['pɔːpə*] *n* pobre *m/f*; **~'s grave** vala comum.
pause [pɔːz] *n* pausa; (*interval*) intervalo ♦ *vi* fazer uma pausa; **to ~ for breath** tomar fôlego; (*fig*) fazer uma pausa.
pave [peɪv] *vt* pavimentar; **to ~ the way for** preparar o terreno para.
pavement ['peɪvmənt] *n* (*BRIT*) calçada (*BR*), passeio (*PT*); (*US*) pavimento.
pavilion [pə'vɪlɪən] *n* pavilhão *m*; (*for band etc*) coreto; (*SPORT*) barraca.
paving ['peɪvɪŋ] *n* pavimento, calçamento.
paving stone *n* laje *f*, paralelepípedo.
paw [pɔː] *n* pata; (*of cat*) garra ♦ *vt* passar a pata em; (*touch*) manusear; (*amorously*) apalpar.
pawn [pɔːn] *n* (*CHESS*) peão *m*; (*fig*) títere *m* ♦ *vt* empenhar.
pawnbroker ['pɔːnbrəukə*] *n* agiota *m/f*.
pawnshop ['pɔːnʃɔp] *n* loja de penhores.
pay [peɪ] (*pt, pp* **paid**) *n* salário; (*of manual worker*) paga ♦ *vt* pagar; (*debt*) liquidar, saldar; (*visit*) fazer; (*respect*) apresentar ♦ *vi* pagar; (*be profitable*) valer a pena, render; **how much did you ~ for it?** quanto você pagou por isso?; **I paid £5 for that record** paguei *or* dei £5 por esse disco; **to ~ one's way** pagar sua parte; (*company*) render; **to ~ dividends** (*fig*) trazer vantagens *or* benefícios; **it won't ~ you to do that** não vale a pena você fazer isso; **to ~ attention (to)** prestar atenção (a).
pay back *vt* (*money*) devolver; (*person*) pagar; (*debt*) saldar.
pay in *vt* depositar.
pay off *vt* (*debts*) saldar, liquidar; (*mortgage*) resgatar; (*creditor*) pagar, reembolsar; (*worker*) despedir ♦ *vi* (*plan, patience*) valer a pena; **to ~ sth off in instalments** pagar algo a prazo.
pay out *vt* (*money*) pagar, desembolsar; (*rope*) dar.
pay up *vt* (*debts*) pagar, liquidar; (*amount*) pagar.
payable ['peɪəbl] *adj* pagável; **to make a**

cheque ~ to sb emitir um cheque nominal em favor de alguém.
pay day *n* dia *m* do pagamento.
PAYE (*BRIT*) *n abbr* (= *pay as you earn*) *tributação na fonte*.
payee [peɪ'iː] *n* beneficiário/a.
pay envelope (*US*) *n* envelope *m* de pagamento.
paying ['peɪɪŋ] *adj* pagador(a); (*business*) rendoso; **~ guest** pensionista *m/f*.
payload ['peɪləud] *n* carga paga.
payment ['peɪmənt] *n* pagamento; (*of debt, bill*) liquidação *f*; **advance ~** (*part sum*) entrada; (*total sum*) pagamento adiantado; **deferred ~, ~ by instalments** pagamento a prazo; **monthly ~** mensalidade *f*; **in ~ for** *or* **of** em pagamento por; **on ~ of £5** contra pagamento de £5.
pay packet (*BRIT*) *n* envelope *m* de pagamento.
payphone ['peɪfəun] *n* telefone *m* público.
payroll ['peɪrəul] *n* folha de pagamento; **to be on a firm's ~** fazer parte do quadro de pessoal assalariado de uma firma.
pay slip (*BRIT*) *n* contracheque *m*.
pay station (*US*) *n* cabine *f* telefônica, orelhão *m* (*BR*).
PBS (*US*) *n abbr* = **Public Broadcasting Service**.
PC *n abbr* (= *personal computer*) PC *m*; (*BRIT*) = **police constable** ♦ *abbr* (*BRIT*) = **Privy Councillor**.
pc *abbr* = **per cent**; **postcard**.
p/c *abbr* = **petty cash**.
PCB *n abbr* = **printed circuit board**.
PD (*US*) *n abbr* = **police department**.
pd *abbr* = **paid**.
PDSA (*BRIT*) *n abbr* = **People's Dispensary for Sick Animals**.
PDT (*US*) *abbr* (= *Pacific Daylight Time*) *hora de verão do Pacífico*.
PE *n abbr* = **physical education** ♦ *abbr* (*CANADA*) = **Prince Edward Island**.
pea [piː] *n* ervilha.
peace [piːs] *n* paz *f*; (*calm*) tranqüilidade *f*, quietude *f*; **to be at ~ with sb/sth** estar em paz com alguém/algo; **to keep the ~** (*subj*: *policeman*) manter a ordem; (: *citizen*) não perturbar a ordem pública.
peaceable ['piːsəbl] *adj* pacato.
peaceful ['piːsful] *adj* (*gentle*) pacífico; (*calm*) tranqüilo, sossegado.
peace-keeping [-'kiːpɪŋ] *n* pacificação *f*.
peace offering *n* proposta de paz.
peach [piːtʃ] *n* pêssego.
peacock ['piːkɔk] *n* pavão *m*.
peak [piːk] *n* (*of mountain*: *top*) cume *m*; (: *point*) pico; (*of cap*) pala, viseira; (*fig*: *of career*, *fame*) apogeu *m*; (: *highest level*) máximo.
peak-hour *adj* (*traffic etc*) no horário de maior movimento, na hora de pique.
peak hours *npl* horário de maior movimento.
peak period *n* período de pique.
peaky ['piːkɪ] (*BRIT*: *inf*) *adj* adoentado.
peal [piːl] *n* (*of bells*) repique *m*, toque *m*; **~ of laughter** gargalhada.
peanut ['piːnʌt] *n* amendoim *m*.
peanut butter *n* manteiga de amendoim.
pear [pɛə*] *n* pêra; **~ tree** pereira.
pearl [pəːl] *n* pérola.
peasant ['pɛznt] *n* camponês/esa *m/f*.
peat [piːt] *n* turfa.
pebble ['pɛbl] *n* seixo, calhau *m*.
peck [pɛk] *vt* (*also*: **~ at**) bicar, dar bicadas em; (*food*) beliscar ♦ *n* bicada; (*kiss*) beijoca.
pecking order ['pɛkɪŋ-] *n* ordem *f* de hierarquia.
peckish ['pɛkɪʃ] (*BRIT*: *inf*) *adj*: **I feel ~** estou a fim de comer alguma coisa.
peculiar [pɪ'kjuːlɪə*] *adj* (*odd*) estranho, esquisito; (*typical*) próprio, característico; (*marked*) especial; **~ to** próprio de.
peculiarity [pɪkjuːlɪ'ærɪtɪ] *n* peculiaridade *f*; (*oddity*) excentricidade *f*, singularidade *f*.
pecuniary [pɪ'kjuːnɪərɪ] *adj* pecuniário.
pedal ['pɛdl] *n* pedal *m* ♦ *vi* pedalar.
pedal bin (*BRIT*) *n* lata de lixo com pedal.
pedantic [pɪ'dæntɪk] *adj* pedante.
peddle ['pɛdl] *vt* vender nas ruas, mascatear; (*drugs*) traficar, fazer tráfico de.
peddler ['pɛdlə*] *n* mascate *m/f*, camelô *m*.
pedestal ['pɛdəstl] *n* pedestal *m*.
pedestrian [pɪ'dɛstrɪən] *n* pedestre *m/f* (*BR*), peão *m* (*PT*) ♦ *adj* pedestre (*BR*), para peões (*PT*); (*fig*) prosaico.
pedestrian crossing (*BRIT*) *n* passagem *f* para pedestres (*BR*), passadeira (*PT*).
pedestrian precinct (*BRIT*) *n* zona para pedestres (*BR*) *or* peões (*PT*), calçadão *m* (*BR*).
pediatrics [piːdɪ'ætrɪks] (*US*) *n* = **paediatrics**.
pedigree ['pɛdɪgriː] *n* genealogia; (*of animal*) raça ♦ *cpd* (*animal*) de raça.
pedlar ['pɛdlə*] *n* = **peddler**.
pee [piː] (*inf*) *vi* fazer xixi, mijar.
peek [piːk] *vi* espiar, espreitar.
peel [piːl] *n* casca ♦ *vt* descascar ♦ *vi* (*paint etc*) descascar; (*wallpaper*) desprender-se.
peel back *vt* descascar.
peeler ['piːlə*] *n* (*potato etc ~*) descascador *m*.
peelings ['piːlɪŋz] *npl* cascas *fpl*.
peep [piːp] *n* (*BRIT*: *look*) espiadela; (*sound*) pio ♦ *vi* (*BRIT*: *look*) espreitar; (*sound*) piar.
peep out (*BRIT*) *vi* mostrar-se, surgir.
peephole ['piːphəul] *n* vigia.
peer [pɪə*] *vi*: **to ~ at** perscrutar, fitar ♦ *n* (*noble*) par *m/f*; (*equal*) igual *m/f*.
peerage ['pɪərɪdʒ] *n* pariato.
peerless ['pɪəlɪs] *adj* sem igual.
peeved [piːvd] *adj* irritado.
peevish ['piːvɪʃ] *adj* rabugento.
peg [pɛg] *n* cavilha; (*for coat etc*) cabide *m*;

NB: European Portuguese adds the following consonants to certain words: **b** (sú(b)dito, su(b)til); **c** (a(c)ção, a(c)cionista, a(c)to); **m** (inde(m)ne); **p** (ado(p)ção, ado(p)tar); *for further details see p. xiii.*

(*BRIT*: *also*: *clothes* ~) pregador *m*; (*tent* ~) estaca ♦ *vt* (*clothes*) prender; (*BRIT*: *groundsheet*) segurar com estacas; (*fig*: *prices, wages*) fixar, tabelar.
pejorative [pɪ'dʒɔrətɪv] *adj* pejorativo.
Pekin [piː'kɪn] *n* Pequim.
Peking [piː'kɪŋ] *n* = **Pekin**.
pekingese [piːkɪ'niːz] *n* pequinês *m*.
pelican ['pɛlɪkən] *n* pelicano.
pelican crossing (*BRIT*) *n* (*AUT*) passagem *f* protegida de pedestres (*BR*), passadeira para peões (*PT*).
pellet ['pɛlɪt] *n* bolinha; (*bullet*) pelota de chumbo.
pell-mell ['pɛl'mɛl] *adv* a esmo.
pelmet ['pɛlmɪt] *n* sanefa.
pelt [pɛlt] *vt*: **to ~ sb with sth** atirar algo em alguém ♦ *vi* (*rain*) chover a cântaros ♦ *n* pele *f* (não curtida).
pelvis ['pɛlvɪs] *n* pelvis *f*, bacia.
pen [pɛn] *n* caneta; (*for sheep*) redil *m*, cercado; (*US*: *inf*: *prison*) cadeia; **to put ~ to paper** escrever.
pen in *vt* encurralar.
penal ['piːnl] *adj* penal.
penalize ['piːnəlaɪz] *vt* impor penalidade a; (*SPORT*) penalizar; (*fig*) prejudicar.
penal servitude [-'səːvɪtjuːd] *n* pena de trabalhos forçados.
penalty ['pɛnltɪ] *n* pena, penalidade *f*; (*fine*) multa; (*SPORT*) punição *f*; (*FOOTBALL*) pênalti *m*; **to take a ~** cobrar um pênalti.
penalty area (*BRIT*) *n* área de pênalti.
penalty clause *n* cláusula penal.
penalty kick *n* (*FOOTBALL*) cobrança de pênalti.
penance ['pɛnəns] *n* penitência.
pence [pɛns] (*BRIT*) *npl of* **penny**.
penchant ['pɑ̃ːʃɑ̃ːŋ] *n* pendor *m*, queda.
pencil ['pɛnsl] *n* lápis *m* ♦ *vt*: **to ~ sth in** anotar algo a lápis.
pencil case *n* lapiseira, porta-lápis *m inv*.
pencil sharpener *n* apontador *m* (de lápis) (*BR*), apara-lápis *m inv* (*PT*).
pendant ['pɛndnt] *n* pingente *m*.
pending ['pɛndɪŋ] *prep* (*during*) durante; (*until*) até ♦ *adj* pendente.
pendulum ['pɛndjuləm] *n* pêndulo.
penetrate ['pɛnɪtreɪt] *vt* penetrar.
penetrating ['pɛnɪtreɪtɪŋ] *adj* penetrante.
penetration [pɛnɪ'treɪʃən] *n* penetração *f*.
penfriend ['pɛnfrɛnd] (*BRIT*) *n* amigo/a por correspondência, correspondente *m/f*.
penguin ['pɛŋgwɪn] *n* pingüim *m*.
penicillin [pɛnɪ'sɪlɪn] *n* penicilina.
peninsula [pə'nɪnsjulə] *n* península.
penis ['piːnɪs] *n* pênis *m*.
penitence ['pɛnɪtns] *n* penitência.
penitent ['pɛnɪtnt] *adj* arrependido; (*REL*) penitente.
penitentiary [pɛnɪ'tɛnʃərɪ] (*US*) *n* penitenciária, presídio.
penknife ['pɛnnaɪf] (*irreg*) *n* canivete *m*.
pen name *n* pseudônimo.
pennant ['pɛnənt] *n* flâmula.
penniless ['pɛnɪlɪs] *adj* sem dinheiro, sem um tostão.
Pennines ['pɛnaɪnz] *npl*: **the ~** as Pennines.
penny ['pɛnɪ] (*pl* **pennies** *or* **pence**) *n* pêni *m* (*new*: *100 in a pound*; *old*: *12 in a shilling*; *a tendência é de se utilizar "pennies" ou "two-pence piece" etc para as moedas, "pence" para o valor*); (*US*) = **cent**.
penpal ['pɛnpæl] *n* amigo/a por correspondência, correspondente *m/f*.
pension ['pɛnʃən] *n* pensão *f*; (*old-age* ~) aposentadoria *f*; (*MIL*) reserva.
pension off *vt* aposentar.
pensionable ['pɛnʃnəbl] *adj* (*person*) com direito a uma pensão; (*age*) de aposentadoria.
pensioner ['pɛnʃənə*] (*BRIT*) *n* aposentado/a (*BR*), reformado/a (*PT*).
pension fund *n* fundo da aposentadoria.
pensive ['pɛnsɪv] *adj* pensativo; (*withdrawn*) absorto.
pentagon ['pɛntəgən] *n* pentágono.
Pentecost ['pɛntɪkɔst] *n* Pentecostes *m*.
penthouse ['pɛnthaus] (*irreg*) *n* cobertura.
pent-up [pɛnt-] *adj* (*feelings*) reprimido.
penultimate [pɛ'nʌltɪmət] *adj* penúltimo.
penury ['pɛnjurɪ] *n* pobreza, miséria.
people ['piːpl] *npl* gente *f*, pessoas *fpl*; (*citizens*) povo ♦ *n* (*nation, race*) povo ♦ *vt* povoar; **several ~ came** vieram várias pessoas; **I know ~ who ...** conheço gente que ...; **~ say that ...** dizem que ...; **old ~** os idosos; **young ~** os jovens; **a man of the ~** um homem do povo.
pep [pɛp] (*inf*) *n* pique *m*, energia, dinamismo.
pep up *vt* animar.
pepper ['pɛpə*] *n* pimenta; (*vegetable*) pimentão *m* ♦ *vt* apimentar; (*fig*) salpicar.
peppermint ['pɛpəmɪnt] *n* hortelã-pimenta; (*sweet*) bala de hortelã.
pepperpot ['pɛpəpɔt] *n* pimenteiro.
peptalk ['pɛptɔːk] (*inf*) *n* conversa para levantar o espírito.
per [pəː*] *prep* por; **~ day/person** por dia/pessoa; **as ~ your instructions** conforme suas instruções.
per annum *adv* por ano.
per capita *adj, adv* per capita, por pessoa.
perceive [pə'siːv] *vt* perceber.
per cent *adv* por cento; **a 20 ~ discount** um desconto de 20 por cento.
percentage [pə'sɛntɪdʒ] *n* porcentagem *f*, percentagem *f*; **on a ~ basis** na base de percentagem.
perceptible [pə'sɛptɪbl] *adj* perceptível, sensível.
perception [pə'sɛpʃən] *n* percepção *f*; (*insight*) perspicácia.
perceptive [pə'sɛptɪv] *adj* perceptivo.
perch [pəːtʃ] (*pl* **~es**) *n* (*for bird*) poleiro; (*pl*: *inv or* **~es**: *fish*) perca ♦ *vi* empoleirar-se, pousar.
percolate ['pəːkəleɪt] *vt, vi* passar.
percolator ['pəːkəleɪtə*] *n* cafeteira de filtro.
percussion [pə'kʌʃən] *n* percussão *f*.
peremptory [pə'rɛmptərɪ] *adj* peremptório;

(*person*: *imperious*) autoritário.
perennial [pə'rɛnɪəl] *adj* perene ♦ *n* planta perene.
perfect [*adj*, *n* 'pə:fɪkt, *vt* pə'fɛkt] *adj* perfeito ♦ *n* (*also*: ~ *tense*) perfeito ♦ *vt* aperfeiçoar; **a ~ stranger** uma pessoa completamente desconhecida.
perfection [pə'fɛkʃən] *n* perfeição *f*.
perfectionist [pə'fɛkʃənɪst] *n* perfeccionista *m/f*.
perfectly ['pə:fɪktlɪ] *adv* perfeitamente; **I'm ~ happy with the situation** estou completamente satisfeito com a situação; **you know ~ well** você sabe muito bem.
perforate ['pə:fəreɪt] *vt* perfurar.
perforated ['pə:fəreɪtɪd] *adj* (*stamp*) picotado.
perforated ulcer *n* (*MED*) úlcera perfurada.
perforation [pə:fə'reɪʃən] *n* perfuração *f*; (*line of holes*) picote *m*.
perform [pə'fɔ:m] *vt* (*carry out*) realizar, fazer; (*concert etc*) executar; (*piece of music*) interpretar ♦ *vi* (*animal*) fazer truques de amestramento; (*THEATRE*) representar; (*TECH*) funcionar.
performance [pə'fɔ:məns] *n* (*of task*) cumprimento, realização *f*; (*of artist*, *player etc*) atuação *f*; (*of car engine*, *function*) desempenho; (*of car*) performance *f*.
performer [pə'fɔ:mə*] *n* (*actor*) artista *m/f*, ator/atriz *m/f*; (*MUS*) intérprete *m/f*.
performing [pə'fɔ:mɪŋ] *adj* (*animal*) amestrado, adestrado.
perfume ['pə:fju:m] *n* perfume *m* ♦ *vt* perfumar.
perfunctory [pə'fʌŋktərɪ] *adj* superficial, negligente.
perhaps [pə'hæps] *adv* talvez; **~ he'll come** talvez ele venha; **~ so/not** talvez seja assim/talvez não.
peril ['pɛrɪl] *n* perigo, risco.
perilous ['pɛrɪləs] *adj* perigoso.
perilously ['pɛrɪləslɪ] *adv*: **they came ~ close to being caught** não foram presos por um triz.
perimeter [pə'rɪmɪtə*] *n* perímetro.
perimeter wall *n* muro periférico.
period ['pɪərɪəd] *n* período; (*HISTORY*) época; (*time limit*) prazo; (*SCH*) aula; (*full stop*) ponto final; (*MED*) menstruação *f*, regra ♦ *adj* (*costume*, *furniture*) da época; **for a ~ of three weeks** por um período de três semanas; **the holiday ~** (*BRIT*) o período de férias.
periodic [pɪərɪ'ɔdɪk] *adj* periódico.
periodical [pɪərɪ'ɔdɪkl] *adj*, *n* periódico.
periodically [pɪərɪ'ɔdɪklɪ] *adv* periodicamente, de vez em quando.
period pains (*BRIT*) *npl* cólicas *fpl* menstruais.
peripatetic [pɛrɪpə'tɛtɪk] *adj* (*salesman*) viajante; (*teacher*) que trabalha em vários lugares.
peripheral [pə'rɪfərəl] *adj* periférico ♦ *n* (*COMPUT*) periférico.
periphery [pə'rɪfərɪ] *n* periferia.
periscope ['pɛrɪskəup] *n* periscópio.
perish ['pɛrɪʃ] *vi* perecer; (*decay*) deteriorar-se, estragar.
perishable ['pɛrɪʃəbl] *adj* perecível, deteriorável.
perishables ['pɛrɪʃəblz] *npl* perecíveis *mpl*.
perishing ['pɛrɪʃɪŋ] (*BRIT*: *inf*) *adj* (*cold*) gelado, glacial.
peritonitis [pɛrɪtə'naɪtɪs] *n* peritonite *f*.
perjure ['pə:dʒə*] *vt*: **to ~ o.s.** prestar falso testemunho.
perjury ['pə:dʒərɪ] *n* (*LAW*) perjúrio, falso testemunho.
perk [pə:k] (*inf*) *n* mordomia, regalia.
perk up (*inf*) *vi* (*cheer up*) animar-se; (*in health*) recuperar-se.
perky ['pə:kɪ] *adj* (*cheerful*) animado, alegre.
perm [pə:m] *n* permanente *f* ♦ *vt*: **to have one's hair ~ed** fazer permanente (no cabelo).
permanence ['pə:mənəns] *n* permanência, continuidade *f*.
permanent ['pə:mənənt] *adj* permanente; **I'm not ~ here** não estou aqui em caráter permanente.
permanently ['pə:mənəntlɪ] *adv* permanentemente.
permeable ['pə:mɪəbl] *adj* permeável.
permeate ['pə:mɪeɪt] *vi* difundir-se ♦ *vt* penetrar.
permissible [pə'mɪsɪbl] *adj* permissível, lícito.
permission [pə'mɪʃən] *n* permissão *f*; (*authorization*) autorização *f*; **to give sb ~ to do sth** dar permissão a alguém para fazer algo.
permissive [pə'mɪsɪv] *adj* permissivo.
permit [*n* 'pə:mɪt, *vt* pə'mɪt] *n* permissão *f*; (*for fishing*, *export etc*) licença; (*to enter*) passe *m* ♦ *vt* permitir; (*authorize*) autorizar; **to ~ sb to do sth** permitir a alguém fazer *or* que faça algo; **weather ~ting** se o tempo permitir.
permutation [pə:mju'teɪʃən] *n* permutação *f*.
pernicious [pə:'nɪʃəs] *adj* nocivo; (*MED*) pernicioso, maligno.
pernickety [pə'nɪkɪtɪ] (*inf*) *adj* cheio de nove-horas *or* luxo; (*task*) minucioso.
perpendicular [pə:pən'dɪkjulə*] *adj* perpendicular ♦ *n* perpendicular *f*.
perpetrate ['pə:pɪtreɪt] *vt* cometer.
perpetual [pə'pɛtjuəl] *adj* perpétuo.
perpetuate [pə'pɛtjueɪt] *vt* perpetuar.
perpetuity [pə:pɪ'tju:ɪtɪ] *n*: **in ~** para sempre.
perplex [pə'plɛks] *vt* deixar perplexo.
perplexing [pə:'plɛksɪŋ] *adj* desconcertante.
perquisites ['pə:kwɪzɪts] *npl* (*also*: *perks*) mordomias *fpl*, regalias *fpl*.
persecute ['pə:sɪkju:t] *vt* (*pursue*) perseguir; (*harass*) importunar.
persecution [pə:sɪ'kju:ʃən] *n* perseguição *f*.

perseverance [pəːsɪ'vɪərəns] *n* perseverança.
persevere [pəːsɪ'vɪə*] *vi* perseverar.
Persia ['pəːʃə] *n* Pérsia.
Persian ['pəːʃən] *adj* persa ♦ *n* (LING) persa *m*; **the (~) Gulf** o golfo Pérsico.
persist [pə'sɪst] *vi*: **to ~ (in doing sth)** persistir (em fazer algo).
persistence [pə'sɪstəns] *n* persistência; (*of disease*) insistência; (*obstinacy*) teimosia.
persistent [pə'sɪstənt] *adj* persistente; (*determined*) teimoso; (*disease*) insistente, persistente; **~ offender** (LAW) infrator(a) *m/f* contumaz.
persnickety [pə'snɪkɪtɪ] (US: *inf*) *adj* = **pernickety**.
person ['pəːsn] *n* pessoa; **in ~** em pessoa; **on** *or* **about one's ~** consigo; **~ to ~ call** (TEL) chamada pessoal.
personable ['pəːsənəbl] *adj* atraente, bem apessoado.
personal ['pəːsənəl] *adj* pessoal; (*private*) particular; (*visit*) em pessoa, pessoal; **~ belongings** *or* **effects** pertences *mpl* particulares; **~ hygiene** higiene *f* íntima; **a ~ interview** uma entrevista particular.
personal allowance *n* (TAX) abatimento da renda de pessoa física.
personal assistant *n* secretário/a particular.
personal call *n* (TEL) chamada pessoal.
personal column *n* anúncios *mpl* pessoais.
personal computer *n* computador *m* pessoal.
personal details *npl* (*on form etc*) dados *mpl* pessoais.
personal identification number *n* (COMPUT, BANKING) senha, número de identificação individual.
personality [pəːsə'nælɪtɪ] *n* personalidade *f*.
personally ['pəːsənəlɪ] *adv* pessoalmente.
personal property *n* bens *mpl* móveis.
personify [pəː'sɔnɪfaɪ] *vt* personificar.
personnel [pəːsə'nɛl] *n* pessoal *m*.
personnel department *n* departamento de pessoal.
personnel manager *n* gerente *m/f* de pessoal.
perspective [pə'spɛktɪv] *n* perspectiva; **to get sth into ~** colocar algo em perspectiva.
perspex ['pəːspɛks] ® (BRIT) *n* Blindex *m* ®.
perspicacity [pəːspɪ'kæsɪtɪ] *n* perspicácia.
perspiration [pəːspɪ'reɪʃən] *n* transpiração *f*.
perspire [pə'spaɪə*] *vi* transpirar.
persuade [pə'sweɪd] *vt* persuadir; **to ~ sb to do sth** persuadir alguém a fazer algo; **to ~ sb that/of sth** persuadir alguém que/de algo.
persuasion [pə'sweɪʒən] *n* persuasão *f*; (*persuasiveness*) poder *m* de persuasão; (*creed*) convicção *f*, crença.
persuasive [pə'sweɪsɪv] *adj* persuasivo.
pert [pəːt] *adj* atrevido, descarado.
pertaining to [pəː'teɪnɪŋ-] *prep* relativo a.
pertinent ['pəːtɪnənt] *adj* pertinente, a propósito.
perturb [pə'təːb] *vt* inquietar.
perturbing [pə'təːbɪŋ] *adj* inquietante.
Peru [pə'ruː] *n* Peru *m*.
perusal [pə'ruːzl] *n* leitura.
peruse [pə'ruːz] *vt* ler com atenção, examinar.
Peruvian [pə'ruːvjən] *adj*, *n* peruano/a.
pervade [pə'veɪd] *vt* impregnar, penetrar em.
pervasive [pə'veɪsɪv] *adj* (*smell*) penetrante; (*influence, ideas, gloom*) difundido.
perverse [pə'vəːs] *adj* perverso; (*stubborn*) teimoso; (*wayward*) caprichoso.
perversion [pə'vəːʃən] *n* perversão *f*.
perversity [pə'vəːsɪtɪ] *n* perversidade *f*.
pervert [*n* 'pəːvəːt, *vt* pə'vəːt] *n* pervertido/a ♦ *vt* perverter, corromper.
pessary ['pɛsərɪ] *n* pessário.
pessimism ['pɛsɪmɪzəm] *n* pessimismo.
pessimist ['pɛsɪmɪst] *n* pessimista *m/f*.
pessimistic [pɛsɪ'mɪstɪk] *adj* pessimista.
pest [pɛst] *n* peste *f*, praga; (*insect*) inseto nocivo; (*fig*) peste *f*.
pest control *n* dedetização *f*; (*for mice*) desratização *f*.
pester ['pɛstə*] *vt* incomodar.
pesticide ['pɛstɪsaɪd] *n* pesticida *m*.
pestilent ['pɛstɪlənt] (*inf*) *adj* (*exasperating*) chato.
pestilential [pɛstɪ'lɛnʃəl] (*inf*) *adj* (*exasperating*) chato.
pestle ['pɛsl] *n* mão *f* (de almofariz).
pet [pɛt] *n* animal *m* de estimação; (*favourite*) preferido/a ♦ *vt* acariciar ♦ (*inf*) *vi* acariciar-se, emburrar ♦ *adj*: **~ lion** *etc* leão *m etc* de estimação; **my ~ hate** a coisa que eu mais odeio.
petal ['pɛtl] *n* pétala.
peter out ['piːtə*-] *vi* esgotar-se, acabar-se.
petite [pə'tiːt] *adj* diminuto.
petition [pə'tɪʃən] *n* petição *f*; (*list of signatures*) abaixo-assinado ♦ *vt* apresentar uma petição a ♦ *vi*: **to ~ for divorce** requerer divórcio.
pet name (BRIT) *n* apelido carinhoso.
petrified ['pɛtrɪfaɪd] *adj* (*fig*) petrificado, paralisado.
petrify ['pɛtrɪfaɪ] *vt* paralisar; (*frighten*) petrificar.
petrochemical [pɛtrə'kɛmɪkl] *adj* petroquímico.
petrodollars ['pɛtrəudɔləz] *npl* petrodólares *mpl*.
petrol ['pɛtrəl] (BRIT) *n* gasolina.
petrol can (BRIT) *n* lata de gasolina.
petrol engine (BRIT) *n* motor *m* a gasolina.
petroleum [pə'trəulɪəm] *n* petróleo.
petroleum jelly *n* vaselina.
petrol pump (BRIT) *n* (*in car, at garage*) bomba de gasolina.
petrol station (BRIT) *n* posto (BR) *or* bomba (PT) de gasolina.
petrol tank (BRIT) *n* tanque *m* de gasolina.
petticoat ['pɛtɪkəut] *n* anágua; (*slip*) combinação *f*.
pettifogging ['pɛtɪfɔgɪŋ] *adj* chicaneiro.
pettiness ['pɛtɪnɪs] *n* mesquinharia *f*.
petty ['pɛtɪ] *adj* (*mean*) mesquinho; (*unimportant*) insignificante.

petty cash *n* fundo para despesas miúdas, caixa pequena, fundo de caixa.
petty officer *n* suboficial *m* da marinha.
petulant ['pɛtjulənt] *adj* irascível.
pew [pjuː] *n* banco (de igreja).
pewter ['pjuːtə*] *n* peltre *m*.
Pfc (*US*) *abbr* (*MIL*) = **private first class**.
PG *n abbr* (*CINEMA*: = *parental guidance*) *aviso dos pais recomendado*.
PGA *n abbr* = **Professional Golfers' Association**.
PH (*US*) *n abbr* (*MIL*: = *Purple Heart*) *condecoração para feridos em combate*.
p & h (*US*) *abbr* = **postage and handling**.
PHA (*US*) *n abbr* (= *Public Housing Administration*) *órgão que supervisiona a construção*.
phallic ['fælɪk] *adj* fálico.
phantom ['fæntəm] *n* fantasma *m*.
Pharaoh ['fɛərəu] *n* faraó *m*.
pharmaceutical [fɑːmə'sjuːtɪkl] *adj* farmacêutico.
pharmaceuticals [fɑːmə'sjuːtɪklz] *npl* farmacêuticos *mpl*.
pharmacist ['fɑːməsɪst] *n* farmacêutico/a.
pharmacy ['fɑːməsɪ] *n* farmácia.
phase [feɪz] *n* fase *f* ♦ *vt*: **to ~ sth in/out** introduzir/retirar algo por etapas.
PhD *abbr* = **Doctor of Philosophy** ♦ *n* ≈ doutorado.
pheasant ['fɛznt] *n* faisão *m*.
phenomena [fə'nɔmɪnə] *npl of* **phenomenon**.
phenomenon [fə'nɔmɪnən] (*pl* **phenomena**) *n* fenômeno.
phew [fjuː] *excl* ufa!
phial ['faɪəl] *n* frasco.
philanderer [fɪ'lændərə*] *n* mulherengo.
philanthropic [fɪlən'θrɔpɪk] *adj* filantrópico.
philanthropist [fɪ'lænθrəpɪst] *n* filantropo/a.
philatelist [fɪ'lætəlɪst] *n* filatelista *m/f*.
philately [fɪ'lætəlɪ] *n* filatelia.
Philippines ['fɪlɪpiːnz] *npl* (*also*: *Philippine Islands*): **the ~** as Filipinas.
philosopher [fɪ'lɔsəfə*] *n* filósofo/a.
philosophical [fɪlə'sɔfɪkl] *adj* filosófico.
philosophy [fɪ'lɔsəfɪ] *n* filosofia.
phlegm [flɛm] *n* fleuma.
phlegmatic [flɛg'mætɪk] *adj* fleumático.
phobia ['fəubjə] *n* fobia.
phone [fəun] *n* telefone *m* ♦ *vt* telefonar a, ligar para ♦ *vi* telefonar, ligar; **to be on the ~** ter telefone; (*be calling*) estar no telefone.
phone back *vt, vi* ligar de volta.
phone book *n* lista telefônica.
phone booth *n* cabine *f* telefônica.
phone box *n* cabine *f* telefônica.
phone call *n* telefonema *m*, ligada.
phone-in (*BRIT*) *n* (*RADIO*) *programa com participação dos ouvintes*; (*TV*) *programa com participação dos espectadores*.
phonetics [fə'nɛtɪks] *n* fonética.
phoney ['fəunɪ] *adj* falso; (*person*) fingido ♦ *n* (*person*) impostor(a) *m/f*.
phonograph ['fəunəgrɑːf] (*US*) *n* vitrola.
phony ['fəunɪ] *adj, n* = **phoney**.
phosphate ['fɔsfeɪt] *n* fosfato.
phosphorus ['fɔsfərəs] *n* fósforo.
photo ['fəutəu] *n* foto *f*.
photo... ['fəutəu] *prefix* foto....
photocopier ['fəutəukɔpɪə*] *n* fotocopiadora *f*.
photocopy ['fəutəukɔpɪ] *n* fotocópia, xerox *m* ♦ *vt* fotocopiar, xerocar.
photoelectric [fəutəuɪ'lɛktrɪk] *adj* fotoelétrico; **~ cell** célula fotoelétrica.
photogenic [fəutəu'dʒɛnɪk] *adj* fotogênico.
photograph ['fəutəgrɑːf] *n* fotografia ♦ *vt* fotografar; **to take a ~ of sb** bater *or* tirar uma foto de alguém.
photographer [fə'tɔgrəfə*] *n* fotógrafo/a.
photographic [fəutə'græfɪk] *adj* fotográfico.
photography [fə'tɔgrəfɪ] *n* fotografia.
photostat ['fəutəustæt] *n* cópia fotostática.
photosynthesis [fəutəu'sɪnθəsɪs] *n* fotossíntese *f*.
phrase [freɪz] *n* frase *f* ♦ *vt* expressar; (*letter*) redigir.
phrasebook ['freɪzbuk] *n* livro de expressões idiomáticas (para turistas).
physical ['fɪzɪkl] *adj* físico; **~ examination** exame *m* físico; **~ education** educação *f* física; **~ exercise** exercício físico, movimento.
physically ['fɪzɪklɪ] *adv* fisicamente.
physician [fɪ'zɪʃən] *n* médico/a.
physicist ['fɪzɪsɪst] *n* físico/a.
physics ['fɪzɪks] *n* física.
physiological [fɪzɪə'lɔdʒɪkl] *adj* fisiológico.
physiology [fɪzɪ'ɔlədʒɪ] *n* fisiologia.
physiotherapist [fɪzɪəu'θɛrəpɪst] *n* fisioterapeuta *m/f*.
physiotherapy [fɪzɪəu'θɛrəpɪ] *n* fisioterapia.
physique [fɪ'ziːk] *n* físico.
pianist ['piːənɪst] *n* pianista *m/f*.
piano [pɪ'ænəu] *n* piano.
piano accordion (*BRIT*) *n* acordeão *m*, sanfona.
piccolo ['pɪkələu] *n* flautim *m*.
pick [pɪk] *n* (*tool*: *also*: *~-axe*) picareta ♦ *vt* (*select*) escolher, selecionar; (*gather*) colher; (*lock*) forçar; **take your ~** escolha o que quiser; **the ~ of** o melhor de; **to ~ a bone** roer um osso; **to ~ one's nose** colocar o dedo no nariz; **to ~ one's teeth** palitar os dentes; **to ~ sb's brains** aproveitar os conhecimentos de alguém; **to ~ pockets** roubar *or* bater carteira; **to ~ a quarrel** *or* **a fight with sb** comprar uma briga com alguém; **to ~ and choose** ser exigente.
pick off *vt* (*kill*) matar de um tiro.
pick on *vt fus* (*person*) azucrinar, aporrinhar.
pick out *vt* escolher; (*distinguish*) distinguir.
pick up *vi* (*improve*) melhorar ♦ *vt* (*from floor*) apanhar; (*telephone*) atender, tirar do gancho; (*collect*) buscar; (*learn*) aprender;

NB: *European Portuguese adds the following consonants to certain words:* **b** (sú(b)dito, su(b)til); **c** (a(c)ção, a(c)cionista, a(c)to); **m** (inde(m)ne); **p** (ado(p)ção, ado(p)tar); *for further details see p. xiii.*

(*RADIO*, *TV*, *TEL*) pegar; **to ~ up speed** acelerar; **to ~ o.s. up** levantar-se; **to ~ up where one left off** continuar do ponto onde se parou.

pickaxe ['pɪkæks] (*US* **pickax**) *n* picareta.

picket ['pɪkɪt] *n* (*in strike*) piquete *m*; (*person*) piqueteiro/a ♦ *vt* formar piquete em frente de.

picket line *n* piquete *m*.

pickings ['pɪkɪŋz] *npl*: **there are rich ~ to be had for investors in gold** os investidores em ouro vão se dar bem.

pickle ['pɪkl] *n* (*also*: *~s*: *as condiment*) picles *mpl*; (*fig*: *mess*) apuro ♦ *vt* (*in vinegar*) conservar em vinagre.

pick-me-up *n* estimulante *m*.

pickpocket ['pɪkpɔkɪt] *n* batedor(a) *m/f* de carteira (*BR*), carteirista *m/f* (*PT*).

pickup ['pɪkʌp] *n* (*on record player*) pick-up *m*; (*small truck*: *also*: *~ truck*, *~ van*) camioneta, pick-up *m*.

picnic ['pɪknɪk] *n* piquenique *m* ♦ *vi* fazer um piquenique.

picnicker ['pɪknɪkə*] *n* pessoa que faz piquenique.

pictorial [pɪk'tɔːrɪəl] *adj* pictórico; (*magazine etc*) ilustrado.

picture ['pɪktʃə*] *n* quadro; (*TV*) imagem *f*; (*painting*) pintura; (*drawing*) desenho; (*photograph*) foto(grafia) *f*; (*film*) filme *m* ♦ *vt* imaginar-se; (*describe*) retratar; **the ~s** *npl* (*BRIT*) o cinema; **to take a ~ of sb/sth** tirar uma foto de alguém/algo; **the overall ~** o quadro geral; **to put sb in the ~** pôr alguém a par da situação.

picture book *n* livro de figuras.

picturesque [pɪktʃə'rɛsk] *adj* pitoresco.

picture window *n* janela panorâmica.

piddling ['pɪdlɪŋ] (*inf*) *adj* irrisório.

pidgin ['pɪdʒɪn] *adj*: **~ English** *forma achinesada do inglês usada entre comerciantes*.

pie [paɪ] *n* pastelão *m*; (*open*) torta; (*of meat*) empadão *m*.

piebald ['paɪbɔːld] *adj* malhado.

piece [piːs] *n* pedaço; (*of land*) lote *m*, parcela; (*CHESS etc*) peça; (*item*): **a ~ of furniture/advice** um móvel/um conselho ♦ *vt*: **to ~ together** juntar; (*TECH*) montar; **in ~s** (*broken*) em pedaços; (*not yet assembled*) desmontado; **to fall to ~s** cair aos pedaços; **to take to ~s** desmontar; **in one ~** (*object*) inteiro; (*person*) ileso; **a 10p ~** (*BRIT*) uma moeda de 10p; **~ by ~** pedaço por pedaço; **a six-~ band** um sexteto; **to say one's ~** vender o seu peixe.

piecemeal ['piːsmiːl] *adv* pouco a pouco.

piece rate *n* salário por peça.

piecework ['piːswəːk] *n* trabalho por empreitada *or* peça.

pie chart *n* gráfico de setores.

pier [pɪə*] *n* cais *m*; (*jetty*) embarcadouro, molhe *m*; (*of bridge etc*) pilar *m*, pilastra.

pierce [pɪəs] *vt* furar, perfurar; **to have one's ears ~d** furar as orelhas.

piercing ['pɪəsɪŋ] *adj* (*cry*) penetrante, agudo.

piety ['paɪətɪ] *n* piedade *f*.

piffling ['pɪflɪŋ] *adj* irrisório.

pig [pɪg] *n* porco; (*fig*) porcalhão/lhona *m/f*.

pigeon ['pɪdʒən] *n* pombo.

pigeonhole ['pɪdʒənhəul] *n* escaninho.

pigeon-toed [-təud] *adj* com pé de pombo.

piggy bank ['pɪgɪ-] *n* *cofre em forma de porquinho*.

pigheaded ['pɪg'hɛdɪd] *adj* teimoso, cabeçudo.

piglet ['pɪglɪt] *n* porquinho, leitão *m*.

pigment ['pɪgmənt] *n* pigmento.

pigmentation [pɪgmən'teɪʃən] *n* pigmentação *f*.

pigmy ['pɪgmɪ] *n* = **pygmy**.

pigskin ['pɪgskɪn] *n* couro de porco.

pigsty ['pɪgstaɪ] *n* chiqueiro.

pigtail ['pɪgteɪl] *n* (*girl's*) trança; (*Chinese*) rabicho, rabo-de-cavalo.

pike [paɪk] (*pl* **~s**) *n* (*spear*) lança, pique *m*; (*pl*: *inv*: *fish*) lúcio.

pilchard ['pɪltʃəd] *n* sardinha.

pile [paɪl] *n* (*of books*) pilha; (*heap*) monte *m*; (*of carpet*) pêlo; (*of cloth*) lado felpudo; (*support*: *in building*) estaca ♦ *vt* (*also*: *~ up*) empilhar; (*heap*) amontoar; (*fig*) acumular ♦ *vi* (*also*: *~ up*) amontoar-se; **~s** *npl* (*MED*) hemorróidas *fpl*; **in a ~** numa pilha.

pile on *vt*: **to ~ it on** (*inf*) exagerar.

pileup ['paɪlʌp] *n* (*AUT*) engavetamento.

pilfer ['pɪlfə*] *vt*, *vi* furtar, afanar, surripiar.

pilfering ['pɪlfərɪŋ] *n* furto.

pilgrim ['pɪlgrɪm] *n* peregrino/a.

pilgrimage ['pɪlgrɪmɪdʒ] *n* peregrinação *f*, romaria.

pill [pɪl] *n* pílula; **the ~** a pílula; **to be on the ~** usar *or* tomar a pílula.

pillage ['pɪlɪdʒ] *vt* saquear, pilhar.

pillar ['pɪlə*] *n* pilar *m*; (*concrete*) coluna.

pillar box (*BRIT*) *n* caixa coletora (do correio) (*BR*), marco do correio (*PT*).

pillion ['pɪljən] *n* (*of motor cycle*) garupa ♦ *adv*: **to ride ~** andar na garupa.

pillory ['pɪlərɪ] *n* pelourinho ♦ *vt* expor ao ridículo.

pillow ['pɪləu] *n* travesseiro (*BR*), almofada (*PT*).

pillowcase ['pɪləukeɪs] *n* fronha.

pillowslip ['pɪləuslɪp] *n* fronha.

pilot ['paɪlət] *n* piloto/a ♦ *cpd* (*scheme etc*) piloto *inv* ♦ *vt* pilotar; (*fig*) guiar.

pilot boat *n* barco-piloto.

pilot light *n* piloto.

pimento [pɪ'mɛntəu] *n* pimentão-doce *m*.

pimp [pɪmp] *n* cafetão *m* (*BR*), cáften *m* (*PT*).

pimple ['pɪmpl] *n* espinha.

pimply ['pɪmplɪ] *adj* espinhento.

PIN *n abbr* = **personal identification number**.

pin [pɪn] *n* alfinete *m*; (*TECH*) cavilha; (*wooden*, *BRIT*: *ELEC*: *of plug*) pino ♦ *vt* alfinetar; **~s and needles** comichão *f*, sensação *f* de formigamento; **to ~ sb against** *or* **to** apertar alguém contra; **to ~ sth on sb** (*fig*) culpar alguém de algo.

pin down *vt* (*fig*): **to ~ sb down** conseguir

que alguém se defina *or* tome atitude; **there's something strange here but I can't quite ~ it down** há alguma coisa estranha aqui, mas não consigo precisar o quê.

pinafore ['pınəfɔː*] *n* avental *m*.

pinafore dress *n* avental *m*.

pinball ['pınbɔːl] *n* fliper *m*, fliperama *m*.

pincers ['pınsəz] *npl* pinça, tenaz *f*.

pinch [pıntʃ] *n* beliscão *m*; (*of salt etc*) pitada ♦ *vt* beliscar; (*inf*: *steal*) furtar ♦ *vi* (*shoe*) apertar; **at a ~** em último caso; **to feel the ~** (*fig*) apertar o cinto, passar por um aperto.

pinched [pıntʃt] *adj* (*drawn*) abatido; **~ with cold** transido de frio; **~ for money** desprovido de dinheiro; **to be ~ for space** não dispor de muito espaço.

pincushion ['pınkuʃən] *n* alfineteira.

pine [paın] *n* (*also*: *~ tree*) pinho ♦ *vi*: **to ~ for** ansiar por.

pine away *vi* consumir-se, definhar.

pineapple ['paınæpl] *n* abacaxi *m* (*BR*), ananás *m* (*PT*).

ping [pıŋ] *n* (*noise*) silvo, sibilo.

ping-pong *n* pingue-pongue *m*.

pink [pıŋk] *adj* cor de rosa *inv* ♦ *n* (*colour*) cor *f* de rosa; (*BOT*) cravo, cravina.

pinking scissors ['pıŋkıŋ-] *npl* tesoura para picotar.

pinking shears ['pıŋkıŋ-] *npl* tesoura para picotar.

pin money (*BRIT*) *n* dinheiro extra.

pinnacle ['pınəkl] *n* cume *m*; (*fig*) auge *m*.

pinpoint ['pınpɔınt] *vt* localizar com precisão.

pinstripe ['pınstraıp] *n* tecido listrado ♦ *adj* listrado.

pint [paınt] *n* quartilho; **to go for a ~** (*BRIT*: *inf*) ir tomar uma cerveja.

pin-up *n* pin-up *f*, *retrato de mulher atraente*.

pioneer [paıə'nıə*] *n* pioneiro/a ♦ *vt* ser pioneiro de.

pious ['paıəs] *adj* pio, devoto.

pip [pıp] *n* (*seed*) caroço, semente *f*; (*BRIT*: *time signal on radio*): **the ~s** ≈ o tope de oito segundos.

pipe [paıp] *n* cano, tubo; (*for smoking*) cachimbo; (*MUS*) flauta ♦ *vt* canalizar, encanar; **~s** *npl* (*also*: *bag~s*) gaita de foles.

pipe down (*inf*) *vi* calar o bico, meter a viola no saco.

pipe cleaner *n* limpa-cachimbo.

piped music [paıpt-] *n* música enlatada.

pipe dream *n* sonho impossível, castelo no ar.

pipeline ['paıplaın] *n* (*for oil*) oleoduto; (*for gas*) gaseoduto; **it's in the ~** (*fig*) está na bica (*inf*).

piper ['paıpə*] *n* (*gen*) flautista *m/f*; (*of bagpipes*) gaiteiro/a.

pipe tobacco *n* fumo (*BR*) *or* tabaco (*PT*) para cachimbo.

piping ['paıpıŋ] *adv*: **~ hot** chiando de quente.

piquant ['piːkənt] *adj* picante.

pique [piːk] *n* ressentimento, melindre *m*.

piracy ['paırəsı] *n* pirataria.

pirate ['paıərət] *n* pirata *m* ♦ *vt* (*record, video, book*) piratear.

pirate radio (*BRIT*) *n* rádio pirata.

pirouette [pıru'ɛt] *n* pirueta ♦ *vi* fazer pirueta(s).

Pisces ['paısiːz] *n* Pisces *m*, Peixes *mpl*.

piss [pıs] (*col!*) *vi* mijar; **~ off!** vai à merda (*!*).

pissed [pıst] (*BRIT*: *inf*) *adj* (*drunk*) bêbado, de porre.

pistol ['pıstl] *n* pistola.

piston ['pıstən] *n* pistão *m*, êmbolo.

pit [pıt] *n* cova, fossa; (*also*: *coal ~*) mina de carvão; (*also*: *orchestra ~*) fosso ♦ *vt*: **to ~ A against B** opor A a B; **~s** *npl* (*AUT*) box *m*; **to ~ o.s. against** opor-se a.

pitapat ['pıtə'pæt] (*BRIT*) *adv*: **to go ~** (*heart*) disparar; (*rain*) tiquetaquear.

pitch [pıtʃ] *n* (*throw*) arremesso, lance *m*; (*MUS*) tom *m*; (*of voice*) altura; (*fig*: *degree*) intensidade *f*; (*also*: *sales ~*) papo (de vendedor); (*SPORT*) campo; (*tar*) piche *m*, breu *m*; (*NAUT*) arfada; (*in market etc*) barraca ♦ *vt* (*throw*) arremessar, lançar; (*tent*) armar; (*set*: *price, message*) adaptar ♦ *vi* (*fall*) tombar, cair; (*NAUT*) jogar, arfar; **to be ~ed forward** ser jogado para frente; **at this ~** neste pique *or* ritmo; **to ~ one's aspirations too high** colocar as aspirações alto demais.

pitch in *vi* contribuir.

pitch-black [pıtʃ'blæk] *adj* escuro como o breu.

pitched battle [pıtʃt-] *n* batalha campal.

pitcher ['pıtʃə*] *n* jarro, cântaro; (*US*: *BASEBALL*) arremessador *m*.

pitchfork ['pıtʃfɔːk] *n* forcado.

piteous ['pıtıəs] *adj* lastimável.

pitfall ['pıtfɔːl] *n* perigo (imprevisto), armadilha.

pith [pıθ] *n* (*of orange*) casca interna e branca; (*fig*) essência, parte *f* essencial.

pithead ['pıthɛd] (*BRIT*) *n* boca do poço.

pithy ['pıθı] *adj* substancial, rico.

pitiable ['pıtıəbl] *adj* deplorável.

pitiful ['pıtıful] *adj* (*touching*) comovente, tocante; (*contemptible*) desprezível, lamentável.

pitifully ['pıtıfəlı] *adv* lamentavelmente, deploravelmente.

pitiless ['pıtılıs] *adj* impiedoso.

pittance ['pıtns] *n* ninharia, miséria.

pitted ['pıtıd] *adj*: **~ with** (*chickenpox*) marcado com; (*rust*) picado de; **~ with potholes** esburacado.

pity ['pıtı] *n* (*compassion*) compaixão *f*, piedade *f*; (*shame*) pena ♦ *vt* ter pena de, compadecer-se de; **what a ~!** que pena!; **it's a ~ (that) you can't come** é uma pena que você não possa vir; **to have** *or* **take ~ on sb**

NB: European Portuguese adds the following consonants to certain words: **b** (sú(b)dito, su(b)til); **c** (a(c)ção, a(c)cionista, a(c)to); **m** (inde(m)ne); **p** (ado(p)ção, ado(p)tar); *for further details see p. xiii.*

ter pena de alguém.
pitying ['pɪtɪɪŋ] *adj* compassivo, compadecido.
pivot ['pɪvət] *n* pino, eixo; (*fig*) pivô *m* ♦ *vi*: **to ~ on** girar sobre; (*fig*) depender de.
pixel ['pɪksl] *n* (*COMPUT*) píxel *m*.
pixie ['pɪksɪ] *n* duende *m*.
pizza ['pi:tsə] *n* pizza.
P&L *abbr* = **profit and loss**.
placard ['plækɑ:d] *n* (*sign*) placar *m*; (*in march etc*) cartaz *m*.
placate [plə'keɪt] *vt* apaziguar, aplacar.
placatory [plə'keɪtərɪ] *adj* apaziguador(a), aplacador(a).
place [pleɪs] *n* lugar *m*; (*rank*) posição *f*; (*post*) posto; (*home*): **at/to his ~** na/para a casa dele ♦ *vt* (*object*) pôr, colocar; (*identify*) identificar, situar; (*find a post for*) colocar; **to take ~** realizar-se; (*occur*) ocorrer; **from ~ to ~** de lugar em lugar; **all over the ~** em tudo quanto é lugar; **out of ~** (*not suitable*) fora de lugar, deslocado; **I feel out of ~ here** eu me sinto deslocado aqui; **in the first ~** em primeiro lugar; **to change ~s with sb** trocar de lugar com alguém; **to put sb in his ~** (*fig*) pôr alguém no seu lugar; **he's going ~s** (*fig*) ele vai se dar bem; **it's not my ~ to do it** não me compete fazê-lo; **to ~ an order with sb for sth** (*COMM*) encomendar algo a alguém; **to be ~d** (*in race, exam*) classificar-se; **how are you ~d next week?** você tem tempo na semana que vem?
placebo [plə'si:bəu] *n* placebo.
place mat *n* descanso.
placement ['pleɪsmənt] *n* (*placing*) colocação *f*; (*job*) cargo.
place name *n* topônimo.
placenta [plə'sɛntə] *n* placenta.
placid ['plæsɪd] *adj* plácido, sereno.
placidity [plə'sɪdɪtɪ] *n* placidez *f*.
plagiarism ['pleɪdʒjərɪzm] *n* plágio.
plagiarist ['pleɪdʒjərɪst] *n* plagiário/a.
plagiarize ['pleɪdʒjəraɪz] *vt* plagiar.
plague [pleɪg] *n* praga; (*MED*) peste *f* ♦ *vt* (*fig*) atormentar, importunar; **to ~ sb with questions** importunar alguém com perguntas.
plaice [pleɪs] *n inv* solha.
plaid [plæd] *n* (*material*) tecido enxadrezado; (*pattern*) xadrez *m* escocês.
plain [pleɪn] *adj* (*clear*) claro, evidente; (*simple*) simples *inv*, despretensioso; (*frank*) franco, sem rodeios; (*not handsome*) sem atrativos; (*pure*) puro, natural; (*in one colour*) liso ♦ *adv* claramente, com franqueza ♦ *n* planície *f*, campina; **in ~ clothes** (*police*) à paisana; **to make sth ~ to sb** dar claramente a entender algo a alguém.
plain chocolate *n* chocolate *m* amargo.
plainly ['pleɪnlɪ] *adv* claramente, obviamente; (*frankly*) francamente, sem rodeios.
plainness ['pleɪnnɪs] *n* clareza; (*simplicity*) simplicidade *f*; (*frankness*) franqueza.
plaintiff ['pleɪntɪf] *n* querelante *m/f*, queixoso/a.
plaintive ['pleɪntɪv] *adj* (*voice, tone*) queixoso; (*song*) lamentoso; (*look*) tristonho.
plait [plæt] *n* trança, dobra ♦ *vt* trançar.
plan [plæn] *n* plano; (*scheme*) projeto; (*schedule*) programa *m* ♦ *vt* planejar (*BR*), planear (*PT*), programar ♦ *vi* fazer planos; **to ~ to do** tencionar fazer, propor-se fazer; **how long do you ~ to stay?** quanto tempo você pretende ficar?
plane [pleɪn] *n* (*AVIAT*) avião *m*; (*tree*) plátano; (*tool*) plaina; (*ART, MATH*) plano ♦ *adj* plano ♦ *vt* (*with tool*) aplainar.
planet ['plænɪt] *n* planeta *m*.
planetarium [plænɪ'tɛərɪəm] *n* planetário.
plank [plæŋk] *n* tábua; (*POL*) item *m* da plataforma política.
plankton ['plæŋktən] *n* plâncton *m*.
planner ['plænə*] *n* planejador(a) *m/f* (*BR*), planeador(a) *m/f* (*PT*); (*chart*) agenda (*quadro*); **town** (*BRIT*) *or* **city** (*US*) **~** urbanista *m/f*.
planning ['plænɪŋ] *n* planejamento (*BR*), planeamento (*PT*).
planning permission (*BRIT*) *n* autorização *f* para construir.
plant [plɑ:nt] *n* planta; (*machinery*) maquinaria; (*factory*) usina, fábrica ♦ *vt* plantar; (*field*) semear; (*bomb*) colocar, pôr; (*inf*) pôr às escondidas.
plantation [plæn'teɪʃən] *n* plantação *f*; (*estate*) fazenda.
plant hire *n* locação *f* de equipamentos.
plant pot (*BRIT*) *n* vaso para planta.
plaque [plæk] *n* placa, insígnia; (*also*: *dental ~*) placa dental.
plasma ['plæzmə] *n* plasma *m*.
plaster ['plɑ:stə*] *n* (*for walls*) reboco; (*on leg etc*) gesso; (*BRIT*: *also*: *sticking ~*) esparadrapo, band-aid *m* ♦ *vt* rebocar; (*cover*): **to ~ with** encher *or* cobrir de; **in ~** (*BRIT*: *leg etc*) engessado; **~ of Paris** gesso.
plaster cast *n* (*MED*) aparelho de gesso; (*ART*) molde *m* de gesso.
plastered ['plɑ:stəd] (*inf*) *adj* bêbado, de porre.
plasterer ['plɑ:stərə*] *n* rebocador(a) *m/f*, caiador(a) *m/f*.
plastic ['plæstɪk] *n* plástico ♦ *adj* de plástico; (*flexible*) plástico; (*art*) plástico.
plastic bag *n* sacola de plástico.
plasticine ['plæstɪsi:n] ® *n* plasticina ®.
plastic surgery *n* cirurgia plástica.
plate [pleɪt] *n* (*dish*) prato; (*metal*) placa, chapa; (*PHOT, on door*) chapa; (*dental*) dentadura; (*TYP*) clichê *m*; (*in book*) gravura; (*AUT*: *number ~*) placa; **gold/silver ~** (*dishes*) baixela de ouro/prata.
plateau ['plætəu] (*pl* **~s** *or* **~x**) *n* planalto.
plateaux ['plætəuz] *npl of* **plateau**.
plateful ['pleɪtful] *n* pratada.
plate glass *n* vidro laminado.
platelayer ['pleɪtleɪə*] (*BRIT*) *n* (*RAIL*) assentador *m* de trilhos.
platen ['plætən] *n* (*on typewriter, printer*) rolo.
plate rack *n* escorredor *m* de pratos.
platform ['plætfɔ:m] *n* (*RAIL*) plataforma (*BR*),

cais *m* (*PT*); (*stage*) estrado; (*at meeting*) tribuna; (*POL*) programa *m* partidário.
platform ticket (*BRIT*) *n* bilhete *m* de plataforma (*BR*) *or* cais (*PT*).
platinum ['plætɪnəm] *n* platina.
platitude ['plætɪtjuːd] *n* lugar *m* comum, chavão *m*.
platoon [plə'tuːn] *n* pelotão *m*.
platter ['plætə*] *n* travessa.
plaudits ['plɔːdɪts] *npl* aclamações *fpl*, aplausos *mpl*.
plausible ['plɔːzɪbl] *adj* plausível; (*person*) convincente.
play [pleɪ] *n* jogo; (*THEATRE*) obra, peça ♦ *vt* (*game*) jogar; (*team, opponent*) jogar contra; (*instrument, music*) tocar; (*THEATRE*) representar; (: *part*) fazer o papel de; (*fig*) desempenhar ♦ *vi* (*sport, game*) jogar; (*music*) tocar; (*frolic*) brincar; **to bring** *or* **call into ~** (*plan*) acionar; (*emotions*) detonar; **~ on words** jogo de palavras, trocadilho; **to ~ a trick on sb** pregar uma peça em alguém; **they're ~ing at soldiers** eles estão brincando de soldados; **to ~ for time** (*fig*) tentar ganhar tempo, protelar; **to ~ into sb's hands** (*fig*) fazer o jogo de alguém; **to ~ the fool/innocent** bancar o tolo/inocente.
play about *vi* brincar.
play along *vi* (*fig*): **to ~ along with sb** fazer o jogo de alguém ♦ *vt* (*fig*): **to ~ sb along** fazer alguém de criança.
play around *vi* brincar.
play back *vt* repetir.
play down *vt* minimizar.
play on *vt fus* (*sb's feelings, credulity*) tirar proveito de, usar.
play up *vi* (*person*) dar trabalho; (*TV, car*) estar com defeito.
playact ['pleɪækt] *vi* fazer fita.
playboy ['pleɪbɔɪ] *n* playboy *m*.
played-out [pleɪd-] *adj* gasto.
player ['pleɪə*] *n* jogador(a) *m/f*; (*THEATRE*) ator/atriz *m/f*; (*MUS*) músico/a.
playful ['pleɪful] *adj* brincalhão/lhona.
playgoer ['pleɪgəuə*] *n* freqüentador(a) *m/f* de teatro.
playground ['pleɪgraund] *n* pátio de recreio.
playgroup ['pleɪgruːp] *n espécie de jardim de infância*.
playing card ['pleɪɪŋ-] *n* carta de baralho.
playing field ['pleɪɪŋ-] *n* campo de esportes (*BR*) *or* jogos (*PT*).
playmate ['pleɪmeɪt] *n* colega *m/f*, camarada *m/f*.
play-off ['pleɪɔf] *n* (*SPORT*) partida de desempate.
playpen ['pleɪpɛn] *n* cercado para crianças.
playroom ['pleɪruːm] *n* sala de jogos.
plaything ['pleɪθɪŋ] *n* brinquedo; (*fig*) joguete *m*.
playtime ['pleɪtaɪm] *n* (*SCH*) recreio.
playwright ['pleɪraɪt] *n* dramaturgo/a.
plc (*BRIT*) *abbr* = **public limited company**.
plea [pliː] *n* (*request*) apelo, petição *f*; (*excuse*) justificativa; (*LAW*: *defence*) defesa.
plead [pliːd] *vt* (*LAW*) defender, advogar; (*give as excuse*) alegar ♦ *vi* (*LAW*) declarar-se; (*beg*): **to ~ with sb (for sth)** suplicar *or* rogar (algo) a alguém; **to ~ guilty/not guilty** declarar-se culpado/inocente.
pleasant ['plɛznt] *adj* agradável; (*person*) simpático.
pleasantly ['plɛzntlɪ] *adv* agradavelmente.
pleasantness ['plɛzntnɪs] *n* (*of person*) amabilidade *f*, simpatia; (*of place*) encanto.
pleasantry ['plɛzntrɪ] *n* (*joke*) brincadeira; **pleasantries** *npl* (*polite remarks*) amenidades *fpl* (na conversa).
please [pliːz] *vt* (*give pleasure to*) agradar a, dar prazer a ♦ *vi* (*think fit*): **do as you ~** faça o que *or* como quiser; **~!** por favor!; **~ yourself!** como você quiser!, você que sabe!
pleased [pliːzd] *adj* (*happy*) satisfeito, contente; **~ (with)** satisfeito (com); **~ to meet you** prazer (em conhecê-lo); **we are ~ to inform you that ...** temos a satisfação de informá-lo de que ....
pleasing ['pliːzɪŋ] *adj* agradável.
pleasurable ['plɛʒərəbl] *adj* agradável.
pleasure ['plɛʒə*] *n* prazer *m*; **it's a ~** não tem de quê; **with ~** com muito prazer; **is this trip for business or ~?** esta viagem é de negócios ou de recreio?
pleasure steamer *n* vapor *m* de recreio.
pleat [pliːt] *n* prega.
plebiscite ['plɛbɪsɪt] *n* plebiscito.
plebs [plɛbz] (*pej*) *npl* plebe *f*.
plectrum ['plɛktrəm] *n* plectro.
pledge [plɛdʒ] *n* (*object*) penhor *m*; (*promise*) promessa ♦ *vt* (*invest*) empenhar; (*promise*) prometer; **to ~ support for sb** empenhar-se a apoiar alguém; **to ~ sb to secrecy** comprometer alguém a guardar sigilo.
plenary ['pliːnərɪ] *adj*: **in ~ session** no plenário.
plentiful ['plɛntɪful] *adj* abundante, profuso.
plenty ['plɛntɪ] *n* abundância; **~ of** (*enough*) bastante; (*many*) muitos/as; **we've got ~ of time** temos tempo de sobra.
pleurisy ['pluərɪsɪ] *n* pleurisia.
Plexiglas ['plɛksɪglɑːs] ® (*US*) *n* Blindex *m* ®.
pliable ['plaɪəbl] *adj* flexível.
pliers ['plaɪəz] *npl* alicate *m*.
plight [plaɪt] *n* situação *f* difícil, apuro.
plimsolls ['plɪmsəlz] (*BRIT*) *npl* tênis *mpl*.
PLO *n abbr* (= *Palestine Liberation Organization*) OLP *f*.
plod [plɔd] *vi* caminhar pesadamente; (*fig*) trabalhar laboriosamente.
plodder ['plɔdə*] *n* burro-de-carga *m*.
plodding ['plɔdɪŋ] *adj* mourejador(a).
plonk [plɔŋk] (*inf*) *n* (*BRIT*: *wine*) zurrapa ♦ *vt*: **to ~ sth down** deixar cair algo (pesada-

NB: European Portuguese adds the following consonants to certain words: **b** (sú(b)dito, su(b)til); **c** (a(c)ção, a(c)cionista, a(c)to); **m** (inde(m)ne); **p** (ado(p)ção, ado(p)tar); *for further details see p. xiii.*

mente).
plot [plɔt] *n* (*scheme*) conspiração *f*, complô *m*; (*of story, play*) enredo, trama; (*of land*) lote *m* ♦ *vt* (*mark out*) traçar; (*conspire*) tramar, planejar (*PT*: planear) ♦ *vi* conspirar; **a vegetable ~** (*BRIT*) uma horta.
plotter ['plɔtə*] *n* conspirador(a) *m/f*; (*COMPUT*) plotter *f*, plotadora.
plough [plau] (*US* **plow**) *n* arado ♦ *vt* (*earth*) arar.
plough back *vt* (*COMM*) reinvestir.
plough through *vt fus* (*crowd*) abrir caminho por; (*snow*) avançar penosamente por.
ploughing ['plauɪŋ] (*US* **plowing**) *n* aradura.
ploughman ['plaumən] (*US* **plowman**) (*irreg*) *n* lavrador *m*; **~'s lunch** (*BRIT*) *lanche de pão, queijo e picles*.
plow *etc* [plau] (*US*) = **plough** *etc*.
ploy [plɔɪ] *n* estratagema *m*.
pluck [plʌk] *vt* (*fruit*) colher; (*musical instrument*) dedilhar; (*bird*) depenar ♦ *n* coragem *f*, puxão *m*; **to ~ one's eyebrows** fazer as sobrancelhas; **to ~ up courage** criar coragem.
plucky ['plʌkɪ] *adj* corajoso, valente.
plug [plʌg] *n* tampão *m*; (*ELEC*) tomada (*BR*), ficha (*PT*); (*AUT*: *also*: *spark(ing)* ~) vela (de ignição) ♦ *vt* (*hole*) tapar; (*inf*: *advertise*) fazer propaganda de; **to give sb/sth a ~** (*inf*) fazer propaganda de alguém/algo.
plug in *vt* (*ELEC*) ligar.
plughole ['plʌghəul] (*BRIT*) *n* (*in sink*) escoadouro.
plum [plʌm] *n* (*fruit*) ameixa ♦ *adj* (*inf*): **a ~ job** um emprego jóia.
plumage ['plu:mɪdʒ] *n* plumagem *f*.
plumb [plʌm] *adj* vertical ♦ *n* prumo ♦ *adv* (*exactly*) exatamente ♦ *vt* sondar.
plumb in *vt* (*washing machine*) instalar.
plumber ['plʌmə*] *n* bombeiro/a (*BR*), encanador(a) *m/f* (*BR*), canalizador(a) *m/f* (*PT*).
plumbing ['plʌmɪŋ] *n* (*trade*) ofício de encanador; (*piping*) encanamento.
plumbline ['plʌmlaɪn] *n* fio de prumo.
plume [plu:m] *n* pluma; (*on helmet*) penacho.
plummet ['plʌmɪt] *vi* despencar.
plump [plʌmp] *adj* roliço, rechonchudo ♦ *vt*: **to ~ sth (down) on** deixar cair algo em.
plump for (*inf*) *vt fus* (*choose*) optar por.
plump up *vt* (*cushion*) afofar.
plunder ['plʌndə*] *n* saque *m*, pilhagem *f*; (*loot*) despojo ♦ *vt* pilhar, espoliar.
plunge [plʌndʒ] *n* (*dive*) salto; (*submersion*) mergulho ♦ *vt* mergulhar, afundar ♦ *vi* (*fall*) despencar; (*dive*) mergulhar; **to take the ~** topar a parada; **to ~ a room into darkness** mergulhar um aposento na escuridão.
plunger ['plʌndʒə*] *n* êmbolo; (*for blocked sink*) desentupidor *m*.
plunging ['plʌndʒɪŋ] *adj* (*neckline*) decotado.
pluperfect [plu:'pə:fɪkt] *n* mais-que-perfeito.
plural ['pluərl] *adj* plural ♦ *n* plural *m*.
plus [plʌs] *n* (*also*: *~ sign*) sinal *m* de adição ♦ *prep* mais ♦ *adj*: **ten/twenty ~** dez/vinte e tantos; **it's a ~** é uma vantagem.
plus fours *npl* calça (*BR*) *or* calças *fpl* (*PT*) de golfe.
plush [plʌʃ] *adj* de pelúcia; (*fig*) suntuoso ♦ *n* pelúcia.
plutonium [plu:'təunɪəm] *n* plutônio.
ply [plaɪ] *n* (*of wool*) fio; (*of wood*) espessura ♦ *vt* (*a trade*) exercer ♦ *vi* (*ship*) ir e vir; **three ~** (*wool*) de três fios; **to ~ sb with drink** dar muita bebida a alguém; **to ~ sb with questions** bombardear alguém com perguntas.
plywood ['plaɪwud] *n* madeira compensada.
PM (*BRIT*) *n abbr* = **Prime Minister**.
p.m. *adv abbr* (= *post meridiem*) da tarde, da noite.
pneumatic [nju:'mætɪk] *adj* pneumático; **~ drill** perfuratriz *f*.
pneumonia [nju:'məunɪə] *n* pneumonia.
PO *n abbr* = **Post Office**; (*MIL*) = **petty officer**.
po *abbr* = **postal order**.
POA (*BRIT*) *n abbr* = **Prison Officers' Association**.
poach [pəutʃ] *vt* (*cook*) escaldar, escalfar; (*eggs*) fazer pochê (*BR*), escalfar (*PT*); (*steal*) furtar ♦ *vi* caçar (*or* pescar) em propriedade alheia.
poached [pəutʃt] *adj* (*egg*) pochê (*BR*), escalfado (*PT*).
poacher ['pəutʃə*] *n* caçador *m* (*or* pescador *m*) furtivo.
poaching ['pəutʃɪŋ] *n* caça (*or* pesca) furtiva.
PO Box *n abbr* = **Post Office Box**.
pocket ['pɔkɪt] *n* bolso; (*BILLIARDS*) caçapa, ventanilha ♦ *vt* embolsar, meter no bolso; (*BILLIARDS*) encaçapar; **to be out of ~** (*BRIT*) perder, ter prejuízo; **~ of resistance** foco de resistência.
pocketbook ['pɔkɪtbuk] *n* carteira.
pocket knife (*irreg*) *n* canivete *m*.
pocket money *n* dinheiro para despesas miúdas; (*for child*) mesada.
pockmarked ['pɔkmɑ:kt] *adj* (*face*) com marcas de varíola.
pod [pɔd] *n* vagem *f* ♦ *vt* descascar.
podgy ['pɔdʒɪ] *adj* nédio, mole.
podiatrist [pɔ'di:ətrɪst] (*US*) *n* pedicuro/a.
podiatry [pɔ'di:ətrɪ] (*US*) *n* podiatria.
podium ['pəudɪəm] *n* pódio.
POE *n abbr* = **port of embarkation**; **port of entry**.
poem ['pəuɪm] *n* poema *m*.
poet ['pəuɪt] *n* poeta/poetisa *m/f*.
poetess ['pəuɪtɪs] *n* poetisa.
poetic [pəu'ɛtɪk] *adj* poético.
poet laureate [-'lɔ:rɪət] *n* poeta *m* laureado.
poetry ['pəuɪtrɪ] *n* poesia.
POEU (*BRIT*) *n abbr* (= *Post Office Engineering Union*) *sindicato dos técnicos do correio*.
poignant ['pɔɪnjənt] *adj* comovente; (*sharp*) agudo.
point [pɔɪnt] *n* ponto; (*tip*) ponta; (*purpose*) finalidade *f*; (*BRIT*: *ELEC*: *also*: *power* ~) tomada; (*also*: *decimal* ~): **2 ~ 3 (2.3)** dois vírgula três ♦ *vt* (*window, wall*) tomar com

argamassa; (*gun etc*): **to ~ sth at sb** apontar algo para alguém ♦ *vi* apontar; **to ~ to** apontar para; (*fig*) indicar; **~s** *npl* (*AUT*) platinado, contato; (*RAIL*) agulhas *fpl*; **good ~s** qualidades; **to make a ~** fazer uma observação; **to make a ~ of** fazer questão de, insistir em; **to make one's ~** dar sua opinião; **you've made your ~** você já disse o que queria, você já falou (*inf*); **to get the ~** compreender; **to come to the ~** ir ao assunto; **when it comes to the ~** na hora; **there's no ~ (in doing)** não adianta nada (fazer); **to be on the ~ of doing sth** estar prestes a *or* a ponto de fazer algo; **that's the whole ~!** aí é que está a questão!, aí é que 'tá! (*inf*); **to be beside the ~** estar fora do assunto; **you've got a ~ there!** você tem razão!; **in ~ of fact** na verdade, na realidade; **~ of departure** ponto de partida; **~ of order** questão *f* de ordem; **~ of sale** (*COMM*) ponto de venda; **~ of view** ponto de vista.

point out *vt* (*indicate*) indicar; (*emphasize*) ressaltar.

point-blank [pɔɪnt'blæŋk] *adv* (*also*: *at ~ range*) à queima-roupa ♦ *adj* (*fig*) categórico.

point duty (*BRIT*) *n*: **to be on ~** estar de serviço no controle do trânsito.

pointed ['pɔɪntɪd] *adj* (*shape*) pontudo, aguçado; (*remark*) mordaz.

pointedly ['pɔɪntɪdlɪ] *adv* sugestivamente.

pointer ['pɔɪntə*] *n* (*stick*) indicador *m*, ponteiro; (*needle*) agulha; (*dog*) pointer *m*; (*clue, advice*) dica.

pointless ['pɔɪntlɪs] *adj* (*useless*) inútil; (*senseless*) sem sentido; (*motiveless*) sem razão.

poise [pɔɪz] *n* (*balance*) equilíbrio; (*of head, body*) porte *m*; (*calmness*) serenidade *f* ♦ *vt* pôr em equilíbrio; **to be ~d for** (*fig*) estar pronto para.

poison ['pɔɪzn] *n* veneno ♦ *vt* envenenar.

poisoning ['pɔɪznɪŋ] *n* envenenamento.

poisonous ['pɔɪzənəs] *adj* venenoso; (*fumes etc*) tóxico; (*fig*) pernicioso.

poke [pəuk] *vt* (*fire*) atiçar; (*jab with finger, stick etc*) cutucar; (*put*): **to ~ sth in(to)** enfiar *or* meter algo em ♦ *n* (*to fire*) remexida; (*jab*) cutucada; (*with elbow*) cotovelada; **to ~ one's nose into** meter o nariz em; **to ~ one's head out of the window** meter a cabeça para fora da janela; **to ~ fun at sb** ridicularizar *or* fazer troça de alguém.

poke about *vi* escarafunchar, espionar.

poker ['pəukə*] *n* atiçador *m*; (*CARDS*) pôquer *m*.

poker-faced [-feɪst] *adj* com rosto impassível.

poky ['pəukɪ] *adj* acanhado, apertado.

Poland ['pəulənd] *n* Polônia.

polar ['pəulə*] *adj* polar.

polar bear *n* urso polar.

polarize ['pəuləraɪz] *vt* polarizar.

Pole [pəul] *n* polonês/esa *m/f*.

pole [pəul] *n* vara; (*GEO*) pólo; (*TEL*) poste *m*; (*flag~*) mastro; (*tent~*) estaca.

pole bean (*US*) *n* feijão-trepador *m*.

polecat ['pəulkæt] *n* furão-bravo.

Pol. Econ. ['pɔlɪkɔn] *n abbr* = **political economy**.

polemic [pɔ'lɛmɪk] *n* polêmica.

pole star *n* estrela Polar.

pole vault *n* salto com vara.

police [pə'liːs] *npl* polícia ♦ *vt* policiar.

police car *n* rádio-patrulha *f*.

police constable (*BRIT*) *n* policial *m/f* (*BR*), polícia *m/f* (*PT*).

police department (*US*) *n* polícia.

police force *n* polícia.

policeman [pə'liːsmən] (*irreg*) *n* policial *m* (*BR*), polícia *m* (*PT*).

police officer *n* policial *m/f* (*BR*), polícia *m/f* (*PT*).

police record *n* ficha na polícia.

police state *n* estado policial.

police station *n* delegacia (de polícia) (*BR*), esquadra (*PT*).

policewoman [pə'liːswumən] (*irreg*) *n* policial *f* (feminina) (*BR*), mulher *f* polícia (*PT*).

policy ['pɔlɪsɪ] *n* política; (*also*: *insurance ~*) apólice *f*; (*of newspaper, company*) orientação *f*; **to take out a ~** (*INSURANCE*) fazer uma apólice *or* um contrato de seguro.

policy holder *n* segurado/a.

polio ['pəulɪəu] *n* poliomielite *f*, polio *f*.

Polish ['pəulɪʃ] *adj* polonês/esa ♦ *n* (*LING*) polonês *m*.

polish ['pɔlɪʃ] *n* (*for shoes*) graxa; (*for floor*) cera (para encerar); (*for nails*) esmalte *m*; (*shine*) brilho; (*fig*: *refinement*) refinamento, requinte *m* ♦ *vt* (*shoes*) engraxar; (*make shiny*) lustrar, dar brilho a; (*fig*: *improve*) refinar, polir.

polish off *vt* (*work*) dar os arremates a; (*food*) raspar.

polished ['pɔlɪʃt] *adj* (*fig*: *person*) culto; (: *manners*) refinado.

polite [pə'laɪt] *adj* educado; (*formal*) cortês; **it's not ~ to do that** é falta de educação fazer isso.

politely [pə'laɪtlɪ] *adv* educadamente.

politeness [pə'laɪtnɪs] *n* gentileza, cortesia.

politic ['pɔlɪtɪk] *adj* prudente.

political [pə'lɪtɪkl] *adj* político.

political asylum *n* asilo político; **to seek ~** pedir asilo político.

politically [pə'lɪtɪklɪ] *adv* politicamente.

politician [pɔlɪ'tɪʃən] *n* político.

politics ['pɔlɪtɪks] *npl* política.

polka ['pɔlkə] *n* polca.

polka dot *n* bolinha.

poll [pəul] *n* (*votes*) votação *f*; (*also*: *opinion ~*) pesquisa, sondagem *f* ♦ *vt* (*votes*) receber, obter; **to go to the ~s** (*voters*) ir às urnas; (*government*) convocar eleições.

pollen ['pɔlən] *n* pólen *m*.

NB: *European Portuguese adds the following consonants to certain words:* **b** (sú(b)dito, su(b)til); **c** (a(c)ção, a(c)cionista, a(c)to); **m** (inde(m)ne); **p** (ado(p)ção, ado(p)tar); *for further details see p. xiii.*

pollen count *n* contagem *f* de pólen.
pollination [pɔlɪ'neɪʃən] *n* polinização *f*.
polling ['pəulɪŋ] *n* (*BRIT*: *POL*) votação *f*; (*TEL*) apuração *f*.
polling booth (*BRIT*) *n* cabine *f* de votar.
polling day (*BRIT*) *n* dia *m* de eleição.
polling station (*BRIT*) *n* centro eleitoral.
pollute [pə'lu:t] *vt* poluir.
pollution [pə'lu:ʃən] *n* poluição *f*.
polo ['pəuləu] *n* (*sport*) pólo.
polo-neck *adj* de gola rolê ♦ *n* gola rolê.
poly ['pɔlɪ] (*BRIT*) *n abbr* = **polytechnic**.
polyester [pɔlɪ'ɛstə*] *n* poliéster *m*.
polyethylene [pɔlɪ'ɛθɪli:n] (*US*) *n* polietileno.
polygamy [pə'lɪgəmɪ] *n* poligamia.
Polynesia [pɔlɪ'ni:zɪə] *n* Polinésia.
Polynesian [pɔlɪ'ni:zɪən] *adj*, *n* polinésio/a.
polyp ['pɔlɪp] *n* (*MED*) pólipo.
polystyrene [pɔlɪ'staɪri:n] *n* isopor *m* ®.
polytechnic [pɔlɪ'tɛknɪk] *n* politécnico, escola politécnica.
polythene ['pɔlɪθi:n] (*BRIT*) *n* politeno.
polythene bag *n* bolsa de plástico.
polyurethane [pɔlɪ'ju:rəθeɪn] *n* poliuretano.
pomegranate ['pɔmɪgrænɪt] *n* (*fruit*) romã *f*.
pommel ['pɔml] *n* botão *m*; (*saddle*) maçaneta ♦ *vt* = **pummel**.
pomp [pɔmp] *n* pompa, fausto.
pompom ['pɔmpɔm] *n* pompom *m*.
pompon ['pɔmpɔn] *n* = **pompom**.
pompous ['pɔmpəs] *adj* pomposo.
pond [pɔnd] *n* (*natural*) lago pequeno; (*artificial*) tanque *m*.
ponder ['pɔndə*] *vt*, *vi* ponderar, meditar (sobre).
ponderous ['pɔndərəs] *adj* pesado.
pong [pɔŋ] (*BRIT*: *inf*) *n* fedor *m*, fartum *m* (*inf*), catinga (*inf*) ♦ *vi* feder.
pontiff ['pɔntɪf] *n* pontífice *m*.
pontificate [pɔn'tɪfɪkeɪt] *vi* (*fig*): **to ~ (about)** pontificar (sobre).
pontoon [pɔn'tu:n] *n* pontão *m*; (*BRIT*: *card game*) vinte-e-um *m*.
pony ['pəunɪ] *n* pônei *m*.
ponytail ['pəunɪteɪl] *n* rabo-de-cavalo.
pony trekking [-'trɛkɪŋ] (*BRIT*) *n* excursão *f* em pônei.
poodle ['pu:dl] *n* cão-d'água *m*.
pooh-pooh [pu:'pu:] *vt* desprezar.
pool [pu:l] *n* (*of rain*) poça, charco; (*pond*) lago; (*also*: *swimming ~*) piscina; (*billiards*) sinuca; (*sth shared*) fundo comum; (*money at cards*) bolo; (*COMM*: *consortium*) consórcio, pool *m*; (*US*: *monopoly trust*) truste *m* ♦ *vt* juntar; **(football) ~s** *npl* (*BRIT*) loteria esportiva (*BR*), totobola (*PT*); **typing** (*BRIT*) *or* **secretary** (*US*) **~** seção *f* de datilografia.
poor [puə*] *adj* pobre; (*bad*) inferior, mau ♦ *npl*: **the ~** os pobres.
poorly ['puəlɪ] *adj* adoentado, indisposto ♦ *adv* mal.
pop [pɔp] *n* (*sound*) estalo, estouro; (*MUS*) pop *m*; (*US*: *inf*: *father*) papai *m*; (*inf*: *lemonade*) bebida gasosa ♦ *vt* (*put*) pôr ♦ *vi* estourar; (*cork*) saltar; **she ~ped her head out of the window** ela meteu a cabeça fora da janela.
pop in *vi* dar um pulo.
pop out *vi* dar uma saída.
pop up *vi* surgir, aparecer inesperadamente.
pop concert *n* concerto pop.
popcorn ['pɔpkɔ:n] *n* pipoca.
pope [pəup] *n* papa *m*.
poplar ['pɔplə*] *n* álamo, choupo.
poplin ['pɔplɪn] *n* popeline *f*.
popper ['pɔpə*] (*BRIT*) *n* presilha.
poppy ['pɔpɪ] *n* papoula.
poppycock ['pɔpɪkɔk] (*inf*) *n* conversa fiada, papo furado.
popsicle ['pɔpsɪkl] ® (*US*) *n* picolé *m*.
populace ['pɔpjuləs] *n* povo.
popular ['pɔpjulə*] *adj* popular; (*fashionable*) badalado; **to be ~ (with)** (*person*) fazer sucesso (com); (*decision*) ser aplaudido (por).
popularity [pɔpju'lærɪtɪ] *n* popularidade *f*.
popularize ['pɔpjuləraɪz] *vt* popularizar; (*science*) vulgarizar.
populate ['pɔpjuleɪt] *vt* povoar.
population [pɔpju'leɪʃən] *n* população *f*.
population explosion *n* explosão *f* demográfica.
populous ['pɔpjuləs] *adj* populoso.
porcelain ['pɔ:slɪn] *n* porcelana.
porch [pɔ:tʃ] *n* pórtico; (*US*: *verandah*) varanda.
porcupine ['pɔ:kjupaɪn] *n* porco-espinho.
pore [pɔ:*] *n* poro ♦ *vi*: **to ~ over** examinar minuciosamente.
pork [pɔ:k] *n* carne *f* de porco.
pork chop *n* costeleta de porco.
pornographic [pɔ:nə'græfɪk] *adj* pornográfico.
pornography [pɔ:'nɔgrəfɪ] *n* pornografia.
porous ['pɔ:rəs] *adj* poroso.
porpoise ['pɔ:pəs] *n* golfinho, boto.
porridge ['pɔrɪdʒ] *n* mingau *m* (de aveia).
port [pɔ:t] *n* (*harbour*) porto; (*NAUT*: *left side*) bombordo; (*wine*) vinho do Porto; (*COMPUT*) porta, port *m* ♦ *cpd* portuário; **to ~** (*NAUT*) a bombordo; **~ of call** porto de escala.
portable ['pɔ:təbl] *adj* portátil.
portal ['pɔ:tl] *n* portal *m*.
portcullis [pɔ:t'kʌlɪs] *n* grade *f* levadiça.
portend [pɔ:'tɛnd] *vt* pressagiar.
portent ['pɔ:tɛnt] *n* presságio, portento.
porter ['pɔ:tə*] *n* (*for luggage*) carregador *m*; (*doorkeeper*) porteiro.
portfolio [pɔ:t'fəulɪəu] *n* pasta.
porthole ['pɔ:thəul] *n* vigia.
portico ['pɔ:tɪkəu] *n* pórtico.
portion ['pɔ:ʃən] *n* porção *f*, quinhão *m*; (*of food*) ração *f*.
portly ['pɔ:tlɪ] *adj* corpulento.
portrait ['pɔ:treɪt] *n* retrato.
portray [pɔ:'treɪ] *vt* retratar; (*in writing*) descrever.
portrayal [pɔ:'treɪəl] *n* representação *f*.
Portugal ['pɔ:tjugl] *n* Portugal *m* (*no article*).
Portuguese [pɔ:tju'gi:z] *adj* português/esa ♦ *n*

inv português/esa *m/f*; (LING) português *m*.
Portuguese man-of-war (*irreg*: *like* **man**) *n* (*jellyfish*) urtiga-do-mar *f*, caravela.
pose [pəuz] *n* postura, pose *f*; (*pej*) pose, afetação *f* ♦ *vi* posar; (*pretend*): **to ~ as** fazer-se passar por ♦ *vt* (*question*) pôr; **to strike a ~** fazer pose.
poser ['pəuzə*] *n* problema *m*, abacaxi *m* (BR: *inf*); (*person*) = **poseur**.
poseur [pəu'zə:*] (*pej*) *n* posudo/a, pessoa afetada.
posh [pɔʃ] (*inf*) *adj* fino, chique; **to talk ~** falar com sotaque fino.
position [pə'zɪʃən] *n* posição *f*; (*job*) cargo ♦ *vt* colocar, situar; **to be in a ~ to do sth** estar em posição de fazer algo.
positive ['pɔzɪtɪv] *adj* positivo; (*certain*) certo; (*definite*) definitivo; **I'm ~** tenho certeza absoluta.
posse ['pɔsɪ] (US) *n* pelotão *m* de civis armados.
possess [pə'zɛs] *vt* possuir; **like one ~ed** como um possuído do demônio; **whatever can have ~ed you?** o que é que te deu?
possession [pə'zɛʃən] *n* posse *f*, possessão *f*; (*object*) bem *m*, posse; **to take ~ of sth** tomar posse de algo.
possessive [pə'zɛsɪv] *adj* possessivo.
possessively [pə'zɛsɪvlɪ] *adv* possessivamente.
possessor [pə'zɛsə*] *n* possuidor(a) *m/f*.
possibility [pɔsɪ'bɪlɪtɪ] *n* possibilidade *f*.
possible ['pɔsɪbl] *adj* possível; **it is ~ to do it** é possível fazê-lo; **as far as ~** tanto quanto possível, na medida do possível; **if ~** se for possível; **as big as ~** o maior possível.
possibly ['pɔsɪblɪ] *adv* (*perhaps*) pode ser, talvez; **if you ~ can** se lhe for possível; **could you ~ come over?** será qué você podia vir para ca?; **I cannot ~ come** estou impossibilitado de vir.
post [pəust] *n* (BRIT: *mail*) correio; (*job, situation*) cargo, posto; (*pole*) poste *m*; (*trading ~*) entreposto comercial ♦ *vt* (BRIT: *send by ~*) pôr no correio; (: MIL) nomear; (*bills*) afixar, pregar; (BRIT: *appoint*): **to ~ to** destinar a; **by ~** (BRIT) pelo correio; **by return of ~** (BRIT) na volta do correio; **to keep sb ~ed** manter alguém informado.
post- [pəust] *prefix* pós...; **~1990** depois de 1990.
postage ['pəustɪdʒ] *n* porte *m*, franquia; **~ paid** porte pago; **~ prepaid** (US) franquia de porte.
postage stamp *n* selo postal.
postal ['pəustəl] *adj* postal.
postal order *n* vale *m* postal.
postbag ['pəustbæg] (BRIT) *n* mala de correio; (*postman's*) sacola.
postbox ['pəustbɔks] (BRIT) *n* caixa de correio.
postcard ['pəustkɑ:d] *n* cartão *m* postal.
postcode ['pəustkəud] (BRIT) *n* código postal, ≈ CEP *m* (BR).
postdate [pəust'deɪt] *vt* (*cheque*) pós-datar.
poster ['pəustə*] *n* cartaz *m*; (*as decoration*) pôster *m*.
poste restante [pəust'rɛstɑ̃:nt] (BRIT) *n* posta-restante *f*.
posterior [pɔs'tɪərɪə*] (*inf*) *n* traseiro, nádegas *fpl*.
posterity [pɔs'tɛrɪtɪ] *n* posteridade *f*.
poster paint *n* guache *m*.
post exchange (US) *n* (MIL) loja do exército.
post-free (BRIT) *adj* franco de porte.
postgraduate [pəust'grædjuət] *n* pós-graduado/a.
posthumous ['pɔstjuməs] *adj* póstumo.
posthumously ['pɔstjuməslɪ] *adv* postumamente.
posting ['pəustɪŋ] (BRIT) *n* nomeação *f*.
postman ['pəustmən] (*irreg*) *n* carteiro.
postmark ['pəustmɑ:k] *n* carimbo do correio.
postmaster ['pəustmɑ:stə*] *n* agente *m* (BR) *or* chefe *m* (PT) do correio.
Postmaster General *n* ≈ Superintendente *m* Geral dos Correios.
postmen ['pəustmɛn] *npl of* **postman**.
postmistress ['pəustmɪstrɪs] *n* agente *f* (BR) *or* chefe *f* (PT) do correio.
post-mortem [-'mɔ:təm] *n* autópsia.
postnatal [pəust'neɪtl] *adj* pós-natal.
post office *n* (*building*) agência do correio, correio; (*organization*) Empresa Nacional dos Correios e Telégrafos (BR), Correios, Telégrafos e Telefones (PT).
post office box *n* caixa postal.
post-paid (BRIT) *adj* porte pago.
postpone [pəs'pəun] *vt* adiar.
postponement [pəs'pəunmənt] *n* adiamento.
postscript ['pəustskrɪpt] *n* pós-escrito.
postulate ['pɔstjuleɪt] *vt* postular.
posture ['pɔstʃə*] *n* postura, atitude *f* ♦ *vi* posar.
postwar [pəust'wɔ:*] *adj* de após-guerra.
posy ['pəuzɪ] *n* ramalhete *m*.
pot [pɔt] *n* (*for cooking*) panela; (*for flowers*) vaso; (*for jam, piece of pottery*) pote *m*; (*inf*: *marijuana*) maconha ♦ *vt* (*plant*) plantar em vaso; (*conserve*) pôr em conserva; **to go to ~** (*country, economy*) arruinar-se, degringolar; **the town has gone to ~** a cidade mixou; **~s of ...** (BRIT: *inf*) ... aos potes.
potash ['pɔtæʃ] *n* potassa.
potassium [pə'tæsɪəm] *n* potássio.
potato [pə'teɪtəu] (*pl* **~es**) *n* batata.
potato crisps (US **potato chips**) *npl* batatinhas *fpl* fritas.
potato flour *n* fécula (de batata).
potato peeler *n* descascador *m* de batatas.
potbellied ['pɔtbɛlɪd] *adj* barrigudo.
potency ['pəutənsɪ] *n* potência; (*of drink*) teor *m* alcoólico.
potent ['pəutnt] *adj* potente, poderoso; (*drink*) forte.

NB*: European Portuguese adds the following consonants to certain words:* **b** (sú(b)dito, su(b)til); **c** (a(c)ção, a(c)cionista, a(c)to); **m** (inde(m)ne); **p** (ado(p)ção, ado(p)tar); *for further details see p. xiii.*

potentate ['pəutnteɪt] *n* potentado.
potential [pə'tɛnʃl] *adj* potencial, latente ♦ *n* potencial *m*; **to have ~** ser promissor.
potentially [pə'tɛnʃəlɪ] *adv* potencialmente.
pothole ['pɔthəul] *n* (*in road*) buraco; (*BRIT*: *underground*) caldeirão *m*, cova.
potholer ['pɔthəulə*] (*BRIT*) *n* espeleologista *m/f*.
potholing ['pɔthəulɪŋ] (*BRIT*) *n*: **to go ~** dedicar-se à espeleologia.
potion ['pəuʃən] *n* poção *f*.
potluck [pɔt'lʌk] *n*: **to take ~** contentar-se com o que houver.
potpourri [pəu'puri:] *n* potpourri *m* (*de pétalas e folhas secas para perfumar o ambiente*).
pot roast *n* carne *f* assada.
potshot ['pɔtʃɔt] *n*: **to take a ~ at sth** atirar em algo a esmo.
potted ['pɔtɪd] *adj* (*food*) em conserva; (*plant*) de vaso; (*fig*: *shortened*) resumido.
potter ['pɔtə*] *n* (*artistic*) ceramista *m/f*; (*artisan*) oleiro/a ♦ *vi* (*BRIT*): **to ~ around, ~ about** ocupar-se com pequenos trabalhos; **~'s wheel** roda *or* torno de oleiro.
pottery ['pɔtərɪ] *n* cerâmica, olaria; **a piece of ~** uma cerâmica.
potty ['pɔtɪ] *adj* (*BRIT*: *inf*: *mad*) maluco, doido ♦ *n* penico.
potty-training *n* treino (da criança) para o uso do urinol.
pouch [pautʃ] *n* (*ZOOL*) bolsa; (*for tobacco*) tabaqueira.
pouf(fe) [pu:f] *n* pufe *m*.
poultice ['pəultis] *n* cataplasma.
poultry ['pəultrɪ] *n* aves *fpl* domésticas.
poultry farm *n* granja avícola.
poultry farmer *n* avicultor(a) *m/f*.
pounce [pauns] *vi*: **to ~ on** lançar-se sobre ♦ *n* salto, arremetida.
pound [paund] *n* libra (*weight = 453g, 16 ounces; money = 100 pence*); (*for dogs*) canil *m*; (*for cars*) depósito ♦ *vt* (*beat*) socar, esmurrar; (*crush*) triturar ♦ *vi* (*beat*) dar pancadas; **half a ~ (of)** meia libra (de); **a five-~ note** uma nota de cinco libras.
pounding ['paundɪŋ] *n*: **to take a ~** (*fig*) levar uma surra.
pound sterling *n* libra esterlina.
pour [pɔ:*] *vt* despejar; (*tea*) servir ♦ *vi* fluir, correr; (*rain*) chover a cântaros.
  pour away *vt* esvaziar, decantar.
  pour in *vi*: **to come ~ing in** (*water, people*) entrar numa enxurrada; (*letters*) chegar numa enxurrada.
  pour off *vt* esvaziar, decantar.
  pour out *vi* (*people*) sair aos borbotões ♦ *vt* (*drink*) servir; (*water etc*) esvaziar.
pouring ['pɔ:rɪŋ] *adj*: **~ rain** chuva torrencial.
pout [paut] *vi* fazer beicinho *or* biquinho.
poverty ['pɔvətɪ] *n* pobreza, miséria.
poverty-stricken *adj* indigente, necessitado.
poverty trap (*BRIT*) *n* armadilha da pobreza.
POW *n abbr* = **prisoner of war**.
powder ['paudə*] *n* pó *m*; (*face ~*) pó-de-arroz *m*; (*gun~*) pólvora ♦ *vt* pulverizar; (*face*) empoar, passar pó em; **to ~ one's nose** empoar-se; (*euphemism*) ir ao banheiro; **~ed milk** leite *m* em pó.
powder compact *n* estojo (de pó-de-arroz).
powder puff *n* esponja de pó-de-arroz.
powder room *n* toucador *m*, banheiro de senhoras.
powdery ['paudərɪ] *adj* poeirento.
power ['pauə*] *n* poder *m*; (*strength*) força; (*nation*) potência; (*ability*, *POL*: *of party, leader*) poder, poderio; (*of speech, thought*) faculdade *f*; (*MATH, TECH*) potência; (*ELEC*) força ♦ *vt* (*ELEC*) alimentar; (*engine, machine*) acionar; (*car, plane*) propulsionar; **to do all in one's ~ to help sb** fazer tudo que tiver ao seu alcance para ajudar alguém; **the world ~s** as grandes potências; **to be in ~** estar no poder; **~ of attorney** procuração *f*.
powerboat ['pauəbəut] (*BRIT*) *n* barco a motor.
power cut (*BRIT*) *n* corte *m* de energia, blecaute *m* (*BR*).
power-driven *adj* movido a motor; (*ELEC*) elétrico.
powered ['pauəd] *adj*: **~ by** movido a; **nuclear-~ submarine** submarino nuclear.
power failure *n* deficiência de força.
powerful ['pauəful] *adj* poderoso; (*engine*) potente; (*build*) vigoroso; (*emotion*) intenso.
powerhouse ['pauəhaus] (*irreg*) *n* (*fig*: *person*) poço de energia; **a ~ of ideas** um poço de idéias.
powerless ['pauəlɪs] *adj* impotente.
power line *n* fio de alta tensão.
power point (*BRIT*) *n* tomada.
power station *n* central *f* elétrica.
power steering *n* direção *f* hidráulica.
powwow ['pauwau] *n* reunião *f*.
pox [pɔks] (*inf*) *n* sífilis *f*; *see also* **chickenpox**; **smallpox**.
pp *abbr* (= *per procurationem*: *by proxy*) p.p.
p&p (*BRIT*) *abbr* (= *postage and packing*) porte e embalagem.
PPE (*BRIT*) *n abbr* (*SCH*) = **philosophy, politics and economics**.
PPS *n abbr* (= *post postscriptum*) PPS; (*BRIT*: = *parliamentary private secretary*) *parlamentário no serviço de um ministro*.
PQ (*CANADA*) *abbr* = **Province of Quebec**.
PR *n abbr* = **proportional representation**; **public relations** ♦ *abbr* (*US*: *POST*) = **Puerto Rico**.
Pr. *abbr* (= *prince*) Princ.
practicability [præktɪkə'bɪlɪtɪ] *n* viabilidade *f*.
practicable ['præktɪkəbl] *adj* (*scheme*) praticável, viável.
practical ['præktɪkl] *adj* prático.
practicality [præktɪ'kælɪtɪ] *n* (*of plan*) viabilidade *f*; (*of person*) índole *f* prática; **practicalities** *npl* aspectos *mpl* práticos.
practical joke *n* brincadeira, peça.
practically ['præktɪkəlɪ] *adv* (*almost*) praticamente.

practice ['præktɪs] *n* (*habit*) costume *m*, hábito; (*exercise*) prática; (*of profession*) exercício; (*training*) treinamento; (*MED*) consultório ♦ *vt*, *vi* (*US*) = **practise; in ~** (*in reality*) na prática; **out of ~** destreinado; **it's common ~** é comum; **to put sth into ~** pôr algo em prática; **to set up in ~** abrir consultório.
practice match *n* jogo de treinamento.
practise ['præktɪs] (*US* **practice**) *vt* praticar; (*profession*) exercer; (*train at*) treinar ♦ *vi* (*doctor*, *lawyer*) ter consultório; (*train*) treinar, praticar.
practised ['præktɪst] (*BRIT*) *adj* (*person*) experiente, experimentado; (*performance*) competente; (*liar*) contumaz; **with a ~ eye** com olhar de entendedor.
practising ['præktɪsɪŋ] *adj* (*Christian etc*) praticante; (*lawyer*) que exerce; (*homosexual*) assumido.
practitioner [præk'tɪʃənə*] *n* praticante *m/f*; (*MED*) médico/a.
pragmatic [præg'mætɪk] *adj* pragmático.
Prague [prɑːg] *n* Praga.
prairie ['prɛərɪ] *n* campina, pradaria.
praise [preɪz] *n* louvor *m*, elogio ♦ *vt* elogiar, louvar.
praiseworthy ['preɪzwəːðɪ] *adj* louvável, digno de elogio.
pram [præm] (*BRIT*) *n* carrinho de bebê.
prance [prɑːns] *vi* (*horse*) curvetear, fazer cabriolas.
prank [præŋk] *n* travessura, peça.
prattle ['prætl] *vi* tagarelar; (*child*) balbuciar.
prawn [prɔːn] *n* pitu *m*; (*small*) camarão *m*.
pray [preɪ] *vi* rezar.
prayer [prɛə*] *n* oração *f*, prece *f*; (*entreaty*) súplica, rogo.
prayer book *n* missal *m*, livro de orações.
pre- ['priː] *prefix* pré-; **~1970** antes de 1970.
preach [priːtʃ] *vt*, *vi* pregar; **to ~ at sb** fazer sermões a alguém.
preacher ['priːtʃə*] *n* pregador(a) *m/f*; (*US*: *clergyman*) pastor *m*.
preamble [prɪ'æmbl] *n* preâmbulo.
prearranged [priːə'reɪndʒd] *adj* combinado de antemão.
precarious [prɪ'kɛərɪəs] *adj* precário.
precaution [prɪ'kɔːʃən] *n* precaução *f*.
precautionary [prɪ'kɔːʃənrɪ] *adj* (*measure*) de precaução.
precede [prɪ'siːd] *vt*, *vi* preceder.
precedence ['prɛsɪdəns] *n* precedência; (*priority*) prioridade *f*.
precedent ['prɛsɪdənt] *n* precedente *m*; **to establish** *or* **set a ~** estabelecer *or* abrir precedente.
preceding [prɪ'siːdɪŋ] *adj* precedente.
precept ['priːsɛpt] *n* preceito.
precinct ['priːsɪŋkt] *n* (*round church*) recinto; (*US*: *district*) distrito policial; **~s** *npl* arredores *mpl*; **shopping ~** (*BRIT*) zona comercial.
precious ['prɛʃəs] *adj* precioso; (*stylized*) afetado ♦ *adv* (*inf*): **~ little** muito pouco, pouquíssimo; **your ~ dog** (*ironic*) seu adorado cãozinho.
precipice ['prɛsɪpɪs] *n* precipício.
precipitate [*adj* prɪ'sɪpɪtɪt, *vt* prɪ'sɪpɪteɪt] *adj* (*hasty*) precipitado, apressado ♦ *vt* (*hasten*) precipitar, acelerar; (*bring about*) causar.
precipitation [prɪsɪpɪ'teɪʃən] *n* precipitação *f*.
precipitous [prɪ'sɪpɪtəs] *adj* (*steep*) íngreme, escarpado.
précis ['preɪsiː, *pl* 'preɪsiːz] *n inv* resumo, sumário.
precise [prɪ'saɪs] *adj* exato, preciso; (*person*) escrupuloso, meticuloso.
precisely [prɪ'saɪslɪ] *adv* exatamente.
precision [prɪ'sɪʒən] *n* precisão *f*.
preclude [prɪ'kluːd] *vt* excluir; **to ~ sb from doing** impedir que alguém faça.
precocious [prɪ'kəuʃəs] *adj* precoce.
preconceived [priːkən'siːvd] *adj* (*idea*) preconcebido.
preconception [priːkən'sɛpʃən] *n* preconceito.
precondition [priːkən'dɪʃən] *n* condição *f* prévia.
precursor [priː'kəːsə*] *n* precursor(a) *m/f*.
predate ['priː'deɪt] *vt* (*precede*) preceder.
predator ['prɛdətə*] *n* predador *m*.
predatory ['prɛdətərɪ] *adj* predatório, rapace.
predecessor ['priːdɪsɛsə*] *n* predecessor(a) *m/f*, antepassado/a.
predestination [priːdɛstɪ'neɪʃən] *n* predestinação *f*, destino.
predetermine [priːdɪ'təːmɪn] *vt* predeterminar, predispor.
predicament [prɪ'dɪkəmənt] *n* situação *f* difícil, apuro.
predicate ['prɛdɪkɪt] *n* (*LING*) predicado.
predict [prɪ'dɪkt] *vt* prever, predizer, prognosticar.
predictable [prɪ'dɪktəbl] *adj* previsível.
predictably [prɪ'dɪktəblɪ] *adv* (*behave*, *react*) de maneira previsível; **~ she didn't come** como era de se esperar, ela não veio.
prediction [prɪ'dɪkʃən] *n* previsão *f*, prognóstico.
predispose [priːdɪs'pəuz] *vt* predispor.
predominance [prɪ'dɔmɪnəns] *n* predominância, preponderância.
predominant [prɪ'dɔmɪnənt] *adj* predominante, preponderante.
predominantly [prɪ'dɔmɪnəntlɪ] *adv* (*for the most part*) na maioria; (*above all*) sobretudo.
predominate [prɪ'dɔmɪneɪt] *vi* predominar.
pre-eminent *adj* preeminente.
pre-empt [-ɛmt] (*BRIT*) *vt* (*obtain*) adquirir por preempção *or* de antemão; (*fig*): **to ~ sb/sth** antecipar-se a alguém/antecipar algo.
pre-emptive [-ɛmtɪv] *adj*: **~ strike** ataque *m* preventivo.
preen [priːn] *vt*: **to ~ itself** (*bird*) limpar e

NB: *European Portuguese adds the following consonants to certain words:* **b** (sú(b)dito, su(b)til); **c** (a(c)ção, a(c)cionista, a(c)to); **m** (inde(m)ne); **p** (ado(p)ção, ado(p)tar); *for further details see p. xiii.*

alisar as penas (com o bico); **to ~ o.s.** enfeitar-se, envaidecer-se.
prefab ['pri:fæb] *n* casa pré-fabricada.
prefabricated [pri:'fæbrɪkeɪtɪd] *adj* pré-fabricado.
preface ['prɛfəs] *n* prefácio.
prefect ['pri:fɛkt] *n* (*BRIT*: *SCH*) monitor(a) *m/f*, tutor(a) *m/f*; (*in Brazil*) prefeito/a.
prefer [prɪ'fə:*] *vt* preferir; (*LAW*): **to ~ charges** intentar uma ação judicial; **to ~ coffee to tea** preferir café a chá.
preferable ['prɛfrəbl] *adj* preferível.
preferably ['prɛfrəblɪ] *adv* de preferência.
preference ['prɛfrəns] *n* preferência; **in ~ to sth** de preferência a algo.
preference shares (*BRIT*) *npl* ações *fpl* preferenciais.
preferential [prɛfə'rɛnʃəl] *adj* preferencial; **~ treatment** preferência.
preferred stock [prɪ'fə:d-] (*US*) *npl* ações *fpl* preferenciais.
prefix ['pri:fɪks] *n* prefixo.
pregnancy ['prɛgnənsɪ] *n* gravidez *f*.
pregnant ['prɛgnənt] *adj* grávida; **3 months ~** grávida de 3 meses; **~ with** rico de, cheio de.
prehistoric [pri:hɪs'tɔrɪk] *adj* pré-histórico.
prehistory [pri:'hɪstərɪ] *n* pré-história.
prejudge [pri:'dʒʌdʒ] *vt* fazer um juízo antecipado de, prejulgar.
prejudice ['prɛdʒudɪs] *n* (*bias*) preconceito; (*harm*) prejuízo ♦ *vt* (*predispose*) predispor; (*harm*) prejudicar; **to ~ sb in favour of/against** predispor alguém a favor de/contra.
prejudiced ['prɛdʒudɪst] *adj* (*person*) cheio de preconceitos; (*view*) parcial, preconcebido; **to be ~ against sb/sth** estar com prevenção contra alguém/algo.
prelate ['prɛlət] *n* prelado.
preliminaries [prɪ'lɪmɪnərɪz] *npl* preliminares *fpl*.
preliminary [prɪ'lɪmɪnərɪ] *adj* preliminar, prévio.
prelude ['prɛlju:d] *n* prelúdio.
premarital [pri:'mærɪtl] *adj* pré-nupcial.
premature ['prɛmətʃuə*] *adj* prematuro, precoce; **to be ~ (in doing sth)** precipitar-se (em fazer algo).
premeditated [pri:'mɛdɪteɪtɪd] *adj* premeditado.
premeditation [pri:mɛdɪ'teɪʃən] *n* premeditação *f*.
premenstrual [pri:'mɛnstruəl] *adj* pré-menstrual.
premenstrual tension *n* tensão *f* pré-menstrual.
premier ['prɛmɪə*] *adj* primeiro, principal ♦ *n* (*POL*) primeiro-ministro/primeira-ministra.
première ['prɛmɪɛə*] *n* estréia.
premise ['prɛmɪs] *n* premissa; **~s** *npl* local *m*; (*house*) casa; (*shop*) loja; **on the ~s** no local; **business ~s** local utilizado para fins comerciais.
premium ['pri:mɪəm] *n* prêmio, recompensa; (*COMM*) prêmio; **to be at a ~** ser difícil de obter; **to sell at a ~** (*shares*) vender acima do par.
premium bond (*BRIT*) *n obrigação qué dá direito a prêmio mediante sorteio.*
premium deal *n* (*COMM*) oferta especial.
premium gasoline (*US*) *n* gasolina azul *or* super.
premonition [prɛmə'nɪʃən] *n* presságio, pressentimento.
preoccupation [pri:ɔkju'peɪʃən] *n* preocupação *f*.
preoccupied [pri:'ɔkjupaɪd] *adj* (*worried*) preocupado, apreensivo; (*absorbed*) absorto.
prep [prɛp] *adj abbr*: **~ school = preparatory school** ♦ *n* (*SCH*: = *preparation*) deveres *mpl*.
prepackaged [pri:'pækɪdʒd] *adj* embalado para venda ao consumidor.
prepaid [pri:'peɪd] *adj* com porte pago.
preparation [prɛpə'reɪʃən] *n* preparação *f*; **~s** *npl* preparativos *mpl*; **in ~ for** em preparação para.
preparatory [prɪ'pærətərɪ] *adj* preparatório; **~ to** antes de.
preparatory school *n* escola preparatória.
prepare [prɪ'pɛə*] *vt* preparar ♦ *vi*: **to ~ for** preparar-se *or* aprontar-se para; (*make preparations*) fazer preparativos para.
prepared [prɪ'pɛəd] *adj*: **~ to** pronto para, disposto a.
preponderance [prɪ'pɔndərns] *n* preponderância, predomínio.
preposition [prɛpə'zɪʃən] *n* preposição *f*.
prepossessing [pri:pə'zɛsɪŋ] *adj* atraente.
preposterous [prɪ'pɔstərəs] *adj* absurdo, disparatado.
prep school *n* = **preparatory school**.
prerecorded ['pri:rɪ'kɔ:dɪd] *adj* pré-gravado.
prerequisite [pri:'rɛkwɪzɪt] *n* pré-requisito, condição *f* prévia.
prerogative [prɪ'rɔgətɪv] *n* prerrogativa.
presbyterian [prɛzbɪ'tɪərɪən] *adj*, *n* presbiteriano/a.
presbytery ['prɛzbɪtərɪ] *n* presbitério.
preschool ['pri:'sku:l] *adj* (*education*) pré-escolar; (*child*) de idade pré-escolar.
prescribe [prɪ'skraɪb] *vt* prescrever; (*MED*) receitar; **~d books** (*BRIT*: *SCH*) livros *mpl* requisitados.
prescription [prɪ'skrɪpʃən] *n* prescrição *f*, ordem *f*; (*MED*) receita; **to make up** (*BRIT*) *or* **fill** (*US*) **a ~** aviar uma receita; **"only available on ~"** "venda exclusivamente mediante receita médica".
prescription charges (*BRIT*) *npl* participação *f* no preço das receitas médicas.
prescriptive [prɪ'skrɪptɪv] *adj* prescritivo.
presence ['prɛzns] *n* presença; **~ of mind** presença de espírito.
present [*adj*, *n* 'prɛznt, *vt* prɪ'zɛnt] *adj* (*in attendance*) presente; (*current*) atual ♦ *n* (*gift*) presente *m*; (*also*: **~** *tense*) presente *m* ♦ *vt* (*introduce*) apresentar; (*expound*) expor; (*prize*) entregar; (*THEATRE*) representar; **to ~ sb with sth** (*as gift*) presentear

alguém com algo; (*as prize etc*) entregar algo a alguém; **at ~** no momento, agora; **for the ~** por enquanto; **to be ~ at** estar presente a, presenciar; **to give sb a ~** presentear alguém.
presentable [prɪ'zɛntəbl] *adj* apresentável.
presentation [prɛzn'teɪʃən] *n* apresentação *f*; (*gift*) presente *m*; (*ceremony*) entrega; (*of case*) exposição *f*; (*THEATRE*) representação *f*; **on ~ of** mediante apresentação de.
present-day ['prɛznt'deɪ] *adj* atual, de hoje.
presenter [prɪ'zɛntə*] (*BRIT*) *n* (*RADIO, TV*) apresentador(a) *m/f*.
presently ['prɛzntlɪ] *adv* (*soon*) logo, em breve; (*now*) atualmente.
preservation [prɛzə'veɪʃən] *n* conservação *f*, preservação *f*.
preservative [prɪ'zəːvətɪv] *n* preservativo.
preserve [prɪ'zəːv] *vt* (*keep safe*) preservar, proteger; (*maintain*) conservar, manter; (*food*) pôr em conserva; (*in salt*) conservar em sal, salgar ♦ *n* (*for game*) reserva de caça, coutada; (*often pl: jam*) geléia; (*: fruit*) compota, conserva.
preshrunk ['priː'ʃrʌŋk] *adj* pré-encolhido.
preside [prɪ'zaɪd] *vi* presidir.
presidency ['prɛzɪdənsɪ] *n* presidência.
president ['prɛzɪdənt] *n* presidente/a *m/f*.
presidential [prɛzɪ'dɛnʃl] *adj* presidencial.
press [prɛs] *n* (*tool, machine*) prensa; (*printer's*) imprensa, prelo; (*newspapers*) imprensa; (*crowd*) turba, apinhamento; (*of hand*) apertão *m* ♦ *vt* (*push*) apertar; (*squeeze: fruit etc*) espremer; (*clothes: iron*) passar; (*TECH*) prensar; (*harry*) assediar; (*insist*): **to ~ sth on sb** insistir para que alguém aceite algo; (*urge*): **to ~ sb to do** *or* **into doing sth** impelir *or* pressionar alguém a fazer algo ♦ *vi* (*squeeze*) apertar; (*pressurize*) fazer pressão, pressionar; **we are ~ed for time** estamos com pouco tempo; **to ~ for sth** pressionar por algo; **to ~ sb for an answer** pressionar alguém por uma resposta; **to ~ charges against sb** (*LAW*) intentar ação judicial contra alguém; **to go to ~** (*newspaper*) ir para o prelo; **to be in the ~** estar no prelo; **to appear in the ~** sair no jornal.
press on *vi* continuar.
press agency *n* agência de informações.
press clipping *n* recorte *m* de jornal.
press conference *n* entrevista coletiva (para a imprensa).
press cutting *n* recorte *m* de jornal.
press-gang *n pelotão de recrutamento da marinha* ♦ *vt*: **to be ~ed into doing** ser impelido a fazer.
pressing ['prɛsɪŋ] *adj* urgente ♦ *n* ação *f* (*or* serviço *etc*) de passar roupa.
pressman ['prɛsmæn] (*irreg*) *n* jornalista *m*.
press release *n* release *m or* comunicado à imprensa.
press stud (*BRIT*) *n* botão *m* de pressão.
press-up (*BRIT*) *n* flexão *f*.
pressure ['prɛʃə*] *n* pressão *f* ♦ *vt* = **to put ~ on**; **to put ~ on sb (to do sth)** pressionar alguém (a fazer algo).
pressure cooker *n* panela de pressão.
pressure gauge *n* manômetro.
pressure group *n* grupo de pressão.
pressurize ['prɛʃəraɪz] *vt* pressurizar; (*BRIT: fig*): **to ~ sb (into doing sth)** pressionar alguém (a fazer algo).
pressurized ['prɛʃəraɪzd] *adj* pressurizado.
Prestel ['prɛstɛl] ® *n serviço de videotexto*.
prestige [prɛs'tiːʒ] *n* prestígio.
prestigious [prɛs'tɪdʒəs] *adj* prestigioso.
presumably [prɪ'zjuːməblɪ] *adv* presumivelmente, provavelmente; **~ he did it** é de se presumir que ele o fez.
presume [prɪ'zjuːm] *vt* presumir, supor; **to ~ to do** (*dare*) ousar fazer, atrever-se a fazer; (*set out to*) pretender fazer.
presumption [prɪ'zʌmpʃən] *n* suposição *f*; (*pretension*) presunção *f*; (*boldness*) atrevimento, audácia.
presumptuous [prɪ'zʌmpʃəs] *adj* presunçoso.
presuppose [priːsə'pəuz] *vt* pressupor, implicar.
pre-tax *adj* antes de impostos.
pretence [prɪ'tɛns] (*US* **pretense**) *n* (*claim*) pretensão *f*; (*display*) ostentação *f*; (*pretext*) pretexto; (*make-believe*) fingimento; **on the ~ of** sob o pretexto de; **to make a ~ of doing** fingir fazer.
pretend [prɪ'tɛnd] *vt* fingir ♦ *vi* (*feign*) fingir; (*claim*): **to ~ to sth** aspirar a *or* pretender a algo; **to ~ to do** fingir fazer.
pretense [prɪ'tɛns] (*US*) *n* = **pretence**.
pretension [prɪ'tɛnʃən] *n* (*presumption*) presunção *f*; (*claim*) pretensão *f*; **to have no ~s to sth/to being sth** não ter pretensão a algo/ a ser algo.
pretentious [prɪ'tɛnʃəs] *adj* pretensioso, presunçoso.
preterite ['prɛtərɪt] *n* pretérito.
pretext ['priːtɛkst] *n* pretexto; **on** *or* **under the ~ of doing sth** sob o *or* a pretexto de fazer algo.
pretty ['prɪtɪ] *adj* bonito ♦ *adv* (*quite*) bastante.
prevail [prɪ'veɪl] *vi* (*win*) triunfar; (*be current*) imperar; (*be usual*) prevalecer, vigorar; (*persuade*): **to ~ (up)on sb to do sth** persuadir alguém a fazer algo.
prevailing [prɪ'veɪlɪŋ] *adj* (*dominant*) predominante; (*usual*) corrente.
prevalent ['prɛvələnt] *adj* (*dominant*) predominante; (*usual*) corrente; (*fashionable*) da moda.
prevarication [prɪværɪ'keɪʃən] *n* embromação *f*.
prevent [prɪ'vɛnt] *vt*: **to ~ sb from doing sth** impedir alguém de fazer algo.

***NB**: European Portuguese adds the following consonants to certain words:* **b** (sú(b)dito, su(b)til); **c** (a(c)ção, a(c)cionista, a(c)to); **m** (inde(m)ne); **p** (ado(p)ção, ado(p)tar); *for further details see p. xiii.*

preventable [prɪ'vɛntəbl] *adj* evitável.
preventative [prɪ'vɛntətɪv] *adj* preventivo.
prevention [prɪ'vɛnʃən] *n* prevenção *f*.
preventive [prɪ'vɛntɪv] *adj* preventivo.
preview ['pri:vju:] *n* (*of film*) pré-estréia; (*fig*) antecipação *f*.
previous ['pri:vɪəs] *adj* (*experience, notice*) prévio; (*earlier*) anterior; **I have a ~ engagement** já tenho compromisso; **~ to doing** antes de fazer.
previously ['pri:vɪəslɪ] *adv* (*in advance*) previamente, antecipadamente; (*earlier*) antes, anteriormente.
prewar [pri:'wɔ:*] *adj* anterior à guerra.
prey [preɪ] *n* presa ♦ *vi*: **to ~ on** viver às custas de; (*feed on*) alimentar-se de; (*plunder*) saquear, pilhar; **it was ~ing on his mind** preocupava-o, atormentava-o.
price [praɪs] *n* preço; (*of shares*) cotação *f* ♦ *vt* (*goods*) fixar o preço de; **what is the ~ of ...?** qual é o preço de ...?, quanto é ...?; **to go up** *or* **rise in ~** subir de preço; **to put a ~ on sth** determinar o preço de algo; **to be ~d out of the market** (*article*) não ser competitivo; (*producer, country*) perder freguesia por causa de preços muito altos; **what ~ his promises now?** que valem suas promessas agora?; **he regained his freedom, but at a ~** ele recobrou a liberdade, mas pagou caro; **at any ~** por qualquer preço.
price control *n* controle *m* de preços.
price-cutting *n* corte *m* de preços.
priceless ['praɪslɪs] *adj* inestimável; (*inf*: *amusing*) impagável.
price list *n* lista *or* tabela de preços.
price range *n* gama de preços; **it's within my ~** está dentro do meu preço.
price tag *n* etiqueta de preço.
price war *n* guerra de preços.
pricey ['praɪsɪ] (*inf*) *adj* salgado.
prick [prɪk] *n* picada; (*with pin*) alfinetada; (*inf!*: *penis*) pau *m* (*!*); (*inf!*: *person*) filho-da-puta *m* (*!*) ♦ *vt* picar; **to ~ up one's ears** aguçar os ouvidos.
prickle ['prɪkl] *n* (*sensation*) comichão, ardência; (*BOT*) espinho.
prickly ['prɪklɪ] *adj* espinhoso; (*fig*: *person*) irritadiço.
prickly heat *n* brotoeja.
prickly pear *n* opúncia.
pride [praɪd] *n* orgulho; (*pej*) soberba ♦ *vt*: **to ~ o.s. on** orgulhar-se de; **to take (a) ~ in** orgulhar-se de, sentir orgulho em; **to have ~ of place** (*BRIT*) ocupar o lugar de destaque, ter destaque; **her ~ and joy** seu tesouro.
priest [pri:st] *n* sacerdote *m*, padre *m*.
priestess ['pri:stɪs] *n* sacerdotisa.
priesthood ['pri:sthud] *n* (*practice*) sacerdócio; (*priests*) clero.
prig [prɪg] *n* pedante *m/f*.
prim [prɪm] *adj* (*formal*) empertigado; (*affected*) afetado.
prima facie ['praɪmə'feɪʃɪ] *adj*: **to have a ~ case** (*LAW*) ter uma causa convincente.
primarily ['praɪmərɪlɪ] *adv* (*above all*) principalmente; (*firstly*) em primeiro lugar.
primary ['praɪmərɪ] *adj* primário; (*first in importance*) principal ♦ *n* (*US*: *election*) eleição *f* primária.
primary colour *n* cor *f* primária.
primary products *npl* produtos *mpl* básicos.
primary school (*BRIT*) *n* escola primária.
primate[1] ['praɪmɪt] *n* (*REL*) primaz *m*.
primate[2] ['praɪmeɪt] *n* (*ZOOL*) primata *m*.
prime [praɪm] *adj* primeiro, principal; (*basic*) fundamental, primário; (*excellent*) de primeira ♦ *vt* (*gun, pump*) escorvar; (*fig*) aprontar, preparar ♦ *n*: **in the ~ of life** na primavera da vida.
prime minister *n* primeiro-ministro/primeira-ministra.
primer ['praɪmə*] *n* (*book*) livro de leitura; (*paint*) pintura de base; (*of gun*) escorva.
prime time *n* (*RADIO, TV*) horário nobre.
primeval [praɪ'mi:vl] *adj* primitivo.
primitive ['prɪmɪtɪv] *adj* primitivo; (*crude*) rudimentar; (*uncivilized*) grosseiro, inculto.
primrose ['prɪmrəuz] *n* prímula, primavera.
primus (stove) ['praɪməs-] ® (*BRIT*) *n* fogão *m* portátil a petróleo.
prince [prɪns] *n* príncipe *m*.
princess [prɪn'sɛs] *n* princesa.
principal ['prɪnsɪpl] *adj* principal ♦ *n* (*head teacher*) diretor(a) *m/f*; (*in play*) papel *m* principal; (*money*) principal *m*.
principality [prɪnsɪ'pælɪtɪ] *n* principado.
principally ['prɪnsɪplɪ] *adv* principalmente.
principle ['prɪnsɪpl] *n* princípio; **in ~** em princípio; **on ~** por princípio.
print [prɪnt] *n* (*impression*) impressão *f*, marca; (*letters*) letra de forma; (*fabric*) estampado; (*ART*) estampa, gravura; (*PHOT*) cópia ♦ *vt* imprimir; (*write in capitals*) escrever em letra de imprensa; **out of ~** esgotado.
print out *vt* (*COMPUT*) imprimir.
printed circuit board ['prɪntɪd-] *n* placa de circuito impresso.
printed matter ['prɪntɪd-] *n* impressos *mpl*.
printer ['prɪntə*] *n* impressor(a) *m/f*; (*machine*) impressora.
printhead ['prɪnthɛd] *n* cabeçote *m* de impressão.
printing ['prɪntɪŋ] *n* (*art*) imprensa; (*act*) impressão *f*; (*quantity*) tiragem *f*.
printing press *n* prelo, máquina impressora.
print-out *n* cópia impressa.
print wheel *n* margarida.
prior ['praɪə*] *adj* anterior, prévio ♦ *n* (*REL*) prior *m*; **~ to doing** antes de fazer; **without ~ notice** sem aviso prévio; **to have a ~ claim to sth** ter prioridade na reivindicação de algo.
priority [praɪ'ɔrɪtɪ] *n* prioridade *f*; **to have** *or* **take ~ over sth/sb** ter prioridade sobre algo/alguém.
priory ['praɪərɪ] *n* priorado.
prise [praɪz] *vt*: **to ~ open** arrombar.
prism ['prɪzəm] *n* prisma *m*.
prison ['prɪzn] *n* prisão *f* ♦ *cpd* carcerário.

prison camp *n* campo de prisioneiros.
prisoner ['prɪzənə*] *n* (*in prison*) preso/a, presidiário/a; (*under arrest*) detido/a; (*in dock*) acusado/a, réu/ré *m/f*; **to take sb ~** aprisionar alguém, prender alguém; **~ of war** prisioneiro de guerra.
prissy ['prɪsɪ] *adj* fresco, cheio de luxo.
pristine ['prɪstiːn] *adj* imaculado.
privacy ['prɪvəsɪ] *n* (*seclusion*) isolamento, solidão *f*; (*intimacy*) intimidade *f*, privacidade *f*.
private ['praɪvɪt] *adj* (*personal*) particular; (*confidential*) confidencial, reservado; (*lesson, car*) particular; (*intimate*) privado, íntimo; (*sitting etc*) a portas fechadas ♦ *n* soldado raso; **"~"** (*on envelope*) "confidencial"; (*on door*) "privativo"; **in ~** em particular; **in (his) ~ life** em (sua) vida particular; **he is a very ~ person** ele é uma pessoa muito reservada; **to be in ~ practice** ter clínica particular; **~ hearing** (*LAW*) audiência em segredo da justiça.
private enterprise *n* iniciativa privada.
private eye *n* detetive *m/f* particular.
private limited company (*BRIT*) *n* sociedade *f* anônima fechada.
privately ['praɪvɪtlɪ] *adv* em particular; (*in oneself*) no fundo.
private parts *npl* partes *fpl* (pudendas).
private property *n* propriedade *f* privada.
private school *n* escola particular.
privation [praɪ'veɪʃən] *n* privação *f*.
privatize ['praɪvɪtaɪz] *vt* privatizar.
privet ['prɪvɪt] *n* alfena.
privilege ['prɪvɪlɪdʒ] *n* privilégio.
privileged ['prɪvɪlɪdʒd] *adj* privilegiado.
privy ['prɪvɪ] *adj*: **to be ~ to** estar inteirado de.
Privy Council (*BRIT*) *n* Conselho Privado.
prize [praɪz] *n* prêmio ♦ *adj* (*bull, novel*) premiado; (*first class*) de primeira classe; (*example*) perfeito ♦ *vt* valorizar.
prize fight *n* luta de boxe profissional.
prize giving [-'gɪvɪŋ] *n* distribuição *f* dos prêmios.
prize money *n* dinheiro do prêmio.
prizewinner ['praɪzwɪnə*] *n* premiado/a.
prizewinning ['praɪzwɪnɪŋ] *adj* premiado.
PRO *n abbr* (= *public relations officer*) RP *m/f inv*.
pro [prəu] *n* (*SPORT*) profissional *m/f*; (*advantage*): **the ~s and cons** os prós e os contras.
pro- [prəu] *prefix* (*in favour of*) pró-.
probability [prɔbə'bɪlɪtɪ] *n* probabilidade *f*; **in all ~** com toda a probabilidade.
probable ['prɔbəbl] *adj* provável; (*plausible*) verossímil; **it is ~/hardly ~ that ...** é provável/pouco provável que ....
probably ['prɔbəblɪ] *adv* provavelmente.
probate ['prəubɪt] *n* (*LAW*) homologação *f*, legitimação *f*.
probation [prə'beɪʃən] *n* (*in employment*) estágio probatório; (*LAW*) liberdade *f* condicional; (*REL*) noviciado; **on ~** (*employee*) em estágio probatório; (*LAW*) em liberdade condicional.
probationary [prə'beɪʃənrɪ] *adj* (*period*) probatório.
probe [prəub] *n* (*MED, SPACE*) sonda; (*enquiry*) pesquisa ♦ *vt* sondar; (*investigate*) investigar, esquadrinhar.
probity ['prəubɪtɪ] *n* probidade *f*.
problem ['prɔbləm] *n* problema *m*; **what's the ~?** qual é o problema?; **I had no ~ in finding her** não foi difícil encontrá-la; **no ~!** não tem problema!
problematic [prɔblə'mætɪk] *adj* problemático.
procedure [prə'siːdʒə*] *n* (*ADMIN, LAW*) procedimento; (*method*) método, processo; **cashing a cheque is a simple ~** descontar um cheque é uma operação simples.
proceed [prə'siːd] *vi* proceder; (*continue*): **to ~ (with)** continuar *or* prosseguir (com); **to ~ to** passar a; **to ~ to do** passar a fazer; **I am not sure how to ~** não sei como proceder; **to ~ against sb** (*LAW*) processar alguém, instaurar processo contra alguém.
proceeding [prə'siːdɪŋ] *n* processo; **~s** *npl* procedimento; (*lawsuit*) processo.
proceeds ['prəusiːdz] *npl* produto, proventos *mpl*.
process [*n, vt* 'prəusɛs, *vi* prə'sɛs] *n* processo ♦ *vt* processar, elaborar ♦ *vi* (*BRIT*: *formal*: *go in procession*) desfilar; **in ~** em andamento; **we are in the ~ of moving to Rio** estamos de mudança para o Rio.
processed cheese ['prəusɛst-] *n* ≈ requeijão *m*.
processing ['prəusɛsɪŋ] *n* processamento.
procession [prə'sɛʃən] *n* desfile *m*, procissão *f*; **funeral ~** cortejo fúnebre.
proclaim [prə'kleɪm] *vt* proclamar; (*announce*) anunciar.
proclamation [prɔklə'meɪʃən] *n* proclamação *f*; (*written*) promulgação *f*.
proclivity [prə'klɪvɪtɪ] *n* inclinação *f*.
procrastination [prəukræstɪ'neɪʃən] *n* protelação *f*.
procreation [prəukrɪ'eɪʃən] *n* procriação *f*.
procure [prə'kjuə*] *vt* obter.
procurement [prə'kjuəmənt] *n* obtenção *f*; (*purchase*) compra.
prod [prɔd] *vt* (*push*) empurrar; (*with elbow*) cutucar, acotovelar; (*jab*) espetar ♦ *n* empurrão *m*; cotovelada; espetada.
prodigal ['prɔdɪgl] *adj* pródigo.
prodigious [prə'dɪdʒəs] *adj* prodigioso, extraordinário.
prodigy ['prɔdɪdʒɪ] *n* prodígio.
produce [*n* 'prɔdjuːs, *vt* prə'djuːs] *n* (*AGR*) produtos *mpl* agrícolas ♦ *vt* produzir; (*profit*) render; (*cause*) provocar; (*show*) apresentar, exibir; (*THEATRE*) pôr em cena *or* em cartaz;

***NB**: European Portuguese adds the following consonants to certain words:* **b** (sú(b)dito, su(b)til); **c** (a(c)ção, a(c)cionista, a(c)to); **m** (inde(m)ne); **p** (ado(p)ção, ado(p)tar); *for further details see p. xiii.*

(*offspring*) dar à luz.
producer [prə'djuːsə*] *n* (*THEATRE*) diretor(a) *m/f*; (*AGR, CINEMA*) produtor(a) *m/f*.
product ['prɔdʌkt] *n* produto.
production [prə'dʌkʃən] *n* (*act*) produção *f*; (*thing*) produto; (*THEATRE*) encenação *f*; **to put into ~** (*goods*) passar a fabricar.
production agreement (*US*) *n* acórdo sobre produtividade.
production control *n* controle *m* de produção.
production line *n* linha de produção *or* de montagem.
production manager *n* gerente *m/f* de produção.
productive [prə'dʌktɪv] *adj* produtivo.
productivity [prɔdʌk'tɪvɪtɪ] *n* produtividade *f*.
productivity agreement (*BRIT*) *n* acordo sobre produtividade.
productivity bonus *n* prêmio de produção.
Prof. [prɔf] *abbr* (= *professor*) Prof.
profane [prə'feɪn] *adj* profano; (*language etc*) irreverente, sacrílego.
profess [prə'fɛs] *vt* professar; (*regret*) manifestar; **I do not ~ to be an expert** não me tenho na conta de entendido.
professed [prə'fɛst] *adj* (*self-declared*) assumido.
profession [prə'fɛʃən] *n* profissão *f*; **the ~s** *npl* as profissões liberais.
professional [prə'fɛʃənl] *n* profissional *m/f* ♦ *adj* profissional; (*work*) de profissional; **he's a ~ man** ele exerce uma profissão liberal; **to take ~ advice** consultar um perito.
professionalism [prə'fɛʃnəlɪzm] *n* profissionalismo.
professionally [prə'fɛʃnəlɪ] *adv* profissionalmente; (*as a job*) de profissão; **I only know him ~** eu só conheço ele pelo trabalho.
professor [prə'fɛsə*] *n* catedrático/a; (*US: teacher*) professor(a) *m/f*.
professorship [prə'fɛsəʃɪp] *n* cátedra.
proffer ['prɔfə*] *vt* (*hand*) estender; (*remark*) fazer; (*apologies*) apresentar.
proficiency [prə'fɪʃənsɪ] *n* competência, proficiência.
proficient [prə'fɪʃənt] *adj* competente, proficiente.
profile ['prəufaɪl] *n* perfil *m*; **to keep a high ~** destacar-se; **to keep a low ~** sair de circulação.
profit ['prɔfɪt] *n* (*COMM*) lucro; (*fig*) proveito, vantagem *f* ♦ *vi*: **to ~ by** *or* **from** (*financially*) lucrar com; (*benefit*) aproveitar-se de, tirar proveito de; **~ and loss account** conta de lucros e perdas; **to make a ~** lucrar; **to sell sth at a ~** vender algo com lucro.
profitability [prɔfɪtə'bɪlɪtɪ] *n* rentabilidade *f*.
profitable ['prɔfɪtəbl] *adj* (*ECON*) lucrativo, rendoso; (*useful*) proveitoso.
profit centre *n* centro de lucro.
profiteering [prɔfɪ'tɪərɪŋ] *n* mercantilismo, exploração *f*.
profit-making *adj* com fins lucrativos.
profit margin *n* margem *f* de lucro.
profit-sharing [-'ʃɛərɪŋ] *n* participação *f* nos lucros.
profits tax (*BRIT*) *n* imposto sobre os lucros.
profligate ['prɔflɪgɪt] *adj* (*behaviour, person*) devasso; (*extravagant*): **~ (with)** pródigo (de).
pro forma [-'fɔːmə] *adj*: **~ invoice** fatura pro-forma *or* simulada.
profound [prə'faund] *adj* profundo.
profuse [prə'fjuːs] *adj* abundante.
profusely [prə'fjuːslɪ] *adv* profusamente.
profusion [prə'fjuːʒən] *n* profusão *f*, abundância.
progeny ['prɔdʒɪnɪ] *n* prole *f*, progênie *f*.
programme ['prəugræm] (*US* **program**) *n* programa *m* ♦ *vt* programar.
program(m)er ['prəugræmə*] *n* programador(a) *m/f*.
program(m)ing ['prəugræmɪŋ] *n* programação *f*.
program(m)ing language *n* linguagem *f* de programação.
progress [*n* 'prəugrɛs, *vi* prə'grɛs] *n* progresso ♦ *vi* progredir, avançar; **in ~** em andamento; **to make ~** fazer progressos; **as the match ~ed** à medida que o jogo se desenvolvia.
progression [prə'grɛʃən] *n* progressão *f*.
progressive [prə'grɛsɪv] *adj* progressivo; (*person*) progressista.
progressively [prə'grɛsɪvlɪ] *adv* progressivamente.
progress report *n* (*MED*) boletim *m* médico; (*ADMIN*) relatório sobre o andamento dos trabalhos.
prohibit [prə'hɪbɪt] *vt* proibir; **to ~ sb from doing sth** proibir alguém de fazer algo; **"smoking ~ed"** "proibido fumar".
prohibition [prəuɪ'bɪʃən] *n* proibição *f*; (*US: ban on alcohol*) lei *f* seca.
prohibitive [prə'hɪbɪtɪv] *adj* (*price etc*) proibitivo.
project [*n* 'prɔdʒɛkt, *vt*, *vi* prə'dʒɛkt] *n* projeto; (*SCH: research*) pesquisa ♦ *vt* projetar ♦ *vi* (*stick out*) ressaltar, sobressair.
projectile [prə'dʒɛktaɪl] *n* projétil *m*.
projection [prə'dʒɛkʃən] *n* projeção *f*; (*overhang*) saliência.
projectionist [prə'dʒɛkʃənɪst] *n* operador(a) *m/f* de projetor.
projection room *n* (*CINEMA*) sala de projeção.
projector [prə'dʒɛktə*] *n* projetor *m*.
proletarian [prəulɪ'tɛərɪən] *adj*, *n* proletário/a.
proletariat [prəulɪ'tɛərɪət] *n* proletariado.
proliferate [prə'lɪfəreɪt] *vi* proliferar.
proliferation [prəlɪfə'reɪʃən] *n* proliferação *f*.
prolific [prə'lɪfɪk] *adj* prolífico.
prologue ['prəulɔg] *n* prólogo.
prolong [prə'lɔŋ] *vt* prolongar.
prom [prɔm] *n abbr* = **promenade**; **promenade concert**; (*US: ball*) baile *m* de estudantes.
promenade [prɔmə'nɑːd] *n* (*by sea*) passeio

(à orla marítima).

promenade concert *n* concerto (de música clássica).

promenade deck *n* (*NAUT*) convés *m* superior.

prominence ['prɔmɪnəns] *n* (*fig*) eminência, importância.

prominent ['prɔmɪnənt] *adj* (*standing out*) proeminente; (*important*) eminente, notório; **he is ~ in the field of ...** ele é muito conhecido no campo de ....

prominently ['prɔmɪnəntlɪ] *adv* (*display, set*) bem à vista; **he figured ~ in the case** ele teve um papel importante no caso.

promiscuity [prɔmɪ'skjuːɪtɪ] *n* promiscuidade *f*.

promiscuous [prə'mɪskjuəs] *adj* promíscuo.

promise ['prɔmɪs] *n* promessa ♦ *vt, vi* prometer; **to make sb a ~** fazer uma promessa a alguém; **to ~ (sb) to do sth** prometer (a alguém) fazer algo; **a young man of ~** um jovem que promete; **to ~ well** prometer.

promising ['prɔmɪsɪŋ] *adj* prometedor(a).

promissory note ['prɔmɪsərɪ-] *n* (nota) promissória.

promontory ['prɔməntrɪ] *n* promontório.

promote [prə'məut] *vt* promover; (*new product*) promover, fazer propaganda de; (*event*) patrocinar.

promoter [prə'məutə*] *n* (*of sporting event etc*) patrocinador(a) *m/f*; (*of cause etc*) partidário/a.

promotion [prə'məuʃən] *n* promoção *f*.

prompt [prɔmpt] *adj* pronto, rápido ♦ *n* (*COMPUT*) sinal *m* de orientação, prompt *m* ♦ *vt* (*urge*) incitar, impelir; (*cause*) provocar, ocasionar; (*THEATRE*) servir de ponto a; **to ~ sb to do sth** induzir alguém a fazer algo; **he's very ~** (*punctual*) ele é pontual; **at 8 o'clock ~** às 8 horas em ponto; **he was ~ to accept** ele não hesitou em aceitar.

prompter ['prɔmptə*] *n* (*THEATRE*) ponto.

promptly ['prɔmptlɪ] *adv* (*punctually*) pontualmente; (*rapidly*) rapidamente.

promptness ['prɔmptnɪs] *n* (*punctuality*) pontualidade *f*; (*rapidity*) rapidez *f*.

promulgate ['prɔməlgeɪt] *vt* promulgar.

prone [prəun] *adj* (*lying*) inclinado, de bruços; **~ to** propenso a, predisposto a; **she is ~ to burst into tears if ...** ela tende a desatar a chorar se ....

prong [prɔŋ] *n* ponta; (*of fork*) dente *m*.

pronoun ['prəunaun] *n* pronome *m*.

pronounce [prə'nauns] *vt* pronunciar; (*declare*) declarar ♦ *vi*: **to ~ (up)on** pronunciar-se sobre.

pronounced [prə'naunst] *adj* (*marked*) marcado, nítido.

pronouncement [prə'naunsmənt] *n* pronunciamento.

pronunciation [prənʌnsɪ'eɪʃən] *n* pronúncia.

proof [pruːf] *n* prova; (*of alcohol*) teor *m* alcoólico ♦ *adj*: **~ against** à prova de ♦ *vt* (*BRIT*: *tent, anorak*) impermeabilizar; **to be 70° ~** ter 70° de gradação.

proofreader ['pruːfriːdə*] *n* revisor(a) *m/f* de provas.

Prop. *abbr* (*COMM*) = **proprietor**.

prop [prɔp] *n* suporte *m*, escora; (*fig*) amparo, apoio ♦ *vt* (*also*: **~ up**) apoiar, escorar; (*lean*): **to ~ sth against** apoiar algo contra.

propaganda [prɔpə'gændə] *n* propaganda.

propagate ['prɔpəgeɪt] *vt* propagar.

propel [prə'pɛl] *vt* propelir, propulsionar.

propeller [prə'pɛlə*] *n* hélice *f*.

propelling pencil [prə'pɛlɪŋ-] (*BRIT*) *n* lapiseira.

propensity [prə'pɛnsɪtɪ] *n* propensão *f*.

proper ['prɔpə*] *adj* (*suited, right*) próprio; (*seemly*) correto, conveniente; (*authentic*) genuíno; (*inf*: *real*) autêntico; **physics ~** a física propriamente dita; **to go through the ~ channels** (*ADMIN*) seguir os trâmites oficiais.

properly ['prɔpəlɪ] *adv* direito; (*really*) bem.

proper noun *n* nome *m* próprio.

property ['prɔpətɪ] *n* (*possessions, quality*) propriedade *f*; (*goods*) posses *fpl*, bens *mpl*; (*buildings*) imóveis *mpl*; (*estate*) propriedade *f*, fazenda; **it's their ~** é deles, pertence a eles.

property developer (*BRIT*) *n* empresário/a de imóveis.

property owner *n* proprietário/a.

property tax *n* imposto predial e territorial.

prophecy ['prɔfɪsɪ] *n* profecia.

prophesy ['prɔfɪsaɪ] *vt* profetizar; (*fig*) predizer ♦ *vi* profetizar.

prophet ['prɔfɪt] *n* profeta *m/f*.

prophetic [prə'fɛtɪk] *adj* profético.

proportion [prə'pɔːʃən] *n* proporção *f*; (*share*) parte *f*, porção *f* ♦ *vt* proporcionar; **in ~ to** *or* **with sth** em proporção *or* proporcional a algo; **out of ~** desproporcionado; **to see sth in ~** (*fig*) ter a visão adequada de algo.

proportional [prə'pɔːʃənl] *adj* proporcional.

proportional representation *n* (*POL*) representação *f* proporcional.

proportionate [prə'pɔːʃənɪt] *adj* proporcionado.

proposal [prə'pəuzl] *n* proposta; (*of marriage*) pedido.

propose [prə'pəuz] *vt* propor ♦ *vi* propor casamento; **to ~ to do** propor-se fazer.

proposer [prə'pəuzə*] (*BRIT*) *n* (*of motion etc*) apresentador(a) *m/f*.

proposition [prɔpə'zɪʃən] *n* proposta, proposição *f*; **to make sb a ~** fazer uma proposta a alguém.

propound [prə'paund] *vt* propor.

proprietary [prə'praɪətrɪ] *adj*: **~ brand** marca registrada; **~ product** produto patenteado.

proprietor [prə'praɪətə*] *n* proprietário/a,

NB: *European Portuguese adds the following consonants to certain words:* **b** (sú(b)dito, su(b)til); **c** (a(c)ção, a(c)cionista, a(c)to); **m** (inde(m)ne); **p** (ado(p)ção, ado(p)tar); *for further details see p. xiii.*

dono/a.
propriety [prə'praɪətɪ] *n* propriedade *f*.
propulsion [prə'pʌlʃən] *n* propulsão *f*.
pro rata [-'rɑːtə] *adv* pro rata, proporcionalmente.
prosaic [prəu'zeɪɪk] *adj* prosaico.
Pros. Atty. (*US*) *abbr* = **prosecuting attorney**.
proscribe [prə'skraɪb] *vt* proscrever.
prose [prəuz] *n* prosa.
prosecute ['prɔsɪkjuːt] *vt* (*LAW*) processar.
prosecuting attorney ['prɔsɪkjuːtɪŋ-] (*US*) *n* promotor(a) *m/f* público/a.
prosecution [prɔsɪ'kjuːʃən] *n* acusação *f*; (*accusing side*) autor *m* da demanda.
prosecutor ['prɔsɪkjuːtə*] *n* promotor(a) *m/f*; (*also*: *public* ~) promotor(a) *m/f* público/a.
prospect [*n* 'prɔspɛkt, *vt*, *vi* prə'spɛkt] *n* (*chance*) probabilidade *f*; (*outlook, potential*) perspectiva ♦ *vt* explorar ♦ *vi* prospectar; **~s** *npl* perspectivas *fpl*; **we are faced with the ~ of ...** nós estamos diante da perspectiva de ...; **there is every ~ of an early victory** há toda probabilidade de uma vitória rápida.
prospecting [prə'spɛktɪŋ] *n* prospecção *f*.
prospective [prə'spɛktɪv] *adj* (*possible*) provável; (*future*) em perspectiva.
prospector [prə'spɛktə*] *n* garimpeiro/a.
prospectus [prə'spɛktəs] *n* prospecto, programa *m*.
prosper ['prɔspə*] *vi* prosperar.
prosperity [prɔ'spɛrɪtɪ] *n* prosperidade *f*.
prosperous ['prɔspərəs] *adj* próspero.
prostate ['prɔsteɪt] *n* (*also*: ~ *gland*) próstata.
prostitute ['prɔstɪtjuːt] *n* prostituta; **male ~** prostituto.
prostitution [prɔstɪ'tjuːʃən] *n* prostituição *f*.
prostrate [*adj* 'prɔstreɪt, *vt* prɔ'streɪt] *adj* prostrado; (*fig*) abatido, aniquilado ♦ *vt*: **to ~ o.s. (before sb)** prostrar-se (diante de alguém).
protagonist [prə'tægənɪst] *n* protagonista *m/f*.
protect [prə'tɛkt] *vt* proteger.
protection [prə'tɛkʃən] *n* proteção *f*; **to be under sb's ~** estar sob a proteção de alguém.
protectionism [prə'tɛkʃənɪzm] *n* protecionismo.
protection racket *n* extorsão *f*.
protective [prə'tɛktɪv] *adj* protetor(a); **~ custody** (*LAW*) prisão *f* preventiva.
protector [prə'tɛktə*] *n* protetor(a) *m/f*.
protégé ['prəutɛʒeɪ] *n* protegido.
protégée ['prəutɛʒeɪ] *n* protegida.
protein ['prəutiːn] *n* proteína.
pro tem [-tɛm] *adv abbr* (= *pro tempore*: *for the time being*) provisoriamente.
protest [*n* 'prəutɛst, *vi*, *vt* prə'tɛst] *n* protesto ♦ *vi* protestar ♦ *vt* (*affirm*) afirmar, declarar.
Protestant ['prɔtɪstənt] *adj*, *n* protestante *m/f*.
protester [prə'tɛstə*] *n* manifestante *m/f*.
protest march *n* passeata.
protestor [prə'tɛstə*] *n* = **protester**.
protocol ['prəutəkɔl] *n* protocolo.
prototype ['prəutətaɪp] *n* protótipo.
protracted [prə'træktɪd] *adj* prolongado, demorado.
protractor [prə'træktə*] *n* (*GEOM*) transferidor *m*.
protrude [prə'truːd] *vi* projetar-se, sobressair, ressaltar.
protuberance [prə'tjuːbərəns] *n* protuberância.
proud [praud] *adj* orgulhoso; (*pej*) vaidoso, soberbo; **to be ~ to do sth** sentir-se orgulhoso de fazer algo; **to do sb ~** (*inf*) fazer muita festa a alguém.
proudly ['praudlɪ] *adv* orgulhosamente.
prove [pruːv] *vt* comprovar ♦ *vi*: **to ~ correct** vir a ser correto; **to ~ o.s.** pôr-se à prova; **to ~ itself (to be) useful** *etc* revelar-se *or* mostrar-se útil *etc*; **he was ~d right in the end** no final deram-lhe razão.
proverb ['prɔvəːb] *n* provérbio.
proverbial [prə'vəːbɪəl] *adj* proverbial.
provide [prə'vaɪd] *vt* fornecer, proporcionar; **to ~ sb with sth** fornecer alguém de algo, fornecer algo a alguém; **to be ~d with** estar munido de.
provide for *vt fus* (*person*) prover à subsistência de; (*emergency*) prevenir.
provided (that) [prə'vaɪdɪd-] *conj* contanto que + *sub*, sob condição de (que) + *sub*.
Providence ['prɔvɪdəns] *n* a Divina Providência.
providing [prə'vaɪdɪŋ] *conj* contanto que + *sub*.
province ['prɔvɪns] *n* província; (*fig*) esfera.
provincial [prə'vɪnʃəl] *adj* provincial; (*pej*) provinciano.
provision [prə'vɪʒən] *n* provisão *f*; (*supply*) fornecimento; (*supplying*) abastecimento; (*in contract*) cláusula, condição *f*; **~s** *npl* (*food*) mantimentos *mpl*; **to make ~ for** fazer provisão para; **there's no ~ for this in the contract** não há cláusula nesse sentido no contrato.
provisional [prə'vɪʒənəl] *adj* provisório, interino; (*agreement, licence*) provisório ♦ *n*: **P~** (*IRISH*: *POL*) *militante do braço armado do IRA*.
provisional licence (*BRIT*) *n* (*AUT*) licença prévia para aprendizagem.
provisionally [prə'vɪʒnəlɪ] *adv* provisoriamente.
proviso [prə'vaɪzəu] *n* condição *f*; (*reservation*) ressalva; (*LAW*) cláusula; **with the ~ that** com a ressalva que.
Provo ['prɔvəu] (*inf*) *n abbr* = **Provisional**.
provocation [prɔvə'keɪʃən] *n* provocação *f*.
provocative [prə'vɔkətɪv] *adj* provocante; (*stimulating*) sugestivo.
provoke [prə'vəuk] *vt* provocar; **to ~ sb to sth/to do** *or* **into doing sth** provocar alguém a algo/a fazer algo.
provoking [prə'vəukɪŋ] *adj* provocante.
provost ['prɔvəst] *n* (*BRIT*: *of university*) reitor(a) *m/f*; (*SCOTTISH*) prefeito/a.
prow [prau] *n* proa.
prowess ['prauɪs] *n* destreza, perícia.

prowl [praul] *vi* (*also*: ~ *about*, ~ *around*) rondar, andar à espreita ♦ *n*: **on the** ~ de ronda, rondando.
prowler ['praulə*] *n* tarado/a.
proximity [prɔk'sɪmɪtɪ] *n* proximidade *f*.
proxy ['prɔksɪ] *n* procuração *f*; (*person*) procurador(a) *m/f*; **by** ~ por procuração.
prude [pru:d] *n* pudico/a.
prudence ['pru:dns] *n* prudência.
prudent ['pru:dənt] *adj* prudente.
prudish ['pru:dɪʃ] *adj* pudico/a.
prune [pru:n] *n* ameixa seca ♦ *vt* podar.
pry [praɪ] *vi*: **to** ~ **into** intrometer-se em.
PS *n abbr* (= *postscript*) PS *m*.
psalm [sɑ:m] *n* salmo.
PSAT (*US*) *n abbr* = **Preliminary Scholastic Aptitude Test**.
PSBR (*BRIT*) *n abbr* (= *public sector borrowing requirement*) necessidade *f* de empréstimos no setor público.
pseud [sju:d] (*BRIT*: *inf*) *n* posudo/a.
pseudo- [sju:dəu] *prefix* pseudo-.
pseudonym ['sju:dənɪm] *n* pseudônimo.
PST (*US*) *abbr* (= *Pacific Standard Time*) *hora de inverno do Pacífico*.
PSV (*BRIT*) *n abbr* = **public service vehicle**.
psyche ['saɪkɪ] *n* psiquismo.
psychiatric [saɪkɪ'ætrɪk] *adj* psiquiátrico.
psychiatrist [saɪ'kaɪətrɪst] *n* psiquiatra *m/f*.
psychiatry [saɪ'kaɪətrɪ] *n* psiquiatria.
psychic ['saɪkɪk] *adj* (*also*: ~*al*) paranormal; (*person*) sensível a forças psíquicas ♦ *n* médium *m/f*.
psychoanalyse [saɪkəu'ænəlaɪz] *vt* psicanalisar.
psychoanalysis [saɪkəuə'nælɪsɪs] *n* psicanálise *f*.
psychoanalyst [saɪkəu'ænəlɪst] *n* psicanalista *m/f*.
psychological [saɪkə'lɔdʒɪkl] *adj* psicológico.
psychologist [saɪ'kɔlədʒɪst] *n* psicólogo/a.
psychology [saɪ'kɔlədʒɪ] *n* psicologia.
psychopath ['saɪkəupæθ] *n* psicopata *m/f*.
psychoses [saɪ'kəusi:z] *npl of* **psychosis**.
psychosis [saɪ'kəusɪs] (*pl* **psychoses**) *n* psicose *f*.
psychosomatic [saɪkəusə'mætɪk] *adj* psicossomático.
psychotherapy [saɪkəu'θɛrəpɪ] *n* psicoterapia.
psychotic [saɪ'kɔtɪk] *adj*, *n* psicótico/a.
PT (*BRIT*) *n abbr* = **physical training**.
Pt. *abbr* (*in place names* = *Point*) Pto.
pt *abbr* = **pint**; **point**.
PTA *n abbr* = **Parent-Teacher Association**.
Pte. (*BRIT*) *abbr* (*MIL*) = **private**.
PTO *abbr* (= *please turn over*) v.v., vire.
PTV (*US*) *n abbr* = **pay television**; **public television**.
pub [pʌb] *n abbr* (= *public house*) pub *m*, bar *m*, botequim *m*.
puberty ['pju:bətɪ] *n* puberdade *f*.
pubic ['pju:bɪk] *adj* púbico, pubiano.
public ['pʌblɪk] *adj*, *n* público; **in** ~ em público; **the general** ~ o grande público; **to be** ~ **knowledge** ser de conhecimento público; **to go** ~ (*COMM*) tornar-se uma companhia de capital aberto, passar a ser cotado na Bolsa de Valores.
public address system *n* sistema *m* (de reforço) de som.
publican ['pʌblɪkən] *n* dono/a de pub.
publication [pʌblɪ'keɪʃən] *n* publicação *f*.
public company *n* sociedade *f* anônima aberta.
public convenience (*BRIT*) *n* banheiro público.
public holiday (*BRIT*) *n* feriado.
public house (*BRIT*: *irreg*) *n* pub *m*, bar *m*, taberna.
publicity [pʌb'lɪsɪtɪ] *n* publicidade *f*.
publicize ['pʌblɪsaɪz] *vt* divulgar; (*product*) promover.
public limited company *n* sociedade *f* anônima aberta.
publicly ['pʌblɪklɪ] *adv* publicamente.
public opinion *n* opinião *f* pública.
public ownership *n*: **to be taken into** ~ ser estatizado.
public relations *n* relações *fpl* públicas.
public relations officer *n* relações-públicas *m/f inv*.
public school *n* (*BRIT*) escola particular; (*US*) escola pública.
public sector *n* setor *m* público.
public service vehicle (*BRIT*) *n* veículo para o transporte público.
public-spirited [-'spɪrɪtɪd] *adj* zeloso pelo bem-estar público.
public transport (*US* **public transportation**) *n* transporte *m* coletivo.
public utility *n* (serviço de) utilidade *f* pública.
public works *npl* obras *fpl* públicas.
publish ['pʌblɪʃ] *vt* publicar.
publisher ['pʌblɪʃə*] *n* editor(a) *m/f*; (*company*) editora.
publishing ['pʌblɪʃɪŋ] *n* (*industry*) a indústria editorial.
publishing company *n* editora.
puce [pju:s] *adj* roxo.
puck [pʌk] *n* (*elf*) duende *m*; (*ICE HOCKEY*) disco.
pucker ['pʌkə*] *vt* (*fabric*) amarrotar; (*brow etc*) franzir.
pudding ['pudɪŋ] *n* (*BRIT*: *dessert*) sobremesa; (*cake*) pudim *m*, doce *m*; **black** (*BRIT*) *or* **blood** (*US*) ~ morcela; **rice** ~ pudim de arroz.
puddle ['pʌdl] *n* poça.
puerile ['pjuəraɪl] *adj* infantil.
Puerto Rico ['pwə:təu'ri:kəu] *n* Porto Rico (*no article*).
Puerto Rican ['pwə:tə'ri:kən] *adj*, *n* porto-riquenho/a.

***NB**: European Portuguese adds the following consonants to certain words:* **b** (sú(b)dito, su(b)til); **c** (a(c)ção, a(c)cionista, a(c)to); **m** (inde(m)ne); **p** (ado(p)ção, ado(p)tar); *for further details see p. xiii.*

puff [pʌf] *n* sopro; (*from mouth*) baforada; (*gust*) rajada, lufada; (*sound*) sopro; (*also*: *powder* ~) pompom *m* ♦ *vt*: **to ~ one's pipe** tirar baforadas do cachimbo ♦ *vi* soprar; (*pant*) arquejar.
puff out *vt* (*sails*) enfunar; (*cheeks*) encher; **to ~ out smoke** lançar baforadas.
puff up *vt* inflar.
puffed [pʌft] (*inf*) *adj* (*out of breath*) sem fôlego.
puffin ['pʌfɪn] *n* papagaio-do-mar *m*.
puff pastry (*US* **puff paste**) *n* massa folhada.
puffy ['pʌfɪ] *adj* inchado, entumecido.
pugnacious [pʌg'neɪʃəs] *adj* pugnaz, brigão/ona.
pull [pul] *n* (*of magnet, sea etc*) atração *f*; (*influence*) influência; (*tug*): **to give sth a ~** dar um puxão em algo ♦ *vt* puxar; (*muscle*) distender ♦ *vi* puxar, dar um puxão; **to ~ a face** fazer careta; **to ~ to pieces** picar em pedacinhos; **to ~ one's punches** não usar toda a força; **to ~ one's weight** fazer a sua parte; **to ~ o.s. together** recompor-se; **to ~ sb's leg** (*fig*) brincar com alguém, sacanear alguém (*inf*); **to ~ strings for sb** mexer os pauzinhos para alguém.
pull about (*BRIT*) *vt* (*handle roughly*) maltratar.
pull apart *vt* separar; (*break*) romper.
pull down *vt* abaixar; (*house*) demolir, derrubar; (*tree*) abater, derrubar.
pull in *vi* (*AUT*: *at the kerb*) encostar; (*RAIL*) chegar (na plataforma).
pull off *vt* tirar; (*deal etc*) acertar.
pull out *vi* arrancar, partir; (*withdraw*) retirar-se; (*AUT*: *from kerb*) sair ♦ *vt* tirar, arrancar; **to ~ out in front of sb** (*AUT*) dar uma fechada em alguém.
pull over *vi* (*AUT*) encostar.
pull round *vi* (*unconscious person*) voltar a si; (*sick person*) recuperar-se.
pull through *vi* sair-se bem (de um aperto); (*MED*) sobreviver.
pull up *vi* (*stop*) deter-se, parar ♦ *vt* levantar; (*uproot*) desarraigar, arrancar; (*stop*) parar.
pulley ['pulɪ] *n* roldana.
pull-out *n* (*withdrawal*) retirada; (*section*: *in magazine, newspaper*) encarte *m* ♦ *cpd* (*magazine, pages*) destacável.
pullover ['puləuvə*] *n* pulôver *m*.
pulp [pʌlp] *n* (*of fruit*) polpa; (*for paper*) pasta, massa; **to reduce sth to a ~** amassar algo.
pulpit ['pulpɪt] *n* púlpito.
pulsate [pʌl'seɪt] *vi* pulsar, palpitar; (*music*) vibrar.
pulse [pʌls] *n* (*ANAT*) pulso; (*of music, engine*) cadência; **~s** *npl* (*CULIN*) legumes *mpl*; **to feel** *or* **take sb's ~** tomar o pulso de alguém; **~ rate** freqüência de pulsos.
pulverize ['pʌlvəraɪz] *vt* pulverizar; (*fig*) esmagar, aniquilar.
puma ['pju:mə] *n* puma, onça-parda.
pumice ['pʌmɪs] *n* (*also*: ~ *stone*) pedra-pomes *f*.
pummel ['pʌml] *vt* esmurrar, socar.
pump [pʌmp] *n* bomba; (*shoe*) sapatilha (de dança) ♦ *vt* bombear; (*fig*: *inf*) sondar; **to ~ sb for information** tentar extrair informações de alguém.
pump up *vt* encher.
pumpkin ['pʌmpkɪn] *n* abóbora.
pun [pʌn] *n* jogo de palavras, trocadilho.
punch [pʌntʃ] *n* (*blow*) soco, murro; (*tool*) punção *m*; (*for tickets*) furador *m*; (*drink*) ponche *m*; (*fig*: *force*) vigor *m*, força ♦ *vt* (*make a hole in*) perfurar, picotar; (*hit*): **to ~ sb/sth** esmurrar *or* socar alguém/algo.
punch in (*US*) *vi* assinar o ponto na entrada.
punch out (*US*) *vi* assinar o ponto na saída.
punch-drunk (*BRIT*) *adj* estupidificado.
punch(ed) card [pʌntʃ(t)-] *n* cartão *m* perfurado.
punch line *n* (*of joke*) remate *m*.
punch-up (*inf*) *n* briga.
punctual ['pʌŋktjuəl] *adj* pontual.
punctuality [pʌŋktju'ælɪtɪ] *n* pontualidade *f*.
punctually ['pʌŋktjuəlɪ] *adv* pontualmente; **it will start ~ at 6** começará às 6 horas em ponto.
punctuate ['pʌŋktjueɪt] *vt* pontuar.
punctuation [pʌŋktju'eɪʃən] *n* pontuação *f*.
punctuation marks *npl* sinais *mpl* de pontuação.
puncture ['pʌŋktʃə*] (*BRIT*) *n* picada, furo; (*flat tyre*) pneu *m* furado ♦ *vt* picar, furar; (*tyre*) furar; **I have a ~** (*AUT*) estou com um pneu furado.
pundit ['pʌndɪt] *n* entendedor(a) *m/f*.
pungent ['pʌndʒənt] *adj* pungente, acre; (*fig*) mordaz.
punish ['pʌnɪʃ] *vt* punir, castigar; **to ~ sb for sth/for doing sth** punir alguém por algo/por ter feito algo.
punishable ['pʌnɪʃəbl] *adj* punível, castigável.
punishing ['pʌnɪʃɪŋ] *adj* (*fig*: *exhausting*) desgastante ♦ *n* punição *f*.
punishment ['pʌnɪʃmənt] *n* castigo, punição *f*; (*fig*: *wear*) desgaste *m*.
punk [pʌŋk] *n* (*person*: *also*: ~ *rocker*) punk *m/f*; (*music*: *also*: ~ *rock*) punk *m*; (*US*: *inf*: *hoodlum*) pinta-brava *m*.
punt [pʌnt] *n* (*boat*) chalana.
punter ['pʌntə*] (*BRIT*) *n* (*gambler*) jogador(a) *m/f*; (*inf*: *client*) cliente *m/f*.
puny ['pju:nɪ] *adj* débil, fraco.
pup [pʌp] *n* (*dog*) cachorrinho (*BR*), cachorro (*PT*); (*seal etc*) filhote *m*.
pupil ['pju:pl] *n* aluno/a.
puppet ['pʌpɪt] *n* marionete *f*, títere *m*.
puppet government *n* governo fantoche *or* títere.
puppy ['pʌpɪ] *n* cachorrinho (*BR*), cachorro (*PT*).
purchase ['pə:tʃɪs] *n* compra; (*grip*) ponto de apoio ♦ *vt* comprar; **to get a ~ on** apoiar-se em.
purchase order *n* ordem *f* de compra.

purchase price *n* preço de compra.
purchaser ['pəːtʃɪsə*] *n* comprador(a) *m/f*.
purchase tax (*BRIT*) *n* ≈ imposto de circulação de mercadorias.
purchasing power ['pəːtʃɪsɪŋ-] *n* poder *m* aquisitivo.
pure [pjuə*] *adj* puro; **a ~ wool jumper** um pulôver de pura lã; **~ and simple** puro e simples.
purebred ['pjuəbrɛd] *adj* de sangue puro.
purée ['pjuəreɪ] *n* purê *m*.
purely ['pjuəlɪ] *adv* puramente; (*only*) meramente.
purge [pəːdʒ] *n* (*MED*) purgante *m*; (*POL*) expurgo ♦ *vt* purgar; (*POL*) expurgar.
purification [pjuərɪfɪ'keɪʃən] *n* purificação *f*, depuração *f*.
purify ['pjuərɪfaɪ] *vt* purificar, depurar.
purist ['pjuərɪst] *n* purista *m/f*.
puritan ['pjuərɪtən] *n* puritano/a.
puritanical [pjuərɪ'tænɪkl] *adj* puritano.
purity ['pjuərɪtɪ] *n* pureza.
purl [pəːl] *n* ponto reverso ♦ *vt* fazer ponto de tricô.
purloin [pəː'lɔɪn] *vt* surripiar.
purple ['pəːpl] *adj* roxo, purpúreo.
purport [pəː'pɔːt] *vi*: **to ~ to be/do** dar a entender que é/faz.
purpose ['pəːpəs] *n* propósito, objetivo; **on ~** de propósito; **for teaching ~s** para fins pedagógicos; **for the ~s of this meeting** para esta reunião; **to no ~** em vão.
purpose-built (*BRIT*) *adj* feito sob medida.
purposeful ['pəːpəsful] *adj* decidido, resoluto.
purposely ['pəːpəslɪ] *adv* de propósito.
purr [pəː*] *n* ronrom *m* ♦ *vi* ronronar.
purse [pəːs] *n* carteira; (*US*: *bag*) bolsa ♦ *vt* enrugar, franzir.
purser ['pəːsə*] *n* (*NAUT*) comissário de bordo.
purse snatcher [-'snætʃə*] *n* trombadinha *m/f*.
pursue [pə'sjuː] *vt* perseguir; (*profession*) exercer; (*inquiry*, *matter*) prosseguir.
pursuer [pə'sjuːə*] *n* perseguidor(a) *m/f*.
pursuit [pə'sjuːt] *n* (*chase*) caça; (*persecution*) perseguição *f*; (*occupation*) ocupação *f*, atividade *f*; (*pastime*) passatempo; **in (the) ~ of sth** em busca de algo.
purveyor [pə'veɪə*] *n* fornecedor(a) *m/f*.
pus [pʌs] *n* pus *m*.
push [puʃ] *n* empurrão *m*; (*attack*) ataque *m*, arremetida; (*advance*) avanço ♦ *vt* empurrar; (*button*) apertar; (*promote*) promover; (*thrust*): **to ~ sth (into)** enfiar algo (em) ♦ *vi* empurrar; **to ~ a door open/shut** abrir/fechar uma porta empurrando-a; **"~"** (*on door*) "empurre"; (*on bell*) "aperte"; **to ~ for** (*better conditions*, *pay*) reivindicar; **to be ~ed for time/money** estar com pouco tempo/dinheiro; **she is ~ing fifty** (*inf*) ela está beirando os 50; **at a ~** (*BRIT*: *inf*) em último caso.
push aside *vt* afastar com a mão.
push in *vi* introduzir-se à força.
push off (*inf*) *vi* dar o fora.
push on *vi* (*continue*) prosseguir.
push over *vt* derrubar.
push through *vt* (*measure*) forçar a aceitação de.
push up *vt* (*total*, *prices*) forçar a alta de.
push-bike (*BRIT*) *n* bicicleta.
push-button *adj* por botões de pressão.
pushchair ['puʃtʃɛə*] (*BRIT*) *n* carrinho.
pusher ['puʃə*] *n* (*also*: *drug ~*) traficante *m/f or* passador(a) *m/f* de drogas.
pushing ['puʃɪŋ] *adj* empreendedor(a).
pushover ['puʃəuvə*] (*inf*) *n*: **it's a ~** é sopa.
push-up (*US*) *n* flexão *f*.
pushy ['puʃɪ] (*pej*) *adj* intrometido, agressivo.
puss [pus] *n* gatinho.
pussy(-cat) ['pusɪ-] *n* gatinho.
put [put] (*pt*, *pp* **put**) *vt* (*place*) pôr, colocar; (*~ into*) meter; (*say*) dizer, expressar; (*a question*) fazer; (*estimate*) avaliar, calcular; **to ~ sb in a good/bad mood** deixar alguém de bom/mau humor; **to ~ sb to bed** pôr alguém para dormir; **to ~ sb to a lot of trouble** incomodar alguém; **how shall I ~ it?** como dizer?; **to ~ a lot of time into sth** investir muito tempo em algo; **to ~ money on a horse** apostar num cavalo; **I ~ it to you that ...** (*BRIT*) eu gostaria de colocar que ...; **to stay ~** não se mexer.
put about *vi* (*NAUT*) mudar de rumo ♦ *vt* (*rumour*) espalhar.
put across *vt* (*ideas etc*) comunicar.
put aside *vt* deixar de lado.
put away *vt* (*store*) guardar.
put back *vt* (*replace*) repor; (*postpone*) adiar; (*delay*, *also*: *watch*, *clock*) atrasar.
put by *vt* (*money*) poupar, pôr de lado.
put down *vt* (*parcel etc*) pôr no chão; (*pay*) pagar; (*animal*) sacrificar; (*in writing*) anotar, inscrever; (*suppress*: *revolt etc*) sufocar; (*attribute*) atribuir.
put forward *vt* (*ideas*) apresentar, propor; (*date*, *clock*) adiantar.
put in *vt* (*application*, *complaint*) apresentar; (*gas*, *electricity*) instalar.
put in for *vt fus* (*job*) candidatar-se a; (*promotion*, *pay rise*) solicitar.
put off *vt* (*light*) apagar; (*postpone*) adiar, protelar; (*discourage*) desencorajar.
put on *vt* (*clothes*, *lipstick etc*) pôr; (*light etc*) acender; (*play etc*) encenar; (*food*, *meal*) preparar; (*weight*) ganhar; (*brake*) aplicar; (*attitude*) fingir, simular; (*accent*, *manner*) assumir; (*inf*: *tease*) fazer de criança; (*inform*): **to ~ sb on to sth** indicar algo a alguém.
put out *vt* pôr para fora; (*fire*, *light*) apagar; (*one's hand*) estender; (*news*) anunciar; (*rumour*) espalhar; (*tongue etc*) mostrar; (*person*: *inconvenience*) incomodar;

***NB**: European Portuguese adds the following consonants to certain words:* **b** (sú(b)dito, su(b)til); **c** (a(c)ção, a(c)cionista, a(c)to); **m** (inde(m)ne); **p** (ado(p)ção, ado(p)tar); *for further details see p. xiii.*

(*BRIT*: *dislocate*) deslocar ♦ *vi* (*NAUT*): **to ~ out to sea** fazer-se ao mar; **to ~ out from Plymouth** zarpar de Plymouth.
put through *vt* (*caller, call*) transferir; **I'd like to ~ a call through to Brazil** eu gostaria de fazer uma ligação para o Brasil.
put together *vt* colocar junto(s); (*assemble*) montar; (*meal*) preparar.
put up *vt* (*raise*) levantar, erguer; (*hang*) prender; (*build*) construir, edificar; (*tent*) armar; (*increase*) aumentar; (*accommodate*) hospedar; **to ~ sb up to doing sth** incitar alguém a fazer algo; **to ~ sth up for sale** pôr algo à venda.
put upon *vt fus*: **to be ~ upon** sofrer abusos.
put up with *vt fus* suportar, agüentar.
putrid ['pju:trɪd] *adj* pútrido, podre.
putt [pʌt] *vt* (*GOLF*) fazer um putt ♦ *n* putt *m*, tacada leve.
putter ['pʌtə*] *n* (*GOLF*) putter *m*.
putting green ['pʌtɪŋ-] *n* campo de golfe em miniatura.
putty ['pʌtɪ] *n* massa de vidraceiro, betume *m*.
put-up *adj*: **~ job** embuste *m*.
puzzle ['pʌzl] *n* (*riddle*) charada; (*jigsaw*) quebra-cabeça *m*; (*also*: *crossword* ~) palavras cruzadas *fpl*; (*mystery*) enigma *m* ♦ *vt* desconcertar, confundir ♦ *vi* estar perplexo; **to ~ over** tentar entender; **to be ~d about sth** estar perplexo com algo.
puzzling ['pʌzlɪŋ] *adj* (*mysterious*) enigmático, misterioso; (*unnerving*) desconcertante; (*incomprehensible*) incompreensível.
PVC *n abbr* (= *polyvinyl chloride*) PVC *m*.
Pvt. (*US*) *abbr* (*MIL*) = **private**.
pw *abbr* (= *per week*) por semana.
PX (*US*) *n abbr* (*MIL*) = **post exchange**.
pygmy ['pɪgmɪ] *n* pigmeu/méia *m/f*.
pyjamas [pɪ'dʒɑ:məz] (*BRIT*) *npl* pijama *m or f*.
pylon ['paɪlən] *n* pilono, poste *m*, torre *f*.
pyramid ['pɪrəmɪd] *n* pirâmide *f*.
Pyrenees [pɪrə'ni:z] *npl*: **the ~** os Pirineus.
Pyrex ['paɪrɛks] ® *n* Pirex *m* ® ♦ *cpd*: **a ~ dish** um pirex.
python ['paɪθən] *n* pitão *m*.

Q

Q, q [kju:] *n* (*letter*) Q, q *m*; **Q for Queen** Q de Quinteta.
Qatar [kæ'tɑ:*] *n* Catar *m*.
QC (*BRIT*) *n abbr* (= *Queen's Counsel*) *título dado a certos advogados*.
QED *abbr* (= *quod erat demonstrandum*) QED.
QM *n abbr* = **quartermaster**.
q.t. (*inf*) *n abbr* (= *quiet*): **on the ~** de fininho.
qty *abbr* (= *quantity*) quant.
quack [kwæk] *n* (*of duck*) grasnido; (*pej*: *doctor*) curandeiro/a, charlatão/tã *m/f* ♦ *vi* grasnar.
quad [kwɔd] *abbr* = **quadrangle**; **quadruplet**.
quadrangle ['kwɔdræŋgl] *n* (*courtyard*) pátio quadrangular.
quadruped ['kwɔdrupɛd] *n* quadrúpede *m*.
quadruple [kwɔ'drupl] *adj*, *n* quádruplo ♦ *vt*, *vi* quadruplicar.
quadruplets [kwɔ:'dru:plɪts] *npl* quadrigêmeos *mpl*, quádruplos *mpl*.
quagmire ['kwægmaɪə*] *n* lamaçal *m*, atoleiro.
quail [kweɪl] *n* (*bird*) codorniz *f*, codorna (*BR*) ♦ *vi* acovardar-se.
quaint [kweɪnt] *adj* curioso, esquisito; (*picturesque*) pitoresco.
quake [kweɪk] *vi* tremer, estremecer ♦ *n abbr* = **earthquake**.
Quaker ['kweɪkə*] *n* quacre *m/f*.
qualification [kwɔlɪfɪ'keɪʃən] *n* (*reservation*) restrição *f*, ressalva; (*modification*) modificação *f*; (*act*) qualificação *f*; (*degree*) título, qualificação; **what are your ~s?** quais são as suas qualificações?
qualified ['kwɔlɪfaɪd] *adj* (*trained*) habilitado, qualificado; (*fit*) apto, capaz; (*limited*) limitado; (*professionally*) diplomado; **~ for/to do** credenciado *or* qualificado para/para fazer.
qualify ['kwɔlɪfaɪ] *vt* qualificar; (*capacitate*) capacitar; (*modify*) modificar; (*limit*) restringir, limitar ♦ *vi* (*SPORT*) classificar-se; **to ~ (as)** *vt* classificar (como) ♦ *vi* formar-se *or* diplomar-se (em); **to ~ (for)** reunir os requisitos (para).
qualifying ['kwɔlɪfaɪɪŋ] *adj*: **~ exam** exame *m* de habilitação; **~ round** eliminatórias *fpl*.
qualitative ['kwɔlɪteɪtɪv] *adj* qualitativo.
quality ['kwɔlɪtɪ] *n* qualidade *f* ♦ *cpd* de qualidade; **of good/poor ~** de boa/má qualidade.
quality control *n* controle *m* de qualidade.
quality papers (*BRIT*) *npl*: **the ~** os jornais de categoria.
qualm [kwɑ:m] *n* (*doubt*) dúvida; (*scruple*) escrúpulo; **to have ~s about sth** ter dúvidas sobre a retidão de algo.
quandary ['kwɔndrɪ] *n*: **to be in a ~** estar num dilema.
quango ['kwæŋgəu] (*BRIT*) *n abbr* (= *quasi-autonomous non-governmental organization*) *comissão nomeada pelo governo*.
quantitative ['kwɔntɪtətɪv] *adj* quantitativo.
quantity ['kwɔntɪtɪ] *n* quantidade *f*; **in ~** em quantidade.
quantity surveyor (*BRIT*) *n* calculista *m/f* de obra.
quarantine ['kwɔrnti:n] *n* quarentena.
quarrel ['kwɔrl] *n* (*argument*) discussão *f*; (*fight*) briga ♦ *vi* brigar, discutir; **to have a ~ with sb** ter uma briga *or* brigar com alguém; **I have no ~ with him** não tenho nada contra ele; **I can't ~ with that** não

posso discordar disso.
quarrelsome ['kwɔrlsəm] *adj* brigão/gona.
quarry ['kwɔrɪ] *n* (*for stone*) pedreira; (*animal*) presa, caça ♦ *vt* (*marble etc*) extrair.
quart [kwɔ:t] *n quarto de galão* (= *1.136 l*).
quarter ['kwɔ:tə*] *n* quarto, quarta parte *f*; (*of year*) trimestre *m*; (*district*) bairro; (*US, CANADA*: *25 cents*) (moeda de) 25 centavos *mpl* de dólar ♦ *vt* dividir em quatro; (*MIL*: *lodge*) aquartelar; **~s** *npl* (*MIL*) quartel *m*; (*living* ~*s*) alojamento; **a ~ of an hour** um quarto de hora; **it's a ~ to** (*BRIT*) *or* **of** (*US*) **3** são quinze para as três (*BR*), são três menos um quarto (*PT*); **it's a ~ past** (*BRIT*) *or* **after** (*US*) **3** são três e quinze (*BR*), são três e um quarto (*PT*); **from all ~s** de toda parte; **at close ~s** de perto.
quarter-deck *n* (*NAUT*) tombadilho superior.
quarter final *n* quarta de final.
quarterly ['kwɔ:təlɪ] *adj* trimestral ♦ *adv* trimestralmente ♦ *n* (*PRESS*) revista trimestral.
quartermaster ['kwɔ:təmɑ:stə*] *n* (*MIL*) quartel-mestre *m*; (*NAUT*) contramestre *m*.
quartet(te) [kwɔ:'tɛt] *n* quarteto.
quarto ['kwɔ:təu] *adj, n* in-quarto *inv*.
quartz [kwɔ:ts] *n* quartzo ♦ *cpd* de quartzo.
quash [kwɔʃ] *vt* (*verdict*) anular.
quasi- ['kweɪzaɪ] *prefix* quase-.
quaver ['kweɪvə*] *n* (*BRIT*: *MUS*) colcheia ♦ *vi* tremer.
quay [ki:] *n* (*also*: ~*side*) cais *m*.
queasy ['kwi:zɪ] *adj* (*sickly*) enjoado.
Quebec [kwɪ'bɛk] *n* Quebec.
queen [kwi:n] *n* rainha; (*CARDS etc*) dama.
queen mother *n* rainha-mãe *f*.
queer [kwɪə*] *adj* (*odd*) esquisito, estranho; (*suspect*) suspeito, duvidoso; (*BRIT*: *sick*): **I feel ~** não estou bem ♦ *n* (*inf!*: *highly offensive*) bicha *m* (*BR*), maricas *m* (*PT*).
quell [kwɛl] *vt* abrandar, acalmar; (*put down*) sufocar.
quench [kwɛntʃ] *vt* apagar; (*thirst*) matar.
querulous ['kwɛruləs] *adj* lamuriante.
query ['kwɪərɪ] *n* (*question*) pergunta; (*doubt*) dúvida; (*question mark*) ponto de interrogação ♦ *vt* questionar.
quest [kwɛst] *n* busca; (*journey*) expedição *f*.
question ['kwɛstʃən] *n* pergunta; (*matter*) questão *f* ♦ *vt* (*plan, idea*) duvidar, questionar; (*person*) interrogar, inquirir; **to ask sb a ~, to put a ~ to sb** fazer uma pergunta a alguém; **to bring** *or* **call sth into ~** colocar algo em questão, pôr algo em dúvida; **the ~ is ...** a questão é ...; **it is a ~ of** é questão de; **beyond ~** sem dúvida; **out of the ~** fora de cogitação, impossível.
questionable ['kwɛstʃənəbl] *adj* discutível; (*doubtful*) duvidoso.
questioner ['kwɛstʃənə*] *n* pessoa que faz uma pergunta (*or* que fez a pergunta *etc*).
questioning ['kwɛstʃənɪŋ] *adj* interrogador(a) ♦ *n* interrogatório.
question mark *n* ponto de interrogação.
questionnaire [kwɛstʃə'nɛə*] *n* questionário.
queue [kju:] (*BRIT*) *n* fila (*BR*), bicha (*PT*) ♦ *vi* fazer fila (*BR*) *or* bicha (*PT*); **to jump the ~** furar a fila (*BR*), pôr-se à frente (*PT*).
quibble ['kwɪbl] *vi* embromar, tergiversar.
quick [kwɪk] *adj* rápido; (*temper*) vivo; (*agile*) ágil; (*mind*) sagaz, despachado ♦ *adv* rápido ♦ *n*: **to cut sb to the ~** ferir alguém; **be ~!** ande depressa!, vai rápido!; **to be ~ to act** agir com rapidez; **she was ~ to see that ...** ela não tardou a ver que ....
quicken ['kwɪkən] *vt* apressar ♦ *vi* apressar-se.
quicklime ['kwɪklaɪm] *n* cal *f* viva.
quickly ['kwɪklɪ] *adv* rapidamente, depressa.
quickness ['kwɪknɪs] *n* rapidez *f*; (*agility*) agilidade *f*; (*liveliness*) vivacidade *f*.
quicksand ['kwɪksænd] *n* areia movediça.
quickstep ['kwɪkstɛp] *n dança de ritmo rápido*.
quick-tempered *adj* irritadiço, de pavio curto.
quick-witted [-'wɪtɪd] *adj* perspicaz, vivo.
quid [kwɪd] (*BRIT*: *inf*) *n inv* libra.
quid pro quo [-kwəu] *n* contrapartida.
quiet ['kwaɪət] *adj* (*tranquil*) tranqüilo, calmo; (*person*: *still*) quieto; (*not noisy*: *engine*) silencioso; (: *person*) calado; (*not busy*: *day, business*) calmo; (*ceremony, colour*) discreto ♦ *n* sossego, quietude *f* ♦ *vt, vi* (*US*) = **quieten**; **keep ~!** cale-se!, fique quieto!; **on the ~** de fininho.
quieten ['kwaɪətən] (*also*: ~ *down*) *vi* (*grow calm*) acalmar-se; (*grow silent*) calar-se ♦ *vt* (*calm*) tranqüilizar; (*make quiet*) fazer calar.
quietly ['kwaɪətlɪ] *adv* tranqüilamente; (*silently*) silenciosamente; (*talk*) baixo.
quietness ['kwaɪətnɪs] *n* (*silence*) quietude *f*; (*calm*) tranqüilidade *f*.
quill [kwɪl] *n* pena (de escrever).
quilt [kwɪlt] *n* acolchoado, colcha; **(continental) ~** (*BRIT*) edredom (*PT*: -dão) *m*.
quin [kwɪn] *n abbr* = **quintuplet**.
quince [kwɪns] *n* (*fruit*) marmelo; (*tree*) marmeleiro.
quinine [kwɪ'ni:n] *n* quinina.
quintet(te) [kwɪn'tɛt] *n* quinteto.
quintuplets [kwɪn'tju:plɪts] *npl* quíntuplos *mpl*.
quip [kwɪp] *n* escárnio, dito espirituoso ♦ *vt*: **... he ~ped ...** soltou.
quire ['kwaɪə*] *n* mão *f* (*de papel*).
quirk [kwə:k] *n* peculiaridade *f*; **by some ~ of fate** por uma singularidade do destino, por uma dessas coisas que acontecem.
quit [kwɪt] (*pt, pp* **quit** *or* **~ted**) *vt* deixar; (*premises*) desocupar ♦ *vi* parar; (*give up*) desistir; (*resign*) demitir-se; **to ~ doing** parar *or* deixar de fazer; **~ stalling!** (*US*: *inf*) chega de evasivas!; **notice to ~** (*BRIT*) aviso

***NB**: European Portuguese adds the following consonants to certain words:* **b** (sú(b)dito, su(b)til); **c** (a(c)ção, a(c)cionista, a(c)to); **m** (inde(m)ne); **p** (ado(p)ção, ado(p)tar); *for further details see p. xiii.*

para desocupar (um imóvel).

quite [kwaɪt] *adv* (*rather*) bastante; (*entirely*) completamente, totalmente; ~ **new** novinho; **she's ~ pretty** ela é bem bonita; **I ~ understand** eu entendo completamente; ~ **a few of them** um bom número deles; **that's not ~ right** não é bem assim; **not ~ as many as last time** um pouco menos do que da vez passada; ~ **(so)!** exatamente!, isso mesmo!

Quito ['kiːtəu] *n* Quito.

quits [kwɪts] *adj*: ~ **(with)** quite (com); **let's call it ~** ficamos quites.

quiver ['kwɪvə*] *vi* estremecer ♦ *n* (*for arrows*) carcás *m*, aljava.

quiz [kwɪz] *n* (*game*) concurso (de cultura geral); (*in magazine etc*) questionário, teste *m* ♦ *vt* interrogar.

quizzical ['kwɪzɪkəl] *adj* zombeteiro.

quoits [kwɔɪts] *npl* jogo de malha.

quorum ['kwɔːrəm] *n* quorum *m*.

quota ['kwəutə] *n* cota, quota.

quotation [kwəu'teɪʃən] *n* citação *f*; (*estimate*) orçamento; (*of shares*) cotação *f*.

quotation marks *npl* aspas *fpl*.

quote [kwəut] *n* citação *f*; (COMM) orçamento ♦ *vt* (*sentence*) citar; (*price*) propor; (*shares*) cotar ♦ *vi*: **to ~ from** citar; **~s** *npl* aspas *fpl*; **to ~ for a job** propor um preço para um trabalho; **in ~s** entre aspas; ~ ... **unquote** (*in dictation*) abre aspas ... fecha aspas.

quotient ['kwəuʃənt] *n* quociente *m*.

qv *abbr* (= *quod vide*: *which see*) vide.

qwerty keyboard ['kwəːtɪ-] *n* teclado qwerty.

R

R, r [ɑː*] *n* (*letter*) R, r *m*; **R for Robert** (BRIT) *or* **Roger** (US) R de Roberto.

R *abbr* (= *right*) dir.; (= *river*) R.; (= *Réaumur (scale)*) R; (US: CINEMA: = *restricted*) *proibido para menores de 17 anos*; (US: POL) = **republican**; (BRIT) = **Rex**; **Regina**.

RA *abbr* = **rear admiral** ♦ *n abbr* (BRIT) = **Royal Academy**; **Royal Academician**.

RAAF *n abbr* = **Royal Australian Air Force**.

Rabat [rə'bɑːt] *n* Rabat.

rabbi ['ræbaɪ] *n* rabino.

rabbit ['ræbɪt] *n* coelho ♦ *vi*: **to ~ (on)** (BRIT) tagarelar.

rabbit hole *n* toca, lura.

rabbit hutch *n* coelheira.

rabble ['ræbl] (*pej*) *n* povinho, ralé *f*.

rabid ['ræbɪd] *adj* raivoso.

rabies ['reɪbiːz] *n* raiva.

RAC (BRIT) *n abbr* (= *Royal Automobile Club*) ≈ TCB *m* (BR), ≈ ACP *m* (PT).

raccoon [rə'kuːn] *n* mão-pelada *m*, guaxinim *m*.

race [reɪs] *n* (*competition, rush*) corrida; (*species*) raça ♦ *vt* (*person*) apostar corrida com; (*horse*) fazer correr; (*engine*) acelerar ♦ *vi* (*compete*) competir; (*run*) correr; (*pulse*) bater rapidamente; **the human ~** a raça humana; **to ~ in/out** *etc* entrar/sair *etc* correndo.

race car (US) *n* = **racing car**.

race car driver (US) *n* = **racing driver**.

racecourse ['reɪskɔːs] *n* hipódromo.

racehorse ['reɪshɔːs] *n* cavalo de corridas.

race relations *npl* relações *fpl* entre as raças.

racetrack ['reɪstræk] *n* pista de corridas; (*for cars*) autódromo.

racial ['reɪʃl] *adj* racial.

racialism ['reɪʃəlɪzəm] *n* racismo.

racialist ['reɪʃəlɪst] *adj*, *n* racista *m/f*.

racing ['reɪsɪŋ] *n* corrida.

racing car (BRIT) *n* carro de corrida.

racing driver (BRIT) *n* piloto/a de corrida.

racism ['reɪsɪzəm] *n* racismo.

racist ['reɪsɪst] (*pej*) *adj*, *n* racista *m/f*.

rack [ræk] *n* (*also*: *luggage* ~) bagageiro; (*shelf*) estante *f*; (*also*: *roof* ~) xalmas *fpl*, porta-bagagem *m*; (*clothes* ~) cabide *m* ♦ *vt* (*cause pain to*) atormentar; **to ~ one's brains** quebrar a cabeça; **to go to ~ and ruin** (*building*) cair aos pedaços; (*business*) falir.

rack up *vt* acumular.

rack-and-pinion [-'pɪnjən] *n* (TECH) cremalheira e pinhão.

racket ['rækɪt] *n* (*for tennis*) raquete *f* (BR), raqueta (PT); (*noise*) barulheira, zoeira; (*swindle*) negócio ilegal, fraude *f*.

racketeer [rækɪ'tɪə*] (*esp* US) *n* chantagista *m/f*.

racoon [rə'kuːn] *n* = **raccoon**.

racquet ['rækɪt] *n* raquete *f* (BR), raqueta (PT).

racy ['reɪsɪ] *adj* ousado, picante.

RADA ['rɑːdə] (BRIT) *n abbr* = **Royal Academy of Dramatic Art**.

radar ['reɪdɑː*] *n* radar *m* ♦ *cpd* de radar.

radar trap *n* radar *m* rodoviário.

radial ['reɪdɪəl] *adj* (*also*: ~*-ply*) radial.

radiance ['reɪdɪəns] *n* brilho, esplendor *m*.

radiant ['reɪdɪənt] *adj* radiante, brilhante; (PHYS) radiante.

radiate ['reɪdɪeɪt] *vt* (*heat*) irradiar; (*emit*) emitir ♦ *vi* (*lines*) difundir-se, estender-se.

radiation [reɪdɪ'eɪʃən] *n* radiação *f*.

radiation sickness *n* radiointoxicação *f*, intoxicação *f* radioativa.

radiator ['reɪdɪeɪtə*] *n* radiador *m*.

radiator cap *n* tampa do radiador.

radiator grill *n* (AUT) grade *f* do radiador.

radical ['rædɪkl] *adj* radical.

radii ['reɪdɪaɪ] *npl of* **radius**.

radio ['reɪdɪəu] *n* rádio ♦ *vi*: **to ~ to sb** comunicar com alguém por rádio ♦ *vt* (*informa-

tion) transmitir por rádio; (*position*) comunicar por rádio; **on the ~** no rádio.
radioactive [reɪdɪəu'æktɪv] *adj* radioativo.
radioactivity [reɪdɪəuæk'tɪvɪtɪ] *n* radioatividade *f*.
radio announcer *n* locutor(a) *m/f* de rádio.
radio-controlled [-kən'trəuld] *adj* controlado por rádio.
radiographer [reɪdɪ'ɔgrəfə*] *n* radiógrafo/a.
radiography [reɪdɪ'ɔgrəfɪ] *n* radiografia.
radiologist [reɪdɪ'ɔlədʒɪst] *n* radiologista *m/f*.
radiology [reɪdɪ'ɔlədʒɪ] *n* radiologia.
radio station *n* emissora, estação *f* de rádio.
radio taxi *n* rádio-táxi *m*.
radiotelephone [reɪdɪəu'tɛlɪfəun] *n* radiotelefone *m*.
radiotherapist [reɪdɪəu'θɛrəpɪst] *n* radioterapeuta *m/f*.
radiotherapy [reɪdɪəu'θɛrəpɪ] *n* radioterapia.
radish ['rædɪʃ] *n* rabanete *m*.
radium ['reɪdɪəm] *n* rádio.
radius ['reɪdɪəs] (*pl* **radii**) *n* raio; (ANAT) rádio; **within a 50-mile ~** dentro de um raio de 50 milhas.
RAF (BRIT) *n abbr* = **Royal Air Force**.
raffia ['ræfɪə] *n* ráfia.
raffish ['ræfɪʃ] *adj* reles *inv*, ordinário.
raffle ['ræfl] *n* rifa ♦ *vt* rifar.
raft [rɑːft] *n* (*also*: *life ~*) balsa; (*logs*) flutuante *m* de árvores.
rafter ['rɑːftə*] *n* viga, caibro.
rag [ræg] *n* (*piece of cloth*) trapo; (*torn cloth*) farrapo; (*pej*: *newspaper*) jornaleco; (*for charity*) *atividades estudantis beneficentes* ♦ *vt* (BRIT) encarnar em, zombar de; **~s** *npl* trapos *mpl*, farrapos *mpl*; **in ~s** em farrapos.
rag-and-bone man (*irreg*) *n* negociante *m* de trastes.
ragbag ['rægbæg] *n* (*fig*) salada.
rag doll *n* boneca de trapo.
rage [reɪdʒ] *n* (*fury*) raiva, furor *m* ♦ *vi* (*person*) estar furioso; (*storm*) bramar; **to fly into a ~** enfurecer-se; **it's all the ~** é a última moda.
ragged ['rægɪd] *adj* (*edge*) irregular, desigual; (*cuff*) puído, gasto; (*appearance*) esfarrapado, andrajoso; (*coastline*) acidentado.
raging ['reɪdʒɪŋ] *adj* furioso; (*fever, pain*) violento; **~ toothache** dor de dente alucinante; **in a ~ temper** enfurecido.
ragman ['rægmæn] (*irreg*) *n* negociante *m* de trastes.
rag trade (*inf*) *n*: **the ~** a confecção e venda de roupa.
raid [reɪd] *n* (MIL) incursão *f*; (*criminal*) assalto; (*attack*) ataque *m*; (*by police*) batida ♦ *vt* (MIL) invadir, atacar; (*bank etc*) assaltar; (*subj*: *police*) fazer uma batida em.
raider ['reɪdə*] *n* atacante *m/f*; (*criminal*) assaltante *m/f*.
rail [reɪl] *n* (*on stair*) corrimão *m*; (*on bridge, balcony*) parapeito, anteparo; (*of ship*) amurada; **~s** *npl* (*for train*) trilhos *mpl*; **by ~** de trem (BR), por caminho de ferro (PT).
railing(s) ['reɪlɪŋ(z)] *n(pl)* grade *f*.
railroad ['reɪlrəud] (US) *n* estrada (BR) *or* caminho (PT) de ferro.
railway ['reɪlweɪ] *n* estrada (BR) *or* caminho (PT) de ferro.
railway engine *n* locomotiva.
railway line *n* linha de trem (BR) *or* de comboio (PT).
railwayman ['reɪlweɪmən] (*irreg*) *n* ferroviário.
railway station *n* estação *f* ferroviária (BR) *or* de caminho de ferro (PT).
rain [reɪn] *n* chuva ♦ *vi* chover; **in the ~** na chuva; **it's ~ing** está chovendo (BR), está a chover (PT); **it's ~ing cats and dogs** chove a cântaros.
rainbow ['reɪnbəu] *n* arco-íris *m inv*.
raincoat ['reɪnkəut] *n* impermeável *m*, capa de chuva.
raindrop ['reɪndrɔp] *n* gota de chuva.
rainfall ['reɪnfɔːl] *n* chuva; (*measurement*) pluviosidade *f*.
rainproof ['reɪnpruːf] *adj* impermeável.
rainstorm ['reɪnstɔːm] *n* chuvada torrencial.
rainwater ['reɪnwɔːtə*] *n* água pluvial.
rainy ['reɪnɪ] *adj* chuvoso; **a ~ day** um dia de chuva.
raise [reɪz] *n* aumento ♦ *vt* (*lift*) levantar; (*end*: *siege, embargo*) levantar, terminar; (*build*) erguer, edificar; (*increase*) aumentar; (*doubts*) suscitar, despertar; (*a question*) fazer, expor; (*cattle, family*) criar; (*crop*) cultivar, plantar; (*army*) recrutar, alistar; (*funds*) angariar; (*loan*) levantar, obter; **to ~ one's voice** levantar a voz; **to ~ one's glass to sb/sth** brindar à saúde de alguém/brindar algo; **to ~ sb's hopes** dar esperanças a alguém; **to ~ a laugh/smile** provocar risada/sorrisos.
raisin ['reɪzn] *n* passa, uva seca.
Raj [rɑːdʒ] *n*: **the ~** o império (na Índia).
rajah ['rɑːdʒə] *n* rajá *m*.
rake [reɪk] *n* (*tool*) ancinho; (*person*) libertino ♦ *vt* (*garden*) revolver *or* limpar com o ancinho; (*fire*) remover as cinzas de; (*with machine gun*) varrer ♦ *vi*: **to ~ through** (*fig*: *search*) vasculhar.
rake-off (*inf*) *n* comissão *f*.
rakish ['reɪkɪʃ] *adj* (*dissolute*) devasso, dissoluto; **at a ~ angle** de banda, inclinado.
rally ['rælɪ] *n* (POL *etc*) comício; (AUT) rally *m*, rali *m*; (TENNIS) rebatida ♦ *vt* reunir ♦ *vi* reorganizar-se; (*sick person, Stock Exchange*) recuperar-se.
rally round *vi* dar apoio ♦ *vt fus* dar apoio a.
rallying point ['rælɪɪŋ-] *n* (POL, MIL) ponto de encontro.
RAM [ræm] *n abbr* (COMPUT: = *random access*

NB*: European Portuguese adds the following consonants to certain words:* **b** (sú(b)dito, su(b)til); **c** (a(c)ção, a(c)cionista, a(c)to); **m** (inde(m)ne); **p** (ado(p)ção, ado(p)tar); *for further details see p. xiii.*

memory) RAM *f*.
ram [ræm] *n* carneiro; (*TECH*) êmbolo, aríete *m* ♦ *vt* (*push*) cravar; (*crash into*) colidir com; (*tread down*) pisar, calcar.
ramble ['ræmbl] *n* caminhada, excursão *f* a pé ♦ *vi* (*pej*: *also*: ~ *on*) divagar.
rambler ['ræmblə*] *n* caminhante *m/f*; (*BOT*) roseira trepadeira.
rambling ['ræmblɪŋ] *adj* (*speech*) desconexo, incoerente; (*house*) cheio de recantos; (*plant*) rastejante ♦ *n* excursionismo.
RAMC (*BRIT*) *n abbr* = **Royal Army Medical Corps**.
ramification [ræmɪfɪ'keɪʃən] *n* ramificação *f*.
ramp [ræmp] *n* (*incline*) rampa; (*in road*) lombada.
rampage [ræm'peɪdʒ] *n*: **to be on the** ~ alvoroçar-se ♦ *vi*: **they went rampaging through the town** correram feito loucos pela cidade.
rampant ['ræmpənt] *adj* (*disease etc*) violento, implacável.
rampart ['ræmpɑːt] *n* baluarte *m*; (*wall*) muralha.
ramshackle ['ræmʃækl] *adj* caindo aos pedaços.
RAN *n abbr* = **Royal Australian Navy**.
ran [ræn] *pt of* **run**.
ranch [rɑːntʃ] *n* rancho, fazenda, estância.
rancher ['rɑːntʃə*] *n* rancheiro/a, fazendeiro/a.
rancid ['rænsɪd] *adj* rançoso, râncio.
rancour ['ræŋkə*] (*US* **rancor**) *n* rancor *m*.
random ['rændəm] *adj* ao acaso, casual, fortuito; (*COMPUT*, *MATH*) aleatório ♦ *n*: **at** ~ a esmo, aleatoriamente.
random access memory *n* (*COMPUT*) memória de acesso randômico *or* aleatório.
randy ['rændɪ] (*BRIT*: *inf*) *adj* de fogo.
rang [ræŋ] *pt of* **ring**.
range [reɪndʒ] *n* (*of mountains*) cadeia, cordilheira; (*of missile*) alcance *m*; (*of voice*) extensão *f*; (*series*) série *f*; (*of products*) gama, sortimento; (*MIL*: *also*: *shooting* ~) estande *m*; (*also*: *kitchen* ~) fogão *m* ♦ *vt* (*place*) colocar; (*arrange*) arrumar, ordenar ♦ *vi*: **to** ~ **over** (*wander*) percorrer; (*extend*) estender-se por; **to** ~ **from ... to ...** variar de ... a ..., oscilar entre ... e ...; **do you have anything else in this price** ~**?** você tem outras coisas dentro desta faixa de preço?; **within (firing)** ~ ao alcance de tiro; ~**d left/right** (*text*) alinhado à esquerda/direita.
ranger ['reɪndʒə*] *n* guarda-florestal *m/f*.
Rangoon [ræŋ'guːn] *n* Rangum.
rank [ræŋk] *n* (*row*) fila, fileira; (*MIL*) posto; (*status*) categoria, posição *f*; (*BRIT*: *also*: *taxi* ~) ponto de táxi ♦ *vi*: **to** ~ **among** figurar entre ♦ *vt*: **I** ~ **him sixth** eu o coloco em sexto lugar ♦ *adj* (*stinking*) fétido, malcheiroso; (*hypocrisy*, *injustice*) total; **the** ~**s** *npl* (*MIL*) a tropa; **the** ~ **and file** (*fig*) a gente comum; **to close** ~**s** (*MIL*, *fig*) cerrar fileiras.
rankle ['ræŋkl] *vi* (*insult*) doer, magoar.
ransack ['rænsæk] *vt* (*search*) revistar; (*plunder*) saquear, pilhar.
ransom ['rænsəm] *n* resgate *m*; **to hold sb to** ~ (*fig*) encostar alguém contra a parede.
rant [rænt] *vi* arengar.
ranting ['ræntɪŋ] *n* palavreado oco.
rap [ræp] *n* batida breve e seca, tapa ♦ *vt* bater de leve.
rape [reɪp] *n* estupro; (*BOT*) colza ♦ *vt* violentar, estuprar.
rape(seed) oil ['reɪp(siːd)-] *n* óleo de colza.
rapid ['ræpɪd] *adj* rápido.
rapidity [rə'pɪdɪtɪ] *n* rapidez *f*.
rapidly ['ræpɪdlɪ] *adv* rapidamente.
rapids ['ræpɪdz] *npl* (*GEO*) cachoeira.
rapist ['reɪpɪst] *n* estuprador *m*.
rapport [ræ'pɔː*] *n* harmonia, afinidade *f*.
rapt [ræpt] *adj* absorvido; **to be** ~ **in contemplation** estar contemplando embevecido.
rapture ['ræptʃə*] *n* êxtase *m*, arrebatamento; **to go into** ~**s over** extasiar-se com.
rapturous ['ræptʃərəs] *adj* extático; (*applause*) entusiasta.
rare [rɛə*] *adj* raro; (*CULIN*: *steak*) mal passado.
rarebit ['rɛəbɪt] *n see* **Welsh rarebit**.
rarefied ['rɛərɪfaɪd] *adj* (*air*, *atmosphere*) rarefeito.
rarely ['rɛəlɪ] *adv* raramente.
raring ['rɛərɪŋ] *adj*: **to be** ~ **to go** (*inf*) estar louco para começar.
rarity ['rɛərɪtɪ] *n* raridade *f*.
rascal ['rɑːskl] *n* maroto, malandro.
rash [ræʃ] *adj* impetuoso, precipitado ♦ *n* (*MED*) exantema *m*, erupção *f* cutânea; **he came out in a** ~ apareceu-lhe uma irritação na pele.
rasher ['ræʃə*] *n* fatia fina.
rashness ['ræʃnɪs] *n* impetuosidade *f*.
rasp [rɑːsp] *n* (*tool*) lima, raspadeira ♦ *vt* (*speak*: *also*: ~ *out*) falar em voz áspera.
raspberry ['rɑːzbərɪ] *n* framboesa.
raspberry bush *n* framboeseira.
rasping ['rɑːspɪŋ] *adj*: **a** ~ **noise** um ruído áspero *or* irritante.
rat [ræt] *n* rato (*BR*), ratazana (*PT*).
ratable ['reɪtəbl] *adj* = **rateable**.
ratchet ['rætʃɪt] *n* (*TECH*) roquete *m*, catraca.
rate [reɪt] *n* (*ratio*) razão *f*; (*percentage*) percentagem *f*, proporção *f*; (*price*) preço, taxa; (: *of hotel*) diária; (*of interest*) taxa; (*speed*) velocidade *f* ♦ *vt* (*value*) taxar; (*estimate*) avaliar; ~**s** *npl* (*BRIT*) imposto predial e territorial; **to** ~ **as** ser considerado como; **to** ~ **sb/sth as** considerar alguém/algo como; **to** ~ **sth among** considerar algo como um(a) dos/das; **to** ~ **sb/sth highly** valorizar alguém/algo; **at a** ~ **of 60 kph** à velocidade de 60 kph; **at any** ~ de qualquer modo; ~ **of exchange** taxa de câmbio; ~ **of growth** taxa de crescimento; ~ **of return** taxa de retorno.
rateable value ['reɪtəbl-] (*BRIT*) *n* valor *m* tributável (*de um imóvel*).
ratepayer ['reɪtpeɪə*] (*BRIT*) *n* contribuinte *m/f* de imposto predial.
rather ['rɑːðə*] *adv* (*somewhat*) um tanto,

meio; **it's ~ expensive** é meio caro; **there's ~ a lot** há bastante *or* muito; **~ than** em vez de; **I would** *or* **I'd ~ go** preferiria *or* preferia ir; **I'd ~ not leave** eu preferiria *or* preferia não sair; **or ~** (*more accurately*) ou melhor; **I ~ think he won't come** eu estou achando que ele não vem.

ratification [rætɪfɪ'keɪʃən] *n* ratificação *f*.

ratify ['rætɪfaɪ] *vt* ratificar.

rating ['reɪtɪŋ] *n* (*valuation*) avaliação *f*; (*value*) valor *m*; (*standing*) posição *f*; (*NAUT*: *category*) posto; (: *sailor*) marinheiro; **~s** *npl* (*RADIO*, *TV*) índice(s) *m(pl)* de audiência.

ratio ['reɪʃɪəu] *n* razão *f*, proporção *f*; **in the ~ of 100 to 1** na proporção *or* razão de 100 para 1.

ration ['ræʃən] *n* ração *f* ♦ *vt* racionar; **~s** *npl* mantimentos *mpl*, víveres *mpl*.

rational ['ræʃənl] *adj* racional; (*solution, reasoning*) lógico; (*person*) sensato, razoável.

rationale [ræʃə'nɑːl] *n* razão *f* fundamental.

rationalization [ræʃnəlaɪ'zeɪʃən] *n* racionalização *f*.

rationalize ['ræʃənəlaɪz] *vt* racionalizar.

rationally ['ræʃənəlɪ] *adv* racionalmente; (*logically*) logicamente.

rationing ['ræʃnɪŋ] *n* racionamento.

rat poison *n* raticida *m*.

rat race *n* corre-corre *m* diário.

rattan [ræ'tæn] *n* rotim *m*.

rattle ['rætl] *n* batida, rufar *m*; (*of train etc*) chocalhada; (*of hail*) saraivada; (*object*: *of baby*) chocalho; (: *of sports fan*) matraca; (*of snake*) guizo ♦ *vi* chocalhar; (*small objects*) tamborilar ♦ *vt* sacudir, fazer bater; (*inf*: *disconcert*) desconcertar; (: *annoy*) encher.

rattlesnake ['rætlsneɪk] *n* cascavel *f*.

ratty ['rætɪ] (*inf*) *adj* rabugento.

raucous ['rɔːkəs] *adj* áspero, rouco.

raucously ['rɔːkəslɪ] *adv* em voz rouca.

ravage ['rævɪdʒ] *vt* devastar, estragar.

ravages ['rævɪdʒɪz] *npl* estragos *mpl*.

rave [reɪv] *vi* (*in anger*) encolerizar-se; (*with enthusiasm*, *MED*) delirar ♦ *cpd*: **~ review** (*inf*) crítica estrondosa.

raven ['reɪvən] *n* corvo.

ravenous ['rævənəs] *adj* morto de fome, esfaimado.

ravine [rə'viːn] *n* ravina, barranco.

raving ['reɪvɪŋ] *adj*: **~ lunatic** doido/a varrido/a.

ravings ['reɪvɪŋz] *npl* delírios *mpl*.

ravioli [rævɪ'əulɪ] *n* raviòli *m*.

ravish ['rævɪʃ] *vt* arrebatar; (*delight*) encantar.

ravishing ['rævɪʃɪŋ] *adj* encantador(a).

raw [rɔː] *adj* (*uncooked*) cru; (*not processed*) bruto; (*sore*) vivo; (*inexperienced*) inexperiente, novato; **to get a ~ deal** (*inf*) levar a pior.

raw material *n* matéria-prima.

ray [reɪ] *n* raio; **~ of hope** fio de esperança.

rayon ['reɪɔn] *n* raiom *m*.

raze [reɪz] *vt* (*also*: **~** *to the ground*) arrasar, aniquilar.

razor ['reɪzə*] *n* (*open*) navalha; (*safety* **~**) aparelho de barbear.

razor blade *n* gilete *m* (*BR*), lâmina de barbear (*PT*).

razzle(-dazzle) ['ræzl-] (*BRIT*: *inf*) *n*: **to go on the ~** cair na farra.

razzmatazz ['ræzmə'tæz] (*inf*) *n* alvoroço.

R&B *n abbr* = **rhythm and blues**.

RC *abbr* = **Roman Catholic**.

RCAF *n abbr* = **Royal Canadian Air Force**.

RCMP *n abbr* = **Royal Canadian Mounted Police**.

RCN *n abbr* = **Royal Canadian Navy**.

RD (*US*) *abbr* (*POST*) = **rural delivery**.

Rd *abbr* = **road**.

R&D *n abbr* = **research and development**.

RDC (*BRIT*) *n abbr* = **rural district council**.

RE (*BRIT*) *n abbr* = **religious education**; (*MIL*) = **Royal Engineers**.

re [riː] *prep* referente a.

reach [riːtʃ] *n* alcance *m*; (*BOXING*) campo de ação; (*of river etc*) extensão *f* ♦ *vt* alcançar, atingir; (*arrive at*) chegar em; (*achieve*) conseguir; (*stretch out*) estender, esticar ♦ *vi* alcançar; (*stretch*) estender-se; **within ~** (*object*) ao alcance (da mão); **within easy ~ (of)** (*place*) ao alcance (de); **out of** *or* **beyond ~** fora de alcance; **to ~ out for sth** estender *or* esticar a mão para pegar (em) algo; **to ~ sb by phone** comunicar-se com alguém por telefone; **can I ~ you at your hotel?** posso entrar em contato com você no seu hotel?

react [riː'ækt] *vi* reagir.

reaction [riː'ækʃən] *n* reação *f*.

reactionary [riː'ækʃənrɪ] *adj*, *n* reacionário/a.

reactor [riː'æktə*] *n* reator *m*.

read [riːd, *pt*, *pp* rɛd] *vi* ler ♦ *vt* ler; (*understand*) compreender; (*study*) estudar; **to take sth as read** (*fig*) considerar algo como garantido; **do you ~ me?** (*TEL*) está me ouvindo?; **to ~ between the lines** ler nas entrelinhas.

read out *vt* ler em voz alta.

read over *vt* reler.

read through *vt* (*quickly*) dar uma lida em; (*thoroughly*) ler até o fim.

read up (on) *vt fus* estudar.

readable ['riːdəbl] *adj* (*writing*) legível; (*book*) que merece ser lido.

reader ['riːdə*] *n* leitor(a) *m/f*; (*book*) livro de leituras; (*BRIT*: *at university*) professor(a) *m/f* adjunto/a.

readership ['riːdəʃɪp] *n* (*of paper*: *readers*) leitores *mpl*; (: *number of readers*) número de leitores.

readily ['rɛdɪlɪ] *adv* (*willingly*) de boa vontade; (*easily*) facilmente; (*quickly*) sem demo-

NB: European Portuguese adds the following consonants to certain words: **b** (sú(b)dito, su(b)til); **c** (a(c)ção, a(c)cionista, a(c)to); **m** (inde(m)ne); **p** (ado(p)ção, ado(p)tar); *for further details see p. xiii.*

ra, prontamente.
readiness ['rɛdɪnɪs] *n* boa vontade *f*, prontidão *f*; (*preparedness*) preparação *f*; **in ~** (*prepared*) preparado, pronto.
reading ['ri:dɪŋ] *n* leitura; (*understanding*) compreensão *f*; (*on instrument*) indicação *f*.
reading lamp *n* lâmpada de leitura.
reading room *n* sala de leitura.
readjust [ri:ə'dʒʌst] *vt* reajustar ♦ *vi* (*person*): **to ~ to** reorientar-se para.
ready ['rɛdɪ] *adj* pronto, preparado; (*willing*) disposto; (*available*) disponível ♦ *adv*: **~-cooked** pronto para comer ♦ *n*: **at the ~** (*MIL*) pronto para atirar; (*fig*) pronto; **~ for use** pronto para o uso; **to be ~ to do sth** estar pronto *or* preparado para fazer algo; **to get ~** *vi* preparar-se ♦ *vt* preparar.
ready cash *n* dinheiro vivo.
ready-made *adj* (já) feito; (*clothes*) pronto.
ready-mix *n* (*for cakes etc*) massa pronta.
ready reckoner [-'rɛkənə*] (*BRIT*) *n* tabela de cálculos feitos.
ready-to-wear *adj* pronto.
reaffirm [ri:ə'fə:m] *vt* reafirmar.
reagent [ri:'eɪdʒənt] *n* reagente *m*, reativo.
real [rɪəl] *adj* real; (*genuine*) verdadeiro, autêntico; (*proper*) de verdade ♦ *adv* (*US*: *inf*: *very*) bem; **in ~ life** na vida real; **in ~ terms** em termos reais.
real estate *n* bens *mpl* imobiliários *or* de raiz.
realism ['rɪəlɪzəm] *n* realismo.
realist ['rɪəlɪst] *n* realista *m/f*.
realistic [rɪə'lɪstɪk] *adj* realista.
reality [ri:'ælɪtɪ] *n* realidade *f*; **in ~** na verdade, na realidade.
realization [rɪəlaɪ'zeɪʃən] *n* (*fulfilment*) realização *f*; (*understanding*) compreensão *f*; (*COMM*) conversão *f* em dinheiro, realização.
realize ['rɪəlaɪz] *vt* (*understand*) perceber; (*a project*, *COMM*: *asset*) realizar; **I ~ that ...** eu concordo que ....
really ['rɪəlɪ] *adv* realmente, na verdade; **~?** é mesmo?
realm [rɛlm] *n* reino.
real-time *adj* (*COMPUT*) em tempo real.
realtor ['rɪəltə*] (*US*) *n* corretor(a) *m/f* de imóveis (*BR*), agente *m/f* imobiliário/a (*PT*).
ream [ri:m] *n* resma; **~s** *npl* (*fig*: *inf*) páginas *fpl* e páginas.
reap [ri:p] *vt* segar, ceifar; (*fig*) colher.
reaper ['ri:pə*] *n* segador(a) *m/f*, ceifeiro/a; (*machine*) segadora.
reappear [ri:ə'pɪə*] *vi* reaparecer.
reappearance [ri:ə'pɪərəns] *n* reaparição *f*.
reapply [ri:ə'plaɪ] *vi*: **to ~ for** requerer de novo; (*job*) candidatar-se de novo a.
reappraisal [ri:ə'preɪzl] *n* reavaliação *f*.
rear [rɪə*] *adj* traseiro, de trás ♦ *n* traseira; (*inf*: *bottom*) traseiro ♦ *vt* (*cattle*, *family*) criar ♦ *vi* (*also*: **~ up**: *animal*) empinar-se.
rear-engined [-'ɛndʒɪnd] *adj* (*AUT*) com motor traseiro.
rearguard ['rɪəgɑ:d] *n* retaguarda.
rearm [ri:'ɑ:m] *vt*, *vi* rearmar.
rearmament [ri:'ɑ:məmənt] *n* rearmamento *m*.
rearrange [ri:ə'reɪndʒ] *vt* arrumar de novo, reorganizar.
rear-view mirror *n* (*AUT*) espelho retrovisor.
reason ['ri:zn] *n* razão *f* ♦ *vi*: **to ~ with sb** argumentar com *or* persuadir alguém; **the ~ for/why** a razão de/pela qual; **to have ~ to think** ter motivo para pensar; **it stands to ~ that** é razoável *or* lógico que; **she claims with good ~ that ...** ela afirma com toda a razão que ...; **all the more ~ why you should not sell it** mais uma razão para você não vendê-lo.
reasonable ['ri:zənəbl] *adj* razoável; (*sensible*) sensato.
reasonably ['ri:zənəblɪ] *adv* razoavelmente; **one can ~ assume that ...** tudo indica que ....
reasoned ['ri:zənd] *adj* (*argument*) fundamentado.
reasoning ['ri:zənɪŋ] *n* raciocínio, argumentação *f*.
reassemble [ri:ə'sɛmbl] *vt* (*people*) reunir; (*machine*) montar de novo ♦ *vi* reunir-se de novo.
reassert [ri:ə'sə:t] *vt* reafirmar.
reassurance [ri:ə'ʃuərəns] *n* garantia; (*comfort*) reconforto.
reassure [ri:ə'ʃuə*] *vt* tranqüilizar, animar; **to ~ sb of** reafirmar a confiança de alguém acerca de.
reassuring [ri:ə'ʃuərɪŋ] *adj* animador(a), tranqüilizador(a).
reawakening [ri:ə'weɪknɪŋ] *n* despertar *m*.
rebate ['ri:beɪt] *n* (*on product*) abatimento; (*on tax etc*) devolução *f*; (*refund*) reembolso.
rebel [*n* 'rɛbl, *vi* rɪ'bɛl] *n* rebelde *m/f* ♦ *vi* rebelar-se.
rebellion [rɪ'bɛljən] *n* rebelião *f*, revolta.
rebellious [rɪ'bɛljəs] *adj* insurreto; (*child*) rebelde.
rebirth [ri:'bə:θ] *n* renascimento.
rebound [*vi* rɪ'baund, *n* 'ri:baund] *vi* (*ball*) ressaltar ♦ *n* ressalto.
rebuff [rɪ'bʌf] *n* repulsa, recusa ♦ *vt* repelir.
rebuild [ri:'bɪld] (*irreg*) *vt* reconstruir.
rebuke [rɪ'bju:k] *n* reprimenda, censura ♦ *vt* repreender.
rebut [rɪ'bʌt] *vt* refutar.
rebuttal [rɪ'bʌtl] *n* refutação *f*.
recalcitrant [rɪ'kælsɪtrənt] *adj* recalcitrante, teimoso.
recall [rɪ'kɔ:l] *vt* (*remember*) recordar, lembrar; (*ambassador etc*) mandar voltar ♦ *n* chamada (de volta); (*memory*) recordação *f*; **it is beyond ~** caiu no esquecimento.
recant [rɪ'kænt] *vi* retratar-se.
recap ['ri:kæp] *vt*, *vi* recapitular ♦ *n* recapitulação *f*.
recapture [ri:'kæptʃə*] *vt* (*town*) retomar, recobrar; (*atmosphere*) recriar.
recd. *abbr* = **received**.
recede [rɪ'si:d] *vi* (*go back*) retroceder; (*go

away) afastar-se.

receding [rɪ'siːdɪŋ] *adj* (*forehead, chin*) metido *or* puxado para dentro; ~ **hairline** entradas *fpl* (no cabelo).

receipt [rɪ'siːt] *n* (*document*) recibo; (*act of receiving*) recebimento (*BR*), recepção *f* (*PT*); ~**s** *npl* (*COMM*) receitas *fpl*; **on ~ of** ao receber; **to acknowledge ~ of** acusar o recebimento (*BR*) *or* a recepção (*PT*) de; **we are in ~ of ...** recebimos ....

receivable [rɪ'siːvəbl] *adj* (*COMM*) a receber.

receive [rɪ'siːv] *vt* receber; (*guest*) acolher; (*wound*) sofrer; **"~d with thanks"** (*COMM*) "recebido".

receiver [rɪ'siːvə*] *n* (*TEL*) fone *m* (*BR*), auscultador *m* (*PT*); (*RADIO*) receptor *m*; (*of stolen goods*) receptador(a) *m/f*; (*COMM*) curador(a) *m/f or* síndico/a de massa falida.

recent ['riːsnt] *adj* recente; **in ~ years** nos últimos anos.

recently ['riːsntlɪ] *adv* (*a short while ago*) recentemente; (*in recent times*) ultimamente; **as ~ as yesterday** ainda ontem; **until ~** até recentemente.

receptacle [rɪ'sɛptɪkl] *n* receptáculo, recipiente *m*.

reception [rɪ'sɛpʃən] *n* recepção *f*; (*welcome*) acolhida.

reception centre (*BRIT*) *n* centro de recepção.

reception desk *n* (mesa de) recepção *f*.

receptionist [rɪ'sɛpʃənɪst] *n* recepcionista *m/f*.

receptive [rɪ'sɛptɪv] *adj* receptivo.

recess [rɪ'sɛs] *n* (*in room*) recesso, vão *m*; (*for bed*) nicho; (*secret place*) esconderijo; (*POL etc: holiday*) férias *fpl*; (*US*: *LAW*: *short break*) recesso; (*SCH*: *esp US*) recreio.

recession [rɪ'sɛʃən] *n* recessão *f*.

recharge [riː'tʃɑːdʒ] *vt* (*battery*) recarregar.

rechargeable [riː'tʃɑːdʒəbl] *adj* recarregável.

recipe ['rɛsɪpɪ] *n* receita.

recipient [rɪ'sɪpɪənt] *n* recipiente *m/f*, recebedor(a) *m/f*; (*of letter*) destinatário/a.

reciprocal [rɪ'sɪprəkl] *adj* recíproco.

reciprocate [rɪ'sɪprəkeɪt] *vt* retribuir ♦ *vi* (*in hospitality etc*) retribuir; (*in aggression etc*) revidar.

recital [rɪ'saɪtl] *n* recital *m*.

recite [rɪ'saɪt] *vt* (*poem*) recitar; (*complaints etc*) enumerar.

reckless ['rɛkləs] *adj* (*driver*) imprudente; (*speed*) imprudente, excessivo; (*spender*) irresponsável.

recklessly ['rɛkləslɪ] *adv* temerariamente, sem prudência; (*spend*) irresponsavelmente.

reckon ['rɛkən] *vt* (*count*) calcular, contar; (*consider*) considerar; (*think*): **I ~ that ...** acho que ... ♦ *vi*: **he is somebody to be ~ed with** ele é alguém que não pode ser esquecido; **to ~ without sb/sth** não levar alguém/algo em conta, não contar com alguém/algo.
 reckon on *vt fus* contar com.

reckoning ['rɛkənɪŋ] *n* (*calculation*) cálculo; **the day of ~** o dia do Juízo Final.

reclaim [rɪ'kleɪm] *vt* (*get back*) recuperar; (*land*) desbravar; (: *from sea*) aterrar; (*demand back*) reivindicar.

reclamation [rɛklə'meɪʃən] *n* recuperação *f*; (*of land from sea*) aterro.

recline [rɪ'klaɪn] *vi* reclinar-se; (*lean*) apoiar-se, recostar-se.

reclining [rɪ'klaɪnɪŋ] *adj* (*seat*) reclinável.

recluse [rɪ'kluːs] *n* recluso/a.

recognition [rɛkəg'nɪʃən] *n* reconhecimento; **transformed beyond ~** tão transformado que está irreconhecível; **in ~ of** em reconhecimento de; **to gain ~** ser reconhecido.

recognizable ['rɛkəgnaɪzəbl] *adj* reconhecível.

recognize ['rɛkəgnaɪz] *vt* reconhecer; (*accept*) aceitar; **to ~ by/as** reconhecer por/como.

recoil [*vi* rɪ'kɔɪl, *n* 'riːkɔɪl] *vi* recuar ♦ *n* (*of gun*) coice *m*; **to ~ from doing sth** recusar-se a fazer algo.

recollect [rɛkə'lɛkt] *vt* lembrar, recordar.

recollection [rɛkə'lɛkʃən] *n* recordação *f*, lembrança; **to the best of my ~** se não me falha a memória.

recommend [rɛkə'mɛnd] *vt* recomendar; **she has a lot to ~ her** ela tem muito a seu favor.

recommendation [rɛkəmɛn'deɪʃən] *n* recomendação *f*.

recommended retail price [rɛkə'mɛndɪd-] (*BRIT*) *n* preço máximo consumidor.

recompense ['rɛkəmpɛns] *vt* recompensar ♦ *n* recompensa.

reconcilable [rɛkən'saɪləbl] *adj* (*ideas*) conciliável.

reconcile ['rɛkənsaɪl] *vt* (*two people*) reconciliar; (*two facts*) conciliar, harmonizar; **to ~ o.s. to sth** resignar-se a *or* conformar-se com algo.

reconciliation [rɛkənsɪlɪ'eɪʃən] *n* reconciliação *f*.

recondite [rɪ'kɔndaɪt] *adj* obscuro.

recondition [riːkən'dɪʃən] *vt* recondicionar.

reconnaissance [rɪ'kɔnɪsns] *n* (*MIL*) reconhecimento.

reconnoitre [rɛkə'nɔɪtə*] (*US* **reconnoiter**) *vt* (*MIL*) reconhecer ♦ *vi* fazer um reconhecimento.

reconsider [riːkən'sɪdə*] *vt* reconsiderar.

reconstitute [riː'kɔnstɪtjuːt] *vt* reconstituir.

reconstruct [riːkən'strʌkt] *vt* reconstruir.

reconstruction [riːkən'strʌkʃən] *n* reconstrução *f*.

record [*n, adj* 'rɛkɔːd, *vt* rɪ'kɔːd] *n* (*MUS*) disco; (*of meeting etc*) ata, minuta; (*register, proof, COMPUT*) registro (*BR*), registo (*PT*); (*file*) arquivo; (*also*: *police ~*) ficha na polícia; (*written*) história; (*SPORT*) recorde *m* ♦ *vt* (*set down*) assentar, registrar (*BR*), registar (*PT*); (*relate*) relatar, referir; (*MUS*: *song etc*) gravar ♦ *adj*: **in ~ time** num

NB: European Portuguese adds the following consonants to certain words: **b** (sú(b)dito, su(b)til); **c** (a(c)ção, a(c)cionista, a(c)to); **m** (inde(m)ne); **p** (ado(p)ção, ado(p)tar); *for further details see p. xiii.*

tempo recorde; **public ~s** arquivo público; **to keep a ~ of** anotar; **to put the ~ straight** (*fig*) corrigir um equívoco; **he is on ~ as saying that ...** ele declarou publicamente que ...; **Italy's excellent ~** o excelente desempenho da Itália; **off the ~** *adj* confidencial ♦ *adv* confidencialmente.

record card *n* (*in file*) ficha.

recorded delivery letter [rɪ'kɔːdɪd-] (*BRIT*) *n* (*POST*) ≈ carta registrada (*BR*) *or* registada (*PT*).

recorder [rɪ'kɔːdə*] *n* (*MUS*) flauta; (*TECH*) indicador *m* mecânico; (*official*) escrivão/vã *m/f*.

record holder *n* (*SPORT*) detentor(a) *m/f* do recorde.

recording [rɪ'kɔːdɪŋ] *n* (*MUS*) gravação *f*.

recording studio *n* estúdio de gravação.

record library *n* discoteca.

record player *n* toca-discos *m inv* (*BR*), gira-discos *m inv* (*PT*).

recount [rɪ'kaunt] *vt* relatar.

re-count [*n* 'riːkaunt, *vt* riː'kaunt] *n* (*POL*: *of votes*) nova contagem *f*, recontagem *f* ♦ *vt* recontar.

recoup [rɪ'kuːp] *vt*: **to ~ one's losses** recuperar-se dos prejuízos.

recourse [rɪ'kɔːs] *n* recurso; **to have ~ to** recorrer a.

recover [rɪ'kʌvə*] *vt* recuperar; (*rescue*) resgatar ♦ *vi* (*from illness*) recuperar-se; (*from shock*) refazer-se.

re-cover *vt* (*chair etc*) revestir.

recovery [rɪ'kʌvərɪ] *n* recuperação *f*, restabelecimento; (*MED*) melhora.

recreate [riːkrɪ'eɪt] *vt* recriar.

recreation [rɛkrɪ'eɪʃən] *n* recreação *f*; (*play*) recreio.

recreational [rɛkrɪ'eɪʃənl] *adj* recreativo.

recreational vehicle (*US*) *n* kombi *m*.

recrimination [rɪkrɪmɪ'neɪʃən] *n* recriminação *f*.

recruit [rɪ'kruːt] *n* recruta *m/f* ♦ *vt* recrutar.

recruiting office [rɪ'kruːtɪŋ-] *n* centro de recrutamento.

recruitment [rɪ'kruːtmənt] *n* recrutamento.

rectangle ['rɛktæŋgl] *n* retângulo.

rectangular [rɛk'tæŋgjulə*] *adj* retangular.

rectify ['rɛktɪfaɪ] *vt* retificar.

rector ['rɛktə*] *n* (*REL*) pároco; (*SCH*) reitor(a) *m/f*.

rectory ['rɛktərɪ] *n* presbitério, residência paroquial.

rectum ['rɛktəm] *n* (*ANAT*) reto.

recuperate [rɪ'kuːpəreɪt] *vi* restabelecer-se, recuperar-se.

recur [rɪ'kəː*] *vi* repetir-se, ocorrer outra vez; (*opportunity*) surgir de novo; (*symptoms*) reaparecer.

recurrence [rɪ'kʌrəns] *n* repetição *f*; (*of symptoms*) reaparição *f*.

recurrent [rɪ'kʌrənt] *adj* repetido, periódico.

recurring [rɪ'kəːrɪŋ] *adj* (*MATH*) periódico.

red [rɛd] *n* vermelho; (*POL*: *pej*) vermelho/a ♦ *adj* vermelho; (*hair*) ruivo; **to be in the ~** (*person*) estar no vermelho; (*account*) não ter fundos.

red carpet treatment *n*: **she was given the ~** ela foi recebida com todas as honras.

Red Cross *n* Cruz *f* Vermelha.

redcurrant ['rɛd'kʌrənt] *n* groselha.

redden ['rɛdən] *vt* avermelhar ♦ *vi* corar, ruborizar-se.

reddish ['rɛdɪʃ] *adj* avermelhado; (*hair*) arruivado.

redecorate [riː'dɛkəreɪt] *vt* decorar de novo, redecorar.

redecoration [riːdɛkə'reɪʃən] *n* remodelação *f*.

redeem [rɪ'diːm] *vt* (*REL*) redimir; (*sth in pawn*) tirar do prego; (*debt, shares, also: fig*) resgatar.

redeemable [rɪ'diːməbl] *adj* resgatável.

redeeming [rɪ'diːmɪŋ] *adj*: **~ feature** lado bom *or* que salva.

redeploy [riːdɪ'plɔɪ] *vt* (*resources, troops*) redistribuir.

redeployment [riːdɪ'plɔɪmənt] *n* redistribuição *f*.

redevelop [riːdɪ'vɛləp] *vt* renovar.

redevelopment [riːdɪ'vɛləpmənt] *n* renovação *f*.

red-haired *adj* ruivo.

red-handed [-'hændɪd] *adj*: **to be caught ~** ser apanhado em flagrante, ser flagrado.

redhead ['rɛdhɛd] *n* ruivo/a.

red herring *n* (*fig*) pista falsa.

red-hot *adj* incandescente.

redid [riː'dɪd] *pt of* **redo**.

redirect [riːdaɪ'rɛkt] *vt* (*mail*) endereçar de novo.

redistribute [riːdɪ'strɪbjuːt] *vt* redistribuir.

red-letter day *n* dia *m* memorável.

red light *n*: **to go through a ~** (*AUT*) avançar o sinal.

red-light district *n* zona (de meretrício).

redness ['rɛdnɪs] *n* vermelhidão *f*.

redo [riː'duː] (*irreg*) *vt* refazer.

redolent ['rɛdələnt] *adj*: **~ of** que cheira a; (*fig*) que evoca.

redone [riː'dʌn] *pp of* **redo**.

redouble [riː'dʌbl] *vt*: **to ~ one's efforts** redobrar os esforços.

redraft [riː'drɑːft] *vt* redigir de novo.

redress [rɪ'drɛs] *n* reparação *f* ♦ *vt* retificar, remediar; **to ~ the balance** restituir o equilíbrio.

Red Sea *n*: **the ~** o mar Vermelho.

redskin ['rɛdskɪn] *n* pele-vermelha *m/f*.

red tape *n* (*fig*) papelada, burocracia.

reduce [rɪ'djuːs] *vt* reduzir; (*lower*) rebaixar; **"~ speed now"** (*AUT*) "diminua a velocidade"; **to ~ sth by/to** diminuir algo em/reduzir algo a; **to ~ sb to tears/despair** levar alguém às lagrimas/ao desespero.

reduced [rɪ'djuːst] *adj*: **"greatly ~ prices"** "preços altamente reduzidos"; **at a ~ price** a preço reduzido.

reduction [rɪ'dʌkʃən] *n* redução *f*; (*of price*) abatimento; (*discount*) desconto.

redundancy [rɪ'dʌndənsɪ] *n* redundância;

(*BRIT*: *of worker*) demissão *f*; **compulsory ~** demissão; **voluntary ~** demissão voluntária.

redundancy payment (*BRIT*) *n indenização paga aos empregados dispensados sem justa causa.*

redundant [rɪ'dʌndnt] *adj* (*BRIT*: *worker*) desempregado; (*detail, object*) redundante, supérfluo; **to be made ~** ficar sem trabalho *or* desempregado.

reed [ri:d] *n* (*BOT*) junco; (*MUS*: *of clarinet etc*) palheta.

reedy ['ri:dɪ] *adj* (*voice, instrument*) agudo.

reef [ri:f] *n* (*at sea*) recife *m*.

reek [ri:k] *vi*: **to ~ (of)** cheirar (a), feder (a).

reel [ri:l] *n* carretel *m*, bobina; (*of film*) rolo, filme *m* ♦ *vt* (*TECH*) bobinar; (*also*: *~ up*) enrolar ♦ *vi* (*sway*) cambalear, oscilar; **my head is ~ing** estou completamente confuso.

reel off *vt* (*say*) enumerar, recitar.

re-election *n* reeleição *f*.

re-enter *vt* reentrar em.

re-entry *n* reentrada.

re-export [*vt* ri:ɪks'pɔ:t, *n* ri:'ɛkspɔ:t] *vt* reexportar ♦ *n* reexportação *f*.

ref [rɛf] (*inf*) *n abbr* = **referee**.

ref. *abbr* (*COMM*: = *reference*) ref.

refectory [rɪ'fɛktərɪ] *n* refeitório.

refer [rɪ'fə:*] *vt*: **to ~ sth to** (*dispute, decision*) submeter algo à apreciação de; **to ~ sb to** (*inquirer*: *for information*) encaminhar alguém a; (*reader*: *to text*) remeter alguém a.

refer to *vt fus* (*allude to*) referir-se *or* aludir a; (*apply to*) aplicar-se a; (*consult*) recorrer a; **~ring to your letter** (*COMM*) com referência à sua carta.

referee [rɛfə'ri:] *n* árbitro/a; (*BRIT*: *for job application*) referência ♦ *vt* arbitrar; (*football match*) apitar.

reference ['rɛfrəns] *n* referência; **with ~ to** com relação a; (*COMM*: *in letter*) com referência a; **"please quote this ~"** (*COMM*) "queira citar esta referência".

reference book *n* livro de consulta.

reference number *n* (*COMM*) número de referência.

referenda [rɛfə'rɛndə] *npl of* **referendum**.

referendum [rɛfə'rɛndəm] (*pl* **referenda**) *n* referendum *m*, plebiscito.

refill [*vt* ri:'fɪl, *n* 'ri:fɪl] *vt* reencher; (*lighter etc*) reabastecer ♦ *n* (*for pen*) carga nova; (*COMM*) refill *m*.

refine [rɪ'faɪn] *vt* (*sugar, oil*) refinar.

refined [rɪ'faɪnd] *adj* (*person, taste*) refinado, culto.

refinement [rɪ'faɪnmənt] *n* (*of person*) cultura, refinamento, requinte *m*.

refinery [rɪ'faɪnərɪ] *n* refinaria.

refit [*n* 'ri:fɪt, *vt* ri:'fɪt] *n* (*NAUT*) reequipamento ♦ *vt* reequipar.

reflate [ri:'fleɪt] *vt* (*economy*) reflacionar.

reflation [ri:'fleɪʃən] *n* reflação *f*.

reflationary [ri:'fleɪʃənrɪ] *adj* reflacionário.

reflect [rɪ'flɛkt] *vt* (*light, image*) refletir ♦ *vi* (*think*) refletir, meditar.

reflect on *vt fus* (*discredit*) prejudicar.

reflection [rɪ'flɛkʃən] *n* (*act*) reflexão *f*; (*image*) reflexo; (*criticism*): **~ on** crítica de; **on ~** pensando bem.

reflector [rɪ'flɛktə*] *n* (*also*: *AUT*) refletor *m*.

reflect stud (*US*) *n* (*AUT*) olho de gato.

reflex ['ri:flɛks] *adj*, *n* reflexo.

reflexive [rɪ'flɛksɪv] *adj* (*LING*) reflexivo.

reform [rɪ'fɔ:m] *n* reforma ♦ *vt* reformar.

reformat [ri:'fɔ:mæt] *vt* (*COMPUT*) reformatar.

Reformation [rɛfə'meɪʃən] *n*: **the ~** a Reforma.

reformatory [rɪ'fɔ:mətərɪ] (*US*) *n* reformatório.

reformed [rɪ'fɔ:md] *adj* emendado, reformado.

reformer [rɪ'fɔ:mə*] *n* reformador(a) *m/f*.

reformist [rɪ'fɔ:mɪst] *n* reformista *m/f*.

refrain [rɪ'freɪn] *vi*: **to ~ from doing** abster-se de fazer ♦ *n* estribilho, refrão *m*.

refresh [rɪ'frɛʃ] *vt* refrescar.

refresher course [rɪ'frɛʃə*-] (*BRIT*) *n* curso de reciclagem.

refreshing [rɪ'frɛʃɪŋ] *adj* refrescante; (*sleep*) repousante; (*change*) agradável; (*idea, thought*) original.

refreshment [rɪ'frɛʃmənt] *n* (*eating*): **for some ~** para comer alguma coisa; (*resting etc*): **in need of ~** precisando se refazer, precisando refazer as suas forças; **~s** *npl* (*drinks*) refrescos *mpl*.

refrigeration [rɪfrɪdʒə'reɪʃən] *n* refrigeração *f*.

refrigerator [rɪ'frɪdʒəreɪtə*] *n* refrigerador *m*, geladeira (*BR*), frigorífico (*PT*).

refuel [ri:'fjuəl] *vt*, *vi* reabastecer.

refuge ['rɛfju:dʒ] *n* refúgio; **to take ~ in** refugiar-se em.

refugee [rɛfju'dʒi:] *n* refugiado/a.

refugee camp *n* campo de refugiados.

refund [*n* 'ri:fʌnd, *vt* rɪ'fʌnd] *n* reembolso ♦ *vt* devolver, reembolsar.

refurbish [ri:'fə:bɪʃ] *vt* renovar.

refurnish [ri:'fə:nɪʃ] *vt* colocar móveis novos em.

refusal [rɪ'fju:zəl] *n* recusa, negativa; **first ~** primeira opção.

refuse [*n* 'rɛfju:s, *vt*, *vi* rɪ'fju:z] *n* refugo, lixo ♦ *vt* recusar; (*order*) recusar-se a ♦ *vi* recusar-se, negar-se; **to ~ to do sth** recusar-se a fazer algo.

refuse bin *n* lata de lixo.

refuse collection *n* remoção *f* de lixo.

refuse collector *n* lixeiro/a, gari *m/f* (*BR*).

refuse disposal *n* destruição *f* de lixo.

refuse tip *n* depósito de lixo.

refute [rɪ'fju:t] *vt* refutar.

regain [rɪ'geɪn] *vt* recuperar, recobrar.

regal ['ri:gl] *adj* real, régio.

regale [rɪ'geɪl] *vt*: **to ~ sb with sth** regalar alguém com algo.

regalia [rɪ'geɪlɪə] *n*, *npl* insígnias *fpl* reais.

NB: European Portuguese adds the following consonants to certain words: **b** (sú(b)dito, su(b)til); **c** (a(c)ção, a(c)cionista, a(c)to); **m** (inde(m)ne); **p** (ado(p)ção, ado(p)tar); *for further details see p. xiii.*

regard [rɪ'gɑːd] *n* (*aspect*) respeito; (*attention*) atenção *f*; (*esteem*) estima, consideração *f* ♦ *vt* (*consider*) considerar; **to give one's ~s to** dar lembranças a; **"with kindest ~s"** "cordialmente"; **as ~s, with ~ to** com relação a, com respeito a, quanto a.
regarding [rɪ'gɑːdɪŋ] *prep* com relação a.
regardless [rɪ'gɑːdlɪs] *adv* apesar de tudo; **~ of** apesar de.
regatta [rɪ'gætə] *n* regata.
regency ['riːdʒənsɪ] *n* regência.
regenerate [rɪ'dʒɛnəreɪt] *vt* regenerar ♦ *vi* regenerar-se.
regent ['riːdʒənt] *n* regente *m/f*.
régime [reɪ'ʒiːm] *n* regime *m*.
regiment [*n* 'rɛdʒɪmənt, *vt* 'rɛdʒɪmɛnt] *n* regimento ♦ *vt* regulamentar; (*children etc*) subordinar a disciplina rígida.
regimental [rɛdʒɪ'mɛntl] *adj* regimental.
regimentation [rɛdʒɪmɛn'teɪʃən] *n* organização *f*.
region ['riːdʒən] *n* região *f*; **in the ~ of** (*fig*) por volta de, ao redor de.
regional ['riːdʒənl] *adj* regional.
regional development *n* desenvolvimento regional.
register ['rɛdʒɪstə*] *n* registro (*BR*), registo (*PT*); (*list*) lista ♦ *vt* registrar (*BR*), registar (*PT*); (*subj*: *instrument*) marcar, indicar ♦ *vi* (*at hotel*) registrar-se (*BR*), registar-se (*PT*); (*sign on*) inscrever-se; (*make impression*) causar impressão; **to ~ for a course** matricular-se num curso; **to ~ a protest** registrar (*BR*) *or* registar (*PT*) uma queixa.
registered ['rɛdʒɪstəd] *adj* (*design, letter*) registrado (*BR*), registado (*PT*); (*student*) matriculado; (*voter*) inscrito.
registered company *n* sociedade *f* registrada (*BR*) *or* registada (*PT*).
registered nurse (*US*) *n* enfermeiro/a formado/a.
registered office *n* sede *f* social.
registered trademark *n* marca registrada (*BR*) *or* registada (*PT*).
registrar ['rɛdʒɪstrɑː*] *n* oficial *m/f* de registro (*BR*) *or* registo (*PT*), escrivão/vã *m/f*.
registration [rɛdʒɪs'treɪʃən] *n* (*act*) registro (*BR*), registo (*PT*); (*AUT*: *also*: *~ number*) número da placa.
registry ['rɛdʒɪstrɪ] *n* registro (*BR*), registo (*PT*), cartório.
registry office (*BRIT*) *n* registro (*BR*) *or* registo (*PT*) civil, cartório; **to get married in a ~** casar-se no civil.
regret [rɪ'grɛt] *n* desgosto, pesar *m*; (*remorse*) remorso ♦ *vt* (*deplore*) lamentar; (*repent of*) arrepender-se de; **to ~ that** ... lamentar que ... + *sub*; **we ~ to inform you that** ... lamentamos informá-lo de que ....
regretfully [rɪ'grɛtfulɪ] *adv* com pesar, pesarosamente.
regrettable [rɪ'grɛtəbl] *adj* deplorável; (*loss*) lamentável.
regrettably [rɪ'grɛtəblɪ] *adv* lamentavelmente; **~, he was unable** ... infelizmente, ele não pôde ....
regroup [riː'gruːp] *vt* reagrupar ♦ *vi* reagrupar-se.
regt *abbr* = **regiment**.
regular ['rɛgjulə*] *adj* (*verb, service, shape*) regular; (*usual*) normal, habitual; (*soldier*) de linha; (*listener, reader*) assíduo; (*COMM*: *size*) médio ♦ *n* (*client etc*) habitual *m/f*.
regularity [rɛgju'lærɪtɪ] *n* regularidade *f*.
regularly ['rɛgjuləlɪ] *adv* regularmente.
regulate ['rɛgjuleɪt] *vt* regular; (*TECH*) ajustar.
regulation [rɛgju'leɪʃən] *n* (*rule*) regra, regulamento; (*adjustment*) ajuste *m* ♦ *cpd* regulamentar.
rehabilitation [riːhəbɪlɪ'teɪʃən] *n* reabilitação *f*.
rehash [riː'hæʃ] (*inf*) *vt* retocar.
rehearsal [rɪ'həːsəl] *n* ensaio; *see also* **dress**.
rehearse [rɪ'həːs] *vt, vi* ensaiar.
rehouse [riː'hauz] *vt* realojar.
reign [reɪn] *n* reinado; (*fig*) domínio ♦ *vi* reinar; (*fig*) imperar.
reigning ['reɪnɪŋ] *adj* (*monarch*) reinante; (*champion*) atual.
reimburse [riːɪm'bəːs] *vt* reembolsar.
reimbursement [riːɪm'bəːsmənt] *n* reembolso.
rein [reɪn] *n* (*for horse*) rédea; **to give ~ to** dar rédeas a, dar rédea larga a; **to give sb free ~** (*fig*) dar carta branca a alguém.
reincarnation [riːɪnkɑː'neɪʃən] *n* reencarnação *f*.
reindeer ['reɪndɪə*] *n inv* rena.
reinforce [riːɪn'fɔːs] *vt* reforçar.
reinforced [riːɪn'fɔːst] *adj* (*concrete*) armado.
reinforcement [riːɪn'fɔːsmənt] *n* (*action*) reforço; **~s** *npl* (*MIL*) reforços *mpl*.
reinstate [riːɪn'steɪt] *vt* (*worker*) readmitir; (*official*) reempossar.
reinstatement [riːɪn'steɪtmənt] *n* readmissão *f*.
reissue [riː'ɪʃuː] *vt* (*book*) reeditar; (*film*) relançar.
reiterate [riː'ɪtəreɪt] *vt* reiterar, repetir.
reject [*n* 'riːdʒɛkt, *vt* rɪ'dʒɛkt] *n* (*COMM*) artigo defeituoso ♦ *vt* rejeitar; (*COMM*: *goods*) refugar.
rejection [rɪ'dʒɛkʃən] *n* rejeição *f*.
rejoice [rɪ'dʒɔɪs] *vi*: **to ~ at** *or* **over** regozijar-se *or* alegrar-se de.
rejoinder [rɪ'dʒɔɪndə*] *n* (*retort*) réplica.
rejuvenate [rɪ'dʒuːvəneɪt] *vt* rejuvenescer.
rekindle [riː'kɪndl] *vt* reacender; (*fig*) despertar, reanimar.
relapse [rɪ'læps] *n* (*MED*) recaída; (*into crime*) reincidência.
relate [rɪ'leɪt] *vt* (*tell*) contar, relatar; (*connect*) relacionar ♦ *vi*: **to ~ to** relacionar-se com.
related [rɪ'leɪtɪd] *adj* (*connected*) afim, ligado; (*person*) aparentado.
relating [rɪ'leɪtɪŋ]: **~ to** *prep* relativo a, acerca de.
relation [rɪ'leɪʃən] *n* (*person*) parente *m/f*; (*link*) relação *f*; **diplomatic/international ~s**

relações diplomáticas/internacionais; **in ~ to** em relação a; **to bear no ~ to** não ter relação com.

relationship [rɪ'leɪʃənʃɪp] *n* relacionamento; (*personal ties*) relações *fpl*; (*also*: *family ~*) parentesco; (*affair*) caso.

relative ['rɛlətɪv] *n* parente *m/f* ♦ *adj* relativo; (*respective*) respectivo.

relatively ['rɛlətɪvlɪ] *adv* relativamente.

relax [rɪ'læks] *vi* (*rest*) descansar; (*unwind*) descontrair-se; (*calm down*) acalmar-se ♦ *vt* relaxar; (*mind, person*) descansar; **~!** (*calm down*) calma!; **to ~ one's grip** *or* **hold** afrouxar um pouco.

relaxation [ri:læk'seɪʃən] *n* (*rest*) descanso; (*ease*) relaxamento, relax *m*; (*amusement*) passatempo; (*entertainment*) diversão *f*.

relaxed [rɪ'lækst] *adj* relaxado; (*tranquil*) descontraído.

relaxing [rɪ'læksɪŋ] *adj* calmante, relaxante.

relay ['ri:leɪ] *n* (*race*) (corrida de) revezamento ♦ *vt* (*message*) retransmitir.

release [rɪ'li:s] *n* (*from prison*) libertação *f*; (*from obligation*) liberação *f*; (*of shot*) disparo; (*of gas etc*) escape *m*; (*of film, book etc*) lançamento; (*device*) desengate *m* ♦ *vt* (*prisoner*) pôr em liberdade; (*book, film*) lançar; (*report, news*) publicar; (*gas etc*) soltar; (*free*: *from wreckage etc*) soltar; (*TECH*: *catch, spring etc*) desengatar, desapertar; (*let go*) soltar; **to ~ one's grip** *or* **hold** afrouxar; **to ~ the clutch** (*AUT*) desembrear.

relegate ['rɛləgeɪt] *vt* relegar, afastar; (*SPORT*): **to be ~d** descer.

relent [rɪ'lɛnt] *vi* abrandar-se; (*yield*) ceder.

relentless [rɪ'lɛntlɪs] *adj* implacável.

relevance ['rɛləvəns] *n* pertinência; (*importance*) relevância; **~ of sth to sth** relação de algo com algo.

relevant ['rɛləvənt] *adj* (*fact*) pertinente; (*apt*) apropriado; (*important*) relevante; **~ to** relacionado com.

reliability [rɪlaɪə'bɪlɪtɪ] *n* (*of person*) confiabilidade *f*, seriedade *f*; (*of method, machine*) segurança; (*of news*) fidedignidade *f*.

reliable [rɪ'laɪəbl] *adj* (*person, firm*) (digno) de confiança, confiável, sério; (*method, machine*) seguro; (*news*) fidedigno.

reliably [rɪ'laɪəblɪ] *adv*: **to be ~ informed that ...** saber de fonte segura que ....

reliance [rɪ'laɪəns] *n*: **~ (on)** (*trust*) confiança (em), esperança (em); (*dependence*) dependência (de).

reliant [rɪ'laɪənt] *adj*: **to be ~ on sth/sb** depender de algo/alguém.

relic ['rɛlɪk] *n* (*REL*) relíquia; (*of the past*) vestígio.

relief [rɪ'li:f] *n* (*from pain, anxiety*) alívio; (*help, supplies*) ajuda, socorro; (*of guard*) rendição *f*; (*ART, GEO*) relevo; **by way of light ~** como forma de diversão.

relief map *n* mapa *m* em relevo.

relief road (*BRIT*) *n* estrada alternativa.

relieve [rɪ'li:v] *vt* (*pain, patient*) aliviar; (*bring help to*) ajudar, socorrer; (*burden*) abrandar, mitigar; (*take over from*: *gen*) substituir, revezar; (: *guard*) render; **to ~ sb of sth** tirar algo de alguém; **to ~ sb of his command** exonerar alguém, destituir alguém de sua função; **to ~ o.s.** fazer as necessidades.

religion [rɪ'lɪdʒən] *n* religião *f*.

religious [rɪ'lɪdʒəs] *adj* religioso.

reline [ri:'laɪn] *vt* (*brakes*) trocar o forro de.

relinquish [rɪ'lɪŋkwɪʃ] *vt* abandonar; (*plan, habit*) renunciar a.

relish ['rɛlɪʃ] *n* (*CULIN*) condimento, tempero; (*enjoyment*) entusiasmo ♦ *vt* (*food etc*) saborear; **to ~ doing** gostar de fazer.

relive [ri:'lɪv] *vt* reviver.

reload [ri:'ləud] *vt* recarregar.

relocate [ri:ləu'keɪt] *vt* deslocar ♦ *vi* deslocar-se; **to ~ in** instalar-se em.

reluctance [rɪ'lʌktəns] *n* relutância.

reluctant [rɪ'lʌktənt] *adj* relutante; **to be ~ to do sth** relutar em fazer algo.

reluctantly [rɪ'lʌktəntlɪ] *adv* relutantemente, de má vontade.

rely [rɪ'laɪ]: **to ~ on** *vt fus* confiar em, contar com; (*be dependent on*) depender de.

remain [rɪ'meɪn] *vi* (*stay*) ficar, permanecer; (*be left*) sobrar; (*continue*) continuar, manter-se; **to ~ silent** ficar calado; **I ~, yours faithfully** (*BRIT*: *in letters*) subscrevo-me, atenciosamente.

remainder [rɪ'meɪndə*] *n* resto, restante *m*.

remaining [rɪ'meɪnɪŋ] *adj* restante.

remains [rɪ'meɪnz] *npl* (*mortal*) restos *mpl*; (*leftovers*) sobras *fpl*.

remand [rɪ'mɑ:nd] *n*: **on ~** sob prisão preventiva ♦ *vt*: **to ~ in custody** recolocar em prisão preventiva, manter sob custódia.

remand home (*BRIT*) *n* instituição *f* do juizado de menores, reformatório.

remark [rɪ'mɑ:k] *n* observação *f*, comentário ♦ *vt* comentar ♦ *vi*: **to ~ on sth** comentar algo, fazer um comentário sobre algo.

remarkable [rɪ'mɑ:kəbl] *adj* notável; (*outstanding*) extraordinário.

remarry [ri:'mærɪ] *vi* casar-se de novo.

remedial [rɪ'mi:dɪəl] *adj* (*tuition, classes*) de reforço.

remedy ['rɛmədɪ] *n*: **~ (for)** remédio (contra *or* a) ♦ *vt* remediar.

remember [rɪ'mɛmbə*] *vt* lembrar-se de, lembrar; (*memorize*) guardar; **I ~ seeing it, I ~ having seen it** eu me lembro de ter visto aquilo; **she ~ed to do it** ela se lembrou de fazer aquilo; **~ me to your wife** dê lembranças minhas à sua esposa.

remembrance [rɪ'mɛmbrəns] *n* (*memory*) memória; (*souvenir*) lembrança, recordação *f*.

remind [rɪ'maɪnd] *vt*: **to ~ sb to do sth** lembrar a alguém que tem de fazer algo; **to ~**

***NB**: European Portuguese adds the following consonants to certain words:* **b** (sú(b)dito, su(b)til); **c** (a(c)ção, a(c)cionista, a(c)to); **m** (inde(m)ne); **p** (ado(p)ção, ado(p)tar); *for further details see p. xiii.*

sb of sth lembrar algo a alguém; **she ~s me of her mother** ela me lembra a mãe dela; **that ~s me, ...** falando nisso, ...
reminder [rɪ'maɪndə*] *n* lembrete *m*; (*souvenir*) lembrança.
reminisce [rɛmɪ'nɪs] *vi* relembrar velhas histórias; **to ~ about sth** relembrar algo.
reminiscences [rɛmɪ'nɪsnsɪz] *npl* recordações *fpl*, lembranças *fpl*.
reminiscent [rɛmɪ'nɪsənt] *adj*: **to be ~ of sth** lembrar algo.
remiss [rɪ'mɪs] *adj* negligente, desleixado; **it was ~ of him** foi um descuido seu.
remission [rɪ'mɪʃən] *n* remissão *f*; (*of sentence*) diminuição *f*.
remit [rɪ'mɪt] *vt* (*send*: *money*) remeter, enviar, mandar.
remittance [rɪ'mɪtəns] *n* remessa.
remnant ['rɛmnənt] *n* resto; (*of cloth*) retalho; **~s** *npl* (COMM) retalhos *mpl*.
remonstrate ['rɛmənstreɪt] *vi*: **to ~ (with sb about sth)** reclamar (a alguém de algo).
remorse [rɪ'mɔːs] *n* remorso.
remorseful [rɪ'mɔːsful] *adj* arrependido.
remorseless [rɪ'mɔːslɪs] *adj* (*fig*) desapiedado, implacável.
remote [rɪ'məut] *adj* (*distant*) remoto, distante; (*person*) reservado, afastado; **there is a ~ possibility that ...** existe uma possibilidade remota de que ....
remote control *n* controle *m* remoto.
remote-controlled [-kən'trəuld] *adj* (*plane*) telecomandado; (*missile*) teleguiado.
remotely [rɪ'məutlɪ] *adv* remotamente; (*slightly*) levemente.
remoteness [rɪ'məutnɪs] *n* afastamento, isolamento.
remould ['riːməuld] (BRIT) *n* (*tyre*) pneu *m* recauchutado.
removable [rɪ'muːvəbl] *adj* (*detachable*) removível.
removal [rɪ'muːvəl] *n* (*taking away*) remoção *f*; (BRIT: *from house*) mudança; (*from office*: *sacking*) afastamento, demissão *f*; (MED) extração *f*.
removal man (*irreg*) *n* homem *m* da companhia de mudanças.
removal van (BRIT) *n* caminhão *m* (BR) *or* camião *m* (PT) de mudanças.
remove [rɪ'muːv] *vt* tirar, retirar; (*employee*) afastar, demitir; (*name*: *from list*) eliminar, remover; (*doubt, abuse*) afastar; (TECH) retirar, separar; (MED) extrair, extirpar; **first cousin once ~d** primo/a em segundo grau.
remover [rɪ'muːvə*] *n* (*substance*) removedor *m*; **~s** *npl* (BRIT: *company*) companhia de mudanças.
remunerate [rɪ'mjuːnəreɪt] *vt* remunerar.
remuneration [rɪmjuːnə'reɪʃən] *n* remuneração *f*.
rename [riː'neɪm] *vt* dar novo nome a.
rend [rɛnd] (*pt, pp* **rent**) *vt* rasgar, despedaçar.
render ['rɛndə*] *vt* (*give*: *help*) dar, prestar; (: *account*) entregar; (*make*) fazer, tornar; (*translate*) traduzir; (*fat*: *also*: ~ *down*) clarificar; (*wall*) rebocar.
rendering ['rɛndərɪŋ] *n* (MUS *etc*) interpretação *f*.
rendezvous ['rɔndɪvuː] *n* encontro; (*place*) ponto de encontro ♦ *vi* encontrar-se; **to ~ with sb** encontrar-se com alguém.
renegade ['rɛnɪgeɪd] *n* renegado/a.
renew [rɪ'njuː] *vt* renovar; (*resume*) retomar, recomeçar; (*loan etc*) prorrogar; (*negotiations, acquaintance*) reatar.
renewable [rɪ'njuːəbl] *adj* renovável.
renewal [rɪ'njuːəl] *n* renovação *f*; (*resumption*) retomada; (*of loan*) prorrogação *f*.
renounce [rɪ'nauns] *vt* renunciar a; (*disown*) repudiar, rejeitar.
renovate ['rɛnəveɪt] *vt* renovar; (*house, room*) reformar.
renovation [rɛnə'veɪʃən] *n* renovação *f*; (*of house etc*) reforma.
renown [rɪ'naun] *n* renome *m*.
renowned [rɪ'naund] *adj* renomado, famoso.
rent [rɛnt] *pt, pp of* **rend** ♦ *n* aluguel *m* (BR), aluguer *m* (PT) ♦ *vt* (*also*: ~ *out*) alugar.
rental ['rɛntəl] *n* (*for television, car*) aluguel *m* (BR), aluguer *m* (PT).
renunciation [rɪnʌnsɪ'eɪʃən] *n* renúncia.
reopen [riː'əupən] *vt* reabrir.
reopening [riː'əupənɪŋ] *n* reabertura.
reorder [riː'ɔːdə*] *vt* encomendar novamente; (*rearrange*) reorganizar.
reorganize [riː'ɔːgənaɪz] *vt* reorganizar.
Rep. (US) *abbr* (POL) = **representative**; **republican**.
rep [rɛp] *n abbr* (COMM) = **representative**; (THEATRE) = **repertory**.
repaid [riː'peɪd] *pt, pp of* **repay**.
repair [rɪ'pɛə*] *n* reparação *f*, conserto; (*patch*) remendo ♦ *vt* consertar; **beyond ~** irreparável; **in good/bad ~** em bom/mau estado; **under ~** no conserto.
repair kit *n* (*tool box*) caixa de ferramentas.
repair man (*irreg*) *n* consertador *m*.
repair shop *n* oficina de reparos.
repartee [rɛpɑː'tiː] *n* resposta arguta e engenhosa; (*skill*) presteza em replicar.
repast [rɪ'pɑːst] *n* (*formal*) repasto.
repatriate [riː'pætrɪeɪt] *vt* repatriar.
repay [riː'peɪ] (*irreg*) *vt* (*money*) reembolsar, restituir; (*person*) pagar de volta; (*debt*) saldar, liquidar; (*sb's efforts*) corresponder, retribuir.
repayment [riː'peɪmənt] *n* reembolso, retribuição *f*; (*of debt*) pagamento; (*of mortgage etc*) prestação *f*.
repeal [rɪ'piːl] *n* (*of law*) revogação *f*; (*of sentence*) anulação *f* ♦ *vt* revogar; anular.
repeat [rɪ'piːt] *n* (RADIO, TV) repetição *f* ♦ *vt* repetir; (COMM: *order*) renovar ♦ *vi* repetir-se.
repeatedly [rɪ'piːtɪdlɪ] *adv* repetidamente.
repel [rɪ'pɛl] *vt* repelir.
repellent [rɪ'pɛlənt] *adj* repelente ♦ *n*: **insect ~** repelente *m* de insetos.

repent [rɪ'pɛnt] *vi*: **to ~ (of)** arrepender-se (de).
repentance [rɪ'pɛntəns] *n* arrependimento.
repercussion [ri:pə'kʌʃən] *n* (*consequence*) repercussão *f*; **to have ~s** repercutir.
repertoire ['rɛpətwɑ:*] *n* repertório.
repertory ['rɛpətərɪ] *n* (*also*: ~ *theatre*) teatro de repertório.
repertory company *n* companhia teatral.
repetition [rɛpɪ'tɪʃən] *n* repetição *f*.
repetitious [rɛpɪ'tɪʃəs] *adj* (*speech*) repetitivo.
repetitive [rɪ'pɛtɪtɪv] *adj* repetitivo.
replace [rɪ'pleɪs] *vt* (*put back*) repor, devolver; (*take the place of*) substituir; (*TEL*): **"~ the receiver"** "desligue".
replacement [rɪ'pleɪsmənt] *n* (*substitution*) substituição *f*; (*putting back*) reposição *f*; (*person*) substituto/a.
replacement part *n* peça sobressalente.
replay ['ri:pleɪ] *n* (*of match*) partida decisiva; (*TV*: *also*: *action* ~) replay *m*.
replenish [rɪ'plɛnɪʃ] *vt* (*glass*) reencher; (*stock etc*) completar, prover; (*with fuel*) reabastecer.
replete [rɪ'pli:t] *adj* repleto; (*well-fed*) cheio, empanturrado.
replica ['rɛplɪkə] *n* réplica, cópia, reprodução *f*.
reply [rɪ'plaɪ] *n* resposta ♦ *vi* responder; **in ~ (to)** em resposta (a); **there's no ~** (*TEL*) ninguém atende.
reply coupon *n* cartão-resposta *m*.
report [rɪ'pɔ:t] *n* relatório; (*PRESS etc*) reportagem *f*; (*also*: *school* ~) boletim *m* escolar; (*of gun*) estampido, detonação *f* ♦ *vt* informar sobre; (*PRESS etc*) fazer uma reportagem sobre; (*bring to notice*: *occurrence*) comunicar, anunciar; (: *person*) denunciar ♦ *vi* (*make a report*): **to ~ (on)** apresentar um relatório (sobre); (*for newspaper*) fazer uma reportagem (sobre); (*present o.s.*): **to ~ (to sb)** apresentar-se (a alguém); **it is ~ed that** dizem que; **it is ~ed from Berlin that** há notícias de Berlim de que.
report card (*US*, *SCOTTISH*) *n* boletim *m* escolar.
reportedly [rɪ'pɔ:tɪdlɪ] *adv*: **she is ~ living in Spain** dizem que ela mora na Espanha.
reported speech [rɪ'pɔ:tɪd-] *n* (*LING*) discurso indireto.
reporter [rɪ'pɔ:tə*] *n* (*PRESS*) jornalista *m/f*, repórter *m/f*; (*RADIO*, *TV*) repórter.
repose [rɪ'pəuz] *n*: **in ~** em repouso.
repossess [ri:pə'zɛs] *vt* retomar.
reprehensible [rɛprɪ'hɛnsɪbl] *adj* repreensível, censurável, condenável.
represent [rɛprɪ'zɛnt] *vt* representar; (*fig*) falar em nome de; (*COMM*) ser representante de; (*explain*): **to ~ to sb that** explicar a alguém que.
representation [rɛprɪzɛn'teɪʃən] *n* representação *f*; (*petition*) petição *f*; **~s** *npl* (*protest*) reclamação *f*, protesto.
representative [rɛprɪ'zɛntətɪv] *n* representante *m/f*; (*US*: *POL*) deputado/a ♦ *adj*: **~ (of)** representativo (de).
repress [rɪ'prɛs] *vt* reprimir, subjugar.
repression [rɪ'prɛʃən] *n* repressão *f*.
repressive [rɪ'prɛsɪv] *adj* repressivo.
reprieve [rɪ'pri:v] *n* (*LAW*) suspensão *f* temporária; (*fig*) alívio ♦ *vt* suspender temporariamente; aliviar.
reprimand ['rɛprɪmɑ:nd] *n* reprimenda ♦ *vt* repreender, censurar.
reprint [*n* 'ri:prɪnt, *vt* ri:'prɪnt] *n* reimpressão *f* ♦ *vt* reimprimir.
reprisal [rɪ'praɪzl] *n* represália; **to take ~s** fazer *or* exercer represálias.
reproach [rɪ'prəutʃ] *n* repreensão *f*, censura ♦ *vt*: **to ~ sb with sth** repreender alguém por algo; **beyond ~** irrepreensível, impecável.
reproachful [rɪ'prəutʃful] *adj* repreensivo, acusatório.
reproduce [ri:prə'dju:s] *vt* reproduzir ♦ *vi* reproduzir-se.
reproduction [ri:prə'dʌkʃən] *n* reprodução *f*.
reproductive [ri:prə'dʌktɪv] *adj* reprodutivo.
reproof [rɪ'pru:f] *n* reprovação *f*, repreensão *f*.
reprove [rɪ'pru:v] *vt* (*action*) reprovar; **to ~ sb for sth** repreender alguém por algo.
reproving [rɪ'pru:vɪŋ] *adj* (*look*) de reprovação; (*tone*) de censura.
reptile ['rɛptaɪl] *n* réptil *m*.
Repub. (*US*) *abbr* (*POL*) = **republican**.
republic [rɪ'pʌblɪk] *n* república.
republican [rɪ'pʌblɪkən] *adj*, *n* republicano/a.
repudiate [rɪ'pju:dɪeɪt] *vt* (*accusation*) rejeitar, negar; (*friend*) repudiar; (*obligation*) desconhecer.
repugnant [rɪ'pʌgnənt] *adj* repugnante, repulsivo.
repulse [rɪ'pʌls] *vt* repelir.
repulsion [rɪ'pʌlʃən] *n* repulsa; (*PHYS*) repulsão *f*.
repulsive [rɪ'pʌlsɪv] *adj* repulsivo.
reputable ['rɛpjutəbl] *adj* (*make etc*) bem conceituado, de confiança; (*person*) honrado, respeitável.
reputation [rɛpju'teɪʃən] *n* reputação *f*; **to have a ~ for** ter fama por; **he has a ~ for being cruel** ele tem fama de ser cruel.
repute [rɪ'pju:t] *n* reputação *f*, renome *m*.
reputed [rɪ'pju:tɪd] *adj* suposto, pretenso; **he is ~ to be rich** dizem que ele é rico.
reputedly [rɪ'pju:tɪdlɪ] *adv* segundo se diz, supostamente.
request [rɪ'kwɛst] *n* pedido; (*formal*) petição *f* ♦ *vt*: **to ~ sth of** *or* **from sb** pedir algo a alguém; (*formally*) solicitar algo a alguém; **on ~** a pedido; **at the ~ of** a pedido de; **"you are ~ed not to smoke"** "pede-se *or* favor não fumar".
request stop (*BRIT*) *n* (*for bus*) parada não

NB: *European Portuguese adds the following consonants to certain words:* **b** (sú(b)dito, su(b)til); **c** (a(c)ção, a(c)cionista, a(c)to); **m** (inde(m)ne); **p** (ado(p)ção, ado(p)tar); *for further details see p. xiii.*

obrigatória.
requiem ['rɛkwɪəm] *n* réquiem *m*.
require [rɪ'kwaɪə*] *vt* (*need*: *subj*: *person*) precisar de, necessitar; (: *thing, situation*) requerer, exigir; (*want*) pedir; (*order*): **to ~ sb to do sth/sth of sb** exigir que alguém faça algo/algo de alguém; **if ~d** se for necessário; **what qualifications are ~d?** quais são as qualificações necessárias?; **~d by law** exigido por lei.
required [rɪ'kwaɪəd] *adj* (*necessary*) necessário; (*desired*) desejado.
requirement [rɪ'kwaɪəmənt] *n* requisito; (*need*) necessidade *f*.
requisite ['rɛkwɪzɪt] *n* requisito ♦ *adj* necessário, indispensável; **toilet ~s** artigos de toalete pessoal.
requisition [rɛkwɪ'zɪʃən] *n*: **~ (for)** requerimento (para) ♦ *vt* (*MIL*) requisitar, confiscar.
reroute [riː'ruːt] *vt* (*train etc*) desviar.
resale ['riː'seɪl] *n* revenda.
resale price maintenance *n* manutenção *f* de preços de revenda.
rescind [rɪ'sɪnd] *vt* (*contract*) rescindir; (*law*) revogar; (*verdict*) anular.
rescue ['rɛskjuː] *n* salvamento, resgate *m* ♦ *vt* (*survivors, wounded etc*) resgatar; (*save, fig*) salvar; **to come to sb's ~** ir ao socorro de alguém.
rescue party *n* grupo *or* expedição *f* de resgate.
rescuer ['rɛskjuə*] *n* (*in disaster etc*) resgatador(a) *m/f*; (*fig*) salvador(a) *m/f*.
research [rɪ'səːtʃ] *n* pesquisa ♦ *vt* pesquisar ♦ *vi*: **to ~ (into sth)** pesquisar (algo), fazer pesquisas (sobre algo); **a piece of ~** uma pesquisa; **~ and development** pesquisa e desenvolvimento.
researcher [rɪ'səːtʃə*] *n* pesquisador(a) *m/f*.
research work *n* trabalho de pesquisa.
resell [riː'sɛl] (*irreg*) *vt* revender.
resemblance [rɪ'zɛmbləns] *n* semelhança; **to bear a strong ~ to** ser muito parecido com.
resemble [rɪ'zɛmbl] *vt* parecer-se com.
resent [rɪ'zɛnt] *vt* (*thing*) ressentir-se de; (*person*) estar ressentido com.
resentful [rɪ'zɛntful] *adj* ressentido.
resentment [rɪ'zɛntmənt] *n* ressentimento.
reservation [rɛzə'veɪʃən] *n* (*booking, doubt, protected area*) reserva; (*BRIT*: *AUT*: *also*: *central ~*) canteiro divisor; **to make a ~** fazer reserva; **with ~s** (*doubts*) com reservas.
reservation desk (*US*) *n* (*in hotel*) recepção *f*.
reserve [rɪ'zəːv] *n* (*restraint, protected area*) reserva; (*SPORT*) suplente *m/f*, reserva *m/f* (*BR*) ♦ *vt* (*seats etc*) reservar; **~s** *npl* (*MIL*) (tropas *fpl* da) reserva; **in ~** de reserva.
reserve currency *n* moeda de reserva.
reserved [rɪ'zəːvd] *adj* reservado.
reserve price (*BRIT*) *n* preço mínimo de venda.
reserve team (*BRIT*) *n* time *m* reserva.
reservist [rɪ'zəːvɪst] *n* reservista *m*.
reservoir ['rɛzəvwɑː*] *n* (*large*) reservatório, represa; (*small*) depósito.
reset [riː'sɛt] (*irreg*) *vt* reajustar; (*COMPUT*) dar reset em, restabelecer.
reshape [riː'ʃeɪp] *vt* (*policy*) reformar, remodelar.
reshuffle [riː'ʃʌfl] *n see* **cabinet**.
reside [rɪ'zaɪd] *vi* residir.
residence ['rɛzɪdəns] *n* residência; (*formal: home*) domicílio; **to take up ~** instalar-se; **in ~** (*monarch*) em residência; (*doctor*) residente.
residence permit (*BRIT*) *n* autorização *f* de residência.
resident ['rɛzɪdənt] *n* (*of house, area*) morador(a) *m/f*; (*in hotel*) hóspede *m/f* ♦ *adj* (*population*) permanente; (*doctor*) interno, residente.
residential [rɛzɪ'dɛnʃəl] *adj* residencial.
residue ['rɛzɪdjuː] *n* resto; (*COMM*) montante *m* líquido; (*CHEM, PHYS*) resíduo.
resign [rɪ'zaɪn] *vt* (*one's post*) renunciar a, demitir-se de ♦ *vi*: **to ~ (from)** demitir-se (de); **to ~ o.s. to** (*endure*) resignar-se a.
resignation [rɛzɪg'neɪʃən] *n* demissão *f*; (*state of mind*) resignação *f*; **to tender one's ~** pedir demissão.
resigned [rɪ'zaɪnd] *adj* resignado.
resilience [rɪ'zɪlɪəns] *n* (*of material*) elasticidade *f*; (*of person*) resistência.
resilient [rɪ'zɪlɪənt] *adj* (*person*) resistente.
resin ['rɛzɪn] *n* resina.
resist [rɪ'zɪst] *vt* resistir a.
resistance [rɪ'zɪstəns] *n* resistência.
resistant [rɪ'zɪstənt] *adj*: **~ (to)** resistente (a).
resold [riː'səuld] *pt, pp of* **resell**.
resolute ['rɛzəluːt] *adj* resoluto, firme.
resolution [rɛzə'luːʃən] *n* resolução *f*; **to make a ~** tomar uma resolução.
resolve [rɪ'zɔlv] *n* resolução *f*; (*purpose*) intenção *f* ♦ *vt* resolver; **to ~ to do** resolver-se a fazer.
resolved [rɪ'zɔlvd] *adj* decidido.
resonance ['rɛzənəns] *n* ressonância.
resonant ['rɛzənənt] *adj* ressonante.
resort [rɪ'zɔːt] *n* (*town*) local *m* turístico, estação *f* de veraneio; (*recourse*) recurso ♦ *vi*: **to ~ to** recorrer a; **seaside/winter sports ~** balneário/estação de inverno; **in the last ~** em último caso, em última instância.
resound [rɪ'zaund] *vi* ressoar, retumbar; **the room ~ed with shouts** os gritos ressoaram no quarto.
resounding [rɪ'zaundɪŋ] *adj* retumbante.
resource [rɪ'sɔːs] *n* recurso; **~s** *npl* recursos *mpl*; **natural ~s** recursos naturais.
resourceful [rɪ'sɔːsful] *adj* desembaraçado, engenhoso, expedito.
resourcefulness [rɪ'sɔːsfəlnɪs] *n* desembaraço, engenho.
respect [rɪs'pɛkt] *n* respeito ♦ *vt* respeitar; **~s** *npl*: **to pay one's ~s to sb** fazer visita de cortesia a alguém; **to pay one's last ~s to sb** prestar a última homenagem a alguém; **to have** *or* **show ~ for sb/sth** ter *or* mostrar respeito por alguém/algo; **out of ~ for** por

respeito a; **with ~ to** com respeito a; **in ~ of** a respeito de; **in this ~** neste respeito; **in some ~s** em alguns pontos; **with all due ~, I** ... com todo respeito, eu ....
respectability [rɪspɛktə'bɪlɪtɪ] *n* respeitabilidade *f*.
respectable [rɪs'pɛktəbl] *adj* respeitável; (*large*) considerável; (*quite good*: *result, player*) razoável.
respectful [rɪs'pɛktful] *adj* respeitoso.
respective [rɪs'pɛktɪv] *adj* respectivo.
respectively [rɪs'pɛktɪvlɪ] *adv* respectivamente.
respiration [rɛspɪ'reɪʃən] *n* respiração *f*.
respiratory [rɛs'pɪrətərɪ] *adj* respiratório.
respite ['rɛspaɪt] *n* pausa, folga; (*LAW*) adiamento, suspensão *f*.
resplendent [rɪs'plɛndənt] *adj* resplandecente.
respond [rɪs'pɔnd] *vi* (*answer*) responder; (*react*) reagir.
respondent [rɪs'pɔndənt] *n* (*in survey*) respondedor(a) *m/f*; (*LAW*) réu/ré *m/f*.
response [rɪs'pɔns] *n* (*answer*) resposta; (*reaction*) reação *f*; **in ~ to** em resposta a.
responsibility [rɪspɔnsɪ'bɪlɪtɪ] *n* responsabilidade *f*; **to take ~ for sth/sb** assumir a responsabilidade por algo/alguém.
responsible [rɪs'pɔnsɪbl] *adj* (*character*) sério, responsável; (*job*) de responsabilidade; (*liable*): **~ (for)** responsável (por); **to be ~ to sb (for sth)** ser responsável diante de alguém (por algo); **to hold sb ~ (for sth)** responsabilizar alguém (por algo).
responsibly [rɪs'pɔnsɪblɪ] *adv* com responsabilidade.
responsive [rɪs'pɔnsɪv] *adj* sensível.
rest [rɛst] *n* descanso, repouso; (*MUS*) pausa; (*break*) intervalo; (*support*) apoio; (*remainder*) resto ♦ *vi* descansar; (*be supported*): **to ~ on** apoiar-se em ♦ *vt* (*lean*): **to ~ sth on/against** apoiar algo em *or* sobre/contra; **the ~ of them** os outros; **to set sb's mind at ~** tranqüilizar alguém; **it ~s with him to do it** cabe a ele fazê-lo; **~ assured that** ... tenha certeza de que ....
restart [ri:'stɑ:t] *vt* (*engine*) arrancar de novo; (*work*) reiniciar, recomeçar.
restaurant ['rɛstərɔŋ] *n* restaurante *m*.
restaurant car (*BRIT*) *n* vagão-restaurante *m*.
rest cure *n* repouso forçado (*para tratamento de saúde*).
restful ['rɛstful] *adj* sossegado, tranqüilo, repousante.
rest home *n* asilo, casa de repouso.
restitution [rɛstɪ'tju:ʃən] *n*: **to make ~ to sb for sth** restituir *or* indenizar alguém de algo.
restive ['rɛstɪv] *adj* inquieto, impaciente; (*horse*) rebelão/ona, teimoso.
restless ['rɛstlɪs] *adj* desassossegado, irrequieto; **to get ~** impacientar-se.
restlessly ['rɛstlɪslɪ] *adv* inquietamente.
restock [ri:'stɔk] *vt* reabastecer.
restoration [rɛstə'reɪʃən] *n* restauração *f*.
restorative [rɪ'stɔrətɪv] *adj* reconstituinte ♦ *n* reconstituinte *m*.
restore [rɪ'stɔ:*] *vt* (*building*) restaurar; (*sth stolen*) restituir; (*peace, health*) restabelecer.
restorer [rɪ'stɔ:rə*] *n* (*ART etc*) restaurador(a) *m/f*.
restrain [rɪs'treɪn] *vt* (*feeling*) reprimir, refrear; (*person*): **to ~ (from doing)** impedir (de fazer).
restrained [rɪs'treɪnd] *adj* (*style*) moderado, comedido.
restraint [rɪs'treɪnt] *n* (*restriction*) restrição *f*; (*moderation*) moderação *f*, comedimento; (*of style*) sobriedade *f*; **wage ~** restrição salarial.
restrict [rɪs'trɪkt] *vt* restringir, limitar.
restricted area [rɪ'strɪktɪd-] *n* (*AUT*) zona com limite de velocidade.
restriction [rɪs'trɪkʃən] *n* restrição *f*, limitação *f*.
restrictive [rɪs'trɪktɪv] *adj* restritivo.
restrictive practices *npl* (*INDUSTRY*) práticas *fpl* restritivas.
rest room (*US*) *n* banheiro (*BR*), lavabo (*PT*).
restructure [ri:'strʌktʃə*] *vt* reestruturar.
result [rɪ'zʌlt] *n* resultado ♦ *vi*: **to ~ (from)** resultar (de); **to ~ in** resultar em; **as a ~ of** como resultado *or* conseqüência de.
resultant [rɪ'zʌltənt] *adj* resultante.
resume [rɪ'zju:m] *vt* (*work, journey*) retomar, recomeçar; (*sum up*) resumir ♦ *vi* (*work etc*) recomeçar.
résumé ['reɪzju:meɪ] *n* (*summary*) resumo; (*US*: *curriculum vitae*) curriculum vitae *m*, currículo.
resumption [rɪ'zʌmpʃən] *n* retomada.
resurgence [rɪ'sə:dʒəns] *n* ressurgimento.
resurrection [rɛzə'rɛkʃən] *n* ressurreição *f*.
resuscitate [rɪ'sʌsɪteɪt] *vt* (*MED*) ressuscitar, reanimar.
resuscitation [rɪsʌsɪ'teɪʃən] *n* ressuscitação *f*.
retail ['ri:teɪl] *n* varejo (*BR*), venda a retalho (*PT*) ♦ *cpd* no varejo (*BR*), a retalho (*PT*) ♦ *vt* vender no varejo (*BR*) *or* a retalho (*PT*) ♦ *vi*: **to ~ at $10** ser vendido no varejo (*BR*) *or* a retalho (*PT*) por $10.
retailer ['ri:teɪlə*] *n* varejista *m/f* (*BR*), retalhista *m/f* (*PT*).
retail outlet *n* ponto de venda.
retail price *n* preço no varejo (*BR*) *or* de venda a retalho (*PT*).
retail price index *n* ≈ índice *m* de preços ao consumidor.
retain [rɪ'teɪn] *vt* (*keep*) reter, conservar; (*employ*) contratar.
retainer [rɪ'teɪnə*] *n* (*servant*) empregado; (*fee*) adiantamento.
retaliate [rɪ'tælɪeɪt] *vi*: **to ~ (against)** revidar (contra).
retaliation [rɪtælɪ'eɪʃən] *n* represálias *fpl*,

NB: European Portuguese adds the following consonants to certain words: **b** (sú(b)dito, su(b)til); **c** (a(c)ção, a(c)cionista, a(c)to); **m** (inde(m)ne); **p** (ado(p)ção, ado(p)tar); *for further details see p. xiii.*

vingança; **in ~ for** em retaliação por.
retaliatory [rɪ'tælɪətərɪ] *adj* retaliativo, retaliatório.
retarded [rɪ'tɑːdɪd] *adj* retardado.
retch [rɛtʃ] *vi* fazer esforço para vomitar.
retentive [rɪ'tɛntɪv] *adj* (*memory*) retentivo, fiel.
rethink ['riː'θɪŋk] (*irreg*) *vt* reconsiderar, repensar.
reticence ['rɛtɪsns] *n* reserva.
reticent ['rɛtɪsnt] *adj* reservado.
retina ['rɛtɪnə] *n* retina.
retinue ['rɛtɪnjuː] *n* séquito, comitiva.
retire [rɪ'taɪə*] *vi* (*give up work*) aposentar-se; (*withdraw*) retirar-se; (*go to bed*) deitar-se.
retired [rɪ'taɪəd] *adj* (*person*) aposentado (*BR*), reformado (*PT*).
retiree [rɪtaɪə'riː] (*US*) *n* aposentado/a (*BR*), reformado/a (*PT*).
retirement [rɪ'taɪəmənt] *n* (*state, act*) aposentadoria (*BR*), reforma (*PT*).
retirement age *n* idade *f* de aposentadoria (*BR*) *or* de reforma (*PT*).
retiring [rɪ'taɪərɪŋ] *adj* (*leaving*) de saída; (*shy*) acanhado, retraído.
retort [rɪ'tɔːt] *n* (*reply*) réplica; (*container*) retorta ♦ *vi* replicar, retrucar.
retrace [riː'treɪs] *vt*: **to ~ one's steps** voltar sobre (os) seus passos, refazer o mesmo caminho.
retract [rɪ'trækt] *vt* (*statement*) retirar, retratar; (*claws*) encolher; (*undercarriage, aerial*) recolher ♦ *vi* retratar-se.
retractable [rɪ'træktəbl] *adj* retrátil.
retrain [riː'treɪn] *vt* reciclar ♦ *vi* ser reciclado.
retraining [riː'treɪnɪŋ] *n* readaptação *f* profissional, reciclagem *f*.
retread [*n* 'riːtrɛd, *vt* riː'trɛd] *vt* (*AUT: tyre*) recauchutar ♦ *n* pneu *m* recauchutado.
retreat [rɪ'triːt] *n* (*place*) retiro; (*act*) retirada ♦ *vi* retirar-se; (*flood*) retroceder; **to beat a hasty ~** bater em retirada.
retrial [riː'traɪəl] *n* revisão *f* do processo.
retribution [rɛtrɪ'bjuːʃən] *n* desforra, revide *m*, vingança.
retrieval [rɪ'triːvəl] *n* recuperação *f*.
retrieve [rɪ'triːv] *vt* (*sth lost*) reaver, recuperar; (*situation, honour*) salvar; (*error, loss*) reparar; (*COMPUT*) recuperar.
retriever [rɪ'triːvə*] *n* cão *m* de busca, perdigueiro.
retroactive [rɛtrəu'æktɪv] *adj* retroativo.
retrograde ['rɛtrəgreɪd] *adj* retrógrado.
retrospect ['rɛtrəspɛkt] *n*: **in ~** retrospectivamente, em retrospecto.
retrospective [rɛtrə'spɛktɪv] *adj* (*law*) retrospectivo, retroativo ♦ *n* (*ART*) retrospectiva.
return [rɪ'təːn] *n* (*going or coming back*) regresso, volta; (*of sth stolen etc*) devolução *f*; (*recompense*) recompensa; (*FINANCE: from land, shares*) rendimento; (*report*) relatório ♦ *cpd* (*journey*) de volta; (*BRIT: ticket*) de ida e volta; (*match*) de revanche ♦ *vi* (*person etc: come or go back*) voltar, regressar; (*symptoms etc*) voltar ♦ *vt* devolver; (*favour, love etc*) retribuir; (*verdict*) proferir, anunciar; (*POL: candidate*) eleger; **~s** *npl* (*COMM*) receita; (: *~ed goods*) mercadorias *fpl* devolvidas; **in ~ (for)** em troca (de); **many happy ~s (of the day)!** parabéns!; **by ~ (of post)** por volta do correio.
returnable [rɪ'təːnəbl] *adj* (*bottle etc*) restituível.
return key *n* (*COMPUT*) tecla de retorno.
reunion [riː'juːnɪən] *n* reunião *f*.
reunite [riːjuː'naɪt] *vt* reunir; (*reconcile*) reconciliar.
rev [rɛv] *n abbr* (*AUT: = revolution*) revolução *f* ♦ *vt* (*also: ~ up*) aumentar a velocidade de ♦ *vi* acelerar.
revaluation [riːvælju'eɪʃən] *n* reavaliação *f*.
revamp ['riː'væmp] *vt* dar um jeito em.
rev counter (*BRIT*) *n* tacômetro.
Rev(d). *abbr* = **reverend.**
reveal [rɪ'viːl] *vt* revelar.
revealing [rɪ'viːlɪŋ] *adj* revelador(a).
reveille [rɪ'vælɪ] *n* (*MIL*) toque *m* de alvorada.
revel ['rɛvl] *vi*: **to ~ in sth/in doing sth** deleitar-se com algo/em fazer algo.
revelation [rɛvə'leɪʃən] *n* revelação *f*.
reveller ['rɛvlə*] *n* farrista *m/f*, folião/liã *m/f*.
revelry ['rɛvəlrɪ] *n* festança, folia.
revenge [rɪ'vɛndʒ] *n* vingança, desforra; (*in sport*) revanche *f* ♦ *vt* vingar; **to take ~ on** vingar-se de.
revengeful [rɪ'vɛndʒful] *adj* vingativo.
revenue ['rɛvənjuː] *n* receita, renda; (*on investment*) rendimento.
reverberate [rɪ'vəːbəreɪt] *vi* (*sound*) ressoar, repercutir, ecoar; (*light*) reverberar.
reverberation [rɪvəːbə'reɪʃən] *n* repercussão *f*.
revere [rɪ'vɪə*] *vt* reverenciar, venerar.
reverence ['rɛvərəns] *n* reverência.
reverend ['rɛvrənd] *adj* reverendo; **the R~ John Smith** o reverendo John Smith.
reverent ['rɛvərənt] *adj* reverente.
reverie ['rɛvərɪ] *n* devaneio, sonho.
reversal [rɪ'vəːsl] *n* (*of order*) reversão *f*; (*of direction*) mudança em sentido contrário; (*of decision*) revogação *f*; (*of opinion*) reviravolta.
reverse [rɪ'vəːs] *n* (*opposite*) contrário; (*back: of cloth*) avesso; (: *of coin*) reverso; (: *of paper*) dorso; (*AUT: also: ~ gear*) marcha à ré (*BR*), marcha atrás (*PT*) ♦ *adj* (*order*) inverso, oposto; (*direction*) contrário ♦ *vt* (*turn over*) virar do lado do avesso; (*invert*) inverter; (*change*) mudar (totalmente) de; (*LAW: judgment*) revogar ♦ *vi* (*BRIT: AUT*) dar (marcha à) ré (*BR*), fazer marcha atrás (*PT*); **to go into ~** dar ré (*BR*), fazer marcha atrás (*PT*); **in ~ order** na ordem inversa.
reversed charge call [rɪ'vəːst-] (*BRIT*) *n* (*TEL*) ligação *f* a cobrar.
reverse video *n* vídeo reverso.
reversible [rɪ'vəːsəbl] *adj* reversível.
reversing lights [rɪ'vəːsɪŋ-] *npl* luzes *fpl* de ré

(*BR*), luzes *fpl* de marcha atrás (*PT*).
reversion [rɪ'vəːʃən] *n* volta.
revert [rɪ'vəːt] *vi*: **to ~ to** voltar a.
review [rɪ'vjuː] *n* (*magazine, MIL*) revista; (*of book, film*) crítica, resenha; (*examination*) recapitulação *f*, exame *m* ♦ *vt* rever, examinar; (*MIL*) passar em revista; (*book, film*) fazer a crítica *or* resenha de; **to come under ~** ser estudado.
reviewer [rɪ'vjuːə*] *n* crítico/a.
revile [rɪ'vaɪl] *vt* ultrajar, injuriar, vilipendiar.
revise [rɪ'vaɪz] *vt* (*manuscript*) corrigir; (*opinion*) alterar, modificar; (*study: subject*) recapitular; (*look over*) revisar, rever; **~d edition** edição *f* revista.
revision [rɪ'vɪʒən] *n* correção *f*, modificação *f*, revisão *f*; (*revised version*) revisão *f*.
revitalize [riː'vaɪtəlaɪz] *vt* revitalizar, revivificar.
revival [rɪ'vaɪvəl] *n* (*recovery*) restabelecimento; (*of interest*) renascença, renascimento; (*THEATRE*) reestréia; (*of faith*) despertar *m*.
revive [rɪ'vaɪv] *vt* (*person*) reanimar, ressuscitar; (*custom*) restabelecer, restaurar; (*hope, courage*) despertar; (*play*) reapresentar ♦ *vi* (*person*) voltar a si, recuperar os sentidos; (*hope, activity*) renascer.
revoke [rɪ'vəuk] *vt* revogar; (*decision, promise*) voltar atrás com.
revolt [rɪ'vəult] *n* revolta, rebelião *f*, insurreição *f* ♦ *vi* revoltar-se ♦ *vt* causar aversão a, repugnar.
revolting [rɪ'vəultɪŋ] *adj* revoltante, repulsivo.
revolution [rɛvə'luːʃən] *n* revolução *f*.
revolutionary [rɛvə'luːʃənərɪ] *adj*, *n* revolucionário/a.
revolutionize [rɛvə'luːʃənaɪz] *vt* revolucionar.
revolve [rɪ'vɔlv] *vi* girar.
revolver [rɪ'vɔlvə*] *n* revólver *m*.
revolving [rɪ'vɔlvɪŋ] *adj* (*chair etc*) giratório.
revolving credit *n* crédito rotativo.
revolving door *n* porta giratória.
revue [rɪ'vjuː] *n* (*THEATRE*) revista.
revulsion [rɪ'vʌlʃən] *n* aversão *f*, repugnância.
reward [rɪ'wɔːd] *n* recompensa ♦ *vt*: **to ~ (for)** recompensar *or* premiar (por).
rewarding [rɪ'wɔːdɪŋ] *adj* (*fig*) gratificante, compensador(a).
rewind [riː'waɪnd] (*irreg*) *vt* (*watch*) dar corda em; (*tape*) voltar para trás.
rewire [riː'waɪə*] *vt* (*house*) renovar a instalação elétrica de.
reword [riː'wəːd] *vt* reformular, exprimir em outras palavras.
rewound [riː'waund] *pt, pp of* **rewind**.
rewrite [riː'raɪt] (*irreg*) *vt* reescrever, escrever de novo.
Reykjavik ['reɪkjəviːk] *n* Reikjavik.
RFD (*US*) *abbr* (*POST*) = **rural free delivery**.
Rh *abbr* (= *rhesus*) Rh.
rhapsody ['ræpsədɪ] *n* (*MUS*) rapsódia; (*fig*) elocução *f* exagerada *or* empolada.
rhesus factor ['riːsəs-] *n* (*MED*) fator *m* Rh.
rhetoric ['rɛtərɪk] *n* retórica.
rhetorical [rɪ'tɔrɪkl] *adj* retórico.
rheumatic [ruː'mætɪk] *adj* reumático.
rheumatism ['ruːmətɪzəm] *n* reumatismo.
rheumatoid arthritis ['ruːmətɔɪd-] *n* artrite *f* reumatóide.
Rhine [raɪn] *n*: **the ~** o (rio) Reno.
rhinestone ['raɪnstəun] *n* diamante *m* postiço.
rhinoceros [raɪ'nɔsərəs] *n* rinoceronte *m*.
Rhodes [rəudz] *n* (ilha de) Rodes.
Rhodesia [rəu'diːʒə] *n* Rodésia.
Rhodesian [rəu'diːʒən] *adj*, *n* rodésio/a.
rhododendron [rəudə'dɛndrən] *n* rododendro.
Rhone [rəun] *n*: **the ~** o (rio) Ródano.
rhubarb ['ruːbɑːb] *n* ruibarbo.
rhyme [raɪm] *n* rima; (*verse*) verso(s) *m(pl)* rimado(s), poesia ♦ *vi*: **to ~ (with)** rimar (com); **without ~ or reason** sem pé nem cabeça.
rhythm ['rɪðm] *n* ritmo, cadência.
rhythmic(al) ['rɪðmɪk(l)] *adj* rítmico, compassado.
rhythmically ['rɪðmɪklɪ] *adv* ritmicamente.
RI *n abbr* (*BRIT*) = **religious instruction** ♦ *abbr* (*US: POST*) = **Rhode Island**.
rib [rɪb] *n* (*ANAT*) costela ♦ *vt* (*mock*) zombar de, encarnar em.
ribald ['rɪbəld] *adj* vulgarmente engraçado, irreverente.
ribbed [rɪbd] *adj* (*knitting*) em ponto de meia.
ribbon ['rɪbən] *n* fita; (*strip*) faixa, tira; **in ~s** (*torn*) em tirinhas, esfarrapado.
rice [raɪs] *n* arroz *m*.
ricefield ['raɪsfiːld] *n* arrozal *m*.
rice pudding *n* arroz *m* doce.
rich [rɪtʃ] *adj* rico; (*banquet*) suntuoso, opulento; (*soil*) fértil; (*food*) suculento, forte; (: *sweet*) rico; **the ~** *npl* os ricos; **~es** *npl* riquezas *fpl*; **to be ~ in sth** ser rico em algo.
richly ['rɪtʃlɪ] *adv* (*decorated*) suntuosamente; (*deserved*) tanto.
richness ['rɪtʃnɪs] *n* riqueza, opulência; (*of soil etc*) fertilidade *f*.
rickets ['rɪkɪts] *n* raquitismo.
rickety ['rɪkɪtɪ] *adj* sem firmeza, vacilante.
rickshaw ['rɪkʃɔː] *n* jinriquixá *m*.
ricochet ['rɪkəʃeɪ] *n* ricochete *m* ♦ *vi* ricochetear.
rid [rɪd] (*pt, pp* **rid**) *vt*: **to ~ sb of sth** livrar alguém de algo; **to get ~ of** livrar-se *or* desembaraçar-se de.
riddance ['rɪdns] *n*: **good ~!** bons ventos o levem!
ridden ['rɪdn] *pp of* **ride**.
riddle ['rɪdl] *n* (*conundrum*) adivinhação *f*; (*mystery*) enigma *m*, charada ♦ *vt*: **to be ~d with** estar cheio *or* crivado de.
ride [raɪd] (*pt* **rode**, *pp* **ridden**) *n* (*gen*) passeio; (*on horse*) passeio a cavalo; (*distance covered*) percurso, trajeto ♦ *vi* (*as*

NB: *European Portuguese adds the following consonants to certain words:* **b** (sú(b)dito, su(b)til); **c** (a(c)ção, a(c)cionista, a(c)to); **m** (inde(m)ne); **p** (ado(p)ção, ado(p)tar); *for further details see p. xiii.*

sport) montar; (*go somewhere*: *on horse*, *bicycle*) ir (a cavalo, de bicicleta); (*journey*: *on bicycle*, *motor cycle*, *bus*) viajar ♦ *vt* (*a horse*) montar a; (*distance*) percorrer; **to ~ a bicycle** andar de bicicleta; **can you ~ a bike?** você sabe andar de bicicleta?; **to ~ at anchor** (*NAUT*) estar ancorado; **horse/car ~** passeio a cavalo/de carro; **to go for a ~** dar um passeio *or* uma volta (de carro *or* de bicicleta *etc*); **to take sb for a ~** (*fig*) enganar alguém.

ride out *vt*: **to ~ out the storm** (*fig*) superar as dificuldades.

rider ['raɪdə*] *n* (*on horse*: *male*) cavaleiro; (: *female*) amazona; (*on bicycle*) ciclista *m/f*; (*on motorcycle*) motociclista *m/f*; (*in document*) cláusula adicional.

ridge [rɪdʒ] *n* (*of hill*) cume *m*, topo; (*of roof*) cumeeira; (*wrinkle*) ruga.

ridicule ['rɪdɪkjuːl] *n* escárnio, zombaria, mofa ♦ *vt* ridicularizar, zombar de; **to hold sb/sth up to ~** ridicularizar alguém/algo.

ridiculous [rɪ'dɪkjuləs] *adj* ridículo.

riding ['raɪdɪŋ] *n* equitação *f*.

riding school *n* escola de equitação.

rife [raɪf] *adj*: **to be ~** ser comum; **to be ~ with** estar repleto de, abundar em.

riffraff ['rɪfræf] *n* plebe *f*, ralé *f*, povinho.

rifle ['raɪfl] *n* rifle *m*, fuzil *m* ♦ *vt* saquear.

rifle through *vt fus* vasculhar.

rifle range *n* campo de tiro; (*at fair*) tiro ao alvo.

rift [rɪft] *n* (*fig*: *disagreement*: *between friends*) desentendimento; (: *in party*) rompimento, divergência.

rig [rɪg] *n* (*also*: *oil ~*) torre *f* de perfuração ♦ *vt* (*election etc*) adulterar *or* falsificar os resultados de.

rig out (*BRIT*) *vt* ataviar, vestir.

rig up *vt* instalar, montar, improvisar.

rigging ['rɪgɪŋ] *n* (*NAUT*) cordame *m*.

right [raɪt] *adj* (*true, correct*) certo, correto; (*suitable*) adequado, conveniente; (*just*) justo; (*morally good*) bom; (*not left*) direito ♦ *n* (*title*, *claim*) direito; (*not left*) direita ♦ *adv* (*correctly*) bem, corretamente; (*not on the left*) à direita; (*to the ~*) para a direita ♦ *vt* endireitar ♦ *excl* bom!; **all ~!** tudo bem!, está bem!; (*enough*) chega!, basta!; **the ~ time** (*precise*) a hora exata; (*not wrong*) a hora certa; **to be ~** (*person*) ter razão; (: *in guess etc*) acertar; (*answer*) estar certo; **to get sth ~** acertar em algo; **let's get it ~ this time!** vamos acertar desta vez; **you did the ~ thing** você fez a coisa certa; **to put a mistake ~** (*BRIT*) consertar um erro; **~ now** agora mesmo; **~ before/after** logo antes/depois; **~ against the wall** rente à parede; **~ in the middle** bem no meio; **~ away** imediatamente, logo, já; **to go ~ to the end of sth** ir até o finalzinho de algo; **by ~s** por direito; **on the ~** à direita; **to be in the ~** ter razão; **film ~s** direitos de adaptação para o cinema; **~ of way** (*AUT*) preferência.

right angle *n* ângulo reto.

righteous ['raɪtʃəs] *adj* justo, honrado; (*anger*) justificado.

righteousness ['raɪtʃəsnɪs] *n* justiça.

rightful ['raɪtful] *adj* (*heir*) legítimo.

rightfully ['raɪtfəlɪ] *adv* legitimamente.

right-hand *adj* à direita.

right-handed [-'hændɪd] *adj* (*person*) destro.

right-hand man (*irreg*) *n* braço direito.

right-hand side *n* lado direito.

rightly ['raɪtlɪ] *adv* corretamente, devidamente; (*with reason*) com razão; **if I remember ~** (*BRIT*) se me lembro bem, se não me engano.

right-minded *adj* sensato, ajuizado.

rights issue *n* (*STOCK EXCHANGE*) emissão *f* de bônus de subscrição.

right wing *n* (*POL*) direita; (*SPORT*) ponta direita; (*MIL*) ala direita ♦ *adj*: **right-wing** de direita.

right-winger *n* (*POL*) direitista *m/f*; (*SPORT*) ponta-direita *m*.

rigid ['rɪdʒɪd] *adj* rígido; (*principle*) inflexível.

rigidity [rɪ'dʒɪdɪtɪ] *n* rigidez *f*, inflexibilidade *f*.

rigidly ['rɪdʒɪdlɪ] *adv* rigidamente; (*behave*) inflexivelmente.

rigmarole ['rɪgmərəul] *n* (*process*) processo; (*story*) ladainha.

rigor ['rɪgə*] (*US*) *n* = **rigour**.

rigor mortis [-'mɔːtɪs] *n* rigidez *f* cadavérica.

rigorous ['rɪgərəs] *adj* rigoroso.

rigorously ['rɪgərəslɪ] *adv* rigorosamente.

rigour ['rɪgə*] (*US* **rigor**) *n* rigor *m*.

rig-out (*BRIT*: *inf*) *n* roupa, traje *m*.

rile [raɪl] *vt* irritar, aborrecer.

rim [rɪm] *n* borda, beira, orla; (*of spectacles*, *wheel*) aro.

rimless ['rɪmlɪs] *adj* (*spectacles*) sem aro.

rind [raɪnd] *n* (*of bacon*) couro, pele *f*; (*of lemon etc*) casca; (*of cheese*) crosta, casca.

ring [rɪŋ] (*pt* **rang**, *pp* **rung**) *n* (*of metal*) aro; (*on finger*) anel *m*; (*also*: *wedding ~*) aliança; (*of people*, *objects*) círculo, grupo; (*of spies*) grupo; (*for boxing*) ringue *m*; (*of circus*) pista, picadeiro; (*bull~*) picadeiro, arena; (*sound*: *of small bell*) toque *m*; (: *of large bell*) badalada, repique *m*; (*telephone call*) chamada (telefônica), ligada ♦ *vi* (*on telephone*) telefonar; (*bell*) tocar; (*also*: *~ out*: *voice*, *words*) soar; (*ears*) zumbir ♦ *vt* (*BRIT*: *TEL*: *also*: *~ up*) telefonar a, ligar para; (*bell etc*) badalar; (*doorbell*) tocar; **to give sb a ~** (*TEL*) dar uma ligada *or* ligar para alguém; **that has the ~ of truth about it** isso tem jeito de ser verdade; **the name doesn't ~ a bell (with me)** o nome não me diz nada.

ring back (*BRIT*) *vi* (*TEL*) telefonar *or* ligar de volta ♦ *vt* telefonar *or* ligar de volta para.

ring off (*BRIT*) *vi* (*TEL*) desligar.

ring binder *n* fichário (*pasta*).

ring finger *n* dedo anelar.

ringing ['rɪŋɪŋ] *n* (*of large bell*) repicar *m*; (*of doorbell*) tocar *m*; (*in ears*) zumbido.

ringing tone (*BRIT*) *n* (*TEL*) sinal *m* de chamada.

ringleader ['rɪŋli:də*] *n* (*of gang*) cabeça *m/f*, cérebro.

ringlets ['rɪŋlɪts] *npl* caracóis *mpl*, argolinhas *fpl*.

ring road (*BRIT*) *n* estrada periférica *or* perimetral.

rink [rɪŋk] *n* (*also*: *ice* ~) pista de patinação, rinque *m*; (*for roller skating*) rinque.

rinse [rɪns] *n* enxaguada ♦ *vt* enxaguar.

Rio (de Janeiro) ['ri:əu(dədʒə'nɪərəu)] *n* o Rio (de Janeiro).

riot ['raɪət] *n* distúrbio, motim *m*, desordem *f* ♦ *vi* provocar distúrbios, amotinar-se; **a ~ of colours** uma orgia de cores; **to run ~** desenfrear-se.

rioter ['raɪətə*] *n* desordeiro/a, amotinador(a) *m/f*.

riotous ['raɪətəs] *adj* (*crowd*) desordeiro; (*party*) tumultuado, barulhento; (*uncontrolled*) desenfreado.

riotously ['raɪətəslɪ] *adv*: **~ funny** hilariante.

riot police *n* polícia anti-motim.

RIP *abbr* (= *rest in peace*) RIP.

rip [rɪp] *n* rasgão *m*; (*opening*) abertura ♦ *vt* rasgar ♦ *vi* rasgar-se.

rip up *vt* rasgar.

ripcord ['rɪpkɔ:d] *n* corda de abertura (de pára-quedas).

ripe [raɪp] *adj* (*fruit*) maduro; (*ready*) pronto.

ripen ['raɪpən] *vt*, *vi* amadurecer.

ripeness ['raɪpnɪs] *n* maturidade *f*, amadurecimento.

rip-off (*inf*) *n*: **this is a ~** isso é roubo.

riposte [rɪ'pɔst] *n* riposta.

ripple ['rɪpl] *n* ondulação *f*, encrespação *f*; (*sound*) murmúrio ♦ *vi* encrespar-se ♦ *vt* ondular.

rise [raɪz] (*pt* **rose**, *pp* **risen**) *n* (*slope*) elevação *f*, ladeira; (*hill*) colina, rampa; (*increase*: *in wages*: *BRIT*) aumento; (: *in prices, temperature*) subida; (*fig*: *to power etc*) ascensão *f* ♦ *vi* (*gen*) levantar-se, erguer-se; (*prices, waters*) subir; (*river*) encher; (*sun*) nascer; (*wind, person*: *from bed etc*) levantar(-se); (*also*: *~ up*: *rebel*) sublevar-se; (*in rank*) ascender, subir; **to give ~ to** ocasionar, dar origem a; **to ~ to the occasion** mostrar-se à altura da situação.

rising ['raɪzɪŋ] *adj* (*increasing*: *prices*) em alta; (: *number*) crescente, cada vez maior; (: *unemployment*) crescente; (*tide*) montante; (*sun, moon*) nascente ♦ *n* (*uprising*) insurreição *f*.

rising damp *n* umidade *f* que sobe.

risk [rɪsk] *n* risco, perigo ♦ *vt* arriscar; (*dare*) atrever-se a; **to take** *or* **run the ~ of doing** correr o risco de fazer; **at ~** em perigo; **at one's own ~** por sua própria conta e risco; **a fire/health/security ~** um risco de incêndio/à saúde/à segurança; **I'll ~ it** eu vou me arriscar.

risk capital *n* capital *m* de risco.

risky ['rɪskɪ] *adj* arriscado.

risqué ['ri:skeɪ] *adj* (*joke*) picante.

rissole ['rɪsəul] *n* rissole *m*.

rite [raɪt] *n* rito; **funeral ~s** exéquias, cerimônia fúnebre; **last ~s** últimos sacramentos.

ritual ['rɪtjuəl] *adj* ritual ♦ *n* ritual *m*, rito.

rival ['raɪvl] *adj*, *n* rival *m/f*; (*in business*) concorrente *m/f* ♦ *vt* rivalizar *or* competir com; **to ~ sb/sth in** rivalizar com alguém/algo em.

rivalry ['raɪvəlrɪ] *n* rivalidade *f*; (*between companies*) concorrência.

river ['rɪvə*] *n* rio ♦ *cpd* (*port, traffic*) fluvial; **up/down ~** rio acima/abaixo.

riverbank ['rɪvəbæŋk] *n* margem *f* (do rio).

riverbed ['rɪvəbɛd] *n* leito (do rio).

riverside ['rɪvəsaɪd] *n* beira, orla (do rio).

rivet ['rɪvɪt] *n* rebite *m*, cravo ♦ *vt* rebitar; (*fig*) cravar.

riveting ['rɪvɪtɪŋ] *adj* (*fig*) fascinante.

Riviera [rɪvɪ'ɛərə] *n*: **the (French) ~** a Costa Azul (francesa), a Riviera francesa.

Riyadh [rɪ'jɑ:d] *n* Riad.

RN *n abbr* (*BRIT*) = **Royal Navy**; (*US*) = **registered nurse**.

RNA *n abbr* (= *ribonucleic acid*) ARN *m*.

RNLI (*BRIT*) *n abbr* (= *Royal National Lifeboat Institution*) ≈ Salvamar.

RNZAF *n abbr* = **Royal New Zealand Air Force**.

RNZN *n abbr* = **Royal New Zealand Navy**.

road [rəud] *n* via; (*motorway etc*) estrada (de rodagem); (*in town*) rua; (*fig*) caminho; **main ~** estrada principal; **major ~** via preferencial; **minor ~** via secundária; **it takes four hours by ~** leva quatro horas de carro; **"~ up"** (*BRIT*) "obras".

roadblock ['rəudblɔk] *n* barricada.

road haulage *n* transportes *mpl* rodoviários.

roadhog ['rəudhɔg] *n* dono da estrada.

road map *n* mapa *m* rodoviário.

road safety *n* segurança do trânsito.

roadside ['rəudsaɪd] *n* beira da estrada ♦ *cpd* à beira da estrada; **by the ~** à beira da estrada.

roadsign ['rəudsaɪn] *n* placa de sinalização.

roadsweeper ['rəudswi:pə*] (*BRIT*) *n* (*person*) gari *m/f* (*BR*), varredor(a) *m/f* (*PT*).

road transport *n* transportes *mpl* rodoviários.

road user *n* usuário/a da via pública.

roadway ['rəudweɪ] *n* pista, estrada.

roadworks ['rəudwə:ks] *npl* obras *fpl* (na estrada).

roadworthy ['rəudwə:ðɪ] *adj* (*car*) em bom estado de conservação e segurança.

roam [rəum] *vi* vagar, perambular, errar ♦ *vt* vagar *or* vadiar por.

roar [rɔ:*] *n* (*of animal*) rugido, urro; (*of crowd*) bramido; (*of vehicle, storm*) estrondo; (*of laughter*) barulho ♦ *vi* rugir, bramar, bradar; **to ~ with laughter** dar garga-

NB: European Portuguese adds the following consonants to certain words: **b** (sú(b)dito, su(b)til); **c** (a(c)ção, a(c)cionista, a(c)to); **m** (inde(m)ne); **p** (ado(p)ção, ado(p)tar); *for further details see p. xiii.*

lhadas.

roaring ['rɔːrɪŋ] *adj*: **a ~ fire** labaredas; **a ~ success** um sucesso estrondoso; **to do a ~ trade** fazer um bom negócio.

roast [rəust] *n* carne *f* assada, assado ♦ *vt* (*meat*) assar; (*coffee*) torrar.

roast beef *n* rosbife *m*.

rob [rɔb] *vt* roubar; (*bank*) assaltar; **to ~ sb of sth** roubar algo de alguém; (*fig*: *deprive*) despojar alguém de algo.

robber ['rɔbə*] *n* ladrão/ladra *m/f*.

robbery ['rɔbərɪ] *n* roubo.

robe [rəub] *n* (*for ceremony etc*) toga, beca; (*also*: *bath ~*) roupão *m* (de banho) ♦ *vt* revestir.

robin ['rɔbɪn] *n* pisco-de-peito-ruivo (*BR*), pintarroxo (*PT*).

robot ['rəubɔt] *n* robô *m*.

robotics [rə'bɔtɪks] *n* robótica.

robust [rəu'bʌst] *adj* robusto, forte.

rock [rɔk] *n* (*gen*) rocha; (*boulder*) penhasco, rochedo; (*BRIT*: *sweet*) pirulito ♦ *vt* (*swing gently*: *cradle*) balançar, oscilar; (: *child*) embalar, acalentar; (*shake*) sacudir ♦ *vi* balançar-se; (*child*) embalar-se; (*shake*) sacudir-se; **on the ~s** (*drink*) com gelo; (*marriage etc*) arruinado, em dificuldades; **to ~ the boat** (*fig*) criar confusão.

rock and roll *n* rock-and-roll *m*.

rock-bottom *adj* (*fig*) mínimo, ínfimo ♦ *n*: **to hit** *or* **reach ~** (*prices*) chegar ao nível mais baixo; (*person*) chegar ao fundo do poço.

rock climber *n* alpinista *m/f*.

rock climbing *n* alpinismo.

rockery ['rɔkərɪ] *n jardim de plantas rasteiras entre pedras.*

rocket ['rɔkɪt] *n* foguete *m* ♦ *vi* (*prices*) disparar.

rocket launcher [-'lɔːntʃə*] *n* dispositivo lança-foguetes.

rock face *n* rochedo a pique.

rock fall *n* queda de pedras.

rocking chair ['rɔkɪŋ-] *n* cadeira de balanço.

rocking horse ['rɔkɪŋ-] *n* cavalo de balanço.

rocky ['rɔkɪ] *adj* rochoso; (*unsteady*: *table*) bambo, instável.

Rocky Mountains *npl*: **the ~** as Montanhas Rochosas.

rod [rɔd] *n* vara, varinha; (*TECH*) haste *f*; (*also*: *fishing ~*) vara de pescar.

rode [rəud] *pt of* **ride**.

rodent ['rəudnt] *n* roedor *m*.

rodeo ['rəudɪəu] *n* rodeio.

roe [rəu] *n* (*of fish*): **hard/soft ~** ova/esperma *m* de peixe.

roe (deer) *n inv* corça, cerva.

rogue [rəug] *n* velhaco, maroto.

roguish ['rəugɪʃ] *adj* travesso, brincalhão/lhona.

role [rəul] *n* papel *m*.

roll [rəul] *n* rolo; (*of banknotes*) maço; (*also*: *bread ~*) pãozinho; (*register*) rol *m*, lista; (*sound*: *of drums etc*) rufar *m*; (*movement*: *of ship*) jogo ♦ *vt* rolar; (*also*: *~ up*: *string*) enrolar; (: *sleeves*) arregaçar; (*cigarettes*) enrolar; (*also*: *~ out*: *pastry*) esticar, alisar ♦ *vi* rolar; (*drum*) rufar; (*in walking*) gingar; (*ship*) balançar, jogar; **cheese ~** sanduíche de queijo (*num pãozinho*).

roll about *vi* ficar rolando.

roll around *vi* ficar rolando.

roll by *vi* (*time*) passar.

roll in *vi* (*mail*, *cash*) chegar em grande quantidade.

roll over *vi* dar uma volta.

roll up *vi* (*inf*: *arrive*) pintar, chegar, aparecer ♦ *vt* (*carpet*) enrolar; (*sleeves*) arregaçar; **to ~ o.s. up into a ball** enrolar-se.

roll call *n* chamada, toque *m* de chamada.

rolled gold [rəuld-] *n* plaquê *m*.

roller ['rəulə*] *n* rolo; (*wheel*) roda, roldana.

roller blind (*BRIT*) *n* estore *m*.

roller coaster *n* montanha-russa.

roller skates *npl* patins *mpl* de roda.

rollicking ['rɔlɪkɪŋ] *adj* alegre, brincalhão/lhona, divertido.

rolling ['rəulɪŋ] *adj* (*landscape*) ondulado.

rolling mill *n* laminador *m*.

rolling pin *n* rolo de pastel.

rolling stock *n* (*RAIL*) material *m* rodante.

roll-on-roll-off (*BRIT*) *adj* (*ferry*) para veículos.

roly-poly ['rəulɪ'pəulɪ] (*BRIT*) *n* (*CULIN*) bolo de rolo.

ROM [rɔm] *n abbr* (*COMPUT*: = *read-only memory*) ROM *m*.

Roman ['rəumən] *adj*, *n* romano/a.

Roman Catholic *adj*, *n* católico/a (romano/a).

romance [rə'mæns] *n* (*love affair*) aventura amorosa, romance *m*; (*book etc*) história de amor; (*charm*) romantismo.

Romania [ruː'meɪnɪə] *n* Romênia.

Romanian [ruː'meɪnɪən] *adj* romeno ♦ *n* romeno/a; (*LING*) romeno.

Roman numeral *n* número romano.

romantic [rə'mæntɪk] *adj* romântico.

romanticism [rə'mæntɪsɪzəm] *n* romantismo.

Romany ['rəumənɪ] *adj* cigano ♦ *n* cigano/a; (*LING*) romani *m*.

romp [rɔmp] *n* brincadeira, travessura ♦ *vi* (*also*: *~ about*) brincar ruidosamente; **to ~ home** (*horse*) ganhar fácil.

rompers ['rɔmpəz] *npl* macacão *m* de bebê.

rondo ['rɔndəu] *n* (*MUS*) rondó.

roof [ruːf, *pl* ruːfs *or* ruːvz] *n* (*of house*) telhado; (*of car*) capota, teto; (*of tunnel*, *cave*) teto ♦ *vt* telhar, cobrir com telhas; **the ~ of the mouth** o céu da boca.

roof garden *n* jardim *m* em terraço.

roofing ['ruːfɪŋ] *n* cobertura.

roof rack *n* (*AUT*) bagageiro.

rook [ruk] *n* (*bird*) gralha; (*CHESS*) torre *f*.

room [ruːm] *n* (*in house*) quarto, aposento; (*also*: *bed~*) quarto, dormitório; (*in school etc*) sala; (*space*) espaço, lugar *m*; **~s** *npl* (*lodging*) alojamento; **"~s to let"** (*BRIT*), **"~s for rent"** (*US*) "alugam-se quartos *or* apartamentos"; **single ~** quarto individual;

double ~ quarto duplo *or* de casal *or* para duas pessoas; **is there ~ for this?** tem lugar para isto aqui?; **to make ~ for sb** dar lugar a alguém; **there is ~ for improvement** isso podia estar melhor.
rooming house ['ru:mıŋ-] (*US*: *irreg*) *n* casa de cômodos.
roommate ['ru:mmeıt] *n* companheiro/a de quarto.
room service *n* serviço de quarto.
room temperature *n* temperatura ambiente.
roomy ['ru:mı] *adj* espaçoso; (*garment*) folgado.
roost [ru:st] *n* poleiro ♦ *vi* empoleirar-se, pernoitar.
rooster ['ru:stə*] *n* galo.
root [ru:t] *n* (*BOT*, *MATH*) raiz *f*; (*fig*: *of problem*) origem *f* ♦ *vi* (*plant*, *belief*) enraizar, arraigar; **to take ~** (*plant*) enraizar; (*idea*) criar raizes.
root about *vi* (*fig*): **to ~ about in** (*drawer*) vasculhar; (*house*) esquadrinhar.
root for (*inf*) *vt fus* torcer por.
root out *vt* desarraigar, extirpar.
rope [rəup] *n* corda; (*NAUT*) cabo ♦ *vt* (*climbers*, *box*) atar *or* amarrar com uma corda; (*horse*, *cow*) laçar; **to know the ~s** (*fig*) estar por dentro (do assunto).
rope in *vt* (*fig*): **to ~ sb in** persuadir alguém a tomar parte.
rope ladder *n* escada de corda.
rosary ['rəuzərı] *n* rosário.
rose [rəuz] *pt of* **rise** ♦ *n* rosa; (*also*: *~bush*) roseira; (*on watering can*) crivo ♦ *adj* rosado, cor de rosa *inv*.
rosé ['rəuzeı] *n* rosado, rosé *m*.
rosebed ['rəuzbɛd] *n* roseiral *m*.
rosebud ['rəuzbʌd] *n* botão *m* de rosa.
rosebush ['rəuzbuʃ] *n* roseira.
rosemary ['rəuzmərı] *n* alecrim *m*.
rosette [rəu'zɛt] *n* rosácea, roseta.
ROSPA ['rɔspə] (*BRIT*) *n abbr* = **Royal Society for the Prevention of Accidents**.
roster ['rɔstə*] *n*: **duty ~** lista de tarefas, escala de serviço.
rostrum ['rɔstrəm] *n* tribuna.
rosy ['rəuzı] *adj* rosado, rosáceo; **a ~ future** um futuro promissor.
rot [rɔt] *n* (*decay*) putrefação *f*, podridão *f*; (*fig*: *pej*) decadência ♦ *vt*, *vi* apodrecer; **to stop the ~** (*BRIT*: *fig*) acabar com a onda de fracassos; **dry ~** apodrecimento seco (*de madeira*); **wet ~** putrefação fungosa.
rota ['rəutə] *n* lista de tarefas, escala de serviço; **on a ~ basis** em rodízio.
rotary ['rəutərı] *adj* rotativo.
rotate [rəu'teıt] *vt* (*revolve*) fazer girar, dar voltas em; (*change round*: *crops*) alternar; (: *jobs*) alternar, revezar ♦ *vi* (*revolve*) girar, dar voltas.
rotating [rəu'teıtıŋ] *adj* (*movement*) rotativo.
rotation [rəu'teıʃən] *n* rotação *f*; **in ~** por turnos.
rote [rəut] *n*: **by ~** de cor.
rotor ['rəutə*] *n* rotor *m*.
rotten ['rɔtn] *adj* (*decayed*) podre; (*wood*) carcomido; (*fig*) corrupto; (*inf*: *bad*) péssimo; **to feel ~** (*ill*) sentir-se podre.
rotting ['rɔtıŋ] *adj* podre.
rotund [rəu'tʌnd] *adj* rotundo; (*person*) rechonchudo.
rouble ['ru:bl] (*US* **ruble**) *n* rublo.
rouge [ru:ʒ] *n* rouge *m*, blush *m*, carmim *m*.
rough [rʌf] *adj* (*skin*, *surface*) áspero; (*terrain*) acidentado; (*road*) desigual; (*voice*) áspero, rouco; (*person*, *manner*: *coarse*) grosseiro, grosso; (: *violent*) violento; (*weather*) tempestuoso; (*treatment*) brutal, mau/má; (*cloth*) grosseiro; (*plan*) preliminar; (*guess*) aproximado ♦ *n* (*person*) grosseirão *m*; (*GOLF*): **in the ~** na grama crescida; **the sea is ~ today** o mar está agitado hoje; **to have a ~ time (of it)** passar maus bocados; **~ estimate** estimativa aproximada; **to ~ it** passar aperto; **to play ~** jogar bruto; **to sleep ~** (*BRIT*) dormir na rua; **to feel ~** (*BRIT*) passar mal.
rough out *vt* (*draft*) rascunhar.
roughage ['rʌfıdʒ] *n* fibras *fpl*.
rough-and-ready *adj* improvisado, feito às pressas.
rough-and-tumble *n* luta, confusão *f*.
roughcast ['rʌfkɑ:st] *n* reboco.
rough copy *n* rascunho.
rough draft *n* rascunho.
roughen ['rʌfən] *vt* (*surface*) tornar áspero.
rough justice *n* justiça sumária.
roughly ['rʌflı] *adv* (*handle*) bruscamente; (*make*) toscamente; (*approximately*) aproximadamente.
roughness ['rʌfnıs] *n* aspereza; (*rudeness*) grosseria.
roughshod ['rʌfʃɔd] *adv*: **to ride ~ over** (*person*) tratar a pontapés; (*objection*) passar por cima de.
rough work *n* (*at school etc*) rascunho.
roulette [ru:'lɛt] *n* roleta.
Roumania *etc* [ru:'meınıə] *n* = **Romania** *etc*.
round [raund] *adj* redondo ♦ *n* círculo; (*BRIT*: *of toast*) rodela; (*of drinks*) rodada; (*of policeman*) ronda; (*of milkman*) trajeto; (*of doctor*) visitas *fpl*; (*game*: *of cards*, *in competition*) partida; (*stage of competition*) rodada, turno; (*of ammunition*) cartucho; (*BOXING*) rounde *m*, assalto; (*of talks*) ciclo ♦ *vt* (*corner*) virar, dobrar; (*bend*) fazer; (*cape*) dobrar ♦ *prep* ao/em redor de, em/à volta de ♦ *adv*: **right ~, all ~** por todos os lados; **the long way ~** o caminho mais comprido; **all the year ~** durante todo o ano; **in ~ figures** em números redondos; **it's just ~ the corner** está logo depois de virar a esquina; (*fig*) está pertinho; **to ask sb ~** convidar alguém (para sua casa); **I'll be ~ at 6**

***NB:** European Portuguese adds the following consonants to certain words:* **b** (sú(b)dito, su(b)til); **c** (a(c)ção, a(c)cionista, a(c)to); **m** (inde(m)ne); **p** (ado(p)ção, ado(p)tar); *for further details see p. xiii.*

o'clock estarei aí às 6 horas; **to go ~** dar a volta; **to go ~ to sb's (house)** dar um pulinho na casa de alguém; **to go ~ an obstacle** contornar um obstáculo; **to go ~ the back** passar por detrás; **to go ~ a house** visitar uma casa; **enough to go ~** suficiente para todos; **she arrived ~ (about) noon** (*BRIT*) ela chegou por volta do meio-dia; **~ the clock** ininterrupto; **to go the ~s** (*story*) divulgar-se; **the daily ~** (*fig*) o cotidiano; **a ~ of applause** uma salva de palmas; **a ~ of drinks** uma rodada de bebidas; **~ of sandwiches** (*BRIT*) sanduíche *m* (*BR*), sandes *f inv* (*PT*).

round off *vt* (*speech etc*) terminar, completar.

round up *vt* (*cattle*) encurralar; (*people*) reunir; (*prices*) arredondar.

roundabout ['raundəbaut] *n* (*BRIT*: *AUT*) rotatória; (*at fair*) carrossel *m* ♦ *adj* (*route, means*) indireto.

rounded ['raundɪd] *adj* arredondado; (*style*) expressivo.

rounders ['raundəz] *npl* (*game*) ≈ beisebol *m*.

roundly ['raundlɪ] *adv* (*fig*) energicamente, totalmente.

round-shouldered [-'ʃəuldəd] *adj* encurvado.

roundsman ['raundzmən] (*BRIT*: *irreg*) *n* entregador *m* a domicílio.

round trip *n* viagem *f* de ida e volta.

roundup ['raundʌp] *n* rodeio; (*of criminals*) batida; **a ~ of the latest news** um resumo das últimas notícias.

rouse [rauz] *vt* (*wake up*) despertar, acordar; (*stir up*) suscitar.

rousing ['rauzɪŋ] *adj* emocionante, vibrante.

rout [raut] *n* (*MIL*) derrota; (*flight*) fuga, debandada ♦ *vt* derrotar.

route [ru:t] *n* caminho, rota; (*of bus*) trajeto; (*of shipping*) rumo, rota; **"all ~s"** (*AUT*) "todas as direções"; **the best ~ to London** o melhor caminho para Londres; **en ~ for** a caminho de; **en ~ from ... to** a caminho de ... para.

route map *n* (*BRIT*: *for journey*) mapa *m* rodoviário; (*for trains etc*) mapa da rede.

routine [ru:'ti:n] *adj* (*work*) rotineiro; (*procedure*) de rotina ♦ *n* rotina; (*THEATRE*) número; **daily ~** cotidiano.

roving ['rəuvɪŋ] *adj* (*wandering*) errante.

roving reporter *n* correspondente *m/f*.

row[1] [rəu] *n* (*line*) fila, fileira; (*KNITTING*) carreira, fileira ♦ *vi, vt* remar; **two days in a ~** dois dias a fio.

row[2] [rau] *n* (*noise, racket*) barulho, balbúrdia; (*dispute*) discussão *f*, briga; (*fuss*) confusão *f*, bagunça; (*scolding*) repreensão *f* ♦ *vi* brigar; **to have a ~** ter uma briga.

rowboat ['rəubəut] (*US*) *n* barco a remo.

rowdiness ['raudɪnɪs] *n* barulheira; (*fighting*) brigas *fpl*.

rowdy ['raudɪ] *adj* (*person*: *noisy*) barulhento; (: *quarrelsome*) brigão/ona; (*occasion*) tumultuado ♦ *n* encrenqueiro, criador *m* de caso.

rowdyism ['raudɪɪzəm] *n* violência.

rowing ['rəuɪŋ] *n* remo.

rowing boat (*BRIT*) *n* barco a remo.

rowlock ['rɔlək] (*BRIT*) *n* toleteira, forqueta.

royal ['rɔɪəl] *adj* real.

Royal Air Force (*BRIT*) *n força aérea britânica.*

royal blue *adj* azul vivo *inv*.

royalist ['rɔɪəlɪst] *adj, n* monarquista *m/f* (*BR*), monárquico/a (*PT*).

Royal Navy (*BRIT*) *n marinha de guerra britânica.*

royalty ['rɔɪəltɪ] *n* (*persons*) família real, realeza; (*payment*: *to author*) direitos *mpl* autorais; (: *to inventor*) direitos *mpl* de exploração de patente.

RP (*BRIT*) *n abbr* (= *received pronunciation*) *norma de pronúncia.*

rpm *abbr* (= *revolutions per minute*) rpm.

RR (*US*) *abbr* = **railroad.**

R&R (*US*) *n abbr* (*MIL*) = **rest and recreation.**

RSA (*BRIT*) *n abbr* = **Royal Society of Arts; Royal Scottish Academy.**

RSPB (*BRIT*) *n abbr* = **Royal Society for the Protection of Birds.**

RSPCA (*BRIT*) *n abbr* = **Royal Society for the Prevention of Cruelty to Animals.**

RSVP *abbr* (= *répondez s'il vous plaît*) ER.

Rt Hon. (*BRIT*) *abbr* (= *Right Honourable*) *título honorífico de conselheiro do estado ou juiz.*

Rt Rev. *abbr* (= *Right Reverend*) *reverendíssimo.*

rub [rʌb] *vt* esfregar; (*hard*) friccionar ♦ *n* esfregadela; (*hard*) fricção *f*; (*touch*) roçar *m*; **to ~ sb up** (*BRIT*) *or* **~ sb** (*US*) **the wrong way** irritar alguém.

rub down *vt* (*person*) esfregar; (*horse*) almofaçar.

rub in *vt* (*ointment*) esfregar.

rub off *vi* sair esfregando; **to ~ off on** transmitir-se para, influir sobre.

rub out *vt* apagar ♦ *vi* apagar-se.

rubber ['rʌbə*] *n* borracha; (*BRIT*: *eraser*) borracha.

rubber band *n* elástico, tira elástica.

rubber plant *n* (*tree*) seringueira; (*plant*) figueira.

rubber ring *n* (*for swimming*) bóia.

rubber stamp *n* carimbo ♦ *vt*: **to rubber-stamp** (*fig*) aprovar sem questionar.

rubbery ['rʌbərɪ] *adj* elástico.

rubbish ['rʌbɪʃ] *n* (*from household*) lixo; (*fig*: *pej*) porcarias *fpl*; (*nonsense*) disparates *mpl*, asneiras *fpl* ♦ *vt* (*BRIT*: *inf*) desprezar; **what you've just said is ~** você acabou de dizer uma besteira; **~!** que nada!, nado disso!

rubbish bin (*BRIT*) *n* lata de lixo.

rubbish dump *n* (*in town*) depósito (de lixo).

rubbishy ['rʌbɪʃɪ] (*BRIT*: *inf*) *adj* micha, chinfrim.

rubble ['rʌbl] *n* escombros *mpl*.

ruble ['ru:bl] (*US*) *n* = **rouble.**

ruby ['ru:bɪ] *n* rubi *m*.

RUC (*BRIT*) *n abbr* = **Royal Ulster Constabulary**.
rucksack ['rʌksæk] *n* mochila.
ructions ['rʌkʃənz] *npl* confusão *f*, tumulto.
rudder ['rʌdə*] *n* leme *m*.
ruddy ['rʌdɪ] *adj* (*face*) corado, avermelhado; (*inf*: *damned*) maldito, desgraçado.
rude [ru:d] *adj* (*impolite*: *person*) grosso, mal-educado; (: *word, manners*) grosseiro; (*sudden*) brusco; (*shocking*) obsceno, chocante; **to be ~ to sb** ser grosso com alguém.
rudely ['ru:dlɪ] *adv* grosseiramente.
rudeness ['ru:dnɪs] *n* falta de educação.
rudiment ['ru:dɪmənt] *n* rudimento; **~s** *npl* primeiras noções *fpl*.
rudimentary [ru:dɪ'mɛntərɪ] *adj* rudimentar.
rue [ru:] *vt* arrepender-se de.
rueful ['ru:ful] *adj* arrependido.
ruff [rʌf] *n* rufo.
ruffian ['rʌfɪən] *n* brigão *m*, desordeiro.
ruffle ['rʌfl] *vt* (*hair*) despentear, desmanchar; (*clothes*) enrugar, amarrotar; (*fig*: *person*) perturbar, irritar.
rug [rʌg] *n* tapete *m*; (*BRIT*: *for knees*) manta (de viagem).
rugby ['rʌgbɪ] *n* (*also*: ~ *football*) rúgbi *m* (*BR*), râguebi *m* (*PT*).
rugged ['rʌgɪd] *adj* (*landscape*) acidentado, irregular; (*features*) marcado; (*character*) severo, austero; (*determination*) teimoso.
rugger ['rʌgə*] (*BRIT*: *inf*) *n* rúgbi *m* (*BR*), râguebi *m* (*PT*).
ruin ['ru:ɪn] *n* ruína ♦ *vt* arruinar; (*spoil*) estragar; **~s** *npl* ruínas *fpl*; **in ~s** em ruínas.
ruination [ru:ɪ'neɪʃən] *n* ruína.
ruinous ['ru:ɪnəs] *adj* desastroso.
rule [ru:l] *n* (*norm*) regra; (*government*) governo, domínio; (*ruler*) régua ♦ *vt* (*country, person*) governar; (*decide*) decidir; (*draw*: *lines*) traçar ♦ *vi* (*monarch*) reger; (*government*) governar; (*LAW*) decretar; **to ~ in favour of/against** decidir oficialmente a favor de/contra; **to ~ that** (*umpire, judge*) decidir que; **under British ~** sob domínio britânico; **it's against the ~s** não é permitido; **by ~ of thumb** empiricamente; **as a ~** por via de regra, geralmente.
rule out *vt* excluir.
ruled [ru:ld] *adj* (*paper*) pautado.
ruler ['ru:lə*] *n* (*sovereign*) soberano/a; (*for measuring*) régua.
ruling ['ru:lɪŋ] *adj* (*party*) dominante; (*class*) dirigente ♦ *n* (*LAW*) parecer *m*, decisão *f*.
rum [rʌm] *n* rum *m* ♦ *adj* (*BRIT*: *inf*) esquisito.
Rumania *etc* [ru:'meɪnɪə] *n* = **Romania** *etc*.
rumble ['rʌmbl] *n* ruído surdo, barulho; (*of thunder*) estrondo, ribombo ♦ *vi* ribombar, ressoar; (*stomach*) roncar; (*pipe*) fazer barulho.
rumbunctious [rʌm'bʌŋkʃəs] (*US*) = **rumbustious**.
rumbustious [rʌm'bʌstʃəs] (*BRIT*) *adj* (*person*) enérgico.
rummage ['rʌmɪdʒ] *vi* remexer, dar busca; **to ~ in** (*drawer*) vasculhar.
rumour ['ru:mə*] (*US* **rumor**) *n* rumor *m*, boato ♦ *vt*: **it is ~ed that ...** corre o boato de que ....
rump [rʌmp] *n* (*of animal*) anca, garupa; (*also*: ~ *steak*) alcatra.
rumple ['rʌmpl] *vt* (*hair*) despentear; (*clothes*) amarrotar.
rumpus ['rʌmpəs] (*inf*) *n* barulho, confusão *f*, zorra; (*quarrel*) bate-boca *m*; **to kick up a ~** fazer um escândalo.
run [rʌn] (*pt* **ran**, *pp* **run**) *n* (*race etc*) corrida; (*outing*) passeio (de carro); (*distance travelled*) trajeto, percurso; (*series*) série *f*; (*THEATRE*) temporada; (*SKI*) pista; (*in stockings*) fio puxado ♦ *vt* (*operate*: *business*) dirigir; (: *competition, course*) organizar; (: *hotel, house*) administrar; (*water*) deixar correr; (*bath*) encher; (*COMPUT*: *program*) rodar; (*pass*: *hand, finger*): **to ~ sth over** passar algo em ♦ *vi* correr; (*pass*: *road etc*) passar; (*work*: *machine*) funcionar; (*bus, train*: *operate*) circular; (: *travel*) ir; (*continue*: *play*) continuar em cartaz; (: *contract*) ser válido; (*slide*: *drawer*) deslizar; (*flow*: *river, bath*) fluir, correr; (*colours, washing*) desbotar; (*in election*) candidatar-se; **to go for a ~** fazer cooper; (*in car*) dar uma volta (de carro); **to break into a ~** pôr-se a correr; **a ~ of luck** um período de sorte; **to have the ~ of sb's house** ter a casa de alguém à sua disposição; **there was a ~ on** (*meat, tickets*) houve muita procura de; **in the long ~** no final das contas, mais cedo ou mais tarde; **on the ~** em fuga, fugindo; **to ~ for the bus** correr até o ônibus; **we'll have to ~ for it** vamos ter que correr atrás; **I'll ~ you to the station** vou te levar à estação; **to ~ a risk** correr um risco; **to ~ errands** fazer recados; **to make a ~ for it** fugir, dar no pé; **the train ~s between Gatwick and Victoria** o trem faz o percurso entre Gatwick e Victoria; **the bus ~s every 20 minutes** o ônibus passa a cada 20 minutos; **it's very cheap to ~** (*car, machine*) é muito econômico; **to ~ on petrol** (*BRIT*) *or* **gas** (*US*)/**on diesel/off batteries** funcionar a gasolina/a óleo diesel/a pilhas; **to ~ for president** candidatar-se à presidência, ser presidenciável; **their losses ran into millions** suas perdas se elevaram a milhões; **to be ~ off one's feet** (*BRIT*) não ter descanso, não parar um minuto; **my salary won't ~ to a car** meu salário não é suficiente para comprar um carro.
run about *vi* (*children*) correr por todos os lados.
run across *vt fus* (*find*) encontrar por acaso, topar com, dar com.
run away *vi* fugir.

NB: *European Portuguese adds the following consonants to certain words:* **b** (sú(b)dito, su(b)til); **c** (a(c)ção, a(c)cionista, a(c)to); **m** (inde(m)ne); **p** (ado(p)ção, ado(p)tar); *for further details see p. xiii.*

run down *vi* (*clock*) parar ♦ *vt* (*AUT*) atropelar; (*BRIT*: *reduce*: *production*) reduzir; (: *factory*) reduzir a produção de; (*criticize*) falar mal de, criticar; **to be ~ down** estar enfraquecido *or* exausto.
run in (*BRIT*) *vt* (*car*) rodar.
run into *vt fus* (*meet*: *person*) dar com, topar com; (: *trouble*) esbarrar em; (*collide with*) bater em; **to ~ into debt** endividar-se.
run off *vt* (*water*) deixar correr ♦ *vi* fugir.
run out *vi* (*person*) sair correndo; (*liquid*) escorrer, esgotar-se; (*lease*) caducar, vencer; (*money*) acabar.
run out of *vt fus* ficar sem; **I've ~ out of petrol** (*BRIT*) *or* **gas** (*US*) estou sem gasolina.
run over *vt* (*AUT*) atropelar ♦ *vt fus* (*revise*) recapitular.
run through *vt fus* (*instructions*) examinar, recapitular.
run up *vt* (*debt*) acumular ♦ *vi*: **to ~ up against** (*difficulties*) esbarrar em.
runaway ['rʌnəweɪ] *adj* (*horse*) desembestado; (*truck*) desgovernado; (*person*) fugitivo; (*inflation*) galopante.
rundown ['rʌndaun] (*BRIT*) *n* (*of industry etc*) redução *f* progressiva.
rung [rʌŋ] *pp of* **ring** ♦ *n* (*of ladder*) degrau *m*.
run-in (*inf*) *n* briga, bate-boca *m*.
runner ['rʌnə*] *n* (*in race*: *person*) corredor(a) *m/f*; (: *horse*) corredor *m*; (*on sledge*) patim *m*, lâmina; (*on curtain*) anel *m*; (*wheel*) roldana, roda; (*for drawer etc*) corrediça; (*carpet*: *in hall etc*) passadeira.
runner bean (*BRIT*) *n* (*BOT*) vagem *f* (*BR*), feijão *m* verde (*PT*).
runner-up *n* segundo/a colocado/a.
running ['rʌnɪŋ] *n* (*sport, race*) corrida; (*of business*) direção *f*; (*of event*) organização *f*; (*of machine etc*) funcionamento ♦ *adj* (*water*) corrente; (*commentary*) contínuo, seguido; **6 days ~** 6 dias seguidos *or* consecutivos; **to be in/out of the ~ for sth** disputar algo/estar fora da disputa por algo.
running costs *npl* (*of business*) despesas *fpl* operacionais; (*of car*) custos *mpl* de manutenção.
running head *n* (*TYP*, *WORD PROCESSING*) título corrido.
running mate (*US*) *n* (*POL*) companheiro/a de chapa.
runny ['rʌnɪ] *adj* (*sauce*, *paint*) aguado; (*ice cream*) derretido, mole; **to have a ~ nose** estar com coriza, estar com o nariz escorrendo.
run-off *n* (*in contest*, *election*) segundo turno; (*extra race etc*) corrida decisiva.
run-of-the-mill *adj* comum, normal.
runt [rʌnt] (*also*: *pej*) *n* nanico, anão/anã *m/f*.
run-through *n* ensaio.
run-up (*BRIT*) *n*: **~ to sth** período que antecede algo; **during** *or* **in the ~ to** nas vésperas de.
runway ['rʌnweɪ] *n* (*AVIAT*) pista (de decolagem *or* de pouso).
rupee [ru:'pi:] *n* rupia.
rupture ['rʌptʃə*] *n* (*MED*) hérnia ♦ *vt*: **to ~ o.s.** provocar-se uma hérnia.
rural ['ruərl] *adj* rural, campestre.
ruse [ru:z] *n* ardil *m*, manha.
rush [rʌʃ] *n* ímpeto, investida; (*hurry*) pressa; (*COMM*) grande procura *or* demanda; (*BOT*) junco; (*current*) corrente *f* forte, torrente *f* ♦ *vt* apressar; (*work*) fazer depressa; (*attack*: *town etc*) assaltar; (*BRIT*: *inf*: *charge*) cobrar ♦ *vi* apressar-se, precipitar-se; **don't ~ me!** não me apresse!; **is there any ~ for this?** isso é urgente?; **to ~ sth off** (*do quickly*) fazer algo às pressas; (*send*) enviar depressa; **we've had a ~ of orders** recebimos uma enxurrada de pedidos; **to be in a ~** estar com pressa; **to do sth in a ~** fazer algo às pressas; **to be in a ~ to do sth** ter urgência em fazer algo.
rush through *vt fus* (*work*) fazer às pressas ♦ *vt* (*COMM*: *order*) executar com toda a urgência.
rush hour *n* rush *m* (*BR*), hora de ponta (*PT*).
rush job *n* trabalho urgente.
rush matting *n* tapete *m* de palha.
rusk [rʌsk] *n* rosca.
Russia ['rʌʃə] *n* Rússia.
Russian ['rʌʃən] *adj* russo ♦ *n* russo/a; (*LING*) russo.
rust [rʌst] *n* ferrugem *f* ♦ *vi* enferrujar.
rustic ['rʌstɪk] *adj* rústico, camponês/esa ♦ *n* (*pej*) caipira *m/f*.
rustle ['rʌsl] *vi* sussurrar ♦ *vt* (*paper*) farfalhar; (*US*: *cattle*) roubar, afanar.
rustproof ['rʌstpru:f] *adj* inoxidável, à prova de ferrugem.
rustproofing ['rʌstpru:fɪŋ] *n* tratamento contra ferrugem.
rusty ['rʌstɪ] *adj* enferrujado.
rut [rʌt] *n* sulco; (*ZOOL*) cio; **to be in a ~** ser escravo da rotina.
rutabaga [ru:tə'beɪgə] (*US*) *n* rutabaga.
ruthless ['ru:θlɪs] *adj* implacável, sem piedade.
ruthlessness ['ru:θlɪsnɪs] *n* crueldade *f*, desumanidade *f*, insensibilidade *f*.
RV *abbr* (= *revised version*) *tradução inglesa da Bíblia de 1885* ♦ *n abbr* (*US*) = **recreational vehicle**.
rye [raɪ] *n* centeio.
rye bread *n* pão *m* de centeio.

S

S, s [ɛs] *n* (*letter*) S, s *m*; (*US*: *SCH*: = *satisfactory*) satisfatório; **S for Sugar** S de Sandra.
S *abbr* (= *south*) S; (= *saint*) S, Sto, Sta.

SA *n abbr* = **South Africa; South America.**
Sabbath ['sæbəθ] *n* (*Christian*) domingo; (*Jewish*) sábado.
sabbatical [sə'bætıkl] *adj*: ~ **year** ano sabático *or* de licença.
sabotage ['sæbətɑ:ʒ] *n* sabotagem *f* ♦ *vt* sabotar.
saccharin(e) ['sækərın] *n* sacarina.
sachet ['sæʃeı] *n* sachê *m*.
sack [sæk] *n* (*bag*) saco, saca ♦ *vt* (*dismiss*) despedir; (*plunder*) saquear; **to get the ~** ser demitido; **to give sb the ~** pôr alguém no olho da rua, despedir alguém.
sackful ['sækful] *n*: **a ~ of** um saco de.
sacking ['sækıŋ] *n* (*dismissal*) demissão *f*; (*material*) aniagem *f*.
sacrament ['sækrəmənt] *n* sacramento.
sacred ['seıkrıd] *adj* sagrado.
sacrifice ['sækrıfaıs] *n* sacrifício ♦ *vt* sacrificar; **to make ~s (for sb)** fazer um sacrifício (por alguém).
sacrilege ['sækrılıdʒ] *n* sacrilégio.
sacrosanct ['sækrəusæŋkt] *adj* sacrossanto.
sad [sæd] *adj* (*unhappy*) triste; (*deplorable*) deplorável, triste.
sadden ['sædn] *vt* entristecer.
saddle ['sædl] *n* sela; (*of cycle*) selim *m* ♦ *vt* (*horse*) selar; **to ~ sb with sth** (*inf*: *task, bill*) pôr algo nas costas de alguém; (: *responsibility*) sobrecarregar alguém com algo.
saddlebag ['sædlbæg] *n* alforje *m*.
sadism ['seıdızm] *n* sadismo.
sadist ['seıdıst] *n* sádico/a.
sadistic [sə'dıstık] *adj* sádico.
sadly ['sædlı] *adv* tristemente; (*regrettably*) infelizmente; **~ lacking (in)** muito carente (de).
sadness ['sædnıs] *n* tristeza.
sae (BRIT) *abbr* (= *stamped addressed envelope*) *envelope selado e sobrescritado*.
safari [sə'fɑ:rı] *n* safári *m*.
safari park *n parque com animais selvagens*.
safe [seıf] *adj* (*out of danger*) fora de perigo; (*not dangerous*) seguro; (*unharmed*) ileso, incólume; (*trustworthy*) digno de confiança ♦ *n* cofre *m*, caixa-forte *f*; **~ and sound** são e salvo; **(just) to be on the ~ side** por via das dúvidas; **to play ~** não correr riscos; **it is ~ to say that ...** posso afirmar que ...; **~ journey!** boa viagem!
safe-breaker (BRIT) *n* arrombador *m* de cofres.
safe-conduct *n* salvo-conduto.
safe-cracker *n* arrombador *m* de cofres.
safe-deposit *n* (*vault*) cofre *m* de segurança; (*box*) caixa-forte *f*.
safeguard ['seıfgɑ:d] *n* salvaguarda, proteção *f* ♦ *vt* proteger, defender.
safekeeping [seıf'ki:pıŋ] *n* custódia, proteção.
safely ['seıflı] *adv* com segurança, a salvo; (*without mishap*) sem perigo; **I can ~ say ...** posso seguramente dizer ....
safety ['seıftı] *n* segurança.
safety belt *n* cinto de segurança.
safety curtain *n* cortina de ferro.
safety net *n* rede *f* de segurança.
safety pin *n* alfinete *m* de segurança.
safety valve *n* válvula de segurança.
saffron ['sæfrən] *n* açafrão *m*.
sag [sæg] *vi* afrouxar.
saga ['sɑ:gə] *n* saga; (*fig*) novela.
sage [seıdʒ] *n* (*herb*) salva; (*man*) sábio.
Sagittarius [sædʒı'tεərıəs] *n* Sagitário.
sago ['seıgəu] *n* sagu *m*.
Sahara [sə'hɑ:rə] *n*: **the ~ (Desert)** o Saara.
said [sεd] *pt, pp of* **say**.
sail [seıl] *n* (*on boat*) vela; (*trip*): **to go for a ~** dar um passeio de barco a vela ♦ *vt* (*boat*) governar ♦ *vi* (*travel*: *ship*) navegar, velejar; (: *passenger*) ir de barco; (*set off*) zarpar; **to set ~** zarpar; **they ~ed into Rio de Janeiro** entraram no porto do Rio de Janeiro.
sail through *vt fus* (*fig*) fazer com facilidade ♦ *vi* fazer de letra, fazer com um pé nas costas.
sailboat ['seılbəut] (US) *n* barco a vela.
sailing ['seılıŋ] *n* (SPORT) navegação *f* a vela, vela; **to go ~** ir velejar.
sailing boat *n* barco a vela.
sailing ship *n* veleiro.
sailor ['seılə*] *n* marinheiro, marujo.
saint [seınt] *n* santo/a; **S~ John** São João.
saintly ['seıntlı] *adj* santo, santificado.
sake [seık] *n*: **for the ~ of** por (causa de), em consideração a; **for my ~** por mim; **arguing for arguing's ~** brigar por brigar; **for the ~ of argument** por exemplo; **for heaven's ~!** pelo amor de Deus!
salad ['sæləd] *n* salada.
salad bowl *n* saladeira.
salad cream (BRIT) *n* maionese *f*.
salad dressing *n* tempero *or* molho da salada.
salad oil *n* azeite *m* de mesa.
salami [sə'lɑ:mı] *n* salame *m*.
salaried ['sælərıd] *adj* (*staff*) assalariado.
salary ['sælərı] *n* salário.
salary scale *n* escala salarial.
sale [seıl] *n* venda; (*at reduced prices*) liquidação *f*, saldo; **"for ~"** "vende-se"; **on ~** à venda; **on ~ or return** em consignação; **~ and lease back** *venda com cláusula de aluguel ao vendedor do item vendido*.
saleroom ['seılrum] *n* sala de vendas.
sales assistant (BRIT) *n* vendedor(a) *m/f*.
sales clerk (US) *n* vendedor(a) *m/f*.
sales conference *n* conferência de vendas.
sales drive *n* campanha de vendas.
sales force *n* equipe *m* de vendas.
salesman ['seılzmən] (*irreg*) *n* vendedor *m*; (*representative*) vendedor *m* viajante.
sales manager *n* gerente *m/f* de vendas.
salesmanship ['seılzmənʃıp] *n* arte *f* de

***NB**: European Portuguese adds the following consonants to certain words:* **b** (sú(b)dito, su(b)til); **c** (a(c)ção, a(c)cionista, a(c)to); **m** (inde(m)ne); **p** (ado(p)ção, ado(p)tar); *for further details see p. xiii.*

vender.
salesmen ['seɪlzmɛn] *npl of* **salesman.**
sales tax (*US*) *n* ≈ ICM *m* (*BR*), ≈ IVA *m* (*PT*).
saleswoman ['seɪlzwumən] (*irreg*) *n* vendedora; (*representative*) vendedora viajante.
salient ['seɪlɪənt] *adj* saliente.
saline ['seɪlaɪn] *adj* salino.
saliva [sə'laɪvə] *n* saliva.
sallow ['sæləu] *adj* amarelado.
sally forth ['sælɪ-] *vi* partir, pôr-se em marcha.
sally out ['sælɪ-] *vi* partir, pôr-se em marcha.
salmon ['sæmən] *n inv* salmão *m.*
saloon [sə'lu:n] *n* (*US*) bar *m*, botequim *m*; (*AUT*) sedã *m*; (*ship's lounge*) salão *m.*
Salop ['sæləp] (*BRIT*) *n abbr* = **Shropshire.**
SALT [sɔ:lt] *n abbr* (= *Strategic Arms Limitation Talks/Treaty*) SALT *m.*
salt [sɔ:lt] *n* sal *m* ♦ *vt* salgar ♦ *cpd* de sal; (*CULIN*) salgado; **an old** ~ um lobo-do-mar.
salt away *vt* pôr de lado.
salt cellar *n* saleiro.
salt-free *adj* sem sal.
saltwater ['sɔ:ltwɔ:tə*] *adj* de água salgada.
salty ['sɔ:ltɪ] *adj* salgado.
salubrious [sə'lu:brɪəs] *adj* salubre, sadio.
salutary ['sæljutərɪ] *adj* salutar.
salute [sə'lu:t] *n* (*tribute*) saudação *f*; (*of guns*) salva; (*MIL*) continência ♦ *vt* saudar; (*guns*) receber com salvas; (*MIL*) fazer continência a.
salvage ['sælvɪdʒ] *n* (*saving*) salvamento, recuperação *f*; (*things saved*) salvados *mpl* ♦ *vt* salvar.
salvage vessel *n* navio de salvamento.
salvation [sæl'veɪʃən] *n* salvação *f.*
Salvation Army *n* Exército da Salvação.
salve [sælv] *n* (*cream etc*) ungüento, pomada.
salver ['sælvə*] *n* bandeja, salva.
salvo ['sælvəu] *n* salva.
Samaritan [sə'mærɪtən] *n*: **the ~s** (*organization*) os Samaritanos.
same [seɪm] *adj* mesmo ♦ *pron*: **the** ~ o mesmo/a mesma; **the ~ book as** o mesmo livro que; **at the ~ time** ao mesmo tempo; **on the ~ day** no mesmo dia; **all** *or* **just the ~** apesar de tudo, mesmo assim; **it's all the ~** dá no mesmo, tanto faz; **they're one and the ~** (*people*) são os mesmos; (*things*) são idênticos; **to do the ~ (as sb)** fazer o mesmo (que alguém); **the ~ to you!** igualmente!; **~ here!** eu também!; **the ~ again!** (*in bar etc*) mais um ... por favor!
sample ['sɑ:mpl] *n* amostra ♦ *vt* (*food, wine*) provar, experimentar; **to take a ~** tirar uma amostra; **free ~** amostra grátis.
sanatoria [sænə'tɔ:rɪə] *npl of* **sanatorium.**
sanatorium [sænə'tɔ:rɪəm] (*pl* **sanatoria**) *n* sanatório.
sanctify ['sæŋktɪfaɪ] *vt* santificar.
sanctimonious [sæŋktɪ'məunɪəs] *adj* santarrão/rona, sacripanta.
sanction ['sæŋkʃən] *n* sanção *f* ♦ *vt* sancionar, ratificar; **to impose economic ~s on** *or* **against** impor sanções econômicas a.
sanctity ['sæŋktɪtɪ] *n* santidade *f*, divindade *f*; (*inviolability*) inviolabilidade *f.*
sanctuary ['sæŋktjuərɪ] *n* (*holy place*) santuário; (*refuge*) refúgio, asilo; (*for animals*) reserva.
sand [sænd] *n* areia ♦ *vt* arear, jogar areia em; (*also*: ~ *down*: *wood etc*) lixar; **~s** *npl* praia.
sandal ['sændl] *n* sandália; (*wood*) sândalo.
sandbag ['sændbæg] *n* saco de areia.
sandbank ['sændbæŋk] *n* banco de areia.
sandblast ['sændblɑ:st] *vt* limpar com jato de areia.
sandbox ['sændbɔks] (*US*) *n* (*for children*) caixa de areia.
sandcastle ['sændkɑ:sl] *n* castelo de areia.
sand dune *n* duna (de areia).
sandpaper ['sændpeɪpə*] *n* lixa.
sandpit ['sændpɪt] (*BRIT*) *n* (*for children*) caixa de areia.
sandstone ['sændstəun] *n* arenito, grés *m.*
sandstorm ['sændstɔ:m] *n* tempestade *f* de areia.
sandwich ['sændwɪtʃ] *n* sanduíche *m* (*BR*), sandes *f inv* (*PT*) ♦ *vt* (*also*: ~ *in*) intercalar; **~ed between** encaixado entre; **cheese/ham ~** sanduíche (*BR*) *or* sandes (*PT*) de queijo/presunto.
sandwich board *n* cartaz *m* ambulante.
sandwich course (*BRIT*) *n* *curso profissionalizante de teoria e prática alternadas.*
sandy ['sændɪ] *adj* arenoso; (*colour*) vermelho amarelado.
sane [seɪn] *adj* são/sã do juízo; (*sensible*) ajuizado, sensato.
sang [sæŋ] *pt of* **sing.**
sanguine ['sæŋgwɪn] *adj* otimista.
sanitaria [sænɪ'tɛərɪə] (*US*) *npl of* **sanitarium.**
sanitarium [sænɪ'tɛərɪəm] (*US*: *pl* **sanitaria**) *n* = **sanatorium.**
sanitary ['sænɪtərɪ] *adj* (*system, arrangements*) sanitário; (*clean*) higiênico.
sanitary towel (*US* **sanitary napkin**) *n* toalha higiênica *or* absorvente.
sanitation [sænɪ'teɪʃən] *n* (*in house*) instalações *fpl* sanitárias; (*in town*) saneamento.
sanitation department (*US*) *n* comissão *f* de limpeza urbana.
sanity ['sænɪtɪ] *n* sanidade *f*, equilíbrio mental; (*common sense*) juízo, sensatez *f.*
sank [sæŋk] *pt of* **sink.**
San Marino ['sænmə'ri:nəu] *n* San Marino (*no article*).
Santa Claus [sæntə'klɔ:z] *n* Papai Noel *m.*
Santiago [sæntɪ'ɑ:gəu] *n* (*also*: ~ *de Chile*) Santiago (do Chile).
sap [sæp] *n* (*of plants*) seiva ♦ *vt* (*strength*) esgotar, minar.
sapling ['sæplɪŋ] *n* árvore *f* nova.
sapphire ['sæfaɪə*] *n* safira.
sarcasm ['sɑ:kæzm] *n* sarcasmo.
sarcastic [sɑ:'kæstɪk] *adj* sarcástico.
sarcophagi [sɑ:'kɔfəgaɪ] *npl of* **sarcophagus.**

sarcophagus [sɑː'kɔfəgəs] (*pl* **sarcophagi**) *n* sarcófago.
sardine [sɑː'diːn] *n* sardinha.
Sardinia [sɑː'dɪnɪə] *n* Sardenha.
Sardinian [sɑː'dɪnɪən] *adj* sardo ♦ *n* sardo/a; (*LING*) sardo.
sardonic [sɑː'dɔnɪk] *adj* sardônico.
sari ['sɑːrɪ] *n* sári *m*.
sartorial [sɑː'tɔːrɪəl] *adj* indumentário.
SAS (*BRIT*) *n abbr* (*MIL*) = **Special Air Service**.
SASE (*US*) *n abbr* (= *self-addressed stamped envelope*) *envelope selado e sobrescritado*.
sash [sæʃ] *n* faixa, banda; (*belt*) cinto.
sash window *n* janela de guilhotina.
SAT (*US*) *n abbr* = **Scholastic Aptitude Test**.
Sat. *abbr* = (*Saturday*) sáb.
sat [sæt] *pt, pp of* **sit**.
Satan ['seɪtn] *n* Satanás *m*, Satã *m*.
satanic [sə'tænɪk] *adj* satânico, diabólico.
satchel ['sætʃl] *n* sacola.
sated ['seɪtɪd] *adj* saciado, farto.
satellite ['sætəlaɪt] *n* satélite *m*.
satiate ['seɪʃɪeɪt] *vt* saciar.
satin ['sætɪn] *n* cetim *m* ♦ *adj* acetinado; **with a ~ finish** acetinado.
satire ['sætaɪə*] *n* sátira.
satirical [sə'tɪrɪkl] *adj* satírico.
satirist ['sætɪrɪst] *n* (*writer*) satirista *m/f*; (*cartoonist*) chargista *m/f*.
satirize ['sætɪraɪz] *vt* satirizar.
satisfaction [sætɪs'fækʃən] *n* satisfação *f*; **has it been done to your ~?** você está satisfeito?
satisfactory [sætɪs'fæktərɪ] *adj* satisfatório.
satisfy ['sætɪsfaɪ] *vt* satisfazer; (*convince*) convencer, persuadir; **to ~ the requirements** satisfazer as exigências; **to ~ sb (that)** convencer alguém (de que); **to ~ o.s. of sth** convencer-se de algo.
satisfying ['sætɪsfaɪɪŋ] *adj* satisfatório.
saturate ['sætʃəreɪt] *vt*: **to ~ (with)** saturar *or* embeber (de).
saturation [sætʃə'reɪʃən] *n* saturação *f*.
Saturday ['sætədɪ] *n* sábado; *see also* **Tuesday**.
sauce [sɔːs] *n* molho; (*sweet*) calda; (*fig: cheek*) atrevimento.
saucepan ['sɔːspən] *n* panela (*BR*), caçarola (*PT*).
saucer ['sɔːsə*] *n* pires *m inv*.
saucy ['sɔːsɪ] *adj* atrevido, descarado; (*flirtatious*) flertivo, provocante.
Saudi Arabia ['saudɪ-] *n* Arábia Saudita.
Saudi (Arabian) ['saudɪ-] *adj, n* saudita *m/f*.
sauna ['sɔːnə] *n* sauna.
saunter ['sɔːntə*] *vi* caminhar devagar, perambular.
sausage ['sɔsɪdʒ] *n* salsicha, lingüiça; (*cold meat*) frios *mpl*.
sausage roll *n* folheado de salsicha.
sauté ['səuteɪ] *adj* (*CULIN*: *potatoes*) sauté; (: *onions*) frito rapidamente ♦ *vt* fritar levemente.
savage ['sævɪdʒ] *adj* (*cruel, fierce*) cruel, feroz; (*primitive*) selvagem ♦ *n* selvagem *m/f* ♦ *vt* (*attack*) atacar ferozmente.
savagery ['sævɪdʒrɪ] *n* selvageria, ferocidade *f*.
save [seɪv] *vt* (*rescue*) salvar, resgatar; (*money*) poupar, economizar; (*time*) ganhar; (*put by*: *food*) guardar; (*SPORT*) impedir; (*avoid*: *trouble*) evitar; (*COMPUT*) salvar ♦ *vi* (*also*: **~ up**) poupar ♦ *n* (*SPORT*) salvamento ♦ *prep* salvo, exceto; **it will ~ me an hour** vou ganhar uma hora; **to ~ face** salvar as aparências; **God ~ the Queen!** Deus salve a Rainha!
saving ['seɪvɪŋ] *n* (*on price etc*) economia ♦ *adj*: **the ~ grace of** o único mérito de; **~s** *npl* economias *fpl*; **to make ~s** economizar.
savings account *n* (caderneta de) poupança.
savings bank *n* caixa econômica, caderneta de poupança.
saviour ['seɪvjə*] (*US* **savior**) *n* salvador(a) *m/f*.
savour ['seɪvə*] (*US* **savor**) *n* sabor *m* ♦ *vt* saborear.
savo(u)ry ['seɪvərɪ] *adj* saboroso; (*dish*: *not sweet*) salgado.
savvy ['sævɪ] (*inf*) *n* juízo.
saw [sɔː] (*pt* **~ed**, *pp* **~ed** *or* **sawn**) *pt of* **see** ♦ *n* (*tool*) serra ♦ *vt* serrar; **to ~ sth up** serrar algo em pedaços.
sawdust ['sɔːdʌst] *n* serragem *f*, pó *m* de serra.
sawed-off shotgun [sɔːd-] (*US*) *n* = **sawn-off shotgun**.
sawmill ['sɔːmɪl] *n* serraria.
sawn [sɔːn] *pp of* **saw**.
sawn-off shotgun (*BRIT*) *n* espingarda de cano serrado.
saxophone ['sæksəfəun] *n* saxofone *m*.
say [seɪ] (*pt, pp* **said**) *n*: **to have one's ~** exprimir sua opinião, vender seu peixe (*inf*) ♦ *vt* dizer, falar; **to have a** *or* **some ~ in sth** opinar sobre algo, ter que ver com algo; **~ after me ...** repita comigo ...; **to ~ yes/no** dizer (que) sim/não; **she said (that) I was to give you this** ela disse que eu deveria te dar isso; **my watch ~s 3 o'clock** meu relógio marca 3 horas; **shall we ~ Tuesday?** marcamos para terça?; **I should ~ it's worth about £100** acho que vale mais ou menos £100; **that doesn't ~ much for him** aquilo não o favorece; **when all is said and done** afinal das contas; **there is something** *or* **a lot to be said for it** isto tem muitas vantagens; **that is to ~** ou seja; **to ~ nothing of ...** por não falar em ...; **~ that ...** vamos supor que ...; **that goes without ~ing** é óbvio, nem é preciso dizer.
saying ['seɪɪŋ] *n* ditado, provérbio.

NB: *European Portuguese adds the following consonants to certain words:* **b** (sú(b)dito, su(b)til); **c** (a(c)ção, a(c)cionista, a(c)to); **m** (inde(m)ne); **p** (ado(p)ção, ado(p)tar); *for further details see p. xiii.*

SBA (*US*) *n abbr* (= *Small Business Administration*) *órgão de auxílio às pequenas empresas.*
SC (*US*) *n abbr* = **supreme court** ♦ *abbr* (*POST*) = **South Carolina.**
s/c *abbr* = **self-contained.**
scab [skæb] *n* casca, crosta (de ferida); (*pej*) fura-greve *m/f inv*.
scabby ['skæbɪ] *adj* cheio de casca *or* cicatrizes.
scaffold ['skæfəuld] *n* (*for execution*) cadafalso, patíbulo.
scaffolding ['skæfəuldɪŋ] *n* andaime *m*.
scald [skɔːld] *n* escaldadura ♦ *vt* escaldar, queimar.
scalding ['skɔːldɪŋ] *adj* (*also*: ~ *hot*) escaldante.
scale [skeɪl] *n* (*gen, MUS*) escala; (*of fish*) escama; (*of salaries, fees etc*) tabela; (*of map, also size, extent*) escala ♦ *vt* (*mountain*) escalar; (*fish*) escamar; **~s** *npl* balança; **pay** ~ tabela de salários; **on a large** ~ em grande escala; ~ **of charges** tarifa, lista de preços; **to draw sth to** ~ desenhar algo em escala; **small-~ model** modelo reduzido.
scale down *vt* reduzir.
scale drawing *n* desenho em escala.
scale model *n* maquete *f* em escala.
scallion ['skæljən] *n* cebola.
scallop ['skɔləp] *n* (*ZOOL*) vieira, venera; (*SEWING*) barra, arremate *m*.
scalp [skælp] *n* couro cabeludo ♦ *vt* escalpar.
scalpel ['skælpl] *n* bisturi *m*.
scalper ['skælpə*] (*US*: *inf*) *n* (*of tickets*) cambista *m/f*.
scamp [skæmp] *n* moleque *m*.
scamper ['skæmpə*] *vi*: **to ~ away, ~ off** sair correndo.
scampi ['skæmpɪ] *npl* camarões *mpl* fritos.
scan [skæn] *vt* (*examine*) esquadrinhar, perscrutar; (*glance at quickly*) passar uma vista de olhos por; (*TV, RADAR*) explorar ♦ *n* (*MED*) exame *m*.
scandal ['skændl] *n* escândalo; (*gossip*) fofocas *fpl*.
scandalize ['skændəlaɪz] *vt* escandalizar.
scandalous ['skændələs] *adj* escandaloso; (*libellous*) difamatório, calunioso.
Scandinavia [skændɪ'neɪvɪə] *n* Escandinávia.
Scandinavian [skændɪ'neɪvɪən] *adj, n* escandinavo/a.
scanner ['skænə*] *n* (*RADAR, MED*) antena.
scant [skænt] *adj* escasso, insuficiente.
scantily ['skæntɪlɪ] *adv*: ~ **clad** *or* **dressed** precariamente vestido.
scanty ['skæntɪ] *adj* escasso.
scapegoat ['skeɪpgəut] *n* bode *m* expiatório.
scar [skɑː] *n* cicatriz *f* ♦ *vt* marcar (com uma cicatriz).
scarce [skɛəs] *adj* escasso, raro.
scarcely ['skɛəslɪ] *adv* mal, quase não; ~ **anybody** quase ninguém; **I can ~ believe it** mal posso acreditar.
scarcity ['skɛəsɪtɪ] *n* escassez *f*.
scarcity value *n* valor *m* de escassez.
scare [skɛə*] *n* susto; (*panic*) pânico ♦ *vt* assustar; **to ~ sb stiff** deixar alguém morrendo de medo; **bomb** ~ alarme de bomba.
scare away *vt* espantar.
scare off *vt* espantar.
scarecrow ['skɛəkrəu] *n* espantalho.
scared [skɛəd] *adj*: **to be** ~ estar assustado *or* com medo.
scaremonger ['skɛəmʌŋgə*] *n* alarmista *m/f*.
scarf [skɑːf] (*pl* **scarves**) *n* (*long*) cachecol *m*; (*square*) lenço (de cabeça).
scarlet ['skɑːlɪt] *adj* escarlate.
scarlet fever *n* escarlatina.
scarves [skɑːvz] *npl of* **scarf**.
scary ['skɛərɪ] (*inf*) *adj* assustador(a).
scathing ['skeɪðɪŋ] *adj* mordaz, severo; **to be ~ about sth** fazer uma crítica mordaz sobre algo.
scatter ['skætə*] *vt* (*spread*) espalhar; (*put to flight*) dispersar ♦ *vi* espalhar-se.
scatterbrained ['skætəbreɪnd] *adj* desmiolado, avoado; (*forgetful*) esquecido.
scattered ['skætəd] *adj* espalhado.
scatty ['skætɪ] (*BRIT*: *inf*) *adj* maluquinho.
scavenge ['skævəndʒ] *vi* (*person*): **to ~ (for)** filar; **to ~ for food** (*hyenas etc*) procurar comida.
scavenger ['skævəndʒə*] *n* (*person*) filante *m/f*; (*ZOOL*) animal *m* (*or* ave *f*) que se alimenta de carniça.
SCE *n abbr* = **Scottish Certificate of Education.**
scenario [sɪ'nɑːrɪəu] *n* cenário.
scene [siːn] *n* (*THEATRE, fig*) cena; (*of crime, accident*) cenário; (*sight, view*) vista, panorama *m*; (*fuss*) escândalo; **behind the ~s** nos bastidores; **to make a ~** (*inf*: *fuss*) fazer um escândalo; **to appear on the ~** entrar em cena; **the political ~** o panorama político.
scenery ['siːnərɪ] *n* (*THEATRE*) cenário; (*landscape*) paisagem *f*.
scenic ['siːnɪk] *adj* (*picturesque*) pitoresco.
scent [sɛnt] *n* perfume *m*; (*smell*) aroma; (*fig*: *track*) pista, rastro; (*sense of smell*) olfato ♦ *vt* perfumar; **to put** *or* **throw sb off the ~** despistar alguém.
scepter ['sɛptə*] (*US*) *n* = **sceptre.**
sceptic ['skɛptɪk] (*US* **skeptic**) *n* cético/a.
sceptical ['skɛptɪkl] (*US* **skeptical**) *adj* cético.
scepticism ['skɛptɪsɪzm] (*US* **skepticism**) *n* ceticismo.
sceptre ['sɛptə*] (*US* **scepter**) *n* cetro.
schedule ['ʃɛdjuːl, (*US*) 'skɛdjuːl] *n* (*of trains*) horário; (*of events*) programa *m*; (*plan*) plano; (*list*) lista ♦ *vt* (*timetable*) planejar; (*visit*) marcar (a hora de); **as ~d** como previsto; **the meeting is ~d for 7.00** a reunião está programada para as 7.00h; **on ~** na hora, sem atraso; **to be ahead of/behind ~** estar adiantado/atrasado; **we are working to a very tight ~** nosso horário está muito apertado; **everything went according to ~**

tudo correu como planejado.
scheduled ['ʃɛdju:ld, (*US*) 'skɛdju:ld] *adj* (*date, time*) marcado; (*visit, event*) programado; (*train, bus, flight*) de linha.
schematic [skɪ'mætɪk] *adj* esquemático.
scheme [ski:m] *n* (*plan*) plano, esquema *m*; (*method*) método; (*plot*) conspiração *f*; (*trick*) ardil *m*; (*arrangement*) disposição *f* ♦ *vi* conspirar.
scheming ['ski:mɪŋ] *adj* intrigante ♦ *n* intrigas *fpl*.
schism ['skɪzəm] *n* cisma *m*.
schizophrenia [skɪtsəu'fri:nɪə] *n* esquizofrenia.
schizophrenic [skɪtsə'frɛnɪk] *adj* esquizofrênico.
scholar ['skɔlə*] *n* (*pupil*) aluno/a, estudante *m/f*; (*learned person*) sábio/a, erudito/a.
scholarly ['skɔləlɪ] *adj* erudito, douto.
scholarship ['skɔləʃɪp] *n* erudição *f*; (*grant*) bolsa de estudos.
school [sku:l] *n* escola; (*in university*) faculdade *f*; (*secondary* ~) colégio; (*of fish*) cardume *m* ♦ *cpd* escolar ♦ *vt* (*animal*) adestrar, treinar.
school age *n* idade *f* escolar.
schoolbook ['sku:lbuk] *n* livro escolar.
schoolboy ['sku:lbɔɪ] *n* aluno.
schoolchild ['sku:ltʃaɪld] (*irreg*) *n* aluno/a.
schooldays ['sku:ldeɪz] *npl* anos *mpl* escolares.
schoolgirl ['sku:lgə:l] *n* aluna.
schooling ['sku:lɪŋ] *n* educação *f*, ensino.
school-leaving age [-'li:vɪŋ-] *n* idade *f* em que se termina a escola.
schoolmaster ['sku:lmɑ:stə*] *n* professor *m*.
schoolmistress ['sku:lmɪstrɪs] *n* professora.
school report (*BRIT*) *n* boletim *m* escolar.
schoolroom ['sku:lrum] *n* sala de aula.
schoolteacher ['sku:lti:tʃə*] *n* professor(a) *m/f*.
schooner ['sku:nə*] *n* (*ship*) escuna; (*glass*) caneca, canecão *m*.
sciatica [saɪ'ætɪkə] *n* ciática.
science ['saɪəns] *n* ciência.
science fiction *n* ficção *f* científica.
scientific [saɪən'tɪfɪk] *adj* científico.
scientist ['saɪəntɪst] *n* cientista *m/f*.
sci-fi ['saɪfaɪ] (*inf*) *n abbr* = **science fiction**.
Scillies ['sɪlɪz] *npl*: **the** ~ as ilhas Scilly.
Scilly Isles ['sɪlɪ'aɪlz] *npl*: **the** ~ as ilhas Scilly.
scintillating ['sɪntɪleɪtɪŋ] *adj* (*wit etc*) brilhante.
scissors ['sɪzəz] *npl* tesoura; **a pair of** ~ uma tesoura.
sclerosis [sklɪ'rəusɪs] *n* esclerose *f*.
scoff [skɔf] *vt* (*BRIT*: *inf*: *eat*) engolir ♦ *vi*: **to** ~ **(at)** (*mock*) zombar (de).
scold [skəuld] *vt* ralhar.
scolding ['skəuldɪŋ] *n* repreensão *f*.
scone [skɔn] *n* bolinho.
scoop [sku:p] *n* colherona; (*for flour etc*) pá *f*; (*PRESS*) furo (jornalístico).
scoop out *vt* escavar.
scoop up *vt* recolher.
scooter ['sku:tə*] *n* (*motor cycle*) moto *f*, lambreta; (*toy*) patinete *m*.
scope [skəup] *n* (*of plan, undertaking*) âmbito; (*reach*) alcance *m*; (*of person*) competência; (*opportunity*) oportunidade *f*; **within the** ~ **of** dentro dos limites de; **there is plenty of** ~ **for improvement** (*BRIT*) poderia ser muito melhor.
scorch [skɔ:tʃ] *vt* (*clothes*) chamuscar; (*earth, grass*) secar, queimar.
scorched earth policy [skɔ:tʃt-] *n* tática da terra arrasada.
scorcher ['skɔ:tʃə*] (*inf*) *n* (*hot day*) dia *m* muito quente.
scorching ['skɔ:tʃɪŋ] *adj* ardente.
score [skɔ:*] *n* (*points etc*) escore *m*, contagem *f*; (*MUS*) partitura; (*reckoning*) conta; (*twenty*) vintena ♦ *vt* (*goal, point*) fazer; (*mark*) marcar, entalhar ♦ *vi* (*FOOTBALL*) marcar *or* fazer um gol; (*keep score*) marcar o escore; **on that** ~ a esse respeito, por esse motivo; **to have an old** ~ **to settle with sb** (*fig*) ter umas contas a ajustar com alguém; ~**s of** (*fig*) um monte de; **to keep (the)** ~ marcar os pontos; **to** ~ **6 out of 10** conseguir um escore de 6 num total de 10.
score out *vt* riscar.
scoreboard ['skɔ:bɔ:d] *n* marcador *m*, placar *m*.
scorecard ['skɔ:kɑ:d] *n* (*SPORT*) cartão *m* de marcação.
scorer ['skɔ:rə*] *n* marcador(a) *m/f*.
scorn [skɔ:n] *n* desprezo ♦ *vt* desprezar, rejeitar.
scornful ['skɔ:nful] *adj* desdenhoso, zombador(a).
Scorpio ['skɔ:pɪəu] *n* Escorpião *m*.
scorpion ['skɔ:pɪən] *n* escorpião *m*.
Scot [skɔt] *n* escocês/esa *m/f*.
Scotch [skɔtʃ] *n* uísque *m* (*BR*) *or* whisky *m* (*PT*) escocês.
scotch [skɔtʃ] *vt* (*rumour*) desmentir; (*plan*) estragar.
Scotch tape ® *n* fita adesiva, durex *m* ® (*BR*).
scot-free *adj*: **to get off** ~ (*unpunished*) sair impune; (*unhurt*) sair ileso.
Scotland ['skɔtlənd] *n* Escócia.
Scots [skɔts] *adj* escocês/esa.
Scotsman ['skɔtsmən] (*irreg*) *n* escocês *m*.
Scotswoman ['skɔtswumən] (*irreg*) *n* escocesa.
Scottish ['skɔtɪʃ] *adj* escocês/esa.
scoundrel ['skaundrəl] *n* canalha *m/f*, patife *m*.
scour ['skauə*] *vt* (*clean*) limpar, esfregar; (*search*) esquadrinhar, procurar em.
scourer ['skaurə*] *n* esponja de aço, bombril *m* ® (*BR*).

***NB**: European Portuguese adds the following consonants to certain words:* **b** (sú(b)dito, su(b)til); **c** (a(c)ção, a(c)cionista, a(c)to); **m** (inde(m)ne); **p** (ado(p)ção, ado(p)tar); *for further details see p. xiii.*

scourge [skəːdʒ] *n* açoite *m*, flagelo.
scout [skaut] *n* (*also*: *boy* ~) escoteiro; (*MIL*) explorador *m*, batedor *m*.
scout around *vi* explorar.
scowl [skaul] *vi* franzir a testa; **to ~ at sb** olhar alguém carrancudamente.
scrabble ['skræbl] *vi*: **to ~ about** *or* **around for sth** tatear procurando algo ♦ *n*: **S~** ® mexe-mexe *m*.
scraggy ['skrægɪ] *adj* magricela, descarnado.
scram [skræm] (*inf*) *vi* dar o fora, safar-se.
scramble ['skræmbl] *n* (*climb*) escalada (difícil); (*struggle*) luta ♦ *vi*: **to ~ out** *or* **through** conseguir sair com dificuldade; **to ~ for** lutar por.
scrambled eggs ['skræmbld-] *npl* ovos *mpl* mexidos.
scrap [skræp] *n* (*bit*) pedacinho; (*fight*) rixa, luta; (*also*: ~ *iron*) ferro velho, sucata ♦ *vt* sucatar, jogar no ferro velho; (*discard*) descartar ♦ *vi* brigar; **~s** *npl* (*waste*) sobras *fpl*, restos *mpl*; **to sell sth for ~** vender algo como sucata.
scrapbook ['skræpbuk] *n* álbum *m* de recortes.
scrap dealer *n* ferro-velho *m*, sucateiro/a.
scrape [skreɪp] *n* (*fig*) aperto, enrascada ♦ *vt* raspar; (*skin etc*) arranhar; (~ *against*) roçar.
scrape through *vi* (*in exam*) passar raspando.
scraper ['skreɪpə*] *n* raspador *m*.
scrap heap *n* (*fig*): **on the ~** rejeitado, jogado fora.
scrap merchant (*BRIT*) *n* sucateiro/a.
scrap metal *n* sucata, ferro-velho.
scrap paper *n* papel *m* de rascunho.
scrappy ['skræpɪ] *adj* (*speech*) incoerente, desconexo; (*bitty*) fragmentário.
scrap yard *n* ferro-velho.
scratch [skrætʃ] *n* arranhão *m*; (*from claw*) arranhadura ♦ *adj*: **~ team** time improvisado, escrete ♦ *vt* (*record*) marcar, riscar; (*with claw, nail*) arranhar, unhar; (*COMPUT*) apagar ♦ *vi* coçar(-se); **to start from ~** partir do zero; **to be up to ~** estar à altura (das circunstâncias).
scratchpad ['skrætʃpæd] (*US*) *n* bloco de rascunho.
scrawl [skrɔːl] *n* garrancho, garatujas *fpl* ♦ *vi* garatujar, rabiscar.
scrawny ['skrɔːnɪ] *adj* magricela.
scream [skriːm] *n* grito ♦ *vi* gritar; **it was a ~** (*inf*) foi engraçadíssimo; **to ~ at sb** gritar com alguém.
scree [skriː] *n* seixos *mpl*.
screech [skriːtʃ] *vi* guinchar ♦ *n* guincho.
screen [skriːn] *n* (*CINEMA*, *TV*) tela (*BR*), écran *m* (*PT*); (*movable*) biombo; (*wall*) tapume *m*; (*also*: *wind*~) pára-brisa *m*; (*fig*) cortina ♦ *vt* (*conceal*) esconder, tapar; (*from the wind etc*) proteger; (*film*) projetar; (*candidates etc*, *MED*) examinar.
screen editing [-'ɛdɪtɪŋ] *n* (*COMPUT*) edição *f* na tela.
screening ['skriːnɪŋ] *n* (*MED*) exame *m* médico; (*of film*) exibição *f*; (*for security*) controle *m*.
screen memory *n* (*COMPUT*) memória da tela.
screenplay ['skriːnpleɪ] *n* roteiro.
screen test *n* teste *m* de cinema.
screw [skruː] *n* parafuso; (*propeller*) hélice *f* ♦ *vt* aparafusar; (*also*: ~ *in*) apertar, atarraxar; (*inf!*: *have sex with*) comer (*!*), trepar com (*!*); **to ~ sth to the wall** pregar algo na parede; **to have one's head ~ed on** (*fig*) ter juízo.
screw up *vt* (*paper*, *material*) amassar; (*inf*: *ruin*) estragar; **to ~ up one's face** contrair as feições.
screwdriver ['skruːdraɪvə*] *n* chave *f* de fenda *or* de parafuso.
screwy ['skruːɪ] (*inf*) *adj* maluco, estranho.
scribble ['skrɪbl] *n* garrancho ♦ *vt* escrevinhar, rabiscar; **to ~ sth down** anotar algo apressadamente.
scribe [skraɪb] *n* escriba *m/f*.
script [skrɪpt] *n* (*CINEMA etc*) roteiro, script *m*; (*writing*) escrita, caligrafia.
scripted ['skrɪptɪd] *adj* (*RADIO*, *TV*) com script.
Scripture ['skrɪptʃə*] *n* Sagrada Escritura.
scriptwriter ['skrɪptraɪtə*] *n* roteirista *m/f*.
scroll [skrəul] *n* rolo de pergaminho ♦ *vt* (*COMPUT*) passar na tela.
scrotum ['skrəutəm] *n* escroto.
scrounge [skraundʒ] (*inf*) *vt*: **to ~ sth off** *or* **from sb** filar algo de alguém ♦ *vi*: **to ~ on sb** viver às custas de alguém.
scrounger ['skraundʒə*] (*inf*) *n* filão/lona *m/f*.
scrub [skrʌb] *n* (*clean*) esfregação *f*, limpeza; (*land*) mato, cerrado ♦ *vt* esfregar; (*reject*) cancelar, eliminar.
scrubbing brush ['skrʌbɪŋ-] *n* escova de esfrega.
scruff [skrʌf] *n*: **by the ~ of the neck** pelo cangote.
scruffy ['skrʌfɪ] *adj* desmazelado.
scrum(mage) ['skrʌm(ɪdʒ)] *n* rolo.
scruple ['skruːpl] *n* escrúpulo; **to have no ~s about doing sth** não ter escrúpulos em fazer algo.
scrupulous ['skruːpjuləs] *adj* escrupuloso.
scrupulously ['skruːpjələslɪ] *adv* escrupulosamente.
scrutinize ['skruːtɪnaɪz] *vt* examinar minuciosamente; (*votes*) escrutinar.
scrutiny ['skruːtɪnɪ] *n* escrutínio, exame *m* cuidadoso; **under the ~ of** vigiado por.
scuba ['skuːbə] *n* equipamento de mergulho.
scuba diving *n* mergulho.
scuff [skʌf] *vt* desgastar.
scuffle ['skʌfl] *n* tumulto.
scull [skʌl] *n* ginga.
scullery ['skʌlərɪ] *n* copa.
sculptor ['skʌlptə*] *n* escultor(a) *m/f*.
sculpture ['skʌlptʃə*] *n* escultura.
scum [skʌm] *n* (*on liquid*) espuma; (*pej*: *people*) ralé *f*, gentinha; (*fig*) escória.
scupper ['skʌpə*] *vt* (*BRIT*: *ship*) afundar;

(*fig*: *plans*) estragar.
scurrilous ['skʌrɪləs] *adj* calunioso.
scurry off ['skʌrɪ-] *vi* sair correndo, dar no pé.
scurvy ['skə:vɪ] *n* escorbuto.
scuttle ['skʌtl] *n* (*also*: *coal* ~) balde *m* para carvão ♦ *vt* (*ship*) afundar voluntariamente, fazer ir a pique ♦ *vi* (*scamper*): **to ~ away, ~ off** sair em disparada.
scythe [saɪð] *n* segadeira, foice *f* grande.
SD (*US*) *abbr* (*POST*) = **South Dakota.**
SDI *n abbr* (= *Strategic Defense Initiative*) IDE *f*.
SDLP (*BRIT*) *n abbr* (*POL*) = **Social Democratic and Labour Party.**
sea [si:] *n* mar *m* ♦ *cpd* do mar, marino; **on the ~** (*boat*) no mar; (*town*) junto ao mar; **by** *or* **beside the ~** (*holiday*) na praia; (*village*) à beira-mar; **to go by ~** viajar por mar; **out to** (*or* **at**) **~** em alto mar; **heavy** *or* **rough ~(s)** mar agitado; **a ~ of faces** (*fig*) uma grande quantidade de pessoas; **to be all at ~** (*fig*) estar confuso *or* desorientado.
sea anemone *n* anêmona-do-mar *f*.
sea bed *n* fundo do mar.
sea bird *n* ave *f* marinha.
seaboard ['si:bɔ:d] *n* costa, litoral *m*.
sea breeze *n* brisa marítima, viração *f*.
seafarer ['si:fɛərə*] *n* marinheiro, homem *m* do mar.
seafaring ['si:ʃɛərɪŋ] *adj* (*life*) de marinheiro; **~ people** povo navegante.
seafood ['si:fu:d] *n* mariscos *mpl*.
sea front *n* orla marítima.
seagoing ['si:gəuɪŋ] *adj* (*ship*) de longo curso.
seagull ['si:gʌl] *n* gaivota.
seal [si:l] *n* (*animal*) foca; (*stamp*) selo ♦ *vt* (*close*) fechar; (: *with* ~) selar; (*decide*: *sb's fate*) decidir; (: *bargain*) fechar; **~ of approval** aprovação *f*.
seal off *vt* (*close*) fechar; (*cordon off*) isolar.
sea level *n* nível *m* do mar.
sealing wax ['si:lɪŋ-] *n* lacre *m*.
sea lion *n* leão-marinho *m*.
sealskin ['si:lskɪn] *n* pele *f* de foca.
seam [si:m] *n* costura; (*of metal*) junta, junção *f*; (*of coal*) veio, filão *m*; **the hall was bursting at the ~s** a sala estava apinhada de gente.
seaman ['si:mən] (*irreg*) *n* marinheiro.
seamanship ['si:mənʃɪp] *n* náutica.
seamen ['si:mɛn] *npl of* **seaman.**
seamless ['si:mlɪs] *adj* sem costura.
seamstress ['sɛmstrɪs] *n* costureira.
seamy ['si:mɪ] *adj* sórdido.
seance ['seɪɔns] *n* sessão *f* espírita.
seaplane ['si:pleɪn] *n* hidroavião *m*.
seaport ['si:pɔ:t] *n* porto de mar.
search [sə:tʃ] *n* (*for person, thing*) busca, procura; (*of drawer, pockets*) revista; (*inspection*) exame *m*, investigação *f* ♦ *vt* (*look in*) procurar em; (*examine*) examinar; (*person, place*) revistar ♦ *vi*: **to ~ for** procurar; **in ~ of** à procura de; **"~ and replace"** (*COMPUT*) "procura e substituição".
search through *vt fus* dar busca em.
searching ['sə:tʃɪŋ] *adj* penetrante, perscrutador(a); (*study*) minucioso.
searchlight ['sə:tʃlaɪt] *n* holofote *m*.
search party *n* equipe *f* de salvamento.
search warrant *n* mandado de busca.
searing ['sɪərɪŋ] *adj* (*heat*) ardente; (*pain*) agudo.
seashore ['si:ʃɔ:*] *n* praia, beira-mar *f*, litoral *m*; **on the ~** na praia.
seasick ['si:sɪk] *adj* enjoado, mareado; **to be** *or* **get ~** enjoar.
seaside ['si:saɪd] *n* praia.
seaside resort *n* balneário.
season ['si:zn] *n* (*of year*) estação *f*; (*sporting etc*) temporada ♦ *vt* (*food*) temperar; **to be in/out of ~** (*fruit*) estar na época/fora de época; **the busy ~** (*shops*) a época de muito movimento; (*hotels*) a temporada de férias; **the open ~** (*HUNTING*) a temporada de caça.
seasonal ['si:zənəl] *adj* sazonal.
seasoned ['si:znd] *adj* (*wood*) tratado; (*fig*: *worker, troops*) calejado; **a ~ campaigner** um combatente experiente.
seasoning ['si:zənɪŋ] *n* tempero.
season ticket *n* bilhete *m* de temporada.
seat [si:t] *n* (*in bus, train*: *place*) assento; (*chair*) cadeira; (*POL*) lugar *m*, cadeira; (*of bicycle*) selim *m*; (*buttocks*) traseiro, nádegas *fpl*; (*of government*) sede *f*; (*of trousers*) fundilhos *mpl* ♦ *vt* sentar; (*have room for*) ter capacidade para; **to be ~ed** estar sentado; **are there any ~s left?** há algum lugar vago?; **to take one's ~** sentar-se; **please be ~ed** sentem-se.
seat belt *n* cinto de segurança.
seating ['si:tɪŋ] *n* lugares *mnpl* sentados ♦ *cpd*: **~ arrangements** distribuição *f* dos lugares sentados.
seating capacity *n* lotação *f*.
seating room *n* lugares *mpl* sentados.
SEATO ['si:təu] *n abbr* (= *Southeast Asia Treaty Organization*) OTSA *f*.
sea urchin *n* ouriço-do-mar *m*.
sea water *n* água do mar.
seaweed ['si:wi:d] *n* alga marinha.
seaworthy ['si:wə:ðɪ] *adj* em condições de navegar, resistente.
SEC (*US*) *n abbr* (= *Securities and Exchange Commission*) *órgão que supervisiona o funcionamento da Bolsa de Valores*.
sec. *abbr* (= *second*) seg.
secateurs [sɛkə'tə:z] *npl* tesoura para podar plantas.
secede [sɪ'si:d] *vi* separar-se.
secluded [sɪ'klu:dɪd] *adj* retirado; (*place*) afastado.

seclusion [sɪ'klu:ʒən] *n* reclusão *f*, isolamento.
second¹ ['sɛkənd] *adj* segundo ♦ *adv* (*in race etc*) em segundo lugar ♦ *n* segundo; (AUT: *also*: ~ *gear*) segunda; (COMM) artigo defeituoso ♦ *vt* (*motion*) apoiar, secundar; **Charles the S~** Carlos II; **just a ~!** (só) um minuto *or* minutinho!; ~ **floor** (BRIT) segundo andar; (US) primeiro andar; **to ask for a ~ opinion** (MED) querer uma segunda opinião; **to have ~ thoughts (about doing sth)** pensar duas vezes (antes de fazer algo); **on ~ thoughts** (BRIT) *or* **thought** (US) pensando bem.
second² [sɪ'kɔnd] *vt* (*employee*) transferir temporariamente.
secondary ['sɛkəndərɪ] *adj* secundário.
secondary picket *n* piquete *m* secundário.
secondary school *n* escola secundária, colégio.
second-best *n* segunda opção *f*.
second-class *adj* de segunda classe ♦ *adv*: **to send sth ~** remeter algo em segunda classe; **to travel ~** viajar em segunda classe; ~ **citizen** cidadão/dã da segunda classe.
second cousin *n* primo/a em segundo grau.
seconder ['sɛkəndə*] *n* pessoa que secunda uma moção.
secondhand [sɛkənd'hænd] *adj* de (BR) *or* em (PT) segunda mão, usado ♦ *adv* (*buy*) de (BR) *or* em (PT) segunda mão; **to hear sth ~** ouvir algo de fonte indireta.
second hand *n* (*on clock*) ponteiro de segundos.
second-in-command *n* suplente *m/f*.
secondly ['sɛkəndlɪ] *adv* em segundo lugar.
secondment [sɪ'kɔndmənt] *n* substituição *f* temporária.
second-rate *adj* de segunda categoria.
secrecy ['si:krəsɪ] *n* sigilo; **in ~** sob sigilo, sigilosamente.
secret ['si:krɪt] *adj* secreto ♦ *n* segredo; **in ~** em segredo; **to keep sth ~ from sb** esconder algo de alguém; **keep it ~** não diz nada a ninguém; **to make no ~ of sth** não esconder algo de ninguém.
secret agent *n* agente *m/f* secreto/a.
secretarial [sɛkrɪ'tɛərɪəl] *adj* de secretário/a, secretarial.
secretariat [sɛkrɪ'tɛərɪət] *n* secretaria, secretariado.
secretary ['sɛkrətərɪ] *n* secretário/a; **S~ of State** (POL: BRIT) Ministro/a de Estado; **Foreign S~** (: US) Ministro das Relações Exteriores.
secrete [sɪ'kri:t] *vt* (ANAT, BIO, MED) secretar; (*hide*) esconder.
secretion [sɪ'kri:ʃən] *n* secreção *f*.
secretive ['si:krətɪv] *adj* sigiloso, reservado, secretório.
secretly ['si:krətlɪ] *adv* secretamente.
sect [sɛkt] *n* seita.
sectarian [sɛk'tɛərɪən] *adj* sectário.
section ['sɛkʃən] *n* seção *f*; (*part*) parte *f*, porção *f*; (*of document*) parágrafo, artigo; (*of opinion*) setor *m* ♦ *vt* secionar; **the business** *etc* ~ (PRESS) a seção de negócios *etc*.
sectional ['sɛkʃənəl] *adj* (*drawing*) transversal, secional.
sector ['sɛktə*] *n* setor *m*.
secular ['sɛkjulə*] *adj* secular, leigo.
secure [sɪ'kjuə*] *adj* (*free from anxiety*) seguro; (*firmly fixed*) firme, rígido; (*in safe place*) a salvo, em segurança ♦ *vt* (*fix*) prender; (*get*) conseguir, obter; (COMM: *loan*) garantir; **to make sth ~** firmar algo, segurar algo; **to ~ sth for sb** arranjar algo para alguém.
secured creditor [sɪ'kjuəd-] *n* credor *m* com garantia.
security [sɪ'kjurɪtɪ] *n* segurança; (*for loan*) fiança, garantia; (: *object*) penhor *m*; **securities** *npl* (STOCK EXCHANGE) títulos *mpl*, valores *mpl*; **to increase** *or* **tighten ~** aumentar a segurança.
security forces *npl* forças *fpl* de segurança.
security guard *n* (guarda *m/f* de) segurança *m/f*.
security risk *n* risco à segurança.
secy *abbr* (= *secretary*) secr.
sedan [sɪ'dæn] (US) *n* (AUT) sedã *m*.
sedate [sɪ'deɪt] *adj* (*calm*) sossegado, tranqüilo; (*formal*) sério, ponderado ♦ *vt* sedar, tratar com calmantes.
sedation [sɪ'deɪʃən] *n* (MED) sedação *f*; **to be under ~** estar sob o efeito de sedativos.
sedative ['sɛdɪtɪv] *n* calmante *m*, sedativo.
sedentary ['sɛdntrɪ] *adj* sedentário.
sediment ['sɛdɪmənt] *n* sedimento.
sedition [sɪ'dɪʃən] *n* sedição *f*.
seduce [sɪ'dju:s] *vt* seduzir.
seduction [sɪ'dʌkʃən] *n* sedução *f*.
seductive [sɪ'dʌktɪv] *adj* sedutor(a).
see [si:] (*pt* **saw**, *pp* **seen**) *vt* ver; (*make out*) enxergar; (*understand*) entender; (*accompany*): **to ~ sb to the door** acompanhar *or* levar alguém até a porta ♦ *vi* ver ♦ *n* sé *f*, sede *f*; **to ~ that** (*ensure*) assegurar que; **there was nobody to be ~n** não havia ninguém; **let me ~** deixa eu ver; **to go and ~ sb** ir visitar alguém; **~ for yourself** veja você mesmo, confira; **I don't know what she ~s in him** não sei o que ela vê nele; **as far as I can ~** que eu saiba; **~ you!** até logo! (BR), adeus! (PT); **~ you soon/later/tomorrow!** até logo/mais tarde/amanhã!
  see about *vt fus* tratar de.
  see off *vt* despedir-se de.
  see through *vt fus* enxergar através de ♦ *vt* levar a cabo.
  see to *vt fus* providenciar.
seed [si:d] *n* semente *f*; (*fig*) germe *m*; (TENNIS) pré-selecionado/a; **to go to ~** produzir sementes; (*fig*) deteriorar-se.
seedless ['si:dlɪs] *adj* sem caroças.
seedling ['si:dlɪŋ] *n* planta brotada da semente, muda.
seedy ['si:dɪ] *adj* (*shabby*) gasto, surrado; (*person*) maltrapilho.
seeing ['si:ɪŋ] *conj*: **~ (that)** visto (que), considerando (que).
seek [si:k] (*pt, pp* **sought**) *vt* procurar; (*post*)

solicitar; **to ~ advice/help from sb** pedir um conselho a alguém/procurar ajuda de alguém.
seek out *vt* (*person*) procurar.
seem [siːm] *vi* parecer; **it ~s (that)** ... parece que ...; **what ~s to be the trouble?** qual é o problema?; **I did what ~ed best** fiz o que me pareceu melhor.
seemingly ['siːmɪŋlɪ] *adv* aparentemente, pelo que aparenta.
seen [siːn] *pp of* **see**.
seep [siːp] *vi* filtrar-se, penetrar.
seer [sɪə*] *n* vidente *m/f*, profeta *m/f*.
seersucker ['sɪəsʌkə*] *n* tecido listrado de algodão.
seesaw ['siːsɔː] *n* gangorra, balanço.
seethe [siːð] *vi* ferver; **to ~ with anger** estar danado (da vida).
see-through *adj* transparente.
segment ['sɛgmənt] *n* segmento.
segregate ['sɛgrɪgeɪt] *vt* segregar.
segregation [sɛgrɪ'geɪʃən] *n* segregação *f*.
Seine [seɪn] *n*: **the ~** o Sena.
seismic ['saɪzmɪk] *adj* sísmico.
seize [siːz] *vt* (*grasp*) agarrar, pegar; (*take possession of*) apoderar-se de, confiscar; (: *territory*) tomar posse de; (*opportunity*) aproveitar.
seize up *vi* (*TECH*) gripar.
seize (up)on *vt fus* valer-se de.
seizure ['siːʒə*] *n* (*MED*) ataque *m*, acesso; (*LAW*) confisco, embargo.
seldom ['sɛldəm] *adv* raramente.
select [sɪ'lɛkt] *adj* seleto, escolhido; (*hotel, restaurant*) fino ♦ *vt* escolher, selecionar; (*SPORT*) selecionar, escalar; **a ~ few** uns poucos escolhidos.
selection [sɪ'lɛkʃən] *n* seleção *f*, escolha; (*COMM*) sortimento.
selection committee *n* comissão *f* de seleção.
selective [sɪ'lɛktɪv] *adj* seletivo.
selector [sɪ'lɛktə*] *n* (*person*) selecionador(a) *m/f*, seletor(a) *m/f*; (*TECH*) selecionador *m*.
self [sɛlf] (*pl* **selves**) *pron see* **herself**; **himself**; **itself**; **myself**; **oneself**; **ourselves**; **themselves**; **yourself** ♦ *n*: **the ~** o eu ♦ *prefix* auto....
self-addressed [-ə'drɛst] *adj*: **~ envelope** envelope *m* endereçado ao remetente.
self-adhesive *adj* auto-adesivo.
self-appointed [-ə'pɔɪntɪd] *adj* auto-nomeado.
self-assertive *adj* autoritário.
self-assurance *n* autoconfiança.
self-assured [-ə'ʃuəd] *adj* seguro de si.
self-catering (*BRIT*) *adj* (*flat*) com cozinha; (*holiday*) em casa alugada.
self-centred [-'sɛntəd] (*US* **self-centered**) *adj* egocêntrico.
self-cleaning *adj* de limpeza automática.
self-coloured (*US* **self-colored**) *adj* de cor natural; (*of one colour*) de uma só cor.
self-confessed [-kən'fɛst] *adj* assumido.
self-confidence *n* autoconfiança, confiança em si.
self-conscious *adj* inibido, constrangido.
self-contained [-kən'teɪnd] *adj* (*gen*) independente; (*flat*) completo, autônomo.
self-control *n* autocontrole *m*, autodomínio.
self-defeating [-dɪ'fiːtɪŋ] *adj* contraproducente.
self-defence (*US* **self-defense**) *n* legítima defesa, autodefesa.
self-discipline *n* autodisciplina.
self-employed [-ɪm'plɔɪd] *adj* autônomo.
self-esteem *n* amor *m* próprio.
self-evident *adj* patente.
self-explanatory *adj* que se explica por si mesmo.
self-governing *adj* autônomo.
self-help *n* iniciativa própria, esforço pessoal.
self-importance *n* presunção *f*.
self-important *adj* presunçoso, que se dá muita importância.
self-indulgent *adj* que se permite excessos.
self-inflicted [-ɪn'flɪktɪd] *adj* infligido a si mesmo.
self-interest *n* egoísmo.
selfish ['sɛlfɪʃ] *adj* egoísta.
selfishness ['sɛlfɪʃnɪs] *n* egoísmo.
selfless ['sɛlflɪs] *adj* desinteressado.
selflessly ['sɛlflɪslɪ] *adv* desinteressadamente.
self-made man (*irreg*) *n* homem *m* que se fez por conta própria.
self-pity *n* pena de si mesmo.
self-portrait *n* auto-retrato.
self-possessed [-pə'zɛst] *adj* calmo, senhor(a) de si.
self-preservation *n* auto-preservação *f*.
self-raising [-'reɪzɪŋ] (*BRIT*) *adj*: **~ flour** farinha de trigo com fermento acrescentado.
self-reliant *adj* seguro de si, independente.
self-respect *n* amor *m* próprio.
self-respecting [-rɪs'pɛktɪŋ] *adj* que se respeita.
self-righteous *adj* farisaico, santarrão/rona.
self-rising (*US*) *adj*: **~ flour** farinha de trigo com fermento acrescentado.
self-sacrifice *n* abnegação *f*, altruísmo.
self-same *adj* mesmo.
self-satisfied [-'sætɪsfaɪd] *adj* satisfeito consigo mesmo.
self-sealing *adj* (*envelope*) auto-adesivo.
self-service *adj* de auto-serviço ♦ *n* auto-serviço.
self-styled [-staɪld] *adj* pretenso.
self-sufficient *adj* auto-suficiente.
self-supporting [-sə'pɔːtɪŋ] *adj* financeiramente independente.
self-taught *adj* autodidata.
self-test *n* (*COMPUT*) auto-teste *m*.
sell [sɛl] (*pt, pp* **sold**) *vt* vender ♦ *vi* vender-se; **to ~ at** *or* **for £10** vender a *or* por 10 libras; **to ~ sb an idea** (*fig*) convencer alguém de uma idéia.

NB: *European Portuguese adds the following consonants to certain words:* **b** (sú(b)dito, su(b)til); **c** (a(c)ção, a(c)cionista, a(c)to); **m** (inde(m)ne); **p** (ado(p)ção, ado(p)tar); *for further details see p. xiii.*

sell off *vt* liquidar.
sell out *vi* vender todo o estoque ♦ *vt*: **the tickets are all sold out** todos os ingressos já foram vendidos; **to ~ out (to)** (*COMM*) vender o negócio (a); (*fig*) vender-se (a).
sell up *vi* vender o negócio.
sell-by date *n* vencimento.
seller ['sɛlə*] *n* vendedor(a) *m/f*; **~'s market** mercado de vendedor.
selling price ['sɛlɪŋ-] *n* preço de venda.
sellotape ['sɛləuteɪp] ® *n* fita adesiva, durex *m* ® (*BR*).
sellout ['sɛlaut] *n* traição *f*; (*of tickets*): **it was a ~** foi um sucesso de bilheteria.
selves [sɛlvz] *npl of* **self**.
semantic [sə'mæntɪk] *adj* semântico.
semantics [sə'mæntɪks] *n* semântica.
semaphore ['sɛməfɔː*] *n* semáforo.
semblance ['sɛmbləns] *n* aparência.
semen ['siːmən] *n* sêmen *m*.
semester [sə'mɛstə*] *n* semestre *m*.
semi ['sɛmɪ] (*BRIT*: *inf*) *n* (casa) geminada.
semi... [sɛmɪ] *prefix* semi..., meio....
semibreve ['sɛmɪbriːv] (*BRIT*) *n* semibreve *f*.
semicircle ['sɛmɪsəːkl] *n* semicírculo.
semicircular [sɛmɪ'səːkjulə*] *adj* semicircular.
semi-colon *n* ponto e vírgula.
semiconductor [sɛmɪkən'dʌktə*] *n* semicondutor *m*.
semi-conscious *adj* semiconsciente.
semi-detached (house) (*BRIT*: *irreg*) *n* (casa) geminada.
semi-final *n* semifinal *f*.
seminar ['sɛmɪnɑː*] *n* seminário.
seminary ['sɛmɪnərɪ] *n* (*for priests*) seminário.
semiprecious [sɛmɪ'prɛʃəs] *adj* semiprecioso.
semiquaver ['sɛmɪkweɪvə*] (*BRIT*) *n* semicolcheia.
semiskilled [sɛmɪ'skɪld] *adj*: **~ worker** operário/a semi-especializado/a.
semitone ['sɛmɪtəun] *n* (*MUS*) semitom *m*.
semolina [sɛmə'liːnə] *n* sêmola, semolina.
SEN (*BRIT*) *n abbr* = **State Enrolled Nurse**.
Sen. *abbr* = **Senator**; **Senior**.
sen. *abbr* = **senator**; **senior**.
senate ['sɛnɪt] *n* senado.
senator ['sɛnətə*] *n* senador(a) *m/f*.
send [sɛnd] (*pt*, *pp* **sent**) *vt* mandar, enviar; (*dispatch*) expedir, remeter; (*telegram*) passar; **to ~ by post** (*BRIT*) *or* **mail** (*US*) mandar pelo correio; **to ~ sb for sth** mandar alguém buscar algo; **to ~ word that ...** mandar dizer que ...; **she ~s (you) her love** ela lhe envia lembranças; **to ~ sb to Coventry** (*BRIT*) colocar alguém em ostracismo; **to ~ sb to sleep** dar sono a alguém; **to ~ sb into fits of laughter** dar um ataque de riso a alguém; **to ~ sth flying** derrubar algo.
send away *vt* (*letter*, *goods*) expedir, mandar.
send away for *vt fus* encomendar, pedir pelo correio.
send back *vt* devolver, mandar de volta.
send for *vt fus* mandar buscar; (*by post*) pedir pelo correio, encomendar.
send in *vt* (*report*, *application*) entregar.
send off *vt* (*goods*) despachar, expedir; (*BRIT*: *SPORT*: *player*) expulsar.
send on *vt* (*BRIT*: *letter*) remeter; (*luggage etc*: *in advance*) mandar com antecedência.
send out *vt* (*invitation*) distribuir; (*signal*) emitir.
send round *vt* (*letter*, *document*) circular.
send up *vt* (*person*, *price*) fazer subir; (*parody*) parodiar.
sender ['sɛndə*] *n* remetente *m/f*.
send-off *n*: **a good ~** uma boa despedida.
Senegal [sɛnɪ'gɔːl] *n* Senegal *m*.
Senegalese [sɛnɪgə'liːz] *adj*, *n inv* senegalês/esa *m/f*.
senile ['siːnaɪl] *adj* senil.
senility [sɪ'nɪlɪtɪ] *n* senilidade *f*.
senior ['siːnɪə*] *adj* (*older*) mais velho *or* idoso; (: *on staff*) mais antigo; (*of higher rank*) superior ♦ *n* o/a mais velho/a; (*on staff*) o/a mais antigo/a; **P. Jones ~** P. Jones Sênior.
senior citizen *n* idoso/a.
senior high school (*US*) *n* ≈ colégio.
seniority [siːnɪ'ɔrɪtɪ] *n* antiguidade *f*.
sensation [sɛn'seɪʃən] *n* sensação *f*; **to cause a ~** causar sensação.
sensational [sɛn'seɪʃənəl] *adj* sensacional.
sensationalism [sɛn'seɪʃənəlɪzəm] *n* sensacionalismo.
sense [sɛns] *n* sentido; (*feeling*) sensação *f*; (*good ~*) bom senso ♦ *vt* sentir, perceber; **~s** *npl* juízo; **it makes ~** faz sentido; **~ of humour** senso de humor; **there is no ~ in (doing) that** não há sentido em (fazer) isso; **to come to one's ~s** (*regain consciousness*) recobrar os sentidos; (*become reasonable*) recobrar o juízo; **to take leave of one's ~s** enlouquecer.
senseless ['sɛnslɪs] *adj* insensato, estúpido; (*unconscious*) sem sentidos, inconsciente.
sensibility [sɛnsɪ'bɪlɪtɪ] *n* sensibilidade *f*; **sensibilities** *npl* suscetibilidade *f*.
sensible ['sɛnsɪbl] *adj* sensato, de bom senso; (*reasonable*) lógico, razoável; (*shoes etc*) prático.
sensitive ['sɛnsɪtɪv] *adj* sensível; (*touchy*) suscetível.
sensitivity [sɛnsɪ'tɪvɪtɪ] *n* sensibilidade *f*; (*touchiness*) suscetibilidade *f*.
sensual ['sɛnsjuəl] *adj* sensual.
sensuous ['sɛnsjuəs] *adj* sensual.
sent [sɛnt] *pt*, *pp of* **send**.
sentence ['sɛntəns] *n* (*LING*) frase *f*, oração *f*; (*LAW*: *verdict*) sentença; (: *punishment*) pena ♦ *vt*: **to ~ sb to death/to 5 years** condenar alguém à morte/a 5 anos de prisão; **to pass ~ on sb** sentenciar alguém.
sentiment ['sɛntɪmənt] *n* sentimento; (*opinion*) opinião *f*.
sentimental [sɛntɪ'mɛntl] *adj* sentimental.
sentimentality [sɛntɪmɛn'tælɪtɪ] *n* sentimentalismo.
sentry ['sɛntrɪ] *n* sentinela *f*.
sentry duty *n*: **to be on ~** estar de guarda.

Seoul [səul] *n* Seul.
separable ['sɛprəbl] *adj* separável.
separate [*adj* 'sɛprɪt, *vt, vi* 'sɛpəreɪt] *adj* separado; (*distinct*) diferente ♦ *vt* separar; (*part*) dividir ♦ *vi* separar-se; ~ **from** separado de; **under ~ cover** (*COMM*) em separado; **to ~ into** dividir em.
separated ['sɛpəreɪtɪd] *adj* (*from spouse*) separado.
separately ['sɛprɪtlɪ] *adv* separadamente.
separates ['sɛprɪts] *npl* (*clothes*) roupas *fpl* que fazem jogo.
separation [sɛpə'reɪʃən] *n* separação *f*.
Sept. *abbr* (= *September*) set.
September [sɛp'tɛmbə*] *n* setembro; *see also* **July**.
septic ['sɛptɪk] *adj* sético; (*wound*) infeccionado.
septicaemia [sɛptɪ'si:mɪə] (*US* **septicemia**) *n* septicemia.
septic tank *n* fossa sética.
sequel ['si:kwl] *n* conseqüência, resultado; (*of story*) continuação *f*.
sequence ['si:kwəns] *n* série *f*, seqüência; (*CINEMA*) série; **in ~** em seqüência.
sequential [sɪ'kwɛnʃəl] *adj*: ~ **access** (*COMPUT*) acesso seqüencial.
sequin ['si:kwɪn] *n* lantejoula, paetê *m*.
Serbo-Croat ['sə:bəu'krəuæt] *n* (*LING*) serbo-croata *m*.
serenade [sɛrə'neɪd] *n* serenata ♦ *vt* fazer serenata para.
serene [sɪ'ri:n] *adj* sereno, tranqüilo.
serenity [sə'rɛnɪtɪ] *n* serenidade *f*, tranqüilidade *f*.
sergeant ['sɑ:dʒənt] *n* sargento.
sergeant major *n* sargento-ajudante *m*.
serial ['sɪərɪəl] *n* (*TV*) seriado; (*in newspaper*) história em folhetim ♦ *adj* (*COMPUT*: *interface, printer*) serial; (: *access*) seqüencial.
serialize ['sɪərɪəlaɪz] *vt* (*book*) publicar em folhetim; (*TV*) seriar.
serial number *n* número de série.
series ['sɪəri:z] *n inv* série *f*.
serious ['sɪərɪəs] *adj* sério; (*grave*) grave; **are you ~ (about it)?** você está falando sério?
seriously ['sɪərɪəslɪ] *adv* a sério, com seriedade; (*gravely*) gravemente; **to take sth/sb ~** levar algo/alguém a sério.
seriousness ['sɪərɪəsnɪs] *n* seriedade *f*; gravidade *f*.
sermon ['sə:mən] *n* sermão *m* .
serrated [sɪ'reɪtɪd] *adj* serrado, dentado.
serum ['sɪərəm] *n* soro.
servant ['sə:vənt] *n* empregado/a *m/f*; (*fig*) servidor(a) *m/f*.
serve [sə:v] *vt* servir; (*customer*) atender; (*subj*: *train*) passar por; (*treat*) tratar; (*apprenticeship*) fazer; (*prison term*) cumprir ♦ *vi* (*TENNIS etc*) sacar; (*be useful*): **to ~ as/for/to do** servir como/para/para fazer ♦ *n* (*TENNIS*) saque *m*; **are you being ~d?** você já foi atendido?; **to ~ on a committee/jury** fazer parte de um comitê/júri; **it ~s him right** é bem feito por ele; **it ~s my purpose** isso me serve.
serve out *vt* (*food*) servir.
serve up *vt* (*food*) servir.
service ['sə:vɪs] *n* serviço; (*REL*) culto; (*AUT*) revisão *f*; (*also*: *dinner ~*) aparelho de jantar ♦ *vt* (*car, washing machine*) fazer a revisão de, revisar; (: *repair*) consertar; **the S~s** *npl* as Forças Armadas; **to be of ~ to sb, to do sb a ~** ser útil a alguém.
serviceable ['sə:vɪsəbl] *adj* aproveitável, prático, durável.
service area *n* (*on motorway*) *posto de gasolina com bar, restaurante etc*.
service charge (*BRIT*) *n* serviço.
service industries *npl* setor *m* de serviços.
serviceman ['sə:vɪsmæn] (*irreg*) *n* militar *m*.
service station *n* posto de gasolina (*BR*), estação *f* de serviço (*PT*).
serviette [sə:vɪ'ɛt] *n* guardanapo.
servile ['sə:vaɪl] *adj* servil.
session ['sɛʃən] *n* (*sitting*) sessão *f*; (*SCH*) ano letivo; **to be in ~** estar reunido em sessão.
set [sɛt] (*pt, pp* **set**) *n* (*of tools, glasses*) jogo; (*RADIO, TV*) aparelho; (*of utensils*) bateria de cozinha; (*of cutlery*) talher *m*; (*of books*) coleção *f*; (*group of people*) grupo; (*TENNIS, CINEMA*) set *m*; (*THEATRE*) cenário; (*HAIRDRESSING*) penteado; (*MATH*) conjunto ♦ *adj* (*fixed*) marcado, fixo; (*ready*) pronto; (*resolved*) decidido, estabelecido ♦ *vt* (*place*) pôr, colocar; (*fix*) fixar; (: *a time*) marcar; (*adjust*) ajustar; (*decide*: *rules etc*) estabelecer, decidir; (*record*) estabelecer; (*homework*) passar; (*TYP*) compor ♦ *vi* (*sun*) pôr-se; (*jam, jelly, concrete*) endurecer, solidificar-se; **to be ~ on doing sth** estar decidido a fazer algo; **to be all ~ to do** estar todo pronto para fazer; **to be (dead) ~ against** estar (completamente) contra; **he's ~ in his ways** ele tem opiniões fixas; **to ~ to music** musicar, pôr música em; **to ~ on fire** botar fogo em, incendiar; **to ~ free** libertar; **to ~ sth going** pôr algo em movimento; **to ~ sail** zarpar, alçar velas; **~ phrase** frase *f* feita; **a ~ of false teeth** uma dentadura; **a ~ of dining-room furniture** um conjunto de salade jantar; **a film ~ in Rome** um filme ambientado em Roma.
set about *vt fus* (*task*) começar com; **to ~ about doing sth** começar a fazer algo.
set aside *vt* deixar de lado.
set back *vt* (*in time*): **to ~ back (by)** atrasar (por); (*place*): **a house ~ back from the road** uma casa afastada da estrada.
set in *vi* (*infection*) manifestar-se; (*complications*) surgir; **the rain has ~ in for the day** vai chover o dia inteiro.
set off *vi* partir, ir indo ♦ *vt* (*bomb*) fazer explodir; (*cause to start*) colocar em funcio-

***NB**: European Portuguese adds the following consonants to certain words:* **b** (sú(b)dito, su(b)til); **c** (a(c)ção, a(c)cionista, a(c)to); **m** (inde(m)ne); **p** (ado(p)ção, ado(p)tar); *for further details see p. xiii.*

namento; (*show up well*) ressaltar.

set out *vi*: **to ~ out to do sth** pretender fazer algo ♦ *vt* (*arrange*) colocar, dispor; (*state*) expor, explicar; **to ~ out (from)** sair (de).

set up *vt* (*organization, record*) fundar, estabelecer; **to ~ up shop** (*fig*) estabelecer-se.

setback ['sɛtbæk] *n* (*hitch*) revés *m*, contratempo; (*in health*) piora.

set menu *n* refeição *f* a preço fixo.

set square *n* esquadro.

settee [sɛ'tiː] *n* sofá *m*.

setting ['sɛtɪŋ] *n* (*frame*) moldura; (*placing*) colocação *f*; (*of sun*) pôr(-do-sol) *m*; (*of jewel*) engaste *m*; (*location*) cenário.

setting lotion *n* loção *f* fixadora.

settle ['sɛtl] *vt* (*argument, matter*) resolver, esclarecer; (*accounts*) ajustar, liquidar; (*land*) colonizar; (*MED*: *calm*) acalmar, tranqüilizar ♦ *vi* (*dust etc*) assentar; (*weather*) firmar, melhorar; (*also*: *~ down*) instalar-se, estabilizar-se; **to ~ to sth** concentrar-se em algo; **to ~ for sth** concordar em aceitar algo; **to ~ on sth** optar por algo; **that's ~d then** está resolvido então; **to ~ one's stomach** acomodar o estômago.

settle in *vi* instalar-se.

settle up *vi*: **to ~ up with sb** ajustar as contas com alguém.

settlement ['sɛtlmənt] *n* (*payment*) liquidação *f*; (*agreement*) acordo, convênio; (*village etc*) povoado, povoação *f*; **in ~ of our account** (*COMM*) em liquidação da nossa conta.

settler ['sɛtlə*] *n* colono/a, colonizador(a) *m/f*.

setup ['sɛtʌp] *n* (*arrangement*) organização *f*; (*situation*) situação *f*.

seven ['sɛvn] *num* sete; *see also* **five**.

seventeen ['sɛvn'tiːn] *num* dezessete; *see also* **five**.

seventh ['sɛvnθ] *num* sétimo; *see also* **fifth**.

seventy ['sɛvntɪ] *num* setenta; *see also* **fifty**.

sever ['sɛvə*] *vt* cortar; (*relations*) romper.

several ['sɛvərl] *adj, pron* vários/as; **~ of us** vários de nós; **~ times** várias vezes.

severance ['sɛvərəns] *n* (*of relations*) rompimento.

severance pay *n* indenização *f* pela demissão.

severe [sɪ'vɪə*] *adj* severo; (*serious*) grave; (*hard*) duro; (*pain*) intenso; (*plain*) austero.

severely [sɪ'vɪəlɪ] *adv* severamente; (*wounded, ill*) gravemente.

severity [sɪ'vɛrɪtɪ] *n* severidade *f*; austeridade *f*; intensidade *f*.

sew [səu] (*pt* **~ed**, *pp* **sewn**) *vt, vi* coser, costurar.

sew up *vt* coser, costurar; **it's all sewn up** (*fig*) está no papo.

sewage ['suːɪdʒ] *n* detritos *mpl*.

sewer ['suːə*] *n* (cano do) esgoto, bueiro.

sewing ['səuɪŋ] *n* costura.

sewing machine *n* máquina de costura.

sewn [səun] *pp of* **sew**.

sex [sɛks] *n* sexo; **to have ~ with sb** fazer sexo com alguém.

sex act *n* ato sexual.

sexism ['sɛksɪzm] *n* sexismo.

sexist ['sɛksɪst] *adj* sexista.

sextet [sɛks'tɛt] *n* sexteto.

sexual ['sɛksjuəl] *adj* sexual; **~ assault** atentado ao pudor; **~ intercourse** relações *fpl* sexuais.

sexy ['sɛksɪ] *adj* sexy.

Seychelles [seɪ'ʃɛl(z)] *npl*: **the ~** Seychelles (*no article*).

SF *n abbr* = **science fiction**.

SG (*US*) *n abbr* = **Surgeon General**.

Sgt *abbr* (= *sergeant*) sarg.

shabbiness ['ʃæbɪnɪs] *n* (*of clothes*) pobreza; (*of building*) mau estado de conservação.

shabby ['ʃæbɪ] *adj* (*person*) esfarrapado, maltrapilho; (*clothes*) usado, surrado.

shack [ʃæk] *n* choupana, barraca.

shackles ['ʃæklz] *npl* algemas *fpl*, grilhões *mpl*.

shade [ʃeɪd] *n* sombra; (*for lamp*) quebra-luz *m*; (*for eyes*) viseira; (*of colour*) tom *m*, tonalidade *f*; (*US*: *window ~*) estore *m* ♦ *vt* sombrear, dar sombra a; **~s** *npl* (*US*: *sunglasses*) óculos *mpl* escuros; **in the ~** à sombra; **a ~ smaller** um pouquinho menor.

shadow ['ʃædəu] *n* sombra ♦ *vt* (*follow*) seguir de perto (sem ser visto); **without** *or* **beyond a ~ of doubt** sem sombra de dúvida.

shadow cabinet (*BRIT*) *n* (*POL*) *gabinete paralelo formado pelo partido da oposição*.

shadowy ['ʃædəuɪ] *adj* escuro; (*dim*) vago, indistinto.

shady ['ʃeɪdɪ] *adj* sombreado, à sombra; (*fig*: *dishonest*) suspeito, duvidoso; (: *deal*) desonesto.

shaft [ʃɑːft] *n* (*of arrow, spear*) haste *f*; (*column*) fuste *m*; (*AUT, TECH*) eixo, manivela; (*of mine, of lift*) poço; (*of light*) raio.

shaggy ['ʃægɪ] *adj* peludo, felpudo.

shake [ʃeɪk] (*pt* **shook**, *pp* **shaken**) *vt* sacudir; (*building, confidence*) abalar; (*surprise*) surpreender ♦ *vi* tremer ♦ *n* (*movement*) sacudidela; (*violent*) safanão *m*; **to ~ hands with sb** apertar a mão de alguém; **to ~ one's head** (*in refusal etc*) dizer não com a cabeça; (*in dismay*) sacudir a cabeça.

shake off *vt* sacudir; (*fig*) livrar-se de.

shake up *vt* sacudir.

shake-up *n* reorganização *f*.

shakily ['ʃeɪkɪlɪ] *adv* (*reply*) de voz trêmula; (*walk*) vacilante; (*write*) de mão trêmula.

shaky ['ʃeɪkɪ] *adj* (*hand, voice*) trêmulo; (*person*: *in shock*) abalado; (: *old*) frágil; (*chair*) bambo; (*knowledge*) duvidoso.

shale [ʃeɪl] *n* argila xistosa.

shall [ʃæl] (*conditional* **should**) *aux vb*: **I ~ go** irei.

shallot [ʃə'lɔt] (*BRIT*) *n* cebolinha.

shallow ['ʃæləu] *adj* raso; (*fig*) superficial.

sham [ʃæm] *n* fraude *f*, fingimento ♦ *adj* falso, simulado ♦ *vt* fingir, simular.

shambles ['ʃæmblz] *n* confusão *f*; **the economy is (in) a complete ~** a economia está completamente desorganizada.

shame [ʃeɪm] *n* vergonha; (*pity*) pena ♦ *vt* envergonhar; **it is a ~ (that/to do)** é (uma) pena (que/fazer); **what a ~!** que pena!; **to put sb/sth to ~** deixar alguém/algo envergonhado.

shamefaced ['ʃeɪmfeɪst] *adj* envergonhado.

shameful ['ʃeɪmful] *adj* vergonhoso.

shameless ['ʃeɪmlɪs] *adj* sem vergonha, descarado; (*immodest*) cínico, impudico.

shampoo [ʃæm'puː] *n* xampu *m* (*BR*), champô *m* (*PT*) ♦ *vt* lavar o cabelo (com xampu); **~ and set** lavagem *f* e penteado.

shamrock ['ʃæmrɔk] *n* trevo.

shandy ['ʃændɪ] *n mistura de cerveja com refresco gaseificado.*

shan't [ʃɑːnt] = **shall not.**

shanty town ['ʃæntɪ-] *n* favela.

SHAPE [ʃeɪp] *n abbr* (= *Supreme Headquarters Allied Powers, Europe*) *QG das forças aliadas na Europa.*

shape [ʃeɪp] *n* forma ♦ *vt* formar, modelar; (*clay, stone*) dar forma a; (*sb's ideas*) moldar; (*sb's life, course of events*) determinar ♦ *vi* (*also*: *~ up*) (*events*) desenrolar-se; (*person*) tomar jeito; **to take ~** tomar forma; **in the ~ of a heart** em forma de coração; **I can't bear gardening in any ~ or form** não suporto jardinagem de forma alguma; **to get o.s. into ~** ficar em forma.

-shaped [ʃeɪpt] *suffix*: **heart~** em forma de coração.

shapeless ['ʃeɪplɪs] *adj* informe, sem forma definida.

shapely ['ʃeɪplɪ] *adj* escultural.

share [ʃɛə*] *n* (*part*) parte *f*; (*contribution*) cota; (*COMM*) ação *f* ♦ *vt* dividir; (*have in common*) compartilhar; **to ~ out (among** *or* **between)** distribuir (entre); **to ~ in** participar de; **to have a ~ in the profits** ter uma participação nos lucros.

share capital *n* capital *m* em ações.

share certificate *n* cautela de ação.

shareholder ['ʃɛəhəuldə*] *n* acionista *m/f*.

share index *n* índice *m* da Bolsa de Valores.

share issue *n* emissão *f* de ações.

shark [ʃɑːk] *n* tubarão *m*.

sharp [ʃɑːp] *adj* (*razor, knife*) afiado; (*point*) pontiagudo; (*outline*) definido, bem marcado; (*pain*) agudo; (*curve, bend*) fechado; (*MUS*) desafinado; (*contrast*) marcado; (*voice*) agudo; (*person*: *quick-witted*) perspicaz; (*dishonest*) desonesto ♦ *n* (*MUS*) sustenido ♦ *adv*: **at 2 o'clock ~** às 2 (horas) em ponto; **turn ~ left** vira logo à esquerda; **to be ~ with sb** ser brusco com alguém; **look ~!** rápido!

sharpen ['ʃɑːpən] *vt* afiar; (*pencil*) apontar, fazer a ponta de; (*fig*) aguçar.

sharpener ['ʃɑːpnə*] *n* (*also*: *pencil ~*) apontador *m* (*BR*), apara-lápis *m inv* (*PT*).

sharp-eyed [-aɪd] *adj* de vista aguda.

sharply ['ʃɑːplɪ] *adv* (*abruptly*) bruscamente; (*clearly*) claramente; (*harshly*) severamente.

sharp-tempered *adj* irascível.

sharp-witted [-'wɪtɪd] *adj* perspicaz, observador(a).

shatter ['ʃætə*] *vt* despedaçar, estilhaçar; (*fig*: *ruin*) destruir, acabar com; (: *upset*) arrasar ♦ *vi* despedaçar-se, estilhaçar-se.

shattered ['ʃætəd] *adj* (*overwhelmed*) arrasado; (*exhausted*) exausto.

shatterproof ['ʃætəpruːf] *adj* inestilhaçável.

shave [ʃeɪv] *vt* barbear, fazer a barba de ♦ *vi* fazer a barba, barbear-se ♦ *n*: **to have a ~** fazer a barba.

shaven ['ʃeɪvn] *adj* (*head*) raspado.

shaver ['ʃeɪvə*] *n* barbeador *m*; **electric ~** barbeador elétrico.

shaving ['ʃeɪvɪŋ] *n* (*action*) barbeação *f*; **~s** *npl* (*of wood*) aparas *fpl*.

shaving brush *n* pincel *m* de barba.

shaving cream *n* creme *m* de barbear.

shaving soap *n* sabão *m* de barba.

shawl [ʃɔːl] *n* xale *m*.

she [ʃiː] *pron* ela; **there ~ is** lá está ela; **~-elephant** *etc* elefante *etc* fêmea.

sheaf [ʃiːf] (*pl* **sheaves**) *n* (*of corn*) gavela; (*of arrows*) feixe *m*; (*of papers*) maço.

shear [ʃɪə*] (*pt* **~ed**, *pp* **~ed** *or* **shorn**) *vt* (*sheep*) tosquiar, tosar.

shear off *vt* cercear.

shears [ʃɪəz] *npl* (*for hedge*) tesoura de jardim.

sheath [ʃiːθ] *n* bainha; (*contraceptive*) camisa-de-vênus *f*, camisinha.

sheathe [ʃiːð] *vt* embainhar.

sheath knife (*irreg*) *n* faca com bainha.

sheaves [ʃiːvz] *npl of* **sheaf**.

shed [ʃɛd] (*pt, pp* **shed**) *n* alpendre *m*, galpão *m*; (*INDUSTRY, RAIL*) galpão *m* ♦ *vt* (*skin*) mudar; (*leaves, fur*) perder; (*tears*) derramar; **to ~ light on** (*problem, mystery*) esclarecer.

she'd [ʃiːd] = **she had; she would.**

sheen [ʃiːn] *n* brilho.

sheep [ʃiːp] *n inv* ovelha.

sheepdog ['ʃiːpdɔg] *n* cão *m* pastor.

sheep farmer *n* criador(a) *m/f* de ovelhas.

sheepish ['ʃiːpɪʃ] *adj* tímido, acanhado.

sheepskin [ʃiːpskɪn] *n* pele *f* de carneiro, pelego.

sheepskin jacket *n* casaco de pele de carneiro.

sheer [ʃɪə*] *adj* (*utter*) puro, completo; (*steep*) íngreme, empinado; (*almost transparent*) fino, translúcido ♦ *adv* a pique; **by ~ chance** totalmente por acaso.

sheet [ʃiːt] *n* (*on bed*) lençol *m*; (*of paper*) folha; (*of glass, metal*) lâmina, chapa.

sheet feed *n* (*on printer*) alimentação *f* de papel (em folhas soltas).

sheet lightning *n* relâmpago difuso.

***NB**: European Portuguese adds the following consonants to certain words:* **b** (sú(b)dito, su(b)til); **c** (a(c)ção, a(c)cionista, a(c)to); **m** (inde(m)ne); **p** (ado(p)ção, ado(p)tar); *for further details see p. xiii.*

sheet metal *n* metal *m* em chapa.
sheet music *n* música.
sheik(h) [ʃeɪk] *n* xeque *m*.
shelf [ʃelf] (*pl* **shelves**) *n* prateleira; **set of shelves** estante *f*.
shelf life *n* (COMM) validade *f* (de produtos perecíveis).
shell [ʃɛl] *n* (*on beach*) concha; (*of egg, nut etc*) casca; (*explosive*) obus *m*; (*of building*) armação *f*, esqueleto ♦ *vt* (*peas*) descascar; (MIL) bombardear.
shell out (*inf*) *vi*: **to ~ out (for)** pagar.
she'll [ʃi:l] = **she will; she shall.**
shellfish ['ʃɛlfɪʃ] *n inv* crustáceo, molusco; (*pl*: *as food*) frutos *mpl* do mar, mariscos *mpl*.
shelter ['ʃɛltə*] *n* abrigo, refúgio ♦ *vt* (*aid*) amparar, proteger; (*give lodging to*) abrigar; (*hide*) esconder ♦ *vi* abrigar-se, refugiar-se; **to take ~ from** abrigar-se de.
sheltered ['ʃɛltəd] *adj* (*life*) protegido; (*spot*) abrigado, protegido.
shelve [ʃɛlv] *vt* (*fig*) pôr de lado, engavetar.
shelves [ʃɛlvz] *npl of* **shelf**.
shelving ['ʃɛlvɪŋ] *n* (*shelves*) prateleiras *fpl*.
shepherd ['ʃɛpəd] *n* pastor *m* ♦ *vt* (*guide*) guiar, conduzir.
shepherdess ['ʃɛpədɪs] *n* pastora.
shepherd's pie *n* empadão *m* de carne e batata.
sherbet ['ʃə:bət] *n* (BRIT: *powder*) *pó doce e efervescente*; (US: *water ice*) *sorvete de frutas à base de água*.
sheriff ['ʃɛrɪf] *n* xerife *m*.
sherry ['ʃɛrɪ] *n* (vinho de) Xerez *m*.
she's [ʃi:z] = **she is; she has.**
Shetland ['ʃɛtlənd] *n* (*also*: *the ~s, the ~ Isles or Islands*) as ilhas Shetland.
shield [ʃi:ld] *n* escudo; (TECH) blindagem *f* ♦ *vt*: **to ~ (from)** proteger contra.
shift [ʃɪft] *n* (*change*) mudança; (*of place*) transferência; (*of workers*) turno ♦ *vt* transferir; (*remove*) tirar ♦ *vi* mudar; (*change place*) mudar de lugar; **the wind has ~ed to the south** o vento virou para o sul; **a ~ in demand** (COMM) um deslocamento de demanda.
shift key *n* (*on typewriter*) tecla para maiúsculas.
shiftless ['ʃɪftlɪs] *adj* indolente.
shift work *n* trabalho em turnos; **to do ~** trabalhar em turnos.
shifty ['ʃɪftɪ] *adj* esperto, trapaceiro; (*eyes*) velhaco, maroto.
shilling ['ʃɪlɪŋ] (BRIT) *n* xelim *m* (= *12 old pence*; *20 in a pound*).
shilly-shally ['ʃɪlɪʃælɪ] *vi* vacilar.
shimmer ['ʃɪmə*] *n* reflexo trêmulo ♦ *vi* cintilar, tremeluzir.
shin [ʃɪn] *n* canela (da perna) ♦ *vi*: **to ~ up/down a tree** subir em/descer de um árvore com mãos e pernas.
shindig ['ʃɪndɪg] (*inf*) *n* arrasta-pé *m*.
shine [ʃaɪn] (*pt, pp* **shone**) *n* brilho, lustre *m* ♦ *vi* brilhar ♦ *vt* (*shoes*) lustrar; **to ~ a torch on sth** apontar uma lanterna para algo.
shingle ['ʃɪŋgl] *n* (*on beach*) pedrinhas *fpl*, seixinhos *mpl*; (*on roof*) telha.
shingles ['ʃɪŋglz] *n* (MED) herpes-zoster *m*.
shining ['ʃaɪnɪŋ] *adj* brilhante.
shiny ['ʃaɪnɪ] *adj* brilhante, lustroso.
ship [ʃɪp] *n* barco; (*large*) navio ♦ *vt* (*goods*) embarcar; (*send*) transportar *or* mandar (por via marítima); **on board ~** a bordo.
shipbuilder ['ʃɪpbɪldə*] *n* construtor *m* naval.
shipbuilding ['ʃɪpbɪldɪŋ] *n* construção *f* naval.
ship canal *n* canal *m* de navegação.
ship chandler [-'tʃændlə*] *n* fornecedor *m* de provisões para navios.
shipment ['ʃɪpmənt] *n* (*act*) embarque *m*; (*goods*) carregamento.
shipowner ['ʃɪpəunə*] *n* armador(a) *m/f*.
shipper ['ʃɪpə*] *n* exportador(a) *m/f*, expedidor(a) *m/f*.
shipping ['ʃɪpɪŋ] *n* (*ships*) navios *mpl*; (*traffic*) navegação *f*.
shipping agent *n* agente *m/f* marítimo/a.
shipping company *n* companhia de navegação.
shipping lane *n* rota de navegação.
shipping line *n* companhia de navegação.
shipshape ['ʃɪpʃeɪp] *adj* em ordem.
shipwreck ['ʃɪprɛk] *n* naufrágio ♦ *vt*: **to be ~ed** naufragar.
shipyard ['ʃɪpjɑ:d] *n* estaleiro.
shire ['ʃaɪə*] (BRIT) *n* condado.
shirk [ʃə:k] *vt* (*work*) esquivar-se de; (*obligations*) não cumprir, faltar a.
shirt [ʃə:t] *n* camisa, blusa; **in ~ sleeves** em manga de camisa.
shirty ['ʃə:tɪ] (BRIT: *inf*) *adj* chateado, sem graça.
shit [ʃɪt] (*inf!*) *excl* merda (*!*).
shiver ['ʃɪvə*] *n* tremor *m*, arrepio ♦ *vi* tremer, estremecer, tiritar.
shoal [ʃəul] *n* (*of fish*) cardume *m*.
shock [ʃɔk] *n* (*impact*) choque *m*; (ELEC) descarga; (*emotional*) comoção *f*, abalo; (*start*) susto, sobressalto; (MED) trauma *m* ♦ *vt* dar um susto em, chocar; (*offend*) escandalizar; **suffering from ~** (MED) traumatizado; **it gave us a ~** ficamos chocados; **it came as a ~ to hear that ...** ficamos atônitos ao saber que ....
shock absorber [-əb'zɔ:bə*] *n* amortecedor *m*.
shocking ['ʃɔkɪŋ] *adj* (*awful*) chocante, lamentável; (*improper*) escandaloso; (*very bad*) péssimo.
shockproof ['ʃɔkpru:f] *adj* à prova de choque.
shock therapy *n* terapia de choque.
shock treatment *n* terapia de choque.
shod [ʃɔd] *pt, pp of* **shoe** ♦ *adj* calçado.
shoddy ['ʃɔdɪ] *adj* ordinário, de má qualidade.
shoe [ʃu:] (*pt, pp* **shod**) *n* sapato; (*for horse*) ferradura; (*also*: *brake ~*) sapata ♦ *vt* (*horse*) ferrar.
shoebrush ['ʃu:brʌʃ] *n* escova de sapato.
shoehorn ['ʃu:hɔ:n] *n* calçadeira.

shoelace ['ʃuːleɪs] *n* cadarço, cordão *m* (de sapato).
shoemaker ['ʃuːmeɪkə*] *n* sapateiro/a.
shoe polish *n* graxa de sapato.
shoe rack *n* porta-sapatos *m inv*.
shoeshop ['ʃuːʃɔp] *n* sapataria.
shoestring ['ʃuːstrɪŋ] *n*: **on a ~** (*fig*) com muito pouco dinheiro.
shoetree ['ʃuːtriː] *n* fôrma de sapato.
shone [ʃɔn] *pt, pp of* **shine.**
shoo [ʃuː] *excl* xô! ♦ *vt* (*also*: *~ away*, *~ off*) enxotar.
shook [ʃuk] *pt of* **shake.**
shoot [ʃuːt] (*pt, pp* **shot**) *n* (*on branch, seedling*) rebento, broto ♦ *vt* disparar; (*kill*) matar à bala, balear; (*wound*) ferir à bala, balear; (*execute*) fuzilar; (*film*) filmar, rodar ♦ *vi* (*with gun, bow*): **to ~ (at)** atirar (em); (*FOOTBALL*) chutar; **to ~ past sb** passar disparado por alguém; **to ~ in/out** entrar correndo/sair disparado.
shoot down *vt* (*plane*) derrubar, abater.
shoot up *vi* (*fig*) subir vertiginosamente.
shooting ['ʃuːtɪŋ] *n* (*shots*) tiros *mpl*, tiroteio; (*HUNTING*) caçada (com espingarda); (*attack*) tiroteio; (: *murder*) assassinato; (*CINEMA*) filmagens *fpl*.
shooting range *n* estande *m*.
shooting star *n* estrela cadente.
shop [ʃɔp] *n* loja; (*workshop*) oficina ♦ *vi* (*also*: *go ~ping*) ir fazer compras; **to talk ~** (*fig*) falar de negócios.
shop around *vi* comparar preços; (*fig*) estudar todas as possibilidades.
shop assistant (*BRIT*) *n* vendedor(a) *m/f*.
shop floor (*BRIT*) *n* operários *mpl*.
shopkeeper ['ʃɔpkiːpə*] *n* lojista *m/f*.
shoplift ['ʃɔplɪft] *vi* furtar (em lojas).
shoplifter ['ʃɔplɪftə*] *n* larápio/a de loja.
shoplifting ['ʃɔplɪftɪŋ] *n* furto (em lojas).
shopper ['ʃɔpə*] *n* comprador(a) *m/f*.
shopping ['ʃɔpɪŋ] *n* (*goods*) compras *fpl*.
shopping bag *n* bolsa (de compras).
shopping centre (*US* **shopping center**) *n* shopping (center) *m*.
shop-soiled (*BRIT*) *adj* manuseado.
shop steward *n* (*INDUSTRY*) representante *m/f* sindical.
shop window *n* vitrine *f* (*BR*), montra (*PT*).
shopworn ['ʃɔpwɔːn] (*US*) *adj* manuseado.
shore [ʃɔː*] *n* (*of sea*) costa, praia; (*of lake*) margem *f* ♦ *vt*: **to ~ (up)** reforçar, escorar; **on ~** em terra.
shore leave *n* (*NAUT*) licença para desembarcar.
shorn [ʃɔːn] *pp of* **shear.**
short [ʃɔːt] *adj* (*not long*) curto; (*in time*) breve, de curta duração; (*person*) baixo; (*curt*) seco, brusco; (*insufficient*) insuficiente, em falta ♦ *n* (*also*: *~ film*) curta-metragem *m*; **~s** *npl* (*also*: *a pair of ~s*) um calção (*BR*), um short (*BR*), uns calções (*PT*); **to be ~ of sth** estar em falta de algo; **to be in ~ supply** estar em falta; **I'm 3 ~** estão me faltando três; **in ~** em resumo; **~ of doing** a não ser fazer; **everything ~ of** tudo a não ser; **a ~ time ago** pouco tempo atrás; **in the ~ term** a curto prazo; **I'm ~ of time** tenho pouco tempo; **it is ~ for** é a abreviatura de; **to cut ~** (*speech, visit*) encurtar; (*person*) interromper; **to fall ~** ser deficiente; **to fall ~ of** não ser à altura de; **to run ~ of sth** ficar sem algo; **to stop ~** parar de repente; **to stop ~ of** chegar quase a.
shortage ['ʃɔːtɪdʒ] *n* escassez *f*, falta.
shortbread ['ʃɔːtbrɛd] *n* biscoito amanteigado.
short-change *vt*: **to ~ sb** roubar alguém no troco.
short-circuit *n* curto-circuito ♦ *vt* provocar um curto-circuito ♦ *vi* entrar em curto-circuito.
shortcoming ['ʃɔːtkʌmɪŋ] *n* defeito, imperfeição *f*, falha.
short(crust) pastry ['ʃɔːt(krʌst)-] (*BRIT*) *n* massa amanteigada.
shortcut ['ʃɔːtkʌt] *n* atalho.
shorten ['ʃɔːtən] *vt* encurtar; (*visit*) abreviar.
shortening ['ʃɔːtnɪŋ] *n* (*CULIN*) gordura.
shortfall ['ʃɔːtfɔːl] *n* déficit *m*.
shorthand ['ʃɔːthænd] (*BRIT*) *n* estenografia.
shorthand notebook (*BRIT*) *n* bloco para estenografia.
shorthand typist (*BRIT*) *n* estenodatilógrafo/a.
short list (*BRIT*) *n* (*for job*) lista dos candidatos escolhidos.
short-lived [-lɪvd] *adj* de curta duração.
shortly ['ʃɔːtlɪ] *adv* em breve, dentro em pouco.
shortness ['ʃɔːtnɪs] *n* (*of distance*) curteza; (*of time*) brevidade *f*; (*manner*) maneira brusca, secura.
short-sighted (*BRIT*) *adj* míope; (*fig*) imprevidente.
short-staffed [-stɑːft] *adj* com falta de pessoal.
short story *n* conto.
short-tempered *adj* irritadiço.
short-term *adj* (*effect*) a curto prazo.
short time *n*: **to work ~, to be on ~** trabalhar em regime de semana reduzida.
short wave *n* (*RADIO*) onda curta.
shot [ʃɔt] *pt, pp of* **shoot** ♦ *n* (*sound*) tiro, disparo; (*pellets*) chumbo; (*person*) atirador(a) *m/f*; (*try*) tentativa; (*injection*) injeção *f*; (*PHOT*) fotografia; **to fire a ~ at sb/sth** atirar em alguém/algo; **to have a ~ at (doing) sth** tentar fazer algo; **like a ~** disparado; (*very readily*) na hora; **to get ~ of sb/sth** (*inf*) livrar-se de alguém/algo; **a big ~** (*inf*) um mandachuva, um figurão.
shotgun ['ʃɔtgʌn] *n* espingarda.
should [ʃud] *aux vb*: **I ~ go now** devo ir embora agora; **he ~ be there now** ele já

***NB:** European Portuguese adds the following consonants to certain words:* **b** (sú(b)dito, su(b)til); **c** (a(c)ção, a(c)cionista, a(c)to); **m** (inde(m)ne); **p** (ado(p)ção, ado(p)tar); *for further details see p. xiii.*

deve ter chegado; **I ~ go if I were you** se eu fosse você eu iria; **I ~ like to** eu gostaria de; **~ he phone ...** caso ele telefone ....

shoulder ['ʃəuldə*] *n* ombro; (*BRIT*: *of road*): **hard ~** acostamento (*BR*), berma (*PT*) ♦ *vt* (*fig*) arcar com; **to look over one's ~** olhar para trás; **to rub ~s with sb** (*fig*) andar com alguém; **to give sb the cold ~** (*fig*) desprezar alguém, dar uma fria em alguém (*inf*).

shoulder bag *n* sacola a tiracolo.

shoulder blade *n* omoplata *m*.

shoulder strap *n* alça.

shouldn't ['ʃudnt] = **should not**.

shout [ʃaut] *n* grito ♦ *vt* gritar ♦ *vi* gritar, berrar; **to give sb a ~** chamar alguém.

shout down *vt* fazer calar com gritos.

shouting *n* gritaria, berreiro.

shove [ʃʌv] *n* empurrão *m* ♦ *vt* empurrar; (*inf*: *put*): **to ~ sth in** botar algo em; **he ~d me out of the way** ele me empurrou para o lado.

shove off *vi* (*NAUT*) zarpar, partir; (*fig*: *inf*) dar o fora.

shovel ['ʃʌvl] *n* pá *f*; (*mechanical*) escavadeira ♦ *vt* cavar com pá.

show [ʃəu] (*pt* **~ed**, *pp* **shown**) *n* (*of emotion*) demonstração *f*; (*semblance*) aparência; (*exhibition*) exibição *f*; (*THEATRE*) espetáculo, representação *f*; (*CINEMA*) sessão *f* ♦ *vt* mostrar; (*courage etc*) demonstrar, dar prova de; (*exhibit*) exibir, expor; (*film*) exibir ♦ *vi* mostrar-se; (*appear*) aparecer; **it doesn't ~** não parece; **I've nothing to ~ for it** não consegui nada; **to ~ sb to his seat/to the door** levar alguém ao seu lugar/até a porta; **to ~ a profit/loss** (*COMM*) apresentar lucros/prejuízo; **it just goes to ~ (that) ...** isso só mostra (que) ...; **to ask for a ~ of hands** pedir uma votação pelo levantamento das mãos; **to be on ~** estar em exposição; **it's just for ~** isso é só para fazer efeito, isso é só pra bonito (*inf*); **who's running the ~ here?** (*inf*) quem é que manda aqui?

show in *vt* mandar entrar.

show off *vi* (*pej*) mostrar-se, exibir-se ♦ *vt* (*display*) exibir, mostrar; (*pej*) fazer ostentação de.

show out *vt* levar até a porta.

show up *vi* (*stand out*) destacar-se; (*inf*: *turn up*) aparecer, pintar ♦ *vt* descobrir; (*unmask*) desmascarar.

show business *n* o mundo do espetáculo.

showcase ['ʃəukeɪs] *n* vitrina.

showdown ['ʃəudaun] *n* confrontação *f*.

shower ['ʃauə*] *n* (*rain*) pancada de chuva; (*of stones etc*) chuva, enxurrada; (*also*: **~** *bath*) chuveiro ♦ *vi* tomar banho (de chuveiro) ♦ *vt*: **to ~ sb with** (*gifts etc*) cumular alguém de; **to have** *or* **take a ~** tomar banho (de chuveiro).

shower cap *n* touca de banho.

showerproof ['ʃauəpru:f] *adj* impermeável.

showery ['ʃauərɪ] *adj* (*weather*) chuvoso.

showground ['ʃəugraund] *n* recinto da feira.

showing ['ʃəuɪŋ] *n* (*of film*) projeção *f*, exibição *f*.

show jumping [-'dʒʌmpɪŋ] *n* hipismo.

showman ['ʃəumən] (*irreg*) *n* artista *mf*; (*fig*) pessoa expansiva.

showmanship ['ʃəumənʃɪp] *n* senso teatral.

showmen ['ʃəumɛn] *npl of* **showman**.

shown [ʃəun] *pp of* **show**.

show-off (*inf*) *n* (*person*) exibicionista *m/f*, faroleiro/a.

showpiece ['ʃəupi:s] *n* (*of exhibition etc*) obra mais importante; **that hospital is a ~** aquele é um hospital modelo.

showroom ['ʃəurum] *n* sala de exposição.

showy ['ʃəuɪ] *adj* vistoso, chamativo.

shrank [ʃræŋk] *pt of* **shrink**.

shrapnel ['ʃræpnl] *n* estilhaços *mpl*.

shred [ʃrɛd] *n* (*gen pl*) tira, pedaço ♦ *vt* rasgar em tiras, retalhar; (*CULIN*) desfiar, picar; (*documents*) fragmentar; **not a ~ of evidence** prova alguma.

shredder ['ʃrɛdə*] *n* (*for documents*) fragmentadora.

shrew [ʃru:] *n* (*ZOOL*) musaranho; (*pej*: *woman*) megera.

shrewd [ʃru:d] *adj* astuto, perspicaz, sutil.

shrewdness ['ʃru:dnɪs] *n* astúcia.

shriek [ʃri:k] *n* grito ♦ *vt*, *vi* gritar, berrar.

shrift [ʃrɪft] *n*: **to give sb short ~** dar uma resposta a alguém sem maiores explicações.

shrill [ʃrɪl] *adj* agudo, estridente.

shrimp [ʃrɪmp] *n* camarão *m*.

shrine [ʃraɪn] *n* santuário, relicário.

shrink [ʃrɪŋk] (*pt* **shrank**, *pp* **shrunk**) *vi* encolher; (*be reduced*) reduzir-se ♦ *vt* fazer encolher ♦ *n* (*inf*: *pej*) psicanalista *m/f*; **to ~ from doing sth** não se atrever a fazer algo.

shrinkage ['ʃrɪŋkɪdʒ] *n* encolhimento, redução *f*.

shrink-wrap *vt* embalar a vácuo.

shrivel ['ʃrɪvl] *vt* (*also*: **~ up**: *dry*) secar; (: *crease*) enrugar ♦ *vi* secar-se, enrugar-se, murchar.

shroud [ʃraud] *n* mortalha ♦ *vt*: **~ed in mystery** envolto em mistério.

Shrove Tuesday [ʃrəuv-] *n* terça-feira gorda.

shrub [ʃrʌb] *n* arbusto.

shrubbery ['ʃrʌbərɪ] *n* arbustos *mpl*.

shrug [ʃrʌg] *n* encolhimento dos ombros ♦ *vt*, *vi*: **to ~ (one's shoulders)** encolher os ombros, dar de ombros (*BR*).

shrug off *vt* negar a importância de.

shrunk [ʃrʌŋk] *pp of* **shrink**.

shrunken ['ʃrʌŋkn] *adj* encolhido.

shudder ['ʃʌdə*] *n* estremecimento, tremor *m* ♦ *vi* estremecer, tremer de medo.

shuffle ['ʃʌfl] *vt* (*cards*) embaralhar; **to ~ (one's feet)** arrastar os pés.

shun [ʃʌn] *vt* evitar, afastar-se de.

shunt [ʃʌnt] *vt* (*RAIL*) manobrar, desviar ♦ *vi*: **to ~ (to and fro)** ir e vir.

shunting ['ʃʌntɪŋ] *n* (*RAIL*) manobras *fpl*.

shunting yard *n* pátio de manobras.

shush [ʃuʃ] *excl* psiu!

shut [ʃʌt] (*pt*, *pp* **shut**) *vt* fechar ♦ *vi*

fechar(-se).
shut down *vt* fechar; (*machine*) parar ♦ *vi* fechar.
shut off *vt* (*supply etc*) cortar, interromper.
shut out *vt* (*person, cold*) impedir que entre; (*noise*) abafar; (*memory*) reprimir.
shut up *vi* (*inf*: *keep quiet*) calar-se, calar a boca ♦ *vt* (*close*) fechar; (*silence*) calar.
shutdown ['ʃʌtdaun] *n* paralização *f*.
shutter ['ʃʌtə*] *n* veneziana; (*PHOT*) obturador *m*.
shuttle ['ʃʌtl] *n* (*in weaving*) lançadeira; (*plane*: *also*: ~ *service*) ponte *f* aérea ♦ *vi* (*vehicle, person*) ir e vir ♦ *vt* (*passengers*) transportar de ida e volta.
shuttlecock ['ʃʌtlkɔk] *n* peteca.
shy [ʃaɪ] *adj* tímido ♦ *vi*: **to ~ away from doing sth** (*fig*) não se atrever a fazer algo.
shyness ['ʃaɪnɪs] *n* timidez *f*.
Siam [saɪ'æm] *n* Sião *m*.
Siamese [saɪə'mi:z] *adj*: ~ **cat** gato siamês; ~ **twins** irmãos *mpl* siameses/irmãs *fpl* siamesas.
Siberia [saɪ'bɪərɪə] *n* Sibéria *f*.
siblings ['sɪblɪŋz] *npl* (*formal*) irmãos *mpl*.
Sicilian [sɪ'sɪlɪən] *adj, n* siciliano/a.
Sicily ['sɪsɪlɪ] *n* Sicília.
sick [sɪk] *adj* (*ill*) doente; (*nauseated*) enjoado; (*humour*) negro; (*vomiting*): **to be ~** vomitar; **to feel ~** estar enjoado; **to fall ~** ficar doente; **to be (off) ~** estar ausente por motivo de doença; **to be ~ of** (*fig*) estar cheio *or* farto de; **he makes me ~** (*fig*: *inf*) ele me enche o saco.
sick bay *n* enfermaria.
sicken ['sɪkən] *vt* dar náuseas a ♦ *vi*: **to be ~ing for sth** (*cold, flu etc*) estar no começo de algo.
sickening ['sɪkənɪŋ] *adj* (*fig*) repugnante.
sickle ['sɪkl] *n* foice *f*.
sick leave *n* licença por doença.
sickly ['sɪklɪ] *adj* doentio; (*causing nausea*) nauseante.
sickness ['sɪknɪs] *n* doença, indisposição *f*; (*vomiting*) náusea, enjôo.
sickness benefit *n* auxílio-enfermidade *m*, auxílio-doença *m*.
sick pay *n salário pago em período de doença.*
sickroom ['sɪkru:m] *n* enfermaria.
side [saɪd] *n* (*gen*) lado; (*of body*) flanco; (*of lake*) margem *f*; (*aspect*) aspecto; (*team*) time *m* (*BR*), equipa (*PT*); (*of hill*) declive *m*; (*page*) página; (*of meat*) costela ♦ *cpd* (*door, entrance*) lateral ♦ *vi*: **to ~ with sb** tomar o partido de alguém; **by the ~ of** ao lado de; **~ by ~** lado a lado, juntos; **on this/that** *or* **the other ~** do lado de cá/do lado de lá; **they are on our ~** (*in game*) fazem parte do nosso time; (*in discussion*) concordam com nós; **from ~ to ~** para lá e para cá; **from all ~s** de todos os lados; **to take ~s with** pôr-se ao lado de.
sideboard ['saɪdbɔ:d] *n* aparador *m*; **~s** *npl* (*BRIT*) suiças *fpl*, costeletas *fpl*.
sideburns ['saɪdbə:nz] *npl* suiças *fpl*, costeletas *fpl*.
sidecar ['saɪdkɑ:*] *n* sidecar *m*.
side dish *n* guarnição *f*.
side drum *n* (*MUS*) caixa clara.
side effect *n* efeito colateral.
sidekick ['saɪdkɪk] (*inf*) *n* camarada *m/f*.
sidelight ['saɪdlaɪt] *n* (*AUT*) luz *f* lateral.
sideline ['saɪdlaɪn] *n* (*SPORT*) linha lateral; (*fig*) linha adicional de produtos; (: *job*) emprego suplementar.
sidelong ['saɪdlɔŋ] *adj* de soslaio.
side plate *n* pequeno prato.
side road *n* rua lateral.
sidesaddle ['saɪdsædl] *adv* de silhão.
side show *n* (*stall*) barraca.
sidestep ['saɪdstɛp] *vt* evitar ♦ *vi* (*BOXING etc*) dar um passo para o lado.
sidetrack ['saɪdtræk] *vt* (*fig*) desviar (do seu propósito).
sidewalk ['saɪdwɔ:k] (*US*) *n* calçada.
sideways ['saɪdweɪz] *adv* de lado.
siding ['saɪdɪŋ] *n* (*RAIL*) desvio, ramal *m*.
sidle ['saɪdl] *vi*: **to ~ up (to)** aproximar-se furtivamente (de).
siege [si:dʒ] *n* sítio, assédio; **to lay ~ to** assediar.
siege economy *n* economia de guerra.
Sierra Leone [sɪ'ɛrəlɪ'əun] *n* Serra Leoa (*no article*).
sieve [sɪv] *n* peneira ♦ *vt* peneirar.
sift [sɪft] *vt* peneirar; (*fig*: *information*) esquadrinhar, analisar minuciosamente ♦ *vi* (*fig*): **to ~ through** examinar minuciosamente.
sigh [saɪ] *n* suspiro ♦ *vi* suspirar.
sight [saɪt] *n* (*faculty*) vista, visão *f*; (*spectacle*) espetáculo; (*on gun*) mira ♦ *vt* avistar; **in ~** à vista; **out of ~** longe dos olhos; **at ~** (*COMM*) à vista; **at first ~** à primeira vista; **I know her by ~** conheço-a de vista; **to catch ~ of sb/sth** avistar alguém/algo; **to lose ~ of sb/sth** perder alguém/algo de vista; **to set one's ~s on sth** visar algo.
sighted ['saɪtɪd] *adj* que enxerga; **partially ~** com vista parcial.
sightseeing ['saɪtsi:ɪŋ] *n* turismo; **to go ~** fazer turismo, passear.
sightseer ['saɪtsi:ə*] *n* turista *m/f*.
sign [saɪn] *n* (*with hand*) sinal *m*, aceno; (*indication*) indício; (*trace*) vestígio; (*notice*) letreiro, tabuleta; (*also*: *road* ~) placa; (*of zodiac, LING*) signo ♦ *vt* assinar; **as a ~ of** como sinal de; **it's a good/bad ~** é um bom/mau sinal; **plus/minus ~** sinal de mais/menos; **there's no ~ of a change of mind** não há sinal *or* indícios de uma mudança de atitude; **he was showing ~s of improvement** ele estava começando a melhorar; **to ~ one's name** assinar.
sign away *vt* (*rights etc*) abrir mão de.

NB*: European Portuguese adds the following consonants to certain words:* **b** (sú(b)dito, su(b)til); **c** (a(c)ção, a(c)cionista, a(c)to); **m** (inde(m)ne); **p** (ado(p)ção, ado(p)tar); *for further details see p. xiii.*

sign off *vi* (*RADIO*, *TV*) terminar a transmissão.
sign on *vi* (*MIL*) alistar-se; (*as unemployed*) cadastrar-se para receber auxílio-desemprego; (*enrol*): **to ~ on for a course** matricular-se num curso ♦ *vt* (*MIL*) alistar; (*employee*) efetivar.
sign out *vi* assinar o registro na partida.
sign over *vt*: **to ~ sth over to sb** assinar a transferência de algo para alguém.
sign up *vi* (*MIL*) alistar-se ♦ *vt* alistar.
signal ['sɪgnl] *n* sinal *m*, aviso; (*US*: *TEL*) ruído discal ♦ *vi* (*AUT*) sinalizar, dar sinal ♦ *vt* (*person*) fazer sinais para; (*message*) transmitir; **to ~ a left/right turn** (*AUT*) dar sinal para esquerda/direita; **to ~ to sb (to do sth)** fazer sinais para alguém (fazer algo).
signal box *n* (*RAIL*) cabine *f* de sinaleiro.
signalman ['sɪgnlmən] (*irreg*) *n* sinaleiro.
signatory ['sɪgnətərɪ] *n* signatário/a.
signature ['sɪgnətʃə*] *n* assinatura.
signature tune *n* tema *m* (de abertura).
signet ring ['sɪgnət-] *n* anel *m* com o sinete *or* a chancela.
significance [sɪg'nɪfɪkəns] *n* significado; (*importance*) importância; **that is of no ~** isto não tem importância alguma.
significant [sɪg'nɪfɪkənt] *adj* significativo, importante.
significantly [sɪg'nɪfɪkəntlɪ] *adv* (*improve, increase*) significativamente; (*smile*) sugestivamente; **and, ~, ...** e, significativamente, ...
signify ['sɪgnɪfaɪ] *vt* significar.
sign language *n* mímica, linguagem *f* através de sinais.
signpost ['saɪnpəust] *n* indicador *m*; (*traffic*) placa de sinalização.
silage ['saɪlɪdʒ] *n* (*fodder*) silagem *f*; (*method*) ensilagem *f*.
silence ['saɪləns] *n* silêncio ♦ *vt* silenciar, impor silêncio a; (*guns*) silenciar.
silencer ['saɪlənsə*] *n* (*on gun*) silenciador *m*; (*AUT*) silencioso.
silent ['saɪlənt] *adj* silencioso; (*not speaking*) calado; (*film*) mudo; **to keep** *or* **remain ~** manter-se em silêncio.
silently ['saɪləntlɪ] *adv* silenciosamente.
silent partner *n* (*COMM*) sócio/a comanditário/a.
silhouette [sɪlu:'ɛt] *n* silhueta ♦ *vt*: **~d against** em silhueta contra.
silicon ['sɪlɪkən] *n* silício.
silicon chip *n* placa *or* chip *m* de silício.
silicone ['sɪlɪkəun] *n* silicone *m*.
silk [sɪlk] *n* seda ♦ *cpd* de seda.
silky ['sɪlkɪ] *adj* sedoso.
sill [sɪl] *n* (*also*: *window ~*) parapeito, peitoril *m*; (*AUT*) soleira.
silly ['sɪlɪ] *adj* (*person*) bobo, idiota, imbecil; (*idea*) absurdo, ridículo; **to do something ~** fazer uma besteira.
silo ['saɪləu] *n* silo.
silt [sɪlt] *n* sedimento, aluvião *m*.
silver ['sɪlvə*] *n* prata; (*money*) moedas *fpl*; (*also*: *~ware*) prataria ♦ *cpd* de prata.
silver foil *n* papel *m* de prata.
silver paper (*BRIT*) *n* papel *m* de prata.
silver-plated [-'pleɪtɪd] *adj* prateado, banhado a prata.
silversmith ['sɪlvəsmɪθ] *n* prateiro/a.
silverware ['sɪlvəwɛə*] *n* prataria.
silver wedding (anniversary) *n* bodas *fpl* de prata.
silvery ['sɪlvərɪ] *adj* prateado.
similar ['sɪmɪlə*] *adj*: **~ to** parecido com, semelhante a.
similarity [sɪmɪ'lærɪtɪ] *n* semelhança.
similarly ['sɪmɪləlɪ] *adv* da mesma maneira.
simmer ['sɪmə*] *vi* cozer em fogo lento, ferver lentamente.
simmer down (*inf*) *vi* (*fig*) acalmar-se.
simper ['sɪmpə*] *vi* sorrir afetadamente.
simpering ['sɪmpərɪŋ] *adj* idiota.
simple ['sɪmpl] *adj* simples *inv*; (*foolish*) ingênuo; **the ~ truth** a pura verdade.
simple interest *n* juros *mpl* simples.
simple-minded *adj* simplório.
simpleton ['sɪmpltən] *n* simplório/a, pateta *m/f*.
simplicity [sɪm'plɪsɪtɪ] *n* simplicidade *f*.
simplification [sɪmplɪfɪ'keɪʃən] *n* simplificação *f*.
simplify ['sɪmplɪfaɪ] *vt* simplificar.
simply ['sɪmplɪ] *adv* simplesmente.
simulate ['sɪmjuleɪt] *vt* simular.
simulation [sɪmju'leɪʃən] *n* simulação *f*.
simultaneous [sɪməl'teɪnɪəs] *adj* simultâneo.
simultaneously [sɪməl'teɪnɪəslɪ] *adv* simultaneamente.
sin [sɪn] *n* pecado ♦ *vi* pecar.
Sinai ['saɪneɪaɪ] *n* Sinai *m*.
since [sɪns] *adv* desde então, depois ♦ *prep* desde ♦ *conj* (*time*) desde que; (*because*) porque, visto que, já que; **~ then** desde então; **~ Monday** desde segunda-feira; **(ever) ~ I arrived** desde que eu cheguei.
sincere [sɪn'sɪə*] *adj* sincero.
sincerely [sɪn'sɪəlɪ] *adv* sinceramente; **Yours ~** (*at end of letter*) atenciosamente.
sincerity [sɪn'sɛrɪtɪ] *n* sinceridade *f*.
sine [saɪn] *n* (*MATH*) seno.
sinew ['sɪnju:] *n* tendão *m*.
sinful ['sɪnful] *adj* (*thought*) pecaminoso; (*person*) pecador(a).
sing [sɪŋ] (*pt* **sang**, *pp* **sung**) *vt*, *vi* cantar.
Singapore [sɪŋgə'pɔ:*] *n* Cingapura (*no article*).
singe [sɪndʒ] *vt* chamuscar.
singer ['sɪŋə*] *n* cantor(a) *m/f*.
Singhalese [sɪŋə'li:z] *adj* = **Sinhalese**.
singing ['sɪŋɪŋ] *n* (*gen*) canto; (*songs*) canções *fpl*; (*in the ears*) zumbido.
single ['sɪŋgl] *adj* único, só; (*unmarried*) solteiro; (*not double*) simples *inv* ♦ *n* (*also*: *~ ticket*) passagem *f* de ida; (*record*) compacto; **~s** *npl* (*TENNIS*) simples *f inv*: (*US*: *~ people*) solteiros *mpl*; **not a ~ one was left** não sobrou nenhum; **every ~ day** todo santo dia.

single out *vt* (*choose*) escolher; (*point out*) distinguir.
single bed *n* cama de solteiro.
single-breasted [-'brɛstɪd] *adj* não trespassado.
single file *n*: **in** ~ em fila indiana.
single-handed [-'hændɪd] *adv* sem ajuda, sozinho.
single-minded *adj* determinado.
single parent *n* pai *m* solteiro/mãe *f* solteira.
single room *n* quarto individual.
singlet ['sɪŋglɪt] *n* camiseta.
singly ['sɪŋglɪ] *adv* separadamente.
singsong ['sɪŋsɔŋ] *adj* (*tone*) cantado ♦ *n* (*songs*): **to have a** ~ cantar.
singular ['sɪŋgjulə*] *adj* (*odd*) esquisito; (LING) singular ♦ *n* (LING) singular *m*; **in the feminine** ~ no feminino singular.
singularly ['sɪŋgjuləlɪ] *adv* particularmente.
Sinhalese [sɪnhə'li:z] *adj* cingalês/esa.
sinister ['sɪnɪstə*] *adj* sinistro.
sink [sɪŋk] (*pt* **sank**, *pp* **sunk**) *n* pia ♦ *vt* (*ship*) afundar; (*foundations*) escavar; (*piles etc*): **to** ~ **sth** enterrar algo ♦ *vi* afundar-se, ir a pique; (*share prices*) cair; **he sank into a chair/the mud** ele afundou na cadeira/na lama; **a ~ing feeling** um vazio no estômago.
sink in *vi* (*fig*) penetrar, entranhar-se; **it took a long time to** ~ **in** demorou muito para ser entendido.
sinking fund ['sɪŋkɪŋ-] *n* fundo de amortização.
sink unit *n* pia.
sinner ['sɪnə*] *n* pecador(a) *m/f*.
Sino- ['saɪnəu] *prefix* sino-.
sinuous ['sɪnjuəs] *adj* sinuoso.
sinus ['saɪnəs] *n* (ANAT) seio (nasal).
sinusitis [saɪnə'saɪtəs] *n* sinusite *f*.
sip [sɪp] *n* gole *m* ♦ *vt* sorver, bebericar.
siphon ['saɪfən] *n* sifão *m* ♦ *vt* (*also*: ~ *off*) extrair com sifão; (*fig*: *funds*) desviar.
sir [sə*] *n* senhor *m*; **S~ John Smith** Sir John Smith; **yes** ~ sim, senhor; **Dear S~** (*in letter*) (Prezado) Senhor.
siren ['saɪərn] *n* sirena.
sirloin ['sə:lɔɪn] *n* lombo de vaca.
sirloin steak *n* filé *m* de alcatra.
sisal ['saɪsəl] *n* sisal *m*.
sissy ['sɪsɪ] (*inf*) *n* fresco.
sister ['sɪstə*] *n* irmã *f*; (*nurse*) enfermeira-chefe *f*; (*nun*) freira ♦ *cpd*: ~ **organization** organização *f* congênere; ~ **ship** navio gêmeo.
sister-in-law (*pl* **sisters-in-law**) *n* cunhada.
sit [sɪt] (*pt, pp* **sat**) *vi* sentar-se; (*be sitting*) estar sentado; (*assembly*) reunir-se; (*for painter*) posar; (*dress*) cair ♦ *vt* (*exam*) prestar; **to** ~ **on a committee** ser membro de um comitê; **to** ~ **tight** não se mexer; (*fig*) esperar.
sit about *vi* ficar sentado não fazendo nada.
sit around *vi* ficar sentado não fazendo nada.
sit back *vi* acomodar-se num assento.
sit down *vi* sentar-se; **to be ~ting down** estar sentado.
sit in *vi*: **to** ~ **in on a discussion** assistir a uma discussão.
sit up *vi* endireitar-se; (*not go to bed*) aguardar acordado, velar.
sitcom ['sɪtkɔm] *n abbr* (TV: = *situation comedy*) comédia de costumes.
sit-down *adj*: ~ **strike** greve *f* de braços cruzados; **a** ~ **meal** uma refeição servida à mesa.
site [saɪt] *n* local *m*, sítio; (*also*: *building* ~) lote *m* (de terreno) ♦ *vt* situar, localizar.
sit-in *n* (*demonstration*) *ocupação de um local como forma de protesto*, manifestação *f* pacífica.
siting ['saɪtɪŋ] *n* (*location*) localização *f*.
sitter ['sɪtə*] *n* (*for painter*) modelo; (*also*: *baby~*) baby-sitter *m/f*.
sitting ['sɪtɪŋ] *n* (*of assembly etc*) sessão *f*; (*in canteen*) turno.
sitting member *n* (POL) parlamentar *m/f*.
sitting room *n* sala de estar.
sitting tenant (BRIT) *n* inquilino/a.
situate ['sɪtjueɪt] *vt* situar.
situated ['sɪtjueɪtɪd] *adj* situado.
situation [sɪtju'eɪʃən] *n* situação *f*; **"~s vacant/wanted"** (BRIT) "empregos oferecem-se/procurados".
situation comedy *n* (THEATRE, TV) comédia de costumes.
six [sɪks] *num* seis; *see also* **five**.
sixteen ['sɪks'ti:n] *num* dezesseis; *see also* **five**.
sixth [sɪksθ] *num* sexto; **the upper/lower** ~ (BRIT: SCH) *os dois últimos anos do colégio*; *see also* **fifth**.
sixty ['sɪkstɪ] *num* sessenta; *see also* **fifty**.
size [saɪz] *n* (*gen*) tamanho; (*extent*) extensão *f*; (*of clothing*) tamanho, medida; (*of shoes*) número; (*glue*) goma; **I take** ~ **14** (*of dress*) ≈ meu tamanho é 44; **the small/large** ~ (*of soap powder etc*) o tamanho pequeno/grande; **what** ~ **do you take in shoes?** que número você calça?; **it's the** ~ **of ...** é do tamanho de ....
size up *vt* avaliar, formar uma opinião sobre.
sizeable ['saɪzəbl] *adj* considerável, importante.
sizzle ['sɪzl] *vi* chiar.
SK (CANADA) *abbr* = **Saskatchewan**.
skate [skeɪt] (*pl* **~s**) *n* patim *m*; (*fish*: *pl*: *inv*) arraia ♦ *vi* patinar.
skate around *vt fus* (*problem*) evitar.
skate over *vt fus* (*problem*) evitar.
skateboard ['skeɪtbɔ:d] *n* skate *m*, patim-tábua *m*.
skater ['skeɪtə*] *n* patinador(a) *m/f*.
skating ['skeɪtɪŋ] *n* patinação *f*.

skating rink *n* rinque *m* de patinação.
skeleton ['skɛlɪtn] *n* esqueleto; (*TECH*) armação *f*; (*outline*) esquema *m*, esboço.
skeleton key *n* chave *f* mestra.
skeleton staff *n* pessoal *m* reduzido (ao mínimo).
skeptic *etc* ['skɛptɪk] (*US*) = **sceptic** *etc*.
sketch [skɛtʃ] *n* (*drawing*) desenho; (*outline*) esboço, croqui *m*; (*THEATRE*) quadro, esquete *m* ♦ *vt* desenhar, esboçar.
sketch book *n* caderno de rascunho.
sketch pad *n* bloco de desenho.
sketchy ['skɛtʃɪ] *adj* incompleto, superficial.
skew [skju:] (*BRIT*) *n*: **on the ~** fora de esquadria.
skewer ['skju:ə*] *n* espetinho.
ski [ski:] *n* esqui *m* ♦ *vi* esquiar.
ski boot *n* bota de esquiar.
skid [skɪd] *n* derrapagem *f* ♦ *vi* derrapar, deslizar.
skid mark *n* marca de derrapagem.
skier ['ski:ə*] *n* esquiador(a) *m/f*.
skiing ['ski:ɪŋ] *n* esqui *m*; **to go ~** ir esquiar.
ski instructor *n* instrutor(a) *m/f* de esqui.
ski jump *n* pista para saltos de esqui; (*event*) salto de esqui.
skilful ['skɪlful] (*US* **skillful**) *adj* habilidoso, jeitoso.
skilfully ['skɪlfəlɪ] (*US* **skillfully**) *adv* habilmente.
ski lift *n* ski lift *m*.
skill [skɪl] *n* habilidade *f*, perícia; (*technique*) técnica.
skilled [skɪld] *adj* hábil, perito; (*worker*) especializado, qualificado.
skillet ['skɪlɪt] *n* frigideira.
skillful *etc* ['skɪlful] (*US*) = **skilful** *etc*.
skim [skɪm] *vt* (*milk*) desnatar; (*glide over*) roçar ♦ *vi*: **to ~ through** (*book*) folhear.
skimmed milk [skɪmd-] *n* leite *m* desnatado.
skimp [skɪmp] *vt* (*work*) atamancar; (*cloth etc*) economizar, regatear.
skimpy ['skɪmpɪ] *adj* (*meagre*) escasso, insuficiente; (*skirt*) sumário.
skin [skɪn] *n* (*gen*) pele *f*; (*of fruit, vegetable*) casca; (*on pudding, paint*) película ♦ *vt* (*fruit etc*) descascar; (*animal*) tirar a pele de; **wet** *or* **soaked to the ~** encharcado, molhado como um pinto.
skin-deep *adj* superficial.
skin diver *n* mergulhador(a) *m/f*.
skin diving *n* caça-submarina.
skinflint ['skɪnflɪnt] *n* pão-duro *m*.
skin graft *n* enxerto de pele.
skinny ['skɪnɪ] *adj* magro, descarnado.
skin test *n* cutirreação *f*.
skintight ['skɪn'taɪt] *adj* (*dress etc*) justo, grudado (no corpo).
skip [skɪp] *n* salto, pulo; (*container*) balde *m* ♦ *vi* saltar; (*with rope*) pular corda ♦ *vt* (*pass over*) omitir, saltar; **to ~ school** (*esp US*) matar aula.
ski pants *npl* calça (*BR*) *or* calças *fpl* (*PT*) de esquiar.
ski pole *n* vara de esqui.
skipper ['skɪpə*] *n* (*NAUT, SPORT*) capitão *m* ♦ *vt* capitanear.
skipping rope ['skɪpɪŋ-] (*BRIT*) *n* corda (de pular).
ski resort *n* estação *f* de esqui.
skirmish ['skə:mɪʃ] *n* escaramuça.
skirt [skə:t] *n* saia ♦ *vt* (*surround*) rodear; (*go round*) orlar, circundar.
skirting board ['skə:tɪŋ-] (*BRIT*) *n* rodapé *m*.
ski run *n* pista de esqui.
ski suit *n* traje *m* de esqui.
skit [skɪt] *n* paródia, sátira.
ski tow *n* ski lift *m*.
skittle ['skɪtl] *n* pau *m*; **~s** *n* (*game*) (jogo de) boliche *m* (*BR*), jogo da bola (*PT*).
skive [skaɪv] (*BRIT*: *inf*) *vi* evitar trabalhar.
skulk [skʌlk] *vi* esconder-se.
skull [skʌl] *n* caveira; (*ANAT*) crânio.
skullcap ['skʌlkæp] *n* solidéu *m*; (*worn by Pope*) barrete *m*.
skunk [skʌŋk] *n* gambá *m*; (*fig*: *person*) cafajeste *m/f*, pessoa vil.
sky [skaɪ] *n* céu *m*; **to praise sb to the skies** pôr alguém nas nuvens.
sky-blue *adj* azul-celeste *inv*.
sky-high *adv* muito alto ♦ *adj*: **prices are ~** os preços dispararam.
skylark ['skaɪlɑ:k] *n* (*bird*) cotovia.
skylight ['skaɪlaɪt] *n* clarabóia, escotilha.
skyline ['skaɪlaɪn] *n* (*horizon*) linha do horizonte; (*of city*) silhueta.
skyscraper ['skaɪskreɪpə*] *n* arranha-céu *m*.
slab [slæb] *n* (*stone*) bloco; (*flat*) laje *f*; (*of cake*) fatia grossa.
slack [slæk] *adj* (*loose*) frouxo; (*slow*) lerdo; (*careless*) descuidoso, desmazelado; (*COMM*: *market*) inativo, frouxo; (: *demand*) fraco ♦ *n* (*in rope*) brando; **~s** *npl* calça (*BR*), calças *fpl* (*PT*); **business is ~** os negócios vão mal.
slacken ['slækən] *vi* (*also*: **~ off**) afrouxar-se ♦ *vt* afrouxar; (*speed*) diminuir.
slag [slæg] *n* escória, escombros *mpl*.
slag heap *n* monte *m* de escória *or* de escombros.
slain [sleɪn] *pp of* **slay**.
slake [sleɪk] *vt* (*one's thirst*) matar.
slalom ['slɑ:ləm] *n* slalom *m*.
slam [slæm] *vt* (*door*) bater *or* fechar (com violência); (*throw*) atirar violentamente; (*criticize*) malhar, criticar ♦ *vi* fechar-se (com violência).
slander ['slɑ:ndə*] *n* calúnia, difamação *f* ♦ *vt* caluniar, difamar.
slanderous ['slɑ:ndərəs] *adj* calunioso, difamatório.
slang [slæŋ] *n* gíria; (*jargon*) jargão *m*.
slant [slɑ:nt] *n* declive *m*, inclinação *f*; (*fig*) ponto de vista.
slanted ['slɑ:ntɪd] *adj* tendencioso.
slanting ['slɑ:ntɪŋ] *adj* inclinado, de esguelha.
slap [slæp] *n* tapa *m or f* ♦ *vt* dar um(a) tapa em ♦ *adv* (*directly*) diretamente, exatamente.
slapdash ['slæpdæʃ] *adj* impetuoso, descuidado.
slapstick ['slæpstɪk] *n* (*comedy*) (comédia-)

pastelão *m*.
slap-up (*BRIT*) *adj*: **a ~ meal** uma refeição suntuosa.
slash [slæʃ] *vt* cortar, talhar; (*fig*: *prices*) cortar.
slat [slæt] *n* (*of wood*) ripa.
slate [sleɪt] *n* ardósia ♦ *vt* (*fig*: *criticize*) criticar duramente, arrasar.
slaughter ['slɔːtə*] *n* (*of animals*) matança; (*of people*) carnificina ♦ *vt* (*animals*) abater; (*people*) matar, massacrar.
slaughterhouse ['slɔːtəhaus] (*irreg*) *n* matadouro.
Slav [slɑːv] *adj*, *n* eslavo/a.
slave [sleɪv] *n* escravo ♦ *vi* (*also*: ~ *away*) trabalhar como escravo; **to ~ (away) at sth/at doing sth** trabalhar feito condenado em algo/fazendo algo.
slave labour *n* trabalho escravo.
slaver ['slævə*] *vi* (*dribble*) babar.
slavery ['sleɪvərɪ] *n* escravidão *f*.
Slavic ['slɑːvɪk] *adj* eslavo.
slavish ['sleɪvɪʃ] *adj* servil.
Slavonic [slə'vɔnɪk] *adj* eslavo.
slay [sleɪ] (*pt* **slew**, *pp* **slain**) *vt* (*literary*) matar.
SLD (*BRIT*) *n abbr* (*POL*) = **Social and Liberal Democratic Party**.
sleazy ['sliːzɪ] *adj* (*fig*: *place*) sórdido.
sled [slɛd] (*US*) *n* trenó *m*.
sledge [slɛdʒ] (*BRIT*) *n* trenó *m*.
sledgehammer ['slɛdʒhæmə*] *n* marreta, malho.
sleek [sliːk] *adj* (*gen*) macio, lustroso; (*car*, *boat*) aerodinâmico.
sleep [sliːp] (*pt*, *pp* **slept**) *n* sono ♦ *vi* dormir ♦ *vt*: **we can ~ 4** podemos acomodar 4 pessoas; **to go to ~** dormir, adormecer; **to have a good night's ~** ter uma boa noite de sono; **to put to ~** (*patient*) fazer dormir; (*animal*: *euphemism*: *kill*) sacrificar; **to ~ lightly** ter sono leve; **to ~ with sb** (*euphemism*) dormir com alguém.
sleep in *vi* (*oversleep*) dormir demais; (*lie in*) dormir até tarde.
sleeper ['sliːpə*] *n* (*person*) dorminhoco/a; (*RAIL*: *on track*) dormente *m*; (: *train*) vagão-leitos *m* (*BR*), carruagem-camas *f* (*PT*).
sleepily ['sliːpɪlɪ] *adv* sonolentamente.
sleeping ['sliːpɪŋ] *adj* adormecido, que dorme.
sleeping bag *n* saco de dormir.
sleeping car *n* vagão-leitos *m* (*BR*), carruagem-camas *f* (*PT*).
sleeping partner (*BRIT*) *n* (*COMM*) sócio comanditário.
sleeping pill *n* pílula para dormir.
sleepless ['sliːplɪs] *adj*: **a ~ night** uma noite em claro.
sleeplessness ['sliːplɪsnɪs] *n* insônia.
sleepwalker ['sliːpwɔːkə*] *n* sonâmbulo.
sleepy ['sliːpɪ] *adj* sonolento; **to be** *or* **feel ~** estar com sono.
sleet [sliːt] *n* chuva com neve *or* granizo.
sleeve [sliːv] *n* manga; (*of record*) capa.
sleeveless ['sliːvlɪs] *adj* (*garment*) sem manga.
sleigh [sleɪ] *n* trenó *m*.
sleight [slaɪt] *n*: **~ of hand** prestidigitação *f*.
slender ['slɛndə*] *adj* magro, delgado; (*means*) escasso, insuficiente.
slept [slɛpt] *pt*, *pp of* **sleep**.
sleuth [sluːθ] (*inf*) *n* detetive *m*.
slew [sluː] *pt of* **slay** ♦ *vi* (*also*: ~ *round*) virar.
slice [slaɪs] *n* (*of meat*, *bread*) fatia; (*of lemon*) rodela; (*of fish*) posta; (*utensil*) pá *f or* espátula de bolo ♦ *vt* cortar em fatias; **~d bread** pão *m* em fatias.
slick [slɪk] *adj* (*skilful*) jeitoso, ágil, engenhoso; (*quick*) rápido; (*astute*) astuto ♦ *n* (*also*: *oil* ~) mancha de óleo.
slid [slɪd] *pt*, *pp of* **slide**.
slide [slaɪd] (*pt*, *pp* **slid**) *n* (*in playground*) escorregador *m*; (*PHOT*) slide *m*; (*BRIT*: *also*: *hair* ~) passador *m*; (*microscope* ~) lâmina; (*in prices*) queda, baixa ♦ *vt* deslizar ♦ *vi* (*slip*) escorregar; (*glide*) deslizar; **to let things ~** (*fig*) deixar tudo ir por água abaixo.
slide projector *n* (*PHOT*) projetor *m* de slides.
slide rule *n* régua de cálculo.
sliding ['slaɪdɪŋ] *adj* (*door*) corrediço; **~ roof** (*AUT*) teto deslizante.
sliding scale *n* escala móvel.
slight [slaɪt] *adj* (*slim*) fraco, franzino; (*frail*) delicado; (*pain etc*) leve; (*trifling*) insignificante; (*small*) pequeno ♦ *n* desfeita, desconsideração *f* ♦ *vt* (*offend*) desdenhar, menosprezar; **not in the ~est** em absoluto, de maneira alguma; **the ~est** o/a menor; **a ~ improvement** uma pequena melhora.
slightly ['slaɪtlɪ] *adv* ligeiramente, um pouco; **~ built** magrinho.
slim [slɪm] *adj* magro, esbelto ♦ *vi* emagrecer.
slime [slaɪm] *n* lodo, limo, lama.
slimming ['slɪmɪŋ] *n* emagrecimento ♦ *adj* (*diet*, *pills*) para emagrecer.
slimy ['slaɪmɪ] *adj* pegajoso; (*covered with mud*) lodoso; (*fig*) falso.
sling [slɪŋ] (*pt*, *pp* **slung**) *n* (*MED*) tipóia; (*weapon*) estilingue *m*, funda ♦ *vt* atirar, arremessar, lançar; **to have one's arm in a ~** estar com o braço na tipóia.
slink [slɪŋk] (*pt*, *pp* **slunk**) *vi*: **to ~ away** *or* **off** escapulir.
slip [slɪp] *n* (*slide*) tropeção *m*; (*fall*) escorregão *m*; (*mistake*) erro, lapso; (*underskirt*) combinação *f*; (*of paper*) tira ♦ *vt* (*slide*) deslizar ♦ *vi* (*slide*) deslizar; (*lose balance*) escorregar; (*decline*) decair; **to let a chance ~ by** deixar passar uma oportunidade; **to ~ sth on/off** enfiar/tirar algo; **it ~ped from her hand** escorregou da mão dela; **to give sb**

the ~ esgueirar-se de alguém; **a ~ of the tongue** um lapso da língua; *see also* **Freudian**.

slip away *vi* escapulir.

slip in *vt* meter ♦ *vi* meter-se.

slip out *vi* (*go out*) sair (um momento).

slip-on *adj* sem fecho ou botões; ~ **shoes** mocassins *mpl*.

slipped disc [slɪpt-] *n* disco deslocado.

slipper ['slɪpə*] *n* chinelo.

slippery ['slɪpərɪ] *adj* escorregadio.

slip road (BRIT) *n* (*to motorway*) entrada para a rodovia.

slipshod ['slɪpʃɔd] *adj* descuidoso, desmazelado.

slip-up *n* (*error*) equívoco, mancada; (*by neglect*) descuido.

slipway ['slɪpweɪ] *n* carreira.

slit [slɪt] (*pt, pp* **slit**) *n* fenda; (*cut*) corte *m* ♦ *vt* rachar, cortar, fender; **to ~ sb's throat** cortar o pescoço de alguém.

slither ['slɪðə*] *vi* escorregar, deslizar.

sliver ['slɪvə*] *n* (*of glass, wood*) lasca; (*of cheese, sausage*) fatia fina.

slob [slɔb] (*inf*) *n* (*in manners*) porco/a; (*in appearance*) maltrapilho/a.

slog [slɔg] *vi* mourejar ♦ *n*: **it was a ~** deu um trabalho louco.

slogan ['sləugən] *n* lema *m*, slogan *m*.

slop [slɔp] *vi* (*also*: ~ *over*) transbordar, derramar ♦ *vt* transbordar, entornar.

slope [sləup] *n* (*up*) ladeira, rampa; (*down*) declive *m*; (*side of mountain*) encosta, vertente *f* ♦ *vi*: **to ~ down** estar em declive; **to ~ up** inclinar-se.

sloping ['sləupɪŋ] *adj* inclinado, em declive.

sloppy ['slɔpɪ] *adj* (*work*) descuidado; (*appearance*) relaxado; (*film etc*) piegas *inv*.

slosh [slɔʃ] (*inf*) *vi*: **to ~ about** *or* **around** (*children*) patinhar; (*liquid*) esparrinhar.

sloshed [slɔʃt] (*inf*) *adj* (*drunk*) com a cara cheia.

slot [slɔt] *n* (*in machine*) fenda; (*opening*) abertura; (*fig*: *in timetable*, RADIO, TV) horário ♦ *vt*: **to ~ into** encaixar em ♦ *vi*: **to ~ into** encaixar-se em.

sloth [sləuθ] *n* (*vice*, ZOOL) preguiça.

slot machine *n* (*for gambling*) caça-níqueis *m inv*; (BRIT: *vending machine*) distribuidora automática.

slot meter (BRIT) *n* contador *m* (*de eletricidade ou gás*) operado por moedas.

slouch [slautʃ] *vi* ter má postura.

slouch about *vi* vadiar.

slouch around *vi* vadiar.

slovenly ['slʌvənlɪ] *adj* (*dirty*) desalinhado, sujo; (*careless*) desmazelado.

slow [sləu] *adj* lento, vagaroso; (*watch*): **to be ~** atrasar ♦ *adv* lentamente, devagar ♦ *vi* (*also*: ~ *down*, ~ *up*) ir mais devagar; **"~"** (*road sign*) "devagar"; **at a ~ speed** devagar; **to be ~ to act/decide** ser lento nas ações/decisões, vacilar; **my watch is 20 minutes ~** meu relógio está atrasado vinte minutos; **business is ~** os negócios vão mal; **to go ~** (*driver*) dirigir devagar; (*in industrial dispute*) fazer uma greve tartaruga; **the ~ lane** a faixa da direita; **bake for 2 hours in a ~ oven** asse durante 2 horas em fogo brando.

slow-acting *adj* de ação lenta.

slowdown (US) *n* greve *f* de trabalho lento, operação *f* tartaruga.

slowly ['sləulɪ] *adv* lentamente, devagar.

slow motion *n*: **in ~** em câmara lenta.

slowness ['sləunɪs] *n* lentidão *f*.

sludge [slʌdʒ] *n* lama, lodo.

slug [slʌg] *n* lesma; (*bullet*) bala.

sluggish ['slʌgɪʃ] *adj* (*slow*) lerdo; (*lazy*) preguiçoso; (*business*) lento.

sluice [slu:s] *n* (*gate*) comporta, eclusa; (*channel*) canal *m* ♦ *vt*: **to ~ down** *or* **out** lavar com jorro d'água.

slum [slʌm] *n* (*area*) favela; (*house*) cortiço, barraco.

slumber ['slʌmbə*] *n* sono.

slump [slʌmp] *n* (*economic*) depressão *f*; (*in prices*) baixa, queda ♦ *vi* baixar repentinamente; **he was ~ed over the wheel** estava caído sobre a direção.

slung [slʌŋ] *pt, pp of* **sling**.

slunk [slʌŋk] *pt, pp* of **slink**.

slur [slə:*] *n* calúnia ♦ *vt* difamar, caluniar; (*word*) pronunciar indistintamente; **to cast a ~ on sb** manchar a reputação de alguém.

slurred [slə:d] *adj* (*pronunciation*) indistinto, ininteligível.

slush [slʌʃ] *n* neve *f* meio derretida.

slush fund *n* verba para suborno.

slushy ['slʌʃɪ] *adj* (*snow*) meio derretido; (*street*) lamacento; (BRIT: *fig*) piegas *inv*.

slut [slʌt] *n* mulher *f* desmazelada; (*whore*) prostituta.

sly [slaɪ] *adj* (*clever*) astuto; (*nasty*) malicioso, velhaco; **on the ~** às escondidas.

smack [smæk] *n* (*slap*) palmada; (*blow*) tabefe *m* ♦ *vt* dar uma palmada (*or* um tabefe) em ♦ *vi*: **to ~ of** cheirar a, saber a ♦ *adv* (*inf*): **it fell ~ in the middle** caiu exatamente no meio.

smacker ['smækə*] (*inf*) *n* (*kiss*) beijoca; (BRIT: *pound note*) libra; (US: *dollar bill*) dólar *m*.

small [smɔ:l] *adj* pequeno; (*short*) baixo; (*letter*) minúsculo ♦ *n*: **the ~ of the back** os rins; **to get** *or* **grow ~er** diminuir; **to make ~er** diminuir; **a ~ shopkeeper** um pequeno comerciante.

small ads (BRIT) *npl* classificados *mpl*.

small arms *npl* armas *fpl* leves.

small change *n* trocado.

smallholder ['smɔ:lhəuldə*] (BRIT) *n* pequeno/a proprietário/a.

smallholding ['smɔ:lhəuldɪŋ] (BRIT) *n* minifúndio.

small hours *npl*: **in the ~** na madrugada, lá pelas tantas (*inf*).

smallish ['smɔ:lɪʃ] *adj* de pequeno porte.

small-minded *adj* mesquinho.

smallpox ['smɔ:lpɔks] *n* varíola.

small print *n* tipo miúdo.
small-scale *adj* (*model, map*) reduzido; (*business, farming*) de pequeno porte.
small talk *n* conversa fiada.
small-time *adj* (*farmer etc*) pequeno; **a ~ thief** um ladrão de galinha.
smart [smɑ:t] *adj* elegante; (*clever*) inteligente, astuto; (*quick*) vivo, esperto ♦ *vi* arder, coçar; **the ~ set** a alta sociedade; **to look ~** estar elegante; **my eyes are ~ing** meus olhos estão ardendo.
smarten up ['smɑ:tən-] *vi* arrumar-se ♦ *vt* arrumar.
smash [smæʃ] *n* (*also*: *~-up*) colisão *f*, choque *m*; (*sound*) estrondo ♦ *vt* (*break*) escangalhar, despedaçar; (*SPORT*: *record*) quebrar ♦ *vi* (*break*) despedaçar-se; (*against wall etc*) espatifar-se.
smash up *vt* destruir.
smash hit *n* sucesso absoluto.
smashing ['smæʃɪŋ] (*inf*) *adj* excelente.
smattering ['smætərɪŋ] *n*: **a ~ of** um conhecimento superficial de.
smear [smɪə*] *n* mancha, nódoa; (*MED*) esfregaço; (*insult*) difamação *f* ♦ *vt* untar, lambuzar; (*fig*) caluniar, difamar; **his hands were ~ed with oil/ink** as mãos dele estavam manchadas de óleo/tinta.
smear campaign *n* campanha de desmoralização.
smear test (*BRIT*) *n* (*MED*) esfregaço.
smell [smɛl] (*pt, pp* **smelt** *or* **~ed**) *n* cheiro; (*sense*) olfato ♦ *vt* cheirar ♦ *vi* (*food etc*) cheirar; (*pej*) cheirar mal; **it ~s of garlic** cheira a alho; **it ~s good** cheira bem, tem um bom cheiro.
smelly ['smɛlɪ] *adj* fedorento, malcheiroso.
smelt [smɛlt] *pt, pp of* **smell** ♦ *vt* (*ore*) fundir.
smile [smaɪl] *n* sorriso ♦ *vi* sorrir.
smiling ['smaɪlɪŋ] *adj* sorridente, risonho.
smirk [smə:k] *n* sorriso falso *or* afetado.
smith [smɪθ] *n* ferreiro.
smithy ['smɪðɪ] *n* forja, oficina de ferreiro.
smitten ['smɪtn] *adj*: **~ with** (*charmed by*) encantado por; (*grief etc*) tomado por.
smock [smɔk] *n* guarda-pó *m*; (*children's*) avental *m*.
smog [smɔg] *n* nevoeiro com fumaça, poluição *f*.
smoke [sməuk] *n* fumaça (*BR*), fumo (*PT*) ♦ *vi* fumar; (*chimney*) fumegar ♦ *vt* (*cigarettes*) fumar; **to have a ~** fumar; **do you ~?** você fuma?; **to go up in ~** (*house etc*) queimar num incêndio; (*fig*) não dar em nada.
smoked [sməukt] *adj* (*bacon*) defumado; (*glass*) fumée.
smokeless fuel ['sməuklɪs-] *n* combustível *m* não poluente.
smokeless zone ['sməuklɪs-] (*BRIT*) *n zona onde não é permitido o uso de combustíveis poluentes.*
smoker ['sməukə*] *n* (*person*) fumante *m/f*; (*RAIL*) vagão *m* para fumantes.
smoke screen *n* cortina de fumaça.
smoke shop
smoking ['sməukɪŋ] *n*: **"no ~"** (*sign*) "proibido fumar"; **he's given up ~** ele deixou de fumar.
smoking compartment (*US* **smoking car**) *n* vagão *m* para fumantes.
smoky ['sməukɪ] *adj* fumegante; (*room*) cheio de fumaça (*BR*) *or* fumo (*PT*).
smolder ['sməuldə*] (*US*) *vi* = **smoulder**.
smooth [smu:ð] *adj* liso, macio; (*sea*) tranqüilo, calmo; (*flat*) plano; (*flavour, movement*) suave; (*person*) culto, refinado; (: *pej*) meloso; (*flight, landing*) tranqüilo; (*cigarette*) suave ♦ *vt* alisar; (*also*: *~ out*: *difficulties*) aplainar.
smooth over *vt*: **to ~ things over** (*fig*) arranjar as coisas.
smoothly ['smu:ðlɪ] *adv* (*easily*) facilmente, sem problemas; **everything went ~** tudo correu muito bem.
smother ['smʌðə*] *vt* sufocar; (*repress*) reprimir.
smoulder ['sməuldə*] (*US* **smolder**) *vi* arder sem chamas.
smudge [smʌdʒ] *n* mancha ♦ *vt* manchar, sujar.
smug [smʌg] *adj* metido, convencido.
smuggle ['smʌgl] *vt* contrabandear; **to ~ in/out** (*goods etc*) fazer entrar/sair de contrabando.
smuggler ['smʌglə*] *n* contrabandista *m/f*.
smuggling ['smʌglɪŋ] *n* contrabando.
smut [smʌt] *n* (*of soot*) marca de fuligem; (*mark*) mancha; (*in conversation etc*) obscenidades *fpl*.
smutty ['smʌtɪ] *adj* (*fig*) obsceno, indecente.
snack [snæk] *n* lanche *m* (*BR*), merenda (*PT*); **to have a ~** fazer um lanche.
snack bar *n* lanchonete *f* (*BR*), snackbar *m* (*PT*).
snag [snæg] *n* dificuldade *f*, obstáculo.
snail [sneɪl] *n* caracol *m*; (*water ~*) caramujo.
snake [sneɪk] *n* cobra.
snap [snæp] *n* (*sound*) estalo; (*of whip*) estalido; (*click*) clique *m*; (*photograph*) foto *f* ♦ *adj* repentino ♦ *vt* (*fingers, whip*) estalar; (*break*) quebrar; (*photograph*) tirar uma foto de ♦ *vi* (*break*) quebrar; (*fig*: *person*) retrucar asperamente; (*sound*) estalar; **to ~ shut** fechar com um estalo; **to ~ at sb** (*subj*: *person*) retrucar bruscamente a alguém; (: *dog*) tentar morder alguém; **to ~ one's fingers** estalar os dedos; **a cold ~** uma onda de frio.
snap off *vt* (*break*) partir.
snap up *vt* arrebatar, comprar rapidamente.
snap fastener *n* colchete *m* de mola.
snappy ['snæpɪ] *adj* rápido; (*slogan*) vigoroso; **he's a ~ dresser** ele está sempre chique;

NB: European Portuguese adds the following consonants to certain words: **b** (sú(b)dito, su(b)til); **c** (a(c)ção, a(c)cionista, a(c)to); **m** (inde(m)ne); **p** (ado(p)ção, ado(p)tar); *for further details see p. xiii.*

make it ~! vai rápido!
snapshot ['snæpʃɔt] *n* foto *f* (instantânea).
snare [snɛə*] *n* armadilha, laço ♦ *vt* apanhar no laço *or* na armadilha.
snarl [snɑːl] *n* grunhido ♦ *vi* grunhir ♦ *vt*: **to get ~ed up** (*wool, plans*) ficar embaralhado; (*traffic*) ficar engarrafado.
snatch [snætʃ] *n* (*fig*) roubo; (*small amount*): **~es of** pedacinhos *mpl* de ♦ *vt* (~ *away*) arrebatar; (*grasp*) agarrar ♦ *vi*: **don't ~!** não tome as coisas dos outros!; **to ~ a sandwich** fazer um lanche rapidinho; **to ~ some sleep** dormir um pouco.
snatch up *vt* agarrar.
sneak [sniːk] *vi*: **to ~ in/out** entrar/sair furtivamente ♦ *vt*: **to ~ a look at sth** olhar disfarçadamente para algo.
sneakers ['sniːkəz] *npl* tênis *m* (*BR*), sapatos *mpl* de treino (*PT*).
sneaking ['sniːkɪŋ] *adj*: **to have a ~ suspicion that ...** ter uma vaga suspeita de que ....
sneaky ['sniːkɪ] *adj* sorrateiro.
sneer [snɪə*] *n* sorriso de desprezo ♦ *vi* rir-se com desdém; **to ~ at** zombar de, desprezar.
sneeze [sniːz] *n* espirro ♦ *vi* espirrar.
snide [snaɪd] *adj* sarcástico.
sniff [snɪf] *n* (*of dog*) farejada; (*of person*) fungadela ♦ *vi* fungar ♦ *vt* fungar, farejar; (*glue, drug*) cheirar.
sniff at *vt fus*: **it's not to be ~ed at** isso não deve ser desprezado.
snigger ['snɪgə*] *n* riso dissimulado ♦ *vi* rir-se com dissimulação.
snip [snɪp] *n* tesourada; (*piece*) pedaço, retalho; (*bargain*) pechincha ♦ *vt* cortar com tesoura.
sniper ['snaɪpə*] *n* franco-atirador(a) *m/f*.
snippet ['snɪpɪt] *n* pedacinho.
snivelling ['snɪvlɪŋ] *adj* (*whimpering*) chorão/rona, lamuriento.
snob [snɔb] *n* esnobe *m/f*.
snobbery ['snɔbərɪ] *n* esnobismo.
snobbish ['snɔbɪʃ] *adj* esnobe.
snooker ['snuːkə*] *n* sinuca.
snoop [snuːp] *vi*: **to ~ about** bisbilhotar.
snooper ['snuːpə*] *n* bisbilhoteiro/a, xereta *m/f*.
snooty ['snuːtɪ] *adj* arrogante.
snooze [snuːz] *n* soneca ♦ *vi* tirar uma soneca, dormitar.
snore [snɔː*] *vi* roncar ♦ *n* ronco.
snoring ['snɔːrɪŋ] *n* roncadura, roncaria.
snorkel ['snɔːkl] *n* tubo snorkel.
snort [snɔːt] *n* bufo, bufido ♦ *vi* bufar ♦ *vt* (*drugs*) cheirar.
snot [snɔt] (*inf*) *n* ranho.
snotty ['snɔtɪ] *adj* ranhoso; (*fig*) altivo, arrogante.
snout [snaut] *n* focinho.
snow [snəu] *n* neve *f* ♦ *vi* nevar ♦ *vt*: **to be ~ed under with work** estar atolado *or* sobrecarregado de trabalho.
snowball ['snəubɔːl] *n* bola de neve ♦ *vi* acumular-se.
snowbound ['snəubaund] *adj* bloqueado pela neve.
snow-capped [-kæpt] *adj* coberto de neve.
snowdrift ['snəudrɪft] *n* monte *m* de neve (formado pelo vento).
snowdrop ['snəudrɔp] *n* campainha branca.
snowfall ['snəufɔːl] *n* nevada.
snowflake ['snəufleɪk] *n* floco de neve.
snowman ['snəumæn] (*irreg*) *n* boneco de neve.
snowplough ['snəuplau] (*US* **snowplow**) *n* máquina limpa-neve, removedor *m* de neve.
snowshoe ['snəuʃuː] *n* raquete *f* de neve.
snowstorm ['snəustɔːm] *n* nevasca, tempestade *f* de neve.
Snow White *n* Branca de Neve.
snowy ['snəuɪ] *adj* nevoso.
SNP (*BRIT*) *n abbr* (*POL*) = **Scottish National Party**.
snub [snʌb] *vt* desdenhar, menosprezar ♦ *n* repulsa.
snub-nosed [-'nəuzd] *adj* de nariz arrebitado.
snuff [snʌf] *n* rapé *m* ♦ *vt* (*also*: ~ *out*: *candle*) apagar.
snug [snʌg] *adj* (*sheltered*) abrigado, protegido; (*fitted*) justo, cômodo.
snuggle ['snʌgl] *vi*: **to ~ up to sb** aconchegar-se *or* aninhar-se a alguém.
snugly ['snʌglɪ] *adv* (*fit*) perfeitamente.
SO *abbr* (*BANKING*) = **standing order**.
so [səu] *adv* (*degree*) tão; (*manner*: *thus*) assim, deste modo ♦ *conj* conseqüentemente, portanto; **~ as to do** para fazer; **~ that** (*purpose*) para que, a fim de que; (*result*) de modo que; **~ that's the reason!** então, esta é a razão!; **~ do I** eu também; **~ it is!**, **~ it does!** é verdade!; **if ~** se for assim, se assim é; **I hope ~** espero que sim; **10 or ~** 10 mais ou menos; **quite ~!** exatamente!; **even ~** mesmo assim; **~ far** até aqui; **~ long!** tchau!; **~ many** tantos; **~ much** tanto; **she didn't ~ much as send me a birthday card** ela nem me mandou um cartão no meu aniversário; **~ to speak** por assim dizer; **~ (what)?** (*inf*) e daí?
soak [səuk] *vt* (*drench*) embeber, ensopar; (*put in water*) pôr de molho ♦ *vi* estar de molho, impregnar-se.
soak in *vi* infiltrar.
soak up *vt* absorver.
soaking ['səukɪŋ] *adj* (*also*: ~ *wet*) encharcado.
so and so *n* fulano/a.
soap [səup] *n* sabão *m*.
soapflakes ['səupfleɪks] *npl* flocos *mpl* de sabão.
soap opera *n* novela.
soap powder *n* sabão *m* em pó.
soapsuds ['səupsʌdz] *n* água de sabão.
soapy ['səupɪ] *adj* ensaboado.
soar [sɔː*] *vi* (*on wings*) elevar-se em vôo; (*building etc*) levantar-se; (*price*) disparar; (*morale, spirits*) renascer.
soaring ['sɔːrɪŋ] *adj* (*flight*) a grande altura; (*prices, inflation*) disparado.
sob [sɔb] *n* soluço ♦ *vi* soluçar.

s.o.b. (US: *inf!*) *n abbr* (= *son of a bitch*) filho da puta (!).
sober ['səubə*] *adj* (*serious*) sério; (*sensible*) sensato; (*moderate*) moderado; (*not drunk*) sóbrio; (*colour, style*) discreto.
sober up *vi* tornar-se sóbrio.
sobriety [sə'braɪətɪ] *n* sobriedade *f*.
Soc. *abbr* = **society**.
so-called [-kɔːld] *adj* chamado.
soccer ['sɔkə*] *n* futebol *m*.
soccer pitch *n* campo de futebol.
soccer player *n* jogador *m* de futebol.
sociable ['səuʃəbl] *adj* sociável.
social ['səuʃl] *adj* social; (*sociable*) sociável ♦ *n* reunião *f* social.
social climber *n* arrivista *m/f*.
social club *n* clube *m*.
Social Democrat *n* democrata-social *m/f*.
social insurance (US) *n* seguro social.
socialism ['səuʃəlɪzəm] *n* socialismo.
socialist ['səuʃəlɪst] *adj*, *n* socialista *m/f*.
socialite ['səuʃəlaɪt] *n* socialite *m/f*, colunável *m/f*.
socialize ['səuʃəlaɪz] *vi* socializar.
socially ['səuʃəlɪ] *adv* socialmente.
social science *n* ciências *fpl* sociais.
social security *n* previdência social; **Department of S~ S~** (BRIT) ≈ Instituto Nacional de Assistência Médica e Previdência Social.
social welfare *n* bem-estar *m* social.
social work *n* assistência social, serviço social.
social worker *n* assistente *m/f* social.
society [sə'saɪətɪ] *n* sociedade *f*; (*club*) associação *f*; (*also*: *high* ~) alta sociedade ♦ *cpd* (*party, column*) da alta sociedade.
socio-economic ['səusɪəu-] *adj* sócio-econômico.
sociological [səusɪə'lɔdʒɪkl] *adj* sociológico.
sociologist [səusɪ'ɔlədʒɪst] *n* sociólogo/a.
sociology [səusɪ'ɔlədʒɪ] *n* sociologia.
sock [sɔk] *n* meia (BR), peúga (PT) ♦ *vt* (*inf*: *hit*) socar, dar um soco em; **to pull one's ~s up** (*fig*) tomar jeito.
socket ['sɔkɪt] *n* (ELEC) tomada.
sod [sɔd] *n* (*of earth*) gramado, torrão *m*; (BRIT: *inf!*) imbecil *m/f* ♦ *vt*: ~ **it!** (*inf!*) droga!
soda ['səudə] *n* (CHEM) soda; (*also*: ~ *water*) água com gás; (US: *also*: ~ *pop*) soda.
sodden ['sɔdn] *adj* encharcado.
sodium ['səudɪəm] *n* sódio.
sodium chloride *n* cloreto de sódio.
sofa ['səufə] *n* sofá *m*.
Sofia ['səufɪə] *n* Sófia.
soft [sɔft] *adj* (*gen*) macio; (*spongy*) mole; (*gentle, not loud*) suave; (*kind*) meigo, bondoso; (*weak*) fraco; (*stupid*) idiota.
soft-boiled egg [-bɔɪld-] *n* ovo quente.
soft currency *n* moeda fraca.
soft drink *n* refrigerante *m*.
soft drugs *n* drogas *fpl* leves.
soften ['sɔfn] *vt* amolecer, amaciar, enternecer ♦ *vi* abrandar-se, enternecer-se, suavizar-se.
softener ['sɔfnər] *n* amaciante *m*.
soft fruit (BRIT) *n* bagas *fpl*.
soft furnishings *npl* cortinas *fpl* e estofados *mpl*.
soft-hearted *adj* bondoso, caridoso.
softly ['sɔftlɪ] *adv* suavemente; (*gently*) delicadamente.
softness ['sɔftnɪs] *n* suavidade *f*, maciez *f*.
soft sell *n* venda de forma não agressiva.
soft toy *n* brinquedo de pelúcia.
software ['sɔftwɛə*] *n* software *m*.
software package *n* soft *m*, pacote *m*.
SOGAT ['səugæt] (BRIT) *n abbr* (= *Society of Graphical and Allied Trades*) *sindicato dos impressores*.
soggy ['sɔgɪ] *adj* ensopado, encharcado.
soil [sɔɪl] *n* (*earth*) terra, solo ♦ *vt* sujar, manchar.
soiled [sɔɪld] *adj* sujo.
sojourn ['sɔdʒəːn] *n* (*formal*) estada *f*.
solace ['sɔlɪs] *n* consolo.
solar ['səulə*] *adj* solar.
solaria [sə'lɛərɪə] *npl of* **solarium**.
solarium [sə'lɛərɪəm] (*pl* **solaria**) *n* solário.
solar plexus [-'plɛksəs] *n* plexo solar.
sold [səuld] *pt*, *pp of* **sell**.
solder ['səuldə*] *vt* soldar ♦ *n* solda.
soldier ['səuldʒə*] *n* soldado; (*army man*) militar *m*; **toy** ~ soldado de chumbo.
soldier on *vi* agüentar firme (*inf*), perseverar.
sold out *adj* (COMM) esgotado.
sole [səul] (*pl* **~s**) *n* (*of foot, of shoe*) sola; (*pl*: *inv*: *fish*) solha, linguado ♦ *adj* único; **the ~ reason** a única razão.
solely ['səullɪ] *adv* somente, unicamente; **I will hold you ~ responsible** vou apontar-lhe como o único responsável.
solemn ['sɔləm] *adj* solene.
sole trader *n* (COMM) comerciante *m/f* independente.
solicit [sə'lɪsɪt] *vt* (*request*) solicitar ♦ *vi* (*prostitute*) aliciar fregueses.
solicitor [sə'lɪsɪtə*] *n* (*for wills etc*) tabelião/lioa *m/f*; (*in court*) ≈ advogado/a.
solid ['sɔlɪd] *adj* (*not hollow*) sólido; (*gold etc*) maciço; (*person*) sério; (*line*) contínuo; (*vote*) unânime ♦ *n* sólido; **we waited 2 ~ hours** esperamos durante 2 horas a fio; **to be on ~ ground** estar em terra firme; (*fig*) ter base.
solidarity [sɔlɪ'dærɪtɪ] *n* solidariedade *f*.
solidify [sə'lɪdɪfaɪ] *vi* solidificar-se.
solidity [sə'lɪdɪtɪ] *n* solidez *f*.
solid-state *adj* de estado sólido.
soliloquy [sə'lɪləkwɪ] *n* monólogo.
solitaire [sɔlɪ'tɛə*] *n* (*gem*) solitário; (*game*) solitário, jogo de paciência.
solitary ['sɔlɪtərɪ] *adj* solitário, só; (*isolated*)

***NB:** European Portuguese adds the following consonants to certain words:* **b** (sú(b)dito, su(b)til); **c** (a(c)ção, a(c)cionista, a(c)to); **m** (inde(m)ne); **p** (ado(p)ção, ado(p)tar); *for further details see p. xiii.*

isolado, retirado; (*only*) único.
solitary confinement *n* (*LAW*) prisão *f* celular, solitária.
solitude ['sɔlɪtjuːd] *n* solidão *f*.
solo ['səuləu] *n* solo.
soloist ['səuləuist] *n* solista *m/f*.
Solomon Islands ['sɔləmən-] *npl*: **the** ~ as ilhas Salomão.
solstice ['sɔlstɪs] *n* solstício.
soluble ['sɔljubl] *adj* solúvel.
solution [sə'luːʃən] *n* solução *f*.
solve [sɔlv] *vt* resolver, solucionar.
solvency ['sɔlvənsɪ] *n* (*COMM*) solvência.
solvent ['sɔlvənt] *adj* (*COMM*) solvente ♦ *n* (*CHEM*) solvente *m*.
solvent abuse *n* abuso de solventes alucinógenos.
Som. (*BRIT*) *abbr* = **Somerset**.
Somali [sə'mɑːlɪ] *adj*, *n* somaliano/a.
Somalia [sə'mɑːlɪə] *n* Somália.
sombre ['sɔmbə*] (*US* **somber**) *adj* sombrio, lúgubre.
some [sʌm] *adj* (*a few*) alguns/algumas; (*certain*) algum(a); (*a certain number or amount*) *see phrases below*; (*unspecified*) um pouco de ♦ *pron* alguns/algumas; (*a bit*) um pouco ♦ *adv*: ~ **10 people** umas 10 pessoas; ~ **children came** algumas crianças vieram; ~ **people say that ...** algumas pessoas dizem que ...; **have** ~ **tea** tome um pouco de chá; **there's** ~ **milk in the fridge** há leite na geladeira; ~ **(of it) was left** ficou um pouco; **could I have** ~ **of that cheese?** pode me dar um pouco daquele queijo?; **I've got** ~ (*books etc*) tenho alguns; (*milk, money etc*) tenho um pouco; **would you like** ~**?** você quer um pouco?; **after** ~ **time** depois de algum tempo; **at** ~ **length** com certa extensão; **in** ~ **form or other** de uma forma ou de outra.
somebody ['sʌmbədɪ] *pron* alguém; ~ **or other** um ou outro.
someday ['sʌmdeɪ] *adv* algum dia.
somehow ['sʌmhau] *adv* de alguma maneira; (*for some reason*) por uma razão ou outra.
someone ['sʌmwʌn] *pron* alguém.
someplace ['sʌmpleɪs] (*US*) *adv* (*be*) em algum lugar; (*go*) para algum lugar; ~ **else** (*be*) em outro lugar; (*go*) para outro lugar.
somersault ['sʌməsɔːlt] *n* (*deliberate*) salto mortal; (*accidental*) cambalhota ♦ *vi* dar um salto mortal *or* uma cambalhota.
something ['sʌmθɪŋ] *pron* alguma coisa, algo (*BR*); ~ **to do** alguma coisa para fazer; ~ **else** (*in addition*) alguma coisa a mais; (~ *different*) outra coisa; **he's** ~ **like me** ele é um pouco como eu; **it's** ~ **of a problem** é de certo modo um problema.
sometime ['sʌmtaɪm] *adv* (*in future*) algum dia, em outra oportunidade; (*in past*): ~ **last month** durante o mês passado; **I'll finish it** ~ vou terminar uma hora dessas.
sometimes ['sʌmtaɪmz] *adv* às vezes, de vez em quando.
somewhat ['sʌmwɔt] *adv* um tanto.
somewhere ['sʌmwɛə*] *adv* (*be*) em algum lugar; (*go*) para algum lugar; ~ **else** (*be*) em outro lugar; (*go*) para outro lugar.
son [sʌn] *n* filho.
sonar ['səunɑː*] *n* sonar *m*.
sonata [sə'nɑːtə] *n* sonata.
song [sɔŋ] *n* canção *f*.
songbook ['sɔŋbuk] *n* cancioneiro.
songwriter ['sɔŋraɪtə*] *n* compositor(a) *m/f* de canções.
sonic ['sɔnɪk] *adj* (*boom*) sônico.
son-in-law ['sʌnɪnlɔː] (*pl* **sons-in-law**) *n* genro.
sonnet ['sɔnɪt] *n* soneto.
sonny ['sʌnɪ] (*inf*) *n* meu filho.
soon [suːn] *adv* logo, brevemente; (*early*) cedo; ~ **afterwards** pouco depois; **very/quite** ~ logo/daqui a pouco; **how** ~ **can you be ready?** quando você estará pronto?; **it's too** ~ **to tell** é muito cedo para dizer; **see you** ~! até logo!; *see also* **as**.
sooner ['suːnə*] *adv* (*time*) antes, mais cedo; (*preference*): **I would** ~ **do that** preferia fazer isso; ~ **or later** mais cedo ou mais tarde; **no** ~ **said than done** dito e feito; **the** ~ **the better** quanto mais cedo melhor; **no** ~ **had we left than he ...** mal partimos, ele ....
soot [sut] *n* fuligem *f*.
soothe [suːð] *vt* acalmar, sossegar; (*pain*) aliviar, suavizar.
soothing ['suːðɪŋ] *adj* calmante.
SOP *n abbr* = **standard operating procedure**.
sop [sɔp] *n* paliativo.
sophisticated [sə'fɪstɪkeɪtɪd] *adj* sofisticado.
sophistication [səfɪstɪ'keɪʃən] *n* sofisticação *f*.
sophomore ['sɔfəmɔː*] (*US*) *n* segundanista *m/f*.
soporific [sɔpə'rɪfɪk] *adj* soporífico.
sopping ['sɔpɪŋ] *adj*: ~ **wet** encharcado.
soppy ['sɔpɪ] (*pej*) *adj* piegas *inv*.
soprano [sə'prɑːnəu] *n* soprano *m/f*.
sorbet ['sɔːbeɪ] *n sorvete de frutas à base de água*.
sorcerer ['sɔːsərə*] *n* feiticeiro.
sordid ['sɔːdɪd] *adj* (*dirty*) imundo, sórdido; (*wretched*) miserável.
sore [sɔː*] *adj* (*painful*) dolorido; (*offended*) magoado, ofendido ♦ *n* chaga, ferida; **it's a** ~ **point** é um ponto delicado; **my eyes are** ~, **I've got** ~ **eyes** meus olhos estão doloridos.
sorely ['sɔːlɪ] *adv*: **I am** ~ **tempted** estou muito tentado.
sore throat *n* dor *f* de garganta.
sorrel ['sɔrəl] *n* azeda.
sorrow ['sɔrəu] *n* tristeza, mágoa, dor *f*.
sorrowful ['sɔrəuful] *adj* triste, aflito, magoado.
sorry ['sɔrɪ] *adj* (*regretful*) arrependido; (*condition, sight*) lamentável; ~! desculpe!, perdão!, sinto muito!; **to feel** ~ **for sb** sentir pena de alguém; **I feel** ~ **for him** estou com pena dele; **I'm** ~ **to hear that ...** lamento saber que ...; **to be** ~ **about sth** arrepender-se de algo.
sort [sɔːt] *n* tipo; (*brand*: *of coffee etc*) marca ♦ *vt* (*also*: ~ *out*: *papers*) classificar; (:

problems) solucionar, resolver; **what ~ do you want?** que tipo você quer?; **what ~ of car?** que tipo de carro?; **I'll do nothing of the ~!** não farei nada do gênero!; **it's ~ of awkward** (*inf*) é meio difícil.
sortie ['sɔ:tɪ] *n* surtida.
sorting office ['sɔ:tɪŋ-] *n* departamento de distribuição.
SOS *n abbr* (= *save our souls*) S.O.S. *m*.
so-so *adv* mais ou menos, regular.
soufflé ['su:fleɪ] *n* suflê *m*.
sought [sɔ:t] *pt*, *pp of* **seek**.
sought-after *adj* desejado.
soul [səul] *n* alma; **I didn't see a ~** não vi uma alma; **God rest his ~** que a sua alma descanse em paz; **the poor ~ had nowhere to sleep** o pobre coitado não tinha onde dormir.
soul-destroying [-dɪs'trɔɪɪŋ] *adj* desalentador(a).
soulful ['səulful] *adj* emocional, sentimental.
soulless ['səullɪs] *adj* desalmado.
soul mate *n* companheiro/a ideal.
soul-searching *n*: **after much ~** depois de muita ponderação.
sound [saund] *adj* (*healthy*) saudável, sadio; (*safe, not damaged*) sólido, completo; (*secure*) seguro; (*reliable*) confiável; (*sensible*) sensato; (*argument, policy*) válido; (*move*) acertado ♦ *adv*: **~ asleep** dormindo profundamente ♦ *n* (*noise*) som *m*, ruído, barulho; (*GEO*) estreito, braço (de mar) ♦ *vt* (*alarm*) soar; (*also*: **~ out**: *opinions*) sondar ♦ *vi* soar, tocar; (*fig*: *seem*) parecer; **to be of ~ mind** estar em juízo perfeito; **I don't like the ~ of it** eu não estou gostando disso; **to ~ like** parecer; **it ~s as if ...** parece que ....
 sound off (*inf*) *vi*: **to ~ off (about)** pontificar (sobre).
sound barrier *n* barreira do som.
sound effects *npl* efeitos *mpl* sonoros.
sound engineer *n* engenheiro/a de som.
sounding ['saundɪŋ] *n* (*NAUT etc*) sondagem *f*.
sounding board *n* (*MUS*) caixa de ressonância; (*fig*): **to use sb as a ~ for one's ideas** testar suas idéias em alguém.
soundly ['saundlɪ] *adv* (*sleep*) profundamente; (*beat*) completamente.
soundproof ['saundpru:f] *adj* à prova de som ♦ *vt* insonorizar.
soundtrack ['saundtræk] *n* (*of film*) trilha sonora.
sound wave *n* onda sonora.
soup [su:p] *n* (*thick*) sopa; (*thin*) caldo; **in the ~** (*fig*) numa encrenca.
soup kitchen *n local onde se distribui comida aos pobres*.
soup plate *n* prato fundo (para sopa).
soupspoon ['su:pspu:n] *n* colher *f* de sopa.
sour ['sauə*] *adj* azedo, ácido; (*milk*) talhado; (*fig*) mal-humorado, rabugento; **to go** *or* **turn ~** (*milk, wine*) azedar; (*fig*: *relationship, plan*) azedar, dar errado.
source [sɔ:s] *n* fonte *f*; **I have it from a reliable ~ that ...** uma fonte confiável me assegura que ....
south [sauθ] *n* sul *m* ♦ *adj* do sul, meridional ♦ *adv* ao *or* para o sul; **(to the) ~ of** ao sul de; **the S~ of France** o Sul da França; **to travel ~** viajar para o sul.
South Africa *n* África do Sul.
South African *adj*, *n* sul-africano/a.
South America *n* América do Sul.
South American *adj*, *n* sul-americano/a.
southbound ['sauθbaund] *adj* em direção ao sul.
south-east *n* sudeste *m* ♦ *adj* do sudeste.
South-East Asia *n* o Sudeste da Ásia.
southerly ['sʌðəlɪ] *adj* meridional; (*from the south*) do sul.
southern ['sʌðən] *adj* meridional, do sul, sulista; **the ~ hemisphere** o Hemisfério Sul.
South Pole *n* Pólo Sul.
South Sea Islands *npl*: **the ~** as ilhas dos Mares do Sul.
South Seas *npl*: **the ~** os Mares do Sul.
southward(s) ['sauθwəd(z)] *adv* para o sul.
south-west *n* sudoeste *m*.
souvenir [su:və'nɪə*] *n* lembrança.
sovereign ['sɔvrɪn] *adj*, *n* soberano/a.
sovereignty ['sɔvrɪntɪ] *n* soberania.
soviet ['səuvɪət] *adj* soviético.
Soviet Union *n*: **the ~** a União Soviética.
sow[1] [sau] *n* porca.
sow[2] [səu] (*pt* **~ed**, *pp* **sown**) *vt* (*gen*) semear; (*spread*) disseminar, espalhar.
sown [səun] *pp of* **sow**[2].
soy [sɔɪ] (*US*) *n* = **soya**.
soya ['sɔɪə] (*BRIT*) *n* soja; **~ bean** semente *f* de soja; **~ sauce** molho de soja.
spa [spɑ:] *n* (*town*) estância hidro-mineral; (*US*: *also*: *health ~*) estância balnear.
space [speɪs] *n* (*gen*) espaço; (*room*) lugar *m* ♦ *vt* (*also*: **~ out**) espaçar; **in a confined ~** num espaço confinado; **in a short ~ of time** num curto espaço de tempo; **(with)in the ~ of an hour** dentro do espaço de uma hora; **to clear a ~ for sth** abrir espaço para algo.
space bar *n* tecla de espacejamento.
spacecraft ['speɪskrɑ:ft] *n inv* nave *f* espacial.
spaceman ['speɪsmæn] (*irreg*) *n* astronauta *m*, cosmonauta *m*.
spaceship ['speɪsʃɪp] *n* nave *f* espacial.
space shuttle *n* ônibus *m* espacial.
spacesuit ['speɪssu:t] *n* traje *m* espacial.
spacewoman ['speɪswumən] (*irreg*) *n* astronauta, cosmonauta.
spacing ['speɪsɪŋ] *n* espacejamento, espaçamento; **single/double ~** espacejamento simples/duplo.
spacious ['speɪʃəs] *adj* espaçoso.
spade [speɪd] *n* (*tool*) pá *f*; **~s** *npl* (*CARDS*) espadas *fpl*.
spadework ['speɪdwə:k] *n* (*fig*) trabalho preli-

NB: *European Portuguese adds the following consonants to certain words:* **b** (sú(b)dito, su(b)til); **c** (a(c)ção, a(c)cionista, a(c)to); **m** (inde(m)ne); **p** (ado(p)ção, ado(p)tar); *for further details see p. xiii.*

minar.

spaghetti [spə'gɛtɪ] *n* espaguete *m*.

Spain [speɪn] *n* Espanha.

span [spæn] *n* (*also*: *wing~*) envergadura; (*of hand*) palma; (*of arch*) vão *m*; (*in time*) lapso, espaço ♦ *vt* estender-se sobre, atravessar; (*fig*) abarcar.

Spaniard ['spænjəd] *n* espanhol(a) *m/f*.

spaniel ['spænjəl] *n* spaniel *m*.

Spanish ['spænɪʃ] *adj* espanhol(a) ♦ *n* (LING) espanhol *m*, castelhano; **the ~** *npl* os espanhóis; **~ omelette** omelete *m* à espanhola.

spank [spæŋk] *vt* bater, dar palmadas.

spanner ['spænə*] *n* chave *f* inglesa.

spar [spɑː*] *n* mastro, verga ♦ *vi* (BOXING) treinar.

spare [spɛə*] *adj* (*free*) vago, desocupado; (*surplus*) de sobra, a mais; (*available*) disponível, de reserva ♦ *n* (*part*) peça sobressalente ♦ *vt* (*do without*) dispensar, passar sem; (*afford to give*) dispor de, ter de sobra; (*refrain from hurting*) perdoar, poupar; (*be grudging with*) dar frugalmente; **there are 2 going ~** (BRIT) há 2 sobrando; **to ~ no expense** não poupar despesas; **can you ~ (me) £10?** pode me ceder £10?; **can you ~ the time?** você tem tempo?; **there is no time to ~** não há tempo a perder; **I've a few minutes to ~** tenho alguns minutos de sobra.

spare part *n* peça sobressalente.

spare room *n* quarto de hóspedes.

spare time *n* tempo livre.

spare tyre *n* estepe *m*.

spare wheel *n* estepe *m*.

sparing ['spɛərɪŋ] *adj*: **to be ~ with** ser econômico com.

sparingly ['spɛərɪŋlɪ] *adv* escassamente.

spark [spɑːk] *n* chispa, faísca; (*fig*) centelha.

spark(ing) plug ['spɑːk(ɪŋ)-] *n* vela (de ignição).

sparkle ['spɑːkl] *n* cintilação *f*, brilho ♦ *vi* cintilar; (*shine*) brilhar, faiscar.

sparkling ['spɑːklɪŋ] *adj* cintilante; (*wine*) espumante.

sparrow ['spærəu] *n* pardal *m*.

sparse [spɑːs] *adj* escasso; (*hair*) ralo.

spartan ['spɑːtən] *adj* (*fig*) espartano.

spasm ['spæzəm] *n* (MED) espasmo; (*fig*) acesso, ataque *m*.

spasmodic [spæz'mɔdɪk] *adj* espasmódico.

spastic ['spæstɪk] *n* espástico/a.

spat [spæt] *pt*, *pp of* **spit** ♦ *n* (US) bate-boca *m*.

spate [speɪt] *n* série *f*; **in ~** (*river*) em cheia.

spatial ['speɪʃəl] *adj* espacial.

spatter ['spætə*] *n* borrifo ♦ *vt* borrifar, salpicar ♦ *vi* borrifar.

spatula ['spætjulə] *n* espátula.

spawn [spɔːn] *vi* desovar, procriar ♦ *vt* gerar; (*pej*: *create*) gerar, criar ♦ *n* ovas *fpl*.

SPCA (US) *n abbr* = **Society for the Prevention of Cruelty to Animals**.

SPCC (US) *n abbr* = **Society for the Prevention of Cruelty to Children**.

speak [spiːk] (*pt* **spoke**, *pp* **spoken**) *vt* (*language*) falar; (*truth*) dizer ♦ *vi* falar; (*make a speech*) discursar; **to ~ to sb/of** *or* **about sth** falar com alguém/de *or* sobre algo; **~ up!** fale alto!; **~ing!** (*on phone*) é ele/ela mesmo!; **to ~ one's mind** desabafar; **he has no money to ~ of** ele quase não tem dinheiro.

speak for *vt fus*: **to ~ for sb** falar por alguém; **that picture is already spoken for** aquele quadro já está vendido.

speaker ['spiːkə*] *n* (*in public*) orador(a) *m/f*; (*also*: *loud~*) alto-falante *m*; (POL): **the S~** o Presidente da Câmara; **are you a Welsh ~?** você fala galês?

speaking ['spiːkɪŋ] *adj* falante; **Italian-~ people** pessoas de língua italiana.

spear [spɪə*] *n* lança; (*for fishing*) arpão *m* ♦ *vt* lancear, arpoar.

spearhead ['spɪəhɛd] *n* ponta-de-lança ♦ *vt* (*attack*) encabeçar.

spearmint ['spɪəmɪnt] *n* hortelã *f*.

spec [spɛk] (BRIT: *inf*) *n*: **to buy sth on ~** comprar algo por acaso.

special ['spɛʃl] *adj* especial; (*edition etc*) extra ♦ *n* (*train*) trem *m* especial; **take ~ care** tome muito cuidado; **nothing ~** nada especial; **today's ~** (*at restaurant*) especialidade do dia, prato do dia.

special delivery *n*: **by ~** por entrega rápida.

specialist ['spɛʃəlɪst] *n* especialista *m/f*; **heart ~** especialista em doenças do coração.

speciality [spɛʃɪ'ælɪtɪ] (BRIT) *n* especialidade *f*.

specialize ['spɛʃəlaɪz] *vi*: **to ~ (in)** especializar-se (em).

specially ['spɛʃəlɪ] *adv* especialmente.

special offer *n* oferta especial.

specialty ['spɛʃəltɪ] (US) *n* = **speciality**.

species ['spiːʃiːz] *n inv* espécie *f*.

specific [spə'sɪfɪk] *adj* específico.

specifically [spə'sɪfɪklɪ] *adv* especificamente.

specification [spɛsɪfɪ'keɪʃən] *n* especificação *f*; **~s** *npl* (*of car, machine*) ficha técnica; (*of building*) especificações *fpl*.

specify ['spɛsɪfaɪ] *vt*, *vi* especificar, pormenorizar; **unless otherwise specified** salvo indicação em contrário.

specimen ['spɛsɪmən] *n* espécime *m*, amostra; (*fig*) exemplar *m*.

specimen copy *n* exemplar *m* de amostra.

specimen signature *n* modelo de assinatura.

speck [spɛk] *n* mancha, pinta; (*particle*) grão *m*.

speckled ['spɛkld] *adj* manchado.

specs [spɛks] (*inf*) *npl* óculos *mpl*.

spectacle ['spɛktəkl] *n* espetáculo; **~s** *npl* óculos *mpl*.

spectacle case *n* estojo de óculos.

spectacular [spɛk'tækjulə*] *adj* espetacular ♦ *n* (CINEMA *etc*) superprodução *f*.

spectator [spɛk'teɪtə*] *n* espectador(a) *m/f*.

specter ['spɛktə*] (US) *n* = **spectre**.

spectra ['spɛktrə] *npl of* **spectrum**.

spectre ['spɛktə*] (US **specter**) *n* espectro, aparição *f*.

spectrum ['spɛktrəm] (*pl* **spectra**) *n* espectro.

speculate ['spɛkjuleɪt] *vi* especular; (*try to*

guess): **to ~ about** especular sobre.
speculation [spɛkju'leɪʃən] *n* especulação *f*.
speculative ['spɛkjulətɪv] *adj* especulativo.
speculator ['spɛkjuleɪtə*] *n* especulador(a) *m*/*f*.
sped [spɛd] *pt*, *pp of* **speed**.
speech [spi:tʃ] *n* (*faculty*, *language*) fala; (*formal talk*) discurso.
speech day (*BRIT*) *n* (*SCH*) dia *m* de distribuição de prêmios.
speech impediment *n* defeito *m* de articulação.
speechless ['spi:tʃlɪs] *adj* estupefato, emudecido.
speech therapy *n* ortofonia.
speed [spi:d] (*pt*, *pp* **sped**) *n* velocidade *f*, rapidez *f*; (*haste*) pressa; (*promptness*) prontidão *f*; (*gear*) marcha ♦ *vi* (*in car*) correr; **the years sped by** os anos voaram; **at full** *or* **top ~** a toda a velocidade; **at a ~ of 70 km/h** a uma velocidade de 70 km/h; **shorthand/typing ~** velocidade de estenografia/datilografia; **at ~** em alta velocidade; **a five-~ gearbox** uma caixa de mudanças com cinco marchas.
speed up (*pt*, *pp* **~ed up**) *vi* acelerar ♦ *vt* acelerar.
speedboat ['spi:dbəut] *n* lancha.
speedily ['spi:dɪlɪ] *adv* depressa, rapidamente.
speeding ['spi:dɪŋ] *n* (*AUT*) excesso de velocidade.
speed limit *n* limite *m* de velocidade, velocidade *f* máxima.
speedometer [spɪ'dɔmɪtə*] *n* velocímetro.
speed trap *n área de fiscalização contra motoristas que dirigem em alta velocidade*.
speedway ['spi:dweɪ] *n* (*SPORT*) pista de corrida, rodovia de alta velocidade; (: *also*: *~ racing*) corrida de motocicleta.
speedy ['spi:dɪ] *adj* (*fast*) veloz, rápido; (*prompt*) pronto, imediato.
speleologist [spi:lɪ'ɔlədʒɪst] *n* espeleologista *m*/*f*.
spell [spɛl] (*pt*, *pp* **~ed** *or* **spelt**) *n* (*also*: *magic ~*) encanto, feitiço; (*period of time*) período, temporada ♦ *vt* (*also*: *~ out*) soletrar; (*fig*) pressagiar, ser sinal de; **to cast a ~ on sb** enfeitiçar alguém; **he can't ~** não sabe escrever bem, comete erros de ortografia; **how do you ~ your name?** como você escreve o seu nome?; **can you ~ it for me?** pode soletrar isso para mim?
spellbound ['spɛlbaund] *adj* enfeitiçado, fascinado.
spelling ['spɛlɪŋ] *n* ortografia.
spelling mistake *n* erro ortográfico.
spelt [spɛlt] *pt*, *pp of* **spell**.
spend [spɛnd] (*pt*, *pp* **spent**) *vt* (*money*) gastar; (*time*) passar; **to ~ time/money on sth** gastar tempo/dinheiro em algo.
spending ['spɛndɪŋ] *n* gastos *mpl*; **government ~** gastos públicos.
spending money *n* dinheiro para pequenas despesas.
spending power *n* poder *m* aquisitivo.
spendthrift ['spɛndθrɪft] *n* esbanjador(a) *m*/*f*, perdulário/a.
spent [spɛnt] *pt*, *pp of* **spend** ♦ *adj* gasto.
sperm [spə:m] *n* esperma.
sperm whale *n* cachalote *m*.
spew [spju:] *vt* vomitar, lançar.
sphere [sfɪə*] *n* esfera.
spherical ['sfɛrɪkl] *adj* esférico.
sphinx [sfɪŋks] *n* esfinge *f*.
spice [spaɪs] *n* especiaria ♦ *vt* condimentar.
spick-and-span [spɪk-] *adj* tudo arrumado.
spicy ['spaɪsɪ] *adj* condimentado; (*fig*) picante.
spider ['spaɪdə*] *n* aranha; **~'s web** teia de aranha.
spiel [spi:l] *n* lengalenga.
spike [spaɪk] *n* (*point*) ponta, espigão *m*; (*BOT*) espiga; **~s** *npl* (*SPORT*) ferrões *mpl*.
spike heel (*US*) *n* salto alto e fino.
spiky ['spaɪkɪ] *adj* espinhoso.
spill [spɪl] (*pt*, *pp* **spilt** *or* **~ed**) *vt* entornar, derramar; (*blood*) derramar ♦ *vi* derramar-se; **to ~ the beans** (*inf*) dar com a língua nos dentes.
spill out *vi* (*come out*) sair; (*fall out*) cair.
spill over *vi* transbordar.
spin [spɪn] (*pt*, *pp* **spun**) *n* (*revolution of wheel*) volta, rotação *f*; (*AVIAT*) parafuso; (*trip in car*) volta *or* passeio de carro ♦ *vt* (*wool etc*) fiar, tecer; (*wheel*) girar; (*clothes*) torcer ♦ *vi* girar, rodar; **the car spun out of control** o carro se desgovernou.
spin out *vt* prolongar, alargar.
spinach ['spɪnɪtʃ] *n* espinafre *m*.
spinal ['spaɪnl] *adj* espinhal.
spinal column *n* coluna vertebral.
spinal cord *n* espinha dorsal.
spindly ['spɪndlɪ] *adj* alto e magro, espigado.
spin-dry *vt* torcer (na máquina).
spin-dryer (*BRIT*) *n* secadora.
spine [spaɪn] *n* espinha dorsal; (*thorn*) espinho.
spine-chilling [-'tʃɪlɪŋ] *adj* arrepiante.
spineless ['spaɪnlɪs] *adj* (*fig*) fraco, covarde.
spinner ['spɪnə*] *n* (*of thread*) fiandeiro/a.
spinning ['spɪnɪŋ] *n* (*of thread*, *art*) fiação *f*.
spinning top *n* pião *m*.
spinning wheel *n* roca de fiar.
spin-off *n* subproduto.
spinster ['spɪnstə*] *n* solteira; (*pej*) solteirona.
spiral ['spaɪərl] *n* espiral *f* ♦ *adj* em espiral, helicoidal ♦ *vi* (*prices*) disparar; **the inflationary ~** a espiral inflacionária.
spiral staircase *n* escada em caracol.
spire ['spaɪə*] *n* flecha, agulha.
spirit ['spɪrɪt] *n* espírito; (*soul*) alma; (*ghost*) fantasma *m*; (*humour*) humor *m*; (*courage*) coragem *f*, ânimo; **~s** *npl* (*drink*) álcool *m*; **in good ~s** alegre, de bom humor; **Holy S~** Espírito Santo; **community/public ~** espírito

NB*: European Portuguese adds the following consonants to certain words:* **b** (sú(b)dito, su(b)til); **c** (a(c)ção, a(c)cionista, a(c)to); **m** (inde(m)ne); **p** (ado(p)ção, ado(p)tar); *for further details see p. xiii.*

comunitário/público.
spirit duplicator *n* duplicador *m* a álcool.
spirited ['spɪrɪtɪd] *adj* animado, espirituoso.
spirit level *n* nível *m* de bolha.
spiritual ['spɪrɪtjuəl] *adj* espiritual ♦ *n* (*also*: *Negro* ~) *canto religioso dos negros*.
spiritualism ['spɪrɪtjuəlɪzəm] *n* espiritualismo.
spit [spɪt] (*pt, pp* **spat**) *n* (*for roasting*) espeto; (GEOG) restinga; (*spittle*) cuspe *m*, cusparada; (*saliva*) saliva ♦ *vi* cuspir; (*sound*) escarrar.
spite [spaɪt] *n* rancor *m*, ressentimento ♦ *vt* contrariar; **in ~ of** apesar de, a despeito de.
spiteful ['spaɪtful] *adj* maldoso, malévolo.
spitting ['spɪtɪŋ] *n*: **"~ prohibited"** "proibido cuspir" ♦ *adj*: **to be the ~ image of sb** ser a imagem escarrada de alguém.
spittle ['spɪtl] *n* cuspe *m*.
spiv [spɪv] (BRIT: *inf*) *n* negocista *m*.
splash [splæʃ] *n* (*sound*) borrifo, respingo; (*of colour*) mancha ♦ *vt*: **to ~ (with)** salpicar (de) ♦ *vi* (*also*: ~ *about*) borrifar, respingar ♦ *excl* pluft.
splashdown ['splæʃdaun] *n* amerissagem *f*.
spleen [spli:n] *n* (ANAT) baço.
splendid ['splɛndɪd] *adj* esplêndido.
splendour ['splɛndə*] (US **splendor**) *n* esplendor *m*; (*of achievement*) pompa, glória.
splice [splaɪs] *vt* juntar.
splint [splɪnt] *n* tala.
splinter ['splɪntə*] *n* (*of wood*) lasca; (*in finger*) farpa ♦ *vi* lascar-se, estilhaçar-se, despedaçar-se.
splinter group *n* grupo dissidente.
split [splɪt] (*pt, pp* **split**) *n* fenda, brecha; (*fig*) rompimento; (POL) divisão *f* ♦ *vt* partir, fender; (*party*) dividir; (*work, profits*) rachar, repartir ♦ *vi* (*divide*) dividir-se, repartir-se; **the ~s** *npl*: **to do the ~s** abrir *or* fazer espaguete; **to ~ sth down the middle** partir algo ao meio; (*fig*) dividir algo (pela metade).
split up *vi* (*couple*) separar-se, acabar; (*meeting*) terminar.
split-level *adj* em vários níveis.
split peas *npl* ervilhas secas *fpl*.
split personality *n* dupla personalidade *f*.
split second *n* fração *f* de segundo.
splitting ['splɪtɪŋ] *adj* (*headache*) lancinante.
splutter ['splʌtə*] *vi* crepitar; (*person*) balbuciar, gaguejar.
spoil [spɔɪl] (*pt, pp* **spoilt** *or* **~ed**) *vt* (*damage*) danificar; (*mar*) estragar, arruinar; (*child*) mimar; (*ballot paper*) violar ♦ *vi*: **to be ~ing for a fight** estar querendo comprar uma briga.
spoils [spɔɪlz] *npl* desojo, saque *m*.
spoilsport ['spɔɪlspɔ:t] *n* desmancha-prazeres *m/f inv*.
spoilt [spɔɪlt] *pt, pp of* **spoil** ♦ *adj* (*child*) mimado; (*ballot paper*) violado.
spoke [spəuk] *pt of* **speak** ♦ *n* (*of wheel*) raio.
spoken ['spəukn] *pp of* **speak**.
spokesman ['spəuksmən] (*irreg*) *n* porta-voz *m*.
spokeswoman ['spəukswumən] (*irreg*) *n* porta-voz *f*.
sponge [spʌndʒ] *n* esponja; (*cake*) pão-de-ló *m* ♦ *vt* (*wash*) lavar com esponja ♦ *vi*: **to ~ on sb** viver às custas de alguém.
sponge bag (BRIT) *n* bolsa de toalete.
sponge cake *n* pão-de-ló *m*.
sponger ['spʌndʒə*] (*pej*) *n* parasito/a.
spongy ['spʌndʒɪ] *adj* esponjoso.
sponsor ['spɔnsə*] *n* (RADIO, TV) patrocinador(a) *m/f*; (*for membership*) padrinho/madrinha; (COMM) fiador(a) *m/f*, financiador(a) *m/f* ♦ *vt* patrocinar; apadrinhar; fiar; (*idea etc*) promover; **I ~ed him at 3p a mile** eu o patrocinei à razão de 3p por milha.
sponsorship ['spɔnsəʃɪp] *n* patrocínio.
spontaneity [spɔntə'neɪɪtɪ] *n* espontaneidade *f*.
spontaneous [spɔn'teɪnɪəs] *adj* espontâneo.
spooky ['spu:kɪ] *adj* arrepiante.
spool [spu:l] *n* carretel *m*; (*of sewing machine*) bobina, novelo.
spoon [spu:n] *n* colher *f*.
spoon-feed ['spu:nfi:d] (*irreg*) *vt* dar de comer com colher; (*fig*) dar tudo mastigado a.
spoonful ['spu:nful] *n* colherada.
sporadic [spə'rædɪk] *adj* esporádico.
sport [spɔ:t] *n* esporte *m* (BR), desporto (PT); (*person*) bom/boa perdedor(a) *m/f*; **indoor/outdoor ~s** esportes de salão/ao ar livre; **to say sth in ~** dizer algo de brincadeira.
sporting ['spɔ:tɪŋ] *adj* esportivo (BR), desportivo (PT).
sport jacket (US) *n* = **sports jacket**.
sports car *n* carro esporte (BR), carro de sport (PT).
sports ground *n* campo de esportes (BR) *or* de desportos (PT).
sports jacket *n* casaco esportivo (BR) *or* desportivo (PT).
sportsman ['spɔ:tsmən] (*irreg*) *n* esportista *m* (BR), desportista *m* (PT).
sportsmanship ['spɔ:tsmənʃɪp] *n* espírito esportivo (BR) *or* desportivo (PT).
sportsmen ['spɔ:tsmɛn] *npl of* **sportsman**.
sports page *n* página de esportes.
sportswear ['spɔ:tswɛə*] *n* roupa esportiva (BR) *or* desportiva (PT) *or* esporte.
sportswoman ['spɔ:tswumən] (*irreg*) *n* esportista (BR), desportista (PT).
sporty ['spɔ:tɪ] *adj* esportivo (BR), desportivo (PT).
spot [spɔt] *n* (*place*) lugar *m*, local *m*; (*dot: on pattern*) mancha, ponto; (*pimple*) espinha; (*freckle*) sarda, pinta; (*small amount*): **a ~ of** um pouquinho de ♦ *vt* (*notice*) notar; **on the ~** (*at once*) na hora; (*there*) ali mesmo; (*in difficulty*) em apuros.
spot check *n* fiscalização *f* de surpresa.
spotless ['spɔtlɪs] *adj* sem mancha, imaculado.
spotlight ['spɔtlaɪt] *n* holofote *m*, refletor *m*.
spot-on (BRIT: *inf*) *adj* acertado em cheio.
spot price *n* preço à vista.
spotted ['spɔtɪd] *adj* (*pattern*) com bolinhas.
spotty ['spɔtɪ] *adj* (*face*) manchado.

spouse [spauz] *n* cônjuge *m/f*.
spout [spaut] *n* (*of jug*) bico; (*pipe*) cano ♦ *vi* jorrar.
sprain [spreɪn] *n* distensão *f*, torcedura ♦ *vt*: **to ~ one's ankle** torcer o tornozelo.
sprang [spræŋ] *pt of* **spring**.
sprawl [sprɔːl] *vi* esparramar-se ♦ *n*: **urban ~** crescimento urbano; **to send sb ~ing** jogar alguém no chão.
spray [spreɪ] *n* (*of sea*) borrifo; (*container*) spray *m*, atomizador *m*; (*of paint*) pistola borrifadora; (*of flowers*) ramalhete *m* ♦ *vt* pulverizar; (*crops*) borrifar, regar ♦ *cpd* (*deodorant etc*) em spray.
spread [sprɛd] (*pt, pp* **spread**) *n* extensão *f*; (*distribution*) expansão *f*, difusão *f*; (*PRESS, TYP*: *two pages*) chapada; (*CULIN*) pasta ♦ *vt* espalhar; (*butter*) untar, passar; (*wings, sails*) abrir, desdobrar; (*scatter*) disseminar; (*payments*) espaçar ♦ *vi* espalhar-se, alastrar-se, difundir-se.
spread-eagled [-'iːgld] *adj*: **to be** *or* **lie ~** estar estirado.
spreadsheet ['sprɛdʃiːt] *n* (*COMPUT*) planilha.
spree [spriː] *n*: **to go on a ~** cair na farra.
sprig [sprɪg] *n* raminho.
sprightly ['spraɪtlɪ] *adj* vivo, desembaraçado.
spring [sprɪŋ] (*pt* **sprang**, *pp* **sprung**) *n* (*leap*) salto, pulo; (*coiled metal*) mola; (*bounciness*) elasticidade *f*; (*season*) primavera; (*of water*) fonte *f* ♦ *vi* pular, saltar ♦ *vt*: **to ~ a leak** (*pipe etc*) furar; **he sprang the news on me** ele me pegou de surpresa com a notícia; **in ~, in the ~** na primavera; **to ~ from** provir de; **to ~ into action** partir para ação; **to walk with a ~ in one's step** andar espevitado.
spring up *vi* nascer *or* aparecer de repente.
springboard ['sprɪŋbɔːd] *n* trampolim *m*.
spring-clean *n* (*also*: *~ing*) limpeza total, faxina (geral).
spring onion (*BRIT*) *n* cebolinha.
springtime ['sprɪŋtaɪm] *n* primavera.
springy ['sprɪŋɪ] *adj* elástico, flexível.
sprinkle ['sprɪŋkl] *vt* (*pour*) salpicar, borrifar; **to ~ water on, ~ with water** borrifar *or* salpicar de água; **~d with** (*fig*) salpicado *or* polvilhado de.
sprinkler ['sprɪŋklə*] *n* (*for lawn etc*) regador *m*; (*to put out fire*) sprinkler *m*.
sprinkling ['sprɪŋklɪŋ] *n* (*of water*) borrifo; (*of salt*) pitada; (*of sugar*) bocado.
sprint [sprɪnt] *n* corrida de pequena distância ♦ *vi* correr a toda velocidade.
sprinter ['sprɪntə*] *n* corredor(a) *m/f*.
sprite [spraɪt] *n* duende *m*, elfo.
sprocket ['sprɔkɪt] *n* (*on printer etc*) dente *m* (de roda).
sprout [spraut] *vi* brotar, germinar.
sprouts [sprauts] *npl* (*also*: *Brussels ~*) couves-de-Bruxelas *fpl*.
spruce [spruːs] *n* (*BOT*) abeto ♦ *adj* arrumado, limpo, elegante.
spruce up *vt* arrumar; **to ~ o.s. up** arrumar-se.
sprung [sprʌŋ] *pp of* **spring**.
spry [spraɪ] *adj* vivo, ativo, ágil.
SPUC *n abbr* = **Society for the Protection of Unborn Children.**
spud [spʌd] (*inf*) *n* batata.
spun [spʌn] *pt, pp of* **spin**.
spur [spəː*] *n* espora; (*fig*) estímulo ♦ *vt* (*also*: *~ on*) incitar, estimular; **on the ~ of the moment** de improviso, de repente.
spurious ['spjuərɪəs] *adj* espúrio, falso.
spurn [spəːn] *vt* desdenhar, desprezar.
spurt [spəːt] *n* (*of energy*) acesso; (*of water*) jorro ♦ *vi* (*water*) jorrar; **to put in** *or* **on a ~** (*runner*) dar uma arrancada; (*fig*: *in work etc*) dar uma virada.
sputter ['spʌtə*] *vi* crepitar; (*person*) balbuciar, gaguejar.
spy [spaɪ] *n* espião/espiã *m/f* ♦ *vi*: **to ~ on** espiar, espionar ♦ *vt* (*see*) enxergar, avistar ♦ *cpd* (*film, story*) de espionagem.
spying ['spaɪɪŋ] *n* espionagem *f*.
Sq. *abbr* (*in address*) = **square.**
sq. *abbr* (*MATH etc*) = **square.**
squabble ['skwɔbl] *n* briga, bate-boca *m* ♦ *vi* brigar, discutir.
squad [skwɔd] *n* (*MIL, POLICE*) pelotão *m*, esquadra; (*FOOTBALL*) seleção *f*; **flying ~** (*POLICE*) polícia de prontidão.
squad car (*BRIT*) *n* (*POLICE*) radiopatrulha.
squadron ['skwɔdrən] *n* (*MIL*) esquadrão *m*; (*AVIAT*) esquadrilha; (*NAUT*) esquadra.
squalid ['skwɔlɪd] *adj* sórdido.
squall [skwɔːl] *n* (*storm*) tempestade *f*; (*wind*) pé *m* (de vento), rajada.
squalor ['skwɔlə*] *n* sordidez *f*.
squander ['skwɔndə*] *vt* (*money*) esbanjar, dissipar; (*chances*) desperdiçar.
square [skwɛə*] *n* quadrado; (*in town*) praça; (*MATH*: *instrument*) esquadro ♦ *adj* quadrado; (*inf*: *ideas, tastes*) careta, antiquado ♦ *vt* (*arrange*) ajustar, acertar; (*MATH*) elevar ao quadrado ♦ *vi* (*agree*) ajustar-se; **all ~** igual, quite; **a ~ meal** uma refeição substancial; **2 metres ~** um quadrado de dois metros de lado; **1 ~ metre** um metro quadrado; **we're back to ~ one** voltamos à estaca zero.
square up (*BRIT*) *vi* (*settle*) ajustar; **to ~ up with sb** acertar as contas com alguém.
square bracket *n* (*TYP*) colchete *m*.
squarely ['skwɛəlɪ] *adv* em forma quadrada; (*fully*) em cheio.
square root *n* raiz *f* quadrada.
squash [skwɔʃ] *n* (*BRIT*: *drink*): **lemon/orange ~** suco (*BR*) *or* sumo (*PT*) de limão/laranja; (*SPORT*) squash *m*; (*vegetable*) abóbora ♦ *vt* esmagar; **to ~ together** apinhar.
squat [skwɔt] *adj* agachado; (*short*) atarracado ♦ *vi* agachar-se, acocorar-se; (*on property*) ocupar ilegalmente.

***NB**: European Portuguese adds the following consonants to certain words:* **b** (sú(b)dito, su(b)til); **c** (a(c)ção, a(c)cionista, a(c)to); **m** (inde(m)ne); **p** (ado(p)ção, ado(p)tar); *for further details see p. xiii.*

squatter ['skwɔtə*] *n* posseiro/a.
squawk [skwɔːk] *vi* grasnar.
squeak [skwiːk] *n* grunhido, chiado; (*of shoe*) rangido; (*of mouse*) guincho ♦ *vi* grunhir, chiar; ranger; guinchar.
squeal [skwiːl] *vi* guinchar, gritar agudamente; (*inf*: *inform*) delatar.
squeamish ['skwiːmɪʃ] *adj* melindroso, delicado.
squeeze [skwiːz] *n* aperto, compressão *f*; (*of hand*) apertão *m*; (*in bus etc*) apinhamento; (*also*: *credit* ~) arrocho (ao crédito) ♦ *vt* comprimir, socar; (*hand, arm*) apertar ♦ *vi*: **to ~ past/under sth** espremer-se para passar algo/para passar por baixo de algo; **a ~ of lemon** umas gotas de limão.
squeeze out *vt* espremer; (*fig*) extorquir.
squelch [skwɛltʃ] *vi* fazer ruído de passos na lama.
squib [skwɪb] *n* busca-pé *m*.
squid [skwɪd] (*pl inv or* **~s**) *n* lula.
squiggle ['skwɪgl] *n* garatuja.
squint [skwɪnt] *vi* olhar *or* ser vesgo ♦ *n* (MED) estrabismo; **to ~ at sth** olhar algo de soslaio *or* de esguelha.
squire ['skwaɪə*] (BRIT) *n* proprietário rural.
squirm [skwəːm] *vi* retorcer-se.
squirrel ['skwɪrəl] *n* esquilo.
squirt [skwəːt] *vi* jorrar, esguichar.
Sr *abbr* = **senior;** (REL) = **sister.**
SRC (BRIT) *n abbr* = **Students' Representative Council.**
Sri Lanka [srɪ'læŋkə] *n* Sri Lanka *m*.
SRN (BRIT) *n abbr* = **State Registered Nurse.**
SRO (US) *abbr* = **standing room only.**
SS *abbr* = **steamship.**
SSA (US) *abbr* = **Social Security Administration.**
SST (US) *abbr* = **supersonic transport.**
ST (US) *abbr* = **Standard Time.**
St *abbr* (= *saint*) S.; = **street.**
stab [stæb] *n* (*with knife etc*) punhalada; (*of pain*) pontada; (*inf*: *try*): **to have a ~ at (doing) sth** tentar (fazer) algo ♦ *vt* apunhalar; **to ~ sb to death** matar alguém a facadas, esfaquear alguém.
stabbing ['stæbɪŋ] *n*: **there's been a ~** houve um esfaqueamento ♦ *adj* (*pain*) cortante.
stability [stə'bɪlɪtɪ] *n* estabilidade *f*.
stabilization [steɪbəlaɪ'zeɪʃən] *n* estabilização *f*.
stabilize ['steɪbəlaɪz] *vt* estabilizar ♦ *vi* estabilizar-se.
stabilizer ['steɪbəlaɪzə*] *n* estabilizador *m*.
stable ['steɪbl] *adj* estável ♦ *n* estábulo, cavalariça; **riding ~s** clube *m* de equitação.
staccato [stə'kɑːtəu] *adv* destacado, staccato ♦ *adj* (MUS) destacado, staccato; (*noise*) interrupto; (*voice*) quebrado.
stack [stæk] *n* montão *m*, pilha ♦ *vt* amontoar, empilhar; **there's ~s of time** (BRIT: *inf*) tem tempo de sobra.
stadium ['steɪdɪəm] *n* estádio.
staff [stɑːf] *n* (*work force*) pessoal *m*, quadro; (BRIT: SCH: *also*: *teaching* ~) corpo docente; (*stick*) cajado, bastão *m* ♦ *vt* prover de pessoal; **the office is ~ed by women** o escritório está composto de mulheres.
staffroom ['stɑːfruːm] *n* sala dos professores.
Staffs (BRIT) *abbr* = **Staffordshire.**
stag [stæg] *n* veado, cervo.
stage [steɪdʒ] *n* (*in theatre*) palco, cena; (*point*) etapa, fase *f*; (*platform*) plataforma, estrado; (*profession*): **the ~** o palco, o teatro ♦ *vt* (*play*) pôr em cena, representar; (*demonstration*) montar, organizar; (*fig*: *perform*: *recovery etc*) realizar; **in ~s** por etapas; **to go through a difficult ~** passar por uma fase difícil; **in the early/final ~s** na fase inicial/final.
stagecoach ['steɪdʒkəutʃ] *n* diligência.
stage door *n* entrada dos artistas.
stage fright *n* medo da platéia.
stagehand ['steɪdʒhænd] *n* ajudante *m/f* de teatro.
stage-manage *vt* (*fig*) orquestrar.
stage manager *n* diretor(a) *m/f* de cena.
stagger ['stægə*] *vi* cambalear ♦ *vt* (*amaze*) surpreender, chocar; (*hours, holidays*) escalonar.
staggering ['stægərɪŋ] *adj* (*amazing*) surpreendente, chocante.
stagnant ['stægnənt] *adj* estagnado.
stagnate [stæg'neɪt] *vi* estagnar.
stagnation [stæg'neɪʃən] *n* estagnação *f*.
stag party *n* despedida de solteiro.
staid [steɪd] *adj* sério, sóbrio.
stain [steɪn] *n* mancha; (*colouring*) tinta, tintura ♦ *vt* manchar; (*wood*) tingir.
stained glass window [steɪnd-] *n* janela com vitral.
stainless ['steɪnlɪs] *adj* (*steel*) inoxidável.
stain remover *n* tira-manchas *m*.
stair [stɛə*] *n* (*step*) degrau *m*; **~s** *npl* escada.
staircase ['stɛəkeɪs] *n* escadaria, escada.
stairway ['stɛəweɪ] *n* escadaria, escada.
stairwell ['stɛəwɛl] *n* caixa de escada.
stake [steɪk] *n* estaca, poste *m*; (BETTING) aposta ♦ *vt* apostar; **to be at ~** estar em jogo; **to have a ~ in sth** ter interesse em algo; **to ~ a claim to sth** reivindicar algo.
stalactite ['stæləktaɪt] *n* estalactite *f*.
stalagmite ['stæləgmaɪt] *n* estalagmite *f*.
stale [steɪl] *adj* (*bread*) amanhecido; (*food*) passado, estragado.
stalemate ['steɪlmeɪt] *n* empate *m*; (*fig*) impasse *m*, beco sem saída.
stalk [stɔːk] *n* caule *m*, talo, haste *f* ♦ *vt* caçar de tocaia; **to ~ off** andar com arrogância.
stall [stɔːl] *n* (*in market*) barraca; (*in stable*) baia ♦ *vt* (AUT) fazer morrer ♦ *vi* (AUT) morrer; (*fig*) esquivar-se, ganhar tempo; **~s** *npl* (BRIT: *in cinema, theatre*) platéia; **a newspaper/flower ~** uma banca de jornais/uma barraca de flores.
stallholder ['stɔːlhəuldə*] *n* feirante *m/f*.
stallion ['stælɪən] *n* garanhão *m*.
stalwart ['stɔːlwət] *adj* (*in build*) robusto; (*in spirit*) leal, firme ♦ *n* partidário leal.
stamen ['steɪmən] *n* estame *m*.

stamina ['stæmɪnə] *n* resistência.

stammer ['stæmə*] *n* gagueira ♦ *vi* gaguejar, balbuciar.

stamp [stæmp] *n* selo; (*mark, also fig*) marca, impressão *f*; (*on document*) timbre *m*, sinete *m* ♦ *vi* (*also*: ~ *one's foot*) bater com o pé ♦ *vt* (*letter*) selar; (*with rubber* ~) carimbar; **~ed addressed envelope** envelope *m* selado e sobrescritado.

stamp out *vt* (*fire*) apagar com os pés; (*crime*) eliminar; (*opposition*) esmagar.

stamp album *n* álbum *m* de selos.

stamp collecting [-kə'lɛktɪŋ] *n* filatelia.

stamp duty (*BRIT*) *n* imposto de selo.

stampede [stæm'pi:d] *n* debandada, estouro (da boiada).

stamp machine *n* máquina de selos.

stance [stæns] *n* postura, posição *f*.

stand [stænd] (*pt, pp* **stood**) *n* (*position*) posição *f*, postura; (*for taxis*) ponto; (*also*: *hall* ~) pedestal *m*; (*also*: *music* ~) estante *f*; (*SPORT*) tribuna, palanque *m*; (*also*: *news* ~) banca de jornais ♦ *vi* (*be*) estar, encontrar-se; (*be on foot*) estar em pé; (*rise*) levantar-se; (*remain*) ficar em pé ♦ *vt* (*place*) pôr, colocar; (*tolerate, withstand*) agüentar, suportar; (*cost*) pagar; **to make a ~** resistir; (*fig*) ater-se a um princípio; **to take a ~ on an issue** tomar posição definida sobre um assunto; **to ~ for parliament** (*BRIT*) apresentar-se como candidato ao parlamento; **to ~ guard** *or* **watch** (*MIL*) montar guarda; **it ~s to reason** é lógico; **as things ~** como as coisas estão; **to ~ sb a drink/meal** pagar uma bebida/refeição para alguém; **I can't ~ him** não o agüento; **to ~ still** ficar parado.

stand aside *vi* pôr-se de lado.

stand by *vi* (*be ready*) estar a postos ♦ *vt fus* (*opinion*) aferrar-se a.

stand down *vi* (*withdraw*) retirar-se; (*MIL*) deixar o serviço.

stand for *vt fus* (*defend*) apoiar; (*signify*) significar; (*tolerate*) tolerar, permitir.

stand in for *vt fus* substituir.

stand out *vi* (*be prominent*) destacar-se.

stand up *vi* (*rise*) levantar-se.

stand up for *vt fus* defender.

stand up to *vt fus* enfrentar.

stand-alone *adj* (*COMPUT*) autônomo, stand-alone.

standard ['stændəd] *n* padrão *m*, critério; (*flag*) estandarte *m*; (*level*) nível *m* ♦ *adj* (*size etc*) padronizado, regular, normal; **~s** *npl* (*morals*) valores *mpl* morais; **to be** *or* **come up to ~** alcançar os padrões exigidos; **to apply a double ~** ter dois pesos e duas medidas; **~ of living** padrão de vida; **the gold ~** (*COMM*) o padrão ouro.

standardization [stændədaɪ'zeɪʃən] *n* padronização *f*.

standardize ['stændədaɪz] *vt* padronizar.

standard lamp (*BRIT*) *n* abajur *m* de pé.

standard time *n* hora legal *or* oficial.

stand-by *adj* de reserva; (*ticket, passenger*) stand-by ♦ *n*: **to be on ~** estar de sobreaviso *or* de prontidão.

stand-in *n* suplente *m/f*; (*CINEMA*) dublê *m/f*.

standing ['stændɪŋ] *adj* (*upright*) ereto vertical; (*on foot*) em pé; (*permanent*) permanente ♦ *n* posição *f*, reputação *f*; **of 6 months' ~** de 6 meses de duração; **of many years' ~** de muitos anos; **he was given a ~ ovation** ele foi ovacionado; **it's a ~ joke** é uma piada famosa; **a man of some ~** um homem de posição.

standing order *n* (*at bank*) instrução *f* permanente; **~s** *npl* (*MIL*) regulamento geral.

standing room *n* lugar *m* em pé.

stand-offish [-'ɔfɪʃ] *adj* incomunicativo, reservado.

standpat ['stændpæt] (*US*) *adj* inflexível, conservador(a).

standpipe ['stændpaɪp] *n* tubo de subida.

standpoint ['stændpɔɪnt] *n* ponto de vista.

standstill ['stændstɪl] *n*: **at a ~** paralisado, parado; **to come to a ~** (*car*) parar; (*factory, traffic*) ficar paralisado.

stank [stæŋk] *pt of* **stink**.

stanza ['stænzə] *n* estância, estrofe *f*.

staple ['steɪpl] *n* (*for papers*) grampo; (*chief product*) produto básico ♦ *adj* (*food etc*) básico ♦ *vt* grampear.

stapler ['steɪplə*] *n* grampeador *m*.

star [stɑ:*] *n* estrela; (*celebrity*) astro/estrela ♦ *vi*: **to ~ in** ser a estrela em, estrelar ♦ *vt* (*CINEMA*) ser estrelado por; **4-~ hotel** hotel 4 estrelas; **2-~ petrol** gasolina simples (*BR*) *or* normal (*PT*); **4-~ petrol** (*BRIT*) (gasolina) azul (*BR*) *or* súper (*PT*).

star attraction *n* atração *f* principal.

starboard ['stɑ:bəd] *n* estibordo; **to ~** a estibordo.

starch [stɑ:tʃ] *n* (*in food*) amido, fécula; (*for clothes*) goma.

starched ['stɑ:tʃt] *adj* (*collar*) engomado.

starchy ['stɑ:tʃɪ] *adj* amiláceo.

stardom ['stɑ:dəm] *n* estrelato.

stare [stɛə*] *n* olhar *m* fixo ♦ *vi*: **to ~ at** olhar fixamente, fitar.

starfish ['stɑ:fɪʃ] *n inv* estrela-do-mar *f*.

stark [stɑ:k] *adj* (*bleak*) severo, áspero; (*colour*) sóbrio; (*reality, truth, simplicity*) cru; (*contrast*) gritante ♦ *adv*: **~ naked** completamente nu, em pêlo.

starlet ['stɑ:lɪt] *n* (*CINEMA*) vedete *f*.

starlight ['stɑ:laɪt] *n*: **by ~** à luz das estrelas.

starling ['stɑ:lɪŋ] *n* estorninho.

starlit ['stɑ:lɪt] *adj* iluminado pelas estrelas.

starry ['stɑ:rɪ] *adj* estrelado.

starry-eyed *adj* (*innocent*) deslumbrado.

star-studded [-'stʌdɪd] *adj*: **a ~ cast** um elenco cheio de estrelas.

start [stɑ:t] *n* (*beginning*) princípio, começo; (*departure*) partida; (*sudden movement*) so-

***NB:** European Portuguese adds the following consonants to certain words:* **b** (sú(b)dito, su(b)til); **c** (a(c)ção, a(c)cionista, a(c)to); **m** (inde(m)ne); **p** (ado(p)ção, ado(p)tar); *for further details see p. xiii.*

bressalto, susto; (*advantage*) vantagem *f* ♦ *vt* começar, iniciar; (*cause*) causar; (*found*) fundar; (*engine*) ligar; (*fire*) provocar ♦ *vi* (*begin*) começar, iniciar; (*with fright*) sobressaltar-se, assustar-se; (*train etc*) sair; **to ~ doing sth** começar a fazer algo; **at the ~** no início; **for a ~** para início de conversa; **to make an early ~** sair *or* começar cedo; **to ~ (off) with ...** (*firstly*) para começar ...; (*at the beginning*) no início ...; **to give sb a ~** dar um susto em alguém.

start off *vi* começar, principiar; (*leave*) sair, pôr-se a caminho.

start over (*US*) *vi* começar de novo.

start up *vi* começar; (*car*) pegar, pôr-se em marcha ♦ *vt* começar; (*car*) ligar.

starter ['stɑːtə*] *n* (*AUT*) arranque *m*; (*SPORT*: *official*) juiz(a) *m/f* da partida; (: *runner*) corredor(a) *m/f*; (*BRIT*: *CULIN*) entrada.

starting handle ['stɑːtɪŋ-] (*BRIT*) *n* manivela de arranque.

starting point ['stɑːtɪŋ-] *n* ponto de partida.

starting price ['stɑːtɪŋ-] *n* preço inicial.

startle ['stɑːtl] *vt* assustar, aterrar.

startling ['stɑːtlɪŋ] *adj* surpreendente.

star turn (*BRIT*) *n* rei *m*/rainha *f* do show.

starvation [stɑː'veɪʃən] *n* fome *f*; (*MED*) inanição *f*.

starve ['stɑːv] *vi* passar fome; (*to death*) morrer de fome ♦ *vt* fazer passar fome; (*fig*): **to ~ (of)** privar (*of* de); **I'm starving** estou morrendo de fome.

starving ['stɑːvɪŋ] *adj* faminto, esfomeado.

state [steɪt] *n* estado; (*pomp*): **in ~** com grande pompa ♦ *vt* (*say, declare*) afirmar, declarar; (*a case*) expor, apresentar; **the S~s** *npl* os Estados Unidos; **to be in a ~** estar agitado; **~ of emergency** estado de emergência; **~ of mind** estado de espírito; **the ~ of the art** a última palavra; **to lie in ~** estar exposto em câmara ardente.

State Department (*US*) *n* Departamento de Estado, ≈ Ministério das Relações Exteriores.

state education (*BRIT*) *n* educação *f* pública.

stateless ['steɪtlɪs] *adj* desnacionalizado.

stately ['steɪtlɪ] *adj* majestoso, imponente.

statement ['steɪtmənt] *n* afirmação *f*; (*LAW*) depoimento; (*ECON*) balanço; **official ~** comunicado oficial; **~ of account** extrato de conta, extrato bancário.

state-owned [-əund] *adj* estatal.

state secret *n* segredo de estado.

statesman ['steɪtsmən] (*irreg*) *n* estadista *m*.

statesmanship ['steɪtsmənʃɪp] *n* arte *f* de governar.

statesmen ['steɪtsmɛn] *npl of* **statesman**.

static ['stætɪk] *n* (*RADIO*) interferência; (*also*: *~ electricity*) (eletricidade *f*) estática ♦ *adj* estático.

station ['steɪʃən] *n* estação *f*; (*place*) posto, lugar *m*; (*POLICE*) delegacia; (*RADIO*) emissora; (*rank*) posição *f* social ♦ *vt* colocar; **to be ~ed in** (*MIL*) estar estacionado em.

stationary ['steɪʃnərɪ] *adj* estacionário.

stationer's (shop) ['steɪʃənəz-] *n* papelaria.

stationery ['steɪʃnərɪ] *n* artigos *mpl* de papelaria; (*writing paper*) papel *m* de carta.

station master *n* (*RAIL*) chefe *m* da estação.

station wagon (*US*) *n* perua (*BR*), canadiana (*PT*).

statistic [stə'tɪstɪk] *n* estatística; **~s** *n* (*science*) estatística.

statistical [stə'tɪstɪkl] *adj* estatístico.

statue ['stætjuː] *n* estátua.

statuesque [stætju'ɛsk] *adj* escultural.

statuette [stætju'ɛt] *n* estatueta.

stature ['stætʃə*] *n* estatura, altura; (*fig*) estatura, envergadura.

status ['steɪtəs] *n* posição *f*, categoria; (*reputation*) reputação *f*, status *m*; (*ADMIN*: *also*: *marital ~*) estado civil.

status quo [-kwəu] *n*: **the ~** o status quo.

status symbol *n* símbolo de prestígio.

statute ['stætjuːt] *n* estatuto, lei *f*; **~s** *npl* (*of club etc*) estatuto.

statute book *n* ≈ Código.

statutory ['stætjutərɪ] *adj* (*according to statutes*) estatutário; (*holiday etc*) regulamentar.

staunch [stɔːntʃ] *adj* firme, constante ♦ *vt* estancar.

stave [steɪv] *n* (*MUS*) pauta.

stave off *vt* (*attack*) repelir; (*threat*) evitar, protelar.

stay [steɪ] *n* (*period of time*) estadia, estada; (*LAW*): **~ of execution** adiamento de execução ♦ *vi* (*remain*) ficar; (*as guest*) hospedar-se; (*spend some time*) demorar-se; **to ~ put** não se mexer; **to ~ the night** pernoitar.

stay behind *vi* ficar atrás.

stay in *vi* (*at home*) ficar em casa.

stay on *vi* ficar.

stay out *vi* (*of house*) ficar fora de casa; (*strikers*) continuar em greve.

stay up *vi* (*at night*) velar, ficar acordado.

staying power ['steɪɪŋ-] *n* resistência, raça.

STD *n abbr* (*BRIT*: = *subscriber trunk dialling*) DDD *f*; (= *sexually transmitted disease*) DST *f*.

stead [stɛd] (*BRIT*) *n*: **in sb's ~** em lugar de alguém; **to stand sb in good ~** prestar bons serviços a alguém.

steadfast ['stɛdfɑːst] *adj* firme, estável, resoluto.

steadily ['stɛdɪlɪ] *adv* (*firmly*) firmemente; (*unceasingly*) sem parar, constantemente; (*drive*) a uma velocidade constante.

steady ['stɛdɪ] *adj* (*constant*) constante, fixo; (*unswerving*) firme; (*regular*) regular; (*person, character*) sensato, equilibrado; (*diligent*) diligente; (*boyfriend, job etc*) firme, estável; (*calm*) calmo, sereno ♦ *vt* (*hold*) manter firme; (*stabilize*) estabilizar; (*nerves*) acalmar; **to ~ o.s. on** *or* **against sth** firmar-se em algo.

steak [steɪk] *n* filé *m*; (*beef*) bife *m*.

steakhouse ['steɪkhaus] (*irreg*) *n* ≈ churrascaria.

steal [stiːl] (*pt* **stole**, *pp* **stolen**) *vt, vi* roubar.

steal away *vi* sair às escondidas.

steal off *vi* sair às escondidas.
stealth [stɛlθ] *n*: **by ~** furtivamente, às escondidas.
stealthy ['stɛlθɪ] *adj* furtivo.
steam [stiːm] *n* vapor *m* ♦ *vt* (*CULIN*) cozinhar no vapor ♦ *vi* fumegar; (*ship*): **to ~ along** avançar *or* mover-se (a vapor); **under one's own ~** (*fig*) por esforço próprio; **to run out of ~** (*fig*: *person*) perder o pique; **to let off ~** (*fig*: *inf*) desabafar.
steam up *vi* (*window*) embaçar; **to get ~ed up about sth** irritar-se com algo.
steam engine *n* máquina a vapor.
steamer ['stiːmə*] *n* vapor *m*, navio (a vapor).
steam iron *n* ferro a vapor.
steamroller ['stiːmrəulə*] *n* rolo compressor (a vapor).
steamy ['stiːmɪ] *adj* vaporoso; (*room*) cheio de vapor, úmido (*PT*: hu-).
steed [stiːd] *n* (*literary*) corcel *m*.
steel [stiːl] *n* aço ♦ *cpd* de aço.
steel band *n banda de percussão do Caribe*.
steel industry *n* indústria siderúrgica.
steel mill *n* (usina) siderúrgica.
steelworks ['stiːlwəːks] *n* (usina) siderúrgica.
steely ['stiːli] *adj* (*determination*) inflexível; (*gaze, eyes*) duro, frio; **~-grey** cor de aço *inv*.
steep [stiːp] *adj* íngreme, escarpado; (*stair*) empinado; (*price*) exorbitante ♦ *vt* ensopar, embeber, impregnar.
steeple ['stiːpl] *n* campanário, torre *f*.
steeplechase ['stiːpltʃeɪs] *n* corrida de obstáculos.
steeplejack ['stiːpldʒæk] *n* consertador *m* de torres *or* de chaminés altas.
steeply ['stiːplɪ] *adv* escarpadamente, a pique.
steer [stɪə*] *n* boi *m* ♦ *vt* guiar, dirigir, pilotar ♦ *vi* conduzir; **to ~ clear of sb/sth** (*fig*) evitar alguém/algo.
steering ['stɪərɪŋ] *n* (*AUT*) direção *f*.
steering column *n* (*AUT*) coluna da direção.
steering committee *n* comitê *m* dirigente.
steering wheel *n* volante *m*.
stellar ['stɛlə*] *adj* estelar.
stem [stɛm] *n* (*of plant*) caule *m*, haste *f*; (*of glass*) pé *m*; (*of pipe*) tubo ♦ *vt* deter, reter; (*blood*) estancar.
stem from *vt fus* originar-se de.
stench [stɛntʃ] *n* fedor *m*.
stencil ['stɛnsl] *n* (*typed*) estêncil *m*; (*lettering*) gabarito de letra ♦ *vt* imprimir com estêncil.
stenographer [stɛ'nɔgrəfə*] (*US*) *n* estenógrafo/a.
stenography [stɛ'nɔgrəfɪ] (*US*) *n* estenografia.
step [stɛp] *n* passo; (*stair*) degrau *m*; (*action*) medida, providência ♦ *vi*: **to ~ forward** avançar, dar um passo em frente; **~s** *npl* (*BRIT*) escada portátil *or* de abrir; **to ~ on** pisar, calcar; **~ by ~** passo a passo; **to be in ~ (with)** (*fig*) manter a paridade (com); **to be out of ~ (with)** (*fig*) estar em disparidade (com); **to take ~s** tomar providências.
step down *vi* (*fig*) retirar-se.
step in *vi* (*fig*) intervir.
step off *vt fus* descer de.
step over *vt fus* passar por cima de.
step up *vt* (*increase*) aumentar; (*intensify*) intensificar.
stepbrother ['stɛpbrʌðə*] *n* meio-irmão *m*.
stepchild ['stɛptʃaɪld] (*irreg*) *n* enteado/a.
stepdaughter ['stɛpdɔːtə*] *n* enteada.
stepfather ['stɛpfɑːðə*] *n* padrasto.
stepladder ['stɛplædə*] (*BRIT*) *n* escada portátil *or* de abrir.
stepmother ['stɛpmʌðə*] *n* madrasta.
stepping stone ['stɛpɪŋ-] *n* pedra utilizada em passarelas; (*fig*) trampolim *m*.
stepsister ['stɛpsɪstə*] *n* meia-irmã *f*.
stepson ['stɛpsʌn] *n* enteado.
stereo ['stɛrɪəu] *n* estéreo; (*record player*) (aparelho de) som *m* ♦ *adj* (*also*: **~***phonic*) estereofônico; **in ~** em estéreo.
stereotype ['stɪərɪətaɪp] *n* estereótipo ♦ *vt* estereotipar.
sterile ['stɛraɪl] *adj* estéril.
sterility [stɛ'rɪlɪtɪ] *n* esterilidade *f*.
sterilization [stɛrɪlaɪ'zeɪʃən] *n* esterilização *f*.
sterilize ['stɛrɪlaɪz] *vt* esterilizar.
sterling ['stəːlɪŋ] *adj* esterlino; (*silver*) de lei; (*fig*) genuíno, puro ♦ *n* (*currency*) libra esterlina; **a pound ~** uma libra esterlina.
sterling area *n* zona esterlina.
stern [stəːn] *adj* severo, austero ♦ *n* (*NAUT*) popa, ré *f*.
sternum ['stəːnəm] *n* esterno.
steroid ['stɪərɔɪd] *n* esteróide *m*.
stethoscope ['stɛθəskəup] *n* estetoscópio.
stevedore ['stiːvədɔː*] *n* estivador *m*.
stew [stjuː] *n* guisado, ensopado ♦ *vt*, *vi* guisar, ensopar; (*fruit*) cozinhar; **~ed tea** chá muito forte; **~ed fruit** compota de frutas.
steward ['stjuːəd] *n* (*AVIAT*) comissário de bordo; (*also*: *shop* ~) delegado/a sindical.
stewardess ['stjuːədɪs] *n* aeromoça (*BR*), hospedeira de bordo (*PT*).
stewing steak ['stjuːɪŋ-] (*US* **stew meat**) *n* carne *f* para ensopado.
St. Ex. *abbr* = **stock exchange**.
stg *abbr* = **sterling**.
stick [stɪk] (*pt, pp* **stuck**) *n* pau *m*; (*as weapon*) cacete *m*; (*walking* ~) bengala, cajado ♦ *vt* (*glue*) colar; (*thrust*): **to ~ sth into** cravar *or* enfiar algo em; (*inf*: *put*) meter; (*tolerate*) agüentar, suportar ♦ *vi* colar-se, aderir-se; (*get jammed*) emperrar; (*in mind etc*) gravar-se; **to get hold of the wrong end of the ~** (*BRIT*: *fig*) confundir-se; **to ~ to** (*promise, principles*) manter.
stick around (*inf*) *vi* ficar.
stick out *vi* estar saliente, projetar-se ♦ *vt*: **to ~ it out** (*inf*) agüentar firme.
stick up *vi* estar saliente, projetar-se.

NB: *European Portuguese adds the following consonants to certain words:* **b** (sú(b)dito, su(b)til); **c** (a(c)ção, a(c)cionista, a(c)to); **m** (inde(m)ne); **p** (ado(p)ção, ado(p)tar); *for further details* *see p. xiii.*

stick up for *vt fus* defender.
sticker ['stɪkə*] *n* adesivo.
sticking plaster ['stɪkɪŋ-] *n* esparadrapo.
stickleback ['stɪklbæk] *n* espinhela.
stickler ['stɪklə*] *n*: **to be a ~ for** insistir em, exigir.
stick-on *adj* adesivo.
stick-up (*inf*) *n* assalto a mão armada.
sticky ['stɪkɪ] *adj* pegajoso; (*label*) adesivo; (*fig*) espinhoso.
stiff [stɪf] *adj* rígido; (*strong*) forte; (*hard*) duro; (*difficult*) difícil; (*door*) empenado; **to be** *or* **feel ~** (*person*) ter dores musculares; **to have a ~ neck** estar com torcicolo; **~ upper lip** (*BRIT*: *fig*) fleuma britânica.
stiffen ['stɪfən] *vt* endurecer; (*limb*) entumecer ♦ *vi* enrijecer-se; (*grow stronger*) fortalecer-se.
stiffness ['stɪfnɪs] *n* rigidez *f*.
stifle ['staɪfl] *vt* sufocar, abafar.
stifling ['staɪflɪŋ] *adj* (*heat*) sufocante, abafado.
stigma ['stɪgmə] (*pl* **~ta**) *n* (*BOT*, *MED*, *REL*) estigma *m*; (*pl*: **~s**: *fig*) estigma *m*.
stigmata [stɪg'mɑːtə] *npl of* **stigma**.
stile [staɪl] *n degraus para passar por uma cerca ou muro.*
stiletto [stɪ'lɛtəu] (*BRIT*) *n* (*also*: *~ heel*) salto alto e fino.
still [stɪl] *adj* (*motionless*) imóvel; (*calm*) quieto; (*BRIT*: *orange drink etc*) sem gás ♦ *adv* (*up to this time*) ainda; (*even*) ainda; (*nonetheless*) entretanto, contudo ♦ *n* (*CINEMA*) still *m*; **to stand ~** ficar parado; **keep ~!** não se mexa!; **he ~ hasn't arrived** ele ainda não chegou.
stillborn ['stɪlbɔːn] *adj* nascido morto, natimorto.
still life *n* natureza morta.
stilt [stɪlt] *n* perna de pau; (*pile*) estaca, suporte *m*.
stilted ['stɪltɪd] *adj* afetado.
stimulant ['stɪmjulənt] *n* estimulante *m*.
stimulate ['stɪmjuleɪt] *vt* estimular.
stimulating ['stɪmjuleɪtɪŋ] *adj* estimulante.
stimulation [stɪmju'leɪʃən] *n* estimulação *f*.
stimuli ['stɪmjulaɪ] *npl of* **stimulus**.
stimulus ['stɪmjuləs] (*pl* **stimuli**) *n* estímulo, incentivo.
sting [stɪŋ] (*pt*, *pp* **stung**) *n* (*wound*) picada; (*pain*) ardência; (*of insect*) ferrão *m*; (*inf*: *confidence trick*) conto-do-vigário ♦ *vt* picar ♦ *vi* arder.
stingy ['stɪndʒɪ] *adj* pão-duro, sovina.
stink [stɪŋk] (*pt* **stank**, *pp* **stunk**) *n* fedor *m*, catinga ♦ *vi* feder, cheirar mal.
stinker ['stɪŋkə*] (*inf*) *n* (*problem*, *person*) osso duro de roer.
stinking ['stɪŋkɪŋ] *adj* fedorento, fétido; **~ rich** ricaço.
stint [stɪnt] *n* tarefa, parte *f* ♦ *vi*: **to ~ on** ser parco com; **to do one's ~** fazer a sua parte.
stipend ['staɪpɛnd] *n* (*of vicar etc*) estipêndio, remuneração *f*.
stipendiary [staɪ'pɛndɪərɪ] *adj*: **~ magistrate** juiz/juíza *m/f* estipendiário/a.
stipulate ['stɪpjuleɪt] *vt* estipular.
stipulation [stɪpju'leɪʃən] *n* estipulação *f*, cláusula.
stir [stəː*] *n* (*fig*: *agitation*) comoção *f*, rebuliço ♦ *vt* (*tea etc*) mexer; (*fig*: *emotions*) comover ♦ *vi* mover-se, remexer-se; **to give sth a ~** mexer algo; **to cause a ~** causar sensação *or* um rebuliço.
stir up *vt* excitar; (*trouble*) provocar.
stirring ['stəːrɪŋ] *adj* comovedor(a).
stirrup ['stɪrəp] *n* estribo.
stitch [stɪtʃ] *n* (*SEWING*, *KNITTING*, *MED*) ponto; (*pain*) pontada ♦ *vt* costurar; (*MED*) dar pontos em, suturar.
stoat [stəut] *n* arminho.
stock [stɔk] *n* (*COMM*: *reserves*) estoque *m*, provisão *f*; (: *selection*) sortimento; (*AGR*) gado; (*CULIN*) caldo; (*fig*: *lineage*) estirpe *f*, linhagem *f*; (*FINANCE*) valores *mpl*, títulos *mpl*; (: *shares*) ações *fpl*; (*RAIL*: *also*: *rolling ~*) material *m* circulante ♦ *adj* (*fig*: *reply etc*) de sempre, costumeiro; (: *greeting*) habitual ♦ *vt* (*have in ~*) ter em estoque, estocar; (*sell*) vender; **well-~ed** bem sortido; **in ~** em estoque; **out of ~** esgotado; **to take ~** (*fig*) fazer um balanço; **~s and shares** valores e títulos mobiliários; **government ~** títulos do governo, fundos públicos.
stock up *vi*: **to ~ up with** abastecer-se de.
stockade [stɔ'keɪd] *n* estacada.
stockbroker ['stɔkbrəukə*] *n* corretor(a) *m/f* de valores *or* da Bolsa.
stock control *n* (*COMM*) controle *m* de estoque.
stock cube (*BRIT*) *n* (*CULIN*) cubo de caldo.
stock exchange *n* Bolsa de Valores.
stockholder ['stɔkhəuldə*] (*US*) *n* acionista *m/f*.
Stockholm ['stɔkhəum] *n* Estocolmo.
stocking ['stɔkɪŋ] *n* meia.
stock-in-trade *n* (*tool*) instrumento de trabalho; (*fig*) arma.
stockist ['stɔkɪst] (*BRIT*) *n* estoquista *m/f*.
stock market *n* Bolsa, mercado de valores.
stock phrase *n* frase *f* feita.
stockpile ['stɔkpaɪl] *n* reservas *fpl*, estocagem *f* ♦ *vt* acumular reservas de, estocar.
stockroom ['stɔkruːm] *n* almoxarifado.
stocktaking ['stɔkteɪkɪŋ] (*BRIT*) *n* (*COMM*) inventário.
stocky ['stɔkɪ] *adj* (*strong*) robusto; (*short*) atarracado.
stodgy ['stɔdʒɪ] *adj* pesado.
stoic ['stəuɪk] *n* estóico/a.
stoical ['stəuɪkəl] *adj* estóico.
stoke [stəuk] *vt* atiçar, alimentar.
stoker ['stəukə*] *n* (*RAIL*, *NAUT etc*) foguista *m*.
stole [stəul] *pt of* **steal** ♦ *n* estola.
stolen ['stəuln] *pp of* **steal**.
stomach ['stʌmək] *n* (*ANAT*) estômago; (*belly*) barriga, ventre *m* ♦ *vt* suportar, tolerar.
stomach ache *n* dor *f* de estômago.
stomach pump *n* bomba gástrica.

stomach ulcer *n* úlcera gástrica.
stomp [stɔmp] *vi*: **to ~ in/out** entrar/sair como um furacão.
stone [stəun] *n* pedra; (*in fruit*) caroço; (*BRIT*: *weight*) = *6.348kg; 14 pounds* ♦ *cpd* de pedra ♦ *vt* apedrejar; **within a ~'s throw of the station** pertinho da estação.
Stone Age *n*: **the ~** a Idade da Pedra.
stone-cold *adj* gelado.
stoned [stəund] (*inf*) *adj* (*on drugs*) doidão/dona, baratinado.
stone-deaf *adj* surdo como uma porta.
stonemason ['stəunmeɪsn] *n* pedreiro/a.
stonework ['stəunwəːk] *n* cantaria.
stony ['stəunɪ] *adj* pedregoso; (*glance*) glacial.
stood [stud] *pt, pp of* **stand**.
stool [stuːl] *n* tamborete *m*, banco.
stoop [stuːp] *vi* (*also*: *have a ~*) ser corcunda; (*bend*) debruçar-se, curvar-se; (*fig*): **to ~ to sth/doing sth** rebaixar-se para algo/fazer algo.
stop [stɔp] *n* parada, interrupção *f*; (*for bus etc*) parada (*BR*), ponto (*BR*), paragem *f* (*PT*); (*in punctuation*) ponto ♦ *vt* parar, deter; (*break off*) interromper; (*also*: *put a ~ to*) terminar, pôr fim a ♦ *vi* parar, deter-se; (*end*) acabar; **to ~ doing sth** deixar de fazer algo; **to ~ sb (from) doing sth** impedir alguém de fazer algo; **to ~ dead** parar de repente; **~ it!** para com isso!
stop by *vi* dar uma passada.
stop off *vi* fazer pausa.
stop up *vt* (*hole*) tapar.
stopcock ['stɔpkɔk] *n* torneira de passagem.
stopgap ['stɔpgæp] *n* (*person*) tapa-buraco *m/f*; (*also*: *~ measure*) paliativo.
stoplights ['stɔplaɪts] *npl* (*AUT*) luzes *fpl* do freio (*BR*), faróis *mpl* de stop (*PT*).
stopover ['stɔpəuvə*] *n* escala.
stoppage ['stɔpɪdʒ] *n* (*strike*) greve *f*; (*temporary stop*) paralisação *f*; (*of pay*) suspensão *f*; (*blockage*) obstrução *f*.
stopper ['stɔpə*] *n* tampa, rolha.
stop press *n* notícia de última hora.
stopwatch ['stɔpwɔtʃ] *n* cronômetro.
storage ['stɔːrɪdʒ] *n* armazenagem *f*.
storage heater (*BRIT*) *n tipo de aquecimento que armazena calor durante a noite, emitindo-o durante o dia*.
store [stɔː*] *n* (*stock*) suprimento; (*depot, large shop*) armazém *m*; (*reserve*) estoque *m*; (*US*: *shop*) loja ♦ *vt* armazenar; (*keep*) guardar; **~s** *npl* víveres *mpl*, provisões *fpl*; **who knows what is in ~ for us?** quem sabe o que nos espera?; **to set great/little ~ by sth** dar grande/pouca importância a algo.
store up *vt* acumular.
storehouse ['stɔːhaus] (*irreg*) *n* depósito, armazém *m*.
storekeeper ['stɔːkiːpə*] (*US*) *n* lojista *m/f*.
storeroom ['stɔːruːm] *n* depósito, almoxarifado.
storey ['stɔːrɪ] (*US* **story**) *n* andar *m*.
stork [stɔːk] *n* cegonha.
storm [stɔːm] *n* tempestade *f*; (*wind*) borrasca, vendaval *m*; (*fig*) tumulto ♦ *vi* (*fig*) enfurecer-se ♦ *vt* tomar de assalto, assaltar.
storm cloud *n* nuvem *f* de tempestade.
storm door *n* porta adicional.
stormy ['stɔːmɪ] *adj* tempestuoso.
story ['stɔːrɪ] *n* história, estória; (*PRESS*) matéria; (*plot*) enredo; (*lie*) mentira; (*US*) = **storey**.
storybook ['stɔːrɪbuk] *n* livro de contos.
storyteller ['stɔːrɪtɛlə*] *n* contador(a) *m/f* de estórias.
stout [staut] *adj* (*strong*) sólido, forte; (*fat*) gordo, corpulento ♦ *n* cerveja preta.
stove [stəuv] *n* (*for cooking*) fogão *m*; (*for heating*) estufa, fogareiro; **gas/electric ~** (*cooker*) fogão a gás/elétrico.
stow [stəu] *vt* guardar; (*NAUT*) estivar.
stowaway ['stəuəweɪ] *n* passageiro/a clandestino/a.
straddle ['strædl] *vt* cavalgar.
strafe [strɑːf] *vt* metralhar.
straggle ['strægl] *vi* (*wander*) vagar, perambular; (*lag behind*) ficar para trás.
straggler ['stræglə*] *n* pessoa que fica para trás.
straggling ['stræglɪŋ] *adj* (*hair*) rebelde, emaranhado.
straggly ['stræglɪ] *adj* (*hair*) rebelde, emaranhado.
straight [streɪt] *adj* reto; (*frank*) franco, direto; (*simple*) simples *inv*; (*THEATRE*: *part, play*) sério; (*inf*: *conventional*) quadrado, careta (*inf*); (: *heterosexual*) heterossexual ♦ *adv* reto; (*drink*) puro ♦ *n*: **the ~** (*SPORT*) a reta; **to put** *or* **get ~** pôr em ordem, dar um jeito em; **let's get this ~** (*explaining*) então, vamos fazer assim; (*warning*) eu quero que isso fique bem claro; **10 ~ wins** 10 vitórias consecutivas; **to go ~ home** ir direto para casa; **~ away, ~ off** (*at once*) imediatamente; **~ off, ~ out** sem mais nem menos.
straighten ['streɪtən] *vt* (*also*: *~ out*) endireitar; **to ~ things out** arrumar as coisas.
straight-faced [-feɪst] *adj* impassível ♦ *adv* com cara séria.
straightforward [streɪt'fɔːwəd] *adj* (*simple*) simples *inv*, direto; (*honest*) honesto, franco.
strain [streɪn] *n* tensão *f*; (*TECH*) esforço; (*MED*) distensão *f*, luxação *f*; (*breed*) raça, estirpe *f*; (*of virus*) classe *f* ♦ *vt* (*back etc*) forçar, torcer, distender; (*tire*) extenuar; (*stretch*) puxar, estirar; (*filter*) filtrar ♦ *vi* esforçar-se; **~s** *npl* (*MUS*) acordes *mpl*; **he's been under a lot of ~** ele tem estado sob muita tensão.
strained [streɪnd] *adj* (*muscle*) distendido; (*laugh*) forçado; (*relations*) tenso.
strainer ['streɪnə*] *n* (*for tea, coffee*) coador *m*; (*sieve*) peneira.

strait [streɪt] *n* (*GEO*) estreito; **to be in dire ~s** (*fig*) estar em apuros.
straitjacket ['streɪtdʒækɪt] *n* camisa-de-força.
strait-laced [-'leɪst] *adj* puritano, austero.
strand [strænd] *n* (*of thread*) fio ♦ *vt* (*boat*) encalhar.
stranded ['strændɪd] *adj* desamparado.
strange [streɪndʒ] *adj* (*not known*) desconhecido; (*odd*) estranho, esquisito.
strangely ['streɪndʒlɪ] *adv* estranhamente.
stranger ['streɪndʒə*] *n* desconhecido/a; (*from another area*) forasteiro/a.
strangle ['stræŋgl] *vt* estrangular; (*sobs etc*) sufocar.
stranglehold ['stræŋglhəuld] *n* (*fig*) domínio total.
strangulation [stræŋgju'leɪʃən] *n* estrangulação *f*.
strap [stræp] *n* correia; (*of slip, dress*) alça ♦ *vt* prender com correia.
straphanging ['stræphæŋɪŋ] *n* viajar *m* em pé (no metrô *etc*).
strapless ['stræplɪs] *adj* (*bra, dress*) sem alças.
strapping ['stræpɪŋ] *adj* corpulento, robusto, forte.
Strasbourg ['stræzbə:g] *n* Estrasburgo.
strata ['strɑ:tə] *npl of* **stratum**.
stratagem ['strætɪdʒəm] *n* estratagema *m*.
strategic [strə'ti:dʒɪk] *adj* estratégico.
strategist ['strætɪdʒɪst] *n* estrategista *m/f*.
strategy ['strætɪdʒɪ] *n* estratégia.
stratosphere ['strætəsfɪə*] *n* estratosfera.
stratum ['strɑ:təm] (*pl* **strata**) *n* estrato, camada.
straw [strɔ:] *n* palha; (*drinking* ~) canudo; **that's the last ~!** essa foi a última gota!
strawberry ['strɔ:bərɪ] *n* morango; (*plant*) morangueiro.
stray [streɪ] *adj* (*animal*) extraviado; (*bullet*) perdido ♦ *vi* extraviar-se, perder-se.
streak [stri:k] *n* listra, traço; (*fig: of madness etc*) sinal *m* ♦ *vt* listrar ♦ *vi*: **to ~ past** passar como um raio; **to have ~s in one's hair** fazer mechas no cabelo; **a winning/losing ~** uma fase de sorte/azar.
streaky ['stri:kɪ] *adj* listrado.
streaky bacon (*BRIT*) *n* toicinho *or* bacon *m* em fatias (*entremeado com gordura*).
stream [stri:m] *n* riacho, córrego; (*current*) fluxo, corrente *f*; (*of people*) fluxo ♦ *vt* (*SCH*) classificar ♦ *vi* correr, fluir; **to ~ in/out** (*people*) entrar/sair em massa; **against the ~** contra a corrente; **on ~** (*power plant etc*) em funcionamento.
streamer ['stri:mə*] *n* serpentina; (*pennant*) flâmula.
stream feed *n* (*on photocopier etc*) alimentação *f* contínua.
streamline ['stri:mlaɪn] *vt* aerodinamizar; (*fig*) agilizar.
streamlined ['stri:mlaɪnd] *adj* aerodinâmico.
street [stri:t] *n* rua; **the back ~s** as ruelas; **to be on the ~s** (*homeless*) estar desabrigado; (*as prostitute*) fazer a vida.
streetcar ['stri:tkɑ:*] (*US*) *n* bonde *m* (*BR*), eléctrico (*PT*).
street lamp *n* poste *m* de iluminação.
street lighting *n* iluminação *f* pública.
street map *n* mapa *m*.
street market *n* feira.
street plan *n* mapa *m*.
streetwise ['stri:twaɪz] (*inf*) *adj* malandro.
strength [strɛŋθ] *n* força; (*of girder, knot etc*) firmeza, resistência; (*of chemical solution*) concentração *f*; (*of wine*) teor *m* alcoólico; **on the ~ of** com base em; **at full ~** completo; **below ~** desfalcado.
strengthen ['strɛŋθən] *vt* fortalecer, intensificar.
strenuous ['strɛnjuəs] *adj* (*tough*) árduo, estrênuo; (*energetic*) enérgico; (*determined*) tenaz.
stress [strɛs] *n* (*force, pressure*) pressão *f*; (*mental strain*) tensão *f*, stress *m*; (*accent*) acento; (*emphasis*) ênfase *f*; (*TECH*) tensão ♦ *vt* realçar, dar ênfase a; **to lay great ~ on sth** dar muita ênfase a algo; **to be under ~** estar com estresse.
stressful ['strɛsful] *adj* (*job*) desgastante.
stretch [strɛtʃ] *n* (*of sand etc*) trecho, extensão *f*; (*of time*) período ♦ *vi* esticar-se; (*extend*): **to ~ to** *or* **as far as** estender-se até; (*be enough: money, food*): **to ~ to** dar para ♦ *vt* estirar, esticar; (*make demands of*) exigir o máximo de; **at a ~** sem parar; **to ~ one's legs** esticar as pernas.
stretch out *vi* esticar-se ♦ *vt* (*arm etc*) esticar; (*spread*) estirar.
stretcher ['strɛtʃə*] *n* maca, padiola.
stretcher-bearer *n* padioleiro.
stretch marks *npl* estrias *fpl*.
strewn [stru:n] *adj*: **~ with** coberto *or* cheio de.
stricken ['strɪkən] *adj* (*wounded*) ferido; (*devastated*) arrasado; (*ill*) acometido; **~ with grief, grief-~** tomado pela dor.
strict [strɪkt] *adj* (*person*) severo, rigoroso; (*precise*) exato, estrito; **in ~ confidence** muito confidencialmente.
strictly ['strɪktlɪ] *adv* (*exactly*) estritamente; (*severely*) severamente; (*definitively*) rigorosamente; **~ confidential** estritamente confidencial; **~ speaking** a rigor; **~ between ourselves** ... cá entre nós ....
strictness ['strɪktnɪs] *n* rigor *m*, severidade *f*.
stridden ['strɪdn] *pp of* **stride**.
stride [straɪd] (*pt* **strode**, *pp* **stridden**) *n* passo largo ♦ *vi* andar a passos largos; **to take in one's ~** (*fig: changes etc*) não se perturbar com.
strident ['straɪdnt] *adj* estridente; (*colour*) berrante.
strife [straɪf] *n* conflito.
strike [straɪk] (*pt, pp* **struck**) *n* greve *f*; (*of oil etc*) descoberta; (*attack*) ataque *m* ♦ *vt* bater em; (*oil etc*) descobrir; (*obstacle*) esbarrar em; (*deal*) fechar, acertar ♦ *vi* estar em greve; (*attack*) atacar; (*clock*) bater, dar (as horas); **to go on** *or* **come out on ~** entrar

em greve; **to call a ~** convocar uma greve; **to ~ a match** acender um fósforo; **to ~ a balance** (*fig*) encontrar um equilíbrio; **the clock struck nine** o relógio bateu nove horas.
strike back *vi* (MIL) contra-atacar; (*fig*) revidar.
strike down *vt* derrubar.
strike off *vt* (*from list*) tirar, cortar; (*doctor*) suspender.
strike out *vt* cancelar, rasurar.
strike up *vt* (MUS) começar a tocar; (*conversation, friendship*) travar.
strikebreaker ['straɪkbreɪkə*] *n* fura-greve *m/f inv*.
striker ['straɪkə*] *n* grevista *m/f*; (SPORT) atacante *m/f*.
striking ['straɪkɪŋ] *adj* impressionante; (*colour*) chamativo.
string [strɪŋ] (*pt, pp* **strung**) *n* (*cord*) barbante *m* (BR), cordel *m* (PT); (MUS) corda; (*series*) série *f*; (*of people, cars*) fila (BR), bicha (PT); (COMPUT) string *m* ♦ *vt*: **to ~ out** esticar; **the ~s** *npl* (MUS) os instrumentos de corda; **to ~ together** (*words*) unir; (*ideas*) concatenar; **to get a job by pulling ~s** (*fig*) usar pistolão; **with no ~s attached** (*fig*) sem condições.
string bean *n* vagem *f*.
string(ed) instrument [strɪŋ(d)-] *n* (MUS) instrumento de corda.
stringent ['strɪndʒənt] *adj* rigoroso.
string quartet *n* quarteto de cordas.
strip [strɪp] *n* tira; (*of land*) faixa; (*of metal*) lâmina, tira; (SPORT) cores *fpl* ♦ *vt* despir; (*fig*): **to ~ sb of sth** despojar alguém de algo; (*also*: ~ *down* : *machine*) desmontar ♦ *vi* despir-se.
strip cartoon *n* história em quadrinhos (BR), banda desenhada (PT).
stripe [straɪp] *n* listra; (MIL) galão *m*.
striped [straɪpt] *adj* listrado, com listras.
strip light (BRIT) *n* lâmpada fluorescente.
stripper ['strɪpə*] *n* artista *m/f* de striptease.
striptease ['strɪptiːz] *n* striptease *m*.
strive [straɪv] (*pt* **strove**, *pp* **striven**) *vi*: **to ~ to do sth** esforçar-se por *or* batalhar para fazer algo.
striven ['strɪvn] *pp of* **strive**.
strode [strəud] *pt of* **stride**.
stroke [strəuk] *n* (*blow*) golpe *m*; (MED) derrame *m* cerebral; (*caress*) carícia; (*of pen*) traço; (SWIMMING: *style*) nado; (: *movement*) braçada; (*of piston*) curso ♦ *vt* acariciar, afagar; **at a ~** de repente, de golpe; **on the ~ of 5** às cinco em ponto; **a ~ of luck** um golpe de sorte; **a 2-~ engine** um motor de dois tempos.
stroll [strəul] *n* volta, passeio ♦ *vi* passear, dar uma volta; **to go for a ~** dar uma volta.
stroller ['strəulə*] (US) *n* carrinho (de criança).
strong [strɔŋ] *adj* forte; (*object, material*) sólido; (*chemical*) concentrado ♦ *adv*: **to be going ~** (*company*) estar prosperando; (*person*) estar com boa saúde; **they are 50 ~** são 50.
strong-arm *adj* (*tactics, methods*) repressivo, violento.
strongbox ['strɔŋbɔks] *n* cofre-forte *m*.
strong drink *n* bebida alcoólica.
stronghold ['strɔŋhəuld] *n* fortaleza; (*fig*) baluarte *m*.
strong language *n* palavrões *mpl*.
strongly ['strɔŋlɪ] *adv* fortemente, vigorosamente; (*believe*) firmemente; **I feel ~ about it** tenho uma opinião firme sobre isso.
strongman ['strɔŋmæn] (*irreg*) *n* homem *m* forte.
strongroom ['strɔŋruːm] *n* casa-forte *f*.
strove [strəuv] *pt of* **strive**.
struck [strʌk] *pt, pp of* **strike**.
structural ['strʌktʃərəl] *adj* estrutural.
structurally ['strʌktʃrəlɪ] *adv* estruturalmente.
structure ['strʌktʃə*] *n* estrutura; (*building*) construção *f*.
struggle ['strʌgl] *n* luta, contenda ♦ *vi* lutar, batalhar; **to have a ~ to do sth** ter que batalhar para fazer algo.
strum [strʌm] *vt* (*guitar*) dedilhar.
strung [strʌŋ] *pt, pp of* **string**.
strut [strʌt] *n* escora, suporte *m* ♦ *vi* pavonear-se, empertigar-se.
strychnine ['strɪkniːn] *n* estricnina.
stub [stʌb] *n* (*of ticket etc*) canhoto; (*of cigarette*) toco, ponta; **to ~ one's toe (on sth)** dar uma topada (em algo).
stub out *vt* apagar.
stubble ['stʌbl] *n* restolho; (*on chin*) barba por fazer.
stubborn ['stʌbən] *adj* teimoso, cabeçudo, obstinado.
stubby ['stʌbɪ] *adj* atarracado.
stucco ['stʌkəu] *n* estuque.
stuck [stʌk] *pt, pp of* **stick** ♦ *adj* (*jammed*) emperrado; **to get ~** emperrar.
stuck-up *adj* convencido, metido, esnobe.
stud [stʌd] *n* (*shirt ~*) botão *m*; (*of boot*) cravo; (*of horses*) haras *m*; (*also*: ~ *horse*) garanhão *m* ♦ *vt* (*fig*): **~ded with** salpicado de.
student ['stjuːdənt] *n* estudante *m/f* ♦ *cpd* estudantil; **law/medical ~** estudante de direito/medicina.
student driver (US) *n* aprendiz *m/f*.
students' union (BRIT) *n* (*association*) união *f* dos estudantes; (*building*) centro estudantil.
studied ['stʌdɪd] *adj* estudado, calculado.
studio ['stjuːdɪəu] *n* estúdio; (*sculptor's*) ateliê *m*.
studio flat (US **studio apartment**) *n* (apartamento) conjugado.
studious ['stjuːdɪəs] *adj* estudioso, aplicado; (*studied*) calculado.
studiously ['stjuːdɪəslɪ] *adv* (*carefully*) com esmero.

NB: *European Portuguese adds the following consonants to certain words:* **b** (sú(b)dito, su(b)til); **c** (a(c)ção, a(c)cionista, a(c)to); **m** (inde(m)ne); **p** (ado(p)ção, ado(p)tar); *for further details see p. xiii.*

study ['stʌdɪ] *n* estudo; (*room*) gabinete *m* ♦ *vt* estudar; (*examine*) examinar, investigar ♦ *vi* estudar; **to make a ~ of sth** estudar algo; **to ~ for an exam** estudar para um exame.
stuff [stʌf] *n* (*inf*: *substance*) troço; (: *things*) troços *mpl*, coisas *fpl* ♦ *vt* encher; (CULIN) rechear; (*animals*) empalhar; **my nose is ~ed up** meu nariz está entupido; **get ~ed!** (*inf!*) vai tomar banho!; **~ed toy** brinquedo de pelúcia.
stuffing ['stʌfɪŋ] *n* recheio.
stuffy ['stʌfɪ] *adj* (*room*) abafado, mal ventilado; (*person*) rabujento, melindroso.
stumble ['stʌmbl] *vi* tropeçar.
stumble across *vt fus* (*fig*) topar com.
stumbling block ['stʌmblɪŋ-] *n* pedra no caminho.
stump [stʌmp] *n* (*of tree*) toco; (*of limb*) coto ♦ *vt*: **to be ~ed** ficar perplexo.
stun [stʌn] *vt* aturdir, pasmar.
stung [stʌŋ] *pt*, *pp of* **sting**.
stunk [stʌŋk] *pp of* **stink**.
stunning ['stʌnɪŋ] *adj* (*fig*) atordoante.
stunt [stʌnt] *n* façanha sensacional; (AVIAT) vôo acrobático; (*publicity* ~) truque *m* publicitário ♦ *vt* tolher.
stunted ['stʌntɪd] *adj* atrofiado, retardado.
stuntman ['stʌntmæn] (*irreg*) *n* dublê *m*.
stupefaction [stju:pɪ'fækʃən] *n* estupefação *f*, assombro.
stupefy ['stju:pɪfaɪ] *vt* deixar estupefato.
stupendous [stju:'pɛndəs] *adj* assombroso, prodigioso, monumental.
stupid ['stju:pɪd] *adj* estúpido, idiota.
stupidity [stju:'pɪdɪtɪ] *n* estupidez *f*.
stupidly ['stju:pɪdlɪ] *adv* estupidamente.
stupor ['stju:pə*] *n* estupor *m*.
sturdy ['stə:dɪ] *adj* robusto.
sturgeon ['stə:dʒən] *n inv* esturjão *m*.
stutter ['stʌtə*] *n* gagueira, gaguez *f* ♦ *vi* gaguejar.
sty [staɪ] *n* (*for pigs*) chiqueiro.
stye [staɪ] *n* (MED) terçol *m*.
style [staɪl] *n* estilo; (*allure*) charme *m*; **in the latest ~** na última moda; **hair ~** penteado.
styli ['staɪlaɪ] *npl of* **stylus**.
stylish ['staɪlɪʃ] *adj* elegante, chique.
stylist ['staɪlɪst] *n* (*hair* ~) cabeleireiro/a; (*literary*) estilista *m/f*.
stylized ['staɪlaɪzd] *adj* estilizado.
stylus ['staɪləs] (*pl* **styli** *or* **~es**) *n* (*of record player*) agulha.
suave [swɑ:v] *adj* suave, melífluo.
sub [sʌb] *n abbr* = **submarine; subscription**.
sub... [sʌb] *prefix* sub....
subcommittee ['sʌbkəmɪtɪ] *n* subcomissão *f*.
subconscious [sʌb'kɔnʃəs] *adj* do subconsciente ♦ *n* subconsciente *m*.
subcontinent [sʌb'kɔntɪnənt] *n*: **the (Indian) ~** o subcontinente (da Índia).
subcontract [*n* sʌb'kɔntrækt, *vt* sʌbkən'trækt] *n* subcontrato ♦ *vt* subcontratar.
subcontractor [sʌbkən'træktə*] *n* subempreiteiro/a.
subdivide [sʌbdɪ'vaɪd] *vt* subdividir.
subdivision [sʌbdɪ'vɪʒən] *n* subdivisão *f*.
subdue [səb'dju:] *vt* subjugar; (*passions*) dominar.
subdued [səb'dju:d] *adj* (*light*) tênue; (*person*) desanimado.
subeditor ['sʌb'ɛdɪtə*] (BRIT) *n* subeditor(a) *m/f*.
subject [*n* 'sʌbdʒɪkt, *vt* səb'dʒɛkt] *n* (*of king*) súdito/a; (*theme*) assunto; (SCH) matéria ♦ *vt*: **to ~ sb to sth** submeter alguém a algo ♦ *adj*: **to be ~ to** (*law*) estar sujeito a; **~ to confirmation in writing** sujeito a confirmação por escrito; **to change the ~** mudar de assunto.
subjection [səb'dʒɛkʃən] *n* submissão *f*, dependência.
subjective [səb'dʒɛktɪv] *adj* subjetivo.
subject matter *n* assunto; (*content*) conteúdo.
sub judice [-'dju:dɪsɪ] *adj* (LAW) sob apreciação judicial, sub judice.
subjugate ['sʌbdʒugeɪt] *vt* subjugar, submeter.
subjunctive [səb'dʒʌŋktɪv] *adj*, *n* subjuntivo.
sublet [sʌb'lɛt] *vt* sublocar.
sublime [sə'blaɪm] *adj* sublime.
subliminal [sʌb'lɪmɪnl] *adj* subliminar.
submachine gun ['sʌbmə'ʃi:n-] *n* metralhadora de mão.
submarine ['sʌbməri:n] *n* submarino.
submerge [səb'mə:dʒ] *vt* submergir; (*flood*) inundar ♦ *vi* submergir-se.
submersion [səb'mə:ʃən] *n* submersão *f*, imersão *f*.
submission [səb'mɪʃən] *n* submissão *f*; (*to committee*) petição *f*.
submissive [səb'mɪsɪv] *adj* submisso.
submit [səb'mɪt] *vt* submeter ♦ *vi* submeter-se.
subnormal [sʌb'nɔ:məl] *adj* anormal, subnormal; (*backward*) atrasado.
subordinate [sə'bɔ:dɪnət] *adj*, *n* subordinado/a.
subpoena [səb'pi:nə] *n* (LAW) intimação *f*, citação *f* judicial ♦ *vt* intimar a comparecer judicialmente, citar.
subroutine [sʌbru:'ti:n] *n* (COMPUT) subrotina.
subscribe [səb'skraɪb] *vi* subscrever; **to ~ to** (*opinion*) concordar com; (*fund*) contribuir para; (*newspaper*) assinar.
subscriber [səb'skraɪbə*] *n* (*to periodical, telephone*) assinante *m/f*.
subscript ['sʌbskrɪpt] *n* (TYP) subscrito.
subscription [səb'skrɪpʃən] *n* subscrição *f*; (*to magazine etc*) assinatura; (*to club*) cota, mensalidade *f*; **to take out a ~ to** fazer uma assinatura de.
subsequent ['sʌbsɪkwənt] *adj* subseqüente, posterior; **~ to** posterior a.
subsequently ['sʌbsɪkwəntlɪ] *adv* posteriormente, depois.
subside [səb'saɪd] *vi* baixar; (*flood*) descer; (*wind*) acanhar-se.
subsidence [səb'saɪdns] *n* baixa.
subsidiary [səb'sɪdɪərɪ] *adj* subsidiário; (*BRIT*:

SCH: *subject*) suplementar ♦ *n* subsidiária.
subsidize ['sʌbsɪdaɪz] *vt* subsidiar.
subsidy ['sʌbsɪdɪ] *n* subsídio.
subsist [səb'sɪst] *vi*: **to ~ on sth** subsistir de algo.
subsistence [səb'sɪstəns] *n* subsistência; (*allowance*) subsídio, ajuda de custo.
subsistence allowance *n* diária.
subsistence level *n* nível *m* de subsistência.
subsistence wage *n* salário de fome.
substance ['sʌbstəns] *n* substância; (*fig*) essência; **a man of ~** um homem de recursos; **to lack ~** não ter substância.
substandard [sʌb'stændəd] *adj* (*goods*) de qualidade inferior; (*housing*) inferior ao padrão.
substantial [səb'stænʃl] *adj* substancial, essencial; (*fig*) importante.
substantially [səb'stænʃəlɪ] *adv* substancialmente.
substantiate [səb'stænʃɪeɪt] *vt* comprovar, justificar.
substitute ['sʌbstɪtju:t] *n* substituto/a; (*person*) suplente *m/f* ♦ *vt*: **to ~ A for B** substituir B por A.
substitute teacher (*US*) *n* professor(a) *m/f* suplente.
substitution [sʌbstɪ'tju:ʃən] *n* substituição *f*, troca.
subterfuge ['sʌbtəfju:dʒ] *n* subterfúgio.
subterranean [sʌbtə'reɪnɪən] *adj* subterrâneo.
subtitle ['sʌbtaɪtl] *n* (*CINEMA*) legenda.
subtle ['sʌtl] *adj* sutil.
subtlety ['sʌtltɪ] *n* sutileza.
subtly ['sʌtlɪ] *adv* sutilmente.
subtotal [sʌb'təutl] *n* total *m* parcial, subtotal *m*.
subtract [səb'trækt] *vt* subtrair, deduzir.
subtraction [səb'trækʃən] *n* subtração *f*.
subtropical [sʌb'trɔpɪkl] *adj* subtropical.
suburb ['sʌbə:b] *n* subúrbio.
suburban [sə'bə:bən] *adj* suburbano; (*train etc*) de subúrbio.
suburbia [sə'bə:bɪə] *n* os subúrbios.
subvention [səb'vɛnʃən] *n* subvenção *f*, subsídio.
subversion [səb'və:ʃən] *n* subversão *f*.
subversive [səb'və:sɪv] *adj* subversivo.
subway ['sʌbweɪ] *n* (*BRIT*) passagem *f* subterrânea; (*US*) metrô *m* (*BR*), metro(-politano) (*PT*).
sub-zero *adj* abaixo de zero.
succeed [sək'si:d] *vi* (*person*) ser bem sucedido, ter êxito; (*plan*) sair bem ♦ *vt* suceder a; **to ~ in doing** conseguir fazer.
succeeding [sək'si:dɪŋ] *adj* (*following*) sucessivo, posterior.
success [sək'sɛs] *n* sucesso, êxito; (*gain*) triunfo.
successful [sək'sɛsful] *adj* (*venture*) bem sucedido; **to be ~ (in doing)** conseguir (fazer).
successfully [sək'sɛsfulɪ] *adv* com sucesso, com êxito.
succession [sək'sɛʃən] *n* (*series*) sucessão *f*, série *f*; (*descendants*) descendência; **in ~** em sucessão; **3 years in ~** três anos consecutivos.
successive [sək'sɛsɪv] *adj* sucessivo; **on 3 ~ days** em 3 dias consecutivos.
successor [sək'sɛsə*] *n* sucessor(a) *m/f*.
succinct [sək'sɪŋkt] *adj* sucinto.
succulent ['sʌkjulənt] *adj* suculento ♦ *n* (*BOT*): **~s** suculentos *mpl*.
succumb [sə'kʌm] *vi* sucumbir.
such [sʌtʃ] *adj* tal, semelhante; (*of that kind*: *sg*): **~ a book** um livro parecido, tal livro; (: *pl*): **~ books** tais livros; (*so much*): **~ courage** tanta coragem ♦ *adv* tão; **~ a long trip** uma viagem tão longa; **~ good books** livros tão bons; **~ a lot of** tanto; **making ~ a noise that** fazendo tanto barulho que; **~ a long time ago** há tanto tempo atrás; **~ as** (*like*) tal como; **a noise ~ as to** um ruído tal que; **~ books as I have** os poucos livros que eu tenho; **I said no ~ thing** eu não disse tal coisa; **as ~** como tal; **until ~ time as** até que.
such-and-such *adj* tal e qual.
suchlike ['sʌtʃlaɪk] (*inf*) *pron*: **and ~** e coisas assim.
suck [sʌk] *vt* chupar; (*breast*) mamar; (*subj*: *pump, machine*) sugar.
sucker ['sʌkə*] *n* (*BOT*) rebento; (*ZOOL*) ventosa; (*inf*) trouxa *m/f*, otário/a.
suckle ['sʌkl] *vt* amamentar.
sucrose ['su:krəuz] *n* sucrose *f*.
suction ['sʌkʃən] *n* sucção *f*.
suction pump *n* bomba de sucção.
Sudan [su'dɑ:n] *n* Sudão *m*.
Sudanese [su:də'ni:z] *adj*, *n inv* sudanês/esa *m/f*.
sudden ['sʌdn] *adj* (*rapid*) repentino, súbito; (*unexpected*) imprevisto; **all of a ~** de repente; (*unexpectedly*) inesperadamente.
suddenly ['sʌdnlɪ] *adv* de repente; (*unexpectedly*) inesperadamente.
suds [sʌdz] *npl* água de sabão.
sue [su:] *vt* processar ♦ *vi*: **to ~ (for)** processar (por), promover ação (por); **to ~ for divorce** requerer divórcio; **to ~ sb for damages** intentar uma ação de perdas e danos contra alguém.
suede [sweɪd] *n* camurça ♦ *cpd* de camurça.
suet ['suɪt] *n* sebo.
Suez Canal ['su:ɪz-] *n* Canal *m* de Suez.
Suff. (*BRIT*) *abbr* = **Suffolk**.
suffer ['sʌfə*] *vt* sofrer; (*bear*) agüentar, suportar ♦ *vi* sofrer, padecer; **to ~ from** (*illness*) sofrer de, estar com; **to ~ from the effects of alcohol** sofrer os efeitos do álcool.
sufferance ['sʌfrəns] *n*: **he was only there on ~** ele estava lá por tolerância.
sufferer ['sʌfərə*] *n* sofredor(a) *m/f*; (*MED*) doente *m/f*, paciente *m/f*.

***NB:** European Portuguese adds the following consonants to certain words:* **b** (sú(b)dito, su(b)til); **c** (a(c)ção, a(c)cionista, a(c)to); **m** (inde(m)ne); **p** (ado(p)ção, ado(p)tar); *for further details see p. xiii.*

suffering ['sʌfərɪŋ] *n* sofrimento; (*pain*) dor *f*.
suffice [sə'faɪs] *vi* bastar, ser suficiente.
sufficient [sə'fɪʃənt] *adj* suficiente, bastante.
sufficiently [sə'fɪʃəntlɪ] *adv* suficientemente.
suffix ['sʌfɪks] *n* sufixo.
suffocate ['sʌfəkeɪt] *vt* sufocar, asfixiar ♦ *vi* sufocar(-se), asfixiar(-se).
suffocation [sʌfə'keɪʃən] *n* sufocação *f*; (*MED*) asfixia.
suffrage ['sʌfrɪdʒ] *n* sufrágio; (*vote*) direito de voto.
suffuse [sə'fjuːz] *vt* banhar; **~d with light/joy** banhado de luz/alegria.
sugar ['ʃugə*] *n* açúcar *m* ♦ *vt* pôr açúcar em, açucarar.
sugar beet *n* beterraba (sacarina).
sugar bowl *n* açucareiro.
sugar cane *n* cana-de-açúcar *f*.
sugar-coated [-'kəutɪd] *adj* cristalizado.
sugar lump *n* torrão *m* de açúcar.
sugar refinery *n* refinaria de açúcar.
sugary ['ʃugərɪ] *adj* açucarado.
suggest [sə'dʒɛst] *vt* sugerir; (*advise*) aconselhar; **what do you ~ I do?** o que você sugere que eu faça?
suggestion [sə'dʒɛstʃən] *n* sugestão *f*.
suggestive [sə'dʒɛstɪv] *adj* sugestivo; (*pej*) indecente.
suicidal [suɪ'saɪdl] *adj* suicida.
suicide ['suɪsaɪd] *n* suicídio; (*person*) suicida *m/f*; **to commit ~** suicidar-se.
suicide attempt *n* tentativa de suicídio.
suicide bid *n* tentativa de suicídio.
suit [suːt] *n* (*man's*) terno (*BR*), fato (*PT*); (*woman's*) conjunto; (*LAW*) processo; (*CARDS*) naipe *m* ♦ *vt* (*gen*) convir a; (*clothes*) ficar bem a; (*adapt*): **to ~ sth to** adaptar *or* acomodar algo a; **to be ~ed to sth** ser apto para algo; **they are well ~ed** fazem um bom par; **to bring a ~ against sb** mover um processo contra alguém; **to follow ~** (*fig*) seguir o exemplo.
suitable ['suːtəbl] *adj* conveniente; (*apt*) apropriado; **would tomorrow be ~?** amanhã lhe convém?
suitably ['suːtəblɪ] *adv* convenientemente, apropriadamente.
suitcase ['suːtkeɪs] *n* mala.
suite [swiːt] *n* (*of rooms*) conjunto de salas; (*MUS*) suite *f*; (*furniture*): **bedroom/dining room ~** conjunto de quarto/de sala de jantar; **a three-piece ~** um conjunto estofado (sofá e duas poltronas).
suitor ['suːtə*] *n* pretendente *m*.
sulfate ['sʌlfeɪt] (*US*) *n* = **sulphate**.
sulfur *etc* ['sʌlfə*] (*US*) = **sulphur** *etc*.
sulk [sʌlk] *vi* ficar emburrado, fazer beicinho *or* biquinho (*inf*).
sulky ['sʌlkɪ] *adj* emburrado.
sullen ['sʌlən] *adj* rabugento, teimoso.
sulphate ['sʌlfeɪt] (*US* **sulfate**) *n* sulfato; *see also* **copper sulphate**.
sulphur ['sʌlfə*] (*US* **sulfur**) *n* enxofre *m*.
sulphuric [sʌl'fjuərɪk] (*US* **sulfuric**) *adj*: **~ acid** ácido sulfúrico.
sultan ['sʌltən] *n* sultão *m*.
sultana [sʌl'tɑːnə] *n* (*fruit*) passa branca.
sultry ['sʌltrɪ] *adj* (*weather*) abafado, mormacento; (*seductive*) sedutor(a).
sum [sʌm] *n* soma; (*SCH etc*) cálculo.
sum up *vt* sumariar, fazer um resumo de; (*evaluate*) avaliar ♦ *vi* resumir.
Sumatra [su'mɑːtrə] *n* Sumatra.
summarize ['sʌməraɪz] *vt* resumir.
summary ['sʌmərɪ] *n* resumo ♦ *adj* (*justice*) sumário.
summer ['sʌmə*] *n* verão *m* ♦ *cpd* de verão; **in (the) ~** no verão.
summer camp (*US*) *n* colônia de férias.
summerhouse ['sʌməhaus] (*irreg*) *n* (*in garden*) pavilhão *m*.
summertime ['sʌmətaɪm] *n* (*season*) verão *m*.
summer time *n* (*by clock*) horário de verão.
summery ['sʌmərɪ] *adj* estival, de verão.
summing-up ['sʌmɪŋ-] *n* resumo, recapitulação *f*.
summit ['sʌmɪt] *n* topo, cume *m*; (*also*: **~** *conference*) (conferência de) cúpula.
summon ['sʌmən] *vt* (*person*) mandar chamar; (*meeting*) convocar; **to ~ a witness** citar uma testemunha.
summon up *vt* (*forces*) concentrar; (*courage*) criar.
summons ['sʌmənz] *n* citação *f*, intimação *f* ♦ *vt* citar, intimar; **to serve a ~ on sb** entregar uma citação a alguém.
sump [sʌmp] (*BRIT*) *n* (*AUT*) cárter *m*.
sumptuous ['sʌmptjuəs] *adj* suntuoso.
Sun. *abbr* (= *Sunday*) dom.
sun [sʌn] *n* sol *m*; **in the ~** ao sol; **everything under the ~** cada coisa.
sunbathe ['sʌnbeɪð] *vi* tomar sol.
sunbeam ['sʌnbiːm] *n* raio de sol.
sunbed ['sʌnbɛd] *n* espreguiçadeira; (*with sunlamp*) cama para bronzeamento artificial.
sunburn ['sʌnbəːn] *n* queimadura do sol.
sunburned ['sʌnbəːnd] *adj* queimado.
sunburnt ['sʌnbəːnt] *adj* queimado.
sun cream *n* creme *m* solar.
sundae ['sʌndeɪ] *n* sorvete *m* (*BR*) *or* gelado (*PT*) com frutas e nozes.
Sunday ['sʌndɪ] *n* domingo; *see also* **Tuesday**.
Sunday school *n* escola dominical.
sundial ['sʌndaɪəl] *n* relógio de sol.
sundown ['sʌndaun] *n* pôr *m* do sol.
sundries ['sʌndrɪz] *npl* gêneros *mpl* diversos.
sundry ['sʌndrɪ] *adj* vários, diversos; **all and ~** todos.
sunflower ['sʌnflauə*] *n* girassol *m*.
sung [sʌŋ] *pp of* **sing**.
sunglasses ['sʌnglɑːsɪz] *npl* óculos *mpl* de sol.
sunk [sʌŋk] *pp of* **sink**.
sunken ['sʌŋkn] *adj* (*ship*) afundado; (*eyes, cheeks*) cavado; (*bath*) enterrado.
sunlamp ['sʌnlæmp] *n* lâmpada ultravioleta.
sunlight ['sʌnlaɪt] *n* (luz *f* do) sol *m*.
sunlit ['sʌnlɪt] *adj* ensolarado, iluminado pelo sol.
sunny ['sʌnɪ] *adj* cheio de sol; (*day*) ensolarado, de sol; (*fig*) alegre; **it's ~** faz sol.

sunrise ['sʌnraɪz] *n* nascer *m* do sol.
sun roof *n* (*AUT*) teto solar.
sunset ['sʌnsɛt] *n* pôr *m* do sol.
sunshade ['sʌnʃeɪd] *n* (*over table*) pára-sol *m*; (*on beach*) barraca.
sunshine ['sʌnʃaɪn] *n* (luz *f* do) sol *m*.
sunspot ['sʌnspɔt] *n* mancha solar.
sunstroke ['sʌnstrəuk] *n* insolação *f*.
suntan ['sʌntæn] *n* bronzeado.
suntanned ['sʌntænd] *adj* bronzeado, moreno.
suntan oil *n* óleo de bronzear, bronzeador *m*.
suntrap ['sʌntræp] *n* lugar *m* muito ensolarado.
super ['su:pə*] (*inf*) *adj* bacana (*BR*), muito giro (*PT*).
superannuation [su:pərænju'eɪʃən] *n* pensão *f* de aposentadoria.
superb [su:'pə:b] *adj* excelente.
supercilious [su:pə'sɪlɪəs] *adj* (*disdainful*) arrogante, desdenhoso; (*haughty*) altivo.
superficial [su:pə'fɪʃəl] *adj* superficial.
superficially [su:pə'fɪʃəlɪ] *adv* superficialmente.
superfluous [su'pə:fluəs] *adj* supérfluo, desnecessário.
superhuman [su:pə'hju:mən] *adj* sobre-humano.
superimpose [su:pərɪm'pəuz] *vt* sobrepor.
superintend [su:pərɪn'tɛnd] *vt* superintender, dirigir.
superintendent [su:pərɪn'tɛndənt] *n* superintendente *m/f*; (*POLICE*) chefe *m/f* de polícia.
superior [su'pɪərɪə*] *adj* superior; (*smug*) desdenhoso ♦ *n* superior *m*; **Mother S~** (*REL*) Madre Superiora.
superiority [supɪərɪ'ɔrɪtɪ] *n* superioridade *f*.
superlative [su'pə:lətɪv] *adj*, *n* superlativo.
superman ['su:pəmæn] (*irreg*) *n* super-homem *m*.
supermarket ['su:pəma:kɪt] *n* supermercado.
supernatural [su:pə'nætʃərəl] *adj* sobrenatural.
superpower ['su:pəpauə*] *n* (*POL*) superpotência.
supersede [su:pə'si:d] *vt* suplantar.
supersonic [su:pə'sɔnɪk] *adj* supersônico.
superstition [su:pə'stɪʃən] *n* superstição *f*.
superstitious [su:pə'stɪʃəs] *adj* supersticioso.
superstore ['su:pəstɔ:*] (*BRIT*) *n* hipermercado.
supertanker ['su:pətæŋkə*] *n* superpetroleiro.
supertax ['su:pətæks] *n* sobretaxa.
supervise ['su:pəvaɪz] *vt* supervisar, supervisionar.
supervision [su:pə'vɪʒən] *n* supervisão *f*; **under medical ~** a critério médico.
supervisor ['su:pəvaɪzə*] *n* supervisor(a) *m/f*; (*academic*) orientador(a) *m/f*.
supervisory [su:pə'vaɪzərɪ] *adj* fiscalizador(a).
supine ['su:paɪn] *adj* em supinação.
supper ['sʌpə*] *n* jantar *m*; **to have ~** jantar.
supplant [sə'pla:nt] *vt* suplantar.
supple ['sʌpl] *adj* flexível.
supplement [*n* 'sʌplɪmənt, *vt* sʌplɪ'mɛnt] *n* suplemento ♦ *vt* suprir, completar.
supplementary [sʌplɪ'mɛntərɪ] *adj* suplementar.
supplementary benefit (*BRIT*) *n auxílio suplementar pago aos de renda baixa.*
supplier [sə'plaɪə*] *n* abastecedor(a) *m/f*, fornecedor(a) *m/f*; (*stockist*) distribuidor(a) *m/f*.
supply [sə'plaɪ] *vt* (*provide*) abastecer, fornecer; (*need*) suprir a; (*equip*): **to ~ (with)** suprir (de) ♦ *n* fornecimento, provisão *f*; (*supplying*) abastecimento ♦ *adj* (*teacher etc*) suplente; **supplies** *npl* (*food*) víveres *mpl*; (*MIL*) apetrechos *mpl*; **office supplies** material *m* de escritório; **to be in short ~** estar escasso; **the electricity/water/gas ~** o abastecimento de força/água/gás; **~ and demand** oferta e procura.
supply teacher (*BRIT*) *n* professor(a) *m/f* suplente.
support [sə'pɔ:t] *n* (*moral*, *financial etc*) apoio; (*TECH*) suporte *m* ♦ *vt* apoiar; (*financially*) manter; (*uphold*) sustentar; (*SPORT*: *team*) torcer por; **to ~ o.s.** (*financially*) ganhar a vida.
supporter [sə'pɔ:tə*] *n* (*POL etc*) partidário/a; (*SPORT*) torcedor(a) *m/f*.
supporting [sə'pɔ:tɪŋ] *adj* (*THEATRE etc*: *role*) secundário; (: *actor*) coadjuvante.
suppose [sə'pəuz] *vt*, *vi* (*gen*) supor; (*imagine*) imaginar; **to be ~d to do sth** dever fazer algo; **he's ~d to be an expert** dizem que ele é um perito; **I don't ~ she'll come** eu acho que ela não virá.
supposedly [sə'pəuzɪdlɪ] *adv* supostamente, pretensamente.
supposing [sə'pəuzɪŋ] *conj* caso, supondo-se que; **always ~ he comes** caso ele venha.
supposition [sʌpə'zɪʃən] *n* suposição *f*.
suppository [sə'pɔzɪtərɪ] *n* supositório.
suppress [sə'prɛs] *vt* (*publication*) suprimir; (*feelings*, *revolt*) reprimir; (*yawn*) conter; (*scandal*) abafar, encobrir.
suppression [sə'prɛʃən] *n* repressão *f*.
suppressor [sə'prɛsə*] *n* (*ELEC etc*) supressor *m*.
supremacy [su'prɛməsɪ] *n* supremacia.
supreme [su'pri:m] *adj* supremo.
Supreme Court (*US*) *n* Corte *f* Suprema.
Supt. *abbr* (*POLICE*) = **superintendent**.
surcharge ['sə:tʃa:dʒ] *n* sobrecarga: (*extra tax*) sobretaxa.
sure [ʃuə*] *adj* (*gen*) seguro; (*definite*) certo; (*aim*) certeiro ♦ *adv* (*inf*: *esp US*): **that ~ is pretty** é bonito mesmo; **~!** (*of course*) claro que sim!; **~ enough** efetivamente; **I'm not ~ how/why/when** não tenho certeza como/por que/quando; **to be ~ of sth** ter certeza de alguma coisa; **to be ~ of o.s.** estar segu-

***NB**: European Portuguese adds the following consonants to certain words:* **b** (sú(b)dito, su(b)til); **c** (a(c)ção, a(c)cionista, a(c)to); **m** (inde(m)ne); **p** (ado(p)ção, ado(p)tar); *for further details see p. xiii.*

ro de si; **to make ~ of** assegurar-se de, verificar.
sure-footed [-'futɪd] *adj* de andar seguro.
surely ['ʃuəlɪ] *adv* (*certainly*) certamente; **~ you don't mean that!** não acredito que você queira dizer isso.
surety ['ʃuərətɪ] *n* garantia, fiança; (*person*) fiador(a) *m/f*; **to go** *or* **stand ~ for sb** afiançar alguém, prestar fiança por alguém.
surf [səːf] *n* (*foam*) espuma; (*waves*) ondas *fpl*, arrebentação *f* ♦ *vi* fazer surfe, pegar onda (*inf*).
surface ['səːfɪs] *n* superfície *f* ♦ *vt* (*road*) revestir ♦ *vi* vir à superfície *or* à tona; **on the ~** (*fig*) à primeira vista.
surface area *n* área da superfície.
surface mail *n* correio comum.
surfboard ['səːfbɔːd] *n* prancha de surfe.
surfeit ['səːfɪt] *n*: **a ~ of** um excesso de.
surfer ['səːfə*] *n* surfista *m/f*.
surfing ['səːfɪŋ] *n* surfe *m*; **to go ~** fazer surfe, pegar onda (*inf*).
surge [səːdʒ] *n* onda; (ELEC) surto ♦ *vi* (*sea*) encapelar-se; (*feeling*) crescer de repente; **to ~ forward** avançar em tropel.
surgeon ['səːdʒən] *n* cirurgião/giã *m/f*.
Surgeon General (US) *n* diretor(a) *m/f* nacional de saúde.
surgery ['səːdʒərɪ] *n* cirurgia; (BRIT: *room*) consultório; **to undergo ~** operar-se.
surgery hours (BRIT) *npl* horas *fpl* de consulta.
surgical ['səːdʒɪkl] *adj* cirúrgico.
surgical spirit (BRIT) *n* álcool *m*.
surly ['səːlɪ] *adj* malcriado, rude.
surmise [sə'maɪz] *vt* conjeturar.
surmount [sə'maunt] *vt* superar, sobrepujar, vencer.
surname ['səːneɪm] *n* sobrenome *m* (BR), apelido (PT).
surpass [səː'pɑːs] *vt* superar, exceder, ultrapassar.
surplus ['səːpləs] *n* excedente *m*; (COMM) superávit *m* ♦ *adj* excedente, de sobra; **~ to my requirements** que me sobram; **~ stock** estoque *m* excedente.
surprise [sə'praɪz] *n* surpresa; (*astonishment*) assombro ♦ *vt* surpreender; **to take by ~** (*person*) pegar de surpresa; (MIL: *town, fort*) atacar de surpresa.
surprising [sə'praɪzɪŋ] *adj* surpreendente; (*unexpected*) inesperado.
surprisingly [sə'praɪzɪŋlɪ] *adv* (*easy, helpful*) surpreendentemente; **(somewhat) ~, he agreed** para surpresa de todos, ele concordou.
surrealism [sə'rɪəlɪzm] *n* surrealismo.
surrealist [sə'rɪəlɪst] *adj, n* surrealista *m/f*.
surrender [sə'rɛndə*] *n* rendição *f*, entrega ♦ *vi* render-se, entregar-se ♦ *vt* (*claim, right*) renunciar a.
surrender value *n* valor *m* de resgate.
surreptitious [sʌrəp'tɪʃəs] *adj* clandestino, furtivo.
surrogate ['sʌrəgɪt] *n* (BRIT: *substitute*) substituto ♦ *adj* substituto.
surrogate mother *n* mãe *f* portadora.
surround [sə'raund] *vt* circundar, rodear; (MIL *etc*) cercar.
surrounding [sə'raundɪŋ] *adj* circundante, adjacente.
surroundings [sə'raundɪŋz] *npl* arredores *mpl*, cercanias *fpl*.
surtax ['səːtæks] *n* sobretaxa.
surveillance [səː'veɪləns] *n* vigilância.
survey [*n* 'səːveɪ, *vt* səː'veɪ] *n* (*inspection*) inspeção *f*, vistoria; (*inquiry*) pesquisa, levantamento; (*of land*) levantamento ♦ *vt* inspecionar, vistoriar; (*look at*) observar, contemplar; (*make inquiries about*) pesquisar, fazer um levantamento de; (*land*) fazer o levantamento de.
surveying [səː'veɪɪŋ] *n* agrimensura.
surveyor [səː'veɪə*] *n* (*of land*) agrimensor(a) *m/f*; (*of building*) inspetor(a) *m/f*.
survival [sə'vaɪvl] *n* sobrevivência ♦ *cpd* (*course, kit*) de sobrevivência.
survive [sə'vaɪv] *vi* sobreviver; (*custom etc*) perdurar ♦ *vt* sobreviver a.
survivor [sə'vaɪvə*] *n* sobrevivente *m/f*.
susceptible [sə'sɛptəbl] *adj*: **~ (to)** suscetível *or* sensível a.
suspect [*adj, n* 'sʌspɛkt, *vt* səs'pɛkt] *adj, n* suspeito/a ♦ *vt* suspeitar, desconfiar.
suspend [səs'pɛnd] *vt* suspender.
suspended sentence [səs'pɛndɪd-] *n* condenação *f* condicional.
suspender belt [səs'pɛndə*-] (BRIT) *n* cinta-liga.
suspenders [səs'pɛndəz] *npl* (BRIT) ligas *fpl*; (US) suspensórios *mpl*.
suspense [səs'pɛns] *n* incerteza, ansiedade *f*; (*in film etc*) suspense *m*.
suspense account *n* conta provisória.
suspension [səs'pɛnʃən] *n* (*gen*, AUT) suspensão *f*; (*of driving licence*) cassação *f*.
suspension bridge *n* ponte *f* pênsil.
suspicion [səs'pɪʃən] *n* suspeita; (*trace*) traço, vestígio; **to be under ~** estar sob suspeita; **arrested on ~ of murder** preso sob suspeita de homicídio.
suspicious [səs'pɪʃəs] *adj* (*suspecting*) suspeitoso; (*causing suspicion*) suspeito; **to be ~ of** *or* **about sb/sth** desconfiar de alguém/algo.
suss out [sʌs-] (BRIT: *inf*) *vt* (*discover*) descobrir; (*understand*) sacar.
sustain [səs'teɪn] *vt* sustentar, manter; (*suffer*) sofrer, agüentar.
sustained [səs'teɪnd] *adj* (*effort*) contínuo.
sustenance ['sʌstɪnəns] *n* sustento.
suture ['suːtʃə*] *n* sutura.
SW *abbr* (= *short wave*) OC.
swab [swɔb] *n* (MED) mecha de algodão ♦ *vt* (NAUT: *also*: **~ *down***) lambazar.
swagger ['swægə*] *vi* andar com ar de superioridade.
swallow ['swɔləu] *n* (*bird*) andorinha; (*of food etc*) bocado; (*of drink*) trago ♦ *vt* engolir, tragar.

swallow up *vt* (*savings etc*) consumir.
swam [swæm] *pt of* **swim**.
swamp [swɔmp] *n* pântano, brejo ♦ *vt* atolar, inundar.
swampy ['swɔmpɪ] *adj* pantanoso.
swan [swɔn] *n* cisne *m*.
swank [swæŋk] (*inf*) *vi* esnobar.
swan song *n* (*fig*) canto do cisne.
swap [swɔp] *n* troca, permuta ♦ *vt*: **to ~ (for)** trocar (por).
swarm [swɔ:m] *n* (*of bees*) enxame *m*; (*gen*) multidão *f* ♦ *vi* (*bees*) enxamear; (*gen*) formigar, aglomerar-se.
swarthy ['swɔ:ðɪ] *adj* moreno.
swashbuckling ['swɔʃbʌklɪŋ] *adj* (*film*) de capa e espada.
swastika ['swɔstɪkə] *n* suástica.
swat [swɔt] *vt* esmagar, bater ♦ *n* (*BRIT*: *also*: *fly* ~) pá *f* para matar mosca.
swathe [sweɪð] *vt*: **to ~ in** (*bandages*, *blankets*) enfaixar em, envolver em.
swatter ['swɔtə*] *n* (*also*: *fly* ~) pá *f* para matar mosca.
sway [sweɪ] *vi* balançar-se, oscilar ♦ *vt* (*influence*) influenciar ♦ *n* (*rule*, *power*) domínio (sobre); **to hold ~ over sb** dominar alguém.
Swaziland ['swɑ:zɪlænd] *n* Suazilândia.
swear [swɛə*] (*pt* **swore**, *pp* **sworn**) *vi* (*by oath*) jurar; (*curse*) xingar ♦ *vt*: **to ~ an oath** prestar juramento; **to ~ to sth** afirmar algo sob juramento.
swear in *vt* (*witness*) ajuramentar; (*president*) empossar.
swearword ['swɛəwə:d] *n* palavrão *m*.
sweat [swɛt] *n* suor *m* ♦ *vi* suar.
sweatband ['swɛtbænd] *n* (*SPORT*) tira elástica (para o cabelo).
sweater ['swɛtə*] *n* suéter *m or f* (*BR*), camisola (*PT*).
sweatshirt ['swɛtʃə:t] *n* moletom *m*.
sweatshop ['swɛtʃɔp] *n oficina onde os trabalhadores são explorados*.
sweaty ['swɛtɪ] *adj* suado.
Swede [swi:d] *n* sueco/a.
swede [swi:d] *n tipo de nabo*.
Sweden ['swi:dən] *n* Suécia.
Swedish ['swi:dɪʃ] *adj* sueco ♦ *n* (*LING*) sueco.
sweep [swi:p] (*pt*, *pp* **swept**) *n* (*act*) varredura; (*of arm*) movimento circular; (*range*) extensão *f*, alcance *m*; (*also*: *chimney* ~) limpador *m* de chaminés ♦ *vt* varrer; (*fashion*, *craze*) espalhar-se por; (*disease*) arrasar ♦ *vi* varrer; (*person*) passar majestosamente.
sweep away *vt* varrer; (*rub out*) apagar.
sweep past *vi* passar rapidamente; (*brush by*) roçar.
sweep up *vt*, *vi* varrer.
sweeping ['swi:pɪŋ] *adj* (*gesture*) abarcador(a); (*reform*) radical; (*statement*) generalizado.
sweepstake ['swi:psteɪk] *n* sweepstake *m*.
sweet [swi:t] *n* (*candy*) bala (*BR*), rebuçado (*PT*); (*pudding*) sobremesa ♦ *adj* doce; (*sugary*) açucarado; (*fresh*) fresco; (*kind*) meigo; (*cute*) bonitinho ♦ *adv*: **to smell ~** ter bom cheiro; **to taste ~** estar doce; **~ and sour** agridoce.
sweetbread ['swi:tbrɛd] *n* moleja.
sweetcorn ['swi:tkɔ:n] *n* milho.
sweeten ['swi:tən] *vt* adoçar; (*add sugar to*) pôr açúcar em.
sweetener ['swi:tnə*] *n* (*CULIN*) adoçante *m*.
sweetheart ['swi:thɑ:t] *n* namorado/a; (*as address*) amor *m*.
sweetly ['swi:tlɪ] *adv* docemente; (*gently*) suavemente.
sweetness ['swi:tnɪs] *n* doçura.
sweet pea *n* ervilha-de-cheiro *f*.
sweet potato (*irreg*) *n* batata doce.
sweetshop ['swi:tʃɔp] *n* confeitaria.
swell [swɛl] (*pt* **~ed**, *pp* **swollen** *or* **~ed**) *n* (*of sea*) vaga, onda ♦ *adj* (*inf*: *excellent*) bacana ♦ *vt* engrossar ♦ *vi* engrossar; (*MED*) inchar(-se).
swelling ['swɛlɪŋ] *n* (*MED*) inchação *f*.
sweltering ['swɛltərɪŋ] *adj* sufocante, mormacento.
swept [swɛpt] *pt*, *pp of* **sweep**.
swerve [swə:v] *vi* dar uma guinada, desviar-se.
swift [swɪft] *n* (*bird*) andorinhão *m* ♦ *adj* rápido, veloz.
swiftly ['swɪftlɪ] *adv* rapidamente, velozmente.
swiftness ['swɪftnɪs] *n* rapidez *f*, ligeireza.
swig [swɪg] (*inf*) *n* (*drink*) trago, gole *m*.
swill [swɪl] *n* lavagem *f* ♦ *vt* (*also*: ~ *out*, ~ *down*) lavar, limpar com água.
swim [swɪm] (*pt* **swam**, *pp* **swum**) *n*: **to go for a ~** ir nadar ♦ *vi* nadar; (*fig*): **my head/the room is ~ming** estou com a cabeça zonza/sinto o quarto rodar ♦ *vt* atravessar a nado; (*distance*) percorrer (a nado); **to go ~ming** ir nadar; **to ~ a length** nadar uma volta.
swimmer ['swɪmə*] *n* nadador(a) *m/f*.
swimming ['swɪmɪŋ] *n* natação *f*.
swimming baths (*BRIT*) *npl* piscina.
swimming cap *n* touca de natação.
swimming costume (*BRIT*) *n* (*woman's*) maiô *m* (*BR*), fato de banho (*PT*); (*man's*) calção *m* de banho (*BR*), calções *mpl* de banho (*PT*).
swimming pool *n* piscina.
swimming trunks *npl* sunga (*BR*), calções *mpl* de banho (*PT*).
swimsuit ['swɪmsu:t] *n* (*woman's*) maiô *m* (*BR*), fato de banho (*PT*); (*man's*) calção *m* de banho (*BR*), calções *mpl* de banho (*PT*).
swindle ['swɪndl] *n* fraude *f* ♦ *vt* defraudar.
swindler ['swɪndlə*] *n* vigarista *m/f*.
swine [swaɪn] *n inv* porcos *mpl*; (*inf*) canalha *m*, calhorda *m*.

NB*: European Portuguese adds the following consonants to certain words:* **b** (sú(b)dito, su(b)til); **c** (a(c)ção, a(c)cionista, a(c)to); **m** (inde(m)ne); **p** (ado(p)ção, ado(p)tar); *for further details see p. xiii.*

swing [swɪŋ] (*pt, pp* **swung**) *n* (*in playground*) balanço; (*movement*) balanceio, oscilação *f*; (*change of direction*) virada; (*rhythm*) ritmo ♦ *vt* balançar; (*also*: ~ *round*) girar, rodar ♦ *vi* balançar(-se), oscilar; (*also*: ~ *round*) voltar-se bruscamente; **a ~ to the left** (*POL*) uma guinada para a esquerda; **to be in full ~** estar em plena atividade; **to get into the ~ of things** familiarizar-se com tudo; **the road ~s south** a estrada vira em direção ao sul.
swing bridge *n* ponte *f* giratória.
swing door (*BRIT*) *n* porta de vaivém.
swingeing ['swɪndʒɪŋ] (*BRIT*) *adj* esmagador(a).
swinging ['swɪŋɪŋ] *adj* rítmico; (*person*) badalativo; ~ **door** (*US*) porta de vaivém.
swipe [swaɪp] *n* pancada violenta ♦ *vt* (*hit*) bater com violência; (*inf*: *steal*) afanar, roubar.
swirl [swəːl] *vi* redemoinhar ♦ *n* redemoinho.
swish [swɪʃ] *adj* (*BRIT*: *inf*: *smart*) chique ♦ *n* (*of whip*) silvo; (*of skirt, grass*) ruge-ruge *m*.
Swiss [swɪs] *adj, n inv* suiço/a.
Swiss roll *n* bolo de rolo, rocambole *m* doce.
switch [swɪtʃ] *n* (*for light, radio etc*) interruptor *m*; (*change*) mudança ♦ *vt* (*change*) trocar.
switch off *vt* apagar; (*engine*) desligar; (*BRIT*: *gas, water*) fechar.
switch on *vt* acender; (*engine, machine*) ligar; (*BRIT*: *gas, water*) abrir.
switchback ['swɪtʃbæk] (*BRIT*) *n* montanha-russa.
switchblade ['swɪtʃbleɪd] *n* (*also*: ~ *knife*) canivete *m* de mola.
switchboard ['swɪtʃbɔːd] *n* (*TEL*) mesa telefônica.
switchboard operator *n* (*TEL*) telefonista *m/f*.
Switzerland ['swɪtsələnd] *n* Suiça.
swivel ['swɪvl] *vi* (*also*: ~ *round*) girar (sobre um eixo), fazer pião.
swollen ['swəulən] *pp of* **swell** ♦ *adj* inchado.
swoon [swuːn] *vi* desmaiar.
swoop [swuːp] *n* (*by police etc*) batida; (*of bird*) vôo picado ♦ *vi* (*also*: ~ *down*) precipitar-se, cair.
swop [swɔp] *n, vt* = **swap**.
sword [sɔːd] *n* espada.
swordfish ['sɔːdfɪʃ] *n inv* peixe-espada *m*.
swore [swɔː*] *pt of* **swear**.
sworn [swɔːn] *pp of* **swear**.
swot [swɔt] *vi* queimar as pestanas.
swum [swʌm] *pp of* **swim**.
swung [swʌŋ] *pt, pp of* **swing**.
sycamore ['sɪkəmɔː*] *n* sicômoro.
sycophant ['sɪkəfænt] *n* bajulador(a) *m/f*.
sycophantic [sɪkə'fæntɪk] *adj* (*person*) bajulador(a); (*behaviour*) bajulatório.
Sydney ['sɪdnɪ] *n* Sydney.
syllable ['sɪləbl] *n* sílaba.
syllabus ['sɪləbəs] *n* programa *m* de estudos; **on the ~** no roteiro.
symbol ['sɪmbl] *n* símbolo.
symbolic(al) [sɪm'bɔlɪk(l)] *adj* simbólico.
symbolism ['sɪmbəlɪzəm] *n* simbolismo.
symbolize ['sɪmbəlaɪz] *vt* simbolizar.
symmetrical [sɪ'mɛtrɪkl] *adj* simétrico.
symmetry ['sɪmɪtrɪ] *n* simetria.
sympathetic [sɪmpə'θɛtɪk] *adj* (*showing pity*) compassivo; (*understanding*) compreensivo; ~ **towards** favorável a.
sympathetically [sɪmpə'θɛtɪklɪ] *adv* (*with pity*) com compaixão; (*understandingly*) compreensivamente.
sympathize ['sɪmpəθaɪz] *vi*: **to ~ with sb** compadecer-se de alguém; **to ~ with** (*sb's feelings*) compreender.
sympathizer ['sɪmpəθaɪzə*] *n* (*POL*) simpatizante *m/f*.
sympathy ['sɪmpəθɪ] *n* (*pity*) compaixão *f*; **in ~ with** em acordo com; (*strike*) em solidariedade com; **with our deepest ~** com nossos mais profundos pêsames.
symphonic [sɪm'fɔnɪk] *adj* sinfônico.
symphony ['sɪmfənɪ] *n* sinfonia.
symphony orchestra *n* orquestra sinfônica.
symposium [sɪm'pəuzɪəm] *n* simpósio.
symptom ['sɪmptəm] *n* sintoma *m*; (*sign*) indício.
symptomatic [sɪmptə'mætɪk] *adj* sintomático.
synagogue ['sɪnəgɔg] *n* sinagoga.
synchromesh ['sɪŋkrəumɛʃ] *n* (*AUT*) engrenagem *f* sincronizada.
synchronize ['sɪŋkrənaɪz] *vt* sincronizar ♦ *vi*: **to ~ with** sincronizar-se com.
syncopated ['sɪŋkəpeɪtɪd] *adj* sincopado.
syndicate ['sɪndɪkɪt] *n* sindicato; (*of newspapers*) cadeia.
syndrome ['sɪndrəum] *n* síndrome *f*.
synonym ['sɪnənɪm] *n* sinônimo.
synonymous [sɪ'nɔnɪməs] *adj*: ~ **(with)** sinônimo (de).
synopses [sɪ'nɔpsiːz] *npl of* **synopsis**.
synopsis [sɪ'nɔpsɪs] (*pl* **synopses**) *n* sinopse *f*, resumo.
syntax ['sɪntæks] *n* sintaxe *f*.
syntheses ['sɪnθəsiːz] *npl of* **synthesis**.
synthesis ['sɪnθəsɪs] (*pl* **syntheses**) *n* síntese *f*.
synthesizer ['sɪnθəsaɪzə*] *n* (*MUS*) sintetizador *m*.
synthetic [sɪn'θɛtɪk] *adj* sintético ♦ *n*: **~s** matérias *fpl* sintéticas.
syphilis ['sɪfɪlɪs] *n* sífilis *f*.
syphon ['saɪfən] = **siphon**.
Syria ['sɪrɪə] *n* Síria.
Syrian ['sɪrɪən] *adj, n* sírio/a.
syringe [sɪ'rɪndʒ] *n* seringa.
syrup ['sɪrəp] *n* xarope *m*; (*BRIT*: *also*: *golden ~*) melaço.
syrupy ['sɪrəpɪ] *adj* xaroposo.
system ['sɪstəm] *n* sistema *m*; (*method*) método; (*ANAT*) organismo.
systematic [sɪstə'mætɪk] *adj* sistemático.
system disk *n* (*COMPUT*) disco sistema.
systems analyst *n* analista *m/f* de sistemas.

T

T, t [tiː] *n* (*letter*) T, t *m*; **T for Tommy** T de Tereza.
TA (*BRIT*) *n abbr* = **Territorial Army**.
ta [tɑː] (*BRIT*: *inf*) *excl* obrigado/a.
tab [tæb] *n abbr* = **tabulator** ♦ *n* lingüeta, aba; (*label*) etiqueta; **to keep ~s on** (*fig*) vigiar.
tabby ['tæbɪ] *n* (*also*: ~ *cat*) gato malhado *or* listrado.
table ['teɪbl] *n* mesa; (*of statistics etc*) quadro, tabela ♦ *vt* (*motion etc*) apresentar; **to lay** *or* **set the ~** pôr a mesa; **to clear the ~** tirar a mesa; **league ~** (*BRIT*: *FOOTBALL*) classificação *f* dos times; **~ of contents** índice *m* das matérias.
tablecloth ['teɪblklɔθ] *n* toalha de mesa.
table d'hôte [tɑːbl'dəut] *n* refeição *f* comercial.
table lamp *n* abajur *m* (*BR*), candeeiro (*PT*).
tableland ['teɪbllænd] *n* planalto.
tablemat ['teɪblmæt] *n* descanso.
table salt *n* sal *m* fino.
tablespoon ['teɪblspuːn] *n* colher *f* de sopa; (*also*: *~ful*: *as measurement*) colherada.
tablet ['tæblɪt] *n* (*MED*) comprimido; (: *for sucking*) pastilha; (*for writing*) bloco; (*of stone*) lápide *f*; **~ of soap** (*BRIT*) sabonete *m*.
table tennis *n* pingue-pongue *m*, tênis *m* de mesa.
table wine *n* vinho de mesa.
tabloid ['tæblɔɪd] *n* (*newspaper*) tablóide *m*; **the ~s** os jornais populares.
taboo [tə'buː] *n* tabu *m* ♦ *adj* tabu.
tabulate ['tæbjuleɪt] *vt* (*data, figures*) dispor em forma de tabela.
tabulator ['tæbjuleɪtə*] *n* tabulador *m*.
tachograph ['tækəgrɑːf] *n* tacógrafo.
tachometer [tæ'kɔmɪtə*] *n* tacômetro.
tacit ['tæsɪt] *adj* tácito, implícito.
taciturn ['tæsɪtəːn] *adj* taciturno.
tack [tæk] *n* (*nail*) tachinha, percevejo; (*BRIT*: *stitch*) alinhavo; (*NAUT*) amura ♦ *vt* prender com tachinha; alinhavar ♦ *vi* virar de bordo; **to change ~** virar de bordo; (*fig*) mudar de tática; **to ~ sth on to (the end of) sth** anexar algo a algo.
tackle ['tækl] *n* (*gear*) equipamento; (*also*: *fishing* ~) apetrechos *mpl*; (*for lifting*) guincho; (*FOOTBALL*) ato de tirar a bola de adversário ♦ *vt* (*difficulty*) atacar; (*grapple with*) atracar-se com; (*FOOTBALL*) tirar a bola de.
tacky ['tækɪ] *adj* pegajoso, grudento; (*inf*: *tasteless*) cafona.
tact [tækt] *n* tato, diplomacia.
tactful ['tæktful] *adj* com tato, diplomático; **to be ~** ser diplomata.
tactfully ['tæktfulɪ] *adv* discretamente, com tato.
tactical ['tæktɪkl] *adj* tático.
tactics ['tæktɪks] *n, npl* tática.
tactless ['tæktlɪs] *adj* sem tato, sem diplomacia.
tactlessly ['tæktlɪslɪ] *adv* indiscretamente.
tadpole ['tædpəul] *n* girino.
taffy ['tæfɪ] (*US*) *n* puxa-puxa *m* (*BR*), caramelo (*PT*).
tag [tæg] *n* (*label*) etiqueta; **price/name ~** etiqueta de preço/com o nome.
tag along *vi* seguir.
Tahiti [tɑː'hiːtɪ] *n* Taiti (*no article*).
tail [teɪl] *n* rabo; (*of bird, comet etc*) cauda; (*of shirt, coat*) aba ♦ *vt* (*follow*) seguir bem de perto; **to turn ~** dar no pé; *see also* **head**.
tail away *vi* (*in size, quality etc*) diminuir gradualmente.
tail off *vi* (*in size, quality etc*) diminuir gradualmente.
tailback ['teɪlbæk] (*BRIT*) *n* fila (de carros).
tail coat *n* fraque *m*.
tail end *n* cauda, parte *f* final.
tailgate ['teɪlgeɪt] *n* (*AUT*) porta traseira.
tailor ['teɪlə*] *n* alfaiate *m* ♦ *vt*: **to ~ sth (to)** adaptar algo (a); **~'s (shop)** alfaiataria.
tailoring ['teɪlərɪŋ] *n* (*cut*) feitio.
tailor-made *adj* feito sob medida; (*fig*) especial.
tailwind ['teɪlwɪnd] *n* vento de popa *or* de cauda.
taint [teɪnt] *vt* (*meat, food*) estragar; (*fig*: *reputation*) manchar.
tainted ['teɪntɪd] *adj* (*food*) estragado, passado; (*water, air*) poluído; (*fig*) manchado.
Taiwan ['taɪ'wɑːn] *n* Taiuan (*no article*).
take [teɪk] (*pt* **took**, *pp* **taken**) *vt* (*gen*) tomar; (*grab*) pegar (em); (*gain*: *prize*) ganhar; (*require*: *effort, courage*) requerer, exigir; (*tolerate*) agüentar; (*accompany, bring, carry*) levar; (*exam*) prestar; (*hold*: *passengers etc*): **it ~s 50 people** cabem 50 pessoas ♦ *vi* (*dye, fire*) pegar ♦ *n* (*CINEMA*) tomada; **to ~ sth from** (*drawer etc*) tirar algo de; (*person*) pegar algo de; **I ~ it that** ... suponho que ...; **I took him for a doctor** eu o tomei por médico; **to ~ sb's hand** pegar a mão de alguém; **to ~ for a walk** levar a passeio; **to be taken ill** adoecer, ficar doente; **to ~ it upon o.s. to do sth** assumir a responsabilidade de fazer algo; **~ the first (street) on the left** pega a primeira (rua) à esquerda; **it won't ~ long** não vai demorar muito; **I was quite taken with it/her** gostei muito daquilo/dela.
take after *vt fus* parecer-se com.
take apart *vt* desmontar.

***NB**: European Portuguese adds the following consonants to certain words:* **b** (sú(b)dito, su(b)til); **c** (a(c)ção, a(c)cionista, a(c)to); **m** (inde(m)ne); **p** (ado(p)ção, ado(p)tar); *for further details see p. xiii.*

take away *vt* (*extract*) tirar; (*carry off*) levar; (*subtract*) subtrair ♦ *vi*: **to ~ away from** diminuir.
take back *vt* (*return*) devolver; (*one's words*) retirar.
take down *vt* (*building*) demolir; (*dismantle*) desmontar; (*letter etc*) tomar por escrito.
take in *vt* (*deceive*) enganar; (*understand*) compreender; (*include*) abranger; (*lodger*) receber; (*orphan, stray dog*) acolher; (*dress etc*) apertar.
take off *vi* (*AVIAT*) decolar ♦ *vt* (*remove*) tirar; (*imitate*) imitar.
take on *vt* (*work*) empreender; (*employee*) empregar; (*opponent*) desafiar.
take out *vt* tirar; (*extract*) extrair; (*licence*) tirar; **to ~ sth out of** tirar algo de; **don't ~ it out on me!** não descarregue em cima de mim!
take over *vt* (*business*) tomar posse de ♦ *vi*: **to ~ over from sb** suceder a alguém.
take to *vt fus* (*person*) simpatizar com; (*activity*) afeiçoar-se a; **to ~ to doing sth** criar o hábito de fazer algo.
take up *vt* (*dress*) encurtar; (*story*) continuar; (*occupy*: *time, space*) ocupar; (*engage in*: *hobby etc*) dedicar-se a; (*accept*: *offer, challenge*) aceitar; (*absorb*: *liquids*) absorver ♦ *vi*: **to ~ up with sb** fazer amizade com alguém.
takeaway ['teɪkəweɪ] (*BRIT*) *adj* (*food*) para levar.
take-home pay *n* salário líquido.
taken ['teɪkən] *pp of* **take**.
takeoff ['teɪkɔf] *n* (*AVIAT*) decolagem *f*.
takeout ['teɪkaut] (*US*) *adj* (*food*) para levar.
takeover ['teɪkəuvə*] *n* (*COMM*) aquisição *f* de controle.
takeover bid *n* oferta pública de aquisição de controle.
takings ['teɪkɪŋz] *npl* (*COMM*) receita, renda.
talc [tælk] *n* (*also*: *~um powder*) talco.
tale [teɪl] *n* (*story*) conto; (*account*) narrativa; **to tell ~s** (*fig*: *lie*) dizer mentiras; (: *sneak*) dedurar.
talent ['tælənt] *n* talento.
talented ['tæləntɪd] *adj* talentoso.
talent scout *n* caçador(a) *m/f* de talentos.
talk [tɔːk] *n* conversa, fala; (*gossip*) mexerico, fofocas *fpl*; (*conversation*) conversa, conversação *f* ♦ *vi* (*speak*) falar; (*chatter*) bater papo, conversar; **~s** *npl* (*POL etc*) negociações *fpl*; **to give a ~** dar uma palestra; **to ~ about** falar sobre; **~ing of films, have you seen ...?** por falar em filmes, você viu ...?; **to ~ sb into doing sth** convencer alguém a fazer algo; **to ~ sb out of doing sth** dissuadir alguém de fazer algo.
talk over *vt* discutir.
talkative ['tɔːkətɪv] *adj* loquaz, tagarela.
talker ['tɔːkə*] *n* falador(a) *m/f*.
talking point ['tɔːkɪŋ-] *n* assunto para discussão.
talking-to ['tɔːkɪŋ-] *n*: **to give sb a good ~** passar um sabão em alguém.
talk show *n* (*TV, RADIO*) programa *m* de entrevistas.
tall [tɔːl] *adj* alto; (*tree*) grande; **to be 6 feet ~** medir 6 pés, ter 6 pés de altura; **how ~ are you?** qual é a sua altura?
tallboy ['tɔːlbɔɪ] (*BRIT*) *n* cômoda alta.
tallness ['tɔːlnɪs] *n* altura.
tall story *n* estória inverossímil.
tally ['tælɪ] *n* conta ♦ *vi*: **to ~ (with)** conferir (com); **to keep a ~ of sth** fazer um registro de algo.
talon ['tælən] *n* garra.
tambourine [tæmbə'riːn] *n* tamborim *m*, pandeiro.
tame [teɪm] *adj* (*mild*) manso; (*tamed*) domesticado; (*fig*: *story, style*) sem graça, insípido.
tamper ['tæmpə*] *vi*: **to ~ with** mexer em.
tampon ['tæmpən] *n* tampão *m* higiénico.
tan [tæn] *n* (*also*: *sun~*) bronzeado ♦ *vt* bronzear ♦ *vi* bronzear-se ♦ *adj* (*colour*) bronzeado, marrom claro; **to get a ~** bronzear-se.
tandem ['tændəm] *n* tandem *m*.
tang [tæŋ] *n* sabor *m* forte.
tangent ['tændʒənt] *n* (*MATH*) tangente *f*; **to go off at a ~** (*fig*) sair pela tangente.
tangerine [tændʒə'riːn] *n* tangerina, mexerica.
tangible ['tændʒəbl] *adj* tangível; **~ assets** ativos *mpl* tangíveis.
tangle ['tæŋgl] *n* emaranhado ♦ *vt* emaranhar; **to get in(to) a ~** meter-se num rolo.
tango ['tæŋgəu] *n* tango.
tank [tæŋk] *n* (*water ~*) depósito, tanque *m*; (*for fish*) aquário; (*MIL*) tanque *m*.
tankard ['tæŋkəd] *n* canecão *m*.
tanker ['tæŋkə*] *n* (*ship*) navio-tanque *m*; (: *for oil*) petroleiro; (*truck*) caminhão-tanque *m*.
tanned [tænd] *adj* (*skin*) moreno, bronzeado.
tannin ['tænɪn] *n* tanino.
tanning ['tænɪŋ] *n* (*of leather*) curtimento.
tannoy ['tænɔɪ] ® (*BRIT*) *n* alto-falante *m*; **over the ~** nos alto-falantes.
tantalizing ['tæntəlaɪzɪŋ] *adj* tentador(a).
tantamount ['tæntəmaunt] *adj*: **~ to** equivalente a.
tantrum ['tæntrəm] *n* chilique *m*, acesso (de raiva); **to throw a ~** ter um chilique *or* acesso.
Tanzania [tænzə'nɪə] *n* Tanzânia.
Tanzanian [tænzə'nɪən] *adj, n* tanzaniano/a.
tap [tæp] *n* (*on sink etc*) torneira; (*gentle blow*) palmadinha; (*gas ~*) chave *f* ♦ *vt* dar palmadinha em, bater de leve; (*resources*) utilizar, explorar; (*telephone*) grampear; **on ~** (*beer*) de barril; (*resources*) disponível.
tap-dancing *n* sapateado.
tape [teɪp] *n* fita; (*also*: *magnetic ~*) fita magnética; (*sticky ~*) fita adesiva ♦ *vt* (*record*) gravar (em fita); **on ~** (*song etc*) em fita.
tape deck *n* gravador *m*, toca-fitas *m inv*.
tape measure *n* fita métrica, trena.

taper ['teɪpə*] *n* círio ♦ *vi* afilar-se, estreitar-se.
tape-record *vt* gravar (em fita).
tape recorder *n* gravador *m*.
tape recording *n* gravação *f* (em fita).
tapered ['teɪpəd] *adj* afilado.
tapering ['teɪpərɪŋ] *adj* afilado.
tapestry ['tæpɪstrɪ] *n* (*object*) tapete *m* de parede; (*art*) tapeçaria.
tapeworm ['teɪpwəːm] *n* solitária.
tapioca [tæpɪ'əukə] *n* tapioca.
tappet ['tæpɪt] *n* (*AUT*) tucho (*BR*), ponteiro de válvula (*PT*).
tar [tɑː] *n* alcatrão *m*; (*on road*) piche *m*; **low-/middle-~ cigarettes** cigarros com baixo/médio teor de alcatrão.
tarantula [tə'ræntjulə] *n* tarântula.
tardy ['tɑːdɪ] *adj* tardio.
target ['tɑːgɪt] *n* alvo; (*fig*: *objective*) objetivo; **to be on ~** (*project*) progredir segundo as previsões.
target practice *n* exercício de tiro ao alvo.
tariff ['tærɪf] *n* tarifa.
tariff barrier *n* barreira alfandegária.
tarmac ['tɑːmæk] *n* (*BRIT*: *on road*) macadame *m*; (*AVIAT*) pista ♦ *vt* (*BRIT*) asfaltar.
tarnish ['tɑːnɪʃ] *vt* empanar o brilho de.
tarpaulin [tɑː'pɔːlɪn] *n* lona alcatroada.
tarragon ['tærəgən] *n* estragão *m*.
tart [tɑːt] *n* (*CULIN*) torta; (*BRIT*: *inf*: *pej*: *woman*) piranha ♦ *adj* (*flavour*) ácido, azedo.
tart up (*inf*) *vt* arrumar, dar um jeito em; **to ~ o.s. up** arrumar-se; (*pej*) empetecar-se.
tartan ['tɑːtn] *n* pano escocês axadrezado, tartan *m* ♦ *adj* axadrezado.
tartar ['tɑːtə*] *n* (*on teeth*) tártaro.
tartar(e) sauce ['tɑːtə*-] *n* molho tártaro.
task [tɑːsk] *n* tarefa; **to take to ~** repreender.
task force *n* (*MIL*, *POLICE*) força-tarefa.
taskmaster ['tɑːskmɑːstə*] *n*: **he's a hard ~** ele é muito exigente.
Tasmania [tæz'meɪnɪə] *n* Tasmânia *f*.
tassel ['tæsl] *n* borla, pendão *m*.
taste [teɪst] *n* gosto; (*also*: *after~*) gosto residual; (*sip*) golinho; (*fig*: *glimpse, idea*) amostra, idéia ♦ *vt* experimentar ♦ *vi*: **to ~ of** *or* **like** (*fish etc*) ter gosto de, saber a; **you can ~ the garlic (in it)** sente-se o gosto de alho; **can I have a ~ of this wine?** posso provar o vinho?; **to have a ~ for** sentir predileção por; **in good/bad ~** de bom/mau gosto.
taste bud *n* papila gustativa.
tasteful ['teɪstful] *adj* de bom gosto.
tastefully ['teɪstfulɪ] *adv* com bom gosto.
tasteless ['teɪstlɪs] *adj* (*food*) insípido, insosso; (*remark*) de mau gosto.
tasty ['teɪstɪ] *adj* saboroso, delicioso.
tattered ['tætəd] *adj* esfarrapado.
tatters ['tætəz] *npl*: **in ~** esfarrapado.
tattoo [tə'tuː] *n* tatuagem *f*; (*spectacle*) espetáculo militar ♦ *vt* tatuar.
tatty ['tætɪ] (*BRIT*: *inf*) *adj* (*worn*) surrado; (*dirty*) enxovalhado.
taught [tɔːt] *pt, pp of* **teach**.
taunt [tɔːnt] *n* zombaria, escárnio ♦ *vt* zombar de, mofar de.
Taurus ['tɔːrəs] *n* Touro.
taut [tɔːt] *adj* esticado, retesado.
tavern ['tævən] *n* taverna.
tawdry ['tɔːdrɪ] *adj* de mau gosto, espalhafatoso, berrante.
tawny ['tɔːnɪ] *adj* moreno, trigueiro.
tax [tæks] *n* imposto ♦ *vt* tributar; (*fig*: *test*) sobrecarregar; (: *patience*) esgotar; **before/after ~** antes/depois de impostos; **free of ~** isento de impostos.
taxable ['tæksəbl] *adj* (*income*) tributável.
tax allowance *n* abatimento da renda.
taxation [tæk'seɪʃən] *n* tributação *f*; **system of ~** sistema fiscal.
tax avoidance *n* evasão *f* de impostos.
tax collector *n* cobrador(a) *m/f* de impostos.
tax disc (*BRIT*) *n* (*AUT*) ≈ plaqueta.
tax evasion *n* sonegação *f* fiscal.
tax exemption *n* isenção *f* de impostos.
tax exile *n pessoa que se expatria para evitar impostos excessivos*.
tax-free *adj* isento de impostos.
tax haven *n* refúgio fiscal.
taxi ['tæksɪ] *n* táxi *m* ♦ *vi* (*AVIAT*) taxiar.
taxidermist ['tæksɪdəːmɪst] *n* taxidermista *m/f*.
taxi driver *n* motorista *m/f* de táxi.
taximeter ['tæksɪmiːtə*] *n* taxímetro.
tax inspector (*BRIT*) *n* fiscal *m/f* de imposto de renda.
taxi rank (*BRIT*) *n* ponto de táxi.
taxi stand *n* ponto de táxi.
tax payer *n* contribuinte *m/f*.
tax rebate *n* devolução *f* de imposto de renda.
tax relief *n* isenção *f* de imposto.
tax return *n* declaração *f* de rendimentos.
tax year *n* ano fiscal, exercício.
TB *abbr of* **tuberculosis.**
TD (*US*) *n abbr* = **Treasury Department;** (*FOOTBALL*) = **touchdown.**
tea [tiː] *n* chá *m*; (*snack*) lanche *m*; **high ~** (*BRIT*) jantar-lanche *m*.
tea bag *n* saquinho (*BR*) *or* carteira (*PT*) de chá.
tea break (*BRIT*) *n* pausa (para o chá).
teacake ['tiːkeɪk] (*BRIT*) *n* pãozinho doce.
teach [tiːtʃ] (*pt, pp* **taught**) *vt*: **to ~ sb sth, ~ sth to sb** ensinar algo a alguém ♦ *vi* ensinar; (*be a teacher*) lecionar (*PT*: -cc-); **it taught him a lesson** (*fig*) isto lhe serviu de lição.
teacher ['tiːtʃə*] *n* professor(a) *m/f*.
teacher training college *n* faculdade *f* de formação de professores.
teaching ['tiːtʃɪŋ] *n* ensino; (*as profession*) magistério.
teaching aids *npl* recursos *mpl* de ensino.
teaching hospital (*BRIT*) *n* hospital *m* esco-

NB: European Portuguese adds the following consonants to certain words: **b** (sú(b)dito, su(b)til); **c** (a(c)ção, a(c)cionista, a(c)to); **m** (inde(m)ne); **p** (ado(p)ção, ado(p)tar); *for further details see p. xiii.*

la.
teaching staff (*BRIT*) *n* corpo docente.
tea cosy *n* coberta do bule, abafador *m*.
teacup ['ti:kʌp] *n* xícara (*BR*) *or* chávena (*PT*) de chá.
teak [ti:k] *n* (madeira de) teca ♦ *cpd* de teca.
tea leaves *npl* folhas *fpl* de chá.
team [ti:m] *n* (*SPORT*) time *m* (*BR*), equipa (*PT*); (*group*) equipe *f* (*BR*), equipa (*PT*); (*of animals*) parelha.
team up *vi*: **to ~ up (with)** agrupar-se (com).
team games *npl* jogos *mpl* de equipe.
teamwork ['ti:mwə:k] *n* trabalho de equipe.
tea party *n* chá *m* (*reunião*).
teapot ['ti:pɔt] *n* bule *m* de chá.
tear[1] [tɪə*] *n* lágrima; **in ~s** chorando, em lágrimas; **to burst into ~s** romper em lágrimas.
tear[2] [tɛə*] (*pt* **tore**, *pp* **torn**) *n* rasgão *m* ♦ *vt* rasgar ♦ *vi* rasgar-se; **to ~ to pieces** *or* **to bits** *or* **to shreds** despedaçar, estraçalhar; (*fig*) arrasar com.
tear along *vi* (*rush*) precipitar-se.
tear apart *vt* rasgar; (*fig*) arrasar.
tear away *vt*: **to ~ o.s. away (from sth)** desgrudar-se (de algo).
tear out *vt* (*sheet of paper, cheque*) arrancar.
tear up *vt* rasgar.
tearaway ['tɛərəweɪ] (*inf*) *n* bagunceiro/a.
teardrop ['tɪədrɔp] *n* lágrima.
tearful ['tɪəful] *adj* choroso.
tear gas *n* gás *m* lacrimogênio.
tearoom ['ti:ru:m] *n* salão *m* de chá.
tease [ti:z] *n* implicante *m/f* ♦ *vt* implicar com.
tea set *n* aparelho de chá.
teashop ['ti:ʃɔp] *n* salão *m* de chá.
teaspoon ['ti:spu:n] *n* colher *f* de chá; (*also*: *~ful*: *as measurement*) (conteúdo de) colher de chá.
tea strainer *n* coador *m* (de chá).
teat [ti:t] *n* (*of bottle*) bico (de mamadeira).
teatime ['ti:taɪm] *n* hora do chá.
tea towel (*BRIT*) *n* pano de prato.
tea urn *n* samovar *m*.
tech [tɛk] (*inf*) *n abbr* = **technology**; **technical college**.
technical ['tɛknɪkl] *adj* técnico.
technical college (*BRIT*) *n* escola técnica.
technicality [tɛknɪ'kælɪtɪ] *n* detalhe *m* técnico; (*quality*) tecnicidade *f*; **on a legal ~** devido a uma particularidade jurídica.
technically ['tɛknɪklɪ] *adv* tecnicamente.
technician [tɛk'nɪʃn] *n* técnico/a.
technique [tɛk'ni:k] *n* técnica.
technocrat ['tɛknəkræt] *n* tecnocrata *m/f*.
technological [tɛknə'lɔdʒɪkl] *adj* tecnológico.
technologist [tɛk'nɔlədʒɪst] *n* tecnólogo/a.
technology [tɛk'nɔlədʒɪ] *n* tecnologia.
teddy (bear) ['tɛdɪ-] *n* ursinho de pelúcia.
tedious ['ti:dɪəs] *adj* maçante, chato.
tedium ['ti:dɪəm] *n* tédio.
tee [ti:] *n* (*GOLF*) tee *m*.
teem [ti:m] *vi* abundar, pulular; **to ~ with** abundar em; **it is ~ing (with rain)** está chovendo a cântaros.
teenage ['ti:neɪdʒ] *adj* (*fashions etc*) de *or* para adolescentes.
teenager ['ti:neɪdʒə*] *n* adolescente *m/f*, jovem *m/f*.
teens [ti:nz] *npl*: **to be in one's ~** estar entre os 13 e 19 anos, estar na adolescência.
tee-shirt *n* = **T-shirt**.
teeter ['ti:tə*] *vi* balançar-se.
teeth [ti:θ] *npl of* **tooth**.
teethe [ti:ð] *vi* começar a ter dentes.
teething ring ['ti:ðɪŋ-] *n* mastigador *m* para a dentição.
teething troubles ['ti:ðɪŋ-] *npl* (*fig*) dificuldades *fpl* iniciais.
teetotal ['ti:'təutl] *adj* (*person*) abstêmio.
teetotaller ['ti:'təutlə*] (*US* **teetotaler**) *n* abstêmio/a.
TEFL ['tɛfl] *n abbr* = **Teaching of English as a Foreign Language**.
Teheran [tɛə'rɑ:n] *n* Teerã (*BR*), Teerão (*PT*).
tel. *abbr* (= *telephone*) tel.
Tel Aviv ['tɛlə'vi:v] *n* Telavive.
telecast ['tɛlɪkɑ:st] (*irreg*: *like* **cast**) *vt* televisionar, transmitir por televisão.
telecommunications [tɛlɪkəmju:nɪ'keɪʃənz] *n* telecomunicações *fpl*.
telegram ['tɛlɪgræm] *n* telegrama *m*.
telegraph ['tɛlɪgrɑ:f] *n* telégrafo.
telegraphic [tɛlɪ'græfɪk] *adj* telegráfico.
telegraph pole *n* poste *m* telegráfico.
telegraph wire *n* fio telegráfico.
telepathic [tɛlɪ'pæθɪk] *adj* telepático.
telepathy [tə'lɛpəθɪ] *n* telepatia.
telephone ['tɛlɪfəun] *n* telefone *m* ♦ *vt* (*person*) telefonar para; (*message*) telefonar; **to be on the ~** (*BRIT*), **to have a ~** (*subscriber*) ter telefone; **to be on the ~** (*be speaking*) estar falando no telefone.
telephone booth (*BRIT* **telephone box**) *n* cabine *f* telefônica.
telephone call *n* telefonema *m*.
telephone directory *n* lista telefônica, catálogo (*BR*).
telephone exchange *n* estação *f* telefônica.
telephone kiosk (*BRIT*) *n* cabine *f* telefônica.
telephone number *n* (número de) telefone *m*.
telephone operator *n* telefonista *m/f*.
telephone tapping [-'tæpɪŋ] *n* escuta telefônica.
telephonist [tə'lɛfənɪst] (*BRIT*) *n* telefonista *m/f*.
telephoto ['tɛlɪfəutəu] *adj*: **~ lens** teleobjetivo.
teleprinter ['tɛlɪprɪntə*] *n* teletipo.
Teleprompter ['tɛlɪprɔmptə*] ® (*US*) *n* ponto mecânico.
telescope ['tɛlɪskəup] *n* telescópio ♦ *vt, vi* abrir (*or* fechar) como um telescópio.
telescopic [tɛlɪ'skɔpɪk] *adj* telescópico.
Teletex ['tɛlətɛks] ® *n* (*TEL*) videotexto.
televiewer ['tɛlɪvju:ə*] *n* telespectador(a) *m/f*.

televise ['tɛlɪvaɪz] *vt* televisar, televisionar.
television ['tɛlɪvɪʒən] *n* televisão *f*.
television licence (*BRIT*) *n licença para utilizar um televisor*.
television programme *n* programa *m* de televisão.
television set *n* (aparelho de) televisão *f*, televisor *m*.
telex ['tɛlɛks] *n* telex *m* ♦ *vt* (*message*) enviar por telex, telexar; (*person*) mandar um telex para ♦ *vi* enviar um telex.
tell [tɛl] (*pt, pp* **told**) *vt* dizer; (*relate*: *story*) contar; (*distinguish*): **to ~ sth from** distinguir algo de ♦ *vi* (*have effect*) ter efeito; (*talk*): **to ~ (of)** falar (de *or* em); **to ~ sb to do sth** dizer para alguém fazer algo; (*order*) mandar alguém fazer algo; **to ~ sb about sth** falar a alguém de algo; (*what happened*) contar algo a alguém; **to ~ the time** (*know how to*) dizer as horas; (*clock*) marcar as horas; **can you ~ me the time?** pode me dizer a hora?; **(I) ~ you what ...** escuta ...; **I can't ~ them apart** não consigo diferenciar um do outro; **to ~ the difference** sentir a diferença; **how can you ~?** como você sabe?
tell off *vt* repreender, dar uma bronca em.
tell on *vt fus* (*inform against*) delatar, dedurar.
teller ['tɛlə*] *n* (*in bank*) caixa *m/f*.
telling ['tɛlɪŋ] *adj* (*remark, detail*) revelador(a).
telltale ['tɛlteɪl] *adj* (*sign*) denunciador(a), revelador(a).
telly ['tɛlɪ] (*BRIT*: *inf*) *n abbr* = **television**.
temerity [tə'mɛrɪtɪ] *n* temeridade *f*.
temp [tɛmp] (*BRIT*: *inf*) *abbr* (= *temporary*) *n* temporário/a ♦ *vi* trabalhar como temporário/a.
temper ['tɛmpə*] *n* (*nature*) temperamento; (*mood*) humor *m*; (*bad* ~) mau gênio; (*fit of anger*) cólera; (*of child*) birra ♦ *vt* (*moderate*) moderar; **to be in a ~** estar de mau humor; **to lose one's ~** perder a paciência *or* a calma, ficar zangado; **to keep one's ~** controlar-se.
temperament ['tɛmprəmənt] *n* (*nature*) temperamento.
temperamental [tɛmprə'mɛntl] *adj* temperamental.
temperance ['tɛmpərəns] *n* moderação *f*; (*in drinking*) sobriedade *f*.
temperate ['tɛmprət] *adj* moderado; (*climate*) temperado.
temperature ['tɛmprətʃə*] *n* temperatura; **to have** *or* **run a ~** ter febre.
temperature chart *n* (*MED*) tabela de temperatura.
tempered ['tɛmpəd] *adj* (*steel*) temperado.
tempest ['tɛmpɪst] *n* tempestade *f*.
tempestuous [tɛm'pɛstjuəs] *adj* (*relationship*) tempestuoso.
tempi ['tɛmpi:] *npl of* **tempo**.
template ['tɛmplɪt] *n* molde *m*.
temple ['tɛmpl] *n* (*building*) templo; (*ANAT*) têmpora.
templet ['tɛmplɪt] *n* = **template**.
tempo ['tɛmpəu] (*pl* **~s** *or* **tempi**) *n* tempo; (*fig*: *of life etc*) ritmo.
temporal ['tɛmpərəl] *adj* temporal.
temporarily ['tɛmpərərɪlɪ] *adv* temporariamente; (*closed*) provisoriamente.
temporary ['tɛmpərərɪ] *adj* temporário; (*passing*) transitório; (*worker*) provisório; **~ secretary** secretária temporária; **~ teacher** professor suplente.
temporize ['tɛmpəraɪz] *vi* temporizar.
tempt [tɛmpt] *vt* tentar; **to ~ sb into doing sth** tentar *or* induzir alguém a fazer algo; **to be ~ed to do sth** ser tentado a fazer algo.
temptation [tɛmp'teɪʃən] *n* tentação *f*.
tempting ['tɛmptɪŋ] *adj* tentador(a).
ten [tɛn] *num* dez ♦ *n*: **~s of thousands** milhares *mpl* e milhares; *see also* **five**.
tenable ['tɛnəbl] *adj* sustentável.
tenacious [tə'neɪʃəs] *adj* tenaz.
tenacity [tə'næsɪtɪ] *n* tenacidade *f*.
tenancy ['tɛnənsɪ] *n* aluguel *m*; (*of house*) locação *f*.
tenant ['tɛnənt] *n* inquilino/a, locatário/a.
tend [tɛnd] *vt* (*sick etc*) cuidar de; (*machine*) vigiar ♦ *vi*: **to ~ to do sth** tender a fazer algo.
tendency ['tɛndənsɪ] *n* tendência.
tender ['tɛndə*] *adj* macio, tenro; (*delicate*) delicado; (*gentle*) terno; (*sore*) sensível, dolorido; (*affectionate*) carinhoso, afetuoso ♦ *n* (*COMM*: *offer*) oferta, proposta; (*money*): **legal ~** moeda corrente *or* legal ♦ *vt* oferecer; **to ~ one's resignation** pedir demissão; **to put in a ~ (for)** apresentar uma proposta (para); **to put work out to ~** (*BRIT*) abrir concorrência para uma obra.
tenderize ['tɛndəraɪz] *vt* (*CULIN*) amaciar.
tenderly ['tɛndəlɪ] *adv* afetuosamente.
tenderness ['tɛndənɪs] *n* ternura; (*of meat*) maciez *f*.
tendon ['tɛndən] *n* tendão *m*.
tenement ['tɛnəmənt] *n* conjunto habitacional.
Tenerife [tɛnə'ri:f] *n* Tenerife (*no article*).
tenet ['tɛnət] *n* princípio.
tenner ['tɛnə*] (*BRIT*: *inf*) *n* nota de dez libras.
tennis ['tɛnɪs] *n* tênis *m* ♦ *cpd* (*match, racket etc*) de tênis.
tennis ball *n* bola de tênis.
tennis court *n* quadra de tênis.
tennis elbow *n* (*MED*) sinovite *f* do cotovelo.
tennis shoes *npl* tênis *m*.
tenor ['tɛnə*] *n* (*MUS*) tenor *m*; (*of speech etc*) teor *m*.
tenpin bowling ['tɛnpɪn-] (*BRIT*) *n* boliche *m* com 10 paus.
tense [tɛns] *adj* tenso; (*stretched*) estirado, esticado; (*stiff*) rígido, teso ♦ *n* (*LING*) tempo

***NB**: European Portuguese adds the following consonants to certain words:* **b** (sú(b)dito, su(b)til); **c** (a(c)ção, a(c)cionista, a(c)to); **m** (inde(m)ne); **p** (ado(p)ção, ado(p)tar); *for further details see p. xiii.*

♦ *vt* (*tighten*: *muscles*) retesar.
tenseness ['tɛnsnɪs] *n* tensão *f*.
tension ['tɛnʃən] *n* tensão *f*.
tent [tɛnt] *n* tenda, barraca.
tentacle ['tɛntəkl] *n* tentáculo.
tentative ['tɛntətɪv] *adj* (*conclusion*) provisório, tentativo; (*person*) hesitante, indeciso.
tenterhooks ['tɛntəhuks] *npl*: **on ~** em suspense.
tenth [tɛnθ] *num* décimo; *see also* **fifth**.
tent peg *n* estaca.
tent pole *n* pau *m*.
tenuous ['tɛnjuəs] *adj* tênue.
tenure ['tɛnjuə*] *n* (*of property*) posse *f*; (*of job*) estabilidade *f*.
tepid ['tɛpɪd] *adj* tépido, morno.
term [tə:m] *n* (COMM) prazo; (*word*) termo; (*period*) período; (SCH) trimestre *m*; (LAW) sessão *f* ♦ *vt* denominar; **~s** *npl* (*conditions*) condições *fpl*; (COMM) cláusulas *fpl*, termos *mpl*; **in ~s of ...** em função de ...; **~ of imprisonment** pena de prisão; **his ~ of office** seu mandato; **in the short/long ~** a curto/longo prazo; **to be on good ~s with sb** dar-se bem com alguém; **to come to ~s with** (*person*) chegar a um acordo com; (*problem*) adaptar-se a.
terminal ['tə:mɪnl] *adj* terminal ♦ *n* (ELEC) borne *m*; (BRIT: *also*: *air* ~) terminal *m*; (*for oil, ore etc, also*: COMPUT) terminal *m*; (BRIT: *also*: *coach* ~) estação *f* rodoviária.
terminate ['tə:mɪneɪt] *vt* terminar, pôr fim a ♦ *vi*: **to ~ in** acabar em.
termination [tə:mɪ'neɪʃən] *n* término; (*of contract*) rescisão *f*; **~ of pregnancy** (MED) interrupção da gravidez.
termini ['tə:mɪnaɪ] *npl of* **terminus**.
terminology [tə:mɪ'nɔlədʒɪ] *n* terminologia.
terminus ['tə:mɪnəs] (*pl* **termini**) *n* término, terminal *m*.
termite ['tə:maɪt] *n* cupim *m*.
Ter(r). *abbr* = **terrace**.
terrace ['tɛrəs] *n* terraço; (BRIT: *row of houses*) lance *m* de casas; **the ~s** *npl* (BRIT: SPORT) a arquibancada (BR), a geral (PT).
terraced ['tɛrəst] *adj* (*house*) ladeado por outras casas; (*garden*) em dois níveis.
terracotta ['tɛrə'kɔtə] *n* terracota.
terrain [tɛ'reɪn] *n* terreno.
terrible ['tɛrɪbl] *adj* terrível, horroroso; (*weather*, *job*) horrível.
terribly ['tɛrɪblɪ] *adv* terrivelmente; (*very badly*) pessimamente.
terrier ['tɛrɪə*] *n* terrier *m*.
terrific [tə'rɪfɪk] *adj* terrível, magnífico; (*wonderful*) maravilhoso, sensacional.
terrify ['tɛrɪfaɪ] *vt* apavorar.
territorial [tɛrɪ'tɔ:rɪəl] *adj* territorial.
territorial waters *npl* águas *fpl* territoriais.
territory ['tɛrɪtərɪ] *n* território.
terror ['tɛrə*] *n* terror *m*.
terrorism ['tɛrərɪzəm] *n* terrorismo.
terrorist ['tɛrərɪst] *n* terrorista *m/f*.
terrorize ['tɛrəraɪz] *vt* aterrorizar.
terse [tə:s] *adj* (*style*) conciso, sucinto; (*reply*) brusco.
tertiary ['tə:ʃərɪ] *adj* terciário; **~ education** (BRIT) ensino superior.
Terylene ['tɛrɪli:n] ® (BRIT) *n* tergal *m* ®.
TESL ['tɛsl] *n abbr* = **Teaching of English as a Second Language**.
test [tɛst] *n* (*trial, check*) prova, ensaio; (: *of goods in factory*) controle *m*; (*of courage etc*, CHEM) prova; (MED) exame *m*; (*exam*) teste *m*, prova; (*also*: *driving* ~) exame de motorista ♦ *vt* testar, pôr à prova; **to put sth to the ~** pôr algo à prova.
testament ['tɛstəmənt] *n* testamento; **the Old/New T~** o Velho/Novo Testamento.
test ban *n* (*also*: *nuclear* ~) proibição *f* de testes nucleares.
test case *n* (LAW, *fig*) caso exemplar.
test flight *n* teste *m* de vôo.
testicle ['tɛstɪkl] *n* testículo.
testify ['tɛstɪfaɪ] *vi* (LAW) depor, testemunhar; **to ~ to sth** (LAW) atestar algo; (*gen*) testemunhar algo.
testimonial [tɛstɪ'məunɪəl] *n* (*reference*) carta de recomendação; (*gift*) obséquio, tributo.
testimony ['tɛstɪmənɪ] *n* (LAW) testemunho, depoimento.
testing ['tɛstɪŋ] *adj* (*situation, period*) difícil.
testing ground *n* campo de provas.
test match *n* (CRICKET, RUGBY) jogo internacional.
test paper *n* (SCH) prova escrita.
test pilot *n* piloto de prova.
test tube *n* proveta, tubo de ensaio.
test-tube baby *n* bebê *m* de proveta.
testy ['tɛstɪ] *adj* rabugento, irritável.
tetanus ['tɛtənəs] *n* tétano.
tetchy ['tɛtʃɪ] *adj* irritável.
tether ['tɛðə*] *vt* amarrar ♦ *n*: **at the end of one's ~** a ponto de perder a paciência *or* as estribeiras.
text [tɛkst] *n* texto.
textbook ['tɛkstbuk] *n* livro didático; (SCH) livro escolar.
textiles ['tɛkstaɪlz] *npl* têxteis *mpl*.
texture ['tɛkstʃə*] *n* textura.
TGIF (*inf*) *abbr* = **thank God it's Friday**.
TGWU (BRIT) *n abbr* (= *Transport and General Workers' Union*) *sindicato dos transportadores*.
Thai [taɪ] *adj* tailandês/esa ♦ *n* tailandês/esa *m/f*; (LING) tailandês *m*.
Thailand ['taɪlænd] *n* Tailândia.
thalidomide [θə'lɪdəmaɪd] ® *n* talidomida ®.
Thames [tɛmz] *n*: **the ~** o Tâmisa (BR), o Tamisa (PT).
than [ðæn, ðən] *conj* do que; (*with numerals*): **more ~ 10/once** mais de 10/uma vez; **I have more/less ~ you** tenho mais/menos do que você; **she has more apples ~ pears** ela tem mais maçãs do que peras; **it is better to phone ~ to write** é melhor telefonar do que escrever; **no sooner did he leave ~ the phone rang** ele acabou de sair quando o telefone tocou.
thank [θæŋk] *vt* agradecer; **~ you (very**

much) muito obrigado/a; ~ **heavens**, ~ **God** graças a Deus; **to** ~ **sb for sth** agradecer a alguém (por) algo; **to say** ~ **you** agradecer.
thankful ['θæŋkful] *adj*: ~ **(for)** agradecido (por); ~ **that** (*relieved*) aliviado que.
thankfully ['θæŋkfəlı] *adv* (*gratefully*) agradecidamente; (*fortunately*) felizmente.
thankless ['θæŋklıs] *adj* ingrato.
thanks [θæŋks] *npl* agradecimentos *mpl*; (*to God etc*) graças *fpl* ♦ *excl* obrigado/a!; ~ **to** graças a.
Thanksgiving (Day) ['θæŋksgıvıŋ-] *n* Dia *m* de Ação de Graças.
that [ðæt, ðət] (*pl* **those**) *conj* que ♦ *adj* esse/essa; (*more remote*) aquele/aquela ♦ *pron* esse/essa, aquele/aquela; (*neuter*) isso, aquilo; (*relative*) que, quem, o qual/a qual *etc*; (*with time*): **on the day** ~ **he came** no dia em que ele veio ♦ *adv*: ~ **high** dessa altura, até essa altura; **it's about** ~ **high** é mais ou menos dessa altura; ~ **one** esse/essa; **what's** ~**?** o que é isso?; **who's** ~**?** quem é?; **is** ~ **you?** é você?; ~**'s what he said** foi isso o que ele disse; ~ **is ...** isto é ...; **all** ~ tudo isso; **I can't work** ~ **much** não posso trabalhar tanto; **at** *or* **with** ~, **she ...** e assim, ela ..., aí, ela ... (*inf*); **do it like** ~ faz assim; **not** ~ **I know of** que eu saiba, não.
thatched [θætʃt] *adj* (*roof*) de sapê; ~ **cottage** chalé *m* com telhado de sapê *or* de colmo.
thaw [θɔ:] *n* degelo ♦ *vi* (*ice*) derreter-se; (*food*) descongelar-se ♦ *vt* (*food*) descongelar; **it's** ~**ing** (*weather*) degela.
the [ði:, ðə] *def art* (*sg*) o/a; (*pl*) os/as; (*in titles*): **Richard** ~ **Second** Ricardo II ♦ *adv*: ~ **sooner** ~ **better** quanto mais cedo, melhor; ~ **more he works** ~ **more he earns** quanto mais ele trabalha, mais ele ganha; ~ **rich and** ~ **poor** os ricos e os pobres; **do you know** ~ **Smiths?** você conhece os Smith?
theatre ['θıətə*] (*US* **theater**) *n* teatro.
theatre-goer ['θıətəgəuə*] *n* freqüentador(a) *m/f* de teatro.
theatrical [θı'ætrıkl] *adj* teatral; ~ **company** companhia de teatro.
theft [θɛft] *n* roubo.
their [ðɛə*] *adj* seu/sua, deles/delas.
theirs [ðɛəz] *pron* (o) seu/(a) sua; **a friend of** ~ um amigo seu/deles; **it's** ~ é deles.
them [ðɛm, ðəm] *pron* (*direct*) os/as; (*indirect*) lhes; (*stressed, after prep*) a eles/a elas; **I see** ~ eu os vejo; **give** ~ **the book** dê o livro a eles; **give me some of** ~ me dê alguns deles.
theme [θi:m] *n* tema *m*.
theme song *n* tema *m* musical.
themselves [ðəm'sɛlvz] *pron* (*subject*) eles mesmos/elas mesmas; (*complement*) se; (*after prep*) si (mesmos/as).
then [ðɛn] *adv* (*at that time*) então; (*next*) em seguida; (*later*) logo, depois; (*and also*) além disso ♦ *conj* (*therefore*) então, nesse caso, portanto ♦ *adj*: **the** ~ **president** o então presidente; **by** ~ (*past*) até então; (*future*) até lá; **from** ~ **on** a partir de então; **before** ~ antes (disso); **until** ~ até lá; **and** ~ **what?** e então?, e daí?; **what do you want me to do** ~**?** (*afterwards*) o que você quer que eu faça depois?; (*in that case*) então, o que você quer que eu faça?
theologian [θıə'ləudʒən] *n* teólogo/a.
theological [θıə'lɔdʒıkl] *adj* teológico.
theology [θı'ɔlədʒı] *n* teologia.
theorem ['θıərəm] *n* teorema *m*.
theoretical [θıə'rɛtıkl] *adj* teórico.
theoretically [θıə'rɛtıklı] *adv* teoricamente.
theorize ['θıəraız] *vi* teorizar, elaborar uma teoria.
theory ['θıərı] *n* teoria; **in** ~ em teoria, teoricamente.
therapeutic(al) [θɛrə'pju:tık(l)] *adj* terapêutico.
therapist ['θɛrəpıst] *n* terapeuta *m/f*.
therapy ['θɛrəpı] *n* terapia.
there [ðɛə*] *adv* aí, ali, lá; ~, ~! calma!; **it's** ~ está aí; **he went** ~ ele foi lá; ~ **is**, ~ **are** há, tem; ~ **he is** lá está ele; **on/in** ~ lá *or* aí encima/dentro; **back** ~ lá atrás; **down** ~ lá embaixo; **over** ~ ali; **through** ~ por aí; **to go** ~ **and back** ir e voltar.
thereabouts ['ðɛərəbauts] *adv* por aí.
thereafter [ðɛər'ɑ:ftə*] *adv* depois disso.
thereby ['ðɛəbaı] *adv* assim, deste modo.
therefore ['ðɛəfɔ:] *adv* portanto.
there's [ðɛəz] = **there is**; **there has**.
thereupon [ðɛərə'pɔn] *adv* (*at that point*) após o que; (*formal: on that subject*) a respeito.
thermal ['θə:ml] *adj* térmico; ~ **paper/printer** papel térmico/impressora térmica.
thermodynamics [θə:mədaı'næmıks] *n* termodinâmica.
thermometer [θə'mɔmıtə*] *n* termômetro.
thermonuclear [θə:məu'nju:klıə*] *adj* termonuclear.
Thermos ['θə:məs] ® *n* (*also*: ~ *flask*) garrafa térmica (*BR*), termo (*PT*).
thermostat ['θə:məustæt] *n* termostato.
thesaurus [θı'sɔ:rəs] *n* tesouro, dicionário de sinônimos.
these [ði:z] *pl adj, pron* estes/estas.
theses ['θi:si:z] *npl of* **thesis**.
thesis ['θi:sıs] (*pl* **theses**) *n* tese *f*.
they [ðeı] *pl pron* eles/elas; ~ **say that ...** (*it is said that*) diz-se que ..., dizem que ....
they'd [ðeıd] = **they had**; **they would**.
they'll [ðeıl] = **they shall**; **they will**.
they're [ðeıə*] = **they are**.
they've [ðeıv] = **they have**.
thick [θık] *adj* espesso, grosso; (*dense*) denso, compacto; (*stupid*) burro ♦ *n*: **in the** ~ **of the battle** em plena batalha; **it's 20 cm** ~ tem 20 cm de espessura.

NB: *European Portuguese adds the following consonants to certain words:* **b** (sú(b)dito, su(b)til); **c** (a(c)ção, a(c)cionista, a(c)to); **m** (inde(m)ne); **p** (ado(p)ção, ado(p)tar); *for further details see p. xiii.*

thicken ['θɪkən] *vi* espessar-se ♦ *vt* (*sauce etc*) engrossar.
thicket ['θɪkɪt] *n* matagal *m*.
thickly ['θɪklɪ] *adv* (*spread*) numa camada espessa; (*cut*) em fatias grossas.
thickness ['θɪknɪs] *n* espessura, grossura.
thickset [θɪk'sɛt] *adj* troncudo.
thick-skinned [-'skɪnd] *adj* (*fig*) insensível, indiferente.
thief [θi:f] (*pl* **thieves**) *n* ladrão/ladra *m/f*.
thieves [θi:vz] *npl of* **thief**.
thieving ['θi:vɪŋ] *n* roubo, furto.
thigh [θaɪ] *n* coxa.
thighbone ['θaɪbəun] *n* fêmur *m*.
thimble ['θɪmbl] *n* dedal *m*.
thin [θɪn] *adj* magro; (*watery*) aguado; (*light*) tênue; (*hair, crowd*) escasso, ralo; (*fog*) pouco denso ♦ *vt* (*also*: ~ *down*: *sauce, paint*) diluir ♦ *vi* (*fog*) rarefazer-se; (*also*: ~ *out*: *crowd*) dispersar; **his hair is** ~ o cabelo dele está caindo.
thing [θɪŋ] *n* coisa; (*object*) negócio; (*matter*) assunto, negócio; (*mania*) mania; **~s** *npl* (*belongings*) pertences *mpl*; **the best ~ would be to ...** o melhor seria ...; **how are ~s?** como vai?, tudo bem?; **first ~ (in the morning)** de manhã, antes de mais nada; **last ~ (at night), he ...** logo antes de dormir, ele ...; **the ~ is ...** é que ..., o negócio é o seguinte ...; **for one ~** primeiro; **she's got a ~ about ...** ela detesta ...; **poor ~!** coitadinho/a!
think [θɪŋk] (*pt, pp* **thought**) *vi* pensar ♦ *vt* pensar, achar; (*imagine*) imaginar; **what did you ~ of them?** o que você achou deles?; **to ~ about sth/sb** pensar em algo/alguém; **I'll ~ about it** vou pensar sobre isso; **to ~ of doing sth** pensar em fazer algo; **I ~ so/not** acho que sim/não; **to ~ well of sb** fazer bom juízo de alguém; **~ again!** pensa bem!; **to ~ aloud** pensar em voz alta.
think out *vt* (*plan*) arquitetar; (*solution*) descobrir.
think over *vt* refletir sobre, meditar sobre; **I'd like to ~ things over** eu gostaria de pensar sobre isso com cuidado.
think through *vt* considerar todos os aspectos de.
think up *vt* inventar, bolar.
thinking ['θɪŋkɪŋ] *n*: **to my (way of) ~** na minha opinião.
think tank *n* comissão *f* de peritos.
thinly ['θɪnlɪ] *adv* (*cut*) em fatias finas; (*spread*) numa camada fina.
thinness ['θɪnnɪs] *n* magreza.
third [θə:d] *adj* terceiro ♦ *n* terceiro/a; (*fraction*) terço; (*SCH*: *degree*) terceira categoria; *see also* **fifth**.
third-degree burns *npl* queimaduras *fpl* de terceiro grau.
thirdly ['θə:dlɪ] *adv* em terceiro lugar.
third party insurance *n* seguro contra terceiros.
third-rate *adj* medíocre.
Third World *n*: **the ~** o Terceiro Mundo.
thirst [θə:st] *n* sede *f*.
thirsty ['θə:stɪ] *adj* (*person*) sedento, com sede; **to be ~** estar com sede.
thirteen ['θə:'ti:n] *num* treze; *see also* **five**.
thirteenth [θə:'ti:nθ] *num* décimo terceiro; *see also* **fifth**.
thirtieth ['θə:tɪəθ] *num* trigésimo; *see also* **fifth**.
thirty ['θə:tɪ] *num* trinta; *see also* **fifty**.
this [ðɪs] (*pl* **these**) *adj* este/esta ♦ *pron* este/esta; (*neuter*) isto ♦ *adv*: **~ high** dessa altura; **who is ~?** quem é esse?; **what is ~?** o que é isso?; **~ is Mr Brown** (*in photo, introduction*) este é o Sr Brown; (*on phone*) aqui é o Sr Brown; **~ is what he said** foi isto o que ele disse; **~ time** desta vez; **~ time last year** nessa época do ano passado; **~ way** (*in this direction*) por aqui; (*in this fashion*) assim, desta maneira; **they were talking of ~ and that** estavam falando disso e daquilo.
thistle ['θɪsl] *n* cardo.
thong [θɔŋ] *n* correia, tira de couro.
thorn [θɔ:n] *n* espinho.
thorny ['θɔ:nɪ] *adj* espinhoso.
thorough ['θʌrə] *adj* (*search*) minucioso; (*knowledge, research*) profundo; (*work*) meticuloso; (*cleaning*) completo.
thoroughbred ['θʌrəbrɛd] *adj* (*horse*) de puro sangue.
thoroughfare ['θʌrəfɛə*] *n* via, passagem *f*; **"no ~"** "passagem proibida".
thoroughly ['θʌrəlɪ] *adv* minuciosamente, profundamente, a fundo; **he ~ agreed** concordou completamente.
thoroughness ['θʌrənɪs] *n* (*of person*) meticulosidade *f*; (*of search etc*) minuciosidade *f*.
those [ðəuz] *pl pron, adj* esses/essas; (*more remote*) aqueles/aquelas.
though [ðəu] *conj* embora, se bem que ♦ *adv* no entanto; **even ~** mesmo que; **it's not easy, ~** se bem que não é fácil.
thought [θɔ:t] *pt, pp of* **think** ♦ *n* pensamento; (*opinion*) opinião *f*; (*intention*) intenção *f*; **after much ~** depois de muito pensar; **I've just had a ~** acabei de pensar em alguma coisa; **to give sth some ~** pensar sobre algo.
thoughtful ['θɔ:tful] *adj* pensativo; (*considerate*) atencioso.
thoughtfully ['θɔ:tfəlɪ] *adv* pensativamente; atenciosamente.
thoughtless ['θɔ:tlɪs] *adj* descuidado, desatento.
thoughtlessly ['θɔ:tlɪslɪ] *adv* desconsideradamente.
thousand ['θauzənd] *num* mil; **two ~** dois mil; **~s (of)** milhares *mpl* (de).
thousandth ['θauzənθ] *adj* milésimo.
thrash [θræʃ] *vt* surrar, malhar; (*defeat*) derrotar.
thrash about *vi* debater-se.
thrash out *vt* discutir exaustivamente.
thrashing ['θræʃɪŋ] *n*: **to give sb a ~** dar uma surra em alguém.
thread [θrɛd] *n* fio, linha; (*of screw*) rosca ♦

vt (*needle*) enfiar; **to ~ one's way between** passar por.
threadbare ['θrɛdbɛə*] *adj* surrado, puído.
threat [θrɛt] *n* ameaça; **to be under ~ of** estar sob ameaça de.
threaten ['θrɛtən] *vi* ameaçar ♦ *vt*: **to ~ sb with sth/to do** ameaçar alguém com algo/de fazer.
threatening ['θrɛtnɪŋ] *adj* ameaçador(a).
three [θri:] *num* três; *see also* **five**.
three-dimensional *adj* tridimensional, em três dimensões.
threefold ['θri:fəuld] *adv*: **to increase ~** triplicar.
three-piece suit *n* terno (3 peças) (*BR*), fato de 3 peças (*PT*).
three-piece suite *n* conjunto de sofá e duas poltronas.
three-ply *adj* (*wool*) triple, com três fios; (*wood*) com três espessuras.
three-quarters *npl* três quartos *mpl*; **~ full** cheio até os três quartos.
three-wheeler *n* (*car*) carro de três rodas.
thresh [θrɛʃ] *vt* (*AGR*) debulhar.
threshing machine ['θrɛʃɪŋ-] *n* debulhadora.
threshold ['θrɛʃhəuld] *n* limiar *m*; **to be on the ~ of** (*fig*) estar no limiar de.
threshold agreement *n* (*ECON*) acordo sobre a indexação de salários.
threw [θru:] *pt of* **throw**.
thrift [θrɪft] *n* economia, poupança.
thrifty ['θrɪftɪ] *adj* econômico, frugal.
thrill [θrɪl] *n* (*excitement*) emoção *f*; (*shudder*) estremecimento ♦ *vi* vibrar ♦ *vt* emocionar, vibrar; **to be ~ed** (*with gift etc*) estar emocionado.
thriller ['θrɪlə*] *n* romance *m* (*or* filme *m*) de suspense.
thrilling ['θrɪlɪŋ] *adj* (*book, play etc*) excitante; (*news, discovery*) emocionante.
thrive [θraɪv] (*pt* **~d** *or* **throve**, *pp* **~d** *or* **thriven**) *vi* (*grow*) vicejar; (*do well*) prosperar, florescer.
thriven ['θrɪvn] *pp of* **thrive**.
thriving ['θraɪvɪŋ] *adj* próspero, florescente.
throat [θrəut] *n* garganta; **to have a sore ~** estar com dor de garganta.
throb [θrɔb] *n* (*of heart*) batida; (*of engine*) vibração *f*; (*of pain*) latejo ♦ *vi* (*heart*) bater, palpitar; (*pain*) dar pontadas; (*engine*) vibrar; **my head is ~bing** minha cabeça está latejando.
throes [θrəuz] *npl*: **in the ~ of** no meio de.
thrombosis [θrɔm'bəusɪs] *n* trombose *f*.
throne [θrəun] *n* trono.
throng [θrɔŋ] *n* multidão *f* ♦ *vt* apinhar, apinhar-se em.
throttle ['θrɔtl] *n* (*AUT*) acelerador *m* ♦ *vt* estrangular.
through [θru:] *prep* por, através de; (*time*) durante; (*by means of*) por meio de, por intermédio de; (*owing to*) devido a ♦ *adj* (*ticket, train*) direto ♦ *adv* através; **(from) Monday ~ Friday** (*US*) de segunda a sexta; **to let sb ~** deixar alguém passar; **to put sb ~ to sb** (*TEL*) ligar alguém com alguém; **to be ~** (*TEL*) estar na linha; (*have finished*) acabar; **"no ~ traffic"** (*US*) "trânsito proibido"; **"no ~ way"** "rua sem saída"; **I'm halfway ~ the book** estou na metade do livro.
throughout [θru:'aut] *prep* (*place*) por todo/a o/a; (*time*) durante todo/a o/a ♦ *adv* por *or* em todas as partes.
throughput ['θru:put] *n* (*of goods, materials*) quantidade *f* tratada; (*COMPUT*) capacidade *f* de processamento.
throve [θrəuv] *pt of* **thrive**.
throw [θrəu] (*pt* **threw**, *pp* **thrown**) *n* arremesso, tiro; (*SPORT*) lançamento ♦ *vt* jogar, atirar; (*SPORT*) lançar; (*rider*) derrubar; (*fig*) desconcertar; (*pot*) afeiçoar; **to ~ a party** dar uma festa.
throw about *vt* (*litter etc*) esparramar.
throw around *vt* (*litter etc*) esparramar.
throw away *vt* (*dispose of*) jogar fora; (*waste*) desperdiçar.
throw in *vt* (*SPORT*) pôr em jogo.
throw off *vt* desfazer-se de.
throw out *vt* (*person*) expulsar; (*things*) jogar fora; (*reject*) rejeitar.
throw together *vt* (*clothes, meal etc*) arranjar às pressas.
throw up *vi* vomitar, botar para fora.
throwaway ['θrəuəweɪ] *adj* descartável.
throwback ['θrəubæk] *n*: **it's a ~ to** é um retrocesso a.
throw-in *n* (*SPORT*) lance *m*.
thru [θru:] (*US*) *prep, adj, adv* = **through**.
thrush [θrʌʃ] *n* (*ZOOL*) tordo; (*MED*) monília.
thrust [θrʌst] (*pt, pp* **thrust**) *n* impulso; (*TECH*) empuxo ♦ *vt* empurrar; (*push in*) enfiar, meter.
thrusting ['θrʌstɪŋ] *adj* dinâmico.
thud [θʌd] *n* baque *m*, som *m* surdo.
thug [θʌg] *n* (*criminal*) criminoso/a; (*pej*) facínora *m/f*.
thumb [θʌm] *n* (*ANAT*) polegar *m*; (*inf*) dedão *m* ♦ *vt* (*book*) folhear; **to ~ a lift** pegar carona (*BR*), arranjar uma boléia (*PT*); **to give sb/sth the ~s up** (*approve*) dar luz verde a alguém/algo.
thumb index *n* índice *m* de dedo.
thumbnail ['θʌmneɪl] *n* unha do polegar.
thumbnail sketch *n* descrição *f* resumida.
thumbtack ['θʌmtæk] (*US*) *n* percevejo, tachinha.
thump [θʌmp] *n* murro, pancada; (*sound*) baque *m* ♦ *vt* dar um murro em ♦ *vi* bater.
thunder ['θʌndə*] *n* trovão *m*; (*sudden noise*) trovoada; (*of applause etc*) estrondo ♦ *vi* trovejar; (*train etc*): **to ~ past** passar como um raio.
thunderbolt ['θʌndəbəult] *n* raio.
thunderclap ['θʌndəklæp] *n* estampido do tro-

***NB:** European Portuguese adds the following consonants to certain words:* **b** (sú(b)dito, su(b)til); **c** (a(c)ção, a(c)cionista, a(c)to); **m** (inde(m)ne); **p** (ado(p)ção, ado(p)tar); *for further details see p. xiii.*

vão.

thunderous ['θʌndərəs] *adj* estrondoso.

thunderstorm ['θʌndəstɔːm] *n* tempestade *f* com trovoada, temporal *m*.

thunderstruck ['θʌndəstrʌk] *adj* estupefato.

thundery ['θʌndərɪ] *adj* tempestuoso.

Thur(s). *abbr* (= *Thursday*) qui, 5ª.

Thursday ['θəːzdɪ] *n* quinta-feira; *see also* **Tuesday**.

thus [ðʌs] *adv* assim, desta maneira.

thwart [θwɔːt] *vt* frustrar.

thyme [taɪm] *n* tomilho.

thyroid ['θaɪrɔɪd] *n* tireóide *f*.

tiara [tɪ'ɑːrə] *n* tiara, diadema *m*.

Tibet [tɪ'bɛt] *n* Tibete *m*.

Tibetan [tɪ'bɛtən] *adj* tibetano ♦ *n* tibetano/a; (*LING*) tibetano.

tibia ['tɪbɪə] *n* tíbia.

tic [tɪk] *n* tique *m*.

tick [tɪk] *n* (*sound*: *of clock*) tique-taque *m*; (*mark*) tique *m*, marca; (*ZOOL*) carrapato; (*BRIT*: *inf*): **in a ~** num instante; (: *credit*): **to buy sth on ~** comprar algo a crédito ♦ *vi* fazer tique-taque ♦ *vt* marcar, ticar; **to put a ~ against sth** marcar *or* ticar algo.

tick off *vt* assinalar, ticar; (*person*) dar uma bronca em.

tick over (*BRIT*) *vi* (*engine*) funcionar em marcha lenta; (*fig*) ir indo.

ticker tape ['tɪkə*-] *n* fita de teleimpressor; (*US*: *in celebrations*) chuva de papel.

ticket ['tɪkɪt] *n* (*for bus*, *plane*) passagem *f*, bilhete *m*; (*for cinema*) entrada, ingresso; (*in shop*: *on goods*) etiqueta; (: *receipt*) ficha, nota fiscal; (*for library*) cartão *m*; (*US*: *POL*) chapa; **to get a (parking) ~** (*AUT*) ganhar uma multa (por estacionamento ilegal).

ticket agency *n* agência de ingressos teatrais.

ticket collector *n* revisor(a) *m/f*.

ticket holder *n* portador(a) *m/f* de um bilhete *or* ingresso.

ticket inspector *n* revisor(a) *m/f*.

ticket office *n* bilheteria (*BR*), bilheteira (*PT*).

tickle ['tɪkl] *n* cócegas *fpl* ♦ *vt* fazer cócegas em; (*captivate*) encantar; (*make laugh*) fazer rir.

ticklish ['tɪklɪʃ] *adj* (*person*) coceguento; (*which tickles*: *blanket etc*) que pica, que faz cócegas; (: *cough*) irritante; **to be ~** (*person*) ter cócegas.

tidal ['taɪdl] *adj* de maré.

tidal wave *n* macaréu *m*, onda gigantesca.

tidbit ['tɪdbɪt] (*esp US*) *n* = **titbit**.

tiddlywinks ['tɪdlɪwɪŋks] *n* jogo de fichas.

tide [taɪd] *n* maré *f*; (*fig*: *of events*) marcha, curso ♦ *vt*: **to ~ sb over** dar para alguém agüentar; **high/low ~** maré alta/baixa; **the ~ of public opinion** a corrente da opinião pública.

tidily ['taɪdɪlɪ] *adv* com capricho.

tidiness ['taɪdɪnɪs] *n* (*good order*) ordem *f*; (*neatness*) asseio, limpeza.

tidy ['taɪdɪ] *adj* (*room*) arrumado; (*dress*, *work*) limpo; (*person*) bem arrumado; (*mind*) metódico ♦ *vt* (*also*: **~ up**) pôr em ordem, arrumar; **to ~ o.s. up** arrumar-se.

tie [taɪ] *n* (*string etc*) fita, corda; (*BRIT*: *also*: *neck~*) gravata; (*fig*: *link*) vínculo, laço; (*SPORT*: *draw*) empate *m*; (*US*: *RAIL*) dormente *m* ♦ *vt* amarrar, atar ♦ *vi* (*SPORT*) empatar; **to ~ in a bow** dar um laço em; **to ~ a knot in sth** dar um nó em algo; **family ~s** laços de família; **"black/white ~"** "smoking/traje a rigor".

tie down *vt* amarrar; (*fig*): **to ~ sb down to** obrigar alguém a.

tie in *vi*: **to ~ in (with)** combinar com.

tie on (*BRIT*) *vt* (*label etc*) prender (com barbante).

tie up *vt* (*parcel*) embrulhar; (*dog*) prender; (*boat*) amarrar; (*arrangements*) concluir; **to be ~d up** (*busy*) estar ocupado.

tie-break(er) *n* (*TENNIS*) tie-break *m*; (*in quiz etc*) decisão *f* de empate.

tie-on (*BRIT*) *adj* (*label*) para atar.

tie-pin (*BRIT*) *n* alfinete *m* de gravata.

tier [tɪə*] *n* fileira; (*of cake*) camada.

Tierra del Fuego [tɪ'ɛrədɛl'fweɪgəu] *n* Terra do Fogo.

tie tack (*US*) *n* alfinete *m* de gravata.

tie-up (*US*) *n* engarrafamento.

tiff [tɪf] *n* briga; (*lover's ~*) arrufo.

tiger ['taɪgə*] *n* tigre *m*.

tight [taɪt] *adj* (*rope*) esticado, firme; (*money*) escasso; (*clothes*) justo; (*budget*, *programme*) apertado; (*control*) rigoroso; (*inf*: *drunk*) bêbado ♦ *adv* (*squeeze*) bem forte; (*shut*) hermeticamente; **to be packed ~** (*suitcase*) estar abarrotado; (*people*) estar apinhado; **everybody hold ~!** segurem firme!

tighten ['taɪtən] *vt* (*rope*) esticar; (*screw*, *security*) apertar ♦ *vi* apertar-se; esticar-se.

tight-fisted [-'fɪstɪd] *adj* pão-duro.

tightly ['taɪtlɪ] *adv* (*grasp*) firmemente.

tight-rope *n* corda (bamba).

tight-rope walker *n* funâmbulo/a.

tights [taɪts] (*BRIT*) *npl* collant *m*.

tigress ['taɪgrɪs] *n* tigre fêmea.

tilde ['tɪldə] *n* til *m*.

tile [taɪl] *n* (*on roof*) telha; (*on floor*) ladrilho; (*on wall*) azulejo, ladrilho ♦ *vt* (*floor*) ladrilhar; (*wall*, *bathroom*) azulejar.

tiled [taɪld] *adj* ladrilhado; (*roof*) de telhas.

till [tɪl] *n* caixa (registradora) ♦ *vt* (*land*) cultivar ♦ *prep*, *conj* = **until**.

tiller ['tɪlə*] *n* (*NAUT*) cana do leme.

tilt [tɪlt] *vt* inclinar ♦ *vi* inclinar-se ♦ *n* (*slope*) inclinação *f*; **(at) full ~** a toda velocidade.

timber ['tɪmbə*] *n* (*material*) madeira; (*trees*) mata, floresta.

time [taɪm] *n* tempo; (*epoch*: *often pl*) época; (*by clock*) hora; (*moment*) momento; (*occasion*) vez *f*; (*MUS*) compasso ♦ *vt* calcular *or* medir o tempo de; (*race*) cronometrar; (*remark etc*) escolher o momento para; **a long ~** muito tempo; **3 at a ~** três de uma vez; **for the ~ being** por enquanto; **from ~ to ~** de vez em quando; **~ after ~**, **~ and again**

repetidamente; **in ~** (*soon enough*) a tempo; (*after some time*) com o tempo; (*MUS*) no compasso; **in a week's ~** dentro de uma semana; **in no ~** num abrir e fechar de olhos; **on ~** na hora; **to be 30 minutes behind/ahead of ~** estar atrasado/adiantado de 30 minutos; **by the ~ he arrived** até ele chegar; **5 ~s 5 is 25** 5 vezes 5 são 25; **what ~ is it?** que horas são?; **what ~ do you make it?** que horas você tem?; **to have a good ~** divertir-se; **we had a hard ~** foi difícil para nós; **he'll do it in his own (good) ~** (*without being hurried*) ele vai fazer isso quando tiver tempo; **he'll do it in** (*BRIT*) *or* **on** (*US*) **his own ~** (*out of working hours*) ele vai fazer isso fora do expediente; **to be behind the ~s** estar antiquado.

time-and-motion study *n* estudo de tempos e movimentos.

time bomb *n* bomba-relógio *f*.

time clock *n* relógio de ponto.

time-consuming [-kən'sju:mɪŋ] *adj* que exige muito tempo.

time difference *n* fuso horário.

time-honoured [-'ɔnəd] (*US* **time-honored**) *adj* consagrado pelo tempo.

timekeeper ['taɪmki:pə*] *n* (*SPORT*) cronometrista *m/f*.

time lag (*BRIT*) *n* defasagem *f*; (*in travel*) fuso horário.

timeless ['taɪmlɪs] *adj* eterno.

time limit *n* limite *m* de tempo; (*COMM*) prazo.

timely ['taɪmlɪ] *adj* oportuno.

time off *n* tempo livre.

timer ['taɪmə*] *n* (*in kitchen*) cronômetro; (*switch*) timer *m*.

time-saving *adj* que economiza tempo.

time scale *n* prazos *mpl*.

time-sharing [-'ʃɛərɪŋ] *n* (*COMPUT*) tempo compartilhado.

time sheet *n* folha de ponto.

time signal *n* tope *m*, sinal *m* horário.

time switch (*BRIT*) *n* interruptor *m* horário.

timetable ['taɪmteɪbl] *n* horário; (*of project*) cronograma *m*.

time zone *n* fuso horário.

timid ['tɪmɪd] *adj* tímido.

timidity [tɪ'mɪdɪtɪ] *n* timidez *f*.

timing ['taɪmɪŋ] *n* escolha do momento; (*SPORT*) cronometragem *f*; **the ~ of his resignation** o momento que escolheu para se demitir.

timing device *n* (*on bomb*) dispositivo de retardamento.

Timor ['ti:mɔ:*] *n* Timor (*no article*).

timpani ['tɪmpənɪ] *npl* tímbales *mpl*.

tin [tɪn] *n* estanho; (*also*: **~** *plate*) folha-de-flandres *f*; (*BRIT*: *can*) lata; (: *for baking*) fôrma.

tin foil *n* papel *m* de estanho.

tinge [tɪndʒ] *n* matiz *m*, toque *m* ♦ *vt*: **~d with** tingido de.

tingle ['tɪŋgl] *n* comichão *f* ♦ *vi* formigar.

tinker ['tɪŋkə*] *n* funileiro/a; (*gipsy*) cigano/a.

tinker with *vt* mexer com.

tinkle ['tɪŋkl] *vi* tilintar, tinir ♦ *n* (*inf*): **to give sb a ~** dar uma ligada para alguém.

tin mine *n* mina de estanho.

tinned [tɪnd] (*BRIT*) *adj* (*food*) em lata, em conserva.

tinny ['tɪnɪ] *adj* metálico.

tin opener (*BRIT*) *n* abridor *m* de latas (*BR*), abre-latas *m inv* (*PT*).

tinsel ['tɪnsl] *n* ouropel *m*.

tint [tɪnt] *n* matiz *m*; (*for hair*) tintura, tinta ♦ *vt* (*hair*) pintar.

tinted ['tɪntɪd] *adj* (*hair*) pintado; (*spectacles, glass*) fumê *inv*.

tiny ['taɪnɪ] *adj* pequenininho, minúsculo.

tip [tɪp] *n* (*end*) ponta; (*gratuity*) gorjeta; (*BRIT*: *for rubbish*) depósito; (*advice*) dica ♦ *vt* (*waiter*) dar uma gorjeta a; (*tilt*) inclinar; (*winner*) apostar em; (*overturn*: *also*: **~** *over*) virar, emborcar; (*empty*: *also*: **~** *out*) esvaziar, entornar; **he ~ped out the contents of the box** esvaziou a caixa.

tip off *vt* avisar.

tip-off *n* (*hint*) aviso, dica.

tipped [tɪpt] *adj* (*BRIT*: *cigarette*) com filtro; **steel-~** com ponta de aço.

Tipp-Ex ['tɪpɛks] ® (*BRIT*) *n* líquido corretor.

tipple ['tɪpl] (*BRIT*) *vt* bebericar ♦ *n*: **to have a ~** beber um gole.

tipsy ['tɪpsɪ] *adj* embriagado, tocado, alto, alegre.

tiptoe ['tɪptəu] *n*: **on ~** na ponta dos pés.

tiptop ['tɪp'tɔp] *adj*: **in ~ condition** em perfeitas condições.

tire ['taɪə*] *n* (*US*) = **tyre** ♦ *vt* cansar ♦ *vi* cansar-se; (*become bored*) chatear-se.

tire out *vt* esgotar, exaurir.

tired ['taɪəd] *adj* cansado; **to be ~ of sth** estar farto *or* cheio de algo.

tiredness ['taɪədnɪs] *n* cansaço.

tireless ['taɪəlɪs] *adj* incansável.

tiresome ['taɪəsəm] *adj* enfadonho, chato.

tiring ['taɪərɪŋ] *adj* cansativo.

tissue ['tɪʃu:] *n* tecido; (*paper handkerchief*) lenço de papel.

tissue paper *n* papel *m* de seda.

tit [tɪt] *n* (*bird*) passarinho; (*inf*: *breast*) teta; **to give ~ for tat** pagar na mesma moeda.

titanium [tɪ'teɪnɪəm] *n* titânio.

titbit ['tɪtbɪt] *n* (*food*) guloseima; (*news*) boato, rumor *m*.

titillate ['tɪtɪleɪt] *vt* titilar, excitar.

titivate ['tɪtɪveɪt] *vt* arrumar.

title ['taɪtl] *n* título; (*LAW*: *right*): **~ (to)** direito (a).

title deed *n* (*LAW*) título de propriedade.

title page *n* página de rosto.

title role *n* papel *m* principal.

titter ['tɪtə*] *vi* rir-se com riso sufocado.

NB: European Portuguese adds the following consonants to certain words: **b** (sú(b)dito, su(b)til); **c** (a(c)ção, a(c)cionista, a(c)to); **m** (inde(m)ne); **p** (ado(p)ção, ado(p)tar); *for further details see p. xiii.*

tittle-tattle ['tɪtltætl] *n* fofocas *fpl* (*BR*), mexericos *mpl* (*PT*).
titular ['tɪtjulə*] *adj* (*in name only*) nominal, titular.
tizzy ['tɪzɪ] *n*: **to be in a ~** estar muito nervoso.
T-junction *n* bifurcação *f* em T.
TM *n abbr* = **trademark; transcendental meditation.**
TN (*US*) *abbr* (*POST*) = **Tennessee.**
TNT *n abbr* (= *trinitrotoluene*) Tnt *m*, trotil *m*.
to [tuː, tə] *prep* a, para; (*towards*) para; (*of time*) até ♦ *with vb* (*purpose, result*) para; (*simple infin*): **~ go/eat** ir/comer; (*following another vb*): **to want/try ~ do** querer/tentar fazer; **to give sth ~ sb** dar algo a alguém; **give it ~ me** me dá isso; **the key ~ the front door** a chave da porta da frente; **it belongs ~ him** pertence a ele, é dele; **the main thing is ~** ... o principal é ...; **to go ~ France/school** ir à França/ao colégio; **8 apples ~ the kilo** 8 maçãs por quilo; **a quarter ~ 5** quinze para as 5 (*BR*), 5 menos um quarto (*PT*); **pull/push the door ~** puxar/empurrar a porta; **to go ~ and fro** ir de um lado para outro; **he did it ~ help you** ele fez isso para ajudar você; **I don't want ~** eu não quero; **I have things ~ do** eu tenho coisas para fazer; **ready ~ go** pronto para ir.
toad [təud] *n* sapo.
toadstool ['təudstuːl] *n* chapéu-de-cobra *m*, cogumelo venenoso.
toady ['təudɪ] *vi* ser bajulador(a), puxar saco (*inf*).
toast [təust] *n* (*CULIN*) torradas *fpl*; (*drink, speech*) brinde *m* ♦ *vt* (*CULIN*) torrar; (*drink to*) brindar; **a piece** *or* **slice of ~** uma torrada.
toaster ['təustə*] *n* torradeira.
toastmaster ['təustmɑːstə*] *n* mestre *m* de cerimônias.
toast rack *n* porta-torradas *m inv*.
tobacco [tə'bækəu] *n* tabaco, fumo (*BR*).
tobacconist [tə'bækənɪst] *n* vendedor(a) *m/f* de tabaco; **~'s (shop)** tabacaria, charutaria (*BR*).
Tobago [tə'beɪgəu] *n see* **Trinidad.**
toboggan [tə'bɔgən] *n* tobogã *m*.
today [tə'deɪ] *adv, n* (*also*: *fig*) hoje *m*; **what day is it ~?** que dia é hoje?; **what date is it ~?** qual é a data de hoje?; **~ is the 4th of March** hoje é dia 4 de março; **a week ago ~** há uma semana atrás; **a fortnight ~** daqui a quinze dias; **~'s paper** o jornal de hoje.
toddler ['tɔdlə*] *n criança que começa a andar*.
toddy ['tɔdɪ] *n* ponche *m* quente.
to-do *n* (*fuss*) rebuliço, alvoroço.
toe [təu] *n* dedo do pé; (*of shoe*) bico ♦ *vt*: **to ~ the line** (*fig*) conformar-se, cumprir as obrigações; **big ~** dedão *m* do pé; **little ~** dedo mindinho do pé.
toehold ['təuhəuld] *n* apoio.
toenail ['təuneɪl] *n* unha do pé.
toffee ['tɔfɪ] *n* puxa-puxa *m* (*BR*), caramelo (*PT*).
toffee apple (*BRIT*) *n* maçã *f* do amor.
toga ['təugə] *n* toga.
together [tə'gɛðə*] *adv* juntos; (*at same time*) ao mesmo tempo; **~ with** junto com.
togetherness [tə'gɛðənɪs] *n* companheirismo, camaradagem *f*.
toggle switch ['tɔgl-] *n* (*COMPUT*) (interruptor *m*) teimoso.
Togo ['təugəu] *n* Togo.
togs [tɔgz] (*inf*) *npl* (*clothes*) roupa.
toil [tɔɪl] *n* faina, labuta ♦ *vi* labutar, trabalhar arduamente.
toilet ['tɔɪlət] *n* (*BRIT*: *lavatory*) banheiro (*BR*), casa de banho (*PT*) ♦ *cpd* (*bag, soap etc*) de toalete; **to go to the ~** ir ao banheiro.
toilet bag (*BRIT*) *n* bolsa de toucador.
toilet bowl *n* vaso sanitário.
toilet paper *n* papel *m* higiênico.
toiletries ['tɔɪlɪtrɪz] *npl* artigos *mpl* de toalete; (*make-up etc*) artigos de toucador.
toilet roll *n* rolo de papel higiênico.
toilet water *n* água de colônia.
to-ing and fro-ing ['tuːɪŋən'frəuɪŋ] (*BRIT*) *n* vaivém *m*.
token ['təukən] *n* (*sign*) sinal *m*, símbolo, prova; (*souvenir*) lembrança; (*voucher*) cupom *m*, vale *m* ♦ *cpd* (*fee, strike*) simbólico; **by the same ~** (*fig*) pela mesma razão; **book/record ~** (*BRIT*) vale para comprar livros/discos.
Tokyo ['təukjəu] *n* Tóquio.
told [təuld] *pt, pp of* **tell.**
tolerable ['tɔlərəbl] *adj* (*bearable*) suportável; (*fairly good*) passável.
tolerably ['tɔlərəblɪ] *adv*: **~ good** razoável.
tolerance ['tɔlərəns] *n* (*also*: *TECH*) tolerância.
tolerant ['tɔlərənt] *adj*: **~ of** tolerante com.
tolerate ['tɔləreɪt] *vt* suportar; (*MED, TECH*) tolerar.
toleration [tɔlə'reɪʃən] *n* tolerância.
toll [təul] *n* (*of casualties*) número de baixas; (*tax, charge*) pedágio (*BR*), portagem *f* (*PT*) ♦ *vi* (*bell*) dobrar, tanger.
tollbridge ['təulbrɪdʒ] *n* ponte *f* de pedágio (*BR*) *or* de portagem (*PT*).
tomato [tə'mɑːtəu] (*pl* **~es**) *n* tomate *m*.
tomb [tuːm] *n* tumba.
tombola [tɔm'bəulə] *n* tômbola.
tomboy ['tɔmbɔɪ] *n* menina moleque.
tombstone ['tuːmstəun] *n* lápide *f*.
tomcat ['tɔmkæt] *n* gato.
tomorrow [tə'mɔrəu] *adv, n* (*also fig*) amanhã *m*; **the day after ~** depois de amanhã; **~ morning** amanhã de manhã.
ton [tʌn] *n* tonelada (*BRIT*: = *1016 kg*; *US* = *907 kg*; *metric* = *1000 kg*); (*NAUT*: *also*: *register ~*) tonelagem *f* de registro; **~s of** (*inf*) um monte de.
tonal ['təunl] *adj* tonal.
tone [təun] *n* tom *m*; (*BRIT*: *TEL*) sinal *m* ♦ *vi* harmonizar.
tone down *vt* (*colour, criticism*) suavizar; (*sound*) baixar; (*MUS*) entoar.

tone up *vt* (*muscles*) tonificar.

tone-deaf *adj* que não tem ouvido.

toner ['təunə*] *n* (*for photocopier*) tinta.

Tonga ['tɔŋgə] *n* Tonga (*no article*).

tongs [tɔŋz] *npl* (*for coal*) tenaz *f*; (*for hair*) pinças *fpl*.

tongue [tʌŋ] *n* língua; **~ in cheek** ironicamente.

tongue-tied [-taɪd] *adj* (*fig*) calado.

tongue-twister [-'twɪstə*] *n* trava-língua *m*.

tonic ['tɔnɪk] *n* (*MED*) tônico; (*MUS*) tônica; (*also*: *~ water*) (água) tônica.

tonight [tə'naɪt] *adv*, *n* esta noite, hoje à noite; **(I'll) see you ~!** até a noite!

tonnage ['tʌnɪdʒ] *n* (*NAUT*) tonelagem *f*.

tonne [tʌn] (*BRIT*) *n* (*metric ton*) tonelada.

tonsil ['tɔnsəl] *n* amígdala; **to have one's ~s out** tirar as amígdalas.

tonsillitis [tɔnsɪ'laɪtɪs] *n* amigdalite *f*; **to have ~** estar com uma amigdalite.

too [tu:] *adv* (*excessively*) demais; (*very*) muito; (*also*) também; **~ much** *adv* demais ♦ *adj* demasiado; **~ many** *adj* muitos/as, demasiados/as; **~ sweet** doce demais; **I went ~** eu fui também.

took [tuk] *pt of* **take**.

tool [tu:l] *n* ferramenta; (*fig*: *person*) joguete *m* ♦ *vt* trabalhar.

tool box *n* caixa de ferramentas.

tool kit *n* jogo de ferramentas.

toot [tu:t] *n* (*of horn*) buzinada; (*of whistle*) apito ♦ *vi* (*with car horn*) buzinar; (*whistle*) apitar.

tooth [tu:θ] (*pl* **teeth**) *n* (*ANAT*, *TECH*) dente *m*; (*molar*) molar *m*; **to have a ~ out** (*BRIT*) *or* **pulled** (*US*) arrancar um dente; **to brush one's teeth** escovar os dentes; **by the skin of one's teeth** (*fig*) por um triz.

toothache ['tu:θeɪk] *n* dor *f* de dente; **to have ~** estar com dor de dente.

toothbrush ['tu:θbrʌʃ] *n* escova de dentes.

toothpaste ['tu:θpeɪst] *n* pasta de dentes, creme *m* dental.

toothpick ['tu:θpɪk] *n* palito.

tooth powder *n* pó *m* dentifrício.

top [tɔp] *n* (*of mountain*) cume *m*, cimo; (*of head*) cocuruto; (*of cupboard, table*) superfície *f*, topo; (*of box, jar, bottle*) tampa; (*of list etc*) cabeça *m*; (*toy*) pião *m*; (*DRESS*: *blouse etc*) top *m*, blusa; (: *of pyjamas*) paletó *m* ♦ *adj* mais alto, máximo; (*in rank*) principal, superior; (*best*) melhor ♦ *vt* (*exceed*) exceder; (*be first in*) estar à cabeça de; **the ~ of the milk** (*BRIT*) a nata do leite; **at the ~ of the stairs/page/street** no alto da escada/no alto da página/no começo da rua; **on ~ of** sobre, em cima de; **from ~ to toe** (*BRIT*) da cabeça aos pés; **at the ~ of the list** à cabeça da lista; **at the ~ of one's voice** aos gritos; **at ~ speed** a toda velocidade; **a ~ surgeon** um dos melhores cirurgiões; **over the ~** (*inf*: *behaviour etc*) extravagante.

top up (*US* **top off**) *vt* completar.

topaz ['təupæz] *n* topázio.

topcoat ['tɔpkəut] *n* sobretudo.

topflight ['tɔpflaɪt] *adj* de primeira categoria.

top floor *n* último andar *m*.

top hat *n* cartola.

top-heavy *adj* (*object*) desequilibrado.

topic ['tɔpɪk] *n* tópico, assunto.

topical ['tɔpɪkl] *adj* atual.

topless ['tɔplɪs] *adj* (*bather etc*) topless *inv*, *sem a parte superior do biquíni*.

top-level *adj* (*talks*) de alto nível.

topmost ['tɔpməust] *adj* o mais alto.

topography [tə'pɔgrəfɪ] *n* topografia.

topping ['tɔpɪŋ] *n* (*CULIN*) cobertura.

topple ['tɔpl] *vt* derrubar, desabar ♦ *vi* cair para frente, ruir.

top-ranking [-'ræŋkɪŋ] *adj* de alto escalão.

TOPS [tɔps] (*BRIT*) *n abbr* (= *Training Opportunities Scheme*) *programa de formação profissional*.

top-secret *adj* ultra-secreto, supersecreto.

top-security (*BRIT*) *adj* de alta segurança.

topsy-turvy ['tɔpsɪ'tə:vɪ] *adj*, *adv* de pernas para o ar, confuso, às avessas.

top-up *n*: **would you like a ~?** você quer mais?

torch [tɔ:tʃ] *n* tocha, archote *m*; (*BRIT*: *electric ~*) lanterna.

tore [tɔ:*] *pt of* **tear**.

torment [*n* 'tɔ:mɛnt, *vt* tɔ:'mɛnt] *n* tormento, suplício ♦ *vt* atormentar; (*fig*: *annoy*) chatear, aborrecer.

torn [tɔ:n] *pp of* **tear** ♦ *adj*: **~ between** (*fig*) dividido entre.

tornado [tɔ:'neɪdəu] (*pl* **~es**) *n* tornado.

torpedo [tɔ:'pi:dəu] (*pl* **~es**) *n* torpedo ♦ *vt* torpedear.

torpedo boat *n* torpedeiro.

torpor ['tɔ:pə*] *n* torpor *m*.

torque [tɔ:k] *n* momento de torção.

torrent ['tɔrənt] *n* torrente *f*.

torrential [tɔ'rɛnʃl] *adj* torrencial.

torrid ['tɔrɪd] *adj* tórrido; (*fig*) abrasador(a).

torso ['tɔ:səu] *n* torso.

tortoise ['tɔ:təs] *n* tartaruga.

tortoiseshell ['tɔ:təʃɛl] *cpd* de tartaruga.

tortuous ['tɔ:tjuəs] *adj* tortuoso.

torture ['tɔ:tʃə*] *n* tortura ♦ *vt* torturar; (*fig*) atormentar.

torturer ['tɔ:tʃərə*] *n* torturador(a) *m/f*.

Tory ['tɔ:rɪ] (*BRIT*) *adj*, *n* (*POL*) conservador(a) *m/f*.

toss [tɔs] *vt* atirar, arremessar; (*head*) lançar para trás ♦ *n* (*of head*) meneio; (*of coin*) lançamento ♦ *vi*: **to ~ and turn in bed** virar de um lado para o outro na cama; **to ~ a coin** tirar cara ou coroa; **to ~ up for sth** (*BRIT*) jogar cara ou coroa por algo; **to win/lose the ~** ganhar/perder no cara ou coroa; (*SPORT*) ganhar/perder o sorteio.

***NB**: European Portuguese adds the following consonants to certain words:* **b** (sú(b)dito, su(b)til); **c** (a(c)ção, a(c)cionista, a(c)to); **m** (inde(m)ne); **p** (ado(p)ção, ado(p)tar); *for further details see p. xiii.*

tot [tɔt] *n* (*BRIT*: *drink*) copinho, golinho; (*child*) criancinha.
tot up (*BRIT*) *vt* (*figures*) somar, adicionar.
total ['təutl] *adj* total ♦ *n* total *m*, soma ♦ *vt* (*add up*) somar; (*amount to*) montar a; **in ~** em total.
totalitarian [təutælı'tɛərıən] *adj* totalitário.
totality [təu'tælıtı] *n* totalidade *f*.
totally ['təutəlı] *adv* totalmente.
tote bag [təut-] *n* sacola.
totem pole ['təutəm-] *n* mastro totêmico.
totter ['tɔtə*] *vi* cambalear; (*object, government*) vacilar.
touch [tʌtʃ] *n* toque *m*; (*sense*) tato; (*contact*) contato; (*FOOTBALL*): **in ~** fora do campo ♦ *vt* tocar (em); (*emotionally*) comover; **the personal ~** o toque pessoal; **to put the finishing ~es to sth** dar os últimos retoques em algo; **a ~ of** (*fig*) uma pitada de, um pouquinho de; **to get in ~ with sb** entrar em contato com alguém; **to lose ~** (*friends*) perder o contato; **to be out of ~ with events** não estar a par dos acontecimentos; **no artist in the country can ~ him** nenhum artista no país se compara a ele.
touch on *vt fus* (*topic*) tocar em, fazer menção de.
touch up *vt* (*paint*) retocar.
touch-and-go *adj* arriscado; **it was ~ whether we did it** por pouco fizemos aquilo.
touchdown ['tʌtʃdaun] *n* aterrissagem *f* (*BR*), aterragem *f* (*PT*); (*on sea*) amerissagem *f* (*BR*), amaragem *f* (*PT*); (*US*: *FOOTBALL*) touchdown *m* (*colocação da bola no chão atrás da linha de gol*).
touched [tʌtʃt] *adj* comovido; (*inf*) tocado, muito louco.
touching ['tʌtʃıŋ] *adj* comovedor(a).
touchline ['tʌtʃlaın] *n* (*SPORT*) linha de fundo.
touch-type *vi* datilografar sem olhar para as teclas.
touchy ['tʌtʃı] *adj* (*person*) suscetível, sensitivo.
tough [tʌf] *adj* duro; (*difficult*) difícil; (*resistant*) resistente; (*person*) tenaz, obstinado; (*exam, experience*) brabo ♦ *n* (*gangster etc*) bandido, capanga *m*; **~ luck!** azar!; **they got ~ with the workers** começaram a falar grosso com os trabalhadores.
toughen ['tʌfən] *vt* endurecer.
toughness ['tʌfnıs] *n* dureza; (*difficulty*) dificuldade *f*; (*resistance*) resistência; (*of person*) tenacidade *f*.
toupee ['tu:peı] *n* peruca.
tour ['tuə*] *n* viagem *f*, excursão *f*; (*also*: *package ~*) excursão organizada; (*of town, museum*) visita; (*by artist*) turnê *f* ♦ *vt* excursionar por; **to go on a ~ of** (*museum, region*) visitar; **to go on ~** fazer turnê.
touring ['tuərıŋ] *n* viagens *fpl* turísticas, turismo.
tourism ['tuərızm] *n* turismo.
tourist ['tuərıst] *n* turista *m/f* ♦ *cpd* turístico; **the ~ trade** o turismo.
tourist office *n* agência de turismo.
tournament ['tuənəmənt] *n* torneio.
tourniquet ['tuənıkeı] *n* (*MED*) torniquete *m*.
tour operator (*BRIT*) *n* empresa de viagens.
tousled ['tauzld] *adj* (*hair*) despenteado.
tout [taut] *vi*: **to ~ for** angariar clientes para ♦ *vt* (*BRIT*): **to ~ sth (around)** tentar vender algo ♦ *n* (*BRIT*: *ticket ~*) cambista *m/f*.
tow [təu] *n*: **to give sb a ~** (*AUT*) rebocar alguém ♦ *vt* rebocar; **"on ~"** (*BRIT*), **"in ~"** (*US*) (*AUT*) "rebocado"; **with her husband in ~** com o marido a tiracolo.
toward(s) [tə'wɔ:d(z)] *prep* em direção a; (*of attitude*) para com; (*of purpose*) para; **~ noon/the end of the year** perto do meio-dia/do fim do ano; **to feel friendly ~ sb** sentir amizade em relação a alguém.
towel ['tauəl] *n* toalha; (*also*: *tea ~*) pano; **to throw in the ~** (*fig*) dar-se por vencido.
towelling ['tauəlıŋ] *n* (*fabric*) tecido para toalhas.
towel rail (*US* **towel rack**) *n* toalheiro.
tower ['tauə*] *n* torre *f* ♦ *vi* (*building, mountain*) elevar-se; **to ~ above** *or* **over sb/sth** dominar alguém/algo.
tower block (*BRIT*) *n* prédio alto, espigão *m*, cortiço (*BR*).
towering ['tauərıŋ] *adj* elevado, eminente.
towline ['təulaın] *n* cabo de reboque.
town [taun] *n* cidade *f*; **to go to ~** ir à cidade; (*fig*) fazer com entusiasmo, mandar brasa (*BR*); **in the ~** na cidade; **to be out of ~** (*person*) estar fora da cidade.
town centre *n* centro (da cidade).
town clerk *n* administrador(a) *m/f* municipal.
town council *n* câmara municipal.
town hall *n* prefeitura (*BR*), concelho (*PT*).
town plan *n* mapa *m* da cidade.
town planner *n* urbanista *m/f*.
town planning *n* urbanismo.
townspeople ['taunzpi:pl] *npl* habitantes *mpl* da cidade.
towpath ['təupɑ:θ] *n* caminho de sirga.
towrope ['təurəup] *n* cabo de reboque.
tow truck (*US*) *n* reboque *m* (*BR*), pronto socorro (*PT*).
toxic ['tɔksık] *adj* tóxico.
toxin ['tɔksın] *n* toxina.
toy [tɔı] *n* brinquedo ♦ *cpd* de brinquedo.
toy with *vt fus* jogar com; (*idea*) andar com.
toyshop ['tɔıʃɔp] *n* loja de brinquedos.
trace [treıs] *n* traço, rasto ♦ *vt* (*through paper*) decalcar; (*draw*) traçar, esboçar; (*follow*) seguir a pista de; (*locate*) encontrar; **without ~** (*disappear*) sem deixar vestígios; **there was no ~ of it** não havia nenhum vestígio disso.
trace element *n* elemento traço.
trachea [trə'kıə] *n* (*ANAT*) traquéia.
tracing paper ['treısıŋ-] papel *m* de decalque.
track [træk] *n* (*mark*) pegada, vestígio; (*path*: *gen*) caminho, vereda; (: *of bullet etc*) trajetória; (: *of suspect, animal*) pista, rasto; (*RAIL*) trilhos (*BR*), carris *mpl* (*PT*); (*on tape*) trilha; (*SPORT*) pista; (*on record*) faixa

♦ *vt* seguir a pista de; **to keep ~ of** não perder de vista; (*fig*) manter-se informado sobre; **to be on the right ~** (*fig*) estar no caminho certo.

track down *vt* (*prey*) seguir a pista de; (*sth lost*) procurar e encontrar.

tracked [trækt] *adj* com lagarta.

tracker dog ['trækə-] (*BRIT*) *n* cão *m* policial.

track events *npl* (*SPORT*) corridas *fpl*.

tracking station ['trækɪŋ-] *n* (*SPACE*) estação *f* de rastreamento.

track record *n*: **to have a good ~** (*fig*) ter uma boa folha de serviço.

track suit *n* roupa de jogging.

tract [trækt] *n* (*GEO*) região *f*; (*pamphlet*) folheto; **respiratory ~** (*ANAT*) aparelho respiratório.

traction ['trækʃən] *n* tração *f*.

tractor ['træktə*] *n* trator *m*.

tractor feed *n* (*on printer*) alimentação *f* a trator.

trade [treɪd] *n* comércio; (*skill, job*) ofício ♦ *vi* negociar, comerciar; **to ~ with/in** comerciar com/em; **foreign ~** comércio exterior; **Department of T~ and Industry** (*BRIT*) Ministério de Indústria e Comércio.

trade in *vt* (*old car etc*) dar como parte do pagamento.

trade barrier *n* barreira comercial.

trade deficit *n* déficit *m* na balança comercial.

Trade Descriptions Act (*BRIT*) *n lei contra a publicidade mentirosa.*

trade discount *n* desconto de revendedor.

trade fair *n* feira industrial.

trade-in *n* venda.

trade-in price *n valor de um objeto usado que se desconta do preço do outro novo.*

trademark ['treɪdmɑːk] *n* marca de fábrica *or* comércio.

trade mission *n* missão *f* comercial.

trade name *n* (*of product*) marca registrada; (*of company*) razão *f* social.

trader ['treɪdə*] *n* comerciante *m/f*.

trade secret *n* segredo do ofício.

tradesman ['treɪdzmən] (*irreg*) *n* (*shopkeeper*) lojista *m*.

trade union *n* sindicato.

trade unionism [-'juːnjənɪzəm] *n* sindicalismo.

trade unionist [-'juːnjənɪst] *n* sindicalista *m/f*.

trade wind *n* vento alísio.

trading ['treɪdɪŋ] *n* comércio.

trading estate (*BRIT*) *n* parque *m* industrial.

trading stamp *n* selo de bonificação.

tradition [trə'dɪʃən] *n* tradição *f*.

traditional [trə'dɪʃənl] *adj* tradicional.

traffic ['træfɪk] *n* trânsito; (*air ~ etc*) tráfego; (*illegal*) tráfico ♦ *vi*: **to ~ in** (*pej*: *liquor, drugs*) traficar com, fazer tráfico com.

traffic circle (*US*) *n* rotatória.

traffic island *n* refúgio de segurança (para pedestres).

traffic jam *n* engarrafamento, congestionamento.

traffic lights *npl* sinal *m* luminoso.

trafficker ['træfɪkə*] *n* traficante *m/f*.

traffic offence (*BRIT*) *n* infração *f* de trânsito.

traffic sign *n* placa de sinalização.

traffic violation (*US*) *n* infração *f*.

traffic warden *n* guarda *m/f* de trânsito.

tragedy ['trædʒədɪ] *n* tragédia.

tragic ['trædʒɪk] *adj* trágico.

trail [treɪl] *n* (*tracks*) rasto, pista; (*path*) caminho, trilha; (*wake*) esteira ♦ *vt* (*drag*) arrastar; (*follow*) seguir a pista de; (*follow closely*) vigiar ♦ *vi* arrastar-se; **to be on sb's ~** estar no encalço de alguém.

trail away *vi* (*sound, voice*) ir-se perdendo; (*interest*) diminuir.

trail behind *vi* atrasar-se.

trail off *vi* (*sound, voice*) ir-se perdendo; (*interest*) diminuir.

trailer ['treɪlə*] *n* (*AUT*) reboque *m*; (*US*: *caravan*) trailer *m* (*BR*), rulote *f* (*PT*); (*CINEMA*) trailer.

trailer truck (*US*) *n* caminhão-reboque *m*.

train [treɪn] *n* trem *m* (*BR*), comboio (*PT*); (*of dress*) cauda; (*series*) seqüência, série *f*; (*followers*) séqüito, comitiva ♦ *vt* (*professionals etc*) formar; (*teach skills to*) instruir; (*SPORT*) treinar; (*dog*) adestrar, amestrar; (*point*: *gun etc*): **to ~ on** apontar para ♦ *vi* (*SPORT*) treinar; (*be educated*) ser treinado; **to lose one's ~ of thought** perder o fio; **to go by ~** ir de trem; **to ~ sb to do sth** treinar alguém para fazer algo.

train attendant (*US*) *n* revisor(a) *m/f*.

trained [treɪnd] *adj* (*worker*) especializado; (*teacher*) formado; (*animal*) adestrado.

trainee [treɪ'niː] *n* estagiário/a; (*in trade*) aprendiz *m/f*.

trainer ['treɪnə*] *n*; (*SPORT*) treinador(a) *m/f*; (*of animals*) adestrador(a) *m/f*; **~s** *npl* (*shoes*) tênis *m*.

training ['treɪnɪŋ] *n* instrução *f*; (*SPORT*) treinamento; (*professional*) formação.

training college *n* (*for teachers*) Escola Normal.

training course *n* curso de formação profissional.

training shoes *npl* tênis *m*.

traipse [treɪps] *vi* arrastar os pés.

trait [treɪt] *n* traço.

traitor ['treɪtə*] *n* traidor(a) *m/f*.

trajectory [trə'dʒɛktərɪ] *n* trajetória.

tram [træm] (*BRIT*) *n* (*also*: *~car*) bonde *m* (*BR*), eléctrico (*PT*).

tramline ['træmlaɪn] *n* trilho para bondes.

tramp [træmp] *n* (*person*) vagabundo/a ♦ *vi* caminhar pesadamente ♦ *vt* (*walk through*: *town, streets*) percorrer, andar por.

trample ['træmpl] *vt*: **to ~ (underfoot)** calcar aos pés.

trampoline ['træmpəliːn] *n* trampolim *m*.
trance [trɑːns] *n* estupor *m*; (*MED*) transe *m* hipnótico; **to go into a** ~ cair em transe.
tranquil ['træŋkwɪl] *adj* tranqüilo.
tranquillity [træŋ'kwɪlɪtɪ] *n* tranqüilidade *f*.
tranquillizer ['træŋkwɪlaɪzə*] *n* (*MED*) tranqüilizante *m*.
transact [træn'zækt] *vt* (*business*) negociar.
transaction [træn'zækʃən] *n* transação *f*, negócio; **~s** *npl* (*minutes*) ata; **cash** ~ transação à vista.
transatlantic [trænzət'læntɪk] *adj* transatlântico.
transcend [træn'sɛnd] *vt* transcender, exceder; (*excel over*) ultrapassar.
transcendental [trænsɛn'dɛntl] *adj*: ~ **meditation** meditação *f* transcendental.
transcribe [træn'skraɪb] *vt* transcrever.
transcript ['trænskrɪpt] *n* cópia, traslado.
transcription [træn'skrɪpʃən] *n* transcrição *f*.
transept ['trænsɛpt] *n* transepto.
transfer [*n* 'trænsfə*, *vt* træns'fəː*] *n* transferência; (*picture, design*) decalcomania ♦ *vt* transferir, trasladar; **to ~ the charges** (*BRIT*: *TEL*) ligar a cobrar; **by bank ~** por transferência bancária.
transferable [træns'fəːrəbl] *adj* transferível; **not** ~ intransferível.
transfix [træns'fɪks] *vt* trespassar; (*fig*): **~ed with fear** paralisado de medo.
transform [træns'fɔːm] *vt* transformar.
transformation [trænsfə'meɪʃən] *n* transformação *f*.
transformer [træns'fɔːmə*] *n* (*ELEC*) transformador *m*.
transfusion [træns'fjuːʒən] *n* transfusão *f*.
transgress [træns'grɛs] *vt* transgredir.
transient ['trænzɪənt] *adj* transitório.
transistor [træn'zɪstə*] *n* (*ELEC*: *also*: ~ *radio*) transistor *m*.
transit ['trænzɪt] *n*: **in** ~ em trânsito, de passagem.
transit camp *n* campo de trânsito.
transition [træn'zɪʃən] *n* transição *f*.
transitional [træn'zɪʃənl] *adj* de transição, transicional.
transitive ['trænzɪtɪv] *adj* (*LING*) transitivo.
transit lounge *n* salão *m* de trânsito.
transitory ['trænzɪtərɪ] *adj* transitório.
translate [trænz'leɪt] *vt*: **to ~ (from/into)** traduzir (do/para o).
translation [trænz'leɪʃən] *n* tradução *f*.
translator [trænz'leɪtə*] *n* tradutor(a) *m/f*.
translucent [trænz'luːsnt] *adj* translúcido.
transmission [trænz'mɪʃən] *n* transmissão *f*.
transmit [trænz'mɪt] *vt* transmitir.
transmitter [trænz'mɪtə*] *n* transmissor *m*; (*station*) emissora.
transparency [træns'pɛərnsɪ] (*BRIT*) *n* (*PHOT*) transparência, diapositivo.
transparent [træns'pærnt] *adj* transparente.
transpire [træns'paɪə*] *vi* (*happen*) ocorrer, acontecer; (*become known*): **it finally ~d that ...** no final soube-se que ....
transplant [*vt* træns'plɑːnt, *n* 'trænsplɑːnt] *vt* transplantar ♦ *n* (*MED*) transplante *m*; **to have a heart ~** ter um transplante de coração.
transport [*n* 'trænspɔːt, *vt* træns'pɔːt] *n* transporte *m* ♦ *vt* transportar; (*carry*) acarretar; **public ~** transportes coletivos; **Department of T~** (*BRIT*) ministérioda dos Transportes.
transportation [trænspɔː'teɪʃən] *n* transporte *m*; **Department of T~** (*US*) ministério da Infra-estrutura.
transport café (*BRIT*) *n* lanchonete *f* de estrada.
transpose [træns'pəuz] *vt* transpor.
transship [træns'ʃɪp] *vt* baldear.
transverse ['trænzvəːs] *adj* transversal.
transvestite [trænz'vɛstaɪt] *n* travesti *m/f*.
trap [træp] *n* (*snare, trick*) armadilha, cilada; (*carriage*) aranha, charrete *f* ♦ *vt* pegar em armadilha; (*immobilize*) bloquear; (*jam*) emperrar; **to set** *or* **lay a ~ (for sb)** montar uma armadilha (para alguém); **to shut one's ~** (*inf*) calar a boca; **to ~ one's finger in the door** prender o dedo na porta.
trap door *n* alçapão *m*.
trapeze [trə'piːz] *n* trapézio.
trapper ['træpə*] *n* caçador *m* de peles.
trappings ['træpɪŋz] *npl* adornos *mpl*, enfeites *mpl*.
trash [træʃ] *n* (*pej*: *goods*) refugo, escória; (: *nonsense*) besteiras *fpl*; (*US*: *rubbish*) lixo.
trash can (*US*) *n* lata de lixo.
trauma ['trɔːmə] *n* trauma *m*.
traumatic [trɔː'mætɪk] *adj* traumático.
travel ['trævl] *n* viagem *f* ♦ *vi* viajar; (*move*) deslocar-se ♦ *vt* (*distance*) percorrer.
travel agency *n* agência de viagens.
travel agent *n* agente *m/f* de viagens.
travel brochure *n* prospecto turístico.
traveller ['trævələ*] (*US* **traveler**) *n* viajante *m/f*; (*COMM*) caixeiro/a viajante.
traveller's cheque (*US* **traveler's check**) *n* cheque *m* de viagem.
travelling ['trævəlɪŋ] (*US* **traveling**) *n* as viagens, viajar *m* ♦ *adj* (*circus, exhibition*) itinerante; (*salesman*) viajante ♦ *cpd* (*bag, clock, expenses*) de viagem.
travel(l)ing salesman (*irreg*) *n* caixeiro viajante.
travelogue ['trævəlɔg] *n* (*book*) livro de viagem; (*film*) documentário de viagem.
travel sickness *n* enjôo.
traverse ['trævəs] *vt* atravessar.
travesty ['trævəstɪ] *n* paródia.
trawler ['trɔːlə*] *n* traineira.
tray [treɪ] *n* bandeja; (*on desk*) cesta.
treacherous ['trɛtʃərəs] *adj* traiçoeiro; **road conditions are ~** as estradas estão perigosas.
treachery ['trɛtʃərɪ] *n* traição *f*.
treacle ['triːkl] *n* melado.
tread [trɛd] (*pt* **trod**, *pp* **trodden**) *n* (*step*) passo, pisada; (*sound*) passada; (*of tyre*) banda de rodagem ♦ *vi* pisar.
tread on *vt fus* pisar (em).
treadle ['trɛdl] *n* pedal *m*.

treas. *abbr* = **treasurer.**
treason ['tri:zn] *n* traição *f*.
treasure ['trɛʒə*] *n* tesouro ♦ *vt* (*value*) apreciar, estimar.
treasure hunt *n* caça ao tesouro.
treasurer ['trɛʒərə*] *n* tesoureiro/a.
treasury ['trɛʒərɪ] *n* tesouraria; **the T~** (*BRIT*: *POL*) *or* **T~ Department** (*US*: *POL*) ≈ o Tesouro Nacional.
treasury bill *n* letra do Tesouro (Nacional).
treat [tri:t] *n* (*present*) regalo, deleite *m*; (*pleasure*) prazer *m* ♦ *vt* tratar; **to ~ sb to sth** convidar alguém para algo; **to give sb a ~** dar um prazer a alguém; **to ~ sth as a joke** não levar algo a sério.
treatise ['tri:tɪz] *n* tratado.
treatment ['tri:tmənt] *n* tratamento; **to have ~ for sth** (*MED*) fazer tratamento para algo.
treaty ['tri:tɪ] *n* tratado, acordo.
treble ['trɛbl] *adj* tríplice ♦ *n* (*MUS*) soprano ♦ *vt* triplicar ♦ *vi* triplicar(-se).
treble clef *n* clave *f* de sol.
tree [tri:] *n* árvore *f*.
tree-lined *adj* ladeado de árvores.
treetop ['tri:tɔp] *n* copa (de árvore).
tree trunk *n* tronco de árvore.
trek [trɛk] *n* (*long journey*) jornada; (*walk*) caminhada; (*as holiday*) excursão *f* (a pé) ♦ *vi* (*as holiday*) caminhar.
trellis ['trɛlɪs] *n* grade *f* de ripas, latada.
tremble ['trɛmbl] *vi* tremer.
trembling ['trɛmblɪŋ] *n* tremor *m* ♦ *adj* trêmulo, trepidante.
tremendous [trɪ'mɛndəs] *adj* tremendo; (*enormous*) enorme; (*excellent*) sensacional, fantástico.
tremendously [trɪ'mɛndəslɪ] *adv* (*well, clever etc*) extraordinariamente; (*very much*) muitíssimo; (*very well*) muito bem.
tremor ['trɛmə*] *n* tremor *m*; (*also*: *earth ~*) tremor de terra.
trench [trɛntʃ] *n* trincheira.
trench coat *n* capa (de chuva).
trench warfare *n* guerra de trincheiras.
trend [trɛnd] *n* (*tendency*) tendência; (*of events*) curso; (*fashion*) modismo, tendência; **~ towards/away from doing** tendência a/contra fazer; **to set the ~** dar o tom; **to set a ~** lançar uma moda.
trendy ['trɛndɪ] *adj* (*idea*) de acordo com a tendência atual; (*clothes*) da última moda.
trepidation [trɛpɪ'deɪʃən] *n* trepidação *f*; (*fear*) apreensão *f*.
trespass ['trɛspəs] *vi*: **to ~ on** invadir; **"no ~ing"** "entrada proibida".
trespasser ['trɛspəsə*] *n* intruso/a; **"~s will be prosecuted"** "aqueles que invadirem esta área serão punidos".
tress [trɛs] *n* trança.
trestle ['trɛsl] *n* cavalete *m*.
trestle table *n* mesa de cavaletes.
trial ['traɪəl] *n* (*LAW*) processo; (*test*: *of machine etc*) prova, teste *m*; (*hardship*) provação *f*; **~s** *npl* (*SPORT*) eliminatórias *fpl*; **horse ~s** provas *fpl* de equitação; **by ~ and error** por tentativas; **~ by jury** julgamento por júri; **to be sent for ~** ser levado a julgamento; **to be on ~** ser julgado.
trial balance *n* (*COMM*) balancete *m*.
trial basis *n*: **on a ~** em experiência.
trial run *n* ensaio.
triangle ['traɪæŋgl] *n* (*MATH, MUS*) triângulo.
triangular [traɪ'æŋgjulə*] *adj* triangular.
tribal ['traɪbəl] *adj* tribal.
tribe [traɪb] *n* tribo *f*.
tribesman ['traɪbzmən] (*irreg*) *n* membro da tribo.
tribulation [trɪbju'leɪʃən] *n* tribulação *f*, aflição *f*.
tribunal [traɪ'bju:nl] *n* tribunal *m*.
tributary ['trɪbju:tərɪ] *n* (*river*) afluente *m*.
tribute ['trɪbju:t] *n* homenagem *f*; (*payment*) tributo; **to pay ~ to** prestar homenagem a, homenagear.
trice [traɪs] *n*: **in a ~** num instante.
trick [trɪk] *n* truque *m*; (*deceit*) fraude *f*, trapaça; (*joke*) peça, brincadeira; (*CARDS*) vaza ♦ *vt* enganar; **to play a ~ on sb** pregar uma peça em alguém; **to ~ sb into doing sth** induzir alguém a fazer algo pela astúcia; **to ~ sb out of sth** obter algo de alguém pela astúcia; **it's a ~ of the light** é uma ilusão de ótica; **that should do the ~** (*inf*) isso deveria dar resultado.
trickery ['trɪkərɪ] *n* trapaça, astúcia.
trickle ['trɪkl] *n* (*of water etc*) fio (de água) ♦ *vi* gotejar, pingar; **to ~ in/out** (*people*) ir entrando/saindo aos poucos.
trick question *n* pergunta capciosa.
trickster ['trɪkstə*] *n* vigarista *m/f*.
tricky ['trɪkɪ] *adj* difícil, complicado.
tricycle ['traɪsɪkl] *n* triciclo.
trifle ['traɪfl] *n* bagatela; (*CULIN*) *tipo de bolo com fruta e creme* ♦ *adv*: **a ~ long** um pouquinho longo ♦ *vi*: **to ~ with** brincar com.
trifling ['traɪflɪŋ] *adj* insignificante.
trigger ['trɪgə*] *n* (*of gun*) gatilho.
  trigger off *vt* desencadear.
trigonometry [trɪgə'nɔmətrɪ] *n* trigonometria.
trilby ['trɪlbɪ] (*BRIT*) *n* (*also*: *~ hat*) chapéu *m* de feltro.
trill [trɪl] *n* (*of bird, MUS*) trinado, trilo.
trilogy ['trɪlədʒɪ] *n* trilogia.
trim [trɪm] *adj* (*elegant*) elegante; (*house*) arrumado; (*garden*) bem cuidado; (*figure*) esbelto ♦ *n* (*haircut etc*) aparada; (*on car*) estofamento; (*embellishment*) acabamento, remate *m* ♦ *vt* (*cut*) aparar, cortar; (*decorate*) enfeitar; (*NAUT*: *sail*) ajustar; **to keep in (good) ~** manter em bom estado.
trimmings ['trɪmɪŋz] *npl* decoração *f*; (*extras*: *gen CULIN*) acompanhamentos *mpl*.
Trinidad and Tobago ['trɪnɪdæd-] *n* Trinidad e Tobago (*no article*).

Trinity ['trɪnɪtɪ] *n*: **the ~** a Trindade.
trinket ['trɪŋkɪt] *n* bugiganga; (*piece of jewellery*) berloque *m*, bijuteria.
trio ['tri:əu] *n* trio.
trip [trɪp] *n* viagem *f*; (*excursion*) excursão *f*; (*stumble*) tropeção *m* ♦ *vi* (*also*: **~ up**) tropeçar; (*go lightly*) andar com passos ligeiros ♦ *vt* fazer tropeçar; **on a ~** de viagem.
trip up *vi* tropeçar ♦ *vt* passar uma rasteira em.
tripartite [traɪ'pɑ:taɪt] *adj* (*in three parts*) tripartido; (*POL*) tripartidário.
tripe [traɪp] *n* (*CULIN*) bucho, tripa; (*pej*: *rubbish*) bobagem *f*.
triple ['trɪpl] *adj* triplo, tríplice ♦ *adv*: **~ the distance/the speed** três vezes a distância/a velocidade.
triplets ['trɪplɪts] *npl* trigêmeos/as *m/fpl*.
triplicate ['trɪplɪkət] *n*: **in ~** em triplicata, em três vias.
tripod ['traɪpɔd] *n* tripé *m*.
Tripoli ['trɪpəlɪ] *n* Trípoli.
tripper ['trɪpə*] (*BRIT*) *n* excursionista *m/f*.
tripwire ['trɪpwaɪə*] *n* fio de disparo.
trite [traɪt] *adj* gasto, banal.
triumph ['traɪʌmf] *n* triunfo ♦ *vi*: **to ~ (over)** triunfar (sobre).
triumphal [traɪ'ʌmfl] *adj* triunfal.
triumphant [traɪ'ʌmfənt] *adj* triunfante.
trivia ['trɪvɪə] *npl* trivialidades *fpl*.
trivial ['trɪvɪəl] *adj* insignificante; (*commonplace*) trivial.
triviality [trɪvɪ'ælɪtɪ] *n* trivialidade *f*.
trivialize ['trɪvɪəlaɪz] *vt* banalizar, trivializar.
trod [trɔd] *pt of* **tread**.
trodden ['trɔdn] *pp of* **tread**.
trolley ['trɔlɪ] *n* carrinho.
trolley bus *n* ônibus *m* elétrico (*BR*), trólei *m* (*PT*).
trollop ['trɔləp] *n* rameira.
trombone [trɔm'bəun] *n* trombone *m*.
troop [tru:p] *n* bando, grupo ♦ *vi*: **to ~ in/out** entrar/sair em bando; **~s** *npl* (*MIL*) tropas *fpl*; (: *men*) homens *mpl*; **~ing the colour** (*BRIT*: *ceremony*) a saudação da bandeira.
troop carrier *n* (*plane*) avião *m* de transporte de tropas; (*NAUT*: *also*: *troopship*) navio-transporte *m*.
trooper ['tru:pə*] *n* (*MIL*) soldado de cavalaria; (*US*: *policeman*) ≈ policial *m* militar, PM *m*.
troopship ['tru:pʃɪp] *n* navio-transporte *m*.
trophy ['trəufɪ] *n* troféu *m*.
tropic ['trɔpɪk] *n* trópico; **in the ~s** nos trópicos; **T~ of Cancer/Capricorn** Trópico de Câncer/Capricórnio.
tropical ['trɔpɪkl] *adj* tropical.
trot [trɔt] *n* trote *m* ♦ *vi* trotar; **on the ~** (*fig*: *inf*) a fio.
trot out *vt* (*excuse, reason*) apresentar, dar; (*names, facts*) recitar.
trouble ['trʌbl] *n* problema(s) *m(pl)*, dificuldade(s) *f(pl)*; (*worry*) preocupação *f*; (*bother, effort*) incômodo, trabalho; (*POL*) distúrbios *mpl*; (*MED*): **stomach ~** *etc* problemas *mpl* gástricos *etc* ♦ *vt* perturbar; (*worry*) preocupar, incomodar ♦ *vi*: **to ~ to do sth** incomodar-se *or* preocupar-se de fazer algo; **~s** *npl* (*POL etc*) distúrbios *mpl*; **to be in ~** (*in difficulty*) estar num aperto; (*for doing sth wrong*) estar numa encrenca; **to go to the ~ of doing sth** dar-se ao trabalho de fazer algo; **to have ~ doing sth** ter dificuldade em fazer algo; **it's no ~!** não tem problema!; **please don't ~ yourself** por favor, não se dê trabalho!; **the ~ is ...** o problema é ...; **what's the ~?** qual é o problema?
troubled ['trʌbld] *adj* (*person*) preocupado; (*epoch, life*) agitado.
trouble-free *adj* sem problemas.
troublemaker ['trʌblmeɪkə*] *n* criador(a)-de-casos *m/f*; (*child*) encrenqueiro/a.
troubleshooter ['trʌblʃu:tə*] *n* (*in conflict*) conciliador(a) *m/f*; (*solver of problems*) solucionador(a) *m/f* de problemas.
troublesome ['trʌblsəm] *adj* incômodo, importuno.
trouble spot *n* área de conflito.
trough [trɔf] *n* (*also*: *drinking ~*) bebedouro, cocho; (*also*: *feeding ~*) gamela; (*channel*) canal *m*; **~ of low pressure** (*METEOROLOGY*) cavado de baixa pressão.
trounce [trauns] *vt* (*defeat*) dar uma surra *or* um banho em.
troupe [tru:p] *n* companhia teatral.
trouser press *n* passadeira de calças.
trousers ['trauzəz] *npl* calça (*BR*), calças *fpl* (*PT*).
trouser suit (*BRIT*) *n* terninho (*BR*), conjunto de calças casaco (*PT*).
trousseau ['tru:səu] (*pl* **~x** *or* **~s**) *n* enxoval *m*.
trousseaux ['tru:səuz] *npl of* **trousseau**.
trout [traut] *n inv* truta.
trowel ['trauəl] *n* colher *f* de jardineiro *or* de pedreiro.
truancy ['truənsɪ] *n* evasão *f* escolar.
truant ['truənt] (*BRIT*) *n*: **to play ~** matar aula (*BR*), fazer gazeta (*PT*).
truce [tru:s] *n* trégua, armistício.
truck [trʌk] *n* caminhão *m* (*BR*), camião *m* (*PT*); (*RAIL*) vagão *m*.
truck driver *n* caminhoneiro/a (*BR*), camionista *m/f* (*PT*).
trucker ['trʌkə*] (*esp US*) *n* caminhoneiro (*BR*), camionista *m/f* (*PT*).
truck farm (*US*) *n* horta.
trucking ['trʌkɪŋ] (*esp US*) *n* transporte *m* rodoviário.
trucking company (*US*) *n* transportadora.
truck stop (*US*) *n* bar *m* de estrada.
truculent ['trʌkjulənt] *adj* agressivo.
trudge [trʌdʒ] *vi* andar com dificuldade, arrastar-se.
true [tru:] *adj* verdadeiro; (*accurate*) exato; (*genuine*) autêntico; (*faithful*) fiel, leal; (*wall*) aprumado; (*beam*) nivelado; (*wheel*) alinhado; **to come ~** realizar-se, tornar-se realidade; **~ to life** realista, fiel à realidade; **it's ~** é verdade.

truffle ['trʌfl] *n* trufa.
truly ['tru:lɪ] *adv* (*really*) realmente; (*truthfully*) verdadeiramente; (*faithfully*) fielmente; **yours ~** (*in letter*) atenciosamente.
trump [trʌmp] *n* trunfo; **to turn** *or* **come up ~s** (*fig*) salvar a pátria.
trump card *n* (*also*: *fig*) trunfo.
trumped-up [trʌmpt-] *adj* inventado, forjado.
trumpet ['trʌmpɪt] *n* trombeta.
truncated [trʌŋ'keɪtɪd] *adj* truncado.
truncheon ['trʌntʃən] *n* cassetete *m*.
trundle ['trʌndl] *vt, vi*: **to ~ along** rolar *or* rodar fazendo ruído.
trunk [trʌŋk] *n* (*of tree, person*) tronco; (*of elephant*) tromba; (*case*) baú *m*; (*US*: *AUT*) mala (*BR*), porta-bagagens *m* (*PT*); **~s** *npl* (*also*: *swimming* ~*s*) sunga (*BR*), calções *mpl* de banho (*PT*).
trunk call (*BRIT*) *n* (*TEL*) ligação *f* interurbana.
trunk road (*BRIT*) *n* ≈ rodovia nacional.
truss [trʌs] *n* (*MED*) funda ♦ *vt*: **to ~ (up)** atar, amarrar.
trust [trʌst] *n* confiança; (*COMM*) truste *m*; (*LAW*) fideicomisso ♦ *vt* (*rely on*) confiar em; (*entrust*): **to ~ sth to sb** confiar algo a alguém; (*hope*): **to ~ (that)** esperar que; **to take sth on ~** aceitar algo sem verificação prévia; **in ~** (*LAW*) em fideicomisso.
trust company *n* companhia fiduciária.
trusted ['trʌstɪd] *adj* de confiança.
trustee [trʌs'ti:] *n* (*LAW*) fideicomissário/a, depositário/a; (*of school etc*) administrador(a) *m/f*.
trustful ['trʌstful] *adj* confiante.
trust fund *n* fundo de fideicomisso.
trusting ['trʌstɪŋ] *adj* confiante.
trustworthy ['trʌstwə:ðɪ] *adj* digno de confiança.
trusty ['trʌstɪ] *adj* fidedigno, fiel.
truth [tru:θ, *pl* tru:ðz] *n* verdade *f*.
truthful ['tru:θful] *adj* (*person*) sincero, honesto; (*account*) verídico.
truthfully ['tru:θfulɪ] *adv* sinceramente.
truthfulness ['tru:θfulnɪs] *n* veracidade *f*.
try [traɪ] *n* tentativa; (*RUGBY*) ensaio ♦ *vt* (*LAW*) julgar; (*test*: *sth new*) provar, pôr à prova; (*attempt*) tentar; (*food etc*) experimentar; (*strain*) cansar ♦ *vi* tentar; **to ~ to do sth** tentar fazer algo; **to ~ one's (very) best** *or* **one's (very) hardest** fazer (todo) o possível; **to give sth a ~** tentar algo.
try on *vt* (*clothes*) experimentar, provar; **to ~ it on with sb** (*fig*: *test sb's patience*) testar a paciência de alguém; (: *try to trick*) tentar engambelar alguém.
try out *vt* experimentar, provar.
trying ['traɪɪŋ] *adj* penoso, árduo.
tsar [zɑ:*] *n* czar *m*.
T-shirt *n* camiseta (*BR*), T-shirt *f* (*PT*).
T-square *n* régua em T.
TT *adj abbr* (*BRIT*: *inf*) = **teetotal** ♦ *abbr* (*US*: *POST*) = **Trust Territory**.
tub [tʌb] *n* tina; (*bath*) banheira.
tuba ['tju:bə] *n* tuba.
tubby ['tʌbɪ] *adj* gorducho.
tube [tju:b] *n* tubo; (*BRIT*: *underground*) metrô *m* (*BR*), metro(-politano) (*PT*); (*for tyre*) câmara-de-ar *f*.
tubeless ['tju:blɪs] *adj* sem câmara.
tuber ['tju:bə*] *n* (*BOT*) tubérculo.
tuberculosis [tjubə:kju'ləusɪs] *n* tuberculose *f*.
tube station (*BRIT*) *n* estação *f* de metrô.
tubing ['tju:bɪŋ] *n* tubulação *f*, encanamento; **a piece of ~** um pedaço de tubo.
tubular ['tju:bjulə*] *adj* tubular; (*furniture*) tubiforme.
TUC (*BRIT*) *n abbr* (= *Trades Union Congress*) ≈ CUT *f*.
tuck [tʌk] *n* (*SEWING*) prega, dobra ♦ *vt* (*put*) enfiar, meter.
tuck away *vt* esconder.
tuck in *vt* enfiar a beirada de; (*child*) aconchegar ♦ *vi* (*eat*) comer com apetite.
tuck up *vt* (*child*) aconchegar.
tuck shop *n* loja de balas.
Tue(s). *abbr* (= *Tuesday*) ter, 3ª.
Tuesday ['tju:zdɪ] *n* terça-feira; **(the date) today is ~ 23rd March** hoje é terça-feira, 23 de março; **on ~** na terça(-feira); **on ~s** nas terças(-feiras); **every ~** todas as terças(-feiras); **every other ~** terça-feira sim, terça-feira não; **last/next ~** na terça-feira passada/na terça-feira que vem; **~ next** na terça-feira que vem; **the following ~** na terça-feira seguinte; **a week on ~** sem ser essa terça, a outra; **the ~ before last** na terça-feira retrasada; **the ~ after next** sem ser essa terça, a outra; **~ morning/lunchtime/afternoon/evening** na terça-feira de manhã/ao meio-dia/à tarde/à noite; **~ night** na terça-feira à noite; **~'s newspaper** o jornal de terça-feira.
tuft [tʌft] *n* penacho; (*of grass etc*) tufo.
tug [tʌg] *n* (*ship*) rebocador *m* ♦ *vt* puxar.
tug-of-war *n* cabo-de-guerra *m*; (*fig*) disputa.
tuition [tju:'ɪʃən] *n* ensino; (*private ~*) aulas *fpl* particulares; (*US*: *fees*) taxas *fpl* escolares.
tulip ['tju:lɪp] *n* tulipa.
tumble ['tʌmbl] *n* (*fall*) queda ♦ *vi* cair, tombar ♦ *vt* derrubar; **to ~ to sth** (*inf*) sacar algo.
tumbledown ['tʌmbldaun] *adj* em ruínas.
tumble dryer (*BRIT*) *n* máquina de secar roupa.
tumbler ['tʌmblə*] *n* copo.
tummy ['tʌmɪ] (*inf*) *n* (*belly*) barriga; (*stomach*) estômago.
tumour ['tju:mə*] (*US* **tumor**) *n* tumor *m*.
tumult ['tju:mʌlt] *n* tumulto.
tumultuous [tju:'mʌltjuəs] *adj* tumultuado.
tuna ['tju:nə] *n inv* (*also*: *~ fish*) atum *m*.

tune [tju:n] *n* melodia ♦ *vt* (MUS) afinar; (RADIO, TV) sintonizar; (AUT) regular; **to be in/out of ~** (*instrument*) estar afinado/desafinado; (*singer*) cantar afinado/desafinar; **to be in/out of ~ with** (*fig*) harmonizar-se com/destoar de; **she was robbed to the ~ of £10,000** ela foi roubada em mais de £10,000.
tune in *vi* (RADIO, TV): **to ~ in(to)** sintonizar (com).
tune up *vi* (*musician*) afinar (seu instrumento).
tuneful ['tju:nful] *adj* melodioso.
tuner ['tju:nə*] *n* (*radio set*) sintonizador *m*; **piano ~** afinador(a) *m/f* de pianos.
tuner amplifier *n* sintonizador *m* amplificador.
tungsten ['tʌŋstən] *n* tungstênio.
tunic ['tju:nɪk] *n* túnica.
tuning ['tju:nɪŋ] *n* (*of radio*) sintonia; (MUS) afinação *f*; (*of car*) regulagem *f*.
tuning fork *n* diapasão *m*.
Tunis ['tju:nɪs] *n* Túnis.
Tunisia [tju:'nɪzɪə] *n* Tunísia.
Tunisian [tju:'nɪzɪən] *adj, n* tunisiano/a.
tunnel ['tʌnl] *n* túnel *m*; (*in mine*) galeria ♦ *vi* abrir um túnel (*or* uma galeria).
tunny ['tʌnɪ] *n* atum *m*.
turban ['tə:bən] *n* turbante *m*.
turbid ['tə:bɪd] *adj* turvo.
turbine ['tə:baɪn] *n* turbina.
turbojet [tə:bəu'dʒɛt] *n* turbojato (PT: -ct-).
turboprop [tə:bəu'prɔp] *n* (*engine*) turboélice *m*.
turbot ['tə:bət] *n inv* rodovalho.
turbulence ['tə:bjuləns] *n* (AVIAT) turbulência.
turbulent ['tə:bjulənt] *adj* turbulento.
tureen [tə'ri:n] *n* terrina.
turf [tə:f] *n* torrão *m* ♦ *vt* relvar, gramar; **the T~** o turfe.
turf out (*inf*) *vt* (*thing*) jogar fora; (*person*) pôr no olho da rua.
turf accountant (BRIT) *n* corretor *m* de apostas.
turgid ['tə:dʒɪd] *adj* (*speech*) pomposo.
Turk [tə:k] *n* turco/a.
Turkey ['tə:kɪ] *n* Turquia.
turkey ['tə:kɪ] *n* peru(a) *m/f*.
Turkish ['tə:kɪʃ] *adj* turco/a ♦ *n* (LING) turco.
Turkish bath *n* banho turco.
Turkish delight *n* lokum *m*.
turmeric ['tə:mərɪk] *n* açafrão-da-terra *m*.
turmoil ['tə:mɔɪl] *n* tumulto, distúrbio, agitação *f*.
turn [tə:n] *n* volta, turno; (*in road*) curva; (*go*) vez *f*, turno; (*tendency*: *of mind, events*) propensão *f*, tendência; (THEATRE) número; (MED) choque *m* ♦ *vt* dar volta a, fazer girar; (*collar*) virar; (*steak*) virar; (*milk*) azedar; (*shape*: *wood*) tornear; (*change*): **to ~ sth into** converter algo em ♦ *vi* virar; (*person*: *look back*) voltar-se; (*reverse direction*) mudar de direção; (*milk*) azedar; (*change*) mudar; (*become*) tornar-se, virar; **to ~ into** converter-se em; **a good ~** um favor; **it gave me quite a ~** me deu um susto enorme; **"no left ~"** (AUT) "proibido virar à esquerda"; **it's your ~** é a sua vez; **in ~** por sua vez; **to take ~s (at)** revezar (em); **at the ~ of the year/century** no final do ano/século; **to take a ~ for the worse** (*situation, patient*) piorar; **to ~ left** (AUT) virar à esquerda; **she has no one to ~ to** ela não tem a quem recorrer.
turn about *vi* dar meia-volta.
turn away *vi* virar a cabeça ♦ *vt* (*reject*: *person*) rejeitar; (: *business*) recusar.
turn back *vi* voltar atrás.
turn down *vt* (*refuse*) recusar; (*reduce*) baixar; (*fold*) dobrar, virar para baixo.
turn in *vi* (*inf*: *go to bed*) ir dormir ♦ *vt* (*fold*) dobrar para dentro.
turn off *vi* (*from road*) virar, sair do caminho ♦ *vt* (*light, radio etc*) apagar; (*engine*) desligar.
turn on *vt* (*light*) acender; (*engine, radio*) ligar.
turn out *vt* (*light, gas*) apagar; (*produce*) produzir ♦ *vi* (*troops*) ser mobilizado; **to ~ out to be ...** revelar-se (ser) ..., resultar (ser) ...., vir a ser ....
turn over *vi* (*person*) virar-se ♦ *vt* (*object*) virar.
turn round *vi* voltar-se, virar-se ♦ *vt* girar.
turn up *vi* (*person*) aparecer, pintar; (*lost object*) aparecer ♦ *vt* (*collar*) subir; (*volume, radio etc*) aumentar.
turnabout ['tə:nəbaut] *n* reviravolta.
turnaround ['tə:nəraund] *n* reviravolta.
turncoat ['tə:nkəut] *n* vira-casaca *m/f*.
turned-up [tə:nd-] *adj* (*nose*) arrebitado.
turning ['tə:nɪŋ] *n* (*in road*) via lateral; **the first ~ on the right** a primeira à direita.
turning circle (BRIT) *n* raio de viragem.
turning point *n* (*fig*) momento decisivo, virada.
turning radius (US) *n* raio de viragem.
turnip ['tə:nɪp] *n* nabo.
turnout ['tə:naut] *n* assistência; (*in election*) afluência às urnas.
turnover ['tə:nəuvə*] *n* (COMM: *amount of money*) volume *m* de negócios; (: *of goods*) movimento; (CULIN) *espécie de pastel*; **there is a rapid ~ in staff** há uma alta rotatividade no quadro de pessoal.
turnpike ['tə:npaɪk] (US) *n* estrada *or* rodovia com pedágio (BR) *or* portagem (PT).
turnstile ['tə:nstaɪl] *n* borboleta (BR), torniquete *m* (PT).
turntable ['tə:nteɪbl] *n* (*on record player*) prato.
turn-up (BRIT) *n* (*on trousers*) volta, dobra.
turpentine ['tə:pəntaɪn] *n* (*also*: *turps*) aguarrás *f*.
turquoise ['tə:kwɔɪz] *n* (*stone*) turquesa ♦ *adj* azul-turquesa *inv*.
turret ['tʌrɪt] *n* torrinha.
turtle ['tə:tl] *n* tartaruga, cágado.
turtleneck (sweater) ['tə:tlnɛk-] *n* pulôver *m* (BR) *or* camisola (PT) de gola alta.
tusk [tʌsk] *n* defesa (de elefante).

tussle ['tʌsl] *n* (*fight*) luta; (*scuffle*) contenda, rixa.
tutor ['tju:tə*] *n* professor(a) *m/f*.
tutorial [tju:'tɔ:rɪəl] *n* (*SCH*) seminário.
tuxedo [tʌk'si:dəu] (*US*) *n* smoking *m*.
TV *n abbr* (= *television*) TV *f*.
twaddle ['twɔdl] *n* bobagens *fpl*, disparates *mpl*.
twang [twæŋ] *n* (*of instrument*) dedilhado; (*of voice*) timbre *m* nasal *or* fanhoso ♦ *vi* vibrar ♦ *vt* (*guitar*) dedilhar.
tweak [twi:k] *vt* (*nose*, *ear*) beliscar; (*hair*) puxar.
tweed [twi:d] *n* tweed *m*, *pano grosso de lã*.
tweezers ['twi:zəz] *npl* pinça (pequena).
twelfth [twɛlfθ] *num* décimo segundo; *see also* **fifth**.
Twelfth Night *n* noite *f* de Reis, Epifania.
twelve [twɛlv] *num* doze; **at ~ (o'clock)** (*midday*) ao meio-dia; (*midnight*) à meia-noite; *see also* **five**.
twentieth ['twɛntɪɪθ] *num* vigésimo; *see also* **fifth**.
twenty ['twɛntɪ] *num* vinte; *see also* **five**.
twerp [twə:p] (*inf*) *n* imbecil *m/f*.
twice [twaɪs] *adv* duas vezes; **~ as much** duas vezes mais; **~ a week** duas vezes por semana; **she is ~ your age** ela tem duas vezes a sua idade.
twiddle ['twɪdl] *vt*, *vi*: **to ~ (with) sth** mexer em algo; **to ~ one's thumbs** (*fig*) chupar o dedo.
twig [twɪg] *n* graveto, varinha ♦ *vt*, *vi* (*inf*) sacar.
twilight ['twaɪlaɪt] *n* crepúsculo, meia-luz *f*; **in the ~** na penumbra.
twill [twɪl] *n* sarja.
twin [twɪn] *adj*, *n* gêmeo/a ♦ *vt* irmanar.
twin(-bedded) room [-'bɛdɪd-] *n* quarto com duas camas.
twin beds *npl* camas *fpl* separadas.
twin-carburettor *adj* de dois carburadores.
twine [twaɪn] *n* barbante *m* (*BR*), cordel *m* (*PT*) ♦ *vi* (*plant*) enroscar-se, enrolar-se.
twin-engined [-'ɛndʒɪnd] *adj* bimotor; **~ aircraft** (avião *m*) bimotor *m*.
twinge [twɪndʒ] *n* (*of pain*) pontada; (*of conscience*) remorso.
twinkle ['twɪŋkl] *n* cintilação *f* ♦ *vi* cintilar; (*eyes*) pestanejar.
twin town *n* cidade *f* irmã.
twirl [twə:l] *n* giro, volta ♦ *vt* fazer girar ♦ *vi* girar rapidamente.
twist [twɪst] *n* (*action*) torção *f*; (*in road, coil*) curva; (*in wire, flex*) virada; (*in story*) mudança imprevista ♦ *vt* torcer, retorcer; (*weave*) entrelaçar; (*roll around*) enrolar; (*fig*) deformar ♦ *vi* serpentear; **to ~ one's ankle/wrist** torcer o tornozelo/pulso.
twisted ['twɪstɪd] *adj* (*wire*, *rope*, *ankle*) torcido; (*fig*: *mind*, *logic*) deturpado.
twit [twɪt] (*inf*) *n* idiota *m/f*, bobo/a.
twitch [twɪtʃ] *n* puxão *m*; (*nervous*) tique *m* nervoso ♦ *vi* contrair-se.
two [tu:] *num* dois; **~ by ~, in ~s** de dois em dois; **to put ~ and ~ together** (*fig*) tirar conclusões; *see also* **five**.
two-door *adj* (*AUT*) de duas portas.
two-faced [-feɪst] (*pej*) *adj* (*person*) falso.
twofold ['tu:fəuld] *adv*: **to increase ~** duplicar ♦ *adj* (*increase*) em cem por cento; (*reply*) duplo.
two-piece *n* (*also*: **~** *suit*) traje *m* de duas peças; (*also*: **~** *swimsuit*) maiô *m* de duas peças, biquíni *m*.
two-seater [-'si:tə*] *n* (*plane*) avião *m* de dois lugares; (*car*) carro de dois lugares.
twosome ['tu:səm] *n* (*people*) casal *m*.
two-stroke *n* (*also*: **~** *engine*) motor *m* de dois tempos ♦ *adj* de dois tempos.
two-tone *adj* em dois tons.
two-way *adj*: **~ radio** rádio emissor-receptor; **~ traffic** trânsito em mão dupla.
TX (*US*) *abbr* (*POST*) = **Texas**.
tycoon [taɪ'ku:n] *n*: **(business) ~** magnata *m*.
type [taɪp] *n* (*category*) tipo, espécie *f*; (*model*) modelo; (*TYP*) tipo, letra ♦ *vt* (*letter etc*) datilografar, bater (à máquina); **what ~ do you want?** que tipo você quer?; **in bold/italic ~** em negrito/itálico.
typecast ['taɪpkɑ:st] *adj* que representa sempre o mesmo papel.
typeface ['taɪpfeɪs] *n* tipo, letra.
typescript ['taɪpskrɪpt] *n* texto datilografado.
typeset ['taɪpsɛt] (*irreg*) *vt* compor (*para imprimir*).
typesetter ['taɪpsɛtə*] *n* compositor(a) *m/f*.
typewriter ['taɪpraɪtə*] *n* máquina de escrever.
typewritten ['taɪprɪtn] *adj* datilografado.
typhoid ['taɪfɔɪd] *n* febre *f* tifóide.
typhoon [taɪ'fu:n] *n* tufão *m*.
typhus ['taɪfəs] *n* tifo.
typical ['tɪpɪkl] *adj* típico.
typify ['tɪpɪfaɪ] *vt* tipificar, simbolizar.
typing ['taɪpɪŋ] *n* datilografia.
typing error *n* erro de datilografia.
typing pool *n* seção *f* de datilografia.
typist ['taɪpɪst] *n* datilógrafo/a *m/f*.
typo ['taɪpəu] (*inf*) *n abbr* (= *typographical error*) erro tipográfico.
typography [taɪ'pɔgrəfɪ] *n* tipografia.
tyranny ['tɪrənɪ] *n* tirania.
tyrant ['taɪərənt] *n* tirano/a.
tyre ['taɪə*] (*US* **tire**) *n* pneu *m*.
tyre pressure *n* pressão *f* dos pneus.
Tyrrhenian Sea [tɪ'ri:nɪən-] *n*: **the ~** o mar Tirreno.
tzar [zɑ:*] *n* = **tsar**.

***NB:** European Portuguese adds the following consonants to certain words:* **b** (sú(b)dito, su(b)til); **c** (a(c)ção, a(c)cionista, a(c)to); **m** (inde(m)ne); **p** (ado(p)ção, ado(p)tar); *for further details see p. xiii.*

U

U, u [juː] *n* (*letter*) U, u *m*; **U for Uncle** U de Úrsula.
U (*BRIT*) *n abbr* (*CINEMA*: = *universal*) ≈ livre.
UAW (*US*) *n abbr* (= *United Automobile Workers*) *sindicato dos trabalhadores na indústria automobilística.*
UB40 (*BRIT*) *n abbr* (= *unemployment benefit form 40*) *carteira que comprova que o portador recebe o auxílio-desemprego.*
U-bend *n* (*in pipe*) curva em U.
ubiquitous [juː'bɪkwɪtəs] *adj* ubíquo, onipresente.
UCCA ['ʌkə] (*BRIT*) *n abbr* = **Universities Central Council on Admissions**.
UDA (*BRIT*) *n abbr* = **Ulster Defence Association**.
UDC (*BRIT*) *n abbr* = **Urban District Council**.
udder ['ʌdə*] *n* ubre *f*.
UDI (*BRIT*) *n abbr* (*POL*) = **unilateral declaration of independence**.
UDR (*BRIT*) *n abbr* = **Ulster Defence Regiment**.
UEFA [juː'eɪfə] *n abbr* (= *Union of European Football Associations*) UEFA *f*.
UFO ['juːfəu] *n abbr* (= *unidentified flying object*) óvni *m*.
Uganda [juː'gændə] *n* Uganda (*no article*).
Ugandan [juː'gændən] *adj*, *n* ugandense *m/f*.
ugh [əːh] *excl* uh!
ugliness ['ʌglɪnɪs] *n* feiúra.
ugly ['ʌglɪ] *adj* feio; (*dangerous*) perigoso.
UHF *abbr* (= *ultra-high frequency*) UHF, freqüência ultra-alta.
UHT *adj abbr* (= *ultra-heat treated*): **~ milk** leite *m* longa-vida.
UK *n abbr* = **United Kingdom**.
ulcer ['ʌlsə*] *n* úlcera; **mouth ~** afta.
Ulster ['ʌlstə*] *n* Ulster *m*, Irlanda do Norte.
ulterior [ʌl'tɪərɪə*] *adj* ulterior; **~ motive** segundas intenções *fpl*.
ultimata [ʌltɪ'meɪtə] *npl of* **ultimatum**.
ultimate ['ʌltɪmət] *adj* último, final; (*authority*) máximo ♦ *n*: **the ~ in luxury** o máximo em luxo.
ultimately ['ʌltɪmətlɪ] *adv* (*in the end*) no final, por último; (*fundamentally*) no fundo.
ultimatum [ʌltɪ'meɪtəm] (*pl* **~s** *or* **ultimata**) *n* ultimato.
ultrasonic [ʌltrə'sɔnɪk] *adj* ultra-sônico.
ultrasound ['ʌltrəsaund] *n* (*MED*) ultra-som *m*.
ultraviolet [ʌltrə'vaɪəlɪt] *adj* ultravioleta.
umbilical cord [ʌmbɪ'laɪkl-] *n* cordão *m* umbilical.
umbrage ['ʌmbrɪdʒ] *n*: **to take ~** ofender-se.
umbrella [ʌm'brɛlə] *n* guarda-chuva *m*; (*fig*): **under the ~ of** sob a égide de.
umpire ['ʌmpaɪə*] *n* árbitro ♦ *vt* arbitrar.
umpteen [ʌmp'tiːn] *adj* inúmeros/as.
umpteenth [ʌmp'tiːnθ] *adj*: **for the ~ time** pela enésima vez.
UMW *n abbr* (= *United Mineworkers of America*) *sindicato dos mineiros.*
UN *n abbr* (= *United Nations*) ONU *f*.
unabashed [ʌnə'bæʃt] *adj* imperturbado.
unabated [ʌnə'beɪtɪd] *adj* sem diminuir.
unable [ʌn'eɪbl] *adj*: **to be ~ to do sth** não poder fazer algo; (*be incapable*) ser incapaz de fazer algo.
unabridged [ʌnə'brɪdʒd] *adj* integral.
unacceptable [ʌnək'sɛptəbl] *adj* (*behaviour*) insuportável; (*price*, *proposal*) inaceitável.
unaccompanied [ʌnə'kʌmpənɪd] *adj* desacompanhado; (*singing*, *song*) sem acompanhamento.
unaccountably [ʌnə'kauntəblɪ] *adv* inexplicavelmente.
unaccounted [ʌnə'kauntɪd] *adj*: **two passengers are ~ for** dois passageiros estão desaparecidos.
unaccustomed [ʌnə'kʌstəmd] *adj* desacostumado; **to be ~ to** não estar acostumado a.
unacquainted [ʌnə'kweɪntɪd] *adj*: **to be ~ with** (*person*) não conhecer; (*facts etc*) não estar familiarizado com.
unadulterated [ʌnə'dʌltəreɪtɪd] *adj* puro, natural.
unaffected [ʌnə'fɛktɪd] *adj* (*person*, *behaviour*) natural, simples *inv*; (*emotionally*): **to be ~ by** não se comover com.
unafraid [ʌnə'freɪd] *adj*: **to be ~** não ter medo.
unaided [ʌn'eɪdɪd] *adj* sem ajuda, por si só.
unanimity [juːnə'nɪmɪtɪ] *n* unanimidade *f*.
unanimous [juː'nænɪməs] *adj* unânime.
unanimously [juː'nænɪməslɪ] *adv* unanimemente.
unanswered [ʌn'ɑːnsəd] *adj* sem resposta.
unappetizing [ʌn'æpɪtaɪzɪŋ] *adj* pouco apetitoso.
unappreciative [ʌnə'priːʃɪətɪv] *adj* (*ungrateful*) ingrato.
unarmed [ʌn'ɑːmd] *adj* (*without a weapon*) desarmado; (*defenceless*) indefeso.
unashamed [ʌnə'ʃeɪmd] *adj* (*open*) desembaraçado; (*impudent*) descarado.
unassisted [ʌnə'sɪstɪd] *adj*, *adv* sem ajuda.
unassuming [ʌnə'sjuːmɪŋ] *adj* modesto, despretencioso.
unattached [ʌnə'tætʃt] *adj* (*person*) livre; (*part etc*) solto, separado.
unattended [ʌnə'tɛndɪd] *adj* (*car*, *luggage*) sem vigilância, abandonado.
unattractive [ʌnə'træktɪv] *adj* sem atrativos, pouco atraente.
unauthorized [ʌn'ɔːθəraɪzd] *adj* não autorizado, sem autorização.
unavailable [ʌnə'veɪləbl] *adj* (*article*, *room*, *book*) indisponível; (*person*) não disponível.
unavoidable [ʌnə'vɔɪdəbl] *adj* inevitável.
unavoidably [ʌnə'vɔɪdəblɪ] *adv* inevita-

velmente.

unaware [ʌnə'wɛə*] *adj*: **to be ~ of** ignorar, não perceber.

unawares [ʌnə'wɛəz] *adv* improvisadamente, de surpresa.

unbalanced [ʌn'bælənst] *adj* desequilibrado.

unbearable [ʌn'bɛərəbl] *adj* insuportável.

unbeatable [ʌn'bi:təbl] *adj* (*team*) invencível; (*price*) sem igual.

unbeaten [ʌn'bi:tn] *adj* invicto; (*record*) não batido.

unbecoming [ʌnbɪ'kʌmɪŋ] *adj* (*unseemly*: *language*, *behaviour*) inconveniente; (*unflattering*: *garment*) que não fica bem.

unbeknown(st) [ʌnbɪ'nəun(st)] *adv*: **~ to me** sem eu saber.

unbelief [ʌnbɪ'li:f] *n* incredulidade *f*.

unbelievable [ʌnbɪ'li:vəbl] *adj* inacreditável, incrível.

unbelievingly [ʌnbɪ'li:vɪŋlɪ] *adv* incredulamente.

unbend [ʌn'bɛnd] (*irreg*) *vi* relaxar-se ♦ *vt* (*wire*) desentortar.

unbending [ʌn'bɛndɪŋ] *adj* inflexível.

unbent [ʌn'bɛnt] *pt*, *pp of* **unbend**.

unbias(s)ed [ʌn'baɪəst] *adj* imparcial.

unblemished [ʌn'blɛmɪʃt] *adj* imaculado.

unblock [ʌn'blɔk] *vt* (*pipe*) desentupir.

unborn [ʌn'bɔ:n] *adj* por nascer.

unbounded [ʌn'baundɪd] *adj* ilimitado, infinito, imenso.

unbreakable [ʌn'breɪkəbl] *adj* inquebrável.

unbridled [ʌn'braɪdld] *adj* (*fig*) desenfreado.

unbroken [ʌn'brəukən] *adj* (*seal*) intacto; (*line*) contínuo; (*series*) ininterrupto; (*record*) mantido; (*spirit*) indômito.

unbuckle [ʌn'bʌkl] *vt* desafivelar.

unburden [ʌn'bə:dn] *vt*: **to ~ o.s.** desabafar.

unbutton [ʌn'bʌtn] *vt* desabotoar.

uncalled-for [ʌn'kɔ:ld-] *adj* desnecessário, gratuito.

uncanny [ʌn'kænɪ] *adj* (*strange*) estranho; (*mysterious*) sobrenatural.

unceasing [ʌn'si:sɪŋ] *adj* ininterrupto.

unceremonious [ʌnsɛrɪ'məunɪəs] *adj* (*abrupt*) incerimonioso.

uncertain [ʌn'sə:tn] *adj* incerto; (*character*) indeciso; **we were ~ whether ...** não tínhamos certeza se ...; **in no ~ terms** em termos precisos.

uncertainty [ʌn'sə:tntɪ] *n* incerteza.

unchallenged [ʌn'tʃæləndʒd] *adj* incontestado; **to go ~** não ser contestado.

unchanged [ʌn'tʃeɪndʒd] *adj* sem mudar, inalterado.

uncharitable [ʌn'tʃærɪtəbl] *adj* sem caridade.

uncharted [ʌn'tʃɑ:tɪd] *adj* inexplorado.

unchecked [ʌn'tʃɛkt] *adj* desenfreado.

uncivilized [ʌn'sɪvəlaɪzd] *adj* incivilizado, primitivo.

uncle ['ʌŋkl] *n* tio.

unclear [ʌn'klɪə*] *adj* (*not obvious*) pouco evidente; (*confused*) confuso; (*indistinct*) indistinto; **I'm still ~ about what I'm supposed to do** ainda não sei exatamente o que devo fazer.

uncoil [ʌn'kɔɪl] *vt* desenrolar ♦ *vi* desenrolar-se.

uncomfortable [ʌn'kʌmfətəbl] *adj* incômodo; (*uneasy*) pouco à vontade; (*situation*) desagradável.

uncomfortably [ʌn'kʌmftəblɪ] *adv* desconfortavelmente; (*uneasily*) sem graça; (*unpleasantly*) desagradavelmente.

uncommitted [ʌnkə'mɪtɪd] *adj* não comprometido.

uncommon [ʌn'kɔmən] *adj* raro, incomum, excepcional.

uncommunicative [ʌnkə'mju:nɪkətɪv] *adj* reservado.

uncomplicated [ʌn'kɔmplɪkeɪtɪd] *adj* descomplicado, simples *inv*.

uncompromising [ʌn'kɔmprəmaɪzɪŋ] *adj* intransigente, inflexível.

unconcerned [ʌnkən'sə:nd] *adj* indiferente, despreocupado; **to be ~ (about)** não estar preocupado (com).

unconditional [ʌnkən'dɪʃənl] *adj* incondicional.

uncongenial [ʌnkən'dʒi:nɪəl] *adj* desagradável.

unconnected [ʌnkə'nɛktɪd] *adj* não relacionado.

unconscious [ʌn'kɔnʃəs] *adj* sem sentidos, desacordado; (*unaware*) inconsciente ♦ *n*: **the ~** o inconsciente; **to knock sb ~** pôr alguém nocaute, nocautear alguém.

unconsciously [ʌn'kɔnʃəslɪ] *adv* inconscientemente.

unconstitutional [ʌnkɔnstɪ'tju:ʃənl] *adj* inconstitucional.

uncontested [ʌnkən'tɛstɪd] *adj* incontestado.

uncontrollable [ʌnkən'trəuləbl] *adj* (*temper*) ingovernável; (*laughter*) incontrolável.

uncontrolled [ʌnkən'trəuld] *adj* descontrolado.

unconventional [ʌnkən'vɛnʃənl] *adj* (*person*) inconvencional; (*approach*) heterodoxo.

unconvinced [ʌnkən'vɪnst] *adj*: **to be ~** não estar convencido.

unconvincing [ʌnkən'vɪnsɪŋ] *adj* pouco convincente.

uncork [ʌn'kɔ:k] *vt* desarrolhar.

uncorroborated [ʌnkə'rɔbəreɪtɪd] *adj* não confirmado.

uncouth [ʌn'ku:θ] *adj* rude, grosseiro, inculto.

uncover [ʌn'kʌvə*] *vt* descobrir; (*take lid off*) destapar, destampar.

unctuous ['ʌŋktjuəs] *adj* untuoso, pegajoso.

undamaged [ʌn'dæmɪdʒd] *adj* (*goods*) intacto; (*fig*: *reputation*) incólume.

undaunted [ʌn'dɔ:ntɪd] *adj* impávido, inabalável.

undecided [ʌndɪ'saɪdɪd] *adj* (*character*) inde-

***NB**: European Portuguese adds the following consonants to certain words:* **b** (sú(b)dito, su(b)til); **c** (a(c)ção, a(c)cionista, a(c)to); **m** (inde(m)ne); **p** (ado(p)ção, ado(p)tar); *for further details see p. xiii.*

ciso; (*question*) não respondido, pendente.
undelivered [ʌndɪ'lɪvəd] *adj* não entregue.
undeniable [ʌndɪ'naɪəbl] *adj* inegável.
under ['ʌndə*] *prep* embaixo de (*BR*), debaixo de (*PT*); (*fig*) sob; (*less than*) menos de, inferior a; (*according to*) segundo, de acordo com ♦ *adv* embaixo; (*movement*) por baixo; **from ~ sth** de embaixo de algo; **~ there** ali embaixo; **in ~ 2 hours** em menos de 2 horas; **~ anaesthetic** sob anestesia; **~ discussion** em discussão; **~ the circumstances** nas circunstâncias; **~ repair** em conserto.
under... [ʌndə*] *prefix* sub-.
under-age *adj* menor de idade.
underarm ['ʌndərɑːm] *adv* com a mão por baixo ♦ *adj* (*throw*) com a mão por baixo; (*deodorant*) para as axilas.
undercapitalized [ʌndə'kæpɪtəlaɪzd] *adj* subcapitalizado.
undercarriage ['ʌndəkærɪdʒ] (*BRIT*) *n* (*AVIAT*) trem *m* de aterrissagem.
undercharge [ʌndə'tʃɑːdʒ] *vt* não cobrar o suficiente.
underclothes ['ʌndəkləuðz] *npl* roupa de baixo, roupa íntima.
undercoat ['ʌndəkəut] *n* (*paint*) primeira mão *f*.
undercover ['ʌndəkʌvə*] *adj* secreto, clandestino.
undercurrent ['ʌndəkʌrənt] *n* corrente *f* submarina; (*fig*) tendência.
undercut [ʌndə'kʌt] (*irreg*) *vt* vender por menos que.
underdeveloped [ʌndədɪ'vɛləpt] *adj* subdesenvolvido.
underdog ['ʌndədɔg] *n* o mais fraco.
underdone [ʌndə'dʌn] *adj* (*CULIN*) mal passado.
under-employment *n* subemprego.
underestimate [ʌndər'ɛstɪmeɪt] *vt* subestimar.
underexposed [ʌndərɪk'spəuzd] *adj* (*PHOT*) sem exposição suficiente.
underfed [ʌndə'fɛd] *adj* subnutrido.
underfoot [ʌndə'fut] *adv* sob os pés.
undergo [ʌndə'gəu] (*irreg*) *vt* sofrer; (*treatment*) receber; **the car is ~ing repairs** o carro está sendo consertado.
undergraduate [ʌndə'grædjuət] *n* universitário/a ♦ *cpd*: **~ courses** profissões *fpl* universitárias.
underground ['ʌndəgraund] *n* (*BRIT*) metrô *m* (*BR*), metro(-politano) (*PT*); (*POL*) organização *f* clandestina ♦ *adj* subterrâneo; (*fig*) clandestino.
undergrowth ['ʌndəgrəuθ] *n* vegetação *f* rasteira.
underhand(ed) [ʌndə'hænd(ɪd)] *adj* (*fig*) esperto.
underinsured [ʌndərɪn'ʃuəd] *adj* segurado abaixo do valor corrente.
underlie [ʌndə'laɪ] (*irreg*) *vt* (*fig*) ser a base de.
underline [ʌndə'laɪn] *vt* sublinhar.
underling ['ʌndəlɪŋ] (*pej*) *n* subalterno/a.
underlying [ʌndə'laɪɪŋ] *adj*: **the ~ cause** a causa subjacente.
undermanning [ʌndə'mænɪŋ] *n* falta de mão-de-obra.
undermentioned [ʌndə'mɛnʃənd] *adj* abaixo mencionado.
undermine [ʌndə'maɪn] *vt* minar, solapar.
underneath [ʌndə'niːθ] *adv* embaixo, debaixo, por baixo ♦ *prep* embaixo de (*BR*), debaixo de (*PT*).
undernourished [ʌndə'nʌrɪʃt] *adj* subnutrido.
underpaid [ʌndə'peɪd] *adj* mal pago.
underpants ['ʌndəpænts] (*BRIT*) *npl* cueca (*BR*), cuecas *fpl* (*PT*).
underpass ['ʌndəpɑːs] (*BRIT*) *n* passagem *f* inferior.
underpin [ʌndə'pɪn] *vt* (*argument, case*) sustentar.
underplay [ʌndə'pleɪ] (*BRIT*) *vt* minimizar.
underpopulated [ʌndə'pɔpjuleɪtɪd] *adj* de população reduzida.
underprice [ʌndə'praɪs] *vt* vender abaixo do preço.
underprivileged [ʌndə'prɪvɪlɪdʒd] *adj* menos favorecido.
underrate [ʌndə'reɪt] *vt* depreciar, subestimar.
underscore [ʌndə'skɔː*] *vt* sublinhar.
underseal [ʌndə'siːl] (*BRIT*) *vt* fazer bronzina em.
undersecretary [ʌndə'sɛkrətərɪ] *n* subsecretário/a.
undersell [ʌndə'sɛl] (*irreg*) *vt* (*competitors*) vender por preço mais baixo que.
undershirt ['ʌndəʃəːt] (*US*) *n* camiseta.
undershorts ['ʌndəʃɔːts] (*US*) *npl* cueca (*BR*), cuecas *fpl* (*PT*).
underside ['ʌndəsaɪd] *n* parte *f* inferior.
undersigned ['ʌndəsaɪnd] *adj*, *n* abaixo assinado/a.
underskirt ['ʌndəskəːt] (*BRIT*) *n* anágua.
understaffed [ʌndə'stɑːft] *adj* com falta de pessoal.
understand [ʌndə'stænd] (*irreg*) *vt* entender, compreender; (*assume*) subentender; **I ~ that ...** (*I hear*) ouço dizer que ...; (*I sympathize*) eu compreendo que ...; **to make o.s. understood** fazer-se entender.
understandable [ʌndə'stændəbl] *adj* compreensível.
understanding [ʌndə'stændɪŋ] *adj* compreensivo ♦ *n* compreensão *f*, entendimento; (*agreement*) acordo; **to come to an ~** chegar a um acordo; **on the ~ that ...** sob condição que ..., contanto que ....
understate [ʌndə'steɪt] *vt* minimizar.
understatement [ʌndə'steɪtmənt] *n* subestimação *f*; (*euphemism*) eufemismo.
understood [ʌndə'stud] *pt, pp of* **understand** ♦ *adj* entendido; (*implied*) subentendido, implícito.
understudy ['ʌndəstʌdɪ] *n* ator *m* substituto/atriz *f* substituta.
undertake [ʌndə'teɪk] (*irreg*) *vt* (*job, project*) empreender; (*task, duty*) incumbir-se de,

encarregar-se de; **to ~ to do sth** comprometer-se a fazer algo.
undertaker ['ʌndəteɪkə*] *n* agente *m/f* funerário/a.
undertaking [ʌndə'teɪkɪŋ] *n* empreendimento; (*promise*) promessa.
undertone ['ʌndətəun] *n* (*of criticism etc*) sugestão *f*; (*low voice*): **in an ~** em meia voz.
undertook [ʌndə'tuk] *pt of* **undertake**.
undervalue [ʌndə'vælju:] *vt* subestimar.
underwater [ʌndə'wɔ:tə*] *adv* sob a água ♦ *adj* subaquático.
underwear ['ʌndəwɛə*] *n* roupa de baixo.
underweight [ʌndə'weɪt] *adj* de peso inferior ao normal; (*person*) magro.
underwent [ʌndə'wɛnt] *pt of* **undergo**.
underworld ['ʌndəwə:ld] *n* (*of crime*) submundo.
underwrite [ʌndə'raɪt] (*irreg*) *vt* (*COMM*) subscrever.
underwriter ['ʌndəraɪtə*] *n* (*INSURANCE*) subscritor(a) *m/f* (que faz resseguro).
underwritten [ʌndə'rɪtn] *pp of* **underwrite**.
underwrote [ʌndə'rəut] *pt of* **underwrite**.
undeserving [ʌndɪ'zə:vɪŋ] *adj*: **to be ~ of** não merecer.
undesirable [ʌndɪ'zaɪərəbl] *adj* indesejável.
undeveloped [ʌndɪ'vɛləpt] *adj* (*land, resources*) não desenvolvido.
undid [ʌn'dɪd] *pt of* **undo**.
undies ['ʌndɪz] (*inf*) *npl* roupa de baixo, roupa íntima.
undignified [ʌn'dɪgnɪfaɪd] *adj* sem dignidade, indecoroso.
undiluted [ʌndaɪ'lu:tɪd] *adj* não diluído, puro; (*pleasure*) puro.
undiplomatic [ʌndɪplə'mætɪk] *adj* pouco diplomático, inábil.
undischarged [ʌndɪs'tʃɑ:dʒd] *adj*: **~ bankrupt** falido/a não reabilitado/a.
undisciplined [ʌn'dɪsɪplɪnd] *adj* indisciplinado.
undisguised [ʌndɪs'gaɪzd] *adj* (*dislike etc*) patente.
undisputed [ʌndɪ'spju:tɪd] *adj* incontestável, evidente.
undistinguished [ʌndɪs'tɪŋgwɪʃt] *adj* medíocre, regular.
undisturbed [ʌndɪs'tə:bd] *adj* (*sleep*) tranqüilo; **to leave sth ~** não mexer em algo.
undivided [ʌndɪ'vaɪdɪd] *adj*: **can I have your ~ attention?** quero a sua total atenção.
undo [ʌn'du:] (*irreg*) *vt* desfazer.
undoing [ʌn'du:ɪŋ] *n* ruína, desgraça.
undone [ʌn'dʌn] *pp of* **undo** ♦ *adj*: **to come ~** desfazer-se.
undoubted [ʌn'dautɪd] *adj* indubitável.
undoubtedly [ʌn'dautɪdlɪ] *adv* sem dúvida, indubitavelmente.
undress [ʌn'drɛs] *vi* despir-se, tirar a roupa ♦ *vt* despir, tirar a roupa de.
undrinkable [ʌn'drɪŋkəbl] *adj* (*unpalatable*) intragável; (*poisonous*) impotável.
undue [ʌn'dju:] *adj* indevido, excessivo.
undulating ['ʌndjuleɪtɪŋ] *adj* ondulante.
unduly [ʌn'dju:lɪ] *adv* indevidamente, impropriamente.
undying [ʌn'daɪɪŋ] *adj* eterno.
unearned [ʌn'ə:nd] *adj* (*praise, respect*) imerecido; **~ income** rendimento não ganho com o trabalho individual.
unearth [ʌn'ə:θ] *vt* desenterrar.
unearthly [ʌn'ə:θlɪ] *adj* sobrenatural; **at an ~ hour of the night** na calada da noite.
uneasy [ʌn'i:zɪ] *adj* inquieto, desassossegado; (*worried*) preocupado; **to feel ~ about doing sth** estar apreensivo quanto a fazer algo.
uneconomic(al) [ʌni:kə'nɔmɪk(l)] *adj* antieconômico; (*unprofitable*) não rentável.
uneducated [ʌn'ɛdjukeɪtɪd] *adj* inculto, sem instrução, não escolarizado.
unemployed [ʌnɪm'plɔɪd] *adj* desempregado ♦ *npl*: **the ~** os desempregados.
unemployment [ʌnɪm'plɔɪmənt] *n* desemprego.
unemployment benefit (*US* **unemployment compensation**) *n* auxílio-desemprego.
unending [ʌn'ɛndɪŋ] *adj* interminável.
unenthusiastic [ʌnɪnθu:zɪ'æstɪk] *adj* sem entusiasmo.
unenviable [ʌn'ɛnvɪəbl] *adj* nada invejável.
unequal [ʌn'i:kwəl] *adj* desigual.
unequalled [ʌn'i:kwəld] (*US* **unequaled**) *adj* inigualável, sem igual.
unequivocal [ʌnə'kwɪvəkl] *adj* (*answer*) inequívoco; (*person*) categórico.
unerring [ʌn'ə:rɪŋ] *adj* infalível.
UNESCO [ju:'nɛskəu] *n abbr* (= *United Nations Educational, Scientific and Cultural Organization*) UNESCO *f*.
unethical [ʌn'ɛθɪkl] *adj* (*methods*) imoral; (*professional behaviour*) contrário à ética.
uneven [ʌn'i:vn] *adj* desigual; (*road etc*) irregular, acidentado.
uneventful [ʌnɪ'vɛntful] *adj* tranqüilo, rotineiro.
unexceptional [ʌnɪk'sɛpʃənl] *adj* regular, corriqueiro.
unexciting [ʌnɪk'saɪtɪŋ] *adj* monótono.
unexpected [ʌnɪk'spɛktɪd] *adj* inesperado.
unexpectedly [ʌnɪk'spɛktɪdlɪ] *adv* inesperadamente.
unexplained [ʌnɪk'spleɪnd] *adj* inexplicado.
unexploded [ʌnɪk'spləudɪd] *adj* não explodido.
unfailing [ʌn'feɪlɪŋ] *adj* inexaurível.
unfair [ʌn'fɛə*] *adj*: **~ (to)** injusto (com); **it's ~ that ...** não é justo que ....
unfair dismissal *n* demissão *f* injusta *or* infundada.
unfairly [ʌn'fɛəlɪ] *adv* injustamente.
unfaithful [ʌn'feɪθful] *adj* infiel.
unfamiliar [ʌnfə'mɪlɪə*] *adj* pouco familiar, desconhecido; **to be ~ with sth** não estar familiarizado com algo.
unfashionable [ʌn'fæʃnəbl] *adj* fora da moda.

NB: European Portuguese adds the following consonants to certain words: **b** (sú(b)dito, su(b)til); **c** (a(c)ção, a(c)cionista, a(c)to); **m** (inde(m)ne); **p** (ado(p)ção, ado(p)tar); *for further details see p. xiii.*

unfasten [ʌn'fɑːsn] *vt* desatar.
unfathomable [ʌn'fæðəməbl] *adj* insondável.
unfavourable [ʌn'feɪvərəbl] (*US* **unfavorable**) *adj* desfavorável.
unfavo(u)rably [ʌn'feɪvrəblɪ] *adv*: **to look ~ upon** não ser favorável a.
unfeeling [ʌn'fiːlɪŋ] *adj* insensível.
unfinished [ʌn'fɪnɪʃt] *adj* incompleto, inacabado.
unfit [ʌn'fɪt] *adj* (*physically*) sem preparo físico; (*incompetent*) incompetente, incapaz; **~ for work** inapto para trabalhar.
unflagging [ʌn'flægɪŋ] *adj* incansável.
unflappable [ʌn'flæpəbl] *adj* imperturbável, sereno.
unflattering [ʌn'flætərɪŋ] *adj* (*dress, hairstyle*) que não fica bem; (*remark*) pouco elogioso.
unflinching [ʌn'flɪntʃɪŋ] *adj* destemido, intrépido.
unfold [ʌn'fəuld] *vt* desdobrar; (*fig*) revelar ♦ *vi* (*story, situation*) desdobrar-se.
unforeseeable [ʌnfɔː'siːəbl] *adj* imprevisível.
unforeseen [ʌnfɔː'siːn] *adj* imprevisto.
unforgettable [ʌnfə'gɛtəbl] *adj* inesquecível.
unforgivable [ʌnfə'gɪvəbl] *adj* imperdoável.
unformatted [ʌn'fɔːmætɪd] *adj* (*disk, text*) não formatado.
unfortunate [ʌn'fɔːtʃənət] *adj* infeliz; (*event, remark*) inoportuno.
unfortunately [ʌn'fɔːtʃənətlɪ] *adv* infelizmente.
unfounded [ʌn'faundɪd] *adj* infundado.
unfriendly [ʌn'frɛndlɪ] *adj* antipático.
unfulfilled [ʌnful'fɪld] *adj* (*ambition, prophecy*) não realizado; (*desire*) não satisfeito; (*promise, terms of contract*) não cumprido; (*person*) que não se realizou.
unfurl [ʌn'fəːl] *vt* desfraldar.
unfurnished [ʌn'fəːnɪʃt] *adj* desmobiliado, sem mobília.
ungainly [ʌn'geɪnlɪ] *adj* desalinhado.
ungodly [ʌn'gɔdlɪ] *adj* ímpio; **at an ~ hour** às altas horas da madrugada.
ungrateful [ʌn'greɪtful] *adj* mal-agradecido, ingrato.
unguarded [ʌn'gɑːdɪd] *adj*: **~ moment** momento de inatenção.
unhappily [ʌn'hæpəlɪ] *adv* tristemente; (*unfortunately*) infelizmente.
unhappiness [ʌn'hæpɪnɪs] *n* tristeza.
unhappy [ʌn'hæpɪ] *adj* (*sad*) triste; (*unfortunate*) desventurado; (*childhood*) infeliz; **~ with** (*arrangements etc*) descontente com, insatisfeito com.
unharmed [ʌn'hɑːmd] *adj* ileso.
unhealthy [ʌn'hɛlθɪ] *adj* insalubre; (*person*) doentio.
unheard-of [ʌn'həːd-] *adj* (*extraordinary*) inaudito, insólito; (*unknown*) desconhecido.
unhelpful [ʌn'hɛlpful] *adj* (*person*) imprestável; (*advice*) inútil.
unhesitating [ʌn'hɛzɪteɪtɪŋ] *adj* (*loyalty*) firme; (*reply*) imediato.
unhook [ʌn'huk] *vt* desenganchar; (*from wall*) despendurar; (*dress*) abrir, soltar.
unhurt [ʌn'həːt] *adj* ileso.
unhygienic [ʌnhaɪ'dʒiːnɪk] *adj* anti-higiênico.
UNICEF ['juːnɪsɛf] *n abbr* (= *United Nations International Children's Emergency Fund*) Unicef *m*.
unicorn ['juːnɪkɔːn] *n* licorne *m*, unicórnio.
unidentified [ʌnaɪ'dɛntɪfaɪd] *adj* não-identificado.
uniform ['juːnɪfɔːm] *n* uniforme *m* ♦ *adj* uniforme.
uniformity [juːnɪ'fɔːmɪtɪ] *n* uniformidade *f*.
unify ['juːnɪfaɪ] *vt* unificar, unir.
unilateral [juːnɪ'lætərəl] *adj* unilateral.
unimaginable [ʌnɪ'mædʒɪnəbl] *adj* inimaginável, inconcebível.
unimaginative [ʌnɪ'mædʒɪnətɪv] *adj* sem imaginação.
unimpaired [ʌnɪm'pɛəd] *adj* inalterado.
unimportant [ʌnɪm'pɔːtənt] *adj* sem importância.
unimpressed [ʌnɪm'prɛst] *adj* indiferente.
uninhabited [ʌnɪn'hæbɪtɪd] *adj* inabitado.
uninhibited [ʌnɪn'hɪbɪtɪd] *adj* sem inibições.
uninjured [ʌn'ɪndʒəd] *adj* ileso.
uninspired [ʌnɪn'spaɪəd] *adj* insípido.
unintelligent [ʌnɪn'tɛlɪdʒənt] *adj* ininteligente.
unintentional [ʌnɪn'tɛnʃənəl] *adj* involuntário, não intencional.
unintentionally [ʌnɪn'tɛnʃənəlɪ] *adv* sem querer.
uninvited [ʌnɪn'vaɪtɪd] *adj* (*guest*) não convidado.
uninviting [ʌnɪn'vaɪtɪŋ] *adj* (*place*) pouco convidativo; (*food*) pouco apetitoso.
union ['juːnjən] *n* união *f*; (*also*: *trade ~*) sindicato (de trabalhadores) ♦ *cpd* sindical.
unionize ['juːnjənaɪz] *vt* sindicalizar.
Union Jack *n* bandeira britânica.
Union of Soviet Socialist Republics *n* União *f* das Repúblicas Socialistas Soviéticas.
union shop *n empresa onde todos os trabalhadores têm que filiar-se ao sindicato.*
unique [juː'niːk] *adj* único, sem igual.
unisex ['juːnɪsɛks] *adj* unissex *inv*.
unison ['juːnɪsn] *n*: **in ~** em harmonia, em uníssono.
unit ['juːnɪt] *n* unidade *f*; (*team, squad*) grupo; **sink ~** pia de cozinha; **production ~** unidade de produção.
unit cost *n* custo unitário.
unite [juː'naɪt] *vt* unir ♦ *vi* unir-se.
united [juː'naɪtɪd] *adj* unido.
United Arab Emirates *npl* Emirados *mpl* Árabes Unidos.
United Kingdom *n* Reino Unido.
United Nations (Organization) *n* (Organização *f* das) Nações *fpl* Unidas.
United States (of America) *n* Estados Unidos *mpl* (da América).
unit price *n* preço unitário.
unit trust (*BRIT*) *n* (*COMM*) fundo de investimento.
unity ['juːnɪtɪ] *n* unidade *f*.
Univ. *abbr* = **university**.

universal [juːnɪˈvəːsl] *adj* universal.
universe [ˈjuːnɪvəːs] *n* universo.
university [juːnɪˈvəːsɪtɪ] *n* universidade *f*, faculdade *f* ♦ *cpd* universitário.
unjust [ʌnˈdʒʌst] *adj* injusto.
unjustifiable [ʌndʒʌstɪˈfaɪəbl] *adj* injustificável.
unjustified [ʌnˈdʒʌstɪfaɪd] *adj* injustificado; (*text*) não alinhado.
unkempt [ʌnˈkɛmpt] *adj* desleixado, descuidado; (*hair*) despenteado.
unkind [ʌnˈkaɪnd] *adj* maldoso; (*comment etc*) cruel.
unkindly [ʌnˈkaɪndlɪ] *adv* (*treat, speak*) maldosamente.
unknown [ʌnˈnəun] *adj* desconhecido; ~ **to me** sem eu saber; ~ **quantity** (*MATH, fig*) incógnita.
unladen [ʌnˈleɪdn] *adj* (*ship, weight*) sem carga.
unlawful [ʌnˈlɔːful] *adj* ilegal.
unleash [ʌnˈliːʃ] *vt* soltar; (*fig*) desencadear.
unleavened [ʌnˈlɛvənd] *adj* sem fermento.
unless [ʌnˈlɛs] *conj* a menos que, a não ser que; ~ **he comes** a menos que ele venha; ~ **otherwise stated** salvo indicação contrária; ~ **I am mistaken** se não me engano.
unlicensed [ʌnˈlaɪsnst] (*BRIT*) *adj* sem licença para a venda de bebidas alcoólicas.
unlike [ʌnˈlaɪk] *adj* diferente ♦ *prep* diferentemente de, ao contrário de.
unlikelihood [ʌnˈlaɪklɪhud] *n* improbabilidade *f*.
unlikely [ʌnˈlaɪklɪ] *adj* (*result, event*) improvável; (*explanation*) inverossímil.
unlimited [ʌnˈlɪmɪtɪd] *adj* ilimitado.
unlisted [ʌnˈlɪstɪd] *adj* (*STOCK EXCHANGE*) não cotado na Bolsa de Valores; (*US*: *TEL*): **an** ~ **number** um número que não consta na lista telefônica.
unlit [ʌnˈlɪt] *adj* (*room*) sem luz.
unload [ʌnˈləud] *vt* descarregar.
unlock [ʌnˈlɔk] *vt* destrancar.
unlucky [ʌnˈlʌkɪ] *adj* infeliz; (*object, number*) de mau agouro; **to be** ~ ser azarado, ter azar.
unmanageable [ʌnˈmænɪdʒəbl] *adj* (*unwieldy*: *tool*) de difícil manuseio, difícil de manejar; (: *situation*) difícil de controlar.
unmanned [ʌnˈmænd] *adj* não tripulado, sem tripulação.
unmarked [ʌnˈmɑːkt] *adj* (*unstained*) sem marca; ~ **police car** carro policial sem identificação.
unmarried [ʌnˈmærɪd] *adj* solteiro.
unmask [ʌnˈmɑːsk] *vt* desmascarar.
unmatched [ʌnˈmætʃt] *adj* sem igual, inigualável.
unmentionable [ʌnˈmɛnʃnəbl] *adj* (*topic*) que não se deve mencionar; (*word*) que não se diz.
unmerciful [ʌnˈməːsɪful] *adj* impiedoso.
unmistakable [ʌnmɪsˈteɪkəbl] *adj* inconfundível.
unmitigated [ʌnˈmɪtɪgeɪtɪd] *adj* não mitigado, absoluto.
unnamed [ʌnˈneɪmd] *adj* (*nameless*) sem nome; (*anonymous*) anônimo.
unnatural [ʌnˈnætʃrəl] *adj* antinatural, artificial; (*manner*) afetado; (*habit*) depravado.
unnecessary [ʌnˈnɛsəsərɪ] *adj* desnecessário, inútil.
unnerve [ʌnˈnəːv] *vt* amedrontar.
unnoticed [ʌnˈnəutɪst] *adj*: **to go** ~ passar despercebido.
UNO [ˈjuːnəu] *n abbr* (= *United Nations Organization*) ONU *f*.
unobservant [ʌnəbˈzəːvənt] *adj* desatento.
unobtainable [ʌnəbˈteɪnəbl] *adj* inalcançável.
unobtrusive [ʌnəbˈtruːsɪv] *adj* discreto.
unoccupied [ʌnˈɔkjupaɪd] *adj* (*seat etc*) desocupado, livre; (*house*) desocupado, vazio.
unofficial [ʌnəˈfɪʃl] *adj* não-oficial, informal; (*strike*) desautorizado.
unopened [ʌnˈəupənd] *adj* por abrir.
unopposed [ʌnəˈpəuzd] *adj* incontestado, sem oposição.
unorthodox [ʌnˈɔːθədɔks] *adj* pouco ortodoxo, heterodoxo.
unpack [ʌnˈpæk] *vi* desfazer as malas, desembrulhar.
unpaid [ʌnˈpeɪd] *adj* (*bill*) a pagar, não pago; (*holiday*) não pago, sem salário; (*work, worker*) não remunerado.
unpalatable [ʌnˈpælətəbl] *adj* (*truth*) desagradável.
unparalleled [ʌnˈpærəlɛld] *adj* (*unequalled*) sem paralelo; (*unique*) único, incomparável.
unpatriotic [ʌnpætrɪˈɔtɪk] *adj* (*person*) antipatriota; (*speech, attitude*) antipatriótico.
unplanned [ʌnˈplænd] *adj* (*visit*) imprevisto; (*baby*) não previsto.
unpleasant [ʌnˈplɛznt] *adj* (*disagreeable*) desagradável; (*person, manner*) antipático.
unplug [ʌnˈplʌg] *vt* desligar.
unpolluted [ʌnpəˈluːtɪd] *adj* impoluído.
unpopular [ʌnˈpɔpjulə*] *adj* impopular.
unprecedented [ʌnˈprɛsɪdəntɪd] *adj* sem precedentes.
unpredictable [ʌnprɪˈdɪktəbl] *adj* imprevisível.
unprejudiced [ʌnˈprɛdʒudɪst] *adj* (*not biased*) imparcial; (*having no prejudices*) sem preconceitos.
unprepared [ʌnprɪˈpɛəd] *adj* (*person*) despreparado; (*speech*) improvisado.
unprepossessing [ʌnpriːpəˈzɛsɪŋ] *adj* pouco atraente.
unpretentious [ʌnprɪˈtɛnʃəs] *adj* despretensioso.
unprincipled [ʌnˈprɪnsɪpld] *adj* sem princípios.
unproductive [ʌnprəˈdʌktɪv] *adj* improdutivo.

***NB:** European Portuguese adds the following consonants to certain words:* **b** (sú(b)dito, su(b)til); **c** (a(c)ção, a(c)cionista, a(c)to); **m** (inde(m)ne); **p** (ado(p)ção, ado(p)tar); *for further details see p. xiii.*

unprofessional [ʌnprə'fɛʃənl] *adj* (*conduct*) pouco profissional.
unprofitable [ʌn'prɔfɪtəbl] *adj* não lucrativo.
unprovoked [ʌnprə'vəukt] *adj* sem provocação.
unpunished [ʌn'pʌnɪʃt] *adj* impune.
unqualified [ʌn'kwɔlɪfaɪd] *adj* (*teacher*) não qualificado, inabilitado; (*success*) irrestrito, absoluto.
unquestionably [ʌn'kwɛstʃənəblɪ] *adv* indubitavelmente.
unquestioning [ʌn'kwɛstʃənɪŋ] *adj* (*obedience, acceptance*) incondicional, total.
unravel [ʌn'rævl] *vt* desemaranhar.
unreal [ʌn'rɪəl] *adj* irreal, ilusório.
unrealistic [ʌnrɪə'lɪstɪk] *adj* pouco realista.
unreasonable [ʌn'ri:znəbl] *adj* despropositado; (*demand*) absurdo, injusto.
unrecognizable [ʌnrɛkəg'naɪzəbl] *adj* irreconhecível.
unrecognized [ʌn'rɛkəgnaɪzd] *adj* (*talent, genius*) não reconhecido.
unrecorded [ʌnrə'kɔ:dɪd] *adj* não registrado.
unrefined [ʌnrə'faɪnd] *adj* (*sugar, petroleum*) não refinado.
unrehearsed [ʌnrɪ'hə:st] *adj* improvisado.
unrelated [ʌnrɪ'leɪtɪd] *adj* sem relação; (*family*) sem parentesco.
unrelenting [ʌnrɪ'lɛntɪŋ] *adj* implacável.
unreliable [ʌnrɪ'laɪəbl] *adj* (*person*) indigno de confiança; (*machine*) incerto, perigoso.
unrelieved [ʌnrɪ'li:vd] *adj* (*monotony*) invariável.
unremitting [ʌnrɪ'mɪtɪŋ] *adj* constante, incessante.
unrepeatable [ʌnrɪ'pi:təbl] *adj* (*offer*) irrepetível.
unrepentant [ʌnrɪ'pɛntənt] *adj* convicto, impenitente.
unrepresentative [ʌnrɛprɪ'zɛntətɪv] *adj* pouco representativo *or* característico.
unreserved [ʌnrɪ'zə:vd] *adj* (*seat*) não reservado; (*approval, admiration*) total, integral.
unresponsive [ʌnrɪs'pɔnsɪv] *adj* indiferente, impassível.
unrest [ʌn'rɛst] *n* inquietação *f*, desassossego; (POL) distúrbios *mpl*.
unrestricted [ʌnrɪ'strɪktɪd] *adj* irrestrito, ilimitado.
unrewarded [ʌnrɪ'wɔ:dɪd] *adj* sem sucesso.
unripe [ʌn'raɪp] *adj* verde, imaturo.
unrivalled [ʌn'raɪvəld] (*US* **unrivaled**) *adj* sem igual, incomparável.
unroll [ʌn'rəul] *vt* desenrolar.
unruffled [ʌn'rʌfld] *adj* (*person*) sereno, imperturbável; (*hair*) liso.
unruly [ʌn'ru:lɪ] *adj* indisciplinado.
unsafe [ʌn'seɪf] *adj* perigoso; ~ **to eat/drink** não comestível/potável.
unsaid [ʌn'sɛd] *adj*: **to leave sth** ~ deixar algo sem dizer.
unsaleable [ʌn'seɪləbl] (*US* **unsalable**) *adj* invendável, invendível.
unsatisfactory [ʌnsætɪs'fæktərɪ] *adj* insatisfatório.
unsatisfied [ʌn'sætɪsfaɪd] *adj* descontente.
unsavoury [ʌn'seɪvərɪ] (*US* **unsavory**) *adj* (*fig*) repugnante, vil.
unscathed [ʌn'skeɪðd] *adj* ileso.
unscientific [ʌnsaɪən'tɪfɪk] *adj* não científico.
unscrew [ʌn'skru:] *vt* desparafusar.
unscrupulous [ʌn'skru:pjuləs] *adj* inescrupuloso, imoral.
unsecured [ʌnsə'kjuəd] *adj*: ~ **creditor** credor(a) *m/f* quirografário/a.
unseemly [ʌn'si:mlɪ] *adj* inconveniente.
unseen [ʌn'si:n] *adj* (*person*) despercebido; (*danger*) escondido.
unselfish [ʌn'sɛlfɪʃ] *adj* desinteressado.
unsettled [ʌn'sɛtld] *adj* (*uncertain*) incerto, duvidoso; (*weather*) variável, instável; (*person*) inquieto.
unsettling [ʌn'sɛtlɪŋ] *adj* inquietador(a), inquietante.
unshak(e)able [ʌn'ʃeɪkəbl] *adj* inabalável.
unshaven [ʌn'ʃeɪvn] *adj* com a barba por fazer.
unsightly [ʌn'saɪtlɪ] *adj* feio, disforme.
unskilled [ʌn'skɪld] *adj*: ~ **worker** operário/a não-especializado/a.
unsociable [ʌn'səuʃəbl] *adj* anti-social.
unsocial [ʌn'səuʃl] *adj* (*hours*) fora do horário normal.
unsold [ʌn'səuld] *adj* não vendido.
unsolicited [ʌnsə'lɪsɪtɪd] *adj* não solicitado, espontâneo.
unsophisticated [ʌnsə'fɪstɪkeɪtɪd] *adj* simples *inv*, natural.
unsound [ʌn'saund] *adj* (*health*) mau; (*floor, foundations*) em mau estado; (*policy, advice*) infundado.
unspeakable [ʌn'spi:kəbl] *adj* indizível; (*bad*) inqualificável.
unspoken [ʌn'spəukən] *adj* (*agreement, approval*) tácito.
unsteady [ʌn'stɛdɪ] *adj* instável.
unstinting [ʌn'stɪntɪŋ] *adj* (*support*) irrestrito, total; (*generosity*) ilimitado.
unstuck [ʌn'stʌk] *adj*: **to come** ~ despregar-se; (*fig*) fracassar.
unsubstantiated [ʌnsəb'stænʃɪeɪtɪd] *adj* (*rumour*) que não foi confirmado; (*accusation*) sem provas.
unsuccessful [ʌnsək'sɛsful] *adj* (*attempt*) frustrado, vão/vã; (*writer, proposal*) sem êxito; **to be** ~ (*in attempting sth*) ser mal sucedido, não conseguir; (*application*) ser recusado.
unsuccessfully [ʌnsək'sɛsfulɪ] *adv* em vão, debalde.
unsuitable [ʌn'su:təbl] *adj* inadequado, inconveniente.
unsuited [ʌn'su:tɪd] *adj*: **to be** ~ **for** *or* **to** ser inadequado *or* impróprio para.
unsupported [ʌnsə'pɔ:tɪd] *adj* (*claim*) não verificado; (*theory*) não sustentado.
unsure [ʌn'ʃuə*] *adj* inseguro, incerto; **to be** ~ **of o.s.** não ser seguro de si.
unsuspecting [ʌnsə'spɛktɪŋ] *adj* confiante,

insuspeitado.

unsweetened [ʌn'swi:tənd] *adj* não adoçado, sem açúcar.

unswerving [ʌn'swə:vɪŋ] *adj* inabalável, firme, resoluto.

unsympathetic [ʌnsɪmpə'θɛtɪk] *adj* insensível; (*unpleasant*) antipático; ~ **to** indiferente a.

untangle [ʌn'tæŋgl] *vt* desemaranhar, desenredar.

untapped [ʌn'tæpt] *adj* (*resources*) inexplorado.

untaxed [ʌn'tækst] *adj* (*goods*) isento de impostos; (*income*) não tributado.

unthinkable [ʌn'θɪŋkəbl] *adj* impensável, inconcebível, incalculável.

untidy [ʌn'taɪdɪ] *adj* (*room*) desarrumado, desleixado; (*appearance*) desmazelado, desalinhado.

untie [ʌn'taɪ] *vt* desatar, desfazer; (*dog, prisoner*) soltar.

until [ən'tɪl] *prep* até ♦ *conj* até que; ~ **he comes** até que ele venha; ~ **now** até agora; ~ **then** até então; **from morning** ~ **night** de manhã à noite.

untimely [ʌn'taɪmlɪ] *adj* inoportuno, intempestivo; (*death*) prematuro.

untold [ʌn'təuld] *adj* (*story*) inédito; (*suffering*) incalculável; (*wealth*) inestimável.

untouched [ʌn'tʌtʃt] *adj* (*not used*) intacto; (*safe: person*) ileso; ~ **by** indiferente a.

untoward [ʌntə'wɔ:d] *adj* desfavorável, inconveniente.

untrammelled [ʌn'træmld] *adj* sem entraves.

untranslatable [ʌntræns'leɪtəbl] *adj* impossível de traduzir, intraduzível.

untrue [ʌn'tru:] *adj* falso.

untrustworthy [ʌn'trʌstwə:ðɪ] *adj* indigno de confiança.

unusable [ʌn'ju:zəbl] *adj* inutilizável, imprestável.

unused[1] [ʌn'ju:zd] *adj* novo, sem uso.

unused[2] [ʌn'ju:st] *adj*: **to be** ~ **to sth/to doing sth** não estar acostumado com algo/a fazer algo.

unusual [ʌn'ju:ʒuəl] *adj* incomum, extraordinário, insólito.

unusually [ʌn'ju:ʒəlɪ] *adv* extraordinariamente.

unveil [ʌn'veɪl] *vt* (*statue*) desvelar, descobrir.

unwanted [ʌn'wɔntɪd] *adj* não desejado, indesejável.

unwarranted [ʌn'wɔrəntɪd] *adj* injustificado.

unwary [ʌn'wɛərɪ] *adj* imprudente.

unwavering [ʌn'weɪvərɪŋ] *adj* firme, inabalável.

unwelcome [ʌn'wɛlkəm] *adj* (*at a bad time*) inoportuno, indesejável; (*unpleasant*) desagradável; **to feel** ~ não se sentir à vontade.

unwell [ʌn'wɛl] *adj*: **to be** ~ estar doente; **to feel** ~ estar indisposto.

unwieldy [ʌn'wi:ldɪ] *adj* difícil de manejar, pesado.

unwilling [ʌn'wɪlɪŋ] *adj*: **to be** ~ **to do sth** relutar em fazer algo, não querer fazer algo.

unwillingly [ʌn'wɪlɪŋlɪ] *adv* de má vontade.

unwind [ʌn'waɪnd] (*irreg*) *vt* desenrolar ♦ *vi* (*relax*) relaxar-se.

unwise [ʌn'waɪz] *adj* imprudente.

unwitting [ʌn'wɪtɪŋ] *adj* inconsciente, involuntário.

unworkable [ʌn'wə:kəbl] *adj* (*plan etc*) inviável, inexequível.

unworthy [ʌn'wə:ðɪ] *adj* indigno.

unwound [ʌn'waund] *pt, pp of* **unwind**.

unwrap [ʌn'ræp] *vt* desembrulhar.

unwritten [ʌn'rɪtən] *adj* (*agreement*) tácito.

unzip [ʌn'zɪp] *vt* abrir (o fecho ecler de).

up [ʌp] *prep*: **to go/be** ~ **sth** subir algo/estar em cima de algo ♦ *adv* em cima, para cima ♦ *vi* (*inf*): **she** ~**ped and left** ela foi embora ♦ *vt* (*inf: price etc*) aumentar; ~ **there** lá em cima; ~ **above** em cima; ~ **to** até; **"this side** ~**"** "este lado para cima"; **to be** ~ (*out of bed*) estar levantado; **prices are** ~ **by 10%** os preços aumentaram em 10%; **when the year was** ~ no fim do ano; **time's** ~ o tempo acabou; **it is** ~ **to you** você é quem sabe, você decide; **what is he** ~ **to?** o que ele está querendo?, o que ele está tramando?; **he is not** ~ **to it** ele não é capaz de fazê-lo; **he's well** ~ **in** *or* **on** ... (BRIT: *knowledgeable*) ele entende de ...; ~ **with Celtic!** pra frente, Celtic!; **what's** ~**?** (*inf*) o que é que é?, o que é que houve?; **what's** ~ **with him?** (*inf*) qual é o problema com ele?

up-and-coming *adj* prometedor(a).

upbeat ['ʌpbi:t] *adj* (MUS) movimentado; (*optimistic*) otimista.

upbraid [ʌp'breɪd] *vt* repreender, censurar.

upbringing ['ʌpbrɪŋɪŋ] *n* educação *f*, criação *f*.

update [ʌp'deɪt] *vt* atualizar, pôr em dia; (*contract etc*) atualizar.

upend [ʌp'ɛnd] *vt* colocar em pé.

upgrade [ʌp'greɪd] *vt* (*person*) promover; (*job*) revalorizar; (*property, equipment*) atualizar; (COMPUT) fazer um upgrade de.

upheaval [ʌp'hi:vl] *n* transtorno; (*unrest*) convulsão *f*.

upheld [ʌp'hɛld] *pt, pp of* **uphold**.

uphill [ʌp'hɪl] *adj* ladeira acima; (*fig: task*) trabalhoso, árduo ♦ *adv*: **to go** ~ ir morro acima.

uphold [ʌp'həuld] (*irreg*) *vt* suster, sustentar.

upholstery [ʌp'həulstərɪ] *n* estofamento.

upkeep ['ʌpki:p] *n* manutenção *f*.

up-market *adj* (*product*) requintado.

upon [ə'pɔn] *prep* sobre.

upper ['ʌpə*] *adj* superior, de cima ♦ *n* (*of shoe*) gáspea, parte *f* superior.

upper class *n*: **the** ~ a classe alta ♦ *adj*: **upper-class** da classe alta.

uppermost ['ʌpəməust] *adj* mais elevado;

NB*: European Portuguese adds the following consonants to certain words:* **b** (sú(b)dito, su(b)til); **c** (a(c)ção, a(c)cionista, a(c)to); **m** (inde(m)ne); **p** (ado(p)ção, ado(p)tar); *for further details see p. xiii.*

what was ~ in my mind o que me preocupava mais.
Upper Volta [-'vɔltə] *n* Alto Volta *m*.
upright ['ʌpraɪt] *adj* vertical; (*fig*) honrado, honesto ♦ *n* viga vertical.
uprising ['ʌpraɪzɪŋ] *n* revolta, rebelião *f*, sublevação *f*.
uproar ['ʌprɔː*] *n* tumulto, algazarra.
uproot [ʌp'ruːt] *vt* desarraigar, arrancar.
ups [ʌps] *npl*: **~ and downs** (*fig*) altos e baixos *mpl*.
upset [*n* 'ʌpsɛt, *vt*, *adj* ʌp'sɛt] (*irreg*: *like* **set**) *n* (*to plan etc*) revés *m*, reviravolta; (MED) indisposição *f* ♦ *vt* (*glass etc*) virar; (*spill*) derramar; (*plan*) perturbar; (*person*: *annoy*) aborrecer, perturbar; (: *sadden*) afligir ♦ *adj* aborrecido, contrariado; (*sad*) aflito; (*stomach*) indisposto.
upset price (US, SCOTTISH) *n* preço mínimo.
upsetting [ʌp'sɛtɪŋ] *adj* desconcertante.
upshot ['ʌpʃɔt] *n* resultado, conclusão *f*.
upside down ['ʌpsaɪd-] *adv* de cabeça para baixo.
upstairs [ʌp'stɛəz] *adv* em cima, lá em cima ♦ *adj* (*room*) de cima ♦ *n* andar *m* de cima.
upstart ['ʌpstɑːt] *n* novo-rico, pessoa sem classe.
upstream [ʌp'striːm] *adv* rio acima.
upsurge ['ʌpsəːdʒ] *n* (*of enthusiasm etc*) explosão *f*.
uptake ['ʌpteɪk] *n*: **he is quick on the ~** ele vê longe; **he is slow on the ~** ele tem raciocínio lento.
uptight [ʌp'taɪt] (*inf*) *adj* nervoso.
up-to-date *adj* moderno, atualizado; **to be ~ with the facts** estar a par dos fatos.
upturn ['ʌptəːn] *n* (*in luck*) virada; (*in economy*) retomada.
upturned ['ʌptəːnd] *adj* (*nose*) arrebitado.
upward ['ʌpwəd] *adj* ascendente, para cima.
upward(s) ['ʌpwəd(z)] *adv* para cima.
URA (US) *n abbr* = **Urban Renewal Administration**.
Ural Mountains ['juərəl-] *npl*: **the ~** (*also*: *the Urals*) as montanhas Urais, os Urais.
uranium [juə'reɪnɪəm] *n* urânio.
Uranus [juə'reɪnəs] *n* Urano.
urban ['əːbən] *adj* urbano, da cidade.
urbane [əː'beɪn] *adj* gentil, urbano.
urbanization [əːbənaɪ'zeɪʃən] *n* urbanização *f*.
urchin ['əːtʃɪn] *n* moleque *m*, criança maltrapilha.
urge [əːdʒ] *n* (*force*) impulso; (*desire*) desejo ♦ *vt*: **to ~ sb to do sth** incitar alguém a fazer algo.
urge on *vt* animar, encorajar.
urgency ['əːdʒənsɪ] *n* urgência; (*of tone*) insistência.
urgent ['əːdʒənt] *adj* urgente; (*tone*, *plea*) insistente.
urgently ['əːdʒəntlɪ] *adv* urgentemente.
urinal ['juərɪnl] (BRIT) *n* urinol *m*, mictório.
urinate ['juərɪneɪt] *vi* urinar, mijar.
urine ['juərɪn] *n* urina.
urn [əːn] *n* urna; (*also*: *tea ~*) samovar *m*.
Uruguay ['juərəgwaɪ] *n* Uruguai *m*.
Uruguayan [juərə'gwaɪən] *adj*, *n* uruguaio/a.
US *n abbr* (= *United States*) EUA *mpl*.
us [ʌs] *pron* nos; (*after prep*) nós.
USA *n abbr* (= *United States* (*of America*)) EUA *mpl*; (MIL) = **United States Army**.
usable ['juːzəbl] *adj* usável, utilizável.
USAF *n abbr* = **United States Air Force**.
usage ['juːzɪdʒ] *n* uso, costume *m*.
USCG *n abbr* = **United States Coast Guard**.
USDA *n abbr* = **United States Department of Agriculture**.
USDAW ['ʌzdɔː] (BRIT) *n abbr* (= *Union of Shop, Distributive and Allied Workers*) *sindicato dos varejistas e distribuidores*.
USDI *n abbr* = **United States Department of the Interior**.
use [*n* juːs, *vt* juːz] *n* uso, emprego; (*usefulness*) utilidade *f* ♦ *vt* usar, utilizar, empregar; **she ~d to do it** ela costumava fazê-lo; **in ~** em uso; **out of ~** fora de uso; **ready for ~** pronto para ser usado; **to be of ~** ser útil; **it's no ~** (*pointless*) é inútil; (*not useful*) não serve; **to have ~ of** ter uso de; **to make ~ of** fazer uso de.
use up *vt* esgotar, consumir.
used[1] [juːzd] *adj* (*car*) usado.
used[2] [juːst] *adj*: **to be ~ to** estar acostumado a; **to get ~ to** acostumar-se a.
useful ['juːsful] *adj* útil; **to come in ~** ser útil.
usefulness ['juːsfəlnɪs] *n* utilidade *f*.
useless ['juːslɪs] *adj* inútil.
user ['juːzə*] *n* usuário/a (BR), utente *m/f* (PT).
user-friendly *adj* de fácil utilização, user-friendly.
USES *n abbr* = **United States Employment Service**.
usher ['ʌʃə*] *n* (*in cinema*) lanterninha *m* (BR), arrumador *m* (PT); (LAW) oficial *m* de justiça ♦ *vt*: **to ~ sb in** fazer alguém entrar.
usherette [ʌʃə'rɛt] *n* (*in cinema*) lanterninha (BR), arrumadora (PT).
USIA *n abbr* = **United States Information Agency**.
USM *n abbr* = **United States Mail**; **United States Mint**.
USN *n abbr* = **United States Navy**.
USPHS *n abbr* = **United States Public Health Service**.
USPO *n abbr* = **United States Post Office**.
USS *n abbr* = **United States Ship; United States Steamer**.
USSR *n abbr* (= *Union of Soviet Socialist Republics*) URSS *f*.
usu. *abbr* = **usually**.
usual ['juːʒuəl] *adj* usual, habitual; **as ~** como de hábito, como sempre.
usually ['juːʒuəlɪ] *adv* normalmente.
usurer ['juːʒərə*] *n* usurário/a.
usurp [juː'zəːp] *vt* usurpar.
UT (US) *abbr* (POST) = **Utah**.
utensil [juː'tɛnsl] *n* utensílio.
uterus ['juːtərəs] *n* útero.
utilitarian [juːtɪlɪ'tɛərɪən] *adj* utilitário.

utility [ju:'tılıtı] *n* utilidade *f*.
utility room *n* copa.
utilization [ju:tılaı'zeıʃən] *n* utilização *f*.
utilize ['ju:tılaız] *vt* utilizar.
utmost ['ʌtməust] *adj* maior ♦ *n*: **to do one's ~** fazer todo o possível; **of the ~ importance** da maior importância.
utter ['ʌtə*] *adj* completo, total ♦ *vt* proferir, pronunciar.
utterance ['ʌtərəns] *n* declaração *f*.
utterly ['ʌtəlı] *adv* completamente, totalmente.
U-turn *n* retorno; (*fig*) reviravolta.

V

V, v [vi:] *n* (*letter*) V, v *m*; **V for Victor** V de Vera.
v *abbr* = **verse**; (= *vide*: *see*) vide; (= *versus*) x; (= *volt*) v.
VA (*US*) *abbr* (*POST*) = **Virginia**.
vac [væk] (*BRIT*: *inf*) *n abbr* = **vacation**.
vacancy ['veıkənsı] *n* (*BRIT*: *job*) vaga; (*room*) quarto livre; **"no vacancies"** "cheio".
vacant ['veıkənt] *adj* (*house*) vazio; (*post*) vago; (*seat etc*) desocupado, livre; (*expression*) distraído.
vacant lot *n* terreno vago; (*uncultivated*) terreno baldio.
vacate [və'keıt] *vt* (*house*) desocupar; (*job*) deixar; (*throne*) renunciar a.
vacation [və'keıʃən] (*esp US*) *n* férias *fpl*; **to take a ~** tirar férias; **on ~** de férias.
vacation course *n* curso de férias.
vacationer [və'keıʃənə*] (*US*) *n* veranista *m/f*.
vaccinate ['væksıneıt] *vt* vacinar.
vaccination [væksı'neıʃən] *n* vacinação *f*.
vaccine ['væksi:n] *n* vacina.
vacuum ['vækjum] *n* vácuo *m*.
vacuum bottle (*US*) *n* garrafa térmica (*BR*), termo (*PT*).
vacuum cleaner *n* aspirador *m* de pó.
vacuum flask (*BRIT*) *n* garrafa térmica (*BR*), termo (*PT*).
vacuum-packed *adj* embalado a vácuo.
vagabond ['vægəbɔnd] *n* vagabundo/a.
vagary ['veıgərı] *n* extravagância, capricho.
vagina [və'dʒaınə] *n* vagina.
vagrancy ['veıgrənsı] *n* vadiagem *f*.
vagrant ['veıgrənt] *n* vagabundo/a, vadio/a.
vague [veıg] *adj* vago; (*blurred*: *memory*) fraco; (*person*) que divaga; **I haven't the ~st idea** não tenho a mínima idéia.
vaguely ['veıglı] *adv* vagamente.
vain [veın] *adj* (*conceited*) vaidoso; (*useless*) vão/vã, inútil; **in ~** em vão.
valance ['væləns] *n* sanefa.
vale [veıl] *n* vale *m*.
valedictory [vælı'dıktərı] *adj* de despedida.
valentine ['væləntaın] *n* (*also*: *~ card*) cartão *m* do Dia dos Namorados; **V~'s Day** Dia *m* dos Namorados.
valet ['vælıt] *n* (*of lord*) criado pessoal; (*in hotel*) camareiro.
valet parking *n* estacionamento por manobrista.
valet service *n* (*for clothes*) lavagem *f* a seco; (*for car*) limpeza completa.
valiant ['vælıənt] *adj* valente.
valid ['vælıd] *adj* válido.
validate ['vælıdeıt] *vt* (*contract, document*) validar, legitimar; (*argument, claim*) confirmar, corroborar.
validity [və'lıdıtı] *n* validade *f*.
valise [və'li:z] *n* maleta.
valley ['vælı] *n* vale *m*.
valour ['vælə*] (*US* **valor**) *n* valor *m*, valentia.
valuable ['væljuəbl] *adj* (*jewel*) de valor; (*time*) valioso.
valuables ['væljuəblz] *npl* objetos *mpl* de valor.
valuation [vælju'eıʃən] *n* avaliação *f*.
value ['vælju:] *n* valor *m*; (*importance*) importância ♦ *vt* (*fix price of*) avaliar; (*esteem*) valorizar, estimar; (*cherish*) apreciar; **you get good ~ (for money) in that shop** o seu dinheiro rende mais naquela loja; **to lose (in) ~** desvalorizar-se; **to gain (in) ~** valorizar-se; **to be of great ~ to sb** (*fig*) ser de grande utilidade para alguém; **to be ~d at $8** ser avaliado em $8.
value added tax [-'ædıd-] (*BRIT*) *n* imposto sobre a circulação de mercadorias (*BR*), imposto sobre valor acrescentado (*PT*).
valued ['vælju:d] *adj* (*appreciated*) valorizado.
valuer ['væljuə*] *n* avaliador(a) *m/f*.
valve [vælv] *n* válvula; (*in radio*) lâmpada.
vampire ['væmpaıə*] *n* vampiro/a.
van [væn] *n* (*AUT*) camionete *f* (*BR*), camioneta (*PT*).
V and A (*BRIT*) *n abbr* = **Victoria and Albert Museum**.
vandal ['vændl] *n* vândalo/a.
vandalism ['vændəlızəm] *n* vandalismo.
vandalize ['vændəlaız] *vt* destruir, depredar.
vanguard ['vængɑ:d] *n* vanguarda.
vanilla [və'nılə] *n* baunilha ♦ *cpd* (*ice cream*) de baunilha.
vanish ['vænıʃ] *vi* desaparecer, sumir.
vanity ['vænıtı] *n* vaidade *f*.
vanity case *n* bolsa de maquilagem.
vantage point ['vɑ:ntıdʒ-] *n* posição *f* estratégica.
vapor *etc* ['veıpə*] (*US*) *n* = **vapour** *etc*.
vaporize ['veıpəraız] *vt* vaporizar ♦ *vi* vaporizar-se.
vapour ['veıpə*] (*US* **vapor**) *n* vapor *m*.

NB: *European Portuguese adds the following consonants to certain words:* **b** (sú(b)dito, su(b)til); **c** (a(c)ção, a(c)cionista, a(c)to); **m** (inde(m)ne); **p** (ado(p)ção, ado(p)tar); *for further details see p. xiii.*

vapo(u)r trail *n* (AVIAT) esteira de vapor.
variable ['vɛərɪəbl] *adj* variável ♦ *n* variável *f*.
variance ['vɛərɪəns] *n*: **to be at ~ (with)** estar em desacordo (com).
variant ['vɛərɪənt] *n* variante *f*.
variation [vɛərɪ'eɪʃən] *n* variação *f*; (*variant*) variante *f*; (*in opinion*) mudança.
varicose veins ['værɪkəus-] *npl* varizes *fpl*.
varied ['vɛərɪd] *adj* variado.
variety [və'raɪətɪ] *n* variedade *f*, diversidade *f*; (*quantity*): **a wide ~ of** uma grande variedade de; **for a ~ of reasons** por várias *or* diversas razões.
variety show *n* espetáculo de variedades.
various ['vɛərɪəs] *adj* vários/as, diversos/as; (*several*) vários/as; **at ~ times** (*different*) em horas variadas; (*several*) várias vezes.
varnish ['vɑːnɪʃ] *n* verniz *m*; (*nail ~*) esmalte *m* ♦ *vt* envernizar; (*nails*) pintar (com esmalte).
vary ['vɛərɪ] *vt* variar; (*change*) mudar ♦ *vi* variar; (*deviate*) desviar-se; **to ~ with** *or* **according to** variar de acordo com.
varying ['vɛərɪɪŋ] *adj* variado.
vase [vɑːz] *n* vaso.
vasectomy [væ'sɛktəmɪ] *n* vasectomia.
vaseline ['væsɪliːn] ® *n* vaselina ®.
vast [vɑːst] *adj* vasto, enorme; (*success*) imenso.
vastly ['vɑːstlɪ] *adv* (*underestimate etc*) enormemente; (*different*) completamente.
vastness ['vɑːstnɪs] *n* imensidão *f*.
VAT [væt] (BRIT) *n abbr* (= *value added tax*) ≈ ICM *m* (BR), IVA *m* (PT).
vat [væt] *n* tina, cuba.
Vatican ['vætɪkən] *n*: **the ~** o Vaticano.
vault [vɔːlt] *n* (*of roof*) abóbada; (*tomb*) sepulcro; (*in bank*) caixa-forte *f*; (*jump*) salto ♦ *vt* (*also*: *~ over*) saltar (por cima de).
vaunted ['vɔːntɪd] *adj*: **much-~** tão alardeado.
VC *n abbr* = **vice-chairman**; (BRIT: = *Victoria Cross*) *distinção militar*.
VCR *n abbr* = **video cassette recorder**.
VD *n abbr* = **venereal disease**.
VDU *n abbr* = **visual display unit**.
veal [viːl] *n* carne *f* de vitela.
veer [vɪə*] *vi* virar.
veg. [vɛdʒ] (BRIT: *inf*) *n abbr* = **vegetable(s)**.
vegetable ['vɛdʒtəbl] *n* (BOT) vegetal *m*; (*edible plant*) legume *m*, hortaliça ♦ *adj* vegetal; **~s** *npl* (*cooked*) verduras *fpl*.
vegetable garden *n* horta.
vegetarian [vɛdʒɪ'tɛərɪən] *adj*, *n* vegetariano/a.
vegetate ['vɛdʒɪteɪt] *vi* vegetar.
vegetation [vɛdʒɪ'teɪʃən] *n* vegetação *f*.
vehemence ['viːɪməns] *n* veemência, violência.
vehement ['viːɪmənt] *adj* veemente; (*impassioned*) apaixonado.
vehicle ['viːɪkl] *n* veículo.
vehicular [vɪ'hɪkjulə*] *adj*: **"no ~ traffic"** "proibido trânsito de veículos automotores".
veil [veɪl] *n* véu *m* ♦ *vt* velar; **under a ~ of secrecy** (*fig*) sob um manto de sigilo.
veiled [veɪld] *adj* velado.
vein [veɪn] *n* veia; (*of ore etc*) filão *m*; (*on leaf*) nervura; (*fig*: *mood*) tom *m*.
vellum ['vɛləm] *n* papel *m* velino.
velocity [vɪ'lɔsɪtɪ] *n* velocidade *f*.
velvet ['vɛlvɪt] *n* veludo ♦ *adj* aveludado.
vendetta [vɛn'dɛtə] *n* vendeta.
vending machine ['vɛndɪŋ-] *n* vendedor *m* automático.
vendor ['vɛndə*] *n* vendedor(a) *m/f*; **street ~** camelô *m*.
veneer [və'nɪə*] *n* capa exterior, folheado; (*wood*) compensado; (*fig*) aparência.
venerable ['vɛnərəbl] *adj* venerável.
venereal [vɪ'nɪərɪəl] *adj*: **~ disease** doença venérea.
Venetian blind [vɪ'niːʃən-] *n* persiana.
Venezuela [vɛnɛ'zweɪlə] *n* Venezuela.
Venezuelan [vɛnɛ'zweɪlən] *adj*, *n* venezuelano/a.
vengeance ['vɛndʒəns] *n* vingança; **with a ~** (*fig*) para valer.
vengeful ['vɛndʒful] *adj* vingativo.
Venice ['vɛnɪs] *n* Veneza.
venison ['vɛnɪsn] *n* carne *f* de veado.
venom ['vɛnəm] *n* veneno.
venomous ['vɛnəməs] *adj* venenoso.
vent [vɛnt] *n* (*opening*, *in jacket*) abertura; (*air-hole*) respiradouro; (*in wall*) abertura para ventilação ♦ *vt* (*fig*: *feelings*) desabafar, descarregar.
ventilate ['vɛntɪleɪt] *vt* ventilar.
ventilation [vɛntɪ'leɪʃən] *n* ventilação *f*.
ventilation shaft *n* poço de ventilação.
ventilator ['vɛntɪleɪtə*] *n* ventilador *m*.
ventriloquist [vɛn'trɪləkwɪst] *n* ventríloquo.
venture ['vɛntʃə*] *n* empreendimento ♦ *vt* aventurar; (*opinion*) arriscar ♦ *vi* arriscar-se, ousar; **a business ~** um empreendimento comercial; **to ~ to do sth** aventurar-se *or* arriscar-se a fazer algo.
venture capital *n* capital *m* de especulação.
venue ['vɛnjuː] *n* local *m*; (*meeting place*) ponto de encontro; (*theatre etc*) espaço.
Venus ['viːnəs] *n* (*planet*) Vênus *f*.
veracity [və'ræsɪtɪ] *n* veracidade *f*.
veranda(h) [və'rændə] *n* varanda.
verb [vəːb] *n* verbo.
verbal ['vəːbəl] *adj* verbal.
verbally ['vəːbəlɪ] *adv* verbalmente.
verbatim [vəː'beɪtɪm] *adj*, *adv* palavra por palavra.
verbose [vəː'bəus] *adj* prolixo.
verdict ['vəːdɪkt] *n* veredicto, decisão *f*; (*fig*) opinião *f*, parecer *m*; **~ of guilty/not guilty** veredicto de culpado/não culpado.
verge [vəːdʒ] *n* beira, margem *f*; (*on road*) acostamento (BR), berma (PT); **to be on the ~ of doing sth** estar a ponto *or* à beira de fazer algo.
verge on *vt fus* beirar em.
verger ['vəːdʒə*] *n* (REL) sacristão *m*.
verification [vɛrɪfɪ'keɪʃən] *n* verificação *f*.
verify ['vɛrɪfaɪ] *vt* verificar.
veritable ['vɛrɪtəbl] *adj* verdadeiro.

vermin ['vəːmɪn] *npl* (*animals*) bichos *mpl*; (*insects, fig*) insetos *mpl* nocivos.
vermouth ['vəːməθ] *n* vermute *m*.
vernacular [və'nækjulə*] *n* vernáculo; **in the ~** na língua corrente.
versatile ['vəːsətaɪl] *adj* (*person*) versátil; (*machine, tool etc*) polivalente; (*mind*) ágil, flexível.
verse [vəːs] *n* verso, poesia; (*stanza*) estrofe *f*; (*in bible*) versículo; **in ~** em verso.
versed [vəːst] *adj*: **(well-)~ in** versado em.
version ['vəːʃən] *n* versão *f*.
versus ['vəːsəs] *prep* contra, versus.
vertebra ['vəːtɪbrə] (*pl* **~e**) *n* vértebra.
vertebrae ['vəːtɪbriː] *npl of* **vertebra**.
vertebrate ['vəːtɪbrɪt] *n* vertebrado.
vertical ['vəːtɪkl] *adj* vertical ♦ *n* vertical *f*.
vertically ['vəːtɪklɪ] *adv* verticalmente.
vertigo ['vəːtɪgəu] *n* vertigem *f*; **to suffer from ~** ter vertigens.
verve [vəːv] *n* garra, pique *m*.
very ['vɛrɪ] *adv* muito ♦ *adj*: **the ~ book which** o mesmo livro que; **the ~ thought (of it)** ... só de pensar (nisso) ...; **at the ~ end** bem no final; **the ~ last** o último (de todos), bem o último; **at the ~ least** no mínimo; **~ much** muitíssimo; **~ little** muito pouco, pouquíssimo.
vespers ['vɛspəz] *npl* vésperas *fpl*.
vessel ['vɛsl] *n* (*ANAT*) vaso; (*NAUT*) navio, barco; (*container*) vaso, vasilha.
vest [vɛst] *n* (*BRIT*) camiseta (*BR*), camisola interior (*PT*); (*US*: *waistcoat*) colete *m* ♦ *vt*: **to ~ sb with sth, to ~ sth in sb** investir alguém de algo, conferir algo a alguém.
vested interest ['vɛstɪd-] *n*: **to have a ~ in doing** ter um interesse em fazer; **~s** *npl* (*COMM*) direitos *mpl* adquiridos.
vestibule ['vɛstɪbjuːl] *n* vestíbulo.
vestige ['vɛstɪdʒ] *n* vestígio.
vestry ['vɛstrɪ] *n* sacristia.
Vesuvius [vɪ'suːvɪəs] *n* Vesúvio.
vet [vɛt] *n abbr* (= *veterinary surgeon*) veterinário/a ♦ *vt* examinar.
veteran ['vɛtərn] *n* veterano/a; (*also*: *war ~*) veterano de guerra ♦ *adj*: **she's a ~ campaigner for** ... ela é uma veterana nas campanhas de ....
veteran car *n* carro antigo.
veterinarian [vɛtrɪ'nɛərɪən] (*US*) *n* veterinário/a.
veterinary ['vɛtrɪnərɪ] *adj* veterinário.
veterinary surgeon (*BRIT*) *n* veterinário/a.
veto ['viːtəu] (*pl* **~es**) *n* veto ♦ *vt* vetar; **to put a ~ on** opor seu veto a.
vex [vɛks] *vt* (*irritate*) irritar, apoquentar; (*make impatient*) impacientar.
vexed [vɛkst] *adj* (*question*) controvertido, discutido.
VFD (*US*) *n abbr* = **voluntary fire department**.
VG (*BRIT*) *n abbr* (*SCH*) = **very good**.
VHF *abbr* (= *very high frequency*) VHF, freqüência muito alta.
VI (*US*) *abbr* (*POST*) = **Virgin Islands**.
via ['vaɪə] *prep* por, via.
viability [vaɪə'bɪlɪtɪ] *n* viabilidade *f*.
viable ['vaɪəbl] *adj* viável.
viaduct ['vaɪədʌkt] *n* viaduto.
vibrant ['vaɪbrənt] *adj* (*sound, colour*) vibrante.
vibrate [vaɪ'breɪt] *vi* vibrar.
vibration [vaɪ'breɪʃən] *n* vibração *f*.
vicar ['vɪkə*] *n* vigário.
vicarage ['vɪkərɪdʒ] *n* vicariato.
vicarious [vɪ'kɛərɪəs] *adj* (*pleasure, existence*) indireto.
vice [vaɪs] *n* (*evil*) vício; (*TECH*) torno mecânico.
vice- [vaɪs] *prefix* vice-.
vice-chairman (*irreg*) *n* vice-presidente *m/f*.
vice-chancellor (*BRIT*) *n* reitor(a) *m/f*.
vice-president *n* vice-presidente *m/f*.
vice squad *n* delegacia de costumes.
vice versa ['vaɪsɪ'vəːsə] *adv* vice-versa.
vicinity [vɪ'sɪnɪtɪ] *n* (*area*) vizinhança; (*nearness*) proximidade *f*.
vicious ['vɪʃəs] *adj* (*violent*) violento; (*depraved*) depravado, vicioso; (*cruel*) cruel; (*bitter*) rancoroso; **a ~ circle** um círculo vicioso.
viciousness ['vɪʃəsnɪs] *n* violência; depravação *f*; crueldade *f*; rancor *m*.
vicissitudes [vɪ'sɪsɪtjuːdz] *npl* vicissitudes *fpl*.
victim ['vɪktɪm] *n* vítima *f*.
victimization [vɪktɪmaɪ'zeɪʃən] *n* perseguição *f*; (*in strike*) represálias *fpl*.
victimize ['vɪktɪmaɪz] *vt* (*strikers etc*) fazer represália contra.
victor ['vɪktə*] *n* vencedor(a) *m/f*.
Victorian [vɪk'tɔːrɪən] *adj* vitoriano.
victorious [vɪk'tɔːrɪəs] *adj* vitorioso.
victory ['vɪktərɪ] *n* vitória; **to win a ~ over sb** conseguir uma vitória sobre alguém.
video ['vɪdɪəu] *n* (*~ film*) vídeo; (*pop ~*) videoclipe *m*; (*also*: *~ cassette*) videocassete *m*; (*also*: *~ cassette recorder*) videocassete *m* ♦ *cpd* de vídeo.
video cassette *n* videocassete *m*.
video cassette recorder *n* videocassete *m*.
video recording *n* gravação *f* em vídeo.
video tape *n* videoteipe *m*; (*cassette*) videocassete *m*.
vie [vaɪ] *vi*: **to ~ with** competir com.
Vienna [vɪ'ɛnə] *n* Viena.
Viet Nam ['vjɛt'næm] *n* = **Vietnam**.
Vietnam ['vjɛt'næm] *n* Vietnã *m* (*BR*), Vietname *m* (*PT*).
Vietnamese [vjɛtnə'miːz] *adj* vietnamita ♦ *n inv* vietnamita *m/f*; (*LING*) vietnamita *m*.
view [vjuː] *n* vista, perspectiva; (*landscape*) paisagem *f*; (*opinion*) opinião *f*, parecer *m* ♦ *vt* (*look at*) olhar; (*examine*) examinar; **on ~** (*in museum etc*) em exposição; **in full ~ (of)** à plena vista (de); **an overall ~ of the**

***NB**: European Portuguese adds the following consonants to certain words:* **b** (sú(b)dito, su(b)til); **c** (a(c)ção, a(c)cionista, a(c)to); **m** (inde(m)ne); **p** (ado(p)ção, ado(p)tar); *for further details see p. xiii.*

situation uma visão geral da situação; **in my ~** na minha opinião; **in ~ of the fact that** em vista do fato de que; **with a ~ to doing sth** com a intenção de fazer algo.
viewdata ['vju:deɪtə] (*BRIT*) *n* teletexto, videotexto.
viewer ['vju:ə*] *n* (*small projector*) visor *m*; (*TV*) telespectador(a) *m/f*.
viewfinder ['vju:faɪndə*] *n* visor *m*.
viewpoint ['vju:pɔɪnt] *n* ponto de vista.
vigil ['vɪdʒɪl] *n* vigília; **to keep ~** velar.
vigilance ['vɪdʒɪləns] *n* vigilância.
vigilance committee *n* comitê *m* de vigilância.
vigilant ['vɪdʒɪlənt] *adj* vigilante.
vigor ['vɪgə*] (*US*) *n* = **vigour**.
vigorous ['vɪgərəs] *adj* enérgico, vigoroso.
vigour ['vɪgə*] (*US* **vigor**) *n* energia, vigor *m*.
vile [vaɪl] *adj* (*action*) vil, infame; (*smell*) repugnante, repulsivo; (*temper*) violento.
vilify ['vɪlɪfaɪ] *vt* vilipendiar.
villa ['vɪlə] *n* (*country house*) casa de campo; (*suburban house*) vila, quinta.
village ['vɪlɪdʒ] *n* aldeia, povoado.
villager ['vɪlɪdʒə*] *n* aldeão/aldeã *m/f*.
villain ['vɪlən] *n* (*scoundrel*) patife *m*; (*criminal*) marginal *m/f*; (*in novel etc*) vilão *m*.
VIN (*US*) *n abbr* = **vehicle identification number**.
vindicate ['vɪndɪkeɪt] *vt* vingar, desagravar.
vindication [vɪndɪ'keɪʃən] *n*: **in ~ of** em defesa de.
vindictive [vɪn'dɪktɪv] *adj* vingativo.
vine [vaɪn] *n* vinha, videira; (*climbing plant*) planta trepadeira.
vinegar ['vɪnɪgə*] *n* vinagre *m*.
vine grower *n* vinhateiro/a, viticultor(a) *m/f*.
vine-growing *adj* vitícola ♦ *n* viticultura.
vineyard ['vɪnjɑ:d] *n* vinha, vinhedo.
vintage ['vɪntɪdʒ] *n* vindima; (*year*) safra, colheita; **the 1970 ~** a safra de 1970.
vintage car *n* carro antigo.
vintage wine *n* vinho velho.
vinyl ['vaɪnl] *n* vinil *m*.
viola [vɪ'əulə] *n* viola.
violate ['vaɪəleɪt] *vt* violar.
violation [vaɪə'leɪʃən] *n* violação *f*; **in ~ of** (*rule, law*) em violação de.
violence ['vaɪələns] *n* violência.
violent ['vaɪələnt] *adj* violento; (*intense*) intenso; **a ~ dislike of sb/sth** uma forte aversão a alguém/algo.
violently ['vaɪələntlɪ] *adv* violentemente; (*ill, angry*) extremamente.
violet ['vaɪələt] *adj* violeta ♦ *n* (*plant*) violeta.
violin [vaɪə'lɪn] *n* violino.
violinist [vaɪə'lɪnɪst] *n* violinista *m/f*.
VIP *n abbr* (= *very important person*) VIP *m/f*.
viper ['vaɪpə*] *n* víbora.
virgin ['və:dʒɪn] *n* virgem *m/f* ♦ *adj* virgem; **the Blessed V~** a Virgem Santíssima.
virginity [və:'dʒɪnɪtɪ] *n* virgindade *f*.
Virgo ['və:gəu] *n* Virgem *f*.
virile ['vɪraɪl] *adj* viril.
virility [vɪ'rɪlɪtɪ] *n* virilidade *f*.
virtual ['və:tjuəl] *adj* (*COMPUT, PHYSICS*) virtual; (*in effect*): **it's a ~ impossibility** é praticamente impossível; **the ~ leader** o líder na prática.
virtually ['və:tjuəlɪ] *adv* (*almost*) praticamente.
virtue ['və:tju:] *n* virtude *f*; (*advantage*) vantagem *f*; **by ~ of** em virtude de.
virtuoso [və:tju'əuzəu] *n* virtuoso/a.
virtuous ['və:tjuəs] *adj* virtuoso.
virulent ['vɪrulənt] *adj* virulento.
virus ['vaɪərəs] *n* vírus *m*.
visa ['vi:zə] *n* visto.
vis-à-vis [vi:zə'vi:] *prep* com relação a.
viscount ['vaɪkaunt] *n* visconde *m*.
viscous ['vɪskəs] *adj* viscoso.
vise [vaɪs] (*US*) *n* (*TECH*) = **vice**.
visibility [vɪzɪ'bɪlɪtɪ] *n* visibilidade *f*.
visible ['vɪzəbl] *adj* visível; **~ exports/imports** exportações *fpl*/importações *fpl* visíveis.
visibly ['vɪzəblɪ] *adv* visivelmente.
vision ['vɪʒən] *n* (*sight*) vista, visão *f*; (*foresight, in dream*) visão *f*.
visionary ['vɪʒənərɪ] *n* visionário/a.
visit ['vɪzɪt] *n* visita ♦ *vt* (*person*) visitar, fazer uma visita a; (*place*) ir a, ir conhecer; **on a private/official ~** em visita particular/oficial.
visiting ['vɪzɪtɪŋ] *adj* (*speaker, team*) visitante.
visiting card *n* cartão *m* de visita.
visiting hours *npl* horário de visita.
visiting professor *n* professor(a) *m/f* de outra faculdade.
visitor ['vɪzɪtə*] *n* visitante *m/f*; (*to one's house*) visita; (*tourist*) turista *m/f*; (*tripper*) excursionista *m/f*.
visitors' book *n* livro de visitas.
visor ['vaɪzə*] *n* viseira.
VISTA ['vɪstə] *n abbr* (= *Volunteers in Service to America*) *programa de assistência às regiões pobres*.
vista ['vɪstə] *n* vista, perspectiva.
visual ['vɪzjuəl] *adj* visual.
visual aid *n* meio visual (de ensino).
visual display unit *n* terminal *m* de vídeo.
visualize ['vɪzjuəlaɪz] *vt* visualizar; (*foresee*) prever.
visually ['vɪzjuəlɪ] *adv* visualmente; **~ handicapped** deficiente visual.
vital ['vaɪtl] *adj* (*essential*) essencial, indispensável; (*important*) de importância vital; (*crucial*) crucial; (*of life*) vital; **of ~ importance** de importância vital.
vitality [vaɪ'tælɪtɪ] *n* energia, vitalidade *f*.
vitally ['vaɪtəlɪ] *adv*: **~ important** de importância vital.
vital statistics *npl* (*of population*) estatística demográfica; (*inf*: *woman's*) medidas *fpl*.
vitamin ['vɪtəmɪn] *n* vitamina.
vitiate ['vɪʃɪeɪt] *vt* viciar.
vitreous ['vɪtrɪəs] *adj* vítreo.
vitriolic [vɪtrɪ'ɔlɪk] *adj* (*fig*) mordaz.
viva ['vaɪvə] *n* (*also*: *~ voce*) exame *m* oral.
vivacious [vɪ'veɪʃəs] *adj* vivaz, animado.

vivacity [vɪ'væsɪtɪ] *n* vivacidade *f*.
vivid ['vɪvɪd] *adj* (*account*) vívido; (*light*) claro, brilhante; (*imagination*) vivo.
vividly ['vɪvɪdlɪ] *adv* (*describe*) vividamente; (*remember*) distintamente.
vivisection [vɪvɪ'sɛkʃən] *n* vivissecção *f*.
vixen ['vɪksn] *n* raposa; (*pej*: *woman*) megera.
viz *abbr* (= *videlicet*: *namely*) a saber.
VLF *abbr* = **very low frequency**.
V-neck *n* decote *m* em V.
VOA *n abbr* (= *Voice of America*) voz *f* da América, *emissora que transmite para o estrangeiro*.
vocabulary [vəu'kæbjulərɪ] *n* vocabulário.
vocal ['vəukl] *adj* vocal; (*noisy*) clamoroso.
vocal cords *npl* cordas *fpl* vocais.
vocalist ['vəukəlɪst] *n* vocalista *m/f*, cantor(a) *m/f*.
vocals ['vəuklz] *npl* vozes *fpl*.
vocation [vəu'keɪʃən] *n* vocação *f*.
vocational [vəu'keɪʃənl] *adj* vocacional; ~ **guidance/training** orientação *f* vocacional/ensino profissionalizante.
vociferous [və'sɪfərəs] *adj* vociferante.
vodka ['vɔdkə] *n* vodca.
vogue [vəug] *n* voga, moda; **to be in ~** estar na moda.
voice [vɔɪs] *n* voz *f* ♦ *vt* (*opinion*) expressar; **in a low/loud ~** em voz baixa/alta; **to give ~ to** dar voz a.
void [vɔɪd] *n* vazio; (*hole*) oco ♦ *adj* (*null*) nulo; **~ of** destituido de.
voile [vɔɪl] *n* voile *m*.
vol. *abbr* (= *volume*) vol.
volatile ['vɔlətaɪl] *adj* volátil.
volcanic [vɔl'kænɪk] *adj* vulcânico.
volcano [vɔl'keɪnəu] (*pl* **~es**) *n* vulcão *m*.
volition [və'lɪʃən] *n*: **of one's own ~** de livre vontade.
volley ['vɔlɪ] *n* (*of gunfire*) descarga, salva; (*of stones etc*) chuva; (*TENNIS etc*) voleio.
volleyball ['vɔlɪbɔːl] *n* voleibol *m*, vôlei *m* (*BR*).
volt [vəult] *n* volt *m*.
voltage ['vəultɪdʒ] *n* voltagem *f*; **high/low ~** alta/baixa tensão.
voluble ['vɔljubl] *adj* tagarela, loquaz.
volume ['vɔljuːm] *n* volume *m*; (*of tank*) capacidade *f*; **~ one/two** tomo um/dois; **his expression spoke ~s** sua expressão disse tudo.
volume control *n* (*RADIO, TV*) controle *m* de volume.
volume discount *n* (*COMM*) desconto de volume.
voluminous [və'luːmɪnəs] *adj* volumoso.
voluntarily ['vɔləntrɪlɪ] *adv* livremente, voluntariamente.
voluntary ['vɔləntərɪ] *adj* voluntário, intencional; (*unpaid*) (a título) gratuito.
voluntary liquidation *n* (*COMM*) liquidação *f* requerida pela empresa.
voluntary redundancy (*BRIT*) *n* demissão *f* voluntária.
volunteer [vɔlən'tɪə*] *n* voluntário/a ♦ *vi* (*MIL*) alistar-se voluntariamente; **to ~ to do** oferecer-se voluntariamente para fazer.
voluptuous [və'lʌptjuəs] *adj* voluptuoso.
vomit ['vɔmɪt] *n* vômito ♦ *vt, vi* vomitar.
vote [vəut] *n* voto; (*votes cast*) votação *f*; (*right to ~*) direito de votar; (*franchise*) título de eleitor ♦ *vt* (*chairman*) eleger ♦ *vi* votar; **to put sth to the ~, to take a ~ on sth** votar algo, submeter algo à votação; **to ~ for sb** votar em alguém; **to ~ for/against a proposal** votar a favor de/contra uma proposta; **to ~ to do sth** votar a favor de fazer algo; **~ of censure** voto de censura; **~ of confidence** voto de confiança; **~ of thanks** agradecimento.
voter ['vəutə*] *n* votante *m/f*, eleitor(a) *m/f*.
voting ['vəutɪŋ] *n* votação *f*.
voting paper (*BRIT*) *n* cédula eleitoral.
voting right *n* direito de voto.
vouch for [vautʃ-] *vt fus* garantir, responder por.
voucher ['vautʃə*] *n* (*for meal, petrol*) vale *m*; (*receipt*) comprovante *m*.
vow [vau] *n* voto ♦ *vi* fazer votos; **to take** *or* **make a ~ to do sth** fazer voto de fazer algo.
vowel ['vauəl] *n* vogal *f*.
voyage ['vɔɪɪdʒ] *n* (*journey*) viagem *f*; (*crossing*) travessia.
VP *n abbr* = **vice-president**.
vs *abbr* (= *versus*) x.
VSO (*BRIT*) *n abbr* = **Voluntary Service Overseas**.
VT (*US*) *abbr* (*POST*) = **Vermont**.
vulgar ['vʌlgə*] *adj* (*rude*) grosseiro, ordinário; (*in bad taste*) vulgar, baixo.
vulgarity [vʌl'gærɪtɪ] *n* grosseria, vulgaridade *f*.
vulnerability [vʌlnərə'bɪlɪtɪ] *n* vulnerabilidade *f*.
vulnerable ['vʌlnərəbl] *adj* vulnerável.
vulture ['vʌltʃə*] *n* abutre *m*, urubu *m*.

W

W, w ['dʌbljuː] *n* (*letter*) W, w *m*; **W for William** W de William.
W *abbr* (= *west*) o; (*ELEC*: = *watt*) W.
WA (*US*) *abbr* (*POST*) = **Washington**.
wad [wɔd] *n* (*of cotton wool*) chumaço; (*of paper*) bola; (*of banknotes etc*) maço.
wadding ['wɔdɪŋ] *n* enchimento.
waddle ['wɔdl] *vi* andar gingando *or* bambo-

***NB**: European Portuguese adds the following consonants to certain words:* **b** (sú(b)dito, su(b)til); **c** (a(c)ção, a(c)cionista, a(c)to); **m** (inde(m)ne); **p** (ado(p)ção, ado(p)tar); *for further details see* *p. xiii*.

leando.

wade [weɪd] *vi*: **to ~ through** andar em; (*fig*: *a book*) ler com dificuldade ♦ *vt* vadear, atravessar (a vau).

wafer ['weɪfə*] *n* (*biscuit*) bolacha; (*REL*) hóstia; (*COMPUT*) pastilha.

wafer-thin *adj* fininho, finíssimo.

waffle ['wɔfl] *n* (*CULIN*) waffle *m*; (*inf*) lengalenga ♦ *vi* lengalengar.

waffle iron *n* fôrma para fazer waffles.

waft [wɔft] *vt* levar ♦ *vi* flutuar.

wag [wæg] *vt* sacudir, menear ♦ *vi* acenar, abanar; **the dog ~ged its tail** o cachorro abanou o rabo.

wage [weɪdʒ] *n* (*also*: *~s*) salário, ordenado ♦ *vt*: **to ~ war** empreender *or* fazer guerra; **a day's ~s** uma diária.

wage claim *n* reivindicação *f* salarial.

wage differential *n* desnível *m* salarial, diferença de salário.

wage earner ['weɪdʒ'ɜːnə*] *n* assalariado/a.

wage freeze *n* congelamento de salários.

wage packet (*BRIT*) *n* envelope *m* de pagamento.

wager ['weɪdʒə*] *n* aposta, parada ♦ *vt* apostar.

waggle ['wægl] *vt* sacudir, agitar.

wag(g)on ['wægən] *n* (*horse-drawn*) carroça; (*BRIT*: *RAIL*) vagão *m*.

wail [weɪl] *n* lamento, gemido ♦ *vi* lamentar-se, gemer.

waist [weɪst] *n* cintura.

waistcoat ['weɪskəut] (*BRIT*) *n* colete *m*.

waistline ['weɪstlaɪn] *n* cintura.

wait [weɪt] *n* espera ♦ *vi* esperar; **to lie in ~ for** aguardar em emboscada; **I can't ~ to** (*fig*) estou morrendo de vontade de; **to ~ for** esperar, aguardar; **to keep sb ~ing** deixar alguém esperando; **~ a minute!** espera aí!; **"repairs while you ~"** "conserta-se na hora".

wait behind *vi* ficar para trás.

wait on *vt fus* servir.

wait up *vi* esperar, não ir dormir; **don't ~ up for me** vá dormir, não espere por mim.

waiter ['weɪtə*] *n* garçom *m* (*BR*), empregado (*PT*).

waiting ['weɪtɪŋ] *n*: **"no ~"** (*BRIT*: *AUT*) "proibido estacionar".

waiting list ['weɪtɪŋ-] *n* lista de espera.

waiting room *n* sala de espera.

waitress ['weɪtrɪs] *n* garçonete *f* (*BR*), empregada (*PT*).

waive [weɪv] *vt* renunciar a.

waiver ['weɪvə*] *n* desistência.

wake [weɪk] (*pt* **woke**, *pp* **woken**) *vt*, *vi* (*also*: *~ up*) acordar ♦ *n* (*for dead person*) velório; (*NAUT*) esteira; **to ~ up to sth** (*fig*) abrir os olhos *or* acordar para algo; **in the ~ of** (*fig*) na esteira de; **to follow in sb's ~** (*fig*) seguir a esteira *or* o exemplo de alguém.

waken ['weɪkən] *vt*, *vi* = **wake**.

Wales [weɪlz] *n* País *m* de Gales.

walk [wɔːk] *n* passeio; (*hike*) excursão *f* a pé, caminhada; (*gait*) passo, modo de andar; (*in park etc*) alameda, passeio ♦ *vi* andar; (*for pleasure, exercise*) passear ♦ *vt* (*distance*) percorrer a pé, andar; (*dog*) levar para passear; **it's 10 minutes' ~ from here** daqui são 10 minutos a pé; **to go for a ~** (ir) dar uma volta; **I'll ~ you home** vou andar com você até a sua casa; **people from all ~s of life** pessoas de todos os níveis.

walk out *vi* (*go out*) sair; (*strike*) entrar em greve; **to ~ out on sb** abandonar alguém.

walker ['wɔːkə*] *n* (*person*) caminhante *m/f*.

walkie-talkie ['wɔːkɪ'tɔːkɪ] *n* transmissor-receptor *m* portátil, walkie-talkie *m*.

walking ['wɔːkɪŋ] *n* o andar; **it's within ~ distance** dá para ir a pé.

walking holiday *n* férias *fpl* fazendo excursões a pé.

walking shoes *npl* sapatos *mpl* para andar.

walking stick *n* bengala.

walk-on *adj* (*THEATRE*: *part*) de figurante.

walkout ['wɔːkaut] *n* (*of workers*) greve *f* branca.

walkover ['wɔːkəuvə*] (*inf*) *n* barbada.

walkway ['wɔːkweɪ] *n* passeio, passadiço.

wall [wɔːl] *n* parede *f*; (*exterior*) muro; (*city ~ etc*) muralha; **to go to the ~** (*fig*: *firm etc*) falir, quebrar.

wall in *vt* (*garden etc*) cercar com muros.

wall cupboard *n* armário de parede.

walled [wɔːld] *adj* (*city*) cercado por muralhas; (*garden*) murado, cercado.

wallet ['wɔlɪt] *n* carteira.

wallflower ['wɔːlflauə*] *n* goivo-amarelo; **to be a ~** (*fig*) tomar chá de cadeira.

wall hanging *n* tapete *m*.

wallop ['wɔləp] (*BRIT*: *inf*) *vt* surrar, espancar.

wallow ['wɔləu] *vi* chafurdar, deitar e rolar; **to ~ in one's own grief** regozijar-se na própria dor.

wallpaper ['wɔːlpeɪpə*] *n* papel *m* de parede.

wall-to-wall *adj*: **~ carpeting** carpete *m*.

wally ['wɔlɪ] (*inf*) *n* mané *m*, boboca *m*.

walnut ['wɔːlnʌt] *n* noz *f*; (*tree*) nogueira.

walrus ['wɔːlrəs] (*pl* **~** *or* **~es**) *n* morsa, vaca marinha.

waltz [wɔːlts] *n* valsa ♦ *vi* valsar.

wan [wɔn] *adj* pálido.

wand [wɔnd] *n* (*also*: *magic ~*) varinha de condão.

wander ['wɔndə*] *vi* (*person*) vagar, perambular; (*thoughts*) divagar; (*get lost*) extraviar-se ♦ *vt* percorrer.

wanderer ['wɔndərə*] *n* vagabundo/a.

wandering ['wɔndərɪŋ] *adj* errante; (*thoughts*) distraído; (*tribe*) nômade; (*minstrel, actor*) itinerante.

wane [weɪn] *vi* diminuir; (*moon*) minguar.

wangle ['wæŋgl] (*inf*) *vt*: **to ~ sth** conseguir algo através de pistolão.

want [wɔnt] *vt* (*wish for*) querer; (*demand*) exigir; (*need*) precisar de, necessitar; (*lack*) carecer de ♦ *n* (*poverty*) pobreza, miséria;

~s *npl* (*needs*) necessidades *fpl*; **for ~ of** por falta de; **to ~ to do** querer fazer; **to ~ sb to do sth** querer que alguém faça algo; **you're ~ed on the phone** estão querendo falar com você no telefone; **"cook ~ed"** "precisa-se cozinheiro".

want ads (*US*) *npl* classificados *mpl*.

wanting ['wɔntɪŋ] *adj* falto, deficiente; **to be found ~** não estar à altura da situação; **to be ~ in** carecer de.

wanton ['wɔntən] *adj* (*destruction*) gratuito, irresponsável; (*licentious*) libertino, lascivo.

war [wɔː*] *n* guerra; **to make ~** fazer guerra; **to go to ~** entrar na guerra; **~ of attrition** guerra de atrição.

warble ['wɔːbl] *n* gorjeio ♦ *vi* gorjear.

war cry *n* grito de guerra.

ward [wɔːd] *n* (*in hospital*) ala; (*POL*) distrito eleitoral; (*LAW*: *child*) tutelado/a, pupilo/a.
ward off *vt* desviar, aparar; (*attack*) repelir.

warden ['wɔːdn] *n* (*BRIT*: *of institution*) diretor(a) *m/f*; (*of park, game reserve*) administrador(a) *m/f*; (*BRIT*: *also*: *traffic ~*) guarda *m/f*.

warder ['wɔːdə*] (*BRIT*) *n* carcereiro/a.

wardrobe ['wɔːdrəub] *n* (*cupboard*) armário; (*clothes*) guarda-roupa *m*.

warehouse ['wɛəhaus] (*irreg*) *n* armazém *m*, depósito.

wares [wɛəz] *npl* mercadorias *fpl*.

warfare ['wɔːfɛə*] *n* guerra, combate *m*.

war game *n* jogo de estrategia militar.

warhead ['wɔːhɛd] *n* ogiva.

warily ['wɛərɪlɪ] *adv* cautelosamente, com precaução.

warlike ['wɔːlaɪk] *adj* guerreiro, bélico.

warm [wɔːm] *adj* (*clothes, day*) quente; (*thanks, welcome*) caloroso, cordial; (*supporter*) entusiasmado; **it's ~** está quente; **I'm ~** estou com calor; **to keep sth ~** manter algo aquecido.
warm up *vi* (*person, room*) aquecer, esquentar; (*athlete*) fazer aquecimento; (*discussion*) esquentar-se ♦ *vt* esquentar.

warm-blooded [-'blʌdɪd] *adj* de sangue quente.

war memorial *n* monumento aos mortos.

warm-hearted [-'hɑːtɪd] *adj* afetuoso.

warmly ['wɔːmlɪ] *adv* calorosamente, afetuosamente.

warmonger ['wɔːmʌŋgə*] *n* belicista *m/f*.

warmongering ['wɔːmʌŋgərɪŋ] *n* belicismo.

warmth [wɔːmθ] *n* calor *m*.

warm-up *n* (*SPORT*) aquecimento.

warn [wɔːn] *vt* prevenir, avisar; **to ~ sb against sth** prevenir alguém contra algo; **to ~ sb not to do sth** *or* **against doing sth** prevenir alguém de não fazer algo.

warning ['wɔːnɪŋ] *n* advertência, aviso; **without (any) ~** (*suddenly*) de improviso, inopinadamente; (*without notice*) sem aviso prévio, sem avisar; **gale ~** (*METEOROLOGY*) aviso de vendaval.

warning light *n* luz *f* de advertência.

warning triangle *n* (*AUT*) triângulo de advertência.

warp [wɔːp] *n* (*TEXTILES*) urdidura ♦ *vt* deformar ♦ *vi* empenar, deformar-se.

warpath ['wɔːpɑːθ] *n*: **to be on the ~** (*fig*) estar disposto a brigar.

warped [wɔːpt] *adj* (*wood*) empenado; (*fig*: *sense of humour*) pervertido, deformado.

warrant ['wɔrnt] *n* (*guarantee*) garantia; (*LAW*: *to arrest*) mandado de prisão; (: *to search*) mandado de busca ♦ *vt* (*justify*) justificar.

warrant officer *n* (*MIL*) subtenente *m*; (*NAUT*) suboficial *m*.

warranty ['wɔrəntɪ] *n* garantia; **under ~** (*COMM*) sob garantia.

warren ['wɔrən] *n* (*of rabbits*) lura; (*house*) coelheira.

warring ['wɔːrɪŋ] *adj* (*nations*) em guerra; (*interests etc*) antagônico.

warrior ['wɔrɪə*] *n* guerreiro/a.

Warsaw ['wɔːsɔː] *n* Varsóvia.

warship ['wɔːʃɪp] *n* navio de guerra.

wart [wɔːt] *n* verruga.

wartime ['wɔːtaɪm] *n*: **in ~** em tempo de guerra.

wary ['wɛərɪ] *adj* cauteloso, precavido; **to be ~ about** *or* **of doing sth** hesitar em fazer algo.

was [wɔz] *pt of* **be**.

wash [wɔʃ] *vt* lavar; (*sweep, carry*: *sea etc*) levar, arrastar; (: *ashore*) lançar ♦ *vi* lavar-se ♦ *n* (*clothes etc*) lavagem *f*; (*of ship*) esteira; **to have a ~** lavar-se; **to give sth a ~** lavar algo; **he was ~ed overboard** foi arrastado do navio pelas águas.
wash away *vt* (*stain*) tirar ao lavar; (*subj*: *river etc*) levar, arrastar.
wash down *vt* lavar; (*food*) regar.
wash off *vt* tirar lavando ♦ *vi* sair ao lavar.
wash up *vi* lavar a louça; (*US*) lavar-se.

washable ['wɔʃəbl] *adj* lavável.

washbasin ['wɔʃbeɪsn] *n* pia (*BR*), lavatório (*PT*).

washbowl ['wɔʃbəul] (*US*) *n* = **washbasin**.

washcloth ['wɔʃklɔθ] (*US*) *n* pano para lavar o rosto.

washer ['wɔʃə*] *n* (*TECH*) arruela, anilha.

wash-hand basin (*BRIT*) *n* pia (*BR*), lavatório (*PT*).

washing ['wɔʃɪŋ] (*BRIT*) *n* (*dirty*) roupa suja; (*clean*) roupa lavada.

washing line (*BRIT*) *n* corda de estender roupa, varal *m*.

washing machine *n* máquina de lavar roupa, lavadora.

washing powder (*BRIT*) *n* sabão *m* em pó.

Washington ['wɔʃɪŋtən] *n* (*city, state*) Washington.

***NB**: European Portuguese adds the following consonants to certain words:* **b** (sú(b)dito, su(b)til); **c** (a(c)ção, a(c)cionista, a(c)to); **m** (inde(m)ne); **p** (ado(p)ção, ado(p)tar); *for further details see p. xiii.*

washing-up *n*: **to do the ~** lavar a louça.
washing-up liquid (*BRIT*) *n* detergente *m*.
wash-out (*inf*) *n* fracasso, fiasco.
washroom ['wɔʃru:m] *n* banheiro (*BR*), casa de banho (*PT*).
wasn't ['wɔznt] = **was not.**
WASP [wɔsp] (*US*: *inf*) *n abbr* (= *White Anglo-Saxon Protestant*) *apelido, muitas vezes pejorativo, dado aos membros da classe dominante nos EUA*.
Wasp [wɔsp] (*US*: *inf*) = **WASP**.
wasp [wɔsp] *n* vespa.
waspish ['wɔspɪʃ] *adj* irritadiço.
wastage ['weɪstɪdʒ] *n* desgaste *m*, desperdício; (*loss*) perda; **natural ~** desgaste natural.
waste [weɪst] *n* desperdício, esbanjamento; (*wastage*) desperdício; (*of time*) perda; (*food*) sobras *fpl*; (*rubbish*) lixo ♦ *adj* (*material*) de refugo; (*left over*) de sobra; (*land*) baldio ♦ *vt* (*squander*) esbanjar, desperdiçar; (*time, opportunity*) perder; **~s** *npl* ermos *mpl*; **it's a ~ of money** é jogar dinheiro fora; **to go to ~** ser desperdiçado; **to lay ~** (*destroy*) devastar.
waste away *vi* definhar.
wastebin ['weɪstbɪn] (*BRIT*) *n* lata de lixo.
waste disposal (unit) (*BRIT*) *n* triturador *m* de lixo.
wasteful ['weɪstful] *adj* esbanjador(a); (*process*) anti-econômico.
waste ground (*BRIT*) *n* terreno baldio.
wasteland ['weɪstlənd] *n* terra inculta; (*in town*) terreno baldio.
wastepaper basket ['weɪstpeɪpə*-] *n* cesta de papéis.
waste pipe *n* cano de esgoto.
waste products *n* (*INDUSTRY*) resíduos *mpl*.
watch [wɔtʃ] *n* (*clock*) relógio; (*act of ~ing*) vigia; (*guard*: *MIL*) sentinela; (*NAUT*: *spell of duty*) quarto ♦ *vt* (*look at*) observar, olhar; (*programme, match*) assistir a; (*television*) ver; (*spy on, guard*) vigiar; (*be careful of*) tomar cuidado com ♦ *vi* ver, olhar; (*keep guard*) montar guarda; **to keep a close ~ on sb/sth** vigiar alguém/algo, ficar de olho em alguém/algo; **~ what you're doing** presta atenção no que você está fazendo.
watch out *vi* ter cuidado.
watchband ['wɔtʃbænd] (*US*) *n* pulseira de relógio.
watchdog ['wɔtʃdɔg] *n* cão *m* de guarda; (*fig*) vigia *m/f*.
watchful ['wɔtʃful] *adj* vigilante, atento.
watchmaker ['wɔtʃmeɪkə*] *n* relojoeiro/a.
watchman ['wɔtʃmən] (*irreg*) *n* vigia *m*; (*also*: *night ~*) guarda *m* noturno; (: *in factory*) vigia *m* noturno.
watch stem (*US*) *n* botão *m* de corda.
watch strap *n* pulseira de relógio.
watchword ['wɔtʃwə:d] *n* lema *m*, divisa.
water ['wɔ:tə*] *n* água ♦ *vt* (*plant*) regar ♦ *vi* (*eyes*) lacrimejar; **a drink of ~** um copo d'água; **in British ~s** nas águas territoriais britânicas; **to pass ~** urinar; **to make sb's mouth ~** dar água na boca de alguém.
water down *vt* (*milk*) aguar; (*fig*) diluir.
water closet (*BRIT*) *n* privada.
watercolour ['wɔ:təkʌlə*] (*US* **watercolor**) *n* aquarela.
water-cooled [-ku:ld] *adj* refrigerado a água.
watercress ['wɔ:təkrɛs] *n* agrião *m*.
waterfall ['wɔ:təfɔ:l] *n* cascata, cachoeira.
waterfront ['wɔ:təfrʌnt] *n* (*seafront*) orla marítima; (*docks*) zona portuária.
water heater *n* aquecedor *m* de água, boiler *m*.
water hole *n* bebedouro, poço.
water ice (*BRIT*) *n sorvete de frutas à base de água*.
watering can ['wɔ:tərɪŋ-] *n* regador *m*.
water level *n* nível *m* d'água.
water lily *n* nenúfar *m*.
waterline ['wɔ:təlaɪn] *n* (*NAUT*) linha d'água.
waterlogged ['wɔ:təlɔgd] *adj* alagado.
water main *n* adutora.
watermark ['wɔ:təmɑ:k] *n* (*on paper*) filigrana.
watermelon ['wɔ:təmɛlən] *n* melancia.
water polo *n* pólo aquático.
waterproof ['wɔ:təpru:f] *adj* impermeável; (*watch*) à prova d'água.
water-repellent *adj* hidrófugo.
watershed ['wɔ:təʃɛd] *n* (*GEO*) linha divisória das águas; (*fig*) momento crítico.
water-skiing *n* esqui *m* aquático.
water softener *n* abrandador *m* de água.
water tank *n* depósito d'água.
watertight ['wɔ:tətaɪt] *adj* hermético, à prova d'água.
water vapour *n* vapor *m* de água.
waterway ['wɔ:təweɪ] *n* hidrovia.
waterworks ['wɔ:təwə:ks] *npl* usina hidráulica.
watery ['wɔ:tərɪ] *adj* (*colour*) pálido; (*coffee*) aguado; (*eyes*) húmido.
watt [wɔt] *n* watt *m*.
wattage ['wɔtɪdʒ] *n* wattagem *f*.
wattle ['wɔtl] *n* caniçada.
wave [weɪv] *n* (*gen, RADIO*) onda; (*of hand*) aceno, sinal *m*; (*in hair*) onda, ondulação *f* ♦ *vi* acenar com a mão; (*flag*) tremular, flutuar ♦ *vt* (*handkerchief*) acenar com; (*weapon*) brandir; (*hair*) ondular; **to ~ goodbye to sb** despedir-se de alguém com um aceno; **short/medium/long ~** (*RADIO*) ondas curtas/médias/longas; **the new ~** (*CINEMA, MUS*) a nova onda.
wave aside *vt* (*fig*: *suggestion, objection*) rejeitar; (: *doubts*) pôr de lado; (*person*): **to ~ sb aside** fazer sinal para alguém pôr-se de lado.
wave away *vt* (*fig*: *suggestion, objection*) rejeitar; (: *doubts*) pôr de lado; (*person*): **to ~ sb away** fazer sinal para alguém pôr-se de lado.
waveband ['weɪvbænd] *n* faixa de onda.
wavelength ['weɪvlɛŋθ] *n* comprimento de onda.
waver ['weɪvə*] *vi* vacilar.

wavy ['weɪvɪ] *adj* ondulado, ondulante.
wax [wæks] *n* cera ♦ *vt* encerar ♦ *vi* (*moon*) crescer.
waxworks ['wækswəːks] *npl* museu *m* de cera.
way [weɪ] *n* caminho; (*distance*) percurso; (*direction*) direção *f*, sentido; (*manner*) maneira, modo; (*habit*) costume *m*; (*condition*) estado; **which ~? — this ~** por onde? — por aqui; **to crawl one's ~ to ...** arrastar-se até ...; **to lie one's ~ out of it** mentir para livrar-se de apuros; **on the ~ (to)** a caminho (de); **to be on one's ~** estar a caminho; **to be in the ~** atrapalhar; **to keep out of sb's ~** evitar alguém; **it's a long ~ away** é muito longe; **the village is rather out of the ~** o lugarejo é um pouco fora de mão; **to go out of one's ~ to do sth** (*fig*) dar-se ao trabalho de fazer algo; **to lose one's ~** perder-se; **to be under ~** (*work, project*) estar em andamento; **to make ~ (for sb/sth)** abrir caminho (para alguém/algo); **to get one's own ~** conseguir o que quer; **to put sth the right ~ up** (*BRIT*) colocar algo na posição certa; **to be the wrong ~ round** estar às avessas; **he's in a bad ~** ele vai muito mal; **in a ~** de certo modo, até certo ponto; **in some ~s** a certos respeitos; **by the ~** a propósito; **"~ in"** (*BRIT*) "entrada"; **"~ out"** (*BRIT*) "saída"; **the ~ back** o caminho de volta; **"give ~"** (*AUT*) "dê a preferência"; **in the ~ of** em matéria de; **by ~ of** (*through*) por, via; (*as a sort of*) à guisa de; **no ~!** (*inf*) de jeito nenhum!
waybill ['weɪbɪl] *n* (*COMM*) conhecimento.
waylay [weɪ'leɪ] (*irreg*) *vt* armar uma cilada para; (*fig*): **I got waylaid** alguém me deteve.
wayside ['weɪsaɪd] *n* beira da estrada; **to fall by the ~** (*fig*) desistir; (*morally*) corromper-se.
way station (*US*) *n* (*RAIL*) apeadeiro; (*fig*) etapa.
wayward ['weɪwəd] *adj* (*wilful*) voluntarioso, teimoso; (*capricious*) caprichoso; (*naughty*) travesso.
WC ['dʌblju'siː] (*BRIT*) *n abbr* = **water closet**.
WCC *n abbr* = **World Council of Churches**.
we [wiː] *pron* nós.
weak [wiːk] *adj* fraco, débil; (*tea*) aguado, ralo; **to grow ~(er)** enfraquecer, ficar cada vez mais fraco.
weaken ['wiːkən] *vi* enfraquecer(-se); (*give way*) ceder ♦ *vt* enfraquecer; (*lessen*) diminuir.
weak-kneed [-niːd] *adj* (*fig*) covarde.
weakling ['wiːklɪŋ] *n* pessoa fraca *or* delicada.
weakly ['wiːklɪ] *adj* fraco ♦ *adv* fracamente.
weakness ['wiːknɪs] *n* fraqueza; (*fault*) ponto fraco.
wealth [wɛlθ] *n* (*money, resources*) riqueza; (*of details*) abundância.
wealth tax *n* imposto sobre fortunas.
wealthy ['wɛlθɪ] *adj* rico, abastado.
wean [wiːn] *vt* desmamar.
weapon ['wɛpən] *n* arma.
wear [wɛə*] (*pt* **wore**, *pp* **worn**) *n* (*use*) uso; (*deterioration through use*) desgaste *m*; (*clothing*): **baby/sports ~** roupa infantil/de esporte ♦ *vt* (*clothes*) usar; (*shoes*) usar, calçar; (*put on*) vestir; (*damage: through use*) desgastar; (*beard etc*) ter ♦ *vi* (*last*) durar; (*rub etc through*) gastar-se; **~ and tear** desgaste *m*; **to ~ a hole in sth** fazer um buraco em algo pelo uso.
wear away *vt* gastar ♦ *vi* desgastar-se.
wear down *vt* gastar; (*strength*) esgotar.
wear off *vi* (*pain etc*) passar.
wear on *vi* alongar-se.
wear out *vt* desgastar; (*person, strength*) esgotar.
wearable ['wɛərəbl] *adj* que se pode usar.
wearily ['wɪərɪlɪ] *adv* de maneira cansada.
weariness ['wɪərɪnɪs] *n* cansaço, fadiga; (*boredom*) aborrecimento.
wearisome ['wɪərɪsəm] *adj* (*tiring*) cansativo; (*boring*) fastidioso.
weary ['wɪərɪ] *adj* (*tired*) cansado; (*dispirited*) deprimido ♦ *vt* aborrecer ♦ *vi*: **to ~ of** cansar-se de.
weasel ['wiːzl] *n* (*ZOOL*) doninha.
weather ['wɛðə*] *n* tempo ♦ *vt* (*storm, crisis*) resistir a; **what's the ~ like?** como está o tempo?; **under the ~** (*fig: ill*) doente.
weather-beaten *adj* curtido.
weather cock *n* cata-vento.
weather forecast *n* previsão *f* do tempo.
weatherman ['wɛðəmæn] (*irreg*) *n* meteorologista *m*.
weatherproof ['wɛðəpruːf] *adj* (*garment*) impermeável; (*building*) à prova de intempérie.
weather report *n* boletim *m* meteorológico.
weather vane [-veɪn] *n* cata-vento.
weave [wiːv] (*pt* **wove**, *pp* **woven**) *vt* (*cloth*) tecer; (*fig*) compor, criar ♦ *vi* (*fig*: *pt, pp* **~d**: *move in and out*) ziguezaguear.
weaver ['wiːvə*] *n* tecelão/loa *m/f*.
weaving ['wiːvɪŋ] *n* tecelagem *f*.
web [wɛb] *n* (*of spider*) teia; (*on foot*) membrana; (*network*) rede *f*.
webbed [wɛbd] *adj* (*foot*) palmípede.
webbing ['wɛbɪŋ] *n* (*on chair*) tira de tecido forte.
wed [wɛd] (*pt, pp* **~ded**) *vt* casar ♦ *vi* casar-se ♦ *n*: **the newly-~s** os recém-casados.
Wed. *abbr* (= *Wednesday*) qua., 4ª.
we'd [wiːd] = **we had; we would**.
wedded ['wɛdɪd] *pt, pp of* **wed**.
wedding ['wɛdɪŋ] *n* casamento, núpcias *fpl*.
wedding anniversary *n* aniversário de casamento; **silver/golden ~** bodas *fpl* de prata/de ouro.
wedding day *n* dia *m* de casamento.
wedding dress *n* vestido de noiva.
wedding night *n* noite *f* de núpcias.

***NB:** European Portuguese adds the following consonants to certain words:* **b** (sú(b)dito, su(b)til); **c** (a(c)ção, a(c)cionista, a(c)to); **m** (inde(m)ne); **p** (ado(p)ção, ado(p)tar); *for further details see p. xiii.*

wedding present *n* presente *m* de casamento.
wedding ring *n* anel *m or* aliança de casamento.
wedge [wɛdʒ] *n* (*of wood etc*) cunha, calço; (*of cake*) fatia ♦ *vt* (*pack tightly*) socar, apertar; (*door*) pôr calço em.
wedge-heeled shoes [-hi:ld-] *npl* sapatos *mpl* tipo Annabella.
wedlock ['wɛdlɔk] *n* matrimônio, casamento.
Wednesday ['wɛdnzdɪ] *n* quarta-feira; *see also* **Tuesday**.
wee [wi:] (*SCOTTISH*) *adj* pequeno, pequenino.
weed [wi:d] *n* erva daninha ♦ *vt* capinar.
weed-killer *n* herbicida *m*.
weedy ['wi:dɪ] *adj* (*man*) fraquinho.
week [wi:k] *n* semana; **once/twice a ~** uma vez/duas vezes por semana; **in two ~s' time** daqui a duas semanas; **Tuesday ~, a ~ on Tuesday** sem ser essa terça-feira, a outra; **every other ~** uma semana sim, uma semana não.
weekday ['wi:kdeɪ] *n* dia *m* de semana; (*COMM*) dia útil; **on ~s** durante a semana.
weekend ['wi:kɛnd] *n* fim *m* de semana.
weekend case *n* maleta.
weekly ['wi:klɪ] *adv* semanalmente ♦ *adj* semanal ♦ *n* semanário.
weep [wi:p] (pt, *pp* **wept**) *vi* (*person*) chorar; (*MED*: *wound*) supurar.
weeping willow ['wi:pɪŋ-] *n* salgueiro chorão.
weft [wɛft] *n* (*TEXTILES*) trama.
weigh [weɪ] *vt*, *vi* pesar; **to ~ anchor** levantar ferro; **to ~ the pros and cons** pesar os prós e contras.
weigh down *vt* sobrecarregar; (*fig*: *with worry*) deprimir, acabrunhar.
weigh out *vt* (*goods*) pesar.
weigh up *vt* ponderar, avaliar.
weighbridge ['weɪbrɪdʒ] *n* báscula automática.
weighing machine ['weɪɪŋ-] *n* balança.
weight [weɪt] *n* peso ♦ *vt* carregar com peso; (*fig*: *statistic*) ponderar; **to lose/put on ~** emagrecer/engordar; **sold by ~** vendido por peso; **~s and measures** pesos e medidas.
weighting ['weɪtɪŋ] *n*: **~ allowance** indenização *f* de residência.
weightlessness ['weɪtlɪsnɪs] *n* ausência de peso.
weightlifter ['weɪtlɪftə*] *n* levantador *m* de pesos.
weighty ['weɪtɪ] *adj* pesado, importante.
weir [wɪə*] *n* represa, açude *m*.
weird [wɪəd] *adj* esquisito, estranho.
welcome ['wɛlkəm] *adj* bem-vindo ♦ *n* acolhimento, recepção *f* ♦ *vt* dar as boas-vindas a; (*be glad of*) acolher; **you're ~** (*after thanks*) de nada; **to make sb ~** dar bom acolhimento a alguém; **you're ~ to try** pode tentar se quiser.
welcoming ['wɛlkəmɪŋ] *adj* acolhedor(a); (*speech*) de boas-vindas.
weld [wɛld] *n* solda ♦ *vt* soldar, unir.
welder ['wɛldə*] *n* (*person*) soldador(a) *m/f*.
welding ['wɛldɪŋ] *n* soldagem *f*, solda.
welfare ['wɛlfɛə*] *n* bem-estar *m*; (*social aid*) assistência social.
welfare state *n país auto-financiador da sua assistência social.*
welfare work *n* trabalho social.
well [wɛl] *n* poço; (*pool*) nascente *f* ♦ *adv* bem ♦ *adj*: **to be ~** estar bem (de saúde) ♦ *excl* bem!, então!; **as ~** também; **as ~ as** assim como; **~ done!** muito bem!; **get ~ soon!** melhoras!; **to do ~** ir *or* sair-se bem; **to think ~ of sb** ter um bom conceito a respeito de alguém; **I don't feel ~** não estou me sentindo bem; **you might as ~ tell me** é melhor você me contar logo; **~, as I was saying** ... bem, como eu estava dizendo ....
well up *vi* brotar, manar.
we'll [wi:l] = **we will**; **we shall**.
well-behaved [-bɪ'heɪvd] *adj* bem educado, bem comportado.
well-being *n* bem-estar *m*.
well-bred *adj* bem educado.
well-built *adj* (*person*) robusto; (*house*) bem construído.
well-chosen *adj* bem escolhido.
well-deserved [-dɪ'zə:vd] *adj* bem merecido.
well-developed [-dɪ'vɛləpt] *adj* bem desenvolvido.
well-disposed *adj*: **~ to(wards)** favorável a.
well-dressed [-drɛst] *adj* bem vestido.
well-earned *adj* (*rest*) bem merecido.
well-groomed [-gru:md] *adj* bem tratado.
well-heeled [-hi:ld] (*inf*) *adj* (*wealthy*) rico.
well-informed *adj* bem informado, versado.
wellingtons ['wɛlɪŋtənz] *n* (*also*: *wellington boots*) *botas de borracha até os joelhos.*
well-kept *adj* (*house*, *hands etc*) bem tratado; (*secret*) bem guardado.
well-known *adj* conhecido; **it's a ~ fact that** ... é sabido que ....
well-mannered [-'mænəd] *adj* bem educado.
well-meaning *adj* bem intencionado.
well-nigh [-naɪ] *adv*: **~ impossible** praticamente impossível.
well-off *adj* próspero, rico.
well-read *adj* lido, versado.
well-spoken *adj* (*person*) bem-falante.
well-stocked [-stɔkt] *adj* bem abastecido.
well-timed [-taɪmd] *adj* oportuno.
well-to-do *adj* abastado.
well-wisher [-'wɪʃə*] *n* simpatizante *m/f*; (*admirer*) admirador(a) *m/f*.
Welsh [wɛlʃ] *adj* galês/galesa ♦ *n* (*LING*) galês *m*; **the ~** *npl* os galeses.
Welshman ['wɛlʃmən] (*irreg*) *n* galês *m*.
Welsh rarebit *n torradas com queijo derretido.*
Welshwoman ['wɛlʃwumən] (*irreg*) *n* galesa.
welter ['wɛltə*] *n* tumulto.
went [wɛnt] *pt of* **go**.
wept [wɛpt] *pt*, *pp of* **weep**.
were [wə:*] *pt of* **be**.
we're [wɪə*] = **we are**.
weren't [wə:nt] = **were not**.

werewolf ['wɪəwulf] (*irreg*) *n* lobisomem *m*.
west [wɛst] *n* oeste *m* ♦ *adj* ocidental, do oeste ♦ *adv* para o oeste *or* ao oeste; **the W~** o Oeste, o Ocidente.
westbound ['wɛstbaund] *adj* em direção ao oeste.
West Country *n*: **the** ~ o sudoeste da Inglaterra.
westerly ['wɛstəlɪ] *adj* (*situation*) ocidental; (*wind*) oeste.
western ['wɛstən] *adj* ocidental ♦ *n* (*CINEMA*) western *m*, bangue-bangue (*BR*: *inf*).
westernized ['wɛstənaɪzd] *adj* ocidentalizado.
West German *adj*, *n* alemão/ã *m/f* ocidental.
West Germany *n* Alemanha Ocidental.
West Indian *adj*, *n* antilhano/a.
West Indies [-'ɪndɪz] *npl* Antilhas *fpl*.
westward(s) ['wɛstwəd(z)] *adv* para o oeste.
wet [wɛt] (*pt*, *pp* **wet** *or* **~ted**) *adj* molhado; (*damp*) úmido; (~ *through*) encharcado; (*rainy*) chuvoso ♦ *vt* molhar; **to ~ one's pants** *or* **o.s.** fazer xixi na calça; **to get ~** molhar-se; **"~ paint"** "tinta fresca".
wet blanket *n* (*fig*) desmancha-prazeres *m/f inv*.
wetness ['wɛtnɪs] *n* umidade *f*.
wet suit *n* roupa de mergulho.
we've [wi:v] = **we have**.
whack [wæk] *vt* bater.
whacked [wækt] (*inf*) *adj* morto, esgotado.
whale [weɪl] *n* (*ZOOL*) baleia.
whaler ['weɪlə*] *n* baleeiro.
wharf [wɔ:f] (*pl* **wharves**) *n* cais *m inv*.
wharves [wɔ:vz] *npl of* **wharf**.
what [wɔt] *excl* quê!, como! ♦ *adj* que ♦ *pron* (*interrogative*) que, o que; (*relative*, *indirect*: *object*, *subject*) o que; **~ are you doing?** o que é que você está fazendo?; **~'s happened?** o que aconteceu?; **~'s in there?** o que é que tem lá dentro?; **for ~ reason?** por que razão?; **I saw ~ you did** eu vi o que você fez; **I don't know ~ to do** não sei o que fazer; **~ a mess!** que bagunça!; **~ is it called?** como se chama?; **~ about doing ...** que tal fazer ...; **~ about me?** e eu?; **~ is his address?** qual é o endereço dele?; **~ I want is a cup of tea** (o que eu) quero é uma xícara de chá; **~ will it cost?** quanto vai custar?
whatever [wɔt'ɛvə*] *adj*: **~ book you choose** qualquer livro que você escolha ♦ *pron*: **do ~ is necessary** faça tudo o que for preciso; **~ happens** aconteça o que acontecer; **no reason ~** *or* **whatsoever** nenhuma razão seja qual for *or* em absoluto; **nothing ~** nada em absoluto.
wheat [wi:t] *n* trigo.
wheatgerm ['wi:tdʒə:m] *n* germe *m* de trigo.
wheatmeal ['wi:tmi:l] *n* farinha de trigo.
wheedle ['wi:dl] *vt*: **to ~ sth out of sb** conseguir algo de alguém por meio de agrados.
wheel [wi:l] *n* roda; (*AUT*: *also*: *steering ~*) volante *m*; (*NAUT*) roda do leme ♦ *vt* (*pram etc*) empurrar ♦ *vi* (*also*: ~ *round*) girar, dar voltas, virar-se.
wheelbarrow ['wi:lbærəu] *n* carrinho de mão.
wheelbase ['wi:lbeɪs] *n* distância entre os eixos.
wheelchair ['wi:ltʃɛə*] *n* cadeira de rodas.
wheel clamp *n* (*AUT*) *grampo com que se imobiliza carros estacionados ilegalmente*.
wheeler-dealer ['wi:lə*-] *n* negocista *m/f*.
wheelhouse ['wi:lhaus] (*irreg*) *n* casa do leme.
wheeling ['wi:lɪŋ] *n*: **~ and dealing** negociatas *fpl*.
wheeze [wi:z] *n* respiração *f* difícil, chiado ♦ *vi* respirar ruidosamente.
when [wɛn] *adv* quando ♦ *conj* quando; (*whereas*) ao passo que; **on the day ~ I met him** no dia em que o conheci.
whenever [wɛn'ɛvə*] *conj* quando, quando quer que; (*every time that*) sempre que ♦ *adv* quando você quiser.
where [wɛə*] *adv* onde ♦ *conj* onde, aonde; **this is ~** aqui é onde; **~ are you from?** de onde você é?
whereabouts ['wɛərəbauts] *adv* (por) onde ♦ *n*: **nobody knows his ~** ninguém sabe o seu paradeiro.
whereas [wɛər'æz] *conj* uma vez que, ao passo que.
whereby [wɛə'baɪ] *adv* (*formal*) pelo qual (*or* pela qual *etc*).
whereupon [wɛərə'pɔn] *adv* depois do que.
wherever [wɛər'ɛvə*] *adv* onde quer que; (*interrogative*) onde?; **sit ~ you like** sente-se onde quiser.
wherewithal ['wɛəwɪðɔ:l] *n* recursos *mpl*, meios *mpl*.
whet [wɛt] *vt* afiar; (*appetite*) abrir.
whether ['wɛðə*] *conj* se; **I don't know ~ to accept or not** não sei se aceito ou não; **~ you go or not** quer você vá quer não.
whey [weɪ] *n* soro (de leite).
which [wɪtʃ] *adj* (*interrogative*) que, qual ♦ *pron* (*interrogative*) qual; (*relative*: *subject*, *object*) que, o que, o qual, *etc*; **~ one of you?** qual de vocês?; **~ do you want?** qual você quer?; **~ picture do you want?** que quadro você quer?; **I don't mind ~** não me importa qual; **the apple ~ is on the table** a maçã que está sobre a mesa; **the chair on ~ you are sitting** a cadeira na qual você está sentado; **he said he knew, ~ is true** ele disse que sabia, o que é verdade; **in ~ case** em cujo caso; **after ~** depois do que; **by ~ time** momento em que.
whichever [wɪtʃ'ɛvə*] *adj*: **take ~ book you prefer** pegue o livro que preferir; **~ book you take** qualquer livro que você pegue.
whiff [wɪf] *n* baforada, cheiro; **to catch a ~ of sth** tomar o cheiro de algo.
while [waɪl] *n* tempo, momento ♦ *conj*

***NB**: European Portuguese adds the following consonants to certain words:* **b** (sú(b)dito, su(b)til); **c** (a(c)ção, a(c)cionista, a(c)to); **m** (inde(m)ne); **p** (ado(p)ção, ado(p)tar); *for further details see p. xiii.*

enquanto; (*although*) embora; **for a ~** durante algum tempo; **in a ~** daqui a pouco; **all the ~** todo o tempo; **we'll make it worth your ~** faremos com que valha a pena para você.

whilst [waɪlst] *conj* = **while.**

whim [wɪm] *n* capricho, veneta.

whimper ['wɪmpə*] *n* (*weeping*) choradeira; (*moan*) lamúria ♦ *vi* choramingar, soluçar.

whimsical ['wɪmzɪkl] *adj* (*person*) caprichoso, de veneta; (*look*) excêntrico.

whine [waɪn] *n* (*of pain*) gemido; (*of engine*) zunido ♦ *vi* gemer, zunir; (*dog*) ganir.

whip [wɪp] *n* açoite *m*; (*for riding*) chicote *m*; (*BRIT: POL*) líder *m/f* da bancada ♦ *vt* chicotear; (*snatch*) apanhar de repente; (*cream*) bater.

whip up *vt* (*cream*) bater; (*inf: meal*) arrumar; (*stir up: feeling*) atiçar; (*: support*) angariar.

whiplash ['wɪplæʃ] *n* (*MED: also:* ~ *injury*) golpe *m* de chicote, chicotinho.

whipped cream [wɪpt-] *n* (creme *m*) chantilly *m*.

whipping boy ['wɪpɪŋ-] *n* (*fig*) bode *m* expiatório.

whip-round *n* coleta, vaquinha.

whirl [wə:l] *n* remoinho ♦ *vt* fazer rodar, rodopiar ♦ *vi* girar; (*leaves, water etc*) redemoinhar.

whirlpool ['wə:lpu:l] *n* remoinho.

whirlwind ['wə:lwɪnd] *n* furacão *m*, remoinho.

whirr [wə:*] *vi* zumbir.

whisk [wɪsk] *n* (*CULIN*) batedeira ♦ *vt* bater; **to ~ sth away from sb** arrebatar algo de alguém; **to ~ sb away** *or* **off** levar rapidamente alguém.

whiskers ['wɪskəz] *npl* (*of animal*) bigodes *mpl*; (*of man*) suíças *fpl*.

whisky ['wɪskɪ] (*IRISH, US* **whiskey**) *n* uísque *m* (*BR*), whisky *m* (*PT*).

whisper ['wɪspə*] *n* sussurro, murmúrio; (*rumour*) rumor *m* ♦ *vt, vi* sussurrar; **to ~ sth to sb** sussurrar algo para alguém.

whispering ['wɪspərɪŋ] *n* sussurros *mpl*.

whist [wɪst] (*BRIT*) *n* uíste *m* (*BR*), whist *m* (*PT*).

whistle ['wɪsl] *n* (*sound*) assobio; (*object*) apito ♦ *vt, vi* assobiar.

whistle-stop *adj*: **to make a ~ tour** (*POL*) fazer uma viagem eleitoral.

Whit [wɪt] *n* Pentecostes *m*.

white [waɪt] *adj* branco; (*pale*) pálido ♦ *n* branco; (*of egg*) clara; **the ~s** *npl* (*washing*) a roupa branca; **tennis ~s** traje *m* de tênis; **to turn** *or* **go ~** (*person*) ficar branco *or* pálido; (*hair*) ficar grisalho.

whitebait ['waɪtbeɪt] *n* filhote *m* de arenque.

white coffee (*BRIT*) *n* café *m* com leite.

white-collar worker *n* empregado/a de escritório.

white elephant *n* (*fig*) elefante *m* branco.

white goods *n* eletrodomésticos *mpl*.

white-hot *adj* (*metal*) incandescente.

white lie *n* mentira inofensiva *or* social.

whiteness ['waɪtnɪs] *n* brancura.

white noise *n* ruído branco.

whiteout ['waɪtaut] *n* resplendor *m* branco.

white paper *n* (*POL*) livro branco.

whitewash ['waɪtwɔʃ] *n* (*paint*) cal *f* ♦ *vt* caiar; (*fig*) encobrir.

whiting ['waɪtɪŋ] *n inv* pescada-marlonga.

Whit Monday *n* segunda-feira de Pentecostes.

Whitsun ['wɪtsn] *n* Pentecostes *m*.

whittle ['wɪtl] *vt* aparar; **to ~ away, ~ down** reduzir gradualmente, corroer.

whizz [wɪz] *vi* zunir; **to ~ past** *or* **by** passar a toda velocidade.

whizz kid (*inf*) *n* prodígio.

WHO *n abbr* (= *World Health Organization*) OMS *f*.

who [hu:] *pron* (*relative*) que, o qual *etc*, quem; (*interrogative*) quem?

whodunit [hu:'dʌnɪt] (*inf*) *n* romance *m* (*or* filme *m*) policial.

whoever [hu:'ɛvə*] *pron*: **~ finds it** quem quer que *or* seja quem for que o encontre; **ask ~ you like** pergunte a quem quiser; **~ he marries** não importa com quem se case; **~ told you that?** quem te disse isso pelo amor de Deus?

whole [həul] *adj* (*complete*) todo, inteiro; (*not broken*) intacto ♦ *n* (*total*) total *m*; (*sum*) conjunto; **the ~ lot (of it)** tudo; **the ~ lot (of them)** todos/as; **the ~ of the time** o tempo todo; **the ~ of the town** toda a cidade, a cidade inteira; **~ villages were destroyed** lugarejos inteiros foram destruídos; **on the ~, as a ~** como um todo, no conjunto.

wholehearted [həul'hɑ:tɪd] *adj* sincero, irrestrito.

wholemeal ['həulmi:l] (*BRIT*) *adj* (*flour, bread*) integral.

whole note (*US*) *n* semibreve *f*.

wholesale ['həulseɪl] *n* venda por atacado ♦ *adj* por atacado; (*destruction*) em grande escala.

wholesaler ['həulseɪlə*] *n* atacadista *m/f*.

wholesome ['həulsəm] *adj* saudável, sadio.

wholewheat ['həulwi:t] *adj* (*flour, bread*) integral.

wholly ['həulɪ] *adv* totalmente, completamente.

whom [hu:m] *pron* que, o qual, quem; (*interrogative*) quem?; **those to ~ I spoke** aqueles com os quais eu falei.

whooping cough ['hu:pɪŋ-] *n* coqueluche *f*.

whoosh [wuʃ] *n* chio.

whopper ['wɔpə*] (*inf*) *n* (*lie*) lorota; (*large thing*): **it was a ~** era enorme.

whopping ['wɔpɪŋ] (*inf*) *adj* (*big*) imenso.

whore [hɔ:*] (*pej*) *n* puta.

whose [hu:z] *adj*: **~ book is this?** de quem é este livro? ♦ *pron*: **~ is this?** de quem é isto?; **I know ~ it is** eu sei de quem é; **~ pen have you taken?** de quem é a caneta que você pegou?, você pegou a caneta de quem?; **the man ~ son you rescued** o homem cujo filho você salvou; **the girl ~ sister**

you were speaking to a menina com cuja irmã você estava falando.
Who's Who *n* Quem é quem (*registro de notabilidades*).
why [waɪ] *adv* por que (*BR*), porque (*PT*); (*at end of sentence*) por quê (*BR*) porquê (*PT*) ♦ *excl* ora essa!, bem!; **tell me ~** diga-me por quê; **the reason ~** a razão por que.
whyever [waɪ'ɛvə*] *adv* mas por que.
WI *n abbr* (*BRIT*: = *Women's Institute*) *associação de mulheres* ♦ *abbr* (*GEO*) = **West Indies**; (*US*: *POST*) = **Wisconsin.**
wick [wɪk] *n* mecha, pavio.
wicked ['wɪkɪd] *adj* malvado; (*mischievous*) malicioso; (*inf*: *terrible*: *prices*, *waste*) terrível.
wicker ['wɪkə*] *n* (*also*: *~work*) (trabalho de) vime *m*.
wicket ['wɪkɪt] *n* (*CRICKET*) arco.
wicket keeper *n* (*CRICKET*) guarda-meta *m* (no críquete).
wide [waɪd] *adj* largo; (*broad*) extenso, amplo; (*region*, *knowledge*) vasto; (*choice*) variado ♦ *adv*: **to open ~** abrir totalmente; **to shoot ~** atirar longe do alvo; **it is 4 metres ~** tem 4 metros de largura.
wide-angle lens *n* lente *f* grande angular.
wide-awake *adj* bem acordado; (*fig*) vivo, esperto.
wide-eyed [-aɪd] *adj* de olhos arregalados; (*fig*) ingênuo.
widely ['waɪdlɪ] *adv* (*different*) extremamente; **it is ~ believed that ...** há uma convicção generalizada de que ...; **to be ~ read** ser muito lido.
widen ['waɪdən] *vt* alargar.
wideness ['waɪdnɪs] *n* largura; (*breadth*) extensão *f*.
wide open *adj* (*eyes*) arregalado; (*door*) escancarado.
wide-ranging [-'reɪndʒɪŋ] *adj* (*survey*, *report*) abrangente; (*interests*) diversos.
widespread ['waɪdsprɛd] *adj* (*belief etc*) difundido, comum.
widow ['wɪdəu] *n* viúva.
widowed ['wɪdəud] *adj* viúvo.
widower ['wɪdəuə*] *n* viúvo.
width [wɪdθ] *n* largura; **it's 7 metres in ~** tem 7 metros de largura.
widthways ['wɪdθweɪz] *adv* transversalmente.
wield [wi:ld] *vt* (*sword*) brandir, empunhar; (*power*) exercer.
wife [waɪf] (*pl* **wives**) *n* mulher *f*, esposa.
wig [wɪg] *n* peruca.
wigging ['wɪgɪŋ] (*BRIT*: *inf*) *n* sabão *m*, descompostura.
wiggle ['wɪgl] *vt* menear, agitar ♦ *vi* menear, agitar-se.
wiggly ['wɪglɪ] *adj* (*line*) ondulado.
wild [waɪld] *adj* (*animal*) selvagem; (*plant*) silvestre; (*rough*) violento, furioso; (*idea*) disparatado, extravagante; (*person*) louco, insensato; (*enthusiastic*): **to be ~ about** ser louco por ♦ *n*: **the ~** a natureza; **~s** *npl* regiões *fpl* selvagens, terras *fpl* virgens.
wild card *n* (*COMPUT*) carácter *m* de substituição.
wildcat ['waɪldkæt] *n* gato selvagem; (*US*: *lynx*) lince *m*.
wildcat strike *n greve espontânea e não autorizada pelo sindicato.*
wilderness ['wɪldənɪs] *n* ermo; (*in Brazil*) sertão *m*.
wildfire ['waɪldfaɪə*] *n*: **to spread like ~** espalhar-se rapidamente.
wild-goose chase *n* (*fig*) busca inútil.
wildlife ['waɪldlaɪf] *n* animais (e plantas) selvagens.
wildly ['waɪldlɪ] *adv* (*roughly*) violentamente; (*foolishly*) loucamente; (*rashly*) desenfreadamente.
wiles [waɪlz] *npl* artimanhas *fpl*, estratagemas *mpl*.
wilful ['wɪlful] (*US* **willful**) *adj* (*person*) teimoso, voluntarioso; (*action*) deliberado, intencional; (*crime*) premeditado.
will [wɪl] (*conditional* **would**) *aux vb*: **he ~ come** ele virá; ♦ *vt* (*pt*, *pp* **~ed**): **to ~ sb to do sth** desejar que alguém faça algo ♦ *n* vontade *f*; (*testament*) testamento; **you won't lose it, ~ you?** não vai perder isto, tá?; **that ~ be the postman** deve ser o carteiro; **~ you sit down** queira sentar-se; **the car won't start** o carro não quer pegar; **he ~ed himself to go on** reuniu grande força de vontade para continuar; **to do sth of one's own free ~** fazer algo de livre vontade; **against one's ~** a contragosto.
willful ['wɪlful] (*US*) *adj* = **wilful.**
willing ['wɪlɪŋ] *adj* (*with goodwill*) disposto, pronto; (*submissive*) complacente ♦ *n*: **to show ~** mostrar boa vontade; **he's ~ to do it** ele é disposto a fazê-lo.
willingly ['wɪlɪŋlɪ] *adv* de bom grado, de boa vontade.
willingness ['wɪlɪŋnɪs] *n* boa vontade *f*, disposição *f*.
will-o'-the-wisp *n* fogo-fátuo; (*fig*) quimera.
willow ['wɪləu] *n* salgueiro.
will power *n* força de vontade.
willy-nilly ['wɪlɪ'nɪlɪ] *adv* quer queira ou não.
wilt [wɪlt] *vi* murchar, definhar.
Wilts [wɪlts] (*BRIT*) *abbr* = **Wiltshire.**
wily ['waɪlɪ] *adj* esperto, astuto.
wimp [wɪmp] (*inf*) *n* banana *m*.
win [wɪn] (*pt*, *pp* **won**) *n* (*in sports etc*) vitória ♦ *vt* ganhar, vencer; (*obtain*) conseguir, obter ♦ *vi* ganhar.
  win over *vt* conquistar.
  win round (*BRIT*) *vt* conquistar.
wince [wɪns] *vi* encolher-se, estremecer ♦ *n* estremecimento.
winch [wɪntʃ] *n* guincho.
Winchester disk ['wɪntʃɛstə*-] *n* (*COMPUT*)

NB: European Portuguese adds the following consonants to certain words: **b** (sú(b)dito, su(b)til); **c** (a(c)ção, a(c)cionista, a(c)to); **m** (inde(m)ne); **p** (ado(p)ção, ado(p)tar); *for further details see p. xiii.*

(disco) Winchester *m*.
wind[1] [wınd] *n* vento; (*MED*) gases *mpl*, flatulência; (*breath*) fôlego ♦ *vt* (*take breath away from*) deixar sem fôlego; **the ~(s)** (*MUS*) instrumentos *mpl* de sopro; **into** *or* **against the ~** contra o vento; **to get ~ of sth** (*fig*) ter notícia de algo, tomar conhecimento de algo; **to break ~** soltar gases intestinais.
wind[2] [waınd] (*pt, pp* **wound**) *vt* enrolar, bobinar; (*wrap*) envolver; (*clock, toy*) dar corda a ♦ *vi* (*road, river*) serpentear.
wind down *vt* (*car window*) abaixar, abrir; (*fig: production, business*) diminuir gradativamente.
wind up *vt* (*clock*) dar corda em; (*debate*) rematar, concluir.
windbreak ['wındbreık] *n* quebra-ventos *m*.
windbreaker ['wındbreıkə*] (*US*) *n* anoraque *m*.
windcheater ['wındtʃiːtə*] (*BRIT*) *n* anoraque *m*.
winder ['waındə*] (*BRIT*) *n* (*on watch*) botão *m* de corda.
windfall ['wındfɔːl] *n* golpe *m* de sorte.
winding ['waındıŋ] *adj* (*road*) sinuoso, tortuoso; (*staircase*) de caracol, em espiral.
wind instrument *n* (*MUS*) instrumento de sopro.
windmill ['wındmıl] *n* moinho de vento.
window ['wındəu] *n* janela; (*in shop etc*) vitrine *f* (*BR*), montra (*PT*).
window box *n* jardineira (no peitoril da janela).
window cleaner *n* (*person*) limpador(a) *m/f* de janelas.
window dressing *n* decoração *f* de vitrines.
window envelope *n* envelope *m* de janela.
window frame *n* caixilho da janela.
window ledge *n* peitoril *m* da janela.
window pane *n* vidraça, vidro.
window-shopping *n*: **to go ~** ir ver vitrines.
windowsill ['wındəusıl] *n* peitoril *m*, soleira.
windpipe ['wındpaıp] *n* traquéia.
windscreen ['wındskriːn] (*BRIT*) *n* pára-brisa *m*.
windscreen washer (*BRIT*) *n* lavador *m* de pára-brisa.
windscreen wiper [-'waıpə*] (*BRIT*) *n* limpador *m* de pára-brisa.
windshield *etc* ['wındʃiːld] (*US*) *n* = **windscreen** *etc*.
windswept ['wındswɛpt] *adj* varrido pelo vento.
wind tunnel *n* túnel *m* aerodinâmico.
windy ['wındı] *adj* com muito vento, batido pelo vento; **it's ~** está ventando (*BR*), faz vento (*PT*).
wine [waın] *n* vinho ♦ *vt*: **to ~ and dine sb** levar alguém para jantar.
wine cellar *n* adega.
wine glass *n* cálice *m* (de vinho).
wine list *n* lista de vinhos.
wine merchant *n* negociante *m/f* de vinhos.
wine tasting [-'teıstıŋ] *n* degustação *f* de vinhos.
wine waiter *n* garção *m* dos vinhos
wing [wıŋ] *n* asa; (*of building*) ala; (*AUT*) aleta, pára-lamas *m inv*; **~s** *npl* (*THEATRE*) bastidores *mpl*.
winger ['wıŋə*] *n* (*SPORT*) ponta, extremo.
wing mirror (*BRIT*) *n* espelho lateral.
wing nut *n* porca borboleta.
wingspan ['wıŋspæn] *n* envergadura.
wingspread ['wıŋsprɛd] *n* envergadura.
wink [wıŋk] *n* piscadela ♦ *vi* piscar o olho; (*light etc*) piscar.
winkle ['wıŋkl] *n* búzio.
winner ['wınə*] *n* vencedor(a) *m/f*.
winning ['wınıŋ] *adj* (*team*) vencedor(a); (*goal*) decisivo; (*manner*) sedutor(a).
winning post *n* meta de chegada.
winnings ['wınıŋz] *npl* ganhos *mpl*.
winsome ['wınsəm] *adj* encantador(a), cativante.
winter ['wıntə*] *n* inverno ♦ *vi* hibernar.
winter sports *npl* esportes *mpl* (*BR*) *or* desportos *mpl* (*PT*) de inverno.
wintry ['wıntrı] *adj* glacial, invernal.
wipe [waıp] *n*: **to give sth a ~** limpar algo com um pano ♦ *vt* limpar; **to ~ one's nose** limpar o nariz.
wipe off *vt* remover esfregando.
wipe out *vt* (*debt*) liquidar; (*memory*) apagar; (*destroy*) exterminar.
wipe up *vt* (*liquid*) limpar; (*dishes*) enxugar.
wire ['waıə*] *n* arame *m*; (*ELEC*) fio (elétrico); (*TEL*) telegrama *m* ♦ *vt* (*house*) instalar a rede elétrica em; (*also*: **~ up**) conectar; (*TEL*) telegrafar para.
wire brush *n* escova de aço.
wire cutters [-'kʌtəz] *npl* alicate *m* corta-arame.
wireless ['waıəlıs] (*BRIT*) *n* rádio.
wire netting *n* rede *f* de arame.
wire-tapping [-'tæpıŋ] *n* escuta telefônica.
wiring ['waıərıŋ] *n* instalação *f* elétrica.
wiry ['waıərı] *adj* nervoso.
wisdom ['wızdəm] *n* sabedoria, sagacidade *f*; (*good sense*) bom senso; (*care*) prudência.
wisdom tooth (*irreg*) *n* dente *m* do siso.
wise [waız] *adj* sábio; (*sensible*) sensato; (*careful*) prudente; **I'm none the ~r** eu não entendi nada.
wise up (*inf*) *vi*: **to ~ up to** abrir os olhos para.
...wise [waız] *suffix*: **time~** com relação ao tempo.
wisecrack ['waızkræk] *n* piada.
wish [wıʃ] *n* (*desire*) desejo ♦ *vt* desejar; (*want*) querer; **best ~es** (*on birthday etc*) parabéns *mpl*, felicidades *fpl*; **with best ~es** (*in letter*) cumprimentos; **give her my best ~es** dá um abraço para ela; **to ~ sb goodbye** despedir-se de alguém; **he ~ed me well** me desejou boa sorte; **to ~ to do/sb to do sth** querer fazer/que alguém faça algo; **to ~ for** desejar; **to ~ sth on sb** desejar algo a

alguém.

wishful ['wɪʃful] *adj*: **it's ~ thinking** é doce ilusão.

wishy-washy ['wɪʃɪ'wɔʃɪ] (*inf*) *adj* (*person*) sem caráter; (*ideas, thinking*) aguado.

wisp [wɪsp] *n* mecha, tufo; (*of smoke*) fio.

wistful ['wɪstful] *adj* melancólico, saudoso.

wit [wɪt] *n* (*wittiness*) presença de espírito, engenho; (*intelligence*) entendimento; (*person*) espirituoso/a; **to be at one's ~s' end** (*fig*) não saber para onde se virar; **to have one's ~s about one** ter uma presença de espírito; **to ~** a saber.

witch [wɪtʃ] *n* bruxa.

witchcraft ['wɪtʃkrɑːft] *n* bruxaria.

witch doctor *n* médico feiticeiro, pajé *m* (*BR*).

witch-hunt *n* caça às bruxas.

with [wɪð, wɪθ] *prep* com; **red ~ anger** vermelho de raiva; **the man ~ the grey hat** o homem do chapéu cinza; **to tremble ~ fear** tremer de medo; **to stay overnight ~ friends** dormir na casa de amigos; **to be ~ it** (*fig: aware*) estar a par da situação; **I am ~ you** (*I understand*) compreendo.

withdraw [wɪð'drɔː] (*irreg*) *vt* tirar, remover ♦ *vi* retirar-se; (*go back on promise*) voltar atrás; **to ~ money (from the bank)** retirar dinheiro (do banco); **to ~ into o.s.** introverter-se.

withdrawal [wɪð'drɔːəl] *n* retirada.

withdrawal symptoms *npl* síndrome *f* de abstinência; **to have ~** ter uma reação.

withdrawn [wɪð'drɔːn] *pp of* **withdraw** ♦ *adj* (*person*) reservado, introvertido.

wither ['wɪðə*] *vi* murchar.

withered ['wɪðəd] *adj* murcho.

withhold [wɪð'həuld] (*irreg*) *vt* (*money*) reter; (*decision*) adiar; (*permission*) negar; (*information*) esconder.

within [wɪð'ɪn] *prep* dentro de ♦ *adv* dentro; **~ reach** ao alcance da mão; **~ sight** à vista; **~ the week** antes do fim da semana; **~ an hour from now** daqui a uma hora; **to be ~ the law** estar dentro da lei.

without [wɪð'aut] *prep* sem; **~ anybody knowing** sem ninguém saber; **to go** *or* **do ~ sth** passar sem algo.

withstand [wɪð'stænd] (*irreg*) *vt* resistir a.

witness ['wɪtnɪs] *n* (*person*) testemunha; (*evidence*) testemunho ♦ *vt* (*event*) testemunhar, presenciar; (*document*) legalizar; **to bear ~ to sth** testemunhar algo; **~ for the prosecution/defence** testemunha para acusação/defesa; **to ~ to sth/having seen sth** testemunhar algo/ter visto algo.

witness box (*US* **witness stand**) *n* banco das testemunhas.

witticism ['wɪtɪsɪzm] *n* observação *f* espirituosa, chiste *m*.

witty ['wɪtɪ] *adj* espirituoso, engenhoso.

wives [waɪvz] *npl of* **wife**.

wizard ['wɪzəd] *n* feiticeiro, mago.

wizened ['wɪznd] *adj* encarquilhado.

wk *abbr* = **week**.

Wm. *abbr* = **William**.

WO *n abbr* = **warrant officer**.

wobble ['wɔbl] *vi* oscilar; (*chair*) balançar.

wobbly ['wɔblɪ] *adj* (*table*) balançante, bambo.

woe [wəu] *n* dor *f*, mágoa.

woke [wəuk] *pt of* **wake**.

woken ['wəukən] *pp of* **wake**.

wolf [wulf] (*pl* **wolves**) *n* lobo.

wolves [wulvz] *npl of* **wolf**.

woman ['wumən] (*pl* **women**) *n* mulher *f* ♦ *cpd*: **~ doctor** médica; **~ teacher** professora; **young ~** mulher jovem; **women's page** (*PRESS*) página da mulher.

womanize ['wumənaɪz] *vi* paquerar as mulheres.

womanly ['wumənlɪ] *adj* feminino.

womb [wuːm] *n* (*ANAT*) matriz *f*, útero.

women ['wɪmɪn] *npl of* **woman**.

Women's (Liberation) Movement *n* (*also*: *women's lib*) Movimento pela Libertação da Mulher.

won [wʌn] *pt, pp of* **win**.

wonder ['wʌndə*] *n* maravilha, prodígio; (*feeling*) espanto ♦ *vi*: **to ~ whether** perguntar-se a si mesmo se; **to ~ at** admirar-se de; **to ~ about** pensar sobre *or* em; **it's no ~ that** não é de admirar que.

wonderful ['wʌndəful] *adj* maravilhoso.

wonderfully ['wʌndəfulɪ] *adv* maravilhosamente.

wonky ['wɔŋkɪ] (*BRIT*) *adj* errado, torto.

won't [wəunt] = **will not**.

woo [wuː] *vt* (*woman*) namorar, cortejar.

wood [wud] *n* (*timber*) madeira; (*forest*) floresta, bosque *m*; (*firewood*) lenha ♦ *cpd* de madeira.

wood carving *n* escultura em madeira, entalhe *m*.

wooded ['wudɪd] *adj* arborizado.

wooden ['wudən] *adj* de madeira; (*fig*) inexpressivo.

woodland ['wudlənd] *n* floresta, bosque *m*.

woodpecker ['wudpɛkə*] *n* pica-pau *m*.

wood pigeon *n* pombo torcaz.

woodwind ['wudwɪnd] *n* (*MUS*) instrumentos *mpl* de sopro de madeira.

woodwork ['wudwəːk] *n* carpintaria.

woodworm ['wudwəːm] *n* carcoma, caruncho.

woof [wuf] *n* (*of dog*) latido ♦ *vi* latir; **~, ~!** au-au!

wool [wul] *n* lã *f*; **to pull the ~ over sb's eyes** (*fig*) enganar alguém, vender a alguém gato por lebre.

woollen ['wulən] (*US* **woolen**) *adj* de lã.

woollens ['wulənz] (*US* **woolens**) *npl* artigos *mpl* de lã.

woolly ['wulɪ] (*US* **wooly**) *adj* lanoso; (*fig: ideas*) confuso.

word [wəːd] *n* palavra; (*news*) notícia; (*message*) aviso ♦ *vt* (*express*) expressar; (*document*) redigir; **in other ~s** em outras palavras, ou seja; **to break/keep one's ~** faltar à palavra/cumprir a promessa; **~ for ~** ao pé da letra; **what's the ~ for "pen" in Portuguese?** como se fala "pen" em português?; **to put sth into ~s** expressar algo; **to have a ~ with sb** falar com alguém; **to have ~s with sb** discutir com alguém; **I'll take your ~ for it** acredito em você; **to send ~ that ...** mandar dizer que ...; **to leave ~ that ...** deixar recado dizendo que ....

wording ['wəːdɪŋ] *n* fraseio.

word-perfect *adj*: **he was ~ in his speech** *etc*, **his speech** *etc* **was ~** ele sabia o discurso de cor.

word processing *n* processamento de textos.

word processor [-'prəusɛsə*] *n* processador *m* de textos.

wordwrap ['wəːdræp] *n* (*COMPUT*) marginação *f* automática.

wordy ['wəːdɪ] *adj* prolixo, verboso.

wore [wɔː*] *pt of* **wear**.

work [wəːk] *n* trabalho; (*job*) emprego, trabalho; (*ART*, *LITERATURE*) obra ♦ *vi* trabalhar; (*mechanism*) funcionar; (*medicine*) surtir efeito, ser eficaz; (*plan*) dar certo ♦ *vt* (*wood etc*) talhar; (*mine etc*) explorar; (*machine*) fazer trabalhar, manejar; **~s** *n* (*BRIT*: *factory*) fábrica, usina ♦ *npl* (*of clock*, *machine*) mecanismo; **road ~s** obras *fpl* (na estrada); **to go to ~** ir trabalhar; **to set to ~**, **to start ~** começar a trabalhar; **to be at ~ (on sth)** estar trabalhando (em algo); **to be out of ~** estar desempregado; **to ~ hard** trabalhar muito; **to ~ loose** (*part*) soltar-se; (*knot*) afrouxar-se.

work on *vt fus* trabalhar em, dedicar-se a; (*principle*) basear-se em.

work out *vi* (*plans etc*) dar certo, surtir efeito ♦ *vt* (*problem*) resolver; (*plan*) elaborar, formular; **it ~s out at £100** monta *or* soma a 100 libras.

workable ['wəːkəbl] *adj* (*solution*) viável.

workaholic [wəːkə'hɔlɪk] *n* burro de carga.

workbench ['wəːkbɛntʃ] *n* banco, bancada.

worked up [wəːkt-] *adj*: **to get ~** ficar exaltado.

worker ['wəːkə*] *n* trabalhador(a) *m/f*, operário/a; **office ~** empregado/a de escritório.

work force *n* força de trabalho.

work-in (*BRIT*) *n* ocupação *f* de fábrica *etc* (*sem paralisação da produção*).

working ['wəːkɪŋ] *adj* (*day*, *tools etc*, *conditions*) de trabalha; (*wife*) que trabalha; (*population*, *partner*) ativo; **in ~ order** em bom estado de funcionamento; **a ~ knowledge of English** um conhecimento prático do inglês.

working capital *n* (*COMM*) capital *m* de giro.

working class ['wəːkɪŋ-] *n* proletariado, classe *f* operária ♦ *adj*: **working-class** do proletariado, da classe operária.

working man (*irreg*) *n* trabalhador *m*.

working model *n* modelo articulado.

working party (*BRIT*) *n* grupo de trabalho.

working week *n* semana de trabalho.

work-in-progress *n* (*COMM*) produção *f* em curso.

workload ['wəːkləud] *n* carga de trabalho.

workman ['wəːkmən] (*irreg*) *n* operário, trabalhador *m*.

workmanship ['wəːkmənʃɪp] *n* (*art*) acabamento; (*skill*) habilidade *f*.

workmate ['wəːkmeɪt] *n* colega *m/f* de trabalho.

workout ['wəːkaut] *n* treinamento, treino.

work permit *n* permissão *f* de trabalho.

works council *n* comissão *f* de operários.

work sheet *n* registro das horas de trabalho; (*COMPUT*) folha de trabalho.

workshop ['wəːkʃɔp] *n* oficina.

work station *n* estação *f* de trabalho.

work study *n* estudo de trabalho.

work-to-rule (*BRIT*) *n* paralisação *f* de trabalho extraordinário.

world [wəːld] *n* mundo ♦ *cpd* mundial; **to think the ~ of sb** (*fig*) ter alguém em alto conceito; **all over the ~** no mundo inteiro; **what in the ~ is he doing?** o que é que ele está fazendo, pelo amor de Deus?; **to do sb a ~ of good** fazer muito bem a alguém; **W~ War One/Two** Primeira/Segunda Guerra Mundial; **out of this ~** sensacional.

World Cup *n*: **the ~** (*FOOTBALL*) a Copa do Mundo.

world-famous *adj* de fama mundial.

worldly ['wəːldlɪ] *adj* mundano.

world-wide *adj* mundial, universal ♦ *adv* no mundo inteiro.

worm [wəːm] *n* verme *m*; (*earth~*) minhoca, lombriga.

worn [wɔːn] *pp of* **wear** ♦ *adj* usado.

worn-out *adj* (*object*) gasto; (*person*) esgotado, exausto.

worried ['wʌrɪd] *adj* preocupado; **to be ~ about sth** estar preocupado com algo.

worrier ['wʌrɪə*] *n*: **he's a ~** ele se preocupa com tudo.

worry ['wʌrɪ] *n* preocupação *f* ♦ *vt* preocupar, inquietar ♦ *vi* preocupar-se, afligir-se; **to ~ about** *or* **over sth/sb** preocupar-se com algo/alguém.

worrying ['wʌrɪɪŋ] *adj* inquietante, preocupante.

worse [wəːs] *adj*, *adv* pior ♦ *n* o pior; **a change for the ~** uma mudança para pior, uma piora; **to get ~** piorar; **he's none the ~ for it** não lhe fez mal; **so much the ~ for you!** pior para você!

worsen ['wəːsən] *vt*, *vi* piorar.

worse off *adj* com menos dinheiro; (*fig*): **you'll be ~ this way** assim você ficará pior que nunca.

worship ['wəːʃɪp] *n* culto; (*act*) adoração *f* ♦ *vt* adorar, venerar; **Your W~** (*BRIT*: *to mayor*) vossa Excelência; (: *to judge*) senhor Juiz.

worshipper ['wəːʃɪpə*] *n* devoto/a, venerador(a) *m/f.*

worst [wəːst] *adj* (o/a) pior ♦ *adv* pior ♦ *n* o pior; **at ~** na pior das hipóteses; **if the ~ comes to the ~** se o pior acontecer.

worsted ['wəːstɪd] *n*: (**wool**) ~ lã *f* penteada.

worth [wəːθ] *n* valor *m*, mérito ♦ *adj*: **to be ~** valer; **it's ~ it** vale a pena; **how much is it ~?** quanto vale?; **50 pence ~ of apples** maçãs no valor de 50 pence.

worthless ['wəːθlɪs] *adj* sem valor; (*useless*) inútil.

worthwhile [wəːθ'waɪl] *adj* (*activity*) que vale a pena; (*cause*) de mérito, louvável; **a ~ book** um livro que vale a pena ler.

worthy ['wəːðɪ] *adj* (*person*) merecedor(a), respeitável; (*motive*) justo; **~ of** digno de.

would [wud] *aux vb*: **she ~ come** ela viria; **he ~ have come** ele teria vindo; **~ you like a biscuit?** você quer um biscoito?; **he ~ go on Mondays** costumava ir às segundas-feiras; **~ you close the door, please?** quer fechar a porta por favor?; **you WOULD say that, ~n't you?** é lógico que você vai dizer isso; **she ~n't leave** ele não queria sair.

would-be (*pej*) *adj* aspirante, que pretende ser.

wound¹ [waund] *pt, pp of* **wind.**

wound² [wuːnd] *n* ferida ♦ *vt* ferir.

wove [wəuv] *pt of* **weave.**

woven ['wəuvən] *pp of* **weave.**

WP *n abbr* = **word processing**; **word processor** ♦ *abbr* (*BRIT*: *inf*) = **weather permitting.**

WPC (*BRIT*) *n abbr* = **woman police constable.**

wpm *abbr* (= *words per minute*) palavras por minuto.

WRAC (*BRIT*) *n abbr* = **Women's Royal Army Corps.**

WRAF (*BRIT*) *n abbr* = **Women's Royal Air Force.**

wrangle ['ræŋgl] *n* briga ♦ *vi* brigar.

wrap [ræp] *n* (*stole*) xale *m*; (*cape*) capa ♦ *vt* (*also*: **~ up**) embrulhar; **under ~s** (*fig*: *plan, scheme*) em sigilo.

wrapper ['ræpə*] *n* envoltório, invólucro; (*BRIT*: *of book*) capa.

wrapping paper ['ræpɪŋ-] *n* papel *m* de embrulho.

wrath [rɔθ] *n* cólera, ira.

wreak [riːk] *vt* (*destruction*) causar; **to ~ havoc** causar estragos; **to ~ vengeance on** vingar-se em, tirar vingança de.

wreath [riːθ, *pl* riːðz] *n* (*funeral ~*) coroa; (*of flowers*) grinalda.

wreathe [riːð] *vt* trançar, cingir.

wreck [rɛk] *n* naufrágio; (*ship*) restos *mpl* do naufrágio; (*pej*: *person*) ruína, caco ♦ *vt* destruir, danificar; (*fig*) arruinar, arrasar.

wreckage ['rɛkɪdʒ] *n* restos *mpl*; (*of building*) escombros *mpl.*

wrecker ['rɛkə*] (*US*) *n* (*breakdown van*) reboque *m* (*BR*), pronto socorro (*PT*).

WREN [rɛn] (*BRIT*) *n abbr membro do WRNS.*

wren [rɛn] *n* (*ZOOL*) carriça.

wrench [rɛntʃ] *n* (*TECH*) chave *f* inglesa; (*tug*) puxão *m*; (*fig*) separação *f* penosa ♦ *vt* arrancar; **to ~ sth from sb** arrancar algo de alguém.

wrest [rɛst] *vt*: **to ~ sth from sb** extorquir algo de *or* a alguém.

wrestle ['rɛsl] *vi*: **to ~ (with sb)** lutar (com *or* contra alguém); **to ~ with** (*fig*) lutar com.

wrestler ['rɛslə*] *n* lutador *m.*

wrestling ['rɛslɪŋ] *n* luta (livre).

wrestling match *n* partida de luta romana.

wretch [rɛtʃ] *n* desgraçado/a; **little ~!** (*often humorous*) seu desgraçado!

wretched ['rɛtʃɪd] *adj* desventurado, infeliz; (*inf*) maldito.

wriggle ['rɪgl] *n* contorção *f* ♦ *vi* retorcer-se, contorcer-se.

wring [rɪŋ] (*pt, pp* **wrung**) *vt* torcer, espremer; (*wet clothes*) torcer; (*fig*): **to ~ sth out of sb** arrancar algo de alguém.

wringer ['rɪŋə*] *n* máquina de espremer roupa.

wringing ['rɪŋɪŋ] *adj* (*also*: **~** *wet*) encharcado, ensopado.

wrinkle ['rɪŋkl] *n* (*on skin*) ruga; (*on paper*) prega ♦ *vt* franzir, preguear ♦ *vi* enrugar-se; (*cloth etc*) franzir-se.

wrinkled ['rɪŋkld] *adj* (*fabric, paper*) franzido, pregueado; (*surface, skin*) enrugado.

wrinkly ['rɪŋklɪ] *adj* (*fabric, paper*) franzido, pregueado; (*surface, skin*) enrugado.

wrist [rɪst] *n* pulso.

wristband ['rɪstbænd] (*BRIT*) *n* (*of shirt*) punho; (*of watch*) pulseira.

wrist watch *n* relógio *m* de pulso.

writ [rɪt] *n* mandado judicial; **to issue a ~ against sb, serve a ~ on sb** demandar judicialmente alguém.

write [raɪt] (*pt* **wrote,** *pp* **written**) *vt, vi* escrever; **to ~ sb a letter** escrever uma carta para alguém.

write away *vi*: **to ~ away for** (*information*) escrever pedindo; (*goods*) encomendar pelo correio.

write down *vt* escrever; (*note*) anotar.

write off *vt* (*debt*) cancelar; (*capital*) reduzir; (*smash up*: *car*) destroçar.

write out *vt* escrever por extenso; (*fair copy*) passar a limpo.

write up *vt* redigir.

write-off *n* perda total; **the car is a ~** o carro virou sucata *or* está destroçado.

write-protect *vt* (*COMPUT*) proteger de escrita *or* contra gravação.

writer ['raɪtə*] *n* escritor(a) *m/f.*

write-up *n* crítica.

writhe [raɪð] *vi* contorcer-se.

writing ['raɪtɪŋ] *n* escrita; (*hand-~*) caligrafia,

***NB**: European Portuguese adds the following consonants to certain words:* **b** (sú(b)dito, su(b)til); **c** (a(c)ção, a(c)cionista, a(c)to); **m** (inde(m)ne); **p** (ado(p)ção, ado(p)tar); *for further details see p. xiii.*

letra; (*of author*) obra; **in ~** por escrito; **to put sth in ~** pôr algo no papel; **in my own ~** do próprio punho.

writing case *n* pasta com material de escrita.

writing desk *n* escrivaninha.

writing paper *n* papel *m* para escrever.

written ['rɪtn] *pp of* **write.**

WRNS (*BRIT*) *n abbr* = **Women's Royal Naval Service.**

wrong [rɔŋ] *adj* (*bad*) errado, mau; (*unfair*) injusto; (*incorrect*) errado, equivocado; (*not suitable*) impróprio, inconveniente ♦ *adv* mal, errado ♦ *n* mal *m*; (*injustice*) injustiça ♦ *vt* ser injusto com; (*hurt*) ofender; **to be ~** estar errado; **you are ~ to do it** você se engana ao fazê-lo; **it's ~ to steal, stealing is ~** é errado roubar; **you are ~ about that, you've got it ~** você está enganado sobre isso; **to be in the ~** não ter razão; **what's ~?** o que é que há?; **there's nothing ~** não há nada de errado, não tem problema; **what's ~ with the car?** qual é o problema com o carro?; **to go ~** (*person*) desencaminhar-se; (*plan*) dar errado; (*machine*) sofrer uma avaria.

wrongful ['rɔŋful] *adj* injusto; **~ dismissal** demissão *f* injusta.

wrongly ['rɔŋlɪ] *adv* (*treat*) injustamente; (*answer, do*) errado.

wrong number *n* (*TEL*): **you have the ~** o número está errado.

wrong side *n* (*of cloth*) avesso.

wrote [rəut] *pt of* **write.**

wrought [rɔːt] *adj*: **~ iron** ferro forjado.

wrung [rʌŋ] *pt, pp of* **wring.**

WRVS (*BRIT*) *n abbr* (= *Women's Royal Voluntary Service*) *instituição de caridade.*

wry [raɪ] *adj* (*smile*) irônico; **to make a ~ face** fazer uma careta.

wt. *abbr* = **weight.**

WV (*US*) *abbr* (*POST*) = **West Virginia.**

WY (*US*) *abbr* (*POST*) = **Wyoming.**

WYSIWYG ['wɪzɪwɪg] *abbr* (*COMPUT*: = *what you see is what you get*) *o documento sairá na impressora exatamente como aparece na tela.*

X

X, x [ɛks] *n* (*letter*) X, x *m*; (*BRIT*: *CINEMA*: *old*) (proibido para menores de) 18 anos; **X for Xmas** X de Xavier; **if you have ~ dollars a year ...** se você tem x dólares por ano ....

Xerox ['zɪərɔks] ® *n* (*also*: *~ machine*) xerox *m* ®; (*photocopy*) xerox *m* ®♦ *vt* xerocar, tirar um xerox de.

XL *abbr* = **extra large.**

Xmas ['ɛksməs] *n abbr* = **Christmas.**

X-rated [-'reɪtɪd] (*US*) *adj* (*film*) proibido para menores de 18 anos.

X-ray [ɛks'reɪ] *n* radiografia ♦ *vt* radiografar, tirar uma chapa de; **~s** *npl* raios *mpl* X; **to have an ~** tirar *or* bater um raio x.

xylophone ['zaɪləfəun] *n* xilofone *m*.

Y

Y, y [waɪ] *n* (*letter*) Y, y *m*; **Y for Yellow** (*BRIT*) *or* **Yoke** (*US*) Y de Yolanda.

yacht [jɔt] *n* iate *m*; (*smaller*) veleiro.

yachting ['jɔtɪŋ] *n* (*sport*) iatismo.

yachtsman ['jɔtsmən] (*irreg*) *n* iatista *m*.

yam [jæm] *n* inhame *m*.

Yank [jæŋk] (*pej*) *n* ianque *m/f*.

yank [jæŋk] *vt* arrancar.

Yankee ['jæŋkɪ] (*pej*) *n* ianque *m/f*.

yap [jæp] *vi* (*dog*) ganir.

yard [jɑːd] *n* pátio, quintal *m*; (*US*: *garden*) jardim *m*; (*measure*) jarda (= *914 mm*; *3 feet*); **builder's ~** depósito de material de construção.

yardstick ['jɑːdstɪk] *n* (*fig*) critério, padrão *m*.

yarn [jɑːn] *n* fio; (*tale*) história inverossímil.

yawn [jɔːn] *n* bocejo ♦ *vi* bocejar.

yawning ['jɔːnɪŋ] *adj* (*gap*) enorme.

yd *abbr* = **yard(s).**

yeah [jɛə] (*inf*) *adv* é.

year [jɪə*] *n* ano; **to be 8 ~s old** ter 8 anos; **every ~** todos os anos, todo ano; **this ~** este ano; **a** *or* **per ~** por ano; **~ in, ~ out** entra ano, sai ano; **an eight-~-old child** uma criança de oito anos (de idade).

yearbook ['jɪəbuk] *n* anuário, almanaque *m*.

yearly ['jɪəlɪ] *adj* anual ♦ *adv* anualmente; **twice ~** duas vezes por ano.

yearn [jəːn] *vi*: **to ~ to do/for sth** ansiar fazer/por algo.

yearning ['jəːnɪŋ] *n* ânsia, desejo ardente.

yeast [jiːst] *n* levedura, fermento.

yell [jɛl] *n* grito, berro ♦ *vi* gritar, berrar.

yellow ['jɛləu] *adj, n* amarelo.

yellow fever *n* febre *f* amarela.

yellowish ['jɛləuɪʃ] *adj* amarelado.

Yellow Sea *n*: **the ~** o mar Amarelo.

yelp [jɛlp] *n* latido ♦ *vi* latir.

Yemen ['jɛmən] *n* Iêmen *m* (*BR*), Iémene *m* (*PT*).

yen [jɛn] *n* (*currency*) iene *m*; (*craving*): **~ for/to do** desejo de/de fazer.

yeoman ['jəumən] (*irreg*) *n*: **Y~ of the Guard** membro da guarda real.

yes [jɛs] *adv, n* sim *m*; **do you speak English? — ~ I do** você fala inglês? — falo (sim); **does the plane leave at six? — ~** o avião sai às seis? — é; **to say ~ to sth/sb** (*ap-*

prove) dar o sim a algo/alguém.

yesterday ['jɛstədɪ] *adv, n* ontem *m*; **the day before** ~ anteontem; ~ **morning/evening** ontem de manhã/à noite; **all day** ~ ontem o dia inteiro.

yet [jɛt] *adv* ainda ♦ *conj* porém, no entanto; **it is not finished** ~ ainda não está acabado; **must you go just** ~? você já tem que ir?; **the best** ~ o melhor até agora; **as** ~ até agora, ainda; **a few days** ~ mais alguns dias; ~ **again** mais uma vez.

yew [ju:] *n* teixo.

YHA (*BRIT*) *n abbr* = **Youth Hostels Association.**

Yiddish ['jɪdɪʃ] *n* (i)ídiche *m*.

yield [ji:ld] *n* produção *f*; (*AGR*) colheita; (*COMM*) rendimento ♦ *vt* (*gen*) produzir; (*profit*) render; (*surrender*) ceder ♦ *vi* (*give way*) render-se, ceder; (*US*: *AUT*) ceder; **a** ~ **of 5%** um rendimento de 5%.

YMCA *n abbr* (= *Young Men's Christian Association*) ≈ ACM *f*.

yob(bo) ['jɔb(əu)] (*BRIT*: *inf*) *n* bagunçeiro.

yodel ['jəudl] *vi* cantar tirolesa.

yoga ['jəugə] *n* ioga.

yog(h)ourt ['jəugət] *n* iogurte *m*.

yog(h)urt ['jəugət] *n* = **yog(h)ourt.**

yoke [jəuk] *n* canga, cangalha; (*pair of oxen*) junta; (*on shoulders*) balancim *m*; (*fig*) jugo ♦ *vt* (*also*: ~ *together*) unir, ligar.

yolk [jəuk] *n* gema (do ovo).

yonder ['jɔndə*] *adv* além, acolá.

Yorks [jɔ:ks] (*BRIT*) *abbr* = **Yorkshire.**

you [ju:] *pron* (*subject*) tu, você; (: *pl*) vós, vocês; (*direct object*) te, o/a; (: *pl*) vos, os/as; (*indirect object*) te, lhe; (: *pl*) vos, lhes; (*after prep*) ti, você; (: *pl*) vós, vocês; (*polite form*) o senhor/a senhora; (: *pl*) os senhores/as senhoras; (*one*): ~ **never know** nunca se sabe; **with** ~ contigo, com você; convosco, com vocês; com o senhor *etc*; **apples do** ~ **good** as maçãs fazem bem à saúde; **if I were** ~ se eu fosse você.

you'd [ju:d] = **you had; you would.**

you'll [ju:l] = **you will; you shall.**

young [jʌŋ] *adj* jovem ♦ *npl* (*of animal*) filhotes *mpl*, crias *fpl*; (*people*): **the** ~ a juventude, os jovens; **a** ~ **man** um jovem; **a** ~ **lady** (*unmarried*) uma jovem, uma moça; (*married*) uma jovem senhora; **my** ~**er brother** o meu irmão mais novo; **the** ~**er generation** a geração mais jovem.

youngish ['jʌŋɪʃ] *adj* bem novo.

youngster ['jʌŋstə*] *n* jovem *m/f*, moço/a.

your [jɔ:*] *adj* teu/tua, seu/sua; (*pl*) vosso, seu/sua; (*formal*) do senhor/da senhora.

you're [juə*] = **you are.**

yours [jɔ:z] *pron* teu/tua, seu/sua; (*pl*) vosso, seu/sua; (*formal*) do senhor/da senhora; ~ **is blue** o teu/a tua é azul; **is it** ~? é teu *etc*?; ~ **sincerely** *or* **faithfully** atenciosamente; **a friend of** ~ um amigo seu.

yourself [jɔ:'sɛlf] *pron* (*subject*) tu mesmo, você mesmo; (*direct/indirect object*) te, se; (*after prep*) ti mesmo, si mesmo; (*formal*) o senhor mesmo/a senhora mesma; **you** ~ **told me** você mesmo me falou; **(all) by** ~ sozinho/a.

yourselves [jɔ:'sɛlvz] *pron* (*subject*) vós mesmos, vocês mesmos; (*direct/indirect object*) vos, se; (*formal*) os senhores mesmos/as senhoras mesmas.

youth [ju:θ, *pl* ju:ðz] *n* mocidade *f*, juventude *f*; (*young man*) jovem *m*; **in my** ~ na minha juventude.

youth club *n* associação *f* de juventude.

youthful ['ju:θful] *adj* juvenil.

youthfulness ['ju:θfəlnəs] *n* juventude *f*.

youth hostel *n* albergue *m* da juventude.

you've [ju:v] = **you have.**

yowl [jaul] *n* uivo ♦ *vi* uivar.

YTS (*BRIT*) *n abbr* (= *Youth Training Scheme*) *programa de ensino profissionalizante.*

Yugoslav ['ju:gəuslɑ:v] *adj, n* iugoslavo/a.

Yugoslavia [ju:gəu'slɑ:vɪə] *n* Iugoslávia.

Yugoslavian [ju:gəu'slɑ:vɪən] *adj* iugoslavo.

Yule [ju:l]: ~ **log** *n* acha de Natal.

Yuletide ['ju:ltaɪd] *n* época natalina *or* do Natal.

yuppie ['jʌpɪ] *n* yuppie *m/f*.

YWCA *n abbr* (= *Young Women's Christian Association*) ≈ ACM *f*.

Z

Z, z [zɛd, (*US*) zi:] *n* (*letter*) Z, z *m*; **Z for Zebra** Z de Zebra.

Zaire [zɑ:'i:ə*] *n* Zaire *m*.

Zambia ['zæmbɪə] *n* Zâmbia.

Zambian ['zæmbɪən] *adj, n* zambiano/a.

zany ['zeɪnɪ] *adj* tolo, bobo.

zap [zæp] *vt* (*COMPUT*) apagar.

zeal [zi:l] *n* zelo, fervor *m*.

zealot ['zɛlət] *n* fanático/a.

zealous ['zɛləs] *adj* zeloso, entusiasta.

zebra ['zi:brə] *n* zebra.

zebra crossing (*BRIT*) *n* faixa (para pedestres) (*BR*), passadeira (*PT*).

zenith ['zɛnɪθ] *n* (*ASTRONOMY*) zênite *m*; (*fig*) apogeu *m*.

zero ['zɪərəu] *n* zero ♦ *vi*: **to** ~ **in on** fazer mira em; **5° below** ~ 5 graus abaixo de zero.

zero hour *n* hora zero.

zero-rated [-'reɪtɪd] (*BRIT*) *adj* isento de IVA.

zest [zɛst] *n* vivacidade *f*, entusiasmo; (*of lemon etc*) zesto.

zigzag ['zɪgzæg] *n* ziguezague *m* ♦ *vi* zigueza-

***NB**: European Portuguese adds the following consonants to certain words:* **b** (sú(b)dito, su(b)til); **c** (a(c)ção, a(c)cionista, a(c)to); **m** (inde(m)ne); **p** (ado(p)ção, ado(p)tar); *for further details see p. xiii.*

guear.
Zimbabwe [zɪm'bɑːbwɪ] *n* Zimbábue *m* (*BR*), Zimbabwe *m* (*PT*).
Zimbabwean [zɪm'bɑːbwɪən] *adj*, *n* zimbabuano/a (*BR*), zimbabweano/a (*PT*).
zinc [zɪŋk] *n* zinco.
Zionism ['zaɪənɪzm] *n* sionismo.
Zionist ['zaɪənɪst] *adj*, *n* sionista *m/f*.
zip [zip] *n* (*also*: ~ *fastener*, ~*per*) fecho ecler (*BR*) *or* éclair (*PT*); (*energy*) vigor *m* ♦ *vt* (*also*: ~ *up*) fechar o fecho ecler de, subir o fecho ecler de.
zip code (*US*) *n* código postal.
zither ['zɪðə*] *n* citara.
zodiac ['zəudɪæk] *n* zodíaco.
zombie ['zɔmbɪ] *n* (*fig*): **like a** ~ como um zumbi.
zone [zəun] *n* zona.
zoo [zuː] *n* (jardim *m*) zoológico.
zoological [zuə'lɔdʒɪkl] *adj* zoológico.
zoologist [zuː'ɔlədʒɪst] *n* zoólogo/a.
zoology [zuː'ɔlədʒɪ] *n* zoologia.
zoom [zuːm] *vi*: **to** ~ **past** passar zunindo; **to** ~ **in (on sb/sth)** (*PHOT*, *CINEMA*) fechar a câmera (em alguém/algo).
zoom lens *n* zoom *m*, zum *m*.
zucchini [zuː'kiːnɪ] (*US*) *n inv* abobrinha.
Zulu ['zuːluː] *adj*, *n* zulu *m/f*.
Zurich ['zjuərɪk] *n* Zurique.

PORTUGUÊS-INGLÊS
PORTUGUESE-ENGLISH

A

A, a [a] (*pl* **as**) *m* A, a; **A de Antônio** A for Andrew (*BRIT*) *ou* Able (*US*).

a [a] *art def* the ♦ *pron* her; (*você*) you; (*coisa*) it ♦ *prep* (*direção*) to; (*tempo*) at; (*com vb*): **começou ~ nevar** it started to snow; (*com infin*: = *gerúndio*): **~ correr** running; (*col*: *usado como substantivo*): **qual é ~ dele?** where's he at?; (*usos pronominais*) *V* **o**; **à direita/esquerda** on the right/left; **ao lado de** beside, at the side of; **~ que horas?** at what time?; **às 5 horas** at 5 o'clock; **à noite** at night; **aos 15 anos** at 15 years of age; **ao vê-lo** when I saw him; **~ cavalo/pé** on horseback/foot; **~ negócios** on business; (*maneira*): **à força** by force; **~ mão/tinta** by hand/in ink; **dia ~ dia** day by day; **pouco ~ pouco** little by little; **aos poucos** gradually; **~ Cr$2000 o quilo** Cr$2000 a kilo.

à [a] = **a** + **a**.

(a) *abr* (= *assinado*) signed.

AAB *abr f* (= *Aliança Anticomunista Brasileira*) *terrorist group*.

aba ['aba] *f* (*de chapéu*) brim; (*de casaco*) tail; (*de montanha*) foot.

abacate [aba'katʃi] *m* avocado (pear).

abacaxi [abaka'ʃi] (*BR*) *m* pineapple; (*col*: *problema*) pain.

abade/abadessa [a'badʒi/aba'desa] *m/f* abbot/abbess.

Abadi [aba'dʒi] *abr f* = **Associação Brasileira das Administradoras de Imóveis**.

abadia [aba'dʒia] *f* abbey.

abafadiço/a [abafa'dʒisu/a] *adj* stifling; (*ar*) stuffy.

abafado/a [aba'fadu/a] *adj* (*ar*) stuffy; (*tempo*) humid, close; (*ocupado*) extremely busy; (*angustiado*) anxious.

abafamento [abafa'mẽtu] *m* fug; (*sufocação*) suffocation.

abafar [aba'fa*] *vt* to suffocate; (*ocultar*) to suppress; (*som*) to muffle; (*encobrir*) to cover up; (*col*) to pilfer ♦ *vi* (*col*: *fazer sucesso*) to steal the show.

abagunçado/a [abagũ'sadu/a] *adj* messy.

abagunçar [abagũ'sa*] *vt* to make a mess of, mess up.

abaixar [abaj'ʃa*] *vt* to lower; (*preço*) to reduce; (*luz, som*) to turn down; **~-se** *vr* to stoop.

abaixo [a'bajʃu] *adv* down ♦ *prep*: **~ de** below; **~ o governo!** down with the government!; **morro ~** downhill; **rio ~** downstream; **mais ~** further down; **~ e acima** up and down; **~ assinado** undersigned.

abaixo-assinado [-asi'nadu] (*pl* **~s**) *m* (*documento*) petition.

abajur [aba'ʒu*] (*BR*) *m* (*cúpula*) lampshade; (*luminária*) table lamp.

abalado/a [aba'ladu/a] *adj* unstable, unsteady; (*fig*) shaken.

abalar [aba'la*] *vt* to shake; (*fig*: *comover*) to affect ♦ *vi* to shake; **~-se** *vr* to be moved.

abalizado/a [abali'zadu/a] *adj* eminent, distinguished; (*opinião*) reliable.

abalo [a'balu] *m* (*comoção*) shock; (*ação*) shaking; **~ sísmico** earth tremor.

abalroar [abawro'a*] *vt* to collide with, run into.

abanar [aba'na*] *vt* to shake; (*rabo*) to wag; (*com leque*) to fan.

abandalhar [abãda'ʎa*] *vt* to debase.

abandonar [abãdo'na*] *vt* (*deixar*) to leave, desert; (*repudiar*) to reject; (*renunciar*) to abandon, give up; (*descuidar*) to neglect; **~-se** *vr*: **~-se a** to abandon o.s. to.

abandono [abã'donu] *m* (*ato*) desertion; (*estado*) neglect.

abarcar [abax'ka*] *vt* (*abranger*) to comprise; (*conter*) to enclose.

abarque [a'baxki] *etc vb V* **abarcar**.

abarrotado/a [abaxo'tadu/a] *adj* crammed full; (*lugar*) crowded, crammed.

abarrotar [abaxo'ta*] *vt*: **~ de** to cram with.

abastado/a [abaʃ'tadu/a] *adj* wealthy.

abastança [abaʃ'tãsa] *f* abundance, surfeit.

abastardar [abaʃtax'da*] *vt* to corrupt.

abastecer [abaʃte'se*] *vt* to supply; (*motor*) to fuel; (*AUTO*) to fill up; (*AER*) to refuel; **~-se** *vr*: **~-se de** to stock up with.

abastecimento [abaʃtesi'mẽtu] *m* supply; (*comestíveis*) provisions *pl*; (*ato*) supplying; (*de carro, avião*) refuelling (*BRIT*), refueling (*US*); **~s** *mpl* supplies.

abater [aba'te*] *vt* (*derrubar*) to knock down; (*gado*) to slaughter; (*preço*) to reduce, lower; (*debilitar*) to weaken; (*desalentar*) to dishearten.

abatido/a [aba'tʃidu/a] *adj* depressed, downcast; (*fisionomia*) haggard.

***NB**: European Portuguese adds the following consonants to certain words:* **b** (sú(b)dito, su(b)til); **c** (a(c)ção, a(c)cionista, a(c)to); **m** (inde(m)ne); **p** (ado(p)ção, ado(p)tar); *for further details see p. xiii.*

abatimento [abatʃi'mẽtu] *m* (*fraqueza*) weakness; (*de preço*) reduction; (*prostração*) depression; **fazer um ~** to give a discount.
abaulado/a [abaw'ladu/a] *adj* convex; (*estrada*) cambered.
abaular-se [abaw'laxsi] *vr* to bulge.
ABBC *abr f* = **Associação Brasileira dos Bancos Comerciais.**
ABBR *abr f* (= *Associação Brasileira Beneficente de Reabilitação*) *charity for the disabled.*
abcesso [ab'sɛsu] *m* tumour (*BRIT*), tumor (*US*); (*de dentes*) abscess.
abdicação [abdʒika'sãw] (*pl* **-ões**) *f* abdication.
abdicar [abdʒi'ka*] *vt*, *vi* to abdicate.
abdômen [ab'domẽ] *m* abdomen.
á-bê-cê [abe'se] *m* alphabet; (*fig*) rudiments *pl*.
abecedário [abese'darju] *m* alphabet, ABC.
Abeenras *abr f* = **Associação Brasileira das Empresas de Engenharia, Reparos e Atividades Subaquáticas.**
abeirar [abej'ra*] *vt* to bring near; **~-se** *vr*: **~-se de** to draw near to.
abelha [a'beʎa] *f* bee.
abelha-mestra (*pl* **abelhas-mestras**) *f* queen bee.
abelhudo/a [abe'ʎudu/a] *adj* nosy.
abençoar [abẽ'swa*] *vt* to bless.
abendiçoar [abẽdʒi'swa*] *vt* to bless.
aberração [abexa'sãw] (*pl* **-ões**) *f* aberration.
aberta [a'bɛxta] *f* opening; (*clareira*) glade; (*intervalo*) break.
aberto/a [a'bɛxtu/a] *pp de* **abrir** ♦ *adj* open; (*céu*) clear; (*sinal*) green; (*torneira*) on; (*desprotegido*) exposed; (*liberal*) open-minded.
abertura [abex'tura] *f* opening; (*FOTO*) aperture; (*ranhura*) gap, crevice; (*POL*) liberalization.
abestalhado/a [abeʃta'ʎadu/a] *adj* stupid.
ABH *abr f* = **Associação Brasileira da Indústria de Hóteis.**
ABI *abr f* = **Associação Brasileira de Imprensa.**
Abifarma *abr f* = **Associação Brasileira da Industria Farmacêutica.**
abilolado/a [abilo'ladu/a] *adj* crazy.
abismado/a [abiʒ'madu/a] *adj* astonished.
abismo [a'biʒmu] *m* abyss, chasm; (*fig*) depths *pl*.
abjeção [abʒe'sãw] (*PT*: **-cç-**) *f* baseness.
abjeto/a [ab'ʒɛtu/a] (*PT*: **-ct-**) *adj* abject, contemptible.
abjudicar [abʒudʒi'ka*] *vt* to seize.
ABL *abr f* = **Academia Brasileira de Letras.**
ABMU *abr f* = **Associação Brasileira de Mulheres Universitárias.**
abnegação [abnega'sãw] *f* self-denial.
abnegado/a [abne'gadu/a] *adj* self-sacrificing.
abnegar [abne'ga*] *vt* to renounce.
abóbada [a'bɔbada] *f* vault; (*telhado*) arched roof.
abobalhado/a [aboba'ʎadu/a] *adj* stupid.
abóbora [a'bɔbora] *f* pumpkin.
abobrinha [abo'briɲa] *f* courgette (*BRIT*), zucchini (*US*).
abocanhar [aboka'ɲa*] *vt* (*apanhar com a boca*) to seize with the mouth; (*morder*) to bite.
abolição [aboli'sãw] *f* abolition.
abolir [abo'li*] *vt* to abolish.
abominação [abomina'sãw] (*pl* **-ões**) *f* abomination.
abominar [abomi'na*] *vt* to loathe, detest.
abominável [abomi'navew] (*pl* **-eis**) *adj* abominable.
abonar [abo'na*] *vt* to guarantee.
abono [a'bɔnu] *m* guarantee; (*JUR*) bail; (*louvor*) praise; **~ de família** child benefit.
abordagem [abox'daʒẽ] (*pl* **-ns**) *f* approach.
abordar [abox'da*] *vt* (*NÁUT*) to board; (*pessoa*) to approach; (*assunto*) to broach, tackle.
aborígene [abo'riʒeni] *adj* native, aboriginal ♦ *m/f* native, aborigine.
aborrecer [aboxe'se*] *vt* (*chatear*) to annoy; (*maçar*) to bore; **~-se** *vr* to get upset; to get bored.
aborrecido/a [aboxe'sidu/a] *adj* boring; (*chateado*) annoyed.
aborrecimento [aboxesi'mẽtu] *m* boredom; (*chateação*) annoyance.
abortar [abox'ta*] *vi* to miscarry ♦ *vt* to abort.
aborto [a'boxtu] *m* (*MED*) miscarriage; (*forçado*) abortion; **fazer um ~** to have an abortion.
abotoadura [abotwa'dura] *f* cufflink.
abotoar [abo'twa*] *vt* to button up ♦ *vi* (*BOT*) to bud.
abr. *abr* (= *abril*) Apr.
abraçar [abra'sa*] *vt* to hug; (*causa*) to embrace; **~-se** *vr* to embrace; **ele abraçou-se a mim** he embraced me.
abraço [a'brasu] *m* embrace, hug; **com um ~** (*em carta*) with best wishes.
abrandar [abrã'da*] *vt* to reduce; (*suavizar*) to soften ♦ *vi* to diminish; (*acalmar*) to calm down.
abranger [abrã'ʒe*] *vt* to include, comprise; (*alcançar*) to reach.
abranjo [a'brãʒu] *etc vb V* **abranger.**
abrasar [abra'za*] *vt* to burn; (*desbastar*) to erode ♦ *vi* to be on fire.
abrasileirado/a [abrazilej'radu/a] *adj* Brazilianized.
ABRATES *abr f* = **Associação Brasileira de Tradutores.**
ABRATT *abr f* = **Associação Brasileira dos Transportadores Exclusivos de Turismo.**
abre-garrafas ['abri-] (*PT*) *m inv* bottle opener.
abre-latas ['abri-] (*PT*) *m inv* tin (*BRIT*) *ou* can opener.
abreugrafia [abrewgra'fia] *f* X-ray.

abreviação [abrevja'sãw] (*pl* **-ões**) *f* abbreviation; (*de texto*) abridgement.
abreviar [abre'vja*] *vt* to abbreviate; (*encurtar*) to shorten; (*texto*) to abridge.
abreviatura [abrevja'tura] *f* abbreviation.
abridor [abri'do*] (*BR*) *m* opener; ~ **(de lata)** tin (*BRIT*) *ou* can opener; ~ **de garrafa** bottle opener.
abrigar [abri'ga*] *vt* to shelter; (*proteger*) to protect; **~-se** *vr* to take shelter.
abrigo [a'brigu] *m* shelter, cover; ~ **anti-aéreo** air-raid shelter; ~ **anti-nuclear** fall-out shelter.
abril [a'briw] (*PT*: **A~**) *m* April; *V tb* **julho**.
abrilhantar [abriʎã'ta*] *vt* to enhance.
abrir [a'bri*] *vt* to open; (*fechadura*) to unlock; (*vestuário*) to unfasten; (*torneiras*) to turn on; (*buraco, exceção*) to make; (*processo*) to start ♦ *vi* to open; (*sinal*) to go green; (*tempo*) to clear up; **~-se** *vr*: **~-se com alguém** to confide in sb, open up to sb.
ab-rogação [abxoga'sãw] (*pl* **~ões**) *f* repeal, annulment.
ab-rogar [abxo'ga*] *vt* to repeal, annul.
abrolho [a'broʎu] *m* thorn.
abrupto/a [a'bruptu/a] *adj* abrupt; (*repentino*) sudden.
abrutalhado/a [abruta'ʎadu/a] *adj* (*pessoa*) coarse; (*sapatos*) heavy.
absenteísta [absẽte'iʃta] *m/f* absentee.
absentismo [absẽ'tʃiʒmu] *m* absenteeism.
abside [ab'sidʒi] *f* apse; (*relicário*) shrine.
absolutamente [absoluta'mẽtʃi] *adv* absolutely; (*de jeito nenhum*) absolutely not, not at all.
absolutismo [absolu'tʃiʒmu] *m* absolutism.
absolutista [absolu'tʃiʃta] *adj, m/f* absolutist.
absoluto/a [abso'lutu/a] *adj* absolute; **em** ~ absolutely not, not at all.
absolver [absow've*] *vt* to absolve; (*JUR*) to acquit.
absolvição [absowvi'sãw] (*pl* **-ões**) *f* absolution; (*JUR*) acquittal.
absorção [absox'sãw] *f* absorption.
absorto/a [ab'soxtu/a] *pp de* **absorver** ♦ *adj* absorbed, engrossed.
absorvente [absox'vẽtʃi] *adj* (*papel etc*) absorbent; (*livro etc*) absorbing.
absorver [absox've*] *vt* to absorb; **~-se** *vr*: **~-se em** to concentrate on.
abstêmio/a [abʃ'temju/a] *adj* abstemious; (*álcool*) teetotal ♦ *m/f* abstainer, teetotaller (*BRIT*), teetotaler (*US*).
abstenção [abʃtẽ'sãw] (*pl* **-ões**) *f* abstention.
abstencionista [abʃtẽsjo'niʃta] *adj* abstaining ♦ *m/f* abstainer.
abstenções [abʃtẽ'sõjʃ] *fpl de* **abstenção**.
abster-se [ab'ʃtexsi] (*irreg*: *como* **ter**) *vr*: ~ **de** to abstain *ou* refrain from.
abstinência [abʃtʃi'nẽsja] *f* abstinence; (*jejum*) fasting.
abstinha [abʃ'tʃiɲa] *etc vb V* **abster-se**.
abstive [abʃ'tʃivi] *etc vb V* **abster-se**.
abstração [abʃtra'sãw] (*PT*: **-cç-**) *f* abstraction; (*concentração*) concentration.
abstrair [abʃtra'i*] *vt* to abstract; (*omitir*) to omit; (*separar*) to separate.
abstrato/a [abʃ'tratu/a] (*PT*: **-ct-**) *adj* abstract.
absurdo/a [abi'suxdu/a] *adj* absurd ♦ *m* nonsense.
abulia [abu'lia] *f* apathy.
abundância [abũ'dãsja] *f* abundance.
abundante [abũ'dãtʃi] *adj* abundant.
abundar [abũ'da*] *vi* to abound.
aburguesado/a [abuxge'zadu/a] *adj* middle-class, bourgeois.
abusar [abu'za*] *vi* (*exceder-se*) to go too far; ~ **de** to abuse.
abuso [a'buzu] *m* abuse; (*JUR*) indecent assault; ~ **de confiança** breach of trust.
abutre [a'butri] *m* vulture.
AC *abr* = **Acre**.
a.C. *abr* (= *antes de Cristo*) B.C.
a/c *abr* (= *aos cuidados de*) c/o.
acabado/a [aka'badu/a] *adj* finished; (*esgotado*) worn out; (*envelhecido*) aged.
acabamento [akaba'mẽtu] *m* finish.
acabar [aka'ba*] *vt* (*terminar*) to finish, complete; (*levar a cabo*) to accomplish; (*aperfeiçoar*) to complete; (*consumir*) to use up; (*rematar*) to finish off ♦ *vi* to finish, end, come to an end; **~-se** *vr* (*terminar*) to be over; (*prazo*) to expire; (*esgotar-se*) to run out; ~ **com** to put an end to; (*destruir*) to do away with; (*namorado*) to finish with; ~ **de chegar** to have just arrived; ~ **por** to end (up) by; **acabou-se!** that's enough!, it's all over!; **ele acabou cedendo** he eventually gave in, he ended up giving in; **... que não acaba mais** no end of ...; **quando acaba** (*no final*) in the end.
acabrunhado/a [akabru'ɲadu/a] *adj* (*abatido*) depressed; (*envergonhado*) embarrassed.
acabrunhar [akabru'ɲa*] *vt* (*entristecer*) to distress; (*envergonhar*) to embarrass.
acácia [a'kasja] *f* acacia.
academia [akade'mia] *f* academy; ~ **(de ginástica)** gym.
acadêmico/a [aka'demiku/a] *adj, m/f* academic.
açafrão [asa'frãw] *m* saffron.
acalcanhar [akawka'ɲa*] *vt* (*sapato*) to put out of shape.
acalentar [akalẽ'ta*] *vt* to rock to sleep; (*esperanças*) to cherish.
acalmar [akaw'ma*] *vt* to calm ♦ *vi* (*vento etc*) to abate; **~-se** *vr* to calm down.
acalorado/a [akalo'radu/a] *adj* heated.
acalorar [akalo'ra*] *vt* to heat; (*fig*) to inflame; **~-se** *vr* (*fig*) to get heated.

NB: *European Portuguese adds the following consonants to certain words:* **b** (sú(b)dito, su(b)til); **c** (a(c)ção, a(c)cionista, a(c)to); **m** (inde(m)ne); **p** (ado(p)ção, ado(p)tar); *for further details see p. xiii.*

acamado/a [aka'madu/a] *adj* bedridden.
açambarcar [asãbax'ka*] *vt* to appropriate; (*mercado*) to corner.
acampamento [akãpa'mẽtu] *m* camping; (MIL) camp, encampment; **levantar ~** to raise camp.
acampar [akã'pa*] *vi* to camp.
acanhado/a [aka'ɲadu/a] *adj* shy.
acanhamento [akaɲa'mẽtu] *m* shyness.
acanhar-se [aka'ɲaxsi] *vr* to be shy.
ação [a'sãw] (*pl* **-ões**) *f* action; (*ato*) act, deed; (MIL) battle; (*enredo*) plot; (JUR) lawsuit; (COM) share; **~ bonificada** (COM) bonus share; **~ de graças** thanksgiving; **~ integralizada/diferida** (COM) fully paid-in/deferred share; **~ ordinária/preferencial** (COM) ordinary/preference share.
acarajé [akara'ʒɛ] *m* (CULIN) *beans fried in palm oil.*
acareação [akarja'sãw] (*pl* **-ões**) *f* confrontation.
acarear [aka'rja*] *vt* to confront.
acariciar [akari'sja*] *vt* to caress; (*fig*) to cherish.
acarinhar [akari'ɲa*] *vt* to caress; (*fig*) to treat with tenderness.
acarretar [akaxe'ta*] *vt* to result in, bring about.
acasalamento [akazala'mẽtu] *m* mating.
acasalar [akaza'la*] *vt* to mate; **~-se** *vr* to mate.
acaso [a'kazu] *m* chance, accident; **ao ~** at random; **por ~** by chance.
acastanhado/a [akaʃta'ɲadu/a] *adj* brownish; (*cabelo*) auburn.
acatamento [akata'mẽtu] *m* respect; (*deferência*) deference.
acatar [aka'ta*] *vt* (*respeitar*) to respect; (*honrar*) to honour (BRIT), honor (US); (*lei*) to obey.
acautelar [akawte'la*] *vt* to warn; **~-se** *vr* to be cautious; **~-se contra** to guard against.
ACC *abr m* = **adiantamento de contratos de câmbio**.
acção [a'sãw] (PT) *f* = **ação**.
accionar *etc* [asjo'na*] (PT) = **acionar** *etc*.
acebolado/a [asebo'ladu/a] *adj* (CULIN) flavoured (BRIT) *ou* flavored (US) with onion.
aceder [ase'de*] *vi*: **~ a** to agree to, accede to.
aceitação [asejta'sãw] *f* acceptance; (*aprovação*) approval.
aceitar [asej'ta*] *vt* to accept; **você aceita uma bebida?** would you like a drink?
aceitável [asej'tavew] (*pl* **-eis**) *adj* acceptable.
aceite [a'sejtʃi] (PT) *pp de* **aceitar** ♦ *adj* accepted ♦ *m* acceptance.
aceito/a [a'sejtu/a] *pp de* **aceitar** ♦ *adj* accepted.
aceleração [aselera'sãw] *f* acceleration; (*pressa*) haste.
acelerado/a [asele'radu/a] *adj* (*rápido*) quick; (*apressado*) hasty.
acelerador [aselera'do*] *m* accelerator.
acelerar [asele'ra*] *vt, vi* to accelerate; **~ o passo** to go faster.
acenar [ase'na*] *vi* (*com a mão*) to wave; (*com a cabeça*) to nod; **~ com** (*oferecer*) to offer, promise.
acendedor [asẽde'do*] *m* lighter.
acender [asẽ'de*] *vt* (*cigarro, fogo*) to light; (*luz*) to switch on; (*fig*) to excite, inflame.
aceno [a'sɛnu] *m* sign, gesture; (*com a mão*) wave; (*com a cabeça*) nod.
acento [a'sẽtu] *m* accent; (*de intensidade*) stress; **~ agudo/circunflexo** acute/circumflex accent.
acentuação [asẽtwa'sãw] *f* accentuation; (*ênfase*) stress.
acentuado/a [asẽ'twadu/a] *adj* (*sílaba*) stressed; (*saliente*) conspicuous.
acentuar [asẽ'twa*] *vt* (*marcar com acento*) to accent; (*salientar*) to stress, emphasize; (*realçar*) to enhance.
acepção [asep'sãw] (*pl* **-ões**) *f* (*de uma palavra*) sense.
acepipe [ase'pipi] *m* tit-bit, delicacy; **~s** *mpl* (PT) hors d'œuvres.
acerca [a'sexka]: **~ de** *prep* about, concerning.
acercar-se [asex'kaxsi] *vr*: **~ de** to approach, draw near to.
acérrimo/a [a'seximu/a] *adj* (*muito acre*) very bitter; (*defensor*) staunch.
acertado/a [asex'tadu/a] *adj* (*certo*) right, correct; (*sensato*) sensible.
acertar [asex'ta*] *vt* (*ajustar*) to put right; (*relógio*) to set; (*alvo*) to hit; (*acordo*) to reach; (*pergunta*) to get right ♦ *vi* to get it right, be right; **~ com** to hit upon; **~ o caminho** to find the right way.
acervo [a'sexvu] *m* heap; (JUR) estate; (*de museu etc*) collection; **um ~ de** vast quantities of.
aceso/a [a'sezu/a] *pp de* **acender** ♦ *adj* (*luz, gás, TV*) on; (*fogo*) alight; (*excitado*) excited; (*furioso*) furious.
acessar [ase'sa*] *vt* (COMPUT) to access.
acessível [ase'sivew] (*pl* **-eis**) *adj* accessible; (*pessoa*) approachable; (*preço*) reasonable, affordable.
acesso [a'sɛsu] *m* access; (MED) fit, attack; **um ~ de cólera** a fit of anger; **de fácil ~** easy to get to; **múltiplo ~** (COMPUT) multiple access; **tempo de ~** (COMPUT) access time.
acessório/a [ase'sɔrju/a] *adj* accessory ♦ *m* accessory.
ACET (BR) *abr f* = **Agência Central dos Teatros**.
acetona [ase'tɔna] *f* nail varnish remover; (QUÍM) acetone.
achacar [aʃa'ka*] (*col*) *vt* (*dinheiro*) to extort.
achado/a [a'ʃadu/a] *adj*: **não se dar por ~** to play dumb ♦ *m* find, discovery; (*pechincha*) bargain; (*sorte*) godsend.
achaque [a'ʃaki] *m* ailment.
achar [a'ʃa*] *vt* (*descobrir*) to find; (*pensar*)

to think; **~-se** *vr* (*considerar-se*) to think (that) one is; (*encontrar-se*) to be; **~ de fazer** (*resolver*) to decide to do; **o que é que você acha disso?** what do you think of it?; **acho que ...** I think (that) ...; **acho que sim** I think so; **~ algo bom/estranho** *etc* to find sth good/strange *etc*; **~ ruim** to be cross.

achatar [aʃa'ta*] *vt* to squash, flatten; (*fig*) to talk round, convince.

achegar-se [aʃe'gaxsi] *vr*: **~ a** *ou* **de** to approach, get closer to.

acidentado/a [asidẽ'tadu/a] *adj* (*terreno*) rough; (*estrada*) bumpy; (*viagem*) eventful; (*vida*) chequered (*BRIT*), checkered (*US*) ♦ *m/f* injured person.

acidental [asidẽ'taw] (*pl* **-ais**) *adj* accidental.

acidente [asi'dẽtʃi] *m* accident; (*acaso*) chance; **por ~** by accident.

acidez [asi'deʒ] *f* acidity.

ácido/a ['asidu/a] *adj* acid; (*azedo*) sour ♦ *m* acid; **~ sulfúrico** sulphuric (*BRIT*) *ou* sulfuric (*US*) acid.

acima [a'sima] *adv* above; (*para cima*) up ♦ *prep*: **~ de** above; (*além de*) beyond; **mais ~** higher up; **rio ~** up river; **passar rua ~** to go up the street; **~ de 1000** more than 1000.

acinte [a'sĩtʃi] *m* provocation ♦ *adv* deliberately, on purpose.

acintosamente [asĩtoza'mẽtʃi] *adv* on purpose.

acinzentado/a [asĩzẽ'tadu/a] *adj* greyish (*BRIT*), grayish (*US*).

acionado/a [asjo'nadu/a] *m/f* (*JUR*) defendant; **~s** *mpl* gestures.

acionar [asjo'na*] *vt* to set in motion; (*máquina*) to operate; (*JUR*) to sue.

acionista [asjo'niʃta] *m/f* shareholder; **~ majoritário/minoritário** majority/minority shareholder.

acirrado/a [asi'xadu/a] *adj* (*luta, competição*) tough.

acirrar [asi'xa*] *vt* to incite, stir up.

aclamação [aklama'sãw] *f* acclamation; (*ovação*) applause.

aclamar [akla'ma*] *vt* to acclaim; (*aplaudir*) to applaud.

aclarado/a [akla'radu/a] *adj* clear.

aclarar [akla'ra*] *vt* to explain, clarify ♦ *vi* to clear up; **~-se** *vr* to become clear.

aclimatação [aklimata'sãw] *f* acclimatization.

aclimatar [aklima'ta*] *vt* to acclimatize (*BRIT*), acclimate (*US*); **~-se** *vr* to become acclimatized *ou* acclimated.

aclive [a'klivi] *m* slope, incline.

ACM *abr f* (= *Associação Cristã de Moços*) YMCA.

aço ['asu] *m* (*metal*) steel; **~ inox** stainless steel.

acocorar-se [akoko'raxsi] *vr* to squat, crouch.

acode [a'kɔdʒi] *etc vb V* **acudir**.

ações [a'sõjʃ] *fpl de* **ação**.

acoitar [akoj'ta*] *vt* to shelter, give refuge to.

açoitar [asoj'ta*] *vt* to whip, lash.

açoite [a'sojtʃi] *m* whip, lash.

acolá [ako'la] *adv* over there.

acolchoado/a [akow'ʃwadu/a] *adj* quilted ♦ *m* quilt.

acolchoar [akow'ʃwa*] *vt* (*costurar*) to quilt; (*forrar*) to pad; (*estofar*) to upholster.

acolhedor(a) [akoʎe'do*(a)] *adj* welcoming; (*hospitaleiro*) hospitable.

acolher [ako'ʎe*] *vt* to welcome; (*abrigar*) to shelter; (*aceitar*) to accept; **~-se** *vr* to shelter.

acolhida [ako'ʎida] *f* (*recepção*) reception, welcome; (*refúgio*) refuge.

acolhimento [akoʎi'mẽtu] *m* (*recepção*) reception, welcome; (*refúgio*) refuge.

acometer [akome'te*] *vt* (*atacar*) to attack; (*suj*: *doença*) to take hold of.

acomodação [akomoda'sãw] (*pl* **-ões**) *f* accommodation; (*arranjo*) arrangement; (*adaptação*) adaptation.

acomodar [akomo'da*] *vt* (*alojar*) to accommodate; (*arrumar*) to arrange; (*tornar cômodo*) to make comfortable; (*adaptar*) to adapt.

acompanhamento [akõpaɲa'mẽtu] *m* attendance; (*cortejo*) procession; (*MÚS*) accompaniment; (*CULIN*) side dish.

acompanhante [akõpa'ɲãtʃi] *m/f* companion; (*MÚS*) accompanist.

acompanhar [akõpa'ɲa*] *vt* to accompany, go along with; (*MÚS*) to accompany; (*assistir*) to watch; (*eventos*) to keep up with; **~ alguém até a porta** to show sb to the door.

aconchegado/a [akõʃe'gadu/a] *adj* snug, cosy (*BRIT*), cozy (*US*).

aconchegante [akõʃe'gãtʃi] *adj* cosy (*BRIT*), cozy (*US*).

aconchegar [akõʃe'ga*] *vt* to bring near; **~-se** *vr* (*acomodar-se*) to make o.s. comfortable; **~-se com** to snuggle up to.

aconchego [akõ'ʃegu] *m* cuddle.

acondicionamento [akõdʒisjona'mẽtu] *m* packaging.

acondicionar [akõdʒisjo'na*] *vt* to condition; (*empacotar*) to pack; (*embrulhar*) to wrap (up).

aconselhar [akõse'ʎa*] *vt* to advise; (*recomendar*) to recommend; **~-se** *vr*: **~-se com** to consult; **~ alguém a fazer** to advise sb to do.

aconselhável [akõse'ʎavew] (*pl* **-eis**) *adj* advisable.

acontecer [akõte'se*] *vi* to happen.

acontecimento [akõtesi'mẽtu] *m* event.

acoplador [akopla'do*] *m*: **~ acústico** (*COMPUT*) acoustic coupler.

acordar [akox'da*] *vt* (*despertar*) to wake

***NB**: European Portuguese adds the following consonants to certain words:* **b** (sú(b)dito, su(b)til); **c** (a(c)ção, a(c)cionista, a(c)to); **m** (inde(m)ne); **p** (ado(p)ção, ado(p)tar); *for further details see p. xiii.*

(up); (*concordar*) to agree (on) ♦ *vi* (*despertar*) to wake up.
acorde [a'kɔrdʒi] *m* chord.
acordeão [akox'dʒjãw] (*pl* **-ões**) *m* accordion.
acordeonista [akoxdʒjo'niʃta] *m/f* accordionist.
acordo [a'koxdu] *m* agreement; **de ~** agreed; **de ~ com** (*pessoa*) in agreement with; (*conforme*) in accordance with; **estar de ~** to agree; **~ de cavalheiros** gentlemen's agreement.
Açores [a'soriʃ] *mpl*: **os ~** the Azores.
açoriano/a [aso'rjanu/a] *adj*, *m/f* Azorean.
acorrentar [akoxẽ'ta*] *vt* to chain (up).
acorrer [ako'xe*] *vi*: **~ a alguém** to come to sb's aid.
acossar [ako'sa*] *vt* (*perseguir*) to pursue; (*atormentar*) to harass.
acostamento [akoʃta'mẽtu] *m* hard shoulder (BRIT), berm (US).
acostar [akoʃ'ta*] *vt* to lean against; (NÁUT) to bring alongside; **~-se** *vr* to lean back.
acostumado/a [akoʃtu'madu/a] *adj* (*habitual*) usual, customary; **estar ~** to be used to it; **estar ~ a algo** to be used to sth.
acostumar [akoʃtu'ma*] *vt* to accustom; **~-se** *vr*: **~-se a** to get used to.
acotovelar [akotove'la*] *vt* to jostle; **~-se** *vr* to jostle.
açougue [a'sogi] *m* butcher's (shop).
açougueiro [aso'gejru] *m* butcher.
acovardado/a [akovax'dadu/a] *adj* intimidated.
acovardar-se [akovax'daxsi] *vr* (*desanimar*) to lose courage; (*amedrontar-se*) to flinch, cower.
acre ['akri] *adj* (*amargo*) bitter; (*ríspido*) harsh; (*aroma*) acrid, strong.
acreano/a [a'krjanu/a] *adj* from Acre ♦ *m/f* native *ou* inhabitant of Acre.
acreditado/a [akredʒi'tadu/a] *adj* accredited.
acreditar [akredʒi'ta*] *vt* to believe; (COM) to credit; (*afiançar*) to guarantee ♦ *vi*: **~ em** to believe in; (*ter confiança em*) to have faith in; "**acredite na sinalização**" "follow traffic signs".
acreditável [akredʒi'tavew] (*pl* **-eis**) *adj* credible.
acre-doce *adj* (CULIN) sweet and sour.
acrescentar [akresẽ'ta*] *vt* to add.
acrescer [akre'se*] *vt* (*aumentar*) to increase; (*juntar*) to add ♦ *vi* to increase; **acresce que** ... add to that the fact that ....
acréscimo [a'krɛsimu] *m* addition; (*aumento*) increase; (*elevação*) rise.
acriançado/a [akrjã'sadu/a] *adj* childish.
acrílico [a'kriliku] *m* acrylic.
acrimônia [akri'monja] *f* acrimony.
acrobacia [akroba'sia] *f* acrobatics *pl*; **~s** *fpl* **aéreas** aerobatics *pl*.
acrobata [akro'bata] *m/f* acrobat.
activo/a *etc* [a'tivu/a] (PT) = **ativo** *etc*.
acto ['atu] (PT) *m* = **ato**.
actor [a'to*] (PT) *m* = **ator**.
actriz [a'triʒ] (PT) *f* = **atriz**.
actual *etc* [a'twaw] (PT) = **atual** *etc*.
actuar *etc* [a'twa*] (PT) = **atuar** *etc*.
acuar [a'kwa*] *vt* to corner.
açúcar [a'suka*] *m* sugar; **~ mascavo** brown sugar.
açucarado/a [asuka'radu/a] *adj* sugary.
açucarar [asuka'ra*] *vt* to sugar; (*adoçar*) to sweeten.
açucareiro [asuka'rejru] *m* (*vaso*) sugar bowl.
açude [a'sudʒi] *m* dam.
acudir [aku'dʒi*] *vi* (*ir em socorro*) to go to help; (*responder*) to reply, respond; **~ a** to come to the aid of.
acuidade [akwi'dadʒi] *f* perceptiveness.
açular [asu'la*] *vt* (*incitar*) to incite; **~ um cachorro contra alguém** to set a dog on sb.
acumulação [akumula'sãw] (*pl* **-ões**) *f* accumulation; (*montão*) heap.
acumulado/a [akumu'ladu/a] *adj* (COM: *juros*, *despesas*) accrued.
acumular [akumu'la*] *vt* to accumulate; (*reunir*) to collect; (*amontoar*) to pile up; (*funções*) to combine.
acúmulo [a'kumulu] *m* accumulation.
acusação [akuza'sãw] (*pl* **-ões**) *f* accusation, charge; (*ato*) accusation; (JUR) prosecution.
acusado/a [aku'zadu/a] *m/f* accused.
acusar [aku'za*] *vt* to accuse; (*revelar*) to reveal; (*culpar*) to blame; **~ o recebimento de** to acknowledge receipt of.
acústica [a'kuʃtʃika] *f* (*ciência*) acoustics *sg*; (*de uma sala*) acoustics *pl*.
acústico/a [a'kuʃtʃiku/a] *adj* acoustic.
adaga [a'daga] *f* dagger.
adágio [a'daʒu] *m* adage; (MÚS) adagio.
adaptabilidade [adaptabili'dadʒi] *f* adaptability.
adaptação [adapta'sãw] (*pl* **-ões**) *f* adaptation.
adaptado/a [adap'tadu/a] *adj* (*criança*) well-adjusted.
adaptar [adap'ta*] *vt* (*modificar*) to adapt; (*acomodar*) to fit; **~-se** *vr*: **~-se a** to adapt to.
ADECIF (BR) *abr f* = **Associação de Diretores de Empresas de Créditos, Investimentos e Financiamento.**
adega [a'dɛga] *f* cellar.
adelgaçado/a [adewga'sadu/a] *adj* thin; (*aguçado*) pointed.
ademais [adʒi'majʃ] *adv* (*além disso*) besides, moreover.
ADEMI (BR) *abr f* = **Associação de Dirigentes de Empresa do Mercado Imobiliário.**
adentro [a'dẽtru] *adv* inside, in; **mata ~** into the woods.
adepto/a [a'dɛptu/a] *m/f* follower; (PT: *de time*) supporter.
adequado/a [ade'kwadu/a] *adj* appropriate.
adequar [ade'kwa*] *vt* to adapt, make suitable.
adereçar [adere'sa*] *vt* to adorn, decorate; **~-**

se *vr* to dress up.
adereço [ade'resu] *m* adornment; **~s** *mpl* (*TEATRO*) stage props.
aderência [ade'rẽsja] *f* adherence.
aderente [ade'rẽtʃi] *adj* adherent, sticking ♦ *m/f* (*partidário*) supporter.
aderir [ade'ri*] *vi* to adhere; (*colar*) to stick; (*a uma moda etc*) to join in.
adesão [ade'zãw] *f* adhesion; (*patrocínio*) support.
adesivo/a [ade'zivu/a] *adj* adhesive, sticky ♦ *m* adhesive tape; (*MED*) sticking plaster.
adestrado/a [adeʃ'tradu/a] *adj* skilful (*BRIT*), skillful (*US*), skilled.
adestrador(a) [adeʃtra'do*(a)] *m/f* trainer.
adestramento [adeʃtra'mẽtu] *m* training.
adestrar [adeʃ'tra*] *vt* to train, instruct; (*cavalo*) to break in.
adeus [a'dewʃ] *excl* goodbye!; **dizer ~** to say goodbye, bid farewell.
adiamento [adʒja'mẽtu] *m* postponement; (*de uma sessão*) adjournment.
adiantado/a [adʒjã'tadu/a] *adj* advanced; (*relógio*) fast; **chegar ~** to arrive ahead of time; **pagar ~** to pay in advance.
adiantamento [adʒjãta'mẽtu] *m* progress; (*dinheiro*) advance payment.
adiantar [adʒjã'ta*] *vt* (*dinheiro, salário*) to advance, pay in advance; (*relógio*) to put forward; (*trabalho*) to advance; (*dizer*) to say in advance ♦ *vi* (*relógio*) to be fast; (*conselho, violência etc*) to be of use; **~-se** *vr* to advance, get ahead; **não adianta reclamar/insistir** there's no point *ou* it's no use complaining/insisting; **~-se a alguém** to get ahead of sb; **~-se para** to go/come up to.
adiante [a'dʒjãtʃi] *adv* (*na frente*) in front; (*para a frente*) forward; **mais ~** further on; (*no futuro*) later on.
adiar [a'dʒja*] *vt* to postpone, put off; (*sessão*) to adjourn.
adição [adʒi'sãw] (*pl* **-ões**) *f* addition; (*MAT*) sum.
adicionar [adʒisjo'na*] *vt* to add.
adições [adʒi'sõjʃ] *fpl de* **adição**.
adido/a [a'dʒidu/a] *m/f* attaché.
adiro [a'diru] *etc vb V* **aderir**.
Adis-Abeba [adʒiza'bɛba] *n* Addis Ababa.
adivinhação [adʒiviɲa'sãw] *f* (*destino*) fortune-telling; (*conjetura*) guessing, guesswork.
adivinhar [adʒivi'ɲa*] *vt, vi* to guess; (*ler a sorte*) to foretell; **~ o pensamento de alguém** to read sb's mind.
adivinho/a [adʒi'viɲu/a] *m/f* fortune-teller.
adjacente [adʒa'sẽtʃi] *adj* adjacent.
adjetivo [adʒe'tʃivu] *m* adjective.
adjudicação [adʒudʒika'sãw] (*pl* **-ões**) *f* grant; (*de contratos*) award; (*JUR*) decision.
adjudicar [adʒudʒi'ka*] *vt* to award, grant.
adjunto/a [ad'ʒũtu/a] *adj* joined, attached ♦ *m/f* assistant.
administração [adʒiminiʃtra'sãw] (*pl* **-ões**) *f* administration; (*direção*) management; (*comissão*) board; **~ de empresas** business administration, management; **~ fiduciária** trusteeship.
administrador(a) [adʒiminiʃtra'do*(a)] *m/f* administrator; (*diretor*) director; (*gerente*) manager.
administrar [adʒiminiʃ'tra*] *vt* to administer, manage; (*governar*) to govern; (*remédio*) to administer.
admiração [adʒimira'sãw] *f* (*assombro*) wonder; (*estima*) admiration; *V tb* **ponto**.
admirado/a [adʒimi'radu/a] *adj* astonished, surprised.
admirador(a) [adʒimira'do*(a)] *adj* admiring.
admirar [adʒimi'ra*] *vt* to admire; **~-se** *vr*: **~-se de** to be astonished *ou* surprised at; **não me admiro!** I'm not surprised; **não é de se ~** it's not surprising.
admirável [adʒimi'ravew] (*pl* **-eis**) *adj* (*assombroso*) amazing.
admissão [adʒimi'sãw] (*pl* **-ões**) *f* admission; (*consentimento para entrar*) admittance; (*de escola*) intake.
admitir [adʒimi'tʃi*] *vt* (*aceitar*) to admit; (*permitir*) to allow; (*funcionário*) to take on.
admoestação [admweʃta'sãw] (*pl* **-ões**) *f* admonition; (*repreensão*) reprimand.
admoestar [admweʃ'ta*] *vt* to admonish.
adoção [ado'sãw] *f* adoption.
adoçar [ado'sa*] *vt* to sweeten.
adocicado/a [adosi'kadu/a] *adj* slightly sweet.
adoecer [adoe'se*] *vi* to fall ill ♦ *vt* to make ill; **~ de** *ou* **com** to fall ill with.
adoidado/a [adoj'dadu/a] *adj* crazy ♦ *adv* (*col*) like mad *ou* crazy.
adolescente [adole'sẽtʃi] *adj, m/f* adolescent.
adoptar *etc* [ado'ta*] (*PT*) = **adotar** *etc*.
adoração [adora'sãw] *f* adoration; (*veneração*) worship.
adorar [ado'ra*] *vt* to adore; (*venerar*) to worship; (*col: gostar muito de*) to love.
adorável [ado'ravew] (*pl* **-eis**) *adj* adorable.
adormecer [adoxme'se*] *vi* to fall asleep; (*entorpecer-se*) to go numb.
adormecido/a [adoxme'sidu/a] *adj* sleeping; (*dormente*) numb ♦ *m/f* sleeper.
adornar [adox'na*] *vt* to adorn, decorate.
adorno [a'doxnu] *m* adornment.
adotar [ado'ta*] *vt* to adopt.
adotivo/a [ado'tʃivu/a] *adj* (*filho*) adopted.
adquirir [adʒiki'ri*] *vt* to acquire; (*obter*) to obtain.
adrede [a'dredʒi] *adv* on purpose, deliberately.
Adriático/a [a'drjatʃiku/a] *adj*: **o (mar) ~** the Adriatic.
adro ['adru] *m* (church) forecourt; (*em volta*

***NB:** European Portuguese adds the following consonants to certain words:* **b** (sú(b)dito, su(b)til); **c** (a(c)ção, a(c)cionista, a(c)to); **m** (inde(m)ne); **p** (ado(p)ção, ado(p)tar); *for further details see p. xiii.*

da igreja) churchyard.
aduana [a'dwana] *f* customs *pl*, customs house.
aduaneiro/a [adwa'nejru/a] *adj* customs *atr* ♦ *m* customs officer.
adubação [aduba'sãw] *f* fertilizing.
adubar [adu'ba*] *vt* to manure; (*fertilizer*) to fertilize.
adubo [a'dubu] *m* (*fertilizante*) fertilizer.
adulação [adula'sãw] *f* flattery.
adulador(a) [adula'do*(a)] *adj* flattering ♦ *m/f* flatterer.
adular [adu'la*] *vt* to flatter.
adulteração [aduwtera'sãw] *f* adulteration; (*de contas*) falsification.
adulterador(a) [aduwtera'do*(a)] *m/f* adulterator.
adulterar [aduwte'ra*] *vt* (*vinho*) to adulterate; (*contas*) to falsify ♦ *vi* to commit adultery.
adultério [aduw'tɛrju] *m* adultery.
adúltero/a [a'duwteru/a] *m/f* adulterer/ adulteress.
adulto/a [a'duwtu/a] *adj*, *m/f* adult.
adunco/a [a'dũku/a] *adj* (*nariz*) hook.
adveio [ad'veju] *etc vb V* **advir**.
adventício/a [advẽ'tʃisju/a] *adj* (*casual*) accidental; (*estrangeiro*) foreign ♦ *m/f* (*estrangeiro*) foreigner.
advento [ad'vẽtu] *m* advent; **o A~** Advent.
advérbio [ad'vɛxbju] *m* adverb.
adversário [adʒivex'sarju/a] *m* adversary, opponent, enemy.
adversidade [adʒivexsi'dadʒi] *f* adversity, misfortune.
adverso/a [adʒi'vɛxsu/a] *adj* adverse, unfavourable; (*oposto*): **~ a** opposed to.
advertência [adʒivex'tẽsja] *f* warning; (*repreensão*) (gentle) reprimand.
advertido/a [adʒivex'tʃidu/a] *adj* prudent; (*informado*) well advised.
advertir [adʒivex'tʃi*] *vt* to warn; (*repreender*) to reprimand; (*chamar a atenção a*) to draw attention to.
advier [ad'vje*] *etc vb V* **advir**.
advindo/a [ad'vĩdu/a] *adj*: **~ de** resulting from.
advir [ad'vi*] (*irreg*: *como* **vir**) *vi*: **~ de** to result from.
advocacia [adʒivoka'sia] *f* legal profession, law.
advogado/a [adʒivo'gadu/a] *m/f* lawyer.
advogar [adʒivo'ga*] *vt* (*promover*) to advocate; (*JUR*) to plead ♦ *vi* to practise (*BRIT*) *ou* practice (*US*) law.
aéreo/a [a'erju/a] *adj* air *atr*; (*pessoa*) vague.
aerobarco [aero'baxku] *m* hovercraft.
aeroclube [aero'klubi] *m* flying club.
aerodinâmica [aerodʒi'namika] *f* aerodynamics *sg*.
aerodinâmico/a [aerodʒi'namiku/a] *adj* aerodynamic.
aerodrómo [aero'drɔmu] *m* airfield.
aeroespacial [aeroiʃpa'sjaw] (*pl* **-ais**) *adj* aerospace *atr*.
aerofagia [aerofa'ʒia] *f* (*MED*) hyperventilation.
aerofoto [aero'fɔtu] *f* aerial photograph.
aeromoço/a [aero'mosu/a] (*BR*) *m/f* steward/ air hostess.
aeromodelismo [aeromode'liʒmu] *m* aeromodelling.
aeronauta [aero'nawta] *m/f* airman/woman.
aeronáutica [aero'nawtʃika] *f* air force; (*ciência*) aeronautics *sg*; **Departamento de A~ Civil** ≈ Civil Aviation Authority.
aeronave [aero'navi] *f* aircraft.
aeroporto [aero'poxtu] *m* airport.
aerossol [aero'sɔw] (*pl* **-óis**) *m* aerosol.
afã [a'fã] *m* (*entusiasmo*) enthusiasm; (*diligência*) diligence; (*ânsia*) eagerness; (*esforço*) effort; (*faina*) task, job; **no seu ~ de agradar** in his eagerness to please.
afabilidade [afabili'dadʒi] *f* friendliness, kindness.
afaço [a'fasu] *etc vb V* **afazer**.
afagar [afa'ga*] *vt* (*acariciar*) to caress; (*cabelo*) to stroke.
afamado/a [afa'madu/a] *adj* renowned, celebrated.
afanar [afa'na*] (*col*) *vt* to nick, pinch.
afanoso/a [afa'nozu/ɔza] *adj* laborious; (*meticuloso*) painstaking.
afasia [afa'zia] *f* aphasia.
afastado/a [afaʃ'tadu/a] *adj* (*distante*) remote; (*isolado*) secluded; (*pernas*) apart; (*amigo*) distant; **manter-se ~** to keep to o.s.
afastamento [afaʃta'mẽtu] *m* removal; (*distância*) distance; (*de emprego solicitado*) rejection; (*de pessoal*) lay-off, sacking.
afastar [afaʃ'ta*] *vt* to remove; (*amigo*) to distance; (*separar*) to separate; (*idéia*) to put out of one's mind; (*pessoal*) to lay off; **~-se** *vr* (*ir-se embora*) to move away, go away; (*de amigo*) to distance o.s.; (*de cargo*) to step down; **~-se do assunto** to stray from the subject; **~ os olhos de** to take one's eyes off.
afável [a'favew] (*pl* **-eis**) *adj* friendly, genial.
afazer [afa'ze*] (*irreg*: *como* **fazer**) *vt* to accustom; **~-se** *vr*: **~-se a** to get used to.
afazeres [afa'zeriʃ] *mpl* business *sg*; (*dever*) duties, tasks; **~ domésticos** household chores.
afectar *etc* [afek'ta*] (*PT*) = **afetar** *etc*.
afegã [afe'gã] *f de* **afegão**.
Afeganistão [afeganiʃ'tãw] *m*: **o ~** Afghanistan.
afegão/gã [afe'gãw/'gã] (*pl* **-ões/~s**) *adj*, *m/f* Afghan.
afeição [afej'sãw] *f* (*amor*) affection, fondness; (*dedicação*) devotion.
afeiçoado/a [afej'swadu/a] *adj* (*amoroso*) fond; (*devotado*) devoted ♦ *m/f* friend.
afeiçoar-se [afej'swaxsi] *vr*: **~ a** (*tomar gosto por*) to take a liking to.

afeito/a [a'fejtu/a] *pp de* **afazer** ♦ *adj*: ~ **a** accustomed to, used to.
afeminado/a [afemi'nadu/a] *adj* effeminate.
aferidor [aferi'do*] *m* (*de pesos e medidas*) inspector; (*verificador*) checker; (*instrumento*) gauge (*BRIT*), gage (*US*).
aferir [afe'ri*] *vt* (*verificar*) to check, inspect; (*comparar*) to compare; (*conhecimentos, resultados*) to assess.
aferrado/a [afe'xadu/a] *adj* obstinate, stubborn.
aferrar [afe'xa*] *vt* (*prender*) to secure; (*NÁUT*) to anchor; (*agarrar*) to grasp; **~-se** *vr*: **~-se a** to cling to.
aferrolhar [afexo'ʎa*] *vt* to bolt; (*pessoa*) to imprison; (*coisas*) to hoard.
aferventar [afexvẽ'ta*] *vt* to bring to the (*BRIT*) *ou* a (*US*) boil.
afetação [afeta'sãw] *f* affectation.
afetado/a [afe'tadu/a] *adj* pretentious, affected.
afetar [afe'ta*] *vt* to affect; (*fingir*) to feign.
afetividade [afetʃivi'dadʒi] *f* affection.
afetivo/a [afe'tʃivu/a] *adj* affectionate; (*problema*) emotional.
afeto [a'fɛtu] *m* affection.
afetuoso/a [afe'twozu/ɔza] *adj* affectionate, tender.
afez [a'feʒ] *etc vb V* **afazer**.
AFI *abr m* (= *Alfabeto Fonético Internacional*) IPA.
afiado/a [a'fjadu/a] *adj* sharp; (*pessoa*) well-trained.
afiançar [afjã'sa*] *vt* (*JUR*) to stand bail for; (*garantir*) to guarantee.
afiar [a'fja*] *vt* to sharpen.
aficionado/a [afisjo'nadu/a] *m/f* enthusiast.
afigurar-se [afigu'raxsi] *vr* to seem, appear; **afigura-se-me que** it seems to me that.
afilado/a [afi'ladu/a] *adj* (*nariz*) thin.
afilhado/a [afi'ʎadu/a] *m/f* godson/goddaughter.
afiliação [afilja'sãw] (*pl* **-ões**) *f* affiliation.
afiliada [afi'ljada] *f* affiliate, affiliated company.
afiliado/a [afi'ljadu/a] *adj* affiliated.
afiliar [afi'lja*] *vt* to affiliate; **~-se** *vr*: **~-se a** to join.
afim [a'fĩ] (*pl* **-ns**) *adj* (*semelhante*) similar; (*consangüíneo*) related ♦ *m/f* relative, relation; **estar ~ de (fazer) algo/alguém** *V* **fim**.
afinação [afina'sãw] *f* (*MÚS*) tuning.
afinado/a [afi'nadu/a] *adj* in tune.
afinal [afi'naw] *adv* at last, finally; ~ **(de contas)** after all.
afinar [afi'na*] *vt* (*MÚS*) to tune ♦ *vi* (*adelgaçar*) to taper.
afinco [a'fĩku] *m* tenacity, persistence; **com ~** tenaciously.
afinidade [afini'dadʒi] *f* affinity.
afins [a'fĩʃ] *m/fpl de* **afim**.
afirmação [afixma'sãw] (*pl* **-ões**) *f* affirmation; (*declaração*) statement.
afirmar [afix'ma*] *vt, vi* to affirm, assert; (*declarar*) to declare.
afirmativo/a [afixma'tʃivu/a] *adj* affirmative.
afiro [a'firu] *etc vb V* **aferir**.
afivelar [afive'la*] *vt* to buckle.
afixar [afik'sa*] *vt* (*cartazes*) to stick, post.
afiz [a'fiʒ] *etc vb V* **afazer**.
afizer [afi'ze*] *etc vb V* **afazer**.
aflição [afli'sãw] *f* (*sofrimento*) affliction; (*ansiedade*) anxiety; (*angústia*) anguish.
afligir [afli'ʒi*] *vt* to distress; (*atormentar*) to torment; (*inquietar*) to worry; **~-se** *vr*: **~-se com** to worry about.
aflijo [a'fliʒu] *etc vb V* **afligir**.
aflito/a [a'flitu/a] *pp de* **afligir** ♦ *adj* distressed, anxious.
aflorar [aflo'ra*] *vi* to emerge, appear.
afluência [a'flwẽsja] *f* affluence; (*corrente copiosa*) great flow; (*de pessoas*) crowd.
afluente [a'flwẽtʃi] *adj* copious; (*rico*) affluent ♦ *m* tributary.
afluir [a'flwi*] *vi* to flow; (*pessoas*) to congregate.
afobação [afoba'sãw] *f* fluster; (*ansiedade*) panic.
afobado/a [afo'badu/a] *adj* flustered; (*ansioso*) panicky, nervous.
afobamento [afoba'mẽtu] *m* fluster; (*ansiedade*) panic.
afobar [afo'ba*] *vt* to fluster; (*deixar ansioso*) to make nervous *ou* panicky ♦ *vi* to get flustered; (*ficar ansioso*) to panic, get nervous; **~-se** *vr* to get flustered.
afofar [afo'fa*] *vt* to fluff.
afogado/a [afo'gadu/a] *adj* drowned.
afogador [afoga'do*] (*BR*) *m* (*AUTO*) choke.
afogar [afo'ga*] *vt* to drown ♦ *vi* (*AUTO*) to flood; **~-se** *vr* to drown, be drowned.
afoito/a [a'fojtu/a] *adj* bold, daring.
afonia [afo'nia] *f* voice loss.
afônico/a [a'foniku/a] *adj*: **estou ~** I've lost my voice.
afora [a'fɔra] *prep* except for, apart from ♦ *adv*: **rua ~** down the street; **pelo mundo ~** throughout the world; **porta ~** out into the street.
aforismo [afo'riʒmu] *m* aphorism.
aforrar [afo'xa*] *vt* (*roupa*) to line; (*poupar*) to save; (*liberar*) to free.
afortunado/a [afoxtu'nadu/a] *adj* fortunate, lucky.
afrescalhado/a [afreʃka'ʎadu/a] (*col*) *adj* effeminate, camp.
afresco [a'freʃku] *m* fresco.
África ['afrika] *f*: **a ~** Africa; **a ~ do Sul** South Africa.
africano/a [afri'kanu/a] *adj, m/f* African.

***NB:** European Portuguese adds the following consonants to certain words:* **b** (sú(b)dito, su(b)til); **c** (a(c)ção, a(c)cionista, a(c)to); **m** (inde(m)ne); **p** (ado(p)ção, ado(p)tar); *for further details see p. xiii.*

AFRMM (*BR*) *abr m* (= *Adicional ao Frete para Renovação da Marinha Mercante*) *tax on goods imported by sea.*

afro-brasileiro/a ['afru-] (*pl* **~s**) *adj* Afro-Brazilian.

afrodisíaco [afrodʒi'ziaku] *m* aphrodisiac.

afronta [a'frõta] *f* insult, affront.

afrontado/a [afrõ'tadu/a] *adj* (*ofendido*) offended; (*com má digestão*) too full.

afrontar [afrõ'ta*] *vt* to insult; (*ofender*) to offend.

afrouxar [afro'ʃa*] *vt* (*desapertar*) to slacken; (*soltar*) to loosen ♦ *vi* (*soltar-se*) to come loose.

afta ['afta] *f* (mouth) ulcer.

afugentar [afuʒẽ'ta*] *vt* to drive away, put to flight.

afundar [afũ'da*] *vt* (*submergir*) to sink; (*cavidade*) to deepen; **~-se** *vr* to sink; (*col: num exame*) to do badly.

agá [a'ga] *m* aitch, h.

agachar-se [aga'ʃaxsi] *vr* (*acaçapar-se*) to crouch, squat; (*curvar-se*) to stoop; (*fig*) to cringe.

agarração [agaxa'sãw] (*col*) *f* necking.

agarrado/a [aga'xadu/a] *adj*: **~ a** (*preso*) stuck to; (*a uma pessoa*) very attached to.

agarramento [agaxa'mẽtu] *m* (*a uma pessoa*) close attachment; (*col: agarração*) necking.

agarrar [aga'xa*] *vt* to seize, grasp; **~-se** *vr*: **~-se a** to cling to, hold on to.

agasalhado/a [agaza'ʎadu/a] *adj* warmly dressed, wrapped up.

agasalhar [agaza'ʎa*] *vt* to dress warmly, wrap up; **~-se** *vr* to wrap o.s. up.

agasalho [aga'zaʎu] *m* (*casaco*) coat; (*suéter*) sweater.

ágeis ['aʒejʃ] *adj pl de* **ágil**.

agência [a'ʒẽsja] *f* agency; (*escritório*) office; (*de banco etc*) branch; **~ de correio** (*BR*) post office; **~ de viagens** travel agency; **~ publicitária** advertising agency.

agenciar [aʒẽ'sja*] *vt* (*negociar*) to negotiate; (*obter*) to procure; (*ser agente de*) to act as an agent for.

agenda [a'ʒẽda] *f* diary.

agente [a'ʒẽtʃi] *m/f* agent; (*de polícia*) policeman/woman; **~ de seguros** (insurance) underwriter.

agigantado/a [aʒigã'tadu/a] *adj* gigantic.

ágil ['aʒiw] (*pl* **-eis**) *adj* agile.

agilidade [aʒili'dadʒi] *f* agility.

agilizar [aʒili'za*] *vt*: **~ algo** (*dar andamento a*) to get sth moving; (*acelerar*) to speed sth up.

ágio ['aʒju] *m* premium.

agiota [a'ʒjɔta] *m/f* moneylender.

agir [a'ʒi*] *vi* to act; **~ bem/mal** to do right/wrong.

agitação [aʒita'sãw] (*pl* **-ões**) *f* agitation; (*perturbação*) disturbance; (*inquietação*) restlessness.

agitado/a [aʒi'tadu/a] *adj* agitated, disturbed; (*inquieto*) restless.

agitar [aʒi'ta*] *vt* to agitate, disturb; (*sacudir*) to shake; (*cauda*) to wag; (*mexer*) to stir; (*os braços*) to swing, wave; **~-se** *vr* to get upset; (*mar*) to get rough.

aglomeração [aglomera'sãw] (*pl* **-ões**) *f* gathering; (*multidão*) crowd.

aglomerado [aglome'radu] *m*: **~ urbano** city.

aglomerar [aglome'ra*] *vt* to heap up, pile up; **~-se** *vr* (*multidão*) to crowd together.

AGO *abr f* (= *assembléia geral ordinária*) AGM.

ago. *abr* (= *agosto*) Aug.

agonia [ago'nia] *f* agony, anguish; (*ânsia da morte*) death throes *pl*; (*indecisão*) indecision.

agoniado/a [ago'njadu/a] *adj* anguished.

agonizante [agoni'zãtʃi] *adj* dying ♦ *m/f* dying person.

agonizar [agoni'za*] *vi* to be dying; (*afligir-se*) to agonize.

agora [a'gɔra] *adv* now; (*hoje em dia*) now, nowadays; **e ~?** now what?; **~ mesmo** right now; (*há pouco*) a moment ago; **a partir de ~, de ~ em diante** from now on; **até ~** so far, up to now; **por ~** for now; **~ que** now that; **eu lhe disse ontem; ~, se ele esquecer** ... I told him yesterday; but if he forgets ....

agorinha [ago'riɲa] *adv* just now.

agosto [a'goʃtu] (*PT*: **A~**) *m* August; *V tb* **julho**.

agourar [ago'ra*] *vt* to predict, foretell ♦ *vi* to augur ill.

agouro [a'goru] *m* omen; (*mau* **~**) bad omen.

agraciar [agra'sja*] *vt* (*condecorar*) to decorate.

agradabilíssimo/a [agradabi'lisimu/a] *adj superl de* **agradável**.

agradar [agra'da*] *vt* (*deleitar*) to please; (*fazer agrados a*) to be nice to ♦ *vi* (*ser agradável*) to be pleasing; (*satisfazer: show, piada etc*) to go down well.

agradável [agra'davew] (*pl* **-eis**) *adj* pleasant.

agradecer [agrade'se*] *vt*: **~ algo a alguém, ~ a alguém por algo** to thank sb for sth.

agradecido/a [agrade'sidu/a] *adj* grateful; **mal ~** ungrateful.

agradecimento [agradesi'mẽtu] *m* gratitude; **~s** *mpl* thanks.

agrado [a'gradu] *m*: **fazer um ~ a alguém** (*afagar*) to be affectionate with sb; (*ser agradável*) to be nice to sb.

agrário/a [a'grarju/a] *adj* agrarian; **reforma agrária** land reform.

agravação [agrava'sãw] (*PT*) *f* aggravation; (*piora*) worsening.

agravamento [agrava'mẽtu] (*BR*) *m* aggravation.

agravante [agra'vãtʃi] *adj* aggravating ♦ *f* aggravating circumstance.

agravar [agra'va*] *vt* to aggravate, make worse; **~-se** *vr* (*piorar*) to get worse.

agravo [a'gravu] *m* (*JUR*) appeal.
agredir [agre'dʒi*] *vt* to attack; (*insultar*) to insult.
agregado/a [agre'gadu/a] *m/f* (*lavrador*) tenant farmer; (*BR*) lodger ♦ *m* aggregate, sum total.
agregar [agre'ga*] *vt* (*juntar*) to collect; (*acrescentar*) to add.
agressão [agre'sãw] (*pl* **-ões**) *f* aggression; (*ataque*) attack; (*assalto*) assault.
agressividade [agresivi'dadʒi] *f* aggressiveness.
agressivo/a [agre'sivu/a] *adj* aggressive.
agressões [agre'sõjʃ] *fpl de* **agressão**.
agressor(a) [agre'so*(a)] *m/f* aggressor.
agreste [a'grɛʃtʃi] *adj* rural, rustic; (*terreno*) wild, uncultivated.
agrião [a'grjãw] *m* watercress.
agrícola [a'grikola] *adj* agricultural.
agricultável [agrikuw'tavew] (*pl* **-eis**) *adj* arable.
agricultor [agrikuw'to*] *m* farmer.
agricultura [agrikuw'tura] *f* agriculture, farming.
agrido [a'gridu] *etc vb V* **agredir**.
agridoce [agri'dosi] *adj* bittersweet.
agronomia [agrono'mia] *f* agronomy.
agrônomo/a [a'gronomu/a] *m/f* agronomist.
agropecuária [agrope'kwarja] *f* farming, agriculture.
agropecuário/a [agrope'kwarju/a] *adj* farming *atr*, agricultural.
agrotóxico [agro'tɔksiku] *m* pesticide.
agrupamento [agrupa'mẽtu] *m* grouping.
agrupar [agru'pa*] *vt* to group; **~-se** *vr* to group together.
agrura [a'grura] *f* bitterness.
água ['agwa] *f* water; **~s** *fpl* (*mar*) waters; (*chuvas*) rain *sg*; (*maré*) tides; **~ abaixo/acima** downstream/upstream; **até debaixo da ~** (*fig*) one thousand per cent; **dar ~ na boca** (*comida*) to be mouthwatering; **estar na ~** (*bêbado*) to be drunk; **fazer ~** (*NÁUT*) to leak; **ir nas ~s de alguém** (*fig*) to follow in sb's footsteps; **~ benta** holy water; **~ corrente** running water; **~ doce** fresh water; **~ dura/leve** hard/soft water; **~ mineral** mineral water; **~ oxigenada** peroxide; **~ salgada** salt water; **~ sanitária** household bleach; **jogar ~ na fervura** (*fig*) to put a damper on things; **mudar como da ~ para o vinho** to change radically; **desta ~ não beberei!** that won't happen to me!; **~s passadas não movem moinhos** it's all water under the bridge.
aguaceiro [agwa'sejru] *m* (*chuva*) heavy shower, downpour; (*com vento*) squall.
água-com-açúcar *adj inv* schmalzy, mushy.
água-de-coco *f* coconut water.
água-de-colônia (*pl* **águas-de-colônia**) *f* eau-de-cologne.
aguado/a [a'gwadu/a] *adj* watery.
água-furtada [-fux'tada] (*pl* **águas-furtadas**) *f* garret, attic.
água-marinha (*pl* **águas-marinhas**) *f* aquamarine.
aguar [a'gwa*] *vt* to water ♦ *vi*: **~ por** (*salivar*) to drool over.
aguardar [agwax'da*] *vt* to wait for, await; (*contar com*) to expect ♦ *vi* to wait.
aguardente [agwax'dẽtʃi] *m* spirit.
aguarrás [agwa'xajʃ] *f* turpentine.
água-viva (*pl* **águas-vivas**) *f* jellyfish.
aguçado/a [agu'sadu/a] *adj* pointed; (*espírito, sentidos*) acute.
aguçar [agu'sa*] *vt* (*afiar*) to sharpen; (*estimular*) to excite; **~ a vista** to keep one's eyes peeled.
agudeza [agu'deza] *f* sharpness; (*perspicácia*) perspicacity; (*de som*) shrillness.
agudo/a [a'gudu/a] *adj* sharp; (*som*) shrill; (*intenso*) acute.
agüentar [agwẽ'ta*] *vt* (*muro etc*) to hold up; (*dor, injustiças*) to stand, put up with; (*peso*) to withstand, stand; (*resistir a*) to stand up to ♦ *vi* to last, hold out; (*resistir a peso*) to hold; **~-se** *vr* (*manter-se*) to remain, hold on; **~ com** to hold, withstand; **~ fazer algo** to manage to do sth; **não ~ de** not to be able to stand; **~ firme** to hold out.
aguerrido/a [age'xidu/a] *adj* warlike, bellicose; (*corajoso*) courageous.
águia ['agja] *f* eagle; (*fig*) genius.
agulha [a'guʎa] *f* (*de coser, tricô*) needle; (*NÁUT*) compass; (*estrada de ferro*) points *pl* (*BRIT*), switch (*US*); **trabalho de ~** needlework.
agulheta [agu'ʎeta] *f* (*bico*) nozzle.
ah [a] *excl* oh!
AI *abr f* = **Anistia Internacional** ♦ *abr m* (*BR*) = **Ato Institucional**; **AI-5** *measure passed in 1968 suspending congress and banning opposition politicians.*
ai [aj] *excl* (*suspiro*) oh!; (*de dor*) ouch! ♦ *m* (*suspiro*) sigh; (*gemido*) groan; **~ de mim** poor me!
aí [a'i] *adv* there; (*então*) then; **por ~** (*em lugar indeterminado*) somewhere over there, thereabouts; **espera ~!** wait!, hang on a minute!; **está ~!** (*col*) right!; **~ é que 'tá!** (*col*) that's just the point; **e por ~ afora** *ou* **vai** and so on; **já não está ~ quem falou** (*col*) I stand corrected; **e ~?** and then what?; **e ~ (como vai)?** (*col*) how are things with you?
aiatolá [ajato'la] *m* ayatollah.
aidético/a [aj'dɛtʃiku/a] *adj* suffering from AIDS ♦ *m/f* person with AIDS.
AIDS ['ajdʒs] *f* AIDS.
ainda [a'ĩda] *adv* still; (*mesmo*) even; **~ ago-**

***NB:** European Portuguese adds the following consonants to certain words:* **b** (sú(b)dito, su(b)til); **c** (a(c)ção, a(c)cionista, a(c)to); **m** (inde(m)ne); **p** (ado(p)ção, ado(p)tar); *for further details see p. xiii.*

ra just now; ~ **assim** even so, nevertheless; ~ **bem** just as well; ~ **por cima** on top of all that, in addition; ~ **não** not yet; ~ **que** even if; **maior** ~ even bigger.
aipim [aj'pĩ] *m* cassava.
aipo ['ajpu] *m* celery.
airado/a [aj'radu/a] *adj* (*frívolo*) frivolous; (*leviano*) dissolute.
airoso/a [aj'rozu/ɔza] *adj* graceful, elegant.
ajantarado [aʒãta'radu] *m* lunch and dinner combined.
ajardinar [aʒaxdʒi'na*] *vt* to make into a garden.
ajeitar [aʒej'ta*] *vt* (*adaptar*) to fit, adjust; (*arranjar*) to arrange, fix; **~-se** *vr* to adapt; **aos poucos as coisas se ajeitam** things will gradually sort themselves out.
ajo ['aʒu] *etc vb V* **agir**.
ajoelhado/a [aʒwe'ʎadu/a] *adj* kneeling.
ajoelhar [aʒwe'ʎa*] *vi* to kneel (down); **~-se** *vr* to kneel down.
ajuda [a'ʒuda] *f* help, aid; (*subsídio*) grant, subsidy; **sem** ~ unaided; **dar ~ a alguém** to lend *ou* give sb a hand; **~ de custo** allowance.
ajudante [aʒu'dãtʃi] *m* assistant, helper; (*MIL*) adjutant.
ajudar [aʒu'da*] *vt* to help.
ajuizado/a [aʒwi'zadu/a] *adj* (*sensato*) sensible; (*sábio*) wise; (*prudente*) discreet.
ajuizar [aʒwi'za*] *vt* to judge; (*calcular*) to calculate.
ajuntamento [aʒũta'mẽtu] *m* gathering.
ajuntar [aʒũ'ta*] *vt* (*unir*) to join, add; (*documentos*) to attach; (*reunir*) to gather.
ajustagem [aʒuʃ'taʒẽ] (*BR*: *pl* **-ns**) *f* (*TEC*) adjustment.
ajustamento [aʒuʃta'mẽtu] *m* adjustment; (*de contas*) settlement.
ajustagens [aʒuʃ'taʒẽʃ] *fpl de* **ajustagem**.
ajustar [aʒuʃ'ta*] *vt* (*regular*) to adjust; (*conta, disputa*) to settle; (*acomodar*) to fit; (*roupa*) to take in; (*contratar*) to contract; (*estipular*) to stipulate; (*preço*) to agree on; **~-se** *vr*: **~-se a** to conform to; (*adaptar-se*) to adapt to.
ajustável [aʒuʃ'tavew] (*pl* **-eis**) *adj* adjustable; (*aplicável*) applicable.
ajuste [a'ʒuʃtʃi] *m* (*acordo*) agreement; (*de contas*) settlement; (*adaptação*) adjustment; ~ **final** (*COM*) settlement of account.
AL *abr* = **Alagoas** ♦ *abr f* (*BR*: = *Aliança Liberal*) *former political party*.
Al. *abr* = **Alameda**.
ala ['ala] *f* (*fileira*) row; (*passagem*) aisle; (*de edifício, exército, ave*) wing.
Alá [a'la] *m* Allah.
ALADI *abr f* = **Associação Latino-Americana de Desenvolvimento e Intercâmbio**.
alagação [alaga'sãw] *f* flooding.
alagadiço/a [alaga'dʒisu/a] *adj* swampy, marshy ♦ *m* swamp, marsh.
alagamento [alaga'mẽtu] *m* flooding; (*arrasamento*) destruction.
alagar [ala'ga*] *vt, vi* to flood.
alagoano/a [ala'gwanu/a] *adj* from Alagoas ♦ *m/f* native *ou* inhabitant of Alagoas.
alambique [alã'biki] *m* still.
alameda [ala'meda] *f* (*avenida*) avenue; (*arvoredo*) grove.
álamo ['alamu] *m* poplar.
alanhar [ala'ɲa*] *vt* to slash; (*peixe*) to gut.
alar [a'la*] *vt* to haul, heave.
alaranjado/a [alarã'ʒadu/a] *adj* orangy.
alarde [a'laxdʒi] *m* (*ostentação*) ostentation; (*jactância*) boasting; **fazer ~ de** to boast about.
alardear [alax'dʒja*] *vt* to show off; (*gabar-se de*) to boast of ♦ *vi* to boast; **~-se** *vr* to boast; ~ **fazer** to boast of doing; **~(-se) de valente** to boast of being strong.
alargamento [alaxga'mẽtu] *m* enlargement.
alargar [alax'ga*] *vt* (*ampliar*) to extend; (*fazer mais largo*) to widen, broaden; (*afrouxar*) to loosen, slacken.
alarido [ala'ridu] *m* (*clamor*) outcry; (*tumulto*) uproar.
alarma [a'laxma] *f* alarm; (*susto*) panic; (*tumulto*) tumult; (*vozearia*) outcry; **dar o sinal de ~** to raise the alarm; **~ de roubo** burglar alarm.
alarmante [alax'mãtʃi] *adj* alarming.
alarmar [alax'ma*] *vt* to alarm; **~-se** *vr* to be alarmed.
alarme [a'laxmi] *m* = **alarma**.
alarmista [alax'miʃta] *adj, m/f* alarmist.
Alasca [a'laʃka] *m*: **o** ~ Alaska.
alastrado/a [alaʃ'tradu/a] *adj*: **~ de** strewn with.
alastrar [alaʃ'tra*] *vt* (*espalhar*) to scatter; (*disseminar*) to spread; (*lastrar*) to ballast; **~-se** *vr* (*epidemia, rumor*) to spread.
alavanca [ala'vãka] *f* lever; (*pé-de-cabra*) crowbar; **~ de mudanças** gear lever.
albanês/esa [awba'neʃ/eza] *adj, m/f* Albanian ♦ *m* (*LING*) Albanian.
Albânia [aw'banja] *f*: **a** ~ Albania.
albergar [awbex'ga*] *vt* (*hospedar*) to provide lodging for; (*abrigar*) to shelter.
albergue [aw'bɛxgi] *m* (*estalagem*) inn; (*refúgio*) hospice, shelter; ~ **noturno** hotel; ~ **para jovens** youth hostel.
albino/a [aw'binu/a] *adj, m/f* albino.
albufeira [awbu'fejra] *f* lagoon.
álbum ['awbũ] (*pl* **-ns**) *m* album; **~ de recortes** scrapbook.
alça ['awsa] *f* strap; (*asa*) handle; (*de fusil*) sight.
alcácer [aw'kase*] *m* fortress.
alcachofra [awka'ʃofra] *f* artichoke.
alcaçuz [awka'suʒ] *m* liquorice.
alçada [aw'sada] *f* (*jurisdição*) jurisdiction; (*competência*) competence; **isso não é da minha ~** that is beyond my control.
alcagüete [awka'gwetʃi] *m/f* informer.
álcali ['awkali] *m* alkali.

alcalino/a [awka'linu/a] *adj* alkaline.
alcançar [awkã'sa*] *vt* to reach; (*estender*) to hand, pass; (*obter*) to obtain, get; (*atingir*) to attain; (*compreender*) to understand ♦ *vi* to reach; **~-se** *vr* (*fazer um desfalque*) to embezzle funds; (*desfalcar*): **~ uma firma em $1 milhão** to embezzle $1 million from a firm.
alcançável [awkã'savew] (*pl* **-eis**) *adj* (*acessível*) reachable; (*atingível*) attainable.
alcance [aw'kãsi] *m* reach; (*competência*) power, competence; (*compreensão*) understanding; (*de tiro, visão*) range; (*desfalque*) embezzlement; **ao ~ de** within reach/range of; **ao ~ da voz** within earshot; **de grande ~** of great consequence; **fora do ~ da mão** out of reach; **fora do ~ de alguém** beyond sb's grasp.
alcantilado/a [awkãtʃi'ladu/a] *adj* (*íngreme*) steep; (*penhascoso*) craggy.
alçapão [awsa'pãw] (*pl* **-ões**) *m* trapdoor; (*arapuca*) trap.
alcaparra [awka'paxa] *f* caper.
alçapões [awsa'põjʃ] *mpl de* **alçapão**.
alçaprema [awsa'prɛma] *f* (*alavanca*) crowbar.
alçar [aw'sa*] *vt* to lift (up); (*voz*) to raise; **~ vôo** to take off.
alcaravia [awkara'via] *f*: **sementes de ~** caraway seeds.
alcatéia [awka'tɛja] *f* (*de lobos*) pack; (*de ladrões*) gang.
alcatra [aw'katra] *f* rump (steak).
alcatrão [awka'trãw] *m* tar.
álcool ['awkɔw] *m* alcohol.
alcoólatra [aw'kɔlatra] *m/f* alcoholic.
alcoólico/a [aw'kɔliku/a] *adj, m/f* alcoholic.
alcoolismo [awko'liʒmu] *m* alcoholism.
Alcorão [awko'rãw] *m* Koran.
alcova [aw'kova] *f* bedroom.
alcoviteiro/a [awkovi'tejru/a] *m/f* pimp/procuress.
alcunha [aw'kuɲa] *f* nickname.
aldeão/eã [aw'dʒjãw/jã] (*pl* **-ões/~s**) *m/f* villager.
aldeia [aw'deja] *f* village.
aldeões [aw'dʒjõjʃ] *mpl de* **aldeão**.
aldraba [aw'draba] *f* (PT: *tranqueta*) latch; (*de bater*) door knocker.
aleatório/a [alea'tɔrju/a] *adj* random.
alecrim [ale'krĩ] *m* rosemary.
alegação [alega'sãw] (*pl* **-ões**) *f* allegation.
alegado [ale'gadu] *m* (JUR) plea.
alegar [ale'ga*] *vt* to allege; (JUR) to plead.
alegoria [alego'ria] *f* allegory.
alegórico/a [ale'gɔriku/a] *adj* allegorical; *V tb* **carro**.
alegrar [ale'gra*] *vt* (*tornar feliz*) to cheer (up), gladden; (*ambiente*) to brighten up; (*animar*) to liven (up); **~-se** *vr* to cheer up.
alegre [a'lɛgri] *adj* (*jovial*) cheerful; (*contente*) happy, glad; (*cores*) bright; (*embriagado*) merry, tight.
alegria [ale'gria] *f* joy, happiness.
aleguei [ale'gej] *etc vb V* **alegar**.
aléia [a'lɛja] *f* (tree-lined) avenue; (*passagem*) alley.
aleijado/a [alej'ʒadu/a] *adj* crippled, disabled ♦ *m/f* cripple.
aleijão [alej'ʒãw] (*pl* **-ões**) *m* deformity.
aleijar [alej'ʒa*] *vt* (*mutilar*) to maim.
aleijões [alej'ʒõjʃ] *mpl de* **aleijão**.
aleitamento [alejta'mẽtu] *m* breast feeding.
aleitar [alej'ta*] *vt, vi* to breast-feed.
além [a'lẽj] *adv* (*lá ao longe*) over there; (*mais adiante*) further on ♦ *m*: **o ~** the hereafter ♦ *prep*: **~ de** beyond; (*no outro lado de*) on the other side of; (*para mais de*) over; (*ademais de*) apart from, besides; **~ disso** moreover; **mais ~** further.
alemã [ale'mã] *f de* **alemão**.
alemães [ale'mãjʃ] *mpl de* **alemão**.
Alemanha [ale'maɲa] *f*: **a ~** Germany; **a ~ Ocidental/Oriental** West/East Germany.
alemão/mã [ale'mãw/'mã] (*pl* **-ães/~s**) *adj, m/f* German ♦ *m* (LING) German.
alentado/a [alẽ'tadu/a] *adj* (*valente*) valiant; (*grande*) great; (*volumoso*) substantial.
alentador(a) [alẽta'do*(a)] *adj* encouraging.
alentar [alẽ'ta*] *vt* to encourage; **~-se** *vr* to cheer up.
alentejano/a [alẽte'ʒanu/a] *adj* from Alentejo ♦ *m/f* native *ou* inhabitant of Alentejo.
alento [a'lẽtu] *m* (*fôlego*) breath; (*ânimo*) courage; **dar ~** to encourage; **tomar ~** to draw breath.
alergia [alex'ʒia] *f*: **~ (a)** allergy (to); (*fig*) aversion (to).
alérgico/a [a'lɛxʒiku/a] *adj*: **~ (a)** allergic (to).
alerta [a'lɛxta] *adj* alert ♦ *adv* on the alert ♦ *m* alert.
alertar [alex'ta*] *vt* to alert; **~-se** *vr* to be alerted.
Alf. *abr* = **Alferes**.
alfabético/a [awfa'bɛtʃiku/a] *adj* alphabetical.
alfabetização [awfabetʃiza'sãw] *f* literacy.
alfabetizado/a [awfabetʃi'zadu/a] *adj* literate.
alfabetizar [awfabetʃi'za*] *vt* to teach to read and write; **~-se** *vr* to learn to read and write.
alfabeto [awfa'bɛtu] *m* alphabet.
alface [aw'fasi] *f* lettuce.
alfaia [aw'faja] *f* (*móveis*) furniture; (*utensílio*) utensil; (*enfeite*) ornament.
alfaiataria [awfajata'ria] *f* tailor's shop.
alfaiate [awfa'jatʃi] *m* tailor.
alfândega [aw'fãdʒiga] *f* customs *pl*, customs house.
alfandegário/a [awfãde'garju/a] *adj* customs *atr* ♦ *m/f* customs officer.

NB*: European Portuguese adds the following consonants to certain words:* **b** (sú(b)dito, su(b)til); **c** (a(c)ção, a(c)cionista, a(c)to); **m** (inde(m)ne); **p** (ado(p)ção, ado(p)tar); *for further details see p. xiii.*

alfanumérico/a [awfanu'mɛriku/a] *adj* alphanumeric.
alfavaca [awfa'vaka] *f* basil.
alfazema [awfa'zɛma] *f* lavender.
alfena [aw'fɛna] *f* privet.
alfinetada [awfine'tada] *f* prick; (*dor aguda*) stabbing pain; (*fig*) dig.
alfinetar [awfine'ta*] *vt* to prick (with a pin); (*marcar costura*) to pin; (*fig*) to needle.
alfinete [awfi'netʃi] *m* pin; ~ **de chapéu** hat pin; ~ **de fralda** nappy (*BRIT*) *ou* diaper (*US*) pin; ~ **de segurança** safety pin.
alfineteira [awfine'tejra] *f* pin cushion; (*caixa*) pin box.
alga ['awga] *f* seaweed; (*BOT*) alga.
algarismo [awga'riʒmu] *m* numeral, digit; ~ **arábico/romano** Arabic/Roman numeral.
Algarve [aw'gaxvi] *m*: **o** ~ the Algarve.
algarvio/a [awgax'viu/a] *adj* from the Algarve ♦ *m/f* native *ou* inhabitant of the Algarve.
algazarra [awga'zaxa] *f* uproar, racket.
álgebra ['awʒebra] *f* algebra.
algemar [awʒe'ma*] *vt* to handcuff.
algemas [aw'ʒɛmaʃ] *fpl* handcuffs.
algibeira [awʒi'bejra] *f* pocket.
algo ['awgu] *adv* somewhat, rather ♦ *pron* something; (*qualquer coisa*) anything.
algodão [awgo'dãw] *m* cotton; ~**(-doce)** candy floss; ~ **(hidrófilo)** cotton wool (*BRIT*), absorbent cotton (*US*).
algodoeiro/a [awgo'dwejru/a] *adj* (*indústria*) cotton *atr* ♦ *m* cotton plant.
algoritmo [awgo'xitʃimu] *m* algorithm.
algoz [aw'goʒ] *m* beast, cruel person.
alguém [aw'gẽj] *pron* someone, somebody; (*em frases interrogativas ou negativas*) anyone, anybody; **ser ~ na vida** to be somebody in life.
algum(a) [aw'gũ/'guma] *adj* some; (*em frases interrogativas ou negativas*) any ♦ *pron* one; (*no plural*) some; (*negativa*): **de modo** ~ in no way; **coisa ~a** nothing; ~ **dia** one day; ~ **tempo** for a while; **~a coisa** something; **~a vez** sometime.
algures [aw'guriʃ] *adv* somewhere.
alheio/a [a'ʎeju/a] *adj* (*de outrem*) someone else's; (*estranho*) alien; (*estrangeiro*) foreign; (*impróprio*) inappropriate; ~ **a** foreign to; (*desatento*) unaware of; ~ **de** (*afastado*) removed from, far from; (*ignorante*) unaware of.
alho ['aʎu] *m* garlic; **confundir ~s com bugalhos** to get things mixed up.
alho-poró [-po'rɔ] (*pl* **alhos-porós**) *m* leek.
ali [a'li] *adv* there; **até** ~ up to there; **por** ~ around there, somewhere there; (*direção*) that way; ~ **por** (*tempo*) round about; **de ~ por diante** from then on; ~ **dentro** in there.
aliado/a [a'ljadu/a] *adj* allied ♦ *m/f* ally.
aliança [a'ljãsa] *f* alliance; (*anel*) wedding ring.
aliar [a'lja*] *vt* to ally; **~-se** *vr* to make an alliance.
aliás [a'ljajʃ] *adv* (*a propósito*) as a matter of fact; (*ou seja*) rather, that is; (*contudo*) nevertheless; (*diga-se de passagem*) incidentally.
álibi ['alibi] *m* alibi.
alicate [ali'katʃi] *m* pliers *pl*; ~ **de unhas** nail clippers *pl*.
alicerçar [alisex'sa*] *vt* (*argumento etc*) to base; (*consolidar*) to consolidate.
alicerce [ali'sɛxsi] *m* (*de edifício*) foundation; (*fig*: *base*) basis.
aliciar [ali'sja*] *vt* (*seduzir*) to entice; (*atrair*) to attract.
alienação [aljena'sãw] *f* alienation; (*de bens*) transfer (of property); ~ **mental** insanity.
alienado/a [alje'nadu/a] *adj* alienated; (*demente*) insane; (*bens*) transferred ♦ *m/f* lunatic.
alienar [alje'na*] *vt* (*bens*) to transfer; (*afastar*) to alienate; **~-se** *vr* to become alienated.
alienígena [alje'niʒena] *adj, m/f* alien.
alijar [ali'ʒa*] *vt* to jettison; (*livrar-se de*) to get rid of; **~-se** *vr*: **~-se de** to free o.s. of.
alimentação [alimẽta'sãw] *f* (*alimentos*) food; (*ação*) feeding; (*nutrição*) nourishment; (*ELET*) supply.
alimentar [alimẽ'ta*] *vt* to feed; (*fig*) to nurture ♦ *adj* (*produto*) food *atr*; (*hábitos*) eating *atr*; **~-se** *vr*: **~-se de** to feed on.
alimentício/a [alimẽ'tʃisju/a] *adj* nourishing; **gêneros ~s** foodstuffs.
alimento [ali'mẽtu] *m* food; (*nutrição*) nourishment.
alínea [a'linja] *f* opening line of a paragraph; (*subdivisão de artigo*) sub-heading.
alinhado/a [ali'ɲadu/a] *adj* (*elegante*) elegant; (*texto*) aligned; ~ **à esquerda/direita** (*texto*) ranged left/right.
alinhamento [aliɲa'mẽtu] *m* alignment; ~ **da margem** justification.
alinhar [ali'ɲa*] *vt* to align; **~-se** *vr* (*enfileirar-se*) to form a line.
alinhavar [aliɲa'va*] *vt* (*COSTURA*) to tack.
alinhavo [ali'ɲavu] *m* tacking.
alinho [a'liɲu] *m* (*alinhamento*) alignment; (*elegância*) neatness.
alíquota [a'likwota] *f* bracket, percentage.
alisar [ali'za*] *vt* (*tornar liso*) to smooth; (*cabelo*) to straighten; (*cariciar*) to stroke.
alistamento [aliʃta'mẽtu] *m* enlistment.
alistar [aliʃ'ta*] *vt* (*MIL*) to recruit; **~-se** *vr* to enlist.
aliteração [alitera'sãw] *f* alliteration.
aliviado/a [ali'vjadu/a] *adj* (*pessoa*) relieved; (: *folgado*) free; (*carga*) lightened; (*dor*) relieved.
aliviar [ali'vja*] *vt* to relieve; (*carga etc*) to lighten ♦ *vi* (*diminuir*) to diminish; (*acalmar*) to give relief; **~-se** *vr*: **~-se de** (*libertar-se*) to unburden o.s. of.
alívio [a'livju] *m* relief.
Alm. *abr* = **Almirante**.

alma ['awma] *f* soul; (*entusiasmo*) enthusiasm; (*caráter*) character; **eu daria a ~ para fazer** I would give anything to do; **sua ~, sua palma** don't say I didn't warn you.
almanaque [awma'naki] *m* almanac; **cultura de ~** superficial knowledge.
almejar [awme'ʒa*] *vt* to long for, yearn for.
almirantado [awmirã'tadu] *m* admiralty.
almirante [awmi'rãtʃi] *m* admiral.
almoçado/a [awmo'sadu/a] *adj*: **ele está ~** he's had lunch.
almoçar [awmo'sa*] *vi* to have lunch ♦ *vt*: **~ peixe** to have fish for lunch.
almoço [aw'mosu] *m* lunch; **pequeno ~** (*PT*) breakfast.
almofada [awmo'fada] *f* cushion; (*PT*: *travesseiro*) pillow.
almofadado/a [awmofa'dadu/a] *adj* cushioned.
almofadinha [awmofa'dʒiɲa] *f* pin cushion.
almôndega [aw'mõdega] *f* meat ball.
almotolia [awmoto'lia] *f* oilcan.
almoxarifado [awmoʃari'fadu] *m* storeroom.
almoxarife [awmoʃa'rifi] *m* storekeeper.
ALN (*BR*) *abr f* (= *Ação Libertadora Nacional*) *former group opposed to junta.*
alô [a'lo] (*BR*) *excl* (*TEL*) hullo.
alocação [aloka'sãw] (*pl* **-ões**) *f* allocation.
alocar [alo'ka*] *vt* to allocate.
aloirado/a [aloj'radu/a] *adj* = **alourado/a**.
alojamento [aloʒa'mẽtu] *m* accommodation (*BRIT*), accommodations (*US*); (*habitação*) housing; (*MIL*) billet.
alojar [alo'ʒa*] *vt* to lodge; (*MIL*) to billet; **~-se** *vr* to stay.
alongamento [alõga'mẽtu] *m* lengthening; (*prazo*) extension; (*ginástica*) stretching.
alongar [alõ'ga*] *vt* (*fazer longo*) to lengthen; (*prazo*) to extend; (*prolongar*) to prolong; (*braço*) to stretch out; **~-se** *vr* (*sobre um assunto*) to dwell.
aloprado/a [alo'pradu/a] (*col*) *adj* nutty.
alourado/a [alo'radu/a] *adj* blondish.
alpaca [aw'paka] *f* alpaca.
alpendre [aw'pẽdri] *m* (*telheiro*) shed; (*pórtico*) porch.
alpercata [awpex'kata] *f* sandal.
Alpes ['awpiʃ] *mpl*: **os ~** the Alps.
alpinismo [awpi'niʒmu] *m* mountaineering, climbing.
alpinista [awpi'niʃta] *m/f* mountaineer, climber.
alq. *abr* = **alqueires**.
alquebrar [awke'bra*] *vt* to bend; (*enfraquecer*) to weaken ♦ *vi* (*curvar*) to stoop, be bent double.
alqueire [aw'kejri] *m* = *4.84 hectares* (*in São Paulo = 2.42 hectares*).
alqueive [aw'kejvi] *m* fallow land.
alquimia [awki'mia] *f* alchemy.
alquimista [awki'miʃta] *m/f* alchemist.
Alsácia [aw'sasja] *f*: **a ~** Alsace.
alta ['awta] *f* (*de preços*) rise; (*de hospital*) discharge; (*na bolsa*) high; **estar em ~** to be on the up; **pessoa da ~** high-class *ou* high-society person.
alta-fidelidade *f* hi-fi, high fidelity.
altaneiro/a [awta'nejru/a] *adj* (*soberbo*) proud.
altar [aw'ta*] *m* altar.
altar-mor [-mɔ*] (*pl* **altares-mores**) *m* high altar.
alta-roda *f* high society.
alta-tensão *f* high tension.
altear [aw'tʃja*] *vt* to raise; (*reputação*) to enhance ♦ *vi* to spread out; **~-se** *vr* (*reputação*) to be enhanced.
alteração [awtera'sãw] (*pl* **-ões**) *f* (*mudança*) alteration; (*desordem*) disturbance; (*falsificação*) falsification.
alterado/a [awte'radu/a] *adj* (*de mau humor*) bad-tempered, irritated.
alterar [awte'ra*] *vt* (*mudar*) to alter; (*falsificar*) to falsify; **~-se** *vr* (*mudar-se*) to become altered; (*enfurecer-se*) to get angry, lose one's temper.
alternado/a [awtex'nadu/a] *adj* alternate.
altercar [awtex'ka*] *vi* to have an altercation ♦ *vt* to argue for, advocate.
alter ego [awter-] *m* alter ego.
alternância [awtex'nãsja] *f* (*AGR*) crop rotation.
alternar [awtex'na*] *vt, vi* to alternate; **~-se** *vr* to alternate; (*por turnos*) to take turns.
alternativa [awtexna'tʃiva] *f* alternative.
alternativo/a [awtexna'tʃivu/a] *adj* alternative; (*ELET*) alternating.
alteroso/a [awte'rozu/ɔza] *adj* towering; (*majestoso*) majestic.
alteza [aw'teza] *f* highness.
altissonante [awtʃiso'nãtʃi] *adj* high-sounding.
altista [aw'tʃiʃta] *m/f* (*BOLSA*) bull ♦ *adj* (*tendência*) bullish; **mercado ~** bull market.
altitude [awtʃi'tudʒi] *f* altitude.
altivez [awtʃi'veʒ] *f* (*arrogância*) haughtiness; (*nobreza*) loftiness.
altivo/a [aw'tʃivu/a] *adj* (*arrogante*) haughty; (*elevado*) lofty.
alto/a ['awtu/a] *adj* high; (*de grande estatura*) tall; (*som*) high, sharp; (*importância, luxo*) great; (*GEO*) upper ♦ *adv* (*falar*) loudly, loud; (*voar*) high ♦ *excl* halt! ♦ *m* (*topo*) top, summit; **~ lá!** just a minute!; **do ~** from above; **por ~** superficially; **estar ~** (*bêbado*) to be tipsy; **alta fidelidade** high fidelity, hi-fi; **alta noite** dead of night; **~s e baixos** ups and downs.
alto-astral (*col*) *m* good vibes *pl*; **estar de ~** to be on good form.
alto-falante (*pl* **~s**) *m* loudspeaker.
altruísmo [awtru'iʒmu] *m* altruism.
altruísta [awtru'iʃta] *adj* altruistic.

***NB**: European Portuguese adds the following consonants to certain words:* **b** (sú(b)dito, su(b)til); **c** (a(c)ção, a(c)cionista, a(c)to); **m** (inde(m)ne); **p** (ado(p)ção, ado(p)tar); *for further details see p. xiii.*

altruístico/a [awtru'iʃtʃiku/a] *adj* altruistic.

altura [aw'tura] *f* height; (*momento*) point, juncture; (*altitude*) altitude; (*de um som*) pitch; (*lugar*) whereabouts; **em que ~ da Rio Branco fica a livraria?** whereabouts in Rio Branco is the bookshop?; **na ~ do banco** near the bank; **nesta ~** at this juncture; **estar à ~ de** (*ser capaz de*) to be up to; **pôr alguém nas ~s** (*fig*) to praise sb to the skies; **ter 1.80 metros de ~** to be 1.80 metres (*BRIT*) *ou* meters (*US*) tall.

alucinação [alusina'sãw] (*pl* **-ões**) *f* hallucination.

alucinado/a [alusi'nadu/a] *adj* (*maluco*) crazy; **~ por** crazy about.

alucinante [alusi'nãtʃi] *adj* crazy; **o tráfego no Rio é ~** the traffic in Rio drives you crazy.

aludir [alu'dʒi*] *vi*: **~ a** to allude to, hint at.

alugar [alu'ga*] *vt* (*tomar de aluguel*) to rent, hire; (*dar de aluguel*) to let, rent out; **~-se** *vr* to let.

aluguei [alu'gej] *etc vb V* **alugar**.

aluguel [alu'gɛw] (*pl* **-éis**) (*BR*) *m* rent; (*ação*) renting; **~ de carro** car hire (*BRIT*) *ou* rental (*US*).

aluguer [alu'gɛ*] (*PT*) *m* = **aluguel**.

aluir [a'lwi*] *vt* (*abalar*) to shake; (*derrubar*) to demolish; (*arruinar*) to ruin ♦ *vi* to collapse; (*ameaçar ruína*) to crumble.

alumiar [alu'mja*] *vt* to light (up) ♦ *vi* to give light.

alumínio [alu'minju] *m* aluminium (*BRIT*), aluminum (*US*).

alunissagem [aluni'saʒẽ] (*pl* **-ns**) *f* moon landing.

alunissar [aluni'sa*] *vi* to land on the moon.

aluno/a [a'lunu/a] *m/f* pupil, student; **~ excepcional** pupil with learning difficulties; **~ externo** day pupil; **~ interno** boarder.

alusão [alu'zãw] (*pl* **-ões**) *f* allusion, reference.

alusivo/a [alu'zivu/a] *adj* allusive.

alusões [alu'zõjʃ] *fpl de* **alusão**.

alvará [awva'ra] *m* permit.

alvejante [awve'ʒãtʃi] *m* bleach.

alvejar [awve'ʒa*] *vt* (*tomar como alvo*) to aim at; (*branquear*) to whiten, bleach ♦ *vi* to whiten.

alvenaria [awvena'ria] *f* masonry, brickwork; **de ~** brick *atr*, brick-built.

alvéolo [aw'vɛolu] *m* cavity; (*de dentes*) socket.

alvitrar [awvi'tra*] *vt* to propose, suggest.

alvitre [aw'vitri] *m* opinion.

alvo/a ['awvu/a] *adj* white ♦ *m* target; **acertar no** *ou* **atingir o ~** to hit the mark; **ser ~ de críticas** *etc* to be the object of criticism *etc*.

alvorada [awvo'rada] *f* dawn.

alvorecer [awvore'se*] *vi* to dawn.

alvoroçar [awvoro'sa*] *vt* (*agitar*) to stir up; (*entusiasmar*) to excite; **~-se** *vr* to get agitated.

alvoroço [awvo'rosu] *m* (*agitação*) commotion; (*entusiasmo*) enthusiasm.

alvura [aw'vura] *f* (*brancura*) whiteness; (*pureza*) purity.

AM *abr* = **Amazonas**; (*RÁDIO*: = *amplitude modulada*) AM.

Amã [a'mã] *n* Amman.

amabilidade [amabili'dadʒi] *f* kindness; (*simpatia*) friendliness.

amabilíssimo/a [amabi'lisimu/a] *adj superl de* **amável**.

amaciante [ama'sjatʃi] *m*: **~ (de roupa)** (fabric) conditioner.

amaciar [ama'sja*] *vt* (*tornar macio*) to soften; (*carro*) to run in.

ama-de-leite ['ama-] (*pl* **amas-de-leite**) *f* wet-nurse.

amado/a [a'madu/a] *m/f* beloved, sweetheart.

amador/a [ama'do*(a)] *adj*, *m/f* amateur.

amadorismo [amado'riʒmu] *m* amateur status.

amadorístico/a [amado'riʃtʃiku/a] *adj* amateurish.

amadurecer [amadure'se*] *vt*, *vi* (*frutos*) to ripen; (*fig*) to mature.

âmago ['amagu] *m* (*centro*) heart, core; (*medula*) pith; (*essência*) essence.

amainar [amaj'na*] *vi* (*tempestade*) to abate; (*cólera*) to calm down.

amaldiçoar [amawdʒi'swa*] *vt* to curse, swear at.

amálgama [a'mawgama] *f* amalgam.

amalgamar [amawga'ma*] *vt* to amalgamate; (*combinar*) to fuse (*BRIT*), fuze (*US*), blend.

amalucado/a [amalu'kadu/a] *adj* crazy, whacky.

amamentação [amamẽta'sãw] *f* breast-feeding.

amamentar [amamẽ'ta*] *vt* to breast-feed.

AMAN (*BR*) *abr f* = **Academia Militar das Agulhas Negras**.

amanhã [ama'ɲã] *adv*, *m* tomorrow; **~ de manhã** tomorrow morning; **~ de tarde** tomorrow afternoon; **~ à noite** tomorrow night; **depois de ~** the day after tomorrow.

amanhecer [amaɲe'se*] *vi* (*alvorecer*) to dawn; (*encontrar-se pela manhã*): **amanhecemos em Paris** we were in Paris at daybreak ♦ *m* dawn; **ao ~** at daybreak.

amansar [amã'sa*] *vt* (*animais*) to tame; (*cavalos*) to break in; (*aplacar*) to placate ♦ *vi* to grow tame.

amante [a'mãtʃi] *m/f* lover.

amanteigado/a [amãtej'gadu/a] *adj V* **biscoito**.

amapaense [amapa'ẽsi] *adj* from Amapá ♦ *m/f* native *ou* inhabitant of Amapá.

amar [a'ma*] *vt* to love.

amarelado/a [amare'ladu/a] *adj* yellowish; (*pele*) sallow.

amarelar [amare'la*] *vt*, *vi* to yellow.

amarelinha [amare'liɲa] *f* (*jogo*) hopscotch.

amarelo/a [ama'rɛlu/a] *adj* yellow ♦ *m* yellow.

amarfanhar [amaxfa'ɲa*] *vt* to screw up.

amargar [amax'ga*] *vt* to make bitter; (*fig*) to embitter; (*sofrer*) to suffer; **ser de ~** to be murder.
amargo/a [a'maxgu/a] *adj* bitter.
amargura [amax'gura] *f* bitterness; (*fig*: *sofrimento*) sadness, suffering.
amargurado/a [amaxgu'radu/a] *adj* sad.
amargurar [amaxgu'ra*] *vt* to embitter, sadden; (*sofrer*) to endure.
amarração [amaxa'sãw] *f*: **ser uma ~** (*col*) to be great.
amarrado/a [ama'xadu/a] *adj* (*cara*) scowling, angry; (*col*: *casado etc*) spoken for.
amarrar [ama'xa*] *vt* to tie (up); (NÁUT) to moor; **~-se** *vr*: **~se em** to like very much; **~ a cara** to frown, scowl.
amarronzado/a [amaxõ'zadu/a] *adj* brownish.
amarrotar [amaxo'ta*] *vt* to crease.
ama-seca ['ama-] (*pl* **amas-secas**) *f* nanny.
amassado/a [ama'sadu/a] *adj* (*roupa*) creased; (*papel*) screwed up; (*carro*) smashed in.
amassar [ama'sa*] *vt* (*pão*) to knead; (*misturar*) to mix; (*papel*) to screw up; (*roupa*) to crease; (*carro*) to dent.
amável [a'mavew] (*pl* **-eis**) *adj* (*afável*) kind.
amazona [ama'zɔna] *f* horsewoman.
Amazonas [ama'zɔnaʃ] *m*: **o ~** the Amazon.
amazonense [amazo'nẽsi] *adj* from Amazonas ♦ *m/f* native *ou* inhabitant of Amazonas.
Amazônia [ama'zonja] *f*: **a ~** the Amazon region.
amazônico/a [ama'zoniku/a] *adj* Amazonian.
âmbar ['ãba*] *m* amber.
ambição [ambi'sãw] (*pl* **-ões**) *f* ambition.
ambicionar [ãbisjo'na*] *vt* (*ter ambição de*) to aspire to; (*desejar*) to crave for.
ambicioso/a [ãbi'sjozu/ɔza] *adj* ambitious.
ambições [ãbi'sõjʃ] *fpl de* **ambição**.
ambidestro/a [ãbi'deʃtru/a] *adj* ambidextrous.
ambiental [ãbjẽ'taw] (*pl* **-ais**) *adj* environmental.
ambientalista [ãbjẽta'liʃta] *m/f* environmentalist.
ambientar [ãbjẽ'ta*] *vt* (*filme etc*) to set; (*adaptar*) to fit in; **~-se** *vr* to fit in.
ambiente [ã'bjẽtʃi] *m* atmosphere; (*meio*, COMPUT) environment; (*de uma casa*) ambience ♦ *adj* surrounding; **meio ~** environment; **temperatura ~** room temperature.
ambigüidade [ambigwi'dadʃi] *f* ambiguity.
ambíguo/a [ã'bigwu/a] *adj* ambiguous.
âmbito ['ãbitu] *m* (*extensão*) extent; (*campo de ação*) scope, range; **no ~ nacional/internacional** at (the) national/international level.
ambivalência [ãbiva'lẽsja] *f* ambivalence.
ambivalente [ãbiva'lẽtʃi] *adj* ambivalent.
ambos/as ['ãbuʃ/aʃ] *adj pl* both; **~ nós** both of us; **~ os lados** both sides.
ambrosia [ãbro'zia] *f eggs and milk cooked in sugar.*
ambulância [ãbu'lãsja] *f* ambulance.
ambulante [ãbu'lãtʃi] *adj* walking; (*errante*) wandering; (*biblioteca*) mobile.
ambulatório [ãbula'tɔrju] *m* outpatient department.
ameaça [ame'asa] *f* threat.
ameaçador(a) [ameasa'do*(a)] *adj* threatening, menacing.
ameaçar [amea'sa*] *vt* to threaten.
ameba [a'mɛba] *f* amoeba (BRIT), ameba (US).
amedrontador(a) [amedrõta'do*(a)] *adj* intimidating, frightening.
amedrontar [amedrõ'ta*] *vt* to scare, intimidate; **~-se** *vr* to be frightened.
ameia [a'meja] *f* battlement.
ameixa [a'mejʃa] *f* plum; (*passa*) prune.
amélia [a'mɛlja] (*col*) *f* long-suffering wife (*ou* girlfriend).
amém [a'mẽj] *excl* amen; **dizer ~ a** (*fig*) to agree to.
amêndoa [a'mẽdwa] *f* almond.
amendoado/a [amẽ'dwadu/a] *adj* (*olhos*) almond-shaped.
amendoeira [amẽ'dwejra] *f* almond tree.
amendoim [amẽdo'ĩ] (*pl* **-ns**) *m* peanut.
amenidade [ameni'dadʒi] *f* wellbeing; **~s** *fpl* small talk *sg*.
amenizar [ameni'za*] *vt* (*abrandar*) to soften; (*tornar agradável*) to make pleasant; (*facilitar*) to ease; (*briga*) to settle.
ameno/a [a'mɛnu/a] *adj* (*agradável*) pleasant; (*clima*) mild, gentle.
América [a'mɛrika] *f*: **a ~** America; **a ~ do Norte/do Sul** North/South America; **a ~ Central/Latina** Central/Latin America.
americanizado/a [amerikani'zadu/a] *adj* Americanized.
americano/a [ameri'kanu/a] *adj*, *m/f* American.
amesquinhar [ameʃki'ɲa*] *vt* to belittle; **~-se** *vr* (*humilhar-se*) to belittle o.s.; (*tornar-se avarento*) to become stingy.
amestrar [ameʃ'tra*] *vt* to train.
ametista [ame'tʃiʃta] *f* amethyst.
amianto [a'mjãtu] *m* asbestos.
amicíssimo/a [ami'sisimu/a] *adj superl de* **amigo/a**.
amido [a'midu] *m* starch.
amigar-se [ami'gaxsi] *vr*: **~ (com)** to become friends (with).
amigável [ami'gavew] (*pl* **-eis**) *adj* amicable.
amígdala [a'migdala] *f* tonsil.
amigdalite [amigda'litʃi] *f* tonsillitis.
amigo/a [a'migu/a] *adj* friendly ♦ *m/f* friend; **ser ~ de** to be friends with; **~ do peito** bosom friend.
amigo/a-da-onça (*pl* **amigos/as-da-onça**) *m/f* false friend.

NB*: European Portuguese adds the following consonants to certain words:* **b** (sú(b)dito, su(b)til); **c** (a(c)ção, a(c)cionista, a(c)to); **m** (inde(m)ne); **p** (ado(p)ção, ado(p)tar); *for further details see p. xiii.*

amistoso/a [amiʃ'tozu/ɔza] *adj* friendly, cordial ♦ *m* (*jogo*) friendly.
AMIU (*BR*) *abr f* (= *Assistência Médica Infantil de Urgencia*) *emergency paediatric* (*BRIT*) *ou pediatric* (*US*) *service*.
amiudar [amju'da*] *vt*, *vi* to repeat; ~ **as visitas** to make frequent visits.
amiúde [a'mjudʒi] *adv* often, frequently.
amizade [ami'zadʒi] *f* (*relação*) friendship; (*simpatia*) friendliness; **fazer ~s** to make friends; ~ **colorida** casual relationship.
amnésia [am'nɛzja] *f* amnesia.
amnistia [amniʃ'tia] (*PT*) *f* = **anistia**.
amofinar [amofi'na*] *vt* to trouble; **~-se** *vr* to fret (over).
amolação [amola'sãw] (*pl* **-ões**) *f* bother, annoyance; (*desgosto*) upset.
amolador(a) [amola'do*(a)] *m/f* knife sharpener.
amolante [amo'lãtʃi] (*BR*) *adj* bothersome.
amolar [amo'la*] *vt* (*afiar*) to sharpen; (*aborrecer*) to annoy, bother ♦ *vi* to be annoying; **~-se** *vr* (*aborrecer-se*) to get annoyed.
amoldar [amow'da*] *vt* to mould (*BRIT*), mold (*US*); **~-se** *vr*: **~-se a** (*conformar-se*) to conform to; (*acostumar-se*) to get used to.
amolecimento [amolesi'mẽtu] *m* softening.
amolecer [amole'se*] *vt* to soften; (*abrandar-se*) to relent ♦ *vi* to soften.
amônia [a'monja] *f* ammonia.
amoníaco [amo'niaku] *m* ammonia.
amontoado [amõ'twadu/a] *m* mass; (*de coisas*) pile.
amontoar [amõ'twa*] *vt* to pile up, accumulate; ~ **riquezas** to amass a fortune.
amor [a'mo*] *m* love; **por ~ de** for the sake of; **fazer ~** to make love; **ela é um ~ (de pessoa)** she's a lovely person; ~ **próprio** self-esteem; (*orgulho*) conceit.
amora [a'mɔra] *f* mulberry; ~ **silvestre** (*PT*) blackberry.
amoral [amo'raw] (*pl* **-ais**) *adj* amoral.
amora-preta (*pl* **amoras-pretas**) *f* blackberry.
amordaçar [amoxda'sa*] *vt* to gag.
amoreco [amo'rɛku] *m*: **ela é um ~** she's a lovely person.
amorenado/a [amore'nadu/a] *adj* darkish.
amorfo/a [a'mɔxfu/a] *adj* (*objeto*) amorphous; (*pessoa*) dull.
amornar [amox'na*] *vt* to warm.
amoroso/a [amo'rozu/ɔza] *adj* loving, affectionate.
amor-perfeito (*pl* **amores-perfeitos**) *m* pansy.
amortecedor [amoxtese'do*] *m* shock absorber.
amortecer [amoxte'se*] *vt* to deaden ♦ *vi* to weaken, fade.
amortecido/a [amoxte'sidu/a] *adj* deadened; (*enfraquecido*) weak.
amortização [amoxtʃiza'sãw] *f* payment in instalments (*BRIT*) *ou* installments (*US*); (*COM*) amortization.
amortizar [amoxtʃi'za*] *vt* to pay in instalments (*BRIT*) *ou* installments (*US*).
amostra [a'mɔʃtra] *f* sample.
amostragem [amoʃ'traʒẽ] *f* sampling.
amotinado/a [amotʃi'nadu/a] *adj* mutinous, rebellious.
amotinar [amotʃi'na*] *vi* to rebel, mutiny; **~-se** *vr* to rebel, mutiny.
amparar [ãpa'ra*] *vt* to support; (*ajudar*) to assist; **~-se** *vr*: **~-se em/contra** (*apoiar-se*) to lean on/against.
amparo [ã'paru] *m* (*apoio*) support; (*auxílio*) help, assistance.
ampère [ã'pɛri] (*BR*) *m* ampere, amp.
ampliação [amplja'sãw] (*pl* **-ões**) *f* (*aumento*) enlargement; (*extensão*) extension.
ampliar [ã'plja*] *vt* to enlarge; (*conhecimento*) to broaden.
amplidão [ãpli'dãw] *f* vastness.
amplificação [amplifika'sãw] (*pl* **-ões**) *f* (*aumento*) enlargement; (*de som*) amplification.
amplificador [ãplifika'do*] *m* amplifier.
amplificar [ãplifi'ka*] *vt* to amplify.
amplitude [ãpli'tudʒi] *f* (*TEC*) amplitude; (*espaço*) spaciousness; (*fig*: *extensão*) extent.
amplo/a ['ãplu/a] *adj* (*sala*) spacious; (*conhecimento*, *sentido*) broad; (*possibilidade*) ample.
ampola [ã'pola] *f* ampoule (*BRIT*), ampule (*US*).
amputação [ãputa'sãw] (*pl* **-ões**) *f* amputation.
amputar [ãpu'ta*] *vt* to amputate.
Amsterdã [amiʃtex'dã] *n* Amsterdam.
amuado/a [a'mwadu/a] *adj* sulky.
amuar [a'mwa*] *vi* to sulk.
amuleto [amu'lɛtu] *m* charm.
amuo [a'muu] *m* sulkiness.
anã [a'nã] *f de* **anão**.
anacrônico/a [ana'kroniku/a] *adj* anachronistic.
anacronismo [anakro'niʒmu] *m* anachronism.
anagrama [ana'grama] *m* anagram.
anágua [a'nagwa] *f* petticoat.
ANAI *abr f* = **Associação Nacional de Apoio ao Índio**.
anais [a'najʃ] *mpl* annals.
analfabetismo [anawfabe'tʃiʒmu] *m* illiteracy.
analfabeto/a [anawfa'bɛtu/a] *adj*, *m/f* illiterate.
analgésico/a [anaw'ʒɛziku/a] *adj* analgesic ♦ *m* painkiller.
analisar [anali'za*] *vt* to analyse.
análise [a'nalizi] *f* analysis.
analista [ana'liʃta] *m/f* analyst; ~ **de sistemas** systems analyst.
analítico/a [ana'litʃiku/a] *adj* analytical.
analogia [analo'ʒia] *f* analogy.
análogo/a [a'nalogu/a] *adj* analogous.
ananás [ana'naʃ] (*pl* **ananases**) *m* (*BR*) *va-*

riety of pineapple; (*PT*) pineapple.
anão/anã [a'nãw/a'nã] (*pl* **-ões/~s**) *m/f* dwarf.
anarquia [anax'kia] *f* anarchy; (*fig*) chaos.
anárquico/a [a'naxkiku/a] *adj* anarchic.
anarquista [anax'kiʃta] *m/f* anarchist.
anarquizar [anaxki'za*] *vt* (*povo*) to incite to anarchy; (*desordenar*) to mess up; (*ridicularizar*) to ridicule.
anátema [a'natema] *m* anathema.
anatomia [anato'mia] *f* anatomy.
anatômico/a [ana'tomiku/a] *adj* anatomical.
anavalhar [anava'ʎa*] *vt* to slash.
Anbid (*BR*) *abr f* = **Associação Nacional de Bancos de Investimentos e Desenvolvimento.**
anca ['ãka] *f* (*de pessoa*) hip; (*de animal*) rump.
Ancara [ã'kara] *n* Ankara.
ancestrais [ãseʃ'trajʃ] *mpl* ancestors.
anchova [ã'ʃova] *f* anchovy.
ancião/anciã [ã'sjãw/ã'sjã] (*pl* **-ões/~s**) *adj* old ♦ *m/f* old man/woman; (*de uma tribo*) elder.
ancinho [ã'siɲu] *m* rake.
anciões [a'sjõjʃ] *mpl de* **ancião.**
âncora ['ãkora] *f* anchor.
ancoradouro [ãkora'doru] *m* anchorage.
ancorar [ãko'ra*] *vt*, *vi* to anchor.
andada [ã'dada] *f* walk; **dar uma ~** to go for a walk.
andaime [ã'dajmi] *m* (*ARQ*) scaffolding.
Andaluzia [ãdalu'zia] *f*: **a ~** Andalucia.
andamento [ãda'mẽtu] *m* (*progresso*) progress; (*rumo*) course; (*MÚS*) tempo; **em ~** in progress; **dar ~ a algo** to set sth in motion.
andanças [ã'dãsaʃ] *fpl* wanderings.
andar [ã'da*] *vi* (*ir a pé*) to walk; (*a cavalo*) to ride; (*máquina*) to work; (*progredir*) to go, progress ♦ *m* (*modo de caminhar*) gait; (*pavimento*) floor, storey (*BRIT*), story (*US*); **anda!** hurry up!; **~ com alguém** to have an affair with sb; **~ de trem/avião/bicicleta** to travel by train/fly/ride a bike; **ela anda triste** she's been sad lately.
andarilho/a [ãda'riʎu/a] *m/f* good walker.
ANDC (*BR*) *abr f* = **Associação Nacional de Defesa do Consumidor.**
Andes ['ãdʒiʃ] *mpl*: **os ~** the Andes.
Andima (*BR*) *abr f* = **Associação Nacional das Instituições de Mercado Aberto.**
andorinha [ãdo'riɲa] *f* (*pássaro*) swallow.
Andorra [ã'dɔxa] *f* Andorra.
andrógino/a [ã'drɔʒinu/a] *adj* androgynous.
anedota [ane'dɔta] *f* anecdote.
anedótico/a [ane'dɔtʃiku/a] *adj* anecdotal.
anel [a'nɛw] (*pl* **-éis**) *m* ring; (*elo*) link; (*de cabelo*) curl; **~ de casamento** wedding ring.
anelado/a [ane'ladu/a] *adj* curly.
anemia [ane'mia] *f* anaemia (*BRIT*), anemia (*US*).
anêmico/a [a'nemiku/a] *adj* anaemic (*BRIT*), anemic (*US*).
anestesia [aneʃte'zia] *f* anaesthesia (*BRIT*), anesthesia (*US*); (*anestésico*) anaesthetic (*BRIT*), anesthetic (*US*).
anestesiar [aneʃte'zja*] *vt* to anaesthetize (*BRIT*), anesthetize (*US*).
anestésico [aneʃ'tɛziku] *m* (*MED*) anaesthetic (*BRIT*), anesthetic (*US*).
anestesista [aneʃte'ziʃta] *m/f* anaesthetist (*BRIT*), anesthetist (*US*).
anexação [aneksa'sãw] (*pl* **-ões**) *f* annexation; (*de documento*) enclosure.
anexar [anek'sa*] *vt* to annex; (*juntar*) to attach; (*documento*) to enclose.
anexo/a [a'nɛksu/a] *adj* attached ♦ *m* annexe; (*de igreja*) hall; (*em carta*) enclosure; **segue em ~** please find enclosed.
Anfavea (*BR*) *abr f* = **Associação Nacional dos Fabricantes de Veículos Automotores.**
anfetamina [ãfeta'mina] *f* amphetamine.
anfíbio/a [ã'fibju/a] *adj* amphibious ♦ *m* amphibian.
anfiteatro [ãfi'tʃjatru] *m* amphitheatre (*BRIT*), amphitheater (*US*); (*no teatro*) dress circle.
anfitrião/anfitriã [ãfi'trjãw/'trjã] (*pl* **-ões/~s**) *m/f* host/hostess.
angariar [ãga'rja*] *vt* (*fundos, donativos*) to raise; (*adeptos*) to attract; (*reputação, simpatia*) to gain; **~ votos** to canvass (for votes).
angelical [ãʒeli'kaw] (*pl* **-ais**) *adj* angelic.
angina [ã'ʒina] *f*: **~ do peito** angina (pectoris).
anglicano/a [ãgli'kanu/a] *adj*, *m/f* Anglican.
anglicismo [ãgli'siʒmu] *m* Anglicism.
anglo-saxão/-saxôni(c)a [ãglosak'sãw/sak'soni(k)a] (*pl* **-ões/~s**) *m/f* Anglo-Saxon.
anglo-saxônico/a [ãglosak'soniku/a] *adj* Anglo-Saxon.
Angola [ã'gɔla] *f* Angola.
angolano/a [ãgo'lanu/a] *adj*, *m/f* Angolan.
angolense [ãgo'lẽsi] *adj*, *m/f* Angolan.
angorá [ãgo'ra] *adj* angora.
angra ['ãgra] *f* inlet, cove.
angu [ã'gu] *m* corn-meal purée.
angular [ãgu'la*] *adj* angular.
ângulo ['ãgulu] *m* angle; (*canto*) corner; (*fig*) angle, point of view.
angústia [ã'guʃtʃja] *f* anguish, distress.
angustiado/a [ãguʃ'tʃjadu/a] *adj* distressed.
angustiante [ãguʃ'tʃjãtʃi] *adj* distressing; (*momentos*) anxious, nerve-racking.
angustiar [ãguʃ'tʃja*] *vt* to distress.
anil [a'niw] *m* (*cor*) indigo.
animação [anima'sãw] *f* (*vivacidade*) liveliness; (*movimento*) bustle; (*entusiasmo*) enthusiasm.
animado/a [ani'madu/a] *adj* (*vivo*) lively;

***NB:** European Portuguese adds the following consonants to certain words:* **b** (sú(b)dito, su(b)til); **c** (a(c)ção, a(c)cionista, a(c)to); **m** (inde(m)ne); **p** (ado(p)ção, ado(p)tar); *for further details see p. xiii.*

(*alegre*) cheerful; ~ **com** enthusiastic about.
animador(a) [anima'do*(a)] *adj* encouraging ♦ *m/f* (BR: TV) presenter.
animal [ani'maw] (*pl* **-ais**) *adj*, *m* animal; ~ **de estimação** pet (animal).
animalesco/a [anima'leʃku/a] *adj* bestial, brutish.
animar [ani'ma*] *vt* (*dar vida*) to liven up; (*encorajar*) to encourage; **~-se** *vr* (*alegrar-se*) to cheer up; (*festa etc*) to liven up; **~-se a** to bring o.s. to.
ânimo ['animu] *m* (*coragem*) courage; ~! cheer up!; **perder o** ~ to lose heart; **recobrar o** ~ to pluck up courage; (*alegrar-se*) to cheer up.
animosidade [animozi'dadʒi] *f* animosity.
aninhar [ani'ɲa*] *vt* to nestle; **~-se** *vr* to nestle.
aniquilação [anikila'sãw] *f* annihilation.
aniquilar [aniki'la*] *vt* to annihilate; (*destruir*) to destroy; (*prostrar*) to shatter; **~-se** *vr* to be annihilated; (*moralmente*) to be shattered.
anis [a'niʃ] *m* aniseed.
anistia [aniʃ'tʃia] *f* amnesty.
aniversariante [anivexsa'rjãtʃi] *m/f* birthday boy/girl.
aniversário [anivex'sarju] *m* anniversary; (*de nascimento*) birthday; (: *festa*) birthday party; ~ **de casamento** wedding anniversary.
anjo ['ãʒu] *m* angel; ~ **da guarda** guardian angel.
ANL (BR) *abr f* (= *Aliança Nacional Libertadora*) *1930's left-wing movement.*
ano ['anu] *m* year; **Feliz A~ Novo!** Happy New Year!; **o ~ passado** last year; **o ~ que vem** next year; **por** ~ per annum; **fazer ~s** to have a birthday; **ele faz ~s hoje** it's his birthday today; **ter dez ~s** to be ten (years old); ~ **bissexto** leap year; ~ **civil** calendar year; ~ **corrente** current year; ~ **financeiro** financial year; ~ **letivo** academic year; (*da escola*) school year.
ano-bom *m* New Year.
anões [a'nõjʃ] *mpl de* **anão**.
anoitecer [anojte'se*] *vi* to grow dark ♦ *m* nightfall; **ao** ~ at nightfall.
anomalia [anoma'lia] *f* anomaly.
anômalo/a [a'nomalu/a] *adj* anomalous.
anonimato [anoni'matu] *m* anonymity.
anônimo/a [a'nonimu/a] *adj* anonymous; (COM): **sociedade anônima** limited company (BRIT), stock company (US).
anoraque [ano'raki] *m* anorak.
anorexia [ano'rɛksja] *f* anorexia.
anoréxico/a [ano'rɛksiku/a] *adj* anorexic.
anormal [anox'maw] (*pl* **-ais**) *adj* abnormal; (*incomum*) unusual; (*excepcional*) handicapped.
anormalidade [anoxmali'dadʒi] *f* abnormality.
anotação [anota'sãw] (*pl* **-ões**) *f* (*comentário*) annotation; (*nota*) note.
anotar [ano'ta*] *vt* (*tomar nota*) to note down; (*esclarecer*) to annotate.
anseio [ã'seju] *etc vb V* **ansiar**.
ânsia ['ãsja] *f* (*ansiedade*) anxiety; (*desejo*): ~ **(de)** longing (for); **ter ~s (de vômito)** to feel sick.
ansiado/a [ã'sjadu/a] *adj* longed for.
ansiar [ã'sja*] *vi*: ~ **por** (*desejar*) to yearn for; ~ **por fazer** to long to do.
ansiedade [ãsje'dadʒi] *f* anxiety; (*desejo*) eagerness.
ansioso/a [ã'sjozu/ɔza] *adj* anxious; (*desejoso*) eager.
antagônico/a [ãta'goniku/a] *adj* antagonistic; (*rival*) opposing.
antagonismo [ãtago'niʒmu] *m* (*hostilidade*) antagonism; (*oposição*) opposition.
antagonista [ãtago'niʃta] *m/f* antagonist; (*adversário*) opponent.
antártico/a [ã'taxtʃiku/a] *adj* antarctic ♦ *m*: **o A~** the Antarctic.
ante ['ãtʃi] *prep* (*na presença de*) before; (*em vista de*) in view of, faced with.
antebraço [ãtʃi'brasu] *m* forearm.
antecedência [ãtese'dẽsja] *f*: **com** ~ in advance; **3 dias de** ~ three days' notice.
antecedente [ãtese'dẽtʃi] *adj* (*anterior*) preceding ♦ *m* antecedent; **~s** *mpl* record *sg*, background *sg*; **~s criminais** criminal record *sg ou* past *sg*.
anteceder [ãtese'de*] *vt* to precede.
antecessor(a) [ãtese'so*(a)] *m/f* predecessor.
antecipação [ãtesipa'sãw] *f* anticipation; **com um mês de** ~ a month in advance; ~ **de pagamento** advance payment.
antecipadamente [ãtesipada'mẽtʃi] *adv* in advance, beforehand; **pagar** ~ to pay in advance.
antecipado/a [ãtesi'padu/a] *adj* (*pagamento*) (in) advance.
antecipar [ãtesi'pa*] *vt* to anticipate, forestall; (*adiantar*) to bring forward; **~-se** *vr* (*adiantar-se*) to be previous.
antegozar [ãtego'za*] *vt* to anticipate.
antemão [ante'mãw]: **de** ~ *adv* beforehand.
antena [ã'tɛna] *f* (BIO) antenna, feeler; (RADIO, TV) aerial; ~ **direcional** directional aerial; ~ **parabólica** satellite dish.
anteontem [ãtʃi'õtẽ] *adv* the day before yesterday.
anteparo [ãte'paru] *m* (*proteção*) screen.
antepassado [ãtʃipa'sadu] *m* ancestor.
antepor [ãte'po*] (*irreg*: *como* **pôr**) *vt* (*pôr antes*) to put before; **~-se** *vr* to anticipate.
anteprojeto [ãtepro'ʒɛtu] (PT: **-ect-**) *m* outline, draft; ~ **de lei** draft bill.
antepunha [ãte'puɲa] *etc vb V* **antepor**.
antepus [ãte'puʃ] *etc vb V* **antepor**.
antepuser [ãtepu'ze*] *etc vb V* **antepor**.
anterior [ãte'rjo*] *adj* (*prévio*) previous; (*antigo*) former; (*de posição*) front.
antes ['ãtʃiʃ] *adv* before; (*antigamente*) formerly; (*ao contrário*) rather; **o quanto ~** as soon as possible; ~ **de** before; ~ **de partir**

before leaving; ~ **do tempo** ahead of time; ~ **de tudo** above all; ~ **que** before.
ante-sala *f* ante-room.
antever [ãte've*] (*irreg*: *como* **ver**) *vt* to anticipate, foresee.
antevisto/a [ãte'viʃtu/a] *pp de* **antever**.
anti- [ãtʃi] *prefixo* anti-.
antiácido/a [ã'tʃjasidu/a] *adj* antacid ♦ *m* antacid.
antiaéreo/a [ãtʃja'ɛrju/a] *adj* anti-aircraft.
antiamericano/a [ãtʃjameri'kanu/a] *adj* anti-American.
antibiótico/a [ãtʃi'bjɔtʃiku/a] *adj* antibiotic ♦ *m* antibiotic.
anticaspa [ãtʃi'kaʃpa] *adj inv* anti-dandruff.
anticiclone [ãtʃisi'klɔni] *m* anticyclone.
anticlímax [ãtʃi'klimaks] *m* anticlimax.
anticoncepcional [ãtʃikõsepsjo'naw] (*pl* **-ais**) *adj*, *m* contraceptive.
anticongelante [ãtʃikõʒe'lãtʃi] *m* antifreeze.
anticonstitucional [ãtʃikõʃtʃitusjo'naw] (*pl* **-ais**) *adj* unconstitutional.
anticorpo [ãtʃi'koxpu] *m* antibody.
antidemocrático/a [ãtʃidemo'kratʃiku/a] *adj* undemocratic.
antidepressivo/a [ãtʃidepre'sivu/a] *adj* anti-depressant ♦ *m* anti-depressant.
antiderrapante [ãtʃidexa'pãtʃi] *adj* (*pneu*) non-skid.
antídoto [ã'tʃidotu] *m* antidote.
antiestético/a [ãtʃjeʃ'tɛtʃiku/a] *adj* tasteless.
antiético/a [ã'tʃjɛtʃiku/a] *adj* unethical.
antigamente [ãtʃiga'mẽtʃi] *adv* formerly; (*no passado*) in the past.
antigo/a [ã'tʃigu/a] *adj* old; (*histórico*) ancient; (*de estilo*) antique; (*chefe etc*) former; **ele é muito ~ na firma** he's been with the firm for many years; **os ~s** (*gregos etc*) the ancients.
Antígua [ã'tʃigwa] *f* Antigua.
antiguidade [ãtʃigi'dadʒi] *f* antiquity, ancient times *pl*; (*de emprego*) seniority; **~s** *fpl* (*monumentos*) ancient monuments; (*artigos*) antiques.
anti-higiênico/a *adj* unhygienic.
anti-histamínico/a [-iʃta'miniku/a] *adj* antihistamine ♦ *m* antihistamine.
anti-horário/a *adj* anticlockwise.
antilhano/a [ãtʃi'ʎanu/a] *adj*, *m/f* West Indian.
Antilhas [ã'tʃiʎaʃ] *fpl*: **as ~** the West Indies.
antílope [ã'tʃilopi] *m* antelope.
antipatia [ãtʃipa'tʃia] *f* antipathy, dislike.
antipático/a [ãtʃi'patʃiku/a] *adj* unpleasant, unfriendly.
antipatizar [ãtʃipatʃi'za*] *vi*: ~ **com alguém** to dislike sb.
antipatriótico/a [ãtʃipa'trjɔtʃiku/a] *adj* unpatriotic.
antipoluente [ãtʃipo'lwẽtʃi] *adj* non-pollutant.
antiquado/a [ãtʃi'kwadu/a] *adj* antiquated; (*fora de moda*) out of date, old-fashioned.
antiquário/a [ãtʃi'kwarju/a] *m/f* antique dealer ♦ *m* (*loja*) antique shop.
antiquíssimo/a [ãtʃi'kisimu/a] *adj superl de* **antigo/a**.
anti-semita *adj* anti-Semitic.
anti-semitismo [-semi'tʃiʒmu] *m* anti-Semitism.
anti-séptico/a *adj* antiseptic ♦ *m* antiseptic.
anti-social (*pl* **-ais**) *adj* antisocial.
antítese [ã'tʃitezi] *f* antithesis.
antitruste [ãtʃi'truʃtʃi] *adj V* **legislação**.
antolhos [ã'tɔʎuʃ] *mpl* (*pala*) eye-shade *sg*; (*de cavalo*) blinkers.
antologia [ãtolo'ʒia] *f* anthology.
antônimo [ã'tonimu] *m* antonym.
antro ['ãtru] *m* cave, cavern; (*de animal*) lair; (*de ladrões*) den.
antropofagia [ãtropofa'ʒia] *f* cannibalism.
antropófago/a [ãtro'pɔfagu/a] *m/f* cannibal.
antropologia [ãtropolo'ʒia] *f* anthropology.
antropólogo/a [ãtro'pɔlogu/a] *m/f* anthropologist.
ANTTUR (BR) *abr f* = **Associação Nacional de Transportadores de Turismo e Agências de Viagens**.
anual [a'nwaw] (*pl* **-ais**) *adj* annual, yearly.
anuário [a'nwarju] *m* yearbook.
anuidade [anwi'dadʒi] *f* annuity.
anuir [a'nwi*] *vi*: ~ **a** to agree to; ~ **com** to comply with.
anulação [anula'sãw] (*pl* **-ões**) *f* cancellation; (*de contrato, casamento*) annulment.
anular [anu'la*] *vt* to cancel; (*contrato, casamento*) to annul; (*efeito*) to cancel out ♦ *m* ring finger.
anunciante [anũ'sjãtʃi] *m* (COM) advertiser.
anunciar [anũ'sja*] *vt* to announce; (COM: *produto*) to advertise.
anúncio [a'nũsju] *m* announcement; (COM) advertisement, advert; (*cartaz*) notice; ~ **luminoso** neon sign; **~s classificados** small *ou* classified ads.
ânus ['anuʃ] *m inv* anus.
anverso [ã'vɛxsu] *m* (*de moeda*) obverse.
anzol [ã'zɔw] (*pl* **-óis**) *m* fish-hook.
ao [aw] = **a** + **o**; *V* **a**.
aonde [a'õdʒi] *adv* where; ~ **quer que** wherever.
aos [awʃ] = **a** + **os**; *V* **a**.
AP *abr* = **Amapá**.
Ap. *abr* = **apartamento**.
apadrinhar [apadri'ɲa*] *vt* (*ser padrinho*) to act as godfather to; (: *de noivo*) to be best man to; (*proteger*) to protect; (*patrocinar*) to support.
apagado/a [apa'gadu/a] *adj* (*fogo*) out; (*luz elétrica*) off; (*indistinto*) faint; (*pessoa*) dull.
apagar [apa'ga*] *vt* (*fogo*) to put out; (*luz elétrica*) to switch off; (*vela*) to blow out; (*com*

***NB**: European Portuguese adds the following consonants to certain words:* **b** (sú(b)dito, su(b)til); **c** (a(c)ção, a(c)cionista, a(c)to); **m** (inde(m)ne); **p** (ado(p)ção, ado(p)tar); *for further details see p. xiii.*

borracha) to rub out, erase; (*quadro-negro*) to clean; (COMPUT) to delete, erase; **~-se** *vr* to go out; (*desmaiar*) to pass out; (*col: dormir*) to nod off.

apaguei [apa'gej] *etc vb V* **apagar**.

apaixonado/a [apajʃo'nadu/a] *adj* (*pessoa*) in love; (*discurso*) impassioned; **ele está ~ por ela** he is in love with her; **ele é ~ por tênis** he's mad about tennis.

apaixonar-se [apajʃo'naxsi] *vr*: **~ por** to fall in love with.

apaixonante [apajʃo'nãtʃi] *adj* captivating.

Apalaches [apa'laʃiʃ] *mpl*: **os ~** the Appalachians.

apalermado/a [apalex'madu/a] *adj* silly.

apalpadela [apawpa'dɛla] *f* touch.

apalpar [apaw'pa*] *vt* to touch, feel; (MED) to examine.

apanhado [apa'ɲadu] *m* (*de flores*) bunch; (*resumo*) summary; (*pregas*) gathering.

apanhar [apa'ɲa*] *vt* to catch; (*algo à mão, do chão*) to pick up; (*ir buscar, surra, táxi*) to get; (*colher*) to pick; (*agarrar*) to grab; (*sol*) to take ♦ *vi* (*ser espancado*) to get a beating; (*em jogo*) to take a beating; **~ chuva** to get soaked.

apaniguado/a [apani'gwadu/a] *m/f* (*protegido*) protégé(e).

apapagaiado/a [apapaga'jadu/a] *adj* loud, garish.

apara [a'para] *f* (*de madeira*) shaving; (*de papel*) clipping.

aparador [apara'do*] *m* sideboard.

aparafusar [aparafu'za*] *vt* to screw.

apara-lápis [apara'lapiʃ] (PT) *m* pencil sharpener.

aparar [apa'ra*] *vt* (*cabelo*) to trim; (*lápis*) to sharpen; (*o que é atirado ou cai*) to catch; (*pancada*) to parry; (*madeira*) to plane.

aparato [apa'ratu] *m* pomp; (*coleção*) array.

aparatoso/a [apara'tozu/ɔza] *adj* grand.

aparecer [apare'se*] *vi* to appear; (*apresentar-se*) to turn up; (*ser publicado*) to be published; **~ em casa de alguém** to drop in on sb, call on sb.

aparecimento [aparesi'mẽtu] *m* appearance; (*publicação*) publication.

aparelhado/a [apare'ʎadu/a] *adj* (*preparado*) ready, prepared; (*madeira*) planed.

aparelhagem [apare'ʎaʒẽ] *f* equipment; (*carpintaria*) finishing; (NÁUT) rigging.

aparelhar [apare'ʎa*] *vt* (*preparar*) to prepare, get ready; (NÁUT) to rig; **~-se** *vr* to get ready.

aparelho [apa'reʎu] *m* apparatus; (*equipamento*) equipment; (PESCA) tackle, gear; (*máquina*) machine; (BR: *fone*) telephone; (POL) hide-out; **~ de barbear** electric shaver; **~ de chá** tea set; **~ de rádio/TV** radio/TV set; **~ digestivo** digestive system; **~ doméstico** domestic appliance; **~ fonador** vocal tract; **~ sanitário** bathroom suite.

aparência [apa'rẽsja] *f* appearance; (*aspecto*) aspect; **na ~** apparently; **sob a ~ de** under the guise of; **manter as ~s** to keep up appearances; **salvar as ~s** to save face; **as ~s enganam** appearances are deceptive.

aparentado/a [aparẽ'tadu/a] *adj* related; **bem ~** well connected.

aparentar [aparẽ'ta*] *vt* (*fingir*) to feign; (*parecer*) to give the appearance of.

aparente [apa'rẽtʃi] *adj* apparent; (*concreto, madeira*) exposed.

aparição [apari'sãw] (*pl* **-ões**) *f* (*visão*) apparition; (*fantasma*) ghost.

aparo [a'paru] (PT) *m* (*de caneta*) (pen) nib.

apartamento [apaxta'mẽtu] *m* apartment, flat (BRIT).

apartar [apax'ta*] *vt* to separate; **~-se** *vr* to separate.

aparte [a'paxtʃi] *m* aside.

apartheid [apax'tajdʒi] *m* apartheid.

aparvalhado/a [apaxva'ʎadu/a] *adj* idiotic.

apatetado/a [apate'tadu/a] *adj* sluggish.

apatia [apa'tʃia] *f* apathy.

apático/a [a'patʃiku/a] *adj* apathetic.

apátrida [a'patrida] *m/f* stateless person.

apavorado/a [apavo'radu/a] *adj* terrified.

apavoramento [apavora'mẽtu] *m* terror.

apavorante [apavo'rãtʃi] *adj* terrifying.

apavorar [apavo'ra*] *vt* to terrify ♦ *vi* to be terrifying; **~-se** *vr* to be terrified.

apaziguar [apazi'gwa*] *vt* to appease; **~-se** *vr* to calm down.

apear-se [a'pjaxsi] *vr*: **~ de** (*cavalo*) to dismount from.

apedrejar [apedre'ʒa*] *vt* to stone.

apegado/a [ape'gadu/a] *adj* attached.

apegar-se [ape'gaxsi] *vr*: **~ a** (*afeiçoar-se*) to become attached to.

apego [a'pegu] *m* (*afeição*) attachment.

apeguei [ape'gej] *etc vb V* **apegar**.

apelação [apela'sãw] (*pl* **-ões**) *f* appeal.

apelante [ape'lãtʃi] *m/f* appellant.

apelar [ape'la*] *vi* to appeal; **~ da sentença** (JUR) to appeal against the sentence; **~ para** to appeal to; **~ para a ignorância/violência** to resort to abuse/violence.

apelidar [apeli'da*] *vt* (BR) to nickname; (PT) to give a surname to; **~-se** *vr*: **~-se de** to go by the name of; **Eduardo, apelidado de Dudu** Eduardo, nicknamed Dudu.

apelido [ape'lidu] *m* (PT: *nome de família*) surname; (BR: *alcunha*) nickname; **feio é ~!** (*col*) ugly is not the word for it!

apelo [a'pelu] *m* appeal.

apenas [a'pɛnaʃ] *adv* only.

apêndice [a'pẽdʒisi] *m* appendix; (*anexo*) supplement.

apendicite [apẽdʒi'sitʃi] *f* appendicitis.

Apeninos [ape'ninuʃ] *mpl*: **os ~** the Apennines.

apenso/a [a'pẽsu/a] *adj* attached.

apequenar [apeke'na*] *vt* to belittle.

aperceber-se [apexse'bexsi] *vr*: **~ de** to notice, see.

aperfeiçoamento [apexfejswa'mẽtu] *m* (*perfeição*) perfection; (*melhoramento*) improvement.
aperfeiçoar [apexfej'swa*] *vt* to perfect; (*melhorar*) to improve; **~-se** *vr* to improve o.s.
aperitivo [aperi'tʃivu] *m* aperitif.
aperreação [apexja'sãw] *f* annoyance.
aperreado/a [ape'xjadu/a] *adj* fed up.
aperrear [ape'xja*] *vt* to annoy.
apertado/a [apex'tadu/a] *adj* tight; (*estreito*) narrow; (*sem dinheiro*) hard-up; (*vida*) hard.
apertar [apex'ta*] *vt* (*agarrar*) to hold tight; (*roupa*) to take in; (*cinto*) to tighten; (*esponja*) to squeeze; (*botão*) to press; (*despesas*) to limit; (*vigilância*) to step up; (*coração*) to break; (*fig*: *pessoa*) to put pressure on ♦ *vi* (*sapatos*) to pinch; (*chuva, frio*) to get worse; (*estrada*) to narrow; **~-se** *vr* (*com roupa*) to corset o.s.; (*reduzir despesas*) to cut down (on expenses); (*ter problemas financeiros*) to feel the pinch; **~ em** (*insistir*) to insist on, press; **~ a mão de alguém** (*cumprimentar*) to shake hands with sb.
aperto [a'pextu] *m* (*pressão*) pressure; (*situação difícil*) spot of bother, jam; **um ~ de mãos** a handshake.
apesar [ape'za*] *prep*: **~ de** in spite of, despite; **~ disso** nevertheless; **~ de que** in spite of the fact that, even though.
apetecer [apete'se*] *vi* (*comida*) to be appetizing; **esse prato não me apetece** I don't fancy that dish.
apetecível [apete'sivew] (*pl* **-eis**) *adj* tempting.
apetite [ape'tʃitʃi] *m* appetite; (*desejo*) desire; (*fig*: *ânimo*) go; **abrir o ~** to get up an appetite; **bom ~!** enjoy your meal!
apetitoso/a [apeti'tozu/ɔza] *adj* appetizing.
apetrechar [apetre'ʃa*] *vt* to fit out, equip.
apetrechos [ape'treʃuʃ] *mpl* gear *sg*; (*de pesca*) tackle *sg*.
ápice ['apisi] *m* (*cume*) summit, top; (*vértice*) apex; **num ~** (*PT*) in a trice.
apicultura [apikuw'tura] *f* beekeeping, apiculture.
apiedar-se [apje'daxsi] *vr*: **~ de** (*ter piedade*) to pity; (*compadecer-se*) to take pity on.
apimentado/a [apimẽ'tadu/a] *adj* peppery.
apimentar [apimẽ'ta*] *vt* to pepper.
apinhado/a [api'ɲadu/a] *adj* crowded.
apinhar [api'ɲa*] *vt* to crowd, pack; **~-se** *vr* (*aglomerar-se*) to crowd together; **~-se de** (*gente*) to be filled *ou* packed with.
apitar [api'ta*] *vi* to whistle; (*col*): **ele não apita em nada em casa** he doesn't have a say in anything at home ♦ *vt* (*jogo*) to referee.
apito [a'pitu] *m* whistle.
aplacar [apla'ka*] *vt* to placate ♦ *vi* to calm down; **~-se** *vr* to calm down.
aplainar [aplaj'na*] *vt* (*madeira*) to plane; (*nivelar*) to level out.
aplanar [apla'na*] *vt* (*alisar*) to smooth; (*nivelar*) to level; (*dificuldades*) to smooth over.
aplaudir [aplaw'dʒi*] *vt* to applaud.
aplauso [a'plawzu] *m* applause; (*apoio*) support; (*elogio*) praise; (*aprovação*) approval; **~s** applause *sg*.
aplicação [aplika'sãw] (*pl* **-ões**) *f* application; (*esforço*) effort; (*COSTURA*) appliqué; (*da lei*) enforcement; (*de dinheiro*) investment; (*de aluno*) diligence; **pacote de aplicações** (*COMPUT*) applications package.
aplicado/a [apli'kadu/a] *adj* hard-working.
aplicar [apli'ka*] *vt* to apply; (*dinheiro*) to invest; (*lei*) to enforce; **~-se** *vr*: **~-se a** to devote o.s. to, apply o.s. to.
aplicativo/a [aplika'tʃivu/a] *adj*: **pacote/software ~** applications package/software ♦ *m* (*COMPUT*) applications program.
aplicável [apli'kavew] (*pl* **-eis**) *adj* applicable.
aplique [a'pliki] *m* (*luz*) wall light; (*peruca*) hairpiece.
apliquei [apli'kej] *etc vb V* **aplicar**.
apocalipse [apoka'lipsi] *f* apocalypse.
apócrifo/a [a'pɔkrifu/a] *adj* apocryphal.
apoderar-se [apode'raxsi] *vr*: **~ de** to seize, take possession of.
apodrecer [apodre'se*] *vt* to rot; (*dente*) to decay ♦ *vi* to rot, decay.
apodrecimento [apodresi'mẽtu] *m* rottenness, decay; (*de dentes*) decay.
apogeu [apo'ʒew] *m* (*ASTRONOMIA*) apogee; (*fig*) height, peak.
apoiar [apo'ja*] *vt* to support; (*basear*) to base; (*moção*) to second; **~-se** *vr*: **~-se em** to rest on.
apoio [a'poju] *m* support; (*financeiro*) backing; **~ moral** moral support.
apólice [a'pɔlisi] *f* (*certificado*) policy, certificate; (*ação*) share, bond; **~ de seguro** insurance policy.
apologia [apolo'ʒia] *f* (*elogio*) eulogy; (*defesa*) defence (*BRIT*), defense (*US*).
apologista [apolo'ʒiʃta] *m/f* apologist.
apontador [apõta'do*] *m* pencil sharpener.
apontamento [apõta'mẽtu] *m* (*nota*) note.
apontar [apõ'ta*] *vt* (*fusil*) to aim; (*erro*) to point out; (*com o dedo*) to point at *ou* to; (*razão*) to put forward; (*nomes*) to name ♦ *vi* (*aparecer*) to begin to appear; (*brotar*) to sprout; (*com o dedo*) to point; **~!** take aim!; **~ para** to point to; (*com arma*) to aim at.
apoplético/a [apo'plɛtʃiku/a] *adj* apoplectic.
apoquentar [apokẽ'ta*] *vt* to annoy, pester; **~-se** *vr* to get annoyed.
aporrinhação [apoxiɲa'sãw] *f* annoyance.

NB: European Portuguese adds the following consonants to certain words: **b** (sú(b)dito, su(b)til); **c** (a(c)ção, a(c)cionista, a(c)to); **m** (inde(m)ne); **p** (ado(p)ção, ado(p)tar); *for further details see p. xiii.*

aporrinhar [apoxi'ɲa*] *vt* to pester, annoy.
aportar [apox'ta*] *vi* to dock.
aportuguesado/a [apoxtuge'zadu/a] *adj* made Portuguese.
após [a'pɔjʃ] *prep* after.
aposentado/a [apozẽ'tadu/a] *adj* retired ♦ *m/f* retired person, pensioner; **ficar** ~ to be retired.
aposentadoria [apozẽtado'ria] *f* retirement; (*dinheiro*) pension.
aposentar [apozẽ'ta*] *vt* to retire; **~-se** *vr* to retire.
aposento [apo'zẽtu] *m* room.
após-guerra *m* post-war period; **a Alemanha do** ~ post-war Germany.
apossar-se [apo'saxsi] *vr*: ~ **de** to take possession of, seize.
aposta [a'pɔʃta] *f* bet.
apostar [apoʃ'ta*] *vt* to bet ♦ *vi*: ~ **em** to bet on.
a posteriori [apoʃte'rjɔri] *adv* afterwards.
apostila [apoʃ'tʃila] *f* students' notes *pl*, study aid.
apóstolo [a'pɔʃtolu] *m* apostle.
apóstrofo [a'pɔʃtrofu] *m* apostrophe.
apoteose [apote'ɔzi] *f* apotheosis.
aprazar [apra'za*] *vt* to allow.
aprazer [apra'ze*] *vi* to be pleasing; ~ **a alguém** to please sb; **ele faz o que lhe apraz** he does as he pleases; **aprazia-lhe escrever cartas** he liked to write letters.
aprazível [apra'zivew] (*pl* **-eis**) *adj* pleasant.
apreçar [apre'sa*] *vt* to value, price.
apreciação [apresja'sãw] *f* appreciation.
apreciar [apre'sja*] *vt* to appreciate; (*gostar de*) to enjoy.
apreciativo/a [apresja'tʃivu/a] *adj* appreciative.
apreciável [apre'sjavew] (*pl* **-eis**) *adj* appreciable.
apreço [a'presu] *m* (*estima*) esteem, regard; (*consideração*) consideration; **em** ~ in question.
apreender [aprjẽ'de*] *vt* to apprehend; (*tomar*) to seize; (*entender*) to grasp.
apreensão [aprjẽ'sãw] (*pl* **-ões**) *f* (*percepção*) perception; (*tomada*) seizure, arrest; (*receio*) apprehension.
apreensivo/a [aprjẽ'sivu/a] *adj* apprehensive.
apreensões [aprjẽ'sõjʃ] *fpl de* **apreensão**.
apregoar [apre'gwa*] *vt* to proclaim, announce; (*mercadorias*) to cry.
aprender [aprẽ'de*] *vt, vi* to learn; ~ **a ler** to learn to read; ~ **de cor** to learn by heart.
aprendiz [aprẽ'dʒiʒ] *m* apprentice; (*condutor*) learner.
aprendizado [aprendʒi'zadu] *m* (*num ofício*) apprenticeship; (*numa profissão*) training; (*escolar*) learning.
aprendizagem [aprẽdʒi'zaʒẽ] *f* (*num ofício*) apprenticeship; (*numa profissão*) training; (*escolar*) learning.
apresentação [aprezẽta'sãw] (*pl* **-ões**) *f* presentation; (*de peça, filme*) performance; (*de pessoas*) introduction; (*porte pessoal*) appearance; ~ **de contas** (*COM*) rendering of accounts.
apresentador(a) [aprezẽta'do*(a)] *m/f* presenter.
apresentar [aprezẽ'ta*] *vt* to present; (*pessoas*) to introduce; (*entregar*) to hand; (*trabalho, documento*) to submit; (*queixa*) to lodge; **~-se** *vr* (*identificar-se*) to introduce o.s.; (*problema*) to present itself; (*à polícia etc*) to report; **quero ~-lhe** may I introduce you to.
apresentável [aprezẽ'tavew] (*pl* **-eis**) *adj* presentable.
apressado/a [apre'sadu/a] *adj* hurried, hasty; **estar** ~ to be in a hurry.
apressar [apre'sa*] *vt* to hurry, hasten; **~-se** *vr* to hurry (up).
aprestar [apreʃ'ta*] *vt* (*aparelhar*) to equip, fit out; (*aprontar*) to get ready; **~-se** *vr* to get ready.
aprestos [a'prɛʃtuʃ] *mpl* (*preparativos*) preparations.
aprimorado/a [aprimo'radu/a] *adj* (*trabalho*) polished; (*pessoa*) elegant.
aprimorar [aprimo'ra*] *vt* to improve; **~-se** *vr* (*no vestir*) to make o.s. look nice.
a priori [a'prjɔri] *adv* beforehand.
aprisionamento [aprizjona'mẽtu] *m* imprisonment.
aprisionar [aprizjo'na*] *vt* (*cativar*) to capture; (*encarcerar*) to imprison.
aprofundar [aprofũ'da*] *vt* to deepen, make deeper; **~-se** *vr*: **~-se em** to go deeper into.
aprontar [aprõ'ta*] *vt* to get ready, prepare; (*briga*) to pick ♦ *vi* (*col*) to play up; **~-se** *vr* to get ready; ~ **alguma** (*col*) to be up to something.
apropriação [aproprja'sãw] (*pl* **-ões**) *f* appropriation; (*tomada*) seizure; ~ **de custos** (*COM*) cost appropriation.
apropriado/a [apro'prjadu/a] *adj* appropriate, suitable.
apropriar [apro'prja*] *vt* to appropriate; **~-se** *vr*: **~-se de** to seize, take possession of.
aprovação [aprova'sãw] *f* approval; (*louvor*) praise; (*num exame*) pass.
aprovado/a [apro'vadu/a] *adj* approved; **ser ~ num exame** to pass an exam; **o índice de ~s** the pass rate.
aprovar [apro'va*] *vt* to approve of; (*aluno*) to pass ♦ *vi* to make the grade, come up to scratch.
aproveitador(a) [aprovejta'do*(a)] *m/f* opportunist.
aproveitamento [aprovejta'mẽtu] *m* use, utilization; (*nos estudos*) progress.
aproveitar [aprovej'ta*] *vt* (*tirar proveito de*) to take advantage of; (*utilizar*) to use; (*não desperdiçar*) to make the most of; (*oportunidade*) to take; (*fazer bom uso de*) to make good use of ♦ *vi* to make the most of it;

(*PT*) to be of use; **não aproveita** it's no use; **aproveite!** enjoy yourself!, have a good time!
aproveitável [aprovej'tavew] (*pl* **-eis**) *adj* usable.
aprovisionamento [aprovizjona'mẽtu] *m* supply, provision.
aprovisionar [aprovizjo'na*] *vt* to supply; (*estocar*) to stock.
aproximação [aprosima'sãw] (*pl* **-ões**) *f* (*estimativa*) approximation; (*chegada*) approach; (*proximidade*) nearness, closeness.
aproximado/a [aprosi'madu/a] *adj* (*cálculo*) approximate; (*perto*) nearby.
aproximar [aprosi'ma*] *vt* to bring near; (*aliar*) to bring together; **~-se** *vr*: **~-se de** (*acercar-se*) to approach.
aprumado/a [apru'madu/a] *adj* vertical; (*altivo*) upright; (*elegante*) well-dressed.
aprumo [a'prumu] *m* vertical position; (*elegância*) elegance; (*altivez*) haughtiness.
aptidão [aptʃi'dãw] *f* aptitude, ability; (*jeito*) knack; **~ física** physical fitness.
aptitude [aptʃi'tudʒi] *f* aptitude, ability; (*jeito*) knack.
apto/a ['aptu/a] *adj* apt; (*capaz*) capable.
apto. *abr* = **apartamento.**
APU (*PT*) *abr f* (= *Aliança Povo Unido*) *political party*.
apunhalar [apuɲa'la*] *vt* to stab.
apuração [apura'sãw] *f* (*de votos*) counting; (*descoberta*) ascertainment; (*averiguação*) investigation; **~ de contas** (*COM*) settlement of accounts; **~ de custos** (*COM*) costing.
apurado/a [apu'radu/a] *adj* refined.
apurar [apu'ra*] *vt* (*aperfeiçoar*) to perfect; (*descobrir*) to find out; (*averiguar*) to investigate; (*dinheiro*) to raise, get; (*votos*) to count; **~-se** *vr* (*no trajar*) to dress up.
apuro [a'puru] *m* (*elegância*) refinement, elegance; (*dificuldade*) difficulty; **estar em ~s** to be in trouble.
aquarela [akwa'rɛla] *f* watercolour (*BRIT*), watercolor (*US*).
aquário [a'kwarju] *m* aquarium; **A~** (*ASTROLOGIA*) Aquarius.
aquartelar [akwaxte'la*] *vt* (*MIL*) to billet, quarter.
aquático/a [a'kwatʃiku/a] *adj* aquatic, water *atr*.
aquecedor(a) [akese'do*(a)] *adj* warming ♦ *m* heater.
aquecer [ake'se*] *vt* to heat ♦ *vi* to heat up; **~-se** *vr* to heat up.
aquecido/a [ake'sidu/a] *adj* heated.
aquecimento [akesi'mẽtu] *m* heating; (*da economia*) acceleration; **~ central** central heating.
aqueduto [ake'dutu] *m* aqueduct.
aquele/ela [a'keli/ɛla] *adj* (*sg*) that; (*pl*) those ♦ *pron* (*sg*) that one; (*pl*) those; **sem mais aquela** (*inesperadamente*) all of a sudden; (*sem cerimônia*) without so much as a "by your leave"; **foi aquela confusão** it was a real mess.
àquele/ela [a'keli/ɛla] = **a** + **aquele/ela.**
aquém [a'kẽj] *adv* on this side; **~ de** on this side of.
aqui [a'ki] *adv* here; **eis ~** here is/are; **~ mesmo** right here; **até ~** up to here; **por ~** hereabouts; (*nesta direção*) this way; **por ~ e por ali** here and there; **estou por ~!** (*col*) I've had it up to here!; *V tb* **daqui.**
aquiescência [akje'sẽsja] *f* consent.
aquiescer [akje'se*] *vi*: **~ (a)** to consent (to).
aquietar [akje'ta*] *vt* to calm, quieten; **~-se** *vr* to calm down.
aquilatar [akila'ta*] *vt* (*metais*) to value; (*avaliar*) to evaluate.
aquilo [a'kilu] *pron* that; **~ que** what.
àquilo [a'kilu] = **a** + **aquilo.**
aquisição [akizi'sãw] (*pl* **-ões**) *f* acquisition.
aquisitivo/a [akizi'tʃivu/a] *adj V* **poder.**
ar [a*] *m* air; (*aspecto*) look; (*brisa*) breeze; (*PT*: *AUTO*) choke; **~es** *mpl* airs; (*clima*) climate *sg*; **ao ~ livre** in the open air; **ir ao/sair do ~** (*TV*, *RÁDIO*) to go on/off the air; **no ~** (*TV*, *RÁDIO*) on air; (*fig*: *planos*) up in the air; **dar-se ~es** to put on airs; **ir pelos ~es** (*explodir*) to blow up; **tomar ~** to get some air; **~ condicionado** (*aparelho*) air conditioner; (*sistema*) air conditioning.
árabe ['arabi] *adj*, *m/f* Arab ♦ *m* (*LING*) Arabic.
Arábia [a'rabja] *f*: **a ~ Saudita** Saudi Arabia.
arado [a'radu] *m* plough (*BRIT*), plow (*US*).
aragem [a'raʒẽ] (*pl* **-ns**) *f* breeze.
arame [a'rami] *m* wire; **~ farpado** barbed wire.
aranha [a'raɲa] *f* spider.
aranha-caranguejeira [-karãge'ʒejra] (*pl* **aranhas-caranguejeiras**) *f* bird-eating spider.
arar [a'ra*] *vt* to plough (*BRIT*), plow (*US*).
arapuca [ara'puka] *f* trap; (*truque*) trick.
araque [a'raki] *m*: **de ~** (*col*) phony, bogus.
arara [a'rara] *f* parrot; **estar/ficar uma ~** (*fig*) to be/get angry.
arbitragem [axbi'traʒẽ] *f* arbitration; (*ESPORTE*) refereeing.
arbitrar [axbi'tra*] *vt* to arbitrate; (*ESPORTE*) to referee; (*adjudicar*) to award.
arbitrariedade [axbitrarje'dadʒi] *f* arbitrariness; (*ato*) arbitrary act.
arbitrário/a [axbi'trarju/a] *adj* arbitrary.
arbítrio [ax'bitrju] *m* decision; **ao ~ de** at the discretion of.
árbitro ['axbitru] *m* (*juiz*) arbiter; (*JUR*) arbitrator; (*FUTEBOL*) referee; (*TÊNIS*) umpire.
arborizado/a [axbori'zadu/a] *adj* green, wooded; (*rua*) tree-lined.

***NB**: European Portuguese adds the following consonants to certain words:* **b** (sú(b)dito, su(b)til); **c** (a(c)ção, a(c)cionista, a(c)to); **m** (inde(m)ne); **p** (ado(p)ção, ado(p)tar); *for further details see p. xiii.*

arborizar [axbori'za*] *vt* to plant with trees.
arbusto [ax'buʃtu] *m* shrub, bush.
arca ['axka] *f* chest, trunk; ~ **de Noé** Noah's Ark.
arcabouço [axka'bosu] *m* outline(s).
arcada [ax'kada] *f* (*série de arcos*) arcade; (*arco*) arch, span; ~ **dentária** dental ridge.
arcaico/a [ax'kajku/a] *adj* archaic; (*antiquado*) antiquated.
arcanjo [ax'kãʒu] *m* archangel.
arcar [ax'ka*] *vt*: ~ **com** (*responsabilidades*) to shoulder; (*despesas*) to handle; (*conseqüencias*) to take.
arcebispo [arse'biʃpu] *m* archbishop.
arco ['axku] *m* (ARQ) arch; (MIL, MÚS) bow; (ELET, MAT) arc; (*de barril*) hoop.
arco-da-velha *m*: **coisa/história do** ~ amazing thing/story.
arco-íris *m inv* rainbow.
ardente [ax'dẽtʃi] *adj* burning; (*intenso*) fervent; (*apaixonado*) ardent.
arder [ax'de*] *vi* to burn; (*pele, olhos*) to sting; ~ **de febre** to burn up with fever; ~ **de raiva** to seethe (with rage).
ardido/a [ax'dʒidu/a] *adj* (*picante*) hot.
ardil [ax'dʒiw] (*pl* **-is**) *m* trick, ruse.
ardiloso/a [axdʒi'lozu/ɔza] *adj* cunning.
ardis [ax'dʒiʃ] *mpl de* **ardil**.
ardor [ax'do*] *m* (*paixão*) ardour (BRIT), ardor (US), passion.
ardoroso/a [axdo'rozu/ɔza] *adj* ardent.
ardósia [ax'dɔzja] *f* slate.
árduo/a ['axdwu/a] *adj* arduous; (*difícil*) hard, difficult.
área ['arja] *f* area; (ESPORTE) penalty area; (*fig*) field; ~ **(de serviço)** balcony (*for hanging washing etc*).
arear [a'rja*] *vt* to polish.
areia [a'reja] *f* sand; ~ **movediça** quicksand.
arejado/a [are'ʒadu/a] *adj* aired, ventilated.
arejar [are'ʒa*] *vt* to air ♦ *vi* to get some air; (*descansar*) to have a breather; **~-se** *vr* to get some air; to have a break.
ARENA (BR) *abr f* (= *Aliança Renovadora Nacional*) *former political party*.
arena [a'rɛna] *f* arena; (*de circo*) ring.
arenito [are'nitu] *m* sandstone.
arenoso/a [are'nozu/ɔza] *adj* sandy.
arenque [a'rẽki] *m* herring.
aresta [a'rɛʃta] *f* edge.
arfar [ax'fa*] *vi* (*ofegar*) to pant, gasp for breath; (NÁUT) to pitch.
argamassa [axga'masa] *f* mortar.
argamassar [axgama'sa*] *vt* to cement.
Argel [ax'ʒɛw] *n* Algiers.
Argélia [ax'ʒɛlja] *f*: **a** ~ Algeria.
argelino/a [axʒe'linu/a] *adj, m/f* Algerian.
Argentina [axʒẽ'tʃina] *f*: **a** ~ Argentina.
argentino/a [axʒẽ'tʃinu/a] *adj, m/f* Argentinian.
argila [ax'ʒila] *f* clay.
argiloso/a [axʒi'lozu/ɔza] *adj* (*terreno*) clay.
argola [ax'gɔla] *f* ring; **~s** *fpl* (*brincos*) hooped earrings; ~ **(de porta)** door-knocker.
argúcia [ax'gusja] *f* (*sutileza*) subtlety; (*agudeza*) astuteness.
argüição [axgwi'sãw] (*pl* **-ões**) *f* oral test.
argüir [ax'gwi*] *vt* (*examinar*) to test, examine.
argumentação [axgumẽta'sãw] *f* argumentation.
argumentador(a) [axgumẽta'do*(a)] *adj* argumentative ♦ *m/f* arguer.
argumentar [axgumẽ'ta*] *vt, vi* to argue.
argumento [axgu'mẽtu] *m* argument; (*de obra*) theme.
arguto/a [ax'gutu/a] *adj* (*sutil*) subtle; (*astuto*) shrewd.
ária ['arja] *f* aria.
ariano/a [a'rjanu/a] *adj, m/f* Aryan; (*do signo Áries*) Arian.
aridez [ari'deʒ] *f* (*secura*) dryness; (*esterilidade*) barrenness; (*falta de interesse*) dullness.
árido/a ['aridu/a] *adj* (*seco*) arid, dry; (*estéril*) barren; (*maçante*) dull, boring.
Áries ['ariʃ] *f* Aries.
arisco/a [a'riʃku/a] *adj* unsociable.
aristocracia [ariʃtokra'sia] *f* aristocracy.
aristocrata [ariʃto'krata] *m/f* aristocrat.
aristocrático/a [ariʃto'kratʃiku/a] *adj* aristocratic.
aritmética [aritʃ'mɛtʃika] *f* arithmetic.
aritmético/a [aritʃ'mɛtʃiku/a] *adj* arithmetical.
arma ['axma] *f* weapon; **~s** *fpl* (*nucleares etc*) arms; (*brasão*) coat *sg* of arms; **de ~s e bagagem** with all one's belongings; **depor as ~s** to lay down arms; **passar pelas ~s** to shoot, execute; ~ **branca** cold steel; ~ **convencional/nuclear** conventional/nuclear weapon; ~ **de fogo** firearm.
armação [axma'sãw] (*pl* **-ões**) *f* (*armadura*) frame; (PESCA) tackle; (NÁUT) rigging; (*de óculos*) frames *pl*.
armada [ax'mada] *f* navy.
armadilha [axma'dʒiʎa] *f* trap.
armado/a [ax'madu/a] *adj* armed; ~ **até os dentes** armed to the teeth.
armador [axma'do*] *m* (NÁUT) shipowner; (*operário*) frame-layer.
armadura [axma'dura] *f* armour (BRIT), armor (US); (ELET) armature; (CONSTR) framework.
armamento [axma'mẽtu] *m* (*armas*) armaments *pl*, weapons *pl*; (NÁUT) equipment; (*ato*) arming.
armar [ax'ma*] *vt* to arm; (*montar*) to assemble; (*barraca*) to pitch; (*um aparelho*) to set up; (*armadilha*) to set; (*maquinar*) to hatch; (NÁUT) to fit out; **~-se** *vr* to arm o.s.; ~ **uma briga com** to pick a quarrel with; ~ **uma confusão** to cause chaos.
armarinho [axma'riɲu] *m* haberdashery (BRIT), notions *pl* (US).
armário [ax'marju] *m* cupboard; (*de roupa*) wardrobe.

armazém [axma'zẽj] (*pl* **-ns**) *m* (*depósito*) warehouse; (*loja*) grocery store.
armazenagem [axmaze'naʒẽ] *f* storage.
armazenamento [axmazena'mẽtu] *m* storage.
armazenar [axmaze'na*] *vt* to store; (*provisões*) to stock; (COMPUT) to store.
armazéns [axma'zẽʃ] *mpl de* **armazém**.
armeiro [ax'mejru] *m* gunsmith.
Armênia [ax'menja] *f*: **a** ~ Armenia.
arminho [ax'miɲu] *m* ermine.
armistício [axmiʃ'tʃisju] *m* armistice.
aro ['aru] *m* (*argola*) ring; (*de óculos, roda*) rim; (*de porta*) frame.
aroma [a'rɔma] *f* (*de comida, café*) aroma; (*de perfume*) fragrance.
aromático/a [aro'matʃiku/a] *adj* (*comida*) aromatic; (*perfume*) fragrant.
arpão [ax'pãw] (*pl* **-ões**) *m* harpoon.
arpejo [ax'peʒu] *m* arpeggio.
arpoar [ax'pwa*] *vt* to harpoon.
arpões [ax'põjʃ] *mpl de* **arpão**.
arqueado/a [ax'kjadu/a] *adj* arched.
arquear [ax'kja*] *vt* to arch; **~-se** *vr* to bend, arch; (*entortar-se*) to warp.
arquei [ax'kej] *etc vb V* **arcar**.
arqueiro/a [ax'kejru/a] *m/f* archer; (*goleiro*) goalkeeper.
arquejar [axke'ʒa*] *vi* to pant, wheeze.
arquejo [ax'keʒu] *m* panting, gasping.
arqueologia [axkjolo'ʒia] *f* archaeology (BRIT), archeology (US).
arqueológico/a [axkjo'lɔʒiku/a] *adj* archaeological (BRIT), archeological (US).
arqueólogo/a [ax'kjɔlogu/a] *m/f* archaeologist (BRIT), archeologist (US).
arquétipo [ax'kɛtʃipu] *m* archetype.
arquibancada [axkibã'kada] *f* terrace.
arquipélago [axki'pɛlagu] *m* archipelago.
arquitetar [axkite'ta*] (PT: **-ect-**) *vt* to think up.
arquiteto/a [axki'tɛtu/a] (PT: **-ect-**) *m/f* architect.
arquitetônico/a [axkite'toniku/a] (PT: **-ect-**) *adj* architectural.
arquitetura [axkite'tura] (PT: **-ect-**) *f* architecture.
arquivamento [axkiva'mẽtu] *m* filing; (*de projeto*) shelving.
arquivar [axki'va*] *vt* to file; (*suspender*) to shelve.
arquivista [axki'viʃta] *m/f* archivist.
arquivo [ax'kivu] *m* file; (*lugar*) archive; (*de empresa*) files *pl*; (*móvel*) filing cabinet; (COMPUT) file; **abrir/fechar um** ~ (COMPUT) to open/close a file; **nome do** ~ (COMPUT) file name; ~ **ativo** (COMPUT) active file.
arrabaldes [axa'bawdʒiʃ] *mpl* suburbs.
arraia [a'xaja] *f* (*peixe*) ray.
arraial [axa'jaw] (*pl* **-ais**) *m* (*povoação*) village; (PT: *festa*) fair.
arraia-miúda *f* masses *pl*.
arraigado/a [axaj'gadu/a] *adj* deep-rooted; (*fig*) ingrained.
arraigar [axaj'ga*] *vi* to root; **~-se** *vr* (*enraizar-se*) to take root; (*estabelecer-se*) to settle.
arrancada [axã'kada] *f* (*puxão*) pull, jerk; (*partida*) start; (*investida*) charge; (*de atleta*) burst of speed.
arrancar [axã'ka*] *vt* to pull out; (*botão etc*) to pull off; (*arrebatar*) to snatch (away); (*fig*: *confissão*) to extract; (: *aplausos*) to get ♦ *vi* to start (off); **~-se** *vr* (*partir*) to leave; (*fugir*) to run off.
arranco [a'xãku] *m* (*puxão*) pull, jerk; (*partida*) sudden start.
arranha-céu [a'xaɲa-] (*pl* **~s**) *m* skyscraper.
arranhadura [axaɲa'dura] *f* scratch.
arranhão [axa'ɲãw] (*pl* **-ões**) *m* scratch.
arranhar [axa'ɲa*] *vt* to scratch; ~ **(n)uma língua** to know a smattering of a language.
arranhões [axa'ɲõjʃ] *mpl de* **arranhão**.
arranjador(a) [axãʒa'do*(a)] *m/f* (MÚS) arranger.
arranjar [axã'ʒa*] *vt* to arrange; (*emprego etc*) to get, find; (*doença*) to get, catch; (*namorado*) to find; (*questão*) to settle; **~-se** *vr* (*virar-se*) to manage; (*conseguir emprego*) to get a job; **~-se sem** to do without.
arranjo [a'xãʒu] *m* arrangement; (*negociata*) shady deal; (*col*: *caso*) affair.
arranque [a'xãki] *m V* **motor**.
arranquei [axã'kej] *etc vb V* **arrancar**.
arrasador(a) [axaza'do*(a)] *adj* devastating.
arrasar [axa'za*] *vt* to devastate; (*demolir*) to demolish; (*estragar*) to ruin; (*verbalmente*) to lambast; **~-se** *vr* to be devastated; (*destruir-se*) to destroy o.s.; (*arruinar-se*) to lose everything; (*nos exames*) to do terribly.
arrastado/a [axaʃ'tadu/a] *adj* (*rasteiro*) crawling; (*demorado*) dragging; (*voz*) drawling.
arrastão [axaʃ'tãw] (*pl* **-ões**) *m* tug, jerk; (*rede*) dragnet.
arrasta-pé [a'xaʃta-] (*pl* **~s**) (*col*) *m* knees-up, shindig.
arrastar [axaʃ'ta*] *vt* to drag; (*atrair*) to draw ♦ *vi* to trail; **~-se** *vr* (*rastejar*) to crawl; (*andar a custo*) to drag o.s.; (*tempo*) to drag; (*processo*) to drag on.
arrasto [a'xaʃtu] *m* (*ação*) dragging; (*rede*) trawl-net; (TEC) drag.
arrazoado/a [axa'zwadu/a] *adj* (*argumento*) reasoned ♦ *m* (JUR) defence (BRIT), defense (US).
arrazoar [axa'zwa*] *vi* (*discutir*) to argue.
arrear [a'xja*] *vt* (*cavalo etc*) to bridle.
arrebanhar [axeba'ɲa*] *vt* (*gado*) to herd; (*juntar*) to gather.
arrebatado/a [axeba'tadu/a] *adj* (*impetuoso*) rash, impetuous; (*enlevado*) entranced.

***NB**: European Portuguese adds the following consonants to certain words:* **b** (sú(b)dito, su(b)til); **c** (a(c)ção, a(c)cionista, a(c)to); **m** (inde(m)ne); **p** (ado(p)ção, ado(p)tar); *for further details* *see p. xiii.*

arrebatador(a) [axebata'do*(a)] *adj* enchanting.

arrebatamento [axebata'mẽtu] *m* (*impetuosidade*) impetuosity; (*enlevo*) ecstasy.

arrebatar [axeba'ta*] *vt* (*arrancar*) to snatch (away); (*levar*) to carry off; (*enlevar*) to entrance; (*enfurecer*) to enrage; **~-se** *vr* (*entusiasmar-se*) to be entranced.

arrebentação [axebẽta'sãw] *f* (*na praia*) surf.

arrebentado/a [axebẽ'tadu/a] *adj* (*quebrado*) broken; (*vaso etc*) smashed; (*estafado*) worn out.

arrebentar [axebẽ'ta*] *vi* to smash; (*porta*) to break down; (*corda*) to snap, break ♦ *vi* to smash; to snap, break; (*guerra*) to break out; (*bomba*) to explode; (*ondas*) to break.

arrebitado/a [axebi'tadu/a] *adj* turned-up; (*nariz*) snub.

arrebitar [axebi'ta*] *vt* to turn up.

arrecadação [axekada'sãw] *f* (*de impostos etc*) collection; (*impostos arrecadados*) tax revenue, taxes *pl*.

arrecadar [axeka'da*] *vt* (*impostos etc*) to collect.

arrecife [axe'sifi] *m* reef.

arredar [axe'da*] *vt* to move away, move back; **~-se** *vr* to move away; **não ~ pé** not to budge, to stand one's ground.

arredio/a [axe'dʒiu/a] *adj* (*pessoa*) withdrawn.

arredondado/a [axedõ'dadu/a] *adj* round, rounded.

arredondar [axedõ'da*] *vt* to round (off); (*conta*) to round up.

arredores [axe'dɔriʃ] *mpl* suburbs; (*cercanias*) outskirts.

arrefecer [axefe'se*] *vt* to cool; (*febre*) to lower; (*desanimar*) to discourage ♦ *vi* to cool (off); to get discouraged.

arrefecimento [axefesi'mẽtu] *m* cooling.

ar-refrigerado (*pl* **ares-refrigerados**) *m* (*aparelho*) air conditioner; (*sistema*) air conditioning.

arregaçar [axega'sa*] *vt* to roll up.

arregalado/a [axega'ladu/a] *adj* (*olhos*) wide; **com os olhos ~s** pop-eyed.

arregalar [axega'la*] *vt*: **~ os olhos** to stare in amazement.

arreganhar [axega'ɲa*] *vt* (*dentes*) to bare; (*lábios*) to draw back.

arreios [a'xejuʃ] *mpl* harness *sg*.

arrematar [axema'ta*] *vt* (*dizer concluindo*) to conclude; (*comprar*) to buy by auction; (*vender*) to sell by auction; (COSTURA) to finish off.

arremate [axe'matʃi] *m* (COSTURA) finishing off; (*conclusão*) conclusion; (FUTEBOL) finishing.

arremedar [axeme'da*] *vt* to mimic.

arremedo [axe'medu] *m* mimicry.

arremessar [axeme'sa*] *vt* to throw, hurl; **~-se** *vr* to hurl o.s.

arremesso [axe'mesu] *m* (*lançamento*) throw; **~ de peso** shot-put.

arremeter [axeme'te*] *vi* to lunge; **~ contra** (*acometer*) to attack, assail.

arremetida [axeme'tʃida] *f* attack, onslaught.

arrendador(a) [axẽda'do*(a)] *m/f* landlord/landlady.

arrendamento [axẽda'mẽtu] *m* (*ação*) leasing; (*contrato*) lease.

arrendar [axẽ'da*] *vt* to lease.

arrendatário/a [axẽda'tarju/a] *m/f* tenant.

arrepender-se [axepẽ'dexsi] *vr* to repent; (*mudar de opinião*) to change one's mind; **~ de** to regret, be sorry for.

arrependido/a [axepẽ'dʒidu/a] *adj* (*pessoa*) sorry.

arrependimento [axepẽdʒi'mẽtu] *m* regret; (REL, *de crime*) repentance.

arrepiado/a [axe'pjadu/a] *adj* (*cabelo*) standing on end; (*pele, pessoa*) goose-pimply; (*horrorizado*) horrified.

arrepiar [axe'pja*] *vt* (*amedrontar*) to horrify; (*cabelo etc*) to cause to stand on end; **~-se** *vr* (*sentir calafrios*) to shiver; (*cabelo*) to stand on end; **isso me arrepia** it gives me goose flesh; **(ser) de ~ os cabelos** (to be) hair-raising.

arrepio [axe'piu] *m* shiver; (*de frio*) chill; **isso me dá ~s** it gives me the creeps.

arresto [a'xɛʃtu] *m* (JUR) seizure, confiscation.

arrevesado/a [axeve'zadu/a] *adj* (*obscuro*) obscure; (*intricado*) intricate.

arrevesar [axeve'za*] *vt* (*complicar*) to complicate.

arriado/a [a'xjadu/a] *adj* (*exausto*) exhausted; (*por doença*) very weak.

arriar [a'xja*] *vt* (*baixar*) to lower; (*depor*) to lay down ♦ *vi* (*cair*) to drop; (*vergar*) to sag; (*desistir*) to give up; (*fig*) to collapse; (AUTO: *bateria*) to go flat.

arribação [axiba'sãw] (BR: *pl* **-ões**) *f* (*de aves*) migration.

arribar [axi'ba*] *vi* (*recuperar-se*) to recuperate.

arrimo [a'ximu] *m* support; **~ de família** breadwinner.

arriscado/a [axiʃ'kadu/a] *adj* risky; (*audacioso*) daring.

arriscar [axiʃ'ka*] *vt* to risk; (*pôr em perigo*) to endanger, jeopardize; **~-se** *vr* to take a risk; **~-se a fazer** to risk doing.

arrisquei [axiʃ'kej] *etc vb V* **arriscar**.

arrivista [axi'viʃta] *m/f* upstart; (*oportunista*) opportunist.

arroba [a'xoba] *f* = *15 kg*.

arrochado/a [axo'ʃadu/a] *adj* (*vestido*) skin-tight; (*fig*) tough.

arrochar [axo'ʃa*] *vt* (*apertar*) to tighten up ♦ *vi* (*ser exigente*) to be demanding.

arrocho [a'xoʃu] *m* squeeze; (*fig*) predicament; **~ salarial/ao crédito** wage/credit squeeze.

arrogância [axo'gãsja] *f* arrogance, haughtiness.

arrogante [axo'gãtʃi] *adj* arrogant, haughty.

arrogar-se [axo'gaxsi] *vr* (*direitos, privilégios*) to claim.
arroio [a'xɔju] *m* stream.
arrojado/a [axo'ʒadu/a] *adj* (*design*) bold; (*temerário*) rash; (*ousado*) daring.
arrojar [axo'ʒa*] *vt* (*lançar*) to hurl.
arrojo [a'xoʒu] *m* (*ousadia*) boldness.
arrolamento [axola'mẽtu] *m* list.
arrolar [axo'la*] *vt* to list.
arrolhar [axo'ʎa*] *vt* to cork.
arromba [a'xõba] *f*: **de ~** great.
arrombar [axõ'ba*] *vt* (*porta*) to break down; (*cofre*) to crack.
arrotar [axo'ta*] *vi* to belch ♦ *vt* (*alardear*) to boast of.
arroto [a'xotu] *m* burp.
arroubo [a'xobu] *m* ecstasy, rapture.
arroz [a'xoʒ] *m* rice; **~ doce** rice pudding.
arrozal [axo'zaw] (*pl* **-ais**) *m* rice field.
arruaça [a'xwasa] *f* street riot.
arruaceiro/a [axwa'sejru/a] *m/f* rioter.
arruela [a'xwɛla] *f* (TEC) washer.
arruinar [axwi'na*] *vt* to ruin; (*destruir*) to destroy; **~-se** *vr* to be ruined; (*perder a saúde*) to ruin one's health.
arrulhar [axu'ʎa*] *vi* (*pombos*) to coo.
arrulho [a'xuʎu] *m* cooing.
arrumação [axuma'sãw] *f* (*arranjo*) arrangement; (*de um quarto etc*) tidying up; (*de malas*) packing.
arrumadeira [axuma'dejra] *f* cleaning lady; (*num hotel*) chambermaid.
arrumar [axu'ma*] *vt* (*pôr em ordem*) to put in order, arrange; (*quarto etc*) to tidy up; (*malas*) to pack; (*emprego*) to get; (*vestir*) to dress up; (*desculpa*) to make up, find; (*vida*) to sort out; **~-se** *vr* (*aprontar-se*) to get dressed, get ready; (*na vida*) to sort o.s. out; (*virar-se*) to manage.
arsenal [axse'naw] (*pl* **-ais**) *m* (MIL) arsenal; **~ de Marinha** naval dockyard.
arsênio [ax'senju] *m* arsenic.
arte ['axtʃi] *f* art; (*habilidade*) skill; (*ofício*) trade, craft; **fazer ~** (*fig*) to get up to mischief.
artefato [axtʃi'fatu] (PT: **-act-**) *m* (manufactured) article; **~s de couro** leather goods, leatherware *sg*.
arteiro/a [ax'tejru/a] *adj* (*criança*) mischievous.
artéria [ax'tɛrja] *f* (ANAT) artery.
arterial [axte'rjaw] (*pl* **-ais**) *adj V* **pressão**.
arteriosclerose [axterjoʃkle'rɔzi] *f* hardening of the arteries, arteriosclerosis.
artesã [axte'zã] *f de* **artesão**.
artesanal [axteza'naw] (*pl* **-ais**) *adj* craft.
artesanato [axteza'natu] *m* craftwork; **artigos de ~** craft items.
artesão/sã [axte'zãw/zã] (*pl* **~s/~s**) *m/f* artisan, craftsman/woman.
ártico/a ['axtʃiku/a] *adj* Arctic ♦ *m*: **o A~** the Arctic.
articulação [axtʃikula'sãw] (*pl* **-ões**) *f* articulation; (MED) joint.
articulado/a [axtʃiku'ladu/a] *adj* articulated, jointed.
articular [axtʃiku'la*] *vt* (*pronunciar*) to articulate; (*ligar*) to join together.
artífice [ax'tʃifisi] *m/f* craftsman/woman; (*inventor*) inventor.
artificial [axtʃifi'sjaw] (*pl* **-ais**) *adj* artificial; (*pessoa*) affected.
artifício [axtʃi'fisju] *m* stratagem, trick.
artificioso/a [axtʃifi'sjozu/ɔza] *adj* (*hábil*) skilful (BRIT), skillful (US); (*astucioso*) artful.
artigo [ax'tʃigu] *m* article; (COM) item; **~s** *mpl* goods; **~ definido/indefinido** (LING) definite/indefinite article; **~ de fundo** leading article, editorial; **~s de toucador** toiletries.
artilharia [axtʃiʎa'ria] *f* artillery.
artilheiro [axtʃi'ʎejru] *m* gunner, artilleryman; (FUTEBOL) striker.
artimanha [axtʃi'maɲa] *f* (*ardil*) stratagem; (*astúcia*) cunning.
artista [ax'tʃiʃta] *m/f* artist.
artístico/a [ax'tʃiʃtʃiku/a] *adj* artistic.
artrite [ax'tritʃi] *f* (MED) arthritis.
arvorar [axvo'ra*] *vt* (*bandeira*) to hoist; (*elevar*): **~ alguém em** to promote *ou* elevate sb to; **~-se** *vr*: **~-se em** to set o.s. up as.
árvore ['axvori] *f* tree; (TEC) shaft; **~ de Natal** Christmas tree.
arvoredo [axvo'redu] *m* grove.
as [aʃ] *art def V* **a**.
ás [ajʃ] *m* ace.
às [ajʃ] = **a** + **as**.
asa ['aza] *f* wing; (*de xícara etc*) handle; **dar ~s à imaginação** to give free rein to one's imagination.
asa-delta *f* hang-glider.
asbesto [aʒ'bɛʃtu] *m* asbestos.
ascendência [asẽ'dẽsja] *f* (*antepassados*) ancestry; (*domínio*) ascendency, sway.
ascendente [asẽ'dẽtʃi] *adj* rising, upward.
ascender [asẽ'de*] *vi* (*subir*) to rise, ascend.
ascensão [asẽ'sãw] (*pl* **-ões**) *f* ascent; (*fig*) rise; **dia da A~** Ascension Day.
ascensor [asẽ'so*] *m* elevator (US), lift (BRIT).
ascensorista [asẽso'riʃta] *m/f* lift operator.
asceta [a'sɛta] *m/f* ascetic.
asco ['aʃku] *m* loathing, revulsion; **dar ~** to be revolting *ou* disgusting.
asfaltar [aʃfaw'ta*] *vt* to asphalt.
asfalto [aʃ'fawtu] *m* asphalt.
asfixia [aʃfik'sia] *f* asphyxia, suffocation.
asfixiar [aʃfik'sja*] *vt* to asphyxiate, suffocate.
Ásia ['azja] *f*: **a ~** Asia.
asiático/a [a'zjatʃiku/a] *adj, m/f* Asian.
asilar [azi'la*] *vt* to give refuge to; **~-se** *vr* to

***NB**: European Portuguese adds the following consonants to certain words:* **b** (sú(b)dito, su(b)til); **c** (a(c)ção, a(c)cionista, a(c)to); **m** (inde(m)ne); **p** (ado(p)ção, ado(p)tar); *for further details see p. xiii.*

take refuge.
asilo [a'zilu] *m* (*refúgio*) refuge; (*estabelecimento*) home; ~ **político** political asylum.
asma ['aʒma] *f* asthma.
asmático/a [aʒ'matʃiku/a] *adj*, *m/f* asthmatic.
asneira [aʒ'nejra] *f* (*tolice*) stupidity; (*ato, dito*) stupid thing.
asno ['aʒnu] *m* donkey; (*fig*) ass.
aspas ['aʃpaʃ] *fpl* inverted commas; **entre** ~ in inverted commas.
aspargo [aʃ'paxgu] *m* asparagus.
aspecto [aʃ'pɛktu] *m* (*de uma questão*) aspect; (*aparência*) look, appearance; (*característica*) feature; (*ponto de vista*) point of view; **ter bom** ~ to look good; **tomar um** ~ to take on an aspect.
aspereza [aʃpe'reza] *f* roughness; (*severidade*) harshness; (*rudeza*) rudeness.
aspergir [aʃpex'ʒi*] *vt* to sprinkle.
áspero/a ['aʃperu/a] *adj* rough; (*severo*) harsh; (*rude*) rude.
asperso/a [aʃ'pɛxsu/a] *pp de* **aspergir** ♦ *adj* scattered.
aspiração [aʃpira'sãw] (*pl* **-ões**) *f* aspiration; (*inalação*) inhalation.
aspirador [aʃpira'do*] *m*: ~ **(de pó)** vacuum cleaner; **passar o** ~ **(em)** to vacuum.
aspirante [aʃpi'rãtʃi] *adj* aspiring ♦ *m/f* candidate; (*MIL*) cadet; (*NÁUT*) midshipman.
aspirar [aʃpi'ra*] *vt* to breathe in; (*bombear*) to suck up; (*LING*) to aspirate ♦ *vi* to breathe; (*soprar*) to blow; (*desejar*): ~ **a algo** to aspire to sth.
aspirina [aʃpi'rina] *f* aspirin.
aspirjo [aʃ'pixʒu] *etc vb V* **aspergir**.
asqueroso/a [aʃke'rozu/ɔza] *adj* disgusting, revolting.
assadeira [asa'dejra] *f* roasting tin.
assado/a [a'sadu/a] *adj* roasted; (*CULIN*) roast ♦ *m* roast; **carne assada** roast beef.
assadura [asa'dura] *f* rash; (*em bebê*) nappy rash.
assalariado/a [asala'rjadu/a] *adj* salaried ♦ *m/f* wage-earner.
assaltante [asaw'tãtʃi] *m/f* assailant; (*de banco*) robber; (*de casa*) burglar; (*na rua*) mugger.
assaltar [asaw'ta*] *vt* (*atacar*) to attack; (*casa*) to break into; (*banco*) to rob; (*pessoa na rua*) to mug.
assalto [a'sawtu] *m* (*ataque*) attack, raid; (*a um banco etc*) raid, robbery; (*BOXE*) round; (*a uma casa*) burglary, break-in; (*a uma pessoa na rua*) mugging.
assanhado/a [asa'ɲadu/a] *adj* excited; (*criança*) excitable; (*desavergonhado*) brazen; (*namorador*) amorous.
assanhar [asa'ɲa*] *vt* to excite; **~-se** *vr* to get excited.
assar [a'sa*] *vt* to roast; (*na grelha*) to grill.
assassinar [asasi'na*] *vt* to murder, kill; (*POL*) to assassinate.
assassinato [asasi'natu] *m* murder, killing; (*POL*) assassination.
assassínio [asa'sinju] *m* murder, killing; (*POL*) assassination.
assassino/a [asa'sinu/a] *m/f* murderer; (*POL*) assassin.
assaz [a'saʒ] *adv* (*suficientemente*) sufficiently; (*muito*) rather.
asseado/a [a'sjadu/a] *adj* clean.
assediar [ase'dʒja*] *vt* (*sitiar*) to besiege; (*importunar*) to pester.
assédio [a'sɛdʒu] *m* siege; (*insistência*) insistence.
assegurar [asegu'ra*] *vt* (*tornar seguro*) to secure; (*garantir*) to ensure; (*afirmar*) to assure; **~-se** *vr*: **~-se de** to make sure of.
asseio [a'seju] *m* cleanliness.
assembléia [asẽ'blɛja] *f* assembly; (*reunião*) meeting; ~ **geral** (*ordinária*) annual general meeting; ~ **geral extraordinária** extraordinary general meeting.
assemelhar [aseme'ʎa*] *vt* to liken; **~-se** *vr* (*ser parecido*) to be alike; **~-se a** to resemble, look like.
assenhorear-se [aseɲo'rjaxsi] *vr*: ~ **de** to take possession of.
assentado/a [asẽ'tadu/a] *adj* (*firme*) fixed, secure; (*combinado*) agreed; (*ajuizado*) sensible.
assentamento [asẽta'mẽtu] *m* registration; (*nota*) entry, record.
assentar [asẽ'ta*] *vt* (*fazer sentar*) to seat; (*colocar*) to place; (*tijolos*) to lay; (*estabelecer*) to establish; (*decidir*) to decide upon; (*determinar*) to fix, settle; (*soco*) to land ♦ *vi* (*pó etc*) to settle; **~-se** *vr* to sit down; ~ **com** to go with; ~ **em** *ou* **a** (*roupa*) to suit.
assente [a'sẽtʃi] *pp de* **assentar** ♦ *adj* agreed, decided.
assentimento [asẽtʃi'mẽtu] *m* assent, agreement.
assentir [asẽ'tʃi*] *vi* to agree; ~ **(em)** to consent *ou* agree (to); ~ **(a)** to accede (to).
assento [a'sẽtu] *m* seat; (*base*) base; **tomar** ~ (*sentar*) to take a seat; (*pó*) to settle.
assertiva [asex'tʃiva] *f* assertion.
assessor(a) [ase'so*(a)] *m/f* adviser; (*POL*) aide; (*assistente*) assistant.
assessoramento [asesora'mẽtu] *m* assistance.
assessorar [aseso'ra*] *vt* to advise.
assessoria [aseso'ria] *f* advisory body.
assestar [aseʃ'ta*] *vt* to aim, point.
asseveração [asevera'sãw] (*pl* **-ões**) *f* assertion.
asseverar [aseve'ra*] *vt* to affirm, assert.
assexuado/a [asek'swadu/a] *adj* asexual.
assiduidade [asidwi'dadʒi] *f* (*às aulas, etc*) regular attendance; (*diligência*) assiduity.
assíduo/a [a'sidwu/a] *adj* (*aluno*) who attends regularly; (*diligente*) assiduous; (*constante*) constant; **ser** ~ **num lugar** to be a regular visitor to a place.
assim [a'sĩ] *adv* (*deste modo*) like this, in this way, thus; (*portanto*) therefore; (*igualmente*)

likewise; ~ ~ so-so; ~ **mesmo** in any case; **e ~ por diante** and so on; ~ **como** as well as; **como ~?** how do you mean?; ~ **que** (*logo que*) as soon as; **nem tanto ~** not as much as that.

assimétrico/a [asi'mɛtriku/a] *adj* asymmetrical.

assimilação [asimila'sãw] *f* assimilation.

assimilar [asimi'la*] *vt* to assimilate; (*apreender*) to take in; (*assemelhar*) to compare.

assinalado/a [asina'ladu/a] *adj* (*marcado*) marked; (*notável*) notable; (*célebre*) eminent.

assinalar [asina'la*] *vt* (*marcar*) to mark; (*distinguir*) to distinguish; (*especificar*) to point out.

assin. *abr* = **assinatura**.

assinante [asi'nãtʃi] *m/f* (*de jornal etc*) subscriber.

assinar [asi'na*] *vt* to sign.

assinatura [asina'tura] *f* (*nome*) signature; (*de jornal etc*) subscription; (*TEATRO*) season ticket; **fazer a ~ de** (*revista etc*) to take out a subscription to.

assinto [a'sĩtu] *etc vb V* **assentir**.

assistência [asiʃ'tẽsja] *f* (*presença*) presence; (*público*) audience; (*auxílio*) aid, assistance; ~ **médica** medical aid; ~ **social** social work; (*serviços*) social services *pl*; ~ **técnica** technical back-up.

assistente [asiʃ'tẽtʃi] *adj* assistant ♦ *m/f* (*pessoa presente*) spectator, onlooker; (*ajudante*) assistant; ~ **social** social worker.

assistir [asiʃ'tʃi*] *vt, vi*: ~ **(a)** (*auxiliar*) to assist; (*MED*) to attend to; (*TV, filme, jogo*) to watch; (*reunião*) to attend; ~ **a** (*caber*) to fall to.

assoalho [aso'aʎu] *m* (wooden) floor.

assoar [aso'a*] *vt*: ~ **o nariz** to blow one's nose; **~-se** *vr* (*PT*) to blow one's nose.

assoberbado/a [asobex'badu/a] *adj* (*pessoa: de serviço*) snowed under with work.

assoberbar [asobex'ba*] *vt* (*de serviço*) to overload.

assobiar [aso'bja*] *vi* to whistle.

assobio [aso'biu] *m* whistle; (*instrumento*) whistle; (*de vapor*) hiss.

associação [asosja'sãw] (*pl* **-ões**) *f* association; (*organização*) society; (*parceria*) partnership; ~ **de moradores** residents' association.

associado/a [aso'sjadu/a] *adj* associate ♦ *m/f* associate, member; (*COM*) associate; (*sócio*) partner.

associar [aso'sja*] *vt* to associate; **~-se** *vr* (*COM*) to form a partnership; **~-se a** to associate with.

assolador(a) [asola'do*(a)] *adj* devastating.

assolar [aso'la*] *vt* to devastate.

assomar [aso'ma*] *vi* (*aparecer*) to appear; ~ **a** (*subir*) to climb to the top of.

assombração [asõbra'sãw] (*pl* **-ões**) *f* (*fantasma*) ghost.

assombrado/a [asõ'bradu/a] *adj* astonished, amazed.

assombrar [asõ'bra*] *vt* to astonish, amaze; **~-se** *vr* to be amazed.

assombro [a'sõbru] *m* amazement, astonishment; (*maravilha*) marvel.

assombroso/a [asõ'brozu/ɔza] *adj* (*espantoso*) astonishing, amazing.

assoprar [aso'pra*] *vi* to blow ♦ *vt* to blow; (*velas*) to blow out.

assoviar [aso'vja*] *vt* = **assobiar**.

assovio [aso'viu] *m* = **assobio**.

assumir [asu'mi*] *vt* to assume, take on; (*reconhecer*) to accept, admit ♦ *vi* to take office.

Assunção [asũ'sãw] *n* (*no Paraguai*) Asunción.

assuntar [asũ'ta*] *vt* (*prestar atenção*) to pay attention to; (*verificar*) to find out ♦ *vi* (*meditar*) to cogitate.

assunto [a'sũtu] *m* (*tema*) subject, matter; (*enredo*) plot.

assustadiço/a [asuʃta'dʒisu/a] *adj* timorous.

assustador(a) [asuʃta'do*(a)] *adj* (*alarmante*) startling; (*amedrontador*) frightening.

assustar [asuʃ'ta*] *vt* to frighten, scare, startle; **~-se** *vr* to be frightened.

asteca [aʃ'tɛka] *adj, m/f* Aztec.

asterisco [aʃte'riʃku] *m* asterisk.

astigmatismo [aʃtʃigma'tʃiʒmu] *m* astigmatism.

astral [aʃ'traw] (*pl* **-ais**) *m* state of mind.

astro ['aʃtru] *m* star.

astrologia [aʃtrolo'ʒia] *f* astrology.

astrólogo/a [aʃ'trɔlogu/a] *m/f* astrologer.

astronauta [aʃtro'nawta] *m/f* astronaut.

astronave [aʃtro'navi] *f* spaceship.

astronomia [aʃtrono'mia] *f* astronomy.

astronômico/a [aʃtro'nomiku/a] *adj* (*preço*) astronomical.

astrônomo/a [aʃ'tronomu/a] *m/f* astronomer.

astúcia [aʃ'tusja] *f* cunning.

astuto/a [aʃ'tutu/a] *adj* astute; (*esperto*) cunning.

ata ['ata] *f* (*de reunião*) minutes *pl*.

atacadista [ataka'dʒiʃta] *adj* wholesale ♦ *m/f* wholesaler.

atacado/a [ata'kadu/a] *adj* (*col: pessoa*) in a bad mood ♦ *m*: **por ~** wholesale.

atacante [ata'kãtʃi] *adj* attacking ♦ *m/f* attacker, assailant ♦ *m* (*FUTEBOL*) forward.

atacar [ata'ka*] *vt* to attack; (*problema etc*) to tackle.

atado/a [a'tadu/a] *adj* (*desajeitado*) clumsy, awkward; (*perplexo*) puzzled.

atadura [ata'dura] *f* bandage.

atalaia [ata'laja] *f* lookout post.

atalhar [ata'ʎa*] *vt* (*impedir*) to prevent;

(*abreviar*) to shorten ♦ *vi* (*tomar um atalho*) to take a short cut.
atalho [a'taʎu] *m* (*caminho*) short cut.
atapetar [atape'ta*] *vt* to carpet.
ataque [a'taki] *m* attack; **ter um ~ (de raiva)** to have a fit; **ter um ~ de riso** to burst out laughing; **~ aéreo** air raid.
ataquei [ata'kej] *etc vb V* **atacar**.
atar [a'ta*] *vt* to tie (up), fasten; **não ~ nem desatar** (*pessoa*) to waver; (*negócio*) to be in the air.
atarantado/a [atarã'tadu/a] *adj* (*pessoa*) flustered, in a flap.
atarantar [atarã'ta*] *vt* to fluster.
atarefado/a [atare'fadu/a] *adj* busy.
atarracado/a [ataxa'kadu/a] *adj* stocky.
atarraxar [ataxa'ʃa*] *vt* to screw.
ataúde [ata'udʒi] *m* coffin.
ataviar [ata'vja*] *vt* to adorn, decorate; **~-se** *vr* to get dressed up.
atavio [ata'viu] *m* adornment.
atazanar [ataza'na*] *vt* to pester.
até [a'tɛ] *prep* (*PT*: + **a**): (*lugar*) up to, as far as; (*tempo etc*) until, till ♦ *adv* (*tb*: **~** *mesmo*) even; **~ agora** up to now; **~ certo ponto** to a certain extent; **~ em cima** to the top; **~ já** see you soon; **~ logo** bye!; **~ onde** as far as; **~ que** until; **~ que enfim!** at last!
atear [ate'a*] *vt* (*fogo*) to kindle; (*fig*) to incite, inflame; **~-se** *vr* (*fogo*) to blaze; (*paixões*) to flare up; **~ fogo a** to set light to.
atéia [a'tɛja] *f de* **ateu**.
ateísmo [ate'iʒmu] *m* atheism.
ateliê [ate'lje] *m* studio.
atemorizador(a) [atemoriza'do*(a)] *adj* frightening.
atemorizar [atemori'za*] *vt* to frighten; (*intimidar*) to intimidate.
Atenas [a'tenaʃ] *n* Athens.
atenção [atẽ'sãw] (*pl* **-ões**) *f* attention; (*cortesia*) courtesy; (*bondade*) kindness; **~!** be careful!; **chamar a ~** to attract attention; **chamar a ~ de alguém** to tell sb off.
atencioso/a [atẽ'sjozu/ɔza] *adj* considerate.
atenções [atẽ'sõjʃ] *fpl de* **atenção**.
atender [atẽ'de*] *vt*: **~ (a)** to attend to; (*receber*) to receive; (*em loja*) to serve; (*deferir*) to grant; (*telefone etc*) to answer; (*paciente*) to see ♦ *vi* (*ao telefone, porta*) to answer; (*dar atenção*) to pay attention.
atendimento [atẽdʒi'mẽtu] *m* service; (*recepção*) reception; answering; **horário de ~** opening hours; (*em consultório*) surgery (*BRIT*) *ou* office (*US*) hours.
atenho [a'teɲu] *etc vb V* **ater-se**.
atentado [atẽ'tadu] *m* (*ataque*) attack; (*crime*) crime; (*contra a vida de alguém*) attempt on sb's life; **~ ao pudor** indecent exposure.
atentar [atẽ'ta*] *vt* (*empreender*) to undertake ♦ *vi* to make an attempt; **~ a** *ou* **em** *ou* **para** to pay attention to; **~ contra a vida de alguém** to make an attempt on sb's life; **~ contra a moral** to offend against morality.
atento/a [a'tẽtu/a] *adj* attentive; (*exame*) careful; **estar ~ a** to be aware *ou* mindful of.
atenuação [atenwa'sãw] (*pl* **-ões**) *f* reduction, lessening.
atenuante [ate'nwãtʃi] *adj* extenuating ♦ *m* extenuating circumstance.
atenuar [ate'nwa*] *vt* (*diminuir*) to reduce, lessen.
aterrador(a) [atexa'do*(a)] *adj* terrifying.
aterragem [ate'xaʒẽj] (*PT*: *pl* **-ns**) *f* (*AER*) landing.
aterrar [ate'xa*] *vt* (*cobrir com terra*) to cover with earth; (*praia*) to reclaim ♦ *vi* (*PT*: *AER*) to land.
aterrissagem [atexi'saʒẽ] (*BR*: *pl* **-ns**) *f* (*AER*) landing.
aterrissar [atexi'sa*] (*BR*) *vi* (*AER*) to land.
aterrizar [atexi'za*] *vi* = **aterrissar**.
aterro [a'texu] *m* landfill.
aterrorizado/a [atexori'zadu/a] *adj* terrified.
aterrorizador(a) [atexoriza'do*(a)] *adj* terrifying.
aterrorizante [atexori'zãtʃi] *adj* terrifying.
aterrorizar [atexori'za*] *vt* to terrorize.
ater-se [a'texsi] (*irreg*: *como* **ter**) *vr*: **~ a** (*prender-se*) to get caught up in; (*limitar-se*) to restrict o.s. to.
atestado/a [ateʃ'tadu/a] *adj* certified ♦ *m* certificate; (*prova*) proof; (*JUR*) testimony.
atestar [ateʃ'ta*] *vt* (*certificar*) to certify; (*testemunhar*) to bear witness to; (*provar*) to prove.
ateu/atéia [a'tew/a'tɛja] *adj, m/f* atheist.
ateve [a'tevi] *etc vb V* **ater-se**.
atiçador [atʃisa'do*] *m* (*utensílio*) poker.
atiçar [atʃi'sa*] *vt* (*fogo*) to poke; (*incitar*) to incite; (*provocar*) to provoke; (*sentimento*) to induce.
atilado/a [atʃi'ladu/a] *adj* (*esperto*) clever.
atinado/a [atʃi'nadu/a] *adj* (*sensato*) wise, sensible.
atinar [atʃi'na*] *vt* (*acertar*) to guess correctly ♦ *vi*: **~ com** (*solução*) to find; **~ em** to notice; **~ a fazer algo** to succeed in doing sth.
atingir [atʃĩ'ʒi*] *vt* to reach; (*acertar*) to hit; (*afetar*) to affect; (*objetivo*) to achieve; (*compreender*) to grasp.
atingível [atʃĩ'ʒivew] (*pl* **-eis**) *adj* attainable.
atinha [a'tʃiɲa] *etc vb V* **ater-se**.
atinjo [a'tʃĩʒu] *etc vb V* **atingir**.
atípico/a [a'tʃipiku/a] *adj* atypical, untypical.
atirador(a) [atʃira'do*(a)] *m/f* marksman/woman; **~ de tocaia** sniper.
atirar [atʃi'ra*] *vt* (*lançar*) to throw, fling, hurl ♦ *vi* (*arma*) to shoot; **~-se** *vr*: **~-se a** (*lançar-se a*) to hurl o.s. at; **~ (em)** to shoot (at).
atitude [atʃi'tudʒi] *f* attitude; (*postura*) posture; **tomar uma ~** (*reagir*) to do something about it.
ativa [a'tʃiva] *f* (*MIL*) active service.

ativar [atʃi'va*] *vt* to activate; (*apressar*) to hasten.

ative [a'tʃivi] *etc vb V* **ater-se**.

atividade [atʃivi'dadʒi] *f* activity.

ativo/a [a'tʃivu/a] *adj* active ♦ *m* (*COM*) assets *pl*.

atlântico/a [at'lãtʃiku/a] *adj* Atlantic ♦ *m*: **o A~** the Atlantic.

atlas ['atlaʃ] *m inv* atlas.

atleta [at'lɛta] *m/f* athlete.

atlético/a [at'lɛtʃiku/a] *adj* athletic.

atletismo [atle'tʃiʒmu] *m* athletics *sg*.

atmosfera [atmoʃ'fɛra] *f* atmosphere.

ato ['atu] *m* act; (*ação*) action; (*cerimônia*) ceremony; (*TEATRO*) act; **em ~ contínuo** straight after; **no ~** on the spot; **no mesmo ~** at the same time; **~ falho** Freudian slip; **~ público** public ceremony.

à-toa *adj* (*insignificante*) insignificant; (*simples*) simple, easy ♦ *adv V* **toa**.

atoalhado/a [atoa'ʎadu/a] *adj*: **(tecido) ~** towelling.

atolado/a [ato'ladu/a] *adj* (*tb fig*) bogged down.

atolar [ato'la*] *vt* to bog down; **~-se** *vr* to get bogged down.

atoleiro [ato'lejru] *m* bog, quagmire; (*fig*) quandary, fix.

atômico/a [a'tomiku/a] *adj* atomic.

atomizador [atomiza'do*] *m* atomizer.

átomo ['atomu] *m* atom.

atônito/a [a'tonitu/a] *adj* astonished, amazed.

ator [a'to*] *m* actor.

atordoado/a [atox'dwadu/a] *adj* dazed.

atordoador(a) [atoxdwa'do*(a)] *adj* stunning.

atordoamento [atoxdwa'mẽtu] *m* daze.

atordoar [atox'dwa*] *vt* to daze, stun.

atormentar [atoxmẽ'ta*] *vt* to torment; (*importunar*) to plague.

atracação [atraka'sãw] (*pl* **-ões**) *f* (*NÁUT*) mooring; (*briga*) fight; (*col*: *agarração*) necking.

atração [atra'sãw] (*pl* **-ões**) *f* attraction.

atracar [atra'ka*] *vt, vi* (*NÁUT*) to moor; **~-se** *vr* to grapple; (*col*: *abraçar-se*) to neck.

atrações [atra'sõjʃ] *fpl de* **atração**.

atractivo/a [atra'tivu/a] (*PT*) *adj* = **atrativo**.

atraente [atra'ẽtʃi] *adj* attractive.

atraiçoar [atraj'swa*] *vt* to betray.

atrair [atra'i*] *vt* to attract; (*fascinar*) to fascinate.

atrapalhação [atrapaʎa'sãw] *f* (*confusão*) confusion.

atrapalhar [atrapa'ʎa*] *vt* (*confundir*) to confuse; (*perturbar*) to disturb; (*dificultar*) to hinder ♦ *vi* to disturb; to be a hindrance; **~-se** *vr* to get confused.

atrás [a'trajʃ] *adv* behind; (*no fundo*) at the back; **~ de** behind; (*no tempo*) after; (*em busca de*) after; **um ~ de outro** one after the other; **dois meses ~** two months ago; **não ficar ~** (*fig*) not to be far behind.

atrasado/a [atra'zadu/a] *adj* late; (*país etc*) backward; (*relógio etc*) slow; (*pagamento*) overdue; (*costumes, pessoa*) antiquated; (*número de revista*) back; **estar ~ nos pagamentos** to be in arrears.

atrasados [atra'zaduʃ] *mpl* (*COM*) arrears.

atrasar [atra'za*] *vt* to delay; (*progresso, desenvolvimento*) to hold back; (*relógio*) to put back; (*pagamento*) to be late with ♦ *vi* (*relógio etc*) to be slow; (*avião, pessoa*) to be late; **~-se** *vr* (*chegar tarde*) to be late; (*num trabalho*) to fall behind; (*num pagamento*) to get into arrears.

atraso [a'trazu] *m* delay; (*de país etc*) backwardness; **~s** *mpl* (*COM*) arrears; **chegar com ~** to arrive late; **com 20 minutos de ~** 20 minutes late; **com um ~ de 6 meses** (*COM*: *pagamento*) six months in arrears; **um ~ de vida** a hindrance.

atrativo/a [atra'tʃivu/a] *adj* attractive ♦ *m* attraction, appeal; (*incentivo*) incentive; **~s** *mpl* charms.

atravancar [atravã'ka*] *vt* to block, obstruct; (*encher*) to fill up.

através [atra'vɛʃ] *adv* across; **~ de** (*de lado a lado*) across; (*pelo centro de*) through; (*por meio de*) through.

atravessado/a [atrave'sadu/a] *adj* (*na garganta*) stuck; **estar com alguém ~ na garganta** to be peeved with sb.

atravessar [atrave'sa*] *vt* (*cruzar*) to cross; (*pôr ao través*) to put *ou* lay across; (*traspassar*) to pass through; (*crise etc*) to go through.

atrelar [atre'la*] *vt* (*cão*) to put on a leash; (*cavalo*) to harness; (*duas viaturas*) to couple up.

atrever-se [atre'vexsi] *vr*: **~ a** to dare to.

atrevido/a [atre'vidu/a] *adj* (*petulante*) cheeky, impudent; (*corajoso*) bold.

atrevimento [atrevi'mẽtu] *m* (*ousadia*) boldness; (*insolência*) cheek, insolence.

atribuição [atribwi'sãw] (*pl* **-ões**) *f* attribution; **atribuições** *fpl* rights, powers.

atribuir [atri'bwi*] *vt*: **~ algo a** to attribute sth to; (*prêmios, regalias*) to confer sth on.

atribulação [atribula'sãw] (*pl* **-ões**) *f* tribulation.

atribular [atribu'la*] *vt* to trouble, distress; **~-se** *vr* to be distressed.

atributo [atri'butu] *m* attribute.

átrio ['atrju] *m* hall; (*pátio*) courtyard.

atrito [a'tritu] *m* (*fricção*) friction; (*desentendimento*) disagreement.

atriz [a'triʒ] *f* actress.

atrocidade [atrosi'dadʒi] *f* atrocity.

atrofia [atro'fia] *f* atrophy.

atrofiar [atro'fja*] *vt* to atrophy; **~-se** *vr* to

NB: European Portuguese adds the following consonants to certain words: **b** (sú(b)dito, su(b)til); **c** (a(c)ção, a(c)cionista, a(c)to); **m** (inde(m)ne); **p** (ado(p)ção, ado(p)tar); *for further details see p. xiii.*

atrophy.

atropeladamente [atropelada'mẽtʃi] *adv* haphazardly.

atropelamento [atropela'mẽtu] *m* (*de pedestre*) running over.

atropelar [atrope'la*] *vt* to knock down, run over; (*empurrar*) to jostle.

atropelo [atro'pelu] *m* bustle, scramble; (*confusão*) confusion.

atroz [a'trɔʒ] *adj* (*cruel*) merciless; (*crime*) heinous; (*dor, lembrança, feiúra*) terrible, awful.

attaché [ata'ʃe] *m* attaché.

atuação [atwa'sãw] (*pl* **-ões**) *f* acting; (*de ator etc*) performance.

atuado/a [a'twadu/a] *adj* (*pessoa*) in a bad mood.

atual [a'twaw] (*pl* **-ais**) *adj* current; (*pessoa, carro*) modern.

atualidade [atwali'dadʒi] *f* present (time); **~s** *fpl* news *sg*.

atualização [atwaliza'sãw] (*pl* **-ões**) *f* updating.

atualizado/a [atwali'zadu/a] *adj* up-to-date.

atualizar [atwali'za*] *vt* to update; **~-se** *vr* to bring o.s. up to date.

atualmente [atwaw'mẽtʃi] *adv* at present, currently; (*hoje em dia*) nowadays.

atuante [a'twãtʃi] *adj* active.

atuar [a'twa*] *vi* to act; **~ para** to contribute to; **~ sobre** to influence.

atulhar [atu'ʎa*] *vt* (*encher*) to cram full; (*meter*) to stuff, cram.

atum [a'tũ] (*pl* **-ns**) *m* tuna (fish).

aturar [atu'ra*] *vt* (*suportar*) to endure, put up with.

aturdido/a [atux'dʒidu/a] *adj* stunned; (*com barulho*) deafened; (*com confusão, movimento*) bewildered.

aturdimento [atuxdʒi'mẽtu] *m* bewilderment.

aturdir [atux'dʒi*] *vt* to stun; (*suj: barulho*) to deafen; (*: confusão, movimento*) to bewilder.

atxim [a'tʃĩ] *excl* achoo!

audácia [aw'dasja] *f* boldness; (*insolência*) insolence; **que ~!** what a cheek!

audacioso/a [awda'sjozu/ɔza] *adj* daring; (*insolente*) insolent.

audaz [aw'daʒ] *adj* daring; (*insolente*) insolent.

audição [awdʒi'sãw] (*pl* **-ões**) *f* audition; (*concerto*) recital.

audiência [aw'dʒjẽsja] *f* audience; (*de tribunal*) session, hearing.

audiovisual [awdʒjovi'zwaw] (*pl* **-ais**) *adj* audiovisual.

auditar [awdʒi'ta*] *vt* (COM) to audit.

auditivo/a [awdʒi'tʃivu/a] *adj* hearing *atr*, auditory.

auditor(a) [awdʒi'to*(a)] *m/f* (COM) auditor; (*juiz*) judge; (*ouvinte*) listener.

auditoria [awdʒito'ria] *f* auditing; **fazer a ~ de** to audit.

auditório [awdʒi'tɔrju] *m* (*ouvintes*) audience; (*recinto*) auditorium; **programa de ~** program(me) recorded before a live audience.

audível [aw'dʒivew] (*pl* **-eis**) *adj* audible.

auferir [awfe'ri*] *vt* (*lucro*) to derive.

auge ['awʒi] *m* height, peak.

augurar [awgu'ra*] *vt* to augur; (*felicidades*) to wish.

augúrio [aw'gurju] *m* omen.

aula ['awla] *f* (PT: *sala*) classroom; (*lição*) lesson, class; **dar ~** to teach.

aumentar [awmẽ'ta*] *vt* to increase; (*salários, preços*) to raise; (*sala, casa*) to expand, extend; (*suj: lente*) to magnify; (*acrescentar*) to add ♦ *vi* to increase; (*preço, salário*) to rise, go up; **~ de peso** (*pessoa*) to put on weight.

aumento [aw'mẽtu] *m* increase; (*de preços*) rise; (*ampliação*) enlargement; (*crescimento*) growth.

áureo/a ['awrju/a] *adj* golden.

auréola [aw'rɛola] *f* halo.

aurora [aw'rɔra] *f* dawn.

auscultar [awʃkuw'ta*] *vt* (*opinião pública*) to sound out; (*paciente*): **~ alguém** to sound sb's chest.

ausência [aw'zẽsja] *f* absence.

ausentar-se [awzẽ'taxsi] *vr* (*ir-se*) to go away; (*afastar-se*) to stay away.

ausente [aw'zẽtʃi] *adj* absent ♦ *m/f* missing person.

auspiciar [awʃpi'sja*] *vt* to augur.

auspício [aw'ʃpisju] *m*: **sob os ~s de** under the auspices of.

auspicioso/a [awʃpi'sjozu/ɔza] *adj* auspicious.

austeridade [awʃteri'dadʒi] *f* austerity.

austero/a [awʃ'tɛru/a] *adj* austere.

austral [awʃ'traw] (*pl* **-ais**) *adj* southern.

Austrália [awʃ'tralja] *f*: **a ~** Australia.

australiano/a [awʃtra'ljanu/a] *adj, m/f* Australian.

Áustria ['awʃtrja] *f*: **a ~** Austria.

austríaco/a [awʃ'triaku/a] *adj, m/f* Austrian.

autarquia [awtax'kia] *f* quango (BRIT), non-governmental organization.

autárquico/a [aw'taxkiku/a] *adj* non-governmental.

autenticar [awtẽtʃi'ka*] *vt* to authenticate; (COM, JUR) to certify.

autenticidade [awtẽtʃisi'dadʒi] *f* authenticity.

autêntico/a [aw'tẽtʃiku/a] *adj* authentic; (*pessoa*) genuine; (*verdadeiro*) true, real.

autismo [aw'tʃiʒmu] *m* autism.

autista [aw'tʃiʃta] *adj* autistic ♦ *m/f* autistic person.

auto ['awtu] *m* (*automóvel*) car; **~s** *mpl* (JUR: *processo*) legal proceedings; (*documentos*) legal papers.

auto-adesivo/a *adj* self-adhesive.

auto-afirmação *f* self-assertion.

autobiografia [awtobjogra'fia] *f* autobiography.

autobiográfico/a [awtobjo'grafiku/a] *adj* autobiographical.

autocarro [awto'kaxu] (PT) *m* bus.
autocontrole [awtokõ'troli] *m* self-control.
autocrata [awto'krata] *adj* autocratic.
autóctone [aw'tɔktoni] *adj* indigenous ♦ *m/f* native.
autodefesa [awtode'feza] *f* self-defence (BRIT), self-defense (US).
autodestruição [awtodeʃ'trwisãw] *f* self-destruction.
autodeterminação [awtodetexmina'sãw] *f* self-determination.
autodidata [awtodʒi'data] *adj* self-taught ♦ *m/f* autodidact.
autodisciplina [awtodʒisi'plina] *f* self-discipline.
autodomínio [awtodo'minju] *m* self-control.
autódromo [aw'tɔdromu] *m* race track.
auto-escola *f* driving school.
auto-estrada *f* motorway (BRIT), expressway (US).
autografar [awtogra'fa*] *vt* to autograph.
autógrafo [aw'tɔgrafu] *m* autograph.
automação [awtoma'sãw] *f* automation; ~ **de escritórios** office automation.
automático/a [awto'matʃiku/a] *adj* automatic.
automatização [awtomatʃiza'sãw] *f* = **automação**.
automatizar [awtomatʃi'za*] *vt* to automate.
autômato [aw'tomatu] *m* automaton.
automedicar-se [awtomedʒi'kaxsi] *vr* to treat o.s.
automobilismo [awtomobi'liʒmu] *m* motoring; (ESPORTE) motor car racing.
automóvel [awto'mɔvew] (*pl* **-eis**) *m* motor car (BRIT), automobile (US).
autonomia [awtono'mia] *f* autonomy.
autônomo/a [aw'tonomu/a] *adj* autonomous; (*trabalhador*) self-employed ♦ *m/f* self-employed person.
autopeça [awto'pɛsa] *f* car spare.
autópsia [aw'tɔpsja] *f* autopsy, post-mortem.
autor(a) [aw'to*(a)] *m/f* author(ess); (*de um crime*) perpetrator; (JUR) plaintiff.
autoral [awto'raw] (*pl* **-ais**) *adj V* **direito**.
auto-retrato *m* self-portrait.
autoridade [awtori'dadʒi] *f* authority.
autoritário/a [awtori'tarju/a] *adj* authoritarian.
autoritarismo [awtorita'riʒmu] *m* authoritarianism.
autorização [awtoriza'sãw] (*pl* **-ões**) *f* permission, authorization; **dar ~ a alguém para** to give sb permission to, authorize sb to.
autorizar [awtori'za*] *vt* to authorize.
auto-serviço *m* self-service.
auto-suficiente *adj* self-sufficient.
auto-sugestão *f* autosuggestion.
autuar [aw'twa*] *vt* to sue.
auxiliar [awsi'lja*] *adj* auxiliary ♦ *m/f* assistant ♦ *vt* to help, assist.
auxílio [aw'silju] *m* help, assistance, aid.
auxílio-doença (*pl* **auxílios-doença**) *m* sickness benefit.
Av *abr* (= *avenida*) Ave.
avacalhado/a [avaka'ʎadu/a] *adj* sloppy.
avacalhar [avaka'ʎa*] (*col*) *vt* to screw up.
aval [a'vaw] (*pl* **-ais**) *m* guarantee; (COM) surety.
avalancha [ava'lãʃa] *f* avalanche.
avalanche [ava'lãʃi] *f* = **avalancha**.
avaliação [avalja'sãw] (*pl* **-ões**) *f* valuation; (*apreciação*) assessment, evaluation.
avaliador(a) [avalja'do*(a)] *m/f*: ~ **de danos** loss adjuster.
avaliar [ava'lja*] *vt* to value; (*apreciar*) to assess, evaluate; (*imaginar*) to imagine; ~ **algo em $100** to value sth at $100.
avalista [ava'liʃta] *m/f* guarantor.
avalizar [avali'za*] *vt* to guarantee.
avançada [avã'sada] *f* advance.
avançado/a [avã'sadu/a] *adj* advanced; (*idéias, pessoa*) progressive.
avançar [avã'sa*] *vt* to move forward ♦ *vi* to advance.
avanço [a'vãsu] *m* advancement; (*progresso*) progress; (*melhora*) improvement, advance.
avantajado/a [avãta'ʒadu/a] *adj* (*corpulento*) stout.
avante [a'vãtʃi] *adv* forward.
avarento/a [ava'rẽtu/a] *adj* mean ♦ *m/f* miser.
avareza [ava'reza] *f* meanness.
avaria [ava'ria] *f* damage; (TEC) breakdown.
avariado/a [ava'rjadu/a] *adj* damaged; (*máquina*) out of order; (*carro*) broken down.
avariar [ava'rja*] *vt* to damage ♦ *vi* to suffer damage; (TEC) to break down.
avaro/a [a'varu/a] *adj* mean ♦ *m/f* miser.
ave ['avi] *f* bird; ~ **de rapina** bird of prey.
aveia [a'veja] *f* oats *pl*.
aveio [a'veju] *etc vb V* **avir-se**.
avelã [ave'lã] *f* hazelnut.
aveludado/a [avelu'dadu/a] *adj* velvety; (*voz*) smooth.
avenho [a'veɲu] *etc vb V* **avir-se**.
avenida [ave'nida] *f* avenue.
avental [avẽ'taw] (*pl* **-ais**) *m* apron; (*vestido*) pinafore dress.
aventar [avẽ'ta*] *vt* (*idéia etc*) to put forward.
aventura [avẽ'tura] *f* adventure; (*proeza*) exploit.
aventurar [avẽtu'ra*] *vt* (*ousar*) to risk, venture; **~-se** *vr*: **~-se a** to dare to.
aventureiro/a [avẽtu'rejru/a] *adj* adventurous ♦ *m/f* adventurer.
averiguação [averigwa'sãw] (*pl* **-ões**) *f* investigation, inquiry; (*verificação*) verification.
averiguar [averi'gwa*] *vt* (*inquirir*) to investigate, ascertain; (*verificar*) to verify.
avermelhado/a [avexme'ʎadu/a] *adj* reddish.
aversão [avex'sãw] (*pl* **-ões**) *f* aversion.

NB: *European Portuguese adds the following consonants to certain words:* **b** (sú(b)dito, su(b)til); **c** (a(c)ção, a(c)cionista, a(c)to); **m** (inde(m)ne); **p** (ado(p)ção, ado(p)tar); *for further details see p. xiii.*

averso/a [a'vɛxsu/a] *adj*: ~ **a** averse to.
aversões [avex'sõjʃ] *fpl de* **aversão**.
avesso/a [a'vesu/a] *adj* (*lado*) opposite, reverse ♦ *m* wrong side, reverse; **ao** ~ inside out; **às avessas** (*inverso*) upside down; (*oposto*) the wrong way round; **virar pelo** ~ to turn inside out.
avestruz [aveʃ'truʒ] *m* ostrich.
aviação [avja'sãw] *f* aviation, flying.
aviado/a [a'vjadu/a] *adj* (*executado*) ready; (*apressado*) hurried.
aviador(a) [avja'do*(a)] *m/f* aviator, airman/woman.
aviamento [avja'mẽtu] *m* (*COSTURA*) haberdashery (*BRIT*), notions *pl* (*US*); (*de receita médica*) filling; (*COM*) goodwill.
avião [a'vjãw] (*pl* **-ões**) *m* aeroplane; ~ **a jato** jet.
aviar [a'vja*] *vt* (*receita médica*) to make up.
avicultor(a) [avikuw'to*(a)] *m/f* poultry farmer.
avicultura [avikuw'tura] *f* poultry farming.
avidez [avi'deʒ] *f* (*cobiça*) greediness; (*desejo*) eagerness.
ávido/a ['avidu/a] *adj* (*cobiçoso*) greedy; (*desejoso*) eager.
aviltamento [aviwta'mẽtu] *m* debasement.
aviltar [aviw'ta*] *vt* to debase; **~-se** *vr* to demean o.s.
avim [a'vĩ] *etc vb V* **avir-se**.
avinagrado/a [avina'gradu/a] *adj* vinegary.
aviões [a'vjõjʃ] *mpl de* **avião**.
avir-se [a'vixsi] (*irreg*: *como* **vir**) *vr* (*conciliar-se*) to reach an understanding.
avisar [avi'za*] *vt* (*advertir*) to warn; (*informar*) to tell, let know; **ele avisou que chega amanhã** he said he's arriving tomorrow.
aviso [a'vizu] *m* (*comunicação*) notice; (*advertência*) warning; ~ **prévio** notice.
avistar [aviʃ'ta*] *vt* to catch sight of; **~-se** *vr*: **~-se com** (*ter entrevista*) to have an interview with.
avitaminose [avitami'nɔzi] *f* vitamin deficiency.
avivar [avi'va*] *vt* (*intensificar*) to intensify, heighten; (*memória*) to bring back.
avizinhar-se [avizi'ɲaxsi] *vr* (*aproximar-se*) to approach, come near.
avo ['avu] *m*: **um doze ~s** one twelfth.
avô/avó [a'vo/a'vɔ] *m/f* grandfather/mother; **avós** *mpl* grandparents.
avoado/a [avo'adu/a] *adj* (*pessoa*) absent-minded.
avolumar [avolu'ma*] *vt* (*aumentar*: *em volume*) to swell; (: *em número*) to accumulate; (*ocupar espaço*) to fill; **~-se** *vr* to increase; to swell.
avulso/a [a'vuwsu/a] *adj* separate, detached ♦ *m* single copy.
avultado/a [avuw'tadu/a] *adj* large, bulky.
avultar [avuw'ta*] *vt* to enlarge, expand ♦ *vi* (*sobressair*) to stand out; (*aumentar*) to increase.
axila [ak'sila] *f* armpit.
axioma [a'sjɔma] *m* axiom.
azáfama [a'zafama] *f* bustle; (*pressa*) hurry.
azaléia [aza'lɛja] *f* azalea.
azar [a'za*] *m* bad luck; ~! too bad, bad luck!; **estar com** ~ to be unlucky; **ter** ~ to be unlucky.
azarado/a [aza'radu/a] *adj* unlucky.
azarento/a [aza'rẽtu/a] *adj* unlucky.
azedar [aze'da*] *vt* to turn sour; (*pessoa*) to put in a bad mood ♦ *vi* to turn sour; (*leite*) to go off.
azedo/a [a'zedu/a] *adj* (*sabor*) sour; (*leite*) off; (*fig*) grumpy, bad-tempered.
azedume [aze'dumi] *m* (*sabor*) sourness; (*fig*) grumpiness.
azeitar [azej'ta*] *vt* (*untar*) to grease; (*lubrificar*) to oil.
azeite [a'zejtʃi] *m* oil; (*de oliva*) olive oil.
azeitona [azej'tɔna] *f* olive.
Azerbaijão [azexbaj'ʒãw] *m*: **o** ~ Azerbaijan.
azeviche [aze'viʃi] *m* (*cor*) jet black.
azevinho [aze'viɲu] *m* holly.
azia [a'zia] *f* heartburn.
aziago/a [a'zjagu/a] *adj* (*de mau agouro*) ominous.
azinhaga [azi'ɲaga] *f* (country) lane.
azinhavre [azi'ɲavri] *m* verdigris.
azo ['azu] *m* (*oportunidade*) opportunity; (*pretexto*) pretext; **dar** ~ **a** to give occasion to.
azougue [a'zogi] *m* quicksilver; (*QUÍM*) mercury; (*fig*: *pessoa*: *inquieta*) livewire; (: *esperta*) sharp person.
azucrinar [azukri'na*] *vt* to bother, pester.
azul [a'zuw] (*pl* **-uis**) *adj* blue; **tudo** ~ (*fig*) everything's rosy.
azular [azu'la*] *vi* to flee.
azulejar [azule'ʒa*] *vt* to tile.
azulejo [azu'leʒu] *m* (glazed) tile.
azul-marinho *adj inv* navy blue.
azul-turquesa *adj inv* turquoise.

B

B, b [be] (*pl* **bs**) *m* B, b; **B de Beatriz** B for Benjamin (*BRIT*) *ou* Baker (*US*).
baba ['baba] *f* saliva, dribble.
babá [ba'ba] *f* nanny.
babaca [ba'baka] (*col*) *adj* stupid ♦ *m/f* idiot.
baba-de-moça (*pl* **babas-de-moça**) *f sweet made with sugar, coconut milk and eggs*.
babado [ba'badu] *m* frill; (*col*) piece of gossip.
babador [baba'do*] *m* bib.
babaquice [baba'kisi] *f* stupidity; (*ato, dito*)

stupid thing.

babar [ba'ba*] *vt* to dribble on ♦ *vi* to dribble; **~-se** *vr* to dribble; **~(-se) por** to drool over.

babeiro [ba'bejru] (*PT*) *m* bib.

babel [ba'bɛw] (*pl* **-éis**) *f* (*fig*) muddle.

baby-sitter ['bejbisite*] (*pl* **~s**) *m/f* baby-sitter.

bacalhau [baka'ʎaw] *m* (dried) cod.

bacalhoada [bakaʎo'ada] *f* salt cod stew.

bacana [ba'kana] (*col*) *adj* great.

bacanal [baka'naw] (*pl* **-ais**) *m* orgy.

bacharel [baʃa'rɛw] (*pl* **-éis**) *m* bachelor, graduate.

bacharelado [baʃare'ladu] *m* bachelor's degree.

bacharelar-se [baʃare'laxsi] *vr* to graduate.

bacia [ba'sia] *f* basin; (*sanitária*) bowl; (*ANAT*) pelvis.

background [bɛk'grãwdʒi] (*pl* **~s**) *m* background.

backup [ba'kapi] (*pl* **~s**) *m* (*COMPUT*) backup; **tirar um ~ de** to back up.

baço/a ['basu/a] *adj* dull; (*metal*) tarnished ♦ *m* (*ANAT*) spleen.

bacon ['bejkõ] *m* bacon.

bactéria [bak'tɛrja] *f* germ, bacterium; **~s** *fpl* bacteria.

badalado/a [bada'ladu/a] (*col*) *adj* talked about, famous.

badalar [bada'la*] *vt* (*sino*) to ring ♦ *vi* to ring; (*col*) to go out and about.

badalativo/a [badala'tʃivu/a] (*col*) *adj* fun-loving.

badalo [ba'dalu] *m* clapper.

badejo [ba'deʒu] *m* sea bass.

baderna [ba'dɛxna] *f* commotion.

badulaque [badu'laki] *m* trinket; **~s** *mpl* junk *sg*.

bafafá [bafa'fa] (*col*) *m* kerfuffle.

bafejar [bafe'ʒa*] *vt* (*aquecer com o bafo*) to blow; (*fortuna*) to smile upon.

bafejo [ba'feʒu] *m* (*sopro*) whiff; **~ da sorte** stroke of luck.

bafio [ba'fiu] *m* musty smell.

bafo ['bafu] *m* (*hálito*) (bad) breath; **isso é ~ dele** (*col*) he's just making it up.

bafômetro [ba'fometru] *m* Breathalyser ®.

baforada [bafo'rada] *f* (*fumaça*) puff.

bagaço [ba'gasu] *m* (*de frutos*) pulp; (*PT*: *cachaça*) brandy; **estar/ficar um ~** (*fig*: *pessoa*) to be/get run down.

bagageiro [baga'ʒejru] *m* (*AUTO*) roofrack; (*PT*) porter.

bagagem [ba'gaʒẽ] *f* luggage; (*fig*) baggage; **recebimento de ~** (*AER*) baggage reclaim.

bagatela [baga'tɛla] *f* trinket; (*fig*) trifle.

Bagdá [bagi'da] *n* Baghdad.

bago ['bagu] *m* (*fruto*) berry; (*uva*) grape; (*de chumbo*) pellet; (*col!*) ball (*!*).

bagulho [ba'guʎu] *m* (*objeto*) piece of junk; (*pessoa*): **ser um ~** to be as ugly as sin.

bagunça [ba'gũsa] *f* (*confusão*) mess, shambles *sg*.

bagunçado/a [bagũ'sadu/a] *adj* in a mess.

bagunçar [bagũ'sa*] *vt* to mess up.

bagunceiro/a [bagũ'sejru/a] *adj* messy.

Bahamas [ba'amaʃ] *fpl*: **as ~** the Bahamas.

baia ['baja] *f* bail.

baía [ba'ia] *f* bay.

baiano/a [ba'janu/a] *adj*, *m/f* Bahian.

baila ['bajla] *f*: **trazer/vir à ~** to bring/come up.

bailado [baj'ladu] *m* dance; (*balé*) ballet.

bailar [baj'la*] *vt*, *vi* to dance.

bailarino/a [bajla'rinu/a] *m/f* ballet dancer.

baile ['bajli] *m* dance; (*formal*) ball; **dar um ~ em alguém** to pull sb's leg; **~ à fantasia** fancy-dress ball.

bainha [ba'iɲa] *f* (*de arma*) sheath; (*de costura*) hem.

baioneta [bajo'neta] *f* bayonet; **~ calada** fixed bayonet.

bairrista [baj'xiʃta] *adj* loyal to one's neighbo(u)rhood ♦ *m/f* proud local.

bairro ['bajxu] *m* district.

baita ['bajta] *adj* huge; (*gripe*) bad.

baixa ['bajʃa] *f* decrease; (*de preço*) reduction, fall; (*diminuição*) drop; (*BOLSA*) low; (*em combate*) casualty; (*do serviço*) discharge; **dar** *ou* **ter ~** to be discharged.

baixada [baj'ʃada] *f* lowland.

baixa-mar *f* low tide.

baixar [baj'ʃa*] *vt* to lower; (*bandeira*) to take down; (*ordem*) to issue; (*lei*) to pass; (*COMPUT*) to download ♦ *vi* to go (*ou* come) down; (*temperatura, preço*) to drop, fall; (*col*: *aparecer*) to show up; **~ ao hospital** to go into hospital.

baixaria [bajʃa'ria] *f* vulgarity; (*ação*) cheap trick.

baixela [baj'ʃɛla] *f* serving set.

baixeza [baj'ʃeza] *f* meanness, baseness.

baixinho [baj'ʃiɲu] *adv* (*em voz baixa*) softly, quietly; (*em segredo*) secretly.

baixio [baj'ʃiu] *m* sandbank, sandbar.

baixista [baj'ʃiʃta] *adj*, *m/f* (*COM*) bear *atr*.

baixo/a ['bajʃu/a] *adj* low; (*pessoa*) short, small; (*rio*) shallow; (*linguagem*) common; (*cabeça, olhos*) lowered; (*som*) quiet; (*atitude*) mean, base; (*metal*) base ♦ *adv* low; (*em posição baixa*) low down; (*falar*) softly ♦ *m* (*MÚS*) bass; **em ~** below; (*em casa*) downstairs; **para ~** down, downwards; (*em casa*) downstairs; **por ~ de** under, underneath; **altos e ~s** ups and downs; **estar por ~** to be down on one's luck.

baixo-astral (*col*) *m* bad vibes *pl*; **estar num ~** to be at a low ebb.

baixote/a [baj'ʃɔtʃi/ta] *adj* shortish.

bajulador(a) [baʒula'do*(a)] *adj* obsequious.

NB: *European Portuguese adds the following consonants to certain words:* **b** (sú(b)dito, su(b)til); **c** (a(c)ção, a(c)cionista, a(c)to); **m** (inde(m)ne); **p** (ado(p)ção, ado(p)tar); *for further details see p. xiii.*

bajular [baʒu'la*] *vt* to fawn over.
bala ['bala] *f* bullet; (*BR*: *doce*) sweet; **estar em ponto de ~** (*fig*) to be in tip-top condition; **estar/ficar uma ~** (*fig*) to be/get furious.
balada [ba'lada] *f* ballad.
balaio [ba'laju] *m* straw basket.
balança [ba'lãsa] *f* scales *pl*; **B~** (*ASTROLOGIA*) Libra; **~ comercial** balance of trade; **~ de pagamentos** balance of payments.
balançar [balã'sa*] *vt* (*fazer oscilar*) to swing; (*pesar*) to weigh (up) ♦ *vi* (*oscilar*) to swing; (*carro, avião*) to shake; (*navio*) to roll; (*em cadeira*) to rock; **~-se** *vr* to swing.
balancear [balã'sja*] *vt* to balance.
balancete [balã'setʃi] *m* (*COM*) trial balance.
balanço [ba'lãsu] *m* (*movimento*) swinging; (*brinquedo*) swing; (*de navio*) rolling; (*de carro, avião*) shaking; (*COM*: *registro*) balance (sheet); (: *verificação*) audit; **fazer um ~ de** (*fig*) to take stock of.
balangandã [balãgã'dã] *m* bauble.
balão [ba'lãw] (*pl* **-ões**) *m* balloon; (*em história em quadrinhos*) speech bubble; (*AUTO*) turning area; **~ de oxigênio** oxygen tank.
balão-de-ensaio (*pl* **balões-de-ensaio**) *m*: **soltar um ~** (*fig*) to put out feelers.
balar [ba'la*] *vi* to bleat.
balaustrada [balawʃ'trada] *f* balustrade.
balaústre [bala'uʃtri] *m* bannister.
balbuciar [bawbu'sja*] *vt, vi* to babble.
balbucio [bawbu'siu] *m* babbling.
balbúrdia [baw'buxdʒja] *f* uproar, bedlam.
balcão [baw'kãw] (*pl* **-ões**) *m* balcony; (*de loja*) counter; (*TEATRO*) circle.
balconista [bawko'niʃta] *m/f* shop assistant.
baldado/a [baw'dadu/a] *adj* unsuccessful, fruitless.
baldar [baw'da*] *vt* to frustrate, foil.
balde ['bawdʒi] *m* bucket, pail.
baldeação [bawdʒja'sãw] (*pl* **-ões**) *f* transfer; **fazer ~** to change.
baldio/a [baw'dʒiu/a] *adj* fallow, uncultivated; **(terreno) ~** (a piece of) waste ground.
balé [ba'lɛ] *m* ballet.
baleeira [bale'ejra] *f* whaler.
baleia [ba'leja] *f* whale.
baleiro/a [ba'lejru/a] *m/f* confectioner.
balido [ba'lidu] *m* bleating; (*um só*) bleat.
balística [ba'liʃtʃika] *f* ballistics *sg*.
balístico/a [ba'liʃtʃiku/a] *adj* ballistic.
baliza [ba'liza] *f* (*estaca*) post; (*bóia*) buoy; (*luminosa*) beacon; (*ESPORTE*) goal.
balizar [bali'za*] *vt* to mark out.
balneário [baw'njarju] *m* bathing resort.
balões [ba'lõjʃ] *mpl de* **balão**.
balofo/a [ba'lofu/a] *adj* (*fofo*) fluffy; (*gordo*) plump, tubby.
baloiço [ba'lojsu] (*PT*) *m* (*de criança*) swing; (*ação*) swinging.
balouçar [balo'sa*] (*PT*) *vt, vi* to swing, sway.
balouço [ba'losu] (*PT*) *m* = **baloiço**.
balsa ['bawsa] *f* raft; (*barca*) ferry.
bálsamo ['bawsamu] *m* balm.
báltico/a ['bawtʃiku/a] *adj* Baltic ♦ *m*: **o B~** the Baltic.
baluarte [ba'lwaxtʃi] *m* rampart, bulwark; (*fig*) supporter.
balzaquiana [bawza'kjana] *f* woman in her thirties.
bamba ['bãba] *adj, m/f* expert.
bambear [bã'bja*] *vt* to loosen ♦ *vi* to work loose; (*pessoa*) to grow weak.
bambo/a ['bãbu/a] *adj* slack, loose; (*pernas*) limp, wobbly.
bambolê [bãbo'le] *m* hula hoop.
bamboleante [bãbo'ljãtʃi] *adj* swaying; (*sem firmeza*) wobbly.
bambolear [bãbo'lja*] *vt* to swing ♦ *vi* (*pessoa*) to sway, totter; (*coisa*) to wobble.
bambu [bã'bu] *m* bamboo.
banal [ba'naw] (*pl* **-ais**) *adj* banal.
banalidade [banali'dadʒi] *f* banality.
banana [ba'nana] *f* banana ♦ *m/f* (*col*) wimp; **dar uma ~** ≈ to stick two fingers up.
bananada [bana'nada] *f* banana paste.
bananeira [bana'nejra] *f* banana tree.
bananosa [bana'nɔza] (*col*) *f*: **estar numa ~** to be in a fix.
banca ['bãka] *f* (*de trabalho*) bench; (*escritório*) office; (*em jogo*) bank; **~ (de jornais)** newsstand; **botar ~** (*col*) to show off; **botar ~ em** *ou* **para cima de** (*col*) to lay down the law to; **~ examinadora** examining body, examination board.
bancada [bã'kada] *f* (*banco, POL*) bench; (*de cozinha*) work surface.
bancar [bã'ka*] *vt* (*financiar*) to finance; **~ o idiota** *etc* to play the fool *etc*; **~ que** to pretend that.
bancário/a [bã'karju/a] *adj* bank *atr* ♦ *m/f* bank employee.
bancarrota [bãka'xota] *f* bankruptcy; **ir à ~** to go bankrupt.
banco ['bãku] *m* (*assento*) bench; (*COM*) bank; (*de cozinha*) stool; **~ de areia** sandbank; **~ de dados** (*COMPUT*) database.
banda ['bãda] *f* band; (*lado*) side; (*cinto*) sash; **de ~** sideways; **pôr de ~** to put aside; **nestas ~s** in these parts; **~ de percussão** steel band; **~ desenhada** (*PT*) cartoon.
bandear-se [bãde'axsi] *vr*: **~ para** *ou* **a** to go over to.
bandeira [bã'dejra] *f* flag; (*estandarte, fig*) banner; (*de porta*) fanlight; **~ a meio pau** flag at half mast; **dar uma ~ em alguém** (*col*) to give sb the brush-off; **levar uma ~** to get the brush-off; **dar ~** (*col*) to give o.s. away.
bandeirante [bãdej'rãtʃi] *m* pioneer ♦ *f* girl guide.
bandeirinha [bãdej'riɲa] *m* (*ESPORTE*) linesman.
bandeja [bã'deʒa] *f* tray; **dar algo de ~ a alguém** (*col*) to give sb sth on a plate.
bandido [bã'dʒidu/a] *m* bandit ♦ *m/f* (*fig*)

rascal.
bando ['bãdu] *m* band; (*grupo*) group; (*de malfeitores*) gang; (*de ovelhas*) flock; (*de gado*) herd; **um ~ de livros** a pile of books.
bandô [bã'do] *m* pelmet.
bandoleiro [bãdo'lejru] *m* robber, bandit.
bandolim [bãdo'lĩ] (*pl* **-ns**) *m* mandolin.
bangalô [bãga'lo] *m* bungalow.
Bangcoc [bãŋ'kɔki] *n* Bangkok.
Bangladesh [bãgla'dɛʃ] *m* Bangladesh.
bangue-bangue [bãgi'bãgi] *m*: **(filme de) ~** western.
banguela [bã'gɛla] *adj* toothless.
banha ['baɲa] *f* fat; (*de porco*) lard.
banhar [ba'ɲa*] *vt* (*molhar*) to wet; (*mergulhar*) to dip; (*lavar*) to wash, bathe; **~-se** *vr* (*no mar*) to bathe.
banheira [ba'ɲejra] *f* bath.
banheiro [ba'ɲejru] *m* bathroom; (*PT*) lifeguard.
banhista [ba'ɲiʃta] *m/f* bather; (*salva-vidas*) lifeguard.
banho ['baɲu] *m* (*TEC*: *na banheira*) bath; (*mergulho*) dip; **dar um ~ de cerveja** *etc* **em alguém** to spill beer *etc* all over sb; **tomar ~** to have a bath; (*de chuveiro*) to have a shower; **tomar um ~ de** (*fig*) to have a heavy dose of; **vai tomar ~!** (*col*) get lost!; **~ de chuveiro** shower; **~ de espuma** bubble bath; **tomar ~ de mar** to have a swim (in the sea); **~ de sol** sunbathing.
banho-maria (*pl* **banhos-marias** *ou* **banhos-maria**) *m* (*CULIN*) bain-marie.
banimento [bani'mẽtu] *m* banishment.
banir [ba'ni*] *vt* to banish.
banjo ['bãʒu] *m* banjo.
banquei [bã'kej] *etc vb V* **bancar**.
banqueiro/a [bã'kejru/a] *m/f* banker.
banqueta [bã'keta] *f* stool.
banquete [bã'ketʃi] *m* banquet; (*fig*) feast.
banquetear [bãke'tʃja*] *vt* to feast; **~-se** *vr*: **~-se com** to feast on.
banqueteiro/a [bãke'tejru/a] *m/f* caterer.
banzé [bã'zɛ] (*col*) *m* kerfuffle.
baptismo *etc* [ba'tiʒmu] (*PT*) = **batismo** *etc*.
baptizar [bati'za*] *etc* (*PT*) = **batizar** *etc*.
baque ['baki] *m* thud, thump; (*contratempo*) setback; (*queda*) fall; **levar um ~** to be hard hit.
baquear [ba'kja*] *vi* to topple over.
bar [ba*] *m* bar.
barafunda [bara'fũda] *f* confusion; (*de coisas*) hotch-potch.
barafustar [barafuʃ'ta*] *vi*: **~ por** to burst through.
baralhada [bara'ʎada] *f* muddle.
baralhar [bara'ʎa*] *vt* (*fig*) to mix up, confuse.
baralho [ba'raʎu] *m* pack of cards.
barão [ba'rãw] (*pl* **-ões**) *m* baron.
barata [ba'rata] *f* cockroach; **entregue às ~s** (*pessoa*) gone to the dogs; (*plano*) gone out the window.
baratear [bara'tʃja*] *vt* to cut the price of; (*menosprezar*) to belittle.
barateiro/a [bara'tejru/a] *adj* cheap.
baratinado/a [baratʃi'nadu/a] (*col*) *adj* in a flap; (*transtornado*) shaken up.
baratinar [baratʃi'na*] (*col*) *vt* to drive crazy; (*transtornar*) to shake up.
barato/a [ba'ratu/a] *adj* cheap ♦ *adv* cheaply ♦ *m* (*col*): **a festa foi um ~** the party was great.
barba ['baxba] *f* beard; **~s** *fpl* whiskers; **nas ~s de** (*fig*) under the nose of; **fazer a ~** to shave; **pôr as ~s de molho** to take precautions.
barbada [bax'bada] (*col*) *f* cinch, piece of cake; (*TURFE*) favourite.
barbado/a [bax'badu/a] *adj* bearded.
Barbados [bax'baduʃ] *m* Barbados.
barbante [bax'bãtʃi] (*BR*) *m* string.
barbaramente [baxbara'mẽtʃi] *adv* (*muito*) a lot.
barbaridade [baxbari'dadʒi] *f* barbarity, cruelty; (*disparate*) nonsense; **que ~!** good heavens!
barbárie [bax'barie] *f* barbarism.
barbarismo [baxba'riʒmu] *m* barbarism.
bárbaro/a ['baxbaru/a] *adj* barbaric; (*dor, calor*) terrible; (*maravilhoso*) great.
barbatana [baxba'tana] *f* fin.
barbeador [baxbja'do*] *m* razor; (*elétrico*) shaver.
barbear [bax'bja*] *vt* to shave; **~-se** *vr* to shave.
barbearia [baxbja'ria] *f* barber's (shop).
barbeiragem [baxbej'raʒẽ] *f* bad driving; **fazer uma ~** to drive badly; (*fig*) to bungle it.
barbeiro [bax'bejru] *m* barber; (*loja*) barber's; (*motorista*) bad driver, Sunday driver.
barbitúrico [baxbi'turiku] *m* barbiturate.
barbudo/a [bax'budu/a] *adj* bearded.
barca ['baxka] *f* barge; (*de travessia*) ferry.
barcaça [bax'kasa] *f* barge.
barco ['baxku] *m* boat; **estar no mesmo ~** (*fig*) to be in the same boat; **deixar o ~ correr** (*fig*) to let things take their course; **tocar o ~ para a frente** (*fig*) to struggle on; **~ a motor** motorboat; **~ a remo** rowing boat; **~ a vela** sailing boat.
Barein [ba'rẽj] *m*: **o ~** Bahrain.
barganha [bax'gaɲa] *f* bargain.
barganhar [baxga'ɲa*] *vt, vi* to negotiate.
barítono [ba'ritonu] *m* baritone.
barlavento [baxla'vẽtu] *m* (*NÁUT*) windward; **a ~** to windward.
barman [bax'mã] (*pl* **-men**) *m* barman.
barnabé [baxna'bɛ] (*col*) *m* petty civil servant.

NB: European Portuguese adds the following consonants to certain words: **b** (sú(b)dito, su(b)til); **c** (a(c)ção, a(c)cionista, a(c)to); **m** (inde(m)ne); **p** (ado(p)ção, ado(p)tar); *for further details see p. xiii.*

barões [ba'rõjʃ] *mpl de* **barão**.
barômetro [ba'rometru] *m* barometer.
baronesa [baro'neza] *f* baroness.
barqueiro [bax'kejru] *m* boatman.
barra ['baxa] *f* bar; (*faixa*) strip; (*traço*) stroke; (*alavanca*) lever; (*col: situação*) scene; **agüentar** *ou* **segurar a ~** to hold out; **forçar a ~** (*col*) to force the issue; **ser uma ~** (*pessoa, entrevista*) to be tough; **~ de direção** steering column; **~ fixa** high bar; **~s paralelas** parallel bars.
barraca [ba'xaka] *f* (*tenda*) tent; (*de feira*) stall; (*de madeira*) hut; (*de praia*) sunshade.
barracão [baxa'kãw] (*pl* **-ões**) *m* (*de madeira*) shed.
barraco [ba'xaku] *m* shack, shanty.
barracões [baxa'kõjʃ] *mpl de* **barracão**.
barragem [ba'xaʒẽ] (*pl* **-ns**) *f* (*represa*) dam; (*impedimento*) barrier.
barranco [ba'xãku] *m* ravine, gully; (*de rio*) bank.
barra-pesada *adj inv* (*lugar*) rough; (*pessoa*) shady; (*difícil*) difficult ♦ *m/f* (*pl*: **barras-pesadas**) shady character.
barrar [ba'xa*] *vt* to bar.
barreira [ba'xejra] *f* barrier; (*cerca*) fence; (*ESPORTE*) hurdle; **pôr ~s a** to put obstacles in the way of; **~ do som** sound barrier.
barrento/a [ba'xẽtu/a] *adj* muddy.
barrete [ba'xetʃi] (*PT*) *m* cap.
barricada [baxi'kada] *f* barricade.
barriga [ba'xiga] *f* belly; **estar de ~** to be pregnant; **falar** *ou* **chorar de ~ cheia** to complain for no reason; **fazer ~** to bulge; **~ da perna** calf.
barrigudo/a [baxi'gudu/a] *adj* paunchy, pot-bellied.
barril [ba'xiw] (*pl* **-is**) *m* barrel, cask.
barro ['baxu] *m* clay; (*lama*) mud.
barroco/a [ba'xoku/a] *adj* baroque; (*ornamentado*) extravagant.
barrote [ba'xɔtʃi] *m* beam.
barulhada [baru'ʎada] *f* racket, din.
barulhento/a [baru'ʎẽtu/a] *adj* noisy.
barulho [ba'ruʎu] *m* (*ruído*) noise; (*tumulto*) din.
base ['bazi] *f* base; (*fig*) basis; **sem ~** groundless; **com ~ em** based on; **na ~ de** (*por meio de*) by means of.
baseado/a [ba'zjadu/a] *adj* well-founded ♦ *m* (*col*) joint.
basear [ba'zja*] *vt* to base; **~-se** *vr*: **~-se em** to be based on.
básico/a ['baziku/a] *adj* basic.
basquete [baʃ'kɛtʃi] *m* = **basquetebol**.
basquetebol [baʃkete'bɔw] *m* basketball.
basta ['baʃta] *m*: **dar um ~ em** to call a halt to.
bastante [baʃ'tãtʃi] *adj* (*suficiente*) enough; (*muito*) quite a lot (of) ♦ *adv* (*suficientemente*) enough; (*muito*) a lot.
bastão [baʃ'tãw] (*pl* **-ões**) *m* stick.
bastar [baʃ'ta*] *vi* to be enough, be sufficient; **~-se** *vr* to be self-sufficient; **basta!** (that's) enough!; **~ para** to be enough to.
bastardo/a [baʃ'taxdu/a] *adj, m/f* bastard.
bastidor [baʃtʃi'do*] *m* frame; **~es** *mpl* (*TEATRO*) wings; **nos ~es** (*fig*) behind the scenes.
basto/a ['baʃtu/a] *adj* (*espesso*) thick; (*denso*) dense.
bastões [baʃ'tõjʃ] *mpl de* **bastão**.
bata ['bata] *f* (*de mulher*) smock; (*de médico*) overall.
batalha [ba'taʎa] *f* battle.
batalhador(a) [bataʎa'do*(a)] *adj* struggling ♦ *m/f* fighter.
batalhão [bata'ʎãw] (*pl* **-ões**) *m* battalion.
batalhar [bata'ʎa*] *vi* to battle, fight; (*esforçar-se*) to make an effort, try hard ♦ *vt* (*emprego*) to go after.
batalhões [bata'ʎõjʃ] *mpl de* **batalhão**.
batata [ba'tata] *f* potato; **~ doce** sweet potato; **~ frita** chips *pl* (*BRIT*), French fries *pl*; (*de pacote*) crisps *pl* (*BRIT*), (potato) chips *pl* (*US*).
bate-boca ['batʃi-] (*pl* **~s**) *m* row, quarrel.
bate-bola ['batʃi-] (*pl* **~s**) *m* kick around.
batedeira [bate'dejra] *f* beater; (*elétrica*) mixer; (*de manteiga*) churn.
batedor [bate'do*] *m* beater; (*polícia*) escort; (*CRIQUETE*) batsman; **~ de carteiras** pickpocket.
bátega ['batega] *f* downpour.
batelada [bate'lada] *f*: **uma ~ de** a whole bunch of.
batente [ba'tẽtʃi] *m* doorpost; (*col*) job; **no ~** at work.
bate-papo ['batʃi-] (*pl* **~s**) (*BR*) *m* chat.
bater [ba'te*] *vt* to beat; (*golpear*) to hit; (*horas*) to strike; (*o pé*) to stamp; (*foto*) to take; (*datilografar*) to type; (*porta*) to slam; (*asas*) to flap; (*recorde*) to break; (*roupa: usar muito*) to wear all the time ♦ *vi* (*porta*) to slam; (*sino*) to ring; (*janela*) to bang; (*coração*) to beat; (*sol*) to beat down; **~-se** *vr*: **~-se para fazer/por** to fight to do/for; **~ (à porta)** to knock at the door; **~ à maquina** to type; **~ em** to hit; (*lugar*) to arrive in; (*assunto*) to harp on; **~ com o carro** to crash one's car; **~ com a cabeça** to bang one's head; **~ com o pé (em)** to kick; **ele não bate bem** (*col*) he is a bit crazy; **~ a carteira de alguém** (*col*) to nick sb's wallet.
bateria [bate'ria] *f* battery; (*MÚS*) drums *pl*; **~ de cozinha** kitchen utensils *pl*.
baterista [bate'riʃta] *m/f* drummer.
batida [ba'tʃida] *f* beat; (*da porta*) slam; (*à porta*) knock; (*da polícia*) raid; (*AUTO*) crash; (*bebida*) *cocktail of cachaça, fruit and sugar*; **dar uma ~ em** (*polícia*) to raid; (*colidir com*) to bump into; **dar uma ~ com o carro** to crash one's car; **dar uma ~ no carro de alguém** to crash into sb's car.
batido/a [ba'tʃidu/a] *adj* beaten; (*roupa*) worn; (*assunto*) hackneyed ♦ *m*: **~ de leite** (*PT*) milkshake.

batina [ba'tʃina] *f* (*REL*) cassock.
batismal [batʃiʒ'maw] (*pl* **-ais**) *adj V* **pia**.
batismo [ba'tʃiʒmu] *m* baptism, christening.
batizado [batʃi'zadu] *m* christening.
batizar [batʃi'za*] *vt* to baptize, christen; (*vinho*) to dilute.
batom [ba'tõ] (*pl* **-ns**) *m* lipstick.
batucada [batu'kada] *f* dance percussion group.
batucar [batu'ka*] *vt, vi* to drum.
batuque [ba'tuki] *m* drumming.
batuta [ba'tuta] *f* baton ♦ *adj* (*col*) clever.
baú [ba'u] *m* trunk.
baunilha [baw'niʎa] *f* vanilla.
bazar [ba'za*] *m* bazaar; (*loja*) shop.
bazófia [ba'zɔfja] *f* boasting, bragging.
BB *abr m* = **Banco do Brasil**.
BBF *abr f* = **Bolsa Brasileira de Futuros**.
BC *abr m* = **Banco Central do Brasil**.
BCG *abr m* (= *Bacilo Calmette-Guerin*) BCG.
bê-á-bá [bea'ba] *m* ABC.
beatitude [beatʃi'tudʒi] *f* bliss.
beato/a [be'atu/a] *adj* blessed; (*devoto*) over-pious.
bêbado/a ['bebadu/a] *adj, m/f* drunk.
bebê [be'be] *m* baby.
bebedeira [bebe'dejra] *f* drunkenness; **tomar uma ~** to get drunk.
bêbedo/a ['bebedu/a] *adj, m/f* = **bêbado**.
bebedor(a) [bebe'do*(a)] *m/f* drinker; (*ébrio*) drunkard.
bebedouro [bebe'douru] *m* drinking fountain.
beber [be'be*] *vt* to drink; (*absorver*) to drink up, soak up ♦ *vi* to drink.
bebericar [beberi'ka*] *vt, vi* to sip.
bebida [be'bida] *f* drink.
beca ['bɛka] *f* gown.
beça ['bɛsa] (*col*) *f*: **à ~** (*com vb*) a lot; (*com n*) a lot of; (*com adj*) really.
beco ['beku] *m* alley, lane; **~ sem saída** cul-de-sac; (*fig*) dead end.
bedelho [be'deʎu] *m* kid; **meter o ~ em** to poke one's nose into.
bege ['bɛʒi] *adj inv* beige.
beicinho [bej'siɲu] *m*: **fazer ~** to sulk.
beiço ['bejsu] *m* lip; **fazer ~** to pout.
beiçudo/a [bej'sudu/a] *adj* thick-lipped.
beija-flor [bejʒa-'flɔ*] (*pl* **~es**) *m* humming-bird.
beijar [bej'ʒa*] *vt* to kiss; **~-se** *vr* to kiss (one another).
beijo ['bejʒu] *m* kiss; **dar ~s em alguém** to kiss sb.
beijoca [bej'ʒɔka] *f* kiss.
beijocar [bejʒo'ka*] *vt*: **~ alguém** to kiss sb.
beira ['bejra] *f* (*borda*) edge; (*de rio*) bank; (*orla*) border; **à ~ de** on the edge of; (*ao lado de*) beside, by; (*fig*) on the verge of; **~ do telhado** eaves *pl*.
beirada [bej'rada] *f* edge.
beira-mar *f* seaside.
beirar [bej'ra*] *vt* (*ficar à beira de*) to be at the edge of; (*caminhar à beira de*) to skirt; (*desespero*) to be on the verge of; (*idade*) to approach, near ♦ *vi*: **~ com** to border on; **~ por** (*idade*) to approach.
Beirute [bej'rutʃi] *n* Beirut.
beisebol [bejsi'bɔw] *m* baseball.
belas-artes *fpl* fine arts.
beldade [bew'dadʒi] *f* beauty.
beleléu [bele'lɛw] (*col*) *m*: **ir para o ~** to go wrong.
belenense [bele'nẽsi] *adj* from Belém ♦ *m/f* native *ou* inhabitant of Belém.
beleza [be'leza] *f* beauty; **que ~!** how lovely!; **ser uma ~** to be lovely; **concurso de ~** beauty contest.
belga ['bɛwga] *adj, m/f* Belgian.
Bélgica ['bɛwʒika] *f*: **a ~** Belgium.
Belgrado [bew'gradu] *n* Belgrade.
beliche [be'liʃi] *m* bunk.
bélico/a ['bɛliku/a] *adj* war *atr*.
belicoso/a [beli'kozu/ɔza] *adj* warlike.
beligerante [beliʒe'rãtʃi] *adj* belligerent.
beliscão [beliʃ'kãw] (*pl* **-ões**) *m* pinch.
beliscar [beliʃ'ka*] *vt* to pinch, nip; (*comida*) to nibble.
beliscões [beliʃ'kõjʃ] *mpl de* **beliscão**.
Belize [be'lizi] *m* Belize.
belo/a ['bɛlu/a] *adj* beautiful.
belo-horizontino/a [-orizõ'tʃinu/a] *adj* from Belo Horizonte ♦ *m/f* person from Belo Horizonte.
bel-prazer [bɛw-] *m*: **a seu ~** at one's own convenience.
beltrano [bew'tranu] *m* so-and-so.
belvedere [bewve'deri] *m* lookout point.
bem [bẽj] *adv* well; (*muito*) very; (*bastante*) quite; (*cheirar*) good, nice ♦ *m* (*ventura, utilidade*) good; (*amado*) love; **o ~ comum** the common good; **bens** *mpl* property *sg*; **bens de consumo** consumer goods; **~ ali** right there; **não é ~ assim** it's not quite like that; **está ~** OK; **fazer ~ a** to be good for; **fazer ~ em fazer** to do well to do; **ficar ~** to look good; **ficar ~ em** (*roupa*) to suit; **tudo ~?** how's it going?; **tudo ~** (*como resposta*) fine; **~ como** as well as; **se ~ que** though; **por ~ ou por mal** for better or worse; **nem ~** as soon as, no sooner; **de ~ com alguém** on good terms with sb; **para o ~ de** for the good of; **~ feito!** (*col*) it serves you right!; **~ que eu falei** I told you so; **muito ~!** well done!; **~ de família** family home; **bens móveis/imóveis** moveable property/real estate; **bens de capital** capital goods.
bem-agradecido/a *adj* grateful.
bem-apessoado/a [-ape'swadu/a] *adj* smart, well-groomed.
bem-arrumado/a [-axu'madu/a] *adj* well-

***NB:** European Portuguese adds the following consonants to certain words:* **b** (sú(b)dito, su(b)til); **c** (a(c)ção, a(c)cionista, a(c)to); **m** (inde(m)ne); **p** (ado(p)ção, ado(p)tar); *for further details see p. xiii.*

dressed.
bem-casado/a [-ka'zadu/a] *adj* happily married.
bem-comportado/a [-kõpox'tadu/a] *adj* well-behaved.
bem-conceituado/a *adj* highly regarded.
bem-disposto/a *adj* well, in good form.
bem-educado/a *adj* well-mannered.
bem-estar *m* well-being.
bem-humorado/a [-umo'radu/a] *adj* good-tempered.
bem-intencionado/a *adj* well-intentioned.
bem-me-quer (*pl* **~es**) *m* daisy.
bem-passado/a *adj* (CULIN) well-done.
bem-sucedido/a *adj* successful.
bem-vindo/a *adj* welcome.
bem-visto/a *adj* well thought of.
bênção ['bẽsãw] (*pl* **~s**) *f* blessing.
bendigo [bẽ'dʒigu] *etc vb V* **bendizer**.
bendisse [bẽ'dʒisi] *etc vb V* **bendizer**.
bendito/a [bẽ'dʒitu/a] *pp de* **bendizer** ♦ *adj* blessed.
bendizer [bẽdʒi'ze*] (*irreg*: *como* **dizer**) *vt* (*louvar*) to praise; (*abençoar*) to bless.
beneficência [benefi'sẽsja] *f* (*bondade*) kindness; (*caridade*) charity; **obra de ~** charity.
beneficente [benefi'sẽtʃi] *adj* (*organização*) charitable; (*feira*) charity *atr*.
beneficiado/a [benefi'sjadu/a] *m/f* beneficiary.
beneficiar [benefi'sja*] *vt* (*favorecer*) to benefit; (*melhorar*) to improve; **~-se** *vr* to benefit.
benefício [bene'fisju] *m* (*proveito*) benefit, profit; (*favor*) favour (BRIT), favor (US); **em ~ de** in aid of; **em ~ próprio** for one's own benefit.
benéfico/a [be'nɛfiku/a] *adj* (*benigno*) beneficial; (*generoso*) generous.
Benelux [bene'luks] *m* Benelux.
benemérito/a [bene'mɛritu/a] *adj* (*digno*) worthy.
beneplácito [bene'plasitu] *m* consent, approval.
benevolência [benevo'lẽsja] *f* benevolence, kindness.
benévolo/a [be'nɛvolu/a] *adj* benevolent, kind.
Benfam [bẽ'fami] *abr f* = **Sociedade Brasileira de Bem-Estar da Família**.
benfazejo/a [bẽfa'zeʒu/a] *adj* benevolent.
benfeitor(a) [bẽfej'to*(a)] *m/f* benefactor/benefactress.
benfeitoria [bẽfejto'ria] *f* improvement.
bengala [bẽ'gala] *f* walking stick.
benigno/a [be'nignu/a] *adj* (*bondoso*) kind; (*agradável*) pleasant; (MED) benign.
Benin [be'nĩ] *m*: **o ~** Benin.
benquisto/a [bẽ'kiʃtu/a] *adj* well-loved, well-liked.
bens [bẽjʃ] *mpl de* **bem**.
bento/a ['bẽtu/a] *pp de* **benzer** ♦ *adj* blessed; (*água*) holy.
benzedeiro/a [bẽze'dejru/a] *m/f* sorcerer/sorceress.
benzer [bẽ'ze*] *vt* to bless; **~-se** *vr* to cross o.s.
berçário [bex'sarju] *m* nursery.
berço ['bexsu] *m* (*com balanço*) cradle; (*cama*) cot; (*origem*) birthplace; **nascer em ~ de ouro** (*fig*) to be born with a silver spoon in one's mouth; **ter ~** to be from a good family.
berimbau [berĩ'baw] *m percussion instrument*.
berinjela [berĩ'ʒɛla] *f* aubergine (BRIT), eggplant (US).
Berlim [bex'lĩ] *n* Berlin.
berlinda [bex'lĩda] *f*: **estar na ~** to be in the firing-line.
berma ['bɛxma] (PT) *f* hard shoulder (BRIT), berm (US).
bermuda [bex'muda] *f* Bermuda shorts *pl*.
Bermudas [bex'mudaʃ] *fpl*: **as ~** Bermuda *sg*.
Berna ['bɛxna] *n* Berne.
berrante [be'xãtʃi] *adj* flashy, gaudy.
berrar [be'xa*] *vi* to bellow; (*criança*) to bawl.
berreiro [be'xejru] *m* yelling; **abrir o ~** to burst out crying.
berro ['bɛxu] *m* yell.
besouro [be'zoru] *m* beetle.
besta ['beʃta] *adj* (*tolo*) stupid; (*convencido*) full of oneself; (*pretensioso*) pretentious ♦ *f* (*animal*) beast; (*pessoa*) fool; **~ de carga** beast of burden; **ficar ~** (*col*: *surpreso*) to be amazed; **fazer alguém de ~** (*col*) to make a fool of sb.
bestar [beʃ'ta*] *vi* to laze around.
besteira [beʃ'tejra] *f* (*tolice*) foolishness; (*insignificância*) small thing; **dizer ~s** to talk nonsense; **fazer uma ~** to do something silly.
bestial [beʃ'tʃjaw] (*pl* **-ais**) *adj* bestial; (*repugnante*) repulsive.
bestialidade [beʃtʃjali'dadʒi] *f* bestiality.
bestificar [beʃtʃifi'ka*] *vt* to astonish, dumbfound.
best-seller ['bɛst'sɛle*] (*pl* **~s**) *m* best seller.
besuntar [bezũ'ta*] *vt* to smear, daub.
betão [be'tãw] (PT) *m* concrete.
beterraba [bete'xaba] *f* beetroot.
betoneira [beto'nejra] *f* cement mixer.
betume [be'tumi] *m* asphalt.
bexiga [be'ʃiga] *f* (*órgão*) bladder.
bezerro/a [be'zexu/a] *m/f* calf.
bianual [bja'nwaw] (*pl* **-ais**) *adj* biannual, twice yearly.
bibelô [bibe'lo] *m* ornament.
Bíblia ['biblja] *f* Bible.
bíblico/a ['bibliku/a] *adj* biblical.
bibliografia [bibljogra'fia] *f* bibliography.
biblioteca [bibljo'tɛka] *f* library; (*estante*) bookcase.
bibliotecário/a [bibljote'karju/a] *m/f* librarian.
biblioteconomia [bibljotekono'mia] *f* librarianship.
bica ['bika] *f* tap; (PT) black coffee, expresso; **suar em ~s** to drip with sweat.
bicada [bi'kada] *f* peck.
bicama [bi'kama] *f* pull-out bed.

bicar [bi'ka*] *vt* to peck.
bicarbonato [bikaxbo'natu] *m* bicarbonate.
bíceps ['biseps] *m inv* biceps.
bicha ['biʃa] *f* (*lombriga*) worm; (*PT*: *fila*) queue; (*BR*: *col*, *pej*: *homossexual*) queer.
bichado/a [bi'ʃadu/a] *adj* eaten away.
bicheiro [bi'ʃejru] *m* (*illegal*) bookie.
bicho ['biʃu] *m* animal; (*inseto*) insect, bug; (*col*: *pessoa*: *intratável*) pain (in the neck); (: *feio*): **ela é um ~ (feio)** she's as ugly as sin; **virar ~** (*col*) to get mad; **ver que ~ dá** (*col*) to see what happens; **que ~ te mordeu?** what's got into you?
bicho-da-seda (*pl* **bichos-da-seda**) *m* silk worm.
bicho-de-sete-cabeças *m*: **fazer um ~** to make a mountain out of a molehill.
bicho-do-mato (*pl* **bichos-do-mato**) *m* extremely shy person.
bicho-papão [-pa'pãw] (*pl* **bichos-papões**) *m* bogeyman.
bicicleta [bisi'klɛta] *f* bicycle; (*col*) bike; **andar de ~** to cycle.
bico ['biku] *m* (*de ave*) beak; (*ponta*) point; (*de chaleira*) spout; (*boca*) mouth; (*de pena*) nib; (*do peito*) nipple; (*de gás*) jet; (*col*: *emprego*) job; (*chupeta*) dummy; **calar o ~** to shut up; **não abrir o ~** not to say a word; **fazer ~** to sulk.
bicudo/a [bi'kudu/a] *adj* pointed; (*difícil*) tricky.
BID *abr m* = **Banco Interamericano de Desenvolvimento**.
bidê [bi'de] *m* bidet.
bidimensional [bidʒimẽsjo'naw] (*pl* **-ais**) *adj* two-dimensional.
bidirecional [bidʒiresjo'naw] (*pl* **-ais**) *adj* bidirectional.
biela ['bjɛla] *f* con(necting) rod.
bienal [bje'naw] (*pl* **-ais**) *adj* biennial ♦ *f* (biennial) art exhibition.
bife ['bifi] *m* (beef) steak; **~ a cavalo** steak with fried eggs; **~ à milanesa** beef escalope; **~ de panela** beef stew.
bifocal [bifo'kaw] (*pl* **-ais**) *adj* bifocal.
bifurcação [bifuxka'sãw] (*pl* **-ões**) *f* fork.
bifurcar-se [bifux'kaxsi] *vr* to fork, divide.
bigamia [biga'mia] *f* bigamy.
bígamo/a ['bigamu/a] *adj* bigamous ♦ *m/f* bigamist.
bigode [bi'gɔdʒi] *m* moustache.
bigodudo/a [bigo'dudu/a] *adj* with a big moustache.
bigorna [bi'gɔxna] *f* anvil.
bijuteria [biʒute'ria] *f* (costume) jewellery (*BRIT*) *ou* jewelry (*US*).
bilateral [bilate'raw] (*pl* **-ais**) *adj* bilateral.
bilhão [bi'ʎãw] (*pl* **-ões**) *m* billion.
bilhar [bi'ʎa*] *m* (*jogo*) billiards *sg*.
bilhete [bi'ʎetʃi] *m* ticket; (*cartinha*) note; **~ de ida** single (*BRIT*) *ou* one-way ticket; **~ de ida e volta** return (*BRIT*) *ou* round-trip (*US*) ticket; **o ~ azul** (*fig*) the sack.
bilheteira [biʎe'tejra] (*PT*) *f* = **bilheteria**; *V tb* **bilheteiro**.
bilheteiro/a [biʎe'tejru/a] *m/f* ticket seller.
bilheteria [biʎete'ria] *f* ticket office; (*TEATRO*) box office; **sucesso de ~** box-office success.
bilhões [bi'ʎõjʃ] *mpl de* **bilhão**.
bilíngüe [bi'lĩgwi] *adj* bilingual.
bilionário/a [biljo'narju/a] *adj*, *m/f* billionaire.
bilioso/a [bi'ljozu/ɔza] *adj* bilious, liverish; (*fig*) bad-tempered.
bílis ['biliʃ] *m* bile.
bimensal [bimẽ'saw] (*pl* **-ais**) *adj* twice-monthly.
bimestral [bimeʃ'traw] (*pl* **-ais**) *adj* two-monthly.
bimotor [bimo'to*] *adj* twin-engined.
binário/a [bi'narju/a] *adj* binary.
bingo ['bĩgu] *m* bingo.
binóculo [bi'nɔkulu] *m* binoculars *pl*; (*para teatro*) opera glasses *pl*.
biodegradável [bjodegra'davew] (*pl* **-eis**) *adj* biodegradable.
biografia [bjogra'fia] *f* biography.
biográfico/a [bjo'grafiku/a] *adj* biographical.
biógrafo/a ['bjɔgrafu/a] *m/f* biographer.
biologia [bjolo'ʒia] *f* biology.
biológico/a [bjo'lɔʒiku/a] *adj* biological.
biólogo/a ['bjɔlogu/a] *m/f* biologist.
biombo ['bjõbu] *m* (*tapume*) screen.
biônico/a ['bjoniku/a] *adj* bionic; (*POL*: *senador*) non-elected.
biópsia ['bjɔpsja] *f* biopsy.
bioquímica [bjo'kimika] *f* biochemistry.
bipartidarismo [bipaxtʃida'riʒmu] *m* two-party system.
bipartidário/a [bipaxtʃi'darju/a] *adj* two-party *atr*, bipartite.
biquíni [bi'kini] *m* bikini.
BIRD *abr m* = **Banco Internacional de Reconstrução e Desenvolvimento**.
birita [bi'rita] (*col*) *f* drink.
birmanês/esa [bixma'neʃ/eza] *adj*, *m/f* Burmese ♦ *m* (*LING*) Burmese.
Birmânia [bix'manja] *f*: **a ~** Burma.
birô [bi'ro] *m* (*COMPUT*) bureau.
birra ['bixa] *f* (*teima*) wilfulness (*BRIT*), willfulness (*US*), obstinacy; (*aversão*) aversion; **fazer ~** to have a tantrum; **ter ~ com** to dislike.
birrento/a [bi'xẽtu/a] *adj* stubborn, obstinate.
biruta [bi'ruta] *adj* crazy ♦ *f* windsock.
bis [biʃ] *excl* encore!
bisar [bi'za*] *vt* (*suj*: *público*) to ask for an encore of; (: *artista*) to do an encore of.
bisavô/ó [biza'vo/ɔ] *m/f* great-grandfather/great-grandmother.
bisavós [biza'vɔʃ] *mpl* great-grandparents.

***NB**: European Portuguese adds the following consonants to certain words:* **b** (sú(b)dito, su(b)til); **c** (a(c)ção, a(c)cionista, a(c)to); **m** (inde(m)ne); **p** (ado(p)ção, ado(p)tar); *for further details see p. xiii.*

bisbilhotar [biʒbiʎo'ta*] *vt* to pry into ♦ *vi* to snoop.
bisbilhoteiro/a [biʒbiʎo'tejru/a] *adj* prying ♦ *m/f* snoop.
bisbilhotice [biʒbiʎo'tʃisi] *f* prying.
Biscaia [biʃ'kaja] *f*: **o golfo de ~** the Bay of Biscay.
biscate [biʃ'katʃi] *m* odd job.
biscateiro/a [biʃka'tejru/a] *m/f* odd-job person.
biscoito [biʃ'kojtu] *m* biscuit (*BRIT*), cookie (*US*); **~ amanteigado** shortbread.
bisnaga [biʒ'naga] *f* (*tubo*) tube; (*pão*) French stick.
bisneto/a [biʒ'nɛtu/a] *m/f* great-grandson/great-granddaughter; **~s** *mpl* great-grandchildren.
bisonho/a [bi'zɔɲu/a] *adj* inexperienced ♦ *m/f* newcomer.
bispado [biʃ'padu] *m* bishopric.
bispo ['biʃpu] *m* bishop.
bissemanal [bisema'naw] (*pl* **-ais**) *adj* twice-weekly.
bissexto/a [bi'seʃtu/a] *adj V* **ano**.
bissexual [bisek'swaw] (*pl* **-ais**) *adj*, *m/f* bisexual.
bisturi [biʃtu'ri] *m* scalpel.
bit ['bitʃi] *m* (*COMPUT*) bit.
bitola [bi'tɔla] *f* gauge (*BRIT*), gage (*US*); (*padrão*) pattern; (*estalão*) standard.
bitolado/a [bito'ladu/a] *adj* narrow-minded.
bizarro/a [bi'zaxu/a] *adj* bizarre.
blablablá [blabla'bla] (*col*) *m* chitchat.
black-tie ['blɛktaj] *m* evening dress.
blasé [bla'zɛ] *adj* blasé.
blasfemar [blaʃfe'ma*] *vt* to curse ♦ *vi* to blaspheme, curse.
blasfêmia [blaʃ'femja] *f* blasphemy; (*ultraje*) swearing.
blasfemo/a [blaʃ'femu/a] *adj* blasphemous ♦ *m/f* blasphemer.
blazer ['blejze*] (*pl* **~s**) *m* blazer.
blecaute [ble'kawtʃi] *m* power cut.
blefar [ble'fa*] *vi* to bluff.
blefe ['blɛfi] *m* bluff.
blindado/a [blĩ'dadu/a] *adj* armoured (*BRIT*), armored (*US*).
blindagem [blĩ'daʒẽ] *f* armo(u)r(-plating).
blitz [blits] *f* police raid; (*na estrada*) police spot-check.
bloco ['blɔku] *m* block; (*POL*) bloc; (*de escrever*) writing pad; **voto em ~** block vote; **~ de carnaval** carnival troupe; **~ de cilindros** cylinder block.
bloquear [blo'kja*] *vt* to blockade; (*obstruir*) to block.
bloqueio [blo'keju] *m* (*MIL*) blockade; (*obstrução*) blockage; (*PSICO*) mental block.
blusa ['bluza] *f* (*de mulher*) blouse; (*de homem*) shirt; **~ de lã** jumper.
blusão [blu'zãw] (*pl* **-ões**) *m* jacket.
BMeF (*BR*) *abr f* = **Bolsa Mercantil e de Futuros**.
BMSP *abr f* = **Bolsa de Mercadorias de São Paulo**.
BNDES *abr m* (= *Banco Nacional de Desenvolvimento Econômico e Social*) Brazilian development bank.
BNH (*BR*) *abr m* (= *Banco Nacional da Habitação*) home-funding bank.
boa ['boa] *adj f de* **bom** ♦ *f* boa constrictor.
boa-gente *adj inv* nice.
boa-pinta (*pl* **boas-pintas**) *adj* handsome.
boa-praça (*pl* **boas-praças**) *adj* nice.
boate ['bwatʃi] *f* nightclub.
boateiro/a [bwa'tejru/a] *adj* gossipy ♦ *m/f* gossip.
boato ['bwatu] *m* rumour (*BRIT*), rumor (*US*).
boa-vida (*pl* **boas-vidas**) *m/f* loafer.
bobagem [bo'baʒẽ] (*pl* **-ns**) *f* silliness, nonsense; (*dito, ato*) silly thing; **deixe de bobagens!** stop being silly!
bobeada [bo'bjada] *f* slip-up.
bobear [bo'bja*] *vi* to miss out.
bobice [bo'bisi] *f* silliness, nonsense; (*dito, ato*) silly thing.
bobina [bo'bina] *f* reel, bobbin; (*ELET*) coil; (*FOTO*) spool; (*de papel*) roll.
bobo/a ['bobu/a] *adj* silly, daft ♦ *m/f* fool ♦ *m* (*de corte*) jester; **fazer-se de ~** to act the fool.
bobó [bo'bɔ] *m beans, palm oil and manioc.*
boboca [bo'bɔka] *adj* silly ♦ *m/f* fool.
boca ['boka] *f* mouth; (*entrada*) entrance; (*de fogão*) ring; **de ~** orally; **de ~ aberta** open-mouthed, amazed; **bater ~** to argue; **botar a ~ no mundo** (*berrar*) to scream; (*revelar*) to spill the beans; **falar da ~ para fora** to say one thing and mean another; **ser boa ~** to eat anything; **vira essa ~ para lá!** don't tempt providence!; **~ da noite** nightfall.
boca-de-fumo (*pl* **bocas-de-fumo**) *f* drug den.
boca-de-sino *adj inv* bell-bottomed.
bocadinho [boka'dʒiɲu] *m*: **um ~** (*pouco tempo*) a little while; (*pouquinho*) a little bit.
bocado [bo'kadu] *m* (*quantidade na boca*) mouthful, bite; (*pedaço*) piece, bit; **um ~ de tempo** quite some time.
bocal [bo'kaw] (*pl* **-ais**) *m* (*de vaso*) mouth; (*MÚS, de aparelho*) mouthpiece; (*de cano*) nozzle.
boçal [bo'saw] (*pl* **-ais**) *adj* ignorant; (*grosseiro*) uncouth.
boçalidade [bosali'dadʒi] *f* coarseness; (*ignorância*) ignorance.
boca-livre (*pl* **bocas-livres**) *f* free meal.
bocejar [bose'ʒa*] *vi* to yawn.
bocejo [bo'seʒu] *m* yawn.
bochecha [bo'ʃeʃa] *f* cheek.
bochechar [boʃe'ʃa*] *vi* to rinse one's mouth.
bochecho [bo'ʃeʃu] *m* mouthwash.
bochechudo/a [boʃe'ʃudu/a] *adj* puffy-cheeked.
boda ['boda] *f* wedding; **~s** *fpl* wedding anniversary *sg*; **~s de prata/ouro** silver/golden wedding *sg*.

bode ['bɔdʒɪ] *m* goat; ~ **expiatório** scapegoat; **vai dar** ~ (*col*) there'll be trouble.
bodega [bo'dɛga] *f* piece of rubbish.
bodum [bo'dũ] *m* stink.
boêmio/a [bo'emju/a] *adj*, *m/f* Bohemian.
bofetada [bofe'tada] *f* slap.
bofetão [bofe'tãw] (*pl* **-ões**) *m* punch.
Bogotá [bogo'ta] *n* Bogota.
boi [boj] *m* ox; **pegar o** ~ **pelos chifres** (*fig*) to take the bull by the horns.
bói [bɔj] *m* office boy.
bóia ['bɔja] *f* buoy; (*col*) grub; (*de braço*) armband, water wing.
boiada [bo'jada] *f* herd of cattle.
bóia-fria (*pl* **bóias-frias**) *m/f* (*itinerant*) farm labourer (*BRIT*) *ou* laborer (*US*).
boiar [bo'ja*] *vt* to float ♦ *vi* to float; (*col*) to be lost; ~ **em** (*inglês etc*) to be hopeless at.
boicotar [bojko'ta*] *vt* to boycott.
boicote [boj'kɔtʃi] *m* boycott.
boiler ['bɔjla*] (*pl* **~s**) *m* boiler.
boina ['bojna] *f* beret.
bojo ['boʒu] *m* (*saliência*) bulge.
bojudo/a [bo'ʒudu/a] *adj* bulging; (*arredondado*) rounded.
bola ['bɔla] *f* ball; (*confusão*) confusion; **dar** ~ **(para)** (*col*) to care (about); (*dar atenção*) to pay attention (to); **dar** ~ **para** (*flertar*) to flirt with; **não dar** ~ **para alguém** to ignore sb; **ela não dá a menor** ~ **(para isso)** she couldn't care less (about it); **pisar na** ~ (*fig*) to make a mistake; **ser bom de** ~ to be good at football; **não ser certo da** ~ (*col*) not to be right in the head; **ser uma** ~ (*pessoa*: *gordo*) to be fat; (: *engraçado*) to be a real character; ~ **de futebol** football; ~ **de gude** marble; ~ **de neve** snowball.
bolacha [bo'laʃa] *f* biscuit (*BRIT*), cookie (*US*); (*col*: *bofetada*) wallop; (*para chope*) beermat.
bolada [bo'lada] *f* (*dinheiro*) lump sum.
bolar [bo'la*] *vt* to think up; **bem bolado** clever.
bole ['bɔli] *etc vb V* **bulir**.
boleia [bo'leja] *f* driver's seat; **dar uma** ~ (*PT*) to give a lift.
boletim [bole'tʃĩ] (*pl* **-ns**) *m* report; (*publicação*) newsletter; (*EDUC*) report; ~ **meteorológico** weather forecast.
bolha ['boʎa] *f* (*na pele*) blister; (*de ar, sabão*) bubble ♦ *m/f* (*col*) fool.
boliche [bo'liʃi] *m* (*jogo*) bowling, skittles *sg*.
bolinar [boli'na*] *vt*: ~ **alguém** (*col*) to feel sb up.
bolinho [bo'liɲu] *m*: ~ **de carne** meat ball; ~ **de arroz/bacalhau** rice/dry cod cake.
Bolívia [bo'livja] *f*: **a** ~ Bolivia.
boliviano/a [boli'vjanu/a] *adj*, *m/f* Bolivian.
bolo ['bolu] *m* cake; **dar o** ~ **em alguém** to stand sb up; **vai dar** ~ (*col*) there's going to be trouble; **um** ~ **de gente/papéis** a bundle of people/papers.
bolor [bo'lo*] *m* mould (*BRIT*), mold (*US*); (*nas plantas*) mildew; (*bafio*) mustiness.
bolorento/a [bolo'rẽtu/a] *adj* mouldy (*BRIT*), moldy (*US*).
bolota [bo'lɔta] *f* acorn.
bolsa ['bowsa] *f* bag; (*COM*: *tb*: ~ *de valores*) stock exchange; ~ **(de estudos)** scholarship; ~ **de mercadorias** commodities market.
bolsista [bow'siʃta] *m/f* scholarship holder.
bolso ['bowsu] *m* pocket; **dicionário de** ~ pocket dictionary.
bom/boa [bõ/'boa] *adj* good; (*bondoso*) nice, kind; (*de saúde*) well; (*tempo*) fine; **um** ~ **quarto de hora** a good quarter of an hour; **essa é boa!** that's a good one!; **numa boa** (*col*) well; **metido numa boa** in a tight spot; **estar numa boa** (*col*) to be doing fine; **~, ...** right, ...; **está ~?** OK?; **tudo ~?** how's it going?; **ficar** ~ (*trabalho*) to turn out well; (*de saúde*) to get better; **acho** ~ **você não fazer** I think it's better if you don't do; ~ **dia** good morning; **dar** ~ **dia em alguém** to say good morning to sb.
bomba ['bõba] *f* (*MIL*) bomb; (*TEC*) pump; (*CULIN*) éclair; (*fig*) bombshell; ~ **atômica/de fumaça/relógio** atomic/smoke/time bomb; ~ **de gasolina** petrol (*BRIT*) *ou* gas (*US*) pump; ~ **de incêndio** fire extinguisher; **levar** ~ (*em exame*) to fail.
bombada [bõ'bada] *f* (*prejuízo*) loss.
Bombaim [bõba'ĩ] *n* Bombay.
bombardear [bõbax'dʒja*] *vt* to bomb, bombard; (*fig*) to bombard.
bombardeio [bõbax'deju] *m* bombing, bombardment.
bomba-relógio (*pl* **bombas-relógio**) *f* time bomb.
bombástico/a [bõ'baʃtʃiku/a] *adj* pompous.
bombear [bõ'bja*] *vt* to pump.
bombeiro [bõ'bejru] *m* fireman; (*BR*: *encanador*) plumber; **o corpo de ~s** fire brigade.
bombom [bõ'bõ] (*pl* **-ns**) *m* chocolate.
bombordo [bõ'bɔxdu] *m* (*NÁUT*) port.
bonachão/chona [bona'ʃãw/'ʃɔna] (*pl* **-ões/~s**) *adj* simple and kind-hearted.
bonança [bo'nãsa] *f* fair weather; (*fig*) calm.
bondade [bõ'dadʒi] *f* goodness, kindness; **tenha a** ~ **de vir** would you please come.
bonde ['bõdʒi] (*BR*) *m* tram.
bondoso/a [bõ'dozu/ɔza] *adj* kind, good.
boné [bo'nɛ] *m* cap.
boneca [bo'nɛka] *f* doll.
boneco [bo'neku] *m* dummy.
bonificação [bonifika'sãw] (*pl* **-ões**) *f* bonus.
bonina [bo'nina] (*PT*) *f* daisy.
boníssimo/a [bo'nisimu/a] *adj superl de* **bom/boa**.

***NB**: European Portuguese adds the following consonants to certain words:* **b** (sú(b)dito, su(b)til); **c** (a(c)ção, a(c)cionista, a(c)to); **m** (inde(m)ne); **p** (ado(p)ção, ado(p)tar); *for further details see p. xiii.*

bonitão/tona [boni'tãw/'tɔna] (*pl* **-ões/~s**) *adj* very attractive.
bonito/a [bo'nitu/a] *adj* (*belo*) pretty; (*gesto, dia*) nice ♦ *m* (*peixe*) tunny; **fazer um ~** to do a good deed.
bonitões [boni'tõjʃ] *mpl de* **bonitão**.
bonitona [boni'tɔna] *f de* **bonitão**.
bônus ['bonuʃ] *m inv* bonus.
boquiaberto/a [bokja'bɛxtu/a] *adj* dumbfounded, astonished.
borboleta [boxbo'leta] *f* butterfly; (*BR*: *roleta*) turnstile.
borboletear [boxbole'tʃja*] *vi* to flutter, flit.
borbotão [boxbo'tãw] (*pl* **-ões**) *m* gush, spurt; **sair aos borbotões** to gush out.
borbulhante [boxbu'ʎãtʃi] *adj* bubbling.
borbulhar [boxbu'ʎa*] *vi* to bubble; (*jorrar*) to gush out.
borco ['boxku] *m*: **de ~** (*coisa*) upside down; (*pessoa*) face down.
borda ['bɔxda] *f* edge; (*do rio*) bank; **à ~ de** on the edge of.
bordado [box'dadu] *m* embroidery.
bordão [box'dãw] (*pl* **-ões**) *m* staff; (*MÚS*) bass string; (*arrimo*) support; (*frase*) catch-phrase.
bordar [box'da*] *vt* to embroider.
bordejar [boxde'ʒa*] *vi* (*NÁUT*) to tack.
bordel [box'dɛw] (*pl* **-éis**) *m* brothel.
bordo ['bɔxdu] *m* (*ao bordejar*) tack; (*de navio*) side; **a ~** on board.
bordoada [box'dwada] *f* blow.
bordões [box'dõjʃ] *mpl de* **bordão**.
borla ['bɔxla] *f* tassel.
borocoxô [boroko'ʃo] *adj* dispirited.
borra ['boxa] *f* dregs *pl*.
borracha [bo'xaʃa] *f* rubber.
borracheiro [boxa'ʃejru] *m* tyre (*BRIT*) *ou* tire (*US*) specialist.
borracho/a [bo'xaʃu/a] *adj* drunk ♦ *m/f* drunk(ard).
borrador [boxa'do*] *m* (*COM*) day book.
borrão [bo'xãw] (*pl* **-ões**) *m* (*rascunho*) rough draft; (*mancha*) blot.
borrar [bo'xa*] *vt* to blot; (*riscar*) to cross out; (*pintar*) to daub; (*sujar*) to dirty.
borrasca [bo'xaʃka] *f* storm; (*no mar*) squall.
borrifar [boxi'fa*] *vt* to sprinkle.
borrifo [bo'xifu] *m* spray.
borrões [bo'xõjʃ] *mpl de* **borrão**.
bosque ['bɔʃki] *m* wood, forest.
bossa ['bɔsa] *f* (*charme*) charm; (*inchaço*) swelling; (*no crânio*) bump; (*corcova*) hump; **ter ~ para** to have an aptitude for.
bosta ['bɔʃta] *f* dung; (*de humanos*) excrement.
bota ['bɔta] *f* boot; **~s de borracha** wellingtons; **bater as ~s** (*col*) to kick the bucket.
bota-fora (*pl* **~s**) *f* (*despedida*) send-off.
botânica [bo'tanika] *f* botany; *V tb* **botânico**.
botânico/a [bo'taniku/a] *adj* botanical ♦ *m/f* botanist.
botão [bo'tãw] (*pl* **-ões**) *m* button; (*flor*) bud; **dizer com os seus botões** (*fig*) to say to o.s.
botar [bo'ta*] *vt* to put; (*PT*: *lançar*) to throw; (*roupa, sapatos*) to put on; (*mesa*) to set; (*defeito*) to find; (*ovos*) to lay; **~ para quebrar** (*col*) to go for broke, go all out; **~ em dia** to get up to date.
bote ['bɔtʃi] *m* (*barco*) boat; (*com arma*) thrust; (*salto*) spring; (*de cobra*) strike.
boteco [bo'tɛku] (*col*) *m* bar.
botequim [botʃi'kĩ] (*pl* **-ns**) *m* bar.
boticário/a [botʃi'karju/a] *m/f* pharmacist, chemist (*BRIT*).
botija [bo'tʃiʒa] *f* (earthenware) jug.
botina [bo'tʃina] *f* ankle boot.
botoeira [bo'twejra] *f* buttonhole.
botões [bo'tõjʃ] *mpl de* **botão**.
Botsuana [bot'swana] *f*: **a ~** Botswana.
Bovespa [bo'vɛʃpa] *abr f* = **Bolsa de Valores do Estado de São Paulo**.
bovino/a [bo'vinu/a] *adj* bovine.
boxe ['bɔksi] *m* boxing.
boxeador [boksja'do*] *m* boxer.
boy [bɔj] *m* = **bói**.
brabo/a ['brabu/a] *adj* (*feroz*) fierce; (*zangado*) angry; (*ruim*) bad; (*calor*) unbearable; (*gripe*) bad.
braça ['brasa] *f* (*NÁUT*) fathom.
braçada [bra'sada] *f* armful; (*NATAÇÃO*) stroke.
braçadeira [brasa'dejra] *f* armband; (*de cortina*) tie-back; (*metálica*) bracket; (*ESPORTE*) sweatband.
braçal [bra'saw] (*pl* **-ais**) *adj* manual.
bracejar [brase'ʒa*] *vi* to wave one's arms about.
bracelete [brase'letʃi] *m* bracelet.
braço ['brasu] *m* arm; (*trabalhador*) hand; **~ direito** (*fig*) right-hand man; **a ~s com** struggling with; **de ~s cruzados** with arms folded; (*fig*) without lifting a finger; **de ~ dado** arm-in-arm; **cruzar os ~s** (*fig*) to down tools; **não dar o ~ a torcer** (*fig*) not to give in; **meter o ~ em** (*col*) to clobber; **receber de ~s abertos** (*fig*) to welcome with open arms.
bradar [bra'da*] *vt, vi* to shout, yell.
brado ['bradu] *m* shout, yell.
braguilha [bra'giʎa] *f* flies *pl*.
braile ['brajli] *m* braille.
bramido [bra'midu] *m* roar.
bramir [bra'mi*] *vi* to roar.
branco/a ['brãku/a] *adj* white ♦ *m/f* white man/woman ♦ *m* (*espaço*) blank; **em ~** blank; **noite em ~** sleepless night; **deu um ~ nele** he drew a blank.
brancura [brã'kura] *f* whiteness.
brandir [brã'dʒi*] *vt* to brandish.
brando/a ['brãdu/a] *adj* gentle; (*mole*) soft.
brandura [brã'dura] *f* gentleness; (*moleza*) softness.
branquear [brã'kja*] *vt* to whiten; (*alvejar*) to bleach ♦ *vi* to turn white.

brasa ['braza] *f* hot coal; **em ~** red-hot; **pisar em ~** to be on tenterhooks; **mandar ~** (*col*) to go for it; **puxar a ~ para a sua sardinha** (*col*) to look out for o.s.
brasão [bra'zãw] (*pl* **-ões**) *m* coat of arms.
braseiro [bra'zejru] *m* brazier.
Brasil [bra'ziw] *m*: **o ~** Brazil.
brasileirismo [brazilej'riʒmu] *m* Brazilianism.
brasileiro/a [brazi'lejru/a] *adj*, *m/f* Brazilian.
Brasília [bra'zilja] *n* Brasília.
brasilianista [brazilja'niʃta] *m/f* Brazilianist.
brasiliense [brazi'ljẽsi] *adj* from Brasília ♦ *m/f* person from Brasília.
brasões [bra'zõjʃ] *mpl de* **brasão**.
bravata [bra'vata] *f* bravado, boasting.
bravatear [brava'tʃja*] *vi* to boast, brag.
bravio/a [bra'viu/a] *adj* (*selvagem*) wild, untamed; (*feroz*) ferocious.
bravo/a ['bravu/a] *adj* (*corajoso*) brave; (*furioso*) angry; (*mar*) rough, stormy ♦ *m* brave man; **~!** bravo!
bravura [bra'vura] *f* courage, bravery.
breca ['brɛka] *f*: **ser levado da ~** to be very naughty.
brecar [bre'ka*] *vt* (*carro*) to stop; (*reprimir*) to curb ♦ *vi* to brake.
brecha ['brɛʃa] *f* breach; (*abertura*) opening; (*dano*) damage; (*meio de escapar*) loophole; (*col*) chance.
brega ['brɛga] (*col*) *adj* tacky.
brejeiro/a [bre'ʒejru/a] *adj* impish.
brejo ['brɛʒu] *m* marsh, swamp; **ir para o ~** (*fig*) to go down the drain.
brenha ['brɛɲa] *f* (*mata*) dense wood.
breque ['brɛki] *m* (*freio*) brake.
breu [brew] *m* tar, pitch; **escuro como ~** pitch black.
breve ['brɛvi] *adj* short; (*conciso, rápido*) brief ♦ *adv* soon; **em ~** soon, shortly; **até ~** see you soon.
brevê [bre've] *m* pilot's licence (*BRIT*) *ou* license (*US*).
brevidade [brevi'dadʒi] *f* brevity, shortness.
bridge ['bridʒi] *m* bridge.
briga ['briga] *f* (*luta*) fight; (*verbal*) quarrel.
brigada [bri'gada] *f* brigade.
brigadeiro [briga'dejru] *m* brigadier; (*doce*) chocolate truffle.
brigão/ona [bri'gãw/ɔna] (*pl* **-ões/~s**) *adj* quarrelsome ♦ *m/f* troublemaker.
brigar [bri'ga*] *vi* (*lutar*) to fight; (*altercar*) to quarrel.
brigões [bri'gõjʃ] *mpl de* **brigão**.
brigona [bri'gɔna] *f de* **brigão**.
briguei [bri'gej] *etc vb V* **brigar**.
brilhante [bri'ʎãtʃi] *adj* brilliant ♦ *m* diamond.
brilhar [bri'ʎa*] *vi* to shine.
brilho ['briʎu] *m* (*luz viva*) brilliance; (*esplendor*) splendour (*BRIT*), splendor (*US*); (*nos sapatos*) shine; (*de metais, olhos*) gleam.
brincadeira [brĩka'dejra] *f* (*divertimento*) fun; (*gracejo*) joke; (*de criança*) game; **deixe de ~s!** stop fooling!; **de ~** for fun; **fora de ~** joking apart; **não é ~** it's no joke.
brincalhão/ona [brĩka'ʎãw/ɔna] (*pl* **-ões/~s**) *adj* playful ♦ *m/f* joker, teaser.
brincar [brĩ'ka*] *vi* to play; (*gracejar*) to joke; **estou brincando** I'm only kidding; **~ de soldados** to play (at) soldiers; **~ com alguém** (*mexer com*) to tease sb.
brinco ['brĩku] *m* (*jóia*) earring; **estar um ~** to be spotless.
brindar [brĩ'da*] *vt* (*beber*) to drink to; (*presentear*) to give a present to.
brinde ['brĩdʒi] *m* (*saudação*) toast; (*presente*) free gift.
brinquedo [brĩ'kedu] *m* toy.
brinquei [brĩ'kej] *etc vb V* **brincar**.
brio ['briu] *m* self-respect, dignity.
brioso/a ['brjozu/ɔza] *adj* self-respecting.
brisa ['briza] *f* breeze.
britânico/a [bri'taniku/a] *adj* British ♦ *m/f* Briton.
broca ['brɔka] *f* drill.
broche ['brɔʃi] *m* brooch.
brochura [bro'ʃura] *f* (*livro*) paperback; (*folheto*) brochure, pamphlet.
brócolis ['brɔkoliʃ] *mpl* broccoli *sg*.
brócolos ['brɔkoluʃ] (*PT*) *mpl* = **brócolis**.
bronca ['brõka] (*col*) *f* telling off; **dar uma ~ em** to tell off; **levar uma ~** to get told off.
bronco/a ['brõku/a] *adj* (*rude*) coarse; (*burro*) thick.
bronquear [brõ'kja*] (*col*) *vi* to get angry; **~ com** to tell off.
bronquite [brõ'kitʃi] *f* bronchitis.
bronze ['brõzi] *m* bronze.
bronzeado/a [brõ'zjadu/a] *adj* (*da cor do bronze*) bronze; (*pelo sol*) suntanned ♦ *m* suntan.
bronzear [brõ'zja*] *vt* to tan; **~-se** *vr* to get a tan.
brotar [bro'ta*] *vt* to produce ♦ *vi* (*manar*) to flow; (*BOT*) to sprout; (*nascer*) to spring up.
brotinho/a [bro'tʃiɲu/a] *m/f* teenager.
broto ['brotu] *m* bud; (*fig*) youngster.
broxa ['brɔʃa] *f* (large) paint brush.
bruços ['brusuʃ]: **de ~** *adv* face down.
bruma ['bruma] *f* mist, haze.
brumoso/a [bru'mozu/ɔza] *adj* misty, hazy.
brunido/a [bru'nidu/a] *adj* polished.
brunir [bru'ni*] *vt* to polish.
brusco/a ['bruʃku/a] *adj* brusque; (*súbito*) sudden.
brutal [bru'taw] (*pl* **-ais**) *adj* brutal.
brutalidade [brutali'dadʒi] *f* brutality.
brutamontes [bruta'mõtʃiʃ] *m inv* (*corpulento*) hulk; (*bruto*) brute.
bruto/a ['brutu/a] *adj* brutish; (*grosseiro*)

NB*: European Portuguese adds the following consonants to certain words:* **b** (sú(b)dito, su(b)til); **c** (a(c)ção, a(c)cionista, a(c)to); **m** (inde(m)ne); **p** (ado(p)ção, ado(p)tar); *for further details see p. xiii.*

coarse; (*móvel*) heavy; (*diamante*) uncut; (*petróleo*) crude; (*peso*, *COM*) gross; (*agressivo*) aggressive ♦ *m* brute; **em ~** raw, unworked; **um ~ resfriado** an awful cold.
bruxa ['bruʃa] *f* witch; (*velha feia*) hag.
bruxaria [bruʃa'ria] *f* witchcraft.
Bruxelas [bru'ʃelaʃ] *n* Brussels.
bruxo ['bruʃu] *m* wizard.
bruxulear [bruʃu'lja*] *vi* to flicker.
BTN (*BR*) *abr m* (= *Bônus do Tesouro Nacional*) *government bond used to quote prices*.
Bucareste [buka'rɛʃtʃi] *n* Bucharest.
bucha ['buʃa] *f* (*para parafuso*) rawlplug ®; (*para buracos*) bung; **acertar na ~** (*fig*) to hit the nail on the head.
bucho ['buʃu] (*col*) *m* gut; **ela é um ~ (feio)** she's as ugly as sin.
buço ['busu] *m* down.
Budapest [buda'pɛʃtʃi] *n* Budapest.
budismo [bu'dʒiʒmu] *m* Buddhism.
budista [bu'dʒiʃta] *adj*, *m/f* Buddhist.
bueiro [bu'ejru] *m* storm drain.
Buenos Aires ['bwɛnuz'ajriʃ] *n* Buenos Aires.
búfalo ['bufalu] *m* buffalo.
bufante [bu'fãtʃi] *adj* puffed, full.
bufar [bu'fa*] *vi* to puff, pant; (*com raiva*) to snort; (*reclamar*) to moan, grumble.
bufê [bu'fe] *m* (*móvel*) sideboard; (*comida*) buffet; (*serviço*) catering service.
buffer ['bafe*] (*pl* **~s**) *m* (*COMPUT*) buffer.
bugiganga [buʒi'gãga] *f* trinket; **~s** *fpl* knicknacks.
bujão [bu'ʒãw] (*pl* **-ões**) *m* (*TEC*) cap; **~ de gás** gas cylinder.
bula ['bula] *f* (*REL*) papal bull; (*MED*) directions *pl* for use.
bulbo ['buwbu] *m* bulb.
buldôzer [buw'doze*] (*pl* **~es**) *m* bulldozer.
bule ['buli] *m* (*de chá*) tea pot; (*de café*) coffeepot.
Bulgária [buw'garja] *f*: **a ~** Bulgaria.
búlgaro/a ['buwgaru/a] *adj*, *m/f* Bulgarian ♦ *m* (*LING*) Bulgarian.
bulha ['buʎa] *f* row.
bulhufas [bu'ʎufaʃ] (*col*) *pron* nothing.
bulício [bu'lisju] *m* (*agitação*) bustle; (*sussurro*) rustling.
buliçoso/a [buli'sozu/ɔza] *adj* (*vivo*) lively; (*agitado*) restless.
bulir [bu'li*] *vt* to move ♦ *vi* to move, stir; **~ com** to tease; **~ em** to touch, meddle with.
bumbum [bũ'bũ] (*pl* **-ns**) (*col*) *m* bottom.
bunda ['bũda] (*col*) *f* bottom, backside.
buquê [bu'ke] *m* bouquet.
buraco [bu'raku] *m* hole; (*de agulha*) eye; (*jogo*) rummy; **ser um ~** (*difícil*) to be tough; **~ da fechadura** keyhole.
burburinho [buxbu'riɲu] *m* hubbub; (*murmúrio*) murmur.
burguês/guesa [bux'geʃ/'geza] *adj* middle-class, bourgeois.
burguesia [buxge'zia] *f* middle class, bourgeoisie.
buril [bu'riw] (*pl* **-is**) *m* chisel.
burilar [buri'la*] *vt* to chisel.
buris [bu'riʃ] *mpl de* **buril**.
Burkina [bux'kina] *m*: **o ~** Burkina Faso.
burla ['buxla] *f* trick, fraud; (*zombaria*) mockery.
burlar [bux'la*] *vt* (*enganar*) to cheat; (*defraudar*) to swindle; (*a lei*, *impostos*) to evade.
burlesco/a [bux'leʃku/a] *adj* burlesque.
burocracia [burokra'sia] *f* bureaucracy; (*excessiva*) red tape.
burocrata [buro'krata] *m/f* bureaucrat.
burocrático/a [buro'kratʃiku/a] *adj* bureaucratic.
burrice [bu'xisi] *f* stupidity.
burro/a ['buxu/a] *adj* stupid; (*pouco inteligente*) dim, thick ♦ *m/f* (*ZOOL*) donkey; (*pessoa*) fool, idiot; **pra ~** (*col*) a lot; (*com adj*) really; **dar com os ~s n'água** (*fig*) to come a cropper; **~ de carga** (*fig*) hard worker.
Burundi [burũ'dʒi] *m*: **o ~** Burundi.
busca ['buʃka] *f* search; **em ~ de** in search of; **dar ~ a** to search for.
busca-pé [buʃka'pɛ] (*pl* **~s**) *m* banger.
buscar [buʃ'ka*] *vt* to fetch; (*procurar*) to look *ou* search for; **ir ~** to fetch, go for; **mandar ~** to send for.
busquei [buʃ'kej] *etc vb V* **buscar**.
bússola ['busola] *f* compass.
bustiê [buʃtʃi'e*] *m* boob tube.
busto ['buʃtu] *m* bust.
butique [bu'tʃiki] *m* boutique.
buzina [bu'zina] *f* horn.
buzinada [buzi'nada] *f* toot, hoot.
buzinar [buzi'na*] *vi* to sound one's horn, toot the horn ♦ *vt* to hoot; **~ nos ouvidos de alguém** (*fig*) to hassle sb; **~ algo nos ouvidos de alguém** (*fig*) to drum sth into sb.
búzio ['buzju] *m* (*concha*) conch.
BVRJ *abr f* = **Bolsa de Valores do Rio de Janeiro**.

C

C [se] (*pl* **cs**) *m* C, c; **C de Carlos** C for Charlie.
c/ *abr* = **com**.
Ca *abr* (= *companhia*) Co.
cá [ka] *adv* here; **de ~** on this side; **para ~** here, over here; **para lá e para ~** back and forth; **de lá para ~** since then; **de um ano para ~** in the last year; **~ entre nós** just between us.

caatinga [ka'tʃĩga] (*BR*) *f* scrub(-land).
cabal [ka'baw] (*pl* **-ais**) *adj* (*completo*) complete; (*exato*) exact.
cabala [ka'bala] *f* (*maquinação*) conspiracy, intrigue.
cabalar [kaba'la*] *vt* (*votos etc*) to canvass (for) ♦ *vi* to canvass.
cabana [ka'bana] *f* hut.
cabaré [kaba'rɛ] *m* (*boate*) night club.
cabeça [ka'besa] *f* head; (*inteligência*) brain; (*de uma lista*) top ♦ *m/f* (*de uma revolta*) leader; (*de uma organização*) brains *sg*; **cinqüenta ~s de gado** fifty head of cattle; **de ~** out of one's head, off the top of one's head; (*calcular*) in one's head; **de ~ para baixo** upside down; **por ~** per person, per head; **deu-lhe na ~ de** he took it into his head to; **esquentar a ~** (*col*) to lose one's cool; **não estar com a ~ para fazer** not to feel like doing; **fazer a ~ de alguém** (*col*) to talk sb into it; **levar na ~** (*col*) to come a cropper; **meter na ~** to get into one's head; **tirar algo da ~** to put sth out of one's mind; **perder a ~** to lose one's head; **quebrar a ~** to rack one's brains; **subir à ~** (*sucesso etc*) to go to sb's head; **com a ~ no ar** absent-minded; **~ fria** cool-headedness.
cabeçada [kabe'sada] *f* (*pancada com cabeça*) butt; (*FUTEBOL*) header; (*asneira*) blunder; **dar uma ~ (em)** to bang one's head (on); **dar uma ~** (*fazer asneira*) to make a blunder; **dar uma ~ na bola** (*FUTEBOL*) to head the ball.
cabeça-de-casal (*pl* **cabeças-de-casal**) *m* dominant partner.
cabeça-de-porco (*pl* **cabeças-de-porco**) (*col*) *f* tenement building.
cabeça-de-vento (*pl* **cabeças-de-vento**) *m/f* scatterbrain.
cabeçalho [kabe'saʎu] *m* (*de livro*) title page; (*de página, capítulo*) heading.
cabecear [kabe'sja*] *vt* (*FUTEBOL*) to head ♦ *vi* to nod; to play a header.
cabeceira [kabe'sejra] *f* (*de cama*) head; (*de mesa*) end; **leitura de ~** bedtime reading.
cabeçudo/a [kabe'sudu/a] *adj* big-headed; (*teimoso*) pigheaded.
cabedal [kabe'daw] (*pl* **-ais**) *m* wealth.
cabeleira [kabe'lejra] *f* head of hair; (*postiça*) wig.
cabeleireiro/a [kabelej'rejru/a] *m/f* hairdresser.
cabelo [ka'belu] *m* hair; **~ liso/crespo/pixaim** straight/curly/frizzy hair; **~ à escovinha** crew cut; **cortar/fazer o ~** to have one's hair cut/done; **ter ~ na venta** to be short-tempered.
cabeludo/a [kabe'ludu/a] *adj* hairy; (*difícil*) complicated; (*obsceno*) obscene.
caber [ka'be*] *vi*: **~ (em)** (*poder entrar*) to fit, go; (*roupa*) to fit; (*ser compatível*) to be appropriate (in); **~ a** (*em partilha*) to fall to; **cabe a alguém fazer** it is up to sb to do; **~ por** to fit through; **não cabe aqui fazer comentários** this is not the time or place to comment; **acho que cabe exigir um explicação** I think it is reasonable to demand an explanation; **são fatos que cabe apurar** they are facts which should be investigated; **tua dúvida cabe perfeitamente** your doubt is perfectly in order; **não ~ em si de** to be beside o.s. with.
cabide [ka'bidʒi] *m* (coat) hanger; (*móvel*) hat stand; (*fixo à parede*) coat rack; **~ de empregos** person who has several jobs.
cabideiro [kabi'dejru] *m* hatstand; (*na parede*) coat rack; (*para sapatos*) rack.
cabimento [kabi'mẽtu] *m* suitability; **ter ~** to be fitting *ou* appropriate; **não ter ~** to be inconceivable.
cabine [ka'bini] *f* cabin; (*em loja*) fitting room; **~ do piloto** (*AER*) cockpit; **~ telefônica** telephone booth.
cabisbaixo/a [kabiʒ'bajʃu/a] *adj* (*deprimido*) dispirited, crestfallen; (*com a cabeça para baixo*) head down.
cabível [ka'bivew] (*pl* **-eis**) *adj* conceivable.
cabo ['kabu] *m* (*extremidade*) end; (*de faca, vassoura etc*) handle; (*corda*) rope; (*elétrico etc*) cable; (*GEO*) cape; (*MIL*) corporal; **ao ~ de** at the end of; **de ~ a rabo** from beginning to end; **levar a ~** to carry out; **dar ~ de** to do away with; **~ eleitoral** canvasser.
caboclo/a [ka'boklu/a] (*BR*) *adj* copper-coloured (*BRIT*), copper-colored (*US*) ♦ *m/f* mestizo.
cabotino/a [kabo'tʃinu/a] *adj* ostentatious ♦ *m/f* show-off.
Cabo Verde *m* Cape Verde.
cabo-verdiano/a [-vex'dʒjanu/a] *adj, m/f* Cape Verdean.
cabra ['kabra] *f* goat ♦ *m* (*BR*: *sujeito*) guy; (: *capanga*) hired gun.
cabra-cega *f* blind man's buff.
cabra-macho (*pl* **cabras-machos**) *m* tough guy.
cabreiro/a [ka'brejru/a] (*col*) *adj* suspicious.
cabresto [kab'reʃtu] *m* (*de cavalos*) halter.
cabrito [ka'britu] *m* kid.
cabrocha [ka'brɔʃa] *f* mulatto girl.
caça ['kasa] *f* hunting; (*busca*) hunt; (*animal*) quarry, game ♦ *m* (*AER*) fighter (plane); **à ~ de** in pursuit of.
caçada [ka'sada] *f* (*jornada de caçadores*) hunting trip.
caçador(a) [kasa'do*(a)] *m/f* hunter.
caçamba [ka'sãba] *f* (*balde*) bucket.
caça-minas *m inv* minesweeper.
caça-níqueis *m inv* slot machine.
cação [ka'sãw] (*pl* **-ões**) *m* shark.

***NB**: European Portuguese adds the following consonants to certain words:* **b** (sú(b)dito, su(b)til); **c** (a(c)ção, a(c)cionista, a(c)to); **m** (inde(m)ne); **p** (ado(p)ção, ado(p)tar); *for further details see p. xiii.*

caçapa [ka'sapa] *f* pocket.
caçar [ka'sa*] *vt* to hunt; (*com espingarda*) to shoot; (*procurar*) to seek ♦ *vi* to hunt, go hunting.
cacareco [kaka'rɛku] *m* piece of junk; **~s** *mpl* junk *sg*.
cacarejar [kakare'ʒa*] *vi* (*galinhas etc*) to cluck.
cacarejo [kaka'reʒu] *m* clucking.
caçarola [kasa'rɔla] *f* (sauce)pan.
cacau [ka'kaw] *m* cocoa; (*BOT*) cacao.
cacaueiro [kaka'wejru] *m* cocoa tree.
cacetada [kase'tada] *f* blow (with a stick).
cacete [ka'setʃi] *adj* tiresome, boring ♦ *m/f* bore ♦ *m* club, stick; **está quente pra ~** (*col!*) it's bloody hot (*!*).
caceteação [kasetʃja'sãw] *f* annoyance.
cacetear [kase'tʃja*] *vt* to annoy.
Cacex [ka'sɛks] *abr f* (= *Carteira do Comércio Exterior*) *part of Banco do Brasil which helps to finance foreign trade.*
cachaça [ka'ʃasa] *f* (white) rum.
cachaceiro/a [kaʃa'sejru/a] *adj* drunk ♦ *m/f* drunkard.
cachaço [ka'ʃasu] *m* neck.
cachê [ka'ʃe] *m* fee.
cachecol [kaʃe'kɔw] (*pl* **-óis**) *m* scarf.
cachepô [kaʃe'po] *m* plant pot.
cachimbo [ka'ʃĩbu] *m* pipe.
cacho ['kaʃu] *m* bunch; (*de cabelo*) curl, lock; (*longo*) ringlet; (*col*: *caso*) affair.
cachoeira [kaʃ'wejra] *f* waterfall.
cachorra [ka'ʃoxa] *f* bitch; (*PT*) (female) puppy; **estar com a ~** (*col*) to be in a foul mood.
cachorrada [kaʃo'xada] *f* pack of dogs; (*sujeira*) dirty trick.
cachorrinho/a [kaʃo'xiɲu/a] *m/f* puppy ♦ *m* (*nado*) doggy paddle.
cachorro [ka'ʃoxu] *m* dog; (*PT*) puppy; (*filhote de animal*) cub; (*patife*) rascal; **soltar os ~s em cima de alguém** (*fig*) to lash out at sb; **estar matando ~ a grito** (*col*) to be scraping the barrel.
cachorro-quente (*pl* **cachorros-quentes**) *m* hot dog.
cacilda [ka'siwda] *excl* wow!, crikey!
cacique [ka'siki] *m* (Indian) chief; (*mandachuva*) local boss.
caco ['kaku] *m* bit, fragment; (*pessoa velha*) old relic; **chegamos ~s humanos** we arrived dead on our feet.
caçoada [ka'swada] *f* jibe.
caçoar [ka'swa*] *vt* to mock, make fun of ♦ *vi* to mock.
cações [ka'sõjʃ] *mpl de* **cação**.
cacoete [ka'kwetʃi] *m* twitch.
cacto ['kaktu] *m* cactus.
caçula [ka'sula] *m/f* youngest child.
cada ['kada] *adj inv* each; (*todo*) every; **$10 ~** $10 each; **~ um** each one; **~ semana** each week; **a ~ 3 horas** every 3 hours; **em ~ 3 crianças, uma já teve sarampo** out of every 3 children, one has already had measles; **~ vez mais** more and more; **~ vez mais barato** cheaper and cheaper; **tem ~ museu em Londres!** there are so many different museums in London; **tem ~ um!** it takes all sorts!
cadafalso [kada'fawsu] *m* (*forca*) gallows.
cadarço [ka'daxsu] *m* shoelace.
cadastrar [kadaʃ'tra*] *vt* (*COMPUT*: *banco de dados*) to set up.
cadastro [ka'daʃtru] *m* (*registro*) register; (*ato*) registration; (*de criminosos*) criminal record; (*de banco etc*) client records *pl*; (*de imóveis*) land registry; **~ bancário** (*de pessoa*) credit rating.
cadáver [ka'dave*] *m* corpse, dead body; **só passando por cima do meu ~** over my dead body; **ao chegar ao hospital, o motorista já era ~** the driver was dead on arrival at hospital.
cadavérico/a [kada'vɛriku/a] *adj* (*exame*) post-mortem; (*pessoa*) emaciated.
CADE (*BR*) *abr m* = **Conselho Administrativo de Defesa Econômica.**
cadê [ka'de] (*col*) *adv*: **~ ...?** where's/where are ...?, what's happened to ...?
cadeado [ka'dʒjadu] *m* padlock.
cadeia [ka'deja] *f* chain; (*prisão*) prison; (*rede*) network.
cadeira [ka'dejra] *f* (*móvel*) chair; (*disciplina*) subject; (*TEATRO*) stall; (*função*) post; **~s** *fpl* (*ANAT*) hips; **~ cativa** private seat; **~ de balanço** rocking chair; **~ de rodas** wheelchair; **falar de ~** (*fig*) to speak with authority.
cadeirudo/a [kadej'rudu/a] *adj* big-hipped.
cadela [ka'dɛla] *f* (*cão*) bitch.
cadência [ka'dẽsja] *f* cadence; (*ritmo*) rhythm.
cadenciado/a [kadẽ'sjadu/a] *adj* rhythmic; (*pausado*) slow.
cadente [ka'dẽtʃi] *adj* (*estrela*) falling.
caderneta [kadex'neta] *f* notebook; **~ de poupança** savings account.
caderno [ka'dɛxnu] *m* exercise book; (*de notas*) notebook; (*de jornal*) section.
cadete [ka'detʃi] *m* cadet.
cadinho [ka'dʒiɲu] *m* crucible; (*fig*) melting pot.
caducar [kadu'ka*] *vi* (*documentos*) to lapse, expire; (*pessoa*) to become senile.
caduco/a [ka'duku/a] *adj* (*nulo*) invalid, expired; (*senil*) senile; (*BOT*) deciduous.
caduquice [kadu'kisi] *f* senility.
cães [kãjʃ] *mpl de* **cão.**
cafajeste [kafa'ʒɛʃtʃi] (*col*) *adj* roguish; (*vulgar*) vulgar, coarse ♦ *m/f* rogue; rough customer.
café [ka'fɛ] *m* coffee; (*estabelecimento*) café; **~ com leite** white coffee (*BRIT*), coffee with cream (*US*); **~ preto** black coffee; **~ da manhã** (*BR*) breakfast; **é ~ pequeno** it's child's play.
café-com-leite *adj inv* coffee-coloured (*BRIT*),

coffee-colored (*US*).

cafeeiro/a [kafe'ejru/a] *adj* coffee *atr* ♦ *m* coffee plant.

cafeicultor [kafejkuw'to*] *m* coffee-grower.

cafeicultura [kafejkuw'tura] *f* coffee-growing.

cafeína [kafe'ina] *f* caffein(e).

cafetã [kafe'tã] *m* caftan.

cafetão [kafe'tãw] (*pl* **-ões**) *m* pimp.

cafeteira [kafe'tejra] *f* (*vaso*) coffee pot; (*máquina*) percolator.

cafetina [kafe'tʃina] *f* madam.

cafetões [kafe'tõjʃ] *mpl de* **cafetão**.

cafezal [kafe'zaw] (*pl* **-ais**) *m* coffee plantation.

cafezinho [kafe'ziɲu] *m small black coffee*.

cafona [ka'fɔna] *adj* tacky ♦ *m/f* tacky person.

cafonice [kafo'nisi] *f* tackiness; (*coisa*) tacky thing.

cafundó-do-judas [kafũ'dɔ-] *m*: **no ~** out in the sticks.

cafuné [kafu'nɛ] *m*: **fazer ~ em alguém** to stroke sb's hair.

cagaço [ka'gasu] (*col!*) *m* shits *pl* (*!*).

cagada [ka'gada] (*col!*) *f* shit (*!*); (*coisa malfeita*) cock-up (*!*).

cágado ['kagadu] *m* turtle; **a passos de ~** (*fig*) at a snail's pace.

caganeira [kaga'nejra] (*col*) *f* runs *pl*.

cagão/gona [ka'gãw/'gɔna] (*pl* **-ões/~s**) (*col*) *m/f*: **ser ~** to be a chicken.

cagar [ka'ga*] (*col!*) *vi* to (have a) shit (*!*) ♦ *vt*: **~ regras** to tell others what to do; **~-se** *vr*: **~-se de medo** to be shit scared (*!*); **~ (para)** not to give a shit (about) (*!*).

cagões [ka'gõjʃ] *mpl de* **cagão**.

cagona [ka'gɔna] *f de* **cagão**.

cagüetar [kagwe'ta*] *vt* to inform on.

cagüete [ka'gwetʃi] *m* informer.

caiaque [ka'jaki] *m* kayak.

caiar [kaj'a*] *vt* to whitewash.

caiba ['kajba] *etc vb V* **caber**.

cãibra ['kãjbra] *f* (*MED*) cramp.

caibro ['kajbru] *m* joist.

caída [ka'ida] *f* = **queda**.

caído/a [ka'idu/a] *adj* (*deprimido*) dejected; (*derrubado*) fallen; (*pendente*) droopy; **~ por** (*apaixonado*) in love with.

câimbra ['kãjbra] *f* = **cãibra**.

caimento [kaj'mẽtu] *m* hang, fall.

caipira [kaj'pira] *adj* countrified; (*sem traquejo social*) provincial ♦ *m/f* yokel.

caipirinha [kajpi'riɲa] *f cocktail of cachaça, lemon and sugar*.

cair [ka'i*] *vi* to fall; (*ser vítima de logro*) to be taken in; **~ bem/mal** (*roupa*) to fit well/badly; (*col*: *pessoa*) to look good/bad; **~ em si** to come to one's senses; **~ de quatro** to land on all fours; **estou caindo de sono** I'm really sleepy; **~ para trás** (*fig*) to be taken aback; **ao ~ da noite** at nightfall; **o Natal caiu num domingo** Christmas fell on a Sunday; **essa comida me caiu mal** that food did not agree with me.

Cairo ['kajru] *m*: **o ~** Cairo.

cais [kajʃ] *m* (*NÁUT*) quay; (*PT*: *FERRO*) platform.

caixa ['kajʃa] *f* box; (*cofre*) safe; (*de uma loja*) cashdesk ♦ *m/f* (*pessoa*) cashier; **de alta/baixa ~** (*col*) well-off/poor; **fazer a ~** (*COM*) to cash up; **pequena ~** petty cash; **~ acústica** loudspeaker; **~ de correio** letter box; **~ de mudanças** (*BR*) *ou* **de velocidades** (*PT*) gear box; **~ econômica** savings bank; **~ postal** P.O. box; **~ registradora** cash register.

caixa-alta (*pl* **caixas-altas**) (*col*) *adj* rich ♦ *m/f* fat cat.

caixa-d'água (*pl* **caixas-d'água**) *f* water tank.

caixa-forte (*pl* **caixas-fortes**) *f* vault.

caixão [kaj'ʃãw] (*pl* **-ões**) *m* (*ataúde*) coffin; (*caixa grande*) large box.

caixa-preta (*pl* **caixas-pretas**) *f* (*AER*) black box.

caixeiro/a [kaj'ʃejru/a] *m/f* shop assistant; (*entregador*) delivery man/woman.

caixeiro/a-viajante (*pl* **caixeiros/as-viajantes**) *m/f* commercial traveller (*BRIT*) *ou* traveler (*US*).

caixilho [kaj'ʃiʎu] *m* (*moldura*) frame.

caixões [kaj'ʃõjʃ] *mpl de* **caixão**.

caixote [kaj'ʃɔtʃi] *m* packing case; **~ do lixo** (*PT*) dustbin (*BRIT*), garbage can (*US*).

caju [ka'ʒu] *m* cashew fruit.

cajueiro [ka'ʒwejru] *m* cashew tree.

cal [kaw] *f* lime; (*na água*) chalk; (*para caiar*) whitewash.

calabouço [kala'bosu] *m* dungeon.

calada [ka'lada] *f*: **na ~ da noite** at dead of night.

calado/a [ka'ladu/a] *adj* quiet.

calafetar [kalafe'ta*] *vt* to stop up.

calafrio [kala'friu] *m* shiver; **ter ~s** to shiver.

calamar [kala'ma*] *m* squid.

calamidade [kalami'dadʒi] *f* calamity, disaster.

calamitoso/a [kalami'tozu/ɔza] *adj* disastrous.

calão [ka'lãw] *m*: **(baixo) ~** (*BR*) bad language; (*PT*) slang.

calar [ka'la*] *vt* (*não dizer*) to keep quiet about; (*impor silêncio a*) to silence ♦ *vi* to go quiet; (*manter-se calado*) to keep quiet; **~-se** *vr* to go quiet; to keep quiet; **~ em** (*penetrar*) to mark; **cala a boca!** shut up!

calça ['kawsa] *f* (*tb*: **~s**) trousers *pl* (*BRIT*), pants *pl* (*US*).

calçada [kaw'sada] *f* (*PT*: *rua*) roadway; (*BR*: *passeio*) pavement (*BRIT*), sidewalk (*US*).

calçadão [kawsa'dãw] (*pl* **-ões**) *m* pedestrian precinct (*BRIT*).

calçadeira [kawsa'dejra] *f* shoe-horn.

calçado/a [kaw'sadu/a] *adj* (*rua*) paved ♦ *m* shoe; **~s** *mpl* footwear *sg*.
calçadões [kawsa'dõjʃ] *mpl de* **calçadão**.
calçamento [kawsa'mẽtu] *m* paving.
calcanhar [kawka'ɲa*] *m* (ANAT) heel.
calcanhar-de-aquiles [-dʒia'kiliʃ] *m* Achilles' heel.
calção [kaw'sãw] (*pl* **-ões**) *m* shorts *pl*; **~ de banho** swimming trunks *pl*.
calcar [kaw'ka*] *vt* (*pisar em*) to tread on; (*espezinhar*) to trample (on); (*comprimir*) to press; (*reprimir*) to repress.
calçar [kaw'sa*] *vt* (*sapatos, luvas*) to put on; (*pavimentar*) to pave; (*pôr calço*) to wedge; **~-se** *vr* to put on one's shoes; **o sapato calça bem?** does the shoe fit?; **ela calça (número) 28** she takes size 28 (in shoes).
calcário/a [kaw'karju/a] *adj* (*água*) hard ♦ *m* limestone.
calceiro/a [kaw'sejru/a] *m/f* shoe-maker.
calcinha [kaw'siɲa] *f* panties *pl*.
cálcio ['kawsju] *m* calcium.
calço ['kawsu] *m* (*cunha*) wedge.
calções [kaw'sõjʃ] *mpl de* **calção**.
calculadora [kawkula'dora] *f* calculator.
calcular [kawku'la*] *vt* to calculate; (*imaginar*) to imagine ♦ *vi* to make calculations; **~ que** to reckon that.
calculável [kawku'lavew] (*pl* **-eis**) *adj* calculable.
calculista [kawku'liʃta] *adj* calculating ♦ *m/f* opportunist.
cálculo ['kawkulu] *m* calculation; (MAT) calculus; (MED) stone.
calda ['kawda] *f* (*de doce*) syrup; **~s** *fpl* hot springs.
caldeira [kaw'dejra] *f* (TEC) boiler.
caldeirada [kawdej'rada] (PT) *f* (*guisado*) fish stew.
caldeirão [kawdej'rãw] (*pl* **-ões**) *m* cauldron.
caldo ['kawdu] *m* (*sopa*) broth; (*de fruta*) juice; **~ de carne/galinha** beef/chicken stock; **~ verde** potato and cabbage broth.
calefação [kalefa'sãw] *f* heating.
caleidoscópio [kalejdo'ʃkɔpju] *m* kaleidoscope.
calejado/a [kale'ʒadu/a] *adj* calloused; (*fig: experiente*) experienced; (: *endurecido*) callous.
calejar [kale'ʒa*] *vt* (*mãos*) to callous; (*pessoa*) to harden; **~-se** *vr* (*mãos*) to get calluses; (*insensibilizar-se*) to become callous; (*tornar-se experiente*) to get experience.
calendário [kalẽ'darju] *m* calendar.
calha ['kaʎa] *f* (*sulco*) channel; (*para água*) gutter.
calhamaço [kaʎa'masu] *m* tome.
calhambeque [kaʎã'bɛki] (*col*) *m* old banger.
calhar [ka'ʎa*] *vi*: **calhou viajarmos no mesmo avião** we happened to travel on the same plane; **calhou que** it so happened that; **ele calhou de chegar** he happened to arrive; **~ a** (*cair bem*) to suit; **vir a ~** to come at the right time; **se ~** (PT) perhaps, maybe.
calhau [ka'ʎaw] *m* stone, pebble.
calibrado/a [kali'bradu/a] *adj* (*meio bêbado*) tipsy.
calibrar [kali'bra*] *vt* to gauge (BRIT), gage (US), calibrate.
calibre [ka'libri] *m* (*de cano*) bore, calibre (BRIT), caliber (US); (*fig*) calibre.
cálice ['kalisi] *m* (*copinho*) wine glass; (REL) chalice.
calidez [kali'deʒ] *f* warmth.
cálido/a ['kalidu/a] *adj* warm.
caligrafia [kaligra'fia] *f* (*arte*) calligraphy; (*letra*) handwriting.
calista [ka'liʃta] *m/f* chiropodist (BRIT), podiatrist (US).
calma ['kawma] *f* calm; **conservar/perder a ~** to keep/lose one's temper; **~!** take it easy!
calmante [kaw'mãtʃi] *adj* soothing ♦ *m* (MED) tranquillizer.
calmo/a ['kawmu/a] *adj* calm, tranquil.
calo ['kalu] *m* callus; (*no pé*) corn; **pisar nos ~s de alguém** (*fig*) to hit a (raw) nerve.
calombo [ka'lõbu] *m* lump; (*na estrada*) bump.
calor [ka'lo*] *m* heat; (*agradável*) warmth; (*fig*) warmth; **está** *ou* **faz ~** it is hot; **estar com ~** to be hot.
calorento/a [kalo'rẽtu/a] *adj* (*pessoa*) sensitive to heat; (*lugar*) hot.
caloria [calo'ria] *f* calorie.
caloroso/a [kalo'rozu/ɔza] *adj* warm; (*entusiástico*) enthusiastic; (*protesto*) fervent.
calota [ka'lɔta] *f* (AUTO) hubcap.
calote [ka'lɔtʃi] (*col*) *m* (*dívida*) bad debt; **dar o ~** to welsh (on one's debts).
caloteiro/a [kalo'tejru/a] (*col*) *adj* unreliable ♦ *m/f* bad payer.
calouro/a [ka'loru/a] *m/f* (EDUC) fresher; (: US) freshman; (*noviço*) novice.
calúnia [ka'lunja] *f* slander.
caluniador(a) [kalunja'do*(a)] *adj* slanderous ♦ *m/f* slanderer.
caluniar [kalu'nja*] *vt* to slander.
calunioso/a [kalu'njozu/ɔza] *adj* slanderous.
calvície [kaw'visi] *f* baldness.
calvo/a ['kawvu/a] *adj* bald.
cama ['kama] *f* bed; **~ de casal** double bed; **~ de solteiro** single bed; **de ~** (*doente*) ill (in bed); **ficar de ~** to take to one's bed.
cama-beliche (*pl* **camas-beliches**) *f* bunk bed.
camada [ka'mada] *f* layer; (*de tinta*) coat.
camafeu [kama'few] *m* cameo.
câmara ['kamara] *f* chamber; (FOTO) camera; **~ municipal** (BR) town council; (PT) town hall; **em ~ lenta** in slow motion.
câmara-ardente *f*: **estar exposto em ~** to lie in state.
camarada [kama'rada] *adj* friendly, nice; (*preço*) good ♦ *m/f* comrade; (*sujeito*) guy/woman.

camaradagem [kamara'daʒẽ] *f* comradeship, camaraderie; **por ~** out of friendliness.
câmara-de-ar (*pl* **câmaras-de-ar**) *f* inner tube.
camarão [kama'rãw] (*pl* **-ões**) *m* shrimp; (*graúdo*) prawn.
camareiro/a [kama'rejru/a] *m/f* cleaner/chambermaid.
camarilha [kama'riʎa] *f* clique.
camarim [kama'rĩ] (*pl* **-ns**) *m* (*TEATRO*) dressing room.
Camarões [kama'rõjʃ] *m*: **o ~** Cameroon.
camarões [kama'rõjʃ] *mpl de* **camarão.**
camarote [kama'rɔtʃi] *m* (*NÁUT*) cabin; (*TEATRO*) box.
cambada [kã'bada] *f* bunch, gang.
cambaio/a [kã'baju/a] *adj* (*mesa*) wobbly, rickety.
cambalacho [kãba'laʃu] *m* scam.
cambaleante [kãba'ljãtʃi] *adj* unsteady (on one's feet).
cambalear [kãba'lja*] *vi* to stagger, reel.
cambalhota [kãba'ʎɔta] *f* somersault.
cambar [kã'ba*] *vi* to lean.
cambial [kã'bjaw] (*pl* **-ais**) *adj* exchange *atr.*
cambiante [kã'bjãtʃi] *adj* changing, variable ♦ *m* (*cor*) shade.
cambiar [kã'bja*] *vt* to change; (*trocar*) to exchange.
câmbio ['kãbju] *m* (*dinheiro etc*) exchange; (*preço de câmbio*) rate of exchange; **~ livre** free trade; **~ negro** black market; **~ oficial/paralelo** official/black market.
cambista [kã'biʃta] *m* (*de dinheiro*) money changer; (*BR*: *de ingressos*) (ticket-)tout.
Camboja [kã'bɔja] *m*: **o ~** Cambodia.
cambojano/a [kãbo'ʒanu/a] *adj, m/f* Cambodian.
camburão [kãbu'rãw] (*pl* **-ões**) *m* police van.
camélia [ka'mɛlja] *f* camelia.
camelo [ka'melu] *m* camel; (*fig*) dunce.
camelô [kame'lo] *m* street pedlar.
camião [ka'mjãw] (*pl* **-ões**) (*PT*) *m* lorry (*BRIT*), truck (*US*).
caminhada [kami'ɲada] *f* walk.
caminhante [kami'ɲãtʃi] *m/f* walker.
caminhão [kami'ɲãw] (*pl* **-oẽs**) (*BR*) *m* lorry (*BRIT*), truck (*US*).
caminhar [kami'ɲa*] *vi* (*ir a pé*) to walk; (*processo*) to get under way; (*negócios*) to go, progress.
caminho [ka'miɲu] *m* way; (*vereda*) road, path; **~ de ferro** (*PT*) railway (*BRIT*), railroad (*US*); **a meio ~** halfway (there); **ser meio ~ andado** (*fig*) to be halfway there; **a ~** on the way, en route; **cortar ~** to take a short cut; **ir pelo mesmo ~** to go the same way; **pôr-se a ~** to set off.
caminhões [kami'ɲõjʃ] *mpl de* **caminhão.**
caminhoneiro/a [kamiɲo'nejru/a] *m/f* lorry driver (*BRIT*), truck driver (*US*).
caminhonete [kamiɲo'nɛtʃi] *m* (*AUTO*) van.
camiões [ka'mjõjʃ] *mpl de* **camião.**
camioneta [kamjo'neta] (*PT*) *f* (*para passageiros*) coach; (*comercial*) van.
camionista [kamjo'niʃta] (*PT*) *m/f* lorry driver (*BRIT*), truck driver (*US*).
camisa [ka'miza] *f* shirt; **~ de dormir** nightshirt; **~ esporte/pólo/social** sports/polo/dress shirt; **mudar de ~** (*ESPORTE*) to change sides.
camisa-de-força (*pl* **camisas-de-força**) *f* straitjacket.
camisa-de-vênus (*pl* **camisas-de-vênus**) *f* condom.
camiseta [kami'zɛta] (*BR*) *f* T-shirt; (*interior*) vest.
camisinha [kami'ziɲa] (*col*) *f* condom.
camisola [kami'zɔla] *f* (*BR*) nightdress; (*PT*: *pulôver*) sweater; **~ interior** (*PT*) vest.
camomila [kamo'mila] *f* camomile.
campa ['kãpa] *f* (*de sepultura*) gravestone.
campainha [kampa'iɲa] *f* bell.
campal [kã'paw] (*pl* **-ais**) *adj*: **batalha ~** pitched battle; **missa ~** open-air mass.
campanário [kãpa'narju] *m* (*torre*) church tower, steeple.
campanha [kã'paɲa] *f* (*MIL etc*) campaign; (*planície*) plain.
campeão/peã [kã'pjãw/'pjã] (*pl* **-ões/~s**) *m/f* champion.
campeonato [kãpjo'natu] *m* championship.
campestre [kã'pɛʃtri] *adj* rural, rustic.
campina [kã'pina] *f* prairie, grassland.
camping ['kãpĩŋ] (*BR*: *pl* **~s**) *m* camping; (*lugar*) campsite.
campismo [kã'piʒmu] (*PT*) *m* camping; **parque de ~** campsite.
campista [kã'piʃta] *m/f* camper.
campo [kãpu] *m* field; (*fora da cidade*) countryside; (*ESPORTE*) ground; (*acampamento*) camp; (*âmbito*) field; (*TÊNIS*) court.
camponês/esa [kãpo'neʃ/eza] *m/f* countryman/woman; (*agricultor*) farmer.
campus ['kãpuʃ] *m inv* campus.
camuflagem [kamu'flaʒẽ] *f* camouflage.
camuflar [kamu'fla*] *vt* to camouflage.
camundongo [kamũ'dõgu] (*BR*) *m* mouse.
camurça [ka'muxsa] *f* suede.
CAN (*BR*) *abr m* = **Correio Aéreo Nacional.**
cana ['kana] *f* cane; (*col*: *cadeia*) nick; (*de açúcar*) sugar cane; **ir em ~** to be put behind bars.
Canadá [kana'da] *m*: **o ~** Canada.
canadense [kana'dẽsi] *adj, m/f* Canadian.
canal [ka'naw] (*pl* **-ais**) *m* channel; (*de navegação*) canal; (*ANAT*) duct.
canalha [ka'naʎa] *f* rabble, mob ♦ *m/f* wretch, scoundrel.
canalização [kanaliza'sãw] *f* (*de água*) plumb-

***NB:** European Portuguese adds the following consonants to certain words:* **b** (sú(b)dito, su(b)til); **c** (a(c)ção, a(c)cionista, a(c)to); **m** (inde(m)ne); **p** (ado(p)ção, ado(p)tar); *for further details see p. xiii.*

ing; (*de gás*) piping.
canalizador(a) [kanaliza'do*(a)] (*PT*) *m/f* plumber.
canalizar [kanali'za*] *vt* (*água, esforços*) to channel; (*colocar canos*) to lay pipes in.
canapé [kana'pɛ] *m* sofa.
canapê [kana'pe] *m* (*CULIN*) canapé.
canário [ka'narju] *m* canary.
canastra [ka'naʃtra] *f* (big) basket; (*jogo*) canasta.
canastrão/trona [kanaʃ'trãw/'trɔna] (*pl* **-ões/~s**) *m/f* ham actor/actress.
canavial [kana'vjaw] (*pl* **-ais**) *m* cane field.
canavieiro/a [kana'vjejru/a] *adj* sugar cane *atr.*
canção [kã'sãw] (*pl* **-ões**) *f* song; **~ de ninar** lullaby.
cancela [kã'sɛla] *f* gate.
cancelamento [kãsela'mẽtu] *m* cancellation.
cancelar [kãse'la*] *vt* to cancel; (*invalidar*) to annul; (*riscar*) to cross out.
câncer ['kãse*] *m* cancer; **C~** (*ASTROLOGIA*) Cancer.
canceriano/a [kãse'rjanu/a] *adj, m/f* Cancerian.
cancerígeno/a [kãse'riʒenu/a] *adj* carcinogenic.
cancerologista [kãserolo'ʒiʃta] *m/f* cancer specialist, oncologist.
canceroso/a [kãse'rozu/ɔza] *adj* (*célula*) cancerous ♦ *m/f* cancer sufferer.
canções [kã'sõjʃ] *fpl de* **canção.**
cancro ['kãkru] (*PT*) *m* cancer.
candango/a [kã'dãgu/a] *m/f* person from Brasília.
candeeiro [kãdʒi'ejru] *m* (*BR*) oil-lamp (*ou* gas-lamp); (*PT*) lamp.
candelabro [kãde'labru] *m* (*castiçal*) candlestick; (*lustre*) chandelier.
candente [kã'dẽtʃi] *adj* white hot; (*fig*) inflamed.
candidatar-se [kãdʒida'taxsi] *vr*: **~ a** (*vaga*) to apply for; (*presidência*) to stand for.
candidato/a [kãdʒi'datu/a] *m/f* candidate; (*a cargo*) applicant.
candidatura [kãdʒida'tura] *f* candidature; (*a cargo*) application.
cândido/a ['kãdʒidu/a] *adj* (*ingênuo*) naive; (*inocente*) innocent.
candomblé [kãdõ'blɛ] *m* candomblé (*Afro-Brazilian religion*); (*local*) candomblé shrine.
candura [kã'dura] *f* (*simplicidade*) simplicity; (*inocência*) innocence.
caneca [ka'nɛka] *f* mug.
caneco [ka'nɛku] *m* tankard; **pintar os ~s** (*col*) to play up.
canela [ka'nɛla] *f* (*especiaria*) cinnamon; (*ANAT*) shin.
canelada [kane'lada] *f* kick in the shins; **dei uma ~ na mesa** I hit my shins on the table.
caneta [ka'neta] *f* pen; **~ esferográfica** ballpoint pen; **~ pilot** felt-tip pen; **~ seletora** (*COMPUT*) light pen.
caneta-tinteiro (*pl* **canetas-tinteiro**) *f* fountain pen.
canga ['kãga] *f* beach wrap.
cangaceiro [kãga'sejru] (*BR*) *m* bandit.
cangote [kã'gotʃi] *m* (back of the) neck.
canguru [kãgu'ru] *m* kangaroo.
cânhamo ['kaɲamu] *m* hemp.
canhão [ka'ɲãw] (*pl* **-ões**) *m* (*MIL*) cannon; (*GEO*) canyon.
canhestro/a [ka'ɲeʃtru/a] *adj* awkward.
canhões [ka'ɲõjʃ] *mpl de* **canhão.**
canhoto/a [ka'ɲotu/a] *adj* left-handed ♦ *m/f* left-handed person ♦ *m* (*de cheque*) stub.
canibal [kani'baw] (*pl* **-ais**) *m/f* cannibal.
canibalismo [kaniba'liʒmu] *m* cannibalism.
caniço/a [ka'nisu/a] *adj* (*col*) skinny ♦ *m* reed.
canícula [ka'nikula] *f* searing heat.
canil [ka'niw] (*pl* **-is**) *m* kennel.
caninha [ka'niɲa] (*col*) *f* rum.
canino/a [ka'ninu/a] *adj* canine; (*fome*) terrible ♦ *m* canine.
canis [ka'niʃ] *mpl de* **canil.**
canivete [kani'vɛtʃi] *m* penknife; **nem que chovam ~s** whatever happens, come what may.
canja ['kãʒa] *f* (*sopa*) chicken broth; (*col*) cinch, pushover.
canjica [kã'ʒika] *f* maize porridge.
cano ['kanu] *m* pipe; (*tubo*) tube; (*de arma de fogo*) barrel; (*de bota*) top; **~ de esgoto** sewer; **entrar pelo ~** (*col*) to come off badly.
canoa [ka'noa] *f* canoe.
canoagem [ka'nwaʒẽ] *f* canoeing.
canoeiro/a [ka'nwejru/a] *m/f* canoeist.
canoísta [kano'iʃta] *m/f* canoeist.
canonizar [kanoni'za*] *vt* to canonize.
cansaço [kã'sasu] *m* tiredness.
cansado/a [kã'sadu/a] *adj* tired.
cansar [kã'sa*] *vt* (*fatigar*) to tire; (*entediar*) to bore ♦ *vi* (*ficar cansado*) to get tired; **~-se** *vr* to get tired.
cansativo/a [kãsa'tʃivu/a] *adj* tiring; (*tedioso*) tedious.
canseira [kã'sejra] *f* (*cansaço*) weariness; (*trabalho árduo*) toil; **dar ~ em alguém** to wear sb out.
cantada [kã'tada] (*col*) *f* sweet talk; **dar uma ~ em** to sweet-talk.
cantado/a [kã'tadu/a] *adj* (*missa*) sung; (*sotaque*) sing-song.
cantar [kã'ta*] *vt* to sing; (*respostas etc*) to sing out; (*col: seduzir*) to sweet-talk ♦ *vi* to sing ♦ *m* song.
cantarolar [kãtaro'la*] *vt* to hum.
canteiro [kã'tejru] *m* stonemason; (*de flores*) flower bed; (*de obra*) site office.
cantiga [kã'tʃiga] *f* ballad; **~ de ninar** lullaby.
cantil [kã'tʃiw] (*pl* **-is**) *m* canteen, flask.
cantina [kã'tʃina] *f* canteen.
cantis [kã'tʃiʃ] *mpl de* **cantil.**
canto ['kãtu] *m* corner; (*lugar*) place; (*canção*) song.
cantor(a) [kã'to*(a)] *m/f* singer.

cantoria [kãto'ria] *f* singing.
canudo [ka'nudu] *m* tube; (*para beber*) straw.
cão [kãw] (*pl* **cães**) *m* dog; (*pessoa*) rascal; **ser** *ou* **estar um ~ de ruim** (*col*) to be awful.
caolho/a [ka'oʎu/a] *adj* cross-eyed.
caos ['kaoʃ] *m* chaos.
caótico/a [ka'ɔtʃiku/a] *adj* chaotic.
capa ['kapa] *f* (*roupa*) cape; (*cobertura*) cover; **livro de ~ dura/mole** hardback/paperback (book).
capacete [kapa'setʃi] *m* helmet.
capacho [ka'paʃu] *m* door mat; (*fig*) toady.
capacidade [kapasi'dadʒi] *f* capacity; (*aptidão*) ability, competence; **ser uma ~** (*pessoa*) to be brilliant; **~ ociosa** (*COM*) idle capacity.
capacíssimo/a [kapa'sisimu/a] *adj superl de* **capaz.**
capacitar [kapasi'ta*] *vt*: **~ alguém a fazer/para algo** to prepare sb to do/for sth; **~-se** *vr*: **~-se de/de que** to convince o.s. of/that.
capar [ka'pa*] *vt* to castrate, geld.
capataz [kapa'taʒ] *m* foreman.
capaz [ka'paʒ] *adj* able, capable; **ser ~ de** to be able to (*ou* capable of); **sou ~ de ...** (*talvez*) I might ...; **é ~ de chover hoje** it might rain today.
capcioso/a [kap'sjozu/ɔza] *adj* (*pergunta*) trick; (*pessoa*) tricky.
capela [ka'pɛla] *f* chapel.
capelão [kape'lãw] (*pl* **-ães**) *m* (*REL*) chaplain.
Capemi [kape'mi] (*BR*) *abr f* (= *Caixa de Pecúlios, Pensões e Montepios dos Militares*) *military pension fund.*
capenga [ka'pẽga] *adj* lame ♦ *m/f* cripple.
capengar [kapẽ'ga*] *vi* to limp.
Capes (*BR*) *abr f* (*EDUC*: = *Coordenação de Aperfeiçoamento de Pessoal de Nível Superior*) *grant-awarding body.*
capeta [ka'peta] *m* devil; **ele é um ~** he's a little devil.
capilar [kapi'la*] *adj* hair *atr*.
capim [ka'pĩ] *m* grass.
capinar [kapi'na*] *vt* to weed ♦ *vi* to weed; (*col*) to clear off.
capitães [kapi'tãjʃ] *mpl de* **capitão.**
capital [kapi'taw] (*pl* **-ais**) *adj*, *m* capital ♦ *f* (*cidade*) capital; **~ circulante** (*COM*) circulating capital; **~ de giro** (*COM*) working capital; **~ investido** (*COM*) investment capital; **~ (em) ações** (*COM*) share capital; **~ imobilizado** *ou* **fixo** (*COM*) fixed capital; **~ integralizado** (*COM*) paid-up capital; **~ próprio** *ou* **social** (*COM*) equity capital; **~ de risco** (*COM*) venture capital.
capitalismo [kapita'liʒmu] *m* capitalism.
capitalista [kapita'liʃta] *m/f* capitalist.
capitalizar [kapitali'za*] *vt* (*tirar proveito de*) to capitalize on; (*COM*) to capitalize.
capitanear [kapita'nja*] *vt* to command, head.
capitania [kapita'nia] *f*: **~ do porto** port authority.
capitão [kapi'tãw] (*pl* **-ães**) *m* captain.
capitulação [kapitula'sãw] *f* capitulation, surrender.
capitular [kapitu'la*] *vt* (*falhas*, *causas*) to list; (*descrever*) to characterize; (*rendição*) to fix the terms of ♦ *vi* to capitulate; **~ alguém de algo** to brand sb (as) sth.
capítulo [ka'pitulu] *m* chapter; (*de novela*) episode.
capô [ka'po] *m* (*AUTO*) bonnet (*BRIT*), hood (*US*).
capoeira [ka'pwejra] *f* (*PT*) hencoop; (*mata*) brushwood; (*jogo*) capoeira (*foot-fighting dance*).
capota [ka'pɔta] *f* (*AUTO*) hood, top.
capotar [kapo'ta*] *vi* to overturn.
capote [ka'pɔtʃi] *m* overcoat.
caprichar [kapri'ʃa*] *vi*: **~ em** to take trouble over.
capricho [ka'priʃu] *m* whim, caprice; (*teimosia*) obstinacy; (*apuro*) care.
caprichoso/a [kapri'ʃozu/ɔza] *adj* capricious; (*com apuro*) meticulous.
Capricórnio [kapri'kɔxnju] *m* Capricorn.
capricorniano/a [kaprikox'njanu/a] *adj*, *m/f* Capricorn.
cápsula ['kapsula] *f* capsule.
captar [kap'ta*] *vt* (*atrair*) to win; (*RÁDIO*) to pick up; (*águas*) to collect, dam up; (*compreender*) to catch.
captura [kap'tura] *f* capture.
capturar [kaptu'ra*] *vt* to capture, seize.
capuz [ka'puʒ] *m* hood.
caquético/a [ka'kɛtʃiku/a] *adj* doddery.
caqui [ka'ki] *m* persimmon.
cáqui ['kaki] *adj* khaki.
cara ['kara] *f* (*de pessoa*) face; (*aspecto*) appearance ♦ *m* (*col*) guy; (*coragem*) courage, heart; **~ ou coroa?** heads or tails?; **de ~** straightaway; **está na ~** it's obvious; **dar de ~ com** to bump into; **estar com boa ~** to look well; (*comida*) to look good; **não vou com a ~ dele** (*col*) I'm not very keen on him; **meter a ~** (*col*) to put one's back into it; **ser a ~ de** (*col*) to be the spitting image of; **ter ~ de** to look (like).
carabina [kara'bina] *f* rifle.
Caracas [ka'rakaʃ] *n* Caracas.
caracol [kara'kɔw] (*pl* **-óis**) *m* snail; (*de cabelo*) curl; *V tb* **escada.**
caracteres [karak'tɛriʃ] *mpl de* **caráter.**
característica [karakte'riʃtʃika] *f* characteristic, feature.
característico/a [karakte'riʃtʃiku/a] *adj* characteristic.
caracterização [karakteriza'sãw] *f* characterization; (*de ator*) make-up.
caracterizar [karakteri'za*] *vt* to characterize,

***NB:** European Portuguese adds the following consonants to certain words:* **b** (sú(b)dito, su(b)til); **c** (a(c)ção, a(c)cionista, a(c)to); **m** (inde(m)ne); **p** (ado(p)ção, ado(p)tar); *for further details see p. xiii.*

typify; (*ator*) to make up; **~-se** *vr* to be characterized; (*ator*) to get in character.
cara-de-pau (*pl* **caras-de-pau**) *adj* brazen ♦ *m/f*: **ele é ~** he's very forward.
caraíba [kara'iba] *adj* Caribbean.
caramanchão [karamã'ʃãw] (*pl* **-ões**) *m* summerhouse.
caramba [ka'rãba] *excl* blimey (*BRIT*), gee (*US*); **quente pra ~** (*col*) really hot.
carambola [karã'bɔla] *f* carambole (*fruit*).
caramelo [kara'mɛlu] *m* caramel; (*bala*) toffee.
cara-metade (*pl* **caras-metades**) *f* better half.
caranguejo [karã'geʒu] *m* crab.
carão [ka'rãw] (*pl* **-ões**) *m* telling-off; **passar/levar um ~** to give/get a telling-off.
carapuça [kara'pusa] *f* cap; **enfiar a ~** to take the hint personally.
caratê [kara'te] *m* karate.
caráter [ka'rate*] (*pl* **caracteres**) *m* character; **de ~ social** of a social nature; **a ~** in character; **uma pessoa de ~** a person of hono(u)r.
caravana [kara'vana] *f* caravan.
carboidrato [kaxboi'dratu] *m* carbohydrate.
carbônico/a [kax'boniku/a] *adj* carbon *atr*.
carbonizar [kaxboni'za*] *vt* to carbonize; (*queimar*) to char.
carbono [kax'bɔnu] *m* carbon.
carburador [kaxbura'do*] *m* carburettor (*BRIT*), carburator (*US*).
carcaça [kax'kasa] *f* (*esqueleto*) carcass; (*armação*) frame; (*de navio*) hull.
carcamano/a [kaxka'manu/a] *m/f* Italian-Brazilian.
cárcere ['kaxseri] *m* prison.
carcereiro/a [kaxse'rejru/a] *m/f* jailer, warder.
carcomido/a [kaxko'midu/a] *adj* worm-eaten; (*rosto*) pock-marked, pitted.
cardápio [kax'dapju] (*BR*) *m* menu.
cardeal [kax'dʒjaw] (*pl* **-ais**) *adj*, *m* cardinal.
cardíaco/a [kax'dʒiaku/a] *adj* cardiac ♦ *m/f* person with a heart condition; **ataque ~** heart attack; **parada cardíaca** cardiac arrest.
cardigã [kaxdʒi'gã] *m* cardigan.
cardinal [kaxdʒi'naw] (*pl* **-ais**) *adj* cardinal.
cardiológico/a [kaxdʒjo'lɔʒiku/a] *adj* heart *atr*.
cardiologista [kaxdʒjolo'ʒiʃta] *m/f* heart specialist, cardiologist.
cardume [kax'dumi] *m* (*peixes*) shoal.
careca [ka'rɛka] *adj* bald ♦ *f* baldness; **estar ~ de fazer/saber** (*col*) to be used to doing/know full well.
carecer [kare'se*] *vi*: **~ de** (*ter falta*) to lack; (*precisar*) to need.
careiro/a [ka'rejru/a] *adj* expensive.
carência [ka'rẽsja] *f* (*falta*) lack, shortage; (*necessidade*) need; (*privação*) deprivation.
carente [ka'rẽtʃi] *adj* wanting; (*pessoa*) needy, deprived; (*de carinho*) in need of affection.
carestia [kareʃ'tʃia] *f* high cost; (*preços altos*) high prices *pl*; (*escassez*) scarcity.
careta [ka'reta] *adj* (*col*) straight, square ♦ *f* grimace; **fazer uma ~** to pull a face.
carga ['kaxga] *f* load; (*de um navio*) cargo; (*ato de carregar*) loading; (*ELET*) charge; (*fig*: *peso*) burden; (*MIL*) attack, charge; **dar ~ em** (*COMPUT*) to boot (up); **voltar à ~** to insist; **~ d'água** heavy downpour; **~ horária** workload; **~ aérea** air cargo.
cargo ['kaxgu] *m* (*responsabilidade*) responsibility; (*função*) post; **a ~ de** in charge of; **ter a ~** to be in charge of; **tomar a ~** to take charge of; **~ honorífico** honorary post; **~ de confiança** position of trust; **~ público** public office.
cargueiro [kax'gejru] *m* cargo ship.
cariar [ka'rja*] *vt*, *vi* to decay.
Caribe [ka'ribi] *m*: **o ~** the Caribbean (Sea).
caricatura [karika'tura] *f* caricature.
caricatural [karikatu'raw] (*pl* **-ais**) *adj* (*fig*) grotesque.
caricaturar [karikatu'ra*] *vt* to caricature.
caricaturista [karikatu'riʃta] *m/f* caricaturist.
carícia [ka'risja] *f* caress.
caridade [kari'dadʒi] *f* charity; **obra de ~** charity.
caridoso/a [kari'dozu/ɔza] *adj* charitable.
cárie ['kari] *f* tooth decay; (*MED*) caries.
carimbar [karĩ'ba*] *vt* to stamp; (*no correio*) to postmark.
carimbo [ka'rĩbu] *m* stamp; (*postal*) postmark.
carinho [ka'riɲu] *m* affection, fondness; (*carícia*) caress; **fazer ~** to caress; **com ~** affectionately; (*com cuidado*) with care.
carinhoso/a [kari'ɲozu/ɔza] *adj* affectionate.
carioca [ka'rjɔka] *adj* of Rio de Janeiro ♦ *m/f* native of Rio de Janeiro ♦ *m* (*PT*: *café*) *type of weak coffee.*
carisma [ka'riʒma] *m* charisma.
carismático/a [kariʒ'matʃiku/a] *adj* charismatic.
caritativo/a [karita'tʃivu/a] *adj* charitable.
carnal [kax'naw] (*pl* **-ais**) *adj* carnal; **primo ~** first cousin.
carnaval [kaxna'vaw] (*pl* **-ais**) *m* carnival; (*fig*) mess; **conhecer alguém de outros carnavais** (*col*) to know sb from way back.
carnavalesco/a [kaxnava'leʃku/a] *adj* (*festa*) carnival *atr*; (*pessoa*) keen on carnival; (*fig*) grotesque ♦ *m/f* carnival organizer.
carne ['kaxni] *f* flesh; (*CULIN*) meat; **em ~ e osso** in the flesh; **ser de ~ e osso** to be human; **~ assada** roast beef.
carnê [kax'ne] *m* (*para compras*) payment book.
carneiro [kax'nejru] *m* sheep; (*macho*) ram; **perna/costeleta de ~** leg of lamb/lamb chop.
carniça [kax'nisa] *f* carrion; **pular ~** to play leapfrog.
carnificina [kaxnifi'sina] *f* slaughter.
carnívoro/a [kax'nivoru/a] *adj* carnivorous ♦ *m* carnivore.

carnudo/a [kax'nudu/a] *adj* plump, fleshy; (*col*) beefy; (*lábios*) thick; (*fruta*) fleshy.
caro/a ['karu/a] *adj* dear, expensive; (*estimado*) dear; **sair ~** to work out expensive; **cobrar/pagar ~** to charge a lot/ pay dearly.
carochinha [karo'ʃiɲa] *f V* **conto.**
caroço [ka'rosu] *m* (*de frutos*) stone; (*endurecimento*) lump.
carões [ka'rõjʃ] *mpl de* **carão.**
carola [ka'rɔla] (*col*) *m/f* pious person.
carona [ka'rɔna] *f* lift; **viajar de ~** to hitchhike; **pegar uma ~** to get a lift.
carpete [kax'pɛtʃi] *m* (fitted) carpet.
carpintaria [kaxpĩta'ria] *f* carpentry.
carpinteiro [kaxpĩ'tejru] *m* carpenter; (TEATRO) stagehand.
carranca [ka'xãka] *f* frown, scowl.
carrancudo/a [kaxã'kudu/a] *adj* (*soturno*) sullen; (*semblante*) scowling.
carrapato [kaxa'patu] *m* (*inseto*) tick; (*pessoa*) hanger-on.
carrapicho [kaxa'piʃu] *m* (*do cabelo*) bun.
carrasco [ka'xaʃku] *m* executioner; (*fig*) tyrant.
carrear [ka'xja*] *vt* (*transportar*) to transport; (*arrastar*) to carry; (*acarretar*) to bring on.
carreata [kaxe'ata] *f* motorcade.
carregado/a [kaxe'gadu/a] *adj* loaded, laden; (*semblante*) sullen; (*céu*) dark; (*ambiente*) tense.
carregador [kaxega'do*] *m* porter.
carregamento [kaxega'mẽtu] *m* (*ação*) loading; (*carga*) load, cargo.
carregar [kaxe'ga*] *vt* to load; (*levar*) to carry; (*bateria*) to charge; (PT: *apertar*) to press; (*levar para longe*) to take away ♦ *vi*: **~ em** (*pôr em demasia*) to overdo, put too much; (*pôr enfase*) to bring out.
carreira [ka'xejra] *f* (*ação de correr*) run, running; (*profissão*) career; (TURFE) race; (NÁUT) slipway; (*fileira*) row; **às ~s** in a hurry; **dar uma ~** to go quickly; **fazer ~** to make a career; **arrepiar ~** to abandon one's career.
carreirista [kaxej'riʃta] *adj, m/f* careerist.
carreta [ka'xeta] *f* cart.
carreteiro [kaxe'tejru] *m* cart driver.
carretel [kaxe'tɛw] (*pl* **-éis**) *m* spool, reel.
carreto [ka'xetu] *m* freight.
carril [ka'xiw] (*pl* **-is**) (PT) *m* (FERRO) rail.
carrilhão [kaxi'ʎãw] (*pl* **-ões**) *m* chime.
carrinho [ka'xiɲu] *m* (*para bagagem, compras*) trolley; (*brinquedo*) toy car; **~ (de criança)** pram; **~ de mão** wheelbarrow; **~ de chá** tea trolley.
carris [ka'xiʃ] *mpl de* **carril.**
carro ['kaxo] *m* (*automóvel*) car; (*de bois*) cart; (*de mão*) handcart, barrow; (*de máquina de escrever*) carriage; **pôr o ~ adiante dos bois** (*fig*) to put the cart before the horse; **~ alegórico** float; **~ de corrida** racing car; **~ de passeio** saloon car; **~ de praça** cab; **~ de bombeiro** fire engine; **~ esporte** sports car.
carroça [ka'xɔsa] *f* cart, waggon.
carroçeria [kaxose'ria] *f* (AUTO) bodywork.
carro-chefe (*pl* **carros-chefes**) *m* (*de desfile*) main float; (*fig*) flagship, centrepiece (BRIT), centerpiece (US).
carrocinha [kaxo'siɲa] *f* wagon.
carro-forte (*pl* **carros-fortes**) *m* security van.
carrossel [kaxo'sɛw] (*pl* **-éis**) *m* merry-go-round.
carruagem [ka'xwaʒẽ] (*pl* **-ns**) *f* carriage, coach.
carta ['kaxta] *f* letter; (*de jogar*) card; (*mapa*) chart; **~ aberta** open letter; **~ aérea** airmail letter; **~ registrada** registered letter; **~ de apresentação** letter of introduction; **~ de crédito/intenção** letter of credit/intent; **~ de condução** (PT) driving licence (BRIT), driver's license (US); **dar as ~s** to deal; **dar/ter ~ branca** to give/have carte blanche; **pôr as ~s na mesa** (*fig*) to put one's cards on the table; **~ magna** charter; **~ patente** patent.
carta-bomba (*pl* **cartas-bomba**) *f* letter bomb.
cartada [kax'tada] *f* (*fig*) move.
cartão [kax'tãw] (*pl* **-ões**) *m* card; (PT: *material*) cardboard; **~ de visita** (calling) card; **~ de crédito** credit card; **~ comercial** business card.
cartão-postal (*pl* **cartões-postais**) *m* postcard.
cartaz [kax'taʒ] *m* poster, bill (US); **ter ~** (*ser famoso*) to be well-known; (*ter popularidade*) to be popular; **(estar) em ~** (TEATRO, CINEMA) (to be) showing.
cartear [kax'tʃja*] *vt* to play ♦ *vi* to play cards.
carteira [kax'tejra] *f* (*móvel*) desk; (*para dinheiro*) wallet; (*de ações*) portfolio; **~ de identidade** identity card; **~ de motorista** driving licence (BRIT), driver's license (US).
carteiro [kax'tejru] *m* postman (BRIT), mailman (US).
cartel [kax'tɛw] (*pl* **-éis**) *m* cartel.
cartilagem [kaxtʃi'laʒẽ] (*pl* **-ns**) *f* (ANAT) cartilage.
cartões [kax'tõjʃ] *mpl de* **cartão.**
cartografia [kaxtogra'fia] *f* cartography.
cartola [kax'tɔla] *f* top hat.
cartolina [kaxto'lina] *f* card.
cartomante [kaxto'mãtʃi] *m/f* fortune-teller.
cartório [kax'tɔrju] *m* registry office.
cartucho [kax'tuʃu] *m* cartridge; (*saco de papel*) packet.
cartum [kax'tũ] (*pl* **-ns**) *m* cartoon.
cartunista [kaxtu'niʃta] *m/f* cartoonist.

NB: European Portuguese adds the following consonants to certain words: **b** (sú(b)dito, su(b)til); **c** (a(c)ção, a(c)cionista, a(c)to); **m** (inde(m)ne); **p** (ado(p)ção, ado(p)tar); *for further details see p. xiii.*

cartuns [kax'tũʃ] *mpl de* **cartum.**
caruncho [ka'rũʃu] *m* (*inseto*) woodworm.
carvalho [kax'vaʎu] *m* oak.
carvão [kax'vãw] (*pl* **-ões**) *m* coal; (*de madeira*) charcoal.
carvoeiro [kaxvo'ejru] *m* coal merchant.
carvões [kax'võjʃ] *mpl de* **carvão.**
casa ['kaza] *f* house; (*lar*) home; (*COM*) firm; (*MAT*: *decimal*) place; ~ **de botão** buttonhole; ~ **de câmbio** exchange bureau; ~ **de pensão** boarding house; ~ **de saúde** hospital; ~ **da moeda** mint; ~ **de banho** (*PT*) bathroom; **em/para** ~ (at) home/home; ~ **e comida** board and lodging; **ser de** ~ to be like one of the family; **ter dez anos de** ~ (*numa firma*) to have ten years' service behind one; ~ **de campo** country house; ~ **de cômodos** tenement; ~ **de máquinas** engine room; ~ **popular** ≈ council house.
casaca [ka'zaka] *f* tails *pl*; **virar a** ~ to become a turncoat.
casacão [kaza'kãw] (*pl* **-ões**) *m* overcoat.
casaco [ka'zaku] *m* coat; (*paletó*) jacket; ~ **de peles** fur coat.
casacões [kaza'kõjʃ] *mpl de* **casacão.**
casa-forte (*pl* **casas-fortes**) *f* vault.
casa-grande (*pl* **casas-grandes**) *f* plantation owner's house.
casal [ka'zaw] (*pl* **-ais**) *m* couple.
casamenteiro/a [kazamẽ'tejru/a] *adj* wedding *atr*.
casamento [kaza'mẽtu] *m* marriage; (*boda*) wedding; (*fig*) combination.
casar [ka'za*] *vt* to marry; (*combinar*) to match (up); **~-se** *vr* to get married; (*harmonizar-se*) to combine well.
casarão [kaza'rãw] (*pl* **-ões**) *m* mansion.
casca ['kaʃka] *f* (*de árvore*) bark; (*de banana*) skin; (*de ferida*) scab; (*de laranja*) peel; (*de nozes, ovos*) shell; (*de milho etc*) husk; (*de pão*) crust.
casca-grossa (*pl* **cascas-grossas**) *adj* coarse, uneducated.
cascalho [kaʃ'kaʎu] *m* gravel; (*na praia*) shingle.
cascão [kaʃ'kãw] *m* crust; (*sujeira*) grime.
cascata [kaʃ'kata] *f* waterfall; (*col*: *mentira*) tall story.
cascateiro/a [kaʃka'tejru/a] (*col*) *adj* bigmouthed ♦ *m/f* storyteller.
cascavel [kaʃka'vɛw] (*pl* **-éis**) *m* (*serpente*) rattlesnake.
casco ['kaʃku] *m* (*crânio*) skull; (*de animal*) hoof; (*de navio*) hull; (*para bebidas*) empty bottle; (*de tartaruga*) shell.
cascudo [kaʃ'kudu] *m* rap on the head.
casebre [ka'zɛbri] *m* hovel, shack.
caseiro/a [ka'zejru/a] *adj* (*produtos*) homemade; (*pessoa, vida*) domestic ♦ *m/f* housekeeper.
caserna [ka'zɛxna] *f* barracks *pl*.
casmurro/a [kaʒ'muxu/a] *adj* introverted.
caso ['kazu] *m* case; (*tb*: ~ *amoroso*) affair; (*estória*) story ♦ *conj* in case, if; **de** ~ **pensado** deliberately; **no** ~ **de** in case (of); **em todo** ~ in any case; **neste** ~ in that case; ~ **necessário** if necessary; **criar** ~ to cause trouble; **fazer pouco** ~ **de** to belittle; **não fazer** ~ **de** to ignore; **vir ao** ~ to be relevant; ~ **de emergência** emergency.
casório [ka'zɔrju] (*col*) *m* wedding.
caspa ['kaʃpa] *f* dandruff.
casquinha [kaʃ'kiɲa] *f* (*de sorvete*) cone; (*pele*) skin.
cassação [kasa'sãw] *f* withholding; (*de políticos*) banning.
cassar [ka'sa*] *vt* (*direitos, licença*) to cancel, withhold; (*políticos*) to ban.
cassete [ka'sɛtʃi] *m* cassette.
cassetete [kase'tɛtʃi] *m* truncheon (*BRIT*), nightstick (*US*).
cassino [ka'sinu] *m* casino.
casta ['kaʃta] *f* caste; (*estirpe*) lineage.
castanha [kaʃ'taɲa] *f* chestnut; ~ **de caju** cashew nut.
castanha-do-pará [-pa'ra] (*pl* **castanhas-do-pará**) *f* Brazil nut.
castanho/a [kaʃ'taɲu/a] *adj* brown.
castanheiro [kaʃta'ɲejru] *m* chestnut tree.
castanholas [kaʃta'ɲɔlaʃ] *fpl* castanets.
castelo [kaʃ'tɛlu] *m* castle; **fazer ~s no ar** (*fig*) to build castles in the air.
castiçal [kaʃtʃi'saw] (*pl* **-ais**) *m* candlestick.
castiço/a [kaʃ'tʃisu/a] *adj* pure; (*de boa casta*) of good stock, pedigree *atr*.
castidade [kaʃtʃi'dadʒi] *f* chastity.
castigar [kaʃtʃi'ga*] *vt* to punish; (*aperfeiçoar*) to perfect; (*col*: *tocar*) to play.
castigo [kaʃ'tʃigu] *m* punishment; (*fig*: *mortificação*) pain; **estar/ficar de** ~ (*criança*) to be getting punished/be punished.
casto/a ['kaʃtu/a] *adj* chaste.
castor [kaʃ'to*] *m* beaver.
castrar [kaʃ'tra*] *vt* to castrate.
casual [ka'zwaw] (*pl* **-ais**) *adj* chance *atr*, accidental; (*fortuito*) fortuitous.
casualidade [kazwali'dadʒi] *f* chance; (*acidente*) accident; **por** ~ by chance, accidentally.
casulo [ka'zulu] *m* (*de sementes*) pod; (*de insetos*) cocoon.
cata ['kata] *f*: **à** ~ **de** in search of.
cataclismo [kata'kliʒmu] *m* cataclysm.
catacumbas [kata'kũbaʃ] *fpl* catacombs.
catalizador(a) [kataliza'do*(a)] *adj* catalytic ♦ *m* catalyst.
catalogar [katalo'ga*] *vt* to catalogue (*BRIT*), catalog (*US*).
catálogo [ka'talogu] *m* catalogue (*BRIT*), catalog (*US*); ~ **(telefônico)** telephone directory.
Catalunha [kata'luɲa] *f*: **a** ~ Catalonia.
catapora [kata'pɔra] (*BR*) *f* chickenpox.
Catar [ka'ta*] *m*: **o** ~ Qatar.
catar [ka'ta*] *vt* to pick (up); (*procurar*) to look for, search for; (*arroz*) to clean; (*re-*

colher) to collect, gather.
catarata [kata'rata] *f* waterfall; (MED) cataract.
catarro [ka'taxu] *m* catarrh.
catártico/a [ka'taxtʃiku/a] *adj* cathartic.
catástrofe [ka'taʃtrofi] *f* catastrophe.
catastrófico/a [kataʃ'trɔfiku/a] *adj* catastrophic.
catatau [kata'tau] *m*: **um ~ de** a lot of.
cata-vento *m* weathercock.
catecismo [kate'siʒmu] *m* catechism.
cátedra ['katedra] *f* chair.
catedral [kate'draw] (*pl* **-ais**) *f* cathedral.
catedrático/a [kate'dratʃiku/a] *m/f* professor.
categoria [katego'ria] *f* category; (*social*) rank; (*qualidade*) quality; **de alta ~** first-rate.
categórico/a [kate'gɔriku/a] *adj* categorical.
categorizar [kategori'za*] *vt* to categorize.
catequizar [kateki'za*] *vt* to talk round; (REL) to catechize.
catinga [ka'tʃĩga] *f* stench, stink.
catinguento/a [katʃĩ'gẽtu/a] *adj* smelly.
catiripapo [katʃiri'papu] *m* punch.
cativante [katʃi'vãtʃi] *adj* captivating; (*atraente*) charming.
cativar [katʃi'va*] *vt* (*escravizar*) to enslave; (*fascinar*) to captivate; (*atrair*) to charm.
cativeiro [katʃi'vejru] *m* captivity; (*escravidão*) slavery; (*cadeia*) prison.
cativo/a [ka'tʃivu/a] *m/f* (*escravo*) slave; (*prisioneiro*) prisoner.
catolicismo [katoli'siʒmu] *m* catholicism.
católico/a [ka'tɔliku/a] *adj*, *m/f* catholic.
catorze [ka'toxzi] *num* fourteen; *V tb* **cinco**.
catucar [katu'ka*] *vt* = **cutucar**.
caturrice [katu'xisi] *f* obstinacy.
caução [kaw'sãw] (*pl* **-ões**) *f* security, guarantee; (JUR) bail; **prestar ~** to give bail; **sob ~** on bail.
caucionante [kawsjo'nãtʃi] *m/f* guarantor.
caucionar [kawsjo'na*] *vt* to guarantee, stand surety for; (JUR) to stand bail for.
cauções [kaw'sõjʃ] *fpl de* **caução**.
cauda ['kawda] *f* tail; (*de vestido*) train.
caudal [kaw'daw] (*pl* **-ais**) *m* torrent.
caudaloso/a [kawda'lozu/ɔza] *adj* torrential.
caudilho [kaw'dʒiʎu] *m* leader, chief.
caule ['kauli] *m* stalk, stem.
causa ['kawza] *f* cause; (*motivo*) motive, reason; (JUR) lawsuit, case; **por ~ de** because of; **em ~** in question.
causador(a) [kawza'do*(a)] *adj* which caused ♦ *m* cause.
causar [kaw'za*] *vt* to cause, bring about.
cáustico/a ['kawʃtʃiku/a] *adj* caustic.
cautela [kaw'tɛla] *f* caution; (*senha*) ticket; (*título*) share certificate; **~ (de penhor)** pawn ticket.
cautelar [kawte'la*] *adj* precautionary.
cauteloso/a [kawte'lozu/ɔza] *adj* cautious, wary.
cauterizar [kawteri'za*] *vt* to cauterize.
cava ['kava] *f* (*de manga*) armhole.
cavação [kava'sãw] (*col*) *f* wheeling and dealing.
cavaco [ka'vaku] *m*: **~s do ofício** occupational hazards.
cavado/a [ka'vadu/a] *adj* (*olhos*) sunken; (*roupa*) low-cut.
cavador(a) [kava'do*(a)] *adj* go-getting ♦ *m/f* go-getter.
cavala [ka'vala] *f* mackerel.
cavalar [kava'la*] *adj* enormous, huge.
cavalaria [kavala'ria] *f* (MIL) cavalry; (*instituição medieval*) chivalry.
cavalariça [kavala'risa] *f* stable.
cavaleiro [kava'lejru] *m* rider, horseman; (*medieval*) knight.
cavalete [kava'letʃi] *m* stand; (FOTO) tripod; (*de pintor*) easel; (*de mesa*) trestle; (*do violino*) bridge.
cavalgar [kavaw'ga*] *vt* to ride ♦ *vi*: **~ em** to ride on; **~ (sobre)** to jump over.
cavalheiresco/a [kavaʎej'reʃku/a] *adj* courteous, gallant, gentlemanly.
cavalheiro/a [kava'ʎejru/a] *adj* courteous, gallant ♦ *m* gentleman; (DANÇA) partner.
cavalinho-de-pau [kava'liɲu-] (*pl* **cavalinhos-de-pau**) *m* rocking horse.
cavalo [ka'valu] *m* horse; (XADREZ) knight; (*pessoa*): **ser um ~** to be rude; **a ~** on horseback; **50 ~s(-vapor), 50 ~s (de força)** 50 horsepower; **quantos ~s tem esse carro?** how many horsepower is that car?; **fazer de algo um ~ de batalha** to make a mountain out of a molehill about sth; **tirar o ~ da chuva** (*fig*) to drop the idea; **~ de corrida** racehorse.
cavalo-marinho (*pl* **cavalos-marinhos**) *m* seahorse.
cavanhaque [kava'ɲaki] *m* goatee (beard).
cavaquinho [kava'kiɲu] *m* small guitar.
cavar [ka'va*] *vt* to dig; (*decote*) to lower; (*esforçar-se para obter*) to try to get ♦ *vi* to dig; (*animal*) to burrow; (*esforçar-se*) to try hard; (*fig*) to delve; **~ a vida** to earn one's living.
cave ['kavi] (PT) *f* wine-cellar.
caveira [ka'vejra] *f* skull; **fazer a ~ de alguém** (*col*) to blacken sb's name.
caverna [ka'vɛxna] *f* cavern.
cavernoso/a [kavex'nozu/ɔza] *adj* (*voz*) booming; (*pessoa*) horrible.
caviar [ka'vja*] *m* caviar.
cavidade [kavi'dadʒi] *f* cavity.
cavilha [ka'viʎa] *f* (*de madeira*) peg, dowel; (*de metal*) bolt.
cavo/a ['kavu/a] *adj* (*côncavo*) concave.
caxias [ka'ʃiaʃ] *adj inv* overdisciplined ♦ *m/f*

***NB:** European Portuguese adds the following consonants to certain words:* **b** (sú(b)dito, su(b)til); **c** (a(c)ção, a(c)cionista, a(c)to); **m** (inde(m)ne); **p** (ado(p)ção, ado(p)tar); *for further details see p. xiii.*

inv stickler for discipline.

caxumba [ka'ʃũba] *f* mumps *sg*.

CBA *abr f* = **Confederação Brasileira de Automobilismo.**

CBAt *abr f* = **Confederação Brasileira de Atletismo.**

CBD *abr f* = **Confederação Brasileira de Desportos.**

CBF *abr f* = **Confederação Brasileira de Futebol.**

CBT *abr m* = **Código Brasileiro de Telecomunicações.**

CBTU *abr f* = **Companhia Brasileira de Trens Urbanos.**

CCT (*BR*) *abr m* = **Conselho Científico e Tecnológico.**

c/c *abr* (= *conta corrente*) c/a.

CDB *abr m* = **Certificado de Depósito Bancário.**

CDC (*BR*) *abr m* = **Conselho de Desenvolvimento Comercial.**

CDDPH (*BR*) *abr m* = **Conselho de Defesa dos Direitos da Pessoa Humana.**

CDI (*BR*) *abr m* = **Certificado de Depósito Interbancário**; = **Conselho de Desenvolvimento Industrial.**

cê [se] (*col*) *pron* = **você.**

cear [sja*] *vt* to have for supper ♦ *vi* to dine.

cearense [sea'rẽsi] *adj* from Ceará ♦ *m/f* person from Ceará.

cebola [se'bola] *f* onion.

cebolinha [sebo'liɲa] *f* spring onion.

Cebrae (*BR*) *abr f* = **Centro de Apoio à Pequena e Média Empresa.**

Cebrap *abr m* = **Centro Brasileiro de Análise e Planejamento.**

cecear [se'sja*] *vi* to lisp.

cê-cedilha (*pl* **cês-cedilhas**) *m* c cedilla.

ceceio [se'seju] *m* lisp.

cê-dê-efe [-'ɛfi] (*col*: *pl* **~s**) *m/f* swot.

ceder [se'de*] *vt* to give up; (*dar*) to hand over; (*emprestar*) to lend ♦ *vi* to give in, yield; (*porta*, *calça etc*) to give (way); **~ a** to give in to.

cedilha [se'dʒiʎa] *f* cedilla.

cedo ['sedu] *adv* early; (*em breve*) soon; **mais ~ ou mais tarde** sooner or later; **o mais ~ possível** as soon as possible.

cedro ['sɛdru] *m* cedar.

cédula ['sɛdula] *f* (*moeda-papel*) banknote; (*eleitoral*) ballot paper.

CEE *abr f* (= *Comunidade Econômica Européia*) EEC.

CEF (*BR*) *abr f* (= *Caixa Econômica Federal*) federal bank.

cegar [se'ga*] *vt* to blind; (*ofuscar*) to dazzle; (*tesoura*) to blunt ♦ *vi* (*ofuscar*) to be dazzling.

cego/a ['sɛgu/a] *adj* blind; (*total*) complete, total; (*tesoura*) blunt ♦ *m/f* blind man/woman; **às cegas** blindly; **ser ~ por alguém** to be mad about sb.

cegonha [se'gɔɲa] *f* stork.

cegueira [se'gejra] *f* blindness.

CEI (*BR*) *abr f* (= *Comissão Especial de Inquérito*) *commission of inquiry*.

ceia ['seja] *f* supper.

ceifa ['sejfa] *f* harvest; (*fig*) destruction.

ceifar [sej'fa*] *vt* to reap, harvest; (*vidas*) to destroy.

cela ['sɛla] *f* cell.

celebração [selebra'sãw] (*pl* **-ões**) *f* celebration.

celebrar [sele'bra*] *vt* to celebrate; (*exaltar*) to praise; (*acordo*) to seal.

célebre ['sɛlebri] *adj* famous, well-known.

celebridade [selebri'dadʒi] *f* celebrity.

celebrizar [selebri'za*] *vt* to make famous; **~-se** *vr* to become famous.

celeiro [se'lejru] *m* granary; (*depósito*) barn.

célere ['sɛleri] *adj* swift, quick.

celeste [se'lɛʃtʃi] *adj* celestial, heavenly.

celeuma [se'lewma] *f* pandemonium, uproar.

celibatário/a [seliba'tarju/a] *adj* unmarried, single ♦ *m/f* bachelor/spinster.

celibato [seli'batu] *m* celibacy.

celofane [selo'fani] *m* cellophane.

celta ['sɛwta] *adj* Celtic ♦ *m/f* Celt.

célula ['sɛlula] *f* (*BIO*, *ELET*) cell.

celular [selu'la*] *adj* cellular.

celulite [selu'litʃi] *f* cellulite.

celulose [selu'lɔzi] *f* cellulose.

cem [sẽ] *num* hundred; **ser ~ por cento** (*fig*) to be great; *V tb* **cinqüenta.**

cemitério [semi'tɛrju] *m* cemetery, graveyard.

cena ['sɛna] *f* scene; (*palco*) stage; **em ~** on the stage; **levar à ~** to stage; **fazer uma ~** to make a scene.

cenário [se'narju] *m* (*TEATRO*) scenery; (*CINEMA*) scenario; (*de um acontecimento*) scene, setting; (*panorama*) view.

cenho ['sɛɲu] *m* face.

cênico/a ['seniku/a] *adj* (*TEATRO*) stage *atr*; (*CINEMA*) set *atr*.

cenografia [senogra'fia] *f* set design.

cenógrafo/a [se'nɔgrafu/a] *m/f* (*TEATRO*) set designer.

cenoura [se'nora] *f* carrot.

censo ['sẽsu] *m* census.

censor(a) [sẽ'so*(a)] *m/f* censor.

censura [sẽ'sura] *f* (*POL etc*) censorship; (*reprovação*) censure, criticism; (*repreensão*) reprimand.

censurar [sẽsu'ra*] *vt* (*reprovar*) to censure; (*filme*, *livro etc*) to censor.

censurável [sẽsu'ravew] (*pl* **-eis**) *adj* reprehensible.

centavo [sẽ'tavu] *m* cent; **estar sem um ~** to be penniless.

centeio [sẽ'teju] *m* rye.

centelha [sẽ'teʎa] *f* spark; (*fig*) flash.

centena [sẽ'tɛna] *f* hundred; **às ~s** in hundreds.

centenário/a [sẽte'narju/a] *adj* centenary ♦ *m/f* centenarian ♦ *m* centenary, centennial.

centésimo/a [sẽ'tɛzimu/a] *adj* hundredth ♦ *m*

hundredth (part).

centígrado [sẽ'tʃigradu] *m* centigrade.

centilitro [sẽtʃi'litru] *m* centilitre (*BRIT*), centiliter (*US*).

centímetro [sẽ'tʃimetru] *m* centimetre (*BRIT*), centimeter (*US*).

cento ['sẽtu] *m*: **~ e um** one hundred and one; **por ~** per cent.

centopeia [sẽto'peja] *f* centipede.

central [sẽ'traw] (*pl* **-ais**) *adj* central ♦ *f* (*de polícia etc*) head office; **~ elétrica** (electric) power station; **~ telefônica** telephone exchange.

centralização [sẽtraliza'sãw] *f* centralization.

centralizar [sẽtrali'za*] *vt* to centralize; **~-se** *vr* to be centralized.

centrar [sẽ'tra*] *vt* to centre (*BRIT*), center (*US*).

centro ['sẽtru] *m* centre (*BRIT*), center (*US*); (*de uma cidade*) town centre; **~ das atenções** centre of attention; **~ de custo/ lucro** (*COM*) cost/profit centre; **~ de mesa** centrepiece (*BRIT*), centerpiece (*US*).

centroavante [sẽtroa'vãtʃi] *m* (*FUTEBOL*) centre forward.

CEP ['sɛpi] (*BR*) *abr m* (= *Código de Endereçamento Postal*) postcode (*BRIT*), zip code (*US*).

cepo ['sepu] *m* (*toco*) stump; (*toro*) log.

céptico/a *etc* ['sɛptiku/a] (*PT*) = **cético** *etc*.

ceptro ['sɛtru] (*PT*) *m* = **cetro**.

cera ['sera] *f* wax; **fazer ~** (*fig*) to dawdle, waste time.

cerâmica [se'ramika] *f* pottery; (*arte*) ceramics *sg*.

cerâmico/a [se'ramiku/a] *adj* ceramic.

ceramista [sera'miʃta] *m/f* potter.

cerca ['sexka] *f* (*de madeira, arame*) fence ♦ *prep*: **~ de** (*aproximadamente*) around, about; **~ viva** hedge.

cercado/a [sex'kadu/a] *adj* surrounded; (*com cerca*) fenced in ♦ *m* enclosure; (*para animais*) pen; (*para crianças*) playpen.

cercanias [sexka'niaʃ] *fpl* (*arredores*) outskirts; (*vizinhança*) neighbourhood *sg* (*BRIT*), neighborhood *sg* (*US*).

cercar [sex'ka*] *vt* to enclose; (*pôr cerca em*) to fence in; (*rodear*) to surround; (*assediar*) to besiege.

cercear [sex'sja*] *vt* (*liberdade*) to curtail, restrict.

cerco ['sexku] *m* encirclement; (*MIL*) siege; **pôr ~ a** to besiege.

cereal [se'rjaw] (*pl* **-ais**) *m* cereal.

cerebral [sere'braw] (*pl* **-ais**) *adj* cerebral, brain *atr*.

cérebro ['sɛrebru] *m* brain; (*fig*) intelligence, brains *pl*.

cereja [se'reʒa] *f* cherry.

cerejeira [sere'ʒejra] *f* cherry tree.

cerimônia [seri'monja] *f* ceremony; **de ~** formal; **sem ~** informal; **fazer ~** to stand on ceremony; **~ de posse** swearing-in ceremony, investiture.

cerimonial [serimo'njaw] (*pl* **-ais**) *adj*, *m* ceremonial.

cerimonioso/a [serimo'njozu/ɔza] *adj* ceremonious.

ceroulas [se'rolaʃ] *fpl* long johns.

cerração [sexa'sãw] *f* (*nevoeiro*) fog.

cerrado/a [se'xadu/a] *adj* shut, closed; (*punho*) clenched; (*denso*) dense, thick ♦ *m* (*vegetação*) scrub(land).

cerrar [se'xa*] *vt* to close, shut; **~-se** *vr* to close, shut.

certame [sex'tami] *m* (*concurso*) contest, competition.

certeiro/a [sex'tejru/a] *adj* (*tiro*) accurate, well-aimed; (*acertado*) correct.

certeza [sex'teza] *f* certainty; **com ~** certainly, surely; (*provavelmente*) probably; **ter ~ de** to be certain *ou* sure of; **ter ~ de que** to be sure that; **tem ~?** are you sure?

certidão [sextʃi'dãw] (*pl* **-ões**) *f* certificate.

certificado [sextʃifi'kadu] *m* (*garantia*) certificate.

certificar [sextʃifi'ka*] *vt* to certify; (*assegurar*) to assure; **~-se** *vr*: **~-se de** to make sure of.

certo/a ['sɛxtu/a] *adj* certain, sure; (*exato, direito*) right; (*um, algum*) a certain ♦ *adv* correctly; **na certa** certainly; **ao ~** for certain; **dar ~** to work; **está ~** okay, all right.

cerveja [sex'veʒa] *f* beer.

cervejaria [sexveʒa'ria] *f* (*fábrica*) brewery; (*bar*) bar, public house.

cervical [sexvi'kaw] (*pl* **-ais**) *adj* cervical.

cérvice ['sɛxvisi] *f* cervix.

cervo ['sɛxvu] *m* deer.

cerzir [sex'zi*] *vt* to darn.

cesariana [seza'rjana] *f* Caesarian (*BRIT*), Cesarian (*US*).

cessão [se'sãw] (*pl* **-ões**) *f* (*cedência*) surrender; (*transferência*) transfer.

cessação [sesa'sãw] *f* halting, ceasing.

cessar [se'sa*] *vi* to cease, stop; **sem ~** continually.

cessar-fogo *m inv* cease-fire.

cessões [se'sõjʃ] *fpl de* **cessão**.

cesta ['seʃta] *f* basket.

cesto ['seʃtu] *m* basket; (*com tampa*) hamper.

ceticismo [setʃi'siʒmu] *m* scepticism (*BRIT*), skepticism (*US*).

cético/a ['sɛtʃiku/a] *adj* sceptical (*BRIT*), skeptical (*US*) ♦ *m/f* sceptic (*BRIT*), skeptic (*US*).

cetim [se'tʃĩ] *m* satin.

cetro ['sɛtru] *m* sceptre (*BRIT*), scepter (*US*).

céu [sɛw] *m* sky; (*REL*) heaven; (*da boca*) roof; **cair do ~** (*fig*) to come at the right time; **mover ~s e terra** (*fig*) to move heaven

NB: European Portuguese adds the following consonants to certain words: **b** (sú(b)dito, su(b)til); **c** (a(c)ção, a(c)cionista, a(c)to); **m** (inde(m)ne); **p** (ado(p)ção, ado(p)tar); *for further details see p. xiii.*

and earth.
cevada [se'vada] *f* barley.
cevar [se'va*] *vt* (*engordar*) to fatten; (*alimentar*) to feed; (*engodar*) to bait.
CGC (*BR*) *abr m* (= *Cadastro Geral de Contribuintes*) *roll of tax payers.*
CGT (*BR*) *abr f* (= *Central Geral dos Trabalhadores*) *trade union.*
chá [ʃa] *m* tea; (*reunião*) tea party; **dar um ~ de sumiço** (*col*) to disappear; **tomar ~ de cadeira** (*fig*) to be a wallflower.
chacal [ʃa'kaw] (*pl* **-ais**) *m* jackal.
chácara ['ʃakara] *f* (*granja*) farm; (*casa de campo*) country house.
chacina [ʃa'sina] *f* slaughter.
chacinar [ʃasi'na*] *vt* (*matar*) to slaughter.
chacoalhar [ʃakwa'ʎa*] *vt* to shake; (*col: amolar*) to bug ♦ *vi* to shake about; to be annoying.
chacota [ʃa'kɔta] *f* (*zombaria*) mockery.
chacrinha [ʃa'kriɲa] (*col*) *f* get-together.
Chade ['ʃadʒi] *m*: **o ~** Chad.
chã-de-dentro [ʃã-] (*pl* **chãs-de-dentro**) *f* round of beef.
chá-de-panela *m* ≈ hen night, ≈ wedding shower (*US*).
chafariz [ʃafa'riʒ] *m* fountain.
chafurdar [ʃafux'da*] *vi*: **~ em** to wallow in; **~-se** *vr*: **~-se em** to wallow in.
chaga ['ʃaga] *f* (*MED*) wound; (*fig*) disease.
chalé [ʃa'lɛ] *m* chalet.
chaleira [ʃa'lejra] *f* kettle; (*bajulador*) crawler, toady.
chaleirar [ʃalej'ra*] *vt* to crawl to.
chama ['ʃama] *f* flame; **em ~s** on fire.
chamada [ʃa'mada] *f* call; (*MIL*) roll call; (*EDUC*) register; (*no jornal*) headline; **dar uma ~ em alguém** (*repreender*) to tell sb off.
chamar [ʃa'ma*] *vt* to call; (*convidar*) to invite; (*atenção*) to attract ♦ *vi* to call; (*telefone*) to ring; **~-se** *vr* to be called; **chamo-me João** my name is John; **~ alguém de idiota/Dudu** to call sb an idiot/Dudu; **mandar ~** to summon, send for.
chamariz [ʃama'riʒ] *m* decoy; (*fig*) lure.
chamativo/a [ʃama'tʃivu/a] *adj* showy, flashy.
chamego [ʃa'megu] *m* cuddle.
chaminé [ʃami'nɛ] *f* chimney; (*de navio*) funnel.
champanha [ʃã'paɲa] *m ou f* champagne.
champanhe [ʃã'paɲi] *m ou f* = **champanha**.
champu [ʃã'pu] (*PT*) *m* shampoo.
chamuscar [ʃamuʃ'ka*] *vt* to scorch, singe; **~-se** *vr* to scorch o.s.
chance ['ʃãsi] *f* chance.
chancela [ʃã'sɛla] *f* seal, official stamp.
chancelaria [ʃãsela'ria] *f* chancellery.
chanceler [ʃãse'le*] *m* chancellor.
chanchada [ʃã'ʃada] *f* second-rate film (*ou* play).
chantagear [ʃãta'ʒja*] *vt* to blackmail.
chantagem [ʃã'taʒẽ] *f* blackmail.
chantagista [ʃãta'ʒiʃta] *m/f* blackmailer.
chão [ʃãw] (*pl* **~s**) *m* ground; (*terra*) soil; (*piso*) floor.
chapa ['ʃapa] *f* (*placa*) plate; (*eleitoral*) list ♦ *m/f* (*col*) mate, friend; **~ de matrícula** (*PT: AUTO*) number (*BRIT*) *ou* license (*US*) plate; **bife na ~** grilled steak; **oi, meu ~!** hi, mate!
chapa-branca (*pl* **chapas-brancas**) *m* civil service car.
chapelaria [ʃapela'ria] *f* (*loja*) hatshop.
chapeleira [ʃape'lejra] *f* hat box; *V tb* **chapeleiro.**
chapeleiro/a [ʃape'lejru/a] *m/f* milliner.
chapéu [ʃa'pɛw] *m* hat.
chapéu-coco (*pl* **chapéus-cocos**) *m* bowler hat.
chapinha [ʃa'piɲa] *f*: **~ (de garrafa)** (bottle) top.
chapinhar [ʃapi'ɲa*] *vi* to splash.
charada [ʃa'rada] *f* (*quebra-cabeça*) puzzle.
charco ['ʃaxku] *m* marsh, bog.
charge ['ʃaxʒi] *f* (political) cartoon.
chargista [ʃax'ʒiʃta] *m/f* (political) cartoonist.
charlatão [ʃaxla'tãw] (*pl* **-ães**) *m* charlatan; (*curandeiro*) quack.
charme ['ʃaxmi] *m* charm; **fazer ~** to be nice, use one's charm.
charmoso/a [ʃax'mozu/ɔza] *adj* charming.
charneca [ʃax'nɛka] *f* moor, heath.
charrete [ʃa'xɛtʃi] *f* cart.
charter ['tʃaxte*] *adj inv* charter ♦ *m* (*pl*: **~s**) charter flight.
charuto [ʃa'rutu] *m* cigar.
chassis [ʃa'si] *m* (*AUTO, ELET*) chassis.
chata ['ʃata] *f* (*embarcação*) barge; *V tb* **chato.**
chateação [ʃatʃja'sãw] (*pl* **-ões**) *f* bother, upset; (*maçada*) bore.
chatear [ʃa'tʃja*] *vt* (*aborrecer*) to bother, upset; (*importunar*) to pester; (*entediar*) to bore; (*irritar*) to annoy ♦ *vi* to be upsetting; to be boring; to be annoying; **~-se** *vr* to get upset; to get bored; to get annoyed.
chatice [ʃa'tʃisi] (*PT*) *f* nuisance.
chato/a ['ʃatu/a] *adj* (*plano*) flat, level; (*pé*) flat; (*tedioso*) boring; (*irritante*) annoying; (*que fica mal*) bad, rude ♦ *m/f* bore; (*quem irrita*) pain.
chatura [ʃa'tura] (*col*) *f* pain (in the neck).
chauvinismo [ʃawvi'niʒmu] *m* chauvinism.
chauvinista [ʃawvi'niʃta] *adj* chauvinistic ♦ *m/f* chauvinist.
chavão [ʃa'vãw] (*pl* **-ões**) *m* cliché.
chave ['ʃavi] *f* key; (*ELET*) switch; (*TIP*) curly bracket; **~ de porcas** spanner; **~ inglesa** (monkey) wrench; **~ de fenda** screwdriver.
-chave *sufixo* key *atr.*
chaveiro [ʃa'vejru] *m* (*utensílio*) key ring; (*pessoa*) locksmith.
chávena ['ʃavena] (*PT*) *f* cup.
checar [ʃe'ka*] *vt* to check.
check-up [tʃe'kapi] (*pl* **~s**) *m* check-up.
chefatura [ʃefa'tura] *f*: **~ de polícia** police

headquarters *sg*.
chefe ['ʃɛfi] *m/f* head, chief; (*patrão*) boss; ~ **de turma** foreman; ~ **de estação** stationmaster.
chefia [ʃe'fia] *f* (*liderança*) leadership; (*direção*) management; (*repartição*) headquarters *sg*; **estar com a** ~ **de** to be in charge of.
chefiar [ʃe'fja*] *vt* to lead.
chega ['ʃega] (*col*) *m*: **dar um** ~ **em alguém** to tell sb off ♦ *prep* even.
chegada [ʃe'gada] *f* arrival; **dar uma** ~ to drop by.
chegado/a [ʃe'gadu/a] *adj* (*próximo*) near; (*íntimo*) close; **ser** ~ **a** (*bebidas, comidas*) to be keen on.
chegar [ʃe'ga*] *vt* (*aproximar*) to bring near ♦ *vi* to arrive; (*ser suficiente*) to be enough; **~-se** *vr*: **~-se a** to approach; **chega!** that's enough!; ~ **a** (*atingir*) to reach; (*conseguir*) to manage to; ~ **algo para cá/para lá** to bring sth closer/move sth over; **chega (mais) para cá/para lá!** come closer!/move over!; **vou chegando** I'm leaving.
cheia ['ʃeja] *f* flood.
cheio/a ['ʃeju/a] *adj* full; (*repleto*) full up; (*col*: *farto*) fed up; ~ **de si** self-important; ~ **de dedos** all fingers and thumbs; (*inibido*) awkward; ~ **de frescura** (*col*) fussy; ~ **da nota** (*col*) rich, loaded; **acertar em** ~ to be exactly right, hit the nail on the head; **estar** ~ **de algo** (*col*) to be fed up with sth.
cheirar [ʃej'ra*] *vt, vi* to smell; ~ **a** to smell of; **isto não me cheira bem** there's something fishy about this.
cheiro ['ʃejru] *m* smell; **ter** ~ **de** to smell of.
cheiroso/a [ʃej'rozu/ɔza] *adj*: **ser** *ou* **estar** ~ to smell nice.
cheiro-verde *m* bunch of parsley and spring onion.
cheque ['ʃɛki] *m* cheque (*BRIT*), check (*US*); (*XADREZ*) check; ~ **cruzado** crossed cheque; ~ **em branco** blank cheque; ~ **sem fundos** uncovered cheque, rubber cheque (*col*); ~ **voador** rubber cheque.
chequei [ʃɛ'kej] *etc vb V* **checar**.
cheque-mate *m* checkmate.
cherne ['ʃɛxni] *m* grouper.
chiado ['ʃjadu] *m* squeak(ing); (*de vapor*) hiss(ing).
chiar [ʃja*] *vi* to squeak; (*porta*) to creak; (*vapor*) to hiss; (*fritura*) to sizzle; (*col*: *reclamar*) to grumble.
chibata [ʃi'bata] *f* (*vara*) cane.
chiclete [ʃi'klɛtʃi] *m* chewing gum; ~ **de bola** bubble gum.
chicória [ʃi'kɔrja] *f* chicory.
chicote [ʃi'kɔtʃi] *m* whip.
chicotear [ʃiko'tʃja*] *vt* to whip, lash.
chifrada [ʃi'frada] *f* (*golpe*) butt; **dar uma** ~ to cheat.
chifrar [ʃi'fra*] *vt* to two-time.
chifre ['ʃifri] *m* (*corno*) horn; **pôr** ~ **em alguém** (*col*) to be unfaithful to sb, cheat on sb.
chifrudo/a [ʃi'frudu/a] (*col*) *adj* cuckolded.
Chile ['ʃili] *m*: **o** ~ Chile.
chileno/a [ʃi'lɛnu/a] *adj, m/f* Chilean.
chilique [ʃi'liki] (*col*) *m* fit.
chilrear [ʃiw'xja*] *vi* to chirp, twitter.
chilreio [ʃiw'xeju] *m* chirping.
chimarrão [ʃima'xãw] (*pl* **-ões**) *m* *maté tea without sugar taken from a pipe-like cup*.
chimpanzé [ʃĩpã'zɛ] *m* chimpanzee.
China ['ʃina] *f*: **a** ~ China.
china ['ʃina] *m/f* Chinese.
chinelo [ʃi'nɛlu] *m* slipper; **botar no** ~ (*fig*) to put to shame.
chinês/esa [ʃi'neʃ/eza] *adj, m/f* Chinese ♦ *m* (*LING*) Chinese.
chinfrim [ʃĩ'frĩ] (*pl* **-ns**) *adj* cheap and cheerful.
chio ['ʃiu] *m* squeak; (*de rodas*) screech.
chip ['ʃipi] *m* (*COMPUT*) chip.
Chipre ['ʃipri] *f* Cyprus.
chique ['ʃiki] *adj* stylish, chic.
chiqueiro [ʃi'kejru] *m* pigsty.
chispa ['ʃiʃpa] *f* spark.
chispada [ʃiʃ'pada] (*BR*) *f* dash.
chispar [ʃiʃ'pa*] *vi* (*correr*) to dash.
chita ['ʃita] *f* printed cotton, calico.
choça ['ʃɔsa] *f* shack, hut.
chocalhar [ʃoka'ʎa*] *vt, vi* to rattle.
chocalho [ʃo'kaʎu] *m* (*MÚS, brinquedo*) rattle; (*para animais*) bell.
chocante [ʃo'kãtʃi] *adj* shocking; (*col*) amazing.
chocar [ʃo'ka*] *vt* (*incubar*) to hatch, incubate; (*ofender*) to shock, offend ♦ *vi* to shock; **~-se** *vr* to crash, collide; to be shocked.
chocho/a ['ʃoʃu/a] *adj* hollow, empty; (*fraco*) weak; (*sem graça*) dull.
chocolate [ʃoko'latʃi] *m* chocolate.
chofer [ʃo'fe*] *m* driver.
chofre ['ʃofri] *m*: **de** ~ all of a sudden.
chongas ['ʃõgaʃ] (*col*) *pron* nothing, bugger all (*col*).
chopada [ʃo'pada] *f* drinking session.
chope ['ʃopi] *m* draught beer.
choque ['ʃɔki] *etc vb V* **chocar** ♦ *m* (*abalo*) shock; (*colisão*) collision; (*MED, ELET*) shock; (*impacto*) impact; (*conflito*) clash, conflict; ~ **cultural** culture shock.
choradeira [ʃora'dejra] *f* fit of crying.
chorado/a [ʃo'radu/a] *adj* (*canto*) sad; (*gol*) hard-won.
choramingar [ʃoramĩ'ga*] *vi* to whine, whimper.
choramingas [ʃora'mĩgaʃ] *m/f inv* crybaby.

NB: *European Portuguese adds the following consonants to certain words:* **b** (sú(b)dito, su(b)til); **c** (a(c)ção, a(c)cionista, a(c)to); **m** (inde(m)ne); **p** (ado(p)ção, ado(p)tar); *for further details see p. xiii.*

choramingo [ʃora'mĩgu] *m* whine, whimper.

chorão/rona [ʃo'rãw/rɔna] (*pl* **-ões/~s**) *adj* tearful ♦ *m/f* crybaby ♦ *m* (BOT) weeping willow.

chorar [ʃo'ra*] *vt, vi* to weep, cry.

chorinho [ʃo'riɲu] *m type of Brazilian music.*

choro ['ʃoru] *m* crying; (MÚS) *type of Brazilian music.*

choroso/a [ʃo'rozu/ɔza] *adj* tearful.

choupana [ʃo'pana] *f* shack, hut.

chouriço [ʃo'risu] *m* (BR) black pudding; (PT) spicy sausage.

chove-não-molha [ʃɔvinãw'mɔʎa] (*col*) *m* shilly-shallying.

chover [ʃo've*] *vi* to rain; ~ **a cântaros** to rain cats and dogs; **choveram cartas** letters poured in.

chuchu [ʃu'ʃu] *m* chayote (*vegetable*); **ele fala/está quente pra ~** (*col*) he talks a lot/ it's really hot.

chucrute [ʃu'krutʃi] *m* sauerkraut.

chué [ʃu'ɛ] (*col*) *adj* lousy.

chulé [ʃu'lɛ] *m* foot odour (BRIT) *ou* odor (US).

chulear [ʃu'lja*] *vt* to hem.

chulo/a ['ʃulu/a] *adj* vulgar.

chumaço [ʃu'masu] *m* (*de papel, notas*) wad; (*material*) wadding.

chumbado/a [ʃũ'badu/a] (*col*) *adj* (*cansado*) dog-tired; (*doente*) laid out.

chumbar [ʃũ'ba*] *vt* to fill with lead; (*soldar*) to solder; (*atirar em*) to fire at ♦ *vi* (PT: *reprovar*) to fail.

chumbo ['ʃũbu] *m* lead; (*de caça*) gunshot; (PT: *de dente*) filling; **esta mala está um ~** this case weighs a ton.

chupado/a [ʃu'padu/a] (*col*) *adj* (*cara, pessoa*) drawn.

chupar [ʃu'pa*] *vt* to suck; (*absorver*) to absorb.

chupeta [ʃu'peta] *f* (*para criança*) dummy (BRIT), pacifier (US).

churrascaria [ʃuxaʃka'ria] *f* barbecue restaurant.

churrasco [ʃu'xaʃku] *m* barbecue.

churrasqueira [ʃuxaʃ'kejra] *f* barbecue.

churrasquinho [ʃuxaʃ'kiɲu] *m* kebab.

chutar [ʃu'ta*] *vt* to kick; (*col*: *adivinhar*) to guess at; (: *dar o fora em*) to dump ♦ *vi* to kick; to guess; (*col*: *mentir*) to lie.

chute ['ʃutʃi] *m* kick; (*para o gol*) shot; (*col*: *mentira*) lie; **dar o ~ em alguém** (*col*) to give sb the boot.

chuteira [ʃu'tejra] *f* football boot; **pendurar as ~s** (*col*) to retire.

chuva ['ʃuva] *f* rain; **tomar ~** to get caught in the rain; **estar na ~** (*fig*) to be drunk; **~ de pedra** hailstorm.

chuvarada [ʃuva'rada] *f* torrential rain.

chuveirada [ʃuvej'rada] *f* shower.

chuveiro [ʃu'vejru] *m* shower.

chuviscar [ʃuviʃ'ka*] *vi* to drizzle.

chuvisco [ʃu'viʃku] *m* drizzle.

chuvoso/a [ʃu'vozu/ɔza] *adj* rainy.

CIA *abr f* (= *Central Intelligence Agency*) CIA.

Cia. *abr* (= *companhia*) Co.

cibernética [sibex'nɛtʃika] *f* cybernetics *sg.*

CIC (BR) *abr m* = **Cartão de Identificação do Contribuinte.**

cica ['sika] *f* sharpness.

cicatriz [sika'triʒ] *f* scar.

cicatrização [sikatriza'sãw] *f* scarring.

cicatrizar [sikatri'za*] *vt* (*rosto*) to scar; (*ferida*) to heal; (*fig*) to cure, heal ♦ *vi* to heal; to scar.

cicerone [sise'rɔni] *m* tourist guide.

ciciar [si'sja*] *vi* to whisper; (*rumorejar*) to murmur.

cíclico/a ['sikliku/a] *adj* cyclical.

ciclismo [si'kliʒmu] *m* cycling.

ciclista [si'kliʃta] *m/f* cyclist.

ciclo ['siklu] *m* cycle; **~ básico** foundation year.

ciclone [si'klɔni] *m* cyclone.

ciclovia [siklo'via] *f* cycle path.

cidadã [sida'dã] *f de* **cidadão.**

cidadania [sidada'nia] *f* citizenship.

cidadão/cidadã [sida'dãw/sida'dã] (*pl* **~s/~s**) *m/f* citizen.

cidade [si'dadʒi] *f* town; (*grande*) city.

cidadela [sida'dɛla] *f* citadel.

cidra ['sidra] *f* citron.

CIE (BR) *abr m* = **Centro de Informações do Exército.**

ciência ['sjẽsja] *f* science; (*erudição*) knowledge; **~s humanas/socias** business studies/ social sciences.

ciente ['sjẽtʃi] *adj* aware.

científico/a [sjẽ'tʃifiku/a] *adj* scientific.

cientista [sjẽ'tʃiʃta] *m/f* scientist.

CIEP (BR) *abr m* (= *Centro Integrado de Educação Popular*) *combined school and community centre.*

cifra ['sifra] *f* (*escrita secreta*) cipher; (*algarismo*) number, figure; (*total*) sum.

cifrão [si'frãw] (*pl* **-ões**) *m* money sign.

cifrar [si'fra*] *vt* to write in code.

cifrões [si'frõjʃ] *mpl de* **cifrão.**

cigano/a [si'ganu/a] *adj, m/f* gypsy.

cigarra [si'gaxa] *f* cicada; (ELET) buzzer.

cigarreira [siga'xejra] *f* (*estojo*) cigarette case.

cigarrilha [siga'xiʎa] *f* cheroot.

cigarro [si'gaxu] *m* cigarette.

cilada [si'lada] *f* (*emboscada*) ambush; (*armadilha*) trap; (*embuste*) trick.

cilíndrico/a [si'lĩdriku/a] *adj* cylindrical.

cilindro [si'lĩdru] *m* cylinder; (*rolo*) roller.

cílio ['silju] *m* eyelash.

cima ['sima] *f*: **de ~ para baixo** from top to bottom; **para ~** up; **em ~ de** on, on top of; **por ~ de** over; **de ~** from above; **lá em ~** up there; (*em casa*) upstairs; **ainda por ~** on top of that; **estar por ~** to be better off; **dar em ~ de alguém** (*col*) to be after sb; **tudo em ~?** (*col*) how's it going?

cimeira [si'mejra] (PT) *f* summit.

cimentar [simẽ'ta*] *vt* to cement.

cimento [si'mẽtu] *m* cement; (*chão*) concrete floor; (*fig*) foundation; ~ **armado** reinforced concrete.
cimo ['simu] *m* top, summit.
cinco ['sĩku] *num* five; **somos** ~ there are five of us; **ela tem** ~ **anos** she is five (years old); **aos** ~ **anos (de idade)** at the age of five; **são** ~ **horas** it's five o'clock; **às** ~ **(horas)** at five (o'clock); **hoje é dia** ~ **de julho** today is the fifth of July; **no dia** ~ **de julho** on the fifth of July, on July the fifth; **eles moram no número** ~**/na Barata Ribeiro número** ~ they live at number five/number five Barata Ribeiro Street; ~ **e um quarto/meio** five and a quarter/a half.
Cindacta [sĩ'dakta] (*BR*) *abr m* = **Centro Integrado de Defesa Aérea e Controle de Tráfego Aéreo.**
cindir [sĩ'dʒi*] *vt* to split; (*cortar*) to cut.
cineasta [sine'aʃta] *m/f* film maker.
cinegrafista [sinegra'fiʃta] *m/f* cameraman/woman.
cinema [si'nεma] *f* cinema.
cinematográfico/a [sinemato'grafiku/a] *adj* cinematographic.
Cingapura [sĩga'pura] *f* Singapore.
cingir [sin'ʒi*] *vt* (*pôr à cintura*) to fasten round one's waist; (*prender em volta*) to tie round; (*cercar*) to encircle, ring; (*coroa, espada*) to put on; ~**-se** *vr*: ~**-se a** (*restringir-se*) to restrict o.s. to.
cínico/a ['siniku/a] *adj* cynical ♦ *m/f* cynic.
cinismo [si'niʒmu] *m* cynicism.
cinjo ['sĩʒu] *etc vb V* **cingir.**
cinqüenta [sĩ'kwẽta] *num* fifty; **umas** ~ **pessoas** about fifty people; **ele tem uns** ~ **anos** he's about fifty; **ele está na casa dos** ~ **anos** he's in his fifties; **nos anos** ~ in the fifties; **ir a** ~ (*AUTO*) to do fifty (km/h).
cinqüentão/tona [sĩkwẽ'tãw/'tɔna] (*pl* **-tões/**~**s**) *m/f* person in his/her fifties ♦ *adj* in his/her fifties.
cinta ['sĩta] *f* (*faixa*) sash; (*de mulher*) girdle.
cintado/a [sĩ'tadu/a] *adj* gathered at the waist.
cintilante [sĩtʃi'lãtʃi] *adj* sparkling.
cintilar [sĩtʃi'la*] *vi* to sparkle, glitter.
cinto ['sĩtu] *m* belt; ~ **de segurança** safety belt; (*AUTO*) seatbelt.
cintura [sĩ'tura] *f* waist; (*linha*) waistline.
cinturão [sĩtu'rãw] (*pl* **-ões**) *m* belt; ~ **verde** green belt.
cinza ['sĩza] *adj inv* grey (*BRIT*), gray (*US*) ♦ *f* ash, ashes *pl*.
cinzeiro [sĩ'zejru] *m* ashtray.
cinzel [sĩ'zεw] (*pl* **-éis**) *m* chisel.
cinzelar [sĩze'la*] *vt* to chisel; (*gravar*) to carve, engrave.
cinzento/a [sĩ'zẽtu/a] *adj* grey (*BRIT*), gray (*US*).
cio [siu] *m* mating season; **no** ~ on heat, in season.
cioso/a ['sjozu/ɔza] *adj* conscientious.
CIP (*BR*) *abr m* = **Conselho Interministerial de Preços.**
cipreste [si'prεʃtʃi] *m* cypress (tree).
cipriota [si'prjɔta] *adj, m/f* Cypriot.
circense [six'sẽsi] *adj* circus *atr*.
circo ['sixku] *m* circus.
circuito [six'kwitu] *m* circuit.
circulação [sixkula'sãw] *f* circulation.
circular [sixku'la*] *adj* circular, round ♦ *f* (*carta*) circular ♦ *vi* to circulate; (*girar, andar*) to go round ♦ *vt* to circulate; (*estar em volta de*) to surround; (*percorrer em roda*) to go round.
círculo ['sixkulu] *m* circle.
circunavegar [sixkunave'ga*] *vt* to circumnavigate, sail round.
circuncidar [sixkũsi'da*] *vt* to circumcise.
circuncisão [sixkũsi'zãw] *f* circumcision.
circundante [sixkũ'dãtʃi] *adj* surrounding.
circundar [sixkũ'da*] *vt* to surround.
circunferência [sixkũfe'rẽsja] *f* circumference.
circunflexo/a [sixkũ'flεksu/a] *adj* circumflex ♦ *m* circumflex.
circunlóquio [sixkũ'lɔkju] *m* circumlocution.
circunscrever [sixkũʃkre've*] *vt* to circumscribe, limit; (*epidemia*) to contain; (*abranger*) to cover; ~**-se** *vr* to be limited.
circunscrição [sixkũʃkri'sãw] (*pl* **-ões**) *f* district; ~ **eleitoral** constituency.
circunscrito/a [sixkũʃ'kritu/a] *pp de* **circunscrever.**
circunspecção [sixkũʃpe'sãw] *f* seriousness.
circunspeto/a [sixkũ'ʃpεtu/a] *adj* serious.
circunstância [sixkũ'ʃtãsja] *f* circumstance; ~**s atenuantes** mitigating circumstances.
circunstanciado/a [sixkũʃtã'sjadu/a] *adj* detailed.
circunstancial [sixkũʃtã'sjaw] (*pl* **-ais**) *adj* circumstantial.
circunstante [sixkũ'ʃtãtʃi] *m/f* onlooker, bystander; ~**s** *mpl* audience *sg*.
cirrose [si'xɔzi] *f* cirrhosis.
cirurgia [sirux'ʒia] *f* surgery; ~ **plástica/estética** plastic/cosmetic surgery.
cirurgião/cirurgiã [sirux'ʒjãw/sirux'ʒjã] (*pl* **-ões/**~**s**) *m/f* surgeon.
cirúrgico/a [si'ruxʒiku/a] *adj* surgical.
cirurgiões [sirux'ʒjõjʃ] *mpl de* **cirurgião.**
cirzo ['sixzu] *etc vb V* **cerzir.**
cisão [si'zãw] (*pl* **-ões**) *f* (*divisão*) split, division; (*desacordo*) disagreement.
cisco ['siʃku] *m* speck.
cisma ['siʒma] *m* schism ♦ *f* (*mania*) silly idea; (*suspeita*) suspicion; (*antipatia*) dislike; (*devaneio*) dream.
cismado/a [siʒ'madu/a] *adj* with fixed ideas.
cismar [siʒ'ma*] *vi* (*pensar*): ~ **em** to brood over; (*antipatizar*): ~ **com** to take a dislike

NB: European Portuguese adds the following consonants to certain words: **b** (sú(b)dito, su(b)til); **c** (a(c)ção, a(c)cionista, a(c)to); **m** (inde(m)ne); **p** (ado(p)ção, ado(p)tar); *for further details see p. xiii.*

to ♦ *vt*: ~ **que** to be convinced that; ~ **de** *ou* **em fazer** (*meter na cabeça*) to get into one's head to do; (*insistir*) to insist on doing.
cisne ['siʒni] *m* swan.
cisões [si'zõjʃ] *fpl de* **cisão**.
cisterna [siʃ'tɛxna] *f* cistern, tank.
cistite [siʃ'tʃitʃi] *f* cystitis.
citação [sita'sãw] (*pl* **-ões**) *f* quotation; (*JUR*) summons *sg*.
citadino/a [sita'dʒinu/a] *adj* town *atr*.
citar [si'ta*] *vt* to quote; (*JUR*) to summon.
cítrico/a ['sitriku/a] *adj* (*fruta*) citrus; (*ácido*) citric.
ciumada [sju'mada] *f* fit of jealousy.
ciúme ['sjumi] *m* jealousy; **ter ~s de** to be jealous of.
ciumeira [sju'mejra] (*col*) *f* = **ciumada**.
ciumento/a [sju'mẽtu/a] *adj* jealous.
cívico/a ['siviku/a] *adj* civic.
civil [si'viw] (*pl* **-is**) *adj* civil ♦ *m/f* civilian.
civilidade [sivili'dadʒi] *f* politeness.
civilização [siviliza'sãw] (*pl* **-ões**) *f* civilization.
civilizador(a) [siviliza'do*(a)] *adj* civilizing.
civilizar [sivili'za*] *vt* to civilize.
civis [si'viʃ] *pl de* **civil**.
civismo [si'viʒmu] *m* public spirit.
clamar [kla'ma*] *vt* to clamour (*BRIT*) *ou* clamor (*US*) for ♦ *vi* to cry out, clamo(u)r.
clamor [kla'mo*] *m* outcry, uproar.
clamoroso/a [klamo'rozu/ɔza] *adj* noisy.
clandestino/a [klãdeʃ'tʃinu/a] *adj* clandestine; (*ilegal*) underground.
clara ['klara] *f* egg white.
clarabóia [klara'bɔja] *f* skylight.
clarão [kla'rãw] (*pl* **-ões**) *m* (*cintilação*) flash; (*claridade*) gleam.
clarear [kla'rja*] *vi* (*dia*) to dawn; (*tempo*) to clear up, brighten up ♦ *vt* to clarify.
clareira [kla'rejra] *f* (*na mata*) clearing.
clareza [kla'reza] *f* clarity.
claridade [klari'dadʒi] *f* (*luz*) brightness.
clarim [kla'rĩ] (*pl* **-ns**) *m* bugle.
clarinete [klari'netʃi] *m* clarinet.
clarinetista [klarine'tʃiʃta] *m/f* clarinet player.
clarins [kla'rĩʃ] *mpl de* **clarim**.
clarividente [klarivi'dẽtʃi] *adj* (*prudente*) far-sighted, prudent.
claro/a ['klaru/a] *adj* clear; (*luminoso*) bright; (*cor*) light; (*evidente*) clear, evident ♦ *m* (*na escrita*) space; (*clareira*) clearing ♦ *adv* clearly; ~! of course!; ~ **que sim!/não!** of course!/of course not!; **às claras** openly; (*publicamente*) publicly; **dia** ~ daylight; **passar a noite em** ~ not to sleep a wink all night; ~ **como água** crystal clear.
clarões [kla'rõjʃ] *mpl de* **clarão**.
classe ['klasi] *f* class; ~ **média/operária** middle/working class.
clássico/a ['klasiku/a] *adj* classical; (*fig*) classic; (*habitual*) usual ♦ *m* classic.
classificação [klasifika'sãw] (*pl* **-ões**) *f* classification; (*ESPORTE*) place, placing.
classificado/a [klasifi'kadu/a] *adj* (*em exame*) successful; (*anúncio*) classified; (*ESPORTE*) placed, qualified ♦ *m* (*anúncio*) classified ad.
classificar [klasifi'ka*] *vt* to classify; **~-se** *vr*: **~-se de algo** to call o.s. sth, describe o.s. as sth.
classificatório/a [klasifika'tɔrju/a] *adj* qualifying.
classudo/a [kla'sudu/a] (*col*) *adj* classy.
claudicar [klawdʒi'ka*] *vi* (*mancar*) to limp; (*errar*) to err.
claustro ['klawʃtru] *m* cloister.
claustrofobia [klawʃtrofo'bia] *f* claustrophobia.
claustrofóbico/a [klawʃtro'fɔbiku/a] *adj* claustrophobic.
cláusula ['klawzula] *f* clause.
clausura [klaw'zura] *f* (*recinto*) enclosure; (*vida*) cloistered existence.
clave ['klavi] *f* (*MÚS*) clef.
clavícula [kla'vikula] *f* collar bone.
clemência [kle'mẽsja] *f* mercy.
clemente [kle'mẽtʃi] *adj* merciful.
cleptomaníaco/a [kleptoma'niaku/a] *m/f* kleptomaniac.
clérigo ['klɛrigu] *m* clergyman.
clero ['klɛru] *m* clergy.
clichê [kli'ʃe] *m* (*FOTO*) plate; (*chavão*) cliché.
cliente ['kljẽtʃi] *m* client; (*de loja*) customer; (*de médico*) patient.
clientela [kljẽ'tɛla] *f* clientele; (*de loja*) customers *pl*; (*de médico*) patients *pl*.
clima ['klima] *m* climate.
climático/a [kli'matʃiku/a] *adj* climatic.
clímax ['klimaks] *m inv* climax.
clínica ['klinika] *f* clinic; ~ **geral** general practice; *V tb* **clínico**.
clinicar [klini'ka*] *vi* to have a practice.
clínico/a ['kliniku/a] *adj* clinical ♦ *m/f* doctor; ~ **geral** general practitioner, GP.
clipe ['klipi] *m* clip; (*para papéis*) paper clip.
clitóris [kli'tɔriʃ] *m inv* clitoris.
clone ['klɔni] *m* clone.
clorar [klo'ra*] *vt* to chlorinate.
cloro ['klɔru] *m* chlorine.
clorofórmio [kloro'fɔxmju] *m* chloroform.
close ['klozi] *m* close-up.
clube ['klubi] *m* club.
CMB *abr f* (= *Casa da Moeda do Brasil*) Brazilian National Mint.
CMN (*BR*) *abr m* = **Conselho Monetário Nacional**.
CNA *abr m* (= *Congresso Nacional Africano*) ANC; (*BR*) = **Conselho Nacional do Álcool**.
CNB (*BR*) *abr m* = **Conselho Nacional da Borracha**.
CNBB *abr f* = **Confederação Nacional dos Bispos do Brasil**.
CNBV (*BR*) *abr f* = **Comissão Nacional da Bolsa de Valores**.
CND (*BR*) *abr m* = **Conselho Nacional de Desportos**.
CNDC (*BR*) *abr m* = **Conselho Nacional de Defesa ao Consumidor**.

CNDM (BR) *abr m* = **Conselho Nacional dos Direitos da Mulher**.
CNDU (BR) *abr m* = **Conselho Nacional de Desenvolvimento Urbano**.
CNEN (BR) *abr f* (= *Comissão Nacional de Energia Nuclear*) ≈ AEA (BRIT), ≈ AEC (US).
CNPq (BR) *abr m* (= *Conselho Nacional de Desenvolvimento Científico*) *organization supporting higher education*.
CNS (BR) *abr m* = **Conselho Nacional de Saúde**.
CNT (BR) *abr m* = **Conselho Nacional de Transportes**.
CNV (BR) *abr m* = **Cadastro Nacional de Veículos**.
coabitar [koabi'ta*] *vi* to live together, cohabit.
coação [koa'sãw] (PT: **-cç-**) *f* coercion.
coadjuvante [koadʒu'vãtʃi] *adj* supporting ♦ *m/f* (*num crime*) accomplice; (TEATRO, CINEMA) co-star.
coadjuvar [koadʒu'va*] *vt* to aid; (TEATRO, CINEMA) to support.
coador [koa'do*] *m* strainer; (*de café*) filter bag; (*para legumes*) colander.
coadunar [koadu'na*] *vt* to combine; **~-se** *vr* to combine.
coagir [koa'ʒi*] *vt* to coerce, compel.
coagular [koagu'la*] *vt, vi* to coagulate; (*sangue*) to clot; **~-se** *vr* to congeal.
coágulo [ko'agulu] *m* clot.
coajo [ko'aʒu] *etc vb V* **coagir**.
coalhada [koa'ʎada] *f* live yoghurt.
coalhado/a [koa'ʎadu/a] *adj* curdled; **~ de gente** packed.
coalhar [koa'ʎa*] *vt, vi* (*leite*) to curdle; **~-se** *vr* to curdle.
coalizão [koali'zãw] (*pl* **-ões**) *f* coalition.
coar [ko'a*] *vt* (*líquido*) to strain.
co-autor(a) [ko-] *m/f* (*de livro*) co-author; (*de crime*) accomplice.
coaxar [koa'ʃa*] *vi* to croak ♦ *m* croaking.
COB *abr m* = **Comitê Olímpico Brasileiro**.
cobaia [ko'baja] *f* guinea pig.
cobalto [ko'bawtu] *m* cobalt.
coberta [ko'bɛxta] *f* cover, covering; (NÁUT) deck.
coberto/a [ko'bɛxtu/a] *pp de* **cobrir** ♦ *adj* covered.
cobertor [kobex'to*] *m* blanket.
cobertura [kobex'tura] *f* covering; (*telhado*) roof; (*apartamento*) penthouse; (TV, RÁDIO, JORNALISMO) coverage; (SEGUROS) cover.
cobiça [ko'bisa] *f* greed.
cobiçar [kobi'sa*] *vt* to covet.
cobiçoso/a [kobi'sozu/ɔza] *adj* covetous.
cobra ['kɔbra] *f* snake ♦ *m/f* (*col*) expert ♦ *adj* (*col*) expert; **dizer ~s e lagartos de alguém** to say bad things about sb.
cobrador(a) [kobra'do*(a)] *m/f* collector; (*em transporte*) conductor; **~ de impostos** tax collector.
cobrança [ko'brãsa] *f* collection; (*ato de cobrar*) charging; **~ de pênalti/falta** penalty/free kick.
cobrar [ko'bra*] *vt* to collect; (*preço*) to charge; (*pênalti*) to take; **~ o prometido** to remind sb of what they promised; **~ uma falta** (FUTEBOL) to take a free kick.
cobre ['kɔbri] *m* copper; **~s** *mpl* money *sg*.
cobrir [ko'bri*] *vt* to cover; **~-se** *vr* to cover o.s.
coca ['kɔka] *f* (*arbusto*) coca bush.
coça ['kɔsa] (*col*) *f* wallop.
cocada [ko'kada] *f* coconut sweet.
cocaína [koka'ina] *f* cocaine.
coçar [ko'sa*] *vt* to scratch ♦ *vi* (*comichar*) to itch; **~-se** *vr* to scratch o.s.; **não ter tempo nem para se ~** to have no time to breathe.
cócegas ['kɔsegaʃ] *fpl*: **fazer ~ em** to tickle; **tenho ~ nos pés** my feet tickle; **sentir ~** to be ticklish; **estar em ~ para fazer** to be itching to do.
coceira [ko'sejra] *f* itch; (*qualidade*) itchiness.
cocheira [ko'ʃejra] *f* stable.
cochichar [koʃi'ʃa*] *vi* to whisper.
cochicho [ko'ʃiʃu] *m* whispering.
cochilada [koʃi'lada] *f* snooze; **dar uma ~** to have a snooze.
cochilar [koʃi'la*] *vi* to snooze, doze.
cochilo [ko'ʃilu] *m* nap.
coco ['koku] *m* coconut.
cocô [ko'ko] (*col*) *m* pooh.
cócoras ['kɔkoraʃ] *fpl*: **de ~** squatting; **ficar de ~** to squat (down).
cocoricar [kokori'ka*] *vi* to crow.
cocuruto [koku'rutu] *m* top.
côdea ['kodʒja] *f* crust.
codeína [kode'ina] *f* codeine.
Codici [kodʒi'si] (BR) *abr f* = **Comissão de Defesa dos Direitos do Cidadão**.
codificador [kodʒifika'do*] *m* (COMPUT) encoder.
codificar [kodʒifi'ka*] *vt* (*leis*) to codify; (*mensagem*) to encode, code.
código ['kɔdʒigu] *m* code; **~ de barras** bar code; **~ de ética profissional** code of practice.
codinome [kodʒi'nɔmi] *m* code name.
codorna [ko'dɔxna] *f* quail.
co-editar [ko-] *vt* to co-publish.
coeficiente [koefi'sjẽtʃi] *m* (MAT) coefficient; (*fig*) factor.
coelho [ko'eʎu] *m* rabbit; **matar dois ~s de uma cajadada só** (*fig*) to kill two birds with one stone.
coentro [ko'ẽtru] *m* coriander.
coerção [koex'sãw] *f* coercion.
coerência [koe'rẽsja] *f* coherence; (*conseqüência*) consistency.

NB: European Portuguese adds the following consonants to certain words: **b** (sú(b)dito, su(b)til); **c** (a(c)ção, a(c)cionista, a(c)to); **m** (inde(m)ne); **p** (ado(p)ção, ado(p)tar); *for further details see p. xiii.*

coerente [koe'rẽtʃi] *adj* coherent; (*conseqüente*) consistent.
coesão [koe'zãw] *f* cohesion.
coeso/a ['kwɛzu/a] *adj* cohesive.
coexistência [koeziʃ'tẽsja] *f* coexistence.
coexistir [koeziʃ'tʃi*] *vi* to coexist.
Cofie (*BR*) *abr f* = **Comissão de Fusão e Incorporação de Empresas**.
cofre ['kɔfri] *m* safe; (*caixa*) strongbox; **os ~s públicos** public funds.
cogitação [koʒita'sãw] *f* contemplation; **estar fora de ~** to be out of the question.
cogitar [koʒi'ta*] *vt, vi* to contemplate.
cognominar [kognomi'na*] *vt* to nickname.
cogumelo [kogu'mɛlu] *m* mushroom; **~ venenoso** toadstool.
COHAB (*BR*) *abr f* = **Companhia de Habitação Popular**.
coibição [koibi'sãw] (*pl* **-ões**) *f* restraint, restriction.
coibir [koi'bi*] *vt* to restrain; **~ de** to restrain from; **~-se** *vr*: **~-se de** to abstain from.
coice ['kojsi] *m* kick; (*de arma*) recoil; **dar ~s em** to kick; (*fig*) to be aggressive with.
coincidência [koĩsi'dẽsja] *f* coincidence.
coincidir [koĩsi'dʒi*] *vi* to coincide; (*concordar*) to agree.
coisa ['kojza] *f* thing; (*assunto*) matter; **~s** *fpl* things; (*col*: *órgãos genitais*) privates; **~ de** about; **ser uma ~** (*col*) to be really something; (*ruim*) to be terrible; **que ~!** gosh!; **não dizer ~ com ~** not to make any sense; **deu uma ~ nele** something strange got into him.
coisíssima [koj'zisima] *f*: **~ nenhuma** (*nada*) nothing; (*de modo algum*) not at all.
coitado/a [koj'tadu/a] *adj* poor, wretched; **~!** poor thing!; **~ do João** poor John.
coito ['kojtu] *m* intercourse, coitus.
cola ['kɔla] *f* glue; (*BR*: *cópia*) crib.
colaboração [kolabora'sãw] (*pl* **-ões**) *f* collaboration; (*num jornal etc*) contribution.
colaborador(a) [kolabora'do*(a)] *m/f* collaborator; (*em jornal*) contributor.
colaborar [kolabo'ra*] *vi* to collaborate; (*ajudar*) to help; (*escrever artigos etc*) to contribute.
colagem [ko'laʒẽ] *f* collage.
colante [ko'lãtʃi] *adj* (*roupa*) skin-tight.
colapso [ko'lapsu] *m* collapse; **~ cardíaco** heart failure.
colar [ko'la*] *vt* to stick, glue; (*BR*: *copiar*) to crib ♦ *vi* to stick; to cheat; (*col*: *ser acreditado*) to stand up, stick ♦ *m* necklace; **~ grau** to graduate .
colarinho [kola'riɲu] *m* collar; (*col*: *na cerveja*) head.
colarinho-branco (*pl* **colarinhos-brancos**) *m* white-collar worker.
colateral [kolate'raw] (*pl* **-ais**) *adj V* **efeito**.
colcha ['kowʃa] *f* bedspread.
colchão [kow'ʃãw] (*pl* **-ões**) *m* mattress.
colcheia [kow'ʃeja] *f* (*MÚS*) quaver.
colchete [kow'ʃetʃi] *m* clasp, fastening; (*parêntese*) square bracket; **~ de gancho** hook and eye; **~ de pressão** press stud.
colchões [kow'ʃõjʃ] *mpl de* **colchão**.
colchonete [kowʃo'nɛtʃi] *m* (portable) mattress.
coleção [kole'sãw] (*PT*: **-cç-**: *pl* **-ões**) *f* collection.
colecionador(a) [kolesjona'do*(a)] (*PT*: **-cc-**) *m/f* collector.
colecionar [kolesjo'na*] (*PT*: **-cc-**) *vt* to collect.
coleções [kole'sõjʃ] *fpl de* **coleção**.
colectar *etc* [kolek'ta*] (*PT*) = **coletar** *etc*.
colega [ko'lɛga] *m/f* (*de trabalho*) colleague; (*de escola*) classmate; (*amigo*) friend.
colegial [kole'ʒjaw] (*pl* **-ais**) *adj* school *atr* ♦ *m/f* schoolboy/girl.
colégio [ko'lɛʒu] *m* school; **~ eleitoral** electoral college.
coleguismo [kole'giʒmu] *m* loyalty to one's colleagues.
coleira [ko'lejra] *f* collar.
cólera ['kɔlera] *f* (*ira*) anger; (*fúria*) rage ♦ *m ou f* (*MED*) cholera.
colérico/a [ko'lɛriku/a] *adj* (*irado*) angry; (*furioso*) furious ♦ *m/f* (*MED*) cholera patient.
colesterol [koleʃte'rɔw] *m* cholesterol.
coleta [ko'lɛta] *f* collection; (*imposto*) levy.
coletânea [kole'tanja] *f* collection.
coletar [kole'ta*] *vt* to tax; (*arrecadar*) to collect.
colete [ko'letʃi] *m* waistcoat (*BRIT*), vest (*US*); **~ salva-vidas** life jacket (*BRIT*), life preserver (*US*).
coletividade [koletʃivi'dadʒi] *f* community.
coletivo/a [kole'tʃivu/a] *adj* collective; (*transportes*) public ♦ *m* bus.
coletor(a) [kole'to*(a)] *m/f* collector.
coletoria [koleto'ria] *f* tax office.
colheita [ko'ʎejta] *f* harvest; (*produto*) crop.
colher [ko'ʎe*] *vt* (*recolher*) to gather, pick; (*dados*) to gather ♦ *f* spoon; **~ de chá/sopa** teaspoon/tablespoon; **dar uma ~ de chá a alguém** (*fig*) to do sb a favo(u)r; **de ~** (*col*) on a silver platter.
colherada [koʎe'rada] *f* spoonful.
colibri [koli'bri] *m* hummingbird.
cólica ['kɔlika] *f* colic.
colidir [koli'dʒi*] *vi*: **~ com** to collide with, crash into.
coligação [koliga'sãw] (*pl* **-ões**) *f* coalition.
coligar [koli'ga*] *vt* to bring together, unit; **~-se** *vr* to join forces.
coligir [koli'ʒi*] *vt* to collect.
colina [ko'lina] *f* hill.
colírio [ko'lirju] *m* eyewash.
colisão [koli'zãw] (*pl* **-ões**) *f* collision.
colis postaux [ko'li pos'to] *mpl* small packets.
colite [ko'litʃi] *f* colitis.
collant [ko'lã] (*pl* **~s**) *m* tights *pl* (*BRIT*), pantihose (*US*); (*blusa*) leotard.

colmeia [kow'meja] *f* beehive.
colo ['kɔlu] *m* neck; (*regaço*) lap; **no** ~ on one's lap, in one's arms.
colocação [koloka'sãw] (*pl* **-ões**) *f* placing; (*emprego*) job, position; (*de pneus, tapete etc*) fitting; (*de uma questão, idéia*) positing; (*opinião*) position.
colocar [kolo'ka*] *vt* to put, place; (*empregar*) to find a job for, place; (*COM*) to market; (*pneus, tapetes*) to fit; (*questão, idéia*) to put forward, state; **~-se** *vr* to place o.s.; **coloque-se no meu lugar** put yourself in my position.
Colômbia [ko'lõbja] *f*: **a** ~ Colombia.
colombiano/a [kolõ'bjanu/a] *adj, m/f* Colombian.
cólon ['kɔlõ] *m* colon.
colônia [ko'lonja] *f* colony; (*perfume*) cologne.
colonial [kolo'njaw] (*pl* **-ais**) *adj* colonial.
colonialismo [kolonja'liʒmu] *m* colonialism.
colonização [koloniza'sãw] *f* colonization.
colonizador(a) [koloniza'do*(a)] *adj* colonizing ♦ *m/f* colonist, settler.
colonizar [koloni'za*] *vt* to colonize.
colono [ko'lɔnu/a] *m/f* settler; (*cultivador*) tenant farmer.
coloquei [kolo'kej] *etc vb V* **colocar**.
coloquial [kolo'kjaw] (*pl* **-ais**) *adj* colloquial.
colóquio [ko'lɔkju] *m* conversation; (*congresso*) conference.
coloração [kolora'sãw] *f* colouration (*BRIT*), coloration (*US*).
colorido/a [kolo'ridu/a] *adj* colourful (*BRIT*), colorful (*US*) ♦ *m* colouring (*BRIT*), coloring (*US*).
colorir [kolo'ri*] *vt* to colour (*BRIT*), color (*US*).
colossal [kolo'saw] (*pl* **-ais**) *adj* colossal.
colosso [ko'losu] *m* (*pessoa*) giant; (*coisa*) extraordinary thing.
coluna [ko'luna] *f* column; (*pilar*) pillar; ~ **dorsal** *ou* **vertebral** spine.
colunável [kolu'navew] (*pl* **-eis**) *adj* famous ♦ *m/f* celebrity.
colunista [kolu'niʃta] *m/f* columnist.
com [kõ] *prep* with; **estar ~ fome** to be hungry; ~ **cuidado** carefully; **estar ~ dinheiro/câncer** to have some money on one/have cancer; **"não ultrapasse ~ faixa contínua"** "do not overtake when centre line is unbroken".
coma ['kɔma] *f* coma.
comadre [ko'madri] *f* (*urinol*) bedpan; **minha** ~ the godmother of my child (*ou* the mother of my godchild).
comandante [komã'dãtʃi] *m* commander; (*MIL*) commandant; (*NÁUT*) captain.
comandar [komã'da*] *vt* to command.
comando [ko'mãdu] *m* command.
combate [kõ'batʃi] *m* combat, fight; (*fig*) battle.
combatente [kõba'tẽtʃi] *m/f* combatant.
combater [kõba'te*] *vt* to fight, combat; (*opor-se a*) to oppose ♦ *vi* to fight; **~-se** *vr* to fight.
combinação [kõbina'sãw] (*pl* **-ões**) *f* combination; (*QUÍM*) compound; (*acordo*) arrangement; (*plano*) scheme; (*roupa*) slip.
combinar [kõbi'na*] *vt* to combine; (*jantar etc*) to arrange; (*fuga etc*) to plan ♦ *vi* (*roupas etc*) to go together; **~-se** *vr* to combine; (*pessoas*) to get on well together; (*temperamentos*) to go well together; ~ **com** (*harmonizar-se*) to go with; ~ **de fazer** to arrange to do; **combinado!** agreed!
comboio [kõ'boju] *m* (*PT*) train; (*de navios*) convoy.
combustão [kõbuʃ'tãw] (*pl* **-ões**) *f* combustion.
combustível [kõbuʃ'tʃivew] *m* fuel.
combustões [kõbuʃ'tõjʃ] *fpl de* **combustão**.
começar [kome'sa*] (*irreg*) *vt, vi* to begin, start; ~ **a fazer** to begin *ou* start to do.
começo [ko'mesu] *etc vb V* **comedir-se** ♦ *m* beginning, start.
comédia [ko'mɛdʒja] *f* comedy.
comediante [kome'dʒjãtʃi] *m/f* (comic) actor/actress.
comedido/a [kome'dʒidu/a] *adj* moderate; (*prudente*) prudent.
comedir-se [kome'dʒixsi] *vr* to control o.s.
comedorias [komedo'riaʃ] *fpl* food.
comemoração [komemora'sãw] (*pl* **-ões**) *f* commemoration.
comemorar [komemo'ra*] *vt* to commemorate; (*celebrar: sucesso etc*) to celebrate.
comemorativo/a [komemora'tʃivu/a] *adj* commemorative.
comensal [komẽ'saw] (*pl* **-ais**) *m/f* diner.
comentar [komẽ'ta*] *vt* to comment on; (*maliciosamente*) to make comments about.
comentário [komẽ'tarju] *m* comment, remark; (*análise*) commentary; **sem** ~ no comment.
comentarista [komẽta'riʃta] *m/f* commentator.
comer [ko'me*] *vt* to eat; (*damas, xadrez*) to take, capture; (*dinheiro*) to eat up; (*corroer*) to eat away ♦ *vi* to eat; **~-se** *vr*: **~-se (de)** to be consumed (with); **dar de ~ a** to feed; ~ **por quatro** (*fig*) to eat like a horse; ~ **fogo** (*col*) to go through hell.
comercial [komex'sjaw] (*pl* **-ais**) *adj* commercial; (*relativo ao negócio*) business *atr* ♦ *m* commercial.
comercialização [komexsjaliza'sãw] *f* marketing.
comercializar [komexsjali'za*] *vt* to market.
comercializável [komexsjali'zavew] (*pl* **-eis**) *adj* marketable.
comerciante [komex'sjãtʃi] *m/f* trader.
comerciar [komex'sja*] *vi* to trade, do busi-

***NB**: European Portuguese adds the following consonants to certain words:* **b** (sú(b)dito, su(b)til); **c** (a(c)ção, a(c)cionista, a(c)to); **m** (inde(m)ne); **p** (ado(p)ção, ado(p)tar); *for further details see p. xiii.*

ness.

comerciário/a [komex'sjarju/a] *m/f* employee in business.

comércio [ko'mɛxsju] *m* commerce; (*tráfico*) trade; (*negócio*) business; (*lojas*) shops *pl*; **de fechar o ~** (*col*) really stunning.

comes ['kɔmiʃ] *mpl*: **~ e bebes** food and drink.

comestíveis [komeʃ'tʃiveis] *mpl* foodstuffs, food *sg*.

comestível [komeʃ'tʃivew] (*pl* **-eis**) *adj* edible.

cometa [ko'meta] *m* comet.

cometer [kome'te*] *vt* to commit.

cometimento [kometʃi'mẽtu] *m* undertaking, commitment.

comichão [komi'ʃãw] *f* itch, itching.

comichar [komi'ʃa*] *vt*, *vi* to itch.

comício [ko'misju] *m* (POL) rally, meeting; (*assembléia*) assembly.

comicidade [komisi'dadʒi] *f* comic quality.

cômico/a ['komiku/a] *adj* comic(al) ♦ *m* comedian; (*de teatro*) actor.

comida [ko'mida] *f* (*alimento*) food; (*refeição*) meal; **~ caseira** home cooking.

comigo [ko'migu] *pron* with me; (*reflexivo*) with myself.

comilança [komi'lãsa] *f* overeating.

comilão/lona [komi'lãw/lɔna] (*pl* **-ões/~s**) *adj* greedy ♦ *m/f* glutton.

cominho [ko'miɲu] *m* cumin.

comiserar [komize'ra*] *vt* to move to pity; **~-se** *vr*: **~-se (de)** to sympathize (with).

comissão [komi'sãw] (*pl* **-ões**) *f* commission; (*comitê*) committee.

comissário [komi'sarju] *m* commissioner; (COM) agent; **~ de bordo** (AER) steward; (NÁUT) purser.

comissionar [komisjo'na*] *vt* to commission.

comissões [komi'sõjʃ] *fpl de* **comissão**.

comitê [komi'te] *m* committee.

comitiva [komi'tʃiva] *f* entourage.

como ['kɔmu] *adv* as; (*assim como*) like; (*de que maneira*) how ♦ *conj* (*porque*) as, since; (*da mesma maneira que*) as; **~?** pardon?; **~ assim?** how do you mean?; **~!** what!; **~ não!** of course!; **~ se** as if; **~ quer que** however; **seja ~ for** be that as it may; **assim ~** as well as; **~ quiser** as you wish; **e ~!** and how.

comoção [komo'sãw] (*pl* **-ões**) *f* (*abalo*) distress; (*revolta*) commotion.

cômoda ['komoda] *f* chest of drawers (BRIT), bureau (US).

comodidade [komodʒi'dadʒi] *f* (*conforto*) comfort; (*conveniência*) convenience.

comodismo [komo'dʒiʒmu] *m* complacency.

comodista [komo'dʒiʃta] *adj* complacent.

cômodo/a ['komodu/a] *adj* (*confortável*) comfortable; (*conveniente*) convenient ♦ *m* (*aposento*) room.

comovedor(a) [komove'do*(a)] *adj* moving, touching.

comovente [komo'vẽtʃi] *adj* moving, touching.

comover [komo've*] *vt* to move ♦ *vi* to be moving; **~-se** *vr* to be moved.

comovido/a [komo'vidu/a] *adj* moved.

compacto/a [kõ'paktu/a] *adj* (*pequeno*) compact; (*espesso*) thick; (*sólido*) solid ♦ *m* (*disco*) single.

compadecer-se [kõpade'sexsi] *vr*: **~-se de** to be sorry for, pity.

compadecido/a [kõpade'sidu/a] *adj* sympathetic.

compadecimento [kõpadesi'mẽtu] *m* sympathy; (*piedade*) pity.

compadre [kõ'padri] *m* (*col*: *companheiro*) buddy, pal, crony; **meu ~** the godfather of my child (*ou* the father of my godchild).

compaixão [kõpaj'ʃãw] *m* (*piedade*) compassion, pity; (*misericórdia*) mercy.

companheirão/rona [kõpaɲej'rãw/'rɔna] (*pl* **-ões/~s**) *m/f* good friend.

companheirismo [kõpaɲej'riʒmu] *m* companionship.

companheiro/a [kõpa'ɲejru/a] *m/f* companion; (*colega*) friend; (*col*) buddy, mate; **~ de viagem** fellow traveller (BRIT) *ou* traveler (US), travelling (BRIT) *ou* traveling (US) companion.

companheirões [kõpaɲej'rõjʃ] *mpl de* **companheirão**.

companheirona [kõpaɲej'rɔna] *f de* **companheirão**.

companhia [kõpa'ɲia] *f* (COM) company, firm; (*convivência*) company; **fazer ~ a alguém** to keep sb company; **em ~ de** accompanied by; **dama de ~** companion.

comparação [kõpara'sãw] (*pl* **-ões**) *f* comparison.

comparar [kõpa'ra*] *vt* to compare; **~-se** *vr*: **~-se com** to bear comparison with; **~ a** to liken to; **~ com** to compare with.

comparativo/a [kõpara'tʃivu/a] *adj* comparative.

comparável [kõpa'ravew] (*pl* **-eis**) *adj* comparable.

comparecer [kõpare'se*] *vi* to appear, make an appearance; **~ a uma reunião** to attend a meeting.

comparecimento [kõparesi'mẽtu] *m* (*presença*) attendance.

comparsa [kõ'paxsa] *m/f* (TEATRO) extra; (*cúmplice*) accomplice.

compartilhar [kõpaxtʃi'ʎa*] *vt* (*partilhar*) to share; **~ de** (*participar de*) to share in, participate in; **~ com alguém** to share with sb.

compartimentar [kõpaxtʃimẽ'ta*] *vt* to compartmentalize.

compartimento [kõpaxtʃi'mẽtu] *m* compartment; (*aposento*) room.

compartir [kõpax'tʃi*] *vt* (*dividir*) to share out ♦ *vi*: **~ de** to share in.

compassado/a [kõpa'sadu/a] *adj* (*medido*) measured; (*moderado*) moderate;

(*cadenciado*) regular; (*pausado*) slow.

compassivo/a [kõpa'sivu/a] *adj* compassionate.

compasso [kõ'pasu] *m* (*instrumento*) a pair of compasses; (*MÚS*) time; (*ritmo*) beat; **dentro do** ~ in time with the music; **fora do** ~ out of time.

compatibilidade [kõpatʃibili'dadʒi] *f* compatibility.

compatível [kõpa'tʃivew] (*pl* **-eis**) *adj* compatible; ~ **com o IBM-PC** IBM compatible.

compatriota [kõpa'trjɔta] *m/f* fellow countryman/woman, compatriot.

compelir [kõpe'li*] *vt* to force, compel.

compêndio [kõ'pẽdʒju] *m* (*sumário*) compendium; (*livro de texto*) text book.

compenetração [kõpenetra'sãw] (*pl* **-ões**) *f* conviction.

compenetrar [kõpene'tra*] *vt* to convince; **~-se** *vr* to be convinced.

compensação [kõpẽsa'sãw] (*pl* **-ões**) *f* compensation; (*de cheques*) clearance; **em** ~ on the other hand.

compensado [kõpẽ'sadu] *m* hardboard.

compensador(a) [kõpẽsa'do*(a)] *adj* compensatory.

compensar [kõpẽ'sa*] *vt* (*reparar o dano*) to make up for, compensate for; (*equilibrar*) to offset, counterbalance; (*cheque*) to clear.

competência [kõpe'tẽsja] *f* competence, ability; **isto é de minha** ~ this is my responsibility.

competente [kõpe'tẽtʃi] *adj* (*capaz*) competent, able; (*apropriado*) appropriate.

competição [kõpetʃi'sãw] (*pl* **-ões**) *f* competition.

competidor(a) [kõpetʃi'do*(a)] *m/f* competitor.

competir [kõpe'tʃi*] *vi* to compete; ~ **a alguém** (*ser da competência de*) to be sb's responsibility; (*caber*) to be up to sb; ~ **com** to compete with.

competitividade [kõpetʃitʃivi'dadʒi] *f* competitiveness.

competitivo/a [kõpetʃi'tʃivu/a] *adj* competitive.

compilação [kõpila'sãw] (*pl* **-ões**) *f* compilation.

compilar [kõpi'la*] *vt* to compile.

compilo [kõ'pilu] *etc vb V* **compelir**.

compito [kõ'pitu] *etc vb V* **competir**.

complacência [kõpla'sẽsja] *f* complaisance.

complacente [kõpla'sẽtʃi] *adj* obliging.

compleição [kõplej'sãw] (*pl* **-ões**) *f* build.

complementar [kõplemẽ'ta*] *adj* complementary ♦ *vt* to supplement.

complemento [kõple'mẽtu] *m* complement.

completamente [kõpleta'mẽtʃi] *adv* completely, quite.

completar [kõple'ta*] *vt* to complete; (*tanque, água*) to fill up, top up; ~ **dez anos** to be ten.

completo/a [kõ'plɛtu/a] *adj* complete; (*cheio*) full (up); **por** ~ completely.

complexado/a [kõplek'sadu/a] *adj* hung-up; **estar/ficar** ~ to have/get a complex.

complexidade [kõpleksi'dadʒi] *f* complexity.

complexo/a [kõ'plɛksu/a] *adj* complex ♦ *m* complex; ~ **de Édipo** Oedipus complex.

complicação [kõplika'sãw] (*pl* **-ões**) *f* complication.

complicado/a [kõpli'kadu/a] *adj* complicated.

complicar [kõpli'ka*] *vt* to complicate; **~-se** *vr* to become complicated; (*enredo*) to thicken.

complô [kõ'plo] *m* plot, conspiracy.

compõe [kõ'põj] *etc vb V* **compor**.

compomos [kõ'pomoʃ] *etc vb V* **compor**.

componho [kõ'poɲu] *etc vb V* **compor**.

componente [kõpo'nẽtʃi] *adj*, *m* component.

compor [kõ'po*] (*irreg*: *como* **pôr**) *vt* to compose; (*discurso, livro*) to write; (*arranjar*) to arrange; (*TIP*) to set ♦ *vi* to compose; **~-se** *vr* (*controlar-se*) to compose o.s.; **~-se de** to be made up of, be composed of.

comporta [kõ'pɔxta] *f* floodgate; (*de canal*) lock.

comportamento [kõpoxta'mẽtu] *m* behaviour (*BRIT*), behavior (*US*); (*conduta*) conduct; **mau** ~ misbehavio(u)r.

comportar [kõpox'ta*] *vt* (*suportar*) to put up with, bear; (*conter*) to hold; **~-se** *vr* (*portar-se*) to behave; **~-se mal** to misbehave, behave badly.

compôs [kõ'poʃ] *vb V* **compor**.

composição [kõpozi'sãw] (*pl* **-ões**) *f* composition; (*TIP*) typesetting; (*conciliação*) compromise.

compositor(a) [kõpozi'to*(a)] *m/f* composer; (*TIP*) typesetter.

composto/a [kõ'poʃtu/'pɔʃta] *pp de* **compor** ♦ *adj* (*sério*) serious; (*de muitos elementos*) composite, compound ♦ *m* compound; ~ **de** made up of, composed of.

compostura [kõpoʃ'tura] *f* composure.

compota [kõ'pɔta] *f* fruit in syrup; ~ **de laranja** oranges in syrup.

compra ['kõpra] *f* purchase; **fazer ~s** to go shopping.

comprador(a) [kõpra'do*(a)] *m/f* buyer, purchaser.

comprar [kõ'pra*] *vt* to buy; (*subornar*) to bribe; ~ **briga** to look for trouble; ~ **a briga de alguém** to fight sb's battle for him.

comprazer-se [kõpra'zexsi] *vr*: ~ **com/em fazer** to take pleasure in/in doing.

compreender [kõprjen'de*] *vt* (*entender*) to understand; (*constar de*) to be comprised of, consist of; (*abranger*) to cover.

***NB**: European Portuguese adds the following consonants to certain words:* **b** (sú(b)dito, su(b)til); **c** (a(c)ção, a(c)cionista, a(c)to); **m** (inde(m)ne); **p** (ado(p)ção, ado(p)tar); *for further details see p. xiii.*

compreensão [kõprjẽ'sãw] *f* understanding, comprehension.

compreensível [kõprjẽ'sivew] (*pl* **-eis**) *adj* understandable, comprehensible.

compreensivo/a [kõprjẽ'sivu/a] *adj* understanding.

compressa [kõ'prεsa] *f* compress.

compressão [kõpre'sãw] (*pl* **-ões**) *f* compression.

compressor(a) [kõpre'so*(a)] *adj V* **rolo**.

comprido/a [kõ'pridu/a] *adj* long; (*alto*) tall; **ao ~** lengthways.

comprimento [kõpri'mẽtu] *m* length.

comprimido/a [kõpri'midu/a] *adj* compressed ♦ *m* (*pílula*) pill; (*pastilha*) tablet.

comprimir [kõpri'mi*] *vt* to compress; (*apertar*) to squeeze.

comprometedor(a) [kõpromete'do*(a)] *adj* compromising.

comprometer [kõprome'te*] *vt* to compromise; (*envolver*) to involve; (*arriscar*) to jeopardize; (*empenhar*) to pledge; **~-se** *vr* to commit o.s.; **~-se a** to undertake to, promise to; **~-se com alguém** to make a commitment to sb.

comprometido/a [kõprome'tʃidu/a] *adj* (*ocupado*) busy; (*noivo etc*) spoken for.

compromisso [kõpro'misu] *m* (*promessa*) promise; (*obrigação*) commitment; (*hora marcada*) appointment, engagement; (*acordo*) agreement; **sem ~** without obligation.

comprovação [kõprova'sãw] (*pl* **-ões**) *f* proof, evidence; (ADMIN) receipts *pl*.

comprovante [kõpro'vãtʃi] *adj* of proof ♦ *m* receipt, voucher.

comprovar [kõpro'va*] *vt* to prove; (*confirmar*) to confirm.

compulsão [kõpuw'sãw] (*pl* **-ões**) *f* compulsion.

compulsivo/a [kõpuw'sivu/a] *adj* compulsive.

compulsões [kõpuw'sõjʃ] *fpl de* **compulsão**.

compulsório/a [kõpuw'sɔrju/a] *adj* compulsory.

compunção [kõpũ'sãw] *f* compunction.

compungir [kõpũ'ʒi*] *vt* to pain ♦ *vi* to be painful.

compunha [kõ'puɲa] *etc vb V* **compor**.

compus [kõ'puʃ] *etc vb V* **compor**.

compuser [kõpu'ze*] *etc vb V* **compor**.

computação [kõputa'sãw] *f* computation; (*ciência, curso*) computer science, computing.

computador [kõputa'do*] *m* computer.

computadorizar [kõputadori'za*] *vt* to computerize.

computar [kõpu'ta*] *vt* to compute; (*calcular*) to calculate; (*contar*) to count.

cômputo ['kõputu] *m* computation.

comum [ko'mũ] (*pl* **-ns**) *adj* (*pessoa*) ordinary, common; (*habitual*) usual ♦ *m* the usual thing; **o ~ é partirmos às 8** we usually set off at 8; **fora do ~** unusual; **temos muito em ~** we have a lot in common.

comuna [ko'muna] (*col*) *m/f* communist.

comungar [komũ'ga*] *vi* to take communion.

comunhão [komu'ɲãw] (*pl* **-ões**) *f* communion; (REL) Holy Communion; **~ de bens** joint ownership.

comunicação [komunika'sãw] (*pl* **-ões**) *f* communication; (*mensagem*) message; (*curso*) media studies *sg*; (*acesso*) access.

comunicado [komuni'kadu] *m* notice; (*oficial*) communiqué.

comunicar [komuni'ka*] *vt* to communicate; (*unir*) to join ♦ *vi* to communicate; **~-se** *vr* to communicate; **~ algo a alguém** to inform sb of sth; **~-se com** (*entrar em contato*) to get in touch with.

comunicativo/a [comunika'tʃivu/a] *adj* communicative; (*riso*) infectious.

comunidade [komuni'dadʒi] *f* community; **C~ Econômica Européia** European (Economic) Community.

comunismo [komu'niʒmu] *m* communism.

comunista [komu'niʃta] *adj, m/f* communist.

comunitário/a [komuni'tarju/a] *adj* community *atr*.

comuns [ko'mũʃ] *pl de* **comum**.

comutador [komuta'do*] *m* switch.

comutar [komu'ta*] *vt* (JUR) to commute; (*trocar*) to exchange.

concatenar [kõkate'na*] *vt* (*idéias*) to string together.

côncavo/a ['kõkavu/a] *adj* concave; (*cavado*) hollow ♦ *m* hollow.

conceber [kõse'be*] *vt* to conceive; (*imaginar*) to conceive of, imagine; (*entender*) to understand ♦ *vi* to become pregnant.

concebível [kõse'bivew] (*pl* **-eis**) *adj* conceivable.

conceder [kõse'de*] *vt* (*permitir*) to allow; (*outorgar*) to grant, accord; (*admitir*) to concede; (*dar*) to give ♦ *vi*: **~ em** to agree to.

conceito [kõ'sejtu] *m* (*idéia*) concept, idea; (*fama*) reputation; (*opinião*) opinion.

conceituado/a [kõsej'twadu/a] *adj* well thought of, highly regarded.

conceituar [kõsej'twa*] *vt* to conceptualize.

concentração [kõsẽtra'sãw] (*pl* **-ões**) *f* concentration; (ESPORTE) training camp.

concentrado/a [kõsẽ'tradu/a] *adj* concentrated ♦ *m* concentrate.

concentrar [kõsẽ'tra*] *vt* to concentrate; (*atenção*) to focus; (*reunir*) to bring together; (*molho*) to thicken; **~-se** *vr* to concentrate; **~-se em** to concentrate on.

concepção [kõsep'sãw] (*pl* **-ões**) *f* (*geração*) conception; (*noção*) idea, concept; (*opinião*) opinion.

concernente [kõsex'nẽtʃi] *adj*: **~ a** concerning.

concernir [kõsex'ni*] *vi*: **~ a** to concern.

concertar [kõsex'ta*] *vt* (*endireitar*) to adjust; (*conciliar*) to reconcile.

concerto [kõ'sextu] *m* concert.
concessão [kõse'sãw] (*pl* **-ões**) *f* concession; (*permissão*) permission.
concessionária [kõsesjo'narja] *f* dealer, dealership.
concessionário [kõsesjo'narju] *m* concessionaire.
concessões [kõse'sõjʃ] *fpl de* **concessão**.
concha ['kõʃa] *f* (*moluscos*) shell; (*para líquidos*) ladle.
conchavo [kõ'ʃavu] *m* conspiracy.
conciliação [kõsilja'sãw] (*pl* **-ões**) *f* reconciliation.
conciliador(a) [kõsilja'do*(a)] *adj* conciliatory ♦ *m/f* conciliator.
conciliar [kõsi'lja*] *vt* to reconcile; ~ **o sono** to get to sleep.
conciliatório/a [kõsilja'tɔrju/a] *adj* conciliatory.
conciliável [kõsi'ljavew] (*pl* **-eis**) *adj* reconcilable.
concílio [kõ'silju] *m* (*REL*) council.
concisão [kõsi'zãw] *f* concision, conciseness.
conciso/a [kõ'sizu/a] *adj* brief, concise.
concitar [kõsi'ta*] *vt* (*estimular*) to stir up, arouse; (*incitar*) to incite.
conclamar [kõkla'ma*] *vt* to shout; (*aclamar*) to acclaim; (*convocar*) to call together.
Conclat [kõ'klatʃi] (*BR*) *abr f* (= *Conferência Nacional da Classe Trabalhadora*) *trade union*.
conclave [kõ'klavi] *m* conclave.
concludente [kõklu'dẽtʃi] *adj* conclusive.
concluir [kõ'klwi*] *vt* (*terminar*) to end, conclude ♦ *vi* (*deduzir*) to conclude.
conclusão [kõklu'zãw] (*pl* **-ões**) *f* (*término*) end; (*dedução*) conclusion; **chegar a uma** ~ to come to a conclusion; ~, **ele não veio** (*col*) the upshot is, he didn't come.
conclusivo/a [kõklu'zivu/a] *adj* conclusive.
conclusões [kõklu'zõjʃ] *fpl de* **conclusão**.
concomitante [kõkomi'tãtʃi] *adj* concomitant.
concordância [kõkox'dãsja] *f* agreement.
concordante [kõkox'dãtʃi] *adj* (*fatos*) concordant.
concordar [kõkox'da*] *vi, vt* to agree; **não concordo!** I disagree!; ~ **com** to agree with; ~ **em** to agree to.
concordata [kõkox'data] *f* liquidation agreement.
concórdia [kõ'kɔxdʒja] *f* (*acordo*) agreement; (*paz*) peace.
concorrência [kõko'xẽsja] *f* competition; (*a um cargo*) application.
concorrente [kõko'xẽtʃi] *m/f* (*competidor*) contestant; (*candidato*) candidate.
concorrer [kõko'xe*] *vi* (*competir*) to compete; ~ **a** (*candidatar-se*) to apply for; ~ **para** (*contribuir*) to contribute to.
concorrido/a [kõko'xidu/a] *adj* popular.
concretização [kõkretʃiza'sãw] *f* realization.
concretizar [kõkretʃi'za*] *vt* to make real; **~-se** *vr* (*sonho*) to come true; (*ambições*) to be realized.
concreto/a [kõ'krɛtu/a] *adj* concrete; (*verdadeiro*) real; (*sólido*) solid ♦ *m* concrete; ~ **armado** reinforced concrete.
concupiscência [kõkupi'sẽsja] *f* greed; (*lascívia*) lust.
concurso [kõ'kuxsu] *m* contest; (*exame*) competition; ~ **público** open competition.
concussão [kõku'sãw] *f* concussion; (*desfalque*) embezzlement.
condado [kõ'dadu] *m* county.
condão [kõ'dãw] *m V* **varinha**.
conde ['kõdʒi] *m* count.
condecoração [kõdekora'sãw] (*pl* **-ões**) *f* decoration.
condecorar [kõdeko'ra*] *vt* to decorate.
condenação [kõdena'sãw] (*pl* **-ões**) *f* condemnation; (*JUR*) conviction.
condenar [kõde'na*] *vt* to condemn; (*JUR*: *sentenciar*) to sentence; (: *declarar culpado*) to convict.
condenável [kõde'navew] (*pl* **-eis**) *adj* reprehensible.
condensação [kõdẽsa'sãw] *f* condensation.
condensar [kõdẽ'sa*] *vt* to condense; **~-se** *vr* to condense.
condescendência [kõdesẽ'dẽsja] *f* acquiescence.
condescendente [kõdesẽ'dẽtʃi] *adj* condescending.
condescender [kõdesẽ'de*] *vi* to acquiesce; ~ **a** *ou* **em** to condescend to, deign to.
condessa [kõ'desa] *f* countess.
condição [kõdʒi'sãw] (*pl* **-ões**) *f* condition; (*social*) status; (*qualidade*) capacity; **com a** ~ **de que** on condition that, provided that; **ter** ~ *ou* **condições para fazer** to be able to do; **em condições de fazer** (*pessoa*) able to do; (*carro etc*) in condition to do; **em sua** ~ **de líder** in his capacity as leader.
condicionado/a [kõdʒisjo'nadu/a] *adj* conditioned; *V tb* **ar**.
condicional [kõdʒisjo'naw] (*pl* **-ais**) *adj* conditional.
condicionamento [kõdʒisjona'mẽtu] *m* conditioning.
condições [kõdʒi'sõjʃ] *fpl de* **condição**.
condigno/a [kõ'dʒignu/a] *adj* (*apropriado*) fitting; (*merecido*) deserved.
condigo [kõ'dʒigu] *etc vb V* **condizer**.
condimentar [kõdʒimẽ'ta*] *vt* to season.
condimento [kõdʒi'mẽtu] *m* seasoning.
condisse [kõ'dʒisi] *etc vb V* **condizer**.
condito [kõ'dʒitu] *pp de* **condizer**.
condizente [kõdʒi'zẽtʃi] *adj*: ~ **com** in keeping with.
condizer [kõdʒi'ze*] (*irreg*: *como* **dizer**) *vi*: ~

NB: European Portuguese adds the following consonants to certain words: **b** (sú(b)dito, su(b)til); **c** (a(c)ção, a(c)cionista, a(c)to); **m** (inde(m)ne); **p** (ado(p)ção, ado(p)tar); *for further details see p. xiii.*

com to match.
condoer-se [kõdo'exsi] *vr*: ~ **de** to pity.
condolência [kõdo'lẽsja] *f* condolence.
condomínio [kõdo'minju] *m* condominium; (*contribuição*) service charge.
condução [kõdu'sãw] *f* (*ato de conduzir*) driving; (*transporte*) transport; (*ônibus*) bus; (FÍS) conduction.
conducente [kõdu'sẽtʃi] *adj*: ~ **a** conducive to.
conduta [kõ'duta] *f* conduct; **má** ~ misconduct.
conduto [kõ'dutu] *m* (*tubo*) tube; (*cano*) pipe; (*canal*) channel.
condutor(a) [kõdu'to*(a)] *m/f* (*de veículo*) driver ♦ *m* (ELET) conductor.
conduzir [kõdu'zi*] *vt* (PT: *veículo*) to drive; (*levar*) to lead; (*negócio*) to manage; (FÍS) to conduct ♦ *vi* (PT) to drive; **~-se** *vr* to behave; ~ **a** to lead to.
cone ['kɔni] *m* cone.
conectar [konek'ta*] *vt* to connect.
cônego ['konegu] *m* (REL) canon.
conexão [konek'sãw] (*pl* **-ões**) *f* connection.
conexo/a [ko'nɛksu/a] *adj* connected.
conexões [konek'sõjʃ] *fpl de* **conexão**.
confabular [kõfabu'la*] *vi* to talk; ~ **com** to talk to.
confecção [kõfek'sãw] (*pl* **-ões**) *f* (*feitura*) making; (*de um boletim*) production; (*roupa*) ready-to-wear clothes *pl*; (*negócio*) *business selling ready-to-wear clothes*.
confeccionar [kõfeksjo'na*] *vt* (*fazer*) to make; (*fabricar*) to manufacture.
confeccionista [kõfeksjo'niʃta] *m/f maker of ready-to-wear clothes*.
confecções [kõfek'sõjʃ] *fpl de* **confecção**.
confederação [kõfedera'sãw] (*pl* **-ões**) *f* confederation; (*liga*) league.
confederar [kõfede'ra*] *vt* to unite; **~-se** *vr* to form an alliance.
confeitar [kõfej'ta*] *vt* (*bolo*) to ice.
confeitaria [kõfejta'ria] *f* patisserie.
confeiteiro/a [kõfej'tejru/a] *m/f* confectioner.
conferência [kõfe'rẽsja] *f* conference; (*discurso*) lecture; **fazer uma** ~ to give a lecture.
conferencista [kõferẽ'siʃta] *m/f* (*que fala*) speaker.
conferente [kõfe'rẽtʃi] *m/f* (*verificador*) checker.
conferir [kõfe'ri*] *vt* (*verificar*) to check; (*comparar*) to compare; (*outorgar*) to grant; (*título*) to confer ♦ *vi* (*estar certo*) to tally; **confira!** see for yourself, check it out (*col*).
confessar [kõfe'sa*] *vt, vi* to confess; **~-se** *vr* to confess; ~ **alguém** (REL) to hear sb's confession; **~-se culpado** (JUR) to plead guilty.
confessionário [kõfesjo'narju] *m* confessional.
confessor [kõfe'so*] *m* confessor.
confete [kõ'fɛtʃi] *m* confetti; **jogar** ~ (*col*) to be flattering.
confiabilidade [kõfjabili'dadʒi] *f* reliability.
confiado/a [kõ'fjadu/a] (*col*) *adj* cheeky.
confiança [kõ'fjãsa] *f* confidence; (*fé*) trust; (*familiaridade*) familiarity; **de** ~ reliable; **digno de** ~ trustworthy; **ter** ~ **em alguém** to trust sb; **dar** ~ **a alguém** (*no tratamento*) to be on informal terms with sb.
confiante [kõ'fjãtʃi] *adj* confident; ~ **em** confident of.
confiar [kõ'fja*] *vt* to entrust; (*segredo*) to confide ♦ *vi*: ~ **em** to trust; (*ter fé*) to have faith in.
confiável [kõ'fjavew] (*pl* **-eis**) *adj* reliable.
confidência [kõfi'dẽsja] *f* secret; **em** ~ in confidence.
confidencial [kõfidẽ'sjaw] (*pl* **-ais**) *adj* confidential.
confidenciar [kõfidẽ'sja*] *vt* to tell in confidence.
confidente [kõfi'dẽtʃi] *m/f* confidant/confidante.
configuração [kõfigura'sãw] (*pl* **-ões**) *f* configuration; (*forma*) shape, form.
configurar [kõfigu'ra*] *vt* to shape, form; (*representar*) to represent; (COMPUT) to configure.
confinamento [kõfina'mẽtu] *m* confinement.
confinar [kõfi'na*] *vt* (*limitar*) to limit; (*enclausurar*) to confine ♦ *vi*: ~ **com** to border on; **~-se** *vr*: **~-se a** to confine o.s. to.
confins [kõ'fĩʃ] *mpl* limits, boundaries; **nos** ~ **de judas** (*col*) out in the sticks.
confirmação [kõfixma'sãw] (*pl* **-ões**) *f* confirmation.
confirmar [kõfix'ma*] *vt* to confirm; **~-se** *vr* (REL) to be confirmed; (*realizar-se*) to come true.
confiro [kõ'firu] *etc vb V* **conferir**.
confiscar [kõfiʃ'ka*] *vt* to confiscate, seize.
confisco [kõ'fiʃku] *m* confiscation.
confissão [kõfi'sãw] (*pl* **-ões**) *f* confession.
conflagração [kõflagra'sãw] (*pl* **-ões**) *f* conflagration.
conflagrar [kõfla'gra*] *vt* to inflame, set alight; (*fig*) to plunge into turmoil.
conflitante [kõfli'tãtʃi] *adj* conflicting.
conflito [kõ'flitu] *m* conflict; **entrar em** ~ **(com)** to clash (with).
confluente [kõ'flwẽtʃi] *m* tributary.
conformação [kõfoxma'sãw] (*pl* **-ões**) *f* (*resignação*) resignation; (*forma*) form.
conformado/a [kõfox'madu/a] *adj* resigned.
conformar [kõfox'ma*] *vt* (*formar*) to form; **~-se** *vr*: **~-se com** to resign o.s. to; (*acomodar-se*) to conform to; ~ **com** to conform to.
conforme [kõ'fɔxmi] *prep* according to ♦ *conj* (*logo que*) as soon as; (*como*) as, according to what; (*à medida que*) as; (*dependendo de*) depending on; **você vai?** — ~ are you going? — it depends.
conformidade [kõfoxmi'dadʒi] *f* agreement; **em** ~ **com** in accordance with.
conformismo [kõfox'miʒmu] *m* conformity.

conformista [kõfox'miʃta] *m/f* conformist.
confortante [kõfox'tãtʃi] *adj* comforting.
confortar [kõfox'ta*] *vt* (*consolar*) to comfort, console.
confortável [kõfox'tavew] (*pl* **-eis**) *adj* comfortable.
conforto [kõ'foxtu] *m* comfort.
confraria [kõfra'ria] *f* fraternity.
confraternizar [kõfratexni'za*] *vi* to fraternize.
confrontação [kõfrõta'sãw] (*pl* **-ões**) *f* (*acareação*) confrontation; (*comparação*) comparison.
confrontar [kõfrõ'ta*] *vt* (*acarear*) to confront; (*comparar*) to compare; **~-se** *vr* to face each other.
confronto [kõ'frõtu] *m* confrontation; (*comparação*) comparison.
confundir [kõfũ'dʒi*] *vt* to confuse; **~-se** *vr* to get mixed up, get confused.
confusão [kõfu'zãw] (*pl* **-ões**) *f* confusion; (*tumulto*) uproar; (*problemas*) trouble; (*barafunda*) chaos; **isso vai dar tanta ~** this will cause so much trouble; **fazer ~** (*confundir-se*) to get mixed up *ou* confused.
confuso/a [kõ'fuzu/a] *adj* confused; (*problema*) confusing; **está tudo muito ~ aqui hoje** it's all very chaotic in here today.
confusões [kõfu'zõjʃ] *fpl de* **confusão**.
congelado/a [kõʒe'ladu/a] *adj* frozen.
congelador [kõʒela'do*] *m* freezer, deep freeze.
congelamento [kõʒela'mẽtu] *m* freezing; (*ECON*) freeze.
congelar [kõʒe'la*] *vt* to freeze; **~-se** *vr* to freeze.
congênere [kõ'ʒeneri] *adj* similar.
congênito/a [kõ'ʒenitu/a] *adj* congenital.
congestão [kõʒeʃ'tãw] *f* congestion.
congestionado/a [kõʒeʃtʃjo'nadu/a] *adj* (*trânsito*) congested; (*olhos*) bloodshot; (*rosto*) flushed.
congestionamento [kõʒeʃtʃjona'mẽtu] *m* congestion; **um ~ (de tráfego)** a traffic jam.
congestionar [kõʒeʃtʃjo'na*] *vt* to congest; **~-se** *vr* (*rosto*) to go red.
conglomeração [kõglomera'sãw] (*pl* **-ões**) *f* conglomeration.
conglomerado [kõglome'radu] *m* conglomerate.
conglomerar [kõglome'ra*] *vt* to heap together; **~-se** *vr* (*unir-se*) to join together, group together.
Congo ['kõgu] *m*: **o ~** the Congo.
congratular [kõgratu'la*] *vt*: **~ alguém por** to congratulate sb on.
congregação [kõgrega'sãw] (*pl* **-ões**) *f* (*REL*) congregation; (*reunião*) gathering.
congregar [kõgre'ga*] *vt* to bring together; **~-se** *vr* to congregate.
congressista [kõgre'siʃta] *m/f* congressman/woman.
congresso [kõ'grɛsu] *m* congress, conference.
conhaque [ko'ɲaki] *m* cognac, brandy.
conhecedor(a) [koɲese'do*(a)] *adj* knowing ♦ *m/f* connoisseur, expert.
conhecer [koɲe'se*] *vt* to know; (*travar conhecimento com*) to meet; (*descobrir*) to discover; **~-se** *vr* (*travar conhecimento*) to meet; (*ter conhecimento*) to know each other; **~ alguém de nome/vista** to know sb by name/sight; **quero ~ sua casa** I'd like to see your house; **você conhece Paris?** have you ever been to Paris?
conhecido/a [koɲe'sidu/a] *adj* known; (*célebre*) well-known ♦ *m/f* acquaintance.
conhecimento [koɲesi'mẽtu] *m* knowledge; (*idéia*) idea; (*conhecido*) acquaintance; (*COM*) bill of lading; **~s** *mpl* knowledge *sg*; **levar ao ~ de alguém** to bring to sb's notice; **ter ~ de** to know; **tomar ~ de** to learn about; **não tomar ~ de** (*não dar atenção a*) to take no notice of; **é de ~ geral** it is common knowledge; **~ aéreo** air waybill.
cônico/a ['koniku/a] *adj* conical.
conivência [koni'vẽsja] *f* connivance.
conivente [koni'vẽtʃi] *adj* conniving; **ser ~ em** to connive in.
conjetura [kõʒe'tura] (*PT*: **-ct-**) *f* conjecture, supposition; **fazer ~ (sobre)** to guess (at).
conjeturar [kõʒetu'ra*] (*PT*: **-ct-**) *vt* to guess at ♦ *vi* to conjecture.
conjugação [kõʒuga'sãw] (*pl* **-ões**) *f* conjugation.
conjugado [kõʒu'gadu] *m* bed-sitter.
conjugal [kõʒu'gaw] (*pl* **-ais**) *adj* conjugal; **vida ~** married life.
conjugar [kõʒu'ga*] *vt* (*verbo*) to conjugate; (*unir*) to join; **~-se** *vr* to join together.
cônjuge ['kõʒuʒi] *m* spouse.
conjunção [kõʒũ'sãw] (*pl* **-ões**) *f* (*união*) union; (*LING*) conjunction.
conjuntivite [kõʒũtʃi'vitʃi] *f* conjunctivitis.
conjuntivo [kõʒũ'tʃivu] (*PT*) *m* (*LING*) subjunctive.
conjunto/a [kõ'ʒũtu/a] *adj* joint ♦ *m* (*totalidade*) whole; (*coleção*) collection; (*músicos*) group; (*roupa*) outfit; **em ~** together.
conjuntura [kõʒũ'tura] *f* situation.
conluio [kõ'luju] *m* collusion.
conosco [ko'noʃku] *pron* with us.
conotação [konota'sãw] (*pl* **-ões**) *f* connotation.
conotar [kono'ta*] *vt* to connote.
conquanto [kõ'kwantu] *conj* although, though.
conquista [kõ'kiʃta] *f* conquest; (*da ciência*) achievement.
conquistador(a) [kõkiʃta'do*(a)] *adj* conquering ♦ *m* conqueror; (*namorador*) ladies' man.

***NB**: European Portuguese adds the following consonants to certain words:* **b** (sú(b)dito, su(b)til); **c** (a(c)ção, a(c)cionista, a(c)to); **m** (inde(m)ne); **p** (ado(p)ção, ado(p)tar); *for further details see p. xiii.*

conquistar [kõkiʃ'ta*] *vt* (*subjugar*) to conquer; (*alcançar*) to achieve; (*ganhar*) to win, gain; (*pessoa*) to win over.

consagração [kõsagra'sãw] (*pl* **-ões**) *f* (*REL*) consecration; (*aclamação*) acclaim; (*exaltação*) praise; (*dedicação*) dedication; (*de uma expressão*) establishment.

consagrado/a [kõsa'gradu/a] *adj* (*estabelecido*) established.

consagrar [kõsa'gra*] *vt* (*REL*) to consecrate; (*aclamar*) to acclaim; (*dedicar*) to dedicate; (*tempo*) to devote; (*expressão*) to establish; (*exaltar*) to glorify; **~-se** *vr*: **~-se a** to devote o.s. to.

consangüíneo/a [kõsã'gwinju/a] *adj* related by blood ♦ *m/f* blood relation.

consciência [kõ'sjẽsja] *f* (*moral*) conscience; (*percepção*) awareness; (*senso de responsabilidade*) conscientiousness; **estar com a ~ limpa/pesada** to have a clear/guilty conscience; **ter ~ de** to be conscious of.

consciencioso/a [kõsjẽ'sjozu/ɔza] *adj* conscientious.

consciente [kõ'sjẽtʃi] *adj* conscious.

conscientizar [kõsjẽtʃi'za*] *vt*: **~ alguém** (*politicamente*) to raise sb's awareness; **~-se** *vr* to become more aware; **~-se de** to be aware of; **~ alguém de algo** to make sb aware of sth.

cônscio/a ['kõsju/a] *adj* aware.

conscrição [kõʃkri'sãw] *f* conscription.

consecução [kõseku'sãw] *f* attainment.

consecutivo/a [kõseku'tʃivu/a] *adj* consecutive.

conseguinte [kõse'gĩtʃi] *adj*: **por ~** consequently.

conseguir [kõse'gi*] *vt* (*obter*) to get, obtain; **~ fazer** to manage to do, succeed in doing; **não consigo abrir a porta** I can't open the door.

conselheiro/a [kõse'ʎejru/a] *m/f* (*que aconselha*) counsellor (*BRIT*), counselor (*US*), adviser; (*POL*) councillor.

conselho [kõ'seʎu] *m* piece of advice; (*corporação*) council; **~s** *mpl* advice *sg*; **~ de guerra** court martial; **C~ de ministros** (*POL*) Cabinet; **C~ de Diretoria** board of directors.

consenso [kõ'sẽsu] *m* consensus, agreement.

consensual [kõsẽ'swaw] (*pl* **-ais**) *adj* agreed.

consentimento [kõsẽtʃi'mẽtu] *m* consent, permission.

consentir [kõsẽ'tʃi*] *vt* (*admitir*) to allow, permit; (*aprovar*) to agree to ♦ *vi*: **~ em** to agree to.

conseqüência [kõse'kwẽsja] *f* consequence; **por ~** consequently; **em ~ de** as a consequence of.

conseqüente [kõse'kwẽtʃi] *adj* consequent; (*coerente*) consistent.

consertar [kõsex'ta*] *vt* to mend, repair; (*remediar*) to put right.

conserto [kõ'sextu] *m* repair.

conserva [kõ'sexva] *f* pickle; **em ~** pickled; **fábrica de ~s** cannery.

conservação [kõsexva'sãw] *f* conservation; (*de vida, alimentos*) preservation.

conservacionista [kõsexvasjo'niʃta] *adj*, *m/f* conservationist.

conservado/a [kõsex'vadu/a] *adj* (*pessoa*) well-preserved.

conservador(a) [kõsexva'do*(a)] *adj* conservative ♦ *m/f* (*POL*) conservative.

conservadorismo [kõsexvado'riʒmu] *m* conservatism.

conservante [kõsex'vãtʃi] *m* preservative.

conservar [kõsex'va*] *vt* (*preservar*) to preserve, maintain; (*reter, manter*) to keep, retain; **~-se** *vr* to keep; **"conserve-se à direita"** "keep right".

conservatório [kõsexva'tɔrju] *m* conservatory.

consideração [kõsidera'sãw] (*pl* **-ões**) *f* consideration; (*estima*) respect, esteem; (*reflexão*) thought; **levar em ~** to take into account.

considerado/a [kõside'radu/a] *adj* respected, well thought of.

considerar [kõside'ra*] *vt* to consider; (*prezar*) to respect ♦ *vi* to consider; **~-se** *vr* to consider o.s.

considerável [kõside'ravew] (*pl* **-eis**) *adj* considerable.

consignação [kõsigna'sãw] (*pl* **-ões**) *f* consignment; (*registro*) recording; (*de verbas*) assignment.

consignar [kõsig'na*] *vt* (*mercadorias*) to send, dispatch; (*registrar*) to record; (*verba etc*) to assign.

consigo [kõ'sigu] *pron* (*m*) with him; (*f*) with her; (*pl*) with them; (*com você*) with you ♦ *vb V* **conseguir**.

consinto [kõ'sĩtu] *etc vb V* **consentir**.

consistência [kõsiʃ'tẽsja] *f* consistency.

consistente [kõsiʃ'tẽtʃi] *adj* (*sólido*) solid; (*espesso*) thick.

consistir [kõsiʃ'tʃi*] *vi*: **~ em** to be made up of, consist of.

consoante [kõso'ãtʃi] *f* consonant ♦ *prep* according to ♦ *conj* as; **~ prometera** as he had promised.

consolação [kõsola'sãw] (*pl* **-ões**) *f* consolation.

consolador(a) [kõsola'do*(a)] *adj* consoling.

consolar [kõso'la*] *vt* to console; **~-se** *vr* to console o.s.

console [kõ'sɔli] *f* (*COMPUT*) console.

consolidar [kõsoli'da*] *vt* to consolidate; (*fratura*) to mend, knit ♦ *vi* to become solid; to mend, knit together.

consolo [kõ'solu] *m* consolation.

consome [kõ'somi] *etc vb V* **consumir**.

consomê [kõso'me] *m* consommé.

consonância [kõso'nãsja] *f* (*harmonia*) harmony; (*concordância*) agreement.

consorciar [kõsox'sja*] *vt* to join; (*combinar*) to combine ♦ *vi*: **~ a** to unite with.

consórcio [kõ'sɔxsju] *m* (*união*) partnership; (*COM*) consortium.
consorte [kõ'sɔxtʃi] *m/f* consort.
conspícuo/a [kõ'ʃpikwu/a] *adj* conspicuous.
conspiração [kõʃpira'sãw] (*pl* **-ões**) *f* plot, conspiracy.
conspirador(a) [kõʃpira'do*(a)] *m/f* plotter, conspirator.
conspirar [kõʃpi'ra*] *vt* to plot ♦ *vi* to plot, conspire.
constância [kõʃ'tãsja] *f* constancy; (*estabilidade*) steadiness.
constante [kõʃ'tãtʃi] *adj* constant; (*estável*) steady ♦ *f* constant.
constar [kõʃ'ta*] *vi* to be in; **consta que** it says that; ~ **de** to consist of; **não me constava que ...** I was not aware that ...; **ao que me consta** as far as I know.
constatação [kõʃtata'sãw] (*pl* **-ões**) *f* observation.
constatar [kõʃta'ta*] *vt* (*estabelecer*) to establish; (*notar*) to notice; (*evidenciar*) to show up; (*óbito*) to certify; **pudemos ~ que** we could see that.
constelação [kõʃtela'sãw] (*pl* **-ões**) *f* constellation; (*grupo*) cluster.
constelado/a [kõʃte'ladu/a] *adj* (*estrelado*) starry.
consternação [kõʃtexna'sãw] *f* (*desalento*) depression; (*desolação*) distress.
consternado/a [kõʃtex'nadu/a] *adj* (*desalentado*) depressed; (*desolado*) distressed.
consternar [kõʃtex'na*] *vt* (*desolar*) to distress; (*desalentar*) to depress; **~-se** *vr* to be distressed; to be depressed.
constipação [kõʃtʃipa'sãw] (*pl* **-ões**) *f* constipation; (*PT*) cold.
constipado/a [kõʃtʃi'padu/a] *adj*: **estar ~** to be constipated; (*PT*) to have a cold.
constipar-se [kõʃtʃi'paxsi] (*PT*) *vr* to catch a cold.
constitucional [kõʃtʃitusjo'naw] (*pl* **-ais**) *adj* constitutional.
constituição [kõʃtʃitwi'sãw] (*pl* **-ões**) *f* constitution.
constituinte [kõʃtʃi'twĩtʃi] *adj* constituent ♦ *m/f* (*deputado*) member ♦ *f*: **a C~** the Constituent Assembly.
constituir [kõʃtʃi'twi*] *vt* (*representar*) to constitute; (*formar*) to form; (*estabelecer*) to establish, set up; (*nomear*) to appoint; **~-se** *vr*: **~-se em** to set o.s. up as; (*representar*) to constitute.
constrangedor(a) [kõʃtrãʒe'do*(a)] *adj* restricting; (*que acanha*) embarrassing.
constranger [kõʃtrã'ʒe*] *vt* to constrain; (*acanhar*) to embarrass; **~-se** *vr* (*acanhar-se*) to feel embarrassed.
constrangimento [kõʃtrãʒi'mẽtu] *m* constraint; (*acanhamento*) embarrassment.
constranjo [kõʃ'trãʒu] *etc vb V* **constranger**.
construção [kõʃtru'sãw] (*pl* **-ões**) *f* building, construction.
construir [kõʃ'trwi*] *vt* to build, construct.
construtivo/a [kõʃtru'tʃivu/a] *adj* constructive.
construtor(a) [kõʃtru'to*(a)] *adj* building *atr*, construction *atr* ♦ *m/f* builder ♦ *f* building contractor.
cônsul ['kõsuw] (*pl* **~es**) *m* consul.
consulado [kõsu'ladu] *m* consulate.
consulesa [kõsu'leza] *f* lady consul; (*esposa*) consul's wife.
consulta [kõ'suwta] *f* consultation; **livro de ~** reference book; **horário de ~** surgery hours *pl* (*BRIT*), office hours *pl* (*US*).
consultar [kõsuw'ta*] *vt* to consult; **~ alguém sobre** to ask sb's opinion about.
consultivo/a [kõsuw'tʃivu/a] *adj* advisory.
consultor(a) [kõsuw'to*(a)] *m/f* adviser, consultant.
consultoria [kõsuwto'ria] *f* consultancy.
consultório [kõsuw'tɔrju] *m* surgery.
consumação [kõsuma'sãw] (*pl* **-ões**) *f* consummation; (*em restaurante etc*) minimum order.
consumado/a [kõsu'madu/a] *adj* consummate; *V tb* **fato**.
consumar [kõsu'ma*] *vt* to consummate; **~-se** *vr* to be consummated.
consumidor(a) [kõsumi'do*(a)] *adj* consumer *atr* ♦ *m/f* consumer.
consumir [kõsu'mi*] *vt* to consume; (*devorar*) to eat away; (*gastar*) to use up; **~-se** *vr* to waste away.
consumismo [kõsu'miʒmu] *m* consumerism
consumista [kõsu'miʃta] *adj*, *m/f* consumerist.
consumo [kõ'sumu] *m* consumption; **artigos de ~** consumer goods.
conta ['kõta] *f* (*cálculo*) count; (*em restaurante*) bill; (*fatura*) invoice; (*bancária*) account; (*de colar*) bead; (*responsabilidade*) responsibility; **~s** *fpl* (*COM*) accounts; **à ~ de** to the account of; **ajustar ~s com** (*fig*) to settle an account with; **fazer de ~ que** to pretend that; **levar** *ou* **ter em ~** to take into account; **por ~ própria** of one's own accord; **trabalhar por ~ própria** to work for oneself; **prestar ~s de** to account for; **não é da sua ~** it's none of your business; **tomar ~ de** (*criança etc*) to look after; (*encarregar-se de*) to take care of; (*dominar*) to take hold of; **afinal de ~s** after all; **dar-se ~ de** to realize; (*notar*) to notice; **isso fica por sua ~** this is for you to deal with; **dar ~ de** (*notar*) to notice; (*prestar ~s de*) to account for; (*de tarefa*) to handle, cope with; **ficar por ~** (*furioso*) to get mad; **ser a ~** to be just enough; **dar ~ do recado** (*col*) to deliver the goods; **~ bancária** bank account; ~

***NB**: European Portuguese adds the following consonants to certain words:* **b** (sú(b)dito, su(b)til); **c** (a(c)ção, a(c)cionista, a(c)to); **m** (inde(m)ne); **p** (ado(p)ção, ado(p)tar); *for further details see p. xiii.*

conjunta joint account; ~ **corrente** current account.
contábil [kõ'tabiw] (*pl* **-eis**) *adj* accounting *atr*.
contabilidade [kõtabili'dadʒi] *f* book-keeping, accountancy; (*departamento*) accounts department; ~ **de custos** cost accounting.
contabilista [kõtabi'liʃta] (*PT*) *m/f* accountant.
contabilizar [kõtabili'za*] *vt* to write up, book; **valor contabilizado** (*COM*) book value.
contacto *etc* [kõ'tatu] (*PT*) = **contato** *etc*.
contado/a [kõ'tadu/a] *adj*: **dinheiro de** ~ (*PT*) cash payment; **estamos com dinheiro** ~ **para só três meses** we've got just enough money for three months.
contador(a) [kõta'do*(a)] *m/f* (*COM*) accountant ♦ *m* (*TEC*: *medidor*) meter; ~ **de estórias** story-teller.
contadoria [kõtado'ria] *f* audit department.
contagem [kõ'taʒẽ] (*pl* **-ns**) *f* (*de números*) counting; (*escore*) score; **abrir a** ~ (*FUTEBOL*) to open the scoring.
contagiante [kõta'ʒjãtʃi] *adj* contagious.
contagiar [kõta'ʒja*] *vt* to infect; **~-se** *vr* to become infected.
contágio [kõ'taʒju] *m* infection.
contagioso/a [kõta'ʒjozu/ɔza] *adj* contagious.
conta-gotas *m inv* dropper.
contaminação [kõtamina'sãw] *f* contamination.
contaminar [kõtami'na*] *vt* to contaminate.
contanto que [kõ'tãtu ki] *conj* provided that.
conta-quilômetros (*PT*) *m inv* speedometer.
contar [kõ'ta*] *vt* to count; (*narrar*) to tell; (*pretender*) to intend; (*imaginar*) to think ♦ *vi* to count; ~ **com** to count on; (*esperar*) to expect; **ela contava que a fossem ajudar** she expected them to help her; ~ **em fazer** to count on doing, expect to do.
contatar [kõta'ta*] *vt* to contact.
contato [kõ'tatu] *m* contact; **entrar em** ~ **com** to get in touch with, contact.
contêiner [kõ'tejne*] *m* container.
contemplação [kõtẽpla'sãw] *f* contemplation.
contemplar [kõtẽ'pla*] *vt* to contemplate; (*olhar*) to gaze at ♦ *vi* to meditate; **~-se** *vr* to look at o.s.
contemplativo/a [kõtẽpla'tʃivu/a] *adj* (*pessoa*) thoughtful; (*vida, literatura*) contemplative.
contemporâneo/a [kõtẽpo'ranju/a] *adj, m/f* contemporary.
contemporizar [kõtẽpori'za*] *vt* (*situação*) to ease ♦ *vi* to ease the situation.
contenção [kõtẽ'sãw] (*pl* **-ões**) *f* restriction, containment; ~ **de despesas** cutbacks *pl*.
contencioso/a [kõtẽ'sjozu/ɔza] *adj* contentious.
contenções [kõtẽ'sõjʃ] *fpl de* **contenção**.
contenda [kõ'tẽda] *f* quarrel, dispute.
contenho [kõ'teɲu] *etc vb V* **conter**.
contentamento [kõtẽta'mẽtu] *m* (*felicidade*) happiness; (*satisfação*) contentment.
contentar [kõtẽ'ta*] *vt* (*dar prazer*) to please; (*dar satisfação*) to content; **~-se** *vr* to be satisfied.
contente [kõ'tẽtʃi] *adj* (*alegre*) happy; (*satisfeito*) pleased, satisfied.
contento [kõ'tẽtu] *m*: **a** ~ satisfactorily.
conter [kõ'te*] (*irreg*: *como* **ter**) *vt* (*encerrar*) to contain, hold; (*refrear*) to restrain, hold back; (*gastos*) to curb; **~-se** *vr* to restrain o.s.
conterrâneo/a [kõte'xanju/a] *adj* fellow ♦ *m/f* compatriot, fellow countryman/woman.
contestação [kõteʃta'sãw] (*pl* **-ões**) *f* challenge; (*negação*) denial.
contestar [kõteʃ'ta*] *vt* (*contrariar*) to dispute, contest, question; (*impugnar*) to challenge.
contestável [kõteʃ'tavew] (*pl* **-eis**) *adj* questionable.
conteúdo [kõte'udu] *m* contents *pl*; (*de um texto*) content.
conteve [kõ'tevi] *etc vb V* **conter**.
contexto [kõ'teʃtu] *m* context.
contido/a [kõ'tʃidu/a] *pp de* **conter** ♦ *adj* contained; (*raiva*) repressed.
contigo [kõ'tʃigu] *pron* with you.
contigüidade [kõtʃigwi'dadʒi] *f* proximity.
contíguo/a [kõ'tʃigwu/a] *adj*: ~ **a** next to.
continência [kõtʃi'nẽsja] *f* (*militar*) salute; **fazer** ~ **a** to salute.
continental [kõtʃinẽ'taw] (*pl* **-ais**) *adj* continental.
continente [kõtʃi'nẽtʃi] *m* continent.
contingência [kõtʃĩ'ʒẽsja] *f* contingency.
contingente [kõtʃĩ'ʒẽtʃi] *adj* uncertain ♦ *m* (*MIL*) contingent; (*COM*) contingency, reserve.
continuação [kõtʃinwa'sãw] *f* continuation.
continuar [kõtʃi'nwa*] *vt* to continue ♦ *vi* to continue, go on; ~ **falando** *ou* **a falar** to go on talking, continue talking *ou* to talk; **continue!** carry on!; **ela continua doente** she is still sick.
continuidade [kõtʃinwi'dadʒi] *f* continuity.
contínuo/a [kõ'tʃinwu/a] *adj* (*persistente*) continual; (*sem interrupção*) continuous ♦ *m* office boy.
contista [kõ'tʃiʃta] *m/f* story writer.
contive [kõ'tʃivi] *etc vb V* **conter**.
contiver [kõtʃi've*] *etc vb V* **conter**.
conto ['kõtu] *m* story, tale; (*PT*: *dinheiro*) 1000 escudos; ~ **da carochinha** *ou* **de fadas** fairy tale.
conto-do-vigário (*pl* **contos-do-vigário**) *m* confidence trick.
contorção [kõtox'sãw] (*pl* **-ões**) *f* contortion; (*dos músculos*) twitch.
contorcer [kõtox'se*] *vt* to twist; **~-se** *vr* to writhe.
contorções [kõtox'sõjʃ] *fpl de* **contorção**.
contornar [kõtox'na*] *vt* (*rodear*) to go round; (*ladear*) to skirt; (*fig*: *problema*) to get round.

contornável [kõtox'navew] (*pl* **-eis**) *adj* avoidable.
contorno [kõ'toxnu] *m* outline; (*da terra*) contour; (*da cara*) profile.
contra ['kõtra] *prep* against ♦ *m*: **os prós e os ~s** the pros and cons; **dar o ~ (a)** to be opposed (to); **ser do ~** to be against it.
contra-almirante *m* rear-admiral.
contra-argumento *m* counter-argument.
contra-atacar *vt* to counterattack.
contra-ataque *m* counterattack.
contrabaixo [kõtra'bajʃu] *m* double bass.
contrabalançar [kõtrabalã'sa*] *vt* to counterbalance; (*compensar*) to compensate.
contrabandear [kõtrabã'dʒja*] *vt, vi* to smuggle.
contrabandista [kõtrabã'dʒiʃta] *m/f* smuggler.
contrabando [kõtra'bãdu] *m* smuggling; (*artigos*) contraband.
contrabarra [kõtra'baxa] *f* (COMPUT) backslash.
contração [kõtra'sãw] (*pl* **-ões**) *f* contraction.
contracapa [kõtra'kapa] *f* inside cover.
contracenar [kõtrase'na*] *vi*: **~ com** to act alongside, star with.
contraceptivo/a [kõtrasep'tʃivu/a] *adj* contraceptive ♦ *m* contraceptive.
contracheque [kõtra'ʃɛki] *m* pay slip (BRIT), check stub (US).
contrações [kõtra'sõjʃ] *fpl de* **contração**.
contradição [kõtradʒi'sãw] (*pl* **-ões**) *f* contradiction.
contradigo [kõtra'dʒigu] *etc vb V* **contradizer**.
contradisse [kõtra'dʒisi] *etc vb V* **contradizer**.
contradito [kõtra'dʒitu] *pp de* **contradizer**.
contraditório/a [kõtradʒi'tɔrju/a] *adj* contradictory.
contradizer [kõtradʒi'ze*] (*irreg*: *como* **dizer**) *vt* to contradict; **~-se** *vr* (*pessoa*) to contradict o.s.; (*atitudes*) to be contradictory.
contrafazer [kõtrafa'ze*] (*irreg*: *como* **fazer**) *vt* to forge, counterfeit; (*pessoa*) to imitate, take off.
contrafeito/a [kõtra'fejtu/a] *pp de* **contrafazer** ♦ *adj* constrained.
contrafez [kõtra'feʒ] *etc vb V* **contrafazer**.
contrafilé [kõtrafi'lɛ] *m* rump steak.
contrafiz [kõtra'fiʒ] *etc vb V* **contrafazer**.
contrafizer [kõtrafi'ze*] *etc vb V* **contrafazer**.
contragosto [kõtra'goʃtu] *m*: **a ~** against one's will, unwillingly.
contraído/a [kõtra'idu/a] *adj* (*tímido*) timid, shy.
contra-indicação (*pl* **-ões**) *f* contra-indication.
contra-indicado/a *adj* inadvisable.
contrair [kõtra'i*] *vt* to contract; (*doença*) to contract, catch; (*hábito*) to form; **~-se** *vr* to contract; **~ matrimônio** to get married.
contralto [kõ'trawtu] *m* contralto.
contramão [kõtra'mãw] *adj* one-way ♦ *f*: **na ~** the wrong way down a one-way street.
contramestre/tra [kõtra'mɛʃtri/tra] *m/f* (*em fábrica*) supervisor ♦ *m* (NÁUT) boatswain.
Contran [kõ'trã] (BR) *abr m* = **Conselho Nacional de Trânsito**.
contra-ofensiva *f* counteroffensive.
contra-oferta *f* counteroffer.
contraparente/a [kõtrapa'rẽtʃi/ta] *m/f* distant relative; (*afim*) in-law.
contrapartida [kõtrapax'tʃida] *f* (COM) counterentry; (*fig*) compensation; **em ~ a** in the face of.
contrapesar [kõtrape'za*] *vt* to counterbalance; (*fig*) to compensate for.
contrapeso [kõtra'pezu] *m* counterbalance; (TEC) counterweight; (COM) makeweight.
contrapor [kõtra'po*] (*irreg*: *como* **pôr**) *vt* (*comparar*) to compare; **~ algo a algo** to set sth against sth; **~-se** *vr*: **~-se a** to be in opposition to; (*atitude*) to go against.
contraproducente [kõtraprodu'sẽtʃi] *adj* counterproductive, self-defeating.
contrapunha [kõtra'puɲa] *etc vb V* **contrapor**.
contrapus [kõtra'puʃ] *etc vb V* **contrapor**.
contrapuser [kõtrapu'ze*] *etc vb V* **contrapor**.
contra-regra (*pl* **~s**) *m/f* stage manager.
contra-revolução (*pl* **-ões**) *f* counter-revolution.
contrariar [kõtra'rja*] *vt* (*contradizer*) to contradict; (*aborrecer*) to annoy.
contrariedade [kõtrarje'dadʒi] *f* (*aborrecimento*) annoyance, vexation.
contrário/a [kõ'trarju/a] *adj* (*oposto*) opposite; (*pessoa*) opposed; (*desfavorável*) unfavourable (BRIT), unfavorable (US), adverse ♦ *m* opposite; **do ~** otherwise; **pelo** *ou* **ao ~** on the contrary; **ao ~** (*do outro lado*) the other way round; **muito pelo ~** on the contrary, quite the opposite.
contra-senso *m* nonsense.
contrastante [kõtraʃ'tãtʃi] *adj* contrasting.
contrastar [kõtraʃ'ta*] *vt* to contrast.
contraste [kõ'traʃtʃi] *m* contrast.
contratante [kõtra'tãtʃi] *adj* contracting ♦ *m/f* contractor.
contratação [kõtrata'sãw] *f* (*de pessoal*) employment.
contratar [kõtra'ta*] *vt* (*serviços*) to contract; (*empregar*) to employ, take on.
contratempo [kõtra'tẽpu] *m* (*imprevisto*) setback; (*aborrecimento*) upset; (*dificuldade*) difficulty.
contrato [kõ'tratu] *m* contract; (*acordo*) agreement.
contratual [kõtra'twaw] (*pl* **-ais**) *adj* contractual.
contravapor [kõtrava'po*] (*col*) *m* rebuff.
contravenção [kõtravẽ'sãw] (*pl* **-ões**) *f* con-

***NB**: European Portuguese adds the following consonants to certain words:* **b** (sú(b)dito, su(b)til); **c** (a(c)ção, a(c)cionista, a(c)to); **m** (inde(m)ne); **p** (ado(p)ção, ado(p)tar); *for further details see p. xiii.*

travention, violation.
contraventor(a) [kõtravẽ'to*(a)] *m/f* offender.
contribuição [kõtribwi'sãw] (*pl* **-ões**) *f* contribution; (*imposto*) tax.
contribuinte [kõtri'bwĩtʃi] *m/f* contributor; (*que paga impostos*) taxpayer.
contribuir [kõtri'bwi*] *vt* to contribute ♦ *vi* to contribute; (*pagar impostos*) to pay taxes.
contrição [kõtri'sãw] *f* contrition.
contrito/a [kõ'tritu/a] *adj* contrite.
controlar [kõtro'la*] *vt* to control; **~-se** *vr* to control o.s.
controlável [kõtro'lavew] (*pl* **-eis**) *adj* controllable.
controle [kõ'troli] *m* control; **~ remoto** remote control; **~ de crédito** (*COM*) credit control; **~ de qualidade** (*COM*) quality control.
controvérsia [kõtro'vɛxsja] *f* controversy; (*discussão*) debate.
controverso/a [kõtro'vɛxsu/a] *adj* controversial.
contudo [kõ'tudu] *conj* nevertheless, however.
contumácia [kõtu'masja] *f* obstinacy; (*JUR*) contempt of court.
contumaz [kõtu'majʒ] *adj* obstinate, stubborn ♦ *m/f* (*JUR*) defaulter.
contundente [kõtũ'dẽtʃi] *adj* bruising; (*argumento*) cutting; **instrumento ~** blunt instrument.
contundir [kõtũ'dʒi*] *vt* to bruise; **~-se** *vr* to bruise o.s.
conturbação [kõtuxba'sãw] (*pl* **-ões**) *f* disturbance, unrest; (*motim*) riot.
conturbado/a [kõtux'badu/a] *adj* disturbed.
conturbar [kõtux'ba*] *vt* to disturb; (*amotinar*) to stir up.
contusão [kõtu'zãw] (*pl* **-ões**) *f* bruise.
contuso/a [kõ'tuzu/a] *adj* bruised.
contusões [kõtu'zõjʃ] *fpl de* **contusão**.
convalescença [kõvale'sẽsa] *f* convalescence.
convalescer [kõvale'se*] *vi* to convalesce.
conveio [kõ'veju] *etc vb V* **convir**.
convenção [kõvẽ'sãw] (*pl* **-ões**) *f* convention; (*acordo*) agreement.
convencer [kõvẽ'se*] *vt* to convince; (*persuadir*) to persuade; **~-se** *vr*: **~-se de** to be convinced about.
convencido/a [kõvẽ'sidu/a] *adj* (*convicto*) convinced; (*col*: *imodesto*) conceited, smug.
convencimento [kõvẽsi'mẽtu] *m* (*convicção*) conviction; (*col*: *imodéstia*) conceit, smugness.
convencional [kõvẽsjo'naw] (*pl* **-ais**) *adj* conventional.
convenções [kõvẽ'sõjʃ] *fpl de* **convenção**.
convenha [kõ'veɲa] *etc vb V* **convir**.
conveniência [kõve'njẽsja] *f* convenience.
convencionar [kõvẽsjo'na*] *vt* to agree on; **~-se** *vr*: **~-se em** to agree to.
conveniente [kõve'njẽtʃi] *adj* convenient, suitable; (*vantajoso*) advantageous.
convênio [kõ'venju] *m* (*reunião*) convention; (*acordo*) agreement.
convento [kõ'vẽtu] *m* convent.
convergir [kõvex'ʒi*] *vi* to converge.
conversa [kõ'vɛxsa] *f* conversation; **~ fiada** idle chat; (*promessa falsa*) hot air; **ir na ~ de alguém** (*col*) to be taken in by sb; **~ vai, ~ vem** in the course of conversation; **ele não tem muita ~** he hasn't got a lot to say for himself.
conversação [kõvexsa'sãw] (*pl* **-ões**) *f* (*ato*) conversation.
conversadeira [kõvexsa'dejra] *f de* **conversador**.
conversado/a [kõvex'sadu/a] *adj* (*assunto*) talked about; (*pessoa*) talkative, chatty; **estamos ~s** we've said all we had to say.
conversador/deira [kõvexsa'do*/'dejra] *adj* talkative, chatty.
conversa-fiada (*pl* **conversas-fiadas**) *m/f*: **ser um ~** to be all talk.
conversão [kõvex'sãw] (*pl* **-ões**) *f* conversion.
conversar [kõvex'sa*] *vi* to talk.
conversibilidade [kõvexsibili'dadʒi] *f* convertibility.
conversível [kõvex'sivew] (*pl* **-eis**) *adj* convertible ♦ *m* (*AUTO*) convertible.
conversões [kõvex'sõjʃ] *fpl de* **conversão**.
converter [kõvex'te*] *vt* to convert; **~-se** *vr* to be converted.
convertido/a [kõvex'tʃidu/a] *adj* converted ♦ *m/f* convert.
convés [kõ'vɛʃ] (*pl* **-eses**) *m* (*NÁUT*) deck.
convexo/a [kõ'vɛksu/a] *adj* convex.
convicção [kõvik'sãw] (*pl* **-ões**) *f* conviction; (*certeza*) certainty.
convicto/a [kõ'viktu/a] *adj* (*convencido*) convinced; (*réu*) convicted; (*patriota etc*) staunch.
convidado/a [kõvi'dadu/a] *adj* invited ♦ *m/f* guest.
convidar [kõvi'da*] *vt* to invite; **~-se** *vr* to invite o.s.
convidativo/a [kõvida'tʃivu/a] *adj* inviting.
convier [kõ'vje*] *etc vb V* **convir**.
convincente [kõvĩ'sẽtʃi] *adj* convincing.
convir [kõ'vi*] (*irreg*: *como* **vir**) *vi* (*ser conveniente*) to suit, be convenient; (*ficar bem*) to be appropriate; **convém fazer isso o mais rápido possível** we must do this as soon as possible; **você há de ~ que ...** you must agree that ....
convirjo [kõ'vixʒu] *etc vb V* **convergir**.
convite [kõ'vitʃi] *m* invitation.
conviva [kõ'viva] *m/f* guest.
convivência [kõvi'vẽsja] *f* living together; (*familiaridade*) familiarity, intimacy.
conviver [kõvi've*] *vi* (*viver em comum*) to live together; (*ter familiaridade*) to be on familiar terms.
convívio [kõ'vivju] *m* (*viver em comum*) living together; (*familiaridade*) familiarity.
convocar [kõvo'ka*] *vt* to summon, call upon; (*reunião, eleições*) to call; (*para o serviço militar*) to call up.

convosco [kõ'voʃku] *adv* with you.
convulsão [kõvuw'sãw] (*pl* **-ões**) *f* convulsion; (*fig*) upheaval.
convulsionar [kõvuwsjo'na*] *vt* (*abalar*) to shake; (*excitar*) to stir up.
convulsivo/a [kõvuw'sivu/a] *adj* convulsive.
convulsões [kõvuw'sõjʃ] *fpl de* **convulsão**.
cooper ['kupe*] *m* jogging, running; **fazer ~** to go jogging *ou* running.
cooperação [koopera'sãw] *f* cooperation.
cooperante [koope'rãtʃi] *adj* cooperative, helpful.
cooperar [koope'ra*] *vi* to cooperate.
cooperativa [koopera'tʃiva] *f* (COM) cooperative.
cooperativo/a [koopera'tʃivu/a] *adj* cooperative.
coordenação [kooxdena'sãw] *f* co-ordination.
coordenada [kooxde'nada] *f* coordinate.
coordenar [kooxde'na*] *vt* to co-ordinate.
copa ['kɔpa] *f* (*de árvore*) top; (*dum chapéu*) crown; (*compartimento*) pantry; (*torneio*) cup; **~s** *fpl* (CARTAS) hearts.
copeira [ko'pejra] *f* kitchen maid.
Copenhague [kope'ɲagi] *n* Copenhagen.
cópia ['kɔpja] *f* copy; **tirar ~ de** to copy.
copiadora [kopja'dora] *f* (*máquina*) duplicating machine.
copiar [ko'pja*] *vt* to copy.
copidesque [kopi'dɛʃki] *m* copy editing ♦ *m/f* copy editor.
co-piloto [kopi'lotu] *m* co-pilot.
copioso/a [ko'pjozu/ɔza] *adj* abundant, numerous; (*refeição*) large; (*provas*) ample.
copirraite [kopi'xajtʃi[*m* copyright.
copo ['kɔpu] *m* glass; **ser um bom ~** (*col*) to be a good drinker.
copyright [kopi'xajtʃi] *m* = **copirraite**.
coque ['kɔki] *m* (*penteado*) bun.
coqueiro [ko'kejru] *m* (BOT) coconut palm.
coqueluche [koke'luʃi] *f* (MED) whooping cough; (*mania*) rage.
coquete [ko'kɛtʃi] *adj* coquettish.
coquetel [koke'tɛw] (*pl* **-éis**) *m* cocktail; (*festa*) cocktail party.
cor¹ [kɔ*] *m*: **de ~** by heart.
cor² [ko*] *f* colour (BRIT), color (US); **de ~** colo(u)red.
coração [kora'sãw] (*pl* **-ões**) *m* heart; **de bom ~** kind-hearted; **de todo o ~** wholeheartedly.
corado/a [ko'radu/a] *adj* ruddy.
coragem [ko'raʒẽ] *f* courage; (*atrevimento*) nerve.
corais [ko'rajʃ] *mpl* de **coral**.
corajoso/a [kora'ʒozu/ɔza] *adj* courageous.
coral [ko'raw] (*pl* **-ais**) *adj* choral ♦ *m* (MÚS) choir; (ZOOL) coral.
corante [ko'rãtʃi] *adj*, *m* colouring (BRIT), coloring (US).
corar [ko'ra*] *vt* (*pintar*) to paint; (*roupa*) to bleach (in the sun) ♦ *vi* (*ruborizar-se*) to blush; (*tornar-se branco*) to bleach.
corbelha [kox'bɛʎa] *f* basket.
corcova [kox'kɔva] *f* hump.
corcunda [kox'kũda] *adj* hunchbacked ♦ *m/f* hump; (*pessoa*) hunchback.
corda ['kɔxda] *f* (*cabo*) rope, line; (MÚS) string; (*varal*) clothes line; (*de relógio*) spring; **dar ~ em** to wind up; **roer a ~** to go back on one's word; **~s vocais** vocal chords; **estar com toda a ~** (*pessoa*) to be really wound up; **dar ~ a alguém** (*deixar falar*) to set sb off; (*flertar*) to flirt with sb.
cordão [kox'dãw] (*pl* **-ões**) *m* string, twine; (*jóia*) chain; (*no carnaval*) group; (ELET) lead; (*fileira*) row; **~ de sapato** shoestring; **~ umbilical** umbilical cord.
cordeiro [kox'dejru] *m* lamb; (*fig*) sheep.
cordel [kox'dɛw] (PT: *pl* **-éis**) *m* string; **literatura de ~** pamphlet literature.
cor-de-rosa *adj inv* pink.
cordial [kox'dʒjaw] (*pl* **-ais**) *adj* cordial ♦ *m* (*bebida*) cordial.
cordialidade [koxdʒjali'dadʒi] *f* warmth, cordiality.
cordilheira [koxdʒi'ʎejra] *f* chain of mountains.
cordões [kox'dõjʃ] *mpl de* **cordão**.
coreano/a [ko'rjanu/a] *adj* Korean ♦ *m/f* Korean ♦ *m* (LING) Korean.
Coréia [ko'rɛja] *f*: **a ~ do Norte/Sul** North/South Korea.
coreografia [korjogra'fia] *f* choreography.
coreógrafo/a [ko'rjɔgrafu/a] *m/f* choreographer.
coreto [ko'retu] *m* bandstand; **bagunçar o ~ (de alguém)** (*col*) to spoil things (for sb).
corisco [ko'riʃku] *m* (*faísca*) flash.
corista [ko'riʃta] *m/f* chorister ♦ *f* (TEATRO) chorus girl.
coriza [ko'riza] *f* runny nose.
corja ['kɔxʒa] *f* (PT: *canalha*) rabble; (*bando*) gang.
córnea ['kɔxnja] *f* cornea.
córner ['kɔxne*] *m* (FUTEBOL) corner.
corneta [kox'neta] *f* cornet; (MIL) bugle.
corneteiro [koxne'tejru] *m* bugler.
cornetim [koxne'tʃĩ] *m* (MÚS) french horn.
coro ['koru] *m* chorus; (*conjunto de cantores*) choir; **em ~** in chorus.
coroa [ko'roa] *f* crown; (*de flores*) garland ♦ *m/f* (BR: *col*) old timer.
coroação [korwa'sãw] (*pl* **-ões**) *f* coronation.
coroar [koro'a*] *vt* to crown; (*premiar*) to reward.
coronel [koro'nɛw] (*pl* **-éis**) *m* colonel; (*político*) local political boss.
coronha [ko'rɔɲa] *f* (*de um fuzil*) butt; (*de um revólver*) handle.
corpete [kox'petʃi] *m* bodice.

corpo ['koxpu] *m* body; (*aparência física*) figure; (: *de homem*) build; (*de vestido*) bodice; (*MIL*) corps *sg*; **de ~ e alma** (*fig*) wholeheartedly; **lutar ~ a ~** to fight hand to hand; **fazer ~ mole** to get out of it; **tirar o ~ fora** (*col*) to duck out; **~ diplomático** diplomatic corps *sg*; **~ discente** student body; **~ docente** teaching staff (*BRIT*), faculty (*US*); **~ estranho** (*MED*) foreign body.

corporal [koxpo'raw] (*pl* **-ais**) *adj* physical.

corpulência [koxpu'lẽsja] *f* stoutness.

corpulento/a [koxpu'lẽtu/a] *adj* stout.

correção [koxe'sãw] (*PT*: **-cç-**: *pl* **-ões**) *f* correction; (*exatidão*) correctness; **casa de ~** reformatory; **~ salarial/monetária** wage/monetary correction.

corre-corre [kɔxi'kɔxi] (*pl* **~s**) *m* rush.

correcto/a *etc* [ko'xektu/a] (*PT*) = **correto** *etc*.

corrediço/a [koxe'dʒisu/a] *adj* sliding.

corredor(a) [koxe'do*(a)] *m/f* runner ♦ *m* (*passagem*) corridor, passageway; (*em avião etc*) aisle; (*cavalo*) racehorse.

córrego ['kɔxegu] *m* stream, brook.

correia [ko'xeja] *f* strap; (*de máquina*) belt; (*para cachorro*) leash.

correio [ko'xeju] *m* mail, post; (*local*) post office; (*carteiro*) postman (*BRIT*), mailman (*US*); **~ aéreo** air mail; **pôr no ~** to post; **pelo ~** by post; **~ eletrônico** electronic mail.

correlação [koxela'sãw] (*pl* **-ões**) *f* correlation.

correlacionar [koxelasjo'na*] *vt* to correlate.

correlações [koxela'sõjʃ] *fpl de* **correlação**.

correligionário/a [koxeliʒjo'narju/a] *m/f* (*POL*) fellow party member.

corrente [ko'xẽtʃi] *adj* (*atual*) current; (*águas*) running; (*fluente*) flowing; (*comum*) usual, common ♦ *f* current; (*cadeia, jóia*) chain; **~ de ar** draught (*BRIT*), draft (*US*).

correnteza [koxẽ'teza] *f* (*de ar*) draught (*BRIT*), draft (*US*); (*de rio*) current.

correr [ko'xe*] *vt* to run; (*viajar por*) to travel across; (*cortina*) to draw; (*expulsar*) to drive out ♦ *vi* to run; (*em carro*) to drive fast, speed; (*líquido*) to flow, run; (*o tempo*) to elapse; (*boato*) to go round; (*atuar com rapidez*) to rush; **está tudo correndo bem** everything is going well; **as despesas correrão por minha conta** I will handle the expenses.

correria [koxe'ria] *f* rush.

correspondência [koxeʃpõ'dẽsja] *f* correspondence.

correspondente [koxeʃpõ'dẽtʃi] *adj* corresponding ♦ *m* correspondent.

corresponder [koxeʃpõ'de*] *vi*: **~ a** to correspond to; (*ser igual*) to match (up to); (*retribuir*) to reciprocate; **~-se** *vr*: **~-se com** to correspond with.

corretagem [koxe'taʒẽ] *f* brokerage.

corretivo/a [koxe'tʃivu/a] *adj* corrective ♦ *m* punishment.

correto/a [ko'xɛtu/a] *adj* correct; (*conduta*) right; (*pessoa*) straight.

corretor(a) [koxe'to*(a)] *m/f* broker ♦ *m* (*para datilografia*) correction strip; **~ de fundos** *ou* **de bolsa** stockbroker; **~ de imóveis** estate agent (*BRIT*), realtor (*US*).

corrida [ko'xida] *f* (*ato de correr*) running; (*certame*) race; (*de taxi*) fare; **~ de cavalos** horse race; **~ armamentista** arms race.

corrido/a [ko'xidu/a] *adj* (*rápido*) quick; (*expulso*) driven out ♦ *adv* quickly.

corrigir [koxi'ʒi*] *vt* to correct; (*defeito, injustiça*) to put right.

corrimão [koxi'mãw] (*pl* **~s**) *m* handrail.

corriqueiro/a [koxi'kejru/a] *adj* common; (*problema*) trivial.

corroa [ko'xoa] *etc vb V* **corroer**.

corroboração [koxobora'sãw] (*pl* **-ões**) *f* confirmation.

corroborar [koxobo'ra*] *vt* to corroborate, confirm.

corroer [koxo'e*] (*irreg*) *vt* (*metais*) to corrode; (*fig*) to eat away; **~-se** *vr* to corrode; to be eaten away.

corromper [koxõ'pe*] *vt* to corrupt; (*subornar*) to bribe; **~-se** *vr* to be corrupted.

corrosão [koxo'zãw] *f* (*de metais*) corrosion; (*fig*) erosion.

corrosivo/a [koxo'zivu/a] *adj* corrosive.

corrupção [koxup'sãw] *f* corruption.

corrupto/a [ko'xuptu/a] *adj* corrupt.

Córsega ['kɔxsega] *f*: **a ~** Corsica.

cortada [kox'tada] *f* (*ESPORTE*) smash; **dar uma ~ em alguém** (*fig*) to cut sb short.

cortado [kox'tadu] *m* (*aperto*) tight spot; **trazer alguém num ~** to keep sb under one's thumb.

cortadura [koxta'dura] *f* (*corte*) cut; (*entre montes*) gap.

cortante [kox'tãtʃi] *adj* cutting.

cortar [kox'ta*] *vt* to cut; (*eliminar*) to cut out; (*água, telefone etc*) to cut off; (*efeito*) to stop; (*AUTO*) to cut up ♦ *vi* to cut; (*encurtar caminho*) to take a short cut; **~-se** *vr* to cut o.s.; **~ o cabelo** (*no cabeleireiro*) to have one's hair cut; **~ a palavra de alguém** to interrupt sb.

corte[1] ['kɔxtʃi] *m* cut; (*gume*) cutting edge; (*de luz*) cut-out; **~ de cabelo** haircut; **esta tesoura está sem ~** these scissors are blunt.

corte[2] ['koxtʃi] *f* (*de um monarca*) court; (*de uma pessoa*) retinue; **~s** *fpl* (*PT*) parliament *sg*.

cortejar [koxte'ʒa*] *vt* to court.

cortejo [kox'teʒu] *m* (*procissão*) procession.

cortês [kox'teʃ] (*pl* **-eses**) *adj* polite.

cortesão/tesã [koxte'zãw/te'zã] (*pl* **~s/~s**) *adj* courtly ♦ *m/f* courtier/courtesan.

cortesia [koxte'zia] *f* politeness; (*de empresa*) free offer.

cortiça [kox'tʃisa] *f* (*matéria*) cork.

cortiço [kox'tʃisu] *m* (*habitação*) slum tenement.

cortina [kox'tʃina] *f* curtain; **~ de rolo** roller blind; **~ de voile** net curtain.

cortisona [koxtʃi'zɔna] *f* cortisone.
coruja [ko'ruʒa] *adj*: **pai/mãe** ~ proud father/mother ♦ *f* owl; **sessão** ~ late show.
coruscar [koruʃ'ka*] *vi* to sparkle, glitter.
corvo ['koxvu] *m* crow.
cós [kɔʃ] *m inv* waistband; (*cintura*) waist.
cosca ['kɔʃka] *f*: **fazer** ~ to tickle.
coser [ko'ze*] *vt, vi* to sew, stitch.
cosmético/a [koʒ'mɛtʃiku/a] *adj* cosmetic ♦ *m* cosmetic.
cósmico/a ['kɔʒmiku/a] *adj* cosmic.
cosmo ['kɔʒmu] *m* cosmos.
cosmonauta [koʒmo'nawta] *m/f* cosmonaut.
cosmopolita [koʒmopo'lita] *adj* cosmopolitan.
cospe ['kɔʃpi] *etc vb V* **cuspir**.
costa ['kɔʃta] *f* coast; **~s** *fpl* back *sg*; **dar as ~s a** to turn one's back on; **ter ~s largas** (*fig*) to be thick-skinned; **ter ~s quentes** (*fig*) to have powerful backing, have friends in high places.
costado [koʃ'tadu] *m* back; **de quatro ~s** through and through.
Costa do Marfim *f*: **a** ~ the Ivory Coast.
Costa Rica *f*: **a** ~ Costa Rica.
costarriquenho/a [koʃtaxi'kɛɲu/a] *adj, m/f* Costa Rican.
costear [koʃ'tʃja*] *vt* (*rodear*) to go round; (*gado*) to round up; (NÁUT) to follow ♦ *vi* to follow the coast.
costela [koʃ'tɛla] *f* rib.
costeleta [koʃte'leta] *f* chop, cutlet; **~s** *fpl* (*suíças*) side-whiskers.
costumar [koʃtu'ma*] *vt* (*habituar*) to accustom ♦ *vi*: **ele costuma chegar às 6.00** he usually arrives at 6.00; **costumava dizer** ... he used to say ....
costume [koʃ'tumi] *m* custom, habit; (*traje*) costume; **~s** *mpl* behaviour *sg* (BRIT), behavior *sg* (US), conduct *sg*; (*de um povo*) customs; **de** ~ usual; **como de** ~ as usual; **ter o ~ de fazer** to have a habit of doing.
costumeiro/a [koʃtu'mejru/a] *adj* usual, habitual.
costura [koʃ'tura] *f* sewing, needlework; (*sutura*) seam; **sem** ~ seamless.
costurar [koʃtu'ra*] *vt, vi* to sew.
costureira [koʃtu'rejra] *f* dressmaker; (*móvel*) sewing box.
cota ['kɔta] *f* (*quinhão*) quota, share; (GEO) height.
cotação [kota'sãw] (*pl* **-ões**) *f* (*de preços*) list, quotation; (*na bolsa*) price; (*consideração*) esteem; ~ **bancária** bank rate.
cotado/a [ko'tadu/a] *adj* (*ação*) quoted; (*bem-conceituado*) well thought of; (*num concurso*) fancied.
cotar [ko'ta*] *vt* (*ações*) to quote; ~ **algo em** to value sth at.
cotejar [kote'ʒa*] *vt* to compare.
cotejo [ko'teʒu] *m* comparison.
cotidiano/a [kotʃi'dʒjanu/a] *adj* daily, everyday ♦ *m*: **o** ~ daily life.
cotoco [ko'toku] *m* (*do corpo*) stump; (*de uma vela etc*) stub.
cotonete [koto'nɛtʃi] *m* cotton bud.
cotovelada [kotove'lada] *f* (*pancada*) shove; (*cutucada*) nudge.
cotovelo [koto'velu] *m* (ANAT) elbow; (*curva*) bend; **falar pelos ~s** to talk non-stop.
coube ['kobi] *etc vb V* **caber**.
couraça [ko'rasa] *f* (*para o peito*) breastplate; (*de navio etc*) armour-plate (BRIT), armor-plate (US); (*de animal*) plating, shell.
couraçado [kora'sadu] (PT) *m* battleship.
couro ['koru] *m* leather; (*de um animal*) hide; ~ **cabeludo** scalp.
couve ['kovi] *f* spring greens *pl*.
couve-de-bruxelas (*pl* **couves-de-bruxelas**) *f* Brussels sprout.
couve-flor (*pl* **couves-flores**) *f* cauliflower.
couvert [ku'vɛx] *m* cover charge.
cova ['kɔva] *f* (*escavação*) pit; (*caverna*) cavern; (*sepultura*) grave.
covarde [ko'vaxdʒi] *adj* cowardly ♦ *m/f* coward.
covardia [kovax'dʒia] *f* cowardice.
coveiro [ko'vejru] *m* gravedigger.
covil [ko'viw] (*pl* **-is**) *m* den, lair.
covinha [ko'viɲa] *f* dimple.
covis [ko'viʃ] *mpl de* **covil**.
coxa ['koʃa] *f* thigh.
coxear [ko'ʃja*] *vi* to limp, hobble.
coxia [ko'ʃia] *f* (*passagem*) aisle, gangway.
coxo/a ['koʃu/a] *adj* lame.
cozer [ko'ze*] *vt, vi* to cook.
cozido [ko'zidu] *m* stew.
cozinha [ko'ziɲa] *f* (*compartimento*) kitchen; (*arte*) cookery; (*modo de cozinhar*) cuisine.
cozinhar [kozi'ɲa*] *vt* to cook; (*remanchar*) to put off ♦ *vi* to cook.
cozinheiro/a [kozi'ɲejru/a] *m/f* cook.
CP *abr* = **Caminhos de Ferro Portugueses** ♦ *abr m* (BR: = *certificado de privatização*) share in state company.
CPF (BR) *abr m* (= *Cadastro de Pessoa Física*) identification number.
CPI (BR) *abr f* = **Comissão Parlamentar de Inquérito**.
CPJ (BR) *abr m* (= *Cadastro de Pessoa Jurídica*) register of companies.
Cr$ *abr* = **cruzeiro**.
crachá [kra'ʃa] *m* badge.
crânio ['kranju] *m* skull; **ser um** ~ (*col*) to be a whizz kid.
craque ['kraki] *m/f* ace, expert ♦ *m* (*jogador de futebol*) soccer star.
crasso/a ['krasu/a] *adj* crass.
cratera [kra'tɛra] *f* crater.
cravar [kra'va*] *vt* (*prego etc*) to drive (in); (*pedras*) to set; (*com os olhos*) to stare at;

NB: European Portuguese adds the following consonants to certain words: **b** (sú(b)dito, su(b)til); **c** (a(c)ção, a(c)cionista, a(c)to); **m** (inde(m)ne); **p** (ado(p)ção, ado(p)tar); *for further details see p. xiii.*

~-se *vr* to penetrate.
cravejar [krave'ʒa*] *vt* (*com cravos*) to nail; (*pedras*) to set; ~ **alguém de balas** to spray sb with bullets.
cravo ['kravu] *m* (*flor*) carnation; (*MÚS*) harpsichord; (*especiaria*) clove; (*na pele*) blackhead; (*prego*) nail.
creche ['krɛʃi] *f* crèche.
Creci [krɛ'si] (*BR*) *abr m* (= *Conselho Regional dos Corretores de Imóveis*) *regulatory body of estate agents.*
credenciais [kredẽ'sjajʃ] *fpl* credentials.
credenciar [kredẽ'sja*] *vt* to accredit; (*habilitar*) to qualify.
crediário [kre'dʒjarju] *m* credit plan.
credibilidade [kredʒibili'dadʒi] *f* credibility.
creditar [kredʒi'ta*] *vt* to guarantee; ~ **algo a alguém** (*quantia*) to credit sb with sth; (*garantir*) to assure sb of sth; ~ **alguém em** to credit sb with; ~ **uma quantia numa conta** to deposit an amount into an account.
crédito ['krɛdʒitu] *m* credit; **a** ~ on credit; **digno de** ~ reliable.
credo ['krɛdu] *m* creed; ~! (*PT*) heavens!
credor(a) [kre'do*(a)] *adj* worthy, deserving; (*COM*: *saldo*) credit *atr* ♦ *m/f* creditor.
credulidade [kreduli'dadʒi] *f* credulity.
crédulo/a ['krɛdulu/a] *adj* credulous.
creio ['kreju] *etc vb V* **crer**.
cremação [krema'sãw] (*pl* **-ões**) *f* cremation.
cremalheira [krema'ʎejra] *f* ratchet.
cremar [kre'ma*] *vt* to cremate.
crematório [krema'tɔrju] *m* crematorium.
creme ['krɛmi] *adj inv* cream-coloured (*BRIT*), cream-colored (*US*) ♦ *m* cream; (*CULIN*: *doce*) custard; ~ **dental** toothpaste; ~ **de leite** single cream.
cremoso/a [kre'mozu/ɔza] *adj* creamy.
crença ['krẽsa] *f* belief.
crendice [krẽ'dʒisi] *f* superstition.
crente ['krẽtʃi] *adj* believing ♦ *m/f* believer; (*protestante*) Protestant; **estar** ~ **que** to think (that).
creosoto [kreo'zotu] *m* creosote.
crepitação [krepita'sãw] *f* crackling.
crepitante [krepi'tãtʃi] *adj* crackling.
crepitar [krepi'ta*] *vi* to crackle.
crepom [kre'põ] *adj V* **papel**.
crepuscular [krepuʃku'la*] *adj* twilight *atr*.
crepúsculo [kre'puʃkulu] *m* dusk, twilight.
crer [kre*] *vt*, *vi* to believe; **~-se** *vr* to believe o.s. to be; ~ **em** to believe in; ~ **que** to think (that); **creio que sim** I think so.
crescendo [kre'sẽdu[*m* crescendo.
crescente [kre'sẽtʃi] *adj* growing; (*forma*) crescent ♦ *m* crescent.
crescer [kre'se*] *vi* to grow; (*CULIN*: *massa*) to rise.
crescido/a [kre'sidu/a] *adj* (*pessoa*) grown up.
crescimento [kresi'mẽtu] *m* growth.
crespo/a ['kreʃpu/a] *adj* (*cabelo*) curly.
cretinice [kretʃi'nisi] *f* stupidity; (*ato*, *dito*) stupid thing.
cretino [kre'tʃinu] *m* cretin, imbecile.
cria ['kria] *f* (*animal*) baby animal, young.
criação [krja'sãw] (*pl* **-ões**) *f* creation; (*de animais*) raising, breeding; (*educação*) upbringing; (*animais domésticos*) livestock; **filho de** ~ adopted child.
criado/a ['krjadu/a] *m/f* servant.
criado-mudo (*pl* **criados-mudos**) *m* bedside table.
criador(a) [krja'do*(a)] *m/f* creator; ~ **de gado** cattle breeder.
criança ['krjãsa] *adj* childish; **ela é muito** ~ **para entender certas coisas** she's too young to understand certain things ♦ *f* child.
criançada [krjã'sada] *f*: **a** ~ the kids.
criancice [krjã'sisi] *f* (*ato*, *dito*) childish thing; (*qualidade*) childishness.
criar [krja*] *vt* to create; (*crianças*) to bring up; (*animais*) to raise, breed; (*amamentar*) to suckle, nurse; (*planta*) to grow; **~-se** *vr*: **~-se (com)** to grow up (with); ~ **fama/coragem** to achieve notoriety/pluck up courage; ~ **caso** to make trouble.
criatividade [kriatʃivi'dadʒi] *f* creativity.
criativo/a [kria'tʃivu/a] *adj* creative.
criatura [kria'tura] *f* creature; (*indivíduo*) individual.
crime ['krimi] *m* crime.
criminal [krimi'naw] (*pl* **-ais**) *adj* criminal.
criminalidade [kriminali'dadʒi] *f* crime.
criminoso/a [krimi'nozu/ɔza] *adj*, *m/f* criminal.
crina ['krina] *f* mane.
crioulo/a ['krjolu/a] *adj* creole ♦ *m/f* creole; (*BR*: *negro*) black (person).
críquete ['kriketʃi] *m* cricket.
crisálida [kri'zalida] *f* chrysalis.
crisântemo [kri'zãtemu] *m* chrysanthemum.
crise ['krizi] *f* crisis; (*escassez*) shortage; (*MED*) attack, fit; ~ **de choro** fit of hysterical crying.
crisma ['kriʒma] *f* (*REL*) confirmation.
crismar [kriʒ'ma*] *vt* (*REL*) to confirm; **~-se** *vr* (*REL*) to be confirmed.
crista ['kriʃta] *f* (*de serra*, *onda*) crest; (*de galo*) cock's comb; **estar na** ~ **da onda** (*fig*) to enjoy a prominent position.
cristal [kriʃ'taw] (*pl* **-ais**) *m* crystal; (*vidro*) glass; **cristais** *mpl* glassware *sg*.
cristalino/a [kriʃta'linu/a] *adj* crystal-clear.
cristalizar [kriʃtali'za*] *vi* to crystallize.
cristandade [kriʃtã'dadʒi] *f* Christianity.
cristão/tã [kriʃ'tãw/'tã] (*pl* **~s/~s**) *adj*, *m/f* Christian.
cristianismo [kriʃtʃja'niʒmu] *m* Christianity.
Cristo ['kriʃtu] *m* Christ.
critério [kri'tɛrju] *m* (*norma*) criterion; (*juízo*) discretion, judgement; **deixo isso a seu** ~ I'll leave that to your discretion.
criterioso/a [krite'rjozu/ɔza] *adj* thoughtful, careful.
crítica ['kritʃika] *f* criticism; (*artigo*) critique; (*conjunto de críticos*) critics *pl*; *V tb* **crítico**.

criticar [kritʃi'ka*] *vt* to criticize; (*um livro*) to review.
crítico/a ['kritʃiku/a] *adj* critical ♦ *m/f* critic.
critiquei [kritʃi'kej] *etc vb V* **criticar**.
crivar [kri'va*] *vt* (*com balas etc*) to riddle; (*de perguntas, de insultos*) to bombard.
crível ['krivew] (*pl* **-eis**) *adj* credible.
crivo ['krivu] *m* sieve; (*fig*) scrutiny.
crocante [kro'kãtʃi] *adj* crunchy.
crochê [kro'ʃe] *m* crochet.
crocodilo [kroko'dʒilu] *m* crocodile.
cromo ['krɔmu] *m* chrome.
cromossomo [kromo'sɔmu] *m* chromosome.
crônica ['kronika] *f* chronicle; (*coluna de jornal*) newspaper column; (*texto jornalístico*) feature; (*conto*) short story.
crônico/a ['kroniku/a] *adj* chronic.
cronista [kro'niʃta] *m/f* (*de jornal*) columnist; (*historiógrafo*) chronicler; (*contista*) short story writer.
cronologia [kronolo'ʒia] *f* chronology.
cronológico/a [krono'lɔʒiku/a] *adj* chronological.
cronometrar [kronome'tra*] *vt* to time.
cronômetro [kro'nometru] *m* stopwatch.
croquete [kro'kɛtʃi] *m* croquette.
croqui [kro'ki] *m* sketch.
crosta ['kroʃta] *f* crust; (*MED*) scab.
cru(a) [kru/'krua] *adj* raw; (*não refinado*) crude; (*ignorante*) not very good; (*realidade*) harsh, stark.
crucial [kru'sjaw] (*pl* **-ais**) *adj* crucial.
crucificação [krusifika'sãw] (*pl* **-ões**) *f* crucifixion.
crucificar [krusifi'ka*] *vt* to crucify.
crucifixo [krusi'fiksu] *m* crucifix.
crudelíssimo/a [krude'lisimu/a] *adj superl de* **cruel**.
cruel [kru'ɛw] (*pl* **-éis**) *adj* cruel.
crueldade [kruew'dadʒi] *f* cruelty.
cruento/a [kru'ẽtu/a] *adj* bloody.
crupe ['krupi] *m* (*MED*) croup.
crustáceos [kruʃ'tasjuʃ] *mpl* crustaceans.
cruz [kruʒ] *f* cross; (*infortúnio*) undoing; **~ gamada** swastika; **C~ Vermelha** Red Cross; **estar entre a ~ e a caldeirinha** (*fig*) to be between the devil and the deep (*BRIT*), be between a rock and a hard place (*US*).
cruzada [kru'zada] *f* crusade.
cruzado/a [kru'zadu/a] *adj* crossed ♦ *m* crusader; (*moeda*) cruzado.
cruzador [kruza'do*] *m* (*navio*) cruiser.
cruzamento [kruza'mẽtu] *m* (*de estradas*) crossroads; (*mestiçagem*) cross.
cruzar [kru'za*] *vt* to cross ♦ *vi* (*NÁUT*) to cruise; **~-se** *vr* to cross; (*pessoas*) to pass by each other; **~ com** to meet.
cruzeiro [kru'zejru] *m* (*cruz*) (monumental) cross; (*moeda*) cruzeiro; (*viagem de navio*) cruise.
cu [ku] (*col!*) *m* arse (*!*); **vai tomar no ~** fuck off (*!*).
CSN (*BR*) *abr m* = **Conselho de Segurança Nacional**.
CTB *abr f* = **Companhia Telefônica Brasileira**.
Cuba ['kuba] *f* Cuba.
cubano/a [ku'banu/a] *adj*, *m/f* Cuban.
cúbico/a ['kubiku/a] *adj* cubic.
cubículo [ku'bikulu] *m* cubicle.
cubismo [ku'biʒmu] *m* cubism.
cubo ['kubu] *m* cube; (*de roda*) hub.
cubro ['kubru] *etc vb V* **cobrir**.
cuca ['kuka] (*col*) *f* head; **fundir a ~** (*quebrar a cabeça*) to rack one's brain; (*baratinar*) to boggle the mind; (*perturbar*) to drive crazy.
cuca-fresca (*pl* **cucas-frescas**) (*col*) *m/f* cool guy/girl.
cuco ['kuku] *m* cuckoo.
cucuia [ku'kuja] *f*: **ir para a ~** (*col*) to go down the drain.
cu-de-ferro (*pl* **cus-de-ferro**) (*col*) *m/f* swot.
cueca ['kwɛka] (*BR*) *f* underpants *pl*; **~s** (*PT*: *para homens*) underpants *pl*; (: *para mulheres*) panties *pl*.
cueiro [ku'ejru] *m* wrap.
cuíca ['kwika] *f kind of musical instrument*.
cuidado [kwi'dadu] *m* care; **aos ~s de** in the care of; **ter ~** to be careful; **~!** watch out!, be careful!; **tomar ~ (de)** to be careful (of); **~ para não se cortar** be careful you don't cut yourself.
cuidadoso/a [kwida'dozu/ɔza] *adj* careful.
cuidar [kwi'da*] *vi*: **~ de** to take care of, look after; **~-se** *vr* to look after o.s.
cujo/a ['kuʒu/a] *pron* (*de quem*) whose; (*de que*) of which.
culatra [ku'latra] *f* (*de arma*) breech.
culinária [kuli'narja] *f* cookery.
culinário/a [kuli'narju/a] *adj* culinary.
culminância [kuwmi'nãsja] *f* culmination.
culminante [kuwmi'nãtʃi] *adj V* **ponto**.
culminar [kuwmi'na*] *vi*: **~ (com)** to culminate (in).
culote [ku'lɔtʃi] *m* (*calça*) jodhpurs *pl*; (*gordura*) flab on the thighs.
culpa ['kuwpa] *f* fault; (*JUR*) guilt; **ter ~ de** to be to blame for; **por ~ de** because of; **pôr a ~ em** to put the blame on; **sentimento de ~** guilty conscience.
culpabilidade [kuwpabili'dadʒi] *f* guilt.
culpado/a [kuw'padu/a] *adj* guilty ♦ *m/f* culprit.
culpar [kuw'pa*] *vt* to blame; (*acusar*) to accuse; **~-se** *vr* to take the blame.
culpável [kuw'pavew] (*pl* **-eis**) *adj* guilty.
cultivar [kuwtʃi'va*] *vt* to cultivate; (*plantas*) to grow.
cultivável [kuwtʃi'vavew] (*pl* **-eis**) *adj* cultivable.
cultivo [kuw'tʃivu] *m* cultivation.

***NB**: European Portuguese adds the following consonants to certain words:* **b** (sú(b)dito, su(b)til); **c** (a(c)ção, a(c)cionista, a(c)to); **m** (inde(m)ne); **p** (ado(p)ção, ado(p)tar); *for further details see p. xiii.*

culto/a ['kuwtu/a] *adj* cultured ♦ *m* (*homenagem*) worship; (*religião*) cult.
cultura [kuw'tura] *f* culture; (*da terra*) cultivation.
cultural [kuwtu'raw] (*pl* **-ais**) *adj* cultural.
cumbuca [kũ'buka] *f* pot.
cume ['kumi] *m* top, summit; (*fig*) climax.
cúmplice ['kũplisi] *m/f* accomplice.
cumplicidade [kũplisi'dadʒi] *f* complicity.
cumpridor(a) [kũpri'do*(a)] *adj* punctilious, responsible.
cumprimentar [kũprimẽ'ta*] *vt* (*saudar*) to greet; (*dar parabéns*) to congratulate; **~-se** *vr* to greet one another.
cumprimento [kũpri'mẽtu] *m* (*realização*) fulfilment; (*saudação*) greeting; (*elogio*) compliment; **~s** *mpl* best wishes; **~ de uma lei/ordem** compliance with a law/an order.
cumprir [kũ'pri*] *vt* (*desempenhar*) to carry out; (*promessa*) to keep (*lei*) to obey ♦ *vi* (*convir*) to be necessary; **~-se** *vr* to be fulfilled; **~ a palavra** to keep one's word; **fazer ~** to enforce; **~ pena** to serve a sentence.
cumulativo/a [kumula'tʃivu/a] *adj* cumulative.
cúmulo ['kumulu] *m* height; **é o ~!** that's the limit!
cunha ['kuɲa] *f* wedge.
cunhado/a [ku'ɲadu/a] *m/f* brother-in-law/sister-in-law.
cunhar [ku'ɲa*] *vt* (*moedas*) to mint; (*palavras*) to coin.
cunho ['kuɲu] *m* (*marca*) hallmark; (*caráter*) nature.
cupê [ku'pe] *m* coupé.
cupim [ku'pĩ] (*pl* **-ns**) *m* termite.
cupincha [ku'pĩʃa] *m/f* mate, friend.
cupins [ku'pĩʃ] *mpl de* **cupim**.
cupom [ku'põ] (*pl* **-ns**) *m* coupon.
cúpula ['kupula] *f* (*ARQ*) dome; (*de abajur*) shade; (*de partido etc*) leadership; **(reunião de) ~** summit (meeting).
cura ['kura] *f* (*ato de curar*) cure; (*tratamento*) treatment; (*de carnes etc*) curing, preservation ♦ *m* priest.
curador(a) [kura'do*(a)] *m/f* (*de menores, órfãos*) guardian; (*de instituição*) trustee.
curandeiro [kurã'dejru] *m* (*feiticeiro*) healer, medicine man; (*charlatão*) quack.
curar [ku'ra*] *vt* (*doença*) to cure; (*ferida*) to treat; (*carne etc*) to cure, preserve; **~-se** *vr* to get well.
curativo [kura'tʃivu] *m* dressing.
curável [ku'ravew] (*pl* **-eis**) *adj* curable.
curetagem [kure'taʒẽ] *f* curettage.
curinga [ku'rĩga] *m* wild card.
curingão [kurĩ'gãw] (*pl* **-ões**) *m* joker.
curiosidade [kurjozi'dadʒi] *f* curiosity; (*objeto raro*) curio.
curioso/a [ku'rjozu/ɔza] *adj* curious ♦ *m/f* snooper, inquisitive person; **~s** *mpl* (*espectadores*) onlookers; **o ~ é ...** the strange thing is ....
curitibano/a [kuritʃi'banu/a] *adj* from Curitiba ♦ *m/f* person from Curitiba.
curral [ku'xaw] (*pl* **-ais**) *m* pen, enclosure.
currar [ku'xa*] (*col*) *vt* to rape.
currículo [ku'xikulu] *m* curriculum; (*curriculum*) curriculum vitae, CV.
curriculum vitae [ku'xikulũ 'vite] *m* curriculum vitae.
cursar [kux'sa*] *vt* (*aulas, escola*) to attend; (*cursos*) to follow; **ele está cursando História** he's studying *ou* doing history.
cursivo [kux'sivu] *m* (*TIP*) script.
curso ['kuxsu] *m* course; (*direção*) direction; **em ~** (*ano etc*) current; (*processo*) in progress; (*dinheiro*) in circulation; **~ primário/secundário/superior** primary school/secondary school/degree course; **~ normal** teacher-training course.
cursor [kux'so*] *m* (*COMPUT*) cursor.
curta ['kuxta] *m* (*CINEMA*) short.
curta-metragem (*pl* **curtas-metragens**) *m* short film.
curtição [kuxtʃi'sãw] *f* (*col*) fun; (*de couro*) tanning.
curtido/a [kux'tʃidu/a] *adj* (*fig*) hardened.
curtir [kux'tʃi*] *vt* (*couro*) to tan; (*tornar rijo*) to toughen up; (*padecer*) to suffer, endure; (*col*) to enjoy.
curto/a ['kuxtu/a] *adj* short; (*inteligência*) limited ♦ *m* (*ELET*) short (circuit).
curto-circuito (*pl* **curtos-circuitos**) *m* short circuit.
curva ['kuxva] *f* curve; (*de estrada, rio*) bend; **~ fechada** hairpin bend.
curvar [kux'va*] *vt* to bend, curve; (*submeter*) to put down; **~-se** *vr* (*abaixar-se*) to stoop; **~-se a** (*submeter-se*) to submit to.
curvatura [kuxva'tura] *f* curvature.
curvo/a ['kuxvu/a] *adj* curved; (*estrada*) winding.
cuscuz [kuʃ'kuʒ] *m* couscous.
cusparada [kuʃpa'rada] *f* spit; **dar uma ~** to spit.
cuspe ['kuʃpi] *m* spit, spittle.
cuspido/a [kuʃ'pidu/a] *adj* covered in spittle; **ele é o pai ~ e escarrado** (*col*) he's the spitting image of his father.
cuspir [kuʃ'pi*] *vt, vi* to spit; **~ no prato em que se come** to bite the hand that feeds one.
custa ['kuʃta] *f*: **à ~ de** at the expense of; **~s** *fpl* (*JUR*) costs.
custar [kuʃ'ta*] *vi* to cost; (*ser difícil*) to be difficult; (*demorar*) to take a long time; **~ caro** to be expensive; **~ a fazer** (*ter dificuldade*) to have trouble doing; (*demorar*) to take a long time to do; **não custa nada perguntar** there's no harm in asking.
custear [kuʃ'tʃja*] *vt* to bear the cost of.
custeio [kuʃ'teju] *m* funding; (*relação de custos*) costing.
custo ['kuʃtu] *m* cost; **a ~** with difficulty; **a todo ~** at all costs; **~/benefício** (*COM*) cost/benefit.

custódia [kuʃ'tɔdʒja] *f* custody.
CUT (*BR*) *abr f* (= *Central Única de Trabalhadores*) *trade union.*
cutelaria [kutela'ria] *f* knife-making.
cutelo [ku'tɛlu] *m* cleaver.
cutícula [ku'tʃikula] *f* cuticle.
cútis ['kutʃiʃ] *f inv* (*pele*) skin; (*tez*) complexion.
cutucada [kutu'kada] *f* nudge; (*com o dedo*) prod.
cutucar [kutu'ka*] *vt* (*com o dedo*) to prod, poke; (*com o cotovelo*) to nudge.
CVV (*BR*) *abr m* (= *Centro de Valorização da Vida*) *Samaritan organization.*
Cz$ *abr* = **cruzado.**

D

D, d [de] (*pl* **ds**) D, d ♦ *abr* = **Dom**; **Dona**; (= *direito*) r; (= *deve*) d; **D de dado** D for David (*BRIT*) *ou* dog (*US*).
d/ *abr* = **dia.**
da [da] = **de** + **a.**
dá [da] *vb V* **dar.**
dádiva ['dadʒiva] *f* (*donativo*) donation; (*oferta*) gift.
DAC (*BR*) *abr m* = **Departamento de Aviação Civil.**
dactilografar *etc* [datilogra'fa*] (*PT*) = **datilografar** *etc.*
dadaísmo [dada'iʒmu] *m* Dadaism.
dadivoso/a [dadʒi'vozu/ɔza] *adj* generous.
dado/a ['dadu/a] *adj* given; (*sociável*) sociable ♦ *m* (*em jogo*) die; (*fato*) fact; (*COMPUT*) piece of data; **~s** *mpl* (*em jogo*) dice; (*fatos, COMPUT*) data *sg*; **ser ~ a algo** to be prone *ou* given to sth; **em ~ momento** at a given moment; **~ que** (*suposto que*) supposing that; (*uma vez que*) given that.
daí [da'ji] *adv* (= **de** + **aí**) (*desse lugar*) from there; (*desse momento*) from then; (*col: num relato*) then; **~ a um mês** a month later; **~ por** *ou* **em diante** from then on; **e ~?** (*col*) so what?
dali [da'li] *adv* (= **de** + **ali**) from there.
dália ['dalja] *f* dahlia.
daltônico/a [daw'toniku/a] *adj* colour-blind (*BRIT*), color-blind (*US*).
daltonismo [dawto'niʒmu] *m* colour (*BRIT*) *ou* color (*US*) blindness.
dama ['dama] *f* lady; (*XADREZ, CARTAS*) queen; **~s** *fpl* draughts (*BRIT*), checkers (*US*); **~ de honra** bridesmaid.
Damasco [da'maʃku] *n* Damascus.
damasco [da'maʃku] *m* (*fruta*) apricot; (*tecido*) damask.
danação [dana'sãw] *f* damnation; (*travessura*) mischief, naughtiness.
danado/a [da'nadu/a] *adj* (*condenado*) damned; (*zangado*) furious, angry; (*menino*) mischievous, naughty; **cão ~** mad dog; **ela está com uma fome/dor danada** she's really hungry/got a terrible pain; **uma gripe danada/um susto ~** a really bad case of flu/ a hell of a fright; **ele é ~ de bom** (*col*) he's really good; **ser ~ em algo** to be really good at sth.
danar-se [dã'naxsi] *vr* (*enfurecer-se*) to get furious; **dane-se!** (*col*) damn it!; **danou-se!** (*col*) oh, gosh!
dança ['dãsa] *f* dance; **entrar na ~** to get involved.
dançar [dã'sa*] *vi* to dance; (*col: pessoa: sair-se mal*) to lose out; (*: em exame*) to fail; (*: coisa*) to go by the board.
dançarino/a [dãsa'rinu/a] *m/f* dancer.
danceteria [dãsete'ria] *f* disco(theque).
dancing ['dãsĩŋ] *m* dance hall.
danificar [danifi'ka*] *vt* (*objeto*) to damage.
daninho/a [da'niɲu/a] *adj* harmful; (*gênio*) nasty.
dano ['danu] *m* (*tb*: **~s**) damage; (*moral*) harm; (*a uma pessoa*) injury.
danoso/a [da'nozu/ɔza] *adj* (*a uma pessoa*) harmful; (*a uma coisa*) damaging.
dantes ['dãtʃiʃ] *adv* before, formerly.
Danúbio [da'nubju] *m*: **o ~** the Danube.
daquela [da'kɛla] = **de** + **aquela**; *V* **aquele.**
daquele [da'keli] = **de** + **aquele**; *V* **aquele.**
daqui [da'ki] *adv* (= **de** + **aqui**) (*deste lugar*) from here; **~ a pouco** soon, in a little while; **~ a uma semana** a week from now, in a week's time; **~ em diante** from now on.
daquilo [da'kilu] = **de** + **aquilo**; *V* **aquilo.**
dar [da*] *vt* (*ger*) to give; (*flor, leite, fruta*) to produce; (*cheiro*) to give off; (*notícias no jornal*) to publish; (*cartas*) to deal; (*problemas*) to cause; (*matemática, francês etc*) to teach ♦ *vi* to give; (*impess: ser possível*) to be possible; (*ser suficiente*): **~ para/para fazer** to be enough for/to do; **~-se** *vr* (*acontecer*) to happen; (*sair-se*) to get on; **~ algo por acabado** *etc* to consider sth finished *etc*; **(não) dá tempo para fazer** there's (no) time to do; **dez libras dão** *ou* **dá 100 francs** ten pounds is equivalent to 100 francs; **a sala dele dá duas da minha** his lounge is twice as big as mine; **ter roupa** *etc* **para ~ e vender** to have loads of clothes *etc*; **~ de beber/comer a** to give a drink to/feed; **~ (a alguém)** (*col: sexualmente*) to go all the way (with sb); **~ com** (*coisa*) to find; (*pessoa*) to meet; **~ de** *ou* **para fazer**

***NB:** European Portuguese adds the following consonants to certain words:* **b** (sú(b)dito, su(b)til); **c** (a(c)ção, a(c)cionista, a(c)to); **m** (inde(m)ne); **p** (ado(p)ção, ado(p)tar); *for further details see p. xiii.*

(*começar*) to take to doing; ~ **em** (*bater*) to hit; (*resultar*) to lead to; (*lugar*) to come to; **não deu em nada** it came to nothing; **o que deu nela?** what got into her?; **ele dá para médico/para tomar conta de crianças** he'll make a good doctor/he's good at looking after children; **dá para você vir amanhã? — não, amanhã não vai** ~ can you come tomorrow? — no, tomorrow I can't; **dá para trocar dinheiro aqui?** is it possible to change money here?; ~ **por** to notice; **~-se bem/mal** (*sair-se*) to get on well/badly; **~-se bem (com alguém)** to get on well (with sb); **~-se ao luxo/trabalho de fazer algo** to allow o.s. the luxury of doing sth/take the trouble to do sth; **~-se com alguém** (*ter amizade*) to be acquainted with sb; **~-se por** to consider o.s.; **~-se por vencido** to give up; **não me dou bem com o clima** the climate doesn't agree with me; **pouco se me dá** I don't care.

Dardanelos [daxda'nɛluʃ] *mpl*: **os** ~ the Dardanelles.

dardo ['daxdu] *m* dart; (*grande*) spear.

das [daʃ] = **de** + **as**; *V* **de**.

data ['data] *f* date; (*época*) time; **de longa** ~ of long standing.

datação [data'sãw] *f* dating.

datar [da'ta*] *vt* to date ♦ *vi*: ~ **de** to date from.

datilografar [datʃilogra'fa*] *vt* to type.

datilografia [datʃilogra'fia] *f* typing.

datilógrafo/a [datʃi'lɔgrafu/a] *m/f* typist (*BRIT*), stenographer (*US*).

dativo/a [da'tʃivu/a] *adj* dative ♦ *m* dative.

d.C. *abr* (= *depois de Cristo*) AD.

DDD *abr f* (= *discagem direta a distância*) STD (*BRIT*), ≈ direct dialling.

DDI *abr f* (= *discagem direta internacional*) IDD.

de [dʒi] *prep* of; (*movimento, procedência*) from; **venho ~ São Paulo** I come from São Paulo; **a casa ~ João** John's house; **um romance** ~ a novel by; **o infeliz do homem** the poor man; **um vestido ~ seda** a silk dress; ~ **manhã** in the morning; ~ **dia** by day; **vestido ~ branco** dressed in white; **um homem ~ cabelo comprido** a man with long hair; ~ **dois em dois dias** every other day; ~ **trem** by train.

dê [de] *etc vb V* **dar**.

deão [dʒi'ãw] (*pl* **~s**) *m* dean.

debaixo [de'bajʃu] *adv* below, underneath ♦ *prep*: ~ **de** under, beneath.

debalde [de'bawdʒi] *adv* in vain.

debandada [debã'dada] *f* stampede; **em** ~ in confusion.

debandar [debã'da*] *vt* to put to flight ♦ *vi* to disperse.

debate [de'batʃi] *m* (*discussão*) discussion, debate; (*disputa*) argument.

debater [deba'te*] *vt* to debate; (*discutir*) to discuss; **~-se** *vr* to struggle.

débeis ['debejʃ] *pl de* **débil**.

debelar [debe'la*] *vt* to put down, suppress; (*crise*) to overcome; (*doença*) to cure.

debênture [de'bẽturi] *f* (*COM*) debenture.

debicar [debi'ka*] *vt* (*caçoar*) to make fun of.

débil ['debiw] (*pl* **-eis**) *adj* (*pessoa*) weak, feeble; (*PSICO*) retarded ♦ *m*: ~ **mental** mentally handicapped person; (*col*: *ofensivo*) moron.

debilidade [debili'dadʒi] *f* weakness; ~ **mental** mental handicap.

debilitação [debilita'sãw] *f* weakening.

debilitante [debili'tãtʃi] *adj* debilitating.

debilitar [debili'ta*] *vt* to weaken; **~-se** *vr* to become weak, weaken.

debilóide [debi'lɔjdʒi] (*col*) *m/f* idiot ♦ *adj* idiotic.

debique [de'biki] *m* mockery, ridicule.

debitar [debi'ta*] *vt* to debit; ~ **a conta de alguém em $40** to debit sb's account by $40; ~ **$40 à** *ou* **na conta de alguém** to debit $40 to sb's account.

débito ['dɛbitu] *m* debit.

debochado/a [debo'ʃadu/a] *adj* (*pessoa*) sardonic; (*jeito, tom*) mocking ♦ *m/f* sardonic person.

debochar [debo'ʃa*] *vt* to mock ♦ *vi*: ~ **de** to mock.

deboche [de'bɔʃi] *m* gibe.

debruar [de'brwa*] *vt* (*roupa*) to edge; (*desenho*) to adorn.

debruçar [debru'sa*] *vt* to bend over; **~-se** *vr* to bend over; (*inclinar-se*) to lean over; **~-se na janela** to lean out of the window.

debrum [de'brũ] *m* edging.

debulha [de'buʎa] *f* (*de trigo*) threshing.

debulhar [debu'ʎa*] *vt* (*grão*) to thresh; (*descascar*) to shell; **~-se** *vr*: **~-se em lágrimas** to burst into tears.

debutante [debu'tãtʃi] *f* débutante.

debutar [debu'ta*] *vi* to appear for the first time, make one's début.

década ['dɛkada] *f* decade.

decadência [deka'dẽsja] *f* decadence.

decadente [deka'dẽtʃi] *adj* decadent.

decair [deka'i*] *vi* to decline; (*restaurante etc*) to go downhill; (*pressão, velocidade*) to drop; (*planta*) to wilt.

decalcar [dekaw'ka*] *vt* to trace; (*fig*) to copy.

decalque [de'kawki] *m* tracing.

decano [de'kanu] *m* oldest member.

decantar [dekã'ta*] *vt* (*líquido*) to decant; (*purificar*) to purify.

decapitar [dekapi'ta*] *vt* to behead, decapitate.

decatlo [de'katlu] *m* decathlon.

decência [de'sẽsja] *f* decency.

decênio [de'senju] *m* decade.

decente [de'sẽtʃi] *adj* decent; (*apropriado*) proper; (*honrado*) honourable (*BRIT*), honorable (*US*); (*trabalho*) neat, presentable.

decentemente [desẽtʃi'mẽtʃi] *adv* (*com decoro*) decently; (*apropriadamente*) properly; (*honradamente*) honourably (*BRIT*), honorably (*US*).

decepar [dese'pa*] *vt* to cut off, chop off.

decepção [desep'sãw] (*pl* **-ões**) *f* disappointment; (*desilusão*) disillusionment.

decepcionar [desepsjo'na*] *vt* to disappoint, let down; (*desiludir*) to disillusion; **~-se** *vr* to be disappointed; to be disillusioned; **o filme decepcionou** the film was disappointing.

decepções [desep'sõjʃ] *fpl de* **decepção**.

decerto [dʒi'sɛxtu] *adv* certainly.

decidido/a [desi'dʒidu/a] *adj* (*pessoa*) determined; (*questão*) resolved.

decidir [desi'dʒi*] *vt* (*determinar*) to decide; (*solucionar*) to resolve; **~-se** *vr*: **~-se a** to make up one's mind to; **~-se por** to decide on, go for.

decíduo/a [de'sidwu/a] *adj* (*BOT*) deciduous.

decifrar [desi'fra*] *vt* to decipher; (*futuro*) to foretell; (*compreender*) to understand.

decifrável (*pl* **-eis**) *adj* decipherable.

decimal [desi'maw] (*pl* **-ais**) *adj* decimal ♦ *m* (*número*) decimal.

décimo/a ['dɛsimu/a] *adj* tenth ♦ *m* tenth; *V tb* **quinto**.

decisão [desi'zãw] (*pl* **-ões**) *f* decision; (*capacidade de decidir*) decisiveness, resolution.

decisivo/a [desi'zivu/a] *adj* (*fator*) decisive; (*jogo*) deciding.

decisões [desi'zõjʃ] *fpl de* **decisão**.

declamação [deklama'sãw] *f* (*de poema*) recitation; (*pej*) ranting.

declamar [dekla'ma*] *vt* (*poemas*) to recite ♦ *vi* (*pej*) to rant.

declaração [deklara'sãw] (*pl* **-ões**) *f* declaration; (*depoimento*) statement; (*revelação*) revelation; **~ de amor** proposal; **~ de imposto de renda** income tax return; **~ juramentada** affidavit.

declarado/a [dekla'radu/a] *adj* (*intenção*) declared; (*opinião*) professed; (*inimigo*) sworn; (*alcoólatra*) self-confessed; (*cristão etc*) avowed.

declarante [dekla'rãtʃi] *m/f* (*JUR*) witness.

declarar [dekla'ra*] *vt* to declare; (*confessar*) to confess.

Dec-lei [dek-] *abr m* = **decreto-lei**.

declinação [deklina'sãw] (*pl* **-ões**) *f* (*LING*) declension.

declinar [dekli'na*] *vt* (*recusar*) to decline, refuse; (*nomes*) to give; (*LING*) to decline ♦ *vi* (*sol*) to go down; (*terreno*) to slope down.

declínio [de'klinju] *m* decline.

declive [de'klivi] *m* slope, incline.

decô [de'ko] *adj inv* Art-Deco.

decodificador [dekodʒifika'do*] *m* (*COMPUT*) decoder.

decodificar [dekodʒifi'ka*] *vt* to decode.

decolagem [deko'laʒẽ] (*pl* **-ns**) *f* (*AER*) take-off.

decolar [deko'la*] *vi* (*AER*) to take off.

decompor [dekõ'po*] (*irreg*: *como* **pôr**) *vt* (*analisar*) to analyse; (*apodrecer*) to rot; (*rosto*) to contort; **~-se** *vr* to rot, decompose.

decomposição [dekõpozi'sãw] (*pl* **-ões**) *f* (*apodrecimento*) decomposition; (*análise*) dissection; (*do rosto*) contortion.

decomposto [dekõ'poʃtu] *pp de* **decompor**.

decompunha [dekõ'puɲa] *etc vb V* **decompor**.

decompus [dekõ'puʃ] *etc vb V* **decompor**.

decompuser [dekõpu'ze*] *etc vb V* **decompor**.

decoração [dekora'sãw] *f* decoration; (*TEATRO*) scenery.

decorar [deko'ra*] *vt* to decorate; (*aprender*) to learn by heart.

decorativo/a [dekora'tʃivu/a] *adj* decorative.

decoro [de'koru] *m* (*decência*) decency; (*dignidade*) decorum.

decoroso/a [deko'rozu/ɔza] *adj* decent, respectable.

decorrência [deko'xẽsja] *f* consequence, result; **em ~ de** as a result of.

decorrente [deko'xẽtʃi] *adj*: **~ de** resulting from.

decorrer [deko'xe*] *vi* (*tempo*) to pass; (*acontecer*) to take place, happen ♦ *m*: **no ~ de** in the course of; **~ de** to result from.

decotado/a [deko'tadu/a] *adj* (*roupa*) low-cut.

decote [de'kɔtʃi] *m* (*vestido*) low neckline.

decrépito/a [de'krɛpitu/a] *adj* decrepit.

decrescente [dekre'sẽtʃi] *adj* decreasing, diminishing.

decrescer [dekre'se*] *vi* to decrease, diminish.

decréscimo [de'krɛsimu] *m* decrease, decline.

decretação [dekreta'sãw] (*pl* **-ões**) *f* announcement; (*de estado de sítio*) declaration.

decretar [dekre'ta*] *vt* to decree, order; (*estado de sítio*) to declare; (*anunciar*) to announce; (*determinar*) to determine.

decreto [de'krɛtu] *m* decree, order; **nem por ~** not for love nor money.

decreto-lei (*pl* **decretos-leis**) *m* act, law.

decúbito [de'kubitu] *m*: **em ~** recumbent.

decurso [de'kuxsu] *m* (*tempo*) course; **no ~ de** in the course of, during.

dedal [de'daw] (*pl* **-ais**) *m* thimble.

dedão [de'dãw] (*pl* **-ões**) *m* thumb; (*do pé*) big toe.

dedetização [dedetʃiza'sãw] *f* spraying with insecticide.

dedetizar [dedetʃi'za*] *vt* to spray with insecticide.

dedicação [dedʒika'sãw] *f* dedication; (*devotamento*) devotion.

dedicado/a [dedʒi'kadu/a] *adj* (*tb*: *COMPUT*) dedicated.

dedicar [dedʒi'ka*] *vt* (*poema*) to dedicate; (*tempo, atenção*) to devote; **~-se** *vr*: **~-se a** to devote o.s. to.

dedicatória [dedʒika'tɔrja] *f* (*de obra*) dedication.
dedilhar [dedʒi'ʎa*] *vt* (*MÚS*: *no braço*) to finger; (: *nas cordas*) to pluck.
dedo ['dedu] *m* finger; (*do pé*) toe; **dois ~s (de)** a little bit (of); **escolher a ~** to handpick; **~ anular** ring finger; **~ indicador** index finger; **~ mínimo** *ou* **mindinho** little finger; **~ polegar** thumb.
dedo-duro (*pl* **dedos-duros**) (*col*) *m* (*criminoso*) grass; (*criança*) sneak, tell-tale.
dedões [de'dõjʃ] *mpl de* **dedão**.
dedução [dedu'sãw] (*pl* **-ões**) *f* deduction.
dedurar [dedu'ra*] (*col*) *vt*: **~ alguém** (*criminoso*) to grass on sb; (*colega etc*) to drop sb in it.
dedutivo/a [dedu'tʃivu/a] *adj* deductive.
deduzir [dedu'zi*] *vt* to deduct; (*concluir*): **~ (de)** to deduce, infer (from) ♦ *vi* (*concluir*) to deduce, infer.
defasado/a [defa'zadu/a] *adj*: **~ (de)** out of step (with).
defasagem [defa'zaʒẽ] (*pl* **-ns**) *f* discrepancy.
defecar [defe'ka*] *vi* to defecate.
defecção [defek'sãw] (*pl* **-ões**) *f* defection; (*deserção*) desertion.
defectivo/a [defek'tʃivu/a] *adj* faulty, defective; (*LING*) defective.
defeito [de'fejtu] *m* defect, flaw; **pôr ~s em** to find fault with; **com ~** broken, out of order; **para ninguém botar ~** (*col*) perfect.
defeituoso/a [defej'twozu/ɔza] *adj* defective, faulty.
defender [defẽ'de*] *vt* (*ger, JUR*) to defend; (*proteger*) to protect; **~-se** *vr* to stand up for o.s.; (*numa língua*) to get by; **~-se de** (*de ataque*) to defend o.s. against; (*do frio etc*) to protect o.s. against.
defensável [defẽ'savew] (*pl* **-eis**) *adj* defensible.
defensiva [defẽ'siva] *f* defensive; **estar** *ou* **ficar na ~** to be on the defensive.
defensor(a) [defẽ'so*(a)] *m/f* defender; (*JUR*) defending counsel.
deferência [defe'rẽsja] *f* (*condescendência*) deference; (*respeito*) respect.
deferente [defe'rẽtʃi] *adj* deferential.
deferimento [deferi'mẽtu] *m* (*concessão*) granting; (*de prêmio, condecoração*) awarding; (*aceitação*) acceptance.
deferir [defe'ri*] *vt* (*pedido, petição*) to grant; (*prêmio, condecoração*) to award ♦ *vi*: **~ a** (*pedido, petição*) to grant; (*sugestão*) to accept.
defesa [de'feza] *f* defence (*BRIT*), defense (*US*); (*JUR*) counsel for the defence ♦ *m* (*PT*: *FUTEBOL*) back.
deficiência [defi'sjẽsja] *f* deficiency.
deficiente [defi'sjẽtʃi] *adj* (*imperfeito*) defective; (*carente*): **~ (em)** deficient (in).
déficit ['dɛfisitʃi] (*pl* **~s**) *m* deficit.
deficitário/a [defisi'tarju/a] *adj*: **empresa/conta deficitária** company/account in deficit.
definhar [defi'ɲa*] *vt* to debilitate ♦ *vi* (*consumir-se*) to waste away; (*BOT*) to wither.
definição [defini'sãw] (*pl* **-ões**) *f* definition.
definir [defi'ni*] *vt* to define; **~-se** *vr* (*decidir-se*) to make a decision; (*explicar-se*) to make one's position clear; **~-se contra/a favor de algo** to come out against/in favo(u)r of sth; **~-se como** to describe o.s. as.
definitivamente [definitʃiva'mẽtʃi] *adv* (*finalmente*) definitively; (*permanentemente*) for good; (*sem dúvida*) definitely.
definitivo/a [defini'tʃivu/a] *adj* (*final*) final, definitive; (*permanente*) permanent; (*resposta, data*) definite.
definível (*pl* **-eis**) *adj* definable.
defira [defi'ra] *etc vb V* **deferir**.
defiro [de'firu] *etc vb V* **deferir**.
deflação [defla'sãw] *f* deflation.
deflacionar [deflasjo'na*] *vt* to deflate.
deflacionário/a [deflasjo'narju/a] *adj* deflationary.
deflagração [deflagra'sãw] (*pl* **-ões**) *f* explosion; (*fig*) outbreak.
deflagrar [defla'gra*] *vi* to explode; (*fig*) to break out ♦ *vt* to set off; (*fig*) to trigger.
deflorar [deflo'ra*] *vt* to deflower.
deformação [defoxma'sãw] (*pl* **-ões**) *f* loss of shape; (*de corpo*) deformation; (*de imagem, pensamento*) distortion.
deformar [defox'ma*] *vt* to put out of shape; (*corpo*) to deform; (*imagem, pensamento*) to distort; **~-se** *vr* to lose shape; to be deformed; to become distorted.
deformidade [defoxmi'dadʒi] *f* deformity.
defraudação [defrawda'sãw] (*pl* **-ões**) *f* fraud; (*de dinheiro*) embezzlement.
defraudar [defraw'da*] *vt* (*dinheiro*) to embezzle; (*uma pessoa*) to defraud; **~ alguém de algo** to cheat sb of sth.
defrontar [defrõ'ta*] *vt* to face ♦ *vi*: **~ com** to face; (*dar com*) to come face to face with; **~-se** *vr* to face each other.
defronte [de'frõtʃi] *adv* opposite ♦ *prep*: **~ de** opposite.
defumado/a [defu'madu/a] *adj* smoked.
defumar [defu'ma*] *vt* (*presunto*) to smoke; (*perfumar*) to perfume.
defunto/a [de'fũtu/a] *adj* dead ♦ *m/f* dead person.
degelar [deʒe'la*] *vt* to thaw; (*geladeira*) to defrost ♦ *vi* to thaw out; to defrost.
degelo [de'ʒelu] *m* thaw.
degeneração [deʒenera'sãw] *f* (*processo*) degeneration; (*estado*) degeneracy.
degenerar [deʒene'ra*] *vi*: **~ (em)** to degenerate (into); **~-se** *vr* to become degenerate.
deglutir [deglu'tʃi*] *vt, vi* to swallow.
degolação [degola'sãw] (*pl* **-ões**) *f* beheading, decapitation.
degolar [dego'la*] *vt* to decapitate.
degradação [degrada'sãw] *f* degradation.
degradante [degra'dãtʃi] *adj* degrading.
degradar [degra'da*] *vt* to degrade, debase;

~**-se** *vr* to demean o.s.
dégradé [degra'de] *adj inv* (*cor*) shaded off.
degrau [de'graw] *m* step; (*de escada de mão*) rung.
degredar [degre'da*] *vt* to exile.
degredo [de'gredu] *m* exile.
degringolar [degrĩgo'la*] *vi* (*cair*) to tumble down; (*fig*) to collapse; (: *deteriorar-se*) to deteriorate; (*desorganizar-se*) to get messed up.
degustação [deguʃta'sãw] (*pl* **-ões**) *f* tasting, sampling; (*saborear*) savouring (*BRIT*), savoring (*US*).
degustar [deguʃ'ta*] *vt* (*provar*) to taste; (*saborear*) to savour (*BRIT*), savor (*US*).
dei [dej] *etc vb V* **dar**.
deificar [dejfi'ka*] *vt* to deify.
deitada [dej'tada] (*col*) *f*: **dar uma** ~ to have a lie-down.
deitado/a [dej'tadu/a] *adj* (*estendido*) lying down; (*na cama*) in bed.
deitar [dej'ta*] *vt* to lay down; (*na cama*) to put to bed; (*colocar*) to put, place; (*lançar*) to cast; (*PT*: *líquido*) to pour; ~**-se** *vr* to lie down; to go to bed; ~ **sangue** (*PT*) to bleed; ~ **abaixo** to knock down, flatten; ~ **a fazer algo** to start doing sth; ~ **uma carta** (*PT*) to post a letter; ~ **fora** (*PT*) to throw away *ou* out; ~ **e rolar** (*col*) to do as one likes.
deixa ['dejʃa] *f* clue, hint; (*TEATRO*) cue; (*chance*) chance.
deixar [dej'ʃa*] *vt* to leave; (*abandonar*) to abandon; (*permitir*) to let, allow ♦ *vi*: ~ **de** (*parar*) to stop; (*não fazer*) to fail to; **não posso** ~ **de ir** I must go; **não posso** ~ **de rir** I can't help laughing; ~ **cair** to drop; ~ **alguém louco** to drive sb crazy *ou* mad; ~ **alguém cansado/nervoso** *etc* to make sb tired/nervous *etc*; ~ **a desejar** to leave something to be desired; **deixa disso!** (*col*) come off it!; **deixa para lá!** (*col*) forget it!
dela ['dɛla] = **de** + **ela**; *V* **ela**.
delação [dela'sãw] (*pl* **-ões**) *f* (*de pessoa*: *denúncia*) accusation; (: *traição*) betrayal; (*de abusos*) disclosure.
delatar [dela'ta*] *vt* (*pessoa*) to inform on; (*abusos*) to reveal; (*à polícia*) to report.
delator(a) [dela'to*(a)] *m/f* informer.
délavé [dela've] *adj inv* (*jeans*) faded.
dele ['deli] = **de** + **ele**; *V* **ele**.
delegação [delega'sãw] (*pl* **-ões**) *f* delegation.
delegacia [delega'sia] *f* office; ~ **de polícia** police station.
delegado/a [dele'gadu/a] *m/f* delegate, representative; ~ **de polícia** police chief.
delegar [dele'ga*] *vt* to delegate.
deleitar [delej'ta*] *vt* to delight; ~**-se** *vr*: ~**-se com** to delight in.
deleite [de'lejtʃi] *m* delight.
deleitoso/a [delej'tozu/ɔza] *adj* delightful.
deletar [dele'ta*] *vt* (*COMPUT*) to delete.
deletério/a [dele'tɛrju/a] *adj* harmful.
delével [de'lɛvew] (*pl* **-eis**) *adj* erasable.
delgado/a [dew'gadu/a] *adj* thin; (*esbelto*) slim, slender; (*fino*) fine.
Délhi ['dɛli] *n*: **(Nova)** ~ (New) Delhi.
deliberação [delibera'sãw] (*pl* **-ões**) *f* deliberation; (*decisão*) decision.
deliberar [delibe'ra*] *vt* to decide, resolve ♦ *vi* to deliberate.
deliberativo/a [delibera'tʃivu/a] *adj* (*conselho*) deliberative.
delicadeza [delika'deza] *f* delicacy; (*cortesia*) kindness.
delicado/a [deli'kadu/a] *adj* delicate; (*frágil*) fragile; (*cortês*) polite; (*sensível*) sensitive.
delícia [de'lisja] *f* delight; (*prazer*) pleasure; **esse bolo é uma** ~ this cake is delicious; **que** ~! how lovely!
deliciar [deli'sja*] *vt* to delight; ~**-se** *vr*: ~**-se com algo** to take delight in sth.
delicioso/a [deli'sjozu/ɔza] *adj* lovely; (*comida, bebida*) delicious.
delimitação [delimita'sãw] *f* delimitation.
delimitar [delimi'ta*] *vt* to delimit.
delineador [delinja'do*] *m* (*de olhos*) eyeliner.
delinear [deli'nja*] *vt* to outline.
delinqüência [delĩ'kwẽsja] *f* delinquency.
delinqüente [delĩ'kwẽtʃi] *adj, m/f* delinquent, criminal.
delinqüir [delĩ'kwi*] *vi* to commit an offence (*BRIT*) *ou* offense (*US*).
delir [de'li*] *vt* to erase.
delirante [deli'rãtʃi] *adj* delirious; (*show, atuação*) thrilling.
delirar [deli'ra*] *vi* (*com febre*) to be delirious; (*de ódio, prazer*) to go mad, go wild.
delírio [de'lirju] *m* (*MED*) delirium; (*êxtase*) ecstasy; (*excitação*) excitement.
delirium tremens [de'liriũ 'trɛmẽs] *m* delirium tremens.
delito [de'litu] *m* (*crime*) crime; (*pecado*) offence (*BRIT*), offense (*US*).
delonga [de'lõga] *f* delay; **sem mais** ~**s** without more ado.
delongar [delõ'ga*] *vt* to delay; ~**-se** *vr* (*conversa*) to wear on; ~**-se em** to dwell on.
delta ['dɛwta] *f* delta.
demagogia [demago'ʒia] *f* demagogy.
demagógico/a [dema'gɔʒiku/a] *adj* demagogic.
demagogo [dema'gogu] *m* demagogue.
demais [dʒi'majʃ] *adv* (*em demasia*) too much; (*muitíssimo*) a lot, very much ♦ *pron*: **os/as** ~ the rest (of them); **já é** ~! this is too much!; **é bom** ~ it's really good; **foi** ~ (*col*: *bacana*) it was great.
demanda [de'mãda] *f* (*JUR*) lawsuit; (*disputa*) claim; (*requisição*) request; (*ECON*) demand; **em** ~ **de** in search of.

NB: European Portuguese adds the following consonants to certain words: **b** (sú(b)dito, su(b)til); **c** (a(c)ção, a(c)cionista, a(c)to); **m** (inde(m)ne); **p** (ado(p)ção, ado(p)tar); *for further details see p. xiii.*

demandar [demã'da*] *vt* (*JUR*) to sue; (*exigir, reclamar*) to demand; (*porto*) to head for.
demão [de'mãw] (*pl* **~s**) *f* (*de tinta*) coat, layer.
demarcação [demaxka'sãw] *f* demarcation.
demarcar [demax'ka*] *vt* (*delimitar*) to demarcate; (*fixar*) to mark out.
demarcatório/a [demaxka'tɔrju/a] *adj V* **linha**.
demasia [dema'zia] *f* excess, surplus; (*imoderação*) lack of moderation; **em ~** (*dinheiro, comida etc*) too much; (*cartas, problemas etc*) too many.
demasiadamente [demazjada'mẽtʃi] *adv* too much; (*com adj*) too.
demasiado/a [dema'zjadu/a] *adj* too much; (*pl*) too many ♦ *adv* too much; (*com adj*) too.
demência [de'mẽsja] *f* dementia.
demente [de'mẽtʃi] *adj* insane, demented.
demérito/a [de'mɛritu/a] *adj* unworthy ♦ *m* demerit.
demissão [demi'sãw] (*pl* **-ões**) *f* dismissal; **pedido de ~** resignation; **pedir ~** to resign.
demissionário/a [demisjo'narju/a] *adj* resigning, outgoing.
demissões [demi'sõjʃ] *fpl de* **demissão**.
demitir [demi'tʃi*] *vt* to dismiss; (*col*) to sack, fire; **~-se** *vr* to resign.
democracia [demokra'sia] *f* democracy.
democrata [demo'krata] *m/f* democrat.
democrático/a [demo'kratʃiku/a] *adj* democratic.
democratização [demokratʃiza'sãw] *f* democratization.
democratizar [demokratʃi'za*] *vt* to democratize.
démodé [demo'de] *adj inv* old-fashioned.
demografia [demogra'fia] *f* demography.
demográfico/a [demo'grafiku/a] *adj* demographic.
demolição [demoli'sãw] (*pl* **-ões**) *f* demolition.
demolir [demo'li*] *vt* to demolish, knock down; (*fig*) to destroy.
demoníaco/a [demo'niaku/a] *adj* devilish.
demônio [de'monju] *m* devil, demon; (*col: criança*) brat.
demonstração [demõʃtra'sãw] (*pl* **-ões**) *f* (*lição prática*) demonstration; (*de amizade*) show, display; (*prova*) proof; **~ de contas** (*COM*) statement of account; **~ de lucros e perdas** (*COM*) profit and loss statement.
demonstrar [demõʃ'tra*] *vt* (*mostrar*) to demonstrate; (*provar*) to prove; (*amizade etc*) to show.
demonstrativo/a [demõʃtra'tʃivu/a] *adj* demonstrative.
demonstrável [demõ'ʃtravew] (*pl* **-eis**) *adj* demonstrable.
demora [de'mɔra] *f* delay; (*parada*) stop; **sem ~** at once, without delay; **qual é a ~ disso?** how long will this take?
demorado/a [demo'radu/a] *adj* slow.
demorar [demo'ra*] *vt* to delay, slow down ♦ *vi* (*permanecer*) to stay; (*tardar a vir*) to be late; (*conserto*) to take (a long) time; **~-se** *vr* to stay for a long time, linger; **~ a chegar** to be a long time coming; **vai ~ muito?** will it take long?; **não vou ~** I won't be long.
demover [demo've*] *vt*: **~ alguém de algo** to talk sb out of sth; **~-se** *vr*: **~-se de algo** to be talked out of sth.
Denatran [dena'trã] (*BR*) *abr m* (= *Departamento Nacional de Trânsito*) ≈ Ministry of Transport.
dendê [dẽ'de] *m* (*CULIN*: *óleo*) palm oil; (*BOT*) oil palm.
denegrir [dene'gri*] *vt* to blacken; (*difamar*) to denigrate.
dengo [dẽgu] *m* coyness; (*choro*) whimpering.
dengoso/a [dẽ'gozu/ɔza] *adj* coy; (*criança: choraminguento*): **ser ~** to be a crybaby.
dengue ['dẽgi] *m* (*MED*) dengue.
denigro [de'nigru] *etc vb V* **denegrir**.
denodado/a [deno'dadu/a] *adj* brave, daring.
denominação [denomina'sãw] (*pl* **-ões**) *f* (*REL*) denomination; (*título*) name; (*ato*) naming.
denominador [denomina'do*] *m*: **~ comum** (*MAT, fig*) common denominator.
denominar [denomi'na*] *vt*: **~ algo/alguém** ... to call sth/sb ...; **~-se** *vr* to be called; (*a si mesmo*) to call o.s.
denotar [deno'ta*] *vt* (*indicar*) to show, indicate; (*significar*) to signify.
densidade [dẽsi'dadʒi] *f* density; **disco de alta ~** (*COMPUT*) high-density disk; **disco de ~ simples/dupla** (*COMPUT*) single-/double-density disk.
denso/a [dẽsu/a] *adj* (*cerrado*) dense; (*espesso*) thick; (*compacto*) compact.
dentada [dẽ'tada] *f* bite.
dentado/a [dẽ'tadu/a] *adj* serrated.
dentadura [dẽta'dura] *f* teeth *pl*, set of teeth; (*artificial*) dentures *pl*.
dental [dẽ'taw] (*pl* **-ais**) *adj* dental.
dentário/a [dẽ'tarju/a] *adj* dental.
dente ['dẽtʃi] *m* tooth; (*de animal*) fang; (*de elefante*) tusk; (*de alho*) clove; **falar entre os ~s** to mutter, mumble; **~ de leite/do siso** milk/wisdom tooth; **~ postiço** false tooth.
dente-de-leão (*pl* **dentes-de-leão**) *m* dandelion.
Dentel [dẽ'tɛw] (*BR*) *abr m* = **Departamento Nacional de Telecomunicações**.
dentição [dẽtʃi'sãw] *f* (*formação dos dentes*) teething; (*dentes*) teeth *pl*; **primeira ~** milk teeth; **segunda ~** second teeth.
dentifrício [dẽtʃi'frisju] *m* toothpaste.
dentina [dẽ'tʃina] *f* dentine.
dentista [dẽ'tʃiʃta] *m/f* dentist.
dentre ['dẽtri] *prep* (from) among.
dentro ['dẽtru] *adv* inside; **aí ~** in there ♦ *prep*: **~ de** inside; (*tempo*) (with)in; **~ pouco** *ou* **em breve** soon, before long; **de ~ para fora** inside out; **dar uma ~** (*col*) to get it right; **por ~** on the inside; **estar por ~** (*col:*

fig) to be in the know; **estar por ~ de algo** (*col*: *fig*) to know the ins and outs of sth.

dentuça [dẽ'tusa] *f* buck teeth *pl*; *V tb* **dentuço**.

dentuço/a [dẽ'tusu/a] *adj* buck-toothed ♦ *m/f* buck-toothed person; **ser ~** to have buck teeth.

denúncia [de'nũsja] *f* denunciation; (*acusação*) accusation; (*de roubo*) report.

denunciar [denũ'sja*] *vt* to denounce, inform against; (*revelar*) to reveal.

deparar [depa'ra*] *vt* (*revelar*) to reveal; (*fazer aparecer*) to present ♦ *vi*: **~ com** to come across, meet; **~-se** *vr*: **~-se com** to come across, meet.

departamental [depaxtamẽ'taw] (*pl* **-ais**) *adj* departmental.

departamento [depaxta'mẽtu] *m* department; **D~ de Marcas e Patentes** Patent Office.

depauperar [depawpe'ra*] *vt*: **~ algo/alguém** to bleed sth/sb dry.

depenar [depe'na*] *vt* to pluck; (*col*: *roubar*) to clean out.

dependência [depẽ'dẽsja] *f* dependence; (*edificação*) annexe (BRIT), annex (US); (*colonial*) dependency; (*cômodo*) room.

dependente [depẽ'dẽtʃi] *m/f* dependant.

depender [depẽ'de*] *vi*: **~ de** to depend on.

dependurar [depẽdu'ra*] *vi* to hang.

depilação [depila'sãw] (*pl* **-ões**) *f* depilation.

depilador(a) [depila'do*(a)] *m/f* beauty therapist.

depilar [depi'la*] *vt* to wax; **~ as pernas** (*mandar fazer*) to have one's legs done; (*fazer sozinho*) to do one's legs.

depilatório [depila'tɔrju] *m* hair-remover.

deplorar [deplo'ra*] *vt* (*lamentar*) to regret; (*morte, perda*) to lament.

deplorável [deplo'ravew] (*pl* **-eis**) *adj* deplorable; (*lamentável*) regrettable.

depoente [de'pwẽtʃi] *m/f* witness.

depoimento [depoj'mẽtu] *m* testimony, evidence; (*na polícia*) statement.

depois [de'pojʃ] *adv* afterwards ♦ *prep*: **~ de** after; **~ de comer** after eating; **~ que** after.

depor [de'po*] (*irreg*: *como* **pôr**) *vt* (*pôr*) to place; (*indicar*) to indicate; (*rei*) to depose; (*governo*) to overthrow ♦ *vi* (JUR) to testify, give evidence; (*na polícia*) to give a statement; **esses fatos depõem contra/a favor dele** these facts speak against him/in his favo(u)r.

deportação [depoxta'sãw] (*pl* **-ões**) *f* deportation.

deportar [depox'ta*] *vt* to deport.

deposição [depozi'sãw] (*pl* **-ões**) *f* deposition; (*governo*) overthrow.

depositante [depozi'tãtʃi] *m/f* depositor ♦ *adj* depositing.

depositar [depozi'ta*] *vt* to deposit; (*voto*) to cast; (*colocar*) to place; **~-se** *vr* (*líquido*) to form a deposit; **~ confiança em** to place one's confidence in.

depositário/a [depozi'tarju/a] *m/f* trustee; (*fig*) confidant(e).

depósito [de'pɔzitu] *m* deposit; (*armazém*) warehouse, depot; (*de lixo*) dump; (*reservatório*) tank; **~ a prazo fixo** fixed-term deposit; **~ de bagagens** left-luggage office.

depravação [deprava'sãw] *f* depravity, corruption.

depravado/a [depra'vadu/a] *adj* depraved ♦ *m/f* degenerate.

depravar [depra'va*] *vt* to deprave, corrupt; (*estragar*) to ruin; **~-se** *vr* to become depraved.

deprecar [depre'ka*] *vt* to beg for, pray for ♦ *vi* to plead.

depreciação [depresja'sãw] *f* depreciation.

depreciador(a) [depresja'do*(a)] *adj* deprecatory.

depreciar [depre'sja*] *vt* (*desvalorizar*) to devalue; (COM) to write down; (*menosprezar*) to belittle; **~-se** *vr* to depreciate, lose value; (*menosprezar-se*) to belittle o.s.

depredação [depreda'sãw] *f* depredation.

depredador(a) [depreda'do*(a)] *adj* destructive ♦ *m/f* vandal.

depredar [depre'da*] *vt* to wreck.

depreender [deprjẽ'de*] *vt*: **~ algo/que ... (de algo)** to gather sth/that ... (from sth).

depressa [dʒi'prɛsa] *adv* fast, quickly; **vamos ~** let's get a move on!

depressão [depre'sãw] (*pl* **-ões**) *f* (*ger*) depression.

depressivo/a [depre'sivu/a] *adj* depressive.

depressões [depre'sõjʃ] *fpl de* **depressão**.

deprimente [depri'mẽtʃi] *adj* depressing.

deprimido/a [depri'midu/a] *adj* depressed, low.

deprimir [depri'mi*] *vt* to depress; **~-se** *vr* to get depressed.

depuração [depura'sãw] *f* purification.

depurar [depu'ra*] *vt* to purify; (COMPUT: *programa*) to debug.

deputado/a [depu'tadu/a] *m/f* deputy; (*agente*) agent; (POL) ≈ Member of Parliament (BRIT), Representative (US).

deputar [depu'ta*] *vt* to delegate.

deque ['dɛki] *m* deck.

DER (BR) *abr m* (= *Departamento de Estradas de Rodagem*) *state highways dept.*

der [de*] *etc vb V* **dar**.

deriva [de'riva] *f* drift; **ir à ~** to drift; **ficar à ~** to be adrift.

derivação [deriva'sãw] (*pl* **-ões**) *f* derivation.

derivar [deri'va*] *vt* (*desviar*) to divert; (LING) to derive ♦ *vi* (*ir à deriva*) to drift; **~-se** *vr* (*palavra*) to be derived; (*ir à deriva*) to drift; (*provir*): **~(-se) (de)** to derive *ou* be derived (from).

NB: *European Portuguese adds the following consonants to certain words:* **b** (sú(b)dito, su(b)til); **c** (a(c)ção, a(c)cionista, a(c)to); **m** (inde(m)ne); **p** (ado(p)ção, ado(p)tar); *for further details see p. xiii.*

dermatologia [dexmatolo'ʒia] *f* dermatology.
dermatologista [dexmatolo'ʒiʃta] *m/f* dermatologist.
dernier cri [dex'nje 'kri] *m* last word.
derradeiro/a [dexa'dejru/a] *adj* last, final.
derramamento [dexama'mẽtu] *m* spilling; (*de sangue, lágrimas*) shedding.
derramar [dexa'ma*] *vt* (*sem querer*) to spill; (*entornar*) to pour; (*sangue, lágrimas*) to shed; **~-se** *vr* to pour out.
derrame [de'xami] *m* haemorrhage (BRIT), hemorrhage (US).
derrapagem [dexa'paʒẽ] (*pl* **-ns**) *f* skid; (*ação*) skidding.
derrapar [dexa'pa*] *vi* to skid.
derredor [dexe'do*] *adv, prep*: **em ~ (de)** around.
derreter [dexe'te*] *vt* to melt; **~-se** *vr* to melt; (*coisa congelada*) to thaw; (*enternecer-se*) to be touched; **~ alguém** to win sb's heart; **~-se por alguém** to fall for sb.
derretido/a [dexe'tʃidu/a] *adj* melted; (*enternecido*) touched; (*apaixonado*) smitten; **estar ~ por alguém** to be crazy about sb.
derrocada [dexo'kada] *f* downfall; (*ruína*) collapse.
derrogação [dexoga'sãw] (*pl* **-ões**) *f* amendment.
derrota [de'xɔta] *f* defeat, rout; (NÁUT) route.
derrotar [dexo'ta*] *vt* (*vencer*) to defeat; (*em jogo*) to beat.
derrubar [dexu'ba*] *vt* to knock down; (*governo*) to bring down; (*suj*: *doença*) to lay low; (*col*: *prejudicar*) to put down.
desabafar [dʒizaba'fa*] *vt* (*sentimentos*) to give vent to ♦ *vi*: **~ (com)** to unburden o.s. (to); **~-se** *vr*: **~-se (com)** to unburden o.s. (to).
desabafo [dʒiza'bafu] *m* confession.
desabalado/a [dʒizaba'ladu/a] *adj*: **correr/sair ~** to run headlong/rush out.
desabamento [dʒizaba'mẽtu] *m* collapse.
desabar [dʒiza'ba*] *vi* (*edifício, ponte*) to collapse; (*chuva*) to pour down; (*tempestade*) to break.
desabilitar [dʒizabili'ta*] *vt*: **~ alguém a** *ou* **para (fazer) algo** to bar sb from (doing) sth.
desabitado/a [dʒizabi'tadu/a] *adj* uninhabited.
desabituar [dʒizabi'twa*] *vt*: **~ alguém de (fazer) algo** to get sb out of the habit of (doing) sth; **~-se** *vr*: **~-se de (fazer) algo** to get out of the habit of (doing) sth.
desabonar [dʒizabo'na*] *vt* to discredit; **~-se** *vr* to be discredited.
desabotoar [dʒizabo'twa*] *vt* to unbutton.
desabrido/a [dʒiza'bridu/a] *adj* rude, brusque.
desabrigado/a [dʒizabri'gadu/a] *adj* (*sem casa*) homeless; (*exposto*) exposed.
desabrigar [dʒizabri'ga*] *vt* to make homeless.
desabrochar [dʒizabro'ʃa*] *vi* (*flores, fig*) to blossom ♦ *m* blossoming.
desabusado/a [dʒizabu'zadu/a] *adj* (*sem preconceitos*) unprejudiced; (*atrevido*) impudent.
desacatar [dʒizaka'ta*] *vt* (*desrespeitar*) to have *ou* show no respect for; (*afrontar*) to defy; (*desprezar*) to scorn ♦ *vi* (*col*) to be amazing.
desacato [dʒiza'katu] *m* (*falta de respeito*) disrespect; (*desprezo*) disregard; (*col*): **ele é um ~** he's amazing.
desaceleração [dʒizaselera'sãw] *f* (*tb*: ECON) slowing down.
desacelerar [dʒizasele'ra*] *vt* to slow down.
desacerto [dʒiza'sextu] *m* mistake, blunder.
desacomodar [dʒizakomo'da*] *vt* to move out.
desacompanhado/a [dʒizakõpa'ɲadu/a] *adj* on one's own, alone.
desaconselhar [dʒizakõse'ʎa*] *vt*: **~ algo (a alguém)** to advise (sb) against sth.
desaconselhável [dʒizakõse'ʎavew] (*pl* **-eis**) *adj* inadvisable.
desacordado/a [dʒizakox'dadu/a] *adj* unconscious.
desacordo [dʒiza'koxdu] *m* (*falta de acordo*) disagreement; (*desarmonia*) discord.
desacostumado/a [dʒizakoʃtumadu/a] *adj* unaccustomed.
desacostumar [dʒizakoʃtu'ma*] *vt*: **~ alguém de algo** to get sb out of the habit of sth; **~-se** *vr*: **~-se de algo** to give sth up.
desacreditado/a [dʒizakredʒi'tadu/a] *adj* discredited.
desacreditar [dʒizakredʒi'ta*] *vt* to discredit; **~-se** *vr* to lose one's reputation.
desafeto [dʒiza'fɛtu] *m* coldness.
desafiador(a) [dʒizafja'do*(a)] *adj* challenging; (*pessoa*) defiant ♦ *m/f* challenger.
desafiar [dʒiza'fja*] *vt* (*propor combate*) to challenge; (*afrontar*) to defy.
desafinação [dʒizafina'sãw] *f* dissonance.
desafinado/a [dʒizafi'nadu/a] *adj* out of tune.
desafinar [dʒizafi'na*] *vt* to put out of tune ♦ *vi* to play out of tune; (*cantor*) to sing out of tune.
desafio [dʒiza'fiu] *m* challenge; (PT: ESPORTE) match, game.
desafivelar [dʒizafive'la*] *vt* to unbuckle.
desafogado/a [dʒizafo'gadu/a] *adj* (*desimpedido*) clear; (*desembaraçado*) free.
desafogar [dʒizafo'ga*] *vt* (*libertar*) to free; (*desapertar*) to relieve; (*desabafar*) to give vent to; **~-se** *vr* (*desapertar-se*) to free o.s.; (*desabafar-se*) to unburden o.s.
desafogo [dʒiza'fogu] *m* (*alívio*) relief; (*folga*) leisure.
desaforado/a [dʒizafo'radu/a] *adj* rude, insolent.
desaforo [dʒiza'foru] *m* insolence, abuse.
desafortunado/a [dʒizafoxtu'nadu/a] *adj* unfortunate, unlucky.
desafronta [dʒiza'frõta] *f* (*satisfação*) redress; (*vingança*) revenge.
desagasalhado/a [dʒizagaza'ʎadu/a] *adj*

scantily clad.

desagradar [dʒizagra'da*] *vt* to displease ♦ *vi*: ~ **a alguém** to displease sb.

desagradável [dʒizagra'davew] (*pl* **-eis**) *adj* unpleasant.

desagrado [dʒiza'gradu] *m* displeasure.

desagravar [dʒizagra'va*] *vt* (*insulta*) to make amends for; (*pessoa*) to make amends to; **~-se** *vr* to avenge o.s.

desagravo [dʒiza'gravu] *m* amends *pl*.

desagregação [dʒizagrega'sãw] *f* (*separação*) separation; (*dissolução*) disintegration.

desagregar [dʒizagre'ga*] *vt* (*desunir*) to break up, split; (*separar*) to separate; **~-se** *vr* to break up, split; to separate.

desaguar [dʒiza'gwa*] *vt* to drain ♦ *vi*: ~ **(em)** to flow *ou* empty (into).

desairoso/a [dʒizaj'rozu/ɔza] *adj* inelegant.

desajeitado/a [dʒizaʒej'tadu/a] *adj* clumsy, awkward.

desajuizado/a [dʒizaʒwi'zadu/a] *adj* foolish, unwise.

desajustado/a [dʒizaʒuʃ'tadu/a] *adj* (PSICO) maladjusted; (*peças*) in need of adjustment ♦ *m/f* maladjusted person.

desajustamento [dʒizaʒuʃta'mẽtu] *m* (PSICO) maladjustment.

desajustar [dʒizaʒuʃ'ta*] *vt* (*peças*) to mess up.

desajuste [dʒiza'ʒuʃtʃi] *m* (PSICO) maladjustment; (*mecânico*) problem.

desalentado/a [dʒizalẽ'tadu/a] *adj* disheartened.

desalentar [dʒizalẽ'ta*] *vt* to discourage; (*deprimir*) to depress.

desalento [dʒiza'lẽtu] *m* discouragement.

desalinhado/a [dʒizali'ɲadu/a] *adj* untidy.

desalinho [dʒiza'liɲu] *m* untidiness.

desalmado/a [dʒizaw'madu/a] *adj* cruel, inhuman.

desalojar [dʒizalo'ʒa*] *vt* (*expulsar*) to oust; **~-se** *vr* to move out.

desamarrar [dʒizama'xa*] *vt* to untie ♦ *vi* (NÁUT) to cast off.

desamarrotar [dʒizamaxo'ta*] *vt* to smooth out.

desamassar [dʒizama'sa*] *vt* (*papel*) to smooth out; (*chapéu etc*) to straighten out; (*carro*) to beat out.

desambientado/a [dʒizãbjẽ'tadu/a] *adj* unsettled.

desamor [dʒiza'mo*] *m* dislike.

desamparado/a [dʒizãpa'radu/a] *adj* (*abandonado*) abandoned; (*sem apoio*) helpless.

desamparar [dʒizãpa'ra*] *vt* to abandon.

desamparo [dʒizã'paru] *m* helplessness.

desandar [dʒizã'da*] *vi* (*maionese, clara*) to separate; ~ **a fazer** to begin to do; ~ **a correr** to break into a run; ~ **a chorar** to burst into tears.

desanimação [dʒizanima'sãw] *f* dejection.

desanimado/a [dʒizani'madu/a] *adj* (*pessoa*) fed up, dispirited; (*festa*) dull; **ser** ~ (*pessoa*) to be apathetic.

desanimar [dʒizani'ma*] *vt* (*abater*) to dishearten; (*desencorajar*): ~ **(de fazer)** to discourage (from doing) ♦ *vi* to lose heart; (*ser desanimador*) to be discouraging; ~ **de fazer algo** to lose the will to do sth; (*desistir*) to give up doing sth.

desânimo [dʒi'zanimu] *m* dejection.

desanuviado/a [dʒizanu'vjadu/a] *adj* cloudless, clear.

desanuviar [dʒizanu'vja*] *vt* (*céu*) to clear; **~-se** *vr* to clear; (*fig*) to stop; ~ **alguém** to put sb's mind at rest.

desapaixonado/a [dʒizapajʃo'nadu/a] *adj* dispassionate.

desaparafusar [dʒizaparafu'za*] *vt* to unscrew.

desaparecer [dʒizapare'se*] *vi* to disappear, vanish.

desaparecido/a [dʒizapare'sidu/a] *adj* lost, missing ♦ *m/f* missing person.

desaparecimento [dʒizaparesi'mẽtu] *m* disappearance; (*falecimento*) death.

desapegado/a [dʒizape'gadu/a] *adj* indifferent, detached.

desapegar [dʒizape'ga*] *vt* to detach; **~-se** *vr*: **~-se de** to go off.

desapego [dʒiza'pegu] *m* indifference, detachment.

desapercebido/a [dʒizapexse'bidu/a] *adj* unnoticed.

desapertar [dʒizapex'ta*] *vt* (*afrouxar*) to loosen; (*livrar*) to free.

desapiedado/a [dʒizapje'dadu/a] *adj* pitiless, ruthless.

desapontador(a) [dʒizapõta'do*(a)] *adj* disappointing.

desapontamento [dʒizapõta'mẽtu] *m* disappointment.

desapontar [dʒizapõ'ta*] *vt* to disappoint.

desapossar [dʒizapo'sa*] *vt*: ~ **alguém de algo** to take sth away from sb; **~-se** *vr*: **~-se de algo** to give sth up.

desaprender [dʒizaprẽ'de*] *vt* to forget ♦ *vi*: ~ **a fazer** to forget how to do.

desapropriação [dʒizaproprja'sãw] *f* (*de bens*) expropriation; (*de pessoa*) dispossession.

desapropriar [dʒizapro'prja*] *vt* (*bens*) to expropriate; (*pessoa*) to dispossess.

desaprovação [dʒizaprova'sãw] *f* disapproval.

desaprovar [dʒizapro'va*] *vt* (*reprovar*) to disapprove of; (*censurar*) to object to.

desaproveitado/a [dʒizaprovej'tadu/a] *adj* wasted; (*terras*) undeveloped.

desaquecimento [dʒizakesi'mẽtu] *m* (ECON) cooling.

desarmamento [dʒizaxma'mẽtu] *m* disarmament.
desarmar [dʒizax'ma*] *vt* to disarm; (*desmontar*) to dismantle; (*bomba*) to defuse.
desarmonia [dʒizaxmo'nia] *f* discord.
desarraigar [dʒizaxaj'ga*] *vt* to uproot.
desarranjado/a [dʒizaxã'ʒadu/a] *adj* (*intestino*) upset; (*TEC*) out of order; **estar ~** (*pessoa*) to have diarrhoea (*BRIT*) *ou* diarrhea (*US*).
desarranjar [dʒizaxã'ʒa*] *vt* (*transtornar*) to upset, disturb; (*desordenar*) to mess up.
desarranjo [dʒiza'xãʒu] *m* (*desordem*) disorder; (*enguiço*) breakdown; (*diarréia*) diarrhoea (*BRIT*), diarrhea (*US*).
desarregaçar [dʒizaxega'sa*] *vt* (*mangas*) to roll down.
desarrumado/a [dʒizaxu'madu/a] *adj* untidy, messy.
desarrumar [dʒizaxu'ma*] *vt* to mess up; (*mala*) to unpack.
desarticulado/a [dʒizaxtʃiku'ladu/a] *adj* dislocated.
desarticular [dʒizaxtʃiku'la*] *vt* (*osso*) to dislocate.
desarvorado/a [dʒizaxvo'radu/a] *adj* disoriented, at a loss.
desassociar [dʒizaso'sja*] *vt* to disassociate; **~-se** *vr*: **~-se de algo** to disassociate o.s. from sth.
desassossego [dʒizaso'segu] *m* (*inquietação*) disquiet; (*perturbação*) restlessness.
desastrado/a [dʒizaʃ'tradu/a] *adj* clumsy.
desastre [dʒi'zaʃtri] *m* disaster; (*acidente*) accident; (*de avião*) crash.
desastroso/a [dʒizaʃ'trozu/ɔza] *adj* disastrous.
desatar [dʒiza'ta*] *vt* (*nó*) to undo, untie ♦ *vi*: **~ a fazer** to begin to do; **~ a chorar** to burst into tears; **~ a rir** to burst out laughing.
desatarraxar [dʒizataxa'ʃa*] *vt* to unscrew.
desatencioso/a [dʒizatẽ'sjozu/ɔza] *adj* inattentive; (*descortês*) impolite.
desatender [dʒizatẽ'de*] *vt* (*não fazer caso de*) to pay no attention to, ignore ♦ *vi*: **~ a** to ignore.
desatento/a [dʒiza'tẽtu/a] *adj* inattentive.
desatinado/a [dʒizatʃi'nadu/a] *adj* crazy, wild ♦ *m/f* lunatic.
desatinar [dʒizatʃi'na*] *vi* to behave foolishly.
desatino [dʒiza'tʃinu] *m* (*loucura*) madness; (*ato*) folly.
desativar [dʒizatʃi'va*] *vt* (*firma, usina*) to shut down; (*veículos*) to withdraw from service; (*bomba*) to deactivate, defuse.
desatracar [dʒizatra'ka*] *vt* (*navio*) to unmoor; (*brigões*) to separate ♦ *vi* (*navio*) to cast off.
desatravancar [dʒizatravã'ka*] *vt* to clear.
desatrelar [dʒizatre'la*] *vt* to unhitch.
desatualizado/a [dʒizatwali'zadu/a] *adj* out of date; (*pessoa*) out of touch.
desautorizar [dʒizawtori'za*] *vt* (*prática*) to disallow; (*desacreditar*) to discredit; **~ alguém** (*tirar a autoridade de*) to undermine sb's authority.
desavença [dʒiza'vẽsa] *f* (*briga*) quarrel; (*discórdia*) disagreement; **em ~** at loggerheads.
desavergonhado/a [dʒizavexgo'ɲadu/a] *adj* insolent, impudent, shameless.
desavir-se [dʒiza'vixsi] (*irreg*: *como* **vir**) *vr*: **~ (com alguém em algo)** to quarrel *ou* disagree (with sb about sth).
desavisado/a [dʒizavi'zadu/a] *adj* careless.
desbancar [dʒiʒbã'ka*] *vt*: **~ alguém (em algo)** to outdo sb (in sth).
desbaratar [dʒiʒbara'ta*] *vt* to ruin; (*desperdiçar*) to waste, squander; (*vencer*) to crush; (*pôr em desordem*) to mess up.
desbarrigado/a [dʒiʒbaxi'gadu/a] *adj* flatbellied.
desbastar [dʒiʒbaʃ'ta*] *vt* (*cabelo, plantas*) to thin (out); (*vegetação*) to trim.
desbocado/a [dʒiʒbo'kadu/a] *adj* (*pessoa*) foul-mouthed, crude.
desbotar [dʒiʒbo'ta*] *vt* to discolour (*BRIT*), discolor (*US*) ♦ *vi* to fade.
desbragadamente [dʒiʒbragada'mẽtʃi] *adv* (*beber*) to excess; (*mentir*) blatantly.
desbravador(a) [dʒiʒbrava'do*(a)] *m/f* explorer.
desbravar [dʒiʒbra'va*] *vt* (*terras desconhecidas*) to explore.
desbundante [dʒiʒbũ'dãtʃi] (*col*) *adj* fantastic.
desbundar [dʒiʒbũ'da*] (*col*) *vt* to knock out ♦ *vi* to flip, freak out.
desbunde [dʒiʒ'bũdʒi] (*col*) *m* knockout.
desburocratizar [dʒiʒburokratʃi'za*] *vt*: **~ algo** to remove the bureaucracy from sth.
descabelar [dʒiʃkabe'la*] *vt*: **~ alguém** to mess up sb's hair; **~-se** *vr* to get one's hair messed up.
descabido/a [dʒiʃka'bidu/a] *adj* (*impróprio*) improper; (*inoportuno*) inappropriate.
descadeirado/a [dʒiʃkadej'radu/a] *adj* (*cansado*) weary; **ficar ~** (*com dor*) to get backache.
descalabro [dʒiʃka'labru] *m* disaster.
descalçar [dʒiʃkaw'sa*] *vt* (*sapatos*) to take off; **~-se** *vr* to take off one's shoes.
descalço/a [dʒiʃ'kawsu/a] *adj* barefoot.
descambar [dʒiʃkã'ba*] *vi*: **~ (de algo) para algo** to sink *ou* deteriorate (from sth) to sth; **~ para** *ou* **em** to degenerate into.
descampado [dʒiʃkã'padu] *m* open country.
descansado/a [dʒiʃkã'sadu/a] *adj* (*tranqüilo*) calm, quiet; (*vagaroso*) slow; **fique ~** don't worry; **pode ficar ~ que** ... you can rest assured that ....
descansar [dʒiʃkã'sa*] *vt* to rest; (*apoiar*) to lean ♦ *vi* to rest.
descanso [dʒiʃ'kãsu] *m* (*repouso*) rest; (*folga*) break; (*para prato*) mat; **sem ~** without a break.
descapitalização [dʒiʃkapitaliza'sãw] *f* (*COM*)

decapitalization.
descarado/a [dʒiʃka'radu/a] *adj* cheeky, impudent.
descaramento [dʒiʃkara'mẽtu] *m* cheek, impudence.
descarga [dʒiʃ'kaxga] *f* unloading; (*vaso sanitário*) flushing; (*MIL*) volley; (*ELET*) discharge; **dar a ~** to flush the toilet.
descarnado/a [dʒiʃkax'nadu/a] *adj* scrawny, skinny.
descaroçar [dʒiʃkaro'sa*] *vt* (*semente*) to seed; (*fruto*) to stone, core; (*algodão*) to gin.
descarregadouro [dʒiʃkaxega'doru] *m* wharf.
descarregamento [dʒiʃkaxega'mẽtu] *m* (*de carga*) unloading; (*ELET*) discharge.
descarregar [dʒiʃkaxe'ga*] *vt* (*carga*) to unload; (*ELET*) to discharge; (*aliviar*) to relieve; (*raiva*) to vent, give vent to; (*arma*) to fire ♦ *vi* to unload; (*bateria*) to run out; **~ a raiva em alguém** to take it out on sb.
descarrilhamento [dʒiʃkaxiʎa'mẽtu] *m* derailment.
descarrilhar [dʒiʃkaxi'ʎa*] *vt* to derail ♦ *vi* to run off the rails; (*fig*) to go off the rails.
descartar [dʒiʃkax'ta*] *vt* to discard; **~-se** *vr*: **~-se de** to get rid of.
descartável [dʒiʃkax'tavew] (*pl* **-eis**) disposable.
descascador [dʒiʃkaʃka'do*] *m* peeler.
descascar [dʒiʃkaʃ'ka*] *vt* (*fruta*) to peel; (*ervilhas*) to shell ♦ *vi* (*depois do sol*) to peel; **o feijão descascou** the skin came off the beans; **a cobra descascou** the snake shed its skin.
descaso [dʒiʃ'kazu] *m* disregard.
descendência [desẽ'dẽsja] *f* descendants *pl*, offspring *pl*.
descendente [desẽ'dẽtʃi] *adj* descending, going down ♦ *m/f* descendant.
descender [desẽ'de*] *vi*: **~ de** to descend from.
descentralização [dʒisẽtraliza'sãw] *f* decentralization.
descentralizar [dʒisẽtrali'za*] *vt* to decentralize.
descer [de'se*] *vt* (*escada*) to go (*ou* come) down; (*bagagem*) to take down ♦ *vi* (*saltar*) to get off; (*baixar*) to go (*ou* come) down; **~ a pormenores** to get down to details.
descida [de'sida] *f* descent; (*declive*) slope; (*abaixamento*) fall, drop.
desclassificação [dʒiʃklasifika'sãw] *f* disqualification.
desclassificar [dʒiʃklasifi'ka*] *vt* (*eliminar*) to disqualify; (*desacreditar*) to discredit.
descoberta [dʒiʃko'bɛxta] *f* discovery; (*invenção*) invention.
descoberto/a [dʒiʃko'bɛxtu/a] *pp de* **descobrir** ♦ *adj* (*nu*) bare, naked; (*exposto*) exposed; (*COM*: *conta*) overdrawn; (: *saldo, compra*) uncovered ♦ *m* overdraft; **a ~** openly; **pôr** *ou* **sacar a ~** (*conta*) to overdraw.
descobridor(a) [dʒiʃkobri'do*(a)] *m/f* discoverer; (*explorador*) explorer.
descobrimento [dʒiʃkobri'mẽtu] *m* discovery.
descobrir [dʒiʃko'bri*] *vt* to discover; (*tirar a cobertura de*) to uncover; (*panela*) to take the lid off; (*averiguar*) to find out; (*enigma*) to solve.
descolar [dʒiʃko'la*] *vt* to unstick; (*cól*: *arranjar*) to get hold of; (: *dar*) to give ♦ *vi*: **a criança não descola da mãe** the child won't leave its mother's side.
descoloração [dʒiʃkolora'sãw] *f* discolouration (*BRIT*), discoloration (*US*).
descolorante [dʒiʃkolo'rãtʃi] *adj* bleaching ♦ *m* bleach.
descolorar [dʒiʃkolo'ra*] *vt*, *vi* = **descorar**.
descolorir [dʒiʃkolo'ri*] *vt* to discolour (*BRIT*), discolor (*US*); (*cabelo*) to bleach ♦ *vi* to fade.
descomedimento [dʒiʃkomedʒi'mẽtu] *m* lack of moderation.
descompassado/a [dʒiʃkõpa'sadu/a] *adj* (*exagerado*) out of all proportion; (*ritmo*) out of step.
descompor (*irreg*: *como* **pôr**) *vt* to disarrange; (*insultar*) to abuse; (*repreender*) to scold, tell off; (*fisionomia*) to distort, twist; **~-se** *vr* (*desordinar-se*) to fall into disarray; (*fisionomia*) to be twisted; (*desarrumar-se*) to expose o.s.
descomposto/a [dʒiʃkõ'poʃtu/'pɔʃta] *pp de* **descompor** ♦ *adj* (*desalinhado*) dishevelled; (*fisionomia*) twisted.
descompostura [dʒiʃkõpoʃ'tura] *f* (*repreensão*) dressing-down; (*insulto*) abuse; **passar uma ~ em alguém** (*repreender*) to give sb a dressing-down; (*insultar*) to hurl abuse at sb.
descompressão [dʒiʃkõpre'sãw] *f* decompression.
descomprometido/a [dʒiʃkõprome'tʃidu/a] *adj* (*sem namorado*) free.
descomunal [dʒiʃkomu'naw] (*pl* **-ais**) *adj* (*fora do comum*) extraordinary; (*colossal*) huge, enormous.
desconcentrar [dʒiʃkõsẽ'tra*] *vt* to distract; **~-se** *vr* to lose one's concentration.
desconcertado/a [dʒiʃkõsex'tadu/a] *adj* disconcerted.
desconcertante [dʒiʃkõsex'tãtʃi] *adj* disconcerting.
desconcertar [dʒiʃkõsex'ta*] *vt* (*atrapalhar*) to confuse, baffle; **~-se** *vr* to get upset.
desconexo/a [dʒiʃko'nɛksu/a] *adj* (*desunido*) disconnected, unrelated; (*incoerente*) incoherent.
desconfiado/a [dʒiʃkõ'fjadu/a] *adj* suspicious, distrustful ♦ *m/f* suspicious person.
desconfiança [dʒiʃkõ'fjãsa] *f* suspicion, dis-

***NB**: European Portuguese adds the following consonants to certain words:* **b** (sú(b)dito, su(b)til); **c** (a(c)ção, a(c)cionista, a(c)to); **m** (inde(m)ne); **p** (ado(p)ção, ado(p)tar); *for further details see p. xiii.*

trust.

desconfiar [dʒiʃkõ'fja*] *vi* to be suspicious; ~ **de alguém** (*não ter confiança em*) to distrust sb; (*suspeitar*) to suspect sb; ~ **que** ... to have the feeling that ....

desconforme [dʒiʃkõ'fɔxmi] *adj* disagreeing, at variance.

desconfortável [dʒiʃkõfox'tavew] (*pl* **-eis**) *adj* uncomfortable.

desconforto [dʒiʃkõ'foxtu] *m* discomfort.

descongelar [dʒiʃkõʒe'la*] *vt* (*degelar*) to thaw out; ~**-se** *vr* (*derreter-se*) to melt.

descongestionante [dʒiʃkõʒeʃtʃjo'nãtʃi] *adj*, *m* decongestant.

descongestionar [dʒiʃkõʃeʃtʃjo'na*] *vt* (*cabeça, trânsito*) to clear; (*rua, cidade*) to relieve congestion in.

desconhecer [dʒiʃkoɲe'se*] *vt* (*ignorar*) not to know; (*não reconhecer*) not to recognise; (*um benefício*) not to acknowledge; (*não admitir*) not to accept.

desconhecido/a [dʒiʃkoɲe'sidu/a] *adj* unknown ♦ *m/f* stranger.

desconhecimento [dʒiʃkoɲesi'mẽtu] *m* ignorance.

desconjuntado/a [dʒiʃkõʒũ'tadu/a] *adj* disjointed; (*ossos*) dislocated.

desconjuntar [dʒiʃkõʒũ'ta*] *vt* (*ossos*) to dislocate; ~**-se** *vr* to come apart.

desconsideração [dʒiʃkõsidera'sãw] *f*: ~ **(de algo)** disregard (for sth).

desconsiderar [dʒiʃkõside'ra*] *vt*: ~ **alguém** to show a lack of consideration for sb; ~ **algo** to fail to take sth into consideration.

desconsolado/a [dʒiʃkõso'ladu/a] *adj* miserable, disconsolate.

desconsolador(a) [dʒiʃkõsola'do*(a)] *adj* distressing.

desconsolar [dʒiʃkõso'la*] *vt* to sadden, depress; ~**-se** *vr* to despair.

descontar [dʒiʃkõ'ta*] *vt* (*abater*) to deduct; (*não levar em conta*) to discount; (*não fazer caso de*) to make light of.

descontentamento [dʒiʃkõtẽta'mẽtu] *m* discontent; (*desprazer*) displeasure.

descontentar [dʒiʃkõtẽ'ta*] *vt* to displease.

descontente [dʒiʃkõ'tẽtʃi] *adj* discontented, dissatisfied.

descontínuo/a [dʒiʃkõ'tʃinwu/a] *adj* broken.

desconto [dʒiʃ'kõtu] *m* discount; **com** ~ at a discount; **dar um** ~ (*fig*) to make allowances.

descontração [dʒiʃkõtra'sãw] *f* casualness.

descontraído/a [dʒiʃkõtra'idu/a] *adj* casual, relaxed.

descontrair [dʒiʃkõtra'i*] *vt* to relax; ~**-se** *vr* to relax.

descontrolar-se [dʒiʃkõtro'laxsi] *vr* (*situação*) to get out of control; (*pessoa*) to lose one's self-control.

descontrole [dʒiʃkõ'troli] *m* lack of control.

desconversar [dʒiʃkõvex'sa*] *vi* to change the subject.

descorar [dʒiʃko'ra*] *vt* to discolour (*BRIT*), discolor (*US*) ♦ *vi* to pale, fade.

descortês/esa [dʒiʃkox'teʃ/teza] *adj* rude, impolite.

descortesia [dʒiʃkoxte'zia] *f* rudeness, impoliteness.

descortinar [dʒiʃkoxtʃi'na*] *vt* (*retrato*) to unveil; (*avistar*) to catch sight of; (*notar*) to notice.

descoser [dʒiʃko'ze*] *vt* (*descosturar*) to unstitch; (*rasgar*) to rip apart; ~**-se** *vr* to come apart at the seams.

descosturar [dʒiʃkoʃtu'ra*] (*BR*) *vt* to unstitch; (*rasgar*) to pull apart; ~**-se** *vr* to come apart at the seams.

descrédito [dʒiʃ'krɛdʒitu] *m* discredit.

descrença [dʒiʃ'krẽsa] *f* disbelief, incredulity.

descrente [dʒiʃ'krẽtʃi] *adj* sceptical (*BRIT*), skeptical (*US*) ♦ *m/f* sceptic (*BRIT*), skeptic (*US*).

descrer [dʒiʃ'kre*] (*irreg*: *como* **crer**) *vt* to disbelieve ♦ *vi*: ~ **de** not to believe in.

descrever [dʒiʃkre've*] *vt* to describe.

descrição [dʒiʃkri'sãw] (*pl* **-ões**) *f* description.

descritivo/a [dʒiʃkri'tʃivu/a] *adj* descriptive.

descrito/a [dʒiʃ'kritu/a] *pp de* **descrever**.

descubro [dʒiʃ'kubru] *etc vb V* **descobrir**.

descuidado/a [dʒiʃkwi'dadu/a] *adj* careless.

descuidar [dʒiʃkwi'da*] *vt* to neglect ♦ *vi*: ~ **de** to neglect, disregard.

descuido [dʒiʃ'kwidu] *m* (*falta de cuidado*) carelessness; (*negligência*) neglect; (*erro*) oversight, slip; **por** ~ inadvertently.

desculpa [dʒiʃ'kuwpa] *f* (*pretexto, escusa*) excuse; (*perdão*) pardon; **pedir ~s a alguém por** *ou* **de algo** to apologise to sb for sth.

desculpar [dʒiʃkuw'pa*] *vt* (*justificar*) to excuse; (*perdoar*) to pardon, forgive; ~**-se** *vr* to apologize; ~ **algo a alguém** to forgive sb for sth; **desculpe!** (I'm) sorry, I beg your pardon.

desculpável [dʒiʃkuw'pavew] (*pl* **-eis**) *adj* excusable.

desde ['deʒdʒi] *prep* (*tempo*) from, since; (*lugar*) from ♦ *conj*: ~ **que** since; ~ **então** from that time, ever since; ~ **há muito** for a long time (now); ~ **já** (*de agora*) from now; (*imediatamente*) at once, right now; ~ ... **a** ... from ... to ....

desdém [deʒ'dẽ] *m* scorn, disdain.

desdenhar [deʒde'ɲa*] *vt* to scorn, disdain.

desdenhoso/a [deʒdeɲozu/ɔza] *adj* disdainful, scornful.

desdentado/a [dʒiʒdẽ'tadu/a] *adj* toothless.

desdigo [dʒiʒ'dʒigu] *etc vb V* **desdizer**.

desdisse [dʒiʒ'dʒisi] *etc vb V* **desdizer**.

desdita [dʒiʒ'dʒita] *f* (*desventura*) misfortune; (*infelicidade*) unhappiness.

desdizer [dʒiʒdʒi'ze*] (*irreg*: *como* **dizer**) *vt* to contradict; ~**-se** *vr* to go back on one's word.

desdobramento [dʒiʒdobra'mẽtu] *m* (*de aventura, crise*) ramification; (*de obra etc*)

spin-off; (*COM*: *de conta*) breakdown.
desdobrar [dʒiʒdo'bra*] *vt* (*abrir*) to unfold; (*esforços*) to increase, redouble; (*tropas*) to deploy; (*COM*: *conta*) to break down; (*bandeira*) to unfurl; (*dividir em grupos*) to split up; **~-se** *vr* to unfold; (*empenhar-se*) to work hard, make a big effort.
deseducar [dʒizedu'ka*] *vt*: **~ alguém** to neglect sb's education.
desejar [dese'ʒa*] *vt* to want, desire; **~ ardentemente** to long for; **que deseja?** what would you like?; **~ algo a alguém** to wish sb sth.
desejável [dese'ʒavew] (*pl* **-eis**) *adj* desirable.
desejo [de'zeʒu] *m* wish, desire.
desejoso/a [deze'ʒozu/ɔza] *adj*: **~ de algo** wishing for sth; **~ de fazer** keen to do.
deselegância [dʒizele'gãsja] *f* lack of elegance.
deselegante [dʒizele'gãtʃi] *adj* inelegant.
desemaranhar [dʒizimara'ɲa*] *vt* to disentangle.
desembainhar [dʒizẽbaj'ɲa*] *vt* (*espada*) to draw.
desembalar [dʒizẽba'la*] *vt* to unwrap.
desembaraçado/a [dʒizẽbara'sadu/a] *adj* (*livre*) free, clear; (*desinibido*) uninhibited, free and easy; (*expedito*) efficient; (*cabelo*) untangled.
desembaraçar [dʒizẽbara'sa*] *vt* (*livrar*) to free; (*COM*: *navio, remessa*) to clear; (*cabelo*) to untangle; **~-se** *vr* (*desinibir-se*) to lose one's inhibitions; (*tornar-se expedito*) to show initiative; **~-se de** to get rid of.
desembaraço [dʒizẽba'rasu] *m* liveliness; (*facilidade*) ease; (*confiança*) self-assurance; **~ alfandegário** customs clearance.
desembarcar [dʒizẽbax'ka*] *vt* (*carga*) to unload; (*passageiros*) to let off ♦ *vi* to disembark.
desembargador(a) [dʒizẽbaxga'do*(a)] *m/f* High Court judge.
desembarque [dʒizẽ'baxki] *m* landing, disembarkation; **"~"** (*no aeroporto*) "arrivals".
desembestado/a [dʒizẽbeʃ'tadu/a] *adj*: **sair ~** to rush off *ou* out.
desembocadura [dʒizẽboka'dura] *f* mouth.
desembocar [dʒizẽbo'ka*] *vi*: **~ em** (*rio*) to flow into; (*rua*) to lead into.
desembolsar [dʒizẽbow'sa*] *vt* to spend.
desembolso [dʒizẽ'bowsu] *m* expenditure.
desembrulhar [dʒizẽbru'ʎa*] *vt* to unwrap.
desembuchar [dʒizẽbu'ʃa*] (*col*) *vt* to get off one's chest ♦ *vi* to get things off one's chest.
desempacotar [dʒizẽpako'ta*] *vt* to unpack.
desempatar [dʒizẽpa'ta*] *vt* to decide ♦ *vi* to decide the match (*ou* race *etc*).
desempate [dʒizẽ'patʃi] *m*: **partida de ~** (*jogo*) play-off, decider.
desempenar [dʒizẽpe'na*] *vt* (*endireitar*) to straighten; **~-se** *vr* to stand up straight.
desempenhar [dʒizẽpe'ɲa*] *vt* (*cumprir*) to carry out, fulfil (*BRIT*), fulfill (*US*); (*papel*) to play.
desempenho [dʒizẽ'pɛɲu] *m* performance; (*de obrigações etc*) fulfilment (*BRIT*), fulfillment (*US*).
desemperrar [dʒizẽpe'xa*] *vt, vi* to loosen.
desempregado/a [dʒizẽpre'gadu/a] *adj* unemployed ♦ *m/f* unemployed person.
desempregar-se [dʒizẽpre'gaxsi] *vr* to lose one's job.
desemprego [dʒizẽ'pregu] *m* unemployment.
desencadear [dʒizẽka'dʒja*] *vt* to unleash; (*despertar*) to provoke, trigger off ♦ *vi* (*chuva*) to pour; **~-se** *vr* to break loose; (*tempestade*) to break.
desencaixado/a [dʒizẽkaj'ʃadu/a] *adj* misplaced.
desencaixar [dʒizẽkaj'ʃa*] *vt* to put out of joint; (*deslocar*) to dislodge, gouge out; **~-se** *vr* to become dislodged.
desencaixotar [dʒizẽkajʃo'ta*] *vt* to unpack.
desencalhar [dʒizẽka'ʎa*] *vt* (*navio*) to refloat ♦ *vi* to be refloated; (*col*: *moça*) to find a husband.
desencaminhar [dʒizẽkami'ɲa*] *vt* to lead astray; (*dinheiro*) to embezzle; **~-se** *vr* to go astray.
desencantar [dʒizẽkã'ta*] *vt* to disenchant; (*desiludir*) to disillusion.
desencardir [dʒizẽkax'dʒi*] *vt* to clean.
desencargo [dʒizẽ'kaxgu] *m* fulfilment (*BRIT*), fulfillment (*US*); **para ~ de consciência** to clear one's conscience.
desencarregar-se [dʒizẽkaxe'gaxsi] *vr* (*de obrigação*) to discharge o.s.
desencavar [dʒizẽka'va*] *vt* to unearth.
desencontrar [dʒizẽkõ'tra*] *vt* to keep apart; **~-se** *vr* (*não se encontrar*) to miss each other; (*perder-se um do outro*) to lose each other; **~-se de** to miss; to get separated from.
desencontro [dʒizẽ'kõtru] *m* failure to meet.
desencorajar [dʒizẽkora'ʒa*] *vt* to discourage.
desencostar [dʒizẽkoʃ'ta*] *vt* to move away; **~-se** *vr*: **~-se de** to move away from.
desenfastiar [dʒizẽfaʃ'tʃja*] *vt* to amuse; **~-se** *vr* to amuse o.s.
desenferrujar [dʒizẽfexu'za*] *vt* (*metal*) to clean the rust off; (*pernas*) to stretch; (*língua*) to brush up.
desenfreado/a [dʒizẽ'frjadu/a] *adj* wild.
desenganado/a [dʒizẽga'nadu/a] *adj* (*sem cura*) incurable; (*desiludido*) disillusioned.
desenganar [dʒizẽga'na*] *vt*: **~ alguém** to disillusion sb; (*de falsas crenças*) to open sb's eyes; (*doente*) to give up hope of curing; **~-se** *vr* to become disillusioned; (*sair de erro*) to realize the truth.
desengano [dʒizẽ'ganu] *m* disillusionment; (*desapontamento*) disappointment.

NB: *European Portuguese adds the following consonants to certain words:* **b** (sú(b)dito, su(b)til); **c** (a(c)ção, a(c)cionista, a(c)to); **m** (inde(m)ne); **p** (ado(p)ção, ado(p)tar); *for further details see p. xiii.*

desengarrafar [dʒizẽgaxa'fa*] *vt* (*trânsito*) to unblock; (*vinho*) to pour out.
desengatar [dʒizẽga'ta*] *vt* to unhitch; (FERRO) to uncouple.
desengonçado/a [dʒizẽgõ'sadu/a] *adj* (*mal-seguro*) rickety; (*pessoa*) ungainly.
desengrenado/a [dʒizẽgre'nadu/a] *adj* (AUTO) out of gear, in neutral.
desengrenar [dʒizẽgre'na*] *vt* to disengage; (*carro*) to put in neutral.
desengrossar [dʒizẽgro'sa*] *vt* to thin.
desenhar [deze'ɲa*] *vt* to draw; (TEC) to design; **~-se** *vr* (*destacar-se*) to stand out; (*figurar-se*) to take shape.
desenhista [deze'ɲiʃta] *m/f* (TEC) designer.
desenho [de'zɛɲu] *m* drawing; (*modelo*) design; (*esboço*) sketch; (*plano*) plan; **~ animado** cartoon; **~ industrial** industrial design.
desenlace [dʒizẽ'lasi] *m* outcome.
desenredar [dʒizẽxe'da*] *vt* to disentangle; (*mistério*) to unravel; (*questão*) to sort out, resolve; (*dúvida*) to clear up; (*explicação*) to clarify; **~-se** *vr*: **~-se de algo** to extricate o.s. from sth; **~ alguém de algo** to extricate sb from sth.
desenrolar [dʒizẽxo'la*] *vt* to unroll; (*narrativa*) to develop; **~-se** *vr* to unfold.
desentender [dʒizẽtẽ'de*] *vt* (*não entender*) to misunderstand; **~-se** *vr*: **~-se com** to have a disagreement with.
desentendido/a [dʒizẽtẽ'dʒidu/a] *adj*: **fazer-se de ~** to pretend not to understand.
desentendimento [dʒizẽtẽdʒi'mẽtu] *m* misunderstanding.
desenterrar [dʒizẽte'xa*] *vt* (*cadáver*) to exhume; (*tesouro*) to dig up; (*descobrir*) to bring to light.
desentoado/a [dʒizẽ'twadu/a] *adj* (*desafinado*) out of tune.
desentranhar [dʒizẽtra'ɲa*] *vt* to disembowel; (*raiz*) to draw out; (*lembranças*) to dredge up; (*mistério*) to fathom.
desentrosado/a [dʒizẽtro'zadu/a] *adj* unintegrated.
desentupir [dʒizẽtu'pi*] *vt* to unblock.
desenvolto/a [dʒizẽ'vowtu/a] *adj* (*desembaraçado*) self-assured, confident; (*desinibido*) uninhibited.
desenvoltura [dʒizẽvow'tura] *f* (*desembaraço*) self-confidence.
desenvolver [dʒizẽvow've*] *vt* to develop; **~-se** *vr* to develop.
desenvolvido/a [dʒizẽvow'vidu/a] *adj* developed.
desenvolvimento [dʒizẽvowvi'mẽtu] *m* development; (*crescimento*) growth; **país em ~** developing country.
desenxabido/a [dʒizẽʃa'bidu/a] *adj* dull.
desequilibrado/a [dʒizekili'bradu/a] *adj* unbalanced.
desequilibrar [dʒizekili'bra*] *vt* (*pessoa*) to throw off balance; (*objeto*) to tip over; (*fig*) to unbalance; **~-se** *vr* to lose one's balance; to tip over.
desequilíbrio [dʒizeki'librju] *m* imbalance.
deserção [dezex'sãw] *f* desertion.
desertar [desex'ta*] *vt* to desert, abandon ♦ *vi* to desert.
deserto/a [de'zɛxtu/a] *adj* deserted ♦ *m* desert.
desertor(a) [dezex'to*(a)] *m/f* deserter.
desesperado/a [dʒizeʃpe'radu/a] *adj* desperate; (*furioso*) furious.
desesperador(a) [dʒizeʃpera'do*(a)] *adj* desperate; (*enfurecedor*) maddening.
desesperança [dʒizeʃpe'rãsa] *f* despair.
desesperançar [dʒizeʃperã'sa*] *vt*: **~ alguém** to make sb despair.
desesperar [dʒizeʃpe'ra*] *vt* to drive to despair; (*enfurecer*) to infuriate; **~-se** *vr* to despair; (*enfurecer-se*) to become infuriated.
desespero [dʒizeʃ'peru] *m* despair, desperation; (*raiva*) fury; **levar ao ~** to drive to despair.
desestabilizar [dʒizeʃtabili'za*] *vt* to destabilize.
desestimulador(a) [dʒizeʃtʃimula'do*(a)] *adj* discouraging.
desestimular [dʒizeʃtʃimu'la*] *vt* to discourage.
desfaçatez [dʒiʃfasa'teʒ] *f* impudence, cheek.
desfalcar [dʒiʃfaw'ka*] *vt* (*aparelho de jantar*) to spoil; (*dinheiro*) to embezzle; (*reduzir*): **~ (de)** to reduce (by); **~ uma firma em $400** to embezzle $400 from a firm.
desfalecer [dʒiʃfale'se*] *vt* (*enfraquecer*) to weaken ♦ *vi* (*enfraquecer*) to weaken; (*desmaiar*) to faint.
desfalecimento [dʒiʃfalesi'mẽtu] *m* (*enfraquecimento*) weakening; (*desmaio*) faint.
desfalque [dʒiʃ'fawki] *m* (*de dinheiro*) embezzlement; (*diminuição*) reduction.
desfavor [dʒiʃfa'vo*] *m* disfavour (BRIT), disfavor (US).
desfavorável [dʒiʃfavo'ravew] (*pl* **-eis**) *adj* unfavourable (BRIT), unfavorable (US).
desfavorecer [dʒiʃfavore'se*] *vt* to discriminate against.
desfazer [dʒiʃfa'ze*] (*irreg*: *como* **fazer**) *vt* (*costura*) to undo; (*dúvidas*) to dispel; (*agravo*) to redress; (*grupo*) to break up; (*contrato*) to dissolve; (*noivado*) to break off ♦ *vi*: **~ de alguém** to belittle sb; **~-se** *vr* (*desaparecer*) to vanish; (*tecido*) to come to pieces; (*grupo*) to break up; (*vaso*) to break; **~-se de** (*livrar-se*) to get rid of; **~-se em lágrimas/gentilezas** to burst into tears/go out of one's way to please.
desfechar [dʒiʃfe'ʃa*] *vt* (*disparar*) to fire; (*setas*) to shoot; (*golpe*) to deal; (*insultos*) to hurl.
desfecho [dʒiʃ'feʃu] *m* ending, outcome.
desfeita [dʒiʃ'fejta] *f* affront, insult.
desfeito/a [dʒiʃ'fejtu/a] *pp de* **desfazer** ♦ *adj* (*desmanchado*) undone; (*cama*) unmade; (*contrato*) broken.

desferir [dʒiʃfe'ri*] *vt* (*golpe*) to strike; (*sons*) to emit; (*lançar*) to throw.

desfiar [dʒiʃ'fja*] *vt* (*tecido*) to unravel; (*galinha*) to strip; **~-se** *vr* to become frayed; **~ o rosário** to say one's rosary.

desfiguração [dʒiʃfigura'sãw] *f* distortion.

desfigurar [dʒiʃfigu'ra*] *vt* (*pessoa, cidade*) to disfigure; (*texto*) to mutilate; **~-se** *vr* to be disfigured.

desfiladeiro [dʒiʃfila'dejru] *m* (*de montanha*) pass.

desfilar [dʒiʃfi'la*] *vi* to parade.

desfile [dʒiʃ'fili] *m* parade, procession.

desflorestamento [dʒiʃfloreʃta'mẽtu] *m* deforestation.

desflorestar [dʒiʃfloreʃ'ta*] *vt* to clear of forest.

desforra [dʒiʃ'fɔxa] *f* (*vingança*) revenge; (*reparação*) redress; **tirar ~** to get even.

desfraldar [dʒiʃfraw'da*] *vt* to unfurl.

desfranzir [dʒiʃfrã'zi*] *vt* to smooth out.

desfrutar [dʒiʃfru'ta*] *vt* to enjoy ♦ *vi*: **~ de** to enjoy; **~ de bom conceito** to have a good reputation, be well thought of.

desfrute [dʒiʃ'frutʃi] *m* (*deleite*) enjoyment; (*desplante*): **ter o ~ de fazer algo** to have the nerve to do sth.

desgarrado/a [dʒiʒga'xadu/a] *adj* stray; (*navio*) off course.

desgarrar-se [dʒiʒga'xaxsi] *vr*: **~ de** to stray from.

desgastante [dʒiʒgaʃ'tãtʃi] *adj* (*fig*) stressful.

desgastar [dʒiʒgaʃ'ta*] *vt* to wear away, erode; (*pessoa*) to wear out, get down; **~-se** *vr* to be worn away; (*pessoa*) to get worn out.

desgaste [dʒiʒ'gaʃtʃi] *m* wear and tear; (*mental*) stress.

desgostar [dʒiʒgoʃ'ta*] *vt* to upset ♦ *vi*: **~ de** to dislike; **~-se** *vr*: **~-se de** to lose one's liking for; **~-se com** to take offence at.

desgosto [dʒiʒ'goʃtu] *m* (*desprazer*) displeasure; (*pesar*) sorrow, unhappiness.

desgostoso/a [dʒiʒgoʃ'tozu/ɔza] *adj* sad, sorrowful.

desgraça [dʒiʒ'grasa] *f* (*desventura*) misfortune; (*miséria*) misery; (*desfavor*) disgrace.

desgraçado/a [dʒiʒgra'sadu/a] *adj* poor; (*col*: *admirável*) amazing ♦ *m/f* wretch; **estou com uma gripe desgraçada** (*col*) I've got a hell of a cold.

desgraçar [dʒiʒgra'sa*] *vt* to disgrace.

desgraceira [dʒiʒgra'sejra] *f* series of misfortunes.

desgravar [dʒiʒgra'va*] *vt* (*música*) to wipe, rub off.

desgrenhado/a [dʒiʒgre'ɲadu/a] *adj* dishevelled, tousled.

desgrenhar [dʒiʒgre'ɲa*] *vt* to tousle; **~-se** *vr* to get tousled.

desgrudar [dʒiʒgru'da*] *vt* to unstick ♦ *vi*: **~ de** to tear o.s. away from; **~ algo de algo** to take sth off sth.

desguarnecer [dʒiʒgwaxne'se*] *vt* to strip.

desguiar [dʒiʒ'gja*] (*col*) *vi* to go away.

desidratação [dʒizidrata'sãw] *f* dehydration.

desidratante [dʒizidra'tãtʃi] *adj* dehydrating.

desidratar [dʒizidra'ta*] *vt* to dehydrate.

design [dʒi'zãjn] *m* design.

designação [dezigna'sãw] (*pl* **-ões**) *f* designation; (*nomeação*) appointment.

designar [dezig'na*] *vt* to designate; (*nomear*) to name, appoint; (*dia, data*) to fix.

designer [dʒi'zajne*] (*pl* **~s**) *m/f* designer.

desígnio [de'zignju] *m* (*propósito*) purpose; (*intenção*) intention.

desigual [dezi'gwaw] (*pl* **-ais**) *adj* unequal; (*terreno*) uneven.

desigualdade [dʒizigwaw'dadʒi] *f* inequality.

desiludir [dʒizilu'dʒi*] *vt* (*desenganar*) to disillusion; (*causar decepção a*) to disappoint; **~-se** *vr* to lose one's illusions.

desilusão [dʒizilu'zãw] *f* disillusionment, disenchantment.

desimpedido/a [dʒizĩpe'dʒidu/a] *adj* free.

desimpedir [dʒizĩpe'dʒi*] *vt* (*desobstruir*) to unblock; (*trânsito*) to ease.

desinchar [dʒizin'ʃa*] *vt* (MED) to get rid of the swelling on ♦ *vi*: **meu pé desinchou** the swelling in my foot went down.

desincumbir-se [dʒizĩkũ'bixsi] *vr*: **~ de algo** to carry sth out.

desinfeccionar [dʒizĩfeksjo'na*] *vt* to disinfect.

desinfetante [dʒizĩfe'tãtʃi] (PT: **-ct-**) *adj, m* disinfectant.

desinfetar [dʒizĩfe'ta*] (PT: **-ct-**) *vt* to disinfect.

desinflamar [dʒizĩfla'ma*] *vt* to remove *ou* get rid of the inflammation on; **~-se** *vr* to become less inflamed.

desinibido/a [dʒizini'bidu/a] *adj* uninhibited.

desinibir [dʒizini'bi*] *vt* to make less inhibited; **~-se** *vr* to lose one's inhibitions.

desintegração [dʒizintegra'sãw] *f* disintegration, break-up.

desintegrar [dʒizĩte'gra*] *vt* to separate; **~-se** *vr* to disintegrate, fall to pieces.

desinteressado/a [dʒizĩtere'sadu/a] *adj* disinterested.

desinteressar [dʒizĩtere'sa*] *vt*: **~ alguém de algo** to make sb lose interest in sth; **~-se** *vr* to lose interest.

desinteresse [dʒizĩte'resi] *m* (*falta de interesse*) lack of interest.

desintoxicar [dʒizĩtoksi'ka*] *vt* to detoxify.

desistência [deziʃ'tẽsja] *f* giving up; (*cancelamento*) cancellation.

desistir [deziʃ'tʃi*] *vi* to give up; **~ de fumar**

NB: *European Portuguese adds the following consonants to certain words:* **b** (sú(b)dito, su(b)til); **c** (a(c)ção, a(c)cionista, a(c)to); **m** (inde(m)ne); **p** (ado(p)ção, ado(p)tar); *for further details see* *p. xiii.*

to stop smoking; **ele ia, mas no final desistiu** he was going, but in the end he gave up the idea *ou* he decided not to.
desjejum [dʒiʒe'ʒũ] *m* breakfast.
deslanchar [dʒiʒlã'ʃa*] *vi* (*carro*) to move off; (*projeto*) to get off the ground, take off.
deslavado/a [dʒiʒla'vadu/a] *adj* (*pessoa, atitude*) shameless; (*mentira*) blatant.
desleal [dʒiʒle'aw] (*pl* **-ais**) *adj* disloyal.
deslealdade [dʒiʒleaw'dadʒi] *f* disloyalty.
desleixado/a [dʒiʒlej'ʃadu/a] *adj* sloppy.
desleixo [dʒiʒ'lejʃu] *m* sloppiness.
desligado/a [dʒiʒli'gadu/a] *adj* (*eletricidade*) off; (*pessoa*) absent-minded; **estar ~** to be miles away.
desligar [dʒiʒli'ga*] *vt* (TEC) to disconnect; (*luz, TV, motor*) to switch off; (*telefone*) to hang up; **~-se** *vr*: **~-se de algo** (*afastar-se*) to leave sth; (*problemas etc*) to turn one's back on sth; **não desligue** (TEL) hold the line.
deslizante [dʒiʒli'zãtʃi] *adj* slippery.
deslizar [dʒiʒli'za*] *vi* to slide; (*por acidente*) to slip; (*passar de leve*) to glide.
deslize [dʒiʒ'lizi] *m* (*lapso*) lapse; (*escorregadela*) slip.
deslocado/a [dʒiʒlo'kadu/a] *adj* (*membro*) dislocated; (*desambientado*) out of place.
deslocamento [dʒiʒloka'mẽtu] *m* moving; (*de membro*) dislocation; (*de funcionário*) transfer.
deslocar [dʒiʒlo'ka*] *vt* (*mover*) to move; (*articulação*) to dislocate; (*funcionário*) to transfer; **~-se** *vr* (*mover-se*) to move; (*membro*) to be dislocated; **eu me desloquei até lá à toa** I went all the way there for nothing.
deslumbrado/a [dʒiʒlũ'bradu/a] *adj* (*ofuscado*) dazzled; (*maravilhado*) amazed ♦ *m/f* impressionable person.
deslumbramento [dʒiʒlũbra'mẽtu] *m* dazzle; (*fascinação*) fascination.
deslumbrante [dʒiʒlũ'brãtʃi] *adj* (*ofuscante*) dazzling; (*casa, festa*) amazing.
deslumbrar [dʒiʒlũ'bra*] *vt* (*ofuscar*) to dazzle; (*maravilhar*) to amaze; (*fascinar*) to fascinate ♦ *vi* (*ofuscar*) to be dazzling; (*maravilhar*) to be amazing; **~-se** *vr*: **~-se com** to be fascinated by.
deslustrar [dʒiʒluʃ'tra*] *vt* to tarnish.
desmaiado/a [dʒiʒma'jadu/a] *adj* (*sem sentidos*) unconscious; (*cor*) pale.
desmaiar [dʒiʒma'ja*] *vi* to faint.
desmaio [dʒiʒ'maju] *m* faint.
desmamar [dʒiʒma'ma*] *vt* to wean.
desmancha-prazeres [dʒiʒ'manʃa-] *m/f inv* kill-joy, spoilsport.
desmanchar [dʒiʒman'ʃa*] *vt* (*costura*) to undo; (*contrato*) to break; (*noivado*) to break off; (*penteado*) to mess up; **~-se** *vr* (*costura*) to come undone.
desmantelar [dʒiʒmãte'la*] *vt* (*demolir*) to demolish; (*desmontar*) to dismantle, take apart.
desmarcar [dʒiʒmax'ka*] *vt* (*compromisso*) to cancel.
desmascarar [dʒiʒmaʃka'ra*] *vt* to unmask.
desmatamento [dʒiʒmata'mẽtu] *m* deforestation.
desmatar [dʒiʒma'ta*] *vt* to clear the forest from.
desmazelado/a [dʒiʒmaze'ladu/a] *adj* slovenly, untidy.
desmazelar-se [dʒiʒmaze'laxsi] *vr* to get untidy.
desmedido/a [dʒiʒme'dʒidu/a] *adj* excessive.
desmembramento [dʒiʒmẽbra'mẽtu] *m* dismemberment.
desmembrar [dʒiʒmẽ'bra*] *vt* to dismember.
desmemoriado/a [dʒiʒmemo'rjadu/a] *adj* forgetful.
desmentido [dʒiʒmẽ'tʃidu] *m* (*negação*) denial; (*contradição*) contradiction.
desmentir [dʒiʒmẽ'tʃi*] *vt* (*contradizer*) to contradict; (*negar*) to deny.
desmerecer [dʒiʒmere'se*] *vt* (*não merecer*) not to deserve; (*desfazer de*) to belittle.
desmesurado/a [dʒiʒmezu'radu/a] *adj* immense, enormous.
desmilingüido/a [dʒiʒmilĩ'gwidu/a] (*col*) *adj* spent.
desmiolado/a [dʒiʒmjo'ladu/a] *adj* brainless; (*esquecido*) forgetful.
desmistificar [dʒiʒmiʃtʃifi'ka*] *vt* to demystify; **~ alguém** to remove the mystery surrounding sb.
desmitificar [dʒiʒmitʃifi'ka*] *vt*: **~ algo/alguém** to dispel the myth(s) surrounding sth/sb.
desmontar [dʒiʒmõ'ta*] *vt* (*máquina*) to take to pieces ♦ *vi* (*do cavalo*) to dismount, get off.
desmoralização [dʒiʒmoraliza'sãw] *f* demoralization.
desmoralizante [dʒiʒmorali'zãtʃi] *adj* demoralizing.
desmoralizar [dʒiʒmorali'za*] *vt* to demoralize.
desmoronamento [dʒiʒmorona'mẽtu] *m* collapse.
desmoronar [dʒiʒmoro'na*] *vt* to knock down ♦ *vi* to collapse.
desmotivado/a [dʒiʒmotʃi'vadu/a] *adj* despondent.
desmunhecar [dʒiʒmuɲe'ka*] (*col*) *vi* (*declarar-se homossexual*) to come out; (*fazer gestos efeminados*) to be camp.
desnatar [dʒiʒna'ta*] *vt* to skim.
desnaturado/a [dʒiʒnatu'radu/a] *adj* inhumane ♦ *m/f* monster.
desnecessário/a [dʒiʒnese'sarju/a] *adj* unnecessary.
desnível [dʒiʒ'nivew] *m* unevenness; (*fig*) difference.
desnorteado/a [dʒiʒnox'tʃjadu/a] *adj* (*perturbado*) bewildered, confused; (*desori-*

entado) off course.
desnortear [dʒiʒnox'tʃja*] *vt* (*desorientar*) to throw off course; (*perturbar*) to bewilder; **~-se** *vr* to lose one's way; (*perturbar-se*) to become confused.
desnudar [dʒiʒnu'da*] *vt* to strip; (*revelar*) to expose; **~-se** *vr* to undress.
desnutrição [dʒiʒnutri'sãw] *f* malnutrition.
desnutrido/a [dʒiʒnu'tridu/a] *adj* malnourished.
desobedecer [dʒizobede'se*] *vt* to disobey.
desobediência [dʒizobe'dʒjẽsja] *f* disobedience.
disobediente [dʒizobe'dʒjẽtʃi] *adj* disobedient.
desobrigar [dʒizobri'ga*] *vt*: **~ (de)** to free (from); **~ de fazer algo** to free from doing sth.
desobstruir [dʒizobiʃ'trwi*] *vt* to unblock.
desocupação [dʒizokupa'sãw] *f* (*de casa*) vacating; (*falta de ocupação*) leisure; (*desemprego*) unemployment.
desocupado/a [dʒizoku'padu/a] *adj* (*casa*) empty, vacant; (*disponível*) free; (*sem trabalho*) unemployed.
desocupar [dʒizoku'pa*] *vt* (*casa*) to vacate; (*liberar*) to free.
desodorante [dʒizodo'rãtʃi] (*PT*: **-dorizante**) *m* deodorant.
desodorizar [dʒizodori'za*] *vt* to deodorize.
desolação [dezola'sãw] *f* (*consternação*) grief; (*de um lugar*) desolation.
desolado/a [dezo'ladu/a] *adj* (*consternado*) distressed; (*lugar*) desolate.
desolar [dezo'la*] *vt* (*consternar*) to distress; (*lugar*) to devastate.
desonestidade [dezoneʃtʃi'dadʒi] *f* dishonesty.
desonesto/a [dezo'nɛʃtu/a] *adj* dishonest.
desonra [dʒi'zõxa] *f* dishonour (*BRIT*), dishonor (*US*); (*descrédito*) disgrace.
desonrar [dʒizõ'xa*] *vt* (*infamar*) to disgrace; (*mulher*) to seduce; **~-se** *vr* to disgrace o.s.
desonroso/a [dʒizõ'xozu/ɔza] *adj* dishonourable (*BRIT*), dishonorable (*US*).
desopilar [dʒizopi'la*] *vt* (*MED*) to flush out; (*mente*) to clear.
desoprimir [dʒizopri'mi*] *vt* to relieve; **~-se** *vr* to be relieved.
desordeiro/a [dʒizox'dejru/a] *adj* troublemaking ♦ *m/f* troublemaker, hooligan.
desordem [dʒi'zoxdẽ] *f* disorder, confusion; **em ~** (*casa*) untidy.
desordenar [dʒizoxde'na*] *vt* (*tirar da ordem*) to put out of order; (*desarrumar*) to mess up.
desorganização [dʒizoxganiza'sãw] *f* disorganization.
desorganizar [dʒizoxgani'za*] *vt* to disorganize; (*dissolver*) to break up; **~-se** *vr* to become disorganized; to break up.
desorientação [dʒizorjẽta'sãw] *f* bewilderment, confusion.
desorientar [dʒizorjẽ'ta*] *vt* (*desnortear*) to throw off course; (*perturbar*) to confuse; (*desvairar*) to unhinge; **~-se** *vr* (*perder-se*) to lose one's way; (*perturbar-se*) to get confused; (*desvairar-se*) to go mad.
desossar [dʒizo'sa*] *vt* (*galinha*) to bone.
desovar [dʒizo'va*] *vt* to lay; (*peixe*) to spawn.
despachado/a [dʒiʃpa'ʃadu/a] *adj* (*pessoa*) efficient.
despachante [dʒiʃpa'ʃãtʃi] *m/f* (*de mercadorias*) forwarding agent; (*de documentos*) agent (*who handles official bureaucracy*).
despachar [dʒiʃpa'ʃa*] *vt* (*expedir*) to dispatch, send off; (*atender, resolver*) to deal with; (*despedir*) to sack ♦ *vi* (*funcionário*) to work; **~-se** *vr* to hurry (up).
despacho [dʒiʃ'paʃu] *m* dispatch; (*de negócios*) handling; (*nota em requerimento*) ruling; (*reunião*) consultation; (*macumba*) witchcraft.
desparafusar [dʒiʃparafu'sa*] *vt* to unscrew.
despeço [dʒiʃ'pɛsu] *etc vb V* **despedir**.
despedaçar [dʒiʃpeda'sa*] *vt* (*quebrar*) to smash; (*rasgar*) to tear apart; **~-se** *vr* to smash; (*rasgar-se*) to tear.
despedida [dʒiʃpe'dʒida] *f* (*adeus*) farewell; (*de trabalhador*) dismissal.
despedir [dʒiʃpe'dʒi*] *vt* (*de emprego*) to dismiss, sack; **~-se** *vr*: **~-se (de)** to say goodbye (to).
despeitado/a [dʒiʃpej'tadu/a] *adj* spiteful; (*ressentido*) resentful.
despeito [dʒiʃ'pejtu] *m* spite; **a ~ de** in spite of, despite.
despejar [dʒiʃpe'ʒa*] *vt* (*água*) to pour; (*esvaziar*) to empty; (*inquilino*) to evict.
despejo [dʒiʃ'peʒu] *m* (*de casa*) eviction; **quarto de ~** junk room.
despencar [dʒiʃpẽ'ka*] *vi* to fall down, tumble down.
despender [dʒiʃpẽ'de*] *vt* (*dinheiro*) to spend; (*energia*) to expend.
despenhadeiro [dʒiʃpeɲa'dejro] *m* cliff, precipice.
despensa [dʒiʃ'pẽsa] *f* larder.
despentear [dʒiʃpẽ'tʃja*] *vt* (*cabelo: sem querer*) to mess up; (*: de propósito*) to let down; **~-se** *vr* to mess one's hair up; to let one's hair down.
despercebido/a [dʒiʃpexse'bidu/a] *adj* unnoticed.
desperdiçar [dʒiʃpexdʒi'sa*] *vt* to waste; (*dinheiro*) to squander.
desperdício [dʒiʃpex'dʒisju] *m* waste.
despersonalizar [dʒiʃpexsonali'za*] *vt* to depersonalize.
despersuadir [dʒiʃpexswa'dʒi*] *vt*: **~ alguém de fazer algo** to dissuade sb from doing sth.

NB: *European Portuguese adds the following consonants to certain words:* **b** (sú(b)dito, su(b)til); **c** (a(c)ção, a(c)cionista, a(c)to); **m** (inde(m)ne); **p** (ado(p)ção, ado(p)tar); *for further details see p. xiii.*

despertador [dʒiʃpexta'do*] *m* (*tb*: *relogio* ~) alarm clock.
despertar [dʒiʃpex'ta*] *vt* (*pessoa*) to wake; (*suspeitas*, *interesse*) to arouse; (*reminiscências*) to revive; (*apetite*) to whet ♦ *vi* to wake up, awake ♦ *m* awakening.
desperto/a [dʒiʃ'pɛxtu/a] *adj* awake.
despesa [dʒiʃ'peza] *f* expense; **~s** *fpl* expenses, costs; **~s antecipadas** prepayments; **~s gerais** (*COM*) overheads; **~s mercantis** sales and marketing expenses; **~s não-operacionais** non-operating expenses *ou* costs; **~s operacionais** operating expenses *ou* costs; **~s tributárias** (*de uma empresa*) corporation tax.
despido/a [dʒiʃ'pidu/a] *adj* (*nu*) naked, bare; (*livre*) free.
despir [dʒiʃ'pi*] *vt* (*roupa*) to take off; (*pessoa*) to undress; (*despojar*) to strip; **~-se** *vr* to undress.
despistar [dʒiʃpiʃ'ta*] *vt* to throw off the scent.
desplante [dʒiʃ'plãtʃi] *m* (*fig*) nerve.
despojado/a [dʒiʃpo'ʒadu/a] *adj* (*pessoa*) unambitious; (*lugar*) spartan, basic.
despojar [dʒiʃpo'ʒa*] *vt* (*casas*) to loot, sack; (*pessoas*) to rob; **~ alguém de algo** to strip sb of sth.
despojo [dʒiʃ'poʒu] *m* loot, booty; **~s** *mpl*: **~s mortais** mortal remains.
despoluir [dʒiʃpo'lwi*] *vt* to clean up.
despontar [dʒiʃpõ'ta*] *vi* to emerge; (*sol*) to come out; (: *ao amanhecer*) to come up; **ao ~ do dia** at daybreak.
desporto [dʒiʃ'poxtu] (*PT*) *m* sport.
déspota ['dɛʃpota] *m/f* despot.
despotismo [deʃpo'tʃiʒmu] *m* despotism.
despovoado/a [dʒiʃpo'vwadu/a] *adj* uninhabited ♦ *m* wilderness.
despovoar [dʒiʃpo'vwa*] *vt* to depopulate.
desprazer [dʒiʃpra'ze*] *m* displeasure.
desprecavido/a [dʒiʃpreka'vidu/a] *adj* unprepared, careless.
despregar [dʒiʃpre'ga*] *vt* to take off, detach; **~-se** *vr* to come off; **~ os olhos de algo** to take one's eyes off sth.
desprender [dʒiʃprẽ'de*] *vt* (*soltar*) to loosen; (*desatar*) to unfasten; (*emitir*) to emit; **~-se** *vr* (*botão*) to come off; (*cheiro*) to be given off; **~-se dos braços de alguém** to extricate o.s. from sb's arms.
desprendido/a [dʒiʃprẽ'dʒidu/a] *adj* (*abnegado*) disinterested.
despreocupado/a [dʒiʃpreoku'pado/a] *adj* carefree, unconcerned; **com a notícia ele ficou mais ~** after hearing the news he was less concerned *ou* worried.
despreocupar [dʒiʃpreoku'pa*] *vt*: **~ alguém (de algo)** to set sb's mind at rest (about sth); **~-se** *vr*: **~-se (de algo)** to stop worrying (about sth).
despreparado/a [dʒiʃprepa'radu/a] *adj* unprepared.
despretensioso/a [dʒiʃpretẽ'sjozu/ɔza] *adj* unpretentious, modest.
desprestigiar [dʒiʃpreʃtʃi'ʒja*] *vt* to discredit; **~-se** *vr* to lose prestige.
desprevenido/a [dʒiʃpreve'nidu/a] *adj* unprepared, unready; **apanhar ~** to catch unawares.
desprezar [dʒiʃpre'za*] *vt* (*desdenhar*) to despise, disdain; (*não dar importância a*) to disregard, ignore.
desprezível [dʒiʃpre'zivew] (*pl* **-eis**) *adj* despicable.
desprezo [dʒiʃ'prezu] *m* scorn, contempt; **dar ao ~** to ignore.
desproporção [dʒiʃpropox'sãw] *f* disproportion.
desproporcionado/a [dʒiʃpropoxsjo'nadu/a] *adj* disproportionate; (*desigual*) unequal.
desproporcional [dʒiʃpropoxsjo'naw] *adj* disproportionate.
despropositado/a [dʒiʃpropozi'tadu/a] *adj* (*absurdo*) preposterous.
despropósito [dʒiʃpro'pɔzitu] *m* nonsense.
desproteger [dʒiʃprote'ʒe*] *vt* to leave unprotected.
desprover [dʒiʃpro've*] *vt*: **~ alguém (de algo)** to deprive sb (of sth).
desprovido/a [dʒiʃpro'vidu/a] *adj* deprived; **~ de** without.
despudorado/a [dʒiʃpudo'radu/a] *adj* shameless.
desqualificar [dʒiʃkwalifi'ka*] *vt* (*ESPORTE etc*) to disqualify; (*tornar indiguo*) to disgrace, lower.
desquitar-se [dʒiʃki'taxsi] *vr* to get a legal separation.
desquite [dʒiʃ'kitʃi] *m* legal separation.
desregrado/a [dʒiʒxe'gradu/a] *adj* (*desordenado*) disorderly, unruly; (*devasso*) immoderate.
desregrar-se [dʒiʒxe'graxsi] *vr* to run riot.
desregular [dʒiʒxegu'la*] *vt* (*mercado*) to deregulate.
desrespeitar [dʒiʒxeʃpej'ta*] *vt* to have no respect for.
desrespeito [dʒiʒxe'ʃpejtu] *m* disrespect.
desrespeitoso/a [dʒiʒxeʃpej'tozu/ɔza] *adj* disrespectful.
desse ['desi] *etc vb V* **dar** ♦ = **de** + **esse**.
destacado/a [dʒiʃta'kadu/a] *adj* outstanding; (*separado*) detached.
destacamento [dʒiʃtaka'mẽtu] *m* (*MIL*) detachment.
destacar [dʒiʃta'ka*] *vt* (*MIL*) to detail; (*separar*) to detach; (*fazer sobressair*) to highlight; (*enfatizar*) to emphasize ♦ *vi* to stand out; **~-se** *vr* to stand out; (*pessoa*) to be outstanding.
destampar [dʒiʃtã'pa*] *vt* to take the lid off.
destapar [dʒiʃta'pa*] *vt* to uncover.
destaque [dʒiʃ'taki] *m* distinction; (*pessoa, coisa*) highlight; (*do noticiário*) main point; **pessoa de ~** distinguished person.

deste ['deʃtʃi] *etc* = **de** + **este**; *V* **este**.
destemido/a [deʃte'midu/a] *adj* fearless, intrepid.
destemperar [dʒiʃtẽpe'ra*] *vt* (*diluir*) to dilute, weaken ♦ *vi* (*perder a cabeça*) to go mad.
desterrar [dʒiʃte'xa*] *vt* (*exilar*) to exile; (*fig*) to banish.
desterro [dʒiʃ'texu] *m* exile.
destilação [deʃtʃila'sãw] *f* distillation.
destilar [deʃtʃi'la*] *vt* to distil (BRIT), distill (US).
destilaria [deʃtʃila'ria] *f* distillery.
destinação [deʃtʃina'sãw] (*pl* **-ões**) *f* destination.
destinar [deʃ'tʃina*] *vt* to destine; **~-se** *vr*: **~-se a** to be intended for, be addressed to; **~ dinheiro para** to set aside money for.
destinatário/a [deʃtʃina'tarju/a] *m/f* addressee.
destino [deʃ'tʃinu] *m* destiny, fate; (*lugar*) destination; **com ~ a** bound for; **sem ~** *adj* aimless ♦ *adv* aimlessly.
destituição [deʃtʃitwi'sãw] (*pl* **-ões**) *f* (*demissão*) dismissal.
destituir [deʃtʃi'twi*] *vt* (*demitir*) to dismiss; **~ de** (*privar de*) to deprive of; (*demitir de*) to dismiss from.
destoante [dʒiʃto'ãtʃi] *adj* (*som*) discordant; (*opiniões*) diverging.
destoar [dʒiʃto'a*] *vi* (*som*) to jar; **~ (de)** (*não condizer*) to be out of keeping (with); (*traje, cor*) to clash (with); (*pessoa: discordar*) to disagree (with).
destorcer [dʒiʃtox'se*] *vt* to straighten out.
destrambelhado/a [dʒiʃtrãbe'ʎadu/a] *adj* scatterbrained.
destrancar [dʒiʃtrã'ka*] *vt* to unlock.
destratar [dʒiʃtra'ta*] *vt* to abuse, insult.
destravar [dʒiʃtra'va*] *vt* (*veículo*) to take the brake off; (*fechadura*) to unlatch.
destreza [deʃ'treza] *f* (*habilidade*) skill; (*agilidade*) dexterity.
destrinchar [dʒiʃtrĩ'ʃa*] *vt* (*desenredar*) to unravel; (*esmiuçar*) to treat in detail; (*problema*) to solve, resolve.
destro/a ['deʃtru/a] *adj* (*hábil*) skilful (BRIT), skillful (US); (*ágil*) agile; (*não canhoto*) right-handed.
destrocar [dʒiʃtro'ka*] *vt* to give back, return.
destroçar [dʒiʃtro'sa*] *vt* (*destruir*) to destroy; (*quebrar*) to smash, break; (*devastar*) to ruin, wreck.
destroços [dʒiʃ'trɔsuʃ] *mpl* wreckage *sg*.
destróier [dʒiʃ'trɔje*] *m* destroyer.
destronar [dʒiʃtro'na*] *vt* to depose.
destroncar [dʒiʃtrõ'ka*] *vt* to dislocate.
destruição [dʒiʃtrwi'sãw] *f* destruction.
destruidor(a) [dʒiʃtrwi'do*(a)] *adj* destructive.
destruir [dʒiʃ'trwi*] *vt* to destroy.
desumano/a [dʒizu'manu/a] *adj* inhuman; (*bárbaro*) cruel.
desunião [dʒizun'jãw] *f* disunity; (*separação*) separation.
desunir [dʒizu'ni*] *vt* (*separar*) to separate; (TEC) to disconnect; (*fig*: *desavir*) to cause a rift between.
desusado/a [dʒizu'zadu/a] *adj* (*não usado*) disused; (*incomum*) unusual.
desuso [dʒi'zuzu] *m* disuse; **em ~** outdated.
desvairado/a [dʒiʒvaj'radu/a] *adj* (*louco*) crazy, demented; (*desorientado*) bewildered.
desvairar [dʒiʒvaj'ra*] *vt* to drive mad.
desvalido/a [dʒiʒva'lidu/a] *adj* (*desamparado*) helpless; (*miserável*) destitute.
desvalorização [dʒiʒvaloriza'sãw] (*pl* **-ões**) *f* devaluation.
desvalorizar [dʒiʒvalori'za*] *vt* to devalue; **~-se** *vr* (*pessoa*) to undervalue o.s.; (*carro*) to depreciate; (*moeda*) to lose value.
desvanecer [dʒiʒvane'se*] *vt* (*envaidecer*) to make proud; (*sentimentos*) to dispel; **~-se** *vr* (*envaidecer-se*) to feel proud; (*sentimentos*) to vanish.
desvanecido/a [dʒiʒvane'sidu/a] *adj* proud.
desvantagem [dʒiʒvã'taʒẽ] (*pl* **-ns**) *f* disadvantage.
desvantajoso/a [dʒiʒvãta'ʒozu/ɔza] *adj* disadvantageous.
desvão [dʒiʒ'vãw] (*pl* **-s**) *m* loft.
desvario [dʒiʒva'riu] *m* madness, folly.
desvelar [dʒiʒve'la*] *vt* (*noiva, estátua*) to unveil; (*corpo, trama*) to uncover; (*segredo*) to reveal; (*problema*) to clarify; **~-se** *vr* (*pessoa*) to go to a lot of trouble.
desvelo [dʒiʒ'velu] *m* (*cuidado*) care; (*dedicação*) devotion.
desvencilhar [dʒiʒvẽsi'ʎa*] *vt* to free, extricate; **~-se** *vr* to free o.s., extricate o.s.
desvendar [dʒiʒvẽ'da*] *vt* (*tirar a venda*) to remove the blindfold from; (*revelar*) to disclose; (*mistério*) to solve.
desventura [dʒiʒvẽ'tura] *f* (*infortúnio*) misfortune; (*infelicidade*) unhappiness.
desventurado/a [dʒiʒvẽtu'radu/a] *adj* (*desafortunado*) unfortunate; (*infeliz*) unhappy ♦ *m/f* wretch.
desviar [dʒiʒ'vja*] *vt* to divert; (*golpe*) to deflect; (*dinheiro*) to embezzle; **~-se** *vr* (*afastar-se*) to turn away; **~-se de** (*evitar*) to avoid; **~-se do assunto** to digress; **~ os olhos** to look away; **desviei o carro para a direita** I pulled the car over to the right; **tentei desviá-lo do assunto** I tried to get *ou* steer him off the subject.
desvincular [dʒiʒvĩku'la*] *vt*: **~ algo de algo** to divest sth of sth; **~-se** *vr*: **~-se de algo** to disassociate o.s. from sth.
desvio [dʒiʒ'viu] *m* diversion, detour; (*curva*) bend; (*fig*) deviation; (*de dinheiro*) embezzle-

ment; (*de mercadorias*) misappropriation; (FERRO) siding; (*da coluna vertebral*) dislocation.
desvirar [dʒiʒvi'ra*] *vt* to turn back.
desvirginar [dʒiʒvixʒi'na*] *vt* to deflower.
desvirtuar [dʒiʒvix'twa*] *vt* (*fatos*) to misrepresent.
detalhadamente [detaʎada'mẽtʃi] *adv* in detail.
detalhado/a [deta'ʎadu/a] *adj* detailed.
detalhar [deta'ʎa*] *vt* to (give in) detail.
detalhe [de'taʎi] *m* detail; **entrar em ~** to go into detail.
detalhista [deta'ʎiʃta] *adj* painstaking, meticulous.
detectar [detek'ta*] *vt* to detect.
detective [detek'tivə] (PT) *m* = **detetive**.
detector [detek'to*] *m* detector.
detenção [detẽ'sãw] (*pl* **-ões**) *f* detention.
détente [de'tãtʃi] *f* détente.
detento/a [de'tẽtu/a] *m/f* detainee.
detentor(a) [detẽ'to*(a)] *m/f* (*de título, recorde*) holder.
deter [de'te*] (*irreg*: *como* **ter**) *vt* (*fazer parar*) to stop; (*prender*) to arrest, detain; (*documento*) to keep; (*reter*) to keep; (*conter*: *riso*) to contain; **~-se** *vr* (*parar*) to stop; (*ficar*) to stay; (*conter-se*) to restrain o.s.; **~-se em minúcias** *etc* to get bogged down in details *etc*.
detergente [detex'ʒẽtʃi] *m* detergent.
deterioração [deterjora'sãw] *f* deterioration.
deteriorar [deterjo'ra*] *vt* to spoil, damage; **~-se** *vr* to deteriorate; (*relações*) to worsen.
determinação [detexmina'sãw] *f* (*firmeza*) determination; (*decisão*) decision; (*ordem*) order; **por ~ de** by order of.
determinado/a [detexmi'nadu/a] *adj* (*resoluto*) determined; (*certo*) certain, given.
determinar [detexmi'na*] *vt* (*fixar, precisar*) to determine; (*decretar*) to order; (*resolver*) to decide (on); (*causar*) to cause; (*fronteiras*) to mark out.
detestar [deteʃ'ta*] *vt* to hate, detest.
detestável [deteʃ'tavew] (*pl* **-eis**) *adj* horrible, hateful.
detetive [dete'tʃivi] *m* detective.
detidamente [detʃida'mẽtʃi] *adv* carefully, thoroughly.
detido/a [de'tʃidu/a] *adj* (*preso*) under arrest; (*minucioso*) thorough.
detonação [detona'sãw] (*pl* **-ões**) *f* explosion.
detonar [deto'na*] *vi* to detonate, go off ♦ *vt* to detonate.
Detran [de'trã] (BR) *abr m* (= *Departamento de Trânsito*) *state traffic department*.
detrás [de'trajʃ] *adv* behind ♦ *prep*: **~ de** behind; **por ~** (from) behind.
detrimento [detri'mẽtu] *m*: **em ~ de** to the detriment of.
detrito [de'tritu] *m* debris *sg*; (*de comida*) remains *pl*; (*resíduo*) dregs *pl*.
deturpação [detuxpa'sãw] *f* corruption; (*de palavras*) distortion.
deturpar [detux'pa*] *vt* to corrupt; (*desfigurar*) to disfigure; **você deturpou minhas palavras** you twisted my words.
deu [dew] *vb V* **dar**.
deus(a) [dewʃ(sa)] *m/f* god/goddess; **D~ me livre!** God forbid!; **graças a D~** thank goodness; **se D~ quiser** God willing; **meu D~!** good Lord!; **D~ e o mundo** everybody.
deus-dará [-da'ra] *adv*: **viver ao ~** to live from hand to mouth; **estar ao ~** (*casa*) to be unattended.
deus-nos-acuda [-a'kuda] *m* commotion.
devagar [dʒiva'ga*] *adv* slowly ♦ *adj inv* (*col*): **ele é um cara tão ~** he's such an old fogey.
devagarinho [dʒivaga'riɲu] *adv* nice and slowly.
devanear [deva'nja*] *vt* to imagine, dream of ♦ *vi* to daydream; (*divagar*) to wander, digress.
devaneio [deva'neju] *m* daydream.
devassa [de'vasa] *f* investigation, inquiry.
devassado/a [deva'sadu/a] *adj* (*casa*) exposed.
devassidão [devasi'dãw] *f* debauchery.
devasso/a [de'vasu/a] *adj* dissolute.
devastar [devaʃ'ta*] *vt* (*destruir*) to devastate; (*arruinar*) to ruin.
deve ['dɛvi] *m* (*débito*) debit; (*coluna*) debit column.
devedor(a) [deve'do*(a)] *adj* (*pessoa*) in debt ♦ *m/f* debtor; **saldo ~** debit balance.
dever [de've*] *m* duty ♦ *vt* to owe ♦ *vi* (*suposição*): **deve (de) estar doente** he must be ill; (*obrigação*): **devo partir às oito** I must go at eight; **você devia ir ao médico** you should go to the doctor; **ele devia ter vindo** he should have come; **que devo fazer?** what shall I do?
deveras [dʒi'vɛraʃ] *adv* really, truly.
devidamente [devida'mẽtʃi] *adv* properly; (*preencher formulário etc*) duly.
devido/a [de'vidu/a] *adj* (*maneira*) proper; (*respeito*) due; **~ a** due to, owing to; **no ~ tempo** in due course.
devoção [devo'sãw] *f* devotion.
devolução [devolu'sãw] *f* devolution; (*restituição*) return; (*reembolso*) refund; **~ de impostos** tax rebate.
devolver [devow've*] *vt* to give back, return; (COM) to refund.
devorar [devo'ra*] *vt* to devour; (*destruir*) to destroy.
devotar [devo'ta*] *vt* to devote; **~-se** *vr*: **~-se a** to devote o.s. to.
devoto/a [de'vɔtu/a] *adj* devout ♦ *m/f* devotee.
dez [dɛʒ] *num* ten; *V tb* **cinco**.
dez. *abr* (= *dezembro*) Dec.
dezanove [deza'nɔvə] (PT) *num* = **dezenove**.
dezasseis [deza'sejʃ] (PT) *num* = **dezesseis**.
dezassete [deza'sɛtə] (PT) *num* = **dezessete**.
dezembro [de'zẽbru] (PT: **D-**) *m* December; *V tb* **julho**.

dezena [de'zena] *f*: **uma** ~ ten.
dezenove [deze'nɔvi] *num* nineteen; *V tb* **cinco**.
dezesseis [deze'sejʃ] *num* sixteen; *V tb* **cinco**.
dezessete [dezi'setʃi] *num* seventeen; *V tb* **cinco**.
dezoito [dʒi'zojtu] *num* eighteen; *V tb* **cinco**.
DF (*BR*) *abr* = **Distrito Federal**.
dia ['dʒia] *m* day; (*claridade*) daylight; ~ **a** ~ day by day; ~ **de anos** (*PT*) birthday; ~ **de folga** day off; ~ **santo** holy day; ~ **útil** weekday; **estar** *ou* **andar em** ~ (**com**) to be up to date (with); **de** ~ in the daytime, by day; **mais** ~ **menos** ~ sooner or later; **todo** ~, **todos os** ~**s** every day; **o** ~ **inteiro** all day (long); ~ **sim**, ~ **não** every other day; **de dois em dois** ~**s** every two days; **no** ~ **seguinte** the next day; ~ **após** ~ day after day; **do** ~ **para a noite** (*fig*) overnight; **bom** ~ good morning; **um** ~ **desses** one of these days; ~**s a fio** days on end; ~ **cheio/morto** busy/quiet *ou* slow day; **todo santo** ~ (*col*) every single day, day after day; **recebo por** ~ I'm paid by the day; **um bebê de** ~**s** a newborn baby; **ele está com os** ~**s contados** his days are numbered.
dia-a-dia *m* daily life, everyday life.
diabete(s) [dʒja'bɛtʃi(ʃ)] *f* diabetes.
diabético/a [dʒja'bɛtʃiku/a] *adj*, *m/f* diabetic.
diabo ['dʒjabu] *m* devil; **que** ~! (*col*) damn it!; **por que** ~ **...?** why the devil ...?; **o** ~ **é que ...** (*col*) the darnedest thing is that ...; **o** ~ **do eletricista não apareceu** (*col*) the damned electricity man didn't turn up; **estar um calor do** ~ (*col*) it's damned *ou* bloody (*!*) hot; **deu um trabalho dos** ~**s** (*col*) it was a hell of a job; **quente pra** ~ (*col*) damned hot; **dizer o** ~ **de alguém** to slag sb off.
diabólico/a [dʒja'bɔliku/a] *adj* diabolical.
diabrete [dʒja'bretʃi] *m* imp.
diabrura [dʒja'brura] *f* prank; ~**s** *fpl* mischief *sg*.
diacho ['dʒjaʃu] (*col*) *excl* hell!
diadema [dʒja'dema] *m* diadem; (*jóia*) tiara.
diáfano/a ['dʒjafanu/a] *adj* (*tecido*) diaphanous; (*águas*) clear.
diafragma [dʒja'fragma] *m* diaphragm; (*anticoncepcional*) diaphragm, cap.
diagnosticar [dʒjagnoʃtʃi'ka*] *vt* to diagnose.
diagnóstico [dʒjag'nɔʃtʃiku] *m* diagnosis.
diagonal [dʒjago'naw] (*pl* **-ais**) *adj*, *f* diagonal.
diagrama [dʒja'grama] *m* diagram.
diagramador(a) [dʒjagrama'do*(a)] *m/f* designer.
diagramar [dʒjagra'ma*] *vt* to design.
dialecto [dja'lɛktu] (*PT*) *m* = **dialeto**.
dialética [dʒja'lɛtʃika] *f* dialectics *sg*.
dialeto [dʒja'lɛtu] *m* dialect.
dialogar [dʒjalo'ga*] *vi*: ~ **(com alguém)** to talk (to sb); (*POL*) to have *ou* hold talks (with sb).
diálogo ['dʒjalogu] *m* dialogue; (*conversa*) talk, conversation.
diamante [dʒja'mãtʃi] *m* diamond.
diâmetro ['dʒjametru] *m* diameter.
diante ['dʒjãtʃi] *prep*: ~ **de** before; (*na frente de*) in front of; (*problemas etc*) in the face of; **e assim por** ~ and so on; **para** ~ forward.
dianteira [dʒjã'tejra] *f* front, vanguard; **tomar a** ~ to get ahead.
dianteiro/a [dʒjã'tejru/a] *adj* front.
diapasão [dʒjapa'zãw] (*pl* **-ões**) *m* (*afinador*) tuning fork; (*tom*) pitch; (*extensão de voz ou instrumento*) range.
diapositivo [dʒjapozi'tʃivu] *m* (*FOTO*) slide.
diária ['dʒjarja] *f* (*de hotel*) daily rate.
diário/a ['dʒjarju/a] *adj* daily ♦ *m* diary; (*jornal*) (daily) newspaper; (*COM*) daybook; ~ **de bordo** log book.
diarista [dʒja'riʃta] *m/f* casual worker, worker paid by the day; (*em casa*) cleaner.
diarréia [dʒja'xɛja] *f* diarrhoea (*BRIT*), diarrhea (*US*).
dica ['dʒika] (*col*) *f* hint.
dicção [dʒik'sãw] *f* diction.
dicionário [dʒisjo'narju] *m* dictionary.
dicionarista [dʒisjona'riʃta] *m/f* lexicographer.
dicotomia [dʒikoto'mia] *f* dichotomy.
didata [dʒi'data] (*PT*: **-ct-**) *m/f* teacher.
didática [dʒi'datʃika] (*PT*: **-ct-**) *f* education, teaching.
didático/a [dʒi'datʃiku/a] (*PT*: **-ct-**) *adj* (*livro*) educational; (*método*) teaching; (*modo*) didactic.
diesel ['dʒizew] *m*: **motor a** ~ diesel engine.
dieta ['dʒjɛta] *f* diet; **fazer** ~ to go on a diet.
dietético/a [dʒje'tɛtʃiku/a] *adj* dietetic.
dietista [dʒje'tʃiʃta] *m/f* dietician.
difamação [dʒifama'sãw] *f* (*falada*) slander; (*escrita*) libel.
difamador(a) [dʒifama'do*(a)] *adj* defamatory ♦ *m/f* slanderer.
difamar [dʒifa'ma*] *vt* to slander; (*por escrito*) to libel.
difamatório/a [dʒifama'tɔrju/a] *adj* defamatory.
diferença [dʒife'rẽsa] *f* difference; **ela tem uma** ~ **comigo** she's got something against me.
diferenciação [dʒiferẽsja'sãw] *f* (*tb*: *MAT*) differentiation.
diferenciar [dʒiferẽ'sja*] *vt* to differentiate.
diferente [dʒife'rẽtʃi] *adj* different; **estar** ~ **com alguém** to be at odds with sb.
diferimento [dʒiferi'mẽtu] *m* deferment.
diferir [dʒife'ri*] (*irreg*) *vi*: ~ **(de)** to differ (from) ♦ *vt* (*adiar*) to defer.
difícil [dʒi'fisiw] (*pl* **-eis**) *adj* (*trabalho, vida*) difficult, hard; (*problema, situação*) difficult;

NB*: European Portuguese adds the following consonants to certain words:* **b** (sú(b)dito, su(b)til); **c** (a(c)ção, a(c)cionista, a(c)to); **m** (inde(m)ne); **p** (ado(p)ção, ado(p)tar); *for further details see p. xiii.*

(*pessoa*: *intratável*) difficult; (: *exigente*) hard to please; (*improvável*) unlikely; **o ~ é** ... the difficult thing is ...; **acho ~ ela aceitar nossa proposta** I think it's unlikely she will accept our proposal; **falar ~** to use big words; **bancar o ~** to play hard to get.

dificílimo/a [dʒifi'silimu/a] *adj superl de* **difícil**.

dificilmente [dʒifisiw'mẽtʃi] *adv* with difficulty; (*mal*) hardly; (*raramente*) hardly ever; **~ ele poderá** ... it won't be easy for him to ....

dificuldade [dʒifikuw'dadʒi] *f* difficulty; (*aperto*) trouble; **em ~s** in trouble.

dificultar [dʒifikuw'ta*] *vt* to make difficult; (*complicar*) to complicate.

difteria [dʒifte'ria] *f* diphtheria.

difundir [dʒifũ'dʒi*] *vt* (*luz*) to diffuse; (*espalhar*) to spread; (*notícia*) to spread, circulate; (*idéias*) to disseminate.

difusão [dʒifu'zãw] *f* (*de luz*) diffusion; (*espalhamento*) spreading; (*de notícias*) circulation; (*de idéias*) dissemination.

difuso/a [dʒi'fuzu/a] *adj* diffuse.

diga ['dʒiga] *etc vb V* **dizer**.

digerir [dʒiʒe'ri*] *vt*, *vi* to digest.

digestão [dʒiʒeʃ'tãw] *f* digestion.

digital [dʒiʒi'taw] (*pl* **-ais**) *adj* digital; **impressão ~** fingerprint.

digitar [dʒiʒi'ta*] *vt* (COMPUT: *dados*) to key (in).

dígito ['dʒiʒitu] *m* digit.

digladiar [dʒigla'dʒja*] *vi* to fight, fence; **~-se** *vr*: **~ (com alguém)** to do battle (with sb).

dignar-se [dʒig'naxsi] *vr*: **~ de** to deign to, condescend to.

dignidade [dʒigni'dadʒi] *f* dignity.

dignificar [dʒignifi'ka*] *vt* to dignify.

digno/a ['dʒignu/a] *adj* (*merecedor*) worthy; (*nobre*) dignified.

digo ['dʒigu] *etc vb V* **dizer**.

digressão [dʒigre'sãw] (*pl* **-ões**) *f* digression.

dilaceração [dʒilasera'sãw] (*pl* **-ões**) *f* laceration.

dilacerante [dʒilase'rãtʃi] *adj* (*dor*) excruciating; (*cruel*) cruel.

dilacerar [dʒilase'ra*] *vt* to tear to pieces, lacerate; **~-se** *vr* to tear one another to pieces.

dilapidação [dʒilapida'sãw] *f* (*de casas etc*) demolition; (*de dinheiro*) squandering.

dilapidar [dʒilapi'da*] *vt* (*fortuna*) to squander; (*casa*) to demolish.

dilatação [dʒilata'sãw] *f* dilation.

dilatar [dʒila'ta*] *vt* to dilate, expand; (*prolongar*) to prolong; (*retardar*) to delay.

dilatório/a [dʒila'tɔrju/a] *adj* dilatory.

dilema [dʒi'lɛma] *m* dilemma.

diletante [dʒile'tãtʃi] *adj*, *m/f* amateur; (*pej*) dilettante.

diletantismo [dʒiletã'tʃiʒmu] *m* amateurism; (*pej*) dilettantism.

diligência [dʒili'ʒẽsja] *f* diligence; (*pesquisa*) inquiry; (*veículo*) stagecoach.

diligenciar [dʒiliʒẽ'sja*] *vt* to strive for; **~ (por) fazer** to strive to do.

diligente [dʒili'ʒẽtʃi] *adj* hardworking, industrious.

diluição [dʒilwi'sãw] *f* dilution.

diluir [dʒi'lwi*] *vt* to dilute.

dilúvio [dʒi'luvju] *m* flood.

dimensão [dʒimẽ'sãw] (*pl* **-ões**) *f* dimension; **dimensões** *fpl* measurements.

dimensionar [dʒimẽsjo'na*] *vt*: **~ algo** to calculate the size of sth; (*fig*) to assess the extent of sth.

diminuição [dʒiminwi'sãw] *f* reduction.

diminuir [dʒimi'nwi*] *vt* to reduce; (*som*) to turn down; (*interesse*) to lessen ♦ *vi* to lessen, diminish; (*preço*) to go down; (*dor*) to wear off; (*barulho*) to die down.

diminutivo/a [dʒiminu'tʃivu/a] *adj* diminutive ♦ *m* diminutive.

diminuto/a [dʒimi'nutu/a] *adj* minute, tiny.

Dinamarca [dʒina'maxka] *f* Denmark.

dinamarquês/quesa [dʒinamax'keʃ/'keza] *adj* Danish ♦ *m/f* Dane ♦ *m* (LING) Danish.

dinâmico/a [dʒi'namiku/a] *adj* dynamic.

dinamismo [dʒina'miʒmu] *m* (*fig*) energy, drive.

dinamitar [dʒinami'ta*] *vt* to blow up.

dinamite [dʒina'mitʃi] *f* dynamite.

dínamo ['dʒinamu] *m* dynamo.

dinastia [dʒinaʃ'tʃia] *f* dynasty.

dinda ['dʒĩda] (*col*) *f* godmother.

dinheirão [dʒiɲej'rãw] *m*: **um ~** loads *pl* of money.

dinheiro [dʒi'ɲejru] *m* money; **~ à vista** ready cash; **sem ~** penniless; **em ~** in cash; **~ em caixa** ready cash; **~ em espécie** cash; **~ vivo** hard cash.

dinossauro [dʒino'sawru] *m* dinosaur.

diocese [dʒjo'sɛzi] *f* diocese.

dióxido ['dʒjɔksidu] *m* dioxide; **~ de carbono** carbon dioxide.

DIP (BR) *abr m* = **Departamento de Imprensa e Propaganda**.

diploma [dʒip'lɔma] *m* diploma.

diplomacia [dʒiploma'sia] *f* diplomacy; (*fig*) tact.

diplomando/a [dʒiplo'mãdu/a] *m/f* diploma candidate.

diplomar [dʒiplo'ma*] *vt* to graduate; **~-se** *vr*: **~-se (em algo)** to get one's diploma (in sth).

diplomata [dʒiplo'mata] *m/f* diplomat.

diplomático/a [dʒiplo'matʃiku/a] *adj* diplomatic; (*discreto*) tactful.

dique ['dʒiki] *m* dam; (GEO) dike.

direção [dʒire'sãw] (PT: **-cç-**: *pl* **-ões**) *f* direction; (*endereço*) address; (AUTO) steering; (*administração*) management; (*comando*) leadership; (*diretoria*) board of directors; **em ~ a** towards.

directo/a [di'rɛktu/a] *etc* (PT) = **direto** *etc*.

direi [dʒi'rej] *etc vb V* **dizer**.

direita [dʒi'rejta] *f* (*mão*) right hand; (*lado*) right-hand side; (*POL*) right wing; **à ~** on the right; **"mantenha-se à ~"** "keep right".
direitinho [dʒirej'tʃiɲu] *adv* properly, just right; (*diretamente*) directly.
direitista [dʒirej'tʃiʃta] *adj* right-wing ♦ *m/f* right-winger.
direito/a [dʒi'rejtu/a] *adj* (*lado*) right-hand; (*mão*) right; (*honesto*) honest; (*devido*) proper; (*justo*) right, just ♦ *m* (*prerrogativa*) right; (*JUR*) law; (*de tecido*) right side ♦ *adv* (*em linha reta*) straight; (*bem*) right; (*de maneira certa*) properly; **~s** *mpl* rights; (*alfandegários*) duty *sg*; **~ civil** civil law; **~s autorais** copyright *sg*; **~s civis** civil rights; **~s de importação** import duty; **~s humanos** human rights; **livre de ~s** duty-free; **ter ~ a** to have a right to, be entitled to; **minha roupa está direita?/meu cabelo está ~?** are my clothes/is my hair all right?
diretas [dʒi'rɛtaʃ] *fpl* (*POL*) direct elections.
direto/a [dʒi'rɛtu/a] *adj* direct ♦ *adv* straight; **transmissão direta** (*TV*) live broadcast; **ir ~ ao assunto** to get straight to the point.
diretor(a) [dʒire'to*(a)] *adj* directing, guiding ♦ *m/f* (*COM, de cinema*) director; (*de jornal*) editor; (*de escola*) head teacher.
diretor(a)-gerente *m/f* managing director.
diretoria [dʒireto'ria] *f* (*cargo*) directorship; (*: em escola*) headship; (*direção: COM*) management; (*sala*) boardroom.
diretório [dʒire'tɔrju] *m* directorate; (*COMPUT*) directory; **~ acadêmico** students' union.
diretriz [dʒire'triʒ] *f* directive.
dirigente [dʒiri'ʒẽtʃi] *adj* (*classe*) ruling ♦ *m/f* (*de país, partido*) leader; (*diretor*) director; (*gerente*) manager.
dirigir [dʒiri'ʒi*] *vt* to direct; (*COM*) to manage, run; (*veículo*) to drive; (*atenção*) to turn ♦ *vi* to drive; **~-se** *vr*: **~-se a** (*falar com*) to speak to, address; (*ir, recorrer*) to go to; (*esforços*) to be directed towards.
dirimir [dʒiri'mi*] *vt* (*dúvida, contenda*) to settle, clear up.
discagem [dʒiʃ'kaʒẽ] *f* (*TEL*) dialling; **~ direta** direct dialling.
discar [dʒiʃ'ka*] *vt* to dial.
discente [dʒi'sẽtʃi] *adj V* **corpo**.
discernimento [dʒisexni'mẽtu] *m* discernment.
discernir [dʒisex'ni*] *vt* (*perceber*) to discern, perceive; (*diferenciar*) to discriminate, distinguish.
discernível [dʒisex'nivew] (*pl* **-eis**) *adj* discernible.
disciplina [dʒisi'plina] *f* discipline.
disciplinador(a) [dʒisiplina'do*(a)] *adj* disciplinary.
disciplinar [dʒisipli'na*] *vt* to discipline; **~-se** *vr* to discipline o.s.
discípulo/a [dʒi'sipulu/a] *m/f* disciple; (*aluno*) pupil.
disc-jóquei [dʒiʃk-] *m/f* disc jockey, DJ.
disco ['dʒiʃku] *m* disc; (*COMPUT*) disk; (*MÚS*) record; (*de telefone*) dial; **~ laser** (*máquina*) compact disc player, CD player; (*disco*) compact disc, CD; **~ flexível/rígido** (*COMPUT*) floppy/hard disk; **~ mestre** (*COMPUT*) master disk; **~ do sistema** system disk; **~ voador** flying saucer; **mudar o ~** (*col*) to change the subject.
discordância [dʒiʃkox'dasja] *f* disagreement; (*de opiniões*) difference.
discordante [dʒiʃkox'dãtʃi] *adj* divergent, conflicting.
discordar [dʒiʃkox'da*] *vi*: **~ de alguém em algo** to disagree with sb on sth.
discórdia [dʒiʃ'kɔxdʒja] *f* discord, strife.
discorrer [dʒiʃko'xe*] *vi*: **~ (sobre)** (*falar*) to talk (about).
discoteca [dʒiʃko'tɛka] *f* (*boate*) discotheque, disco (*col*); (*coleção de discos*) record library.
discotecário/a [dʒiʃkote'karju/a] *m/f* disc jockey, DJ.
discrepância [dʒiʃkre'pãsja] *f* discrepancy; (*desacordo*) disagreement.
discrepante [dʒiʃkre'pãtʃi] *adj* conflicting.
discrepar [dʒiʃkre'pa*] *vi*: **~ de** to differ from.
discreto/a [dʒiʃ'krɛtu/a] *adj* discreet; (*modesto*) modest; (*prudente*) shrewd; (*roupa*) plain, sober.
discrição [dʒiʃkri'sãw] *f* discretion, good sense.
discricionário/a [dʒiʃkrisjo'narju/a] *adj* discretionary.
discriminação [dʒiʃkrimina'sãw] *f* discrimination; (*especificação*) differentiation; **~ racial** racial discrimination.
discriminar [dʒiʃkrimi'na*] *vt* to distinguish ♦ *vi*: **~ entre** to discriminate between.
discriminatório/a [dʒiʃkrimina'tɔrju/a] *adj* discriminatory.
discursar [dʒiʃkux'sa*] *vi* (*em público*) to make a speech; (*falar*) to speak.
discurso [dʒiʃ'kuxsu] *m* speech; (*LING*) discourse.
discussão [dʒiʃku'sãw] (*pl* **-ões**) *f* (*debate*) discussion, debate; (*contenda*) argument.
discutir [dʒiʃku'tʃi*] *vt* to discuss ♦ *vi*: **~ (sobre algo)** (*debater*) to talk (about sth); (*contender*) to argue (about sth).
discutível [dʒiʃku'tʃivew] (*pl* **-eis**) *adj* debatable.
disenteria [dʒizẽte'ria] *f* dysentery.
disfarçar [dʒiʃfax'sa*] *vt* to disguise ♦ *vi* to pretend; **~-se** *vr*: **~-se em** *ou* **de algo** to disguise o.s. as sth.
disfarce [dʒiʃ'faxsi] *m* disguise; (*máscara*) mask.

***NB**: European Portuguese adds the following consonants to certain words:* **b** (sú(b)dito, su(b)til); **c** (a(c)ção, a(c)cionista, a(c)to); **m** (inde(m)ne); **p** (ado(p)ção, ado(p)tar); *for further details* *see p. xiii.*

disfasia [dʒiʃfa'zia] *f* (MED) speech defect.
disforme [dʒiʃ'fɔxmi] *adj* deformed, hideous.
disfunção [dʒiʃfũ'sãw] (*pl* **-ões**) *f* (MED) dysfunction.
disléticо/a [dʒiʒ'lɛtʃiku/a] *adj*, *m/f* dyslexic.
dislexia [dʒiʒlek'sia] *f* dyslexia.
disléxico/a [dʒiʒ'lɛksiku/a] *adj*, *m/f* dyslexic.
díspar ['dʒiʃpa*] *adj* dissimilar.
disparada [dʒiʃpa'rada] *f*: **dar uma ~** to surge ahead; **em ~** at full tilt.
disparado/a [dʒiʃpa'radu/a] *adj* very fast ♦ *adv* by a long way.
disparar [dʒiʃpa'ra*] *vt* to shoot, fire ♦ *vi* to fire; (*arma*) to go off; (*correr*) to shoot off, bolt.
disparatado/a [dʒiʃpara'tadu/a] *adj* silly, absurd.
disparate [dʒiʃpa'ratʃi] *m* nonsense, rubbish; (*ação*) blunder.
disparidade [dʒiʃpari'dadʒi] *f* disparity.
dispêndio [dʒiʃ'pẽdʒu] *m* expenditure.
dispendioso/a [dʒiʃpẽ'dʒjozu/ɔza] *adj* costly, expensive.
dispensa [dʒiʃ'pẽsa] *f* exemption; (REL) dispensation.
dispensar [dʒiʃpẽ'sa*] *vt* (*desobrigar*) to excuse; (*prescindir de*) to do without; (*conferir*) to grant.
dispensário [dʒiʃpẽ'sarju] *m* dispensary.
dispensável [dʒiʃpẽ'savew] (*pl* **-eis**) *adj* expendable.
dispepsia [dʒiʃpep'sia] *f* dyspepsia.
dispersão [dʒiʃpex'sãw] *f* dispersal.
dispersar [dʒiʃpex'sa*] *vt*, *vi* to disperse.
dispersivo/a [dʒiʃpex'sivu/a] *adj* (*pessoa*) scatterbrained.
disperso/a [dʒiʃ'pɛxsu/a] *adj* scattered.
displicência [dʒiʃpli'sensja] (BR) *f* (*descuido*) negligence, carelessness.
displicente [dʒiʃpli'sẽtʃi] *adj* careless.
dispo ['dʒiʃpu] *etc vb V* **despir**.
disponibilidade [dʒiʃponibili'dadʒi] *f* availability; (*finanças*) liquid *ou* available assets *pl*; **~ de caixa** cash in hand.
disponível [dʒiʃpo'nivew] (*pl* **-eis**) *adj* available.
dispor [dʒiʃ'po*] (*irreg*: *como* **pôr**) *vt* (*arranjar*) to arrange; (*colocar em ordem*) to put in order ♦ *vi*: **~ de** (*usar*) to have the use of; (*ter*) to have, own; (*pessoas*) to have at one's disposal; **~-se** *vr*: **~-se a** (*estar pronto a*) to be prepared to, be willing to; (*decidir*) to decide to; **~ sobre** to talk about; **não disponho de tempo para ...** I can't afford the time to ...; **disponha!** feel free!
disposição [dʒiʃpozi'sãw] (*pl* **-ões**) *f* arrangement; (*humor*) disposition; (*inclinação*) inclination; **à sua ~** at your disposal.
dispositivo [dʒiʃpozi'tʃivu] *m* (*mecanismo*) gadget, device; (*determinação de lei*) provision; (*conjunto de meios*): **~ de segurança** security operation; **~ intra-uterino** intrauterine device.
disposto/a [dʒiʃ'poʃtu/'pɔʃta] *pp de* **dispor** ♦ *adj* (*arranjado*) arranged; **estar ~ a** to be willing to; **estar bem ~** to look well; **sentir-se ~ a fazer algo** to feel like doing sth.
disputa [dʒiʃ'puta] *f* (*contenda*) dispute, argument; (*competição*) contest.
disputar [dʒiʃpu'ta*] *vt* to dispute; (*lutar por*) to fight over; (*concorrer a*) to compete for ♦ *vi* (*discutir*) to quarrel, argue; (*competir*) to compete; **~ uma corrida** to run a race.
disquete [dʒiʃ'ketʃi] *m* (COMPUT) floppy disk, diskette.
dissabor [dʒisa'bo*] *m* (*desgosto*) sorrow; (*aborrecimento*) annoyance.
disse ['dʒisi] *etc vb V* **dizer**.
dissecar [dʒise'ka*] *vt* to dissect.
disseminação [dʒisemina'sãw] *f* (*de pólen etc*) spread(ing); (*de idéias*) dissemination.
disseminar [dʒisemi'na*] *vt* to disseminate; (*espalhar*) to spread.
dissensão [dʒisẽ'sãw] *f* dissension, discord.
dissentir [dʒisẽ'tʃi*] *vi*: **~ de alguém (em algo)** to be in disagreement with sb (over sth); **~ de algo** (*não combinar*) to be at variance with sth.
disse-que-disse *m* gossip, tittle-tattle.
dissertação [dʒisexta'sãw] (*pl* **-ões**) *f* dissertation; (*discurso*) lecture.
dissertar [dʒisex'ta*] *vi* to speak.
dissidência [dʒisi'dẽsja] *f* (*divergência*) dissension; (*dissidentes*) dissidents *pl*: (*cisão*) split, difference of opinion.
dissidente [dʒisi'dẽtʃi] *adj*, *m/f* dissident.
dissídio [dʒi'sidʒu] *m* (JUR): **~ coletivo/individual** collective/individual dispute.
dissimilar [dʒisimi'la*] *adj* dissimilar.
dissimulação [dʒisimula'sãw] *f* (*fingimento*) pretence (BRIT), pretense (US); (*disfarce*) disguise.
dissimular [dʒisimu'la*] *vt* (*ocultar*) to hide; (*fingir*) to feign ♦ *vi* to dissemble.
dissinto [dʒi'sĩtu] *etc vb V* **dissentir**.
dissipação [dʒisipa'sãw] *f* waste, squandering.
dissipar [dʒisi'pa*] *vt* (*dispersar*) to disperse, dispel; (*malgastar*) to squander, waste; **~-se** *vr* to vanish.
disso ['dʒisu] = **de** + **isso**.
dissociar [dʒiso'sja*] *vt*: **~ algo (de/em algo)** to separate sth (from sth)/break sth up (into sth); **~-se** *vr*: **~-se de algo** to dissociate o.s. from sth.
dissolução [dʒisolu'sãw] *f* (*dissolvência*) dissolving; (*libertinagem*) debauchery; (*de casamento*) dissolution.
dissoluto/a [dʒiso'lutu/a] *adj* dissolute, debauched.
dissolver [dʒisow've*] *vt* to dissolve; (*dispersar*) to disperse; (*motim*) to break up.
dissonância [dʒiso'nãsja] *f* dissonance; (*discordância*) discord.
dissonante [dʒiso'nãtʃi] *adj* (*som*) dissonant, discordant; (*fig*) discordant.
dissuadir [dʒiswa'dʒi*] *vt* to dissuade; ~

alguém de fazer algo to talk sb out of doing sth, dissuade sb from doing sth.
dissuasão [dʒiswa'zãw] *f* dissuasion.
dissuasivo/a [dʒiswa'zivu/a] *adj* dissuasive.
distância [dʒiʃ'tãsja] *f* distance; **a grande ~** far away; **a 3 quilômetros de ~** 3 kilometres (*BRIT*) *ou* kilometers (*US*) away.
distanciamento [dʒiʃtãsja'mẽtu] *m* distancing.
distanciar [dʒiʃtã'sja*] *vt* (*afastar*) to distance, set apart; (*colocar por intervalos*) to space out; **~-se** *vr* to move away; (*fig*) to distance o.s.
distante [dʒiʃ'tãtʃi] *adj* distant, far-off; (*fig*) aloof.
distar [dʒiʃ'ta*] *vi* to be far away; **o aeroporto dista 10 quilômetros da cidade** the airport is 10 km away from the city.
distender [dʒiʃtẽ'de*] *vt* (*estender*) to expand; (*estirar*) to stretch; (*dilatar*) to distend; (*músculo*) to pull; **~-se** *vr* (*estender-se*) to expand; (*dilatar-se*) to distend.
distinção [dʒiʃtʃĩ'sãw] (*pl* **-ões**) *f* distinction; **fazer ~** to make a distinction.
distinguir [dʒiʃtʃĩ'gi*] *vt* (*diferenciar*) to distinguish, differentiate; (*avistar, ouvir*) to make out; (*enobrecer*) to distinguish; **~-se** *vr* to stand out; **~ algo de algo/entre** to distinguish sth from sth/between.
distintivo/a [dʒiʃtʃĩ'tʃivu/a] *adj* distinctive ♦ *m* (*insígnia*) badge; (*emblema*) emblem.
distinto/a [dʒiʃ'tʃĩtu/a] *adj* (*diferente*) different; (*eminente*) distinguished; (*claro*) distinct; (*refinado*) refined.
disto ['dʒiʃtu] = **de** + **isto**.
distorção [dʒiʃtox'sãw] (*pl* **-ões**) *f* distortion.
distorcer [dʒiʃtox'se*] *vt* to distort.
distorções [dʒiʃtox'sõjʃ] *fpl de* **distorção**.
distração [dʒiʃtra'sãw] (*PT*: **-cç-**: *pl* **-ões**) *f* (*alheamento*) absent-mindedness; (*divertimento*) pastime; (*descuido*) oversight.
distraído/a [dʒiʃtra'idu/a] *adj* absent-minded; (*não atento*) inattentive.
distrair [dʒiʃtra'i*] *vt* (*tornar desatento*) to distract; (*divertir*) to amuse; **~-se** *vr* to amuse o.s.
distribuição [dʒiʃtribwi'sãw] *f* distribution; (*de cartas*) delivery.
distribuidor(a) [dʒiʃtribwi'do*(a)] *m/f* distributor ♦ *m* (*AUTO*) distributor ♦ *f* (*COM*) distribution company, distributor.
distribuir [dʒiʃtri'bwi*] *vt* to distribute; (*repartir*) to share out; (*cartas*) to deliver.
distrito [dʒiʃ'tritu] *m* district; (*delegacia*) police station; **~ eleitoral** constituency; **~ federal** federal area.
distúrbio [dʒiʃ'tuxbju] *m* disturbance; **~s** *mpl* (*POL*) riots.
ditado [dʒi'tadu] *m* dictation; (*provérbio*) saying.
ditador [dʒita'do*] *m* dictator.
ditadura [dʒita'dura] *f* dictatorship.
ditame [dʒi'tami] *m* (*da consciência*) dictate; (*regra*) rule.
ditar [dʒi'ta*] *vt* to dictate; (*impor*) to impose.
ditatorial [dʒitato'rjaw] (*pl* **-ais**) *adj* dictatorial.
dito/a ['dʒitu/a] *pp de* **dizer** ♦ *m*: **~ espirituoso** witticism; **~ e feito** no sooner said than done.
dito-cujo (*pl* **ditos-cujos**) (*col*) *m* said person.
ditongo [dʒi'tõgu] *m* diphthong.
ditoso/a [dʒi'tozu/ɔza] *adj* (*feliz*) happy; (*venturoso*) lucky.
DIU *abr m* (= *dispositivo intra-uterino*) IUD.
diurético/a [dʒju'rɛtʃiku/a] *adj* diuretic ♦ *m* diuretic.
diurno/a ['dʒjuxnu/a] *adj* daytime *atr*.
divã [dʒi'vã] *m* couch, divan.
divagação [dʒivaga'sãw] (*pl* **-ões**) *f* (*andança*) wandering; (*digressão*) digression; (*devaneio*) rambling.
divagar [dʒiva'ga*] *vi* (*vaguear*) to wander; (*falar sem nexo*) to ramble (on); **~ do assunto** to wander off the subject, digress.
divergência [dʒivex'ʒẽsja] *f* divergence; (*desacordo*) disagreement.
divergente [dʒivex'ʒẽtʃi] *adj* divergent.
divergir [dʒivex'ʒi*] (*irreg*) *vi* to diverge; **~ (de alguém)** to disagree (with sb).
diversão [dʒivex'sãw] (*pl* **-ões**) *f* (*divertimento*) amusement; (*passatempo*) pastime.
diversidade [dʒivexsi'dadʒi] *f* diversity.
diversificação [dʒivexsifika'sãw] *f* diversification.
diversificar [dʒivexsifi'ka*] *vt* to diversify ♦ *vi* to vary.
diverso/a [dʒi'vɛxsu/a] *adj* (*diferente*) different; (*pl*) various.
diversões [divex'sõjʃ] *fpl de* **diversão**.
diversos/as [dʒi'vɛxsuʃ/aʃ] *adj* several ♦ *mpl* (*na contabilidade*) sundries.
divertido/a [dʒivex'tʃidu/a] *adj* amusing, funny.
divertimento [dʒivextʃi'mẽtu] *m* amusement, entertainment.
divertir [dʒivex'tʃi*] *vt* to amuse, entertain; **~-se** *vr* to enjoy o.s., have a good time.
dívida ['dʒivida] *f* debt; (*obrigação*) indebtedness; **contrair ~s** to run into debt; **~ externa** foreign debt.
dividendo [dʒivi'dẽdu] *m* dividend.
dividido/a [dʒivi'dʒidu/a] *adj* divided; **sentir-se ~ entre duas coisas** to feel torn between two things.
dividir [dʒivi'dʒi*] *vt* to divide; (*despesas, lucro, comida etc*) to share; (*separar*) to separate ♦ *vi* (*MAT*) to divide; **~-se** *vr* to divide, split up; **as opiniões se dividem** opinions are divided; **ele tem que se ~ entre**

***NB**: European Portuguese adds the following consonants to certain words:* **b** (sú(b)dito, su(b)til); **c** (a(c)ção, a(c)cionista, a(c)to); **m** (inde(m)ne); **p** (ado(p)ção, ado(p)tar); *for further details see p. xiii.*

a família e o trabalho he has to divide his time between the family and work; ~ **21 por 7** to divide 21 by 7; ~ **algo em 3 partes** to divide sth into 3 parts; ~ **algo pela metade** to divide sth in half *ou* in two.

divindade [dʒivĩ'dadʒi] *f* divinity.

divino/a [dʒi'vinu/a] *adj* divine; (*col*) gorgeous ♦ *m* Holy Ghost.

divirjo [dʒi'vixʒu] *etc vb V* **divergir**.

divisa [dʒi'viza] *f* (*emblema*) emblem; (*frase*) slogan; (*fronteira*) border; (*MIL*) stripe; **~s** *fpl* foreign exchange *sg*, foreign currency *sg*.

divisão [dʒivi'zãw] (*pl* **-ões**) *f* division; (*discórdia*) split; (*partilha*) sharing.

divisar [dʒivi'za*] *vt* (*avistar*) to see, make out.

divisível [dʒivi'zivew] (*pl* **-eis**) *adj* divisible.

divisões [dʒivi'zõjʃ] *fpl de* **divisão**.

divisória [dʒivi'zɔrja] *f* partition.

divisório/a [dʒivi'zɔrju/a] *adj* (*linha*) dividing.

divorciado/a [dʒivox'sjadu/a] *adj* divorced ♦ *m/f* divorcé(e).

divorciar [dʒivox'sja*] *vt* to divorce; **~-se** *vr* to get divorced.

divórcio [dʒi'vɔxsju] *m* divorce.

divulgação [dʒivuwga'sãw] *f* (*de notícias*) spread; (*de segredo*) divulging; (*de produto*) marketing.

divulgar [dʒivuw'ga*] *vt* (*notícias*) to spread; (*segredo*) to divulge; (*produto*) to market; (*tornar conhecido*) to publish; **~-se** *vr* to leak out.

dizer [dʒi'ze*] *vt* to say ♦ *m* saying; **~-se** *vr* to claim to be; **diz-se** *ou* **dizem que ...** it is said that ...; **diga-se de passagem** by the way; ~ **algo a alguém** (*informar, avisar*) to tell sb sth; (*falar*) to say sth to sb; ~ **a alguém que ...** to tell sb that ...; **o que você diz da minha sugestão?** what do you think of my suggestion?; ~ **para alguém fazer** to tell sb to do; **o filme não me disse nada** (*não interessou*) the film left me cold; **o nome não me diz nada** (*não significa*) the name means nothing to me; ~ **bem com** to go well with; **querer** ~ to mean; **quer** ~ that is to say; **nem é preciso** ~ that goes without saying; **não** ~ **coisa com coisa** to make no sense; **digo** (*ou seja*) I mean; **diga!** what is it?; **não diga!** you don't say!; **digamos** let's say; **bem que eu te disse, eu não disse?** I told you so; **ele tem dificuldade em acordar às sete, que dirá às cinco** he finds it difficult to wake at seven, let alone *ou* never mind five; **por assim** ~ so to speak; **até** ~ **chega** as much as possible.

dizimar [dʒizi'ma*] *vt* to decimate; (*herança*) to fritter away.

Djibuti [dʒibu'tʃi] *m*: **o** ~ Djibouti.

DNER (*BR*) *abr m* (= *Departamento Nacional de Estradas de Rodagem*) *national highways department*.

DNOCS (*BR*) *abr m* = **Departamento Nacional de Obras contra as Secas**.

DNPM (*BR*) *abr m* = **Departamento Nacional de Produção Mineral**.

do [du] = **de** + **o**.

dó [dɔ] *m* (*lástima*) pity; (*MÚS*) do; **ter** ~ **de** to feel sorry for.

doação [doa'sãw] (*pl* **-ões**) *f* donation, gift.

doador(a) [doa'do*(a)] *m/f* donor.

doar [do'a*] *vt* to donate, give.

dobra ['dɔbra] *f* fold; (*prega*) pleat; (*de calças*) turn-up.

dobradiça [dobra'dʒisa] *f* hinge.

dobradiço/a [dobra'dʒisu/a] *adj* flexible.

dobradinha [dobra'dʒiɲa] *f* (*CULIN*) tripe stew; (*col*: *dupla*) pair, partnership.

dobrar [do'bra*] *vt* (*duplicar*) to double; (*papel*) to fold; (*joelho*) to bend; (*esquina*) to turn, go round; (*fazer ceder*): ~ **alguém** to bring sb round ♦ *vi* (*duplicar-se*) to double; (*sino*) to toll; (*vergar*) to bend; **~-se** *vr* to double (up).

dobro ['dobru] *m* double.

DOC (*BR*) *abr f* = **Diretoria de Obras de Cooperação**.

doca ['dɔka] *f* (*NÁUT*) dock.

doce ['dosi] *adj* sweet; (*terno*) gentle ♦ *m* sweet; **ele é um** ~ he's a sweetie; **fazer** ~ (*col*) to play hard to get.

doce-de-coco (*pl* **doces-de-coco**) *m* (*pessoa*) sweetie.

doceiro/a [do'sejru/a] *m/f* sweet-seller.

docemente [dose'mẽtʃi] *adv* gently.

docência [do'sẽsja] *f* teaching.

docente [do'sẽtʃi] *adj* teaching; **o corpo** ~ teaching staff.

dócil ['dɔsiw] *adj* docile.

documentação [dokumẽta'sãw] *f* documentation; (*documentos*) papers *pl*.

documentar [dokumẽ'ta*] *vt* to document.

documentário/a [dokumẽ'tarju/a] *adj* documentary ♦ *m* documentary.

documento [doku'mẽtu] *m* document; **não é** ~ (*col*) it doesn't mean a thing.

doçura [do'sura] *f* sweetness; (*brandura*) gentleness.

Dodecaneso [dodeka'nɛzu] *m*: **o** ~ the Dodecanese.

dodói [do'dɔj] (*col*) *m*: **você tem ~?** does it hurt? ♦ *adj inv* ill, under the weather.

doença [do'ẽsa] *f* illness.

doente [do'ẽtʃi] *adj* ill, sick ♦ *m/f* sick person; (*cliente*) patient.

doentio/a [doẽ'tʃiu/a] *adj* (*pessoa*) sickly; (*clima*) unhealthy; (*curiosidade*) morbid.

doer [do'e*] *vi* to hurt, ache; ~ **a alguém** (*pesar*) to grieve sb; **dói ver tanta pobreza** it's sad to see so much poverty.

dogma ['dɔgma] *m* dogma.

dogmático/a [dog'matʃiku/a] *adj* dogmatic.

DOI (*BR*) *abr m* (= *Destacamento de Operações Internas*) *military secret police*.

Doi-Codi ['dɔi-'kɔdʒi] (*BR*) *abr m* (= *Departamento de Operações e Informações — Centro de Operação e Defesa Interna*) *secret police*

HQ during the military dictatorship.

doidão/dona [doj'dãw/'dɔna] (*pl* **-ões/-s**) *adj*: **(ser)** ~ (to be) completely crazy; **(estar)** ~ (to be) high.

doideira [doj'dejra] *f* madness, foolishness.

doidice [doj'dʒisi] *f* madness, foolishness.

doidivanas [dojdʒi'vanaʃ] *m/f inv* hothead.

doido/a ['dojdu/a] *adj* mad, crazy; ~ **por** mad/crazy about ♦ *m/f* madman/woman; ~ **de pedras** *or* **varrido** (*col*) raving loony.

doído/a [do'idu/a] *adj* sore, painful; (*moralmente*) hurt; (*que causa dor*) painful.

doidões [doj'dõjʃ] *adj pl de* **doidão**.

doidona [doj'dɔna] *f de* **doidão**.

doirar [doj'ra*] *vt* = **dourar**.

dois [dojʃ] *num* two; **conversa a** ~ tête-à-tête; *V tb* **cinco**.

dólar ['dɔla*] *m* dollar; ~ **oficial/paralelo** dollar at the official/black-market rate; ~-**turismo** dollar at the special tourist rate.

doleiro/a [do'lejru/a] *m/f* (black market) dollar dealer.

dolo ['dɔlu] *m* fraud.

dolorido/a [dolo'ridu/a] *adj* painful, sore; (*fig*) sorrowful.

dolorosa [dolo'rɔza] *f* bill.

doloroso/a [dolo'rozu/ɔza] *adj* painful.

dom [dõ] *m* gift; (*aptidão*) knack; **o** ~ **da palavra** the gift of the gab.

dom. *abr* (= *domingo*) Sun.

domador(a) [domado*(a)] *m/f* tamer.

domar [do'ma*] *vt* to tame.

doméstica [do'mɛʃtʃika] *f* maid.

domesticado/a [domeʃtʃi'kadu/a] *adj* domesticated; (*manso*) tame.

domesticar [domeʃtʃi'ka*] *vt* to domesticate; (*povo*) to tame.

doméstico/a [do'mɛʃtʃiku/a] *adj* domestic; (*vida*) home *atr*.

domiciliar [domisi'lja*] *adj* home *atr*.

domicílio [domi'silju] *m* home, residence; **vendas/entrega a** ~ home sales/delivery; **"entregamos a ~"** "we deliver".

dominação [domina'sãw] *f* domination.

dominador(a) [domina'do*(a)] *adj* (*pessoa*) domineering; (*olhar*) imposing ♦ *m/f* ruler.

dominante [domi'nãtʃi] *adj* dominant; (*predominante*) predominant.

dominar [domi'na*] *vt* to dominate; (*reprimir*) to overcome ♦ *vi* to dominate, prevail; ~-**se** *vr* to control o.s.

domingo [do'mĩgu] *m* Sunday; *V tb* **terça-feira**.

domingueiro/a [domĩ'gejru/a] *adj* Sunday *atr*; *V tb* **traje**.

Dominica [domi'nika] *f* Dominica.

dominicano/a [domini'kanu/a] *adj, m/f* Dominican; **República Dominicana** Dominican Republic.

domínio [do'minju] *m* (*poder*) power; (*dominação*) control; (*território*) domain; (*esfera*) sphere; ~ **próprio** self-control.

dom-juan [-'jwã] *m* ladies' man, Don Juan.

domo ['dɔmu] *m* dome.

dona ['dɔna] *f* (*proprietária*) owner; (*col*: *mulher*) lady; ~ **de casa** housewife; **D~ Luísa** *etc corresponde ao uso de Mrs ou Miss seguido do sobrenome da mulher em inglês.*

donatário/a [dona'tarju/a] *m/f* recipient.

donde ['dõdə] (*PT*) *adv* from where; (*daí*) thus; ~ **vem?** where do you come from?

dondoca [dõ'dɔka] (*col*) *f* society lady, lady of leisure.

dono ['donu] *m* (*proprietário*) owner.

donzela [dõ'zɛla] *f* (*mulher*) maiden.

dopar [do'pa*] *vt* to drug; ~-**se** *vr* (*atleta*) to take drugs.

DOPS (*BR*) *abr m* (= *Departamento de Ordem Política e Social*) *internal security agency*.

dor [do*] *f* ache; (*aguda*) pain; (*fig*) grief, sorrow; ~ **de cabeça** headache; ~ **de dentes** toothache; ~ **de estômago** stomach ache.

doravante [dora'vãtʃi] *adv* henceforth.

dor-de-cotovelo (*col*) *m* jealousy; **estar com** ~ to be jealous.

dormência [dox'mẽsja] *f* numbness.

dormente [dox'mẽtʃi] *adj* numb ♦ *m* (*FERRO*) sleeper.

dormida [dox'mida] *f* sleep; (*lugar*) place to sleep; **dar uma** ~ to have a sleep.

dormideira [doxmi'dejra] *f* drowsiness.

dorminhoco/a [doxmi'ɲoku/a] *adj* dozy ♦ *m/f* sleepyhead.

dormir [dox'mi*] *vi* to sleep; ~ **como uma pedra** *ou* **a sono solto** to sleep like a log *ou* soundly; **hora de** ~ bedtime; ~ **no ponto** (*fig*) to miss the boat; ~ **fora** to spend the night away.

dormitar [doxmi'ta*] *vi* to doze.

dormitório [doxmi'tɔrju] *m* bedroom; (*coletivo*) dormitory.

dorsal [dox'saw] (*pl* **-ais**) *adj V* **coluna**.

dorso ['doxsu] *m* back.

dos [duʃ] = **de** + **os**.

dosagem [do'zaʒẽ] *m* dosage.

dosar [do'za*] *vt* (*medicamento*) to judge the correct dosage of; (*graduar*) to give in small doses; **você tem que** ~ **bem o que diz para ele** you have to be careful what you say to him.

dose ['dɔzi] *f* dose; ~ **cavalar** huge dose; ~ **excessiva** overdose; **é** ~ **para leão** *or* **cavalo** (*col*) it's too much.

dossiê [do'sje] *m* dossier, file.

dotação [dota'sãw] (*pl* **-ões**) *f* endowment, allocation.

dotado/a [do'tadu/a] *adj* gifted; ~ **de** endowed with.

dotar [do'ta*] *vt* (*filha*) to give a dowry to; ~

***NB**: European Portuguese adds the following consonants to certain words:* **b** (sú(b)dito, su(b)til); **c** (a(c)ção, a(c)cionista, a(c)to); **m** (inde(m)ne); **p** (ado(p)ção, ado(p)tar); *for further details see p. xiii.*

alguém de algo to endow sb with sth.
dote ['dɔtʃi] *m* dowry; (*fig*) gift.
DOU *abr m* (= *Diário Oficial da União*) *official journal of Brazilian government.*
dou [do] *vb V* **dar.**
dourado/a [do'radu/a] *adj* golden; (*com camada de ouro*) gilt, gilded ♦ *m* gilt; (*cor*) golden colour (*BRIT*) *ou* color (*US*).
dourar [do'ra*] *vt* to gild.
douto/a ['dotu/a] *adj* learned.
doutor(a) [do'to*(a)] *m/f* doctor; **D~** (*forma de tratamento*) Sir; **D~ Eduardo** *etc corresponde ao uso de Mr com o sobrenome do homem em inglês.*
doutorado [doto'radu] *m* doctorate.
doutrina [do'trina] *f* doctrine.
doze ['dozi] *num* twelve; *V tb* **cinco.**
DP (*BR*) *abr f* = **delegacia policial.**
DPF (*BR*) *abr m* = **Departamento de Polícia Federal.**
DPNRE (*BR*) *abr m* = **Departamento de Parques Nacionais e Reservas Equivalentes.**
Dr. *abr* (= *Doutor*) Dr.
Dra. *abr* (= *Doutora*) Dr.
dracma ['drakma] *f* drachma.
draga ['draga] *f* dredger.
dragagem [dra'gaʒẽ] *f* dredging.
dragão [dra'gãw] (*pl* **-ões**) *m* dragon; (*MIL*) dragoon.
dragar [dra'ga*] *vt* to dredge.
drágea ['draʒja] *f* pastille.
dragões [dra'gõjʃ] *mpl de* **dragão.**
drama ['drama] *m* (*teatro*) drama; (*peça*) play; **fazer ~** (*col*) to make a scene; **ser um ~** (*col*) to be an ordeal.
dramalhão [drama'ʎãw] (*pl* **-ões**) *m* melodrama.
dramático/a [dra'matʃiku/a] *adj* dramatic.
dramatização [dramatʃiza'sãw] (*pl* **-ões**) *f* dramatization.
dramatizar [dramatʃi'za*] *vt, vi* (*tb fig*) to dramatize.
dramaturgo/a [drama'tuxgu/a] *m/f* playwright, dramatist.
drapeado/a [dra'pjadu/a] *adj* draped ♦ *m* hang.
drástico/a ['draʃtʃiku/a] *adj* drastic.
drenagem [dre'naʒẽ] *f* drainage.
drenar [dre'na*] *vt* to drain.
dreno ['drɛnu] *m* drain.
driblar [dri'bla*] *vt* (*FUTEBOL*) to dribble round; (*fig*) to get round ♦ *vi* to dribble.
drinque ['drĩki] *m* drink.
drive ['drajvi] *m* (*COMPUT*) (disk) drive.
droga ['drɔga] *f* drug; (*fig*) rubbish ♦ *excl*: **~!** damn!, blast!; **ser uma ~** (*col*: *filme, caneta etc*) to be a dead loss; (*obrigação, atividade*) to be a drag.
drogado/a [dro'gadu/a] *m/f* drug addict.
drogar [dro'ga*] *vt* to drug; **~-se** *vr* to take drugs.
drogaria [droga'ria] *f* chemist's shop (*BRIT*), drugstore (*US*).
dromedário [drome'darju] *m* dromedary.
duas ['duaʃ] *f de* **dois.**
duas-peças *m inv* two-piece.
dúbio/a ['dubju/a] *adj* dubious; (*vago*) uncertain.
dublagem [du'blaʒẽ] *f* (*de filme*) dubbing.
dublar [du'bla*] *vt* to dub.
dublê [du'ble] *m/f* double.
ducentésimo/a [dusẽ'tɛzimu/a] *num* two-hundredth.
ducha ['duʃa] *f* shower; (*MED*) douche.
ducto ['duktu] *m* duct.
duelo ['dwɛlu] *m* duel.
duende ['dwẽdʒi] *m* elf, sprite.
dueto ['dwetu] *m* duet.
dulcíssimo/a [duw'sisimu/a] *adj superl de* **doce.**
dumping ['dãpĩŋ] *m* (*ECON*) dumping.
duna ['duna] *f* dune.
duodécimo/a [dwo'dɛsimu/a] *num* twelfth.
duodeno [dwo'dɛnu] *m* duodenum.
dupla ['dupla] *f* pair; (*ESPORTE*): **~ masculina/feminina/mista** men's/women's/mixed doubles.
dúplex ['dupleks] *adj inv* two-storey (*BRIT*), two-story (*US*) ♦ *m inv* luxury maisonette, duplex.
duplicação [duplika'sãw] *f* (*repetição*) duplication; (*aumento*) doubling.
duplicar [dupli'ka*] *vt* (*repetir*) to duplicate ♦ *vi* (*dobrar*) to double.
duplicidade [duplisi'dadʒi] *f* (*fig*) duplicity.
duplicata [dupli'kata] *f* (*cópia*) duplicate; (*título*) trade note, bill.
duplo/a ['duplu/a] *adj* double ♦ *m* double.
duque ['duki] *m* duke.
duquesa [du'keza] *f* duchess.
durabilidade [durabili'dadʒi] *f* durability.
duração [dura'sãw] *f* duration; **de pouca ~** short-lived.
duradouro/a [dura'doru/a] *adj* lasting.
durante [du'rãtʃi] *prep* during; **~ uma hora** for an hour.
durão/rona [du'rãw/'rɔna] (*col*: *pl* **-ões/~s**) *adj* strict, tough.
durar [du'ra*] *vi* to last.
durável [du'ravew] (*pl* **-eis**) *adj* lasting.
durex [du'rɛks] *adj V* **fita.**
dureza [du'reza] *f* hardness; (*severidade*) harshness; (*col*: *falta de dinheiro*) lack of funds.
durmo ['duxmu] *etc vb V* **dormir.**
duro/a ['duru/a] *adj* hard; (*som*) harsh; (*resistente*) tough; (*sentença, palavras*) harsh, tough; (*inverno*) hard, harsh; (*fig*: *difícil*) hard, tough; **ser ~ com alguém** to be hard on sb; **estar ~** (*col*) to be broke; **dar um ~** (*col*: *trabalhar*) to work hard; **dar um ~ em alguém** (*col*) to come down hard on sb; **~ de roer** (*fig*) hard to take; **no ~** (*col*) really; **a praia estava dura de gente** the beach was packed.
durões [du'rõjʃ] *adj pl de* **durão.**
durona [du'rɔna] *f de* **durão.**

DUT (*BR*) *abr m* (= *documento único de trânsito*) *vehicle licensing document*.
dúvida ['duvida] *f* doubt; **sem ~** undoubtedly, without a doubt.
duvidar [duvi'da*] *vt* to doubt ♦ *vi* to have one's doubts; **~ de alguém/algo** to doubt sb/sth; **~ que ...** to doubt that ...; **duvido!** I doubt it!; **duvido que você consiga correr a maratona** I bet you don't manage to run the marathon.
duvidoso/a [duvi'dozu/ɔza] *adj* (*incerto*) doubtful; (*suspeito*) dubious.
duzentos/as [du'zẽtuʃ/aʃ] *num* two hundred.
dúzia ['duzja] *f* dozen; **meia ~** half a dozen.
dz. *abr* = **dúzia**.

E

E, e [ɛ] *m* (*pl* **es**) E, e ♦ *abr* (= *esquerda*) L.; (= *este*) E; (= *editor*) Ed.; **E de Eliane** E for Edward (*BRIT*) *ou* Easy (*US*).
e [i] *conj* and; **~ a bagagem?** what about the luggage?
é [ɛ] *vb V* **ser**.
EAPAC (*BR*) *abr f* (= *Escola de Aperfeiçoamento e Preparação Civil*) *civil service training school*.
ébano ['ɛbanu] *m* ebony.
EBN *abr f* = **Empresa Brasileira de Notícias**.
ébrio/a ['ɛbrju/a] *adj* drunk ♦ *m/f* drunkard.
EBTU *abr f* = **Empresa Brasileira de Transportes Urbanos**.
ebulição [ebuli'sãw] *f* boiling; (*fig*) ferment.
ebuliente [ebu'ljẽtʃi] *adj* boiling.
ECEME (*BR*) *abr f* (= *Escola de Comando e Estado-Maior do Exército*) *officer training school*.
eclesiástico/a [ekle'zjastʃiku/a] *adj* ecclesiastical, church *atr* ♦ *m* clergyman.
eclético/a [e'klɛtʃiku/a] *adj* eclectic.
eclipsar [eklip'sa*] *vt* (*tb fig*) to eclipse.
eclipse [e'klipsi] *m* eclipse.
eclodir [eklo'dʒi*] *vi* (*aparecer*) to emerge; (*revolução*) to break out; (*flor*) to open.
eclusa [e'kluza] *f* (*de canal*) lock; (*comporta*) floodgate.
eco ['ɛku] *m* echo; **ter ~** to catch on.
ecoar [e'kwa*] *vt* to echo ♦ *vi* (*ressoar*) to echo; (*fig*: *repercutir*) to have repercussions.
ecologia [ekolo'ʒia] *f* ecology.
ecológico/a [eko'lɔʒiku/a] *adj* ecological.
ecologista [ekolo'ʒiʃta] *m/f* ecologist.
economia [ekono'mia] *f* economy; (*ciência*) economics *sg*; **~s** *fpl* savings; **fazer ~ (de)** to economize (with).
econômico/a [eko'nomiku/a] *adj* (*barato*) cheap; (*que consome pouco*) economical; (*pessoa*) thrifty; (*COM*) economic.
economista [ekono'miʃta] *m/f* economist.
economizar [ekonomi'za*] *vt* (*gastar com economia*) to economize on; (*poupar*) to save (up) ♦ *vi* to economize; to save up.
écran ['ɛkrã] (*PT*) *m* screen.
ECT *abr f* = **Empresa Brasileira de Correios e Telégrafos**.
ecumênico/a [eku'meniku/a] *adj* ecumenical.
eczema [eg'zema] *m* eczema.
Ed. *abr* = **edifício**.
ed. *abr* = **edição**.
éden ['ɛdẽ] *m* (*tb fig*) paradise.
edição [ɛdʒi'sãw] (*pl* **-ões**) *f* (*publicação*) publication; (*conjunto de exemplares*) edition; (*TV, CINEMA*) editing; **~ atualizada/revista** updated/revised edition; **~ extra** special edition; **~ de imagem** video editing.
edicto [e'ditu] (*PT*) *m* = **edito**.
edificação [edʒifika'sãw] *f* construction, building; (*fig*: *moral*) edification.
edificante [edʒifi'kãtʃi] *adj* edifying.
edificar [edʒifi'ka*] *vt* (*construir*) to build; (*fig*) to edify ♦ *vi* to be edifying.
edifício [edʒi'fisju] *m* building; **~ garagem** multistorey car park (*BRIT*), multistory parking lot (*US*).
Edimburgo [edʒĩ'buxgu] *n* Edinburgh.
Édipo ['ɛdʒipu] *m V* **complexo**.
edital [edʒi'taw] (*pl* **-ais**) *m* announcement.
editar [edʒi'ta*] *vt* to publish; (*COMPUT etc*) to edit.
edito [e'dʒitu] *m* edict, decree.
editor(a) [edʒi'to*(a)] *adj* publishing *atr* ♦ *m/f* publisher; (*redator*) editor ♦ *f* publishing company; **casa ~a** publishing house; **~ de imagem** video editor; **~ de texto** (*COMPUT*) text editor.
editoração [edʒitora'sãw] *f*: **~ eletrônica** desktop publishing.
editoria [edʒito'ria] *f* section; **~ de esportes** (*em jornal*) sports desk.
editorial [edʒitor'jaw] (*pl* **-ais**) *adj* publishing *atr* ♦ *m* editorial.
edredão [ədrə'dãw] (*pl* **-ões**) (*PT*) *m* = **edredom**.
edredom [edre'dõ] (*pl* **-ns**) *m* eiderdown.
educação [eduka'sãw] *f* (*ensino*) education; (*criação*) upbringing; (*de animais*) training; (*maneiras*) good manners *pl*; **é falta de ~ falar com a boca cheia** it's rude to talk with your mouth full.
educacional [edukasjo'naw] (*pl* **-ais**) *adj* education *atr*.
educado/a [edu'kadu/a] *adj* (*bem-educado*) polite.

***NB**: European Portuguese adds the following consonants to certain words:* **b** (sú(b)dito, su(b)til); **c** (a(c)ção, a(c)cionista, a(c)to); **m** (inde(m)ne); **p** (ado(p)ção, ado(p)tar); *for further details see p. xiii.*

educador(a) [eduka'do*(a)] *m/f* educator.
educandário [edukã'darju] *m* educational establishment.
educar [edu'ka*] *vt* (*instruir*) to educate; (*criar*) to bring up; (*animal*) to train.
educativo/a [eduka'tʃivu/a] *adj* educational.
efectivamente [efektʃiva'mẽtə] (*PT*) *adv* = **efetivamente**.
efectivo/a *etc* [efek'tivu/a] (*PT*) *adj* = **efetivo** *etc*.
efectuar [efek'twa*] (*PT*) *vt* = **efetuar**.
efeito [e'fejtu] *m* effect; **fazer ~** to work; **levar a ~** to put into effect; **com ~** indeed; **para todos os ~s** to all intents and purposes; **~ colateral** side effect; **~ estufa** greenhouse effect.
efêmero/a [e'femeru/a] *adj* ephemeral, short-lived.
efeminado [efemi'nadu] *adj* effeminate ♦ *m* effeminate man.
efervescência [efexve'sẽsja] *f* effervescence; (*fig*) ferment.
efervescente [efexve'sẽtʃi] *adj* fizzy.
efervescer [efexve'se*] *vi* to fizz; (*fig*) to hum.
efetivamente [efetʃiva'mẽtʃi] *adv* effectively; (*realmente*) really, in fact.
efetivar [efetʃi'va*] *vt* (*mudanças, cortes*) to bring into effect; (*professor, estagiário*) to take on permanently.
efetividade [efetʃivi'dadʒi] *f* effectiveness; (*realidade*) reality.
efetivo/a [efe'tʃivu/a] *adj* effective; (*real*) actual, real; (*cargo, funcionário*) permanent ♦ *m* (*COM*) liquid assets *pl*.
efetuar [efe'twa*] *vt* to carry out; (*soma*) to do, perform.
eficácia [efi'kasja] *f* (*de pessoa*) efficiency; (*de tratamento*) effectiveness.
eficacíssimo/a [efika'sisimu/a] *adj superl de* **eficaz**.
eficaz [efi'kaʒ] *adj* (*pessoa*) efficient; (*tratamento*) effective.
eficiência [efi'sjẽsja] *f* efficiency.
eficiente [efi'sjẽtʃi] *adj* efficient, competent.
efígie [e'fiʒi] *f* effigy.
efusão [efu'zãw] (*pl* **-ões**) *f* effusion.
efusivo/a [efu'zivu/a] *adj* effusive.
efusões [efu'zõjʃ] *fpl de* **efusão**.
Egeu [e'ʒew] *m*: **o (mar) ~** the Aegean (Sea).
EGF (*BR*) *abr m* = **empréstimo do governo federal**.
égide ['ɛʒidʒi] *f*: **sob a ~ de** under the aegis (*BRIT*) *ou* egis (*US*) of.
egípcio/a [e'ʒipsju/a] *adj, m/f* Egyptian.
Egito [e'ʒitu] (*PT*: **-pt-**) *m*: **o ~** Egypt.
ego ['ɛgu] *m* ego.
egocêntrico/a [ego'sẽtriku/a] *adj* self-centred (*BRIT*), self-centered (*US*), egocentric.
egoísmo [ego'iʒmu] *m* selfishness, egoism.
egoísta [ego'iʃta] *adj* selfish, egoistic ♦ *m/f* egoist ♦ *m* earplug.
egolatria [egola'tria] *f* self-admiration.
egotismo [ego'tʃiʒmu] *m* egotism.
egotista [ego'tʃiʃta] *m/f* egotist ♦ *adj* egotistical.
egrégio/a [e'grɛʒju/a] *adj* distinguished.
egresso [e'grɛsu] *m* (*preso*) ex-prisoner; (*frade*) former monk; (*universidade*) graduate.
égua ['ɛgwa] *f* mare.
ei [ej] *excl* hey!
ei-lo *etc* = **eis** + **o**; *V* **eis**.
eira ['ejra] (*PT*) *f* threshing floor; **sem ~ nem beira** down and out.
eis [ejʃ] *adv* (*sg*) here is; (*pl*) here are; **~ aí** there is; there are.
eivado/a [ej'vadu/a] *adj* (*fig*) full.
eixo ['ejʃu] *m* (*de rodas*) axle; (*MAT*) axis; (*de máquina*) shaft; **~ de transmissão** drive shaft; **entrar nos ~s** (*pessoa*) to get back on the straight and narrow; (*situação*) to get back to normal; **pôr algo/alguém nos ~s** to set sth/sb straight; **sair dos ~s** to step out of line; **o ~ Rio-São Paulo** the Rio-São Paulo area.
ejacular [eʒaku'la*] *vt* (*sêmen*) to ejaculate; (*líquido*) to spurt ♦ *vi* to ejaculate.
ejetar [eʒe'ta*] *vt* to eject.
ela ['ɛla] *pron* (*pessoa*) she; (*coisa*) it; (*com prep: pessoa*) her; (*: coisa*) it; **~s** *fpl* they; (*com prep*) them; **~s por ~s** (*col*) tit for tat; **aí é que são ~s** (*col*) that's just the point.
elã [e'lã] *m* enthusiasm, drive.
elaboração [elabora'sãw] (*pl* **-ões**) *f* (*de uma teoria*) working out; (*preparo*) preparation.
elaborador(a) [elabora'do*(a)] *m/f* maker.
elaborar [elabo'ra*] *vt* (*preparar*) to prepare; (*fazer*) to make.
elasticidade [elaʃtʃisi'dadʒi] *f* elasticity; (*flexibilidade*) suppleness.
elástico/a [e'laʃtʃiku/a] *adj* elastic; (*flexível*) flexible; (*colchão*) springy ♦ *m* elastic band.
ele ['elɪ] *pron* he; (*coisa*) it; (*com prep: pessoa*) him; (*: coisa*) it; **~s** *mpl* they; (*com prep*) them.
electri... *etc* [elektri...] (*PT*) = **eletri...** *etc*.
eléctrico/a [e'lɛktriku/a] (*PT*) *adj* = **elétrico** ♦ *m* tram (*BRIT*), streetcar (*US*).
electro... *etc* [elektru...] (*PT*) = **eletro...** *etc*.
eléctrodo [e'lɛktrodu] (*PT*) *m* = **eletrodo**.
elefante/ta [ele'fãtʃi/ta] *m/f* elephant; (*col: pessoa gorda*) fatso, fatty; **~ branco** (*fig*) white elephant.
elefantino/a [elefã'tʃinu/a] *adj* elephantine.
elegância [ele'gãsja] *f* elegance.
elegante [ele'gãtʃi] *adj* elegant; (*da moda*) fashionable.
eleger [ele'ʒe*] *vt* (*por votação*) to elect; (*escolher*) to choose.
elegia [ele'ʒia] *f* elegy.
elegibilidade [eleʒibili'dadʒi] *f* eligibility.
elegível [ele'ʒivɛw] (*pl* **-eis**) *adj* eligible.
eleição [elej'sãw] (*pl* **-ões**) *f* (*por votação*) election; (*escolha*) choice.
eleito/a [e'lejtu/a] *pp de* **eleger** ♦ *adj* (*por*

votação) elected; (*escolhido*) chosen.
eleitor(a) [elej'to*(a)] *m/f* voter.
eleitorado [elejto'radu] *m* electorate; **conhecer o seu ~** (*fig*: *col*) to know what one is up against.
eleitoral [elejto'raw] (*pl* **-ais**) *adj* electoral.
elejo [ele'ʒu] *etc vb V* **eleger**.
elementar [elemẽ'ta*] *adj* (*simples*) elementary; (*fundamental*) basic, fundamental.
elemento [ele'mẽtu] *m* element; (*parte*) component; (*ambiente*) element; (*recurso*) means; (*informação*) grounds *pl*; **~s** *mpl* rudiments; **ele é mau ~** he's a bad lot.
elenco [e'lẽku] *m* list; (*de atores*) cast.
elepê [eli'pe] *m* LP, album.
eletivo/a [ele'tʃivu/a] *adj* elective.
eletricidade [eletrisi'dadʒi] *f* electricity.
eletricista [eletri'siʃta] *m/f* electrician.
elétrico/a [e'lɛtriku/a] *adj* electric; (*fig*: *agitado*) worked up.
eletrificar [eletrifi'ka*] *vt* to electrify.
eletrizar [eletri'za*] *vt* to electrify; (*fig*) to thrill.
eletro [e'lɛtru] *m* (*MED*) ECG.
eletro... [eletru] *prefixo* electro....
Eletrobrás [eletro'braʃ] *abr f Brazilian state electricity company.*
eletrocutar [eletroku'ta*] *vt* to electrocute.
eletrodo [ele'trodu] *m* electrode.
eletrodomésticos [eletrodo'mɛʃtʃikuʃ] (*BR*) *mpl* (electrical) household appliances.
eletrônica [ele'tronika] *f* electronics *sg*.
eletrônico/a [ele'troniku/a] *adj* electronic.
elevação [eleva'sãw] (*pl* **-ões**) *f* (*ARQ*) elevation; (*aumento*) rise; (*ato*) raising; (*altura*) height; (*promoção*) elevation, promotion; (*ponto elevado*) bump.
elevado/a [ele'vadu/a] *adj* high; (*pensamento, estilo*) elevated ♦ *m* (*via*) elevated road.
elevador [eleva'do*] *m* lift (*BRIT*), elevator (*US*); **~ de serviço** service lift.
elevar [ele'va*] *vt* (*levantar*) to lift up; (*voz, preço*) to raise; (*exaltar*) to exalt; (*promover*) to elevate, promote; **~-se** *vr* to rise.
eliminação [elimina'sãw] *f* elimination.
eliminar [elimi'na*] *vt* to remove, eliminate; (*suprimir*) to delete; (*possibilidade*) to eliminate, rule out; (*MED*, *banir*) to expel; (*ESPORTE*) to eliminate.
eliminatória [elimina'tɔrja] *f* (*ESPORTE*) heat, preliminary round; (*exame*) test.
eliminatório/a [elimina'tɔrju/a] *adj* eliminatory.
elipse [e'lipsi] *f* ellipse; (*LING*) ellipsis.
elite [e'litʃi] *f* elite.
elitismo [eli'tʃiʒmu] *m* elitism.
elitista [eli'tʃiʃta] *adj*, *m/f* elitist.
elitizar [elitʃi'za*] *vt* (*arte, ensino*) to make elitist.
elixir [elik'si*] *m* elixir.
elo ['ɛlu] *m* link.
elocução [eloku'sãw] *f* elocution.
elogiar [elo'ʒja*] *vt* to praise; **~ alguém por algo** to compliment sb on sth.
elogio [elo'ʒiu] *m* praise; (*cumprimento*) compliment.
elogioso/a [elo'ʒozu/ɔza] *adj* complimentary.
eloqüência [elo'kwẽsja] *f* eloquence.
eloqüente [elo'kwẽtʃi] *adj* eloquent; (*persuasivo*) persuasive.
El Salvador [ew-] *n* El Salvador.
elucidação [elusida'sãw] *f* elucidation.
elucidar [elusi'da*] *vt* to elucidate, clarify.
elucidativo/a [elusida'tʃivu/a] *adj* elucidatory.
elucubração [elukubra'sãw] (*pl* **-ões**) *f* cogitation, musing.
em [ẽ] *prep* in; (*sobre*) on; **no bolso** in the pocket; **na mesa** on the table; **no Brasil** in Brazil; **~ casa** at home; **~ São Paulo** in São Paulo; **nessa altura** at that time; **~ breve** soon; **nessa ocasião** on that occasion; **tudo aconteceu ~ 6 dias** it all happened in *or* within six days; **fui lá na vizinha** I went to my neighbour's; **estou na vizinha** I'm at my neighbour's; **ir de porta ~ porta** to go from door to door; **reduzir/aumentar ~ 20%** to reduce/increase by 20%.
Emaer [ema'e*] (*BR*) *abr m* = **Estado-Maior da Aeronáutica**.
emagrecer [imagre'se*] *vt* to make thin ♦ *vi* to grow thin; (*mediante regime*) to slim.
emagrecimento [imagresi'mẽtu] *m* (*mediante regime*) slimming.
emanar [ema'na*] *vi*: **~ de** to come from, emanate from.
emancipação [imãsipa'sãw] (*pl* **-ões**) *f* emancipation; (*atingir a maioridade*) coming of age.
emancipar [imãsi'pa*] *vt* to emancipate; **~-se** *vr* (*atingir a maioridade*) to come of age.
emaranhado/a [imara'ɲadu/a] *adj* tangled ♦ *m* tangle.
emaranhar [imara'ɲa*] *vt* to tangle; (*complicar*) to complicate; **~-se** *vr* to get entangled; (*fig*) to get mixed up.
emassar [ema'sa*] *vt* (*parede*) to plaster; (*janela*) to putty.
Emater [ema'te*] (*BR*) *abr f* (= *Empresa de Assistência Técnica e Extensão Rural*) *company giving aid to farmers.*
embaçado/a [ẽba'sadu/a] *adj* (*vidro*) steamed up.
embaçar [ẽba'sa*] *vt* to steam up.
embaciado/a [ẽba'sjadu/a] *adj* dull; (*vidro*) misted; (*janela*) steamed up; (*olhos*) misty.
embaciar [ẽba'sja*] *vt* (*vidro*) to steam up; (*olhos*) to cloud ♦ *vi* to steam up; (*olhos*) to grow misty.
embainhar [ẽbaj'ɲa*] *vt* (*espada*) to put

***NB**: European Portuguese adds the following consonants to certain words:* **b** (sú(b)dito, su(b)til); **c** (a(c)ção, a(c)cionista, a(c)to); **m** (inde(m)ne); **p** (ado(p)ção, ado(p)tar); *for further details see p. xiii.*

away, sheathe; (*calça etc*) to hem.
embaixada [ẽbaj'ʃada] *f* embassy.
embaixador(a) [ẽbajʃa'do*(a)] *m/f* ambassador.
embaixatriz [ẽbajʃa'triʒ] *f* ambassador; (*mulher de embaixador*) ambassador's wife.
embaixo [ẽ'bajʃu] *adv* below, underneath ♦ *prep*: ~ **de** under, underneath; **(lá)** ~ (*em andar inferior*) downstairs.
embalado/a [ẽba'ladu/a] *adj* (*acelerado*) fast; (*drogado*) high; **ir** ~ to race (along).
embalagem [ẽba'laʒẽ] *f* packing; (*de produto*: *caixa etc*) packaging.
embalar [ẽba'la*] *vt* to pack; (*balançar*) to rock.
embalo [ẽ'balu] *m* (*balanço*) rocking; (*impulso*) rush; (*col*: *com drogas*) high; **aproveitar o** ~ to take the opportunity.
embalsamar [ẽbawsa'ma*] *vt* (*perfumar*) to perfume; (*cadáver*) to embalm.
embananado/a [ẽbana'nadu/a] (*col*) *adj* (*confuso*) muddled; (*em dificuldades*) in trouble.
embananamento [ẽbanana'mẽtu] (*col*) *m* muddle; (*bananosa*) jam.
embananar [ẽbana'na*] (*col*) *vt* (*tornar confuso*) to muddle up; (*complicar*) to complicate; (*meter em dificuldades*) to get into trouble; **~-se** *vr* to get tied up in knots.
embaraçar [ẽbara'sa*] *vt* (*impedir*) to hinder; (*complicar*) to complicate; (*encabular*) to embarrass; (*confundir*) to confuse; (*obstruir*) to block; **~-se** *vr* to become embarrassed.
embaraço [ẽba'rasu] *m* (*estorvo*) hindrance; (*cábula*) embarrassment.
embaraçoso/a [ẽbara'sozu/ɔza] *adj* embarrassing.
embarafustar [ẽbarafuʃ'ta*] *vi*: ~ **por** to burst *ou* barge into.
embaralhar [ẽbara'ʎa*] *vt* (*confundir*) to muddle up; (*cartas*) to shuffle; **~-se** *vr* to get mixed up.
embarcação [ẽbaxka'sãw] (*pl* **-ões**) *f* vessel.
embarcadiço [ẽbaxka'dʒisu] *m* seafarer.
embarcadouro [ẽbaxka'doru] *m* wharf.
embarcar [ẽbax'ka*] *vt* to embark, put on board; (*mercadorias*) to ship, stow ♦ *vi* to go on board, embark; ~ **em algo** (*fig*: *col*) to fall for sth.
embargar [ẽbax'ga*] *vt* (JUR) to seize; (*pôr obstáculos a*) to hinder; (*reprimir*: *voz*) to keep down; (*impedir*) to forbid.
embargo [ẽ'baxgu] *m* (*de navio*) embargo; (JUR) seizure; (*impedimento*) impediment; **sem** ~ nevertheless.
embarque [ẽ'baxkɪ] *m* (*de pessoas*) boarding, embarkation; (*de mercadorias*) shipment.
embasamento [ẽbaza'mẽtu] *m* (ARQ) foundation; (*de coluna*) base; (*fig*) basis.
embasbacado/a [ẽbaʒba'kadu/a] *adj* gaping, open-mouthed.
embasbacar [ẽbaʒba'ka*] *vt* to leave open-mouthed; **~-se** *vr* to be taken aback, be dumbfounded.
embate [ẽ'batʃi] *m* clash; (*choque*) shock.
embatucar [ẽbatu'ka*] *vt* to dumbfound ♦ *vi* to be speechless.
embebedar [ẽbebe'da*] *vt* to make drunk ♦ *vi*: **o vinho embebeda** wine makes you drunk; **~-se** *vr* to get drunk.
embeber [ẽbe'be*] *vt* to soak up, absorb; **~-se** *vr*: **~-se em** to become absorbed in.
embelezador(a) [ẽbeleza'do*(a)] *adj* cosmetic.
embelezar [ẽbele'za*] *vt* to make beautiful; (*casa*) to brighten up; **~-se** *vr* to make o.s. beautiful.
embevecer [ẽbeve'se*] *vt* to captivate; **~-se** *vr* to be captivated.
embicar [ẽbi'ka*] *vi* (NÁUT) to enter port, dock; (*fig*): ~ **para** to head for; ~ **com alguém** to quarrel with sb.
embirrar [ẽbi'xa*] *vi* to sulk; ~ **em** to insist on; ~ **com** to dislike.
emblema [ẽ'blɛma] *m* emblem; (*na roupa*) badge.
embocadura [ẽboka'dura] *f* (*de rio*) mouth; (MÚS) mouthpiece; (*de freio*) bit.
emboço [ẽ'bosu] *m* roughcast, render.
embolar [ẽbo'la*] *vt* (*confundir*) to confuse ♦ *vi*: ~ **com** to grapple with; **~-se** *vr*: **~-se (com)** to grapple (with).
êmbolo ['ẽbolu] *m* piston.
embolorar [ẽbolo'ra*] *vi* to go musty.
embolsar [ẽbow'sa*] *vt* to pocket; (*herança etc*) to come by; (*indenizar*) to refund.
embonecar [ẽbone'ka*] *vt* to doll up; **~-se** *vr* to doll o.s. up, get dolled up.
embora [ẽ'bɔra] *conj* though, although ♦ *excl* even so, what of it?; **ir(-se)** ~ to go away.
emborcar [ẽbox'ka*] *vt* to turn upside down.
emboscada [ẽboʃ'kada] *f* ambush.
embotar [ẽbo'ta*] *vt* (*lâmina*) to blunt; (*fig*) to deaden, dull.
embrabecer [ẽbrabe'se*] *vi* = **embravecer**.
Embraer [ẽbrãe*] *abr f* (= *Empresa Brasileira de Aeronáutica SA*) *aerospace company*.
embranquecer [ẽbrãke'se*] *vt, vi* to turn white.
Embratur [ẽbra'tu*] *abr f* (= *Empresa Brasileira de Turismo*) *state tourist board*.
embravecer [ẽbrave'se*] *vr* to get furious; **~-se** *vr* to get furious.
embreagem [ẽb'rjaʒẽ] (*pl* **-ns**) *f* (AUTO) clutch.
embrear [ẽ'brja*] *vt* (AUTO) to disengage ♦ *vi* to let in the clutch.
embrenhar [ẽbre'ɲa*] *vt* to penetrate; **~-se** *vr*: **~-se (em/por)** to make one's way (into/through).
embriagante [ẽbrja'gãtʃi] *adj* intoxicating.
embriagar [ẽbrja'ga*] *vt* to make drunk, intoxicate; **~-se** *vr* to get drunk.
embriaguez [ẽbrja'geʒ] *f* drunkenness; (*fig*) rapture; ~ **no volante** drunk(en) driving.
embrião [e'brjãw] (*pl* **-ões**) *m* embryo.
embrionário/a [ẽbrjo'narju/a] *adj* (*tb fig*) embryonic.

embromação [ẽbroma'sãw] (*pl* **-ões**) *f* stalling; (*trapaça*) con.
embromador(a) [ẽbroma'do*(a)] *adj* (*remanchador*) slow; (*trapaçeiro*) dishonest, bent ♦ *m/f* (*remanchador*) staller; (*trapaçeiro*) con merchant.
embromar [ẽbro'ma*] *vt* to put off, string along; (*enganar*) to con, cheat ♦ *vi* (*prometer e não cumprir*) to make empty promises, be all talk (and no action); (*protelar*) to stall; (*falar em rodeios*) to beat about the bush.
embrulhada [ẽbru'ʎada] *f* muddle, mess.
embrulhar [ẽbru'ʎa*] *vt* (*pacote*) to wrap; (*enrolar*) to roll up; (*confundir*) to muddle up; (*enganar*) to cheat; (*estômago*) to upset; **~-se** *vr* to get into a muddle; **ao contar a estória, ele embrulhou tudo** when he told the story he got everything mixed up.
embrulho [ẽ'bruʎu] *m* (*pacote*) package, parcel; (*confusão*) mix-up.
embrutecer [ẽbrute'se*] *vt* to brutalize ♦ *vi* to have a brutalizing effect; **~-se** *vr* to be brutalized.
emburrar [ẽbu'xa*] *vi* to sulk.
embuste [ẽ'buʃtʃi] *m* (*engano*) deception; (*ardil*) trick.
embusteiro/a [ẽbuʃ'tejru/a] *adj* deceitful ♦ *m/f* cheat; (*mentiroso*) liar; (*impostor*) impostor.
embutido/a [ẽbu'tʃidu/a] *adj* (*armário*) built-in, fitted.
embutir [ẽbu'tʃi*] *vt* to build in; (*marfim etc*) to inlay.
emenda [e'mẽda] *f* correction; (JUR) amendment; (*de uma pessoa*) improvement; (*ligação*) join; (*sambladura*) joint; (COSTURA) seam.
emendar [emẽ'da*] *vt* (*corrigir*) to correct; (*reparar*) to mend; (*injustiças*) to make amends for; (JUR) to amend; (*ajuntar*) to put together; **~-se** *vr* to mend one's ways.
ementa [e'mẽta] (PT) *f* menu.
emergência [imex'ʒẽsja] *f* (*nascimento*) emergence; (*crise*) emergency.
emergente [imex'ʒẽtʒi] *adj* emerging.
emergir [imex'ʒi*] *vi* to emerge, appear; (*submarino*) to surface.
EMFA (BR) *abr m* = **Estado-maior das Forças Armadas**.
emigração [emigra'sãw] (*pl* **-ões**) *f* emigration; (*de aves*) migration.
emigrado/a [emi'gradu/a] *adj* emigrant.
emigrante [emi'grãtʃi] *m/f* emigrant.
emigrar [emi'gra*] *vi* to emigrate; (*aves*) to migrate.
eminência [emi'nẽsja] *f* eminence; (*altura*) height.
eminente [emi'nẽtʃi] *adj* eminent, distinguished; (GEO) high.
Emirados Árabes Unidos [emi'raduʃ-] *mpl*: **os ~** the United Arab Emirates.
emirjo [e'mixʒu] *etc vb V* **emergir**.
emissão [emi'sãw] (*pl* **-ões**) *f* emission; (RÁDIO) broadcast; (*de moeda, ações*) issue.
emissário/a [emi'sarju/a] *m/f* emissary ♦ *m* outlet.
emissões [emi'sõjʃ] *fpl de* **emissão**.
emissor(a) [emi'so*(a)] *adj* (*de moeda-papel*) issuing ♦ *m* (RÁDIO) transmitter ♦ *f* (*estação*) broadcasting station; (*empresa*) broadcasting company.
emitente [emi'tẽtʃi] *adj* (COM) issuing ♦ *m/f* (COM) issuer.
emitir [emi'tʃi*] *vt* (*som*) to give out; (*cheiro*) to give off; (*moeda, ações*) to issue; (RÁDIO) to broadcast; (*opinião*) to express ♦ *vi* (*emitir moeda*) to print money.
emoção [emo'sãw] (*pl* **-ões**) *f* emotion; (*excitação*) excitement.
emocional [imosjo'naw] (*pl* **-ais**) *adj* emotional.
emocionante [imosjo'nãtʃi] *adj* (*comovente*) moving; (*excitante*) exciting.
emocionar [imosjo'na*] *vt* (*comover*) to move; (*perturbar*) to upset; (*excitar*) to excite, thrill ♦ *vi* to be exciting; (*comover*) to be moving; **~-se** *vr* to get emotional.
emoções [emo'sõjʃ] *fpl de* **emoção**.
emoldurar [emowdu'ra*] *vt* to frame.
emotividade [emotʃivi'dadʒi] *f* emotions *pl*.
emotivo/a [emo'tʃivu/a] *adj* emotional.
empacar [ẽpa'ka*] *vi* (*cavalo*) to baulk; (*fig: negócios etc*) to grind to a halt; (*orador*) to dry up; **~ numa palavra** to get stuck on a word.
empachado/a [ẽpa'ʃadu/a] *adj* full up.
empacotar [ẽpako'ta*] *vt* to pack, wrap up ♦ *vi* (*col: morrer*) to pop one's clogs.
empada [ẽ'pada] *f* pie.
empadão [ẽpa'dãw] (*pl* **-ões**) *m* pie.
empalhar [ẽpa'ʎa*] *vt* (*animal*) to stuff; (*louça, fruta*) to pack with straw.
empalidecer [ẽpalide'se*] *vt, vi* to turn pale.
empanar [ẽpa'na*] *vt* (*fig*) to tarnish; (CULIN) to batter.
empanturrar [ẽpãtu'xa*] *vt*: **~ alguém de algo** to stuff sb full of sth; **~-se** *vr* to gorge o.s., stuff o.s. (*col*).
empanzinado/a [ẽpãzi'nadu/a] *adj* full.
empapar [ẽpa'pa*] *vt* to soak; **~-se** *vr* to get soaked.
empapuçado/a [ẽpapu'sadu/a] *adj* (*olhos*) puffy; (*blusa*) full.
emparedar [ẽpare'da*] *vt* to wall in; (*pessoa*) to shut up.
emparelhar [ẽpare'ʎa*] *vt* to pair; (*equiparar*) to match ♦ *vi*: **~ com** to be equal to.
empastado/a [ẽpaʃ'tadu/a] *adj* (*cabelo*) plastered down.
empastar [ẽpaʃ'ta*] *vt*: **~ algo de algo** to

***NB**: European Portuguese adds the following consonants to certain words:* **b** (sú(b)dito, su(b)til); **c** (a(c)ção, a(c)cionista, a(c)to); **m** (inde(m)ne); **p** (ado(p)ção, ado(p)tar); *for further details see p. xiii.*

plaster sth with sth.

empatar [ẽpa'ta*] *vt* (*embaraçar*) to hinder; (*dinheiro*) to tie up; (*no jogo*) to draw; (*corredores*) to tie; (*tempo*) to take up ♦ *vi* (*no jogo*): ~ **(com)** to draw (with).

empate [ẽ'patʃi] *m* (*no jogo*) draw; (*numa corrida etc*) tie; (XADREZ) stalemate; (*em negociações*) deadlock.

empatia [ẽpa'tʃia] *f* empathy.

empavonar-se [ẽpavo'naxsi] *vr* to strut.

empecilho [ẽpe'siʎu] *m* obstacle; (*col*) snag.

empedernido/a [ẽpedex'nidu/a] *adj* hard-hearted.

empedrar [ẽpe'dra*] *vt* to pave.

empenar [ẽpe'na*] *vt, vi* (*curvar*) to warp.

empenhar [ẽpe'ɲa*] *vt* (*objeto*) to pawn; (*palavra*) to pledge; (*empregar*) to exert; (*compelir*) to oblige; **~-se** *vr*: **~-se em fazer** to strive to do, do one's utmost to do.

empenho [ẽ'peɲu] *m* (*de um objeto*) pawning; (*palavra*) pledge; (*insistência*): ~ **(em)** commitment (to); **ele pôs todo seu ~ neste projeto** he committed himself wholeheartedly to this project .

emperiquitar-se [ẽperiki'taxsi] *vr* to get done up to the nines.

emperrar [ẽpe'xa*] *vt* (*máquina*) to jam; (*porta, junta*) to make stiff; (*fazer calar*) to cut short ♦ *vi* (*máquina*) to jam; (*gaveta, porta*) to stick; (*junta*) to go stiff; (*calar*) to go quiet.

empertigado/a [ẽpextʃi'gadu/a] *adj* upright.

empertigar-se [ẽpextʃi'gaxsi] *vr* to stand up straight.

empestar [ẽpeʃ'ta*] *vt* (*infetar*) to infect; (*tornar desagradável*) to pollute, stink out (*col*).

empetecar [ẽpete'ka*] *vt* to doll up; **~-se** *vr* to doll o.s. up.

empilhar [ẽpi'ʎa*] *vt* to pile up.

empinado/a [ẽpi'nadu/a] *adj* (*direito*) upright; (*cavalo*) rearing; (*colina*) steep.

empinar [ẽpi'na*] *vt* to raise, uplift; (*ressaltar*) to thrust out; (*papagaio*) to fly; (*copo*) to empty.

empipocar [ẽpipo'ka*] *vi* to come out in spots.

empírico/a [ẽ'piriku/a] *adj* empirical.

empistolado/a [ẽpiʃto'ladu/a] *adj* with contacts.

emplacar [ẽpla'ka*] *vt* (*col*: *anos, sucessos*) to notch up; (*carro*) to put number (BRIT) *ou* license (US) plates on; ~ **o ano 2000** to make it to the year 2000.

emplastrar [ẽplaʃ'tra*] *vt* to put in plaster.

emplastro [ẽ'plaʃstru] *m* (MED) plaster.

empobrecer [ẽpobre'se*] *vt* to impoverish ♦ *vi* to become poor.

empobrecimento [ẽpobresi'mẽtu] *m* impoverishment.

empoeirar [ẽpoej'ra*] *vt* to cover in dust.

empola [ẽ'pola] *f* (*na pele*) blister; (*de água*) bubble.

empolado/a [ẽpo'ladu/a] *adj* covered with blisters; (*estilo*) pompous, bombastic.

empolgação [ẽpowga'sãw] *f* excitement; (*entusiasmo*) enthusiasm.

empolgante [ẽpow'gãtʃi] *adj* exciting.

empolgar [ẽpow'ga*] *vt* to stimulate, fill with enthusiasm; (*prender a atenção de*): ~ **alguém** to keep sb riveted.

emporcalhar [ẽpoxka'ʎa*] *vt* to dirty; **~-se** *vr* to get dirty.

empório [ẽ'pɔrju] *m* (*mercado*) market; (*armazém*) department store.

empossar [ẽpo'sa*] *vt* to appoint.

empreendedor(a) [ẽprjẽde'do*(a)] *adj* enterprising ♦ *m/f* entrepreneur.

empreender [ẽprjẽ'de*] *vt* to undertake.

empreendimento [ẽprjẽdʒi'mẽtu] *m* undertaking.

empregada [ẽpre'gada] *f* (BR: *doméstica*) maid; (PT: *de restaurante*) waitress; *V tb* **empregado**.

empregado/a [ẽpre'gadu/a] *m/f* employee; (*em escritório*) clerk ♦ *m* (PT: *de restaurante*) waiter.

empregador(a) [ẽprega'do*(a)] *m/f* employer.

empregar [ẽpre'ga*] *vt* (*pessoa*) to employ; (*coisa*) to use; **~-se** *vr* to get a job.

empregatício/a [ẽprega'tʃisju/a] *adj* *V* **vínculo**.

emprego [ẽ'pregu] *m* (*ocupação*) job; (*uso*) use.

empreguismo [ẽpre'giʒmu] *m* patronage, nepotism.

empreitada [ẽprej'tada] *f* (COM) contract job; (*tarefa*) enterprise, venture.

empreiteira [ẽprej'tejra] *f* (*firma*) contractor.

empreiteiro [ẽprej'tejru] *m* contractor.

empresa [ẽ'preza] *f* undertaking; (COM) enterprise, firm.

empresariado [ẽpreza'rjadu] *m* business community.

empresarial [ẽpreza'rjaw] (*pl*: **-ais**) *adj* business *atr*.

empresário/a [ẽpre'zarju/a] *m/f* businessman/woman; (*de cantor, boxeador etc*) manager; ~ **teatral** impresario.

emprestado/a [ẽpreʃ'tadu/a] *adj* on loan; **pedir ~** to borrow.

emprestar [ẽpreʃ'ta*] *vt* to lend.

empréstimo [ẽ'prɛʃtʃimu] *m* loan.

emproado/a [ẽpro'adu/a] *adj* arrogant.

empulhação [ẽpuʎa'sãw] (*pl* **-ões**) *f* (*ato*) trickery; (*embuste*) con.

empulhar [ẽpu'ʎa*] *vt* to trick, con.

empunhar [ẽpu'ɲa*] *vt* to grasp, seize.

empurrão [ẽpu'xãw] (*pl* **-ões**) *m* push, shove; **aos empurrões** jostling.

empurrar [ẽpu'xa*] *vt* to push.

empurrões [ẽpu'xõjʃ] *mpl de* **empurrão**.

emudecer [emude'se*] *vt* to silence ♦ *vi* to fall silent, go quiet.

emular [emu'la*] *vt* to emulate.

enaltecer [enawte'se*] *vt* (*fig*) to elevate.

enamorado/a [enamo'radu/a] *adj* (*encantar*)

enchanted; (*apaixonado*) in love.

ENAP (*BR*) *abr f* (= **Escola Nacional de Administração Pública**) *civil service training school*.

encabeçar [ẽkabe'sa*] *vt* to head.

encabulação [ẽkabula'sãw] *f* (*vergonha*) embarrassment; (*acanhamento*) shyness.

encabulado/a [ẽkabu'ladu/a] *adj* shy.

encabular [ẽkabu'la*] *vt* to embarrass ♦ *vi* (*fato, situação*) to be embarrassing; (*pessoa*) to get embarrassed; **não se encabule!** don't be shy!

encaçapar [ẽkasa'pa*] *vt* (*bola*) to sink; (*col*: *surrar*) to bash.

encadeamento [ẽkadʒja'mẽtu] *m* (*série*) chain; (*conexão*) link.

encadear [ẽka'dʒja*] *vt* to chain together, link together.

encadernação [ẽkadexna'sãw] (*pl* **-ões**) *f* (*de livro*) binding.

encadernado/a [ẽkadex'nadu/a] *adj* bound; (*de capa dura*) hardback.

encadernador(a) [ẽkadexna'do*(a)] *m/f* bookbinder.

encadernar [ẽkadex'na*] *vt* to bind.

encafuar [ẽka'fwa*] *vt* to hide; **~-se** *vr* to hide.

encaixar [ẽkaj'ʃa*] *vt* (*colocar*) to fit in; (*inserir*) to insert ♦ *vi* to fit.

encaixe [ẽ'kajʃi] *m* (*ato*) fitting; (*ranhura*) groove; (*buraco*) socket.

encaixotar [ẽkajʃo'ta*] *vt* to pack into boxes.

encalacrar [ẽkala'kra*] *vt*: **~ alguém** to get sb into trouble; **~-se** *vr* to get into debt.

encalço [ẽ'kawsu] *m* pursuit; **ir no ~ de** to pursue.

encalhado/a [ẽka'ʎadu/a] *adj* stranded; (*mercadoria*) unsaleable; (*col*: *solteiro*) unmarried.

encalhar [ẽka'ʎa*] *vi* (*embarcação*) to run aground; (*fig*: *processo*) to grind to a halt; (: *mercadoria*) to be returned, not to sell; (*col*: *ficar solteiro*) to be left on the shelf.

encalorado/a [ẽkalo'radu/a] *adj* hot.

encaminhar [ẽkami'ɲa*] *vt* (*dirigir*) to direct; (*no bom caminho*) to put on the right path; (*processo*) to set in motion; **~-se** *vr*: **~-se para/a** to set out for/to; **eu encaminhei-os para a seção devida** I referred them to the appropriate department; **~ uma petição a alguém** to refer an application to sb; **foi minha mãe quem me encaminhou para as letras** it was my mother who steered me towards literature; **as coisas se encaminham bem no momento** things are going well at the moment.

encampar [ẽkã'pa*] *vt* (*empresa*) to expropriate; (*opinião, medida*) to adopt.

encanador [ẽkana'do*] (*BR*) *m* plumber.

encanamento [ẽkana'mẽtu] (*BR*) *m* plumbing.

encanar [ẽka'na*] *vt* to channel; (*BR*: *col*: *prender*) to throw in jail.

encanecido/a [ẽkane'sidu/a] *adj* grey (*BRIT*), gray (*US*); (*cabelo*) white.

encantado/a [ẽkã'tadu/a] *adj* (*contente*) delighted; (*castelo etc*) enchanted; (*fascinado*): **~ (por alguém/algo)** to be smitten (with sb/sth).

encantador(a) [ẽkãta'do*(a)] *adj* delightful, charming ♦ *m/f* enchanter/enchantress.

encantamento [ẽkãta'mẽtu] *m* (*magia*) spell; (*fascinação*) charm.

encantar [ẽkã'ta*] *vt* (*enfeitiçar*) to bewitch; (*cativar*) to charm; (*deliciar*) to delight.

encanto [ẽ'kãtu] *m* (*delícia*) delight; (*fascinação*) charm.

encapar [ẽka'pa*] *vt* (*cobrir*) to cover; (*envolver*) to wrap; (*livro*) to cover.

encapelar [ẽkape'la*] *vt* (*mar*) to swell ♦ *vi* (*mar*) to turn rough.

encapetado/a [ẽkape'tadu/a] *adj* (*criança*) mischievous.

encapotar [ẽkapo'ta*] *vt* to wrap up; **~-se** *vr* to wrap o.s. up.

encaracolar [ẽkarako'la*] *vt, vi* to curl; **~-se** *vr* to curl up.

encarangar [ẽkarã'ga*] *vt* to cripple ♦ *vi* (*pessoa*) to be crippled; (*reumatismo*) to be crippling.

encarapinhado/a [ẽkarapi'ɲadu/a] *adj* (*cabelo*) frizzy.

encarapitar [ẽkarapi'ta*] *vt* to perch; **~-se** *vr*: **~-se em algo** to climb on top of sth; (*num cargo etc*) to get o.s. fixed up in sth.

encarar [ẽka'ra*] *vt* to face; (*olhar*) to look at; (*considerar*) to consider.

encarcerar [ẽkaxse'ra*] *vt* to imprison.

encardido/a [ẽkax'dʒidu/a] *adj* (*roupa, casa*) grimy; (*pele*) sallow.

encardir [ẽkax'dʒi*] *vt* to make grimy ♦ *vi* to get grimy.

encarecer [ẽkare'se*] *vt* (*subir o preço*) to raise the price of; (*louvar*) to praise; (*exagerar*) to exaggerate ♦ *vi* to go up in price, get dearer.

encarecidamente [ẽkaresida'mẽtʃi] *adv* insistently.

encarecimento [ẽkaresi'mẽtu] *m* (*preço*) increase.

encargo [ẽ'kaxgu] *m* (*responsabilidade*) responsibility; (*ocupação*) job, assignment; (*oneroso*) burden; **dar a alguém o ~ de fazer algo** to give sb the job of doing sth.

encarnação [ẽkaxna'sãw] (*pl* **-ões**) *f* incarnation.

encarnado/a [ẽkax'nadu/a] *adj* red, scarlet.

encarnar [ẽkax'na*] *vt* to embody, personify; (*TEATRO*) to play ♦ *vi* to be embodied; **~-se** *vr* to be embodied; **~ em alguém** (*col*) to pick on sb.

encarneirado/a [ẽkaxnej'radu/a] *adj* (*mar*) choppy.
encaroçar [ẽkaro'sa*] *vi* (*molho*) to go lumpy; (*pele*) to come up in bumps.
encarquilhado/a [ẽkaxki'ʎadu/a] *adj* (*fruta*) wizened; (*rosto*) wrinkled.
encarregado/a [ẽkaxe'gadu/a] *adj*: ~ **de** in charge of ♦ *m/f* person in charge ♦ *m* (*de operários*) foreman; ~ **de negócios** chargé d'affaires.
encarregar [ẽkaxe'ga*] *vt*: ~ **alguém de algo** to put sb in charge of sth; **~-se** *vr*: **~-se de fazer** to undertake to do.
encarreirar [ẽkaxej'ra*] *vt* to guide; (*negócios*) to run; (*moralmente*): ~ **alguém** to put sb on the right track.
encarrilhar [ẽkaxi'ʎa*] *vt* to put back on the rails; (*fig*) to put on the right track.
encartar [ẽkax'ta*] *vt* to insert.
encarte [ẽ'kaxtʃi] *m* insert.
encasacar-se [ẽkaza'kaxsi] *vr* to put on one's coat.
encasquetar [ẽkaʃke'ta*] *vt*: ~ **uma idéia** to get an idea into one's head.
encatarrado/a [ẽkata'xadu/a] *adj* congested.
encenação [ẽsena'sãw] (*pl* **-ões**) *f* (*de peça*) staging, putting on; (*produção*) production; (*fingimento*) playacting; (*atitude fingida*) put-on, put-up job (*col*); **fazer** ~ (*col*) to put it on.
encenador(a) [ẽsena'do*(a)] *m/f* (*TEATRO*) director.
encenar [ẽse'na*] *vt* (*TEATRO*: *pôr em cena*) to stage, put on; (: *produzir*) to produce; (*fingir*) to put on.
enceradeira [ẽsera'dejra] *f* floor-polisher.
encerar [ẽse'ra*] *vt* to wax.
encerramento [ẽsexa'mẽtu] *m* (*término*) close, end.
encerrar [ẽse'xa*] *vt* (*confinar*) to shut in, lock up; (*conter*) to contain; (*concluir*) to close.
encestar [ẽseʃ'ta*] *vt* (*BASQUETE*) to put in the basket ♦ *vi* to score a basket.
encetar [ẽse'ta*] *vt* to start, begin.
encharcar [ẽʃax'ka*] *vt* (*alagar*) to flood; (*ensopar*) to soak, drench; **~-se** *vr* to get soaked *ou* drenched; **~-se de algo** (*beber muito*) to drink gallons of sth.
encheção [ẽʃe'sãw] (*col*) *f* annoyance.
enchente [ẽ'ʃẽtʃi] *f* flood.
encher [ẽ'ʃe*] *vt* to fill (up); (*balão*) to blow up; (*tempo*) to fill, take up ♦ *vi* (*col*) to be annoying; **~-se** *vr* to fill up; **~-se (de)** (*col*) to get fed up (with); ~ **de** *ou* **com** to fill up with; ~ **o saco de alguém** (*col*) to bug sb, piss sb off (*!*); **ela enche o filho de presentes** she showers her son with presents.
enchimento [ẽʃi'mẽtu] *m* filling.
enchova [ẽ'ʃova] *f* anchovy.
enciclopédia [ẽsiklo'pɛdʒja] *f* encyclopedia, encyclopaedia (*BRIT*).
enciumar [ẽsju'ma*] *vt* to make jealous; **~-se** *vr* to get jealous.
enclausurar [ẽklawzu'ra*] *vt* to shut away; **~-se** *vr* to shut o.s. away.
encoberto/a [ẽko'bɛxtu/a] *pp de* **encobrir** ♦ *adj* (*escondido*) concealed; (*tempo*) overcast.
encobrir [ẽko'bri*] *vt* to conceal, hide.
encolerizar [ẽkoleri'za*] *vt* to irritate, annoy; **~-se** *vr* to get angry.
encolher [ẽko'ʎe*] *vt* (*pernas*) to draw up; (*os ombros*) to shrug; (*roupa*) to shrink ♦ *vi* to shrink; **~-se** *vr* (*de frio*) to huddle; (*para dar lugar*) to hunch up.
encomenda [ẽko'mẽda] *f* order; **feito de** ~ made to order, custom-made; **vir de** ~ (*fig*) to come just at the right time.
encomendar [ẽkomẽ'da*] *vt* to order; ~ **algo a alguém** to order sth from sb.
encompridar [ẽkõpri'da*] *vt* to lengthen.
encontrão [ẽkõ'trãw] (*pl* **-ões**) *m* (*esbarrão*) collision, impact; (*empurrão*) shove; **dar um** ~ **em** to bump into; **ir aos encontrões pela multidão** to jostle one's way through the crowd.
encontrar [ẽkõ'tra*] *vt* (*achar*) to find; (*inesperadamente*) to come across, meet; (*dar com*) to bump into ♦ *vi*: ~ **com** to bump into; **~-se** *vr* (*achar-se*) to be; (*ter encontro*): **~-se (com alguém)** to meet (sb).
encontro [ẽ'kõtru] *m* (*de pessoas*) meeting; (*MIL*) encounter; ~ **marcado** appointment; **ir/vir ao** ~ **de** to go/come and meet; **ir** *ou* **vir ao** ~ **de** (*aspirações*) to meet, fulfil (*BRIT*), fulfill (*US*); **ir de** ~ **a** to go against, run contrary to; **meu carro foi de** ~ **ao muro** my car ran into the wall.
encontrões [ẽkõ'trõjʃ] *mpl de* **encontrão**.
encorajamento [ẽkoraʒa'mẽtu] *m* encouragement.
encorajar [ẽkora'ʒa*] *vt* to encourage.
encorpado/a [ẽkox'padu/a] *adj* stout; (*vinho*) full-bodied; (*tecido*) closely-woven; (*papel*) thick.
encorpar [ẽkox'pa*] *vt* (*ampliar*) to expand ♦ *vi* (*criança*) to fill out.
encosta [ẽ'kɔʃta] *f* slope.
encostar [ẽkoʃ'ta*] *vt* (*cabeça*) to put down; (*carro*) to park; (*pôr de lado*) to put to one side; (*pôr junto*) to put side by side; (*porta*) to leave ajar ♦ *vi* to pull in; **~-se** *vr*: **~-se em** to lean against; (*deitar-se*) to lie down on; ~ **em** to lean against; ~ **a mão em** (*bater*) to hit; **ele está sempre se encostando nos outros** he's always depending on others.
encosto [ẽ'koʃtu] *m* (*arrimo*) support; (*de cadeira*) back.
encouraçado/a [ẽkora'sadu/a] *adj* armoured (*BRIT*), armored (*US*) ♦ *m* (*NÁUT*) battleship.
encravado/a [ẽkra'vadu/a] *adj* (*unha*) ingrowing.
encravar [ẽkra'va*] *vt*: ~ **algo em algo** to stick sth into sth; (*diamante num anel*) to mount sth in sth.
encrenca [ẽ'krẽka] (*col*) *f* (*problema*) fix,

jam; (*briga*) fight; **meter-se numa ~** to get into trouble.
encrencar [ẽkrẽ'ka*] (*col*) *vt* (*situação*) to complicate; (*pessoa*) to get into trouble ♦ *vi* (*complicar-se*) to get complicated; (*carro*) to break down; **~se** *vr* to get complicated; to get into trouble; **~ (com alguém)** to fall out (with sb).
encrenqueiro/a [ẽkrẽ'kejru/a] (*col*) *m/f* troublemaker ♦ *adj* troublemaking.
encrespado/a [ẽkreʃ'padu/a] *adj* (*cabelo*) curly; (*mar*) choppy; (*água*) rippling.
encrespar [ẽkreʃ'pa*] *vt* (*o cabelo*) to curl; **~-se** *vr* (*o cabelo*) to curl; (*água*) to ripple; (*o mar*) to get choppy.
encruar [ẽkru'a*] *vi* (*negócio*) to grind to a halt.
encruzilhada [ẽkruzi'ʎada] *f* crossroads *sg*.
encucação [ẽkuka'sãw] (*pl* **-ões**) *f* fixation.
encucado/a [ẽku'kadu/a] (*col*) *adj*: **~ (com)** hung up (about).
encucar [ẽku'ka*] (*col*) *vt*: **~ alguém** to give sb a hang-up ♦ *vi*: **~ com** *ou* **em algo/alguém** to be hung up about sth/sb.
encurralar [ẽkura'la*] *vt* (*gado, pessoas*) to herd; (*cercar*) to corner.
encurtar [ẽkux'ta*] *vt* to shorten.
endêmico/a [ẽ'demiku/a] *adj* endemic.
endemoninhado/a [ẽdemoni'ɲadu/a] *adj* (*pessoa*) possessed; (*espíritu*) demoniac; (*fig*: *criança*) naughty.
endentar [ẽdẽ'ta*] *vt* to engage.
endereçamento [ẽderesa'mẽtu] *m* (*tb*: COMPUT) addressing; (*endereço*) address.
endereçar [ẽdere'sa*] *vt* (*carta*) to address; (*encaminhar*) to direct.
endereço [ẽde'resu] *m* address; **~ absoluto/relativo** (COMPUT) absolute/relative address.
endeusar [ẽdew'za*] *vt* to deify; (*amado*) to worship.
endiabrado/a [ẽdʒja'bradu/a] *adj* devilish; (*travesso*) mischievous.
endinheirado/a [ẽdʒiɲej'radu/a] *adj* rich, wealthy, well-off.
endireitar [ẽdʒirej'ta*] *vt* (*objeto*) to straighten; (*retificar*) to put right; (*fig*) to straighten out; **~-se** *vr* to straighten up.
endividado/a [ẽdʒivi'dadu/a] *adj* in debt.
endividamento [ẽdʒivida'mẽtu] *m* debt.
endividar [ẽdʒivi'da*] *vt* to put into debt; **~-se** *vr* to run into debt.
endócrino/a [ẽ'dɔkrinu/a] *adj V* **glândula**.
endoidecer [ẽdojde'se*] *vt* to madden ♦ *vi* to go mad.
endoscopia [ẽdoʃko'pia] *f* (MED) endoscopy.
endossante [ẽdo'sãtʃi] *m/f* endorser.
endossar [ẽdo'sa*] *vt* to endorse.
endossável [ẽdo'savew] (*pl* **-eis**) *adj* endorsable.
endosso [ẽ'dosu] *m* endorsement.
endurecer [ẽdure'se*] *vt, vi* to harden.
endurecido/a [ẽdure'sidu/a] *adj* hardened.
endurecimento [ẽduresi'mẽtu] *m* hardening.
ENE *abr* (= *és-nordeste*) ENE.
enegrecer [enegre'se*] *vt* to darken; (*fig*: *nome*) to blacken ♦ *vi* to darken.
enema [e'nema) *m* enema.
energético/a [enex'ʒɛtʃiku/a] *adj* energy *atr* ♦ *m* energy source.
energia [enɛx'ʒia] *f* (*vigor*) energy, drive; (TEC) power, energy.
enérgico/a [e'nɛxʒiku/a] *adj* energetic, vigorous; **ele é ~ com os filhos** he is hard on his children.
enervação [enexva'sãw] *f* annoyance, irritation.
enervante [enex'vãtʃi] *adj* annoying.
enervar [enex'va*] *vt* to annoy, irritate ♦ *vi* to be irritating; **~-se** *vr* to get annoyed.
enevoado/a [ene'vwadu/a] *adj* misty, hazy.
enfadar [ẽfa'da*] *vt* (*entediar*) to bore; (*incomodar*) to annoy; **~-se** *vr*: **~-se de** to get tired of; **~-se com** (*aborrecer-se*) to get fed up with.
enfado [ẽ'fadu] *m* annoyance.
enfadonho/a [ẽfa'doɲu/a] *adj* (*cansativo*) tiresome; (*aborrecido*) boring.
enfaixar [ẽfaj'ʃa*] *vt* (*perna*) to bandage, bind; (*bebê*) to wrap up.
enfarte [ẽ'faxtʃi] *m* (MED) coronary.
ênfase ['ẽfazi] *f* emphasis, stress.
enfastiado/a [ẽfaʃ'tʃjadu/a] *adj* bored.
enfastiar [ẽfaʃ'tʃja*] *vt* (*cansar*) to weary; (*aborrecer*) to bore; **~-se** *vr*: **~-se de** *ou* **com** (*cansar-se*) to get tired of; (*aborrecer-se*) to get bored with.
enfático/a [ẽ'fatʃiku/a] *adj* emphatic.
enfatizar [ẽfatʃi'za*] *vt* to emphasize.
enfear [ẽfe'a*] *vt* (*pessoa etc*) to make ugly; (*deturpar*) to distort ♦ *vi* to become ugly.
enfeitar [ẽfej'ta*] *vt* to decorate; **~-se** *vr* to dress up.
enfeitiçante [ẽfejtʃi'sãtʃi] *adj* enchanting, charming.
enfeite [ẽ'fejtʃi] *m* decoration.
enfeitiçar [ẽfejtʃi'sa*] *vt* to bewitch, cast a spell on.
enfermagem [ẽfex'maʒẽ] *f* nursing.
enfermaria [ẽfexma'ria] *f* ward.
enfermeiro/a [ẽfex'mejru/a] *m/f* nurse.
enfermidade [ẽfexmi'dadʒi] *f* illness.
enfermo/a [ẽ'fexmu/a] *adj* ill, sick ♦ *m/f* sick person, patient.
enferrujar [ẽfexu'ʒa*] *vt* to rust, corrode ♦ *vi* to go rusty.
enfezado/a [ẽfe'zadu/a] *adj* (*irritadiço*) irritable; (*irritado*) angry, mad.
enfezar [ẽfe'za*] *vt* (*irritar*) to make angry; **~-se** *vr* to become angry.
enfiada [ẽ'fjada] *f* (*de pérolas*) string; (*fila*)

***NB**: European Portuguese adds the following consonants to certain words:* **b** (sú(b)dito, su(b)til); **c** (a(c)ção, a(c)cionista, a(c)to); **m** (inde(m)ne); **p** (ado(p)ção, ado(p)tar); *for further details see p. xiii.*

row.

enfiar [ẽ'fja*] *vt* (*meter*) to put; (*agulha*) to thread; (*pérolas*) to string together; (*vestir*) to slip on; **~-se** *vr*: **~-se em** to slip into.

enfileirar [ẽfilej'ra*] *vt* to line up.

enfim [ẽ'fĩ] *adv* finally, at last; (*em suma*) in short; **até que ~!** at last!

enfocar [ẽfo'ka*] *vt* (*assunto*) to tackle.

enfoque [ẽ'fɔki] *m* approach.

enforcamento [ẽfoxka'mẽtu] *m* hanging.

enforcar [ẽfox'ka*] *vt* to hang; (*trabalho, aulas*) to skip; **~-se** *vr* to hang o.s.; **~ a sexta-feira** to take the Friday off.

enfraquecer [ẽfrake'se*] *vt* to weaken ♦ *vi* to grow weak.

enfraquecimento [ẽfrakesi'mẽtu] *m* weakening.

enfrentar [ẽfrẽ'ta*] *vt* (*encarar*) to face; (*confrontar*) to confront; (*problemas*) to face up to.

enfronhado/a [ẽfro'ɲadu/a] *adj*: **estar bem ~ num assunto** to be well versed in a subject.

enfronhar [ẽfro'ɲa*] *vi*: **~ alguém em algo** to instruct sb in sth; **~-se** *vr*: **~-se em algo** to learn about sth, become well versed in sth.

enfumaçado/a [ẽfuma'sadu/a] *adj* full of smoke, smoky.

enfumaçar [ẽfuma'sa*] *vt* to fill with smoke.

enfurecer [ẽfure'se*] *vt* to infuriate; **~-se** *vr* to get furious.

enfurnar [ẽfux'na*] *vt* to hide away; (*meter*) to stow away; **~-se** *vr* to hide (o.s.) away.

engª *abr* (=*engenheira*) Eng.

engaiolar [ẽgajo'la*] (*col*) *vt* to jail.

engajamento [ẽgaʒa'mẽtu] *m* (*empenho*, *POL*) commitment; (*de trabalhadores*) hiring; (*MIL*) enlistment.

engajar [ẽga'ʒa*] *vt* (*trabalhadores*) to take on, hire; **~-se** *vr* to take up employment; (*MIL*) to enlist; **~-se em algo** to get involved in sth; (*POL*) to be committed to sth.

engalfinhar-se [ẽgawfi'ɲaxsi] *vr* (*atacar-se*) to fight; (*discutir*) to argue.

engambelar [ẽgãbe'la*] *vt* to con, trick.

enganado/a [ẽga'nadu/a] *adj* (*errado*) mistaken; (*traído*) deceived.

enganador(a) [ẽgana'do*(a)] *adj* (*mentiroso*) deceitful; (*artificioso*) fake; (*conselho*) misleading; (*aspecto*) deceptive.

enganar [ẽga'na*] *vt* to deceive; (*desonrar*) to seduce; (*cônjuge*) to be unfaithful to; (*fome*) to stave off; **~-se** *vr* (*cair em erro*) to be wrong, be mistaken; (*iludir-se*) to deceive o.s.; **as aparências enganam** appearances are deceptive.

enganchar [ẽgã'ʃa*] *vt*: **~ algo (em algo)** to hook sth up (to sth).

engano [ẽ'gãnu] *m* (*error*) mistake; (*ilusão*) deception; (*logro*) trick; **é ~** (*TEL*) I've (*ou* you've) got the wrong number.

engarrafado/a [ẽgaxa'fadu/a] *adj* bottled; (*trânsito*) blocked.

engarrafamento [ẽgaxafa'mẽtu] *m* bottling; (*de trânsito*) traffic jam.

engarrafar [ẽgaxa'fa*] *vt* to bottle; (*trânsito*) to block.

engasgar [ẽgaʒ'ga*] *vt* to choke ♦ *vi* to choke; (*carro*) to backfire; **~-se** *vr* to choke.

engasgo [ẽ'gaʒgu] *m* choking.

engastar [ẽgaʃ'ta*] *vt* (*jóias*) to set, mount.

engaste [ẽ'gaʃtʃi] *m* setting, mounting.

engatar [ẽga'ta*] *vt* (*vagões*) to couple, hitch up; (*AUTO*) to put into gear.

engatilhar [ẽgatʃi'ʎa*] *vt* (*revólver*) to cock; (*fig*: *resposta etc*) to prepare.

engatinhar [ẽgatʃi'ɲa*] *vi* to crawl; (*fig*) to be feeling one's way.

engavetamento [ẽgaveta'mẽtu] *m* (*de carros*) pile-up.

engavetar [ẽgave'ta*] *vt* (*fig*: *projeto*) to shelve; **~-se** *vr* to crash into one another; **~-se em algo** to crash into (the back of) sth.

engelhar [ẽʒe'ʎa*] *vt*, *vi* (*pele*) to wrinkle.

engendrar [ẽʒẽ'dra*] *vt* to dream up.

engenharia [ẽʒeɲa'ria] *f* engineering.

engenheiro/a [ẽʒe'ɲejru/a] *m/f* engineer.

engenho [ẽ'ʒeɲu] *m* (*talento*) talent; (*destreza*) skill; (*máquina*) machine; (*moenda*) mill; (*fazenda*) sugar plantation.

engenhoso/a [ẽʃe'ɲozu/ɔza] *adj* clever, ingenious.

engessar [ẽʒe'sa*] *vt* (*perna*) to put in plaster; (*parede*) to plaster.

englobar [ẽglo'ba*] *vt* to include.

engº *abr* (= *engenheiro*) Eng.

engodar [ẽgo'da*] *vt* to lure, entice.

engodo [ẽ'godu] *m* (*para peixe*) bait; (*para pessoas*) lure, enticement.

engolir [ẽgo'li*] *vt* (*tb fig*) to swallow; **até hoje não engoli o que ele me fez** I still haven't forgiven him for what he did to me.

engomar [ẽgo'ma*] *vt* to starch; (*passar*) to iron.

engonço [ẽ'gõsu] *m* hinge.

engordar [ẽgox'da*] *vt* to fatten ♦ *vi* to put on weight; **o açúcar engorda** sugar is fattening.

engordurado/a [ẽgoxdu'radu/a] *adj* (*comida*) fatty; (*mãos*) greasy.

engordurar [ẽgoxdu'ra*] *vt* to cover with grease.

engraçado/a [ẽgra'sadu/a] *adj* funny, amusing.

engraçar-se [ẽgra'saxsi] (*col*) *vr*: **~ com alguém** to take advantage of sb.

engradado [ẽgra'dadu] *m* crate.

engrandecer [ẽgrãde'se*] *vt* to elevate ♦ *vi* to grow; **~-se** *vr* to become great.

engravatar-se [ẽgrava'taxsi] *vr* to put on a tie; (*vestir-se bem*) to dress smartly.

engravidar [ẽgravi'da*] *vt*: **~ alguém** to get sb pregnant; (*MED*) to impregnate sb ♦ *vi* to get pregnant.

engraxador [ẽgraʃa'do*] (*PT*) *m* shoe shiner.

engraxar [ẽgra'ʃa*] *vt* to polish.

engraxate [ẽgra'ʃatʃi] *m* shoe shiner.

engrenagem [ẽgre'naʒẽ] (*pl* **-ns**) *f* (*AUTO*)

gear.
engrenar [ẽgre'na*] *vt* (AUTO) to put into gear; (*fig*: *conversa*) to strike up ♦ *vi*: ~ **com alguém** to get on with sb.
engrolado/a [ẽgro'ladu/a] *adj* (*voz*) slurred.
engrossar [ẽgro'sa*] *vt* (*sopa*) to thicken; (*aumentar*) to swell; (*voz*) to raise ♦ *vi* to thicken; to swell; to rise; (*col*: *pessoa*, *conversa*) to turn nasty.
engrupir [ẽgru'pi*] (*col*) *vt* to con, trick.
enguia [ẽ'gia] *f* eel.
enguiçar [ẽgi'sa*] *vi* (*máquina*) to break down ♦ *vt* to cause to break down.
enguiço [ẽ'gisu] *m* (*empecilho*) snag; (*desarranjo*) breakdown.
engulho [ẽ'guʎu] *m* nausea.
enigma [e'nigima] *m* enigma; (*mistério*) mystery.
enigmático/a [enigi'matʃiku/a] *adj* enigmatic.
enjaular [ẽʒaw'la*] *vt* (*fera*) to cage, cage up; (*prender*: *pessoa*) to imprison.
enjeitado/a [ẽʒej'tadu/a] *m/f* foundling, waif.
enjeitar [ẽʒej'ta*] *vt* (*rejeitar*) to reject; (*abandonar*) to abandon; (*condenar*) to condemn.
enjoado/a [ẽ'ʒwadu/a] *adj* sick; (*enfastiado*) bored; (*enfadonho*) boring; (*mal-humorado*) in a bad mood.
enjoar [ẽ'ʒwa*] *vt* to make sick; (*enfastiar*) to bore ♦ *vi* (*pessoa*) to be sick; (*remédio*, *comida*) to cause nausea; **~-se** *vr*: **~se de** to get sick of; **eu enjôo com o cheiro de fritura** the smell of frying makes me sick; **eu enjoei de ir ao cinema** I'm sick of going to the cinema.
enjoativo/a [ẽʒwa'tʃivu/a] *adj* (*comida*) revolting; (*tedioso*) boring.
enjôo [ẽ'ʒou] *m* sickness; (*em carro*) travel sickness; (*em navio*) seasickness; (*aborrecimento*) boredom; **que ~!** what a bore!
enlaçar [ẽla'sa*] *vt* (*atar*) to tie, bind; (*abraçar*) to hug; (*unir*) to link, join; (*bois*) to hitch; (*cingir*) to wind around; **~-se** *vr* to be linked.
enlace [ẽ'lasi] *m* link, connection; (*casamento*) marriage, union.
enlamear [ẽla'mja*] *vt* to cover in mud; (*reputação*) to besmirch.
enlatado/a [ẽla'tadu/a] *adj* tinned (BRIT), canned ♦ *m* (*pej*: *filme*) foreign import; **~s** *mpl* tinned (BRIT) *ou* canned foods.
enlatar [ẽla'ta*] *vt* (*comida*) to can.
enlevar [ẽle'va*] *vt* (*extasiar*) to enrapture; (*absorver*) to absorb.
enlevo [ẽ'levu] *m* (*êxtase*) rapture; (*deleite*) delight.
enlouquecer [ẽloke'se*] *vt* to drive mad ♦ *vi* to go mad.
enluarado/a [ẽlua'rado/a] *adj* moonlit.
enlutado/a [ẽlu'tadu/a] *adj* in mourning.
enlutar-se [ẽlu'taxsi] *vr* to go into mourning.
enobrecer [enobre'se*] *vt* to ennoble ♦ *vi* to be ennobling.
enojar [eno'ja*] *vt* to disgust, sicken.
enorme [e'nɔxmi] *adj* enormous, huge.
enormidade [enoxmi'dadʒi] *f* enormity; **uma ~ (de)** (*col*) a hell of a lot (of).
enovelar [enove'la*] *vt* to wind into a ball; (*enrolar*) to roll up.
enquadrar [ẽkwa'dra*] *vt* to fit; (*gravura*) to frame ♦ *vi*: ~ **com** (*condizer*) to fit *ou* tie in with.
enquanto [ẽ'kʷwãtu] *conj* while; (*considerado como*) as; ~ **isso** meanwhile; **por ~** for the time being; ~ **ele não vem** until he comes; ~ **que** whereas.
enquête [ã'kɛtʒi] *f* survey.
enrabichar-se [ẽxabi'ʃaxsi] *vr*: ~ **por alguém** to fall for sb.
enraivecer [ẽxajve'se*] *vt* to enrage.
enraizar [ẽxaj'za*] *vi* to take root; **~-se** *vr* (*pessoa*) to settle down.
enrascada [ẽxaʃ'kada] *f* tight spot, predicament; **meter-se numa ~** to get into a spot of bother.
enrascar [ẽxaʃ'ka*] *vt* to embroil; **~-se** *vr* to get embroiled.
enredar [ẽxe'da*] *vt* (*emaranhar*) to entangle; (*complicar*) to complicate; **~-se** *vr* to get entangled.
enredo [ẽ'xedu] *m* (*de uma obra*) plot; (*intriga*) intrigue; **ele faz tanto ~** (*fig*) he makes such a fuss.
enregelado/a [ẽxeʒe'ladu/a] *adj* (*pessoa*, *mão*) frozen; (*muito frio*) freezing.
enrijecer [ẽxiʒe'se*] *vt* to stiffen; **~-se** *vr* to stiffen; (*fortalecer*) to get stronger.
enriquecer [ẽxike'se*] *vt* to make rich; (*fig*) to enrich ♦ *vi* to get rich; **~-se** *vr* to get rich.
enriquecimento [ẽxikesi'mẽtu] *m* enrichment.
enrolado/a [ẽxo'ladu/a] (*col*) *adj* complicated.
enrolar [ẽxo'la*] *vt* to roll up; (*agasalhar*) to wrap up; (*col*: *enganar*) to con ♦ *vi* (*col*) to waffle; **~-se** *vr* to roll up; (*agasalhar-se*) to wrap up; (*col*: *confundir-se*) to get mixed *ou* muddled up.
enroscar [ẽxoʃ'ka*] *vt* (*torcer*) to twist, wind (round); **~-se** *vr* to coil up.
enrouquecer [ẽxoke'se*] *vt* to make hoarse ♦ *vi* to go hoarse.
enrubescer [ẽxube'se*] *vt* to redden, colour (BRIT), color (US) ♦ *vi* (*por vergonha*) to blush, go red.
enrugar [ẽxu'ga*] *vt* (*pele*) to wrinkle; (*testa*) to furrow; (*tecido*) to crease ♦ *vi* (*pele*, *mãos*) to go wrinkly; (*pessoa*) to get wrinkles.
enrustido/a [ẽxuʃ'tʃido/a] (*col*) *adj* withdrawn.
ensaboar [ẽsa'bwa*] *vt* to wash with soap; **~-**

NB: European Portuguese adds the following consonants to certain words: **b** (sú(b)dito, su(b)til); **c** (a(c)ção, a(c)cionista, a(c)to); **m** (inde(m)ne); **p** (ado(p)ção, ado(p)tar); *for further details see p. xiii.*

se *vr* to soap o.s.
ensaiar [ẽsa'ja*] *vt* (*provar*) to test, try out; (*treinar*) to practise (*BRIT*), practice (*US*); (*TEATRO*) to rehearse.
ensaio [ẽ'saju] *m* (*prova*) test; (*tentativa*) attempt; (*treino*) practice; (*TEATRO*) rehearsal; (*literário*) essay.
ensaísta [ẽsaj'iʃta] *m/f* essayist.
ensangüentado/a [ẽsãgwẽ'tadu/a] *adj* bloody.
ensangüentar [ẽsãgwẽ'ta*] *vt* to stain with blood.
enseada [ẽ'sjada] *f* inlet, cove; (*baía*) bay.
ensebado/a [ẽse'badu/a] *adj* greasy; (*sujo*) soiled.
ensejar [ẽse'ʒa*] *vt*: ~ **algo (a alguém)** to provide (sb with) an opportunity for sth.
ensejo [ẽ'seʒu] *m* chance, opportunity.
ensimesmado/a [ẽsimeʒ'madu/a] *adj* lost in thought.
ensimesmar-se [ẽsimeʒ'maxsi] *vr* to be lost in thought; ~ **em** to be lost in.
ensinamento [ẽsina'mẽtu] *m* teaching; (*exemplo*) lesson.
ensinar [ẽsi'na*] *vt, vi* to teach; ~ **alguém a patinar** to teach sb to skate; ~ **algo a alguém** to teach sb sth; ~ **o caminho a alguém** to show sb the way; **você quer ~ o padre a rezar missa?** are you trying to teach your grandmother to suck eggs?
ensino [ẽ'sinu] *m* teaching, tuition; (*educação*) education.
ensolarado/a [ẽsola'radu/a] *adj* sunny.
ensombrecido/a [ẽsõbre'sidu/a] *adj* darkened.
ensopado/a [ẽso'padu/a] *adj* soaked ♦ *m* stew.
ensopar [ẽso'pa*] *vt* to soak, drench.
ensurdecedor(a) [ẽsuxdese'do*(a)] *adj* deafening.
ensurdecer [ẽsuxde'se*] *vt* to deafen ♦ *vi* to go deaf.
entabular [ẽtabu'la*] *vt* (*negociação*) to start, open; (*empreender*) to undertake; (*assunto*) to broach; (*conversa*) to strike up.
entalado/a [ẽta'ladu/a] *adj* (*apertado*) wedged, jammed; (*enrascado*) embroiled, involved; (*engasgado*) choking.
entalar [ẽta'la*] *vt* (*encravar*) to wedge, jam; (*fig*) to put in a fix; **ela me entalou de comida** she stuffed me full of food.
entalhador(a) [ẽtaʎa'do*(a)] *m/f* woodcarver.
entalhar [ẽta'ʎa*] *vt* to carve.
entalhe [ẽ'taʎi] *m* groove, notch.
entalho [ẽ'taʎu] *m* woodcarving.
entanto [ẽ'tãtu]: **no** ~ *adv* yet, however.
então [ẽ'tãw] *adv* then; **até** ~ up to that time; **desde** ~ ever since; **e ~?** well then?; **para** ~ so that; **pois** ~ in that case; **~, você vai ou não?** so, are you going or not?
entardecer [ẽtaxde'se*] *vi* to get late ♦ *m* sunset.
ente ['ẽtʃi] *m* being.
enteado/a [ẽ'tʃjadu/a] *m/f* stepson/stepdaughter.
entediante [ẽte'dʒjãtʃi] *adj* boring, tedious.
entediar [ẽte'dʒja*] *vt* to bore; **~-se** *vr* to get bored.
entendedor(a) [ẽtẽde'do*(a)] *adj* knowledgeable ♦ *m*: **a bom ~ meia palavra basta** a word to the wise is enough.
entender [ẽtẽ'de*] *vt* (*compreender*) to understand; (*pensar*) to think; (*ouvir*) to hear; **~-se** *vr* (*compreender-se*) to understand one another; **dar a ~** to imply; **no meu ~** in my opinion; **~ de música** to know about music; **~ de fazer** to decide to do; **~-se por** to be meant by; **~-se com alguém** to get along with sb; (*dialogar*) to sort things out with sb.
entendido/a [ẽtẽ'dʒidu/a] *adj* (*col*) gay; (*conhecedor*): **~ em** good at ♦ *m* expert; (*col*) homosexual, gay; **bem ~** that is.
entendimento [ẽtẽdʒi'mẽtu] *m* (*compreensão*) understanding; (*opinião*) opinion; (*combinação*) agreement.
enternecedor(a) [ẽtexnese'do*(a)] *adj* touching.
enternecer [ẽtexne'se*] *vt* to move, touch; **~-se** *vr* to be moved.
enterrar [ẽte'xa*] *vt* to bury; (*faca*) to plunge; (*lever à ruina*) to ruin; (*assunto*) to close; **~ o chapéu na cabeça** to put one's hat on.
enterro [ẽ'texu] *m* burial; (*funeral*) funeral.
entidade [ẽtʃi'dadʒi] *f* (*ser*) being; (*corporação*) body; (*coisa que existe*) entity.
entoação [ẽtoa'sãw] *f* singing.
entoar [ẽ'twa*] *vt* (*cantar*) to chant.
entonação [ẽtona'sãw] (*pl* **-ões**) *f* intonation.
entontecer [ẽtõte'se*] *vt* to make dizzy; (*enlouquecer*) to drive mad ♦ *vi* to become *ou* get dizzy; to go mad; **o vinho entontece** wine makes you dizzy.
entornar [ẽtox'na*] *vt* to spill; (*fig*: *copo*) to drink ♦ *vi* to drink a lot.
entorpecente [ẽtoxpe'sẽtʃi] *m* narcotic.
entorpecer [ẽtoxpe'se*] *vt* (*paralisar*) to numb, stupefy; (*retardar*) to slow down.
entorpecimento [ẽtoxpesi'mẽtu] *m* numbness; (*torpor*) lethargy.
entorse [ẽ'tɔxsi] *f* sprain.
entortar [ẽtox'ta*] *vt* (*curvar*) to bend; (*empenar*) to warp; ~ **os olhos** to squint.
entourage [ãtu'raʒi] *m* entourage.
entrada [ẽ'trada] *f* (*ato*) entry; (*lugar*) entrance; (*TEC*) inlet; (*de casa*) doorway; (*começo*) beginning; (*bilhete*) ticket; (*CULIN*) starter, entrée; (*COMPUT*) input; (*pagamento inicial*) down payment; (*corredor de casa*) hall; (*no cabelo*) receding hairline; **~ gratuita** admission free; **"~ proibida"** "no entry", "no admittance"; **meia ~** half-price ticket; **dar ~ a** (*requerimento*) to submit; (*processo*) to institute; **dar uma ~** to go in; **~ de serviço** service entrance.
entrado/a [ẽ'tradu/a] *adj*: **~ em anos** (*PT*) elderly.
entra-e-sai ['ẽtrai'saj] *m* comings and goings

pl.

entranhado/a [ẽtra'ɲadu/a] *adj* deep-rooted.

entranhar-se [ẽtra'ɲaxsi] *vr* to penetrate.

entranhas [ẽ'traɲaʃ] *fpl* bowels, entrails; (*sentimentos*) feelings; (*centro*) heart *sg.*

entrar [ẽ'tra*] *vi* to go *ou* come in, enter; (*conseguir* ~) to get in; **deixar** ~ to let in; ~ **com** (*COMPUT*: *dados etc*) to enter; **eu entrei com £10** I contributed £10; ~ **de férias/licença** to start one's holiday (*BRIT*) *ou* vacation (*US*)/leave; ~ **em** (*casa etc*) to go *ou* come into, enter; (*assunto*) to get onto; (*comida, bebida*) to start in on; (*universidade*) to enter; ~ **em detalhes** to go into details; ~ **em vigor** to come into force; **ele entra às 9 no trabalho** he starts work at 9.00; **o que entra nesta receita?** what goes into this recipe?; ~ **para um clube** to join a club; **quando a primavera entra** when spring comes; ~ **bem** (*col*) to get into trouble.

entravar [ẽtra'va*] *vt* to obstruct, impede.

entrave [ẽ'travi] *m* (*fig*) impediment.

entre ['ẽtri] *prep* (*dois*) between; (*mais de dois*) among(st); ~ **si** amongst themselves.

entreaberto/a [ẽtrja'bɛxtu/a] *pp de* **entreabrir** ♦ *adj* half-open; (*porta*) ajar.

entreabrir [ẽtrja'bri*] *vt* to half open; **~-se** *vr* (*flores*) to open up.

entrechocar-se [ẽtriʃo'kaxsi] *vr* to collide, crash; (*fig*) to clash.

entrecortado/a [ẽtrikox'tadu/a] *adj* intermittent; **região entrecortada de estradas** region intersected by roads.

entrecosto [ẽtri'koʃtu] *m* (*CULIN*) entrecôte.

entrega [ẽ'trɛga] *f* (*de mercadorias*) delivery; (*a alguém*) handing over; (*rendição*) surrender; **caminhão/serviço de** ~ delivery van/service; **pronta** ~ speedy delivery; ~ **rápida** special delivery; ~ **a domicílio** home delivery.

entregar [ẽtre'ga*] *vt* (*dar*) to hand over; (*mercadorias*) to deliver; (*denunciar*) to hand over; (*confiar*) to entrust; (*devolver*) to return; **~-se** *vr* (*render-se*) to give o.s. up; (*dedicar-se*) to devote o.s.; **~-se à dor/bebida** to be overcome by grief/take to drink; **~-se a um homem** to sleep with a man; ~ **os pontos** to give up, throw in the towel.

entregue [ẽ'trɛgi] *pp de* **entregar**.

entrelaçar [ẽtrila'sa*] *vt* to entwine.

entrelinha [ẽtre'liɲa] *f* line spacing; **ler nas ~s** to read between the lines.

entremear [ẽtri'mja*] *vt* to intermingle.

entremostrar [ẽtrimoʃ'tra*] *vt* to give a glimpse of.

entreolhar-se [ẽtrio'ʎaxsɪ] *vr* to exchange glances.

entrepernas [ẽtri'pɛxnaʃ] *adv* between one's legs.

entrepor [ẽtripo*] (*irreg*: *como* **pôr**) *vt* to insert; **~-se** *vr*: **~-se entre** to come between.

entressafra [ẽtri'safra] *f* time between harvests; (*fig*): **as ~s de algo** the periods without sth.

entretanto [ẽtri'tãtu] *conj* however.

entretenimento [ẽtriteni'mẽtu] *m* entertainment; (*distração*) pastime.

entretela [ẽtri'tɛla] *f* (*COSTURA*) interlining, buckram.

entreter [ẽtri'te*] (*irreg*: *como* **ter**) *vt* (*divertir*) to entertain, amuse; (*ocupar*) to occupy; (*manter*) to keep up; (*esperanças*) to cherish; **~-se** *vr* (*divertir-se*) to amuse o.s.; (*ocupar-se*) to occupy o.s.

entrevar [ẽtre'va*] *vt* to paralyse, cripple.

entrever [ẽtri've*] (*irreg*: *como* **ver**) *vt* to glimpse, catch a glimpse of.

entrevista [ẽtre'viʃta] *f* interview; ~ **coletiva (à imprensa)** press conference.

entrevistador(a) [ẽtreviʃta'do*(a)] *m/f* interviewer.

entrevistar [ẽtreviʃ'ta*] *vt* to interview; **~-se** *vr* to have an interview.

entrevisto/a [ẽtre'viʃtu/a] *pp de* **entrever**.

entristecedor(a) [ẽtriʃtese'do*(a)] *adj* saddening, sad.

entristecer [ẽtriʃte'se*] *vt* to sadden, grieve ♦ *vi* to feel sad; **~-se** *vr* to feel sad.

entroncamento [ẽtrõka'mẽtu] *m* junction.

entrosado/a [ẽtro'zadu/a] *adj* (*fig*) integrated.

entrosamento [ẽtroza'mẽtu] *m* (*fig*) integration.

entrosar [ẽtro'za*] *vt* (*rodas*) to mesh; (*peças*) to fit; (*fig*) to integrate ♦ *vi* to mesh; to fit; ~ **com** (*fig*) to fit in with; ~ **em** (*adaptar-se*) to settle into.

entrudo [ẽ'trudu] (*PT*) *m* carnival; (*REL*) Shrovetide.

entulhar [ẽtu'ʎa*] *vt* to cram full; (*suj*: *multidão*) to pack.

entulho [ẽ'tuʎu] *m* rubble, debris *sg.*

entupido/a [ẽtu'pidu/a] *adj* blocked; **estar** ~ (*col*: *congestionado*) to have a blocked-up nose; (*de comida*) to be fit to burst, be full up.

entupimento [ẽtupi'mẽtu] *m* blockage.

entupir [ẽtu'pi*] *vt* to block, clog; **~-se** *vr* to become blocked; (*de comida*) to stuff o.s.

entupitivo/a [ẽtupi'tʃivu/a] *adj* filling.

enturmar-se [ẽtux'maxsi] *vr*: ~ **(com)** to make friends (with).

entusiasmar [ẽtuzjaʒ'ma*] *vt* to fill with enthusiasm; (*animar*) to excite; **~-se** *vr* to get excited.

entusiasmo [ẽtu'zjaʒmu] *m* enthusiasm; (*júbilo*) excitement.

entusiasta [ẽtu'zjaʃta] *adj* enthusiastic ♦ *m/f* enthusiast.

entusiástico/a [ẽtu'zjaʃtʃiku/a] *adj* enthusiastic.

NB*: European Portuguese adds the following consonants to certain words:* **b** (sú(b)dito, su(b)til); **c** (a(c)ção, a(c)cionista, a(c)to); **m** (inde(m)ne); **p** (ado(p)ção, ado(p)tar); *for further details see p. xiii.*

enumeração [enumera'sãw] (*pl* **-ões**) *f* enumeration; (*numeração*) numbering.
enumerar [enume'ra*] *vt* to enumerate; (*com números*) to number.
enunciar [enũ'sja*] *vt* to express, state.
envaidecer [ẽvajde'se*] *vt* to make conceited; **~-se** *vr* to become conceited.
envelhecer [ẽveʎe'se*] *vt* to age ♦ *vi* to grow old, age.
envelhecimento [ẽveʎesi'mẽtu] *m* aging.
envelope [ẽve'lɔpi] *m* envelope.
envenenado/a [ẽvene'nadu/a] *adj* poisoned; (*col*: *festa, roupa*) wild, great; (: *carro*) souped up.
envenenamento [ẽvenena'mẽtu] *m* poisoning; **~ do sangue** blood poisoning.
envenenar [ẽvene'na*] *vt* to poison; (*fig*) to corrupt; (: *declaração, palavras*) to distort, twist; (*tornar amargo*) to sour; (*col*: *carro*) to soup up ♦ *vi* to be poisonous; **~-se** *vr* to poison o.s.
enverdecer [ẽvexde'se*] *vt* to turn green.
enveredar [ẽvere'da*] *vi*: **~ por um caminho** to follow a road; **~ para** to head for.
envergadura [ẽvexga'dura] *f* (*asas, velas*) spread; (*avião*) wingspan; (*fig*) scope; **de grande ~** large-scale.
envergar [ẽvex'ga*] *vt* (*arquear*) to bend; (*vestir*) to wear.
envergonhado/a [ẽvexgo'ɲadu/a] *adj* ashamed; (*tímido*) shy.
envergonhar [ẽvexgo'ɲa*] *vt* to shame; (*degradar*) to disgrace; **~-se** *vr* to be ashamed.
envernizar [ẽvexni'za*] *vt* to varnish.
enviado/a [ẽ'vjadu/a] *m/f* envoy, messenger.
enviar [ẽ'vja*] *vt* to send.
envidar [ẽvi'da*] *vt*: **~ esforços (para fazer algo)** to endeavour (BRIT) *ou* endeavor (US) (to do sth).
envidraçado/a [ẽvidra'sadu/a] *adj* V **varanda**.
envidraçar [ẽvidra'sa*] *vt* to glaze.
enviesado/a [ẽvje'zadu/a] *adj* slanting.
envilecer [ẽvile'se*] *vt* to debase, degrade.
envio [ẽ'viu] *m* sending; (*expedição*) dispatch; (*remessa*) remittance; (*de mercadorias*) consignment.
enviuvar [ẽvju'va*] *vi* to be widowed.
envolto/a [ẽ'vowtu/a] *pp de* **envolver**.
envoltório [ẽvow'tɔrju] *m* cover.
envolvente [ẽvow'vẽtʃi] *adj* compelling.
envolver [ẽvow've*] *vt* (*embrulhar*) to wrap (up); (*cobrir*) to cover; (*comprometer, acarretar*) to involve; (*nos braços*) to embrace; **~-se** *vr* (*intrometer-se*) to become involved; (*cobrir-se*) to wrap o.s. up.
envolvimento [ẽvowvi'mẽtu] *m* involvement.
enxada [ẽ'ʃada] *f* hoe.
enxadrista [ẽʃa'driʃta] *m/f* chess player.
enxaguada [ẽʃa'gwada] *f* rinse.
enxaguar [ẽʃa'gwa*] *vt* to rinse.
enxame [ẽ'ʃami] *m* swarm.
enxaqueca [ẽʃa'keka] *f* migraine.
enxergão [ẽʃex'gãw] (*pl* **-ões**) *m* (straw) mattress.
enxergar [ẽʃex'ga*] *vt* (*avistar*) to catch sight of; (*divisar*) to make out; (*notar*) to observe, see; **~-se** *vr*: **ele não se enxerga** he doesn't know his place.
enxergões [ẽʃex'gõjʃ] *mpl de* **enxergão**.
enxerido/a [ẽʃe'ridu/a] *adj* nosy, interfering.
enxertar [ẽʃex'ta*] *vt* to graft; (*fig*) to incorporate.
enxerto [ẽ'ʃextu] *m* graft.
enxó [ẽ'ʃɔ] *m* adze.
enxofre [ẽ'ʃofri] *m* sulphur (BRIT), sulfur (US).
enxota-moscas [ẽ'ʃɔta-] (PT) *m* fly swatter.
enxotar [ẽʃo'ta*] *vt* (*expulsar*) to drive out.
enxoval [ẽʃo'vaw] (*pl* **-ais**) *m* (*de noiva*) trousseau; (*de recém-nascido*) layette.
enxovalhar [ẽʃova'ʎa*] *vt* (*sujar*) to soil; (*amarrotar*) to crumple; (*reputação*) to blacken; (*insultar*) to insult; **~-se** *vr* to disgrace o.s.
enxugador [ẽʃuga'do*] *m* clothes drier.
enxugar [ẽʃu'ga*] *vt* to dry; (*fig*: *texto*) to tidy up; **~ as lágrimas** to dry one's eyes.
enxurrada [ẽʃu'xada] *f* (*de água*) torrent; (*fig*) spate.
enxuto/a [ẽ'ʃutu/a] *adj* dry; (*corpo*) shapely; (*bonito*) good-looking.
enzima [ẽ'zima] *f* enzyme.
epicentro [epi'sẽtru] *m* epicentre (BRIT), epicenter (US).
épico/a ['ɛpiku/a] *adj* epic ♦ *m* epic poet.
epidemia [epide'mia] *f* epidemic.
epidêmico/a [epi'demiku/a] *adj* epidemic.
Epifania [epifa'nia] *f* Epiphany.
epilepsia [epile'psia] *f* epilepsy.
epiléptico/a [epi'lɛptʃiku/a] *adj, m/f* epileptic.
epílogo [e'pilogu] *m* epilogue.
episcopado [epiʃko'padu] *m* bishopric.
episódio [epi'zɔdʒu] *m* episode.
epístola [e'piʃtola] *f* epistle; (*carta*) letter.
epitáfio [epi'tafju] *m* epitaph.
epítome [e'pitomi] *m* summary; (*fig*) epitome.
época ['ɛpoka] *f* time, period; (*da história*) age, epoch; **~ da colheita** harvest time; **naquela ~** at that time; **fazer ~** to be epoch-making; **fazer segunda ~** to resit one's exams.
epopéia [epo'pɛja] *f* epic.
equação [ekwa'sãw] (*pl* **-ões**) *f* equation.
equacionar [ekwasjo'na*] *vt* to set out.
equações [ekwa'sõjʃ] *fpl de* **equação**.
Equador [ekwa'do*] *m*: **o ~** Ecuador.
equador [ekwa'do*] *m* equator.
equânime [e'kwanimi] *adj* fair; (*caráter*) unbiased, neutral.
equatorial [ekwato'rjaw] (*pl* **-ais**) *adj* equatorial.
equatoriano/a [ekwato'rjanu/a] *adj, m/f* Ecuadorian.
eqüestre [e'kwɛʃtri] *adj* equestrian.
eqüidade [ekwi'dadʒi] *f* equity.
eqüidistante [ekwidʒiʃ'tãtʃi] *adj* equidistant.
eqüilátero/a [ekwi'lateru/a] *adj* equilateral.

equilibrado/a [ekili'bradu/a] *adj* balanced; (*pessoa*) level-headed.
equilibrar [ekili'bra*] *vt* to balance; **~-se** *vr* to balance.
equilíbrio [eki'librju] *m* balance; **perder o ~** to lose one's balance.
eqüino/a [e'kwinu/a] *adj* equine.
equipa [e'kipa] (*PT*) *f* team.
equipamento [ekipa'mẽtu] *m* equipment, kit.
equipar [eki'pa*] *vt* (*navio*) to fit out; (*prover*) to equip.
equiparação [ekipara'sãw] (*pl* **-ões**) *f* comparison.
equiparar [ekipara*] *vt* (*comparar*) to equate; **~-se** *vr*: **~-se a** to equal.
equiparável [ekipa'ravew] (*pl* **-eis**) *adj* comparable, equitable.
equipe [e'kipi] (*BR*) *f* team.
equitação [ekita'sãw] *f* (*ato*) riding; (*arte*) horsemanship.
eqüitativo/a [ekwita'tʃivu/a] *adj* fair, equitable.
equivalência [ekiva'lẽsja] *f* equivalence.
equivalente [ekiva'lẽtʃi] *adj*, *m* equivalent.
equivaler [ekiva'le*] *vi*: **~ a** to be the same as, equal.
equivocado/a [ekivo'kadu/a] *adj* mistaken, wrong.
equivocar-se [ekivo'kaxsi] *vr* to make a mistake, be wrong.
equívoco/a [e'kivoku/a] *adj* ambiguous ♦ *m* (*engano*) mistake.
ER *abr* (= *espera resposta*) RSVP.
era ['ɛra] *etc vb V* **ser** ♦ *f* era, age.
erário [e'rarju] *m* exchequer.
ereção [ere'sãw] (*PT*: **-cç-**: *pl* **-ões**) (*tb*: *FISIOL*) erection.
erecto/a [e'rɛktu/a] (*PT*) *adj* = **ereto**.
eremita [ere'mita] *m/f* hermit.
eremitério [eremi'tɛrju] *m* hermitage.
ereto/a [e'rɛtu/a] *adj* upright, erect.
erguer [ex'ge*] *vt* (*levantar*) to raise, lift; (*edificar*) to build, erect; **~-se** *vr* to rise; (*pessoa*) to stand up.
eriçado/a [eri'sadu/a] *adj* bristling; (*cabelos*) (standing) on end.
eriçar [eri'sa*] *vt*: **~ o cabelo de alguém** to make sb's hair stand on end; **~-se** *vr* to bristle; (*cabelos*) to stand on end.
erigir [eri'ʒi*] (*irreg*) *vt* to erect.
ermo/a ['exmu/a] *adj* (*solitário*) lonely; (*desabitado*) uninhabited ♦ *m* wilderness.
erógeno/a [e'rɔʒenu/a] *adj* erogenous.
erosão [ero'zãw] *f* erosion.
erótico/a [e'rɔtʃiku/a] *adj* erotic.
erotismo [ero'tʃiʒmu] *m* eroticism.
erradicar [exadʒi'ka*] *vt* to eradicate.
errado/a [e'xadu/a] *adj* wrong; **dar ~** to go wrong.
errante [e'xãtʃi] *adj* wandering.
errar [e'xa*] *vt* (*o alvo*) to miss; (*a conta*) to get wrong ♦ *vi* (*vaguear*) to wander, roam; (*enganar-se*) to be wrong, make a mistake; **~ o caminho** to lose one's way.
errata [e'xata] *f* errata.
erro ['exu] *m* mistake; **salvo ~** unless I am mistaken; **~ de imprensa** misprint; **~ de programa** (*COMPUT*) bug; **~ de pronúncia** mispronunciation.
errôneo/a [e'xonju/a] *adj* wrong, mistaken; (*falso*) false, untrue.
erudição [erudʒi'sãw] *f* erudition, learning.
erudito/a [eru'dʒitu/a] *adj* learned, scholarly ♦ *m* scholar.
erupção [erup'sãw] (*pl* **-ões**) *f* eruption; (*na pele*) rash; (*fig*) outbreak.
erva ['ɛxva] *f* herb; **~ daninha** weed; (*col*: *dinheiro*) dosh; (: *maconha*) dope.
erva-cidreira [-si'drejra] (*pl* **ervas-cidreiras**) *f* lemon verbena.
erva-doce (*pl* **ervas-doces**) *f* fennel.
erva-mate [(*pl* **ervas-mates**) *f* matte.
ervilha [ex'viʎa] *f* pea.
ES (*BR*) *abr* = **Espírito Santo**.
ESAO [e'saw] (*BR*) *abr f* (= *Escola Superior de Aperfeiçoamento de Oficiais*) *officer training school*.
esbaforido/a [iʒbafo'ridu/a] *adj* breathless, panting.
esbaldar-se [iʒbaw'daxsi] *vr* to have a great time, really enjoy o.s.
esbandalhado/a [iʒbãda'ʎadu/a] *adj* (*pessoa*) scruffy; (*casa*, *jardim*) untidy.
esbanjador(a) [iʒbãʒa'do*(a)] *adj* extravagant, spendthrift ♦ *m/f* spendthrift.
esbanjamento [iʒbãʒa'mẽtu] *m* (*ato*) squandering; (*qualidade*) extravagance.
esbanjar [iʒbã'ʒa*] *vt* to squander, waste; **estar esbanjando saúde** to be bursting with health.
esbarrão [iʒba'xãw] (*pl* **-ões**) *m* collision.
esbarrar [iʒba'xa*] *vi*: **~ em** to bump into; (*obstáculo*, *problema*) to come up against.
esbarrões [iʒba'xõjʃ] *mpl de* **esbarrão**.
esbeltez [iʒbew'teʒ] *f* slenderness.
esbelto/a [iʒ'bɛwtu/a] *adj* svelte.
esboçar [iʒbo'sa*] *vt* to sketch; (*delinear*) to outline; (*plano*) to draw up; **~ um sorriso** to give a little smile.
esboço [iʒ'bosu] *m* (*desenho*) sketch; (*primeira versão*) draft; (*fig*: *resumo*) outline.
esbodegado/a [iʒbode'gadu/a] *adj* tatty; (*cansado*) worn out.
esbodegar [iʒbode'ga*] (*col*) *vt* to ruin.
esbofar [iʒbo'fa*] *vt* to tire out; **~-se** *vr* to be worn out.
esbofetear [iʒbofe'tʃja*] *vt* to slap, hit.
esbórnia [iʒ'bɔxnja] *f* orgy.
esborrachar [iʒboxa'ʃa*] *vt* to squash; (*esbofetear*) to hit; **~-se** *vr* to go sprawling.

esbranquiçado/a [iʒbrãki'sadu/a] *adj* whitish; (*lábios*) pale.
esbravejar [iʒbrave'ʒa*] *vt*, *vi* to shout.
esbregue [iʒ'brɛgi] (*col*) *m* (*descompostura*) telling-off, dressing-down (*BRIT*); (*rolo*) punch-up, brawl.
esburacado/a [iʒbura'kadu/a] *adj* full of holes, holey; (*rua*) full of potholes.
esburacar [iʒbura'ka*] *vt* to make holes (*ou* a hole) in.
esbugalhado/a [iʒbuga'ʎadu/a] *adj* V **olho**.
esbugalhar-se [iʒbuga'ʎaxsi] *vr* to goggle, boggle.
esc (*PT*) *abr* = **escudo**.
escabeche [iʃka'bɛʃi] *m* (*CULIN*) marinade, *sauce of spiced vinegar and onion*.
escabroso/a [iʃka'brozu/ɔza] *adj* (*difícil*) tough; (*indecoroso*) indecent.
escada [iʃ'kada] *f* (*dentro da casa*) staircase, stairs *pl*; (*fora da casa*) steps *pl*; (*de mão*) ladder; ~ **em caracol** spiral staircase; ~ **de incêndio** fire escape; ~ **rolante** escalator.
escadaria [iʃkada'ria] *f* staircase.
escafandrista [iʃkafã'driʃta] *m/f* deep-sea diver.
escafandro [iʃka'fãdru] *m* diving suit.
escafeder-se [iʃkafe'dexsi] (*col*) *vi* to sneak off.
escala [iʃ'kala] *f* scale; (*NÁUT*) port of call; (*parada*) stop; **fazer ~ em** to call at; **sem ~** non-stop; ~ **móvel** sliding scale.
escalação [iʃkala'sãw] *f* climbing; (*designação*) selection.
escalada [iʃka'lada] *f* (*de guerra*) escalation.
escalafobético/a [iʃkalafo'bɛtʃiku/a] (*col*) *adj* weird, strange.
escalão [eʃka'lãw] (*pl* **-ões**) *m* step; (*MIL*) echelon; **o primeiro ~ do governo** the highest level of government.
escalar [iʃka'la*] *vt* (*montanha*) to climb; (*muro*) to scale; (*designar*) to select.
escalavrar [iʃkala'vra*] *vt* (*pele*) to graze; (*parede*) to damage.
escaldado/a [iʃkaw'dadu/a] *adj* (*fig*) cautious, wary.
escaldar [iʃkaw'da*] *vt* to scald; (*CULIN*) to blanch; **~-se** *vr* to scald o.s.
escaler [iʃka'lɛ*] *m* launch.
escalfar [iʃkaw'fa*] (*PT*) *vt* (*ovos*) to poach.
escalões [ɛʃka'lõjʃ] *mpl de* **escalão**.
escalonamento [iʃkalona'mẽtu] *m* (*COM*: *de dívida*) scheduling.
escalonar [iʃkalo'na*] *vt* (*argumentos*, *opiniões*) to set out; (*dívida*) to spread, schedule.
escalope [iʃka'lɔpi] *m* escalope (*BRIT*), cutlet (*US*).
escama [iʃ'kama] *f* (*de peixe*) scale; (*de pele*) flake.
escamar [iʃka'ma*] *vt* to scale.
escamotear [iʃkamo'tʃja*] *vt* (*furtar*) to pilfer, pinch (*BRIT*); (*empalmar*) to make disappear (by sleight of hand).
escancarado/a [iʃkãka'radu/a] *adj* wide open.
escancarar [iʃkãka'ra*] *vt* to open wide.
escandalizar [iʃkãdali'za*] *vt* to shock; **~-se** *vr* to be shocked; (*ofender-se*) to be offended.
escândalo [iʃ'kãdalu] *m* scandal; (*indignação*) outrage; **fazer** *ou* **dar um ~** to make a scene.
escandaloso/a [iʃkãdalozu/ɔza] *adj* shocking, scandalous.
Escandinávia [iʃkãdʒi'navja] *f*: **a ~** Scandinavia.
escandinavo/a [iʃkãdʒi'navu/a] *adj*, *m/f* Scandinavian.
escangalhar [iʃkãga'ʎa*] *vt* to break, smash (up); (*a saúde*) to ruin; **~-se** *vr*: **~-se de rir** to split one's sides laughing.
escaninho [iʃka'niɲu] *m* (*na secretária*) pigeonhole.
escanteio [iʃkã'teju] *m* (*FUTEBOL*) corner.
escapada [iʃka'pada] *f* escape; (*ato leviano*) escapade.
escapar [iʃka'pa*] *vi*: ~ **a** *ou* **de** to escape from; (*fugir*) to run away from; **~-se** *vr* to run away, flee; **deixar ~** (*uma oportunidade*) to miss; (*palavras*) to blurt out; ~ **da morte/de uma incumbência** to escape death/get out of a task; **ele escapou de ser atropelado** he escaped being run over; **o vaso escapou-lhe das mãos** the vase slipped out of his hands; **nada lhe escapa** (*passar desapercebido*) nothing escapes him, he doesn't miss a thing; **o nome me escapa no momento** the name escapes me for the moment; **não está bom, mas escapa** it's not good, but it'll do; ~ **de boa** (*col*) to have a close shave.
escapatória [iʃkapa'tɔrja] *f* (*saída*) way out; (*desculpa*) excuse.
escape [iʃ'kapi] *m* (*de gás*) leak; (*AUTO*) exhaust.
escapismo [iʃka'piʒmu] *m* escapism.
escapulida [iʃkapu'lida] *f* escape.
escapulir [iʃkapu'li*] *vi*: ~ **(de)** to get away (from); (*suj*: *coisa*) to slip (from).
escarafunchar [iʃkarafũ'ʃa*] *vt*: ~ **algo** (*remexer em*) to rummage in sth; (*com as unhas*) to scratch at sth; (*investigar*) to pore over sth.
escaramuça [iʃkara'musa] *f* skirmish.
escaravelho [iʃkara'veʎu] *m* beetle.
escarcéu [iʃkax'sɛw] *m* (*fig*): **fazer um ~** to make a scene.
escarlate [iʃkax'latʃi] *adj* scarlet.
escarlatina [iʃkaxla'tʃina] *f* scarlet fever.
escarnecer [iʃkaxne'se*] *vt* to mock, make fun of ♦ *vi*: ~ **de** to mock, make fun of.
escárnio [iʃ'kaxnju] *m* mockery; (*desprezo*) derision.
escarpa [iʃ'kaxpa] *f* steep slope.
escarpado/a [iʃkax'padu/a] *adj* steep.
escarrado/a [iʃka'xadu/a] *adj* (*fig*): **ela é o pai ~** she's the spitting image of her father.
escarrapachar-se [iʃkaxapa'ʃaxsi] *vr* to sprawl.

escarrar [iʃka'xa*] *vt* to spit, cough up ♦ *vi* to spit.
escarro [iʃ'kaxu] *m* phlegm, spit.
escasseamento [iʃkasja'mẽtu] *m* (*COM*) shortage.
escassear [iʃka'sja*] *vt* to skimp on ♦ *vi* to become scarce.
escassez [iʃka'seʒ] *f* (*falta*) shortage.
escasso/a [iʃ'kasu/a] *adj* scarce.
escavação [iʃkava'sãw] (*pl* **-ões**) *f* digging, excavation.
escavadeira [iʃkava'dejra] *f* digger.
escavar [iʃka'va*] *vt* to excavate.
esclarecedor(a) [iʃklarese'do*(a)] *adj* explanatory; (*que alarga o conhecimento*) informative.
esclarecer [iʃklare'se*] *vt* (*situação*) to explain; (*mistério*) to clear up, explain; **~-se** *vr*: **~-se (sobre algo)** to find out (about sth); **~ alguém sobre algo** to explain to sb about sth.
esclarecido/a [iʃklare'sidu/a] *adj* (*pessoa*) enlightened.
esclarecimento [iʃklaresi'mẽtu] *m* explanation; (*informação*) information.
esclerosado/a [iʃklero'zadu/a] (*col*) *adj* (*pessoa*) batty, nutty.
esclerótica [iʃkle'rɔtʃika] *f* white of the eye.
escoadouro [iʃkoa'doru] *m* drain; (*cano*) drainpipe.
escoar [iʃko'a*] *vt* to drain off ♦ *vi* to drain away; **~-se** *vr* to seep out.
escocês/esa [iʃko'seʃ/seza] *adj* Scottish ♦ *m/f* Scot, Scotsman/woman.
Escócia [iʃ'kɔsja] *f* Scotland.
escoicear [iʃkoj'sja*] *vt* to kick; (*fig*) to ill-treat ♦ *vi* to kick.
escol [iʃ'kɔw] *m* best; **de ~** of excellence.
escola [iʃ'kɔla] *f* school; **~ naval** naval college; **~ primária/secundária** primary (*BRIT*) *ou* elementary (*US*)/secondary (*BRIT*) *ou* high (*US*) school; **~ particular/pública** private/state (*BRIT*) *ou* public (*US*) school; **~ superior** college; **fazer ~** to win converts.
escolado/a [iʃko'ladu/a] *adj* (*esperto*) shrewd; (*experiente*) experienced.
escolar [iʃko'la*] *adj* school *atr* ♦ *m/f* schoolboy/girl; **~es** *mpl* schoolchildren.
escolaridade [iʃkolari'dadʒi] *f* schooling.
escolarização [iʃkolariza'sãw] *f* education, schooling.
escolarizar [iʃkolari'za*] *vt* to educate (in school).
escolha [iʃ'koʎa] *f* choice.
escolher [iʃko'ʎe*] *vt* to choose, select.
escolho [iʃ'koʎu] *m* (*recife*) reef; (*rocha*) rock.
escolta [iʃ'kɔwta] *f* escort.
escoltar [iʃkow'ta*] *vt* to escort.
escombros [iʃ'kõbruʃ] *mpl* ruins, debris *sg*.
esconde-esconde [iʃkõdʃiʃ'kõdʒi] *m* hide-and-seek.
esconder [iʃkõ'de*] *vt* to hide, conceal; **~-se** *vr* to hide; **brincar de ~** to play hide-and-seek.
esconderijo [iʃkõde'riʒu] *m* hiding place; (*de bandidos*) hideout.
escondidas [iʃkõ'dʒidaʃ] *fpl*: **às ~** secretly.
esconjurar [iʃkõʒu'ra*] *vt* (*o Demônio*) to exorcize; (*afastar*) to keep off; (*amaldiçoar*) to curse; **~-se** *vr* (*lamentar-se*) to complain.
escopo [iʃ'kopu] *m* aim, purpose.
escora [iʃ'kɔra] *f* prop, support; (*cilada*) ambush.
escorar [iʃko'ra*] *vt* to prop (up); (*amparar*) to support; (*esperar de espreita*) to lie in wait for ♦ *vi* to lie in wait; **~-se** *vr*: **~-se em** (*fundamentar-se*) to go by; (*amparar-se*) to live off.
escorbuto [iʃkox'butu] *m* scurvy.
escore [iʃ'kɔri] *m* score.
escória [iʃ'kɔrja] *f* (*de metal*) dross; **a ~ da humanidade** the scum of the earth.
escoriação [iʃkorja'sãw] (*pl* **-ões**) *f* abrasion, scratch.
escorpiano/a [iʃkox'pjanu/a] *adj*, *m/f* (*ASTROLOGIA*) Scorpio.
escorpião [iʃkoxpi'ãw] (*pl* **-ões**) *m* scorpion; **E~** (*ASTROLOGIA*) Scorpio.
escorraçar [iʃkoxa'sa*] *vt* (*tratar mal*) to ill-treat; (*expulsar*) to throw out; **~ alguém de casa** *ou* **para fora de casa** to throw sb out of the house.
escorrega [iʃko'xɛga] *f* slide.
escorregadela [iʃkoxega'dɛla] *f* slip.
escorregadi(ç)o/a [iʃkoxega'dʒi(s)u/a] *adj* slippery.
escorregador [iʃkoxega'do*] *m* slide.
escorregão [iʃkoxe'gãw] (*pl* **-ões**) *m* slip; (*fig*) slip, slip-up.
escorregar [iʃkoxe'ga*] *vi* to slip; (*errar*) to slip up.
escorregões [iʃkoxe'gõjʃ] *mpl de* **escorregão**.
escorrer [iʃko'xe*] *vt* (*fazer correr*) to drain (off); (*verter*) to pour out ♦ *vi* (*pingar*) to drip; (*correr em fio*) to trickle.
escoteiro [iʃko'tejru] *m* scout.
escotilha [iʃko'tʃiʎa] *f* hatch, hatchway.
escova [iʃ'kova] *f* brush; (*penteado*) blow-dry; **~ de dentes** toothbrush; **fazer ~ no cabelo** to blow-dry one's hair; (*por outra pessoa*) to have a blow-dry.
escovar [iʃko'va*] *vt* to brush.
escovinha [iʃko'viɲa] *f V* **cabelo**.
escrachado/a [iʃkra'ʃadu/a] (*col*) *adj* (*desleixado*) scruffy; **estar** *ou* **ser ~** (*ter ficha na polícia*) to have a criminal record.
escravatura [iʃkrava'tura] *f* (*tráfico*) slave trade; (*escravidão*) slavery.
escravidão [iʃkravi'dãw] *f* slavery.

***NB**: European Portuguese adds the following consonants to certain words:* **b** (sú(b)dito, su(b)til); **c** (a(c)ção, a(c)cionista, a(c)to); **m** (inde(m)ne); **p** (ado(p)ção, ado(p)tar); *for further details see p. xiii.*

escravização [iʃkraviza'sãw] *f* enslavement.
escravizar [iʃkravi'za*] *vt* to enslave; (*cativar*) to captivate.
escravo/a [iʃ'kravu/a] *adj* captive ♦ *m/f* slave; **ele é um ~ do amigo/trabalho** he's a slave to his friend/work.
escrete [iʃ'krɛtʃi] *m* team.
escrevente [iʃkre'vẽtʃi] *m/f* clerk.
escrever [iʃkre've*] *vt, vi* to write; **~-se** *vr* to write to each other; **~ à máquina** to type.
escrevinhador(a) [iʃkreviɲa'do*(a)] (*col*) *m/f* hack (writer).
escrevinhar [iʃkrevi'ɲa*] *vt* to scribble.
escrita [eʃ'krita] *f* writing; (*pessoal*) handwriting; **pôr a ~ em dia** to bring one's correspondence up to date.
escrito/a [eʃ'kritu/a] *pp de* **escrever** ♦ *adj* written ♦ *m* piece of writing; **~ à mão** handwritten; **dar por ~** to put in writing; **ela é o pai ~** she's the spitting image of her father.
escritor(a) [iʃkri'to*(a)] *m/f* writer; (*autor*) author.
escritório [iʃkri'tɔrju] *m* office; (*em casa*) study.
escritura [iʃkri'tura] *f* (JUR) deed; (*ato na compra de imóveis*) ≈ exchange of contracts; **as Sagradas E~s** the Scriptures.
escrituração [iʃkritura'sãw] *f* book-keeping; (*de transações, quantias*) entering, recording; **~ por partidas simples/dobradas** (COM) single-entry/double-entry book-keeping.
escriturar [iʃkritu'ra*] *vt* (*contas*) to register, enter up; (*documento*) to draw up.
escriturário/a [iʃkritu'rarju/a] *m/f* clerk.
escrivã [iʃkri'vã] *f de* **escrivão**.
escrivaninha [iʃkriva'niɲa] *f* writing desk.
escrivão/vã [iʃkri'vãw/vã] (*pl* **-ões/~s**) *m/f* registrar, recorder.
escroque [iʃ'krɔki] *m* swindler, conman.
escroto/a [iʃ'krotu/a] *m* scrotum ♦ *adj* (*col!*: *pessoa*) vile, gross; (: *filme etc*) crappy (*!*), shitty (*!*).
escrúpulo [iʃ'krupulu] *m* scruple; (*cuidado*) care; **sem ~** unscrupulous.
escrupuloso/a [iʃkrupu'lozu/ɔza] *adj* scrupulous; (*cuidadoso*) careful.
escrutinar [iʃkrutʃina*] *vi* to act as a scrutineer.
escrutínio [iʃkru'tʃinju] *m* (*votação*) poll; (*apuração de votos*) counting; (*exame atento*) scrutiny; **~ secreto** secret ballot.
escudar [iʃku'da*] *vt* to shield; **~-se** *vr* to shield o.s.; (*apoiar-se*): **~-se em algo** to rely on sth.
escudeiro [iʃku'dejru] *m* squire.
escudo [iʃ'kudu] *m* shield; (*moeda*) escudo.
esculachado/a [iʃkula'ʃadu/a] (*col*) *adj* sloppy.
esculachar [iʃkula'ʃa*] (*col*) *vt* (*bagunçar*) to mess up; (*espancar*) to beat up; (*criticar*) to get at; (*repreender*) to tick off.
esculacho [iʃku'laʃu] (*col*) *m* mess; (*repreensão*) telling-off.
esculhambação [iʃkuʎãba'sãw] (*pl* **-ões**) (*col!*) *f* mess; (*repreensão*) telling-off, bollocking (*!*).
esculhambado/a [iʃkuʎã'badu/a] (*col!*) *adj* (*descuidado*) shabby, slovenly; (*estragado*) messed up, knackered.
esculhambar [iʃkuʎã'ba*] (*col!*) *vt* to mess up, fuck up (*!*); **~ alguém** (*criticar*) to give sb stick; (*descompor*) to give sb a bollocking (*!*).
esculpir [iʃkuw'pi*] *vt* to carve, sculpt; (*gravar*) to engrave.
escultor(a) [iʃkuw'to*(a)] *m/f* sculptor.
escultura [iʃkuw'tura] *f* sculpture.
escultural [iʃkuwtu'raw] (*pl* **-ais**) *adj* sculptural; (*corpo*) statuesque.
escuma [iʃ'kuma] (PT) *f* foam; (*em cerveja*) froth.
escumadeira [iʃkuma'dejra] *f* skimmer.
escuna [iʃ'kuna] *f* (NÁUT) schooner.
escuras [iʃ'kuraʃ] *fpl*: **às ~** in the dark.
escurecer [iʃkure'se*] *vt* to darken ♦ *vi* to get dark; **ao ~** at dusk.
escurecimento [iʃkuresi'mẽtu] *m* darkening.
escuridão [iʃkuri'dãw] *f* (*trevas*) dark.
escuro/a [iʃ'kuru/a] *adj* (*sombrio*) dark; (*dia*) overcast; (*pessoa*) swarthy; (*negócios*) shady ♦ *m* darkness.
escusa [iʃ'kuza] *f* excuse.
escusado/a [iʃku'zadu/a] *adj* unnecessary; **é ~ fazer isso** there's no need to do that.
escusar [iʃku'za*] *vt* (*desculpar*) to excuse, forgive; (*justificar*) to vindicate; (*dispensar*) to exempt; (*não precisar de*) not to need; **~-se** *vr* (*desculpar-se*) to apologise; **~-se de fazer** to refuse to do; **escuso-me de dar maiores explicações** I need not explain further.
escuta [iʃ'kuta] *f* listening; **à ~** listening out; **ficar na ~** to stand by; **~ eletrônica/telefônica** bugging/phone tapping.
escutar [iʃku'ta*] *vt* to listen to; (*sem prestar atenção*) to hear ♦ *vi* to listen; to hear; **escuta!** listen!; **ele não escuta bem** he is hard of hearing; **o médico escutou o paciente** the doctor listened to the patient's chest.
esdrúxulo/a [iʒ'druʃulu/a] *adj* weird, odd.
esfacelar [iʃfase'la*] *vt* (*destruir*) to destroy.
esfaimado/a [iʃfaj'madu/a] *adj* famished, ravenous.
esfalfar [iʃfaw'fa*] *vt* to tire out, exhaust; **~-se** *vr* to tire o.s. out.
esfaquear [iʃfaki'a*] *vt* to stab.
esfarelar [iʃfare'la*] *vt* to crumble; **~-se** *vr* to crumble.
esfarrapado/a [iʃfaxa'padu/a] *adj* ragged, in tatters.
esfarrapar [iʃfaxa'pa*] *vt* to tear to pieces.
esfera [iʃ'fɛra] *f* (*tb fig*) sphere; (*globo*) globe; (TIP, COMPUT) golfball; **máquina de ~** golfball typewriter.
esférico/a [iʃ'fɛriku/a] *adj* spherical.
esferográfico/a [iʃfero'grafiku/a] *adj*: **caneta esferográfica** ballpoint pen.

esfiapar [iʃfja'pa*] *vt* to fray; **~-se** *vr* to fray.
esfinge [iʃ'fĩʒi] *f* sphinx.
esfogueado/a [iʃfo'gjadu/a] *adj* impatient.
esfolar [iʃfo'la*] *vt* to skin; (*arranhar*) to graze; (*cobrar demais a*) to overcharge, fleece.
esfomeado/a [iʃfo'mjadu/a] *adj* famished, starving.
esforçado/a [iʃfox'sadu/a] *adj* committed, dedicated.
esforçar-se [iʃfox'saxsi] *vr*: **~ para** to try hard to, strive to.
esforço [iʃ'foxsu] *m* effort; **fazer ~** to try hard, make an effort.
esfregação [iʃfrega'sãw] *f* rubbing; (*col*) necking, petting.
esfregaço [iʃfre'gasu] *m* smear.
esfregar [iʃfre'ga*] *vt* to rub; (*com água*) to scrub.
esfriamento [iʃfrja'mẽtu] *m* cooling.
esfriar [iʃ'frja*] *vt* to cool, chill ♦ *vi* to get cold; (*fig*) to cool off.
esfumaçar [iʃfuma'sa*] *vt* to fill with smoke.
esfumar [iʃfu'ma*] *vt* to disperse; **~-se** *vr* to fade away.
esfuziante [iʃfu'zjãtʃi] *adj* (*pessoa*) bubbly; (*alegria*) irrepressible.
ESG (*BR*) *abr f* (= *Escola Superior de Guerra*) *military training school.*
esganado/a [iʒga'nadu/a] *adj* (*sufocado*) choked; (*voraz*) greedy; (*avaro*) grasping.
esganar [iʃga'na*] *vt* to strangle, choke.
esganiçado/a [iʒgani'sadu/a] *adj* (*voz*) shrill.
esgaravatar [iʃgarava'ta*] *vt* (*fig*) to delve into.
esgarçar [iʃgax'sa*] *vt, vi* to tear; (*com o uso*) to wear into a hole.
esgazeado/a [iʃga'zjadu/a] *adj* (*olhos, olhar*) crazed.
esgoelar [iʒgoe'la*] *vt* to yell; (*estrangular*) to choke; **~-se** *vr* to yell, scream.
esgotado/a [iʃgo'tadu/a] *adj* (*exausto*) exhausted; (*consumido*) used up; (*livros*) out of print; **os ingressos estão ~s** the tickets are sold out.
esgotamento [iʒgota'mẽtu] *m* exhaustion.
esgotar [iʒgo'ta*] *vt* (*vazar*) to drain, empty; (*recursos*) to use up; (*pessoa, assunto*) to exhaust; **~-se** *vr* (*cansar-se*) to become exhausted; (*mercadorias, edição*) to be sold out; (*recursos*) to run out.
esgoto [iʒ'gotu] *m* drain; (*público*) sewer.
esgrima [iʒ'grima] *f* (*ESPORTE*) fencing.
esgrimir [iʒgri'mi*] *vi* to fence.
esgrouvinhado/a [iʒgrovi'ɲadu/a] *adj* dishevelled.
esgueirar-se [iʒgej'raxsi] *vr* to slip away, sneak off.
esguelha [iʒ'geʎa] *f* slant; **olhar alguém de ~** to look at sb out of the corner of one's eye.
esguichar [iʒgi'ʃa*] *vt* to squirt ♦ *vi* to squirt out.
esguicho [iʃ'giʃu] *m* (*jacto*) jet; (*de mangueira etc*) spout.
esguio/a [eʒ'giu/a] *adj* slender.
eslavo/a [iʃ'lavu/a] *adj* Slavic ♦ *m/f* Slav.
emaecer [iʒmaje'se*] *vi* to fade.
esmagador(a) [iʒmagado*(a)] *adj* crushing; (*provas*) irrefutable; (*maioria*) overwhelming.
esmagar [iʒma'ga*] *vt* to crush.
esmaltado/a [iʒmaw'tadu/a] *adj* enamelled (*BRIT*), enameled (*US*).
esmalte [iʒ'mawtʃi] *m* enamel; (*de unhas*) nail polish.
esmerado/a [iʒme'radu/a] *adj* careful, neat; (*bem acabado*) polished.
esmeralda [iʒme'rawda] *f* emerald.
esmerar-se [iʒme'raxsi] *vr* to take great care.
esmero [iʒ'meru] *m* (great) care.
esmigalhar [iʒmiga'ʎa*] *vt* to crumble; (*despedaçar*) to shatter; (*esmagar*) to crush; **~-se** *vr* (*pão etc*) to crumble; (*vaso*) to smash, shatter.
esmirrado/a [iʒmi'xadu/a] *adj* (*roupa*) skimpy, tight.
esmiuçar [iʒmju'sa*] *vt* (*pão*) to crumble; (*examinar*) to examine in detail.
esmo ['eʒmu] *m*: **a ~** at random; **andar a ~** to walk aimlessly; **falar a ~** to prattle.
esmola [iʒ'mɔla] *f* alms *pl*; (*col: surra*) thrashing; **pedir ~s** to beg.
esmolar [iʒmo'la*] *vt, vi*: **~ (algo a alguém)** to beg (sth from sb).
esmorecer [iʒmore'se*] *vt* to discourage ♦ *vi* (*desanimar-se*) to lose heart.
esmorecimento [iʒmoresi'mẽtu] *m* dismay, discouragement; (*enfraquecimento*) weakening.
esmurrar [iʒmu'xa*] *vt* to punch.
Esni [eʒ'ni] (*BR*) *abr f* (= *Escola Nacional de Informações*) *training school for intelligence services.*
esnobação [iʒnoba'sãw] *f* snobbishness.
esnobar [iʒno'ba*] *vi* to be snobbish ♦ *vt*: **~ alguém** to give sb the cold shoulder.
esnobe [iʒ'nɔbi] *adj* snobbish; (*col*) stuck-up ♦ *m/f* snob.
esnobismo [iʒno'biʒmu] *m* snobbery.
esôfago [e'zofagu] *m* oesophagus (*BRIT*), esophagus (*US*).
esotérico/a [ezo'tɛriku/a] *adj* esoteric.
espaçado/a [iʃpa'sadu/a] *adj* spaced out.
espaçar [iʃpa'sa*] *vt* to space out; **~ visitas/saídas** *etc* to visit/go out *etc* less often.
espacejamento [iʃpaseʃa'mẽtu] *m* (*TIP*) spacing; **~ proporcional** proportional spacing.
espacial [iʃpa'sjaw] (*pl* **-ais**) *adj* spatial, space *atr*; **nave ~** spaceship.

***NB:** European Portuguese adds the following consonants to certain words:* **b** (sú(b)dito, su(b)til); **c** (a(c)ção, a(c)cionista, a(c)to); **m** (inde(m)ne); **p** (ado(p)ção, ado(p)tar); *for further details see p. xiii.*

espaço [iʃ'pasu] *m* space; (*tempo*) period; ~ **para 3 pessoas** room for 3 people; **a ~s** from time to time; **sujeito a ~** (*em avião*) standby.
espaçoso/a [iʃpa'sozu/ɔza] *adj* spacious, roomy.
espada [iʃ'pada] *f* sword; **~s** *fpl* (CARTAS) spades; **estar entre a ~ e a parede** to be between the devil and the deep blue sea.
espadachim [iʃpada'ʃĩ] (*pl* **-ns**) *m* swordsman.
espadarte [iʃpa'daxtʃi] *m* swordfish.
espádua [iʃ'padwa] *f* shoulder blade.
espairecer [iʃpajre'se*] *vt* to amuse, entertain ♦ *vi* to relax; **~-se** *vr* to relax.
espairecimento [iʃpajresi'mẽtu] *m* recreation.
espaldar [iʃpaw'da*] *m* (chair) back.
espalha-brasas [iʃpaʎa'-] *m/f inv* troublemaker.
espalhafato [iʃpaʎa'fatu] *m* din, commotion.
espalhafatoso/a [iʃpaʎafa'tozu/ɔza] *adj* (*pessoa*) loud, rowdy; (*roupa*) loud, garish.
espalhar [iʃpa'ʎa*] *vt* to scatter; (*boato, medo*) to spread; (*luz*) to shed; **~-se** *vr* (*fogo, boato*) to spread; (*refestelar-se*) to lounge.
espanador [iʃpana'do*] *m* duster.
espanar [iʃpa'na*] *vt* to dust.
espancamento [iʃpãka'mẽtu] *m* beating.
espancar [iʃpã'ka*] *vt* to beat up.
espandongado/a [iʃpãdõ'gadu/a] *adj* (*no vestir*) scruffy; (*estragado*) tatty.
Espanha [iʃ'paɲa] *f*: **a ~** Spain.
espanhol(a) [iʃpa'ɲow/ola] (*pl* **-óis/~s**) *adj* Spanish ♦ *m/f* Spaniard ♦ *m* (LING) Spanish; **os espanhóis** the Spanish.
espantado/a [iʃpã'tadu/a] *adj* astonished; (*cor*) loud, garish.
espantalho [iʃpã'taʎu] *m* scarecrow.
espantar [iʃpã'ta*] *vt* (*causar medo a*) to frighten; (*admirar*) to amaze, astonish; (*afugentar*) to frighten away ♦ *vi* to be amazing; **~-se** *vr* (*admirar-se*) to be amazed; (*assustar-se*) to be frightened.
espanto [iʃ'pãtu] *m* (*medo*) fright, fear; (*admiração*) amazement.
espantoso/a [iʃpã'tozu/ɔza] *adj* amazing.
esparadrapo [iʃpara'drapu] *m* (sticking) plaster (BRIT), bandaid ® (US).
espargir [iʃpax'ʒi*] *vt* (*líquido*) to sprinkle; (*flores*) to scatter; (*luz*) to shed.
esparramar [iʃpaxa'ma*] *vt* (*líquido*) to splash; (*espalhar*) to scatter.
esparso/a [iʃ'paxsu/a] *adj* scattered; (*solto*) loose.
espartano/a [iʃpax'tanu/a] *adj* (*fig*) spartan.
espartilho [iʃpax'tʃiʎu] *m* corset.
espasmo [iʃ'paʒmu] *m* spasm, convulsion.
espasmódico/a [iʃpaʒ'mɔdʒiku/a] *adj* spasmodic.
espatifar [iʃpatʃi'fa*] *vt* to smash; **~-se** *vr* to smash; (*avião*) to crash.
espavorir [iʃpavo'ri*] *vt* to terrify.

EsPCEx (BR) *abr f* = **Escola Preparatória de Cadetes do Exército.**
especial [iʃpe'sjaw] (*pl* **-ais**) *adj* special; **em ~** especially.
especialidade [iʃpesjali'dadʒi] *f* speciality (BRIT), specialty (US); (*ramo de atividades*) specialization.
especialista [iʃpesja'liʃta] *m/f* specialist; (*perito*) expert.
especialização [iʃpesjaliza'sãw] (*pl* **-ões**) *f* specialization.
especializado/a [iʃpesjali'zadu/a] *adj* specialized; (*operário, mão de obra*) skilled.
especializar-se [iʃpesjali'zaxsi] *vr*: **~ (em)** to specialize (in).
especiaria [iʃpesja'ria] *f* spice.
espécie [iʃ'pɛsi] *f* (BIO) species; (*tipo*) sort, kind; **causar ~** to be surprising; **pagar em ~** to pay in cash.
especificação [iʃpesifika'sãw] (*pl* **-ões**) *f* specification.
especificar [iʃpesifi'ka*] *vt* to specify.
específico/a [iʃpe'sifiku/a] *adj* specific.
espécime [iʃ'pɛsimi] *m* specimen.
espécimen [iʃ'pɛsimẽ] (*pl* **~s**) *m* = **espécime.**
espectáculo *etc* [iʃpek'takulu] (PT) *m* = **espetáculo** *etc.*
espectador(a) [iʃpekta'do*(a)] *m/f* (*testemunha*) onlooker; (TV) viewer; (ESPORTE) spectator; (TEATRO) member of the audience; **~es** *mpl* audience *sg.*
espectro [iʃ'pɛktru] *m* spectre (BRIT), specter (US); (FÍS) spectrum; (*pessoa*) gaunt figure.
especulação [iʃpekula'sãw] (*pl* **-ões**) *f* speculation.
especulador(a) [iʃpekula'do*(a)] *adj* speculating ♦ *m/f* (*na Bolsa etc*) speculator; (*explorador*) opportunist.
especular [iʃpeku'la*] *vi*: **~ (sobre)** to speculate (on).
especulativo/a [iʃpekula'tʃivu/a] *adj* speculative.
espelhar [iʃpe'ʎa*] *vt* to mirror; **~-se** *vr* to be mirrored; **seus olhos espelham malícia, espelha-se malícia nos seus olhos** there is malice in his eyes.
espelho [iʃ'peʎu] *m* mirror; (*fig*) model; **~ retrovisor** (AUTO) rearview mirror.
espelunca [iʃpe'lũka] (*col*) *f* (*bar*) dive; (*casa*) dump, hole.
espera [iʃ'pɛra] *f* (*demora*) wait; (*expectativa*) expectation; **à ~ de** waiting for; **à minha ~** waiting for me.
espera-marido (*pl* **-s**) *m* (CULIN) *sweet made with burnt sugar and eggs.*
esperança [iʃpe'rãsa] *f* (*confiança*) hope; (*expectativa*) expectation; **dar ~s a alguém** to get sb's hopes up; **que ~!** (*col*) no chance!
esperançar [iʃperã'sa*] *vt*: **~ alguém** to give sb hope.
esperançoso/a [iʃperã'sozu/ɔza] *adj* hopeful.
esperar [iʃpe'ra*] *vt* (*aguardar*) to wait for; (*contar com, bebê*) to expect; (*desejar*) to

hope for ♦ *vi* to wait; (*desejar*) to hope; (*contar com*) to expect; **espero que sim/não** I hope so/not; **fazer alguém** ~ to keep sb waiting; **espera aí!** hold on!; (*col*: *não vem*) come off it!
esperável [iʃpe'ravew] (*pl* **-eis**) *adj* expected, probable.
esperma [iʃ'pɛxma] *f* sperm.
espernear [iʃpex'nja*] *vi* to kick out; (*protestar*) to protest.
espertalhão/lhona [iʃpexta'ʎãw/ʎɔna] (*pl* **-ões/~s**) *m/f* shrewd operator ♦ *adj* crafty, shrewd.
esperteza [iʃpex'teza] *f* cleverness; (*astúcia*) cunning.
esperto/a [iʃ'pɛxtu/a] *adj* clever; (*espertalhão*) crafty; (*col*: *bacana*) great.
espesso/a [iʃ'pesu/a] *adj* thick.
espessura [iʃpe'sura] *f* thickness.
espetacular [iʃpetaku'la*] *adj* spectacular.
espetáculo [iʃpe'takulu] *m* (TEATRO) show; (*vista*) sight; (*cena ridícula*) spectacle; **dar** ~ to make a spectacle of o.s.; **ela/a casa é um** ~ (*col*) she/the house is fabulous.
espetada [iʃpe'tada] *f* prick.
espetar [iʃpe'ta*] *vt* (*carne*) to put on a spit; (*cravar*) to stick; **~-se** *vr* to prick o.s.; ~ **algo em algo** to pin sth to sth.
espetinho [iʃpe'tʃiɲu] *m* skewer.
espeto [iʃ'petu] *m* spit; (*pau*) pointed stick; (*fig*: *pessoa magra*) beanpole; **ser um** ~ (*ser difícil*) to be awkward.
espevitado/a [iʃpevi'tadu/a] *adj* (*fig*: *vivo*) lively.
espezinhar [iʃpezi'ɲa*] *vt* to trample (on); (*humilhar*) to treat like dirt.
espia [iʃ'pia] *m/f* spy.
espiã [iʃ'pjã] *f de* **espião**.
espiada [iʃ'pjada] *f*: **dar uma** ~ to have a look.
espião/piã [iʃ'pjãw/'pjã] (*pl* **-ões/~s**) *m/f* spy.
espiar [iʃ'pja*] *vt* (*espionar*) to spy on; (*uma ocasião*) to watch out for; (*olhar*) to watch ♦ *vi* to spy; (*olhar*) to peer.
espicaçar [iʃpika'sa*] *vt* to trouble, torment.
espichar [iʃpi'ʃa*] *vt* (*couro*) to stretch out; (*pescoço, pernas*) to stretch ♦ *vi* (*col*: *crescer*) to shoot up; **~-se** *vr* to stretch out.
espiga [iʃ'piga] *f* (*de milho*) ear.
espigado/a [iʃpigadu/a] *adj* (*milho*) fully-grown; (*ereto*) upright.
espigueiro [iʃpi'gejru] *m* granary.
espinafração [iʃpinafra'sãw] (*pl* **-ões**) (*col*) *f* telling-off.
espinafrar [iʃpina'fra*] (*col*) *vt*: ~ **alguém** (*repreender*) to give sb a telling-off; (*criticar*) to get at sb; (*ridicularizar*) to jeer at sb.
espinafre [iʃpi'nafri] *m* spinach.
espingarda [iʃpĩ'gaxda] *f* shotgun, rifle; ~ **de ar comprimido** air rifle.
espinha [iʃ'piɲa] *f* (*de peixe*) bone; (*na pele*) spot, pimple; (*coluna vertebral*) spine.
espinhar [iʃpi'ɲa*] *vt* (*picar*) to prick; (*irritar*) to irritate, annoy.
espinheiro [iʃpi'ɲejro] *m* bramble bush.
espinhento/a [iʃpi'ɲẽtu/a] *adj* spotty, pimply.
espinho [iʃ'piɲu] *m* thorn; (*de animal*) spine; (*fig*: *dificuldade*) snag.
espinhoso/a [iʃpi'ɲozu/ɔza] *adj* (*planta*) prickly, thorny; (*fig*: *difícil*) difficult; (: *problema*) thorny.
espinotear [iʃpino'tʃja*] *vi* (*cavalo*) to buck; (*pessoa*) to leap about.
espiões [iʃ'pjõjʃ] *mpl de* **espião**.
espionagem [iʃpio'naʒẽ] *f* spying, espionage.
espionar [iʃpjo'na*] *vt* to spy on ♦ *vi* to spy, snoop.
espiral [iʃpi'raw] (*pl* **-ais**) *adj, f* spiral.
espírita [iʃ'pirita] *adj, m/f* spiritualist.
espiritismo [iʃpiri'tʃiʒmu] *m* spiritualism.
espírito [iʃ'piritu] *m* spirit; (*pensamento*) mind; ~ **de porco** wet blanket; ~ **esportivo** sense of humour (BRIT) *ou* humor (US); ~ **forte/fraco** (*fig*: *pessoa*) freethinker/sheep; **E~ Santo** Holy Spirit.
espiritual [iʃpiri'twaw] (*pl* **-ais**) *adj* spiritual.
espirituoso/a [iʃpiri'twozu/ɔza] *adj* witty.
espirrar [iʃpi'xa*] *vi* to sneeze; (*jorrar*) to spurt out ♦ *vt* (*água*) to spurt.
espirro [iʃ'pixu] *m* sneeze.
esplanada [iʃpla'nada] *f* esplanade.
esplêndido/a [iʃ'plẽdʒidu/a] *adj* splendid.
esplendor [iʃplẽ'do*] *m* splendour (BRIT), splendor (US).
espocar [iʃpo'ka*] *vi* to explode.
espoleta [iʃpo'leta] *f* (*de arma*) fuse.
espoliar [iʃpo'lja*] *vt* to plunder.
espólio [iʃ'pɔlju] *m* (*herança*) estate, property; (*roubado*) booty, spoils *pl*.
esponja [iʃ'põʒa] *f* sponge; (*de pó de arroz*) puff; (*parasita*) sponger; (*col*: *ébrio*) boozer.
esponjoso/a [iʃpõ'ʒozu/ɔza] *adj* spongy.
espontaneidade [iʃpõtanei'dadʒi] *f* spontaneity.
espontâneo/a [iʃpõ'tanju/a] *adj* spontaneous; (*pessoa*: *natural*) straightforward.
espora [iʃ'pɔra] *f* spur.
esporádico/a [iʃpo'radʒiku/a] *adj* sporadic.
esporão [iʃpo'rãw] (*pl* **-ões**) *m* (*de galo*) spur.
esporear [iʃpo'rja*] *vt* (*picar*) to spur on; (*fig*) to incite.
esporões [iʃpo'rõjʃ] *mpl de* **esporão**.
esporte [iʃ'pɔxtʃi] (BR) *m* sport.
esportista [iʃpox'tʃiʃta] *adj* sporting ♦ *m/f* sportsman/woman.
esportiva [iʃpox'tʃiva] *f* sense of humour (BRIT) *ou* humor (US); **perder a** ~ to lose one's sense of humo(u)r.
esportivo/a [iʃpox'tʃivu/a] *adj* sporting.

NB: European Portuguese adds the following consonants to certain words: **b** (sú(b)dito, su(b)til); **c** (a(c)ção, a(c)cionista, a(c)to); **m** (inde(m)ne); **p** (ado(p)ção, ado(p)tar); *for further details see p. xiii.*

esposa [iʃ'poza] *f* wife.
esposar [iʃpo'za*] *vt* to marry; (*causa*) to defend.
esposo [iʃ'pozu] *m* husband.
espoucar [iʃpo'ka*] *vt* = **espocar**.
espraiar [iʃpra'ja*] *vt, vi* to spread; (*dilatar*) to expand; **~-se** *vr* (*mar*) to wash across the beach; (*rio*) to spread out; (*fig*: *epidemia*) to spread.
espreguiçadeira [iʃpregisa'dejra] *f* deck chair; (*com lugar para as pernas*) lounger.
espreguiçar-se [iʃpregi'saxsi] *vr* to stretch.
espreita [iʃ'prejta] *f*: **ficar à ~** to keep watch.
espreitar [iʃprej'ta*] *vt* (*espiar*) to spy on; (*observar*) to observe, watch.
espremedor [iʃpreme'do*] *m* squeezer.
espremer [iʃpre'me*] *vt* (*fruta*) to squeeze; (*roupa molhada*) to wring out; (*pessoas*) to squash; **~-se** *vr* (*multidão*) to be squashed together; (*uma pessoa*) to squash up.
espuma [iʃ'puma] *f* foam; (*de cerveja*) froth, head; (*de sabão*) lather; (*de ondas*) surf; **colchão de ~** foam mattress; **~ de borracha** foam rubber.
espumante [iʃpu'mãtʃi] *adj* frothy, foamy; (*vinho*) sparkling.
espumar [iʃpu'ma*] *vi* to foam; (*fera, cachorro*) to foam at the mouth.
espúrio/a [iʃ'purju/a] *adj* spurious, bogus.
esputinique [iʃputʃi'niki] *m* satellite, sputnik.
esq. *abr* (= *esquerdo/a*) l.; = **esquina**.
esquadra [iʃ'kwadra] *f* (NÁUT) fleet; (PT: *da polícia*) police station.
esquadrão [iʃkwa'drãw] (*pl* **-ões**) *m* squadron.
esquadrilha [iʃkwa'driʎa] *f* squadron.
esquadrinhar [iʃkwadri'ɲa*] *vt* (*casa, área*) to search, scour; (*fatos*) to scrutinize.
esquadro [iʃ'kwadru] *m* set square.
esquadrões [iʃkwa'drõjʃ] *mpl de* **esquadrão**.
esqualidez [iʃkwali'deʃ] *f* squalor.
esquálido/a [iʃ'kwalidu/a] *adj* squalid, filthy.
esquartejar [iʃkwaxte'ʒa*] *vt* to quarter.
esquecer [iʃke'se*] *vt, vi* to forget; **~-se** *vr*: **~-se de** to forget; **~-se de fazer algo** to forget to do sth; **~-se (de) que ...** to forget that ....
esquecido/a [iʃke'sidu/a] *adj* forgotten; (*pessoa*) forgetful.
esquecimento [iʃkesi'mẽtu] *m* (*falta de memória*) forgetfulness; (*olvido*) oblivion; **cair no ~** to fall into oblivion.
esquelético/a [iʃke'lɛtʃiku/a] *adj* (ANAT) skeletal; (*pessoa*) scrawny.
esqueleto [iʃke'letu] *m* skeleton; (*arcabouço*) framework; **ser um ~** (*fig*: *pessoa*) to be just skin and bone.
esquema [iʃ'kɛma] *m* (*resumo*) outline; (*plano*) scheme; (*diagrama*) diagram, plan; **~ de segurança** security operation.
esquemático/a [iʃke'matʃiku/a] *adj* schematic.
esquematizar [iʃkematʃi'za*] *vt* to represent schematically; (*planejar*) to plan.
esquentado/a [iʃkẽ'tadu/a] *adj* (*fig*: *irritado*) annoyed; (: *irritadiço*) irritable.
esquentar [iʃkẽ'ta*] *vt* to heat (up), warm (up); (*fig*: *irritar*) to annoy ♦ *vi* to warm up; (*casaco*) to be warm; **~-se** *vr* to get annoyed; **~ a cabeça** (*col*) to get worked up; **não esquenta!** don't worry!
esquerda [iʃ'kexda] *f* (*tb*: POL) left; **à ~** on the left; **dobrar à ~** to turn left; **políticos de ~** left-wing politicians; **a ~ festiva** the trendy left.
esquerdista [iʃkex'dʒiʃta] *adj* left-wing ♦ *m/f* left-winger.
esquerdo/a [iʃ'kexdu/a] *adj* left.
esquete [iʃ'kɛtʃi] *m* (TEATRO, TV) sketch.
esqui [iʃ'ki] *m* (*patim*) ski; (*esporte*) skiing; **~ aquático** water skiing; **fazer ~** to go skiing.
esquiador(a) [iʃkja'do*(a)] *m/f* skier.
esquiar [iʃ'kja*] *vi* to ski.
esquilo [iʃ'kilu] *m* squirrel.
esquina [iʃ'kina] *f* corner; **fazer ~ com** to join.
esquisitão/ona [iʃkizi'tãw/ɔna] (*pl* **-ões/~s**) *adj* odd, peculiar.
esquisitice [iʃkizi'tʃisi] *f* oddity, peculiarity; (*ato, dito*) strange thing.
esquisito/a [iʃki'zitu/a] *adj* strange, odd.
esquisitões [iʃkizi'tõjʃ] *mpl de* **esquisitão**.
esquisitona [iʃkizi'tɔna] *f de* **esquisitão**.
esquiva [iʃ'kiva] *f* dodge.
esquivar-se [iʃki'vaxsi] *vr*: **~ de** to escape from, get away from; (*deveres*) to get out of.
esquivo/a [iʃ'kivu/a] *adj* aloof, standoffish.
esquizofrenia [iʃkizofre'nia] *f* schizophrenia.
esquizofrênico/a [iʃkizo'freniku/a] *adj, m/f* schizophrenic.
esq° *abr* = **esquerdo**.
essa ['ɛsa] *pron*: **~ é/foi boa** that is/was a good one; **~ não, sem ~** come off it!; **vamos nessa** let's go!; **ainda mais ~!** that's all I need!; **corta ~!** cut it out!; **gostei dessa** I like that; **estou nessa** count me in, I'm game; **por ~s e outras** for these and other reasons; **~ de fazer ...** this business of doing ....
esse ['esi] *adj* (*sg*) that; (*pl*) those; (BR: *este*: *sg*) this; (: *pl*) these ♦ *pron* (*sg*) that one; (*pl*) those; (BR: *este*: *sg*) this one; (: *pl*) these.
essência [e'sẽsja] *f* essence.
essencial [esẽ'sjaw] (*pl* **-ais**) *adj* essential; (*principal*) main ♦ *m*: **o ~** the main thing.
Est. *abr* (= *Estação*) Stn.; (= *Estrada*) ≈ Rd.
esta ['ɛʃta] *f de* **este**.
estabanado/a [iʃtaba'nadu/a] *adj* clumsy.
estabelecer [iʃtabele'se*] *vt* to establish; (*fundar*) to set up; **~-se** *vr* to establish o.s., set o.s. up; **estabeleceu-se que ...** it was established that ...; **o governo estabeleceu que ...** the government decided that ....
estabelecimento [iʃtabelesi'mẽtu] *m* establishment; (*casa comercial*) business.

estabilidade [iʃtabili'dadʒi] *f* stability.
estabilização [iʃtabiliza'sãw] *f* stabilization.
estabilizar [iʃtabili'za*] *vt* to stabilize; **~-se** *vr* to stabilize.
estábulo [iʃ'tabulu] *m* cow-shed.
estaca [iʃ'taka] *f* post, stake; (*de barraca*) peg; **voltar à ~ zero** to go back to square one.
estacada [iʃta'kada] *f* (*defensiva*) stockade; (*fileira de estacas*) fencing.
estação [iʃta'sãw] (*pl* **-ões**) *f* station; (*do ano*) season; **~ de águas** spa; **~ balneária** seaside resort; **~ emissora** broadcasting station.
estacar [iʃta'ka*] *vt* to prop up ♦ *vi* to stop short, halt.
estacionamento [iʃtasjona'mẽtu] *m* (*ato*) parking; (*lugar*) car park (*BRIT*), parking lot (*US*).
estacionar [iʃtasjo'na*] *vt* to park ♦ *vi* to park; (*não mover*) to remain stationary.
estacionário/a [iʃtasjo'narju/a] *adj* (*veículo*) stationary; (*COM*) slack.
estações [iʃta'sõjʃ] *fpl de* **estação**.
estada [iʃ'tada] *f* stay.
estadia [iʃta'dʒia] *f* = **estada**.
estádio [iʃ'tadʒu] *m* stadium.
estadista [iʃta'dʒiʃta] *m/f* statesman/woman.
estado [i'ʃtadu] *m* state; **E~s Unidos (da América)** United States (of America), USA; **~ civil** marital status; **~ de espírito** state of mind; **~ de saúde** condition; **~ maior** staff; **em bom ~** in good condition; **estar em ~ interessante** to be expecting; **estar em ~ de fazer** to be in a position to do.
estadual [iʃta'dwaw] (*pl* **-ais**) *adj* state *atr*.
estadunidense [iʃtaduni'dẽsi] *adj* (North) American, US *atr*.
estafa [iʃ'tafa] *f* fatigue; (*esgotamento*) nervous exhaustion.
estafante [iʃta'fãtʃi] *adj* exhausting.
estafar [iʃta'fa*] *vt* to tire out, fatigue; **~-se** *vr* to tire o.s. out.
estafermo [iʃta'fexmu] (*PT*) *m* scarecrow; (*col*) nincompoop.
estagiar [iʃta'ʒja*] *vi* to work as a trainee, do a traineeship.
estagiário/a [iʃta'ʒjarju/a] *m/f* probationer, trainee; (*professor*) student teacher; (*médico*) junior doctor.
estágio [iʃ'taʒu] *m* (*aprendizado*) traineeship; (*fase*) stage.
estagnação [iʃtagna'sãw] *f* stagnation.
estagnado/a [iʃtag'nadu/a] *adj* stagnant.
estagnar [iʃtag'na*] *vt* to make stagnant; (*país*) to bring to a standstill ♦ *vi* to stagnate; **~-se** *vr* to stagnate.
estalagem [iʃta'laʒẽ] (*pl* **-ns**) *f* inn.
estalar [iʃta'la*] *vt* (*quebrar*) to break; (*os dedos*) to snap ♦ *vi* (*fender-se*) to split, crack; (*crepitar*) to crackle; **estou estalando de dor de cabeça** I've got a splitting headache.
estaleiro [iʃta'lejru] *m* shipyard.
estalido [iʃta'lidu] *m* pop.
estalo [iʃ'talu] *m* (*do chicote*) crack; (*dos dedos*) snap; (*dos lábios*) smack; (*de foguete*) bang; **~ de trovão** thunderclap; **de ~** suddenly; **me deu um ~** it clicked, the penny dropped.
estampa [iʃ'tãpa] *f* (*figura impressa*) print; (*ilustração*) picture; **ter uma bela ~** (*fig*) to be beautiful.
estampado/a [iʃtã'padu/a] *adj* printed ♦ *m* (*tecido*) print; (*num tecido*) pattern; **sua angústia estava estampada no rosto** his anxiety was written on his face.
estampar [iʃtã'pa*] *vt* (*imprimir*) to print; (*marcar*) to stamp.
estamparia [iʃtãpa'ria] *f* (*oficina*) printshop; (*tecido, figura*) print.
estampido [iʃtã'pidu] *m* bang.
estancar [iʃtã'ka*] *vt* (*sangue, água*) to staunch; (*fazer cessar*) to stop; **~-se** *vr* (*parar*) to stop.
estância [iʃ'tãsja] *f* (*fazenda*) ranch, farm; (*versos*) stanza; **~ hidromineral** spa resort.
estandardizar [iʃtãdaxdʒi'za*] *vt* to standardize.
estandarte [iʃtã'daxtʃi] *m* standard, banner.
estande [iʃ'tãdʒi] *m* stand.
estanho [iʃ'taɲu] *m* (*metal*) tin.
estanque [iʃ'tãki] *adj* watertight.
estante [iʃ'tãtʃi] *f* (*armário*) bookcase; (*suporte*) stand.
estapafúrdio/a [iʃtapa'fuxdʒu/a] *adj* outlandish, odd.
estar [iʃ'ta*] *vi* to be; (*em casa*) to be in; (*no telefone*): **a Lúcia está? - não, ela não está** is Lúcia there? — no, she's not here; **a Maria não está** Maria's not in; **~ fora** (*de casa*) to be out; (*de viagem*) to be away; **~ fazendo** (*BR*) *ou* **a fazer** (*PT*) to be doing; **~ bem** (*de saúde*) to be all right; (*de aparência*) to look all right; (*financeiramente*) to be well off; **está bem, 'tá** (*col*) OK; **~ bem com** to be on good terms with; **~ calor/frio** (*o tempo*) to be hot/cold; **~ com fome/sede/medo** to be hungry/thirsty/afraid; **~ doente** to be ill; **você está muito elegante hoje** you look very smart today; **~ sentado** to be sitting down; **ela estava de chapéu** she had a hat on, she was wearing a hat; **~ de férias/licença** to be on holiday (*BRIT*) *ou* vacation (*US*)/leave; **o preço está em 3 milhões** the price is 3 million; **~ na hora de fazer** to be time to do; **estou na minha** (*col*) I'm doing my own thing; **ele está para chegar a qualquer momento** he'll be here any minute; **não ~ para conversas** not to be in the mood for talking; **~ para fazer** to be about to do; **não estou**

***NB:** European Portuguese adds the following consonants to certain words:* **b** (sú(b)dito, su(b)til); **c** (a(c)ção, a(c)cionista, a(c)to); **m** (inde(m)ne); **p** (ado(p)ção, ado(p)tar); *for further details see p. xiii.*

para ninguém I'm not available to see anyone; ~ **por algo** to be in favour (*BRIT*) *ou* favor (*US*) of sth; ~ **por fazer** to be still to be done.
estardalhaço [iʃtaxda'ʎasu] *m* fuss; (*ostentação*) ostentation.
estarrecer [iʃtaxe'se*] *vt* to petrify ♦ *vi* to be petrified.
estas ['ɛʃtaʃ] *adj, pron fpl de* **este**.
estatal [iʃta'taw] (*pl* **-ais**) *adj* nationalized, state-owned ♦ *f* state-owned company.
estatelado/a [iʃtate'ladu/a] *adj* (*cair*) sprawling.
estatelar [iʃtate'la*] *vt* to send sprawling; (*estarrecer*) to stun; **~-se** *vr* (*cair*) to go sprawling.
estática [iʃ'tatʃika] *f* (*TEC*) static.
estático/a [iʃ'tatʃiku/a] *adj* static.
estatística [iʃta'tʃiʃtʃika] *f* statistic; (*ciência*) statistics *sg*.
estatístico/a [iʃta'tʃiʃtʃiku/a] *adj* statistical.
estatização [iʃtatʃiza'sãw] (*pl* **-ões**) *f* nationalization.
estatizar [iʃtatʃi'za*] *vt* to nationalize.
estátua [iʃ'tatwa] *f* statue.
estatueta [iʃta'tweta] *f* statuette.
estatura [iʃta'tura] *f* stature.
estatuto [iʃta'tutu] *m* (*JUR*) statute; (*de cidade*) bye-law; (*de associação*) rule; **~s sociais** *ou* **da empresa** (*COM*) articles of association.
estável [iʃ'tavew] (*pl* **-eis**) *adj* stable.
este ['ɛʃtʃi] *m* east ♦ *adj inv* (*região*) eastern; (*vento, direção*) easterly.
este/ta ['eʃtʃi/'ɛʃta] *adj* (*sg*) this; (*pl*) these ♦ *pron* this one; (*pl*) these; (*a quem/que se referiu por último*) the latter; **esta noite** (*noite passada*) last night; (*noite de hoje*) tonight.
esteio [iʃ'teju] *m* prop, support; (*NÁUT*) stay.
esteira [iʃ'tejra] *f* mat; (*de navio*) wake; (*rumo*) path.
esteja [iʃ'teʒa] *etc vb V* **estar**.
estelionato [iʃteljo'natu] *m* fraud.
estêncil [iʃ'tẽsiw] (*pl* **-eis**) *m* stencil.
estender [iʃtẽ'de*] *vt* to extend; (*mapa*) to spread out; (*pernas*) to stretch; (*massa*) to roll out; (*conversa*) to draw out; (*corda*) to pull tight; (*roupa molhada*) to hang out; **~-se** *vr* (*no chão*) to lie down; (*fila, terreno*) to stretch, extend; **~-se sobre algo** to dwell on sth, expand on sth; **esta lei estende-se a todos** this law applies to all; **o conferencista estendeu-se demais** the speaker went on too long; ~ **a mão** to hold out one's hand; ~ **uma cadeira para alguém** to offer sb a chair; ~ **uma crítica a todos** to extend a criticism to everyone.
estenodatilógrafo/a [iʃtenodatʃi'lɔgrafu/a] *m/f* shorthand typist (*BRIT*), stenographer (*US*).
estenografar [iʃtenogra'fa*] *vt* to write in shorthand.
estenografia [iʃtenogra'fia] *f* shorthand.
estepe [iʃ'tɛpi] *m* spare wheel.
esterco [iʃ'texku] *m* manure, dung.
estéreis [iʃ'tɛrejʃ] *adj pl de* **estéril**.
estereo... [iʃterju-] *prefix* stereo....
estereofônico/a [iʃterjo'foniku/a] *adj* stereo(phonic).
estereotipado/a [iʃterjotʃi'padu/a] *adj* stereotypical.
estereotipar [iʃterjotʃi'pa*] *vt* to stereotype.
estereótipo [iʃte'rjɔtʃipu] *m* stereotype.
estéril [iʃ'tɛriw] (*pl* **-eis**) *adj* sterile; (*terra*) infertile; (*fig*) futile.
esterilidade [iʃterili'dadʒi] *f* sterility; (*de terra*) infertility; (*escassez*) dearth.
esterilização [iʃteriliza'sãw] *f* sterilization.
esterilizar [iʃterili'za*] *vt* to sterilize.
esterlino/a [iʃtex'linu/a] *adj* sterling ♦ *m* sterling; **libra esterlina** pound sterling.
esteróide [iʃte'rɔjdʒi] *m* steroid.
esteta [iʃ'tɛta] *m/f* aesthete (*BRIT*), esthete (*US*).
estética [iʃ'tɛtʃika] *f* aesthetics *sg* (*BRIT*), esthetics *sg* (*US*).
esteticista [iʃtetʃi'siʃta] *m/f* beautician.
estético/a [iʃ'tɛtʃiku/a] *adj* aesthetic (*BRIT*), esthetic (*US*).
estetoscópio [iʃteto'skɔpju] *m* stethoscope.
esteve [iʃ'tevi] *vb V* **estar**.
estiagem [iʃ'tʃjaʒẽ] (*pl* **-ns**) *f* (*depois da chuva*) calm after the storm; (*falta de chuva*) dry spell.
estiar [iʃ'tʃja*] *vi* (*não chover*) to stop raining; (*o tempo*) to clear up.
estibordo [iʃtʃi'bɔxdu] *m* starboard.
esticada [iʃtʃi'kada] *f*: **dar uma** ~ (*esticar-se*) to stretch, have a stretch; **dar uma ~ numa boate** (*col*) to go on to a nightclub.
esticar [iʃtʃi'ka*] *vt* (*uma corda*) to stretch, tighten; (*a perna*) to stretch; **~-se** *vr* to stretch out; ~ **as canelas** (*col*) to pop one's clogs, kick the bucket; **depois da festa esticamos numa boate** (*col*) after the party we went on to a nightclub.
estigma [iʃ'tʃigima] *m* (*marca*) mark, scar; (*fig*) stigma.
estigmatizar [iʃtʃigimatʃi'za*] *vt* to brand; ~ **alguém de algo** to brand sb (as) sth.
estilhaçar [iʃtʃiʎa'sa*] *vt* to splinter; (*despedaçar*) to shatter; **~-se** *vr* to shatter.
estilhaço [iʃtʃi'ʎasu] *m* fragment, chip, splinter.
estilista [iʃtʃi'liʃta] *m/f* stylist; (*de moda*) designer.
estilística [iʃtʃi'liʃtʃika] *f* stylistics *sg*.
estilístico/a [iʃtʃi'liʃtʃiku/a] *adj* stylistic.
estilizar [iʃtʃili'za*] *vt* to stylize.
estilo [iʃ'tʃilu] *m* style; (*TEC*) stylus; ~ **de vida** way of life; **móveis de** ~ stylish furniture; **o vestido não é do meu** ~ *ou* **não faz o meu** ~ the dress isn't my style.
estima [iʃ'tʃima] *f* esteem; (*afeto*) affection.
estimação [iʃtʃima'sãw] *f*: **... de** ~ favourite (*BRIT*) ..., favorite (*US*) ....

estimado/a [iʃtʃi'madu/a] *adj* respected; (*em cartas*): **E~ Senhor** Dear Sir.
estimar [iʃtʃi'ma*] *vt* (*apreciar*) to appreciate; (*avaliar*) to value; (*ter estima a*) to have a high regard for; (*calcular aproximadamente*) to estimate; **~-se** *vr*: **eles se estimam muito** they have a high regard for one another; **estima-se o número de ouvintes em 3 milhões** the number of listeners is estimated to be 3 million; **~ em** (*avaliar*) to value at; (*população*) to estimate to be; **estimo que você tenha exito** I wish you success.
estimativa [iʃtʃima'tʃiva] *f* estimate; **fazer uma ~ de algo** to estimate sth; **~ de custo** estimate, costing.
estimável [iʃtʃi'mavew] (*pl* **-eis**) *adj* (*digno de estima*) decent; **prejuízo ~ em 3 milhões** loss estimated at 3 million.
estimulação [iʃtʃimula'sãw] *f* stimulation.
estimulante [iʃtʃimu'lãtʃi] *adj* stimulating ♦ *m* stimulant.
estimular [iʃtʃimu'la*] *vt* to stimulate; (*incentivar*) to encourage; **~ alguém a fazer algo** to encourage sb to do sth.
estímulo [iʃ'tʃimulu] *m* stimulus; (*ânimo*) encouragement; **falta de ~** lack of incentive; **ele não tem ~ para nada no momento** he has got no incentive to do anything at the moment.
estio [iʃ'tʃiu] *m* summer.
estipêndio [iʃtʃi'pẽdʒu] *m* pay.
estipulação [iʃtʃipula'sãw] (*pl* **-ões**) *f* stipulation, condition.
estipular [iʃtʃipu'la*] *vt* to stipulate.
estirar [iʃtʃi'ra*] *vt* to stretch (out); **~-se** *vr* to stretch.
estirpe [iʃ'tʃixpi] *f* stock, lineage.
estivador(a) [iʃtʃiva'do*(a)] *m/f* docker.
estive [iʃ'tʃivi] *etc vb V* **estar.**
estocada [iʃto'kada] *f* stab, thrust.
estocado/a [iʃto'kadu/a] *adj* (COM) in stock.
estocagem [iʃto'kaʒẽ] *f* (*estocar*) stockpiling; (*estoque*) stock.
estocar [iʃto'ka*] *vt* to stock.
Estocolmo [iʃto'kɔwmu] *n* Stockholm.
estofador(a) [iʃtofa'do*(a)] *m/f* upholsterer.
estofar [iʃto'fa*] *vt* to upholster; (*acolchoar*) to pad, stuff.
estofo [iʃ'tofu] *m* (*tecido*) material; (*para acolchoar*) padding, stuffing.
estóico/a [iʃ'tɔjku/a] *adj* stoic(al) ♦ *m/f* stoic.
estojo [iʃ'toʒu] *m* case; **~ de ferramentas** tool kit; **~ de óculos** glasses case; **~ de tintas** paintbox; **~ de unhas** manicure set.
estola [iʃ'tɔla] *f* stole.
estólido/a [iʃ'tɔlidu/a] *adj* stupid.
estômago [iʃ'tomagu] *m* stomach; **ter ~ para (fazer) algo** to be up to (doing) sth; **estar com o ~ embrulhado** to have an upset stomach; **forrar o ~** to have a little bite to eat.
Estônia [iʃ'tonja] *f*: **a ~** Estonia.
estoniano/a [iʃto'njanu/a] *adj, m/f* Estonian.
estonteante [iʃtõ'tʃjãtʃi] *adj* stunning.
estontear [iʃtõ'tʃja*] *vt* to stun, daze.
estoque [iʃ'tɔki] *m* (COM) stock; **em ~** in stock.
estore [iʃ'tɔri] *m* blind.
estória [iʃ'tɔrja] *f* story.
estorninho [iʃtox'niɲu] *m* starling.
estorricar [iʃtoxi'ka*] *vt, vi* = **esturricar.**
estorvar [iʃtox'va*] *vt* to hinder, obstruct; (*fig*: *importunar*) to bother, disturb; **~ alguém de fazer** to prevent sb from doing.
estorvo [iʃ'toxvu] *m* hindrance, obstacle; (*amolação*) bother, nuisance.
estourado/a [iʃto'radu/a] *adj* (*temperamental*) explosive; (*col*: *cansado*) knackered, worn out.
estoura-peito [iʃtora'-] (*col*: *pl* **~s**) *m* strong cigarette.
estourar [iʃto'ra*] *vi* to explode; (*pneu*) to burst; (*escândalo*) to blow up; (*guerra*) to break out; (BR: *chegar*) to turn up, arrive; **~ (com alguém)** (*zangar-se*) to blow up (at sb); **estou estourando de dor de cabeça** I've got a splitting headache; **eu devo chegar às 9.00, estourando, 9 e meia** I should get there at 9 o'clock, or 9.30 at the latest.
estouro [iʃ'toru] *m* explosion; **ser um ~** (*col*) to be great; **dar o ~** (*fig*: *zangar-se*) to blow up, blow one's top.
estouvado/a [iʃto'vadu/a] *adj* rash, foolhardy.
estrábico/a [iʃ'trabiku/a] *adj* cross-eyed.
estrabismo [iʃtra'biʒmu] *m* squint.
estraçalhar [iʃtrasa'ʎa*] *vt* (*livro, objeto*) to pull to pieces; (*pessoa*) to tear to pieces; **~-se** *vr* to mutilate one another.
estrada [iʃ'trada] *f* road; **~ de contorno** ring road (BRIT), beltway (US); **~ de ferro** (BR) railway (BRIT), railroad (US); **~ de rodagem** (BR) (trunk) road; **~ de terra** dirt road; **~ principal** main road (BRIT), state highway (US); **~ secundária** minor road.
estrado [iʃ'tradu] *m* (*tablado*) platform; (*de cama*) base.
estragado/a [iʃtra'gadu/a] *adj* ruined, wrecked; (*saúde*) ruined; (*fruta*) rotten; (*muito mimado*) spoiled, spoilt (BRIT).
estraga-prazeres [iʃtraga-] *m/f inv* spoilsport.
estragão [iʃtra'gãw] *m* tarragon.
estragar [iʃtra'ga*] *vt* to spoil; (*arruinar*) to ruin, wreck; (*desperdiçar*) to waste; (*saúde*) to damage; (*mimar*) to spoil.
estrago [iʃ'tragu] *m* (*destruição*) destruction; (*desperdício*) waste; (*dano*) damage; **os ~s da guerra** the ravages of war.
estrangeiro/a [iʃtrã'ʒejru/a] *adj* foreign ♦ *m/f* foreigner; **no ~** abroad.

NB: European Portuguese adds the following consonants to certain words: **b** (sú(b)dito, su(b)til); **c** (a(c)ção, a(c)cionista, a(c)to); **m** (inde(m)ne); **p** (ado(p)ção, ado(p)tar); *for further details see p. xiii.*

estrangulação [iʃtrãgula'sãw] *f* strangulation.
estrangulador [iʃtrãgula'do*] *m* strangler.
estrangular [iʃtrãgu'la*] *vt* to strangle; **esta suéter está me estrangulando** this sweater is too tight for me.
estranhar [iʃtra'ɲa*] *vt* (*surpreender-se de*) to be surprised at; (*achar estranho*): ~ **algo** to find sth strange; **estranhei o clima** the climate did not agree with me; **minha filha estranhou a visita/a cama nova** my daughter was shy with the visitor/found it hard to get used to the new bed; **não é de se** ~ it's not surprising; **você não quer um chocolate? — estou te estranhando** you don't want a chocolate? — that's not like you.
estranho/a [iʃ'traɲu/a] *adj* strange, odd; (*influências*) outside ♦ *m/f* (*desconhecido*) stranger; (*de fora*) outsider; **o nome não me é** ~ the name rings a bell.
Estrasburgo [iʃtraʒ'buxgu] *n* Strasbourg.
estratagema [iʃtrata'ʒɛma] *m* (MIL) stratagem; (*ardil*) trick.
estratégia [iʃtra'tɛʒa] *f* strategy.
estratégico/a [iʃtra'tɛʒiku/a] *adj* strategic.
estratificar-se [iʃtratʃifi'kaxsi] *vr* (*fig*: *idéias, opiniões*) to become entrenched.
estrato [iʃ'tratu] *m* layer, stratum.
estratosfera [iʃtratoʃ'fɛra] *f* stratosphere.
estreante [iʃ'trjãtʃi] *adj* new ♦ *m/f* newcomer.
estrear [iʃ'trja*] *vt* (*vestido*) to wear for the first time; (*peça de teatro*) to perform for the first time; (*veículo*) to use for the first time; (*filme*) to show for the first time, première; (*iniciar*): ~ **uma carreira** to embark on *ou* begin a career ♦ *vi* (*ator, jogador*) to make one's first appearance; (*filme, peça*) to open.
estrebaria [iʃtreba'ria] *f* stable.
estrebuchar [iʃtrebu'ʃa*] *vi* to struggle; (*ao morrer*) to shake (in death throes).
estréia [iʃ'trɛja] *f* (*de artista*) debut; (*de uma peça*) first night; (*de um filme*) première, opening; **é a** ~ **do meu carro** it's the first time I've used my car.
estreitamento [iʃtrejta'mẽtu] *m* (*diminuição*) narrowing; (*aperto*) tightening; (*de relações*) strengthening.
estreitar [iʃtrej'ta*] *vt* (*reduzir*) to narrow; (*roupa*) to take in; (*abraçar*) to hug; (*laços de amizade*) to strengthen ♦ *vi* (*estrada*) to narrow; **~-se** *vr* (*laços de amizade*) to deepen.
estreiteza [iʃtrej'teza] *f* narrowness; (*de regulamento*) strictness; ~ **de pontos de vista** narrowmindedness.
estreito/a [iʃ'trejtu/a] *adj* narrow; (*saia*) straight; (*vínculo, relação*) close; (*medida*) strict ♦ *m* strait; **ter convivência estreita com alguém** to live at close quarters with sb.
estrela [iʃ'trela] *f* star; ~ **cadente** shooting star; ~ **de cinema** film (BRIT) *ou* movie (US) star; **ter boa** ~ to be lucky.
estrelado/a [iʃtre'ladu/a] *adj* (*céu*) starry; (PT: *ovo*) fried; **um filme** ~ **por Marilyn Monroe** a film starring Marilyn Monroe.
estrela-do-mar (*pl* **estrelas-do-mar**) *f* starfish.
estrelar [iʃtre'la*] *vt* (PT: *ovos*) to fry; **~-se** *vr* (*céu*) to fill with stars; ~ **um filme/uma peça** to star in a film/play.
estrelato [iʃtre'latu] *m*: **o** ~ stardom.
estrelinha [iʃtre'liɲa] *f* (*fogo de artifício*) sparkler.
estrelismo [iʃtre'liʒmu] *m* star quality.
estremadura [iʃtrema'dura] *f* frontier.
estremecer [iʃtreme'se*] *vt* (*sacudir*) to shake; (*amizade*) to strain; (*fazer tremer*): ~ **alguém** to make sb shudder ♦ *vi* (*vibrar*) to shake; (*tremer*) to tremble; (*horrorizar-se*) to shudder; (*amizade*) to be strained; **ela estremeceu de susto, o susto estremeceu-a** the fright made her jump.
estremecido/a [iʃtreme'sidu/a] *adj* (*sacudido*) shaken; (*sobressaltado*) startled; (*amizade*) strained.
estremecimento [iʃtremesi'mẽtu] *m* (*sacudida*) shaking, trembling; (*tremor*) tremor; (*abalo numa amizade*) tension.
estremunhado/a [iʃtremu'ɲadu/a] *adj* half-asleep.
estrepar-se [iʃtre'paxsi] *vr* (*fig*) to come unstuck.
estrepe [iʃ'trɛpi] (*col*) *m* (*mulher*) dog.
estrépito [iʃ'trɛpitu] *m* din, racket; **com** ~ with a lot of noise, noisily; **fazer** ~ to make a din.
estrepitoso/a [iʃtrepitozu/ɔza] *adj* noisy, rowdy; (*fig*) sensational.
estressante [iʃtre'sãtʃi] *adj* stressful.
estressar [iʃtre'sa*] *vt* to stress.
estresse [iʃ'trɛsi] *m* stress.
estria [iʃ'tria] *f* groove; (*na pele*) stretch mark.
estribar [iʃtri'ba*] *vt* to base; **~-se** *vr*: **~-se em** to be based on.
estribeira [iʃtri'bejra] *f*: **perder as ~s** (*col*) to fly off the handle, lose one's temper.
estribilho [iʃtri'biʎu] *m* (MÚS) chorus.
estribo [iʃ'tribu] *m* (*de cavalo*) stirrup; (*degrau*) step; (*fig*: *apoio*) support.
estricnina [iʃtrik'nina] *f* strychnine.
estridente [iʃtri'dẽtʃi] *adj* shrill, piercing.
estrilar [iʃtri'la*] (*col*) *vi* (*zangar-se*) to get mad; (*reclamar*) to moan.
estrilo [iʃ'trilu] *m*: **dar um** ~ to blow one's top.
estripulia [iʃtripu'lia] *f* prank.
estrito/a [iʃ'tritu/a] *adj* (*rigoroso*) strict; (*restrito*) restricted; **no sentido** ~ **da palavra** in the strict sense of the word.
estrofe [iʃ'trɔfi] *f* stanza.
estrogonofe [iʃtrogo'nɔfi] *m* (CULIN) stroganoff.
estrompado/a [iʃtrõ'padu/a] *adj* worn out; (*pessoa*) exhausted.
estrondar [iʃtrõ'da*] *vi* to boom; (*fig*) to resound.

estrondo [iʃ'trõdu] *m* (*de trovão*) rumble; (*de armas*) din; ~ **sônico** sonic boom.
estrondoso/a [iʃtrõ'dozu/ɔza] *adj* (*ovação*) tumultuous, thunderous; (*sucesso*) resounding; (*notícia*) sensational.
estropiar [iʃtro'pja*] *vt* (*aleijar*) to maim, cripple; (*fatigar*) to wear out, exhaust; (*texto*) to mutilate; (*pronunciar mal*) to mispronounce.
estrumar [iʃtru'ma*] *vt* to spread manure on.
estrume [iʃ'trumi] *m* manure.
estrutura [iʃtru'tura] *f* structure; (*armação*) framework; (*de edifício*) fabric.
estrutural [iʃtrutu'raw] (*pl* **-ais**) *adj* structural.
estruturalismo [iʃtrutura'liʒmu] *m* structuralism.
estruturar [iʃtrutu'ra*] *vt* to structure.
estuário [iʃtu'arju] *m* estuary.
estudado/a [iʃtu'dadu/a] *adj* (*fig*) studied, affected.
estudantada [iʃtudã'tada] *f* students *pl*.
estudante [iʃtu'dãtʃi] *m/f* student.
estudantil [iʃtudã'tʃiw] (*pl* **-is**) *adj* student *atr*.
estudar [iʃtu'da*] *vt*, *vi* to study.
estúdio [iʃ'tudʒu] *m* studio.
estudioso/a [iʃtudʒozu/ɔza] *adj* studious ♦ *m/f* student.
estudo [iʃ'tudu] *m* study; ~ **de caso** case study; ~ **de viabilidade** feasibility study.
estufa [iʃ'tufa] *f* (*fogão*) stove; (*de plantas*) greenhouse; (*de fogão*) plate warmer; **este quarto é uma** ~ this room is like an oven.
estufado [iʃtu'fadu] (*PT*) *m* stew.
estufar [iʃtu'fa*] *vt* (*peito*) to puff up; (*almofada*) to stuff.
estulto/a [iʃ'tuwtu/a] *adj* foolish, silly.
estupefação [iʃtupefa'sãw] (*PT*: **-cç-**) *f* amazement, astonishment.
estupefato/a [iʃtupe'fatu/a] (*PT*: **-ct-**) *adj* dumbfounded; **ele me olhou** ~ he looked at me in astonishment.
estupendo/a [iʃtu'pẽdu/a] *adj* wonderful; (*col*) fantastic, terrific.
estupidamente [iʃtupida'mẽtʃi] *adv* stupidly; **uma cerveja** ~ **gelada** (*col*) an ice-cold beer.
estupidez [iʃtupi'deʒ] *f* stupidity; (*ato*, *dito*) stupid thing; (*grosseria*) rudeness; **que** ~! what a stupid thing to do! (*ou* to say!).
estúpido/a [iʃ'tupidu/a] *adj* stupid; (*grosseiro*) rude, churlish ♦ *m/f* idiot; (*grosseiro*) oaf; **calor** ~ incredible heat.
estupor [iʃtu'po*] *m* stupor; (*fig*: *pessoa de mau caráter*) bad lot; (: *pessoa feia*) fright.
estuporado/a [iʃtupo'radu/a] *adj* (*estragado*) ruined; (*cansado*) tired out; (*ferido*) seriously injured.
estuporar-se [iʃtupo'raxsi] (*col*) *vr* (*num acidente*) to be seriously injured.
estuprador [iʃtupra'do*] *m* rapist.
estuprar [iʃtu'pra*] *vt* to rape.
estupro [iʃ'tupru] *m* rape.
estuque [iʃ'tuki] *m* stucco; (*massa*) plaster.
esturricado/a [iʃtuxi'kadu/a] *adj* (*seco*) shrivelled, dried out; (*roupa*) skimpy, tight.
esturricar [iʃtuxi'ka*] *vt*, *vi* to shrivel, dry out.
esvaecer-se [iʒvaje'sexsi] *vr* to fade away, vanish.
esvair-se [iʒva'jixsi] *vr* to vanish, disappear; ~ **em sangue** to lose a lot of blood.
esvaziamento [iʒvazja'mẽtu] *m* emptying.
esvaziar [iʒva'zja*] *vt* to empty; **~-se** *vr* to empty.
esverdeado/a [iʒvex'dʒjado/a] *adj* greenish.
esvoaçante [iʒvwa'sãtʃi] *adj* billowing.
esvoaçar [iʒvoa'sa*] *vi* to flutter.
ETA ['ɛta] *abr m* (= *Euskadi Ta Askatasuna*) ETA.
eta ['eta] (*col*) *excl*: ~ **filme chato!** what a boring film!; ~ **ferro!** gosh!
etapa [e'tapa] *f* (*fase*) stage; **por ~s** in stages.
etário/a [e'tarju/a] *adj* age *atr*.
etc. *abr* (= *et cetera*) etc.
éter ['ɛte*] *m* ether.
eternidade [etexni'dadʒi] *f* eternity.
eternizar [etexni'za*] *vt* (*fazer eterno*) to make eternal; (*nome*, *pessoa*) to immortalize; (*discussão*, *processo*) to drag out; **~-se** *vr* to be immortalized; to drag on.
eterno/a [e'texnu/a] *adj* eternal.
ética ['ɛtʃika] *f* ethics *pl*.
ético/a ['ɛtʃiku/a] *adj* ethical.
etimologia [etʃimolo'ʒia] *f* etymology.
etíope [e'tʃiopi] *adj*, *m/f* Ethiopian.
Etiópia [e'tʃjɔpja] *f*: **a** ~ Ethiopia.
etiqueta [etʃi'keta] *f* (*maneiras*) etiquette; (*rótulo*) label; (*que se amarra*) tag; (*em roupa*) label; ~ **adesiva** adhesive *ou* stick-on label.
etiquetar [etʃike'ta*] *vt* to label.
étnico/a ['ɛtʃniku/a] *adj* ethnic.
etnocêntrico/a [etʃno'sẽtriku/a] *adj* ethnocentric.
etnografia [etʃnogra'fia] *f* ethnography.
etnologia [etʃnolo'ʒia] *f* ethnology.
etos ['ɛtuʃ] *m inv* ethos.
eu [ew] *pron* I ♦ *m* self; **sou** ~ it's me; ~ **mesmo** I myself; **~, hein?** I don't know ... (how strange!).
EUA *abr mpl* (= *Estados Unidos da América*) USA; **nos** ~ in the USA.
eucalipto [ewka'liptu] *m* eucalyptus.
eucaristia [ewkariʃ'tʃia] *f* Holy Communion.
eufemismo [ewfe'miʒmu] *m* euphemism.
eufonia [ewfo'nia] *f* euphony.
euforia [ewfo'ria] *f* euphoria.
eunuco [ew'nuku] *m* eunuch.
Europa [ew'rɔpa] *f*: **a** ~ Europe.
européia [euro'pɛja] *f de* **europeu**.
europeizar [ewropeji'za*] *vt* to Europeanize; **~-se** *vr* to become Europeanized.

europeu/péia [ewro'peu/'pɛja] *adj, m/f* European.
eutanásia [ewta'nazja] *f* euthanasia.
evacuação [evakwa'sãw] (*pl* **-ões**) *f* evacuation.
evacuar [eva'kwa*] *vt* to evacuate; (*sair de*) to leave; (*MED*) to discharge ♦ *vi* to defecate.
evadir [eva'dʒi*] *vt* to evade; (*col*) to dodge; **~-se** *vr* to escape.
evanescente [evane'sẽtʃi] *adj* fading, vanishing.
evangelho [evã'ʒeʎu] *m* gospel.
evangélico/a [evã'ʒɛliku/a] *adj* evangelical.
evaporação [evapora'sãw] *f* evaporation.
evaporar [evapo'ra*] *vt, vi* to evaporate; **~-se** *vr* to evaporate; (*desaparecer*) to vanish.
evasão [eva'zãw] (*pl* **-ões**) *f* escape, flight; (*fig*) evasion; **~ de impostos** tax avoidance.
evasê [eva'ze] *adj* (*saia*) flared.
evasiva [eva'ziva] *f* excuse.
evasivo/a [eva'zivu/a] *adj* evasive.
evasões [eva'zõjʃ] *fpl de* **evasão**.
evento [e'vẽtu] *m* (*acontecimento*) event; (*eventualidade*) eventuality.
eventual [evẽ'tuaw] (*pl* **-ais**) *adj* fortuitous, accidental.
eventualidade [evẽtwali'dadʒi] *f* eventuality.
evicção [evik'sãw] (*pl* **-ões**) *f* (*JUR*) eviction.
evidência [evi'dẽsja] *f* evidence, proof.
evidenciar [evidẽ'sja*] *vt* (*comprovar*) to prove; (*mostrar*) to show; **~-se** *vr* to be evident, be obvious.
evidente [evi'dẽtʃi] *adj* obvious, evident.
evitar [evi'ta*] *vt* to avoid; **~ de fazer algo** to avoid doing sth.
evitável [evi'tavew] (*pl* **-eis**) *adj* avoidable.
evocação [evoka'sãw] (*pl* **-ões**) *f* evocation; (*de espíritos*) invocation.
evocar [evo'ka*] *vt* to evoke; (*espíritos*) to invoke.
evolução [evolu'sãw] (*pl* **-ões**) *f* (*desenvolvimento*) development; (*MIL*) manoeuvre (*BRIT*), maneuver (*US*); (*movimento*) movement; (*BIO*) evolution.
evoluído/a [evo'lwidu/a] *adj* advanced; (*pessoa*) broad-minded.
evoluir [evo'lwi*] *vi* to evolve; **~ para** to evolve into; **ela não evolviu com os tempos** she hasn't moved with the times.
ex- [eʃ-, eʒ-] *prefixo* ex-, former.
Ex.ª *abr* = **Excelência**.
exacerbação [ezasexba'sãw] *f* worsening; (*exasperação*) irritation.
exacerbante [ezasex'bãtʃi] *adj* exacerbating.
exacerbar [ezasex'ba*] *vt* (*irritar*) to irritate, annoy; (*agravar*) to aggravate, worsen; (*revolta, indignação*) to deepen.
exacto/a *etc* [e'zatu/a] (*PT*) = **exato** *etc*.
exagerado/a [ezaʒe'radu/a] *adj* (*relato*) exaggerated; (*maquilagem etc*) overdone; (*pessoa*): **ele é ~** (*na maneira de falar*) he exaggerates; (*nos gestos*) he overdoes it *ou* things.
exagerar [ezaʒe'ra*] *vt* to exaggerate ♦ *vi* to exaggerate; (*agir com exagero*) to overdo it.
exagero [eza'ʒeru] *m* exaggeration.
exalação [ezala'sãw] (*pl* **-ões**) *f* fume.
exalar [eza'la*] *vt* (*odor*) to give off.
exaltação [ezawta'sãw] *f* (*de virtudes etc*) exaltation; (*excitamento*) excitement; (*irritação*) annoyance.
exaltado/a [ezaw'tadu/a] *adj* (*fanático*) fanatical; (*apaixonado*) overexcited.
exaltar [ezaw'ta*] *vt* (*elevar: pessoa, virtude*) to exalt; (*louvar*) to praise; (*excitar*) to excite; (*irritar*) to annoy; **~-se** *vr* (*irritar-se*) to get worked up; (*arrebatar-se*) to get carried away.
exame [e'zami] *m* (*EDUC*) examination, exam; (*MED etc*) examination; **fazer um ~** (*EDUC*) to take an exam; (*MED*) to have an examination; **~ de direção** driving test; **~ de sangue** blood test; **~ médico** medical (examination); **(~) vestibular** university entrance exam.
examinador(a) [ezamina'do*(a)] *m/f* examiner ♦ *adj* examining.
examinando/a [ezami'nãdu/a] *m/f* (exam) candidate.
examinar [ezami'na*] *vt* to examine.
exangue [e'zãgi] *adj* (*sem sangue*) bloodless.
exasperação [ezaʃpera'sãw] *f* exasperation.
exasperador(a) [ezaʃpera'do*(a)] *adj* exasperating.
exasperante [ezaʃpe'rãtʃi] *adj* exasperating.
exasperar [ezaʃpe'ra*] *vt* to exasperate; **~-se** *vr* to get exasperated.
exatidão [ezatʃi'dãw] *f* (*precisão*) accuracy; (*perfeição*) correctness.
exato/a [e'zatu/a] *adj* (*certo*) right, correct; (*preciso*) exact; **~!** exactly!
exaurir [ezaw'ri*] *vt* to exhaust, drain; **~-se** *vr* to become exhausted.
exaustão [ezaw'ʃtãw] *f* exhaustion.
exaustar [ezaw'ʃta*] *vt* to exhaust, drain; **~-se** *vr* to become exhausted.
exaustivo/a [ezaw'ʃtʃivu/a] *adj* (*tratado*) exhaustive; (*trabalho*) exhausting.
exausto/a [e'zawʃtu/a] *pp de* **exaurir** ♦ *adj* exhausted.
exaustor [ezaw'ʃto*] *m* extractor fan.
exceção [ese'sãw] (*pl* **-ões**) *f* exception; **com ~ de** with the exception of; **abrir ~** to make an exception.
excedente [ese'dẽtʃi] *adj* excess; (*COM*) surplus ♦ *m* (*COM*) surplus; **(aluno) ~** *pupil who cannot be given a place because the school is full*.
exceder [ese'de*] *vt* to exceed; (*superar*) to surpass; **~-se** *vr* (*cometer excessos*) to go too far; (*cansar-se*) to overdo things; **~ em peso/brilho** to outweigh/outshine.
excelência [ese'lẽsja] *f* excellence; **por ~** par excellence; **Vossa E~** Your Excellency.
excelente [ese'lẽtʃi] *adj* excellent.
excelentíssimo/a [eselẽ'tʃisimu/a] *adj superl de* **excelente**; (*tratamento*) honourable

(*BRIT*), honorable (*US*).

excelso/a [e'sɛwsu/a] *adj* (*sublime*) sublime; (*excelente*) excellent.

excentricidade [esẽtrisi'dadʒi] *f* eccentricity.

excêntrico/a [e'sẽtriku/a] *adj, m/f* eccentric.

excepção [ese'sãw] (*PT*) *f* = **exceção**.

excepcional [esepsjo'naw] (*pl* **-ais**) *adj* (*extraordinário*) exceptional; (*especial*) special; (*MED*) handicapped.

excepcionalidade [esepsjonali'dadʒi] *f* exceptional nature.

excepto *etc* [e'sɛtu] (*PT*) = **exceto** *etc*.

excerto [e'sɛxtu] *m* fragment, excerpt.

excessivo/a [ese'sivu/a] *adj* excessive.

excesso [e'sɛsu] *m* excess; (*COM*) surplus; **em ~** in excess; **~ de peso** excess weight; **~ de velocidade** excessive speed.

exceto [e'sɛtu] *prep* except (for), apart from.

excetuar [ese'twa*] *vt* to except, make an exception of; **todos, excetuando você** everyone except you.

excitação [esita'sãw] *f* excitement.

excitado/a [esi'tadu/a] *adj* excited; (*estimulado*) aroused.

excitante [esi'tãtʃi] *adj* exciting.

excitar [esi'ta*] *vt* to excite; (*estimular*) to arouse; **~-se** *vr* to get excited.

excitável [esi'tavew] (*pl* **-eis**) *adj* excitable.

exclamação [iʃklama'sãw] (*pl* **-ões**) *f* exclamation.

exclamar [iʃkla'ma*] *vi* to exclaim.

exclamativo/a [iʃklama'tʃivu/a] *adj* exclamatory; *V tb* **ponto**.

excluir [iʃ'klwi*] *vt* to exclude; (*deixar fora*) to leave out; (*eliminar*) to rule out; (*ser incompatível com*) to preclude.

exclusão [iʃklu'zãw] *f* exclusion.

exclusividade [iʃkluzivi'dadʒi] *f* exclusiveness; (*COM*) exclusive rights *pl*; **com ~ no "Globo"** only in the "Globo".

exclusivo/a [iʃklu'zivu/a] *adj* exclusive; **para uso ~ de** for the sole use of.

excluso/a [iʃ'kluzu/a] *adj* excluded.

excomungar [iʃkomũ'ga*] *vt* to excommunicate.

excremento [iʃkre'mẽtu] *m* excrement.

excruciante [iʃkru'sjãtʃi] *adj* excruciating.

excursão [iʃkux'sãw] (*pl* **-ões**) *f* trip, outing; (*em grupo*) excursion; **~ a pé** hike.

excursionar [iʃkuxsjo'na*] *vi* to go on a trip; **~ pela Europa** *etc* to tour Europe *etc*.

excursionista [iʃkuxsjo'niʃta] *m/f* tourist; (*para o dia*) day-tripper; (*a pé*) hiker.

excursões [iʃkux'sõjʃ] *fpl de* **excursão**.

execrável [eze'kravew] (*pl* **-eis**) *adj* execrable, deplorable.

execução [ezeku'sãw] (*pl* **-ões**) *f* execution; (*de música*) performance; **~ de hipoteca** (*COM*) foreclosure.

executante [ezeku'tãtʃi] *m/f* player, performer.

executar [ezeku'ta*] *vt* to execute; (*MÚS*) to perform; (*plano*) to carry out; (*papel teatral*) to play; **~ uma hipoteca** (*COM*) to foreclose on a mortgage.

executivo/a [ezeku'tʃivu/a] *adj, m/f* executive.

executor(a) [ezeku'to*(a)] *m/f* executioner.

exemplar [ezẽ'pla*] *adj* exemplary ♦ *m* model, example; (*BIO*) specimen; (*livro*) copy; (*peça*) piece.

exemplificar [ezẽplifi'ka*] *vt* to exemplify.

exemplo [e'zẽplu] *m* example; **por ~** for example; **dar o ~** to set an example; **servir de ~ a alguém** to be an example to sb; **a ~ de** just like; **a ~ do que** just as; **ela é um ~ de bondade** she's a model of kindness.

exéquias [e'zɛkjaʃ] *fpl* funeral rites.

exeqüível [eze'kwivew] (*pl* **-eis**) *adj* feasible.

exercer [ezex'se*] *vt* to exercise; (*influência, pressão*) to exert; (*função*) to perform; (*profissão*) to practise (*BRIT*), practice (*US*); (*obrigações*) to carry out.

exercício [ezex'sisju] *m* (*ginástica*, *EDUC*) exercise; (*de medicina*) practice; (*de direitos*) exercising; (*MIL*) drill; (*COM*) financial year; **em ~** (*funcionário*) in office; (*professor etc*) in service; **em pleno ~ de suas faculdades mentais** in full command of one's mental faculties; **~ anterior/corrente** (*COM*) previous/current (financial) year.

exercitar [ezexsi'ta*] *vt* (*profissão*) to practise (*BRIT*), practice (*US*); (*direitos, músculos*) to exercise; (*adestrar*) to train.

exército [e'zɛxsito] *m* army.

exibição [ezibi'sãw] (*pl* **-ões**) *f* show, display; (*de filme*) showing.

exibicionismo [ezibisjo'niʒmu] *m* flamboyance; (*PSICO*) exhibitionism.

exibicionista [ezibisjo'niʃta] *adj* flamboyant; (*PSICO*) exhibitionist ♦ *m/f* flamboyant character; exhibitionist.

exibições [ezibi'sõjʃ] *fpl de* **exibição**.

exibido/a [ezi'bidu/a] *adj* (*exibicionista*) flamboyant ♦ *m/f* show-off.

exibidor(a) [ezibi'do*(a)] *m/f* exhibitor; (*CINEMA*) cinema owner.

exibir [ezi'bi*] *vt* to show, display; (*alardear*) to show off; (*filme*) to show, screen; **~-se** *vr* to show off; (*indecentemente*) to expose o.s.

exigência [ezi'ʒẽsja] *f* demand; (*o necessário*) requirement.

exigente [ezi'ʒẽtʃi] *adj* demanding; **ser ~ com alguém** to be hard on sb.

exigibilidades [eziʒibili'dadʒiʃ] *fpl* (*COM*) liabilities.

exigir [ezi'ʒi*] *vt* to demand; **~ que alguém faça algo** to demand that sb do sth; **o médico exigiu-lhe repouso absoluto** the doctor ordered him to have complete rest.

exigível [ezi'ʒivew] (*pl* **-eis**) *adj* (*COM*:

NB: *European Portuguese adds the following consonants to certain words:* **b** (sú(b)dito, su(b)til); **c** (a(c)ção, a(c)cionista, a(c)to); **m** (inde(m)ne); **p** (ado(p)ção, ado(p)tar); *for further details see p. xiii.*

passivo): ~ **a curto/longo prazo** current/long-term liabilities *pl*.

exíguo/a [e'zigwu/a] *adj* (*diminuto*) small; (*escasso*) scanty.

exilado/a [ezi'ladu/a] *adj* exiled ♦ *m/f* exile.

exilar [ezi'la*] *vt* to exile; (*pessoa indesejável*) to deport; ~**-se** *vr* to go into exile.

exílio [e'zilju] *m* exile; (*forçado*) deportation.

exímio/a [e'zimju/a] *adj* (*eminente*) famous, distinguished; (*excelente*) excellent.

eximir [ezi'mi*] *vt*: ~ **de** to exempt from; (*obrigação*) to free from; (*culpa*) to clear of; ~**-se** *vr*: ~**-se de** to avoid, shun.

existência [eziʃ'tẽsja] *f* existence; (*vida*) life.

existencial [eziʃtẽ'sjaw] (*pl* **-ais**) *adj* existential.

existencialismo [eziʃtẽsja'liʒmu] *m* existentialism.

existencialista [eziʃtẽsja'liʃta] *adj*, *m/f* existentialist.

existente [eziʃ'tẽtʃi] *adj* extant; (*vivente*) living.

existir [eziʃ'tʃi*] *vi* to exist; **existe/existem ...** (*há*) there is/are ...; **ela não existe** (*col*) she's incredible.

êxito ['ezitu] *m* (*resultado*) result; (*sucesso*) success; (*música, filme etc*) hit; **ter** ~ **(em)** to succeed (in), be successful (in); **não ter** ~ **(em)** to fail (in), be unsuccessful (in).

Exmo(s)/a(s) *abr* (= *Excelentíssimo(s)/a(s)*) Dear.

êxodo ['ezodu] *m* exodus.

exoneração [ezonera'sãw] (*pl* **-ões**) *f* dismissal.

exonerar [ezone'ra*] *vt* (*demitir*) to dismiss; ~ **de uma obrigação** to free from an obligation.

exorbitante [ezoxbi'tãtʃi] *adj* (*preço*) exorbitant; (*pretensões*) extravagant; (*exigências*) excessive.

exorcismo [ezox'siʒmu] *m* exorcism.

exorcista [ezox'siʃta] *m/f* exorcist.

exorcizar [ezoxsi'za*] *vt* to exorcise.

exortação [ɛzoxta'sãw] (*pl* **-ões**) *f* exhortation.

exortar [ezox'ta*] *vt*: ~ **alguém a fazer algo** to urge sb to do sth.

exortativo/a [ezoxta'tʃivu/a] *adj* (*tom*) encouraging.

exótico/a [e'zɔtʃiku/a] *adj* exotic.

exotismo [ezo'tʃiʒmu] *m* exoticism, exotic nature.

expandir [iʃpã'dʒi*] *vt* to expand; (*espalhar*) to spread; ~**-se** *vr* (*dilatar-se*) to expand; ~**-se com alguém** to be frank with sb.

expansão [iʃpã'sãw] *f* expansion, spread; (*de alegria*) effusiveness.

expansividade [iʃpãsivi'dadʒi] *f* outgoing nature.

expansivo/a [iʃpã'sivu/a] *adj* (*pessoa*) outgoing.

expatriação [iʃpatrja'sãw] *f* expatriation.

expatriado/a [iʃpa'trjadu/a] *adj*, *m/f* expatriate.

expatriar [iʃpa'trja*] *vt* to expatriate.

expeça [iʃ'pɛsa] *etc vb V* **expedir**.

expectativa [iʃpekta'tʃiva] *f* (*esperança*) expectation; **na** ~ **de** in expectation of; **estar na** ~ to be expectant; (*em suspense*) to be in suspense; ~ **de vida** life expectancy.

expectorante [iʃpekto'rãtʃi] *adj*, *m* expectorant.

expectorar [iʃpekto'ra*] *vt* to cough up ♦ *vi* to expectorate.

expedição [iʃpedʒi'sãw] (*pl* **-ões**) *f* (*viagem*) expedition; (*de mercadorias*) despatch; (*por navio*) shipment; (*de passaporte etc*) issue.

expediência [iʃpe'dʒjẽsja] *f* (*desembaraço*) efficiency.

expediente [iʃpe'dʒjẽtʃi] *m* means; (*serviço*) working day; (*correspondência*) correspondence ♦ *adj* expedient; ~ **bancário** banking hours *pl*; ~ **do escritório** office hours *pl*; **meio** ~ part-time working; **só trabalho meio** ~ I only work part-time; **viver de** ~**s** to live on one's wits; **ser** *ou* **ter** ~ (*pessoa*) to be resourceful, have initiative.

expedir [iʃpe'dʒi*] *vt* (*enviar*) to send, despatch; (*bilhete, passaporte, decreto*) to issue.

expedito/a [iʃpe'dʒitu/a] *adj* prompt, speedy; (*pessoa*) efficient.

expelir [iʃpe'li*] *vt* (*expulsar*) to expel; (*sangue*) to spit.

experiência [iʃpe'rjẽsja] *f* (*prática*) experience; (*prova*) experiment, test; **em** ~ on trial.

experienciar [iʃperjẽ'sja*] *vt* to experience.

experiente [iʃpe'rjẽtʃi] *adj* experienced.

experimentação [iʃperimẽta'sãw] *f* experimentation.

experimentado/a [iʃperimẽ'tadu/a] *adj* (*experiente*) experienced; (*testado*) tried; (*provado*) tested.

experimental [iʃperimẽ'taw] (*pl* **-ais**) *adj* experimental.

experimentar [iʃperimẽ'ta*] *vt* (*comida*) to taste; (*vestido*) to try on; (*pôr à prova*) to try out, test; (*conhecer pela experiência*) to experience; (*sofrer*) to suffer, undergo; ~ **fazer algo** to try doing sth, have a go at doing sth.

experimento [iʃperi'mẽtu] *m* (*científico*) experiment.

expiar [iʃ'pja*] *vt* to atone for.

expiatório/a [iʃpja'tɔrju/a] *adj V* **bode**.

expilo [iʃ'pilu] *etc vb V* **expelir**.

expiraçao [iʃpira'sãw] (*pl* **-ões**) *f* (*de ar*) exhalation; (*termo*) expiry.

expirar [iʃpi'ra*] *vt* (*ar*) to exhale, breathe out ♦ *vi* (*morrer*) to die; (*terminar*) to end.

explanação [iʃplana'sãw] (*pl* **-ões**) *f* explanation.

explanar [iʃpla'na*] *vt* to explain.

explicação [iʃplika'sãw] (*pl* **-ões**) *f* explanation; (*PT*: *lição*) private lesson.

explicar [iʃpli'ka*] *vt*, *vi* to explain; ~**-se** *vr* to

explain o.s.; **isto não se explica** this does not make sense.
explicável [iʃpli'kavew] (*pl* **-eis**) *adj* explicable, explainable.
explícito/a [iʃ'plisitu/a] *adj* explicit, clear.
explodir [iʃplo'dʒi*] *vi* to explode, blow up ♦ *vt* (*bomba*) to explode.
exploração [iʃplora'sãw] *f* (*de um país*) exploration; (*abuso*) exploitation; (*de uma mina*) running.
explorador(a) [iʃplora'do*(a)] *adj* exploitative ♦ *m/f* (*descobridor*) explorer; (*de outros*) exploiter.
explorar [iʃplo'ra*] *vt* (*região*) to explore; (*mina*) to work, run; (*ferida*) to probe; (*trabalhadores etc*) to exploit.
explosão [iʃplo'zãw] (*pl* **-ões**) *f* explosion, blast; (*fig*) outburst.
explosivo/a [iʃplo'zivu/a] *adj* explosive; (*pessoa*) hot-headed ♦ *m* explosive.
explosões [iʃplo'sõjʃ] *fpl de* **explosão**.
Expoagro [eʃpu'agru] *abr f* = **Exposição Agropecuária Internacional do Rio de Janeiro**.
expor [iʃ'po*] (*irreg: como* **pôr**) *vt* to expose; (*a vida*) to risk; (*teoria*) to explain; (*revelar*) to reveal; (*mercadorias*) to display; (*quadros*) to exhibit; **~-se** *vr* to expose o.s.; **~(-se) a algo** to expose (o.s.) to sth; **seu rosto expõe sinais de cansaço** his face shows signs of tiredness.
exportação [iʃpoxta'sãw] *f* (*ato*) export(ing); (*mercadorias*) exports *pl*.
exportador(a) [iʃpoxta'do*(a)] *adj* exporting ♦ *m/f* exporter.
exportar [iʃpox'ta*] *vt* to export.
expôs [iʃ'poʃ] *etc vb V* **expor**.
exposição [iʃposi'sãw] (*pl* **-ões**) *f* (*exibição*) exhibition; (*explicação*) explanation; (*declaração*) statement; (*narração*) account; (FOTO) exposure.
expositor(a) [iʃpozi'to*(a)] *m/f* exhibitor.
exposto/a [iʃ'poʃtu/'pɔʃta] *pp de* **expor** ♦ *adj* (*lugar*) exposed; (*quadro, mercadoria*) on show *ou* display ♦ *m*: **o acima ~** the above; **estar ~ a algo** to be open *ou* exposed to sth.
expressão [iʃpre'sãw] (*pl* **-ões**) *f* expression.
expressar [iʃpre'sa*] *vt* to express; **~-se** *vr* to express o.s.
expressividade [iʃpresivi'dadʒi] *f* expressiveness.
expressivo/a [iʃpre'sivu/a] *adj* expressive; (*pessoa*) demonstrative.
expresso/a [iʃ'prɛsu/a] *pp de* **exprimir** ♦ *adj* (*manifesto*) definite, clear; (*trem, ordem, carta*) express ♦ *m* express.
expressões [iʃpre'sõjʃ] *fpl de* **expressão**.
exprimir [iʃpri'mi*] *vt* to express; **~-se** *vr* to express o.s.
expropriar [iʃpro'prja*] *vt* to expropriate.
expugnar [iʃpugi'na*] *vt* to take by storm.
expulsado/a [iʃpuw'sadu/a] *pp de* **expulsar**.
expulsão [iʃpul'sãw] (*pl* **-ões**) *f* expulsion; (ESPORTE) sending off.
expulsar [iʃpuw'sa*] *vt* to expel; (*de uma festa, clube etc*) to throw out; (*inimigo*) to drive out; (*estrangeiro*) to expel, deport; (*jogador*) to send off.
expulso/a [iʃ'puwsu/a] *pp de* **expulsar**.
expulsões [iʃpul'sõjʃ] *fpl de* **expulsão**.
expunha [iʃ'puɲa] *etc vb V* **expor**.
expus [iʃ'puʃ] *etc vb V* **expor**.
expuser [iʃpu'ze*] *etc vb V* **expor**.
expurgar [iʃpux'ga*] *vt* to expurgate.
êxtase ['eʃtazi] *m* ecstasy; (*transe*) trance; **estar em ~** to be in a trance.
extasiado/a [iʃta'zjadu/a] *adj* entranced.
extensão [iʃtẽ'sãw] (*pl* **-ões**) *f* (*ger*, TEL) extension; (*de uma empresa*) expansion; (*terreno*) expanse; (*tempo*) length, duration; (*de conhecimentos*) extent.
extensivo/a [iʃtẽ'sivu/a] *adj* extensive; **ser ~ a** to extend to.
extenso/a [iʃ'tẽsu/a] *adj* (*amplo*) extensive, wide; (*comprido*) long; (*conhecimentos*) extensive; (*artigo*) full, comprehensive; **por ~** in full.
extensões [iʃtẽ'sõjʃ] *fpl de* **extensão**.
extenuado/a [iʃte'nwadu/a] *adj* (*esgotado*) worn out.
extenuante [iʃte'nwãtʃi] *adj* exhausting; (*debilitante*) debilitating.
extenuar [iʃte'nwa*] *vt* to exhaust; (*debilitar*) to weaken.
exterior [iʃte'rjo*] *adj* (*de fora*) outside, exterior; (*aparência*) outward; (*comércio*) foreign ♦ *m* (*da casa*) outside; (*aspecto*) outward appearance; **do ~** (*do estrangeiro*) from abroad; **no ~** abroad.
exteriorizar [iʃterjori'za*] *vt* to show, manifest.
exteriormente [iʃterjox'mẽtʃi] *adv* on the outside.
exterminação [iʃtexmina'sãw] *f* extermination.
exterminar [iʃtexmi'na*] *vt* (*inimigo*) to wipe out, exterminate; (*acabar com*) to do away with.
extermínio [iʃtex'minju] *m* extermination, wiping out.
externato [iʃtex'natu] *m* day school.
externo/a [iʃ'tɛxnu/a] *adj* external; (*aparente*) outward; **"para uso ~"** "external use only".
extinção [iʃtʃĩ'sãw] *f* extinction.
extinguir [iʃtʃĩ'gi*] *vt* (*fogo*) to put out, extinguish; (*um povo*) to wipe out; **~-se** *vr* (*fogo, luz*) to go out; (BIO) to become extinct.
extinto/a [iʃ'tʃĩtu/a] *adj* (*fogo*) extinguished; (*língua*) dead; (*animal, vulcão*) extinct; (*associação etc*) defunct; (*pessoa*) dead.
extintor [iʃtĩ'to*] *m* (fire) extinguisher.

***NB**: European Portuguese adds the following consonants to certain words:* **b** (sú(b)dito, su(b)til); **c** (a(c)ção, a(c)cionista, a(c)to); **m** (inde(m)ne); **p** (ado(p)ção, ado(p)tar); *for further details see p. xiii.*

extirpar [iʃtix'pa*] *vt* (*desarraigar*) to uproot; (*corrupção*) to eradicate; (*tumor*) to remove.
extorquir [iʃtox'ki*] *vt* to extort.
extorsão [iʃtox'sãw] *f* extortion.
extorsivo/a [iʃtox'sivu/a] *adj* extortionate.
extra ['ɛʃtra] *adj* extra ♦ *m/f* extra person; (*TEATRO*) extra; *V tb* **hora**.
extração [iʃtra'sãw] (*PT*: **-cç-**: *pl* **-ões**) *f* extraction; (*de loteria*) draw.
extraconjugal [eʃtrakõʒu'gaw] (*pl* **-ais**) *adj* extramarital.
extracto [iʃ'tratu] (*PT*) *m* = **extrato**.
extracurricular [eʃtrakuxiku'la*] *adj* extracurricular.
extradição [eʃtradʒi'sãw] *f* extradition.
extraditar [eʃtradʒi'ta*] *vt* to extradite.
extrafino/a [eʃtra'finu/a] *adj* extra high-quality.
extrair [iʃtra'ji*] *vt* to extract, take out.
extra-oficial (*pl* **-ciais**) *adj* unofficial.
extraordinário/a [iʃtraoxdʒi'narju/a] *adj* extraordinary; (*despesa*) extra; (*reunião*) special; **nada de ~** nothing out of the ordinary.
extrapolar [iʃtrapo'la*] *vt* to extrapolate.
extraterrestre [eʃtrate'xɛʃtri] *adj* extraterrestrial.
extrato [iʃ'tratu] *m* extract; (*resumo*) summary; **~ (bancário)** (bank) statement.
extravagância [iʃtrava'gãsja] *f* extravagance.
extravagante [iʃtrava'gãtʃi] *adj* extravagant; (*roupa*) outlandish; (*conduta*) wild.
extravasar [iʃtrava'za*] *vi* to overflow.
extraviado/a [iʃtra'vjadu/a] *adj* lost, missing.
extraviar [iʃtra'vja*] *vt* (*perder*) to mislay; (*pessoa*) to lead astray; (*dinheiro*) to embezzle; **~-se** *vr* to get lost.
extravio [iʃtra'viu] *m* (*perda*) loss; (*roubo*) embezzlement; (*fig*) deviation.
extremado/a [iʃtre'madu/a] *adj* extreme.
extremar-se [iʃtre'maxsi] *vt* to do one's utmost, make every effort; (*distinguir-se*) to distinguish o.s.; **~ em gentilezas** to show extreme kindness.
extrema-unção [iʃtrɛmaũ'sãw] (*pl* **extrema-unções**) *f* (*REL*) extreme unction.
extremidade [iʃtremi'dadʒi] *f* extremity; (*do dedo*) tip; (*ponta*) end; (*beira*) edge.
extremo/a [iʃ'trɛmu/a] *adj* extreme ♦ *m* extreme; **~s** *mpl* (*carinho*) doting *sg*; (*descomedimento*) extremes; **ao ~** extremely; **de um ~ a outro** from one extreme to another; **o E~ Oriente** the Far East.
extremoso/a [iʃtre'mozu/ɔza] *adj* doting.
extroversão [eʃtrovex'sãw] *f* extroversion.
extroverso/a [eʃtro'vɛxsu/a] *adj* extrovert.
extroverter-se [eʃtrovex'texsi] *vr* to be outgoing.
extrovertido/a [eʃtrovex'tʃidu/a] *adj* extrovert, outgoing ♦ *m/f* extrovert.
exu [e'ʃu] *m* devil (*in voodoo rituals*).
exuberância [ezube'rãsja] *f* exuberance.
exuberante [ezube'rãtʃi] *adj* exuberant.
exultação [ezuwta'sãw] *f* joy, exultation.
exultante [ezuw'tãtʃi] *adj* jubilant, exultant.
exultar [ezuw'ta*] *vi* to rejoice.
exumar [ezu'ma*] *vt* (*corpo*) to exhume; (*fig*) to dig up.
ex-voto *m* votive offering.

F

F, f ['ɛfi] (*pl* **fs**) *m* F, f; **F de Francisco** F for Frederick (*BRIT*) *ou* Fox (*US*).
f *abr* = **folha**.
F-1 *abr* = **Fórmula Um**.
fá [fa] *m* (*MÚS*) F.
fã [fã] (*col*) *m/f* fan.
FAB ['fabi] *abr f* = **Força Aérea Brasileira**.
fábrica ['fabrika] *f* factory; **~ de cerveja** brewery; **~ de conservas** cannery; **~ de papel** paper mill; **a preço de ~** wholesale.
fabricação [fabrika'sãw] *f* manufacture; **de ~ caseira/própria** home-made/own-make; **~ em série** mass production.
fabricante [fabri'kãtʃi] *m/f* manufacturer.
fabricar [fabri'ka*] *vt* to manufacture, make; (*inventar*) to fabricate.
fabrico [fa'briku] *m* production.
fabril [fa'briw] (*pl* **-is**) *adj V* **industria**.
fábula ['fabula] *f* fable; (*conto*) tale; (*BR*: *grande quantia*) fortune.
fabuloso/a [fabu'lozu/ɔza] *adj* fabulous.
faca ['faka] *f* knife; **é uma ~ de dois gumes** (*fig*) it's a two-edged sword; **entrar na ~** (*col*) to be operated on, go under the knife; **ter a ~ e o queijo na mão** (*fig*) to have things in hand.
facada [fa'kada] *f* stab, cut; **dar uma ~ em alguém** to stab sb; (*fig*: *col*) to touch sb for money.
façanha [fa'saɲa] *f* exploit, deed.
facão [fa'kãw] (*pl* **-ões**) *m* carving knife; (*para cortar o mato*) machete.
facção [fak'sãw] (*pl* **-ões**) *f* faction.
faccioso/a [fak'sjozu/ɔza] *adj* factious.
facções [fak'sõjʃ] *fpl de* **facção**.
face ['fasi] *f* (*rosto, de moeda*) face; (*bochecha*) cheek; **em ~ de** in view of; **fazer ~ a** to face up to; **~ a ~** face to face; **disquete de ~ simples/dupla** (*COMPUT*) single-/double-sided disk.
faceiro/a [fa'sejru/a] *adj* (*elegante*) smart; (*alegre*) cheerful.
fáceis ['fasejʃ] *adj pl de* **fácil**.
faceta [fa'seta] *f* (*tb fig*) facet.
fachada [fa'ʃada] *f* (*tb fig*) façade, front; (*col*: *rosto*) face, mug (*col*).

facho ['faʃu] *m* beam.
facial [fa'sjaw] (*pl* **-ais**) *adj* facial.
fácil ['fasiw] (*pl* **-eis**) *adj* easy; (*temperamento, pessoa*) easy-going; (*mulher*) easy ♦ *adv* easily.
facilidade [fasili'dadʒi] *f* ease; (*jeito*) facility; **~s** *fpl* facilities; **ter ~ para algo** to have a talent *ou* a facility for sth; **com ~** easily.
facílimo/a [fa'silimu/a] *adj superl de* **fácil**.
facilitação [fasilita'sãw] *f* facilitation; (*fornecimento*) provision.
facilitar [fasili'ta*] *vt* to facilitate, make easy; (*fornecer*) to provide ♦ *vi* (*agir sem cautela*) to be careless.
facínora [fa'sinora] *m* criminal.
fã-clube [fã'klubi] (*pl* **fãs-clubes**) *m* fan club.
faço ['fasu] *etc vb V* **fazer**.
facões [fa'kõjʃ] *fpl de* **facão**.
fac-símile [fak-] (*pl* **~s**) *m* (*cópia*) facsimile; (*carta*) fax; (*máquina*) fax (machine); **enviar por ~** to fax.
factício/a [fak'tʃisju/a] *adj* unnatural.
facto ['faktu] (*PT*) *m* = **fato**.
factor [fak'to*] (*PT*) *m* = **fator**.
factótum [fak'tɔtũ] *m* factotum.
factual [fak'twaw] (*pl* **-ais**) *adj* factual.
factura *etc* [fak'tura] (*PT*) = **fatura** *etc*.
faculdade [fakuw'dadʒi] *f* faculty; (*poder*) power; (*BR*: *escola*) university, college; (*corpo docente*) teaching staff (*BRIT*), faculty (*US*); **fazer ~** to go to university *ou* college.
facultar [fakuw'ta*] *vt* (*permitir*) to allow; (*conceder*) to grant.
facultativo/a [fakuwta'tʃivu/a] *adj* optional ♦ *m/f* doctor.
fada ['fada] *f* fairy.
fadado/a [fa'dadu/a] *adj* fated, destined, doomed.
fada-madrinha (*pl* **fadas-madrinhas**) *f* fairy godmother.
fadiga [fa'dʒiga] *f* fatigue.
fadista [fa'dʒiʃta] (*PT*) *m/f* "fado" singer ♦ *m* ruffian.
fado ['fadu] *m* fate; (*canção*) *traditional song of Portugal*.
Faferj [fa'fɛxʒi] *abr f* = **Federação das Associações das Favelas do Estado do Rio de Janeiro**.
fagueiro/a [fa'gejru/a] *adj* (*contente*) happy; (*agradável*) pleasant.
fagulha [fa'guʎa] *f* spark.
fahrenheit [farẽ'ajtʃi] *adj inv* Fahrenheit.
faia ['faja] *f* beech (tree).
faina ['fajna] *f* toil, work; (*tarefa*) task, job.
fair-play ['fɛxplej] *m* fair play.
faisão [faj'zãw] (*pl* **-ães** *ou* **-ões**) *m* pheasant.
faísca [fa'iʃka] *f* spark; (*brilho*) flash.
faiscante [faj'ʃkãtʃi] *adj* flashing; (*fogo*) flickering.
faiscar [fajʃ'ka*] *vi* to sparkle; (*brilhar*) to flash.
faisões [faj'zõjʃ] *mpl de* **faisão**.
faixa ['fajʃa] *f* (*cinto*) belt; (*tira*) strip; (*área*) zone; (*AUTO*: *pista*) lane; (*BR*: *para pedestres*) zebra crossing (*BRIT*), crosswalk (*US*); (*MED*) bandage; (*num disco*) track; (*JUDÔ*) belt; **~ etária** age group.
faixa-título *f* (*MÚS*) title track.
fajuto/a [fa'ʒutu/a] (*col*) *adj* (*pão*) rough; (*falso*: *nota*) fake.
fala ['fala] *f* speech; **chamar às ~s** to call to account; **sem ~** speechless; **perder a ~** to be struck dumb.
falação [fala'sãw] (*pl* **-ões**) *f* (*ato*) talk; (*discurso*) speech.
falácia [fa'lasja] *f* fallacy.
falações [fala'sõjʃ] *fpl de* **falação**.
faladeira [fala'dejra] *f de* **falador**.
falado/a [fa'ladu/a] *adj* (*caso etc*) talked about, much discussed; (*famoso*) well-known; (*de má fama*) notorious; (*CINEMA*) talking.
falador/deira [fala'do*/dejra] *adj* talkative ♦ *m/f* chatterbox.
falante [fa'lãtʃi] *adj* talkative.
falar [fa'la*] *vt* (*língua*) to speak; (*besteira etc*) to talk; (*dizer*) to say; (*verdade, mentira*) to tell ♦ *vi* to speak, talk; (*discursar*) to speak; **~-se** *vr* to talk to one another; **~ algo a alguém** to tell sb sth; **~ que** to say that; **~ de** *ou* **em algo** to talk about sth; **~ com alguém** to talk to sb; **por ~ em** speaking of; **por ~ nisso** by the way; **sem ~ em** not to mention; **~ alto** to talk loudly; **~ alto com alguém** (*fig*) to give sb a good talking-to; **sua consciência falou mais alto** his conscience got the better of him; **falou!, 'tá falado!** (*col*) OK!; **falando sério ...** but seriously ...; **~ sozinho** to talk to o.s.; **ele está falando da boca para fora** (*col*) he's just saying that, he doesn't mean it; **ele falou por ~** he was just saying that; **dar que ~** to cause a stir; **~ para dentro** to talk into one's beard; **~ pelos cotovelos** to talk one's head off; **eles não se falam** (*estão de mal*) they are not speaking to one another; **nem se fala!** definitely not!
falatório [fala'tɔrju] *m* (*ruído de vozes*) voices *pl*, talking; (*falar demorado*) diatribe; (*maledicência*) rumour (*BRIT*), rumor (*US*).
falaz [fa'laʒ] *adj* deceptive, misleading; (*falso*) false.
falcão [faw'kãw] (*pl* **-ões**) *m* falcon.
falcatrua [fawka'trua] *f* fraud.
falcões [faw'kõjʃ] *mpl de* **falcão**.
falecer [fale'se*] *vi* to die.
falecido/a [fale'sidu/a] *adj* dead, late ♦ *m/f* deceased.
falecimento [falesi'mẽtu] *m* death.
falência [fa'lẽsja] *f* bankruptcy; **abrir ~** to declare o.s. bankrupt; **ir à ~** to go bankrupt;

***NB**: European Portuguese adds the following consonants to certain words:* **b** (sú(b)dito, su(b)til); **c** (a(c)ção, a(c)cionista, a(c)to); **m** (inde(m)ne); **p** (ado(p)ção, ado(p)tar); *for further details see p. xiii.*

levar à ~ to bankrupt.
falésia [fa'lɛzja] *f* cliff.
falha ['faʎa] *f* (*defeito*, GEO *etc*) fault; (*lacuna*) omission; (*de caráter*) flaw.
falhar [fa'ʎa*] *vi* to fail; (*não acertar*) to miss; (*errar*) to be wrong; **o motor está falhando** the engine is missing.
falho/a ['faʎu/a] *adj* faulty; (*deficiente*) wanting.
fálico/a ['faliku/a] *adj* phallic.
falido/a [fa'lidu/a] *adj*, *m/f* bankrupt.
falir [fa'li*] *vi* to fail; (COM) to go bankrupt.
falível [fa'livew] (*pl* **-eis**) *adj* fallible.
falo ['falu] *m* phallus.
falsário/a [faw'sarju/a] *m/f* forger.
falsear [faw'sja*] *vt* to forge, falsify; (*verdade*) to twist; **~ o pé** to put a foot wrong.
falseta [faw'sɛta] (*col*) *f* dirty trick.
falsete [faw'setʃi] *m* falsetto.
falsidade [fawsi'dadʒi] *f* falsehood; (*fingimento*) pretence (BRIT), pretense (US); (*mentira*) lie.
falsificação [fawsifika'sãw] (*pl* **-ões**) *f* (*ato*) falsification; (*efeito*) forgery; (*falsa interpretação*) misrepresentation.
falsificador(a) [fawsifika'do*(a)] *m/f* forger.
falsificar [fawsifi'ka*] *vt* to forge, falsify; (*adulterar*) to adulterate; (*desvirtuar*) to misrepresent.
falsificações [fawsifika'sõjʃ] *fpl de* **falsificação**.
falso/a ['fawsu/a] *adj* false; (*fraudulento*) dishonest; (*errôneo*) wrong; (*jóia*, *moeda*, *quadro*) fake; (*pessoa*: *insincero*) two-faced; **pisar em ~** to miss one's step, put a foot wrong.
falta ['fawta] *f* (*carência*) lack; (*ausência*) absence; (*defeito*, *culpa*) fault; (FUTEBOL) foul; **por** *ou* **na ~ de** for lack of; **sem ~** without fail; **cometer/cobrar uma ~** (FUTEBOL) to commit a foul/take a free kick; **estar em ~ com alguém** to feel guilty about sb; **fazer ~** to be lacking, be needed; **ela faz ~** she is missed; **este livro não vai te fazer ~?** won't you need this book?; **sentir ~ de alguém/algo** to miss sb/sth; **ter ~ de** to lack, be in need of; **~ de água** water shortage; **~ de ânimo** lack of enthusiasm; **~ de educação** *ou* **modos** rudeness; **~ de tato** tactlessness.
faltar [faw'ta*] *vi* (*escassear*) to be lacking, be wanting; (*pessoa*) to be absent; (*falhar*) to fail; **~ ao trabalho** to be absent from work; **~ à palavra** to break one's word; **falta pouco para ...** it won't be long until ...; **falta uma semana para nossas férias** it's only a week until our holidays; **faltam 10 minutos para as 3** it's ten minutes to three; **faltam 3 páginas (para eu acabar)** there are 3 pages to go (before I finish); **faltam chegar duas pessoas** two people are still to come; **falta fazermos mais algumas coisas** there are still a few things for us to do; **só faltava essa!** that's all I (*ou* we *etc*) needed!; **nada me falta** I have all I need.
falto/a ['fawtu/a] *adj* lacking, deficient.
faltoso/a [faw'tozu/ɔza] *adj* (*culpado*) at fault; (*que costuma faltar*) frequently absent.
fama ['fama] *f* (*renome*) fame; (*reputação*) reputation; **ter ~ de (ser) generoso** to be said to be generous; **de ~** famous; **de má ~** notorious, of ill repute.
Famerj [fa'mɛxʒi] *abr f* = **Federação das Associações de Moradores do Estado do Rio de Janeiro**.
famigerado/a [famiʒe'radu/a] *adj* (*malfeitor*) notorious; (*autor etc*) famous.
família [fa'milja] *f* family; (COMPUT) font ♦ *adj inv* (*col*: *pessoa*) decent; (: *festa*) proper; **de boa ~** from a good family; **estar em ~** to be one of the family, be among friends; **isso é de ~** this runs in the family, this is a family trait.
familiar [fami'lja*] *adj* (*da família*) family *atr*; (*conhecido*) familiar ♦ *m/f* relation, relative.
familiaridade [familjari'dadʒi] *f* familiarity; (*sem-cerimônia*) informality.
familiarização [familjariza'sãw] *f* familiarization.
familiarizar [familjari'za*] *vt* to familiarize; **~-se** *vr*: **~-se com algo** to familiarize o.s. with sth.
faminto/a [fa'mĩtu/a] *adj* hungry; (*fig*): **~ de** eager for.
famoso/a [fa'mozu/ɔza] *adj* famous.
fanático/a [fa'natʃiku/a] *adj* fanatical ♦ *m/f* fanatic.
fanatismo [fana'tʃiʒmu] *m* fanaticism.
fanfarrão/rona [fãfa'xãw/'xɔna] (*pl* **-ões/~s**) *adj* boastful ♦ *m/f* braggart.
fanhoso/a [fa'ɲozu/ɔza] *adj* (*pessoa*) with a nasal voice; (*voz*) nasal; **falar** *ou* **ser ~** to talk through one's nose.
faniquito [fani'kitu] (*col*) *m* fit of nerves.
fantasia [fãta'zia] *f* fantasy; (*imaginação*) imagination; (*capricho*) fancy; (*traje*) fancy dress; **jóia (de) ~** (piece of) costume jewellery (BRIT) *ou* jewelry (US).
fantasiar [fãta'zja*] *vt* to imagine ♦ *vi* to daydream; **~-se** *vr* to dress up (in fancy dress).
fantasioso/a [fãta'zjozu/ɔza] *adj* imaginative.
fantasista [fãta'ziʃta] *adj* imaginative.
fantasma [fã'taʒma] *m* ghost; (*alucinação*) illusion; **ela está um ~** she's like a ghost.
fantasmagórico/a [fãtazma'gɔriku/a] *adj* ghostly.
fantástico/a [fã'taʃtʃiku/a] *adj* fantastic; (*ilusório*) imaginary; (*incrível*) unbelievable.
fantoche [fã'tɔʃi] *m* (*tb fig*) puppet.
fanzoca [fã'zɔka] (*col*) *m/f* great fan.
faqueiro [fa'kejru] *m* (*jogo de talheres*) set of cutlery; (*pessoa*) cutler.
faquir [fa'ki*] *m* fakir.
faraó [fara'ɔ] *m* pharaoh.
faraônico/a [fara'oniku/a] *adj* (*fig*: *obra*) large-scale.
farda ['faxda] *f* uniform.

fardar [fax'da*] *vt* to dress in uniform.
fardo ['faxdu] *m* bundle; (*carga*) load; (*fig*) burden.
farei [fa'rej] *etc vb V* **fazer**.
farejar [fare'ʒa*] *vt* to smell (out), sniff (out); ♦ *vi* to sniff.
farelo [fa'rɛlu] *m* (*de pão*) crumb; (*de madeira*) sawdust; ~ **de trigo** bran.
farfalhante [faxfa'ʎãtʃi] *adj* rustling.
farfalhar [faxfa'ʎa*] *vi* to rustle.
farfalhudo/a [faxfa'ʎudu/a] *adj* ostentatious.
farináceo/a [fari'nasju/a] *adj* (*alimento*) starchy; (*molho etc*) floury.
farináceos [fari'nasjuʃ] *mpl* (*alimentos*) starchy foods.
faringe [fa'rĩʒi] *f* pharynx.
faringite [farĩ'ʒitʃi] *f* pharyngitis.
farinha [fa'riɲa] *f*: ~ **(de mesa)** (manioc) flour; ~ **de arroz** rice flour; ~ **de osso** bonemeal; ~ **de rosca** breadcrumbs *pl*; ~ **de trigo** plain flour.
farmacêutico/a [faxma'sewtʃiku/a] *adj* pharmaceutical ♦ *m/f* pharmacist, chemist (*BRIT*).
farmácia [fax'masja] *f* pharmacy, chemist's (shop) (*BRIT*); (*ciência*) pharmacy.
farnel [fax'nɛw] (*pl* **-éis**) *m* (*provisões*) provisions *pl*; (*saco*) food parcel.
faro ['faru] *m* sense of smell; (*fig*) flair.
faroeste [fa'rwɛʃtʃi] *m* (*filme*) western; (*região*) wild west.
farofa [fa'rɔfa] *f* (*CULIN*) *side dish based on manioc flour*.
farofeiro/a [faro'fejru/a] *m/f* picnicker (*who comes to the beach from far away*).
farol [fa'rɔw] (*pl* **-óis**) *m* lighthouse; (*AUTO*) headlight; (*col*) bragging; ~ **alto/baixo** (*AUTO*) full (*BRIT*) *ou* high (*US*) beam/dipped (*BRIT*) *ou* dimmed (*US*) beam; **contar** ~ (*col*) to brag.
faroleiro [faro'lejru] *m* lighthouse keeper; (*col*) braggart.
farolete [faro'letʃi] *m* (*AUTO*: *dianteiro*) sidelight; (*tb*: ~ *traseiro*) tail-light.
farpa ['faxpa] *f* barb; (*estilha*) splinter.
farpado/a [fax'padu/a] *adj* barbed; *V tb* **arame**.
farra ['faxa] *f* binge, spree; **cair na** ~ to go on the razzle; **só de** *ou* **por** ~ just for the fun of it.
farrapo [fa'xapu] *m* rag; **ela parecia um** ~ she looked like a tramp; **esta blusa está um** ~ this blouse is a sight.
farrear [fa'xja*] *vi* to go on a spree.
farripas [fa'xipaʃ] *fpl* wisps of hair.
farrista [fa'xiʃta] *m/f* raver ♦ *adj* gallivanting.
farsa ['faxsa] *f* farce.
farsante [fax'sãtʃi] *m/f* joker; (*pessoa sem palavra*) smooth operator.
farta ['faxta] *f*: **comer à** ~ to eat one's fill.
fartar [fax'ta*] *vt* to satiate, fill up; ~**-se** *vr* to gorge o.s.; ~**-se de** (*cansar-se*) to get fed up with; **me fartei (de comer)** I'm full up.
farto/a ['faxtu/a] *adj* full, satiated; (*abundante*) plentiful; (*aborrecido*) fed up; **cabeleira farta** full head of hair, shock of hair.
fartum [fax'tũ] (*pl* **-ns**) *m* stench.
fartura [fax'tura] *f* abundance, plenty.
fascículo [fa'sikulu] *m* (*de publicação*) instalment (*BRIT*), installment (*US*).
fascinação [fasina'sãw] *f* fascination; **ter** ~ **por alguém** to be infatuated with sb.
fascinante [fasi'nãtʃi] *adj* fascinating.
fascinar [fasi'na*] *vt* to fascinate; (*encantar*) to charm.
fascínio [fa'sinju] *m* fascination.
fascismo [fa'siʒmu] *m* fascism.
fascista [fa'siʃta] *adj*, *m/f* fascist.
fase ['fazi] *f* phase; (*etapa*) stage.
fastidioso/a [faʃtʃi'dʒjozu/ɔza] *adj* tedious; (*enfadonho*) annoying.
fastígio [faʃ'tʃiʒju] *m* (*fig*) height.
fastio [faʃ'tʃiu] *m* lack of appetite; (*tédio*) boredom.
fatal [fa'taw] (*pl* **-ais**) *adj* (*mortal*) fatal; (*inevitável*) fateful.
fatalidade [fatali'dadʒi] *f* (*destino*) fate; (*desgraça*) disaster.
fatalista [fata'liʃta] *adj* fatalistic ♦ *m/f* fatalist.
fatalmente [fataw'mẽtʃi] *adv* (*de modo fatal*) fatally; (*certamente*) inevitably, doubtlessly.
fatia [fa'tʃia] *f* slice.
fatídico/a [fa'tʃidʒiku/a] *adj* fateful.
fatigante [fatʃi'gãtʃi] *adj* tiring; (*aborrecido*) tiresome.
fatigar [fatʃi'ga*] *vt* to tire; (*aborrecer*) to bore; ~**-se** *vr* to get tired.
fato ['fatu] *m* fact; (*acontecimento*) event; (*PT*: *traje*) suit; ~ **de banho** (*PT*) swimming costume (*BRIT*), bathing suit (*US*); ~ **consumado** fait accompli; **de** ~ in fact, really; **o** ~ **é que** ... the fact remains that ...; **chegar às vias de** ~ to come to blows.
fator [fa'to*] *m* factor; ~ **Rh** (*MED*) Rh *ou* rhesus (*BRIT*) factor.
fátuo/a ['fatwu/a] *adj* (*vão*) fatuous.
fatura [fa'tura] *f* bill, invoice.
faturamento [fatura'mẽtu] *m* (*COM*: *volume de negócios*) turnover; (*faturar*) invoicing.
faturar [fatu'ra*] *vt* to invoice; (*dinheiro*) to make; (*col*: *gol*) to score, notch up ♦ *vi (col*: *ganhar dinheiro*): ~ **(alto)** to rake it in; ~ **algo a alguém** to invoice sb for sth.
fauna ['fawna] *f* fauna.
fausto/a ['fawʃtu/a] *adj* lucky ♦ *m* luxury.
fava ['fava] *f* (broad) bean; **mandar alguém às** ~**s** to send sb packing.
favela [fa'vɛla] *f* slum, shanty town.
favelado/a [fave'ladu/a] *m/f* slum-dweller.

NB: European Portuguese adds the following consonants to certain words: **b** (sú(b)dito, su(b)til); **c** (a(c)ção, a(c)cionista, a(c)to); **m** (inde(m)ne); **p** (ado(p)ção, ado(p)tar); *for further details see p. xiii.*

favo ['favu] *m* honeycomb.
favor [fa'vo*] *m* favour (*BRIT*), favor (*US*); **a ~ de** in favo(u)r of; **em ~ de** on behalf of; **por ~** please; **fazer um ~ para alguém** to do sb a favo(u)r; **faça** *ou* **faz o ~ de ...** would you be so good as to ..., kindly ...; **faça-me o ~!** (*col*) do me a favo(u)r!; **ter a seu ~** to have to one's credit.
favorável [favo'ravew] (*pl* **-eis**) *adj*: **~ (a)** favourable (*BRIT*) *ou* favorable (*US*) (to).
favorecer [favore'se*] *vt* to favour (*BRIT*), favor (*US*); (*beneficiar*) to benefit; (*suj: vestido*) to suit; (: *retrato*) to flatter.
favoritismo [favori'tʃizmu] *m* favouritism (*BRIT*), favoritism (*US*).
favorito/a [favo'ritu/a] *adj*, *m/f* favourite (*BRIT*), favorite (*US*).
faxina [fa'ʃina] *f* (*limpeza*) cleaning (up); **fazer ~** to clean up.
faxineiro/a [faʃi'nejru/a] *m/f* (*pessoa*) cleaner.
faz-de-conta [fajʒ-] *m*: **o ~** make-believe.
fazedor(a) [faze'do*(a)] *m/f* maker.
fazenda [fa'zẽda] *f* farm; (*de café*) plantation; (*de gado*) ranch; (*pano*) cloth, fabric; (*ECON*) treasury, exchequer.
fazendeiro [fazẽ'dejru] *m* farmer; (*de café*) plantation-owner; (*de gado*) rancher, ranch-owner.
fazer [fa'ze*] to make; (*executar*) to do; (*pergunta*) to ask; (*construir*) to build; (*poema*) to write ♦ *vi* (*portar-se*) to act, behave; **~-se** *vr* (*tornar-se*) to become; (*ter êxito*) to make it; **~-se de algo** to pretend to be sth; **ele faz anos hoje** it's his birthday today; **fiz 30 anos ontem** I was 30 yesterday; **~ com que alguém faça algo** to make sb do sth; **~ que** (*fingir*) to pretend that; **~ bem/mal** to do the right/wrong thing; **faz um ano** a year ago; **faz dois anos que ele se formou** it's two years since he graduated; **faz três meses que ele está aqui** he's been here for three months; **não faz mal** never mind; **tanto faz** it's all the same; **não fiz por mal** I didn't mean any harm, I didn't mean it; **isso vai me dar que ~** this will be a tough job; **~ por onde** to work for it.
faz-tudo [fajʒ-] *m/f inv* jack-of-all-trades.
FBI *abr m* (= *Federal Bureau of Investigation*) FBI.
FC *abr m* (= *Futebol Clube*) FC.
FDLP *abr f* (= *Frente Democrática para a Libertação da Palestina*) PFLP.
fé [fɛ] *f* faith; (*crença*) belief; (*confiança*) trust; **de boa/má ~** in good/bad faith; **dar ~ de** to bear witness to; **fazer ~ em** to have faith in; **~ em Deus e pé na tábua** go for it.
fealdade [feaw'dadʒi] *f* ugliness.
FEB ['fɛbi] *abr f* (= *Força Expedicionária Brasileira*) *force sent out in World War II.*
FEBEM [fe'bẽ] (*BR*) *abr f* (= *Fundação Estadual do Bem-Estar do Menor*) *reform school.*
febrão [fe'brãw] (*pl* **-ões**) *m* raging fever.
febre ['fɛbri] *f* fever; (*fig*) excitement; **~ amarela** yellow fever; **~ de poder** *etc* hunger for power *etc*; **~ do feno** hay fever.
febril [fe'briw] (*pl* **-is**) *adj* feverish.
febrões [fe'brõjʃ] *mpl de* **febrão**.
fecal [fe'kaw] (*pl* **-ais**) *adj V* **matéria**.
fechada [fe'ʃada] *f*: **dar uma ~ em alguém** (*AUTO*) to cut sb up; **levar uma ~** to be cut up.
fechado/a [fe'ʃadu/a] *adj* shut, closed; (*pessoa*) reserved; (*sinal*) red; (*luz, torneira*) off; (*tempo*) overcast; (*cara*) stern; **noite fechada** well into the night.
fechadura [feʃa'dura] *f* (*de porta*) lock.
fechamento [feʃa'mẽtu] *m* closure.
fechar [fe'ʃa*] *vt* to close, shut; (*concluir*) to finish, conclude; (*luz, torneira*) to turn off; (*rua*) to close off; (*ferida*) to close up; (*bar, loja*) to close down; (*negócio*) to close, make; (*AUTO*) to cut up ♦ *vi* to close (up), shut; (*ferida*) to heal; (*sinal*) to turn red; (*bar, empresa*) to close down; (*tempo*) to cloud over; **~-se** *vr* to close, shut; (*pessoa*) to withdraw; **~-se no quarto** *etc* to shut o.s. away in one's room *etc;* **~ à chave** to lock; **~ a cara** to look annoyed; **ser de ~ o comércio** (*col*) to be a real show-stopper.
fecho ['feʃu] *m* fastening; (*trinco*) latch; (*término*) close, closing; **~ ecler** zip fastener (*BRIT*), zipper (*US*).
fécula ['fɛkula] *f* starch.
fecundação [fekũda'sãw] *f* fertilization.
fecundar [fekũ'da*] *vt* to fertilize, make fertile.
fecundidade [fekũdʒi'dadʒi] *f* fertility.
fecundo/a [fe'kũdu/a] *adj* fertile; (*produtivo*) fruitful; (*fig*) prolific.
fedelho/a [fe'deʎu/a] *m/f* kid.
feder [fe'de*] *vi* to stink; **não ~ nem cheirar** (*fig*) to be wishy-washy.
federação [federa'sãw] (*pl* **-ões**) *f* federation.
federal [fede'raw] (*pl* **-ais**) *adj* federal; (*col: grande*) huge.
federativo/a [federa'tʃivu/a] *adj* federal.
fedor [fe'do*] *m* stench.
fedorento/a [fedo'rẽtu/a] *adj* stinking.
FEEM (*BR*) *abr f* (= *Fundação Estadual de Educação do Menor*) *children's home.*
Feema [fe'ɛma] (*BR*) *abr f* (= *Fundação Estadual de Engenharia do Meio Ambiente*) *environmental protection agency.*
feérico/a [fe'ɛriku/a] *adj* magical.
feição [fej'sãw] (*pl* **-ões**) *f* form, shape; (*caráter*) nature; (*modo*) manner; **feições** *fpl* (*face*) features; **à ~ de** in the manner of.
feijão [fej'ʒãw] (*pl* **-ões**) *m* bean(s) (*pl*); (*preto*) black bean(s) (*pl*).
feijão-fradinho [-fra'dʒiɲu] (*pl* **feijões-fradinhos**) *m* black-eyed bean(s) (*pl*).
feijão-mulatinho [-mula'tʃiɲu] (*pl* **feijões-mulatinhos**) *m* red kidney bean(s) (*pl*).
feijão-preto (*pl* **feijões-pretos**) *m* black bean(s) (*pl*).
feijão-soja (*pl* **feijões-sojas**) *m* soya bean(s)

(*pl*) (*BRIT*), soybean(s) (*pl*) (*US*).

feijão-tropeiro [-tro'pejru] (*pl* **feijões-tropeiros**) *m* (*CULIN*) bean stew.

feijoada [fej'ʒwada] *f* (*CULIN*) meat, rice and black beans.

feijões [fej'ʒõjʃ] *mpl de* **feijão**.

feijoeiro [fej'ʒwejru] *m* bean plant.

feio/a ['feju/a] *adj* ugly; (*situação*) grim; (*atitude*) bad; (*tempo*) horrible ♦ *adv* (*perder*) badly; **olhar ~** to give a filthy look; **fazer ~** to make a bad impression; **ficar ~** (*dar má impressão*) to look bad; (*situação*) to turn nasty; **quem ama o ~, bonito lhe parece** love is blind.

feioso/a [fe'jozu/ɔza] *adj* plain.

feira ['fejra] *f* fair; (*mercado*) market; **fazer a ~** to go to market; **~ livre** market.

feirante [fej'rãtʃi] *m/f* market trader, stall-holder.

feita ['fejta] *f*: **certa ~** once, on one occasion; **de uma ~** once and for all.

feitiçaria [fejtʃisa'ria] *f* witchcraft, magic.

feiticeira [fejtʃi'sejra] *f* witch.

feiticeiro/a [fejtʃi'sejru/a] *adj* bewitching, enchanting ♦ *m* wizard.

feitiço [fej'tʃisu] *m* charm, spell; **virou o ~ contra o feiticeiro** (*fig*) the tables were turned.

feitio [fej'tʃiu] *m* shape, pattern; (*caráter*) nature, manner; (*TEC*) workmanship.

feito/a ['fejtu/a] *pp de* **fazer** ♦ *adj* (*terminado*) finished, ready ♦ *m* act, deed; (*façanha*) feat ♦ *conj* like; **~ a mão** hand-made; **homem ~** grown man; **que é ~ dela?** what has become of her?; **bem ~ (por você)!** (it) serves you right!; **dito e ~** no sooner said than done; **estar ~** (*pessoa*: *ter dinheiro etc*) to have it made.

feitor(a) [fej'to*(a)] *m/f* administrator; (*capataz*) supervisor.

feitura [fej'tura] *f* work.

feiúra [fe'jura] *f* ugliness.

feixe ['fejʃi] *m* bundle, bunch; (*TEC*) beam.

fel [fɛw] *m* bile, gall; (*fig*) bitterness; **esse remédio é um ~** that medicine is really bitter.

felicidade [felisi'dadʒi] *f* happiness; (*sorte*) good luck; (*êxito*) success; **~s** *fpl* congratulations.

felicíssimo/a [feli'sisimu/a] *adj superl de* **feliz**.

felicitações [felisita'sõjʃ] *fpl* congratulations, best wishes.

felicitar [felisi'ta*] *vt* to congratulate.

felino/a [fe'linu/a] *adj* feline; (*fig*: *traiçoeiro*) treacherous ♦ *m* feline.

feliz [fe'liʒ] *adj* happy; (*afortunado*) fortunate; (*idéia, sugestão*) timely; (*próspero*) successful; (*expressão*) fortunate; **~ aniversário/Natal!** happy birthday/Christmas!; **dar-se por ~** to think o.s. lucky.

felizardo/a [feli'zaxdu/a] *m/f* lucky devil.

felizmente [feliʒ'mẽtʃi] *adv* fortunately.

felonia [felo'nia] *f* (*traição*) treachery.

felpa ['fewpa] *f* (*de animais*) down; (*de tecido*) nap.

felpudo/a [few'pudu/a] *adj* fuzzy, downy.

feltro ['fewtru] *m* felt.

fêmea ['femja] *f* (*BIO, BOT*) female.

feminil [femi'niw] (*pl* **-is**) *adj* feminine.

feminilidade [feminili'dadʒi] *f* femininity.

feminino/a [femi'ninu/a] *adj* feminine; (*sexo*) female; (*equipe, roupas*) women's ♦ *m* (*LING*) feminine.

feminis [femi'niʃ] *adj pl de* **feminil**.

feminismo [femi'niʒmu] *m* feminism.

feminista [femi'niʃta] *adj, m/f* feminist.

fêmur ['femu*] *m* (*ANAT*) femur.

fenda ['fẽda] *f* slit, crack; (*GEO*) fissure.

fender [fẽ'de*] *vt, vi* to split, crack.

fenecer [fene'se*] *vi* to die; (*terminar*) to come to an end.

feno ['fenu] *m* hay.

fenomenal [fenome'naw] (*pl* **-ais**) *adj* phenomenal; (*espantoso*) amazing; (*pessoa*) brilliant.

fenômeno [fe'nomenu] *m* phenomenon.

fera ['fɛra] *f* wild animal; (*fig*: *pessoa cruel*) beast; (: *pessoa severa*) hothead; **ser ~ em algo** to be brilliant at sth; **ficar uma ~ (com alguém)** (*fig*) to get mad (with sb).

féretro ['fɛretru] *m* coffin.

feriado [fe'rjadu] *m* holiday (*BRIT*), vacation (*US*); **~ bancário** bank (*BRIT*) *ou* public holiday.

férias ['fɛrjaʃ] *fpl* holidays, vacation *sg*; **de ~** on holiday; **tirar ~** to have *ou* take a holiday.

ferida [fe'rida] *f* wound, injury; **tocar na ~** (*fig*) to hit home; *V tb* **ferido**.

ferido/a [fe'ridu/a] *adj* injured; (*em batalha*) wounded; (*magoado*) hurt ♦ *m/f* casualty.

ferimento [feri'mẽtu] *m* injury; (*em batalha*) wound.

ferino/a [fe'rinu/a] *adj* (*cruel*) cruel; (*crítica, ironia*) biting.

ferir [fe'ri*] *vt* to injure, wound; (*ofender*) to offend.

fermentar [fexmẽ'ta*] *vt* to ferment; (*fig*) to excite ♦ *vi* to ferment.

fermento [fex'mẽtu] *m* yeast; **~ em pó** baking powder.

ferocidade [ferosi'dadʒi] *f* fierceness, ferocity.

ferocíssimo/a [fero'sisimu/a] *adj superl de* **feroz**.

feroz [fe'rɔʒ] *adj* fierce, ferocious; (*cruel*) cruel.

ferrado/a [fe'xadu/a] *adj* (*cavalgadura*) shod; (*col*: *sem saída*) done for; **~ no sono** sound asleep.

ferradura [fexa'dura] *f* horseshoe.

ferragem [fe'xaʒẽ] (*pl* **-ns**) *f* (*peças*) hardware; (*guarnição*) metalwork.

NB: European Portuguese adds the following consonants to certain words: **b** (sú(b)dito, su(b)til); **c** (a(c)ção, a(c)cionista, a(c)to); **m** (inde(m)ne); **p** (ado(p)ção, ado(p)tar); *for further details see p. xiii.*

ferramenta [fexa'mẽta] *f* tool; (*caixa de ~s*) tool kit.
ferrão [fe'xãw] (*pl* **-ões**) *m* goad; (*de inseto*) sting.
ferrar [fe'xa*] *vt* to spike; (*cavalo*) to shoe; (*gado*) to brand; **~-se** *vr* (*col*) to come to grief.
ferreiro [fe'xejru] *m* blacksmith.
ferrenho/a [fe'xeɲu/a] *adj* (*vontade*) iron; (*marxista etc*) staunch.
férreo/a ['fɛxju/a] *adj* iron *atr*: (*QUÍM*) ferrous; (*vontade*) iron; (*disciplina*) strict.
ferrete [fe'xetʃi] *m* branding iron; (*fig*) stigma.
ferro ['fɛxu] *m* iron; **~s** *mpl* shackles, chains; **~ batido** wrought iron; **~ de passar** iron; **~ fundido** cast iron; **~ ondulado** corrugated iron; **a ~ e fogo** at all costs; **ninguém é/não sou de ~** (*fig*) we're all/I'm only human.
ferrões [fe'xõjʃ] *mpl de* **ferrão**.
ferrolho [fe'xoʎu] *m* (*trinco*) bolt.
ferro-velho (*pl* **ferros-velhos**) *m* (*pessoa*) scrap metal dealer; (*lugar*) scrap metal yard; (*sucata*) scrap metal.
ferrovia [fexo'via] *f* railway (*BRIT*), railroad (*US*).
ferroviário/a [fexo'vjarju/a] *adj* railway *atr* (*BRIT*), railroad *atr* (*US*) ♦ *m/f* railway *ou* railroad worker.
ferrugem [fe'xuʒẽ] *f* rust; (*BOT*) blight.
fértil ['fɛxtʃiw] (*pl* **-eis**) *adj* fertile.
fertilidade [fextʃili'dadʒi] *f* fertility; (*abundância*) fruitfulness.
fertilizante [fextʃili'zãtʃi] *adj* fertilizing ♦ *m* fertilizer.
fertilizar [fextʃili'za*] *vt* to fertilize.
fervente [fex'vẽtʃi] *adj* boiling.
ferver [fex've*] *vt*, *vi* to boil; **~ de raiva/indignação** to seethe with rage/indignation; **~ em fogo baixo** (*CULIN*) to simmer.
fervilhar [fexvi'ʎa*] *vi* (*ferver*) to simmer; (*com excitação*) to hum; (*pulular*): **~ de** to swarm with.
fervor [fex'vo*] *m* fervour (*BRIT*), fervor (*US*).
fervoroso/a [fexvo'rozu/ɔza] *adj* zealous, fervent.
fervura [fex'vura] *f* boiling.
festa ['fɛʃta] *f* (*reunião*) party; (*conjunto de ceremônias*) festival; **~s** *fpl* caresses; **boas ~s** Merry Christmas and a Happy New Year; **dia de ~** public holiday; **fazer ~ a alguém** to make a fuss of sb; **fazer ~(s) em alguém** to caress sb; **fazer a ~** (*fig*) to have a ball, have a whale of a time; **~ caipira** hoedown; **~ de arromba** (*col*) big party; **~ de embalo** (*col*) wild party.
festança [feʃ'tãsa] *f* big party.
festeiro/a [feʃ'tejru/a] *adj* party-going.
festejar [feʃte'ʒa*] *vt* (*celebrar*) to celebrate; (*acolher*) to welcome, greet.
festejo [feʃ'teʒu] *m* (*festividade*) festivity; (*ato*) celebration.
festim [feʃ'tʃĩ] (*pl* **-ns**) *m* feast.
festival [feʃtʃi'vaw] (*pl* **-ais**) *m* festival.
festividade [feʃtʃivi'dadʒi] *f* festivity.
festivo/a [feʃ'tʃivu/a] *adj* festive.
fetiche [fe'tʃiʃi] *m* fetish.
fetichismo [fetʃi'ʃiʒmu] *m* fetishism.
fetichista [fetʃi'ʃiʃta] *adj* fetishistic ♦ *m/f* fetishist.
fétido/a ['fɛtʃidu/a] *adj* foul.
feto ['fɛtu] *m* (*MED*) foetus (*BRIT*), fetus (*US*); (*BOT*) fern.
feudal [few'daw] (*pl* **-ais**) *adj* feudal.
feudalismo [fewda'liʒmu] *m* feudalism.
fev. *abr* = **fevereiro**.
fevereiro [feve'rejru] (*PT*: **F-**) *m* February; *V tb* **julho**.
fez [feʒ] *vb V* **fazer**.
fezes ['fɛziʃ] *fpl* faeces (*BRIT*), feces (*US*).
FGTS (*BR*) *abr m* (= *Fundo de Garantia por Tempo de Serviço*) *pension fund*.
FGV (*BR*) *abr f* (= *Fundação Getúlio Vargas*) *economic research agency*.
fiação [fja'sãw] (*pl* **-ões**) *f* spinning; (*fábrica*) textile mill; (*ELET*) wiring; **fazer a ~ da casa** to rewire the house.
fiada ['fjada] *f* (*fileira*) row, line.
fiado/a ['fjadu/a] *adj* (*a crédito*) on credit; **comprar/vender ~** to buy/sell on credit.
fiador(a) [fja'do*(a)] *m/f* (*JUR*) guarantor; (*COM*) backer.
fiambre ['fjãbri] *m* cold meat; (*presunto*) ham.
fiança ['fjãsa] *f* surety, guarantee; (*JUR*) bail; **prestar ~ por** to stand bail for; **sob ~** on bail.
fiapo ['fjapu] *m* thread.
fiar ['fja*] *vt* (*algodão etc*) to spin; (*confiar*) to entrust; (*vender a crédito*) to sell on credit; **~-se** *vr*: **~-se em** to trust.
fiasco ['fjaʃku] *m* fiasco.
FIBGE *abr f* = **Fundação do Instituto Brasileiro de Geografia e Estatística**.
fibra ['fibra] *f* fibre (*BRIT*), fiber (*US*); (*fig*): **pessoa de ~** person of character; **~ ótica** optical fibre *ou* fiber.
ficar [fi'ka*] *vi* (*permanecer*) to stay; (*sobrar*) to be left; (*tornar-se*) to become; (*estar situado*) to be; (*durar*) to last; (*ser adiado*) to be postponed; **~ cego/surdo/louco** to go blind/deaf/mad; **fiquei contente ao saber a notícia** I was happy when I heard the news; **~ perguntando/olhando** *etc* to keep asking/looking *etc*; **~ com algo** (*guardar*) to keep sth; **~ com raiva/medo** to get angry/frightened; **~ de fazer algo** (*combinar*) to arrange to do sth; (*prometer*) to promise to do sth; **~ por fazer** to be still to be done; **~ bom** (*de saúde*) to get better; (*trabalho, foto etc*) to turn out well; **~ bem** (*roupa, comportamento*) to look good; **esta saia não fica bem para você** that skirt doesn't suit you; **~ para trás** to be left behind; **ficou por isso mesmo** nothing came of it; **~ sem algo** to be left without sth, run out of sth; **~ de**

bem/mal com alguém (*col*) to make up/fall out with sb; ~ **de pé** to stand up.
ficção [fik'sãw] *f* fiction.
ficcionista [fiksjo'niʃta] *m/f* author, fiction writer.
ficha ['fiʃa] *f* (*tb*: ~ *de telefone*) token; (*tb*: ~ *de jogo*) chip; (*de fichário*) (index) card; (*fig*) record; (*PT*: *ELET*) plug; (*em loja, lanchonete*) ticket; **dar a ~ de alguém** (*fig*: *col*) to give the low-down on sb; **ter ~ na polícia** to have a criminal record; **ter ~ limpa** (*col*) to have a clean record; ~ **de identidade** means *sg* of identification, ID.
fichar [fi'ʃa*] *vt* to file, index.
fichário [fi'ʃarju] *m* (*móvel*) filing cabinet; (*caixa*) card index; (*caderno*) file.
ficheiro [fi'ʃejru] (*PT*) *m* = **fichário**.
fictício/a [fik'tʃisju/a] *adj* fictitious.
FIDA (*BR*) *abr m* = **Fundo Internacional para o Desenvolvimento Agrícola**.
fidalgo [fi'dawgu] *m* nobleman.
fidedigno/a [fide'dʒignu/a] *adj* trustworthy.
fidelidade [fideli'dadʒi] *f* (*lealdade*) fidelity, loyalty; (*exatidão*) accuracy.
fidelíssimo/a [fide'lisimu/a] *adj superl de* **fiel**.
fiduciário/a [fidu'sjarju/a] *adj* (*companhia*) trust *atr* ♦ *m/f* trustee.
fiéis [fjɛjʃ] *adj pl de* **fiel** ♦ *mpl*: **os ~** the faithful.
fiel [fjɛw] (*pl* **-éis**) *adj* (*leal*) faithful, loyal; (*tradução*) accurate; (*que não falha*) reliable.
Fiesp [fi'ɛʃpi] *abr f* = **Federação das Indústrias do Estado de São Paulo**.
FIFA ['fifa] *abr f* (= *Fédération Internationale de Football Association*) FIFA.
figa ['figa] *f* talisman; **fazer uma ~** to make a *figa*, ≈ cross one's fingers; **de uma ~** (*col*) damned.
figada [fi'gada] *f* fig jelly.
fígado ['figadu] *m* liver; **de maus ~s** bad-tempered, vindictive.
figo ['figu] *m* fig.
figueira [fi'gejra] *f* fig tree.
figura [fi'gura] *f* figure; (*forma*) form, shape; (*GRAMÁTICA*) figure of speech; (*aspecto*) appearance; (*CARTAS*) face card; (*ilustração*) picture; (*col*: *pessoa*) character; **fazer ~** to cut a figure; **fazer má ~** to make a bad impression; **mudar de ~** to take on a new aspect; **ser uma ~ difícil** (*col*) to be difficult to get hold of; **ele é uma ~** (*col*) he's a real character .
figura-chave (*pl* **figuras-chave**) *f* key figure.
figurado/a [figu'radu/a] *adj* figurative.
figurante [figu'rãtʃi] *m/f* (*CINEMA*) extra.
figurão [figu'rãw] (*pl* **-ões**) *m* big shot.
figurar [figu'ra*] *vi* (*ator*) to appear; (*fazer parte*): ~ **(entre/em)** to figure *ou* appear (among/in) ♦ *vt* (*imaginar*) to imagine; **ela figura ter menos de 30 anos** she looks younger than 30.
figurinha [figu'riɲa] *f* sticker; ~ **difícil** (*col*) person who is difficult to get hold of.
figurinista [figuri'niʃta] *m/f* fashion designer.
figurino [figu'rinu] *m* fashion plate; (*revista*) fashion magazine; (*CINEMA*, *TEATRO*) costume design; (*exemplo*) example; **como manda o ~** as it should be.
figurões [figu'rõjʃ] *mpl de* **figurão**.
Fiji [fi'ʒi] *m* Fiji.
fila ['fila] *f* row, line; (*BR*: *fileira de pessoas*) queue (*BRIT*), line (*US*); (*num teatro, cinema*) row ♦ *m* (*cão*) Brazilian mastiff; **em ~** in a row; **fazer ~** to form a line, queue; ~ **indiana** single file.
Filadélfia [fila'dɛwfja] *f* Philadelphia.
filamento [fila'mẽtu] *m* filament.
filante [fi'lãtʃi] *m/f* sponger ♦ *adj* sponging.
filantropia [filãtro'pia] *f* philanthropy.
filantrópico/a [filã'trɔpiku/a] *adj* philanthropic.
filantropo [filã'tropu] *m* philanthropist.
filão [fi'lãw] (*pl* **-ões**) *m* (*JORNALISMO*) lead.
filar [fi'la*] *vt* (*agarrar*) to seize; (*col*: *pedir/obter gratuitamente*) to scrounge.
filarmônica [filax'monika] *f* philharmonic.
filarmônico/a [filax'moniku/a] *adj* philharmonic.
filatelia [filate'lia] *f* philately.
filé [fi'lɛ] *m* (*bife*) steak; (*peixe*) fillet; ~ **mignon** filet mignon.
fileira [fi'lejru] *f* file, row, line; **~s** *fpl* military service *sg*.
filete [fi'letʃi] *m* fillet; (*de parafuso*) thread.
filharada [fiʎa'rada] *f* herd of children.
filhinho/a [fi'ʎiɲu/a] *m/f* little son/daughter; ~ **de mamãe** mummy's boy; ~ **de papai** rich kid.
filho/a ['fiʎu/a] *m/f* son/daughter; **~s** *mpl* children; (*de animais*) young; **minha filha/meu ~** (*col*) dear, darling; **ter um ~** to have a child; (*fig*: *col*) to have kittens, have a fit; **ele também é ~ de Deus** he is just as good as anyone else; ~ **adotivo** adoptive child; ~ **da mãe** (*col!*) bastard(*!*); ~ **da puta** (*col!*) wanker(*!*), bastard(*!*); ~ **de criação** foster child; ~ **ilegítimo/natural** illegitimate/natural child; ~ **único** only child; ~ **único de mãe viúva** (*fig*) one in a million.
filhote [fi'ʎɔtʃi] *m* (*de leão, urso etc*) cub; (*cachorro*) pup(py).
filiação [filja'sãw] (*pl* **-ões**) *f* affiliation.
filial [fi'ljaw] (*pl* **-ais**) *f* (*sucursal*) branch ♦ *adj* filial; **gerente de ~** branch manager.
filigrana [fili'grana] *f* filigree.
Filipinas [fili'pinaʃ] *fpl*: **as ~** the Philippines.
filipino/a [fili'pinu/a] *adj*, *m/f* Filipino ♦ *m* (*LING*) Filipino.
filmagem [fiw'maʒẽ] *f* filming.

***NB:** European Portuguese adds the following consonants to certain words:* **b** (sú(b)dito, su(b)til); **c** (a(c)ção, a(c)cionista, a(c)to); **m** (inde(m)ne); **p** (ado(p)ção, ado(p)tar); *for further details* *see p. xiii.*

filmar [fiw'ma*] *vt, vi* to film.
filme ['fiwmi] *m* film (*BRIT*), movie (*US*); ~ **(de) bangue-bangue** *ou* **faroeste** western; ~ **(de) curta/longa metragem** short/feature film; ~ **de época** period film; ~ **de capa e espada** swashbuckling film.
filmoteca [fiwmo'tɛka] *f* (*lugar*) film library; (*coleção*) film collection.
filó [fi'lɔ] *m* tulle.
filões [fi'lõjʃ] *mpl de* **filão**.
filologia [filolo'ʒia] *f* philology.
filólogo/a [fi'lɔlogu/a] *m/f* philologist.
filosofar [filozo'fa*] *vi* to philosophize.
filosofia [filozo'fia] *f* philosophy.
filosófico/a [filo'zɔfiku/a] *adj* philosophical.
filósofo/a [fi'lɔzofu/a] *m/f* philosopher.
filtrar [fiw'tra*] *vt* to filter; **~-se** *vr* (*líquidos*) to filter; (*infiltrar-se*) to infiltrate.
filtro ['fiwtru] *m* (*TEC*) filter.
fim [fĩ] (*pl* **-ns**) *m* end; (*motivo*) aim, purpose; (*de história, filme*) ending; **a** ~ **de** in order to; **por** ~ finally; **ter por** ~ to aim at; **no** ~ **das contas** after all; **levar ao** ~ to carry through; **pôr** *ou* **dar** ~ **a** to put an end to; **ter** ~ to come to an end; **sem** ~ endless; ~ **de semana** weekend; ~ **de mundo** (*fig*) hole; **ele mora no** ~ **do mundo** he lives miles from anywhere; **é o** ~ **(do mundo** *ou* **da picada)** (*fig*) it's the pits; **estar a** ~ **de (fazer) algo** to feel like (doing) sth, fancy (doing) sth; **estar a** ~ **de alguém** (*col*) to fancy sb.
finado/a [fi'nadu/a] *adj, m/f* deceased.
final [fi'naw] (*pl* **-ais**) *adj* final, last ♦ *m* end; (*MÚS*) finale ♦ *f* (*ESPORTE*) final.
finalista [fina'liʃta] *m/f* finalist.
finalização [finaliza'sãw] (*pl* **-ões**) *f* conclusion.
finalizar [finali'za*] *vt* to finish, conclude ♦ *vi* (*FUTEBOL*) to finish; **~-se** *vr* to end.
Finam [fi'nã] *abr m* (= *Fundo de Investimento da Amazônia*) *regional development fund*.
Finame [fi'nami] (*BR*) *abr m* = **Agência Especial de Financiamento Industrial**.
finanças [fi'nãsaʃ] *fpl* finance *sg*.
financeiro/a [finã'sejru/a] *adj* financial ♦ *m/f* financier.
financiamento [finãsja'mẽtu] *m* financing.
financiar [finã'sja*] *vt* to finance.
financista [finã'siʃta] *m/f* financier.
finar-se [fi'naxsi] *vr* (*consumir-se*) to waste away; (*morrer*) to die.
fincar [fĩ'ka*] *vt* (*cravar*) to drive in; (*fixar*) to fix; (*apoiar*) to lean.
findar [fĩ'da*] *vt, vi* to end, finish.
findo/a ['fĩdu/a] *adj* (*ano*) past; (*assunto*) closed.
fineza [fi'neza] *f* fineness; (*gentileza*) kindness.
fingido/a [fĩ'ʒidu/a] *adj* pretend; (*pessoa*) two-faced, insincere ♦ *m/f* hypocrite.
fingimento [fĩʒi'mẽtu] *m* pretence (*BRIT*), pretense (*US*).
fingir [fĩ'ʒi*] *vt* (*simular*) to feign ♦ *vi* to pretend; **~-se** *vr*: **~-se de** to pretend to be; ~ **fazer/que** to pretend to do/that.
finito/a [fi'nitu/a] *adj* finite.
finlandês/esa [fĩlã'deʃ/eza] *adj* Finnish ♦ *m/f* Finn ♦ *m* (*LING*) Finnish.
Finlândia [fĩ'lãdʒja] *f*: **a** ~ Finland.
fino/a ['finu/a] *adj* fine; (*delgado*) slender; (*educado*) polite; (*som, voz*) shrill; (*elegante*) refined, posh (*col*) ♦ *adv*: **falar** ~ to talk in a high voice; **ser o** ~ (*col*) to be the business; **tirar um** ~ **em alguém** to almost drive into sb.
Finor [fi'no*] (*BR*) *abr m* (= *Fundo de Investimento do Nordeste*) *regional development fund*.
finório/a [fi'nɔrju/a] *adj* crafty, sly.
fins [fĩʃ] *mpl de* **fim**.
Finsocial [fĩso'sjaw] (*BR*) *abr m* = **Fundo de Investimento Social**.
finura [fi'nura] *f* fineness; (*elegância*) finesse.
fio ['fiu] *m* thread; (*BOT*) fibre (*BRIT*), fiber (*US*); (*ELET*) wire; (*TEL*) line; (*de líquido*) trickle; (*gume*) edge; (*encadeamento*) series; **horas/dias a** ~ hours/days on end; **de** ~ **a pavio** from beginning to end; **por um** ~ (*fig: escapar*) by the skin of one's teeth; **bater um** ~ (*col*) to make a call; **estar por um** ~ to be on one's last legs; **perder o** ~ **(da meada)** (*fig*) to lose one's thread; **retomar o** ~ **perdido** (*fig*) to take up the thread again; ~ **condutor** (*fig*) connecting thread.
fiorde ['fjoxdʒi] *m* fjord.
Firjan [fix'ʒã] *abr f* = **Federação das Indústrias do Rio de Janeiro**.
firma ['fixma] *f* (*assinatura*) signature; (*COM*) firm, company.
firmamento [fixma'mẽtu] *m* firmament.
firmar [fix'ma*] *vt* (*tornar firme*) to secure, make firm; (*assinar*) to sign; (*estabelecer*) to establish; (*basear*) to base ♦ *vi* (*tempo*) to settle; **~-se** *vr*: **~-se em** (*basear-se*) to rest on, be based on.
firme ['fixmi] *adj* firm; (*estável*) stable; (*sólido*) solid; (*tempo*) settled ♦ *adv* firmly; **agüentar** ~ to hang on; **pisar** ~ to stride out.
firmeza [fix'meza] *f* firmness; (*estabilidade*) stability; (*solidez*) solidity.
FISA ['fiza] *abr f* (= *Federação Internacional de Automobilismo Esportivo*) FISA.
fiscal [fiʃ'kaw] (*pl* **-ais**) *m/f* supervisor; (*aduaneiro*) customs officer; (*de impostos*) tax inspector.
fiscalização [fiʃkaliza'sãw] (*pl* **-ões**) *f* inspection.
fiscalizar [fiʃkali'za*] *vt* (*supervisionar*) to supervise; (*examinar*) to inspect, check.
fisco ['fiʃku] *m*: **o** ~ ≈ the Inland Revenue (*BRIT*), ≈ the Internal Revenue Service (*US*).
Fiset [fi'sɛtʃi] (*BR*) *abr m* = **Fundo de Investimentos Setoriais**.
fisgada [fiʒ'gada] *f* stabbing pain.
fisgar [fiʒ'ga*] *vt* to catch.
física ['fizika] *f* physics *sg*; ~ **nuclear** nuclear

physics; *V tb* **físico**.

físico/a ['fiziku/a] *adj* physical ♦ *m/f* (*cientista*) physicist ♦ *m* (*corpo*) physique.

fisiologia [fizjolo'ʒia] *f* physiology.

fisionomia [fizjono'mia] *f* (*rosto*) face; (*ar*) expression, look; (*aspecto de algo*) physiognomy; (*conjunto de caracteres*) make-up.

fisionomista [fizjono'miʃta] *m/f* person with a good memory for faces.

fisioterapeuta [fizjotera'pewta] *m/f* physiotherapist.

fisioterapia [fizjotera'pia] *f* physiotherapy.

fissura [fi'sura] *f* crack; (*col: ansia*) craving.

fissurado/a [fisu'radu/a] *adj* cracked; **estar ~ em** (*col*) to be wild about.

fissurar [fisu'ra*] *vt* to crack.

fita ['fita] *f* (*tira*) strip, band; (*de seda, algodão*) ribbon, tape; (*filme*) film; (*para máquina de escrever*) ribbon; (*magnética, adesiva*) tape; **~ durex** ® adhesive tape, sellotape ® (*BRIT*), scotchtape ® (*US*); **~ isolante** insulating tape; **~ métrica** tape measure; **fazer ~** (*col*) to put on an act; **isso é ~ dela** (*col*) it's just an act.

fitar [fi'ta*] *vt* (*com os olhos*) to stare at, gaze at; **~-se** *vr* to stare at each other.

fiteiro/a [fi'tejru/a] *adj* melodramatic.

fito/a ['fitu/a] *adj* fixed ♦ *m* aim, intention.

fivela [fi'vɛla] *f* buckle.

fixação [fiksa'sãw] (*pl* **-ões**) *f* fixation.

fixador [fiksa'do*] *m* (*de cabelo*) hair gel; (*: líquido*) setting lotion (*BRIT*).

fixar [fik'sa*] *vt* (*estabelecer: hora, lugar*) to fix; (*: data, regras*) to set; (*colar, prender*) to stick; (*atenção*) to concentrate; **~-se** *vr*: **~-se em** (*assunto*) to concentrate on; (*detalhe*) to fix on; (*apegar-se a*) to be attached to; **~ os olhos em** to stare at; **~ residência** to set up house, settle down; **~ algo na memória** to fix sth in one's mind.

fixo/a ['fiksu/a] *adj* fixed; (*firme*) firm; (*permanente*) permanent; (*cor*) fast.

fiz [fiʒ] *etc vb V* **fazer**.

flacidez [flasi'deʒ] *f* softness, flabbiness.

flácido/a ['flasidu/a] *adj* flabby.

Fla-Flu [fla-] *m* local derby (*football match between rivals Flamengo and Fluminense*).

flagelado/a [flaʒe'ladu/a] *m/f*: **os ~s** the afflicted, the victims.

flagrante [fla'grãtʃi] *adj* flagrant; **apanhar em ~ (delito)** to catch red-handed *ou* in the act.

flagrar [fla'gra*] *vt* to catch.

flambar [flã'ba*] *vt* (*CULIN*) to flambé.

flamejante [flame'ʒãtʃi] *adj* flaming.

flamejar [flame'ʒa*] *vi* to blaze.

flamengo/a [fla'mẽgu/a] *adj* Flemish ♦ *m* (*LING*) Flemish.

flamingo [fla'mĩgu] *m* flamingo.

flâmula ['flamula] *f* pennant.

flanco ['flãku] *m* flank.

Flandres ['flãdriʃ] *f* Flanders.

flanela [fla'nɛla] *f* flannel.

flanquear [flã'kja*] *vt* to flank; (*MIL*) to outflank.

flash [flaʃ] *m* (*FOTO*) flash.

flash-back [flaʃ'baki] (*pl* **~s**) *m* flashback.

flatulência [flatu'lẽsja] *f* flatulence.

flauta ['flawta] *f* flute; **ele leva tudo na ~** (*col*) he doesn't take anything seriously; **~ doce** (*MÚS*) recorder.

flautista [flaw'tʃiʃta] *m/f* flautist.

flecha ['flɛʃa] *f* arrow.

flechada [fle'ʃada] *f* (*golpe*) shot; (*ferimento*) arrow wound.

flertar [flex'ta*] *vi*: **~ (com alguém)** to flirt (with sb).

flerte ['flextʃi] *m* flirtation.

fleu(g)ma ['flewma] *f* phlegm.

flexão [flek'sãw] (*pl* **-ões**) *f* flexing; (*exercício*) press-up; (*LING*) inflection.

flexibilidade [fleksibili'dadʒi] *f* flexibility.

flexionar [fleksjo'na*] *vt, vi* (*LING*) to inflect.

flexível [flek'sivew] (*pl* **-eis**) *adj* flexible.

flexões [flek'sõjʃ] *fpl de* **flexão**.

fliperama [flipe'rama] *m* pinball machine.

floco ['flɔku] *m* flake; **~ de milho** cornflake; **~ de neve** snowflake; **sorvete de ~s** chocolate chip ice-cream.

flor [flo*] *f* flower; (*o melhor*) cream, pick; **em ~** in bloom; **a fina ~** the elite; **a ~ de** on the surface of; **ele não é ~ que se cheire** (*col*) he's a bad lot.

flora ['flɔra] *f* flora.

floreado/a [flo'rjadu/a] *adj* (*jardim*) full of flowers; (*relevo*) ornate; (*estilo*) florid.

floreio [flo'reju] *m* clever turn of phrase.

florescente [flore'sẽtʃi] *adj* (*BOT*) in flower; (*próspero*) flourishing.

florescer [flore'se*] *vi* (*BOT*) to flower; (*prosperar*) to flourish.

floresta [flo'rɛʃta] *f* forest.

florestal [floreʃ'taw] (*pl* **-ais**) *adj* forest *atr*.

florianopolitano/a [florjanopoli'tanu/a] *adj* from Florianópolis ♦ *m/f* native of Florianópolis.

Flórida ['flɔrida] *f*: **a ~** Florida.

florido/a [flo'ridu/a] *adj* (*jardim*) in flower; (*mesa*) decorated with flowers.

florir [flo'ri*] *vi* to flower.

flotilha [flo'tʃiʎa] *f* flotilla.

flozô [flo'zo] (*col*) *m*: **ficar de ~** to lounge around; **viver de ~** to lead a life of leisure.

Flu [flu] *abr m* = **Fluminense Futebol Clube**.

fluência [flu'ẽsja] *f* fluency.

fluente [flu'ẽtʃi] *adj* fluent.

fluidez [flui'deʒ] *f* fluidity.

fluido/a ['flwidu/a] *adj* fluid ♦ *m* fluid.

fluir [flwi*] *vi* to flow.

fluminense [flumi'nẽsi] *adj* from the state of

***NB**: European Portuguese adds the following consonants to certain words:* **b** (sú(b)dito, su(b)til); **c** (a(c)ção, a(c)cionista, a(c)to); **m** (inde(m)ne); **p** (ado(p)ção, ado(p)tar); *for further details see p. xiii.*

Rio de Janeiro ♦ *m/f* native *ou* inhabitant of the state of Rio de Janeiro.

fluorescente [flwore'sẽtʃi] *adj* fluorescent.

flutuação [flutwa'sãw] (*pl* **-ões**) *f* fluctuation.

flutuante [flu'twãtʃi] *adj* floating; (*bandeira*) fluttering; (*fig*: *vacilante*) hesitant, wavering; (*COM*: *câmbio*) floating.

flutuar [flu'twa*] *vi* to float; (*bandeira*) to flutter; (*fig*: *vacilar*) to waver.

fluvial [flu'vjaw] (*pl* **-ais**) *adj* river *atr*.

fluxo ['fluksu] *m* (*corrente*) flow; (*ELET*) flux; ~ **de caixa** (*COM*) cash flow.

fluxograma [flukso'grama] *m* flow chart.

FM *abr* (*RÁDIO*: *freqüencia modulada*) FM ♦ *f* (*pl* ~**s**) FM (radio) station.

FMI *abr m* (= *Fundo Monetário Internacional*) IMF.

FMS *abr f* = **Federação Mundial dos Sindicatos**.

FN (*BR*) *abr m* = **Fuzileiro Naval**.

FND (*BR*) *abr m* = **Fundo Nacional de Desenvolvimento**.

fobia [fo'bia] *f* phobia.

foca ['fɔka] *f* (*animal*) seal ♦ *m/f* (*col*: *jornalista*) cub reporter.

focalização [fokaliza'sãw] *f* focusing.

focalizar [fokali'za*] *vt* to focus (on).

focinho [fo'siɲu] *m* snout; (*col*: *cara*) face, clock (*col*).

foco ['fɔku] *m* focus; (*MED*, *fig*) seat, centre (*BRIT*), center (*US*); **fora de** ~ out of focus.

fofo/a ['fofu/a] *adj* soft; (*col*: *pessoa*) cute.

fofoca [fo'fɔka] *f* piece of gossip; ~**s** *fpl* gossip *sg*; **fazer** ~ to gossip.

fofocar [fofo'ka*] *vi* to gossip.

fofoqueiro/a [fofo'kejru/a] *adj* gossipy ♦ *m/f* gossip.

fofura [fo'fura] (*col*) *f* cutie.

fogão [fo'gãw] (*pl* **-ões**) *m* stove, cooker.

fogareiro [foga'rejru] *m* stove.

foge ['fɔʒi] *etc vb V* **fugir**.

fogo ['fogu] *m* fire; (*fig*) ardour (*BRIT*), ardor (*US*); **você tem** ~**?** have you got a light?; ~**s de artifício** fireworks; **a** ~ **lento** on a low flame; **à prova de** ~ fireproof; **abrir** ~ to open fire; **brincar com** ~ (*fig*) to play with fire; **cessar** ~ (*MIL*) to cease fire; **estar com** ~ (*col*: *pessoa*) to be randy; **estar de** ~ (*col*: *bêbado*) to be drunk; **pegar** ~ to catch fire; (*estar com febre*) to burn up; **pôr** ~ **a** to set fire to; **ser bom para o** ~ (*fig*) to be useless; **ser** ~ **(na roupa)** (*col*: *pessoa*) to be a pain; (: *trabalho etc*) to be murder; (: *ser incrível*) to be amazing.

fogões [fo'gõjʃ] *mpl de* **fogão**.

fogo-fátuo (*pl* **fogos-fátuos**) *m* will-o'-the-wisp.

fogoso/a [fo'gozu/ɔza] *adj* fiery; (*libidinoso*) lustful.

fogueira [fo'gejra] *f* bonfire.

foguete [fo'getʃi] *m* rocket; (*pessoa*) live wire; **soltar os** ~**s antes da festa** (*fig*) to jump the gun.

foi [foj] *vb V* **ir**, **ser**.

foice ['fɔjsɪ] *f* scythe.

folclore [fowk'lɔri] *m* folklore.

folclórico/a [fowk'lɔriku/a] *adj* folkloric.

fole ['fɔli] *m* bellows *sg*.

fôlego ['folegu] *m* breath; (*folga*) breathing space; **perder o** ~ to get out of breath; **tomar** ~ to pause for breath.

folga ['fɔwga] *f* (*descanso*) rest, break; (*espaço livre*) clearance; (*ócio*) inactivity; (*col*: *atrevimento*) cheek; **dia de** ~ day off; **que** ~**!** what a cheek!

folgado/a [fow'gadu/a] *adj* (*roupa*) loose; (*vida*) leisurely; (*col*: *atrevido*) cheeky; (: *boa vida*) easy-living ♦ *m/f* (*col*: *atrevido*) cheeky devil; (: *boa vida*) loafer.

folgar [fow'ga*] *vt* to loosen, slacken ♦ *vi* (*descansar*) to rest, relax; (*divertir-se*) to have fun, amuse o.s.; ~ **em saber que ...** to be pleased to hear that ....

folgazão/zona [fowga'zãw/'zɔna] (*pl* **-ões/~s**) *adj* (*pessoa*) fun-loving; (*gênio*) lively.

folha ['foʎa] *f* leaf; (*de papel, de metal*) sheet; (*página*) page; (*de faca*) blade; (*jornal*) paper; **novo em** ~ brand new; ~ **de estanho** tinfoil (*BRIT*), aluminum foil (*US*); ~ **de pagamento** payroll; ~ **de rosto** imprint page; ~**s soltas** (*COMPUT*) single sheets, cut sheets.

folhagem [fo'ʎaʒẽ] *f* foliage.

folha-seca (*pl* **folhas-secas**) *f* (*FUTEBOL*) swerving shot.

folheado/a [fo'ʎjadu/a] *adj* veneered; ~ **a ouro** gold-plated.

folhear [fo'ʎja*] *vt* to leaf through.

folheto [fo'ʎetu] *m* booklet, pamphlet.

folhinha [fo'ʎiɲa] *f* tear-off calendar.

folhudo/a [fo'ʎudu/a] *adj* leafy.

folia [fo'lia] *f* revelry, merriment.

folião/liona [fo'ʎjãw/'ʎjɔna] (*pl* **-ões/~s**) *m/f* reveller (*in carnival*).

folículo [fo'likulu] *m* follicle.

foliões [fo'ʎõjʃ] *mpl de* **folião**.

foliona [fo'ʎjɔna] *f de* **folião**.

fome ['fɔmi] *f* hunger; (*escassez*) famine; (*fig*: *avidez*) longing; **passar** ~ to go hungry; **estar com** *ou* **ter** ~ to be hungry; **varado de** ~ starving, ravenous.

fomentar [fomẽ'ta*] *vt* to instigate, promote; (*discórdia*) to sow, cause.

fomento [fo'mẽtu] *m* (*MED*) fomentation; (*estímulo*) promotion; (*de discórdia, ódio etc*) stirring up.

fominha [fo'miɲa] (*col*) *adj* stingy ♦ *m/f* skinflint.

fonador(a) [fona'do*(a)] *adj V* **aparelho**.

fone ['fɔni] *m* telephone, phone; (*peça do telefone*) receiver.

fonema [fo'nɛma] *m* (*LING*) phoneme.

fonética [fo'nɛtʃika] *f* phonetics *sg*.

fonético/a [fo'nɛtʃiku/a] *adj* phonetic.

fonfom [fõ'fõ] (*pl* **-ns**) *m* toot.

fonologia [fonolo'ʒia] *f* phonology.

fonte ['fõtʃi] *f* (*nascente*) spring; (*chafariz*) fountain; (*origem*) source; (*ANAT*) temple; **de ~ limpa** from a reliable source; **retido/tributado na ~** (*COM*) deducted/taxed at source.

footing ['futʃiŋ] *m* jogging.

for [fo*] *etc vb V* **ir**; **ser**.

fora ['fɔra] *etc vb V* **ir**; **ser** ♦ *adv* out, outside ♦ *prep* (*além de*) apart from ♦ *m*: **dar o ~** (*bateria, radio*) to give out; (*pessoa*) to leave, be off; **dar um ~** to slip up; **dar um ~ em alguém** (*namorado*) to chuck sb, dump sb; (*esnobar*) to snub sb; **levar um ~** (*de namorado*) to be given the boot; (*ser esnobado*) to get the brush-off; **~ de** outside; **~ de si** beside o.s.; **estar ~** (*viajando*) to be away; **estar ~ (de casa)** to be out; **lá ~** outside; (*no exterior*) abroad; **jantar ~** to eat out; **com os braços de ~** with bare arms; **ser de ~** to be from out of town; **ficar de ~** not to join in; **lá para ~** outside; **ir para ~** (*viajar*) to go out of town; **com a cabeça para ~ da janela** with one's head sticking out of the window; **costurar/cozinhar para ~** to do sewing/cooking for other people; **por ~** on the outside; **cobrar por ~** to charge extra; **~ de dúvida** beyond doubt; **~ de propósito** irrelevant.

fora-de-lei *m/f inv* outlaw.

foragido/a [fora'ʒidu/a] *adj, m/f* (*fugitivo*) fugitive.

foragir-se [fora'ʒixsi] *vr* to go into hiding.

forasteiro/a [foraʃ'tejru/a] *adj* (*estranho*) alien ♦ *m/f* outsider, stranger; (*de outro país*) foreigner.

forca ['foxka] *f* gallows *sg*.

força ['foxsa] *f* (*energia física*) strength; (*TEC, ELET*) power; (*esforço*) effort; (*coerção*) force; **à ~** by force; **à ~ de** by dint of; **com ~** hard; **por ~** of necessity; **dar (uma) ~ a** to back up, encourage; **fazer ~** to try (hard); **como vai essa ~?** (*col*) how's it going?; **F~ Aérea** Air Force; **~ de trabalho** workforce; **~ maior** (*COM*) act of God.

forcado [fox'kadu] *m* pitchfork.

forçado/a [fox'sadu/a] *adj* forced; (*afetado*) false.

forçar [fox'sa*] *vt* to force; (*olhos, voz*) to strain; **~-se** *vr*: **~-se a** to force o.s. to.

força-tarefa (*pl* **forças-tarefa**) *f* task force.

forcejar [foxse'ʒa*] *vi* (*esforçar-se*) to strive; (*lutar*) to struggle.

fórceps ['fɔxsipʃ] *m inv* forceps *pl*.

forçoso/a [fox'sozu/ɔza] *adj* (*necessário*) necessary; (*obrigatório*) obligatory.

forja ['fɔxʒa] *f* forge.

forjar [fox'ʒa*] *vt* to forge; (*pretexto*) to make up.

forma ['fɔxma] *f* form; (*de um objeto*) shape; (*físico*) figure; (*maneira*) way; (*MED*) fitness; **desta ~** in this way; **de (tal) ~ que** in such a way that; **de qualquer ~** anyway; **da mesma ~** likewise; **de outra ~** otherwise; **de ~ alguma** in no way whatsoever; **em ~ de pêra/comprimido** pear-shaped/in tablet form; **estar fora de/em ~** (*pessoa*) to be unfit/fit; **manter a ~** to keep fit; **~ de pagamento** means of payment.

fôrma ['foxma] *f* (*CULIN*) cake tin; (*molde*) mould (*BRIT*), mold (*US*); (*para sapatos*) last.

formação [foxma'sãw] (*pl* **-ões**) *f* formation; (*antecedentes*) background; (*caráter*) make-up; (*profissional*) training.

formado/a [fox'madu/a] *adj* (*modelado*) formed; ♦ *m/f* graduate; **ser ~ de** to consist of; **ser ~ em** to be a graduate in.

formal [fox'maw] (*pl* **-ais**) *adj* formal.

formalidade [foxmali'dadʒi] *f* formality.

formalizar [foxmali'za*] *vt* to formalize.

formando/a [fox'mãdu/a] *m/f* graduating student, graduand.

formão [fox'mãw] (*pl* **-ões**) *m* chisel.

formar [fox'ma*] *vt* to form; (*constituir*) to constitute, make up; (*educar*) to train, educate; (*soldados*) to form up ♦ *vi* to form up; **~-se** *vr* (*tomar forma*) to form; (*EDUC*) to graduate.

formatar [foxma'ta*] *vt* (*COMPUT*) to format.

formato [fox'matu] *m* format; (*de papel*) size.

formatura [foxma'tura] *f* (*MIL*) formation; (*EDUC*) graduation.

fórmica ['fɔxmika] ® *f* formica ®.

formidável [foxmi'davew] (*pl* **-eis**) *adj* tremendous, great.

formiga [fox'miga] *f* ant.

formigar [foxmi'ga*] *vi* (*ser abundante*) to abound; (*sentir comichão*) to itch; **~ de algo** to swarm with sth.

formigueiro [foxmi'gejru] *m* ants' nest; (*multidão*) throng, swarm.

formões [fox'mõjʃ] *mpl de* **formão**.

Formosa [fox'mɔza] *f* Taiwan.

formoso/a [fox'mozu/ɔza] *adj* (*belo*) beautiful; (*esplêndido*) superb.

formosura [foxmo'zura] *f* beauty.

fórmula ['fɔxmula] *f* formula.

formulação [foxmula'sãw] (*pl* **-ões**) *f* formulation.

formular [foxmu'la*] *vt* to formulate; (*queixas*) to voice; **~ votos** to express one's hopes/wishes.

formulário [foxmu'larju] *m* form; **~s** *mpl* **contínuos** (*COMPUT*) continuous stationery *sg*.

fornalha [fox'naʎa] *f* furnace; (*fig*: *lugar quente*) oven.

fornecedor(a) [foxnese'do*(a)] *m/f* supplier ♦ *f* (*empresa*) supplier ♦ *adj* supply *atr*.

fornecer [foxne'se*] *vt* to supply, provide; **~ algo a alguém** to supply sb with sth.

fornecimento [foxnesi'mẽtu] *m* supply.

NB*: European Portuguese adds the following consonants to certain words:* **b** (sú(b)dito, su(b)til); **c** (a(c)ção, a(c)cionista, a(c)to); **m** (inde(m)ne); **p** (ado(p)ção, ado(p)tar); *for further details see p. xiii.*

fornicar [foxni'ka*] *vi* to fornicate.
forno ['foxnu] *m* (*CULIN*) oven; (*TEC*) furnace; (*para cerâmica*) kiln; **alto ~** blast furnace; **cozinheiro/a de ~ e fogão** expert cook.
foro ['foru] *m* forum; (*JUR*) Court of Justice; **~s** *mpl* privileges; **de ~ íntimo** personal, private.
forra ['fɔxa] *f*: **ir à ~** (*col*) to get one's own back.
forragem [fo'xaʒẽ] *f* fodder.
forrar [fo'xa*] *vt* (*cobrir*) to cover; (*: interior*) to line; (*de papel*) to paper.
forro ['foxu] *m* (*cobertura*) covering; (*interior*) lining; **com ~ de pele** fur-lined.
forró [fo'xɔ] (*col*) *m* shindig, dance.
fortalecer [foxtale'se*] *vt* to strengthen.
fortalecimento [foxtalesi'mẽtu] *m* strengthening.
fortaleza [foxta'leza] *f* (*forte*) fortress; (*força*) strength; (*moral*) fortitude; **ser uma ~** to be as strong as an ox.
fortalezense [foxtale'zẽsi] *adj* from Fortaleza ♦ *m/f* native *ou* inhabitant of Fortaleza.
forte ['fɔxtʃi] *adj* strong; (*pancada*) hard; (*chuva*) heavy; (*som*) loud; (*dor*) sharp, strong; (*filme*) powerful; (*pessoa: musculoso*) muscular ♦ *adv* strongly; (*som*) loud(ly) ♦ *m* (*fortaleza*) fort; (*talento*) strength; **ser ~ em algo** (*versado*) to be good at sth *ou* strong in sth.
fortificação [foxtʃifika'sãw] (*pl* **-ões**) *f* fortification; (*fortaleza*) fortress.
fortificante [foxtʃifi'kãtʃi] *adj* fortifying ♦ *m* fortifier.
fortificar [foxtʃifi'ka*] *vt* to fortify; **~-se** *vr* to build o.s. up.
fortuitamente [foxtwita'mẽtʃi] *adv* (*imprevisivelmente*) by chance, unexpectedly; (*ocasionalmente*) casually.
fortuito/a [fox'twitu/a] *adj* accidental.
fortuna [fox'tuna] *f* fortune; (*sorte*) (good) luck; (*riqueza*) fortune, wealth; **custar uma ~** to cost a fortune.
fosco/a ['foʃku/a] *adj* (*sem brilho*) dull; (*opaco*) opaque.
fosfato [foʃ'fatu] *m* phosphate.
fosforescente [foʃfore'sẽtʃi] *adj* phosphorescent.
fósforo ['fɔʃforu] *m* match; (*QUÍM*) phosphorus.
fossa ['fɔsa] *f* pit; (*col*) blues *pl*; **estar/ficar na ~** (*col*) to be/get down in the dumps *ou* depressed; **tirar alguém da ~** (*col*) to cheer sb up; **~ séptica** cesspit, septic tank.
fosse ['fosi] *etc vb V* **ir**; **ser**.
fóssil ['fɔsiw] (*pl* **fósseis**) *m* fossil.
fosso ['fosu] *m* trench, ditch; (*de uma fortaleza*) moat.
foto ['fɔtu] *f* photo.
fotocópia [foto'kɔpja] *f* photocopy.
fotocopiadora [fotokopja'dora] *f* photocopier.
fotocopiar [fotoko'pja*] *vt* to photocopy.
fotogênico/a [foto'ʒeniku/a] *adj* photogenic.
fotografar [fotogra'fa*] *vt* to photograph.
fotografia [fotogra'fia] *f* photography; (*uma foto*) photograph.
fotográfico/a [foto'grafiku/a] *adj* photographic; *V tb* **máquina**.
fotógrafo/a [fo'tɔgrafu/a] *m/f* photographer.
fotonovela [fotono'vɛla] *f* photo story.
fotossíntese [foto'sĩtezi] *f* (*BIOL*) photosynthesis.
foxtrote [foks'trɔtʃi] *m* foxtrot.
foyer [fua'je] *m* foyer.
foz [fɔʒ] *f* river mouth.
FP-25 *abr fpl* (= *Forças Populares do 25 de Abril*) *Portuguese terrorist group*.
fração [fra'sãw] (*pl* **-ões**) *f* fraction.
fracassar [fraka'sa*] *vi* to fail.
fracasso [fra'kasu] *m* failure.
fracção [fra'sãw] (*PT*) *f* = **fração**.
fracionar [frasjo'na*] *vt* to break up; **~-se** *vr* to break up, fragment.
fraco/a ['fraku/a] *adj* weak; (*sol*, *som*) faint ♦ *m* weakness; **estar ~ em algo** to be poor at sth; **ter um ~ por algo** to have a weakness for sth.
frações [fra'sõjʃ] *fpl de* **fração**.
fractura *etc* [fra'tura] (*PT*) *f* = **fratura** *etc*.
frade ['fradʒi] *m* (*REL*) friar; (*: monge*) monk.
fraga ['fraga] *f* crag, rock.
fragata [fra'gata] *f* (*NÁUT*) frigate.
frágil ['fraʒiw] (*pl* **-eis**) *adj* (*débil*) fragile; (*quebradiço*) breakable; (*pessoa*) frail; (*saúde*) delicate, poor.
fragilidade [fraʒili'dadʒi] *f* fragility; (*de uma pessoa*) frailty.
fragílimo/a [fra'ʒilimu/a] *adj superl de* **frágil**.
fragmentar [fragmẽ'ta*] *vt* to break up; **~-se** *vr* to break up.
fragmento [frag'mẽtu] *m* fragment.
fragrância [fra'grãsja] *f* fragrance, perfume.
fragrante [fra'grãtʃi] *adj* fragrant.
frajola [fra'ʒɔla] (*col*) *adj* smart.
fralda ['frawda] *f* (*da camisa*) shirt tail; (*para bebê*) nappy (*BRIT*), diaper (*US*); (*de montanha*) foot; **mal saído das ~s** (*fig*) still wet behind the ears.
framboesa [frã'beza] *f* raspberry.
França ['frãsa] *f* France.
francamente [frãka'mẽtʃi] *adv* (*abertamente*) frankly; (*realmente*) really.
francês/esa [frã'seʃ/eza] *adj* French ♦ *m/f* Frenchman/woman ♦ *m* (*LING*) French.
franco/a ['frãku/a] *adj* (*sincero*) frank; (*isento de pagamento*) free; (*óbvio*) clear ♦ *m* franc; **entrada franca** free admission.
frangalho [frã'gaʎu] *m* (*trapo*) rag, tatter; (*pessoa*) wreck; **em ~s** in tatters.
frango ['frãgu] *m* chicken; (*FUTEBOL*) easy goal.
franja ['frãʒa] *f* fringe (*BRIT*), bangs *pl* (*US*).
franquear [frã'kja*] *vt* (*caminho*) to clear; (*isentar de imposto*) to exempt from duties; (*carta*) to frank; **~ algo a alguém** (*facultar*) to make sth available to sb.

franqueza [frã'keza] *f* frankness.
franquia [frã'kia] *f* (*COM*) franchise; (*isenção*) exemption; ~ **de bagagem** baggage allowance; ~ **diplomática** diplomatic immunity; ~ **postal** freepost.
franzido [frã'zidu] *m* pleat.
franzino/a [frã'zinu/a] *adj* skinny.
franzir [frã'zi*] *vt* (*preguear*) to pleat; (*enrugar*) to wrinkle, crease; (*lábios*) to curl; ~ **as sobrancelhas** to frown.
fraque ['fraki] *m* morning suit.
fraquejar [frake'ʒa*] *vi* to grow weak; (*vontade*) to weaken.
fraqueza [fra'keza] *f* weakness.
frasco ['fraʃku] *m* (*de remédio, perfume*) bottle.
frase ['frazi] *f* sentence; ~ **feita** set phrase.
fraseado [fra'zjadu] *m* wording.
frasqueira [fraʃ'kejra] *f* vanity case.
fraternal [fratex'naw] (*pl* **-ais**) *adj* fraternal.
fraternidade [fratexni'dadʒi] *f* fraternity.
fraternizar [fratexni'za*] *vt* to bring together ♦ *vi* to fraternize.
fraterno/a [fra'tɛxnu/a] *adj* fraternal.
fratura [fra'tura] *f* fracture, break.
fraturar [fratu'ra*] *vt* to fracture.
fraudar [fraw'da*] *vt* to defraud; (*expectativa, esperanças*) to dash.
fraude ['frawdʒi] *f* fraud.
fraudulento/a [frawdu'lẽtu/a] *adj* fraudulent.
freada [fre'ada] (*BR*) *f* burst on the brake; **dar uma** ~ to slam on the brakes.
frear [fre'a*] (*BR*) *vt* (*conter*) to curb, restrain; (*veículo*) to stop ♦ *vi* (*veículo*) to brake.
freelance [fri'lãs] *m/f* freelancer.
freezer ['frize*] *m* freezer.
frege ['frɛʒi] *m* mess.
freguês/guesa [fre'geʃ/'geza] *m/f* (*cliente*) customer; (*PT*) parishioner.
freguesia [frege'zia] *f* customers *pl*; (*PT*) parish.
frei [frej] *m* friar, monk; (*título*) Brother.
freio ['freju] *m* (*BR*: *veículo*) brake; (*cavalo*) bridle; (*bocado do freio*) bit; (*fig*) check; ~ **de mão** handbrake.
freira ['frejra] *f* nun.
freixo ['frejʃu] *m* (*BOT*) ash.
Frelimo [fre'limo] *abr f* (= *Frente de Libertação de Moçambique*) Frelimo.
fremente [fre'mẽtʃi] *adj* (*fig*) rousing.
fremir [fre'mi*] *vi* (*bramar*) to roar; (*tremer*) to tremble.
frêmito ['fremitu] *m* (*fig*: *de alegria etc*) wave.
frenesi [frene'zi] *m* frenzy.
frenético/a [fre'nɛtʃiku/a] *adj* frantic, frenzied.
frente ['frẽtʃi] *f* (*de objeto, POL, MIL*) front; (*rosto*) face; (*fachada*) façade; ~ **a** ~ face to face; **à** ~ **de** at the front of; **de** ~ **para** facing; **em** ~ **de** in front of; (*defronte a*) opposite; **para a** ~ ahead, forward; **de trás para** ~ from back to front; **porta da** ~ front door; **apartamento de** ~ apartment at the front; **seguir em** ~ to continue ahead; **a casa em** ~ the house opposite; **na minha (***ou* **sua** *etc***)** ~ in front of me (*ou* you *etc*); **sair da** ~ to get out of the way; **sai da minha** ~**!** get out of my sight!; **pela** ~ ahead; **pra** ~ (*col*) fashionable, trendy; **fazer** ~ **a algo** to face sth; **ir para a** ~ (*progredir*) to progress; **levar à** ~ to carry through; ~ **de combate** (*MIL*) front; ~ **de trabalho** area of employment; ~ **fria/quente** (*METEOROLOGIA*) cold/warm front.
freqüência [fre'kwẽsja] *f* frequency; **com** ~ often, frequently.
freqüentador(a) [frekwẽta'do*(a)] *m/f* regular visitor; (*de restaurante etc*) regular customer.
freqüentar [frekwẽ'ta*] *vt* to frequent; ~ **a casa de alguém** to go to sb's house a lot; ~ **um curso** to attend a course.
freqüente [fre'kwẽtʃi] *adj* frequent.
fresca ['freʃka] *f* cool breeze.
frescão [freʃ'kãw] (*pl* **-ões**) *m* air-conditioned coach.
fresco/a ['freʃku/a] *adj* fresh; (*vento, tempo*) cool; (*col*: *efeminado*) camp; (: *afetado*) pretentious; (: *cheio de luxo*) fussy ♦ *m* (*ar*) fresh air; (*ARTE*) fresco.
frescobol [freʃko'bɔw] *m* (kind of) racketball (*played mainly on the beach*).
frescões [freʃ'kõjʃ] *mpl de* **frescão**.
frescor [freʃ'ko*] *m* freshness.
frescura [freʃ'kura] *f* freshness; (*frialdade*) coolness; (*col*: *luxo*) fussiness; (: *afetaçao*) pretentiousness; **que** ~! how fussy!; how pretentious!
fresta ['frɛʃta] *f* gap, slit.
fretar [fre'ta*] *vt* (*avião, navio*) to charter; (*caminhão*) to hire.
frete ['frɛtʃi] *m* (*carregamento*) freight, cargo; (*tarifa*) freightage; **a** ~ for hire.
freudiano/a [frɔj'dʒjanu/a] *adj* Freudian.
frevo ['frevu] *m improvised Carnival dance*.
fria ['fria] *f*: **dar uma** ~ **em alguém** to give sb the cold shoulder; **estar/entrar numa** ~ (*col*) to be in/get into a mess; **levar uma** ~ **de alguém** to get the cold shoulder from sb.
friagem ['frjaʒẽ] *f* cold weather.
frialdade [frjaw'dadʒi] *f* coldness; (*indiferença*) indifference, coolness.
fricção [frik'sãw] *f* friction; (*ato*) rubbing; (*MED*) massage.
friccionar [friksjo'na*] *vt* to rub.
fricote [fri'kɔtʃi] (*col*) *m* finickiness.
fricoteiro/a [fiko'tejru/a] (*col*) *adj* finicky ♦ *m/f* fusspot.
frieira ['frjejra] *f* chilblain.

***NB**: European Portuguese adds the following consonants to certain words:* **b** (sú(b)dito, su(b)til); **c** (a(c)ção, a(c)cionista, a(c)to); **m** (inde(m)ne); **p** (ado(p)ção, ado(p)tar); *for further details see p. xiii.*

frieza ['frjeza] *f* coldness; (*indiferença*) coolness.
frigideira [friʒi'dejra] *f* frying pan.
frigidez [friʒi'deʒ] *f* frigidity.
frígido/a ['friʒidu/a] *adj* frigid.
frigir [fri'ʒi*] *vt* to fry.
frigorífico [frigo'rifiku] *m* refrigerator; (*congelador*) freezer.
frincha ['frĩʃa] *f* chink, slit.
frio/a ['friu/a] *adj* cold; (*col*) forged ♦ *m* coldness; **~s** *mpl* cold meats; **estou com ~** I'm cold; **faz** *ou* **está ~** it's cold.
friorento/a [frjo'rẽtu/a] *adj* (*pessoa*) sensitive to the cold; (*lugar*) chilly.
frisar [fri'za*] *vt* (*encrespar*) to curl; (*salientar*) to emphasize.
Frísia ['frizja] *f*: **a ~** Frisia.
friso ['frizu] *m* border; (*na parede*) frieze; (*ARQ*) moulding (*BRIT*), molding (*US*).
fritada [fri'tada] *f* fry-up; **dar uma ~ em algo** to fry sth.
fritar [fri'ta*] *vt* to fry.
fritas ['fritas] *fpl* chips (*BRIT*), French fries (*US*).
frito/a ['fritu/a] *adj* fried; (*col*): **estar ~** to be done for.
fritura [fri'tura] *f* fried food.
frivolidade [frivoli'dadʒi] *f* frivolity.
frívolo/a ['frivolu/a] *adj* frivolous.
fronha ['froɲa] *f* pillowcase.
front [frõ] (*pl* **~s**) *m* (*MIL*, *fig*) front.
fronte ['frõtʃi] *f* (*ANAT*) forehead, brow.
fronteira [frõ'tejra] *f* frontier, border.
fronteiriço/a [frõtej'risu/a] *adj* frontier *atr*.
fronteiro/a [frõ'tejru/a] *adj* front.
frontispício [frõtʃiʃ'pisju] *m* (*de edifício*) main façade; (*de livro*) frontispiece; (*rosto*) face.
frota ['frɔta] *f* fleet.
frouxo/a ['froʃu/a] *adj* loose; (*corda*) slack; (*fraco*) weak; (*indolente*) lax; (*col*: *condescendente*) soft.
frufru [fru'fru] *m* (*enfeite*) ruff.
frugal [fru'gaw] (*pl* **-ais**) *adj* frugal.
fruição [frwi'sãw] *f* enjoyment.
fruir ['frwi*] *vt* to enjoy ♦ *vi*: **~ de algo** to enjoy sth.
frustração [fruʃtra'sãw] *f* frustration.
frustrado/a [fruʃ'tradu/a] *adj* frustrated; (*planos*) thwarted.
frustrante [fruʃ'trãtʃi] *adj* frustrating.
frustrar [fruʃ'tra*] *vt* to frustrate.
fruta ['fruta] *f* fruit.
fruta-de-conde (*pl* **frutas-de-conde**) *f* sweetsop.
fruta-pão (*pl* **frutas-pães** *ou* **frutas-pão**) *f* breadfruit.
fruteira [fru'tejra] *f* fruit bowl.
frutífero/a [fru'tʃiferu/a] *adj* (*proveitoso*) fruitful; (*árvore*) fruit-bearing.
fruto ['frutu] *m* (*BOT*) fruit; (*resultado*) result, product; **dar ~** to bear fruit.
fubá [fu'ba] *m* corn meal.
fubeca [fu'bɛka] (*col*) *f* thrashing.
fubica [fu'bika] (*col*) *f* heap, jalopy.
fuçar [fu'sa*] *vi*: **~ em algo** (*remexer*) to rummage in sth; (*meter-se*) to meddle in sth.
fuças ['fusaʃ] (*col*) *fpl* face *sg*, chops.
fuga ['fuga] *f* flight, escape; (*de gás etc*) leak; (*da prisão*) escape; (*de namorados*) elopement; (*MÚS*) fugue.
fugacíssimo/a [fuga'sisimu/a] *adj superl de* **fugaz**.
fugaz [fu'gaʒ] *adj* fleeting.
fugida [fu'ʒida] *f* sortie; **dar uma ~** *ou* **fugidinha** to pop out for a moment.
fugir [fu'ʒi*] *vi* to flee, escape; (*prisioneiro*) to escape; (*criança*: *de casa*) to run away; (*namorados*) to elope; **~ a algo** to avoid sth.
fugitivo/a [fuʒi'tʃivu/a] *adj*, *m/f* fugitive.
fui [fuj] *vb V* **ir**; **ser**.
fulano/a [fu'lanu/a] *m/f* so-and-so; **~ de tal** what's-his-name/what's-her-name; **~, beltrano e sicrano** Tom, Dick and Harry.
fulcro ['fuwkru] *m* fulcrum.
fuleiro/a [fu'lejru/a] *adj* tacky.
fúlgido/a ['fuwʒidu/a] *adj* brilliant.
fulgir [fuw'ʒi*] *vi* to shine.
fulgor [fuw'go*] *m* brilliance.
fuligem [fu'liʒẽ] *f* soot.
fulminante [fuwmi'nãtʃi] *adj* (*devastador*) devastating; (*palavras*) scathing.
fulminar [fuwmi'na*] *vt* (*ferir*, *matar*) to strike down; (*petrificar*) to stop dead; (*aniquilar*) to annihilate ♦ *vi* to flash with lightning; **fulminado por um raio** struck by lightning.
fulo/a ['fulu/a] *adj*: **estar** *ou* **ficar ~ de raiva** to be furious.
fumaça [fu'masa] (*BR*) *f* (*de fogo*) smoke; (*de gás*) fumes *pl*; **500 e lá vai ~** (*col*) 500 and then some.
fumador(a) [fuma'do*(a)] (*PT*) *m/f* smoker.
fumante [fu'mãtʃi] *m/f* smoker.
fumar [fu'ma*] *vt*, *vi* to smoke.
fumê [fu'me] *adj inv* (*vidro*) smoked.
fumo ['fumu] *m* (*PT*: *de fogo*) smoke; (: *de gás*) fumes *pl*; (*BR*: *tabaco*) tobacco; (*fumar*) smoking; (*BR*: *col*: *maconha*) dope; **~ louro** Virginia tobacco; **puxar ~** (*col*) to smoke dope.
FUNABEM [funa'bẽ] (*BR*) *abr f* (= *Fundação Nacional do Bem-Estar do Menor*) *children's home*.
Funai [fu'naj] (*BR*) *abr f* = **Fundação Nacional do Índio**.
Funarte [fu'naxtʃi] (*BR*) *abr f* = **Fundaçao Nacional de Arte**.
função [fũ'sãw] (*pl* **-ões**) *f* function; (*ofício*) duty; (*papel*) role; (*espetáculo*) performance.
Funcep [fũ'sɛpi] (*BR*) *abr f* = (*Fundação Centro de Formação do Servidor Público*) *civil service training centre*.
funcho ['fũʃu] *m* (*BOT*) fennel.
funcional [fũsjo'naw] (*pl* **-ais**) *adj* functional.
funcionalismo [fũsjona'liʒmu] *m*: **~ público** civil service.

funcionamento [fūsjona'mētu] *m* functioning, working; **pôr em ~** to set going, start.
funcionar [fūsjo'na*] *vi* to function; (*máquina*) to work, run; (*dar bom resultado*) to work.
funcionário/a [fūsjo'narju/a] *m/f* official; **~ (público)** civil servant.
funções [fū'sõjʃ] *fpl de* **função**.
fundação [fūda'sāw] (*pl* **-ões**) *f* foundation.
fundador(a) [fūda'do*(a)] *m/f* founder ♦ *adj* founding.
fundamental [fūdamē'taw] (*pl* **-ais**) *adj* fundamental, basic.
fundamentar [fūdamē'ta*] *vt* (*argumento*) to substantiate; (*basear*): **~ (em)** to base (on).
fundamento [fūda'mētu] *m* (*fig*) foundation, basis; (*motivo*) motive; **sem ~** groundless.
fundar [fū'da*] *vt* to establish, found; (*basear*) to base; **~-se** *vr*: **~-se em** to be based on.
fundear [fū'dʒja*] *vi* to anchor.
fundição [fūdʒi'sāw] (*pl* **-ões**) *f* fusing; (*fábrica*) foundry.
fundilho [fū'dʒiʎu] *m* (*da calça*) seat.
fundir [fū'dʒi*] *vt* to fuse; (*metal*) to smelt, melt down; (*COM*: *empresas*) to merge; (*em molde*) to cast; **~-se** *vr* (*derreter-se*) to melt; (*juntar-se*) to merge, fuse; (*COM*) to merge; **~ a cuca** to crack up.
fundo/a ['fūdu/a] *adj* deep; (*fig*) profound; (*col*: *ignorante*) ignorant; (: *despreparado*) hopeless ♦ *m* (*do mar, jardim*) bottom; (*profundidade*) depth; (*base*) basis; (*da loja, casa, do papel*) back; (*de quadro*) background; (*de dinheiro*) fund ♦ *adv* deeply; **~s** *mpl* (*COM*) funds; (*da casa etc*) back *sg*; **a ~** thoroughly; **ao ~** in the background; **ir ao ~** (*navio*) to sink, go down; **no ~** (*de caixa etc*) at the bottom; (*de casa etc*) at the back; (*de quadro*) in the background; (*fig*) basically, at bottom; **sem ~** (*poço*) bottomless; **dar ~s para** (*casa etc*) to back on to; **~ de contingência** contingency fund; **~ de investimento** investment fund; **F~ Monetário Internacional** International Monetary Fund.
fundura [fū'dura] *f* depth; (*col*) ignorance.
fúnebre ['funebri] *adj* funeral *atr*, funereal; (*fig*: *triste*) gloomy, lugubrious.
funeral [fune'raw] (*pl* **-ais**) *m* funeral.
funerário/a [fune'rarju/a] *adj* funeral *atr*; **casa funerária** undertakers *pl*.
funesto/a [fu'nɛʃtu/a] *adj* (*fatal*) fatal; (*infausto*) disastrous; (*notícia*) fateful.
fungar [fū'ga*] *vt, vi* to sniff.
fungo ['fūgu] *m* (*BOT*) fungus.
funil [fu'niw] (*pl* **-is**) *m* funnel.
Funrural [fūxu'raw] (*BR*) *abr m* = **Fundo de Assistência e Previdência ao Trabalhador Rural.**
Funtevê [fūte've] *abr f* = **Fundação Centro-Brasileira de TV Educativa.**
fura-bolo ['fura-] (*pl* **fura-bolos**) (*col*) *m* index finger.
furacão [fura'kāw] (*pl* **-ões**) *m* hurricane; **entrar/sair como um ~** to stomp in/out.
furado/a [fu'radu/a] *adj* perforated; (*pneu*) flat; (*orelha*) pierced; (*col*: *programa*) crummy.
furão/rona [fu'rāw/'rɔna] (*pl* **-ões/~s**) *m* ferret ♦ *m/f* (*col*) go-getter ♦ *adj* (*col*) hard-working, dynamic.
furar [fu'ra*] *vt* (*perfurar*) to bore, perforate; (*penetrar*) to penetrate; (*frustrar*) to foil; (*fila*) to jump ♦ *vi* (*col*: *programa*) to fall through; **~ uma greve** to break a strike.
furdúncio [fux'dūsju] (*col*) *m* commotion.
furgão [fux'gāw] (*pl* **-ões**) *m* van.
furgoneta [fuxgo'neta] (*PT*) *f* van.
fúria ['furja] *f* fury, rage; **estar uma ~** to be furious.
furibundo/a [furi'būdu/a] *adj* furious.
furioso/a [fu'rjozu/ɔza] *adj* furious.
furo ['furu] *m* hole; (*num pneu*) puncture; **~ jornalístico** scoop; **dar um ~** (*col*) to make a blunder; **estar muitos ~s acima de algo** (*fig*) to be a cut above sth, be a lot better than sth.
furões [fu'rõjʃ] *mpl de* **furão**.
furona [fu'rɔna] *f de* **furão**.
furor [fu'ro*] *m* fury, rage; **causar ~** to cause a furore; **fazer ~** to be all the rage.
furta-cor ['fuxta-] (*pl* **furta-cores**) *adj* iridescent ♦ *m* iridescence.
furtar [fux'ta*] *vt, vi* to steal; **~-se** *vr*: **~-se a** to avoid, evade.
furtivo/a [fux'tʃivu/a] *adj* furtive, stealthy.
furto ['fuxtu] *m* theft.
furúnculo [fu'rūkulu] *m* (*MED*) boil.
fusão [fu'zāw] (*pl* **-ões**) *f* fusion; (*COM*) merger; (*derretimento*) melting; (*união*) union.
fusca ['fuʃka] (*col*) *m* (VW) beetle.
fusco/a ['fuʃku/a] *adj* dark, dusky.
fuselagem [fuze'laʒē] (*pl* **-ns**) *f* fuselage.
fusível [fu'zivew] (*pl* **-eis**) *m* (*ELET*) fuse.
fuso ['fuzu] *m* (*TEC*) spindle; **~ horário** time zone.
fusões [fu'zõjʃ] *fpl de* **fusão**.
fustão [fuʃ'tāw] *m* corduroy.
fustigar [fuʃtʃi'ga*] *vt* (*açoitar*) to flog, whip; (*suj*: *vento*) to lash; (*maltratar*) to lash out at.
futebol [futʃi'bɔw] *m* football; **~ de salão** five-a-side football; **~ totó** table football; **fazer um ~ de algo** (*col*) to get sth all mixed up.
fútil ['futʃiw] (*pl* **-eis**) *adj* (*pessoa*) superficial, shallow; (*insignificante*) trivial.
futilidade [futʃili'dadʒi] *f* (*de pessoa*) shallowness; (*insignificância*) triviality; (*coisa fútil*) trivial thing.
futurismo [futu'riʒmu] *m* futurism.

NB: *European Portuguese adds the following consonants to certain words:* **b** (sú(b)dito, su(b)til); **c** (a(c)ção, a(c)cionista, a(c)to); **m** (inde(m)ne); **p** (ado(p)ção, ado(p)tar); *for further details see p. xiii.*

futuro/a [fu'turu/a] *adj* future ♦ *m* future; **no ~** in the future; **num ~ próximo** in the near future.
fuxicar [fuʃi'ka*] *vi* to gossip.
fuxico [fu'ʃiku] *m* piece of gossip.
fuxiqueiro/a [fuʃi'kejru/a] *m/f* gossip ♦ *adj* gossipy.
fuzil [fu'ziw] (*pl* **-is**) *m* rifle.
fuzilamento [fuzila'mẽtu] *m* shooting.
fuzilante [fuzi'lãtʃi] *adj* (*olhos*) blazing.
fuzilar [fuzi'la*] *vt* to shoot ♦ *vi* (*olhos*) to blaze; (*pessoa*) to fume.
fuzileiro/a [fuzi'lejru/a] *m/f*: **~ naval** (MIL) marine.
fuzis [fu'ziʃ] *mpl de* **fuzil**.
fuzuê [fu'zwe] *m* commotion.

G

G, g [ʒe] (*pl* **gs**) *m* G, g; **G de Gomes** G for George.
g. *abr* (= *grama*) gr.; (= *grau*) deg.
Gabão [ga'bãw] *m*: **o ~** Gabon.
gabar [ga'ba*] *vt* to praise; **~-se** *vr*: **~-se de** to boast about.
gabardine [gabax'dʒini] *f* gabardine.
gabaritado/a [gabari'tadu/a] *adj* (*pessoa*) well-qualified.
gabarito [gaba'ritu] *m* (*fig*): **ter ~ para** to have the ability to; **de ~** (of) high calibre *atr* (BRIT) *ou* caliber *atr* (US).
gabinete [gabi'netʃi] *m* (COM) office; (*escritório*) study; (POL) cabinet.
gado ['gadu] *m* livestock; (*bovino*) cattle; **~ leiteiro** dairy cattle; **~ suíno** pigs *pl*.
gaélico/a [ga'ɛliku/a] *adj* Gaelic ♦ *m* (LING) Gaelic.
gafanhoto [gafa'ɲotu] *m* grasshopper.
gafe ['gafi] *f* gaffe, faux pas; **dar** *ou* **cometer uma ~** to make a faux pas.
gafieira [ga'fjejra] (*col*) *f* (*lugar*) dive; (*baile*) knees-up.
gagá [ga'ga] *adj* senile.
gago/a ['gagu/a] *adj* stuttering ♦ *m/f* stutterer.
gagueira [ga'gejra] *f* stutter.
gaguejar [gage'ʒa*] *vi* to stammer, stutter ♦ *vt* (*resposta*) to stammer.
gaiato/a [ga'jatu/a] *adj* funny.
gaiola [ga'jɔla] *f* (*para pássaro*) cage; (*cadeia*) jail ♦ *m* (*barco*) riverboat.
gaita ['gajta] *f* harmonica; (*col*: *dinheiro*) cash, dough; **cheio/a da ~** (*col*) loaded; **solta a ~!** (*col*) hand over your cash!; **~ de foles** bagpipes *pl*.
gaivota [gaj'vɔta] *f* seagull.
gajo ['gaʒu] (PT: *col*) *m* guy, fellow.

gala ['gala] *f*: **traje de ~** full dress; **festa de ~** gala.
galã [ga'lã] *m* (*ator*) leading man; (*fig*) ladies' man.
galalau [gala'law] *m* giant.
galante [ga'lãtʃi] *adj* (*gracioso*) graceful; (*gentil*) gallant.
galanteador [galãtʃja'do*] *m* suitor, admirer.
galantear [galã'tʃja*] *vt* to court, woo.
galanteio [galã'teju] *m* wooing.
galantina [galã'tʃina] *f* (CULIN): **~ de galinha** chicken in aspic.
galão [ga'lãw] (*pl* **-ões**) *m* (MIL) stripe; (*medida*) gallon; (PT: *café*) white coffee; (*passamanaria*) braid.
Galápagos [ga'lapaguʃ]: **(as) Ilhas** *fpl* **~** (the) Galapagos Islands.
galardão [galax'dãw] (*pl* **-ões**) *m* reward.
galardoar [galax'dwa*] *vt*: **~ alguém (com algo)** to reward sb (with sth).
galardões [galax'dõjʃ] *mpl de* **galardão**.
galáxia [ga'laksja] *m* galaxy.
galé [ga'lɛ] *f* (NÁUT) galley ♦ *m* galley slave.
galego/a [ga'legu/a] *adj* Galician ♦ *m/f* Galician; (*col*, *pej*) Portuguese ♦ *m* (LING) Galician.
galera [ga'lɛra] *f* (NÁUT) galley; (*col*: *pessoas*, *público*) crowd.
galeria [gale'ria] *f* gallery; (TEATRO) circle; (*para águas pluviais*) storm drain.
Gales ['galiʃ] *m*: **País de ~** Wales.
galês/esa [ga'leʃ/eza] *adj* Welsh ♦ *m/f* Welshman/woman ♦ *m* (LING) Welsh; **os galeses** *mpl* the Welsh.
galeto [ga'letu] *m* spring chicken.
galgar [gaw'ga*] *vt* (*saltar*) to leap over; (*subir*) to climb up.
galgo ['gawgu] *m* greyhound.
galhardia [gaʎax'dʒia] *f* (*elegância*) elegance; (*bravura*, *gentileza*) gallantry; **com ~** gallantly.
galhardo/a [ga'ʎaxdu/a] *adj* (*elegante*) elegant; (*bravo*, *gentil*) gallant.
galheteiro [gaʎe'tejru] *m* cruet stand.
galho ['gaʎu] *m* (*de árvore*) branch; (*col*: *bico*) part-time job; (: *problema*): **dar o ~** to cause trouble; **quebrar um** *ou* **o ~** to sort it out.
galicismo [gali'siʒmu] *m* Gallicism.
galináceos [gali'nasjuʃ] *mpl* poultry *sg*.
galinha [ga'liɲa] *f* hen; (CULIN; *fig*: *covarde*) chicken; (*fig*: *puta*) slut; **a ~ do vizinho é sempre mais gorda** (*fig*) the grass is always greener (on the other side of the fence); **matar a ~ dos ovos de ouro** (*fig*) to kill the goose that lays the golden egg.
galinha-d'angola [-dã'gɔla] (*pl* **galinhas-d'angolas**) *f* guinea fowl.
galinha-morta (*pl* **galinhas-mortas**) (*col*) *f* (*pechincha*) bargain; (*coisa fácil*) piece of cake ♦ *m/f* (*pessoa*) weakling.
galinheiro [gali'ɲejru] *m* (*lugar*) hen-house.
galo ['galu] *m* cock, rooster; (*inchação*) bump;

missa do ~ midnight mass; **ouvir cantar o ~ e não saber onde** (*fig*) to jump to conclusions; **~ de briga** fighting cock; (*fig*: *pessoa*) troublemaker.
galocha [ga'lɔʃa] *f* (*bota*) Wellington (boot).
galões [ga'lõjʃ] *mpl de* **galão**.
galopante [galo'pãtʃi] *adj* (*fig*: *inflação*) galloping; (: *doença*) rampant.
galopar [galo'pa*] *vi* to gallop.
galope [ga'lɔpi] *m* gallop.
galpão [gaw'pãw] (*pl* **-ões**) *m* shed.
galvanizar [gawvani'za*] *vt* to galvanize.
gama ['gama] *f* (*MÚS*) scale; (*fig*) range; (*ZOOL*) doe.
gamado/a [ga'madu/a] (*col*) *adj*: **ser** *ou* **estar ~ por** to be crazy about.
gamão [ga'mãw] *m* backgammon.
gamar [ga'ma*] (*col*) *vi*: **~ (por)** to fall in love (with).
gambá [gã'ba] *m* (*ZOO*) opossum; **bêbado/a como um ~** (*col*) pissed as a newt.
Gâmbia ['gãbja] *m*: **o ~** (the) Gambia.
gambito [gã'bitu] *m* (*XADREZ etc*) gambit; (*col*: *perna*) pin.
gamo ['gamu] *m* (fallow) deer.
Gana ['gana] *m* Ghana.
gana ['gana] *f* (*desejo*) craving, desire; (*ódio*) hate; **ter ~s de (fazer) algo** to feel like (doing) sth; **ter ~ de alguém** to hate sb.
ganância [ga'nãsja] *f* greed.
ganancioso/a [ganã'sjozu/ɔza] *adj* greedy.
gancho ['gãʃu] *m* hook; (*de calça*) crotch.
gandaia [gã'daja] *f* (*vadiagem*) idling; (*farra*) living it up; **viver na ~** to lead the life of Riley; **cair na ~** to live it up.
Ganges ['gãʒiʃ] *m*: **o ~** the Ganges.
gânglio ['gãglju] *m* (*MED*) ganglion.
gangorra [gã'goxa] *f* seesaw.
gangrena [gã'grena] *f* gangrene.
gangrenar [gãgre'na*] *vi* to go gangrenous.
gângster ['gãɲʃte*] *m* gangster.
gangue ['gãgi] (*col*) *f* gang.
ganhador(a) [gaɲa'do*(a)] *adj* winning ♦ *m/f* winner.
ganha-pão ['gaɲa-] (*pl* **-ães**) *m* living, livelihood.
ganhar [ga'ɲa*] *vt* to win; (*salário*) to earn; (*adquirir*) to get; (*lugar*) to reach; (*lucrar*) to gain ♦ *vi* (*vencer*) to win; **~ de alguém** (*num jogo*) to beat sb; **~ a alguém em algo** to outdo sb in sth; **~ tempo** to gain time; **sair ganhando** to come out better off, come off better; **ganhei o dia** (*fig*) it made my day.
ganho/a ['gaɲu/a] *pp de* **ganhar** ♦ *m* (*lucro*) profit, gain; **~s** *mpl* (*ao jogo*) winnings; **~ de capital** (*COM*) capital gain.
ganido [ga'nidu] *m* (*de cão*) yelp; (*de pessoa*) squeal.
ganir [ga'ni*] *vi* (*cão*) to yelp; (*pessoa*) to squeal ♦ *vt* (*gemido, gritos*) to let out.
ganso/a ['gãsu/a] *m/f* gander/goose.
garagem [ga'raʒẽ] (*pl* **-ns**) *f* garage.
garagista [gara'ʒiʃta] *m/f* garage owner.
garanhão [gara'ɲãw] (*pl* **-ões**) *m* stallion; (*col*: *homem*) stud.
garantia [garã'tʃia] *f* guarantee; (*de dívida*) surety; **estar na ~** (*compra*) to be under guarantee; **empréstimo sem ~** (*COM*) unsecured loan.
garantir [garã'tʃi*] *vt* to guarantee; **~-se** *vr*: **~-se contra algo** to defend o.s. against sth; **~ algo (a alguém)** (*prometer*) to promise (sb) sth; **~ que** ... to maintain that ...; **~ a alguém que** ... to assure sb that ...; **~ alguém contra algo** to defend sb against sth.
garatujar [garatu'ʒa*] *vt* to scribble, scrawl.
garbo ['gaxbu] *m* (*elegância*) elegance; (*distinção*) distinction.
garboso/a [gax'bozu/ɔza] *adj* (*elegante*) elegant; (*distinto*) distinguished.
garça ['gaxsa] *f* heron.
garçom [gax'sõ] (*BR*: *pl* **-ns**) *m* waiter.
garçonete [gaxso'netʃi] (*BR*) *f* waitress.
garçonnière [gaxso'njɛ*] *f* love nest.
garçons [gax'sõʃ] *mpl de* **garçom**.
garfada [gax'fada] *f* forkful.
garfo ['gaxfu] *m* fork; **ser um bom ~** (*fig*) to enjoy one's food.
gargalhada [gaxga'ʎada] *f* burst of laughter; **rir às ~s** to roar with laughter; **dar** *ou* **soltar uma ~** to burst out laughing; **~ homérica** guffaw.
gargalo [gax'galu] *m* (*tb fig*) bottleneck.
garganta [gax'gãta] *f* (*ANAT*) throat; (*GEO*) gorge, ravine ♦ *m/f* (*col*) braggart, loudmouth ♦ *adj* (*col*) loudmouth(ed); **limpar a ~** to clear one's throat; **molhar a ~** (*col*) to wet one's whistle; **aquilo não me passou pela ~** (*fig*) that stuck in my craw.
gargantilha [gaxgã'tʃiʎa] *f* choker.
gargarejar [gaxgare'ʒa*] *vi* to gargle.
gargarejo [gaxga'reʒu] *m* (*ato*) gargling; (*líquido*) gargle.
gari ['gari] *m/f* (*na rua*) roadsweeper (*BRIT*), streetsweeper (*US*); (*lixeiro*) dustman (*BRIT*), garbage man (*US*).
garimpar [garĩ'pa*] *vi* to prospect.
garimpeiro [garĩ'pejru] *m* prospector.
garoa [ga'roa] *f* drizzle.
garoar [ga'rwa*] *vi* to drizzle.
garota [ga'rota] (*BR*: *col*) *f* (*cerveja*) beer; *V tb* **garoto**.
garotada [garo'tada] *f*: **a ~** the kids *pl*.
garota-de-programa (*pl* **garotas-de-programa**) (*col*) *f* good-time girl.
garoto/a [ga'rotu/a] *m/f* boy/girl; (*namorado*) boyfriend/girlfriend; (*PT*: *café*) coffee with milk.
garoto/a-propaganda (*pl* **garotos/as-**

propaganda) *m/f* publicity boy/girl.

garoupa [ga'ropa] *f* (*peixe*) grouper.

garra ['gaxa] *f* claw; (*de ave*) talon; (*fig*: *entusiasmo*) enthusiasm, drive; **~s** *fpl* (*fig*) clutches.

garrafa [ga'xafa] *f* bottle; **~ térmica** (*BR*) Thermos flask ®.

garrafada [gaxa'fada] *f*: **dar uma ~ em alguém** to hit sb with a bottle.

garrafão [gaxa'fãw] (*pl* **-ões**) *m* flagon.

garrancho [ga'xãʃu] *m* scrawl.

garrido/a [ga'xidu/a] *adj* (*elegante*) smart; (*alegre*) lively; (*vistoso*) showy; (*gracioso*) pretty.

garrote [ga'xɔtʃi] *m* (*MED*) tourniquet; (*tortura*) garrote.

garupa [ga'rupa] *f* (*de cavalo*) hindquarters *pl*; (*de moto*) back seat; **andar na ~** (*de moto*) to ride pillion.

gás [gajʃ] *m* gas; **gases** *mpl* (*do intestino*) wind *sg*; **~ lacrimogêneo** tear gas; **~ natural** natural gas.

gaseificar [gazejfi'ka*] *vt* to vapourize (*BRIT*), vaporize (*US*); **~-se** *vr* to vapo(u)rize.

gasoduto [gazo'dutu] *m* gas pipeline.

gasóleo [ga'zɔlju] *m* diesel oil.

gasolina [gazo'lina] *f* petrol (*BRIT*), gas(oline) (*US*).

gasômetro [ga'zometru] *m* gasometer.

gasosa [ga'zɔza] *f* fizzy drink, soda pop (*US*).

gasoso/a [ga'zozu/ɔza] *adj* (*QUÍM*) gaseous; (*água*) sparkling; (*bebida*) fizzy.

gáspea ['gaʃpja] *f* (*de sapato*) upper.

gastador/deira [gaʃta'do*/'dejra] *adj*, *m/f* spendthrift.

gastar [gaʃ'ta*] *vt* (*dinheiro, tempo*) to spend; (*gasolina, electricidade*) to use; (*roupa, sapato*) to wear out; (*salto, piso etc*) to wear down; (*saúde*) to damage; (*desperdiçar*) to waste ♦ *vi* to spend; to wear out; to wear down; **~-se** *vr* to wear out; to wear down.

gasto/a ['gaʃtu/a] *pp de* **gastar** ♦ *adj* (*dinheiro, tempo, energias*) spent; (*frase*) trite; (*sapato etc, fig*: *pessoa*) worn out; (*salto, piso*) worn down ♦ *m* (*despesa*) expense; **~s** *mpl* expenses, expenditure *sg*; **~s públicos** public spending *sg*; **dar para o ~** (*col*) to do, be OK.

gastrenterite [gaʃtrẽte'ritʃi] *f* (*MED*) gastroenteritis.

gástrico/a ['gaʃtriku/a] *adj* gastric.

gastrite [gaʃ'tritʃi] *f* (*MED*) gastritis.

gastronomia [gaʃtrono'mia] *f* gastronomy.

gastronômico/a [gaʃtro'nomiku/a] *adj* gastronomic.

gata ['gata] *f* (she-)cat; (*col*: *mulher*) sexy lady; **andar de ~s** (*PT*) to go on all fours; **~ borralheira** Cinderella; (*mulher*) stay-at-home.

gatão [ga'tãw] (*col*: *pl* **-ões**) *m* (*homem*) hunk.

gatilho [ga'tʃiʎu] *m* trigger.

gatinha [ga'tʃiɲa] (*col*) *f* (*mulher*) sexy lady.

gatinhas [ga'tʃiɲaʃ] *fpl*: **andar de ~** (*BR*) to go on all fours.

gato ['gatu] *m* cat; (*col*: *homem*) dish, hunk; **ter um ~** (*col*) to have kittens; **~ escaldado tem medo de água fria** once bitten, twice shy; **~ montês** wild cat.

gatões [ga'tõjʃ] *mpl de* **gatão.**

gatos-pingados *mpl* stalwarts.

gato-sapato *m*: **fazer alguém de ~** to walk all over sb, treat sb as a doormat.

GATT *abr m* (= *Acordo Geral sobre Tarifas Aduaneiras e Comércio*) GATT.

gatuno/a [ga'tunu/a] *adj* thieving ♦ *m/f* thief.

gaúcho/a [ga'uʃu/a] *adj* from Rio Grande do Sul ♦ *m/f* native of Rio Grande do Sul.

gaveta [ga'veta] *f* drawer.

gavetão [gave'tãw] (*pl* **-ões**) *m* big drawer.

gavião [ga'vjãw] (*pl* **-ões**) *m* hawk.

Gaza ['gaza] *f*: **a faixa de ~** the Gaza Strip.

gaza ['gaza] *f* gauze.

gaze ['gazi] *f* = **gaza**.

gazela [ga'zɛla] *f* gazelle.

gazeta [ga'zeta] *f* (*jornal*) newspaper, gazette; **fazer ~** to play truant.

gazua [ga'zua] *f* skeleton key.

GB *abr* (= *Guanabara*) *former state, now Rio de Janeiro*.

geada ['ʒjada] *f* frost.

geladeira [ʒela'dejra] (*BR*) *f* refrigerator, icebox (*US*).

gelado/a [ʒe'ladu/a] *adj* frozen ♦ *m* (*PT*: *sorvete*) ice cream.

gelar [ʒe'la*] *vt* to freeze; (*vinho etc*) to chill ♦ *vi* to freeze.

gelatina [ʒela'tʃina] *f* gelatine; (*sobremesa*) jelly (*BRIT*), jello (*US*).

gelatinoso/a [ʒelatʃi'nozu/ɔza] *adj* gooey.

geléia [ʒe'lɛja] *f* jam.

geleira [ʒe'lejra] *f* (*GEO*) glacier.

gélido/a ['ʒɛlidu/a] *adj* chill, icy.

gelo ['ʒelu] *adj inv* light grey (*BRIT*) *or* gray (*US*) ♦ *m* ice; (*cor*) light grey (*BRIT*) *or* gray (*US*); **quebrar o ~** (*fig*) to break the ice; **hoje está um ~** it's freezing today; **dar o ~ em alguém** (*col*) to give sb the cold shoulder.

gelo-seco *m* dry ice.

gema ['ʒɛma] *f* (*de ovo*) yolk; (*pedra preciosa*) gem; **ser da ~** to be genuine; **ela é paulista da ~** she's a real Paulista.

gemada [ʒe'mada] *f* eggnog.

gêmeo/a ['ʒemju/a] *adj*, *m/f* twin; **G~s** *mpl* (*ASTROLOGIA*) Gemini *sg*.

gemer [ʒe'me*] *vt* (*canção*) to croon ♦ *vi* (*de dor*) to groan, moan; (*lamentar-se*) to wail, howl; (*animal*) to whine; (*vento*) to howl.

gemido [ʒe'midu] *m* groan, moan; (*lamento*) wail; (*de animal*) whine.

gen. *abr* (= *general*) Gen.

gene ['ʒɛni] *m* gene.

genealogia [ʒenjalo'ʒia] *f* genealogy.

genealógico/a [ʒenja'lɔʒiku/a] *adj* genealogical; **árvore genealógica** family tree.

Genebra [ʒe'nɛbra] *n* Geneva.

genebra [ʒe'nɛbra] (*PT*) *f* gin.
general [ʒene'raw] (*pl* **-ais**) *m* (*MIL*) general.
generalidade [ʒenerali'dadʒi] *f* generality; (*maioria*) majority; **~s** *fpl* basics, principles.
generalização [ʒeneraliza'sãw] (*pl* **-ões**) *f* generalization.
generalizar [ʒenerali'za*] *vt* (*propagar*) to propagate ♦ *vi* to generalize; **~-se** *vr* to become general, spread.
genérico/a [ʒe'nɛriku/a] *adj* generic.
gênero ['ʒeneru] *m* (*espécie*) type, kind; (*LITERATURA*) genre; (*BIO*) genus; (*GRAMÁTICA*) gender; **~s** *mpl* goods; **~s alimentícios** foodstuffs; **~s de primeira necessidade** essentials; **~ de vida** way of life; **~ humano** humankind, human race; **essa roupa/ele não faz o meu ~** this outfit is not my style/he is not my type.
generosidade [ʒenerozi'dadʒi] *f* generosity.
generoso/a [ʒene'rozu/ɔza] *adj* generous.
gênese ['ʒenezi] *f* origin, beginning; **G~** (*REL*) Genesis.
genética [ʒe'nɛtʃika] *f* genetics *sg*.
genético/a [ʒe'nɛtʃiku/a] *adj* genetic.
gengibre [ʒẽ'ʒibri] *m* ginger.
gengiva [ʒẽ'ʒiva] *f* (*ANAT*) gum.
genial [ʒe'njaw] (*pl* **-ais**) *adj* inspired; (*idéia*) brilliant; (*col*) terrific, fantastic.
gênio ['ʒenju] *m* (*temperamento*) nature; (*irascibilidade*) temper; (*talento*, *pessoa*) genius; **de bom ~** good-natured; **de mau ~** bad-tempered; **um cientista de ~** a scientific genius, a genius at science.
genioso/a [ʒe'njozu/ɔza] *adj* bad-tempered.
genital [ʒeni'taw] (*pl* **-ais**) *adj* genital.
genitivo [ʒeni'tʃivu] *m* (*LING*) genitive.
genitora [ʒeni'tora] *f* mother.
genocídio [ʒeno'sidʒju] *m* genocide.
genro ['ʒẽxu] *m* son-in-law.
gentalha [ʒẽ'taʎa] *f* rabble.
gente ['ʒẽtʃi] *f* (*pessoas*) people *pl*; (*col*) folks *pl*; (*família*) folks *pl*, family; **a ~** (*nós*: *suj*) we; (: *obj*) us; **vai com a ~** come with us; **a casa da ~** our house; **toda a ~** everybody; **ficar ~** to grow up; **ser ~** (*ser alguém*) to be somebody; **também ser ~** (*col*) to be as good as anyone else; **ser ~ boa** *ou* **fina** (*col*) to be a nice person; **a ~ bem** the upper crust; **~ grande** grown-ups *pl*; **tem ~ batendo à porta** there's somebody knocking at the door; **oi/tchau, ~!** hi/bye, folks!; **~!** (*exprime admiração*, *surpresa*) gosh!
gentil [ʒẽ'tʃiw] (*pl* **-is**) *adj* kind.
gentileza [ʒẽtʃi'leza] *f* kindness; **por ~** if you please; **tenha a ~ de fazer ...?** would you be so kind as to do ...?
gentinha [ʒẽ'tʃiɲa] *f* rabble.
gentio/a [ʒẽ'tʃiu/a] *adj*, *m/f* heathen.
gentis [ʒe'tʃiʃ] *adj pl de* **gentil**.
genuflexão [ʒenuflek'sãw] (*pl* **-ões**) *f* (*REL*) genuflection.
genuíno/a [ʒe'nwinu/a] *adj* genuine.
geofísica [ʒeo'fizika] *f* geophysics *sg*.
geografia [ʒeogra'fia] *f* geography.
geográfico/a [ʒeo'grafiku/a] *adj* geographical.
geógrafo/a [ʒe'ɔgrafu/a] *m/f* geographer.
geologia [ʒeolo'ʒia] *f* geology.
geólogo/a [ʒe'ɔlogu/a] *m/f* geologist.
geometria [ʒeome'tria] *f* geometry.
geométrico/a [ʒeo'mɛtriku/a] *adj* geometrical.
geopolítico/a [ʒeopo'litʃiku/a] *adj* geopolitical.
Geórgia ['ʒɔxʒa] *f*: **a ~** Georgia.
georgiano/a [ʒox'ʒanu/a] *adj*, *m/f* Georgian.
geração [ʒera'sãw] (*pl* **-ões**) *f* (*tb*: *COMPUT*) generation; **linguagem de quarta ~** (*COMPUT*) fourth-generation language.
gerador(a) [ʒera'do*(a)] *adj*: **~ de algo** causing sth ♦ *m/f* (*produtor*) creator ♦ *m* (*TEC*) generator.
geral [ʒe'raw] (*pl* **-ais**) *adj* general ♦ *f* (*TEATRO*) gallery; (*revisão*) general overhaul; **dar uma ~ em algo** (*col*) to have a blitz on sth; **em ~** in general, generally; **de um modo ~** on the whole.
geralmente [ʒeraw'mẽtʃi] *adv* generally, usually.
gerânio [ʒe'ranju] *m* geranium.
gerar [ʒe'ra*] *vt* (*produzir*) to produce; (*filhos*) to beget; (*causar*: *ódios etc*) to engender, cause; (*eletricidade*) to generate.
gerativo/a [ʒera'tʃivu/a] *adj* generative.
gerência [ʒe'rẽsja] *f* management.
gerenciador [ʒerẽsja'do*] *m*: **~ de banco de dados** (*COMPUT*) database manager.
gerencial [ʒerẽ'sjaw] (*pl* **-ais**) *adj* management *atr*.
gerenciar [ʒerẽ'sja*] *vt*, *vi* to manage.
gerente [ʒe'rẽtʃi] *adj* managing ♦ *m/f* manager.
gergelim [ʒexʒe'lĩ] *m* (*BOT*) sesame.
geriatria [ʒerja'tria] *f* geriatrics *sg*.
geriátrico/a [ʒe'rjatriku/a] *adj* geriatric.
geringonça [ʒerĩ'gõsa] *f* contraption.
gerir [ʒe'ri*] *vt* to manage, run.
germânico/a [ʒex'maniku/a] *adj* Germanic.
germe ['ʒɛxmi] *m* (*embrião*) embryo; (*micróbio*) germ; (*fig*) origin; **o ~ de uma idéia** the germ of an idea.
germicida [ʒexmi'sida] *adj* germicidal ♦ *m* germicide.
germinação [ʒexmina'sãw] *f* germination.
germinar [ʒexmi'na*] *vi* (*semente*) to germinate; (*fig*) to develop.
gerontologia [ʒerõtolo'ʒia] *f* gerontology.
gerúndio [ʒe'rũdʒju] *m* (*LING*) gerund.
gesso ['ʒesu] *m* plaster (of Paris).
gestação [ʒeʃta'sãw] *f* gestation.
gestante [ʒeʃ'tãtʃi] *f* pregnant woman.

gestão [ʒeʃ'tãw] *f* management.
gesticular [ʒeʃtʃiku'la*] *vi* to make gestures, gesture ♦ *vt*: ~ **um adeus** to wave goodbye.
gesto ['ʒɛʃtu] *m* gesture; **fazer ~s** to gesture.
gibi [ʒi'bi] (*col*) *m* comic; **não estar no ~** (*fig*) to be incredible *ou* amazing.
Gibraltar [ʒibraw'ta*[*f* Gibraltar.
gigante/a [ʒi'gãtʃi] *adj* gigantic, huge ♦ *m* giant.
gigantesco/a [ʒigã'teʃku/a] *adj* gigantic.
gigolô [ʒigo'lo] *m* gigolo.
gilete [ʒi'lɛtʃi] (*BR*) *f* (*lâmina*) razor blade; (*col*) bisexual, bi.
gim [ʒĩ] (*pl* **-ns**) *m* gin.
ginásio [ʒi'nazju] *m* (*para ginástica*) gymnasium; (*escola*) secondary (*BRIT*) *ou* high (*US*) school.
ginasta [ʒi'naʃta] *m/f* gymnast.
ginástica [ʒi'naʃtʃika] *f* (*competitiva*) gymnastics *sg*; (*para fortalecer o corpo*) keep-fit.
ginecologia [ʒinekolo'ʒia] *f* gynaecology (*BRIT*), gynecology (*US*).
ginecologista [ʒinekolo'ʒiʃta] *m/f* gynaecologist (*BRIT*), gynecologist (*US*).
ginete [ʒi'netʃi] *m* thoroughbred.
gingar [ʒĩ'ga*] *vi* to sway.
ginja ['ʒĩʒa] (*PT*) *f* morello cherry.
ginjinha [ʒĩ'ʒiɲa] (*PT*) *f* cherry brandy.
gins [ʒĩʃ] *mpl de* **gim**.
gira ['ʒira] *adj* crazy.
gira-discos (*PT*) *m inv* record-player.
girafa [ʒi'rafa] *f* giraffe; (*col*: *pessoa*) giant.
girar [ʒi'ra*] *vt* to turn, rotate; (*como pião*) to spin ♦ *vi* to go round; to spin; (*vaguear*) to wander; **ele não gira bem** (*col*) he's not all there.
girassol [ʒira'sɔw] (*pl* **-óis**) *m* sunflower.
giratório/a [ʒira'tɔrju/a] *adj* revolving; (*cadeira*) swivel *atr*.
gíria ['ʒirja] *f* (*calão*) slang; (*jargão*) jargon.
giro ['ʒiru] *etc vb V* **gerir** ♦ *m* turn; **dar um ~** to go for a wander; (*em veículo*) to go for a spin; **que ~!** (*PT*) terrific!
giz [ʒiʒ] *m* chalk.
glacê [gla'se] *m* icing.
glacial [gla'sjaw] (*pl* **-ais**) *adj* icy.
gladiador [gladʒja'do*] *m* gladiator.
glamouroso/a [glamu'rozu/ɔza] *adj* glamorous.
glândula ['glãdula] *f* gland; ~ **endócrina** endocrine (gland).
glandular [glãdu'la*] *adj* glandular.
gleba ['glɛba] *f* field.
glicerina [glise'rina] *f* glycerine.
glicose [gli'kɔzi] *f* glucose.
global [glo'baw] (*pl* **-ais**) *adj* (*da terra*) global; (*total*) overall; **quantia ~** lump sum.
globo ['globu] *m* globe; ~ **ocular** eyeball.
globular [globu'la*] *adj* (*forma*) rounded.
glóbulo ['glɔbulu] *m* (*tb*: ~ *sanguíneo*) corpuscle.
glória ['glorja] *f* glory.
gloriar-se [glo'rjaxsi] *vr*: ~ **de** to boast of.
glorificar [glorifi'ka*] *vt* to glorify.
glorioso/a [glo'rjozu/ɔza] *adj* glorious.
glosa ['glɔza] *f* comment.
glosar [glo'za*] *vt* to comment on; (*conta*) to cancel.
glossário [glo'sarju] *m* glossary.
glote ['glɔtʃi] *f* (*ANAT*) glottis.
gluglu [glu'glu] *m* (*de peru*) gobble-gobble; (*de água*) glug-glug.
glutão/tona [glu'tãw/tɔna] (*pl* **-ões/~s**) *adj* greedy ♦ *m/f* glutton.
glúten ['glutẽ] (*pl* **~s**) *m* gluten.
glutões [glu'tõjʃ] *mpl de* **glutão**.
glutona [glu'tɔna] *f de* **glutão**.
gnomo ['gnomu] *m* gnome.
GO *abr* = **Goiás**.
Goa ['goa] *n* Goa.
godê [go'de] *adj* (*saia*) flared.
goela ['gwɛla] *f* throat.
goela-de-pato (*pl* **goelas-de-pato**) *f* (*CULIN*) pasta strand.
gogó [go'gɔ] (*col*) *m* Adam's apple.
goiaba [go'jaba] *f* guava.
goiabada [goja'bada] *f* guava jelly.
goiabeira [goja'bejra] *f* guava tree.
goian(i)ense [goja'n(j)ẽsi] *adj* from Goiânia ♦ *m/f* native of Goiânia.
goiano/a [go'janu/a] *adj* from Goiás ♦ *m/f* native of Goiás.
gol [gow] (*pl* **~s**) *m* goal; **marcar um ~** to score a goal.
gola ['gɔla] *f* collar; ~ **rulê** polo neck.
golaço [go'lasu] *m* (*FUTEBOL*) great goal.
Golan [go'lã] *m*: **as colinas de ~** the Golan heights.
gole ['gɔli] *m* gulp, swallow; (*pequeno*) sip; **de um só ~** at one gulp; **dar um ~** to have a sip.
goleada [go'ljada] *f* (*FUTEBOL*) convincing win.
golear [go'lja*] *vt* to thrash ♦ *vi* to win convincingly.
goleiro [go'lejru] (*BR*) *m* goalkeeper.
golfada [gow'fada] *f* (*jacto*) spurt.
golfar [gow'fa*] *vt* (*vomitar*) to spit up; (*lançar*) to throw out ♦ *vi* (*sair*) to spurt out; (*bebê*) to bring up some milk.
golfe ['gowfi] *m* golf; **campo de ~** golf course.
golfinho [gow'fiɲu] *m* (*ZOOL*) dolphin.
golfista [gow'fiʃta] *m/f* golfer.
golfo ['gowfu] *m* gulf.
golinho [go'liɲu] *m* sip; **beber algo aos ~s** to sip sth.
golo ['golu] (*PT*) *m* = **gol**.
golpe ['gɔwpi] *m* (*tb moral*) blow; (*de mão*) smack; (*de punho*) punch; (*manobra*) ploy; **de um só ~** at a stroke; **dar um ~ em alguém** (*golpear*) to hit sb; (*fig*: *trapacear*) to trick sb; **o ~ é fazer ...** the clever thing is to do ...; **dar o ~ do baú** (*fig*) to marry for money; ~ **baixo** (*fig*, *col*) dirty trick; ~ **(de estado)** coup (d'état); ~ **de mestre** masterstroke; ~ **de vento** gust of wind; ~ **de vista** (*olhar*) glance; (*de motorista*) eye

for distances; ~ **mortal** death blow.

golpear [gow'pja*] *vt* (*tb fig*) to hit; (*com navalha*) to stab; (*com o punho*) to punch.

golpista [gow'piʃta] *adj* tricky.

golquíper [gow'kipe*] *m* goalkeeper.

goma ['gɔma] *f* (*cola*) gum, glue; (*de roupa*) starch; ~ **de mascar** chewing gum.

gomo ['gomu] *m* (*de laranja*) slice.

gôndola ['gõdola] *f* (NÁUT) gondola; (*em supermercado*) rack.

gondoleiro [gõdo'lejru] *m* gondolier.

gongo ['gõgu] *m* (MÚS) gong; (*sineta*) bell.

gonorréia [gono'xɛja] *f* (MED) gonorrhea.

gonzo ['gõzu] *m* hinge.

gorar [go'ra*] *vt* to frustrate, thwart ♦ *vi* (*plano*) to fail, go wrong.

gordo/a ['goxdu/a] *adj* (*pessoa*) fat; (*gordurento*) greasy; (*carne*) fatty; (*fig*: *quantia*) considerable, ample ♦ *m/f* fat man/woman; **nunca vi mais** ~ (*col*) I've never seen him (*ou* her, them *etc*) before in my life.

gorducho/a [gox'duʃu/a] *adj* plump, tubby ♦ *m/f* plump person.

gordura [gox'dura] *f* fat; (*derretida*) grease; (*obesidade*) fatness.

gordurento/a [goxdu'rẽtu/a] *adj* (*ensebado*) greasy; (*gordo*) fatty.

gorduroso/a [goxdu'rozu/ɔza] *adj* (*pele*) greasy, oily; (*comida*) fatty, greasy; (*mãos*) greasy.

gorgolejar [goxgole'ʒa*] *vi* to gurgle.

gorila [go'rila] *m* gorilla.

gorjear [gox'ʒja*] *vi* to chirp, twitter.

gorjeio [gox'ʒeju] *m* twittering, chirping.

gorjeta [gox'ʒeta] *f* tip, gratuity.

gororoba [goro'rɔba] (*col*) *f* (*comida*) grub; (*comida ruim*) muck.

gorro ['goxu] *m* cap; (*de lã*) hat.

gosma ['gɔʒma] *f* spittle; (*fig*) slime.

gosmento/a [goʒ'mẽtu/a] *adj* slimy.

gostar [goʃ'ta*] *vi*: ~ **de** to like; (*férias, viagem etc*) to enjoy; **~-se** *vr* to like each other; ~ **de fazer algo** to like *ou* enjoy doing sth; **eu ~ia de ir** I would like to go; **gosto de sua companhia** I enjoy your company; **gosto de nadar** I like *ou* enjoy swimming; **gostei muito de falar com você** it was very nice talking to you; ~ **mais de** ... to prefer ..., to like ... better.

gosto ['goʃtu] *m* taste; (*prazer*) pleasure; **falta de** ~ lack of taste; **a seu** ~ to your liking; **com** ~ willingly; (*vestir-se*) tastefully; (*comer*) heartily; **de bom/mau** ~ in good/bad taste; **para o meu** ~ for my liking; **ter** ~ **de** to taste of; **tenho muito** ~ **em** ... it gives me a lot of pleasure to ...; **tomar** ~ **por** to take a liking to.

gostosão/sona [goʃto'zaw/'zɔna] (*col*: *pl* **-ões/~s**) *m/f* stunner.

gostoso/a [goʃ'tozu/ɔza] *adj* (*comida*) tasty; (*ambiente*) pleasant; (*cheiro*) lovely; (*risada*) good; (*col*: *pessoa*) gorgeous ♦ *m/f* (*col*) cracker; **é** ~ **viajar** it's really nice to travel.

gostosões [goʃto'zõjʃ] *mpl de* **gostosão**.

gostosona [goʃto'zɔna] *f de* **gostosão**.

gostosura [goʃto'zura] *f*: **ser uma** ~ (*comida*) to be delicious; (*bebê, jogo etc*) to be lovely.

gota ['gota] *f* drop; (*de suor*) bead; (MED) gout; ~ **a** ~ drop by drop; **ser a** ~ **d'água** *ou* **a última** ~ (*fig*) to be the last straw; **ser uma** ~ **d'água no oceano** (*fig*) to be a drop in the ocean.

goteira [go'tejra] *f* (*cano*) gutter; (*buraco*) leak.

gotejante [gote'ʒãtʃi] *adj* dripping.

gotejar [gote'ʒa*] *vt* to drip ♦ *vi* to drip; (*telhado*) to leak.

gótico/a ['gɔtʃiku/a] *adj* Gothic.

gotícula [go'tʃikula] *f* droplet.

gourmet [gux'me] (*pl* **~s**) *m/f* gourmet.

governador(a) [govexnado*(a)] *m/f* governor.

governamental [govexnamẽ'taw] (*pl* **-ais**) *adj* government *atr*.

governanta [govex'nãta] *f* (*de casa*) housekeeper; (*de criança*) governess.

governante [govex'nãtʃi] *adj* ruling ♦ *m/f* ruler ♦ *f* governess.

governar [govex'na*] *vt* (POL) to govern, rule; (*barco*) to steer.

governista [govex'niʃta] *adj* pro-government ♦ *m/f* government supporter.

governo [go'vexnu] *m* government; (*controle*) control; (NÁUT) steering; **para o seu** ~ (*col*) for the record, for your information.

gozação [goza'sãw] (*pl* **-ões**) *f* (*desfrute*) enjoyment; (*zombaria*) teasing; (*uma* ~) joke.

gozada [go'zada] *f*: **dar uma** ~ **em alguém** to pull sb's leg.

gozado/a [go'zadu/a] *adj* funny; (*estranho*) strange, odd.

gozador(a) [goza'do*(a)] *adj* (*caçoador*) comical; (*boa-vida*) happy-go-lucky ♦ *m/f* joker; loafer.

gozar [go'za*] *vt* to enjoy; (*col*: *rir de*) to make fun of ♦ *vi* to enjoy o.s.; (*ao fazer sexo*) to have an orgasm; ~ **de** to enjoy; to make fun of.

gozo ['gozu] *m* (*prazer*) pleasure; (*uso*) enjoyment, use; (*orgasmo*) orgasm; **estar em pleno** ~ **de suas faculdades mentais** to be in full possession of one's faculties; **ser um** ~ (*ser engraçado*) to be a laugh.

G/P *abr* (COM) = **ganhos e perdas**.

gr. *abr* = **grátis**; (= *grau*) deg.; (= *gross*) gr.

Grã-Bretanha [grã-bre'taɲa] *f* Great Britain.

graça ['grasa] *f* (REL) grace; (*charme*) charm; (*gracejo*) joke; (JUR) pardon; **de** ~ (*grátis*) for nothing; (*sem motivo*) for no reason; **sem** ~ dull, boring; **fazer** *ou* **ter** ~ to be funny;

NB: *European Portuguese adds the following consonants to certain words:* **b** (sú(b)dito, su(b)til); **c** (a(c)ção, a(c)cionista, a(c)to); **m** (inde(m)ne); **p** (ado(p)ção, ado(p)tar); *for further details see* *p. xiii.*

ficar sem ~ to be embarrassed; **~s a** thanks to; **não tem ~ fazer** (*é chato*) it's no fun to do; (*não é certo*) it's not right to do; **deixa de ~** don't be cheeky; **não sei que ~ você vê nele/nisso** I don't know what you see in him/it; **ser uma ~** to be lovely.

gracejar [grase'ʒa*] *vi* to joke.

gracejo [gra'seʒu] *m* joke.

gracinha [gra'siɲa] *f*: **ser uma ~** to be sweet *ou* cute; **que ~!** how sweet!

gracioso/a [gra'sjozu/ɔza] *adj* (*pessoa*) charming; (*gestos*) gracious.

gradação [grada'sãw] (*pl* **-ões**) *f* gradation.

gradativo/a [grada'tʃivu/a] *adj* gradual.

grade ['gradʒi] *f* (*no chão*) grating; (*grelha*) grill; (*na janela*) bars *pl*; (*col*: *cadeia*) prison.

gradear [gra'dʒja*] *vt* (*janela*) to put bars up at; (*jardim*) to fence off.

grado/a ['gradu/a] *adj* (*importante*) important ♦ *m*: **de bom/mau ~** willingly/unwillingly.

graduação [gradwa'sãw] (*pl* **-ões**) *f* gradation; (*classificação*) grading; (*EDUC*) graduation; (*MIL*) rank; **curso de ~** degree course.

graduado/a [gra'dwadu/a] *adj* (*dividido em graus*) graduated; (*diplomado*) graduate; (*eminente*) highly thought of.

gradual [gra'dwaw] (*pl* **-ais**) *adj* gradual.

graduando/a [gra'dwandu/a] *m/f* graduating student, graduand.

graduar [gra'dwa*] *vt* (*termômetro*) to graduate; (*classificar*) to grade; (*luz, fogo*) to regulate; **~-se** *vr* to graduate; **~ alguém em algo** (*EDUC*) to confer a degree in sth on sb; **~ alguém em coronel** *etc* (*MIL*) to make sb a colonel *etc*.

graduável [gra'dwavew] (*pl* **-eis**) *adj* adjustable.

grafia [gra'fia] *f* (*escrita*) writing; (*ortografia*) spelling.

gráfica ['grafika] *f* (*arte*) graphics *sg*; (*estabelecimento*) printer's; (*seção*: *de jornal etc*) production department; *V tb* **gráfico**.

gráfico/a ['grafiku/a] *adj* graphic ♦ *m/f* printer ♦ *m* (*MAT*) graph; (*diagrama*) diagram, chart; **~s** *mpl* (*COMPUT*) graphics; **~ de barras** bar chart.

grã-finagem [grãfi'naʒẽ] *f*: **a ~** the upper crust.

grã-finismo [grãfi'niʒmu] *m* (*qualidade*) poshness; (*ato*) thing which posh people do; **o ~** (*pessoas*) the upper crust.

grã-fino/a [grã-] *adj* posh ♦ *m/f* nob, toff.

grafite [gra'fitʃi] *f* (*lápis*) lead; (*pichação*) (piece of) graffiti.

grafologia [grafolo'ʒia] *f* graphology.

grama ['grama] *m* (*peso*) gramme ♦ *f* (*BR*: *capim*) grass.

gramado [gra'madu] (*BR*) *m* lawn; (*FUTEBOL*) pitch.

gramar [gra'ma*] *vt* to plant *ou* sow with grass; (*PT*: *col*) to be fond of ♦ *vi* (*PT*: *col*) to cry out.

gramática [gra'matʃika] *f* grammar; *V tb* **gramático**.

gramatical [gramatʃi'kaw] (*pl* **-ais**) *adj* grammatical.

gramático/a [gra'matʃiku/a] *adj* grammatical ♦ *m/f* grammarian.

gramofone [gramo'fɔni] *m* gramophone.

grampeador [grãpja'do*] *m* stapler.

grampear [grã'pja*] *vt* to staple; (*BR*: *TEL*) to tap; (*col*: *prender*) to nick.

grampo ['grãpu] *m* staple; (*no cabelo*) hairgrip; (*de carpinteiro*) clamp; (*de chapéu*) hatpin.

grana ['grana] (*col*) *f* cash.

Granada [gra'nada] *f* Grenada.

granada [gra'nada] *f* (*MIL*) shell; (*pedra*) garnet; **~ de mão** hand grenade.

grandalhão/lhona [grãda'ʎãw/'ʎɔna] (*pl* **-ões/~s**) *adj* enormous.

grandão/dona [grã'dãw/'dɔna] (*pl* **-ões/~s**) *adj* huge.

grande ['grãdʒi] *adj* big, large; (*alto*) tall; (*notável, intenso*) great; (*longo*) long; (*adulto*) grown-up; **mulher ~** big woman; **~ mulher** great woman; **a G~ Londres** Greater London.

grandessíssimo/a [grãdʒi'sisimu/a] *adj superl de* **grande**.

grandeza [grã'deza] *f* (*tamanho*) size; (*fig*) greatness; (*ostentação*) grandeur; **ter mania de ~** to have delusions of grandeur.

grandiloqüente [grãdʒilo'kwẽtʃi] *adj* grandiloquent.

grandiosidade [grãdʒjozi'dadʒi] *f* grandeur, magnificence.

grandioso/a [grã'dʒjozu/ɔza] *adj* magnificent, grand.

grandíssimo/a [grã'dʒisimu/a] *adj superl de* **grande**.

grandões [grã'dõjʃ] *mpl de* **grandão**.

grandona [grã'dɔna] *f de* **grandão**.

granel [gra'nɛw] *m*: **a ~** (*COM*) in bulk; **compra a ~** bulk buying.

granfa ['grãfa] (*col*) *adj* posh ♦ *m/f* nob, toff.

granito [gra'nitu] *m* (*GEO*) granite.

granizo [gra'nizu] *m* hail; **chover ~** to hail; **chuva de ~** hail.

granja ['grãʒa] *f* farm; (*de galinhas*) chicken farm.

granjear [gra'ʒja*] *vt* (*simpatia, amigos*) to win, gain; (*bens, fortuna*) to procure; **~ algo a** *ou* **para alguém** to win sb sth.

granulado/a [granu'ladu/a] *adj* grainy; (*açúcar*) granulated.

grânulo ['granulu] *m* granule.

grão ['grãw] (*pl* **~s**) *m* grain; (*semente*) seed; (*de café*) bean.

grão-de-bico (*pl* **grãos-de-bico**) *m* chick pea.

grapefruit [greip'frutʃi] (*pl* **~s**) *m* grapefruit.

grasnar [graʒ'na*] *vi* (*corvo*) to caw; (*pato*) to quack; (*rã*) to croak.

gratidão [gratʃi'dãw] *f* gratitude.

gratificação [gratʃifika'sãw] (*pl* **-ões**) *f*

(*gorjeta*) gratuity, tip; (*bônus*) bonus; (*recompensa*) reward.
gratificado/a [gratʃifi'kadu/a] *adj* (*grato*) grateful.
gratificante [gratʃifi'kãtʃi] *adj* rewarding.
gratificar [gratʃifi'ka*] *vt* (*dar gorjeta a*) to tip; (*dar bônus a*) to give a bonus to; (*recompensar*) to reward.
gratinado/a [gratʃi'nadu/a] *adj* (*CULIN*) au gratin ♦ *m* (*prato*) gratin; (*crosta*) crust.
grátis ['gratʃiʃ] *adj* free.
grato/a ['gratu/a] *adj* (*agradecido*) grateful; (*agradável*) pleasant; **ficar ~ a alguém por** to be grateful to sb for.
gratuidade [gratwi'dadʒi] *f* gratuity.
gratuito/a [gra'twitu/a] *adj* (*grátis*) free; (*infundado*) gratuitous.
grau [graw] *m* degree; (*nível*) level; (*EDUC*) class; **a temperatura é de 38 ~s** the temperature is 38 degrees; **primo/a em segundo ~** second cousin; **em alto ~** to a high degree; **primeiro/segundo ~** (*EDUC*) primary/secondary level; **ensino de primeiro/segundo ~** primary (*BRIT*) *ou* elementary (*US*)/secondary education; **estar no 1°/2° ~** (*EDUC*) to be at primary/secondary (*BRIT*) *ou* high (*US*) school.
graúdo/a [gra'udu/a] *adj* (*grande*) big; (*pessoa*: *influente*) important ♦ *m/f* bigwig.
gravação [grava'sãw] *f* (*em madeira*) carving; (*em disco, fita*) recording.
gravador(a) [grava'do*(a)] *m* tape recorder ♦ *m/f* engraver ♦ *f* (*empresa*) record company.
gravame [gra'vami] *m* (*imposto*) duty; (*JUR*) lien.
gravar [gra'va*] *vt* (*madeira*) to carve; (*metal, pedra*) to engrave; (*na memória*) to memorize; (*disco, fita*) to record; **~ algo/alguém com impostos** to mark sth up/burden sb with taxes; **aquele dia ficou gravado na minha mente/memória** that day remained fixed in my mind/memory.
gravata [gra'vata] *f* tie; **dar** *ou* **aplicar uma ~ em alguém** to get sb in a stranglehold; **~ borboleta** bow tie.
grave ['gravi] *adj* (*situação, falta*) serious, grave; (*doença*) serious; (*tom*) deep; (*LING*) grave.
gravemente [grave'mẽtʃi] *adv* (*doente, ferido*) seriously.
graveto [gra'vetu] *m* piece of kindling.
grávida ['gravida] *adj* pregnant.
gravidade [gravi'dadʒi] *f* (*FÍS*) gravity; (*de doença, situação*) seriousness.
gravidez [gravi'deʒ] *f* pregnancy; **~ tubária** ectopic pregnancy.
gravitação [gravita'sãw] *f* gravitation.
gravura [gra'vura] *f* (*em madeira*) engraving; (*estampa*) print.
graxa ['graʃa] *f* (*para sapatos*) polish; (*lubrificante*) grease.
Grécia ['grɛsja] *f*: **a ~** Greece.
grega ['grega] *f* (*galão*) braid; *V tb* **grego**.
gregário/a [gre'garju/a] *adj* gregarious.
grego/a ['gregu/a] *adj, m/f* Greek ♦ *m* (*LING*) Greek.
grei [grej] *f* flock.
grelar [gre'la*] *vt* to stare at.
grelha ['grɛʎa] *f* grill; (*de fornalha*) grate; **bife na ~** grilled steak.
grelhado/a [gre'ʎadu/a] *adj* grilled ♦ *m* (*prato*) grill.
grelhar [gre'ʎa*] *vt* to grill.
grêmio ['gremju] *m* (*associação*) guild; (*clube*) club.
grená [gre'na] *adj, m* dark red.
greta ['greta] *f* crack.
gretado/a [gre'tadu/a] *adj* cracked.
greve ['grɛvi] *f* strike; **fazer ~** to go on strike; **~ de fome** hunger strike; **~ branca** go-slow.
grevista [gre'viʃta] *m/f* striker.
grifado/a [gri'fadu/a] *adj* in italics.
grifar [gri'fa*] *vt* to italicize; (*sublinhar*) to underline; (*fig*) to emphasize.
griffe ['grifi] *m* designer label.
grifo ['grifu] *m* italics *pl*.
grilado/a [gri'ladu/a] (*col*) *adj* full of hang-ups; **estar ~ com algo** to be hung-up about sth.
grilar [gri'la*] (*col*) *vt*: **~ alguém** to get sb worked up; **~-se** *vr* to get worked up.
grilhão [gri'ʎãw] (*pl* **-ões**) *m* chain; **grilhões** *mpl* (*fig*) fetters.
grilo ['grilu] *m* cricket; (*AUTO*) squeak; (*col*: *de pessoa*) hang-up; **qual é o ~?** what's the matter?; **dar ~** (*col*) to cause problems; **se der ~** (*impess*) if there's a problem; **não tem ~!** (*col*) (there's) no problem!
grimpar [grĩ'pa*] *vi* to climb.
grinalda [gri'nawda] *f* garland.
gringada [grĩ'gada] *f* (*grupo*) bunch of foreigners; (*gringos*) foreigners *pl*.
gringo/a ['grĩgu/a] (*col*: *pej*) *m/f* foreigner.
gripado/a [gri'padu/a] *adj*: **estar/ficar ~** to have/get a cold.
gripar-se [gri'paxsi] *vr* to catch flu.
gripe ['gripi] *f* flu, influenza.
grisalho/a [gri'zaʎu/a] *adj* (*cabelo*) grey (*BRIT*), gray (*US*).
grita ['grita] *f* uproar.
gritante [gri'tãtʃi] *adj* glaring, gross, blatant; (*cor*) loud, garish.
gritar [gri'ta*] *vt* to shout, yell ♦ *vi* to shout; (*de dor, medo*) to scream; (*protestar*) to speak out; **~ com alguém** to shout at sb.
gritaria [grita'ria] *f* shouting, din.
grito ['gritu] *m* shout; (*de medo*) scream; (*de dor*) cry; (*de animal*) call; **dar um ~** to cry out; **falar/protestar aos ~s** to shout/shout protests; **no ~** (*col*) by force.

Groenlândia [grwẽ'lãdʒja] *f*: **a ~** Greenland.
grogue ['grɔgi] *adj* groggy.
groom [grũ] (*pl* **~s**) *m* groom.
grosa ['grɔza] *f* gross.
groselha [gro'zɛʎa] *f* (red)currant.
grosseiro/a [gro'sejru/a] *adj* (*pessoa, comentário*) rude; (*piada*) crude; (*modos*) coarse; (*tecido*) coarse, rough; (*móvel*) roughly-made.
grosseria [grose'ria] *f* rudeness; (*ato, dito*) rude thing; **fazer uma ~** to be rude; **dizer uma ~** to be rude, say something rude.
grosso/a ['grosu/'grɔsa] *adj* (*tamanho, consistência*) thick; (*áspero*) rough; (*voz*) deep; (*col: pessoa, piada*) rude ♦ *m*: **o ~ de** the bulk of ♦ *adv*: **falar ~** to talk in a deep voice; **falar ~ com alguém** (*fig*) to get tough with sb; **a ~ modo** roughly.
grossura [gro'sura] *f* thickness.
grotão [gro'tãw] (*pl* **-ões**) *m* gorge.
grotesco/a [gro'teʃku/a] *adj* grotesque.
grotões [gro'tõjʃ] *mpl de* **grotão**.
grua ['grua] *f* (MEC) crane.
grudado/a [gru'dadu/a] *adj* (*fig*): **ser ~ com** *ou* **em alguém** to be very attached to sb.
grudar [gru'da*] *vt* to glue, stick ♦ *vi* to stick.
grude ['grudʒi] *f* glue; (*col: comida*) grub; (*ligação entre pessoas*): **ficar numa ~** to cling to sb.
grudento/a [gru'dẽtu/a] *adj* sticky.
gruja ['gruʒa] (*col*) *f* tip.
grunhido [gru'ɲidu] *m* grunt.
grunhir [gru'ɲi*] *vi* (*porco*) to grunt; (*tigre*) to growl; (*resmungar*) to grumble.
grupo ['grupu] *m* group; (TEC) unit, set; **~ sanguíneo** blood group.
gruta ['gruta] *f* grotto.
guache ['gwaʃi] *m* gouache.
guapo/a ['gwapu/a] *adj* beautiful.
guaraná [gwara'na] *m* guarana; (*bebida*) *soft drink flavoured with guarana*.
guarani [gwara'ni] *adj, m/f* Guarani ♦ *m* (LING) Guarani; (*moeda*) guarani.
guarda ['gwaxda] *f* (*polícia*) policewoman; (*vigilância*) guarding; (*de objeto*) safekeeping; ♦ *m* (MIL) guard; (*polícia*) policeman; **estar de ~** to be on guard; **pôr-se em ~** to be on one's guard; **a velha ~** the old guard; **a G~ Civil** the Civil Guard.
guarda-chuva (*pl* **~s**) *m* umbrella.
guarda-civil (*pl* **guardas-civis**) *m* civil guard.
guarda-costas *m inv* (NÁUT) coastguard boat; (*capanga*) bodyguard.
guardador(a) [gwaxda'do*(a)] *m/f* car attendant.
guardados [gwax'daduʃ] *mpl* keepsakes, valuables.
guarda-florestal (*pl* **guardas-florestais**) *m/f* forest ranger.
guarda-fogo (*pl* **~s**) *m* fireguard.
guarda-louça [gwaxda-'losa] (*pl* **~s**) *m* sideboard.
guarda-marinha (*pl* **guardas-marinha(s)**) *m* naval ensign.
guarda-mor [-mɔ*] (*pl* **guardas-mores**) *m* inspector of customs.
guardamoria [gwaxdamo'ria] *f* customs authorities *pl*.
guarda-móveis *m inv* furniture storage warehouse.
guardanapo [gwaxda'napu] *m* napkin.
guarda-noturno (*pl* **guardas-noturnos**) *m* night watchman.
guardar [gwax'da*] *vt* (*pôr em algum lugar*) to put away; (*zelar por*) to guard; (*conservar; segredo*) to keep; (*vigiar*) to watch over; (*gravar na memória*) to remember; **~-se** *vr* (*defender-se*) to protect o.s.; **~-se de** (*acautelar-se*) to guard against; **~ silêncio** to keep quiet; **~ o lugar para alguém** to keep sb's seat; **vou ~ este resto de bolo para ele** I'll keep this last piece of cake for him.
guarda-redes (PT) *m inv* goalkeeper.
guarda-roupa (*pl* **~s**) *m* wardrobe.
guarda-sol (*pl* **-óis**) *m* sunshade, parasol.
guardião/diã [gwax'dʒjãw/'dʒjã] (*pl* **-ães** *ou* **-ões/~s**) *m/f* guardian.
guarida [gwa'rida] *f* refuge.
guarita [gwa'rita] *f* (*casinha*) sentry box; (*torre*) watch tower.
guarnecer [gwaxne'se*] *vt* (MIL: *fronteira*) to garrison; (*comida*) to garnish; (NÁUT: *tripular*) to crew; **~ alguém (de algo)** to equip sb (with sth); **~ a despensa** *etc* **(de algo)** to stock the pantry *etc* (with sth).
guarnição [gwaxni'sãw] (*pl* **-ões**) *f* (MIL) garrison; (NÁUT) crew; (CULIN) garnish.
Guatemala [gwate'mala] *f*: **a ~** Guatemala.
guatemalteco/a [gwatemaw'tɛku/a] *adj, m/f* Guatemalan.
gude ['gudʒi] *m*: **bola de ~** marble; (*jogo*) marbles *pl*.
gueixa ['gejʃa] *f* geisha.
guelra ['gɛwxa] *f* (*de peixe*) gill.
guerra ['gɛxa] *f* war; **em ~** at war; **declarar ~ (a alguém)** to declare war (on sb); **estar em pé de ~ (com)** (*países, facções*) to be at war (with); (*vizinhos, casal*) to be at loggerheads (with); **fazer ~** to wage war; **~ atômica** *ou* **nuclear** nuclear war; **~ civil** civil war; **~ de nervos** war of nerves; **~ fria** cold war; **~ mundial** world war; **~ santa** holy war.
guerrear [ge'xja*] *vi* to wage war.
guerreiro/a [ge'xejru/a] *adj* (*espírito*) fighting; (*belicoso*) warlike ♦ *m* warrior.
guerrilha [ge'xiʎa] *f* (*luta*) guerrilla warfare; (*tropa*) guerrilla band.
guerrilhar [gexi'ʎa*] *vi* to engage in guerilla warfare.
guerrilheiro/a [gexi'ʎejru/a] *adj* guerrilla *atr* ♦ *m/f* guerrilla.
gueto ['getu] *m* ghetto.
guia ['gia] *f* (*orientação*) guidance; (COM) permit, bill of lading; (*formulário*) advice slip ♦ *m* (*livro*) guide(book) ♦ *m/f* (*pessoa*) guide; **para que lhe sirva de ~** as a guide.

Guiana ['gjana] *f*: **a ~** Guyana; **a ~ Francesa** French Guyana.
guiar [gja*] *vt* (*orientar*) to guide; (*AUTO*) to drive; (*cavalos*) to steer ♦ *vi* (*AUTO*) to drive; **~-se** *vr*: **~-se por** to go by.
guichê [gi'ʃe] *m* ticket window; (*em banco, repartição*) window, counter.
guidão [gi'dãw] (*pl* **-ões**) *m* = **guidom**.
guidom [gi'dõ] (*pl* **-ns**) *m* handlebar.
guilder [giw'de*] *m* guilder.
guilhotina [giʎo'tʃina] *f* guillotine.
guimba ['gĩba] (*col*) *f* (cigarette) butt.
guinada [gi'nada] *f* (*NÁUT*) lurch; (*virada*) swerve; **dar uma ~** (*com o carro*) to swerve; (*fig*: *governo etc*) to do a U-turn.
guinchar [gĩ'ʃa*] *vt* (*carro*) to tow.
guincho ['gĩʃu] *m* (*de animal, rodas*) squeal; (*de pessoa*) shriek.
guindar [gĩ'da*] *vt* to hoist, lift; (*fig*): **~ alguém a** to promote sb to.
guindaste [gĩ'daʃtʃi] *m* hoist, crane.
Guiné [gi'nɛ] *f*: **a ~** Guinea.
Guiné-Bissau [-bi'saw] *f*: **a ~** Guinea-Bissau.
guisa ['giza] *f*: **à ~ de** like, by way of.
guisado [gi'zadu] *m* stew.
guisar [gi'za*] *vt* to stew.
guitarra [gi'taxa] *f* (electric) guitar.
guitarrista [gita'xiʃta] *m/f* guitarist; (*col*) forger (*of money*).
guizo ['gizu] *m* bell.
gula ['gula] *f* gluttony, greed.
gulodice [gulo'dʒisi] *f* greed.
guloseima [gulo'zejma] *f* delicacy, titbit.
guloso/a [gu'lozu/ɔza] *adj* greedy.
gume ['gumi] *m* cutting edge; (*fig*) sharpness.
guri(a) [gu'ri(a)] *m/f* kid ♦ *f* (*namorada*) girlfriend.
gurizote [guri'zɔtʃi] *m* lad.
guru [gu'ru] *m/f* guru.
gustação [guʃta'sãw] *f* tasting.
gutural [gutu'raw] (*pl* **-ais**) *adj* guttural.

H

NB: initial H is usually silent in Portuguese.
H, h [a'ga] (*pl* **hs**) *m* H, h; **H de Henrique** H for Harry (*BRIT*) *ou* How (*US*).
há [a] *vb V* **haver**.
hã [ã] *excl*: **~!** aha!
habeas-corpus ['abjas-'kɔxpus] *m* habeas corpus.
hábil ['abiw] (*pl* **-eis**) *adj* (*competente*) competent, capable; (*com as mãos*) clever; (*astucioso, esperto*) clever, shrewd; (*sutil*) diplomatic; (*JUR*) qualified; **em tempo ~** in reasonable time.
habilidade [abili'dadʒi] *f* (*aptidão, competência*) skill, ability; (*astúcia, esperteza*) shrewdness; (*tato*) discretion; (*JUR*) qualification; **ele não teve a menor ~ com ela** (*tato*) he wasn't at all tactful with her; **ela não tem a menor ~ com crianças** (*jeito*) she's hopeless with children; **ter ~ manual** to be good with one's hands.
habilidoso/a [abili'dozu/ɔza] *adj* skilful (*BRIT*), skillful (*US*), clever.
habilitação [abilita'sãw] (*pl* **-ões**) *f* (*aptidão*) competence; (*ato*) qualification; (*JUR*) attestation; **habilitações** *fpl* (*conhecimentos*) qualifications *pl*.
habilitado/a [abili'tadu/a] *adj* qualified; (*manualmente*) skilled.
habilitar [abili'ta*] *vt* (*tornar apto*) to enable; (*dar direito a*) to qualify, entitle; (*preparar*) to prepare; (*JUR*) to qualify.
habitação [abita'sãw] (*pl* **-ões**) *f* dwelling, residence; (*POL*: *alojamento*) housing.
habitacional [abitasjo'naw] (*pl* **-ais**) *adj* housing *atr*.
habitações [abita'sõjʃ] *fpl de* **habitação**.
habitante [abi'tãtʃi] *m/f* inhabitant.
habitar [abi'ta*] *vt* (*viver em*) to live in; (*povoar*) to inhabit ♦ *vi* to live.
hábitat ['abitatʃi] *m* habitat.
habitável [abi'tavew] (*pl* **-eis**) *adj* (in)habitable.
hábito ['abitu] *m* habit; (*social*) custom; (*REL*: *traje*) habit; **adquirir/perder o ~ de (fazer) algo** to get into/out of the habit of (doing) sth; **ter o ~ de (fazer) algo** to be in the habit of (doing) sth; **por força do ~** by force of habit.
habituação [abitwa'sãw] *f* acclimatization (*BRIT*), acclimatation (*US*), adjustment.
habituado/a [abi'twadu/a] *adj*: **~ a (fazer) algo** used to (doing) sth.
habitual [abi'twaw] (*pl* **-ais**) *adj* usual.
habituar [abi'twa*] *vt*: **~ alguém a** to get sb used to, accustom sb to; **~-se** *vr*: **~-se a** to get used to.
habitué [abi'twe] *m* habitué.
hacker ['ake*] (*pl* **~s**) *m* (*COMPUT*) hacker.
hadoque [a'dɔki] *m* haddock.
Haia ['aja] *n* the Hague.
Haiti [aj'tʃi] *m*: **o ~** Haiti.
haitiano/a [aj'tʃjanu/a] *adj*, *m/f* Haitian.
haja ['aʒa] *etc vb V* **haver**.
hálito ['alitu] *m* breath; **mau ~** bad breath.
halitose [ali'tɔzi] *f* halitosis.
hall [xɔw] (*pl* **~s**) *m* hall; (*de teatro, hotel*) foyer; **~ de entrada** entrance hall.
halo ['alu] *m* halo.
haltere [aw'tɛri] *m* dumbbell.
halterofilismo [awterofi'liʒmu] *m* weight

***NB:** European Portuguese adds the following consonants to certain words:* **b** (sú(b)dito, su(b)til); **c** (a(c)ção, a(c)cionista, a(c)to); **m** (inde(m)ne); **p** (ado(p)ção, ado(p)tar); *for further details see p. xiii.*

lifting.

halterofilista [awterofi'liʃta] *m/f* weight lifter.

hambúrguer [ã'buxge*] *m* hamburger.

handicap [ãdʒi'kapi] *m* handicap.

hangar [ã'ga*] *m* hangar.

hão [ãw] *vb V* **haver**.

haras ['araʃ] *m inv* stud.

hardware ['xadwe*] *m* (COMPUT) hardware.

harém [a'rẽ] (*pl* **-ns**) *m* harem.

harmonia [axmo'nia] *f* harmony.

harmônica [ax'monika] *f* concertina.

harmonioso/a [axmo'njozu/ɔza] *adj* harmonious.

harmonizar [axmoni'za*] *vt* (MÚS) to harmonize; (*conciliar*): ~ **algo (com algo)** to reconcile sth with sth; **~-se** *vr*: **~(-se) (com algo)** (*idéias etc*) to coincide (with sth); (*pessoas*) to be in agreement (with sth); (*música*) to fit in (with sth); (*tapete*) to match (sth).

harpa ['axpa] *f* harp.

harpista [ax'piʃta] *m/f* harpist.

hasta ['aʃta] *f*: ~ **pública** auction.

haste ['aʃtʃi] *f* (*de bandeira*) flagpole; (TEC) shaft, rod; (BOT) stem.

hastear [aʃ'tʃja*] *vt* to raise, hoist.

Havaí [avaj'i] *m*: **o** ~ Hawaii.

havaiano/a [avaj'anu/a] *adj*, *m/f* Hawaiian ♦ *m* (LING) Hawaiian.

Havana [a'vana] *n* Havana.

havana [a'vana] *adj inv* light brown ♦ *m* (*charuto*) Havana cigar.

haver [a've*] *vb impess*: **há** (*sg*) there is; (*pl*) there are ♦ *vb aux*: **ele havia saido** he had left ♦ *m* (COM) credit; **~-se** *vr*: **~-se com alguém** to sort things out with sb; **~es** *mpl* property *sg*, possessions; (*riqueza*) wealth *sg*; **havia** (*sg*) there was; (*pl*) there were; **haja o que houver** come what may; **o que é que há?** what's the matter?; **o que é que houve?** what happened, what was that?; **não há como ...** there's no way to ...; **não há de quê** you're welcome, don't mention it; **o que há de novo?** what's new?; **o que há com ela?** what's up with her?; **há séculos/cinco dias que não o vejo** I haven't seen him for ages/five days; **há um ano que ela chegou** it's a year since she arrived; **há cinco dias (atrás)** five days ago; **você há de ver** you'll see; **quem ~ia de dizer que ...** who would have thought that ....

haxixe [a'ʃiʃi] *m* hashish.

hebraico/a [e'brajku/a] *adj*, *m/f* Hebrew ♦ *m* (LING) Hebrew.

hebreu/bréia [e'brew/'brɛja] *adj*, *m/f* Hebrew.

Hébridas ['ɛbridaʃ] *fpl*: **as (ilhas)** ~ the Hebrides.

hecatombe [eka'tõbi] *f* (*fig*) massacre.

hectare [ek'tari] *m* hectare.

hectograma [ekto'grama] *m* hectogram.

hectolitro [ekto'litru] *m* hectolitre (BRIT), hectoliter (US).

hediondo/a [e'dʒjõdu/a] *adj* (*repulsivo*) vile, revolting; (*crime*) heinous; (*horrendo*) hideous.

hedonista [edo'niʃta] *adj* hedonistic ♦ *m/f* hedonist.

hegemonia [eʒemo'nia] *f* hegemony.

hei [ej] *vb V* **haver**.

hein [ẽj] *excl* eh?; (*exprimindo indignação*) hmm.

hélice ['ɛlisi] *f* propeller.

helicóptero [eli'kɔpteru] *m* helicopter.

hélio ['ɛlju] *m* helium.

heliporto [eli'poxtu] *m* heliport.

Helsinque [ew'sĩki] *n* Helsinki.

hem [ẽj] *excl* = **hein**.

hematologia [ematolo'ʒia] *f* haematology (BRIT), hematology (US).

hematoma [ema'tɔma] *m* bruise.

hemisférico/a [emiʃ'fɛriku/a] *adj* hemispherical.

hemisfério [emiʃ'fɛrju] *m* hemisphere.

hemofilia [emofi'lia] *f* haemophilia (BRIT), hemophilia (US).

hemofílico/a [emo'filiku/a] *adj*, *m/f* haemophiliac (BRIT), hemophiliac (US).

hemoglobina [emoglo'bina] *f* haemoglobin (BRIT), hemoglobin (US).

hemograma [emo'grama] *m* blood count.

hemorragia [emoxa'ʒia] *f* haemorrhage (BRIT), hemorrhage (US); ~ **nasal** nosebleed.

hemorróidas [emo'xɔjdaʃ] *fpl* haemorrhoids (BRIT), hemorrhoids (US), piles.

hena ['ɛna] *f* henna.

henê [e'ne] *m* henna.

hepatite [epa'tʃitʃi] *f* hepatitis.

heptágono [ep'tagonu] *m* heptagon.

hera ['ɛra] *f* ivy.

heráldica [e'rawdʒika] *f* heraldry.

herança [e'rãsa] *f* inheritance; (*fig*) heritage.

herbáceo/a [ex'basju/a] *adj* herbaceous.

herbicida [exbi'sida] *m* weed-killer, herbicide.

herbívoro/a [ex'bivoru/a] *adj* herbivorous ♦ *m/f* herbivore.

herdade [ex'dadʒi] (PT) *f* large farm.

herdar [ex'da*] *vt*: ~ **algo (de)** to inherit sth (from); ~ **a** to bequeath to.

herdeiro/a [ex'dejru/a] *m/f* heir(ess).

hereditário/a [eredʒi'tarju/a] *adj* hereditary.

herege [e'reʒi] *m/f* heretic.

heresia [ere'zia] *f* heresy.

herético/a [e'rɛtʃiku/a] *adj* heretical.

hermafrodita [exmafro'dʒita] *m/f* hermaphrodite.

hermético/a [ex'mɛtʃiku/a] *adj* airtight; (*fig*) obscure, impenetrable.

hérnia ['ɛxnja] *f* hernia; ~ **de hiato** hiatus hernia.

herói [e'rɔj] *m* hero.

heróico/a [e'rɔjku/a] *adj* heroic.

heroína [ero'ina] *f* heroine; (*droga*) heroin.

heroismo [ero'iʒmu] *m* heroism.

herpes ['ɛxpiʃ] *m inv* herpes *sg*.

herpes-zoster [-'zɔʃte*] *m* (MED) shingles *sg*.

hertz ['ɛxtzi] *m inv* hertz.

hesitação [ezita'sãw] *f* (*pl* **-ões**) hesitation.
hesitante [ezi'tãtʃi] *adj* hesitant.
hesitar [ezi'ta*] *vi* to hesitate; ~ **em (fazer) algo** to hesitate in (doing) sth.
heterodoxo/a [etero'dɔksu/a] *adj* unorthodox.
heterogêneo/a [etero'ʒenju/a] *adj* heterogeneous.
heterônimo [ete'ronimu] *m* pen name, nom de plume.
heterossexual [eterosek'swaw] (*pl* **-ais**) *adj*, *m/f* heterosexual.
heterossexualidade [eterosekswali'dadʒi] *f* heterosexuality.
hexagonal [eksago'naw] (*pl* **-ais**) *adj* hexagonal.
hexágono [ek'sagonu] *m* hexagon.
hiato ['jatu] *m* hiatus.
hibernação [ibexna'sãw] *f* hibernation.
hibernar [ibex'na*] *vi* to hibernate.
hibisco [i'biʃku] *m* (BOT) hibiscus.
híbrido/a ['ibridu/a] *adj* hybrid.
hidramático/a [idra'matʃiku/a] *adj* (*mudança*) hydraulic; (*carro*) with hydraulic transmission.
hidratante [idra'tãtʃi] *adj* moisturizing ♦ *m* moisturizer.
hidratar [idra'ta*] *vt* to hydrate; (*pele*) to moisturize.
hidrato [i'dratu] *m*: ~ **de carbono** carbohydrate.
hidráulica [i'drawlika] *f* hydraulics *sg*.
hidráulico/a [i'drawliku/a] *adj* hydraulic; **força hidráulica** hydraulic power.
hidrelétrica [idre'lɛtrika] (PT: **-ct-**) *f* (*usina*) hydroelectric power station; (*empresa*) hydroelectric power company.
hidreletricidade [idreletrisi'dadʒi] (PT: **-ct-**) *f* hydroelectric power.
hidrelétrico/a [idre'lɛtriku/a] (PT: **-ct-**) *adj* hydroelectric.
hidro... [idru] *prefixo* hydro..., water... *atr*.
hidroavião [idrua'vjãw] (*pl* **-ões**) *m* seaplane.
hidrocarboneto [idrokaxbo'netu] *m* hydrocarbon.
hidrófilo/a [i'drɔfilu/a] *adj* absorbent; **algodão** ~ cotton wool (BRIT), absorbent cotton (US).
hidrofobia [idrofo'bia] *f* rabies *sg*.
hidrogênio [idro'ʒenju] *m* hydrogen.
hidroterapia [idrotera'pia] *f* hydrotherapy.
hidrovia [idro'via] *f* waterway.
hiena ['jena] *f* hyena.
hierarquia [jerax'kia] *f* hierarchy.
hierárquico/a [je'raxkiku/a] *adj* hierarchical.
hierarquizar [jeraxki'za*] *vt* to place in a hierarchy.
hieroglífico/a [jero'glifiku/a] *adj* hieroglyphic.
hieróglifo [je'rɔglifu] *m* hieroglyph(ic).
hífen ['ifẽ] (*pl* ~**s**) *m* hyphen.
higiene [i'ʒjeni] *f* hygiene; ~ **mental** (mental) rest.
higiênico/a [i'ʒjeniku/a] *adj* hygienic; (*pessoa*) clean; **papel** ~ toilet paper.
hilariante [ila'rjãtʃi] *adj* hilarious.
Himalaia [ima'laja] *m*: **o** ~ the Himalayas *pl*.
hímen ['imẽ] (*pl* ~**s**) *m* (ANAT) hymen.
hindi [ĩ'dʒi] *m* (LING) Hindi.
hindu [ĩ'du] *adj*, *m/f* Hindu; (*indiano*) Indian.
hinduismo [ĩ'dwiʒmu] *m* Hinduism.
hino ['inu] *m* hymn; ~ **nacional** national anthem.
hinterlândia [ĩtex'lãdʒja] *f* hinterland.
hiper... [ipe*] *prefixo* hyper...; (*col*) really.
hipérbole [i'pɛxboli] *f* hyperbole.
hipermercado [ipexmex'kadu] *m* hypermarket.
hipersensível [ipexsẽ'sivew] (*pl* **-eis**) *adj* hypersensitive.
hipertensão [ipextẽ'sãw] *f* high blood pressure.
hípico/a ['ipiku/a] *adj* riding *atr*; **clube** ~ riding club.
hipismo [i'piʒmu] *m* (*turfe*) horse racing; (*esporte*) (horse) riding.
hipnose [ip'nɔzi] *f* hypnosis.
hipnótico/a [ip'nɔtʃiku/a] *adj* hypnotic; (*substância*) sleep-inducing ♦ *m* sleeping drug.
hipnotismo [ipno'tʃiʒmu] *m* hypnotism.
hipnotizador(a) [ipnotʃizado*(a)] *m/f* hypnotist.
hipnotizar [ipnotʃi'za*] *vt* to hypnotize.
hipocondríaco/a [ipokõ'driaku/a] *adj*, *m/f* hypochondriac.
hipocrisia [ipokri'sia] *f* hypocrisy.
hipodérmico/a [ipo'dɛxmiku/a] *adj* hypodermic.
hipócrita [i'pɔkrita] *adj* hypocritical ♦ *m/f* hypocrite.
hipódromo [i'pɔdromu] *m* racecourse.
hipopótamo [ipo'pɔtamu] *m* hippopotamus.
hipoteca [ipo'tɛka] *f* mortgage.
hipotecar [ipote'ka*] *vt* to mortgage.
hipotecário/a [ipote'karju/a] *adj* mortgage *atr*; **credor/devedor** ~ mortgagee/mortgager.
hipotermia [ipotex'mia] *f* hypothermia.
hipótese [i'pɔtezi] *f* hypothesis; **na** ~ **de** in the event of; **em** ~ **alguma** under no circumstances; **na melhor/pior das** ~**s** at best/worst.
hipotético/a [ipo'tɛtʃiku/a] *adj* hypothetical.
hirsuto/a [ix'sutu/a] *adj* (*cabeludo*) hairy, hirsute; (*barba*) spiky; (*fig*: *ríspido*) harsh.
hirto/a ['ixtu/a] *adj* stiff, rigid; **ficar** ~ (*pessoa*) to stand stock still.
hispânico/a [iʃ'paniku/a] *adj* Hispanic.
hispanista [iʃpa'niʃta] *m/f* Hispanist.
hispano-americano/a [iʃ'pano-] *adj* Spanish American.
histamina [iʃta'mina] *f* histamine.
histerectomia [iʃterekto'mia] *f* hysterectomy.
histeria [iʃte'ria] *f* hysteria; ~ **coletiva** mass

***NB**: European Portuguese adds the following consonants to certain words:* **b** (sú(b)dito, su(b)til); **c** (a(c)ção, a(c)cionista, a(c)to); **m** (inde(m)ne); **p** (ado(p)ção, ado(p)tar); *for further details see p. xiii.*

hysteria.

histérico/a [iʃ'tɛriku/a] *adj* hysterical.

histerismo [iʃte'riʒmu] *m* hysteria.

história [iʃ'tɔrja] *f* (*estudo, ciência*) history; (*conto*) story; **~s** *fpl* (*chateação*) bother *sg*, fuss *sg*; **a mesma ~ de sempre** the same old story; **isso é outra ~** that's a different matter; **é tudo ~ dela** she's making it all up; **deixe de ~**! come off it!; **que ~ é essa**? what's going on?; **essa ~ de ...** (*col*: *troço*) this business of ...; **~ antiga/natural** ancient/natural history; **~ da carochinha** nursery story; **~ do arco-da-velha** apocryphal story; **~ em quadrinhos** comic strip.

historiador(a) [iʃtorja'do*(a)] *m/f* historian.

historiar [iʃto'rja*] *vt* to recount.

histórico/a [iʃ'tɔriku/a] *adj* (*personagem, pesquisa etc*) historical; (*fig*: *notável*) historic ♦ *m* history.

historieta [iʃto'rjeta] *f* anecdote, very short story.

histrionismo [iʃtrjo'niʒmu] *m* histrionics *pl*.

hobby ['xɔbi] (*pl* **-bies**) *m* hobby.

hodierno/a [o'dʒjɛxnu/a] *adj* today's, present.

hoje ['oʒi] *adv* today; (*atualmente*) now(adays); **~ à noite** tonight; **de ~ a uma semana** in a week's time; **de ~ em diante** from now on; **~ em dia** nowadays; **~ faz uma semana** a week ago today; **ainda ~** (before the end of) today; **de ~ para amanhã** in one day; **por ~ é só** that's all for today.

Holanda [o'lãda] *f*: **a ~** Holland.

holandês/esa [olã'deʃ/eza] *adj* Dutch ♦ *m/f* Dutchman/woman ♦ *m* (*LING*) Dutch.

holding ['xowdiŋ] (*pl* **~s**) *m* holding company.

holocausto [olo'kawʃtu] *m* holocaust.

holofote [olo'fɔtʃi] *m* searchlight; (*em campo de futebol etc*) floodlight.

holograma [olo'grama] *m* hologram.

homem ['omẽ] (*pl* **-ns**) *m* man; (*a humanidade*) mankind; **uma conversa de ~ para ~** a man-to-man talk; **ser o ~ da casa** (*fig*) to wear the trousers; **ser outro ~** (*fig*) to be a changed man; **~ da lei** lawyer; **~ da rua** man in the street; **~ de ação** man of action; **~ de bem** honest man; **~ de empresa** *ou* **negócios** businessman; **~ de estado** statesman; **~ de letras** man of letters; **~ de palavra** man of his word; **~ de peso** influential man; **~ de recursos** man of means; **~ público** public servant.

homem-feito (*pl* **homens-feitos**) *m* grown man.

homem-rã (*pl* **homens-rã(s)**) *m* frogman.

homem-sanduíche (*pl* **homens-sanduíche**) *m* sandwich board man.

homenageado/a [omena'ʒjadu/a] *adj* honoured (*BRIT*), honored (*US*) ♦ *m/f* person hono(u)red.

homenageante [omena'ʒjãtʃi] *adj* respectful.

homenagear [omena'ʒja*] *vt* (*pessoa*) to pay tribute to, honour (*BRIT*), honor (*US*).

homenagem [ome'naʒẽ] *f* tribute; (*REL*) homage; **prestar ~ a alguém** to pay tribute to sb; **em ~ a** in honour (*BRIT*) *ou* honor (*US*) of.

homenzarrão [omẽza'xãw] (*pl* **-ões**) *m* hulk (of a man).

homenzinho [omẽ'ziɲu] *m* little man; (*jovem*) young man.

homens ['omẽʃ] *mpl de* **homem**.

homeopata [omjo'pata] *m/f* homoeopath(ic doctor) (*BRIT*), homeopath(ic doctor) (*US*).

homeopatia [omjopa'tʃia] *f* homoeopathy (*BRIT*), homeopathy (*US*).

homeopático/a [omjo'patʃiku/a] *adj* homoeopathic (*BRIT*), homeopathic (*US*); (*fig*): **em doses homeopáticas** in tiny quantities.

homérico/a [o'mɛriku/a] *adj* (*fig*) phenomenal.

homicida [omi'sida] *adj* (*pessoa*) homicidal ♦ *m/f* murderer.

homicídio [omi'sidʒju] *m* murder; **~ involuntário** manslaughter.

homiziado/a [omi'zjadu/a] *adj* in hiding ♦ *m/f* fugitive.

homiziar [omi'zja*] *vt* (*esconder*) to hide; **~-se** *vr* to hide.

homogeneidade [omoʒenej'dadʒi] *f* homogeneity.

homogeneizado/a [omoʒenej'zadu/a] *adj V* **leite**.

homogêneo/a [omo'ʒenju/a] *adj* homogeneous; (*CULIN*) blended.

homologar [omolo'ga*] *vt* to ratify.

homólogo/a [o'mɔlogu/a] *adj* homologous; (*fig*) equivalent ♦ *m/f* opposite number.

homônimo [o'monimu] *m* (*de pessoa*) namesake; (*LING*) homonym.

homossexual [omosek'swal] (*pl* **-ais**) *adj, m/f* homosexual.

homossexualismo [omosekswa'liʒmu] *m* homosexuality.

Honduras [õ'duraʃ] *f* Honduras.

hondurenho/a [õdu'rɛɲu/a] *adj, m/f* Honduran.

honestidade [oneʃtʃi'dadʒi] *f* honesty; (*decência*) decency; (*justeza*) fairness.

honesto/a [o'nɛʃtu/a] *adj* honest; (*decente*) decent; (*justo*) fair, just.

Hong Kong [oŋ'koŋ] *f* Hong Kong.

honorário/a [ono'rarju/a] *adj* honorary.

honorários [ono'rarjuʃ] *mpl* fees.

honorífico/a [ono'rifiku/a] *adj* honorific.

honra ['õxa] *f* honour (*BRIT*), honor (*US*); **~s** *fpl* **fúnebres** funeral rites; **convidado de ~** guest of hono(u)r; **em ~ de** in hono(u)r of; **por ~ da firma** (*por obrigação*) out of a sense of duty; (*para salvar as aparências*) to save face; **fazer as ~s da casa** to do the hono(u)rs, attend to the guests.

honradez [õxa'deʒ] *f* honesty; (*de pessoa*) integrity.

honrado/a [õ'xadu/a] *adj* honest; (*respeitado*)

honourable (*BRIT*), honorable (*US*).

honrar [õ'xa*] *vt* to honour (*BRIT*), honor (*US*); **~-se** *vr*: **~-se em fazer** to be hono(u)red to do.

honraria [õxa'ria] *f* honour (*BRIT*), honor (*US*).

honroso/a [õ'xozu/ɔza] *adj* honourable (*BRIT*), honorable (*US*).

hóquei ['ɔkej] *m* hockey; **~ sobre gelo** ice hockey.

hora ['ɔra] *f* (*60 minutos*) hour; (*momento*) time; **a que ~s?** (at) what time?; **que ~s são?** what time is it?; **são duas ~s** it's two o'clock; **você tem as ~s?** have you got the time?; **isso são ~s?** what time do you call this?; **dar as ~s** (*relógio*) to strike the hour; **fazer ~** to kill time; **fazer ~ com alguém** (*col*) to tease sb; **marcar ~** to make an appointment; **perder a ~** to be late; **não vejo a ~ de ...** I can't wait to ...; **às altas ~s da noite** *ou* **da madrugada** in the small hours; **de ~ em ~** every hour; **em boa/má ~** at the right/wrong time; **chegar em cima da ~** to arrive just in time *ou* on the dot; **fora de ~** at the wrong moment; **na ~** (*no ato, em seguida*) on the spot; (*em boa hora*) at the right moment; (*na hora H*) at the moment of truth; **na ~ H** (*no momento certo*) in the nick of time; (*na hora crítica*) at the moment of truth, when it comes (*ou* came) to it; **está na ~ de ...** it's time to ...; **bem na ~** just in time; **chegar na ~** to be on time; **de última ~** *adj* last-minute ♦ *adv* at the last minute; **~ de dormir** bedtime; **meia ~** half an hour; **~ local** local time; **~s extras** overtime *sg*; **trabalhei 2 ~s extras** I worked 2 hours overtime; **você recebe por ~ extra?** do you get paid overtime?; **~s vagas** spare time *sg*.

horário/a [o'rarju/a] *adj*: **100 km ~s** 100 km an hour ♦ *m* (*tabela*) timetable; (*hora*) time; **~ de expediente** working hours *pl*; (*de um escritório*) office hours *pl*; **~ de verão** summer time; **~ integral** full time; **~ nobre** (*TV*) prime time.

horda ['ɔxda] *f* horde.

horista [o'riʃta] *adj* paid by the hour ♦ *m/f* hourly-paid worker.

horizontal [orizõ'taw] (*pl* **-ais**) *adj* horizontal ♦ *f*: **estar na ~** (*col*) to be lying down.

horizonte [ori'zõtʃi] *m* horizon.

hormonal [oxmo'naw] (*pl* **-ais**) *adj* hormonal.

hormônio [ox'monju] *m* hormone.

horóscopo [o'rɔʃkopu] *m* horoscope.

horrendo/a [o'xẽdu/a] *adj* horrendous, frightful.

horripilante [oxipi'lãtʃi] *adj* horrifying, hair-raising.

horripilar [oxipi'la*] *vt* to horrify; **~-se** *vr* to be horrified.

horrível [o'xivew] (*pl* **-eis**) *adj* awful, horrible.

horror [o'xo*] *m* horror; **que ~!** how awful!; **ser um ~** to be awful; **ter ~ a algo** to hate sth; **um ~ de** (*porção*) a lot of; **dizer/fazer ~es** to say/do terrible things; **~es de** (*muitos*) loads of; **ele está faturando ~es** he's raking it in, he's making a fortune.

horrorizar [oxori'za*] *vt* to horrify, frighten ♦ *vi*: **cenas de ~** horrifying scenes; **~-se** *vr* to be horrified.

horroroso/a [oxo'rozu/ɔza] *adj* horrible, ghastly.

horta ['ɔxta] *f* vegetable garden.

hortaliças [oxta'lisaʃ] *fpl* vegetables.

hortelã [oxte'lã] *f* mint; **~ pimenta** peppermint.

hortelão/loa [oxte'lãw/loa] (*pl* **~s** *ou* **-ões/~s**) (*PT*) *m/f* (market) gardener.

hortênsia [ox'tẽsja] *f* hydrangea.

horticultor(a) [oxtʃikuw'to*(a)] *m/f* market gardener (*BRIT*), truck farmer (*US*).

horticultura [oxtʃikuw'tura] *f* horticulture.

hortifrutigranjeiros [oxtʃifrutʃigrã'ʒejruʃ] *mpl* fruit and vegetables.

hortigranjeiros [oxtʃigrã'ʒejruʃ] *mpl* garden vegetables.

horto ['oxtu] *m* market garden (*BRIT*), truck farm (*US*).

hospedagem [oʃpe'daʒẽ] *f* lodging.

hospedar [oʃpe'da*] *vt* to put up, lodge; **~-se** *vr* to stay, lodge.

hospedaria [oʃpeda'ria] *f* inn.

hóspede ['ɔʃpedʒi] *m* (*amigo*) guest; (*estranho*) lodger.

hospedeira [oʃpe'dejra] *f* landlady; (*PT*: *de bordo*) stewardess, air hostess (*BRIT*).

hospedeiro/a [oʃpe'dejru/a] *adj* hospitable ♦ *m* (*dono*) landlord.

hospício [oʃ'pisju] *m* mental hospital.

hospital [oʃpi'taw] (*pl* **-ais**) *m* hospital.

hospitalar [oʃpita'la*] *adj* hospital *atr*.

hospitaleiro/a [oʃpita'lejru/a] *adj* hospitable.

hospitalidade [oʃpitali'dadʒi] *f* hospitality.

hospitalização [oʃpitaliza'sãw] (*pl* **-ões**) *f* hospitalization.

hospitalizar [oʃpitali'za*] *vt* to hospitalize, take to hospital.

hostess ['ɔʃtes] (*pl* **~es**) *f* hostess.

hóstia ['ɔʃtʃia] *f* Host, wafer.

hostil [oʃ'tʃiw] (*pl* **-is**) *adj* hostile.

hostilidade [oʃtʃili'dadʒi] *f* hostility.

hostilizar [oʃtʃili'za*] *vt* to antagonize; (*MIL*) to wage war on.

hostis [oʃ'tʃiʃ] *pl de* **hostil**.

hotel [o'tɛw] (*pl* **-éis**) *m* hotel; **~ de alta rotatividade** *motel for sexual encounters*.

hotelaria [otela'ria] *f* (*curso*) hotel management; (*conjunto de hotéis*) hotels *pl*.

hoteleiro/a [ote'lejru/a] *adj* hotel *atr* ♦ *m/f* hotelier; **rede hoteleira** hotel chain.

houve ['ovi] *etc vb V* **haver**.

NB: *European Portuguese adds the following consonants to certain words:* **b** (sú(b)dito, su(b)til); **c** (a(c)ção, a(c)cionista, a(c)to); **m** (inde(m)ne); **p** (ado(p)ção, ado(p)tar); *for further details see p. xiii.*

h(s). *abr* (= *hora(s)*) o'clock.
humanidade [umani'dadʒi] *f* (*os homens*) man(kind); (*compaixão*) humanity; **~s** *fpl* (*EDUC*) humanities.
hui [wi] *excl* (*de dor*) ow!; (*de susto, surpresa*) ah!; (*de repugnância*) ugh!
hum [ũ] *excl* hmm.
humanismo [uma'niʒmu] *m* humanism.
humanista [uma'niʃta] *adj, m/f* humanist.
humanitário/a [umani'tarju/a] *adj* humanitarian; (*benfeitor*) humane ♦ *m/f* humanitarian.
humanizar [umani'za*] *vt* to humanize; **~-se** *vr* to become more human.
humano/a [u'manu/a] *adj* human; (*bondoso*) humane.
humanos [u'manuʃ] *mpl* humans.
húmido/a (*PT*) *adj* = **úmido**.
humildade [umiw'dadʒi] *f* humility; (*pobreza*) humbleness.
humilde [u'miwdʒi] *adj* humble; (*pobre*) poor.
humildes [u'miwdʒiʃ] *m/fpl*: **os** (*ou* **as**) ~ the poor.
humilhação [umiʎa'sãw] *f* humiliation.
humilhante [umi'ʎãtʃi] *adj* humiliating.
humilhar [umi'ʎa*] *vt* to humiliate ♦ *vi* to be humiliating; **~-se** *vr* to humble o.s.
humor [u'mo*] *m* (*disposição*) mood, temper; (*graça*) humour (*BRIT*), humor (*US*); **de bom/mau** ~ in a good/bad mood.
humorismo [umo'riʒmu] *m* humour (*BRIT*), humor (*US*).
humorista [umo'riʃta] *m/f* (*escritor*) humorist; (*na TV, no palco*) comedian.
humorístico/a [umo'riʃtʃiku/a] *adj* humorous.
húmus ['umuʃ] *m inv* humus.
húngaro/a ['ũgaru/a] *adj, m/f* Hungarian.
Hungria [ũ'gria] *f*: **a** ~ Hungary.
hurra ['uxa] *m* cheer ♦ *excl* hurrah!
Hz *abr* (= *hertz*) Hz.

I

I, i [i:] (*pl* **is**) *m* I, i; **I de Irene** I for Isaac (*BRIT*) *ou* Item (*US*).
ia ['ia] *etc vb V* **ir**.
IAB *abr m* = **Instituto dos Advogados do Brasil; Instituto dos Arquitetos do Brasil**.
ialorixá [jalori'ʃa] *f* macumba priestess.
IAPAS (*BR*) *abr m* = **Instituto de Administração da Previdência e Assistência Social**.
iate ['jatʃi] *m* yacht; ~ **clube** yacht club.
iatista [ja'tʃiʃta] *m/f* yachtsman/woman.
iatismo [ja'tʃiʒmu] *m* yachting.
IBAM *abr m* = **Instituto Brasileiro de Administração Municipal**.
IBDF *abr m* = **Instituto Brasileiro de Desenvolvimento Florestal**.
ibérico/a [i'bɛriku/a] *adj, m/f* Iberian.
ibero/a [i'bɛru/a] *adj, m/f* Iberian.
ibero-americano/a [iberu-] *adj, m/f* Ibero-American.
IBGE *abr m* = **Instituto Brasileiro de Geografia e Estatística**.
IBMC *abr m* = **Instituto Brasileiro do Mercado de Capitais**.
Ibope [i'bɔpi] *abr m* = **Instituto Brasileiro de Opinião Pública e Estatística**; **dar i~** (*TV*) to get high ratings; (*fig*: *ser popular*) to be popular.
IBV *abr m* = **Índice da Bolsa de Valores (do Rio de Janeiro)**.
içar [i'sa*] *vt* to hoist, raise.
iceberg [ajs'bɛxgi] (*pl* **~s**) *m* iceberg.
ICM (*BR*) *abr m* (= *Imposto sobre Circulação de Mercadorias*) ≈ VAT.
ICM/S (*BR*) *abr m* (*Imposto sobre Circulação de Mercadorias e Serviços*) ≈ VAT.
icone ['ikoni] *m* icon.
iconoclasta [ikono'klaʃta] *adj* iconoclastic ♦ *m/f* iconoclast.
icterícia [ikte'risja] *f* jaundice.
ida ['ida] *f* going, departure; ~ **e volta** round trip, return; **a (viagem de)** ~ the outward journey; **na** ~ on the way there; **~s e vindas** comings and goings; **comprei só a** ~ I only bought a single *ou* one-way (*US*) (ticket).
idade [i'dadʒi] *f* age; **ter cinco anos de** ~ to be five (years old); **de meia** ~ middle-aged; **qual é a** ~ **dele**? how old is he?; **na minha** ~ at my age; **ser menor/maior de** ~ to be under/of age; **pessoa de** ~ elderly person; **estar na** ~ **de trabalhar** to be (of) working age; **já não estou mais em** ~ **de fazer** I'm past doing; ~ **atômica** atomic age; ~ **da pedra** Stone Age; **I~ Média** Middle Ages *pl*.
ideação [idea'sãw] (*pl* **-ões**) *f* conception.
ideal [ide'jaw] (*pl* **-ais**) *adj, m* ideal.
idealismo [idea'liʒmu] *m* idealism.
idealista [idea'liʃta] *m/f* idealist ♦ *adj* idealistic.
idealização [idealiza'sãw] (*pl* **-ões**) *f* idealization; (*planejamento*) creation.
idealizar [ideali'za*] *vt* to idealize; (*planejar*) to devise, create.
idear [ide'a*] *vt* (*imaginar*) to imagine, think up; (*idealizar*) to create.
ideário [i'dʒjarju] *m* ideas *pl*, thinking.
idéia [i'dɛja] *f* idea; (*mente*) mind; **mudar de** ~ to change one's mind; **não ter a mínima** ~ to have no idea; **não faço** ~ I can't imagine; **estar com** ~ **de fazer** to plan to do; **fazer uma** ~ **errada de algo** to get the wrong idea about sth; ~ **fixa** obsession; ~ **genial** brilliant idea.
idem ['idẽ] *pron* ditto.
idêntico/a [i'dẽtʃiku/a] *adj* identical.
identidade [idẽtʃi'dadʒi] *f* identity; **carteira de** ~ identity (*BRIT*) *ou* identification (*US*) card.
identificação [idẽtʃifika'sãw] *f* identification.

identificar [idẽtʃifi'ka*] *vt* to identify; **~-se** *vr*: **~-se com** to identify with.
ideologia [ideolo'ʒia] *f* ideology.
ideológico/a [ideo'lɔʒiku/a] *adj* ideological.
ideólogo/a [ide'ɔlogu/a] *m/f* ideologue.
ídiche ['idiʃi] *m* = **iídiche**.
idílico/a [i'dʒiliku/a] *adj* idyllic.
idílio [i'dʒilju] *m* idyll.
idioma [i'dʒɔma] *m* language.
idiomático/a [idʒo'matʃiku/a] *adj* idiomatic.
idiossincrasia [idʒosĩkra'zia] *f* character.
idiota [i'dʒɔta] *adj* idiotic ♦ *m/f* idiot.
idiotice [idʒo'tʃisi] *f* idiocy.
ido/a ['idu/a] *adj* past.
idólatra [i'dɔlatra] *adj* idolatrous ♦ *m/f* idolater/tress.
idolatrar [idola'tra*] *vt* to idolize.
idolatria [idola'tria] *f* idolatry.
ídolo ['idolu] *m* idol.
idoneidade [idonej'dadʒi] *f* suitability; (*competência*) competence; **~ moral** moral probity.
idôneo/a [i'donju/a] *adj* (*adequado*) suitable, fit; (*pessoa*) able, capable.
idos ['iduʃ] *mpl* bygone days.
idoso/a [i'dozu/ɔza] *adj* elderly, old.
Iemanjá [jemã'ʒa] *f* Iemanjá (*Afro-Brazilian sea goddess*).
Iêmen ['jemẽ] *m*: **o ~ (do Sul)** (South) Yemen.
iemenita [jeme'nita] *adj*, *m/f* Yemeni.
iene ['jɛni] *m* yen.
iglu [i'glu] *m* igloo.
IGC (*BR*) *abr m* = **Imposto sobre Ganhos de Capital**.
ignaro/a [igi'naru/a] *adj* ignorant.
ignição [igni'sãw] (*pl* **-ões**) *f* ignition.
ignóbil [ig'nɔbiw] (*pl* **-eis**) *adj* ignoble.
ignomínia [igno'minja] *f* disgrace, ignominy.
ignominioso/a [ignomi'njozu/ɔza] *adj* ignominious.
ignorado/a [igno'radu/a] *adj* unknown.
ignorância [igno'rãsja] *f* ignorance; **apelar para a ~** (*col*) to lose one's rag.
ignorante [igno'rãtʃi] *adj* ignorant, uneducated ♦ *m/f* ignoramus.
ignorar [igno'ra*] *vt* not to know; (*não dar atenção a*) to ignore.
ignoto/a [ig'nɔtu/a] *adj* (*formal*) unknown.
IGP (*BR*) *abr m* = **Índice Geral de Preços**.
igreja [i'greʒa] *f* church.
igual [i'gwaw] (*pl* **-ais**) *adj* equal; (*superfície*) even ♦ *m/f* equal; **em partes iguais** in equal parts; **ser ~** to be the same; **ser ~ a** to be the same as, be like; **~ se ...** as if ...; **por ~** equally; **sem ~** unequalled, without equal; **de ~ para ~** on equal terms; **tratar alguém de ~ para ~** to treat sb as an equal; **nunca vi coisa ~** I've never seen anything like it.
igualar [igwa'la*] *vt* (*ser igual a*) to equal; (*fazer igual*) to make equal; (*nivelar*) to level ♦ *vi*: **~ a** *ou* **com** to be equal to, be the same as; (*ficar no mesmo nível*) to be level with; **~-se** *vr*: **~-se a alguém** to be sb's equal; **~ algo com** *ou* **a algo** to equal sth to sth; **~ algo com algo** (*terreno etc*) to level sth with sth.
igualdade [igwaw'dadʒi] *f* (*paridade*) equality; (*uniformidade*) evenness, uniformity.
igualitário/a [igwali'tarju/a] *adj* egalitarian.
igualmente [igwaw'mẽtʃi] *adv* equally; (*também*) likewise, also; **~!** (*saudação*) the same to you!
iguana [i'gwana] *m* iguana.
iguaria [igwa'ria] *f* (*CULIN*) delicacy.
ih [i:] *excl* (*de admiração, surpresa*) cor (*BRIT*), gee (*US*); (*de perigo próximo*) ooh.
iídiche ['jidiʃi] *m* (*LING*) Yiddish.
ilação [ila'sãw] (*pl* **-ões**) *f* inference, deduction.
I.L. Ano (*BR*) *abr* (*COM*) = **Índice de Lucratividade no Ano**.
ilegal [ile'gaw] (*pl* **-ais**) *adj* illegal.
ilegalidade [ilegali'dadʒi] *f* illegality.
ilegítimo/a [ile'ʒitʃimu/a] *adj* illegitimate; (*ilegal*) unlawful.
ilegível [ile'ʒivew] (*pl* **-eis**) *adj* illegible.
ileso/a [i'lɛzu/a] *adj* unhurt; **sair ~** to escape unhurt.
iletrado/a [ile'tradu/a] *adj*, *m/f* illiterate.
ilha ['iʎa] *f* island.
ilhar [i'ʎa*] *vt* to cut off, isolate.
ilharga [i'ʎaxga] *f* (*ANAT*) side.
ilhéu/ilhoa [i'ʎɛw/i'ʎoa] *m/f* islander.
ilhós [i'ʎɔʃ] (*pl* **ilhoses**) *m* eyelet.
ilhota [i'ʎɔta] *f* small island.
ilícito/a [i'lisitu/a] *adj* illicit.
ilimitado/a [ilimi'tadu/a] *adj* unlimited.
ilógico/a [i'lɔʒiku/a] *adj* illogical; (*absurdo*) absurd.
iludir [ilu'dʒi*] *vt* to delude; (*enganar*) to deceive; (*a lei*) to evade; **~-se** *vr* to delude o.s.
iluminação [ilumina'sãw] (*pl* **-ões**) *f* lighting; (*fig*) enlightenment.
iluminado/a [ilumi'nadu/a] *adj* illuminated, lit; (*estádio*) floodlit; (*fig*) enlightened.
iluminante [ilumi'nãtʃi] *adj* bright.
iluminar [ilumi'na*] *vt* to light up; (*estádio etc*) to floodlight; (*fig*) to enlighten.
ilusão [ilu'zãw] (*pl* **-ões**) *f* illusion; (*quimera*) delusion; **~ de ótica** optical illusion; **viver de ilusões** to live in a dream-world.
ilusionista [iluzjo'niʃta] *m/f* conjurer; (*que escapa*) escapologist.
ilusões [ilu'zõjʃ] *f pl de* **ilusão**.
ilusório/a [ilu'zɔrju/a] *adj* (*enganoso*) deceptive.
ilustração [iluʃtra'sãw] (*pl* **-ões**) *f* (*figura, exemplo*) illustration; (*saber*) learning.
ilustrado/a [iluʃ'tradu/a] *adj* (*com gravuras*)

NB: European Portuguese adds the following consonants to certain words: **b** (sú(b)dito, su(b)til); **c** (a(c)ção, a(c)cionista, a(c)to); **m** (inde(m)ne); **p** (ado(p)ção, ado(p)tar); *for further details see p. xiii.*

illustrated; (*instruído*) learned.
ilustrador(a) [iluʃtra'do*(a)] *m/f* illustrator.
ilustrar [iluʃ'tra*] *vt* (*com gravuras*) to illustrate; (*instruir*) to instruct; (*exemplificar*) to illustrate; **~-se** *vr* (*distinguir-se*) to excel; (*instruir-se*) to inform o.s.
ilustrativo/a [iluʃtra'tʃivu/a] *adj* illustrative.
ilustre [i'luʃtri] *adj* famous, illustrious; **um ~ desconhecido** a complete stranger.
ilustríssimo/a [iluʃ'trisimu/a] *adj superl de* **ilustre**; (*tratamento*): **~ senhor** dear Sir.
ímã ['imã] *m* magnet.
imaculado/a [imaku'ladu/a] *adj* immaculate.
imagem [i'maʒẽ] (*pl* **-ns**) *f* image; (*semelhança*) likeness; (*TV*) picture; **imagens** *fpl* (*LITERATURA*) imagery *sg*; **ela é a ~ do pai** she's the image of her father.
imaginação [imaʒina'sãw] (*pl* **-ões**) *f* imagination.
imaginar [imaʒi'na*] *vt* to imagine; (*supor*) to suppose; **~-se** *vr* to imagine o.s.; **imagine só**! just imagine!; **obrigado — imagina!** thank you — don't worry about it!
imaginário/a [imaʒi'narju/a] *adj* imaginary.
imaginativo/a [imaʒina'tʃivu/a] *adj* imaginative.
imaginável [imaʒi'navew] (*pl* **-eis**) *adj* imaginable.
imaginoso/a [imaʒi'nozu/ɔza] *adj* (*pessoa*) imaginative.
íman ['imã] (*PT*) *m* = **ímã**.
imanente [ima'nẽtʃi] *adj*: **~ (a)** inherent (in).
imantar [imã'ta*] *vt* to magnetize.
imaturidade [imaturi'dadʒi] *f* immaturity.
imaturo/a [ima'turu/a] *adj* immature.
imbatível [ĩba'tʃivew] (*pl* **-eis**) *adj* invincible.
imbecil [ĩbe'siw] (*pl* **-is**) *adj* stupid ♦ *m/f* imbecile, half-wit.
imbecilidade [ĩbesili'dadʒi] *f* stupidity.
imbecis [ĩbe'siʃ] *pl de* **imbecil**.
imberbe [ĩ'bɛxbi] *adj* (*sem barba*) beardless; (*jovem*) youthful.
imbricar [ĩbri'ka*] *vt* to overlap; **~-se** *vr* to overlap.
imbuir [ĩ'bwi*] *vt*: **~ alguém de** (*sentimentos*) to imbue sb with.
IME (*BR*) *abr m* = **Instituto Militar de Engenharia**.
imediações [imedʒa'sõjʃ] *fpl* vicinity *sg*, neighbourhood *sg* (*BRIT*), neighborhood *sg* (*US*).
imediatamente [imedʒata'mẽtʃi] *adv* immediately, right away.
imediato/a [ime'dʒatu/a] *adj* immediate; (*seguinte*) next ♦ *m* second-in-command; **~ a** next to; **de ~** straight away.
imemorial [imemo'rjaw] (*pl* **-ais**) *adj* immemorial.
imensidade [imẽsi'dadʒi] *f* immensity.
imensidão [imẽsi'dãw] *f* hugeness, enormity.
imenso/a [i'mẽsu/a] *adj* immense, huge; (*ódio, amor*) great.
imensurável [imẽsu'ravew] (*pl* **-eis**) *adj* immeasurable.
imerecido/a [imere'sidu/a] *adj* undeserved.
imergir [imex'ʒi*] *vt* to immerse; (*fig*) to plunge ♦ *vi* to be immersed; to plunge.
imersão [imex'sãw] (*pl* **-ões**) *f* immersion.
imerso/a [i'mɛxsu/a] *adj* (*tb fig*) immersed.
imersões [imex'sõjʃ] *fpl de* **imersão**.
imigração [imigra'sãw] (*pl* **-ões**) *f* immigration.
imigrante [imi'grãtʃi] *adj*, *m/f* immigrant.
imigrar [imi'gra*] *vi* to immigrate.
iminência [imi'nẽsja] *f* imminence.
iminente [imi'nẽtʃi] *adj* imminent.
imiscuir-se [imiʃ'kwixsi] *vr* to meddle, interfere.
imitação [imita'sãw] (*pl* **-ões**) *f* imitation, copy; **jóia de ~** imitation jewel.
imitador(a) [imita'do*(a)] *adj* imitative ♦ *m/f* imitator.
imitar [imi'ta*] *vt* to imitate; (*assinatura*) to copy.
imobiliária [imobi'ljarja] *f* estate agent's (*BRIT*), real estate broker's (*US*).
imobiliário/a [imobi'ljarju/a] *adj* property *atr*, real estate *atr*.
imobilidade [imobili'dadʒi] *f* immobility.
imobilizar [imobili'za*] *vt* to immobilize; (*fig*: *economia, progresso*) to bring to a standstill; (*COM*: *capital*) to tie up.
imoderação [imodera'sãw] *f* lack of moderation.
imoderado/a [imode'radu/a] *adj* immoderate.
imodéstia [imo'dɛʃtʃja] *f* immodesty.
imodesto/a [imo'dɛʃtu/a] *adj* immodest.
imódico/a [i'mɔdʒiku/a] *adj* exorbitant.
imolar [imo'la*] *vt* (*sacrificar*) to sacrifice; (*prejudicar*) to harm.
imoral [imo'raw] (*pl* **-ais**) *adj* immoral.
imoralidade [imorali'dadʒi] *f* immorality.
imortal [imox'taw] (*pl* **-ais**) *adj* immortal ♦ *m/f* (*membro da ABL*) *member of the Brazilian Academy of Letters*.
imortalidade [imoxtali'dadʒi] *f* immortality.
imortalizar [imoxtali'za*] *vt* to immortalize.
imóvel [i'mɔvew] (*pl* **-eis**) *adj* (*parado*) motionless, still; (*não movediço*) immovable ♦ *m* property; (*edifício*) building; **imóveis** *mpl* real estate *sg*, property *sg*.
impaciência [ĩpa'sjẽsja] *f* impatience.
impacientar-se [ĩpasjẽ'taxsi] *vr* to lose one's patience.
impaciente [ĩpa'sjẽtʃi] *adj* impatient; (*inquieto*) anxious.
impacto [ĩ'paktu] (*PT*: **-cte**) *m* impact.
impagável [ĩpa'gavew] (*pl* **-eis**) *adj* (*fig*) priceless.
impaludismo [ĩpalu'dʒiʒmu] *m* malaria.
ímpar ['ĩpa*] *adj* (*números*) odd; (*sem igual*) unique, unequalled.
imparcial [ĩpax'sjaw] (*pl* **-ais**) *adj* fair, impartial.
imparcialidade [ĩpaxsjali'dadʒi] *f* impartiality.
impasse [ĩ'pasi] *m* impasse, deadlock.

impassível [ĩpa'sivew] (*pl* **-eis**) *adj* impassive.
impávido/a [ĩ'pavidu/a] *adj* (*formal*) fearless, intrepid.
impecável [ĩpe'kavew] (*pl* **-eis**) *adj* perfect, impeccable.
impeço [ĩ'pɛsu] *etc vb V* **impedir**.
impedido/a [ĩpe'dʒidu/a] *adj* hindered; (*estrada*) blocked; (FUTEBOL) offside; (PT: TEL) engaged (BRIT), busy (US).
impedimento [ĩpedʒi'mẽtu] *m* impediment; (FUTEBOL) offside; (POL) impeachment.
impedir [ĩpe'dʒi*] *vt* to obstruct; (*estrada, passagem, tráfego*) to block; (*movimento, execução, progresso*) to impede; ~ **alguém de fazer** to prevent sb from doing; (*proibir*) to forbid sb from doing; ~ **(que aconteça) algo** to prevent sth (happening).
impelir [ĩpe'li*] *vt* to drive (on); (*obrigar*) to force; (*incitar*) to impel.
impenetrável [ĩpene'travew] (*pl* **-eis**) *adj* impenetrable.
impenitência [ĩpeni'tẽsja] *f* unrepentance.
impenitente [ĩpeni'tẽtʃi] *adj* unrepentant.
impensado/a [ĩpẽ'sadu/a] *adj* (*imprevidente*) thoughtless; (*não calculado*) unpremeditated; (*imprevisto*) unforeseen.
impensável [ĩpẽ'savew] (*pl* **-eis**) *adj* unthinkable.
imperador [ĩpera'do*] *m* emperor.
imperar [ĩpe'ra*] *vi* to reign, rule; (*fig*: *prevalecer*) to prevail.
imperativo/a [ĩpera'tʃivu/a] *adj* (*tb* LING) imperative ♦ *m* absolute necessity; imperative.
imperatriz [ĩpera'triʒ] *f* empress.
imperceptível [ĩpexsep'tʃivew] (*pl* **-eis**) *adj* imperceptible.
imperdível [ĩpex'dʒivew] (*pl* **-eis**) *adj* (*questão*) impossible to lose; (*filme*) unmissable.
imperdoável [ĩpex'dwavew] (*pl* **-eis**) *adj* unforgivable, inexcusable.
imperecível [ĩpere'sivew] (*pl* **-eis**) *adj* imperishable.
imperfeição [ĩmpexfej'sãw] (*pl* **-ões**) *f* imperfection; (*falha*) flaw.
imperfeito/a [ĩpex'fejtu/a] *adj* imperfect ♦ *m* (LING) imperfect.
imperial [ĩpe'rjaw] (*pl* **-ais**) *adj* imperial.
imperialismo [ĩperja'liʒmu] *m* imperialism.
imperícia [ĩpe'risja] *f* (*inabilidade*) inability; (*inexperiência*) inexperience.
imperialista [ĩperja'liʃta] *adj, m/f* imperialist.
império [ĩ'pɛrju] *m* empire.
imperioso/a [ĩpe'rjozu/ɔza] *adj* (*dominador*) domineering; (*necessidade*) pressing, urgent; (*tom, olhar*) imperious.
impermeabilidade [ĩpexmjabili'dadʒi] *f* imperviousness.
impermeabilizar [ĩpexmjabili'za*] *vt* to waterproof.
impermeável [ĩpex'mjavew] (*pl* **-eis**) *adj* impervious; (*à água*) waterproof ♦ *m* raincoat; ~ **a** (*tb fig*) impervious to.
impertinência [ĩpextʃi'nẽsja] *f* impertinence; (*irrelevância*) irrelevance.
impertinente [ĩpextʃi'nẽtʃi] *adj* (*alheio*) irrelevant; (*insolente*) impertinent.
imperturbável [ĩpextux'bavew] (*pl* **-eis**) *adj* imperturbable; (*impassível*) impassive.
impessoal [ĩpe'swaw] (*pl* **-ais**) *adj* impersonal.
impetigo [ĩpe'tʃigo] *m* impetigo.
ímpeto ['ĩpetu] *m* (TEC: *força*) impetus; (*movimento súbito*) start; (*de cólera*) fit; (*de emoção*) surge; (*de chamas*) fury; **agir com** ~ to act on impulse; **levantar-se num** ~ to get up with a start; **senti um** ~ **de sair correndo** I felt an urge to run away.
impetrante [ĩpe'trãtʃi] *m/f* (JUR) petitioner.
impetrar [ĩpe'tra*] *vt* (JUR): ~ **algo** to petition for sth.
impetuosidade [ĩpetwozi'dadʒi] *f* impetuosity.
impetuoso/a [ĩpe'twozu/ɔza] *adj* (*pessoa*) headstrong, impetuous; (*ato*) rash, hasty; (*rio*) fast-moving.
impiedade [ĩpje'dadʒi] *f* irreverence; (*crueldade*) cruelty.
impiedoso/a [ĩpje'dozu/ɔza] *adj* merciless, cruel.
impilo [ĩ'pilu] *etc vb V* **impelir**.
impingir [ĩpĩ'ʒi*] *vt*: ~ **algo a alguém** (*mentiras, mercadorias*) to palm sth off on sb; ~ **algo em alguém** (*bofetada, pontapé etc*) to land sth on sb.
implacável [ĩpla'kavew] (*pl* **-eis**) *adj* (*pessoa*) unforgiving; (*destino, doença, perseguição*) relentless.
implantação [ĩplãta'sãw] (*pl* **-ões**) *f* introduction; (MED) implant.
implantar [ĩplã'ta*] *vt* to introduce; (MED) to implant.
implante [ĩ'plãtʃi] *m* (MED) implant.
implausível [ĩplaw'zivew] (*pl* **-eis**) *adj* implausible.
implementação [ĩplemẽta'sãw] (*pl* **-ões**) *f* implementation.
implementar [ĩplemẽ'ta*] *vt* to implement.
implemento [ĩple'mẽtu] *m* implement.
implicação [ĩplika'sãw] (*pl* **-ões**) *f* implication; (*envolvimento*) involvement.
implicância [ĩpli'kãsja] *f* (*ato de chatear*) teasing; (*antipatia*) horribleness; **estar de** ~ **com alguém** to pick on sb, have it in for sb.
implicante [ĩpli'kãtʃi] *adj* horrible ♦ *m/f* stirrer.
implicar [ĩpli'ka*] *vt* (*envolver*) to implicate; (*pressupor*) to imply; **~-se** *vr* (*envolver-se*) to get involved; ~ **com alguém** (*antipatizar*) to be horrible to sb; (*chatear*) to tease sb, pick on sb; ~ **(em) algo** to involve sth.
implícito/a [ĩ'plisitu/a] *adj* implicit.

***NB**: European Portuguese adds the following consonants to certain words:* **b** (sú(b)dito, su(b)til); **c** (a(c)ção, a(c)cionista, a(c)to); **m** (inde(m)ne); **p** (ado(p)ção, ado(p)tar); *for further details see p. xiii.*

impliquei [ĩpli'kej] *etc vb V* **implicar**.
implodir [ĩplo'dʒi*] *vi* to implode.
imploração [ĩplora'sãw] *f* begging.
implorar [ĩplo'ra*] *vt*: ~ **(algo a alguém)** to beg *ou* implore (sb for sth).
impõe [ĩ'põj] *etc vb V* **impor**.
impoluto/a [ĩpo'lutu/a] *adj* immaculate; (*pessoa*) beyond reproach.
impomos [ĩ'pomoʃ] *vb V* **impor**.
imponderado/a [ĩpõde'radu/a] *adj* rash.
imponderável [ĩpõde'ravew] (*pl* **-eis**) *adj* imponderable.
imponência [ĩpo'nẽsja] *f* impressiveness.
imponente [ĩpo'nẽtʃi] *adj* impressive, imposing.
imponho [ĩ'poɲu] *etc vb V* **impor**.
impontual [ĩpõ'twaw] (*pl* **-ais**) *adj* unpunctual.
impopular [ĩpopu'la*] *adj* unpopular.
impopularidade [ĩpopulari'dadʒi] *f* unpopularity.
impor [ĩ'po*] (*irreg*: *como* **pôr**) *vt* to impose; (*respeito*) to command; **~-se** *vr* to assert o.s.; ~ **algo a alguém** to impose sth on sb.
importação [impoxta'sãw] (*pl* **-ões**) *f* (*ato*) importing; (*mercadoria*) import.
importador(a) [ĩpoxta'do*(a)] *adj* import *atr* ♦ *m/f* importer ♦ *f* (*empresa*) import company; (*loja*) shop selling imported goods.
importância [ĩpox'tãsja] *f* importance; (*de dinheiro*) sum, amount; **não tem** ~ it doesn't matter, never mind; **ter** ~ to be important; **dar** ~ **a algo/alguém** to attach importance to sth/show consideration for sb; **sem** ~ unimportant; **não dê** ~ **ao que ele disse** take no notice of what he said; **de certa** ~ of some importance.
importante [ĩpox'tãtʃi] *adj* important; (*arrogante*) self-important ♦ *m*: **o (mais)** ~ the (most) important thing.
importar [ĩpox'ta*] *vt* (*COM*) to import; (*trazer*) to bring in; (*causar*: *prejuízos etc*) to cause; (*implicar*) to imply, involve ♦ *vi* to matter, be important; **~-se** *vr*: **~-se com algo** to mind sth; **não me importo** I don't care; **não** *ou* **pouco importa!** it doesn't matter!; ~ **em** (*preço*) to add up to, amount to; (*resultar*) to lead to; **eu pouco me importo que ela venha ou não** I don't care whether she comes or not.
importe [ĩ'pɔxtʃi] *m* (*soma*) amount; (*custo*) cost.
importunação [ĩpoxtuna'sãw] (*pl* **-ões**) annoyance.
importunar [ĩpoxtu'na*] *vt* to bother, annoy.
importuno/a [ĩpox'tunu/a] *adj* (*maçante*) annoying; (*inoportuno*) inopportune ♦ *m/f* nuisance.
impôs [ĩ'poʃ] *vb V* **impor**.
imposição [ĩpozi'sãw] (*pl* **-ões**) *f* imposition.
impossibilidade [ĩposibili'dadʒi] *f* impossibility.
impossibilitado/a [ĩposibili'tadu/a] *adj*: ~ **de fazer** unable to do.
impossibilitar [ĩposibili'ta*] *vt*: ~ **algo** to make sth impossible; ~ **alguém de fazer,** ~ **a alguém fazer** to prevent sb doing; ~ **algo a alguém,** ~ **alguém para algo** to make sth impossible for sb.
impossível [ĩpo'sivew] (*pl* **-eis**) *adj* impossible; (*insuportável*: *pessoa*) insufferable; (*incrível*) incredible.
impostação [ĩpoʃta'sãw] *f* (*da voz*) diction, delivery.
impostar [ĩpoʃ'ta*] *vt* (*voz*) to throw.
imposto/a [ĩ'poʃtu/'pɔʃta] *pp de* **impor** ♦ *m* tax; **antes/depois de ~s** before/after tax; ~ **de renda** (*BR*) income tax; ~ **predial** rates *pl*; ~ **sobre ganhos de capital** capital transfer tax (*BRIT*), inheritance tax (*US*); ~ **sobre os lucros** profits tax; ~ **sobre transferência de capital** capital transfer tax; **I~ sobre Circulação de Mercadorias (e Serviços)** (*BR*), ~ **sobre valor agregado** (*PT*) value added tax (*BRIT*), sales tax (*US*).
impostor [ĩpoʃ'to*] *m* impostor.
impostura [ĩpoʃ'tura] *f* deception.
impotência [ĩpo'tẽʃja] *f* impotence.
impotente [ĩpo'tẽtʃi] *adj* powerless; (*MED*) impotent.
impraticabilidade [ĩpratʃikabili'dadʒi] *f* impracticability.
impraticável [ĩpratʃi'kavew] (*pl* **-eis**) *adj* impracticable; (*rua, rio etc*) impassable.
imprecisão [ĩpresi'zãw] (*pl* **-ões**) *f* inaccuracy.
impreciso/a [ĩpre'sizu/a] *adj* vague; (*falto de rigor*) inaccurate.
imprecisões [ĩpresi'zõjʃ] *fpl de* **imprecisão**.
impregnar [ĩpreg'na*] *vt* to impregnate; ~ **algo de** to impregnate sth with; (*fig*: *mente etc*) to fill sth with.
imprensa [ĩ'prẽsa] *f* (*a arte*) printing; (*máquina, jornais*) press; ~ **marrom** tabloid press, gutter press.
imprensar [ĩprẽ'sa*] *vt* (*no prelo*) to stamp; (*apertar*) to squash; (*fig*): ~ **alguém (contra a parede)** to press sb.
imprescindível [ĩpresĩ'dʒivew] (*pl* **-eis**) *adj* essential, indispensable.
impressão [impre'sãw] (*pl* **-ões**) *f* impression; (*de livros*) printing; (*marca*) imprint; **causar boa** ~ to make a good impression; **ficar com/ter a** ~ **(de) que** to get/have the impression that; **ter má** ~ **de algo** to have a bad impression of sth; ~ **digital** fingerprint.
impressionante [ĩpresjo'nãtʃi] *adj* impressive; (*abalador*) amazing.
impressionar [ĩpresjo'na*] *vt* to impress; (*abalar*) to affect ♦ *vi* to be impressive; to make an impression; **~-se** *vr*: **~-se (com algo)** (*comover-se*) to be moved (by sth).
impressionável [ĩpresjo'navew] (*pl* **-eis**) *adj* impressionable.
impressionismo [ĩpresjo'niʒmu] *m* impressionism.
impressionista [ĩpresjo'niʃta] *adj, m/f* impressionist.

impresso/a [ĩ'prɛsu/a] *pp de* **imprimir** ♦ *adj* printed ♦ *m* (*para preencher*) form; (*folheto*) leaflet; **~s** *mpl* printed matter *sg*.

impressões [impre'sõjʃ] *fpl de* **impressão**.

impressor [ĩpre'so*] *m* printer.

impressora [ĩpre'sora] *f* printing machine; (*COMPUT*) printer; **~ a laser** laser printer; **~ de linha** line printer; **~ margarida** daisy-wheel printer; **~ matricial** dot-matrix printer.

imprestável [ĩpreʃ'tavew] (*pl* **-eis**) *adj* (*inútil*) useless; (*pessoa*) unhelpful.

impreterível [ĩprete'rivew] (*pl* **-eis**) *adj* (*compromisso*) essential; (*prazo*) final.

imprevidente [ĩprevi'dẽtʃi] *adj* short-sighted.

imprevisão [ĩprevi'zãw] *f* lack of foresight, short-sightedness.

imprevisível [ĩprevi'zivew] (*pl* **-eis**) *adj* unforeseeable.

imprevisto/a [ĩpre'viʃtu/a] *adj* unexpected, unforeseen ♦ *m*: **um ~** something unexpected.

imprimir [ĩpri'mi*] *vt* to print; (*marca*) to stamp; (*infundir*) to instil (*BRIT*), instill (*US*); (*COMPUT*) to print out; **~-se** *vr* to be stamped, be impressed; **~-se na memória** to impress o.s. on the memory; **~ algo a algo** to stamp sth on sth.

improbabilidade [ĩprobabili'dadʒi] *f* improbability.

improcedente [ĩprose'dẽtʃi] *adj* groundless, unjustified.

improdutivo/a [ĩprodu'tʃivu/a] *adj* unproductive.

improfícuo/a [impro'fikwu/a] *adj* useless, futile.

impropério [ĩpro'pɛrju] *m* insult; **dizer ~s** to swear.

impropriedade [ĩproprje'dadʒi] *f* inappropriateness; (*moral*) impropriety.

impróprio/a [ĩ'prɔprju/a] *adj* (*inadequado*) inappropriate; (*indecente*) improper; **filme ~ para menores de 18 anos** X-certificate *ou* X-rated film.

improrrogável [ĩproxo'gavew] (*pl* **-eis**) *adj* non-extendible.

improvável [ĩpro'vavew] (*pl* **-eis**) *adj* unlikely.

improvidência [ĩprovi'dẽsja] *f* lack of foresight.

improvidente [ĩprovi'dẽtʃi] *adj* lacking foresight.

improvisado/a [ĩprovi'zadu/a] *adj* improvised, impromptu.

improvisação [ĩproviza'sãw] (*pl* **-ões**) *f* improvisation.

improvisar [ĩprovi'za*] *vt, vi* to improvise; (*TEATRO*) to ad-lib.

improviso [ĩpro'vizu] *m* impromptu talk; **de ~** (*de repente*) suddenly; (*sem preparação*) without preparation; **falar de ~** to talk off the cuff.

imprudência [ĩpru'dẽsja] *f* rashness; (*descuido*) carelessness.

imprudente [ĩpru'dẽtʃi] *adj* (*irrefletido*) rash; (*motorista*) careless.

impudico/a [ĩpu'dʒiku/a] *adj* shameless.

impugnar [ĩpug'na*] *vt* (*refutar*) to refute; (*opor-se a*) to oppose.

impulsionar [ĩpuwsjo'na*] *vt* (*impelir*) to drive, impel; (*fig: estimular*) to urge.

impulsividade [ĩpuwsivi'dadʒi] *f* impulsiveness.

impulsivo/a [ĩpuw'sivu/a] *adj* impulsive.

impulso [ĩ'puwsu] *m* impulse; (*fig: estímulo*) urge, impulse; **tomar ~** (*fig: empresa, negócio*) to take off; **compra por ~** (*ato*) impulse buying.

impune [ĩ'puni] *adj* unpunished.

impunemente [ĩpune'mẽtʃi] *adv* with impunity.

impunha [ĩ'puɲa] *etc vb V* **impor**.

impunidade [ĩpuni'dadʒi] *f* impunity.

impureza [ĩpu'reza] *f* impurity.

impuro/a [ĩ'puru/a] *adj* impure.

impus [ĩ'puʃ] *etc vb V* **impor**.

impuser [ĩpu'ze*] *etc vb V* **impor**.

imputação [imputa'sãw] (*pl* **-ões**) *f* accusation.

imputar [ĩpu'ta*] *vt*: **~ algo a** (*atribuir*) to attribute sth to; **~ algo a alguém** to blame sb for sth.

imputável [ĩpu'tavew] (*pl* **-eis**) *adj* attributable.

imundice [imũ'dʒisi] *f* = **imundície**.

imundície [imũ'dʒisji] *f* filth.

imundo/a [i'mũdu/a] *adj* filthy; (*obsceno*) dirty.

imune [i'muni] *adj*: **~ a** immune to.

imunidade [imuni'dadʒi] *f* immunity.

imunizar [imuni'za*] *vt*: **~ alguém (contra algo)** (*MED*) to immunize sb (against sth); (*fig*) to protect sb (from sth).

imutável [imu'tavew] (*pl* **-eis**) *adj* fixed, unalterable, unchanging.

inabalável [inaba'lavew] (*pl* **-eis**) *adj* unshakeable.

inábil [i'nabiw] (*pl* **-eis**) *adj* (*incapaz*) incapable; (*desajeitado*) clumsy.

inabilidade [inabili'dadʒi] *f* (*incompetência*) incompetence; (*falta de destreza*) clumsiness.

inabilidoso/a [inabili'dozu/ɔza] *adj* clumsy, awkward.

inabilitação [inabilita'sãw] (*pl* **-ões**) *f* disqualification.

inabilitar [inabili'ta*] *vt* (*incapacitar*) to incapacitate; (*em exame*) to disqualify.

inabitado/a [inabi'tadu/a] *adj* uninhabited.

inabitável [inabi'tavew] (*pl* **-eis**) *adj* uninhabitable.

inacabado/a [inaka'badu/a] *adj* unfinished.

inacabável [inaka'bavew] (*pl* **-eis**) *adj* interminable, unending.

***NB:** European Portuguese adds the following consonants to certain words:* **b** (sú(b)dito, su(b)til); **c** (a(c)ção, a(c)cionista, a(c)to); **m** (inde(m)ne); **p** (ado(p)ção, ado(p)tar); *for further details see p. xiii.*

inação [ina'sãw] (*PT*: **-cç-**) *f* (*inércia*) inactivity; (*irresolução*) indecision.
inaceitável [inasej'tavew] (*pl* **-eis**) *adj* unacceptable.
Inacen [ina'sẽ] (*BR*) *abr m* = **Instituto Nacional de Artes Cênicas**.
inacessível [inase'sivew] (*pl* **-eis**) *adj* inaccessible.
inacreditável [inakredʒi'tavew] (*pl* **-eis**) *adj* unbelievable, incredible.
inactivo/a *etc* [ina'tivu/a] (*PT*) = **inativo/a** *etc*.
inadaptado/a [inadap'tadu/a] *adj* maladjusted.
inadequação [inadekwa'sãw] (*pl* **-ões**) *f* inadequacy; (*impropriedade*) unsuitability.
inadequado/a [inade'kwadu/a] *adj* inadequate; (*impróprio*) unsuitable.
inadiável [ina'dʒjavew] (*pl* **-eis**) *adj* pressing.
inadimplência [inadʒĩ'plẽsja] *f* (*JUR*) breach of contract, default.
inadimplente [inadʒĩ'plẽtʃi] *adj* (*JUR*) in breach of contract, at fault.
inadimplir [inadʒĩ'pli*] *vt, vi*: ~ **(algo)** to default (on sth).
inadmissível [inadʒimi'sivew] (*pl* **-eis**) *adj* inadmissible.
inadquirível [inadʒiki'rivew] (*pl* **-eis**) *adj* unobtainable.
inadvertência [inadʒivex'tẽsja] *f* oversight; **por** ~ by mistake.
inadvertido/a [inadʒivex'tʃidu/a] *adj* inadvertent.
inalação [inala'sãw] (*pl* **-ões**) *f* inhalation.
inalar [ina'la*] *vt* to inhale, breathe in.
inalcançável [inawkã'savew] (*pl* **-eis**) *adj* out of reach; (*sucesso, ambição*) unattainable.
inalterado/a [inawte'radu/a] *adj* unchanged; (*sereno*) unperturbed.
inalterável [inawte'ravew] (*pl* **-eis**) *adj* unchangeable; (*impassível*) imperturbable.
Inamps [i'nãps] (*BR*) *abr m* = **Instituto Nacional de Assistência Médica e Previdência Social**.
inanição [inani'sãw] (*pl* **-ões**) *f* starvation.
inanimado/a [inani'madu/a] *adj* inanimate.
inapetência [inape'tẽsja] *f* loss of appetite.
inapetente [inape'tẽtʃi] *adj* off one's food.
inaplicado/a [inapli'kadu/a] *adj* (*aluno*) idle, lazy.
inaplicável [inapli'kavew] (*pl* **-eis**) *adj* inapplicable.
inapreciável [inapre'sjavew] (*pl* **-eis**) *adj* invaluable.
inaproveitável [inaprovej'tavew] (*pl* **-eis**) *adj* useless.
inaptidão [inaptʃi'dãw] (*pl* **-ões**) *f* inability.
inapto/a [i'naptu/a] *adj* (*incapaz*) unfit, incapable; (*inadequado*) unsuited.
inarticulado/a [inaxtʃiku'ladu/a] *adj* inarticulate.
inatacável [inata'kavew] (*pl* **-eis**) *adj* unassailable.
inatenção [inatẽ'sãw] *f* inattention.
inatingido/a [inatʃĩ'ʒidu/a] *adj* unconquered.
inatingível [inatʃĩ'ʒivew] (*pl* **-eis**) *adj* unattainable.
inatividade [inatʃivi'dadʒi] *f* inactivity; (*aposentadoria*) redundancy (*BRIT*), dismissal (*US*); (*MIL*: *reforma*) retirement (on health grounds).
inativo/a [ina'tʃivu/a] *adj* inactive; (*aposentado, reformado*) retired.
inato/a [i'natu/a] *adj* innate, inborn.
inaudito/a [inaw'dʒitu/a] *adj* unheard-of.
inaudível [inaw'dʒivew] (*pl* **-eis**) *adj* inaudible.
inauguração [inawgura'sãw] (*pl* **-ões**) *f* inauguration; (*de exposição*) opening; (*de estátua*) unveiling.
inaugural [inawgu'raw] (*pl* **-ais**) *adj* inaugural.
inaugurar [inawgu'ra*] *vt* to inaugurate; (*exposição*) to open; (*estátua*) to unveil.
inca ['ĩka] *adj, m/f* Inca.
incabível [ĩka'bivew] (*pl* **-eis**) *adj* unacceptable.
incalculável [ĩkawku'lavew] (*pl* **-eis**) *adj* incalculable.
incandescente [ĩkãde'sẽtʃi] *adj* incandescent.
incansável [ĩkã'savew] (*pl* **-eis**) *adj* tireless, untiring.
incapacidade [ĩkapasi'dadʒi] *f* incapacity; (*incompetência*) incompetence; ~ **de fazer** inability to do.
incapacitado/a [ĩkapasi'tadu/a] *adj* (*inválido*) disabled, handicapped ♦ *m/f* handicapped person; **estar** ~ **de fazer** to be unable to do.
incapacitar [ĩkapasi'ta*] *vt*: ~ **alguém (para)** to make sb unable (to).
incapaz [ĩka'pajʒ] *adj, m/f* incompetent; ~ **de fazer** incapable of doing; ~ **para** unfit for.
incauto/a [in'kawtu/a] *adj* (*imprudente*) rash.
incendiar [ĩsẽ'dʒja*] *vt* to set fire to; (*fig*) to inflame; **~-se** *vr* to catch fire.
incendiário/a [ĩsẽ'dʒjarju/a] *adj* incendiary; (*fig*) inflammatory ♦ *m/f* arsonist; (*agitador*) agitator.
incêndio [ĩ'sẽdʒju] *m* fire; ~ **criminoso** *ou* **premeditado** arson.
incenso [ĩ'sẽsu] *m* incense.
incentivador(a) [ĩsẽtʃiva'do*(a)] *adj* stimulating, encouraging.
incentivar [ĩsẽtʃi'va*] *vt* to stimulate, encourage.
incentivo [ĩsẽ'tʃivu] *m* incentive; ~ **fiscal** tax incentive.
incerteza [ĩsex'teza] *f* uncertainty.
incerto/a [ĩ'sɛxtu/a] *adj* uncertain.
incessante [ĩse'sãtʃi] *adj* incessant.
incesto [ĩ'sɛʃtu] *m* incest.
incestuoso/a [ĩseʃ'twozu/ɔza] *adj* incestuous.
inchação [ĩʃa'sãw] (*pl* **-ões**) *f* swelling.
inchado/a [ĩ'ʃadu/a] *adj* swollen; (*fig*) conceited.
inchar [ĩ'ʃa*] *vt* to swell ♦ *vi* to swell; **~-se** *vr* to swell (up); (*fig*) to become conceited.
incidência [ĩsi'dẽsja] *f* incidence, ocurrence.
incidente [ĩsi'dẽtʃi] *m* incident.

incidir [ĩsi'dʒi*] *vi*: ~ **em erro** to go wrong; ~ **em** *ou* **sobre algo** (*luz*) to fall on sth; (*influir*) to affect sth; (*imposto*) to be payable on sth.

incinerar [ĩsine'ra*] *vt* to burn.

incipiente [ĩsi'pjẽtʃi] *adj* incipient.

incisão [insi'zãw] (*pl* **-ões**) *f* cut; (MED) incision.

incisivo/a [ĩsi'zivu/a] *adj* cutting, sharp; (*fig*) incisive ♦ *m* incisor.

incisões [insi'zõjʃ] *fpl de* **incisão**.

incitação [ĩsita'sãw] (*pl* **-ões**) *f* incitement.

incitamento [ĩsita'mẽtu] *m* incitement.

incitar [ĩsi'ta*] *vt* to incite; (*pessoa, animal*) to drive on; (*instigar*) to rouse; ~ **alguém a (fazer) algo** to urge sb on to (do) sth, incite sb to (do) sth.

incivil [ĩsi'viw] (*pl* **-is**) *adj* rude, ill-mannered.

incivilidade [ĩsivili'dadʒi] *f* rudeness.

incivilizado/a [ĩsivili'zadu/a] *adj* uncivilized.

incivis [ĩsi'viʃ] *adj pl de* **incivil**.

inclemência [ĩkle'mẽsja] *f* harshness, rigour (BRIT), rigor (US); (*tempo*) inclemency.

inclemente [ĩkle'mẽtʃi] *adj* severe, harsh; (*tempo*) inclement.

inclinação [ĩklina'sãw] (*pl* **-ões**) *f* (*tb fig*) inclination; (*da terra*) slope; (*simpatia*) liking; ~ **da cabeça** nod.

inclinado/a [ĩkli'nadu/a] *adj* (*terreno, estrada*) sloping; (*corpo, torre*) leaning; **estar ~/pouco ~ a** to be inclined/loath to.

inclinar [ĩkli'na*] *vt* (*objeto*) to tilt; (*cabeça*) to nod ♦ *vi* (*terra*) to slope; (*objeto*) to tilt; **~-se** *vr* (*objeto*) to tilt; (*dobrar o corpo*) to bow, stoop; ~ **para** (*propensão*) to lean towards; **~-se sobre algo** to lean over sth; **~(-se) para trás** to lean back.

ínclito/a ['ĩklitu/a] *adj* illustrious, renowned.

incluir [ĩ'klwi*] *vt* to include; (*em carta*) to enclose; **~-se** *vr* to be included; **tudo incluído** (COM) all in.

inclusão [ĩklu'zãw] *f* inclusion.

inclusive [ĩklu'zivi] *prep* including ♦ *adv* inclusive; (*até mesmo*) even; **de segunda à sexta ~** from Monday to Friday inclusive; **e ~ falou que ...** and furthermore he said that ....

incluso/a [ĩ'kluzu/a] *adj* included; (*em carta*) enclosed.

incobrável [ĩko'bravew] (*pl* **-eis**) *adj* (COM): **dívida ~** bad debt.

incoercível [ĩkoex'sivew] (*pl* **-eis**) *adj* uncontrollable.

incoerência [ĩkoe'rẽsja] *f* incoherence; (*contradição*) inconsistency.

incoerente [ĩkoe'rẽtʃi] *adj* incoherent; (*contraditório*) inconsistent.

incógnita [ĩ'kɔgnita] *f* (MAT) unknown; (*fato incógnito*) mystery.

incógnito/a [ĩ'kɔgnitu/a] *adj* unknown ♦ *adv* incognito.

incolor [ĩko'lo*] *adj* colourless (BRIT), colorless (US).

incólume [ĩ'kɔlumi] *adj* safe and sound; (*ileso*) unharmed.

incomensurável [ĩkomẽsu'ravew] (*pl* **-eis**) *adj* immense.

incomodada [ĩkomo'dada] *adj* (*menstruada*) having one's period.

incomodar [ĩkomo'da*] *vt* (*importunar*) to bother, trouble; (*aborrecer*) to annoy ♦ *vi* to be bothersome; **~-se** *vr* to bother, put o.s. out; **~-se com algo** to be bothered by sth, mind sth; **não se incomode!** don't worry!; **você se incomoda se eu abrir a janela?** do you mind if I open the window?

incômodo/a [ĩ'komodu/a] *adj* (*desconfortável*) uncomfortable; (*incomodativo*) troublesome; (*inoportuno*) inconvenient ♦ *m* (*menstruação*) period; (*maçada*) nuisance, trouble; (*amolação*) inconvenience.

incomparável [ĩkõpa'ravew] (*pl* **-eis**) *adj* incomparable.

incompatibilidade [ĩkõpatʃibili'dadʒi] *f* incompatibility.

incompatibilizar [ĩkõpatʃibili'za*] *vt*: ~ **alguém (com alguém)** to alienate sb (from sb); **~-se** *vr*: **~-se (com alguém)** to alienate o.s. (from sb).

incompatível [ĩkõpa'tʃivew] (*pl* **-eis**) *adj* incompatible.

incompetência [ĩkõpe'tẽsja] *f* incompetence.

incompetente [ĩkõpe'tẽtʃi] *adj, m/f* incompetent.

incompleto/a [ĩkõ'plɛtu/a] *adj* incomplete, unfinished.

incompreendido/a [ĩkõprjẽ'dʒidu/a] *adj* misunderstood.

incompreensão [ĩkõprjẽ'sãw] *f* incomprehension.

incompreensível [ĩkõprjẽ'sivew] (*pl* **-eis**) *adj* incomprehensible.

incompreensivo/a [ĩkõprjẽ'sivu/a] *adj* uncomprehending.

incomum [ĩko'mũ] *adj* uncommon.

incomunicável [ĩkomuni'kavew] (*pl* **-eis**) *adj* cut off; (*privado de comunicação, fig*) incommunicado; (*preso*) in solitary confinement.

inconcebível [ĩkõse'bivew] (*pl* **-eis**) *adj* inconceivable; (*incrível*) incredible.

inconciliável [ĩkõsi'ljavew] (*pl* **-eis**) *adj* irreconcilable.

inconcludente [ĩkõklu'dẽtʃi] *adj* inconclusive.

inconcluso/a [ĩkõ'kluzu/a] *adj* unfinished.

incondicional [ĩkõdʒisjo'naw] (*pl* **-ais**) *adj* unconditional; (*apoio*) wholehearted; (*partidário*) staunch; (*amizade, fã*) loyal.

inconfesso/a [ĩkõ'fɛsu/a] *adj* closet *atr*.

inconfidência [ĩkõfi'dẽsja] *f* disloyalty; (JUR)

***NB:** European Portuguese adds the following consonants to certain words:* **b** (sú(b)dito, su(b)til); **c** (a(c)ção, a(c)cionista, a(c)to); **m** (inde(m)ne); **p** (ado(p)ção, ado(p)tar); *for further details see p. xiii.*

treason.

inconfidente [ĩkõfi'dẽtʃi] *adj* disloyal ♦ *m* conspirator.

inconformado/a [ĩkõfox'madu/a] *adj* bitter; ~ **com** unreconciled to.

inconfundível [ĩkõfũ'dʒivew] (*pl* **-eis**) *adj* unmistakeable.

incongruência [ĩkõ'grwẽsja] *f*: **ser uma** ~ to be incongruous.

incongruente [ĩkõ'grwẽtʃi] *adj* incongruous.

incôngruo/a [ĩ'kõgrwu/a] *adj* incongruous.

inconsciência [ĩkõ'sjẽsja] *f* (*MED*) unconsciousness; (*irreflexão*) thoughtlessness.

inconsciente [ĩkõ'sjẽtʃi] *adj* (*MED*, *PSICO*) unconscious; (*involuntário*) unwitting; (*irresponsável*) irresponsible ♦ *m* (*PSICO*) unconscious ♦ *m/f* (*irresponsável*) irresponsible person.

inconseqüência [ĩkõse'kwẽsja] *f* (*irresponsabilidade*) irresponsibility; (*incoerência*) inconsistency.

inconseqüente [ĩkõse'kwẽtʃi] *adj* (*incoerente*) inconsistent; (*contraditório*) illogical; (*irresponsável*) irresponsible.

inconsistência [ĩkõsiʃ'tẽsja] *f* inconsistency; (*falta de solidez*) runny consistency.

inconsistente [ĩkõsiʃ'tẽtʃi] *adj* inconsistent; (*sem solidez*) runny.

inconsolável [ĩkõso'lavew] (*pl* **-eis**) *adj* inconsolable.

inconstância [ĩkõʃ'tãsja] *f* fickleness; (*do tempo*) changeability.

inconstante [ĩkõʃ'tãtʃi] *adj* fickle; (*tempo*) changeable.

inconstitucional [ĩkõʃtʃitusjo'naw] (*pl* **-ais**) *adj* unconstitutional.

incontável [ĩkõ'tavew] (*pl* **-eis**) *adj* countless.

incontestável [ĩkõteʃ'tavew] (*pl* **-eis**) *adj* undeniable.

incontinência [ĩkõtʃi'nẽsja] *f* (*MED*) incontinence; (*sensual*) licentiousness.

incontinente [ĩkõtʃi'nẽtʃi] *adj* (*MED*) incontinent; (*sensual*) licentious.

incontinenti [ĩkõtʃi'nẽtʃi] *adv* immediately.

incontrolável [ĩkõtro'lavew] (*pl* **-eis**) *adj* uncontrollable.

incontroverso/a [ĩkõtro'vɛxsu/a] *adj* incontrovertible.

inconveniência [ĩkõve'njẽsja] *f* (*inadequação*) inconvenience; (*impropriedade*) inappropriateness; (*descortesia*) impoliteness; (*ato, dito*) indiscretion.

inconveniente [ĩkõve'njẽtʃi] *adj* (*incômodo*) inconvenient; (*inoportuno*) awkward; (*grosseiro*) rude; (*importuno*) annoying ♦ *m* (*desvantagem*) disadvantage; (*obstáculo*) difficulty, problem.

Incor [ĩ'ko*] *abr m* (= *Instituto do Coração*) *hospital in São Paulo*.

incorporação [ĩkoxpora'sãw] (*pl* **-ões**) *f* (*tb*: *COM*) incorporation; (*no espiritismo*) embodiment, incorporation.

incorporado/a [ĩkoxpo'radu/a] *adj* (*TEC*) built-in.

incorporar [ĩkoxpo'ra*] *vt* to incorporate; (*juntar*) to add; (*COM*) to merge; **~-se** *vr* (*espírito*) to be embodied; ~ **-se a** *ou* **em** to join.

incorreção [ĩkoxe'sãw] (*PT*: **-cç-**; *pl* **-ões**) *f* (*erro*) inaccuracy.

incorrecto/a [ĩko'xɛktu/a] (*PT*) *adj* = **incorreto/a**.

incorrer [ĩko'xe*] *vi*: ~ **em** to incur.

incorreto/a [ĩko'xɛtu/a] *adj* incorrect; (*desonesto*) dishonest.

incorrigível [ĩkoxi'ʒivew] (*pl* **-eis**) *adj* incorrigible.

incorruptível [ĩkoxup'tʃivew] (*pl* **-eis**) *adj* incorruptible.

incorrupto/a [ĩko'xuptu/a] *adj* incorrupt.

INCRA ['ĩkra] (*BR*) *abr m* = **Instituto Nacional de Colonização e Reforma Agrária**.

incredulidade [ĩkreduli'dadʒi] *f* incredulity; (*ceticismo*) scepticism (*BRIT*), skepticism (*US*).

incrédulo/a [ĩ'krɛdulu/a] *adj* incredulous; (*cético*) sceptical (*BRIT*), skeptical (*US*) ♦ *m/f* sceptic (*BRIT*), skeptic (*US*).

incrementado/a [ĩkremẽ'tadu/a] *adj* (*indústria*) well-developed; (*col*: *festa*) lively; (: *roupa*) trendy; (: *carro*) expensive.

incrementar [ĩkremẽ'ta*] *vt* (*desenvolver*) to develop; (*aumentar*) to increase; (*col*: *festa*, *roupa*) to liven up.

incremento [ĩkre'mẽtu] *m* (*desenvolvimento*) growth; (*aumento*) increase.

incriminação [ĩkrimina'sãw] *f* criminalization.

incriminar [ĩkrimi'na*] *vt* to criminalize; ~ **alguém de algo** to accuse sb of sth.

incrível [ĩ'krivew] (*pl* **-eis**) *adj* incredible.

incrustar [ĩkruʃ'ta*] *vt* to encrust; (*móveis etc*) to inlay.

incubadora [ĩkuba'dora] *f* incubator.

incubar [ĩku'ba*] *vt* (*ovos*, *doença*) to incubate; (*plano*) to hatch ♦ *vi* (*ovos*) to incubate.

inculpar [ĩkuw'pa*] *vt*: ~ **alguém de algo** (*culpar*) to blame sb for sth; (*acusar*) to accuse sb of sth; **~-se** *vr*: **~-se de algo** to blame o.s. for sth.

inculto/a [ĩ'kuwtu/a] *adj* (*pessoa*) uncultured, uneducated; (*terreno*) uncultivated.

incumbência [ĩkũ'bẽsja] *f* task, duty; **não é da minha** ~ it is not part of my duty.

incumbir [ĩkũ'bi*] *vt*: ~ **alguém de algo** *ou* **algo a alguém** to put sb in charge of sth ♦ *vi*: ~ **a alguém** to be sb's duty; **~-se** *vr*: **~-se de** to undertake, take charge of.

incurável [ĩku'ravew] (*pl* **-eis**) *adj* incurable.

incúria [ĩ'kurja] *f* carelessness.

incursão [ĩkux'sãw] (*pl* **-ões**) *f* (*invasão*) raid, attack; (*penetração*) foray.

incursionar [ĩkuxsjo'na*] *vi*: ~ **por algo** to make forays into sth.

incursões [ĩkux'sõjʃ] *fpl de* **incursão**.

incutir [ĩku'tʃi*] *vt*: ~ **algo (em** *ou* **a alguém)**

to instil (*BRIT*) *ou* instill (*US*) *ou* inspire sth (in sb).

inda ['īda] *adv*= **ainda.**

indagação [īdaga'sãw] (*pl* **-ões**) *f* (*investigação*) investigation; (*pergunta*) inquiry, question.

indagar [īda'ga*] *vt* (*investigar*) to investigate, inquire into ♦ *vi* to inquire; **~-se** *vr*: **~-se a si mesmo** to ask o.s.; **~ algo de alguém** to ask sb about sth; **~ (de alguém) sobre** *ou* **de algo** to inquire (of sb) about sth.

indébito/a [ī'dɛbitu/a] *adj* undue; (*queixa*) unfounded.

indecência [īde'sēsja] *f* indecency; (*ato, dito*) vulgar thing.

indecente [īde'sētʃi] *adj* indecent, improper; (*obsceno*) rude, vulgar.

indecifrável [īdesi'fravew] (*pl* **-eis**) *adj* undecipherable; (*pessoa*) inscrutable.

indecisão [īdesi'zãw] *f* indecision.

indeciso/a [īde'sizu/a] *adj* (*irresoluto*) undecided, hesitant; (*indistinto*) vague; (*por decidir*) undecided.

indeclinável [īdekli'navew] (*pl* **-eis**) *adj* indeclinable.

indecoroso/a [īdeko'rozu/ɔza] *adj* indecent, improper.

indefensável [īdefē'savew] (*pl* **-eis**) *adj* indefensible.

indeferido/a [īdefe'ridu/a] *adj* refused, rejected.

indeferir [īdefe'ri*] *vt* (*desatender*) to reject; (*requerimento*) to turn down.

indefeso/a [īde'fezu/a] *adj* undefended; (*fraco*) defenceless.

indefinição [īdefini'sãw] (*pl* **-ões**) *f* (*de pessoa*) vague stance.

indefinido/a [īdefi'nidu/a] *adj* indefinite; (*vago*) vague, undefined; **por tempo ~** indefinitely.

indefinível [īdefi'nivew] (*pl* **-eis**) *adj* indefinable.

indefiro [īde'firu] *etc vb V* **indeferir.**

indelével [īde'lɛvew] (*pl* **-eis**) *adj* indelible.

indelicadeza [īdelika'deza] *f* impoliteness; (*ação, dito*) rude thing.

indelicado/a [īdeli'kadu/a] *adj* impolite, rude.

indene [ī'dɛni] (*PT*: **-mn-**) *adj* (*pessoa*) unharmed; (*objeto*) undamaged.

indenização [indeniza'sãw] (*PT*: **-mn-**; *pl* **-ões**) *f* compensation; (*COM*) indemnity; (*de demissão*) redundancy (*BRIT*) *ou* severance (*US*) payment.

indenizar [īdeni'za*] (*PT*: **-mn-**) *vt*: **~ alguém por** *ou* **de algo** (*compensar*) to compensate sb for sth; (*por gastos*) to reimburse sb for sth.

independência [īdepē'dēsja] *f* independence.

independente [īdepē'dētʃi] *adj* independent; (*auto-suficiente*) self-sufficient; **quarto ~** room with private entrance.

independer [īdepē'de*] *vi*: **~ de algo** not to depend on sth.

indescritível [īdeʃkri'tʃivew] (*pl* **-eis**) *adj* indescribable.

indesculpável [īdʒiʃkuw'pavew] (*pl* **-eis**) *adj* inexcusable.

indesejável [īdeze'ʒavew] (*pl* **-eis**) *adj* undesirable.

indestrutível [īdʒiʃtru'tʃivew] (*pl* **-eis**) *adj* indestructible.

indeterminado/a [īdetexmi'nadu/a] *adj* indeterminate.

indevassável [īdeva'savew] (*pl* **-eis**) *adj* impenetrable.

indevido/a [īde'vidu/a] *adj* (*imerecido*) unjust; (*impróprio*) inappropriate.

índex ['īdeks] (*pl* **índices**) *m* = **índice.**

indexar [īdek'sa*] *vt* to index.

Índia ['īdʒa] *f*: **a ~** India; **as ~s Ocidentais** the West Indies.

indiano/a [ī'dʒjanu/a] *adj, m/f* Indian.

indicação [indʒika'sãw] (*pl* **-ões**) *f* indication; (*de termômetro*) reading; (*para um cargo, prêmio*) nomination; (*recomendação*) recommendation; (*de um caminho*) directions *pl*.

indicado/a [īdʒi'kadu/a] *adj* (*apropriado*) appropriate.

indicador(a) [īdʒika'do*(a)] *m* indicator; (*TEC*) gauge; (*dedo*) index finger; (*ponteiro*) pointer ♦ *adj*: **~ de** indicative of; **~ econômico** economic indicator.

indicar [īdʒi'ka*] *vt* (*mostrar*) to indicate; (*apontar*) to point to; (*temperatura*) to register; (*recomendar*) to recommend; (*para um cargo*) to nominate; (*determinar*) to determine; **~ o caminho a alguém** to give sb directions; **ao que tudo indica ...** by the looks of things ....

indicativo/a [īdʒika'tʃivu/a] *adj* (*tb*: *LING*) indicative.

índice ['indʒisi] *m* (*de livro*) index; (*dedo*) index finger; (*taxa*) rate; **~ do custo de vida** cost of living index; **~ de audiência** (*TV*) rating.

índices ['indʒisiʃ] *mpl de* **índex.**

indiciado/a [īdʒi'sjadu/a] *m/f* defendant.

indiciar [īdʒi'sja*] *vt* (*acusar*) to charge; (*submeter a inquérito*) to investigate.

indício [in'dʒisju] *m* (*sinal*) sign; (*vestígio*) trace; (*JUR*) clue.

indiferença [īdʒife'rēsa] *f* indifference.

indiferente [īdʒife'rētʃi] *adj*: **~ (a)** indifferent (to); **isso me é ~** it's all the same to me.

indígena [ī'dʒiʒena] *adj, m/f* native; (*índio*) Indian.

indigência [īdʒi'ʒēsja] *f* poverty; (*fig*) lack, need.

indigente [īdʒi'ʒētʃi] *adj* destitute, indigent.

***NB:** European Portuguese adds the following consonants to certain words:* **b** (sú(b)dito, su(b)til); **c** (a(c)ção, a(c)cionista, a(c)to); **m** (inde(m)ne); **p** (ado(p)ção, ado(p)tar); *for further details see p. xiii.*

indigestão [ĩdʒiʒeʃ'tãw] *f* indigestion.
indigesto/a [ĩdʒi'ʒɛʃtu/a] *adj* indigestible; (*fig*: *aborrecido*) dull, boring; (: *obscuro*) turgid.
indignação [ĩdʒigna'sãw] *f* indignation.
indignado/a [ĩdʒig'nadu/a] *adj* indignant.
indignar [ĩdʒig'na*] *vt* to anger, incense; **~-se** *vr* to get angry; **~-se com** to get indignant about.
indignidade [ĩdʒigni'dadʒi] *f* indignity; (*ultraje*) outrage.
indigno/a [ĩ'dʒignu/a] *adj* (*não merecedor*) unworthy; (*desprezível*) disgraceful, despicable.
índio/a ['ĩdʒju/a] *adj*, *m/f* (*da América*) Indian.
indiquei [ĩdʒi'kej] *etc vb V* **indicar**.
indireta [ĩdʒi'rɛta] (*PT*: **-ct-**) *f* insinuation; **dar uma ~** to drop a hint.
indireto/a [ĩdʒi'rɛtu/a] (*PT*: **-ct-**) *adj* indirect; (*olhar*) sidelong; (*procedimento*) roundabout.
indisciplina [ĩdʒisi'plina] *f* indiscipline.
indisciplinado/a [ĩdʒisipli'nadu/a] *adj* undisciplined.
indiscreto/a [ĩdʒiʃ'krɛtu/a] *adj* indiscreet.
indiscrição [ĩdʒiʃkri'sãw] (*pl* **-ões**) *f* indiscretion.
indiscriminado/a [ĩdʒiʃkrimi'nadu/a] *adj* indiscriminate.
indiscutível [ĩdʒiʃku'tʃivew] (*pl* **-eis**) *adj* indisputable.
indispensável [ĩdʒiʃpẽ'savew] (*pl* **-eis**) *adj* essential, vital ♦ *m* essentials *pl*.
indispõe [ĩdʒiʃ'põj] *etc vb V* **indispor**.
indispomos [ĩdʒiʃ'pomoʃ] *etc vb V* **indispor**.
indisponho [ĩdʒiʃ'poɲu] *etc vb V* **indispor**.
indisponível [ĩdʒiʃpo'nivew] (*pl* **-eis**) *adj* unavailable.
indispor [ĩdʒiʃ'po*] (*irreg*: *como* **pôr**) *vt* (*de saúde*) to make ill; (*aborrecer*) to upset; **~-se** *vr*: **~-se com um amigo** to fall out with a friend; **~-se com** *ou* **contra alguém** (*governo etc*) to turn against sb; **~ alguém com** *ou* **contra alguém** to turn sb against sb.
indisposição [ĩdʒiʃpozi'sãw] (*pl* **-ões**) *f* illness.
indisposto/a [ĩdʒiʃ'poʃtu/'pɔʃta] *pp de* **indispor** ♦ *adj* (*doente*) unwell, poorly.
indispunha [ĩdʒiʃ'puɲa] *etc vb V* **indispor**.
indispus [ĩdʒiʃ'puʃ] *etc vb V* **indispor**.
indispuser [ĩdʒiʃpu'ze*] *etc vb V* **indispor**.
indisputável [ĩdʒiʃpu'tavew] (*pl* **-eis**) *adj* indisputable.
indissolúvel [ĩdʒiso'luvew] (*pl* **-eis**) *adj* (*material*) insoluble; (*contrato*) indissoluble.
indistinguível [ĩdʒiʃtʃĩ'givew] (*pl* **-eis**) *adj* indistinguishable.
indistinto/a [ĩdʒiʃ'tʃĩtu/a] *adj* indistinct.
individual [ĩdʒivi'dwaw] (*pl* **-ais**) *adj* individual.
individualidade [ĩdʒividwali'dadʒi] *f* individuality.
individualismo [ĩdʒividwa'liʒmu] *m* individualism.
individualista [ĩdʒividwa'liʃta] *adj* individualist(ic) ♦ *m/f* individualist.
individualizar [ĩdʒividwali'za*] *vt* to individualize.
indivíduo [ĩdʒi'vidwu] *m* individual; (*col*: *sujeito*) person.
indivisível [ĩdʒivi'zivew] (*pl* **-eis**) *adj* indivisible.
indiviso/a [ĩdʒi'vizu/a] *adj* undivided; (*propriedade*) joint.
indizível [ĩdʒi'zivew] (*pl* **-eis**) *adj* unspeakable; (*indescritível*) indescribable.
Ind. Lucr. (*BR*) *abr* (*COM*) = **Índice de Lucratividade.**
indóceis [ĩ'dɔsejʃ] *adj pl de* **indócil**.
Indochina [ĩdo'ʃina] *f*: **a ~** Indochina.
indócil [ĩ'dɔsiw] (*pl* **-eis**) *adj* (*rebelde*) unruly, wayward; (*impaciente*) restless.
indo-europeu/péia [ĩdu-] *adj* Indo-European.
índole ['ĩdoli] *f* (*temperamento*) nature; (*tipo*) sort, type.
indolência [ĩdo'lẽsja] *f* laziness, indolence; (*apatia*) apathy.
indolente [ĩdo'lẽtʃi] *adj* indolent; (*apático*) apathetic.
indolor [ĩdo'lo*] *adj* painless.
indomável [ĩdo'mavew] (*pl* **-eis**) *adj* (*animal*) untameable; (*coragem*) indomitable; (*criança*) unmanageable; (*paixão*) consuming.
indômito/a [ĩ'domitu/a] *adj* untamed, wild.
Indonésia [ĩdo'nɛzja] *f*: **a ~** Indonesia.
indonésio/a [ĩdo'nɛzju/a] *adj*, *m/f* Indonesian.
indoor [ĩ'do*] *adj inv* (*ESPORTE*) indoor.
indubitável [ĩdubi'tavew] (*pl* **-eis**) *adj* indubitable.
indução [ĩdu'sãw] (*pl* **-ões**) *f* induction; (*persuasão*) inducement.
indulgência [ĩduw'ʒẽsja] *f* indulgence; (*tolerância*) leniency; (*JUR*) clemency.
indulgente [ĩduw'ʒẽtʃi] *adj* (*juiz*, *atitude*) lenient; (*olhar*) indulgent.
indultar [ĩduw'ta*] *vt* (*JUR*) to reprieve.
indulto [ĩ'duwtu] *m* (*JUR*) reprieve.
indumentária [ĩdumẽ'tarja] *f* costume.
indústria [ĩ'duʃtrja] *f* industry; **"~ brasileira"** "made in Brazil"; **~ automobilística** car industry; **~ de consumo** *ou* **de ponta** *ou* **leve** light industry; **~ de base** key industry; **~ pesada** heavy industry; **~ de transformação** process industry; **~ fabril** manufacturing industry.
industrial [ĩduʃ'trjaw] (*pl* **-ais**) *adj* industrial ♦ *m/f* industrialist.
industrialização [ĩduʃtrjaliza'sãw] *f* industrialization.
industrializado/a [ĩduʃtrjali'zadu/a] *adj* (*país*) industrialized; (*produto*) manufactured; (*gêneros*) processed; (*pão*) sliced.
industrializar [ĩduʃtrjali'za*] *vt* (*país*) to industrialize; (*aproveitar*) to process; **~-se** *vr* to become industrialized.
industriar [ĩduʃ'trja*] *vt* (*orientar*) to instruct; (*amestrar*) to train.
industrioso/a [ĩduʃ'trjozu/ɔza] *adj* (*traba-*

lhador) hard-working, industrious; (*hábil*) clever, skilful (*BRIT*), skillful (*US*).

indutivo/a [ĩdu'tʃivu/a] *adj* inductive.

induzir [ĩdu'zi*] *vt* to induce; ~ **alguém a fazer** to persuade sb to do; ~ **alguém em erro** to mislead sb; ~ **(algo de algo)** to infer (sth from sth).

inebriante [ine'brjãtʃi] *adj* intoxicating.

inebriar [ine'brja*] *vt* (*fig*) to intoxicate; **~-se** *vr* to be intoxicated.

inédito/a [i'nɛdʒitu/a] *adj* (*livro*) unpublished; (*incomum*) unheard-of, rare.

inefável [ine'favew] (*pl* **-eis**) *adj* indescribable.

ineficácia [inefi'kasja] *f* (*de remédio, medida*) ineffectiveness; (*de empregado, máquina*) inefficiency.

ineficaz [inefi'kajʒ] *adj* (*remédio, medida*) ineffective; (*empregado, máquina*) inefficient.

ineficiência [inefi'sjẽsja] *f* inefficiency.

ineficiente [inefi'sjẽtʃi] *adj* inefficient.

inegável [ine'gavew] (*pl* **-eis**) *adj* undeniable.

inelutável [inelu'tavew] (*pl* **-eis**) *adj* inescapable.

inépcia [i'nɛpsja] *f* ineptitude.

inepto/a [i'nɛptu/a] *adj* inept, incompetent.

inequívoco/a [ine'kivoku/a] *adj* (*evidente*) clear; (*inconfundível*) unmistakeable.

inércia [i'nɛxsja] *f* (*torpor*) lassitude, lethargy; (*FÍS*) inertia.

inerente [ine'rẽtʃi] *adj* inherent.

inerme [i'nɛxmi] *adj* (*formal: não armado*) unarmed; (*indefeso*) defenceless (*BRIT*), defenseless (*US*).

inerte [i'nɛxtʃi] *adj* lethargic; (*FÍS*) inert.

INES (*BR*) *abr m* = **Instituto Nacional de Educação dos Surdos.**

inescrupuloso/a [ineʃkrupu'lozu/ɔza] *adj* unscrupulous.

inescrutável [ineʃkru'tavew] (*pl* **-eis**) *adj* inscrutable.

inescusável [ineʃku'zavew] (*pl* **-eis**) *adj* (*indesculpável*) inexcusable; (*indispensável*) essential.

inesgotável [ineʒgo'tavew] (*pl* **-eis**) *adj* inexhaustible; (*superabundante*) boundless, abundant.

inesperado/a [ineʃpe'radu/a] *adj* unexpected, unforeseen ♦ *m*: **o** ~ the unexpected.

inesquecível [ineʃke'sivew] (*pl* **-eis**) *adj* unforgettable.

inestimável [ineʃtʃi'mavew] (*pl* **-eis**) *adj* invaluable.

inevitável [inevi'tavew] (*pl* **-eis**) *adj* inevitable.

inexatidão [inezatʃi'dãw] (*PT*: **-ct-**; *pl* **-ões**) *f* inaccuracy.

inexato/a [ine'zatu/a] (*PT*: **-ct-**) *adj* inaccurate.

inexaurível [inezaw'rivew] (*pl* **-eis**) *adj* inexhaustible.

inexcedível [inese'dʒivew] (*pl* **-eis**) *adj* unsurpassed.

inexeqüível [ineze'kwivew] (*pl* **-eis**) *adj* impracticable, unworkable.

inexistência [ineziʃ'tẽsja] *f* lack.

inexistente [ineziʃ'tẽtʃi] *adj* non-existent.

inexistir [ineziʃ'tʃi*] *vi* not to exist.

inexorável [inezo'ravew] (*pl* **-eis**) *adj* implacable.

inexperiência [ineʃpe'rjẽsja] *f* inexperience, lack of experience.

inexperiente [ineʃpe'rjẽtʃi] *adj* inexperienced; (*ingênuo*) naive.

inexplicável [ineʃpli'kavew] (*pl* **-eis**) *adj* inexplicable.

inexplorado/a [ineʃplo'radu/a] *adj* unexplored.

inexpressivo/a [ineʃpre'sivu/a] *adj* expressionless.

inexpugnável [ineʃpug'navew] (*pl* **-eis**) *adj* (*fortaleza*) impregnable; (*invencível*) invincible.

inextinto/a [ineʃ'tʃĩtu/a] *adj* unextinguished.

inextricável [ineʃtri'kavew] (*pl* **-eis**) *adj* inextricable.

infalível [ĩfa'livew] (*pl* **-eis**) *adj* infallible; (*sucesso*) guaranteed.

infame [ĩ'fami] *adj* (*pessoa, procedimento*) mean, nasty; (*comida, trabalho*) awful.

infâmia [ĩ'famja] *f* (*desonra*) disgrace; (*vileza*) villainy; (*dito*) nasty thing.

infância [ĩ'fãsja] *f* childhood; **primeira** ~ infancy, early childhood.

infantaria [ĩfãta'ria] *f* infantry.

infante/a [ĩ'fãtʃi/a] *m/f* (*filho dos reis*) prince/princess ♦ *m* (*soldado*) foot soldier.

infanticídio [ĩfãtʃi'sidʒu] *m* infanticide.

infantil [ĩfã'tʃiw] (*pl* **-is**) *adj* (*ingênuo*) childlike; (*pueril*) childish; (*para crianças*) children's.

infantilidade [ĩfãtʃili'dadʒi] *f* childishness; (*dito, ação*) childish thing.

infantis [ĩfã'tʃiʃ] *adj pl de* **infantil.**

infanto-juvenil [ĩfãto-] (*pl* **-is**) *adj* children's.

infarto [ĩ'faxtu] *m* heart attack.

infatigável [ĩfatʃi'gavew] (*pl* **-eis**) *adj* untiring.

infausto/a [ĩ'fawʃtu/a] *adj* unlucky.

infecção [ĩfek'sãw] (*pl* **-ões**) *f* infection; (*contaminação*) contamination.

infeccionar [ĩfeksjo'na*] *vt* (*ferida*) to infect; (*contaminar*) to contaminate.

infeccioso/a [ĩfek'sjozu/ɔza] *adj* infectious.

infecções [ĩfek'sõjʃ] *fpl de* **infecção.**

infectar [ĩfek'ta*] (*PT*) *vt* = **infetar.**

infelicidade [ĩfelisi'dadʒi] *f* unhappiness; (*desgraça*) misfortune.

infelicíssimo/a [ĩfeli'sisimu/a] *adj superl de* **infeliz.**

infeliz [ĩfe'liʒ] *adj* (*triste*) unhappy; (*infausto*) unfortunate; (*ação, medida*) unfortunate; (*sugestão, idéia*) inappropriate ♦ *m/f* unhappy

NB: *European Portuguese adds the following consonants to certain words:* **b** (sú(b)dito, su(b)til); **c** (a(c)ção, a(c)cionista, a(c)to); **m** (inde(m)ne); **p** (ado(p)ção, ado(p)tar); *for further details see p. xiii.*

person; **como um** ~ (*col*) like there's no tomorrow.

infelizmente [ĩfeliʒ'mẽtʃi] *adv* unfortunately.

infenso/a [ĩ'fẽsu/a] *adj* adverse.

inferior [ĩfe'rjo*] *adj*: ~ **(a)** (*em valor, qualidade*) inferior (to); (*mais baixo*) lower (than) ♦ *m/f* inferior, subordinate.

inferioridade [ĩferjori'dadʒi] *f* inferiority.

inferiorizar [ĩferjori'za*] *vt* to put down; **~-se** *vr* to become inferior.

inferir [ĩfe'ri*] *vt* to infer, deduce.

infernal [ĩfex'naw] (*pl* **-ais**) *adj* infernal; (*col: excepcional*) amazing.

inferninho [ĩfex'niɲu] *m* club.

infernizar [ĩfexni'za*] *vt*: ~ **a vida de alguém** to make sb's life hell.

inferno [ĩ'fɛxnu] *m* hell; **é um** ~ (*fig*) it's hell; **vá pro** ~! (*col*) piss off!

infértil [ĩ'fɛxtʃiw] (*pl* **-eis**) *adj* infertile.

infertilidade [ĩfextʃili'dadʒi] *f* infertility.

infestar [ĩfeʃ'ta*] *vt* to infest.

infetar [ĩfe'ta*] *vt* to infect, contaminate.

infidelidade [ĩfideli'dadʒi] *f* infidelity, unfaithfulness; (*REL*) disbelief; ~ **conjugal** marital infidelity.

infidelíssimo/a [ĩfide'lisimu/a] *adj superl de* **infiel**.

infiel [ĩ'fjɛw] (*pl* **-éis**) *adj* (*desleal*) disloyal; (*marido*) unfaithful; (*texto*) inaccurate ♦ *m/f* (*REL*) non-believer.

infiltração [ĩfiwtra'sãw] (*pl* **-ões**) *f* infiltration.

infiltrar [ĩfiw'tra*] *vt* to permeate; **~-se** *vr* (*água, luz, odor*) to permeate; **~-se em algo** (*pessoas*) to infiltrate sth.

ínfimo/a ['ĩfimu/a] *adj* lowest; (*qualidade*) poorest.

infindável [ĩfĩ'davew] (*pl* **-eis**) *adj* unending, constant.

infinidade [ĩfini'dadʒi] *f* infinity; **uma** ~ **de** countless.

infinitesimal [ĩfinitezi'maw] (*pl* **-ais**) *adj* infinitesimal.

infinitivo/a [ĩfini'tʃivu/a] *adj* (*LING*) infinitive ♦ *m* infinitive.

infinito/a [ĩfi'nitu/a] *adj* infinite ♦ *m* infinity.

infiro [ĩ'firu] *etc vb V* **inferir**.

inflação [ĩfla'sãw] *f* inflation.

inflacionar [ĩflasjo'na*] *vt* (*ECON*) to inflate.

inflacionário/a [ĩflasjo'narju/a] *adj* inflationary.

inflacionista [ĩflasjo'niʃta] *adj, m/f* inflationist.

inflamação [ĩflama'sãw] (*pl* **-ões**) *f* (*MED*) inflammation; (*de madeira etc*) combustion.

inflamado/a [ĩfla'madu/a] *adj* (*MED*) inflamed; (*discurso*) heated.

inflamar [ĩfla'ma*] *vt* (*madeira, pólvora*) to set fire to; (*MED, fig*) to inflame; **~-se** *vr* to catch fire; (*fig*) to get worked up; **~-se de algo** to be consumed with sth.

inflamatório/a [ĩflama'tɔrju/a] *adj* inflammatory.

inflamável [ĩfla'mavew] (*pl* **-eis**) *adj* inflammable.

inflar [ĩ'fla*] *vt* to inflate, blow up; **~-se** *vr* to swell (up); ~ **algo de algo** to inflate sth *ou* fill sth up with sth.

inflexibilidade [ĩfleksibili'dadʒi] *f* inflexibility.

inflexível [ĩflek'sivew] (*pl* **-eis**) *adj* stiff, rigid; (*fig*) unyielding.

infligir [ĩfli'ʒi*] *vt*: ~ **algo (a alguém)** to inflict sth (upon sb).

influência [ĩ'flwẽsja] *f* influence; **sob a** ~ **de** under the influence of.

influenciar [ĩflwẽ'sja*] *vt* to influence ♦ *vi*: ~ **em algo** to influence sth, have an influence on sth; **~-se** *vr*: **~-se por** to be influenced by.

influenciável [ĩflwẽ'sjavew] (*pl* **-eis**) *adj* open to influence.

influente [ĩ'flwẽtʃi] *adj* influential.

influir [ĩ'flwi*] *vi* (*importar*) to matter, be important; ~ **em** *ou* **sobre** to influence, have an influence on.

influxo [ĩ'fluksu] *m* influx; (*maré-cheia*) high tide.

informação [ĩfoxma'sãw] (*pl* **-ões**) *f* (piece of) information; (*notícia*) news; (*MIL*) intelligence; (*JUR*) inquiry; (*COMPUT*) piece of data; (*instrução*) instruction; **informações** *fpl* information *sg*; **Informações** (*TEL*) directory enquiries (*BRIT*), information (*US*); **pedir informações sobre** to ask about, inquire about; **serviço de** ~ intelligence service.

informado/a [ĩfox'madu/a] *adj* informed.

informal [ĩfox'maw] (*pl* **-ais**) *adj* informal.

informalidade [ĩfoxmali'dadʒi] *f* informality.

informante [ĩfox'mãtʃi] *m* informant; (*JUR*) informer.

informar [ĩfox'ma*] *vt*: ~ **alguém (de/sobre algo)** to inform sb (of/about sth) ♦ *vi* to inform, be informative; ~ **de** to report on; **~-se** *vr*: **~-se de** to find out about, inquire about; ~ **algo a alguém** to tell sb sth.

informática [ĩfox'matʃika] *f* (*ciência*) computer science; (*ramo*) computing, computers *pl*.

informativo/a [ĩfoxma'tʃivu/a] *adj* informative.

informatização [ĩfoxmatʃiza'sãw] *f* computerization.

informatizar [ĩfoxmatʃi'za*] *vt* to computerize.

informe [ĩ'fɔxmi] *m* (piece of) information; (*MIL*) briefing; **~s** *mpl* information *sg*.

infortúnio [ĩfox'tunju] *m* misfortune.

infração [ĩfra'sãw] (*PT*: **-cç-**; *pl* **-ões**) *f* breach, infringement; (*FUTEBOL*) foul; ~ **de trânsito** traffic offence (*BRIT*) *ou* violation (*US*).

infractor(a) [ĩfra'to*(a)] (*PT*) *m/f* = **infrator(a)**.

infra-estrutura [ĩfra-] *f* infrastructure.

infrator(a) [ĩfra'to*(a)] *m/f* offender.

infravermelho/a [ĩfravex'meʎu/a] *adj* infrared.

infreqüente [ĩfre'kwẽtʃi] *adj* infrequent.

infringir [ĩfrĩ'ʒi*] *vt* to infringe, contravene.

infrutífero/a [ĩfru'tʃiferu/a] *adj* fruitless.

infundado/a [ĩfũ'dadu/a] *adj* groundless, unfounded.

infundir [ĩfũ'dʒi*] *vt* to infuse; (*terror*) to strike; (*incutir*) to instil (*BRIT*), instill (*US*).
infusão [ĩfu'zãw] (*pl* **-ões**) *f* infusion.
ingenuidade [ĩʒenwi'dadʒi] *f* ingenuousness.
ingênuo/a [ĩ'ʒenwu/a] *adj* ingenuous, naïve; (*comentário*) harmless ♦ *m/f* naïve person.
ingerência [ĩʒe'rẽsja] *f* interference.
ingerir [ĩʒe'ri*] *vt* to ingest; (*engolir*) to swallow; **~-se** *vr*: **~-se em algo** to interfere in sth.
Inglaterra [ĩgla'tɛxa] *f*: **a ~** England.
inglês/esa [ĩ'gleʃ/eza] *adj* English ♦ *m/f* Englishman/woman ♦ *m* (*LING*) English; **os ingleses** *mpl* the English; **(só) para ~ ver** (*col*) (just) for show.
inglesar [ĩgle'za*] *vt* to Anglicize; **~-se** *vr* to become Anglicized.
inglório/a [ĩ'glɔrju/a] *adj* inglorious.
ingovernável [ĩgovex'navew] (*pl* **-eis**) *adj* ungovernable.
ingratidão [ĩgratʒi'dãw] *f* ingratitude.
ingrato/a [ĩ'gratu/a] *adj* ungrateful.
ingrediente [ĩgre'dʒjẽtʃi] *m* ingredient.
íngreme ['ĩgremi] *adj* steep.
ingressar [ĩgre'sa*] *vi*: **~ em** to enter, go into; (*um clube*) to join.
ingresso [ĩ'grɛsu] *m* (*entrada*) entry; (*admissão*) admission; (*bilhete*) ticket.
inhaca [i'ɲaka] (*col*) *f* (*fedor*) stink.
inhame [i'ɲami] *m* yam.
inibição [inibi'sãw] (*pl* **-ões**) *f* inhibition.
inibido/a [ini'bidu/a] *adj* inhibited.
inibidor(a) [inibi'do*(a)] *adj* inhibiting.
inibir [ini'bi*] *vt*: **~ alguém (de fazer)** to inhibit sb (from doing); **~-se** *vr*: **~-se (de fazer)** to be inhibited (from doing).
iniciação [inisja'sãw] (*pl* **-ões**) *f* initiation.
iniciado/a [ini'sjadu/a] *m/f* initiate.
iniciador(a) [inisja'do*(a)] *adj* initiating ♦ *m/f* initiator.
inicial [ini'sjaw] (*pl* **-ais**) *adj* initial, first ♦ *f* initial.
inicializar [inisjali'za*] *vt* (*COMPUT*) to initialize.
iniciar [ini'sja*] *vt*, *vi* (*começar*) to begin, start; **~ alguém em algo** (*arte*, *seita*) to initiate sb into sth.
iniciativa [inisja'tʃiva] *f* initiative; **tomar a ~** to take the initiative; **por ~ própria** on one's own initiative, off one's own bat (*BRIT*); **a ~ privada** (*ECON*) private enterprise; **não ter ~** to lack initiative.
início [i'nisju] *m* beginning, start; **no ~** at the start.
inigualável [inigwa'lavew] (*pl* **-eis**) *adj* unequalled.
inimaginável [inimaʒi'navew] (*pl* **-eis**) *adj* unimaginable.
inimigo/a [ini'migu/a] *adj*, *m/f* enemy.
inimizade [inimi'zadʒi] *f* enmity, hatred.
inimizar [inimi'za*] *vt*: **~ alguém com alguém** to set sb against sb; **~-se** *vr*: **~-se com** to fall out with.
ininteligível [inĩteli'ʒivew] (*pl* **-eis**) *adj* unintelligible.
ininterrupto/a [inĩte'xuptu/a] *adj* continuous; (*esforço*) unstinting; (*vôo*) non-stop; (*serviço*) 24-hour.
iniqüidade [inikwi'dadʒi] *f* iniquity.
iníquo/a [i'nikwu/a] *adj* iniquitous.
injeção [inʒe'sãw] (*PT*: **-cç-**; *pl* **-ões**) *f* injection.
injetado/a [ĩʒe'tadu/a] (*PT*: **-ct-**) *adj* (*olhos*) bloodshot.
injetar [ĩʒe'ta*] (*PT*: **-ct-**) *vt* to inject.
injunção [ĩʒũ'sãw] (*pl* **-ões**) *f* (*ordem*) order; (*pressão*) pressure.
injúria [ĩ'ʒurja] *f* (*insulto*) insult.
injuriar [ĩʒu'rja*] *vt* to insult.
injurioso/a [ĩʒu'rjozu/ɔza] *adj* insulting; (*ofensivo*) offensive.
injustiça [ĩʒuʃ'tʃisa] *f* injustice.
injustiçado/a [ĩʒuʃtʃi'sadu/a] *adj* wronged ♦ *m/f* victim of injustice.
injustificável [ĩʒuʃtʃifi'kavew] (*pl* **-eis**) *adj* unjustifiable.
injusto/a [ĩ'ʒuʃtu/a] *adj* unfair, unjust.
INM (*BR*) *abr m* = **Instituto Nacional de Meteorologia**.
inobservado/a [inobizex'vadu/a] *adj* unobserved; (*nunca visto*) never witnessed.
inobservância [inobizex'vãsja] *f* nonobservance.
inobservante [inobizex'vãtʃi] *adj* inobservant.
inocência [ino'sẽsja] *f* innocence.
inocentar [inosẽ'ta*] *vt*: **~ alguém (de algo)** to clear sb (of sth).
inocente [ino'sẽtʃi] *adj* innocent ♦ *m/f* innocent man/woman; **os ~s** the innocent.
inoculação [inokula'sãw] (*pl* **-ões**) *f* inoculation.
inocular [inoku'la*] *vt* to inoculate.
inócuo/a [i'nɔkwu/a] *adj* harmless.
inodoro/a [ino'dɔru/a] *adj* odourless (*BRIT*), odorless (*US*).
inofensivo/a [inofẽ'sivu/a] *adj* harmless, inoffensive.
inolvidável [inowvi'davew] (*pl* **-eis**) *adj* unforgettable.
inoperante [inope'rãtʃi] *adj* inoperative.
inopinado/a [inopi'nadu/a] *adj* unexpected.
inoportuno/a [inopox'tunu/a] *adj* inconvenient, inopportune.
inorgânico/a [inox'ganiku/a] *adj* inorganic.
inóspito/a [i'nɔʃpitu/a] *adj* inhospitable.
inovação [inova'sãw] (*pl* **-ões**) *f* innovation.
inovar [ino'va*] *vt* to innovate.
inoxidável [inoksi'davew[(*pl* **-eis**) *adj*: **aço ~** stainless steel.
INPC (*BR*) *abr m* (= *Indice Nacional de Pre-*

NB*: European Portuguese adds the following consonants to certain words:* **b** (sú(b)dito, su(b)til); **c** (a(c)ção, a(c)cionista, a(c)to); **m** (inde(m)ne); **p** (ado(p)ção, ado(p)tar); *for further details see p. xiii.*

ços ao Consumidor) RPI.

INPS (*BR*) *abr m* (= *Instituto Nacional de Previdência Social*) ≈ DSS (*BRIT*), ≈ Welfare Dept (*US*).

inqualificável [ĩkwalifi'kavew] (*pl* **-eis**) *adj* incalculable; (*vil*) unacceptable.

inquebrantável [ĩkebrã'tavew] (*pl* **-eis**) *adj* unbreakable; (*fig*) unshakeable.

inquestionável [ĩkeʃtʃjo'navew] (*pl* **-eis**) *adj* unquestionable.

inquérito [ĩ'kɛritu] *m* inquiry; (*JUR*) inquest.

inquietação [ĩkjeta'sãw] *f* (*preocupação*) anxiety, uneasiness; (*agitação*) restlessness.

inquietador(a) [ĩkjeta'do*(a)] *adj* worrying, disturbing.

inquietante [ĩkje'tãtʃi] *adj* worrying, disturbing.

inquietar [ĩkje'ta*] *vt* to worry, disturb; **~-se** *vr* to worry, bother.

inquieto/a [ĩ'kjɛtu/a] *adj* (*ansioso*) anxious, worried; (*agitado*) restless.

inquietude [ĩkje'tudʒi] *f* (*preocupação*) anxiety, uneasiness; (*agitação*) restlessness.

inquilino/a [ĩki'linu/a] *m/f* tenant.

inquirição [ĩkiri'sãw] (*pl* **-ões**) *f* investigation; (*JUR*) cross-examination.

inquirir [ĩki'ri*] *vt* (*investigar*) to investigate; (*perguntar*) to question; (*JUR*) to cross-examine ♦ *vi* to enquire.

inquisição [ĩkizi'sãw] (*pl* **-ões**) *f*: **a I~** the Inquisition.

inquisitivo/a [ĩkizi'tʃivu/a] *adj* inquisitive.

insaciável [ĩsa'sjavew] (*pl* **-eis**) *adj* insatiable.

insalubre [ĩsa'lubri] *adj* unhealthy.

insanidade [ĩsani'dadʒi] *f* madness, insanity.

insano/a [ĩ'sanu/a] *adj* insane; (*fig*: *trabalho*) exhaustive.

insatisfação [ĩsatʃiʃfa'sãw] *f* dissatisfaction.

insatisfatório/a [ĩsatʃiʃfa'tɔrju/a] *adj* unsatisfactory.

insatisfeito/a [ĩsatʃiʃ'fejtu/a] *adj* dissatisfied, unhappy.

inscrever [ĩʃkre've*] *vt* (*gravar*) to inscribe; (*aluno*) to enrol (*BRIT*), enroll (*US*); (*em registro*) to register; **~-se** *vr* to enrol(l); to register.

inscrição [ĩʃkri'sãw] (*pl* **-ões**) *f* (*legenda*) inscription; (*EDUC*) enrolment (*BRIT*), enrollment (*US*); (*em lista etc*) registration.

inscrito/a [ĩ'ʃkritu/a] *pp de* **inscrever**.

insecto *etc* [ĩ'sɛktu] (*PT*) = **inseto** *etc*.

insegurança [ĩsegu'rãsa] *f* insecurity.

inseguro/a [ĩse'guru/a] *adj* insecure.

inseminação [ĩsemina'sãw] *f*: **~ artificial** artificial insemination.

inseminar [ĩsemi'na*] *vt* to inseminate.

insensatez [ĩsẽsa'teʒ] *f* folly, madness.

insensato/a [ĩsẽ'satu/a] *adj* unreasonable, foolish.

insensibilidade [ĩsẽsibili'dadʒi] *f* insensitivity; (*dormência*) numbness.

insensível [ĩsẽ'sivew] (*pl* **-eis**) *adj* insensitive; (*dormente*) numb.

inseparável [ĩsepa'ravew] (*pl* **-eis**) *adj* inseparable.

inserção [ĩsex'sãw] (*pl* **-ões**) *f* insertion; (*COMPUT*) entry.

inserir [ĩse'ri*] *vt* to insert, put in; (*COMPUT*: *dados*) to enter; **~-se** *vr*: **~-se em** to become part of.

inseticida [ĩsetʃi'sida] *m* insecticide.

inseto [ĩ'sɛtu] *m* insect.

insidioso/a [ĩsi'dʒjozu/ɔza] *adj* insidious.

insigne [ĩ'signi] *adj* distinguished, eminent.

insígnia [ĩ'signia] *f* (*sinal distintivo*) badge; (*emblema*) emblem.

insignificância [ĩsignifi'kãsja] *f* insignificance.

insignificante [ĩsignifi'kãtʃi] *adj* insignificant.

insinceridade [ĩsĩseri'dadʒi] *f* insincerity.

insincero/a [ĩsĩ'sɛru/a] *adj* insincere.

insinuação [ĩsinwa'sãw] (*pl* **-ões**) *f* insinuation; (*sugestão*) hint.

insinuante [ĩsi'nwãtʃi] *adj* ingratiating.

insinuar [ĩsi'nwa*] *vt* to insinuate, imply ♦ *vi* to make insinuations; **~-se** *vr*: **~-se por** *ou* **entre** to slip through; **~-se na confiança de alguém** to worm one's way into sb's confidence.

insípido/a [ĩ'sipidu/a] *adj* insipid; (*fig*) dull.

insiro [ĩ'siru] *etc vb V* **inserir**.

insistência [ĩsiʃ'tẽsja] *f*: **~ (em)** insistence (on); (*obstinação*) persistence (in).

insistente [ĩsiʃ'tẽtʃi] *adj* (*pessoa*) insistent; (*apelo*) urgent.

insistir [ĩsiʃ'tʃi*] *vi*: **~ (em)** (*exigir*) to insist (on); (*perseverar*) to persist (in); **~ por algo** to stand up for sth; **~ sobre algo** to dwell on sth; **~ (para) que alguém faça** to insist that sb do *ou* on sb doing; **~ (em) que** to insist that.

insociável [ĩso'sjavew] (*pl* **-eis**) *adj* unsociable, antisocial.

insofismável [ĩsofiʒ'mavew] (*pl* **-eis**) *adj* simple.

insofrido/a [ĩso'fridu/a] *adj* impatient, restless.

insolação [insola'sãw] *f* sunstroke; **pegar uma ~** to get sunstroke.

insolência [ĩso'lẽsja] *f* insolence.

insolente [ĩso'lẽtʃi] *adj* insolent.

insólito/a [ĩ'sɔlitu/a] *adj* unusual.

insolúvel [ĩso'luvew] (*pl* **-eis**) *adj* insoluble.

insolvência [ĩsow'vẽsja] *f* insolvency.

insolvente [ĩsow'vẽtʃi] *adj* insolvent.

insondável [ĩsõ'davew] (*pl* **-eis**) *adj* unfathomable.

insone [ĩ'sɔni] *adj* (*pessoa*) insomniac; (*noite*) sleepless.

insônia [ĩ'sonja] *f* insomnia.

insosso/a [ĩ'sosu/a] *adj* unsalted; (*sem sabor*) tasteless; (*pessoa*) uninteresting, dull.

inspeção [ĩʃpe'sãw] (*PT*: **-cç-**; *pl* **-ões**) *f* inspection, check; (*departamento*) inspectorate.

inspecionar [ĩʃpesjo'na*] (*PT*: **-cc-**) *vt* to inspect.

inspeções [ĩʃpe'sõjʃ] *fpl de* **inspeção**.

inspetor(a) [ĩʃpe'to*(a)] (*PT*: **-ct-**) *m/f* inspector.
inspetoria [ĩʃpeto'ria] (*PT*: **-ct-**) *f* inspectorate.
inspiração [ĩʃpira'sãw] (*pl* **-ões**) *f* inspiration; (*nos pulmões*) inhalation.
inspirador(a) [ĩʃpira'do*(a)] *adj* inspiring.
inspirar [ĩʃpi'ra*] *vt* to inspire; (*MED*) to inhale; **~-se** *vr* to be inspired; **ele não me inspira confiança** he does not inspire me with confidence.
instabilidade [ĩʃtabili'dadʒi] *f* instability.
instalação [ĩʃtala'sãw] (*pl* **-ões**) *f* installation; **~ elétrica** electrics *pl*, electrical system; **~ hidráulica** waterworks *sg*.
instalar [ĩʃta'la*] *vt* (*equipamento*) to install; (*estabelecer*) to set up; (*alojar*) to accommodate, put up; (*num cargo*) to place, install; **~-se** *vr* (*numa cadeira*) to install o.s.; (*alojar-se*) to settle in; (*num cargo*) to take up office.
instância [ĩʃ'tãsja] *f* (*insistência*) persistence; (*súplica*) entreaty; (*legislativa*) authority; (*JUR*): **tribunal de primeira ~** ≈ magistrate's court (*BRIT*), ≈ district court (*US*); **em última ~** as a last resort.
instantâneo/a [ĩʃtã'tanju/a] *adj* instant, instantaneous; (*café*) instant ♦ *m* (*FOTO*) snapshot.
instante [ĩʃ'tãtʃi] *m* moment ♦ *adj* urgent; **nesse ~** just a moment ago; **num ~** in an instant, quickly; **a cada ~** (at) any moment; **só um ~!** just a moment!
instar [ĩʃ'ta*] *vt* to urge ♦ *vi* to insist; **~ com alguém para que faça algo** to urge sb to do sth.
instauração [ĩʃtawra'sãw] *f* establishment; (*de processo, inquérito*) institution.
instaurar [ĩʃtaw'ra*] *vt* to establish, set up; (*processo, inquérito*) to institute.
instável [ĩʃ'tavew] (*pl* **-eis**) *adj* unstable; (*tempo*) unsettled; (*mesa*) unsteady.
instigação [ĩʃtʃiga'sãw] *f* instigation; **por ~ de alguém** at sb's instigation.
instigar [ĩʃtʃi'ga*] *vt* (*incitar*) to urge; (*provocar*) to provoke; **~ alguém contra alguém** to set sb against sb.
instilar [ĩʃtʃi'la*] *vt*: **~ algo em algo** (*veneno*) to inject sth into sth; **~ algo em alguém** (*fig*: *ódio etc*) to instil (*BRIT*) *ou* instill (*US*) sth in sb.
instintivo/a [ĩʃtʃĩ'tʃivu/a] *adj* instinctive.
instinto [ĩʃ'tʃĩtu] *m* instinct; **por ~** instinctively; **~ de conservação** survival instinct.
institucional [ĩʃtʃitusjo'naw] (*pl* **-ais**) *adj* institutional.
instituição [ĩʃtʃitwi'sãw] (*pl* **-ões**) *f* institution.
instituir [ĩʃtʃi'twi*] *vt* to institute; (*fundar*) to establish, found; (*prazo*) to set.
instituto [ĩʃtʃi'tutu] *m* (*escola*) institute; (*instituição*) institution; **~ de beleza** beauty salon; **I~ de Pesos e Medidas** ≈ British Standards Institution.
instrução [ĩʃtru'sãw] (*PT*: **-cç-**; *pl* **-ões**) *f* education; (*erudição*) learning; (*diretriz*) instruction; (*MIL*) training; **instruções** *fpl* (*para o uso*) instructions (for use); **manual de instruções** instruction manual.
instructor(a) [ĩʃtru'to*(a)] (*PT*) *m/f* = **instrutor(a)**.
instruído/a [ĩʃ'trwidu/a] *adj* educated.
instruir [ĩʃ'trwi*] *vt* to instruct; (*MIL*) to train; (*JUR*: *processo*) to prepare; **~-se** *vr*: **~-se em algo** to learn sth; **~ alguém de** *ou* **sobre algo** to inform sb about sth.
instrumentação [ĩʃtrumẽta'sãw] *f* (*MÚS*) instrumentation.
instrumental [ĩʃtrumẽ'taw] (*pl* **-ais**) *adj* instrumental ♦ *m* instruments *pl*.
instrumentar [ĩʃtrumẽ'ta*] *vt* (*MÚS*) to score.
instrumentista [ĩʃtrumẽ'tʃiʃta] *m/f* instrumentalist.
instrumento [ĩʃtru'mẽtu] *m* instrument; (*ferramenta*) implement; (*JUR*) deed, document; **~ de cordas/percussão/sopro** stringed/percussion/wind instrument; **~ de trabalho** tool.
instrutivo/a [ĩʃtru'tʃivu/a] *adj* instructive.
instrutor(a) [ĩʃtru'to*(a)] *m/f* instructor; (*ESPORTE*) coach.
insubordinação [ĩsuboxdʒina'sãw] *f* rebellion; (*MIL*) insubordination.
insubordinado/a [ĩsuboxdʒi'nadu/a] *adj* unruly; (*MIL*) insubordinate.
insubordinar-se [ĩsuboxdʒi'naxsi] *vr* to rebel; (*NÁUT*) to mutiny.
insubstituível [ĩsubiʃtʃi'twivew] (*pl* **-eis**) *adj* irreplaceable.
insucesso [ĩsu'sesu] *m* failure.
insuficiência [ĩsufi'sjẽsja] *f* inadequacy; (*carência*) shortage; (*MED*) deficiency; **~ cardíaca** heart failure.
insuficiente [ĩsufi'sjẽtʃi] *adj* (*não bastante*) insufficient; (*EDUC*: *nota*) ≈ fail; (*pessoa*) incompetent.
insuflar [ĩsu'fla*] *vt* to blow up, inflate; (*ar*) to blow; (*fig*): **~ algo (em** *ou* **a alguém)** to instil (*BRIT*) *ou* instill (*US*) sth (in sb).
insular [ĩsu'la*] *vt* (*TEC*) to insulate ♦ *adj* insular.
insulina [ĩsu'lina] *f* insulin.
insultar [ĩsuw'ta*] *vt* to insult.
insulto [ĩ'suwtu] *m* insult.
insultuoso/a [ĩsuw'twozu/ɔza] *adj* insulting.
insumo [ĩ'sumu] *m* raw materials *pl*; (*ECON*) input.
insuperável [ĩsupe'ravew] (*pl* **-eis**) *adj* (*dificuldade*) insuperable; (*qualidade*) unsurpassable.
insuportável [ĩsupox'tavew] (*pl* **-eis**) *adj* unbearable.

NB: *European Portuguese adds the following consonants to certain words:* **b** (sú(b)dito, su(b)til); **c** (a(c)ção, a(c)cionista, a(c)to); **m** (inde(m)ne); **p** (ado(p)ção, ado(p)tar); *for further details see p. xiii.*

insurgente [ĩsux'ʒẽtʃi] *adj* rebellious ♦ *m/f* rebel.
insurgir-se [ĩsux'ʒixsi] *vr* to rebel, revolt.
insurreição [ĩsuxej'sãw] (*pl* **-ões**) *f* rebellion, insurrection.
insurreto/a [ĩsu'xɛtu/a] *adj* rebellious ♦ *m/f* insurgent.
insuspeito/a [ĩsuʃ'pejtu/a] *adj* unsuspected; (*imparcial*) impartial.
insustentável [ĩsuʃtẽ'tavew] (*pl* **-eis**) *adj* untenable.
intacto/a [ĩ'tatu/a] (*PT*) *adj* = **intato/a**.
intangível [ĩtã'ʒivew] (*pl* **-eis**) *adj* intangible.
intato/a [ĩ'tatu/a] *adj* intact; (*ileso*) unharmed; (*fig*) pure.
íntegra ['ĩtegra] *f* full text; **na ~** in full.
integração [ĩtegra'sãw] *f* integration.
integral [ĩte'graw] (*pl* **-ais**) *adj* whole ♦ *f* (*MAT*) integral; **arroz ~** brown rice; **pão ~** wholemeal (*BRIT*) *ou* wholewheat (*US*) bread.
integralismo [ĩtegra'liʒmu] *m Brazilian fascism.*
integralmente [ĩtegraw'mẽtʃi] *adv* in full, fully.
integrante [ĩte'grãtʃi] *adj* integral ♦ *m/f* member.
integrar [ĩte'gra*] *vt* to unite, combine; (*completar*) to form, make up; (*MAT, raças*) to integrate; **~-se** *vr* to become complete; **~-se em** *ou* **a algo** (*juntar-se*) to join sth; (*adaptar-se*) to integrate into sth.
integridade [ĩtegri'dadʒi] *f* (*totalidade*) entirety; (*fig*: *de pessoa*) integrity.
íntegro/a ['ĩtegru/a] *adj* entire; (*honesto*) upright, honest.
inteiramente [ĩtejra'mẽtʃi] *adv* completely.
inteirar [ĩtej'ra*] *vt* (*completar*) to complete; **~-se** *vr*: **~-se de** to find out about; **~ alguém de** to inform sb of.
inteireza [ĩtej'reza] *f* entirety; (*moral*) integrity.
inteiriçado/a [ĩtejri'sadu/a] *adj* stiff.
inteiriço/a [ĩtej'risu/a] *adj* (*pedaço de pano*) single; (*vestido*) one-piece.
inteiro/a [ĩ'tejru/a] *adj* (*todo*) whole, entire; (*ileso*) unharmed; (*não quebrado*) undamaged; (*completo, ilimitado*) complete; (*vestido*) one-piece; (*fig*: *caráter*) upright.
intelecto [ĩte'lɛktu] *m* intellect.
intelectual [ĩtelek'twaw] (*pl* **-ais**) *adj, m/f* intellectual.
intelectualidade [ĩtelektwali'dadʒi] *f* (*qualidade*) intellect; (*pessoas*) intellectuals *pl*.
inteligência [ĩteli'ʒẽsja] *f* intelligence; (*interpretação*) interpretation; (*pessoa*) intellect, thinker; **~ artificial** artificial intelligence.
inteligente [ĩteli'ʒẽtʃi] *adj* (*pessoa*) intelligent, clever; (*decisão, romance, filme etc*) clever.
inteligível [ĩteli'ʒivew] (*pl* **-eis**) *adj* intelligible.
intempérie [ĩtẽ'pɛri] *f* bad weather.
intempestivo/a [ĩtẽpeʃ'tʃivu/a] *adj* ill-timed.
intenção [ĩtẽ'sãw] (*pl* **-ões**) *f* intention; **segundas intenções** ulterior motives; **ter a ~ de** to intend to; **com boa ~** with good intent; **com má ~** maliciously; (*JUR*) with malice aforethought.
intencionado/a [ĩtẽsjo'nadu/a] *adj*: **bem ~** well-meaning; **mal ~** ill-intentioned.
intencional [ĩtẽsjo'naw] (*pl* **-ais**) *adj* intentional, deliberate.
intencionar [ĩtẽsjo'na*] *vt*: **~ fazer** to intend to do.
intenções [ĩtẽ'sõjʃ] *fpl de* **intenção**.
intendência [ĩtẽ'dẽsja] (*PT*) *f* management, administration.
intendente [ĩtẽ'dẽtʃi] *m/f* manager; (*MIL*) quartermaster.
intensidade [ĩtẽsi'dadʒi] *f* intensity.
intensificação [ĩtẽsifika'sãw] *f* intensification.
intensificar [ĩtẽsifi'ka*] *vt* to intensify; **~-se** *vr* to intensify.
intensivo/a [ĩtẽ'sivu/a] *adj* intensive.
intenso/a [ĩ'tẽsu/a] *adj* intense; (*emoção*) deep; (*impressão*) vivid; (*trabalho*) intensive; (*vida social*) full.
intentar [ĩtẽ'ta*] *vt* (*obra*) to plan; (*assalto*) to commit; (*tentar*) to attempt; **~ fazer** to intend to do; **~ uma ação contra** (*JUR*) to sue.
intento [ĩ'tẽtu] *m* aim, purpose.
intentona [ĩtẽ'tɔna] *f* (*POL*) plot, conspiracy.
interação [ĩtera'sãw] (*PT*: **-cç-**) *f* interaction.
interagir [ĩtera'ʒi*] *vi*: **~ (com)** to interact (with).
interamericano/a [ĩter-] *adj* inter-American.
interativo/a [ĩtera'tʃivu/a] *adj* (*COMPUT*) interactive.
intercalar [ĩtexka'la*] *vt* to insert; (*COMPUT*: *arquivos*) to merge.
intercâmbio [ĩtex'kãbju] *m* exchange.
interceder [ĩtexse'de*] *vi*: **~ por** to intercede on behalf of.
interceptar [ĩtexsep'ta*] *vt* to intercept; (*fazer parar*) to stop; (*ligação telefônica*) to cut off; (*ser obstáculo a*) to hinder.
intercessão [ĩtexse'sãw] (*pl* **-ões**) *f* intercession.
interconexão [ĩtexkonek'sãw] (*pl* **-ões**) *f* interconnection.
intercontinental [ĩtexkõtʃinẽ'taw] (*pl* **-ais**) *adj* intercontinental.
intercostal [ĩtexkoʃ'taw] (*pl* **-ais**) *adj* (*MED*) intercostal.
interdependência [ĩtexdepẽ'dẽsja] *f* interdependence.
interdição [ĩtexdʒi'sãw] (*pl* **-ões**) *f* (*de estrada, porta*) closure; (*JUR*) injunction; **~ de direitos civis** removal of civil rights.
interdisciplinar [ĩtexdʒisipli'na*] *adj* interdisciplinary.
interditado/a [ĩtexdʒi'tadu/a] *adj* closed, sealed off.
interditar [ĩtexdʒi'ta*] *vt* (*importação etc*) to ban; (*estrada, praia*) to close off; (*cinema etc*) to close down; (*JUR*) to interdict.
interdito/a [ĩtex'dʒitu/a] *adj* (*JUR*) interdicted

♦ *m* (*JUR*: *interdição*) injunction.

interessado/a [ĩtere'sadu/a] *adj* interested; (*amizade*) based on self-interest ♦ *m/f* interested party.

interessante [ĩtere'sãtʃi] *adj* interesting; **estar em estado** ~ to be expecting *ou* pregnant.

interessar [ĩtere'sa*] *vt* to interest, be of interest to ♦ *vi* to be interesting; **~-se** *vr*: **~-se em** *ou* **por** to take an interest in, be interested in; **a quem possa** ~ to whom it may concern.

interesse [ĩte'resi] *m* interest; (*próprio*) self-interest; (*proveito*) advantage; **no ~ de** for the sake of; **por ~ (próprio)** for one's own ends.

interesseiro/a [ĩtere'sejru/a] *adj* self-seeking.

interestadual [ĩtereʃta'dwaw] (*pl* **-ais**) *adj* interstate.

interface [ĩtex'fasi] *f* (*COMPUT*) interface.

interferência [ĩtexfe'rẽsja] *f* interference.

interferir [ĩtexfe'ri*] *vi*: ~ **em** to interfere in; (*rádio*) to jam.

interfone [ĩtex'fɔni] *m* intercom.

ínterim ['ĩterĩ] *m* interim; **nesse** ~ in the meantime.

interino/a [ĩte'rinu/a] *adj* temporary, interim.

interior [ĩte'rjo*] *adj* inner, inside; (*vida*) inner; (*COM*) domestic, internal ♦ *m* inside, interior; (*coração*) heart; (*do país*): **no** ~ inland, in the country; **Ministério do I~** Home Office (*BRIT*), Department of the Interior (*US*); **Ministro do I~** Home Secretary (*BRIT*), Secretary of the Interior (*US*); **na parte** ~ inside.

interiorizar [ĩterjori'za*] *vt* to internalize.

interjeição [ĩtexʒej'sãw] (*pl* **-ões**) *f* interjection.

interligar [ĩtexli'ga*] *vt* to interconnect; **~-se** *vr* to be interconnected.

interlocutor(a) [ĩtexloku'to*(a)] *m/f* speaker; **meu** ~ the person I was speaking to.

interlúdio [ĩtex'ludʒu] *m* interlude.

intermediário/a [ĩtexme'dʒjarju/a] *adj* intermediary ♦ *m/f* (*COM*) middleman; (*mediador*) intermediary, mediator.

intermédio [ĩtex'mɛdʒu] *m*: **por ~ de** through.

interministerial [ĩtexminiʃte'rjaw] (*pl* **-ais**) *adj* interministerial.

interminável [ĩtexmi'navew] (*pl* **-eis**) *adj* endless.

intermissão [ĩtexmi'sãw] (*pl* **-ões**) *f* interval.

intermitente [ĩtexmi'tẽtʃi] *adj* intermittent.

internação [ĩtexna'sãw] (*pl* **-ões**) *f* internment; (*de aluno*) sending to boarding school.

internacional [ĩtexnasjo'naw] (*pl* **-ais**) *adj* international.

internacionalismo [ĩtexnasjona'liʒmu] *m* internationalism.

internacionalizar [ĩtexnasjonali'za*] *vt* to internationalize; **~-se** *vr* to become international.

internações [ĩtexna'sõjʃ] *fpl de* **internação**.

internar [ĩtex'na*] *vt* (*aluno*) to put into boarding school; (*doente*) to take into hospital; (*MIL*, *POL*) to intern.

internato [ĩtex'natu] *m* boarding school.

interno/a [ĩ'tɛxnu/a] *adj* internal, interior; (*do país*) internal, domestic; (*aluno*) boarding ♦ *m/f* (*aluno*) boarder; (*MED*: *estudante*) houseman (*BRIT*), intern (*US*); **de uso** ~ (*MED*) for internal use.

interpelação [ĩtexpela'sãw] (*pl* **-ões**) *f* questioning; (*JUR*) summons *sg*.

interpelar [ĩtexpe'la*] *vt*: ~ **alguém sobre algo** to question sb about sth; (*pedir explicações*) to challenge sb about sth.

interplanetário/a [ĩtexplane'tarju/a] *adj* interplanetary.

interpõe [ĩtex'põj] *etc vb V* **interpor**.

interpolar [ĩtexpo'la*] *vt* to interpolate.

interpor [ĩtex'po*] (*irreg*: *como* **pôr**) *vt* to put in, interpose; **~-se** *vr* to intervene; **~-se a algo** (*contrapor-se*) to militate against sth; ~ **A (a B)** (*argumentos etc*) to counter (B) with A.

interposto/a [ĩtex'poʃtu/'pɔʃta] *pp de* **interpor**.

interpretação [ĩtexpreta'sãw] (*pl* **-ões**) *f* interpretation; (*TEATRO*) performance; **má** ~ misinterpretation.

interpretar [ĩtexpre'ta*] *vt* to interpret; (*um papel*) to play; ~ **mal** to misinterpret.

intérprete [ĩ'tɛxpretʃi] *m/f* (*LING*) interpreter; (*TEATRO*) performer, artist.

interpunha [ĩtex'puɲa] *etc vb V* **interpor**.

interpus [ĩtex'puʃ] *etc vb V* **interpor**.

interpuser [ĩtexpu'ze*] *etc vb V* **interpor**.

inter-racial [ĩtex-] (*pl* **-ais**) *adj* interracial.

interrogação [ĩtexoga'sãw] (*pl* **-ões**) *f* questioning, interrogation; **ponto de** ~ question mark.

interrogador(a) [ĩtexoga'do*(a)] *m/f* interrogator.

interrogar [ĩtexo'ga*] *vt* to question, interrogate; (*JUR*) to cross-examine.

interrogativo/a [ĩtexoga'tʃivu/a] *adj* interrogative.

interrogatório [ĩtexoga'tɔrju] *m* cross-examination.

interromper [ĩtexõ'pe*] *vt* to interrupt; (*parar*) to stop; (*ELET*) to cut off.

interrupção [ĩtexup'sãw] (*pl* **-ões**) *f* interruption; (*intervalo*) break.

interruptor [ĩtexup'to*] *m* (*ELET*) switch.

interseção [ĩtexse'sãw] (*PT*: **-cç-**; *pl* **-ões**) *f* intersection.

interstício [ĩtexʃ'tʃisju] *m* gap.

interurbano/a [ĩterux'banu/a] *adj* (*TEL*) long-distance ♦ *m* long-distance *ou* trunk call.

intervalado/a [ĩtexva'ladu/a] *adj* spaced out.
intervalo [ĩtex'valu] *m* interval; (*descanso*) break; **a ~s** every now and then.
interveio [ĩtex'veju] *etc vb V* **intervir**.
intervenção [ĩtexvẽ'sãw] (*pl* **-ões**) *f* intervention; **~ cirúrgica** (MED) operation.
interventor(a) [ĩtexvẽ'to*(a)] *m/f* inspector; (POL) caretaker governor.
intervir [ĩtex'vi*] (*irreg*: *como* **vir**) *vi* to intervene; (*sobrevir*) to come up.
intestinal [ĩteʃtʃi'naw] (*pl* **-ais**) *adj* intestinal.
intestino [ĩteʃ'tʃinu] *m* intestine; **~ delgado/grosso** small/large intestine; **~ solto** loose bowels *pl*, diarrhoea (BRIT), diarrhea (US).
inti [ĩ'tʃi] *m* inti (*Peruvian currency*).
intimação [ĩtʃima'sãw] (*pl* **-ões**) *f* (*ordem*) order; (JUR) summons.
intimar [ĩtʃi'ma*] *vt* (JUR) to summon; **~ alguém a fazer** *ou* **a alguém que faça** to order sb to do.
intimidação [ĩtʃimida'sãw] *f* intimidation.
intimidade [ĩtʃimi'dadʒi] *f* intimacy; (*vida privada*) private life; (*familiaridade*) familiarity; **ter ~ com alguém** to be close to sb; **ela é pessoa de minha ~** she's a close friend of mine.
intimidar [ĩtʃimi'da*] *vt* to intimidate; **~-se** *vr* to be intimidated.
íntimo/a ['ĩtʃimu/a] *adj* intimate; (*sentimentos*) innermost; (*amigo*) close; (*vida*) private ♦ *m/f* close friend; **no ~** at heart; **festa íntima** small gathering.
intitular [ĩtʃitu'la*] *vt* (*livro*) to title; **~-se** *vr* to be called; (*livro*) to be entitled; (*a si mesmo*) to call oneself; **~ algo de algo** to call sth sth.
intocável [ĩto'kavew] (*pl* **-eis**) *adj* untouchable.
intolerância [ĩtole'rãsja] *f* intolerance.
intolerante [ĩtole'rãtʃi] *adj* intolerant.
intolerável [ĩtole'ravew] (*pl* **-eis**) *adj* intolerable, unbearable.
intoxicação [ĩtoksika'sãw] *f* poisoning; **~ alimentar** food poisoning.
intoxicar [ĩtoksi'ka*] *vt* to poison.
intraduzível [ĩtradu'zivew] (*pl* **-eis**) *adj* untranslateable.
intragável [ĩtra'gavew] (*pl* **-eis**) *adj* unpalatable; (*pessoa*) unbearable.
intranqüilidade [ĩtrãkwili'dadʒi] *f* disquiet.
intranqüilo/a [ĩtrã'kwilu/a] *adj* (*aflito*) worried; (*desassossegado*) restless.
intransferível [ĩtrãʃfe'rivew] (*pl* **-eis**) *adj* non-transferable.
intransigência [ĩtrãsi'ʒẽsja] *f* intransigence.
intransigente [ĩtrãsi'ʒẽtʃi] *adj* uncompromising; (*fig*: *rígido*) strict.
intransitável [ĩtrãsi'tavew] (*pl* **-eis**) *adj* impassable.
intransitivo/a [ĩtrãsi'tʃivu/a] *adj* intransitive.
intransponível [ĩtrãʃpo'nivew] (*pl* **-eis**) *adj* (*rio*) impossible to cross; (*problema*) insurmountable.
intratável [ĩtra'tavew] (*pl* **-eis**) *adj* (*pessoa*) contrary, awkward; (*doença*) untreatable; (*problema*) insurmountable.
intra-uterino/a ['ĩtra-] *adj*: **dispositivo ~** intra-uterine device.
intravenoso/a [ĩtrave'nozu/ɔza] *adj* intravenous.
intrepidez [ĩtrepi'deʒ] *f* courage, bravery.
intrépido/a [ĩ'trɛpidu/a] *adj* daring, intrepid.
intriga [ĩ'triga] *f* intrigue; (*enredo*) plot; (*fofoca*) piece of gossip; **~ amorosa** (PT) love affair; **~s** (*fofocas*) gossip *sg*.
intrigante [ĩtri'gãtʃi] *m/f* troublemaker ♦ *adj* intriguing.
intrigar [ĩtri'ga*] *vt* to intrigue ♦ *vi* to be intriguing.
intrincado/a [ĩtrĩ'kadu/a] *adj* intricate.
intrínseco/a [ĩ'trĩseku/a] *adj* intrinsic.
introdução [ĩtrodu'sãw] (*pl* **-ões**) *f* introduction.
introdutório/a [ĩtrodu'tɔrju/a] *adj* introductory.
introduzir [ĩtrodu'zi*] *vt* to introduce; (*prego*) to insert.
intróito [ĩ'trɔjtu] *m* beginning; (REL) introit.
intrometer-se [ĩtrome'texsi] *vr* to interfere, meddle.
intrometido/a [ĩtrome'tʃidu/a] *adj* interfering; (*col*) nosey ♦ *m/f* busybody.
intromissão [ĩtromi'sãw] (*pl* **-ões**) *f* interference, meddling.
introspecção [ĩtroʃpek'sãw] *f* introspection.
introspectivo/a [ĩtroʃpek'tʃivu/a] *adj* introspective.
introversão [ĩtrovex'sãw] *f* introversion.
introvertido/a [ĩtrovex'tʃidu/a] *adj* introverted ♦ *m/f* introvert.
intrujão/jona [ĩtru'ʒãw/'ʒɔna] (*pl* **-ões/~s**) *m/f* swindler.
intrujar [ĩtru'ʒa*] *vt* to trick, swindle.
intrujões [ĩtru'ʒõjʃ] *mpl de* **intrujão**.
intrujona [ĩtru'ʒɔna] *f de* **intrujão**.
intruso/a [ĩ'truzu/a] *m/f* intruder.
intuição [ĩtwi'sãw] (*pl* **-ões**) *f* intuition; (*pressentimento*) feeling; **por ~** by intuition, intuitively.
intuir [ĩ'twi*] *vt*, *vi* to intuit.
intuitivo/a [ĩtwi'tʃivu/a] *adj* intuitive.
intuito [ĩ'tuito] *m* (*intento*) intention; (*fim*) aim, purpose.
intumescência [ĩtume'sẽsja] *f* swelling.
intumescer-se [ĩtume'sexsi] *vr* to swell (up).
intumescido/a [ĩtume'sidu/a] *adj* swollen.
inumano/a [inu'manu/a] *adj* inhuman.
inumerável [inume'ravew] (*pl* **-eis**) *adj* countless, innumerable.
inúmero/a [i'numeru/a] *adj* countless, innumerable.
inundação [inũda'sãw] (*pl* **-ões**) *f* (*enchente*) flood; (*ato*) flooding.
inundar [inũ'da*] *vt* to flood; (*fig*) to inundate ♦ *vi* (*rio*) to flood.
inusitado/a [inuzi'tadu/a] *adj* unusual.
inútil [i'nutʃiw] (*pl* **-eis**) *adj* useless; (*esforço*)

futile; (*desnecessário*) pointless ♦ *m/f* good-for-nothing; **ser ~** to be of no use, be no good.
inutilidade [inutʃili'dadʒi] *f* uselessness.
inutilizar [inutʃili'za*] *vt* to make useless, render useless; (*incapacitar*) to put out of action; (*danificar*) to ruin; (*esforços*) to thwart; **~-se** *vr* (*pessoa*) to become incapacitated.
inutilizável [inutʃili'zavew] (*pl* **-eis**) *adj* unusable.
inutilmente [inutʃiw'mẽtʃi] *adv* in vain.
invadir [ĩva'dʒi*] *vt* to invade; (*suj*: *água*) to overrun; (: *sentimento*) to overtake.
invalidação [ĩvalida'sãw] *f* invalidation.
invalidar [ĩvali'da*] *vt* to invalidate; (*pessoa*) to make an invalid.
invalidez [ĩvali'deʒ] *f* disability.
inválido/a [ĩ'validu/a] *adj, m/f* invalid; **~ de guerra** wounded war veteran.
invariável [ĩva'rjavew] (*pl* **-eis**) *adj* invariable.
invasão [ĩva'zãw] (*pl* **-ões**) *f* invasion.
invasor(a) [ĩva'zo*(a)] *adj* invading ♦ *m/f* invader.
inveja [ĩ'vɛʒa] *f* envy.
invejar [ĩve'ʒa*] *vt* to envy; (*cobiçar: bens*) to covet ♦ *vi* to be envious.
invejável [ĩve'ʒavew] (*pl* **-eis**) *adj* enviable.
invejoso/a [ĩve'ʒozu/ɔza] *adj* envious ♦ *m/f* envious person.
invenção [ĩvẽ'sãw] (*pl* **-ões**) *f* invention.
invencível [ĩvẽ'sivew] (*pl* **-eis**) *adj* invincible.
invenções [ĩvẽ'sõjʃ] *fpl de* **invenção**.
inventar [ĩvẽ'ta*] *vt* to invent; (*história, desculpa*) to make up; (*nome*) to think up ♦ *vi* to make things up; **~ de fazer** to take it into one's head to do.
inventariação [ĩvẽtarja'sãw] (*pl* **-ões**) *f* (COM) stocktaking.
inventariar [ĩvẽta'rja*] *vt*: **~ algo** to make an inventory of sth.
inventário [ĩvẽ'tarju] *m* inventory.
inventiva [ĩvẽ'tʃiva] *f* inventiveness.
inventivo/a [ĩvẽ'tʃivu/a] *adj* inventive.
inventor(a) [ĩvẽ'to*(a)] *m/f* inventor.
inverdade [ĩvex'dadʒi] *f* untruth.
inverificável [ĩverifi'kavew] (*pl* **-eis**) *adj* impossible to verify.
invernada [ĩvex'nada] *f* winter pasture.
invernar [ĩvex'na*] *vi* to spend the winter.
inverno [ĩ'vɛxnu] *m* winter.
inverossímil [ĩvero'simiw] (PT: **-osí-**; *pl* **-eis**) *adj* (*improvável*) unlikely, improbable; (*inacreditável*) implausible.
inversão [ĩvex'sãw] (*pl* **-ões**) *f* reversal, inversion.
inverso/a [ĩ'vɛxsu/a] *adj* inverse; (*oposto*) opposite; (*ordem*) reverse ♦ *m* opposite, reverse; **ao ~ de** contrary to.
inversões [ĩvex'sõjʃ] *fpl de* **inversão**.
invertebrado/a [ĩvexte'bradu/a] *adj* invertebrate ♦ *m* invertebrate.
inverter [ĩvex'te*] *vt* (*mudar*) to alter; (*ordem*) to invert, reverse; (*colocar às avessas*) to turn upside down, invert; **~ a marcha** (AUTO) to reverse.
invés [ĩ'vɛʃ] *m*: **ao ~ de** instead of.
investida [ĩveʃ'tʃida] *f* attack; (*tentativa*) attempt.
investidura [ĩveʃtʃi'dura] *f* investiture.
investigação [ĩveʃtʃiga'sãw] (*pl* **-ões**) *f* investigation; (*pesquisa*) research.
investigar [ĩveʃtʃi'ga*] *vt* to investigate; (*examinar*) to examine; (*pesquisar*) to research into.
investimento [ĩveʃtʃi'mẽtu] *m* investment.
investir [ĩveʃ'tʃi*] *vt* (*dinheiro*) to invest ♦ *vi* to invest; **~ contra** *ou* **para alguém** (*atacar*) to attack sb; **~ alguém no cargo de presidente** to install sb in the presidency; **~ para algo** (*atirar-se*) to rush towards sth.
inveterado/a [ĩvete'radu/a] *adj* (*mentiroso*) inveterate; (*criminoso*) hardened; (*hábito*) deep-rooted.
inviabilidade [ĩvjabili'dadʒi] *f* impracticality.
inviabilizar [ĩvjabili'za*] *vt*: **~ algo** to make sth impracticable.
inviável [ĩ'vjavew] (*pl* **-eis**) *adj* impracticable.
invicto/a [ĩ'viktu/a] *adj* unconquered; (*invencível*) unbeatable.
inviolabilidade [ĩvjolabili'dadʒi] *f* inviolability; (JUR) immunity.
inviolável [ĩvjo'lavew] (*pl* **-eis**) *adj* inviolable; (JUR) immune.
invisível [ĩvi'zivew] (*pl* **-eis**) *adj* invisible.
invisto [ĩ'viʃtu] *etc vb V* **investir**.
invocado/a [ĩvo'kadu/a] *adj*: **estar/ficar ~ com alguém** to dislike/take a dislike to sb.
invocar [ĩvo'ka*] *vt* to invoke; (*col*: *irritar*) to provoke; (: *impressionar*) to have a profound effect on ♦ *vi*: **~ com alguém** (*col*: *antipatizar*) to take a dislike to sb.
invólucro [ĩ'vɔlukru] *m* (*cobertura*) covering; (*envoltório*) wrapping; (*caixa*) box.
involuntário/a [ĩvolũ'tarju/a] *adj* (*movimento*) involuntary; (*ofensa*) unintentional.
invulnerável [ĩvuwne'ravew] (*pl* **-eis**) *adj* invulnerable.
iodo ['jodu] *m* iodine.
IOF (BR) *abr m* = **Imposto sobre Operações Financeiras**.
ioga ['jɔga] *f* yoga.
iogurte [jo'guxtʃi] *m* yogurt.
ioiô [jo'jo] *m* yoyo.
íon ['iõ] (*pl* **~s**) *m* ion.
iônico/a ['joniku/a] *adj* ionic.
IPC (BR) *abr m* (= *Indice de Preços ao Consumidor*) RPI.
IPEA (BR) *abr m* = **Instituto de Planejamento Econômico Social**.

NB: *European Portuguese adds the following consonants to certain words:* **b** (sú(b)dito, su(b)til); **c** (a(c)ção, a(c)cionista, a(c)to); **m** (inde(m)ne); **p** (ado(p)ção, ado(p)tar); *for further details see p. xiii.*

ipecacuanha [ipeka'kwaɲa] *f* ipecac.
IPI (*BR*) *abr m* = **Imposto sobre Produtos Industrializados.**
IPM (*BR*) *abr m* = **Inquérito Policial-Militar.**
IPT (*BR*) *abr m* = **Instituto de Pesquisas Tecnológicas.**
IPTU (*BR*) *abr m* (= *Imposto Predial e Territorial Urbano*) ≈ rates *pl* (*BRIT*), ≈ property tax (*US*).
IPVA (*BR*) *abr m* (= *Imposto Sobre Veículos Automóveis*) road (*BRIT*) *ou* motor-vehicle (*US*) tax.
IR (*BR*) *abr m* = **Imposto de Renda.**
ir [i*] *vi* to go; (+ *infin*): **vou fazer** I will do, I am going to do; (+ *gerúndio*): ~ **fazendo** to keep on doing; **~-se** *vr* to go away, leave; **vamos!** let's go!; **vamos lá!** let's get started!; **já vou!** I'm coming!; ~ **bem** (*negócio*) to go well; (*pessoa*: *de saúde*) to be well; (: *na escola etc*) to get on well; ~ **a cavalo/a pé** to ride/walk; ~ **atrás de alguém** (*seguir*) to follow sb; (*confiar*) to take sb's word for it; ~ **com alguém** (*fig*: *simpatizar*) to like sb; **eu vou de cerveja** (*col*) I'll have a beer; **vamos nessa!** (*col*: *vamos embora*) let's go!; (: *vamos tentar*) let's go for it!; **já vai para dez anos que ele morreu** it's getting on for ten years since he died; **vai por mim** (*col*) take my word for it, believe you me; **vá lá!** go on!; **vá lá que seja** all right then; **vai daí que ela tem ...** that's why she has ...; **vamos que ...** (*suponhamos*) let's suppose (that) ...; **e vão 3** (*MAT*) carry 3; **lá se foram meus planos** that was the end of my plans.
IRA *abr m* (= *Irish Republican Army*) IRA.
ira ['ira] *f* anger, rage.
Irã [i'rã] *m*: **o** ~ Iran.
irado/a [i'radu/a] *adj* angry, irate.
iraniano/a [ira'njanu/a] *adj*, *m/f* Iranian.
Irão [i'rãw] (*PT*) *m* = **Irã.**
Iraque [i'raki] *m*: **o** ~ Iraq.
iraquiano/a [ira'kjanu/a] *adj*, *m/f* Iraqi.
irascibilidade [irasibili'dadʒi] *f* irritability.
irascível [ira'sivew] (*pl* **-eis**) *adj* irritable, short-tempered.
ir-e-vir (*pl* **ires-e-vires**) *m* coming and going.
íris ['iriʃ] *f inv* iris.
Irlanda [ix'lãda] *f*: **a** ~ Ireland; **a** ~ **do Norte** Northern Ireland.
irlandês/esa [ixlã'deʃ/eza] *adj* Irish ♦ *m/f* Irishman/woman ♦ *m* (*LING*) Irish.
irmã [ix'mã] *f* sister ♦ *adj* (*empresa etc*) sister; **almas ~s** kindred souls; ~ **Paula** (*fig*) good Samaritan; ~ **gêmea/de criação** twin-/half-sister.
irmanar [ixma'na*] *vt* to join together, unite.
irmandade [ixmã'dadʒi] *f* brotherhood; (*confraternidade*) fraternity; (*associação*) brotherhood.
irmão [ix'mãw] (*pl* **~s**) *m* brother; (*fig*: *similar*) twin; (*col*: *companheiro*) mate; ~ **de criação** half-brother; ~ **gêmeo** twin brother; **~s siameses** Siamese twins.
ironia [iro'nia] *f* irony; (*sarcasmo*) sarcasm; **com** ~ ironically; (*com sarcasmo*) sarcastically; **por** ~ **do destino** by a quirk of fate.
irônico/a [i'roniku/a] *adj* ironic(al); (*sarcástico*) sarcastic.
ironizar [ironi'za*] *vt* to be ironic about ♦ *vi* to be ironic.
IRPF (*BR*) *abr m* (= *Imposto de Renda Pessoa Física*) personal income tax.
IRPJ (*BR*) *abr m* (= *Imposto de Renda Pessoa Jurídica*) corporation tax.
irra! ['ixa] (*PT*) *excl* damn!
irracional [ixasjo'naw] (*pl* **-ais**) *adj* irrational.
irracionalidade [ixasjonali'dadʒi] *f* irrationality.
irradiação [ixadʒja'sãw] (*pl* **-ões**) *f* (*de luz*) radiation; (*espalhamento*) spread; (*RÁDIO*) broadcasting; (*MED*) radiation treatment.
irradiar [ixa'dʒja*] *vt* (*luz*) to radiate; (*espalhar*) to spread; (*RÁDIO*) to broadcast, transmit; (*simpatia*) to radiate, exude ♦ *vi* to radiate; (*RÁDIO*) to be on the air; **~-se** *vr* to spread; to be transmitted.
irreais [ixe'ajʃ] *adj pl de* **irreal.**
irreajustável [ixeaʒuʃ'tavew] (*pl* **-eis**) *adj* fixed.
irreal [ixe'aw] (*pl* **-ais**) *adj* unreal.
irrealizado/a [ixeali'zadu/a] *adj* (*pessoa*) unfulfilled; (*sonhos*) unrealized.
irrealizável [ixeali'zavew] (*pl* **-eis**) *adj* unrealizable.
irreconciliável [ixekõsi'ljavew] (*pl* **-eis**) *adj* irreconcilable.
irreconhecível [ixekõɲe'sivew] (*pl* **-eis**) *adj* unrecognizable.
irrecorrível [ixeko'xivew] (*pl* **-eis**) *adj* (*JUR*) unappealable.
irrecuperável [ixekupe'ravew] (*pl* **-eis**) *adj* irretrievable.
irrecusável [ixeku'zavew] (*pl* **-eis**) *adj* (*incontestável*) irrefutable; (*convite*) which cannot be turned down.
irrefletido/a [ixefle'tʃidu/a] *adj* rash; **de maneira irrefletida** rashly.
irrefreável [ixe'frjavew] (*pl* **-eis**) *adj* uncontrollable.
irrefutável [ixefu'tavew] (*pl* **-eis**) *adj* irrefutable.
irregular [ixegu'la*] *adj* irregular; (*vida*) unconventional; (*feições*) unusual; (*aluno, gênio*) erratic.
irregularidade [ixegulari'dadʒi] *f* irregularity.
irrelevância [ixele'vãsja] *f* irrelevance.
irrelevante [ixele'vãtʃi] *adj* irrelevant.
irremediável [ixeme'dʒjavew] (*pl* **-eis**) *adj* irremediable; (*sem remédio*) incurable.
irreparável [ixepa'ravew] (*pl* **-eis**) *adj* irreparable.
irrepreensível [ixeprjẽ'sivew] (*pl* **-eis**) *adj* irreproachable, impeccable.
irreprimível [ixepri'mivew] (*pl* **-eis**) *adj* irrepressible.

irrequietação [ixekjeta'sãw] *f* restlessness.
irrequieto/a [ixe'kjɛtu/a] *adj* restless.
irresgatável [ixeʒga'tavew] (*pl* **-eis**) *adj* (COM) irredeemable.
irrevogável [ixevo'gavew] (*pl* **-eis**) *adj* irrevocable.
irresistível [ixeziʃ'tʃivew] (*pl* **-eis**) *adj* irresistible; (*desejo*) overwhelming.
irresoluto/a [ixezo'lutu/a] *adj* (*pessoa*) irresolute, indecisive; (*problema*) unresolved.
irresponsabilidade [ixeʃpõsabili'dadʒi] *f* irresponsibility.
irresponsável [ixeʃpõ'savew] (*pl* **-eis**) *adj* irresponsible.
irrestrito/a [ixeʃ'tritu/a] *adj* unrestricted.
irreverente [ixeve'rẽtʃi] *adj* irreverent.
irreversível [ixevex'sivew] (*pl* **-eis**) *adj* irreversible.
irrigação [ixiga'sãw] *f* irrigation.
irrigar [ixi'ga*] *vt* to irrigate.
irrisório/a [ixi'zɔrju/a] *adj* derisory, ludicrous; (*quantia*) derisory, paltry.
irritabilidade [ixitabili'dadʒi] *f* irritability.
irritação [ixita'sãw] (*pl* **-ões**) *f* irritation.
irritadiço/a [ixita'dʒisu/a] *adj* irritable.
irritante [ixi'tãtʃi] *adj* irritating, annoying.
irritar [ixi'ta*] *vt* to irritate, annoy; (MED) to irritate; **~-se** *vr* to get angry, get annoyed.
irritável [ixi'tavew] (*pl* **-eis**) *adj* irritable.
irromper [ixõ'pe*] *vi*: **~ (em)** to burst in(to); (*epidemia*) to break out; (*surgir*) to emerge; (*lágrimas*) to well; (*voz*) to be heard.
irrupção [ixup'sãw] (*pl* **-ões**) *f* invasion; (*de idéias*) emergence; (*de doença*) outbreak.
isca ['iʃka] *f* (PESCA) bait; (*fig*) lure, bait.
iscambau [iʃkã'baw] (*col*) *m*: **e o ~** and what not.
isenção [izẽ'sãw] (*pl* **-ões**) *f* exemption; **~ de impostos** tax exemption.
isentar [izẽ'ta*] *vt* (*dispensar*) to exempt; (*livrar*) to free.
isento/a [i'zẽtu/a] *adj* (*dispensado*) exempt; (*livre*) free; **~ de taxas** duty-free; **~ de impostos** tax-free.
Islã [iʒ'lã] *m* Islam.
islâmico/a [iʒ'lamiku/a] *adj* Islamic.
islamismo [iʒla'miʒmu] *m* Islam.
islamita [iʒla'mita] *adj*, *m/f* Muslim.
islandês/esa [iʒlã'deʃ/eza] *adj* Icelandic ♦ *m/f* Icelander ♦ *m* (LING) Icelandic.
Islândia [iʒ'lãdʒa] *f*: **a ~** Iceland.
isolado/a [izo'ladu/a] *adj* (*separado*) isolated; (*solitário*) lonely; (ELET) insulated.
isolamento [izola'mẽtu] *m* isolation; (MED) isolation ward; (ELET) insulation; **~ acústico** soundproofing.
isolante [izo'lãtʃi] *adj* (ELET) insulating.
isolar [izo'la*] *vt* to isolate; (ELET) to insulate ♦ *vi* (*afastar mau agouro*) to touch wood (BRIT), knock on wood (US); **~-se** *vr* to isolate o.s., cut o.s. off.
isonomia [izono'mia] *f* equality.
isopor [izo'po*] ® *m* polystyrene.
isqueiro [iʃ'kejru] *m* (cigarette) lighter.
Israel [iʒxa'ɛw] *m* Israel.
israelense [iʒxae'lẽsi] *adj*, *m/f* Israeli.
israelita [iʒxae'lita] *adj*, *m/f* Israelite.
ISS (BR) *abr m* = **Imposto Sobre Serviços**.
isso ['isu] *pron* that; (*col*: *isto*) this; **~ mesmo** exactly; **por ~** therefore, so; **por ~ mesmo** for that very reason; **só ~?** is that all?; **~!** that's it!; **é ~, é ~ aí** (*col*) (*você tem razão*) that's right; (*é tudo*) that's it, that's all; **é ~ mesmo** exactly, that's right; **não seja por ~** that's no big deal; **eu não tenho nada com ~** it's got nothing to do with me; **que é ~?** (*exprime indignação*) what's going on?, what's all this?; **~ de fazer ...** this business of doing ....
Istambul [iʃtã'buw] *n* Istanbul.
istmo ['iʃtʃimu] *m* isthmus.
isto ['iʃtu] *pron* this; **~ é** that is, namely.
ITA (BR) *abr m* = **Instituto Tecnológico da Aeronáutica**.
Itália [i'talja] *f*: **a ~** Italy.
italiano/a [ita'ljanu/a] *adj*, *m/f* Italian ♦ *m* (LING) Italian.
itálico [i'taliku] *m* italics *pl*.
Itamarati [itamara'tʃi] *m*: **o ~** the Brazilian Foreign Ministry.
item ['itẽ] (*pl* **-ns**) *m* item.
iterar [ite'ra*] *vt* to repeat.
itinerante [itʃine'rãtʃi] *adj*, *m/f* itinerant.
itinerário [itʃine'rarju] *m* (*plano*) itinerary; (*caminho*) route.
Iugoslávia [jugoʒ'lavja] *f*: **a ~** Yugoslavia.
iugoslavo/a [jugoʒ'lavu/a] *adj*, *m/f* Yugoslav(ian).

J

J, j ['ʒɔta] (*pl* **js**) *m* J, j; **J de José** J for Jack (BRIT) *ou* Jig (US).
já [ʒa] *adv* already; (*em perguntas*) yet; (*agora*) now; (*imediatamente*) right now, at once; (*agora mesmo*) right away ♦ *conj* on the other hand; **até ~** bye; **desde ~** from now on; **desde ~ lhe agradeço** thanking you in anticipation; **é para ~** it won't be a minute; **~ esteve na Inglaterra?** have you ever been to England?; **~ não** no longer; **ele ~ não vem mais aqui** he doesn't come here any more; **~ que** as, since; **~ se vê** of

NB: European Portuguese adds the following consonants to certain words: **b** (sú(b)dito, su(b)til); **c** (a(c)ção, a(c)cionista, a(c)to); **m** (inde(m)ne); **p** (ado(p)ção, ado(p)tar); *for further details see p. xiii.*

course; ~ **vou** I'm coming; ~ **até** even; ~, ~ right away; ~ **era** (*col*) it's been and gone; **você** ~ **viu o filme?** — ~ have you seen the film? — yes.

jabaculê [ʒabaku'le] (*col*) *m* backhander.

jabota [ʒa'bɔta] *f* giant tortoise.

jabuti [ʒabu'tʃi] *m* giant tortoise.

jabuticaba [ʒabutʃi'kaba] *f* jaboticaba (*type of berry*).

jaca ['ʒaka] *f* jack fruit.

jacarandá [ʒakarã'da] *m* jacaranda.

jacaré [ʒaka'rɛ] *m* alligator; **fazer** *ou* **pegar** ~ to body-surf.

Jacarta [ʒa'kaxta] *n* Jakarta.

jacente [ʒa'sẽtʃi] *adj* lying; (*herança*) unclaimed.

jacinto [ʒa'sĩtu] *m* hyacinth.

jactância [ʒak'tãsja] *f* boasting.

jactar-se [ʒak'taxsi] *vr*: ~ **de** to boast about.

jacto ['ʒaktu] (*PT*) *m* = **jato**.

jade ['ʒadʒi] *m* jade.

jaez [ʒa'eʒ] *m* harness; (*fig*: *categoria*) sort.

jaguar [ʒa'gwa*] *m* jaguar.

jaguatirica [ʒagwatʃi'rika] *f* leopard cat.

jagunço [ʒa'gũsu] *m* hired gun(man).

jaleco [ʒa'lɛku] *m* jacket.

jamais [ʒa'majʃ] *adv* never; (*com palavra negativa*) ever; **ninguém** ~ **o tratou assim** nobody ever treated him like that.

Jamaica [ʒa'majka] *f*: **a** ~ Jamaica.

jamaicano/a [ʒamaj'kanu/a] *adj*, *m/f* Jamaican.

jamanta [ʒa'mãta] *f* juggernaut (*BRIT*), truck-trailer (*US*).

jamegão [ʒame'gãw] (*pl* **-ões**) (*col*) *m* signature.

jan. *abr* = **janeiro**.

janeiro [ʒa'nejru] (*PT*: **J-**) *m* January; *V tb* **julho**.

janela [ʒa'nɛla] *f* window; (~) **basculante** louvre (*BRIT*) *ou* louver (*US*) window.

janelão [ʒane'lãw] (*pl* **-ões**) *m* picture window.

jangada [ʒã'gada] *f* raft.

jangadeiro [ʒãga'dejru] *m* jangada fisherman.

janota [ʒa'nɔta] *adj* foppish ♦ *m* dandy.

janta ['ʒãta] (*col*) *f* dinner.

jantar [ʒã'ta*] *m* dinner ♦ *vt* to have for dinner ♦ *vi* to have dinner; ~ **americano** buffet dinner; ~ **dançante** dinner dance.

jantarado [ʒãta'radu] *m* tea.

Japão [ʒa'pãw] *m*: **o** ~ Japan.

japona [ʒa'pɔna] *f* (*casaco*) three-quarter length coat ♦ *m/f* (*col*) Japanese.

japonês/esa [ʒapo'neʃ/eza] *adj*, *m/f* Japanese ♦ *m* (*LING*) Japanese.

jaqueira [ʒa'kejra] *f* jack tree.

jaqueta [ʒa'keta] *f* jacket.

jaquetão [ʒake'tãw] (*pl* **-ões**) *m* double-breasted coat.

jararaca [ʒara'raka] *f* (*cobra*) jararaca (*snake*); (*fig*: *mulher*) shrew.

jarda ['ʒaxda] *f* yard.

jardim [ʒax'dʒĩ] (*pl* **-ns**) *m* garden; ~ **zoológico** zoo.

jardim-de-infância (*pl* **jardins-de-infância**) *m* kindergarten.

jardim-de-inverno (*pl* **jardins-de-inverno**) *m* conservatory.

jardinagem [ʒaxdʒi'naʒẽ] *f* gardening.

jardinar [ʒaxdʒi'na*] *vt* to cultivate ♦ *vi* to garden.

jardineira [ʒaxdʒi'nejra] *f* (*móvel*) flower-stand; (*caixa*) trough; (*ônibus*) open bus; (*calça*) dungarees *pl*; (*vestido*) pinafore dress (*BRIT*), jumper (*US*); *V tb* **jardineiro**.

jardineiro/a [ʒaxdʒi'nejru/a] *m/f* gardener.

jardins [ʒax'dʒĩʃ] *mpl de* **jardim**.

jargão [ʒax'gãw] *m* jargon.

jarra ['ʒaxa] *f* pot.

jarro ['ʒaxu] *m* jug.

jasmim [ʒaʒ'mĩ] *m* jasmine.

jato ['ʒatu] *m* jet; (*de luz*) flash; (*de ar*) blast; **a** ~ at top speed.

jaula ['ʒawla] *f* cage.

Java ['ʒava] *f* Java.

javali [ʒava'li] *m* wild boar.

jazer [ʒa'ze*] *vi* to lie.

jazida [ʒa'zida] *f* deposit.

jazigo [ʒa'zigu] *m* grave; (*monumento*) tomb; ~ **de família** family tomb.

jazz [dʒɛz] *m* jazz.

jazzista [dʒa'ziʃta] *m/f* (*músico*) jazz artist; (*fã*) jazz fan.

jazzístico/a [dʒa'ziʃtʃiku/a] *adj* jazzy.

JB *abr m* = **Jornal do Brasil**.

JEC (*BR*) *abr f* = **Juventude Estudantil Católica**.

jeca ['ʒɛka] *m/f Brazilian hillbilly* ♦ *adj* rustic; (*cafona*) tacky.

jeca-tatu (*pl* **jecas-tatus**) *m/f Brazilian hillbilly*.

jeitão [ʒej'tãw] (*col*: *pl* **-ões**) *m* (*aspecto*) look; (*modo de ser*) style, way.

jeitinho [ʒej'tʃiɲu] *m* knack.

jeito ['ʒejtu] *m* (*maneira*) way; (*aspecto*) appearance; (*aptidão, habilidade*) skill, knack; (*modos pessoais*) manner; **falta de** ~ clumsiness; **ter** ~ **de** to look like; **ter** *ou* **levar** ~ **para** to have a gift for, be good at; **não ter** ~ (*pessoa*) to be awkward; (*situação*) to be hopeless; **dar um** ~ **em algo** (*pé*) to twist sth; (*quarto, casa, papéis*) to tidy sth up; (*consertar*) to fix sth; **dar um** ~ **em alguém** to sort sb out; **dar um** ~ to find a way; **tomar** ~ to pull one's socks up; **o** ~ **é ...** the thing to do is ...; **é o** ~ it's the best way; **ao** ~ **de** in the style of; **com** ~ tactfully; **daquele** ~ (in) that way; (*col*: *em desordem, mal*) anyhow; **de qualquer** ~ anyway; **de** ~ **nenhum!** no way!; **ficar sem** ~ to feel awkward.

jeitões [ʒej'tõjʃ] *mpl de* **jeitão**.

jeitoso/a [ʒej'tozu/ɔza] *adj* (*hábil*) skilful (*BRIT*), skillful (*US*); (*elegante*) handsome; (*apropriado*) suitable.

jejuar [ʒe'ʒwa*] *vi* to fast.

jejum [ʒe'ʒũ] (*pl* **-ns**) *m* fast; **em ~** fasting.
Jeová [ʒeo'va] *m*: **testemunha de ~** Jehovah's witness.
jequice [ʒe'kisi] *f* country ways *pl*; (*cafonice*) tackiness.
jerico [ʒe'riku] *m* donkey; **idéia de ~** stupid idea.
jérsei ['ʒɛxsej] *m* jersey.
Jerusalém [ʒeruza'lẽ] *n* Jerusalem.
jesuíta [ʒe'zwita] *m* Jesuit.
Jesus [ʒe'zuʃ] *m* Jesus ♦ *excl* heavens!
jetom [ʒe'tõ] (*pl* **-ns**) *m* (*ficha*) token; (*remuneração*) fee.
jibóia [ʒi'bɔja] *f* boa (constrictor).
jiboiar [ʒibo'ja*] *vi* to let one's dinner go down.
jiló [ʒi'lɔ] *m kind of vegetable.*
jingle ['dʒĩgew] *m* jingle.
jipe ['ʒipi] *m* jeep.
jirau [ʒi'raw] *m* (*na cozinha*) rack; (*palanque*) platform.
jiu-jitsu [ʒu'ʒitsu] *m* jiu-jitsu.
joalheiro/a [ʒoa'ʎejru/a] *m/f* jeweller (*BRIT*), jeweler (*US*).
joalheria [ʒoaʎe'ria] *f* jeweller's (shop) (*BRIT*), jewelry store (*US*).
joanete [ʒwa'netʃi] *m* bunion.
joaninha [ʒwa'niɲa] *f* ladybird (*BRIT*), ladybug (*US*).
joão-ninguém *m* nonentity.
JOC (*BR*) *abr f* = **Juventude Operária Católica.**
joça ['ʒɔsa] (*col*) *f* thing, contraption.
jocoso/a [ʒo'kozu/ɔza] *adj* jocular, humorous.
joelhada [ʒoe'ʎada] *f*: **dar uma ~ em alguém** to knee sb.
joelheira [ʒoe'ʎejra] *f* (*ESPORTE*) kneepad.
joelho [ʒo'eʎu] *m* knee; **de ~s** kneeling; **ficar de ~s** to kneel down.
jogada [ʒo'gada] *f* (*num jogo*) move; (*lanço*) throw; (*negócio*) scheme; (*col*: *modo de agir*) move; **a ~ é a seguinte** (*col*) this is the situation; **morar na ~** (*col*) to catch on.
jogado/a [ʒo'gadu/a] *adj* (*prostrado*) flat out; (*abandonado*) abandoned.
jogador(a) [ʒoga'do*(a)] *m/f* player; (*de jogo de azar*) gambler; **~ de futebol** footballer.
jogão [ʒo'gãw] (*pl* **-ões**) *m* great game.
jogar [ʒo'ga*] *vt* to play; (*em jogo de azar*) to gamble; (*atirar*) to throw; (*indiretas*) to drop ♦ *vi* to play; (*em jogo de azar*) to gamble; (*barco*) to pitch; **~-se** *vr* to throw o.s.; **~ fora** to throw away; **~ na Bolsa** to play the markets; **~ no bicho** to play the numbers game; **~ com** (*combinar*) to match.
jogatina [ʒoga'tʃina] *f* gambling.
jogging ['ʒɔgĩŋ] *m* jogging; (*roupa*) track suit; **fazer ~** to go jogging, jog.
jogo ['ʒogu] *m* game; (*jogar*) play; (*de azar*) gambling; (*conjunto*) set; (*artimanha*) trick; **abrir o ~** (*fig*) to lay one's cards on the table, come clean; **esconder o ~** to play one's cards close to one's chest; **estar em ~** (*fig*) to be at stake; **fazer o ~ de alguém** to play sb's game, go along with sb; **ter ~ de cintura** (*fig*) to be flexible; **~ de armar** construction set; **~ de cartas** card game; **~ de damas** draughts *sg* (*BRIT*), checkers *sg* (*US*); **~ de luz** lighting effects *pl*; **~ de salão** indoor game; **~ do bicho** (illegal) numbers game; **J~s Olímpicos** Olympic Games; **~ limpo/sujo** fair play/dirty tricks *pl*; **o ~ político** political manoeuvring (*BRIT*) *ou* maneuvering (*US*).
jogo-da-velha *m* noughts and crosses.
jogões [ʒo'gõjʃ] *mpl de* **jogão**.
joguei [ʒo'gej] *etc vb V* **jogar**.
joguete [ʒo'getʃi] *m* plaything; **fazer alguém de ~** to toy with sb.
jóia ['ʒɔja] *f* jewel; (*taxa*) entry fee ♦ *adj* (*col*) great; **tudo ~?** (*col*) how's things?
jóquei ['ʒɔkej] *m* (*clube*) jockey club; (*cavaleiro*) jockey.
jóquei-clube (*pl* **jóqueis-clubes**) *m* jockey club.
Jordânia [ʒox'danja] *f*: **a ~** Jordan.
jordaniano/a [ʒoxda'njanu/a] *adj*, *m/f* Jordanian.
Jordão [ʒox'dãw] *m*: **o (rio) ~** the Jordan (River).
jornada [ʒox'nada] *f* (*viagem*) journey; (*percurso diário*) day's journey; **~ de trabalho** working day.
jornal [ʒox'naw] (*pl* **-ais**) *m* newspaper; (*TV*, *RÁDIO*) news.
jornaleiro/a [ʒoxna'lejru/a] *m/f* newsagent (*BRIT*), newsdealer (*US*).
jornalismo [ʒoxna'liʒmu] *m* journalism.
jornalista [ʒoxna'liʃta] *m/f* journalist.
jornalístico/a [ʒoxna'liʃtʃiku/a] *adj* journalistic.
jorrante [ʒo'xãtʃi] *adj* gushing.
jorrar [ʒo'xa*] *vi* to gush, spurt out.
jorro ['ʒoxu] *m* jet; (*de sangue*) spurt; (*fig*) stream, flood.
jovem ['ʒɔvẽ] (*pl* **-ns**) *adj* young; (*aspecto*) youthful; (*música*) youth *atr* ♦ *m/f* young person, youngster.
jovial [ʒo'vjaw] (*pl* **-ais**) *adj* jovial, cheerful.
jovialidade [ʒovjali'dadʒi] *f* joviality.
JPCCC (*BR*) *abr f* = **Justiça de Pequenas Causas Civis e Criminais.**
Jr *abr* = **Júnior.**
JT (*BR*) *abr m* = **Jornal da Tarde.**
juba ['ʒuba] *f* (*de leão*) mane; (*col*: *cabelo*) mop.
jubilação [ʒubila'sãw] *f* (*aposentadoria*) retirement; (*de estudante*) sending down.
jubilar [ʒubi'la*] *vt* (*aposentar*) to retire, pension off; (*aluno*) to send down.
jubileu [ʒubi'lew] *m* jubilee; **~ de prata** silver

***NB:** European Portuguese adds the following consonants to certain words:* **b** (sú(b)dito, su(b)til); **c** (a(c)ção, a(c)cionista, a(c)to); **m** (inde(m)ne); **p** (ado(p)ção, ado(p)tar); *for further details see p. xiii.*

jubilee.
júbilo ['ʒubilu] *m* rejoicing; **com ~** jubilantly.
jubiloso/a [ʒubi'lozu/ɔza] *adj* jubilant.
JUC (*BR*) *abr f* = **Juventude Universitária Católica**.
judaico/a [ʒu'dajku/a] *adj* Jewish.
judaísmo [ʒuda'iʒmu] *m* Judaism.
judas ['ʒudaʃ] *m* (*fig*) Judas; (*boneco*) effigy; **onde J~ perdeu as botas** (*col*) at the back of beyond.
judeu/judia [ʒu'dew/ʒu'dʒia] *adj* Jewish ♦ *m/f* Jew.
judiação [ʒudʒja'sãw] *f* ill-treatment.
judiar [ʒu'dʒja*] *vi*: **~ de alguém/algo** to ill-treat sb/sth.
judiaria [ʒudʒja'ria] *f* ill-treatment; **que ~!** how cruel!
judicatura [ʒudʒika'tura] *f* (*cargo*) office of judge; (*magistratura*) judicature.
judicial [ʒudʒi'sjaw] (*pl* **-ais**) *adj* judicial.
judiciário/a [ʒudʒi'sjarju/a] *adj* judicial; **o (poder) ~** the judiciary.
judicioso/a [ʒudʒi'sjozu/ɔza] *adj* judicious, wise.
judô [ʒu'do] *m* judo.
jugo ['ʒugu] *m* yoke.
juiz/íza [ʒwiʒ/'iza] *m/f* judge; (*em jogos*) referee; **~ de menores** juvenile judge; **~ de paz** justice of the peace.
juizado [ʒwi'zado] *m* court; **J~ de Menores** Juvenile Court; **J~ de Pequenas Causas** small claims court.
juízo ['ʒwizu] *m* judgement; (*parecer*) opinion; (*siso*) common sense; (*foro*) court; **J~ Final** Day of Judgement, doomsday; **perder o ~** to lose one's mind; **não ter ~** to be foolish; **tomar** *ou* **criar ~** to come to one's senses; **chamar/levar a ~** to summon/take to court; **~!** behave yourself!
jujuba [ʒu'ʒuba] *f* (*BOT*) jujube; (*bala*) jujube sweet.
jul. *abr* = **julho**.
julgador(a) [ʒuwga'do*(a)] *adj* judging ♦ *m/f* judge.
julgamento [ʒuwga'mẽtu] *m* judgement; (*audiência*) trial; (*sentença*) sentence.
julgar [ʒuw'ga*] *vt* to judge; (*achar*) to think; (*JUR*: *sentenciar*) to sentence; **~-se** *vr*: **~-se algo** to consider o.s. sth, think of o.s. as sth.
julho ['ʒuʎu] (*PT*: **J-**) *m* July; **dia primeiro de ~** the first of July (*BRIT*), July first (*US*); **dia dois/onze de ~** the second/eleventh of July (*BRIT*), July second/eleventh (*US*); **ele chegou no dia cinco de ~** he arrived on 5th July *ou* July 5th; **em ~** in July; **no começo/fim de ~** at the beginning/end of July; **em meados de ~** in mid July; **todo ano em ~** every July; **em ~ do ano que vem/do ano passado** next/last July.
jumento/a [ʒu'mẽtu/a] *m/f* donkey.
jun. *abr* = **junho**.
junção [ʒũ'sãw] (*pl* **-ões**) *f* (*ato*) joining; (*junta*) join.
junco ['ʒũku] *m* reed, rush.
junções [ʒũ'sõjʃ] *fpl de* **junção**.
junho ['ʒuɲu] (*PT*: **J-**) *m* June; *V tb* **julho**.
junino/a [ʒu'ninu/a] *adj* June; **festa junina** St John's day party.
júnior ['ʒunjo*] (*pl* **juniores**) *adj* younger ♦ *m/f* (*ESPORTE*) junior; **Eduardo Autran J~** Eduardo Autran Junior.
junta ['ʒũta] *f* (*comissão*) board, committee; (*POL*) junta; (*articulação, juntura*) joint; **~ comercial** board of trade; **~ médica** medical team.
juntar [ʒũ'ta*] *vt* (*por junto*) to join; (*reunir*) to bring together; (*aglomerar*) to gather together; (*recolher*) to collect up; (*acrescentar*) to add; (*dinheiro*) to save up ♦ *vi* to gather; **~-se** *vr* to gather; (*associar-se*) to join up; **~-se a alguém** to join sb; **~-se com alguém** to (go and) live with sb.
junto/a ['ʒũtu/a] *adj* joined; (*chegado*) near; **ir ~s** to go together; **~ a/de** near/next to; **segue ~** (*COM*) please find enclosed.
juntura [ʒũ'tura] *f* join; (*articulação*) joint.
Júpiter ['ʒupite*] *m* Jupiter.
jura ['ʒura] *f* vow.
jurado/a [ʒu'radu/a] *adj* sworn ♦ *m/f* juror.
juramentado/a [ʒuramẽ'tadu/a] *adj* accredited, legally certified.
juramento [ʒura'mẽtu] *m* oath.
jurar [ʒu'ra*] *vt, vi* to swear; **jura?** really?
júri ['ʒuri] *m* jury.
jurídico/a [ʒu'ridʒiku/a] *adj* legal.
jurisconsulto/a [ʒuriʃkõ'suwtu/a] *m/f* legal advisor.
jurisdição [ʒuriʃdʒi'sãw] *f* jurisdiction.
jurisprudência [ʒuriʃpru'dẽsja] *f* jurisprudence.
jurista [ʒu'riʃta] *m/f* jurist.
juros ['ʒuruʃ] *mpl* (*ECON*) interest *sg*; **a/sem ~** at interest/interest-free; **render ~** to yield *ou* bear interest; **~ fixos/variáveis** fixed/variable interest; **~ simples/compostos** simple/compound interest.
jururu [ʒuru'ru] *adj* melancholy, wistful.
jus [ʒuʃ] *m*: **fazer ~ a algo** to live up to sth.
jusante [ʒu'zãtʃi] *f*: **a ~ (de)** downstream (from).
justamente [ʒuʃta'mẽtʃi] *adv* (*com justiça*) fairly, justly; (*precisamente*) exactly.
justapor [ʒuʃta'po*] (*irreg*: *como* **pôr**) *vt* to juxtapose; **~-se** *vr* to be juxtaposed; **~ algo a algo** to juxtapose sth with sth.
justaposição [ʒuʃtapozi'sãw] (*pl* **-ões**) *f* juxtaposition.
justaposto [ʒuʃta'poʃtu] *pp de* **justapor**.
justapunha [ʒuʃta'puɲa] *etc vb V* **justapor**.
justapus [ʒuʃta'puʃ] *etc vb V* **justapor**.
justapuser [ʒuʃtapu'ze*] *etc vb V* **justapor**.
justeza [ʒuʃ'teza] *f* fairness; (*precisão*) precision.
justiça [ʒuʃ'tʃisa] *f* justice; (*poder judiciário*) judiciary; (*eqüidade*) fairness; (*tribunal*) court; **com ~** justly, fairly; **ir à ~** to go to

court; **fazer ~ a** to do justice to; **J~ Eleitoral** Electoral Court; **J~ do Trabalho** industrial tribunal (*BRIT*), labor relations board (*US*).

justiceiro/a [ʒuʃtʃi'sejru/a] *adj* righteous; (*inflexível*) inflexible.

justificação [ʒuʃtʃifika'sãw] (*pl* **-ões**) *f* justification.

justificar [ʒuʃtʃifi'ka*] *vt* to justify; **~-se** *vr* to justify o.s.

justificativa [ʒuʃtʃifika'tʃiva] *f* (*JUR*) justification.

justificável [ʒuʃtʃifi'kavew] (*pl* **-eis**) *adj* justifiable.

justo/a ['ʒuʃtu/a] *adj* just, fair; (*legítimo*: *queixa*) legitimate, justified; (*exato*) exact; (*apertado*) tight ♦ *adv* just.

juta ['ʒuta] *f* jute.

juvenil [ʒuve'niw] (*pl* **-is**) *adj* (*ar*) youthful; (*roupa*) young; (*livro*) for young people; (*ESPORTE*: *equipe*, *campeonato*) youth *atr*, junior ♦ *m* (*ESPORTE*) junior championship.

juventude [ʒuvẽ'tudʒi] *f* youth; (*jovialidade*) youthfulness; (*jovens*) young people *pl*, youth.

K

K, k [ka] (*pl* **ks**) *m* K, k; **K de Kátia** K for king.

kanga ['kãga] *f* beach wrap.

karaokê [karao'ke] *m* karaoke; (*lugar*) karaoke bar.

kart ['kaxtʃi] (*pl* **~s**) *m* go-kart.

ketchup [ke'tʃupi] *m* ketchup.

kg *abr* (= *quilograma*) kg.

KGB *abr f* KGB.

kHz *abr* (= *quilohertz*) kHz.

kibutz [ki'butz] *m inv* kibbutz.

kilt ['kiwtʃi] (*pl* **~s**) *m* kilt.

kirsch [kixʃ] *m* kirsch.

kit ['kitʃi] (*pl* **~s**) *m* kit; **~ de sobrevivência** survival kit.

kitchenette [kitʃe'netʃi] *f* studio flat.

kitsch [kitʃ] *adj inv*, *m* kitsch.

kl *abr* (= *quilolitro*) kl.

km *abr* (= *quilômetro*) km.

km/h *abr* (= *quilômetros por hora*) km/h.

know-how ['now'haw] *m* know-how.

Kremlin [krẽ'lĩ] *m*: **a ~** the Kremlin.

Kuweit [ku'wejtʃi] *m*: **a ~** Kuwait.

kW *abr* (= *quilowatt*) kW.

kwh *abr* (= *quilowatt-hora*) kwh.

L

L, L ['eli] (*pl* **ls**) *m* L, l; **L de Lúcia** L for Lucy (*BRIT*) *ou* Love (*US*).

L *abr* = **Largo**.

-la [la] *pron* her; (*você*) you; (*coisa*) it.

lá [la] *adv* there ♦ *m* (*MÚS*) A; **~ fora** outside; **~ em baixo** down there; **por ~** (*direção*) that way; (*situação*) over there; **até ~** (*no espaço*) there; (*no tempo*) until then; **~ pelas tantas** in the small hours; **para ~ de** (*mais do que*) more than; **diga ~ ...** come on and say ...; **sei ~!** don't ask me!; **ela sabe ~** she's got no idea; **ele pode ~ pagar um aluguel tão caro** there's no way he can pay such a high rent; **o apartamento não é ~ essas coisas** the apartment is nothing special; **estar mais para ~ do que para cá** (*de cansaço*) to be dead on one's feet; (*prestes a morrer*) to be at death's door.

lã [lã] *f* wool; **de ~** woollen (*BRIT*), woolen (*US*); **de pura ~** pure wool; **~ de camelo** camel hair.

labareda [laba'reda] *f* flame; (*fig*) ardour (*BRIT*), ardor (*US*).

labia ['labja] *f* (*astúcia*) cunning; **ter ~** to have the gift of the gab.

labial [la'bjaw] (*pl* **-ais**) *adj* lip *atr*; (*LING*) labial ♦ *f* (*LING*) labial.

lábio ['labju] *m* lip; **~ leporino** hare lip.

labirinto [labi'rĩtu] *m* labyrinth, maze.

labor [la'bo*] *m* work, labour (*BRIT*), labor (*US*).

laborar [labo'ra*] *vi*: **~ em erro** to labour (*BRIT*) *ou* labor (*US*) under a misconception.

laboratório [labora'tɔrju] *m* laboratory.

laborioso/a [labo'rjozu/ɔza] *adj* (*diligente*) hard-working; (*árduo*) laborious.

LABRE *abr f* = **Liga de Amadores Brasileiros de Radio Emissão**.

labuta [la'buta] *f* toil, drudgery.

labutar [labu'ta*] *vi* to toil; (*esforçar-se*) to struggle, strive.

laca ['laka] *f* lacquer.

laçada [la'sada] *f* (*nó*) slipknot; (*no tricô*) loop.

laçar [la'sa*] *vt* to bind, tie; (*boi*) to rope.

laçarote [lasa'rɔtʃi] *m* big bow.

laço ['lasu] *m* bow; (*de gravata*) knot; (*armadilha*) snare; (*fig*) bond, tie; **dar um ~** to tie a bow; **~s de família** family ties.

lacônico/a [la'koniku/a] *adj* laconic.

lacraia [la'kraja] *f* centipede.

NB*: European Portuguese adds the following consonants to certain words:* **b** (sú(b)dito, su(b)til); **c** (a(c)ção, a(c)cionista, a(c)to); **m** (inde(m)ne); **p** (ado(p)ção, ado(p)tar); *for further details see p. xiii.*

lacrar [la'kra*] *vt* to seal (with wax).
lacre ['lakri] *m* sealing wax.
lacrimal [lakri'maw] (*pl* **-ais**) *adj* (*canal*) tear *atr*.
lacrimejante [lakrime'ʒãtʃi] *adj* weeping.
lacrimejar [lakrime'ʒa*] *vi* (*olhos*) to water; (*chorar*) to weep.
lacrimogêneo/a [lakrimo'ʒenju/a] *adj* tear-jerking; *V tb* **gás**.
lacrimoso/a [lakri'mozu/ɔza] *adj* tearful.
lactação [lakta'sãw] *f* lactation; (*amamentação*) breastfeeding.
lácteo/a ['laktju/a] *adj* milk *atr*; **Via Láctea** Milky Way.
lacticínio [laktʃi'sinju] *m* dairy product.
lactose [lak'tɔzi] *f* lactose.
lacuna [la'kuna] *f* gap; (*omissão*) omission; (*espaço em branco*) blank.
ladainha [lada'iɲa] *f* litany; (*fig*) rigmarole.
ladear [la'dʒja*] *vt* to flank; (*problema*) to get round; **o rio ladeia a estrada** the river runs by the side of the road.
ladeira [la'dejra] *f* slope.
ladino/a [la'dʒinu/a] *adj* cunning, crafty.
lado ['ladu] *m* side; (MIL) flank; (*rumo*) direction; **ao ~** (*perto*) close by; **a casa ao ~** the house next door; **ao ~ de** beside; **de ~** sideways; **deixar de ~** to set aside; (*fig*) to leave out; **de um ~ para outro** back and forth; **do ~ de dentro/fora** on the inside/outside; **do ~ de cá/lá** on this/that side; **no outro ~ da rua** across the road; **ela foi para aqueles ~s** she went that way; **por um ~ ... por outro ~** on the one hand ... on the other hand; **por todos os ~s** all around; **~ a ~** side by side; **o meu ~** (*col*: *interesses*) my interests.
ladra ['ladra] *f* thief, robber; (*picareta*) crook.
ladrão/ona [la'drãw/ɔna] (*pl* **-ões/~s**) *adj* thieving ♦ *m/f* thief, robber; (*picareta*) crook ♦ *m* (*tubo*) overflow pipe; **pega ~!** stop thief!
ladrar [la'dra*] *vi* to bark.
ladrilhar [ladri'ʎa*] *vt*, *vi* to tile.
ladrilheiro/a [ladri'ʎejru/a] *m/f* tiler.
ladrilho [la'driʎu] *m* tile; (*chão*) tiled floor, tiles *pl*.
ladro ['ladru] *m* (*latido*) bark; (*ladrão*) thief.
ladroagem [la'drwaʒẽ] (*pl* **-ns**) *f* robbery.
ladroeira [la'drwejra] *f* robbery.
ladrões [la'drõjʃ] *mpl de* **ladrão**.
ladrona [la'drɔna] *f de* **ladrão**.
lagarta [la'gaxta] *f* caterpillar.
lagartixa [lagax'tʃiʃa] *f* gecko.
lagarto [la'gaxtu] *m* lizard; (*carne*) silverside.
lago ['lagu] *m* lake; (*de jardim*) pond; (*de sangue*) pool.
lagoa [la'goa] *f* pool, pond; (*lago*) lake.
lagosta [la'goʃta] *f* lobster.
lagostim [lagoʃ'tʃĩ] (*pl* **-ns**) *m* crayfish.
lágrima ['lagrima] *f* tear; **~s de crocodilo** crocodile tears; **chorar ~s de sangue** to cry bitterly.
laguna [la'guna] *f* lagoon.
laia ['laja] *f* kind, sort, type.
laico/a ['lajku/a] *adj* (*pessoa*) lay; (*ensino etc*) secular.
laivos ['lajvuʃ] *mpl* hints, traces.
laje ['laʒi] *f* paving stone, flagstone.
lajedo [la'ʒedu] *m* rock.
lajear [la'ʒja*] *vt* to pave.
lajota [la'ʒɔta] *f* paving stone.
lama ['lama] *f* mud; **tirar alguém da ~** (*fig*) to rescue sb from poverty.
lamaçal [lama'saw] (*pl* **-ais**) *m* quagmire; (*pântano*) bog, marsh.
lamaceiro [lama'sejru] *m* = **lamaçal**.
lamacento/a [lama'sẽtu/a] *adj* muddy.
lambança [lã'bãsa] *f* mess.
lambão/bona [lam'bãw/'bɔna] (*pl* **-ões/~s**) *adj* (*guloso*) greedy; (*no trabalho*) sloppy; (*ao comer*) messy; (*tolo*) idiotic.
lamber [lã'be*] *vt* to lick; **de ~ os beiços** (*comida*) delicious.
lambida [lã'bida] *f* lick; **dar uma ~ em algo** to lick sth.
lambido/a [lã'bidu/a] *adj* (*cara*) without make-up; (*cabelo*) plastered down.
lambiscar [lãbiʃ'ka*] *vt*, *vi* to nibble, pick at.
lambisgóia [lãbiʒ'gɔja] *f* haggard person.
lambões [lã'bõjʃ] *mpl de* **lambão**.
lambona [lã'bɔna] *f de* **lambão**.
lambreta [lã'breta] *f* scooter.
lambri(s) [lã'bri(ʃ)] *m(pl)* panelling *sg* (BRIT), paneling *sg* (US).
lambuja [lã'buʒa] *f* start, advantage.
lambujem [lã'buʒẽ] (*pl* **-ns**) *f* start, advantage.
lambuzar [lãbu'za*] *vt* to smear.
lambuzeira [lãbu'zejra] *f* sticky mess.
lamentação [lamẽta'sãw] (*pl* **-ões**) *f* lamentation.
lamentar [lamẽ'ta*] *vt* to lament; (*sentir*) to regret; **~-se** *vr*: **~-se (de algo)** to lament (sth); **~ (que)** to be sorry (that).
lamentável [lamẽ'tavew] (*pl* **-eis**) *adj* regrettable; (*deplorável*) deplorable.
lamentavelmente [lamẽtavew'mẽtʃi] *adv* regrettably.
lamento [la'mẽtu] *m* lament; (*gemido*) moan.
lamentoso/a [lamẽ'tozu/ɔza] *adj* (*voz*, *som*) sorrowful; (*lamentável*) lamentable.
lâmina ['lamina] *f* (*chapa*) sheet; (*placa*) plate; (*de faca*) blade; (*de persiana*) slat.
laminado/a [lami'nadu/a] *adj* laminated ♦ *m* laminate.
laminar [lami'na*] *vt* to laminate.
lâmpada ['lãpada] *f* lamp; (*tb*: **~** *elétrica*) light bulb; **~ de mesa** table lamp; **~ fluorescente** fluorescent light.
lamparina [lãpa'rina] *f* lamp.
lampejante [lãpe'ʒãtʃi] *adj* flashing, glittering.
lampejar [lãpe'ʒa*] *vi* to glisten, flash ♦ *vt* to give off.
lampejo [lã'peʒu] *m* flash.
lampião [lã'pjãw] (*pl* **-ões**) *m* lantern; (*de rua*) street lamp.
lamúria [la'murja] *f* whining, lamentation.

lamuriante [lamu'rjãtʃi] *adj* whining.
lamuriar-se [lamu'rjaxsi] *vr*: ~ **de algo** to moan about sth.
lança ['lãsa] *f* lance, spear.
lançadeira [lãsa'dejra] *f* shuttle.
lançador(a) [lãsa'do*(a)] *m/f* (*ESPORTE*) thrower; (*em leilão*) bidder; (*COM*) *company which* (ou *person who*) *launches a product*.
lançamento [lãsa'mẽtu] *m* throwing; (*COM*: *em livro*) entry; (*NÁUT*, *COM*: *de produto*, *campanha*) launch; (: *de disco*, *filme*) release; **novo** ~ (*livro*) new title; (*filme*, *disco*) new release; (*produto*) new product; ~ **do dardo** (*ESPORTE*) javelin; ~ **do disco** (*ESPORTE*) discus; ~ **do martelo** (*ESPORTE*) hammer.
lança-perfume (*pl* ~**s**) *m* ether spray (*used as a drug in carnival*).
lançar [lã'sa*] *vt* to throw; (*NÁUT*, *COM*) to launch; (*disco*, *filme*) to release; (*em livro comercial*) to enter; (*em leilão*) to bid; (*imposto*) to assess; ~**-se** *vr* to throw o.s.; ~ **ações no mercado** to float shares on the market; ~ **mão de algo** to make use of sth.
lance ['lãsi] *m* (*arremesso*) throw; (*incidente*) incident; (*história*) story; (*situação*) position; (*fato*) fact; (*ESPORTE*: *jogada*) shot; (*em leilão*) bid; (*de escada*) flight; (*de casas*) row; (*episódio*) moment; (*de muro*, *estrada*) stretch.
lancha ['lãʃa] *f* launch; (*col*: *sapato*, *pé*) clodhopper; ~ **torpedeira** torpedo boat.
lanchar [lã'ʃa*] *vi* to have a snack ♦ *vt* to have as a snack.
lanche ['lãʃi] *m* snack.
lanchonete [lãʃo'netʃi] (*BR*) *f* snack bar.
lancinante [lãsi'nãtʃi] *adj* (*dor*) stabbing; (*grito*) piercing.
langanho [lã'gaɲu] *m* rake.
languidez [lãgi'deʒ] *f* languor, listlessness.
lânguido/a ['lãgidu/a] *adj* languid, listless.
lanhar [la'ɲa*] *vt* to slash, gash; (*peixe*) to gut; ~**-se** *vr* to cut o.s.
lanho ['laɲu] *m* slash, gash.
lanígero/a [la'niʒeru/a] *adj* (*gado*) wool-producing; (*planta*) downy.
lanolina [lano'lina] *f* lanolin.
lantejoula [lãte'ʒola] *f* sequin.
lanterna [lã'tɛxna] *f* lantern; (*portátil*) torch (*BRIT*), flashlight (*US*).
lanternagem [lãtex'naʒẽ] (*pl* **-ns**) *f* (*AUTO*) panel-beating; (*oficina*) bodyshop.
lanterneiro/a [lãtex'nejru/a] *m/f* panel-beater.
lanterninha [lãtex'niɲa] (*BR*) *m/f* usher(ette).
lanugem [la'nuʒẽ] *f* down, fluff.
Laos ['lawʃ] *m*: **o** ~ Laos.
lapão/pona [la'pãw/'pɔna] (*pl* **-ões/~s**) *adj*, *m/f* Lapp.
lapela [la'pɛla] *f* lapel.
lapidador(a) [lapida'do*(a)] *m/f* cutter.
lapidar [lapi'da*] *vt* (*jóias*) to cut; (*fig*) to polish, refine ♦ *adj* (*fig*) masterful.
lápide ['lapidʒi] *f* (*tumular*) tombstone; (*comemorativa*) memorial stone.
lápis ['lapiʃ] *m inv* pencil; **escrever a** ~ to write in pencil; ~ **de cor** coloured (*BRIT*) *ou* colored (*US*) pencil, crayon; ~ **de olho** eyebrow pencil.
lapiseira [lapi'zejra] *f* propelling (*BRIT*) *ou* mechanical (*US*) pencil; (*caixa*) pencil case.
lápis-lazúli [-la'zuli] *m* lapis-lazuli.
lapões [la'põjʃ] *mpl de* **lapão**.
lapona [la'pɔna] *f de* **lapão**.
Lapônia [la'ponja] *f*: **a** ~ Lappland.
lapso ['lapsu] *m* lapse; (*de tempo*) interval; (*erro*) slip.
laquê [la'ke] *m* lacquer.
laquear [la'kja*] *vt* to lacquer.
lar [la*] *m* home.
laranja [la'rãʒa] *adj inv* orange ♦ *f* orange ♦ *m* (*cor*) orange.
laranjada [larã'ʒada] *f* orangeade.
laranjal [larã'ʒaw] (*pl* **-ais**) *m* orange grove.
laranjeira [larã'ʒejra] *f* orange tree.
larápio [la'rapju] *m* thief.
lardo ['laxdu] *m* bacon.
lareira [la'rejra] *f* hearth, fireside.
larga ['laxga] *f*: **à** ~ lavishly; **dar ~s a** to give free rein to; **viver à** ~ to lead a lavish life.
largada [lax'gada] *f* start; **dar a** ~ to start; (*fig*) to make a start.
largado/a [lax'gadu/a] *adj* spurned; (*no vestir*) scruffy.
largar [lax'ga*] *vt* (*soltar*) to let go of, release; (*deixar*) to leave; (*deixar cair*) to drop; (*risada*) to let out; (*velas*) to unfurl; (*piada*) to tell; (*pôr em liberdade*) to let go ♦ *vi* (*NÁUT*) to set sail; ~**-se** *vr* (*desprender-se*) to free o.s.; (*ir-se*) to go off; (*pôr-se*) to proceed; **ele não a larga** *ou* **não larga dela um instante** he won't leave her alone for a moment; **me larga!** leave me alone!; ~ **a mão em alguém** to wallop sb; ~ **de fazer** to stop doing; **largue de besteira** stop being stupid.
largo/a ['laxgu/a] *adj* wide, broad; (*amplo*) extensive; (*roupa*) loose, baggy; (*conversa*) long ♦ *m* (*praça*) square; (*alto-mar*) open sea; **ao** ~ at a distance, far off; **fazer-se ao** ~ to put out to sea; **passar de** ~ **sobre um assunto** to gloss over a subject; **passar ao** ~ **de algo** (*fig*) to sidestep sth.
larguei [lax'gej] *etc vb V* **largar**.
largueza [lax'geza] *f* largesse.
largura [lax'gura] *f* width, breadth.
laringe [la'rĩʒi] *f* larynx.
laringite [larĩ'ʒitʃi] *f* laryngitis.
larva ['laxva] *f* larva, grub.
lasanha [la'zaɲa] *f* lasagna.
lasca ['laʃka] *f* (*de madeira*, *metal*) splinter;

(*de pedra*) chip; (*fatia*) slice.

lascado/a [laʃ'kadu/a] (*col*) *adj* in a hurry *ou* rush.

lascar [laʃ'ka*] *vt* to chip; (*pergunta*) to throw in; (*tapa*) to let go ♦ *vi* to chip; **ser** *ou* **estar de** ~ to be horrible.

lascívia [la'sivja] *f* lewdness.

lascivo/a [la'sivu/a] *adj* lewd; (*movimentos*) sensual.

laser ['lejze*] *m* laser; **raio** ~ laser beam.

lassidão [lasi'dãw] *f* lassitude, weariness.

lassitude [lasi'tudʒi] *f* lassitude, weariness.

lasso/a ['lasu/a] *adj* lax; (*cansado*) weary.

lástima ['laʃtʃima] *f* pity, compassion; (*infortúnio*) misfortune; **é uma ~ (que)** it's a shame (that).

lastimar [laʃtʃi'ma*] *vt* to lament; **~-se** *vr* to complain, be sorry for o.s.

lastimável [laʃtʃi'mavew] (*pl* **-eis**) *adj* lamentable.

lastimoso/a [laʃtʃi'mozu/ɔza] *adj* (*lamentável*) pitiful; (*plangente*) mournful.

lastro ['laʃtru] *m* ballast.

lata ['lata] *f* tin, can; (*material*) tin-plate; ~ **de lixo** rubbish bin (*BRIT*), garbage can (*US*); ~ **velha** (*col: carro*) old banger (*BRIT*) *ou* clunker (*US*).

latada [la'tada] *f* trellis.

latão [la'tãw] *m* brass.

lataria [lata'ria] *f* (*AUTO*) bodywork; (*enlatados*) canned food.

látego ['lategu] *m* whip.

latejante [late'ʒãtʃi] *adj* throbbing.

latejar [late'ʒa*] *vi* to throb.

latejo [la'teʒu] *m* throbbing, beat.

latente [la'tẽtʃi] *adj* latent, hidden.

lateral [late'raw] (*pl* **-ais**) *adj* side, lateral ♦ *f* (*FUTEBOL*) sideline ♦ *m* (*FUTEBOL*) throw-in.

látex ['lateks] *m inv* latex.

laticínio [latʃi'sinju] *m* = **lacticínio**.

latido [la'tʃidu] *m* bark(ing), yelp(ing).

latifundiário/a [latʃifũ'dʒjarju/a] *adj* landowning ♦ *m/f* landowner.

latifúndio [latʃi'fũdʒju] *m* large estate.

latim [la'tʃĩ] *m* (*LING*) Latin; **gastar o seu** ~ to waste one's breath.

latino/a [la'tʃinu/a] *adj* Latin.

latino-americano/a *adj*, *m/f* Latin-American.

latir [la'tʃi*] *vi* to bark, yelp.

latitude [latʃi'tudʒi] *f* latitude; (*largura*) breadth; (*fig*) scope.

lato/a ['latu/a] *adj* broad.

latrina [la'trina] *f* latrine.

latrocínio [latro'sinju] *m* armed robbery.

lauda ['lawda] *f* page.

laudatório/a [lawda'tɔrju/a] *adj* laudatory.

laudo ['lawdu] *m* (*JUR*) decision; (*resultados*) findings *pl*; (*peça escrita*) report.

laureado/a [law'rjadu/a] *adj* honoured (*BRIT*), honored (*US*) ♦ *m* laureate.

laurear [law'rja*] *vt* to honour (*BRIT*), honor (*US*).

laurel [law'rɛw] (*pl* **-éis**) *m* laurel wreath; (*fig*) prize, reward.

lauto/a ['lawtu/a] *adj* sumptuous; (*abundante*) lavish, abundant.

lava ['lava] *f* lava.

lavabo [la'vabu] *m* toilet.

lavadeira [lava'dejra] *f* washerwoman.

lavadora [lava'dora] *f* washing machine.

lavadouro [lava'doru] *m* washing place.

lavagem [la'vaʒẽ] *f* washing; ~ **a seco** dry cleaning; ~ **cerebral** brainwashing; **dar uma ~ em alguém** (*col: ESPORTE*) to thrash sb.

lavanda [la'vãda] *f* (*BOT*) lavender; (*colônia*) lavender water; (*para lavar os dedos*) fingerbowl.

lavanderia [lavãde'ria] *f* laundry; (*aposento*) laundry room.

lavar [la'va*] *vt* to wash; (*culpa*) to wash away; ~ **a seco** to dry clean; ~ **a égua** (*col: ESPORTE*) to win hands down; ~ **as mãos de algo** (*fig*) to wash one's hands of sth.

lavatório [lava'tɔrju] *m* washbasin; (*aposento*) toilet.

lavoura [la'vora] *f* tilling; (*agricultura*) farming; (*terreno*) plantation.

lavra ['lavra] *f* ploughing (*BRIT*), plowing (*US*); (*de minerais*) mining; (*mina*) mine; **ser da ~ de** to be the work of.

lavradio/a [lavra'dʒiu/a] *adj* workable, arable ♦ *m* farming.

lavrador(a) [lavra'do*(a)] *m/f* farmhand, farm labourer.

lavrar [la'vra*] *vt* to work; (*esculpir*) to carve; (*redigir*) to draw up.

laxante [la'ʃãtʃi] *adj*, *m* laxative.

laxativo/a [laʃa'tʃivu/a] *adj* laxative ♦ *m* laxative.

lazer [la'ze*] *m* leisure.

LBA *abr f* (= *Legião Brasileira de Assistência*) *charity*.

LBC (*BR*) *abr f* = **Letra do Banco Central**.

leal [le'aw] (*pl* **-ais**) *adj* loyal.

lealdade [leaw'dadʒi] *f* loyalty.

leão [le'ãw] (*pl* **-ões**) *m* lion; **L~** (*ASTROLOGIA*) Leo; **o L~** (*BR: fisco*) ≈ the Inland Revenue (*BRIT*), the IRS (*US*).

leão-de-chácara (*pl* **leões-de-chácara**) *m* bouncer.

lebre ['lɛbri] *f* hare.

lecionar [lesjo'na*] (*PT*: **-cc-**) *vt*, *vi* to teach.

lecitina [lesi'tʃina] *f* lecithin.

lectivo/a [lek'tivu/a] (*PT*) *adj* = **letivo/a**.

legação [lega'sãw] (*pl* **-ões**) *f* legation.

legado [le'gadu] *m* envoy, legate; (*herança*) legacy, bequest.

legal [le'gaw] (*pl* **-ais**) *adj* legal, lawful; (*col*) fine; (: *pessoa*) nice ♦ *adv* (*col*) well; **(tá) ~!** OK!

legalidade [legali'dadʒi] *f* legality, lawfulness.

legalização [legaliza'sãw] *f* legalization; (*de documento*) authentication.

legalizar [legali'za*] *vt* to legalize; (*documento*) to authenticate.

legar [le'ga*] *vt* to bequeath, leave.

legatário/a [lega'tarju/a] *m/f* legatee.

legenda [le'ʒẽda] *f* inscription; (*texto explicativo*) caption; (CINEMA) subtitle; (POL) party.

legendário/a [leʒẽ'darju/a] *adj* legendary.

legião [le'ʒjãw] (*pl* **-ões**) *f* legion; **a L~ Estrangeira** the Foreign Legion.

legionário/a [leʒjo'narju/a] *adj* legionary ♦ *m* legionary.

legislação [leʒiʒla'sãw] *f* legislation; **~ antitruste** (COM) antitrust legislation.

legislador(a) [leʒiʒla'do*(a)] *m/f* legislator.

legislar [leʒiʒ'la*] *vi* to legislate ♦ *vt* to pass.

legislativo/a [leʒiʒla'tʃivu/a] *adj* legislative ♦ *m* legislature.

legislatura [leʒiʒla'tura] *f* legislature; (*período*) term of office.

legista [le'ʒiʃta] *adj*: **médico ~** expert in medical law ♦ *m/f* legal expert; (*médico*) expert in medical law.

legitimar [leʒitʃi'ma*] *vt* to legitimize; (*justificar*) to legitimate; (*filho*) to adopt legally.

legitimidade [leʒitʃimi'dadʒi] *f* legitimacy.

legítimo/a [le'ʒitʃimu/a] *adj* legitimate; (*justo*) rightful; (*autêntico*) genuine; **legítima defesa** self-defence (BRIT), self-defense (US).

legível [le'ʒivew] (*pl* **-eis**) *adj* legible, readable; **~ por máquina** machine readable.

légua ['lɛgwa] *f* league.

legume [le'gumi] *m* vegetable.

lei [lej] *f* law; (*regra*) rule; (*metal*) standard; **prata de ~** sterling silver; **ditar a ~** to lay down the law; **~ marcial** martial law.

leiaute [lej'awtʃi] *m* layout.

leigo/a ['lejgu/a] *adj* (REL) lay, secular ♦ *m* layman; **ser ~ em algo** (*fig*) to be no expert at sth, be unversed in sth.

leilão [lej'lãw] (*pl* **-ões**) *m* auction; **vender em ~** to sell by auction, auction off.

leiloamento [lejlwa'mẽtu] *m* auctioning.

leiloar [lej'lwa*] *vt* to auction.

leiloeiro/a [lej'lwejru/a] *m/f* auctioneer.

leilões [lej'lõjʃ] *mpl de* **leilão**.

leio ['leju] *etc vb V* **ler**.

leitão/toa [lej'tãw/'toa] (*pl* **-ões/~s**) *m/f* sucking (BRIT) *ou* suckling (US) pig.

leite ['lejtʃi] *m* milk; **~ em pó** powdered milk; **~ desnatado** *ou* **magro** skimmed milk; **~ de magnésia** milk of magnesia; **~ condensado/evaporado/homogeneizado** condensed/evaporated/homogenized milk; **~ de vaca** cow's milk.

leite-de-onça *m milk with cachaça.*

leiteira [lej'tejra] *f* (*para ferver*) milk pan; (*para servir*) milk jug.

leiteiro/a [lej'tejru/a] *adj* (*vaca, gado*) dairy; (*trem*) milk *atr* ♦ *m/f* milkman/woman.

leiteria [lejte'ria] *f* dairy.

leito ['lejtu] *m* bed.

leitoa [lej'toa] *f de* **leitão**.

leitões [lej'tõjʃ] *mpl de* **leitão**.

leitor(a) [lej'to*(a)] *m/f* reader; (*professor*) lector.

leitoso/a [lej'tozu/ɔza] *adj* milky.

leitura [lej'tura] *f* reading; (*livro etc*) reading matter; **pessoa de muita ~** well-read person; **~ dinâmica** speed reading.

lelé [le'lɛ] (*col*) *adj* nuts, crazy; **~ da cuca** out of one's mind.

lema ['lɛma] *m* motto; (POL) slogan.

lembrança [lẽ'brãsa] *f* recollection, memory; (*presente*) souvenir; **~s** *fpl*: **~s a sua mãe!** regards to your mother!

lembrar [lẽ'bra*] *vt, vi* to remember; **~-se** *vr*: **~(-se) de** to remember; **~(-se) (de) que** to remember that; **~ algo a alguém**, **~ alguém de algo** to remind sb of sth; **~ alguém de que**, **~ a alguém que** to remind sb that; **esta rua lembra a rua onde eu ...** this street reminds me of the street where I ...; **ele lembra meu irmão** he reminds me of my brother, he is like my brother.

lembrete [lẽ'bretʃi] *m* reminder.

leme ['lɛmi] *m* rudder; (NÁUT) helm; (*fig*) control.

lenço ['lẽsu] *m* handkerchief; (*de pescoço*) scarf; (*de cabeça*) headscarf; **~ de papel** tissue.

lençol [lẽ'sɔw] (*pl* **-óis**) *m* sheet; **estar em maus lençóis** to be in a fix; **~ de água** water table.

lenda ['lẽda] *f* legend; (*fig*: *mentira*) lie.

lendário/a [lẽ'darju/a] *adj* legendary.

lengalenga [lẽga'lẽga] *f* rigmarole.

lenha ['lɛɲa] *f* firewood; **fazer ~** (*de carro*) to have a race; **meter a ~ em alguém** (*col*: *surrar*) to give sb a beating; (: *criticar*) to run sb down; **ser uma ~** (*col*) to be tough; **botar ~ no fogo** (*fig*) to fan the flames, make things worse.

lenhador [leɲa'do*] *m* woodcutter.

lenho ['lɛɲu] *m* (*tora*) log; (*material*) timber.

Leningrado [lenĩ'gradu] *n* Leningrad.

leninista [leni'niʃta] *adj, m/f* Leninist.

lenitivo/a [leni'tʃivu/a] *adj* soothing ♦ *m* palliative; (*fig*: *alívio*) relief.

lenocínio [leno'sinju] *m* living off immoral earnings.

lente ['lẽtʃi] *f* lens *sg*; **~ de aumento** magnifying glass; **~s de contato** contact lenses.

lentidão [lẽtʃi'dãw] *f* slowness.

lentilha [lẽ'tʃiʎa] *f* lentil.

lento/a ['lẽtu/a] *adj* slow.

leoa [le'oa] *f* lioness.

leões [le'õjʃ] *mpl de* **leão**.

leopardo [ljo'paxdu] *m* leopard.

lépido/a ['lɛpidu/a] *adj* (*alegre*) sprightly, bright; (*ágil*) nimble, agile.

leporino/a [lepo'rinu/a] *adj V* **lábio**.
lepra ['lɛpra] *f* leprosy.
leprosário [lepro'zarju] *m* leprosy hospital.
leproso/a [le'prozu/ɔza] *adj* leprous ♦ *m/f* leper.
leque ['lɛki] *m* fan; (*fig*) array.
ler [le*] *vt, vi* to read; ~ **a sorte de alguém** to tell sb's fortune; ~ **nas entrelinhas** (*fig*) to read between the lines.
lerdeza [lex'deza] *f* sluggishness.
lerdo/a ['lɛxdu/a] *adj* slow, sluggish.
lero-lero [lɛru'lɛru] (*col*) *m* chit-chat, idle talk.
lés [lɛʃ] (PT) *m*: **de** ~ **a** ~ from one end to the other.
lesão [le'zãw] (*pl* **-ões**) *f* harm, injury; (JUR) violation; (MED) lesion; ~ **corporal** (JUR) bodily harm.
lesar [le'za*] *vt* to harm, damage; (*direitos*) to violate; ~ **alguém** (*financeiramente*) to leave sb short; ~ **o fisco** to withhold one's taxes.
lesbianismo [leʒbja'niʒmu] *m* lesbianism.
lésbica ['lɛʒbika] *f* lesbian.
lesco-lesco [lɛʃku'lɛʃku] (*col*) *m* daily grind; **estar no** ~ to be on the go *ou* hard at it.
leseira [le'zejra] *f* lethargy.
lesionar [lezjo'na*] *vt* to injure.
lesivo/a [le'zivu/a] *adj* harmful.
lesma ['leʒma] *f* slug; (*fig*: *pessoa*) slowcoach.
lesões [le'zõjʃ] *fpl de* **lesão**.
Lesoto [le'zotu] *m*: **o** ~ Lesotho.
lesse ['lesi] *etc vb V* **ler**.
leste ['lɛʃtʃi] *m* east.
letal [le'taw] (*pl* **-ais**) *adj* lethal.
letargia [letax'ʒia] *f* lethargy.
letárgico/a [le'taxʒiku/a] *adj* lethargic.
letivo/a [le'tʃivu/a] *adj* school *atr*; **ano** ~ academic year.
Letônia [le'tonja] *f*: **a** ~ Latvia.
letra ['letra] *f* letter; (*caligrafia*) handwriting; (*de canção*) lyrics *pl*; **L~s** *fpl* (*curso*) language and literature; **à** ~ literally; **seguir à** ~ to follow to the letter; **ao pé da** ~ literally, word for word; **fazer** *ou* **tirar algo de** ~ (*col*) to be able to do sth standing on one's head; ~ **de câmbio** (COM) bill of exchange; ~ **de fôrma** block letter; ~ **de imprensa** print; ~ **de médico** (*fig*) scrawl; ~ **maiúscula/minúscula** capital/small letter.
letrado/a [le'tradu/a] *adj* learned, erudite ♦ *m/f* scholar; **ser** ~ **em algo** to be well-versed in sth.
letreiro [le'trejru] *m* sign, notice; (*inscrição*) inscription; (CINEMA) subtitle; ~ **luminoso** neon sign.
leu [lew] *etc vb V* **ler**.
léu [lɛw] *m*: **ao** ~ (*à toa*) aimlessly; (*à mostra*) uncovered.
leucemia [lewse'mia] *f* leukaemia (BRIT), leukemia (US).
leva ['lɛva] *f* (*de pessoas*) group.
levadiço/a [leva'dʒisu/a] *adj V* **ponte**.
levado/a [le'vadu/a] *adj* mischievous; (*criança*) naughty; ~ **da breca** naughty.
leva-e-traz [-'trajʒ] *m/f inv* gossip, stirrer.
levantador(a) [levãta'do*(a)] *adj* lifting ♦ *m/f*: ~ **de pesos** weightlifter.
levantamento [levãta'mẽtu] *m* lifting, raising; (*revolta*) uprising, rebellion; (*arrolamento*) survey; ~ **de pesos** weightlifting.
levantar [levã'ta*] *vt* to lift, raise; (*voz, capital*) to raise; (*apanhar*) to pick up; (*suscitar*) to arouse; (*ambiente*) to brighten up ♦ *vi* to stand up; (*da cama*) to get up; (*dar vida*) to brighten; **~-se** *vr* to stand up; (*da cama*) to get up; (*rebelar-se*) to rebel; ~ **vôo** to take off; ~ **a mão** to raise *ou* put up one's hand.
levante [le'vãtʃi] *m* east; (*revolta*) revolt.
levar [le'va*] *vt* to take; (*portar*) to carry; (*tempo*) to pass, spend; (*roupa*) to wear; (*lidar com*) to handle; (*induzir*) to lead; (*filme*) to show; (*peça teatral*) to do, put on ♦ *vi* to get a beating; ~ **a** to lead to; ~ **a mal** to take amiss; ~ **a cabo** to carry out; ~ **adiante** to go ahead with; ~ **uma vida feliz** to lead a happy life; ~ **a melhor/pior** to get a good/raw deal; ~ **pancadas/um susto/uma bronca** to get hit/a fright/told off; ~ **a educação a todos** to bring education to all; **deixar-se** ~ **por** to be carried along by.
leve ['lɛvi] *adj* light; (*insignificante*) slight; **de** ~ lightly, softly.
levedo [le'vedu] *m* yeast.
levedura [leve'dura] *f* = **levedo**.
leveza [le'veza] *f* lightness.
levezinho [leve'ziɲu] *adj*: **de** ~ very lightly.
leviandade [levjã'dadʒi] *f* frivolity.
leviano/a [le'vjanu/a] *adj* frivolous.
levitação [levita'sãw] *f* levitation.
levitar [levi'ta*] *vi* to levitate.
lexical [leksi'kaw] (*pl* **-ais**) *adj* lexical.
léxico/a ['lɛksiku/a] *adj* lexical ♦ *m* lexicon.
lexicografia [leksikogra'fia] *f* lexicography.
lexicógrafo/a [leksi'kɔgrafu/a] *m/f* lexicographer.
lezíria [le'zirja] (PT) *f* marshland.
LFT (BR) *abr f* = **Letra Financeira do Tesouro**.
lha(s) [ʎa(ʃ)] = **lhe** + **a(s)**.
lhama ['ʎama] *m* llama.
lhaneza [ʎa'neza] *f* amiability.
lhano/a ['ʎanu/a] *adj* amiable.
lhe [ʎi] *pron* (*a ele*) to him; (*a ela*) to her; (*a você*) to you.
lhes [ʎiʃ] *pron pl* (*a eles/elas*) to them; (*a vocês*) to you.
lho(s) [ʎu(ʃ)] = **lhe** + **o(s)**.
lhufas ['ʎufaʃ] (*col*) *pron* nothing, bugger all (!).
li [li] *etc vb V* **ler**.
lia ['lia] *f* dregs *pl*, sediment.
liame ['ljami] *m* tie, bond.
libanês/esa [liba'neʃ/eza] *adj* Lebanese.
Líbano ['libanu] *m*: **o** ~ (the) Lebanon.
libelo [li'bɛlu] *m* satire, lampoon; (JUR) formal indictment.
libélula [li'bɛlula] *f* dragonfly.

liberação [libera'sãw] *f* liberation.
liberal [libe'raw] (*pl* **-ais**) *adj, m/f* liberal.
liberalidade [liberali'dadʒi] *f* liberality.
liberalismo [libera'liʒmu] *m* liberalism.
liberalização [liberaliza'sãw] *f* liberalization.
liberalizante [liberali'zãtʃi] *adj* liberalizing.
liberalizar [liberali'za*] *vt* to liberalize.
liberar [libe'ra*] *vt* to release; (*libertar*) to free; (*COMPUT*: *dados*) to output.
liberdade [libex'dadʒi] *f* freedom; **~s** *fpl* (*direitos*) liberties; **tomar ~s com alguém** to take liberties with sb; **pôr alguém em ~** to set sb free; **estar em ~** to be free; **tomar a ~ de fazer** to take the liberty of doing; **~ condicional** probation; **~ de expressão** freedom of expression; **~ de cultos** freedom of worship; **~ de palavra** freedom of speech; **~ de pensamento** freedom of thought; **~ de imprensa** press freedom; **~ sob palavra** parole.
Libéria [li'bɛrja] *f*: **a ~** Liberia.
líbero ['liberu] *m* (*FUTEBOL*) sweeper.
libérrimo/a [li'bɛximu/a] *adj superl de* **livre**.
libertação [libexta'sãw] *f* release.
libertador(a) [libexta'do*(a)] *m/f* liberator.
libertar [libex'ta*] *vt* to free.
libertinagem [libextʃi'naʒẽ] *f* licentiousness, loose living.
libertino/a [libex'tʃinu/a] *adj* loose-living ♦ *m/f* libertine.
liberto/a [li'bɛxtu/a] *pp de* **libertar**.
Líbia ['libja] *f*: **a ~** Libya.
líbio/a ['libju/a] *adj, m/f* Libyan.
libidinoso/a [libidʒi'nozu/ɔza] *adj* lecherous, lustful.
libido [li'bidu] *f* libido.
libra ['libra] *f* pound; **~ esterlina** pound sterling; **L~** (*ASTROLOGIA*) Libra.
librar [li'bra*] *vt* to support.
libreto [li'bretu] *m* libretto.
libriano/a [li'brjanu/a] *adj, m/f* Libran.
lição [li'sãw] (*pl* **-ões**) *f* lesson; **que isto lhe sirva de ~** let this be a lesson to you.
licença [li'sẽsa] *f* licence (*BRIT*), license (*US*); (*permissão*) permission; (*do trabalho, MIL*) leave; **estar de ~** to be on leave; **com ~** excuse me; **dá ~?** may I?; **tirar ~** to go on leave; **sob ~** under licence; **~ poética** poetic licence.
licença-prêmio (*pl* **licenças-prêmio**) *f* long paid leave.
licenciado/a [lisẽ'sjadu/a] *m/f* graduate.
licenciar [lisẽ'sja*] *vt* to license; **~-se** *vr* (*EDUC*) to graduate; (*ficar de licença*) to take leave; **~ alguém** to give sb leave.
licenciatura [lisẽsja'tura] *f* (*título*) degree; (*curso*) degree course.
licencioso/a [lisẽ'sjozu/ɔza] *adj* licentious.
liceu [li'sew] (*PT*) *m* secondary (*BRIT*) *ou* high (*US*) school.
licitação [lisita'sãw] (*pl* **-ões**) *f* auction; (*concorrência*) tender; **abrir ~** to put out to tender.
licitante [lisi'tãtʃi] *m/f* bidder.
licitar [lisi'ta*] *vt* (*pôr em leilão*) to put up for auction ♦ *vi* to bid.
lícito/a ['lisitu/a] *adj* (*JUR*) lawful; (*justo*) fair, just; (*permissível*) permissible.
lições [li'sõjʃ] *fpl de* **lição**.
licor [li'ko*] *m* liqueur.
licoroso/a [liko'rozu/ɔza] *adj* (*vinho*) fortified.
lida ['lida] *f* toil; (*col*: *leitura*): **dar uma ~ em** to have a read of.
lidar [li'da*] *vi*: **~ com** (*ocupar-se*) to deal with; (*combater*) to struggle against; **~ em algo** to work in sth.
lide ['lidʒi] *f* (*trabalho*) work, chores *pl*; (*luta*) fight; (*JUR*) case.
líder ['lide*] *m/f* leader.
liderança [lide'rãsa] *f* leadership; (*ESPORTE*) lead.
liderar [lide'ra*] *vt* to lead.
lido/a ['lidu/a] *pp de* **ler** ♦ *adj* (*pessoa*) well-read.
lifting ['liftĩŋ] (*pl* **~s**) *m* face lift.
liga ['liga] *f* league; (*de meias*) garter, suspender; (*metal*) alloy.
ligação [liga'sãw] (*pl* **-ões**) *f* connection; (*fig*: *de amizade*) bond; (*TEL*) call; (*relação amorosa*) liaison; **fazer uma ~ para alguém** to call sb; **não consigo completar a ~** (*TEL*) I can't get through; **caiu a ~** (*TEL*) I (*ou* he *etc*) was cut off.
ligada [li'gada] *f* (*TEL*) ring, call; **dar uma ~ para alguém** (*col*) to give sb a ring.
ligado/a [li'gadu/a] *adj* (*TEC*) connected; (*luz, rádio etc*) on; (*metal*) alloy; **estar ~ (em)** (*col*: *absorto*) to be wrapped up (in); (: *em droga*) to be hooked (on); (*afetivamente*) to be attached (to).
ligadura [liga'dura] *f* bandage; (*MÚS*) ligature.
ligamento [liga'mẽtu] *m* ligament.
ligar [li'ga*] *vt* to tie, bind; (*unir*) to join, connect; (*luz, TV*) to switch on; (*afetivamente*) to bind together; (*carro*) to start (up) ♦ *vi* (*telefonar*) to ring; **~-se** *vr* to join; **~-se com alguém** to join with sb; **~-se a algo** to be connected with sth; **~ para alguém** to ring sb up; **~ para fora** to ring out; **~ para** *ou* **a algo** (*dar atenção*) to take notice of sth; (*dar importância*) to care about sth; **eu nem ligo** it doesn't bother me; **não ligo a mínima (para)** I couldn't care less (about).
ligeireza [liʒej'reza] *f* lightness; (*rapidez*) swiftness; (*agilidade*) nimbleness.
ligeiro/a [li'ʒejru/a] *adj* light; (*ferimento*) slight; (*referência*) passing; (*conhecimentos*) scant; (*rápido*) quick, swift; (*ágil*) nimble ♦ *adv* swiftly, nimbly.
liguei [li'gej] *etc vb V* **ligar**.

***NB**: European Portuguese adds the following consonants to certain words:* **b** (sú(b)dito, su(b)til); **c** (a(c)ção, a(c)cionista, a(c)to); **m** (inde(m)ne); **p** (ado(p)ção, ado(p)tar); *for further details see p. xiii.*

lilás [li'laʃ] *adj, m* lilac.
lima ['lima] *f* (*laranja*) type of (very sweet) orange; (*ferramenta*) file; ~ **de unhas** nail file.
limão [li'mãw] (*pl* **-ões**) *m* lime.
limão(-galego) (*pl* **limões(-galegos)**) *m* lemon.
limar [li'ma*] *vt* to file.
limbo ['lĩbu] *m*: **estar no** ~ to be in limbo.
limeira [li'mejra] *f* lime tree.
limiar [li'mja*] *m* threshold.
liminar [limi'na*] *f* (*JUR*) preliminary verdict.
limitação [limita'sãw] (*pl* **-ões**) *f* limitation, restriction.
limitado/a [limi'tadu/a] *adj* limited; **ele é meio** *ou* **bem** ~ he's not very bright.
limitar [limi'ta*] *vt* to limit, restrict; **~-se** *vr*: **~-se a** to limit o.s. to; **~(-se) com** to border on; **ele limitava-se a dizer ...** he did nothing more than say ....
limite [li'mitʃi] *m* (*de terreno etc*) limit, boundary; (*fig*) limit; **passar dos ~s** to go too far; ~ **de crédito** credit limit; ~ **de idade** age limit.
limo ['limu] *m* (*BOT*) water weed; (*lodo*) slime.
limoeiro [li'mwejru] *m* lemon tree.
limões [li'mõjʃ] *mpl de* **limão**.
limonada [limo'nada] *f* lemonade (*BRIT*), lemon soda (*US*).
limpa ['lĩpa] (*col*) *f* clean; (*roubo*): **fazer uma ~ em** to clean out.
limpação [lĩpa'sãw] *f* cleaning.
limpador [lĩpa'do*] *m*: ~ **de pára-brisas** windscreen wiper (*BRIT*), windshield wiper (*US*).
limpa-pés *m inv* shoe scraper.
limpar [lĩ'pa*] *vt* to clean; (*lágrimas, suor*) to wipe away; (*polir*) to shine, polish; (*fig*) to clean up; (*arroz, peixe*) to clean; (*roubar*) to rob.
limpa-trilhos *m inv* cowcatcher.
limpeza [lĩ'peza] *f* cleanliness; (*esmero*) neatness; (*ato*) cleaning; (*fig*) clean-up; (*roubo*): **fazer uma ~ em** to clean out; ~ **de pele** facial; ~ **pública** rubbish (*BRIT*) *ou* garbage (*US*) collection, sanitation.
límpido/a ['lĩpidu/a] *adj* limpid.
limpo/a ['lĩpu/a] *pp de* **limpar** ♦ *adj* clean; (*céu, consciência*) clear; (*COM*) net, clear; (*fig*) pure; (*col: pronto*) ready; **passar a ~** to make a fair copy; **tirar a ~** to find out the truth about, clear up; **estar ~ com alguém** (*col*) to be in with sb.
limusine [limu'zini] *f* limousine.
lince ['lĩsi] *m* lynx; **ter olhos de ~** to have eyes like a hawk.
linchar [lĩ'ʃa*] *vt* to lynch.
lindeza [lĩ'deza] *f* beauty.
lindo/a ['lĩdu/a] *adj* lovely; ~ **de morrer** (*col*) stunning.
linear [li'nja*] *adj* linear.
linfático/a [lĩ'fatʃiku/a] *adj* lymphatic.
lingerie [lĩʒe'ri] *m* lingerie.
lingote [lĩ'gɔtʃi] *m* ingot.
língua ['lĩgwa] *f* tongue; (*linguagem*) language; **botar a ~ para fora** to stick out one's tongue; **dar com a ~ nos dentes** to let the cat out of the bag; **dobrar a ~** to bite one's tongue; **estar na ponta da ~** to be on the tip of one's tongue; **ficar de ~ de fora** (*exausto*) to be pooped; **pagar pela ~** to live to regret one's words; **saber algo na ponta da ~** to know sth inside out; **ter uma ~ comprida** (*fig*) to have a big mouth; **em ~ da gente** (*col*) in plain English; ~ **franca** lingua franca; ~ **materna** mother tongue.
linguado [lĩ'gwadu] *m* (*peixe*) sole.
linguagem [lĩ'gwaʒẽ] (*pl* **-ns**) *f* (*tb*: *COMPUT*) language; (*falada*) speech; ~ **de alto nível** (*COMPUT*) high-level language; ~ **de máquina** (*COMPUT*) machine language; ~ **de montagem** (*COMPUT*) assembly language; ~ **de programação** (*COMPUT*) programming language.
linguajar [lĩgwa'ʒa*] *m* speech, language.
linguarudo/a [lĩgwa'rudu/a] *adj* gossiping ♦ *m/f* gossip.
lingüeta [lĩ'gweta] *f* (*fechadura*) bolt; (*balança*) pointer.
lingüiça [lĩ'gwisa] *f* sausage; **encher ~** (*col*) to waffle on.
lingüista [lĩ'gwiʃta] *m/f* linguist.
lingüística [lĩ'gwiʃtʃika] *f* linguistics *sg*.
lingüístico/a [lĩ'gwiʃtʃiku/a] *adj* linguistic.
linha ['liɲa] *f* line; (*para costura*) thread; (*barbante*) string, cord; (*fila*) row; **~s** *fpl* (*carta*) letter *sg*; **as ~s gerais de um projeto** the outlines of a project; **em ~** in line, in a row; (*COMPUT*) on line; **fora de ~** (*COMPUT*) off line; **andar na ~** (*fig*) to toe the line; **sair da ~** (*fig*) to step out of line; **comportar-se com muita ~** to behave very correctly; **manter/perder a ~** to keep/lose one's cool; **o telefone não deu ~** the line was dead; ~ **aérea** airline; ~ **de ataque** (*FUTEBOL*) forward line, forwards *pl*; ~ **de conduta** course of action; ~ **de crédito** (*COM*) credit line; ~ **de fogo** firing line; ~ **demarcatória** demarcation line; ~ **de mira** sights *pl*; ~ **de montagem** assembly line; ~ **de partido** party line; ~ **de saque** (*TÊNIS*) baseline; ~ **férrea** railway (*BRIT*), railroad (*US*).
linhaça [li'ɲasa] *f* linseed.
linha-dura (*pl* **linhas-duras**) *m/f* hardliner.
linhagem [li'ɲaʒẽ] *f* lineage.
linho ['liɲu] *m* linen; (*planta*) flax.
linóleo [li'nɔlju] *m* linoleum.
lipoaspiração [lipuaʃpira'sãw] *f* liposuction.
liquefazer [likefa'ze*] (*irreg*: *como* **fazer**) *vt* to liquefy.
líquen ['likẽ] *m* lichen.
liquidação [likida'sãw] (*pl* **-ões**) *f* liquidation; (*em loja*) (clearance) sale; (*de conta*) settlement; **em ~** on sale; **entrar em ~** to go into liquidation.
liquidante [liki'dãtʃi] *m/f* liquidator.
liquidar [liki'da*] *vt* to liquidate; (*conta*) to settle; (*mercadoria*) to sell off; (*assunto*) to

lay to rest ♦ *vi* (*loja*) to have a sale; **~-se** *vr* (*destruir-se*) to be destroyed; **~ (com) alguém** (*fig*: *arrasar*) to destroy sb; (: *matar*) to do away with sb.

liquidez [liki'deʒ] *f* (COM) liquidity.

liqüidificador [likwidʒifika'do*] *m* liquidizer.

liqüidificar [likwidʒifi'ka*] *vt* to liquidize.

líquido/a ['likidu/a] *adj* liquid, fluid; (COM) net ♦ *m* liquid.

lira ['lira] *f* lyre; (*moeda*) lira.

lírica ['lirika] *f* (MÚS) lyrics *pl*; (*poesia*) lyric poetry.

lírico/a ['liriku/a] *adj* lyric(al).

lírio ['lirju] *m* lily.

lírio-do-vale (*pl* **lírios-do-vale**) *m* lily of the valley.

lirismo [li'riʒmu] *m* lyricism.

Lisboa [liʒ'boa] *n* Lisbon.

lisboeta [liʒ'bweta] *adj* Lisbon *atr* ♦ *m/f* inhabitant *ou* native of Lisbon.

liso/a ['lizu/a] *adj* smooth; (*tecido*) plain; (*cabelo*) straight; (*col*: *sem dinheiro*) broke; **estar ~, leso e louco** (*col*) to be flat broke.

lisonja [li'zõʒa] *f* flattery.

lisonjeador(a) [lizõʒja'do*(a)] *adj* flattering ♦ *m/f* flatterer.

lisonjear [lizõ'ʒja*] *vt* to flatter.

lisonjeiro/a [lizõ'ʒejru/a] *adj* flattering.

lista ['liʃta] *f* list; (*listra*) stripe; (PT: *menu*) menu; **~ civil** civil list; **~ negra** black list; **~ telefônica** telephone directory.

listado/a [li'ʃtadu/a] *adj* = **listrado/a**.

listagem [liʃ'taʒẽ] (*pl* **-ns**) *f* (COMPUT) listing.

listar [liʃ'ta*] *vt* (COMPUT) to list.

listra ['liʃtra] *f* stripe.

listrado/a [liʃ'tradu/a] *adj* striped.

literal [lite'raw] (*pl* **-ais**) *adj* literal.

literário/a [lite'rarju/a] *adj* literary.

literato [lite'ratu] *m* man of letters.

literatura [litera'tura] *f* literature.

litigante [litʃi'gãtʃi] *m/f* (JUR) litigant.

litigar [litʃi'ga*] *vt* to contend ♦ *vi* to go to law.

litígio [li'tʃiʒju] *m* (JUR) lawsuit; (*contenda*) dispute.

litigioso/a [litʃi'ʒozu/ɔza] *adj* (JUR) disputed.

litografia [litogra'fia] *f* (*processo*) lithography; (*gravura*) lithograph.

litogravura [litogra'vura] *f* lithograph.

litoral [lito'raw] (*pl* **-ais**) *adj* coastal ♦ *m* coast, seaboard.

litorâneo/a [lito'ranju/a] *adj* coastal.

litro ['litru] *m* litre (BRIT), liter (US).

Lituânia [li'twanja] *f*: **a ~** Lithuania.

liturgia [litux'ʒia] *f* liturgy.

litúrgico/a [li'tuxʒiku/a] *adj* liturgical.

lívido/a ['lividu/a] *adj* livid.

living ['livĩŋ] (*pl* **~s**) *m* living room.

livramento [livra'mẽtu] *m* release; **~ condicional** parole.

livrar [li'vra*] *vt* to release, liberate; (*salvar*) to save; **~-se** *vr* to escape; **~-se de** to get rid of; (*compromisso*) to get out of; **Deus me livre!** Heaven forbid!

livraria [livra'ria] *f* bookshop (BRIT), bookstore (US).

livre ['livri] *adj* free; (*lugar*) unoccupied; (*desimpedido*) clear, open; **~ de impostos** tax-free; **estar ~ de algo** to be free of sth; **de ~ e espontânea vontade** of one's own free will.

livre-arbítrio *m* free will.

livreiro/a [liv'rejru/a] *m/f* bookseller.

livresco/a [li'vreʃku/a] *adj* book *atr*; (*pessoa*) bookish.

livrete [li'vretʃi] *m* booklet.

livro ['livru] *m* book; **~ brochado** paperback; **~ caixa** (COM) cash book; **~ de bolso** pocket-sized book; **~ de cabeceira** favo(u)rite book; **~ de cheques** cheque book (BRIT), check book (US); **~ de consulta** reference book; **~ de cozinha** cookery book (BRIT), cookbook (US); **~ de mercadorias** stock book; **~ de registro** catalogue (BRIT), catalog (US); **~ de texto** *ou* **didático** text book; **~ encadernado** *ou* **de capa dura** hardback.

lixa ['liʃa] *f* sandpaper; (*de unhas*) nail-file; (*peixe*) dogfish.

lixadeira [liʃa'dejra] *f* sander.

lixar [li'ʃa*] *vt* to sand; **~-se** *vr* (*col*): **estou me lixando com isso** I couldn't care less about it.

lixeira [li'ʃejra] *f* dustbin (BRIT), garbage can (US).

lixeiro [li'ʃejru] *m* dustman (BRIT), garbage man (US).

lixo ['liʃu] *m* rubbish, garbage (US); **ser um ~** (*col*) to be rubbish; **~ atômico** nuclear waste.

Lj. *abr* = **loja**.

lj. *abr* = **loja**.

-lo [lu] *pron* him; (*você*) you; (*coisa*) it.

lobby ['lɔbi] (*pl* **-ies**) *m* (POL) lobby.

lobinho [lo'biɲu] *m* (ZOOL) wolf cub; (*escoteiro*) cub.

lóbi ['lɔbi] *m* = **lobby**.

lobisomem [lobi'somẽ] (*pl* **-ns**) *m* werewolf.

lobista [lo'biʃta] *m/f* lobbyist.

lobo ['lobu] *m* wolf.

lobo-do-mar (*pl* **lobos-do-mar**) *m* old salt.

lobo-marinho (*pl* **lobos-marinhos**) *m* sea lion.

lobrigar [lobri'ga*] *vt* to glimpse.

lóbulo ['lɔbulu] *m* lobe.

locação [loka'sãw] (*pl* **-ões**) *f* lease; (*de vídeo etc*) rental.

locador(a) [loka'do*(a)] *m/f* (*de casa*) landlord; (*de carro, filme*) rental agent ♦ *f* rental company; **~a de vídeo** video rental shop.

local [lo'kaw] (*pl* **-ais**) *adj* local ♦ *m* site, place

NB: European Portuguese adds the following consonants to certain words: **b** (sú(b)dito, su(b)til); **c** (a(c)ção, a(c)cionista, a(c)to); **m** (inde(m)ne); **p** (ado(p)ção, ado(p)tar); *for further details see p. xiii.*

♦ *f* (*notícia*) story.
localidade [lokali'dadʒi] *f* (*lugar*) locality; (*povoação*) town.
localização [lokaliza'sãw] (*pl* **-ões**) *f* location.
localizar [lokali'za*] *vt* to locate; (*situar*) to place; **~-se** *vr* (*estabelecer-se*) to be located; (*orientar-se*) to get one's bearings.
loção [lo'sãw] (*pl* **-ões**) *f* lotion; **~ após-barba** aftershave (lotion).
locatário/a [loka'tarju/a] *m/f* (*de casa*) tenant; (*de carro, filme*) hirer.
locaute [lo'kawtʃi] *m* lockout.
loções [lo'sõjʃ] *fpl de* **loção**.
locomoção [lokomo'sãw] (*pl* **-ões**) *f* locomotion.
locomotiva [lokomo'tʃiva] *f* railway (*BRIT*) *ou* railroad (*US*) engine, locomotive.
locomover-se [lokomo'vexsi] *vr* to move around.
locução [loku'sãw] (*pl* **-ões**) *f* (*LING*) phrase; (*dicção*) diction.
locutor(a) [loku'to*(a)] *m/f* (*TV, RÁDIO*) announcer.
lodacento/a [loda'sẽtu/a] *adj* muddy.
lodo ['lodu] *m* mud, slime.
lodoso/a [lo'dozu/ɔza] *adj* muddy.
logaritmo [loga'ritʃimo] *m* logarithm.
lógica ['lɔʒika] *f* logic.
lógico/a ['lɔʒiku/a] *adj* logical; **(é) ~!** of course!
logística [lo'ʒiʃtʃika] *f* logistics *sg*.
logo ['lɔgu] *adv* (*imediatamente*) right away, at once; (*em breve*) soon; (*justamente*) just, right; (*mais tarde*) later; **~, ~** straightaway, without delay; **~ mais** later; **~ no começo** right at the start; **~ que, tão ~** as soon as; **até ~!** bye!; **~ antes/depois** just before/ shortly afterwards; **~ de saída** *ou* **de cara** straightaway, right away.
logopedia [logope'dʒia] *f* speech therapy.
logopedista [logope'dʒiʃta] *m/f* speech therapist.
logotipo [logo'tʃipu] *m* logo.
logradouro [logra'doru] *m* public area.
lograr [lo'gra*] *vt* (*alcançar*) to achieve; (*obter*) to get, obtain; (*enganar*) to cheat; **~ fazer** to manage to do.
logro ['logru] *m* fraud.
loiro/a ['lojru/a] *adj* = **louro/a**.
loja ['lɔʒa] *f* shop; (*maçônica*) lodge; **~ de antiguidades** antique shop; **~ de brinquedos** toy shop; **~ de departamentos** department store; **~ de ferragens** ironmonger's (*BRIT*), hardware store; **~ de produtos naturais** health food shop.
lojista [lo'ʒiʃta] *m/f* shopkeeper.
lomba ['lõba] *f* ridge; (*ladeira*) slope.
lombada [lõ'bada] *f* (*de animal*) back; (*de livro*) spine; (*na estrada*) ramp.
lombar [lõ'ba*] *adj* lumbar.
lombeira [lõ'bejra] *f* listlessness.
lombinho [lõ'biɲu] *m* (*carne*) tenderloin.
lombo ['lõbu] *m* back; (*carne*) loin.
lombriga [lõ'briga] *f* ringworm.
lona ['lɔna] *f* canvas; **estar na última ~** (*col*) to be broke.
Londres ['lõdriʃ] *n* London.
londrino/a [lõ'drinu/a] *adj* London *atr* ♦ *m/f* Londoner.
longa-metragem (*pl* **longas-metragens**) *m*: **(filme de) ~** feature (film).
longe ['lõʒi] *adv* far, far away ♦ *adj* distant; **ao ~** in the distance; **de ~** from far away; (*sem dúvida*) by a long way; **~ dos olhos, ~ do coração** out of sight, out of mind; **~ de** a long way *ou* far from; **~ disso** far from it; **ir ~ demais** (*fig*) to go too far; **essa sua mania vem de ~** he's had this habit for a long time; **ver ~** (*fig*) to have vision.
longevidade [lõʒevi'dadʒi] *f* longevity.
longínquo/a [lõ'ʒĩkwu/a] *adj* distant, remote.
longíquo/a [lõ'ʒikwu/a] *adj* = **longínquo/a**.
longitude [lõʒi'tudʒi] *f* (*GEO*) longitude.
longitudinal [lõʒitudʒi'naw] (*pl* **-ais**) *adj* longitudinal.
longo/a ['lõgu/a] *adj* long ♦ *m* (*vestido*) long dress, evening dress; **ao ~ de** along, alongside.
lontra ['lõtra] *f* otter.
loquacidade [lokwasi'dadʒi] *f* loquacity.
loquaz [lo'kwaʒ] *adj* talkative.
lorde ['lɔxdʒi] *m* lord.
lorota [lo'rɔta] (*col*) *f* fib.
losango [lo'zãgu] *m* lozenge, diamond.
lotação [lota'sãw] *f* capacity; (*vinho*) blending; (*de funcionários*) complement; (*BR*: *ônibus*) bus; **~ completa** *ou* **esgotada** (*TEATRO*) sold out.
lotado/a [lo'tadu/a] *adj* (*TEATRO*) full; (*ônibus*) full up; (*bar, praia*) packed, crowded.
lotar [lo'ta*] *vt* to fill, pack; (*funcionário*) to place ♦ *vi* to fill up.
lote ['lɔtʃi] *m* (*porção*) portion, share; (*em leilão*) lot; (*terreno*) plot; (*de ações*) parcel, batch.
loteamento [lotʃja'mẽtu] *m* division into lots.
lotear [lo'tʃja*] *vt* to divide into lots.
loteca [lo'tɛka] (*col*) *f* pools *pl* (*BRIT*), lottery (*US*).
loteria [lote'ria] *f* lottery; **ganhar na ~** to win the lottery; **~ esportiva** football pools *pl* (*BRIT*), lottery (*US*).
loto¹ ['lɔtu] *m* lotus.
loto² ['lotu] *m* bingo.
lótus ['lɔtuʃ] *m inv* lotus.
louça ['losa] *f* china; (*conjunto*) crockery; (*tb*: *~ sanitária*) bathroom suite; **de ~** china *atr*; **~ de barro** earthenware; **~ de jantar** dinner service; **lavar a ~** to do the washing up (*BRIT*) *ou* the dishes.
louçaria [losa'ria] *f* china; (*loja*) china shop.
louco/a ['loku/a] *adj* crazy, mad; (*sucesso*) runaway; (*frio*) freezing ♦ *m/f* lunatic; **~ varrido** raving mad; **~ de fome/raiva** ravenous/hopping mad; **~ por** crazy about; **deixar alguém ~** to drive sb crazy; **ser uma**

coisa de ~ (*col*) to be really something; **estar/ficar** ~ **da vida (com)** to be/get mad (at); ~ **de pedra** (*col*) stark staring mad; **deu uma louca nele e ...** something strange came over him and ...; **cada** ~ **com sua mania** whatever turns you on.

loucura [lo'kura] *f* madness; (*ato*) crazy thing; **ser** ~ **(fazer)** to be crazy (to do); **ser uma** ~ to be crazy; (*col*: *ser muito bom*) to be fantastic; **ter** ~ **por** to be crazy about.

louquice [lo'kisi] *f* madness; (*ato, dito*) crazy thing.

louro/a ['loru/a] *adj* blond, fair ♦ *m* laurel; (*CULIN*) bay leaf; (*cor*) blondness; (*papagaio*) parrot; ~**s** *mpl* (*fig*) laurels.

lousa ['loza] *f* flagstone; (*tumular*) gravestone; (*quadro-negro*) blackboard.

louva-a-deus ['lova-] *m inv* praying mantis.

louvação [lova'sãw] (*pl* **-ões**) *f* praise.

louvar [lo'va*] *vt, vi*: ~ **(a) Deus** to praise God.

louvável [lo'vavew] (*pl* **-eis**) *adj* praiseworthy.

louvor [lo'vo*] *m* praise.

LP *abr m* LP.

lpm *abr* (= *linhas por minuto*) lpm.

Ltda. *abr* (= *Limitada*) Ltd.

lua ['lua] *f* moon; **estar** *ou* **viver no mundo da** ~ to have one's head in the clouds; **estar de** ~ (*col*) to be in a mood; **ser de** ~ (*col*) to be moody; ~ **cheia/nova** full/new moon.

lua-de-mel *f* honeymoon.

Luanda ['lwãda] *n* Luanda.

luar ['lwa*] *m* moonlight; **banhado de** ~ moonlit.

luarento/a [lwa'rẽtu/a] *adj* moonlit.

lubrificação [lubrifika'sãw] (*pl* **-ões**) *f* lubrication.

lubrificante [lubrifi'kãtʃi] *m* lubricant ♦ *adj* lubricating.

lubrificar [lubrifi'ka*] *vt* to lubricate.

lucidez [lusi'deʒ] *f* lucidity, clarity.

lúcido/a ['lusidu/a] *adj* lucid.

lúcio ['lusju] *m* (*peixe*) pike.

lucrar [lu'kra*] *vt* (*tirar proveito*) to profit from *ou* by; (*dinheiro*) to make; (*gozar*) to enjoy ♦ *vi* to make a profit; ~ **com** *ou* **em** to profit by.

lucratividade [lukratʃivi'dadʒi] *f* profitability.

lucrativo/a [lukra'tʃivu/a] *adj* lucrative, profitable.

lucro ['lukru] *m* gain; (*COM*) profit; ~ **bruto/líquido** (*COM*) gross/net profit; **participação nos** ~**s** (*COM*) profit-sharing; ~**s e perdas** (*COM*) profit and loss.

lucubração [lukubra'sãw] (*pl* **-ões**) *f* meditation, pondering.

ludibriar [ludʒi'brja*] *vt* (*enganar*) to dupe, deceive; (*escarnecer*) to mock, deride.

lúdico/a ['ludʒiku/a] *adj* playful.

lufada [lu'fada] *f* gust (of wind).

lugar [lu'ga*] *m* place; (*espaço*) space, room; (*para sentar*) seat; (*emprego*) job; (*ocasião*) opportunity; **em** ~ **de** instead of; **dar** ~ **a** (*causar*) to give rise to; ~ **comum** commonplace; **em primeiro** ~ in the first place; **em algum/nenhum/outro/todo** ~ somewhere/nowhere/somewhere else, elsewhere/everywhere; **ter** ~ (*acontecer*) to take place; **ponha-se em meu** ~ put yourself in my position; **ponha-se no seu** ~ don't get ideas above your station; **ele foi no meu** ~ he went instead of me *ou* in my place; **tirar o primeiro** ~ to come first; **conhecer o seu** ~ to know one's place; ~ **de nascimento** place of birth.

lugarejo [luga'reʒu] *m* village.

lúgubre ['lugubri] *adj* mournful; (*escuro*) gloomy.

lula ['lula] *f* squid.

lumbago [lũ'bagu] *m* lumbago.

lume ['lumi] *m* fire; (*luz*) light.

luminária [lumi'narja] *f* lamp; ~**s** *fpl* illuminations.

luminosidade [luminozi'dadʒi] *f* brightness.

luminoso/a [lumi'nozu/ɔza] *adj* luminous, bright; (*fig*: *raciocínio*) clear; (: *idéia, talento*) brilliant; (*letreiro*) illuminated.

lunar [lu'na*] *adj* lunar ♦ *m* (*na pele*) mole.

lunático/a [lu'natʃiku/a] *adj* mad.

luneta [lu'neta] *f* eye-glass; (*telescópio*) telescope.

lupa ['lupa] *f* magnifying glass.

lúpulo ['lupulu] *m* (*BOT*) hop.

lusco-fusco ['luʃku-] *m* twilight.

lusitano/a [luzi'tanu/a] *adj* Portuguese, Lusitanian.

luso/a ['luzu/a] *adj* Portuguese.

luso-brasileiro/a (*pl* ~**s**) *adj* Luso-Brazilian.

lustra-móveis ['luʃtra-] *m inv* furniture polish.

lustrar [luʃ'tra*] *vt* to polish, clean.

lustre ['luʃtri] *m* gloss, sheen; (*fig*) lustre (*BRIT*), luster (*US*); (*luminária*) chandelier.

lustroso/a [luʃ'trozu/ɔza] *adj* shiny.

luta ['luta] *f* fight, struggle; ~ **armada** armed combat; ~ **de boxe** boxing; ~ **de classes** class struggle; ~ **livre** wrestling; **foi uma** ~ **convencê-lo** it was a struggle to convince him.

lutador(a) [luta'do*(a)] *m/f* fighter; (*atleta*) wrestler.

lutar [lu'ta*] *vi* to fight, struggle; (*luta livre*) to wrestle ♦ *vt* (*caratê, judô*) to do; ~ **contra/por algo** to fight against/for sth; ~ **para fazer algo** to fight *ou* struggle to do sth; ~ **com** (*dificuldades*) to struggle against; (*competir*) to fight with.

luto ['lutu] *m* mourning; (*tristeza*) grief; **de** ~ in mourning; **pôr** ~ to go into mourning.

luva ['luva] *f* glove; ~**s** *fpl* (*pagamento*) pay-

NB: European Portuguese adds the following consonants to certain words: **b** (sú(b)dito, su(b)til); **c** (a(c)ção, a(c)cionista, a(c)to); **m** (inde(m)ne); **p** (ado(p)ção, ado(p)tar); *for further details see p. xiii.*

ment *sg*; (*ao locador*) fee *sg*; **caber como uma ~** to fit like a glove.
luxação [luʃa'sãw] (*pl* **-ões**) *f* dislocation.
luxar [lu'ʃa*] *vi* to show off.
Luxemburgo [luʃẽ'buxgu] *m*: **o ~** Luxembourg.
luxento/a [lu'ʃẽtu/a] *adj* fussy, finnicky.
luxo ['luʃu] *m* luxury; **de ~** luxury *atr*; **dar-se ao ~ de** to allow o.s. to; **poder dar-se ao ~ de** to be able to afford to; **cheio de ~** (*col*) prissy, finnicky; **deixe de ~** (*col*) don't come it; **fazer ~** (*col*) to play hard to get; **com ~** luxurious(ly); (*vestir-se*) fancily.
luxuosidade [luʃwozi'dadʒi] *f* luxuriousness.
luxuoso/a [lu'ʃwozu/ɔza] *adj* luxurious.
luxúria [lu'ʃurja] *f* lust.
luxuriante [luʃu'rjãtʃi] *adj* lush.
luz [luʒ] *f* light; (*eletricidade*) electricity; **à ~ de** by the light of; (*fig*) in the light of; **a meia ~** with subdued lighting; **dar à ~ (um filho)** to give birth (to a son); **deu-me uma ~** I had an idea; **~ artificial/natural** artificial/natural light; **~ de vela** candlelight; **pessoa de muita ~** enlightened person.
luzidio/a [luzi'dʒiu/a] *adj* shining, glossy.
luzir [lu'zi*] *vi* to shine, gleam; (*fig*) to be successful.
Lx.a *abr* = **Lisboa**.
lycra ['lajkra] ® *f* lycra ®.

M

M, m ['emi] (*pl* **ms**) *m* M, m; **M de Maria** M for Mike.
MA *abr* = **Maranhão**.
ma [ma] *pron* = **me** + **a**.
má [ma] *adj f de* **mau**.
maca ['maka] *f* stretcher.
maçã [ma'sã] *f* apple; **~ do rosto** cheekbone.
macabro/a [ma'kabru/a] *adj* macabre.
macaca [ma'kaka] *f* she-monkey; **estar com a ~** (*col*) to be in a foul mood.
macacada [maka'kada] *f* (*turma*): **a ~** the gang.
macacão [maka'kãw] (*pl* **-ões**) *m* (*de trabalhador*) overalls *pl* (*BRIT*), coveralls *pl* (*US*); (*da moda*) jump-suit.
macaco [ma'kaku] *m* monkey; (*MEC*) jack; **(fato) ~** (*PT*) overalls *pl* (*BRIT*), coveralls *pl* (*US*); (*pessoa feia*) ugly mug; (*tb*: **~** *de imitação*) copycat; **~ velho** (*fig*) old hand; **~s me mordam** (*col*) blow me down.
macacões [maka'kõjʃ] *mpl de* **macacão**.
maçada [ma'sada] *f* bore.
macadame [maka'dami] *m* asphalt, tarmac (*BRIT*).
maçador(a) [masa'do*(a)] (*PT*) *adj* boring.
macambúzio/a [makã'buzju/a] *adj* sullen.
maçaneta [masa'neta] *f* knob.
maçante [ma'sãtʃi] (*BR*) *adj* boring.
macaquear [maka'kja*] *vt* to ape.
macaquice [maka'kisi] *f*: **fazer ~s** to clown around.
maçar [ma'sa*] *vt* to bore.
maçarico [masa'riku] *m* (*tubo*) blowpipe; (*ave*) curlew.
maçaroca [masa'rɔka] *f* wad.
macarrão [maka'xãw] *m* pasta; (*em forma de canudo*) spaghetti.
macarronada [makaxo'nada] *f* pasta with cheese and tomato sauce.
macarrônico/a [maka'xoniku/a] *adj* (*francês etc*) broken, halting.
Macau [ma'kaw] *n* Macao.
maceioense [masej'wẽsi] *adj* from Maceió ♦ *m/f* person from Maceió.
macerado/a [mase'radu/a] *adj* (*rosto*) haggard.
macerar [mase'ra*] *vt* (*amolecer*) to soften; (*fig*: *mortificar*) to mortify; (: *rosto*) to make haggard.
macérrimo/a [ma'sɛximu/a] *adj superl de* **magro**.
macete [ma'setʃi] *m* mallet; (*col*) trick; **dar o ~ a alguém** (*col*) to show sb the way.
maceteado/a [mase'tʃjadu/a] (*col*) *adj* (*plano*) clever; (*casa*) well-designed.
machadada [maʃa'dada] *f* blow with an axe (*BRIT*) *ou* ax (*US*).
machado [ma'ʃadu] *m* axe (*BRIT*), ax (*US*).
machão/ona [ma'ʃãw/ɔna] (*pl* **-ões/~s**) *adj* tough; (*mulher*) butch ♦ *m* macho man; (*valentão*) tough guy.
machê [ma'ʃe] *adj*: **papel ~** papier-mâché.
machete [ma'ʃetʃi] *m* machete.
machismo [ma'ʃiʒmu] *m* male chauvinism, machismo; (*col*) toughness.
machista [ma'ʃiʃta] *adj* chauvinistic, macho ♦ *m* male chauvinist.
macho ['maʃu] *adj* male; (*fig*) virile, manly; (*valentão*) tough ♦ *m* male; (*TEC*) tap.
machões [ma'ʃõjʃ] *mpl de* **machão**.
machona [ma'ʃɔna] *f* butch woman; (*col*: *ofensivo*: *lésbica*) dyke.
machucado/a [maʃu'kadu/a] *adj* hurt; (*pé, braço*) bad ♦ *m* injury; (*lugar*) sore patch.
machucar [maʃu'ka*] *vt* to hurt; (*produzir contusão*) to bruise ♦ *vi* to hurt; **~-se** *vr* to hurt o.s.; (*col*: *estrepar-se*) to come a cropper, mess up.
maciço/a [ma'sisu/a] *adj* solid; (*espesso*) thick; (*quantidade*) massive ♦ *m* (*GEO*) massif; **ouro ~** solid gold; **uma dose maciça** a massive dose.
macieira [ma'sjejra] *f* apple tree.
maciez [ma'sjeʒ] *f* softness.
macilento/a [masi'lẽtu/a] *adj* gaunt, haggard.
macio/a [ma'siu/a] *adj* soft; (*liso*) smooth.
maciota [ma'sjɔta] *f*: **na ~** without problems.

maço ['masu] *m* (*de folhas, notas*) bundle; (*de cigarros*) packet.
maçom [ma'sõ] (*pl* **-ns**) *m* freemason.
maçonaria [masona'ria] *f* freemasonry.
maconha [ma'kɔɲa] *f* dope; **cigarro de ~** joint.
maconhado/a [mako'ɲadu/a] *adj* stoned.
maconheiro/a [mako'ɲejru/a] *m/f* (*viciado*) dope fiend; (*vendedor*) dope peddler.
maçônico/a [ma'soniku/a] *adj* masonic; **loja maçônica** masonic lodge.
maçons [ma'sõʃ] *mpl de* **maçom**.
má-criação (*pl* **-ões**) *f* rudeness; (*ato, dito*) rude thing.
macrobiótica [makro'bjɔtʃika] *f* (*dieta*) macrobiotic diet.
macrobiótico/a [makro'bjɔtʃiku/a] *adj* macrobiotic.
macroeconomia [makroekono'mia] *f* macroeconomics.
mácula ['makula] *f* stain, blemish.
macumba [ma'kũba] *f* voodoo; (*despacho*) voodoo offering.
macumbeiro/a [makũ'bejru/a] *adj* voodoo ♦ *m/f* follower of macumba.
madama [ma'dama] *f* = **madame**.
madame [ma'dami] *f* (*senhora*) lady; (*col: dona-de-casa*) lady of the house; (: *esposa*) missus; (: *de bordel*) madame.
Madeira [ma'dejra] *f*: **a ~** Madeira.
madeira [ma'dejra] *f* wood ♦ *m* Madeira (wine); **~ compensada** plywood; **de ~** wooden; **~ de lei** hardwood; **bater na ~** (*fig*) to touch (*BRIT*) *ou* knock on (*US*) wood.
madeira-branca (*pl* **madeiras-brancas**) *f* softwood.
madeiramento [madejra'mẽtu] *m* woodwork.
madeirense [madej'rẽsi] *adj, m/f* Madeiran.
madeiro [ma'dejru] *m* (*lenho*) log; (*viga*) beam.
madeixa [ma'dejʃa] *f* (*de cabelo*) lock; **~s** *fpl* locks.
madona [ma'dɔna] *f* madonna.
madrasta [ma'draʃta] *f* stepmother; (*fig*) heartless mother.
madre ['madri] *f* (*freira*) nun; (*superiora*) mother superior.
madrepérola [madre'pɛrola] *f* mother of pearl.
madressilva [madre'siwva] *f* honeysuckle.
Madri [ma'dri] *n* Madrid.
Madrid [ma'drid] (*PT*) *n* Madrid.
madrinha [ma'driɲa] *f* godmother; (*fig: patrocinadora*) patron.
madrugada [madru'gada] *f* (early) morning; (*alvorada*) dawn, daybreak; **duas horas da ~** two in the morning.
madrugador(a) [madruga'do*(a)] *m/f* early riser; (*fig*) early bird ♦ *adj* early-rising.
madrugar [madru'ga*] *vi* to get up early; (*aparecer cedo*) to be early.
madurar [madur'a*] *vt, vi* (*fruta*) to ripen; (*fig*) to mature.
madureza [madu'reza] *f* (*de pessoa*) maturity.
maduro/a [ma'duro/a] *adj* (*fruta*) ripe; (*fig*) mature; (: *prudente*) prudent.
mãe [mãj] *f* mother; **~ adotiva/de criação** adoptive/foster mother; **~ de família** wife and mother.
mãe-benta (*pl* **mães-bentas**) *f* (*CULIN*) coconut cookie.
mãe-de-santo (*pl* **mães-de-santo**) *f* voodoo priestess.
MAer (*BR*) *abr m* = **Ministério da Aeronáutica.**
maestria [majʃ'tria] *f* mastery; **com ~** in a masterly way.
maestro/trina [ma'ɛʃtru/'trina] *m/f* conductor.
má-fé *f* bad faith, malicious intent.
máfia ['mafja] *f* mafia.
mafioso/a [ma'fjozu/ɔza] *adj* gangsterish ♦ *m* mobster.
mafuá [ma'fwa] *m* fair; (*bagunça*) mess.
magarefe [maga'rɛfi] (*PT*) *m* butcher, slaughterer.
magazine [maga'zini] *m* magazine; (*loja*) department store.
magia [ma'ʒia] *f* magic; **~ negra** black magic.
mágica ['maʒika] *f* magic; (*truque*) magic trick; *V tb* **mágico**.
mágico/a ['maʒiku/a] *adj* magic ♦ *m/f* magician.
magistério [maʒiʃ'tɛrju] *m* (*ensino*) teaching; (*profissão*) teaching profession; (*professorado*) teachers *pl*.
magistrado [maʒiʃ'tradu] *m* magistrate.
magistral [maʒiʃ'traw] (*pl* **-ais**) *adj* magisterial; (*fig*) masterly.
magistratura [maʒiʃtra'tura] *f* magistracy.
magnanimidade [magnanimi'dadʒi] *f* magnanimity.
magnânimo/a [mag'nanimu/a] *adj* magnanimous.
magnata [mag'nata] *m* magnate, tycoon.
magnésia [mag'nɛzja] *f* magnesia.
magnésio [mag'nɛzju] *m* magnesium.
magnético/a [mag'nɛtʃiku/a] *adj* magnetic.
magnetismo [magne'tʃizmu] *m* magnetism.
magnetizar [magnetʃi'za*] *vt* to magnetize; (*fascinar*) to mesmerize.
magnificência [magnifi'sẽsja] *f* magnificence, splendour (*BRIT*), splendor (*US*).
magnífico/a [mag'nifiku/a] *adj* splendid, magnificent.
magnitude [magni'tudʒi] *f* magnitude.
magno/a ['magnu/a] *adj* (*grande*) great; (*importante*) important.
magnólia [mag'nɔlja] *f* magnolia.
mago ['magu] *m* magician; **os reis ~s** the Three Wise Men, the Three Kings.

NB: *European Portuguese adds the following consonants to certain words:* **b** (sú(b)dito, su(b)til); **c** (a(c)ção, a(c)cionista, a(c)to); **m** (inde(m)ne); **p** (ado(p)ção, ado(p)tar); *for further details see p. xiii.*

mágoa ['magwa] *f* (*tristeza*) sorrow, grief; (*fig*: *desagrado*) hurt.
magoado/a [ma'gwadu/a] *adj* hurt.
magoar [ma'gwa*] *vt*, *vi* to hurt; **~-se** *vr*: **~-se com algo** to be hurt by sth.
MAgr (*BR*) *abr m* = **Ministério da Agricultura.**
magreza [ma'greza] *f* slimness; (*de carne*) leanness; (*fig*) meagreness (*BRIT*), meagerness (*US*).
magricela [magri'sɛla] *adj* skinny.
magrinho/a [ma'griɲu/a] *adj* thin, skinny.
magro/a ['magru/a] *adj* (*pessoa*) slim; (*carne*) lean; (*fig*: *parco*) meagre (*BRIT*), meager (*US*); (*leite*) skimmed; **ser ~ como um palito** to be like a beanpole.
mai. *abr* = **maio.**
mainframe [mẽj'frejm] *m* mainframe.
maio ['maju] (*PT*: **M-**) *m* May; *V tb* **julho.**
maiô [ma'jo] (*BR*) *m* swimsuit.
maionese [majo'nezi] *f* mayonnaise.
maior [ma'jɔ*] *adj* (*compar*: *de tamanho*) bigger; (: *de importância*) greater; (*superl*: *de tamanho*) biggest; (: *de importância*) greatest ♦ *m/f* adult; **tive a ~ discussão com ela** I had a real argument with her; **foi o ~ barato** (*col*) it was really great; **tenho a ~ para te contar, não te conto a ~** the best is yet to come; **~ de idade** of age, adult; **~ de 21 anos** over 21; **ser de ~** (*col*) to be of age *ou* grown up; **ser ~ e vacinado** (*col*) to be one's own master.
maioral [majo'raw] (*pl* **-ais**) *m* boss; **o ~** the greatest.
Maiorca [maj'ɔxka] *f* Majorca.
maioria [majo'ria] *f* majority; **a ~ de** most of; **~ absoluta** absolute majority.
maioridade [majori'dadʒi] *f* adulthood; **atingir a ~** to come of age.
mais [majʃ] *adv*, *adj*, *pron* more ♦ *conj* plus, and ♦ *m*: **o ~** the rest; **~ um livro** another book; **~ cerveja** more beer; **ela é quem tem ~ livros** she has the most books; **~ alguma coisa?** anything else?; **nada/ninguém ~** nothing/no-one else; **~ alto/interessante** higher/more interesting; **o ~ alto** the highest; **correr/durar ~** to run faster/last longer; **~ de** more than; **~ dois** two more; **~ ou menos** more or less; **~ uma vez** once more; **não ~** no longer, not anymore; **nunca ~** never again; **a ~** too much; **um dia a ~** one more day; **cada vez ~** more and more; **não estudo ~** I don't study any more *ou* any longer; **por ~ que** however much; **quanto ~ ganha, ~ gasta** the more he earns, the more he spends; **e no ~, tudo bem?** how are you otherwise?; **até ~!** bye!; **~ adiante** further on; **logo ~** a bit later; **de ~ a ~** besides, anyhow; **~ a tempo** sooner; **~ cedo ou ~ tarde, ~ dia menos dia** sooner or later; **~ essa!** not that too!; **no ~ tardar** at the latest; **para ~ de** over; **não tem nada de ~ você fazer ...** there's nothing wrong with you doing ...; **sem ~ nem menos** out of the blue; **nem ~ nem menos** nothing more, nothing less; **que lugar ~ feio!** what a horrible place!
maisena [maj'zena] *f* cornflower.
mais-valia (*pl* **~s**) *f* surplus value.
maître ['mɛtrə] *m* head waiter.
maiúscula [ma'juʃkula] *f* capital letter.
majestade [maʒeʃ'tadʒi] *f* majesty; **Sua/Vossa M~** His (*ou* Her)/Your Majesty.
majestoso/a [maʒeʃ'tozu/ɔza] *adj* majestic.
major [ma'ʒɔ*] *m* (*MIL*) major.
majoritário/a [maʒori'tarju/a] *adj* majority *atr*.
mal [maw] (*pl* **~es**) *m* harm; (*MED*) illness ♦ *adv* badly; (*quase não*) hardly ♦ *conj* hardly; **~ desliguei o fone, a campainha tocou** I had hardly put the phone down when the doorbell rang; **o bem e o ~** good and bad; **o ~ é que ...** the bad thing is that ...; **falar ~ de alguém** to speak ill of sb, run sb down; **desejar ~ a alguém** to wish sb ill; **fazer ~ a alguém** to harm sb; (*deflorar*) to deflower sb; **fazer ~ à saúde de alguém** to damage sb's health; **fazer ~ em fazer** to be wrong to do; **não faz ~** never mind; **não fiz por ~** I meant no harm, I didn't mean it; **levar algo a ~** to take offence (*BRIT*) *ou* offense (*US*) at sth; **querer ~ a alguém** to bear sb ill; **estar ~** (*doente*) to be ill; **passar ~** to be sick; **estar ~ da vida** to be in a bad way; **viver ~ com alguém** not to get on with sb; **~ e porcamente** in a slapdash way; **estar de ~ com alguém** not to be speaking to sb; **dos ~es o menor** the lesser of two evils.
mal- [mal-] *prefixo* badly.
mala ['mala] *f* suitcase; (*BR*: *AUTO*) boot, trunk (*US*); **~s** *fpl* luggage *sg*; **fazer as ~s** to pack; **~ aérea** air courier; **~ de mão** piece of hand luggage; **~ direta** (*COM*) direct mail; **~ postal** mail bag.
malabarismo [malaba'riʒmu] *m* juggling; (*fig*) shrewd manoeuvre (*BRIT*) *ou* maneuver (*US*).
malabarista [malaba'riʃta] *m/f* juggler; (*fig*) smooth operator.
mal-acabado/a *adj* badly finished; (*pessoa*) deformed.
mal-acostumado/a *adj* maladjusted.
mal-afamado/a *adj* notorious, of ill repute.
malagradecido/a [malagrade'sidu/a] *adj* ungrateful.
malagueta [mala'geta] *f* chilli pepper.
malaio/a [ma'laju/a] *adj*, *m/f* Malay ♦ *m* (*LING*) Malay.
Malaísia [mala'izja] *f*: **a ~** Malaysia.
malaísio/a [mala'izju/a] *adj*, *m/f* Malaysian.
mal-ajambrado/a [-aʒã'bradu/a] *adj* scruffy.
mal-amada *adj* unloved ♦ *f* single woman.
malandragem [malã'draʒẽ] *f* (*patifaria*) double-dealing; (*preguiça*) idleness; (*esperteza*) cunning.
malandrear [malã'drja*] *vi* to loaf.
malandrice [malã'drisi] *f* = **malandragem.**

malandro/a [ma'lãdru/a] *adj* (*patife*) double-dealing; (*preguiçoso*) idle; (*esperto*) wily, cunning ♦ *m/f* (*patife*) crook; (*preguiçoso*) idler, layabout; (*esperto*) streetwise person.
mal-apanhado/a *adj* unpleasant-looking.
mal-apessoado/a [-ape'swadu/a] *adj* unpleasant-looking.
malária [ma'larja] *f* malaria.
mal-arrumado/a [-axu'madu/a] *adj* untidy.
mal-assombrado/a *adj* haunted.
Malavi [mala'vi] *m*: **o** ~ Malawi.
mal-avisado/a [-avi'zadu/a] *adj* rash.
malbaratar [mawbara'ta*] *vt* (*dinheiro*) to squander, waste.
malcasado/a [mawka'zadu/a] *adj* unhappily married; (*com pessoa inferior*) married to sb below one's class.
malcheiroso/a [mawʃej'rozu/ɔza] *adj* evil-smelling.
malcomportado/a [mawkõpox'tadu/a] *adj* badly behaved.
malconceituado/a [mawkõsej'twadu/a] *adj* badly thought of.
malcriado/a [maw'krjadu/a] *adj* rude ♦ *m/f* slob.
maldade [maw'dadʒi] *f* cruelty; (*malícia*) malice; **é uma** ~ it is cruel.
maldição [mawdʒi'sãw] (*pl* **-ões**) *f* curse.
maldigo [maw'dʒigu] *etc vb V* **maldizer**.
maldisposto/a [mawdʒiʃ'poʃtu/'pɔʃta] *adj* indisposed.
maldisse [maw'dʒisi] *etc vb V* **maldizer**.
maldito/a [maw'dʒitu/a] *pp de* **maldizer** ♦ *adj* damned.
Maldivas [maw'dʒivaʃ] *fpl*: **as (ilhas)** ~ the Maldives.
maldiz [maw'dʒiʒ] *etc vb V* **maldizer**.
maldizente [mawdʒi'zẽtʃi] *m/f* slanderer.
maldizer [mawdʒi'ze*] (*irreg*: *como* **dizer**) *vt* to curse.
maldoso/a [maw'dozu/ɔza] *adj* wicked; (*malicioso*) malicious.
maldotado/a [mawdo'tadu/a] *adj* untalented.
maleável [ma'ljavew] (*pl* **-eis**) *adj* malleable.
maledicência [maledʒi'sẽsja] *f* slander.
maledicente [maledʒi'sẽtʃi] *m/f* slanderer.
mal-educado/a *adj* rude ♦ *m/f* slob.
malefício [male'fisju] *m* harm.
maléfico/a [ma'lɛfiku/a] *adj* (*pessoa*) malicious; (*prejudicial*) harmful, injurious.
mal-empregado/a *adj* wasted.
mal-encarado/a *adj* shady, shifty.
mal-entendido/a *adj* misunderstood ♦ *m* misunderstanding.
mal-estar *m* (*indisposição*) indisposition, discomfort; (*embaraço*) uneasiness.
maleta [ma'leta] *f* small suitcase, grip.
malevolência [malevo'lẽsja] *f* malice, spite.
malevolente [malevo'lẽtʃi] *adj* malicious.
malévolo/a [ma'lɛvolu/a] *adj* malicious, spiteful.
malfadado/a [mawfa'dadu/a] *adj* unlucky; (*viagem*) fateful.
malfeito/a [mal'fejtu/a] *adj* (*roupa*) poorly made; (*corpo*) misshapen; (*fig*: *injusto*) wrong, unjust.
malfeitor/a [mawfej'to*(a)] *m/f* wrong-doer.
malgastar [mawgaʃ'ta*] *vt* to waste.
malgasto/a [maw'gaʃtu/a] *adj* wasted.
malgrado [maw'gradu] *prep* despite.
malha ['maʎa] *f* (*de rede*) mesh; (*tecido*) jersey; (*suéter*) sweater; (*de ginástica*) leotard; **fazer** ~ (*PT*) to knit; **artigos de** ~ knitwear; ~ **perdida** ladder, run; **vestido de** ~ jersey dress.
mal-habituado/a *adj* maladjusted.
malhado/a [ma'ʎadu/a] *adj* spotted, mottled, dappled; (*roque*) heavy.
malhar [ma'ʎa*] *vt* (*bater*) to beat; (*cereais*) to thresh; (*col*: *criticar*) to knock, run down ♦ *vi* (*col*: *fazer ginástica*) to work out.
malharia [maʎa'ria] *f* (*fábrica*) mill; (*artigos de malha*) knitted goods *pl*.
malho ['maʎu] *m* (*maço*) mallet; (*grande*) sledgehammer.
mal-humorado/a [-umo'radu/a] *adj* grumpy, sullen.
Mali [ma'li] *m*: **o** ~ Mali.
malícia [ma'lisja] *f* malice; (*astúcia*) slyness; (*esperteza*) cleverness; **pôr** ~ **em algo** to give sth a double meaning.
maliciar [mali'sja*] *vt* (*ação*) to see malice in; (*palavras*) to misconstrue.
malicioso/a [mali'sjozu/ɔza] *adj* malicious; (*astuto*) sly; (*esperto*) clever; (*quem interpreta erradamente*) dirty-minded.
malignidade [maligni'dadʒi] *f* malice, spite; (*MED*) malignancy.
maligno/a [ma'lignu/a] *adj* (*maléfico*) evil, malicious; (*danoso*) harmful; (*MED*) malignant.
má-língua (*pl* **más-línguas**) *f* backbiting ♦ *m/f* backbiter.
mal-intencionado/a *adj* malicious.
malmequer [mawme'ke*] *m* marigold.
maloca [ma'lɔka] *f* (*casa*) communal hut; (*aldeia*) (Indian) village; (*esconderijo*) bolthole.
malocar [malo'ka*] (*col*) *vt* to hide.
malogrado/a [malo'gradu/a] *adj* (*plano*) abortive, frustrated; (*sem êxito*) unsuccessful.
malograr [malo'gra*] *vt* (*planos*) to spoil, upset; (*frustrar*) to thwart, frustrate ♦ *vi*, **~-se** *vr* (*planos*) to fall through; (*fracassar*) to fail.
malogro [ma'logru] *m* failure.
malote [ma'lɔtʃi] *m* pouch; (*serviço*) express courier.
mal-passado/a *adj* underdone; (*bife*) rare.
malproporcionado/a [mawpropoxsjo'nadu/a]

NB: European Portuguese adds the following consonants to certain words: **b** (sú(b)dito, su(b)til); **c** (a(c)ção, a(c)cionista, a(c)to); **m** (inde(m)ne); **p** (ado(p)ção, ado(p)tar); *for further details see p. xiii.*

adj ill-proportioned.
malquerença [mawke'rẽsa] *f* ill will, enmity.
malquisto/a [maw'kiʃtu/a] *adj* disliked.
malsão/sã [maw'sãw/'sã] (*pl* **~s**) *adj* (*insalubre*) unhealthy; (*nocivo*) harmful.
malsucedido/a [mawsuse'dʒidu/a] *adj* unsuccessful.
Malta ['mawta] *f* Malta.
malta ['mawta] (PT) *f* gang, mob.
malte ['mawtʃi] *m* malt.
maltrapilho/a [mawtra'piʎu/a] *adj* in rags, ragged ♦ *m/f* ragamuffin.
maltratar [mawtra'ta*] *vt* to ill-treat; (*com palavras*) to abuse; (*estragar*) to ruin, damage.
maluco/a [ma'luku/a] *adj* crazy, daft ♦ *m/f* madman/woman.
maluquice [malu'kisi] *f* madness; (*ato, dito*) crazy thing.
malvadez [mawva'deʒ] *f* = **malvadeza**.
malvadeza [mawva'deza] *f* wickedness; (*ato*) wicked thing.
malvado/a [maw'vadu/a] *adj* wicked.
malversação [mawvexsa'sãw] *f* (*de dinheiro*) embezzlement; (*má administração*) mismanagement.
malversar [mawvex'sa*] *vt* (*dinheiro*) to embezzle, misappropriate; (*administrar mal*) to mismanage.
Malvinas [maw'vinaʃ] *fpl*: **as (ilhas) ~** the Falklands, the Falkland Islands.
MAM (BR) *abr m* = **Museu de Arte Moderna** (*no Rio*).
mama ['mama] *f* breast.
mamada [ma'mada] *f* feeding.
mamadeira [mama'dejra] (BR) *f* feeding bottle.
mamãe [ma'mãj] *f* mum, mummy.
mamão [ma'mãw] (*pl* **-ões**) *m* papaya.
mamar [ma'ma*] *vt* to suck; (*dinheiro*) to extort, get; (*empresa*) to milk (dry) ♦ *vi* (*bebê*) to be breastfed; **~ numa empresa** to get a rake-off from a company; **dar de ~ a um bebê** to (breast)feed a baby.
mamata [ma'mata] *f* (*negociata*) racket; (*boa vida*) cushy number.
mambembe [mã'bẽbi] *m/f* amateur thespian ♦ *adj* shoddy, second-rate.
mameluco/a [mame'luku/a] *m/f* half-breed (*of Indian and white*).
mamífero [ma'miferu] *m* mammal.
mamilo [ma'milu] *m* nipple.
mamoeiro [ma'mwejru] *m* papaya tree.
mamões [ma'mõjʃ] *mpl de* **mamão**.
mana ['mana] *f* sister.
manada [ma'nada] *f* herd, drove.
manancial [manã'sjaw] (*pl* **-ais**) *m* spring; (*fig: fonte*) source; (: *abundância*) wealth.
manar [ma'na*] *vt, vi* to pour.
manauense [manaw'ẽsi] *adj* from Manaus ♦ *m/f* person from Manaus.
mancada [mã'kada] *f* (*erro*) mistake; (*gafe*) blunder; **dar uma ~** to make a blunder.
mancar [mã'ka*] *vt* to cripple ♦ *vi* to limp; **~-se** *vr* (*col*) to get the message, take the hint.
manceba [mã'seba] *f* young woman; (*concubina*) concubine.
mancebo [mã'sebu] *m* young man, youth.
Mancha ['mãʃa] *f*: **o canal da ~** the English Channel.
mancha ['mãʃa] *f* (*nódoa*) stain; (*na pele*) mark, spot; (*em pintura*) blotch; **sem ~s** (*reputação*) spotless.
manchado/a [mã'ʃadu/a] *adj* (*sujo*) soiled; (*malhado*) mottled, spotted.
manchar [mã'ʃa*] *vt* to stain, mark; (*reputação*) to soil.
manchete [mã'ʃɛtʃi] *f* headline; **virar ~** to make *ou* hit (*col*) the headlines.
manco/a ['mãku/a] *adj* crippled, lame ♦ *m/f* cripple.
mancomunar [mãkomu'na*] *vt* to contrive; **~-se** *vr*: **~-se (com)** to conspire (with).
mandachuva [mãda'ʃuva] *m* (*figurão*) big shot; (*chefe*) boss.
mandado [mã'dadu] *m* (*ordem*) order; (JUR) writ, injunction; **~ de arresto** repossession order; **~ de prisão/busca** warrant for sb's arrest/search warrant; **~ de segurança** injunction.
mandamento [mãda'mẽtu] *m* order, command; (REL) commandment.
mandante [mã'dãtʃi] *m/f* instigator; (*dirigente*) person in charge; (COM) principal.
mandão/dona [mã'dãw/'dɔna] (*pl* **-ões/~s**) *adj* bossy, domineering ♦ *m/f* bossy person.
mandar [mã'da*] *vt* (*ordenar*) to order; (*enviar*) to send ♦ *vi* to be in charge; **~-se** *vr* (*col: partir*) to make tracks, get going; (*fugir*) to take off; **~ buscar** *ou* **chamar** to send for; **~ dizer** to send word; **~ embora** to send away; **~ fazer um vestido** to have a dress made; **~ que alguém faça, ~ alguém fazer** to tell sb to do; **~ alguém passear** (*fig*) to send sb packing; **~ alguém para o inferno** to tell sb to go to hell; **o que é que você manda?** (*col*) what can I do for you?; **~ em alguém** to boss sb around; **manda!** (*col*) fire away!; **~ ver** (*col*) to go to town; **~ a mão, ~ um soco (em alguém)** to hit (sb); **aqui quem manda sou eu** I give the orders around here.
mandarim [mãda'rĩ] *m* (LING) Mandarin; (*fig*) mandarin.
mandatário/a [mãda'tarju/a] *m/f* (*delegado*) delegate; (*representante*) representative, agent.
mandato [mã'datu] *m* (*autorização*) mandate; (*ordem*) order; (POL) term of office.
mandíbula [mã'dʒibula] *f* jaw.
mandinga [mã'dʒĩga] *f* witchcraft.
mandioca [mã'dʒjɔka] *f* cassava, manioc.
mando ['mãdu] *m* (*comando*) command; (*poder*) power; **a ~ de** by order of.
mandões [mã'dõjʃ] *mpl de* **mandão**.

mandona [mã'dɔna] *f de* **mandão**.
mandrião/driona [mã'drjãw/'drjɔna] (*pl* **-ões/~s**) (*PT*) *adj* lazy ♦ *m/f* idler, lazybones *sg*.
mandriar [mã'drja*] *vi* to idle, loaf about.
mandriões [mã'drjõjʃ] *mpl de* **mandrião**.
mandriona [mã'drjɔna] *f de* **mandrião**.
maneira [ma'nejra] *f* (*modo*) way; (*estilo*) style, manner; **~s** *fpl* manners; **à ~ de** like; **de ~ que** so that; **de ~ alguma** *ou* **nenhuma** not at all; **desta ~** in this way; **de qualquer ~** anyway; **não houve ~ de convencê-lo** it was impossible to convince him.
maneirar [manej'ra*] (*col*) *vt* to sort out, fix ♦ *vi* to sort things out; **maneira!** take it easy!
maneiro/a [ma'nejru/a] *adj* (*ferramenta, roupa*) manageable; (*trabalho*) easy; (*pessoa*) capable; (*col: bacana*) great, brilliant.
manejar [mane'ʒa*] *vt* (*instrumento*) to handle; (*máquina*) to work.
manejável [mane'ʒavew] (*pl* **-eis**) *adj* manageable.
manejo [ma'neʒu] *m* handling.
manequim [mane'kĩ] (*pl* **-ns**) *m* (*boneco*) dummy ♦ *m/f* model.
maneta [ma'neta] *adj* one-handed ♦ *m/f* one-handed person.
manga ['mãga] *f* sleeve; (*fruta*) mango; (*filtro*) filter; **em ~s de camisa** in (one's) shirt sleeves.
manganês [mãga'neʃ] *m* manganese.
mangue ['mãgi] *m* mangrove swamp; (*planta*) mangrove; (*col: zona*) red-light district.
mangueira [mã'gejra] *f* hose(pipe); (*árvore*) mango tree.
manguinha [mã'giɲa] *f*: **botar as ~s de fora** (*col*) to let one's hair down.
manha ['maɲa] *f* (*malícia*) guile, craftiness; (*destreza*) skill; (*ardil*) trick; (*birra*) tantrum; **fazer ~** to have a tantrum.
manhã [ma'ɲã] *f* morning; **de** *ou* **pela ~** in the morning; **amanhã/hoje de ~** tomorrow/this morning; **de ~ cedo** early in the morning; **4 hs da ~** 4 o'clock in the morning.
manhãzinha [maɲã'ziɲa] *f*: **de ~** early in the morning.
manhoso/a [ma'ɲozu/ɔza] *adj* (*ardiloso*) crafty, sly; (*criança*) whining.
mania [ma'nia] *f* (*MED*) mania; (*obsessão*) craze; **ela é cheia de ~s** she's very compulsive; **estar com ~ de ...** to have a thing about ...; **~ de grandeza** delusions *pl* of grandeur; **~ de perseguição** persecution complex.
maníaco/a [ma'niaku/a] *adj* manic ♦ *m/f* maniac.
maníaco-depressivo (*pl* **~s**) *adj, m/f* manic depressive.
manicômio [mani'komju] *m* asylum, mental hospital.
manicura [mani'kura] *f* (*tratamento*) manicure; (*pessoa*) manicurist.
manicure [mani'kuri] *f* = **manicura**.
manifestação [manifeʃta'sãw] (*pl* **-ões**) *f* demonstration, display; (*expressão*) expression, declaration; (*política*) demonstration.
manifestante [manifeʃ'tãtʃi] *m/f* demonstrator.
manifestar [manifeʃ'ta*] *vt* (*revelar*) to show, display; (*declarar*) to express, declare; **~-se** *vr* to manifest o.s.; (*pronunciar-se*) to express an opinion.
manifesto/a [mani'fɛʃtu/a] *adj* obvious, clear ♦ *m* manifesto.
manilha [ma'niʎa] *f* (ceramic) drain-pipe.
manipulação [manipula'sãw] *f* handling; (*fig*) manipulation.
manipular [manipu'la*] *vt* to manipulate; (*manejar*) to handle.
manivela [mani'vɛla] *f* (*ferramenta*) crank.
manjado/a [mã'ʒadu/a] (*col*) *adj* well-known.
manjar [mã'ʒa*] *m* (*iguaria*) delicacy, titbit ♦ *vt* (*col: conhecer*) to know; (*: entender*) to grasp; (*: observar*) to check out ♦ *vi* (*col*) to catch on; **~ de algo** to know about sth; **manjou?** (*col*) get it?, see?
manjar-branco *m* blancmange.
manjedoura [mãʒe'dora] *f* manger, crib.
manjericão [mãʒeri'kãw] *m* basil.
mano ['manu] *m* brother.
manobra [ma'nɔbra] *f* (*de carro, barco*) manoeuvre (*BRIT*), maneuver (*US*); (*de mecanismo*) operation; (*de trens*) shunting; (*fig*) move; (*: artimanha*) manoeuvre *ou* maneuver, trick; **~s** *mpl* (*MIL*) manoeuvres *ou* maneuvers.
manobrar [mano'bra*] *vt* to manoeuvre (*BRIT*), maneuver (*US*); (*mecanismo*) to operate, work; (*governar*) to take charge of; (*manipular*) to manipulate ♦ *vi* to manoeuvre *ou* maneuver; (*tomar medidas*) to make moves.
manobreiro/a [mano'brejru/a] *m/f* operator.
manobrista [mano'briʃta] *m/f* parking attendant.
manquejar [mãke'ʒa*] *vi* to limp.
mansão [mã'sãw] (*pl* **-ões**) *f* mansion.
mansidão [mãsi'dãw] *f* gentleness, meekness; (*do mar*) calmness; (*de animal*) tameness.
mansinho [mã'siɲu] *adv*: **de ~** (*devagar*) slowly; (*de leve*) gently; (*sorrateiramente*): **sair/entrar de ~** to creep out/in.
manso/a ['mãsu/a] *adj* (*brando*) gentle; (*mar*) calm; (*animal*) tame.
mansões [mã'sõjʃ] *fpl de* **mansão**.
manta ['mãta] *f* (*cobertor*) blanket; (*xale*) shawl; (*agasalho*) cloak; (*de viajar*) travelling rug.
manteiga [mã'tejga] *f* butter; **~ derretida** (*fig*,

col) cry baby; ~ **de cacau** cocoa butter.
manteigueira [mãtej'gejra] *f* butter dish.
mantém [mã'tẽ] *etc vb V* **manter**.
mantenedor(a) [mãtene'do*(a)] *m/f* (*da família*) breadwinner; (*de opinião, princípio*) holder; (*de ordem, ESPORTE*) retainer.
manter [mã'te*] (*irreg: como* **ter**) *vt* to maintain; (*num lugar*) to keep; (*uma família*) to support; (*a palavra*) to keep; (*princípios*) to abide by; **~-se** *vr* (*sustentar-se*) to support o.s.; (*permanecer*) to remain; **~-se firme** to stand firm.
mantilha [mã'tʃiʎa] *f* mantilla; (*véu*) veil.
mantimento [mãtʃi'mẽtu] *m* maintenance; **~s** *mpl* provisions.
mantinha [mã'tʃiɲa] *etc vb V* **manter**.
mantive [mã'tʃivi] *etc vb V* **manter**.
mantiver [mãtʃi've*] *etc vb V* **manter**.
manto ['mãtu] *m* cloak; (*de cerimônia*) robe.
mantô [mã'to] *m* coat.
manual [ma'nwaw] (*pl* **-ais**) *adj* manual ♦ *m* handbook; (*compêndio*) manual; **ter habilidade** ~ to be good with one's hands.
manufatura [manufa'tura] (*PT*: **-ct-**) *f* manufacture.
manufaturados [manufatu'raduʃ] (*PT*: **-ct-**) *mpl* manufactured products.
manufaturar [manufatu'ra*] (*PT*: **-ct-**) *vt* to manufacture.
manuscrever [manuʃkre've*] *vt* to write by hand.
manuscrito/a [manuʃ'kritu/a] *adj* handwritten ♦ *m* manuscript.
manusear [manu'zja*] *vt* (*manejar*) to handle; (*livro*) to leaf through.
manuseio [manu'zeju] *m* handling.
manutenção [manutẽ'sãw] *f* maintenance; (*da casa*) upkeep.
mão [mãw] (*pl* **~s**) *f* hand; (*de animal*) paw; (*demão*) coat; (*de direção*) flow of traffic; **à** ~ by hand; (*perto*) at hand; **feito à** ~ handmade; **de ~s dadas** hand in hand; **de** *ou* **em primeira** ~ first-hand; **de segunda** ~ second-hand; **em** ~ by hand; **fora de** ~ out of the way; **abrir ~ de algo** (*fig*) to give sth up; **agüentar a** ~ (*col: suportar*) to hold out; (*: esperar*) to hang on; **dar a ~ à palmatória** to admit one's mistake; **dar a ~ a alguém** to hold sb's hand; (*cumprimentar*) to shake hands with sb; **dar uma ~ a alguém** to give sb a hand, help sb out; **ficar na** ~ (*col*) to be stood up; **forçar a** ~ to go overboard; **lançar ~ de algo** to have recourse to sth; **largar algo de** ~ to give sth up; **uma ~ lava a outra** (*fig*) one good turn deserves another; **meter a ~ em alguém** to hit sb; **meter** *ou* **passar a ~ em algo** (*col*) to nick sth; **passar a ~ pela cabeça de alguém** (*fig*) to let sb off; **pôr a ~ no fogo por alguém** (*fig*) to vouch for sb; **pôr ~s à obra** to set to work; **ser uma ~ na roda** (*fig*) to be a great help; **ter ~ leve** (*bater facilmente*) to be violent; (*ser ladrão*) to be light-fingered; **ter a ~ pesada** to be heavy-handed; **ter uma boa ~ para** to be good at; **vir com as ~s abanando** (*fig*) to come back empty-handed; **~ única/dupla** one-way/two-way traffic; **esta rua dá ~ para o centro** this street goes to the centre (*BRIT*) *ou* center (*US*); **rua de duas ~s** two-way street; **~s ao alto!** hands up!; **de ~ beijada** (*fig*) for nothing.
mão-aberta (*pl* **mãos-abertas**) *adj* generous ♦ *m/f* generous person.
mão-cheia *f*: **de** ~ first-rate.
mão-de-obra *f* (*trabalho*) workmanship; (*trabalhadores*) labour (*BRIT*), labor (*US*); (*coisa difícil*) tricky thing; ~ **especializada** skilled labo(u)r.
maoísta [maw'iʃta] *adj, m/f* Maoist.
mão-leve (*pl* **mãos-leves**) *m/f* pilferer.
mãozinha [mãw'ziɲa] *f*: **dar uma ~ a alguém** to give sb a hand, help sb out.
mapa ['mapa] *m* map; (*gráfico*) chart; **não estar no** ~ (*fig, col*) to be extraordinary; **sair do** ~ (*col*) to disappear.
mapa-múndi [-'mũdʒi] (*pl* **mapas-múndi**) *m* world map.
Maputo [ma'putu] *n* Maputo.
maquete [ma'kɛtʃi] *f* model.
maquiador(a) [makja'do*(a)] *m/f* make-up artist.
maquiagem [ma'kjaʒẽ] *f* = **maquilagem**.
maquiar [ma'kja*] *vt* to make up; (*fig*) to touch up; **~-se** *vr* to make o.s. up, put on make-up.
maquiavélico/a [makja'vɛliku/a] *adj* Machiavellian.
maquilagem [maki'laʒẽ] (*PT*: **-lha-**) *f* make-up; (*ato*) making up.
maquilar [makila*] (*PT*: **-lha-**) *vt* to make up; **~-se** *vr* to put on one's make-up.
máquina ['makina] *f* machine; (*de trem*) engine; (*de relógio*) movement; (*fig*) machinery; ~ **a vapor** steam engine; **~s agrícolas** agricultural machinery; ~ **de calcular** calculator; ~ **de costura** sewing machine; ~ **fotográfica** *ou* **de filmar** camera; ~ **de escrever** typewriter; ~ **de lavar (roupa)** washing-machine; ~ **de lavar pratos** dishwasher; ~ **de tricotar** knitting machine; **costurar/escrever à** ~ to machine-sew/type; **escrito à** ~ typewritten; **preencher um formulário à** ~ to fill in a form on the typewriter.
maquinação [makina'sãw] (*pl* **-ões**) *f* machination, plot.
maquinal [maki'naw] (*pl* **-ais**) *adj* mechanical, automatic.
maquinar [maki'na*] *vt* to plot ♦ *vi* to conspire.
maquinaria [makina'ria] *f* machinery.
maquinismo [maki'niʒmu] *m* mechanism; (*máquinas*) machinery; (*TEATRO*) stage machinery.
maquinista [maki'niʃta] *m* (*FERRO*) engine driver; (*NÁUT*) engineer.

mar [ma*] *m* sea; **por ~** by sea; **cair no ~** to fall overboard; **fazer-se ao ~** to set sail; **~ aberto** open sea; **pleno ~, ~ alto** high sea; **um ~ de** (*fig*) a sea of; **~ de rosas** calm sea; (*fig*) bed of roses; **nem tanto ao ~ nem tanto à terra** (*fig*) somewhere in between; **o ~ Cáspio** the Caspian Sea; **o ~ Morto** the Dead Sea; **o ~ Negro** the Black Sea; **o ~ Vermelho** the Red Sea.

maraca [ma'raka] *f* maraca.

maracujá [maraku'ʒa] *m* passion fruit; **pé de ~** passion flower.

maracujazeiro [marakuʒa'zejru] *m* passion-fruit plant.

maracutaia [maraku'taja] *f* dirty trick.

marafa [ma'rafa] (*col*) *f* loose living.

marafona [mara'fɔna] (*col*) *f* whore.

marajá [mara'ʒa] *m* maharaja; (*BR*: *POL*) civil service fat-cat.

maranhense [mara'ɲẽsi] *adj* from Maranhão ♦ *m/f* person from Maranhão.

marasmo [ma'raʒmu] *m* (*inatividade*) stagnation; (*apatia*) apathy.

maratona [mara'tona] *f* marathon.

maratonista [marato'niʃta] *m/f* marathon runner.

maravilha [mara'viʎa] *f* marvel, wonder; **às mil ~s** wonderfully.

maravilhar [maravi'ʎa*] *vt* to amaze, astonish ♦ *vi* to be amazing; **~-se** *vr*: **~-se de** to be astonished at, be amazed at.

maravilhoso/a [maravi'ʎozu/ɔza] *adj* marvellous (*BRIT*), marvelous (*US*), wonderful.

marca ['maxka] *f* mark; (*COM*) make, brand; (*carimbo*) stamp; (*da prata*) hallmark; (*fig*: *categoria*) calibre (*BRIT*), caliber (*US*); **de ~ maior** (*fig*) of the first order; **~ de fábrica** trademark; **~ registrada** registered trademark.

marcação [maxka'sãw] (*pl* **-ões**) *f* marking; (*em jogo*) scoring; (*de instrumento*) reading; (*TEATRO*) action; (*PT*: *TEL*) dialling; **estar de ~ com alguém** (*col*) to pick on sb constantly.

marcador [maxka'do*] *m* marker; (*de livro*) bookmark; (*ESPORTE*: *quadro*) scoreboard; (: *jogador*) scorer.

marcante [max'kãtʃi] *adj* outstanding.

marcapasso [maxka'pasu] *m* (*MED*) pacemaker.

marcar [max'ka*] *vt* to mark; (*hora, data*) to fix, set; (*PT*: *discar*) to dial; (*animal*) to brand; (*delimitar*) to demarcate; (*observar*) to keep an eye on; (*gol, ponto*) to score; (*FUTEBOL*: *jogador*) to mark; (*produzir impressão em*) to leave one's mark on ♦ *vi* (*impressionar*) to make one's mark; **~ uma consulta, ~ hora** to make an appointment; **~ um encontro** to arrange to meet; **~ uma reunião/um jantar para sexta-feira** to arrange a meeting/a dinner for Friday; **~ época** to make history; **~ o ponto** to punch the clock; **ter hora marcada com alguém** to have an appointment with sb; **~ o tempo de algo** to time sth.

marcenaria [maxsena'ria] *f* joinery; (*oficina*) joiner's.

marceneiro [maxse'nejru] *m* cabinet-maker, joiner.

marcha ['maxʃa] *f* march; (*ato*) marching; (*de acontecimentos*) course; (*passo*) pace; (*AUTO*) gear; (*progresso*) progress; **~ à ré** (*BR*), **~ atrás** (*PT*) reverse (gear); **primeira (~)** first (gear); **pôr-se em ~** to set off.

marchar [max'ʃa*] *vi* (*ir*) to go; (*andar a pé*) to walk; (*MIL*) to march.

marcha-rancho (*pl* **marchas-rancho**) *f* carnival march.

marchetar [maxʃe'ta*] *vt* to inlay.

marcial [max'sjaw] (*pl* **-ais**) *adj* martial; **lei ~** martial law; **corte ~** court martial.

marciano/a [max'sjanu/a] *adj*, *m* Martian.

marco ['maxku] *m* landmark; (*de janela*) frame; (*fig*) frontier; (*moeda*) mark.

março ['maxsu] (*PT*: **M-**) *m* March; *V tb* **julho**.

maré [ma'rɛ] *f* tide; (*fig*: *oportunidade*) chance; **~ alta/baixa** high/low tide; **estar de boa ~** *ou* **de ~ alta** to be in a good mood; **remar contra a ~** (*fig*) to swim against the tide.

marear [ma'rja*] *vt* to make seasick; (*oxidar*) to dull, stain ♦ *vi* to be seasick.

marechal [mare'ʃaw] (*pl* **-ais**) *m* marshal.

marejar [mare'ʒa*] *vt* to wet ♦ *vi* to get wet.

maremoto [mare'mɔtu] *m* tidal wave.

maresia [mare'zia] *f* smell of the sea, sea air.

marfim [max'fĩ] *m* ivory.

margarida [maxga'rida] *f* daisy; (*COMPUT*) daisy-wheel.

margarina [maxga'rina] *f* margarine.

margear [max'ʒja*] *vt* to border.

margem ['maxʒẽ] (*pl* **-ns**) *f* (*borda*) edge; (*de rio*) bank; (*litoral*) shore; (*de impresso*) margin; (*fig*: *tempo*) time; (: *lugar*) space; (: *oportunidade*) chance; **à ~ de** alongside; **dar ~ a alguém** to give sb a chance; **~ de erro** margin of error; **~ de lucro** profit margin.

marginal [maxʒi'naw] (*pl* **-ais**) *adj* marginal ♦ *m/f* delinquent.

marginalidade [maxʒinali'dadʒi] *f* delinquency.

marginalizar [maxʒinali'za*] *vt* to marginalize.

maria-fumaça [ma'ria-] (*pl* **marias-fumaças**) *f* steam train.

maria-sem-vergonha [ma'ria-] (*pl* **marias-sem-vergonha**) *f* (*BOT*) busy lizzie.

maria-vai-com-as-outras [ma'ria-] *m/f inv* sheep, follower.

maricas [ma'rikaʃ] (*PT*: *col*) *m inv* queer, poof.

***NB**: European Portuguese adds the following consonants to certain words:* **b** (sú(b)dito, su(b)til); **c** (a(c)ção, a(c)cionista, a(c)to); **m** (inde(m)ne); **p** (ado(p)ção, ado(p)tar); *for further details see p. xiii.*

marido [ma'ridu] *m* husband.
marimbondo [marĩ'bõdu] *m* hornet.
marina [ma'rina] *f* marina.
marinha [ma'riɲa] *f* (*tb*: ~ *de guerra*) navy; (*pintura*) seascape; ~ **mercante** merchant navy.
marinheiro [mari'ɲejru] *m* seaman, sailor; ~ **de primeira viagem** (*fig*) beginner.
marinho/a [ma'riɲu/a] *adj* sea, marine.
marionete [marjo'netʃi] *f* puppet.
mariposa [mari'poza] *f* moth.
marisco [ma'riʃku] *m* shellfish.
marital [mari'taw] (*pl* **-ais**) *adj* marital.
maritalmente [maritaw'mẽtʃi] *adv*: **viver ~ (com alguém)** to live (with sb) as man and wife.
marítimo/a [ma'ritʃimu/a] *adj* sea, maritime; **pesca marítima** sea fishing.
marketing ['maxketʃĩŋ] *m* marketing.
marmanjo [max'mãʒu] *m* grown man.
marmelada [maxme'lada] *f* quince jam; (*col*) double-dealing.
marmelo [max'mɛlu] *m* quince.
marmita [max'mita] *f* (*vasilha*) pot.
mármore ['maxmori] *m* marble.
marmóreo/a [max'mɔrju/a] *adj* marble; (*fig*) cold.
marola [ma'rɔla] *f* wave, roller.
maroto/a [ma'rotu/a] *m/f* rogue, rascal; (*criança*) naughty boy/girl ♦ *adj* roguish; (*criança*) naughty.
marquei [max'kej] *etc vb V* **marcar**.
marquês/quesa [max'keʃ/'keza] *m/f* marquis/ marchioness.
marquise [max'kizi] *f* awning, canopy.
marra ['maxa] *f*: **na ~** (*à força*) forcibly; (*a qualquer preço*) whatever the cost.
marreco [ma'xɛku] *m* duck.
Marrocos [ma'xɔkuʃ] *m*: **o ~** Morocco.
marrom [ma'xõ] (*pl* **-ns**) *adj*, *m* brown.
marroquino/a [maxo'kinu/a] *adj*, *m/f* Moroccan.
Marte ['maxtʃi] *m* Mars.
martelada [maxte'lada] *f* (*pancada*) blow (with a hammer); (*ruído*) hammering sound.
martelar [maxte'la*] *vt* to hammer; (*amolar*) to bother ♦ *vi* to hammer; (*insistir*): **~ (em algo)** to keep *ou* harp on (about sth).
martelo [max'tɛlu] *m* hammer.
martíni [max'tʃini] ® *m* martini ®.
Martinica [maxtʃi'nika] *f*: **a ~** Martinique.
mártir ['maxtʃi*] *m/f* martyr.
martírio [max'tʃirju] *m* martyrdom; (*fig*) torment.
martirizante [maxtʃiri'zãtʃi] *adj* agonizing.
martirizar [maxtʃiri'za*] *vt* to martyr; (*atormentar*) to afflict; **~-se** *vr* to agonize.
marujo [ma'ruʒu] *m* sailor.
marulhar [maru'ʎa*] *vi* (*mar*) to surge; (*ondas*) to lap; (*produzir ruído*) to roar.
marulho [ma'ruʎu] *m* (*do mar*) surge; (*das ondas*) lapping.
marxismo [max'ksiʒmu] *m* Marxism.
marxista [max'ksiʃta] *adj*, *m/f* Marxist.
marzipã [maxzi'pã] *m* marzipan.
mas [ma(j)ʃ] *conj* but ♦ *pron* = **me** + **as**.
mascar [maʃ'ka*] *vt* to chew.
máscara ['maʃkara] *f* mask; (*para limpeza de pele*) face-pack; **sob a ~ de** under the guise of; **tirar a ~ de alguém** (*fig*) to unmask sb; **baile de ~s** masked ball; **~ de oxigênio** oxygen mask.
mascarado/a [maʃka'radu/a] *adj* masked; (*convencido*) conceited.
mascarar [maʃka'ra*] *vt* to mask; (*disfarçar*) to disguise; (*encobrir*) to cover up.
mascate [maʃ'katʃi] *m* peddler, hawker (*BRIT*).
mascavo [maʃ'kavu] *adj V* **açúcar**.
mascote [maʃ'kɔtʃi] *f* mascot.
masculinidade [maʃkulini'dadʒi] *f* masculinity.
masculino/a [maʃku'linu/a] *adj* masculine; (*BIO*) male ♦ *m* (*LING*) masculine; **roupa masculina** men's clothes *pl*.
másculo/a ['maʃkulu/a] *adj* masculine; (*viril*) manly.
masmorra [maʒ'mɔxa] *f* dungeon; (*fig*) black hole.
masoquismo [mazo'kiʒmu] *m* masochism.
masoquista [mazo'kiʃta] *m/f* masochist ♦ *adj* masochistic.
MASP *abr m* = **Museu de Arte de São Paulo**.
massa ['masa] *f* (*física*) mass; (*de tomate*) paste; (*CULIN*: *de pão*) dough; (: *macarrão etc*) pasta; (*fig*) mass; **as ~s** the masses; **em ~** en masse; **~ de vidraceiro** putty; **estar com as mãos na ~** (*fig*) to be about *ou* at it.
massacrante [masa'krãtʃi] *adj* annoying.
massacrar [masa'kra*] *vt* to massacre; (*fig*: *chatear*) to annoy; (: *torturar*) to tear apart.
massacre [ma'sakri] *f* massacre; (*fig*) annoyance.
massagear [masa'ʒja*] *vt* to massage ♦ *vi* to do massage.
massagem [ma'saʒẽ] (*pl* **-ns**) *f* massage.
massagista [masa'ʒiʃta] *m/f* masseur/masseuse.
massificar [masifi'ka*] *vt* to influence (through mass communication).
massudo/a [ma'sudu/a] *adj* bulky; (*espesso*) thick; (*com aspecto de massa*) doughy.
mastectomia [maʃtekto'mia] *f* mastectomy.
mastigado/a [maʃtʃi'gadu/a] *adj* (*fig*) well-planned.
mastigar [maʃtʃi'ga*] *vt* to chew; (*pronunciar mal*) to mumble, mutter; (*fig*: *refletir*) to mull over.
mastim [maʃ'tʃĩ] (*pl* **-ns**) *m* watchdog.
mastodonte [maʃto'dõtʃi] *m* (*fig*: *pessoa gorda*) hulk, lump.
mastro ['maʃtru] *m* (*NÁUT*) mast; (*para bandeira*) flagpole.
masturbação [maʃtuxba'sãw] *f* masturbation.
masturbar [maʃtux'ba*] *vt* to masturbate; ~

se *vr* to masturbate.
mata ['mata] *f* forest, wood; ~ **virgem** virgin forest.
mata-bicho *m* tot of brandy, snifter.
mata-borrão *m* blotting paper.
matacão [mata'kãw] (*pl* **-ões**) *m* lump; (*pedra*) boulder.
matado/a [ma'tadu/a] *adj* (*trabalho*) badly done.
matador(a) [mata'do*(a)] *m/f* killer ♦ *m* (*em tourada*) matador.
matadouro [mata'doru] *m* slaughterhouse.
matagal [mata'gaw] (*pl* **-ais**) *m* bush; (*brenha*) thicket, undergrowth.
mata-moscas *m inv* fly-killer.
mata-mosquito (*pl* **~s**) *m* mosquito exterminator.
matança [ma'tãsa] *f* massacre; (*de reses*) slaughter(ing).
mata-piolho (*pl* **~s**) (*col*) *m* thumb.
matar [ma'ta*] *vt* to kill; (*sede*) to quench; (*fome*) to satisfy; (*aula*) to skip; (*trabalho: não aparecer*) to skive off; (*: fazer rápido*) to dash off; (*tempo*) to kill; (*adivinhar*) to guess, get ♦ *vi* to kill; **~-se** *vr* to kill o.s.; (*esfalfar-se*) to wear o.s. out; **um calor/uma dor de** ~ stifling heat/excruciating pain; ~ **saudades** to catch up.
mata-rato (*pl* **~s**) *m* (*veneno*) rat poison; (*cigarro*) throat-scraper.
mate ['matʃi] *adj* matt ♦ *m* (*chá*) maté tea; (*xeque-~*) checkmate.
matelassê [matela'se] *adj* quilted ♦ *m* quilting.
matemática [mate'matʃika] *f* mathematics *sg*, maths *sg* (*BRIT*), math (*US*); *V tb* **matemático**.
matemático/a [mate'matʃiku/a] *adj* mathematical ♦ *m/f* mathematician.
matéria [ma'tɛrja] *f* matter; (*TEC*) material; (*EDUC: assunto*) subject; (*tema*) topic; (*jornalística*) story, article; **em ~ de** on the subject of; ~ **fecal** faeces *pl* (*BRIT*), feces *pl* (*US*); ~ **plástica** plastic.
material [mate'rjaw] (*pl* **-ais**) *adj* material; (*físico*) physical ♦ *m* material; (*TEC*) equipment; (*col: corpo*) body; ~ **humano** manpower; ~ **bélico** armaments *pl*; ~ **de construção** building materials *pl*; ~ **de limpeza** cleaning materials *pl*; ~ **escolar** school materials *pl*.
materialismo [materja'liʒmu] *m* materialism.
materialista [materja'liʃta] *adj* materialistic ♦ *m/f* materialist.
materializar [materjali'za*] *vt* to materialize; **~-se** *vr* to materialize.
matéria-prima (*pl* **matérias-primas**) *f* raw material.
maternal [matex'naw] (*pl* **-ais**) *adj* motherly, maternal; **escola** ~ nursery (school).
maternidade [matexni'dadʒi] *f* motherhood, maternity; (*hospital*) maternity hospital.
materno/a [ma'tɛxnu/a] *adj* motherly, maternal; (*língua*) native; (*avô*) maternal.
matilha [ma'tʃiʎa] *f* (*cães*) pack; (*fig: corja*) rabble.
matina [ma'tʃina] *f* morning.
matinal [matʃi'naw] (*pl* **-ais**) *adj* morning.
matinê [matʃi'ne] *f* matinée.
matiz [ma'tʃiʒ] *m* (*de cor*) shade; (*fig: de ironia*) tinge; (*cor política*) colouring (*BRIT*), coloring (*US*).
matizar [matʃi'za*] *vt* (*colorir*) to tinge, colour (*BRIT*), color (*US*); (*combinar cores*) to blend; ~ **algo de algo** (*fig*) to tinge sth with sth.
mato ['matu] *m* scrubland, bush; (*plantas agrestes*) scrub; (*o campo*) country; **ser** ~ (*col*) to be there for the taking; **estar num ~ sem cachorro** (*col*) to be up the creek without a paddle.
mato-grossano/a [-gro'sanu/a] *adj*, *m/f* = **mato-grossense**.
mato-grossense [-gro'sẽsi] *adj* from Mato Grosso ♦ *m/f* person from Mato Grosso.
matraca [ma'traka] *f* rattle; (*pessoa*) chatterbox; **falar como uma** ~ to talk nineteen to the dozen (*BRIT*) *ou* a blue streak (*US*).
matraquear [matra'kja*] *vi* to rattle, clatter; (*tagarelar*) to chatter, rabbit on.
matreiro/a [ma'trejru/a] *adj* cunning, crafty.
matriarca [ma'trjaxka] *f* matriarch.
matriarcal [matrjax'kaw] (*pl* **-ais**) *adj* matriarchal.
matrícula [ma'trikula] *f* (*lista*) register; (*inscrição*) registration; (*pagamento*) enrolment (*BRIT*) *ou* enrollment (*US*) fee; (*PT: AUTO*) registration number (*BRIT*), license number (*US*); **fazer a** ~ to enrol (*BRIT*), enroll (*US*).
matricular [matriku'la*] *vt*, **~-se** *vr* to enrol (*BRIT*), enroll (*US*), register.
matrimonial [matrimo'njaw] (*pl* **-ais**) *adj* marriage *atr*, matrimonial.
matrimônio [matri'monju] *m* marriage; **contrair ~ (com alguém)** to be joined in marriage (with sb).
matriz [ma'triʒ] *f* (*MED*) womb; (*fonte*) source; (*molde*) mould (*BRIT*), mold (*US*); (*COM*) head office; (*col*) wife; **igreja** ~ mother church.
matrona [ma'trɔna] *f* matron.
maturação [matura'sãw] *f* maturing; (*de fruto*) ripening.
maturidade [maturi'dadʒi] *f* maturity.
matusquela [matuʃ'kɛla] (*col*) *m/f* lunatic.
matutar [matu'ta*] *vt* (*planejar*) to plan ♦ *vi*: ~ **em** *ou* **sobre algo** to turn sth over in one's mind.
matutino/a [matu'tʃinu/a] *adj* morning ♦ *m* morning paper.
matuto/a [ma'tutu/a] *adj*, *m/f* (*caipira*) rustic; (*provinciano*) provincial.

***NB**: European Portuguese adds the following consonants to certain words:* **b** (sú(b)dito, su(b)til); **c** (a(c)ção, a(c)cionista, a(c)to); **m** (inde(m)ne); **p** (ado(p)ção, ado(p)tar); *for further details see p. xiii.*

mau/má [maw/ma] *adj* bad; (*malvado*) evil, wicked ♦ *m* bad; (*REL*) evil; **os ~s** bad people; (*num filme*) the baddies.
mau-caráter (*pl* **maus-carateres**) *m* bad lot ♦ *adj* shady.
mau-olhado [-o'ʎadu] *m* evil eye.
Maurício [maw'risju] *m* Mauritius.
Mauritânia [mawri'tanja] *f*: **a ~** Mauritania.
mausoléu [mawzo'lɛw] *m* mausoleum.
maus-tratos *mpl* ill-treatment *sg*.
mavioso/a [ma'vjozu/ɔza] *adj* tender, soft; (*som*) sweet.
máx. *abr* (= *máximo*) max.
máxi ['maksi] *adj inv* (*saia*) maxi.
maxidesvalorização [maksidʒiʒvaloriza'sãw] (*pl* **-ões**) *f* large-scale devaluation.
maxila [mak'sila] *f* jawbone.
maxilar [maksi'la*] *m* jawbone ♦ *adj* jaw *atr*.
máxima ['masima] *f* maxim, saying.
máxime ['maksimɛ] *adv* especially.
maximizar [masimi'za*] *vt* to maximize; (*superestimar*) to play up.
máximo/a ['masimu/a] *adj* (*maior que todos*) greatest; (*o maior possível*) maximum ♦ *m* maximum; (*o cúmulo*) peak; (*temperature*) high; **o ~ cuidado** the greatest of care; **no ~** at most; **ao ~** to the utmost; **chegar ao ~** (*fig*) to reach a peak; **ele acha-a o ~** (*col*) he thinks she is the greatest.
maxixe [ma'ʃiʃi] *m* gherkin; (*BR*: *dança*) *19th-century dance*.
mazela [ma'zɛla] *f* (*ferida*) sore spot; (*doença*) illness; (*fig*) blemish.
MCE *abr m* = **Mercado Comum Europeu**.
MCom (*BR*) *abr m* = **Ministério das Comunicações**.
MCT (*BR*) *abr m* = **Ministério de Ciência e Tecnologia**.
MD (*BR*) *abr m* = **Ministério da Desburocratização**.
MDB *abr m* (*old*) = **Movimento Democrático Brasileiro**.
me [mi] *pron* (*direto*) me; (*indireto*) (to) me; (*reflexivo*) (to) myself.
meada ['mjada] *f* skein, hank.
meado ['mjadu] *m* middle; **em ~s** *ou* **no(s) ~(s) de julho/do ano** in mid-July/in the middle of the year.
meandro ['mjãdru] *m* meander; **os ~s** (*fig*) the ins and outs.
MEC (*BR*) *abr m* = **Ministério de Educação e Cultura**.
Meca ['mɛka] *n* Mecca.
mecânica [me'kanika] *f* (*ciência*) mechanics *sg*; (*mecanismo*) mechanism; *V tb* **mecânico**.
mecânico/a [me'kaniku/a] *adj* mechanical ♦ *m/f* mechanic; **broca mecânica** power drill.
mecanismo [meka'niʒmu] *m* mechanism.
mecanização [mekaniza'sãw] *f* mechanization.
mecanizar [mekani'za*] *vt* to mechanize.
mecenas [me'sɛnaʃ] *m inv* patron.
mecha ['meʃa] *f* (*de vela*) wick; (*cabelo*) tuft; (*tingida*) highlight; (*MED*) swab; **fazer ~ no cabelo** to put highlights in one's hair, to highlight one's hair.
mechado/a [me'ʃadu/a] *adj* highlighted.
meço ['mɛsu] *etc vb V* **medir**.
méd. *abr* (= *médio*) av.
medalha [me'daʎa] *f* medal.
medalhão [meda'ʎãw] (*pl* **-ões**) *m* medallion; (*fig*: *figurão*) big name; (*jóia*) locket.
média ['mɛdʒja] *f* average; (*café*) coffee with milk; **em ~** on average; **fazer ~** to ingratiate o.s.
mediação [medʒja'sãw] *f* mediation; **por ~ de** through.
mediador(a) [medʒja'do*(a)] *m/f* mediator.
mediano/a [me'dʒjanu/a] *adj* medium, average; (*medíocre*) mediocre.
mediante [me'dʒjãtʃi] *prep* by (means of), through; (*a troco de*) in return for.
mediar [me'dʒja*] *vt* to mediate (for) ♦ *vi* (*ser mediador*) to mediate; **a distância que medeia entre** the distance between.
medicação [medʒika'sãw] (*pl* **-ões**) *f* treatment; (*medicamentos*) medication.
medicamento [medʒika'mẽtu] *m* medicine.
medição [medʒi'sãw] (*pl* **-ões**) *f* measurement.
medicar [medʒi'ka*] *vt* to treat ♦ *vi* to practise (*BRIT*) *ou* practice (*US*) medicine; **~-se** *vr* to take medicine, doctor o.s. up.
medicina [medʒi'sina] *f* medicine; **~ legal** forensic medicine.
medicinal [medʒisi'naw] (*pl* **-ais**) *adj* medicinal.
médico/a ['mɛdʒiku/a] *adj* medical ♦ *m/f* doctor; **receita médica** prescription.
médico-cirurgião/médica-cirurgiã (*pl* **médicos-cirurgiões/médicas-cirurgiãs**) *m/f* surgeon.
medições [medʒi'sõjʃ] *fpl de* **medição**.
médico-hospitalar (*pl* **-es**) *adj* hospital and medical.
médico-legal (*pl* **-ais**) *adj* forensic.
médico-legista (*pl* **médicos-legistas**) *m* forensic expert (*BRIT*), medical examiner (*US*).
medida [me'dʒida] *f* measure; (*providência*) step; (*medição*) measurement; (*moderação*) prudence; **à ~ que** while, as; **tomar ~s** to take steps; **tomar as ~s de** to measure; **feito sob ~** made to measure; **software sob ~** bespoke software; **ir além da ~** to go too far; **encher as ~s** (*satisfazer*) to fit the bill; **encher as ~s de alguém** (*chatear*) to get on sb's wick; **na ~ em que** in so far as; **tirar as ~s de alguém** to take sb's measurements; **~ de emergência/urgência** emergency/urgent measure.
medidor [medʒi'do*] *m*: **~ de pressão** pressure gauge; **~ de gás** gas meter.
medieval [medʒje'vaw] (*pl* **-ais**) *adj* medieval.
médio/a ['mɛdʒju/a] *adj* (*dedo*, *classe*) middle; (*tamanho*, *estatura*) medium; (*mediano*) average; **a ~ prazo** in the medium term;

ensino ~ secondary education; **o brasileiro** ~ the average Brazilian.

medíocre [me'dʒiokri] *adj* mediocre.

mediocridade [medʒjokri'dadʒi] *f* mediocrity.

mediocrizar [medʒjokri'za*] *vt* to make mediocre.

medir [me'dʒi*] *vt* to measure; (*atos, palavras*) to weigh; (*avaliar: conseqüências, distâncias*) to weigh up ♦ *vi* to measure; **~-se** *vr* to measure o.s.; **~-se (com alguém)** (*comparar-se*) to be on a par (with sb); **quanto você mede? — meço 1.60 m** how tall are you? — I'm 1.60 m (tall); **a saia mede 80 cm de comprimento** the skirt is 80 cm long; **meça suas palavras!** watch your language!; **~ alguém dos pés à cabeça** (*fig*) to eye sb up; **não ter mãos a ~** (*fig*) to have one's hands full.

meditação [medʒita'sãw] (*pl* **-ões**) *f* meditation.

meditar [medʒi'ta*] *vi* to meditate; **~ sobre algo** to ponder (on) sth.

meditativo/a [medʒita'tʃivu/a] *adj* thoughtful, reflective.

mediterrâneo/a [medʒite'xanju/a] *adj* Mediterranean ♦ *m*: **o M~** the Mediterranean.

médium ['mɛdʒjũ] (*pl* **-ns**) *m* (*pessoa*) medium.

mediunidade [medʒjuni'dadʒi] *f* second sight.

médiuns ['mɛdʒjũʃ] *mpl de* **médium.**

medo ['medu] *m* fear; **com ~** afraid; **ter ~ de** to be afraid of; **ficar com ~** to get frightened; **meter ~** to be frightening; **meter ~ em alguém** to frighten sb; **com ~ que** for fear that; **ter um ~ que se péla** (*fig*) to be frightened out of one's wits.

medonho/a [me'doɲu/a] *adj* terrible, awful.

medrar [me'dra*] *vi* to thrive, flourish; (*col: ter medo*) to get frightened.

medroso/a [me'drozu/ɔza] *adj* (*com medo*) frightened; (*tímido*) timid.

medula [me'dula] *f* marrow.

megabyte [mega'bajtʃi] *m* megabyte.

megalomania [megaloma'nia] *f* megalomania.

megalomaníaco/a [megaloma'niaku/a] *adj, m/f* megalomaniac.

megaton [mega'tõ] *m* megaton.

megera [me'ʒɛra] *f* shrew; (*mãe*) cruel mother.

meia ['meja] *f* stocking; (*curta*) sock; (*meia-entrada*) half-price ticket ♦ *num* six; **(ponto de) ~** stocking stitch.

meia-calça (*pl* **meias-calças**) *f* tights *pl*, panty hose (*US*).

meia-direita (*pl* **meias-direitas**) *f* (*FUTEBOL*) inside right ♦ *m* (*jogador*) inside right.

meia-entrada (*pl* **meias-entradas**) *f* half-price ticket.

meia-esquerda (*pl* **meias-esquerdas**) *f* (*FUTEBOL*) inside left ♦ *m* (*jogador*) inside left.

meia-estação *f*: **roupa de ~** spring *ou* autumn clothing.

meia-idade *f* middle age; **pessoa de ~** middle-aged person.

meia-lua *f* half moon; (*formato*) semicircle.

meia-luz *f* half light.

meia-noite *f* midnight.

meia-tigela *f*: **de ~** two-bit.

meia-volta (*pl* **meias-voltas**) *f* (*tb*: *MIL*) about-turn (*BRIT*), about-face (*US*).

meigo/a ['mejgu/a] *adj* sweet.

meiguice [mej'gisi] *f* sweetness.

meio/a ['meju/a] *adj* half ♦ *adv* a bit, rather ♦ *m* (*centro*) middle; (*social, profissional*) milieu; (*tb*: *~ ambiente*) environment; (*recurso*) means *pl*; (*maneira*) way; **~s** *mpl* means *pl*; **cortar ao ~** to cut in half; **no ~ (de)** in the middle (of); **o quarto do ~** the middle room, the room in the middle; **dividir algo ~ a ~** to divide sth in half *ou* fifty-fifty; **em ~ a** amid; **deixar algo pelo ~** to leave sth half-finished; **por ~ de** through; **por todos os ~s** by all available means; **não há ~ de chover/de ela chegar cedo** there is no way it's going to rain/she will arrive early; **~ quilo** half a kilo; **um mês e ~** one and a half months; **embolar o ~ de campo** (*fig*) to foul things up; **nos ~s financeiros** in financial circles; **~ de transporte** means of transport; **~s de comunicação (de massa)** (mass) media *pl*; **~s de produção** means *pl* of production.

meio-de-campo (*pl* **meios-de-campo**) *m* (*FUTEBOL*) centre (*BRIT*) *ou* center (*US*) forward; (: *posição*) midfield.

meio-dia *m* midday, noon.

meio-feriado (*pl* **meios-feriados**) *m* half-day holiday.

meio-fio *m* kerb (*BRIT*), curb (*US*).

meio-termo (*pl* **meios-termos**) *m* (*fig*) compromise.

meio-tom (*pl* **meios-tons**) *m* (*MÚS*) semitone; (*nuança*) half-tone.

mel [mɛw] *m* honey.

melaço [me'lasu] *m* molasses *pl*.

melado/a [me'ladu/a] *adj* (*pegajoso*) sticky ♦ *m* (*melaço: US*) molasses; (: *BRIT*) treacle.

melancia [melã'sia] *f* watermelon.

melancieira [melã'sjejra] *f* watermelon plant.

melancolia [melãko'lia] *f* melancholy, sadness.

melancólico/a [melã'kɔliku/a] *adj* sad, melancholy.

Melanésia [mela'nɛzja] *f*: **a ~** Melanesia.

melão [me'lãw] (*pl* **-ões**) *m* melon.

melar [me'la*] *vt* to dirty ♦ *vi* (*gorar*) to flop; **~-se** *vr* to get messy.

meleca [me'lɛka] (*col*) *f* snot; (*uma ~*) bogey; **tirar ~** to pick one's nose; **que ~!** (*col*) what crap!

meleira [me'lejra] *f* sticky mess.
melena [me'lena] *f* long hair.
melhor [me'ʎɔ*] *adj, adv* (*compar*) better; (*superl*) best; ~ **que nunca** better than ever; **quanto mais** ~ the more the better; **seria** ~ **começarmos** we had better begin; **tanto** ~ so much the better; ~ **ainda** even better; **bem** ~ much better; **o** ~ **é** ... the best thing is ...; **levar a** ~ to come off best; **ou** ~ ... (*ou antes*) or rather ...; **fiz o** ~ **que pude** I did the best I could; **no** ~ **da festa** (*fig*: *no melhor momento*) when things are (*ou* were) in full swing; (: *inesperadamente*) all of a sudden.
melhora [me'ʎɔra] *f* improvement; ~**s!** get well soon!
melhorada [meʎo'rada] (*col*) *f*: **dar uma** ~ to get better.
melhoramento [meʎora'mẽtu] *m* improvement.
melhorar [meʎo'ra*] *vt* to improve, make better; (*doente*) to make better ♦ *vi* to improve, get better; (*doente*) to get better; ~ **de vida** to improve one's circumstances; ~ **no emprego** to get better at one's job.
meliante [me'ljãtʃi] *m* scoundrel; (*vagabundo*) tramp.
melindrar [melĩ'dra*] *vt* to offend, hurt; ~**-se** *vr* to take offence (*BRIT*) *ou* offense (*US*), be hurt.
melindre [me'lĩdri] *m* sensitivity.
melindroso/a [melĩ'drozu/ɔza] *adj* (*sensível*) sensitive, touchy; (*problema, situação*) tricky; (*operação*) delicate.
melodia [melo'dʒia] *f* melody; (*composição*) tune.
melódico/a [me'lɔdʒiku/a] *adj* melodic.
melodrama [melo'drama] *m* melodrama.
melodramático/a [melodra'matʃiku/a] *adj* melodramatic.
meloeiro [me'lwejru] *m* melon plant.
melões [me'lõjʃ] *mpl de* **melão**.
meloso/a [me'lozu/ɔza] *adj* sweet; (*voz*) mellifluous; (*fig*: *pessoa*) sweet-talking.
melro ['mɛwxu] *m* blackbird.
membrana [mẽ'brana] *f* membrane.
membro ['mẽbru] *m* member; (*ANAT*: *braço, perna*) limb.
membrudo/a [mẽ'brudu/a] *adj* big; (*fig*) robust.
memento [me'mẽtu] *m* reminder; (*caderneta*) jotter.
memorando [memo'rãdu] *m* (*aviso*) note; (*COM*: *comunicação*) memorandum.
memorável [memo'ravew] (*pl* **-eis**) *adj* memorable.
memória [me'mɔrja] *f* memory; ~**s** *fpl* (*de autor*) memoirs; **de** ~ by heart; **em** ~ **de** in memory of; ~ **fraca** bad memory; **falta de** ~ loss of memory; **digno de** ~ memorable; **vir à** ~ to come to mind; **varrer da** ~ (*fig*) to wipe sth from one's memory; ~ **RAM** RAM memory; ~ **não-volátil** non-volatile memory.
memorial [memo'rjaw] (*pl* **-ais**) *m* memorial; (*JUR*) brief.
memorizar [memori'za*] *vt* to memorize.
menção [mẽ'sãw] (*pl* **-ões**) *f* mention, reference; ~ **honrosa** honours (*BRIT*), honors (*US*), distinction; **fazer** ~ **de algo** to mention sth; **fazer** ~ **de sair** to make as if to leave, begin to leave.
mencionar [mẽsjo'na*] *vt* to mention; **para não** ~ ... not to mention ...; **sem** ~ ... let alone ....
menções [mẽ'sõjʃ] *fpl de* **menção**.
mendicância [mẽdʒi'kãsja] *f* begging.
mendicante [mẽdʒi'kãtʃi] *adj* mendicant ♦ *m/f* beggar.
mendigar [mẽdʒi'ga*] *vt* to beg for ♦ *vi* to beg.
mendigo/a [mẽ'dʒigu/a] *m/f* beggar.
menear [me'nja*] *vt* (*corpo, cabeça*) to shake; (*quadris*) to swing; ~ **a cabeça de modo afirmativo** to nod (one's head).
meneio [me'neju] *m* (*balanço*) swaying.
meninada [meni'nada] *f* kids *pl*.
meningite [menĩ'ʒitʃi] *f* meningitis.
meninice [meni'nisi] *f* (*infância*) childhood; (*modos de criança*) childishness; (*ato, dito*) childish thing.
menino/a [me'ninu/a] *m/f* boy/girl; (*olhos*): **menina do olho** pupil; **ser a menina dos olhos de alguém** (*fig*) to be the apple of sb's eye; **seu sorriso de** ~ his boyish smile.
meninote/a [meni'nɔtʃi/ta] *m/f* boy/girl.
menopausa [meno'pawza] *f* menopause.
menor [me'nɔ*] *adj* (*mais pequeno*: *compar*) smaller; (: *superl*) smallest; (*mais jovem*: *compar*) younger; (: *superl*) youngest; (*o mínimo*) the least, slightest; (*tb*: ~ *de idade*) under age ♦ *m/f* juvenile, young person; (*JUR*) minor; ~ **abandonado** abandoned child; **proibido para** ~**es** over 18s only; (*filme*) X-certificate (*BRIT*), X-rated (*US*); **um** ~ **de 10 anos** a child of ten; **não tenho a** ~ **idéia** I haven't the slightest idea.
menoridade [menori'dadʒi] *f* under-age status.
menos ['menuʃ] *adj* (*compar*: *sg*) less; (: *pl*) fewer; (*superl*: *sg*) least; (: *pl*) fewest ♦ *adv* (*compar*) less; (*superl*) least ♦ *prep* except ♦ *conj* minus, less ♦ *m*: **o** ~ the least; **a** *ou* **de** ~ (*faltando*) missing; **ele me deu £1 a** *ou* **de** ~ he gave me £1 too little; **a** ~ **que** unless; **ao** *ou* **pelo** ~ at least; **mais ou** ~ more or less; ~ **de (***ou* **que)** less than; ~ **cansativo** less tiring; **trabalhar** ~ to work less; **quanto** ~ **você** ... the less you ...; **muito** ~ ... much less ..., let alone ...; **nem ao** ~ not even, not as much as; **quando** ~ **se espera** when you least expect it; **tudo** ~ **isso!** anything but that!; **não é para** ~ it's no wonder; **isso é o de** ~ that's nothing.
menosprezar [menuʃpre'za*] *vt* (*subestimar*) to underrate; (*desprezar*) to despise, scorn.
menosprezível [menuʃpre'zivew] (*pl* **-eis**) *adj* despicable.

menosprezo [menuʃ'prezu] *m* contempt, disdain.
mensageiro/a [mẽsa'ʒejru/a] *adj* messenger *atr* ♦ *m/f* messenger.
mensagem [mẽ'saʒẽ] (*pl* **-ns**) *f* message; ~ **de erro** (COMPUT) error message.
mensal [mẽ'saw] (*pl* **-ais**) *adj* monthly; **ele ganha £1000 mensais** he earns £1000 a month.
mensalidade [mẽsali'dadʒi] *f* monthly payment.
mensalmente [mẽsaw'mẽtʃi] *adv* monthly.
menstruação [mẽʃtrwa'sãw] *f* period, menstruation.
menstruada [mẽʃ'trwada] *adj* having one's period; (MED) menstruating.
menstrual [mẽʃ'trwaw] (*pl* **-ais**) *adj* menstrual.
menstruar [mẽʃ'trwa*] *vi* to menstruate, have a period.
mênstruo ['mẽʃtru] *m* period, menstruation.
menta ['mẽta] *f* mint.
mental [mẽ'taw] (*pl* **-ais**) *adj* mental.
mentalidade [mẽtali'dadʒi] *f* mentality.
mentalizar [mẽtali'za*] *vt* (*plano*) to conceive; ~ **alguém de algo** to make sb realize sth.
mente ['mẽtʃi] *f* mind; **de boa** ~ willingly; **ter em** ~ to bear in mind.
mentecapto/a [mẽtʃi'kaptu/a] *adj* mad, crazy ♦ *m/f* fool, idiot.
mentir [mẽ'tʃi*] *vi* to lie; **minto!** (I) tell a lie!
mentira [mẽ'tʃira] *f* lie; (*ato*) lying; **parece** ~ **que** it seems incredible that; **de** ~ not for real; ~**!** (*acusação*) that's a lie!, you're lying; (*de surpresa*) you don't say!, no!
mentiroso/a [mẽtʃi'rozu/ɔza] *adj* lying; (*enganoso*) deceitful; (*falso*) deceptive ♦ *m/f* liar.
mentol [mẽ'tɔw] (*pl* **-óis**) *m* menthol.
mentolado/a [mẽto'ladu/a] *adj* mentholated.
mentor [mẽ'to*] *m* mentor.
menu [me'nu] *m* (*tb*: COMPUT) menu.
mercadinho [mexka'dʒiɲu] *m* local market.
mercado [mex'kadu] *m* market; **M~ Comum** Common Market; ~ **negro** *ou* **paralelo** black market; ~ **externo/interno** foreign/domestic *ou* home market; ~ **das pulgas** flea market; ~ **de capitais** capital market; ~ **de trabalho** labo(u)r market; ~ **à vista** spot market.
mercadologia [mexkadolo'ʒia] *f* marketing.
mercador [mexka'do*] *m* merchant, trader.
mercadoria [mexkado'ria] *f* commodity; ~**s** *fpl* goods.
mercante [mex'kãtʃi] *adj* merchant *atr*.
mercantil [mexkã'tʃiw] (*pl* **-is**) *adj* mercantile, commercial.
mercê [mex'se] *f* (*favor*) favour (BRIT), favor (US); (*perdão*) mercy; **à** ~ **de** at the mercy of.
mercearia [mexsja'ria] *f* grocer's (shop) (BRIT), grocery store.
merceeiro [mex'sjejru] *m* grocer.
mercenário/a [mexse'narju/a] *adj* mercenary ♦ *m* mercenary.
mercerizado/a [mexseri'zadu/a] *adj* mercerized.
mercúrio [mex'kurju] *m* mercury; **M~** Mercury.
merda ['mɛxda] (*col!*) *f* shit *(!)* ♦ *m/f* (*pessoa*) jerk; **a** ~ **do carro** the bloody (BRIT) *ou* goddamn (US) car *(!)*; **mandar alguém à** ~ to tell sb to piss off *(!)*; **estar numa** ~ to be fucked up *(!)*; ~ **nenhuma** fuck all *(!)*; **ser uma** ~ (*viagem, filme*) to be crap *(!)*.
merecedor(a) [merese'do*(a)] *adj* deserving.
merecer [mere'se*] *vt* to deserve; (*consideração*) to merit; (*valer*) to be worth ♦ *vi* to be worthy.
merecido/a [mere'sidu/a] *adj* deserved; (*castigo, prêmio*) just.
merecimento [meresi'mẽtu] *m* desert; (*valor, talento*) merit.
merenda [me'rẽda] *f* packed lunch; ~ **escolar** free school meal.
merendar [merẽ'da*] *vi* to have school dinner.
merendeira [merẽ'dejra] *f* (*maleta*) lunch-box; (*funcionária*) dinner-lady.
merengue [me'rẽgi] *m* meringue.
meretrício [mere'trisju] *m* prostitution.
meretriz [mere'triʒ] *f* prostitute.
mergulhador(a) [mexguʎa'do*(a)] *adj* diving ♦ *m/f* diver.
mergulhar [mexgu'ʎa*] *vi* (*para nadar*) to dive; (*penetrar*) to plunge ♦ *vt*: ~ **algo em algo** (*num líquido*) to dip sth into sth; (*na terra etc*) to plunge sth into sth; ~ **no trabalho/na floresta** to immerse o.s. in one's work/go deep into the forest.
mergulho [mex'guʎu] *m* dip(ping), immersion; (*em natação*) dive; (*vôo*) nose-dive; **dar um** ~ (*na praia*) to go for a dip.
meridiano [meri'dʒjanu] *m* meridian.
meridional [meridʒjo'naw] (*pl* **-ais**) *adj* southern.
mérito ['mɛritu] *m* merit.
meritório/a [meri'tɔrju/a] *adj* meritorious.
merluza [mex'luza] *f* hake.
mero/a ['mɛru/a] *adj* mere.
mertiolate [mextʃjo'latʒi] *m* antiseptic.
mês [meʃ] *m* month; **pago por** ~ paid by the month; **duas vezes por** ~ twice a month; ~ **corrente** this month; **o** ~ **que vem** next month.
mesa ['meza] *f* table; (*de trabalho*) desk; (*comitê*) board; (*numa reunião*) panel; **pôr/tirar a** ~ to lay/clear the table; **à** ~ at the table; **por baixo da** ~ (*tb fig*) under the table; ~ **de bilhar** billiard table; ~ **de centro** coffee table; ~ **de cozinha/jantar** kitchen/dining table; ~ **de jogo** card table; ~ **de toalete** dressing table; ~ **telefônica**

***NB**: European Portuguese adds the following consonants to certain words:* **b** (sú(b)dito, su(b)til); **c** (a(c)ção, a(c)cionista, a(c)to); **m** (inde(m)ne); **p** (ado(p)ção, ado(p)tar); *for further details see p. xiii.*

switchboard.
mesada [me'zada] *f* monthly allowance; (*de criança*) pocket-money.
mesa-de-cabeceira (*pl* **mesas-de-cabeceira**) *f* bedside table.
mesa-redonda (*pl* **mesas-redondas**) *f* discussion panel.
mescla ['mɛʃkla] *f* mixture, blend.
mesclar [meʃ'kla*] *vt* to mix (up); (*cores*) to blend.
meseta [me'zeta] *f* plateau, tableland.
mesmice [meʒ'misi] *f* sameness.
mesmo/a ['meʒmu/a] *adj* same; (*enfático*) very ♦ *adv* (*exatamente*) right; (*até*) even; (*realmente*) really ♦ *m/f*: **o ~/a mesma** the same (one); **o ~** (*a mesma coisa*) the same (thing); **eu ~** I myself; **este ~ homem** this very man; **ele ~ o fez** he did it himself; **o Rei ~** the King himself; **continuar na mesma** to be just the same; **dá no ~** *ou* **na mesma** it's all the same; **aqui/agora/hoje ~** right here/right now/this very day; **~ que** even if; **é ~** it's true; **é ~?** really?; **(é) isso ~!** exactly!, that's right!; **por isso ~** that's why; **~ assim** even so; **nem ~** not even; **~ quando** even when; **só ~** only; **por si ~** by one's self; (*referindo-se a pessoa já mencionada*): **..., e estive com o ~ ontem** ..., and I was with him yesterday; **ficar na mesma** (*não entender*) to be none the wiser; **isto para mim é o ~** it's all the same to me; **o ~, por favor!** (*num bar etc*) the same again, please.
mesquinharia [meʃkiɲa'ria] *f* meanness; (*ato, dito*) mean thing.
mesquinho/a [meʃ'kiɲu/a] *adj* mean.
mesquita [meʃ'kita] *f* mosque.
messias [me'siaʃ] *m* Messiah.
mestiçar-se [meʃtʃi'saxsi] *vr*: **~ (com)** to interbreed (with).
mestiço/a [meʃ'tʃisu/a] *adj* half-caste, of mixed race; (*animal*) crossbred ♦ *m/f* half-caste; (*animal*) half-breed.
mestrado [meʃ'trado] *m* master's degree; **fazer/tirar o ~** to do/get one's master's (degree).
mestre/a ['mɛʃtri/a] *adj* (*chave, viga*) master; (*linha, estrada*) main; (*qualidade*) masterly ♦ *m/f* master/mistress; (*professor*) teacher; **de ~** masterly; **obra mestra** masterpiece; **ele é ~ em mentir** he's an expert liar.
mestre-cuca (*pl* **mestres-cucas**) (*col*) *m* chef.
mestre-de-cerimônias (*pl* **mestres-de-cerimônias**) *m* master of ceremonies, MC.
mestre-de-obras (*pl* **mestres-de-obras**) *m* foreman.
mestria [meʃ'tria] *f* mastery; (*habilidade*) expertise; **com ~** to perfection.
mesura [me'zura] *f* (*cumprimento*) bow; (*cortesia*) courtesy; **cheio de ~s** cap in hand.
meta ['mɛta] *f* (*em corrida*) finishing post; (*regata*) finishing line; (*gol*) goal; (*objetivo*) aim, goal.
metabolismo [metabo'liʒmu] *m* metabolism.
metade [me'tadʒi] *f* half; (*meio*) middle; **~ de uma laranja** half an orange; **pela ~** halfway through.
metafísica [meta'fizika] *f* metaphysics *sg*.
metafísico/a [meta'fiziku/a] *adj* metaphysical.
metáfora [me'tafora] *f* metaphor.
metafórico/a [meta'fɔriku/a] *adj* metaphorical.
metal [me'taw] (*pl* **-ais**) *m* metal; **metais** *mpl* (MÚS) brass *sg*.
metálico/a [me'taliku/a] *adj* (*som*) metallic; (*de metal*) metal.
metalinguagem [metalĩ'gwaʒẽ] (*pl* **-ns**) *f* metalanguage.
metalizado/a [metali'zadu/a] *adj* metallic.
metalurgia [metalux'ʒia] *f* metallurgy.
metalúrgica [meta'luxʒika] *f* metal works; *V tb* **metalúrgico**.
metalúrgico/a [meta'luxʒiku/a] *adj* metallurgical ♦ *m/f* metalworker.
metamorfose [metamox'fɔzi] *f* metamorphosis.
metamorfosear [metamoxfo'zja*] *vt*: **~ alguém em algo** to transform sb into sth.
metano [me'tanu] *m* methane.
meteórico/a [mete'ɔriku/a] *adj* meteoric.
meteorito [meteo'ritu] *m* meteorite.
meteoro [me'tjɔru] *m* meteor.
meteorologia [meteorolo'ʒia] *f* meteorology.
meteorológico/a [meteoro'lɔʒiku/a] *adj* meteorological.
meteorologista [meteorolo'ʒiʃta] *m/f* meteorologist; (TV, RÁDIO) weather forecaster.
meter [me'te*] *vt* (*colocar*) to put; (*envolver*) to involve; (*introduzir*) to introduce; **~-se** *vr* (*esconder-se*) to hide; (*retirar-se*) to closet o.s.; **~ na cabeça** to take it into one's head; **~-se na cama** to get into bed; **~-se com** (*provocar*) to pick a quarrel with; (*associar-se*) to get involved with; **~-se a médico** to set o.s. up as a doctor; **~-se a fazer** to decide to have a go at doing; **~-se em** to get involved in; (*intrometer-se*) to interfere in; **~-se onde não é chamado** to poke one's nose in(to other people's business); **meta-se com a sua vida** mind your own business.
meticulosidade [metʃikulozi'dadʒi] *f* meticulousness.
meticuloso/a [metʃiku'lozu/ɔza] *adj* meticulous.
metido/a [me'tʃidu/a] *adj* (*envolvido*) involved; (*intrometido*) meddling; **~ (a besta)** snobbish.
metódico/a [me'tɔdʒiku/a] *adj* methodical.
metodismo [meto'dʒiʒmu] *m* (REL) Methodism.
metodista [meto'dʒiʃta] *adj, m/f* Methodist.
método ['mɛtodu] *m* method.
metodologia [metodolo'ʒia] *f* methodology.
metragem [me'traʒẽ] *f* length (in metres

(*BRIT*) *ou* meters (*US*)); (*CINEMA*) footage, length; **filme de longa/curta ~** feature *ou* full-length/short film.
metralhadora [metraʎa'dora] *f* sub-machine gun.
metralhar [metra'ʎa*] *vt* (*ferir, matar*) to shoot; (*fazer fogo contra*) to spray with machine-gun fire.
métrica ['mɛtrika] *f* (*em poesia*) metre (*BRIT*), meter (*US*).
métrico/a ['mɛtriku/a] *adj* metric; **fita métrica** tape measure.
metro ['mɛtru] *m* metre (*BRIT*), meter (*US*); (*PT: metropolitano*) underground (*BRIT*), subway (*US*); **~ quadrado/cúbico** square/cubic metre.
metrô [me'tro] (*BR*) *m* underground (*BRIT*), subway (*US*).
metrópole [me'trɔpoli] *f* metropolis; (*capital*) capital.
metropolitano/a [metropoli'tanu/a] *adj* metropolitan ♦ *m* (*PT*) underground (*BRIT*), subway (*US*).
metroviário/a [metro'vjarju/a] *adj* underground *atr* (*BRIT*), subway *atr* (*US*) ♦ *m/f* underground (*BRIT*) *ou* subway (*US*) worker.
meu/minha [mew/'miɲa] *adj* my ♦ *pron* mine; **um amigo ~** a friend of mine; **este livro é ~** this book is mine; **os ~s** *mpl* (*minha família*) my family *ou* folks (*col*); **estou na minha** I'm doing my own thing.
MEx (*BR*) *abr m* = **Ministério do Exército.**
mexer [me'ʃe*] *vt* (*mover*) to move; (*cabeça: dizendo sim*) to nod; (: *dizendo não*) to shake; (*misturar*) to stir; (*ovos*) to scramble ♦ *vi* (*mover*) to move; **~-se** *vr* to move; (*apressar-se*) to get a move on; **~ em algo** to touch sth; **~ com algo** (*trabalhar*) to work with sth; (*comerciar*) to deal in sth; **~ com alguém** (*provocar*) to tease sb; (*comover*) to have a profound effect on sb, get to sb (*col*); **mexa-se!** get going!, move yourself!
mexerica [meʃe'rika] *f* tangerine.
mexericar [meʃeri'ka*] *vi* to gossip.
mexerico [meʃe'riku] *m* piece of gossip; **~s** *mpl* gossip *sg*.
mexeriqueiro/a [meʃeri'kejru/a] *adj* gossiping ♦ *m/f* gossip, busybody.
mexicano/a [meʃi'kanu/a] *adj, m/f* Mexican.
México ['mɛʃiku] *m*: **o ~** Mexico; **a Cidade do ~** Mexico City.
mexida [me'ʃida] *f* mess, disorder.
mexido/a [me'ʃidu/a] *adj* (*papéis*) mixed up; (*ovos*) scrambled.
mexilhão [meʃi'ʎãw] (*pl* **-ões**) *m* mussel.
mezanino [meza'ninu] *m* mezzanine (floor).
MF (*BR*) *abr m* = **Ministério da Fazenda.**
MG (*BR*) *abr* = **Minas Gerais.**
mg *abr* (= *miligrama*) mg.
mi [mi] *m* (*MÚS*) E.
miado ['mjadu] *m* miaow.
miar [mja*] *vi* to miaow; (*vento*) to whistle.
miasma ['mjaʒma] *m* (*fig*) decay.
miau [mjaw] *m* miaow.
MIC (*BR*) *abr m* = **Ministério de Indústria e Comércio.**
miçanga [mi'sãga] *f* beads *pl*.
micção [mik'sãw] *f* urination.
mico ['miku] *m* capuchin monkey.
micose [mi'kɔzi] *f* mycosis.
micrão [mi'krãw] (*pl* **-ões**) *m* (*COMPUT*) supermicro.
micro ['mikru] *m* (*COMPUT*) micro.
micro- [mikru] *prefixo* micro-.
micróbio [mi'krɔbju] *m* germ, microbe.
microcirurgia [mikrosirux'ʒia] *f* microsurgery.
microcomputador [mikrokõputa'do*] *m* microcomputer.
microcosmo [mikro'kɔʒmu] *m* microcosm.
microempresa [mikroẽ'preza] *f* small business.
micrões [mi'krõjʃ] *mpl de* **micrão.**
microfilme [mikro'fiwmi] *m* microfilm.
microfone [mikro'fɔni] *m* microphone.
microinformática [mikroĩfox'matʃika] *f* microcomputing.
Micronésia [mikro'nɛzja] *f*: **a ~** Micronesia.
microonda [mikro'õda] *f* microwave.
microondas [mikro'õdaʃ] *m inv* (*tb*: *forno de ~*) microwave (oven).
microônibus [mikro'onibuʃ] *m inv* minibus.
microplaqueta [mikropla'keta] *f* microchip; **~ de silicone** silicon chip.
microprocessador [mikroprosesa'do*] *m* microprocessor.
microrganismo [mikroxga'niʒmu] *m* microorganism.
microscópico/a [mikro'ʃkɔpiku/a] *adj* microscopic.
microscópio [mikro'ʃkɔpju] *m* microscope.
mídi ['midʒi] *adj inv* midi.
mídia ['midʒja] *f* media *pl*.
migalha [mi'gaʎa] *f* crumb; **~s** *fpl* scraps.
migração [migra'sãw] (*pl* **-ões**) *f* migration.
migrar [mi'gra*] *vi* to migrate.
migratório/a [migra'tɔrju/a] *adj* migratory; **aves migratórias** birds of passage.
miguel [mi'gɛw] (*pl* **-eis**) (*col*) *m* (*banheiro*) loo (*BRIT*), john (*US*).
mijada [mi'ʒada] (*col*) *f* pee; **dar uma ~** to have a pee.
mijar [mi'ʒa*] (*col*) *vi* to pee; **~-se** *vr* to wet o.s.
mijo ['miʒu] (*col*) *m* pee, piss (*!*).
mil [miw] *num* thousand; **dois ~** two thousand; **estar a ~** (*col*) to be buzzing.
milagre [mi'lagri] *m* miracle; **por ~** miraculously.
milagroso/a [mila'grozu/ɔza] *adj* miraculous.
milenar [mile'na*] *adj* thousand-year-old; (*fig*)

***NB**: European Portuguese adds the following consonants to certain words:* **b** (sú(b)dito, su(b)til); **c** (a(c)ção, a(c)cionista, a(c)to); **m** (inde(m)ne); **p** (ado(p)ção, ado(p)tar); *for further details see p. xiii.*

ancient.
milênio [mi'lenju] *m* millennium.
milésimo/a [mi'lɛzimu/a] *num* thousandth.
mil-folhas *f inv* (*massa*) millefeuille pastry; (*doce*) cream slice.
milha ['miʎa] *f* mile; (*col*: *mil cruzeiros*): **dez ~s** ten grand; ~ **marítima** nautical mile.
milhão [mi'ʎãw] (*pl* **-ões**) *m* million; **um ~ de vezes** hundreds of times; **adorei milhões!** (*col*) I loved it!
milhar [mi'ʎa*] *m* thousand; **turistas aos ~es** tourists in their thousands.
milharal [miʎa'raw] (*pl* **-ais**) *m* maize (*BRIT*) *ou* corn (*US*) field.
milho ['miʎu] *m* maize (*BRIT*), corn (*US*).
milhões [miʎ'õjs] *mpl de* **milhão**.
miliardário/a [miljax'darju/a] *adj*, *m/f* billionaire.
milícia [mi'lisja] *f* (*MIL*) militia; (: *vida*) military life; (: *força*) military force.
milico [mi'liku] (*col*) *m* military type.
miligrama [mili'grama] *m* milligram.
mililitro [mili'litru] *m* millilitre (*BRIT*), milliliter (*US*).
milímetro [mi'limetru] *m* millimetre (*BRIT*), millimeter (*US*).
milionário/a [miljo'narju/a] *adj*, *m/f* millionaire.
militância [mili'tãsja] *f* militancy.
militante [mili'tãtʃi] *adj*, *m/f* militant.
militar [mili'ta*] *adj* military ♦ *m* soldier ♦ *vi* to fight; ~ **em** (*MIL*: *regimento*) to serve in; (*POL*: *partido*) to belong to, be active in; (*profissão*) to work in.
militarismo [milita'riʒmu] *m* militarism.
militarista [milita'riʃta] *adj*, *m/f* militarist.
militarizar [militari'za*] *vt* to militarize.
mil-réis *m inv former unit of currency in Brazil and Portugal.*
mim [mĩ] *pron* me; (*reflexivo*) myself; **de ~ para ~** to myself.
mimado/a [mi'madu/a] *adj* spoiled, spoilt (*BRIT*).
mimar [mi'ma*] *vt* to pamper, spoil.
mimeógrafo [mime'ɔgrafu] *m* duplicating machine.
mimetismo [mime'tʃiʒmu] *m* (*BIO*) mimicry.
mímica ['mimika] *f* mime; (*jogo*) charades; *V tb* **mímico**.
mímico/a ['mimiku/a] *m/f* mime artist.
mimo ['mimu] *m* (*presente*) gift; (*pessoa, coisa encantadora*) delight; (*carinho*) tenderness; (*gentileza*) kindness; **cheio de ~s** (*criança*) spoiled, spoilt (*BRIT*).
mimoso/a [mi'mozu/ɔza] *adj* (*delicado*) delicate; (*carinhoso*) tender, loving, sweet; (*encantador*) delightful.
MIN (*BR*) *abr m* = **Ministério do Interior**.
min. *abr* (= *mínimo*) min.
mina ['mina] *f* mine; (*fig*: *de riquezas*) gold mine; (: *de informações*) mine of information; (*col*: *garota*) girl; ~ **de carvão** coal mine; ~ **de ouro** (*tb fig*) gold mine.
minar [mi'na*] *vt* to mine; (*fig*) to undermine.
minarete [mina'retʃi] *m* minaret.
Minc (*BR*) *abr m* = **Ministério da Cultura**.
mindinho [mĩ'dʒiɲu] *m* (*tb*: *dedo* ~) little finger.
mineiro/a [mi'nejru/a] *adj* mining; (*de Minas Gerais*) from Minas Gerais ♦ *m/f* miner; (*de Minas Gerais*) person from Minas Gerais.
mineração [minera'sãw] *f* mining.
mineral [mine'raw] (*pl* **-ais**) *adj*, *m* mineral.
mineralogia [mineralo'ʒia] *f* mineralogy.
minerar [mine'ra*] *vt*, *vi* to mine.
minério [mi'nɛrju] *m* ore; ~ **de ferro** iron ore.
mingau [mĩ'gaw] *m* porridge; (*fig*) slop; ~ **de aveia** porridge.
míngua ['mĩgwa] *f* lack; **à ~ de** for want of; **viver à ~** to live in poverty.
minguado/a [mĩ'gwadu/a] *adj* scant; (*criança*) stunted; ~ **de algo** short of sth.
minguante [mĩ'gwãtʃi] *adj* waning; **(quarto) ~** (*ASTRONOMIA*) last quarter.
minguar [mĩ'gwa*] *vi* (*diminuir*) to decrease, dwindle; (*faltar*) to run short.
minha ['miɲa] *f de* **meu**.
minhoca [mi'ɲɔka] *f* (earth)worm; (*col*: *bobagem*) daft idea; ~ **da terra** (*fig*: *caipira*) country person.
míni ['mini] *adj inv* mini ♦ *m* minicomputer.
mini- [mini-] *prefixo* mini-.
miniatura [minja'tura] *adj*, *f* miniature.
mínima ['minima] *f* (*temperatura*) low; (*MÚS*) minim.
minicomputador [minikõputa'do*] *m* minicomputer.
minimalista [minima'liʃta] *adj* (*fig*) stark.
minimizar [minimi'za*] *vt* to minimize; (*subestimar*) to play down.
mínimo/a ['minimu/a] *adj* minimum ♦ *m* minimum; (*tb*: *dedo* ~) little finger; **não dou** *ou* **ligo a mínima para isso** I couldn't care less about it; **a mínima importância/idéia** the slightest importance/idea; **o ~ que podem fazer** the least they can do; **no ~** at least; **no ~ às 11 horas** at 11.00 at the earliest.
minissaia [mini'saja] *f* miniskirt.
ministerial [miniʃte'rjaw] (*pl* **-ais**) *adj* ministerial.
ministeriável [miniʃte'rjavew] (*pl* **-eis**) *adj* eligible to be a minister.
ministério [mini'ʃtɛrju] *m* ministry; **M~ das Relações Exteriores** Foreign Office (*BRIT*), State Department (*US*); ~ **da Fazenda** Treasury (*BRIT*), Treasury Department (*US*); **M~ da Marinha/Educação/Saúde** Admiralty/Ministry of Education/Health; ~ **do Trabalho** Department of Employment (*BRIT*) *ou* Labor (*US*); ~ **público** public prosecution service; **M~ do Interior** Home Office (*BRIT*), Department of the Interior (*US*).
ministrar [miniʃ'tra*] *vt* (*dar*) to supply; (*remédio*) to administer; (*aulas*) to give ♦ *vi* to serve as a minister.

ministro/a [mi'niʃtru/a] *m/f* minister; ~ **da Fazenda** Chancellor of the Exchequer (*BRIT*), Head of the Treasury Department (*US*); ~ **das Relações Exteriores** Foreign Secretary (*BRIT*), Head of the State Department (*US*); ~ **do Interior** Home Secretary (*BRIT*); ~ **sem pasta** minister without portfolio.
minorar [mino'ra*] *vt* to lessen, reduce.
Minorca [mi'nɔxka] *f* Menorca.
minoritário/a [minori'tarju/a] *adj* minority *atr*.
minto ['mĩtu] *etc vb V* **mentir**.
minoria [mino'ria] *f* minority.
minúcia [mi'nusja] *f* detail.
minucioso/a [minu'sjozu/ɔza] *adj* (*indivíduo, busca*) thorough; (*explicação*) detailed.
minúsculo/a [mi'nuʃkulu/a] *adj* minute, tiny; **letra minúscula** small letter.
minuta [mi'nuta] *f* (*rascunho*) rough draft; (*CULIN*) dish cooked to order; ~ **de contrato** draft contract.
minutar [minu'ta*] *vt* to draft.
minuto [mi'nutu] *m* minute.
miolo ['mjolu] *m* inside; (*polpa*) pulp; (*de maçã*) core; ~**s** *mpl* (*cérebro, inteligência*) brains.
míope ['miopi] *adj* short-sighted ♦ *m/f* myopic.
miopia [mjo'pia] *f* short-sightedness.
miosótis [mjo'zɔtʃiʃ] *m inv* (*BOT*) forget-me-not.
mira ['mira] *f* (*de fuzil*) sight; (*pontaria*) aim; (*fig*) aim, purpose; **à** ~ **de** on the lookout for; **ter em** ~ to have one's eye on.
mirabolante [mirabo'lãtʃi] *adj* (*roupa*) showy, loud; (*plano*) ambitious; (*surpreendente*) amazing.
mirada [mi'rada] *f* look.
miradouro [mira'doru] *m* viewpoint, belvedere.
miragem [mi'raʒẽ] (*pl* **-ns**) *f* mirage.
miramar [mira'ma*] *m* sea view.
mirante [mi'rãtʃi] *m* viewpoint, belvedere.
mirar [mi'ra*] *vt* to look at; (*observar*) to watch; (*apontar para*) to aim at ♦ *vi*: ~ **em** to aim at; ~**-se** *vr* to look at o.s.; ~ **para** to look onto.
miríade [mi'riadʒi] *f* myriad.
mirim [mi'rĩ] (*pl* **-ns**) *adj* little.
mirrado/a [mi'xadu/a] *adj* (*planta*) withered; (*pessoa*) haggard.
mirrar-se [mi'xaxsi] *vr* (*planta*) to wither, dry up; (*pessoa*) to waste away.
misantropo/a [mizã'tropu/a] *m/f* misanthrope ♦ *adj* misanthropic.
miscelânea [mise'lanja] *f* miscellany; (*confusão*) muddle.
miscigenação [misiʒena'sãw] *f* interbreeding.
mise-en-plis [mizã'pli] *m* shampoo and set.
miserável [mize'ravew] (*pl* **-eis**) *adj* (*digno de compaixão*) wretched; (*pobre*) impoverished; (*avaro*) stingy, mean; (*insignificante*) paltry; (*lugar*) squalid; (*infame*) despicable ♦ *m* (*indigente*) wretch; (*coitado*) poor thing; (*pessoa infame*) rotter.
miserê [mize're] (*col*) *m* poverty, pennilessness.
miséria [mi'zɛrja] *f* (*estado lastimável*) misery; (*pobreza*) poverty; (*avareza*) stinginess; **ganhar/custar uma** ~ to earn/cost a pittance; **chorar** ~ to complain that one is hard up; **fazer** ~**s** (*col*) to do wonders; **ser uma** ~ (*col*) to be awful.
misericórdia [mizeri'kɔxdʒja] *f* (*compaixão*) pity, compassion; (*graça*) mercy.
misógino/a [mi'zɔʒinu/a] *adj* misogynistic ♦ *m* misogynist.
missa ['misa] *f* (*REL*) mass; **não saber da** ~ **a metade** (*col*) not to know the half of it.
missal [mi'saw] (*pl* **-ais**) *m* missal.
missão [mi'sãw] (*pl* **-ões**) *f* mission; (*dever*) duty; (*incumbência*) job.
misse ['misi] *f* beauty queen.
míssil ['misiw] (*pl* **-eis**) *m* missile; ~ **balístico/guiado** ballistic/guided missile; ~ **de curto/médio/longo alcance** short-/medium-/long-range missile.
missionário/a [misjo'narju/a] *m/f* missionary.
missiva [mi'siva] *f* missive.
missões [mi'sõjʃ] *fpl de* **missão**.
mister [miʃ'te*] *m* (*ocupação*) occupation; (*trabalho*) job; **ser** ~ to be necessary; **ter-se** ~ **de algo** to need sth; **não há** ~ **de** there's no need for.
mistério [miʃ'tɛrju] *m* mystery; **fazer** ~ **de algo** to make a mystery of sth; **não ter** ~ to be straightforward.
misterioso/a [miʃte'rjozu/ɔza] *adj* mysterious.
misticismo [miʃtʃi'siʒmu] *m* mysticism.
místico/a ['miʃtʃiku/a] *adj, m/f* mystic.
mistificar [miʃtʃifi'ka*] *vt, vi* to fool.
misto/a ['miʃtu/a] *adj* mixed; (*confuso*) mixed up; (*escola*) mixed ♦ *m* mixture.
misto-quente *m* toasted cheese and ham sandwich.
mistura [miʃ'tura] *f* mixture; (*ato*) mixing.
misturada [miʃtu'rada] *f* jumble.
misturar [miʃtu'ra*] *vt* to mix; (*confundir*) to mix up; ~**-se** *vr*: ~**-se com** to mix in with, mingle with.
mítico/a ['mitʃiku/a] *adj* mythical.
mitificar [mitʃifi'ka*] *vt* to mythicize; (*mulher, estrela*) to idolize.
mitigar [mitʃi'ga*] *vt* (*raiva*) to temper; (*dor*) to relieve; (*sede*) to lessen.
mito ['mitu] *m* myth.
mitologia [mitolo'ʒia] *f* mythology.
mitológico/a [mito'lɔʒiku/a] *adj* mythological.
miudezas [mju'dezaʃ] *fpl* minutiae; (*bugigangas*) odds and ends; (*objetos pequenos*) trinkets.

NB: European Portuguese adds the following consonants to certain words: **b** (sú(b)dito, su(b)til); **c** (a(c)ção, a(c)cionista, a(c)to); **m** (inde(m)ne); **p** (ado(p)ção, ado(p)tar); *for further details see p. xiii.*

miúdo/a ['mjudu/a] *adj* (*pequeno*) tiny, minute ♦ *m/f* (*PT*: *criança*) youngster, kid; **~s** *mpl* (*dinheiro*) change *sg*; (*de aves*) giblets; **dinheiro ~** small change; **trocar em ~s** (*fig*) to spell it out.
mixa ['miʃa] (*col*) *adj* (*insignificante*) measly; (*de má qualidade*) crummy; (*festa*) dull.
mixagem [mik'saʒẽ] *f* mixing.
mixar[1] [mi'ʃa*] *vt* to mess up ♦ *vi* (*gorar*) to go down the drain; (*acabar*) to finish.
mixar[2] [mik'sa*] *vt* (*sons*) to mix.
mixaria [miʃa'ria] (*col*) *f* (*coisa sem valor*) trifle; (*insignificância*) trivial matter.
mixórdia [mi'ʃɔxdʒja] *f* mess, jumble.
MJ *abr m* = **Ministério da Justiça**.
MM *abr m* = **Ministério da Marinha**.
mm *abr* (= *milímetro*) mm.
MME (*BR*) *abr m* = **Ministério de Minas e Energia**.
mnemônico/a [mne'moniku/a] *adj* mnemonic.
mo [mu] *pron* = **me** + **o**.
mó [mɔ] *f* (*de moinho*) millstone; (*para afiar*) grindstone.
moa ['moa] *etc vb V* **moer**.
moagem ['mwaʒẽ] *f* grinding.
móbil ['mɔbiw] (*pl* **-eis**) *adj* = **móvel**.
mobilar [mobi'la*] (*PT*) *vt* to furnish.
móbile ['mɔbili] *m* mobile.
mobília [mo'bilja] *f* furniture.
mobiliar [mobi'lja*] (*BR*) *vt* to furnish.
mobiliária [mobi'ljarja] *f* furniture shop.
mobiliário [mobi'ljarju] *m* furnishings *pl*.
mobilidade [mobili'dadʒi] *f* mobility; (*fig*: *de espírito*) changeability.
mobilização [mobiliza'sãw] *f* mobilization.
mobilizar [mobili'za*] *vt* to mobilize; (*movimentar*) to move.
Mobral [mo'braw] *abr m* = **Movimento Brasileiro de Alfabetização**.
moça ['mosa] *f* girl, young woman.
moçada [mo'sada] *f* (*moços*) boys *pl*; (*moças*) girls *pl*.
moçambicano/a [mosãbi'kanu/a] *adj*, *m/f* Mozambican.
Moçambique [mosã'biki] *m* Mozambique.
moção [mo'sãw] (*pl* **-ões**) *f* motion.
mocassim [moka'sĩ] (*pl* **-ns**) *m* mocassin; (*sapato esporte*) slip-on.
mochila [mo'ʃila] *f* rucksack.
mocidade [mosi'dadʒi] *f* youth; (*os moços*) young people.
mocinho/a [mo'siɲu/a] *m/f* little boy/girl ♦ *m* (*herói*) hero, good guy.
moço/a ['mosu/a] *adj* young ♦ *m* young man, lad; **~ de bordo** ordinary seaman; **~ de cavalariça** groom.
moções [mo'sõjʃ] *fpl de* **moção**.
mocorongo/a [moko'rõgu/a] (*col*) *m/f* country bumpkin.
moda ['mɔda] *f* fashion; **estar na ~** to be in fashion, be all the rage; **fora da ~** old-fashioned; **sair da** *ou* **cair de ~** to go out of fashion; **a última ~** the latest fashion; **à ~ brasileira** in the Brazilian way; **ele faz tudo à sua ~** he does everything his own way; **fazer ~** to make up stories.
modalidade [modali'dadʒi] *f* kind; (*ESPORTE*) event.
modelagem [mode'laʒẽ] *f* modelling; **~ do corpo** bodybuilding.
modelar [mode'la*] *vt* to model; (*assinalar os contornos de*) to shape, highlight; **~(-se) a algo** to model (o.s.) on sth.
modelista [mode'liʃta] *m/f* designer.
modelo [mo'delu] *m* model; (*criação de estilista*) design.
moderação [modera'sãw] (*pl* **-ões**) *f* moderation.
moderado/a [mode'radu/a] *adj* moderate; (*clima*) mild.
moderar [mode'ra*] *vt* to moderate; (*violência*) to control, restrain; (*velocidade*) to reduce; (*voz*) to lower; (*gastos*) to cut down; **~-se** *vr* to control o.s.
modernidade [modexni'dadʒi] *f* modernity.
modernismo [modex'niʒmu] *m* modernism.
modernização [modexniza'sãw] (*pl* **-ões**) *f* modernization.
modernizar [modexni'za*] *vt* to modernize; **~-se** *vr* to modernize.
moderno/a [mo'dɛxnu/a] *adj* modern; (*atual*) present-day.
modernoso/a [modex'nozu/ɔza] *adj* new-fangled.
módess ['mɔdeʃ] ® (*col*) *m inv* sanitary towel (*BRIT*) *ou* napkin (*US*).
modéstia [mo'dɛʃtʃja] *f* modesty.
modesto/a [mo'dɛʃtu/a] *adj* modest; (*simples*) simple, plain; (*vida*) frugal.
módico/a ['mɔdʒiku/a] *adj* moderate; (*preço*) reasonable; (*bens*) scant.
modificação [modʒifika'sãw] (*pl* **-ões**) *f* modification.
modificar [modʒifi'ka*] *vt* to modify, alter.
modinha [mo'dʒiɲa] *f* popular song, tune.
modismo [mo'dʒiʒmu] *m* idiom.
modista [mo'dʒiʃta] *f* dressmaker.
modo ['mɔdu] *m* (*maneira*) way, manner; (*método*) way; (*LING*) mood; (*MÚS*) mode; **~s** *mpl* manners; **~ de pensar** way of thinking; **de (tal) ~ que** so (that); **de ~ nenhum** in no way; **de qualquer ~** anyway, anyhow; **tenha ~s!** behave yourself!; **de ~ geral** in general; **~ de andar** way of walking, walk; **~ de escrever** style of writing; **~ de emprego** instructions *pl* for use; **~ de ser** way (of being), manner; **~ de vida** way of life.
modorra [mo'doxa] *f* (*sonolência*) drowsiness; (*letargia*) lethargy.
modulação [modula'sãw] (*pl* **-ões**) *f* modulation; **~ de freqüência** frequency modulation.
modular [modu'la*] *vt* to modulate ♦ *adj* modular.
módulo ['mɔdulu] *m* module; **~ lunar** lunar module.
moeda ['mwɛda] *f* (*uma*) coin; (*dinheiro*)

currency; **uma ~ de 10p** a 10p piece; **~ corrente** currency; **pagar na mesma ~** to give tit for tat; **Casa da M~** the Mint (*BRIT*), the (US) Mint; **~ falsa** forged money; **~ forte** hard currency.

moedor [moe'do*] *m* (*de café*) grinder; (*de carne*) mincer.

moenda ['mwẽda] *f* grinding equipment.

moer [mwe*] *vt* (*café*) to grind; (*cana*) to crush; (*bater*) to beat; (*cansar*) to tire out.

mofado/a [mo'fadu/a] *adj* mouldy (*BRIT*), moldy (*US*).

mofar [mo'fa*] *vi* to go mouldy (*BRIT*) *ou* moldy (*US*); (*na prisão*) to rot; (*ficar esperando*) to hang around; (*zombar*) to mock, scoff ♦ *vt* to cover in mo(u)ld.

mofo ['mofu] *m* (*BOT*) mould (*BRIT*), mold (*US*); **cheiro de ~** musty smell.

mogno ['mɔgnu] *m* mahogany.

mói [mɔj] *etc vb V* **moer**.

moía [mo'ia] *etc vb V* **moer**.

moído/a [mo'idu/a] *pp de* **moer** ♦ *adj* (*café*) ground; (*carne*) minced; (*cansado*) tired out; (*corpo*) aching.

moinho ['mwiɲu] *m* mill; (*de café*) grinder; **~ de vento** windmill.

moisés [moj'zɛʃ] *m inv* carry-cot.

moita ['mɔjta] *f* thicket; **~!** mum's the word!; **na ~** (*fig*) on the quiet; **ficar na ~** (*fazer segredo*) to keep quiet, not say a word; (*ficar na expectativa*) to stand by.

mola ['mɔla] *f* (*TEC*) spring; (*fig*) motive, motivation.

molambo [mo'lãbu] *m* rag.

molar [mo'la*] *m* molar (tooth).

moldar [mow'da*] *vt* to mould (*BRIT*), mold (*US*); (*metal*) to cast; (*fig*) to mo(u)ld, shape.

Moldávia [mow'davja] *f*: **a ~** Moldavia.

molde ['mɔwdʒi] *m* mould (*BRIT*), mold (*US*); (*de papel*) pattern; (*fig*) model; **~ de vestido** dress pattern.

moldura [mow'dura] *f* (*de pintura*) frame; (*ornato*) moulding (*BRIT*), molding (*US*).

moldurar [mowdu'ra*] *vt* to frame.

mole ['mɔli] *adj* (*macio, fofo*) soft; (*sem energia*) listless; (*carnes*) flabby; (*col*: *fácil*) easy; (*pessoa*: *sentimental*) soft; (*lento*) slow; (*preguiçoso*) sluggish ♦ *adv* (*facilmente*) easily; (*lentamente*) slowly.

moleca [mo'lɛka] *f* urchin; (*menina*) youngster.

molecada [mole'kada] *f* urchins *pl*.

molecagem [mole'kaʒẽ] (*pl* **-ns**) *f* (*de criança*) piece of mischief; (*sujeira*) dirty trick; (*brincadeira*) joke.

molécula [mo'lɛkula] *f* molecule.

molecular [moleku'la*] *adj* molecular.

molejo [mo'leʒu] *m* (*de carro*) suspension; (*col*: *de pessoa*) wiggle.

moleque [mo'lɛki] *m* (*de rua*) urchin; (*menino*) youngster; (*pessoa sem palavra*) unreliable person; (*canalha*) scoundrel ♦ *adj* (*levado*) mischievous; (*brincalhão*) funny.

molestar [moleʃ'ta*] *vt* (*ofender*) to upset; (*enfadar*) to annoy; (*importunar*) to bother.

moléstia [mo'lɛʃtʃja] *f* illness.

molesto/a [mo'lɛʃtu/a] *adj* tiresome; (*prejudicial*) unhealthy.

moletom [mole'tõ] (*pl* **-ns**) *m* (*de lã*) fleece; (*de algodão*) sweatshirt material; **blusa de ~** sweatshirt.

moleza [mo'leza] *f* softness; (*falta de energia*) listlessness; (*falta de força*) weakness; **ser (uma) ~** (*col*) to be easy; **na ~** without exerting oneself.

molhada [mo'ʎada] *f* soaking.

molhado/a [mo'ʎadu/a] *adj* wet, damp.

molhar [mo'ʎa*] *vt* to wet; (*de leve*) to moisten, dampen; (*mergulhar*) to dip; **~-se** *vr* to get wet; (*col*: *urinar*) to wet o.s.

molhe ['moʎi] (*PT*) *m* jetty; (*cais*) wharf, quay.

molheira [mo'ʎejra] *f* sauce boat; (*para carne*) gravy boat.

molho[1] ['mɔʎu] *m* (*de chaves*) bunch; (*de trigo*) sheaf.

molho[2] ['moʎu] *m* (*CULIN*) sauce; (: *de salada*) dressing; (: *de carne*) gravy; **pôr de ~** to soak; **estar/deixar de ~** (*roupa etc*) to be/leave to soak; **estar/ficar de ~** (*fig*) to be/stay in bed; **~ branco** white sauce; **~ inglês** Worcester sauce.

molinete [moli'netʃi] *m* reel; (*caniço*) fishing rod.

molóide [mo'lɔjdʒi] (*col*) *adj* slow ♦ *m/f* lazybones.

molusco [mo'luʃku] *m* mollusc (*BRIT*), mollusk (*US*).

momentâneo/a [momẽ'tanju/a] *adj* momentary.

momento [mo'mẽtu] *m* moment; (*TEC*) momentum; **a todo ~** constantly; **de um ~ para outro** suddenly; **no ~ em que** just as; **no/neste ~** at the/this moment; **a qualquer ~** at any moment.

Mônaco ['monaku] *m* Monaco.

monarca [mo'naxka] *m/f* monarch, ruler.

monarquia [monax'kia] *f* monarchy.

monarquista [monax'kiʃta] *adj, m/f* monarchist.

monastério [monaʃ'tɛrju] *m* monastery.

monástico/a [mo'naʃtʃiku/a] *adj* monastic.

monção [mõ'sãw] (*pl* **-ões**) *f* monsoon.

mondar [mõ'da*] (*PT*) *vt* (*ervas daninhas*) to pull up; (*árvores*) to prune; (*fig*) to weed out.

monetário/a [mone'tarju/a] *adj* monetary; **correção monetária** currency adjustment.

monetarismo [moneta'riʒmu] *m* monetarism.

monetarista [moneta'riʃta] *adj, m/f* monetar-

***NB**: European Portuguese adds the following consonants to certain words:* **b** (sú(b)dito, su(b)til); **c** (a(c)ção, a(c)cionista, a(c)to); **m** (inde(m)ne); **p** (ado(p)ção, ado(p)tar); *for further details see p. xiii.*

ist.

monge ['mõʒɪ] *m* monk.

mongol [mõ'gɔw] (*pl* **-óis**) *adj, m/f* Mongol, Mongolian.

Mongólia [mõ'gɔlja] *f*: **a ~** Mongolia.

mongolismo [mõgo'liʒmu] *m* (*MED*) mongolism.

mongolóide [mõgo'lɔjdʒi] *adj, m/f* mongol.

monitor [moni'to*] *m* monitor; **~ (de vídeo)** (*COMPUT*) monitor, VDU.

monitorar [monito'ra*] *vt* to monitor.

monitorizar [monitori'za*] *vt* = **monitorar**.

monja ['mõʒa] *f* nun.

monocromo/a [mono'krɔmu/a] *adj* monochrome.

monóculo [mo'nɔkulu] *m* monocle.

monocultura [monokuw'tura] *f* monoculture.

monogamia [monoga'mia] *f* monogamy.

monógamo/a [mo'nɔgamu/a] *adj* monogamous.

monograma [mono'grama] *m* monogram.

monologar [monolo'ga*] *vi* to talk to o.s.; (*TEATRO*) to speak a monologue ♦ *vt* to say to o.s.

monólogo [mo'nɔlogu] *m* monologue.

monoplano [mono'planu] *m* monoplane.

monopólio [mono'pɔlju] *m* monopoly.

monopolizar [monopoli'za*] *vt* to monopolize.

monossilábico/a [monosi'labiku/a] *adj* monosyllabic.

monossílabo [mono'silabu] *m* monosyllable; **responder por ~s** to reply in monosyllables.

monotonia [monoto'nia] *f* monotony.

monótono/a [mo'nɔtonu/a] *adj* monotonous.

monotrilho [mono'triʎu] *m* monorail.

monóxido [mo'nɔksidu] *m*: **~ de carbono** carbon monoxide.

monsenhor [mõse'ɲo*] *m* monsignor.

monstro/a ['mõʃtru/a] *adj inv* giant ♦ *m* (*tb fig*) monster; **~ sagrado** superstar.

monstruosidade [mõʃtrwozi'dadʒi] *f* monstrosity.

monstruoso/a [mõ'ʃtrwozu/ɔza] *adj* monstrous; (*enorme*) gigantic, huge.

monta ['mõta] *f*: **de pouca ~** trivial, of little account.

montador(a) [mõta'do*(a)] *m/f* (*CINEMA*) editor.

montagem [mõ'taʒẽ] (*pl* **-ns**) *f* assembly; (*ARQ*) erection; (*CINEMA*) editing; (*TEATRO*) production.

montanha [mõ'taɲa] *f* mountain.

montanha-russa *f* roller coaster.

montanhês/esa [mõta'ɲeʃ/eza] *adj* mountain *atr* ♦ *m/f* highlander.

montanhismo [mõta'ɲiʒmu] *m* mountaineering.

montanhista [mõta'ɲiʃta] *m/f* mountaineer ♦ *adj* mountaineering.

montanhoso/a [mõta'ɲozu/ɔza] *adj* mountainous.

montante [mõ'tãtʃi] *m* amount, sum ♦ *adj* (*maré*) rising; **a ~** upstream.

montão [mõ'tãw] (*pl* **-ões**) *m* heap, pile.

montar [mõ'ta*] *vt* (*subir a*) to mount, get on; (*colocar em*) to put on; (*cavalgar*) to ride; (*peças*) to assemble, put together; (*loja, máquina*) to set up; (*casa*) to put up; (*peça teatral*) to put on ♦ *vi* to ride; **~ a** *ou* **em** (*animal*) to get on; (*cavalgar*) to ride; (*despesa*) to come to.

montaria [mõta'ria] *f* (*cavalgadura*) mount.

monte ['mõtʃi] *m* hill; (*pilha*) heap, pile; **um ~ de** (*muitos*) a lot of, lots of; **gente aos ~s** loads of people.

montepio [mõtʃi'piu] *m* (*pensão*) pension; (*fundo*) trust fund.

montês [mõ'teʃ] *adj*: **cabra ~** mountain goat.

Montevidéu [mõtʃivi'dɛw] *n* Montevideo.

montoeira [mõ'twejra] *f* stack.

montões [mõ'tõjʃ] *mpl de* **montão**.

montra ['mõtra] (*PT*) *f* shop window.

monumental [monumẽ'taw] (*pl* **-ais**) *adj* monumental; (*fig*) magnificent, splendid.

monumento [monu'mẽtu] *m* monument.

moqueca [mo'kɛka] *f fish or seafood simmered in pepper and oil*; **~ de camarão** prawn moqueca.

morada [mo'rada] *f* home, residence; (*PT*: *endereço*) address.

moradia [mora'dʒia] *f* home, dwelling.

morador(a) [mora'do*(a)] *m/f* (*de casa, bairro*) resident; (*de casa alugada*) tenant.

moral [mo'raw] (*pl* **-ais**) *adj* moral ♦ *f* (*ética*) ethics *pl*; (*conclusão*) moral; (*ânimo*) morale ♦ *m* (*de pessoa*) sense of morality; (*ânimo*) morale; **levantar a ~** to raise morale; **estar de ~ baixa** to be demoralized; **~ da história** moral of the story.

moralidade [morali'dadʒi] *f* morality.

moralista [mora'liʃta] *adj* moralistic ♦ *m/f* moralist.

moralizar [morali'za*] *vi* to moralize ♦ *vt* to preach at.

morango [mo'rãgu] *m* strawberry.

morangueiro [morã'gejru] *m* strawberry plant.

morar [mo'ra*] *vi* to live, reside; (*col*: *entender*) to catch on; **~ em algo** (*col*) to grasp sth; **morou?** got it?, see?

moratória [mora'tɔrja] *f* moratorium.

morbidez [moxbi'deʒ] *f* morbidness.

mórbido/a ['mɔxbidu/a] *adj* morbid.

morcego [mox'segu] *m* (*BIO*) bat.

morcela [mox'sɛla] (*PT*) *f* black pudding (*BRIT*), blood sausage (*US*).

mordaça [mox'dasa] *f* (*de animal*) muzzle; (*fig*) gag.

mordaz [mox'daʒ] *adj* scathing.

morder [mox'de*] *vt* to bite; (*corroer*) to corrode; **~-se** *vr* to bite o.s.; **~ a língua** to bite one's tongue; **~-se de inveja** to be green with envy.

mordida [mox'dʒida] *f* bite.

mordomia [moxdo'mia] *f* (*de executivos*) perk; (*col*: *regalia*) luxury, comfort.

mordomo [mox'dɔmu] *m* butler.
morenaço/a [more'nasu/a] *m/f* dark beauty.
moreno/a [mo'renu/a] *adj* dark(-skinned); (*de cabelos*) dark(-haired); (*de tomar sol*) brown ♦ *m/f* dark person; **ela é loura ou morena?** is she a blonde or a brunette?
morfina [mox'fina] *f* morphine.
morfologia [moxfolo'ʒia] *f* morphology.
morgada [mox'gada] *f* heiress.
morgado [mox'gadu] (*PT*) *m* (*herdeiro*) heir; (*filho mais velho*) eldest son; (*propriedade*) entailed estate.
moribundo/a [mori'bũdu/a] *adj* dying.
morigerado/a [moriʒe'radu/a] *adj* upright.
moringa [mo'rĩga] *f* water-cooler.
mormacento/a [moxma'sẽtu/a] *adj* sultry.
mormaço [mox'masu] *m* sultry weather.
mormente [mox'mẽtʃi] *adv* chiefly, especially.
mórmon ['mɔxmõ] *m/f* Mormon.
morno/a ['moxnu/'mɔxna] *adj* lukewarm, tepid.
morosidade [morozi'dadʒi] *f* slowness.
moroso/a [mo'rozu/ɔza] *adj* slow, sluggish.
morrer [mo'xe*] *vi* to die; (*luz, cor*) to fade; (*fogo*) to die down; (*AUTO*) to stall; ~ **de rir** to kill o.s. laughing; **estou morrendo de fome/inveja/medo/saudades** I'm starving/ green with envy/scared stiff/really missing you (*ou* him, home *etc*); ~ **de amores por alguém** to be mad about sb; **estou morrendo de vontade de fazer** I'm dying to do; ~ **atropelado/afogado** to be knocked down and killed/drown; **lindo de** ~ (*col*) stunning; ~ **em** (*col*: *pagar*) to fork out.
morrinha [mo'xiɲa] *f* (*fedor*) stench ♦ *m/f* (*col*: *chato*) pain (in the neck) ♦ *adj* (*col*) boring.
morro ['moxu] *m* hill; (*favela*) shanty-town, slum.
mortadela [moxta'dɛla] *f* salami.
mortal [mox'taw] (*pl* **-ais**) *adj* mortal; (*letal, insuportável*) deadly; (*pecado*) deadly ♦ *m* mortal; **restos mortais** mortal remains.
mortalha [mox'taʎa] *f* shroud.
mortalidade [moxtali'dadʒi] *f* mortality; ~ **infantil** infant mortality.
mortandade [moxtã'dadʒi] *f* slaughter.
morte ['mɔxtʃi] *f* death; **pena de** ~ death penalty; **ser de** ~ (*fig*) to be impossible; **estar às portas da** ~ to be at death's door; **pensar na** ~ **da bezerra** (*fig*) to be miles away.
morteiro [mox'tejru] *m* mortar.
mortiço/a [mox'tʃisu/a] *adj* (*olhar*) dull; (*desanimado*) lifeless; (*luz*) dimming.
mortífero/a [mox'tʃiferu/a] *adj* deadly, lethal.
mortificar [moxtʃifi'ka*] *vt* (*torturar*) to torture; (*afligir*) to annoy, torment.
morto/a ['moxtu/'mɔxta] *pp de* **matar; morrer** ♦ *adj* (*cor*) dull; (*exausto*) exhausted; (*inexpressivo*) lifeless ♦ *m/f* dead man/woman; **cem/os ~s** a hundred/the dead; **estar** ~ to be dead; **ser** ~ to be killed; **estar** ~ **de inveja** to be green with envy; **estar** ~ **de vontade de** to be dying to; ~ **de medo/cansaço** scared stiff/dead tired; **nem ~!** not on your life!, no way!; ~ **da silva** (*col*) dead as a doornail.
mos [muʃ] *pron* = **me** + **os.**
mosaico [mo'zajku] *m* mosaic.
mosca ['moʃka] *f* fly; **estar às ~s** (*bar etc*) to be deserted.
mosca-morta (*pl* **moscas-mortas**) (*col*) *m/f* (*pessoa*) stiff.
Moscou [moʃ'ku] (*BR*) *n* Moscow.
Moscovo [moʃ'kovu] (*PT*) *n* Moscow.
mosquitada [moʃki'tada] *f* load of mosquitos.
mosquiteiro [moʃki'tejru] *m* mosquito net.
mosquito [moʃ'kitu] *m* mosquito.
mossa ['mɔsa] *f* dent; (*fig*) impression.
mostarda [moʃ'taxda] *f* mustard.
mosteiro [moʃ'tejru] *m* monastery; (*de monjas*) convent.
mosto ['moʃtu] *m* (*do vinho*) must.
mostra ['mɔʃtra] *f* (*exibição*) display; (*sinal*) sign, indication; **dar ~s de** to show signs of.
mostrador [moʃtra'do*] *m* (*de relógio*) face, dial.
mostrar [moʃ'tra*] *vt* to show; (*mercadorias*) to display; (*provar*) to demonstrate, prove; **~-se** *vr* to show o.s. to be; (*exibir-se*) to show off.
mostruário [moʃ'trwarju] *m* display case.
mote ['mɔtʃi] *m* motto.
motel [mo'tɛw] (*pl* **-éis**) *m* motel.
motejar [mote'ʒa*] *vi*: ~ **de** (*zombar*) to jeer at, make fun of.
motejo [mo'teʒu] *m* mockery, derision.
motilidade [motʃili'dadʒi] *f* mobility.
motim [mo'tʃĩ] (*pl* **-ns**) *m* riot, revolt; (*militar*) mutiny.
motivação [motʃiva'sãw] (*pl* **-ões**) *f* motivation.
motivado/a [motʃi'vadu/a] *adj* (*causado*) caused; (*pessoa*) motivated.
motivar [motʃi'va*] *vt* (*causar*) to cause, bring about; (*estimular*) to motivate.
motivo [mo'tʃivu] *m* (*causa*): ~ **(de** *ou* **para)** cause (of), reason (for); (*fim*) motive; (*ARTE, MÚS*) motif; **ser** ~ **de riso** *etc* to be a cause of laughter *etc*; **dar** ~ **de algo a alguém** to give sb cause for sth; **por** ~ **de** because of, owing to; **sem** ~ for no reason.
moto ['mɔtu] *f* motorbike ♦ *m* (*lema*) motto; **de** ~ **próprio** of one's own accord.
motoca [mo'tɔka] (*col*) *f* motorbike, bike.
motocicleta [motosi'kleta] *f* motorcycle, motorbike.
motociclismo [motosi'kliʒmu] *m* motorcycling.
motociclista [motosi'kliʃta] *m/f* motorcyclist.

***NB**: European Portuguese adds the following consonants to certain words:* **b** (sú(b)dito, su(b)til); **c** (a(c)ção, a(c)cionista, a(c)to); **m** (inde(m)ne); **p** (ado(p)ção, ado(p)tar); *for further details see p. xiii.*

motociclo [moto'siklu] (PT) *m* = **motocicleta**.
motoneta [moto'neta] *f* (motor-)scooter.
motoniveladora [motonivela'dora] *f* bulldozer.
motoqueiro/a [moto'kejru/a] (*col*) *m/f* biker, motorcyclist.
motor/motriz [mo'to*/mo'triʒ] *adj* (TEC) driving; (ANAT) motor ♦ *m* motor; (*de carro, avião*) engine; ~ **de arranque** starter (motor); ~ **de explosão** internal combustion engine; ~ **de popa** outboard motor; ~ **diesel** diesel engine; **com** ~ motorized.
motorista [moto'riʃta] *m/f* driver.
motorizado/a [motori'zadu/a] *adj* motorized; (*col: com carro*) motorized, driving.
motorizar [motori'za*] *vt* to motorize; **~-se** *vr* to get a car.
motorneiro/a [motox'nejru/a] *m/f* tram (BRIT) *ou* streetcar (US) driver.
motoserra [moto'sɛxa] *f* chain-saw.
motriz [mo'triʒ] *f de* **motor**; **força** ~ driving force.
mouco/a ['moku/a] *adj* deaf, hard of hearing; **fazer ouvido** ~ to pretend not to hear.
movediço/a [move'dʒisu/a] *adj* easily moved; (*instável*) unsteady; *V tb* **areia**.
móvel ['mɔvew] (*pl* **-eis**) *adj* movable ♦ *m* (*peça de mobília*) piece of furniture; **móveis** *mpl* furniture *sg*; **bens móveis** personal property; **móveis e utensílios** (COM) fixtures and fittings.
mover [mo've*] *vt* to move; (*cabeça*) to shake; (*mecanismo: acionar*) to drive; (*campanha*) to set in motion; **~-se** *vr* to move; ~ **uma ação** to start a lawsuit; ~ **alguém a fazer** to move sb to do.
movido/a [mo'vidu/a] *adj* moved; (*impelido*) powered; (*causado*) caused; ~ **a álcool** alcohol-powered.
movimentação [movimẽta'sãw] (*pl* **-ões**) *f* movement; (*na rua*) bustle.
movimentado/a [movimẽ'tadu/a] *adj* (*rua, lugar*) busy; (*pessoa*) active; (*show, música*) up-tempo.
movimentar [movimẽ'ta*] *vt* to move; (*animar*) to liven up.
movimento [movi'mẽtu] *m* movement; (TEC) motion; (*na rua*) activity, bustle; **de muito** ~ (*loja, rua etc*) busy; **pôr algo em** ~ to set sth in motion.
movível [mo'vivew] (*pl* **-eis**) *adj* movable.
MPAS (BR) *abr m* = **Ministério da Previdência e Assistência Social**.
MPB *abr f* = **Música Popular Brasileira**.
MPlan (BR) *abr m* = **Ministério do Planejamento**.
MRE (BR) *abr m* = **Ministério das Relações Exteriores**.
MS (BR) *abr* = **Mato Grosso do Sul** ♦ *abr m* = **Ministério da Saúde**.
MT (BR) *abr* = **Mato Grosso** ♦ *abr m* = **Ministério dos Transportes**.
MTb (BR) *abr m* = **Ministério do Trabalho**.
muamba ['mwãba] (*col*) *f* (*contrabando*) contraband; (*objetos roubados*) loot.
muambeiro/a [mwã'bejru/a] *m/f* smuggler; (*de objetos roubados*) fence.
muar [mwa*] *m/f* mule.
muco ['muku] *m* mucus.
mucosa [mu'kɔza] *f* (ANAT) mucous membrane.
muçulmano/a [musuw'manu/a] *adj, m/f* Moslem.
muda ['muda] *f* (*planta*) seedling; (*vestuário*) outfit; ~ **de roupa** change of clothes.
mudança [mu'dãsa] *f* change; (*de casa*) move; (AUTO) gear.
mudar [mu'da*] *vt* to change; (*deslocar*) to move ♦ *vi* to change; (*ave*) to moult (BRIT), molt (US); **~-se** *vr* (*de casa*) to move (away); ~ **de roupa/de assunto** to change clothes/the subject; ~ **de casa** to move (house); ~ **de idéia** to change one's mind.
mudez [mu'deʒ] *f* muteness; (*silêncio*) silence.
mudo/a ['mudu/a] *adj* dumb; (*calado*, CINEMA) silent; (*telefone*) dead ♦ *m/f* mute.
mugido [mu'ʒidu] *m* moo.
mugir [mu'ʒi*] *vi* (*vaca*) to moo, low.
mugunzá [mugũ'za] *m* = **munguzá**.
muito/a ['mwĩtu/a] *adj* a lot of; (*em frase negativa ou interrogativa: sg*) much, (: *pl*) many ♦ *pron* a lot; (*em frase negativa ou interrogativa: sg*) much; (: *pl*) many ♦ *adv* a lot; (+ *adj*) very; (+ *compar*): ~ **melhor** much *ou* far *ou* a lot better; ~ **admirado** much admired; ~ **tempo** a long time; ~ **depois** long after; **há** ~ a long time ago; **não demorou** ~ it didn't take long; **muitas vezes** often; **por** ~ **que** however much; **quando** ~ at most; **ter** ~ **de alguém** (*parecer-se com*) to look a lot like sb; **ele faz** ~ **erro** he makes a lot of mistakes.
mula ['mula] *f* mule.
mulato/a [mu'latu/a] *adj, m/f* mulatto.
muleta [mu'leta] *f* crutch; (*fig*) support.
mulher [mu'ʎe*] *f* woman; (*esposa*) wife; ~ **da vida** prostitute.
mulheraço [muʎe'rasu] *m* fantastic woman.
mulherão [muʎe'rãw] (*pl* **-ões**) *m* = **mulheraço**.
mulherengo [muʎe'rẽgu] *m* womanizer ♦ *adj* womanizing.
mulherio [muʎe'riu] *m* women *pl*.
multa ['muwta] *f* fine; **levar uma** ~ to get fined.
multar [muw'ta*] *vt* to fine; ~ **alguém em $1000** to fine sb $1000.
multi- [muwtʃi-] *prefixo* multi-.
multicolor [muwtʃiko'lo*] *adj* multicoloured (BRIT), multicolored (US).
multidão [muwtʃi'dãw] (*pl* **-ões**) *f* crowd; **uma** ~ **de** (*muitos*) lots of.
multiforme [muwtʃi'fɔxme] *adj* manifold, multifarious.
multilateral [muwtʃilate'raw] (*pl* **-ais**) *adj* multilateral.

multimilionário/a [muwtʃimiljo'narju/a] *adj, m/f* multimillionaire.
multinacional [muwtʃinasjo'naw] (*pl* **-ais**) *adj, f* multinational.
multiplicação [muwtʃiplika'sãw] *f* multiplication.
multiplicar [muwtʃipli'ka*] *vt* (MAT) to multiply; (*aumentar*) to increase.
multiplicidade [muwtʃiplisi'dadʒi] *f* multiplicity.
múltiplo/a ['muwtʃiplu/a] *adj* multiple ♦ *m* multiple; **múltipla escolha** multiple choice.
multirracial [muwtʃixa'sjaw] (*pl* **-ais**) *adj* multiracial.
multiusuário/a [muwtʃju'zwarju/a] *adj* (COMPUT) multiuser.
múmia ['mumja] *f* mummy; (*fig*) plodder.
mundano/a [mũ'danu/a] *adj* worldly.
mundial [mũ'dʒjaw] (*pl* **-ais**) *adj* worldwide; (*guerra, recorde*) world ♦ *m* (*campeonato*) world championship; **o ~ de futebol** the World Cup.
mundo ['mũdu] *m* world; **todo o ~** everybody; **um ~ de** lots of, a great many; **correr ~** to see the world; **vir ao ~** to come into the world; **como este ~ é pequeno!** (what a) small world!; **desde que o ~ é ~** since time immemorial; **~s e fundos** (*quantia altíssima*) the earth; **prometer ~s e fundos** to promise the earth; **tinha meio ~ no comício** there were loads of people at the rally; **com esta notícia meu ~ veio abaixo** the news shattered my world; **abarcar o ~ com as pernas** (*fig*) to take on too much; **Novo/Velho/Terceiro M~** New/Old/Third World.
munguzá [mũgu'za] *m* corn meal.
munheca [mu'ɲeka] *f* wrist.
munição [muni'sãw] (*pl* **-ões**) *f* (*de armas*) ammunition; (*chumbo*) shot; (MIL) munitions *pl*, supplies *pl*.
municipal [munisi'paw] (*pl* **-ais**) *adj* municipal.
municipalidade [munisipali'dadʒi] *f* local authority.
município [muni'sipju] *m* local authority; (*cidade*) town; (*condado*) county.
munições [muni'sõjʃ] *fpl de* **munição**.
munir [mu'ni*] *vt*: **~ de** to provide with, supply with; **~-se** *vr*: **~-se de** (*provisões*) to equip o.s. with; (*paciência*) to arm o.s. with.
mural [mu'raw] (*pl* **-ais**) *adj, m* mural.
muralha [mu'raʎa] *f* (*de fortaleza*) rampart; (*muro*) wall.
murchar [mux'ʃa*] *vt* (BOT) to wither; (*sentimentos*) to dull; (*pessoa*) to sadden ♦ *vi* (BOT) to wither, wilt; (*fig*) to fade; (: *pessoa*) to grow sad.
murcho/a ['muxʃu/a] *adj* (*planta*) wilting; (*esvaziado*) shrunken; (*fig*) languid, resigned.
murmuração [muxmura'sãw] *f* muttering; (*maledicência*) gossiping.
murmurante [muxmu'rãtʃi] *adj* murmuring.
murmurar [muxmu'ra*] *vi* (*segredar*) to murmur, whisper; (*queixar-se*) to mutter, grumble; (*água*) to ripple; (*folhagem*) to rustle ♦ *vt* to murmur.
murmurinho [muxmu'riɲu] *m* (*de vozes*) murmuring; (*som confuso*) noise; (*de folhas*) rustling; (*de água*) trickling.
murmúrio [mux'murju] *m* murmuring, whispering; (*queixa*) grumbling; (*de água*) rippling; (*de folhagem*) rustling.
muro ['muru] *m* wall.
murro ['muxu] *m* punch, sock; **dar um ~ em alguém** to punch sb; **levar um ~ de alguém** to be punched by sb; **dar ~ em ponta de faca** (*fig*) to bash one's head against a brick wall.
musa ['muza] *f* muse.
musculação [muʃkula'sãw] *f* body-building.
muscular [muʃku'la*] *adj* muscular.
musculatura [muʃkula'tura] *f* musculature.
músculo ['muʃkulu] *m* muscle.
musculoso/a [muʃku'lozu/ɔza] *adj* muscular.
museu [mu'zew] *m* museum; (*de pintura*) gallery.
musgo ['muʒgu] *m* moss.
musgoso/a [muʒ'gozu/ɔza] *adj* mossy.
música ['muzika] *f* music; (*canção*) song; **dançar conforme a ~** (*fig*) to play the game; **~ de câmara** chamber music; **~ de fundo** background music; **~ erudita** classical music; **~ folclórica** folk music; *V tb* **músico**.
musicado/a [muzi'kadu/a] *adj* set to music.
musical [muzi'kaw] (*pl* **-ais**) *adj, m* musical; **fundo ~** background music.
musicalidade [muzikali'dadʒi] *f* musicality.
músico/a ['muziku/a] *adj* musical ♦ *m/f* musician.
musse ['musi] *f* mousse.
musselina [muse'lina] *f* muslin.
mutação [muta'sãw] (*pl* **-ões**) *f* change, alteration; (BIO) mutation.
mutável [mu'tavew] (*pl* **-eis**) *adj* changeable.
mutilação [mutʃila'sãw] *f* mutilation; (*de texto*) cutting.
mutilado/a [mutʃi'ladu/a] *adj* mutilated; (*pessoa*) maimed ♦ *m/f* cripple.
mutilar [mutʃi'la*] *vt* to mutilate; (*pessoa*) to maim; (*texto*) to cut; (*árvore*) to strip.
mutirão [mutʃi'rãw] (*pl* **-ões**) *m* collective effort.
mútua ['mutwa] *f* loan company.
mutuante [mu'twãtʃi] *m/f* lender.
mutuário/a [mu'twarju/a] *m/f* borrower.
mútuo/a ['mutwu/a] *adj* mutual.
muxiba [mu'ʃiba] *f* (*pelancas*) wrinkled flesh; (*carne para cães*) dogmeat; (*seios*) drooping breasts *pl*.
muxoxo [mu'ʃoʃu] *m* tutting; **fazer ~** to tut.

NB: European Portuguese adds the following consonants to certain words: **b** (sú(b)dito, su(b)til); **c** (a(c)ção, a(c)cionista, a(c)to); **m** (inde(m)ne); **p** (ado(p)ção, ado(p)tar); *for further details see p. xiii.*

MVR (*BR*) *abr m* = **Maior Valor de Referência.**

N

N, n ['eni] (*pl* **ns**) *m* N, n; **N de Nair** N for Nelly (*BRIT*) *ou* Nan (*US*).
N *abr* (= *norte*) N.
n. *abr* (= *nascido*) b; (= *nome*) name.
ñ *abr* = **não.**
na [na] = **em** + **a.**
-na [na] *pron* her; (*coisa*) it.
nabo ['nabu] *m* turnip.
nac. *abr* (= *nacional*) nat.
nação [na'sãw] (*pl* **-ões**) *f* nation; **as Nações Unidas** the United Nations.
nácar ['naka*] *m* mother-of-pearl; (*cor*) pink.
nacional [nasjo'naw] (*pl* **-ais**) *adj* national; (*carro, vinho etc*) domestic, home-produced.
nacionalidade [nasjonali'dadʒi] *f* nationality.
nacionalismo [nasjona'liʒmu] *m* nationalism.
nacionalista [nasjona'liʃta] *adj, m/f* nationalist.
nacionalização [nasjonaliza'sãw] (*pl* **-ões**) *f* nationalization.
nacionalizar [nasjonali'za*] *vt* to nationalize.
naco ['naku] *m* piece, chunk.
nações [na'sõjʃ] *fpl de* **nação.**
nada ['nada] *pron* nothing ♦ *m* nothingness; (*pessoa*) nonentity ♦ *adv* at all; **não dizer ~** to say nothing, not to say anything; **antes de mais ~** first of all; **não é ~ difícil** it's not at all hard, it's not hard at all; **~ mais** nothing else; **quase ~** hardly anything; **~ de novo** nothing new; **~ feito** nothing doing; **~ mau** not bad (at all); **obrigado — de ~** thank you — not at all *ou* don't mention it; **(que) ~!, ~ disso!** nonsense!, not at all!, **não foi ~** it was nothing; **por ~ nesse mundo** (not) for love nor money; **ele fez o que você pediu? — fez ~!** did he do as you asked? — no, he did not!; **não ser de ~** (*col*) to be a dead loss; **é uma coisinha de ~** it's nothing; **de ~** (*à-toa*) trifling; **discutimos por um ~** we argued over nothing.
nadada [na'dada] *f* swim; **dar uma ~** to go for a swim.
nadadeira [nada'dejra] *f* (*de peixe*) fin; (*de golfinho, foca, mergulhador*) flipper.
nadador(a) [nada'do*(a)] *adj* swimming ♦ *m/f* swimmer.
nadar [na'da*] *vi* to swim; **~ em** to be dripping with; **estar** *ou* **ficar nadando** (*fig*) to be out of it, be out of one's depth; **ele está nadando em dinheiro** he's rolling in money.
nádegas ['nadegaʃ] *fpl* buttocks.
nadinha [na'dʒiɲa] *pron* absolutely nothing.
nado ['nadu] *m*: **~ livre** freestyle; **~ borboleta** butterfly (stroke); **~ de peito** breaststroke; **~ de cachorrinho** doggy paddle; **~ de costas** backstroke; **a ~** swimming; **atravessar a ~** to swim across.
naftalina [nafta'lina] *f* naphthaline.
náilon ['najilõ] *m* nylon.
naipe ['najpi] *m* (*cartas*) suit; (*fig: categoria*) order.
Nairobi [naj'rɔbi] *n* Nairobi.
namoradeira [namora'dejra] *adj* flirtatious ♦ *f* flirt.
namorado/a [namo'radu/a] *m/f* boyfriend/girlfriend.
namorador(a) [namora'do*(a)] *adj* flirtatious ♦ *m* ladies' man.
namorar [namo'ra*] *vt* (*ser namorado de*) to be going out with; (*cobiçar*) to covet; (*fitar*) to stare longingly at ♦ *vi* (*casal*) to go out together; (*homem, mulher*) to have a boyfriend (*ou* girlfriend).
namoricar [namori'ka*] *vt* to flirt with ♦ *vi* to flirt.
namoro [na'moru] *m* relationship.
nanar [na'na*] (*col*) *vi* to sleep, kip.
nanico/a [na'niku/a] *adj* tiny.
nanquim [nã'kĩ] *m* Indian ink.
não [nãw] *adv* not; (*resposta*) no ♦ *m* no; **~ sei** I don't know; **~ muito** not much; **~ só ... mas também** not only ... but also; **agora ~** not now; **~ tem de quê** don't mention it; **~ é?** isn't it?, won't you? (*etc, segundo o verbo precedente*); **eles são brasileiros, ~ é?** they're Brazilian, aren't they?
não- [nãw-] *prefixo* non-.
não-agressão *f*: **pacto de ~** non-aggression treaty.
não-alinhado/a *adj* non-aligned.
não-conformista *adj, m/f* non-conformist.
não-intervenção *f* non-intervention.
napa ['napa] *f* napa leather.
naquela(s) [na'kɛla(ʃ)] = **em** + **aquela(s).**
naquele(s) [na'keli(ʃ)] = **em** + **aquele(s).**
naquilo [na'kilu] = **em** + **aquilo.**
narcisismo [naxsi'ziʒmu] *m* narcissism.
narcisista [naxsi'ziʃta] *adj* narcissistic.
narciso [nax'sizu] *m* (*BOT*) narcissus; (*pessoa*) narcissist; **~ dos prados** daffodil.
narcótico/a [nax'kɔtʃiku/a] *adj* narcotic ♦ *m* narcotic.
narcotizar [naxkotʃi'za*] *vt* to drug; (*fig*) to bore.
narigudo/a [nari'gudu/a] *adj* with a big nose; **ser ~** to have a big nose.
narina [na'rina] *f* nostril.
nariz [na'riʒ] *m* nose; **~ adunco/arrebitado** hook/snub nose; **meter o ~ em** to poke one's nose into; **torcer o ~ para** to turn one's nose up at; **ser dono/a do seu ~** to know one's own mind; **dar com o ~ na porta** (*fig*) to find (the) doors closed to one.
narração [naxa'sãw] (*pl* **-ões**) *f* narration; (*re-*

lato) account.
narrador(a) [naxa'do*(a)] *m/f* narrator.
narrar [na'xa*] *vt* to narrate, recount.
narrativa [naxa'tʃiva] *f* narrative; (*história*) story.
narrativo/a [naxa'tʃivu/a] *adj* narrative.
nas [naʃ] = **em** + **as.**
-nas [naʃ] *pron* them.
NASA ['naza] *abr f* NASA.
nasal [na'zaw] (*pl* **-ais**) *adj* nasal.
nasalado/a [naza'ladu/a] *adj* nasalized, nasal.
nasalização [nazaliza'sãw] *f* nasalization.
nascença [na'sẽsa] *f* birth; **de ~** by birth; **ele é surdo de ~** he was born deaf.
nascente [na'sẽtʃi] *adj* nascent ♦ *m* East, Orient ♦ *f* (*fonte*) spring.
nascer [na'se*] *vi* to be born; (*plantas*) to sprout; (*o sol*) to rise; (*ave*) to hatch; (*dente*) to come through; (*fig*: *ter origem*) to come into being ♦ *m*: **~ do sol** sunrise; **~ de** (*descender*) to be born of; (*fig*: *originar-se*) to be born out of; **~ de novo** (*fig*) to have a narrow escape, escape with one's life; **não nasci ontem** I wasn't born yesterday; **~ em berço de ouro** to be born with a silver spoon in one's mouth; **ele nasceu para médico** *etc* he's a born doctor *etc*; **não nasci para fazer isto** I wasn't cut out to do this.
nascido/a [na'sidu/a] *adj* born; **bem ~** from a good family.
nascimento [nasi'mẽtu] *m* birth; (*fig*) origin; (*estirpe*) descent.
Nassau [na'saw] *n* Nassau.
nata ['nata] *f* (CULIN) cream; (*elite*) élite.
natação [nata'sãw] *f* swimming.
natais [na'tajʃ] *adj pl de* **natal.**
Natal [na'taw] *m* Christmas; **Feliz ~!** Merry Christmas!
natal [na'taw] (*pl* **-ais**) *adj* (*relativo ao nascimento*) natal; (*país*) native; **cidade ~** home town; **terra ~** birthplace.
natalício/a [nata'lisju/a] *adj*: **aniversário ~** birthday ♦ *m* birthday.
natalidade [natali'dadʒi] *f*: **(índice de) ~** birth rate.
natalino/a [nata'linu/a] *adj* Christmas *atr.*
natividade [natʃivi'dadʒi] *f* nativity.
nativo/a [na'tʃivu/a] *adj, m/f* native.
NATO ['natu] *abr f* NATO.
nato/a ['natu/a] *adj* born.
natural [natu'raw] (*pl* **-ais**) *adj* natural; (*nativo*) native ♦ *m/f* (*nativo*) native; **de tamanho ~** full-scale; **ao ~** (CULIN) fresh, uncooked.
naturalidade [naturali'dadʒi] *f* naturalness; **falar com ~** to talk openly; **agir com a maior ~** to act as if nothing had happened; **de ~ paulista** *etc* born in São Paulo *etc.*
naturalismo [natura'liʒmu] *m* naturalism.
naturalista [natura'liʃta] *adj, m/f* naturalist.
naturalização [naturaliza'sãw] *f* naturalization.
naturalizado/a [naturali'zadu/a] *adj* naturalized ♦ *m/f* naturalized citizen.
naturalizar [naturali'za*] *vt* to naturalize; **~-se** *vr* to become naturalized.
naturalmente [naturaw'mẽtʃi] *adv* naturally; **~!** of course!
natureza [natu'reza] *f* nature; (*espécie*) kind, type; **~ morta** still life; **por ~** by nature.
naturismo [natu'riʒmu] *m* naturism.
naturista [natu'riʃta] *adj, m/f* naturist.
nau [naw] *f* (*literário*) ship.
naufragar [nawfra'ga*] *vi* (*navio*) to be wrecked; (*marinheiro*) to be shipwrecked; (*fig*: *malograr-se*) to fail.
naufrágio [naw'fraʒu] *m* shipwreck; (*fig*) failure.
náufrago/a ['nawfragu/a] *m/f* castaway.
náusea ['nawzea] *f* nausea; **dar ~s a alguém** to make sb feel sick; **sentir ~s** to feel sick.
nauseabundo/a [nawzja'bũdu/a] *adj* nauseating, sickening.
nauseante [naw'zjãtʃi] *adj* nauseating, sickening.
nausear [naw'zja*] *vt* to nauseate, sicken ♦ *vi* to feel sick.
náutica ['nawtʃika] *f* seamanship.
náutico/a ['nawtʃiku/a] *adj* nautical.
naval [na'vaw] (*pl* **-ais**) *adj* naval; **construção ~** shipbuilding.
navalha [na'vaʎa] *f* (*de barba*) razor; (*faca*) knife.
navalhada [nava'ʎada] *f* cut (*with a razor*).
navalhar [nava'ʎa*] *vt* to cut *ou* slash with a razor.
nave ['navi] *f* (*de igreja*) nave; **~ espacial** spaceship.
navegação [navega'sãw] *f* navigation, sailing; **~ aérea** air traffic; **~ costeira** coastal shipping; **~ fluvial** river traffic; **companhia de ~** shipping line.
navegador(a) [navega'do*(a)] *m/f* navigator.
navegante [nave'gãtʃi] *m* navigator, seafarer.
navegar [nave'ga*] *vt* to navigate; (*mares*) to sail ♦ *vi* to sail; (*dirigir o rumo*) to navigate.
navegável [nave'gavew] (*pl* **-eis**) *adj* navigable.
navio [na'viu] *m* ship; **~ aeródromo** aircraft carrier; **~ cargueiro** cargo ship, freighter; **~ de carreira** liner; **~ de guerra** warship; **~ escola** training ship; **~ fábrica** factory ship; **~ mercante** merchant ship; **~ petroleiro** oil tanker; **~ tanque** tanker; **ficar a ver ~s** to be left high and dry.
Nazaré [naza'rɛ] *n* Nazareth.
nazi [na'zi] (PT) *adj, m/f* = **nazista.**
nazismo [na'ziʒmu] *m* Nazism.
nazista [na'ziʃta] (BR) *adj, m/f* Nazi.
NB *abr* (= *note bem*) NB.
n/c *abr* (= *nossa carta*) our letter; (= *nossa*

***NB:** European Portuguese adds the following consonants to certain words:* **b** (sú(b)dito, su(b)til); **c** (a(c)ção, a(c)cionista, a(c)to); **m** (inde(m)ne); **p** (ado(p)ção, ado(p)tar); *for further details see p. xiii.*

conta) our account; (= *nossa casa*) our firm.
N da R *abr* = **nota da redação.**
N do A *abr* = **nota do autor.**
N do E *abr* = **nota do editor.**
N do T *abr* = **nota do tradutor.**
NE *abr* (= *nordeste*) NE.
neblina [ne'blina] *f* fog, mist.
nebulosa [nebu'lɔza] *f* (*ASTRONOMIA*) nebula.
nebulosidade [nebulozi'dadʒi] *f* cloud.
nebuloso/a [nebu'lozu/ɔza] *adj* foggy, misty; (*céu*) cloudy; (*fig*) vague.
neca ['nɛka] (*col*) *pron* nothing ♦ *excl* nope.
necessaire [nese'se*] *m* toilet bag.
necessário/a [nese'sarju/a] *adj* necessary ♦ *m*: **o** ~ the necessities *pl*; **se for** ~ if necessary.
necessidade [nesesi'dadʒi] *f* need, necessity; (*o que se necessita*) need; (*pobreza*) poverty, need; **ter** ~ **de** to need; **não há** ~ **de algo/ de fazer algo** there is no need for sth/to do sth; **em caso de** ~ if need be; **gêneros de primeira** ~ basic foodstuffs; **passar por muitas** ~**s** to suffer many deprivations; **fazer suas** ~**s** (*col*) to go to the toilet.
necessitado/a [nesesi'tadu/a] *adj* needy, poor ♦ *m/f* person in need; **os** ~**s** the needy *pl*; ~ **de** in need of.
necessitar [nesesi'ta*] *vt* to need, require ♦ *vi* to be in need; ~ **de** to need.
necrológio [nekro'lɔʒu] *m* obituary.
necrópole [ne'krɔpoli] *f* cemetery.
necrose [ne'krɔzi] *f* necrosis.
necrotério [nekro'tɛrju] *m* mortuary, morgue (*US*).
néctar ['nɛkta*] *m* nectar.
nectarina [nekta'rina] *f* nectarine.
nédio/a ['nɛdʒu/a] *adj* (*luzidio*) glossy, sleek; (*rechonchudo*) plump.
neerlandês/esa [neexlã'deʃ/eza] *adj* Dutch ♦ *m/f* Dutchman/woman.
Neerlândia [neex'lãdʒa] *f* the Netherlands *pl*.
nefando/a [ne'fãdu/a] *adj* atrocious, heinous.
nefasto/a [ne'faʃtu/a] *adj* (*de mau agouro*) ominous; (*trágico*) tragic.
negaça [ne'gasa] *f* lure, bait; (*engano*) deception; (*recusa*) refusal; (*desmentido*) denial.
negação [nega'sãw] (*pl* **-ões**) *f* negation; (*recusa*) refusal; (*desmentido*) denial; **ele é uma** ~ **em matéria de cozinha** he's hopeless at cooking.
negacear [nega'sja*] *vt* (*atrair*) to entice; (*enganar*) to deceive; (*recusar*) to refuse ♦ *vi* (*cavalo*) to balk; (*HIPISMO*) to refuse.
negações [nega'sõjʃ] *fpl de* **negação**.
negar [ne'ga*] *vt* (*desmentir*) to deny; (*recusar*) to refuse; (*não permitir*) to deny; ~**-se** *vr*: ~**-se a** to refuse to.
negativa [nega'tʃɪva] *f* (*LING*) negative; (*recusa*) denial.
negativo/a [nega'tʃivu/a] *adj* negative ♦ *m* (*TEC*, *FOTO*) negative ♦ *excl* (*col*) nope!
negável [ne'gavew] *adj* (*pl* **-eis**) deniable.
negligé [negli'ge] *m* negligee.
negligência [negli'ʒẽsja] *f* negligence, carelessness.
negligenciar [negliʒẽ'sja*] *vt* to neglect.
negligente [negli'ʒẽtʃi] *adj* negligent, careless.
nego/a ['negu/a] (*col*) *m/f* (*negro*) black; (*camarada*): **tudo bem, (meu)** ~**?** how are you, mate?; (*querido*): **tchau, (meu)** ~ bye, dear *ou* darling.
negociação [negosja'sãw] (*pl* **-ões**) *f* negotiation; (*transação*) transaction.
negociador(a) [negosja'do*(a)] *adj* negotiating ♦ *m/f* negotiator.
negociante [nego'sjãtʃi] *m/f* businessman/ woman; (*comerciante*) merchant.
negociar [nego'sja*] *vt* (*POL etc*) to negotiate; (*COM*) to trade ♦ *vi*: ~ **(com)** to trade *ou* deal (in); to negotiate (with).
negociata [nego'sjata] *f* crooked deal; ~**s** wheeling and dealing *sg*.
negociável [nego'sjavew] (*pl* **-eis**) *adj* negotiable.
negócio [ne'gɔsju] *m* (*COM*) business; (*transação*) deal; (*questão*) matter; (*col*: *troço*) thing; (*assunto*) affair, business; **homem de** ~**s** businessman; **a** ~**s** on business; **fazer um bom** ~ (*pessoa*) to get a good deal; (*loja etc*) to do good business; **fechar um** ~ to make a deal; ~ **fechado!** it's a deal!; **isso não é** ~ it's not worth it; **a casa dela é um** ~ (*col*) her house is really something; **tenho um** ~ **para te contar** I've got something to tell you; **aconteceu um** ~ **estranho comigo** something strange happened to me; **mas que** ~ **é esse?** (*col*) what's the big idea?; **meu** ~ **é outro** (*col*) this isn't my thing; **o** ~ **é o seguinte ...** (*col*) the thing is ....
negocista [nego'siʃta] *m/f* wheeler-dealer ♦ *adj* crooked.
negridão [negri'dãw] *f* blackness.
negrito [ne'gritu] *m* (*TIP*) bold (face).
negritude [negri'tudʒi] *f* (*POL etc*) black awareness.
negro/a ['negru/a] *adj* black; (*raça*) Negro; (*fig*: *lúgubre*) black, gloomy ♦ *m/f* black man/woman; Negro/Negress; **a situação está negra** the situation is bad; **humor** ~ black humo(u)r; **magia negra** black magic.
negrume [ne'grumi] *m* black, darkness.
negrura [ne'grura] *f* blackness.
neguei [ne'gej] *etc vb V* **negar**.
nela(s) ['nɛla(ʃ)] = **em** + **ela(s)**.
nele(s) ['neli(ʃ)] = **em** + **ele(s)**.
nem [nẽj] *conj* nor, neither; ~ **(sequer)** not even; ~ **que** even if; ~ **bem** hardly; ~ **um só** not a single one; ~ **estuda** ~ **trabalha** he neither studies nor works; ~ **eu** nor me; **sem** ~ without even; ~ **todos** not all; ~ **tanto** not so much; ~ **sempre** not always; ~ **por isso** nonetheless; **ele fala português que** ~ **brasileiro** he speaks Portuguese like a Brazilian; ~ **vem (que não tem)** (*col*) don't give me that.
nenê [ne'ne] *m/f* baby.

neném [ne'nẽj] (*pl* **-ns**) *m/f* = **nenê**.
nenhum(a) [ne'ɲũ/'ɲuma] *adj* no, not any ♦ *pron* (*nem um só*) none, not one; (*de dois*) neither; ~ **professor** no teacher; **não vi professor** ~ I didn't see any teachers; ~ **dos professores** none of the teachers; ~ **dos dois** neither of them; ~ **lugar** nowhere; **ele não fez** ~ **comentário** he didn't make any comments, he made no comments; **não vou a** ~ **lugar** I'm not going anywhere; **estar a** ~ (*col*) to be flat broke.
neofascismo [neofa'siʒmu] *m* neofascism.
neolatino/a [neola'tʃinu/a] *adj*: **línguas neolatinas** Romance languages.
neolítico/a [neo'litʃiku/a] *adj* neolithic.
neologismo [neolo'ʒiʒmu] *m* neologism.
néon ['nɛõ] *m* neon.
neônio [ne'onju] *m* = **néon**.
neo-realismo ['neo-] *m* new realism.
neozelandês/esa [neozelã'deʃ/deza] *adj* New Zealand *atr* ♦ *m/f* New Zealander.
Nepal [ne'paw] *m*: **o** ~ Nepal.
nepotismo [nepo'tʃiʒmu] *m* nepotism.
nervo ['nexvu] *m* (*ANAT*) nerve; (*fig*) energy, strength; (*em carne*) sinew; **ser** *ou* **estar uma pilha de** ~**s** to be a bundle of nerves.
nervosismo [nexvo'ziʒmu] *m* (*nervosidade*) nervousness; (*irritabilidade*) irritability.
nervoso/a [nex'vozu/ɔza] *adj* nervous; (*irritável*) touchy, on edge; (*exaltado*) worked up; **isso/ele me deixa** ~ he gets on my nerves; **sistema** ~ nervous system.
nervudo/a [ner'vudu/a] (*PT*) *adj* (*robusto*) robust.
nervura [nex'vura] *f* rib; (*BOT*) vein.
néscio/a ['nɛsju/a] *adj* (*idiota*) stupid; (*insensato*) foolish.
nesga ['neʒga] *f* (*COSTURA*) flare, gore; (*porção: de comida*) portion; (: *de mesa, terra*) corner, patch.
nessa(s) ['nɛsa(ʃ)] = **em** + **essa(s)**.
nesse(s) ['nesi(ʃ)] =**em** + **esse(s)**.
nesta(s) ['nɛʃta(ʃ)] = **em** + **esta(s)**.
neste(s) ['neʃtʃi(ʃ)] = **em** + **este(s)**.
neto/a ['nɛtu/a] *m/f* grandson/daughter; ~**s** *mpl* grandchildren.
neuralgia [newraw'ʒia] *f* neuralgia.
neurastênico/a [newraʃ'teniku/a] *adj* (*PSICO*) neurasthenic; (*col: irritadiço*) irritable.
neurite [new'ritʃi] *f* (*MED*) neuritis.
neurocirurgião/giã [newrosiruxʒjãw/ʒjã] (*pl* **-ões/**~**s**) *m/f* neurosurgeon.
neurologia [newrolo'ʒia] *f* neurology.
neurológico/a [newro'lɔʒiku/a] *adj* neurological.
neurologista [newrolo'ʒiʃta] *m/f* neurologist.
neurose [new'rɔzi] *f* neurosis.
neurótico/a [new'rɔtʃiku/a] *adj*, *m/f* neurotic.
neutralidade [newtrali'dadʒi] *f* neutrality.
neutralização [newtraliza'sãw] *f* neutralization.
neutralizar [newtrali'za*] *vt* to neutralize; (*anular*) to counteract.
neutrão [new'trãw] (*PT*; *pl* **-ões**) *m* = **nêutron**.
neutro/a ['newtru/a] *adj* neuter.
neutrões [new'trõjs] *mpl de* **neutrão**.
nêutron ['newtrõ] (*pl* ~**s**) *m* neutron; **bomba de** ~**s** neutron bomb.
nevada [ne'vada] *f* snowfall.
nevado/a [ne'vadu/a] *adj* snow-covered; (*branco*) snow-white.
nevar [ne'va*] *vi* to snow.
nevasca [ne'vaʃka] *f* snowstorm.
neve ['nɛvi] *f* snow; **clara em** ~ (*CULIN*) beaten egg-white.
névoa ['nɛvoa] *f* fog.
nevoeiro [nevo'ejru] *m* thick fog.
nevralgia [nevraw'ʒia] *f* neuralgia.
nexo ['nɛksu] *m* connection, link; **sem** ~ disconnected, incoherent.
nhenhenhém [ɲeɲe'ɲẽj] *m* (*conversa fiado*) idle talk; (*reclamação*) whinging.
nhoque ['ɲɔki] *m* (*CULIN*) gnocchi.
Nicarágua [nika'ragwa] *f*: **a** ~ Nicaragua.
nicaragüense [nikara'gwẽsi] *adj*, *m/f* Nicaraguan.
nicho ['niʃu] *m* niche.
Nicósia [ni'kɔzja] *n* Nicosia.
nicotina [niko'tʃina] *f* nicotine.
Níger ['niʒe*] *m*: **o** ~ Niger.
Nigéria [ni'ʒɛrja] *f*: **a** ~ Nigeria.
nigeriano/a [niʒe'rjanu/a] *adj*, *m/f* Nigerian.
niilista [nii'liʃta] *adj* nihilistic ♦ *m/f* nihilist.
Nilo ['nilu] *m*: **o** ~ the Nile.
nimbo ['nĩbu] *m* (*nuvem*) rain cloud; (*GEO*) halo.
ninar [ni'na*] *vt* to sing to sleep; ~**-se** *vr*: ~**-se para algo** to ignore sth.
ninfeta [nĩ'feta] *f* nymphette.
ninfomaníaca [nĩfoma'niaka] *f* nymphomaniac.
ninguém [nĩ'gẽj] *pron* nobody, no-one; ~ **o conhece** no-one knows him; **não vi** ~ I saw noone, I didn't see anybody; ~ **mais** nobody else.
ninhada [ni'ɲada] *f* brood.
ninharia [niɲa'ria] *f* trifle.
ninho ['niɲu] *m* (*de aves*) nest; (*toca*) lair; (*lar*) home; ~ **de rato** (*col*) mess, tip.
níquel ['nikew] *m* nickel; **estar sem um** ~ to be penniless.
niquelar [nike'la*] *vt* (*TEC*) to nickel-plate.
nirvana [nix'vana] *f* nirvana.
nisei [ni'zej] *adj*, *m/f* second-generation Japanese Brazilian.
nisso ['nisu] = **em** + **isso**.
nisto ['niʃtu] = **em** + **isto**.
nitidez [nitʃi'deʒ] *f* (*clareza*) clarity; (*brilho*) brightness; (*imagem*) sharpness.
nítido/a ['nitʃidu/a] *adj* clear, distinct;

NB: *European Portuguese adds the following consonants to certain words:* **b** (sú(b)dito, su(b)til); **c** (a(c)ção, a(c)cionista, a(c)to); **m** (inde(m)ne); **p** (ado(p)ção, ado(p)tar); *for further details see p. xiii.*

(*brilhante*) bright; (*imagem*) sharp, clear.

nitrato [ni'tratu] *m* nitrate.

nítrico/a ['nitriku/a] *adj*: **ácido ~** nitric acid.

nitrogênio [nitro'ʒenju] *m* nitrogen.

nitroglicerina [nitroglise'rina] *f* nitroglycerine.

nível ['nivew] (*pl* **-eis**) *m* level; (*fig*: *padrão*) level, standard; (: *ponto*) point, pitch; **~ de vida** standard of living; **~ do mar** sea level; **a ~ de** in terms of; **ao ~ de** level with.

nivelamento [nivela'mẽtu] *m* levelling (*BRIT*), leveling (*US*).

nivelar [nive'la*] *vt* (*terreno etc*) to level ♦ *vi*: **~ com** to be level with; **~-se** *vr*: **~-se com** to be equal to; **a morte nivela os homens** death is the great leveller (*BRIT*) *ou* leveler (*US*).

NO *abr* (= *nordoeste*) NW.

no [nu] = **em** + **o**.

-no [nu] *pron* him; (*coisa*) it.

nº *abr* (= *número*) no.

n/o *abr* = **nossa ordem**.

nó *m* knot; (*de uma questão*) crux; **~ corredio** slipknot; **~ na garganta** lump in the throat; **~s dos dedos** knuckles; **dar um ~** to tie a knot.

nobilíssimo/a [nobi'lisimu/a] *adj superl de* **nobre**.

nobilitar [nobili'ta*] *vt* to ennoble.

nobre ['nɔbri] *adj* noble; (*bairro etc*) exclusive ♦ *m/f* noble; **horário ~** prime time.

nobreza [no'breza] *f* nobility.

noção [no'sãw] (*pl* **-ões**) *f* notion; **noções** *fpl* rudiments, basics; **~ vaga** inkling; **não ter a menor ~ de algo** not to have the slightest idea about sth.

nocaute [no'kawtʃi] *m* knockout; (*soco*) knockout blow ♦ *adv*: **pôr alguém ~** to knock sb out.

nocautear [nokaw'tʃja*] *vt* to knock out.

nocivo/a [no'sivu/a] *adj* harmful.

noções [no'sõjʃ] *fpl de* **noção**.

nocturno/a [no'tuxnu/a] (*PT*) *adj* = **noturno**.

nódoa ['nɔdwa] *f* spot; (*mancha*) stain.

nódulo ['nɔdulu] *m* nodule.

nogueira [no'gejra] *f* (*árvore*) walnut tree; (*madeira*) walnut.

noitada [noj'tada] *f* (*noite inteira*) whole night; (*noite de divertimento*) night out.

noite ['nojtʃi] *f* night; (*início da ~*) evening; **à** *ou* **de ~** at night, in the evening; **ontem/hoje/amanhã à ~** last night/tonight/tomorrow night; **boa ~** good evening; (*despedida*) good night; **da ~ para o dia** overnight; **tarde da ~** late at night; **passar a ~ em claro** to have a sleepless night; **a ~ carioca** Rio nightlife; **~ de estréia** opening night.

noitinha [noj'tʃiɲa] *f*: **à ~s** at nightfall.

noivado [noj'vadu] *m* engagement.

noivar [noj'va*] *vi*: **~ (com)** (*ficar noivo*) to get engaged (to); (*ser noivo*) to be engaged (to).

noivo/a ['nojvu/a] *m/f* (*prometido*) fiancé fiancée; (*no casamento*) bridegroom/bride; **os ~s** *mpl* (*prometidos*) the engaged couple; (*no casamento*) the bride and groom; (*recém-casados*) the newly-weds.

nojeira [no'ʒejra] *f* disgusting thing; (*trabalho*) filthy job.

nojento/a [no'ʒẽtu/a] *adj* disgusting.

nojo ['noʒu] *m* (*náusea*) nausea; (*repulsão*) disgust, loathing; **ela é um ~** she's horrible; **este trabalho está um ~** this work is messy.

no-la = **nos** + **a**.

no-lo = **nos** + **o**.

no-las = **nos** + **as**.

no-los = **nos** + **os**.

nômade ['nomadʒi] *adj* nomadic ♦ *m/f* nomad.

nome ['nɔmi] *m* name; (*fama*) fame; **de ~** by name; **escritor de ~** famous writer; **um restaurante de ~** a restaurant with a good reputation; **em ~ de** in the name of; **dar ~ aos bois** to call a spade a spade; **esse ~ não me é estranho** the name rings a bell; **~ comercial** trade name; **~ completo** full name; **~ de batismo** Christian name; **~ de família** family name; **~ de guerra** nickname; **~ feio** swearword; **~ próprio** (*LING*) proper name.

nomeação [nomja'sãw] (*pl* **-ões**) *f* nomination; (*para um cargo*) appointment.

nomeada [no'mjada] *f* fame.

nomeadamente [nomjada'mẽtʃi] *adv* namely.

nomear [no'mja*] *vt* to nominate; (*conferir um cargo*) to appoint; (*dar nome a*) to name.

nomenclatura [nomẽkla'tura] *f* nomenclature.

nominal [nomi'naw] (*pl* **-ais**) *adj* nominal.

nonagésimo/a [nona'ʒɛzimu/a] *num* ninetieth.

nono/a ['nɔnu/a] *num* ninth; *V tb* **quinto**.

nora ['nɔra] *f* daughter-in-law.

nordeste [nox'dɛʃtʃi] *m* northeast; **o N~** the Northeast.

nordestino/a [noxdeʃ'tʃinu/a] *adj* northeastern ♦ *m/f* Northeasterner.

nórdico/a ['nɔxdʒiku/a] *adj*, *m/f* Nordic.

norma ['nɔxma] *f* standard, norm; (*regra*) rule; **como ~** as a rule.

normal [nox'maw] (*pl* **-ais**) *adj* normal; (*habitual*) usual; **escola ~** ≈ teacher training college; **curso ~** primary (*BRIT*) *ou* elementary (*US*) school teacher training; **está um calor que não é ~** it's incredibly hot.

normalidade [noxmali'dadʒi] *f* normality.

normalista [noxma'liʃta] *m/f* trainee primary (*BRIT*) *ou* elementary (*US*) school teacher.

normalização [noxmaliza'sãw] *f* normalization.

normalizar [noxmali'za*] *vt* to bring back to normal; (*POL*: *relações etc*) to normalize; **~-se** *vr* to return to normal.

normativo/a [noxma'tʃivu/a] *adj* prescriptive.

noroeste [nor'wɛʃtʃi] *adj* northwest, northwestern ♦ *m* northwest.

norte ['nɔxtʃi] *adj* northern, north; (*vento, direção*) northerly ♦ *m* north; **ao ~ de** to the north of.

norte-africano/a *adj*, *m/f* North African.

norte-americano/a *adj*, *m/f* (North) American.

nortear [nox'tʃja*] *vt* to orientate; **~-se** *vr* to orientate o.s.
norte-coreano/a *adj, m/f* North Korean.
norte-vietnamita *adj, m/f* North Vietnamese.
nortista [nox'tʃiʃta] *adj* northern ♦ *m/f* Northerner.
Noruega [nor'wega] *f* Norway.
norueguês/esa [norwe'geʃ/geza] *adj, m/f* Norwegian ♦ *m* (*LING*) Norwegian.
nos[1] [nuʃ] = **em** + **os**.
nos[2] [nuʃ] *pron* (*direto*) us; (*indireto*) us, to us, for us; (*reflexivo*) (to) ourselves; (*recíproco*) (to) each other.
-nos [nuʃ] *pron* them.
nós [nɔʃ] *pron* we; **~ mesmos** we ourselves; **para ~** for us; **~ dois** we two, both of us; **cá entre ~** between the two (*ou* three *etc*) of us.
nossa ['nɔsa] *excl*: **~!** my goodness!
nosso/a ['nɔsu/a] *adj* our ♦ *pron* ours; **um amigo ~** a friend of ours; **Nossa Senhora** (*REL*) Our Lady; **os ~s** (*família*) our family *sg*.
nostalgia [noʃtaw'ʒia] *f* nostalgia; (*saudades da pátria etc*) homesickness.
nostálgico/a [noʃ'tawʒiku/a] *adj* nostalgic.
nota ['nɔta] *f* note; (*EDUC*) mark; (*conta*) bill; (*cédula*) banknote; **digno de ~** noteworthy; **cheio da ~** (*col*) flush; **custar uma ~ (preta)** (*col*) to cost a bomb; **tomar ~** to make a note; **~ de venda** sales receipt; **~ fiscal** receipt; **(~) promissória** promissory note.
notabilidade [notabili'dadʒi] *f* notability; (*pessoa*) notable.
notabilizar [notabili'za*] *vt* to make known; **~-se** *vr* to become known.
notação [nota'sãw] (*pl* **-ões**) *f* notation.
notadamente [notada'mẽtʃi] *adv* especially.
notar [no'ta*] *vt* (*reparar em*) to notice, note; **~-se** *vr* to be obvious; **é de ~ que** it is to be noted that; **fazer ~** to call attention to.
notável [no'tavew] (*pl* **-eis**) *adj* notable, remarkable.
notícia [no'tʃisja] *f* (*uma* **~**) piece of news; (*TV etc*) news item; **~s** *fpl* news *sg*; **pedir ~s de** to inquire about; **ter ~s de** to hear from.
noticiar [notʃi'sja*] *vt* to announce, report.
noticiário [notʃi'sjarju] *m* (*de jornal*) news section; (*CINEMA*) newsreel; (*RÁDIO etc*) news bulletin.
noticiarista [notʃisja'riʃta] *m/f* news writer, reporter; (*TV, RÁDIO*) newsreader, newscaster.
noticioso/a [notʃi'sjozu/ɔza] *adj* news *atr*.
notificação [notʃifika'sãw] (*pl* **-ões**) *f* notification.
notificar [notʃifi'ka*] *vt* to notify, inform.
notívago/a [no'tʃivagu/a] *adj* nocturnal ♦ *m/f* sleepwalker; (*pessoa que gosta da noite*) night bird.
notoriedade [notorje'dadʒi] *f* renown, fame.
notório/a [no'tɔrju/a] *adj* well-known.
noturno/a [no'tuxnu/a] *adj* nocturnal, nightly; (*trabalho*) night *atr* ♦ *m* (*trem*) night train.
nouveau-riche [nuvo'xiʃi] (*pl* **nouveaux-riches**) *m/f* nouveau-riche.
nov. *abr* (= *novembro*) Nov.
nova ['nɔva] *f* piece of news; **~s** *fpl* news *sg*.
novamente [nova'mẽtʃi] *adv* again.
novato/a [no'vatu/a] *adj* inexperienced, raw ♦ *m/f* (*principiante*) beginner, novice; (*EDUC*) fresher.
nove ['nɔvi] *num* nine; *V tb* **cinco**.
novecentos/as [nove'sẽtuʃ/aʃ] *num* nine hundred.
novela [no'vɛla] *f* short novel, novella; (*RÁDIO TV*) soap opera.
novelista [nove'liʃta] *m/f* novella writer.
novelo [no'velu] *m* ball of thread.
novembro [no'vẽbru] (*PT*: **N-**) *m* November; *V tb* **julho**.
novena [no'vena] *f* (*REL*) novena.
noventa [no'vẽta] *num* ninety; *V tb* **cinqüenta**.
noviciado [novi'sjadu] *m* (*REL*) novitiate.
noviço/a [no'visu/a] *m/f* (*REL, fig*) novice.
novidade [novi'dadʒi] *f* novelty; (*notícia*) piece of news; **~s** *fpl* news *sg;* **sem ~** without incident.
novidadeiro/a [novida'dejru/a] *adj* chatty ♦ *m/f* gossip.
novilho/a [no'viʎu/a] *m/f* young bull/heifer.
novo/a ['novu/'nɔva] *adj* new; (*jovem*) young; (*adicional*) further; **de ~** again; **~ em folha** brand new; **o que há de ~?** what's new?; **~ rico** nouveau riche.
noz [nɔʒ] *f* walnut, nut; **~ moscada** nutmeg.
nu(a) [nu/'nua] *adj* (*corpo, pessoa*) naked; (*braço, arvore, sala, parede*) bare ♦ *m* nude; **~ em pêlo** stark naked; **a olho ~** with the naked eye; **a verdade nua e crua** the stark truth *ou* reality; **pôr a ~** (*fig*) to expose.
nuança [nu'ãsa] *f* nuance.
nubente [nu'bẽtʃi] *adj, m/f* betrothed.
nublado/a [nu'bladu/a] *adj* cloudy, overcast.
nublar [nu'bla*] *vt* to darken; **~-se** *vr* to cloud over.
nuca ['nuka] *f* nape (of the neck).
nuclear [nu'klja*] *adj* nuclear; **energia/usina ~** nuclear energy/power station.
núcleo ['nuklju] *m* nucleus *sg*; (*centro*) centre (*BRIT*), center (*US*).
nudez [nu'deʒ] *f* nakedness, nudity; (*de paredes etc*) bareness.
nudismo [nu'dʒiʒmu] *m* nudism.
nudista [nu'dʒiʃta] *adj, m/f* nudist.
nulidade [nuli'dadʒi] *f* nullity, invalidity; (*pessoa*) nonentity.
nulo/a ['nulu/a] *adj* (*JUR*) null, void; (*nenhum*) non-existent; (*sem valor*) worthless; (*esforço*) vain, useless; **ele é ~ em matemática** he's useless at maths (*BRIT*) *ou* math

***NB**: European Portuguese adds the following consonants to certain words:* **b** (sú(b)dito, su(b)til); **c** (a(c)ção, a(c)cionista, a(c)to); **m** (inde(m)ne); **p** (ado(p)ção, ado(p)tar); *for further details see p. xiii.*

(*US*).

num [nũ] = **em** + **um** ♦ *adv* (*col*: *não*) not.

numa(s) ['numa(ʃ)] = **em** + **uma(s)**.

numeração [numera'sãw] *f* (*ato*) numbering; (*números*) numbers *pl*; (*de sapatos etc*) sizes *pl*.

numerado/a [nume'radu/a] *adj* numbered; (*em ordem numérica*) in numerical order.

numeral [nume'raw] (*pl* **-ais**) *m* numeral ♦ *adj* numerical.

numerar [nume'ra*] *vt* to number.

numerário [nume'rarju] *m* cash, money.

numérico/a [nu'mɛriku/a] *adj* numerical.

número ['numeru] *m* number; (*de jornal*) issue; (*TEATRO etc*) act; (*de sapatos*, *roupa*) size; **sem ~** countless; **um sem ~ de vezes** hundreds *ou* thousands of times; **amigo/escritor ~ um** number one friend/writer; **fazer ~** to make up the numbers; **ele é um ~** (*col*) he's a riot; **~ cardinal/ordinal** cardinal/ordinal number; **~ de matrícula** registration (*BRIT*) *ou* license plate (*US*) number; **~ primo** prime number.

numeroso/a [nume'rozu/ɔza] *adj* numerous.

nunca ['nũka] *adv* never; **~ mais** never again; **como ~** as never before; **quase ~** hardly ever; **mais que ~** more than ever.

nuns [nũʃ] = **em** + **uns**.

nupcial [nup'sjaw] *adj* (*pl* **-ais**) wedding *atr*.

núpcias ['nupsjaʃ] *fpl* nuptials, wedding *sg*.

nutrição [nutri'sãw] *f* nutrition.

nutricionista [nutrisjo'niʃta] *m/f* nutritionist.

nutrido/a [nu'tridu/a] *adj* (*bem alimentado*) well-nourished; (*robusto*) robust.

nutrimento [nutri'mẽtu] *m* nourishment.

nutrir [nu'tri*] *vt* (*sentimento*) to harbour (*BRIT*), harbor (*US*); (*fig*) to feed ♦ *vi* to be nourishing; **~ (de)** to nourish (with), feed (on).

nutritivo/a [nutri'tʃivu/a] *adj* nourishing; **valor ~** nutritional value.

nuvem ['nuvẽj] (*pl* **-ns**) *f* cloud; (*de insetos*) swarm; **cair das nuvens** (*fig*) to be astounded; **estar nas nuvens** to be daydreaming, be miles away; **pôr nas nuvens** to praise to the skies; **o aniversário passou em brancas nuvens** the birthday went by without any celebration.

O

O, o [ɔ] (*pl* **os**) *m* O, o; **O de Osvaldo** O for Oliver (*BRIT*) *ou* Oboe (*US*).

o [u] (*pl* **os**) *art def* the ♦ *pron* him; (*coisa*) it; (*usos pronominais*): **~ que** the one (that); **~ quê?** what?; **não entendi ~ que ele falou** I didn't understand what he said; **meu carro é melhor do que ~ dele** my car is better then his; **dos dois carros, eu prefiro ~ verde/~ que tem 4 portas** of the two cars, I prefer the green one/the one which has 4 doors.

ó [ɔ] *excl* oh!; (*olha*) look!; **~ Pedro** hey Pedro.

ô [o] *excl* oh!; **~ Pedro** hey Pedro; **~ de casa!** anyone at home?; **~ criança difícil!** oh, what a difficult child!

OAB *abr f* = **Ordem dos Advogados do Brasil**.

oásis [o'asiʃ] *m inv* oasis.

oba ['oba] *excl* wow! great!; (*saudação*) hi!

obcecado/a [obise'kadu/a] *adj* obsessed.

obcecar [obise'ka*] *vt* to obsess.

obedecer [obede'se*] *vi*: **~ a** to obey; **obedeça!** (*a criança*) do as you're told!

obediência [obe'dʒẽsja] *f* obedience.

obediente [obe'dʒẽtʃi] *adj* obedient.

obelisco [obe'liʃku] *m* obelisk.

obesidade [obezi'dadʒi] *f* obesity.

obeso/a [o'bɛzu/a] *adj* obese.

óbice ['ɔbisi] *m* obstacle.

óbito ['ɔbitu] *m* death; **atestado de ~** death certificate.

obituário [obi'twarju] *m* obituary.

objeção [obʒe'sãw] (*PT*: **-cç-**; *pl* **-ões**) *f* objection; (*obstáculo*) obstacle; **fazer** *ou* **pôr objeções a** to object to.

objetar [obʒe'ta*] (*PT*: **-ct-**) *vt* to object ♦ *vi*: **~ (a algo)** to object (to sth).

objetiva [obʒe'tʃiva] (*PT*: **-ct-**) *f* lens; **sem ~** aimlessly.

objetivar [obʒetʃi'va*] (*PT*: **-ct-**) *vt* (*visar*) to aim at; **~ fazer** to aim to do, set out to do.

objetividade [obʒetʃivi'dadʒi] (*PT*: **-ct-**) *f* objectivity.

objetivo/a [obʒe'tʃivu/a] (*PT*: **-ct-**) *adj* objective ♦ *m* objective, aim.

objeto [ob'ʒɛtu] (*PT*: **-ct-**) *m* object; **~ de uso pessoal** personal effect.

oblíqua [o'blikwa] *f* oblique.

oblíquo/a [o'blikwu/a] *adj* oblique, slanting; (*olhar*) sidelong; (*LING*) oblique.

obliterar [oblite'ra*] *vt* to obliterate; (*MED*) to close off.

oblongo/a [ob'lõgu/a] *adj* oblong.

oboé [o'bwɛ] *m* oboe.

oboísta [o'bwiʃta] *m/f* oboe player.

obra ['ɔbra] *f* work; (*ARQ*) building, construction; (*TEATRO*) play; **em ~s** under repair; **~s públicas** public works; **ser ~ de alguém** to be the work of sb; **ser ~ de algo** to be the result of sth; **~ de arte** work of art; **~ de caridade** charity; **~s completas** complete works.

obra-mestra (*pl* **obras-mestras**) *f* masterpiece.

obra-prima (*pl* **obras-primas**) *f* masterpiece.

obreiro/a [o'brejru/a] *adj* working ♦ *m/f* worker.

obrigação [obriga'sãw] (*pl* **-ões**) *f* obligation,

duty; (*COM*) bond; **cumprir (com) suas obrigações** to fulfil(l) one's obligations; **dever obrigações a alguém** to owe sb favo(u)rs; ~ **ao portador** bearer bond.

obrigado/a [obri'gadu/a] *adj* (*compelido*) obliged, compelled ♦ *excl*: ~! thank you; (*recusa*) no, thank you.

obrigar [obri'ga*] *vt* to oblige, compel; **~-se** *vr*: **~-se a fazer algo** to undertake to do sth.

obrigatoriedade [obrigatorje'dadʒi] *f* compulsory nature.

obrigatório/a [obriga'tɔrju/a] *adj* compulsory, obligatory.

obscenidade [obiseni'dadʒi] *f* obscenity.

obsceno/a [obi'sɛnu/a] *adj* obscene.

obscurecer [obiʃkure'se*] *vt* to darken; (*entendimento, verdade etc*) to obscure; (*prestígio*) to dim ♦ *vi* to get dark.

obscuridade [obiʃkuri'dadʒi] *f* (*falta de luz*) darkness; (*fig*) obscurity.

obscuro/a [obi'ʃkuru/a] *adj* dark; (*fig*) obscure.

obsequiar [obse'kja*] *vt* (*presentear*) to give presents to; (*tratar com agrados*) to treat kindly.

obséquio [ob'sɛkju] *m* favour (*BRIT*), favor (*US*), kindness; **faça o ~ de ...** would you be kind enough to ....

obsequioso/a [obse'kjozu/ɔza] *adj* obliging, courteous.

observação [obisexva'sãw] (*pl* **-ões**) *f* observation; (*comentário*) remark, comment; (*de leis, regras*) observance.

observador(a) [obisexva'do*(a)] *adj* observant ♦ *m/f* observer.

observância [obisex'vãsja] *f* observance.

observar [obisex'va*] *vt* to observe; (*notar*) to notice; (*replicar*) to remark; ~ **algo a alguém** to point sth out to sb.

observatório [obsexva'tɔrju] *m* observatory.

obsessão [obise'sãw] (*pl* **-ões**) *f* obsession.

obsessivo/a [obise'sivu/a] *adj* obsessive.

obsessões [obise'sõjʃ] *fpl de* **obsessão**.

obsoleto/a [obiso'lɛtu/a] *adj* obsolete.

obstáculo [obi'ʃtakulu] *m* obstacle; (*dificuldade*) hindrance, drawback.

obstante [obi'ʃtãtʃi]: **não** ~ *conj* nevertheless, however ♦ *prep* in spite of, notwithstanding.

obstar [obi'ʃta*] *vi*: ~ **a** to hinder; (*opor-se*) to oppose.

obstetra [obi'ʃtɛtra] *m/f* obstetrician.

obstetrícia [obiʃte'trisja] *f* obstetrics *sg*.

obstétrico/a [obi'ʃtɛtriku/a] *adj* obstetric.

obstinação [obiʃtʃina'sãw] *f* obstinacy.

obstinado/a [obiʃtʃi'nadu/a] *adj* obstinate, stubborn.

obstinar-se [obiʃtʃi'naxsi] *vr* to be obstinate; ~ **em** (*insistir em*) to persist in.

obstrução [obiʃtru'sãw] (*pl* **-ões**) *f* obstruction.

obstruir [obi'ʃtrwi*] *vt* to obstruct; (*impedir*) to impede.

obtêm [obi'tẽ] *etc vb V* **obter**.

obtemperar [obitẽpe'ra*] *vt* to reply respectfully ♦ *vi*: ~ **(a algo)** to demur (at sth).

obtenção [obitẽ'sãw] (*pl* **-ões**) *f* acquisition; (*consecução*) attainment.

obtenho [ob'teɲu] *etc vb V* **obter**.

obtenível [obite'nivew] (*pl* **-eis**) *adj* obtainable.

obter [obi'te*] (*irreg*: *como* **ter**) *vt* to obtain, get; (*alcançar*) to gain.

obturação [obitura'sãw] (*pl* **-ões**) *f* (*de dente*) filling.

obturador [obitura'do*] *m* (*FOTO*) shutter.

obturar [obitu'ra*] *vt* to stop up, plug; (*dente*) to fill.

obtuso/a [obi'tuzu/a] *adj* (*ger*) obtuse; (*fig*: *pessoa*) thick, slow, dull.

obviedade [obvje'dadʒi] *f* obviousness; (*coisa óbvia*) obvious fact.

óbvio/a ['ɔbvju/a] *adj* obvious; **(é)** ~! of course!; **é o** ~ **ululante** it's glaringly *ou* screamingly (*col*) obvious.

OC *abr* (= *onda curta*) SW.

ocasião [oka'zjãw] (*pl* **-ões**) *f* (*oportunidade*) opportunity, chance; (*momento, tempo*) occasion, time.

ocasional [okazjo'naw] (*pl* **-ais**) *adj* chance.

ocasionar [okazjo'na*] *vt* to cause, bring about.

ocaso [o'kazu] *m* (*do sol*) sunset; (*ocidente*) the west; (*decadência*) decline.

Oceania [osja'nia] *f*: **a** ~ Oceania.

oceânico/a [o'sjaniku/a] *adj* ocean *atr*.

oceano [o'sjanu] *m* ocean; **O~ Atlântico/Pacífico/Índico** Atlantic/Pacific/Indian Ocean.

oceanografia [osjanogra'fia] *f* oceanography.

ocidental [osidẽ'taw] (*pl* **-ais**) *adj* western ♦ *m/f* westerner.

ocidente [osi'dẽtʃi] *m* west; **o O~** (*POL*) the West.

ócio ['ɔsju] *m* (*lazer*) leisure; (*inação*) idleness.

ociosidade [osjozi'dadʒi] *f* idleness.

ocioso/a [o'sjozu/ɔza] *adj* idle; (*vaga*) unfilled.

oco/a ['oku/a] *adj* hollow, empty; (*cabeça*) empty.

ocorrência [oko'xẽsja] *f* incident, event; (*circunstância*) circumstance.

ocorrer [oko'xe*] *vi* to happen, occur; (*vir ao pensamento*) to come to mind; ~ **a alguém** to happen to sb; (*vir ao pensamento*) to occur to sb.

ocre ['ɔkri] *adj* ochre (*BRIT*), ocher (*US*) ♦ *m* ochre.

octogenário/a [oktoʒe'narju/a] *adj* eighty-year-old ♦ *m/f* octogenarian.

octogonal [oktogo'naw] (*pl* **-ais**) *adj*

***NB**: European Portuguese adds the following consonants to certain words:* **b** (sú(b)dito, su(b)til); **c** (a(c)ção, a(c)cionista, a(c)to); **m** (inde(m)ne); **p** (ado(p)ção, ado(p)tar); *for further details see p. xiii.*

octagonal.
octógono [ok'tɔgonu] *m* octagon.
ocular [oku'la*] *adj* ocular; **testemunha** ~ eye witness.
oculista [oku'liʃta] *m/f* optician.
óculo ['ɔkulu] *m* spyglass; **~s** *mpl* glasses, spectacles; **~s de proteção** goggles.
ocultar [okuw'ta*] *vt* to hide, conceal.
ocultas [o'kuwtaʃ] *fpl*: **às** ~ in secret.
oculto/a [o'kuwtu/a] *adj* hidden; (*desconhecido*) unknown; (*secreto*) secret; (*sobrenatural*) occult.
ocupação [okupa'sãw] (*pl* **-ões**) *f* occupation.
ocupacional [okupasjo'naw] (*pl* **-ais**) *adj* occupational.
ocupações [okupa'sõjʃ] *fpl de* **ocupação**.
ocupado/a [oku'padu/a] *adj* (*pessoa*) busy; (*lugar*) taken, occupied; (*BR*: *telefone*) engaged (*BRIT*), busy (*US*); **sinal de** ~ (*BR*: *TEL*) engaged tone (*BRIT*), busy signal (*US*).
ocupar [oku'pa*] *vt* to occupy; (*tempo*) to take up; (*pessoa*) to keep busy; **~-se** *vr* to keep o.s. occupied; **~-se com** *ou* **de** *ou* **em algo** (*dedicar-se a*) to deal with sth; (*cuidar de*) to look after sth; (*passar seu tempo com*) to occupy o.s. with sth; **posso ~ esta mesa/ cadeira?** can I take this table/chair?
ode ['ɔdʒi] *f* ode.
odiar [o'dʒja*] *vt* to hate.
odiento/a [o'dʒjẽtu/a] *adj* hateful.
ódio ['ɔdʒju] *m* hate, hatred; **que ~!** (*col*) I'm (*ou* was) furious!
odioso/a [o'dʒjozu/ɔza] *adj* hateful.
odontologia [odõtolo'ʒia] *f* dentistry.
odor [o'do*] *m* smell.
OEA *abr f* (= *Organização dos Estados Americanos*) OAS.
oeste ['wɛʃtʃi] *m* west ♦ *adj inv* (*região*) western; (*direção*, *vento*) westerly; **ao ~ de** to the west of; **em direção ao ~** westwards.
ofegante [ofe'gãtʃi] *adj* breathless, panting.
ofegar [ofe'ga*] *vi* to pant, puff.
ofender [ofẽ'de*] *vt* to offend; **~-se** *vr* to take offence (*BRIT*) *ou* offense (*US*).
ofensa [o'fẽsa] *f* insult; (*à lei*, *moral*) offence (*BRIT*), offense (*US*).
ofensiva [ofẽ'siva] *f* (*MIL*) offensive; **tomar a ~** to go on to the offensive.
ofensivo/a [ofẽ'sivu/a] *adj* offensive; (*agressivo*) aggressive; ~ **à moral** morally offensive.
oferecer [ofere'se*] *vt* to offer; (*presentear*) to give; (*jantar*) to give; (*propor*) to propose; (*dedicar*) to dedicate; **~-se** *vr* (*pessoa*) to offer o.s., volunteer; (*oportunidade*) to present o.s., arise; **~-se para fazer** to offer to do.
oferecido/a [ofere'sidu/a] *adj* (*intrometido*) pushy.
oferecimento [oferesi'mẽtu] *m* offer.
oferenda [ofe'rẽda] *f* (*REL*) offering.
oferta [o'fɛxta] *f* (*oferecimento*) offer; (*dádiva*) gift; (*COM*) bid; (*em loja*) special offer; **a ~ e a demanda** (*ECON*) supply and demand; **em ~** (*numa loja*) on special offer.
ofertar [ofex'ta*] *vt* to offer.
office-boy [ɔfis'bɔj] (*pl* **~s**) *m* messenger.
oficial [ofi'sjaw] (*pl* **-ais**) *adj* official ♦ *m/f* official; (*MIL*) officer; ~ **de justiça** bailiff.
oficializar [ofisjali'za*] *vt* to make official.
oficiar [ofi'sja*] *vi* (*REL*) to officiate ♦ *vt*: ~ **(algo) a alguém** to report (sth) to sb.
oficina [ofi'sina] *f* workshop; ~ **mecânica** garage.
ofício [o'fisju] *m* (*profissão*) profession, trade; (*REL*) service; (*carta*) official letter; (*função*) function; (*encargo*) job, task; **bons ~s** good offices; ~ **de notas** notary public.
oficioso/a [ofi'sjozu/ɔza] *adj* (*não oficial*) unofficial.
ofsete [of'sɛtʃi] *m* offset printing.
oftálmico/a [of'tawmiku/a] *adj* ophthalmic.
oftalmologia [oftawmolo'ʒia] *f* ophthalmology.
ofuscante [ofuʃ'kãtʃi] *adj* dazzling.
ofuscar [ofuʃ'ka*] *vt* (*obscurecer*) to blot out; (*deslumbrar*) to dazzle; (*entendimento*) to colour (*BRIT*), color (*US*); (*suplantar em brilho*) to outshine ♦ *vi* to be dazzling.
ogro ['ɔgru] *m* ogre.
ogum [o'gũ] *m Afro-Brazilian god of war*.
oh [ɔ] *excl* oh.
oi [ɔj] *excl* oh; (*saudação*) hi; (*resposta*) yes?
oitava-de-final (*pl* **oitavas-de-final**) *f* round before the quarter finals.
oitavo/a [oj'tavu/a] *adj* eighth ♦ *m* eighth; *V tb* **quinto**.
oitenta [oj'tẽta] *num* eighty; *V tb* **cinqüenta**.
oito ['ojtu] *num* eight; **ou ~ ou oitenta** all or nothing; *V tb* **cinco**.
oitocentos/as [ojtu'sẽtuʃ/aʃ] *num* eight hundred; **os O~** the nineteenth century.
ojeriza [oʒe'riza] *f* dislike; **ter ~ a alguém** to dislike sb.
o.k. [o'ke] *excl*, *adv* OK, okay.
olá [o'la] *excl* hello!
olaria [ola'ria] *f* (*fábrica*: *de louças de barro*) pottery; (*de tijolos*) brickworks *sg*.
oleado [o'ljadu] *m* oil cloth.
oleiro/a [o'lejru/a] *m/f* potter; (*de tijolos*) brickmaker.
óleo ['ɔlju] *m* (*lubricante*) oil; **pintura a ~** oil painting; ~ **combustível** fuel oil; ~ **de bronzear** suntan oil; ~ **de rícino** castor oil; ~ **diesel** diesel oil.
oleoduto [oljo'dutu] *m* (oil) pipeline.
oleoso/a [o'ljozu/ɔza] *adj* oily; (*gorduroso*) greasy.
olfato [ow'fatu] *m* sense of smell.
olhada [o'ʎada] *f* glance, look; **dar uma ~** to have a look.
olhadela [oʎa'dɛla] *f* peep.
olhar [o'ʎa*] *vt* to look at; (*observar*) to watch; (*ponderar*) to consider; (*cuidar de*) to look after ♦ *vi* to look ♦ *m* look; **~-se** *vr* to look at o.s.; (*duas pessoas*) to look at each other; **olha!** look!; ~ **fixamente** to stare at;

~ **para** to look at; ~ **por** to look after; ~ **alguém de frente** to look sb straight in the eye; **e olha lá** (*col*) and that's pushing it; **olha lá o que você vai me arranjar!** careful you don't make things worse for me!; ~ **fixo** stare.

olheiras [o'ʎejraʃ] *fpl* dark rings under the eyes.

olho ['oʎu] *m* (ANAT, *de agulha*) eye; (*vista*) eyesight; (*de queijo*) hole; ~ **nele!** watch him!; ~ **vivo!** keep your eyes open!; **a** ~ (*medir, calcular etc*) by eye; **a** ~ **nu** with the naked eye; **a ~s vistos** visibly; **abrir os ~s de alguém** (*fig*) to open sb's eyes; **andar** *ou* **estar de** ~ **em algo** to have one's eyes on sth; **custar/pagar os ~s da cara** to cost/pay the earth; **ficar de** ~ to keep an eye out; **ficar de** ~ **em algo** to keep an eye on sth; **ficar de** ~ **comprido em algo** to look longingly at sth; **passar os ~s por algo** to scan over sth; **pôr alguém nos ~s da rua** to put sb on the street; (*de emprego*) to fire sb; **não pregar o** ~ not to sleep a wink; **ter bom** ~ **para** to have a good eye for; **ver com bons ~s** to approve of; ~ **clínico** sharp *ou* keen eye; ~ **de lince** sharp eye; **ter** ~ **de peixe morto** to be glassy-eyed; **~s esbugalhados** goggle eyes; ~ **grande** (*fig*) envy; **estar de** ~ **grande em algo** to covet sth; **ter** ~ **grande** to be envious; ~ **mágico** (*na porta*) peephole, magic eye; ~ **roxo** black eye; ~ **por** ~ an eye for an eye; **num abrir e fechar de ~s** in a flash; **longe dos ~s, longe do coração** out of sight, out of mind; **ele tem o** ~ **maior que a barriga** his eyes are bigger than his belly.

oligarquia [oligax'kia] *f* oligarchy.

olimpíada [olĩ'piada] *f*: **as O~s** the Olympics.

olimpicamente [olĩpika'mẽtʃi] *adj* blissfully.

olímpico/a [o'lĩpiku/a] *adj* (*jogos, chama*) Olympic.

olival [oli'vaw] (*pl* **-ais**) *m* olive grove.

olivedo [oli'vedu] *m* = **olival.**

oliveira [oli'vejra] *f* olive tree.

olmeiro [ow'mejru] *m* = **olmo.**

olmo ['ɔwmu] *m* elm.

OLP *abr f* (= *Organização para a Libertação da Palestina*) PLO.

OM *abr* (= *onda média*) MW.

Omã [o'mã] *m*: **(o)** ~ Oman.

ombreira [õ'brejra] *f* (*de porta*) doorpost; (*de roupa*) shoulder pad.

ombro ['õbru] *m* shoulder; **encolher os ~s** *ou* **dar de ~s** to shrug one's shoulders; **chorar no** ~ **de alguém** to cry on sb's shoulder.

omeleta [ome'leta] (PT) *f* = **omelete.**

omelete [ome'letʃi] (BR) *f* omelette (BRIT), omelet (US).

omissão [omi'sãw] (*pl* **-ões**) *f* omission; (*negligência*) negligence; (*ato de não se manifestar*) failure to appear.

omisso/a [o'misu/a] *adj* omitted; (*negligente*) negligent; (*que não se manifesta*) absent.

omissões [omi'sõjʃ] *fpl de* **omissão.**

omitir [omi'tʃi*] *vt* to omit; **~-se** *vr* to fail to appear.

OMM *abr f* (= *Organização Meteorológica Mundial*) WMO.

omnipotente *etc* [omnipo'tẽtə] (PT) = **onipotente** *etc.*

omnipresente [omnipre'zẽtə] (PT) *adj* = **onipresente.**

omnisciente [omni'sjẽtə] (PT) *adj* = **onisciente.**

omnivoro/a [om'nivoru/a] (PT) *adj* = **onivoro.**

omoplata [omo'plata] *f* shoulder blade.

OMS *abr f* (= *Organização Mundial da Saúde*) WHO.

ON *abr* (COM: *de ações*) = **ordinária nominativa.**

onça ['õsa] *f* (*peso*) ounce; (*animal*) jaguar; **ser do tempo da** ~ to be as old as the hills; **ficar uma** *ou* **virar** ~ (*col*) to get furious; **estou numa** ~ **danada** (*col*) I'm flat broke.

onça-parda (*pl* **onças-pardas**) *f* puma.

onda ['õda] *f* wave; (*moda*) fashion; (*confusão*) commotion; ~ **sonora/luminosa** sound/light wave; ~ **curta/média/longa** short/medium/long wave; ~ **de calor** heat wave; **pegar** ~ to go surfing; **ir na** ~ (*col*) to follow the crowd; **ir na** ~ **de alguém** (*col*) to be taken in by sb; **estar na** ~ to be in fashion; **fazer** ~ (*col*) to make a fuss; **deixa de ~!** (*col*) cut the crap!; **isso é** ~ **dela** (*col*) that's just something she's made up; **tirar uma** ~ **de algo** to act like sth.

onde ['õdʒi] *adv* where ♦ *conj* where, in which; **de** ~ **você é?** where are you from?; **por** ~ through which; **por ~?** which way?; ~ **quer que** wherever; **não ter** ~ **cair morto** (*fig*) to have nothing to call one's own; **fazer por** ~ to work for it.

ondeado/a [õ'dʒjadu/a] *adj* wavy ♦ *m* (*de cabelo*) wave.

ondeante [õ'dʒjãtʃi] *adj* waving, undulating.

ondear [õ'dʒja*] *vt* to wave ♦ *vi* to wave; (*água*) to ripple; (*serpear*) to meander, wind.

ondulação [õdula'sãw] (*pl* **-ões**) *f* undulation.

ondulado/a [õdu'ladu/a] *adj* wavy.

ondulante [õdu'lãtʃi] *adj* wavy.

onerar [one'ra*] *vt* to burden; (COM) to charge.

oneroso/a [one'rozu/ɔza] *adj* onerous; (*dispendioso*) costly.

ônibus ['onibuʃ] (BR) *m inv* bus; **ponto de** ~ bus-stop.

onipotência [onipo'tẽsja] *f* omnipotence.

onipotente [onipo'tẽtʃi] *adj* omnipotent.

onipresente [onipre'zẽtʃi] *adj* omnipresent, ever-present.

***NB**: European Portuguese adds the following consonants to certain words:* **b** (sú(b)dito, su(b)til); **c** (a(c)ção, a(c)cionista, a(c)to); **m** (inde(m)ne); **p** (ado(p)ção, ado(p)tar); *for further details see p. xiii.*

onírico/a [o'niriku/a] *adj* dreamlike.
onisciente [oni'sjẽtʃi] *adj* omniscient.
onívoro/a [o'nivoru/a] *adj* omnivorous.
onomástico/a [ono'maʃtʃiku/a] *adj*: **índice ~** index of proper names; **dia ~** name day.
onomatopéia [onomato'pɛja] *f* onomatopoeia.
ônix ['oniks] *m* onyx.
ontem ['õtẽ] *adv* yesterday; **~ à noite** last night; **~ à tarde/de manhã** yesterday afternoon/morning.
ONU ['onu] *abr f* (= *Organização das Nações Unidas*) UNO.
ônus ['onuʃ] *m inv* onus; (*obrigação*) obligation; (*COM*) charge; (*encargo desagradável*) burden; (*imposto*) tax burden.
onze ['õzi] *num* eleven; *V tb* **cinco**.
OP *abr* (*COM*: *açoes*) = **ordinária ao portador**.
opa ['opa] *excl* (*de admiração*) wow!; (*de espanto*) oops!; (*saudação*) hi!
opacidade [opasi'dadʒi] *f* opaqueness; (*escuridão*) blackness.
opaco/a [o'paku/a] *adj* opaque; (*obscuro*) dark.
opala [o'pala] *f* opal; (*tecido*) fine muslin.
opalino/a [opa'linu/a] *adj* bluish white.
opção [op'sãw] (*pl* **-ões**) *f* option, choice; (*preferência*) first claim, right.
open ['opẽ] *m* = **open market**.
open market [-'maxkitʃ] *m* open market.
OPEP [o'pɛpɪ] *abr f* (= *Organização dos Países Exportadores de Petróleo*) OPEC.
ópera ['ɔpera] *f* opera; **~ bufa** comic opera.
operação [opera'sãw] (*pl* **-ões**) *f* operation; (*COM*) transaction.
operacional [operasjo'naw] (*pl* **-ais**) *adj* operational; (*sistema, custos*) operating.
operações [opera'sõjʃ] *fpl de* **operação**.
operado/a [ope'radu/a] *adj* (*MED*) who has (*ou* have) had an operation ♦ *m/f* person who has had an operation.
operador(a) [opera'do*(a)] *m/f* operator; (*cirurgião*) surgeon; (*num cinema*) projectionist.
operante [ope'rãtʃi] *adj* effective.
operar [ope'ra*] *vt* to operate; (*produzir*) to effect, bring about; (*MED*) to operate on ♦ *vi* to operate; (*agir*) to act, function; **~-se** *vr* (*suceder*) to take place; (*MED*) to have an operation.
operariado [opera'rjadu] *m*: **o ~** the working class.
operário/a [ope'rarju/a] *adj* working ♦ *m/f* worker; **classe operária** working class.
opereta [ope'reta] *f* operetta.
opinar [opi'na*] *vt* (*julgar*) to think ♦ *vi* (*dar o seu parecer*) to give one's opinion.
opinião [opi'njãw] (*pl* **-ões**) *f* opinion; **na minha ~** in my opinion; **ser de** *ou* **da ~ (de) que** to be of the opinion that; **ser da ~ de alguém** to think the same as sb, share sb's view; **mudar de ~** to change one's mind; **~ pública** public opinion.
ópio ['ɔpju] *m* opium.
opíparo/a [o'piparu/a] *adj* (*formal*) splendid, lavish.
opõe [o'põj] *etc vb V* **opor**.
opomos [o'pomoʃ] *vb V* **opor**.
oponente [opo'nẽtʃi] *adj* opposing ♦ *m/f* opponent.
opor [o'po*] (*irreg*: *como* **pôr**) *vt* to oppose; (*resistência*) to put up, offer; (*objeção, dificuldade*) to raise; **~-se** *vr*: **~-se a** (*fazer objeção*) to object to; (*resistir*) to oppose; **~ algo a algo** (*colocar em contraste*) to contrast sth with sth.
oportunamente [opoxtuna'mẽtʃi] *adv* at an opportune moment.
oportunidade [opoxtuni'dadʒi] *f* opportunity; **na primeira ~** at the first opportunity.
oportunismo [opoxtu'niʒmu] *m* opportunism.
oportunista [opoxtu'niʃta] *adj*, *m/f* opportunist.
oportuno/a [opox'tunu/a] *adj* (*momento*) opportune, right; (*oferta de ajuda*) well-timed; (*conveniente*) convenient, suitable.
opôs [o'poʃ] *vb V* **opor**.
oposição [opozi'sãw] *f* opposition; **em ~ a** against; **fazer ~ a** to oppose.
oposicionista [opozisjo'niʃta] *adj* opposition *atr* ♦ *m/f* member of the opposition.
oposto/a [o'poʃtu/'pɔʃta] *pp de* **opor** ♦ *adj* (*contrário*) opposite; (*em frente*) facing, opposite; (*opiniões*) opposing, opposite ♦ *m* opposite.
opressão [opre'sãw] (*pl* **-ões**) *f* oppression; (*sufocação*) feeling of suffocation, tightness in the chest.
opressivo/a [opre'sivu/a] *adj* oppressive.
opressões [opre'sõjʃ] *fpl de* **opressão**.
opressor(a) [opre'so*(a)] *m/f* oppressor.
oprimido/a [opri'midu/a] *adj* oppressed ♦ *m*: **os ~s** the oppressed.
oprimir [opri'mi*] *vt* to oppress; (*comprimir*) to press ♦ *vi* to be oppressive.
opróbrio [o'prɔbrju] *m* (*infâmia*) ignominy; (*formal*: *desonra*) shame.
optar [op'ta*] *vi* to choose; **~ por** to opt for; **~ por fazer** to opt to do; **~ entre** to choose between.
optativo/a [opta'tʃivu/a] *adj* optional; (*LING*) optative.
óptico/a *etc* ['ɔtiku/a] (*PT*) = **ótico** *etc*.
óptimo/a *etc* ['ɔtimu/a] (*PT*) *adj* = **ótimo** *etc*.
opulência [opu'lẽsja] *f* opulence.
opulento/a [opu'lẽtu/a] *adj* opulent.
opunha [o'puɲa] *etc vb V* **opor**.
opus [o'puʃ] *etc vb V* **opor**.
opúsculo [o'puʃkulu] *m* (*livreto*) booklet; (*pequena obra*) pamphlet.
opuser [opu'ze*] *etc vb V* **opor**.
ora ['ɔra] *adv* now ♦ *conj* well; **por ~** for the time being; **~ ..., ~ ...** one moment ..., the next ...; **~ sim, ~ não** first yes, then no; **~ essa!** the very idea!, come off it!; **~ bem** now then; **~ viva!** hello there!; **~, que besteira!** well, how stupid!; **~ bolas!** (*col*)

for heaven's sake!

oração [ora'sãw] (*pl* **-ões**) *f* (*reza*) prayer; (*discurso*) speech; (*LING*) clause.

oráculo [o'rakulu] *m* oracle.

orador(a) [ora'do*(a)] *m/f* (*aquele que fala*) speaker.

oral [o'raw] (*pl* **-ais**) *adj* oral ♦ *f* oral (exam).

orangotango [orãgu'tãgu] *m* orang-utan.

orar [o'ra*] *vi* (*REL*) to pray.

oratória [ora'tɔrja] *f* public speaking, oratory.

oratório/a [ora'tɔrju/a] *adj* oratorical ♦ *m* (*MÚS*) oratorio; (*REL*) oratory.

orbe ['ɔxbi] *m* globe.

órbita ['ɔxbita] *f* orbit; (*do olho*) socket; **entrar/colocar em ~** to go/put into orbit; **estar em ~** to be in orbit.

orbital [oxbi'taw] (*pl* **-ais**) *adj* orbital.

Órcades ['ɔxkadʒiʃ] *fpl*: **as ~** the Orkneys.

orçamentário/a [oxsamẽ'tarju/a] *adj* budget *atr*.

orçamento [oxsa'mẽtu] *m* (*do estado etc*) budget; (*avaliação*) estimate; **~ sem compromisso** estimate with no obligation.

orçar [ox'sa*] *vt* to value, estimate ♦ *vi*: **~ em** (*gastos etc*) to be valued at, be put at; **~ a** to reach, go up to; **ele orça por 20 anos** he is around 20; **um projeto orçado em $100** a project valued at $100.

ordeiro/a [ox'dejru/a] *adj* orderly.

ordem ['oxdẽ] (*pl* **-ns**) *f* order; **às suas ordens** at your service; **um lucro da ~ de $60 milhões** a profit in the order of $60 million; **até nova ~** until further notice; **de primeira ~** first-rate; **estar em ~** to be tidy; **pôr em ~** to arrange, tidy; **tudo em ~?** (*col*) everything OK?; **por ~** in order, in turn; **dar/receber ordens** to give/take orders; **dar uma ~ na casa** to tidy the house; **~ alfabética/cronológica** alphabetical/chronological order; **~ bancária** banker's order; **~ de grandeza** order of magnitude; **~ de pagamento** (*COM*) banker's draft; **~ de prisão** (*JUR*) prison order; **~ do dia** agenda; **O~ dos Advogados** Bar Association; **~ público** public order, law and order; **~ social** social order.

ordenação [oxdena'sãw] (*pl* **-ões**) *f* (*REL*) ordination; (*ordem*) order; (*arrumação*) tidiness, orderliness.

ordenado/a [oxde'nadu/a] *adj* (*posto em ordem*) in order; (*metódico*) orderly; (*REL*) ordained ♦ *m* salary, wages *pl*.

ordenança [oxde'nãsa] *m* (*MIL*) orderly ♦ *f* (*regulamento*) ordinance.

ordenar [oxde'na*] *vt* to arrange, put in order; (*determinar*) to order; (*REL*) to ordain; **~-se** *vr* (*REL*) to be ordained; **~ que alguém faça** to order sb to do; **~ algo a alguém** to order sth of sb.

ordenhar [oxde'ɲa*] *vt* to milk.

ordens ['oxdẽʃ] *fpl de* **ordem**.

ordinariamente [oxdʒinarja'mẽte] *adv* ordinarily, usually.

ordinário/a [oxdʒi'narju/a] *adj* ordinary; (*comum*) usual; (*medíocre*) mediocre; (*grosseiro*) coarse, vulgar; (*de má qualidade*) inferior; (*sem caráter*) rough; **de ~** usually.

orégano [o'rɛganu] *m* oregano.

orelha [o'reʎa] *f* (*ANAT*) ear; (*aba*) flap; **de ~s em pé** (*col*) on one's guard; **endividado até as ~s** up to one's ears in debt; **~s de abano** flappy ears.

orelhada [ore'ʎada] (*col*) *f*: **de ~** through the grapevine.

orelhão [ore'ʎãw] (*pl* **-ões**) *m* open telephone booth.

órfã ['ɔxfã] *f de* **órfão**.

orfanato [oxfa'natu] *m* orphanage.

órfão/fã ['ɔxfãw/fã] (*pl* **~s**) *m/f* orphan ♦ *adj* orphan; **~ de pai** with no father; **~ de** (*fig*) starved of.

orfeão [ox'fjãw] (*pl* **-ões**) *m* choral society.

orgânico/a [ox'ganiku/a] *adj* organic.

organismo [oxga'niʒmu] *m* organism; (*entidade*) organization.

organista [oxga'niʃta] *m/f* organist.

organização [oxganiza'sãw] (*pl* **-ões**) *f* organization; **~ de caridade** charity; **~ de fachada** front; **~ sem fins lucrativos** non-profit-making organization.

organizador(a) [oxganiza'do*(a)] *m/f* organizer ♦ *adj* (*comitê*) organizing.

organizar [oxgani'za*] *vt* to organize.

organograma [oxgano'grama] *m* organization chart.

órgão ['ɔxgãw] (*pl* **~s**) *m* organ; (*governamental etc*) institution, body; **~ de imprensa** news publication.

orgasmo [ox'gaʒmu] *m* orgasm.

orgia [ox'ʒia] *f* orgy.

orgulhar [oxgu'ʎa] *vt* to make proud; **~-se** *vr*: **~-se de** to be proud of.

orgulho [ox'guʎu] *m* pride; (*arrogância*) arrogance.

orgulhoso/a [oxgu'ʎozu/ɔza] *adj* proud; (*arrogante*) haughty.

orientação [orjẽta'sãw] *f* (*direção*) direction; (*de tese*) supervision; (*posição*) position; (*tendência*) tendency; **~ educacional** training, guidance; **~ vocacional** careers guidance.

orientador(a) [orjẽta'do*(a)] *m/f* advisor; (*de tese*) supervisor ♦ *adj* guiding; **~ profissional** careers advisor.

oriental [orjẽ'taw] (*pl* **-ais**) *adj* eastern; (*do Extremo Oriente*) oriental ♦ *m/f* oriental.

orientar [orjẽ'ta*] *vt* (*situar*) to orientate; (*indicar o rumo*) to direct; (*aconselhar*) to guide; **~-se** *vr* to get one's bearings; **~-se**

NB: *European Portuguese adds the following consonants to certain words:* **b** (sú(b)dito, su(b)til); **c** (a(c)ção, a(c)cionista, a(c)to); **m** (inde(m)ne); **p** (ado(p)ção, ado(p)tar); *for further details see p. xiii.*

por algo to follow sth.
oriente [o'rjẽtʃi] *m*: **o O~** the East; **Extremo O~** Far East; **O~ Médio/Próximo** Middle/Near East.
orifício [ori'fisju] *m* hole, opening.
origem [o'riʒẽ] (*pl* **-ns**) *f* origin; (*ascendência*) lineage, descent; **lugar de ~** birthplace; **pessoa de ~ brasileira/humilde** person of Brazilian origin/of humble origins; **dar ~ a** to give rise to; **país de ~** country of origin; **ter ~** to originate.
original [oriʒi'naw] (*pl* **-ais**) *adj* original; (*estranho*) strange, odd ♦ *m* original; (*na datilografia*) top copy.
originalidade [oriʒinali'dadʒi] *f* originality; (*excentricidade*) eccentricity.
originar [oriʒi'na*] *vt* to give rise to, start; **~-se** *vr* to arise; **~-se de** to originate from.
originário/a [oriʒi'narju/a] *adj* (*natural*) native; **~ de** (*proveniente*) originating from; **um pássaro ~ do Brasil** a bird native to Brazil.
oriundo/a [o'rjũdu/a] *adj* (*procedente*) arising from; (*natural*) native of.
orixá [ori'ʃa] *m Afro-Brazilian deity*.
orla ['ɔxla] *f* (*borda*) edge, border; (*de roupa*) hem; (*faixa*) strip; **~ marítima** seafront.
orlar [ox'la*] *vt*: **~ algo de algo** to edge sth with sth.
ornamentação [oxnamẽta'sãw] *f* ornamentation.
ornamental [oxnamẽ'taw] (*pl* **-ais**) *adj* ornamental.
ornamentar [oxnamẽ'ta*] *vt* to decorate, adorn.
ornamento [oxna'mẽtu] *m* adornment, decoration.
ornar [ox'na*] *vt* to adorn, decorate.
ornato [ox'natu] *m* adornment, decoration.
ornitologia [oxnitolo'ʒia] *f* ornithology.
ornitologista [oxnitolo'ʒiʃta] *m/f* ornithologist.
orquestra [ox'kɛʃtra] *f* orchestra; **~ de câmara/sinfônica** chamber/symphony orchestra.
orquestração [oxkeʃtra'sãw] *f* (*MÚS*) orchestration; (*fig*) harmonization.
orquestrar [oxkeʃ'tra*] *vt* (*MÚS*) to orchestrate; (*fig*) to harmonize.
orquídea [ox'kidʒja] *f* orchid.
ortodoxia [oxtodok'sia] *f* orthodoxy.
ortodoxo/a [oxto'dɔksu/a] *adj* orthodox.
ortografia [oxtogra'fia] *f* spelling.
ortopedia [oxtope'dʒia] *f* orthopaedics *sg* (*BRIT*), orthopedics *sg* (*US*).
ortopédico/a [oxto'pɛdʒiku/a] *adj* orthopaedic (*BRIT*), orthopedic (*US*).
ortopedista [oxtope'dʒiʃta] *m/f* orthopaedic (*BRIT*) *ou* orthopedic (*US*) specialist.
orvalhar [oxva'ʎa*] *vt* to sprinkle with dew.
orvalho [ox'vaʎu] *m* dew.
os [uʃ] *art def V* **o**.
Osc. *abr* (= *oscilação*) *change in price from previous day*.
oscilação [osila'sãw] (*pl* **-ões**) *f* (*movimento*) oscillation; (*flutuação*) fluctuation; (*hesitação*) hesitation.
oscilante [osi'lãtʃi] *adj* oscillating; (*fig*: *hesitante*) hesitant.
oscilar [osi'la*] *vi* (*balançar-se*) to sway, swing; (*variar*) to fluctuate; (*hesitar*) to hesitate.
ossatura [osa'tura] *f* skeleton, frame.
ósseo/a ['ɔsju/a] *adj* bony; (*ANAT*: *medula etc*) bone *atr*.
osso ['osu] *m* bone; (*dificuldade*) predicament; **um ~ duro de roer** a hard nut to crack; **~s do ofício** occupational hazards.
ossudo/a [o'sudu/a] *adj* bony.
ostensivo/a [oʃtẽ'sivu/a] *adj* ostensible, apparent; (*com alarde*) ostentatious.
ostentação [oʃtẽta'sãw] (*pl* **-ões**) *f* ostentation; (*exibição*) display, show.
ostentar [oʃtẽ'ta*] *vt* to show; (*alardear*) to show off, flaunt.
ostentoso/a [oʃtẽ'tozu/ɔza] *adj* ostentatious, showy.
osteopata [oʃtʃjo'pata] *m/f* osteopath.
ostra ['oʃtra] *f* oyster.
ostracismo [oʃtra'siʒmu] *m* ostracism.
OTAN ['otã] *abr f* (= *Organização do Tratado do Atlântico Norte*) NATO.
otário [o'tarju] (*col*) *m* fool, idiot.
OTE (*BR*) *abr f* = **Obrigação do Tesouro Estadual**.
ótica ['ɔtʃika] *f* optics *sg*; (*loja*) optician's; (*fig*: *ponto de vista*) viewpoint; *V tb* **ótico**.
ótico/a ['ɔtʃiku/a] *adj* optical ♦ *m/f* optician.
otimismo [otʃi'miʒmu] *m* optimism.
otimista [otʃi'miʃta] *adj* optimistic ♦ *m/f* optimist.
otimizar [otʃimi'za*] *vt* to optimize.
ótimo/a ['ɔtʃimu/a] *adj* excellent, splendid ♦ *excl* great!, super!
OTN (*BR*) *abr f* = **Obrigação do Tesouro Nacional**.
otorrino [oto'xinu] *m/f* ear, nose and throat specialist.
ou [o] *conj* or; **~ este ~ aquele** either this one or that one; **~ seja** in other words.
OUA *abr f* (= *Organização da Unidade Africana*) OAU.
ouço ['osu] *etc vb V* **ouvir**.
ourela [o'rela] *f* edge, border.
ouriçado/a [ori'sadu/a] (*col*) *adj* excited.
ouriçar [ori'sa*] *vt* (*col*: *animar*) to liven up; (: *excitar*) to excite; **~-se** *vr* to bristle; (*col*) to get excited.
ouriço [o'risu] *m* (*europeu*) hedgehog; (*casca*) shell; (*col*: *animação*) riot.
ouriço-cacheiro [-ka'ʃejru] (*pl* **ouriços-cacheiros**) *m* coendou.
ouriço-do-mar (*pl* **ouriços-do-mar**) *m* sea urchin.
ourives [o'riviʃ] *m/f inv* (*fabricante*) goldsmith; (*vendedor*) jeweller (*BRIT*), jeweler (*US*).

ourivesaria [oriveza'ria] *f* (*arte*) goldsmith's art; (*loja*) jeweller's (shop) (*BRIT*), jewelry store (*US*).
ouro ['oru] *m* gold; **~s** *mpl* (*CARTAS*) diamonds; **de ~** golden; **nadar em ~** to be rolling in money; **valer ~s** to be worth one's weight in gold.
ousadia [oza'dʒia] *f* daring; (*lance ousado*) daring move; **ter a ~ de fazer** to have the cheek to do.
ousado/a [o'zadu/a] *adj* daring, bold.
ousar [o'za*] *vt, vi* to dare.
out. *abr* (= *Outubro*) Oct.
outdoor [awt'dɔ*] (*pl* **~s**) *m* billboard.
outeiro [o'tejru] *m* hill.
outonal [oto'naw] (*pl* **-ais**) *adj* autumnal.
outono [o'tɔnu] *m* autumn.
outorga [o'tɔxga] *f* granting, concession.
outorgante [otox'gãtʃi] *m/f* grantor.
outorgar [otox'ga*] *vt* to grant.
outrem [o'trẽ] *pron inv* (*sg*) somebody else; (*pl*) other people.
outro/a ['otru/a] *adj* (*sg*) another; (*pl*) other ♦ *pron* another (one); **~s** others; **o ~** the other one; **outra coisa** something else; **~ qualquer** any other; **de ~ modo, de outra maneira** otherwise; **~ tanto** the same again; **na casa dos ~s** in other people's houses; **outra vez** again; **no ~ dia** the next day; **ela está outra** (*mudada*) she's changed; **estar em outra** (*col*) to be into something else; **em ~ lugar** somewhere else; **não deu outra** (*col*) that's exactly what happened.
outrora [o'trɔra] *adv* formerly.
outrossim [otro'sĩ] *adv* likewise, moreover.
outubro [o'tubru] (*PT*: **O-**) *m* October; *V tb* **julho**.
ouvido [o'vidu] *m* (*ANAT*) ear; (*sentido*) hearing; **de ~** by ear; **dar ~s a** to listen to; **entrar por um ~ e sair pelo outro** to go in one ear and out the other; **fazer ~s moucos** *ou* **de mercador** to turn a deaf ear, pretend not to hear; **ser todo ~s** to be all ears; **ter bom ~ para música** to have a good ear for music; **se isso chegar aos ~s dele, ...** if he gets to hear about it, ...
ouvinte [o'vĩtʃi] *m/f* listener; (*estudante*) auditor.
ouvir [o'vi*] *vt* to hear; (*com atenção*) to listen to; (*missa*) to attend ♦ *vi* to hear; to listen; (*levar descompostura*) to catch it; **~ dizer que ...** to hear that ...; **~ falar de** to hear of.
ova ['ɔva] *f* roe; **uma ~!** (*col*) my eye!, no way!
ovação [ova'sãw] (*pl* **-ões**) *f* ovation, acclaim.
ovacionar [ovasjo'na*] *vt* to acclaim; (*pessoa no palco*) to give a standing ovation to.
ovações [ova'sõjʃ] *fpl de* **ovação**.
oval [o'vaw] (*pl* **-ais**) *adj, f* oval.
ovalado/a [ova'ladu/a] *adj* oval.
ovário [o'varju] *m* ovary.
ovelha [o'veʎa] *f* sheep; **~ negra** (*fig*) black sheep.
over ['ove*] *m* overnight market ♦ *adj* overnight.
overnight [ovex'najtʃi] *m, adj* = **over**.
óvni ['ɔvni] *m* UFO.
ovo ['ovu] *m* egg; **~s cozidos duros** hard-boiled eggs; **~s escaldados** (*PT*) *ou* **pochê** (*BR*) poached eggs; **~s estrelados** *ou* **fritos** fried eggs; **~s mexidos** scrambled eggs; **~s quentes** soft-boiled eggs; **~s de granja** free-range eggs; **~ de Páscoa** Easter egg; **estar/acordar de ~ virado** (*col*) to be/wake up in a bad mood; **pisar em ~s** (*fig*) to tread carefully; **ser um ~** (*apartamento etc*) to be a shoebox.
ovulação [ovula'sãw] *f* ovulation.
óvulo ['ɔvulu] *m* egg, ovum.
oxalá [oʃa'la] *excl* let's hope ...; **~ a situação melhore em breve** let's hope the situation improves soon.
oxidação [oksida'sãw] *f* (*QUÍM*) oxidation; (*ferrugem*) rusting.
oxidado/a [oksi'dadu/a] *adj* rusty; (*QUÍM*) oxidized.
oxidar [oksi'da*] *vt* to rust; (*QUÍM*) to oxidize; **~-se** *vr* to rust, go rusty; to oxidize.
óxido ['ɔksidu] *m* oxide; **~ de carbono** carbon monoxide.
oxigenado/a [oksiʒe'nadu/a] *adj* (*cabelo*) bleached; (*QUÍM*) oxygenated; **água oxigenada** peroxide; **uma loura oxigenada** a peroxide blonde.
oxigenar [oksiʒe'na*] *vt* to oxygenate; (*cabelo*) to bleach.
oxigênio [oksi'ʒenju] *m* oxygen.
oxum [o'ʃũ] *m* *Afro-Brazilian river god.*
ozônio [o'zonju] *m* ozone; **camada de ~** ozone layer.

P

P, p [pe] (*pl* **ps**) *m* P, p; **P de Pedro** P for Peter.
P. *abr* (= *Praça*) Sq.; = **Padre**.
p. *abr* (= *página*) p.; (= *parte*) pt; = **por**; = **próximo**.
p/ *abr* = **para**.
PA *abr* = **Pará** ♦ *abr* (*COM*: *de ações*) = **preferencial, classe A**.
p.a. *abr* (= *por ano*) p.a.

***NB**: European Portuguese adds the following consonants to certain words:* **b** (sú(b)dito, su(b)til); **c** (a(c)ção, a(c)cionista, a(c)to); **m** (inde(m)ne); **p** (ado(p)ção, ado(p)tar); *for further details see p. xiii.*

pá [pa] *f* shovel; (*de remo, hélice*) blade; (*de moinho*) sail ♦ *m* (*PT*) pal, mate; ~ **de lixo** dustpan; ~ **mecânica** bulldozer; **uma** ~ **de** lots of; **da** ~ **virada** (*col*) wild.

paca ['paka] *f* (*ZOOL*) paca ♦ *m/f* fool ♦ *adj* stupid ♦ *adv* (*col*): **'tá quente** ~ it's bloody hot.

pacatez [paka'teʒ] *f* (*de pessoa*) quietness; (*de lugar, vida*) peacefulness.

pacato/a [pa'katu/a] *adj* (*pessoa*) quiet; (*lugar*) peaceful.

pachorra [pa'ʃoxa] *f* phlegm, impassiveness; **ter a** ~ **de fazer** to have the gall to do.

pachorrento/a [paʃo'xẽtu/a] *adj* slow, sluggish.

paciência [pa'sjẽsja] *f* patience; (*CARTAS*) patience; **ter** ~ to be patient; ~! we'll (*ou* you'll *etc*) just have to put up with it!; **perder a** ~ to lose one's patience.

paciente [pa'sjẽtʃi] *adj*, *m/f* patient.

pacificação [pasifika'sãw] *f* pacification.

pacificador(a) [pasifika'do*(a)] *adj* calming ♦ *m/f* peacemaker.

pacificar [pasifi'ka*] *vt* to pacify, calm (down); ~**-se** *vr* to calm down.

pacífico/a [pa'sifiku/a] *adj* (*pessoa*) peace-loving; (*aceito sem discussão*) undisputed; (*sossegado*) peaceful; **(Oceano) P**~ Pacific Ocean; **ponto** ~ undisputed point.

pacifismo [pasi'fiʒmu] *m* pacifism.

pacifista [pasi'fiʃta] *m/f* pacifist.

paço ['pasu] *m* palace; (*fig*) court.

paçoca [pa'sɔka] *f* (*doce*) peanut fudge; (*fig*: *misturada*) jumble, hotchpotch; (: *coisa amassada*) crumpled mess.

pacote [pa'kɔtʃi] *m* packet; (*embrulho*) parcel; (*ECON, COMPUT, TURISMO*) package.

pacto ['paktu] *m* pact; (*ajuste*) agreement; ~ **de não-agressão** non-aggression treaty; ~ **de sangue** blood pact; **P**~ **de Varsóvia** Warsaw Pact.

pactuar [pak'twa*] *vt* to agree on ♦ *vi* : ~ **(com)** to make a pact *ou* an agreement with.

padaria [pada'ria] *f* bakery, baker's (shop).

padecer [pade'se*] *vt* to suffer; (*suportar*) to put up with, endure ♦ *vi*: ~ **de** to suffer from.

padecimento [padesi'mẽtu] *m* suffering; (*dor*) pain.

padeiro [pa'dejru] *m* baker.

padiola [pa'dʒjɔla] *f* stretcher.

padrão [pa'drãw] (*pl* **-ões**) *m* standard; (*medida*) gauge; (*desenho*) pattern; (*fig*: *modelo*) model; ~ **de vida** standard of living.

padrasto [pa'draʃtu] *m* stepfather.

padre ['padri] *m* priest; **O Santo P**~ the Holy Father.

padrinho [pa'driɲu] *m* (*REL*) godfather; (*de noivo*) best man; (*fig*) sponsor; (*paraninfo*) guest of honour.

padroeiro/a [pa'drwejru/a] *m/f* patron; (*santo*) patron saint.

padrões [pa'drõjʃ] *mpl de* **padrão**.

padronização [padroniza'sãw] *f* standardization.

padronizado/a [padroni'zadu/a] *adj* standardized, standard.

padronizar [padroni'za*] *vt* to standardize.

pães [pãjʃ] *mpl de* **pão**.

paetê [pae'te] *m* sequin.

pág. *abr* (= *página*) p.

paga ['paga] *f* payment; (*salário*) pay; **em** ~ **de** in return for.

pagã [pa'gã] *f de* **pagão**.

pagador(a) [paga'do*(a)] *adj* paying ♦ *m/f* (*quem paga*) payer; (*de salário*) pay clerk; (*de banco*) teller.

pagadoria [pagado'ria] *f* payment office.

pagamento [paga'mẽtu] *m* payment; ~ **a prazo** *ou* **em prestações** payment in instal(l)ments; ~ **à vista** cash payment; ~ **contra entrega** (*COM*) COD, cash on delivery.

pagão/gã [pa'gãw/gã] (*pl* ~**s/**~**s**) *adj*, *m/f* pagan.

pagar [pa'ga*] *vt* to pay; (*compras, pecados*) to pay for; (*o que devia*) to pay back; (*retribuir*) to repay ♦ *vi* to pay; ~ **por algo** (*tb fig*) to pay for sth; ~ **a prestações** to pay in instal(l)ments; ~ **à vista** (*PT* **a pronto**) to pay on the spot, pay at the time of purchase; ~ **de contado** (*PT*) to pay cash; **a** ~ unpaid; ~ **caro** (*fig*) to pay a high price; ~ **a pena** to pay the penalty; ~ **na mesma moeda** (*fig*) to give tit for tat; ~ **para ver** (*fig*) to call sb's bluff, demand proof; **você me paga!** you'll pay for this!

página ['paʒina] *f* page; ~ **de rosto** frontispiece, title page; ~ **em branco** blank page.

paginação [paʒina'sãw] *f* pagination.

paginar [paʒi'na*] *vt* to paginate.

pago/a ['pagu/a] *pp de* **pagar** ♦ *adj* paid; (*fig*) even ♦ *m* pay.

pagode [pa'gɔdʒi] *m* pagoda; (*fig*) fun, high jinks *pl*; (*festa*) knees-up.

pagto. *abr* = **pagamento**.

paguei [pa'gej] *etc vb V* **pagar**.

pai [paj] *m* father; ~**s** *mpl* parents; ~ **adotivo** adoptive father; ~ **de família** family man; **um idiota de** ~ **e mãe** (*col*) a complete idiot.

pai-de-santo (*pl* **pais-de-santo**) *m* macumba priest.

pai-de-todos (*pl* **pais-de-todos**) (*col*) *m* middle finger.

pai-dos-burros (*pl* **pais-dos-burros**) (*col*) *m* dictionary.

painel [paj'nɛw] (*pl* **-éis**) *m* (*numa parede*) panel; (*quadro*) picture; (*AUTO*) dashboard; (*de avião*) instrument panel; (*reunião de especialistas*) panel (of experts).

paio ['paju] *m* pork sausage.

paiol [pa'jɔw] (*pl* **-óis**) *m* storeroom; (*celeiro*) barn; (*de pólvora*) powder magazine; ~ **de carvão** coal bunker.

pairar [paj'ra*] *vi* to hover; (*embarcação*) to lie to.

país [pa'jiʃ] *m* country; (*região*) land; ~

encantado fairyland; ~ **natal** native land.
paisagem [paj'zaʒẽ] (*pl* **-ns**) *f* scenery, landscape; (*pintura*) landscape.
paisano/a [paj'zanu/a] *adj* civilian ♦ *m/f* (*não militar*) civilian; (*compatriota*) fellow countryman; **à paisana** (*soldado*) in civvies; (*policial*) in plain clothes.
Países Baixos *mpl*: **os** ~ the Netherlands.
paixão [paj'ʃãw] (*pl* **-ões**) *f* passion.
paixonite [pajʃo'nitʃi] (*col*) *f*: ~ **(aguda)** crush, infatuation.
pajé [pa'ʒɛ] *m* medicine man.
pajear [pa'ʒja*] *vt* (*cuidar*) to look after; (*paparicar*) to mollycoddle.
pajem ['paʒẽ] (*pl* **-ns**) *m* (*moço*) page.
pala ['pala] *f* (*de boné*) peak; (*em automóvel*) sun visor; (*de vestido*) yoke; (*de sapato*) strap; (*col*: *dica*) tip.
palacete [pala'setʃi] *m* small palace.
palácio [pa'lasju] *m* palace; ~ **da justiça** courthouse; ~ **real** royal palace.
paladar [pala'da*] *m* taste; (ANAT) palate.
paladino [pala'dʒinu] *m* (*medieval*, *fig*) champion.
palafita [pala'fita] *f* (*estacaria*) stilts *pl*; (*habitação*) stilt house.
palanque [pa'lãki] *m* (*estrado*) stand.
palatável [pala'tavew] (*pl* **-eis**) *adj* palatable.
palato [pa'latu] *m* palate.
palavra [pa'lavra] *f* word; (*fala*) speech; (*promessa*) promise; (*direito de falar*) right to speak; ~! honestly!; **pessoa de/sem** ~ reliable/unreliable person; **em outras** ~**s** in other words; **em poucas** ~**s** briefly; **cumprir a/faltar com a** ~ to keep/break one's word; **dar a** ~ **a alguém** to give sb the chance to speak; **não dar uma** ~ not to say a word; **dirigir a** ~ **a** to address; **estar com a** ~ **na boca** to have the word on the tip of one's tongue; **pedir a** ~ to ask permission to speak; **ter** ~ (*pessoa*) to be reliable; **tirar a** ~ **da boca de alguém** to take the words right out of sb's mouth; **tomar a** ~ to take the floor; **a última** ~ (*tb fig*) the last word; ~ **de honra** word of honour; ~ **de ordem** watchword, formula; ~**s cruzadas** crossword (puzzle) *sg*.
palavra-chave (*pl* **palavras-chaves**) *f* key word.
palavrão [pala'vrãw] (*pl* **-ões**) *m* (*obsceno*) swearword.
palavreado [pala'vrjadu] *m* babble, gibberish; (*loquacidade*) smooth talk.
palavrões [pala'vrõjʃ] *mpl de* **palavrão**.
palco ['palku] *m* (TEATRO) stage; (*fig*: *local*) scene.
paleontologia [paljõtolo'ʒia] *f* palaeontology (BRIT), paleontology (US).
palerma [pa'lɛxma] *adj* silly, stupid ♦ *m/f* fool.
Palestina [paleʃ'tʃina] *f*: **a** ~ Palestine.
palestino/a [paleʃ'tʃinu/a] *adj*, *m/f* Palestinian.
palestra [pa'lɛʃtra] *f* (*conversa*) chat, talk; (*conferência*) lecture, talk.
palestrar [paleʃ'tra*] *vi* to chat, talk.
paleta [pa'leta] *f* palette.
paletó [pale'tɔ] *m* jacket; **abotoar o** ~ (*col*) to kick the bucket.
palha ['paʎa] *f* straw; **chapéu de** ~ straw hat; **não mexer** *ou* **levantar uma** ~ (*col*) not to lift a finger.
palhaçada [paʎa'sada] *f* (*ato*, *dito*) joke; (*cena*) farce.
palhaço [pa'ʎasu] *m* clown.
palheiro [pa'ʎejru] *m* hayloft; (*monte de feno*) haystack.
palheta [pa'ʎeta] *f* (*de veneziana*) slat; (*de turbina*) blade; (*de pintor*) palette.
palhoça [pa'ʎɔsa] *f* thatched hut.
paliar [pa'lja*] *vt* (*disfarçar*) to disguise, gloss over; (*atenuar*) to mitigate, extenuate.
paliativo/a [palja'tʃivu/a] *adj* palliative.
paliçada [pali'sada] *f* fence; (*militar*) stockade; (*para torneio*) enclosure.
palidez [pali'deʒ] *f* paleness.
pálido/a ['palidu/a] *adj* pale.
pálio ['palju] *m* canopy.
palitar [pali'ta*] *vt* to pick ♦ *vi* to pick one's teeth.
paliteiro [pali'tejru] *m* toothpick holder.
palito [pa'litu] *m* stick; (*para os dentes*) toothpick; (*pessoa*) beanpole; (*perna*) pin.
palma ['pawma] *f* (*folha*) palm leaf; (*da mão*) palm; **bater** ~**s** to clap; **conhecer algo como a** ~ **da mão** to know sth like the back of one's hand; **trazer alguém nas** ~**s da mão** (*fig*) to pamper sb.
palmada [paw'mada] *f* slap.
palmatória [pawma'tɔrja] *f*: ~ **do mundo** self-righteous person; *V tb* **mão**.
palmeira [paw'mejra] *f* palm tree.
palmilha [paw'miʎa] *f* inner sole.
palmilhar [pawmi'ʎa*] *vt*, *vi* to walk.
palmito [paw'mitu] *m* palm heart.
palmo ['pawmu] *m* (hand) span; ~ **a** ~ inch by inch; **não enxerga um** ~ **adiante do nariz** he can't see further than the nose on his face.
palpável [paw'pavew] (*pl* **-eis**) *adj* tangible; (*fig*) obvious.
pálpebra ['pawpebra] *f* eyelid.
palpitação [pawpita'sãw] (*pl* **-ões**) *f* beating, throbbing; **palpitações** *fpl* palpitations.
palpitante [pawpi'tãtʃi] *adj* beating, throbbing; (*fig*: *emocionante*) thrilling; (: *de interesse atual*) sensational.
palpitar [pawpi'ta*] *vi* (*coração*) to beat; (*comover-se*) to shiver; (*dar palpite*) to stick one's oar in.
palpite [paw'pitʃi] *m* (*intuição*) hunch; (*em*

NB: *European Portuguese adds the following consonants to certain words:* **b** (sú(b)dito, su(b)til); **c** (a(c)ção, a(c)cionista, a(c)to); **m** (inde(m)ne); **p** (ado(p)ção, ado(p)tar); *for further details see p. xiii.*

jogo, turfe) tip; (*opinião*) opinion; **dar ~** to give one's two cents' worth, stick one's oar in.

palpiteiro/a [pawpi'tejru/a] *adj* meddling ♦ *m/f* meddler.

palude [pa'ludʒi] *m* marsh, swamp.

paludismo [palu'dʒiʒmu] *m* malaria.

palustre [pa'luʃtri] *adj* (*terra*) marshy; (*aves*) marsh-dwelling.

pamonha [pa'mɔɲa] *m/f* nitwit ♦ *adj* idiotic.

pampa ['pãpa] *f* pampas; **às ~s** (+ *n*) (*col*) loads of; (+ *adj, adv*) really.

panaca [pa'naka] *m/f* fool ♦ *adj* stupid.

panacéia [pana'sɛja] *f* panacea.

Panamá [pana'ma] *m*: **o ~** Panama.

panamenho/a [pana'mɛɲu/a] *adj, m/f* Panamanian.

pan-americano/a [pan-] *adj* Pan-American.

pança ['pãsa] *f* belly, paunch.

pancada [pã'kada] *f* (*no corpo*) blow, hit; (*choque*) knock; (*relógio*) stroke ♦ *m/f* (*col*) loony ♦ *adj* crazy; **~ d'água** downpour; **dar uma ~ com a cabeça** to bang one's head; **dar ~ em alguém** to hit sb; **levar uma ~** to get hit.

pancadaria [pãkada'ria] *f* (*surra*) beating; (*tumulto*) fight.

pâncreas ['pãkrjaʃ] *m inv* pancreas.

pançudo/a [pã'sudu/a] *adj* fat, potbellied.

panda ['pãda] *f* panda.

pandarecos [pãda'rɛkuʃ] *mpl*: **em ~** in pieces; (*fig*: *exausto*) worn out; (: *moralmente*) devastated.

pândega ['pãdega] *f* merrymaking, good time.

pândego/a ['pãdegu/a] *adj* (*farrista*) merrymaking; (*engraçado*) jolly ♦ *m/f* (*farrista*) merrymaker; (*pessoa engraçada*) joker.

pandeiro [pã'dejru] *m* tambourine.

pandemônio [pãde'monju] *m* pandemonium.

pane ['pani] *f* breakdown.

panegírico [pane'ʒiriku] *m* panegyric.

panejar [pane'ʒa*] *vi* to flap.

panela [pa'nɛla] *f* (*de barro*) pot; (*de metal*) pan; (*de cozinhar*) saucepan; (*no dente*) large cavity, hole; **~ de pressão** pressure cooker.

panelinha [pane'liɲa] *f* clique.

panfletar [pãfle'ta*] *vi* to distribute pamphlets.

panfleto [pã'fletu] *m* pamphlet.

pangaré [pãga'rɛ] *m* (*cavalo*) nag.

pânico ['paniku] *m* panic; **em ~** panic-stricken; **entrar em ~** to panic.

panificação [panifika'sãw] *f* (*fabricação*) bread-making; (*padaria*) bakery.

panificadora [panifika'dora] *f* baker's.

pano ['panu] *m* cloth; (*TEATRO*) curtain; (*largura de tecido*) width; (*vela*) sheet, sail; **~ de chão** floorcloth; **~ de pratos** tea-towel; **~ de pó** duster; **~ de fundo** (*tb fig*) backdrop; **a todo o ~** at full speed; **por baixo do ~** (*fig*) under the counter; **dar ~ para mangas** (*fig*) to give food for thought; **pôr ~s quentes em algo** (*fig*) to dampen sth down.

panorama [pano'rama] *m* (*vista*) view; (*fig: observação*) survey.

panorâmica [pano'ramika] *f* (*exposição*) survey.

panorâmico/a [pano'ramiku/a] *adj* panoramic.

panqueca [pã'kɛka] *f* pancake.

pantalonas [pãta'lɔnaʃ] *fpl* baggy trousers.

pantanal [pãta'naw] (*pl* **-ais**) *m* swampland.

pântano ['pãtanu] *m* marsh, swamp.

pantanoso/a [pãta'nozu/ɔza] *adj* marshy, swampy.

panteão [pã'tjãw] (*pl* **-ões**) *m* pantheon.

pantera [pã'tɛra] *f* panther.

pantomima [pãto'mima] *f* pantomime.

pantufa [pã'tufa] *f* slipper.

pão [pãw] (*pl* **pães**) *m* bread; **o P~ de Açúcar** (*no Rio*) Sugarloaf Mountain; **~ de carne** meat loaf; **~ de centeio** rye bread; **~ de fôrma** sliced loaf; **~ caseiro** home-made bread; **~ francês** French bread; **~ integral** wholemeal (*BRIT*) *ou* wholewheat (*US*) bread; **~ preto** black bread; **~ torrado** toast; **ganhar o ~** to earn a living; **~ dormido** day-old bread; **dizer ~, ~, queijo, queijo** (*col*) to call a spade a spade, pull no punches; **comer o ~ que o diabo amassou** (*fig*) to have it tough; **tirar o ~ da boca de alguém** (*fig*) to take the food out of sb's mouth.

pão-de-ló [-lɔ] *m* sponge cake.

pão-durismo [-du'riʒmu] (*col*) *m* meanness, stinginess.

pão-duro (*pl* **pães-duros**) (*col*) *adj* mean, stingy ♦ *m/f* miser.

pãozinho [pãw'ziɲu] *m* roll.

papa ['papa] *m* Pope; (*fig*) spiritual leader ♦ *f* mush, pap; (*mingau*) porridge; **não ter ~s na língua** to be outspoken, not to mince one's words.

papada [pa'pada] *f* double chin.

papagaiada [papagaj'ada] (*col*) *f* showing off.

papagaio [papa'gaju] *m* parrot; (*pipa*) kite; (*COM*) accommodation bill; (*AUTO*) provisional licence (*BRIT*), student driver's license (*US*) ♦ *excl* (*col*) heavens!

papai [pa'paj] *m* dad, daddy; **P~ Noel** Santa Claus, Father Christmas; **o ~ aqui** (*col*) yours truly.

papal [pa'paw] (*pl* **-ais**) *adj* papal.

papa-moscas *f inv* (*BIO*) flycatcher.

papar [pa'pa*] (*col*) *vt, vi* (*comer*) to eat; (*extorquir*): **~ algo a alguém** to get sth out of sb.

paparicar [papari'ka*] *vt* to pamper.

paparicos [papa'rikuʃ] *mpl* (*mimos*) pampering *sg*.

papear [pa'pja*] *vi* to chat.

papel [pa'pɛw] (*pl* **-éis**) *m* paper; (*no teatro*) part, role; (*função*) role; **fazer o ~ de** to play the part of; **fazer ~ de idiota** *etc* to play the fool *etc*; **~ aéreo** airmail paper; **~ celofane** cling film; **~ crepom** crêpe paper;

~ **de embrulho** wrapping paper; ~ **de escrever/de alumínio** writing paper/tinfoil; ~ **higiênico** toilet paper; ~ **de parede** wallpaper; ~ **de seda/transparente** tissue paper/tracing paper; ~ **laminado** *ou* **lustroso** coated paper; ~ **ofício** foolscap; ~ **pardo** brown paper; ~ **timbrado** headed paper; ~ **usado** waste paper; ~ **yes** ® tissue, kleenex ®; **ficar no** ~ (*fig*) to stay on the drawing board; **pôr no** ~ to put down on paper *ou* in writing; **de** ~ **passado** officially.

papelada [pape'lada] *f* pile of papers; (*burocracia*) paperwork, red tape.

papelão [pape'lãw] *m* cardboard; (*fig*) fiasco; **fazer um** ~ to make a fool of o.s.

papelaria [papela'ria] *f* stationer's (shop).

papel-carbono *m* carbon paper.

papeleta [pape'leta] *f* (*cartaz*) notice; (*papel avulso*) piece of paper; (*MED*) chart.

papel-moeda (*pl* **papéis-moeda(s)**) *m* paper money, banknotes *pl*.

papel-pergaminho *m* parchment.

papelzinho [papew'ziɲu[*m* scrap of paper.

papiro [pa'piru] *m* papyrus.

papo ['papu] *m* (*de ave*) crop; (*col*: *de pessoa*) double chin; (: *conversa*) chat; (: *chute*) hot air; (*numa roupa*) tuck; **ele é um bom** ~ (*col*) he's a good talker; **bater** *ou* **levar um** ~ (*col*) to have a chat; **ficar de** ~ **para o ar** (*fig*) to laze around; ~ **firme** (*col*: *verdade*) gospel (truth); (: *pessoa*) straight talker; ~ **furado** (*col*: *promessa*) hot air; (: *conversa*) idle chat.

papo-de-anjo (*pl* **papos-de-anjo**) *m sweet made of egg yolks*.

papo-firme (*pl* **papos-firmes**) (*col*) *adj* reliable ♦ *m/f* reliable sort.

papo-furado (*pl* **papos-furados**) (*col*) *adj* unreliable ♦ *m/f*: **ele é um** ~ he never comes up with the goods.

papoula [pa'pola] *f* poppy.

páprica ['paprika] *f* paprika.

Papua Nova Guiné [pa'pua-] *f* Papua New Guinea.

papudo/a [pa'pudu/a] *adj* fat in the face, double-chinned.

paqueração [pakera'sãw] (*col*: *pl* **-ões**) *f* pick-up.

paquerador(a) [pakera'do*(a)] (*col*) *adj* flirtatious ♦ *m/f* flirt.

paquerar [pake'ra*] (*col*) *vi* to flirt ♦ *vt* to chat up.

paquete [pa'ketʃi] *m* steamship.

paquistanês/esa [pakiʃta'neʃ/eza] *adj*, *m/f* Pakistani.

Paquistão [pakiʃ'tãw] *m*: **o** ~ Pakistan.

par [pa*] *adj* (*igual*) equal; (*número*) even ♦ *m* pair; (*casal*) couple; (*pessoa na dança*) partner; ~ **a** ~ side by side, level; **ao** ~ (*COM*) at par; **sem** ~ incomparable; **abaixo de** ~ (*COM, GOLFE*) below par; **estar/ficar a** ~ **de algo** to be/get up to date with sth.

para ['para] *prep* for; (*direção*) to, towards; **bom** ~ **comer** good to eat; ~ **não ser ouvido** so as not to be heard; ~ **que** so that, in order that; ~ **quê?** what for?, why?; **ir** ~ **São Paulo** to go to São Paulo; **ir** ~ **casa** to go home; ~ **com** (*atitude*) towards; **de lá** ~ **cá** since then; ~ **a semana** next week; **estar** ~ to be about to; **é** ~ **nós ficarmos aqui?** should we stay here?

parabenizar [parabeni'za*] *vt*: ~ **alguém por algo** to congratulate sb on sth.

parabens [para'bẽjʃ] *mpl* congratulations; (*no aniversário*) happy birthday; **dar** ~ **a** to congratulate; **você está de** ~ you are to be congratulated.

parábola [par'rabola] *f* parable; (*MAT*) parabola.

pára-brisa ['para-] (*pl* ~**s**) *m* windscreen (*BRIT*), windshield (*US*).

pára-choque ['para-] (*pl* ~**s**) *m* (*AUTO*) bumper.

parada [pa'rada] *f* stop; (*COM*) stoppage; (*militar*, *colegial*) parade; (*col*: *coisa difícil*) ordeal; **ser uma** ~ (*col*: *pessoa*: *difícil*) to be awkward; (: *ser bonito*) to be gorgeous; **agüentar a** ~ (*col*) to stick it out; **topar a** ~ (*col*) to accept the challenge; **topar qualquer** ~ (*col*) to be game for anything; ~ **cardíaca** heart failure.

paradeiro [para'dejru] *m* whereabouts.

paradigma [para'dʒigma] *m* paradigm.

paradisíaco/a [paradʒi'ʒiaku/a] *adj* (*fig*) idyllic.

parado/a [pa'radu/a] *adj* (*pessoa*: *imóvel*) standing still; (: *sem vida*) lifeless; (*carro*) stationary; (*máquina*) out of action; (*olhar*) fixed; (*trabalhador*, *fábrica*) idle; **fiquei** ~ **uma hora no ponto de ônibus** I stood for an hour at the bus stop; **não fique aí** ~**!** don't just stand there!

paradoxal [paradok'saw] (*pl* **-ais**) *adj* paradoxical.

paradoxo [para'dɔksu] *m* paradox.

paraense [para'ẽsi] *adj* from Pará ♦ *m/f* person from Pará.

parafernália [parafex'nalja] *f* (*de uso pessoal*) personal items *pl*; (*equipamento*) equipment; (*tralha*) paraphernalia.

parafina [para'fina] *f* paraffin.

paráfrase [pa'rafrazi] *f* paraphrase.

parafrasear [parafra'zja*] *vt* to paraphrase.

parafusar [parafu'za*] *vt* to screw in ♦ *vi*: ~ (*meditar*) to ponder.

parafuso [para'fuzu] *m* screw; **entrar em** ~ (*col*) to get into a state; **ter um** ~ **de menos** (*col*) to have a screw loose.

paragem [pa'raʒẽ] (*pl* **-ns**) *f* stop; ~ **de eléctrico** (*PT*) tram (*BRIT*) *ou* streetcar (*US*) stop;

NB: European Portuguese adds the following consonants to certain words: **b** (sú(b)dito, su(b)til); **c** (a(c)ção, a(c)cionista, a(c)to); **m** (inde(m)ne); **p** (ado(p)ção, ado(p)tar); *for further details see p. xiii.*

paragens *pl* (*lugares*) places, parts.
parágrafo [pa'ragrafu] *m* paragraph.
Paraguai [para'gwaj] *m*: **o** ~ Paraguay.
paraguaio/a [para'gwaju/a] *adj*, *m/f* Paraguayan.
paraíba [para'iba] (*col*) *m* (*operário*) labourer (*BRIT*), laborer (*US*) ♦ *f* (*mulher macho*) butch woman.
paraibano/a [paraj'banu/a] *adj* from Paraíba ♦ *m/f* person from Paraíba.
paraíso [para'izu] *m* paradise.
pára-lama ['para-] (*pl* ~**s**) *m* wing (*BRIT*), fender (*US*); (*de bicicleta*) mudguard.
paralelamente [paralela'mẽtʃi] *adv* in parallel; (*ao mesmo tempo*) at the same time.
paralela [para'lɛla] *f* parallel line; ~**s** *fpl* (*ESPORTE*) parallel bars.
paralelepípedo [paralele'pipedu] *m* paving stone.
paralelo/a [para'lɛlu/a] *adj* (*tb*: *COMPUT*) parallel ♦ *m* (*GEO*, *comparação*) parallel.
paralisação [paraliza'sãw] (*pl* **-ões**) *f* (*suspensão*) stoppage.
paralisar [parali'za*] *vt* to paralyse; (*trabalho*) to bring to a standstill; ~**-se** *vr* to become paralysed; (*fig*) to come to a standstill.
paralisia [parali'zia] *f* paralysis.
paralítico/a [para'litʃiku/a] *adj*, *m/f* paralytic.
paramédico/a [para'mɛdʒiku/a] *adj* paramedical.
paramentado/a [paramẽ'tadu/a] *adj* smart.
paramento [para'mẽtu] *m* (*adorno*) ornament; ~**s** *mpl* (*vestes*) vestments; (*de igreja*) hangings.
parâmetro [pa'rametru] *m* parameter.
paramilitar [paramili'ta*] *adj* paramilitary.
paranaense [parana'ẽsi] *adj* from Paraná ♦ *m/f* person from Paraná.
paraninfo [para'nĩfu] *m* patron; (*pessoa homenageada*) guest of honour (*BRIT*) *ou* honor (*US*).
paranóia [para'nɔja] *f* paranoia.
paranóico/a [para'nɔjku/a] *adj*, *m/f* paranoid.
paranormal [paranox'maw] (*pl* **-ais**) *adj* paranormal.
parapeito [para'pejtu] *m* (*muro*) wall, parapet; (*da janela*) windowsill.
paraplégico/a [para'plɛʒiku/a] *adj*, *m/f* paraplegic.
pára-quedas ['para-] *m inv* parachute; **saltar de** ~ to parachute.
pára-quedismo [parake'dʒiʒmu] *m* parachuting, sky-diving.
pára-quedista [parake'dʒiʃta] *m/f* parachutist ♦ *m* (*MIL*) paratrooper.
parar [pa'ra*] *vi* to stop; (*ficar*) to stay ♦ *vt* to stop; **fazer** ~ (*deter*) to stop; ~ **na cadeia** to end up in jail; ~ **de fazer** to stop doing.
pára-raios ['para-] *m inv* lightning conductor.
parasita [para'zita] *adj* parasitic ♦ *m* parasite.
parasitar [parazi'ta*] *vi* to sponge ♦ *vt*: ~ **alguém** to sponge off sb.
parasito [para'zitu] *m* parasite.
parceiro/a [pax'sejru/a] *adj* matching ♦ *m/f* partner.
parcela [pax'sɛla] *f* piece, bit; (*de pagamento*) instalment (*BRIT*), installment (*US*); (*de terra*) plot; (*do eleitorado etc*) section; (*MAT*) item.
parcelado/a [paxse'ladu/a] *adj* (*pagamento*) in instalments (*BRIT*) *ou* installments (*US*).
parcelar [paxse'la*] *vt* (*pagamento*, *dívida*) to schedule in instalments (*BRIT*) *ou* installments (*US*).
parceria [paxse'ria] *f* partnership.
parcial [pax'sjaw] (*pl* **-ais**) *adj* (*incompleto*) partial; (*feito por partes*) in parts; (*pessoa*) biased; (*POL*) partisan.
parcialidade [paxsjali'dadʒi] *f* bias, partiality; (*POL*) partisans *pl*.
parcimonioso/a [paxsimo'njozu/ɔza] *adj* parsimonious.
parco/a ['paxku/a] *adj* (*escasso*) scanty; (*econômico*) thrifty; (*refeição*) frugal.
pardal [pax'daw] (*pl* **-ais**) *m* sparrow.
pardieiro [pax'dʒjejru] *m* ruin, heap.
pardo/a ['paxdu/a] *adj* (*cinzento*) grey (*BRIT*), gray (*US*); (*castanho*) brown; (*mulato*) mulatto.
parecença [pare'sẽsa] *f* resemblance.
parecer [pare'se*] *m* (*opinião*) opinion ♦ *vi* (*ter a aparência de*) to look, seem; ~ **(com)** (*ter semelhança com*) to look like; ~**-se** *vr* to look alike, resemble each other; ~**-se com alguém** to look like sb; **ao que parece** apparently; **parece-me que** I think that, it seems to me that; **que lhe parece?** what do you think?; **parece que** it looks as if; ~ **de auditoria** (*COM*) auditors' report.
parecido/a [pare'sidu/a] *adj* alike, similar; ~ **com** like.
paredão [pare'dãw] (*pl* **-ões**) *m* (*de serra*) face.
parede [pa'redʒi] *f* wall; **imprensar** *ou* **pôr alguém contra a** ~ to put sb on the spot, buttonhole sb; ~ **divisória** partition wall.
paredões [pare'dõjʃ] *mpl de* **paredão**.
parelha [pa'reʎa] *f* (*de cavalos*) team; (*par*) pair.
parente/a [pa'rẽtʃi] *m/f* relative, relation; **ser** ~ **de alguém** to be related to sb.
parentela [parẽ'tɛla] *f* relations *pl*.
parentesco [parẽ'teʃku] *m* relationship; (*fig*) connection.
parêntese [pa'rẽtezi] *m* parenthesis; (*na escrita*) bracket; (*fig*: *digressão*) digression.
páreo ['parju] *m* race; (*fig*) competition; **ser um** ~ **duro** to be a hard nut to crack.
pareô [pa'rjo] *m* beach wrap.
pária ['parja] *m* pariah.
paridade [pari'dadʒi] *f* (*igualdade*) equality; (*de câmbio*, *remuneração*) parity; **abaixo/acima da** ~ below/above par.
parir [pa'ri*] *vt* to give birth to ♦ *vi* to give birth; (*mulher*) to have a baby.

Paris [pa'riʃ] *n* Paris.
parisiense [pari'zjẽsi] *adj*, *m/f* Parisian.
parlamentar [paxlamẽ'ta*] *adj* parliamentary ♦ *m/f* parliamentarian, MP ♦ *vi* to parley.
parlamentarismo [paxlamẽta'riʒmu] *m* parliamentary democracy.
parlamentarista [paxlamẽta'riʃta] *adj* in favo(u)r of parliamentary democracy ♦ *m/f* supporter of the parliamentary system.
parlamento [paxla'mẽtu] *m* parliament.
parmesão [paxme'zãw] *adj*: **(queijo)** ~ Parmesan (cheese).
pároco ['paroku] *m* parish priest.
paródia [pa'rɔdʒja] *f* parody.
parodiar [paro'dʒja*] *vt* (*fazer paródia de*) to parody; (*imitar*) to mimic, copy.
paróquia [pa'rɔkja] *f* (*REL*) parish; (*col: localidade*) neighbourhood (*BRIT*), neighborhood (*US*).
paroquial [paro'kjaw] (*pl* **-ais**) *adj* parochial.
paroquiano/a [paro'kjanu/a] *m/f* parishioner.
paroxismo [parok'siʒmu] *m* fit, attack; **~s** *mpl* death throes.
parque ['paxki] *m* park; ~ **industrial** industrial estate; ~ **infantil** children's playground; ~ **nacional** national park.
parqueamento [paxkja'mẽtu] *m* parking.
parquear [pax'kja*] *vt* to park.
parreira [pa'xejra] *f* trellised vine.
parrudo/a [pa'xudu/a] *adj* muscular, well-built.
part. *abr* (= *particular*) priv.
parte ['paxtʃi] *f* part; (*quinhão*) share; (*lado*) side; (*ponto*) point; (*JUR*) party; (*papel*) role; ~ **interna** inside; **a maior ~ de** most of; **a maior ~ das vezes** most of the time; **à ~** aside; (*separado*) separate; (*separadamente*) separately; (*além de*) apart from; **da ~ de alguém** on sb's part; **de ~ a ~** each other; **em ~** in part, partly; **em grande ~** to a great extent; **em alguma/qualquer ~** somewhere/anywhere; **em ~ alguma** nowhere; **por toda (a) ~** everywhere; **por ~s** in parts; **por ~ da mãe** on one's mother's side; **pôr de ~** to set aside; **tomar ~ em** to take part in; **dar ~ de alguém à polícia** to report sb to the police; **fazer ~ de algo** to be part of sth; **mandar alguém àquela ~** (*col!*) to tell sb to go to hell.
parteira [pax'tejra] *f* midwife.
partição [paxtʃi'sãw] *f* splitting.
participação [paxtʃisipa'sãw] *f* participation; (*COM*) stake, share; (*comunicação*) announcement, notification.
participante [paxtʃisi'pãtʃi] *m/f* participant ♦ *adj* participating.
participar [paxtʃisi'pa*] *vt* to announce, notify of ♦ *vi*: ~ **de** *ou* **em** (*tomar parte*) to participate in, take part in; (*compartilhar*) to share in.
participio [paxtʃi'sipju] *m* participle.
partícula [pax'tʃikula] *f* particle.
particular [paxtʃiku'la*] *adj* (*especial*) particular, special; (*privativo, pessoal*) private ♦ *m* particular; (*indivíduo*) individual; **em ~** in private; **~es** *mpl* details.
particularidade [paxtʃikulari'dadʒi] *f* peculiarity.
particularizar [paxtʃikulari'za*] *vt* (*especificar*) to specify; (*detalhar*) to give details of; **~-se** *vr* to distinguish o.s.
particularmente [paxtʃikulax'mẽtʃi] *adv* privately; (*especialmente*) particularly.
partida [pax'tʃida] *f* (*saída*) departure; (*ESPORTE*) game, match; (*COM: quantidade*) lot; (*: remessa*) shipment; (*em corrida*) start; **dar ~ em** to start; **perder a ~** to lose.
partidário/a [paxtʃi'darju/a] *adj* supporting ♦ *m/f* supporter, follower.
partido/a [pax'tʃidu/a] *adj* (*dividido*) divided; (*quebrado*) broken ♦ *m* (*POL*) party; (*em jogo*) handicap; **tirar ~ de** to profit from; **tomar o ~ de** to side with.
partilha [pax'tʃiʎa] *f* share.
partilhar [paxtʃi'ʎa*] *vt* to share; (*distribuir*) to share out.
partir [pax'tʃi*] *vt* (*quebrar*) to break; (*dividir*) to divide, split ♦ *vi* (*pôr-se a caminho*) to set off, set out; (*ir-se embora*) to leave, depart; **~-se** *vr* (*quebrar-se*) to break; ~ **de** (*começar, tomar por base*) to start from; (*originar*) to arise from; **a ~ de** (starting) from; **a ~ de agora** from now on, starting from now; ~ **ao meio** to split down the middle; **eu parto do princípio que ...** I am working on the principle that ...; ~ **para** (*col: recorrer a*) to resort to; ~ **para outra** (*col*) to change tack.
partitura [paxtʃi'tura] *f* score.
parto ['paxtu] *m* (child)birth; **estar em trabalho de ~** to be in labour (*BRIT*) *ou* labor (*US*); ~ **induzido** induced labo(u)r; ~ **prematuro** premature birth.
parturiente [paxtu'rjẽtʃi] *f* woman about to give birth.
parvo/a ['paxvu/a] *adj* stupid, silly ♦ *m/f* fool, idiot.
parvoíce [pax'vwisi] *f* silliness, stupidity.
Pasart [pa'zaxtʃi] (*BR*) *abr m* = **Partido Socialista Agrário e Renovador Trabalhista.**
Páscoa ['paʃkwa] *f* Easter; (*dos judeus*) Passover; **a ilha da ~** Easter Island.
Pasep [pa'zɛpi] (*BR*) *abr m* = **Programa de Formação do Patrimônio do Servidor Público.**
pasmaceira [paʒma'sejra] *f* (*apatia*) indolence.
pasmado/a [paʒ'madu/a] *adj* amazed, astonished.
pasmar [paʒ'ma*] *vt* to amaze, astonish; **~-se** *vr*: **~-se com** to be amazed at.

NB: *European Portuguese adds the following consonants to certain words:* **b** (sú(b)dito, su(b)til); **c** (a(c)ção, a(c)cionista, a(c)to); **m** (inde(m)ne); **p** (ado(p)ção, ado(p)tar); *for further details see p. xiii.*

pasmo/a ['paʒmu/a] *m* amazement ♦ *adj* astonished.

paspalhão/lhona [paʃpa'ʎãw/'ʎɔna] (*pl* **-ões/~s**) *adj* stupid ♦ *m/f* fool.

paspalho [paʃ'paʎu] *m* simpleton.

paspalhões [paʃpa'ʎõjʃ] *mpl de* **paspalhão**.

paspalhona [paʃpa'ʎɔna] *f de* **paspalhão**.

pasquim [paʃ'kĩ] (*pl* **-ns**) *m* (*jornal*) satirical newspaper.

passa ['pasa] *f* raisin.

passada [pa'sada] *f* (*passo*) step; **dar uma ~ em** to call in at.

passadeira [pasa'dejra] *f* (*tapete*) stair carpet; (*mulher*) ironing lady; (*PT*: *para peões*) zebra crossing (*BRIT*), crosswalk (*US*).

passadiço/a [pasa'dʒisu/a] *adj* passing ♦ *m* walkway; (*NÁUT*) bridge.

passado/a [pa'sadu/a] *adj* (*decorrido*) past; (*antiquado*) old-fashioned; (*fruta*) bad; (*peixe*) off ♦ *m* past; **o ano ~** last year; **bem/mal passada** (*carne*) well done/rare; **ficar ~** (*encabulado*) to be very embarrassed.

passageiro/a [pasa'ʒejru/a] *adj* (*transitório*) passing ♦ *m/f* passenger.

passagem [pa'saʒẽ] (*pl* **-ns**) *f* passage; (*preço de condução*) fare; (*bilhete*) ticket; **~ de nível** level (*BRIT*) *ou* grade (*US*) crossing; **~ de ida e volta** return ticket, round trip ticket (*US*); **~ subterrânea** underpass, subway (*BRIT*); **~ de pedestres** pedestrian crossing (*BRIT*), crosswalk (*US*); **de ~** in passing; **estar de ~** to be passing through.

passamanaria [pasamana'ria] *f* trimming.

passamento [pasa'mẽtu] *m* (*morte*) passing.

passaporte [pasa'pɔxtʃi] *m* passport.

passar [pa'sa*] *vt* to pass; (*ponte, rio*) to cross; (*exceder*) to go beyond, exceed; (*coar*: *farinha*) to sieve; (: *líquido*) to strain; (: *café*) to percolate; (*a ferro*) to iron; (*tarefa*) to set; (*telegrama*) to send; (*o tempo*) to spend; (*bife*) to cook; (*a outra pessoa*) to pass on; (*pomada*) to put on; (*contrabandear*) to smuggle ♦ *vi* to pass; (*na rua*) to go past; (*tempo*) to go by; (*dor*) to wear off; (*terminar*) to be over; (*ser razoável*) to pass, be passable; (*mudar*) to change; **~-se** *vr* (*acontecer*) to go on, happen; (*desertar*) to go over; (*tempo*) to go by; **~ bem** (*de saúde*) to be well; **como está passando?** how are you?; **~ a** (*questão*) to move on to; (*suj*: *propriedade*) to pass to; **~ a fazer** to start to do; **~ a ser** to become; **passava das dez horas** it was past ten o' clock; **ele passa dos 50 anos** he's over 50; **não ~ de** to be only; **~ na frente** to go ahead; **~ alguém para trás** to con sb; (*cônjuge*) to cheat on sb; **~ pela casa de** to call in on; **~ pela cabeça de** to occur to; **~ por algo** (*sofrer*) to go through sth; (*transitar*: *estrada*) to go along sth; (*ser considerado como*) to be thought of as sth; **~ por cima de algo** to overlook sth; **~ algo por algo** to put *ou* pass sth through sth; **~ sem** to do without.

passarela [pasa'rɛla] *f* footbridge; (*para modelos*) catwalk.

pássaro ['pasaru] *m* bird.

passatempo [pasa'tẽpu] *m* pastime; **como ~** for fun.

passável [pa'savew] (*pl* **-eis**) *adj* passable, so-so, all right.

passe ['pasi] *m* (*licença*) pass; (*FUTEBOL*: *ato*) pass; (: *contrato*) contract; **~ de mágica** sleight of hand.

passear [pa'sja*] *vt* to take for a walk ♦ *vi* (*a pé*) to go for a walk; (*sair*) to go out; **~ a cavalo** (*ou* **de carro**) to go for a ride; **não moro aqui, estou passeando** I don't live here, I'm on holiday (*BRIT*) *ou* vacation (*US*); **mandar alguém ~** (*col*) to send sb packing.

passeata [pa'sjata] *f* (*marcha coletiva*) protest march; (*passeio*) stroll.

passeio [pa'seju] *m* walk; (*de carro*) drive, ride; (*excursão*) outing; (*calçada*) pavement (*BRIT*), sidewalk (*US*); **dar um ~** to go for a walk; (*de carro*) to go for a drive *ou* ride; **~ público** promenade.

passional [pasjo'naw] (*pl* **-ais**) *adj* passionate; **crime ~** crime of passion.

passista [pa'siʃta] *m/f* dancer (*in carnival parade*).

passível [pa'sivew] (*pl* **-eis**) *adj*: **~ de** (*dor etc*) susceptible to; (*pena, multa*) subject to.

passividade [pasivi'dadʒi] *f* passivity.

passivo/a [pa'sivu/a] *adj* passive ♦ *m* (*COM*) liabilities *pl*.

passo ['pasu] *m* step; (*medida*) pace; (*modo de andar*) walk; (*ruído dos passos*) footstep; (*sinal de pé*) footprint; **~ a ~** one step at a time; **a cada ~** constantly; **a um ~ de** (*fig*) on the verge of; **a dois ~s de** (*perto de*) a stone's throw away from; **ao ~ que** while; **apertar o ~** to hurry up; **ceder o ~ a** to give way to; **dar um ~** to take a step; **dar um mau ~** to slip up; **marcar ~** (*fig*) to mark time; **seguir os ~s de alguém** (*fig*) to follow in sb's footsteps; **~ de cágado** snail's pace.

pasta ['paʃta] *f* paste; (*de couro*) briefcase; (*de cartolina*) folder; (*de ministro*) portfolio; **~ dentifrícia** *ou* **de dentes** toothpaste; **~ de galinha** chicken pâté.

pastagem [paʃ'taʒẽ] (*pl* **-ns**) *f* pasture.

pastar [paʃ'ta*] *vt* to graze on ♦ *vi* to graze.

pastel [paʃ'tɛw] (*pl* **-éis**) *m* samosa; (*desenho*) pastel drawing ♦ *adj inv* (*cor*) pastel.

pastelão [paʃte'lãw] *m* (*comédia*) slapstick.

pastelaria [paʃtela'ria] *f* (*loja*) cake shop; (*comida*) pastry.

pasteurizado/a [paʃtewri'zadu/a] *adj* pasteurized.

pastiche [paʃ'tʃiʃi] *m* pastiche.

pastilha [paʃ'tʃiʎa] *f* (*MED*) tablet; (*doce*) pastille; (*COMPUT*) chip.

pastio [paʃ'tʃiu] *m* pasture; (*ato*) grazing.

pasto ['paʃtu] *m* (*erva*) grass; (*terreno*) pasture; **casa de ~** (*PT*) cheap restaurant, diner.

pastor(a) [paʃ'to*(a)] *m/f* shepherd(ess) ♦ *m* (*REL*) clergyman, pastor.

pastoral [paʃto'raw] (*pl* **-ais**) *adj* pastoral.

pastorear [paʃto'rja*] *vt* (*gado*) to watch over.

pastoril [paʃto'riw] (*pl* **-is**) *adj* pastoral.

pastoso/a [paʃ'tozu/ɔza] *adj* pasty.

pata ['pata] *f* (*pé de animal*) foot, paw; (*ave*) duck; (*col*: *pé*) foot; **meter a ~** to put one's foot in it.

pata-choca (*pl* **patas-chocas**) *f* lump.

patada [pa'tada] *f* kick; **dar uma ~** to kick; (*fig*: *col*) to behave rudely; **levar uma ~** (*fig*) to be treated rudely.

Patagônia [pata'gonja] *f*: **a ~** Patagonia.

patamar [pata'ma*] *m* (*de escada*) landing; (*fig*) level.

patavina [pata'vina] *pron* nothing, (not) anything.

patê [pa'te] *m* pâté.

patente [pa'tẽtʃi] *adj* obvious, evident ♦ *f* (*COM*) patent; (*MIL*: *título*) commission; **altas ~s** high-ranking officers.

patentear [patẽ'tʃja*] *vt* to show, reveal; (*COM*) to patent; **~-se** *vr* to be shown, be evident.

paternal [patex'naw] (*pl* **-ais**) *adj* paternal.

paternalista [patexna'liʃta] *adj* paternalistic.

paternidade [patexni'dadʒi] *f* paternity.

paterno/a [pa'tɛxnu/a] *adj* fatherly, paternal; **casa paterna** family home.

pateta [pa'tɛta] *adj* stupid, daft ♦ *m/f* idiot.

patetice [pate'tʃisi] *f* stupidity; (*ato*, *dito*) daft thing.

patético/a [pa'tɛtʃiku/a] *adj* pathetic, moving.

patíbulo [pa'tʃibulu] *m* gallows *sg*.

patifaria [patʃifa'ria] *f* roguishness; (*ato*) nasty thing.

patife [pa'tʃifi] *m* scoundrel, rogue.

patim [pa'tʃĩ] (*pl* **-ns**) *m* skate; **~ de rodas** roller skate.

patinação [patʃina'sãw] (*pl* **-ões**) *f* skating; (*lugar*) skating rink.

patinador(a) [patʃinado*(a)] *m/f* skater.

patinar [patʃi'na*] *vi* to skate; (*AUTO*: *derrapar*) to skid.

patinhar [patʃi'ɲa*] *vi* (*como um pato*) to dabble; (*em lama*) to splash about, slosh.

patinete [patʃi'nɛtʃi] *f* skateboard.

patinho [pa'tʃiɲu] *m* duckling; (*carne*) leg of beef; (*urinol*) bedpan; **cair como um ~** to be taken in.

patins [pa'tʃĩʃ] *mpl de* **patim**.

pátio ['patʃju] *m* (*de uma casa*) patio, backyard; (*espaço cercado de edifícios*) courtyard; (*de escola*) playground; (*MIL*) parade ground; **~ de recreio** playground.

pato ['patu] *m* duck; (*macho*) drake; (*col*: *otário*) sucker; **pagar o ~** (*col*) to carry the can.

patologia [patolo'ʒia] *f* pathology.

patológico/a [pato'lɔʒiku/a] *adj* pathological.

patologista [patolo'ʒiʃta] *m/f* pathologist.

patota [pa'tɔta] *f* (*col*) gang.

patrão [pa'trãw] (*pl* **-ões**) *m* (*COM*) boss; (*dono de casa*) master; (*proprietário*) landlord; (*NÁUT*) skipper; (*col*: *tratamento*) sir.

pátria ['patrja] *f* homeland; **lutar pela ~** to fight for one's country; **salvar a ~** (*fig*) to save the day.

patriarca [pa'trjaxka] *m* patriarch.

patriarcal [patrjax'kaw] (*pl* **-ais**) *adj* patriarchal.

patrício/a [pa'trisju/a] *adj*, *m/f* patrician.

patrimonial [patrimo'njaw] (*pl* **-ais**) *adj* (*bens*) family *atr*; (*imposto*) wealth *atr*.

patrimônio [patri'monju] *m* (*herança*) inheritance; (*fig*) heritage; (*bens*) property; **~ líquido** equity.

patriota [pa'trjɔta] *m/f* patriot.

patriótico/a [pa'trjɔtʃiku/a] *adj* patriotic.

patriotismo [patrjo'tʃiʒmu] *m* patriotism.

patroa [pa'troa] *f* (*mulher do patrão*) boss's wife; (*dona de casa*) lady of the house; (*proprietária*) landlady; (*col*: *esposa*) missus, wife; (: *tratamento*) madam.

patrocinador(a) [patrosina'do*(a)] *m/f* sponsor, backer ♦ *adj* sponsoring.

patrocinar [patrosi'na*] *vt* to sponsor; (*proteger*) to support.

patrocínio [patro'sinju] *m* sponsorship, backing; (*proteção*) support.

patrões [pa'trõjʃ] *mpl de* **patrão**.

patrono [pa'trɔnu] *m* patron; (*advogado*) counsel.

patrulha [pa'truʎa] *f* patrol.

patrulhar [patru'ʎa*] *vt*, *vi* to patrol.

pau [paw] *m* (*madeira*) wood; (*vara*) stick; (*col*: *briga*) punch-up; (: *cruzeiro*) cruzeiro; (*col!*: *pênis*) cock (*!*); **~s** *mpl* (*CARTAS*) clubs; **~ a ~** neck and neck; **a meio ~** (*bandeira*) at half-mast; **o ~ comeu** (*col*) all hell broke loose; **estar/ficar ~ da vida** (*col*) to be/get mad; **ir ao** *ou* **levar ~** (*em exame*) to fail; **meter o ~ em alguém** (*col*: *espancar*) to beat sb up; (: *criticar*) to run sb down; **mostrar a alguém com quantos ~s se faz uma canoa** (*fig*) to teach sb a lesson; **ser ~** (*col*: *maçante*) to be a drag; **ser ~ para toda obra** to be a jack of all trades; **comida a dar com um ~** tons of food; **~ de bandeira** flagpole.

pau-a-pique *m* wattle and daub.

pau-d'água (*pl* **paus-d'água**) *m* drunkard.

pau-de-arara (*pl* **paus-de-arara**) *m* (*tortura*) upside-down torture ♦ *m/f* migrant (*from North-East*); (*pej*) North-Easterner.

pau-de-cabeleira (*pl* **paus-de-cabeleira**) *m* chaperon.

paulada [paw'lada] *f* blow (with a stick).

NB: *European Portuguese adds the following consonants to certain words:* **b** (sú(b)dito, su(b)til); **c** (a(c)ção, a(c)cionista, a(c)to); **m** (inde(m)ne); **p** (ado(p)ção, ado(p)tar); *for further details see p. xiii.*

paulatinamente [pawlatʃina'mẽtʃi] *adv* gradually.
paulatino/a [pawla'tʃinu/a] *adj* slow, gradual.
paulicéia [pawli'sɛja] *f*: **a P~** São Paulo.
paulificante [pawlifi'kãtʃi] *adj* annoying.
paulificar [pawlifi'ka*] *vt* to annoy, bother.
paulista [paw'liʃta] *adj* from (the state of) São Paulo ♦ *m/f* person from São Paulo.
paulistano/a [pawliʃi'tanu/a] *adj* from (the city of) São Paulo ♦ *m/f* person from São Paulo.
pau-mandado (*pl* **paus-mandados**) *m* yes man.
paupérrimo/a [paw'pɛximu/a] *adj* poverty-stricken.
pausa ['pawza] *f* pause; (*intervalo*) break; (*descanso*) rest.
pausado/a [paw'zadu/a] *adj* (*lento*) slow; (*sem pressa*) leisurely; (*cadenciado*) measured ♦ *adv* (*falar*) in measured tones.
pauta ['pawta] *f* (*linha*) (guide)line; (MÚS) stave; (*lista*) list; (*folha*) ruled paper; (*de programa de TV*) running order; (*ordem do dia*) agenda; (*indicações*) guidelines *pl*; **sem ~** (*papel*) plain; **em ~** on the agenda.
pautado/a [paw'tadu/a] *adj* (*papel*) ruled.
pautar [paw'ta*] *vt* (*papel*) to rule; (*assuntos*) to put in order, list; (*conduta*) to regulate.
pauzinho [paw'ziɲu] *m*: **mexer os ~s** to pull strings.
pavão/voa [pa'vãw/'voa] (*pl* **-ões/~s**) *m/f* peacock/peahen.
pavê [pa've] *m* (CULIN) cream cake.
pavilhão [pavi'ʎãw] (*pl* **-ões**) *m* (*tenda*) tent; (*de madeira*) hut; (*no jardim*) summerhouse; (*em exposição*) pavilion; (*bandeira*) flag; **~ de isolamento** isolation ward.
pavimentação [pavimẽta'sãw] *f* (*da rua*) paving; (*piso*) flooring.
pavimentar [pavimẽ'ta*] *vt* to pave.
pavimento [pavi'mẽtu] *m* (*chão, andar*) floor; (*da rua*) road surface.
pavio [pa'viu] *m* wick.
pavoa [pa'voa] *f de* **pavão**.
pavões [pa'võjʃ] *mpl de* **pavão**.
pavonear [pavo'nja*] *vt* (*ostentar*) to show off ♦ *vi* (*caminhar*) to strut; **~-se** *vr* to show off.
pavor [pa'vo*] *m* dread, terror; **ter ~ de** to be terrified of.
pavoroso/a [pavo'rozu/ɔza] *adj* dreadful, terrible.
paz [pajʒ] *f* peace; **fazer as ~es** to make up, be friends again; **estar em ~** to be at peace; **deixar alguém em ~** to leave sb alone; **ser de boa ~** to be easy-going.
PB *abr f* = **Paraíba** ♦ *abr* (COM: *de ações*) = **preferencial, classe B.**
PC *abr m* = **Partido Comunista**; = **personal computer.**
Pça. *abr* (= *Praça*) Sq.
PCB *abr m* = **Partido Comunista Brasileiro.**
PCBR *abr m* = **Partido Comunista Brasileiro Revolucionário.**
PCC *abr m* = **Partido Comunista Chinês.**
PC do B *abr m* = **Partido Comunista do Brasil.**
PCN (BR) *abr m* = **Partido Comunitário Nacional.**
PCUS *abr m* = **Partido Comunista da União Soviética.**
PDC (BR) *abr m* = **Partido Demócrata-Cristão.**
PDI (BR) *abr m* = **Partido Democrático Independente.**
PDS (BR) *abr m* = **Partido Democrático Social.**
PDT (BR) *abr m* = **Partido Democrático Trabalhista.**
PE *abr m* = **Pernambuco.**
pé [pɛ] *m* foot; (*da mesa*) leg; (*fig*: *base*) footing; (*de alface*) head; (*milho, café*) plant; **ir a ~** to walk, go on foot; **ao ~ de** near, by; **ao ~ da letra** literally; **ao ~ do ouvido** in secret; **~ ante ~** on tip-toe; **com um ~ nas costas** (*com facilidade*) standing on one's head; **estar de ~** (*festa etc*) to be on; **estar de ~ no chão** to be barefoot; **em** *ou* **de ~** standing (up); **em ~ de guerra/igualdade** on a war/an equal footing; **dar no ~** (*col*) to run away, take off; **pôr-se em ~, ficar de ~** to stand up; **arredar ~** to move; **bater o ~** (*fig*) to dig one's heels in; **não chegar aos ~s de** (*fig*) to be nowhere near as good as; **a água dá ~** (NATAÇÃO) you can touch the bottom; **ficar com o ~ atrás** to be suspicious; **ficar no ~ de alguém** to keep on at sb; **larga meu ~!** leave me alone!; **levantar-se** *ou* **acordar com o ~ direito/esquerdo** to wake up in a good mood/get out of bed on the wrong side; **meter os ~s pelas mãos** to mess up; **perder o ~** (*no mar*) to get out of one's depth; **pôr os ~s em** to set foot in; **não ter ~ nem cabeça** (*fig*) to make no sense; **ter os ~s na terra** (*fig*) to be down-to-earth, have one's feet firmly on the ground.
peão [pjãw] (*pl* **-ões**) *m* (PT) pedestrian; (MIL) foot soldier; (XADREZ) pawn; (*trabalhador*) farm labourer (BRIT) *ou* laborer (US).
peça ['pɛsa] *f* (*pedaço*) piece; (AUTO) part; (*aposento*) room; (TEATRO) play; **(serviço) pago por ~** piecework; **~ de reposição** spare part; **~ de roupa** garment; **pregar uma ~ em alguém** to play a trick on sb.
pecado [pe'kadu] *m* sin; **~ mortal** deadly sin.
pecador(a) [peka'do*(a)] *m/f* sinner, wrongdoer.
pecaminoso/a [pekami'nozu/ɔza] *adj* sinful.
pecar [pe'ka*] *vi* to sin; (*cometer falta*) to do wrong; **~ por excesso de zelo** to be overzealous.
pechincha [pe'ʃĩʃa] *f* (*vantagem*) godsend; (*coisa barata*) bargain.
pechinchar [peʃĩ'ʃa*] *vi* to bargain, haggle.
pechincheiro/a [peʃĩ'ʃejru/a] *m/f* bargain hunter.
peço ['pɛsu] *etc vb V* **pedir**.

peçonha [pe'sɔɲa] *f* poison.
pectina [pek'tʃina] *f* pectin.
pecuária [pe'kwarja] *f* cattle-raising.
pecuário/a [pe'kwarju/a] *adj* cattle *atr*.
pecuarista [pekwa'riʃta] *m/f* cattle farmer.
peculiar [peku'lja*] *adj* (*especial*) special, peculiar; (*particular*) particular.
peculiaridade [pekuljari'dadʒi] *f* peculiarity.
pecúlio [pe'kulju] *m* (*acumulado*) savings *pl*; (*bens*) wealth.
pecuniário/a [pecu'njarju/a] *adj* money *atr*, financial.
pedaço [pe'dasu] *m* piece; (*fig*: *trecho*) bit; **aos ~s** in pieces; **caindo aos ~s** (*objeto, carro*) tatty, broken-down; (*casa*) tumble-down; (*pessoa*) worn out.
pedágio [pe'daʒju] (*BR*) *m* (*pagamento*) toll; (*posto*) tollbooth.
pedagogia [pedago'ʒia] *f* pedagogy; (*curso*) education.
pedagógico/a [peda'gɔʒiku/a] *adj* educational, teaching *atr*.
pedagogo/a [peda'gogu/a] *m/f* educationalist.
pé-d'água (*pl* **pés-d'água**) *m* shower, downpour.
pedal [pe'daw] (*pl* **-ais**) *m* pedal.
pedalada [peda'lada] *f* turn of the pedals; **dar uma ~** to pedal.
pedalar [peda'la*] *vt, vi* to pedal.
pedalinho [peda'liɲu] *m* pedalo (boat).
pedante [pe'dãtʃi] *adj* pretentious ♦ *m/f* pseud.
pedantismo [pedã'tʃiʒmu] *m* pretentiousness.
pé-de-atleta *m* athlete's foot.
pé-de-galinha (*pl* **pés-de-galinha**) *m* crow's foot.
pé-de-meia (*pl* **pés-de-meia**) *m* nest egg, savings *pl*.
pé-de-moleque (*pl* **pés-de-moleque**) *m* (*doce*) nut brittle; (*calçamento*) crazy paving.
pé-de-pato (*pl* **pés-de-pato**) *m* flipper.
pederneira [pedex'nejra] *f* flint.
pedestal [pedeʃ'taw] (*pl* **-ais**) *m* pedestal.
pedestre [pe'dɛʃtri] (*BR*) *m* pedestrian.
pé-de-vento (*pl* **pés-de-vento**) *m* gust of wind.
pediatra [pe'dʒjatra] *m/f* paediatrician (*BRIT*), pediatrician (*US*).
pediatria [pedʒja'tria] *f* paediatrics *sg* (*BRIT*), pediatrics *sg* (*US*).
pedicuro/a [pedʒi'kuru/a] *m/f* chiropodist (*BRIT*), podiatrist (*US*).
pedida [pe'dʒida] *f*: **boa ~** (*col*) good idea.
pedido [pe'dʒidu] *m* (*solicitação*) request; (*COM*) order; **a ~ de alguém** at sb's request; **~ de casamento** proposal (of marriage); **~ de demissão** resignation; **~ de desculpa** apology; **~ de informação** inquiry.
pedigree [pedʒi'gri] *m* pedigree.
pedinte [pe'dʒĩtʃi] *m/f* beggar ♦ *adj* begging.
pedir [pe'dʒi*] *vt* to ask for; (*COM, comida*) to order; (*exigir*) to demand ♦ *vi* to ask; (*num restaurante*) to order; **~ algo a alguém** to ask sb for sth; **~ a alguém que faça, ~ para alguém fazer** to ask sb to do; **~ desculpa** to apologize; **~ emprestado** to borrow; **~ $100 por algo** to ask $100 for sth; **~ alguém em casamento** *ou* **a mão de alguém** to ask for sb's hand in marriage, propose to sb.
pedra ['pɛdra] *f* stone; (*rochedo*) rock; (*de granizo*) hailstone; (*de açúcar*) lump; (*quadro-negro*) slate; **~ de amolar** grindstone; **~ de gelo** ice cube; **~ preciosa** precious stone; **~ falsa** (*MED*) stone; **~ de toque** (*fig*) touchstone, benchmark; **doido de ~s** raving mad; **dormir como uma ~** to sleep like a log; **pôr uma ~ em cima de algo** (*fig*) to consider sth dead and buried; **ser de ~** (*fig*) to be hard-hearted; **ser uma ~ no sapato de alguém** (*fig*) to be a thorn in sb's side; **vir** *ou* **responder com quatro ~s na mão** (*fig*) to be aggressive; **uma ~ no caminho** (*fig*) a stumbling block, a hindrance.
pedrada [pe'drada] *f* blow with a stone; **dar ~s em** to throw stones at.
pedra-mármore *f* polished marble.
pedra-pomes [-pɔmiʃ] *f* pumice stone.
pedregal [pedre'gaw] (*pl* **-ais**) *m* stony ground.
pedregoso/a [pedre'gozu/ɔza] *adj* stony, rocky.
pedregulho [pedre'guʎu] *m* gravel.
pedreira [pe'drejra] *f* quarry.
pedreiro [pe'drejru] *m* stonemason.
pedúnculo [pe'dũkulu] *m* stalk.
pê-eme [pe'ɛmi] (*pl* **pê-emes**) *f* military police ♦ *m/f* military policeman/woman.
pé-frio (*pl* **pés-frios**) (*col*) *m* jinx.
pega [*m* 'pɛga, *f* 'pega] *m* (*briga*) quarrel ♦ *f* magpie; (*PT*: *col*: *moça*) bird; (: *meretriz*) tart.
pegada [pe'gada] *f* (*de pé*) footprint; (*no futebol*) save; **ir nas ~s de alguém** (*fig*) to follow in sb's footsteps.
pegado/a [pe'gadu/a] *adj* (*colado*) stuck; (*unido*) together; **a casa pegada** the house next door.
pega-gelo (*pl* **pega-gelos**) *m* ice tongs *pl*.
pegajoso/a [pega'ʒozu/ɔza] *adj* sticky.
pega-pra-capar (*col*) *m inv* scuffle.
pegar [pe'ga*] *vt* to catch; (*selos*) to stick (on); (*segurar*) to take hold of; (*hábito, mania*) to get into; (*compreender*) to take in; (*trabalho*) to take on; (*estação de rádio*) to pick up, get ♦ *vi* (*aderir*) to stick; (*planta*) to take; (*moda*) to catch on; (*doença*) to be catching; (*motor*) to start; (*vacina*) to take; (*mentira*) to stand up, stick; (*fogueira*) to catch; **~-se** *vr* (*brigar*) to have a fight, quarrel; **~ em** (*começar*) to start on; (*segurar*) to grab, pick up; **~ com** (*casa*) to be

***NB:** European Portuguese adds the following consonants to certain words:* **b** (sú(b)dito, su(b)til); **c** (a(c)ção, a(c)cionista, a(c)to); **m** (inde(m)ne); **p** (ado(p)ção, ado(p)tar); *for further details see p. xiii.*

next door to; ~ **a fazer** to start to do; **ir** ~ (*buscar*) to go and get; ~ **um emprego** to get a job; ~ **uma rua** to take a street; ~ **fogo a algo** to set fire to sth; ~ **3 anos de cadeia** to get 3 years in prison; ~ **alguém fazendo** to catch sb doing; **pega, ladrão!** stop thief!; ~ **no sono** to fall asleep; **ele pegou e disse ...** he upped and said ...; **pegue e pague** cash and carry; ~ **bem/mal** (*col*) to go down well/badly.

pega-rapaz (*pl* **~es**) *m* kiss curl.

pego/a ['pɛgu/a] *pp de* **pegar**.

peguei [pe'gej] *etc vb V* **pegar**.

peidar [pej'da*] (*col!*) *vi* to fart (*!*).

peido ['pejdu] (*col!*) *m* fart (*!*).

peitilho [pej'tʃiʎu] *m* shirt front.

peito ['pejtu] *m* (ANAT) chest; (*de ave, mulher*) breast; (*fig*) courage; **dar o ~ a um bebê** to breastfeed a baby; **largar o ~** to be weaned; **meter os ~s** (*col*) to put one's heart into it; **no ~ (e na raça)** (*col*) whatever it takes; ~ **do pé** instep; **amigo do ~** bosom pal, close friend.

peitoril [pejto'riw] (*pl* **-is**) *m* windowsill.

peitudo/a [pej'tudu/a] *adj* big-chested; (*valente*) feisty.

peixada [pej'ʃada] *f* cooked fish.

peixaria [pejʃa'ria] *f* fishmonger's.

peixe ['pejʃi] *m* fish; **P~s** *mpl* (ASTROLOGIA) Pisces *sg*; **como ~ fora d'água** like a fish out of water; **filho de ~, peixinho é** like father, like son; **não ter nada com o ~** (*fig*) to have nothing to do with the matter; **vender seu ~** (*ver seus interesses*) to feather one's nest; (*falar*) to say one's piece, have one's say.

peixeira [pej'ʃejra] *f* fishwife; (*faca*) fish knife.

peixeiro [pej'ʃejru] *m* fishmonger.

pejar-se [pe'ʒaxsi] *vr* to be ashamed.

pejo ['peʒu] *m* shame; **ter ~** to be ashamed.

pejorativo/a [peʒora'tʃivu/a] *adj* pejorative.

pela ['pɛla] = **por** + **a**.

pelada [pe'lada] *f* football game.

pelado/a [pe'ladu/a] *adj* (*sem pele*) skinned; (*sem pêlo, cabelo*) shorn; (*nu*) naked, in the nude; (*sem dinheiro*) broke.

pelanca [pe'lãka] *f* fold of skin; (*de carne*) lump.

pelancudo/a [pelã'kudu/a] *adj* (*pessoa*) flabby.

pelar [pe'la*] *vt* (*tirar a pele*) to skin; (*tirar o pêlo*) to shear; (*col*) to fleece; **~-se** *vr*: **~-se por** to be crazy about, adore; **~-se de medo** to be scared stiff.

pelas ['pɛlaʃ] = **por** + **as**.

pele ['pɛli] *f* (*de pessoa, fruto*) skin; (*couro*) leather; (*como agasalho*) fur (coat); (*de animal*) hide; **cair na ~ de alguém** (*col*) to pester sb; **arriscar/salvar a ~** (*col*) to risk one's neck/save one's skin; **sentir algo na ~** (*fig*) to feel sth at first hand; **estar na ~ de alguém** (*fig*) to be in sb's shoes; **ser** *ou* **estar ~ e osso** to be all skin and bone.

peleja [pe'leʒa] *f* (*luta*) fight; (*briga*) quarrel.

pelejar [pele'ʒa*] *vi* (*lutar*) to fight; (*discutir*) to quarrel; ~ **pela paz** to fight for peace; ~ **para fazer/para que alguém faça** to fight to do/to fight to get sb to do.

pelerine [pele'rini] *f* cape.

peleteiro/a [pele'tejru/a] *m/f* furrier.

peleteria [pelete'ria] *f* furrier's.

pele-vermelha (*pl* **peles-vermelhas**) *m/f* redskin.

pelica [pe'lika] *f* kid (leather).

pelicano [peli'kanu] *m* pelican.

película [pe'likula] *f* film; (*de pele*) film of skin.

pelintra [pe'lĩtra] (PT) *adj* shabby; (*pobre*) penniless.

pelo ['pɛlu] = **por** + **o**.

pêlo ['pelu] *m* hair; (*de animal*) fur, coat; **nu em ~** stark naked; **montar em ~** to ride bareback.

Peloponeso [pelopo'nɛzu] *m*: **o ~** the Peloponnese.

pelos ['pɛluʃ] = **por** + **os**.

pelota [pe'lɔta] *f* ball; (*num molho*) lump; (*na pele*) bump; **dar ~ para** (*col*) to pay attention to.

pelotão [pelo'tãw] (*pl* **-ões**) *m* platoon, squad.

pelúcia [pe'lusja] *f* plush.

peludo/a [pe'ludu/a] *adj* hairy; (*animal*) furry.

pélvico/a ['pɛwviku/a] *adj* pelvic.

pélvis ['pɛwviʃ] *f inv* pelvis.

pena ['pena] *f* (*pluma*) feather; (*de caneta*) nib; (*escrita*) writing; (JUR) penalty, punishment; (*sofrimento*) suffering; (*piedade*) pity; **que ~!** what a shame!; **a duras ~s** with great difficulty; **sob ~ de** under penalty of; **cumprir ~** to serve a term in jail; **dar ~** to be upsetting; **é uma ~ que ...** it is a pity that ...; **ter ~ de** to feel sorry for; **valer a ~** to be worthwhile; **não vale a ~** it's not worth it; ~ **capital** capital punishment.

penacho [pe'naʃu] *m* plume; (*crista*) crest.

penal [pe'naw] (*pl* **-ais**) *adj* penal.

penalidade [penali'dadʒi] *f* (JUR) penalty; (*castigo*) punishment; **impor uma ~ a** to penalize.

penalizar [penali'za*] *vt* (*causar pena a*) to trouble; (*castigar*) to penalize.

pênalti ['penawtʃi] *m* (FUTEBOL) penalty; **cobrar um ~** to take a penalty.

penar [pe'na*] *vt* to grieve ♦ *vi* to suffer.

penca ['pẽka] *f* bunch; **gente em ~** lots of people.

pence ['pẽsi] *f* dart.

pendão [pẽ'dãw] (*pl* **-ões**) *m* pennant; (*fig*) banner; (*do milho*) blossom.

pendência [pẽ'dẽsja] *f* dispute, quarrel.

pendente [pẽ'dẽtʃi] *adj* (*pendurado*) hanging; (*por decidir*) pending; (*inclinado*) sloping ♦ *m* pendant; **~ de** (*dependente*) dependent on.

pender [pẽ'de*] *vt* to hang ♦ *vi* to hang; (*estar para cair*) to sag, droop; **~ de** (*depender de*)

to depend on; (*estar pendurado*) to hang from; ~ **para** (*inclinar*) to lean towards; (*ter tendência para*) to tend towards; ~ **a** (*estar disposto a*) to be inclined to.
pendões [pẽ'dõjʃ] *mpl de* **pendão**.
pendor [pẽ'do*] *m* inclination, tendency.
pêndulo ['pẽdulu] *m* pendulum.
pendura [pẽ'dura] *f*: **estar na** ~ (*col*) to be broke.
pendurado/a [pẽdu'radu/a] *adj* hanging; (*col*: *compra*) on tick.
pendurar [pẽdu'ra*] *vt* to hang; (*conta*) to put on tick ♦ *vi*: ~ **de** to hang from; **não estou com dinheiro hoje, posso** ~**?** (*col*) I haven't got any money today, can I pay you later?
penduricalho [pẽduri'kaʎu] *m* pendant.
pendurucalho [pẽduru'kaʎu] *m* = **penduricalho**.
penedo [pe'nedu] *m* rock, boulder.
peneira [pe'nejra] *f* (*da cozinha*) sieve; (*do jardim*) riddle.
peneirar [penej'ra*] *vt* to sift, sieve ♦ *vi* (*chover*) to drizzle.
penetra [pe'nɛtra] (*col*) *m/f* gatecrasher; **entrar de** ~ to gatecrash.
penetração [penetra'sãw] *f* penetration; (*perspicácia*) insight, sharpness.
penetrante [pene'trãtʃi] *adj* (*olhar*) searching; (*ferida*) deep; (*frio*) biting; (*som, análise*) penetrating; piercing; (*dor, arma*) sharp; (*inteligência, idéias*) incisive.
penetrar [pene'tra*] *vt* to get into, penetrate; (*em segredo*) to steal into; (*compreender*) to understand ♦ *vi*: ~ **em** *ou* **por** *ou* **entre** to penetrate.
penha ['peɲa] *f* (*rocha*) rock; (*penhasco*) cliff.
penhasco [pe'ɲaʃku] *m* cliff, crag.
penhoar [pe'ɲwa*] *m* dressing gown.
penhor [pe'ɲo*] *m* pledge; **casa de** ~**es** pawnshop; **dar em** ~ to pawn.
penhora [pe'ɲɔra] *f* (JUR) seizure.
penhoradamente [peɲorada'mẽtʃi] *adv* gratefully.
penhorado/a [peɲo'radu/a] *adj* pawned.
penhorar [peɲo'ra*] *vt* (*dar em penhor*) to pledge, pawn; (*apreender*) to confiscate; (*fig*) to put under an obligation; **a ajuda do amigo penhorou-a bastante** she was very grateful for her friend's help.
pêni ['peni] *m* penny.
penicilina [penisi'lina] *f* penicillin.
penico [pe'niku] *m* (*col*) potty; **pedir** ~ (*col*) to chicken out.
Peninos [pe'ninuʃ] *mpl*: **os** ~ the Pennines.
península [pe'nĩsula] *f* peninsula.
peninsular [penĩsu'la*] *adj* peninsular.
pênis ['peniʃ] *m inv* penis.
penitência [peni'tẽsja] *f* (*contrição*) penitence; (*expiação*) penance.
penitenciar [penitẽ'sja*] *vt* to impose penance on; (*crime etc*) to pay for; ~**-se** *vr* to castigate o.s.
penitenciária [penitẽ'sjarja] *f* prison; *V tb* **penitenciário**.
penitenciário/a [penitẽ'sjarju/a] *adj* prison *atr* ♦ *m/f* prisoner, inmate.
penitente [peni'tẽtʃi] *adj* repentant ♦ *m/f* penitent.
penosa [pe'nɔza] (*col*) *f* chicken.
penoso/a [pe'nozu/ɔza] *adj* (*assunto, tratamento*) painful; (*trabalho*) hard.
pensado/a [pẽ'sadu/a] *adj* deliberate, intentional.
pensador(a) [pẽsa'do*(a)] *m/f* thinker.
pensamento [pẽsa'mẽtu] *m* thought; (*ato*) thinking; (*mente*) thought, mind; (*opinião*) way of thinking; (*idéia*) idea.
pensante [pẽ'sãtʃi] *adj* thinking.
pensão [pẽ'sãw] (*pl* **-ões**) *f* (*pequeno hotel*) boarding house; (*comida*) board; ~ **completa** full board; ~ **de aposentadoria** (retirement) pension; ~ **alimentícia** alimony, maintenance; ~ **de invalidez** disability allowance.
pensar [pẽ'sa*] *vi* to think; (*imaginar*) to imagine ♦ *vt* to think about; (*ferimento*) to dress; ~ **em** to think of *ou* about; ~ **fazer** (*ter intenção*) to intend to do, be thinking of doing; ~ **sobre** (*meditar*) to ponder over; **pensando bem** on second thoughts; ~ **alto** to think out loud; ~ **melhor** to think better of it.
pensativo/a [pẽsa'tʃivu/a] *adj* thoughtful, pensive.
Pensilvânia [pẽsiw'vanja] *f*: **a** ~ Pennsylvania.
pensionato [pẽsjo'natu] *m* boarding school
pensionista [pẽsjo'niʃta] *m/f* pensioner; (*que mora em pensão*) boarder.
penso/a ['pẽsu/a] *adj* leaning ♦ *m* (*curativo*) dressing.
pensões [pẽ'sõjʃ] *fpl de* **pensão**.
pentágono [pẽ'tagonu] *m* pentagon; **o P**~ the Pentagon.
pentatlo [pẽ'tatlu] *m* pentathlon.
pente ['pẽtʃi] *m* comb.
penteadeira [pẽtʃja'dejra] *f* dressing table.
penteado/a [pẽ'tʃjadu/a] *adj* (*cabelo*) in place; (*pessoa*) groomed ♦ *m* hairdo, hairstyle.
pentear [pẽ'tʃja*] *vt* to comb; (*arranjar o cabelo*) to do, style; ~**-se** *vr* (*com um pente*) to comb one's hair; (*arranjar o cabelo*) to do one's hair.
Pentecostes [pẽtʃi'kɔʃtʃiʃ] *m* Whitsun.
pente-fino [pẽtʃi'finu] (*pl* **pentes-finos**) *m* fine-tooth comb.
penugem [pe'nuʒẽ] *f* (*de ave*) down; (*pêlo*) fluff.
penúltimo/a [pe'nuwtʃimu/a] *adj* last but one, penultimate.
penumbra [pe'nũbra] *f* (*ao cair da tarde*) twi-

***NB**: European Portuguese adds the following consonants to certain words:* **b** (sú(b)dito, su(b)til); **c** (a(c)ção, a(c)cionista, a(c)to); **m** (inde(m)ne); **p** (ado(p)ção, ado(p)tar); *for further details see p. xiii.*

light, dusk; (*sombra*) shadow; (*meia-luz*) half-light.

penúria [pe'nurja] *f* poverty.

peões [pjõjʃ] *mpl de* **peão**.

pepino [pe'pinu] *m* cucumber.

pepita [pe'pita] *f* (*de ouro*) nugget.

pequena [pe'kena] *f* girl; (*namorada*) girlfriend.

pequenez [peke'neʒ] *f* smallness; (*fig: mesquinhez*) meanness; ~ **de sentimentos** pettiness.

pequenininho/a [pekeni'niɲu/a] *adj* tiny.

pequenino/a [peke'ninu/a] *adj* little.

pequeninos [peke'ninuʃ] *mpl*: **os** ~ the little children.

pequeno/a [pe'kenu/a] *adj* small; (*mesquinho*) petty ♦ *m* boy; **em** ~ **eu fazia** ... when I was small I used to do ....

pequeno-burguês/esa (*pl* **-eses/~s**) *adj* petty bourgeois.

pequerrucho/a [peke'xuʃu/a] *adj* tiny ♦ *m* thimble.

Pequim [pe'kĩ] *n* Pekin, Peking.

pequinês [peki'neʃ] *m* (*cão*) Pekinese.

pêra ['pera] *f* pear.

peralta [pe'rawta] *adj* naughty ♦ *m/f* (*menino*) naughty child.

perambular [perãbu'la*] *vi* to wander.

perante [pe'rãtʃi] *prep* before, in the presence of.

pé-rapado [-xa'padu] (*pl* **pés-rapados**) *m* nobody.

percalço [pex'kawsu] *m* (*de uma tarefa*) difficulty; (*de profissão, matrimônio etc*) pitfall.

per capita [pɛx'kapita] *adv, adj* per capita.

perceber [pexse'be*] *vt* (*notar*) to realize; (*por meio dos sentidos*) to perceive; (*compreender*) to understand; (*ver*) to see; (*ouvir*) to hear; (*ver ao longe*) to make out; (*dinheiro: receber*) to receive.

percentagem [pexsẽ'taʒẽ] *f* percentage.

percentual [pexsẽ'twaw] (*pl* **-ais**) *adj* percentage *atr* ♦ *m* percentage.

percepção [pexsep'sãw] *f* perception; (*compreensão*) understanding.

perceptível [pexsep'tʃivew] (*pl* **-eis**) *adj* perceptible, noticeable; (*som*) audible.

perceptividade [pexseptʃivi'dadʒi] *f* perceptiveness, perception.

perceptivo/a [pexsep'tʃivu/a] *adj* perceptive.

percevejo [pexse'veʒu] *m* (*inseto*) bug; (*prego*) drawing pin (*BRIT*), thumbtack (*US*).

perco ['pexku] *etc vb V* **perder**.

percorrer [pexko'xe*] *vt* (*viajar por*) to travel (across *ou* over); (*passar por*) to go through, traverse; (*investigar*) to search through.

percurso [pex'kuxsu] *m* (*espaço percorrido*) distance (covered); (*trajeto*) route; (*viagem*) journey; **fazer o** ~ **entre** to travel between.

percussão [pexku'sãw] *f* (*MÚS*) percussion.

percussionista [pexkusjo'niʃta] *m/f* percussionist, percussion player.

percutir [pexku'tʃi*] *vt* to strike ♦ *vi* to reverberate.

perda ['pexda] *f* loss; (*desperdício*) waste; ~ **de tempo** waste of time;' **~s e danos** damages, losses.

perdão [pex'dãw] *m* pardon, forgiveness; ~! sorry!; **pedir** ~ **a alguém** to ask sb for forgiveness; ~ **da dívida** cancellation of the debt; ~ **da pena** (*JUR*) pardon.

perder [pex'de*] *vt* to lose; (*tempo*) to waste; (*trem, show, oportunidade*) to miss ♦ *vi* to lose; **~-se** *vr* (*extraviar-se*) to get lost; (*arruinar-se*) to be ruined; (*desaparecer*) to disappear; (*em reflexões*) to be lost; (*num discurso*) to lose one's thread; **~-se de alguém** to lose sb; ~ **algo de vista** to lose sight of sth; **a** ~ **de vista** (*fig*) as far as the eye can see; **pôr tudo a** ~ to risk losing everything; **saber** ~ to be a good loser.

perdição [pexdʒi'sãw] *f* perdition, ruin; (*desonra*) depravity; **ser uma** ~ (*col*) to be irresistible.

perdido/a [pex'dʒidu/a] *adj* lost; (*pervertido*) depraved; ~ **por** (*apaixonado*) desperately in love with; **~s e achados** lost and found, lost property.

perdigão [pexdʒi'gãw] (*pl* **-ões**) *m* (*macho*) partridge.

perdigueiro [pexdʒi'gejru] *m* (*cachorro*) pointer, setter.

perdiz [pex'dʒiʒ] *f* partridge.

perdoar [pex'dwa*] *vt* (*desculpar*) to forgive; (*pena*) to lift; (*dívida*) to cancel; ~ **(algo) a alguém** to forgive sb (for sth).

perdoável [pex'dwavew] (*pl* **-eis**) *adj* forgivable.

perdulário/a [pexdu'larju/a] *adj* wasteful ♦ *m/f* spendthrift.

perdurar [pexdu'ra*] *vi* (*durar muito*) to last a long time; (*continuar a existir*) to still exist.

pereba [pe'rɛba] *f* (*ferida pequena*) scratch.

perecer [pere'se*] *vi* to perish; (*morrer*) to die; (*acabar*) to come to nothing.

perecível [pere'sivew] (*pl* **-eis**) *adj* perishable.

peregrinação [peregrina'sãw] (*pl* **-ões**) *f* (*viagem*) travels *pl*; (*REL*) pilgrimage.

peregrinar [peregri'na*] *vi* (*viajar*) to travel; (*REL*) to go on a pilgrimage.

peregrino/a [pere'grinu/a] *adj* (*beleza*) rare ♦ *m/f* pilgrim.

pereira [pe'rejra] *f* pear tree.

peremptório/a [perẽp'tɔrju/a] *adj* (*final*) final; (*decisivo*) decisive.

perene [pe'rɛni] *adj* (*perpétuo*) everlasting; (*BOT*) perennial.

perereca [pere'rɛka] *f* tree frog.

perfazer [pexfa'ze*] (*irreg: como* **fazer**) *vt* (*completar o número de*) to make up; (*concluir*) to complete.

perfeccionismo [pexfeksjo'niʒmu] *m* perfectionism.

perfeccionista [pexfeksjo'niʃta] *adj, m/f* perfectionist.

perfeição [pexfej'sãw] *f* perfection; **à ~** to perfection.
perfeitamente [pexfejta'mẽtʃi] *adv* perfectly ♦ *excl* exactly!
perfeito/a [pex'fejtu/a] *adj* perfect; (*carro etc*) in perfect condition ♦ *m* (LING) perfect.
perfez [pex'feʒ] *vb V* **perfazer**.
perfídia [pex'fidʒja] *f* treachery.
pérfido/a ['pɛxfidu/a] *adj* treacherous.
perfil [pex'fiw] (*pl* **-is**) *m* (*do rosto, fig*) profile; (*silhueta*) silhouette, outline; (ARQ) (cross) section; **de ~** in profile.
perfilar [perfi'la*] *vt* (*soldados*) to line up; (*aprumar*) to straighten up; **~-se** *vr* to stand to attention.
perfilhar [pexfi'ʎa*] *vt* (JUR) to legally adopt; (*princípio, teoria*) to adopt.
perfis [pex'fiʃ] *mpl de* **perfil**.
perfiz [pex'fiʒ] *vb V* **perfazer**.
perfizer [pexfi'ze*] *etc vb V* **perfazer**.
performance [pex'fɔxmãs] *f* performance.
perfumado/a [pexfu'madu/a] *adj* sweet-smelling; (*pessoa*) wearing perfume.
perfumar [pexfu'ma*] *vt* to perfume; **~-se** *vr* to put perfume on.
perfumaria [pexfuma'ria] *f* perfumery; (*col*) idle talk.
perfume [pex'fumi] *m* perfume; (*cheiro*) scent.
perfunctório/a [pexfũk'tɔrju/a] *adj* perfunctory.
perfurado/a [pexfu'radu/a] *adj* (*cartão*) punched.
perfurador [pexfura'do*] *m* punch.
perfurar [pexfu'ra*] *vt* (*o chão*) to drill a hole in; (*papel*) to punch (a hole in).
perfuratriz [pexfura'triʒ] *f* drill.
pergaminho [pexga'miɲu] *m* parchment; (*diploma*) diploma.
pérgula ['pɛxgula] *f* arbour (BRIT), arbor (US).
pergunta [pex'gũta] *f* question; **fazer uma ~ a alguém** to ask sb a question.
perguntador(a) [pexgũta'do*(a)] *adj* inquiring, inquisitive ♦ *m/f* questioner.
perguntar [pexgũ'ta*] *vt* to ask; (*interrogar*) to question ♦ *vi*: **~ por alguém** to ask after sb; **~-se** *vr* to wonder; **~ algo a alguém** to ask sb sth.
perícia [pe'risja] *f* (*conhecimento*) expertise; (*destreza*) skill; (*exame*) investigation; **~ (criminal)** criminal investigation; (*os peritos criminais*) criminal investigators *pl*.
pericial [peri'sjaw] (*pl* **-ais**) *adj* expert.
periclitante [perikli'tãtʃi] *adj* (*situação*) perilous; (*saúde*) shaky.
periclitar [perikli'ta*] *vi* to be in danger; (*negócio etc*) to be at risk.
periculosidade [perikulozi'dadʒi] *f* dangerousness; (JUR) risk factor.
peridural [peridu'raw] (*pl* **-ais**) *f* (MED) epidural.
periferia [perife'ria] *f* periphery; (*da cidade*) outskirts *pl*.
periférico/a [peri'fɛriku/a] *adj* peripheral ♦ *m* (COMPUT) peripheral; **estrada periférica** ring road.
perífrase [pe'rifrazi] *f* circumlocution.
perigar [peri'ga*] *vi* to be at risk; **~ ser ...** to risk being ..., be in danger of being ....
perigo [pe'rigu] *m* danger; **correr ~** to be in danger; **fora de ~** safe, out of danger; **pôr em ~** to endanger; **o carro dele é um ~** his car is a deathtrap; **ser um ~** (*col*: *pessoa*) to be a tease; **estar a ~** (*col*: *sem dinheiro*) to be broke; (: *em situação difícil*) to be in a bad way.
perigoso/a [peri'gozu/ɔza] *adj* dangerous; (*arriscado*) risky.
perímetro [pe'rimetru] *m* perimeter; **~ urbano** city limits *pl*.
periódico/a [pe'rjɔdʒiku/a] *adj* periodic; (*chuvas*) occasional; (*doença*) recurrent ♦ *m* (*revista*) magazine, periodical; (*jornal*) (news)paper.
período [pe'riodu] *m* period; (*estação*) season; **~ letivo** term (time).
peripécia [peri'pɛsja] *f* (*aventura*) adventure; (*incidente*) turn of events.
periquito [peri'kitu] *m* parakeet.
periscópio [periʃ'kɔpju] *m* periscope.
perito/a [pe'ritu/a] *adj* expert; **~ em** (*atividade*) expert at, clever at; (*matéria*) highly knowledgeable in ♦ *m/f* expert; (*quem faz perícia*) investigator; **~ em matéria de** expert in.
peritonite [perito'nitʃi] *f* peritonitis.
perjurar [pexʒu'ra*] *vi* to commit perjury.
perjúrio [pex'ʒurju] *m* perjury.
perjuro/a [pex'ʒuru/a] *m/f* perjurer.
permanecer [pexmane'se*] *vi* to remain; (*num lugar*) to stay; (*continuar a ser*) to remain, keep; **~ parado** to keep still.
permanência [pexma'nẽsja] *f* permanence; (*estada*) stay.
permanente [pexma'nẽtʃi] *adj* (*dor*) constant; (*cor*) fast; (*residência, pregas*) permanent ♦ *m* (*cartão*) pass ♦ *f* perm; **fazer uma ~** to have a perm.
permeável [pex'mjavew] (*pl* **-eis**) *adj* permeable.
permeio [pex'meju]: **de ~** *adv* in between.
permissão [pexmi'sãw] *f* permission, consent.
permissível [pexmi'sivew] (*pl* **-eis**) *adj* permissible.
permissivo/a [pexmi'sivu/a] *adj* permissive.
permitir [pexmi'tʃi*] *vt* to allow, permit; (*conceder*) to grant; **~ a alguém fazer** to let sb do, allow sb to do.
permuta [pex'muta] *f* exchange; (COM) barter.
permutação [pexmuta'sãw] (*pl* **-ões**) *f* (MAT)

***NB**: European Portuguese adds the following consonants to certain words:* **b** (sú(b)dito, su(b)til); **c** (a(c)ção, a(c)cionista, a(c)to); **m** (inde(m)ne); **p** (ado(p)ção, ado(p)tar); *for further details see p. xiii.*

permutation; (*troca*) exchange.
permutar [pexmu'ta*] *vt* to exchange; (*COM*) to barter.
perna ['pexna] *f* leg; **de ~(s) para o ar** upside down, topsy turvy; **em cima da ~** (*col*) sloppily, in a slapdash way; **bater ~s** (*col*) to wander; **passer a ~ em alguém** (*col*) to put one over on sb; **trocar as ~s** (*col*) to stagger; **~ de pau** wooden leg; **~ mecânica** artificial leg; **~s tortas** bow legs.
perna-de-pau (*pl* **pernas-de-pau**) *m/f* pegleg; (*FUTEBOL*) carthorse, bad player.
pernambucano/a [pexnãbu'kanu/a] *adj* from Pernambuco ♦ *m/f* person from Pernambuco.
perneira [pex'nejra] *f* (*de dançarina etc*) legwarmer.
perneta [pex'neta] *m/f* one-legged person.
pernicioso/a [pexni'sjozu/ɔza] *adj* pernicious; (*MED*) malignant.
pernil [pex'niw] (*pl* **-is**) *m* (*de animal*) haunch; (*CULIN*) leg.
pernilongo [pexni'lõgu] *m* mosquito.
pernis [pex'niʃ] *mpl de* **pernil**.
pernoitar [pexnoj'ta*] *vi* to spend the night.
pernóstico/a [pex'nɔʃtʃiku/a] *adj* pedantic ♦ *m/f* pedant.
pérola ['pɛrola] *f* pearl.
perpassar [pexpa'sa*] *vi* (*tempo*) to go by; **~ (por)** to pass by; **~ a mão em/por** to run one's hand through/over.
perpendicular [pexpẽdʒiku'la*] *adj*, *f* perpendicular; **ser ~ a** to be at right angles to.
perpetração [pexpetra'sãw] *f* perpetration.
perpetrar [pexpe'tra*] *vt* to perpetrate, commit.
perpetuar [pexpe'twa*] *vt* to perpetuate.
perpetuidade [pexpetwi'dadʒi] *f* eternity.
perpétuo/a [pex'pɛtwu/a] *adj* perpetual; (*eterno*) eternal; **prisão perpétua** life imprisonment.
perplexidade [pexpleksi'dadʒi] *f* confusion, bewilderment.
perplexo/a [pex'plɛksu/a] *adj* (*confuso*) bewildered, puzzled; (*indeciso*) uncertain; **ficar ~** (*atônito*) to be taken aback.
perquirir [pexki'ri*] *vt* to probe, investigate.
persa ['pɛxsa] *adj*, *m/f* Persian.
perscrutar [pexʃkru'ta*] *vt* to scrutinize, examine.
perseguição [pexsegi'sãw] *f* pursuit; (*REL*, *POL*) persecution.
perseguidor(a) [pexsegi'do*(a)] *m/f* pursuer; (*REL*, *POL*) persecutor.
perseguir [pexse'gi*] *vt* (*seguir*) to pursue; (*correr atrás*) to chase (after); (*REL*, *POL*) to persecute; (*importunar*) to harass, pester.
perseverança [pexseve'rãsa] *f* (*insistência*) persistence; (*constância*) perseverance.
perseverante [pexseve'rãtʃi] *adj* persistent.
perseverar [pexseve'ra*] *vi* to persevere; **~ em** (*conservar-se firme*) to persevere in; **~ corajoso** to keep one's courage up; **~ em erro** to persist in doing wrong.
Pérsia ['pɛxsja] *f*: **a ~** Persia.
persiana [pex'sjana] *f* blind.
Pérsico/a ['pɛxsiku/a] *adj*: **o golfo ~** the Persian Gulf.
persignar-se [pexsig'naxsi] *vr* to cross o.s.
persigo [pex'sigu] *etc vb V* **perseguir**.
persistência [pexsiʃ'tẽsja] *f* persistence.
persistente [pexsiʃ'tẽtʃi] *adj* persistent.
persistir [pexsiʃ'tʃi*] *vi* to persist; **~ em** to persist in; **~ calado** to keep quiet.
personagem [pexso'naʒẽ] (*pl* **-ns**) *m/f* famous person, celebrity; (*num livro, filme*) character.
personalidade [pexsonali'dadʒi] *f* personality; **~ dupla** dual personality.
personalizado/a [pexsonali'zadu/a] *adj* personalized; (*móveis etc*) custom-made.
personalizar [pexsonali'za*] *vt* to personalize; (*personificar*) to personify; (*nomear*) to name.
personificação [pexsonifika'sãw] *f* personification.
personificar [pexsonifi'ka*] *vt* to personify.
perspectiva [pexʃpek'tʃiva] *f* (*na pintura*) perspective; (*panorama*) view; (*probabilidade*) prospect; (*ponto de vista*) point of view; **em ~** in prospect.
perspicácia [pexʃpi'kasja] *f* insight, perceptiveness.
perspicaz [pexʃpi'kajʒ] *adj* (*que observa*) observant; (*sagaz*) shrewd.
persuadir [pexswa'dʒi*] *vt* to persuade; **~-se** *vr* to convince o.s., make up one's mind; **~ alguém de que/alguém a fazer** to persuade sb that/sb to do.
persuasão [pexswa'zãw] *f* persuasion; (*convicção*) conviction.
persuasivo/a [pexswa'zivu/a] *adj* persuasive.
pertencente [pextẽ'sẽtʃi] *adj* belonging; **~ a** (*pertinente*) pertaining to.
pertencer [pextẽ'se*] *vi*: **~ a** to belong to; (*referir-se*) to concern.
pertences [pex'tẽsiʃ] *mpl* (*de uma pessoa*) belongings.
pertinácia [pextʃi'nasja] *f* (*persistência*) persistence; (*obstinação*) obstinacy.
pertinaz [pextʃi'najʒ] *adj* (*persistente*) persistent; (*obstinado*) obstinate.
pertinência [pextʃi'nẽsja] *f* relevance.
pertinente [pextʃi'nẽtʃi] *adj* relevant; (*apropriado*) appropriate.
perto/a ['pɛxtu/a] *adj* nearby ♦ *adv* near; **~ de** near to; (*em comparação com*) next to; **~ da casa** near *ou* close to the house; **~ de 100 cruzeiros** about 100 cruzeiros; **estar ~ de fazer** (*a ponto de*) to be close to doing; **de ~** closely; **conhecer de ~** to know very well; **ela não enxerga bem de ~** she can't see well close up.
perturbação [pextuxba'sãw] (*pl* **-ões**) *f* disturbance; (*desorientação*) perturbation; (*MED*) trouble; (*POL*) disturbance; **~ da**

ordem breach of the peace.

perturbador(a) [pextuxba'do*(a)] *adj* (*pessoa*) disruptive; (*notícia*) perturbing, disturbing.

perturbado/a [pextux'badu/a] *adj* perturbed; (*desvairado*) unbalanced.

perturbar [pextux'ba*] *vt* to disturb; (*abalar*) to upset, trouble; (*atrapalhar*) to put off; (*andamento, trânsito*) to disrupt; (*envergonhar*) to embarrass; (*alterar*) to affect; **não perturba!** do not disturb!; ~ **a ordem** to cause a breach of the peace.

Peru [pe'ru] *m*: **o** ~ Peru.

peru [pe'ru] *m* turkey; (*col!*: *pênis*) cock (*!*).

perua [pe'rua] *f* (*carro*) estate (car) (BRIT), station wagon (US); (ZOOL) turkey.

peruada [pe'rwada] (*col*) *f* (*palpite*) tip.

peruano/a [pe'rwanu/a] *adj, m/f* Peruvian.

peruar [pe'rwa*] *vt* (*jogo*) to watch ♦ *vi* to hang around.

peruca [pe'ruka] *f* wig.

perversão [pexvex'sãw] (*pl* **-ões**) *f* perversion.

perversidade [pexvexsi'dadʒi] *f* perversity.

perverso/a [pex'vɛxsu/a] *adj* perverse; (*malvado*) wicked.

perversões [pexvex'sõjʃ] *fpl de* **perversão**.

perverter [pexvex'te*] *vt* (*corromper*) to corrupt, pervert; **~-se** *vr* to become corrupt.

pervertido/a [pexvex'tʃidu/a] *adj* perverted ♦ *m/f* pervert.

pesada [pe'zada] *f* weighing.

pesadelo [peza'delu] *m* nightmare.

pesado/a [pe'zadu/a] *adj* heavy; (*ambiente*) tense; (*trabalho*) hard; (*estilo*) dull, boring; (*andar*) slow; (*piada*) coarse; (*comida*) stodgy; (*ar*) sultry ♦ *adv* heavily; **pegar no** ~ (*col*) to work hard; **da pesada** (*col*: *legal*) great; (: *barra-pesada*) rough, violent.

pesagem [pe'zaʒẽ] *f* weighing.

pêsames ['pesamiʃ] *mpl* condolences, sympathy *sg*.

pesar [pe'za*] *vt* to weigh; (*fig*) to weigh up ♦ *vi* to weigh; (*ser pesado*) to be heavy; (*influir*) to carry weight; (*causar mágoa*): ~ **a** to hurt, grieve ♦ *m* grief; ~ **sobre** (*recair*) to fall upon; **em que pese a** despite; **apesar dos ~es** despite everything.

pesaroso/a [peza'rozu/ɔza] *adj* (*triste*) sorrowful, sad; (*arrependido*) regretful, sorry.

pesca ['pɛʃka] *f* (*ato*) fishing; (*os peixes*) catch; **ir à** ~ to go fishing; ~ **submarina** skin diving.

pescada [peʃ'kada] *f* whiting.

pescado [peʃ'kadu] *m* fish.

pescador(a) [peʃka'do*(a)] *m/f* fisherman/woman; ~ **à linha** angler.

pescar [peʃ'ka*] *vt* (*peixe*) to catch; (*tentar apanhar*) to fish for; (*retirar como que pescando*) to fish out; (*um marido*) to catch, get ♦ *vi* to fish; (BR: *col*) to understand; ~ **de algo** (*col*) to know about sth; **pescou?** got it?, see?

pescoção [peʃko'sãw] (*pl* **-ões**) *m* slap.

pescoço [peʃ'kosu] *m* neck; **até o** ~ (*endividado*) up to one's neck.

pescoções [peʃko'sõjʃ] *mpl de* **pescoção**.

pescoçudo/a [peʃko'sudu/a] *adj* bull-necked.

peso ['pezu] *m* weight; (*fig*: *ônus*) burden; (*importância*) importance; **pessoa/argumento de** ~ important person/weighty argument; **de pouco** ~ lightweight; **em** ~ in full force; ~ **atômico** atomic weight; ~ **bruto/líquido** gross/net weight; ~ **morto** dead weight; **ter dois ~s e duas medidas** (*fig*) to have double standards.

pespontar [peʃpõ'ta*] *vt* to backstitch.

pesponto [peʃ'põtu] *m* backstitch.

pesquei [peʃ'kej] *etc vb V* **pescar**.

pesqueiro/a [peʃ'kejru/a] *adj* fishing.

pesquisa [peʃ'kiza] *f* inquiry, investigation; (*científica*) research; ~ **de campo** field work; ~ **de mercado** market research; ~ **e desenvolvimento** research and development.

pesquisador(a) [peʃkiza'do*(a)] *m/f* investigator; (*científico, de mercado*) researcher.

pesquisar [peʃki'za*] *vt, vi* to investigate; (*nas ciências etc*) to research.

pêssego ['pesegu] *m* peach.

pessegueiro [pese'gejru] *m* peach tree.

pessimismo [pesi'miʒmu] *m* pessimism.

pessimista [pesi'miʃta] *adj* pessimistic ♦ *m/f* pessimist.

péssimo/a ['pɛsimu/a] *adj* very bad, awful; **estar** ~ (*pessoa*) to be in a bad way.

pessoa [pe'soa] *f* person; **~s** *fpl* people; **em** ~ personally; ~ **de bem** honest person; ~ **física/jurídica** (JUR) individual/legal entity.

pessoal [pe'swaw] (*pl* **-ais**) *adj* personal ♦ *m* personnel *pl*, staff *pl*; (*col*) people *pl*, folks *pl*; **oi, ~!** (*col*) hi, everyone!, hi, folks!

pestana [peʃ'tana] *f* eyelash; **tirar uma** ~ (*col*) to have a nap.

pestanejar [peʃtane'ʒa*] *vi* to blink; **sem** ~ (*fig*) without batting an eyelid.

peste ['pɛʃtʃi] *f* (*epidemia*) epidemic; (*bubônica*) plague; (*fig*) pest, nuisance.

pesticida [peʃtʃi'sida] *m* pesticide.

pestífero/a [peʃ'tʃiferu/a] *adj* (*fig*) pernicious.

pestilência [peʃtʃi'lẽsja] *f* plague; (*epidemia*) epidemic; (*fedor*) stench.

pestilento/a [peʃtʃi'lẽtu/a] *adj* pestilential, plague *atr*; (*malcheiroso*) putrid.

pétala ['pɛtala] *f* petal.

peteca [pe'tɛka] *f* (kind of) shuttlecock; **fazer alguém de** ~ to make a fool of sb; **não deixar a ~ cair** (*col*) to keep the ball rolling.

peteleco [pete'lɛku] *m* flick; **dar um ~ em algo** to flick sth.

petição [petʃi'sãw] (*pl* **-ões**) *f* (*rogo*) request; (*documento*) petition; **em ~ de miséria** in a terrible state.

peticionário/a [petʃisjo'narju/a] *m/f* petitioner; (*JUR*) plaintiff.
petições [petʃi'sõjʃ] *fpl de* **petição**.
petiscar [petʃiʃ'ka*] *vt* to nibble at, peck at ♦ *vi* to have a nibble.
petisco [pe'tʃiʃku] *m* savoury (*BRIT*), savory (*US*), titbit (*BRIT*), tidbit (*US*).
petit-pois [petʃi'pwa] *m inv* pea.
petiz [pe'tʃiʒ] (*PT*) *m* boy.
petrechos [pe'treʃuʃ] *mpl* equipment *sg*; (*MIL*) stores, equipment *sg*; (*de cozinha*) utensils.
petrificar [petrifi'ka*] *vt* to petrify; (*empedernir*) to harden; (*assombrar*) to stun; **~-se** *vr* to be petrified; to be stunned; to become hard.
Petrobrás [petro'brajʃ] *abr f Brazilian state oil company.*
petrodólar [petro'dɔla*] *m* petrodollar.
petroleiro/a [petro'lejru/a] *adj* oil *atr*, petroleum *atr* ♦ *m* (*navio*) oil tanker.
petróleo [pe'trɔlju] *m* oil, petroleum; ~ **bruto** crude oil.
petrolífero/a [petro'liferu/a] *adj* oil-producing.
petroquímica [petro'kimika] *f* petrochemicals *pl*; (*ciência*) petrochemistry.
petroquímico/a [petro'kimiku/a] *adj* petrochemical.
petulância [petu'lãsja] *f* impudence.
petulante [petu'lãtʃi] *adj* impudent.
petúnia [pe'tunja] *f* petunia.
peúga ['pjuga] (*PT*) *f* sock.
pevide [pe'vidʒi] (*PT*) *f* (*de melão*) seed; (*de maçã*) pip.
p. ex. *abr* (= *por exemplo*) e.g.
pexote [pe'ʃɔtʃi] *m/f* (*criança*) little kid; (*novato*) beginner, novice.
PF (*BR*) *abr f* = **Polícia Federal**.
PFL (*BR*) *abr m* = **Partido da Frente Liberal**.
PH (*BR*) *abr m* = **Partido Humanitário**.
PI *abr* = **Piauí**.
pia ['pia] *f* wash basin; (*da cozinha*) sink; ~ **batismal** font.
piada ['pjada] *f* joke.
piadista [pja'dʒiʃta] *m/f* joker.
pianista [pja'niʃta] *m/f* pianist.
piano ['pjanu] *m* piano; ~ **de cauda** grand piano.
pião [pjãw] (*pl* **-ões**) *m* (*brinquedo*) top.
piar [pja*] *vi* (*pinto*) to cheep; (*coruja*) to hoot; **não** ~ not to say a word.
piauiense [pjaw'jẽsi] *adj* from Piauí ♦ *m/f* person from Piauí.
PIB *abr m* (= *Produto Interno Bruto*) GNP.
picada [pi'kada] *f* (*de agulha etc*) prick; (*de abelha*) sting; (*de mosquito, cobra*) bite; (*de avião*) dive; (*de navalha*) stab; (*atalho*) path, trail; (*de droga*) shot.
picadeiro [pika'dejru] *m* (*circo*) ring.
picadinho [pika'dʒiɲu] *m* stew.
picado/a [pi'kadu/a] *adj* (*por agulha*) pricked; (*por abelha*) stung; (*por cobra, mosquito*) bitten; (*papel*) shredded; (*carne*) minced; (*legumes*) chopped.
picante [pi'kãtʃi] *adj* (*tempero*) hot; (*piada*) risqué, blue; (*comentário*) saucy.
pica-pau ['pika-] (*pl* **~s**) *m* woodpecker.
picar [pi'ka*] *vt* (*com agulha*) to prick; (*suj: abelha*) to sting; (*: mosquito*) to bite; (*: pássaro*) to peck; (*um animal*) to goad; (*carne*) to mince; (*papel*) to shred; (*fruta*) to chop up; (*comichar*) to prickle ♦ *vi* (*a isca*) to take the bait; (*comichar*) to prickle; (*avião*) to dive; **~-se** *vr* to prick o.s.
picardia [pikax'dʒia] *f* (*implicância*) spitefulness; (*esperteza*) craftiness.
picaresco/a [pika'reʃku/a] *adj* comic, ridiculous.
picareta [pika'reta] *f* pickaxe (*BRIT*), pickax (*US*) ♦ *m/f* crook.
picaretagem [pikare'taʒẽ] (*pl* **-ns**) *f* con.
pícaro/a ['pikaru/a] *adj* crafty, cunning.
pichação [piʃa'sãw] (*pl* **-ões**) *f* (*ato*) spraying; (*grafite*) piece of graffiti.
pichar [pi'ʃa*] *vt* (*dizeres, muro*) to spray; (*aplicar piche em*) to cover with pitch; (*col: espinafrar*) to run down ♦ *vi* (*col*) to criticize.
piche ['piʃi] *m* pitch.
piclés ['pikliʃ] *mpl* pickles.
pico ['piku] *m* (*cume*) peak; (*ponta aguda*) sharp point; (*PT: um pouco*) a bit; **mil e** ~ just over a thousand; **meio-dia e** ~ just after midday.
picolé [piko'lɛ] *m* lolly.
picotar [piko'ta*] *vt* to perforate; (*bilhete*) to punch.
picote [pi'kɔtʃi] *m* perforation.
pictórico/a [pik'tɔriku/a] *adj* pictorial.
picuinha [pi'kwiɲa] *f*: **estar de** ~ **com alguém** to have it in for sb.
piedade [pje'dadʒi] *f* (*devoção*) piety; (*compaixão*) pity; **ter** ~ **de** to have pity on.
piedoso/a [pje'dozu/ɔza] *adj* (*REL*) pious; (*compassivo*) merciful.
piegas ['pjɛgaʃ] *adj inv* sentimental; (*col*) soppy ♦ *m/f inv* softy.
pieguice [pje'gisi] *f* sentimentality.
píer ['pie*] *m* pier.
pifa ['pifa] (*col*) *m* booze-up; **tomar um** ~ to get smashed.
pifado/a [pi'fadu/a] (*col*) *adj* (*carro*) broken down; (*TV etc*) broken.
pifar [pi'fa*] (*col*) *vi* (*carro*) to break down; (*rádio*) to go wrong; (*plano, programa*) to fall through.
pigarrear [piga'xja*] *vi* to clear one's throat.
pigarro [pi'gaxu] (*col*) *m* frog in the throat.
pigméia [pig'mɛja] *f de* **pigmeu**.
pigmentação [pigmẽta'sãw] *f* pigmentation, colouring (*BRIT*), coloring (*US*).
pigmento [pig'mẽtu] *m* pigment.
pigmeu/méia [pig'mew/'mɛja] *adj, m/f* pigmy.
pijama [pi'ʒama] *m* pyjamas *pl*.
pilantra [pi'lãtra] (*col*) *m/f* crook.
pilantragem [pilã'traʒẽ] *f* rip-off.
pilão [pi'lãw] (*pl* **-ões**) *m* crusher; (*rural*)

mortar.
pilar [pi'la*] *vt* to pound, crush ♦ *m* pillar.
pilastra [pi'laʃtra] *f* pilaster.
pileque [pi'lɛki] *m* booze-up; **tomar um ~** to get smashed *ou* plastered; **estar de ~** to be smashed *ou* plastered.
pilha ['piʎa] *f* (ELET) battery; (*monte*) pile, heap; (COMPUT) stack; **às ~s** in vast quantities; **estar uma ~ (de nervos)** to be a bundle of nerves.
pilhagem [pi'ʎaʒẽ] *f* (*ato*) pillage; (*objetos*) plunder, booty.
pilhar [pi'ʎa] *vt* (*saquear*) to plunder, pillage; (*roubar*) to rob; (*surpreender*) to catch.
pilhéria [pi'ʎɛrja] *f* joke.
pilheriar [piʎe'rja*] *vi* to joke, jest.
pilões [pi'lõjʃ] *mpl de* **pilão**.
pilotagem [pilo'taʒẽ] *f* flying; **escola de ~** flying school.
pilotar [pilo'ta*] *vt* (*avião*) to fly; (*carro de corrida*) to drive ♦ *vi* to fly.
pilotis [pilo'tʃiʃ] *mpl* stilts.
piloto [pi'lotu] *m* (*de avião*) pilot; (*de navio*) first mate; (*motorista*) (racing) driver; (*bico de gás*) pilot light ♦ *adj inv* (*usina, plano*) pilot; (*peça*) sample *atr*; **~ automático** automatic pilot; **~ de prova** test pilot.
pílula ['pilula] *f* pill; **a ~ (anticoncepcional)** the pill.
pimba ['pĩba] *excl* wham!
pimenta [pi'mẽta] *f* (CULIN) pepper; **~ de Caiena** cayenne pepper.
pimenta-do-reino *f* black pepper.
pimenta-malagueta (*pl* **pimentas-malagueta**) *f* chilli (BRIT) *ou* chili (US) pepper.
pimentão [pimẽ'tãw] *m* (BOT) pepper; **~ verde** green pepper.
pimenteira [pimẽ'tejra] *f* (BOT) pepper plant; (*à mesa*) pepper pot; (: *moedor*) pepper mill.
pimpão/pona [pĩ'pãw/'pɔna] (PT: *pl* **-ões/~s**) *adj* smart, flashy ♦ *m/f* show-off.
pimpolho [pĩ'poʎu] *m* (*criança*) youngster.
pimpona [pĩ'pɔna] *f de* **pimpão**.
PIN (BR) *abr m* = **Plano de Integração Nacional**.
pinacoteca [pinako'tɛka] *f* art gallery; (*coleção de quadros*) art collection.
pináculo [pi'nakulu] *m* (*tb fig*) pinnacle.
pinça ['pĩsa] *f* (*de sobrancelhas*) tweezers *pl*; (*de casa*) tongs *pl*; (MED) callipers *pl* (BRIT), calipers *pl* (US).
pinçar [pĩ'sa*] *vt* to pick up; (*sobrancelhas*) to pluck; (*fig*: *exemplos, defeitos*) to pick out.
píncaro ['pĩkaru] *m* summit, peak.
pincel [pĩ'sɛw] (*pl* **-éis**) *m* brush; (*para pintar*) paintbrush; **~ de barba** shaving brush.
pincelada [pĩse'lada] *f* (brush) stroke.
pincelar [pĩse'la*] *vt* to paint.
pincenê [pĩse'ne] *m* pince-nez.
pindaíba [pĩda'iba] *f*: **estar na ~** (*col*) to be broke.
pinel [pi'nɛw] (*pl* **-éis**) (*col*) *m/f*: **ser/ficar ~** to be/go crazy.
pinga ['pĩga] *f* (*cachaça*) rum; (PT: *trago*) drink.
pingado/a [pĩ'gadu/a] *adj*: **~ de** covered in drops of.
pingar [pĩ'ga*] *vi* to drip; (*começar a chover*) to start to rain.
pingente [pĩ'ʒẽtʃi] *m* pendant.
pingo ['pĩgu] *m* (*gota*) drop; (*ortografia*) dot; **~ de gente** (*col*) slip of a child; **um ~ de** (*comida etc*) a spot of; (*educação etc*) a scrap of.
pingue-pongue [pĩgi-'põgi] *m* ping-pong.
pingüim [pĩ'gwĩ] (*pl* **-ns**) *m* penguin.
pinguinho [pĩ'giɲu] *m* little drop; (*pouquinho*): **um ~** a tiny bit.
pingüins [pĩ'gwĩʃ] *mpl de* **pingüim**.
pinha ['piɲa] *f* pine cone.
pinheiral [piɲej'raw] (*pl* **-ais**) *m* pine wood.
pinheiro [pi'ɲejru] *m* pine (tree).
pinho ['piɲu] *m* pine.
pinicada [pini'kada] *f* (*beliscão*) pinch; (*cutucada*) poke; (*de pássaro*) peck.
pinicar [pini'ka*] *vt* (*pele*) to prickle; (*com o bico*) to peck; (*beliscar*) to pinch; (*cutucar*) to poke.
pinimba [pi'nĩba] (*col*) *f*: **estar de ~ com alguém** to have it in for sb.
pino ['pinu] *m* (*peça*) pin; (AUT: *na porta*) lock; **a ~** upright; **sol a ~** noon-day sun; **bater ~** (AUTO) to knock; (*col*) to be in a bad way.
pinóia [pi'nɔja] (*col*) *f* piece of trash; **que ~!** what a drag!
pinote [pi'nɔtʃi] *m* buck.
pinotear [pino'tʃja*] *vi* to buck.
pinta ['pĩta] *f* (*mancha*) spot; (*col*: *aparência*) appearance, looks *pl*; (: *sujeito*) guy; **dar na ~** (*col*) to give o.s. away; **ela tem ~ de (ser) inglesa** she looks English; **está com ~ de chover** it looks like rain.
pinta-braba [pĩta'braba] (*pl* **pintas-brabas**) *m/f* hoodlum, shady character.
pintado/a [pĩ'tadu/a] *adj* painted; (*cabelo*) dyed; (*olhos, lábios*) made up; **é o avô ~** he's the image of his grandfather; **não querer ver alguém nem ~** (*col*) to hate the sight of sb.
pintar [pĩ'ta*] *vt* to paint; (*cabelo*) to dye; (*rosto*) to make up; (*descrever*) to describe; (*imaginar*) to picture ♦ *vi* to paint; (*col*: *aparecer*) to appear, turn up; (: *problemas, oportunidade*) to crop up; **~-se** *vr* to make o.s. up; **~ (o sete)** to paint the town red.
pintarroxo [pĩta'xoʃu] *m* linnet; (PT) robin.
pinto ['pĩtu] *m* chick; (*col!*) prick (*!*); **como**

***NB**: European Portuguese adds the following consonants to certain words:* **b** (sú(b)dito, su(b)til); **c** (a(c)ção, a(c)cionista, a(c)to); **m** (inde(m)ne); **p** (ado(p)ção, ado(p)tar); *for further details see p. xiii.*

um ~ (molhado) like a drowned rat; **ser ~** to be a piece of cake.
pintor(a) [pĩ'to*(a)] *m/f* painter.
pintura [pĩ'tura] *f* painting; (*maquiagem*) make-up; **~ a óleo** oil painting.
pio/a ['piu/a] *adj* (*devoto*) pious; (*caridoso*) charitable ♦ *m* cheep, chirp; **não dar um ~** not to make a sound.
piões [pjõjʃ] *mpl de* **pião**.
piolho ['pjoʎu] *m* louse.
pioneiro/a [pjo'nejru/a] *adj* pioneering ♦ *m* pioneer.
piopio [pju'pju] (*col*) *m* birdie, dicky bird.
pior ['pjɔ*] *adj, adv* (*comparativo*) worse; (*superlativo*) worst ♦ *m*: **o ~** worst of all ♦ *f*: **estar na ~** (*col*) to be in a jam.
piora ['pjɔra] *f* worsening.
piorar [pjo'ra*] *vt* to make worse, worsen ♦ *vi* to get worse.
pipa ['pipa] *f* barrel, cask; (*de papel*) kite.
piparote [pipa'rɔtʃi] *m* (*com o dedo*) flick.
pipi [pi'pi] *m* (*col*: *urina*) pee; **fazer ~** to have a pee, pee.
pipilar [pipi'la*] *vi* to chirp.
pipoca [pi'pɔka] *f* popcorn; (*col*: *na pele*) blister; **~s!** blast!
pipocar [pipo'ka*] *vi* to go pop, pop; (*aparecer*) to spring up.
pipoqueiro/a [pipo'kejru/a] *m/f* popcorn seller.
pique ['piki] *m* (*corte*) nick; (*auge*) peak; (*grande disposição*) keenness, enthusiasm; **a ~** vertically, steeply; **a ~ de** on the verge of; **ir/pôr a ~** to sink; **perder o ~** to lose one's momentum; **estou no maior ~ no momento** I'm really in the mood *ou* keen at the moment.
piquei [pi'kej] *etc vb V* **picar**.
piquenique [piki'niki] *m* picnic; **fazer ~** to have a picnic.
piquete [pi'ketʃi] *m* (*MIL*) squad; (*em greve*) picket.
pira ['pira] (*col*) *f*: **dar o ~** to take off.
pirado/a [pi'radu/a] (*col*) *adj* crazy.
pirâmide [pi'ramidʒi] *f* pyramid.
piranha [pi'raɲa] *f* piranha (fish); (*col*: *mulher*) tart.
pirão [pi'rãw] *m* manioc meal.
pirar [pi'ra*] (*col*) *vi* to go mad; (*com drogas*) to get high; (*ir embora*) to take off.
pirata [pi'rata] *m* pirate; (*namorador*) lady-killer; (*vigarista*) crook ♦ *adj* pirate.
pirataria [pirata'ria] *f* piracy; (*patifaria*) crime.
pires ['piriʃ] *m inv* saucer.
pirilampo [piri'lãpu] *m* glow worm.
Pirineus [piri'newʃ] *mpl*: **os ~** the Pyrenees.
piriri [piri'ri] (*col*) *m* (*diarréia*) the runs *pl*.
pirotecnia [pirotek'nia] *f* pyrotechnics *sg*, art of making fireworks.
pirraça [pi'xasa] *f* spiteful thing; **fazer ~** to be spiteful.
pirracento/a [pixa'sẽtu/a] *adj* spiteful, bloody-minded.
pirralho/a [pi'xaʎu/a] *m/f* child.
pirueta [pi'rweta] *f* pirouette.
pirulito [piru'litu] (*BR*) *m* lollipop.
PISA (*BR*) *abr f* = **Papel de Imprensa SA**.
pisada [pi'zada] *f* (*passo*) footstep; (*rastro*) footprint.
pisar [pi'za*] *vt* (*andar por cima de*) to tread on; (*uvas*) to tread, press; (*esmagar, subjugar*) to crush; (*café*) to pound; (*assunto*) to harp on ♦ *vi* (*andar*) to step, tread; (*acelerar*) to put one's foot down; **~ em** (*grama, pé*) to step *ou* tread on; (*casa de alguém, pátria*) to set foot in; **"não pise na grama"** "do not walk on the grass"; **~ forte** to stomp; **pisa mais leve!** don't stamp your feet!
piscadela [piʃka'dɛla] *f* (*involuntária*) blink; (*sinal*) wink.
pisca-pisca [piʃka-'piʃka] (*pl* **~s**) *m* (*AUTO*) indicator.
piscar [piʃ'ka*] *vt* to blink; (*dar sinal*) to wink; (*estrelas*) to twinkle ♦ *m*: **num ~ de olhos** in a flash.
piscicultor(a) [pisikuw'to*(a)] *m/f* fish farmer.
piscicultura [pisikuw'tura] *f* fish farming.
piscina [pi'sina] *f* swimming pool; (*para peixes*) fish pond.
piscoso/a [piʃ'kozu/ɔza] *adj* rich in fish.
piso ['pizu] *m* floor; **~ salarial** wage floor, lowest wage.
pisotear [pizo'tʃja*] *vt* to trample (on); (*fig*) to ride roughshod over.
pisquei [piʃ'kej] *etc vb V* **piscar**.
píssico/a ['pisiku/a] *adj* crazy, mad.
pista ['piʃta] *f* (*vestígio*) track, trail; (*indicação*) clue; (*de corridas*) track; (*AVIAT*) runway; (*de equitação*) ring; (*de estrada*) lane; (*de dança*) (dance) floor.
pistache [piʃ'taʃi] *m* pistachio (nut).
pistacho [piʃ'taʃu] *m* = **pistache**.
pistão [piʃ'tãw] (*pl* **-ões**) *m* = **pistom**.
pistola [piʃ'tɔla] *f* (*arma*) pistol; (*para tinta*) spray gun.
pistolão [piʃto'lãw] (*pl* **-ões**) *m* contact.
pistoleiro [piʃto'lejru] *m* gunman.
pistolões [piʃto'lõjʃ] *mpl de* **pistolão**.
pistom [piʃ'tõ] (*pl* **-ns**) *m* piston.
pitada [pi'tada] *f* (*porção*) pinch.
pitanga [pi'tãga] *f* Surinam cherry.
pitar [pi'ta*] *vt, vi* to smoke.
piteira [pi'tejra] *f* cigarette-holder.
pito ['pitu] *m* (*cachimbo*) pipe; (*col*: *repreensão*) telling-off; **sossegar o ~** to calm down.
pitonisa [pito'niza] *f* fortune-teller.
pitoresco/a [pito'reʃku/a] *adj* picturesque.
pituitário/a [pitwi'tarju/a] *adj* (*glândula*) pituitary.
pivete [pi'vɛtʃi] *m* child thief.
pivô [pi'vo] *m* (*TEC*) pivot; (*fig*) central figure, prime mover.
pixaim [piʃa'ĩ] *m* frizzy hair ♦ *adj* frizzy.
pixote [pi'ʃɔtʃi] *m/f* = **pexote**.

pizza ['pitsa] *f* pizza.
pizzaria [pitsa'ria] *f* pizzeria.
PJ (*BR*) *abr m* = **Partido da Juventude.**
PL (*BR*) *abr m* = **Partido Liberal.**
PLB *abr m* = **Partido Liberal Brasileiro.**
plá [pla] (*col*) *m* (*dica*) tip; (*papo*) chat.
placa ['plaka] *f* plate; (*AUTO*) number plate (*BRIT*), license plate (*US*); (*comemorativa*) plaque; (*COMPUT*) board; (*na pele*) blotch; ~ **de sinalização** roadsign; ~ **fria** false number *ou* license plate.
placar [pla'ka*] *m* scoreboard; **abrir o** ~ to open the scoring.
placebo [pla'sɛbu] *m* placebo.
placenta [pla'sẽta] *f* placenta.
placidez [plasi'deʒ] *f* peacefulness, serenity.
plácido/a ['plasidu/a] *adj* (*sereno*) calm; (*manso*) placid.
plagiador(a) [plaʒja'do*(a)] *m/f* = **plagiário/a.**
plagiário/a [pla'ʒjarju/a] *m/f* plagiarist.
plagiar [pla'ʒja*] *vt* to plagiarize.
plágio ['plaʒu] *m* plagiarism.
plaina ['plajna] *f* (*instrumento*) plane.
plana ['plana] *f*: **de primeira** ~ first-class.
planador [plana'do*] *m* glider.
planalto [pla'nawtu] *m* tableland, plateau.
planar [pla'na*] *vi* to glide.
planear [pla'nja*] (*PT*) *vt* = **planejar.**
planejador(a) [planeʒa'do*(a)] *m/f* planner.
planejamento [planeʒa'mẽtu] *m* planning; (*ARQ*) design; ~ **familiar** family planning.
planejar [plane'ʒa*] (*BR*) *vt* to plan; (*edifício*) to design.
planeta [pla'neta] *m* planet.
planetário/a [plane'tarju/a] *adj* planetary ♦ *m* planetarium.
plangente [plã'ʒẽtʃi] *adj* plaintive, mournful.
planície [pla'nisi] *f* plain.
planificar [planifi'ka*] *vt* (*programar*) to plan out; (*uma região*) to make a plan of.
planilha [pla'niʎa] *f* (*COMPUT*) spreadsheet.
plano/a ['planu/a] *adj* (*terreno*) flat, level; (*liso*) smooth ♦ *m* plan; (*MAT*) plane; ~ **diretor** master plan; **em primeiro/em último** ~ in the foreground/background.
planta ['plãta] *f* (*BIO*) plant; (*de pé*) sole; (*ARQ*) plan.
plantação [plãta'sãw] *f* (*ato*) planting; (*terreno*) planted land; (*o que se plantou*) crops *pl*.
plantado/a [plã'tadu/a] *adj*: **deixar alguém/ficar ~ em algum lugar** (*col*) to leave sb/be left standing somewhere.
plantão [plã'tãw] (*pl* **-ões**) *m* duty; (*noturno*) night duty; (*plantonista*) person on duty; (*MIL*: *serviço*) sentry duty; (: *pessoa*) sentry; **estar de** ~ to be on duty; **médico/farmácia de** ~ duty doctor/pharmacy *ou* chemist's (*BRIT*).
plantar [plã'ta*] *vt* to plant; (*semear*) to sow; (*estaca*) to drive in; (*estabelecer*) to set up; **~-se** *vr* to plant o.s.
plantio [plã'tʃiu] *m* planting; (*terreno*) planted land.
plantões [plã'tõjʃ] *mpl de* **plantão.**
plantonista [plãto'niʃta] *m/f* person on duty.
planura [pla'nura] *f* plain.
plaquê [pla'ke] (*PT*) *m* gold plate.
plaqueta [pla'keta] *f* plaque; (*AUTO*) licensing badge (*attached to number plate*); (*COMPUT*) chip.
plasma ['plaʒma] *m* plasma.
plasmar [plaʒ'ma*] *vt* to mould (*BRIT*), mold (*US*), shape.
plástica ['plaʃtʃika] *f* (*cirurgia*) piece of plastic surgery; (*do corpo*) build; **fazer uma** ~ to have plastic surgery.
plástico/a ['plaʃtʃiku/a] *adj* plastic ♦ *m* plastic.
plastificado/a [plaʃtʃifi'kadu/a] *adj* plastic-coated.
plataforma [plata'fɔxma] *f* platform; ~ **de exploração de petróleo** oil rig; ~ **de lançamento** launch pad.
plátano ['platanu] *m* plane tree.
platéia [pla'tɛja] *f* (*TEATRO etc*) stalls *pl* (*BRIT*), orchestra (*US*); (*espectadores*) audience.
platina [pla'tʃina] *f* platinum.
platinado/a [platʃi'nadu/a] *adj* platinum *atr*; **loura platinada** platinum blonde.
platinados [platʃi'naduʃ] *mpl* (*AUTO*) points.
platinar [platʃi'na*] *vt* (*cabelo*) to dye platinum blonde.
platô [pla'to] *m* plateau.
platônico/a [pla'toniku/a] *adj* platonic.
plausibilidade [plawzibili'dadʒi] *f* plausibility.
plausível [plaw'zivew] (*pl* **-eis**) *adj* credible, plausible.
playboy [plej'bɔi] (*pl* **~s**) *m* playboy.
playground [plej'grãwdʒi] (*pl* **~s**) *m* children's playground.
plebe ['plɛbi] *f* common people, populace.
plebeu/béia [ple'bew/'bɛja] *adj* plebeian ♦ *m/f* pleb.
plebiscito [plebi'situ] *m* referendum, plebiscite.
plectro ['plɛktru] *m* (*MÚS*) plectrum.
pleitear [plej'tʃja*] *vt* (*JUR*: *causa*) to plead; (*contestar*) to contest; (*tentar conseguir*) to go after; (*concorrer a*) to compete for.
pleito ['plejtu] *m* lawsuit, case; (*fig*) dispute; ~ **(eleitoral)** election.
plenamente [plena'mẽtʃi] *adv* fully, completely.
plenário/a [ple'narju/a] *adj* plenary ♦ *m* plenary session; (*local*) chamber.
plenipotência [plenipo'tẽsja] *f* full powers *pl*.
plenipotenciário/a [plenipotẽ'sjarju/a] *adj, m/f* plenipotentiary.

***NB:** European Portuguese adds the following consonants to certain words:* **b** (sú(b)dito, su(b)til); **c** (a(c)ção, a(c)cionista, a(c)to); **m** (inde(m)ne); **p** (ado(p)ção, ado(p)tar); *for further details see p. xiii.*

plenitude [pleni'tudʒi] *f* plenitude, fullness.
pleno/a ['plenu/a] *adj* full; (*completo*) complete; **em ~ dia** in broad daylight; **em plena rua/Londres** in the middle of the street/London; **em ~ inverno** in the middle *ou* depths of winter; **em ~ mar** out at sea; **ter plena certeza** to be completely sure; **~s poderes** full powers.
pleonasmo [pljo'naʒmu] *m* pleonasm.
pletora [ple'tɔra] *f* plethora.
pleurisia [plewri'zia] *f* pleurisy.
plinto ['plĩtu] *m* plinth.
plissado/a [pli'sadu/a] *adj* pleated.
pluma ['pluma] *f* feather.
plumagem [plu'maʒẽ] *f* plumage.
plural [plu'raw] (*pl* **-ais**) *adj*, *m* plural.
pluralismo [plura'liʒmu] *m* pluralism.
pluralista [plura'liʃta] *adj*, *m/f* pluralist.
Plutão [plu'tãw] *m* Pluto.
plutocrata [pluto'krata] *m/f* plutocrat.
plutônio [plu'tonju] *m* plutonium.
pluvial [plu'vjaw] (*pl* **-ais**) *adj* pluvial, rain *atr*.
PM (*BR*) *abr f*, *m* = **Polícia Militar**.
PMB *abr m* = **Partido Municipalista Brasileiro**.
PMC (*BR*) *abr m* = **Partido Municipalista Comunitário**.
PMDB *abr m* = **Partido do Movimento Democrático Brasileiro**.
PMN (*BR*) *abr m* = **Partido da Mobilização Nacional**.
PN *abr m* (*BR*) = **Partido Nacionalista** ♦ *abr f* (*COM*: *de ações*) = **preferencial nominativa**.
PNA (*BR*) *abr m* = **Plano Nacional de Álcool**.
PNB *abr m* (= *Produto Nacional Bruto*) GNP.
PNC (*BR*) *abr m* = **Partido Nacionalista Comunitário**.
PND (*BR*) *abr m* = **Plano Nacional de Desenvolvimento**; **Partido Nacionalista Democrático**.
pneu ['pnew] *m* tyre (*BRIT*), tire (*US*).
pneumático/a [pnew'matʃiku/a] *adj* pneumatic ♦ *m* tyre (*BRIT*), tire (*US*).
pneumonia [pnewmo'nia] *f* pneumonia.
PNR (*BR*) *abr m* = **Partido da Nova República**.
pó [pɔ] *m* (*partículas*) powder; (*sujeira*) dust; (*col*: *cocaína*) coke; **~ de arroz** face powder; **ouro/sabão em ~** gold dust/soap powder; **tirar o ~ (de algo)** to dust (sth).
pô [po] (*col*) *excl* (*dando ênfase*) blimey; (*mostrando desagrado*) damn it!
pobre ['pɔbri] *adj* poor ♦ *m/f* poor person; **os ~s** *mpl* the poor; **~ de espírito** simple, dull; **um Sinatra dos ~s** a poor man's Sinatra.
pobre-diabo (*pl* **pobres-diabos**) *m* poor devil.
pobretão/tona [pobre'tãw/'tɔna] (*pl* **-ões/~s**) *m/f* pauper.
pobreza [po'breza] *f* poverty; **~ de espírito** simplicity.
poça ['posa] *f* puddle, pool; **~ de sangue** pool of blood.
poção [po'sãw] (*pl* **-ões**) *f* potion.
pocilga [po'siwga] *f* pigsty.
poço ['posu] *m* well; (*de mina*, *elevador*) shaft; **ser um ~ de ciência/bondade** (*fig*) to be a fount of knowledge/kindness; **~ de petróleo** oil well.
poções [po'sõjʃ] *fpl de* **poção**.
poda ['pɔda] *f* pruning.
podadeira [poda'dejra] *f* pruning knife.
podar [po'da*] *vt* to prune.
pôde ['podʒi] *etc vb V* **poder**.
pó-de-arroz *m* face powder.
poder [po'de*] *vi* (*ser capaz de*) to be able to, can; (*ter o direito de*) to be allowed to, may ♦ *m* power; (*autoridade*) authority; **pode ser** maybe; **pode ser que** it may be that; **ele poderá vir amanhã** he might come tomorrow; **até não mais ~** with all one's might; **~ com** (*ser superior a*) to be a match for; **não posso com ele** I cannot cope with him; **pudera!** no wonder!; **como é que pode?** (*col*) you're joking!; **pode entrar?** (*posso*) can I come in?; **a ~ de** by dint of; **em ~ de alguém** in sb's hands; **estar no ~** to be in power; **~ aquisitivo** purchasing power; **~ de fogo** fire power.
poderio [pode'riu] *m* might, power.
poderoso/a [pode'rozu/ɔza] *adj* mighty, powerful; (*COMPUT*) powerful.
pódio ['pɔdʒju] *m* podium.
podre ['podri] *adj* rotten, putrid; (*fig*) rotten, corrupt; **sentir-se ~** (*col*: *mal*) to feel grotty; **~ de rico/cansaço** filthy rich/dog tired.
podres ['podriʃ] *mpl* faults.
podridão [podri'dãw] *f* decay, rottenness; (*fig*) corruption.
põe [põj] *etc vb V* **pôr**.
poeira ['pwejra] *f* dust; **~ radioativa** fall-out.
poeirada [pwej'rada] *f* pile of dust.
poeirento/a [pwej'rẽtu/a] *adj* dusty.
poema ['pwɛma] *m* poem.
poente ['pwẽtʃi] *m* west; (*do sol*) setting.
poesia [poe'zia] *f* poetry; (*poema*) poem.
poeta ['pwɛta] *m* poet.
poética ['pwetʃika] *f* poetics *sg*.
poético/a ['pwɛtʃiku/a] *adj* poetic.
poetisa [pwe'tʃiza] *f* poetess.
poetizar [pwetʃi'za*] *vt* to set to poetry ♦ *vi* to write poetry.
pogrom [po'grõ] (*pl* **~s**) *m* pogrom.
pois [pojʃ] *adv* (*portanto*) so; (*PT*: *assentimento*) yes ♦ *conj* as, since, because; (*mas*) but; **~ bem** well then; **~ é** that's right; **~ não!** (*BR*) of course!; **~ não?** (*numa loja*) what can I do for you?; (*PT*) isn't it?, aren't you?, didn't they? *etc*; **~ sim!** certainly not!; **~ (então)** then.
polaco/a [po'laku/a] (*PT*) *adj* Polish ♦ *m/f* Pole ♦ *m* (*LING*) Polish.
polainas [po'lajnaʃ] *fpl* gaiters.
polar [po'la*] *adj* polar.
polaridade [polari'dadʒi] *f* polarity.

polarizar [polari'za*] *vt* to polarize.
polca ['pɔwka] *f* polka.
poldro/a ['powdru/a] *m/f* colt/filly.
polegada [pole'gada] *f* inch.
polegar [pole'ga*] *m* (*tb*: *dedo* ~) thumb.
poleiro [po'lejru] *m* perch.
polêmica [po'lemika] *f* controversy.
polêmico/a [po'lemiku/a] *adj* controversial.
polemista [pole'miʃta] *adj* argumentative ♦ *m/f* debater.
polemizar [polemi'za*] *vi* to debate, argue.
pólen ['pɔlẽ] *m* pollen.
polia [po'lia] *f* pulley.
poliamida [polja'mida] *f* polyamide.
polichinelo [poliʃi'nɛlu] *m* Mr Punch.
polícia [po'lisja] *f* police, police force ♦ *m/f* policeman/woman; **agente de** ~ police officer; ~ **aduaneira** border police; ~ **militar** military police; ~ **rodoviária** traffic police.
policial [poli'sjaw] (*pl* **-ais**) *adj* police *atr*; **novela** *ou* **romance** ~ detective novel ♦ *m/f* (*BR*) policeman/woman.
policial-militar (*pl* **policiais-militares**) *adj* military police *atr*.
policiamento [polisja'mẽtu] *m* policing.
policiar [poli'sja*] *vt* to police; (*instintos, modos*) to control, keep in check; ~**-se** *vr* to control o.s.
policlínica [poli'klinika] *f* general hospital.
policultura [polikuw'tura] *f* mixed farming.
polidez [poli'deʒ] *f* good manners *pl*, politeness.
polido/a [po'lidu/a] *adj* (*lustrado*) polished, shiny; (*cortês*) well-mannered, polite.
poliéster [po'ljɛʃte*] *m* polyester.
poliestireno [poljeʃtʃi'rɛnu] *m* polystyrene.
polietileno [poljetʃi'lɛnu] *m* polyethylene.
poligamia [poliga'mia] *f* polygamy.
polígamo/a [po'ligamu/a] *adj* polygamous.
poliglota [poli'glɔta] *adj, m/f* polyglot.
polígono [po'ligonu] *m* polygon.
polimento [poli'mẽtu] *m* (*lustração*) polishing; (*finura*) refinement.
Polinésia [poli'nɛzja] *f*: **a** ~ Polynesia.
polinésio/a [poli'nɛzju/a] *adj, m/f* Polynesian.
polinização [poliniza'sãw] *f* pollination.
polinizar [polini'za*] *vt, vi* to pollinate.
pólio ['pɔlju] *f* polio.
poliomielite [poljomje'litʃi] *f* poliomyelitis.
pólipo ['pɔlipu] *m* polyp.
polir [po'li*] *vt* to polish.
polissílabo/a [poli'silabu/a] *adj* polysyllabic ♦ *m* polysyllable.
politécnica [poli'tɛknika] *f* (*EDUC*) polytechnic.
política [po'litʃika] *f* politics *sg*; (*programa*) policy; (*diplomacia*) tact; (*astúcia*) cunning; *V tb* **político**.
politicagem [politʃi'kaʒẽ] *f* politicking.
politicar [politʃi'ka*] *vi* to be involved in politics; (*discorrer*) to talk politics.
político/a [po'litʃiku/a] *adj* political; (*astuto*) crafty ♦ *m/f* politician.
politiqueiro/a [politʃi'kejru/a] *m/f* political wheeler-dealer ♦ *adj* politicking.
politizar [politʃi'za*] *vt* to politicize; (*trabalhadores*) to mobilize politically; ~**-se** *vr* to become politically aware.
pólo ['pɔlu] *m* pole; (*ESPORTE*) polo; ~ **aquático** water polo; ~ **petroquímico** petrochemical complex; **P~ Norte/Sul** North/South Pole.
polonês/esa [polo'neʃ/eza] *adj* Polish ♦ *m/f* Pole ♦ *m* (*LING*) Polish.
Polônia [po'lonja] *f*: **a** ~ Poland.
polpa ['powpa] *f* pulp.
polpudo/a [pow'pudu/a] *adj* (*fruta*) fleshy; (*negócio*) profitable, lucrative; (*quantia*) sizeable, considerable.
poltrão/trona [pow'trãw/'trɔna] (*pl* **-ões/~s**) *adj* cowardly ♦ *m/f* coward.
poltrona [pow'trɔna] *f* armchair; (*em teatro, cinema*) upholstered seat; *V tb* **poltrão.**
poluente [po'lwẽtʃi] *adj, m* pollutant.
poluição [polwi'sãw] *f* pollution.
poluidor(a) [polwi'do*(a)] *adj* pollutant.
poluir [po'lwi*] *vt* to pollute.
polvilhar [powvi'ʎa*] *vt* to sprinkle, powder.
polvilho [pow'viʎu] *m* powder; (*farinha*) manioc flour.
polvo ['powvu] *m* octopus.
pólvora ['pɔwvora] *f* gunpowder.
polvorosa [powvo'rɔza] (*col*) *f* uproar; **em** ~ (*apressado*) in a flap; (*desarrumado*) in a mess.
pomada [po'mada] *f* ointment.
pomar [po'ma*] *m* orchard.
pomba ['põba] *f* dove; ~**(s)!** for heaven's sake!
pombal [põ'baw] (*pl* **-ais**) *m* dovecote.
pombo ['põbu] *m* pigeon.
pombo-correio (*pl* **pombos-correios**) *m* carrier pigeon.
pomo ['pomu] *m*: ~ **de discórdia** bone of contention.
pomo-de-Adão [-a'dãw] *m* Adam's apple.
pomos ['pomoʃ] *vb V* **pôr.**
pompa ['põpa] *f* pomp.
Pompéia [põ'pɛja] *n* Pompeii.
pompom [põ'põ] (*pl* **-ns**) *m* pompom.
pomposo/a [põ'pozu/ɔza] *adj* ostentatious, pompous.
ponche ['põʃi] *m* punch.
poncheira [põ'ʃejra] *f* punchbowl.
poncho ['põʃu] *m* poncho, cape.
ponderação [põdera'sãw] *f* consideration, meditation; (*prudência*) prudence.
ponderado/a [põde'radu/a] *adj* prudent.
ponderar [põde'ra*] *vt* to consider, weigh up ♦ *vi* to meditate, muse; ~ **que** (*alegar*) to point out that.

***NB**: European Portuguese adds the following consonants to certain words:* **b** (sú(b)dito, su(b)til); **c** (a(c)ção, a(c)cionista, a(c)to); **m** (inde(m)ne); **p** (ado(p)ção, ado(p)tar); *for further details see p. xiii.*

pônei ['ponej] *m* pony.
ponho ['poɲu] *etc vb V* **pôr.**
ponta ['põta] *f* tip; (*de faca*) point; (*de sapato*) toe; (*extremidade*) end; (*TEATRO, CINEMA*) walk-on part; (*FUTEBOL: posição*) wing; (: *jogador*) winger; **uma ~ de** (*um pouco*) a touch of; **~ de cigarro** cigarette end; **~ do dedo** fingertip; **na ~ da língua** on the tip of one's tongue; **na(s) ~(s) dos pés** on tiptoe; **de ~ a ~** from one end to the other; (*do princípio ao fim*) from beginning to end; **~ de terra** point; **estar de ~ com alguém** to be at odds with sb; **agüentar as ~s** (*col*) to hold on.
ponta-cabeça *f*: **de ~** upside down; (*cair*) head first.
pontada [põ'tada] *f* (*dor*) twinge.
ponta-de-lança (*pl* **pontas-de-lança**) *m/f* (*fig*) spearhead.
ponta-direita (*pl* **pontas-direitas**) *m* (*FUTEBOL*) right winger.
ponta-esquerda (*pl* **pontas-esquerdas**) *m* (*FUTEBOL*) left winger.
pontal [põ'taw] (*pl* **-ais**) *m* (*de terra*) point, promontory.
pontão [põ'tãw] *m* pontoon.
pontapé [põta'pɛ] *m* kick; **dar ~s em alguém** to kick sb.
pontaria [põta'ria] *f* aim; **fazer ~** to take aim.
ponte ['põtʃi] *f* bridge; **~ aérea** air shuttle, airlift; **~ de safena** (heart) bypass operation; **~ levadiça** drawbridge; **~ móvel** swing bridge; **~ suspensa** *ou* **pênsil** suspension bridge.
ponteado/a [põ'tʃjadu/a] *adj* stippled, dotted ♦ *m* stipple.
pontear [po'tʃja*] *vt* (*pontilhar*) to dot, stipple; (*dar pontos*) to sew, stitch.
ponteira [põ'tejra] *f* ferrule, tip.
ponteiro [põ'tejru] *m* (*indicador*) pointer; (*de relógio*) hand; (*MÚS: plectro*) plectrum.
pontiagudo/a [põtʃja'gudu/a] *adj* sharp, pointed.
pontificado [põtʃifi'kadu] *m* pontificate.
pontificar [põtʃifi'ka*] *vi* to pontificate.
pontífice [põ'tʃifisi] *m* pontiff, Pope.
pontilhado/a [põtʃi'ʎadu/a] *adj* dotted ♦ *m* dotted area.
pontilhar [põtʃi'ʎa*] *vt* to dot, stipple.
pontinha [põ'tʃiɲa] *f*: **uma ~ de** a bit *ou* touch of.
ponto ['põtu] *m* point; (*MED, COSTURA, TRICÔ*) stitch; (*pequeno sinal, do i*) dot; (*na pontuação*) full stop (*BRIT*), period (*US*); (*na pele*) spot; (*TEATRO*) prompter; (*de ônibus*) stop; (*de táxi*) rank (*BRIT*), stand (*US*); (*tb*: *~ cantado*) macumba chant; (*matéria escolar*) subject; (*boca-de-fumo*) drug den; **estar a ~ de fazer** to be on the point of doing; **ao ~** (*bife*) medium; **até certo ~** to a certain extent; **às cinco em ~** at five o'clock on the dot; **em ~ de bala** (*col*) all set; **assinar o ~** to sign in; (*fig*) to put in an appearance; **dar ~s** (*MED*) to put in stitches; **não dar ~ sem nó** (*fig*) to look out for one's own interests; **entregar os ~s** (*fig*) to give up; **fazer ~ em** to hang out at; **pôr um ~ em algo** (*fig*) to put a stop to sth; **dois ~s** colon *sg*; **~ cardeal** cardinal point; **~ culminante** highest point; (*fig*) peak; **~ de admiração** (*PT*) exclamation mark; **~ de equilíbrio** (*COM*) break-even point; **~ de exclamação/interrogação** exclamation/question mark; **~ de meia/de tricô** stocking/plain stitch; **~ de mira** bead; **~ de partida** starting point; **~ de referência** point of reference; **~ de vista** point of view, viewpoint; **~ facultativo** optional day off; **~ final** (*fig*) end; (*de ônibus*) terminus; **~ fraco** weak point.
ponto-de-venda (*pl* **pontos-de-venda**) *m* (*COM*) point of sale, outlet.
ponto-e-vírgula (*pl* **ponto-e-vírgulas**) *m* semicolon.
pontuação [põtwa'sãw] *f* punctuation.
pontual [põ'twaw] (*pl* **-ais**) *adj* punctual.
pontualidade [põtwali'dadʒi] *f* punctuality.
pontuar [põ'twa*] *vt* to punctuate.
pontudo/a [põ'tudu/a] *adj* pointed.
poodle ['pudw] *m* poodle.
pool [puw] *m* pool.
popa ['popa] *f* stern, poop; **à ~** astern, aft.
popelina [pope'lina] *f* poplin.
população [popula'sãw] (*pl* **-ões**) *f* population.
populacional [populasjo'naw] (*pl* **-ais**) *adj* population *atr*.
populações [popula'sõjʃ] *fpl de* **população.**
popular [popu'la*] *adj* popular.
popularidade [populari'dadʒi] *f* popularity.
popularizar [populari'za*] *vt* to popularize, make popular; **~-se** *vr* to become popular.
populista [popu'liʃta] *adj* populist.
populoso/a [popu'lozu/ɔza] *adj* populous.
pôquer ['poke*] *m* poker.
por [po*] *prep* (*a favor de*) for; (*por causa de*) out of, because of, from; (*meio, agente*) by; (*troca*) (in exchange) for; (*através de*) through; **~ hábito/natureza** out of habit/by nature; **soubemos disso ~ carta** we learnt about it by letter; **viemos pelo parque** we came through the park; **faço isso ~ ela** I do it for her; **~ volta das duas horas** at about two o'clock; **~ aqui** this way; **~ isso** therefore; **~ cento** per cent; **~ mais difícil que seja** however difficult it is; **pelo amor de Deus!** for heaven's sake!; **~ escrito** in writing; **~ fora/~ dentro** outside/inside; **~ exemplo** for example; **~ ano** yearly; **~ mês** monthly; **~ semana** weekly; **~ dia** daily; **~ si** by o.s.; **está ~ acontecer** it is about to happen, it is yet to happen; **está ~ fazer** it is still to be done; **~ que** (*BR*) why; **~ quê?** (*BR*) why?
pôr [po*] *vt* to put; (*roupas*) to put on; (*objeções, dúvidas*) to raise; (*ovos, mesa*) to lay; (*defeito*) to find ♦ *m*: **o ~ do sol** sunset; **~-se** *vr* (*sol*) to set; **~ furioso** to infuriate;

~ **de lado** to set aside; ~ **o dedo na ferida** (*fig*) to hit a raw nerve; **você põe açúcar?** do you take sugar?; **ponhamos que ...** let us suppose (that) ..., supposing ...; **~-se de pé** to stand up; **~-se a caminho** to set off; **~-se a chorar** to start crying; **ponha-se no meu lugar** put yourself in my position.

porão [po'rãw] (*pl* **-ões**) *m* (*NÁUT*) hold; (*de casa*) basement; (: *armazém*) cellar.

porca ['pɔxka] *f* (*animal*) sow; (*TEC*) nut.

porcalhão/lhona [poxka'ʎãw/'ʎɔna] (*pl* **-ões/~s**) *adj* filthy ♦ *m/f* pig.

porção [pox'sãw] (*pl* **-ões**) *f* portion, piece; **uma ~ de** a lot of.

porcaria [poxka'ria] *f* filth; (*dito sujo*) obscenity; (*coisa ruim*) piece of junk ♦ *excl* damn!; **o filme era uma ~** the film was a load of rubbish.

porcelana [poxse'lana] *f* porcelain, china.

porcentagem [poxsẽ'taʒẽ] (*pl* **-ns**) *f* percentage.

porco/a ['poxku/'pɔxka] *adj* filthy ♦ *m* (*animal*) pig, hog (*US*); (*carne*) pork; **~ chauvinista** male chauvinist pig.

porções [pox'sõjʃ] *fpl de* **porção**.

porco-espinho (*pl* **porcos-espinhos**) *m* porcupine.

porco-montês [-mõ'teʃ] (*pl* **porcos-monteses**) *m* wild boar.

porejar [pore'ʒa*] *vt* to exude ♦ *vi* to be exuded.

porém [po'rẽ] *conj* however.

porfia [pox'fia] *f* (*altercação*) dispute, wrangle; (*rivalidade*) rivalry.

pormenor [poxme'no*] *m* detail.

pormenorizar [poxmenori'za*] *vt* to detail.

pornô [pox'no] (*col*) *adj inv* porn ♦ *m* (*filme*) porn film.

pornochanchada [poxnoʃã'ʃada] *f* (*filme*) soft porn movie.

pornografia [poxnogra'fia] *f* pornography.

pornográfico/a [poxno'grafiku/a] *adj* pornographic.

poro ['pɔru] *m* pore.

porões [po'rõjs] *mpl de* **porão**.

pororoca [poro'rɔka] *f* bore.

poroso/a [po'rozu/ɔza] *adj* porous.

porquanto [pox'kwãtu] *conj* since, seeing that.

porque ['poxke] *conj* because; (*interrogativo*: *PT*) why.

porquê [pox'ke] *adv* why; **~?** (*PT*) why? ♦ *m* reason, motive.

porquinho-da-índia [pox'kiɲu-] (*pl* **porquinhos-da-índia**) *m* guinea pig.

porra ['poxa] (*col!*) *f* come (*!*), spunk (*!*) ♦ *excl* fuck (*!*), fucking hell (*!*); **para quê ~?** what the fuck for? (*!*).

porrada [po'xada] *f* (*col*: *pancada*) beating; **uma ~ de** (*col!*) fucking loads of (*!*).

porra-louca (*pl* **porras-loucas**) (*col!*) *m/f* fucking maniac (*!*) ♦ *adj* fucking crazy (*!*).

porre ['pɔxi] (*col*) *m* booze-up; **tomar um ~** to get plastered; **estar de ~** to be plastered; **ser um ~** (*ser chato*) to be boring, be a drag.

porretada [poxe'tada] *f* clubbing.

porrete [po'xetʃi] *m* club.

porta ['pɔxta] *f* door; (*vão da ~*) doorway; (*de um jardim*) gate; (*COMPUT*) port; **a ~s fechadas** behind closed doors; **de ~ em ~** from door to door; **~ corrediça** sliding door; **~ da rua/da frente/dos fundos** street/front/back door; **~ de entrada** entrance door; **~ de vaivém** swing door; **~ giratória** revolving door; **~ sanfonada** folding door.

porta-aviões *m inv* aircraft carrier.

porta-bandeira (*pl* **~s**) *m/f* standard-bearer.

porta-chaves *m inv* key-holder.

portador(a) [poxta'do*(a)] *m/f* bearer; **ao ~** (*COM*) payable to the bearer.

porta-espada (*pl* **~s**) *m* sheath.

porta-estandarte (*pl* **~s**) *m/f* standard-bearer.

porta-fólio [-'fɔlju] (*pl* **~s**) *m* portfolio.

portagem [pox'taʒẽ] (*PT*: *pl* **-ns**) *f* toll.

porta-jóias *m inv* jewellery (*BRIT*) *ou* jewelry (*US*) box.

portal [pox'taw] (*pl* **-ais**) *m* doorway.

porta-lápis *m inv* pencil box.

portaló [poxta'lɔ] *m* (*NÁUT*) gangway.

porta-luvas *m inv* (*AUTO*) glove compartment.

porta-malas *m inv* (*AUTO*) boot (*BRIT*), trunk (*US*).

porta-moedas (*PT*) *m* purse.

porta-níqueis *m inv* purse.

portanto [pox'tãtu] *conj* so, therefore.

portão [pox'tãw] (*pl* **-ões**) *m* gate.

porta-partitura (*pl* **~s**) *m* music stand.

portar [pox'ta*] *vt* to carry; **~-se** *vr* to behave.

porta-retratos *m inv* photo frame.

porta-revistas *m inv* magazine rack.

portaria [poxta'ria] *f* (*de um edifício*) entrance hall; (*recepção*) reception desk; (*do governo*) edict, decree; **baixar uma ~** to issue a decree.

porta-seios *m inv* bra, brassiere.

portátil [pox'tatʃiw] (*pl* **-eis**) *adj* portable.

porta-toalhas *m inv* towel rail.

porta-voz (*pl* **~es**) *m/f* (*pessoa*) spokesman/woman.

porte ['pɔxtʃi] *m* (*transporte*) transport; (*custo*) freight charge, carriage; (*NÁUT*) tonnage, capacity; (*atitude*) bearing; **~ pago** post paid; **de grande ~** far-reaching, important; **empresa de ~ medio** medium-sized enterprise; **um autor do ~ de ...** an author of the calibre (*BRIT*) *ou* caliber (*US*) of ....

***NB**: European Portuguese adds the following consonants to certain words:* **b** (sú(b)dito, su(b)til); **c** (a(c)ção, a(c)cionista, a(c)to); **m** (inde(m)ne); **p** (ado(p)ção, ado(p)tar); *for further details see p. xiii.*

porteiro/a [pox'tejru/a] *m/f* caretaker; ~ **eletrônico** entryphone.
portenho/a [pox'tɛɲu/a] *adj* from Buenos Aires ♦ *m/f* person from Buenos Aires.
portento [pox'tẽtu] *m* wonder, marvel.
portentoso/a [poxtẽ'tozu/ɔza] *adj* amazing, marvellous (*BRIT*), marvelous (*US*).
pórtico ['pɔxtʃiku] *m* porch, portico.
portinhola [poxtʃi'ɲɔla] *f* small door; (*de carruagem*) door.
porto ['poxtu] *m* (*do mar*) port, harbour (*BRIT*), harbor (*US*); (*vinho*) port; **o P~** Oporto; ~ **de escala** port of call; ~ **franco** freeport.
porto-alegrense [-ale'grẽsi] *adj* from Porto Alegre ♦ *m/f* person from Porto Alegre.
portões [pox'tõjʃ] *mpl de* **portão**.
Porto Rico *m* Puerto Rico.
porto-riquenho/a [poxtuxi'kɛɲu/a] *adj*, *m/f* Puertorican.
portuense [pox'twẽsi] *adj* from Oporto ♦ *m/f* person from Oporto.
portuga [pox'tuga] *m/f* (*pej*) Portuguese.
Portugal [poxtu'gaw] *m* Portugal.
português/guesa [portu'geʃ/'geza] *adj* Portuguese ♦ *m/f* Portuguese ♦ *m* (*LING*) Portuguese; ~ **de Portugal/do Brasil** European/Brazilian Portuguese.
portunhol [poxtu'ɲɔw] *m mixture of Spanish and Portuguese*.
porventura [poxvẽ'tura] *adj* by chance; **se ~ você** ... if you happen to ....
porvir [pox'vi*] *m* future.
pôs [poʃ] *vb V* **pôr**.
pós- [pɔjʃ-] *prefixo* post-.
posar [po'za*] *vi* (*FOTO*) to pose.
pós-datado/a [-da'tadu/a] *adj* post-dated.
pós-datar *vt* to postdate.
pose ['pozi] *f* pose.
pós-escrito *m* postscript.
pós-graduação *f* postgraduation; **curso de ~** postgraduate course.
pós-graduado/a *adj*, *m/f* postgraduate.
pós-guerra *m* post-war period; **o Brasil do ~** post-war Brazil.
posição [pozi'sãw] (*pl* **-ões**) *f* position; (*social*) standing, status; (*de esportista no mundo*) ranking; **tomar uma ~** to take a stand.
posicionar [pozisjo'na*] *vt* to position; **~-se** *vr* to position o.s.; (*tomar atitude*) to take a position.
positivo/a [pozi'tʃivu/a] *adj* positive ♦ *m* positive ♦ *excl* (*col*) yeah! sure!
posologia [pozolo'ʒia] *f* dosage.
pós-operatório/a [-opera'tɔrju/a] *adj* post-operative.
pospor [poʃ'po*] (*irreg*: *como* **pôr**) *vt* to put after; (*adiar*) to postpone.
possante [po'sãtʃi] *adj* powerful, strong; (*carro*) flashy.
posse ['pɔsi] *f* possession, ownership; (*investidura*) swearing in; **~s** *fpl* possessions, belongings; **tomar ~** to take office; **tomar ~ de** to take possession of; **cerimônia de ~** swearing in ceremony; **pessoa de ~s** person of means; **viver de acordo com suas ~s** to live according to one's means.
posseiro/a [po'sejru/a] *adj* leaseholding ♦ *m/f* leaseholder.
possessão [pose'sãw] *f* possession.
possessivo/a [pose'sivu/a] *adj* possessive.
possesso/a [po'sɛsu/a] *adj* possessed; (*furioso*) furious.
possibilidade [posibili'dadʒi] *f* possibility; (*oportunidade*) chance; **~s** *fpl* means.
possibilitar [posibili'ta*] *vt* to make possible, permit.
possível [po'sivew] (*pl* **-eis**) *adj* possible; **fazer todo o ~** to do one's best; **não é ~!** (*col*) you're joking!
posso ['posu] *etc vb V* **poder**.
possuidor(a) [poswi'do*(a)] *m/f* (*de casa, livro etc*) owner; (*de dinheiro, talento etc*) possessor; **ser ~ de** to be the owner/possessor of.
possuir [po'swi*] *vt* (*casa, livro etc*) to own; (*dinheiro, talento*) to possess; (*dominar*) to possess, grip; (*sexualmente*) to take, have.
posta ['pɔʃta] *f* (*pedaço*) piece, slice.
postal [poʃ'taw] (*pl* **-ais**) *adj* postal ♦ *m* postcard.
postar [poʃ'ta*] *vt* to place, post; **~-se** *vr* to position o.s.
posta-restante (*pl* **postas-restantes**) *f* poste-restante (*BRIT*), general delivery (*US*).
poste ['pɔʃtʃi] *m* pole, post.
pôster ['poʃte*] *m* poster.
postergar [poʃtex'ga*] *vt* (*adiar*) to postpone; (*amigos*) to pass over; (*interesse pessoal*) to set *ou* put aside; (*lei, norma*) to disregard.
posteridade [poʃteri'dadʒi] *f* posterity.
posterior [poʃte'rjo*] *adj* (*mais tarde*) subsequent, later; (*traseiro*) rear, back ♦ *m* (*col*) posterior, bottom.
posteriormente [poʃterjox'mẽtʃi] *adv* later, subsequently.
postiço/a [poʃ'tʃisu/a] *adj* false, artificial; **dentes ~s** false teeth.
postigo [poʃ'tʃigu] *m* (*em porta*) peephole.
posto/a ['poʃtu/'pɔʃta] *pp de* **pôr** ♦ *m* post, position; (*emprego*) job; (*de diplomata: local*) posting; ~ **de comando** command post; ~ **de gasolina** service *ou* petrol station; ~ **que** although; **a ~s** at action stations; ~ **do corpo de bombeiros** fire station; ~ **de saúde** health centre *ou* center.
posto-chave (*pl* **postos-chaves**) *m* key position *ou* post.
postulado [poʃtu'ladu] *m* postulate, assumption.
postulante [poʃtu'lãtʃi] *m/f* petitioner; (*candidato*) candidate.
postular [poʃtu'la*] *vt* (*pedir*) to request; (*teoria*) to postulate.
póstumo/a ['pɔʃtumu/a] *adj* posthumous.

postura [poʃ'tura] *f* (*posição*) posture, position; (*aspecto físico*) appearance; (*fig*) posture.

posudo/a [po'zudu/a] *adj* poseurish.

potassa [po'tasa] *f* potash.

potássio [po'tasju] *m* potassium.

potável [po'tavew] (*pl* **-eis**) *adj* drinkable; **água ~** drinking water.

pote ['pɔtʃi] *m* jug, pitcher; (*de geléia*) jar; (*de creme*) pot; **chover a ~s** (*PT*) to rain cats and dogs; **dinheiro aos ~s** (*fig*) pots of money.

potência [po'tẽsja] *f* power; (*força*) strength; (*nação*) power; (*virilidade*) potency.

potencial [potẽ'sjaw] (*pl* **-ais**) *adj* potential, latent ♦ *m* potential; **riquezas** *etc* **em ~** potential wealth *etc*.

potentado [potẽ'tadu] *m* potentate.

potente [po'tẽtʃi] *adj* powerful, potent.

pot-pourri [popu'xi] *m* (*MÚS*) medley; (*fig*) pot-pourri.

potro/a ['potru/a] *m/f* (*cavalo*) colt/filly, foal.

pouca-vergonha (*pl* **poucas-vergonhas**) *f* (*ato*) shameful act, disgrace; (*falta de vergonha*) shamelessness.

pouco/a ['poku/a] *adj*, *pron* (*sg*) little; (*pl*) few ♦ *adv* not much, little ♦ *m*: **um ~** a little; **há ~ (tempo)** a short time ago; **poucas vezes** rarely; **~ a ~** gradually, bit by bit; **por ~** almost; **aos ~s** gradually; **fazer ~ de** (*desprezar*) to belittle; (*zombar*) to make light of; **nem um ~** not at all; **dentro em ~, daqui a ~** shortly; **~ antes** a short while before; **ouvir poucas e boas** to hear some home truths.

pouco-caso *m* scorn.

poupador(a) [popa'do*(a)] *adj* thrifty.

poupança [po'pãsa] *f* thrift; (*economias*) savings *pl*; (*tb*: *caderneta de ~*) savings bank.

poupar [po'pa*] *vt* to save; (*vida*) to spare; **~ alguém** (*de sofrimentos*) to spare sb; **~ algo a alguém, ~ alguém de algo** (*trabalho etc*) to save sb sth; (*aborrecimentos*) to spare sb sth.

pouquinho [po'kiɲu] *m*: **um ~ (de)** a little.

pouquíssimo/a [po'kisimu/a] *adj*, *adv superl de* **pouco**.

pousada [po'zada] *f* (*hospedagem*) lodging; (*hospedaria*) inn.

pousar [po'za*] *vt* to place; (*mão*) to rest, place ♦ *vi* (*avião, pássaro*) to land; (*pernoitar*) to spend the night.

pouso ['pozu] *m* landing; (*lugar*) resting place.

povão [po'vãw] *m* ordinary people.

povaréu [pova'rɛw] *m* crowd of people.

povo ['povu] *m* people; (*raça*) people *pl*, race; (*plebe*) common people *pl*; (*multidão*) crowd.

povoação [povwa'sãw] (*pl* **-ões**) *f* (*aldeia*) village, settlement; (*habitantes*) population; (*ato de povoar*) settlement, colonization.

povoado/a [po'vwadu/a] *adj* populated ♦ *m* village.

povoamento [povwa'mẽtu] *m* settlement.

povoar [po'vwa*] *vt* (*de habitantes*) to people, populate; (*de animais etc*) to stock.

poxa ['poʃa] *excl* gosh!

PP *abr* (*COM*: *de ações*) = **preferencial ao portador.**

PPB *abr m* = **Partido do Povo Brasileiro.**

PR (*BR*) *abr* = **Paraná** ♦ *abr f* = **Polícia Rodoviária.**

pra [pra] (*col*) *prep* = **para; para a.**

praça ['prasa] *f* (*largo*) square; (*mercado*) marketplace; (*soldado*) soldier; (*cidade*) town ♦ *m* (*MIL*) private; (*polícia*) constable; **sentar ~** to enlist; **~ de touros** bull ring; **~ forte** stronghold.

praça-d'armas (*pl* **praças-d'armas**) *m* officers' mess.

pracinha [pra'siɲa] *m* GI.

prado ['pradu] *m* meadow, grassland; (*BR*: *hipódromo*) racecourse.

pra-frente (*col*) *adj inv* trendy.

prafrentex [prafrẽ'tɛks] (*col*) *adj inv* trendy.

Praga ['praga] *n* Prague.

praga ['praga] *f* (*maldição*) curse; (*coisa, pessoa importuna*) nuisance; (*desgraça*) misfortune; (*erva daninha*) weed; **rogar ~ a alguém** to curse sb.

pragmático/a [prag'matʃiku/a] *adj* (*prático*) pragmatic.

pragmatismo [pragma'tʃiʒmu] *m* pragmatism.

pragmatista [pragma'tʃiʃta] *adj*, *m/f* pragmatist.

praguejar [prage'ʒa*] *vt*, *vi* to curse.

praia ['praja] *f* beach, seashore.

pralina [pra'lina] *f* praline.

prancha ['prãʃa] *f* plank; (*NÁUT*) gangplank; (*de surfe*) board.

prancheta [prã'ʃeta] *f* (*mesa*) drawing board.

prantear [prã'tʃja*] *vt* to mourn ♦ *vi* to weep.

pranto ['prãtu] *m* weeping; **debulhar-se em ~** to weep bitterly.

Prata ['prata] *f*: **o rio da ~** the River Plate.

prata ['prata] *f* silver; (*col*: *cruzeiro*) ≈ quid (*BRIT*), ≈ buck (*US*); **de ~** silver *atr*; **~ de lei** sterling silver.

prataria [prata'ria] *f* silverware; (*pratos*) crockery.

pratarrão [prata'xãw] (*pl* **-ões**) *m* large plate.

prateado/a [pra'tʃjadu/a] *adj* silver-plated; (*brilhante*) silvery; (*cor*) silver ♦ *m* (*cor*) silver; (*de um objeto*) silver-plating; **papel ~** silver paper.

pratear [pra'tʃja*] *vt* to silver-plate; (*fig*) to turn silver.

prateleira [prate'lejra] *f* shelf.

prática ['pratʃika] *f* (*ato de praticar*) practice; (*experiência*) experience, know-how; (*cos-*

***NB:** European Portuguese adds the following consonants to certain words:* **b** (sú(b)dito, su(b)til); **c** (a(c)ção, a(c)cionista, a(c)to); **m** (inde(m)ne); **p** (ado(p)ção, ado(p)tar); *for further details see p. xiii.*

tume) habit, custom; **na ~** in practice; **pôr em ~** to put into practice; **aprender com a ~** to learn with practice; *V tb* **prático**.

praticagem [pratʃi'kaʒẽ] *f* (NÁUT) pilotage.

praticante [pratʃi'kãtʃi] *adj* practising (BRIT), practicing (US) ♦ *m/f* apprentice; (*de esporte*) practitioner.

praticar [pratʃi'ka*] *vt* to practise (BRIT), practice (US); (*profissão, medicina*) to practise *ou* practice; (*roubo, operação*) to carry out.

praticável [pratʃi'kavew] (*pl* **-eis**) *adj* practical, feasible.

prático/a ['pratʃiku/a] *adj* practical ♦ *m/f* expert ♦ *m* (NÁUT) pilot.

prato ['pratu] *m* (*louça*) plate; (*comida*) dish; (*de uma refeição*) course; (*de toca-discos*) turntable; **~s** *mpl* (MÚS) cymbals; **~ raso/fundo/de sobremesa** dinner/soup/dessert plate; **~ do dia** dish of the day; **cuspir no ~ em que comeu** (*fig*) to bite the hand that feeds one; **pôr algo em ~s limpos** to get to the bottom of sth; **~ de resistência** pièce de résistance.

praxe ['praksi] *f* custom, usage; **de ~** usually; **ser de ~** to be the norm.

prazenteiro/a [prazẽ'tejru/a] *adj* cheerful, pleasant.

prazer [pra'ze*] *m* pleasure ♦ *vi*: **~ a alguém** to please sb; **muito ~ em conhecê-lo** pleased to meet you.

prazeroso/a [praze'rozu/ɔza] *adj* (*pessoa*) pleased; (*viagem*) pleasurable.

prazo ['prazu] *m* term, period; (*vencimento*) expiry date, time limit; **a curto/médio/longo ~** in the short/medium/long term; **comprar a ~** to buy on hire purchase (BRIT) *ou* on the installment plan (US); **último** *ou* **~ final** deadline.

pre- [pri-] *prefixo* pre-.

pré- [prɛ-] *prefixo* pre-.

preamar [prea'ma*] (BR) *f* high tide.

preâmbulo [pre'ãbulu] *m* preamble, introduction; **sem mais ~s** without further ado.

preaquecer [prjake'se*] *vt* to preheat.

pré-aviso *m* (prior) notice.

precário/a [pre'karju/a] *adj* precarious, insecure; (*escasso*) failing; (*estado de saúde*) delicate.

precatado/a [preka'tadu/a] *adj* cautious.

precatar-se [preka'taxsi] *vr* to take precautions; **~-se contra** to be wary of; **precate-se para o pior** prepare yourself for the worst.

precatória [preka'tɔrja] *f* (JUR) writ, prerogative order.

precaução [prekaw'sãw] (*pl* **-ões**) *f* precaution.

precaver-se [preka'vexsi] *vr*: **~ (contra** *ou* **de)** to be on one's guard (against); **~ para algo/fazer algo** to prepare o.s for sth/be prepared to do sth.

precavido/a [preka'vidu/a] *adj* cautious.

prece ['prɛsi] *f* prayer; (*súplica*) entreaty.

precedência [prese'dẽsja] *f* precedence; **ter ~ sobre** to take precedence over.

precedente [prese'dẽtʃi] *adj* preceding ♦ *m* precedent; **sem ~(s)** unprecedented.

preceder [prese'de*] *vt, vi* to precede; **~ a algo** to precede sth; (*ter primazia*) to take precedence over sth.

preceito [pre'sejtu] *m* precept, ruling.

preceituar [presej'twa*] *vt* to set down, prescribe.

preceptor [presep'to*] *m* mentor.

preciosidade [presjozi'dadʒi] *f* (*qualidade*) preciousness; (*coisa*) treasure.

preciosismo [presjo'ziʒmu] *m* preciosity.

precioso/a [pre'sjozu/ɔza] *adj* precious; (*de grande importância*) invaluable.

precipício [presi'pisju] *m* precipice; (*fig*) abyss.

precipitação [presipita'sãw] *f* haste; (*imprudência*) rashness.

precipitado/a [presipi'tadu/a] *adj* hasty; (*imprudente*) rash.

precipitar [presipi'ta*] *vt* (*atirar*) to hurl; (*acontecimentos*) to precipitate ♦ *vi* (QUÍM) to precipitate; **~-se** *vr* (*atirar-se*) to hurl o.s.; (*contra, para*) to rush; (*agir com precipitação*) to be rash, act rashly; **~ alguém/~-se em** (*situação*) to plunge sb/be plunged into; (*aventuras, perigos*) to sweep sb/be swept into.

precisado/a [presi'zadu/a] *adj* needy, in need.

precisamente [presiza'mẽtʃi] *adv* precisely.

precisão [presi'zãw] *f* (*exatidão*) precision, accuracy; **ter ~ de** to need.

precisar [presi'za*] *vt* to need; (*especificar*) to specify ♦ *vi* to be in need; **~-se** *vr*: **"precisa-se"** "needed"; **~ de** to need; (*uso impessoal*): **não precisa você se preocupar** you needn't worry; **precisa de um passaporte** a passport is necessary *ou* needed; **preciso ir** I have to go; **~ que alguém faça** to need sb to do.

preciso/a [pre'sizu/a] *adj* (*exato*) precise, accurate; (*necessário*) necessary; (*claro*) concise; **é ~ você ir** you must go.

preclaro/a [pre'klaru/a] *adj* famous, illustrious.

preço ['presu] *m* price; (*custo*) cost; (*valor*) value; **por qualquer ~** at any price; **a ~ de banana** (BR) *ou* **de chuva** (PT) dirt cheap; **não ter ~** (*fig*) to be priceless; **~ por atacado/a varejo** wholesale/retail price; **~ de custo** cost price; **~ de venda** sale price; **~ de fábrica/de revendedor** factory/trade price; **~ à vista** cash price; (*de commodities*) spot price; **~ pedido** asking price.

precoce [pre'kɔsi] *adj* precocious; (*antecipado*) early; (*calvície*) premature.

precocidade [prekosi'dadʒi] *f* precociousness.

preconcebido/a [prekõse'bidu/a] *adj* preconceived.

preconceito [prekõ'sejtu] *m* prejudice.

preconizar [prekoni'za*] *vt* to extol;

(*aconselhar*) to advocate.
precursor(a) [prekux'so*(a)] *m/f* (*predecessor*) precursor, forerunner; (*mensageiro*) herald.
predador [preda'do*] *m* predator.
pré-datado/a [-da'tadu/a] *adj* predated.
pré-datar *vt* to predate.
predatório/a [preda'tɔrju/a] *adj* predatory.
predecessor [predese'so*] *m* predecessor.
predestinado/a [predeʃtʃi'nadu/a] *adj* predestined.
predestinar [predeʃtʃi'na*] *vt* to predestine.
predeterminado/a [predetexmi'nadu/a] *adj* predetermined.
predeterminar [predetexmi'na*] *vt* to predetermine.
predial [pre'dʒjaw] (*pl* **-ais**) *adj* property *atr*, real-estate *atr*; **imposto ~** domestic rates.
prédica ['prɛdʒika] *f* sermon.
predicado [predʒi'kadu] *m* predicate.
predição [predʒi'sãw] (*pl* **-ões**) *f* prediction, forecast.
predigo [pre'dʒigu] *etc vb V* **predizer**.
predileção [predʒile'sãw] (*PT*: **-cç-**: *pl* **-ões**) *f* preference, predilection.
predileto/a [predʒi'lɛtu/a] (*PT*: **-ct-**) *adj* favourite (*BRIT*), favorite (*US*).
prédio ['prɛdʒju] *m* building; **~ de apartamentos** block of flats (*BRIT*), apartment house (*US*).
predispor [predʒiʃ'po*] (*irreg*: *como* **pôr**) *vt*: **~ alguém contra** to prejudice sb against; **~-se** *vr*: **~-se a/para** to get o.s. in the mood to/for; **a natação me predispõe para o trabalho** swimming puts me in the mood for work; **a notícia os predispôs para futuros problemas** the news prepared them for future problems.
predisposição [predʒiʃpozi'sãw] *f* predisposition.
predisposto/a [predʒiʃ'poʃtu/'pɔʃta] *pp de* **predispor** ♦ *adj* predisposed.
predispunha [predʒiʃ'puɲa] *etc vb V* **predispor**.
predispus [predʒiʃ'puʃ] *etc vb V* **predispor**.
predispuser [predʒiʃpu'ze*] *etc vb V* **predispor**.
predizer [predʒi'ze*] (*irreg*: *como* **dizer**) *vt* to predict, forecast.
predominância [predomi'nãsja] *f* predominance, prevalence.
predominante [predomi'nãtʃi] *adj* predominant.
predominar [predomi'na*] *vi* to predominate, prevail.
predomínio [predo'minju] *m* predominance, supremacy.
pré-eleitoral (*pl* **-ais**) *adj* pre-election.
preeminência [preemi'nẽsja] *f* pre-eminence, superiority.
preeminente [preemi'nẽtʃi] *adj* pre-eminent, superior.
preencher [preẽ'ʃe*] *vt* (*formulário*) to fill in (*BRIT*) *ou* out, complete; (*requisitos*) to fulfil (*BRIT*), fulfill (*US*), meet; (*espaço, vaga, tempo, cargo*) to fill; **~ à máquina** (*formulário*) to complete on a typewriter.
preenchimento [preẽʃi'mẽtu] *m* completion; (*de requisitos*) meeting; (*de vaga*) filling.
pré-escolar *adj* pre-school.
preestabelecer [preeʃtabele'se*] *vt* to prearrange.
pré-estréia *f* preview.
preexistir [preeziʃ'tʃi*] *vi* to preexist; **~ a algo** to exist before sth.
pré-fabricado/a [-fabri'kadu/a] *adj* prefabricated.
prefaciar [prefa'sja*] *vt* to preface.
prefácio [pre'fasju] *m* preface.
prefeito/a [pre'fejtu/a] *m/f* mayor.
prefeitura [prefej'tura] *f* town hall.
preferência [prefe'rẽsja] *f* preference; (*AUTO*) priority; **de ~** preferably; **ter ~ por** to have a preference for.
preferencial [preferẽ'sjaw] (*pl* **-ais**) *adj* (*rua*) main; (*ação*) preference *atr* ♦ *f* main road (*with priority*).
preferido/a [prefe'ridu/a] *adj* favourite (*BRIT*), favorite (*US*).
preferir [prefe'ri*] *vt* to prefer; **~ algo a algo** to prefer sth to sth.
preferível [prefe'rivew] (*pl* **-eis**) *adj*: **~ (a)** preferable (to).
prefigurar [prefigu'ra*] *vt* to prefigure.
prefiro [pre'firu] *etc vb V* **preferir**.
prefixo [pre'fiksu] *m* (*LING*) prefix; (*TEL*) code.
prega ['prɛga] *f* pleat, fold.
pregado/a [pre'gadu/a] *adj* exhausted.
pregador [prega'do*] *m* preacher; (*de roupa*) peg.
pregão [pre'gãw] (*pl* **-ões**) *m* proclamation, cry; **o ~** (*na Bolsa*) trading; (*em leilão*) bidding.
pregar[1] [prɛ'ga*] *vt* (*sermão*) to preach; (*anunciar*) to proclaim; (*idéias, virtude*) to advocate ♦ *vi* to preach.
pregar[2] [pre'ga*] *vt* (*com prego*) to nail; (*fixar*) to pin, fasten; (*cosendo*) to sew on ♦ *vi* to give out; **~ uma peça** to play a trick; **~ os olhos em** to fix one's eyes on; **não ~ olho** not to sleep a wink; **~ mentiras em alguém** to fob sb off with lies; **~ um susto em alguém** to give sb a fright.
prego ['prɛgu] *m* nail; (*col*: *casa de penhor*) pawn shop; **dar o ~** (*pessoa, carro*) to give out; **pôr algo no ~** to pawn sth; **não meter ~ sem estopa** (*fig*) to be out for one's own advantage.
pregões [pre'gõjʃ] *mpl de* **pregão**.
pré-gravado/a [-gra'vadu/a] *adj* prerecorded.
pregresso/a [pre'grɛsu/a] *adj* past, previous.

***NB:** European Portuguese adds the following consonants to certain words:* **b** (sú(b)dito, su(b)til); **c** (a(c)ção, a(c)cionista, a(c)to); **m** (inde(m)ne); **p** (ado(p)ção, ado(p)tar); *for further details see p. xiii.*

preguear [pre'gja*] *vt* to pleat, fold.
preguiça [pre'gisa] *f* laziness; (*animal*) sloth; **estar com ~** to feel lazy; **estou com ~ de cozinhar** I can't be bothered to cook.
preguiçar [pregi'sa*] *vi* to laze around.
preguiçoso/a [pregi'sozu/ɔza] *adj* lazy ♦ *m/f* lazybones.
pré-história *f* prehistory.
pré-histórico/a *adj* prehistoric.
preia ['prɛja] *f* prey.
preia-mar (*PT*) *f* high tide.
preito ['prejtu] *m* homage, tribute; **render ~ a** to pay homage to.
prejudicar [preʒudʒi'ka*] *vt* to damage; (*atrapalhar*) to hinder; **~-se** *vr* (*pessoa*) to do o.s. no favours (*BRIT*) *ou* favors (*US*).
prejudicial [preʒudʒi'sjaw] (*pl* **-ais**) *adj* damaging; (*à saúde*) harmful.
prejuízo [pre'ʒwizu] *m* (*dano*) damage, harm; (*em dinheiro*) loss; **com ~** (*COM*) at a loss; **em ~ de** to the detriment of.
prejulgar [preʒuw'ga*] *vt* to prejudge.
prelado [pre'ladu] *m* prelate.
preleção [prele'sãw] (*PT*: **-cç-**: *pl* **-ões**) *f* lecture.
preliminar [prelimi'na*] *adj* preliminary ♦ *f* (*partida*) preliminary ♦ *m* preliminary.
prelo ['prɛlu] *m* (printing) press; **no ~** in the press.
prelúdio [pre'ludʒju] *m* prelude.
prematuro/a [prema'turu/a] *adj* premature.
premeditação [premedʒita'sãw] *f* premeditation.
premeditado/a [premedʒi'tadu/a] *adj* premeditated.
premeditar [premedʒi'ta*] *vt* to premeditate.
premência [pre'mẽsja] *f* urgency, pressing nature.
pré-menstrual (*pl* **-ais**) *adj* premenstrual.
premente [pre'mẽtʃi] *adj* pressing.
premer [pre'me*] *vt* to press.
premiado/a [pre'mjadu/a] *adj* prize-winning; (*bilhete*) winning ♦ *m/f* prize-winner.
premiar [pre'mja*] *vt* to award a prize to; (*recompensar*) to reward.
premiê [pre'mje] *m* (*POL*) premier.
premier [pre'mje] *m* = **premiê**.
prêmio ['premju] *m* prize; (*recompensa*) reward; (*SEGUROS*) premium; **Grande P~** Grand Prix; **~ de consolação** consolation prize.
premir [pre'mi*] *vt* = **premer**.
premissa [pre'misa] *f* premise.
pré-moldado/a [-mow'dadu/a] *adj* precast ♦ *m* breeze block.
premonição [premoni'sãw] (*pl* **-ões**) *f* premonition.
premonitório/a [premoni'tɔrju/a] *adj* premonitory.
pré-natal (*pl* **-ais**) *adj* antenatal (*BRIT*), prenatal (*US*).
prenda ['prẽda] *f* gift, present; (*em jogo*) forfeit; **~s** *fpl* talents; **~s domésticas** housework *sg*.
prendado/a [prẽ'dadu/a] *adj* gifted, talented; (*homem*: *em afazeres domésticos*) domesticated.
prendedor [prẽde'do*] *m* fastener; (*de cabelo, gravata*) clip; **~ de roupa** clothes peg; **~ de papéis** paper clip.
prender [prẽ'de*] *vt* (*pregar*) to fasten, fix; (*roupa, cabelo*) to clip; (*capturar*) to arrest; (*amarrar*) to tie; (*atenção*) to catch; (*afetivamente*) to tie, bind; (*reter*: *suj*: *doença, compromisso*) to keep; (*movimentos*) to restrict; **~-se** *vr* to get caught, stick; **~-se a alguém** (*por amizade*) to be attached to sb; (*casar-se*) to tie o.s. down to sb; **~-se a algo** (*detalhes, maus hábitos*) to get caught up in sth; **~-se com algo** to be connected with sth.
prenhe ['prɛɲi] *adj* pregnant.
prenhez [pre'ɲeʒ] *f* pregnancy.
prenome [pre'nɔmi] *m* first name, Christian name.
prensa ['prẽsa] *f* (*ger*) press.
prensar [prẽ'sa*] *vt* to press, compress; (*fruta*) to squeeze; (*uvas*) to press; **~ alguém contra a parede** to push sb up against the wall.
prenunciar [prenũ'sja*] *vt* to predict, foretell; **as nuvens prenunciam chuva** the clouds suggest rain.
prenúncio [pre'nũsju] *m* forewarning, sign.
preocupação [preokupa'sãw] (*pl* **-ões**) *f* (*idéia fixa*) preoccupation; (*inquietação*) worry, concern.
preocupante [preoku'pãtʃi] *adj* worrying.
preocupar [preoku'pa*] *vt* (*absorver*) to preoccupy; (*inquietar*) to worry; **~-se** *vr*: **~-se com** to worry about, be worried about.
preparação [prepara'sãw] (*pl* **-ões**) *f* preparation.
preparado [prepa'radu] *m* preparation.
preparar [prepa'ra*] *vt* to prepare; **~-se** *vr* to get ready; **~-se para algo/para fazer** to prepare for sth/to do.
preparativos [prepara'tʃivuʃ] *mpl* preparations, arrangements.
preparo [pre'paru] *m* preparation; (*instrução*) ability; **~ físico** physical fitness.
preponderância [prepõde'rãsja] *f* preponderance, predominance.
preponderante [prepõde'rãtʃi] *adj* predominant.
preponderar [prepõde'ra*] *vi*: **~ (sobre)** to prevail (over).
preposição [prepozi'sãw] (*pl* **-ões**) *f* preposition.
preposto/a [pre'poʃtu/'pɔʃta] *m/f* person in charge; (*representante*) representative.
prepotência [prepo'tẽsja] *f* superiority; (*despotismo*) absolutism.
prepotente [prepo'tẽtʃi] *adj* (*poderoso*) predominant; (*despótico*) despotic; (*atitude*) overbearing.

prerrogativa [prexoga'tʃiva] *f* prerogative, privilege.

presa ['preza] *f* (*na guerra*) spoils *pl*; (*vítima*) prey; (*dente de animal*) fang.

presbiteriano/a [preʒbite'rjanu/a] *adj*, *m/f* Presbyterian.

presbitério [preʒbi'tɛrju] *m* presbytery.

presciência [pre'sjẽsja] *f* foreknowledge, foresight.

presciente [pre'sjẽtʃi] *adj* far-sighted, prescient.

prescindir [presĩ'dʒi*] *vi*: ~ **de algo** to do without sth.

prescindível [presĩ'dʒivew] (*pl* **-eis**) *adj* dispensable.

prescrever [preʃkre've*] *vt* to prescribe; (*prazo*) to set ♦ *vi* (JUR: *crime*, *direito*) to lapse; (*cair em desuso*) to fall into disuse.

prescrição [preʃkri'sãw] (*pl* **-ões**) *f* order, rule; (MED) instruction; (: *de um remédio*) prescription; (JUR) lapse.

prescrito/a [preʃ'kritu/a] *pp de* **prescrever**.

presença [pre'zẽsa] *f* presence; (*freqüência*) attendance; ~ **de espírito** presence of mind; **ter boa** ~ to be presentable; **na** ~ **de** in the presence of.

presenciar [prezẽ'sja*] *vt* to be present at; (*testemunhar*) to witness.

presente [pre'zẽtʃi] *adj* present; (*fig*: *interessado*) attentive; (: *evidente*) clear, obvious ♦ *m* present ♦ *f* (COM: *carta*): **a** ~ this letter; **os ~s** *mpl* those present; **ter algo** ~ to bear sth in mind; **dar/ganhar de** ~ to give/get as a present; ~ **de grego** undesirable gift, mixed blessing; **anexamos à** ~ we enclose herewith; **pela** ~ hereby.

presentear [prezẽ'tʃja*] *vt*: ~ **alguém (com algo)** to give sb (sth as) a present.

presentemente [prezẽtʃe'mẽtʃi] *adv* at present.

presepada [preze'pada] *f* (*fanfarrice*) boasting; (*atitude*, *espetáculo ridículo*) joke.

presépio [pre'zɛpju] *m* Nativity scene, crib.

preservação [prezexva'sãw] *f* preservation.

preservar [prezex'va*] *vt* to preserve, protect.

preservativo [prezexva'tʃivu] *m* preservative; (*anticoncepcional*) condom.

presidência [prezi'dẽsja] *f* (*de um país*) presidency; (*de uma assembléia*) chair, presidency; **assumir a** ~ (POL) to become president.

presidencial [prezidẽ'sjaw] (*pl* **-ais**) *adj* presidential.

presidencialismo [prezidẽsja'liʒmu] *m* presidential system.

presidenciável [prezidẽ'sjavew] (*pl* **-eis**) *adj* eligible for the presidency ♦ *m/f* presidential candidate.

presidente/a [prezi'dẽtʃi/ta] *m/f* (*de um país*) president; (*de uma assembléia*, COM) chair, president; **o P~ da República** the President (of Brazil).

presidiário/a [prezi'dʒjarju/a] *m/f* convict.

presídio [pre'zidʒju] *m* prison.

presidir [prezi'dʒi*] *vt*, *vi*: ~ **(a)** to preside over; (*reunião*) to chair; (*suj*: *leis*, *critérios*) to govern.

presilha [pre'ziʎa] *f* fastener; (*para o cabelo*) slide.

preso/a ['prezu/a] *adj* (*em prisão*) imprisoned; (*capturado*) under arrest, captured; (*atado*) bound, tied; (*moralmente*) bound ♦ *m/f* prisoner; **ficar ~ a detalhes** to get bogged down in detail(s); **ficar ~ em casa** (*com filhos pequenos etc*) to be stuck at home; **estar ~ a alguém** to be attached to sb; **você está ~!** you're under arrest!; **com a greve dos ônibus, fiquei ~ na cidade** with the bus strike I got stuck in town.

pressa ['prɛsa] *f* haste, hurry; (*rapidez*) speed; (*urgência*) urgency; **às ~s** hurriedly; **estar com** ~ to be in a hurry; **sem** ~ unhurriedly; **não tem** ~ there's no hurry; **ter ~ de** *ou* **em fazer** to be in a hurry to do.

pressagiar [presa'ʒja*] *vt* to foretell, presage.

presságio [pre'saʒu] *m* omen, sign; (*pressentimento*) premonition.

pressago/a [pre'sagu/a] *adj* (*comentário*) portentous.

pressão [pre'sãw] (*pl* **-ões**) *f* pressure; **(colchete de)** ~ press stud, popper; **fazer ~ (sobre alguém/algo)** to put pressure on (sb/sth); ~ **arterial** *ou* **sanguínea** blood pressure.

pressentimento [presẽtʃi'mẽtu] *m* premonition, presentiment.

pressentir [presẽ'tʃi*] *vt* (*pressagiar*) to foresee; (*suspeitar*) to sense; (*inimigo*) to preempt.

pressionar [presjo'na*] *vt* (*botão*) to press; (*coagir*) to pressure ♦ *vi* to press, put on pressure.

pressões [pre'sõjʃ] *fpl de* **pressão**.

pressupor [presu'po*] (*irreg*: *como* **pôr**) *vt* to presuppose.

pressuposto/a [presu'poʃtu/'pɔʃta] *pp de* **pressupor** ♦ *m* (*conjetura*) presupposition.

pressupunha [presu'puɲa] *etc vb V* **pressupor**.

pressupus [presu'puʃ] *etc vb V* **pressupor**.

pressupuser [presu'puze*] *etc vb V* **pressupor**.

pressurização [presuriza'sãw] *f* pressurization.

pressurizado/a [presuri'zadu/a] *adj* pressurized.

pressuroso/a [presu'rozu/ɔza] *adj* (*apressado*) hurried, in a hurry; (*zeloso*) keen, eager.

prestação [preʃta'sãw] (*pl* **-ões**) *f* instalment (BRIT), installment (US); (*por uma casa*) repayment; **à ~, a prestações** in instal(l)ments; ~ **de contas/serviços** accounts/

NB: *European Portuguese adds the following consonants to certain words:* **b** (sú(b)dito, su(b)til); **c** (a(c)ção, a(c)cionista, a(c)to); **m** (inde(m)ne); **p** (ado(p)ção, ado(p)tar); *for further details see p. xiii.*

services rendered.

prestamente [preʃta'mẽtʃi] *adv* promptly.

prestamista [preʃta'miʃta] *m/f* moneylender; (*comprador*) person paying hire purchase (*BRIT*) *ou* on the installment plan (*US*).

prestar [preʃ'ta*] *vt* (*cuidados*) to give; (*favores, serviços*) to do; (*contas*) to render; (*informações*) to supply; (*uma qualidade a algo*) to lend ♦ *vi*: ~ **a alguém para algo** to be of use to sb for sth; **~-se** *vr*: **~-se a** (*servir*) to be suitable for; (*admitir*) to lend o.s. to; (*dispor-se*) to be willing to; ~ **atenção** to pay attention; ~ **juramento** to take an oath; **isto não presta para nada** it's absolutely useless; **ele não presta** he's good for nothing; ~ **homenagem/culto a** to pay tribute to/worship.

prestativo/a [preʃta'tʃivu/a] *adj* helpful, obliging.

prestável [preʃ'tavew] (*pl* **-eis**) *adj* serviceable.

prestes ['prɛʃtʃiʃ] *adj inv* (*pronto*) ready; (*a ponto de*): ~ **a partir** about to leave.

presteza [preʃ'teza] *f* (*prontidão*) promptness; (*rapidez*) speed; **com** ~ promptly.

prestidigitação [preʃtʃidʒiʒita'sãw] *f* sleight of hand, conjuring, magic tricks *pl*.

prestidigitador [preʃtʃidʒiʒita'do*] *m* conjurer, magician.

prestigiar [preʃtʃi'ʒja*] *vt* to give prestige to.

prestígio [preʃ'tʃiʒu] *m* prestige.

prestigioso/a [preʃtʃi'ʒozu/ɔza] *adj* prestigious, eminent.

préstimo ['prɛʃtʃimu] *m* use, usefulness; **~s** *mpl* favours (*BRIT*), favors (*US*), services; **sem** ~ useless, worthless.

presto/a ['prɛʃtu/a] *adj* swift.

presumido/a [prezu'midu/a] *adj* vain, self-important.

presumir [prezu'mi*] *vt* to presume.

presunção [prezũ'sãw] (*pl* **-ões**) *f* (*suposição*) presumption; (*vaidade*) conceit, self-importance.

presunçoso/a [prezũ'sozu/ɔza] *adj* vain, self-important.

presunto [pre'zũtu] *m* ham; (*col*: *cadáver*) stiff.

pret-à-porter [prɛtapox'te] *adj inv* ready to wear.

pretendente [pretẽ'dẽtʃi] *m/f* claimant; (*candidato*) candidate, applicant ♦ *m* (*de uma mulher*) suitor.

pretender [pretẽ'de*] *vt* to claim; (*cargo, emprego*) to go for; ~ **fazer** to intend to do.

pretensamente [pretẽsa'mẽtʃi] *adv* supposedly.

pretensão [pretẽ'sãw] (*pl* **-ões**) *f* (*reivindicação*) claim; (*vaidade*) pretension; (*propósito*) aim; (*aspiração*) aspiration; **pretensões** *fpl* (*presunção*) pretentiousness.

pretensioso/a [pretẽ'sjozu/ɔza] *adj* pretentious.

pretenso/a [pre'tẽsu/a] *adj* alleged, supposed.

pretensões [pretẽ'sõjʃ] *fpl de* **pretensão**.

preterir [prete'ri*] *vt* (*desprezar*) to ignore; (*deixar de promover*) to pass over; (*ocupar cargo de*) to displace; (*ser usado em lugar de*) to displace; (*omitir*) to disregard.

pretérito/a [pre'tɛritu/a] *adj* past ♦ *m* (*LING*) preterite.

pretextar [preteʃ'ta*] *vt* to give as an excuse.

pretexto [pre'teʃtu] *m* pretext, excuse; **a ~ de** on the pretext of.

preto/a ['pretu/a] *adj* black; ♦ *m/f* black (man/woman); **pôr o ~ no branco** to put it down in writing.

preto-e-branco *adj inv* (*filme, TV*) black and white.

pretume [pre'tumi] *m* blackness.

prevalecente [prevale'sẽtʃi] *adj* prevalent.

prevalecer [prevale'se*] *vi* to prevail; **~-se** *vr*: **~-se de** (*aproveitar-se*) to take advantage of; ~ **sobre** to outweigh.

prevaricar [prevari'ka*] *vi* (*faltar ao dever*) to fail in one's duty; (*proceder mal*) to behave badly; (*cometer adultério*) to commit adultery.

prevê [pre've] *etc vb V* **prever**.

prevejo [pre'veʒu] *etc vb V* **prever**.

prevenção [prevẽ'sãw] (*pl* **-ões**) *f* (*ato de evitar*) prevention; (*preconceito*) prejudice; (*cautela*) caution; **estar de ~ com** *ou* **contra alguém** to be biased against sb.

prevenido/a [preve'nidu/a] *adj* (*cauteloso*) cautious, wary; (*avisado*) forewarned; **estar** ~ (*com dinheiro*) to have cash on one.

prevenir [preve'ni*] *vt* (*evitar*) to prevent; (*avisar*) to warn; (*preparar*) to prepare; **~-se** *vr* (*acautelar-se*): **~-se contra** to be wary of; (*equipar-se*): **~-se de** to equip o.s. with; **~-se para** to prepare (o.s.) for.

preventivo/a [prevẽ'tʃivu/a] *adj* preventive.

prever [pre've*] (*irreg*: *como* **ver**) *vt* to predict, foresee; (*pressupor*) to presuppose.

pré-vestibular [prɛveʃtʃibu'la*] *adj* (*curso*) preparing for university entry ♦ *m* preparation for university entry.

previa [pre'via] *etc vb V* **prever**.

prévia ['prɛvja] *f* opinion poll.

previamente [prevja'mẽtʃi] *adj* previously.

previdência [previ'dẽsja] *f* (*previsão*) foresight; (*precaução*) precaution; ~ **social** social welfare; (*instituição*) welfare department, ≈ DSS (*BRIT*).

previdente [previ'dẽtʃi] *adj* with foresight; **ser** ~ to show foresight.

previno [pre'vinu] *etc vb V* **prevenir**.

prévio/a ['prɛvju/a] *adj* prior; (*preliminar*) preliminary.

previr [pre'vi*] *etc vb V* **prever**.

previsão [previ'zãw] (*pl* **-ões**) *f* (*antevisão*) foresight; (*prognóstico*) prediction, forecast; ~ **do tempo** weather forecast.

previsível [previ'zivew] (*pl* **-eis**) *adj* predictable.

previsões [previ'zõjʃ] *fpl de* **previsão**.

previsto/a [pre'viʃtu/a] *pp de* **prever** ♦ *adj* predicted; (*na lei etc*) prescribed.
prezado/a [pre'zadu/a] *adj* esteemed; (*numa carta*) dear.
prezar [pre'za*] *vt* (*amigos*) to value highly; (*autoridade*) to respect; (*gostar de*) to appreciate; **~-se** *vr* (*ter dignidade*) to have self-respect; **~-se de** (*orgulhar-se*) to pride o.s. on.
primado [pri'madu] *m* (*primazia*) primacy.
prima-dona (*pl* **~s**) *f* leading lady.
primar [pri'ma*] *vi* to excel, stand out.
primário/a [pri'marju/a] *adj* primary; (*elementar*) basic, rudimentary; (*primitivo*) primitive ♦ *m* (*curso*) elementary education.
primata [pri'mata] *m* primate.
primavera [prima'vɛra] *f* spring; (*planta*) primrose.
primaveril [primave'riw] (*pl* **-is**) *adj* spring *atr*; (*pessoa*) youthful, young.
primaz [pri'majʒ] *m* primate.
primazia [prima'zia] *f* primacy; (*prioridade*) priority; (*superioridade*) superiority.
primeira [pri'mejra] *f* (*AUTO*) first gear.
primeira-dama (*pl* **primeiras-damas**) *f* (*POL*) first lady.
primeiranista [primejra'niʃta] *m/f* first-year (student).
primeiro/a [pri'mejru/a] *adj* first; (*fundamental*) fundamental, prime ♦ *adv* first; **de primeira** (*pessoa, restaurante*) first-class; (*carne*) prime; **viajar de primeira** to travel first class; **à primeira vista** at first sight; **em ~ lugar** first of all; **de ~** first; **~s socorros** first aid *sg*; **primeira página** (*de jornal*) front page; **ele foi o ~ que disse isso** he was the first to say this.
primeiro-de-abril (*pl* **primeiros-de-abril**) *m* April fool.
primeiro-time (*col*) *adj inv* top-notch, first rate.
primitivo/a [primi'tʃivu/a] *adj* primitive; (*original*) original.
primo/a ['primu/a] *m/f* cousin; **~ irmão** first cousin; **~ em segundo grau** second cousin; **(número) ~** prime number.
primogênito/a [primo'ʒenitu/a] *adj, m/f* first-born.
primor [pri'mo*] *m* excellence, perfection; (*beleza*) beauty; **com ~** to perfection; **é um ~** it's perfect.
primordial [primox'dʒjaw] (*pl* **-ais**) *adj* (*primitivo*) primordial, primeval; (*principal*) principal, fundamental.
primórdio [pri'mɔxdʒju] *m* origin.
primoroso/a [primo'rozu/ɔza] *adj* (*excelente*) excellent; (*belo*) exquisite.
princesa [prĩ'seza] *f* princess.
principado [prĩsi'padu] *m* principality.
principal [prĩsi'paw] (*pl* **-ais**) *adj* principal; (*entrada, razão, rua*) main ♦ *m* (*chefe*) head, principal; (*essencial, de dívida*) principal ♦ *f* (*LING*) main clause.
príncipe ['prĩsipi] *m* prince.
principiante [prĩsi'pjãtʃi] *m/f* beginner.
principiar [prĩsi'pja*] *vt, vi* to begin; **~ a fazer** to begin to do.
princípio [prĩ'sipju] *m* (*começo*) beginning, start; (*origem*) origin; (*legal, moral*) principle; **~s** *mpl* (*de matéria*) rudiments; **em ~** in principle; **no ~** in the beginning; **por ~** on principle; **do ~ ao fim** from beginning to end; **uma pessoa de ~s** a person of principle.
prior [prjo*] *m* (*sacerdote*) parish priest; (*de convento*) prior.
prioridade [prjori'dadʒi] *f* priority; **ter ~ sobre** to have priority over.
prioritário/a [prjori'tarju/a] *adj* priority *atr*.
prisão [pri'zãw] (*pl* **-ões**) *f* (*encarceramento*) imprisonment; (*cadeia*) prison, jail; (*detenção*) arrest; **ordem de ~** warrant for arrest; **~ perpétua** life imprisonment; **~ preventiva** protective custody; **~ de ventre** constipation.
prisioneiro/a [prizjo'nejru/a] *m/f* prisoner.
prisma ['priʒma] *m* prism; **sob esse ~** (*fig*) in this light, from this angle.
prisões [pri'zõjʃ] *fpl de* **prisão**.
privação [priva'sãw] (*pl* **-ões**) *f* deprivation; **privações** *fpl* (*penúria*) hardship *sg*.
privacidade [privasi'dadʒi] *f* privacy.
privações [priva'sõjʃ] *fpl de* **privação**.
privada [pri'vada] *f* toilet.
privado/a [pri'vadu/a] *adj* (*particular*) private; (*carente*) deprived.
privar [pri'va*] *vt*: **~ alguém de algo** to deprive sb of sth; **~-se** *vr*: **~-se de algo** to deprive o.s. of sth, go without sth.
privativo/a [priva'tʃivu/a] *adj* (*particular*) private; **~ de** peculiar to.
privatização [privatʃiza'sãw] (*pl* **-ões**) *f* privatization.
privatizar [privatʃi'za*] *vt* to privatize.
privilegiado/a [privile'ʒjadu/a] *adj* privileged; (*excepcional*) unique, exceptional.
privilegiar [privile'ʒja*] *vt* to privilege; (*favorecer*) to favour (*BRIT*), favor (*US*).
privilégio [privi'lɛʒu] *m* privilege.
pro [pru] (*col*) = **para** + **o**.
pró [prɔ] *adv* for, in favour (*BRIT*) *ou* favor (*US*) ♦ *m* advantage; **os ~s e os contras** the pros and cons; **em ~ de** in favo(u)r of.
pró- [prɔ] *prefixo* pro-; **~soviético** pro-Soviet.
proa ['proa] *f* prow, bow.
probabilidade [probabili'dadʒi] *f* probability, likelihood; **~s** *fpl* odds; **segundo todas as ~s** in all probability.
probabilíssimo/a [probabi'lisimu/a] *adj superl de* **provável**.

NB: *European Portuguese adds the following consonants to certain words:* **b** (sú(b)dito, su(b)til); **c** (a(c)ção, a(c)cionista, a(c)to); **m** (inde(m)ne); **p** (ado(p)ção, ado(p)tar); *for further details see p. xiii.*

problema [prob'lɛma] *m* problem.
problemática [proble'matʃika] *f* problematics *sg*; (*problemas*) problems *pl*.
problemático/a [proble'matʃiku/a] *adj* problematic.
procedência [prose'dẽsja] *f* (*origem*) origin, source; (*lugar de saída*) point of departure.
procedente [prose'dẽtʃi] *adj* (*oriundo*) derived, rising; (*lógico*) logical.
proceder [prose'de*] *vi* (*ir adiante*) to proceed; (*comportar-se*) to behave; (*agir*) to act; (JUR) to take legal action ♦ *m* conduct; ~ **a** to carry out; ~ **de** (*originar-se*) to originate from; (*descender*) to be descended from.
procedimento [prosedʒi'mẽtu] *m* (*comportamento*) conduct, behaviour (BRIT), behavior (US); (*processo*) procedure; (JUR) proceedings *pl*.
procela [pro'sɛla] *f* storm, tempest.
proceloso/a [prose'lozu/ɔza] *adj* stormy.
prócer ['prɔse*] *m* chief, leader.
processador [prosesa'do*] *m* processor; ~ **de texto** word processor.
processamento [prosesa'mẽtu] *m* (*de requerimentos*, COMPUT) processing; (JUR) prosecution; (*verificação*) verification; (*de depoimentos*) taking down; ~ **de dados** data processing; ~ **por lotes** batch processing; ~ **de texto** word processing.
processar [prose'sa*] *vt* (JUR) to take proceedings against, prosecute; (*verificar*) to check, verify; (*depoimentos*) to take down; (*requerimentos*, COMPUT) to process.
processo [pro'sɛsu] *m* process; (*procedimento*) procedure; (JUR) lawsuit, legal proceedings *pl*; (: *autos*) record; (*conjunto de documentos*) documents *pl*; (*de uma doença*) course, progress; **abrir um ~ (contra alguém)** to start legal proceedings (against sb); ~ **inflamatório** (MED) inflammation.
procissão [prosi'sãw] (*pl* **-ões**) *f* procession.
proclamação [proklama'sãw] (*pl* **-ões**) *f* proclamation.
proclamar [prokla'ma*] *vt* to proclaim.
proclamas [pro'klamaʃ] *mpl* banns.
procrastinar [prokraʃtʃi'na*] *vt* to put off ♦ *vi* to procrastinate.
procriação [prokrja'sãw] *f* procreation.
procriar [pro'krja*] *vt*, *vi* to procreate.
procura [pro'kura] *f* search; (COM) demand; **em ~ de** in search of.
procuração [prokura'sãw] (*pl* **-ões**) *f* power of attorney; (*documento*) letter of attorney; **por ~** by proxy.
procurado/a [proku'radu/a] *adj* sought after, in demand.
procurador(a) [prokura'do*(a)] *m/f* (*advogado*) attorney; (*mandatário*) proxy; **P~ Geral da República** Attorney General.
procurar [proku'ra*] *vt* to look for, seek; (*emprego*) to apply for; (*ir visitar*) to call on, go and see; (*contatar*) to get in touch with; ~ **fazer** to try to do.
prodigalizar [prodʒigali'za*] *vt* (*gastar excessivamente*) to squander; (*dar com profusão*) to lavish.
prodígio [pro'dʒiʒu] *m* prodigy.
prodigioso/a [prodʒi'ʒozu/ɔza] *adj* prodigious, marvellous (BRIT), marvelous (US).
pródigo/a ['prɔdʒigu/a] *adj* (*perdulário*) wasteful; (*generoso*) lavish; **filho ~** prodigal son.
produção [produ'sãw] (*pl* **-ões**) *f* production; (*volume de produção*) output; (*produto*) product; ~ **em massa** *ou* **série** mass production.
produtividade [produtʃivi'dadʒi] *f* productivity.
produtivo/a [produ'tʃivu/a] *adj* productive; (*rendoso*) profitable.
produto [pro'dutu] *m* product; (*renda*) proceeds *pl*, profit; **~s alimentícios** foodstuffs; **~s agrícolas** agricultural produce *sg*; **ser ~ de** to be a product of; ~ **nacional bruto** gross national product; **~s acabados/semi-acabados** finished/semi-finished products.
produtor(a) [produ'to*(a)] *adj* producing ♦ *m/f* producer.
produzido/a [produ'zidu/a] *adj* trendy.
produzir [produ'zi*] *vt* to produce; (*ocasionar*) to cause, bring about; (*render*) to produce, bring in ♦ *vi* to be productive; (ECON) to produce.
proeminência [proemi'nẽsja] *f* prominence; (*protuberância*) protuberance; (*elevação de terreno*) elevation.
proeminente [proemi'nẽtʃi] *adj* prominent.
proeza [pro'eza] *f* achievement, feat.
profanação [profana'sãw] *f* sacrilege, profanation.
profanar [profa'na*] *vt* to desecrate, profane.
profano/a [pro'fanu/a] *adj* profane; (*secular*) secular ♦ *m/f* layman/woman.
profecia [profe'sia] *f* prophecy.
proferir [profe'ri*] *vt* to utter; (*sentença*) to pronounce; ~ **um discurso** to make a speech.
professar [profe'sa*] *vt* to profess; (*profissão*) to practise (BRIT), practice (US) ♦ *vi* (REL) to take religious vows.
professo/a [pro'fɛsu/a] *adj* (*católico etc*) confirmed; (*político etc*) seasoned.
professor(a) [profe'so*(a)] *m/f* teacher; (*universitário*) lecturer; ~ **titular** *ou* **catedrático** (university) professor; ~ **associado** reader.
professorado [profeso'radu] *m* (*professores*) teachers *pl*; (*magistério*) teaching profession.
profeta [pro'fɛta] *m* prophet.
profético/a [pro'fɛtʃiku/a] *adj* prophetic.
profetisa [profe'tʃiza] *f* prophetess.
profetizar [profetʃi'za*] *vt*, *vi* to prophesy, predict.
proficiência [profi'sjẽsja] *f* proficiency, competence.

proficiente [profi'sjẽtʃi] *adj* proficient, competent.
profícuo/a [pro'fikwu/a] *adj* useful, advantageous.
profiro [pro'firu] *etc vb V* **proferir**.
profissão [profi'sãw] (*pl* **-ões**) *f* (*ofício*) profession; (*de fé*) declaration; ~ **liberal** liberal profession.
profissional [profisjo'naw] (*pl* **-ais**) *adj*, *m/f* professional.
profissionalizante [profisjonali'zãtʃi] *adj* (*ensino*) vocational.
profissionalizar [profisjonali'za*] *vt* to professionalize; **~-se** *vr* to turn professional; (*atividade*) to become professional.
profissões [profi'sõjʃ] *fpl de* **profissão**.
profundas [pro'fũdaʃ] *fpl* depths.
profundidade [profũdʒi'dadʒi] *f* depth; (*fig*) profoundness, depth; **tem 4 metros de** ~ it is 4 metres *ou* meters deep.
profundo/a [pro'fũdu/a] *adj* deep; (*fig*) profound.
profusão [profu'zãw] *f* profusion, abundance.
profuso/a [pro'fuzu/a] *adj* (*abundante*) profuse, abundant.
progênie [pro'ʒeni] *f* (*ascendência*) lineage; (*prole*) offspring, progeny.
progenitor(a) [proʒeni'to*(a)] *m/f* ancestor; (*pai/mãe*) father/mother.
prognosticar [prognoʃtʃi'ka*] *vt* to predict, forecast ♦ *vi* (*MED*) to make a prognosis.
prognóstico [prog'nɔʃtʃiku] *m* prediction, forecast; (*MED*) prognosis.
programa [pro'grama] *m* programme (*BRIT*), program (*US*); (*COMPUT*) program; (*plano*) plan; (*diversão*) thing to do; (*de um curso*) syllabus; **fazer um** ~ to go out; ~ **de índio** (*col*) boring thing to do.
programação [programa'sãw] *f* planning; (*TV*, *RADIO*) programming; (*COMPUT*) programming; ~ **visual** graphic design.
programador(a) [programa'do*(a)] *m/f* programmer; ~ **visual** graphic designer.
programar [progra'ma*] *vt* to plan; (*COMPUT*) to program.
programável [progra'mavew] (*pl* **-eis**) *adj* programmable.
progredir [progre'dʒi*] *vi* to progress, make progress; (*avançar*) to move forward; (*infecção*) to progress.
progressão [progre'sãw] *f* progression.
progressista [progre'siʃta] *adj*, *m/f* progressive.
progressivo/a [progre'sivu/a] *adj* progressive; (*gradual*) gradual.
progresso [pro'grɛsu] *m* progress.
progrido [pro'gridu] *etc vb V* **progredir**.
proibição [proibi'sãw] (*pl* **-ões**) *f* prohibition, ban.
proibir [proi'bi*] *vt* to prohibit, forbid; (*livro*, *espetáculo*) to ban; "**é proibido fumar**" "no smoking"; ~ **alguém de fazer**, ~ **que alguém faça** to forbid sb to do.
proibitivo/a [proibi'tʃivu/a] *adj* prohibitive.
projeção [proʒe'sãw] (*PT*: **-cç-**: *pl* **-ões**) *f* projection; (*arremesso*) throwing; (*proeminência*) prominence; **tempo de** ~ (*de filme*) running time.
projetar [proʒe'ta*] (*PT*: **-ct-**) *vt* to project; (*arremessar*) to throw; (*planejar*) to plan; (*ARQ*, *TEC*) to design; **~-se** *vr* (*lançar-se*) to hurl o.s.; (*sombra etc*) to fall; (*delinear-se*) to jut out; ~ **fazer** to plan to do.
projétil [pro'ʒɛtʃiw] (*PT*: **-ct-**: *pl* **-eis**) *m* projectile, missile; (*MIL*) missile.
projetista [proʒe'tʃiʃta] (*PT*: **-ct-**) *m/f* designer ♦ *adj* design *atr*.
projeto [pro'ʒɛtu] (*PT*: **-ct-**) *m* (*empreendimento*) project; (*plano*, *ARQ*) plan; (*TEC*) design; (*de tese etc*) draft; ~ **de lei** bill; ~ **assistido por computador** computer-aided design.
projetor [proʒe'to*] (*PT*: **-ct-**) *m* (*CINEMA*) projector; (*holofote*) searchlight.
prol [prɔw] *m* advantage; **em** ~ **de** on behalf of, for the benefit of.
pró-labore [-la'bɔri] *m* remuneration, fee.
prolapso [pro'lapsu] *m* (*MED*) prolapse.
prole ['prɔli] *f* offspring, progeny.
proletariado [proleta'rjadu] *m* proletariat.
proletário/a [prole'tarju/a] *adj*, *m/f* proletarian.
proliferação [prolifera'sãw] *f* proliferation.
proliferar [prolife'ra*] *vi* to proliferate.
prolífico/a [pro'lifiku/a] *adj* prolific.
prolixo/a [pro'liksu/a] *adj* long-winded, tedious.
prólogo ['prɔlogu] *m* prologue.
prolongação [prolõga'sãw] *f* extension.
prolongado/a [prolõ'gadu/a] *adj* (*demorado*) prolonged; (*alongado*) extended.
prolongamento [prolõga'mẽtu] *m* extension.
prolongar [prolõ'ga*] *vt* (*tornar mais longo*) to extend, lengthen; (*adiar*) to prolong; (*vida*) to prolong; **~-se** *vr* to extend; (*durar*) to last.
promessa [pro'mɛsa] *f* promise; (*compromisso*) pledge.
prometedor(a) [promete'do*(a)] *adj* promising.
prometer [prome'te*] *vt* to promise ♦ *vi* to promise; (*ter potencial*) to show promise; ~ **fazer/que** to promise to do/that.
prometido/a [prome'tʃidu/a] *adj* promised ♦ *m*: **o** ~ what one promised; **cumprir o** ~ to keep to one's promise.
promiscuidade [promiʃkwi'dadʒi] *f* (*sexual*) promiscuity; (*desordem*) untidiness.
promiscuir-se [promiʃ'kwixsi] *vr*: ~ **(com)** to mix (with).

***NB**: European Portuguese adds the following consonants to certain words:* **b** (sú(b)dito, su(b)til); **c** (a(c)ção, a(c)cionista, a(c)to); **m** (inde(m)ne); **p** (ado(p)ção, ado(p)tar); *for further details see p. xiii.*

promíscuo/a [pro'miʃkwu/a] *adj* (*misturado*) disorderly, mixed up; (*comportamento sexual*) promiscuous.

promissor(a) [promi'so*(a)] *adj* promising.

promissório/a [promi'sɔrju/a] *adj*, *f*: **(nota) promissória** promissory note.

promoção [promo'sãw] (*pl* **-ões**) *f* promotion; **fazer ~ de alguém/algo** to promote sb/sth.

promontório [promõ'tɔrju] *m* headland, promontory.

promotor(a) [promo'to*(a)] *adj* promoting ♦ *m/f* promoter; (*JUR*) prosecutor; **~ público** public prosecutor.

promover [promo've*] *vt* (*dar impulso a*) to promote; (*causar*) to cause; (*elevar a cargo superior*) to promote; (*reunião, encontro*) to bring about.

promulgação [promuwga'sãw] *f* promulgation.

promulgar [promuw'ga*] *vt* (*lei etc*) to promulgate; (*tornar público*) to declare publicly.

pronome [pro'nɔmi] *m* pronoun.

pronta-entrega (*pl* **~s**) *f* immediate delivery department.

prontidão [prõtʃi'dãw] *f* (*estar preparado*) readiness; (*rapidez*) promptness, speed; **estar de ~** to be at the ready.

prontificar [prõtʃifi'ka*] *vt* to have ready; **~-se** *vr*: **~-se a fazer/para algo** to volunteer to do/for sth.

pronto/a [prõtu/a] *adj* ready; (*rápido*) quick, speedy; (*imediato*) prompt; (*col*: *sem dinheiro*) broke ♦ *adv* promptly; **de ~** promptly; **estar ~ a ...** to be prepared *ou* willing to ...; **(e) ~!** (and) that's that!

pronto-socorro (*pl* **prontos-socorros**) *m* emergency hospital; (*PT*: *reboque*) towtruck.

prontuário [prõ'twarju] *m* (*manual*) handbook; (*policial*) record.

pronúncia [pro'nũsja] *f* pronunciation; (*JUR*) indictment.

pronunciação [pronũsja'sãw] (*pl* **-ões**) *f* pronouncement; (*LING*) pronunciation.

pronunciamento [pronũsja'mẽtu] *m* proclamation, pronouncement.

pronunciar [pronũ'sja*] *vt* to pronounce; (*discurso*) to make, deliver; (*JUR*: *réu*) to indict; (: *sentença*) to pass; **~-se** *vr* (*expressar opinião*) to express one's opinion; **~ mal** to mispronounce.

propagação [propaga'sãw] *f* propagation; (*fig*: *difusão*) dissemination.

propaganda [propa'gãda] *f* (*POL*) propaganda; (*COM*) advertising; (: *uma ~*) advert, advertisement; **fazer ~ de** to advertise.

propagar [propa'ga*] *vt* to propagate; (*fig*: *difundir*) to disseminate.

propender [propẽ'de*] *vi* to lean; **~ para algo** (*fig*) to incline *ou* tend towards sth.

propensão [propẽ'sãw] (*pl* **-ões**) *f* inclination, tendency.

propenso/a [pro'pẽsu/a] *adj*: **~ a** inclined to, with a tendency to; **ser ~ a** to be inclined to, have a tendency to.

propensões [propẽ'sõjʃ] *fpl de* **propensão**.

propiciar [propi'sja*] *vt* (*tornar favorável*) to favour (*BRIT*), favor (*US*); (*permitir*) to allow; (*proporcionar*) to provide.

propício/a [pro'pisju/a] *adj* (*favorável*) favourable (*BRIT*), favorable (*US*), propitious; (*apropriado*) appropriate.

propina [pro'pina] *f* (*gorjeta*) tip; (*PT*: *cota*) fee.

propor [pro'po*] (*irreg*: *como* **pôr**) *vt* to propose; (*oferecer*) to offer; (*um problema*) to pose; (*JUR*: *ação*) to start, move; **~-se** *vr*: **~-se (a) fazer** (*pretender*) to intend to do; (*visar*) to aim to do; (*dispor-se*) to decide to do; (*oferecer-se*) to offer to do; **~-se a** *ou* **para governador** *etc* to stand for governor *etc*.

proporção [propox'sãw] (*pl* **-ões**) *f* proportion; **proporções** *fpl* dimensions; **à ~ que** as.

proporcionado/a [propoxsjo'nadu/a] *adj* proportionate.

proporcional [propoxsjo'naw] (*pl* **-ais**) *adj* proportional.

proporcionar [propoxsjo'na*] *vt* (*dar*) to provide, give; (*adaptar*) to adjust, adapt.

proporções [propox'sõjʃ] *fpl de* **proporção**.

propôs [pro'poʃ] *vb V* **propor**.

proposição [propozi'sãw] (*pl* **-ões**) *f* proposition, proposal.

propositado/a [propozi'tadu/a] *adj* intentional.

proposital [propozi'taw] (*pl* **-ais**) *adj* intentional.

propósito [pro'pɔzitu] *m* (*intenção*) purpose; (*objetivo*) aim; **a ~** by the way; (*oportunamente*) at an opportune moment; **a ~ de** with regard to; **de ~** on purpose; **fora de ~** irrelevant; **com o ~ de** with the purpose of.

proposta [pro'pɔʃta] *f* proposal; (*oferecimento*) offer.

proposto/a [pro'poʃtu/'pɔʃta] *pp de* **propor**.

propriamente [proprja'mẽtʃi] *adv* properly, exactly; **~ falando** *ou* **dito** strictly speaking; **a Igreja ~ dita** the Church proper.

propriedade [proprje'dadʒi] *f* property; (*direito de proprietário*) ownership; (*o que é apropriado*) appropriateness, propriety; **~ imobiliária** real estate.

proprietário/a [proprje'tarju/a] *m/f* owner, proprietor; (*de casa alugada*) landlord/lady; (*de jornal*) publisher.

próprio/a ['prɔprju/a] *adj* (*possessivo*) own, of one's own; (*mesmo*) very, selfsame; (*hora, momento*) opportune, right; (*nome*) proper; (*característico*) characteristic; (*sentido*) proper, true; (*depois de pronome*) -self; **~ (para)** suitable (for); **eu ~** I myself; **ele ~** he himself; **mora em casa própria** he lives in a house of his own; **por si ~** of one's own accord; **o ~ homem** the very man; **ele é o ~ inglês** he's a typical Englishman; **é o ~** it's him himself.

propulsão [propuw'sãw] *f* propulsion; ~ **a jato** jet propulsion.
propulsor(a) [propuw'so*(a)] *adj* propelling ♦ *m* propellor.
propus [pro'puʃ] *etc vb V* **propor**.
propuser [propu'ze*] *etc vb V* **propor**.
prorrogação [proxoga'sãw] (*pl* **-ões**) *f* extension; (*COM*) deferment; (*JUR*) stay; (*FUTEBOL*) extra time.
prorrogar [proxo'ga*] *vt* to extend, prolong.
prorrogável [proxo'gavel] (*pl* **-eis**) *adj* extendible.
prorromper [proxõ'pe*] *vi* (*águas, lágrimas*) to burst forth; (*vaias*) to break out; ~ **em choro/gargalhadas** to burst into tears/burst out laughing.
prosa ['prɔza] *f* prose; (*conversa*) chatter; (*fanfarrice*) boasting, bragging ♦ *adj* full of oneself; **ter boa** ~ to have the gift of the gab.
prosador(a) [proza'do*(a)] *m/f* prose writer.
prosaico/a [pro'zajku/a] *adj* prosaic.
proscênio [pro'senju] *m* proscenium.
proscrever [proʃkre've*] *vt* to prohibit, ban; (*expulsar*) to ban, exile; (*vícios, usos*) to do away with.
proscrição [proʃkri'sãw] (*pl* **-ões**) *f* proscription; (*proibição*) prohibition, ban; (*desterro*) exile; (*abolição*) abolition.
proscrito/a [proʃ'kritu/a] *pp de* **proscrever** ♦ *m/f* (*desterrado*) exile.
prosear [pro'zja*] *vi* to chat.
prosélito [pro'zɛlitu] *m* convert.
prosódia [pro'zɔdʒja] *f* prosody.
prosopopéia [prozopo'pɛja] *f* (*fig*) diatribe; (*col: pose*) pose.
prospecto [proʃ'pɛktu] *m* (*desdobrável*) leaflet; (*em forma de livro*) brochure.
prospector [proʃpek'to*] *m* prospector.
prosperar [proʃpe'ra*] *vi* to prosper, thrive.
prosperidade [proʃperi'dadʒi] *f* prosperity; (*bom êxito*) success.
próspero/a ['prɔʃperu/a] *adj* prosperous; (*bem sucedido*) successful; (*favorável*) favourable (*BRIT*), favorable (*US*).
prosseguimento [prosegi'mẽtu] *m* continuation.
prosseguir [prose'gi*] *vt* to continue ♦ *vi* to continue, go on; ~ **em** to continue (with).
prostituição [proʃtʃitwi'sãw] *f* prostitution.
próstata ['prɔʃtata] *f* prostate.
prostíbulo [proʃ'tʃibulu] *m* brothel.
prostituir [proʃtʃi'twi*] *vt* to prostitute; (*fig: desonrar*) to debase; **~-se** *vr* (*tornar-se prostituta*) to become a prostitute; (*ser prostituta*) to be a prostitute; (*no trabalho*) to prostitute o.s.; (*corromper-se*) to be corrupted; (*desonrar-se*) to debase o.s.
prostituta [proʃti'tuta] *f* prostitute.
prostração [proʃtra'sãw] *f* (*cansaço*) exhaustion; (*moral*) desolation.
prostrado/a [proʃ'tradu/a] *adj* prostrate.
prostrar [proʃ'tra*] *vt* (*derrubar*) to knock down, throw down; (*extenuar*) to tire out; (*abater*) to lay low; **~-se** *vr* to prostrate o.s.
protagonista [protago'niʃta] *m/f* protagonist.
protagonizar [protagoni'za*] *vt* to play the lead role in; (*fig*) to be at the centre (*BRIT*) *ou* center (*US*) of.
proteção [prote'sãw] (*PT*: **-cç-**) *f* protection; (*amparo*) support, backing.
protecionismo [protesjo'niʒmu] (*PT*: **-cç-**) *m* protectionism.
protector(a) [protek'to*(a)] (*PT*) = **protetor**.
proteger [prote'ʒe*] *vt* to protect.
protegido/a [prote'ʒidu/a] *adj* protected ♦ *m/f* protégé(e).
proteína [prote'ina] *f* protein.
protejo [pro'teʒu] *etc vb V* **proteger**.
protelar [prote'la*] *vt* to postpone, put off.
PROTERRA (*BR*) *abr m* = **Programa de Redistribuição da Terra e de Estímulo Agro-Industrial do Norte e Nordeste.**
protestante [proteʃ'tãtʃi] *adj, m/f* Protestant.
protestantismo [proteʃtã'tʃiʒmu] *m* Protestantism.
protestar [proteʃ'ta*] *vt* to protest; (*declarar*) to declare, affirm ♦ *vi* to protest.
protesto [pro'tɛʃtu] *m* protest; (*declaração*) affirmation.
protetor(a) [prote'to*(a)] *adj* protective ♦ *m/f* protector.
protocolar [protoko'la*] *adj* protocol *atr* ♦ *vt* to record.
protocolo [proto'kɔlu] *m* protocol; (*recibo*) record slip.
protótipo [pro'tɔtʃipu] *m* prototype.
protuberância [protube'rãsja] *f* bump.
protuberante [protube'rãtʃi] *adj* sticking out.
prova ['prɔva] *f* proof; (*TEC: teste*) test, trial; (*EDUC: exame*) examination; (*sinal*) sign; (*de comida, bebida*) taste; (*de roupa*) fitting; (*ESPORTE*) competition; (*TIP*) proof; **~(s)** (*JUR*) evidence *sg*; **à** ~ on trial; **à** ~ **de bala/fogo/água** bulletproof/fireproof/waterproof; **pôr à** ~ to put to the test; ~ **circunstancial/documental** (piece of) circumstantial/documentary evidence.
provação [prova'sãw] *f* (*sofrimento*) trial.
provado/a [pro'vadu/a] *adj* proven.
provar [pro'va*] *vt* to prove; (*comida*) to taste, try; (*roupa*) to try on ♦ *vi* to try.
provável [pro'vavew] (*pl* **-eis**) *adj* probable, likely; **é** ~ **que não venha** he probably won't come.
provê [pro've] *etc vb V* **prover**.
provedor(a) [prove'do*(a)] *m/f* provider.
proveio [pro'veju] *etc vb V* **provir**.
proveito [pro'vejtu] *m* (*vantagem*) advantage; (*ganho*) profit; **em** ~ **de** for the benefit of;

NB: *European Portuguese adds the following consonants to certain words:* **b** (sú(b)dito, su(b)til); **c** (a(c)ção, a(c)cionista, a(c)to); **m** (inde(m)ne); **p** (ado(p)ção, ado(p)tar); *for further details see p. xiii.*

fazer ~ de to make use of; **tirar ~ de** to benefit from.

proveitoso/a [provej'tozu/ɔza] *adj* profitable, advantageous; (*útil*) useful.

provejo [pro'veʒu] *etc vb V* **prover**.

proveniência [prove'njẽsja] *f* source, origin.

proveniente [prove'njẽtʃi] *adj*: ~ **de** originating from; (*que resulta de*) arising from.

proventos [pro'vẽtuʃ] *mpl* proceeds *pl*.

prover [pro've*] (*irreg*: *como* **ver**) *vt* (*fornecer*) to provide, supply; (*vaga*) to fill ♦ *vi*: ~ **a** to take care of, see to; **~-se** *vr*: **~-se de algo** to provide o.s. with sth; ~ **alguém de algo** to provide sb with sth; (*dotar*) to endow sb with sth.

provérbio [pro'vɛxbju] *m* proverb.

proveta [pro'veta] *f* test tube; **bebê de ~** test-tube baby.

provi [pro'vi] *etc vb V* **prover**.

provia [pro'via] *etc vb V* **prover**.

providência [provi'dẽsja] *f* providence; **~s** *fpl* measures, steps; **tomar ~s** to take steps.

providencial [providẽ'sjaw] (*pl* **-ais**) *adj* opportune.

providenciar [providẽ'sja*] *vt* (*prover*) to provide; (*tomar providências*) to arrange ♦ *vi* (*tomar providências*) to make arrangements, take steps; (*prover*) to make provision; ~ **para que** to see to it that.

providente [provi'dẽtʃi] *adj* provident; (*prudente*) prudent, careful.

provido/a [pro'vidu/a] *adj* (*fornecido*) supplied, provided; (*cheio*) full up, fully stocked.

provier [pro'vje*] *etc vb V* **provir**.

provim [pro'vĩ] *etc vb V* **provir**.

provimento [provi'mẽtu] *m* provision; **dar ~** (*JUR*) to grant a petition.

província [pro'vĩsja] *f* province.

provinciano/a [provĩ'sjanu/a] *adj* provincial.

provindo/a [pro'vĩdu/a] *pp de* **provir** ♦ *adj*: ~ **de** coming from, originating from.

provir[1] [pro'vi*] *etc vb V* **prover**.

provir[2] [pro'vi*] (*irreg*: *como* **vir**) *vi*: ~ **de** to come from, derive from.

provisão [provi'zãw] (*pl* **-ões**) *f* provision, supply; **provisões** *fpl* provisions.

provisoriamente [provizorja'mẽtʃi] *adv* provisionally.

provisório/a [provi'zɔrju/a] *adj* provisional, temporary.

provisto/a [pro'viʃtu/a] *pp de* **prover**.

provocação [provoka'sãw] (*pl* **-ões**) *f* provocation.

provocador(a) [provoka'do*(a)] *adj* provocative ♦ *m/f* provoker.

provocante [provo'kãtʃi] *adj* provocative.

provocar [provo'ka*] *vt* to provoke; (*ocasionar*) to cause; (*atrair*) to tempt, attract; (*estimular*) to rouse, stimulate ♦ *vi* to provoke, be provocative.

proximidade [prosimi'dadʒi] *f* proximity, nearness; (*iminência*) imminence; **~s** *fpl* neighbourhood *sg* (*BRIT*), neighborhood *sg* (*US*), vicinity *sg*.

próximo/a ['prɔsimu/a] *adj* (*no espaço*) near, close; (*no tempo*) close; (*seguinte*) next; (*amigo, parente*) close; (*vizinho*) neighbouring (*BRIT*), neighboring (*US*) ♦ *adv* near ♦ *m* fellow man; ~ **a** *ou* **de** near to, close to; **futuro ~** near future; **até a próxima!** see you again soon!

PRP (*BR*) *abr m* = **Partido Renovador Progressista**.

PRT (*BR*) *abr m* = **Partido Reformador Trabalhista**.

prudência [pru'dẽsja] *f* (*comedimento*) care, prudence; (*cautela*) care, caution.

prudente [pru'dẽtʃi] *adj* sensible, prudent; (*cauteloso*) cautious.

prumo ['prumu] *m* plumb line; (*NÁUT*) lead; **a ~** perpendicularly, vertically.

prurido [pru'ridu] *m* itch.

Prússia ['prusja] *f*: **a ~** Prussia.

PS (*BR*) *abr m* = **Partido Socialista**.

PSB *abr m* = **Partido Socialista Brasileiro**.

PSC (*BR*) *abr m* = **Partido Social Cristão**.

PSD (*BR*) *abr m* = **Partido Social Democrático**.

PSDB *abr m* = **Partido Social-Democrata Brasileiro**.

pseudônimo [psew'donimu] *m* pseudonym.

psicanálise [psika'nalizi] *f* psychoanalysis.

psicanalista [psikana'liʃta] *m/f* psychoanalyst.

psicanalítico/a [psikana'litʃiku/a] *adj* psychoanalytic(al).

psicodélico/a [psiko'dɛliku/a] *adj* psychedelic.

psicologia [psikolo'ʒia] *f* psychology.

psicológico/a [psiko'lɔʒiku/a] *adj* psychological.

psicólogo/a [psi'kɔlogu/a] *m/f* psychologist.

psicopata [psiko'pata] *m/f* psychopath.

psicose [psi'kɔzi] *f* psychosis; **estar com ~ de** to be obsessed with *ou* by.

psicossomático/a [psikoso'matʃiku/a] *adj* psychosomatic.

psicoterapeuta [psikotera'pewta] *m/f* psychotherapist.

psicoterapia [psikotera'pia] *f* psychotherapy.

psicótico/a [psi'kɔtʃiku/a] *adj* psychotic.

psique ['psiki] *f* psyche.

psiquiatra [psi'kjatra] *m/f* psychiatrist.

psiquiatria [psikja'tria] *f* psychiatry.

psiquiátrico/a [psi'kjatriku/a] *adj* psychiatric.

psíquico/a ['psikiku/a] *adj* psychological.

psiu [psiw] *excl* hey!

PST (*BR*) *abr m* = **Partido Social Trabalhista**.

PT (*BR*) *abr m* = **Partido dos Trabalhadores**.

PTN (*BR*) *abr m* = **Partido Tancredista Nacional**.

PTR (*BR*) *abr m* = **Partido Trabalhista Renovador**.

PUA (*BR*) *abr m* (= *Pacto de Unidade e Ação*) *workers' movement*.

pua ['pua] *f* (*de broca*) bit; **sentar a ~ em alguém** (*col*) to give sb a beating.

puberdade [pubex'dadʒi] *f* puberty.
púbere ['puberi] *adj* pubescent.
púbis ['pubiʃ] *m inv* pubis.
publicação [publika'sãw] *f* publication.
publicar [publi'ka*] *vt* (*editar*) to publish; (*divulgar*) to divulge; (*proclamar*) to announce.
publicidade [publisi'dadʒi] *f* publicity; (COM) advertising.
publicitário/a [publisi'tarju/a] *adj* publicity *atr*; (COM) advertising *atr* ♦ *m/f* (COM) advertising executive.
público/a ['publiku/a] *adj* public ♦ *m* public; (CINEMA, TEATRO *etc*) audience; **em ~** in public; **o grande ~** the general public.
PUC (BR) *abr f* = **Pontifícia Universidade Católica.**
púcaro ['pukaru] (PT) *m* jug, mug.
pude ['pudʒi] *etc vb V* **poder**.
pudera [pu'dɛra] *etc vb V* **poder**.
pudicícia [pudi'sisja] *f* modesty.
pudico/a [pu'dʒiku/a] *adj* bashful; (*pej*) prudish.
pudim [pu'dʒĩ] (*pl* **-ns**) *m* pudding; **~ de leite** crème caramel.
pudim-flã [pudĩ'flã] (PT) *m* crème caramel.
pudins [pu'dʒĩʃ] *mpl de* **pudim**.
pudor [pu'do*] *m* bashfulness, modesty; (*moral*) decency; **atentado ao ~** indecent assault.
puerícia [pwe'risja] *f* childhood.
puericultura [pwerikuw'tura] *f* child care.
pueril [pwe'riw] (*pl* **-is**) *adj* puerile.
puerilidade [pwerili'dadʒi] *f* childishness, foolishness.
pueris [pwe'riʃ] *adj pl de* **pueril**.
pufe ['pufi] *m* pouf(fe).
pugilismo [puʒi'liʒmu] *m* boxing.
pugilista [puʒi'liʃta] *m* boxer.
pugna ['pugna] *f* fight, struggle.
pugnar [pug'na*] *vi* to fight.
pugnaz [pug'najʒ] *adj* pugnacious.
puído/a ['pwidu/a] *adj* worn.
puir [pwi*] *vt* to wear thin.
pujança [pu'ʒãsa] *f* vigour (BRIT), vigor (US), strength; (*de vegetação*) lushness; **na ~ da vida** in the prime of life.
pujante [pu'ʒãtʃi] *adj* powerful; (*saúde*) robust.
pular [pu'la*] *vi* to jump; (*no Carnaval*) to celebrate ♦ *vt* (*muro*) to jump (over); (*páginas, trechos*) to skip; **~ de alegria** to jump for joy; **~ Carnaval** to celebrate Carnival; **~ corda** to skip.
pulga ['puwga] *f* flea; **estar/ficar com a ~ atrás da orelha** to smell a rat.
pulgão [puw'gãw] (*pl* **-ões**) *m* greenfly.
pulha ['puʎa] *m* rat, creep.
pulmão [puw'mãw] (*pl* **-ões**) *m* lung.
pulmonar [puwmo'na*] *adj* pulmonary, lung *atr*.
pulo ['pulu] *etc vb V* **polir** ♦ *m* jump; **dar ~s (de contente)** to be delighted; **dar um ~ em** to stop off at; **aos ~s** by leaps and bounds; **a um ~ de** a stone's throw away from; **num ~** in a flash.
pulôver [pu'love*] (BR) *m* pullover.
púlpito ['puwpitu] *m* pulpit.
pulsação [puwsa'sãw] *f* pulsation, beating; (MED) pulse.
pulsar [puw'sa*] *vi* (*palpitar*) to pulsate, throb.
pulseira [puw'sejra] *f* bracelet; (*de sapato*) strap.
pulso ['puwsu] *m* (ANAT) wrist; (MED) pulse; (*fig*) vigour (BRIT), vigor (US), energy; **obra de ~** work of great importance; **homem de ~** energetic man; **tomar o ~ de alguém** to take sb's pulse; **tomar o ~ de algo** (*fig*) to look into sth, sound sth out; **a ~** by force.
pulular [pulu'la*] *vi* to abound; (*surgir*) to spring up; **~ de** to teem with; (*de turistas, mendigos*) to be crawling with.
pulverizador [puwveriza'do*] *m* (*para líquidos etc*) spray, spray gun.
pulverizar [puwveri'za*] *vt* to pulverize; (*líquido*) to spray; (*polvilhar*) to dust.
pum [pũ] *excl* bang! ♦ *m* (*col*) fart (*!*), trump.
pumba ['pũba] *excl* zoom!
punção [pũ'sãw] (*pl* **-ões**) *m* (*instrumento*) punch ♦ *f* (MED) puncture.
Pundjab [pũ'dʒabi] *m*: **o ~** the Punjab.
pundonor [pũdo'no*] *m* dignity, self-respect.
pungente [pũ'ʒẽtʃi] *adj* painful.
pungir [pũ'ʒi*] *vt* to afflict ♦ *vi* to be painful.
punguear [pũ'gja*] (*col*) *vt* (*bolso*) to pick; (*bolsa*) to snatch.
punguista [pũ'giʃta] *m* pickpocket.
punha ['puɲa] *etc vb V* **pôr**.
punhado [pu'ɲadu] *m* handful.
punhal [pu'ɲaw] (*pl* **-ais**) *m* dagger.
punhalada [puɲa'lada] *f* stab.
punho ['puɲu] *m* (ANAT) fist; (*de manga*) cuff; (*de espada*) hilt; **de (seu) próprio ~** in one's own hand(writing).
punição [puni'sãw] (*pl* **-ões**) *f* punishment.
punir [pu'ni*] *vt* to punish.
punitivo/a [puni'tʃivu/a] *adj* punitive.
punja ['pũʒa] *etc vb V* **pungir**.
pupila [pu'pila] *f* (ANAT) pupil; (*tutelada*) ward.
pupilo [pu'pilu] *m* (*tutelado*) ward; (*aluno*) pupil.
purê [pu're] *m* purée; **~ de batatas** mashed potatoes.
pureza [pu'reza] *f* purity.
purgação [puxga'sãw] (*pl* **-ões**) *f* purge; (*purificação*) purification.
purgante [pux'gãtʃi] *m* purgative; (*col: pessoa*) bore.
purgar [pux'ga*] *vt* to purge; (*purificar*) to

***NB:** European Portuguese adds the following consonants to certain words:* **b** (sú(b)dito, su(b)til); **c** (a(c)ção, a(c)cionista, a(c)to); **m** (inde(m)ne); **p** (ado(p)ção, ado(p)tar); *for further details see p. xiii.*

purify.

purgativo/a [puxga'tʃivu/a] *adj* purgative ♦ *m* purgative.

purgatório [puxga'tɔrju] *m* purgatory.

purificação [purifika'sãw] *f* purification.

purificar [purifi'ka*] *vt* to purify.

purista [pu'riʃta] *m/f* purist.

puritanismo [purita'niʒmu] *m* puritanism.

puritano/a [puri'tanu/a] *adj* (*atitude*) puritanical; (*seita*) puritan ♦ *m/f* puritan.

puro/a ['puru/a] *adj* pure; (*uísque*) neat; (*verdade*) plain; (*intenções*) honourable (*BRIT*), honorable (*US*); (*estilo*) clear; **isto é pura imaginação sua** it's pure imagination on your part, you're just imagining it; **~ e simples** pure and simple.

puro-sangue (*pl* **puros-sangues**) *adj*, *m* thoroughbred.

púrpura ['puxpura] *f* purple.

purpúreo/a [pux'purju/a] *adj* (*cor*) crimson.

purpurina [puxpu'rina] *f* metallic paint.

purulento/a [puru'lẽtu] *adj* festering, suppurating.

pus¹ [puʃ] *m* pus, matter.

pus² [pujʃ] *etc vb V* **pôr**.

puser [pu'ze*] *etc vb V* **pôr**.

pusilânime [puzi'lanimi] *adj* fainthearted; (*covarde*) cowardly.

pústula ['puʃtula] *f* pustule; (*fig*) rotter.

puta ['puta] (*col!*) *f* whore; **~ que pariu!** fucking hell! (*!*); **mandar alguém para a ~ que (o) pariu** to tell sb to fuck off (*!*); *V tb* **puto**.

putativo/a [puta'tʃivu/a] *adj* supposed.

puto/a ['putu/a] (*col!*) *m/f* (*sem-vergonha*) bastard ♦ *adj* (*zangado*) furious; (*incrível*): **um ~ ...** a hell of a ...; **o ~ de ...** the bloody ....

putrefação [putrefa'sãw] *f* rotting, putrefaction.

putrefato/a [putre'fatu/a] *adj* rotten.

putrefazer [putrefa'ze*] (*irreg*: *como* **fazer**) *vt* to rot ♦ *vi* to putrefy, rot; **~-se** *vr* to putrefy, rot.

pútrido/a ['putridu/a] *adj* putrid, rotten.

puxa ['puʃa] *excl* gosh; **~ vida!** gosh!

puxada [pu'ʃada] *f* pull; (*puxão*) tug; **dar uma ~** (*nos estudos*) to make an effort.

puxado/a [pu'ʃadu/a] *adj* (*col*: *aluguel*) steep, high; (: *curso*) tough; (: *trabalho*) hard.

puxador [puʃa'do*] *m* handle, knob.

puxão [pu'ʃãw] (*pl* **-ões**) *m* tug, jerk.

puxa-puxa (*pl* **~s**) *m* toffee.

puxar [pu'ʃa*] *vt* to pull; (*sacar*) to pull out; (*assunto*) to bring up; (*conversa*) to strike up; (*briga*) to pick ♦ *vi*: **~ de uma perna** to limp; **~ a** to take after; **~ por** (*alunos*, *etc*) to push; **uma coisa puxa a outra** one thing leads to another; **os paulistas puxam pelo esse** the s is very pronounced in São Paulo.

puxa-saco (*pl* **~s**) *m* creep, crawler.

puxo ['puʃu] *m* (*em parto*) push.

puxões [pu'ʃõjʃ] *mpl de* **puxão**.

Q

Q, q [ke] (*pl* **qs**) *m* Q, q; **Q de Quintela** Q for Queen.

q. *abr* (= *quartel*) *60 kg*.

QC *abr m* (= *Quartel-General*) HQ.

QI *abr m* (= *Quociente de Inteligência*) IQ.

ql. *abr* (= *quilate*) ct.

qtd. *abr* (= *quantidade*) qty.

qua. *abr* = (*quarta-feira*) Weds.

quadra ['kwadra] *f* (*quarteirão*) block; (*de tênis etc*) court; (*período*) time, period; (*jogos*) four; (*estrofe*) quatrain.

quadrado/a [kwa'dradu/a] *adj* square; (*col*: *antiquado*) square ♦ *m* square ♦ *m/f* (*col*) square.

quadragésimo/a [kwadra'ʒɛzimu/a] *num* fortieth; *V tb* **quinto**.

quadrangular [kwadrãgu'la*] *adj* quadrangular.

quadrângulo [kwa'drãgulu] *m* quadrangle.

quadrar [kwa'dra*] *vt* to square, make square ♦ *vi*: **~ a** (*ser conveniente*) to suit; **~ com** (*condizer*) to square with.

quadriculado/a [kwadriku'ladu/a] *adj* checkered; **papel ~** squared paper.

quadril [kwa'driw] (*pl* **-is**) *m* hip.

quadrilátero/a [kwadri'lateru/a] *adj* quadrilateral.

quadrilha [kwa'driʎa] *f* gang; (*dança*) square dance.

quadrimotor [kwadrimo'to*] *adj* four-engined ♦ *m* four-engined plane.

quadrinho [kwa'driɲu] *m* (*de tira*) frame; **história em ~s** (*BR*) cartoon.

quadris [kwa'driʃ] *mpl de* **quadril**.

quadro ['kwadru] *m* (*pintura*) painting; (*gravura*, *foto*) picture; (*lista*) list; (*tabela*) chart, table; (*TEC*: *painel*) panel; (*pessoal*) staff; (*time*) team; (*TEATRO*, *fig*) scene; (*fig*: *MED*) patient's condition; **~ de avisos** bulletin board; **~ de reserva** (*MIL*) reserve list; **~ clínico** clinical picture; **o ~ político** (*fig*) the political scene; **~ social** (*de um clube*) members *pl*; (*de uma empresa*) partners *pl*.

quadro-negro (*pl* **quadros-negros**) *m* blackboard.

quadrúpede [kwa'drupedʒi] *adj*, *m* quadruped ♦ *m/f* (*fig*) blockhead.

quadruplicar [kwadrupli'ka*] *vt*, *vi* to quadruple.

quádruplo/a ['kwadruplu/a] *adj*, *m* quadruple ♦ *m/f* (*quadrigêmeo*) quad.

qual [kwaw] (*pl* **-ais**) *pron* which ♦ *conj* as,

like ♦ *excl* what!; ~ **deles** which of them; ~ **é o problema/o seu nome?** what's the problem/your name?; **o** ~ which; (*pessoa: sujeito*) who; (*pessoa: objeto*) whom; **seja** ~ **for** whatever *ou* whichever it may be; **cada** ~ each one; ~ **é?** *ou* ~ **é a tua?** (*col*) what are you up to?; ~ **seja** such as; **tal** ~ just like; ~ **nada!** *ou* ~ **o quê!** no such thing!

qual. *abr* (= *qualidade*) qual.

qualidade [kwali'dadʒi] *f* quality; **na** ~ **de** in the capacity of; **produto de** ~ quality product; **Q~ Carta** (COMPUT) letter quality.

qualificação [kwalifika'sãw] (*pl* **-ões**) *f* qualification.

qualificado/a [kwalifi'kadu/a] *adj* qualified; **não** ~ unqualified.

qualificar [kwalifi'ka*] *vt* to qualify; (*avaliar*) to evaluate; **~-se** *vr* to qualify; ~ **de** *ou* **como** to classify as, regard as.

qualificativo/a [kwalifika'tʃivu/a] *adj* qualifying ♦ *m* qualifier.

qualitativo/a [kwalita'tʃivu/a] *adj* qualitative.

qualquer [kwaw'ke*] (*pl* **quaisquer**) *adj* any ♦ *pron* any; ~ **pessoa** anyone, anybody; ~ **um dos dois** either; ~ **outro** any other; ~ **dia** any day; ~ **que seja** whichever it may be; **um disco** ~ any record at all, any record you like; **a** ~ **momento** at any moment; **a** ~ **preço** at any price; **de** ~ **jeito** *ou* **maneira** anyway; (*a* ~ *preço*) no matter what; (*sem cuidado*) anyhow; **um/uma** ~ (*pej*) any old person.

quando ['kwãdu] *adv* when ♦ *conj* when; (*interrogativo*) when?; (*ao passo que*) whilst; ~ **muito** at most; ~ **quer que** whenever; **de** ~ **em** ~**, de vez em** ~ now and then; **desde** ~**?** how long?, since when?; ~ **mais não seja** if for no other reason; ~ **de** on the occasion of; ~ **menos se esperava** when we (*ou* they, I *etc*) least expected (it).

quant. *abr* (= *quantidade*) quant.

quantia [kwã'tʃia] *f* sum, amount.

quantidade [kwãtʃi'dadʒi] *f* quantity, amount; **uma** ~ **de** a large amount of; **em** ~ in large amounts.

quantificar [kwãtʃifi'ka*] *vt* to quantify.

quantitativo/a [kwãtʃita'tʃivu/a] *adj* quantitative.

quanto/a ['kwãtu/a] *adj, pron* all that, as much as; (*interrogativo: sg*) how much?; (: *pl*) how many?; ~ **tempo?** how long?; ~ **custa?** how much does it cost?; ~ **a** as regards; ~ **a mim** as for me; ~ **antes** as soon as possible; ~ **mais** (*principalmente*) specially; (*muito menos*) let alone; ~ **mais cedo melhor** the sooner the better; ~ **mais trabalha, mais ganha** the more he works, the more he earns; ~ **mais, (tanto) melhor** the more, the better; **tanto** ~ **possível** as much as possible; **tanto/tantos ...** ~ **...** as much/as many ... as ...; **tão ...** ~ **...** as ... as ...; **tudo** ~ everything that, as much as; **um tanto** ~ somewhat, rather; ~ **sofria!** how he suffered!; ~ **sofrimento!** what suffering!; **um Luís não sei dos** ~**s** a Luís something or other; **sei o** ~ **você se esforçou** I know how much you tried; **não saber a quantas anda** not to know how things stand; **a** ~ **está o jogo?** what's the score?; **a** ~ **está o dólar?** what's the rate for the dollar?

quão [kwãw] *adv* how.

quarenta [kwa'rẽta] *num* forty; *V tb* **cinqüenta.**

quarentão/ona [kwarẽ'tãw/'tɔna] (*pl* **-ões/~s**) *adj* in one's forties ♦ *m/f* man/woman in his/her forties.

quarentena [kwarẽ'tɛna] *f* quarantine.

quarentões [kwarẽ'tõjʃ] *mpl de* **quarentão.**

quarentona [kwarẽ'tɔna] *f de* **quarentão.**

quaresma [kwa'reʒma] *f* Lent.

quart. *abr* = **quarteirão.**

quarta ['kwaxta] *f* (*tb*: **~-feira**) Wednesday; (*parte*) quarter; (AUTO) fourth (gear); (MÚS) fourth.

quarta-de-final (*pl* **quartas-de-final**) *f* quarter final.

quarta-feira ['kwaxta-'fejra] (*pl* **quartas-feiras**) *f* Wednesday; ~ **de cinzas** Ash Wednesday; *V tb* **terça-feira.**

quartanista [kwaxta'niʃta] *m/f* fourth-year.

quarteirão [kwaxtej'rãw] (*pl* **-ões**) *m* (*de casas*) block.

quartel [kwax'tɛw] (*pl* **-éis**) *m* barracks *sg.*

quartel-general (*pl* **quartéis-generais**) *m* headquarters *pl.*

quarteto [kwax'tetu] *m* (MÚS) quartet; ~ **de cordas** string quartet.

quarto/a ['kwaxtu/a] *num* fourth ♦ *m* (*quarta parte*) quarter; (*aposento*) room; (MIL) watch; (*anca*) haunch; ~ **de banho** bathroom; ~ **de dormir** bedroom; ~ **de casal** double bedroom; ~ **de solteiro** single room; ~ **crescente/minguante** (ASTRO) first/last quarter; **três** ~**s de hora** three quarters of an hour; **passar um mau** ~ **de hora** (*fig*) to have a rough time; *V tb* **quinto.**

quarto-e-sala (*pl* **~s**) *m* two-room apartment.

quartzo ['kwaxtsu] *m* quartz.

quase ['kwazi] *adv* almost, nearly; ~ **nada** hardly anything; ~ **nunca** hardly ever; ~ **sempre** nearly always.

quaternário/a [kwatex'narju/a] *adj* quaternary.

quatorze [kwa'toxzi] *num* fourteen; *V tb* **cinco.**

quatro ['kwatru] *num* four; **estar/ficar de** ~ to be/get down on all fours; *V tb* **cinco.**

quatrocentos/as [kwatro'sẽtuʃ/aʃ] *num* four hundred.

NB: *European Portuguese adds the following consonants to certain words:* **b** (sú(b)dito, su(b)til); **c** (a(c)ção, a(c)cionista, a(c)to); **m** (inde(m)ne); **p** (ado(p)ção, ado(p)tar); *for further details see p. xiii.*

que [ki] *pron* (*sujeito*) who, that; (: *coisa*) which, that; (*complemento*) whom, that; (: *coisa*) which, that; (*interrogativo*) what? ♦ *conj* that; (*porque*) because; **ele não tem nada ~ fazer** he's got nothing to do; **~ nem** (*BR*) like; **~ pena!** what a pity!; **(do) ~** than; **mais do ~ pensa** more than you think; **não há nada ~ fazer** there's nothing to be done; **~ lindo!** how lovely!; **~ susto!** what a fright!; **espero ~ sim/não** I hope so/not; **dizer ~ sim/não** to say yes/no; *V tb* **tal**.
quê [ke] *m* something ♦ *pron* what; **~!** what!; **não tem de ~** don't mention it; **para ~?** what for?; **por ~?** why?; **sem ~ nem por ~** for no good reason, all of a sudden.
Quebec [ke'bɛk] *n* Quebec.
quebra ['kɛbra] *f* break, rupture; (*falência*) bankruptcy; (*de energia elétrica*) cut; (*de disciplina*) breakdown; **de ~** in addition; **~ de página** (*COMPUT*) page break.
quebra-cabeça (*pl* **~s**) *m* puzzle, problem; (*jogo*) jigsaw puzzle.
quebrada [ke'brada] *f* (*vertente*) slope; (*barranco*) ravine, gully.
quebradiço/a [kebra'dʒisu/a] *adj* fragile, breakable.
quebrado/a [ke'bradu/a] *adj* broken; (*cansado*) exhausted; (*falido*) bankrupt; (*carro, máquina*) broken down; (*telefone*) out of order; (*col: pronto*) broke.
quebrados [ke'braduʃ] *mpl* loose change *sg*.
quebra-galho (*pl* **~s**) (*col*) *m* lifesaver.
quebra-gelos *m inv* (*NÁUT*) icebreaker.
quebra-mar (*pl* **~es**) *m* breakwater, sea wall.
quebra-molas *m inv* speed bump, sleeping policeman.
quebra-nozes *m inv* nutcrackers *pl* (*BRIT*), nutcracker (*US*).
quebrantar [kebrã'ta*] *vt* to break; (*entusiasmo, ânimo*) to dampen; (*debilitar*) to weaken, wear out; **~-se** *vr* (*tornar-se fraco*) to grow weak.
quebranto [ke'brãtu] *m* (*fraqueza*) weakness; (*mau-olhado*) blight, evil eye.
quebra-pau (*pl* **~s**) (*col*) *m* row.
quebra-quebra (*pl* **~s**) *m* riot.
quebrar [ke'bra*] *vt* to break; (*entusiasmo*) to dampen; (*espancar*) to beat; (*dobrar*) to bend ♦ *vi* to break; (*carro*) to break down; (*COM*) to go bankrupt; (*ficar sem dinheiro*) to go broke.
quebra-vento (*pl* **~s**) *m* (*AUTO*) fanlight.
quéchua ['kɛʃwa] *m* (*LING*) Quechua.
queda ['kɛda] *f* fall; (*fig: ruína*) downfall; **ter ~ para algo** to have a bent for sth; **ter uma ~ por alguém** to have a soft spot for sb; **~ de barreira** landslide.
queda-d'água (*pl* **quedas-d'água**) *f* waterfall.
queda-de-braço *f* arm wrestling.
quedê [ke'de] (*col*) *adv* where is/are?
queijada [kej'ʒada] *f* cheesecake.
queijadinha [kejʒa'dʒiɲa] *f* coconut sweet.
queijeira [kej'ʒejra] *f* cheese dish.
queijo ['kejʒu] *m* cheese; **~ prato** ≈ cheddar cheese; **~ ralado** grated cheese.
queijo-de-minas *m* white cheese (≈ *Cheshire*).
queijo-do-reino *m* ≈ Edam cheese.
queima ['kejma] *f* burning; (*COM*) clearance sale.
queimada [kej'mada] *f* burning (of forests).
queimado/a [kej'madu/a] *adj* burnt; (*de sol: machucado*) sunburnt; (: *bronzeado*) brown, tanned; (*plantas, folhas*) dried up; **cheiro/gosto de ~** smell of burning/burnt taste.
queimadura [kejma'dura] *f* burn; (*de sol*) sunburn; **~ de primeiro/terceiro grau** first-/third-degree burn.
queimar [kej'ma*] *vt* to burn; (*roupa*) to scorch; (*com líquido*) to scald; (*bronzear a pele*) to tan; (*planta, folha*) to wither; (*calorias*) to burn off ♦ *vi* to burn; (*estar quente*) to be burning hot; (*lâmpada, fusível*) to blow; **~-se** *vr* (*pessoa*) to burn o.s.; to tan; (*zangar-se*) to get angry.
queima-roupa ['kejma-] *f*: **à ~** point-blank, at point-blank range.
queira ['kejra] *etc vb V* **querer**.
queixa ['kejʃa] *f* complaint; (*lamentação*) lament; **fazer ~ de alguém** to complain about sb; **ter ~ de alguém** to have a problem with sb.
queixa-crime (*pl* **queixas-crime(s)**) *f* (*JUR*) citation.
queixada [kej'ʃada] *f* (*de animal*) jaw; (*queixo grande*) prominent chin.
queixar-se [kej'ʃaxsi] *vr* to complain; **~ de** to complain about; (*dores etc*) to complain of.
queixo ['kejʃu] *m* chin; (*maxilar*) jaw; **ficar de ~ caído** to be open-mouthed; **bater o ~** to shiver.
queixoso/a [kej'ʃozu/ɔza] *adj* complaining; (*magoado*) doleful ♦ *m/f* (*JUR*) plaintiff.
queixume [kej'ʃumi] *m* complaint; (*lamentação*) lament.
quem [kẽj] *pron* who; (*como objeto*) who(m); **~ quer que** whoever; **seja ~ for** whoever it may be; **de ~ é isto?** whose is this?; **~ é?** who is it?; **a pessoa com ~ trabalha** the person he works with; **para ~ você deu o livro?** who did you give the book to?; **convide ~ você quiser** invite whoever you want; **~ disse isso, se enganou** whoever said that was wrong; **~ fez isso fui eu** it was me who did it, the person who did it was me; **~ diria!** who would have thought (it)!; **~ me dera ser rico** if only I were rich; **~ me dera que isso não fosse verdade** I wish it weren't true; **~ sabe** (*talvez*) perhaps; **~ sou eu para negar?** who am I to deny it?
Quênia ['kenja] *m*: **o ~** Kenya.
queniano/a [ke'njanu/a] *adj*, *m/f* Kenyan.
quentão [kẽ'tãw] *m* ≈ mulled wine.
quente ['kẽtʃi] *adj* hot; (*roupa*) warm;

(*notícia*) reliable, solid; **o ~ agora é ...** (*col*) the big thing now is ....
quentinha [kẽ'tʃiɲa] *f* heatproof carton (*for food*).
quentura [kẽ'tura] *f* heat, warmth.
quer [ke*] *vb V* **querer** ♦ *conj* **~ ... ~ ...** whether ... or ...; **~ chova ~ não** whether it rains or not; **~ você queira, ~ não** whether you like it or not; **onde ~ que** wherever; **quando ~ que** whenever; **quem ~ que** whoever; **o que ~ que seja** whatever it is; **~ chova, ~ faça sol** come rain or shine.
querela [ke'rɛla] *f* dispute; (*JUR*) complaint, accusation.
querelado [kere'ladu] *m* (*JUR*) defendant.
querelador(a) [kerela'do*(a)] *m/f* (*JUR*) plaintiff.
querelante [kere'lãtʃi] *m/f* (*JUR*) plaintiff.
querelar [kere'la*] *vt* (*JUR*) to prosecute, sue ♦ *vi*: **~ contra** *ou* **de** (*queixar-se*) to lodge a complaint against.
querer [ke're*] *vt* to want; (*ter afeição*) to be fond of; (*amar*) to love ♦ *m* (*vontade*) wish; (*afeto*) affection; **~-se** *vr* to love one another; **~ bem a** to be fond of; **~ mal a** to dislike; **sem ~** unintentionally, by accident; **por ~** intentionally; **como queira** as you wish; **você quer fechar a janela?** will you shut the window?; **queira entrar/sentar** do come in/sit down; **~ que alguém faça** to want sb to do; **você vai ~ sair amanhã?** do you want to go out tomorrow?; **eu vou ~ uma cerveja** (*num bar etc*) I'd like a beer; **o forno não quer acender** the oven won't light; **~ dizer** (*significar*) to mean; (*pretender dizer*) to mean to say; **quer dizer** (*com outras palavras*) in other words; (*quero dizer*) I mean, that is to say; **está querendo chover** it feels like rain; **não ~ nada com** to want to have nothing to do with; **como quem não quer nada** casually.
querido/a [ke'ridu/a] *adj* dear ♦ *m/f* darling; **~ no grupo/por todos** prized in the group/by all; **o ator ~ das mulheres** the women's favo(u)rite actor; **Q~ João** Dear John.
quermesse [kex'mɛsi] *f* fête.
querosene [kero'zɛni] *m* kerosene oil.
querubim [keru'bĩ] (*pl* **-ns**) *m* cherubim.
quesito [ke'zitu] *m* (*questão*) query, question; (*requisito*) requirement.
questão [keʃ'tãw] (*pl* **-ões**) *f* (*pergunta*) question, inquiry; (*problema*) matter, question; (*JUR*) case; (*contenda*) dispute, quarrel; **fazer ~ (de)** to insist (on); **em ~** in question; **há ~ de um ano** about a year ago; **~ de tempo/de vida ou morte** question of time/matter of life and death; **~ de ordem** point of order; **~ fechada** point of principle.
questionar [keʃtʃjo'na*] *vi* to question, argue ♦ *vt* to question, call into question.
questionário [keʃtʃjo'narju] *m* questionnaire.
questionável [keʃtʃjo'navew] (*pl* **-eis**) *adj* questionable.
questões [keʃ'tõjʃ] *fpl de* **questão**.
qui. *abr* (= *quinta-feira*) Thurs.
quiabo ['kjabu] *m* okra.
quibe ['kibi] *m deep-fried mince with flour and mint.*
quibebe [ki'bɛbi] *m* pumpkin purée.
quicar [ki'ka*] *vi* (*bola*) to bounce; (*col: pessoa*) to go mad ♦ *vt* to bounce.
quiche ['kiʃi] *f* quiche.
quieto/a ['kjɛtu/a] *adj* quiet; (*imóvel*) still; **fica ~!** be quiet!
quietude [kje'tudʒi] *f* calm, tranquillity.
quilate [ki'latʃi] *m* carat; (*fig*) calibre (*BRIT*), caliber (*US*).
quilha ['kiʎa] *f* (*NÁUT*) keel.
quilo ['kilu] *m* kilo.
quilobyte [kilo'bajtʃi] *m* kilobyte.
quilograma [kilo'grama] *m* kilogram.
quilohertz [kilo'hɛxts] *m* kilohertz.
quilometragem [kilome'traʒẽ] *f* number of kilometres *ou* kilometers travelled, ≈ mileage.
quilometrar [kilome'tra*] *vt* to measure in kilometres *ou* kilometers.
quilométrico/a [kilo'mɛtriku/a] *adj* (*distância*) in kilometres *ou* kilometers; (*fig: fila etc*) ≈ mile-long.
quilômetro [ki'lometru] *m* kilometre (*BRIT*), kilometer (*US*).
quilowatt [kilo'watʃi] *m* kilowatt.
quimbanda [kĩ'bãda] *m* (*ritual*) macumba ceremony; (*feiticeiro*) medicine man; (*local*) macumba site.
quimera [ki'mɛra] *f* chimera.
quimérico/a [ki'mɛriku/a] *adj* fantastic.
química ['kimika] *f* chemistry; *V tb* **químico**.
químico/a ['kimiku/a] *adj* chemical ♦ *m/f* chemist.
quimioterapia [kimjotera'pia] *f* chemotherapy.
quimono [ki'mɔnu] *m* kimono; (*penhoar*) robe.
quina ['kina] *f* (*canto*) corner; (*de mesa etc*) edge; **de ~** edgeways (*BRIT*), edgewise (*US*).
quindim [kĩ'dʒĩ] *m sweet made of egg yolks, coconut and sugar.*
quinhão [ki'ɲãw] (*pl* **-ões**) *m* share, portion.
quinhentista [kiɲẽ'tʃiʃta] *adj* sixteenth century *atr*.
quinhentos/as [ki'ɲẽtuʃ/aʃ] *num* five hundred; **isso são outros ~** (*col*) that's a different matter, that's a different kettle of fish.
quinhões [ki'ɲõjʃ] *mpl de* **quinhão**.
quinina [ki'nina] *f* quinine.
qüinquagésimo/a [kwĩkwa'ʒɛzimu/a] *num* fiftieth; *V tb* **quinto**.

***NB:** European Portuguese adds the following consonants to certain words:* **b** (sú(b)dito, su(b)til); **c** (a(c)ção, a(c)cionista, a(c)to); **m** (inde(m)ne); **p** (ado(p)ção, ado(p)tar); *for further details see p. xiii.*

quinquilharias [kĩkiʎa'riaʃ] *fpl* odds and ends; (*miudezas*) knicknacks, trinkets.
quinta ['kĩta] *f* (*tb*: *~-feira*) Thursday; (*propriedade*) estate; (*PT*) farm.
quinta-essência (*pl* **~s**) *f* quintessence.
quinta-feira ['kĩta-'fejra] (*pl* **quintas-feiras**) *f* Thursday; *V tb* **terça-feira.**
quintal [kĩ'taw] (*pl* **-ais**) *m* back yard.
quintanista [kĩta'niʃta] *m/f* fifth-year.
quinteiro [kĩ'tejru] (*PT*) *m* farmer.
quinteto [kĩ'tetu] *m* quintet.
quinto/a ['kĩtu/a] *num* fifth; **ele tirou o ~ lugar** he came fifth; **eu fui o ~ a chegar** I was the fifth to arrive, I arrived fifth; (*numa corrida*) I came fifth.
quintuplo/a [kĩ'tuplu/a] *adj*, *m* quintuple ♦ *m/f*: **~s** (*crianças*) quins.
quinze ['kĩzɪ] *num* fifteen; **duas e ~** a quarter past (*BRIT*) *ou* after (*US*) two; **~ para as sete** a quarter to (*BRIT*) *ou* of (*US*) seven; *V tb* **cinco.**
quinzena [kĩ'zɛna] *f* two weeks, fortnight (*BRIT*); (*salário*) two weeks' wages.
quinzenal [kĩze'naw] (*pl* **-ais**) *adj* fortnightly.
quinzenalmente [kĩzenaw'mẽtʃi] *adv* fortnightly.
quiosque ['kjɔʃki] *m* kiosk; (*de jardim*) gazebo.
qüiproquó [kwipro'kwɔ] *m* misunderstanding, mix-up.
quiromante [kiro'mãtʃi] *m/f* palmist, fortune teller.
quis [kiʒ] *etc vb V* **querer.**
quiser [ki'ze*] *etc vb V* **querer.**
quisto ['kiʃtu] *m* cyst.
quitação [kita'sãw] (*pl* **-ões**) *f* (*remissão*) discharge, remission; (*pagamento*) settlement; (*recibo*) receipt.
quitanda [ki'tãda] *f* (*loja*) grocer's (shop) (*BRIT*), grocery store (*US*).
quitandeiro/a [kitã'dejru/a] *m/f* grocer; (*vendedor de hortaliças*) greengrocer (*BRIT*), produce dealer (*US*).
quitar [ki'ta*] *vt* (*dívida*: *pagar*) to pay off; (: *perdoar*) to cancel; (*devedor*) to release.
quite ['kitʃi] *adj* (*livre*) free; (*com um credor*) squared up; (*igualado*) even; **estar ~ (com alguém)** to be quits (with sb).
quitute [ki'tutʃi] *n* titbit (*BRIT*), tidbit (*US*).
quizumba [ki'zũba] (*col*) *f* punch-up, brawl.
quociente [kwo'sjẽtʃi] *m* quotient; **~ de inteligência** intelligence quotient.
quorum ['kwɔrũ] *m* quorum.
quota ['kwota] *f* quota; (*porção*) share, portion.
quotidiano/a [kwotʃi'dʒjanu/a] *adj* everyday.
q.v. *abr* (= *queira ver*) q.v.

R

R, r ['ɛxi] (*pl* **rs**) *m* R, r; **R de Roberto** R for Robert (*BRIT*) *ou* Roger (*US*).
R *abr* (= *rua*) St.
rã [xã] *f* frog.
rabada [xa'bada] *f* (*rabo*) tail; (*fig*) tail end; (*CULIN*) oxtail stew.
rabanada [xaba'nada] *f* (*CULIN*) cinnamon toast; (*golpe*) blow with the tail; **dar uma ~ em alguém** (*col*) to give sb the brush-off.
rabanete [xaba'netʃi] *m* radish.
rabear [xa'bja*] *vi* (*cão*) to wag one's tail; (*navio*) to wheel around; (*carro*) to skid round.
rabecão [xabe'kãw] (*pl* **-ões**) *m* mortuary wagon.
rabicho [xa'biʃu] *m* pony tail.
rabino [xa'binu] *m* rabbi.
rabiscar [xabiʃ'ka*] *vt* (*escrever*) to scribble; (*papel*) to scribble on ♦ *vi* to doodle; (*escrever mal*) to scribble.
rabisco [xa'biʃku] *m* scribble.
rabo ['xabu] *m* (*cauda*) tail; (*col!*) bum; **meter o ~ entre as pernas** (*fig*) to be left with one's tail between one's legs; **olhar alguém com o ~ do olho** to look at sb out of the corner of one's eye; **pegar em ~ de foguete** (*col*) to stick one's neck out; **ser ~ de foguete** (*col*) to be a minefield.
rabo-de-cavalo (*pl* **rabos-de-cavalo**) *m* ponytail.
rabo-de-saia (*pl* **rabos-de-saia**) (*col*) *m* woman; **não poder ver ~** to be a womanizer.
rabugento/a [xabu'ʒẽtu/a] *adj* grumpy.
rabugice [xabu'ʒisi] *f* grumpiness.
rabujar [xabu'ʒa*] *vi* to be grumpy; (*criança*) to have a tantrum.
raça ['xasa] *f* breed; (*grupo étnico*) race; **cão/cavalo de ~** pedigree dog/thoroughbred horse; **(no peito e) na ~** (*col*) by sheer effort; **ter ~** to have guts; (*ter ascendência africana*) to be of African origin.
ração [xa'sãw] (*pl* **-ões**) *f* ration; (*para animal*) food; **~ de cachorro** dog food.
racha ['xaʃa] *f* (*fenda*) split; (*greta*) crack ♦ *m* (*col*) scrap.
rachadura [xaʃa'dura] *f* (*fenda*) crack.
rachar [xa'ʃa*] *vt* (*fender*) to crack; (*objeto, despesas*) to split; (*lenha*) to chop ♦ *vi* to split; (*cristal*) to crack; **~-se** *vr* to split; to crack; **frio de ~** bitter cold; **sol de ~** scorching sun; **ou vai ou racha** it's make or break.
racial [xa'sjaw] (*pl* **-ais**) *adj* racial; **preconcei-**

to ~ racial prejudice.
raciocinar [xasjosi'na*] *vi* to reason.
raciocínio [xasjo'sinju] *m* reasoning.
racional [xasjo'naw] (*pl* **-ais**) *adj* rational.
racionalização [xasjonaliza'sãw] *f* rationalization.
racionalizar [xasjonali'za*] *vt* to rationalize.
racionamento [xasjona'mẽtu] *m* rationing.
racionar [xasjo'na*] *vt* (*distribuir*) to ration out; (*limitar a venda de*) to ration.
racismo [xa'siʒmu] *m* racism.
racista [xa'siʃta] *adj*, *m/f* racist.
raçoes [xa'sõjʃ] *fpl de* **ração**.
radar [xa'da*] *m* radar.
radiação [xadʒja'sãw] (*pl* **-ões**) *f* radiation; (*raio*) ray.
radiador [xadʒja'do*] *m* radiator.
radialista [xadʒja'liʃta] *m/f* radio announcer; (*na produção*) radio producer.
radiante [xa'dʒjãtʃi] *adj* radiant; (*de alegria*) overjoyed.
radical [xadʒi'kaw] (*pl* **-ais**) *adj* radical ♦ *m* radical; (LING) root.
radicalismo [xadʒika'liʒmu] *m* radicalism.
radicalizar [xadʒikali'za*] *vt* to radicalize; **~-se** *vr* to become radical.
radicar-se [xadʒi'kaxsi] *vr* to take root; (*fixar residência*) to settle.
rádio ['xadʒju] *m* radio; (QUÍM) radium ♦ *f* radio station.
radioactivo/a *etc* [xadjua'tivu/a] (PT) *adj* = **radioativo** *etc*.
radioamador(a) [xadʒjuama'do*(a)] *m/f* radio ham.
radioatividade [xadʒjuatʃivi'dadʒi] *f* radioactivity.
radioativo/a [xadʒjua'tʃivu/a] *adj* radioactive.
radiodifusão [xadʒjodʒifu'zãw] *f* broadcasting.
radiodifusora [xadʒjodʒifu'zora] *f* radio station.
radioemissora [xadʒjuemi'sora] *f* radio station.
radiografar [xadʒjogra'fa*] *vt* (MED) to X-ray; (*notícia*) to radio.
radiografia [xadʒjogra'fia] *f* X-ray.
radiograma [xadʒjo'grama] *m* cablegram.
radiogravador [xadʒjograva'do*] *m* radio cassette.
radiojornal [xadʒjoʒox'naw] (*pl* **-ais**) *m* radio news *sg*.
radiologia [xadʒjolo'ʒia] *f* radiology.
radiologista [xadʒjolo'ʒiʃta] *m/f* radiologist.
radionovela [xadʒjono'vɛla] *f* radio serial.
radiopatrulha [xadʒjopa'truʎa] *f* radio patrol; (*viatura*) patrol car.
radiooperador(a) [xadʒjoopera'do*(a)] *m/f* radio operator.
radiorrepórter [xadʒjoxe'pɔxte*] *m/f* radio reporter.
radioso/a [xa'dʒjozu/ɔza] *adj* radiant, brilliant.
radiotáxi [xadʒjo'taksi] *m* radio taxi *ou* cab.
radioterapia [xadʒjotera'pia] *f* radiotherapy.
radiouvinte [xadʒjo'vĩtʃi] *m/f* (radio) listener.
ragu [xa'gu] *m* stew, ragoût.
raia ['xaja] *f* (*risca*) line; (*fronteira*) boundary; (*limite*) limit; (*de corrida*) lane; (*peixe*) ray; **chegar às ~s** to reach the limit.
raiado/a [xa'jadu/a] *adj* striped.
raiar [xa'ja*] *vi* (*brilhar*) to shine; (*madrugada*) to dawn; (*aparecer*) to appear.
rainha [xa'iɲa] *f* queen; **ela é a ~ da preguiça** (*col*) she's the world's worst for laziness.
rainha-mãe (*pl* **rainhas-mães**) *f* queen mother.
raio ['xaju] *m* (*de sol*) ray; (*de luz*) beam; (*de roda*) spoke; (*relâmpago*) flash of lightning; (*distância*) range; (MAT) radius; **~s X** X-rays; **~ de ação** range; **onde está o ~ da chave?** (*col*) where's the blasted key?
raiva ['xajva] *f* rage, fury; (MED) rabies *sg*; **ter ~ de** to hate; **estar/ficar com ~ (de)** to be/get angry (with); **tomar ~ de** to begin to hate; **estar morto de ~** to be furious; **que ~!** I am (*ou* was *etc*) furious!
raivoso/a [xaj'vozu/ɔza] *adj* furious; (MED) rabid, mad.
raiz [xa'iʒ] *f* root; (*origem*) source; **~ quadrada** square root; **criar raízes** to put down roots.
rajada [xa'ʒada] *f* (*vento*) gust; (*de tiros*) burst.
ralado/a [xa'ladu/a] *adj* grated; (*esfolado*) grazed.
ralador [xala'do*] *m* grater.
ralar [xa'la*] *vt* to grate; (*esfolar*) to graze.
ralé [xa'lɛ] *f* common people *pl*, rabble.
ralhar [xa'ʎa*] *vi* to scold; **~ com alguém** to tell sb off.
rali [xa'li] *m* rally.
ralo/a ['xalu/a] *adj* (*cabelo*) thinning; (*tecido*) thin, flimsy; (*vegetação*) sparse; (*sopa*) thin, watery; (*café*) weak ♦ *m* (*de regador*) rose, nozzle; (*de pia, banheiro*) drain.
rama ['xama] *f* branches *pl*, foliage; **algodão em ~** raw cotton; **pela ~** superficially.
ramagem [xa'maʒẽ] *f* branches *pl*, foliage; (*num tecido*) floral pattern.
ramal [xa'maw] (*pl* **-ais**) *m* (FERRO) branch line; (*telefônico*) extension; (AUTO) branch (road).
ramalhete [xama'ʎetʃi] *m* bouquet, posy.
rameira [xa'mejra] *f* prostitute.
ramerrão [xame'xãw] (*pl* **-ões**) *m* routine, round.
ramificação [xamifika'sãw] (*pl* **-ões**) *f* (*tb*: COMPUT) branching; (*ramo*) branch.
ramificar-se [xamifi'kaxsi] *vr* to branch out.
ramo ['xamu] *m* branch; (*profissão, negócios*) line; (*de flores*) bunch; **Domingo de R~s** Palm Sunday; **um perito do ~** an expert in

***NB**: European Portuguese adds the following consonants to certain words:* **b** (sú(b)dito, su(b)til); **c** (a(c)ção, a(c)cionista, a(c)to); **m** (inde(m)ne); **p** (ado(p)ção, ado(p)tar); *for further details see p. xiii.*

the field.
rampa ['xãpa] *f* ramp; (*ladeira*) slope.
rançar [xã'sa*] *vi* to go rancid.
rancheiro [xã'ʃejru] *m* cook.
rancho ['xãʃu] *m* (*grupo*) group, band; (*cabana*) hut; (*refeição*) meal.
rancor [xã'ko*] *m* (*ressentimento*) bitterness; (*ódio*) hatred.
rancoroso/a [xãko'rozu/ɔza] *adj* bitter, resentful; (*odiento*) hateful.
ranço ['xãsu] *m* rancidness; (*cheiro*) musty smell.
rançoso/a [xã'sozu/ɔza] *adj* rancid; (*cheiro*) musty.
randevu [xãde'vu] *m* brothel.
ranger [xã'ʒe*] *vi* to creak ♦ *vt*: ~ **os dentes** to grind one's teeth.
rangido [xã'ʒidu] *m* creak.
rango ['xãgu] (*col*) *m* grub.
Rangum [xã'gũ] *n* Rangoon.
ranheta [xa'ɲeta] *adj* sullen, surly.
ranhetice [xaɲe'tʃisi] *f* sullenness; (*ato*) surly thing.
ranho ['xaɲu] (*col*) *m* snot.
ranhura [xa'ɲura] *f* groove; (*para moeda*) slot.
ranjo ['xãju] *etc vb V* **ranger**.
ranzinza [xã'zĩza] *adj* surly, bolshy (*col*).
rapa ['xapa] *m* (*de comida*) remains *pl*; (*carro*) illegal trading patrol car; (*policial*) policeman concerned with illegal street trading.
rapadura [xapa'dura] *f* (*doce*) raw brown sugar.
rapagão [xapa'gãw] (*pl* **-ões**) *m* hunk.
rapapé [xapa'pɛ] *m* touch of the forelock; **~s** *mpl* bowing and scraping; (*lisonja*) flattery *sg*; **fazer ~s a alguém** to bow and scrape to sb.
rapar [xa'pa*] *vt* to scrape; (*barbear*) to shave; (*o cabelo*) to crop; ~ **algo a alguém** (*roubar*) to steal sth from sb.
rapariga [xapa'riga] (*PT*) *f* girl.
rapaz [xa'pajʒ] *m* boy; (*col*) lad; **ô, ~, tudo bem?** hi, mate, how's it going?
rapaziada [xapa'zjada] *f* (*grupo*) lads *pl*.
rapazote [xapa'zɔtʃi] *m* little boy.
rapé [xa'pɛ] *m* snuff.
rapidez [xapi'deʒ] *f* speed, rapidity; **com ~** quickly, fast.
rápido/a ['xapidu/a] *adj* quick, fast ♦ *adv* fast, quickly ♦ *m* (*trem*) express.
rapina [xa'pina] *f* robbery; *V tb* **ave**.
raposo/a [xa'pozu/ɔza] *m/f* fox/vixen; (*fig*) crafty person.
rapsódia [xap'sɔdʒja] *f* rhapsody.
raptado/a [xap'tadu/a] *m/f* kidnap victim.
raptar [xap'ta*] *vt* to kidnap.
rapto ['xaptu] *m* kidnapping.
raptor [xap'to*] *m* kidnapper.
raqueta [xa'keta] (*PT*) *f* = **raquete**.
raquetada [xake'tada] *f* stroke with a (*ou* the) racquet.
raquete [xa'ketʃi] *f* (*de tênis*) racquet; (*de pingue-pongue*) bat.
raquidiana [xaki'dʒjana] *f* (*anestesia*) epidural.
raquítico/a [xa'kitʃiku/a] *adj* (*MED*) suffering from rickets; (*franzino*) puny; (*vegetação*) poor.
raquitismo [xaki'tʃiʒmu] *m* (*MED*) rickets *sg*.
raramente [xara'mẽtʃi] *adv* rarely, seldom.
rarear [xa'rja*] *vt* to make rare; (*diminuir*) to thin out ♦ *vi* to become rare; (*cabelos*) to thin; (*casas etc*) to thin out.
rarefazer [xarefa'ze*] (*irreg*: *como* **fazer**) *vt*, *vi* to rarefy; (*nuvens*) to disperse, blow away; (*multidão*) to thin out.
rarefeito/a [xare'fejtu/a] *pp de* **rarefazer** ♦ *adj* rarefied; (*multidão, população*) sparse.
rarefez [xare'feʒ] *vb V* **rarefazer**.
rarefizer [xarefi'ze*] *etc vb V* **rarefazer**.
raridade [xari'dadʒi] *f* rarity.
raro/a ['xaru/a] *adj* rare ♦ *adv* rarely, seldom; **não ~** often.
rasante [xa'zãtʃi] *adj* (*avião*) low-flying; (*vôo*) low.
rascunhar [xaʃku'ɲa*] *vt* to draft, make a rough copy of.
rascunho [xaʃ'kuɲu] *m* rough copy, draft.
rasgado/a [xaʒ'gadu/a] *adj* (*roupa*) torn, ripped; (*cumprimentos, elogio, gesto*) effusive.
rasgão [xaʒ'gãw] (*pl* **-ões**) *m* tear, rip.
rasgar [xaʒ'ga*] *vt* to tear, rip; (*destruir*) to tear up, rip up; **~-se** *vr* to split.
rasgo ['xaʒgu] *m* (*rasgão*) tear, rip; (*risco*) stroke; (*ação*) feat; (*ímpeto*) burst; (*da imaginação*) flight.
rasgões [xaʒ'gõjʃ] *mpl de* **rasgão**.
rasguei [xaʒ'gej] *etc vb V* **rasgar**.
raso/a ['xazu/a] *adj* (*liso*) flat, level; (*sapato*) flat; (*não fundo*) shallow; (*baixo*) low; (*colher*: *como medida*) level ♦ *m*: **o ~** the shallow water; **soldado ~** private.
raspa ['xaʃpa] *f* (*de madeira*) shaving; (*de metal*) filing.
raspadeira [xaʃpa'dejra] *f* scraper.
raspão [xaʃ'pãw] (*pl* **-ões**) *m* scratch, graze; **tocar de ~** to graze.
raspar [xaʃ'pa*] *vt* (*limpar, tocar*) to scrape; (*alisar*) to file; (*tocar de raspão*) to graze; (*arranhar*) to scratch; (*pêlos, cabeça*) to shave; (*apagar*) to rub out ♦ *vi*: ~ **em** to scrape; **passar raspando (num exame)** to scrape through (an exam).
raspões [xaʃ'põjʃ] *mpl de* **raspão**.
rasteira [xaʃ'tejra] *f* (*pernada*) trip; **dar uma ~ em alguém** to trip sb up.
rasteiro/a [xaʃ'tejru/a] *adj* (*que se arrasta*) crawling; (*planta*) creeping; (*a pouca altura*) low-lying; (*ordinário*) common.
rastejante [xaʃte'ʒãtʃi] *adj* trailing; (*arrastando-se*) creeping; (*voz*) slurred.
rastejar [xaʃte'ʒa*] *vi* to crawl; (*furtivamente*) to creep; (*fig*: *rebaixar-se*) to grovel ♦ *vt* (*fu-*

gitivo etc) to track.
rastilho [xaʃ'tʃiʎu] *m* (*de pólvora*) fuse.
rasto ['xaʃtu] *m* (*pegada*) track; (*de veículo*) trail; (*fig*) sign, trace; **de ~s** crawling; **andar de ~s** to crawl; **levar de ~s** to drag along.
rastrear [xaʃ'trja*] *vt* to track; (*investigar*) to scan ♦ *vi* to track.
rastro ['xaʃtru] *m* = **rasto**.
rasura [xa'zura] *f* deletion.
rasurar [xazu'ra*] *vt* to delete items from.
rata ['xata] *f* rat; (*pequena*) mouse; **dar uma ~** to slip up.
ratão [xa'tãw] (*pl* **-ões**) *m* rat.
rataplã [xata'plã] *m* drum roll.
ratazana [xata'zana] *f* rat.
ratear [xa'tʃja*] *vt* (*dividir*) to share ♦ *vi* (*motor*) to miss.
rateio [xa'teju] *m* (*de custos*) sharing, spreading.
ratificação [xatʃifika'sãw] *f* ratification.
ratificar [xatʃifi'ka*] *vt* to confirm, ratify.
rato ['xatu] *m* rat; (~ *pequeno*) mouse; **~ de biblioteca** bookworm; **~ de hotel/praia** hotel/beach thief.
ratoeira [xa'twejra] *f* rat trap; (*pequena*) mousetrap.
ratões [xa'tõjʃ] *mpl de* **ratão**.
ravina [xa'vina] *f* ravine.
ravióli [xa'vjɔli] *m* ravioli.
razão [xa'zãw] (*pl* **-ões**) *f* reason; (*bom senso*) common sense; (*raciocínio, argumento*) reasoning, argument; (*conta*) account; (*MAT*) ratio ♦ *m* (*COM*) ledger; **à ~ de** at the rate of; **com/sem ~** with good reason/for no reason; **em ~ de** on account of; **dar ~ a alguém** to support sb; **ter ~/não ter ~** to be right/be wrong; **ter toda ~ (em fazer)** to be quite right (to do); **estar coberto de ~** to be quite right; **a ~ pela qual ...** the reason why ...; **~ demais para você ficar aqui** all the more reason for you to stay here; **~ de Estado** reason of State.
razoável [xa'zwavew] (*pl* **-eis**) *adj* reasonable.
razões [xa'zõjʃ] *fpl de* **razão**.
r/c (*PT*) *abr* = **rés-do-chão**.
RDA *abr f* (*antes*: = *República Democrática Alemã*) GDR.
ré [xɛ] *f* (*AUTO*) reverse (gear); **dar (marcha à) ~** to reverse, back up; *V tb* **réu**.
reá [xe'a] *vb V* **reaver**.
reabastecer [xeabaʃte'se*] *vt* (*carro, avião*) to refuel; **~-se** *vr*: **~-se de** to replenish one's supply of.
reabastecimento [xeabaʃtesi'mẽtu] *m* (*de carro, avião*) refuelling; (*de uma cidade*) reprovisioning.
reaberto/a [xea'bɛxtu/a] *pp de* **reabrir**.
reabertura [xeabex'tura] *f* reopening.
reabilitação [xeabilita'sãw] *f* rehabilitation; **~ motora** physiotherapy.
reabilitar [xeabili'ta*] *vt* to rehabilitate; (*falido*) to discharge, rehabilitate.
reabrir [xea'bri*] *vt* to reopen.
reaça [xe'asa] (*col*) *m/f* reactionary.
reação [xea'sãw] (*PT*: **-cç-**: *pl* **-ões**) *f* reaction; **~ em cadeia** chain reaction.
reacender [xeasẽ'de*] *vt* to relight; (*fig*) to rekindle.
reacionário/a [xeasjo'narju/a] *adj* reactionary.
reações [xea'sõjʃ] *fpl de* **reação**.
reactor [xea'to*] (*PT*) *m* = **reator**.
readaptar [xeadap'ta*] *vt* to readapt.
readmitir [xeadʒimi'tʃi*] *vt* to readmit; (*funcionário*) to reinstate.
readquirir [xeadʒiki'ri*] *vt* to reacquire.
reafirmar [xeafix'ma*] *vt* to reaffirm.
reagir [xea'ʒi*] *vi* to react; (*doente, time perdedor*) to fight back; **~ a** (*resistir*) to resist; (*protestar*) to rebel against.
reais [xe'ajʃ] *adj pl de* **real**.
reaja [xe'aʒa] *etc vb V* **reagir; reaver**.
reajustar [xeaʒuʃ'ta*] *vt* to readjust; (*MECÂNICA*) to regulate; (*salário, preço*) to adjust (*in line with inflation*).
reajuste [xea'ʒuʃtʃi] *m* adjustment; **~ salarial/de preços** wage/price adjustment (*in line with inflation*).
real [xe'aw] (*pl* **-ais**) *adj* real; (*relativo à realeza*) royal.
realçar [xeaw'sa*] *vt* to highlight.
realce [xe'awsi] *m* (*destaque*) emphasis; (*mais brilho*) highlight; **dar ~ a** to enhance.
realejo [xea'leʒu] *m* barrel organ.
realeza [xea'leza] *f* royalty.
realidade [xeali'dadʒi] *f* reality; **na ~** actually, in fact.
realimentação [xealimẽta'sãw] *f* (*ELET*) feedback.
realismo [xea'liʒmu] *m* realism.
realista [xea'liʃta] *adj* realistic ♦ *m/f* realist.
realização [xealiza'sãw] *f* fulfilment (*BRIT*), fulfillment (*US*), realization; (*de projeto*) execution, carrying out; (*transformação em dinheiro*) conversion into cash.
realizado/a [xeali'zadu/a] *adj* (*pessoa*) fulfilled.
realizador(a) [xealiza'do*(a)] *adj* (*pessoa*) enterprising.
realizar [xeali'za*] *vt* (*um objetivo*) to achieve; (*projeto*) to carry out; (*ambições, sonho*) to fulfil (*BRIT*), fulfill (*US*), realize; (*negócios*) to transact; (*converter em dinheiro*) to realize; (*perceber*) to realize; **~-se** *vr* (*acontecer*) to take place; (*ambições*) to be realized; (*sonhos*) to come true; (*pessoa*) to fulfil(l) o.s.; **o congresso será realizado em Lisboa** the conference will be held in Lisbon.
realizável [xeali'zavew] (*pl* **-eis**) *adj* realizable.
realmente [xeaw'mẽtʃi] *adv* really; (*de fato*)

NB: *European Portuguese adds the following consonants to certain words:* **b** (sú(b)dito, su(b)til); **c** (a(c)ção, a(c)cionista, a(c)to); **m** (inde(m)ne); **p** (ado(p)ção, ado(p)tar); *for further details see p. xiii.*

actually.

reanimar [xeani'ma*] *vt* to revive; (*encorajar*) to encourage; **~-se** *vr* (*pessoa*) to cheer up.

reão [xe'ãw] *vb V* **reaver**.

reaparecer [xeapare'se*] *vi* to reappear.

reaprender [xeaprẽ'de*] *vt* to relearn.

reapresentar [xeaprezẽ'ta*] *vt* to represent; (*espetáculo*) to put on again.

reaproximação [xeaprosima'sãw] (*pl* **-ões**) *f* (*entre pessoas, países*) rapprochement.

reaproximar [xeaprosi'ma*] *vt* to bring back together; **~-se** *vr* to be brought back together.

reaquecer [xeake'se*] *vt* to reheat.

reassumir [xeasu'mi*] *vt, vi* to take over again.

reatar [xea'ta*] *vt* (*continuar*) to resume, take up again; (*nó*) to retie.

reativar [xeatʃi'va*] *vt* to reactivate; (*organização, lei*) to revive.

reator [xea'to*] *m* reactor.

reavaliação [xeavalja'sãw] *f* revaluation.

reaver [xea've*] *vt* to recover, get back.

reavivar [xeavi'va*] *vt* (*cor*) to brighten up; (*lembrança*) to revive; (*sofrimento, dor*) to bring back.

rebaixa [xe'bajʃa] *f* reduction.

rebaixar [xebaj'ʃa*] *vt* (*tornar mais baixo*) to lower; (*o preço de*) to lower the price of; (*humilhar*) to put down, humiliate ♦ *vi* to drop; **~-se** *vr* to demean o.s.

rebanho [xe'baɲu] *m* (*de carneiros, fig*) flock; (*de gado, elefantes*) herd.

rebarbar [xebax'ba*] *vt* (*opor-se a*) to oppose ♦ *vi* (*reclamar*) to complain.

rebarbativo/a [xebaxba'tʃivu/a] *adj* (*pessoa*) disagreeable, unpleasant.

rebate [xe'batʃi] *m* (*sinal*) alarm; (*COM*) discount; **~ falso** false alarm.

rebater [xeba'te*] *vt* (*um golpe*) to ward off; (*acusações, argumentos*) to refute; (*bola*) to knock back; (*à máquina*) to retype.

rebelar [xebe'la*] *vt* to cause to rebel; **~-se** *vr* to rebel.

rebelde [xe'bɛwdʒi] *adj* rebellious; (*indisciplinado*) unruly, wild ♦ *m/f* rebel.

rebeldia [xebew'dʒia] *f* rebelliousness; (*fig: obstinação*) stubbornness; (*: oposição*) defiance.

rebelião [xebe'ljãw] (*pl* **-ões**) *f* rebellion.

rebentar [xebẽ'ta*] *vi* (*guerra*) to break out; (*louça*) to smash; (*corda*) to snap; (*represa*) to burst; (*ondas*) to break ♦ *vt* (*louça*) to smash; (*corda*) to snap; (*porta, ponte*) to break down.

rebento [xe'bẽtu] *m* (*filho*) offspring.

rebite [xe'bitʃi] *m* (*TEC*) rivet.

reboar [xe'bwa*] *vi* to resound, echo.

rebobinar [xebobi'na*] *vt* (*vídeo*) to rewind.

rebocador [xeboka'do*] *m* (*NÁUT*) tug(boat).

rebocar [xebo'ka*] *vt* (*paredes*) to plaster; (*veículo mal estacionado*) to tow away; (*dar reboque a*) to tow.

reboco [xe'boku] *m* plaster.

rebolar [xebo'la*] *vt* to swing ♦ *vi* to sway; (*fig*) to work hard; **~-se** *vr* to sway.

rebolo [xe'bolu] *m* (*mó*) grindstone; (*cilindro*) cylinder.

reboque [xe'bɔki] *etc vb V* **rebocar** ♦ *m* (*ato*) tow; (*veículo*) trailer; (*cabo*) towrope; (*BR: de socorro*) towtruck; **carro ~** trailer; **a ~** in tow.

rebordo [xe'boxdu] *m* rim, edge; **~ da lareira** mantelpiece.

rebordosa [xebox'dɔza] *f* (*situação difícil*) difficult situation; (*doença grave*) serious illness; (*reincidência de moléstia*) recurrence; (*pancadaria*) commotion.

rebu [xe'bu] (*col*) *m* commotion, rumpus.

rebuçado [xebu'sadu] (*PT*) *m* sweet, candy (*US*).

rebuliço [xebu'lisu] *m* commotion, hubbub.

rebuscado/a [xebuʃ'kadu/a] *adj* affected.

recado [xe'kadu] *m* message; **mandar ~** to send word; **menino de ~s** errand boy; **deixar ~** to leave a message; **dar o ~, dar conta do ~** (*fig*) to deliver the goods.

recaída [xeka'ida] *f* relapse.

recair [xeka'i*] *vi* (*doente*) to relapse; **~ em erro** *ou* **falta** to go wrong again; **a culpa recaiu nela** she got the blame; **o acento recai na última sílaba** the accent falls on the last syllable.

recalcado/a [xekaw'kadu/a] *adj* repressed.

recalcar [xekaw'ka*] *vt* to repress.

recalcitrante [xekawsi'trãtʃi] *adj* recalcitrant.

recalque [xe'kawki] *etc vb V* **recalcar** ♦ *m* repression.

recamado/a [xeka'madu/a] *adj* embroidered.

recambiar [xekã'bja*] *vt* to send back.

recanto [xe'kãtu] *m* (*lugar aprazível*) corner, nook; (*esconderijo*) hiding place.

recapitulação [xekapitula'sãw] *f* (*resumo*) recapitulation; (*rememorar*) revision.

recapitular [xekapitu'la*] *vt* (*resumir*) to sum up, recapitulate; (*fatos*) to review; (*matéria escolar*) to revise.

recatado/a [xeka'tadu/a] *adj* (*modesto*) modest; (*reservado*) reserved.

recatar-se [xeka'taxsi] *vr* to become withdrawn; (*ocultar-se*) to hide.

recato [xe'katu] *m* (*modéstia*) modesty.

recauchutado/a [xekawʃu'tadu/a] *adj* (*fig*) revamped; (*col: pessoa*) having had cosmetic surgery; **pneu ~** (*AUTO*) retread, remould (*BRIT*).

recauchutagem [xekawʃu'taʒẽ] (*pl* **-ns**) *f* (*de pneu*) retreading; (*fig*) face-lift.

recauchutar [xekawʃu'ta*] *vt* (*pneu*) to retread; (*fig*) to give a face-lift to.

recear [xe'sja*] *vt* to fear ♦ *vi*: **~ por** to fear for; **~ fazer/que** to be afraid to do/that.

recebedor(a) [xesebe'do*(a)] *m/f* receiver; (*de impostos*) collector.

receber [xese'be*] *vt* to receive; (*ganhar*) to earn, get; (*hóspedes*) to take in; (*con-

vidados) to entertain; (*acolher bem*) to welcome ♦ *vi* (~ *convidados*) to entertain; (*ser pago*) to be paid; **a** ~ (*COM*) receivable.

recebimento [xesebi'mẽtu] (*BR*) *m* reception; (*de uma carta*) receipt; **acusar o** ~ **de** to acknowledge receipt of.

receio [xe'seju] *m* fear; **não tenha** ~ never fear; **ter** ~ **de que** to fear that.

receita [xe'sejta] *f* (*renda*) income; (*do Estado*) revenue; (*MED*) prescription; (*culinária*) recipe; ~ **pública** tax revenue; **R~ Federal** ≈ Inland Revenue (*BRIT*), ≈ IRS (*US*).

receitar [xesej'ta*] *vt* to prescribe ♦ *vi* to write prescriptions.

recém [xe'sẽ] *adv* recently, newly.

recém-casado/a *adj* newly-married; **os ~s** the newlyweds.

recém-chegado/a *m/f* newcomer.

recém-nascido/a *m/f* newborn child.

recém-publicado/a *adj* newly *ou* recently published.

recender [xesẽ'de*] *vt*: ~ **um cheiro** to give off a smell ♦ *vi* to smell; ~ **a** to smell of.

recenseamento [xesẽsja'mẽtu] *m* census.

recensear [xesẽ'sja*] *vt* to take a census of.

recente [xe'sẽtʃi] *adj* recent; (*novo*) new ♦ *adv* recently.

recentemente [xesẽtʃi'mẽtʃi] *adv* recently.

receoso/a [xe'sjozu/ɔza] *adj* (*medroso*) frightened, fearful; (*apreensivo*) afraid; **estar** ~ **de (fazer)** to be afraid of (doing).

recepção [xesep'sãw] (*pl* **-ões**) *f* reception; (*PT*: *de uma carta*) receipt; **acusar a** ~ **de** (*PT*) to acknowledge receipt of.

recepcionar [xesepsjo'na*] *vt* to receive.

recepcionista [xesepsjo'niʃta] *m/f* receptionist.

recepcões [xesep'sõjʃ] *fpl de* **recepção**.

receptáculo [xesep'takulu] *m* receptacle.

receptador(a) [xesepta'do*(a)] *m/f* fence, receiver of stolen goods.

receptar [xesep'ta*] *vt* to fence, receive.

receptivo/a [xesep'tʃivu/a] *adj* receptive; (*acolhedor*) welcoming.

receptor [xesep'to*] *m* (*TEC*) receiver.

recessão [xese'sãw] (*pl* **-ões**) *f* recession.

recesso [xe'sɛsu] *m* recess.

recessões [xese'sõjʃ] *fpl de* **recessão**.

rechaçar [xeʃa'sa*] *vt* (*ataque*) to repel; (*idéias, argumentos*) to oppose; (*oferta*) to turn down.

réchaud [xe'ʃo] *m* (*pl* **~s**) plate-warmer.

recheado/a [xe'ʃjadu/a] *adj* (*ave, carne*) stuffed; (*empada, bolo*) filled; (*cheio*) full, crammed.

rechear [xe'ʃja*] *vt* to fill; (*ave, carne*) to stuff.

recheio [xe'ʃeju] *m* (*para carne assada*) stuffing; (*de empada, de bolo*) filling; (*o conteúdo*) contents *pl*.

rechonchudo/a [xeʃõ'ʃudu/a] *adj* chubby, plump.

recibo [xe'sibu] *m* receipt.

reciclagem [xesi'klaʒẽ] *f* (*de papel etc*) recycling; (*de professores, funcionários*) retraining.

reciclar [xesi'kla*] *vt* (*papel etc*) to recycle; (*professores, funcionários*) to retrain.

recidiva [xesi'dʒiva] *f* recurrence.

recife [xe'sifi] *m* reef.

recifense [xesi'fẽsi] *adj* from Recife ♦ *m/f* person from Recife.

recinto [xe'sĩtu] *m* (*espaço fechado*) enclosure; (*lugar*) area.

recipiente [xesi'pjẽtʃi] *m* container, receptacle.

recíproca [xe'siproka] *f* reverse.

reciprocar [xesipro'ka*] *vt* to reciprocate.

reciprocidade [xesiprosi'dadʒi] *f* reciprocity.

recíproco/a [xe'siproku/a] *adj* reciprocal.

récita ['xɛsita] *f* (*teatral*) performance.

recitação [xesita'sãw] (*pl* **-ões**) *f* recitation.

recital [xesi'taw] (*pl* **-ais**) *m* recital.

recitar [xesi'ta*] *vt* (*declamar*) to recite.

reclamação [xeklama'sãw] (*pl* **-ões**) *f* (*queixa*) complaint; (*JUR*) claim.

reclamante [xekla'mãtʃi] *m/f* claimant.

reclamar [xekla'ma*] *vt* (*exigir*) to demand; (*herança*) to claim ♦ *vi*: ~ **(de)** (*comida etc*) to complain (about); (*dores etc*) to complain (of); ~ **contra** to complain about.

reclame [xe'klami] *m* advertisement.

reclinado/a [xekli'nadu/a] *adj* (*inclinado*) leaning; (*recostado*) lying back.

reclinar [xekli'na*] *vt* to rest, lean; **~-se** *vr* to lie back; (*deitar-se*) to lie down.

reclinável [xekli'navew] (*pl* **-eis**) *adj* (*cadeira*) reclinable.

reclusão [xeklu'zãw] *f* (*isolamento*) seclusion; (*encarceramento*) imprisonment.

recluso/a [xe'kluzu/a] *adj* reclusive ♦ *m/f* recluse; (*prisioneiro*) prisoner.

recobrar [xeko'bra*] *vt* to recover, get back; **~-se** *vr* to recover.

recolher [xeko'ʎe*] *vt* to collect; (*coisas dispersas*) to collect up; (*gado, roupa do varal*) to bring in; (*juntar*) to gather together; (*abrigar*) to give shelter to; (*notas antigas*) to withdraw; (*encolher*) to draw in; **~-se** *vr* (*ir para casa*) to go home; (*deitar-se*) to go to bed; (*ir para o quarto*) to retire; (*em meditações*) to meditate; ~ **alguém a algum lugar** to take sb somewhere.

recolhido/a [xeko'ʎidu/a] *adj* (*lugar*) secluded; (*retraído*) withdrawn.

recolhimento [xekoʎi'mẽtu] *m* (*vida retraída*) retirement; (*arrecadação*) collection; (*ato de levar*) taking.

recomeçar [xekome'sa*] *vt, vi* to restart; ~ **a fazer** to start to do again.

***NB**: European Portuguese adds the following consonants to certain words:* **b** (sú(b)dito, su(b)til); **c** (a(c)ção, a(c)cionista, a(c)to); **m** (inde(m)ne); **p** (ado(p)ção, ado(p)tar); *for further details see p. xiii.*

recomeço [xeko'mesu] *m* restart.
recomendação [xekomẽda'sãw] (*pl* **-ões**) *f* recommendation; **recomendações** *fpl* (*cumprimentos*) regards; **carta de ~** letter of recommendation.
recomendar [xekomẽ'da*] *vt* to recommend; **~ alguém a alguém** (*enviar cumprimentos*) to remember sb to sb, give sb's regards to sb; (*pedir favor*) to put in a word for sb with sb; **~ algo a alguém** (*confiar*) to entrust sth to sb; **~ que alguém faça** to recommend that sb do; (*lembrar, pedir*) to urge that sb do.
recomendável [xekomẽ'davew] (*pl* **-eis**) *adj* advisable.
recompensa [xekõ'pẽsa] *f* (*prêmio*) reward; (*indenização*) recompense.
recompensar [xekõpẽ'sa*] *vt* (*premiar*) to reward; **~ alguém de algo** (*indenizar*) to compensate sb for sth.
recompor [xekõ'po*] (*irreg*: *como* **pôr**) *vt* (*reorganizar*) to reorganize; (*restabelecer*) to restore.
recôncavo [xe'kõkavu] *m* (*enseada*) bay area.
reconciliação [xekõsilja'sãw] (*pl* **-ões**) *f* reconciliation.
reconciliar [xekõsi'lja*] *vt* to reconcile; **~-se** *vr* to become reconciled.
recondicionar [xekõdʒisjo'na*] *vt* to recondition.
recôndito/a [xe'kõdʒitu/a] *adj* (*escondido*) hidden; (*lugar*) secluded.
reconfortar [xekõfox'ta*] *vt* to invigorate; **~-se** *vr* to be invigorated.
reconhecer [xekoɲe'se*] *vt* to recognize; (*admitir*) to admit; (MIL) to reconnoitre (BRIT), reconnoiter (US); (*assinatura*) to witness.
reconhecido/a [xekoɲe'sidu/a] *adj* recognized; (*agradecido*) grateful, thankful.
reconhecimento [xekoɲesi'mẽtu] *m* recognition; (*admissão*) admission; (*gratidão*) gratitude; (MIL) reconnaissance; (*de assinatura*) witnessing.
reconhecível [xekoɲe'sivew] (*pl* **-eis**) *adj* recognizable.
reconquista [xekõ'kiʃta] *f* reconquest.
reconsiderar [xekõside'ra*] *vt, vi* to reconsider.
reconstituinte [xekõʃtʃi'twĩtʃi] *m* tonic.
reconstituir [xekõʃtʃi'twi*] *vt* to reconstitute; (*doente*) to build up; (*crime*) to piece together.
reconstrução [xekõʃtru'sãw] *f* reconstruction.
reconstruir [xekõʃ'trwi*] *vt* to rebuild, reconstruct.
recontar [xekõ'ta*] *vt* (*objetos, pessoas*) to recount; (*história*) to retell.
recordação [xekoxda'sãw] (*pl* **-ões**) *f* (*reminiscência*) memory; (*objeto*) memento.
recordar [xekox'da*] *vt* (*relembrar*) to remember; (*parecer*) to look like; (*lição*) to revise; **~-se** *vr*: **~-se de** to remember; **~ algo a alguém** to remind sb of sth.
recorde [xe'kɔxdʒi] *adj inv* record *atr* ♦ *m* record; **em tempo ~** in record time; **bater um ~** to break a record.
recordista [xekox'dʒiʃta] *m/f* record-breaker; (*quem detém o recorde*) record-holder ♦ *adj* record-breaking; **~ mundial** world record-holder.
recorrer [xeko'xe*] *vi*: **~ a** (*para socorro*) to turn to; (*valer-se de*) to resort to; **~ da sentença/decisão** to appeal against the sentence/decision.
recortar [xekox'ta*] *vt* to cut out.
recorte [xe'kɔxtʃi] *m* (*ato*) cutting out; (*de jornal*) cutting, clipping.
recostar [xekoʃ'ta*] *vt* to lean, rest; **~-se** *vr* to lean back; (*deitar-se*) to lie down.
recosto [xe'koʃtu] *m* back(rest).
recreação [xekrja'sãw] *f* recreation.
recrear [xe'krja*] *vt* to entertain, amuse; **~-se** *vr* to have fun.
recreativo/a [xekrja'tʃivu/a] *adj* recreational.
recreio [xe'kreju] *m* recreation; (EDUC) playtime; **viagem de ~** trip, outing; **hora do ~** break.
recriar [xe'krja*] *vt* to recreate.
recriminação [xekrimina'sãw] (*pl* **-ões**) *f* recrimination.
recriminador(a) [xekrimina'do*(a)] *adj* reproving.
recriminar [xekrimi'na*] *vt* to reproach, reprove.
recrudescência [xekrude'sẽsja] *f* = **recrudescimento**.
recrudescer [xekrude'se*] *vi* to grow worse, worsen.
recrudescimento [xekrudesi'mẽtu] *m* worsening.
recruta [xe'kruta] *m/f* recruit.
recrutamento [xekruta'mẽtu] *m* recruitment.
recrutar [xekru'ta*] *vt* to recruit.
rectângulo *etc* [xek'tãgulu] (PT) = **retângulo** *etc*.
rectificar *etc* [xektifi'ka*] (PT) = **retificar** *etc*.
recto/a *etc* ['xɛkto/a] (PT) = **reto** *etc*.
récua ['xɛkwa] *f* (*de mulas*) pack, train; (*de cavalos*) drove.
recuado/a [xe'kwadu/a] *adj* (*prédio*) set back.
recuar [xe'kwa*] *vt, vi* to move back; (*exército*) to retreat; (*num intento*) to back out; (*num compromisso*) to backpedal; (*ciência*) to regress; **~ de** (*lugar*) to move back from; (*intenções, planos*) to back out of; **~ a** *ou* **para** (*no tempo*) to return *ou* regress to; (*numa decisão, opinião*) to back down to.
recuo [xe'kuu] *m* retreat; (*de ciência*) regression; (*de intento*) climbdown; (*de um prédio*) frontage.
recuperação [xekupera'sãw] *f* recovery.
recuperar [xekupe'ra*] *vt* to recover; (*tempo perdido*) to make up for; (*reabilitar*) to rehabilitate; **~-se** *vr* to recover; **~-se de** to recover *ou* recuperate from.

recurso [xe'kuxsu] *m* (*meio*) resource; (*JUR*) appeal; **~s** *mpl* (*financeiros*) resources; **em último ~** as a last resort; **o ~ à violência** resorting to violence; **não há outro ~ contra a fome** there is no other solution to famine; **~s próprios** (*COM*) own resources.

recusa [xe'kuza] *f* refusal; (*negação*) denial.

recusar [xeku'za*] *vt* to refuse; (*negar*) to deny; **~-se** *vr*: **~-se a** to refuse to; **~ fazer** to refuse to do; **~ algo a alguém** to refuse *ou* deny sb sth.

redação [xeda'sãw] (*PT*: **-cç-**: *pl* **-ões**) *f* (*ato*) writing; (*escolar*) composition, essay; (*redatores*) editorial staff; (*lugar*) editorial office.

redactor(a) *etc* [xeda'to*(a)] (*PT*) *m/f* = **redator(a)** *etc*.

redargüir [xedax'gwi*] *vi* to retort.

redator(a) [xeda'to*(a)] *m/f* journalist; (*editor*) editor; (*quem redige*) writer.

redator(a)-chefe *m/f* editor in chief.

rede ['xedʒi] *f* net; (*de salvamento*) safety net; (*de cabelos*) hairnet; (*de dormir*) hammock; (*cilada*) trap; (*FERRO, TEC, fig*) network; **~ bancária** banking system; **~ de esgotos** drainage system; **comunicar-se em ~ (com)** (*COMPUT*) to network (with); **operação em ~** (*COMPUT*) networking.

rédea ['xɛdʒja] *f* rein; **dar ~ larga a** to give free rein to; **tomar as ~s** (*fig*) to take control, take over; **falar à ~ solta** to talk nineteen to the dozen.

redenção [xedẽ'sãw] *f* redemption.

redentor(a) [xedẽ'to*(a)] *adj* redeeming ♦ *m/f* redeemer.

redigir [xedʒi'ʒi*] *vt, vi* to write.

redime [xe'dʒimi] *etc vb V* **remir**.

redimir [xedʒi'mi*] *vt* (*livrar*) to free; (*REL*) to redeem.

redobrar [xedo'bra*] *vt* (*dobrar de novo*) to fold again; (*aumentar*) to increase; (*esforços*) to redouble; (*sinos*) to ring ♦ *vi* to increase; (*intensificar*) to intensify; to ring out.

redoma [xe'dɔma] *f* glass dome.

redondamente [xedõda'mẽtʃi] *adv* (*completamente*) completely.

redondeza [xedõ'deza] *f* roundness; **~s** *fpl* (*arredores*) surroundings.

redondo/a [xe'dõdu/a] *adj* round; (*gordo*) plump.

redor [xe'dɔ*] *m*: **ao** *ou* **em ~ (de)** around, round about.

redução [xedu'sãw] (*pl* **-ões**) *f* reduction; (*conversão*: *de moeda*) conversion.

redundância [xedũ'dãsja] *f* redundancy.

redundante [xedũ'dãtʃi] *adj* redundant.

redundar [xedũ'da*] *vi*: **~ em** (*resultar em*) to result in.

reduto [xe'dutu] *m* stronghold; (*refúgio*) haven.

reduzido/a [xedu'zidu/a] *adj* reduced; (*limitado*) limited; (*pequeno*) small; **ficar ~ a** to be reduced to.

reduzir [xedu'zi*] *vt* to reduce; (*converter*: *dinheiro*) to convert; (*abreviar*) to abridge; **~-se** *vr*: **~-se a** to be reduced to; (*fig*: *resumir-se em*) to come down to; **"reduza a velocidade"** "reduce speed now".

reedificar [xeedʒifi'ka*] *vt* to rebuild.

reeditar [xeedʒi'ta*] *vt* (*livro*) to republish; (*repetir*) to repeat.

reeducar [xeedu'ka*] *vt* to reeducate.

reeleger [xeele'ʒe*] *vt* to re-elect; **~-se** *vr* to be re-elected.

reeleição [xeelej'sãw] *f* re-election.

reelejo [xee'leʒu] *etc vb V* **reeleger**.

reembolsar [xeẽbow'sa*] *vt* (*reaver*) to recover; (*restituir*) to reimburse; (*depósito*) to refund; **~ alguem de algo** *ou* **algo a alguém** to reimburse sb for sth.

reembolso [xeẽ'bowsu] *m* refund, reimbursement; **~ postal** cash on delivery.

reencarnação [xeẽkaxna'sãw] *f* reincarnation.

reencarnar [xeẽkax'na*] *vi* to be reincarnated.

reencontrar [xeẽkõ'tra*] *vt* to meet again; **~-se** *vr*: **~-se (com)** to meet up (with).

reencontro [xeẽ'kõtru] *m* reunion.

reentrância [xeẽ'trãsja] *f* recess.

reescalonamento [xeeʃkalona'mẽtu] *m* rescheduling.

reescalonar [xeeʃkalo'na*] *vt* (*dívida*) to reschedule.

reescrever [xeeʃkre've*] *vt* to rewrite.

reexaminar [xeezami'na*] *vt* to re-examine.

refaço [xe'fasu] *etc vb V* **refazer**.

refastelado/a [xefaʃte'ladu/a] *adj* stretched out.

refastelar-se [xefaʃte'laxsi] *vr* to stretch out, lounge.

refazer [xefa'ze*] (*irreg*: *como* **fazer**) *vt* (*trabalho*) to redo; (*consertar*) to repair, fix; (*forças*) to restore; (*finanças*) to recover; (*vida*) to rebuild; **~-se** *vr* (*MED etc*) to recover; **~-se de despesas** to recover one's expenses.

refeição [xefej'sãw] (*pl* **-ões**) *f* meal; **na hora da ~** at mealtimes.

refeito/a [xe'fejtu/a] *pp de* **refazer**.

refeitório [xefej'tɔrju] *m* dining hall, refectory.

refém [xe'fẽ] (*pl* **-ns**) *m* hostage.

referência [xefe'rẽsja] *f* reference; **com ~ a** with reference to, about; **fazer ~ a** to make reference to, refer to; **~s** *fpl* references.

referendar [xeferẽ'da*] *vt* to countersign, endorse; (*aprovar*: *tratado etc*) to ratify.

referendum [xefe'rẽdũ] *m* (*POL*) referendum.

referente [xefe'rẽtʃi] *adj*: **~ a** concerning, regarding.

referido/a [xefe'ridu/a] *adj* aforesaid, already

NB: European Portuguese adds the following consonants to certain words: **b** (sú(b)dito, su(b)til); **c** (a(c)ção, a(c)cionista, a(c)to); **m** (inde(m)ne); **p** (ado(p)ção, ado(p)tar); *for further details see p. xiii.*

mentioned.

referir [xefe'ri*] *vt* (*contar*) to relate, tell; **~-se** *vr*: **~-se a** to refer to.

REFESA (*BR*) *f* = **Rede Ferroviária SA.**

refestelar-se [xefeʃte'laxsi] *vr* = **refastelar-se.**

refez [xe'feʒ] *vb V* **refazer.**

refil [xe'fiw] (*pl* **-is**) *m* refill.

refiz [xe'fiʒ] *vb V* **refazer.**

refizer [xefi'ze*] *etc vb V* **refazer.**

refinado/a [xefi'nadu/a] *adj* refined.

refinamento [xefina'mẽtu] *m* refinement.

refinanciamento [xefinãsja'mẽtu] *m* refinancing.

refinanciar [xefinã'sja*] *vt* to refinance.

refinar [xefi'na*] *vt* to refine.

refinaria [xefina'ria] *f* refinery.

refiro [xe'firu] *etc vb V* **referir.**

refis [xe'fiʃ] *mpl de* **refil.**

refletido/a [xefle'tʃidu/a] (*PT*: **-ct-**) *adj* reflected; (*prudente*) thoughtful; (*ação*) prudent, shrewd.

refletir [xefle'tʃi*] (*PT*: **-ct-**) *vt* (*espelhar*) to reflect; (*som*) to echo; (*fig*: *revelar*) to reveal ♦ *vi*: **~ em** *ou* **sobre** (*pensar*) to consider, think about; **~-se** *vr* to be reflected; **~-se em** (*repercutir-se*) to have implications for.

refletor(a) [xefle'to*(a)] (*PT*: **-ct-**) *adj* reflecting ♦ *m* reflector.

reflexão [xeflek'sãw] (*pl* **-ões**) *f* reflection; (*meditação*) thought, reflection.

reflexivo/a [xeflek'sivu/a] *adj* reflexive.

reflexo/a [xe'flɛksu/a] *adj* (*luz*) reflected; (*ação*) reflex ♦ *m* reflection; (*ANAT*) reflex; (*no cabelo*) streak.

reflexões [xeflek'sõjʃ] *fpl de* **reflexão.**

reflito [xe'flitu] *etc vb V* **refletir.**

refluxo [xe'fluksu] *m* ebb.

refogado/a [xefo'gadu/a] *adj* sautéed ♦ *m* (*molho*) sautéed seasonings; (*prato*) stew.

refogar [xefo'ga*] *vt* to sauté.

reforçado/a [xefox'sadu/a] *adj* reinforced; (*pessoa*) strong; (*café da manhã, jantar*) hearty.

reforçar [xefox'sa*] *vt* to reinforce; (*revigorar*) to invigorate.

reforço [xe'foxsu] *m* reinforcement.

reforma [xe'fɔxma] *f* reform; (*ARQ*) renovation; (*REL*) reformation; (*aposentadoria*) retirement; **fazer ~s em casa** to have building work done in the house; **o banheiro está em ~** the bathroom is being done up; **~ agrária** land reform; **~ ministerial** cabinet reshuffle.

reformado/a [xefox'madu/a] *adj* reformed; (*ARQ*) renovated; (*PT*: *MIL*) retired.

reformar [xefox'ma*] *vt* to reform; (*ARQ*) to renovate; (*aposentar*) to retire; (*sentença*) to commute; **~-se** *vr* (*militar*) to retire; (*criminoso*) to reform, mend one's ways.

reformatar [xefoxma'ta*] *vt* to reformat.

reformatório [xefoxma'tɔrju] *m* approved school, borstal.

refractário/a [xefra'tarju/a] (*PT*) *adj* = **refratário/a.**

refrão [xe'frãw] (*pl* **-ãos** *ou* **-ães**) *m* (*cantado*) chorus, refrain; (*provérbio*) saying.

refratário/a [xefra'tarju/a] *adj* (*rebelde*) difficult, unmanageable; (*TEC*) heat-resistant; (*CULIN*) ovenproof; **ser ~ a** (*admoestações etc*) to be impervious to.

refrear [xefre'a*] *vt* (*cavalo*) to rein in; (*inimigo*) to contain, check; (*paixões, raiva*) to control; **~-se** *vr* to restrain o.s.; **~ a língua** to mind one's language.

refrega [xe'frɛga] *f* fight.

refrescante [xefreʃ'kãtʃi] *adj* refreshing.

refrescar [xefreʃ'ka*] *vt* (*ar, ambiente*) to cool; (*pessoa*) to refresh ♦ *vi* to cool down; **~-se** *vr* to refresh o.s.

refresco [xe'freʃku] *m* cool drink; **~s** *mpl* refreshments.

refrigeração [xefriʒera'sãw] *f* cooling; (*de alimentos*) refrigeration; (*de casa*) air conditioning.

refrigerado/a [xefriʒe'radu/a] *adj* cooled; (*casa*) air-conditioned; (*alimentos*) refrigerated; **~ a ar** air-cooled.

refrigerador [xefriʒera'do*] *m* refrigerator, fridge (*BRIT*).

refrigerante [xefriʒe'rãtʃi] *m* soft drink.

refrigerar [xefriʒe'ra*] *vt* to keep cool; (*com geladeira*) to refrigerate.

refrigério [xefri'ʒɛrju] *m* solace, consolation.

refugar [xefu'ga*] *vt* (*alimentos*) to reject; (*proposta, conselho*) to reject, dismiss ♦ *vi* (*cavalo*) to baulk, refuse.

refugiado/a [xefu'ʒjadu/a] *adj, m/f* refugee.

refugiar-se [xefu'ʒjaxsi] *vr* to take refuge; **~ na leitura** *etc* to seek solace in reading *etc*.

refúgio [xe'fuʒju] *m* refuge.

refugo [xe'fugu] *m* waste, rubbish, garbage (*US*); (*mercadoria*) reject.

refulgência [xefuw'ʒẽsja] *f* brilliance.

refulgir [xefuw'ʒi*] *vi* to shine out.

refutação [xefuta'sãw] (*pl* **-ões**) *f* refutation.

refutar [xefu'ta*] *vt* to refute.

reg *abr* = **regimento; regular.**

regº *abr* = **regulamento.**

rega ['xɛga] *f* watering; (*PT*: *irrigação*) irrigation.

regaço [xe'gasu] *m* (*colo*) lap.

regador [xega'do*] *m* watering can.

regalado/a [xega'ladu/a] (*PT*) *adj* (*encantado*) delighted; (*confortável*) comfortable ♦ *adv* comfortably.

regalar [xega'la*] (*PT*) *vt* (*causar prazer*) to delight; **~-se** *vr* (*divertir-se*) to enjoy o.s.; (*alegrar-se*) to be delighted; **~ alguém com algo** to give sb sth, present sb with sth.

regalia [xega'lia] *f* privilege.

regalo [xe'galu] *m* (*presente*) present; (*prazer*) pleasure, treat.

regar [xe'ga*] *vt* (*plantas, jardim*) to water; (*umedecer*) to sprinkle; **~ o jantar a vinho** to wash one's dinner down with wine.

regata [xe'gata] *f* regatta.

regatear [xega'tʃja*] *vt* (*o preço*) to haggle over, bargain for ♦ *vi* to haggle.
regateio [xega'teju] *m* haggling.
regato [xe'gatu] *m* brook, stream.
regência [xe'ʒẽsja] *f* regency; (*LING*) government; (*MÚS*) conducting.
regeneração [xeʒenera'sãw] *f* regeneration; (*de criminosos*) reform.
regenerar [xeʒene'ra*] *vt* to regenerate; (*criminoso*) to reform; **~-se** *vr* to regenerate; to reform.
regente [xe'ʒẽtʃi] *m* (*POL*) regent; (*de orquestra*) conductor; (*de banda*) leader.
reger [xe'ʒe*] *vt* to govern, rule; (*regular, LING*) to govern; (*orquestra*) to conduct; (*empresa*) to run ♦ *vi* (*governar*) to rule; (*maestro*) to conduct; **~ uma cadeira** (*EDUC*) to hold a chair.
região [xe'ʒjãw] (*pl* **-ões**) *f* region; (*de uma cidade*) area.
regime [xe'ʒimi] *m* (*POL*) regime; (*dieta*) diet; (*maneira*) way; **meu ~ agora é levantar cedo** my routine now is to get up early; **fazer ~** to diet; **estar de ~** to be on a diet; **o ~ das prisões/dos hospitais** the prison/hospital system; **~ de vida** way of life.
regimento [xeʒi'mẽtu] *m* regiment; (*regras*) regulations *pl*, rules *pl*; **~ interno** (*de empresa*) company rules *pl*.
régio/a ['xɛʒju/a] *adj* (*real*) royal; (*digno do rei*) regal; (*suntuoso*) princely.
regiões [xe'ʒjõjʃ] *fpl de* **região**.
regional [xeʒjo'naw] (*pl* **-ais**) *adj* regional.
registrador(a) [xeʒiʃtra'do*(a)] (*PT*: **registador(a)**) *m/f* registrar, recorder; **(caixa) registradora** cash register, till.
registrar [xeʒiʃ'tra*] (*PT*: **registar**) *vt* to register; (*anotar*) to record; (*com máquina registradora*) to ring up.
registro [xe'ʒiʃtru] (*PT*: **registo**) *m* (*ato*) registration; (: *anotação*) recording; (*livro, LING*) register; (*histórico, COMPUT*) record; (*relógio*) meter; (*MÚS*) range; (*torneira*) stopcock; **~ civil** registry office.
rego ['xegu] *m* (*para água*) ditch; (*de arado*) furrow; (*col!*) crack.
regozijar [xegozi'ʒa*] *vt* to gladden; **~-se** *vr* to be delighted, rejoice.
regozijo [xego'ziʒu] *m* joy, delight.
regra ['xɛgra] *f* rule; **~s** *fpl* (*MED*) periods; **sair da ~** to step out of line; **em ~** as a rule, usually; **por via de ~** as a rule.
regrado/a [xe'gradu/a] *adj* (*sensato*) sensible.
regredir [xegre'dʒi*] *vi* to regress; (*doença*) to retreat.
regressão [xegre'sãw] *f* regression.
regressar [xegre'sa*] *vi* to come (*ou* go) back, return.
regressivo/a [xegre'sivu/a] *adj* regressive; **contagem regressiva** countdown.
regresso [xe'grɛsu] *m* return.
regrido [xe'gridu] *etc vb V* **regredir**.
régua ['xɛgwa] *f* ruler; **~ de calcular** slide rule.
regulador(a) [xegula'do*(a)] *adj* regulating ♦ *m* regulator.
regulagem [xegu'laʒẽ] *f* (*de motor, carro*) tuning.
regulamentação [xegulamẽta'sãw] *f* regulation; (*regras*) regulations *pl*.
regulamento [xegula'mẽtu] *m* rules *pl*, regulations *pl*.
regular [xegu'la*] *adj* regular; (*estatura*) average, medium; (*tamanho*) normal; (*razoável*) not bad ♦ *vt* to regulate; (*reger*) to govern; (*máquina*) to adjust; (*carro, motor*) to tune; (*relógio*) to put right ♦ *vi* to work, function; **~-se** *vr*: **~-se por** to be guided by; **ele não regula (bem)** he's not quite right in the head; **~ por** to be about; **~ com alguém** to be about the same age as sb.
regularidade [xegulari'dadʒi] *f* regularity.
regularizar [xegulari'za*] *vt* to regularize.
regurgitar [xeguxʒi'ta*] *vt, vi* to regurgitate.
rei [xej] *m* king; **ele é o ~ da bagunça** (*col*) he's the world's worst for untidiness; **ter o ~ na barriga** to be full of oneself; **Dia de R~s** Epiphany; **R~ Momo** carnival king.
reimprimir [xeĩpri'mi*] *vt* to reprint.
reinado [xej'nadu] *m* reign.
reinar [xej'na*] *vi* to reign; (*fig*) to reign, prevail.
reincidência [xeĩsi'dẽsja] *f* backsliding; (*de criminoso*) recidivism.
reincidir [xeĩsi'dʒi*] *vi* to relapse; (*criminoso*) to commit the offence (*BRIT*) *ou* offense (*US*) again; **~ em erro** to do wrong again.
reingressar [xeĩgre'sa*] *vi*: **~ (em)** to reenter.
reiniciar [xejni'sja*] *vt* to restart.
reino ['xejnu] *m* kingdom; (*fig*) realm; **~ animal** animal kingdom; **o R~ Unido** the United Kingdom.
reintegrar [xeĩte'gra*] *vt* (*em emprego*) to reinstate; (*reconduzir*) to return, restore.
reiterar [xeite'ra*] *vt* to reiterate, repeat.
reitor(a) [xej'to*(a)] *m/f* (*de uma universidade*) vice-chancellor (*BRIT*), president (*US*) ♦ *m* (*PT*: *pároco*) rector.
reitoria [xejto'ria] *f* (*de universidade*: *cargo*) vice-chancellorship (*BRIT*), presidency (*US*); (*gabinete*) vice-chancellor's (*BRIT*) *ou* president's (*US*) office.
reivindicação [xejvĩdʒika'sãw] (*pl* **-ões**) *f* claim, demand.
reivindicar [xejvĩdʒi'ka*] *vt* to reclaim; (*aumento salarial, direitos*) to demand.
rejeição [xeʒej'sãw] (*pl* **-ões**) *f* rejection.
rejeitar [xeʒej'ta*] *vt* to reject; (*recusar*) to refuse.

NB: *European Portuguese adds the following consonants to certain words:* **b** (sú(b)dito, su(b)til); **c** (a(c)ção, a(c)cionista, a(c)to); **m** (inde(m)ne); **p** (ado(p)ção, ado(p)tar); *for further details see p. xiii.*

rejo ['xeju] *etc vb V* **reger**.

rejubilar [xeʒubi'la*] *vt* to fill with joy ♦ *vi* to rejoice; **~-se** *vr* to rejoice.

rejuvenescedor(a) [xeʒuvenese'do*(a)] *adj* rejuvenating.

rejuvenescer [xeʒuvene'se*] *vt* to rejuvenate ♦ *vi* to be rejuvenated; **~-se** *vr* to be rejuvenated.

relação [xela'sãw] (*pl* **-ões**) *f* relation; (*conexão*) connection, relationship; (*relacionamento*) relationship; (*MAT*) ratio; (*lista*) list; **com** *ou* **em ~ a** regarding, with reference to; **ter relações com alguém** to have intercourse with sb; **relações públicas** public relations.

relacionado/a [xelasjo'nadu/a] *adj* (*listado*) listed; (*ligado*) related, connected; **uma pessoa bem** *ou* **muito relacionada** a well-connected person.

relacionamento [xelasjona'mẽtu] *m* relationship.

relacionar [xelasjo'na*] *vt* (*listar*) to make a list of; **~-se** *vr* to be connected *ou* related; **~ algo com algo** to connect sth with sth, relate sth to sth; **~ alguém com alguém** to bring sb into contact with sb; **~-se com** (*ligar-se*) to be connected with, have to do with; (*conhecer*) to become acquainted with.

relaçoes [xela'sõjʃ] *fpl de* **relação**.

relações-públicas *m/f inv* PR person.

relâmpago [xe'lãpagu] *m* flash of lightning; **~s** lightning *sg* ♦ *adj* (*visita*) lightning *atr*; **passar como um ~** to flash past; **como um ~** like lightning, as quick as a flash.

relampejar [xelãpe'ʒa*] *vi* to flash; **relampejou** the lightning flashed.

relance [xe'lãsi] *m* glance; **olhar de ~** to glance at.

relapso/a [xe'lapsu/a] *adj* (*reincidente*) lapsed; (*negligente*) negligent.

relatar [xela'ta*] *vt* to give an account of.

relativo/a [xela'tʃivu/a] *adj* relative.

relato [xe'latu] *m* account.

relator(a) [xela'to*(a)] *m/f* storyteller.

relatório [xela'tɔrju] *m* report; **~ anual** (*COM*) annual report.

relaxado/a [xela'ʃadu/a] *adj* relaxed; (*desleixado*) slovenly, sloppy; (*relapso*) complacent.

relaxamento [xelaʃa'mẽtu] *m* relaxation; (*de moral, costumes*) debasement; (*desleixo*) slovenliness; (*de relapsos*) complacency.

relaxante [xela'ʃãtʃi] *adj* relaxing ♦ *m* tranquillizer.

relaxar [xela'ʃa*] *vt* to relax; (*moral, costumes*) to debase ♦ *vi* to relax; (*tornar-se negligente*): **~ (em)** to grow complacent in; **~ com** (*transigir*) to acquiesce in.

relaxe [xe'laʃi] *m* relaxation.

relegar [xele'ga*] *vt* to relegate.

relê [xe'le] *vb V* **reler**.

releio [xe'leju] *etc vb V* **reler**.

relembrar [xelẽ'bra*] *vt* to recall.

relento [xe'lẽtu] *m*: **ao ~** out of doors.

reler [xe'le*] (*irreg*: *como* **ler**) *vt* to reread.

reles ['xɛliʃ] *adj inv* (*gente*) common, vulgar; (*comportamento*) despicable; (*mero*) mere.

relevância [xele'vãsja] *f* relevance.

relevante [xele'vãtʃi] *adj* relevant.

relevar [xele'va*] *vt* (*tornar saliente*) to emphasize; (*atenuar*) to relieve; (*desculpar*) to pardon, forgive.

relevo [xe'levu] *m* relief; (*fig*) prominence, importance; **pôr em ~** to emphasize.

reli [xe'li] *vb V* **reler**.

relicário [xeli'karju] *m* reliquary, shrine.

relido/a [xe'lido/a] *pp de* **reler**.

religião [xeli'ʒãw] (*pl* **-ões**) *f* religion.

religioso/a [xeli'ʒozu/ɔza] *adj* religious; (*casamento*) church ♦ *m/f* religious person; (*frade/freira*) monk/nun ♦ *m* (*casamento*) church wedding.

relinchar [xelĩ'ʃa*] *vi* to neigh.

relincho [xe'lĩʃu] *m* (*som*) neigh; (*ato*) neighing.

relíquia [xe'likja] *f* relic; **~ de família** family heirloom.

relógio [xe'lɔʒu] *m* clock; (*de gás*) meter; **~ de pé** grandfather clock; **~ de ponto** time clock; **~ de sol** sundial; **~ (de pulso)** (wrist)watch; **corrida contra o ~** race against the clock.

relojoaria [xeloʒwa'ria] *f* watchmaker's, watch shop.

relojoeiro/a [xelo'ʒwejru/a] *m/f* watchmaker.

relutância [xelu'tãsja] *f* reluctance.

relutante [xelu'tãtʃi] *adj* reluctant.

relutar [xelu'ta*] *vi*: **~ (em fazer)** to be reluctant (to do); **~ contra algo** to be reluctant to accept sth.

reluzente [xelu'zẽtʃi] *adj* brilliant, shining.

reluzir [xelu'zi*] *vi* to gleam, shine.

relva ['xɛwva] *f* grass; (*terreno gramado*) lawn.

relvado [xew'vadu] (*PT*) *m* lawn.

rem *abr* (= *remetente*) sender.

remador(a) [xema'do*(a)] *m/f* rower, oarsman/woman.

remanchar [xemã'ʃa*] *vi* to delay, take one's time.

remanescente [xemane'sẽtʃi] *adj* remaining ♦ *m* remainder; (*excesso*) surplus.

remanescer [xemane'se*] *vi* to remain.

remanso [xe'mãsu] *m* (*pausa*) pause, rest; (*sossego*) stillness, quiet; (*água*) backwater.

remar [xe'ma*] *vt* to row; (*canoa*) to paddle ♦ *vi* to row; **~ contra a maré** (*fig*) to swim against the tide.

remarcação [xemaxka'sãw] *f* (*de preços*) changing; (*de artigos*) repricing; (*artigos remarcados*) repriced goods *pl*.

remarcar [xemax'ka*] *vt* (*preços*) to adjust; (*artigos*) to reprice.

rematado/a [xema'tadu/a] *adj* (*concluído*) completed.

rematar [xema'ta*] *vt* to finish off.

remate [xe'matʃi] *m* (*fim*) end; (*acabamento*)

finishing touch; (*ARQ*) coping; (*fig*: *cume*) peak; (*de piada*) punch line.
remedeio [xeme'deju] *etc vb V* **remediar**.
remediado/a [xeme'dʒjadu/a] *adj* comfortably off.
remediar [xeme'dʒja*] *vt* (*corrigir*) to put right, remedy.
remediável [xeme'dʒjavew] (*pl* **-eis**) *adj* rectifiable.
remédio [xe'mɛdʒju] *m* (*medicamento*) medicine; (*recurso, solução*) remedy; (*JUR*) recourse; **não tem ~** there's no way; **que ~?** what else can one do?; **~ caseiro** home remedy.
remela [xe'mɛla] *f* (*nos olhos*) sleep.
remelento/a [xeme'lẽtu/a] *adj* bleary-eyed.
remelexo [xeme'leʃu] *m* (*requebro*) swaying.
rememorar [xememo'ra*] *vt* to remember.
rememorável [xememo'ravew] (*pl* **-eis**) *adj* memorable.
remendar [xemẽ'da*] *vt* to mend; (*com pano*) to patch.
remendo [xe'mẽdu] *m* repair; (*de pano*) patch.
remessa [xe'mɛsa] *f* (*COM*) shipment, dispatch; (*de dinheiro*) remittance.
remetente [xeme'tẽtʃi] *m/f* (*de carta*) sender; (*COM*) shipper.
remeter [xeme'te*] *vt* (*expedir*) to send, dispatch; (*dinheiro*) to remit; (*entregar*) to hand over; **~-se** *vr*: **~-se a** (*referir-se*) to refer to.
remexer [xeme'ʃe*] *vt* (*papéis*) to shuffle; (*sacudir*: *braços, folhas*) to shake; (*revolver*: *areia, lama*) to stir up ♦ *vi*: **~ em** to rummage through; **~-se** *vr* (*mover-se*) to move around; (*rebolar-se*) to sway.
reminiscência [xemini'sẽsja] *f* reminiscence.
remição [xemi'sãw] *f* redemption.
remir [xe'mi*] *vt* (*coisa penhorada, REL*) to redeem; (*livrar*) to free; (*danos, perdas*) to make good; **~-se** *vr* (*pecador*) to redeem o.s.
remissão [xemi'sãw] (*pl* **-ões**) *f* (*COM, REL*) redemption; (*compensação*) payment; (*num livro*) cross-reference.
remisso/a [xe'misu/a] *adj* remiss; **~ em fazer** (*lento*) slow to do.
remissões [xemi'sõjʃ] *fpl de* **remissão**.
remível [xe'mivew] (*pl* **-eis**) *adj* redeemable.
remo ['xɛmu] *m* oar; (*de canoa*) paddle; (*ESPORTE*) rowing.
remoa [xe'moa] *etc vb V* **remoer**.
remoção [xemo'sãw] *f* removal.
remoçar [xemo'sa*] *vt* to rejuvenate; ♦ *vi* to be rejuvenated.
remoer [xe'mwe*] *vt* (*café*) to regrind; (*no pensamento*) to turn over in one's mind; (*amofinar*) to eat away; **~-se** *vr* (*amofinar-se*) to be consumed *ou* eaten away.
remoinho [xemo'iɲu] *m* = **rodamoinho**.
remontar [xemõ'ta*] *vt* (*elevar*) to raise; (*tornar a armar*) to re-assemble ♦ *vi* (*em cavalo*) to remount; **~ ao passado** to return to the past; **~ ao século XV** *etc* to date back to the 15th century *etc*; **~ o vôo** to soar.
remoque [xe'mɔki] *m* gibe, taunt.
remorso [xe'mɔxsu] *m* remorse.
remoto/a [xe'mɔtu/a] *adj* remote, far off; (*controle, COMPUT*) remote.
remover [xemo've*] *vt* (*mover*) to move; (*transferir*) to transfer; (*demitir*) to dismiss; (*retirar, afastar*) to remove; (*terra*) to churn up.
remuneração [xemunera'sãw] (*pl* **-ões**) *f* remuneration; (*salário*) wage.
remunerador(a) [xemunera'do*(a)] *adj* remunerative; (*recompensador*) rewarding.
remunerar [xemune'ra*] *vt* to remunerate; (*premiar*) to reward.
rena ['xɛna] *f* reindeer.
renal [xe'naw] (*pl* **-ais**) *adj* renal, kidney *atr*.
Renamo [xe'namu] *abr f* = **Resistência Nacional Moçambicana**.
Renascença [xena'sẽsa] *f*: **a ~** the Renaissance.
renascer [xena'se*] *vi* to be reborn; (*fig*) to be revived.
renascimento [xenasi'mẽtu] *m* rebirth; (*fig*) revival; **o R~** the Renaissance.
Renavam (*BR*) *abr m* = **Registro Nacional de Veículos Automotores**.
renda ['xẽda] *f* income; (*nacional*) revenue; (*de aplicação, locação*) yield; (*tecido*) lace; **~ bruta/líquida** gross/net income; **imposto de ~** income tax; **~ per capita** per capita income.
rendado/a [xẽ'dadu/a] *adj* lace-trimmed; (*com aspecto de renda*) lacy ♦ *m* lacework.
rendeiro/a [xẽ'dejru/a] *m/f* lacemaker.
render [xẽ'de*] *vt* (*lucro, dinheiro*) to bring in, yield; (*preço*) to fetch; (*homenagem*) to pay; (*graças*) to give; (*serviços*) to render; (*armas*) to surrender; (*guarda*) to relieve; (*causar*) to bring ♦ *vi* (*dar lucro*) to pay; (*trabalho*) to be productive; (*comida*) to go a long way; (*conversa, caso*) to go on, last; **~-se** *vr* to surrender.
rendez-vous [xãde'vu] *m inv* = **randevu**.
rendição [xẽdʒi'sãw] *f* surrender.
rendido/a [xẽ'dʒidu/a] *adj* subdued.
rendimento [xẽdʒi'mẽtu] *m* (*renda*) income; (*lucro*) profit; (*juro*) yield, interest; (*produtividade*) productivity; (*de máquina*) efficiency; (*de um produto*) value for money; **~ por ação** (*COM*) earnings per share, earnings yield; **~ de capital** (*COM*) return on capital.
rendoso/a [xẽ'dozu/ɔza] *adj* profitable.
renegado/a [xene'gadu/a] *adj, m/f* renegade.
renegar [xene'ga*] *vt* (*crença*) to renounce;

NB: European Portuguese adds the following consonants to certain words: **b** (sú(b)dito, su(b)til); **c** (a(c)ção, a(c)cionista, a(c)to); **m** (inde(m)ne); **p** (ado(p)ção, ado(p)tar); *for further details see p. xiii.*

(*detestar*) to hate; (*trair*) to betray; (*negar*) to deny; (*desprezar*) to reject.
renhido/a [xe'ɲidu/a] *adj* hard-fought; (*batalha*) bloody.
renitência [xeni'tẽsja] *f* obstinacy.
renitente [xeni'tẽtʃi] *adj* obstinate, stubborn.
Reno ['xenu] *m*: **o** ~ the Rhine.
renomado/a [xeno'madu/a] *adj* renowned.
renome [xe'nɔmi] *m* fame, renown; **de** ~ renowned.
renovação [xenova'sãw] (*pl* **-ões**) *f* renewal; (*ARQ*) renovation.
renovar [xeno'va*] *vt* to renew; (*ARQ*) to renovate; (*ensino, empresa*) to revamp ♦ *vi* to be renewed.
renque ['xẽki] *m* row.
rentabilidade [xẽtabili'dadʒi] *f* profitability.
rentável [xẽ'tavew] (*pl* **-eis**) *adj* profitable.
rente ['xẽtʃi] *adj* (*cabelo*) close-cropped; (*casa*) nearby ♦ *adv* close; (*muito curto*) very short; ~ **a** close by.
renúncia [xe'nũsja] *f* renunciation; (*de cargo*) resignation; ~ **a um direito** waiver (of a right).
renunciar [xenũ'sja*] *vt* to give up, renounce ♦ *vi* to resign; ~ **a algo** to give sth up; (*direito*) to surrender sth; (*fé, crença*) to renounce sth.
reorganizar [xeoxgani'za*] *vt* to reorganize.
reouve [xe'ovi] *etc vb V* **reaver**.
reouver [xeo've*] *etc vb V* **reaver**.
reparação [xepara'sãw] (*pl* **-ões**) *f* (*conserto*) mending, repairing; (*de mal, erros*) remedying; (*de prejuizos, ofensa*) making amends; (*fig*) amends *pl*, reparation.
reparar [xepa'ra*] *vt* (*consertar*) to repair; (*forças*) to restore; (*mal, erros*) to remedy; (*prejuizo, danos, ofensa*) to make amends for; (*notar*) to notice ♦ *vi*: ~ **em** to notice; **não repare em** pay no attention to; **repare em** (*olhe*) look at.
reparo [xe'paru] *m* (*conserto*) repair; (*crítica*) criticism; (*observação*) observation.
repartição [xepaxtʃi'sãw] (*pl* **-ões**) *f* (*ato*) distribution; (*seção*) department; (*escritório*) office; ~ **(pública)** government department.
repartir [xepax'tʃi*] *vt* (*distribuir*) to distribute; (*dividir entre vários*) to share out; (*dividir em várias porções*) to divide up; (*cabelo*) to part; **~-se** *vr* (*dividir-se*) to divide.
repassar [xepa'sa*] *vt* (*ponte, fronteira*) to go over again; (*lição*) to revise, go over ♦ *vi* to go by again; **passar e** ~ to go back and forth.
repasto [xe'paʃtu] *m* (*refeição*) meal, repast; (*banquete*) feast.
repatriar [xepa'trja*] *vt* to repatriate; **~-se** *vr* to go back home.
repelão [xepe'lãw] (*pl* **-ões**) *m* push, shove; **de** ~ brusquely.
repelente [xepe'lẽtʃi] *adj, m* repellent.
repelir [xepe'li*] *vt* to repel; (*curiosos*) to drive away; (*idéias, atitudes*) to reject, repudiate; **seu estômago repele certos alimentos** his stomach cannot take certain foods.
repelões [xepe'lõjʃ] *fpl de* **repelão**.
repensar [xepẽ'sa*] *vi* to reconsider, rethink.
repente [xe'pẽtʃi] *m* outburst; **de** ~ suddenly; (*col: talvez*) maybe.
repentino/a [xepẽ'tʃinu/a] *adj* sudden.
repercussão [xepexku'sãw] (*pl* **-ões**) *f* repercussion.
repercutir [xepexku'tʃi*] *vt* (*som*) to echo ♦ *vi* (*som*) to reverberate, echo; (*fig*): ~ **(em)** to have repercussions (on).
repertório [xepex'tɔrju] *m* (*lista*) list; (*coleção*) collection; (*MÚS*) repertoire.
repetição [xepetʃi'sãw] (*pl* **-ões**) *f* repetition.
repetidamente [xepetʃida'mẽtʃi] *adj* repeatedly.
repetido/a [xepe'tʃidu/a] *adj* repeated; **repetidas vezes** repeatedly, again and again.
repetir [xepe'tʃi*] *vt* to repeat; (*vestido*) to wear again ♦ *vi* (*ao comer*) to have seconds; **~-se** *vr* (*acontecer de novo*) to happen again; (*pessoa*) to repeat o.s.
repetitivo/a [xepetʃi'tʃivu/a] *adj* repetitive.
repicar [xepi'ka*] *vt* (*sinos*) to ring ♦ *vi* to ring (out).
repilo [xe'pilu] *etc vb V* **repelir**.
repimpado/a [xepĩ'padu/a] *adj* (*refestelado*) lolling; (*satisfeito*) full up.
repique [xe'pikɪ] *etc vb V* **repicar** ♦ *m* (*de sinos*) peal; ~ **falso** false alarm.
repisar [xepi'za*] *vt* (*repetir*) to repeat; (*uvas*) to tread ♦ *vi*: ~ **em** (*assunto*) to keep on about, harp on.
repito [xe'pitu] *etc vb V* **repetir**.
replay [xe'plei] (*pl* **~s**) *m* (*TV*) (action) replay.
repleto/a [xe'plɛtu/a] *adj* replete, full up.
réplica ['xɛplika] *f* (*cópia*) replica; (*contestação*) reply, retort.
replicar [xepli'ka*] *vt* to answer, reply to ♦ *vi* to reply, answer back.
repõe [xe'põj] *etc vb V* **repor**.
repolho [xe'poʎu] *m* cabbage.
repomos [xe'pomoʃ] *vb V* **repor**.
reponho [xe'poɲu] *etc vb V* **repor**.
repontar [xepõ'ta*] *vi* (*aparecer*) to appear.
repor [xe'po*] (*irreg*: *como* **pôr**) *vt* to put back, replace; (*restituir*) to return; **~-se** *vr* (*pessoa*) to recover.
reportagem [xepox'taʒẽ] (*pl* **-ns**) *f* (*ato*) reporting; (*notícia*) report; (*repórteres*) reporters *pl*.
reportar [xepox'ta*] *vt*: ~ **a** (*o pensamento*) to take back to; (*atribuir*) to attribute to; **~-se** *vr*: **~-se a** to refer to; (*relacionar-se a*) to be connected with.
repórter [xe'pɔxte*] *m/f* reporter.
repôs [xe'poʃ] *vb V* **repor**.
reposição [xepozi'sãw] (*pl* **-ões**) *f* replacement; (*restituição*) return; ~ **salarial** wage adjustment.

repositório [xepozi'tɔrju] *m* repository.
reposto/a [xe'poʃtu/'pɔʃta] *pp de* **repor**.
repousar [xepo'za*] *vi* to rest.
repouso [xe'pozu] *m* rest.
repreender [xeprjẽ'de*] *vt* to reprimand.
repreensão [xeprjẽ'sãw] (*pl* **-ões**) *f* rebuke, reprimand.
repreensível [xeprjẽ'sivew] (*pl* **-eis**) *adj* reprehensible.
repreensões [xeprjẽ'sõjʃ] *fpl de* **repreensão**.
represa [xe'preza] *f* dam.
represália [xepre'zalja] *f* reprisal.
representação [xeprezẽta'sãw] (*pl* **-ões**) *f* representation; (*representantes*) representatives *pl*; (TEATRO) performance; (*atuação do ator*) acting.
representante [xeprezẽ'tãtʃi] *m/f* representative.
representativo/a [xeprezẽta'tʃivu/a] *adj* representative.
representar [xeprezẽ'ta*] *vt* to represent; (TEATRO: *papel*) to play; (: *encenar*) to put on ♦ *vi* (*ator*) to act; (*tb*: JUR) to make a complaint.
repressão [xepre'sãw] (*pl* **-ões**) *f* repression.
repressivo/a [xepre'sivu/a] *adj* repressive.
repressões [xepre'sõjʃ] *fpl de* **repressão**.
reprimido/a [xepri'midu/a] *adj* repressed.
reprimir [xepri'mi*] *vt* to repress; (*lágrimas*) to keep back.
reprise [xe'prizi] *f* reshowing.
réprobo/a ['xɛprobu/a] *adj*, *m/f* reprobate.
reprodução [xeprodu'sãw] (*pl* **-ões**) *f* reproduction.
reprodutor(a) [xeprodu'to*(a)] *adj* reproductive.
reproduzir [xeprodu'zi*] *vt* to reproduce; (*repetir*) to repeat; **~-se** *vr* to breed, multiply; (*repetir-se*) to be repeated.
reprovação [xeprova'sãw] (*pl* **-ões**) *f* disapproval; (*em exame*) failure.
reprovado/a [xepro'vadu/a] *m/f* failed candidate, failure; **taxa de ~s** failure rate.
reprovador(a) [xeprova'do*(a)] *adj* (*olhar*) disapproving, reproving.
reprovar [xepro'va*] *vt* (*condenar*) to disapprove of; (*aluno*) to fail.
réptil ['xɛptʃiw] (*pl* **-eis**) *m* reptile.
repto ['xɛptu] *m* challenge, provocation.
república [xe'publika] *f* republic; **~ de estudantes** students' house; **~ popular** people's republic.
republicano/a [xepubli'kanu/a] *adj*, *m/f* republican.
repudiar [xepu'dʒja*] *vt* to repudiate, reject; (*abandonar*) to disown.
repúdio [xe'pudʒju] *m* rejection, repudiation.
repugnância [xepug'nãsja] *f* repugnance; (*por comida etc*) disgust; (*aversão*) aversion; (*moral*) abhorrence.
repugnante [xepug'nãtʃi] *adj* repugnant, repulsive.
repugnar [xepug'na*] *vt* to oppose ♦ *vi* to be repulsive; **~ a alguém** to disgust sb; (*moralmente*) to be repugnant to sb.
repulsão [xepuw'sãw] (*pl* **-ões**) *f* repulsion; (*rejeição*) rejection.
repulsa [xɛ'puwsa] *f* (*ato*) rejection; (*sentimento*) repugnance; (*física*) repulsion.
repulsivo/a [xepuw'sivu/a] *adj* repulsive.
repulsões [xepuw'sõjʃ] *fpl de* **repulsão**.
repunha [xe'puɲa] *etc vb V* **repor**.
repus [xe'puʃ] *etc vb V* **repor**.
repuser [xepu'ze*] *etc vb V* **repor**.
reputação [reputa'sãw] (*pl* **-ões**) *f* reputation.
reputado/a [xepu'tadu/a] *adj* renowned.
reputar [xepu'ta*] *vt* to consider, regard as.
repuxado/a [xepu'ʃadu/a] *adj* (*pele*) tight, firm; (*olhos*) slanted.
repuxar [xepu'ʃa*] *vt* (*puxar*) to tug; (*esticar*) to pull tight.
repuxo [xe'puʃu] *m* (*de água*) fountain; **agüentar o ~** (*col*) to bear up.
requebrado [xeke'bradu] *m* (*rebolado*) swing, sway.
requebrar [xeke'bra*] *vt* to wiggle, swing; **~-se** *vr* to wiggle, swing.
requeijão [xekej'ʒãw] *m* cheese spread.
requeira [xe'kejra] *etc vb V* **requerer**.
requentar [xekẽ'ta*] *vt* to reheat, warm up.
requer [xe'ke*] *vb V* **requerer**.
requerente [xeke'rẽtʃi] *m/f* (JUR) petitioner.
requerer [xeke're*] *vt* (*emprego*) to apply for; (*pedir*) to request, ask for; (*exigir*) to require; (JUR) to petition for.
requerimento [xekeri'mẽtu] *m* application; (*pedido*) request; (*petição*) petition.
réquiem ['xɛkjẽ] (*pl* **-ns**) *m* requiem.
requintado/a [xekĩ'tadu/a] *adj* refined, elegant.
requintar [xekĩ'ta*] *vt* to refine ♦ *vi*: **~ em** to be refined in.
requinte [xe'kĩtʃi] *m* refinement, elegance; (*cúmulo*) height.
requisição [xekizi'sãw] (*pl* **-ões**) *f* request, demand.
requisitado/a [xekizi'tadu/a] *adj* (*requerido*) required; (*muito procurado*) sought after.
requisitar [xekizi'ta*] *vt* to make a request for; (MIL) to requisition.
requisito [xeki'zitu] *m* requirement.
rês [xeʃ] *f* head of cattle; **reses** *fpl* cattle, livestock *sg*.
rescindir [xesĩ'dʒi*] *vt* (*contrato*) to rescind.
rescrever [xeʃkre've*] *vt* = **reescrever**.
rés-do-chão [xɛʒ-] (PT) *m inv* (*andar térreo*) ground floor (BRIT), first floor (US).
resenha [xe'zɛɲa] *f* (*relatório*) report; (*resumo*) summary; (*de livro*) review; **fazer a ~ de** (*livro*) to review.

***NB:** European Portuguese adds the following consonants to certain words:* **b** (sú(b)dito, su(b)til); **c** (a(c)ção, a(c)cionista, a(c)to); **m** (inde(m)ne); **p** (ado(p)ção, ado(p)tar); *for further details see p. xiii.*

reserva [xe'zɛxva] *f* reserve; (*para hotel, fig: ressalva*) reservation; (*discrição*) discretion ♦ *m/f* (*ESPORTE*) reserve; ~ **de mercado** (*COM*) protected market; ~ **de petróleo** oil reserve; ~ **natural** nature reserve; ~ **em dinheiro** cash reserve.

reservado/a [xezex'vadu/a] *adj* reserved; (*pej: retraído*) standoffish.

reservar [xezex'va*] *vt* to reserve; (*guardar de reserva*) to keep; (*forças*) to conserve; **~-se** *vr* to save o.s.; **~-se o direito de fazer** to reserve the right to do; **ele não sabe o que o futuro lhe reserva** he does not know what the future has in store for him.

reservatório [xezexva'tɔrju] *m* (*lago*) reservoir.

reservista [xezex'viʃta] *m/f* (*MIL*) member of the reserves.

resfolegar [xeʃfole'ga*] *vi* to pant.

resfriado/a [xeʃ'frjadu/a] (*BR*) *adj*: **estar** ~ to have a cold; **ficar** ~ to catch cold ♦ *m* cold, chill.

resfriar [xeʃ'frja*] *vt* to cool, chill ♦ *vi* (*pessoa*) to catch (a) cold; **~-se** *vr* to catch (a) cold.

resgatar [xeʒga'ta*] *vt* (*prisioneiro*) to ransom; (*salvar*) to rescue; (*retomar*) to get back, recover; (*dívida*) to pay off; (*COM: ação, coisa penhorada*) to redeem.

resgatável [xeʒga'tavew] (*pl* **-eis**) *adj* redeemable.

resgate [xeʒ'gatʃi] *m* (*salvamento*) rescue; (*para livrar reféns*) ransom; (*COM: de ações, coisa penhorada*) redemption; (*retomada*) recovery.

resguardar [xeʒgwax'da*] *vt* to protect; **~-se** *vr*: **~-se de** to guard against.

resguardo [xeʒ'gwaxdu] *m* protection; (*cuidado*) care; (*convalescência*): **estar** *ou* **ficar de** ~ to take *ou* be taking things easy.

residência [xezi'dẽsja] *f* residence.

residencial [xezidẽ'sjaw] (*pl* **-ais**) *adj* (*zona, edifício*) residential; (*computador, telefone etc*) home *atr*.

residente [xezi'dẽtʃi] *adj, m/f* resident; ~ **na memória** (*COMPUT*) memory-resident.

residir [xezi'dʒi*] *vi* to live, reside; (*achar-se*) to reside.

resíduo [xe'zidwu] *m* residue.

resignação [xezigna'sãw] (*pl* **-ões**) *f* resignation.

resignadamente [xezignada'mẽtʃi] *adj* with resignation.

resignado/a [xezig'nadu/a] *adj* resigned.

resignar-se [xezig'naxsi] *vr*: ~ **com** to resign o.s. to.

resiliente [xezi'ljẽtʃi] *adj* resilient.

resina [xe'zina] *f* resin.

resistência [xeziʃ'tẽsja] *f* resistance; (*de atleta*) stamina; (*de material, objeto*) strength; (*moral*) morale.

resistente [xeziʃ'tẽtʃi] *adj* resistant; (*material, objeto*) hard-wearing, strong; ~ **a traças** mothproof.

resistir [xeziʃ'tʃi*] *vi* (*suporte*) to hold; (*pessoa*) to hold out; ~ **a** (*não ceder*) to resist; (*sobreviver*) to survive; ~ **ao uso** to wear well; ~ **(ao tempo)** to endure, stand the test of time.

resma ['xeʒma] *f* ream.

resmungar [xeʒmũ'ga*] *vt, vi* to mutter, mumble.

resmungo [xeʒ'mũgu] *m* grumbling.

resolução [xezolu'sãw] (*pl* **-ões**) *f* resolution; (*coragem*) courage; (*de um problema*) solution; **de alta ~ (gráfica)** (*COMPUT*) high-resolution.

resoluto/a [xezo'lutu/a] *adj* decisive; ~ **a fazer** resolved to do.

resolver [xezow've*] *vt* to sort out; (*problema*) to solve; (*questão*) to resolve; (*decidir*) to decide; **~-se** *vr*: **~-se (a fazer)** (*decidir*) to make up one's mind (to do), decide (to do); **chorar não resolve** crying doesn't help, it's no use crying; **~-se por** to decide on.

resolvido/a [xezow'vidu/a] *adj* (*pessoa*) decisive.

respaldo [xeʃ'pawdu] *m* (*de cadeira*) backrest; (*fig*) support, backing.

respectivo/a [xeʃpek'tʃivu/a] *adj* respective.

respeitador(a) [xeʃpejta'do*(a)] *adj* respectful.

respeitante [xeʃpej'tãtʃi] *adj*: ~ **a** concerning, with regard to.

respeitar [xeʃpej'ta*] *vt* to respect.

respeitável [xeʃpej'tavew] (*pl* **-eis**) *adj* respectable; (*considerável*) considerable.

respeito [xeʃ'pejtu] *m*: ~ (**a** *ou* **por**) respect (for); **~s** *mpl* regards; **a ~ de, com ~ a** as to, as regards; (*sobre*) about; **dizer ~ a** to concern; **faltar ao ~ a** to be rude to; **em ~ a** with respect to; **dar-se ao ~** to command respect; **pessoa de ~** respected person; **ela não me disse nada a seu ~** she didn't tell me anything about you; **não sei nada a ~ (disso)** I know nothing about it.

respeitoso/a [xeʃpej'tozu/ɔza] *adj* respectful.

respingar [xeʃpĩ'ga*] *vt, vi* to splash, spatter.

respingo [xeʃ'pĩgu] *m* splash.

respiração [xeʃpira'sãw] *f* breathing; (*MED*) respiration.

respirador [xeʃpira'do*] *m* respirator.

respirar [xeʃpi'ra*] *vt* to breathe; (*revelar*) to reveal, show ♦ *vi* to breathe; (*descansar*) to have a respite.

respiratório/a [xeʃpira'tɔrju/a] *adj* respiratory.

respiro [xeʃ'piru] *m* breath; (*descanso*) respite; (*abertura*) vent.

resplandecente [xeʃplãde'sẽtʃi] *adj* resplendent.

resplandecer [xeʃplãde'se*] *vi* to gleam, shine (out).

resplendor [xeʃplẽ'do*] *m* brilliance; (*fig*) glory.

respondão/dona [xeʃpõ'dãw/'dɔna] (*pl* **-ões/~s**) *adj* cheeky, insolent.
responder [xeʃpõ'de*] *vt* to answer ♦ *vi* to answer; (*ser respondão*) to answer back; ~ **por** to be responsible for, answer for; (COM) to be liable for; ~ **a** (*tratamento, agressão*) to respond to; (*processo, inquérito*) to undergo.
respondões [xeʃpõ'dõjʃ] *mpl de* **respondão**.
respondona [xeʃpõ'dɔna] *f de* **respondão**.
responsabilidade [xeʃpõsabili'dadʒi] *f* responsibility; (JUR) liability.
responsabilizar [xeʃpõsabili'za*] *vt*: ~ **alguém (por algo)** to hold sb responsible (for sth); **~-se** *vr*: **~-se por** to take responsibility for.
responsável [xeʃpõ'savew] (*pl* **-eis**) *adj*: ~ **(por)** responsible (for) ♦ *m* person responsible *ou* in charge; ~ **a** answerable to, accountable to.
resposta [xeʃ'pɔʃta] *f* answer, reply.
resquício [xeʃ'kisju] *m* (*vestígio*) trace.
ressabiado/a [xesa'bjadu/a] *adj* (*desconfiado*) wary; (*ressentido*) resentful.
ressaca [xe'saka] *f* (*refluxo*) undertow; (*mar bravo*) rough sea; (*fig*: *de quem bebeu*) hangover; **estar de** ~ (*mar*) to be rough; (*pessoa*) to have a hangover.
ressaibo [xe'sajbu] *m* (*mau sabor*) unpleasant taste; (*fig*: *indício*) trace; (: *ressentimento*) ill feeling.
ressaltar [xesaw'ta*] *vt* to emphasize ♦ *vi* to stand out.
ressalva [xe'sawva] *f* (*proteção*) safeguard; (MIL) exemption certificate; (*correção*) correction; (*restrição*) reservation, proviso; (*exceção*) exception.
ressarcir [xesax'si*] *vt* (*pagar*) to compensate; (*compensar*) to compensate for; ~ **alguém de** to compensate sb for.
ressecado/a [xese'kadu/a] *adj* (*terra, lábios*) parched; (*pele, planta*) very dry.
ressecar [xese'ka*] *vt, vi* to dry up.
resseguro [xese'guru] *m* reinsurance.
ressentido/a [xesẽ'tʃidu/a] *adj* resentful.
ressentimento [xesẽtʃi'mẽtu] *m* resentment.
ressentir-se [xesẽ'tʃixsi] *vr*: ~ **de** (*magoar-se*) to resent, be hurt by; (*sofrer*) to suffer from, feel the effects of.
ressequido/a [xese'kidu/a] *adj* = **ressecado/a**.
ressinto [xe'sĩtu] *etc vb V* **ressentir-se**.
ressoar [xe'swa*] *vi* to resound; (*ecoar*) to echo.
ressonância [xeso'nãsja] *f* resonance; (*eco*) echo.
ressonante [xeso'nãtʃi] *adj* resonant.
ressurgimento [xesuxʒi'mẽtu] *m* resurgence, revival.
ressurreição [xesuxej'sãw] (*pl* **-ões**) *f* resurrection.
ressuscitar [xesusi'ta*] *vt* to revive, resuscitate; (*costumes etc*) to revive ♦ *vi* to revive.
restabelecer [xeʃtabele'se*] *vt* to re-establish; (*ordem, forças*) to restore; (*doente*) to restore to health; **~-se** *vr* to recover, recuperate.
restabelecimento [xeʃtabelesi'mẽtu] *m* re-establishment; (*da ordem*) restoration; (MED) recovery.
restante [xeʃ'tãtʃi] *m* rest ♦ *adj* remaining.
restar [xeʃ'ta*] *vi* to remain, be left; (*esperança, dúvida*) to remain; **não lhe resta nada** he has nothing left; **resta-me fechar o negócio** I still have to close the deal; **não resta dúvida de que** there is no longer any doubt that.
restauração [xeʃtawra'sãw] (*pl* **-ões**) *f* restoration; (*de doente*) restoring to health; (*de costumes, usos*) revival.
restaurante [xeʃtaw'rãtʃi] *m* restaurant.
restaurar [xeʃtaw'ra*] *vt* to restore; (*recuperar*: *doente*) to restore to health; (*de costumes, usos*) to revive, restore.
réstia ['xɛʃtʃja] *f* (*de cebolas*) string; (*luz*) ray.
restinga [xeʃ'tʃĩga] *f* spit.
restituição [xeʃtʃitwi'sãw] (*pl* **-ões**) *f* restitution, return; (*de dinheiro*) repayment; (*a cargo*) reinstatement.
restituir [xeʃtʃi'twi*] *vt* to return; (*dinheiro*) to repay; (*forças, saúde*) to restore; (*usos*) to revive; (*reempossar*) to reinstate.
resto ['xɛʃtu] *m* rest; (MAT) remainder; **~s** *mpl* remains; (*de comida*) scraps; **~s mortais** mortal remains; **de** ~ apart from that.
restrição [xeʃtri'sãw] (*pl* **-ões**) *f* restriction.
restringir [xeʃtrĩ'ʒi*] *vt* to restrict; **~-se** *vr*: **~-se a** to be restricted to; (*pessoa*) to restrict o.s. to.
restrito/a [xeʃ'tritu/a] *adj* restricted.
resultado [xezuw'tadu] *m* result; **dar** ~ to work, be effective; ~ ... (*col*) the upshot being ....
resultante [xezuw'tãtʃi] *adj* resultant; ~ **de** resulting from.
resultar [xezuw'ta*] *vi*: ~ **(de/em)** to result (from/in) ♦ *vi (vir a ser)* to turn out to be.
resumido/a [xezu'midu/a] *adj* abbreviated, abridged; (*curto*) concise.
resumir [xezu'mi*] *vt* to summarize; (*livro*) to abridge; (*reduzir*) to reduce; (*conter em resumo*) to sum up; **~-se** *vr*: **~-se a** *ou* **em** to consist in *ou* of.
resumo [xe'zumu] *m* summary, résumé; **em** ~ in short, briefly.
resvalar [xeʒva'la*] *vt* to slide, slip.
resvés [xeʃ'vɛʃ] *adj* tight ♦ *adv* closely; ~ **a** right by; (*na conta*) just.

***NB**: European Portuguese adds the following consonants to certain words:* **b** (sú(b)dito, su(b)til); **c** (a(c)ção, a(c)cionista, a(c)to); **m** (inde(m)ne); **p** (ado(p)ção, ado(p)tar); *for further details see p. xiii.*

reta ['xɛta] *f* (*linha*) straight line; (*trecho de estrada*) straight; ~ **final** *ou* **de chegada** home straight; **na** ~ **final** (*tb fig*) on the home straight.

retaguarda [xeta'gwaxda] *f* rearguard; (*posição*) rear.

retalhar [xeta'ʎa*] *vt* to cut up; (*separar*) to divide; (*despedaçar*) to shred; (*ferir*) to slash.

retalho [xe'taʎu] *m* (*de pano*) scrap, remnant; **vender a** ~ (PT) to sell retail; **colcha de** ~**s** patchwork quilt.

retaliação [xetalja'sãw] (*pl* **-ões**) *f* retaliation.

retaliar [xeta'lja*] *vt* to repay ♦ *vi* to retaliate.

retangular [xetãgu'la*] *adj* rectangular.

retângulo [xe'tãgulu] *m* rectangle.

retardado/a [xetax'dadu/a] *adj* (PSICO) retarded.

retardar [xetax'da*] *vt* to hold up, delay; (*adiar*) to postpone.

retardatário/a [xetaxda'tarju/a] *m/f* latecomer.

retardo [xe'taxdu] *m* (PSICO) retardedness.

retenção [xetẽ'sãw] *f* retention.

reter [xe'te*] (*irreg*: *como* **ter**) *vt* (*guardar*, *manter*) to keep; (*deter*) to stop, detain; (*segurar*) to hold; (*ladrão*, *suspeito*) to detain, hold; (*na memória*) to retain; (*lágrimas*, *impulsos*) to hold back; (*impedir de sair*) to keep back; ~**-se** *vr* to restrain o.s.

retesado/a [xete'zadu/a] *adj* taut.

retesar [xete'za*] *vt* (*músculo*) to flex; (*corda*) to pull taut.

reteve [xe'tevi] *vb V* **reter**.

reticência [xetʃi'sẽsja] *f* reticence, reserve; ~**s** *fpl* suspension points.

reticente [xetʃi'sẽtʃi] *adj* reticent.

retidão [xetʃi'dãw] *f* (*integridade*) rectitude; (*de linha*) straightness.

retificar [xetʃifi'ka*] *vt* to rectify.

retinha [xe'tʃiɲa] *etc vb V* **reter**.

retinir [xetʃi'ni*] *vi* (*ferros*) to clink; (*campainha*) to ring, jingle; (*ressoar*) to resound.

retirada [xetʃi'rada] *f* (MIL) withdrawal, retreat; (*salário*, *saque*) withdrawal; **bater em** ~ to beat a retreat.

retirado/a [xetʃi'radu/a] *adj* (*vida*) solitary; (*lugar*) isolated.

retirante [xetʃi'rãtʃi] *m/f* migrant (*from the NE of Brazil*).

retirar [xetʃi'ra*] *vt* to withdraw; (*tirar*) to take out; (*afastar*) to take away, remove; (*fazer sair*) to get out; (*ganhar*) to make; ~**-se** *vr* to withdraw; (*de uma festa etc*) to leave; (*da política etc*) to retire; (*recolher-se*) to retire, withdraw; (MIL) to retreat.

retiro [xe'tʃiru] *m* retreat.

retitude [xetʃi'tudʒi] *f* rectitude.

retive [xe'tʃivi] *etc vb V* **reter**.

retiver [xetʃi've*] *etc vb V* **reter**.

reto/a ['xɛtu/a] *adj* straight; (*fig*: *justo*) fair; (: *honesto*) honest, upright ♦ *m* (ANAT) rectum.

retocar [xeto'ka*] *vt* (*pintura*) to touch up; (*texto*) to tidy up.

retomar [xeto'ma*] *vt* to take up again; (*reaver*) to get back.

retoque [xe'tɔki] *etc vb V* **retocar** ♦ *m* finishing touch.

retorcer [xetox'se*] *vt* to twist; ~**-se** *vr* to wriggle, writhe; ~**-se de dor** to writhe in pain.

retórica [xe'tɔrika] *f* rhetoric; (*pej*) affectation.

retórico/a [xe'tɔriku/a] *adj* rhetorical; (*pej*) affected.

retornar [xetox'na*] *vi* to return, go back.

retorno [xe'toxnu] *m* return; (COM) barter, exchange; (*em rodovia*) turning area; **dar** ~ to do a U-turn; ~ **sobre investimento** return on investment; ~ **(do carro)** (COMPUT) (carriage) return.

retorquir [xetox'ki*] *vi* to retort, reply ♦ *vt* to reply; **ela não retorquiu nada** she said nothing in reply.

retractação [xetrata'sãw] (PT) *f* = **retratação**.

retraído/a [xetra'idu/a] *adj* retracted; (*fig*) reserved, timid.

retraimento [xetraj'mẽtu] *m* withdrawal; (*contração*) contraction; (*fig*: *de pessoa*) timidity, shyness.

retrair [xetra'i*] *vt* to withdraw; (*contrair*) to contract; (*pessoa*) to make reserved; ~**-se** *vr* to withdraw; (*encolher-se*) to retract.

retrasado/a [xetra'zadu/a] *adj*: **a semana retrasada** the week before last.

retratação [xetrata'sãw] (*pl* **-ões**) *f* retraction.

retratar [xetra'ta*] *vt* to portray, depict; (*mostrar*) to show; (*dito*) to retract; ~**-se** *vr*: ~**-se (de algo)** to retract (sth).

retrátil [xe'tratʃiw] (*pl* **-eis**) *adj* retractable; **cinto de segurança** ~ inertia-reel seat belt.

retratista [xetra'tʃiʃta] *m/f* portraitist.

retrato [xe'tratu] *m* portrait; (FOTO) photo; (*fig*: *efígie*) likeness; (: *representação*) portrayal; **ela é o** ~ **da mãe** she's the image of her mother; **tirar um** ~ **(de alguém)** to take a photo (of sb); ~ **a meio corpo/de corpo inteiro** half/full-length portrait; ~ **falado** identikit picture.

retribuição [xetribwi'sãw] (*pl* **-ões**) *f* reward, recompense; (*pagamento*) remuneration; (*de hospitalidade*, *favor*) return, reciprocation.

retribuir [xetri'bwi*] *vt* (*recompensar*) to reward, recompense; (*pagar*) to remunerate; (*hospitalidade*, *favor*, *sentimento*, *visita*) to return.

retroactivo/a [xetroa'tivu/a] (PT) *adj* = **retroativo**.

retroagir [xetroa'ʒi*] *vi* (*lei*) to be retroactive; (*modificar o que está feito*) to change what has been done.

retroativo/a [xetroa'tʃivu/a] *adj* retroactive; (*pagamento*): ~ **(a)** backdated (to).

retroceder [xetrose'de*] *vi* to retreat, fall back; (*decair*) to decline; (*num intento*) to back down.

retrocesso [xetro'sɛsu] *m* retreat; (*ao passado*) return; (*decadência*) decline; (*tecla*) backspace (key); (*da economia*) slowdown.

retrógrado/a [xe'trɔgradu/a] *adj* retrograde; (*reacionário*) reactionary.

retroprojetor [xetroproʒe'to*] *m* overhead projector.

retrospectiva [xetroʃpek'tʃiva] *f* retrospective.

retrospectivamente [xetroʃpektʃiva'mẽtʃi] *adv* in retrospect.

retrospectivo/a [xetroʃpek'tʃivu/a] *adj* retrospective.

retrospecto [xetro'ʃpɛktu] *m* retrospective look; **em ~** in retrospect.

retrovisor [xetrovi'zo*] *adj*, *m*: **(espelho) ~** (rear-view) mirror.

retrucar [xetru'ka*] *vi* to retort, reply ♦ *vt* to retort.

retumbância [xetũ'bãsja] *f* resonance.

retumbante [xetũ'bãtʃi] *adj* (*tb fig*) resounding.

retumbar [xetũ'ba*] *vi* to resound, echo; (*ribombar*) to rumble, boom.

returco [xe'tuxku] *etc vb V* **retorquir**.

réu/ré [xɛw/xɛ] *m/f* defendant; (*culpado*) culprit, criminal; **~ de morte** condemned man.

reumático/a [xew'matʃiku/a] *adj* rheumatic.

reumatismo [xewma'tʃiʒmu] *m* rheumatism.

reumatologista [xewmatolo'ʒiʃta] *m/f* rheumatologist.

reunião [xeu'njãw] (*pl* **-ões**) *f* meeting; (*ato, reencontro*) reunion; (*festa*) get-together; party; **~ de cúpula** summit (meeting); **~ de diretoria** board meeting.

reunir [xeu'ni*] *vt* (*pessoas*) to bring together; (*partes*) to join, unite; (*qualidades*) to combine; **~-se** *vr* to meet; (*amigos*) to meet, get together; **~-se a** to join.

reutilizar [xeutʃili'za*] *vt* to re-use.

revalorizar [xevalori'za*] *vt* (*moeda*) to revalue.

revanche [xe'vãʃi] *f* revenge; (ESPORTE) return match.

revê [xe've] *etc vb V* **rever**.

reveillon [xeve'jõ] *m* New Year's Eve.

revejo [xe'veʒu] *etc vb V* **rever**.

revelação [xevela'sãw] (*pl* **-ões**) *f* revelation; (FOTO) development; (*novo cantor, ator etc*) promising newcomer.

revelar [xeve'la*] *vt* to reveal; (*mostrar*) to show; (FOTO) to develop; **~-se** *vr* to turn out to be; **ela se revelou nessa crise** she showed her true colo(u)rs in this crisis.

revelia [xeve'lia] *f* default; **à ~** by default; **à ~ de** without the knowledge *ou* consent of.

revendedor(a) [xevẽde'do*(a)] *m/f* dealer.

revender [xevẽ'de*] *vt* to resell.

rever [xe've*] (*irreg*: *como* **ver**) *vt* to see again; (*examinar*) to check; (*revisar*) to check, revise; (*provas tipográficas*) to proofread.

reverberar [xevexbe'ra*] *vt* (*luz*) to reflect ♦ *vi* to be reflected.

reverdecer [xevexde'se*] *vt*, *vi* to turn green again.

reverência [xeve'rẽsja] *f* reverence, respect; (*ato*) bow; (: *de mulher*) curtsey; **fazer uma ~** to bow; to curtsey.

reverenciar [xeverẽ'sja*] *vt* to revere, venerate; (*obedecer*) to obey.

reverendo/a [xeve'rẽdu/a] *adj* venerable ♦ *m* priest, clergyman.

reverente [xeve'rẽtʃi] *adj* reverential.

reversão [xevex'sãw] (*pl* **-ões**) *f* reversion.

reversível [xevex'sivew] (*pl* **-eis**) *adj* reversible.

reverso [xe'vɛxsu] *m* reverse; **o ~ da medalha** (*fig*) the other side of the coin.

reversões [xevex'sõjʃ] *fpl de* **reversão**.

reverter [xevex'te*] *vt* to revert; (*a questão*) to return; **~ em benefício de** to benefit.

revertério [xevex'tɛrju] *m*: **dar o ~** (*col*) to go wrong.

revés [xe'vɛʃ] *m* reverse; (*infortúnio*) setback, mishap; **ao ~** (*roupa*) inside out; **de ~** (*olhar*) askance.

revestimento [xeveʃtʃi'mẽtu] *m* (*da parede*) covering; (*de sofá*) cover; (*de caixa*) lining.

revestir [xeveʃ'tʃi*] *vt* (*traje*) to put on; (*cobrir*: *paredes etc*) to cover; (*interior de uma caixa etc*) to line; **~-se** *vr*: **~-se de** (*poderes*) to assume, take on; (*paciência*) to arm o.s. with; (*coragem*) to take, pluck up; **~ alguém de poderes** *etc* to invest sb with powers *etc*.

revezamento [xeveza'mẽtu] *m* alternation.

revezar [xeve'za*] *vt* to alternate ♦ *vi* to take turns, alternate; **~-se** *vr* to take turns, alternate.

revi [xe'vi] *vb V* **rever**.

revia [xe'via] *etc vb V* **rever**.

revidar [xevi'da*] *vt* (*soco, insulto*) to return; (*retrucar*) to retort; (*crítica*) to rise to, respond to ♦ *vi* to hit back; (*retrucar*) to respond.

revide [xe'vidʒi] *m* response.

revigorar [xevigo'ra*] *vt* to reinvigorate ♦ *vi* to regain one's strength; **~-se** *vr* to regain one's strength.

revir [xe'vi*] *etc vb V* **rever**.

revirado/a [xevi'radu/a] *adj* (*casa*) untidy, upside-down.

revirar [xevi'ra*] *vt* to turn round; (*gaveta*) to turn out, go through; **~-se** *vr* (*na cama*) to toss and turn; **~ os olhos** to roll one's eyes.

reviravolta [xevira'vɔwta] *f* about-turn, U-turn; (*mudança da situação*) turn.

NB: *European Portuguese adds the following consonants to certain words:* **b** (sú(b)dito, su(b)til); **c** (a(c)ção, a(c)cionista, a(c)to); **m** (inde(m)ne); **p** (ado(p)ção, ado(p)tar); *for further details see p. xiii.*

revisão [xevi'zãw] (*pl* **-ões**) *f* revision; (*de máquina*) overhaul; (*de carro*) service; (*JUR*) appeal; ~ **de provas** proofreading.
revisar [xevi'za*] *vt* to revise; (*prova tipográfica*) to proofread.
revisões [xevi'zõjʃ] *fpl de* **revisão**.
revisor(a) [xevi'zo*(a)] *m/f* (*FERRO*) ticket inspector; (*de provas*) proofreader.
revista [xe'viʃta] *f* (*busca*) search; (*MIL, exame*) inspection; (*publicação*) magazine; (: *profissional, erudita*) journal; (*TEATRO*) revue; **passar** ~ **a** to review; (*MIL*) to inspect, review; ~ **em quadrinhos** comic; ~ **literária** literary review; ~ **para mulheres** women's magazine.
revistar [xeviʃ'ta*] *vt* to search; (*tropa*) to review; (*examinar*) to examine.
revisto [xe'viʃtu] *etc vb V* **revestir**.
revisto/a [xe'viʃtu/a] *pp de* **rever**.
revitalizar [xevitali'za*] *vt* to revitalize.
reviu [xe'viu] *vb V* **rever**.
reviver [xevi've*] *vt* to relive; (*costumes, palavras*) to revive ♦ *vi* to come back to life; (*doente*) to pick up.
revocar [xevo'ka*] *vt* (*o passado*) to evoke; (*mandar voltar*) to recall; ~ **alguém a/de** to bring sb back to/from.
revogação [xevoga'sãw] (*pl* **-ões**) *f* (*de lei*) repeal; (*de ordem*) reversal.
revogar [xevo'ga*] *vt* to revoke.
revolta [xe'vɔwta] *f* revolt; (*fig: indignação*) disgust.
revoltado/a [xevow'tadu/a] *adj* (*indignado*) disgusted; (*amargo*) bitter; (*revoltoso*) in revolt.
revoltante [xevow'tãtʃi] *adj* disgusting; (*repugnante*) revolting.
revoltar [xevow'ta*] *vt* to disgust; (*insurgir*) to incite to revolt ♦ *vi* to cause indignation; **~-se** *vr* to rebel, revolt; (*indignar-se*) to be disgusted.
revolto/a [xe'vowtu/a] *pp de* **revolver** ♦ *adj* (*década*) turbulent; (*mundo*) troubled; (*cabelo*) dishevelled; (*mar*) rough; (*desarrumado*) untidy.
revoltoso/a [xevow'tozu/ɔza] *adj* in revolt.
revolução [xevolu'sãw] (*pl* **-ões**) *f* revolution.
revolucionar [xevolusjo'na*] *vt* to revolutionize.
revolucionário/a [xevolusjo'narju/a] *adj, m/f* revolutionary.
revoluções [xevolu'sõjʃ] *fpl de* **revolução**.
revolver [xevow've*] *vt* (*terra*) to turn over, dig over; (*gaveta*) to rummage through; (*olhos*) to roll; (*suj: vento*) to blow around ♦ *vi* (*girar*) to revolve, rotate.
revólver [xe'vɔwve*] *m* revolver, gun.
reza ['xɛza] *f* prayer.
rezar [xe'za*] *vt* (*missa, prece*) to say ♦ *vi* to pray; ~ **(que)** (*contar, dizer*) to state (that).
RFA *abr f* (*antes: República Federal Alemã*) FRG.
RFFSA (*BR*) *abr f* = **Rede Ferroviária Federal SA**.
RG (*BR*) *abr m* (= *Registro Geral*) *identity document*.
rh *abr*: **factor** ~ Rh. *ou* rhesus (*BRIT*) factor; ~ **negativo/positivo** rhesus negative/positive.
riacho ['xjaʃu] *m* stream, brook.
ribalta [xi'bawta] *f* footlights *pl*; (*fig*) boards *pl*.
ribanceira [xibã'sejra] *f* (*margem*) steep river bank; (*rampa*) steep slope; (*precipício*) cliff.
ribeira [xi'bejra] *f* riverside; (*riacho*) river.
ribeirão [xibej'rãw] (*BR*: *pl* **-ões**) *m* stream.
ribeirinho/a [xibej'riɲu/a] *adj* riverside *atr*.
ribeiro [xi'bejru] *m* brook, stream.
ribeirões [xibej'rõjʃ] *mpl de* **ribeirão**.
ribombar [xibõ'ba*] *vi* (*trovão*) to rumble, boom; (*ressoar*) to resound.
ricaço [xi'kasu] *m* plutocrat, very rich man.
rícino ['xisinu] *m* castor-oil plant; **óleo de** ~ castor oil.
rico/a ['xiku/a] *adj* rich; (*PT*: *lindo*) beautiful; (: *excelente*) splendid ♦ *m/f* rich man/woman.
ricochetear [xikoʃe'tʃja*] *vi* to ricochet.
ricota [xi'kɔta] *f* cream cheese.
ridicularizar [xidʒikulari'za*] *vt* to ridicule.
ridículo/a [xi'dʒikulu/a] *adj* ridiculous.
rifa ['xifa] *f* raffle.
rifão [xi'fãw] (*pl* **-ões** *ou* **-ães**) *m* proverb, saying.
rifar [xi'fa*] *vt* to raffle; (*col: abandonar*) to dump.
rififi [xifi'fi] (*col*) *m* fight, brawl.
rifle ['xifli] *m* rifle.
rifões [xi'fõjʃ] *mpl de* **rifão**.
rigidez [xiʒi'deʒ] *f* rigidity, stiffness; (*austeridade*) severity, strictness; (*inflexibilidade*) inflexibility.
rígido/a ['xiʒidu/a] *adj* rigid, stiff; (*fig*) strict.
rigor [xi'go*] *m* rigidity; (*meticulosidade*) rigour (*BRIT*), rigor (*US*); (*severidade*) harshness, severity; (*exatidão*) precision; **a** ~ strictly speaking; **vestido a** ~ in full evening dress; **ser de** ~ to be essential *ou* obligatory; **no** ~ **do inverno** in the depths of winter.
rigoroso/a [xigo'rozu/ɔza] *adj* rigorous, strict; (*severo*) strict; (*exigente*) demanding; (*minucioso*) precise, accurate; (*inverno*) hard, harsh.
rijo/a ['xiʒu/a] *adj* tough, hard; (*severo*) harsh, severe; (*músculos, braços*) firm.
rim [xĩ] (*pl* **-ns**) *m* kidney; **rins** *mpl* (*parte inferior das costas*) small *sg* of the back.
rima ['xima] *f* rhyme; (*poema*) verse, poem.
rimar [xi'ma*] *vt, vi* to rhyme; ~ **com** (*condizer*) to agree with, tally with.
rímel ['ximew] (®: *pl* **-eis**) *m* mascara.
rinçagem [xĩ'saʒẽ] (*pl* **-ns**) *f* rinse.
rinçar [xĩ'sa*] *vt* to rinse.
rinchar [xĩ'ʃa*] *vi* to neigh, whinny.
rincho ['xĩʃu] *m* neigh(ing).
ringue ['xĩgi] *m* ring.
rinha ['xiɲa] *f* cock-fight.
rinoceronte [xinose'rõtʃi] *m* rhinoceros.

rinque ['xĩki] *m* rink.
rins [xĩʃ] *mpl de* **rim**.
Rio ['xiu] *m*: **o ~ (de Janeiro)** Rio (de Janeiro).
rio ['xiu] *m* river.
ripa ['xipa] *f* lath, slat.
riqueza [xi'keza] *f* wealth, riches *pl*; (*qualidade*) richness; (*fartura*) abundance; (*fecundidade*) fertility.
rir [xi*] *vi* to laugh; **~ de** to laugh at; **morrer de ~** to laugh one's head off.
risada [xi'zada] *f* (*riso*) laughter; (*gargalhada*) guffaw.
risca ['xiʃka] *f* stroke; (*listra*) stripe; (*no cabelo*) parting; **à ~** to the letter, exactly.
riscar [xiʃ'ka*] *vt* (*papel*) to draw lines on; (*marcar*) to mark; (*apagar*) to cross out; (*desenhar*) to outline; (*fósforo*) to strike; (*expulsar: sócios*) to expel, throw out; (*eliminar*) to do away with; (*amigo*) to write off.
risco ['xiʃku] *m* (*marca*) mark, scratch; (*traço*) stroke; (*desenho*) drawing, sketch; (*perigo*) risk; **sob o ~ de** at the risk of; **correr o ~ de** to run the risk of; **correr ~s** to take risks; **pôr em ~** to put at risk, risk.
risível [xi'zivew] (*pl* **-eis**) *adj* laughable, ridiculous.
riso ['xizu] *m* laughter; **não ser motivo de ~** to be no laughing matter.
risonho/a [xi'zɔɲu/a] *adj* laughing, smiling; (*contente*) cheerful; **estar muito ~** to be all smiles.
risoto [xi'zotu] *m* risotto.
rispidez [xiʃpi'deʒ] *f* brusqueness; (*aspereza*) harshness.
ríspido/a ['xiʃpidu/a] *adj* brusque; (*áspero*) harsh.
risquei [xiʃ'kej] *etc vb V* **riscar**.
rissole [xi'sɔli] *m* rissole.
riste ['xiʃtʃi] *m*: **em ~** (*dedo*) pointing; (*orelhas*) pointed.
rítmico/a ['xitʃmiku/a] *adj* rhythmic(al)
ritmo ['xitʃmu] *m* rhythm.
rito ['xitu] *m* rite; (*seita*) cult.
ritual [xi'twaw] (*pl* **-ais**) *adj*, *m* ritual.
rival [xi'vaw] (*pl* **-ais**) *adj*, *m/f* rival.
rivalidade [xivali'dadʒi] *f* rivalry.
rivalizar [xivali'za*] *vt* to rival ♦ *vi*: **~ com** to compete with, vie with.
rixa ['xiʃa] *f* quarrel, fight.
RJ *abr* = **Rio de Janeiro**.
RN *abr* = **Rio Grande do Norte**.
RNVA (*BR*) *abr m* = **Registro Nacional de Veículos Automotores**.
RO *abr* = **Rondônia**.
roa ['xoa] *etc vb V* **roer**.
robalo [xo'balu] *m* snook (*type of fish*).
robô [xo'bo] *m* robot.
robustecer [xobuʃte'se*] *vt* to strengthen ♦ *vi* to become stronger; **~-se** *vr* to become stronger.
robustez [xobuʃ'teʒ] *f* strength.
robusto/a [xo'buʃtu/a] *adj* strong, robust.
roça ['xɔsa] *f* plantation; (*no mato*) clearing; (*campo*) country.
roçado [xo'sadu] *m* clearing.
rocambole [xokã'bɔli] *m* roll.
roçar [xo'sa*] *vt* (*terreno*) to clear; (*tocar de leve*) to brush against ♦ *vi*: **~ em** *ou* **por** to brush against.
roceiro [xo'sejru/a] *m/f* (*lavrador*) peasant; (*caipira*) country bumpkin.
rocha ['xɔʃa] *f* rock; (*penedo*) crag.
rochedo [xo'ʃedu] *m* crag, cliff.
rock ['xɔki] *m* = **roque**.
rock-and-roll [-ã'xɔw] *m* rock and roll.
roda ['xɔda] *f* wheel; (*círculo, grupo de pessoas*) circle; (*de saia*) width, fullness; **~ dentada** cog(wheel); **alta ~** high society; **em** *ou* **à ~ de** round, around; **~ de direção** steering wheel; **~ do leme** ship's wheel, helm; **brincar de ~** to play in the round.
rodada [xo'dada] *f* (*de bebidas*, *ESPORTE*) round.
roda-d'água (*pl* **rodas-d'água**) *f* water wheel.
rodado/a [xo'dadu/a] *adj* (*saia*) full, wide; **o carro tem 5000 km ~s** the car has 5000 km on the clock.
rodagem [xo'daʒẽ] (*pl* **-ns**) *f V* **estrada**.
roda-gigante (*pl* **rodas-gigantes**) *f* big wheel.
rodamoinho [xodamo'iɲu] *m* (*na água*) whirlpool; (*de vento*) whirlwind; (*no cabelo*) swirl.
Ródano ['xɔdanu] *m*: **o ~** the Rhône.
rodapé [xoda'pɛ] *m* skirting board (*BRIT*), baseboard (*US*); (*de página*) foot.
rodar [xo'da*] *vt* (*fazer girar*) to turn, spin; (*viajar por*) to tour, travel; (*percorrer de carro*) to drive round; (*a pé*) to walk round; (*quilômetros*) to do; (*filme*) to make; (*imprimir*) to print; (*COMPUT: programa*) to run ♦ *vi* (*girar*) to turn round; (*AUTO*) to drive around; (*col: ser reprovado*) to fail; (*: sair*) to make o.s. scarce; (*: ser excluido*) to be ruled out; **~ por** (*a pé*) to wander around; (*de carro*) to drive around.
roda-viva (*pl* **rodas-vivas**) *f* bustle, commotion; **estou numa ~ danada** I'm in a real flap.
rodear [xo'dʒja*] *vt* to go round; (*circundar*) to encircle, surround; (*pessoa*) to surround.
rodeio [xo'deju] *m* (*em discurso*) circumlocution; (*subterfúgio*) subterfuge; (*de gado*) round-up; **fazer ~s** to beat about the bush; **sem ~s** plainly, frankly.
rodela [xo'dɛla] *f* (*pedaço*) slice.
rodízio [xo'dʒizju] *m* rota; **à ~** (*em restaurante*) at discretion; **em ~** on a rota basis.
rodo ['xodu] *m* rake; (*para puxar água*) water

***NB**: European Portuguese adds the following consonants to certain words:* **b** (sú(b)dito, su(b)til); **c** (a(c)ção, a(c)cionista, a(c)to); **m** (inde(m)ne); **p** (ado(p)ção, ado(p)tar); *for further details see p. xiii.*

rake; **a ~** in abundance.
rododentro [xodo'dẽtru] *m* rhododendron.
rodoferroviário/a [xodofexo'vjarju/a] *adj* road and rail *atr*.
rodopiar [xodo'pja*] *vi* to whirl around, swirl.
rodopio [xodo'piu] *m* spin.
rodovia [xodo'via] *f* highway, ≈ motorway (*BRIT*), ≈ interstate (*US*).
rodoviária [xodo'vjarja] *f* (*tb*: *estação ~*) bus station; *V tb* **rodoviário**.
rodoviário/a [xodo'vjarju/a] *adj* road *atr*; (*polícia*) traffic *atr* ♦ *m/f* roadworker.
roedor(a) [xwe'do*(a)] *adj* gnawing ♦ *m* rodent.
roer [xwe*] *vt* to gnaw, nibble; (*enferrujar*) to corrode; (*afligir*) to eat away; **ser duro de ~** to be a hard nut to crack.
rogado [xo'gadu] *adj*: **fazer-se de ~** to play hard to get.
rogar [xo'ga*] *vi* to ask, request; **~ a alguém que faça** to beg sb to do.
rogo ['xogu] *m* request; **a ~ de** at the request of.
rói [xɔj] *vb V* **roer**.
roía [xo'ia] *etc vb V* **roer**.
róis [xɔjʃ] *mpl de* **rol**.
rojão [xo'ʒãw] (*pl* **-ões**) *m* (*foguete*) rocket; (*fig*: *ritmo intenso*) hectic pace; **agüentar o ~** (*fig*) to stick it out.
rol [xɔw] (*pl* **róis**) *m* roll, list.
rolagem [xo'laʒẽ] *f* (*de uma dívida*) snowballing.
rolar [xo'la*] *vt* to roll; (*dívida*) to run up ♦ *vi* to roll; (*na cama*) to toss and turn; (*col*: *vinho etc*) to flow; (: *estender-se*) to roll on.
roldana [xow'dana] *f* pulley.
roleta [xo'leta] *f* roulette; (*borboleta*) turnstile.
roleta-paulista *f*: **fazer uma ~** (*AUTO*) to go through a red light.
roleta-russa *f* Russian roulette.
rolha ['xoʎa] *f* cork; (*fig*) gag (on free speech).
roliço/a [xo'lisu/a] *adj* (*pessoa*) plump, chubby; (*objeto*) round, cylindrical.
rolo ['xolu] *m* (*de papel etc*) roll; (*para nivelar o solo, para pintura*) roller; (*almofada*) bolster; (*para cabelo*) curler; (*col*: *briga*) brawl, fight; **~ compressor** streamroller; **~ de massa** *ou* **pastel** rolling pin.
Roma ['xoma] *n* Rome.
romã [xo'mã] *f* pomegranate.
romance [xo'mãsi] *m* (*livro*) novel; (*caso amoroso*) romance; (*fig*: *história*) complicated story; **~ policial** detective story; **fazer um ~ (de algo)** (*exagerar*) to dramatize (sth).
romanceado/a [xomã'sjadu/a] *adj* (*biografia*) in the style of a novel; (*exagerado*) exaggerated, fanciful.
romancear [xomã'sja*] *vt* (*biografia*) to write in the style of a novel; (*exagerar*) to exaggerate, embroider ♦ *vi* (*inventar histórias*) to tell tales.
romancista [xomã'siʃta] *m/f* novelist.
românico/a [xo'maniku/a] *adj* (*LING*) Romance; (*ARQ*) romanesque.
romano/a [xo'manu/a] *adj*, *m/f* Roman.
romântico/a [xo'mãtʃiku/a] *adj* romantic.
romantismo [xomã'tʃiʒmu] *m* romanticism; (*romance*) romance.
romaria [xoma'ria] *f* (*peregrinação*) pilgrimage; (*festa*) festival.
rombo ['xõbu] *m* (*buraco*) hole; (*MAT*) rhombus; (*fig*: *desfalque*) embezzlement; (: *prejuízo*) loss, shortfall.
rombudo/a [xõ'budu/a] *adj* very blunt.
romeiro/a [xo'mejru/a] *m/f* pilgrim.
Romênia [xo'menja] *f*: **a ~** Romania.
romeno/a [xo'mɛnu/a] *adj*, *m/f* Rumanian ♦ *m* (*LING*) Rumanian.
romeu-e-julieta [xo'mewiʒu'ljeta] *m* (*CULIN*) *guava jelly with cheese*.
rompante [xõ'pãtʃi] *m* outburst.
romper [xõ'pe*] *vt* to break; (*rasgar*) to tear; (*relações*) to break off ♦ *vi* (*sol*, *manhã*) to break through; **~ com** to break with; **~ de** (*jorrar*) to well up from; **~ em pranto** *ou* **lágrimas** to burst into tears; **~ em soluços** to sob.
rompimento [xõpi'mẽtu] *m* (*ato*) breakage; (*fenda*) break; (*de relações*) breaking off.
roncar [xõ'ka*] *vi* to snore.
ronco ['xõku] *m* snore; (*de motor*) roar; (*de porco*) grunt.
ronda ['xõda] *f* patrol, beat; **fazer a ~** to go the rounds.
rondar [xõ'da*] *vt* to patrol, go the rounds of; (*espreitar*) to prowl, hang around; (*rodear*) to go round ♦ *vi* to prowl about, lurk; (*fazer a ronda*) to patrol, do the rounds; **a inflação ronda os 30% ao mês** inflation is in the region of 30% a month.
rondoniano/a [xõdo'njanu/a] *adj* from Rondônia ♦ *m/f* person from Rondônia.
ronquei [xõ'kej] *etc vb V* **roncar**.
ronqueira [xõ'kejra] *f* wheeze.
ronrom [xõ'xõ] *m* purring.
ronronar [xõxo'na*] *vi* to purr.
roque ['xɔkɪ] *m* (*XADREZ*) rook, castle; (*MÚS*) rock.
roqueiro/a [xo'kejru/a] *m/f* rock musician.
roraimense [xoraj'mẽsi] *adj* from Roraima ♦ *m/f* person from Roraima.
rosa ['xɔza] *f* rose ♦ *adj inv* pink; **a vida não é feita de ~s** life is not a bed of roses.
rosado/a [xo'zadu/a] *adj* rosy, pink.
rosa-dos-ventos *f inv* compass.
rosário [xo'zarju] *m* rosary.
rosa-shocking [-'ʃɔkĩŋ] *adj inv* shocking pink.
rosbife [xoʒ'bifi] *m* roast beef.
rosca ['xoʃka] *f* spiral, coil; (*de parafuso*) thread; (*pão*) *ring-shaped loaf*.
roseira [xo'zejra] *f* rosebush.
róseo/a ['xɔzju/a] *adj* rosy.
roseta [xo'zeta] *f* rosette.
rosetar [xoze'ta*] *vi* to loaf around.

rosnar [xoʒ'na*] *vi* (*cão*) to growl, snarl; (*murmurar*) to mutter, mumble.
rossio [xo'siu] (*PT*) *m* large square.
rosto ['xoʃtu] *m* (*cara*) face; (*frontispício*) title page.
rota ['xɔta] *f* route, course.
rotação [xota'sãw] (*pl* **-ões**) *f* rotation; ~ **de estoques** turnover of stock.
rotativa [xota'tʃiva] *f* rotary printing press.
rotatividade [xotatʃivi'dadʒi] *f* rotation; **hotel de alta** ~ hotel renting rooms by the hour, motel.
rotativo/a [xota'tʃivu/a] *adj* rotary.
roteirista [xotej'riʃta] *m/f* scriptwriter.
roteiro [xo'tejru] *m* (*itinerário*) itinerary; (*ordem*) schedule; (*guia*) guidebook; (*de filme*) script; (*de discussão, trabalho escrito*) list of topics; (*fig*: *norma*) norm.
rotina [xo'tʃina] *f* (*tb*: *COMPUT*) routine.
rotineiro/a [xotʃi'nejru/a] *adj* routine.
roto/a ['xotu/a] *adj* broken; (*rasgado*) torn; (*maltrapilho*) scruffy; **o** ~ **rindo do esfarrapado** the pot calling the kettle black.
rótula ['xɔtula] *f* (*ANAT*) kneecap.
rotular [xotu'la*] *vt* (*tb fig*) to label; ~ **alguém/algo de** to label sb/sth as.
rótulo ['xɔtulu] *m* label, tag; (*fig*) label.
rotunda [xo'tũda] *f* (*ARQ*) rotunda.
rotundo/a [xo'tũdu/a] *adj* (*redondo*) round; (*gorducho*) rotund.
roubalheira [xoba'ʎejra] *f* (*roubo vultoso*) wholesale robbery; (*do Estado, de empresa*) embezzlement.
roubar [xo'ba*] *vt* to steal; (*loja, casa, pessoa*) to rob ♦ *vi* to steal; (*em jogo, no preço*) to cheat; ~ **algo a alguém** to steal sth from sb.
roubo ['xobu] *m* theft, robbery; **$100 é** ~ $100 is daylight robbery.
rouco/a ['roku/a] *adj* hoarse.
round ['xãwdʒi] (*pl* ~**s**) *m BOXE*) round.
roupa ['xopa] *f* clothes *pl*, clothing; ~ **de baixo** underwear; ~ **de cama** bedclothes *pl*, bed linen.
roupagem [xo'paʒẽ] (*pl* **-ns**) *f* clothes *pl*, apparel; (*fig*) appearance.
roupão [xo'pãw] (*pl* **-ões**) *m* dressing gown.
rouquidão [xoki'dãw] *f* hoarseness.
rouxinol [xoʃi'nɔw] (*pl* **-óis**) *m* nightingale.
roxo/a ['xoʃu/a] *adj* purple, violet; ~ **por** (*col*) mad about; ~ **de saudades** pining away.
royalty ['xɔjawtʃi] (*pl* **-ies**) *m* royalty.
RR *abr* = **Roraima**.
RS *abr* = **Rio Grande do Sul**.
rua ['xua] *f* street ♦ *excl*: ~! get out!, clear off!; **botar alguém na** ~ to put sb out on the street; **ir para a** ~ to go out; (*ser despedido*) to get the sack; **viver na** ~ to be out all the time; **estar na** ~ **da amargura** to be going through hell; ~ **principal** main street; ~ **sem saída** no through road, cul-de-sac.
Ruanda ['xwãda] *f* Rwanda.
rubéola [xu'bɛola] *f* (*MED*) German measles.
rubi [xu'bi] *m* ruby.
rublo ['xublu] *m* r(o)uble.
rubor [xu'bo*] *m* blush; (*fig*) shyness, bashfulness.
ruborizar [xubori'za*] *vt* to make blush; ~**-se** *vr* to blush.
rubrica [xu'brika] *f* signed initials *pl*.
rubricar [xubri'ka*] *vt* to initial.
rubro/a ['xubru/a] *adj* ruby-red; (*faces*) rosy, ruddy.
rubro-negro/a *adj* of Flamengo FC.
ruço/a ['xusu/a] *adj* grey (*BRIT*), gray (*US*), dun; (*desbotado*) faded; (*col*) tough, tricky.
rude ['xudʒi] *adj* (*povo*) simple, primitive; (*ignorante*) simple; (*grosseiro*) rude.
rudeza [xu'deza] *f* simplicity; (*grosseria*) rudeness.
rudimentar [xudʒimẽ'ta*] *adj* rudimentary.
rudimento [xudʒi'mẽtu] *m* rudiment; ~**s** *mpl* rudiments, first principles.
ruela ['xwɛla] *f* lane, alley.
rufar [xu'fa*] *vt* (*tambor*) to roll ♦ *m* roll.
rufião [xu'fjãw] (*pl* **-ães** *ou* **-ões**) *m* pimp.
ruflar [xuf'la*] *vt*, *vi* to rustle.
ruga ['xuga] *f* (*na pele*) wrinkle; (*na roupa*) crease.
rúgbi ['xugbi] *m* rugby.
ruge ['xuʒi] *m* rouge.
rugido [xu'ʒidu] *m* roar.
rugir [xu'ʒi*] *vi* to roar, bellow.
ruibarbo [xwi'baxbu] *m* rhubarb.
ruído ['xwidu] *m* noise, din; (*ELET, TEC*) noise.
ruidoso/a [xwi'dozu/ɔza] *adj* noisy.
ruim [xu'ĩ] (*pl* **-ns**) *adj* bad; (*defeituoso*) defective; **achar** ~ (*col*) to get upset.
ruína ['xwina] *f* ruin; (*decadência*) downfall; **levar alguém à** ~ to ruin sb, be sb's downfall.
ruindade [xwĩ'dadʒi] *f* wickedness, evil; (*ação*) bad thing.
ruins [xu'ĩʃ] *adj pl de* **ruim**.
ruir ['xwi*] *vi* to collapse, go to ruin.
ruivo/a ['xwivu/a] *adj* red-haired ♦ *m/f* redhead.
rujo ['xuju] *etc vb V* **rugir**.
rulê [xu'le] *adj*: **gola** ~ roll-neck (collar).
rum [xũ] *m* rum.
rumar [xu'ma*] *vt* (*barco*) to steer ♦ *vi*: ~ **para** to head for.
rumba ['xũba] *f* rumba.
ruminação [xumina'sãw] (*pl* **-ões**) *f* rumination.
ruminante [xumi'nãtʃi] *adj*, *m* ruminant.
ruminar [xumi'na*] *vt* to chew; (*fig*) to ponder ♦ *vi* (*tb fig*) to ruminate.
rumo ['xumu] *m* course, bearing; (*fig*) course; ~ **a** bound for; **sem** ~ adrift.

NB: *European Portuguese adds the following consonants to certain words:* **b** (sú(b)dito, su(b)til); **c** (a(c)ção, a(c)cionista, a(c)to); **m** (inde(m)ne); **p** (ado(p)ção, ado(p)tar); *for further details see p. xiii.*

rumor [xu'mo*] *m* (*ruído*) noise; (*notícia*) rumour (*BRIT*), rumor (*US*), report.
rumorejar [xumore'ʒa*] *vi* to murmur; (*folhas*) to rustle; (*água*) to ripple.
rupia [xu'pia] *f* rupee.
ruptura [xup'tura] *f* break, rupture.
rural [xu'raw] (*pl* **-ais**) *adj* rural.
rusga ['xuʒga] *f* (*briga*) quarrel, row.
rush [xʌʃ] *m* rush; **(a hora do)** ~ rush hour; **o** ~ **imobiliário** the rush to buy property.
Rússia ['xusja] *f*: **a** ~ Russia.
russo/a ['xusu/a] *adj*, *m/f* Russian ♦ *m* (*LING*) Russian.
rústico/a ['xuʃtʃiku/a] *adj* rustic; (*pessoa*) simple; (*utensílio*, *objeto*) rough; (*casa*) rustic-style; (*lugar*) countrified.

S

S, s ['ɛsi] (*pl* **ss**) *m* S, s; **S de Sandra** S for Sugar.
S. *abr* (= *Santo*; *Santa*; *São*) St.
SA *abr* (= *Sociedade Anônima*) Ltd., Inc. (*US*).
sã [sã] *f de* **são.**
Saara [sa'ara] *m*: **o** ~ the Sahara.
sáb. *abr* (= *sábado*) Sat.
sábado ['sabadu] *m* Saturday; (*dos judeus*) Sabbath; ~ **de aleluia** Easter Saturday; *V tb* **terça-feira.**
sabão [sa'bãw] (*pl* **-ões**) *m* soap; (*descompostura*): **passar um** ~ **em alguém/levar um** ~ to give sb a telling-off/get a telling-off; ~ **de coco** coconut soap; ~ **em pó** soap powder.
sabatina [saba'tʃina] *f* revision test.
sabedor(a) [sabe'do*(a)] *adj* informed.
sabedoria [sabedo'ria] *f* wisdom; (*erudição*) learning.
saber [sa'be*] *vt*, *vi* to know; (*descobrir*) to find out ♦ *m* knowledge; ~ **fazer** to know how to do, be able to do; ~ **de cor (e salteado)** to know off by heart; **ele sabe nadar?** can he swim?; **a** ~ namely; **sei lá** (*col*) I've got no idea, heaven knows; **sei** (*col*: *como resposta*) I see; **você é quem sabe, você que sabe** (*col*) it's up to you; **que eu saiba** as far as I know; **sabe de uma coisa?** (*col*) you know what?
Sabesp [sa'bɛʃpi] *abr m* = **Saneamento Básico do Estado de São Paulo.**
sabiá [sa'bja] *m/f* thrush.
sabichão/chona [sabi'ʃãw/'ʃɔna] (*pl* **-ões/~s**) *m/f* know-it-all, smart aleck.
sabido/a [sa'bidu/a] *adj* (*versado*) knowledgeable; (*esperto*) shrewd, clever.
sábio/a ['sabju/a] *adj* wise; (*erudito*) learned ♦ *m/f* wise person; (*erudito*) scholar.
sabões [sa'bõjʃ] *mpl de* **sabão.**
sabonete [sabo'netʃi] *m* toilet soap.
saboneteira [sabone'tejra] *f* soap dish.
sabor [sa'bo*] *m* taste, flavour (*BRIT*), flavor (*US*); **ao** ~ **de** at the mercy of.
saborear [sabo'rja*] *vt* to taste, savour (*BRIT*), savor (*US*); (*fig*) to relish.
saboroso/a [sabo'rozu/ɔza] *adj* tasty, delicious.
sabotador(a) [sabota'do*(a)] *m/f* saboteur.
sabotagem [sabo'taʒẽ] *f* sabotage.
sabotar [sabo'ta*] *vt* to sabotage.
saburrento/a [sabu'xẽtu/a] *adj* (*língua*) furry.
saca ['saka] *f* sack.
sacada [sa'kada] *f* balcony; *V tb* **sacado.**
sacado/a [sa'kadu/a] *m/f* (*COM*) drawee.
sacador(a) [saka'do*(a)] *m/f* (*COM*) drawer.
sacal [sa'kaw] (*col*: *pl* **-ais**) *adj* boring; **ser** ~ to be a pain.
sacana [sa'kana] (*col!*) *adj* (*canalha*) crooked; (*lascivo*) randy.
sacanagem [saka'naʒẽ] (*col*: *pl* **-ns**) *f* (*sujeira*) dirty trick; (*libidinagem*) screwing; **fazer uma** ~ **com alguém** (*sujeira*) to screw sb; **filme de** ~ blue movie.
sacanear [saka'nja*] (*col!*) *vt*: ~ **alguém** (*fazer sujeira*) to screw sb; (*amolar*) to take the piss out of sb (*!*).
sacar [sa'ka*] *vt* to take out, pull out; (*dinheiro*) to withdraw; (*arma*, *cheque*) to draw; (*ESPORTE*) to serve; (*col*: *entender*) to understand ♦ *vi* (*col*: *entender*) to understand; (: *mentir*) to tell fibs; (: *dar palpites*) to talk off the top of one's head; ~ **de um revólver** to pull a gun; ~ **sobre um devedor** to borrow money from sb.
saçaricar [sasari'ka*] *vi* to have fun, fool around.
sacarina [saka'rina] *f* saccharine (*BRIT*), saccharin (*US*).
saca-rolhas *m inv* corkscrew.
sacerdócio [sasex'dɔsju] *m* priesthood.
sacerdote [sasex'dɔtʃi] *m* priest.
sachê [sa'ʃe] *m* sachet.
saci [sa'si] *m* (*in Brazilian folklore*) *one-legged black man who ambushes travellers.*
saciar [sa'sja*] *vt* (*fome etc*) to satisfy; (*sede*) to quench.
saco ['saku] *m* bag; (*enseada*) inlet; (*col*: *testículos*) balls *pl* (*!*); ~**!** (*BR*: *col*) damn!; **que** ~**!** (*BR*: *col*) how boring!; **encher o** ~ **de alguém** (*BR*: *col*) to annoy sb, get on sb's nerves; **estar de** ~ **cheio (de)** to be fed up (with); **haja** ~**!** give me strength!; **puxar o** ~ **de alguém** (*col*) to suck up to sb; **ser um** ~ (*col*) to be a drag; **ter** ~ (*col*) to have patience; **ter** ~ **de fazer algo** to be bothered to do sth; ~ **de água quente** hot water bottle; ~ **de café** coffee filter; ~ **de dormir** sleeping bag.
sacode [sa'kɔdʒi] *etc vb V* **sacudir.**
sacola [sa'kɔla] *f* bag.

sacolejar [sakole'ʒa*] *vt, vi* to shake.
sacramentar [sakramẽ'ta*] *vt* (*documento etc*) to legalize.
sacramento [sakra'mẽtu] *m* sacrament.
sacrificar [sakrifi'ka*] *vt* to sacrifice; (*consagrar*) to dedicate; (*submeter*) to subject; (*animal*) to have put down; **~-se** *vr* to sacrifice o.s.
sacrifício [sakri'fisju] *m* sacrifice.
sacrilégio [sakri'lɛʒu] *m* sacrilege.
sacrílego/a [sa'krilegu/a] *adj* sacrilegious.
sacristão [sakri'ʃtãw] (*pl* **~s** *ou* **-ões**) *m* sacristan, sexton.
sacristia [sakriʃ'tʃia] *f* sacristy.
sacristões [sakriʃ'tõjʃ] *mpl de* **sacristão**.
sacro/a ['sakru/a] *adj* sacred; (*santo*) holy; (*música*) religious.
sacrossanto/a [sakro'sãtu/a] *adj* sacrosanct.
sacudida [saku'dʒida] *f* shake.
sacudidela [sakudʒi'dela] *f* shake, jolt.
sacudido/a [saku'dʒidu/a] *adj* shaken; (*movimento*) rapid, quick; (*robusto*) sturdy.
sacudir [saku'dʒi*] *vt* to shake; **~-se** *vr* to shake.
sádico/a ['sadʒiku/a] *adj* sadistic ♦ *m/f* sadist.
sadio/a [sa'dʒiu/a] *adj* healthy.
sadismo [sa'dʒiʒmu] *m* sadism.
sadomasoquista [sadomazo'kiʃta] *adj* sadomasochistic ♦ *m/f* sadomasochist.
safadeza [safa'deza] *f* (*vileza*) meanness; (*imoralidade*) crudity; (*travessura*) mischief.
safado/a [sa'fadu/a] *adj* (*descarado*) shameless, barefaced; (*imoral*) dirty; (*travesso*) mischievous ♦ *m* rogue; (*imoral*) coarse person; **estar/ficar ~ (da vida) com** to be/get furious with.
safanão [safa'nãw] (*pl* **-ões**) *m* (*puxão*) tug; (*tapa*) slap.
safári [sa'fari] *m* safari.
safira [sa'fira] *f* sapphire.
safo/a ['safu/a] *adj* (*livre*) clear; (*col*: *esperto*) quick, clever.
safra ['safra] *f* harvest; (*fig*: *de músicos etc*) crop.
saga ['saga] *f* saga.
sagacidade [sagasi'dadʒi] *f* sagacity, shrewdness.
sagaz [sa'gajʒ] *adj* sagacious, shrewd.
sagitariano/a [saʒita'rjanu/a] *adj, m/f* Sagittarian.
Sagitário [saʒi'tarju] *m* Sagittarius.
sagrado/a [sa'gradu/a] *adj* sacred, holy.
saguão [sa'gwãw] (*pl* **-ões**) *m* (*pátio*) yard, patio; (*entrada*) foyer, lobby; (*de estação*) entrance hall.
saia ['saja] *f* skirt; (*col*: *mulher*) woman; **viver agarrado às ~s de alguém** (*fig*) to be tied to sb's apron strings; **~ escocesa** kilt.
saibro ['sajbru] *m* gravel.
saia-calça (*pl* **saias-calças**) *f* culottes *pl*.
saiba ['sajba] *etc vb V* **saber**.
saída [sa'ida] *f* (*porta*) exit, way out; (*partida*) departure; (*ato*: *de pessoa*) going out; (*fig*: *solução*) way out; (COMPUT: *de programa*) exit; (: *de dados*) output; **de ~** (*primeiro*) first; (*de cara*) straight away; **estar de ~** to be on one's way out; **na ~ do cinema** on the way out of the cinema; **(não) ter boa ~** (*produto*) (not) to sell well; **uma mercadoria de muita ~** a commodity which sells well; **dar uma ~** to go out; **ter boas ~s** (*réplicas*) to be witty; **não tem ~** (*fig*) there is no escaping it; **~ de emergência** emergency exit.
saideira [saj'dejra] *f* last drink.
saidinha [saj'dʒinha] *f*: **dar uma ~** to pop out.
saiote [sa'jɔtʃi] *m* short skirt.
sair [sa'i*] *vi* to go (*ou* come) out; (*partir*) to leave; (*realizar-se*) to turn out; (COMPUT) to exit; **~-se** *vr*: **~-se bem/mal de** to be successful/unsuccessful in; **~-se com** (*dito*) to come out with; **~ caro/barato** to work out expensive/cheap; **~ ganhando/perdendo** to come out better/worse off; **~ a alguém** (*parecer-se*) to take after sb; **~ de** (*casa etc*) to leave; (*situação difícil*) to get out of; (*doença*) to come out of; **a notícia saiu na TV/no jornal** the news was on TV/in the paper.
sal [saw] (*pl* **sais**) *m* salt; **sem ~** (*comida*) salt-free; (*pessoa*) lacklustre (BRIT), lackluster (US); **~ de banho** bath salts *pl*; **~ de cozinha** cooking salt.
sala ['sala] *f* room; (*num edifício público*) hall; (*classe, turma*) class; **fazer ~ a alguém** to entertain sb; **~ de audiências** (JUR) courtroom; **~ (de aula)** classroom; **~ de conferências** conference room; **~ de embarque** departure lounge; **~ de espera** waiting room; **~ de espetáculo** concert hall; **~ (de estar)** living room, lounge; **~ de jantar** dining room; **~ de operação** (MED) operating theatre (BRIT) *ou* theater (US); **~ de parto** delivery room.
salada [sa'lada] *f* salad; (*fig*) confusion, jumble; **~ de frutas** fruit salad; **~ russa** (CULIN) Russian salad; (*fig*) hotchpotch.
saladeira [sala'dejra] *f* salad bowl.
sala-e-quarto *m* two-room flat *ou* apartment.
salafra [sa'lafra] (*col*) *m/f* rat.
salafrário [sala'frarju] (*col*) *m* crook.
salame [sa'lami] *m* (CULIN) salami.
salaminho [sala'miɲu] *m* pepperoni (sausage).
salão [sa'lãw] (*pl* **-ões**) *m* large room, hall; (*exposição*) show; (*cabeleireiro*) hairdressing salon; **de ~** (*jogos*) indoor; (*anedota*) proper, acceptable; **~ de baile** dance studio; **~ de beleza** beauty salon.
salarial [sala'rjaw] (*pl* **-ais**) *adj* wage *atr*, pay *atr*.

***NB**: European Portuguese adds the following consonants to certain words:* **b** (sú(b)dito, su(b)til); **c** (a(c)ção, a(c)cionista, a(c)to); **m** (inde(m)ne); **p** (ado(p)ção, ado(p)tar); *for further details see p. xiii.*

salário [sa'larju] *m* wages *pl*, salary; ~ **mínimo** minimum wage.

salário-família (*pl* **salários-família**) *m* family allowance.

saldar [saw'da*] *vt* (*contas*) to settle; (*dívida*) to pay off.

saldo ['sawdu] *m* balance; (*sobra*) surplus; (*fig*: *resultado*) result; ~ **anterior/credor/devedor** opening balance/credit balance/debit balance.

saleiro [sa'lejru] *m* salt cellar; (*moedor*) salt mill.

salgadinho [sawga'dʒiɲu] *m* savoury (*BRIT*), savory (*US*), snack.

salgado/a [saw'gadu/a] *adj* salty, salted; (*preço*) exorbitant.

salgar [saw'ga*] *vt* to salt.

salgueiro [saw'gejru] *m* willow; ~ **chorão** weeping willow.

saliência [sa'ljẽsja] *f* projection; (*assanhamento*) forwardness.

salientar [saljẽ'ta*] *vt* to point out; (*acentuar*) to stress, emphasise; ~-**se** *vr* (*pessoa*) to distinguish o.s.

saliente [sa'ljẽtʃi] *adj* jutting out, prominent; (*evidente*) clear, conspicuous; (*importante*) outstanding; (*assanhado*) forward.

salina [sa'lina] *f* salt bed; (*empresa*) salt company.

salino/a [sa'linu/a] *adj* saline.

salitre [sa'litri] *m* saltpetre (*BRIT*), saltpeter (*US*), nitre (*BRIT*), niter (*US*).

saliva [sa'liva] *f* saliva; **gastar** ~ (*col*) to waste one's breath.

salivar [sali'va*] *vi* to salivate.

salmão [saw'mãw] (*pl* **-ões**) *m* salmon ♦ *adj inv* salmon-pink.

salmo ['sawmu] *m* psalm.

salmões [saw'mõjʃ] *mpl de* **salmão**.

salmonela [sawmo'nɛla] *f* salmonella.

salmoura [saw'mora] *f* brine.

salobro/a [sa'lobru/a] *adj* salty, brackish.

salões [sa'lõjʃ] *mpl de* **salão**.

saloio [sa'lɔju] (*PT*) *m* (*camponês*) country bumpkin.

Salomão [salo'mãw]: **(as) ilhas** *fpl* **de** ~ (the) Solomon Islands.

salpicão [sawpi'kãw] (*pl* **-ões**) *m* (*paio*) pork sausage; (*prato*) fricassee.

salpicar [sawpi'ka*] *vt* to splash; (*polvilhar*, *fig*) to sprinkle.

salpicões [sawpi'kõjʃ] *mpl de* **salpicão**.

salsa ['sawsa] *f* parsley.

salsicha [saw'siʃa] *f* sausage.

salsichão [sawsi'ʃãw] (*pl* **-ões**) *m* sausage.

saltado/a [saw'tadu/a] *adj* (*saliente*) protruding.

saltar [saw'ta*] *vt* to jump (over), leap (over); (*omitir*) to skip ♦ *vi* to jump, leap; (*sangue*) to spurt out; (*de ônibus*, *cavalo*): ~ **de** to get off; ~ **à vista** *ou* **aos olhos** to be obvious.

salteado/a [saw'tʃjadu/a] *adj* broken up; (*CULIN*) sautéed.

salteador [sawtʃja'do*] *m* highwayman.

saltear [saw'tʃja*] *vt* (*trechos de um livro*) to skip; (*CULIN*) to sauté.

saltimbanco [sawtʃĩ'bãku] *m* travelling (*BRIT*) *ou* traveling (*US*) player.

saltitante [sawtʃi'tãtʃi] *adj*: ~ **de alegria** as pleased as punch.

saltitar [sawtʃi'ta*] *vi* (*pássaros*) to hop; (*fig*: *de um assunto a outro*) to skip.

salto ['sawtu] *m* jump, leap; (*de calçado*) heel; **dar um** ~ to jump, leap; **dar** ~**s de alegria** *ou* **de contente** to jump for joy; ~ **de vara** pole vault; ~ **em altura** high jump; ~ **em distância** long jump.

salto-mortal (*pl* **saltos-mortais**) *m* somersault.

salubre [sa'lubri] *adj* healthy, salubrious.

salutar [salu'ta*] *adj* salutary, beneficial.

salva ['sawva] *f* salvo; (*bandeja*) tray, salver; (*BOT*) sage; ~ **de palmas** round of applause; ~ **de tiros** round of gunfire.

salvação [sawva'sãw] *f* salvation; ~ **da pátria** *ou* **da lavoura** (*col*) lifesaver.

salvador [sawva'do*] *m* saviour (*BRIT*), savior (*US*).

salvados [saw'vaduʃ] *mpl* salvage *sg*; (*COM*) salvaged goods.

salvaguarda [sawva'gwaxda] *f* protection, safeguard.

salvaguardar [sawvagwax'da*] *vt* to safeguard.

salvamento [sawva'mẽtu] *m* rescue; (*de naufrágio*) salvage.

salvar [saw'va*] *vt* (*tb*: *COMPUT*) to save; (*resgatar*) to rescue; (*objetos*, *de ruína*) to salvage; (*honra*) to defend; ~-**se** *vr* to escape.

salva-vidas *m inv* (*bóia*) lifebuoy; (*pessoa*) lifeguard; **barco** ~ lifeboat.

salve ['sawvi] *excl* hooray (for)!

salvo/a ['sawvu/a] *adj* safe ♦ *prep* except, save; **a** ~ in safety; **pôr-se a** ~ to run to safety; **todos** ~ **ele** all except him.

salvo-conduto (*pl* ~**s** *ou* **salvos-condutos**) *m* safe-conduct.

samambaia [samã'baja] *f* fern.

samaritano [samari'tanu] *m*: **bom** ~ good Samaritan; (*pej*) do-gooder.

samba ['sãba] *m* samba; **cueca** ~ boxer shorts *pl*.

samba-canção (*pl* **sambas-canção**) *m* slow samba.

sambar [sã'ba*] *vi* to dance the samba.

sambista [sã'biʃta] *m/f* (*dançarino*) samba dancer; (*compositor*) samba composer.

sambódromo [sã'bɔdromu] *m* carnival parade ground.

Samoa [sa'moa] *m*: ~ **Ocidental** Western Samoa.

samovar [samo'va*] *m* tea urn.

sanar [sa'na*] *vt* to cure; (*remediar*) to remedy.

sanatório [sana'tɔrju] *m* sanatorium (*BRIT*),

sanitorium (*US*).
sanável [sa'navew] (*pl* **-eis**) *adj* curable; (*remediável*) remediable.
sanca ['sãka] *f* cornice, moulding (*BRIT*), molding (*US*).
sanção [sã'sãw] (*pl* **-ões**) *f* sanction.
sancionar [sansjo'na*] *vt* to sanction; (*autorizar*) to authorize.
sanções [sã'sõjʃ] *fpl de* **sanção**.
sândalo ['sãdalu] *m* sandalwood.
sandália [sã'dalja] *f* sandal.
sandes ['sãdəʃ] (*PT*) *f inv* sandwich.
sanduíche [sand'wiʃi] (*BR*) *m* sandwich; ~ **americano** ham and egg sandwich; ~ **misto** ham and cheese sandwich; ~ **natural** wholemeal sandwich.
saneamento [sanja'mẽtu] *m* sanitation; (*de governo etc*) clean-up.
sanear [sa'nja*] *vt* to clean up; (*pântanos*) to drain.
sanfona [sã'fɔna] *f* (*MÚS*) accordion; (*TRICÔ*) ribbing.
sanfonado/a [sãfo'nadu/a] *adj* (*porta*) folding; (*suéter*) ribbed.
sangrar [sã'gra*] *vt, vi* to bleed; ~ **alguém** (*fig*) to bleed sb dry.
sangrento/a [sã'grẽtu/a] *adj* bloody; (*ensanguentado*) bloodstained; (*CULIN*: *carne*) rare.
sangria [sã'gria] *f* bloodshed; (*extorsão*) extortion; (*bebida*) sangria.
sangue ['sãgi] *m* blood; ~ **pisado** bruise.
sangue-frio *m* cold-bloodedness.
sanguessuga [sãgi'suga] *f* leech.
sanguinário/a [sãgi'narju/a] *adj* bloodthirsty, cruel.
sanguíneo/a [sã'ginju/a] *adj* blood *atr*; **vaso** ~ blood vessel.
sanha ['saɲa] *f* rage, fury.
sanidade [sani'dadʒi] *f* (*saúde*) healthiness; (*mental*) sanity.
sanita [sa'nita] (*PT*) *f* toilet, lavatory.
sanitário/a [sani'tarju/a] *adj* sanitary; **vaso** ~ toilet, lavatory (bowl).
sanitários [sani'tarjuʃ] *mpl* toilets.
sanitarista [sanita'riʃta] *m/f* health worker.
Santiago [sã'tʃjagu] *n*: ~ **(do Chile)** Santiago (de Chile).
santidade [sãtʃi'dadʒi] *f* holiness, sanctity; **Sua S~** His Holiness (the Pope).
santificar [sãtʃifi'ka*] *vt* to sanctify, make holy.
santinho [sã'tʃiɲu] *m* (*imagem*) holy picture; (*col*: *pessoa*) saint.
santista [sã'tʃiʃta] *adj* from Santos ♦ *m/f* person from Santos.
santo/a ['sãtu/a] *adj* holy, sacred; (*pessoa*) saintly; (*remédio*) effective ♦ *m/f* saint; **todo** ~ **dia** every single day; **ter** ~ **forte** (*col*) to have good backing.
santuário [sã'twarju] *m* shrine, sanctuary.
São [sãw] *m* Saint.
são/sã [sãw/sã] (*pl* **~s/~s**) *adj* healthy; (*conselho*) sound; (*atitude*) wholesome; (*mentalmente*) sane; ~ **e salvo** safe and sound.
São Lourenço [-lo'rẽsu] *m*: **o (rio)** ~ the St. Lawrence river.
São Marinho *m* San Marino.
São Paulo [-'pawlu] *n* São Paulo.
são-tomense [-to'mẽsi] *adj* from São Tomé e Príncipe ♦ *m/f* native *ou* inhabitant of São Tomé e Príncipe.
sapata [sa'pata] *m* (*do freio*) shoe.
sapatão [sapa'tãw] (*pl* **-ões**) *m* big shoe; (*col*: *lésbica*) lesbian.
sapataria [sapata'ria] *f* shoe shop.
sapateado [sapa'tʃjadu] *m* tap dancing.
sapateador(a) [sapatʃja'do*(a)] *m/f* tap dancer.
sapatear [sapa'tʃja*] *vi* to tap one's feet; (*dançar*) to tap-dance.
sapateiro [sapa'tejru] *m* shoemaker; (*vendedor*) shoe salesman; (*que conserta*) shoe repairer; (*loja*) shoe repairer's.
sapatilha [sapa'tʃiʎa] *f* (*de balé*) shoe; (*sapato*) pump; (*de atleta*) running shoe.
sapato [sa'patu] *m* shoe.
sapatões [sapa'tõjʃ] *mpl de* **sapatão**.
sapé [sa'pɛ] *m* = **sapê**.
sapê [sa'pe] *m* thatch; **teto de** ~ thatched roof.
sapeca [sa'pɛka] *adj* flirtatious; (*criança*) cheeky.
sapecar [sape'ka*] *vt* (*tapa, pontapé*) to land ♦ *vi* (*flertar*) to flirt.
sapiência [sa'pjẽsja] *f* wisdom, learning.
sapiente [sa'pjẽtʃi] *adj* wise.
sapinho [sa'piɲu] *m* (*MED*) thrush.
sapo ['sapu] *m* toad; **engolir ~s** (*fig*) to sit back and take it.
saque ['saki] *etc vb V* **sacar** ♦ *m* (*de dinheiro*) withdrawal; (*COM*) draft, bill; (*ESPORTE*) serve; (*pilhagem*) plunder, pillage; (*col*: *mentira*) fib; ~ **a descoberto** (*COM*) overdraft.
saquear [sa'kja*] *vt* to pillage, plunder.
saracotear [sarako'tʃja*] *vi* to wiggle one's hips; (*vaguear*) to wander around ♦ *vt* to shake.
Saragoça [sara'gɔsa] *n* Zaragoza.
saraiva [sa'rajva] *f* hail.
saraivada [sarai'vada] *f* hailstorm; **uma** ~ **de** (*fig*) a hail of.
saraivar [sarai'va*] *vi* to hail; (*fig*) to spray.
sarampo [sa'rãpu] *m* measles *sg*.
sarapintado/a [sarapĩ'tadu/a] *adj* spotted, speckled.
sarar [sa'ra*] *vt* to cure; (*ferida*) to heal ♦ *vi* to recover, be cured.
sarau [sa'raw] *m* soirée.

NB: *European Portuguese adds the following consonants to certain words:* **b** (sú(b)dito, su(b)til); **c** (a(c)ção, a(c)cionista, a(c)to); **m** (inde(m)ne); **p** (ado(p)ção, ado(p)tar); *for further details see p. xiii.*

sarcasmo [sax'kaʒmu] *m* sarcasm.
sarcástico/a [sax'kaʃtʃiku/a] *adj* sarcastic.
sarda ['saxda] *f* freckle.
Sardenha [sax'dɛɲa] *f*: **a ~** Sardinia.
sardento/a [sax'dẽtu/a] *adj* freckled, freckly.
sardinha [sax'dʒiɲa] *f* sardine; **como ~ em lata** (*apertado*) like sardines.
sardônico/a [sax'doniku/a] *adj* sardonic, sarcastic.
sargento [sax'ʒẽtu] *m* sergeant.
sári ['sari] *m* sari.
sarjeta [sax'ʒeta] *f* gutter.
sarna ['saxna] *f* scabies *sg*.
sarrafo [sa'xafu] *m*: **baixar o ~ em alguém** (*col*) to let sb have it.
sarro ['saxu] *m* (*de vinho, nos dentes*) tartar; (*na língua*) fur, coating; (*col*) laugh; **tirar um ~** (*col*) to pet, neck.
Satã [sa'tã] *m* Satan, the Devil.
Satanás [sata'naʃ] *m* Satan, the Devil.
satânico/a [sa'taniku/a] *adj* satanic; (*fig*) devilish.
satélite [sa'tɛlitʃi] *adj* satellite *atr* ♦ *m* satellite.
sátira ['satʃira] *f* satire.
satírico/a [sa'tʃiriku/a] *adj* satirical.
satirizar [satʃiri'za*] *vt* to satirize.
satisfação [satʃiʃfa'sãw] (*pl* **-ões**) *f* satisfaction; (*recompensa*) reparation; **dar uma ~ a alguém** to give sb an explanation; **ela não dá satisfações a ninguém** she answers to noone; **tomar satisfações de alguém** to ask sb for an explanation.
satisfaço [satʃiʃ'fasu] *etc vb V* **satisfazer**.
satisfações [satʃiʃfa'sõjʃ] *fpl de* **satisfação**.
satisfatório/a [satʃiʃfa'tɔrju/a] *adj* satisfactory.
satisfazer [satʃiʃfa'ze*] (*irreg*: *como* **fazer**) *vt* to satisfy; (*dívida*) to pay off ♦ *vi* (*ser satisfatório*) to be satisfactory; **~-se** *vr* to be satisfied; (*saciar-se*) to fill o.s. up; **~ a** to satisfy; **~ com** to fulfil (*BRIT*), fulfill (*US*).
satisfeito/a [satʃiʃ'fejtu/a] *pp de* **satisfazer** ♦ *adj* satisfied; (*alegre*) content; (*saciado*) full; **dar-se por ~ com algo** to be content with sth; **dar alguém por ~** to make sb happy.
satisfez [satʃiʃ'feʒ] *vb V* **satisfazer**.
satisfiz [satʃiʃ'fiʒ] *etc vb V* **satisfazer**.
saturado/a [satu'radu/a] *adj* (*de comida*) full; (*aborrecido*) fed up; (*COM*: *mercado*) saturated.
saturar [satu'ra*] *vt* to saturate; (*de comida, aborrecimento*) to fill.
Saturno [sa'tuxnu] *m* Saturn.
saudação [sawda'sãw] (*pl* **-ções**) *f* greeting.
saudade [saw'dadʒi] *f* (*desejo ardente*) longing, yearning; (*lembrança nostálgica*) nostalgia; **deixar ~s** to be greatly missed; **matar as ~s de alguém/algo** to catch up with sb/cure one's nostalgia for sth; **ter ~s de** (*desejar*) to long for; (*sentir falta de*) to miss; **~s (de casa** *ou* **da família** *ou* **da pátria)** homesickness *sg*.
saudar [saw'da*] *vt* (*cumprimentar*) to greet; (*dar as boas vindas*) to welcome; (*aclamar*) to acclaim.
saudável [saw'davew] (*pl* **-eis**) *adj* healthy; (*moralmente*) wholesome.
saúde [sa'udʒi] *f* health; (*brinde*) toast; **~!** (*brindando*) cheers!; (*quando se espirra*) bless you!; **à sua ~!** your health!; **beber à ~ de** to drink to, toast; **estar bem/mal de ~** to be well/ill; **não ter mais ~ para fazer** not to be up to doing; **vender ~** to be bursting with health; **~ pública** public health; (*órgão*) health service.
saudosismo [sawdo'ziʒmu] *m* nostalgia.
saudoso/a [saw'dozu/ɔza] *adj* (*nostálgico*) nostalgic; (*da família ou terra natal*) homesick; (*de uma pessoa*) longing; (*que causa saudades*) much-missed.
sauna ['sawna] *f* sauna; **fazer ~** to have *ou* take a sauna.
saveiro [sa'vejru] *m* sailing boat.
saxofone [sakso'fɔni] *m* saxophone.
saxofonista [saksofo'niʃta] *m/f* saxophonist.
sazonado/a [sazo'nadu/a] *adj* ripe, mature.
sazonal [sazo'naw] (*pl* **-ais**) *adj* seasonal.
SBPC *abr f* = **Sociedade Brasileira para o Progresso da Ciência**.
SBT *abr m* (= *Sistema Brasileiro de Televisão*) *television station*.
SC *abr* = **Santa Catarina**.
SCDF (*BR*) *abr f* = **Sagrada Congregação para a Doutrina da Fé**.
SE *abr* = **Sergipe**.
se [si] *conj* if; (*em pergunta indireta*) whether ♦ *pron* oneself; (*m*) himself; (*f*) herself; (*coisa*) itself; (*você*) yourself; (*vocês*) yourselves; (*eles/elas*) themselves; (*reciprocamente*) each other; **~ bem que** even though; **come-~ bem aqui** you can eat well here; **diz-~ que** ... it is said that ...; **sabe-~ que** ... it is known that ...; **vende(m)-~ jornais naquela loja** they sell newspapers in that shop.
sé [sɛ] *f* cathedral; **Santa S~** Holy See.
sê [se] *vb V* **ser**.
Seade [se'adʒi] (*BR*) *abr m* = **Sistema Estadual de Análise de Dados**.
seara ['sjara] *f* (*campo de cereais*) wheat (*ou* corn) field; (*campo cultivado*) tilled field.
sebe ['sɛbi] (*PT*) *f* fence; **~ viva** hedge.
sebento/a [se'bẽtu/a] *adj* greasy; (*sujo*) dirty, filthy.
sebo ['sebu] *m* fat, tallow; (*livraria*) second-hand bookshop.
seborréia [sebo'xɛja] *f* seborrhoea (*BRIT*), seborrhea (*US*).
seboso/a [se'bozu/ɔza] *adj* greasy; (*sujo*) dirty; (*col*) stuck-up.
seca ['seka] *f* (*estiagem*) drought.
secador [seka'do*] *m* drier; **~ de cabelo/roupa** hairdrier/clothes drier.
secagem [se'kaʒẽ] *f* drying.
seção [se'sãw] (*pl* **-ões**) *f* section; (*em loja, re-*

partição) department; ~ **rítmica** rhythm section.

secar [se'ka*] *vt* to dry; (*planta*) to parch; (*rio*) to dry up ♦ *vi* to dry; (*plantas*) to wither; (*fonte*) to dry up.

secarrão/rrona [seka'xãw/'xɔna] (*pl* **-ões/~s**) *m/f* cold fish.

secção [sek'sãw] (*PT*) *f* = **seção**.

seccionar [seksjo'na*] *vt* to split up.

secessão [sese'sãw] (*pl* **-ões**) *f* secession.

seco/a ['seku/a] *adj* dry; (*árido*) arid; (*fruta, carne*) dried; (*ríspido*) curt, brusque; (*pancada, ruído*) dull; (*magro*) thin; (*pessoa*: *frio*) cold; (: *sério*) serious; **em** ~ (*barco*) aground; **estar** ~ **por algo/para fazer** (*col*) to be dying for sth/to do.

seções [se'sõjʃ] *fpl de* **seção**.

secreção [sekre'sãw] (*pl* **-ões**) *f* secretion.

secretaria [sekreta'ria] *f* (*local*) general office, secretary's office; (*ministério*) ministry.

secretária [sekre'tarja] *f* (*mesa*) writing desk; ~ **eletrônica** (telephone) answering machine; *V tb* **secretário**.

secretariar [sekreta'rja*] *vt* to work as a secretary to ♦ *vi* to work as a secretary.

secretário/a [sekre'tarju/a] *m/f* secretary; ~ **particular** private secretary; **S~ de Estado** Secretary of State.

secretário/a-geral (*pl* **secretários/as-gerais**) *m/f* secretary-general.

secreto/a [se'krɛtu/a] *adj* secret.

sectário/a [sek'tarju/a] *adj* sectarian ♦ *m/f* follower.

sectarismo [sekta'riʒmu] *m* sectarianism.

sector [sek'to*] (*PT*) *m* = **setor**.

secular [seku'la*] *adj* (*leigo*) secular, lay; (*muito antigo*) age-old.

secularizar [sekulari'za*] *vt* to secularize.

século ['sɛkulu] *m* (*cem anos*) century; (*época*) age; **há ~s** (*fig*) for ages; (:*atrás*) ages ago.

secundar [sekũ'da*] *vt* (*apoiar*) to support, back up; (*ajudar*) to help; (*pedido*) to follow up.

secundário/a [sekũ'darju/a] *adj* secondary.

secura [se'kura] *f* dryness; (*fig*) coldness; (*col*: *desejo*) keenness.

seda ['seda] *f* silk; **ser** *ou* **estar uma** ~ to be nice; **bicho da** ~ silkworm.

sedã [se'dã] *m* (*AUTO*) saloon (car) (*BRIT*), sedan (*US*).

sedativo/a [seda'tʃivu/a] *adj* sedative ♦ *m* sedative.

SEDE (*BR*) *abr m* = **Sistema Estadual de Empregos**.

sede¹ ['sɛdʒi] *f* (*de empresa, instituição*) headquarters *sg*; (*de governo*) seat; (*REL*) see, diocese; ~ **social** head office.

sede² ['sedʒi] *f* thirst; (*fig*): ~ **(de)** craving (for); **estar com** *ou* **ter** ~ to be thirsty; **matar a** ~ to quench one's thirst.

sedentário/a [sedẽ'tarju/a] *adj* sedentary.

sedento/a [se'dẽtu/a] *adj* thirsty; (*fig*): ~ **(de)** eager (for).

sediar [se'dʒja*] *vt* to base.

sedição [sedʒi'sãw] *f* sedition.

sedicioso/a [sedʒi'sjozu/ɔza] *adj* seditious.

sedimentar [sedʒimẽ'ta*] *vi* to silt up.

sedimento [sedʒi'mẽtu] *m* sediment.

sedoso/a [se'dozu/ɔza] *adj* silky.

sedução [sedu'sãw] (*pl* **-ões**) *f* seduction; (*atração*) allure, charm.

sedutor(a) [sedu'to*(a)] *adj* seductive; (*oferta etc*) tempting ♦ *m/f* seducer.

seduzir [sedu'zi*] *vt* to seduce; (*fascinar*) to fascinate; (*desencaminhar*) to lead astray.

Sefiti [sefi'tʃi] (*BR*) *abr m* = **Serviço de Fiscalização de Trânsito Interestadual e Internacional**.

seg. *abr* (= *segunda-feira*) Mon.

segmentar [segmẽ'ta*] *vt* to segment.

segmento [seg'mẽtu] *m* segment.

segredar [segre'da*] *vt*, *vi* to whisper.

segredo [se'gredu] *m* secret; (*sigilo*) secrecy; (*de fechadura*) combination; **em** ~ in secret; ~ **de estado** state secret.

segregação [segrega'sãw] *f* segregation.

segregar [segre'ga*] *vt* to segregate, separate.

seguidamente [segida'mẽtʃi] *adv* (*sem parar*) continuously; (*logo depois*) soon afterwards.

seguido/a [se'gidu/a] *adj* following; (*contínuo*) continuous, consecutive; ~ **de** *ou* **por** followed by; **três dias ~s** three days running; **horas seguidas** for hours on end; **em seguida** next; (*logo depois*) soon afterwards; (*imediatamente*) immediately, right away.

seguidor(a) [segi'do*(a)] *m/f* follower.

seguimento [segi'mẽtu] *m* continuation; **dar ~ a** to proceed with; **em ~ de** after.

seguinte [se'gĩtʃi] *adj* following, next; **(o negócio) é o** ~ (*col*) the thing is; **eu lhe disse o** ~ this is what I said to him; **pelo** ~ hereby.

seguir [se'gi*] *vt* to follow; (*continuar*) to continue ♦ *vi* to follow; (*continuar*) to continue, carry on; (*ir*) to go; **~-se** *vr*: **~-se (a)** to follow; **logo a** ~ next; **~-se (de)** to result (from); **ao jantar seguiu-se uma reunião** the dinner was followed by a meeting.

segunda [se'gũda] *f* (*tb*: *~-feira*) Monday; (*MÚS*) second; (*AUTO*) second (gear); **de** ~ second-rate.

segunda-feira (*pl* **segundas-feiras**) *f* Monday; *V tb* **terça-feira**.

segundanista [segũda'niʃta] *m/f* second year.

segundo/a [se'gũdu/a] *adj* second ♦ *prep* according to ♦ *conj* as, from what ♦ *adv* secondly ♦ *m* second; **de segunda mão** second-hand; **de segunda (classe)** second-

NB: *European Portuguese adds the following consonants to certain words:* **b** (sú(b)dito, su(b)til); **c** (a(c)ção, a(c)cionista, a(c)to); **m** (inde(m)ne); **p** (ado(p)ção, ado(p)tar); *for further details see p. xiii.*

class; ~ **ele disse** according to what he said; ~ **dizem** apparently; ~ **me consta** as far as I know; ~ **se afirma** according to what is said, from what is said; **segundas intenções** ulterior motives; ~ **tempo** (*FUTEBOL*) second half; *V tb* **quinto**.

segundo-time *adj inv* (*pessoa*) second-rate.

segurado/a [segu'radu/a] *adj, m/f* (*COM*) insured.

segurador(a) [segura'do*(a)] *m/f* insurer ♦ *f* insurance company.

seguramente [segura'mẽtʃi] *adv* (*com certeza*) certainly; (*muito provavelmente*) surely.

segurança [segu'rãsa] *f* security; (*ausência de perigo*) safety; (*confiança*) confidence; (*convicção*) assurance ♦ *m/f* security guard; **com** ~ assuredly; ~ **nacional** national security.

segurar [segu'ra*] *vt* to hold; (*amparar*) to hold up; (*COM*: *bens*) to insure ♦ *vi*: ~ **em** to hold; ~**-se** *vr* (*COM*: *fazer seguro*) to insure o.s.; ~**-se em** to hold on to.

seguro/a [se'guru/a] *adj* (*livre de perigo*) safe; (*livre de risco, firme*) secure; (*certo*) certain, assured; (*confiável*) reliable; (*de si mesmo*) secure, confident; (*tempo*) settled ♦ *adv* confidently ♦ *m* (*COM*) insurance; ~ **de si** self-assured; ~ **morreu de velho** better safe than sorry; **estar** ~ **de/de que** to be sure of/that; **fazer** ~ to take out an insurance policy; **companhia de ~s** insurance company; ~ **contra acidentes/incêndio** accident/fire insurance; ~ **de vida/automóvel** life/car insurance.

seguro-saúde (*pl* **seguros-saúde**) *m* health insurance.

SEI (*BR*) *abr f* = **Secretaria Especial da Informática**.

sei [sej] *vb V* **saber**.

seio ['seju] *m* breast, bosom; (*âmago*) heart; (~ *paranasal*) sinus; **no** ~ **de** in the heart of.

seis [sejʃ] *num* six; *V tb* **cinco**.

seiscentos/as [sej'sẽtuʃ/aʃ] *num* six hundred.

seita ['sejta] *f* sect.

seiva ['sejva] *f* sap; (*fig*) vigour (*BRIT*), vigor (*US*), vitality.

seixo ['sejʃu] *m* pebble.

seja ['seʒa] *etc vb V* **ser**.

SELA *abr m* = **Sistema Econômico Latino-Americano**.

sela ['sɛla] *f* saddle.

selagem [se'laʒẽ] *f* (*de cartas*) franking; **máquina de** ~ franking machine.

selar [se'la*] *vt* (*carta*) to stamp; (*documento oficial, pacto*) to seal; (*cavalo*) to saddle; (*fechar*) to shut, seal; (*concluir*) to conclude.

seleção [sele'sãw] (*PT*: **-cç-**: *pl* **-ões**) *f* selection; (*ESPORTE*) team.

selecionado [selesjo'nadu] (*PT*: **-cc-**) *m* (*ESPORTE*) team.

selecionador(a) [selesjona'do*(a)] (*PT*: **-cc-**) *m/f* selector.

selecionar [selesjo'na*] (*PT*: **-cc-**) *vt* to select.

seleções [sele'sõjʃ] *fpl de* **seleção**.

seleta [se'lɛta] (*PT*: **-ct-**) *f* anthology.

seletivo/a [sele'tʃivu/a] (*PT*: **-ct-**) *adj* selective.

seleto/a [se'lɛtu/a] (*PT*: **-ct-**) *adj* select.

selim [se'lĩ] (*pl* **-ns**) *m* saddle.

selo ['selu] *m* stamp; (*carimbo, sinete*) seal; (*fig*) stamp, mark.

selva ['sɛwva] *f* (*tb fig*) jungle.

selvagem [sew'vaʒẽ] (*pl* **-ns**) *adj* (*silvestre*) wild; (*feroz*) fierce; (*povo*) savage; (*fig*: *indivíduo, maneiras*) coarse.

selvageria [sewvaʒe'ria] *f* savagery.

sem [sẽ] *prep* without ♦ *conj*: ~ **que eu peça** without my asking; **a casa está** ~ **limpar há duas semanas** the house hasn't been cleaned for two weeks; **estar/ficar** ~ **dinheiro/gasolina** to have no/have run out of money/petrol; ~ **quê nem para quê** for no apparent reason.

SEMA (*BR*) *abr f* = **Secretaria Especial do Meio Ambiente**.

semáforo [se'maforu] *m* (*AUTO*) traffic lights *pl*; (*FERRO*) signal.

semana [se'mana] *f* week.

semanada [sema'nada] *f* (weekly) wages *pl*; (*mesada*) weekly allowance.

semanal [sema'naw] (*pl* **-ais**) *adj* weekly; **ganha $200 semanais** he earns $200 a week.

semanário [sema'narju] *m* weekly (publication).

semântica [se'mãtʃika] *f* semantics *sg*.

semântico/a [se'mãtʃiku/a] *adj* semantic.

semblante [sẽ'blãtʃi] *m* face; (*fig*) appearance, look.

semeadura [semja'dura] *f* sowing.

semear [se'mja*] *vt* to sow; (*fig*) to spread; (*espalhar*) to scatter.

semelhança [seme'ʎãsa] *f* similarity, resemblance; **a** ~ **de** like; **ter** ~ **com** to resemble.

semelhante [seme'ʎãtʃi] *adj* similar; (*tal*) such ♦ *m* fellow creature.

semelhar [seme'ʎa*] *vi*: ~ **a** to look like, resemble ♦ *vt* to look like, resemble; ~**-se** *vr* to be alike.

sêmen ['semẽ] *m* semen.

semente [se'mẽtʃi] *f* seed.

sementeira [semẽ'tejra] *f* sowing, spreading.

semestral [semeʃ'traw] (*pl* **-ais**) *adj* half-yearly.

semestralmente [semeʃtraw'mẽtʃi] *adv* every six months.

semestre [se'mɛʃtri] *m* six months; (*EDUC*) semester.

sem-fim *m*: **um** ~ **de perguntas** *etc* endless questions *etc*.

semi... [semi] *prefixo* semi..., half....

semi-aberto/a *adj* half-open.

semi-analfabeto/a *adj* semiliterate.

semibreve [semi'brɛvi] *f* (*MÚS*) semibreve.

semicírculo [semi'sixkulu] *m* semicircle.

semicondutor [semikõdu'to*] *m* semicon-

ductor.
semiconsciente [semikõ'sjẽtʃi] *adj* semiconscious.
semifinal [semi'finaw] (*pl* **-ais**) *f* semifinal.
semifinalista [semifina'liʃta] *m/f* semifinalist.
semi-internato *m* day school.
semi-interno/a *m/f* (*tb*: *aluno* ~) day pupil.
seminal [semi'naw] (*pl* **-ais**) *adj* seminal.
seminário [semi'narju] *m* (*EDUC*, *congresso*) seminar; (*REL*) seminary.
seminarista [semina'riʃta] *m* seminarist.
seminu(a) [semi'nu(a)] *adj* half-naked.
semiótica [se'mjɔtʃika] *f* semiotics *sg*.
semiprecioso/a [semipre'sjozu/ɔza] *adj* semiprecious.
semita [se'mita] *adj* Semitic.
semítico/a [se'mitʃiku/a] *adj* Semitic.
semitom [semi'tõ] *m* (*MÚS*) semitone.
sem-lar *m/f inv* homeless person.
sem-número *m*: **um ~ de coisas** loads *pl* of things.
semolina [semo'lina] *f* semolina.
sem-par *adj inv* unequalled, unique.
sempre ['sẽpri] *adv* always; **você ~ vai?** (*PT*) are you still going?; **~ que** whenever; **como ~** as always; **a comida/hora** *etc* **de ~** the usual food/time *etc*; **a mesma história de ~** the same old story; **para ~** forever; **para todo o ~** for ever and ever; **quase ~** nearly always.
sem-sal *adj inv* insipid.
sem-terra *m/f inv* landless labourer (*BRIT*) *ou* laborer (*US*).
sem-vergonha *adj inv* shameless ♦ *m/f inv* (*pessoa*) rogue.
Sena ['sɛna] *m*: **o ~** the Seine.
Senac [se'naki] (*BR*) *abr m* = **Serviço Nacional de Aprendizagem Comercial**.
senado [se'nadu] *m* senate.
senador(a) [sena'do*(a)] *m/f* senator.
Senai [se'naj] (*BR*) *abr m* = **Serviço Nacional de Aprendizagem Industrial**.
senão [se'nãw] (*pl* **-ões**) *conj* (*do contrário*) otherwise; (*mas sim*) but, but rather ♦ *prep* (*exceto*) except ♦ *m* flaw, defect; **~ quando** suddenly.
Senav [se'navi] (*BR*) *abr f* = **Superintendência Estadual de Navegação**.
senda ['sẽda] *f* path.
Senegal [sene'gaw] *m*: **o ~** Senegal.
senha ['sɛɲa] *f* (*sinal*) sign; (*palavra de passe*, *COMPUT*) password; (*de caixa automática*) PIN number; (*recibo*) receipt; (*bilhete*) ticket, voucher.
senhor(a) [se'ɲo*(a)] *m* (*homem*) man; (*formal*) gentleman; (*homem idoso*) elderly man; (*REL*) lord; (*dono*) owner; (*tratamento*) Mr(.); (*tratamento respeitoso*) sir ♦ *f* (*mulher*) lady; (*esposa*) wife; (*mulher idosa*) elderly lady; (*dona*) owner; (*tratamento*) Mrs(.), Ms(.); (*tratamento respeitoso*) madam ♦ *adj* marvellous (*BRIT*), marvelous (*US*); **uma ~a gripe** a bad case of flu; **o ~/a ~a** (*você*) you; **nossa ~a!** (*col*) gosh; **sim, ~(a)!** yes indeed; **estar ~ de si** to be cool *ou* collected; **estar ~ da situação** to be in control of the situation; **ser ~ do seu nariz** to be one's own boss; **~ de engenho** plantation owner.
senhoria [seɲo'ria] *f* (*proprietária*) landlady; **Vossa S~** (*em cartas*) you.
senhoril [seɲo'riw] (*pl* **-is**) *adj* (*roupa etc*) gentlemen's/ladies'; (*distinto*) lordly.
senhorio [seɲo'riu] *m* (*proprietário*) landlord; (*posse*) ownership.
senhoris [seɲo'riʃ] *adj pl de* **senhoril**.
senhorita [seɲo'rita] *f* young lady; (*tratamento*) Miss, Ms.; **a ~** (*você*) you.
senil [se'niw] (*pl* **-is**) *adj* senile.
senilidade [senili'dadʒi] *f* senility.
senilizar [senili'za*] *vt* to age.
senis [se'niʃ] *adj pl de* **senil**.
senões [se'nõjʃ] *mpl de* **senão**.
sensação [sẽsa'sãw] (*pl* **-ões**) *f* sensation; **a ~ de que/uma ~ de** the feeling that/a feeling of; **causar ~** to cause a sensation.
sensacional [sẽsasjo'naw] (*pl* **-ais**) *adj* sensational.
sensacionalismo [sẽsasjona'liʒmu] *m* sensationalism.
sensacionalista [sẽsasjona'liʃta] *adj* sensationalist.
sensações [sẽsa'sõjʃ] *fpl de* **sensação**.
sensatez [sẽsa'teʒ] *f* good sense.
sensato/a [sẽ'satu/a] *adj* sensible.
sensibilidade [sẽsibili'dadʒi] *f* sensitivity; (*artística*) sensibility; (*física*) feeling; **estou com muita ~ neste dedo** this finger is very sensitive.
sensibilizar [sẽsibili'za*] *vt* to touch, move; (*opinião pública*) to influence; **~-se** *vr* to be moved.
sensitivo/a [sẽsi'tʃivu/a] *adj* sensory; (*pessoa*) sensitive.
sensível [sẽ'sivew] (*pl* **-eis**) *adj* sensitive; (*visível*) noticeable; (*considerável*) considerable; (*dolorido*) tender.
sensivelmente [sẽsivew'mẽtʃi] *adv* perceptibly, markedly.
senso ['sẽsu] *m* sense; (*juízo*) judgement; **~ comum** *ou* **bom ~** common sense; **~ de humor/responsabilidade** sense of humour (*BRIT*) *ou* humor (*US*)/responsibility.
sensorial [sẽso'rjaw] (*pl* **-ais**) *adj* sensory.
sensual [sẽ'swaw] (*pl* **-ais**) *adj* sensual, sensuous.
sensualidade [sẽswali'dadʒi] *f* sensuality, sensuousness.
sentado/a [sẽ'tadu/a] *adj* sitting; (*almoço*) sit-down.

sentar [sẽ'ta*] *vt* to seat ♦ *vi* to sit; **~-se** *vr* to sit down.
sentença [sẽ'tẽsa] *f* (JUR) sentence; **~ de morte** death sentence.
sentenciar [sẽtẽ'sja*] *vt* (*julgar*) to pass judgement on; (*condenar por sentença*) to sentence ♦ *vi* to pass judgement; to pass sentence.
sentidamente [sẽtʃida'mẽtʃi] *adv* (*chorar*) bitterly; (*desculpar-se*) abjectly.
sentido/a [sẽ'tʃidu/a] *adj* (*magoado*) hurt; (*choro, queixa*) heartfelt ♦ *m* sense; (*significação*) sense, meaning; (*direção*) direction; (*atenção*) attention; (*aspecto*) respect; **~!** (MIL) attention!; **em certo ~** in a sense; **sem ~** meaningless; **fazer ~** to make sense; **perder/recobrar os ~s** to lose/recover consciousness; **(não) ter ~** (not) to be acceptable; **~ figurado** figurative sense; **"~ único"** (PT: *sinal*) "one-way".
sentimental [sẽtʃimẽ'taw] (*pl* **-ais**) *adj* sentimental; **aventura ~** romance; **vida ~** love life.
sentimentalismo [sẽtʃimẽta'liʒmu] *m* sentimentality.
sentimento [sẽtʃi'mẽtu] *m* feeling; (*senso*) sense; **~s** *mpl* (*pêsames*) condolences; **fazer algo com ~** to do sth with feeling; **ter bons ~s** to be good-natured.
sentinela [sẽtʃi'nɛla] *f* sentry, guard; **estar de ~** to be on guard duty; **render ~** to relieve the guard.
sentir [sẽ'tʃi*] *vt* to feel; (*perceber, pressentir*) to sense; (*ser afetado por*) to be affected by; (*magoar-se*) to be upset by ♦ *vi* to feel; (*sofrer*) to suffer; **~-se** *vr* to feel; (*julgar-se*) to consider o.s. (to be); **~ a falta de** to miss; **~ cheiro/gosto (de)** to smell/taste; **~ tristeza** to feel sad; **~ vontade de** to feel like; **você sente a diferença?** can you tell the difference?; **sinto muito** I am very sorry.
senzala [sẽ'zala] *f* slave quarters *pl*.
separação [separa'sãw] (*pl* **-ões**) *f* separation.
separado/a [sepa'radu/a] *adj* separate; (*casal*) separated; **em ~** separately, apart.
separar [sepa'ra*] *vt* to separate; (*dividir*) to divide; (*pôr de lado*) to put aside; **~-se** *vr* to separate; (*dividir-se*) to be divided; **~-se de** to separate from.
separata [sepa'rata] *f* offprint.
separatismo [separa'tʃiʒmu] *m* separatism.
séptico/a ['sɛptʃiku/a] *adj* septic.
septuagésimo/a [septwa'ʒɛzimu/a] (PT) *num* = **setuagésimo**.
sepulcro [se'puwkru] *m* tomb.
sepultamento [sepuwta'mẽtu] *m* burial.
sepultar [sepuw'ta*] *vt* to bury; (*esconder*) to hide, conceal; (*segredo*) to keep quiet.
sepultura [sepuw'tura] *f* grave, tomb.
sequei [se'kej] *etc vb V* **secar**.
seqüela [se'kwɛla] *f* sequel; (*conseqüência*) consequence; (MED) after-effect.
seqüência [se'kwẽsja] *f* sequence.
seqüencial [sekwẽ'sjaw] (*pl* **-ais**) *adj* (COMPUT) sequential.
sequer [se'kɛ*] *adv* at least; **(nem) ~** not even.
seqüestrador(a) [sekweʃtra'do*(a)] *m/f* (*raptor*) kidnapper; (*de avião etc*) hijacker.
seqüestrar [sekweʃ'tra*] *vt* (*bens*) to seize, confiscate; (*raptar*) to kidnap; (*avião etc*) to hijack.
seqüestro [se'kwɛʃtru] *m* seizure; (*rapto*) abduction, kidnapping; (*de avião etc*) hijack.
sequidão [seki'dãw] *f* dryness; (*de pessoa*) coldness.
sequioso/a [se'kjozu/ɔza] *adj* (*sedento*) thirsty; (*fig*: *desejoso*) eager.
séquito ['sɛkitu] *m* retinue.
ser [se*] *vi* to be; (*como aux*): **~ ferido/amado** to be injured/loved ♦ *m* being; **~es** *mpl* creatures; **~ com** (*dizer respeito a*) to concern; (*estar sob a alçada de*) to be up to; (*depender de*) to be dependent on; (*interessar*): **o futebol é com ele** football is his thing; **~ de** (*origem*) to be *ou* come from; (*feito de*) to be made of; (*pertencer*) to belong to; **ela é de uma bondade incrível** she's incredibly kind; **~ de mentir/briga** (*pessoa*) to be the sort to lie/fight; **~ por** to be for, be in favour (BRIT) *ou* favor (US) of; **a não ~** except; **a não ~ por** but for; **a não ~ que** unless; **é** (*resposta afirmativa*) yes; **..., não é?** isn't it?, don't you? *etc*; **ah, é?** really?; **é ou não é?** am I right?; **que foi?** (*o que aconteceu?*) what happened?; (*qual é o problema?*) what's the matter?; **é que ...** it's just that ...; **nós é que pedimos feijoada** it was us who ordered feijoada; **eu quero é viajar** what I want is to travel; **ele está é danado** he's really angry; **seja ... seja ...** whether it is ... or ...; **ou seja** that is to say; **seja quem for** whoever it may be; **se eu fosse você** if I were you; **se não fosse você, ...** if it hadn't been for you, ...; **será que ...?** I wonder if ...?; **ele vem amanhã — será?** he's coming tomorrow — do you think so?; **~ humano** human being.
serão [se'rãw] (*pl* **-ões**) *m* (*trabalho noturno*) night work; (*horas extraordinárias*) overtime; **fazer ~** to work late; (*dormir tarde*) to go to bed late.
sereia [se'reja] *f* mermaid.
serelepe [sere'lɛpi] *adj* frisky.
serenar [sere'na*] *vt* to calm ♦ *vi* (*pessoa*) to calm down; (*mar*) to grow calm; (*dor*) to subside.
serenata [sere'nata] *f* serenade.
serenidade [sereni'dadʒi] *f* serenity, tranquillity.
sereno/a [se'rɛnu/a] *adj* calm; (*olhar*) serene; (*tempo*) fine, clear ♦ *m* (*relento*) damp night air; **no ~** in the open.
seresta [se'rɛʃta] *f* serenade.
SERFA (BR) *abr m* = **Serviço de Fiscalização**

Agrícola.

sergipano/a [sexʒi'panu/a] *adj* from Sergipe ♦ *m/f* person from Sergipe.

seriado/a [se'rjadu/a] *adj* (*número*) serial; (*publicação, filme*) serialized.

serial [se'rjaw] (*pl* **-ais**) *adj* (COMPUT) serial.

série ['sɛri] *f* series; (*seqüência*) sequence, succession; (EDUC) grade; (*categoria*) category; **fora de ~** out of order; (*fig*) extraordinary; **fabricar em ~** to mass-produce.

seriedade [serje'dadʒi] *f* seriousness; (*honestidade*) honesty.

seringa [se'rĩga] *f* syringe.

seringal [serĩ'gaw] (*pl* **-ais**) *m* rubber plantation.

seringalista [serĩga'liʃta] *m* rubber plantation owner.

seringueira [serĩ'gejra] *f* rubber tree; *V tb* **seringueiro.**

seringueiro/a [serĩ'gejru/a] *m/f* rubber tapper.

sério/a ['sɛrju/a] *adj* serious; (*honesto*) honest, decent; (*responsável*) responsible; (*confiável*) reliable; (*roupa*) sober ♦ *adv* seriously; **a ~** seriously; **falando ~ ...** seriously ...; **~?** really?

sermão [sex'mãw] (*pl* **-ões**) *m* sermon; (*fig*) telling-off; **levar um ~ de alguém** to get a telling-off from sb; **passar um ~ em alguém** to give sb a telling-off.

serões [se'rõjʃ] *mpl de* **serão.**

serpeante [sex'pjãtʃi] *adj* wriggling; (*fig: caminho, rio*) winding, meandering.

serpear [sex'pja*] *vi* (*como serpente*) to wriggle; (*fig: caminho, rio*) to wind, meander.

serpente [sex'pẽtʃi] *f* snake; (*pessoa*) snake in the grass.

serpentear [sexpẽ'tʃja*] *vi* = **serpear.**

serpentina [sexpẽ'tʃina] *f* (*conduto*) coil; (*fita de papel*) streamer.

serra ['sɛxa] *f* (*montanha*) mountain range; (TEC) saw; **~ circular** circular saw; **~ de arco** hacksaw; **~ de cadeia** chain saw; **~ tico-tico** fret saw.

serrado/a [se'xadu/a] *adj* serrated.

serragem [se'xaʒẽ] *f* (*pó*) sawdust.

Serra Leoa *f* Sierra Leone.

serralheiro/a [sexa'ʎejru/a] *m/f* locksmith.

serrania [sexa'nia] *f* mountain range.

serrano/a [se'xanu/a] *adj* highland ♦ *m/f* highlander.

serrar [se'xa*] *vt* to saw.

serraria [sexa'ria] *f* sawmill.

serrote [se'xɔtʃi] *m* handsaw.

sertanejo/a [sexta'neʒu/a] *adj* rustic, country *atr* ♦ *m/f* inhabitant of the "sertão".

sertão [sex'tãw] (*pl* **-ões**) *m* backwoods *pl*, bush (country).

servente [sex'vẽtʃi] *m/f* (*criado*) servant; (*operário*) assistant; **~ de pedreiro** bricklayer's mate.

serventuário/a [sexvẽ'twarju/a] *m/f* (JUR) legal official.

serviçal [sexvi'saw] (*pl* **-ais**) *adj* obliging, helpful ♦ *m/f* (*criado*) servant; (*trabalhador*) wage earner.

serviço [sex'visu] *m* service; (*de chá etc*) set; **o ~** (*emprego*) work; **um ~** (*trabalho*) a job; **não brincar em ~** not to waste time; **dar o ~** (*col: confessar*) to blab; **estar de ~** to be on duty; **matar o ~** to cut corners; **prestar ~** to help; **~ ativo** (MIL) active duty; **~ de informações** (MIL) intelligence service; **~ doméstico** housework; **~ militar** military service; **S~ Nacional de Saúde** National Health Service; **S~ Público** Civil Service; **~s públicos** public utilities.

servidão [sexvi'dãw] *f* servitude, serfdom; (JUR: *de passagem*) right of way.

servido/a [sex'vidu/a] *adj* served; **~ de** (*provido*) supplied with, provided with; **você está ~?** (*num bar*) are you all right for a drink?

servidor(a) [sexvi'do*(a)] *m/f* (*criado*) servant; (*funcionário*) employee; **~ público** civil servant.

servil [sex'viw] (*pl* **-is**) *adj* servile.

servir [sex'vi*] *vt* to serve ♦ *vi* to serve; (*ser útil*) to be useful; (*ajudar*) to help; (*roupa: caber*) to fit; **~-se** *vr*: **~-se (de)** (*comida, café*) to help o.s. (to); (*meios*) to use, make use of; **~ de algo** to serve as sth; **para que serve isto?** what is this for?; **ele não serve para trabalhar aqui** he's not suitable to work here; **qualquer ônibus serve** any bus will do.

servis [sex'viʃ] *adj pl de* **servil.**

servível [sex'vivew] (*pl* **-eis**) *adj* serviceable; (*roupa*) wearable.

servo/a ['sɛxvu/a] *m/f* (*feudal*) serf; (*criado*) servant.

servo-croata [sɛxvu'krwata] *m* (LING) Serbo-Croat.

Sesc ['sɛʃki] (BR) *abr m* = **Serviço Social do Comércio.**

Sesi [sɛ'zi] (BR) *abr m* = **Serviço Social da Indústria.**

sessão [se'sãw] (*pl* **-ões**) *f* (*do parlamento etc*) session; (*reunião*) meeting; (*de cinema*) showing; **primeira/segunda ~** first/second show; **~ coruja** late show; **~ da tarde** matinée.

sessenta [se'sẽta] *num* sixty; *V tb* **cinqüenta.**

sessões [se'sõjʃ] *fpl de* **sessão.**

sesta ['sɛʃta] *f* siesta, nap.

set ['sɛtʃi] *m* (TÊNIS) set.

set. *abr* (= *setembro*) Sept.

seta ['sɛta] *f* arrow.

sete ['sɛtʃi] *num* seven; **pintar o ~** (*fig*) to get up to all sorts; *V tb* **cinco.**

setecentos/as [sete'sẽtuʃ/aʃ] *num* seven

NB: European Portuguese adds the following consonants to certain words: **b** (sú(b)dito, su(b)til); **c** (a(c)ção, a(c)cionista, a(c)to); **m** (inde(m)ne); **p** (ado(p)ção, ado(p)tar); *for further details see p. xiii.*

hundred.

sete-e-meio *m* seven-and-a-half (*card game similar to pontoon*).

setembro [se'tẽbru] (*PT*: **S-**) *m* September; *V tb* **julho**.

setenta [se'tẽta] *num* seventy; *V tb* **cinqüenta**.

setentrional [setẽtrjo'naw] (*pl* **-ais**) *adj* northern.

sétima ['sɛtʃima] *f* (*MÚS*) seventh.

sétimo/a ['sɛtʃimu/a] *num* seventh; *V tb* **quinto**.

setor [se'to*] *m* sector.

setuagésimo/a [setwa'ʒɛzimu/a] *num* seventieth; *V tb* **quinto**.

seu/sua [sew/'sua] *adj* (*dele*) his; (*dela*) her; (*de coisa*) its; (*deles, delas*) their; (*de você, vocês*) your ♦ *pron* (*dele*) his; (*dela*) hers; (*deles, delas*) theirs; (*de você, vocês*) yours ♦ *m* (*senhor*) Mr(.); **um homem de ~s 60 anos** a man of about sixty; **~ idiota!** you idiot!

Seul [se'uw] *n* Seoul.

severidade [severi'dadʒi] *f* severity, harshness.

severo/a [se'vɛru/a] *adj* severe, harsh.

seviciar [sevi'sja*] *vt* to ill-treat; (*mulher, criança*) to batter.

sevícias [se'visjaʃ] *fpl* (*maus tratos*) ill treatment *sg*; (*desumanidade*) inhumanity *sg*, cruelty *sg*.

Sevilha [se'viʎa] *n* Seville.

sex. *abr* (= *sexta-feira*) Fri.

sexagésimo/a [seksa'ʒɛzimu/a] *num* sixtieth; *V tb* **quinto**.

sexo ['sɛksu] *m* sex; **de ~ feminino/ masculino** female/male.

sexta ['seʃta] *f* (*tb*: *~-feira*) Friday; (*MÚS*) sixth.

sexta-feira (*pl* **sextas-feiras**) *f* Friday; **S~ Santa** Good Friday; *V tb* **terça-feira**.

sexto/a ['seʃtu/a] *num* sixth; *V tb* **quinto**.

sexual [se'kswaw] (*pl* **-ais**) *adj* sexual; (*vida, ato*) sex *atr*.

sexualidade [sekswali'dadʒi] *f* sexuality.

sexy ['sɛksi] (*pl* **~s**) *adj* sexy.

Seychelles [sej'ʃɛliʃ] *f ou fpl*: **a(s) ~** the Seychelles.

sezão [se'zãw] (*pl* **-ões**) *f* (*febre*) (intermittent) fever; (*malária*) malaria.

s.f.f. (*PT*) *abr* = **se faz favor**.

SFH (*BR*) *abr m* = **Sistema Financeiro de Habitação**.

shopping (center) ['ʃɔpĩŋ('sẽte*)] *m* shopping centre (*BRIT*), (shopping) mall (*US*).

short ['ʃɔxtʃi] *m* (pair of) shorts *pl*.

show [ʃow] (*pl* **~s**) *m* show; (*de cantor, conjunto*) concert, gig; **dar um ~** (*fig*) to put on a real show; (*dar escândalo*) to make a scene; **ser um ~** (*col*) to be a sensation.

showroom [ʃow'rũ] (*pl* **~s**) *m* showroom.

si [si] *pron* oneself; (*ele*) himself; (*ela*) herself; (*coisa*) itself; (*PT*: *você*) yourself, you; (: *vocês*) yourselves; (*eles, elas*) themselves; **em ~** in itself; **fora de ~** beside oneself; **cheio de ~** full of oneself; **voltar a ~** to come round.

siamês/esa [sja'meʃ/eza] *adj* Siamese.

Sibéria [si'bɛrja] *f*: **a ~** Siberia.

sibilar [sibi'la*] *vi* to hiss.

sicário [si'karju] *m* hired assassin.

Sicília [si'silja] *f*: **a ~** Sicily.

sicrano [si'kranu] *m*: **fulano e ~** so-and-so.

SIDA ['sida] (*PT*) *abr f* (= *síndrome de deficiência imunológica adquirida*): **a ~** AIDS.

siderúrgica [side'ruxʒika] *f* steel industry.

siderúrgico/a [side'ruxʒiku/a] *adj* iron and steel *atr*; **(usina) siderúrgica** steelworks.

sidra ['sidra] *f* cider.

SIF (*BR*) *abr m* = **Serviço de Inspeção Federal**.

sifão [si'fãw] (*pl* **-ões**) *m* syphon.

sífilis ['sifiliʃ] *f* syphilis.

sifões [si'fõjʃ] *mpl de* **sifão**.

siga ['siga] *etc vb V* **seguir**.

sigilo [si'ʒilu] *m* secrecy; **guardar ~ sobre algo** to keep quiet about sth.

sigiloso/a [siʒi'lozu/ɔza] *adj* secret.

sigla ['sigla] *f* acronym, abbreviation.

signatário/a [signa'tarju/a] *m/f* signatory.

significação [signifika'sãw] *f* significance.

significado [signifi'kadu] *m* meaning.

significante [signifi'kãtʃi] *adj* significant.

significar [signifi'ka*] *vt* to mean, signify.

significativo/a [signifika'tʃivu/a] *adj* significant.

signo ['signu] *m* sign; **~ do zodíaco** sign of the zodiac.

sigo ['sigu] *etc vb V* **seguir**.

sílaba ['silaba] *f* syllable.

silenciar [silẽ'sja*] *vt* (*pessoa*) to silence; (*escândalo*) to hush up ♦ *vi* to remain silent.

silêncio [si'lẽsju] *m* silence, quiet; **~!** silence!; **ficar em ~** to remain silent.

silencioso/a [silẽ'sjozu/ɔza] *adj* silent, quiet ♦ *m* (*AUTO*) silencer (*BRIT*), muffler (*US*).

silhueta [si'ʎweta] *f* silhouette.

silício [si'lisju] *m* silicon.

silicone [sili'kɔni] *m* silicone.

silo ['silu] *m* silo.

silvar [siw'va*] *vi* to hiss; (*assobiar*) to whistle.

silvestre [siw'vɛʃtri] *adj* wild.

silvícola [siw'vikola] *adj* wild.

silvicultura [siwvikuw'tura] *f* forestry.

sim [sĩ] *adv* yes; **creio que ~** I think so; **isso ~** that's it!; **pelo ~, pelo não** just in case; **dar** *ou* **dizer o ~** to consent, say yes.

simbólico/a [sĩ'bɔliku/a] *adj* symbolic.

simbolismo [sĩbo'liʒmu] *m* symbolism.

simbolizar [sĩboli'za*] *vt* to symbolise.

símbolo ['sĩbolu] *m* symbol.

simetria [sime'tria] *f* symmetry.

simétrico/a [si'mɛtriku/a] *adj* symmetrical.

similar [simi'la*] *adj* similar.

similaridade [similari'dadʒi] *f* similarity.

símile ['simili] *m* simile.
similitude [simili'tudʒi] *f* similarity.
simpatia [sĩpa'tʃia] *f* (*por alguém, algo*) liking; (*afeto*) affection; (*afinidade, solidariedade*) sympathy; **~s** *fpl* (*inclinações*) sympathies; **com ~** sympathetically; **ser uma ~** to be very nice; **ter** *ou* **sentir ~ por** to like.
simpático/a [sĩ'patʃiku/a] *adj* (*pessoa, decoração etc*) nice; (*lugar*) pleasant, nice; (*amável*) kind ♦ *m* (ANAT) nervous system; **ser ~ a** to be sympathetic to.
simpatizante [sĩpatʃi'zãtʃi] *adj* sympathetic ♦ *m/f* sympathizer.
simpatizar [sĩpatʃi'za*] *vi*: **~ com** (*pessoa*) to like; (*causa*) to sympathize with.
simples ['sĩpliʃ] *adj inv* simple; (*único*) single; (*fácil*) easy; (*mero*) mere; (*ingênuo*) naïve ♦ *adv* simply.
simplicidade [sĩplisi'dadʒi] *f* simplicity; (*ingenuidade*) naïveté; (*modéstia*) plainness; (*naturalidade*) naturalness.
simplicíssimo/a [sĩpli'sisimu/a] *adj superl de* **simples**.
simplificação [sĩplifika'sãw] (*pl* **-ões**) *f* simplification.
simplificar [sĩplifi'ka*] *vt* to simplify.
simplíssimo/a [sĩ'plisimu/a] *adj superl de* **simples**.
simplista [sĩ'pliʃta] *adj* simplistic.
simplório/a [sĩ'plɔrju/a] *adj* simple ♦ *m/f* simple person.
simpósio [sĩ'pɔzju] *m* symposium.
simulação [simula'sãw] (*pl* **-ões**) *f* simulation; (*fingimento*) pretence (BRIT), pretense (US), sham.
simulacro [simu'lakru] *m* (*imitação*) imitation; (*fingimento*) pretence (BRIT), pretense (US).
simulado/a [simu'ladu/a] *adj* simulated.
simular [simu'la*] *vt* to simulate.
simultaneamente [simuwtanja'mẽtʃi] *adv* simultaneously.
simultâneo/a [simuw'tanju/a] *adj* simultaneous.
sina ['sina] *f* fate, destiny.
sinagoga [sina'gɔga] *f* synagogue.
Sinai [sina'i] *m* Sinai.
sinal [si'naw] (*pl* **-ais**) *m* (*ger*) sign; (*gesto,* TEL) signal; (*na pele*) mole; (: *de nascença*) birthmark; (*depósito*) deposit; (*tb*: **~** *luminoso*) traffic light; **~ (de tráfego)** traffic light; **~ rodoviário** road sign; **dar de ~** to give as a deposit; **em ~ de** (*fig*) as a sign of; **por ~** (*por falar nisso*) by the way; (*aliás*) as a matter of fact; **avançar o ~** (AUTO) to jump the lights; (*fig*) to jump the gun; **dar ~ de vida** to show up; **fazer ~** to signal; **~ de alarma** alarm; **~ de chamada** (TEL) ringing tone; **~ de discar** (BR) *ou* **de marcar** (PT) dialling (BRIT) *ou* dial (US) tone; **~ de ocupado** (BR) *ou* **de impedido** (PT) engaged tone (BRIT), busy signal (US); **~ de mais/menos** (MAT) plus/minus sign; **~ de perigo** danger signal; **~ de pontuação** punctuation mark; **~ verde** *ou* **aberto/vermelho** *ou* **fechado** green/red light.
sinal-da-cruz *m* sign of the cross; **fazer o ~** to cross o.s.
sinaleiro [sina'lejru] *m* (FERRO) signalman; (*aparelho*) traffic lights *pl*.
sinalização [sinaliza'sãw] *f* (*ato*) signalling; (*para motoristas*) traffic signs *pl*; (FERRO) signals *pl*.
sinalizar [sinali'za*] *vi* to signal.
sinceridade [sĩseri'dadʒi] *f* sincerity.
sincero/a [sĩ'sɛru/a] *adj* sincere; (*opinião, confissão*) honest.
sincopado/a [sĩko'padu/a] *adj* (MÚS) syncopated.
síncope ['sĩkopi] *f* fainting fit.
sincronizar [sĩkroni'za*] *vt* to synchronize.
sindical [sĩdʒi'kaw] (*pl* **-ais**) *adj* (trade) union *atr*.
sindicalismo [sĩdʒika'liʒmu] *m* trade unionism.
sindicalista [sĩdʒika'liʃta] *m/f* trade unionist.
sindicalizar [sĩdʒikali'za*] *vt* to unionize; **~-se** *vr* to become unionized.
sindicância [sĩdʒi'kãsja] *f* inquiry, investigation.
sindicato [sĩdʒi'katu] *m* (*de trabalhadores*) trade union; (*financeiro*) syndicate.
síndico/a ['sĩdʒiku/a] *m/f* (*de condomínio*) manager; (*de massa falida*) receiver.
síndrome ['sĩdromi] *f* syndrome; **~ de deficiência imunológica adquirida** acquired immune deficiency syndrome.
SINE (BR) *abr m* = **Sistema Nacional de Empregos**.
sinecura [sine'kura] *f* sinecure.
sineta [si'neta] *f* bell.
sinfonia [sĩfo'nia] *f* symphony.
sinfônica [sĩ'fonika] *f* (*tb*: *orquestra* ~) symphony orchestra.
sinfônico/a [sĩ'foniku/a] *adj* symphonic.
singeleza [sĩʒe'leza] *f* simplicity.
singelo/a [sĩ'ʒɛlu/a] *adj* simple.
singular [sĩgu'la*] *adj* singular; (*extraordinário*) exceptional; (*bizarro*) odd, peculiar.
singularidade [sĩgulari'dadʒi] *f* peculiarity.
singularizar [sĩgulari'za*] *vt* (*distinguir*) to single out; **~-se** *vr* to stand out, distinguish o.s.
sinistrado/a [siniʃ'tradu/a] *adj* damaged.
sinistro/a [si'niʃtru/a] *adj* sinister ♦ *m* disaster, accident; (*prejuízo*) damage.
sino ['sinu] *m* bell.
sinônimo/a [si'nonimu/a] *adj* synonymous ♦ *m* synonym.

NB: European Portuguese adds the following consonants to certain words: **b** (sú(b)dito, su(b)til); **c** (a(c)ção, a(c)cionista, a(c)to); **m** (inde(m)ne); **p** (ado(p)ção, ado(p)tar); *for further details see p. xiii.*

sinopse [si'nɔpsi] *f* synopsis.
sinta ['sĩta] *etc vb V* **sentir**.
sintático/a [sĩ'tatʃiku/a] *adj* syntactic.
sintaxe [sĩ'tasi] *f* syntax.
síntese ['sĩtezi] *f* synthesis; **em** ~ in short.
sintético/a [sĩ'tɛtʃiku/a] *adj* synthetic; (*resumido*) brief.
sintetizar [sĩtetʃi'za*] *vt* to synthesize; (*resumir*) to summarize.
sinto ['sĩtu] *etc vb V* **sentir**.
sintoma [sĩ'tɔma] *m* symptom.
sintomático/a [sĩto'matʃiku/a] *adj* symptomatic.
sintonizador [sĩtoniza'do*] *m* tuner.
sintonizar [sĩtoni'za*] *vt* (RÁDIO) to tune ♦ *vi* to tune in; ~ **(com)** (*pessoa*) to get on (with); (*opinião*) to coincide (with).
sinuca [si'nuka] *f* snooker; (*mesa*) snooker table; **estar numa** ~ (*col*) to be snookered.
sinuoso/a [si'nwozu/ɔza] *adj* (*caminho*) winding; (*linha*) wavy.
sinusite [sinu'zitʃi] *f* sinusitis.
sionismo [sjo'niʒmu] *m* Zionism.
sionista [sjo'niʃta] *adj*, *m/f* Zionist.
sirena [si'rɛna] *f* siren.
sirene [si'rɛni] *f* = **sirena**.
siri [si'ri] *m* crab; **casquinha de** ~ (CULIN) crab au gratin.
sirigaita [siri'gajta] (*col*) *f* floozy.
Síria ['sirja] *f*: **a** ~ Syria.
sírio/a ['sirju/a] *adj*, *m/f* Syrian.
sirvo ['sixvu] *vb V* **servir**.
siso ['sizu] *m* good sense; **dente de** ~ wisdom tooth.
sísmico/a ['siʒmiku/a] *adj* seismic.
sismógrafo [siʒ'mɔgrafu] *m* seismograph.
sistema [siʃ'tɛma] *m* system; (*método*) method; ~ **operacional** (COMPUT) operating system; ~ **solar** solar system.
sistemático/a [siʃte'matʃiku/a] *adj* systematic.
sistematizar [siʃtematʃi'za*] *vt* to systematize.
sisudo/a [si'zudu/a] *adj* serious, sober.
sitiar [si'tʃja*] *vt* to besiege.
sítio ['sitʃju] *m* (MIL) siege; (*propriedade rural*) small farm; (PT: *lugar*) place; **estado de** ~ state of siege.
situação [sitwa'sãw] (*pl* **-ões**) *f* situation; (*posição*) position; (*social*) standing.
situado/a [si'twadu/a] *adj* situated; **estar** *ou* **ficar** ~ to be situated.
situar [si'twa*] *vt* (*pôr*) to place, put; (*edifício*) to situate, locate; **~-se** *vr* (*pôr-se*) to position o.s.; (*estar situado*) to be situated.
SL *abr* = **sobreloja**.
sl *abr* = **sobreloja**.
slogan [iʃ'lɔgã] (*pl* **~s**) *m* slogan.
smoking [iʒ'mokĩʃ] (*pl* **~s**) *m* dinner jacket (BRIT), tuxedo (US).
SMTU (BR) *abr f* = **Superintendência Municipal de Transportes Urbanos**.
SNI (BR) *abr m* (*antes*: = *Serviço Nacional de Informações*) *state intelligence service*.
só [sɔ] *adj* alone; (*único*) single; (*solitário*) solitary ♦ *adv* only; **um** ~ only one; **a ~s** alone; **por si** ~ by himself (*ou* herself, itself); **é ~!** that's all!; **é** ~ **discar** all you have to do is dial; **veja/imagine** ~ just look/imagine; **não** ~ **... mas também** ... not only ... but also ...; **que** *ou* **como** ~ **ele** *etc* like nobody else; ~ **isso?** is that all?
soalho ['swaʎu] *m* = **assoalho**.
soar [swa*] *vi* to sound; (*cantar*) to sing; (*sinos*, *clarins*) to ring; (*apito*) to blow; (*boato*) to go round ♦ *vt* (*horas*) to strike; (*instrumento*) to play; ~ **a** to sound like; ~ **bem/mal** (*fig*) to go down well/badly.
sob [sob] *prep* under; ~ **emenda** subject to correction; ~ **juramento** on oath; ~ **medida** (*roupa*) made to measure; (*software*) bespoke; ~ **minha palavra** on my word; ~ **pena de** on pain of.
sobe ['sɔbi] *etc vb V* **subir**.
sobejar [sobe'ʒa*] *vi* (*superabundar*) to abound; (*restar*) to be left over.
sobejos [so'beʒuʃ] *mpl* remains, leftovers.
soberania [sobera'nia] *f* sovereignty.
soberano/a [sobe'ranu/a] *adj* sovereign; (*fig*: *supremo*) supreme; (: *altivo*) haughty ♦ *m/f* sovereign.
soberba [so'bexba] *f* haughtiness, arrogance.
soberbo/a [so'bexbu/a] *adj* (*arrogante*) haughty, arrogant; (*magnífico*) magnificent, splendid.
sobra ['sɔbra] *f* surplus, remnant; **~s** *fpl* remains; (*de comida*) leftovers, remains; **ter algo de** ~ to have sth extra; (*tempo*, *comida*, *motivos*) to have plenty of sth; **ficar de** ~ to be left over.
sobraçar [sobra'sa*] *vt* (*levar debaixo do braço*) to carry under one's arm; (*meter debaixo do braço*) to put under one's arm.
sobrado [so'bradu] *m* (*andar*) floor; (*casa*) house (*of two or more storeys*).
sobranceiro/a [sobrã'sejru/a] *adj* (*que está acima de*) lofty, towering; (*proeminente*) prominent; (*arrogante*) haughty, arrogant.
sobrancelha [sobrã'seʎa] *f* eyebrow.
sobrar [so'bra*] *vi* to be left; (*dúvidas*) to remain; **ficar sobrando** (*pessoa*) to be left out; (: *não ter parceiro*) to be the odd one out; **sobram-me cinco** I have five left; **isto dá e sobra** this is more than enough.
sobre ['sobri] *prep* on; (*por cima de*) over; (*acima de*) above; (*a respeito de*) about; **ser meio** ~ **o chato** (*col*) to be a bit boring.
sobreaviso [sobrja'vizu] *m* warning; **estar de** ~ to be alert, be on one's guard.
sobrecapa [sobri'kapa] *f* cover.
sobrecarga [sobri'kaxga] *f* overload.
sobrecarregar [sobrikaxe'ga*] *vt* to overload.
sobreestimar [sobrjeʃtʃi'ma*] *vt* to overestimate.
sobre-humano/a *adj* superhuman.
sobrejacente [sobriʒa'sẽtʃi] *adj*: ~ **a** over.
sobreloja [sobri'lɔʒa] *f* mezzanine (floor).

sobremaneira [sobrema'nejra] *adv* exceedingly.
sobremesa [sobri'meza] *f* dessert.
sobremodo [sobri'mɔdu] *adv* exceedingly.
sobrenatural [sobrinatu'raw] (*pl* **-ais**) *adj* supernatural; (*esforço*) superhuman ♦ *m*: **o ~** the supernatural.
sobrenome [sobri'nɔmi] (*BR*) *m* surname, family name.
sobrepairar [sobripaj'ra*] *vi*: **~ a** to hover above; (*crise*) to rise above.
sobrepor [sobri'po*] (*irreg*: *como* **pôr**) *vt*: **~ algo a algo** (*pôr em cima*) to put sth on top of sth; (*adicionar*) to add sth to sth; (*dar preferência*) to put sth before sth; **~-se** *vr*: **~-se a** (*pôr-se sobre*) to cover, go on top of; (*sobrevir*) to succeed.
sobrepujar [sobripu'ʒa*] *vt* (*exceder em altura*) to rise above; (*superar*) to surpass; (*obstáculos, perigos*) to overcome; (*inimigo*) to overwhelm.
sobrepunha [sobri'puɲa] *etc vb V* **sobrepor**.
sobrepus [sobri'pujʃ] *etc vb V* **sobrepor**.
sobrepuser [sobripu'ze*] *etc vb V* **sobrepor**.
sobrescritar [sobreʃkri'ta*] *vt* to address.
sobrescrito [sobreʃ'kritu] *m* address.
sobressair [sobrisa'i*] *vi* to stand out; **~-se** *vr* to stand out.
sobressalente [sobrisa'lẽtʃi] *adj, m* spare.
sobressaltado/a [sobrisaw'tadu/a] *adj*: **viver ~** to live in fear; **acordar ~** to wake up with a start.
sobressaltar [sobrisaw'ta*] *vt* to startle, frighten; **~-se** *vr* to be startled.
sobressalto [sobri'sawtu] *m* (*movimento brusco*) start; (*temor*) trepidation; **de ~** suddenly; **o seu ~ com aquele estrondo/aquela notícia** his fright at that noise/his shock at that news; **ter um ~** to get a fright.
sobretaxa [sobri'taʃa] *f* surcharge.
sobretudo [sobri'tudu] *m* overcoat ♦ *adv* above all, especially.
sobrevir [sobri'vi*] (*irreg*: *como* **vir**) *vi* to occur, arise; **~ a** (*seguir*) to follow (on from); **sobreveio-lhe uma doença** he was struck down by illness.
sobrevivência [sobrivi'vẽsja] *f* survival.
sobrevivente [sobrivi'vẽtʃi] *adj* surviving ♦ *m/f* survivor.
sobreviver [sobrivi've*] *vi*: **~ (a)** to survive.
sobrevoar [sobrivo'a*] *vt, vi* to fly over.
sobriedade [sobrje'dadʒi] *f* soberness; (*comedimento*) moderation, restraint.
sobrinho/a [so'briɲu/a] *m/f* nephew/niece.
sóbrio/a ['sɔbrju/a] *adj* sober; (*moderado*) moderate, restrained.
socado/a [so'kadu/a] *adj* (*alho*) crushed; (*escondido*) hidden; (*pessoa*) stout.
socador [soka'do*] *m* crusher; **~ de alho** garlic press.
soçaite [so'sajtʃi] (*col*) *m* high society.
socapa [so'kapa] *f*: **à ~** furtively, on the sly.
socar [so'ka*] *vt* (*esmurrar*) to hit, strike; (*calcar*) to crush, pound; (*massa de pão*) to knead.
social [so'sjaw] (*pl* **-ais**) *adj* social; (*entrada, elevador*) private; (*camisa*) dress *atr*.
socialismo [sosja'liʒmu] *m* socialism.
socialista [sosja'liʃta] *adj, m/f* socialist.
socialite [sosja'lajtʃi] *m/f* socialite.
socializar [sosjali'za*] *vt* to socialize.
sociável [so'sjavew] (*pl* **-eis**) *adj* sociable.
sociedade [sosje'dadʒi] *f* society; (*COM*: *empresa*) company; (: *de sócios*) partnership; (*associação*) association; **~ anônima** joint-stock *ou* limited company; **~ anônima aberta/fechada** public/private limited company.
sócio/a ['sɔsju/a] *m/f* (*COM*) partner, associate; (*de clube*) member; **~ comanditário** (*COM*) silent partner.
socio-econômico/a *adj* socio-economic.
sociolingüística [sosjolĩ'gwiʃtʃika] *f* sociolinguistics *sg*.
sociologia [sosjolo'ʒia] *f* sociology.
sociológico/a [sosjo'lɔʒiku/a] *adj* sociological.
sociólogo/a [so'sjɔlogu/a] *m/f* sociologist.
socio-político/a *adj* socio-political.
soco ['soku] *m* punch; **dar um ~ em** to punch.
soçobrar [soso'bra*] *vt* (*afundar*) to sink ♦ *vi* to sink; (*esperanças*) to founder; **~ em** (*fig*: *no vício etc*) to sink into.
soco-inglês (*pl* **socos-ingleses**) *m* knuckle-duster.
socorrer [soko'xe*] *vt* (*ajudar*) to help, assist; (*salvar*) to rescue; **~-se** *vr*: **~-se de** to resort to, have recourse to.
socorro [so'koxu] *m* help, assistance; (*reboque*) breakdown (*BRIT*) *ou* tow (*US*) truck; **ir em ~ de** to come to the aid of; **primeiros ~s** first aid *sg*; **~!** help!; **equipe de ~** rescue team.
soda ['sɔda] *f* soda (water); **pedir ~** (*col*) to back off, back down; **~ cáustica** caustic soda.
sódio ['sɔdʒju] *m* sodium.
sodomia [sodo'mia] *f* sodomy.
sofá [so'fa] *m* sofa, settee.
sofá-cama (*pl* **sofás-camas**) *m* sofa-bed.
Sófia ['sɔfja] *n* Sofia.
sofisma [so'fiʒma] *m* sophism; (*col*) trick.
sofismar [sofiʒ'ma*] *vt* (*fatos*) to twist; (*enganar*) to swindle, cheat.
sofisticação [sofiʃtʃika'sãw] *f* sophistication.
sofisticado/a [sofiʃtʃi'kadu/a] *adj* sophisticated; (*afetado*) pretentious.
sofisticar [sofiʃtʃi'ka*] *vt* to refine.
sôfrego/a ['sofregu/a] *adj* (*ávido*) keen; (*impaciente*) impatient; (*no comer*) greedy.
sofreguidão [sofregi'dãw] *f* keenness; (*im-*

NB: *European Portuguese adds the following consonants to certain words:* **b** (sú(b)dito, su(b)til); **c** (a(c)ção, a(c)cionista, a(c)to); **m** (inde(m)ne); **p** (ado(p)ção, ado(p)tar); *for further details see p. xiii.*

paciência) impatience; (*no comer*) greed.
sofrer [so'fre*] *vt* to suffer; (*acidente*) to have; (*agüentar*) to bear, put up with; (*experimentar*) to undergo, experience ♦ *vi* to suffer; ~ **de reumatismo/do fígado** to suffer from rheumatism/with one's liver.
sofrido/a [so'fridu/a] *adj* long-suffering.
sofrimento [sofri'mẽtu] *m* suffering.
sofrível [so'frivew] (*pl* **-eis**) *adj* bearable; (*razoável*) reasonable.
soft ['sɔftʃi] (*pl* **~s**) *m* (COMPUT) piece of software, software package.
software [sof'twe*] (*pl* **~s**) *m* (COMPUT) software; **um** ~ a piece of software.
sogro/a ['sogru/'sɔgra] *m/f* father-in-law/mother-in-law.
sóis [sɔjʃ] *mpl de* **sol**.
soja ['sɔʒa] *f* soya (BRIT), soy (US); **leite de** ~ soya *ou* soy milk.
sol [sɔw] (*pl* **sóis**) *m* sun; (*luz*) sunshine, sunlight; **ao** *ou* **no** ~ in the sun; **fazer** ~ to be sunny; **pegar** ~ to sunbathe; **tomar (banho de)** ~ to sunbathe.
sola ['sɔla] *f* sole.
solado/a [so'ladu/a] *adj* (*bolo*) flat.
solão [so'lãw] *m* very hot sun.
solapar [sola'pa*] *vt* (*escavar*) to dig into; (*abalar*) to shake; (*fig*: *arruinar*) to destroy.
solar [so'la*] *adj* solar ♦ *m* manor house ♦ *vt* (*sapato*) to sole ♦ *vi* (*bolo*) not to rise; (*cantor*, *músico*) to sing (*ou* play) solo.
solavanco [sola'vãku] *m* jolt, bump; **andar aos ~s** to jog along.
solda ['sɔwda] *f* solder.
soldado [sow'dadu] *m* soldier; ~ **de chumbo** toy soldier; ~ **raso** private soldier.
soldador(a) [sowda'do*(a)] *m/f* welder.
soldadura [sowda'dura] *f* (*ato*) welding; (*parte soldada*) weld.
soldagem [sow'daʒẽ] *f* welding.
soldar [sow'da*] *vt* to weld; (*fig*) to unite, amalgamate.
soldo ['sowdu] *m* (MIL) pay.
soleira [so'lejra] *f* doorstep.
solene [so'lɛni] *adj* solemn.
solenidade [soleni'dadʒi] *f* solemnity; (*cerimônia*) ceremony.
solenizar [soleni'za*] *vt* to solemnize.
solércia [so'lɛxsja] *f* ploy.
soletração [soletra'sãw] *f* spelling.
soletrar [sole'tra*] *vt* to spell; (*ler devagar*) to read out slowly.
solicitação [solisita'sãw] (*pl* **-ões**) *f* request; **solicitações** *fpl* (*apelo*) appeal *sg*.
solicitar [solisi'ta*] *vt* to ask for; (*requerer*: *emprego etc*) to apply for; (*amizade*, *atenção*) to seek; ~ **algo a alguém** to ask sb for sth.
solícito/a [so'lisitu/a] *adj* helpful.
solicitude [solisi'tudʒi] *f* (*zelo*) care; (*boa vontade*) concern, thoughtfulness; (*empenho*) commitment.
solidão [soli'dãw] *f* solitude, isolation; (*sensação*) loneliness; (*de lugar*) desolation; **sentir** ~ to feel lonely.
solidariedade [solidarje'dadʒi] *f* solidarity.
solidário/a [soli'darju/a] *adj* (*pessoas*) who show solidarity; (*a uma causa etc*) sympathetic; (JUR: *obrigação*) mutually binding; (: *devedores*) jointly liable; **ser** ~ **com** to stand by.
solidarizar [solidari'za*] *vt* to bring together; **~-se** *vr* to join forces.
solidez [soli'deʒ] *f* solidity, strength.
solidificar [solidʒifi'ka*] *vt* to solidify; (*fig*) to consolidate; **~-se** *vr* to solidify; to be consolidated.
sólido/a ['sɔlidu/a] *adj* solid.
solilóquio [soli'lɔkju] *m* soliloquy.
solista [so'liʃta] *m/f* soloist.
solitária [soli'tarja] *f* (*verme*) tapeworm; (*cela*) solitary confinement.
solitário/a [soli'tarju/a] *adj* lonely, solitary ♦ *m* hermit; (*jóia*) solitaire.
solo ['sɔlu] *m* ground, earth; (MÚS) solo.
soltar [sow'ta*] *vt* (*tornar livre*) to set free; (*desatar*) to loosen, untie; (*afrouxar*) to slacken, loosen; (*largar*) to let go of; (*emitir*) to emit; (*grito, risada*) to let out; (*foguete*, *fogos de artifício*) to set *ou* let off; (*cabelo*) to let down; (*freio*, *animais*) to release; (*piada*) to tell; **~-se** *vr* (*desprender-se*) to come loose; (*desinibir-se*) to let o.s. go; ~ **palavrão** to swear.
solteira [sol'tejra] *f* single woman, spinster.
solteirão [sowtej'rãw] (*pl* **-ões**) *m* bachelor.
solteiro/a [sow'tejru/a] *adj* unmarried, single ♦ *m* bachelor.
solteirões [sowtej'rõjʃ] *mpl de* **solteirão**.
solteirona [sowtej'rɔna] *f* old maid.
solto/a ['sowtu/a] *pp de* **soltar** ♦ *adj* loose; (*livre*) free; (*sozinho*) alone; (*arroz*) fluffy; **à solta** freely.
soltura [sow'tura] *f* looseness; (*liberdade*) release, discharge.
solução [solu'sãw] (*pl* **-ões**) *f* solution.
soluçar [solu'sa*] *vi* (*chorar*) to sob; (MED) to hiccup.
solucionar [solusjo'na*] *vt* to solve; (*decidir*) to resolve.
soluço [so'lusu] *m* (*pranto*) sob; (MED) hiccup.
soluções [solu'sõjʃ] *fpl de* **solução**.
solúvel [so'luvew] (*pl* **-eis**) *adj* soluble.
solvência [sow'vẽsja] *f* solvency.
solvente [sow'vẽtʃi] *adj*, *m* solvent.
som [sõ] (*pl* **-ns**) *m* sound; (MÚS) tone; (BR: *equipamento*) hi-fi, stereo; (: *música*) music; **ao** ~ **de** (MÚS) to the accompaniment of.
soma ['sɔma] *f* sum.
Somália [so'malja] *f*: **a** ~ Somalia.
somar [so'ma*] *vt* (*adicionar*) to add (up); (*chegar a*) to add up to, amount to ♦ *vi* to add up.
somatório [soma'tɔrju] *m* sum; (*fig*) sum total.
sombra ['sõbra] *f* shadow; (*proteção*) shade;

(*indício*) trace, sign; **à ~ de** in the shade of; (*fig*) under the protection of; **sem ~ de dúvida** without a shadow of a doubt; **querer ~ e água fresca** (*fig*) to want the good things in life.
sombreado/a [sõ'brjadu/a] *adj* shady ♦ *m* shading.
sombrear [sõ'brja*] *vt* to shade.
sombreiro [sõ'brejru] *m* (*chapéu*) sombrero.
sombrinha [sõ'briɲa] *f* parasol, sunshade; (*BR*) lady's umbrella.
sombrio/a [sõ'briu/a] *adj* (*escuro*) shady, dark; (*triste*) gloomy; (*rosto*) grim.
some ['sɔmi] *etc vb V* **sumir**.
somenos [so'menuʃ] *adj* inferior, poor; **de ~ importância** unimportant.
somente [sɔ'mẽtʃi] *adv* only; **tão ~** only.
somos ['somoʃ] *vb V* **ser**.
sonambulismo [sonãbu'liʒmu] *m* sleepwalking.
sonâmbulo/a [so'nãbulu/a] *adj* sleepwalking ♦ *m/f* sleepwalker.
sonante [so'nãtʃi] *adj*: **moeda ~** cash.
sonata [so'nata] *f* sonata.
sonda ['sõda] *f* (*NÁUT*) plummet, sounding lead; (*MED*) probe; (*de petróleo*) drill; (*de alimentação*) drip; **~ espacial** space probe.
sondagem [sõ'daʒẽ] (*pl* **-ns**) *f* (*NÁUT*) sounding; (*de terreno, opinião*) survey; (*para petróleo*) drilling; (*para minerais*) boring; (*atmosférica*) testing.
sondar [sõ'da*] *vt* to probe; (*opinião etc*) to sound out.
soneca [so'nɛka] *f* nap, snooze; **tirar uma ~** to have a nap.
sonegação [sonega'sãw] *f* withholding; (*furto*) theft; **~ de impostos** tax evasion.
sonegar [sone'ga*] *vt* (*dinheiro, valores*) to conceal, withhold; (*furtar*) to steal, pilfer; (*impostos*) to dodge, evade; (*informações, dados*) to withhold.
soneto [so'netu] *m* sonnet.
sonhador(a) [soɲa'do*(a)] *adj* dreamy ♦ *m/f* dreamer.
sonhar [so'ɲa*] *vt, vi* to dream; **~ com** to dream about; **~ em fazer** to dream of doing; **~ acordado** to daydream; **nem sonhando** *ou* **~!** (*col*) no way!
sonho ['sɔɲu] *m* dream; (*CULIN*) doughnut.
sono ['sɔnu] *m* sleep; **estar caindo de ~** to be half-asleep; **estar com** *ou* **ter ~** to be sleepy; **estar sem ~** not to be sleepy; **ferrar no ~** to fall into a deep sleep; **pegar no ~** to fall asleep; **ter o ~ leve/pesado** to be a light/heavy sleeper.
sonolência [sono'lẽsja] *f* drowsiness.
sonolento/a [sono'lẽtu/a] *adj* sleepy, drowsy.
sonoridade [sonori'dadʒi] *f* sound quality.
sonoro/a [so'nɔru/a] *adj* resonant; (*consoante*) voiced.
sonoterapia [sonotera'pia] *f* hypnotherapy.
sons [sõʃ] *mpl de* **som**.
sonso/a ['sõsu/a] *adj* sly, artful.
sopa ['sopa] *f* soup; (*col*) pushover, cinch; **dar ~** (*abundar*) to be plentiful; (*estar disponível*) to go spare; (*descuidar-se*) to be careless; **essa ~ vai acabar** (*col*) all good things come to an end; **~ de legumes** vegetable soup.
sopapear [sopa'pja*] *vt* to slap.
sopapo [so'papu] *m* slap, cuff; **dar um ~ em** to slap.
sopé [so'pɛ] *m* foot, bottom.
sopeira [so'pejra] *f* (*CULIN*) soup dish.
sopitar [sopi'ta*] *vt* (*conter*) to curb, repress.
soporífero/a [sopo'riferu/a] *adj* soporific ♦ *m* sleeping drug.
soporífico/a [sopo'rifiku/a] *adj, m* = **soporífero**.
soprano [so'pranu] *adj, m/f* soprano.
soprar [so'pra*] *vt* to blow; (*balão*) to blow up; (*vela*) to blow out; (*dizer em voz baixa*) to whisper ♦ *vi* to blow.
sopro ['sopru] *m* blow, puff; (*de vento*) gust; (*no coração*) murmur; **instrumento de ~** wind instrument.
soquei [so'kej] *etc vb V* **socar**.
soquete [so'kɛtʃi] *f* ankle sock.
sordidez [soxdʒi'deʒ] *f* sordidness; (*imundície*) squalor.
sórdido/a ['sɔxdʒidu/a] *adj* sordid; (*imundo*) squalid; (*obsceno*) indecent, dirty.
soro ['soru] *m* (*MED*) serum; (*do leite*) whey.
sóror ['sɔro*] *f* (*REL*) sister.
sorrateiro/a [soxa'tejru/a] *adj* sly, sneaky.
sorridente [soxi'dẽtʃi] *adj* smiling.
sorrir [so'xi*] *vi* to smile.
sorriso [so'xizu] *m* smile; **~ amarelo** forced smile.
sorte ['sɔxtʃi] *f* luck; (*casualidade*) chance; (*destino*) fate, destiny; (*condição*) lot; (*espécie*) sort, kind; **de ~** (*pessoa etc*) lucky; **desta ~** so, thus; **de ~ que** so that; **por ~** luckily; **dar ~** (*trazer sorte*) to bring good luck; (*ter sorte*) to be lucky; **estar com** *ou* **ter ~** to be lucky; **tentar a ~** to try one's luck; **ter a ~ de** to be lucky enough to; **tirar a ~** to draw lots; **tirar a ~ grande** (*tb fig*) to hit the jackpot; **~ grande** big prize.
sorteado/a [sox'tʃjadu/a] *adj* (*pessoa, bilhete*) winning; (*MIL*) conscripted.
sortear [sox'tʃja*] *vt* to draw lots for; (*rifar*) to raffle; (*MIL*) to draft.
sorteio [sox'teju] *m* draw; (*rifa*) raffle; (*MIL*) draft.
sortido/a [sox'tʃidu/a] *adj* (*abastecido*) supplied, stocked; (*variado*) assorted; (*loja*) well-stocked.
sortilégio [soxtʃi'lɛʒu] *m* (*bruxaria*) sorcery; (*encantamento*) charm, fascination.

***NB:** European Portuguese adds the following consonants to certain words:* **b** (sú(b)dito, su(b)til); **c** (a(c)ção, a(c)cionista, a(c)to); **m** (inde(m)ne); **p** (ado(p)ção, ado(p)tar); *for further details see p. xiii.*

sortimento [soxtʃi'mẽtu] *m* assortment, stock.
sortir [sox'tʃi*] *vt* (*abastecer*) to supply, stock; (*variar*) to vary, mix.
sortudo/a [sox'tudu/a] (*col*) *adj* lucky ♦ *m/f* lucky beggar.
sorumbático/a [sorũ'batʃiku/a] *adj* gloomy, melancholy.
sorvedouro [soxve'doru] *m* whirlpool; (*abismo*) chasm; **um ~ de dinheiro** (*fig*) a drain on resources.
sorver [sox've*] *vt* (*beber*) to sip; (*inalar*) to inhale; (*tragar*) to swallow up; (*absorver*) to soak up, absorb.
sorvete [sox'vetʃi] (*BR*) *m* (*feito com leite*) ice cream; (*feito com água*) sorbet; **~ de chocolate/creme** chocolate/dairy ice cream.
sorveteiro [soxve'tejru] *m* ice-cream man.
sorveteria [soxvete'ria] *f* ice-cream parlour (*BRIT*) *ou* parlor (*US*).
sorvo ['soxvu] *m* sip.
SOS *abr* SOS.
sósia ['sɔzja] *m/f* double.
soslaio [soʒ'laju]: **de ~** *adv:* sideways, obliquely; **olhar algo de ~** to squint at sth.
sossegado/a [sose'gadu/a] *adj* peaceful, calm.
sossegar [sose'ga*] *vt* to calm, quieten ♦ *vi* to quieten down.
sossego [so'segu] *m* peace (and quiet).
sotaina [so'tajna] *f* cassock, soutane.
sótão ['sɔtãw] (*pl* **~s**) *m* attic, loft.
sotaque [so'taki] *m* accent.
sotavento [sota'vẽtu] *m* (*NÁUT*) lee; **a ~** to leeward.
soterrar [sote'xa*] *vt* to bury.
soturno/a [so'tuxnu/a] *adj* sad, gloomy.
sou [so] *vb V* **ser**.
soube ['sobi] *etc vb V* **saber**.
soutien [su'tʃjã] *m* = **sutiã**.
sova ['sɔva] *f* beating, thrashing; **dar uma ~ em alguém** to beat sb up; **levar uma ~ (de alguém)** to be beaten up (by sb).
sovaco [so'vaku] *m* armpit.
sovaqueira [sova'kejra] *f* body odour (*BRIT*) *ou* odor (*US*).
sovar [so'va*] *vt* (*surrar*) to beat, thrash; (*massa*) to knead; (*uva*) to tread; (*roupa*) to wear out; (*couro*) to soften up.
soviético/a [so'vjɛtʃiku/a] *adj, m/f* Soviet.
sovina [so'vina] *m/f* miser, skinflint ♦ *adj* mean, stingy.
sovinice [sovi'nisi] *f* meanness.
sozinho/a [sɔ'ziɲu/a] *adj* (all) alone, by oneself; (*por si mesmo*) by oneself.
SP *abr* = **São Paulo**.
SPI (*BR*) *abr m* = **Serviço de Proteção ao Índio**.
spot [iʃ'pɔtʃi] (*pl* **~s**) *m* spotlight.
spray [iʃ'prej] (*pl* **~s**) *m* spray.
spread [iʃ'prɛdʒi] *m* (*COM*) spread.
SPU (*BR*) *abr m* = **Serviço de Patrimônio da União; = Serviço Psiquiátrico de Urgência**.
squash [iʃ'kwɛʃ] *m* squash.
Sr. *abr* (= *senhor*) Mr(.).
Sr.ª *abr* (= *senhora*) Mrs(.).
Sri Lanka [ʃri'lãka] *m*: **o ~** Sri Lanka.
Sr.ᵗᵃ *abr* (= *senhorita*) Miss.
SSP (*BR*) *abr f* = **Secretaria de Segurança Pública**.
staff [iʃ'tafi] *m* staff.
standard [iʃ'tãdaxdʒi] *adj inv* standard.
status [iʃ'tatus] *m* status.
STF (*BR*) *abr m* = **Supremo Tribunal Federal**.
STM (*BR*) *abr m* = **Supremo Tribunal Militar**.
sua ['sua] *f de* **seu**.
suado/a ['swadu/a] *adj* sweaty; (*fig: dinheiro etc*) hard-earned.
suadouro [swa'doru] *m* sweat; (*lugar*) sauna.
suar [swa*] *vt* to sweat ♦ *vi* to sweat; (*fig*): **~ por algo/para conseguir algo** to sweat blood for sth/to get sth; **~ em bicas** to sweat buckets; **~ frio** to come out in a cold sweat.
suástica ['swaʃtʃika] *f* swastika.
suave ['swavi] *adj* gentle; (*música, voz*) soft; (*sabor, vinho*) smooth; (*cheiro*) delicate; (*dor*) mild; (*trabalho*) light; (*prestações*) easy.
suavidade [suavi'dadʒi] *f* gentleness; (*de voz*) softness.
suavizar [swavi'za*] *vt* to soften; (*dor, sofrimento*) to alleviate.
subalimentado/a [subalimẽ'tadu/a] *adj* undernourished.
subalterno/a [subaw'tɛxnu/a] *adj* inferior, subordinate ♦ *m/f* subordinate.
subalugar [subalu'ga*] *vt* to sublet.
subarrendar [subaxẽ'da*] (*PT*) *vt* to sublet.
subconsciência [subkõ'sjẽsja] *f* subconscious.
subconsciente [subkõ'sjẽtʃi] *adj, m* subconscious.
subdesenvolvido/a [subdʒizẽvow'vidu/a] *adj* underdeveloped ♦ *m/f* (*pej*) degenerate.
subdesenvolvimento [subdʒizẽvowvi'mẽtu] *m* underdevelopment.
súbdito ['subditu] (*PT*) *m* = **súdito**.
subdividir [subdʒivi'dʒi*] *vt* to subdivide; **~-se** *vr* to subdivide.
subeditor(a) [subedʒi'to*(a)] *m/f* subeditor.
subemprego [subẽ'pregu] *m* low-paid unskilled job.
subentender [subẽtẽ'de*] *vt* to understand, assume.
subentendido/a [subẽtẽ'dʒidu/a] *adj* implied ♦ *m* implication.
subestimar [subeʃtʃi'ma*] *vt* to underestimate.
subida [su'bida] *f* ascent, climb; (*ladeira*) slope; (*de preços*) rise.
subido/a [su'bidu/a] *adj* high.
subir [su'bi*] *vi* to go up; (*preço, de posto etc*) to rise ♦ *vt* (*levantar*) to raise; (*ladeira, escada, rio*) to climb, go up; **~ em** (*morro, árvore*) to climb, go up; (*cadeira, palanque*) to climb onto, get up onto; (*ônibus*) to get on.
súbito/a ['subitu/a] *adj* sudden ♦ *adv* (*tb: de ~*) suddenly.
subjacente [subʒa'sẽtʃi] *adj* (*tb fig*) underly-

ing.
subjetivo/a [subʒe'tʃivu/a] (*PT*: **-ct-**) *adj* subjective.
subjugar [subʒu'ga*] *vt* to subjugate, subdue; (*inimigo*) to overpower; (*moralmente*) to dominate.
subjuntivo/a [subʒũ'tʃivu/a] *adj* subjunctive ♦ *m* subjunctive.
sublevação [subleva'sãw] (*pl* **-ões**) *f* (up)rising, revolt.
sublevar [suble'va*] *vt* to stir up (to revolt), incite (to revolt); **~-se** *vr* to revolt, rebel.
sublimar [subli'ma*] *vt* (*pessoa*) to exalt; (*desejos*) to sublimate.
sublime [su'blimi] *adj* sublime; (*nobre*) noble; (*música, espetáculo*) marvellous (*BRIT*), marvelous (*US*).
sublinhado [subli'ɲadu] *m* underlining.
sublinhar [subli'ɲa*] *vt* (*pôr linha debaixo de*) to underline; (*destacar*) to emphasize, stress.
sublocar [sublo'ka*] *vt, vi* to sublet.
sublocatário/a [subloka'tarju/a] *m/f* subtenant.
submarino/a [subma'rinu/a] *adj* underwater ♦ *m* submarine.
submergir [submex'ʒi*] *vt* to submerge; **~-se** *vr* to submerge.
submerso/a [sub'mɛxsu/a] *adj* submerged; (*absorto*): **~ em** immersed *ou* engrossed in.
submeter [subme'te*] *vt* (*povos, inimigo*) to subdue; (*plano*) to submit; (*sujeitar*): **~ a** to subject to; **~-se** *vr*: **~-se a** to submit to; (*operação*) to undergo.
submirjo [sub'mixju] *etc vb V* **submergir**.
submissão [submi'sãw] *f* submission.
submisso/a [sub'misu/a] *adj* submissive, docile.
submundo [sub'mũdu] *m* underworld.
subnutrição [subnutri'sãw] *f* malnutrition.
subnutrido/a [subnu'tridu/a] *adj* malnourished.
subordinar [suboxdʒi'na*] *vt* to subordinate.
subornar [subox'na*] *vt* to bribe.
suborno [su'boxnu] *m* bribery.
subproduto [subpro'dutu] *m* by-product.
sub-reptício/a [subxep'tʃisju/a] *adj* surreptitious.
subrotina [subxo'tʃina] *f* (*COMPUT*) subroutine.
subscrever [subʃkre've*] *vt* to sign; (*opinião, COM: ações*) to subscribe to; (*contribuir*) to put in ♦ *vi*: **~ a** to endorse; **~-se** *vr* to sign one's name; **~ para** to contribute to; **subscrevemo-nos ...** (*COM: em cartas*) ≈ we remain ....
subscrição [subʃkri'sãw[(*pl* **-ões**) *f* subscription; (*contribuição*) contribution.
subscritar [subʃkri'ta*] *vt* to sign.
subscrito/a [sub'ʃkritu/a] *pp de* **subscrever**.
subsecretário/a [subsekre'tarju/a] *m/f* undersecretary.
subseqüente [subse'kwẽtʃi] *adj* subsequent.
subserviente [subsex'vjẽtʃi] *adj* obsequious, servile.
subsidiar [subsi'dʒja*] *vt* to subsidize.
subsidiária [subsi'dʒjarja] *f* (*COM*) subsidiary (company).
subsidiário/a [subsi'dʒjarju/a] *adj* subsidiary.
subsídio [sub'sidʒu] *m* subsidy; (*ajuda*) aid; **~s** *mpl* data *sg*, information *sg*.
subsistência [subsiʃ'tẽsja] *f* (*sustento*) subsistence; (*meio de vida*) livelihood.
subsistir [subsiʃ'tʃi*] *vi* (*existir*) to exist; (*viver*) to subsist, live; (*estar em vigor*) to be in force; (*perdurar*) to remain, survive.
subsolo [sub'sɔlu] *m* subsoil; (*de prédio*) basement.
substabelecer [subiʃtabele'se*] *vt* to delegate.
substância [sub'ʃtãsja] *f* substance.
substancial [subʃtã'sjaw] (*pl* **-ais**) *adj* substantial.
substantivo/a [subʃtã'tʃivu/a] *adj* substantive ♦ *m* noun.
substituição [subʃtʃitwi'sãw] (*pl* **-ões**) *f* substitution, replacement.
substituir [subʃtʃi'twi*] *vt* to substitute, replace.
substituto/a [subʃti'tutu/a] *adj, m/f* substitute.
subterfúgio [subtex'fuʒu] *m* subterfuge.
subterrâneo/a [subite'xanju/a] *adj* subterranean, underground.
subtil *etc* [sub'tiw] (*PT*) = **sutil** *etc*.
subtítulo [sub'tʃitulu] *m* subtitle.
subtrair [subtra'i*] *vt* (*furtar*) to steal; (*deduzir*) to subtract ♦ *vi* to subtract.
subumano/a [subu'manu/a] *adj* subhuman; (*desumano*) inhuman.
suburbano/a [subux'banu/a] *adj* suburban; (*pej*) uncultivated.
subúrbio [su'buxbju] *m* suburb.
subvenção [subvẽ'sãw] (*pl* **-ões**) *f* subsidy, grant.
subvencionar [subvẽsjo'na*] *vt* to subsidize.
subvenções [subvẽ'sõjʃ] *fpl de* **subvenção**.
subversivo/a [subvex'sivu/a] *adj, m/f* subversive.
subverter [subvex'te*] *vt* to subvert; (*povo*) to incite (to revolt); (*planos*) to upset.
Sucam ['sukã] (*BR*) *abr f* = **Superintendência da Campanha de Saúde Pública**.
sucata [su'kata] *f* scrap metal.
sucatar [suka'ta*] *vt* to scrap.
sucção [suk'sãw] *f* suction.
sucedâneo/a [suse'danju/a] *adj* substitute ♦ *m* (*substância*) substitute.
suceder [suse'de*] *vi* to happen ♦ *vt* to succeed; **~-se** *vr* to succeed one another; **~ a** (*num cargo*) to succeed; (*seguir*) to follow; **~ com** to happen to; **~-se a** to follow.
sucedido [suse'dʒidu] *m* event, occurrence.
sucessão [suse'sãw] (*pl* **-ões**) *f* succession.

***NB:** European Portuguese adds the following consonants to certain words:* **b** (sú(b)dito, su(b)til); **c** (a(c)ção, a(c)cionista, a(c)to); **m** (inde(m)ne); **p** (ado(p)ção, ado(p)tar); *for further details see p. xiii.*

sucessivo/a [suse'sivu/a] *adj* successive.
sucesso [su'sɛsu] *m* success; (*música, filme*) hit; **com/sem ~** successfully/unsuccessfully; **de ~** successful; **fazer** *ou* **ter ~** to be successful.
sucessor(a) [suse'so*(a)] *m/f* successor.
súcia ['susja] *f* gang, band.
sucinto/a [su'sĩtu/a] *adj* succinct.
suco ['suku] (*BR*) *m* juice; **~ de laranja** orange juice.
suculento/a [suku'lẽtu/a] *adj* succulent, juicy; (*substancial*) substantial.
sucumbir [sukũ'bi*] *vi* (*render*) to succumb, yield; (*morrer*) to die, perish.
sucursal [sukux'saw] (*pl* **-ais**) *f* (*COM*) branch.
Sudam ['sudã] *abr f* = **Superintendência de Desenvolvimento da Amazônia.**
Sudão [su'dãw] *m*: **o ~** (the) Sudan.
Sudeco [su'dɛku] (*BR*) *abr f* = **Superintendência de Desenvolvimento do Centro-Oeste.**
Sudene [su'dɛni] (*BR*) *abr f* = **Superintendência de Desenvolvimento do Nordeste.**
Sudepe [su'dɛpi] (*BR*) *abr f* = **Superintendência de Desenvolvimento da Pesca.**
sudeste [su'dɛʃtʃi] *adj* southeast ♦ *m*: **o ~** the South East.
Sudhevea [sude'vɛa] (*BR*) *abr f* = **Superintendência da Borracha.**
súdito ['sudʒitu] *m* (*de rei etc*) subject.
sudoeste [sud'wɛʃtʃi] *adj* southwest ♦ *m*: **o ~** the South West.
Suécia ['swɛsja] *f*: **a ~** Sweden.
sueco/a ['swɛku/a] *adj* Swedish ♦ *m/f* Swede ♦ *m* (*LING*) Swedish.
suéter ['swɛte*] (*BR*) *m ou f* sweater.
Suez [swɛʒ]: **o canal de ~** the Suez canal.
suficiência [sufi'sjẽsja] *f* sufficiency.
suficiente [sufi'sjẽtʃi] *adj* sufficient, enough; **o ~** enough.
sufixo [su'fiksu] *m* suffix.
suflê [su'fle] *m* soufflé.
sufocante [sufo'kãtʃi] *adj* suffocating; (*calor*) sweltering, oppressive.
sufocar [sufo'ka*] *vt* to suffocate; (*revolta*) to put down ♦ *vi* to suffocate.
sufoco [su'foku] *m* (*afã*) eagerness; (*ansiedade*) anxiety; (*dificuldade*) hassle.
sufrágio [su'fraʒu] *m* suffrage, vote; **~ universal** universal suffrage.
sugar [su'ga*] *vt* to suck; (*fig*) to extort.
sugerir [suʒe'ri*] *vt* to suggest.
sugestão [suʒeʃ'tãw] (*pl* **-ões**) *f* suggestion; **dar uma ~** to make a suggestion.
sugestionar [suʒeʃtʃjo'na*] *vt* to influence; **~-se** *vr* to be influenced.
sugestionável [suʒeʃtʃjo'navew] (*pl* **-eis**) *adj* impressionable.
sugestivo/a [suʒeʃ'tʃivu/a] *adj* suggestive.
sugestões [suʒeʃ'tõjʃ] *fpl de* **sugestão.**
sugiro [su'ʒiru] *etc vb V* **sugerir.**
suguei [su'gej] *etc vb V* **sugar.**
Suíça ['swisa] *f*: **a ~** Switzerland.
suíças ['swisaʃ] *fpl* sideburns; *V tb* **suiço.**
suicida [swi'sida] *m/f* suicidal person; (*morto*) suicide ♦ *adj* suicidal.
suicidar-se [swisi'daxsi] *vr* to commit suicide.
suicídio [swi'sidʒju] *m* suicide.
suíço/a ['swisu/a] *adj, m/f* Swiss.
sui generis [swi'ʒɛneris] *adj inv* in a class of one's own, unique.
suíno ['swinu] *m* pig, hog ♦ *adj V* **gado.**
Suipa ['swipa] (*BR*) *abr f* = **Sociedade União Internacional Protetora dos Animais.**
suíte ['switʃi] *f* (*MÚS, em hotel*) suite; (*em residência*) maid's quarters *pl*.
sujar [su'ʒa*] *vt* to dirty; (*fig: honra*) to sully ♦ *vi* to make a mess; **~-se** *vr* to get dirty; (*fig*) to sully o.s.
sujeição [suʒej'sãw] *f* subjection.
sujeira [su'ʒejra] *f* dirt; (*estado*) dirtiness; (*col*) dirty trick; **fazer uma ~ com alguém** to do the dirty on sb.
sujeitar [suʒej'ta*] *vt* to subject; **~-se** *vr* to submit.
sujeito/a [su'ʒejtu/a] *adj*: **~ a** subject to ♦ *m* (*LING*) subject ♦ *m/f* fellow/woman; **~ a espaço** (*AER*) stand-by.
sujidade [suʒi'dadʒi] (*PT*) *f* dirt; (*estado*) dirtiness.
sujo/a ['suʒu/a] *adj* dirty; (*fig: desonesto*) nasty, dishonest ♦ *m* dirt; **estar/ficar ~ com alguém** to be/get into sb's bad books.
sul [suw] *adj inv* south, southern ♦ *m*: **o ~** the south.
sul-africano/a *adj, m/f* South African.
sul-americano/a *adj, m/f* South American.
sulcar [suw'ka*] *vt* to plough (*BRIT*), plow (*US*); (*rosto*) to line, furrow.
sulco [suw'ku] *m* furrow.
sulfato [suw'fatu] *m* sulphate (*BRIT*), sulfate (*US*).
sulfúrico/a [suw'furiku/a] *adj V* **ácido.**
sulista [su'liʃta] *adj* Southern ♦ *m/f* Southerner.
sultão/tana [suw'tãw/'tana] (*pl* **-ões/~s**) *m/f* sultan/sultana.
suma ['suma] *f*: **em ~** in short.
sumamente [suma'mẽtʃi] *adv* extremely.
sumário/a [su'marju/a] *adj* (*breve*) brief, concise; (*JUR*) summary; (*biquíni*) brief, skimpy ♦ *m* summary.
sumiço [su'misu] *m* disappearance; **dar ~ a** *ou* **em** to do away with; (*comida*) to put away.
sumidade [sumi'dadʒi] *f* (*pessoa*) genius.
sumido/a [su'midu/a] *adj* (*apagado*) faint, indistinct; (*voz*) low; (*desaparecido*) vanished; (*escondido*) hidden; **ela anda sumida** she's not around much.
sumir [su'mi*] *vi* to disappear, vanish.
sumo/a ['sumu/a] *adj* (*importância*) extreme; (*qualidade*) supreme ♦ *m* (*PT*) juice.
sumptuoso/a [sũ'twozu/ɔza] (*PT*) *adj* = **suntuoso/a.**
Sunab [su'nabi] (*BR*) *abr f* = **Superintendência Nacional de Abastecimento.**

Sunamam [suna'mami] (*BR*) *abr f* = **Superintendência Nacional da Marinha Mercante.**
sundae ['sãdej] *m* sundae.
sunga ['sũga] *f* swimming trunks *pl.*
sungar [sũ'ga*] *vt* to hitch up.
suntuoso/a [sũ'twozu/ɔza] *adj* sumptuous.
suor [swɔ*] *m* sweat; (*fig*): **com o meu ~** by the sweat of my brow.
super- [supe*-] *prefixo* super-; (*col*) really.
superabundante [superabũ'dãtʃi] *adj* overabundant.
superado/a [supe'radu/a] *adj* (*idéias*) outmoded.
superalimentar [superalimẽ'ta*] *vt* to overfeed.
superaquecer [superake'se*] *vt* to overheat.
superar [supe'ra*] *vt* (*rival*) to surpass; (*inimigo, dificuldade*) to overcome; (*expectativa*) to exceed.
superávit [supe'ravitʃi] *m* (*COM*) surplus.
superdose [supex'dɔzi] *f* overdose.
superdotado/a [supexdo'tadu/a] *adj* exceptionally gifted.
superestimar [supereʃtʃi'ma*] *vt* to overestimate.
superestrutura [supereʃtru'tura] *f* superstructure.
superficial [supexfi'sjaw] (*pl* **-ais**) *adj* superficial; (*pessoa*) shallow.
superfície [supex'fisi] *f* (*parte externa*) surface; (*extensão*) area; (*fig*: *aparência*) appearance.
superfino/a [supex'finu/a] *adj* (*de largura*) extra fine; (*de qualidade*) excellent quality *atr.*
supérfluo/a [su'pɛxflwu/a] *adj* superfluous.
super-homem (*pl* **-ns**) *m* superman.
superintendência [superĩtẽ'dẽsja] *f* (*órgão*) bureau.
superintendente [superĩtẽ'dẽtʃi] *m* superintendent; (*de empresa*) chief executive.
superintender [superĩtẽ'de*] *vt* to superintend.
superior [supe'rjo*] *adj* superior; (*mais elevado*) higher; (*quantidade*) greater; (*mais acima*) upper ♦ *m* superior; (*REL*) superior, abbot; **~ a** superior to; **um número ~ a 10** a number greater *ou* higher than 10; **curso/ensino ~** degree course/higher education; **lábio ~** upper lip.
superiora [supe'rjora] *adj, f*: **(madre) ~** mother superior.
superioridade [superjori'dadʒi] *f* superiority.
superlativo/a [supexla'tʃivu/a] *adj* superlative ♦ *m* superlative.
superlotação [supexlota'sãw] *f* overcrowding.
superlotado/a [supexlo'tadu/a] *adj* (*cheio*) really crowded; (*excessivamente cheio*) overcrowded.
supermercado [supexmex'kadu] *m* supermarket.
supermicro [supex'mikru] *m* (*COMPUT*) supermicro.
supermíni [supex'mini] *m* (*COMPUT*) supermini.
superpor [supex'po*] (*irreg*: *como* **pôr**) *vt*: **~ algo a algo** to put sth before sth.
superpotência [supexpo'tẽsja] *f* superpower.
superpovoado/a [supexpo'vwadu/a] *adj* overpopulated.
superprodução [supexprodu'sãw] *f* overproduction.
superproteger [supexprote'ʒe*] *vt* to overprotect.
superpunha [supex'puɲa] *etc vb V* **superpor.**
superpus [supex'puʃ] *etc vb V* **superpor.**
superpuser [supexpu'ze*] *etc vb V* **superpor.**
supersecreto/a [supexse'krɛtu/a] *adj* top secret.
supersensível [supexsẽ'sivew] (*pl* **-eis**) *adj* oversensitive.
supersimples [supex'sĩpliʃ] *adj inv* extremely simple.
supersônico/a [supex'soniku/a] *adj* supersonic.
superstição [supexʃtʃi'sãw] (*pl* **-ões**) *f* superstition.
supersticioso/a [supexʃtʃi'sjozu/ɔza] *adj* superstitious.
superstições [supexʃtʃi'sõjʃ] *fpl de* **superstição.**
supervisão [supexvi'zãw] *f* supervision.
supervisionar [supexvizjo'na*] *vt* to supervise.
supervisor(a) [supexvi'zo*(a)] *m/f* supervisor.
supetão [supe'tãw] *m*: **de ~** all of a sudden.
suplantar [suplã'ta*] *vt* to supplant, supersede.
suplementar [suplemẽ'ta*] *adj* supplementary ♦ *vt* to supplement.
suplemento [suple'mẽtu] *m* supplement.
suplente [su'plẽtʃi] *m/f* substitute.
súplica ['suplika] *f* supplication, plea.
suplicante [supli'kãtʃi] *m/f* supplicant; (*JUR*) plaintiff.
suplicar [supli'ka*] *vt, vi* to plead, beg; **~ algo a** *ou* **de alguém** to beg sb for sth; **~ a alguém que faça** to beg sb to do.
suplício [su'plisju] *m* torture; (*experiência penosa*) trial.
supor [su'po*] (*irreg*: *como* **pôr**) *vt* to suppose; (*julgar*) to think; **suponhamos que** let us suppose that; **vamos ~** let us suppose *ou* say; **suponho que sim** I suppose so; **era de ~ que** one could assume that.
suportar [supox'ta*] *vt* to hold up, support; (*tolerar*) to bear, tolerate.
suportável [supox'tavew] (*pl* **-eis**) *adj* bearable, tolerable.
suporte [su'pɔxtʃi] *m* support, stand; **~ atlético** athletic support, jockstrap.
suposição [supozi'sãw] (*pl* **-ões**) *f* supposition,

NB: *European Portuguese adds the following consonants to certain words:* **b** (sú(b)dito, su(b)til); **c** (a(c)ção a(c)cionista, a(c)to); **m** (inde(m)ne); **p** (ado(p)ção, ado(p)tar); *for further details see p. xiii.*

presumption.
supositório [supozi'tɔrju] *m* suppository.
supostamente [supoʃta'mẽtʃi] *adv* supposedly.
suposto/a [su'poʃtu/'pɔʃta] *pp de* **supor** ♦ *adj* supposed ♦ *m* assumption.
supracitado/a [suprasi'tadu/a] *adj* foregoing ♦ *m* foregoing.
supra-sumo ['supra-] *m*: **o ~ da beleza** *etc* the pinnacle of beauty *etc*.
supremacia [suprema'sia] *f* supremacy.
supremo/a [su'prɛmu/a] *adj* supreme ♦ *m*: **o S~** the Supreme Court; **S~ Tribunal Federal** (*BR*) Federal Supreme Court.
supressão [supre'sãw] (*pl* **-ões**) *f* suppression; (*omissão*) omission; (*abolição*) abolition.
suprimento [supri'mẽtu] *m* supply.
suprimir [supri'mi*] *vt* to suppress; (*frases de um texto*) to delete; (*abolir*) to abolish.
suprir [su'pri*] *vt* (*fazer as vezes de*) to take the place of; **~ alguém de** to provide *ou* supply sb with; **~ algo por algo** to substitute sth with sth; **~ uma quantia** to make up an amount; **~ a falta de alguém/algo** to make up for sb's absence/the lack of sth; **~ as necessidades/uma família** to provide for needs/a family.
supunha [su'puɲa] *etc vb V* **supor**.
supus [su'puʃ] *etc vb V* **supor**.
supuser [supu'ze*] *etc vb V* **supor**.
supurar [supu'ra*] *vi* to go septic, suppurate.
surdez [sux'deʒ] *f* deafness; **aparelho de ~** hearing aid.
surdina [sux'dʒina] *f* (*MÚS*) mute; **em ~** stealthily, on the quiet.
surdo/a ['suxdu/a] *adj* deaf; (*som*) muffled, dull; (*consoante*) voiceless ♦ *m/f* deaf person; **~ como uma porta** as deaf as a post.
surdo/a-mudo/a *adj* deaf and dumb ♦ *m/f* deaf-mute.
surfe ['suxfi] *m* surfing.
surfista [sux'fiʃta] *m/f* surfer.
surgir [sux'ʒi*] *vi* to appear; (*problema, dificuldade*) to arise, crop up; (*oportunidade*) to arise, come up; **~ de** (*proceder*) to come from; **~ à mente** to come *ou* spring to mind.
Suriname [suri'nami] *m*: **o ~** Surinam.
surjo ['suxju] *etc vb V* **surgir**.
surpreendente [suxprjẽ'dẽtʃi] *adj* surprising.
surpreender [suxprjẽ'de*] *vt* to surprise; (*pegar de surpresa*) to take unawares ♦ *vi* to be surprising; **~-se** *vr*: **~-se (de)** to be surprised (at).
surpresa [sux'preza] *f* surprise; **de ~** by surprise.
surpreso/a [sux'prezu/a] *pp de* **surpreender** ♦ *adj* surprised.
surra ['suxa] *f* (*ger, ESPORTE*) thrashing; **dar uma ~ em** to thrash; **levar uma ~ (de)** to get thrashed (by).
surrado/a [su'xadu/a] *adj* (*espancado*) beaten up; (*roupa*) worn out.
surrar [su'xa*] *vt* to beat, thrash; (*roupa*) to wear out.
surrealismo [suxea'liʒmu] *m* surrealism.
surrealista [suxea'liʃta] *adj, m/f* surrealist.
surrupiar [suxu'pja*] *vt* to steal.
sursis [sux'si] *m inv* (*JUR*) suspended sentence.
surte ['suxtʃi] *etc vb V* **sortir**.
surtir [sux'tʃi*] *vt* to produce, bring about; **~ bem** to turn out well; **~ efeito** to have an effect.
surto ['suxtu] *m* (*de doença*) outbreak; (*de progresso*) surge.
suscetibilidade [susetʃibili'dadʒi] *f* susceptibility; (*sensibilidade*) sensitivity.
suscetível [suse'tʃivew] (*pl* **-eis**) *adj* susceptible; **~ de** liable to.
suscitar [susi'ta*] *vt* to arouse; (*admiração*) to cause; (*dúvidas*) to raise; (*obstáculos*) to throw up.
Susep [su'zɛpi] (*BR*) *abr f* = **Superintendência de Seguros Privados**.
suspeição [suʃpej'sãw] (*pl* **-ões**) *f* suspicion.
suspeita [suʃ'pejta] *f* suspicion.
suspeitar [suʃpej'ta*] *vt* to suspect ♦ *vi*: **~ de algo** to suspect sth; **~ de alguém** to be suspicious of sb.
suspeito/a [suʃ'pejtu/a] *adj* suspect, suspicious ♦ *m/f* suspect.
suspeitoso/a [suʃpej'tozu/ɔza] *adj* suspicious.
suspender [suʃpẽ'de*] *vt* (*levantar*) to lift; (*pendurar*) to hang; (*trabalho, pagamento etc*) to suspend, stop; (*funcionário, aluno*) to suspend; (*jornal*) to suspend publication of; (*encomenda*) to cancel; (*sessão*) to adjourn, defer; (*viagem*) to put off.
suspensão [suʃpẽ'sãw] (*pl* **-ões**) *f* (*ger, AUTO*) suspension; (*de trabalho, pagamento*) stoppage; (*de viagem, sessão*) deferment; (*de encomenda*) cancellation.
suspense [suʃ'pẽsi] *m* suspense; **filme de ~** thriller.
suspenso/a [suʃ'pẽsu/a] *pp de* **suspender**.
suspensões [suʃpẽ'sõjʃ] *fpl de* **suspensão**.
suspensórios [suʃpẽ'sɔrjuʃ] *mpl* braces (*BRIT*), suspenders (*US*).
suspicácia [suʃpi'kasja] *f* distrust, suspicion.
suspicaz [suʃpi'kajʒ] *adj* (*suspeito*) suspect; (*desconfiado*) suspicious.
suspirar [suʃpi'ra*] *vi* to sigh; **~ por algo** to long for sth.
suspiro [suʃ'piru] *m* sigh; (*doce*) meringue.
sussurrar [susu'xa*] *vt, vi* to whisper.
sussurro [su'suxu] *m* whisper.
sustância [suʃ'tãsja] *f* (*força*) strength; (*de comida*) nourishment.
sustar [suʃ'ta*] *vt, vi* to stop.
sustenho [suʃ'teɲu] *etc vb V* **suster**.
sustentáculo [suʃtẽ'takulu] *m* (*tb fig*) support.
sustentar [suʃtẽ'ta*] *vt* to sustain; (*escorar*) to hold up, support; (*manter*) to maintain; (*financeiramente, acusação*) to support; **~-se** *vr* (*alimentar-se*) to sustain o.s.; (*financeiramente*) to support o.s.; (*equilibrar-se*) to balance; **~ que** to maintain that.

sustento [suʃ'tẽtu] *m* sustenance; (*subsistência*) livelihood; (*amparo*) support.
suster [suʃ'te*] (*irreg*: *como* **ter**) *vt* to support, hold up; (*reprimir*) to restrain, hold back.
susto ['suʃtu] *m* fright, scare; **tomar** *ou* **levar um ~** to get a fright; **que ~!** what a fright!
sutiã [su'tʃjã] *m* bra(ssiere).
sutil [su'tʃiw] (*pl* **-is**) *adj* subtle; (*fino*) fine, delicate.
sutileza [sutʃi'leza] *f* subtlety; (*finura*) fineness, delicacy.
sutilizar [sutʃili'za*] *vt* to refine.
sutis [su'tʃiʃ] *adj pl de* **sutil**.
sutura [su'tura] *f* (*MED*) suture.
suturar [sutu'ra*] *vt*, *vi* to suture.

T

T, t [te] (*pl* **ts**) *m* T, t; **T de Tereza** T for Tommy.
ta [ta] = **te** + **a**.
tá [ta] (*col*) *excl* OK; **~ bom** OK, fine; = **está**.
tabacaria [tabaka'ria] *f* tobacconist's (shop).
tabaco [ta'baku] *m* tobacco.
tabefe [ta'bɛfi] (*col*) *m* slap.
tabela [ta'bɛla] *f* table, chart; (*lista*) list; **por ~** indirectly; **estar caindo pelas ~s** (*fig*) to be feeling low; **~ de preços** price table.
tabelado/a [tabe'ladu/a] *adj* (*produto*) price-controlled; (*preço*) controlled.
tabelar [tabe'la*] *vt* (*produto*) to fix the price of; (*preço*) to fix; (*dados*) to tabulate.
tabelião [tabe'ljãw] (*pl* **-ães**) *m* notary public.
taberna [ta'bɛxna] *f* tavern, bar.
tabique [ta'biki] *m* partition.
tablado [ta'bladu] *m* platform; (*para espectadores*) grandstand.
tablete [ta'blɛtʃi] *m* (*de chocolate*) bar; (*de manteiga*) pat.
tablóide [ta'blɔjdʒi] *m* tabloid.
tabu [ta'bu] *adj*, *m* taboo.
tábua ['tabwa] *f* (*de madeira*) plank, board; (*MAT*) list, table; (*de mesa*) leaf; **~ de passar roupa** ironing board; **~ de salvação** (*fig*) last resort.
tabuada [ta'bwada] *f* 'times table; (*livro*) tables book.
tabulador [tabula'do*] *m* tab(ulator key).
tabular [tabu'la*] *vt* to tabulate.
tabuleiro [tabu'lejru] *m* tray; (*XADREZ*) board.
tabuleta [tabu'leta] *f* (*letreiro*) sign, signboard.
taça ['tasa] *f* cup; **~ de champanhe** champagne glass *ou* flute.
tacada [ta'kada] *f* shot; **de uma ~** in one go.
tacanho/a [ta'kaɲu/a] *adj* mean, niggardly; (*de idéias curtas*) narrow-minded; (*baixo*) small.
tacar [ta'ka*] *vt* (*bola*) to hit; (*col*: *jogar*) to chuck; **~ a mão** *ou* **um soco em alguém** to punch sb.
tacha ['taʃa] *f* (*prego*) tack; (*em calça jeans*) stud.
tachar [ta'ʃa*] *vt*: **~ algo de** to brand sth as.
tachinha [ta'ʃiɲa] *f* drawing pin (*BRIT*), thumb tack (*US*).
tácito/a ['tasitu/a] *adj* tacit, implied.
taciturno/a [tasi'tuxnu/a] *adj* taciturn, reserved.
taco ['taku] *m* (*de bilhar*) cue; (*de golfe*) club; (*de hóquei*) stick; (*bucha*) plug, wad; (*de assoalho*) parquet block.
táctico/a *etc* ['tatiku/a] (*PT*) = **tático** *etc*.
táctil ['tatiw] (*PT*) *adj* = **tátil**.
tacto ['tatu] (*PT*) *m* = **tato**.
tadinho/a [ta'dʒiɲu/a] (*col*) *excl* poor thing!; **~ dele!** poor him!
tafetá [tafe'ta] *m* taffeta.
tagarela [taga'rɛla] *adj* talkative ♦ *m/f* chatterbox.
tagarelar [tagare'la*] *vi* to chatter.
tagarelice [tagare'lisi] *f* chat, chatter, gossip.
tailandês/esa [tajlã'deʃ/eza] *adj*, *m/f* Thai ♦ *m* (*LING*) Thai.
Tailândia [taj'lãdʒja] *f*: **a ~** Thailand.
tailleur [taj'ɛ*] *m* suit.
tainha [ta'iɲa] *f* mullet.
taipa ['tajpa] *f*: **parede de ~** mud wall.
tais [tajʃ] *adj pl de* **tal**.
Taiti [taj'tʃi] *m*: **o ~** Tahiti.
tal [taw] (*pl* **tais**) *adj* such; **~ e coisa** this and that; **um ~ de Sr. X** a certain Mr. X; **que ~?** what do you think?; (*PT*) how are things?; **que ~ um cafezinho?** what about a coffee?; **que ~ nós irmos ao cinema?** what about (us) going to the cinema?; **~ pai, ~ filho** like father, like son; **~ como** such as; (*da maneira que*) just as; **~ qual** just like; **o ~ professor** that teacher; **a ~ ponto** to such an extent; **de ~ maneira** in such a way; **e ~** and so on; **o/a ~** (*col*) the greatest; **o Pedro de ~** Peter what's-his-name; **na rua ~** in such and such a street; **foi um ~ de gente ligar lá para casa** there were people ringing home non-stop.
tala ['tala] *f* (*MED*) splint.
talão [ta'lãw] (*pl* **-ões**) *m* (*de recibo*) stub; **~ de cheques** cheque book (*BRIT*), check book (*US*).
talco ['tawku] *m* talc; **pó de ~** (*PT*) talcum powder.

NB: *European Portuguese adds the following consonants to certain words:* **b** (sú(b)dito, su(b)til); **c** (a(c)ção, a(c)cionista, a(c)to); **m** (inde(m)ne); **p** (ado(p)ção, ado(p)tar); *for further details* *see p. xiii.*

talento [ta'lẽtu] *m* talent; (*aptidão*) ability.
talentoso/a [talẽ'tozu/ɔza] *adj* talented.
talha ['taʎa] *f* (*corte*) carving; (*vaso*) pitcher; (*NÁUT*) tackle.
talhado/a [ta'ʎadu/a] *adj* (*apropriado*) appropriate, right; (*leite*) curdled.
talhar [ta'ʎa*] *vt* to cut; (*esculpir*) to carve ♦ *vi* (*coalhar*) to curdle.
talharim [taʎa'rĩ] *m* tagliatelle.
talhe ['taʎi] *m* cut, shape; (*de rosto*) line.
talher [ta'ʎe*] *m* set of cutlery; **~es** *mpl* cutlery *sg*.
talho ['taʎu] *m* (*corte*) cutting, slicing; (*PT*: *açougue*) butcher's (shop).
talismã [taliʒ'mã] *m* talisman.
talo ['talu] *m* stalk, stem; (*ARQ*) shaft.
talões [ta'lõjʃ] *mpl de* **talão**.
talude [ta'ludʒi] *m* slope, incline.
taludo/a [ta'ludu/a] *adj* stocky.
talvez [taw'veʒ] *adv* perhaps, maybe; **~ tenha razão** maybe you're right.
tamanco [ta'mãku] *m* clog, wooden shoe.
tamanduá [tamã'dwa] *m* ant-eater.
tamanho/a [ta'maɲu/a] *adj* such (a) great ♦ *m* size; **em ~ natural** life-size; **de que ~ é?** what size is it?; **uma casa que não tem ~** (*col*) a huge house; **do ~ de um bonde** (*col*) enormous.
tamanho-família *adj inv* family-size; (*fig*) giant-size.
tamanho-gigante *adj inv* giant-size.
tâmara ['tamara] *f* date.
tamarindo [tama'rĩdu] *m* tamarind.
também [tã'bẽj] *adv* also, too, as well; (*além disso*) besides; **~ não** not ... either, nor; **eu ~** me too; **eu ~ não** nor me, neither do (*ou* did, am, have *etc*) I.
tambor [tã'bo*] *m* drum.
tamborilar [tãbori'la*] *vi* (*com os dedos*) to drum; (*chuva*) to pitter-pat.
tamborim [tãbo'rĩ] (*pl* **-ns**) *m* tambourine.
Tâmisa ['tamiza] *m*: **o ~** the Thames.
tampa ['tãpa] *f* lid; (*de garrafa*) cap.
tampão [tã'pãw] (*pl* **-ões**) *m* cover; (*rolha*) stopper, plug; (*vaginal*) tampon; (*para curativos*) compress.
tampar [tã'pa*] *vt* (*lata, garrafa*) to put the lid on; (*cobrir*) to cover.
tampinha [tã'piɲa] *f* lid, top ♦ *m/f* (*col*) shortly.
tampo ['tãpu] *m* lid; (*MÚS*) sounding board.
tampões [tã'põjʃ] *mpl de* **tampão**.
tampouco [tã'poku] *adv* nor, neither.
tanga ['tãga] *f* loincloth; (*biquíni*) bikini.
tangente [tã'ʒẽtʃi] *f* tangent; (*trecho retilíneo*) straight section; **pela ~** (*fig*) narrowly.
tanger [tã'ʒe*] *vt* (*MÚS*) to play; (*sinos*) to ring; (*cordas*) to pluck ♦ *vi* (*sinos*) to ring; **~ a** (*dizer respeito*) to concern; **no que tange a** as regards, with respect to.
tangerina [tãʒe'rina] *f* tangerine.
tangerineira [tãʒeri'nejra] *f* tangerine tree.
tangível [tã'ʒivew] (*pl* **-eis**) *adj* tangible.
tango ['tãgu] *m* tango.
tanjo ['tãʒu] *etc vb V* **tanger**.
tanque ['tãki] *m* (*reservatório, MIL*) tank; (*de lavar roupa*) sink.
tantã [tã'tã] (*col*) *adj* crazy.
tanto/a ['tãtu/a] *adj, pron* (*sg*) so much; (: + *interrogativa/negativa*) as much; (*pl*) so many; (: + *interrogativa/negativa*) as many ♦ *adv* so much; **~ melhor/pior** so much the better/more's the pity; **~ ... como ...** both ... and ...; **~ mais ... quanto mais ...** the more ... the more ...; **~ ... quanto ...** as much ... as ...; **~s ... quanto ...** as many ... as ...; **~ tempo** so long; **quarenta e ~s anos** forty-odd years; **vinte e tantas pessoas** twenty-odd people; **~ a Lúcia, quanto o Luís** both Lúcia and Luís; **~ faz** it's all the same to me, I don't mind; **um ~ vinho** some wine; **um outro ~ de vinho** a little more wine; **um ~ (quanto)** (*como advérbio*) rather, somewhat; **as tantas** the small hours; **lá para as tantas** late, in the small hours; **um médico e ~** quite a doctor; **não é para ~** it's not such a big deal; **não** *ou* **nem ~ assim** not as much as all that; **~ (assim) que** so much so that.
Tanzânia [tã'zanja] *f*: **a ~** Tanzania.
tão [tãw] *adv* so; **~ rico quanto** as rich as.
tão-só *adv* only.
tapa ['tapa] *f ou m* slap; **no ~** (*col*) by force.
tapado/a [ta'padu/a] *adj* (*col*: *bobo*) stupid.
tapar [ta'pa*] *vt* to cover; (*garrafa*) to cork; (*caixa*) to put the lid on; (*ouvidos*) to block; (*orifício*) to block up; (*encobrir*) to block out.
tapeação [tapja'sãw] *f* cheating.
tapear [ta'pja*] *vt, vi* to cheat.
tapeçaria [tapesa'ria] *f* tapestry; (*loja*) carpet shop.
tapetar [tape'ta*] *vt* to carpet.
tapete [ta'petʃi] *m* carpet, rug.
tapioca [ta'pjɔka] *f* tapioca.
tapume [ta'pumi] *m* fencing, boarding.
taquicardia [takikax'dʒia] *f* palpitations *pl*.
taquigrafar [takigra'fa*] *vt, vi* to write in shorthand.
taquigrafia [takigra'fia] *f* shorthand.
taquígrafo/a [ta'kigrafu/a] *m/f* shorthand typist (*BRIT*), stenographer (*US*).
tara ['tara] *f* fetish, mania; (*COM*) tare.
tarado/a [ta'radu/a] *adj* manic; (*sexualmente*) perverted ♦ *m/f* maniac; **~ sexual** sex maniac, pervert; **ser ~ por** to be mad about.
tarar [ta'ra*] *vi*: **~ (por)** to be smitten (with).
tardança [tax'dãsa] *f* delay, slowness.
tardar [tax'da*] *vi* to delay, be slow; (*chegar tarde*) to be late ♦ *vt* to delay; **sem mais ~** without delay; **~ a** *ou* **em fazer** to take a long time to do; **o mais ~** at the latest.
tarde ['taxdʒi] *f* afternoon ♦ *adv* late; **ele chegou ~ (demais)** he got there too late; **mais cedo ou mais ~** sooner or later; **antes ~ do que nunca** better late than never; **boa ~!**

good afternoon!; **hoje à ~** this afternoon; **à** *ou* **de ~** in the afternoon; **às três da ~** at three in the afternoon; **~ da noite** late at night; **ontem/sexta à ~** yesterday/(on) Friday afternoon.

tardinha [tax'dʒiɲa] *f* late afternoon; **de ~** late in the afternoon.

tardio/a [tax'dʒiu/a] *adj* late.

tarefa [ta'rɛfa] *f* task, job; (*faina*) chore.

tarifa [ta'rifa] *f* tariff; (*para transportes*) fare; (*lista de preços*) price list; **~ alfandegária** customs duty; **~ de embarque** (AER) airport tax.

tarimba [ta'rĩba] *f* bunk; (*fig*) army life; (: *experiência*) experience; **ter ~** to be an old hand.

tarimbado/a [tarĩ'badu/a] *adj* experienced.

tartamudear [taxtamu'dʒja*] *vi, vt* to mumble; (*gaguejar*) to stammer, stutter.

tartamudo/a [taxta'mudu/a] *m/f* mumbler; (*gago*) stammerer, stutterer.

tártaro ['taxtaru] *m* tartar.

tartaruga [taxta'ruga] *f* turtle; **pente de ~** tortoiseshell comb.

tas [taʃ] = **te** + **as**.

tasca ['taʃka] (PT) *f* cheap eating place.

tascar [taʃ'ka*] *vt* (*tapa, beijo*) to plant.

tasco ['taʃku] (*col*) *m* bit, mouthful.

Tasmânia [taʒ'manja] *f*: **a ~** Tasmania.

tatear [ta'tʃja*] *vt* to touch, feel; (*fig*) to sound out ♦ *vi* to feel one's way.

táteis ['tatejʃ] *adj pl de* **tátil**.

tática ['tatʃika] *f* tactics *pl*.

tático/a ['tatʃiku/a] *adj* tactical.

tátil ['tatʃiw] (*pl* **-eis**) *adj* tactile.

tato ['tatu] *m* touch; (*fig*: *diplomacia*) tact.

tatu [ta'tu] *m* armadillo.

tatuador(a) [tatwa'do*(a)] *m/f* tattooist.

tatuagem [ta'twaʒẽ] (*pl* **-ns**) *f* tattoo.

tatuar [ta'twa*] *vt* to tattoo.

tauromaquia [tawroma'kia] *f* bullfighting.

tautologia [tawtolo'ʒia] *f* tautology.

tautológico/a [tawto'lɔʒiku/a] *adj* tautological.

taxa ['taʃa] *f* (*imposto*) tax; (*preço*) fee; (*índice*) rate; **~ de câmbio** exchange rate; **~ de juros** interest rate; **~ bancária** bank rate; **~ de desconto** discount rate; **~ de matrícula** *ou* **inscrição** enrol(l)ment *ou* registration fee; **~ de exportação** export duty; **~ rodoviária** road tax; **~ fixa** (COM) flat rate; **~ de retorno** (COM) rate of return; **~ de crescimento** growth rate.

taxação [taʃa'sãw] *f* taxation; (*de preços*) fixing.

taxar [ta'ʃa*] *vt* (*fixar o preço de*) to fix the price of; (*lançar impostos sobre*) to tax.

taxativo/a [taʃa'tʃivu/a] *adj* categorical, firm.

táxi ['taksi] *m* taxi, cab; **~ aéreo** air taxi.

taxímetro [tak'simetru] *m* taxi meter.

taxista [tak'siʃta] *m/f* taxi driver.

tchã [tʃã] (*col*) *m* (*toque*) special touch; (*charme*) charm.

tchau [tʃaw] *excl* bye!

tcheco/a ['tʃɛku/a] *adj, m/f* Czech.

Tcheco-Eslováquia [tʃɛkuiʒlo'vakja] *f* = **Tchecoslováquia**.

Tchecoslováquia [tʃekoʒlo'vakja] *f*: **a ~** Czechoslovakia.

TCU (BR) *abr m* = **Tribunal de Contas da União**.

te [tʃi] *pron* you; (*para você*) (to) you.

té [tɛ] *prep abr de* **até**.

tear [tʃja*] *m* loom.

teatral [tʃja'traw] (*pl* **-ais**) *adj* theatrical; (*grupo*) theatre *atr* (BRIT), theater *atr* (US); (*obra, arte*) dramatic.

teatralizar [tʃjatrali'za*] *vt* to dramatize.

teatro ['tʃjatru] *m* theatre (BRIT), theater (US); (*obras*) plays *pl*, dramatic works *pl*; (*gênero, curso*) drama; **peça de ~** play; **fazer ~** (*fig*) to be dramatic; **~ de arena** theatre-in-the-round; **~ de bolso** small theatre; **~ de marionetes** puppet theatre; **~ de variedades** vaudeville theatre; **~ rebolado** burlesque theatre.

teatrólogo/a [tʃja'trɔlogu/a] *m/f* playwright, dramatist.

teatro-revista (*pl* **teatros-revista**) *m* review theatre (BRIT) *ou* theater (US).

tecelão/lã [tese'lãw/'lã] (*pl* **-ões/~s**) *m/f* weaver.

tecer [te'se*] *vt* to weave; (*fig*: *intrigas*) to weave; (*disputas*) to cause ♦ *vi* to weave.

tecido [te'sidu] *m* cloth, material; (ANAT) tissue.

tecla ['tɛkla] *f* key; **bater na mesma ~** (*fig*) to harp on the same subject; **~ de controle** (COMPUT) control key; **~ de função** (COMPUT) function key; **~ de saída** (COMPUT) exit key.

tecladista [tekla'dʒiʃta] *m/f* (MÚS) keyboards player; (COMPUT) keyboard operator.

teclado [tek'ladu] *m* keyboard; **~ complementar** (COMPUT) keypad.

teclar [tek'la*] *vt* (*dados*) to key (in).

tecnicalidade [teknikali'dadʒi] *f* technicality.

técnica ['tɛknika] *f* technique; *V tb* **técnico**.

técnico/a ['tɛkniku/a] *adj* technical ♦ *m/f* technician; (*especialista*) expert.

tecnicolor [tekniko'lo*] *adj* technicolour (BRIT), technicolor (US) ♦ *m*: **em ~** in technicolo(u)r.

tecnocrata [tekno'krata] *m/f* technocrat.

tecnologia [teknolo'ʒia] *f* technology; **~ de ponta** up-to-the-minute technology.

tecnológico/a [tekno'lɔʒiku/a] *adj* technological.

teco ['tɛku] *m* hit; (*tiro*) shot; (*peteleco*) flick.

teco-teco (*pl* **~s**) *m* small plane, light aircraft.

tecto ['tɛktu] (PT) *m* = **teto**.

tédio ['tɛdʒju] *m* tedium, boredom.

tedioso/a [te'dʒjozu/ɔza] *adj* tedious, boring.

Teerã [tee'rã] *n* Teheran.

teia ['teja] *f* web; (*fig*: *enredo*) intrigue, plot; (: *série*) series; ~ **de aranha** spider's web; ~ **de espionagem** spy ring, web of espionage.

teima ['tejma] *f* insistence.

teimar [tej'ma*] *vi* to insist, keep on; ~ **em** to insist on.

teimosia [tejmo'zia] *f* stubbornness; ~ **em fazer** insistence on doing.

teimoso/a [tej'mozu/ɔza] *adj* obstinate; (*criança*) wilful (BRIT), willful (US).

teixo ['tejʃu] *m* yew.

Tejo ['teʒu] *m*: **o (rio)** ~ the (river) Tagus.

tel. *abr* (= *telefone*) tel.

tela ['tɛla] *f* (*tecido*) fabric, material; (*de pintar*) canvas; (CINEMA, TV) screen.

telão [te'lãw] (*pl* **-ões**) *m* big screen.

Telavive [tela'vivi] *n* Tel Aviv.

tele... [tele] *prefixo* tele....

telecomandar [telekomã'da*] *vt* to operate by remote control.

telecomando [teleko'mãdu] *m* remote control.

telecomunicação [telekomunika'sãw] (*pl* **-ões**) *f* telecommunication; **telecomunicações** *fpl* telecommunications.

teleférico [tele'fɛriku] *m* cable car.

telefonar [telefo'na*] *vi* to telephone, phone; ~ **para alguém** to (tele)phone sb.

telefone [tele'fɔni] *m* phone, telephone; (*número*) (tele)phone number; (*telefonema*) phone call; **estar/falar no** ~ to be/talk on the phone; ~ **público** public phone; ~ **sem fio** cordless (tele)phone.

telefonema [telefo'nɛma] *m* phone call; **dar um** ~ to make a phone call.

telefônico/a [tele'foniku/a] *adj* telephone *atr*; **mesa telefônica** switchboard; **cabine telefônica** telephone box (BRIT) *ou* booth (US).

telefonista [telefo'niʃta] *m/f* telephonist; (*na companhia telefônica*) operator.

telegrafar [telegra'fa*] *vt*, *vi* to telegraph, wire.

telegrafia [telegra'fia] *f* telegraphy.

telegráfico/a [tele'grafiku/a] *adj* telegraphic.

telegrafista [telegra'fiʃta] *m/f* telegraph operator.

telégrafo [te'lɛgrafu] *m* telegraph.

telegrama [tele'grama] *m* telegram, cable; **passar um** ~ to send a telegram; ~ **fonado** telemessage.

teleguiado/a [tele'gjadu/a] *adj* remote-controlled.

teleguiar [tele'gja*] *vt* to operate by remote control.

teleimpressor [teleĩpre'so*] *m* teleprinter.

telejornal [teleʒox'naw] (*pl* **-ais**) *m* television news *sg*.

telêmetro [te'lemetru] *m* rangefinder.

telenovela [teleno'vɛla] *f* (TV) soap opera.

teleobjetiva [teleobʒe'tʃiva] (PT: **-ct-**) *f* telephoto lens.

telepatia [telepa'tʃia] *f* telepathy.

telepático/a [tele'patʃiku/a] *adj* telepathic.

teleprocessamento [teleprosesa'mẽtu] *m* teleprocessing.

Telerj [te'lɛxʒi] *abr f Rio telephone company*.

telescópico/a [tele'skɔpiku/a] *adj* telescopic.

telescópio [tele'skɔpju] *m* telescope.

Telesp [te'lɛʃpi] *abr f São Paulo telephone company*.

telespectador(a) [teleʃpekta'do*(a)] *m/f* viewer ♦ *adj* (*público*) viewing.

teletexto [tele'teʃtu] *m* teletext.

teletipista [teletʃi'piʃta] *m/f* teletypist.

teletipo [tele'tʃipu] *m* teletype.

televisão [televi'zãw] *f* television; ~ **a cores** colo(u)r television; ~ **a cabo** cable television; **aparelho de** ~ television set.

televisar [televi'za*] *vt* = **televisionar**.

televisionar [televizjo'na*] *vt* to televise.

televisivo/a [televi'zivu/a] *adj* television *atr*.

televisor [televi'zo*] *m* (*aparelho*) television (set), TV (set).

telex [te'lɛks] *m* telex.

telha ['teʎa] *f* tile; (*col*: *cabeça*) head; **ter uma** ~ **de menos** to have a screw loose; **não estar bom da** ~ not to be right in the head; **deu-lhe na** ~ **(de) viajar** he got it into his head to go travel(l)ing.

telhado [te'ʎadu] *m* roof.

telões [te'lõjʃ] *mpl de* **telão**.

tema ['tɛma] *m* theme; (*assunto*) subject.

temática [te'matʃika] *f* theme.

temático/a [te'matʃiku/a] *adj* thematic.

temer [te'me*] *vt* to fear, be afraid of ♦ *vi* to be afraid; ~ **por** to fear for; ~ **que** to be afraid that; ~ **fazer** to be afraid of doing.

temerário/a [teme'rarju/a] *adj* reckless; (*arriscado*) risky; (*juízo*) unfounded.

temeridade [temeri'dadʒi] *f* recklessness.

temeroso/a [teme'rozu/ɔza] *adj* fearful, afraid; (*pavoroso*) dreadful.

temido/a [te'midu/a] *adj* fearsome, frightening.

temível [te'mivew] (*pl* **-eis**) *adj* fearsome.

temor [te'mo*] *m* fear.

tempão [tẽ'pãw] *m*: **um** ~ a long time, ages *pl* (*col*).

têmpera ['tẽpera] *f* (*de metais*) tempering; (*caráter*) temperament; (*pintura*) distemper, tempera.

temperado/a [tẽpe'radu/a] *adj* (*metal*) tempered; (*clima*) temperate; (*comida*) seasoned.

temperamental [tẽperamẽ'taw] (*pl* **-ais**) *adj* temperamental.

temperamento [tẽpera'mẽtu] *m* temperament, nature.

temperança [tẽpe'rãsa] *f* moderation.

temperar [tẽpe'ra*] *vt* (*metal*) to temper, harden; (*comida*) to season.

temperatura [tẽpera'tura] *f* temperature.

tempero [tẽ'peru] *m* seasoning, flavouring (*BRIT*), flavoring (*US*).

tempestade [tẽpeʃ'tadʒi] *f* storm, tempest; **fazer uma ~ em copo de água** to make a mountain out of a molehill.

tempestuoso/a [tẽpeʃ'twozu/ɔza] *adj* stormy; (*fig*) tempestuous.

templo ['tẽplu] *m* temple; (*igreja*) church.

tempo ['tẽpu] *m* time; (*meteorológico*) weather; (*LING*) tense; **o ~ todo** the whole time; **a ~** on time; **ao mesmo ~** at the same time; **a um ~** at once; **a ~ e a hora** at the appropriate time; **antes do ~** before time; **com ~** in good time; **de ~ em ~** from time to time; **nesse ~** at that time; **nesse meio ~** in the meantime; **em ~ de fazer** about to do; **em ~ recorde** in record time; **em seu devido ~** in due course; **quanto ~?** how long?; **muito/pouco ~** a long/short time; **mais ~** longer; **ganhar/perder ~** to gain/waste time; **já era ~** it's about time; **não dá ~** there isn't time; **dar ~ ao ~** to bide one's time, wait and see; **matar o ~** to kill time; **nos bons ~s** in the good old days; **o maior de todos os ~s** the greatest of all time; **há ~s** for ages; (*atrás*) ages ago; **com o passar do ~** in time; **primeiro/segundo ~** (*ESPORTE*) first/second half; **~ integral** full time; **~ real** (*COMPUT*) real time.

tempo-quente *m* fight, set-to.

têmpora ['tẽpora] *f* (*ANAT*) temple.

temporada [tẽpo'rada] *f* season; (*tempo*) spell; **~ de ópera** opera season.

temporal [tẽpo'raw] (*pl* **-ais**) *adj* worldly ♦ *m* storm, gale.

temporário/a [tẽpo'rarju/a] *adj* temporary, provisional.

tenacidade [tenasi'dadʒi] *f* tenacity.

tenaz [te'najʒ] *adj* tenacious ♦ *f* tongs *pl*.

tenção [tẽ'sãw] (*pl* **-ões**) *f* intention; **fazer ~ de fazer** to decide to do.

tencionar [tẽsjo'na*] *vt* to intend, plan.

tenções [tẽ'sõjʃ] *fpl de* **tenção**.

tenda ['tẽda] *f* (*barraca*) tent; **~ de oxigênio** oxygen tent.

tendão [tẽ'dãw] (*pl* **-ões**) *m* tendon; **~ de Aquiles** Achilles tendon.

tendência [tẽ'dẽsja] *f* tendency; (*da moda etc*) trend; **a ~ de** *ou* **em** *ou* **a fazer** the tendency to do.

tendencioso/a [tẽdẽ'sjozu/ɔza] *adj* tendentious, bias(s)ed.

tendente [tẽ'dẽtʃi] *adj*: **~ a** tending to.

tender [tẽ'de*] *vi*: **~ para** to tend towards; **~ a fazer** to tend *ou* have a tendency to do; (*encaminhar-se*) to head towards doing; (*visar*) to aim to do.

tendinha [tẽ'dʒiɲa] *f* (*botequim*) dive; (*birosca*) shop.

tendões [tẽ'dõjʃ] *mpl de* **tendão**.

tenebroso/a [tene'brozu/ɔza] *adj* dark, gloomy; (*fig*) horrible.

tenente [te'nẽtʃi] *m* lieutenant.

tenho ['teɲu] *etc vb V* **ter**.

tênis ['teniʃ] *m inv* (*jogo*) tennis; (*sapatos*) training shoes *pl*; (*um sapato*) training shoe; **~ de mesa** table tennis.

tenista [te'niʃta] *m/f* tennis player.

tenor [te'no*] *adj*, *m* tenor.

tenro/a ['tẽxu/a] *adj* tender; (*macio*) soft; (*delicado*) delicate; (*novo*) young.

tensão [tẽ'sãw] *f* tension; (*pressão*) pressure, strain; (*rigidez*) tightness; (*TEC*) stress; (*ELET*: *voltagem*) voltage; **~ nervosa** nervous tension; **~ pré-menstrual** premenstrual tension.

tenso/a ['tẽsu/a] *adj* tense; (*sob pressão*) under stress, strained.

tentação [tẽta'sãw] *f* temptation.

tentáculo [tẽ'takulu] *m* tentacle.

tentado/a [tẽ'tadu/a] *adj* (*pessoa*) tempted; (*crime*) attempted.

tentador(a) [tẽta'do*(a)] *adj* tempting; (*sedutor*) inviting ♦ *m/f* tempter/temptress.

tentar [tẽ'ta*] *vt* to try; (*seduzir*) to tempt, entice ♦ *vi* to try; **~ fazer** to try to do.

tentativa [tẽta'tʃiva] *f* attempt; **~ de fazer** attempt to do; **~ de homicídio/suicídio/roubo** (*JUR*) attempted murder/suicide/robbery; **por ~s** by trial and error.

tentativo/a [tẽta'tʃivu/a] *adj* tentative.

tentear [tẽ'tʃja*] *vt* (*tentar*) to try.

tênue ['tenwi] *adj* tenuous; (*fino*) thin; (*delicado*) delicate; (*luz*, *voz*) faint; (*pequeníssimo*) minute.

tenuidade [tenwi'dadʒi] *f* tenuousness.

teologia [teolo'ʒia] *f* theology.

teológico/a [teo'lɔʒiku/a] *adj* theological.

teólogo/a [te'ɔlogu/a] *m/f* theologian.

teor [te'o*] *m* (*conteúdo*) tenor; (*sentido*) meaning, drift; (*fig*: *norma*) system; (: *modo*) way; (*QUÍM*) grade; **~ alcoólico** alcoholic content; **baixo ~ de nicotina** low tar.

teorema [teo'rɛma] *m* theorem.

teoria [teo'ria] *f* theory.

teoricamente [teorika'mẽtʃi] *adv* theoretically, in theory.

teórico/a [te'ɔriku/a] *adj* theoretical ♦ *m/f* theoretician.

teorizar [teori'za*] *vi* to theorize.

tépido/a ['tɛpidu/a] *adj* tepid, lukewarm.

ter [te*] *vt* to have; (*na mão*) to hold; (*considerar*) to consider; (*conter*) to hold, contain; **~ fome/sorte** to be hungry/lucky; **~ frio/calor** to be cold/hot; **ela tem 5 anos** she is 5 years old; **tem 10 metros de largura** it is 10 metres wide; **~ que** *ou* **de fazer** to have to do; **~ o que dizer/fazer** to have something

***NB:** European Portuguese adds the following consonants to certain words:* **b** (sú(b)dito, su(b)til); **c** (a(c)ção, a(c)cionista, a(c)to); **m** (inde(m)ne); **p** (ado(p)ção, ado(p)tar); *for further details see p. xiii.*

to say/do; **você tem como chegar lá?** have you got some way of getting there?; ~ **a ver com** to have to do with; **tem** (*impess*) there is/are; **tem 3 dias que não saio de casa** I haven't been out for 3 days; **o que é que ele tem?** what's the matter with him?; **o que é que tem isso?** (*col*) so what?; **não tem de quê** don't mention it; **vai ~!** (*col*) there'll be hell to pay!; **ir ~ com** to (go and) meet; **~-se** *vr*: **~-se por** to consider o.s.

ter. *abr* (= *terça-feira*) Tues.

terapeuta [tera'pewta] *m/f* therapist.

terapêutica [tera'pewtʃika] *f* therapeutics *sg*.

terapêutico/a [tera'pewtʃiku/a] *adj* therapeutic.

terapia [tera'pia] *f* therapy; ~ **ocupacional** occupational therapy; ~ **de reposição de estrogênio** hormone replacement therapy.

terça ['texsa] *f* (*tb*: *~-feira*) Tuesday.

terça-feira (*pl* **terças-feiras**) *f* Tuesday; ~ **gorda** Shrove Tuesday; ~ **que vem** next Tuesday; ~ **passada/retrasada** last Tuesday/ Tuesday before last; **hoje é ~ dia 12 de junho** today is Tuesday the 12th of June; **na ~** on Tuesday; **nas terças-feiras** on Tuesdays; **todas as terças-feiras** every Tuesday; ~ **sim, ~ não** every other Tuesday; **na ~ de manhã** on Tuesday morning; **o jornal da ~** Tuesday's newspaper.

terceiranista [texsejra'niʃta] *m/f* third-year.

terceiro/a [tex'sejru/a] *num* third ♦ *m* (JUR) third party; **~s** *mpl* outsiders; **o T~ Mundo** the Third World; *V tb* **quinto**.

terciário/a [tex'sjarju/a] *adj* tertiary.

terço ['texsu] *m* third (part).

terçol [tex'sɔw] (*pl* **-óis**) *m* stye.

tergal [tex'gaw] ® *m* Terylene ®.

tergiversar [texʒivex'sa*] *vi* to prevaricate, evade the issue.

termal [tex'maw] (*pl* **-ais**) *adj* thermal.

termas ['tɛxmaʃ] *fpl* bathhouse *sg*.

térmico/a ['tɛxmiku/a] *adj* thermal; **garrafa térmica** (Thermos ®) flask.

terminação [texmina'sãw] (*pl* **-ões**) *f* (LING) ending.

terminal [texmi'naw] (*pl* **-ais**) *adj* terminal ♦ *m* (*de rede*, ELET, COMPUT) terminal ♦ *f* terminal; ~ **de vídeo** monitor, VDU.

terminante [texmi'nãtʃi] *adj* final; (*categórico*) categorical, firm; (*decisivo*) decisive.

terminantemente [texminãtʃi'mẽtʃi] *adv* categorically, expressly.

terminar [texmi'na*] *vt* to finish ♦ *vi* (*pessoa*) to finish; (*coisa*) to end; ~ **de fazer** to finish doing; (*ter feito há pouco*) to have just done; ~ **por algo/fazer algo** to end with sth/end up doing sth.

término ['tɛxminu] *m* (*fim*) end, termination.

terminologia [texminolo'ʒia] *f* terminology.

termo ['texmu] *m* term; (*fim*) end, termination; (*limite*) limit, boundary; (*prazo*) period; (PT: *garrafa*) (Thermos ®) flask; **pôr ~ a** to put an end to; **meio ~** compromise; **em ~s (de)** in terms (of).

termodinâmica [texmodʒi'namika] *f* thermodynamics *sg*.

termômetro [tex'mometru] *m* thermometer.

termonuclear [texmonukle'a*] *adj* thermonuclear ♦ *f* nuclear power station.

termostato [texmoʃ'tatu] *m* thermostat.

terninho [tex'niɲu] *m* trouser suit (BRIT), pantsuit (US).

terno/a ['tɛxnu/a] *adj* gentle, tender ♦ *m* (BR: *roupa*) suit.

ternura [tex'nura] *f* gentleness, tenderness.

terra ['tɛxa] *f* (*mundo*) earth, world; (AGR, *propriedade*) land; (*pátria*) country; (*chão*) ground; (GEO) soil, earth; (*pó*) dirt; (ELET) earth; ~ **firme** dry land; **por ~** on the ground; **nunca viajei por essas ~s** I've never been to those parts; **ela não é da ~** she's not from these parts; **caminho de ~ batida** dirt road; ~ **de ninguém** no man's land; ~ **natal** homeland; ~ **prometida** promised land; **a T~ Santa** the Holy Land; ~ **vegetal** black earth; **soltar em ~** to disembark.

terraço [te'xasu] *m* terrace.

terracota [texa'kɔta] *f* terracotta.

Terra do Fogo *f* Tierra del Fuego.

terramoto [texa'mɔtu] (PT) *m* earthquake.

Terra Nova *f*: **a ~** Newfoundland.

terraplenagem [texaple'naʒẽ] *f* earth-moving.

terreiro [te'xejru] *m* yard, square; (*de macumba*) shrine.

terremoto [texe'mɔtu] *m* earthquake.

terreno/a [te'xɛnu/a] *m* ground, land; (*porção de terra*) plot of land; (GEO) terrain ♦ *adj* earthly; **ganhar/perder ~** (*fig*) to gain/lose ground; **sondar o ~** (*fig*) to test the ground; ~ **baldio** (piece of) wasteground.

térreo/a ['tɛxju/a] *adj* ground level *atr*; **andar ~** (BR) ground floor (BRIT), first floor (US).

terrestre [te'xɛʃtri] *adj* land *atr*; **globo ~** globe, Earth.

terrificante [texifi'kãtʃi] *adj* terrifying.

terrífico/a [te'xifiku/a] *adj* terrifying.

terrina [te'xina] *f* tureen.

territorial [texito'rjaw] (*pl* **-ais**) *adj* territorial.

território [texi'tɔrju] *m* territory; (*distrito*) district, region.

terrível [te'xivew] (*pl* **-eis**) *adj* terrible, dreadful.

terror [te'xo*] *m* terror, dread.

terrorismo [texo'riʒmu] *m* terrorism.

terrorista [texo'riʃta] *m/f*, *adj* terrorist.

tertúlia [tex'tulja] *f* gathering (of friends).

tesão [te'zãw] (*pl* **-ões**) (*col!*) *m* randiness; (*pessoa*, *coisa*) turn-on; (*ereção*) hard-on; **sentir ~ por alguém** to fancy sb; **estar de ~** to feel randy; (*ter ereção*) to have a hard-on.

tese ['tɛzi] *f* proposition, theory; (EDUC) thesis; **em ~** in theory.

teso/a ['tezu/a] *adj* (*cabo*) taut; (*rígido*) stiff; **estar ~** (*col*) to be broke *ou* skint.

tesões [te'zõjʃ] *mpl de* **tesão**.

tesoura [te'zora] *f* scissors *pl*; (*fig*) backbiter; **uma ~** a pair of scissors.
tesourar [tezo'ra*] *vt* to cut; (*col*) to run down.
tesouraria [tezora'ria] *f* treasury.
tesoureiro/a [tezo'rejru/a] *m/f* treasurer.
tesouro [te'zoru] *m* treasure; (*erário*) treasury, exchequer; (*LITERATURA*) thesaurus; **um ~ (de informações)** a treasure trove of information.
testa ['tɛʃta] *f* brow, forehead; **à ~ de** at the head of.
testa-de-ferro (*pl* **testas-de-ferro**) *f* figurehead, dummy.
testamentário/a [teʃtamẽ'tarju/a] *adj* of a will.
testamento [teʃta'mẽtu] *m* will, testament; **Velho/Novo T~** Old/New Testament.
testar [teʃ'ta*] *vt* to test; (*deixar em testamento*) to bequeath.
teste ['tɛʃtʃi] *m* test; **~ de aptidão** aptitude test.
testemunha [teʃte'muɲa] *f* witness; **~ ocular** eyewitness; **~ de acusação** prosecution witness; **~ de Jeová** Jehovah's witness.
testemunhar [teʃtemu'ɲa*] *vi* to testify ♦ *vt* to give evidence about; (*presenciar*) to witness; (*confirmar*) to demonstrate.
testemunho [teʃte'muɲu] *m* evidence, testimony; (*prova*) evidence; **dar ~** to give evidence.
testículo [teʃ'tʃikulu] *m* testicle.
testificar [teʃtʃifi'ka*] *vt* to testify to; (*comprovar*) to attest; (*assegurar*) to maintain.
testudo/a [teʃ'tudu/a] *adj* big-headed.
teta ['tɛta] *f* teat, nipple.
tétano ['tɛtanu] *m* tetanus.
tête-à-tête [tɛta'tɛtʃi] *m* tête-à-tête.
tetéia [te'tɛja] *f* (*pessoa*) gem.
teto ['tɛtu] *m* ceiling; (*telhado*) roof; (*habitação*) home; (*para preço etc*) ceiling; **~ solar** sun roof.
tetracampeão [tetrakã'pjãw] (*pl* **-ões**) *m* four-times champion.
tétrico/a ['tɛtriku/a] *adj* (*lúgubre*) gloomy, dismal; (*horrível*) horrible.
teu/tua [tew/'tua] *adj* your ♦ *pron* yours.
teve ['tevi] *vb V* **ter**.
tevê [te've] *f* telly (*BRIT*), TV.
têxtil ['teʃtʃiw] (*pl* **-eis**) *m* textile.
texto ['teʃtu] *m* text.
textual [teʃ'twaw] (*pl* **-ais**) *adj* textual; **estas são suas palavras textuais** these are his exact words.
textualmente [teʃtwaw'mẽtʃi] *adv* (*exatamente*) exactly, to the letter.
textura [teʃ'tura] *f* texture.
texugo [te'ʃugu] *m* badger.
tez [teʒ] *f* complexion; (*pele*) skin.

TFR (*BR*) *abr m* = **Tribunal Federal de Recursos**.
thriller ['srila*] (*pl* **~s**) *m* thriller.
ti [tʃi] *pron* you.
tia ['tʃia] *f* aunt.
tia-avó (*pl* **tias-avós**) *f* great aunt.
tiara ['tʃjara] *f* tiara.
Tibete [tʃi'bɛtʃi] *m*: **o ~** Tibet.
tíbia ['tʃibja] *f* shinbone.
ticar [tʃi'ka*] *vt* to tick.
tico ['tʃiku] *m*: **um ~ (de)** a little bit (of).
tido/a [t'ʃidu/a] *pp de* **ter** ♦ *adj*: **~ como** *ou* **por** considered to be.
tiete ['tʃjɛtʃi] (*col*) *m/f* fan.
tifo ['tʃifu] *m* typhoid, typhus.
tigela [tʃi'ʒɛla] *f* bowl; **de meia ~** (*fig*, *col*) second-rate, small-time.
tigre ['tʃigri] *m* tiger.
tigresa [tʃi'greza] *f* tigress.
tijolo [tʃi'ʒolu] *m* brick; **~ furado** air brick.
til [tʃiw] (*pl* **tis**) *m* tilde.
tilintar [tʃilĩ'ta*] *vt*, *vi* to jingle ♦ *m* jingling.
timaço [tʃi'masu] (*col*) *m* great team.
timão [tʃi'mãw] (*pl* **-ões**) *m* (*NÁUT*) helm, tiller; (*time*) great team.
timbre ['tʃĩbri] *m* insignia, emblem; (*selo*) stamp; (*MÚS*) tone, timbre; (*de voz*) tone; (*LING*: *de vogal*) quality; (*em papel de carta*) heading.
time ['tʃimi] (*BR*) *m* team; **de segundo ~** (*fig*) second-rate; **tirar o ~ de campo** (*col*) to get going.
timer ['tajme*] (*pl* **~s**) *m* timer.
timidez [tʃimi'deʒ] *f* shyness, timidity.
tímido/a ['tʃimidu/a] *adj* shy, timid.
timões [tʃi'mõjʃ] *mpl de* **timão**.
timoneiro [tʃimo'nejru] *m* helmsman, coxswain.
tímpano ['tʃĩpanu] *m* eardrum; (*MÚS*) kettledrum.
tina ['tʃina] *f* vat.
tingimento [tʃĩʒi'mẽtu] *m* dyeing.
tingir [tʃĩ'ʒi*] *vt* to dye; (*fig*) to tinge.
tinha ['tʃiɲa] *etc vb V* **ter**.
tinhoso/a [tʃi'ɲozu/ɔza] *adj* single-minded.
tinido [tʃi'nidu] *m* jingle.
tinir [tʃi'ni*] *vi* to jingle, tinkle; (*ouvidos*) to ring; (*de frio*, *febre*) to shiver; (*de raiva*, *fome*) to tremble; **estar tinindo** (*carro*, *atleta*) to be in tip-top condition.
tinjo ['tʃĩʒu] *etc vb V* **tingir**.
tino ['tʃinu] *m* (*juízo*) discernment, judgement; (*intuição*) intuition; (*prudência*) prudence; **perder o ~** to lose one's senses; **ter ~ para algo** to have a flair for sth.
tinta ['tʃĩta] *f* (*de pintar*) paint; (*de escrever*) ink; (*para tingir*) dye; (*fig*: *vestígio*) shade, tinge; **carregar nas ~s** (*fig*) to exaggerate, embroider; **~ a óleo** oil paint; **~ de impressão** printing ink.

NB*: European Portuguese adds the following consonants to certain words:* **b** (sú(b)dito, su(b)til); **c** (a(c)ção, a(c)cionista, a(c)to); **m** (inde(m)ne); **p** (ado(p)ção, ado(p)tar); *for further details see p. xiii.*

tinteiro [tʃĩ'tejru] *m* inkwell.
tintim [tʃĩ'tʃĩ] *m*: **~!** cheers!; **~ por ~** blow by blow.
tinto/a ['tʃĩtu/a] *adj* dyed; (*fig*) stained; **vinho ~** red wine.
tintura [tʃĩ'tura] *f* dye; (*ato*) dyeing; (*fig*) tinge, hint.
tinturaria [tʃĩtura'ria] *f* (*lavanderia a seco*) dry-cleaner's.
tintureiro/a [tʃĩtu'rejru/a] *m/f* dry cleaner ♦ *m* police van.
tio/a ['tʃiu/a] *m/f* uncle/aunt; **meus ~s** my uncle and aunt.
tio-avô (*pl* **tios-avôs**) *m* great uncle.
tipa ['tʃipa] (*col: pej*) *f* dolly bird.
tipão [tʃi'pãw] (*col: pl* **-ões**) *m* good looker.
típico/a ['tʃipiku/a] *adj* typical.
tipificar [tʃipifi'ka*] *vt* to typify.
tipo ['tʃipu] *m* type; (*de imprensa*) print; (*de impressora*) typeface; (*classe*) kind; (*col: sujeito*) guy, chap; (*pessoa*) person.
tipões [tʃi'põjʃ] *mpl de* **tipão**.
tipografia [tʃipogra'fia] *f* printing, typography; (*estabelecimento*) printing office, printer's.
tipógrafo [tʃi'pɔgrafu] *m* printer.
tipóia [tʃi'pɔja] *f* (*tira de pano*) sling.
tique ['tʃiki] *m* (*MED*) twitch, tic; (*sinal*) tick.
tique-taque [-'taki] (*pl* **~s**) *m* tick-tock.
tíquete ['tʃiketʃi] *m* ticket.
tiquinho [tʃi'kiɲu] *m*: **um ~ (de)** a little bit (of).
tira ['tʃira] *f* strip ♦ *m* (*BR: col*) cop.
tiracolo [tʃira'kɔlu] *m*: **a ~** slung from the shoulder; **com o marido a ~** with her husband in tow.
tirada [tʃi'rada] *f* (*dito*) tirade.
tiragem [tʃi'raʒẽ] *f* (*de livro*) print run; (*de jornal, revista*) circulation; (*de chaminé*) draught (*BRIT*), draft (*US*).
tira-gosto (*pl* **~s**) *m* snack, savoury (*BRIT*).
tira-manchas *m inv* stain remover.
tirania [tʃira'nia] *f* tyranny.
tirânico/a [tʃi'raniku/a] *adj* tyrannical.
tiranizar [tʃirani'za*] *vt* to tyrannize.
tirano/a [tʃi'ranu/a] *adj* tyrannical ♦ *m/f* tyrant.
tirante [tʃi'rãtʃi] *m* (*de arreio*) brace; (*MECÂNICA*) driving rod; (*viga*) tie beam ♦ *prep* except; **uma cor ~ a vermelho** *etc* a reddish *etc* colo(u)r.
tirar [tʃi'ra*] *vt* to take away; (*de dentro*) to take out; (*de cima*) to take off; (*roupa, sapatos*) to take off; (*arrancar*) to pull out; (*férias*) to take, have; (*boas notas*) to get; (*salário*) to get, earn; (*curso*) to do, take; (*mancha*) to remove; (*foto, cópia*) to take; (*radiografia*) to have; (*mesa*) to clear; (*música, letra*) to take down; (*libertar*) to get out; **~ algo a alguém** to take sth from sb; **sem ~ nem pôr** exactly, precisely; **~ proveito/conclusões de** to benefit/draw conclusions from; **~ alguém para dançar** to ask sb to dance; **~ a tampa de** to take the lid off.
tiririca [tʃiri'rika] (*col*) *adj* hopping mad.
tiritante [tʃiri'tãtʃi] *adj* shivering.
tiritar [tʃiri'ta*] *vi* to shiver.
tiro ['tʃiru] *m* (*disparo*) shot; (*ato de disparar*) shooting, firing; **~ ao alvo** target practice; **trocar ~s** to fire at one another; **o ~ saiu pela culatra** (*fig*) the plan backfired; **dar um ~ no escuro** (*fig*) to take a shot in the dark; **ser ~ e queda** (*fig*) to be a dead cert.
tirocínio [tʃiro'sinju] *m* apprenticeship, training.
tiroteio [tʃiro'teju] *m* shooting, exchange of shots.
tis [tʃiʃ] *mpl de* **til**.
tísica ['tʃizika] *f* consumption; *V tb* **tísico**.
tísico/a ['tʃiziku/a] *adj, m/f* consumptive.
tisnar [tʃiʒ'na*] *vt* (*enegrecer*) to blacken; (*tostar*) to brown.
titânico/a [tʃi'taniku/a] *adj* titanic.
titânio [tʃi'tanju] *m* titanium.
títere ['tʃiteri] *m* (*tb fig*) puppet.
titia [tʃi'tʃia] *f* aunty; **ficar para ~** to be left on the shelf.
titica [tʃi'tʃika] (*col*) *f* (piece of) junk ♦ *m/f* good-for-nothing.
titio [tʃi'tʃiu] *m* uncle.
tititi [tʃitʃi'tʃi] *m* (*tumulto*) hubbub; (*falatório*) gossip, talk.
titubeante [tʃitu'bjãtʃi] *adj* tottering; (*vacilante*) hesitant.
titubear [tʃitu'bja*] *vi* (*cambalear*) to totter, stagger; (*vacilar*) to hesitate.
titular [tʃitu'la*] *adj* titular ♦ *m/f* holder; (*POL*) minister ♦ *vt* to title.
título ['tʃitulu] *m* title; (*COM*) bond; (*universitário*) degree; **a ~ de** by way of, as; **a ~ de que você fez isso?** what was your reason for doing that?; **a ~ de curiosidade** out of curiosity; **~ ao portador** (*COM*) bearer bond; **~ de propriedade** title deed; **~ de câmbio** (*COM*) bill of exchange.
tive ['tʃivi] *etc vb V* **ter**.
TJ (*BR*) *abr m* = **Tribunal do Júri**; **Tribunal de Justiça**.
tlim [tʃlĩ] *m* ring.
TO *abr* = **Tocantins**.
to [tu] = **te** + **o**.
toa ['toa] *f* towrope; **à ~** (*sem reflexão*) at random; (*sem motivo*) for no reason; (*inutilmente*) in vain, for nothing; (*sem ocupação*) with nothing to do; (*sem mais nem menos*) out of the blue; **andar à ~** to wander aimlessly; **não é à ~ que** it is not for nothing that, it is without reason that.
toada [to'ada] *f* tune, melody.
toalete [twa'lɛtʃi] *f* washing and dressing ♦ *m* (*banheiro*) toilet; (*traje*) outfit; **fazer a ~** to have a wash.
toalha [to'aʎa] *f* towel; **~ de mesa** tablecloth; **~ de banho** bath towel; **~ de rosto** hand towel.

toar [to'a*] *vi* to sound, resound.

tobogã [tobo'gã] *m* toboggan.

toca ['tɔka] *f* burrow, hole; (*fig*: *refúgio*) bolt-hole; (: *casebre*) hovel.

toca-discos (*BR*) *m inv* record-player.

tocado/a [to'kadu/a] *adj* (*col*: *alegre*) tipsy; (*expulso*) thrown out.

toca-fitas *m inv* cassette player.

tocaia [to'kaja] *f* ambush.

tocante [to'kãtʃi] *adj* moving, touching; **no ~ a** regarding, concerning.

tocar [to'ka*] *vt* to touch; (*MÚS*) to play; (*campainha*) to ring; (*comover*) to touch; (*programa*, *campanha*) to conduct; (*ônibus*, *gado*) to drive; (*expulsar*) to drive out; (*chegar a*) to reach ♦ *vi* to touch; (*MÚS*) to play; (*campainha*, *sino*, *telefone*) to ring; (*em carro*) to drive; **~-se** *vr* to touch (each other); (*ir-se*) to head off; (*perceber*) to realize; **~ a** (*dizer respeito*) to concern, affect; **~ em** to touch; (*assunto*) to touch upon; (*NÁUT*) to call at; **~ para alguém** (*telefonar*) to ring sb (up), call sb (up); **~ (o bonde) para frente** (*fig*) to get going, get a move on; **pelo que me toca** as far as I am concerned.

tocha ['tɔʃa] *f* torch.

toco ['toku] *m* (*de cigarro*) stub; (*de árvore*) stump.

todavia [toda'via] *adv* yet, still, however.

todo/a ['todu/'tɔda] *adj* all; (*inteiro*) whole, entire; (*cada*) every; **~s** *mpl* everybody *sg*, everyone *sg*; **a toda (velocidade)** at full speed; **toda a gente** (*PT*), **~ (o) mundo** (*BR*) everyone, everybody; **em toda (a) parte** everywhere; **~s nós** all of us; **~s os dias** *ou* **~ dia** every day; **~ o dia, o dia ~** all day; **ao ~** altogether; (*no total*) in all; **de ~** completely; **não está de ~ ruim** it's not all bad; **para ~ e sempre** for ever more; **em ~ caso** in any case; **~ o Brasil** the whole of Brazil; **como um ~** as a whole; **estar em todas** (*col*) to be all over the place.

todo-poderoso/a *adj* almighty, all-powerful ♦ *m*: **o T~** the Almighty.

tofe ['tɔfi] *m* toffee.

toga ['tɔga] *f* toga; (*EDUC*, *de magistrado*) gown.

toicinho [toj'siɲu] *m* bacon fat.

toldo ['towdu] *m* awning, sun blind.

toleima [to'lɛjma] *f* folly, stupidity.

tolerância [tole'rãsja] *f* tolerance.

tolerante [tole'rãtʃi] *adj* tolerant.

tolerar [tole'ra*] *vt* to tolerate.

tolerável [tole'ravew] (*pl* **-eis**) *adj* tolerable, bearable; (*satisfatório*) passable; (*falta*) excusable.

tolher [to'ʎe*] *vt* to impede, hinder; (*voz*) to cut off; **~ alguém de fazer** to stop sb doing.

tolice [to'lisi] *f* stupidity, foolishness; (*ato*, *dito*) stupid thing.

tolo/a ['tolu/a] *adj* foolish, silly, stupid ♦ *m/f* fool; **fazer alguém/fazer-se de ~** to make a fool of sb/o.s.

tom [tõ] (*pl* **-ns**) *m* tone; (*MÚS*: *altura*) pitch; (: *escala*) key; (*cor*) shade; **ser de bom ~** to be good manners; **~ agudo/grave** high/low note; **~ maior/menor** (*MÚS*) major/minor key.

tomada [to'mada] *f* capture; (*ELET*) socket; (*CINEMA*) shot; **~ de posse** investiture; **~ de preços** tender.

tomar [to'ma*] *vt* to take; (*capturar*) to capture, seize; (*decisão*) to make; (*bebida*) to drink; **~-se** *vr*: **~-se de** to be overcome with; **~ algo emprestado** to borrow sth; **~ alguém por algo** to take sb for sth; **~ algo como** to take sth as; **toma!** here you are!; **quer ~ alguma coisa?** do you want something to drink?; **~ café** (*de manhã*) to have breakfast; **toma lá, dá cá** give and take.

tomara [to'mara] *excl*: **~!** if only!; **~ que venha hoje** I hope he comes today.

tomara-que-caia *adj inv*: **(vestido) ~** strapless dress.

tomate [to'matʃi] *m* tomato.

tombadilho [tõba'dʒiʎu] *m* deck.

tombar [tõ'ba*] *vi* to fall down, tumble down ♦ *vt* to knock down, knock over; (*conservar*: *edifício*) to list.

tombo ['tõbu] *m* (*queda*) tumble, fall; (*registro*) archives *pl*, records *pl*.

tomilho [to'miʎu] *m* thyme.

tomo ['tɔmu] *m* tome, volume.

tona ['tɔna] *f* surface; **vir à ~** to come to the surface; (*fig*) to emerge; **trazer à ~** to bring up; (*recordações*) to bring back.

tonalidade [tonali'dadʒi] *f* (*de cor*) shade; (*MÚS*) tonality; (: *tom*) key.

tonel [to'nɛw] (*pl* **-éis**) *m* cask, barrel.

tonelada [tone'lada] *f* ton; **uma ~ de** (*fig*) tons of.

tonelagem [tone'laʒẽ] *f* tonnage.

toner ['tone*] *m* toner.

tônica ['tonika] *f* (*água*, *MÚS*) tonic; (*LING*) stressed syllable; (*fig*) keynote.

tônico/a ['toniku/a] *adj* tonic; (*sílaba*) stressed ♦ *m* tonic; **acento ~** stress.

tonificante [tonifi'kãtʃi] *adj* invigorating.

tonificar [tonifi'ka*] *vt* to tone up.

tons [tõʃ] *mpl de* **tom**.

tontear [tõ'tʃja*] *vt*: **~ alguém** to make sb dizzy; (*suj*: *barulheira*) to get sb down, give sb a headache; (: *alvoroço*, *notícia*) to stun sb ♦ *vi* (*pessoa*: *com bebida*) to get dizzy; (: *com barulho*) to get a headache; (: *com alvoroço*) to be dazed; (*barulho*) to be wearing; (*alvoroço*) to be upsetting; **~ de sono** to be half-asleep.

tonteira [tõ'tejra] *f* dizziness.

tontice [tõ'tʃisi] *f* stupidity, nonsense.

NB*: European Portuguese adds the following consonants to certain words:* **b** (sú(b)dito, su(b)til); **c** (a(c)ção, a(c)cionista, a(c)to); **m** (inde(m)ne); **p** (ado(p)ção, ado(p)tar); *for further details see p. xiii.*

tonto/a ['tõtu/a] *adj* (*tolo*) stupid, silly; (*zonzo*) dizzy, lightheaded; (*atarantado*) flustered; **às tontas** impulsively.

tontura [tõ'tura] *f* dizziness, lightheadedness.

topada [to'pada] *f* trip; **dar uma ~ em** to stub one's toe on.

topar [to'pa*] *vt* to agree to ♦ *vi*: **~ com** to come across; **~-se** *vr* (*duas pessoas*) to run into one another; **~ em** (*tropeçar*) to stub one's toe on; (*esbarrar*) to run into; (*tocar*) to touch; **você topa ir ao cinema?** do you fancy going to the cinema?; **~ que alguém faça** to agree that sb should do.

topa-tudo ['tɔpa-] *m inv* person who can't say no.

topázio [to'pazju] *m* topaz.

tope ['tɔpi] *m* top.

topete [to'petʃi] *m* quiff; **ter o ~ de fazer** (*fig*) to have the cheek to do.

tópico/a ['tɔpiku/a] *adj* topical ♦ *m* topic.

topless [tɔp'lɛs] *adj inv* topless ♦ *m inv* (*na praia*) topless bikini.

topo ['topu] *m* top; (*extremidade*) end, extremity.

topografia [topogra'fia] *f* topography.

topográfico/a [topo'grafiku/a] *adj* topographical.

topônimo [to'ponimu] *m* place name, toponym.

toque ['tɔkɪ] *etc vb V* **tocar** ♦ *m* touch; (*de instrumento musical*) playing; (*de campainha*) ring; (*fig*: *vestígio*) touch; (*retoque*) finishing touch; **os últimos ~s** the finishing touches; **dar um ~ em alguém** (*col*: *avisar*) to let sb know; (: *falar com*) to have a word with sb; **a ~ de caixa** in all haste.

Tóquio ['tɔkju] *n* Tokyo.

tora ['tɔra] *f* (*pedaço*) piece; (*de madeira*) log; (*sesta*) nap; **tirar uma ~** to have a nap.

toranja [to'rãʒa] *f* grapefruit.

tórax ['tɔraks] *m inv* thorax.

torção [tox'sãw] (*pl* **-ões**) *m* twist, twisting; (*MED*) sprain.

torcedor(a) [toxse'do*(a)] *m/f* supporter, fan.

torcedura [toxse'dura] *f* twist; (*MED*) sprain.

torcer [tox'se*] *vt* to twist; (*deslocar*) to sprain; (*desvirtuar*) to distort, misconstrue; (*roupa*: *espremer*) to wring; (: *na máquina*) to spin; (*vergar*) to bend ♦ *vi*: **~ por** (*time*) to support; (*amigo etc*) to keep one's fingers crossed for; **~-se** *vr* (*contorcer-se*) to squirm, writhe; **~ para** *ou* **por** to cheer for; **~ para que tudo dê certo** to keep one's fingers crossed that everything works out right.

torcicolo [toxsi'kɔlu] *m* stiff neck.

torcida [tox'sida] *f* (*pavio*) wick; (*ESPORTE*: *ato de torcer*) cheering; (: *torcedores*) supporters; **dar uma ~ em algo** to twist sth; (*roupa*) to wring sth out.

torções [tox'sõjʃ] *mpl de* **torção**.

tormenta [tox'mẽta] *f* storm; (*fig*) upset.

tormento [tox'mẽtu] *m* torment, torture; (*angústia*) anguish.

tormentoso/a [toxmẽ'tozu/ɔza] *adj* stormy, tempestuous.

tornado [tox'nadu] *m* tornado.

tornar [tox'na*] *vi* (*voltar*) to return, go back ♦ *vt* to make; **~-se** *vr* to become; **~ algo em algo** to turn *ou* make sth into sth; **~ a fazer algo** to do sth again.

torneado/a [tox'njadu/a] *adj*: **bem ~** (*pernas, pescoço*) shapely.

tornear [tox'nja*] *vt* to turn (on a lathe), shape.

torneio [tox'neju] *m* tournament.

torneira [tox'nejra] *f* tap (*BRIT*), faucet (*US*).

torniquete [toxni'ketʃi] *m* (*MED*) tourniquet; (*PT*: *roleta*) turnstile.

torno ['toxnu] *m* lathe; (*CERÂMICA*) wheel; **em ~ de** (*ao redor de*) around; (*sobre*) about; **em ~ de 5 milhões** around 5 million.

tornozeleira [toxnoze'lejra] *f* ankle support.

tornozelo [toxno'zelu] *m* ankle.

toró [to'rɔ] *m* (*chuva*) downpour, shower; **caiu um ~** there was a sudden downpour.

torpe ['toxpi] *adj* vile.

torpedear [toxpe'dʒja*] *vt* to torpedo.

torpedo [tox'pedu] *m* torpedo.

torpeza [tox'peza] *f* vileness.

torpor [tox'po*] *m* torpor; (*MED*) numbness.

torrada [to'xada] *f* toast.

torradeira [toxa'dejra] *f* toaster.

torrão [to'xãw] (*pl* **-ões**) *m* turf, sod; (*terra*) soil, land; (*de açúcar*) lump; **~ natal** native land.

torrar [to'xa*] *vt* (*pão*) to toast; (*café*) to roast; (*plantação*) to parch; (*dinheiro*) to blow, squander; (*vender*) to sell off cheap; **~ a paciência** *ou* **o saco** (*col*) **de alguém** to try sb's patience; **~ (alguém)** (*col*) to get on sb's nerves.

torre ['toxi] *f* tower; (*XADREZ*) castle, rook; (*ELET*) pylon; **~ de controle** (*AER*) control tower; **~ de vigia** watchtower.

torreão [to'xjãw] (*pl* **-ões**) *m* turret.

torrefação [toxefa'sãw] (*PT*: **-cç-**: *pl* **-ões**) *f* coffee-roasting house.

torrencial [toxẽ'sjaw] (*pl* **-ais**) *adj* torrential.

torrente [to'xẽtʃi] *f* (*tb fig*) torrent.

torreões [to'xjõjʃ] *mpl de* **torreão**.

torresmo [to'xeʒmu] *m* crackling.

tórrido/a ['tɔxidu/a] *adj* torrid.

torrinha [to'xiɲa] *f* (*TEATRO*) gallery; **as ~s** the gods.

torrões [to'xõjʃ] *mpl de* **torrão**.

torrone [to'xɔni] *m* nougat.

torso ['toxsu] *m* torso, trunk.

torta ['tɔxta] *f* pie, tart; **~ de maçã** apple pie.

torto/a ['toxtu/'tɔxta] *adj* twisted, crooked; **a ~ e a direito** indiscriminately; **cometer erros a ~ e a direito** to make mistakes left, right and centre.

tortuoso/a [tox'twozu/ɔza] *adj* winding.

tortura [tox'tura] *f* torture; (*fig*) anguish,

agony.
torturador(a) [toxtura'do*(a)] *m/f* torturer.
torturante [toxtu'rãtʃi] *adj* (*sonhos*) haunting; (*dor*) excruciating.
torturar [toxtu'ra*] *vt* to torture; (*fig*: *afligir*) to torment.
torvelinho [toxve'liɲu] *m* (*de vento*) whirlwind; (*de água*) whirlpool; (*fig*: *de pensamentos*) swirl.
tos [tuʃ] = **te** + **os**.
tosão [to'zãw] (*pl* **-ões**) *m* fleece.
tosar [to'za*] *vt* (*ovelha*) to shear; (*cabelo*) to crop.
tosco/a ['toʃku/a] *adj* rough, unpolished; (*grosseiro*) coarse, crude.
tosões [to'zõjʃ] *mpl de* **tosão**.
tosquiar [toʃ'kja*] *vt* (*ovelha*) to shear, clip.
tosse ['tɔsi] *f* cough; ~ **de cachorro** whooping cough; ~ **seca** dry *ou* tickly cough.
tossir [to'si*] *vi* to cough ♦ *vt* to cough up.
tosta ['tɔʃta] (*PT*) *f* toast; ~ **mista** toasted cheese and ham sandwich.
tostado/a [toʃ'tadu/a] *adj* toasted; (*pessoa*) tanned; (*carne*) browned.
tostão [toʃ'tãw] *m* (*dinheiro*) cash; **estar sem um** ~ to be completely penniless.
tostar [toʃ'ta*] *vt* to toast; (*pele*, *pessoa*) to tan; (*carne*) to brown; **~-se** *vr* to get tanned.
total [to'taw] (*pl* **-ais**) *adj*, *m* total.
totalidade [totali'dadʒi] *f* totality, entirety; **em sua** ~ in its entirety; **a** ~ **da população/dos políticos** the entire population/all politicians.
totalitário/a [totali'tarju/a] *adj* totalitarian.
totalitarismo [totalita'riʒmu] *m* totalitarianism.
totalizar [totali'za*] *vt* to total up.
totalmente [totaw'mẽtʃi] *adv* totally, completely.
touca ['toka] *f* bonnet; (*de freira*) veil; ~ **de banho** bathing hat.
toucador [toka'do*] *m* (*penteadeira*) dressing table.
toucinho [to'siɲu] *m* = **toicinho**.
toupeira [to'pejra] *f* mole; (*fig*) numbskull, idiot.
tourada [to'rada] *f* bullfight.
tourear [to'rja*] *vi* to fight (bulls).
toureiro [to'rejru] *m* bullfighter.
touro ['toru] *m* bull; **T~** (*ASTROLOGIA*) Taurus; **pegar o** ~ **à unha** to take the bull by the horns; **praça de ~s** bullring.
toxemia [tokse'mia] *f* blood poisoning.
tóxico/a ['tɔksiku/a] *adj* poisonous, toxic ♦ *m* (*veneno*) poison; (*droga*) drug.
toxicômano/a [toksi'komanu/a] *m/f* drug addict.
toxina [tok'sina] *f* toxin.
trabalhadeira [trabaʎa'dejra] *f de* **trabalhador**.
trabalhador(a) [trabaʎa'do*(a)] *adj* (*laborioso*) hard-working, industrious; (*POL*: *classe*) working ♦ *m/f* worker; ~ **braçal** manual worker.
trabalhão [traba'ʎãw] (*pl* **-ões**) *m* big job.
trabalhar [traba'ʎa*] *vi* to work; (*TEATRO*) to act ♦ *vt* (*terra*) to till, work; (*madeira*, *metal*) to work; (*texto*) to work at; ~ **com** (*comerciar*) to deal in; ~ **de** *ou* **como** to work as.
trabalheira [traba'ʎejra] *f* big job.
trabalhista [traba'ʎiʃta] *adj* labour *atr* (*BRIT*), labor *atr* (*US*) ♦ *m/f* Labour Party member; **Partido T~** (*BRIT*: *POL*) Labour Party.
trabalho [tra'baʎu] *m* work; (*emprego*, *tarefa*) job; (*ECON*) labour (*BRIT*), labor (*US*); (*EDUC*: *tarefa*) assignment; ~ **braçal** manual work; **~s forçados** hard labo(u)r, forced labo(u)r; **estar sem** ~ to be out of work; **dar** ~ to need work; **dar** ~ **a alguém** to cause sb trouble; **dar-se o** ~ **de fazer** to take the trouble to do; **um** ~ **ingrato** a thankless task; ~ **doméstico** housework; ~ **de parto** labo(u)r.
trabalhões [traba'ʎõjʃ] *mpl de* **trabalhão**.
trabalhoso/a [traba'ʎozu/ɔza] *adj* laborious, arduous.
traça ['trasa] *f* moth.
traçado [tra'sadu] *m* sketch, plan.
tração [tra'sãw] *f* traction.
traçar [tra'sa*] *vt* to draw; (*determinar*) to set out, outline; (*limites*, *fronteiras*) to mark out; (*planos*) to draw up; (*escrever*) to compose; (*col*: *comer*, *beber*) to guzzle down.
tracçao [tra'sãw] (*PT*) *f* = **tração**.
traço ['trasu] *m* (*linha*) line, dash; (*de lápis*) stroke; (*vestígio*) trace, vestige; (*aspecto*) feature, trait; **~s** *mpl* (*do rosto*) features; ~ **(de união)** hyphen; (*entre frases*) dash.
tractor [tra'to*] (*PT*) *m* = **trator**.
tradição [tradʒi'sãw] (*pl* **-ões**) *f* tradition.
tradicional [tradʒisjo'naw] (*pl* **-ais**) *adj* traditional.
tradições [tradʒi'sõjʃ] *fpl de* **tradição**.
tradução [tradu'sãw] (*pl* **-ões**) *f* translation.
tradutor(a) [tradu'to*(a)] *m/f* translator; ~ **juramentado** legally recognized translator.
traduzir [tradu'zi*] *vt* to translate; **~-se** *vr* to come across; ~ **do inglês para o português** to translate from English into Portuguese.
trafegar [trafe'ga*] *vi* to move, go.
trafegável [trafe'gavew] (*pl* **~eis**) *adj* (*rua*) open to traffic.
tráfego ['trafegu] *m* (*trânsito*) traffic; ~ **aéreo/marítimo** air/sea traffic.
traficante [trafi'kãtʃi] *m/f* trafficker, dealer; ~ **de drogas** drug trafficker, pusher (*col*).
traficar [trafi'ka*] *vi*: ~ **(com)** to deal (in), traffic (in).
tráfico ['trafiku] *m* traffic; ~ **de drogas** drug

trafficking.

tragada [tra'gada] *f* (*em cigarro*) drag, puff.

tragar [tra'ga*] *vt* to swallow; (*fumaça*) to inhale; (*suportar*) to tolerate ♦ *vi* to inhale.

tragédia [tra'ʒɛdʒja] *f* tragedy; **fazer ~ de algo** to make a drama out of sth.

trágico/a ['traʒiku/a] *adj* tragic; (*dado a fazer tragédia*) dramatic.

tragicomédia [traʒiko'mɛdʒja] *f* tragicomedy.

tragicômico/a [traʒi'komiku/a] *adj* tragicomic.

trago ['tragu] *etc vb V* **trazer** ♦ *m* mouthful; (*em cigarro*) drag, puff; **tomar um ~** to have a mouthful; (*em cigarro*) to have a drag; **de um ~** in one gulp.

traguei [tra'gej] *etc vb V* **tragar**.

traição [traj'sãw] (*pl* **-ões**) *f* treason, treachery; (*deslealdade*) betrayal, disloyalty; (*infidelidade*) infidelity; **alta ~** high treason.

traiçoeiro/a [traj'swejru/a] *adj* treacherous; (*infiel*) disloyal.

traições [traj'sõjʃ] *fpl de* **traição**.

traidor(a) [traj'do*(a)] *m/f* traitor.

trailer ['trejla*] (*pl* **~s**) *m* trailer; (*tipo casa*) caravan (*BRIT*), trailer (*US*).

traineira [traj'nejra] *f* trawler.

training ['trejnĩŋ] (*pl* **~s**) *m* track suit.

trair [tra'i*] *vt* to betray; (*mulher, marido*) to be unfaithful to; (*esperanças*) not to live up to; **~-se** *vr* to give o.s. away.

trajar [tra'ʒa*] *vt* to wear; **~-se** *vr*: **~-se de preto** to be dressed in black.

traje ['traʒi] *m* dress, clothes *pl*; **~ de banho** bathing costume; **~ de noite** evening gown; **~ a rigor** evening dress; **~ de passeio** smart dress; **~ domingueiro** Sunday best; **em ~s de Adão** in one's birthday suit; **~s menores** smalls, underwear *sg*.

trajeto [tra'ʒɛtu] (*PT*: **-ct-**) *m* course, path.

trajetória [traʒe'tɔrja] (*PT*: **-ct-**) *f* trajectory, path; (*fig*) course.

tralha ['traʎa] *f* fishing net; (*col*) junk.

trama ['trama] *f* (*tecido*) woof; (*enredo, conspiração*) plot.

tramar [tra'ma*] *vt* (*tecer*) to weave; (*maquinar*) to scheme, plot; ♦ *vi*: **~ contra** to conspire against.

trambicar [trãbi'ka*] *vt* to con.

trambique [trã'biki] (*col*) *m* con.

trambiqueiro/a [trãbi'kejru/a] *m/f* con merchant ♦ *adj* slippery.

trambolhão [trambo'ʎãw] (*pl* **-ões**) *m* tumble; **andar aos trambolhões** to stumble along.

trambolho [trã'boʎu] *m* encumbrance.

trambolhões [trambo'ʎõjʃ] *mpl de* **trambolhão**.

tramitar [trami'ta*] *vi* to go through the procedure.

trâmites ['tramitʃiʃ] *mpl* procedure *sg*, channels.

tramóia [tra'mɔja] *f* (*fraude*) swindle, trick; (*trama*) plot, scheme.

trampolim [trãpo'lĩ] (*pl* **-ns**) *m* trampoline; (*de piscina*) diving board; (*fig*) springboard.

trampolinagem [trãpoli'naʒẽ] (*pl* **-ns**) *f* trick, swindle.

trampolineiro [trãpoli'nejru] *m* trickster, swindler.

trampolinice [trãpoli'nisi] *f* trick, swindle.

trampolins [trãpo'lĩʃ] *mpl de* **trampolim**.

tranca ['trãka] *f* (*de porta*) bolt; (*de carro*) lock.

trança ['trãsa] *f* (*cabelo*) plait; (*galão*) braid.

trançado/a [trã'sadu/a] *adj* (*cesto*) woven.

trancafiar [trãka'fja*] *vt* to lock up.

trancão [trã'kãw] (*pl* **-ões**) *m* bump.

trancar [trã'ka*] *vt* to lock; (*matrícula*) to suspend; (*FUTEBOL*) to shove; **~-se** *vr* (*mostrar-se fechado*) to clam up; **~-se no quarto** to lock o.s. (away) in one's room.

trançar [trã'sa*] *vt* to weave; (*cabelo*) to plait, braid ♦ *vi* (*col*) to wander around.

tranco ['trãku] *m* (*solavanco*) jolt; (*esbarrão*) bump; (*de cavalo*) walk; (*col*: *admoestação*) put-down; **aos ~s** jolting; **aos ~s e barrancos** with great difficulty; (*aos saltos*) jolting.

trancões [trã'kõjʃ] *mpl de* **trancão**.

tranqüilamente [trãkwila'mẽtʃi] *adv* calmly; (*facilmente*) easily; (*seguramente*) for sure.

tranqüilidade [trãkwili'dadʒi] *f* tranquillity; (*paz*) peace.

tranqüilizador(a) [trãkwiliza'do*(a)] *adj* reassuring; (*música*) soothing.

tranqüilizante [trãkwili'zãtʃi] *adj* = **tranqüilizador** ♦ *m* (*MED*) tranquillizer.

tranqüilizar [trãkwili'za*] *vt* to calm, quieten; (*despreocupar*): **~ alguém** to reassure sb, put sb's mind at rest; **~-se** *vr* to quieten down; (*pessoa preocupada*) to be reassured.

tranqüilo/a [trã'kwilu/a] *adj* peaceful; (*mar, pessoa*) calm; (*criança*) quiet; (*consciência*) clear; (*seguro*) sure, certain ♦ *adv* with no problems.

transa ['trãza] (*BR*: *col*) *f* (*namoro*) affair; (*combinação*) arrangement; (*trama, negócios*) business; (*ligação*) relationship; (*assunto*) matter; **combinar altas ~s** to be into all sorts of things.

transação [trãza'sãw] (*PT*: **-cç-**; *pl* **-ões**) *f* (*COM*) transaction, deal; (*combinação*) arrangement; (*col*: *maquinação*) business.

transada [trã'zada] *f*: **dar uma ~** (*col*) to have sex.

transado/a [trã'zadu/a] *adj*: **bem ~** (*col*: *objeto*) well made; (*relacionamento*) sorted out, healthy; (*pessoa, casa*) classy.

Transamazônica [trãzama'zonika]: **a ~** the trans-Amazonian highway.

transamazônico/a [trãzama'zoniku/a] *adj* trans-Amazonian.

transar [trã'za*] (*col*) *vt* (*combinar*) to arrange; (*tramar*) to plan; (*drogas*) to do ♦ *vi* (*namorar*) to go out; (*ter relação sexual*) to have sex; **~ com** (*relacionar-se*) to hang out with; (*negociar*) to deal in.

transatlântico/a [trãzat'lãtʃiku/a] *adj* transatlantic ♦ *m* (transatlantic) liner.
transbordar [trãʒbox'da*] *vi* to overflow; ~ **de alegria** to burst with happiness.
transbordo [trãʒ'boxdu] *m* (*de viajantes*) change, transfer.
transcendental [trãsẽdẽ'taw] (*pl* **-ais**) *adj* transcendental.
transcender [trãsẽ'de*] *vt, vi*: ~ **(a)** to transcend.
transcorrer [trãʃko'xe*] *vi* to elapse, go by; (*evento*) to pass off.
transcrever [trãʃkre've*] *vt* to transcribe.
transcrição [trãʃkri'sãw] (*pl* **-ões**) *f* transcription.
transcrito/a [trãʃ'kritu/a] *pp de* **transcrever** ♦ *m* transcript.
transe ['trãzi] *m* ordeal; (*lance*) plight; (*hipnótico*) trance; **a todo** ~ at all costs.
transeunte [trã'zjũtʃi] *m/f* passer-by.
transferência [trãʃfe'rẽsja] *f* transfer; (*JUR*) conveyancing.
transferir [trãʃfe'ri*] *vt* to be transferred; (*adiar*) to postpone.
transferível [trãʃfe'rivew] (*pl* **-eis**) *adj* transferable.
transfigurar [trãʃfigu'ra*] *vt* to transfigure, transform; **~-se** *vr* to be transformed.
transfiro [trãʃ'firu] *etc vb V* **transferir**.
transformação [trãʃfoxma'sãw] (*pl* **-ões**) *f* transformation.
transformador [trãʃfoxma'do*] *m* (*ELET*) transformer.
transformar [trãʃfox'ma*] *vt* to transform, turn; **~-se** *vr* to turn; ~ **algo em algo** to turn *ou* transform sth into sth.
trânsfuga ['trãʃfuga] *m* (*desertor*) deserter; (*político*) renegade, turncoat; (*da Rússia etc*) defector.
transfusão [trãʃfu'zãw] (*pl* **-ões**) *f* transfusion; ~ **de sangue** blood transfusion.
transgredir [trãʒgre'dʒi*] *vt* to infringe.
transgressão [trãʒgre'sãw] (*pl* **-ões**) *f* transgression, infringement.
transgrido [trãʒ'gridu] *etc vb V* **transgredir**.
transição [trãzi'sãw] (*pl* **-ões**) *f* transition; **período** *ou* **fase de** ~ transition period.
transicional [trãzisjo'naw] (*pl* **-ais**) *adj* transitional.
transições [trãzi'sõjʃ] *fpl de* **transição**.
transido/a [trã'zidu/a] *adj* numb.
transigente [trãzi'ʒẽtʃi] *adj* willing to compromise.
transigir [trãzi'ʒi*] *vi* to compromise, make concessions; ~ **com alguém** to compromise with sb, meet sb halfway.
transistor [trãziʃ'to*] *m* transistor.
transitar [trãzi'ta*] *vi*: ~ **por** to move through; (*rua*) to go along.
transitável [trãzi'tavew] (*pl* **-eis**) *adj* (*caminho*) passable.
transitivo/a [trãzi'tʃivu/a] *adj* (*LING*) transitive.
trânsito ['trãzitu] *m* (*ato*) transit, passage; (*na rua: veículos*) traffic; (*: pessoas*) flow; **em** ~ in transit; **sinal de** ~ traffic signal.
transitório/a [trãzi'tɔrju/a] *adj* transitory, passing; (*período*) transitional.
transladar [trãʒla'da*] *vt* = **trasladar**.
translado [trãʒ'ladu] *m* = **traslado**.
translúcido/a [trãʒ'lusidu/a] *adj* translucent.
transmissão [trãʒmi'sãw] (*pl* **-ões**) *f* transmission; (*RÁDIO, TV*) transmission, broadcast; (*transferência*) transfer; ~ **ao vivo** live broadcast; ~ **de dados** data transmission.
transmissível [trãʒmi'sivew] (*pl* **-eis**) *adj* transmittable.
transmissões [trãʒmi'sõjʃ] *fpl de* **transmissão**.
transmissor(a) [trãʒmi'so*(a)] *adj* transmitting ♦ *m* transmitter.
transmitir [trãʒmi'tʃi*] *vt* to transmit; (*RÁDIO, TV*) to broadcast, transmit; (*transferir*) to transfer; (*recado, notícia*) to pass on; (*aroma, som*) to carry; **~-se** *vr* (*doença*) to be transmitted; ~ **algo a alguém** (*paz etc*) to bring sb sth.
transparecer [trãʃpare'se*] *vi* to be visible, appear; (*revelar-se*) to be apparent.
transparência [trãʃpa'rẽsja] *f* transparency; (*de água*) clarity.
transparente [trãʃpa'rẽtʃi] *adj* transparent; (*roupa*) see-through; (*água*) clear; (*evidente*) clear, obvious.
transpassar [trãʃpa'sa*] *vt* = **traspassar**.
transpiração [trãʃpira'sãw] *f* perspiration.
transpirar [trãʃpi'ra*] *vi* (*suar*) to perspire; (*divulgar-se*) to become known; (*verdade*) to come out ♦ *vt* to exude.
transplantar [trãʃplã'ta*] *vt* to transplant.
transplante [trãʃ'plãtʃi] *m* transplant.
transpor [trãʃ'po*] (*irreg*: *como* **pôr**) *vt* to cross; (*inverter*) to transpose.
transportação [trãʃpoxta'sãw] *f* transportation.
transportadora [trãʃpoxta'dora] *f* haulage company.
transportar [trãʃpox'ta*] *vt* to transport; (*levar*) to carry; (*enlevar*) to entrance, enrapture; (*fig*: *remontar*) to take back; **~-se** *vr* to be entranced; (*remontar*) to be transported back; **a** ~ (*COM*: *quantia*) carry forward, c/f.
transporte [trãʃ'pɔxtʃi] *m* transport; (*COM*) haulage; (*em contas*) amount carried forward; (*fig*: *êxtase*) rapture, delight; **despesas de** ~ transport costs; **Ministério dos T~s** Ministry of Transport (*BRIT*), Department of Transportation (*US*); ~ **rodoviário** road transport; **~s coletivos** public transport

NB: European Portuguese adds the following consonants to certain words: **b** (sú(b)dito, su(b)til); **c** (a(c)ção, a(c)cionista, a(c)to); **m** (inde(m)ne); **p** (ado(p)ção, ado(p)tar); *for further details see p. xiii.*

sg.

transposição [trãʃpozi'sãw] *f* transposition; (*de rio*) crossing.

transpôs [trãʃ'poʃ] *vb V* **transpor**.

transposto/a [trãʃ'poʃtu/'pɔʃta] *pp de* **transpor**.

transpunha [trãʃ'puɲa] *etc vb V* **transpor**.

transpus [trãʃ'puʃ] *etc vb V* **transpor**.

transpuser [trãʃpu'ze*] *etc vb V* **transpor**.

transtornar [trãʃtox'na*] *vt* to upset; (*rotina, reunião*) to disrupt; **~-se** *vr* to get upset; (*reunião, rotina*) to be disrupted.

transtorno [trãʃ'toxnu] *m* upset, disruption; (*contrariedade*) hardship; (*mental*) distraction.

transversal [trãʒvex'saw] (*pl* **-ais**) *adj* transverse, cross; **(rua) ~** cross street.

transverso/a [trãʒ'vɛxsu/a] *adj* transverse.

transviado/a [trãʒ'vjadu/a] *adj* wayward, erring.

transviar [trãʒ'vja*] *vt* to lead astray; **~-se** *vr* to go astray.

trapaça [tra'pasa] *f* swindle, fraud.

trapacear [trapa'sja*] *vt, vi* to swindle.

trapaceiro/a [trapa'sejru/a] *adj* crooked, cheating ♦ *m/f* swindler, cheat.

trapalhada [trapa'ʎada] *f* confusion, mix up.

trapalhão/lhona [trapa'ʎãw/'ʎɔna] (*pl* **-ões/~s**) *m/f* bungler, blunderer.

trapézio [tra'pɛzju] *m* trapeze; (*MAT*) trapezium.

trapezista [trape'ziʃta] *m/f* trapeze artist.

trapo ['trapu] *m* rag; **ser** *ou* **estar um ~** (*pessoa*) to be washed up.

traquéia [tra'kɛja] *f* windpipe.

traquejo [tra'keʒu] *m* experience.

traqueotomia [trakjoto'mia] *f* tracheotomy.

traquinas [tra'kinaʃ] *adj inv* mischievous.

trarei [tra'rej] *etc vb V* **trazer**.

trás [trajʃ] *prep, adv*: **para ~** backwards; **por ~ de** behind; **de ~** from behind; **a luz de ~** the back light; **de ~ para frente** back to front; **ano ~ ano** year after year; **dar para ~** (*fig*: *pessoa*) to go wrong.

traseira [tra'zejra] *f* rear; (*ANAT*) bottom.

traseiro/a [tra'zejru/a] *adj* back, rear ♦ *m* (*ANAT*) bottom, behind.

trasladar [traʒla'da*] *vt* to remove, transfer; (*copiar*) to transcribe.

traslado [traʒ'ladu] *m* (*cópia*) copy; (*deslocamento*) removal, transference.

traspassar [traʃpa'sa*] *vt* (*rio etc*) to cross; (*penetrar*) to pierce, penetrate; (*exceder*) to exceed, overstep; (*transferir*) to transmit, transfer; (*PT*: *sublocar*) to sublet.

traspasse [traʃ'pasi] *m* transfer; (*sublocação*) sublease, sublet.

traste ['traʃtʃi] *m* thing; (*coisa sem valor*) piece of junk; (*patife*) rogue, rascal; **estar** *ou* **ficar um ~** to be devastated.

tratado [tra'tadu] *m* treaty; (*LITERATURA*) treatise; **~ de paz** peace treaty.

tratador(a) [trata'do*(a)] *m/f*: **~ de cavalos** groom.

tratamento [trata'mẽtu] *m* treatment; (*título*) title; **forma de ~** form of address; **~ de choque** shock treatment.

tratante [tra'tãtʃi] *m/f* rogue.

tratar [tra'ta*] *vt* to treat; (*tema*) to deal with, cover; (*combinar*) to agree ♦ *vi*: **~ com** to deal with; (*combinar*) to agree with; **~-se** *vr* (*MED*) to take treatment; (*cuidar-se*) to take care of o.s.; **~ de** to deal with; **~ por** *ou* **de** to address as; **de que se trata?** what is it about?; **trata-se de** it is a question of; **~ de fazer** (*esforçar-se*) to try to do; (*resolver*) to resolve to do; **trate da sua vida!** mind your own business!; **~-se a pão e água** to live on bread and water.

tratável [tra'tavew] (*pl* **-eis**) *adj* treatable; (*afável*) approachable, amenable.

trato ['tratu] *m* (*tratamento*) treatment; (*contrato*) agreement, contract; **~s** *mpl* (*relações*) dealings; **maus ~s** ill-treatment *sg*; **pessoa de fino ~** refined person; **dar ~s à bola** to rack one's brains.

trator [tra'to*] *m* tractor.

traulitada [trawli'tada] *f* beating.

trauma ['trawma] *m* trauma.

traumático/a [traw'matʃiku/a] *adj* traumatic.

traumatizante [trawmatʃi'zãtʃi] *adj* traumatic, harrowing.

traumatizar [trawmatʃi'za*] *vt* to traumatize.

travada [tra'vada] *f*: **dar uma ~** to put on the brake.

travão [tra'vãw] (*PT*: *pl* **-ões**) *m* brake.

travar [tra'va*] *vt* (*roda*) to lock; (*iniciar*) to engage in; (*conversa*) to strike up; (*luta*) to wage; (*carro*) to stop; (*passagem*) to block; (*movimentos*) to hinder ♦ *vi* (*PT*) to brake; **~ amizade com** to become friendly with, make friends with.

trave ['travi] *f* beam, crossbeam; (*ESPORTE*) crossbar; **foi na ~** (*col*: *resposta etc*) (it was) close.

través [tra'vɛʃ] *m* slant, incline; **de ~** across, sideways; **olhar de ~** to look sideways (at).

travessa [tra'vɛsa] *f* crossbeam, crossbar; (*rua*) lane, alley; (*prato*) dish; (*para o cabelo*) comb, slide.

travessão [trave'sãw] (*pl* **-ões**) *m* (*de balança*) bar, beam; (*pontuação*) dash.

travesseiro [trave'sejru] *m* pillow; **consultar o ~** to sleep on it.

travessia [trave'sia] *f* (*viagem*) journey, crossing.

travesso/a[1] [tra'vɛsu/a] *adj* cross, transverse.

travesso/a[2] [tra'vesu/a] *adj* mischievous, naughty.

travessões [trave'sõjʃ] *mpl de* **travessão**.

travessura [trave'sura] *f* mischief, prank; **fazer ~s** to get up to mischief.

travesti [traveʃ'tʃi] *m/f* transvestite; (*artista*) drag artist.

travões [tra'võjʃ] *mpl de* **travão**.

trazer [tra'ze*] *vt* to bring; (*roupa*) to wear;

(*causar*) to bring; (*nome, marcas*) to bear; ~ **à memória** to bring to mind; **o jornal traz uma notícia sobre isso** the newspaper has an item about that; ~ **de volta** to bring back.
TRE (*BR*) *abr m* = **Tribunal Regional Eleitoral**.
trecho ['treʃu] *m* passage; (*de rua, caminho*) stretch; (*espaço*) space.
treco ['trɛku] (*col*) *m* (*tralha*) thing; (*indisposição*) bad turn; **~s** *mpl* stuff *sg*; **ter um** ~ (*sentir-se mal*) to be taken bad; (*zangar-se*) to have a fit.
trégua ['trɛgwa] *f* truce; (*descanso*) respite, rest; **não dar ~ a** to give no respite to.
treinado/a [trej'nadu/a] *adj* (*atleta*) fit; (*animal*) trained; (*acostumado*) practised (*BRIT*), practiced (*US*).
treinador(a) [trejna'do*(a)] *m/f* trainer.
treinamento [trejna'mẽtu] *m* training.
treinar [trej'na*] *vt* to train; **~-se** *vr* to train; ~ **seu inglês** to practise (*BRIT*) *ou* practice (*US*) one's English.
treino ['trejnu] *m* training.
trejeito [tre'ʒejtu] *m* (*gesto*) gesture; (*careta*) grimace, face.
trela ['trɛla] *f* (*correia*) lead, leash; (*col: conversa*) chat; **dar ~ a** (*col: conversar*) to chat with; (*encorajar*) to lead on.
treliça [tre'lisa] *f* trellis.
trem [trẽj] (*pl* **-ns**) *m* train; (*PT: carruagem*) carriage, coach; **trens** *mpl* (*col*) gear *sg*, belongings *pl*; **ir de** ~ to go by train; **mudar de** ~ to change trains; **pegar um** ~ to catch a train; **puxar o** ~ (*col*) to make tracks; ~ **de carga/passageiros** freight/passenger train; ~ **correio** mail train; ~ **de aterrissagem** (*avião*) landing gear; ~ **da alegria** (*POL*) jobs *pl* for the boys, nepotism.
trema ['trɛma] *m* di(a)eresis.
tremedeira [treme'dejra] *f* trembling.
tremelicante [tremeli'kãtʃi] *adj* trembling.
tremelicar [tremeli'ka*] *vi* to tremble, shiver.
tremelique [treme'liki] *m* trembling.
tremeluzir [tremelu'zi*] *vi* to twinkle, glimmer.
tremendo/a [tre'mẽdu/a] *adj* tremendous; (*terrível*) terrible, awful.
tremer [tre'me*] *vi* to shudder, quake; (*terra*) to shake; (*de frio, medo*) to shiver.
tremor [tre'mo*] *m* tremor, trembling; ~ **de terra** earth tremor.
tremular [tremu'la*] *vi* (*bandeira*) to flutter, wave; (*luz*) to glimmer, flicker.
trêmulo/a ['tremulu/a] *adj* shaky, trembling; (*voz*) faltering.
trena ['trɛna] *f* tape measure.
trenó [tre'nɔ] *m* sledge (*BRIT*), sled (*US*), sleigh.
trens [trẽjʃ] *mpl de* **trem**.
trepadeira [trepa'dejra] *f* creeper, climbing plant.
trepada [tre'pada] (*col!*) *f* screw (*!*), fuck (*!*).
trepar [tre'pa*] *vt* to climb ♦ *vi*: ~ **(com alguém)** (*col!*) to screw (*!*) (sb); ~ **em** to climb.
trepidação [trepida'sãw] *f* shaking.
trepidar [trepi'da*] *vi* to tremble, shake.
trépido/a ['trɛpidu/a] *adj* fearful.
três [treʃ] *num* three; **a ~ por dois** every five minutes, all the time; *V tb* **cinco**.
tresloucado/a [treʒlo'kadu/a] *adj* crazy, deranged.
três-quartos *adj inv* (*saia, manga*) three-quarter-length ♦ *m inv* (*apartamento*) three-room flat *ou* apartment.
trespassar [treʃpa'sa*] *vt* = **traspassar**.
trespasse [treʃ'pasi] *m* = **traspasse**.
trevas ['trɛvaʃ] *fpl* darkness *sg*.
trevo ['trevu] *m* clover; (*de vias*) intersection.
treze ['trezi] *num* thirteen; *V vb* **cinco**.
trezentos/as [tre'zẽtuʃ/aʃ] *num* three hundred.
tríade ['triadʒi] *f* triad.
triagem ['trjaʒẽ] *f* selection; (*separação*) sorting; **fazer uma ~ de** to make a selection of, sort out.
triangular [trjãgu'la*] *adj* triangular.
triângulo ['trjãgulu] *m* triangle.
tribal [tri'baw] (*pl* **-ais**) *adj* tribal.
tribo ['tribu] *f* tribe.
tribulação [tribula'sãw] (*pl* **-ões**) *f* tribulation, affliction.
tribuna [tri'buna] *f* platform, rostrum; (*REL*) pulpit.
tribunal [tribu'naw] (*pl* **-ais**) *m* court; (*comissão*) tribunal; ~ **de apelação** *ou* **de recursos** court of appeal; **T~ de Justiça/Contas** Court of Justice/Accounts; **T~ do Trabalho** Industrial Tribunal.
tributação [tributa'sãw] *f* taxation.
tributar [tribu'ta*] *vt* to tax; (*pagar*) to pay.
tributário/a [tribu'tarju/a] *adj* tax *atr* ♦ *m* (*de rio*) tributary.
tributável [tribu'tavew] (*pl* **-eis**) *adj* taxable.
tributo [tri'butu] *m* tribute; (*imposto*) tax.
tricampeão/peã [trikã'pjãw/'pjã] (*pl* **-ões/~s**) *m/f* three-times champion.
tricô [tri'ko] *m* knitting; **artigos de** ~ knitted goods, knitwear *sg*; **ponto de** ~ plain stitch.
tricolor [triko'lo*] *adj* three-coloured (*BRIT*), three-colored (*US*).
tricotar [triko'ta*] *vt, vi* to knit.
tridimensional [tridimẽsjo'naw] (*pl* **-ais**) *adj* three-dimensional.
triênio ['trjenju] *m* three-year period.
trigal [tri'gaw] (*pl* **-ais**) *m* wheat field.
trigêmeo/a [tri'ʒemju/a] *m/f* triplet.
trigésimo/a [tri'ʒɛzimu/a] *adj* thirtieth; *V tb* **quinto**.
trigo ['trigu] *m* wheat.
trigonometria [trigonome'tria] *f* trigonometry.

NB: *European Portuguese adds the following consonants to certain words:* **b** (sú(b)dito, su(b)til); **c** (a(c)ção, a(c)cionista, a(c)to); **m** (inde(m)ne); **p** (ado(p)ção, ado(p)tar); *for further details see p. xiii.*

trigueiro/a [tri'gejru/a] *adj* dark, swarthy.
trilátero/a [tri'lateru/a] *adj* trilateral.
trilha ['triʎa] *f* (*caminho*) path; (*rasto*) track, trail; (COMPUT) track; ~ **sonora** soundtrack.
trilhado/a [tri'ʎadu/a] *adj* (*pisado*) well-worn, well-trodden; (*percorrido*) covered.
trilhão [tri'ʎãw] (*pl* **-ões**) *m* billion (BRIT), trillion (US).
trilhar [tri'ʎa*] *vt* (*vereda*) to tread, wear.
trilho ['triʎu] *m* (BR: FERRO) rail; (*vereda*) path, track.
trilhões [tri'ʎõjʃ] *mpl de* **trilhão**.
trilíngüe [tri'lĩgwi] *adj* trilingual.
trilogia [trilo'ʒia] *f* trilogy.
trimestral [trimeʃ'traw] (*pl* **-ais**) *adj* quarterly.
trimestralidade [trimeʃtrali'dadʒi] *f* quarterly payment.
trimestralmente [trimeʃtraw'mẽtʃi] *adv* quarterly.
trimestre [tri'mɛʃtri] *m* (EDUC) term; (COM) quarter.
trinca ['trĩka] *f* set of three; (*col*: *trio*) threesome.
trincar [trĩ'ka*] *vt* to crunch; (*morder*) to bite; (*dentes*) to grit ♦ *vi* to crunch.
trinchar [trĩ'ʃa*] *vt* to carve.
trincheira [trĩ'ʃejra] *f* trench.
trinco ['trĩku] *m* latch.
trindade [trĩ'dadʒi] *f*: **a T~** the Trinity; **~s** *fpl* angelus *sg*.
Trinidad e Tobago [trinidadʒito'bagu] *m* Trinidad and Tobago.
trinta ['trĩta] *num* thirty; *V tb* **cinqüenta**.
trio ['triu] *m* trio; ~ **elétrico** music float.
tripa ['tripa] *f* gut, intestine; **~s** *fpl* bowels, guts; (CULIN) tripe *sg*; **fazer das ~s coração** to make a great effort.
tripé [tri'pɛ] *m* tripod.
tríplex ['tripleks] *adj inv* three-storey (BRIT), three-story (US) ♦ *m inv* three-stor(e)y apartment.
triplicar [tripli'ka*] *vt*, *vi* to treble; **~-se** *vr* to treble.
Trípoli ['tripoli] *n* Tripoli.
tripulação [tripula'sãw] (*pl* **-ões**) *f* crew.
tripulante [tripu'lãtʃi] *m/f* crew member.
tripular [tripu'la*] *vt* to man.
trisavô/vó [triza'vo/'vɔ] *m/f* great-great-grandfather/mother.
triste ['triʃtʃi] *adj* sad; (*lugar*) depressing.
tristeza [triʃ'teza] *f* sadness; (*de lugar*) gloominess; **esse professor é uma** ~ (*col*) this teacher is awful.
tristonho/a [triʃ'tɔɲu/a] *adj* sad, melancholy.
triturar [tritu'ra*] *vt* (*moer*) to grind; (*espancar*) to beat to a pulp; (*afligir*) to beset.
triunfal [trjũ'faw] (*pl* **-ais**) *adj* triumphal.
triunfante [trjũ'fãtʃi] *adj* triumphant.
triunfar [trjũ'fa*] *vi* to triumph.
triunfo ['trjũfu] *m* triumph.
trivial [tri'vjaw] (*pl* **-ais**) *adj* (*comum*) common(place), ordinary; (*insignificante*) trivial, trifling ♦ *m* (*pratos*) everyday food.
trivialidade [trivjali'dadʒi] *f* triviality; **~s** *fpl* trivia *sg*.
triz [triʒ] *m*: **por um** ~ by a hair's breadth; **escapar por um** ~ to have a narrow escape.
troca ['trɔka] *f* exchange, swap; **em ~ de** in exchange for.
troça ['trɔsa] *f* ridicule, mockery; **fazer ~ de** to make fun of.
trocadilho [troka'dʒiʎu] *m* pun, play on words.
trocado/a [tro'kadu/a] *adj* mixed up ♦ *m*: **~(s)** (small) change.
trocador(a) [troka'do*(a)] *m/f* (*em ônibus*) conductor.
trocar [tro'ka*] *vt* to exchange, swap; (*mudar*) to change; (*inverter*) to change *ou* swap round; (*confundir*) to mix up; **~-se** *vr* to change; ~ **dinheiro** to change money; ~ **algo por algo** to exchange *ou* swap sth for sth; ~ **algo de lugar** to move sth; ~ **de roupa/lugar** to change (clothes)/places; ~ **de bem/mal** to make up/fall out.
troçar [tro'sa*] *vi*: ~ **de** to ridicule, make fun of.
troca-troca (*pl* **~s**) *m* swap.
trocista [tro'siʃta] *m/f* joker.
troco ['troku] *m* (*dinheiro*) change; (*revide*) retort, rejoinder; **a ~ de** at the cost of; (*por causa de*) because of; **em ~ de** in exchange for; **dar o ~ a alguém** (*fig*) to pay sb back.
troço ['trɔsu] (BR: *col*) *m* (*coisa inútil*) piece of junk; (*coisa*) thing; **ser** ~ (*pessoa*) to be a big-shot; **ser um** ~ to be amazing; **ter um** ~ (*sentir-se mal*) to be taken bad; (*zangar-se*) to get mad; **senti** *ou* **me deu um** ~ I felt bad; **ele é um ~ de feio** he's incredibly ugly; **meus ~s** my things.
troféu [tro'fɛw] *m* trophy.
tromba ['trõba] *f* (*do elefante*) trunk; (*de outro animal*) snout; (*col*) poker face; **estar de** ~ (*col*) to be poker-faced.
trombada [trõ'bada] *f* crash; **dar uma** ~ to have a crash.
tromba-d'água (*pl* **trombas-d'água**) *f* waterspout; (*chuva*) downpour.
trombadinha [trõba'dʒiɲa] *f* child thief.
trombeta [trõ'beta] *f* (MÚS) trumpet.
trombone [trõ'bɔni] *m* (MÚS) trombone; **botar a boca no** ~ (*fig*: *col*) to tell the world.
trombose [trõ'bɔzi] *f* thrombosis.
trombudo/a [trõ'budu/a] *adj* (*fig*) poker-faced.
trompa ['trõpa] *f* (MÚS) horn; ~ **de Falópio** (ANAT) fallopian tube.
tronchar [trõ'ʃa*] *vt* to cut off, chop off.
troncho/a ['trõʃu/a] *adj* (*torto*) crooked; ~ **de uma perna** one-legged.
tronco ['trõku] *m* (*caule*) trunk; (*ramo*) branch; (*de corpo*) torso, trunk; (*de família*) lineage; (TEL) trunkline.
troncudo/a [trõ'kudu/a] *adj* stocky.
trono ['trɔnu] *m* throne.

tropa ['trɔpa] *f* troop, gang; (*MIL*) troop; (*exército*) army; **ir para a ~** (*PT*) to join the army; **~ de choque** riot police, riot squad.
tropeção [trope'sãw] (*pl* **-ões**) *m* trip-up; (*fig*) faux pas, slip-up; **dar um ~ (em)** to stumble (on).
tropeçar [trope'sa*] *vi* to stumble, trip; (*fig*) to blunder; **~ em dificuldades** to meet with difficulties.
tropeço [tro'pesu] *m* stumbling block.
tropeções [trope'sõjʃ] *mpl de* **tropeção**.
trôpego/a ['tropegu/a] *adj* shaky, unsteady.
tropel [tro'pɛw] (*pl* **-éis**) *m* (*ruído*) uproar, tumult; (*confusão*) confusion; (*estrépito de pés*) stamping of feet; (*turbamulta*) mob.
tropical [tropi'kaw] (*pl* **-ais**) *adj* tropical.
trópico ['trɔpiku] *m* tropic; **T~ de Câncer/Capricórnio** Tropic of Cancer/Capricorn.
troquei [tro'kej] *etc vb V* **trocar**.
trotar [tro'ta*] *vi* to trot.
trote ['trɔtʃi] *m* trot; (*por telefone etc*) hoax; (*em calouro*) trick; **passar um ~** to play a hoax.
trottoir [tro'twa*] *m*: **fazer ~** to go on the streets (as a prostitute).
trouxa ['troʃa] *adj* (*col*) gullible ♦ *f* bundle of clothes ♦ *m/f* (*col*: *pessoa*) sucker.
trouxe ['trosi] *etc vb V* **trazer**.
trova ['trɔva] *f* ballad, folksong.
trovador [trova'do*] *m* troubadour, minstrel.
trovão [tro'vãw] (*pl* **-ões**) *m* clap of thunder.
trovejar [trove'ʒa*] *vi* to thunder.
trovoada [tro'vwada] *f* thunderstorm.
trovoar [tro'vwa*] *vi* to thunder.
trovões [tro'võjʃ] *mpl de* **trovão**.
TRT (*BR*) *abr m* = **Tribunal Regional do Trabalho**.
TRU (*BR*) *abr f* = **Taxa Rodoviária Única**.
trucidar [trusi'da*] *vt* to butcher, slaughter.
truculência [truku'lẽsja] *f* cruelty, barbarism.
truculente [truku'lẽtʃi] *adj* cruel, barbaric.
trufa ['trufa] *f* truffle.
truísmo [tru'iʒmu] *m* truism.
trumbicar-se [trũbi'kaxsi] (*col*) *vr* to come a cropper.
truncar [trũ'ka*] *vt* to chop off, cut off; (*texto*) to garble.
trunfo ['trũfu] *m* trump card.
truque ['truki] *m* trick; (*publicitário*) gimmick.
truste ['truʃtʃi] *m* trust, monopoly.
truta ['truta] *f* trout.
TSE (*BR*) *abr m* = **Tribunal Superior Eleitoral**.
TST (*BR*) *abr m* = **Tribunal Superior do Trabalho**.
tu [tu] (*PT*) *pron* you.
tua ['tua] *f de* **teu**.
tuba ['tuba] *f* tuba.
tubarão [tuba'rãw] (*pl* **-ões**) *m* shark.
tubário/a [tu'barju/a] *adj V* **gravidez**.
tubarões [tuba'rõjʃ] *mpl de* **tubarão**.
tuberculose [tubexku'lɔzi] *f* tuberculosis, TB.
tuberculoso/a [tubexku'lozu/ɔza] *adj* suffering from tuberculosis ♦ *m/f* TB sufferer.
tubinho [tu'biɲu] *m* tube dress.
tubo ['tubu] *m* tube, pipe; **~ de ensaio** test tube; **gastar/custar os ~s** (*col*) to spend/cost a bomb.
tubulação [tubula'sãw] *f* piping, plumbing; **entrar pela ~** to come a cropper.
tubular [tubu'la*] *adj* tubular.
tucano [tu'kanu] *m* toucan.
tudo ['tudu] *pron* everything; **~ quanto** everything that; **antes de ~** first of all; **apesar de ~** despite everything; **acima de ~** above all; **depois de ~** after all; **~ ou nada** all or nothing; **estar com ~** to be sitting pretty.
tufão [tu'fãw] (*pl* **-ões**) *m* typhoon.
tugúrio [tu'gurju] *m* (*cabana*) hut, shack; (*refúgio*) shelter.
tulipa [tu'lipa] *f* tulip; (*copo*) tall glass.
tumba ['tũba] *f* (*sepultura*) tomb; (*lápide*) tombstone.
tumido/a [tu'midu/a] *adj* (*inchado*) swollen.
tumular [tumu'la*] *adj* (*pedra*) tomb *atr*; (*silêncio*) like the grave.
túmulo ['tumulu] *m* tomb; (*sepultura*) burial; **ser um ~** (*pessoa*) to be very discreet.
tumor [tu'mo*] *m* tumour (*BRIT*), tumor (*US*); **~ benigno/maligno** benign/malignant tumo(u)r; **~ cerebral** brain tumo(u)r.
tumulto [tu'muwtu] *m* (*confusão*) uproar, trouble; (*grande movimento*) bustle; (*balbúrdia*) hubbub; (*motim*) riot.
tumultuado/a [tumuw'twadu/a] *adj* riotous, heated.
tumultuar [tumuw'twa*] *vt* (*fazer tumulto em*) to disrupt; (*amotinar*) to rouse, incite.
tumultuoso/a [tumuw'twozu/ɔza] *adj* tumultuous; (*revolto*) stormy.
tunda ['tũda] *f* thrashing, beating; (*fig*) dressing-down.
túnel ['tunew] (*pl* **-eis**) *m* tunnel.
túnica ['tunika] *f* tunic.
Tunísia [tu'nizja] *f*: **a ~** Tunisia.
tupi [tu'pi] *m* Tupi (tribe); (*LING*) Tupi ♦ *m/f* Tupi Indian.
tupiniquim [tupini'kĩ] (*pej*: *pl* **-ns**) *adj* Brazilian (Indian).
turba ['tuxba] *f* throng; (*em desordem*) mob.
turbamulta [tuxba'muwta] *f* mob.
turbante [tux'bãtʃi] *m* turban.
turbar [tux'ba*] *vt* (*escurecer*) to darken, cloud; (*perturbar*) to perturb; **~-se** *vr* to be perturbed.
turbilhão [tuxbi'ʎãw] (*pl* **-ões**) *m* (*de vento*) whirlwind; (*de água*) whirlpool; **um ~ de** a whirl of.
turbina [tux'bina] *f* turbine.
turbulência [tuxbu'lẽsja] *f* turbulence.

***NB**: European Portuguese adds the following consonants to certain words:* **b** (sú(b)dito, su(b)til); **c** (a(c)ção, a(c)cionista, a(c)to); **m** (inde(m)ne); **p** (ado(p)ção, ado(p)tar); *for further details see p. xiii.*

turbulento/a [tuxbu'lẽtu/a] *adj* turbulent, stormy; (*pessoa*) disorderly.
turco/a ['tuxku/a] *adj* Turkish ♦ *m/f* Turk ♦ *m* (LING) Turkish.
turfa ['tuxfa] *f* peat.
turfe ['tuxfi] *m* horse-racing.
túrgido/a ['tuxʒidu/a] *adj* swollen, bloated.
turíbulo [tu'ribulu] *m* incense-burner.
turismo [tu'riʒmu] *m* tourism; (*indústria*) tourist industry; **fazer ~** to go sightseeing; **agência de ~** travel agency.
turista [tu'riʃta] *m/f* tourist; (*aluno*) persistent absentee ♦ *adj* (*classe*) tourist *atr*.
turístico/a [tu'riʃtʃiku/a] *adj* tourist *atr*; (*viagem*) sightseeing *atr*.
turma ['tuxma] *f* group; (EDUC) class; **a ~ da pesada** (*col*) the in crowd.
turnê [tux'ne] *f* tour.
turnedô [tuxne'do] *m* (CULIN) tournedos.
turno ['tuxnu] *m* shift; (*vez*) turn; (ESPORTE, *de eleição*) round; **por ~s** alternately, by turns, in turn; **~ da noite** night shift.
turquesa [tux'keza] *adj inv* turquoise.
Turquia [tux'kia] *f*: **a ~** Turkey.
turra ['tuxa] *f* (*disputa*) argument, dispute; **andar** *ou* **viver às ~s** to be at loggerheads.
turvar [tux'va*] *vt* to cloud; (*escurecer*) to darken; **~-se** *vr* to become clouded; to darken.
turvo/a ['tuxvu/a] *adj* clouded.
tusso ['tusu] *etc vb V* **tossir**.
tusta ['tuʃta] (*col*) *m*: **nem um ~** not a penny.
tutano [tu'tanu] *m* (ANAT) marrow.
tutela [tu'tɛla] *f* protection; (JUR) guardianship; **estar sob a ~ de** (*fig*) to be under the protection of.
tutelar [tute'la*] *adj* protective; (JUR) guardian ♦ *vt* to protect; to act as a guardian to.
tutor(a) [tu'to*(a)] *m/f* guardian.
tutu [tu'tu] *m* (CULIN) *beans, bacon and manioc flour*; (*de balé*) tutu; (*col: dinheiro*) cash.
TV [te've] *abr f* (= *televisão*) TV.
TVE (BR) *abr f* (= *Televisão Educativa*) *educational television station*.
TVS (BR) *abr f* = **Televisão Stúdio Sílvio Santos**.
tweed ['twidʒi] *m* tweed.

U

U, u [u] (*pl* **us**) *m* U, u; **U de Úrsula** U for Uncle.
uai [waj] *excl* ah.
UBE *abr f* = **União Brasileira de Empresários**.
úbere ['uberi] *adj* fertile ♦ *m* udder.
ubérrimo/a [u'bɛximu/a] *adj superl de* **úbere**.
ubiqüidade [ubikwi'dadʒi] *f* ubiquity.
ubíquo/a [u'bikwu/a] *adj* ubiquitous.
Ucrânia [u'kranja] *f*: **a ~** the Ukraine.
UD (BR) *abr f* = **Feira de Utilidades Domésticas**.
UDN *abr f* (= *União Democrática Nacional*) *former Brazilian political party*.
ué [wɛ] *excl* what?, just a minute!
UERJ ['wɛxʒi] *abr f* = **Universidade Estadual do Rio de Janeiro**.
ufa ['ufa] *excl* phew!
ufanar-se [ufa'naxsi] *vr*: **~ de** to take pride in, pride o.s. on.
ufanismo [ufa'niʒmu] (BR) *m* boastful nationalism, chauvinism.
Uferj [u'fɛxʒi] *abr f* = **Unidade Fiscal do Estado do Rio de Janeiro**.
UFF *abr f* = **Universidade Federal Fluminense**.
UFMG *abr f* = **Universidade Federal de Minas Gerais**.
UFPE *abr f* = **Universidade Federal de Pernambuco**.
UFRJ *abr f* = **Universidade Federal do Rio de Janeiro**.
Uganda [u'gãda] *m* Uganda.
ugandense [ugã'dẽsi] *adj, m/f* Ugandan.
uh [uh] *excl* ooh!; (*de repugnância*) ugh!
ui [ui] *excl* (*de dor*) ouch, ow; (*de surpresa*) oh; (*de repugnância*) ugh.
uísque ['wiʃki] *m* whisky (BRIT), whiskey (US).
uisqueria [wiʃke'ria] *f* whisk(e)y bar.
uivada [wi'vada] *f* howl.
uivante [wi'vãtʃi] *adj* howling.
uivar [wi'va*] *vi* to howl; (*berrar*) to yell.
uivo ['wivu] *m* howl; (*fig*) yell.
úlcera ['uwsera] *f* ulcer.
ulceração [uwsera'sãw] *f* ulceration.
ulcerar [uwse'ra*] *vt, vi* to ulcerate; **~-se** *vr* to ulcerate.
ulceroso/a [uwse'rozu/ɔza] *adj* ulcerous.
ulterior [ulte'rjo*] *adj* (*além*) further, farther; (*depois*) later, subsequent.
ulteriormente [uwteriox'mẽtʃi] *adv* later on, subsequently.
ultimamente [uwtʃima'mẽtʃi] *adv* lately.
ultimar [uwtʃi'ma*] *vt* to finish; (*negócio, compra*) to complete.
ultimato [uwtʃi'matu] *m* ultimatum.
ultimátum [uwtʃi'matũ] *m* = **ultimato**.
último/a ['uwtʃimu/a] *adj* last; (*mais recente*) latest; (*qualidade*) lowest; (*fig*) final; **por ~** finally; **fazer algo por ~** to do sth last; **nos ~s anos** in recent years; **em ~ caso** if the worst comes to the worst; **pela última vez** (for) the last time; **a última** (*notícia*) the latest (news); (*absurdo*) the latest folly; **dizer as últimas a alguém** to insult sb; **estar nas últimas** (*na miséria*) to be down and out; (*agoniando*) to be on one's last legs.
ultra- [uwtra-] *prefixo* ultra-.
ultracheio/a [uwtra'ʃeju/a] *adj* packed.
ultrajante [uwtra'ʒãtʃi] *adj* outrageous; (*que*

insulta) insulting.
ultrajar [uwtra'ʒa*] *vt* to outrage; (*insultar*) to insult, offend.
ultraje [uw'traʒi] *m* outrage; (*insulto*) insult, offence (*BRIT*), offense (*US*).
ultraleve [uwtra'lɛvi] *adj* ultralight ♦ *m* microlite.
ultramar [uwtra'ma*] *m* overseas.
ultramarino/a [uwtrama'rinu/a] *adj* overseas *atr*.
ultramoderno/a [uwtramo'dɛxnu/a] *adj* ultramodern.
ultrapassado/a [uwtrapa'sadu/a] *adj* (*idéias etc*) outmoded.
ultrapassagem [uwtrapa'saʒẽ] *f* overtaking (*BRIT*), passing (*US*).
ultrapassar [uwtrapa'sa*] *vt* (*atravessar*) to cross, go beyond; (*ir além de*) to exceed; (*transgredir*) to overstep; (*AUTO*) to overtake (*BRIT*), pass (*US*); (*ser superior a*) to surpass ♦ *vi* (*AUTO*) to overtake (*BRIT*), pass (*US*).
ultra-secreto/a *adj* top secret.
ultra-sensível (*pl* **-eis**) *adj* hypersensitive.
ultra-som *m* ultrasound.
ultra-sônico/a [-'soniku/a] *adj* ultrasonic; (*MED*) ultrasound *atr*.
ultra-sonografia [-sonogra'fia] *f* ultrasound scanning.
ultravioleta [uwtravjo'leta] *adj* ultraviolet.
ululante [ulu'lãtʃi] *adj* howling; (*mentira: óbvio*) blatant.
ulular [ulu'la*] *vi* to howl, wail ♦ *m* howling, wailing.
um(a) [ũ/'uma] (*pl* **uns/~s**) *art indef* (*sg*) a; (*antes de vogal ou 'h' mudo*) an; (*pl*) some ♦ *num* one ♦ *pron* one ♦ *f* (*fato, acontecimento*) a thing, one; **~ e outro** both; **~ a ~** one by one; **~ ao outro** one another; (*entre dois*) each other; **à uma** at once, at the same time; **à uma (hora)** at one (o'clock); (*aproximadamente*): **uns 5** about 5; (*dando ênfase*): **estou com uma fome!** I'm so hungry!; **~ dia sim, ~ dia não** every other day; **ela é de uma beleza incrível** she's incredibly beautiful; **~ de cada vez** one at a time; **dar uma de ator** *etc* (*col*) to do the actor *etc* bit; *V tb* **cinco**.
umbanda [ũ'bãda] *m* umbanda (*Afro-Brazilian cult*).
umbigo [ũ'bigu] *m* navel.
umbilical [ũbili'kaw] (*pl* **-ais**) *adj V* **cordão**.
umbral [ũ'braw] (*pl* **-ais**) *m* (*limiar*) threshold.
umedecer [umede'se*] *vt* to moisten, wet; **~-se** *vr* to get wet.
umedecido/a [umede'sidu/a] *adj* damp.
umidade [umi'dadʒi] *f* dampness; (*clima*) humidity.
úmido/a ['umidu/a] *adj* wet, moist; (*roupa*) damp; (*clima*) humid.
unânime [u'nanimi] *adj* unanimous.
unanimidade [unanimi'dadʒi] *f* unanimity.
unção [ũ'sãw] *f* anointing; (*REL*) unction.
UNE (*BR*) *abr f* = **União Nacional de Estudantes**.
UNESCO [u'nɛʃku] *abr f* UNESCO.
ungir [ũ'ʒi*] *vt* to rub with ointment; (*REL*) to anoint.
ungüento [ũ'gwẽtu] *m* ointment.
unha ['uɲa] *f* nail; (*garra*) claw; **com ~s e dentes** tooth and nail; **ser ~ e carne (com)** to be hand in glove (with); **fazer as ~s** to do one's nails; (*por outra pessoa*) to have one's nails done; **~ encravada** (*no pé*) ingrowing toenail.
unhada [u'ɲada] *f* scratch.
unha-de-fome (*pl* **unhas-de-fome**) *m/f* miser ♦ *adj* mean.
unhar [u'ɲa*] *vt* to scratch.
união [u'njãw] (*pl* **-ões**) *f* union; (*ato*) joining; (*unidade, solidariedade*) unity; (*casamento*) marriage; (*TEC*) joint; **a U~ Soviética** the Soviet Union; **a ~ faz a força** unity is strength; **a U~** (*no Brasil*) the Union, the Federal Government.
unicamente [unika'mẽtʃi] *adv* only.
único/a ['uniku/a] *adj* only; (*sem igual*) unique; (*um só*) single; **mão única** (*sinal*) one-way; **ele é o ~ que ...** he is the only one who ...; **ela é filha única** she's an only child; **um caso ~** a one-off; **preço ~** one price.
unicórnio [uni'kɔxnju] *m* unicorn.
unidade [uni'dadʒi] *f* unity; (*TEC, COM*) unit; **~ de processamento central** (*COMPUT*) central processing unit; **~ de disco** (*COMPUT*) disk drive; **~ de fita** (*COMPUT*) tape streamer.
unido/a [u'nidu/a] *adj* joined, linked; (*fig*) united; **manter-se ~s** to stick together.
Unif [u'nifi] (*BR*) *abr f* = **Unidade Fiscal**.
unificação [unifika'sãw] *f* unification.
unificar [unifi'ka*] *vt* to unite; **~-se** *vr* to join together.
uniforme [uni'fɔxmi] *adj* uniform; (*semelhante*) alike, similar; (*superfície*) even ♦ *m* uniform; **de ~** uniformly.
uniformidade [unifoxmi'dadʒi] *f* uniformity.
uniformizado/a [unifoxmi'zadu/a] *adj* (*uniforme*) uniform, standardized; (*vestido de uniforme*) in uniform.
uniformizar [unifoxmi'za*] *vt* to standardize; (*pessoa*) to put into uniform; **~-se** *vr* to put on one's uniform.
unilateral [unilate'raw] (*pl* **-ais**) *adj* unilateral.
unilíngüe [uni'lĩgwi] *adj* monolingual.
uniões [u'njõjʃ] *fpl de* **união**.
unir [u'ni*] *vt* (*juntar*) to join together; (*ligar*) to link; (*pessoas, fig*) to unite; (*misturar*) to mix together; (*atar*) to tie together; **~-se** *vr* to come together; (*povos etc*) to unite; **~-se**

***NB:** European Portuguese adds the following consonants to certain words:* **b** (sú(b)dito, su(b)til); **c** (a(c)ção, a(c)cionista, a(c)to); **m** (inde(m)ne); **p** (ado(p)ção, ado(p)tar); *for further details see p. xiii.*

a alguém to join forces with sb.
unissex [uni'sɛks] *adj inv* unisex.
uníssono [u'nisonu] *m*: **em** ~ in unison.
Unita [u'nita] *abr f* (= *União Nacional pela Libertação de Angola*) Unita.
unitário/a [uni'tarju/a] *adj* (*preço*) unit *atr*; (*POL*) unitarian ♦ *m/f* (*POL*, *REL*) unitarian.
universal [univex'saw] (*pl* **-ais**) *adj* universal; (*geral*) general; (*mundial*) worldwide; (*espírito*) broad.
universalidade [univexsali'dadʒi] *f* universality.
universalizar [univexsali'za*] *vt* to universalize.
universidade [univexsi'dadʒi] *f* university.
universitário/a [univexsi'tarju/a] *adj* university *atr* ♦ *m/f* (*professor*) lecturer; (*aluno*) university student.
universo [uni'vɛxsu] *m* universe; (*mundo*) world.
unjo ['ũʒu] *etc vb V* **ungir**.
uno/a ['unu/a] *adj* one.
uns [ũʃ] *mpl de* **um**.
untar [ũ'ta*] *vt* (*esfregar*) to rub; (*com óleo, manteiga*) to grease.
upa ['upa] *excl* (*quando algo cai*) whoops!; (*para animar a se levantar*) up you get!; (*de espanto*) wow!
UPC (*BR*) *abr f* = **Unidade Padrão de Capital**.
Urais [u'rajʃ] *mpl*: **os** ~ the Urals.
urânio [u'ranju] *m* uranium.
Urano [u'ranu] *m* Uranus.
urbanidade [uxbani'dadʒi] *f* courtesy, politeness.
urbanismo [uxba'niʒmu] *m* town planning.
urbanista [uxba'niʃta] *m/f* town planner.
urbanístico/a [uxba'niʃtʃiku/a] *adj* town planning *atr*.
urbanização [uxbaniza'sãw] *f* urbanization.
urbanizado/a [uxbani'zadu/a] *adj* (*zona*) built-up.
urbanizar [uxbani'za*] *vt* to urbanize; (*pessoa*) to refine.
urbano/a [ux'banu/a] *adj* (*da cidade*) urban; (*fig*) urbane.
urbe ['uxbi] *f* city.
urdir [ux'dʒi*] *vt* to weave; (*fig*: *maquinar*) to weave, hatch.
urdu [ux'du] *m* (*LING*) Urdu.
uretra [u'rɛtra] *f* urethra.
urgência [ux'ʒẽsja] *f* urgency; **com toda** ~ as quickly as possible; **de** ~ urgent; **pedir algo com** ~ to ask for sth insistently.
urgente [ux'ʒẽtʃi] *adj* urgent.
urgir [ux'ʒi*] *vi* to be urgent; (*tempo*) to be pressing ♦ *vt* to require urgently; **são providências que urge sejam tomadas** they are steps which urgently need to be taken; **urge fazermos** we must do.
urina [u'rina] *f* urine.
urinado/a [uri'nadu/a] *adj* (*molhado*) soaked with urine; (*manchado*) urine-stained.
urinar [uri'na*] *vi* to urinate ♦ *vt* (*sangue*) to pass; (*cama*) to wet; **~-se** *vr* to wet o.s.
urinário/a [uri'narju/a] *adj* urinary.
urinol [uri'nɔw] (*pl* **-óis**) *m* chamber pot.
urna ['uxna] *f* urn; **as ~s** *fpl* (*fig*) the polls; ~ **eleitoral** ballot box.
urologia [urolo'ʒia] *f* urology.
urologista [urolo'ʒiʃta] *m/f* urologist.
URP (*BR*) *abr f* = **Unidade de Referência de Preços**.
URPE (*BR*) *abr fpl* = **Urgências Pediátricas**.
urrar [u'xa*] *vt, vi* to roar; (*de dor*) to yell.
urro ['uxu] *m* roar; (*de dor*) yell.
ursa ['uxsa] *f* bear; **U~ Maior/Menor** Ursa Major/Minor.
urso ['uxsu] *m* bear.
urso-branco (*pl* **ursos-brancos**) *m* polar bear.
URSS *abr f* (= *União das Repúblicas Socialistas Soviéticas*): **a** ~ the USSR.
urticária [uxtʃi'karja] *f* nettle rash.
urtiga [ux'tʃiga] *f* nettle.
urubu [uru'bu] *m* vulture.
urubusservar [urubusex'va*] (*col*) *vt, vi* to watch.
urucubaca [uruku'baka] *f* bad luck; **estar com uma** ~ to be unlucky.
Uruguai [uru'gwaj] *m*: **o** ~ Uruguay.
uruguaio/a [uru'gwaju/a] *adj, m/f* Uruguayan.
urze ['uxzi] *m* heather.
usado/a [u'zadu/a] *adj* used; (*comum*) common; (*roupa*) worn; (*gasto*) worn out; (*de segunda mão*) second-hand; ~ **a** (*acostumado*) accustomed to.
usar [u'za*] *vt* (*servir-se de*) to use; (*vestir*) to wear; (*gastar com o uso*) to wear out; (*barba, cabelo curto*) to have, wear ♦ *vi*: ~ **de** to use; ~ **fazer** to be in the habit of doing; **modo de** ~ directions *pl*.
usina [u'zina] *f* (*fábrica*) factory; (*de energia*) plant; ~ **de açúcar** sugar mill; ~ **de aço** steelworks; ~ **hidrelétrica** hydroelectric power station; ~ **termonuclear** nuclear power plant.
usineiro/a [uzi'nejru/a] *adj* plant *atr* ♦ *m/f* sugar mill owner.
uso ['uzu] *m* (*emprego*) use; (*utilização*) usage; (*prática*) practice; (*moda*) fashion; (*costume*) custom; (*vestir*) wearing; ~ **e desgaste normal** (*COM*) fair wear and tear.
USP ['uʃpi] *abr f* = **Universidade de São Paulo**.
usual [u'zwaw] (*pl* **-ais**) *adj* usual; (*comum*) common.
usuário/a [u'zwarju/a] *m/f* user; ~ **do telefone** telephone subscriber.
usucapião [uzuka'pjãw] *m* (*JUR*) prescription.
usufruir [uzu'frwi*] *vt* to enjoy ♦ *vi*: ~ **de** to enjoy.
usufruto [uzu'frutu] *m* (*JUR*) usufruct.
usura [u'zura] *f* (*juro*) interest; (*avareza*) avarice.
usurário/a [uzu'rarju/a] *m/f* (*avaro*) miser; (*col*: *agiota*) loan shark ♦ *adj* avaricious.

usurpar [uzux'pa*] *vt* to usurp.
úteis ['utejʃ] *adj pl de* **útil**.
utensílio [utẽ'silju] *m* utensil.
uterino/a [ute'rinu/a] *adj* uterine.
útero ['uteru] *m* womb, uterus.
UTI ['utʃi] *abr f* (= *Unidade de Terapia Intensiva*) intensive care (unit), ICU.
útil ['utʃiw] (*pl* **-eis**) *adj* useful; (*vantajoso*) profitable, worthwhile; (*tempo*) working; (*prazo*) stipulated; **dias úteis** weekdays, working days; **em que lhe posso ser ~?** how can I be of assistance (to you)?
utilidade [utʃili'dadʒi] *f* usefulness; (*vantagem*) advantage; (*utensílio*) utility.
utilitário/a [utʃili'tarju/a] *adj* utilitarian, practical; (*pessoa*) matter-of-fact, pragmatic; (*veículo*) general purpose *atr*; **programa ~** (COMPUT) utilities program.
utilização [utʃiliza'sãw] *f* use.
utilizar [utʃili'za*] *vt* to use; **~-se** *vr*: **~-se de** to make use of.
utilizável [utʃili'zavew] (*pl* **-eis**) *adj* usable.
utopia [uto'pia] *f* Utopia.
utópico/a [u'tɔpiku/a] *adj* Utopian.
uva ['uva] *f* grape; (*col*: *mulher*) peach; (: *coisa*) lovely thing; **ser uma ~** (*pessoa, objeto*) to be lovely; **uma ~ de pessoa/broche** a lovely person/brooch.
úvula ['uvula] *f* uvula.

V

V, v [ve] (*pl* **vs**) *m* V, v; **V de Vera** V for Victor.
v *abr de* **volt**.
vá [va] *etc vb V* **ir**.
vã [vã] *f de* **vão**[2].
vaca ['vaka] *f* cow; **carne de ~** beef; **tempo das ~s magras** (*fig*) lean period; **a ~ foi para o brejo** (*fig*) everything went wrong; **voltar à ~ fria** to get back to the subject.
vacância [va'kãsja] *f* vacancy.
vacante [va'kãtʃi] *adj* vacant.
vaca-preta (*pl* **vacas-pretas**) *f coca-cola with ice cream*.
vacilação [vasila'sãw] *f* (*hesitação*) hesitation; (*balanço*) swaying.
vacilada [vasi'lada] *f* slip-up; **dar uma ~** (*col*) to slip up.
vacilante [vasi'lãtʃi] *adj* (*hesitante*) hesitant; (*pouco firme*) unsteady; (*luz*) flickering.
vacilar [vasi'la*] *vi* (*hesitar*) to hesitate; (*balançar*) to sway; (*cambalear*) to stagger; (*luz*) to flicker; (*col*) to slip up.
vacina [va'sina] *f* vaccine.
vacinação [vasina'sãw] (*pl* **-ões**) *f* vaccination.
vacinar [vasi'na*] *vt* to vaccinate; (*fig*) to immunize; **~-se** *vr* to take vaccine.
vacuidade [vakwi'dadʒi] *f* emptiness.
vacum [va'kũ] *adj*: **gado ~** cattle.
vácuo ['vakwu] *m* vacuum; (*fig*) void; (*espaço*) space; **empacotado a ~** vacuum-packed.
vadear [va'dʒja*] *vt* to wade through.
vadiação [vadʒja'sãw] *f* vagrancy.
vadiagem [va'dʒjaʒẽ] *f* vagrancy.
vadiar [va'dʒja*] *vi* to lounge about; (*não trabalhar*) to idle about; (*não estudar*) to skive; (*perambular*) to wander.
vadio/a [va'dʒiu/a] *adj* (*ocioso*) idle, lazy; (*vagabundo*) vagrant ♦ *m/f* idler; (*vagabundo*) vagabond, vagrant.
vaga ['vaga] *f* (*onda*) wave; (*em hotel, trabalho*) vacancy; (*em estacionamento*) parking place; **ser bom de ~** to be good at parking.
vagabundear [vagabũ'dʒja*] *vi* to wander about, roam about; (*vadiar*) to laze around.
vagabundo/a [vaga'bũdu/a] *adj* vagrant; (*vadio*) lazy, idle; (*de má qualidade*) cheap and cheerful; (*canalha*) rotten; (*mulher*) easy ♦ *m/f* tramp; (*canalha*) bum.
vagalhão [vaga'ʎãw] (*pl* **-ões**) *m* big wave, breaker.
vaga-lume [vaga'lumi] (*pl* **~s**) *m* (ZOOL) glow-worm; (*no cinema*) usher.
vagão [va'gãw] (*pl* **-ões**) *m* (*de passageiros*) carriage; (*de cargas*) wagon.
vagão-leito (*pl* **vagões-leitos**) (PT) *m* sleeping car.
vagão-restaurante (*pl* **vagões-restaurantes**) *m* buffet car.
vagar [va'ga*] *vi* to wander about, roam about; (*barco*) to drift; (*ficar vago*) to be vacant ♦ *m* slowness; **fazer algo com mais ~** to do sth at a more leisurely pace.
vagareza [vaga'reza] *f* slowness; **com ~** slowly.
vagaroso/a [vaga'rozu/ɔza] *adj* slow.
vagem ['vaʒẽ] (*pl* **-ns**) *f* green bean.
vagido [va'ʒidu] *m* wail.
vagina [va'ʒina] *f* vagina.
vaginal [vaʒi'naw] (*pl* **-ais**) *adj* vaginal.
vago/a ['vagu/a] *adj* (*indefinido*) vague; (*desocupado*) vacant, free; **tempo ~, horas vagas** spare time.
vagões [va'gõjʃ] *mpl de* **vagão**.
vaguear [va'gja*] *vi* to wander, roam; (*passear*) to ramble.
vai [vaj] *etc vb V* **ir**.
vaia ['vaja] *f* boo.
vaiar [va'ja*] *vt, vi* to boo, hiss.
vaidade [vaj'dadʒi] *f* vanity; (*futilidade*)

***NB:** European Portuguese adds the following consonants to certain words:* **b** (sú(b)dito, su(b)til); **c** (a(c)ção, a(c)cionista, a(c)to); **m** (inde(m)ne); **p** (ado(p)ção, ado(p)tar); *for further details see p. xiii.*

futility.

vai-da-valsa *m*: **ir no ~** to take life as it comes, go with the flow.

vaidoso/a [vaj'dozu/ɔza] *adj* vain.

vai-e-vem [-vẽj] *m inv* = **vaivém**.

vai-não-vai *m inv* shilly-shallying.

vaivém [vaj'vẽj] *m* to-and-fro.

vala ['vala] *f* ditch; **~ comum** pauper's grave.

vale ['vali] *m* valley; (*poético*) vale; (*escrito*) voucher; (*reconhecimento de dívida*) IOU; **~ postal** postal order.

vale-tudo [vali'tudu] *m inv* (*ESPORTE*) all-in wrestling; (*fig*) anything goes principle.

valentão/tona [valẽ'tãw/'tɔna] (*pl* **-ões/~s**) *adj* tough ♦ *m/f* tough nut.

valente [va'lẽtʃi] *adj* brave.

valentia [valẽ'tʃia] *f* courage, bravery; (*proeza*) feat.

valentões [valẽ'tõjʃ] *mpl de* **valentão**.

valentona [valẽ'tɔna] *f de* **valentão**.

valer [va'le*] *vi* to be worth; (*ser válido*) to be valid; (*ter influência*) to carry weight; (*servir*) to serve; (*ser proveitoso*) to be useful; **~-se** *vr*: **~-se de** to use, make use of; **~ a pena** to be worthwhile; **não vale a pena** it isn't worth it; **vale a pena fazer** it is worth doing; **~ a** (*ajudar*) to help; **~ por** (*equivaler*) to be worth the same as; **para ~** (*muito*) very much, a lot; (*realmente*) for real, properly; **vale dizer** in other words; **fazer ~ os seus direitos** to stand up for one's rights; **vale examinar os detalhes** we should examine the details; **mais vale fazê-lo já (do que ...)** it would be better to do it right away (than ...); **não vale empurrar** (*ESPORTE etc*) you're not allowed to push; **assim não vale!** that's not fair!; **vale tudo** anything goes; **ser para ~** (*col*) to be for real; **ou coisa que o valha** or something like it; **valeu!** (*col*) you bet!

valeta [va'leta] *f* gutter.

valete [va'lɛtʃi] *m* (*CARTAS*) jack.

valha ['vaʎa] *etc vb V* **valer**.

valia [va'lia] *f* value; **de grande ~** valuable.

validação [valida'sãw] *f* validation.

validade [vali'dadʒi] *f* validity.

validar [vali'da*] *vt* to validate, make valid.

válido/a ['validu/a] *adj* valid.

valioso/a [va'ljozu/ɔza] *adj* valuable.

valise [va'lizi] *f* case, grip.

valor [va'lo*] *m* value; (*mérito*) merit; (*coragem*) courage; (*preço*) price; (*importância*) importance; **~es** *mpl* values; (*num exame*) marks; (*COM*) securities; **dar ~ a** to value; **sem ~** worthless; **no ~ de** to the value of; **objetos de ~** valuables; **~ nominal** face value; **~ contábil** *ou* **contabilizado** (*COM*) book value; **~ ao par** (*COM*) par value.

valorização [valoriza'sãw] *f* increase in value.

valorizar [valori'za*] *vt* to value; (*aumentar o valor*) to raise the value of; **~-se** *vr* to go up in value; (*pessoa*) to value o.s.

valoroso/a [valo'rozu/ɔza] *adj* brave.

valsa ['vawsa] *f* waltz.

válvula ['vawvula] *f* valve.

vampe ['vãpi] *f* femme fatale.

vampiro/a [vã'piru/a] *m/f* vampire.

vandalismo [vãda'liʒmu] *m* vandalism.

vândalo/a ['vãdalu/a] *m/f* vandal.

vangloriar-se [vãglo'rjaxsi] *vr*: **~ de** to boast of *ou* about.

vanguarda [vã'gwaxda] *f* vanguard, forefront; (*arte*) avant-garde; **artista de ~** avant-garde artist.

vantagem [vã'taʒẽ] (*pl* **-ns**) *f* advantage; (*ganho*) profit, benefit; **contar ~** (*col*) to brag, boast; **levar ~** to get the upper hand; **tirar ~ de** to take advantage of.

vantajoso/a [vãta'ʒozu/ɔza] *adj* advantageous; (*lucrativo*) profitable; (*proveitoso*) beneficial.

vão[1] [vãw] *vb V* **ir**.

vão[2]**/vã** [vãw/vã] (*pl* **~s/~s**) *adj* vain; (*fútil*) futile ♦ *m* (*intervalo*) space; (*de porta etc*) opening; (*ARQ*) empty space; **em ~** in vain.

vapor [va'po*] *m* steam; (*navio*) steamer; (*de gas*) vapour (*BRIT*), vapor (*US*); **cozer no ~** to steam; **ferro a ~** steam iron; **a todo o ~** at full speed.

vaporizador [vaporiza'do*] *m* vaporizer; (*de perfume*) spray.

vaporizar [vapori'za*] *vt* to vaporize; (*perfume*) to spray.

vaporoso/a [vapo'rozu/ɔza] *adj* steamy, misty; (*transparente*) transparent, see-through.

vaqueiro [va'kejru] *m* cowboy, cowhand.

vaquinha [va'kiɲa] *f*: **fazer uma ~** to have a whip-round.

vara ['vara] *f* (*pau*) stick; (*TEC*) rod; (*JUR*) jurisdiction; (*de porcos*) herd; **salto de ~** pole vault; **~ de condão** magic wand.

varal [va'raw] (*pl* **-ais**) *m* clothes line.

varanda [va'rãda] *f* verandah; (*balcão*) balcony; **~ envidraçada** conservatory.

varão/roa [va'rãw/'roa] (*pl* **-ões/~s**) *adj* male ♦ *m* man, male; (*de ferro*) rod.

varapau [vara'paw] (*col*) *m* (*pessoa*) beanpole.

varar [va'ra*] *vt* (*furar*) to pierce; (*passar*) to cross ♦ *vi* to beach, run aground.

varejar [vare'ʒa*] *vt* (*com vara*) to beat; (*revistar*) to search.

varejeira [vare'ʒejra] *f* bluebottle.

varejista [vare'ʒiʃta] (*BR*) *m/f* retailer ♦ *adj* (*mercado*) retail.

varejo [va'reʒu] (*BR*) *m* (*COM*) retail trade; **loja de ~** retail store; **a ~** retail; **preço no ~** retail price.

variação [varja'sãw] (*pl* **-ões**) *f* variation, change.

variado/a [va'rjadu/a] *adj* varied; (*sortido*) assorted.

variante [va'rjãtʃi] *adj, f* variant.

variar [va'rja*] *vt, vi* to vary; **para ~** for a change.

variável [va'rjavew] (*pl* **-eis**) *adj* variable; (*tempo, humor*) changeable ♦ *f* variable.

varicela [vari'sɛla] *f* chickenpox.
variedade [varje'dadʒi] *f* variety; **~s** *fpl* (TEATRO) variety *sg*; **espetáculo/teatro de ~s** variety show/theatre (BRIT) *ou* theater (US).
Varig ['varigi] *abr f* (= *Viação Aérea Rio-Grandense*) *Brazilian national airline*.
varinha [va'riɲa] *f* wand; **~ de condão** magic wand.
vário/a ['varju/a] *adj* (*diverso*) varied; (*pl*) various, several; (COM) sundry.
varíola [va'riola] *f* smallpox.
varizes [va'riziʃ] *fpl* varicose veins.
varoa [va'roa] *f de* **varão**.
varões [va'rõjʃ] *mpl de* **varão**.
varonil [varo'niw] (*pl* **-is**) *adj* manly, virile.
VAR-Palmares *abr f* (= *Vanguarda Armada Revolucionária*) *former Brazilian terrorist movement*.
varredor(a) [vaxe'do*(a)] *adj* sweeping ♦ *m/f* sweeper; **~ de rua** road sweeper.
varrer [va'xe*] *vt* to sweep; (*sala*) to sweep out; (*folhas*) to sweep up; (*fig*) to sweep away.
varrido/a [va'xidu/a] *adj*: **um doido ~** a raving lunatic.
Varsóvia [vax'sɔvja] *n* Warsaw; **pacto de ~** Warsaw Pact.
várzea ['vaxzja] *f* meadow, field.
vascular [vaʃku'la*] *adj* vascular.
vasculhar [vaʃku'ʎa*] *vt* (*pesquisar*) to research; (*remexer*) to rummage through.
vasectomia [vazekto'mia] *f* vasectomy.
vaselina [vaze'lina] ® *f* vaseline ®; (*col*: *pessoa*) smooth talker.
vasilha [va'ziʎa] *f* (*para líquidos*) jug; (*para alimentos*) dish, container; (*barril*) barrel.
vaso ['vazu] *m* pot; (*para flores*) vase; **~ (sanitário)** toilet (bowl); **~ sanguíneo** blood vessel.
Vasp ['vaʃpi] *abr f* (= *Viação Aérea de São Paulo*) *Brazilian internal airline*.
vassoura [va'sora] *f* broom.
vastidão [vaʃtʃi'dãw] *f* vastness, immensity.
vasto/a ['vaʃtu/a] *adj* vast.
vatapá [vata'pa] *m dish of fish or chicken with coconut milk, shrimps, nuts, palm oil and spices*.
Vaticano [vatʃi'kanu] *m*: **o ~** the Vatican; **a Cidade do ~** the Vatican City.
vaticinar [vatʃisi'na*] *vt* to foretell, prophesy.
vaticínio [vatʃi'sinju] *m* prophecy.
vau [vaw] *m* ford, river crossing; (NÁUT) beam.
vazamento [vaza'mẽtu] *m* leak.
vazante [va'zãtʃi] *f* ebb tide.
vazão [va'zãw] (*pl* **-ões**) *f* flow; (*venda*) sale; **dar ~ a** (*expressar*) to give vent to; (COM) to clear; (*atender*) to deal with; (*resolver*) to attend to.
vazar [va'za*] *vt* (*tornar vazio*) to empty; (*derramar*) to spill; (*verter*) to pour out ♦ *vi* to leak; (*maré*) to go out; (*notícia*) to leak; **ser vazado em** (*moldado*) to be modelled on.
vazio/a [va'ziu/a] *adj* empty; (*pessoa*) empty-headed, frivolous; (*cidade*) deserted ♦ *m* (*tb fig*) emptiness; (*deixado por alguém, algo*) void; **~ de** (*fig*: *sem*) devoid of.
vazões [va'zõjʃ] *fpl de* **vazão**.
VBC (BR) *abr m* = **Valor Básico de Custeio**.
vê [ve] *etc vb V* **ver**.
veado ['vjadua] *m* deer; (BR: *col*) poof (BRIT), fag (US); **carne de ~** venison.
vedado/a [ve'dadu/a] *adj* (*proibido*) forbidden; (*fechado*) enclosed.
vedar [ve'da*] *vt* (*proibir*) to ban, prohibit; (*sangue*) to stop (the flow of); (*buraco*) to stop up; (*garrafa*) to cork; (*entrada, passagem*) to block; (*terreno*) to close off.
vedete [ve'dɛtʃi] *f* star.
veemência [vje'mẽsja] *f* vehemence.
veemente [vje'mẽtʃi] *adj* vehement.
vegetação [veʒeta'sãw] *f* vegetation.
vegetal [veʒe'taw] (*pl* **-ais**) *adj* vegetable *atr*; (*reino, vida*) plant *atr* ♦ *m* vegetable; **medicamento ~** herbal remedy.
vegetar [veʒe'ta*] *vi* to vegetate.
vegetariano/a [veʒeta'rjanu/a] *adj, m/f* vegetarian.
vegetativo/a [veʒeta'tʃivu/a] *adj*: **vida vegetativa** (*fig*) insular life.
veia ['veja] *f* (MED, BOT) vein; (*fig*: *pendor*) bent.
veicular [vejku'la*] *vt* to convey; (*anúncios*) to distribute.
veículo [ve'ikulu] *m* vehicle; (*fig: meio*) means *sg*; **~ de propaganda** advertising medium.
veio ['veju] *vb V* **vir** ♦ *m* (*de rocha*) vein; (*na mina*) seam; (*de madeira*) grain; (*eixo*) shaft.
vejo ['veʒu] *etc vb V* **ver**.
vela ['vɛla] *f* candle; (AUTO) spark plug; (NÁUT) sail; **fazer-se à** *ou* **de ~** to set sail; **segurar a ~** (*col*) to play gooseberry; **barco à ~** sailing boat; **~ mestra** mainsail.
velar [ve'la*] *vt* (*cobrir*) to veil; (*ocultar*) to hide; (*vigiar*) to keep watch over; (*um doente*) to sit up with ♦ *vi* (*não dormir*) to stay up; (*vigiar*) to keep watch; **~ por** to look after.
veleidade [velej'dadʒi] *f* (*capricho*) whim, fancy; (*inconstância*) fickleness.
veleiro [ve'lejru] *m* (*barco*) sailing boat.
velejar [vele'ʒa*] *vi* to sail.
velhaco/a [ve'ʎaku/a] *adj* crooked ♦ *m/f* crook.
velha-guarda *f* old guard.
velharia [veʎa'ria] *f* (*os velhos*) old people *pl*; (*coisa*) old thing.
velhice [ve'ʎisi] *f* old age.
velho/a ['vɛʎu/a] *adj* old ♦ *m/f* old man/

NB: *European Portuguese adds the following consonants to certain words:* **b** (sú(b)dito, su(b)til); **c** (a(c)ção, a(c)cionista, a(c)to); **m** (inde(m)ne); **p** (ado(p)ção, ado(p)tar); *for further details see p. xiii.*

woman; (*col*: *pai/mãe*) old man/lady; **meus ~s** (*col*: *pais*) my folks; **meu ~!** (*col*) old chap.

velhote/ta [ve'ʎɔtʃi/ta] *adj* elderly ♦ *m/f* elderly man/woman.

velocidade [velosi'dadʒi] *f* speed, velocity; (*PT*: *AUTO*) gear; **a toda ~** at full speed; **trem de alta ~** high-speed train; **"diminua a ~"** "reduce speed now"; **~ máxima** (*em estrada*) speed limit; **~ de processamento** (*COMPUT*) processing speed.

velocímetro [velo'simetru] *m* speedometer.

velocíssimo/a [velo'sisimu/a] *adj superl de* **veloz**.

velocista [velo'siʃta] *m/f* sprinter.

velódromo [ve'lɔdromu] *m* cycle track.

velório [ve'lɔrju] *m* wake.

veloz [ve'lɔʒ] *adj* fast.

velozmente [velɔʒ'mẽtʃi] *adv* fast.

veludo [ve'ludu] *m* velvet; **~ cotelê** corduroy.

vencedor(a) [vẽse'do*(a)] *adj* winning ♦ *m/f* winner.

vencer [vẽ'se*] *vt* (*num jogo*) to beat; (*competição*) to win; (*inimigo*) to defeat; (*exceder*) to surpass; (*obstáculos*) to overcome; (*percorrer*) to pass; (*dominar*) to overcome ♦ *vi* (*num jogo*) to win; **~(-se)** (*vr*) (*prazo*) to run out; (*promissória*) to become due; (*apólice*) to mature.

vencido/a [vẽ'sidu/a] *adj*: **dar-se por ~** to give in.

vencimento [vẽsi'mẽtu] *m* (*COM*) expiry; (: *de letra*, *dívida*) maturation; (*data*) expiry date; (: *de promissória*) due date; (*salário*) salary; (*de gêneros alimentícios etc*) sell-by date; **~s** *mpl* earnings.

venda ['vẽda] *f* sale; (*pano*) blindfold; (*mercearia*) general store; **à ~** on sale, for sale; **pôr algo à ~** to put sth up for sale; **preço de ~** selling price; **~ a crédito** credit sale; **~ a prazo** *ou* **prestação** sale in instal(l)ments; **~ à vista** cash sale; **~ por atacado** wholesale; **~ pelo correio** mail-order.

vendar [vẽ'da*] *vt* to blindfold.

vendaval [vẽda'vaw] (*pl* **-ais**) *m* gale.

vendável [vẽ'davew] (*pl* **-eis**) *adj* marketable.

vendedor(a) [vẽde'do*(a)] *m/f* seller; (*em loja*) sales assistant; (*de imóvel*) vendor; **~ ambulante** street seller.

vender [vẽ'de*] *vt*, *vi* to sell; **~-se** *vr* (*pessoa*) to allow o.s. to be bribed; **~ por atacado/a varejo** to sell wholesale/retail; **~ fiado/a prestações** *ou* **a prazo** to sell on credit/in instal(l)ments; **~ à vista** to sell for cash; **ela está vendendo saúde** she's bursting with health.

vendeta [vẽ'deta] *f* vendetta.

vendinha [vẽ'dʒiɲa] *f* corner shop.

veneno [ve'nɛnu] *m* poison; (*fig*, *de serpente*) venom; **ser um ~ para** (*fig*) to be very bad for.

venenoso/a [vene'nozu/ɔza] *adj* poisonous; (*fig*) venomous.

veneta [ve'neta] *f*: **ser de ~** (*pessoa*) to be moody; **deu-lhe na ~ (que)** he got it into his head (that).

veneração [venera'sãw] *f* reverence.

venerar [vene'ra*] *vt* to revere; (*REL*) to worship.

venéreo/a [ve'nɛrju/a] *adj* venereal.

Veneza [ve'neza] *n* Venice.

veneziana [vene'zjana] *f* (*porta*) louvre (*BRIT*) *ou* louver (*US*) door; (*janela*) louvre *ou* louver window.

Venezuela [vene'zwɛla] *f*: **a ~** Venezuela.

venezuelano/a [venezwe'lanu/a] *adj*, *m/f* Venezuelan.

venha ['vɛɲa] *etc vb V* **vir**.

vênia ['venja] *f* (*desculpa*) forgiveness; (*licença*) permission.

venial [ve'njaw] (*pl* **-ais**) *adj* venial, forgiveable.

venta ['vẽta] *f* nostril.

ventania [vẽta'nia] *f* gale.

ventar [vẽ'ta*] *vi*: **está ventando** it is windy.

ventarola [vẽta'rɔla] *f* fan.

ventas ['vẽtaʃ] *fpl* nose *sg*.

ventilação [vẽtʃila'sãw] *f* ventilation.

ventilador [vẽtʃila'do*] *m* ventilator; (*elétrico*) fan.

ventilar [vẽtʃi'la*] *vt* to ventilate; (*roupa*, *sala*) to air; (*fig*) to discuss; (: *hipótese*, *possibilidade*) to entertain.

vento ['vẽtu] *m* wind; (*brisa*) breeze; **de ~ em popa** (*fig*) swimmingly, very well.

ventoinha [vẽ'twiɲa] *f* (*cata-vento*) weathercock; (*grimpa*) weather vane; (*PT*: *AUTO*) fan.

ventoso/a [vẽ'tozu/ɔza] *adj* windy.

ventre ['vẽtri] *m* belly; (*literário*: *útero*) womb.

ventríloquo/a [vẽ'trilokwu/a] *m/f* ventriloquist.

ventura [vẽ'tura] *f* fortune; (*felicidade*) happiness; **se por ~** if by any chance.

venturoso/a [vẽtu'rozu/ɔza] *adj* happy.

Vênus ['venuʃ] *f* Venus.

ver [ve*] *vt* to see; (*olhar para*, *examinar*) to look at; (*resolver*) to see to; (*televisão*) to watch ♦ *vi* to see ♦ *m*: **a meu ~** in my opinion; **~-se** *vr* (*achar-se*) to be, find o.s.; (*no espelho*) to see o.s.; (*duas pessoas*) to see each other; **vai ~ que ...** maybe ...; **viu?** (*col*) OK?; **deixa eu ~** let me see; **ele tem um carro que só vendo** (*col*) he's got a car like you wouldn't believe; **não tem nada a ~ (com)** it has nothing to do (with); **não tenho nada que ~ com isto** it is nothing to do with me, it is none of my concern; **~-se com** to settle accounts with; **bem se vê que** it's obvious that; **já se vê** of course; **pelo que se vê** apparently.

veracidade [verasi'dadʒi] *f* truthfulness.

veranear [vera'nja*] *vi* to spend the summer; (*tirar férias*) to take summer holidays (*BRIT*) *ou* a summer vacation (*US*).

veraneio [vera'neju] *m* summer holidays *pl* (*BRIT*) *ou* vacation (*US*).
veranista [vera'niʃta] *m/f* holidaymaker (*BRIT*), (summer) vacationer (*US*).
verão [ve'rãw] (*pl* **-ões**) *m* summer.
veraz [ve'rajʒ] *adj* truthful.
verba ['vɛxba] *f* allowance; **~(s)** *f(pl)* (*recursos*) funds *pl*.
verbal [vex'baw] (*pl* **-ais**) *adj* verbal.
verbalizar [vexbali'za*] *vt, vi* to verbalize.
verbete [vex'betʃi] *m* (*num dicionário*) entry.
verbo ['vɛxbu] *m* verb; **deitar o ~** (*col*) to say a few words; **soltar o ~** (*col*) to start talking.
verborragia [vexboxa'ʒia] *f* verbiage, waffle.
verboso/a [vex'bozu/ɔza] *adj* wordy, verbose.
verdade [vex'dadʒi] *f* truth; **na ~** in fact; **é ~** it's true; **é ~?** (*col*) really?; **uma princesa de ~** a real princess; **de ~** (*falar*) truthfully; (*ameaçar etc*) really; **dizer umas ~s a alguém** to tell sb a few home truths; **a ~ nua e crua** the plain truth; **para falar a ~** to tell the truth; **..., não é ~?** (*col*) ..., isn't that so?
verdadeiramente [vexdadejra'mẽtʃi] *adv* really.
verdadeiro/a [vexda'dejru/a] *adj* true; (*genuíno*) real; (*pessoa*) truthful; **foi um ~ desastre** it was a real disaster.
verde ['vexdʒi] *adj* green; (*fruta*) unripe; (*fig*) inexperienced ♦ *m* green; (*plantas etc*) greenery; **~ de medo** pale with fear; **~ de fome/raiva** terribly hungry/angry; **jogar ~ (para colher maduro)** to fish, ask leading questions; **Partido V~** Green Party.
verde-abacate *adj inv* avocado.
verde-garrafa *adj inv* bottle-green.
verdejar [vexde'ʒa*] *vi* to turn green.
verdor [vex'do*] *m* greenness; (*BOT*) greenery; (*fig*) inexperience.
verdugo [vex'dugu] *m* executioner; (*fig*) beast.
verdura [vex'dura] *f* (*hortaliça*) greens *pl*; (*BOT*) greenery; (*cor verde*) greenness.
verdureiro/a [vexdu'rejru/a] *m/f* greengrocer (*BRIT*), produce dealer (*US*).
vereador(a) [verja'do*(a)] *m/f* councillor (*BRIT*), councilor (*US*).
vereda [ve'reda] *f* path.
veredicto [vere'dʒiktu] *m* verdict.
verga ['vexga] *f* (*vara*) stick; (*de metal*) rod.
vergão [vex'gãw] (*pl* **-ões**) *m* weal.
vergar [vex'ga*] *vt* (*curvar*) to bend ♦ *vi* to bend; (*com um peso*) to sag.
vergões [vex'gõjʃ] *mpl de* **vergão**.
vergonha [vex'gɔɲa] *f* shame; (*timidez*) embarrassment; (*humilhação*) humiliation; (*ato indecoroso*) indecency; (*brio*) self-respect; **é uma ~** it's disgraceful; **ter ~** to be ashamed; (*tímido*) to be shy; **ter ~ de fazer** to be ashamed of doing; (*ser tímido*) to be too shy to do; **não ter ~ na cara** to have a cheek, have no shame.
vergonhoso/a [vexgo'ɲozu/ɔza] *adj* (*infame*) shameful; (*indecoroso*) disgraceful.
verídico/a [ve'ridʒiku/a] *adj* true, truthful.
verificação [verifika'sãw] *f* (*exame*) checking; (*confirmação*) verification.
verificar [verifi'ka*] *vt* to check; (*confirmar*, *COMPUT*) to verify; **~-se** *vr* (*acontecer*) to happen; (*realizar-se*) to come true; **~ se ...** to check that ....
verme ['vɛxmi] *m* worm.
vermelhidão [vexmeʎi'dãw] *f* redness; (*da pele*) rosiness.
vermelho/a [vex'meʎu/a] *adj* red ♦ *m* red; **estar no ~** to be in the red; **ficar ~** to go red.
vermute [vex'mutʃi] *m* vermouth.
vernáculo/a [vex'nakulu/a] *adj*, *m* vernacular; **língua vernácula** vernacular.
vernissage [vexni'saʒ] *m* opening, vernissage.
verniz [vex'niʒ] *m* varnish; (*couro*) patent leather; (*fig*) whitewash; (: *polidez*) veneer; **sapatos de ~** patent shoes.
verões [ve'rõjʃ] *mpl de* **verão**.
verossímil [vero'simiw] (*PT*: **-osí**: *pl* **-eis**) *adj* (*provável*) likely, probable; (*crível*) credible.
verossimilhança [verosimi'ʎãsa] (*PT*: **-osi-**) *f* probability.
verruga [ve'xuga] *f* wart.
versado/a [vex'sadu/a] *adj*: **~ em** clever at, good at.
versão [vex'sãw] (*pl* **-ões**) *f* version; (*tradução*) translation.
versar [vex'sa*] *vi*: **~ sobre** to be about, concern.
versátil [vex'satʃiw] (*pl* **-eis**) *adj* versatile.
versatilidade [vexsatʃili'dadʒi] *f* versatility.
versículo [vex'sikulu] *m* (*REL*) verse; (*de artigo*) paragraph.
verso ['vɛxsu] *m* verse; (*linha*) line of poetry; (*da página*) other side, reverse; **vide ~** see over; **~ solto** blank verse; **~s brancos** blank verse *sg*.
versões [vex'sõjʃ] *fpl de* **versão**.
vértebra ['vɛxtebra] *f* vertebra.
vertebrado/a [vexte'bradu/a] *adj* vertebrate ♦ *m* vertebrate.
vertebral [vexte'braw] (*pl* **-ais**) *adj V* **coluna**.
vertente [vex'tẽtʃi] *f* slope.
verter [vex'te*] *vt* to pour; (*por acaso*) to spill; (*traduzir*) to translate; (*lágrimas, sangue*) to shed ♦ *vi*: **~ de** to spring from; **~ em** (*rio*) to flow into.
vertical [vextʃi'kaw] (*pl* **-ais**) *adj* vertical; (*de pé*) upright, standing ♦ *f* vertical.
vértice ['vɛxtʃisi] *m* apex.
vertigem [vex'tʃiʒẽ] *f* dizziness.
vertiginoso/a [vextʃiʒi'nozu/ɔza] *adj* dizzy,

giddy; (*velocidade*) frenetic.

verve ['vɛxvi] *f* verve.

vesgo/a ['veʒgu/a] *adj* cross-eyed.

vesícula [ve'zikula] *f*: ~ **(biliar)** gall bladder.

vespa ['veʃpa] *f* wasp.

véspera ['vɛʃpera] *f* the day before; **~s** *fpl* (*REL*) vespers *sg*; **a ~ de Natal** Christmas Eve; **nas ~s de** on the eve of; (*de eleição etc*) in the run-up to; **estar nas ~s de** to be about to.

vesperal [veʃpe'raw] (*pl* **-ais**) *adj* afternoon *atr* ♦ *f* matinée.

vespertino/a [veʃpex'tʃinu/a] *adj* evening *atr*.

veste ['vɛʃtʃi] *f* garment; (*REL*) vestment, robe.

vestiário [veʃ'tʃjarju] *m* (*em casa, teatro*) cloakroom; (*ESPORTE*) changing room; (*de ator*) dressing room.

vestibular [veʃtʃibu'la*] *m* college entrance exam.

vestíbulo [veʃ'tʃibulu] *m* hall(-way), vestibule; (*TEATRO*) foyer.

vestido/a [veʃ'tʃidu/a] *adj* dressed ♦ *m* dress; ~ **de branco** *etc* dressed in white *etc*; ~ **de baile** ball gown; ~ **de noiva** wedding dress.

vestidura [veʃtʃi'dura] *f* (*REL*) robe.

vestígio [veʃ'tʃiʒju] *m* (*rastro*) track; (*fig*) sign, trace.

vestimenta [veʃtʃi'mẽta] *f* (*roupa*) garment; (*REL*) vestment.

vestir [veʃ'tʃi*] *vt* (*uma criança*) to dress; (*pôr sobre si*) to put on; (*trajar*) to wear; (*comprar, dar roupa para*) to clothe; (*fazer roupa para*) to make clothes for; **~-se** *vr* to dress; (*pôr roupa*) to get dressed; **~-se de algo** to dress up as sth; **ela se veste naquela butique** she buys her clothes in that boutique; **~-se de preto** *etc* to dress in black *etc*; **este terno veste bem** this suit is a good fit.

vestuário [veʃ'twarju] *m* clothing.

vetar [ve'ta*] *vt* to veto; (*proibir*) to forbid.

veterano/a [vete'ranu/a] *adj, m/f* veteran.

veterinário/a [veteri'narju/a] *adj* veterinary ♦ *m/f* vet(erinary surgeon).

veto ['vɛtu] *m* veto.

véu [vɛw] *m* veil; ~ **do paladar** (*ANAT*) soft palate, velum.

vexame [ve'ʃami] *f* (*vergonha*) shame, disgrace; (*tormento*) affliction; (*humilhação*) humiliation; (*afronta*) insult; **passar um ~** to be disgraced; **dar um ~** to make a fool of o.s.

vexaminoso/a [veʃami'nozu/ɔza] *adj* shameful, disgraceful.

vexar [ve'ʃa*] *vt* (*atormentar*) to upset; (*envergonhar*) to put to shame; **~-se** *vr* to be ashamed.

vez [veʒ] *f* time; (*turno*) turn; **uma ~** once; **duas ~es** twice; **alguma ~** ever; **algumas ~es, às ~es** sometimes; **~ por outra** sometimes; **cada ~ (que)** every time; **cada ~ mais/menos** more and more/less and less; **desta ~** this time; **de ~** once and for all; **de uma ~** (*ao mesmo tempo*) at once; (*de um golpe*) in one go; **de ~ em quando** from time to time; **em ~ de** instead of; **fazer as ~es de** (*pessoa*) to stand in for; (*coisa*) to replace; **mais uma ~, outra ~** again, once more; **raras ~es** seldom; **uma ~ que** since; **3 ~es 6** 3 times 6; **de uma ~ por todas** once and for all; **ter ~** (*pessoa*) to have a chance; (*argumento etc*) to apply; **muitas ~es** many times; (*freqüentemente*) often; **mais ~es** more often; **na maioria das ~es** most times; **toda ~ que** every time; **um de cada ~** one at a time; **repetidas ~es** repeatedly; **uma ~ ou outra** once in a while; **uma ~ na vida, outra na morte** once in a blue moon; **era uma ~ ...** once upon a time there was ....

vi [vi] *vb V* **ver**.

via ['via] *etc vb V* **ver** ♦ *f* road, route; (*meio*) way; (*documento*) copy; (*conduto*) channel ♦ *prep* via, by way of; ~ **aérea** airmail; ~ **de acesso** access road; ~ **férrea** railway (*BRIT*), railroad (*US*); **V~ Láctea** Milky Way; **primeira ~** (*de documento*) top copy; **chegar às ~s de fato** to come to blows; **em ~s de** about to; **por ~ aérea** by airmail; **por ~ das dúvidas** just in case; **por ~ de regra** generally, as a rule; **por ~ terrestre/marítima** by land/sea.

viabilidade [vjabili'dadʒi] *f* feasibility, viability.

viação [vja'sãw] (*pl* **-ões**) *f* transport; (*companhia de ônibus*) bus (*ou* coach) company; (*conjunto de estradas*) roads *pl*.

viaduto [vja'dutu] *m* viaduct.

viageiro/a [vja'ʒejru/a] *adj* travelling (*BRIT*), traveling (*US*).

viagem ['vjaʒẽ] (*pl* **-ns**) *f* journey, trip; (*o viajar*) travel; (*NÁUT*) voyage; (*com droga*) trip; **viagens** *fpl* travels; ~ **de ida e volta** return trip, round trip; ~ **de núpcias** honeymoon; ~ **de ida** outward trip; ~ **de negócios** business trip; ~ **inaugural** (*NÁUT*) maiden voyage; **boa ~!** bon voyage!, have a good trip!

viajado/a [vja'ʒadu/a] *adj* well-travelled (*BRIT*), well-traveled (*US*).

viajante [vja'ʒãtʃi] *adj* travelling (*BRIT*), traveling (*US*) ♦ *m* traveller (*BRIT*), traveler (*US*); (*COM*) commercial travel(l)er.

viajar [vja'ʒa*] *vi* to travel; ~ **por** to travel, tour.

viário/a ['vjarju/a] *adj* road *atr*.

viatura [vja'tura] *f* vehicle.

viável ['vjavew] (*pl* **-eis**) *adj* feasible, viable.

víbora ['vibora] *f* viper; (*fig: pessoa*) snake in the grass.

vibração [vibra'sãw] (*pl* **-ões**) *f* vibration; (*fig*) thrill.

vibrante [vi'brãtʃi] *adj* vibrant; (*discurso*) stirring.

vibrar [vi'bra*] *vt* (*brandir*) to brandish; (*fazer estremecer*) to vibrate; (*cordas*) to strike

♦ *vi* to vibrate, shake; (*som*) to echo; (*col*) to be thrilled.
vice ['visi] *m/f* deputy.
vice- [visi-] *prefixo* vice-.
vice-campeão/peã (*pl* **-ões/~s**) *m/f* runner-up.
vicejar [vise'ʒa*] *vi* to flourish.
vice-presidente/a *m/f* vice president.
vice-rei *m* viceroy.
vice-reitor(a) *m/f* deputy head.
vice-versa [-'vɛxsa] *adv* vice-versa.
viciado/a [vi'sjadu/a] *adj* addicted; (*ar*) foul ♦ *m/f* addict; **um ~ em entorpecentes** a drug addict; **~ em algo** addicted to sth.
viciar [vi'sja*] *vt* (*criar vício em*) to make addicted; (*falsificar*) to falsify; (*taxímetro etc*) to fiddle; **~-se** *vr* to become addicted; **~/~se em algo** to make/become addicted to sth.
vicinal [visi'naw] (*pl* **-ais**) *adj* local.
vício ['visju] *m* vice; (*defeito*) failing; (*costume*) bad habit; (*em entorpecentes*) addiction.
vicioso/a [vi'sjozu/ɔza] *adj* (*defeituoso*) defective; (*círculo*) vicious.
vicissitude [visisi'tudʒi] *f* vicissitude; **~s** *fpl* ups and downs.
viço ['visu] *m* vigour (*BRIT*), vigor (*US*); (*da pele*) freshness.
viçoso/a [vi'sozu/ɔza] *adj* (*plantas*) luxuriant; (*fig*) exuberant.
vida ['vida] *f* life; (*duração*) lifetime; (*fig*) vitality; **com ~** alive; **ganhar a ~** to earn one's living; **modo de ~** way of life; **para toda a ~** forever; **sem ~** dull, lifeless; **na ~ real** in real life; **dar ~ a** (*festa, ambiente*) to liven up; **dar a ~ por algo/por fazer algo** to give one's right arm for sth/to do sth; **estar bem de ~** to be well off; **mete-se com a sua ~** mind your own business; **estar entre a ~ e a morte** to be at death's door; **cair na ~** (*col*) to go on the game; **é a ~!** that's life!; **danado/feliz da ~** really angry/happy; **siga essa rua toda a ~** follow this street as far as you can go; **ele trabalha que não é ~** (*col*) he works really hard; **a ~ mansa** the easy life; **~ civil/privada/pública/sentimental/sexual/social** civilian/private/public/love/sex/social life; **~ conjugal/doméstica** married/home life; **~ útil** (*COM*) useful life.
vidão [vi'dãw] *m* good life.
vide ['vidʒi] *vt* see; **~ verso** see over.
videira [vi'dejra] *f* grapevine.
vidente [vi'dẽtʃi] *m/f* clairvoyant; (*no mundo antigo*) seer.
vídeo ['vidʒju] *m* video; (*televisão*) TV; (*tela*) screen.
videocâmara [vidʒju'kamara] *f* video camera.
videocassete [vidʒjuka'sɛtʃi] *m* (*fita*) video cassette *ou* tape; (*aparelho*) video (recorder).
videoclipe [vidʒju'klipi] *m* video.
videoclube [vidʒju'klubi] *m* video club.
videodisco [vidʒju'dʒiʃku] *m* video disk.
vídeo game [-'gejmi] (*pl* **~s**) *m* video game.
videoteipe [vidʒju'tejpi] *m* (*fita*) video tape; (*processo*) (video-)taping.
videotexto [vidʒju'teʃtu] *m* teletext.
vidraça [vi'drasa] *f* window pane.
vidraçaria [vidrasa'ria] *f* glazier's; (*fábrica*) glass factory; (*conjunto de vidraças*) glasswork.
vidraceiro [vidra'sejru] *m* glazier.
vidrado/a [vi'dradu/a] *adj* glazed; (*porta*) glass *atr*; (*olhos*) glazed, glassy; **estar** *ou* **ser ~ em** *ou* **por** (*col*) to be crazy about.
vidrar [vi'dra*] *vt* to glaze ♦ *vi*: **~ em** *ou* **por** (*col*) to fall in love with.
vidreiro [vi'drejru] *m* glazier, glassmaker.
vidro ['vidru] *m* glass; (*frasco*) bottle; **fibra de ~** fibreglass (*BRIT*), fiberglass (*US*); **~ fosco** frosted glass; **~ fumê** tinted glass; **~ de aumento** magnifying glass.
viela ['vjɛla] *f* alley.
Viena ['vjɛna] *n* Vienna.
vier [vje*] *etc vb V* **vir**.
viés [vjɛʃ] *m* slant; (*COSTURA*) bias strip; **ao** *ou* **de ~** diagonally.
vieste ['vjeʃtʃi] *vb V* **vir**.
viga ['viga] *f* beam; (*de ferro*) girder.
Vietnã [vjet'nã] *m*: **o ~** Vietnam.
vietnamita [vjetna'mita] *adj, m/f* Vietnamese.
vigarice [viga'risi] *f* swindle.
vigário [vi'garju] *m* vicar.
vigarista [viga'riʃta] *m* swindler, confidence trickster.
vigência [vi'ʒẽsja] *f* validity; **durante a ~ da lei** while the law is in force.
vigente [vi'ʒẽtʃi] *adj* in force, valid.
viger [vi'ʒe*] *vi* to be in force.
vigésimo/a [vi'ʒɛzimu/a] *num* twentieth; *V tb* **quinto**.
vigia [vi'ʒia] *f* (*ato*) watching; (*NÁUT*) porthole ♦ *m* night watchman; **de ~** on watch.
vigiar [vi'ʒja*] *vt* to watch, keep an eye on; (*ocultamente*) to spy on; (*velar por*) to keep watch over; (*presos, fronteira*) to guard ♦ *vi* to be on the lookout.
vigilância [viʒi'lãsja] *f* vigilance.
vigilante [viʒi'lãtʃi] *adj* vigilant; (*atento*) alert.
vigília [vi'ʒilja] *f* (*falta de sono*) wakefulness; (*vigilância*) vigilance.
vigor [vi'go*] *m* energy; **em ~** in force; **entrar/pôr em ~** to take effect/put into effect.
vigorar [vigo'ra*] *vi* to be in force; **a ~ a partir de** effective as of.
vigoroso/a [vigo'rozu/ɔza] *adj* vigorous.
vil [viw] (*pl* **vis**) *adj* vile, low.

NB*: European Portuguese adds the following consonants to certain words:* **b** (sú(b)dito, su(b)til); **c** (a(c)ção, a(c)cionista, a(c)to); **m** (inde(m)ne); **p** (ado(p)ção, ado(p)tar); *for further details see p. xiii.*

vila ['vila] *f* town; (*casa*) villa; (*conjunto de casas*) *group of houses round a courtyard*; ~ **militar** military base.
vilã [vi'lã] *f de* **vilão**.
vilania [vila'nia] *f* villainy.
vilão/lã [vi'lãw/'lã] (*pl* **~s/~s**) *m/f* villain.
vilarejo [vila'reʒu] *m* village.
vileza [vi'leza] *f* vileness; (*ação*) mean trick.
vilipendiar [vilipẽ'dʒja*] *vt* to revile; (*desprezar*) to despise.
vim [vĩ] *vb V* **vir**.
vime ['vimi] *m* wicker.
vinagre [vi'nagri] *m* vinegar.
vinagrete [vina'grɛtʃi] *m* vinaigrette.
vincar [vĩ'ka*] *vt* to crease; (*produzir sulco em*) to furrow; (*rosto*) to line.
vinco ['vĩku] *m* crease; (*sulco*) furrow; (*no rosto*) line.
vincular [vĩku'la*] *vt* to link, tie; **~-se** *vr* to be linked *ou* tied.
vínculo ['vĩkulu] *m* bond, tie; (*relação*) link; ~ **de parentesco** blood tie; ~ **empregatício** contract of employment.
vinda ['vĩda] *f* arrival; (*ato de vir*) coming; (*regresso*) return; **dar as boas ~s** to welcome.
vindicar [vĩdʒi'ka*] *vt* to vindicate.
vindima [vĩ'dʒima] *f* grape harvest.
vindique [vĩ'dʒiki] *etc vb V* **vindicar**.
vindouro/a [vĩ'doru/a] *adj* future, coming.
vingador(a) [vĩga'do*(a)] *adj* avenging ♦ *m/f* avenger.
vingança [vĩ'gãsa] *f* vengeance, revenge.
vingar [vĩ'ga*] *vt* to avenge ♦ *vi* (*ter êxito*) to be successful; (*planta*) to grow; **~-se** *vr*: **~-se de** to take revenge on.
vingativo/a [vĩga'tʃivu/a] *adj* vindictive.
vingue ['vĩgi] *etc vb V* **vingar**.
vinha ['viɲa] *etc vb V* **vir** ♦ *f* vineyard; (*planta*) vine.
vinha-d'alho (*pl* **vinhas d'alho**) *f* marinade.
vinhedo [vi'ɲedu] *m* vineyard.
vinho ['viɲu] *m* wine ♦ *adj inv* maroon; ~ **branco/rosado/tinto** white/rosé/red wine; ~ **seco/doce** dry/sweet wine; ~ **espumante/de mesa** sparkling/table wine; ~ **do Porto** port.
vinícola [vi'nikola] *adj inv* wine-producing.
vinicultor(a) [vinikuw'to*(a)] *m/f* wine grower.
vinicultura [vinikuw'tura] *f* wine-growing, viticulture.
vinil [vi'niw] *m* vinyl.
vinte ['vĩtʃi] *num* twenty; **o século** ~ the twentieth century; **as** ~ (*col*: *de cigarro, bebida*) the last bit; *V tb* **cinqüenta**.
vintém [vĩ'tẽj] *m*: **sem um** ~ penniless.
vintena [vĩ'tɛna] *f* twenty, a score.
viola ['vjɔla] *f* viola.
violação [vjola'sãw] (*pl* **-ões**) *f* violation; ~ **da lei** lawbreaking; ~ **de domicílio** housebreaking.
violão [vjo'lãw] (*pl* **-ões**) *m* guitar.
violar [vjo'la*] *vt* to violate; (*a lei*) to break.
violência [vjo'lẽsja] *f* violence.
violentar [vjolẽ'ta*] *vt* to force; (*mulher*) to rape; (*fig*: *sentido*) to distort.
violento/a [vjo'lẽtu/a] *adj* violent; (*furioso*) furious.
violeta [vjo'leta] *f* violet ♦ *adj inv* violet.
violinista [vjoli'niʃta] *m/f* violinist, violin player.
violino [vjo'linu] *m* violin.
violões [vjo'lõjʃ] *mpl de* **violão**.
violoncelista [vjolõse'liʃta] *m/f* 'cellist.
violoncelo [vjolõ'sɛlu] *m* 'cello.
VIP ['vipi] *m/f* VIP ♦ *adj* (*sala*) VIP *atr*.
vir [vi*] *etc vb V* **ver** ♦ *vi* to come; ~ **a ser** to turn out to be; **a semana que vem** next week; ~ **abaixo** to collapse; **mandar** ~ to send for; ~ **fazendo algo** to have been doing sth; ~ **fazer** to come to do; ~ **buscar** to come for; ~ **com** (*alegar*) to come up with; **isso não vem ao caso** that's irrelevant; **veio-lhe uma idéia** he had an idea, an idea came to him; ~ **a saber** to come to know; **venha o que vier** come what may; **vem cá!** come here!; (*col*: *escuta*) listen!; **não vem que não tem!** (*col*) come off it!
viração [vira'sãw] (*pl* **-ões**) *f* breeze.
vira-casaca ['vira-] (*pl* **~s**) *m/f* turncoat.
virada [vi'rada] *f* turning; (*guinada*) swerve; (ESPORTE) turnaround; **dar uma** ~ (*col*) to put on a last burst.
virado/a [vi'radu/a] *adj* (*às avessas*) upside down ♦ *m* (CULIN): ~ **(de feijão)** *fried beans with sausage and eggs*; ~ **para** facing.
vira-lata ['vira-] (*pl* **~s**) *m* (*cão*) mongrel; (*pessoa*) bum.
virar [vi'ra*] *vt* to turn; (*página, disco, barco*) to turn over; (*esquina*) to turn; (*bolsos*) to turn inside out; (*copo*) to empty; (*despejar*) to tip; (*fazer mudar de opinião*) to turn round; (*transformar-se em*) to become ♦ *vi* to turn; (*barco*) to turn over, capsize; (*mudar*) to change; **~-se** *vr* to turn; (*voltar-se*) to turn round; (*defender-se*) to fend for o.s.; ~ **de cabeça para baixo** to turn upside down; ~ **do avesso** to turn inside out; ~ **para** to face; **vira e mexe** every so often; **~(-se) contra** to turn against; **~-se para** (*recorrer a*) to turn to; **~-se de bruços** to turn onto one's stomach.
viravolta [vira'vɔwta] *f* (*fig*) turnabout; (*volta completa*) complete turn; (*giro sobre si mesmo*) about-turn; (*cambalhota*) somersault.
virgem ['vixʒẽ] (*pl* **-ns**) *adj* (*puro*) pure; (*mata*) virgin; (*não usado*) unused; (: *fita*) blank ♦ *f* virgin; **V~** (ASTROLOGIA) Virgo; ~ **de** free of.
virgindade [vixʒĩ'dadʒi] *f* virginity.
vírgula ['vixgula] *f* comma; (*decimal*) point; **uma ~!** (*col*) my eye!
virgular [vixgu'la*] *vt*: ~ **com** *ou* **de** (*entremear*) to punctuate with.
viril [vi'riw] (*pl* **-is**) *adj* virile.

virilha [vi'riʎa] *f* groin.
virilidade [virili'dadʒi] *f* virility.
viris [vi'riʃ] *adj pl de* **viril**.
virose [vi'rɔzi] *f* viral illness.
virtual [vix'twaw] (*pl* **-ais**) *adj* virtual; (*potencial*) potential.
virtualmente [vixtwaw'mẽtʃi] *adv* virtually.
virtude [vix'tudʒi] *f* virtue; **em ~ de** owing to, because of.
virtuosidade [vixtwozi'dadʒi] *f* virtuosity.
virtuosismo [vixtwo'ziʒmu] *m* = **virtuosidade**.
virtuoso/a [vix'twozu/ɔza] *adj* virtuous ♦ *m* virtuoso.
virulência [viru'lẽsja] *f* virulence.
virulento/a [viru'lẽtu/a] *adj* virulent.
vírus ['viruʃ] *m inv* virus.
vis [viʃ] *adj pl de* **vil**.
visado/a [vi'zadu/a] *adj* stamped; (*pessoa*: *pela polícia, imprensa*) under observation.
visão [vi'zãw] (*pl* **-ões**) *f* vision; (*ANAT*) eyesight; (*vista*) sight; (*maneira de perceber*) view; **~ de conjunto** overall view.
visar [vi'za*] *vt* (*alvo*) to aim at; (*ter em vista*) to have in view; (*ter como objetivo*) to aim for; (*passaporte, cheque*) to stamp ♦ *vi*: **~ a** to have in view; to aim for; **~ fazer** to aim to do.
Visc. *abr* = **Visconde**.
vísceras ['viseraʃ] *fpl* innards, bowels; (*fig*) heart *sg*.
visconde [viʃ'kõdʒi] *m* viscount.
viscondessa [viʃkõ'desa] *f* viscountess.
viscoso/a [viʃ'kozu/ɔza] *adj* sticky, viscous.
viseira [vi'zejra] *f* visor.
visibilidade [vizibili'dadʒi] *f* visibility.
visionário/a [vizjo'narju/a] *adj, m/f* visionary.
visita [vi'zita] *f* visit, call; (*pessoa*) visitor; **fazer uma ~ a** to visit; **ter ~s** to have company; **~ de médico** (*col*) flying visit; **horário de ~s** visiting hours *pl*.
visitante [vizi'tãtʃi] *adj* visiting ♦ *m/f* visitor.
visitar [vizi'ta*] *vt* to visit; (*inspecionar*) to inspect.
visível [vi'zivew] (*pl* **-eis**) *adj* visible.
vislumbrar [viʒlũ'bra*] *vt* to glimpse, catch a glimpse of.
vislumbre [viʒ'lũbri] *m* glimpse.
visões [vi'zõjʃ] *fpl de* **visão**.
visom [vi'zõ] (*pl* **-ns**) *m* mink; **casaco de ~** mink coat.
visor [vi'zo*] *m* (*FOTO*) viewfinder.
visse ['visi] *etc vb V* **ver**.
vista ['viʃta] *f* sight; (*MED*) eyesight; (*panorama*) view; (*braguilha*) fly; **à** *ou* **em ~ de** in view of; **conhecer de ~** to know by sight; **dar na ~** to attract attention; **dar uma ~ de olhos em** to glance at; **fazer ~ grossa (a)** to turn a blind eye (to); **pôr à ~** to show; **ter em ~** to have in mind; **à primeira ~** at first sight; **à ~** visible, showing; (*COM*) in cash; **até a ~!** see you!; **na ~ de todos** in view of everyone; **perder de ~** to lose sight of; **a perder de ~** as far as the eye can (*ou* could) see; (*pagamento*) over a long period; **saltar à ~** to be obvious; **fazer ~** to look nice; **~ cansada/curta** eye strain/shortsightedness.
vista-d'olhos *f* glance, quick look; **dar uma ~ em** to have a quick look at.
visto/a ['viʃtu/a] *etc vb V* **vestir** ♦ *pp de* **ver** ♦ *adj* seen ♦ *m* (*em passaporte*) visa; (*em documento*) stamp; **haja ~** witness; **pelo ~** by the looks of things.
vistoria [viʃto'ria] *f* inspection.
vistoriar [viʃto'rja*] *vt* to inspect.
vistoso/a [viʃ'tozu/ɔza] *adj* eye-catching.
visual [vi'zwaw] (*pl* **-ais**) *adj* visual ♦ *m* (*col*: *de pessoa*) look; (*aparência*) appearance; (*vista*) view.
visualizar [vizwali'za*] *vt* to visualize.
vital [vi'taw] (*pl* **-ais**) *adj* vital; (*essencial*) essential.
vitalício/a [vita'lisju/a] *adj* for life.
vitalidade [vitali'dadʒi] *f* vitality.
vitalizar [vitali'za*] *vt* to revitalize.
vitamina [vita'mina] *f* vitamin; (*para beber*) fruit crush.
vitaminado/a [vitami'nadu/a] *adj* with added vitamins.
vitamínico/a [vita'miniku/a] *adj* vitamin *atr*.
vitela [vi'tɛla] *f* calf; (*carne*) veal.
viticultura [vitʃikuw'tura] *f* wine growing.
vítima ['vitʃima] *f* victim; **fazer-se de ~** to play the martyr.
vitimar [vitʃi'ma*] *vt* to sacrifice; (*matar*) to kill, claim the life of; (*danificar*) to damage.
vitória [vi'tɔrja] *f* victory; (*ESPORTE*) win.
vitória-régia (*pl* **vitórias-régias**) *f* giant water lily.
vitorioso/a [vito'rjozu/ɔza] *adj* victorious; (*time*) winning.
vitral [vi'traw] (*pl* **-ais**) *m* stained glass window.
vítreo/a ['vitrju/a] *adj* (*feito de vidro*) glass *atr*; (*com o aspecto de vidro*) glassy; (*água*) clear.
vitrina [vi'trina] *f* = **vitrine**.
vitrine [vi'trini] *f* shop window; (*armário*) display case.
vitrola [vi'trɔla] *f* gramophone.
viuvez [vju've3] *f* widowhood.
viúvo/a ['vjuvu/a] *adj* widowed ♦ *m/f* widower/widow.
viva ['viva] *m* cheer; **~!** hurray!; **~ o rei!** long live the king!
vivacidade [vivasi'dadʒi] *f* vivacity; (*energia*) vigour (*BRIT*), vigor (*US*).
vivalma [vi'vawma] *f*: **não ver ~** not to see a (living) soul.
vivamente [viva'mẽtʃi] *adv* animatedly; (*descrever, sentir*) vividly; (*protestar*) loud-

NB: *European Portuguese adds the following consonants to certain words:* **b** (sú(b)dito, su(b)til); **c** (a(c)ção, a(c)cionista, a(c)to); **m** (inde(m)ne); **p** (ado(p)ção, ado(p)tar); *for further details see p. xiii.*

ly.

vivar [vi'va*] *vt, vi* to cheer.

vivaz [vi'vajʒ] *adj* (*animado*) lively.

viveiro [vi'vejru] *m* nursery.

vivência [vi'vẽsja] *f* existence; (*experiência*) experience.

vivenda [vi'vẽda] *f* (*casa*) residence.

vivente [vi'vẽtʃi] *adj* living ♦ *m/f* living being; **os ~s** the living.

vivido/a [vi'vidu/a] *adj* experienced in life.

vívido/a ['vividu/a] *adj* vivid.

viver [vi've*] *vi* to live; (*estar vivo*) to be alive ♦ *vt* (*vida*) to live; (*experimentar*) to have, experience ♦ *m* life; **~ de** to live on; **~ à custa de** to live off; **ela vive viajando/ cansada** she's always travel(l)ing/tired; **ele vive resfriado/com dor de estômago** he's always got a cold/stomach ache; **vivendo e aprendendo** live and learn.

víveres ['vivereʃ] *mpl* provisions.

vivificar [vivifi'ka*] *vt* to bring to life.

vivissecção [vivisek'sãw] *f* vivisection.

vivo/a ['vivu/a] *adj* living; (*esperto*) clever; (*cor*) bright; (*criança, debate*) lively ♦ *m*: **os ~s** the living; **televisionar ao ~** to televise live; **estar ~** to be alive.

vizinhança [vizi'ɲãsa] *f* neighbourhood (*BRIT*), neighborhood (*US*).

vizinho/a [vi'ziɲu/a] *adj* neighbouring (*BRIT*), neighboring (*US*); (*perto*) nearby ♦ *m/f* neighbour (*BRIT*), neighbor (*US*).

voador(a) [vwa'do*(a)] *adj* flying.

voar [vo'a*] *vi* to fly; (*explodir*) to blow up, explode; **fazer ~ (pelos ares)** (*dinamitar*) to blow up, blast; **~ para cima de alguém** to fly at sb; **estar voando** (*col*) to be in the dark; **~ alto** (*fig*) to aim high; **fazer algo voando** to do sth in a hurry.

vocabulário [vokabu'larju] *m* vocabulary.

vocábulo [vo'kabulu] *m* word.

vocação [voka'sãw] (*pl* **-ões**) *f* vocation.

vocacional [vokasjo'naw] (*pl* **-ais**) *adj* vocational; (*orientação*) careers *atr*.

vocações [voka'sõjʃ] *fpl de* **vocação**.

vocal [vo'kaw] (*pl* **-ais**) *adj* vocal.

você [vo'se] *pron* you.

vocês [vo'seʃ] *pron pl* you.

vociferação [vosifera'sãw] (*pl* **-ões**) *f* shouting; (*censura*) harangue.

vociferar [vosife'ra*] *vt, vi* to shout, yell; **~ contra** to decry.

vodca ['vɔdʒka] *f* vodka.

voga ['vɔga] *f* (*NÁUT*) rowing; (*moda*) fashion; (*popularidade*) popularity; **em ~** popular, fashionable.

vogal [vo'gaw] (*pl* **-ais**) *f* (*LING*) vowel ♦ *m/f* (*votante*) voting member.

vogar [vo'ga*] *vi* to sail; (*boiar*) to float; (*importar*) to matter; (*estar na moda*) to be popular; (*lei*) to be in force; (*palavra*) to be in use.

voile ['vwali] *m* voile; **cortina de ~** net curtain.

vol. *abr* (= *volume*) vol.

volante [vo'lãtʃi] *m* (*AUTO*) steering wheel; (*piloto*) racing driver; (*impresso para apostas*) betting slip; (*roda*) flywheel.

volátil [vo'latʃiw] (*pl* **-eis**) *adj* volatile.

vôlei ['volej] *m* volleyball.

voleibol [volej'bɔw] *m* = **vôlei**.

volt ['vɔwtʃi] (*pl* **~s**) *m* volt.

volta ['vɔwta] *f* turn; (*regresso*) return; (*curva*) bend, curve; (*circuito*) lap; (*resposta*) retort; **passagem de ida e ~** return ticket (*BRIT*), round trip ticket (*US*); **dar uma ~** (*a pé*) to go for a walk; (*de carro*) to go for a drive; **dar ~s** *ou* **uma ~ (a)** to go round; **estar de ~** to be back; **na ~ do correio** by return (post); **por ~ de** about, around; **à** *ou* **em ~ de** around; **na ~** (*no caminho de ~*) on the way back; **vou resolver isso na ~** I'll sort this out when I get back; **estar** *ou* **andar às ~s com** to be tied up with; **fazer a ~, dar meia ~** (*AUTO*) to do a U-turn; **dar meia ~** (*MIL*) to do an about-turn; **dar a ~ por cima** (*fig*) to get over it, pick o.s. up; **~ e meia** every so often.

voltado/a [vow'tadu/a] *adj*: **estar ~ para** to be concerned with.

voltagem [vow'taʒẽ] *f* voltage.

voltar [vow'ta*] *vt* to turn ♦ *vi* to return, go *ou* come back; **~-se** *vr* to turn round; **~ uma arma contra** to turn a weapon on; **~ a fazer** to do again; **~ a si** to come to; **~ atrás** (*fig*) to backtrack; **~-se para** to turn to; **~-se contra** to turn against.

voltear [vow'tʃja*] *vt* to go round; (*manivela*) to turn ♦ *vi* to spin; (*borboleta*) to flit around.

volubilidade [volubili'dadʒi] *f* fickleness.

volume [vo'lumi] *m* volume; (*tamanho*) bulk; (*pacote*) package.

volumoso/a [volu'mozu/ɔza] *adj* bulky, big; (*som*) loud.

voluntário/a [volũ'tarju/a] *adj* voluntary ♦ *m/f* volunteer.

voluntarioso/a [volũta'rjozu/ɔza] *adj* headstrong.

volúpia [vo'lupja] *f* pleasure, ecstasy.

voluptuoso/a [volup'twozu/ɔza] *adj* voluptuous.

volúvel [vo'luvew] (*pl* **-eis**) *adj* fickle, changeable.

volver [vow've*] *vt* to turn ♦ *vi* to go (*ou* come) back.

vomitar [vomi'ta*] *vt, vi* to vomit; (*fig*) to pour out.

vômito ['vomitu] *m* (*ato*) vomiting; (*efeito*) vomit.

vontade [võ'tadʒi] *f* will; (*desejo*) wish; **boa/ má ~** good/ill will; **de boa/má ~** willingly/ grudgingly; **frutas à ~** fruit galore; **coma à ~** eat as much as you like; **fique** *ou* **esteja à ~** make yourself at home; **não estar à ~** to be ill at ease *ou* uncomfortable; **com ~** (*com prazer*) with pleasure; (*com gana*) with gusto; **estar com** *ou* **ter ~ de fazer** to feel like doing; **dar ~ a alguém de fazer** to make sb want to do; **essa música dá ~ de bailar** this music makes you want to dance; **fazer a ~ de alguém** to do what sb wants; **de livre e espontânea ~** of one's own free will; **por ~ própria** off one's own bat; **força de ~** will power; **ser cheio de ~s** to be spoilt.

vôo ['vou] (*PT*: **voo**) *m* flight; **levantar ~** to take off; **~ cego** flying blind, instrument flying; **~ livre** (*ESPORTE*) hang-gliding; **~ picado** nose dive.

voragem [vo'raʒẽ] (*pl* **-ns**) *f* abyss, gulf; (*de águas*) whirlpool; (*fig*: *de paixões*) maelstrom.

voraz [vo'rajʒ] *adj* voracious, greedy.

vórtice ['vɔxtʃisi] *m* vortex.

vos [vuʃ] *pron* you, to you.

vós [vɔʃ] *pron* you.

vosso/a ['vɔsu/a] *adj* your ♦ *pron*: **(o) ~** yours.

votação [vota'sãw] (*pl* **-ões**) *f* vote, ballot; (*ato*) voting; **submeter algo a ~** to put sth to the vote; **~ secreta** secret ballot.

votado/a [vo'tadu/a] *adj*: **o deputado mais ~** the MP (*BRIT*) *ou* Member of Congress (*US*) with the highest number of votes.

votante [vo'tãtʃi] *m/f* voter.

votar [vo'ta*] *vt* (*eleger*) to vote for; (*aprovar*) to pass; (*submeter a votação*) to vote on; (*dedicar*) to devote ♦ *vi* to vote; **~-se** *vr*: **~-se a** to devote o.s. to; **~ em** to vote for; **~ por/contra** to vote for/against.

voto ['vɔtu] *m* vote; (*promessa*) vow; **~s** *mpl* (*desejos*) wishes; **fazer ~s por** to wish for; **fazer ~s que** to hope that; **fazer ~ de castidade** to take a vow of chastity; **~ nulo** *ou* **em branco** blank vote; **~ de confiança** vote of confidence; **~ secreto** secret ballot.

vou [vo] *vb V* **ir**.

vovó [vo'vɔ] *f* grandma.

vovô [vo'vo] *m* grandad.

voz [vɔʒ] *f* voice; (*clamor*) cry; **a meia ~** in a whisper; **dar ~ de prisão a alguém** to tell sb he is under arrest; **de viva ~** orally; **ter ~ ativa** to have a say; **em ~ baixa** in a low voice; **em ~ alta** aloud; **levantar a ~ para alguém** to raise one's voice to sb; **~ de cana rachada** (*col*) screeching voice; **~ de comando** command, order.

vozearia [vozja'ria] *f* = **vozerio**.

vozeirão [vozej'rãw] (*pl* **-ões**) *m* loud voice.

vozerio [voze'riu] *m* shouting, hullabaloo.

VPR *abr f* (= *Vanguarda Popular Revolucionária*) *former Brazilian revolutionary movement*.

vulcânico/a [vuw'kaniku/a] *adj* volcanic.

vulcão [vuw'kãw] (*pl* **~s** *ou* **-ões**) *m* volcano.

vulgar [vuw'ga*] *adj* (*comum*) common; (*reles*) cheap; (*pej*: *pessoa etc*) vulgar.

vulgaridade [vuwgari'dadʒi] *f* commonness; (*pej*) vulgarity.

vulgarizar [vuwgari'za*] *vt* to popularize; (*abandalhar*) to cheapen.

vulgarmente [vuwgax'mẽtʃi] *adv* commonly, popularly.

vulgo ['vuwgu] *m* common people *pl* ♦ *adv* commonly known as.

vulnerabilidade [vuwnerabili'dadʒi] *f* vulnerability.

vulnerável [vuwne'ravew] (*pl* **-eis**) *adj* vulnerable.

vulto ['vuwtu] *m* figure; (*volume*) mass; (*fig*) importance; (*pessoa importante*) important person; **obras de ~** important works; **tomar ~** to take shape.

vultoso/a [vuw'tozu/ɔza] *adj* bulky; (*importante*) important; (*quantia*) considerable.

vulva ['vuwva] *f* vulva.

vupt ['vuptʃi] *excl* wham!

W

W, w ['dablju, *PT* ve'duplu] (*pl* **ws**) *m* W, w; **W de William** W for William.

w. *abr* (= *watt*) w.

walkie-talkie [wɔki'tɔki] (*pl* **~s**) *m* walkie-talkie.

watt ['wɔtʃi] (*pl* **~s**) *m* watt.

watt-hora (*pl* **watts-horas**) *m* watt-hour.

western ['wɛʃtexn] (*pl* **~s**) *m* western.

windsurfe [wĩ'suxfi] *m* windsurfing.

windsurfista [wĩsux'fiʃta] *m/f* windsurfer.

X, x [ʃiʃ] (*pl* **xs**) *m* X, x; **o ~ do problema** the crux of the problem; **X de Xavier** X for Xmas.

xá [ʃa] *m* shah.

xadrez [ʃa'dreʒ] *m* (*jogo*) chess; (*tabuleiro*) chessboard; (*tecido*) checked cloth; (*col*: *cadeia*) clink ♦ *adj inv* check(ered); **tecido de ~** check material.

xale ['ʃali] *m* shawl.

xampu [ʃã'pu] *m* shampoo.

Xangai [ʃã'gaj] *n* Shanghai.

***NB**: European Portuguese adds the following consonants to certain words:* **b** (sú(b)dito, su(b)til); **c** (a(c)ção, a(c)cionista, a(c)to); **m** (inde(m)ne); **p** (ado(p)ção, ado(p)tar); *for further details see p. xiii.*

xangô [ʃã'go] *m* (*orixá*) Afro-Brazilian deity; (*culto*) Afro-Brazilian religion.
xará [ʃa'ra] *m/f* namesake; (*companheiro*) mate.
xaropada [ʃaro'pada] (*col*) *f* bore; (*conversa*) boring talk.
xarope [ʃa'rɔpi] *m* syrup; (*para a tosse*) cough syrup.
xavante [ʃa'vãtʃi] *adj*, *m/f* Shavante Indian.
xaveco [ʃa'vɛku] *m* (*coisa sem valor*) piece of junk.
xaxim [ʃa'ʃĩ] *m* plant fibre (BRIT) *ou* fiber (US) (*used to plant indoor plants*).
xelim [ʃe'lĩ] (*pl* **-ns**) *m* shilling.
xenofobia [ʃenofo'bia] *f* xenophobia.
xenófobo/a [ʃe'nɔfobu/a] *adj* xenophobic ♦ *m/f* xenophobe.
xepa ['ʃepa] (*col*) *f* left-overs *pl*.
xepeiro/a [ʃe'pejru/a] *m/f* rubbish (BRIT) *ou* garbage (US) picker.
xeque ['ʃɛki] *m* (XADREZ) check; (*soberano*) sheikh; **pôr em ~** (*fig*) to call into question.
xeque-mate (*pl* **xeques-mate**) *m* checkmate.
xereta [ʃe'reta] *m/f* busybody ♦ *adj* nosy.
xeretar [ʃere'ta*] *vi* to poke one's nose in.
xerez [ʃe'reʒ] *m* sherry.
xerife [ʃe'rifi] *m* sheriff.
xerocar [ʃero'ka*] *vt* to photocopy, Xerox ®.
xerocópia [ʃero'kɔpja] *f* photocopy.
xerocopiar [ʃeroko'pja*] *vt* = **xerocar**.
xerox [ʃe'rɔks] ® *m* (*copia*) photocopy; (*máquina*) photocopier.
xexelento/a [ʃeʃe'lẽtu/a] (*col*) *adj* scruffy ♦ *m/f* scruff.
xexéu [ʃe'ʃɛw] *m* stink.
xi [ʃi] *excl* cor! (BRIT), gee! (US).
xícara ['ʃikara] (BR) *f* cup.
xicrinha [ʃi'kriɲa] *f* little cup.
xiita [ʃi'ita] *adj*, *m/f* Shiite.
xilindró [ʃilĩ'drɔ] (*col*) *m* clink.
xilofone [ʃilo'fɔni] *m* xylophone.
xilografia [ʃilogra'fia] *f* woodcut.
xingação [ʃĩga'sãw] (*pl* **-ões**) *f* curse.
xingamento [ʃĩga'mẽtu] *m* = **xingação**.
xingar [ʃĩ'ga*] *vt* to swear at ♦ *vi* to swear; **~ alguém de algo** to call sb sth.
xingatório [ʃĩga'tɔrju] *m* stream of invectives.
xinxim [ʃĩ'ʃĩ] *m* (*tb*: *~ de galinha*) chicken ragout.
xixi [ʃi'ʃi] (*col*) *m* wee, pee; **fazer ~** to wee, have a wee.
xô [ʃo] *excl* shoo.
xodó [ʃo'dɔ] *m* (*pessoa*) sweetheart; (*coisa*) passion; **ter ~ por alguém/algo** to have a soft spot for sb/sth.

Z

Z, z [ze] (*pl* **zs**) *m* Z, z; **Z de Zebra** Z for Zebra.
zaga ['zaga] *f* (FUTEBOL) fullback position.
zagueiro [za'gejru] *m* (FUTEBOL) fullback.
Zaire ['zajri] *m*: **o ~** Zaire.
Zâmbia ['zãbja] *f* Zambia.
zanga ['zãga] *f* (*raiva*) anger; (*irritação*) annoyance.
zangado/a [zã'gadu/a] *adj* angry; (*irritado*) annoyed; (*irritadiço*) bad-tempered; **ele está ~ comigo** (*de relações cortadas*) he's not speaking to me.
zangão [zã'gãw] (*pl* **~s** *ou* **-ões**) *m* (*inseto*) drone.
zangar [zã'ga*] *vt* to annoy, irritate ♦ *vi* to get angry; **~-se** *vr* (*aborrecer-se*) to get annoyed; **~-se com** to get cross with.
zangões [zã'gõjʃ] *mpl de* **zangão**.
zanzar [zã'za*] *vi* to wander.
zarolho/a [za'roʎu/a] *adj* blind in one eye.
zarpar [zax'pa*] *vi* (*navio*) to set sail; (*ir-se*) to set off; (*fugir*) to run away.
Zé [zɛ] *abr* (= *José*) Joe.
zebra ['zebra] *f* zebra; (*col*: *pessoa*) silly ass; (*jogo*) upset, turn-up for the books; **deu ~** (*col*) there was an upset.
zebrar [ze'bra*] *vi* to be a turn-up for the books.
zelador(a) [zela'do*(a)] *m/f* caretaker ♦ *adj* caring.
zelar [ze'la*] *vt*, *vi*: **~ (por)** to look after.
zelo ['zelu] *m* devotion, zeal; **~ por alguém/algo** devotion to sb/sth.
zeloso/a [ze'lozu/ɔza] *adj* zealous; (*diligente*) hard-working.
zen-budismo [zẽ-] *m* Zen (Buddhism).
zênite ['zenitʃi] *m* zenith.
zé-povinho [-po'viɲu] (*pl* **~s**) *m* the man in the street; (*o povo*) the masses *pl*; (*ralé*) riffraff.
zerar [ze'ra*] *vt* (*conta*, *inflação*) to reduce to zero; (*déficit*) to pay off, wipe out; (*aluno*) to give no marks to ♦ *vi*: **~ em** (*aluno*) to get no marks in.
zerinho/a [ze'riɲu/a] (*col*) *adj* brand new.
zero ['zɛru] *num* zero; (ESPORTE) nil; **ser um ~ à esquerda** to be useless; **8 graus abaixo/acima de ~** 8 degrees below/above zero; **reduzir alguém a ~** to clean sb out; **ficar a ~** to lose everything; **começar do ~** (*fig*) to start from nothing.
zero-quilômetro *adj inv* brand new ♦ *m inv* brand new car.

ziguezague [zigi'zagi] *m* zigzag.
ziguezagueante [zigiza'gjãtʃi] *adj* zigzag.
ziguezaguear [zigiza'gja*] *vi* to zigzag.
Zimbábue [zĩ'babwi] *m*: **o ~** Zimbabwe.
zinco ['zĩku] *m* zinc; **folha de ~** corrugated iron.
-zinho/a [-'ziɲu/a] *sufixo* little; **florzinha** little flower.
zipe ['zipi] *m* = **zíper**.
zíper ['zipe*] *m* zip (*BRIT*), zipper (*US*).
ziquizira [ziki'zira] (*col*) *f* lurgy.
zoada ['zwada] *f* = **zoeira**.
zodíaco [zo'dʒiaku] *m* zodiac.
zoeira ['zwejra] *f* din.
zombador(a) [zõba'do*(a)] *adj* mocking ♦ *m/f* mocker.
zombar [zõ'ba*] *vi* to mock; **~ de** to make fun of.
zombaria [zõba'ria] *f* mockery, ridicule.
zona ['zɔna] *f* area; (*de cidade*) district; (*GEO*) zone; (*col: local de meretrício*) red-light district; (*: confusão*) mess; (*: tumulto*) free-for-all; **fazer a ~** to go on the game; **fazer uma ~** to raise hell, make a fuss; **~ eleitoral** electoral district, constituency; **~ franca** free-trade area; **Z~ Norte/Sul** (*do Rio, São Paulo etc*) Northern/Southern District; **a Z~ Sul carioca** *the fashionable middle-class suburbs along the beaches in Rio.*
zonear [zo'nja*] *vt* to divide into districts; (*col*) to make a mess in ♦ *vi* (*col*) to raise hell.
zonzeira [zõ'zejra] *f* dizziness; **dar/sentir ~** to make/feel dizzy.
zonzo/a ['zõzu/a] *adj* dizzy.
zôo ['zou] *m* zoo.
zoologia [zolo'ʒia] *f* zoology.
zoológico/a [zo'lɔʒiku/a] *adj* zoological; **jardim ~** zoo.
zoólogo/a [zo'ɔlogu/a] *m/f* zoologist.
zoom [zũ] *m* = **zum**.
zorra ['zoxa] (*col*) *f* mess.
zuarte ['zwaxtʃi] *m* denim.
zulu [zu'lu] *adj*, *m/f* Zulu ♦ *m* (*LING*) Zulu.
zum [zũ] *m* zoom.
zumbido [zũ'bidu] *m* buzz(ing); (*de tráfego*) hum; **um ~ no ouvido** a ringing in one's ear.
zumbir [zũ'bi*] *vi* to buzz; (*ouvido*) to ring ♦ *m* buzzing; ringing.
zunido [zu'nidu] *m* (*vento*) whistling; (*inseto*) buzz.
zunir [zu'ni*] *vi* (*vento*) to whistle; (*seta*) to whizz; (*bala*) to zip; (*inseto*) to buzz.
zunzum [zũ'zũ] *m* buzz(ing); (*boato*) rumour (*BRIT*), rumor (*US*).
zunzunzum [zũzũ'zũ] *m* rumour (*BRIT*), rumor (*US*).
zura ['zura] *m/f inv* miser ♦ *adj inv* mean, stingy.
zureta [zu'reta] (*col*) *m/f* loony.
Zurique [zu'riki] *n* Zurich.
zurrapa [zu'xapa] *f* rough wine, plonk (*col*).
zurrar [zu'xa*] *vi* to bray.
zurro ['zuxu] *m* bray.

***NB:** European Portuguese adds the following consonants to certain words:* **b** (sú(b)dito, su(b)til); **c** (a(c)ção, a(c)cionista, a(c)to); **m** (inde(m)ne); **p** (ado(p)ção, ado(p)tar); *for further details see p. xiii.*